Elements of Land Law

ELEMENTS OF LAND LAW

Second edition

Kevin Gray LLD (Cantab)
Fellow of Trinity College
Professor of Law, University of Cambridge
Of the Middle Temple, Barrister

Butterworths
London, Dublin, Edinburgh
1993

United Kingdom Butterworth & Co (Publishers) Ltd, 88 Kingsway, LONDON WC2B 6AB and 4 Hill Street, EDINBURGH EH2 3JZ

Australia Butterworths, SYDNEY, MELBOURNE, BRISBANE, ADELAIDE, PERTH, CANBERRA and HOBART

Belgium Butterworth & Co (Publishers) Ltd, BRUSSELS

Canada Butterworths Canada Ltd, TORONTO and VANCOUVER

Ireland Butterworth (Ireland) Ltd, DUBLIN

Malaysia Malayan Law Journal Sdn Bhd, KUALA LUMPUR

New Zealand Butterworths of New Zealand Ltd, WELLINGTON and AUCKLAND

Puerto Rico Equity de Puerto Rico, Inc, HATO REY

Singapore Butterworths Asia, SINGAPORE

USA Butterworth Legal Publishers, AUSTIN, Texas; BOSTON, Massachusetts; CLEARWATER, Florida (D & S Publishers); ORFORD, New Hampshire (Equity Publishing); ST PAUL, Minnesota; and SEATTLE, Washington

A CIP Catalogue record for this book is available from the British Library.

First edition 1987

ISBN 0 406 01149 4

Cover picture of JMW Turner's *A Town on a River at Sunset* reproduced by kind permission of Tate Gallery Publications

Typeset by Kerrypress Ltd, Luton
Printed by Butler & Tanner Ltd, Frome and London

Preface to second edition

There is no more effective way to make time gallop past in six-year stages than to write a book which threatens to require a further edition. Yet the logic of experience is that there is life in the law. Even during this all too brief interlude the English law of land has moved on apace.

The preparation of this edition was made possible by a period of leave from Trinity and a Research Fellowship in the Division of Philosophy and Law at the Australian National University's Research School of Social Sciences. I have taken the opportunity to reorganise the material contained in the first edition, both adding to and subtracting from its coverage. Time and the endless patience of Butterworths' editorial staff have allowed account to be taken of very recent innovations and amendments (including the enactment of the Leasehold Reform, Housing and Urban Development Act 1993). As usual Lexis has given access to better reporting of some material than was available anywhere else and, where necessary, I have used direct quotation from Lexis to supplement less adequate reports. Uncharacteristically, however, Lexis proved wholly uninformative about the long-awaited outcome of the pending appeal to the House of Lords in *Barclays Bank Plc v O'Brien.*

This edition owes much to the enormous kindness of a number of friends. I have received unfailing help from the staff of the Squire Law Library (and particularly from Keith McVeigh and Peter Zawada). Quite remarkable technical assistance was rendered in Trinity by Laura Pieters Cordy. Toni Makkai, Sophia Oliver and Jeremy Gray performed amazing electronic wizardry. Much needed intelligence was contributed by Jonathan Aleck, Hilaire Barnett, John Brown, Michael Fealy, Tony Oakley, Geoffrey Samuel, Nicholas Seddon and William Swadling. I am also greatly indebted to John Adams (than whom I could have had no more generous predecessor and friend). I have been the beneficiary of endless encouragement from Gareth Jones, Kurt Lipstein and John Tiley. My deep thanks are, as always, due to Tim Bonyhady and Paul Finn, all three of us being companions on a shared journey.

Trinity College
23 September 1993

Kevin Gray

Preface to first edition

By long tradition land law has acquired a reputation as a highly technical area which many students find both difficult and unrewarding. This book seeks to show that none of this need be true and that even quite complex problems of modern land law can be explained in simple terms which start from underlying 'elements' or first principles. Far from being an uninspiring subject of study, land law—when properly understood—emerges as one of the most exciting and fast-moving branches of contemporary English law.

It is, of course, quite true that the law of land often appears to have a strangely enduring quality. In England and Wales the modern law is still dominated by the vast corpus of legislation which came into effect on 1 January 1926. This legislation was itself the summation of the steady movement towards reform of real property law which had been set in motion almost a century earlier. Against this background it was perhaps inevitable that the structural elements of English land law, so painstakingly gathered together in the 1925 legislation, should have been destined to survive relatively intact to the present day.

This sense of stasis or permanence is, however, largely illusory: modern land law is not the slow-moving subject it is commonly supposed to be. Important developments over the last few years—both judicial and legislative—have begun to refashion even the structural features of the 1925 Acts to accord more closely with the constantly changing needs of the 1980s and 1990s. Significant elements of English land law are nowadays on the move and, as they gather a critical mass, may well push past a tipping point into an area where the law of the future suddenly appears markedly different from the law of the past. Thus, for instance, the unremitting extension of title registration has made it realistic for the first time to contemplate that unregistered land may shortly become a thing of the past. The rights of residential occupiers have been revolutionised by a veritable explosion of housing legislation which confers rights of security, rights to repair, rights to buy and even a so-called 'preserved' right to buy. A recent flurry of Law Commission reports indicates that there may soon be a wholesale reshaping of such areas as the law of leases, mortgages, covenants, and even of the registered land regime itself.

These are indeed interesting times not only for land lawyers but also for those who have any curiosity about the criteria of distributive justice. And it should not go unnoticed that land law, in so far as it allocates the rights and benefits traditionally labelled as 'property', provides an important reflection of our ideas of social justice. With such considerations in mind, it is the aim of this book, while remaining rigorously analytical, to provide a contextual and critical treatment of modern land law. The book says relatively little about the history of land law; nor does it purport to be a manual on conveyancing. It does, however, seek to describe the elements of contemporary land law against the background of the social and political implications of the subject.

The book is divided into two parts. 'The General Part' identifies the basic concepts and principles of land law and integrates them into a framework for comprehensive and systematic analysis. Primary emphasis has been given to those aspects of land law which are of greatest modern relevance—hence the substantial exclusion of such matters as the law of strict settlements and the rule against perpetuities. The second part of the book, 'Special Problems', gives a practical application to many of the concepts which are described in the first part. A number of key issues which illustrate the wider effects of land law are examined. Given that 1987 has been designated as the 'International Year of Shelter for the Homeless', it is perhaps appropriate that this portion of the book should concentrate particularly upon the sphere of residential property.

The book as a whole seeks to make extensive reference to the relevant English and comparative case law. Given the increasing welcome accorded even in English courts to the decisions of other jurisdictions, it seems quite wrong to ignore comparative material which contributes towards a richer understanding of a particular problem. The greater accessibility of unreported case law (through devices such as Lexis) has likewise thrown new light on areas which have hitherto been of somewhat low visibility. Although an attempt has been made to state the law as it existed at the end of July 1987, considerable attention has been given throughout to the reform proposals made by the Law Commission and other bodies.

Many people have contributed either practical help or encouragement towards the completion of this book. I must particularly thank Caroline Amory, Stephen Bellamy, Tim Bonyhady, Paul Finn, Gareth Jones, Kurt Lipstein, David Pearl, Paul Popplewell, John Tiley, Frances Wilson, and Tim Youdan. I am also indebted to the Squire Law Librarian, Keith McVeigh, and to his consistently cheerful and helpful staff, Clive Argent, Brian Humphreys, Trudy Young and Peter Zawada. I must likewise record my gratitude to the Libraries of the Institute for Advanced Legal Studies and the New Zealand High Commission in London. Back at Trinity Laura Cordy and John Hinch gave extremely generous help with computers and word-processors, while at Butterworths nothing was done without the efficient and patient intervention of the editorial staff. Ultimately, perhaps, my greatest debt is to a generation of law students in Cambridge and elsewhere who taught me very much more than I ever taught them.

Trinity College
11 August 1987

Kevin Gray

Contents

Table of Statutes

References in this Table to *Statutes* are to Halsbury's Statutes of England (Fourth Edition) showing the volume and page at which the annotated text of an Act may be found.

PAGE

Table of Foreign Enactments

Table of Cases

A

B

C

D

E

F

H

I

J

K

L

M

N

O

P

Q

R

S

T

W

X

Y

Z

Abbreviations

Bl Comm	W. Blackstone, *Commentaries on the Laws of England* (1st edn London 1765–1769)
BPR	Butterworths Property Reports
Challis	*Law of Real Property* (3rd edn London 1911)
Co Litt	E. Coke, *The First Part of the Institutes of the Laws of England* or *A Commentary upon Littleton* (11th edn London 1719)
Emmet on Title	18th edn by J.T. Farrand, London 1983
Jiro	Journal of the Institute of Rent Officers
Litt	Littleton's Tenures (ed E. Wambaugh, Washington DC 1903)
Sheppard's Touchstone	W. Sheppard, *The Touchstone of Common Assurances* (London 1651)

A. Concepts

CHAPTER 1

Land

The great lawyers of a previous age were supremely conscious of the significance of land in human affairs. They were aware of the paradox of the integrity of man and his utter dependence upon his physical environment; of land as dignified by the habitation of man, yet alone providing the means for his survival; of land as a base for human striving and as an inspiration towards fleeting comprehension of something more.[1] The contemporary legal definition of 'land'—albeit broad in some respects—is but a pale shadow of these elevated perceptions.

1. THE LEGAL DEFINITION OF 'LAND'

For the modern property lawyer the word 'land' bears an extended meaning. According to section 205(1)(ix) of the Law of Property Act 1925, 'land' includes

> land of any tenure, and mines and minerals, whether or not held apart from the surface, buildings or parts of buildings (whether the division is horizontal, vertical or made in any other way) and other corporeal hereditaments; also a manor, an advowson, and a rent and other incorporeal hereditaments, and an easement, right, privilege, or benefit in, over, or derived from land.

As Blackstone said,[2] 'land' is 'a word of a very extensive signification'. For the purpose of the Law of Property Act 1925, it includes both 'corporeal hereditaments' and 'incorporeal hereditaments'. In broad terms 'corporeal hereditaments' refer to the physical and tangible characteristics of land, while 'incorporeal hereditaments' refer to certain intangible rights which may be enjoyed over or in respect of land.

2. CORPOREAL HEREDITAMENTS

Corporeal hereditaments comprise those 'substantial and permanent objects' which 'affect the senses',[3] the only objects which are truly 'permanent' being those constituted by or connected with immovable property. In the extended sense in which the term is used in English law, 'corporeal hereditaments' include not merely the physical clods of earth which make up the surface

1 See eg *Co Litt*, p 4a.
2 *Bl Comm*, Vol II, p 16.
3 *Bl Comm*, Vol II, p 17.

layer of land, but also all physical things which are attached to or are inherent in the ground. Thus the term 'corporeal hereditaments' comprehends such things as buildings, trees and subjacent minerals.[4]

(1) Cuius est solum eius est usque ad coelum et ad inferos

The extended significance of the term 'land' is sometimes more eloquently than accurately expressed in the Latin maxim, *cuius est solum eius est usque ad coelum et ad inferos*: he who owns the land owns everything reaching up to the very heavens and down to the depths of the earth. Whether accurate or not, this maxim articulates a notion of the sacrosanct nature of property rights in the common law,[5] and has tended to be invoked wherever necessary for the purpose of investing the landowner with all the rights required for reasonable enjoyment of his property.

Curiously enough, the maxim *cuius est solum*. . . cannot be traced back to Roman law,[6] and seems to be a brocard of medieval origin.[7] It contains a certain measure of truth as far as English law is concerned, for there is doubtless a general sense in which common lawyers have conceptualised 'land' as having an infinitely extended three-dimensional quality.[8] However, the original Latin maxim is now subject to so many qualifications that it is virtually worthless as a statement of contemporary law.[9] In no sense can it be understood to mean that 'land' in English law comprehends the whole

4 *Mitchell v Mosley* [1914] 1 Ch 438 at 450 (post, p 19).

5 See eg *Lewvest Ltd v Scotia Towers Ltd* (1982) 126 DLR (3d) 239 at 240.

6 See Lord McNair, *The Law of the Air* (3rd edn, London 1964), p 393; J.C. Cooper, *Roman Law and the Maxim 'Cuius est Solum' in International Air Law*, (1952) 1 McGill LJ 23 at 26ff. It is unlikely that the maxim contains any residual trace of a belief in a flat earth. Contrary to popular conception, the medievals were not 'flat-earthers' (see C.S. Lewis, *The Discarded Image* (Cambridge 1964), p 142), but had fully adopted the traditional Aristotelian cosmology. The last educated man to espouse a flat earth theory seems to have been the sixth century Cosmas Indicopleustes, who believed the earth to be a flat parallelogram (see W.E.H. Lecky, *The Rise and Influence of Rationalism in Europe* (2nd edn London 1882), Vol I, p 269).

7 Its first recognised appearance seems to be in the 13th Century *Glossa Ordinaria* on the *Corpus Iuris* (*Digest*, VIII.2.1) by Accursius of Bologna (see H. Guibé, *Essai sur la navigation aérienne en droit interne et en droit international* (Paris 1912), p 35ff). It has been suggested that the maxim may have derived from even earlier Jewish origins (see (1931) 47 LQR 14; *Deuteronomy*, xxx: 11-14, *Isaiah*, vii: 11), but see D.E. Smith, *The Origins of Trespass to Airspace and the Maxim 'Cujus est solum ejus est usque ad coelum'*, (1982) 6 Trent Law Journal 33 at 38. For the earliest English reference, see the terminal note in *Bury v Pope* (1588) Cro Eliz 118, 78 ER 375, where the maxim is said to have been known from the time of Edward I (1239-1307). (It has been pointed out that Franciscus, the son of Accursius, appears to have travelled to England in 1274 at the invitation of Edward I (see McNair, *op cit*, p 397)). The maxim was later incorporated in *Co Litt*, p 4a; *Bl Comm*, Vol II, p 18.

8 Thus, for instance, the mere superaddition of a quantity of dumped soil on the surface layer of Blackacre does not in itself increase the 'land' owned by the proprietor of Blackacre or mark any increase in his interest in that land (see *McClure v Petre* [1988] 1 WLR 1386 at 1390D, 1393E).

9 In *Bernstein of Leigh (Baron) v Skyviews & General Ltd* [1978] QB 479 at 485C, Griffiths J dismissed the maxim as merely 'a colourful phrase'. The formula has been said to be 'imprecise' and 'mainly serviceable as dispensing with analysis' (*Commissioner for Railways et al v Valuer-General* [1974] AC 328 at 351G), and to have 'no place in the modern world' (*United States v Causby*, 328 US 256 at 261, 90 L ed 1206 at 1210 (1946)). See also *Re The Queen in Right of Manitoba and Air Canada* (1978) 86 DLR (3d) 631 at 635, 637.

of the space from the centre of the earth to the heavens, not least since 'so sweeping, unscientific and unpractical a doctrine is unlikely to appeal to the common law mind.'[10] At most the maxim serves nowadays only as an approximate statement of the prima facie extent of the rights pertaining to owners of land[11] and of the extent of that ownership which is transferred by conveyance.[12]

(2) Buildings and other constructions

Another Latin maxim frequently invoked in the present context is the general rule *superficies solo cedit* (a building becomes part of the ground).[13] Thus buildings constructed on foundations placed in the soil become themselves part of the 'land'.[14] Even the top floor of a high-rise block of flats comprises 'land'. A garage or garden shed or wall[15] likewise qualifies as 'land', provided that in each case it is firmly attached to the ground.

The rule *superficies solo cedit* is confirmed in section 62(1) of the Law of Property Act 1925, which provides that any conveyance of land is deemed to include by implication all buildings, erections, and fixtures attached to the land. Likewise, section 62(2) provides that any conveyance of land with houses or other buildings on it is deemed to include by implication 'all outhouses, erections, fixtures, cellars, areas, courts, courtyards, cisterns, sewers, gutters, drains, ways, passages, lights, [and] watercourses' appertaining to the land.[16]

(3) Strata titles

Section 205(1)(ix) of the Law of Property Act 1925 establishes beyond doubt that 'land' is capable of horizontal as well as vertical division, and that a land title can therefore relate to a slice of defined area or cubic space which is not grounded on the surface layer of the earth. A modern example of such an area is an upper-storey flat.

That there can be a horizontal stratification of rights in land is not a new idea. The possibility of horizontal division of land follows almost necessarily from the maxim *cuius est solum eius est usque ad coelum et ad inferos*. However attenuated the force of this maxim today, it is recognised that the landowner is at least to some limited extent competent to convey away

10 *Commissioner for Railways et al v Valuer-General* [1974] AC 328 at 351H–352A per Lord Wilberforce.
11 See eg *Pountney v Clayton* (1883) 11 QBD 820 at 838 per Bowen LJ.
12 See eg *National Carriers Ltd v Panalpina (Northern) Ltd* [1981] AC 675 at 708C, where Lord Russell of Killowen noted that a grant of a freehold estate in fee simple passes the land 'as to its surface and below its surface, and the airspace above, subject to exclusions'.
13 This rule originates in Roman law (*Gaius*, 2.73; *Inst.* 2.1.29). See also S.S. Ball, *The Jural Nature of Land*, 23 Illinois L Rev 45 at 48 (1928–29).
14 *Mitchell v Mosley* [1914] 1 Ch 438 at 450. On demolition the disassembled parts of a building revert to the status of personalty (*R v Leominster DC, Ex p Antique Country Buildings Ltd* (1988) 56 P & CR 240 at 247).
15 *Moody v Steggles* (1879) 12 Ch D 261 at 267.
16 Post, p 1100. Section 62 can be excluded by contrary intention expressed in the conveyance (see section 62(4)).

separate estates in horizontal strata of his 'land'.[17] These strata may be subterranean. It is quite feasible, for instance, that one person should own the freehold estate[18] in the surface layer of the ground,[19] while another person owns the freehold in a subjacent cavern,[20] or layer of minerals,[1] or underground cellar.[2]

As a matter of strict definition it is even possible that 'land' may include a cubic quantum of airspace which is separate from any physical solum.[3] From this there follows the initially improbable notion that an individual can own an interest literally in thin air—a proposition which neatly gives the lie to any assumption that land is necessarily a tangible resource. A three-dimensional quantum of airspace can exist as an 'independent unit of real property'.[4] Such airspace can be conveyed in fee simple;[5] it can be leased;[6] it can be subdivided;[7] and it can even be subjected to land taxes.[8] The exploitability of airspace as a commerciable resource nowadays ensures that a conveyance of airspace in crowded urban locations can often operate as an efficient means of development. New buildings can, for instance, be suspended above street level, thus maximising the utility of existing resources and reconciling otherwise incompatible forms of 'land' user.

(a) *The 'flying freehold'*

Although there is always something controversial in the suggestion that separate freehold titles can be created above ground level, the idea is by no means novel. Coke allowed that 'a man may have an inheritance in an upper chamber though the lower buildings and soil be in another, and

17 The strata need not even be horizontal. There is in principle nothing impossible about the conveyance of an estate in a sloping subterranean area (eg a cave or mineral bed) or in a sloping 'flying freehold' (eg an enclosed walkway across a street between different levels of adjacent buildings).

18 On the meaning of the 'freehold estate', see Chapter 3 (post, p 58).

19 In England if a highway is maintainable by the relevant statutory highway authority at public expense, that authority holds a determinable fee simple interest in the surface of the highway and in so much of the subjacent land and superjacent air-space as is required for the discharge of its statutory duties (see *Coverdale v Charlton* (1878) 4 QBD 104 at 118, 121, 126; *Foley's Charity Trustees v Dudley Corpn* [1910] 1 KB 317 at 322; *Tithe Redemption Commission v Runcorn UDC* [1954] Ch 383 at 398; *Wiltshire County Council v Frazer* (1984) 47 P & CR 69 at 72; Highways Act 1980, s 263). See also *Muswellbrook Coal Co Ltd v Minister for Mineral Resources and Energy* (1986) 6 NSWLR 654 at 657G–658A.

20 *Cox v Colossal Cavern Co*, 276 SW 540 at 542f (1925).

1 *Williams v Usherwood* (1983) 45 P & CR 235 at 253.

2 The possibility that there can, in this sense, be such a thing as a 'subterranean flying freehold' was conceded in *Grigsby v Melville* [1974] 1 WLR 80 at 83D-E. See also *Metropolitan Railway Co v Fowler* [1893] AC 416 at 420, 422.

3 See *Property in Thin Air*, [1991] CLJ 252 at 258f.

4 *Macht v Department of Assessments of Baltimore City*, 296 A2d 162 at 168 (1972); *Re Trizec Manitoba Ltd and City Assessor for the City of Winnipeg* (1986) 25 DLR (4th) 444 at 450.

5 *Reilly v Booth* (1890) 44 Ch D 12 at 23 per Cotton LJ, 26f per Lopes LJ.

6 *Macht v Department of Assessments of Baltimore City*, 296 A2d 162 at 168 (1972); *Re Trizec Manitoba Ltd and City Assessor for the City of Winnipeg* (1986) 25 DLR (4th) 444 at 452.

7 *Bursill Enterprises Pty Ltd v Berger Bros Trading Co Pty Ltd* (1971) 124 CLR 73 at 91 per Windeyer J; *Ratto v Trifid Pty Ltd* [1987] WAR 237 at 255 per Brinsden J.

8 *Re Trizec Manitoba Ltd and City Assessor for the City of Winnipeg* (1986) 25 DLR (4th) 444.

seeing it is an inheritance corporeal it shall pass by livery.'[9] The horizontal stratification of estates in land has more often been achieved through the creation of leasehold rather than freehold estates, but there seems to be nothing wrong in principle with the idea that a landowner may carve out of his own estate a 'flying freehold' which is not contiguous with ground level.[10] Although somewhat unusual in England, such titles do exist in certain parts of London, most notably in parts of Lincoln's Inn.

The principal objection to the 'flying freehold' is not conceptual but practical.[11] Planning considerations apart,[12] a freeholder has an inherent right to destroy his property or allow it to fall into disrepair. Thus a flying freehold is extremely vulnerable to the possibility that a subjacent freeholder may damage or prejudice the subjacent structure on which the 'flying freehold' physically rests. Of course the answer to this dilemma lies in fastening upon the subjacent owner the required positive duties of physical support and repair in relation to superior freeholders. This solution is, however, fraught with further difficulty since, in the current state of English law,[13] it is impossible to cause the burden of such positive covenants to run with the land so as to affect successors in title.[14] The Law Commission has proposed that the law of covenants should be amended to make the burden of positive covenants transmissible as between freeholders,[15] and it seems likely that this change will occur in the fairly near future.

(b) The Australian model

Such a change in the law will almost certainly be accompanied by a movement towards increased use of the freehold estate in the conveyancing of flats.[16] This development would merely mirror the concept of 'strata titles' which was successfully pioneered in New South Wales in 1961[17] and which is now widespread in Australia.[18] Strata titles legislation of the Australian model

9 *Co Litt*, p 48b. Challis adds that it seems 'clear on principle that if the house is burnt down or otherwise destroyed, the rights of the owner of the upper chamber cease, but the point does not appear to have been decided' (see *Challis*, p 54). The Law Commission expressed a contrary view on this point in 1984, observing that conveyances of freehold flats are drafted on the assumption that the freehold estate conferred is capable of lasting beyond the life of the building itself, ie is capable of surviving the destruction of the building. The Law Commission noted the preponderant view that 'an estate can exist in what has become mere airspace' (Law Commission, *Transfer of Land: The Law of Positive and Restrictive Covenants* (Law Com No 127, 26 January 1984), para 4.6). Moreover, it is generally assumed that the leasehold estate granted to a tenant does not end automatically with the destruction of a flat.

10 See S.M. Tolson, *'Land' without earth: Freehold Flats in English Law*, (1950) 14 Conv (NS) 350.

11 See *Bursill Enterprises Pty Ltd v Berger Bros Trading Co Pty Ltd* (1971) 124 CLR 73 at 92 per Windeyer J.

12 Post, p 1166.

13 See Law Com No 127, para 4.6.

14 See Law Commission, *Commonhold: Freehold Flats and freehold ownership of other interdependent buildings* (Cm 179, July 1987), para 1.3.

15 Post, p 1167.

16 In 1984 the Building Societies Association advocated a switch from leasehold to freehold conveyancing of flats (see (1984) 128 SJ 538).

17 See Conveyancing (Strata) Titles Act 1961 (NSW), now replaced by Strata Titles Act 1973.

18 See *Sackville and Neave's Property Law: Cases and Materials* (3rd edn, Sydney 1981), para 7.179; [1986] Conv 222.

has proved to be extremely flexible, even to the extent that it is possible to convey lots within a 'strata plan' which comprise cubic spaces of thin air,[19] or which include not merely a dwelling but also a share of a communal garage, shed and swimming pool.[20]

(c) 'Commonhold' ownership schemes

In view of the steady disenchantment with the leasehold estate as the legal medium of flat ownership, it is possible that English law will soon introduce a new scheme of land ownership known as 'commonhold'. During the 1980s a Working Group of the Law Commission investigated the merits of adopting a modified form of strata title or 'condominium title'[1] as the most appropriate form of ownership for multi-occupied residential units which involve aspects of both private and communal user.[2] The Working Group's recommendations thus relate primarily, but not exclusively, to such properties as a residential block of flats.

Commonhold ownership provides a means of regulating relations between owners of separate properties which lie in close proximity to each other and which are interdependent. The Law Commission's 'commonhold' proposals comprise a significant adaptation of existing notions of freehold ownership. Under the commonhold scheme each 'unit holder' (eg a flat-owner) would take a freehold estate by way of exclusive ownership of his own unit[3] and would also become a member of a management or commonhold association which owned the common parts of the grounds and building (including its structural walls).[4] The commonhold association would be responsible for the repair and maintenance of the common parts and for the provision of services within the commonhold scheme, receiving for this purpose a service charge payable by each unit holder.[5] Each unit holder would also take a proportionate share in the site of the commonhold premises themselves, this share being realisable on the termination of the entire commonhold scheme.[6]

In respect of his or her own unit, the unit holder would be affected by a body of standard rights and obligations defined by statutory instrument.[7] These rights and obligations would thereafter attach automatically by force of statute to each unit, irrespective of subsequent changes in the ownership of the unit.[8] Both the benefit and the burden of rules relating to such matters

19 See Strata Titles Act 1973 (NSW), s 8(1)(f)(iii), resolving the point left open in *Rochester Investments Pty Ltd v Couchman* (1969) 90 WN (NSW) (Pt 1) 371 at 376G. See also *Burgchard v Holroyd Municipal Council* [1984] 2 NSWLR 164 at 169F.

20 *Woollahra Municipal Council v Local Government Appeals Tribunal* [1975] 2 NSWLR 594 at 603E.

1 Post, p 1167. See [1985] Conv 305.

2 Law Commission, *Commonhold: Freehold Flats and freehold ownership of other interdependent buildings* (Cm 179, July 1987). See also B. Denyer-Green, *Commonhold and unitisation*, (1986) 16 CSW 140.

3 Law Commission, *Commonhold* (July 1987), paras 1.10, 5.16, 6.1.

4 Law Commission, *Commonhold* (July 1987), paras 1.12, 8.1ff.

5 Law Commission, *Commonhold* (July 1987), paras 8.20ff.

6 Law Commission, *Commonhold* (July 1987), paras 1.10, 14.4ff.

7 Law Commission, *Commonhold* (July 1987), para 7.3. These rights and duties may be varied or extended, initially by the promoter of the commonhold, and thereafter by a special majority vote of the unit owners (ibid, paras 7.5f).

8 Law Commission, *Commonhold* (July 1987), paras 7.2, 7.22ff.

as support, access, services, defects, repairs and common facilities would thus form a constitutional framework designed to govern the relationship of the unit holders.

The commonhold ownership scheme represents a significantly innovative proposal in English law. It combines the benefits (both legal and psychological) of freehold ownership with a new facility for democratic self-management of co-operatively held premises. It remains to be seen whether some version of the commonhold formula finds legislative approval.[9]

(4) Fixtures

As indicated in section 62 of the Law of Property Act 1925, the statutory definition of 'land' includes 'fixtures' attached to the land. English law has effectively adopted the maxim *quicquid plantatur solo, solo cedit* (whatever is attached to the ground becomes a part of it),[10] but in so doing has had to fashion a slightly uneasy distinction between 'fixtures' and 'chattels'.

(a) The distinction between fixtures and chattels

'Fixtures' comprise that category of material objects which, when attached physically to the land, are regarded as becoming annexed to the realty.[11] Irrespective of its previous ownership, title to such an object thenceforth vests automatically and exclusively in the owner of the realty. As a fixture the annexed object is regarded, by virtue of some curious legal metamorphosis, as having merged with the 'land'. The fixture therefore passes with all subsequent conveyances[12] of the realty unless and until lawfully severed from the land.[13] This merger of chattel with realty automatically extinguishes

9 For further discussion of commonhold schemes, see Chapter 18 (post, p 797) and Chapter 22 (post, p 1168).

10 *Lancaster v Eve* (1859) 5 CB (NS) 717 at 727, 141 ER 288 at 293 per Williams J. Thus the freeholder 'has exactly the same interest in everything attached to the freehold as he has in the bricks and mortar' (*Ex parte Daglish. In re Wilde* (1873) LR 8 Ch App 1072 at 1080 per James LJ).

11 See *New Zealand Government Property Corpn v H. M. & S. Ltd* [1982] QB 1145 at 1160H–1161A. 'The land and the fixtures are one' (*Emanuel (Rundle Mall) Pty Ltd v Commissioner of Stamps* (1986) 39 SASR 582 at 592). Fixtures become 'incorporated with the soil' (*Lancaster v Eve* (1859) 5 CB (NS) 717 at 728, 141 ER 288 at 293) or '*partes soli*' (*Bain v Brand* (1876) 1 App Cas 762 at 769). However, physical connection is not always necessary in order to constitute a particular physical thing an integral part of a freehold. 'Everybody knows that a key, although in its nature a chattel, belongs to the house, and passes with the freehold' (*Moody v Steggles* (1879) 12 Ch D 261 at 267 per Fry J).

12 The relevant conveyance may of course include a mortgage, with the result that the mortgagee takes a security over land inclusive of fixtures. See *Ex parte Daglish. In re Wilde* (1873) LR 8 Ch App 1072 at 1080 per James LJ; *In re Yates* (1888) 38 Ch D 112 at 120 per Cotton LJ, 124f per Lindley LJ; *In re Rogerstone Brick & Stone Co Ltd* [1919] 1 Ch 110 at 124; *Re Penning; Ex parte State Bank of South Australia* (1989) 89 ALR 417 at 427. The mortgagee's security covers fixtures irrespective of the date of their annexation, ie whether before or after the creation of the mortgage (*Sanwa Australia Leasing Ltd v National Westminster Finance Australia Ltd* (1989) NSW ConvR 55-437 at 58,175 per Powell J).

13 *North Shore Gas Co Ltd v Commissioner of Stamp Duties (NSW)* (1940) 63 CLR 52 at 68; *Emanuel (Rundle Mall) Pty Ltd v Commissioner of Stamps* (1986) 39 SASR 582 at 590.

any separate title formerly held in the relevant object.[14] The process of annexation thus expropriates the former owner of the chattel, whilst simultaneously disabling the landowner from claiming any independent title in the fixture which is distinct from his general title in the 'land'.[15]

By contrast, the category of 'chattels' consists of physical objects which never lose their character as mere personalty, but which retain their 'chattel' status even though placed in some close relation with realty. Not being included within the realty, chattels do not automatically pass with conveyances of the 'land'.

The distinction between 'fixtures' and 'chattels' is not entirely straightforward.[16] The distinction seems largely to turn on two separate but related tests as to the intention of the original owner of the object in question. As Blackburn J said in *Holland v Hodgson*,[17] these two tests relate to the degree or mode of annexation present in the given circumstances and to the general purpose of the annexation. The intention of the annexor is material only in so far as it can be presumed from the degree and purpose of the annexation.[18]

(i) Degree of annexation The older of the two tests takes the more primitive form of an enquiry into the degree of the physical attachment between the object and the pre-existing realty. The more firmly or irreversibly the object is affixed to the earth or to a building thereon, the more likely is the object to be classified as a 'fixture'. However, as Blackburn J observed in *Holland v Hodgson*,[19] when 'the article in question is no further attached to the land than by its own weight it is generally considered to be a mere chattel'.[20]

On this basis the courts have been able to assign the status of 'fixture' to spinning looms bolted to the floor of a mill,[1] an automatic car wash machine

14 The title of the former owner is extinguished even if the attachment to the realty is carried out by someone else (*Reynolds v Ashby & Son* [1904] AC 466 at 472f, 475). The former owner has clearly lost any title to the now non-existent chattel, but may have a remedy for the tort of conversion. See also the related discussion of proprietary estoppel (post, p 312).

15 See *Emanuel (Rundle Mall) Pty Ltd v Commissioner of Stamps* (1986) 39 SASR 582 at 587 per White J.

16 Thus, for instance, it can even be said that certain kinds of earth are not 'land'! In *R v Parker; ex parte Mullavey* [1989] WAR 233 at 237f, the Full Court of Western Australia's Supreme Court held that 'tailings' (ie waste residue or 'leavings' of earlier mining operations) constitute chattel property and thus a species of personal property. Brinsden J conceded (at 238) that if the tailings were later to be 'spread upon and. . .mingled with the earth upon which they rest' they might revert to the status of realty. This approach mirrors the old common law rule that a heap of dung was a mere chattel but could, if spread on the ground, merge with the realty (*Yearworth v Pierce* (1647) Aleyn 31 at 32, 82 ER 900, sub nom *Carver v Pierce* Sty 66 at 73, 82 ER 534, 539). See J.H. Baker, *An Introduction to English Legal History* (3rd edn, London 1990), p 429.

17 (1872) LR 7 CP 328 at 334.

18 *Hobson v Gorringe* [1897] 1 Ch 182 at 193; *Stack v T. Eaton Co* (1902) 4 OLR 335 at 338; *Royal Bank of Canada v Beyak* (1981) 119 DLR (3d) 505 at 509.

19 (1872) LR 7 CP 328 at 335.

20 *Wiltshear v Cottrell* (1853) 1 E & B 674 at 689, 118 ER 589 at 595; *Vaudeville Electric Cinema Ltd v Muriset* [1923] 2 Ch 74 at 83. For a modern example, see *Deen v Andrews* [1986] 1 EGLR 262 at 264G. See also *Stack v T. Eaton Co* (1902) 4 OLR 335 at 338; *Plaza Equities Ltd v Bank of Nova Scotia* (1978) 84 DLR (3d) 609 at 631.

1 *Holland v Hodgson* (1872) LR 7 CP 328 at 340.

bolted to the ground,[2] petrol pumps on a station forecourt,[3] and a bridge fixed on either side of a river.[4] Gas mains and service pipes embedded in the soil likewise lose their chattel character.[5] Consistently with principle, however, the courts have regarded as mere 'chattels' those objects which rest by their own weight, such as printing machinery,[6] a 'Dutch barn',[7] a mobile home,[8] and movable greenhouses.[9] Even if an object is attached to the realty only slightly and can be fairly easily removed, its character is prima facie that of a fixture.[10] Fixtures can thus include anything attached to 'land' by bolts, screws or nails. Somewhat to the surprise of the lay person, even such objects as a bathroom cabinet, overhead heater or extractor fan, if attached to a wall, become prima facie part of the 'land'.

(ii) Purpose of annexation The degree of annexation is not in itself a conclusive test of the status of an object as a fixture or chattel. At most it provides a prima facie characterisation, which may be reversed by evidence of a contrary purpose as to the positioning of a given object in relation to the realty.[11] The more recent case law suggests that the relative significance of the degree of annexation has declined and that considerations of purpose are 'now of first importance'.[12] Generally the tests of degree and purpose coincide in result,[13] but this is not always or necessarily true.

It is clear, for instance, that certain objects which rest on the ground by their own weight may nevertheless be regarded as fixtures if the circumstances are such as to show that they were intended to become part of the land.[14] Thus, 'fixtures' can include heavy marble statues of lions,[15]

2 *Lombard and Ulster Banking Ltd v Kennedy* [1974] NI 20 at 23.

3 *Smith v City Petroleum Co Ltd* [1940] 1 All ER 260 at 261G-H; *Costa Investments Pty Ltd v Mobil Oil Australia Ltd* [1979] 1 SR (WA) 137 at 148.

4 *Montague v Long* (1972) 24 P & CR 240 at 246. Compare *Tate & Lyle Food and Distribution Ltd v GLC* [1983] 2 AC 509 at 534F (jetty).

5 *North Shore Gas Co Ltd v Commissioner of Stamp Duties (NSW)* (1940) 63 CLR 52 at 67f, 70.

6 *Hulme v Brigham* [1943] KB 152 at 157. See also *Northern Press & Engineering Co v Shepherd* (1908) 52 SJ 715 (connection to motor or power supply irrelevant).

7 *Culling v Tufnal* (1694) Bull NP 34.

8 *Royal Bank of Canada v Beyak* (1981) 119 DLR (3d) 505 at 508f.

9 *H.E. Dibble Ltd v Moore* [1970] 2 QB 181 at 189A.

10 *Holland v Hodgson* (1872) LR 7 CP 328 at 335; *Stack v T. Eaton Co* (1902) 4 OLR 335 at 338; *Royal Bank of Canada and Saskatchewan Telecommunications* (1985) 20 DLR (4th) 415 at 417f.

11 However, in the absence of a contrary intention, the prima facie inference to be drawn from the mode and degree of annexation will not be displaced (see *Berkley v Poulett* (1976) 120 Sol Jo 836 at 837).

12 *Hamp v Bygrave* (1983) 266 Estates Gazette 720 at 724. See also *Leigh v Taylor* [1902] AC 157 at 162 per Lord Macnaghten ('. . .its relative importance is probably not what it was in ruder or simpler times'); *In re Hulse* [1905] 1 Ch 406 at 411; *Commonwealth of Australia v New South Wales* (1923) 33 CLR 1 at 34.

13 See eg *Royal Bank of Canada v Beyak* (1981) 119 DLR (3d) 505 at 509f.

14 *Reid v Smith* (1905) 3 CLR 656 at 669; *N.H. Dunn Pty Ltd v L.M. Ericsson Pty Ltd* (1979) 2 BPR 9241 at 9243; *McIntosh v Goulburn City Council* (1985) 3 BPR 9367 at 9374.4. The onus of proof that the items were intended to annex to the realty lies on those who assert that they have ceased to be chattels (see *Holland v Hodgson* (1872) LR 7 CP 328 at 335; *Haggert v Town of Brampton* (1897) 28 SCR 174 at 180f).

15 *D'Eyncourt v Gregory* (1866) LR 3 Eq 382 at 397. Compare, however, *Berkley v Poulett* (1976) 120 Sol Jo 836 at 837.

and substantial 'garden ornaments',[16] if the presence of these items was integral to a permanent architectural design or if they were part of a general scheme for the improvement of the realty.[17]

Likewise, items which are firmly fixed to the realty may yet remain chattels if the purpose of the annexation was merely to facilitate enjoyment of them as chattels and if the degree of annexation was no more than was necessary for the achieving of that purpose.[18] The category of affixed objects which thus persist as chattels has been held to include such items as tapestries,[19] display cases of stuffed birds[20] and a private automatic branch telephone exchange switchboard.[1] The chattel character of such items survives if there was clearly no intention that they should attach indefinitely and *gratis* to the realty.[2]

The relevant intention in this context is usually that of the party who affixes the disputed objects to the realty. Yet even this element of intent cannot be assessed on a purely subjective basis. A person who erects a brick-built construction on land with the intention, after a brief occupancy, of demolishing it and perhaps rebuilding on the same location cannot thereby maintain that the first building is a mere chattel.[3] The status of the affixed object or objects cannot be arbitrarily defined by the simple declaration of the proprietor. While subjective intentions are not wholly irrelevant and may indeed be persuasive, greater weight attaches to the objective intention or underlying purpose of the annexation as disclosed by surrounding circumstances, by the duration of the annexation and, in particular, by shared or communal understandings of the function to be served by the annexation.[4]

An important element in the 'purpose test' appears to relate to whether the purpose of attachment was more heavily weighted towards promoting

16 *Hamp v Bygrave* (1983) 266 Estates Gazette 720 at 726 (not garden gnomes but a number of large urns, a statue and a lead trough!)

17 See *D'Eyncourt v Gregory* (1866) LR 3 Eq 382 at 396. It is on this basis, for instance, that a dry stone wall, although resting only by its own weight, is regarded as part of the realty (*Holland v Hodgson* (1872) LR 7 CP 328 at 335). As Sargant J pointed out in *Vaudeville Electric Cinema Ltd v Muriset* [1923] 2 Ch 74 at 83, the same stones, 'if deposited in a builder's yard and for convenience sake stacked on top of each other in the form of a wall', would remain chattels.

18 *Hamp v Bygrave* (1983) 266 Estates Gazette 720 at 724; *Re Royal Bank of Canada and Saskatchewan Telecommunications* (1985) 20 DLR (4th) 415 at 417f. See also *Attorney-General of the Commonwealth v R.T. Co Pty Ltd* (1957) 97 CLR 146 at 156.

19 *Leigh v Taylor* [1902] AC 157 at 161. Compare, however, *In re Whaley* [1908] 1 Ch 615 at 619f, where a fixture classification was accorded to a picture and tapestry displayed in a house which had been rebuilt as a 'complete specimen of an Elizabethan dwelling-house'.

20 *Viscount Hill v Bullock* [1897] 2 Ch 482 at 483ff.

1 *N.H. Dunn Pty Ltd v L.M. Ericsson Pty Ltd* (1979) 2 BPR 9241 at 9245ff (Court of Appeal of New South Wales) (PABX switchboard attached to land merely 'to steady the chattels and prevent damage or inconvenience from their moving while in use').

2 *Leigh v Taylor* [1902] AC 157 at 159. As soon as physical attachment is proved, the onus of proof rests on the party who asserts the continuing chattel status of the object in question (see *Vaudeville Electric Cinema Ltd v Muriset* [1923] 2 Ch 74 at 83).

3 See *State Savings Bank v Kircheval* (1877) 27 Am Rep 310 at 311; *Reid v Smith* (1906) 3 CLR 656 at 667, 681; *N.H. Dunn Pty Ltd v L.M. Ericsson Pty Ltd* (1979) 2 BPR 9241 at 9244.

4 See *N.H. Dunn Pty Ltd v L.M. Ericsson Pty Ltd* (1979) 2 BPR 9241 at 9244f per Mahoney JA; *Sanwa Australia Leasing Ltd v National Westminster Finance Australia Ltd* (1989) NSW ConvR 55-437 at 58,172 per Powell J.

increased enjoyment of the object itself or towards maximising the use which could be made of the land.[5] The 'degree of annexation' test is thus dwarfed in importance by the question whether the purpose of the annexation was to improve the realty or to enhance the chattel.[6] If the purpose of affixing a chattel was to improve the freehold, then the object—even if only somewhat tenuously affixed—is more readily regarded as a fixture.[7] On this basis wall-to-wall carpeting affixed to the floors of a hotel has been considered a fixture since its attachment was intended for the better use of the building as a hotel rather than for the better use of the carpeting.[8] Likewise, the fact that an object is attached to the land in order to increase its commercial value for mortgage purposes may point irresistibly towards a fixture characterisation.[9] By contrast, a mobile home ranks as a mere chattel, since its attachment to the ground is intended to enhance only the enjoyment of the chattel rather than the enjoyment of the land.[10] Likewise, the installation of a television cable and equipment does not so much improve a building as make it possible for its occupiers to receive cable television.[11]

(b) Legal relevance of the distinction between fixtures and chattels

The distinction between fixtures and chattels—although sometimes elusive—is important for several legal purposes. Fixtures but not chattels pass with a conveyance of an estate in the land.[12] Fixtures can be the subject of theft only if severed from the land.[13] Writing is required in order to create an equitable charge over fixtures since they constitute an interest in land.[14] But perhaps the most significant distinction between fixtures and chattels relates to the circumstances in which they can be removed from the land.

(c) Rights of removal

A chattel may be removed from the land at any time by the owner of the chattel, subject to any contractual commitment (eg, a television hire or hire-

5 *Hellawell v Eastwood* (1851) 6 Ex 295 at 312, 155 ER 554 at 561 per Parke B.

6 Even this is not an easy test to apply. 'In a sense every chattel affixed to a building could be said to improve the building or else it would not be affixed' (*Credit Valley Cable TV/FM Ltd v Peel Condominium Corp No 95* (1980) 107 DLR (3d) 266 at 275). See also *Holland v Hodgson* (1872) LR 7 CP 328 at 339f. In *N.H. Dunn Pty Ltd v L.M. Ericsson Pty Ltd* (1979) 2 BPR 9241 at 9245, a PABX switchboard was not regarded as being attached 'for the better enjoyment of the land'. See also *McIntosh v Goulburn City Council* (1985) 3 BPR 9367 at 9273.

7 *Holland v Hodgson* (1872) LR 7 CP 328 at 339; *Re Davis* [1954] OWN 187 at 190 per Spence J.

8 *La Salle Recreations Ltd v Canadian Camdex Investments Ltd* (1969) 4 DLR (3d) 549 at 556. Compare, however, *Holland v Hodgson* (1872) LR 7 CP 328 at 335.

9 *Haggert v Town of Brampton* (1897) 28 SCR 174 at 182; *Bank of Nova Scotia v Mitz* (1980) 106 DLR (3d) 534 at 539f.

10 *Lichty v Voigt* (1978) 80 DLR (3d) 757 at 761f. See also *Turismo Industries Ltd v Kovacs* (1977) 72 DLR (3d) 710 at 715.

11 *Credit Valley Cable TV/FM Ltd v Peel Condominium Corp No 95* (1980) 107 DLR (3d) 266 at 275. See also *Re Davis* [1954] OWN 187 at 190 (installation of bowling alley not for better use of building but for more efficient bowling).

12 Ante, p 11.

13 Theft Act 1968, s 4(2)(b), (c). See also *R v Dowsey* (1903) 29 VLR 453 at 456.

14 *Jarvis v Jarvis* (1893) 9 TLR 631 at 632; *North Shore Gas Co Ltd v Commissioner of Stamp Duties (NSW)* (1940) 63 CLR 52 at 68.

purchase agreement) which may regulate the location and use of the chattel. The right to remove fixtures is more complex.

(i) Removal by the freehold owner The freehold owner who attaches fixtures to his own land may, of course, remove those fixtures at any time before he contracts to sell his estate to a stranger. The removal of his own fixtures is simply part and parcel of his rights of ownership.[15] However, if the freehold owner contracts to sell his estate to another, the conveyance operates to pass to the purchaser all fixtures which were attached to the land at the date of the contract of sale,[16] unless both vendor and purchaser agreed to the contrary.[17]

(ii) Removal by a tenant for years All fixtures attached by a tenant or lessee accede prima facie to the realty, thus representing an uncompensated benefit for the landlord at the expense of the tenant.[18] In order to mitigate the harshness of this rule,[19] the law has conceded certain exceptions from the strict effect of annexation to the realty.[20] Although a tenant is normally under no obligation to remove fixtures,[1] he has a right to remove any fixtures which he has attached for trade,[2] ornamental and domestic,[3] or certain agricultural[4] purposes. However, such fixtures remain the property of the

15 *In re Whaley* [1908] 1 Ch 615 at 620. In certain circumstances removal of a fixture even by the freehold owner may require planning permission or listed building consent.

16 Law of Property Act 1925, s 62(1), (2); *Phillips v Lamdin* [1949] 2 KB 33 at 41f; *Hamp v Bygrave* (1983) 266 Estates Gazette 720 at 726. Between contract and conveyance the vendor is, in some sense, a trustee for the purchaser (post, p 264).

17 See J.E. Adams, (1986) 136 NLJ 652. It is even possible that the doctrine of proprietary estoppel may confer upon the purchaser the right to claim any chattels which were advertised in an estate agent's particulars of sale as being included in the sale of a house (post, p 328).

18 See *North Shore Gas Co Ltd v Commissioner of Stamp Duties (NSW)* (1940) 63 CLR 52 at 68; *D'Arcy v Burelli Investments Pty Ltd* (1987) 8 NSWLR 317 at 320D.

19 See *Lombard and Ulster Banking Ltd v Kennedy* [1974] NI 20 at 23f; *Mancetter Developments Ltd v Garmanson Ltd* [1986] QB 1212 at 1218G–1219A.

20 The proliferation of exceptions has been linked with the growing solicitude towards trade shown by the courts during the years following the Industrial Revolution. As Lord Kenyon observed in *Penton v Robart* (1801) 2 East 88 at 90, 102 ER 302 at 303, the new leaning in favour of the tenant was 'in support of the interests of trade which is become the pillar of the State. What tenant will lay out his money in costly improvements of the land, if he must leave every thing behind...' See also *Concept Projects Ltd v McKay* [1984] 1 NZLR 560 at 567f; *D'Arcy v Burelli Investments Pty Ltd* (1987) 8 NSWLR 317 at 320D-E.

1 See *Never-Stop Railway (Wembley) Ltd v British Empire Exhibition (1924) Incorporated* [1926] Ch 877 at 886f (licensee's fixtures, but the same principle seems applicable to a lessee).

2 *Climie v Wood* (1869) LR 4 Ex 328 at 329f; *New Zealand Government Property Corpn v H. M. & S. Ltd* [1982] QB 1145 at 1157A-B, 1161E-F. The tenant's right to remove trade fixtures may be excluded by sufficiently clear terms in the lease (see *In re British Red Ash Collieries Ltd* [1920] 1 Ch 326 at 333; *Lombard and Ulster Banking Ltd v Kennedy* [1974] NI 20 at 26f). An action may lie for the tort of waste in respect of failure to make good any damage done by the removal of the tenant's fixtures, at least where the building is left no longer weather-proof (see *Mancetter Developments Ltd v Garmanson Ltd* [1986] QB 1212 at 1219D–1220A, 1224D-E).

3 *Spyer v Phillipson* [1931] 2 Ch 183 at 199ff, 208ff (ornamental panelling and fireplaces removable provided no substantial or irreparable damage was done).

4 Agricultural Holdings Act 1986, s 10.

landlord unless and until the tenant severs them from the realty,[5] which he must do (if at all) during his tenancy or within a reasonable time after its expiry.[6] Fixtures not removed are effectively forfeited to the landlord.[7] However, if a lease expires or is surrendered and is followed immediately by the grant of another term to the same tenant in possession, the tenant does not lose his right to remove fixtures installed during the first term. His right of removal is preserved to the end of the new term.[8]

There is a certain judicial ambivalence as to whether the treatment of 'tenant's fixtures' truly represents an exception to a general rule of accession to the realty. It can be argued quite cogently that the case law concerning 'tenant's fixtures' merely comprises instances where the courts, by engaging in a more benevolent interpretation of the purpose of the annexation, have been more difficult to convince that the object attached to the land has lost its chattel character.[9]

(iii) Removal by a tenant for life Any fixtures attached by a tenant for life under a strict settlement likewise become part of the realty.[10] As such they must be left for the person next entitled (ie the remainderman), with the exception of trade and ornamental and domestic fixtures, which the tenant for life is entitled to remove if he wishes.[11]

(iv) Contractual rights to remove fixtures Certain categories of person may be given a contractual right to remove chattels which have been affixed to realty and which have therefore assumed the character of fixtures.[12] For instance, equipment or machinery may be the subject of a contract for hire or hire-purchase. If that equipment or machinery has been attached to the land of the hirer, it becomes annexed to his realty, and the former chattel owner loses his title.[13] However, the latter may well reserve for himself a

5 See *Holland v Hodgson* (1872) LR 7 CP 328 at 336f; *Hobson v Gorringe* [1897] 1 Ch 182 at 191f; *Crossley Brothers Ltd v Lee* [1908] 1 KB 86 at 90; *North Shore Gas Co Ltd v Commissioner of Stamp Duties (NSW)* (1940) 63 CLR 52 at 70. Compare, however, *In re Hulse* [1905] 1 Ch 406 at 411.

6 *Ex parte Stephens. In re Lavies* (1877) 7 Ch D 127 at 130. It may be that the allowance of a reasonable time for removal following the termination of a lease applies only in the case of tenancies of uncertain duration (eg a tenancy for life or tenancy at will). See *D'Arcy v Burelli Investments Pty Ltd* (1987) 8 NSWLR 317 at 323A. If this is so, the tenant under a fixed term of years or periodic tenancy has no right of removal *after* termination unless there is some new lease or the tenant remains in possession under a genuine colour of right (*Concept Projects Ltd v McKay* [1984] 1 NZLR 560 at 568) or there are circumstances, amounting to an estoppel, in which there arose a reasonable expectation that the time limit would not be strictly enforced (see *Reader v Christian*, 234 SW 155 at 158f (1921)).

7 See *Carabin v Offman* (1989) 55 DLR (4th) 135 at 150.

8 *New Zealand Government Property Corpn v H. M. & S. Ltd* [1982] QB 1145 at 1160A. See (1982) 132 NLJ 786 (H.W. Wilkinson); (1982) 98 LQR 342.

9 For the suggestion that more exacting standards of annexation are applied as between landlord and tenant (thereby favouring the tenant), see *Fisher v Dixon* (1845) 12 Cl & Fin 312 at 328, 8 ER 1426 at 1433; *Webb v Frank Bevis Ltd* [1940] 1 All ER 247 at 251G-H; *Doran v Willard* (1873) 14 NBR 358 at 360; *Bank of Nova Scotia v Mitz* (1980) 106 DLR (3d) 534 at 538; *Royal Bank of Canada v Beyak* (1981) 119 DLR (3d) 505 at 506f.

10 On the role of the tenant for life under a strict settlement, see Chapter 15 (post, p 616).

11 *Lawton v Lawton* (1743) 3 Atk 13 at 15f, 26 ER 811 at 812; *In re Hulse* [1905] 1 Ch 406 at 410f; *Registrar of Titles v Spencer* (1909) 9 CLR 641 at 645f.

12 See generally G. McCormack, [1990] Conv 275.

13 Ante, p 11. See also *Lombard and Ulster Banking Ltd v Kennedy* [1974] NI 20 at 27f.

contractual right to remove the equipment or machinery in the event of default in the payment of the relevant hire charges or hire-purchase instalments. Such a contractual right of removal confers on the former chattel owner an equitable interest in the land known as a 'right of entry',[14] and this interest may be binding on third parties to whom the land is later conveyed.[15]

(5) Trees, plants and flowers

'Land' includes for legal purposes all trees, shrubs, hedges, plants and flowers growing thereon, whether cultivated or wild. Such forms of growth attach to the realty and are thus part of the estate owned by the landowner.[16] However, realty is capable of horizontal division and it is, in this sense, feasible to own and to convey a fee simple estate in a tree which is separate from the fee simple estate in the subjacent soil, provided that the tree has not yet been severed from the realty.[17]

Although ownership of living vegetable matter thus vests prima facie in the owner of the soil, it is now clear that no theft is committed by a stranger who, for non-commercial purposes, picks wild mushrooms, or flowers, fruit or foliage from a plant growing wild upon the land.[18] Such actions do not constitute criminal damage either,[19] even if the motive is commercial, but may however comprise the torts of trespass and conversion.[20]

(6) Minerals and other inorganic substances

Minerals and other inorganic substances present in the ground comprise part of the realty and, unless reserved from the original grant to the landowner

14 See *In re Morrison, Jones & Taylor Ltd* [1914] 1 Ch 50 at 58.

15 In unregistered land this right to remove hired fixtures is enforceable against all third parties other than a bona fide purchaser of a legal estate for value without notice (see *Poster v Slough Estates Ltd* [1968] 1 WLR 1515 at 1520G–1521C, post, p 151), and therefore binds a subsequent equitable mortgagee of the land (*In re Samuel Allen & Sons Ltd* [1907] 1 Ch 575 at 582). In registered land the right to remove hired fixtures is neither a minor interest nor an overriding interest, and cannot apparently be made to bind a purchaser at all—a result which has been described as 'unfortunate' (*Poster v Slough Estates Ltd*, supra at 1521F per Cross J). See generally A.G. Guest and J. Lever, *Hire-Purchase, Equipment Leases and Fixtures*, (1963) 27 Conv (NS) 30.

16 *Bl Comm*, Vol II, p 18. See *Stukeley v Butler* (1615) Hob 168 at 170, 80 ER 316 at 317.

17 See *Liford's Case* (1614) 11 Co Rep 46b at 49a, 77 ER 1206 at 1211; *Stukeley v Butler* (1615) Hob 168 at 173, 80 ER 316 at 320; *John Austin & Sons Ltd v Smith* (1982) 132 DLR (3d) 311 at 319). The largest estate which can exist in a growing tree is presumably a fee simple conditional upon the life of the tree (see *Smith v Daly* [1949] 4 DLR 45 at 48). The characterisation of a forest as realty means that the fee simple in the trees may be owned by one person while the fee simple in the surface soil may be owned by someone else (see eg *Herlakenden's Case* (1589) 4 Co Rep 62a at 63b, 76 ER 1025 at 1029f; *Eastern Construction Co Ltd v National Trust Co Ltd* [1914] AC 197 at 208; *Southwestern Lumber Co v Evans*, 275 SW 1078 at 1082 (1925)). See also *Commonwealth of Australia v New South Wales* (1923) 33 CLR 1 at 34.

18 Theft Act 1968, s 4(3). However, theft is committed if the entire plant is uprooted (see Theft Act 1968, s 4(1)). See also Wildlife and Countryside Act 1981, ss 13(1), 21(3).

19 Criminal Damage Act 1971, s 10(1)(b).

20 *Mills v Brooker* [1919] 1 KB 555 at 558 (post, p 21).

or severed from the realty by him, are annexed to the estate of the landowner.[1] Thus substances ranging from stone and mineral ores to gravel, sand and china clay comprise 'land' for legal purposes. To this principle there exist certain exceptions relating to hydrocarbons. Most notably, the ownership of all coal[2] and of all oil and natural gas[3] is vested exclusively in the state, and the landowner has no right to extract such commodities except by licence from the appropriate state agency.[4] The crown also has a prerogative right to mines of gold and silver.[5]

(7) Airspace

The Latin maxim, *cuius est solum eius est usque ad coelum et ad inferos*, has a qualified application to airspace contained within the vertical planes which mark the territorial boundaries of an estate in land.[6] There is no doubt that the rights of the owner extend to limited portions of airspace both above and below the ground level within those physical geographical boundaries.[7] Thus a conveyance of an estate in the land (whether freehold or leasehold) is effective to convey the void space contained within an immediately subjacent cellar,[8] the void space contained between a false ceiling and an original ceiling,[9] and even the vacant underground spaces from which minerals have been worked out.[10] Likewise, a trespass is committed where an adjoining landowner uses a means of access situated on his own land for the purpose of gaining entry to a cave located partly beneath the surface of his neighbour's land.[11]

It is in connection with superjacent airspace that the principal difficulties arise. Some jurists go so far as to deny that such airspace is capable of ownership at all.[12] However, irrespective of viewpoint on this issue, all seem to be agreed that some pragmatic distinction must be drawn between two different strata of airspace.

1 *Bl Comm*, Vol II, p 18. The subterranean limits of the landowner's rights may in some cases be curtailed by legislation. See *Goldblatt v Town of Hempstead*, 369 US 590 at 595f, 8 L Ed 2d 130 at 135 (1962) (Supreme Court of the United States upheld constitutional validity of town ordinance prohibiting, for safety reasons, excavation below the water table).
2 Coal Act 1938, s 3.
3 Petroleum (Production) Act 1934, s 1(1). See, however, *Earl of Lonsdale v Attorney-General* [1982] 1 WLR 887 at 947E.
4 See Petroleum (Production) Act 1934, s 2(1).
5 *Case of Mines* (1568) 1 Plowd 310 at 336, 75 ER 472 at 510.
6 See *Grigsby v Melville* [1974] 1 WLR 80 at 83F-G, 85G.
7 See *Property in Thin Air*, [1991] CLJ 252.
8 *Grigsby v Melville* [1974] 1 WLR 80 at 84F-G, 86G-H.
9 *Graystone Property Investments Ltd v Margulies* (1984) 269 Estates Gazette 538 at 543. (It was sought to use this space for the construction of a mezzanine floor). See [1984] Conv 171.
10 See *Mitchell v Mosley* [1914] 1 Ch 438 at 450.
11 *Edwards v Sims*, 24 SW2d 619 at 629 (1930); *Edwards v Lee's Administrator*, 96 SW2d 1028 at 1029 (1936) (the 'Great Onyx Cave' in Kentucky).
12 See eg *Re The Queen in Right of Manitoba and Air Canada* (1978) 86 DLR (3d) 631 at 635 per Monnin JA ('. . .air and airspace are not the subject of ownership by anyone, either State or individual, but fall into the category of *res omnium communis*'). This ruling had a devastating impact on the attempt by Manitoba to impose a sales tax in respect of transactions on board aircraft flying over the province: the sales did not take place 'within the province'!

(a) The lower stratum

The lower stratum of airspace comprises that portion of the immediately superjacent airspace whose effective control is necessary for the landowner's reasonable enjoyment of his land at ground level.[13] There is no doubt that the landowner's rights extend to this stratum, whether his rights be analysed in terms of ownership or mere possession. As Douglas J once said in the Supreme Court of the United States, the landowner must have 'exclusive control of the immediate reaches of the enveloping atmosphere' since otherwise 'buildings could not be erected, trees could not be planted, and even fences could not be run.'[14]

(i) Vertical extent Courts are notoriously unwilling to quantify the extent of the airspace which thus falls within the dominion of the landowner, but it seems unlikely in most cases to reach beyond an altitude of much more than 200 metres above roof level.[15] Even within this lower stratum the landowner may not enjoy unqualified dominion. He is subject to such restrictions as may be imposed by a local authority or state agency by way of planning or zoning regulation.[16]

(ii) Invasion It would seem to follow that any lateral invasion of airspace at this low altitude is prima facie actionable in trespass.[17] It is well known that where the branches of a neighbour's tree overhang the land of an adjoining owner, the latter is entitled, without giving prior notice,[18] to lop off the branches which intrude into his airspace, so long as he does not enter upon

13 See *Swetland v Curtiss Airports Corporation*, 55 F2d 201 at 203 (1932).

14 *United States v Causby*, 328 US 256 at 264, 90 L ed 1206 at 1212 (1946). See, however, *Cheyenne Airport Board and City of Cheyenne v Rogers*, 707 P2d 717 at 727ff (1985), where the Supreme Court of Wyoming upheld as constitutional a local zoning ordinance restricting the height of trees in properties situated in the approach zone to an airport. It was held that the ordinance could validly require the landowners to cut back a large cottonwood tree from 48 feet to the permissible height limit of 26 feet.

15 In *Smith v New England Aircraft Co*, 170 NE 385 at 393 (1930), the Supreme Court of Massachussetts regarded as trespass the overflight of an aircraft at a height of 100 feet. In Britain no aircraft may ever fly 'closer than 500 feet to any person, vessel, vehicle or structure' (Rules of the Air Regulations 1991 (SI 1991/2437), Sch, Section II, reg 5(1)(e)). An exception is made for aircraft 'while landing or taking off' (reg 5(2)(d)(i)) and for gliders 'while hill-soaring' (reg 5(2)(d)(ii)).

16 Post, p 1166. The United States Supreme Court has upheld the constitutional validity of various kinds of restriction imposed for aesthetic or practical reasons on the 'air rights' of the landowner. See eg *Welch v Swasey*, 214 US 91 at 107, 53 L ed 923 at 930 (1909) (local restriction on height of buildings); *Penn Central Transport Company v City of New York*, 438 US 104 at 130f, 57 L Ed 2d 631 at 652f (1978) (rejection, as contrary to Landmarks Preservation Law, of proposal to cantilever a 55-storey building above facade of Grand Central Terminal held not to constitute a 'taking' of private property without just compensation).

17 There may also be an actionable nuisance (post, p 21). See generally C.L. Bouvé, *Private Ownership of Airspace*, 1 Air L Rev 232 (1930); H.H. Hackley, *Trespassers in the Sky*, 21 Minn L Rev 773 (1936–37); D.E. Smith, *The Origins of Trespass to Airspace and the Maxim 'Cujus est solum ejus est usque ad coelum'*, (1982) 6 Trent Law Journal 33 at 38.

18 *Lemmon v Webb* [1895] AC 1 at 6, 8.

his neighbour's land for the purpose of so doing.[19] Likewise, either trespass or nuisance is committed through the projection of overhanging eaves,[20] advertising signs,[1] overhead cables and wires,[2] and the jibs of sky cranes.[3] Illicit invasion of airspace is caused even by the poking of a horse's head across a dividing fence,[4] and certainly by the intrusion of low-flying aircraft.[5] All trespasses are actionable *per se*,[6] and an injunction may be granted irrespective of whether damage has resulted.[7] However, the courts have tended to deny that trespass has occurred at all if the intrusion is purely trivial.[8]

19 *Lemmon v Webb* [1895] AC 1 at 4; [1894] 3 Ch 1 at 14f, 17f, 24. (This right is probably better founded in the law of nuisance than in trespass: see *Lemmon v Webb* [1894] 3 Ch 1 at 24; *Bernstein of Leigh (Baron) v Skyviews & General Ltd* [1978] QB 479 at 485E). Because of the ever changing nature of the tree, neither the statute of limitations nor the law of prescription can validate the wrong (*Lemmon v Webb* [1895] AC 1 at 6 (post, p 1107)). However, the adjoining owner commits a conversion if he appropriates either the branches or any fruit thereon (see *Mills v Brooker* [1919] 1 KB 555 at 558). Severance of fruit from the branch does not alter the ownership of the fruit. This remains after severance, as before, in the owner of the tree—even if the severance is caused by the action of the wind or the ripeness of the fruit (see *Mills v Brooker*, supra at 558 per Lush J).

20 *Baten's Case* (1610) 9 Co Rep 53b at 54a/b, 77 ER 810 at 811f; *Fay v Prentice* (1845) 1 CB 828 at 838, 840, 135 ER 769 at 773f; *Ward v Gold* (1969) 211 Estates Gazette 155 at 159. See also *Corbett v Hill* (1869–70) LR 9 Eq 671 at 673f.

1 *Gifford v Dent* [1926] WN 336; *Kelsen v Imperial Tobacco Co (of Great Britain and Ireland) Ltd* [1957] 2 QB 334 at 345.

2 *Barker v Corporation of the City of Adelaide* [1900] SALR 29 at 33f; *Graves v Interstate Power Co*, 178 NW 376 at 377 (1920). See also *Wandsworth Board of Works v United Telephone Co* (1884) 13 QBD 904 at 927 per Fry LJ.

3 *Graham v K.D. Morris & Sons Pty Ltd* [1974] Qd R 1 at 4D; *Lewvest Ltd v Scotia Towers Ltd* (1982) 126 DLR (3d) 239 at 240f (where it appeared that by trespassing the defendant building contractor was saving approximately $500,000, but Goodridge J ruled that if 'a third party can gain economic advantage by using the property of another, then it must negotiate with that other to acquire user rights. The Court cannot give it to him'). See also *John Trenberth Ltd v National Westminster Bank Ltd* (1979) 39 P & CR 104 at 106f; *Anchor Brewhouse Developments Ltd v Berkley House (Docklands Developments) Ltd* (1987) 38 BLR 82 at 94f; *London & Manchester Assurance Co Ltd v O & H Construction Ltd* [1989] 2 EGLR 185 at 186M–187A.

4 *Ellis v Loftus Iron Company* (1874) LR 10 CP 10 at 12ff ('That may be a very small trespass, but it is a trespass in law'). Compare *Gifford v Dent* [1926] WN 336, where Romer J thought that an occupier must have a right to 'put his head out of the window' even if his head therefore protruded into someone else's airspace. (The different perceptions here may turn on the presence or absence of actual damage—however irrelevant this variable is to the strict definition of trespass).

5 See *Smith v New England Aircraft Co*, 170 NE 385 at 393 (1930); *Thrasher v City of Atlanta*, 173 SE 817 at 826 (1934).

6 See eg *Woollerton and Wilson Ltd v Richard Costain Ltd* [1970] 1 WLR 411 at 413E.

7 See eg *Lewvest Ltd v Scotia Towers Ltd* (1982) 126 DLR (3d) 239 at 241. In *Woollerton and Wilson Ltd v Richard Costain Ltd* [1970] 1 WLR 411 at 416C, the operation of the injunction was suspended largely because the offending party had at all times offered a substantial sum as compensation for the trespass. Compare, however, *John Trenberth Ltd v National Westminster Bank Ltd* (1979) 39 P & CR 104 at 108.

8 See eg *Pickering v Rudd* (1815) 4 Camp 219 at 220, 171 ER 70 at 71, where Lord Ellenborough CJ thought no trespass was occasioned by 'firing [a gun] across a field *in vacuo*, no part of the contents touching it'. Compare, however, *Clifton v Viscount Bury* (1887) 4 TLR 8 at 9 (bullet fragments fell on land); *Davies v Bennison* (1927) 22 Tas LR 52 at 55ff (shooting of neighbour's cat on hot tin roof). See also *Lemmon v Webb* [1894] 3 Ch 1 at 11, 24 (no trespass by spreading tree roots but possible remedy in nuisance if damage caused).

(b) The higher stratum

Whatever its application to the lower stratum of airspace, it is now clear that the maxim *cuius est solum* . . . has no relevance at all to the higher stratum of airspace which lies beyond any reasonable possibility of purposeful use by the landowner below.[9] The borderline between the strata is inevitably somewhat imprecise, but the landowner's rights in superjacent airspace seem to be restricted to 'such height as is necessary for the ordinary use and enjoyment of his land and the structures upon it.'[10] Above this height the landowner 'has no greater rights in the air space than any other member of the public.'[11] Any other view would lead to 'the absurdity of a trespass at common law being committed by a satellite every time it passes over a suburban garden.'[12]

(i) Civil immunity of overflying aircraft It follows therefore that overflying aircraft commit no trespass when flying at a height of hundreds or thousands of feet,[13] since the mere intrusion of such aircraft into superjacent airspace causes no interference with any reasonable use to which the landowner may wish to put his land.[14] Section 76(1) of the Civil Aviation Act 1982 provides accordingly that no action shall lie in trespass or nuisance in respect of the flight of an aircraft over any property 'at a height above the ground, which, having regard to wind, weather and all the circumstances of the case is reasonable', provided that the aircraft complies with all relevant regulatory legislation.[15]

9 See the distinction indicated by Griffiths J in *Bernstein of Leigh (Baron) v Skyviews & General Ltd* [1978] QB 479 at 486D, 487F. See also S.S. Ball, *The Vertical Extent of Ownership in Land*, 76 U of Penn L Rev 631 (1928).

10 *Bernstein of Leigh (Baron) v Skyviews & General Ltd* [1978] QB 479 at 488A. See also *Staden v Tarjanyi* (1980) 78 LGR 614 at 621f; *Griggs v Allegheny County*, 369 US 84 at 88f, 7 L Ed 2d 585 at 588 (1962); *Laird v Nelms*, 406 US 797 at 799f, 32 L Ed 2d 499 at 503 (1972).

11 *Bernstein of Leigh (Baron) v Skyviews & General Ltd* [1978] QB 479 at 488B. See, for instance, the descriptions of the upper stratum of airspace as that which 'belongs to the world' (*Hinman v Pacific Air Transport*, 84 F2d 755 at 758 (1936), affd 300 US 655, 81 L ed 865 (1936)) and as 'free territory. . .a sort of "no-man's land"' (*Thrasher v City of Atlanta*, 173 SE 817 at 826 (1934)). The Air Commerce Act of 1926 (49 USC, §171) declared a 'public right of freedom of interstate and foreign air navigation' in the navigable air space of the United States (see now 49 USC, §1304 (Supp 1990)).

12 *Bernstein of Leigh (Baron) v Skyviews & General Ltd* [1978] QB 479 at 487G. At a level closer to earth, it is clear that a local authority byelaw cannot validly prohibit hang-gliding at *any* height above prescribed areas. The byelaw must specify a level below which the hang-glider is not allowed to fly (*Staden v Tarjanyi* (1980) 78 LGR 614 at 623). See also Rules of the Air Regulations 1991 (SI 1991/2437), Sch, Section II, reg 5(2)(d)(ii).

13 This was first recognised in relation to overflight in hot air balloons (see eg *Pickering v Rudd* (1815) 4 Camp 219 at 220f, 171 ER 70 at 71), but is now more generally acknowledged in relation to harmless air traffic in navigable airspace.

14 Excessive noise resulting from the overflight may be actionable in negligence (but see *Nova Mink Ltd v Trans-Canada Airlines* [1951] 2 DLR 241 at 244, 246, 266) or in nuisance.

15 See *Bernstein of Leigh (Baron) v Skyviews & General Ltd* [1978] QB 479 at 489H. The current regulations stipulate that, except 'while landing or taking off in accordance with normal aviation practice', no aircraft shall fly at less than 1,500 feet above the highest fixed object within 2,000 feet of the aircraft (Rules of the Air Regulations 1991 (SI 1991/2437), Sch, Section II, regs 5(1)(a)(ii), 5(1)(e)). The Civil Aviation Act 1982, s 76(2) imposes on the owner of the aircraft an absolute liability for any material damage or loss caused by the aircraft in flight. See *Weedair (NZ) Ltd v Walker* [1961] NZLR 153 at 157; *Southgate v Commonwealth of Australia* (1987) 13 NSWLR 188 at 191E-F (rider thrown by horse when frightened by helicopter flying at 50 to 100 feet above ground).

This statutory immunity does not necessarily cover all forms of overflight. It seems to be agreed that the 1982 Act confers only a right of 'innocent passage',[16] and that it would not, for instance, give tort immunity in respect of an aerobatic display in airspace above private property.[17] Slightly more difficult is the use of overflight for the purpose of aerial photography. Such overflight has been held to constitute neither trespass nor nuisance so long as the aircraft does not interfere with the owner's use of his land (eg through the 'harassment of constant surveillance of his house from the air, accompanied by the photographing of his every activity').[18]

(ii) Aerial surveillance More controversial is the use of aerial surveillance as a regular means of law enforcement. Overflight by police helicopters is regularly used not only for the purpose of traffic control, but also for the detection of crime and for the searching of areas which would otherwise be inaccessible in the absence of a properly obtained warrant. There is here a dangerous potential for invasion of the individual's right to privacy, the problem being intensified by the lack of any effective practice of accountability for policing activity.

There appears to be no English decision on the proper balance which requires to be maintained in this context between the individual's legitimate interest in his own freedom and privacy and the general public interest in the detection and due prosecution of crime. In the United States warrantless aerial searches have until recently been upheld as constitutionally valid,[19] at least so long as such searches are 'routine'.[20] However, there are now some indications that the courts may be starting to assert more control over the issue of 'backyard surveillance'. In *People v Cook*[1] the Supreme Court of California held by a majority that a warrantless aerial search conducted by police frustrated the individual's 'reasonable expectation of privacy from

16 Shawcross and Beaumont, *Air Law* (3rd edn 1966), p 561.

17 See J.E. Richardson, *Private Property Rights in the Air Space at Common Law*, (1953) 31 Can Bar Rev 117 at 120.

18 *Bernstein of Leigh (Baron) v Skyviews & General Ltd* [1978] QB 479 at 489G. See (1977) 93 LQR 491 (R. Wacks). (It did not help that the television company of which the plaintiff was chairman had recently made a series of films involving substantial aerial photography over wide areas of private property!) See also *E.I. du Pont de Nemours & Co v Christopher*, 431 F2d 1012 at 1015 (1970), affd 400 US 1024, 27 L Ed 2d 637 (1971) (aerial photography an unlawful means of obtaining a trade secret). It is, however, no trespass either to land or to airspace to photograph someone's property from a position outside that property by standing in a public street or on adjoining land (*Bathurst CC v Saban* (1985) 2 NSWLR 704 at 706B). See *Property in Thin Air*, [1991] CLJ 252 at 263f.

19 See eg *Dean v Superior Court for County of Nevada*, 110 Cal Rptr 585 at 589f (1973) (observation of marijuana field); *People v Superior Court*, 112 Cal Rptr 764 at 765 (1974); *Burkholder v Superior Court*, 158 Cal Rptr 86 at 88f (1979); *People v Lashmett*, 389 NE2d 888 at 890 (1979); *United States v Allen*, 633 F2d 1282 at 1290 (1980); *People v St Amour*, 163 Cal Rptr 187 at 192 (1980). Compare, however, *People v Sneed*, 108 Cal Rptr 146 at 151 (1973) (helicopter search from position 20–25 feet above ground was 'unreasonable governmental intrusion into the serenity and privacy of [defendant's] backyard').

20 For an incisive criticism of American practice, see S.A. Higgins, *Aerial Surveillance: Overlooking the Fourth Amendment*, 50 Fordham L Rev 271 at 279 (1981–82).

1 221 Cal Rptr 499 (1985).

purposeful police surveillance of his backyard from the air'.[2] The Court firmly rejected the contention that 'the air lanes are modern highways' and that aerial surveillance by the police is 'but a form of routine "street patrol" to which the modern public must be deemed to be resigned.'[3]

In the view adopted by the majority in the Supreme Court, purposeful surveillance from the air 'simply lays open everything and everyone below—whether marijuana plants, nude sunbathers, or family members relaxing in their lawn chairs—to minute inspection.'[4] While conceding that 'one may have to put up with the occasional downward glance of a passing pilot or passenger',[5] the majority refused to accept that the police should be allowed arbitrarily to violate the individual's reasonable expectation that his home and private yard would not 'be spied upon from the air by police officers scrutinising the property for evidence of crime.'[6] Accordingly, the Court denounced 'the Orwellian notion that precious liberties derived from the Framers [of the Constitution] simply shrink as the government acquires new means of infringing them.'[7] The Court observed that 'a society where individuals are required to erect opaque cocoons within which to carry on any affairs they wish to conduct in private, and the concomitant chill such a requirement would place on lawful outdoor activity, would be inimical to the vision of legitimate privacy which underlies [the] state Constitution.'[8] The defendant's conviction for the offence of unlawfully cultivating marijuana was therefore overturned.[9]

It seems unlikely that English courts will spring with similar vigilance to the defence of the privacy claims of the landowner.[10]

(8) Water

Although English law can contemplate with equanimity the conveyance of

2 Post, p 895. In *Oliver v United States*, 80 L Ed 2d 214 at 224 (1984), the Supreme Court of the United States seemed to say that both 'the public and police lawfully may survey lands from the air', but this was not read in *People v Cook* as expressing approval of 'intense aerial scrutiny of an enclosed backyard'.
3 221 Cal Rptr 499 at 504.
4 221 Cal Rptr 499 at 505 per Grodin J.
5 221 Cal Rptr 499 at 501.
6 221 Cal Rptr 499 at 504. The police surveillance in this case occurred from a height of 1,600 feet, with the aid of photography using a 200 mm telephoto lens.
7 221 Cal Rptr 499 at 505.
8 221 Cal Rptr 499 at 501. The Supreme Court of the United States has since held by a five-to-four majority in *California v Ciraolo*, 90 L Ed 2d 210 at 217f (1986), that the Fourth Amendment protection of privacy is not violated by 'warrantless naked-eye observation' from an altitude of 1000 feet. See also *Dow Chemical Co v United States*, 90 L Ed 2d 226 at 238 (1986).
9 Lucas J entered a vigorous dissent, arguing that the '*only* privacy interest significantly infringed by such overflights is the interest of the marijuana grower in concealing his illegal crop. . .we are not concerned here with the privacy interests of nude sunbathers, religious cultists, political activists, or *anyone* except marijuana growers. The majority pays lip service to the self-evident principle that no one has a reasonable expectation of privacy in the conduct of his *criminal* affairs. . .but ultimately the majority fails to apply that sound principle here.' (221 Cal Rptr 499 at 508).
10 Post, p 896. In particular it is noteworthy that the prohibition on aircraft flying within 500 feet of any person or structure (ante, p 20) has no application to an aircraft in the service of a police authority (Rules of the Air Regulations 1991 (SI 1991/2437), Sch, Section II, reg 5(2)(b)).

an estate in thin air, it has substantially more difficulty in relation to a conveyance of water.[11] Inland water (whether a river or lake) is considered to be merely 'a species of land',[12] in that lawyers regard such areas of water as simply areas of 'land covered with water'.[13]

(a) Conveyancing implications

A conveyance of an estate in the land carries with it certain rights over the superjacent water,[14] whereas a grant of the water itself without reference to the land would pass merely a right of fishing.[15] In the absence of contrary evidence,[16] a conveyance of riparian land bounded by a non-tidal river carries with it the soil *ad medium filum* (or to the middle point of the river), whether the conveyance be of a freehold or leasehold estate.[17]

(b) Limits of the landowner's rights

The mere fact that rights over water are attributed to the owner of the underlying land does not necessarily confer upon that owner an absolute title to the water itself.[18] It is clear that the landowner does not have any property as such in water which flows through his land in a defined channel (eg a river)[19] or in water which percolates through his land.[20] His right to abstract water is, for instance, strictly controlled by the requirement that

11 In English law water is incapable of being owned (*Alfred F. Beckett Ltd v Lyons* [1967] Ch 449 at 481G–482A; *Attorney-General ex rel Yorkshire Derwent Trust Ltd v Brotherton* [1992] 1 AC 425 at 441A per Lord Goff of Chieveley). See Chapter 21 (post, p 1045).

12 *Bl Comm*, Vol II, p 18.

13 *Ibid*, p 18. 'The solum of a river bed is a property differing in no essential characteristic from other lands' (*Attorney-General for British Columbia v Attorney-General for Canada* [1914] AC 153 at 167 per Viscount Haldane LC).

14 *Bl Comm*, Vol II, p 18.

15 *Bl Comm*, Vol II, p 19.

16 *Tait-Jamieson v G C Smith Metal Contractors Ltd* [1984] 2 NZLR 513 at 514.

17 *Tilbury v Silva* (1890) 45 Ch D 98 at 108f; *City of London Land Tax Commissioners v Central London Railway Co* [1913] AC 364 at 371, 379; *Southern Centre of Theosophy Inc v State of South Australia* [1982] AC 706 at 715G; *Tait-Jamieson v G C Smith Metal Contractors Ltd* [1984] 2 NZLR 513 at 514.

18 The owner of the bed and soil of a lake or river, if he enjoys a corporeal right to fishing, is thereby entitled to restrain canoeing on the water (*Wills' Trustees v Cairngorm Canoeing and Sailing School Ltd* 1976 SC 30 at 63; *Tennent v Clancy* [1987] IR 15 at 20, 22).

19 *Mason v Hill* (1833) 5 B & Ad 1 at 24f, 110 ER 692 at 701. At common law, however, the owner or occupier of land situated upon the banks of a natural water course (whether running on the surface or underground) has a natural right to receive and is bound to accept the flow of water past or through his land. He is not entitled to deprive those lower down the stream of its flow, nor to pen it back upon the lands of his upstream neighbour (*Home Brewery Co Ltd v William Davis & Co (Leicester) Ltd* [1987] QB 339 at 345B-D).

20 *Ballard v Tomlinson* (1885) 29 Ch D 115 at 120f, 126. A higher owner or occupier has no duty to preserve the flow to lower occupiers of water which flows or percolates freely above or below ground level in undefined channels (*Chasemore v Richards* (1859) 7 HL Cas 349 at 382, 11 ER 140 at 153; *Home Brewery Co Ltd v William Davis & Co (Leicester) Ltd* [1987] QB 339 at 345D-G). The lower occupier has no remedy even though he has hitherto enjoyed long user of an undiminished flow (*Broadbent v Ramsbotham* (1856) 11 Ex 602 at 615ff, 156 ER 971 at 976f), and even though the abstraction by the higher occupier be motivated by malice (*Bradford Corpn v Pickles* [1895] AC 587 at 592, 595, 600).

he should obtain a licence to do so from the relevant water authority.[1] However, the landowner does have an exclusive right to fish in any non-tidal river which runs through his land.[2] If he owns only one of the banks of the river, he owns the subjacent land out to the *medium filum*,[3] and each riparian owner may fish as far across the river as he can reach by normal casting or spinning. So long as he stands on his own bank or wades out no further than the *medium filum*, each riparian owner may cast beyond the *medium filum*.[4]

(9) Avulsion and accretion

Titles to land are, in relatively rare cases, affected by the processes of avulsion and accretion. The common law recognises as a matter both of fairness and of convenience that where land is bounded by water the forces of nature are likely to cause changes in the boundary between the land and the water. Where these changes are gradual and imperceptible,[5] the law considers the title to the land as applicable to the land as it may be changed from time to time,[6] even if there still remains a means of identifying the original boundaries of the property.[7]

(a) Effects on title

If part of a landowner's land is removed by erosion or 'diluvion' caused by an advance of the water, the landowner is treated as losing a portion

1 Water Resources Act 1991, s 24(1). No licence is required if the water is abstracted merely for the domestic purposes of the occupier's household or for agricultural purposes other than spray irrigation (Water Resources Act 1991, s 27(4)(b)).

2 'The general principle is that fisheries are in their nature mere profits of the soil over which the water flows, and that the title to a fishery arises from the right to the solum' (*Attorney-General for British Columbia v Attorney-General for Canada* [1914] AC 153 at 167). See also *Ecroyd v Coulthard* [1898] 2 Ch 358 at 366, 374; *Jones v Llanrwst UDC* [1911] 1 Ch 393 at 401. If the right to fish is severed from the solum, it becomes a 'profit *à prendre*' (post, p 1045). The public has no general right of fishing except in the open sea and in tidal waters (see *Blundell v Catterall* (1821) 5 B & Ald 268 at 294, 106 ER 1190 at 1199f), but where there is a public right to fish, the common law recognises a right of bait-digging on the foreshore as ancillary to its exercise (*Anderson v Alnwick DC* (1993) *Times*, 21 January).

3 *Micklethwait v Newlay Bridge Co* (1886) 33 Ch D 133 at 145, 152, 155; *Tait-Jamieson v G C Smith Metal Contractors Ltd* [1984] 2 NZLR 513 at 515f.

4 *Fothringham v Kerr* (1984) 48 P & CR 173 at 186f (House of Lords). See (1984) 134 NLJ 567.

5 The requirement that the relevant change be gradual and imperceptible is widely accepted. See *Bl Comm*, Vol II, p 262; *Attorney-General v McCarthy* [1911] 2 IR 260 at 277ff; *Southern Centre of Theosophy Inc v State of South Australia* [1982] AC 706 at 716C; *Clarke v City of Edmonton* [1929] 4 DLR 1010 at 1015; *Port Franks Properties Ltd v The Queen* (1980) 99 DLR (3d) 28 at 36. Rapid, easily perceived and violent shifts of land by avulsion do not affect pre-existing legal boundaries (*State of Hawaii by Kobayashi v Zimring*, 566 P2d 725 at 734 (1977)).

6 Any change caused by the deliberate action of the claimant falls outside the doctrine of accretion (*Brighton and Hove General Gas Co v Hove Bungalows Ltd* [1924] 1 Ch 372 at 390; *Southern Centre of Theosophy Inc v State of South Australia* [1982] AC 706 at 720A).

7 *Hazlett v Presnell* (1982) 149 CLR 107 at 116.

of his land.[8] If, however, an addition is made to the land by wind-blown or water-borne deposit,[9] the landowner's land is regarded *pro tanto* as extending into the area which was previously water.[10] This doctrine of accretion does not apply to substantial and recognisable changes in boundary which take place suddenly.[11] However, the mere fact that the leading-edge of a sand dune may move forward two or three feet in a perceptible jump over a 24 hour period in conditions of strong winds does not disqualify such an advance as an allowable accretion to the land, if in the long term the movement is imperceptible.[12] The title extended by accretion also confers a right to any minerals situated below the newly claimed land.[13] Land is accordingly conveyed prima facie subject to and with the benefit of such subtractions and additions as may take place over the course of time.[14]

(b) *Mobile estates in land*

It is even possible that land, the ultimate immovable, may in fact 'move', even though this can bring about the improbable result that someone holds title to a constantly mobile piece of land. For instance, it is quite feasible that the pattern of tide levels on a coastline may vary over time, with the result that the foreshore extending between the high- and low-tide marks shifts position. The foreshore is normally vested in the crown,[15] but if a portion of the foreshore has been conveyed to an individual (or more usually a local authority), the title conveyed may well, in the absence of a contrary intention, relate to a moving strip of foreshore.[16]

8 *Southern Centre of Theosophy Inc v State of South Australia* [1982] AC 706 at 716D. See also *Fellowes v Rother DC* [1983] 1 All ER 513 at 515a.

9 The distinction between these forms of deposit, even if possible, is irrelevant (*Southern Centre of Theosophy Inc v State of South Australia* [1982] AC 706 at 719H–720A, 720D).

10 *R v Lord Yarborough* (1824) 3 B & C 91 at 105, 107 ER 668 at 673; *Gifford v Lord Yarborough* (1828) 5 Bing 163, 130 ER 1023; *Dunstan v Hell's Gate Enterprises Ltd* (1986) 22 DLR (4th) 568 at 584. The doctrine of accretion applies equally to lakes and rivers (*Southern Centre of Theosophy Inc v State of South Australia*, supra at 715F; *State of Hawaii by Kobayashi v Zimring*, 566 P2d 725 at 734 (1977)). See H.W. Wilkinson, (1982) 132 NLJ 1164; (1983) 99 LQR 412 (P. Jackson); W. Howarth, [1986] Conv 247.

11 The Supreme Court of Hawaii has held that extensions of land created by catastrophic lava flows should inure, not for the windfall gain of a limited segment of the population of an overcrowded island, but for the public as a whole. The added land is held by the government in public trust (*State of Hawaii by Kobayashi v Zimring*, 566 P2d 725 at 735 (1977)).

12 *Southern Centre of Theosophy Inc v State of South Australia* [1982] AC 706 at 722F, 723B.

13 *Re Eliason and Registrar, Northern Alberta Land Registration District* (1981) 115 DLR (3d) 360 at 364.

14 This rule can be excluded by clear evidence of a contrary intention, but the mere fact that the grant of land was accompanied by a map delineating the boundary is not conclusive against the operation of the rule (see *Southern Centre of Theosophy Inc v State of South Australia* [1982] AC 706 at 716F-G; *Attorney-General v McCarthy* [1911] 2 IR 260 at 284).

15 See *Blundell v Catterall* (1821) 5 B & Ald 268 at 293, 304, 106 ER 1190 at 1199, 1203.

16 See *Baxendale v Instow Parish Council* [1982] Ch 14 at 23B-C (contrary intention shown). See also *Re Monashee Enterprises Ltd and Minister of Recreation and Conservation for British Columbia* (1979) 90 DLR (3d) 521 at 531. A movable fee simple seems not to be a fee simple absolute in possession, and can therefore take effect only under the Settled Land Act 1925 (see R.E. Annand, [1982] Conv 208 at 211). See also *Scratton v Brown* (1825) 4 B & C 485 at 498, 107 ER 1140 at 1145.

(10) Wild animals

It is clearly established that wild animals[17] cannot, while alive, be the subject of absolute ownership in English law.[18] However, the landowner whose land they inhabit has a 'qualified property'[19] which arises *ratione soli*[20] : he has a right to hunt and catch such animals,[1] thereby reducing them into his possession.[2] This 'qualified property' of the landowner in wild animals persists only so long as he 'can keep them in sight' and has 'power to pursue them'.[3] When the animals escape to the land of a neighbour, it is the latter who takes over the 'qualified property' in them.[4]

As soon as wild animals are killed, they become personalty and therefore proper objects of absolute ownership by the owner of the soil.[5] Thus if

17 There is no definition of a 'wild animal' for this purpose, but in its common law usage the phrase is sufficiently narrow to exclude fish and sufficiently broad to encompass birds, insects and reptiles. The criterion of 'wildness' seems to require that an animal should not by habit or training live with or in association with or in the service of man (see *McQuaker v Goddard* [1940] 1 KB 687 at 696). The distinction between domesticated and undomesticated species is highly unsatisfactory. A homing pigeon is 'wild' (*Hamps v Darby* [1948] 2 KB 311 at 320f), as is a circus elephant (*Filburn v People's Palace and Aquarium Co Ltd* (1890) 25 QBD 258 at 260f; *Behrens v Bertram Mills Circus Ltd* [1957] 2 QB 1 at 15), whereas a camel is always 'tame' (*McQuaker v Goddard* [1940] 1 KB 687 at 694f).

18 *Case of Swans* (1592) 7 Co Rep 15b at 17b, 77 ER 435 at 438; *Blades v Higgs* (1865) 11 HLCas 621 at 638, 11 ER 1474 at 1481 per Lord Chelmsford; *Bl Comm*, Vol II, p 391. See generally Tim Bonyhady, *The Law of the Countryside: the Rights of the Public* (Abingdon 1987), pp 215ff.

19 *Bl Comm*, Vol II, p 391.

20 That is, 'in consideration of the property of the soil whereon they are found' (*Bl Comm*, Vol II, p 393). See also *Blades v Higgs* (1865) 11 HLCas 621 at 634, 11 ER 1474 at 1480 per Lord Westbury LC ('...ownership of the game is considered as incident to the property in the land'); *Kearry v Pattinson* [1939] 1 KB 471 at 479.

1 This right can be extended to any person to whom the freehold or leasehold landowner gives consent (*Walden v Hensler* (1987) 163 CLR 561 at 565).

2 *Blades v Higgs* (1865) 11 HLCas 621 at 631, 11 ER 1474 at 1478f. This common law right is nowadays curtailed by conservationist legislation aimed at the protection of rare or endangered species, although such legislation still grants substantial immunity to the landowner or occupier (see eg Wildlife and Countryside Act 1981, ss 2(2), 4(3), 10(4), 27(1)). There are also anomalous exceptions to the landowner's rights which include the little known, but much flouted, provision contained in section 3 of the Game Act 1831 which prohibits hunting for game on Sundays and Christmas Day!

3 *Bl Comm*, Vol II, p 393 (swarm of bees). However, 'power to pursue' was construed in *Kearry v Pattinson* [1939] 1 KB 471 at 479 to mean 'lawful power' to pursue without committing trespass. However, provided the pursuit was lawful, Goddard LJ went so far as to suggest (at 481) that no stranger was entitled to frustrate the pursuit by intercepting the animal and capturing it himself (but compare *Young v Hichens* (1844) 6 QB 606 at 611, 115 ER 228 at 230). See also (1939) 17 Can Bar Rev 130; G.W. Paton, *Bees and the Law*, (1939–41) 2 Res Judicata 22. It is possible that interception of an animal which is in the course of being reduced into possession may now be theft (see Theft Act 1968, s 4(4)).

4 *Sutton v Moody* (1697) 1 Ld Raym 250 at 251, 91 ER 1063 at 1064; *Kearry v Pattinson* [1939] 1 KB 471 at 480f (swarm of bees). It has been suggested that certain distinctive or exotic animals (eg a tiger which has escaped from a zoo) must represent an exception to this rule (see T. Beven, 22 Harvard L Rev 465 at 481f (1908–09)). There may be an ancient doctrine of 'hot pursuit' which gives a landowner immunity from trespass when pursuing vermin from his own land on to a neighbour's land if the purpose of the incursion is merely the destruction of the vermin (see *Earl of Essex v Capel*, Hertford Assizes 1809, cited in *Locke on the Game Laws of England and Wales* (5th edn London 1866), p 45), but even this immunity is now somewhat dubious (see *Paul v Summerhayes* (1878) 4 QBD 9 at 11). See Tim Bonyhady, op cit, p 224.

5 *Blades v Higgs* (1865) 11 HLCas 621 at 631, 11 ER 1474 at 1478f.

A kills a wild animal found on his own land, it belongs to him absolutely.[6] Likewise, if A trespasses on the land of B and there kills a wild animal, the absolute property vests in B, both *ratione soli*[7] and because the trespasser may not profit by his wrong.[8] Anomalously, however, if A starts the chase on the land of B and hunts the animal into the land of C, where he eventually kills it, it seems that the absolute property in the animal vests inexplicably in A,[9] although A may well be liable in trespass to both B and C.[10]

(11) Fish

A landowner who by reason of the ownership of land owns also a right to fish in superjacent water[11] is regarded as having a 'qualified property' in fish found within the limits of his 'fishery'.[12] The fish become his absolute property only when he catches and kills them. If those fish are caught by some unauthorised person, the absolute property in the fish vests—on the analogy of wild animals—not in the trespasser but in the owner of the fishing rights.[13]

(12) Lost and hidden objects

In certain circumstances a landowner may have a right to lost or hidden things found in or on his land where the true owner's identity is unknown.[14] In this context a primary distinction appears to be drawn between those things which are hidden *under* the surface of the land and those which are found merely resting *on* the land surface.

(a) Objects found within the ground

It is presumed that the owner in fee simple has possession of, and is therefore entitled to, all things concealed within the ground itself, even though before the date of discovery he was wholly unaware of the presence of the object

6 *Blades v Higgs* (1865) 11 HLCas 621 at 638, 11 ER 1474 at 1481 per Lord Chelmsford.

7 *Sutton v Moody* (1697) 1 Ld Raym 250 at 251, 91 ER 1063 at 1064, 5 Mod 375 at 376, 87 ER 715; *Earl of Lonsdale v Rigg* (1856) 11 Ex 654 at 675, 679, 682, 156 ER 992 at 1002ff, 1 Hurl & N 923 at 937, 156 ER 1475 at 1481; *Blades v Higgs* (1865) 11 HLCas 621 at 634, 11 ER 1474 at 1480.

8 *Blades v Higgs* (1865) 11 HLCas 621 at 632f, 11 ER 1474 at 1479.

9 *Sutton v Moody* (1697) 1 Ld Raym 250 at 251, 91 ER 1063 at 1064; *Churchward v Studdy* (1811) 14 East 249 at 251, 104 ER 596 at 597; *Blades v Higgs* (1865) 11 HLCas 621 at 633, 11 ER 1474 at 1479, but see the doubts expressed by Lord Chelmsford at 639f, 1482. In any event, A's ownership in this example holds good only so long as B's original entitlement arose merely *ratione soli.* If B were the owner of some special franchise, his rights would persist even if the animal were killed in the land of C (*Blades v Higgs* (1865) 11 HLCas 621 at 632f, 11 ER 1474 at 1479).

10 *Sutton v Moody* (1697) 1 Ld Raym 250 at 251, 91 ER 1063 at 1064.

11 Ante, p 26.

12 *Nicholls v Ely Beet Sugar Factory Ltd* [1936] Ch 343 at 347.

13 *Nicholls v Ely Beet Sugar Factory Ltd* [1936] Ch 343 at 347. The unlawful taking of the fish is not theft as such but may constitute an offence under Theft Act 1968, s 32(1), Sch 1, para 2(1).

14 The law relating to claims of ownership and possession of goods found on someone else's land has been said to be 'in an unsatisfactory state' (*R v Hancock* [1990] 2 QB 242 at 251H–252A per Auld J). For an excellent discussion of the relevant problems, see Tim Bonyhady, op cit, p 268ff. See also D.C. Hoath, *Some Conveyancing Implications of 'Finding' Disputes*, [1990] Conv 348.

and even though he is not the actual finder.[15] This rule has been supported by reference to the maxim *cuius est solum eius est usque ad coelum et ad inferos.*[16] A trespasser can assert no lawful title to things found by him within the ground,[17] and may even be liable to prosecution if his find was facilitated by the use of a metal detector in a 'protected place' of archaeological importance.[18]

(b) Chattels found on the ground

At least until fairly recently the law of finding of chattels has been somewhat unclear.[19] However, it now seems that an 'occupier' of a building has rights superior to those of a finder in respect of chattels found upon or in that building 'if, but only if, before the chattel is found, he has manifested an intention to exercise control over the building and the things which may be upon it or in it.'[20] This intention may be manifested either expressly or impliedly,[1] and the title to the discovered chattel depends on the individual facts of each case. Thus a valuable chattel found by a stranger on the floor of a bank vault belongs to the bank,[2] whereas the same chattel found in a public park belongs prima facie to the finder, there being in the latter instance no manifest intention on the part of the landowner or occupier to exercise the required degree of control.[3]

(i) 'Finders keepers' The case law tends to suggest that there may be unsuspected legal force in the lay person's maxim 'finders keepers', and that the courts will not be easily convinced that the landowner or occupier has formulated the intention to control which is needed to rebut the popular aphorism. In *Parker v British Airways Board*[4] a gold bracelet found by a passenger on the floor of an executive lounge at Heathrow Airport was held to belong to that passenger when attempts to locate the true owner ultimately proved fruitless.[5] In *Bridges v Hawkesworth*[6] money found by a customer

15 *Elwes v Brigg Gas Company* (1886) 33 Ch D 562 at 568f (prehistoric longboat); *Attorney-General of the Duchy of Lancaster v G.E. Overton (Farms) Ltd* [1981] Ch 333 at 338C. *South Staffordshire Water Co v Sharman* [1896] 2 QB 44 is supportable on the ground that the rings found in this case were embedded in mud at the bottom of a pool of water (see *Parker v British Airways Board* [1982] QB 1004 at 1010E, 1013A).

16 *Elwes v Brigg Gas Company* (1886) 33 Ch D 562 at 568. See also *Parker v British Airways Board* [1982] QB 1004 at 1010C ('the chattel is to be treated as an integral part of the realty as against all but the true owner').

17 *Elwes v Brigg Gas Company* (1886) 33 Ch D 562 at 568. In the case of treasure trove, however, he may receive an ex gratia payment of the full value of the find notwithstanding his status as a trespasser (post, p 32).

18 Ancient Monuments and Archaeological Areas Act 1979, s 42(1).

19 *Parker v British Airways Board* [1982] QB 1004 at 1008B.

20 *Parker v British Airways Board* [1982] QB 1004 at 1018A. See also *South Staffordshire Water Co v Sharman* [1896] 2 QB 44 at 47.

1 *Parker v British Airways Board* [1982] QB 1004 at 1018B-C.

2 *Parker v British Airways Board* [1982] QB 1004 at 1019B, 1020C.

3 *Parker v British Airways Board* [1982] QB 1004 at 1019B-C.

4 *Parker v British Airways Board* [1982] QB 1004 at 1019D, 1020G-H, 1021E. See [1982] CLJ 242 (A. Tettenborn); (1982) 45 MLR 683 (S. Roberts).

5 The decision was supported by the argument that if 'finders had no prospect of any reward, they would be tempted to pass by without taking any action or to become concealed keepers of articles which they found' ([1982] QB 1004 at 1017B).

6 (1851) 21 LJ QB 75 at 78.

on the floor of a shop was held to belong to the finder rather than the shopkeeper. The finder's claim will normally prevail except in special circumstances involving, for instance, premises with extremely restricted access (eg a private house or bank vault), where the control exerted by the owner or occupier clearly indicates an overwhelming *animus possidendi* (or intention to possess).[7]

(ii) Trespassing finders The rights of a trespassing finder are 'frail' but not wholly non-existent.[8] Although he cannot resist the claim of the occupier of the land on which the property was found, the common law gives him 'very limited rights' to retain the chattel—if only in order to prevent a 'free-for-all situation. . .in that anyone could take the article from the trespassing finder.'[9]

(13) Treasure trove

At common law the specific kind of find known as 'treasure trove' vests automatically in the crown,[10] irrespective of whose land concealed the treasure.[11]

(a) Scope

The scope of 'treasure trove' is, however, fairly narrowly defined. In *Attorney-General of the Duchy of Lancaster v G.E. Overton (Farms) Ltd*[12] the Court of Appeal held that only objects of gold and silver are capable of constituting 'treasure trove'.[13] Moreover, for the term 'treasure trove' to apply properly to a coin (which is almost necessarily an alloy of some kind), the Court ruled that

7 *Parker v British Airways Board* [1982] QB 1004 at 1020B-C.
8 *Parker v British Airways Board* [1982] QB 1004 at 1009D.
9 *Parker v British Airways Board* [1982] QB 1004 at 1009D-E.
10 The mere fact that ancient coins discovered with a metal detector *may* turn out to be treasure trove does not necessarily justify a conviction for theft from the crown (*R v Hancock* [1990] 2 QB 242 at 251D-G).
11 *Co Inst*, Part III, p 132. The only exception to crown ownership occurs where the landowner can prove that a crown franchise to receive treasure trove had been granted to one of his predecessors in title (see *Attorney-General v Trustees of the British Museum* [1903] 2 Ch 598 at 608). The ownership of goods which fall short of the definition of 'treasure trove' vests in the relevant landowner (see *Attorney-General of the Duchy of Lancaster v G.E. Overton (Farms) Ltd* [1981] Ch 333 at 338C).
12 [1982] Ch 277 at 291E, 293E. See [1981] Conv 385 (A.A. Preece); (1981) 125 SJ 92 (W.A. Greene).
13 This limitation excludes a vast range of other antiquarian finds from the scope of the royal prerogative in respect of treasure trove (see N.E. Palmer, *Treasure Trove and the Protection of Antiquities*, (1981) 44 MLR 178 at 180f). See also *Attorney-General of the Duchy of Lancaster v G.E. Overton (Farms) Ltd* [1982] Ch 277 at 293B-D. In the Supreme Court of Ireland in *Webb v Ireland* [1988] IR 353 at 390f, Walsh J, although disavowing the notion of prerogative rights in treasure trove, suggested that a modern sovereign state, concerned to emphasise its historical origins, may claim rights of ownership in all antiquities of national importance extending beyond those of gold and silver. (*Webb v Ireland* concerned the Derrynaflan hoard, found in 1980, which comprised one of the most significant discoveries ever made of early Christian art.)

the coin must contain a 'substantial' amount of gold or silver.[14] 'Treasure trove' must be found concealed '*in* the earth, or other private place', and the owner of the treasure must be unknown.[15] A claim of 'treasure trove' can succeed only if it is inferable that the original owner hid the property with the intention of later recovery.[16] The crown's claim to the treasure will fail if there is evidence that the original owner simply lost or abandoned it,[17] although a heavy onus rests on the landowner to prove that the goods were lost or abandoned rather than merely temporarily hidden.[18]

The rationale underlying the law of treasure trove thus seems to be that if the original owner hides his treasure in a secret place, intending to reclaim it later, but then dies, his secret 'also dies with him', in which case the property vests in the crown. If, however, the original owner deliberately abandons or casually loses the treasure, he is presumed to have 'returned it into the common stock', in which case it 'belongs, as in a state of nature, to the first occupant, or finder'.[19]

(b) Compensation for finders

It is the practice of the crown to make an ex gratia payment of the full value of the 'treasure trove' to a finder who immediately reports his discovery to the police or relevant local authority.[20] Such payments are intended to provide an incentive to finders to reveal their recovery of objects of archaeological interest and, for this reason, are paid even to those who were trespassers at the time of making the find.[1]

3. INCORPOREAL HEREDITAMENTS

The concept of 'land' also includes 'incorporeal hereditaments'.[2] In contradistinction to 'corporeal hereditaments', which are tangible, 'incorporeal hereditaments' are not 'the object of sensation, can neither be

14 [1982] Ch 277 at 291H, 294A; [1981] Ch 333 at 343B. The Court offered no arithmetic definition of 'substantial' beyond suggesting that the coins would require to be at least 50 per cent gold or silver (compare *Palser v Grinling* [1948] AC 291 at 317). In the present case the highest proportion of silver was only 18 per cent.

15 *Bl Comm*, Vol I, p 285. Goods are not treasure trove if found 'in the sea, or *upon* the earth' (*ibid*). It seems to be enough to establish the character of treasure trove that articles of gold or silver are concealed *in* a building or secreted in some private place (eg hidden in a thatched roof or inside furniture). See *Co Inst*, II, 576, III, 132; N.E. Palmer, (1981) 44 MLR 178 at 183.

16 *R v Hancock* [1990] 2 QB 242 at 247C-E.

17 *R v Hancock* [1990] 2 QB 242 at 247E.

18 See *Attorney-General v Trustees of the British Museum* [1903] 2 Ch 598 at 609f.

19 *Bl Comm*, Vol I, p 285f. The unfortunate nature (see [1980] CLJ 281 (D.E.C. Yale)) of this long accepted distinction is perhaps most clearly apparent in the fact that the Sutton Hoo burial find of 1939 did not qualify as 'treasure trove' because it consisted of abandoned goods. (The landowner in fact donated the hoard to the nation: see N.E. Palmer, (1981) 44 MLR 178 at 182). See also *Attorney-General v Trustees of the British Museum* [1903] 2 Ch 598 at 608f.

20 The payment is made to the finder rather than the landowner or occupier, but see, however, N.E. Palmer, (1981) 44 MLR 178 at 184. If no museum wishes to receive the find, it is returned without payment to the finder.

1 See Bonyhady, op cit, p 277.

2 Ante, p 5.

seen nor handled, are creatures of the mind, and exist only in contemplation.'[3] An important modern example of this category of intangible rights is the right of way which one landowner, A, may have over the land of another, B. There are, however, other kinds of incorporeal hereditament known to English law, and they provide the subject matter of discussion elsewhere in this book.[4]

It is a curious feature of the English land lawyer's mode of thought that the benefit of the intangible rights which A enjoys over the land of B is conceptualised as becoming just as much part of A's 'land' as the very soil on which A's house is built. Thus, for example, the benefit of the right of way which A may have over the land of B is 'reified' and regarded as an integral piece of A's land. It follows that any future conveyance of A's 'land' to C will effectively transfer to C not only A's corporeal hereditaments but also the benefit of A's right of way over B's land.[5]

3 *Bl Comm*, Vol II, p 17.
4 Post, pp 931, 1136.
5 See Law of Property Act 1925, s 62(1) (post, p 1062).

CHAPTER 2

Trust

The great codes of continental law follow Roman law in defining 'property' as the right to enjoy a thing and to dispose of it in the most absolute manner, ie as the right to deal with that thing as one pleases and to exclude strangers from interference.[1] Property or ownership thus expresses itself as an absolute jural relationship between a person and a thing. The *dominium* of Roman law comprised both the legal title and the right of actual beneficial enjoyment. In other words, *dominium* treated as conceptually inseparable the owner's right to use, dispose of, and exclude others from, his property. The idea that *dominium* might be fragmented between a number of owners, each with a separate proprietary right to some aspect of *dominium*, was and still is unacceptable to civilian legal thought. *Dominium* is an indivisible unity.

This rather stolid conception of property and ownership has made it difficult for continental systems of law to accommodate the fragmentation of rights of title, use and enjoyment which is integral to the economic reality of property in a complex modern world. However, these problems have been largely resolved in English law and in most legal systems derived from the common law tradition. English law has been able to develop a more flexible concept of property simply because deeply grounded in the English lawyer's tradition is the institution of the 'trust'. Otto Kahn-Freund observed sagely that, in creating the trust, 'in some ways its most original contribution to jurisprudence', the English legal mind has made it 'unnecessary and impossible for itself to search for a definition of property in the continental sense.'[2] Maitland was able to say

> Of all the exploits of Equity the largest and the most important is the invention and development of the Trust. It is an 'institute' of great elasticity and generality; as elastic, as general as contract. This perhaps forms the most distinctive achievement of English lawyers. It seems to us almost essential to civilisation, and yet there is nothing quite like it in foreign law.[3]

1. DEFINING THE 'TRUST'

Many attempts have been made to define the notion of a 'trust'.[4] The essence of a 'trust' is the idea that the trustee is the nominal owner of property but that the real or beneficial owner of that property is the 'beneficiary'

1 See *Code civil*, art 544; *Bürgerliches Gesetzbuch*, para 903; Swiss Civil Code, art 641.

2 *Introduction* to K. Renner, *The Institutions of Private Law and Their Social Functions* (London and Boston 1949), p 23.

3 *Equity* (2nd edn, London 1936), p 23. See also A. Nussbaum, *Sociological and Comparative Aspects of the Trust*, 38 Columbia L Rev 408 (1938); V. Bolgár, *Why No Trusts in the Civil Law?*, (1953) 2 AJCL 204.

4 See eg W.G. Hart, *What is a Trust?*, (1899) 15 LQR 294.

or 'cestui que trust'. The central feature of a trust lies in the fact that the formal or 'titular' interest in property vests in a nominee (or 'trustee') whose duty it is to deflect the beneficial enjoyment of the property to those who hold the 'equitable interests' under the trust.

(1) The function of a trust

In its classical form the trust is a device created expressly for a specific purpose. It is in effect an obligation arising out of a confidence reposed in one who holds property or who has had property conveyed to him. The obligation binds this person to apply the property faithfully in accordance with the confidence placed in him, ie in accordance with the wishes of the creator of the trust and the expectations engendered in the beneficiaries. The most usual kind of trust may be represented diagrammatically as follows, where A, the owner of a legal estate in property, conveys that property to T as trustee, in order that T should hold at law 'on trust for' B, a named beneficiary whose rights are recognised and enforced only 'in equity':[5]

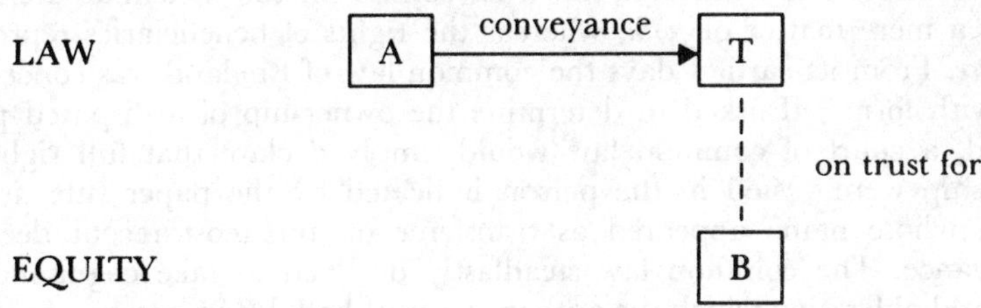

Fig. 1

(2) The functions of a trustee

Once such a trust has been created, its author, A, has no further part to play. The legal title in the trust property is held thereafter by T, who as title-holder is invested with administrative powers of management and disposition. In other words, T is charged with the fiduciary responsibility of managing the trust property in such a way as to render it productive of income or other use value, subject always to the duty to divert the benefit (whether in the form of income or actual enjoyment) to the beneficiary, B.[6] It is a cardinal principle of trust law that, in the absence of proper authorisation, T must never profit himself by reason of his office of trust.[7] His task is simply one of decision-making in the performance of the administrative duties connected with the trust. He manages the trust property

5 It is not impossible that A may declare himself to be a trustee of his own legal title on behalf of B; or even that A himself owns only an equitable interest and can therefore, in effect, create only a sub-trust of that equitable interest for B. However, these are more sophisticated examples of trust than the primary example discussed in Fig 1.

6 The principles outlined here are exactly the same whether there is one trustee alone or several persons acting together as trustees, and whether the beneficiary is one person or many persons collectively.

7 See eg *Keech v Sandford* (1726) 2 Eq Cas Abr 741, 22 ER 629, Sel Cas T King 61 at 62, 25 ER 223 (post, p 414).

and ultimately exercises powers of disposition in relation to that property. However, even the latter function is purely administrative. A disposition of the trust property simply converts that property into cash, which is still governed by the terms of the trust and which therefore requires to be reinvested in another form for the benefit of the person or persons entitled in equity.

2. RELATIONSHIP BETWEEN LAW AND EQUITY

It is easily seen that the fundamental feature of a trust is that it makes possible a separation of the functions of administration and enjoyment. Although the trustee is invested with a formal title in the property, his ownership is purely nominal. If the trustee holds a legal title, that title is only a 'paper title'; the trustee, a mere 'paper owner'. The substance of beneficial enjoyment is reserved at all times for the beneficiary.

(1) Distinction between form and substance

Another important feature of the trust consists in the idea that the legal title is a mere matter of *form*, whereas the rights of beneficiaries represent *substance*. From its earliest days the common law of England was concerned only with form.[8] If asked to determine the ownership of a disputed piece of land, a court of common law would simply declare that full rights of ownership were vested in the person indicated by the paper title, ie the person whose name appeared as transferee on the most recent deed of conveyance. The common law steadfastly declined to take cognisance of the moral obligation which the author of a trust had, by agreement, fastened on the conscience of the transferee of the paper title. The courts of common law regarded the formal title as exclusive of any rights in the supposed beneficiaries and as conclusive of any question relating to use, benefit or enjoyment.

(2) Development of the jurisdiction of equity

It was left to a jurisdiction founded upon conscience to remedy the defects of the common law. It was in the court of the Chancellor, and only in his court, that the moral obligations imposed on, and accepted by, the trustee were capable of enforcement. The court of the Chancellor, or the Court of Chancery as it came to be called, developed a body of rules which supplemented the rules of common law in the interest of achieving a greater equity in the dealings of men.[9] This body of rules became known as 'equity', and it was by virtue of the 'equity' recognised by the Chancellor that the beneficiary of a trust could secure the enforcement of the trust reposed in his trustee. From the 14th century the Chancellors, although never denying that the trustee was the legal owner of the trust property, nevertheless began

8 See A.E.-S. Tay, 'The sense of justice in the Common Law', in E. Kamenka and A.E.-S. Tay (ed), *Justice* (London 1979), p 79.
9 See Pollock and Maitland, *The History of English Law* (2nd edn, London 1968), Vol 2, p 193ff; Maitland, *Equity*, p 2ff.

to give the beneficiary a remedy denied him by the courts of common law. The Court of Chancery insisted that the terms of the trust be observed and that the trust property be dealt with for the benefit of those persons named as beneficiaries or, as it came to be said, for the benefit of those persons 'entitled in equity'.

(3) Conflict between the jurisdictions of common law and equity

The courts of common law and equity thus diverged fundamentally in their approach to trust property. The courts of common law afforded a remedy only to the trustee; the court of equitable jurisdiction gave a remedy to the beneficiary. Not unnaturally conflict arose between these courts. The supremacy of the Court of Chancery became settled by the 17th century, but the mutual antagonism of the courts of common law and equity was not resolved until late in the 19th century. The Supreme Court of Judicature Act 1873 finally established that the rules of law and equity should be administered by all the courts of the land, so that the remedy obtained should no longer depend upon the precise court in which the plaintiff brought his action. Furthermore, in cases of conflict between law and equity, it was enacted that the rules of equity should prevail.[10]

In the orthodox analysis the changes of the late 19th century brought about a fusion merely of administration in respect of law and equity. 'The two streams of jurisdiction, though they run in the same channel, run side by side and do not mingle their waters.'[11] Although all courts may now grant legal and equitable remedies, the principles on which those remedies are granted remain distinct.

(4) Differences between legal and equitable remedies

There is one further procedural difference between law and equity which is of particular importance in land law. The characteristic remedy of the common law is the remedy of damages. The range of equitable remedies extends much more widely, embracing forms of relief which act *in personam* (eg, decrees of specific performance, injunctions and orders for rectification). However, whereas the common law remedy of damages is available as of right once the plaintiff's case has been proved,[12] equitable remedies are always discretionary. Even if the plaintiff has proved his case, he may be denied equitable relief on the ground, for instance, that he has not come to court 'with clean hands'. That is, he may be precluded from relief simply because he has forfeited any claim to the assistance of equity by reason of his own inequitable or unconscionable conduct.[13]

10 Supreme Court of Judicature Act 1873, s 25(11) (post, p 747). See now Supreme Court Act 1981, s 49.

11 *Ashburner's Principles of Equity* (2nd edn by D. Browne, London 1933), p 18. Compare, however, *United Scientific Holdings Ltd v Burnley Borough Council* [1978] AC 904 at 925A-B per Lord Diplock.

12 The quantum of damages awarded remains, of course, a matter to be decided at the discretion of the court.

13 Post, p 744.

3. THE ORIGIN AND TYPES OF TRUST

The modern concept of 'trust' developed from the more ancient institution of the 'use'.[14] Maitland attributed the derivation of the term 'use' not to the Latin *usus* but to the Latin *opus*.[15] In the vulgar or barbarous Latin of the 7th and 8th centuries, the phrase *ad opus* had already acquired a meaning of 'on behalf of'. Thus, if Coemgenus held land *ad opus Johannis*, he was under an obligation to hold land on behalf of Johannes. *Ad opus* became in time *ad oeps* or *ad eops*, emerging later in the form of the law-french *a son oes* and finally as the English 'to the use of'. Thus A might hold lands 'to the use of' B.

(1) The medieval 'use'

It was also Maitland who explained why, in the medieval context, it might be that A should hold lands 'to the use of' B. The device of the use arose in the 13th and 14th centuries because of the restraints imposed by feudal law on the owner of land. The owner of land could not leave his land by will, for every germ of testamentary power in respect of land had been ruthlessly stamped out in the 12th century. Yet the claims of family endowment and the need for spiritual solace were strong. As Maitland pointed out,[16]

> the Englishman would like to leave his land by will. He would like to provide for the weal of his sinful soul, and he would like to provide for his daughters and younger sons. That is the root of the matter...the law is hard upon him at the hour of death, more especially if he is one of the great.

For want of a testamentary alternative, recourse was had to the institution of the 'use'. The landowner typically conveyed his land inter vivos to friends, who were instructed to hold it to his 'use'. They could be directed to allow him enjoyment of the land during his lifetime, and could be given further instructions as to what they should do with the land on his death. They might well be directed in such an event to hold the land 'to the use of' other members of the deceased's family or 'to the use of' the Church. The latter form of use had the two-fold consequence of evading the Statutes of Mortmain, which prohibited the conveyance of lands to the Church, and of securing eternal rest for the soul of the 'feoffor to uses'.

The 'feoffment to uses' thus became a most flexible device.[17] A conveyance (or 'feoffment') of land might be made on terms which would prove highly beneficial to the 'feoffor'. Provided the 'feoffees' survived the 'feoffor', they could hold land to the uses indicated by the 'feoffor'. The utility of this scheme was so extensive, and the scheme itself became so commonplace, that in time it became standard practice to enfeoff a purely fictitious 'feoffee', so that a man of straw was caused to hold land 'to the use of' each beneficiary (or 'cestui que use').[18]

14 See generally A.W.B. Simpson, *A History of The Land Law* (2nd edn, Oxford 1986), p 173ff.
15 *Equity*, p 24.
16 *The Collected Papers of Frederic William Maitland* (ed H.A.L. Fisher, Cambridge 1911), Vol III, p 335.
17 See W.F. Fratcher, *Uses of Uses*, 34 Missouri L Rev 39 (1969).
18 C.R. Noyes, *The Institution of Property* (New York, Toronto and London 1936), p 320.

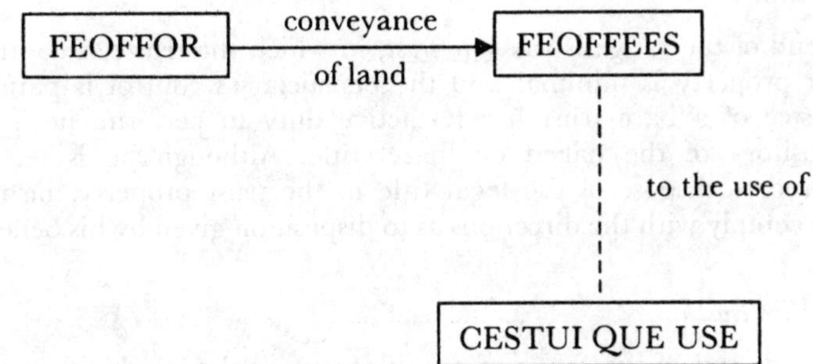

Fig. 2

(2) Development of the trust

Although the courts of common law looked only to the feoffee as the owner of the land, it was the Chancellor who by the 14th century had begun to enforce the use. It was natural of course that restrictions should later be imposed on the use, and in 1535 the Statute of Uses effectively abolished the power to create a use by will. However, within the next two centuries the foundations had been laid for an alternative device which was to perform most of the functions earlier discharged by the use. This device was the trust.[19] From the late 17th century onwards the Court of Chancery began to fashion the principles which were to harden into the bleak and inflexible body of rules known as 'equity'—rules which were primarily (but not exclusively) concerned with the internal administration and external consequences of trusts of both real and personal property.

(3) Historical significance of the trust

In historical terms the major achievement of the trust was without doubt the final dismantling of the feudal system and its replacement by a new and much more flexible mechanism for the distribution of family wealth. In more recent times the trust has also developed a role as an extremely potent instrumentality of capitalism. One commentator has described the trust as 'a device of an individualistic character, conforming to the Anglo-Saxon system of economic liberalism'.[20] As a jural device, the trust is as essential to modern English law as is the institution of contract.

(4) Types of trust

The trust appears in a multiplicity of forms and may be directed towards a variety of purposes. In all its many forms the trust provides a medium by which the administrative and enjoyment functions pertaining to property may be separated and vested in different persons. The possible variations of the trust form depend on the precise way in which these functions are allocated between trustee and beneficiary. The degree of control vested in trustee and beneficiary respectively may vary greatly.

19 On the emergence of the trust, see Maitland, *Equity*, p 43ff.
20 A. Nussbaum, 38 Columbia L Rev 408 at 412 (1938).

(a) Bare trust

At one end of the range is the *bare trust*, in which the trustee's control over the trust property is minimal and the beneficiary's control is paramount. The trustee of a bare trust has no active duty to perform: he is merely the repository of the naked or 'bare' title. Although he is technically empowered to dispose of the legal title in the trust property, he must at all times comply with the directions as to disposition given by his beneficiary.

(b) Protective trust

At the other end of the range of possible trusts is the *spendthrift* or *protective trust*, under which the beneficiary has no alienable interest and therefore no control over the trust property. Such trusts are frequently used to confer upon a beneficiary an interest which is terminable automatically on his insolvency, with the result that the trust estate is protected from the claims of the beneficiary's creditors.

(c) Active trust

At some intermediate point in the range of possible trusts is the *active* or *special trust*—perhaps the most common of all types of trust. This is a trust in which the trustee is charged with the performance of active and substantial duties in respect of the control, management and disposition of the trust property, subject always to the fiduciary duty to deflect the benefit derived from that property towards the nominated beneficiaries.

(d) Other trusts

There also exist many other kinds of trust, such as the *trust for sale*, the *resulting trust*, and the *constructive trust*, but these are best explained later in the context in which they appear.[1]

4. EFFECT OF THE TRUST ON THIRD PARTIES

A trust is a fiduciary relationship with respect to property. The trustee holds typically the legal title to the trust property and exercises the appropriate powers of management and disposition. The beneficiary or 'cestui que trust' has an essentially personal right against his trustee to ensure that the latter carries out the terms of his trust.[2] As Maitland pointed out,[3] the liability of the trustee is almost certainly of contractual origin. He is bound by the terms of the trust because he has bound himself: he has agreed with the author of the trust that he will faithfully observe the conditions on which the trust property was transferred to himself. The right of the cestui que trust is the benefit of an obligation—a right which is enforceable nowadays by appeal to the equitable jurisdiction of the courts. The cestui may apply for a court order directing his trustee to act conformably with the terms

1 Post, pp 518, 384, 413.
2 See *Re Transphere Pty Ltd* (1986) 5 NSWLR 309 at 311E per McLelland J.
3 *Equity*, p 110f.

of his trust, or he may recover damages in respect of any breach of trust which has already occurred.

When stated in this way, it is apparent that the fiduciary relationship created by the trust should in principle affect the rights and obligations of only the trustee and the cestui. Third parties should not be subjected to the onerous liability undertaken voluntarily by the trustee. However, a proper understanding of the rights enjoyed by the cestui que trust begins with the realisation that equity, being a jurisdiction of conscience, gradually extended the ramifications of the use or trust, thereby causing the trust to affect many categories of person other than the original trustee and cestui.[4]

This diffusion of trust liability occurred in the context of transfers of the trust property in favour of various kinds of third party (see *Fig.* 3).

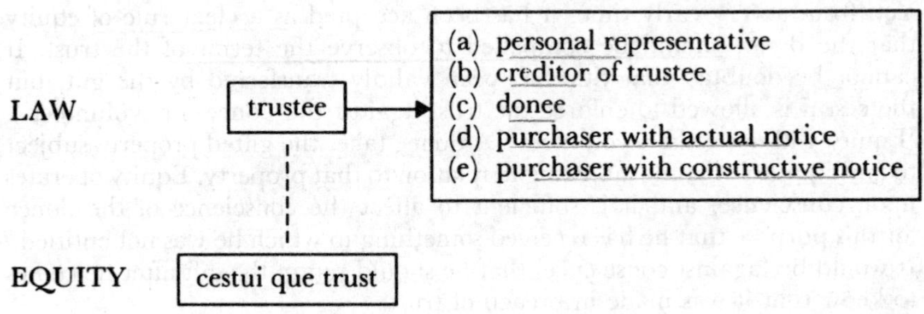

Fig. 3

(1) Persons who succeed to the rights of the trustee

The cestui que trust may enforce the trust against his original trustee. It was but a short step for equity to declare that the cestui que trust may also enforce the terms of the trust against all persons who by succession on the death of the trustee fill the place of that trustee. He may therefore enforce the trust against such persons as the trustee's personal representatives (ie his executors in the case where the trustee dies testate, and his administrators in the case of death intestate). These persons are regarded as 'sustaining wholly or partially the *persona* of the original trustee and being bound by his obligations as regards the proprietary rights to which they have succeeded.'[5]

(2) Creditors of the trustee

The next step is to allow the cestui que trust to enforce the trust against the trustee's creditors.[6] The creditors may not claim the trust property in satisfaction of personal debts owed by the trustee,[7] for the trust property

4 For an excellent historical account, see A.W.B. Simpson, *The Equitable Doctrine of Consideration and the Law of Uses*, (1965–66) 16 U of Toronto LJ 1 at 24ff.

5 Maitland, *Equity*, p 112.

6 *Finch v Earl of Winchelsea* (1715) 1 P Wms 277 at 282, 24 ER 387 at 389.

7 See *Worrall v Harford* (1802) 8 Ves 4 at 8, 32 ER 250 at 252; *In re Morgan* (1881) 18 Ch D 93 at 104.

is that to which the trustee is only nominally entitled as a paper owner. The benefit derived from the trust property belongs to the cestui que trust.[8]

(3) Donees of the trustee

Grave difficulties occur if the trustee, acting in breach of his trust, transfers the trust property to an innocent third party without receiving valuable consideration. There arises here a question of social, ethical and economic priority. Both the donee and the cestui que trust are entirely blameless, yet only one can prevail. It cannot be said that the donee is under any form of contractual liability towards the cestui, since the donee contracted with nobody. He is *ex hypothesi* utterly unaware of the existence of the trust. Yet, from a very early time, it has been accepted as a clear rule of equity that the donee should be compelled to observe the terms of the trust. It cannot be doubted that title has been validly transferred by the gift, but the cestui is allowed to enforce the trust against the donee (or 'volunteer'). 'Equity will not assist a volunteer'. A donee takes the gifted property subject to any equitable claims subsisting in relation to that property. Equity operates upon conscience, and it is sufficient to affect the conscience of the donee for this purpose that he has received something to which he was not entitled.[9] It would be 'against conscience' that he should retain the gift after he comes to know that it was made in breach of trust.

(4) Purchasers from the trustee with actual notice of the trust

At a very early stage in the development of equity, it was also decided that a cestui que trust may enforce the trust against a stranger who purchases the trust property with actual knowledge of the existence of the trust. The ground of liability in the third party is something akin to fraud. It is unconscientious—'against conscience'—to buy what one knows to be held on trust for another. The purchaser is liable *ex delicto vel quasi*.[10] The basis for this conclusion is to be found in the simple but poignant law-French of 1471:

> Si mon feoffee de trust etc enfeoffe un autre, que conust bien que le feoffor rien ad forsque a mon use, subpoena girra vers ambideux: scil auxibien vers le feoffee come vers le feoffor. . .pur ceo que en conscience il purchase ma terre.[11]

Thus the claims of equity operated upon the guilty conscience. If a stranger knowingly bought land held on trust, he did what was unconscientious and

8 Ante, p 35. This principle is currently preserved in Insolvency Act 1986, ss 283(1)(a), (3)(a), 306 (post, p 597).

9 See eg *Burgess v Wheate* (1759) 1 Eden 177 at 195, 28 ER 652 at 659; *Re Diplock* [1948] Ch 465 at 503. The liability of the donee may rest on a theory of unjust enrichment (see J.B. Ames, *Lectures on Legal History* (Cambridge Mass 1913), p 255).

10 Maitland, *Equity*, p 113. A.W. Scott attributed the liability of the purchaser with actual notice to the fact that he was 'colluding with the trustee in a breach of trust' (see *The Nature of the Rights of the Cestui Que Trust*, 17 Columbia L Rev 269 at 281 (1917)).

11 YB 11 Edw IV, fol 8: 'If my trustee conveys the land to a third person who knows well that the trustee holds for my use, I shall have a remedy in the Chancery against both of them: as well against the buyer as against the trustee: for in conscience he buys my land' (see Maitland, *Collected Papers*, Vol III, p 345).

must now be regarded as holding on trust for me, for *en conscience il purchase ma terre*.

(5) Purchasers from the trustee with constructive notice of the trust

If equity had stopped there and gone no further, it would have been possible that purchasers would take good care to ensure that their consciences were not affected by actual notice of any trust which might exist. They would simply have 'shut their eyes' to the possible existence of a trust, and would have relied on the absence of actual notice as their ground of immunity from the obligation of the trust.

Equity accordingly developed the further rule that, in order to take the property free of the trust, the purchaser must not only be honest; he must also be diligent. He must have made all such investigation of the vendor's title and land as a prudent purchaser would have made, and he is affected with 'constructive notice' of all equitable rights of which he would have acquired actual notice had he made the proper enquiries. The trust may be enforced against any purchaser who would have known of the trust had he behaved as prudent purchasers behave in the conduct of their affairs.[12] Thus a standard of diligence has been elaborated by the courts in order to fasten upon the conscience of the unreasonable or disingenuous purchaser. If not actually guilty of *dolus*, such a purchaser is at least 'guilty of that sort of negligence which is equivalent to *dolus*. He had shut his eyes in order that he might not see.'[13]

At this point the long arm of equity stopped. Equity recognised that if the purchaser who acquired ownership from the trustee was excusably ignorant of the rights of the cestui que trust, then he must be left to enjoy the ownership thus obtained. Since his conscience was unaffected, the Chancellor's equity had no hold upon him.[14] In *Pilcher v Rawlins*[15] James LJ regarded it as 'established law' that the purchaser's plea of 'a purchase for valuable consideration without notice is an absolute, unqualified, unanswerable defence, and an unanswerable plea to the jurisdiction of this Court.' James LJ accepted that the purchaser may be 'interrogated and tested to any extent' as to whether he gave valuable consideration or acted mala fide or had notice. But once a purchaser 'has gone through that ordeal', and has successfully maintained his unanswerable defence, then

12 'In the course of time it came to be held in the Court of Chancery that it would be unconscionable for the purchaser to take his stand on the facts that had come to his notice to the exclusion of those which ordinary prudence or circumspection or skill should have called to his attention. When the facts at his command beckoned him to look and inquire further, and he refrained from doing so, equity fixed him with constructive notice of what he would have ascertained if he had pursued the further investigation which a person of reasonable care and skill would have felt proper to make in the circumstances. He would not be allowed to say "I acted in good faith, in ignorance of those facts, of which I learned only after I took the conveyance," if those facts were such as a reasonable man in the circumstances would have brought within his knowledge' (*Somers v W* [1979] IR 94 at 108 per Henchy J).

13 Maitland, *Collected Papers*, Vol III, p 346.

14 *Burgess v Wheate* (1759) 1 Eden 177 at 195, 28 ER 652 at 659 ('A conveyance with consideration without notice bars a trust').

15 (1872) 7 Ch App 259 at 268f.

this Court has no jurisdiction whatever to do anything more than to let him depart in possession of that legal estate, that legal right, that legal advantage which he has obtained. In such a case the purchaser is entitled to hold that which, without breach of duty, he has had conveyed to him.

In these circumstances there is no ground in equity for taking away that to which the purchaser is entitled at law. The purchaser has not himself undertaken any express obligation; he does not participate in the *persona* of the trustee; he has done no wrong; he has acted honestly and with due diligence. As Maitland said, 'Equity cannot touch him, because. . .his conscience is unaffected by the trust.'[16] Maitland added that this result could be formulated in either of two ways:

Formulation A

The cestui que trust may enforce his rights against

(i) the trustee, *and*
(ii) all who claim through the trustee as volunteers (personal representatives, devisees, donees), *and*
(iii) all those who acquire the trust property with actual or constructive notice of the trust.

Formulation B

The cestui que trust may enforce his rights against all persons *except* a bona fide purchaser of a legal title for valuable consideration without notice of the trust (whether actual or constructive).

Formulation B is now the more common means of stating the relevant proposition, and as such constitutes what is generally known as the *equitable doctrine of notice*. However, it is a statement of a negative kind, and it is not without interest that Maitland himself preferred *Formulation A* 'because it puts us at what is historically the right point of view—the benefit of an obligation has been so treated that it has come to look rather like a true proprietary right.'[17]

5. THE INTEREST OF THE CESTUI QUE TRUST

The nature of the rights of the cestui que trust has traditionally been discussed in terms of the distinction between rights *in rem* and rights *in personam*.

(1) Rights in personam

A right *in personam* is a right to enforce the performance of an obligation undertaken by or imposed upon a specific person.[18] Such an obligation arises typically by reason of the law of contract, the law of torts, the law of trusts or indeed the law of property. The contractual promisee has rights *in personam* against his promisor. The victim of a tort has rights *in personam* against the tortfeasor. The cestui que trust has rights *in personam* against his trustee.

16 *Equity*, p 115.
17 *Equity*, p 115.
18 See J.L. Austin, *Lectures On Jurisprudence* (5th edn London 1885), Vol 1, p 370.

It is possible to have rights *in personam* in respect of a thing. In each case, however, the rights concerned are rights enforceable only against the particular individual who has incurred liability by virtue of some transaction in law (whether contract, tort, trust, or licence). The identity or *persona* of the individual against whom enforcement proceedings are brought is highly relevant to the success of these proceedings, because there is no point in A's attempting to enforce against C a contract which A has concluded with B.[19] There is no point in A's attempting to recover damages from E in respect of a tort committed by D.[20]

(2) Rights in rem

A right *in rem* is, by contrast, a right which is enforceable not against merely one person but against the entire world.[1] The assertion of a right *in rem* is ultimately the assertion of some kind of ownership of a thing. A right *in rem* is a right enforceable 'against the world' in respect of that thing; in a sense it represents the summation of all possible rights *in personam*.[2] If, in respect of the thing concerned, A is entitled to assert a right *in personam* against each and every individual in the world, the enforceability of his right is in no way dependent upon the precise identity of the individual against whom enforcement is sought (whether B, C, D, E, F...). A's right *in personam* is equally enforceable against all, and the *persona* of the individual enforced against ceases to be a determinant of A's ability to vindicate his rights. The *persona* no longer represents a relevant variable in the equation which leads to enforcement of what were originally rights *in personam*. A's rights may just as comprehensively be described as rights against the thing itself, that is, as rights *in rem*.[3]

(3) Delineation of the boundaries of 'property'

The difference between rights *in rem* and rights *in personam* may seem academic. If rights are enforceable in any given situation, it matters not whether they are described as rights *in rem* or rights *in personam*. However, the distinction

19 This is, of course, the doctrine of 'privity of contract'.

20 An exception to this proposition arises where E is D's employer and is therefore vicariously liable in respect of torts committed by D.

1 'The phrase *in rem* denotes the *compass*, and not the *subject* of the right' (J.L. Austin, op cit, p 369). 'A right *in rem* is usually defined to be a right available against the world at large, corresponding to a duty imposed upon the world at large; and by the world at large is meant indeterminate persons, an indefinite number of persons, not necessarily every one in the world; and it is to be distinguished from a right *in personam*, or obligation, which is a right available against determinate persons, corresponding to a duty imposed upon determinate persons' (A.W. Scott, 17 Columbia L Rev 269 at 273f (1917)).

2 It has been said that a 'right *in rem* is a name for a large number of rights *in personam*, actual or potential. A violation of a right *in rem* is always a violation of a definite one of these rights *in personam*' (W.W. Cook, *The Powers of Courts of Equity*, 15 Columbia L Rev 37 at 53 (1915)).

3 There is another, and rather different, sense in which the phrase 'right *in rem*' is sometimes used to describe a right in property which may be vindicated by the physical recovery of the physical property or *res* from the person into whose hands that property has come (as distinct from a mere action for money damages). However, this usage of 'right *in rem*' is less common than the meaning which has been attributed here (see W.W. Cook, 15 Columbia L Rev 37 at 43 (1915)).

between rights *in rem* and rights *in personam* has a conventional significance in the law of land, because the borderline between these two categories of rights marks the boundaries of the 'proprietary right'. Only rights *in rem* are traditionally regarded as truly proprietary rights. Rights *in personam* are seen as purely personal rights which remain outside the realm of property law. According to Lord Wilberforce in *National Provincial Bank Ltd v Ainsworth*,[4] 'before a right or interest can be admitted into the category of property, or of a right affecting property, it must be definable, identifiable by third parties, capable in its nature of assumption by third parties, and have some degree of permanence or stability.'[5]

The borderline between rights *in rem* and rights *in personam* is therefore crucial, for it expresses an important social judgment. The designation of a right as 'proprietary' is a kind of social accolade which signifies that a certain importance is attached to the entitlement in question. The interest concerned is sufficiently significant to merit public protection not merely vis à vis the participants in the private transaction which generated the interest, but vis à vis the entire world. It has been said that the 'basic badge of a proprietary right—that is, of an interest in property—is that unlike a personal right it is enforceable against the relevant property in the hands of third parties.'[6]

(4) Fluctuating boundary between rights in rem and rights in personam

The frontier between rights *in rem* and rights *in personam* has not yet been definitively settled. It is not impossible that a purely personal right may undergo a slow juristic metamorphosis, qualifying eventually for full recognition as a proprietary interest. Such an evolution is not unknown in the law of land, a prime example being the development which affected the law of restrictive covenants in the middle of the 19th century.[7] There are indications that a similar development may currently be taking place in the law of contractual licences.[8]

(5) Cause and effect in the definition of 'proprietary status'

One of the most intriguing questions in this general context is whether a given right is enforced against third parties because it is a proprietary right, or whether a given right acquires proprietary status precisely because it is enforced against such parties. Is curial enforcement the cause or the effect of proprietary character? This question is deeply bound up with the way in which the courts conceptualise the underlying issues in the context of property. It may even be that the balance of cause and effect is undergoing a noticeable reversal in some areas of property law today, as increasingly the courts fashion proprietary rights in order to give effect to what are thought

4 [1965] AC 1175 at 1247G–1248A.
5 For an argument that this method of demarcating property rights is flawed by circularity, see [1991] CLJ 252 at 293.
6 F.R. Crane, *Estoppel Interests in Land*, (1967) 31 Conv (NS) 332.
7 Post, p 1136.
8 Post, p 901.

to be the 'legitimate' moral expectations of litigants or the demands of conscionable conduct in their dealings.[9]

(6) Is the interest of the cestui que trust a right in rem or a right in personam?

The debate concerning the precise nature of the interest of the cestui que trust has traditionally centred on whether the cestui has a right *in rem* or merely a right *in personam.*[10] It is tempting, on first analysis of the trust concept, to say that two different forms of ownership are recognised in relation to the property which forms the subject matter of the trust. At law the owner is the trustee; in equity the owner is the cestui que trust. However, this view has not been accepted unqualifiedly in the orthodox teaching on the nature of the cestui's rights, for it seems to assert that the cestui has a right *in rem,* ie that he is the 'equitable owner' of the trust property. Conventional doctrine tends towards the view that the cestui's rights are essentially and ultimately mere rights *in personam.*

(a) The orthodox view

The more generally accepted view of the nature of beneficial rights is that once expressed by Professor J.B. Ames, who observed that

> A *cestui que trust* is frequently spoken of as an equitable owner of the land. This, though a convenient form of expression, is clearly inaccurate. The trustee is the owner of the land, and, of course, two persons with adverse interests cannot be owners of the same thing. What the *cestui que trust* really owns is the obligation of the trustee; for an obligation is as truly the subject-matter of property as any physical *res.*[11]

Maitland went further in his efforts to maintain that equitable estates and interests are not rights *in rem.* According to Maitland, the trustee 'is the owner, the full owner of the thing, while the cestui que trust has no rights in the thing.'[12] In Maitland's view, it was simply not true to say that 'whereas the common law said that the trustee was the owner of the land, equity said that the cestui que trust was the owner.'[13] For Maitland there was an absurdity in the statement that before 1875 there were two courts of co-ordinate jurisdiction, one of which maintained that A was the owner, the other that B was the owner, of Blackacre:

9 Post, pp 314, 413.

10 See eg A.W. Scott, *The Nature of the Rights of the Cestui Que Trust,* 17 Columbia L Rev 269 (1917).

11 *Purchase for Value without Notice,* 1 Harvard L Rev 1 at 9 (1887–88).

12 *Equity,* p 47.

13 See *Re Transphere Pty Ltd* (1986) 5 NSWLR 309 at 311E-F, where McLelland J spoke of 'the imprecision of the notion that absolute ownership of property can properly be divided up into a legal estate and an equitable estate. An absolute owner holds only the legal estate, with all the rights and incidents that attach to that estate. Where a legal owner holds property on trust for another, he has at law all the rights of an absolute owner but the beneficiary has the right to compel him to hold and use those rights which the law gives him in accordance with the obligations which equity has imposed on him by virtue of the existence of the trust. Although this right of the beneficiary constitutes an equitable estate in the property, it is engrafted on to, not carved out of, the legal estate.'

That means civil war and utter anarchy...Equity did not say that the *cestui que trust* was the owner of the land, it said that the trustee was the owner of the land, but added that he was bound to hold the land for the benefit of the *cestui que trust*. There was no conflict here.[14]

In this way Equity fulfilled its historical purpose. 'Equity had not come to destroy the law, but to fulfil it. Every jot and every tittle of the law was to be obeyed, but when all this had been done something might yet be needful, something that equity would require.' But at every point equity presupposed the existence of common law. In Maitland's famous words,

It's of no use for Equity to say that A is a trustee of Blackacre for B, unless there can be some court that can say that A is the owner of Blackacre. Equity without common law would have been a castle in the air, an impossibility.[15]

The Supreme Court of Judicature Acts 1873–1875 declared, of course, that in any case of variance the rules of equity should prevail over the rules of law, but as Maitland shrewdly pointed out this only served to show that there had not been any conflict before 1875 as to the identity of the 'owner' of land held on trust. Had there been a conflict, the legislation would have had the effect of abolishing the entire law of trusts by its confirmation of the supremacy of equitable rules. B would have been recognised, in a situation of conflict, as the only owner of Blackacre. Such a conclusion is, however, patently untenable: the institution of the trust remains alive and well to this day.

Thus, in the conventional view of the matter, the interest of the cestui que trust comprises merely the benefit of an obligation—the obligation binding the trustee to observe and perform the duties of his trust. The right of a cestui is ultimately a right *in personam* against his trustee and against all persons claiming through him to the extent that the trust is fastened upon their conscience.[16]

(b) *The wider view*

To other jurists it has seemed plausible to maintain that the rights of the cestui que trust comprise more than mere rights *in personam*. This wider view attributes greater significance to substance than to form. It recognises that the legal estate of the trustee is in most cases a mere 'shadow' following the equitable estate 'which is the substance'.[17] Support for this view may be found in the range of third parties against whom the cestui can enforce his rights. With the sole exception of the bona fide purchaser for value without notice, all third parties are bound by the trust, and in this sense the cestui

14 *Equity*, p 17. In this sense equity was true to its maxim: 'equity follows the law' (post, p 513). For a view contrary to that of Maitland, compare A.W. Scott, 17 Columbia L Rev 269 at 276 (1917).

15 *Equity*, p 19.

16 It was essentially for this reason that Maitland preferred 'an enumeration of the persons against whom the equitable rights are good to a general statement that they are good against all, followed by an exception of persons who obtain legal rights *bona fide*, for value and without notice' (*Equity*, p 115).

17 See *Town of Cascade v Cascade Co*, 75 Mont 304 at 311 (1925). This wider view was the view typically espoused by Lord Mansfield CJ, who stated quite clearly in *Burgess v Wheate* (1759) 1 Eden 177 at 217, 28 ER 652 at 668, that 'trusts are considered as real estates, as the real ownership of the land.'

is able to assert an 'equitable ownership' of the trust property against almost all the world.[18] Thus for Salmond

If we have regard to the essence of the matter rather than to the form of it, a trustee is not an owner at all, but a mere agent, upon whom the law has conferred the power and imposed the duty of administering the property of another person. In legal theory, however, he is not a mere agent but an owner. He is a person to whom the property of some one else is fictitiously attributed by the law, to the extent that the rights and powers thus vested in a nominal owner shall be used by him on behalf of the real owner. As between trustee and beneficiary, the law recognises the truth of the matter; as between these two, the property belongs to the latter and not to the former. But as between the trustee and third persons, the fiction prevails. The trustee is clothed with the rights of his beneficiary, and is so enabled to personate or represent him in dealings with the world at large.[19]

It is this perception of the cestui's true rights which ultimately underlies the rule in *Saunders v Vautier*[20] under which the beneficiary or beneficiaries of a trust may, if *sui iuris* (of full age and sound mind), terminate the trust and direct the trustee or trustees as to the disposition of the trust property.

Even Maitland was prepared to concede that the cestui has 'rights which in many ways are treated as analogous to true proprietary rights, to *iura in rem*.'[1] In his *Lectures on Equity*, he expressed the view that

The best answer may be that in history, and probably in ultimate analysis, it is *ius in personam*; but that it is so treated (and this for many important purposes) that it is very like *ius in rem*. A right primarily good against *certa persona*, viz the trustee, but so treated as to be almost equivalent to a right good against all—a *dominium*, ownership, which however exists only in equity. And this is so from a remote time.[2]

In his later writings it seems that Maitland mellowed even further towards a recognition that the cestui has rights which may be treated as ownership, or 'as some of those modalities of [*Eigenthum*] in which our medieval land law is so rich.'[3] In considering the question whether the rights of the 'destinatory' (or cestui) are rights *in rem* (*dinglich*) or mere rights *in personam* (*obligatorisch*), Maitland made reference to the wide categories of third party whose conscience is bound by the trust, and concluded:

18 The immunity conferred on the bona fide purchaser is, of course, an undeniable qualification on the 'ownership' of the beneficiary. It was Langdell who pointed out that 'if equitable rights were rights *in rem*, they would follow the *res* into the hands of a purchaser for value and without notice' (*A Brief Survey of Equity Jurisdiction*, 1 Harvard L Rev 55 at 60 (1887–88)). See, however, A.W. Scott, 17 Columbia L Rev 269 at 278f.

19 *Jurisprudence* (12th edn by P.J. Fitzgerald, London 1966), p 256f. See also the statement of Isaacs J in *Hoysted v Federal Commissioner of Taxation* (1920) 27 CLR 400 at 422 that equity 'regards the cestui que trust of property as the true owner of the property itself.'

20 (1841) 4 Beav 115 at 116, 49 ER 282, Cr & Ph 240 at 249, 41 ER 482 at 485 (post, p 541).

1 *Equity*, p 110.

2 *Equity*, p 23.

3 *Collected Papers*, Vol III, p 343. In Maitland's day juristic debate in the area of property law was conducted largely in German—a factor which influenced much of Maitland's writing. Maitland clearly envied the greater expressive capacity of the German language: see for instance his remark that 'we have to envy our neighbours such a word as *Dinglichkeit*', a term which Maitland himself could render in English only in the rather ungainly form of 'thinglikeness' (see Pollock and Maitland, *The History of English Law* (2nd edn, London 1968), Vol 2, p 125).

Thus we come by the idea of an 'equitable ownership' or 'ownership in equity'. Supposing that a man is in equity the owner ('tenant in fee simple') of a piece of land, it makes very little difference to him that he is not also 'owner at law' and that, as we say, 'the legal ownership is outstanding in trustees.' The only serious danger that he is incurring is that this 'legal ownership' may come to a person who acquires it *bona fide*, for value, and without actual or constructive notice of his rights. And that is an uncommon event. . .I believe that for the ordinary thought of Englishmen 'equitable ownership' is just ownership pure and simple, though it is subject to a peculiar, technical and not very intelligible rule in favour of *bona fide* purchasers. A professor of law will tell his pupils that they must not think, or at any rate must not begin by thinking, in this manner. He may tell them that the destinatory's rights are in history and in ultimate analysis not *dinglich* but *obligatorisch*: that they are valid only against those who for some special reason are bound to respect them. But let the Herr Professor say what he likes, so many people are bound to respect these rights that practically they are almost as valuable as if they were *dominium*.[4]

Ultimately the question whether a cestui que trust has rights *in rem* or rights *in personam* may simply be a matter of emphasis and perspective. From the earliest times there has been a willingness to concede that the cestui holds at the very least the benefit of an obligation and that this benefit may well, in some sense, comprise a *form* of 'equitable ownership'. This view receives support from an altogether more modern and more radical conception which sees the very *enforceability* of a claim to be the essence of a property right.[5]

4 *Collected Papers*, Vol III, p 349f.
5 Post, p 361.

CHAPTER 3

Tenures and estates

It is not easy to imagine, *tabula rasa,* how best to fashion a coherent and systematic body of rules governing rights in and over land. During the course of eight centuries, English law has developed a framework of rules which functions today with admirable success, but it is far from obvious that, if the task of construction were begun again, the end result would necessarily resemble the law of real property in its present form. The conceptual points of departure which lie at the back of the law of real property contain little, if anything, of a particularly compelling or *a priori* nature. There is indeed nothing inevitable about the eventual shape of modern land law, but it remains true that the law of today is still heavily impressed with the form of ancient legal and intellectual constructs.

The present chapter is concerned with the basal notions of English land law. From its earliest origins land law has comprised a highly artificial field of concepts, defined with meticulous precision, with the result that the interrelation of these concepts is not unlike a form of mathematical calculus. The intellectual constructs of land law move, as Professor Lawson once said, 'in a world of pure ideas from which everything physical or material is entirely excluded.'[1] The law of land is logical and highly ordered, consisting almost wholly of systematic abstractions which 'seem to move among themselves according to the rules of a game which exists for its own purposes.' It is from this interplay of naked concepts that the creature of modern land law ultimately derives.

English law cannot be properly understood except in the light of its history,[2] and it is in the doctrines relating to tenures and estates that the historical roots of English land law are to be found. The present chapter is devoted to an examination of the way in which these doctrines provided the conceptual underpinnings for the modern law of land.

1. THE DOCTRINE OF TENURES

The origin of the medieval theory of English land law was the Norman invasion of England in 1066. By virtue of this act of conquest the King acquired, in some sense, an ultimate or radical title to all land in England.[3]

1 *The Rational Strength of the English Law* (London 1951), p 79.

2 See generally A.W.B. Simpson, *A History of the Land Law* (2nd edn, Oxford 1986); S.F.C. Milsom, *Historical Foundations of the Common Law* (2nd edn, London 1981); J.H. Baker, *An Introduction to English Legal History* (3rd edn, London 1990).

3 As Brennan J recently observed in the High Court of Australia in *Mabo v Queensland* (1992) 107 ALR 1 at 33, '[t]he radical title is a postulate of the doctrine of tenure and a concomitant of sovereignty'. The *Mabo* case, involving the land rights of the Merriam people of the Murray Islands, provided an unusual—indeed almost unprecedented—forum for the critical examination of the most fundamental concepts of English land law.

On this basis it has sometimes been supposed that the entire property in the land vested exclusively in the King and that to this day the Crown remains the *only* true owner of the land situated within the jurisdiction.[4] It would follow from this assumption that the physical elements of land can never be the subject of any absolute ownership other than that of the Crown,[5] and that the rights of all others in respect of land are confined to mere forms of limited tenure.[6] In retrospect, however, some caution is required. It may not be wholly correct to equate the fact of territorial sovereignty with any more modern notion of absolute beneficial ownership of the land,[7] such a concept being arguably quite alien to the medieval cast of mind.[8]

The subjugation of territory by the King as paramount lord nevertheless provided the foundation for the feudal theory that every parcel of land in England was held either mediately or immediately of that lord: no land was 'allodial'. Since the Normans had brought with them no written law of land, they initiated in their new territory what was effectively a system of landholding in return for the performance of services to a feudal superior.[9] It was this *doctrine of tenures* which was to provide the basal doctrine of English land law.[10]

In effect the term 'tenure' was used primarily to signify the relationship between tenant and lord rather than the relationship between tenant and land.[11] According to the theory of tenures, all land was held by the Crown in virtue of some universal and ultimate title and was granted to subjects of the Crown only upon the continued fulfilment of certain conditions. Land was never granted by way of an actual transfer of ownership, and any notion of absolute or final ownership other than in the Crown was to that extent inconceivable. Pollock and Maitland were later to explain quite simply that all land in England 'must be held of the king of England, otherwise he would not be the king of all England.'[12] In their view, to have wished in

4 See *Bl Comm*, Vol II, p 51. See also Stephen CJ's reference in *Attorney-General v Brown* (1847) 1 Legge 312 at 316, to the Sovereign as the 'universal occupant' of all his or her land—a "fiction [which]. . .is adopted by the Constitution to answer the ends of government, for the good of the people".'

5 See T.C. Williams, (1931) 75 SJ 843 at 844.

6 This was one of the bases of the dissenting judgment of Dawson J in *Mabo v Queensland* (1992) 107 ALR 1 at 93 (note 7, infra).

7 It is the recognition of precisely this distinction which has recently enabled a majority in the High Court of Australia to rule that the colonial appropriation of Australia did not extinguish existing proprietary rights based on native title. On this view, the doctrine of *terra nullius* caused the Crown to acquire absolute beneficial ownership of land only where such land was truly desert and uninhabited (see *Mabo v Queensland* (1992) 107 ALR 1 at 34ff per Brennan J). To his credit Blackstone had already observed, more than two centuries earlier, that the question how far the 'driving out or massacring [of]. . .innocent and defenceless natives. . .was consonant to nature, to reason, or to christianity, deserved well to be considered by those, who have rendered their names immortal by thus civilising mankind' (*Bl Comm*, Vol II, p 7).

8 See A.W.B. Simpson, *A History of the Land Law* (2nd edn Oxford 1986), p 47f.

9 See *Attorney-General v Brown* (1847) 1 Legge 312 at 316 per Stephen CJ.

10 Pollock and Maitland remarked that this 'extensive application' of the feudal formula 'perhaps was possible only in a conquered country' (*The History of English Law* (2nd edn, London 1968), Vol 1, p 236).

11 *Mabo v Queensland* (1992) 107 ALR 1 at 32 per Brennan J.

12 Op cit, Vol 2, p 3.

medieval times for an ownership of land which was not subject to royal rights was 'to wish for the state of nature'.

It was a direct consequence of this theory that all occupiers of land were at best regarded as 'tenants', ie as holders of the land who in return for their respective grants rendered services of some specified kind either to the King himself or to some immediate overlord who, in his turn, owed services ultimately to the Crown. In this way there emerged a feudal pyramid, with the King at its apex, and it was the doctrine of tenures which defined the terms of the grant on which each tenant enjoyed his occupation of 'his' land.

(1) Classification of tenures

The feudal services rendered by 'tenants' were an integral part of early English land law, and in time became standardised and identifiable by the type of service exacted and performed. The different methods of landholding (differentiated according to the form of service required) were known as 'tenures', each tenure indicating the precise terms on which the land was held. The tenures were themselves subdivided into those tenures which were 'free' (and therefore formed part of the strict feudal framework) and those tenures which were 'unfree' (and appertained to tenants of lowly status who were *adscripti glebae*—effectively little better than slaves).

(a) Unfree tenures

The common labourer or 'villein tenant' originally had no place on the feudal ladder at all. He merely occupied land on behalf of his lord, and it was the latter who was deemed by the common law to have 'seisin'[13] of the land thus occupied. Villeinage (later called 'copyhold tenure'), although of an unfree nature, came in practice to enjoy increasing protection. This form of tenure retained its existence in law until the enactment of the property legislation of 1922–1925.

(b) Free tenures

The kinds of service provided by those who enjoyed free tenure included, for instance, the provision of armed horsemen for battle (the tenure of 'knight's service') or the performance of some personal service such as the bearing of high office at the King's court (the tenure of 'grand sergeanty'). These tenures were known as 'tenures in chivalry', and were distinct from the 'spiritual tenures' of 'frankalmoign' and 'divine service' (by which ecclesiastical lands were held in return for the performance of some sacred office) and the somewhat humbler 'tenures in socage' (which obliged the tenant to render agricultural service to his lord).[14]

With the passage of time, the military and socage tenures were commuted for money payments, but all tenures carried with them 'incidents' (or privileges

13 Post, p 61.

14 A much later echo of tenurial service appeared in the practice of granting grazing licences to the early 19th century colonists of New South Wales which were conditioned on the obligation to keep and clothe a stipulated number of convicts per grant of one hundred acres. See A. Buck, *The Peculiarities of Property in Mid-Nineteenth Century New South Wales.*

enjoyed by the lord) which were often more valuable than the services themselves.

(2) The feudal pyramid

The consequence of medieval theory was the emergence of a kind of feudal pyramid of free tenants,[15] with the actual occupiers of the land (the 'tenants in demesne') forming the base, their overlords ('mesne lords') standing in the middle—both receiving services and rendering services in their turn—and with the King at the apex receiving services from his immediate tenants ('tenants in chief').

(a) Subinfeudation

Pollock and Maitland described the system of tenures in terms of a series of 'feudal ladders', noting that 'theoretically there is no limit to the possible number of rungs, and. . .men have enjoyed a large power, not merely of adding new rungs to the bottom of the ladder, but of inserting new rungs in the middle of it.'[16] This process of potentially infinite extension of the feudal ladder was known as *subinfeudation.* However, subinfeudation carried the disadvantage that it tended to make the feudal ladder long and cumbersome, and in time the process of alienating land by *substitution* became more common. Under the latter device the alienee of land simply assumed the rung on the feudal ladder previously occupied by the alienor, and the creation of a new and inferior rung was no longer necessary.

(b) The Statute Quia Emptores

By the end of the 13th century a more modern concept of land as freely alienable property was beginning to displace the restrictive feudal order, and this evolution culminated in the enactment of Quia Emptores in 1290. The Statute Quia Emptores constituted a pre-eminent expression of a new preference for freedom of alienability as a principle of public policy. The major innovation contained in the Statute was the prohibition for the future of alienation by subinfeudation.[17] Following the enactment of 1290 only the Crown could grant new tenures, and the existing network of tenures could only contract with the passage of time. Every conveyance of land henceforth had the effect of substituting the grantee in the tenurial position

15 See *Mabo v Queensland* (1992) 107 ALR 1 at 59 per Deane and Gaudron JJ.

16 Op cit, Vol 1, p 233. In one of the authentic examples provided by Pollock and Maitland, it could be said that '[i]n Edward I's day Roger of St German holds land at Paxton in Huntingdonshire of Robert of Bedford, who holds of Richard of Ilchester, who holds of Alan of Chartres, who holds of William le Boteler, who holds of Gilbert Neville, who holds of Devorguil Balliol, who holds of the king of Scotland, who holds of the king of England'.

17 The participants in the 17th and 18th century plantations of Ulster were commonly dispensed from the impact of the Statute Quia Emptores 1290, and thus had power to subinfeudate by way of 'fee farm grants' (post, p 87). The surviving effects of the subinfeudation which then took place are still obvious today in the extreme complexity of the 'pyramid titles' which create particularly acute difficulties in the conveyancing of urban land (see *Report of the Committee on Registration of Title to Land in Northern Ireland* (Cmd 512, 1967), para 116ff).

formerly occupied by his grantor: no new relationship of lord and tenant was created by the transfer.

It is the Statute Quia Emptores which—quite unnoticed—still regulates every transfer of land in fee simple today. Every such conveyance is merely a process of substitution of the purchaser in the shoes of the vendor, and the effect of the Statute during the last seven centuries has tended towards a gradual levelling of the feudal pyramid so that all tenants in fee simple today are presumed (in the absence of contrary evidence) to hold directly of the Crown as 'tenants in chief'.

(3) Virtual disappearance of the concept of tenure

The dismantling of the old feudal order was later accelerated by more direct measures aimed at a reduction of the forms of tenure. Under the Tenures Abolition Act 1660, almost all free tenures were converted into 'free and common socage' or 'freehold tenure'. By 1925 the only remaining tenures which enjoyed any importance were socage tenure and copyhold tenure. The Law of Property Act 1922 (which came into force on 1 January 1926) enfranchised all copyhold tenure, converting it automatically into freehold (ie socage) tenure.

There is therefore only one surviving form of tenure today—freehold tenure in socage—but the conceptual vestiges of the doctrine of tenures live on. It is still true that every parcel of land in England and Wales is held of some lord—almost invariably the Crown. It is still technically the case that the Crown holds the ultimate or radical title in all land in this jurisdiction, and that all occupiers of land are merely—in the feudal sense—'tenants'. However, for all practical purposes the doctrine of tenures is now obsolete.[18] Tenure of land for an estate in fee simple is now tantamount to absolute ownership of the land[19]—or as close to total control of land as is nowadays possible. The doctrine of tenures has long been overtaken in importance by that other doctrine which explains much of English land law—the 'doctrine of estates'.

2. THE DOCTRINE OF ESTATES

Whereas the doctrine of tenures served within the framework of medieval theory to indicate the conditions on which a grant of land was held, the *doctrine of estates* defined the effective duration of that grant. The doctrine still plays a fundamental role today in the classification of interests in land law.

18 Only in the context of the landlord-tenant relationship does the notion of tenure have much contemporary meaning (see Chapter 17, post, p 673). See also *Warner v Sampson* [1959] 1 QB 297 at 312f; (1959) 75 LQR 310 (P.V. Baker). The ultimate nature of crown ownership of realty also surfaces indirectly in the law of escheat to the crown and in the law relating to the foreshore (ante, p 27). See *Mabo v Queensland* (1992) 107 ALR 1 at 59 per Deane and Gaudron JJ.

19 See *Mabo v Queensland* (1992) 107 ALR 1 at 59 per Deane and Gaudron JJ, 93 per Dawson J.

(1) The concept of the 'estate'

Since it was intrinsic to the structure of medieval land law that the King held the underlying or radical title to all land, it followed that his subjects—be they ever so great—occupied their lands on the terms of some grant derived ultimately from the largesse of the Crown. It was not initially clear what (if anything at all) the individual tenant could say he 'owned'.

(a) *The interposed abstraction*

The answer to the conundrum was provided by the 'doctrine of estates'. As Professor F.H. Lawson pointed out, the solution arrived at in English law was 'to create an abstract entity called the estate in land and to interpose it between the tenant and the land.'[20] The object of the ownership enjoyed by each 'tenant' was not the land itself but a conceptual 'estate' in the land, each 'estate' differing from the others in temporal extent. Consonantly with the feudal metaphor of ultimate sovereign title, the maximum interest which a subject could have in respect of the land was some graded form of estate in fee.[1] In this way, while the doctrine of tenures was apt to describe the relationship between tenant and lord, the doctrine of estates mediated much more directly the relationship between tenant and land.

By resorting to this ingenious compromise, English law resolved at a stroke the apparent contradiction of theory and reality in the ownership of land. Although at one level the 'estate' in the land merely demarcated the temporal extent of the grant to the 'tenant', in practice it provided a functional (and theoretically acceptable) substitute form of ownership in respect of land. The doctrine of estates survives to the present day. Like the medieval 'tenant', the modern proprietor of land owns in some strict sense not the land, but rather an 'estate' in the land which confers specific rights and powers according to the nature of the 'estate'.[2]

(b) *The dimension of time*

The terminology of 'estates' introduced a fourth dimension of *time* into the description of the terms of grant enjoyed by the 'tenant'. Each 'estate' recognised by the common law simply represented a temporal 'slice' of the bundle of rights and powers exercisable in respect of land,[3] and in the doctrine of estates there was developed a coherent set of rules classifying the diverse ways in which rights in land might be carved up in this dimension of time.[4]

It was the concentration on the rights and powers appertinent to differing kinds of 'estate' which so sharply distinguished the common law view of real property from the continental emphasis on full ownership in the abstract

20 Op cit, p 66f.

1 See *Mabo v Queensland* (1992) 107 ALR 1 at 59f per Deane and Gaudron JJ.

2 See *Minister of State for the Army v Dalziel* (1944) 68 CLR 261 at 277 per Latham CJ ('In English law no subject can own lands allodially—he can own only an estate in land'). See also *Stokes v Costain Property Investments Ltd* [1983] 1 WLR 907 at 909E–F.

3 See Deane J's statement in the High Court of Australia in *Corin v Patton* (1990) 169 CLR 540 at 573, that 'at law. . .time, possession, title and interest can be seen as of the stuff of property'.

4 See R. Maudsley, *Escaping the Tyranny of the Common Law Estates*, 42 Missouri L Rev 355 (1977).

sense (*dominium*).[5] An 'estate' denoted the *duration* of a grant of land from a superior owner within the vertical power structure which emanated from the Crown; and no man could grant another any greater 'estate' than that which he himself owned (*nemo dat quod non habet*).

(c) Successive estates in land

Through the doctrine of estates the common law was able to organise the allocation of certain powers of management, enjoyment and disposition over land in respect of particular periods or 'slices' of time. Moreover, as the law of real property became distanced from the physical reality of land and entered a world of almost mathematical abstraction, it was possible to accord an *immediate* conceptual reality to each 'slice' of time represented by an 'estate'. In other words, any particular 'slice' of entitlement in the land could be viewed as having a present existence, notwithstanding that its owner was not entitled to possession of the land until some future date. In a world of concepts it was quite easy to conceive of rights to successive holdings of the land as 'present estates coexisting at the same time'.[6] It was ultimately this feature of the time-related aspect of the 'estate' in land which made it possible for the common lawyer to comprehend the notional reality of immediate dispositions of, and dealings with, future interests in land.

(d) The doctrine of 'waste'

Precisely because the doctrine of estates recognised the feasibility of successive estates in the same land, rules were developed both at common law and in equity in order to restrain the current estate owner (usually a 'tenant for life') from prejudicing the value of the land in the hands of any successor (or 'remainderman'). These rules took the form of a doctrine relating to 'waste', 'waste' being defined as any action or inaction on the part of the estate owner which permanently altered the physical character of the land. The unauthorised commission of waste operates implicitly as a compulsory transfer of wealth from the remainderman to the limited owner, and for this reason the law relating to waste was designed 'primarily to police the temporal boundary' between the two.[7]

Waste can be committed in several ways, although not all forms of waste lead to any legal remedy. The courts have been unwilling, for instance, to restrain the commission by a tenant for life of *ameliorating waste*, which merely has the effect of improving the land and of enhancing its value.[8] Only if the terms of his grant so stipulate can a tenant for life be made

5 Ante, p 34. It was Otto Kahn-Freund who pointed out that '[o]wing to its habit of looking at the powers and rights arising from ownership rather than at ownership in the abstract, English law has been able to introduce the time element into the property concept. The continental notion of property, like the dominium of Roman law, contains, as a matter of principle, the element of eternity' (*Introduction* to Karl Renner, *The Institutions of Private Law and Their Social Functions* (London and Boston 1949), p 23).

6 F.H. Lawson, op cit, p 67.

7 R.A. Epstein, *Past and Future: The Temporal Dimension in the Law of Property*, 64 Wash ULQ 667 at 707 (1986).

8 See eg *Doherty v Allman* (1878) 3 App Cas 709 at 722f (conversion of dilapidated premises into dwelling-houses).

liable for *permissive waste*, which comprises defaults of maintenance and repair leading to the dilapidation of buildings situated on the land.[9] More serious is *voluntary waste*, which includes any positive diminution of the value of the land (for instance, by quarrying or by the cutting of timber). A tenant for life is liable for such waste unless the terms of his grant give him specific exemption by declaring him 'unimpeachable for waste'.[10] Even if a tenant for life is at common law unimpeachable for waste, in equity he can be restrained from the commission of *equitable waste* in the form of wanton destruction of the land to the prejudice of any remainderman.[11]

(2) The freehold estates

The three freehold 'estates' known to the common law were the fee simple, the fee tail and the life estate, and each must now be examined in turn. Only one of these estates (the fee simple) is created with any frequency nowadays, the entailed interest and the life interest effectively requiring to be created behind some form of trust.

The key to the distinctions between them lies in the notion of time. The essence of the doctrine of estates has never been more elegantly captured than in the argument presented before the Court of Exchequer in the 16th century in *Walsingham's Case*.[12] Here it was said that

> the land itself is one thing, and the estate in the land is another thing, for an estate in the land is a time in the land, or land for a time, and there are diversities of estates, which are no more than diversities of time. . .

(a) The estate in fee simple

The estate in fee simple has always been the primary estate in land.[13] It represents the amplest 'estate' which a 'tenant' can have in or over land.[14] As was said in *Walsingham's Case*,[15] 'he who has a fee-simple in land has a time in the land without end, or the land for time without end'. In so far as real property represents a 'bundle of rights' exercisable with respect to the land, 'the tenant of an unencumbered estate in fee simple has the largest possible bundle.'[16]

(i) Infinite transferability of the fee simple estate Although in theory each tenant in fee simple is still merely a tenant in chief of the Crown, the estate in fee simple is nowadays tantamount to absolute ownership of land. In terms of the feudal fiction, an estate in fee simple denotes a grant of land from

9 See eg *In re Cartwright* (1889) 41 Ch D 532 at 535f.
10 *Woodhouse v Walker* (1880) 5 QBD 404 at 406f.
11 See eg *Vane v Lord Barnard* (1716) 2 Vern 738 at 739, 23 ER 1082.
12 (1573) 2 Plowd 547 at 555, 75 ER 805 at 816f.
13 See J.L. Barton, (1976) 92 LQR 108. On the historical evolution of the fee simple estate, see R.A. Epstein, 64 Wash ULQ 667 at 699ff (1986).
14 'A fee simple is the most extensive in quantum, and the most absolute in respect to the rights which it confers, of all the estates known to the law' (*Challis*, p 218, cited with approval by Isaacs J in *Commonwealth of Australia v State of New South Wales* (1923) 33 CLR 1 at 42). See also *City of St John v Saab* (1987) 37 DLR (4th) 160 at 163.
15 (1573) 2 Plowd 547 at 555, 75 ER 805 at 816f.
16 *Minister of State for the Army v Dalziel* (1944) 68 CLR 261 at 285 per Rich J. See also J.H. Merryman, *Ownership and Estate*, 48 Tulane L Rev 916 at 927 (1973-74).

the Crown in perpetuity—a right of tenure which endures for ever and which is capable, more or less indefinitely, of transfer inter vivos or of devolution on death. The owners of the fee simple estate may come and go but the estate remains, since it is of infinite duration. Each new owner steps into the shoes of his predecessor as a tenant in chief of the Crown—the modern effect of the Statute Quia Emptores of 1290.

(ii) Policy of unrestricted alienability The owner of an estate in fee simple is sometimes called a 'freeholder'—the owner of a freehold estate. Although modern legislation often curtails the fee simple owner's rights of use and enjoyment (for environmental and planning purposes[17]), there are relatively few limitations on his power to dispose of an estate in the land whether by will or by alienation inter vivos.[18] There is an important public policy which requires that land should be freely alienable in fee simple, since the unrestricted transferability of land is a vital precondition of a healthy and vibrant economy. Thus any grant or conveyance of an estate in fee simple subject to a condition which completely prohibits alienation by the grantee is in conflict with public policy. The offending condition is liable to be declared void at common law,[19] in which case the conveyance takes effect unconditionally.[20]

(b) The entailed interest

A 'fee tail' or 'entailed interest' is an estate in land which endures so long as the original grantee (the 'tenant in tail') or any of his lineal descendants is alive.[1] Historically the entail provided a form of landholding designedto retain land within the family.[2] However, from the 16th century onwards, this purpose was commonly frustrated by the 'barring' of the entail by the tenant in possession—which usually had the effect of converting the entail into some form of fee simple.[3] The grantor's expressed intention is of course subverted by the barring of an entail,[4] but few tears are shed on this account

17 Post, p 1124.
18 See, however, Inheritance (Provision for Family and Dependants) Act 1975; Race Relations Act 1976, s 21f.
19 *Co Litt*, p 223a.
20 Post, p 90.
1 As was said arguendo in *Walsingham's Case* (1573) 2 Plowd 547 at 555, 75 ER 805 at 817, 'he who has land in tail has a time in the land or the land for time as long as he has issues of his body'. An entailed interest in land can take effect nowadays only under a strict settlement governed by the complex machinery of the Settled Land Act 1925 (post p 611).
2 The fee tail frequently provided an instrument for giving effect to intricate patterns of landholding within an aristocratic dynastic family setting (see A.W.B. Simpson, *Introduction* to W. Blackstone, *Commentaries on the Laws of England* (Facsimile edn, Chicago and London, 1979), Vol 2, pp x-xi). Entails, said Samuel Johnson, 'are good, because it is good to preserve in a country, series of men, whom the people are accustomed to look up to as their leaders' (see A.W.B. Simpson, (1979) 24 Jur Rev (NS) 1).
3 The 'barring' of an entail may now be achieved quite easily either by will (see Law of Property Act 1925, s 176) or by means of a 'disentailing assurance', which comprises simply a declaration by deed executed by the tenant in tail that he henceforth holds a fee simple rather than an entailed interest. See Chapter 15 (post, p 612).
4 Entails may occasionally be rendered unbarrable by statute. Examples are the entails conferred for public services upon the first Duke of Marlborough and the Duke of Wellington (see 6 Anne, c 6 (1706), s 5; 6 Anne c 7 (1706), s 4; 54 Geo 3, c 161 (1814), s 28).

nowadays, partly because it is widely accepted that the 'dead hand' of the grantor should not prevail for ever, and partly because an entailed interest generates an especially onerous liability to taxation.[5]

(c) *The life interest*

A life interest is plainly coextensive and coterminous with the life of the grantee.[6] Since 1925 it has been possible to create a life interest only behind a trust for sale[7] or under a strict settlement of land (in which case the owner of the life interest becomes the 'tenant for life').[8] If a life interest is conveyed to a stranger, it ranks merely as an interest *pur autre vie*, in that it still endures only for the lifetime of the original grantee. Unlike an entailed interest, a life interest cannot be unilaterally transformed into an interest of greater duration.

(3) Words of limitation

In accordance with the rules as to words of limitation now contained in section 60 of the Law of Property Act 1925, a conveyance of freehold land to any person 'without words of limitation, or any equivalent expression' is effective to pass to the grantee 'the fee simple or other the whole interest which the grantor had power to convey in such land, unless a contrary intention appears in the conveyance.'[9]

Thus a conveyance of freehold land without further reference to the estate or interest intended to be granted (eg Blackacre 'to X') is normally effective to invest the grantee with an estate in fee simple in the land.[10] If the grantor wishes to dispose of some lesser estate in the land, he must actually employ 'words of limitation' in his grant (eg Blackacre 'to X in tail' or 'to X for life').[11]

5 The enlargement of the interest of the tenant in tail immediately takes the land outside the clutches of the Settled Land Act 1925 (see *In re Alefounder's Will Trusts* [1927] 1 Ch 360 at 364, post, p 630) and operates to simplify the title to the land by sweeping all limited interests off the land. There has never been much sympathy for any sense of grievance which may be felt by the remainderman who, but for the barring of the entail, would have taken the fee simple in possession. No great injustice is worked against the latter if a right which was initially almost worthless (in view of the possibility of the barring of the entail) is in fact rendered completely worthless (when that possibility materialises).

6 '[H]e who has an estate in land for life has no time in it longer than for his own life' (see *Walsingham's Case* (1573) 2 Plowd 547 at 555, 75 ER 805 at 817).

7 Post, p 519.

8 Post, p 611.

9 Law of Property Act 1925, s 60(1). An exactly parallel provision governs testamentary dispositions (see Wills Act 1837, s 28). Before 1882 a grant in fee simple required the use of the formula 'to X and his heirs'. In this formula the phrase 'to X' comprised *words of purchase* indicating the identity of the grantee. The phrase 'and his heirs' comprised the *words of limitation* which defined the nature of the estate granted, thereby removing any ambiguity between the grant intended and the grant of a life interest. Nowadays a grant 'to X' is sufficient to transfer a fee simple estate. See J. Baalman, *Sacred Cow of the Common Law*, (1965) 39 ALJ 197.

10 The words of limitation 'in fee simple' are never used, for instance, in the transfer of a registered title under the Land Registration Act 1925 (see *A J Dunning & Sons (Shopfitters) Ltd v Sykes & Son (Poole) Ltd* [1987] Ch 287 at 302E).

11 Law of Property Act 1925, s 60(4).

(4) The concept of 'seisin'

The concept of 'seisin' is an early idea which lies at the root of the historical development of English land law. The notion of 'seisin' is part of the common law tradition that proprietary rights in land are based on physical possession rather than on abstract title. In its original form, seisin consisted essentially of the actual or de facto possession of land—quite irrespective of right. Such possession, even if wrongful, was accorded a certain protection by the common law 'in the interests of peace'.[12] Seisin was fact not right, although the right might flow from the fact and be reinforced by the passage of time.[13] As Pollock and Maitland wrote, a man is in 'seisin' of land 'when he is enjoying it or in a position to enjoy it.'[14]

(a) Seisin as intrinsic to estate ownership

Seisin thus expressed the organic element in the relationship between man and land and as such provided presumptive evidence of ownership within the medieval framework of rights in land. Furthermore only the person 'seised of' land could avail himself of an estate owner's rights in respect of that land. Since seisin was a matter of fact, even the thief could enjoy seisin and it is significant that he could be dispossessed only if the rightful estate owner brought against him the action of novel disseisin. In other words, it was the recovery of seisin which provided the first step towards recovery of the full rights of estate ownership.

(b) Feoffments with 'livery of seisin'

From the 15th century onwards, as Lord Mansfield was later to state,[15] seisin was the technical term used to 'denote the completion of that investiture, by which the tenant was admitted into the tenure; and without which, no freehold could be constituted or pass.' Indeed only the person seised could effect a 'feoffment' (or conveyance of freehold land) with 'livery of seisin' in the symbolic sense required by the common law. 'Livery of seisin' took the form of a solemn ceremony. The grantor and grantee entered upon the land conveyed and the feoffor, in the presence of witnesses, delivered the seisin to the feoffee either by some symbolic act, such as handing him a twig or sod of earth, or by expressing appropriate words of alienation and leaving him in possession of the land.[16]

The quaint ritual of feoffment with livery of seisin is no longer effective

12 See *Minister of State for the Army v Dalziel* (1944) 68 CLR 261 at 276 per Latham CJ. Such was the force of the concept of seisin that the wrongful possessor was regarded as having a tortious fee simple which he could alienate and devise.

13 See A.E.-S. Tay, *Property and Law in the Society of Mass Production, Mass Consumption and Mass Allocation*, (1977) 10 ARSP (New Series) 87 at 91ff.

14 Op cit, Vol 2, p 34. See also F. W. Maitland, (1886) 2 LQR 481; (1888) 4 LQR 24, 286.

15 *Taylor d Atkyns v Horde* (1757) 1 Burr 60 at 107, 97 ER 190 at 216.

16 '"What's taking seizin?" said Dan, cautiously. "It's an old custom the people had when they bought and sold land. They used to cut out a clod and hand it over to the buyer, and you weren't lawfully seized of your land—it didn't really belong to you—till the other fellow had actually given you a piece of it—like this." He held out the turves' (Rudyard Kipling, *Puck of Pook's Hill* (London 1906), p 12). See also *Manton v Parabolic Pty Ltd* [1985] 2 NSWLR 361 at 367A-368C (post, p 273).

under English law to transfer an estate in land.[17] All interests in land now 'lie in grant' and may be conveyed 'without actual entry'.[18]

(c) *The modern importance of seisin*

Although seisin in its technical sense is no longer of much importance today, the emphasis which it placed on factual possession rather than abstract title continues to influence several areas of contemporary law.

(i) Relativity of title The pragmatic process of modern conveyancing rests to some degree on the assumption that proof of continued de facto enjoyment of land by the vendor and his predecessors provides a good root of title for the purchaser.[19] The law of adverse possession likewise relies upon the significance of unhindered possession of land, in so far as uninterrupted enjoyment of land over a period of time stipulated by law effectively generates title to the land concerned.[20]

Moreover, the pre-eminent position accorded to de facto possession in English law ensures that there is no such thing as 'absolute title' to land.[1] All title is ultimately relative.[2] The title of the present possessor will customarily be upheld unless and until a better claim is advanced on behalf of somebody else. As Cockburn CJ observed in *Asher v Whitlock*,[3]

> possession is good against all the world except the person who can shew a good title: and it would be mischievous to change this established doctrine...All the old law on the doctrine of disseisin was founded on the principle that the disseisor's title was good against all but the disseisee.

(ii) The common law concept of 'property' It has also been said that the concept of seisin has laid an indelible mark upon the way in which the common lawyer thinks of land. It was to the concept of seisin that Professor Alice Tay attributed 'the Englishman's concept of freedom—of his home as his castle'.[4] In her words, the common law has long maintained

> a bias in favour of the factual situation—the citizen's actual behaviour and powers *against* the claims of privilege and authority as such...The role of the underlying seisin-possession concept in the common law is to recognise and protect those still important areas in which men live, work and plan as user-owners, to set out their rights and obligations, to give them an area of privacy in which they have a right to be free of state and community interference, to repel the unattractive neighbour, the busybody, the officious policeman, and to ensure that they allow their neighbours the same possibility of undisturbed enjoyment. Only in societies that do not have such protection do men realise how important this concept of personal security and

17 That a title in land may be transferred by livery of seisin seems still to be a live possibility in the Canadian province of Ontario (see eg *Re Bouris and Button* (1976) 60 DLR (3d) 233 at 238).
18 Law of Property Act 1925, s 51(1).
19 Post, p 96. See *Minister of State for the Army v Dalziel* (1944) 68 CLR 261 at 277.
20 Post, p 282.
1 Even the artificial concept of 'absolute title' as recorded in the Land Register is something of a misnomer (post, p 229).
2 See B. Rudden, (1964) 80 LQR 63.
3 (1865) LR 1 QB 1 at 5.
4 'Law, the citizen and the state', in E. Kamenka, R. Brown and A.E.-S. Tay (ed), *Law and Society: The Crisis in Legal Ideals* (London 1978), p 11f.

inviolability is. . .It is also the base and shaper of the social sentiment that shrinks with distaste from the forcible eviction.

(iii) Protection of residential security It is not without significance that the primarily physical or factual dimension bound up in the medieval notion of seisin finds a modern counterpart in the importance which is increasingly attached nowadays to the utility-based aspects of land ownership and particularly to the protection of residential security. One of the themes of any account of modern English land law is the emergence of a contemporary emphasis on the use value of land as distinct from its exchange value.

A significant index of this development was provided, for instance, by the decision in *Williams & Glyn's Bank Ltd v Boland*.[5] In the Court of Appeal in this case Lord Denning MR construed the concept of the 'overriding interest' in registered land in language which was highly reminiscent of the concept of seisin.[6] He noted that, for the purpose of protection under the Land Registration Act 1925, 'actual occupation is matter of fact, not matter of law. . .It does not depend on title. A squatter is often in actual occupation.'[7] Thus, just as in the context of seisin the fact was instrumental in establishing the right, similarly in *Boland*'s case it was the fact of physical possession which ultimately conferred overriding status on a legal entitlement.

5 [1981] AC 487 (House of Lords), [1979] Ch 312 (Court of Appeal) (post, p 568f).
6 See Land Registration Act 1925, s 70(1)(g) (post, p 203).
7 [1979] Ch 312 at 332E. Lord Wilberforce ruled similarly in the House of Lords that the statutory phrase 'actual occupation' emphasises 'that what is required is physical presence, not some entitlement in law' ([1981] AC 487 at 505B).

B. Structures

CHAPTER 4

Legal and equitable rights

The historical development of the English law of real property has been based on a fundamental—albeit arbitrarily drawn—distinction between those property rights in land which are designated as 'legal' rights and those which are designated as merely 'equitable'. It is true to say that the distinction between legal and equitable rights no longer retains the importance which it once had, and that it may well fade into relative insignificance with the comprehensive coverage of registered title.[1] Nevertheless any systematic review of English land law must start from a rigorous analysis of the difference between legal and equitable rights.

1. THE DISTINCTION BETWEEN 'LEGAL' AND 'EQUITABLE' RIGHTS

It might reasonably be expected that something fairly basic about land law should appear in section 1 of the Law of Property Act 1925—and indeed it does. In its terms section 1 surveys the entire field of proprietary rights in land,[2] and outlines the way in which either 'legal' or 'equitable' quality can be attached to those rights. The significance of this ascription of 'legal' or 'equitable' character derives, of course, from the days when 'legal' rights were those rights which were recognised exclusively by the courts of common law, while 'equitable' rights were enforced only by the courts of equity.[3] The jurisdictions of law and equity have now been fused for more than a century,[4] and legal and equitable rights are currently recognised and enforced in all courts alike. However, the distinction between these two kinds of right is still highly relevant—even decisive—in certain circumstances. This is particularly true in the case of unregistered land, where the attribution of legal or equitable character may fundamentally determine the effect of rights upon third parties who purchase the land to which they relate.

It is for precisely this reason that section 1 of the Law of Property Act 1925 takes great pains to demarcate legal from equitable rights in land.

1 Post, p 166.

2 For the distinction between 'proprietary' and 'personal' rights in land see Chapter 2 (ante, p 44). It is important to note that section 1 of the Law of Property Act 1925 says nothing about those categories of rights affecting land which are not truly proprietary rights as such but are merely personal rights in land. The difference between 'proprietary' and 'personal' rights in land rests ultimately on some intuitive perception that the former confer on the grantee some kind of 'stake' in the land itself, whereas the latter confer merely a personal and usually transient permission to live on or do something on the land in question. 'Personal' rights affect only the immediate grantor and grantee: they are not normally regarded as capable of binding third parties (post, p 209f).

3 See A.W.B. Simpson, *A History of The Land Law* (2nd edn Oxford 1986), p 192ff.

4 See Supreme Court of Judicature Acts 1873-1875.

(1) The statutory criterion

Section 1 of the Law of Property Act 1925 draws a fairly sharp distinction between certain rights which are 'capable of subsisting or of being conveyed or created at law' and those rights which are capable of existence only in equity.

1. —(1) The only estates in land which are capable of subsisting or of being conveyed or created at law are —
(a) An estate in fee simple absolute in possession;
(b) A term of years absolute.

(2) The only interests or charges in or over land which are capable of subsisting or of being conveyed or created at law are—
(a) An easement, right, or privilege in or over land for an interest equivalent to an estate in fee simple absolute in possession or a term of years absolute;
(b) A rentcharge in possession issuing out of or charged on land being either perpetual or for a term of years absolute;
(c) A charge by way of legal mortgage;
(d) . . .and any other similar charge on land which is not created by an instrument;
(e) Rights of entry exercisable over or in respect of a legal term of years absolute, or annexed, for any purpose, to a legal rentcharge.

(3) All other estates, interests, and charges in or over land take effect as equitable interests.

Section 1 thus distinguishes between
(a) two legal *estates* (section 1(1)) and five legal *interests* or *charges* (section 1(2)),[5] and
(b) all other proprietary rights in land—which must necessarily by reason of their exclusion from the first two subsections be equitable only (section 1(3)).

(2) The proper classification of rights in land

The distinction between 'legal' and 'equitable' rights in land is therefore both artificial and crude; but it is nonetheless clear. Whether an estate, interest or charge can ever be 'legal' depends quite simply on whether reference to it can be found in one or other of the categories contained in section 1(1) or (2). If the right in question is to be found there (eg a term of years absolute or a mortgage), then it is indeed capable of existing

5 The rights referred to in section 1(1) and (2) are alike in that they are all potentially *legal* in character. The difference between estates, interests and charges consists in the fact that an 'estate' is a right in land owned or occupied by oneself, while an 'interest' or 'charge' tends to be a right acquired in or over somebody else's land. However, this formal distinction should not obscure the fact that the estates, interests and charges referred to in section 1(1) and (2) are all potentially legal rather than equitable. In the legislation consolidated in the 1925 enactments, all three kinds of legal right were thrown together in *one* subsection rather than the *two* subsections which appear as section 1(1) and (2) of the Law of Property Act 1925 (see Law of Property Act 1922, s 1(1)).

at law.[6] If it is not referred to within section 1(1) or (2)—as would be the case, for instance, with a restrictive covenant[7]—then the right can only be equitable.[8]

2. LEGAL ESTATES

Section 1(1) marks out two possible *legal estates* in land—the 'freehold' and 'leasehold' estates respectively. Neither of these estates can be held by a minor, ie by a person who has not attained the age of 18 years.[9]

(1) The fee simple absolute in possession

As indicated in section 1(1)(a) of the Law of Property Act 1925, the larger of the two estates which can exist in land at common law is the fee simple absolute in possession. This estate—the freehold estate—nowadays connotes the virtual reality of absolute ownership of land. The fee simple estate was described in outline in Chapter 3,[10] and is subjected to further analysis in Chapter 5.[11]

(2) The term of years absolute

According to section 1(1)(b) of the Law of Property Act 1925, the only other estate in land which is capable of subsisting or of being conveyed or created at law is the 'term of years absolute'.[12] A term of years is the estate which a landlord confers upon his tenant, the qualifier 'absolute' appearing in this context to have no special significance.[13] A term of years is commonly known as a 'leasehold estate' and its owner as a leaseholder as distinct from a freeholder. A term of years is also often called simply a lease or tenancy.

(a) Distinguishing characteristic of the term of years

The distinguishing characteristic of a term of years is that it confers a right to occupy and enjoy land for a period of fixed maximum duration. It matters not whether that period is fixed and therefore self-determining or periodic

6 Section 1 of the Law of Property Act 1925 indicates merely whether a given property right is 'capable' of existing at law. Whether, within a particular context, that right *actually* constitutes a legal right depends usually on whether certain formalities (eg the use of a deed) were observed in the granting of that right (post, p 271f).
7 Post, p 1138.
8 Moreover, the right is equitable in such a case irrespective of its mode of creation (eg even if created by deed).
9 Law of Property Act 1925, s 1(6).
10 Ante, p 58.
11 Post, p 85.
12 Ante, p 68; post, pp 673, 777.
13 As defined in Law of Property Act 1925, s 205(1)(xxvii), a 'term of years absolute' retains its absolute character notwithstanding that it is determinable by notice given by either the landlord or the tenant or is determinable by reason of the landlord's exercise of a right of re-entry in the event of breach of covenant by the tenant.

and therefore capable of extension. The period may be one week or three thousand years: a term of years can exist in either case.[14] Being an estate in land, a term of years provides a flexible base for other transactions with the land. The term may itself become the subject matter of either an 'assignment' (ie transfer) or a subletting.[15]

(b) Social and economic functions of the lease

Leases of land are exceedingly important in both social and commercial terms. The device of the term of years plays a vital role in the provision of business premises for commercial enterprise, in the regulation of land use for agricultural purposes, and in the supply of residential housing.[16] Each of these spheres of operation was originally left to the free play of market forces, but in more recent times the conduct of relations between landlord and tenant has been controlled in some degree by regulatory legislation.[17] Perhaps the most conspicuous aspect of this legislation has tended to be that dealing with private residential tenancies. Historically the landlord, operating from a superior bargaining position, was frequently able to impose oppressive rents and conditions upon his tenants. However, the Rent Act legislation which has prevailed for most of the present century did much to redress the balance of power in the residential context, by affording substantial security of tenure and by establishing effective rent controls. Less extensive forms of protection for the tenant are provided by the statutory codes which govern other leasehold areas, ie in respect of public sector residential tenancies, business tenancies and agricultural tenancies.

Leases are described further in Chapters 17 and 18.[18]

(3) Formal creation of legal estates

With certain exceptions[19] no conveyance of land is effective to confer a legal estate on the grantee unless the conveyance is made by deed (or formal writing).[20] Failure to use a deed in the grant of a fee simple absolute or

14 A 'term of years absolute' is specifically defined as including 'a term for less than a year' (Law of Property Act 1925, s 205(1)(xxvii)). The longest lease on record seems to be one of 10 million years, granted on 3 December 1868 in respect of a plot for a sewage tank adjoining Columb Barracks, Mullingar, County Meath, Ireland (see *Guinness Book of Records 1993* (London 1992), p 186).

15 Post, p 734.

16 In Great Britain almost one third of the available housing stock is occupied by leaseholders under a term of years of some sort (Central Statistical Office, *Social Trends No 22* (London 1992), p 145).

17 Post, pp 873, 887.

18 Post, pp 673, 777.

19 These exceptions are spelt out in Law of Property Act 1925, s 52(2), the most important relating to assents by a personal representative (s 52(2)(a)) and certain kinds of lease not exceeding a term of three years (s 52(2)(d) in conjunction with s 54(2)) (post, pp 272, 736).

20 Law of Property Act 1925, s 52(1). For further details of the rules regarding formalities, see Chapter 9 (post, p 271). The formal documents of conveyance which evidence the transmission of the legal estate through a series of successive owners are collectively termed the 'title deeds'. These title deeds provide 'the essential indicia of title to unregistered land' (*Sen v Headley* [1991] Ch 425 at 437C per Nourse LJ, post, p 131).

a term of years generally results in the creation of only an equitable interest for the grantee.[1]

3. LEGAL INTERESTS AND CHARGES

Section 1(2) of the Law of Property Act 1925 defines five categories of 'interest' or 'charge' capable of existence 'at law'.

(1) Easements, rights and privileges (section 1(2)(a))

An easement is effectively a right to utilise somebody else's land in some limited way, the best example being a right of way over land belonging to a stranger.[2] If A, the owner of an estate in fee simple, grants his neighbour, B, a right of way over A's land, B is regarded in English law as having a proprietary right—of some kind—in or over A's land.

(a) Requirements for legal character

Whether an easement is legal or equitable is determined largely by the terms of section 1(2)(a) of the Law of Property Act 1925, which includes within the rights 'capable' of existence at law any 'easement, right, or privilege in or over land for an interest equivalent to an estate in fee simple absolute in possession or a term of years absolute'. Whether an easement of the kind referred to here is actually legal in any given circumstances will depend on its creation by deed, statute or prescription.[3] However, section 1(2)(a) enables a distinction to be made between legal and equitable easements. It is a necessary, but not sufficient, condition of legal quality that an easement must conform to the characteristics as to duration which are laid down in section 1(2)(a).

(b) Examples

If A by deed grants B an easement without limit of time, B's easement is legal, since its duration corresponds, in the terms of section 1(2)(a), to that of 'an estate in fee simple absolute in possession'. Likewise, if A by deed grants B an easement for a fixed period of time—whether long or short—B's easement is legal, since its duration is framed on the analogy of 'a term of years absolute', as referred to in the statute. However, if A grants B an easement for any period other than the two kinds of time-scale stipulated in section 1(2)(a), B's right can only be equitable. Section 1(2)(a) does not cover any easement granted for an indeterminate period other than in perpetuity, and therefore an easement granted eg for B's life, or until

1 This demonstrates, incidentally, that it is quite possible to hold an *equitable* fee simple absolute in possession or an *equitable* term of years absolute. Section 1(1) of the Law of Property Act 1925 merely provides that it is these estates alone which have even the potentiality of *legal* existence.

2 Post, p 1044.

3 Post, p 1087.

such time as an alternative access is constructed, can only take effect in equity—even if granted by deed.[4]

(2) Rentcharges (section 1(2)(b))

A rentcharge is a right to a periodic payment of money charged on or issuing out of land other than under a lease or mortgage.[5] A rentcharge arises for instance where A has charged his own land with a payment of £100 per annum in favour of B. In such circumstances B is regarded as having a proprietary interest in A's land, and the characterisation of B's interest as legal or equitable turns on section 1(2)(b) of the Law of Property Act 1925. B's rentcharge can be legal only if it is 'either perpetual or for a term of years absolute', being equitable in all other cases.

Rentcharges are today fairly uncommon and are, in any case, in the process of being phased out of existence under the terms of the Rentcharges Act 1977.[6] This legislation recognises the anomalous nature of rentcharges in the modern context and provides that no new rentcharge may be created after 22 August 1977 'whether at law or in equity'.[7] Any instrument which purports to create a new rentcharge is declared void,[8] and all existing rentcharges are liable to be extinguished at the expiry of a period of sixty years beginning with the commencement of the 1977 Act or with the date on which the rentcharge in question first became payable, whichever is the later.[9]

(3) Mortgages (section 1(2)(c))

A mortgage is a form of security in real property taken by one who has advanced money on loan to the owner of land.[10] Although not of course confined to residential property, mortgage transactions have become the primary means of financing home ownership in fee simple or on long lease, the prospective home-owner often raising the bulk of the required purchase price by means of a loan from an institutional mortgagee such as a bank or building society or from a local authority.[11] The purchaser then acquires the fee simple or a long lease in the property purchased, granting a charge

4 Law of Property Act 1925, s 1(3).
5 Rentcharges Act 1977, s 1.
6 See Law Commission, *Report on Rentcharges* (Law Com No 68, August 1975).
7 Rentcharges Act 1977, s 2(1). There are, however, certain exceptions. There is, for instance, no prohibition on the creation of a rentcharge which has the effect of making the land on which the rent is charged settled land by virtue of Settled Land Act 1925, s 1(1)(v) (see Rentcharges Act 1977, s 2(3)(a)). Another exempted class is the 'estate rentcharge' (Rentcharges Act 1977, s 2(3)(c), (4), (5)), which often plays a useful role in the enforcement of freehold covenants (post, p 1136). In effect the embargo on new rentcharges covers only those created in a commercial context for money or money's worth.
8 Rentcharges Act 1977, s 2(2).
9 Rentcharges Act 1977, s 3(1). The owner of land subject to a rentcharge which is liable to extinguishment under section 3(1) may redeem the rentcharge by paying a redemption price calculated according to an algebraic formula contained in section 10(1).
10 Mortgages are dealt with in detail in Chapter 20 (post, p 931).
11 The role of the local authority as a mortgagee has been greatly increased by the 'right to buy' provisions introduced by Part I of the Housing Act 1980 (post, p 772).

by way of legal mortgage as security for the loan.[12] The purchaser retains ownership of the estate throughout the loan term, although he is under a contractual obligation to repay both the capital sum advanced and any interest which it bears. The home-owner—the mortgagor—is thereby enabled to acquire both a family base and a major capital asset by way of instalment purchase over a lengthy period (usually 20 or 25 years). Meanwhile the creditor—the mortgagee—is protected since the charge taken as security can always be enforced by taking possession of the property if the mortgagor becomes unable to discharge his obligations under the terms of the loan.

A charge granted 'by way of legal mortgage' is defined in section 1(2)(c) of the Law of Property Act 1925 as being capable of creation at law. If contained in a deed, such a charge is in fact *legal*.

(4) Miscellaneous charges (section 1(2)(d))

Section 1(2)(d) of the Law of Property Act 1925 refers to a group of legal charges on land not created by the voluntary transactions of individuals but imposed by statute. The categories of charge included here have been gravely diminished by repealing legislation,[13] and are now of little consequence.

(5) Rights of entry (section 1(2)(e))

A 'right of entry' has nothing to do with a right of way or any other easement.[14] A right of entry may be attached to a lease or rentcharge and, if so attached, is penal[15] rather than facultative. It consists essentially of the right to enforce forfeiture of the estate which is the subject matter of the lease or rentcharge. The right of entry becomes exercisable only in the event of default by, respectively, the tenant or the rentchargor, and its exercise results in a vesting or revesting of the delinquent's estate in the party exercising the right.[16] Far from comprising a 'right to use or draw profit from another man's land', the right of entry provides a means 'to take his land altogether away'.[17]

It is an intrinsic feature of a right of entry that it constitutes a proprietary right in the subject land which is somehow distinct from the proprietary right comprised in the lease or rentcharge to which it is appended. Thus A, the owner of an estate in fee simple, may have an extra proprietary right against his tenant, B, in the form of a right of entry expressly conferred on A by the terms of the lease. As a proprietary right in B's land, A's right of entry must be either legal or equitable. Section 1(2)(e) of the Law of

12 This is nowadays a much more common means of creating a legal mortgage than the other mortgage device which is still permitted today, which involves the conferment on the mortgagee of a long lease in the property offered as security (Law of Property Act 1925, ss 85(1), 86(1)) (post, p 939).

13 Tithe rentcharge was abolished by the Tithe Act 1936, s 1, and land tax by the Finance Act 1963, Part V, Sch 14.

14 'To include a right of entry in the description of "equitable easement" offends a sense both of elegance and accuracy' (*Shiloh Spinners Ltd v Harding* [1973] AC 691 at 720B per Lord Wilberforce).

15 *Shiloh Spinners Ltd v Harding* [1973] AC 691 at 719E.

16 The exercise of the right of entry is subject to the court's jurisdiction to afford the defaulting party relief against forfeiture (post, p 812).

17 *Shiloh Spinners Ltd v Harding* [1973] AC 691 at 720C per Lord Wilberforce.

Property Act 1925 specifically provides that a right of entry is legal if it is 'exercisable over or in respect of a legal term of years absolute'. Likewise, if A has annexed a right of entry to a rentcharge undertaken in his favour by B, that right of entry is legal if the rentcharge itself is legal. In all other cases the right of entry must be equitable only.[18]

4. EQUITABLE INTERESTS

In the scheme of the Law of Property Act 1925 equitable interests in or over land are defined essentially by exclusion. Those proprietary rights in or over land which fail to qualify as 'legal' rights under the criteria of section 1(1), (2) take effect merely as 'equitable interests'.[19] These equitable interests and the conveyancing difficulties which they generate provide the subject matter of much of the remainder of this book.

5. SIGNIFICANCE OF THE DISTINCTION BETWEEN LEGAL AND EQUITABLE RIGHTS

A question must inevitably arise as to the reasons which underlie the strenuous efforts made in the Law of Property Act 1925 to distinguish *legal* from *equitable* rights.

The sharpness of the distinction drawn by statute results from the fact that the borderline between legal and equitable rights has traditionally provided the starting point for the resolution of the central question of land law. This central issue relates to whether certain rights in land survive a transfer of that land to a purchaser, thereby remaining valid and enforceable against him. Given the pre-eminent importance of the transferability of land in an exchange economy, this question ranks as one of considerable social and commercial significance. Land law in practice means conveyancing—the quotidian business of effecting dispositions of property—and the scope of the problem becomes even larger once it is recognised that a 'conveyance' is defined broadly as including not merely the outright sale of property, but also a mortgage, charge, lease and assent relating to property.[20]

The fate of legal and equitable rights in the context of a conveyance is, of course, a matter of importance for both the purchaser and the owner of the rights in question. People tend to make the largest investment of their lifetime savings in one or other form of real property. It is a matter of more than marginal concern that the rights which they purchase should not be taken away, superseded or destroyed in any later transaction without proper compensation. Likewise the purchaser of land has a legitimate interest in knowing precisely which rights will be binding upon him in the aftermath of a purchase. Any uncertainty as to the effect of land transactions on various

18 Law of Property Act 1925, s 1(3). See eg *Shiloh Spinners Ltd v Harding* [1973] AC 691 at 719B.

19 Law of Property Act 1925, s 1(3), (8).

20 Law of Property Act 1925, s 205(1)(ii). A 'purchaser' is likewise defined as including 'a lessee, mortgagee or other person who for valuable consideration acquires an interest in property. . .' (section 205(1)(xxi)).

types of real property right has the effect of inhibiting purchasers and of stultifying dealings in land. No purchaser wants to risk his money if there is any real danger that the land purchased may be subject to adverse rights vested in others which render his title effectively or substantially worthless.

The social and economic implications involved here become even more acute if the 'purchaser' concerned is a mortgagee. In most instances mortgagees are large lending institutions which exist to finance the acquisition of realty for a wide range of commercial or residential purposes. Any inhibition placed on the availability of mortgage funds has immediately a potential impact on business life and the living patterns of millions. It was no mere casual afterthought which provoked the statement of Lord Upjohn in *National Provincial Bank Ltd v Ainsworth*[1] that

> It has been the policy of the law for over a hundred years to simplify and facilitate transactions in real property. It is of great importance that persons should be able freely and easily to raise money on the security of their property.

Given these policy motivations, it is clear that the operation of an efficient conveyancing system depends heavily upon the achievement of a high degree of clarity in determining the fate of proprietary rights in the event of transactions with title. At least in historical terms, the answer to the central question of land law has turned ultimately on the characterisation of those rights as either *legal* or *equitable*. Although the importance of this distinction is being steadily eroded by the extension of the system of title registration,[2] it is this watershed between various sorts of right in land which still provides a vital key to resolving disputed issues of priority.

This can best be seen in the operation of two axioms which lie deeply embedded in the sedimentary layers of English land law. At some points today these two axioms still remain exposed to view, and provide an indispensable basis for the construction of solutions to land law problems. At other points they have been overlaid by different strata deposited by the later action of legislative change, although even here the erosive activity of judge-made law has occasionally stripped back the more recent strata to reveal the bed-rock of original principle.

The two most basic axioms of English land law are the following:

(i) legal rights bind the world;

(ii) equitable rights bind all persons except a bona fide purchaser of a legal estate for value without notice of those equitable rights.

(1) Legal rights bind the world

The force of the first axiom is simply explained. If B owns a *legal* right in or over land belonging to A (see *Fig*. 4), and C later acquires any interest in that land, B's right is binding on and effective against C. This result follows irrespective of whether C previously knew of B's right. The outcome rarely works injustice since almost all legal rights in or over land are evident on the face of the documents relating to title, and are therefore open to perusal by an intending purchaser.

1 [1965] AC 1175 at 1233G–1234A.

2 Post, p 166.

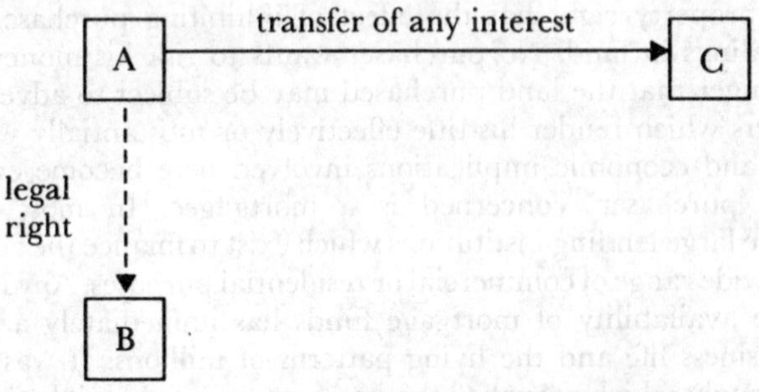

Fig. 4

Legal rights thus effectively take care of themselves. When land (or an interest in land) is transferred to *any* third party, legal rights previously attached to the land remain attached and are therefore binding on that third party. The axiomatic nature of this result works for both efficiency and clarity. The owner of legal rights knows that his position is secure notwithstanding the transfer of the land; likewise the purchaser is in general wholly aware that he takes his disposition subject to any legal rights which belong to others.

The simple logic of land law can be demonstrated in the following way. Suppose that A, the owner of a legal fee simple estate in Blackacre, grants a term of years (or lease) to B, and then transfers his fee simple (or 'freehold reversion'[3]) to C. If the term of years granted to B is a *legal* estate (as defined by the Law of Property Act 1925[4]), then it follows inexorably that C is bound by it.[5] The same result occurs *a fortiori* if C takes some lesser interest than a legal fee simple (eg if C is a mortgagee, or if C's interest is equitable rather than legal), for the binding effect of B's interest is not conditional on the precise nature of the interest taken by C. C is bound by B's legal right even if C is not a purchaser but is an adverse possessor (or 'squatter').[6] It is simply axiomatic that legal rights bind the world, and moreover that they bind the world irrespective of notice. It is entirely irrelevant whether C had any prior knowledge of the existence of B's rights.

The same reasoning is applicable to any other kind of legal interest owned by B. For example, if A, the owner of a legal fee simple estate in Blackacre, grants B a right of way over Blackacre, the effect of this easement on C (a subsequent purchaser from A) depends fundamentally on whether B's easement is characterised as legal or equitable. C is automatically bound by B's easement if the easement is properly classified as *legal* according to the canons contained in section 1(2)(a) of the Law of Property Act 1925 (eg if it was granted in perpetuity or for a fixed period of time).[7] Similarly, a mortgage granted by A to B is binding on C if it constitutes a legal mortgage

3 Post, p 685.
4 Ante, p 68.
5 If B's term of years is not legal but equitable (eg if not created by deed in circumstances where a deed was required (see Law of Property Act 1925, ss 52(2)(d), 54(2)), its effect on C depends on different principles (post, pp 142, 181).
6 *In re Nisbet and Potts' Contract* [1906] 1 Ch 386 at 401.
7 Ante, p 71. If, however, the easement was granted for an indefinite period other than perpetuity or was granted otherwise than by deed, the easement can only be equitable and its impact on C turns on different principles (post, pp 151, 201).

within the terms of section 1(2)(c) of the Law of Property Act 1925 (eg if created by deed).[8] A right of entry, if legal within the terms of section 1(2)(e), is also binding on the world.[9] In all these cases it matters not what precise interest is taken by C. It is likewise irrelevant that C was at the date of purchase unaware of the rights of B, since the doctrine of notice has no application at all to legal rights.

(2) Equitable rights are governed by the doctrine of notice

According to the second axiom of English land law, equitable rights in or over land are binding on all persons *other than* a bona fide purchaser of a legal estate for value without notice of those equitable rights.[10] This basic proposition incorporates what is known as the *equitable doctrine of notice*,[11] and provides the historical method of determining whether an equitable interest granted to B in respect of A's land remains binding on a stranger, C, who later receives some interest in that land.

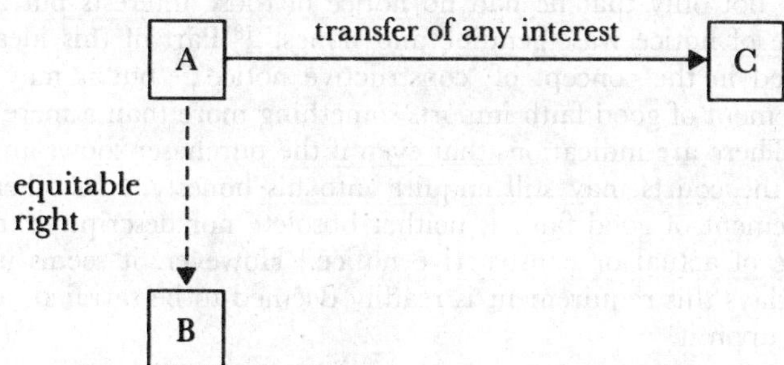

Fig. 5

It must be emphasised that this doctrine of notice, although forming a fundamental stratum of English land law, is nowadays heavily overlaid by various systems of registration of land interests.[12] It has also been superseded by certain statutory mechanisms for 'overreaching' prior equitable rights. To this extent the doctrine is no longer the *comprehensive* arbiter of the binding effect of equitable interests.[13] It tends to play only a residual role in determining questions of priority when other methods have failed or are inapplicable.[14] Nevertheless the doctrine of notice holds a vital key even today to an understanding of the structure and function of the law of real property, and for this reason must be subjected to minute examination.

In terms of the doctrine of notice, equitable rights granted to B in respect of A's land are liable to be defeated by a third party purchaser who at the date of purchase had no notice or knowledge of their existence. In *Midland Bank Trust Co Ltd v Green*[15] Lord Wilberforce explained this doctrine as an

8 Ante, p 73, post, p 939.
9 Post, p 73.
10 *London and South Western Railway Co v Gomm* (1882) 20 Ch D 562 at 583; *In re Nisbet and Potts' Contract* [1906] 1 Ch 386 at 403, 405.
11 Ante, p 44.
12 Post, pp 113, 166.
13 Post, p 104.
14 Post, p 110.
15 [1981] AC 513 at 528D.

instance of equity's tendency to fasten upon conscience, observing that the 'composite expression' of the doctrine was 'used to epitomise the circumstances in which equity would or rather would not do so.'[16]

The full implications of this 'composite expression' must now be investigated. Before the equitable doctrine of notice may operate in his favour and release him from pre-existing equitable rights, the purchaser must discharge a heavy onus. He must establish that he is a bona fide (good faith) purchaser of a legal estate for value without notice. The onus of proof rests clearly on him.[17] A purchaser who demonstrates that he is possessed of all these attributes is sometimes known simply as 'Equity's Darling'—one to whom the favour of equity has been extended.

(a) *Bona fides*

It is generally assumed that the requirement of bona fides or good faith on the part of the purchaser relates primarily to the element of notice. In order that the purchaser may claim immunity from equitable interests, he must show not only that he had no notice of those interests but also that his absence of notice was 'genuine and honest'.[18] Part of this idea is now incorporated in the concept of 'constructive notice',[19] but it may be that the requirement of good faith imports something more than a mere absence of notice. There are indications that even if the purchaser shows an absence of notice, the courts may still enquire into his honesty.[20] In other words, the requirement of good faith is neither obsolete nor descriptive merely of an absence of actual or constructive notice.[1] However, it seems in reality that nowadays this requirement is readily deemed to be satisfied, and little ever turns upon it.

(b) *Purchase of a legal estate*

In order to defeat pre-existing equitable rights, the purchaser must take a legal estate in the land concerned.[2] He must therefore purchase either

16 Ante, p 42.

17 *Attorney-General v Biphosphated Guano Co* (1879) 11 Ch D 327 at 337; *In re Nisbet and Potts' Contract* [1906] 1 Ch 386 at 403f; *Heneghan v Davitt* [1933] IR 375 at 377, 379; *Northern Bank Ltd v Henry* [1981] IR 1 at 19.

18 *Midland Bank Trust Co Ltd v Green* [1981] AC 513 at 528E per Lord Wilberforce.

19 Ante, p 43, post, p 80.

20 See *Pilcher v Rawlins* (1872) 7 Ch App 259 at 269; *Oliver v Hinton* [1899] 2 Ch 264 at 273; *Taylor v London and County Banking Co* [1901] 2 Ch 231 at 256; *Midland Bank Trust Co Ltd v Green* [1981] AC 513 at 528F-G.

1 It is significant that the term 'purchaser', which appears in the statutory formulation of the notice doctrine contained in the Law of Property Act 1925, s 199(1)(ii) (post, p 81), is itself defined as incorporating an element of good faith (see Law of Property Act 1925, s 205(1)(xxi)).

2 Even a purchaser who has paid the purchase money in full is not safe if notice of the adverse equitable interest reaches him before the formal conveyance to him of the legal estate (*Wigg v Wigg* (1739) 1 Atk 382 at 384, 26 ER 244 at 245). However, this is true only in respect of those adverse equitable rights which existed prior to the contract to purchase. Any adverse equitable interest which arises between the date of contract and the date of the conveyance of the legal estate must concede priority to the purchaser, since the purchaser himself acquires an equitable interest at the date of contract (post, p 263). The latter situation is governed by the rule that where the equities are equal, the first in time prevails.

a legal fee simple absolute in possession or a legal term of years.[3] Thus the freedom from prior equitable interests conferred by the doctrine of notice may be acquired by a purchaser of either a freehold or a leasehold. Moreover, by a special statutory fiction a third party lender who takes a charge 'by way of legal mortgage' is also regarded for some purposes as having purchased a legal estate.[4] He is deemed to have 'the same protection. . .as if some form of term of years had been created in his favour by the mortgagor (ie the borrower).[5]

If the purchaser takes only an equitable interest in the land, he is, in principle, subject to all prior equitable interests irrespective of notice.[6] The general rule is that where the equities are equal, the first in time prevails.[7]

(c) *Purchase for value*

The equitable doctrine of notice operates in favour only of a purchaser for value. The concept of a 'purchaser for value' may appear pleonastic, but it should be borne in mind that in the strictest common law sense[8] a 'purchaser' is one who takes property by reason of the act of another (as distinct from one whose title arises by operation of law, eg by descent or escheat).[9] On this basis, even a donee (or 'volunteer') ranks technically as a 'purchaser', since his interest derives from an act of gift; whereas a squatter can never rank as a 'purchaser' *stricto sensu*, since his title derives from the legal effect of the mere effluxion of time.

In terms of the doctrine of notice it is therefore clear that one who seeks immunity from prior equitable interests must show not merely that he is a 'purchaser' in the technical sense, but also that he gave valuable consideration.[10] The status of 'Equity's Darling' can never be achieved by either a donee[11] or a squatter.[12] However, if the purchaser gave value, it is irrelevant whether the consideration given was adequate.[13]

3 Law of Property Act 1925, s 1(1)(a), (b). Even a lessee at a rack rent constitutes a purchaser of a legal estate (*Goodright d Humphreys v Moses* (1775) 2 Wm Bl 1019 at 1022, 96 ER 599 at 600).

4 Law of Property Act 1925, s 87(1).

5 The grant of a long lease to the mortgagee is another method of creating a legal mortgage (post, p 939). See *Cave v Cave* (1880) 15 Ch D 639 at 646.

6 *London and South Western Railway Co v Gomm* (1882) 20 Ch D 562 at 583. See eg *Cave v Cave* (1880) 15 Ch D 639 at 648f (one of purchasers was equitable mortgagee).

7 Post, p 980.

8 See *Powell v Cleland* [1948] 1 KB 262 at 272 for a recognition that, in its old common law significance, 'purchase' covers all means of acquisition otherwise than by descent or escheat. See also Inheritance Act 1833, s 1.

9 See *IRC v Gribble* [1913] 3 KB 212 at 218 per Buckley LJ; *Frederick Lawrence Ltd v Freeman, Hardy & Willis Ltd* [1959] Ch 731 at 744f; *Snape v Kiernan* (1988) 13 NSWLR 88 at 97A.

10 'Value' includes money, money's worth, marriage consideration, and even the satisfaction of an existing debt (*Thorndike v Hunt* (1859) 3 De G & J 563 at 569, 44 ER 1386 at 1388). If the transfer to the purchaser is for a money consideration, the purchaser does not rank as a 'purchaser for value' until he has paid the money over. He cannot plead the doctrine of notice in his own favour merely because a legal estate has been conveyed to him in advance of payment (*Story v Windsor* (1743) 2 Atk 630 at 631, 26 ER 776).

11 *Burgess v Wheate* (1759) 1 Eden 177 at 195, 28 ER 652 at 659.

12 *In re Nisbet and Potts' Contract* [1906] 1 Ch 386 at 406, 408, 410 (It is inconceivable that by his trespass a squatter should put himself in a more favourable position than if he had entered upon the land by right).

13 *Basset v Nosworthy* (1673) Cas temp Finch 102 at 104, 23 ER 55 at 56.

(d) Absence of notice

The crux of the equitable doctrine of notice is, of course, the idea that immunity from prior equitable interests should be conferred only on those purchasers who, at the date of their purchase, had no knowledge or notice of the existence of such interests. Only in the absence of notice can it truly be said that the conscience of the purchaser is unaffected by adverse pre-existing rights.[14]

For this purpose 'notice' is given an extended meaning in the English law of real property. 'Notice' embraces not only 'actual' notice, but also 'constructive' and 'imputed' notice.[15]

(i) Actual notice Actual notice refers to matters of which the purchaser was consciously aware at the date of his purchase or which, in the statutory formulation of the doctrine of notice,[16] were 'within his own knowledge'. Clearly no purchaser can be allowed to take priority over equitable interests whose existence was fully known to him, since otherwise the purchaser would be guilty of a form of equitable fraud.[17]

The source of the purchaser's knowledge is in most cases entirely irrelevant. If the purchaser has actual knowledge of an adverse equitable interest, it seems to matter not that this knowledge is derived from some person other than the vendor or that the purchaser came by the information fortuitously. However, it is probable that knowledge derived from casual conversations does not constitute actual notice except where the mind of the purchaser 'has in some way been brought to an intelligent apprehension of the nature of the incumbrance. . .so that a reasonable man, or an ordinary man of business, would act upon the information and would regulate his conduct by it. . .'[18]

By reason of a statutory fiction the formal registration of an equitable interest may sometimes constitute *actual* notice to the purchaser of the subject matter of the registration.[19]

(ii) Constructive notice Constructive notice relates to matters of which the purchaser would have been consciously aware if he had taken reasonable care to inspect both land and title.[20] It used to be thought that constructive notice arose only in circumstances of 'gross negligence' on the part of the

14 Ante, p 44.

15 *Kemmis v Kemmis* [1988] 1 WLR 1307 at 1333B per Nourse LJ.

16 Law of Property Act 1925, s 199(1)(ii)(a).

17 See *Ware v Lord Egmont* (1854) 4 De GM & G 460 at 473, 43 ER 586 at 592 per Lord Cranworth: 'Where a person has actual notice of any matter of fact, there can be no danger of doing injustice if he is held to be bound by all the consequences of that which he knows to exist.'

18 *Lloyd v Banks* (1868) 3 Ch App 488 at 490f per Lord Cairns LC. See also *Barnhart v Greenshields* (1853) 9 Moo PCC 18 at 36, 14 ER 204 at 211 ('A purchaser is not bound to attend to vague rumours').

19 See eg Law of Property Act 1925, s 198(1) (post, p 118).

20 Ante, p 43. 'The basic concepts are "knowing something" which ought to have stimulated inquiry or "wilfully abstaining from inquiry to avoid notice"' (*Kemmis v Kemmis* [1988] 1 WLR 1307 at 1317H per Purchas LJ).

purchaser,[1] but it seems at least since the Conveyancing Act 1882 that the standard of care required of the purchaser is perhaps somewhat higher.[2] Although phrased in a negative or restrictive form, section 199(1)(ii)(a) of the Law of Property Act 1925 indicates that the purchaser is prejudicially affected by notice of those matters which 'would have come to his knowledge if such inquiries and inspections had been made as ought reasonably to have been made by him. . .'[3]

The classic description of the proper subject matter of the purchaser's inquiries is found in *Jones v Smith*.[4] Here, in a celebrated judgment, Wigram V-C reduced the categories of constructive notice to two classes of circumstances. The first comprises cases in which the purchaser has actual notice of some defect or incumbrance in relation to the property, enquiry into which would disclose others: the purchaser is fixed with constructive notice of such matters as this further enquiry would have revealed.[5] The second category comprises cases in which the purchaser has 'designedly abstained from inquiry for the very purpose of avoiding notice.'[6]

To these two categories there must now be added a third—perhaps today the most important. The purchaser is fixed with constructive notice of all those matters which a reasonable or prudent purchaser, acting with skilled legal advice,[7] would have investigated. He is judged objectively with reference to that which any ordinary purchaser, advised by a competent lawyer, would reasonably have enquired about or inspected for the purpose of obtaining a good title. A reasonable purchaser is one who 'not only consults his own needs or preferences but also has regard to whether the purchase may affect,

1 See eg *Ware v Lord Egmont* (1854) 4 De GM & G 460 at 473, 43 ER 586 at 592 per Lord Cranworth. In *Jones v Smith* (1841) 1 Hare 43 at 56, 66 ER 943 at 949, Wigram V-C thought that a 'mere want of caution, as distinguished from fraudulent and wilful blindness' was not enough.

2 See Conveyancing Act 1882, s 3(1)(i) (now Law of Property Act 1925, s 199(1)(ii)(a)). It is a source of some perplexity (see *Northern Bank Ltd v Henry* [1981] IR 1 at 16) that section 3(3) of the 1882 Act (now section 199(3) of the 1925 Act) appears to provide that the purchaser is not to be affected by notice in any case in which he would not have been regarded as having constructive notice before the enactment of the statutory formula. Some comfort may perhaps be found in the observation of Lindley LJ in *Bailey v Barnes* [1894] 1 Ch 25 at 35 that the 1882 Act 'really does no more than state the law as it was before, but its negative form shews that a restriction rather than an extension of the doctrine of notice was intended by the Legislature.' The truth may be simply that 19th century judges were prone to stigmatise all actionable negligence as 'gross' or 'culpable' (see eg the statement of Rolfe B in *Wilson v Brett* (1843) 11 M & W 113 at 115, 152 ER 737 at 739, that negligence and gross negligence were 'the same thing, with the addition of a vituperative epithet').

3 A purchaser who negligently fails to make any inquiry is unaffected if such inquiries as he might have made would not in any event have revealed the matters with constructive notice of which he is alleged to be fixed (see *Kemmis v Kemmis* [1988] 1 WLR 1307 at 1324B-C per Purchas LJ, 1328E-F per Lloyd LJ, 1333H–1334A per Nourse LJ).

4 (1841) 1 Hare 43 at 55, 66 ER 943 at 948.

5 See eg *Birch v Ellames* (1794) 2 Anst 427 at 431f, 145 ER 924 at 926, where a mortgagee who lent money in the full knowledge that the borrower's title deeds were deposited with a third party was held to take subject to a prior mortgage which was secured by that deposit.

6 See also *Hunt v Luck* [1901] 1 Ch 45 at 52 per Farwell J.

7 See *Northern Bank Ltd v Henry* [1981] IR 1 at 18 for the assertion by Kenny J that no prudent purchaser 'who was without legal qualifications would undertake the investigation of title to land.'

prejudicially and unfairly, the rights of third parties in the property.'[8] Thus a reasonable purchaser can legally be expected to 'make such inquiries and inspections as would normally disclose whether the purchase will trench, fraudulently or unconscionably, on the rights of such third parties in the property.'[9] As Henchy J explained in *Northern Bank Ltd v Henry*,[10] 'the reasonable man, in the eyes of the law, will be expected to look beyond the impact of his decisions on his own affairs, and to consider whether they may unfairly and prejudicially affect his "neighbour", in the sense in which that word has been given juristic currency by Lord Atkin in *Donoghue v Stevenson*.' Because the imposition of this standard of care represents a significant restraint on the ability of the purchaser to take free of adverse equitable interests,[11] the courts have been reluctant to extend the ambit of constructive notice to any large degree. A persuasive element of policy exerts an opposing tendency towards maximising the protection given to the purchaser of land.[12] The classic observation in this context is that of Farwell J, who stated in *Hunt v Luck*[13] the 'doctrine of constructive notice, imputing as it does, knowledge which the person affected does not actually possess, is one which the Courts of late years have been unwilling to extend.'[14]

In consequence the duty of care expected of a purchaser covers only two major areas, concerning respectively an inspection of land and an inspection of title. An inspection of land may reveal facts which are inconsistent with the title offered by the vendor.[15] An inspection of the land may disclose the presence of persons other than the vendor, in which case the purchaser may be fixed with constructive notice of such rights as these persons may have in the property.[16] For instance, the presence of a tenant provides constructive notice of his leasehold interest[17] and of the terms of his lease,[18]

8 *Northern Bank Ltd v Henry* [1981] IR 1 at 9 per Henchy J. It is for this reason that the doctrine of notice is not tied to the standards observed by the prudent man of business. The latter is, almost by definition, no altruist and consequently sees no further than his own interests. As Henchy J said ([1981] IR 1 at 12), the 'test for constructive notice is legal reasonableness, not business prudence.'

9 *Northern Bank Ltd v Henry* [1981] IR 1 at 11.

10 *Northern Bank Ltd v Henry* [1981] IR 1 at 12.

11 See eg the discussion of protection for equitable rights under a trust for sale (post, p 563).

12 Post, p 97.

13 [1901] 1 Ch 45 at 48, affd [1902] 1 Ch 428 at 434f (post, p 564).

14 For evidence of the continued potency of this approach, see *Caunce v Caunce* [1969] 1 WLR 286 at 291H–292F (post, p 565); *Kemmis v Kemmis* [1988] 1 WLR 1307 at 1334G-H per Nourse LJ.

15 In extreme circumstances the scope of constructive notice may go even further. In *Hervey v Smith* (1856) 22 Beav 299 at 302, 52 ER 1123 at 1124, for instance, a purchaser of a house with fourteen chimney pots but only twelve flues was held to have received constructive notice of his neighbour's equitable easement to use the other two flues. See, however, *Allen v Seckham* (1879) 11 Ch D 790 at 794; R.A. Pearce, *Joint Occupation and the Doctrine of Notice*, (1980) 15 Ir Jur (NS) 211 at 213.

16 This possibility has been indirectly accentuated by the decision of the House of Lords in *Williams & Glyn's Bank Ltd v Boland* [1981] AC 487 (post, p 569). In *City of London Building Society v Flegg* [1988] AC 54 at 80F-G, Lord Oliver of Aylmerton observed that this formulation of the constructive notice doctrine is also reflected in the protection accorded by Law of Property Act 1925, s 14, to the interests of persons 'in possession or in actual occupation of land' (post, p 124). See also *Clyne v Lowe* (1968) 69 SR (NSW) 433 at 436.

17 *Hunt v Luck* [1902] 1 Ch 428 at 432. See also *Hayes v Seymour-Johns* (1981) 2 BPR 9366 at 9372.

18 *Taylor v Stibbert* (1794) 2 Ves Jun 437 at 440f, 30 ER 713 at 714f.

but not necessarily of the rights of any person to whom the tenant may be paying rent.[19] It is now also quite likely that the purchaser is bound by the equitable rights of members of the vendor's family (and perhaps even of others) who are in joint occupation of the property with the vendor.[20]

An inspection of title comes within the scope of constructive notice in that the purchaser is fixed with constructive notice of all rights or interests affecting the land which would have been disclosed if he had investigated the vendor's title for the period allowed by statute.[1] The purchaser takes the land subject to any adverse equitable rights arising within that period, even where he has contracted for a shorter period of investigation than he is entitled by statute to require.[2] However, unless he positively chooses to investigate title for a longer period, the purchaser is not bound by equitable interests created before the beginning of the statutory period of title investigation.[3]

(iii) Imputed notice Imputed notice is notice which is attributed to a purchaser in virtue of knowledge possessed actually or constructively by some agent of his. The purchaser is deemed, for instance, to have notice of those matters of which his own solicitor was actually aware or should reasonably have been aware. This extension of the doctrine of notice is clearly necessitated by the widespread practice of employing legal advisers and other agents in the conduct of land transactions.

Imputed notice is now governed by section 199(1)(ii)(b) of the Law of Property Act 1925, which provides that this form of notice arises in respect of knowledge possessed actually or constructively by the purchaser's 'counsel. . .solicitor or other agent'. However, imputed notice is subject to certain restrictions. The knowledge of a solicitor or other agent is imputed to the purchaser only if it arises within the current transaction of purchase, and only if the solicitor or other agent acquired his knowledge while acting in his capacity 'as such'.[4] Notice derived from any other transaction or circumstance is irrelevant and cannot be fastened upon the purchaser.[5]

(e) The destructive effect of purchase for value without notice

If the purchaser succeeds in establishing all the foregoing elements of the 'composite expression' which epitomises the doctrine of notice, he has an 'absolute, unqualified, unanswerable defence'[6] against adverse equitable

19 *Hunt v Luck* [1901] 1 Ch 45 at 51, affd [1902] 1 Ch 428 at 434f (ante, p 82). The question of constructive notice becomes controversial here only if the vendor is not the person to whom the tenant is paying his rent.
20 Post, pp 565, 569.
1 The period of investigation of title fixed by statute now covers at least the 15 years preceding the current transaction. See Law of Property Act 1969, s 23 (post, p 271).
2 *In re Cox and Neve's Contract* [1891] 2 Ch 109 at 118; *In re Nisbet and Potts' Contract* [1906] 1 Ch 386 at 408.
3 Law of Property Act 1925, s 44(8).
4 Law of Property Act 1925, s 199(1)(ii)(b).
5 See eg *Rock Permanent Benefit Building Society v Kettlewell* (1956) 168 Estates Gazette 397. (Although mortgagee's solicitor was mortgagor's brother and was therefore aware of mortgagor's matrimonial difficulties, such knowledge was not to be imputed to mortgagee under section 199(1)(ii)(b)).
6 *Pilcher v Rawlins* (1872) 7 Ch App 259 at 269.

claims. This defence is so complete that the mere fact of purchase for value without notice has the effect of *destroying* the equitable rights involved. The advent of a good faith purchaser of a legal estate is sufficient to obliterate those rights once and for all. They cannot thereafter revive even against a subsequent purchaser who *does* have notice of the fact that equitable rights once existed. This operation of the doctrine of notice was exemplified in *Wilkes v Spooner*[7] (see *Fig*. 6).

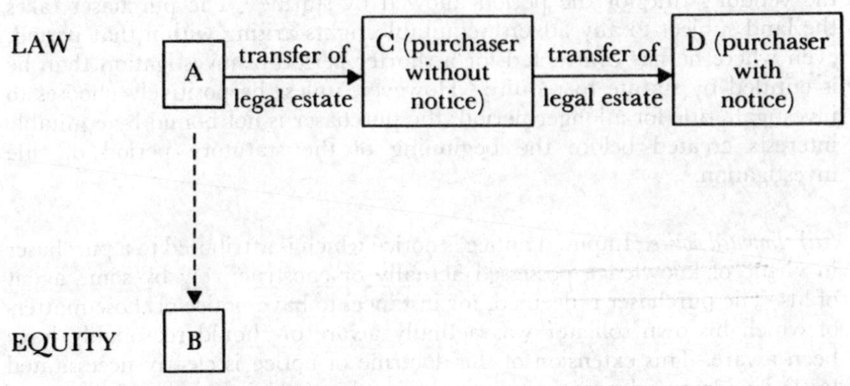

Fig. 6

On the facts presented in *Wilkes v Spooner*, C takes the legal estate free of B's equitable interest, since C is a bona fide purchaser of A's legal estate for value without notice. D likewise takes the legal estate free of B's equitable interest, albeit that he has notice of it, since B's interest has already been destroyed by the earlier transfer to a good faith purchaser who had no notice of its existence.[8] B therefore has no rights *in rem*. Such rights as he retains are rights only *in personam*, ie against A alone deriving from the transaction which gave B his rights in the first place.

7 [1911] 2 KB 473 at 487f. See also *Lowther v Carlton* (1741) 2 Atk 242, 26 ER 549 at 550 per Lord Hardwicke: 'It is certainly the rule of this court, that a man who is a purchaser with notice himself from a person who bought without notice, may shelter himself under the first purchaser, or otherwise it would very much clog the sale of estates.' See likewise *Nottingham Patent Brick and Tile Co v Butler* (1886) 16 QBD 778 at 788.

8 This result does not apply, however, if A and D are the same person. A cannot destroy the equitable interest to which he is subject by selling the land to C and then purchasing that land from C (see eg *Barrow's Case* (1880) 14 Ch D 432 at 445).

CHAPTER 5

Fee simple estates

At common law the primary estate in land is the freehold estate in fee simple.[1] For centuries this estate has provided the basis for the most ample form of ownership known to English law. The fee simple itself can assume several forms and this chapter is therefore devoted to an analysis of the various guises in which the fee simple may appear.

The pre-eminent form of fee simple estate is the 'fee simple absolute in possession'. It is this form of the fee simple estate which is declared, by section 1(1)(a) of the Law of Property Act 1925, to be 'capable of subsisting or of being conveyed or created' as a legal estate in land.[2] The fee simple absolute in possession today provides by far the most common kind of ownership of English realty,[3] and it is therefore important to recognise the full significance of each element in the name of this freehold estate.

1. THE FEE SIMPLE 'ABSOLUTE'

The term 'absolute' qualifies the character of a fee simple estate in such a way as to distinguish it from various forms of modified fee such as the 'determinable' and the 'conditional' fee simple. The fee simple absolute is nowadays much more common than any of the modified fees, but the internal distinctions between these fees may be quite difficult to draw.

(1) The determinable fee simple

A determinable fee simple is an estate of potentially perpetual duration which is, however, liable to be cut short by the occurrence of some specified but unpredictable event. An example would occur in a grant of Blackacre to A in fee simple until A qualifies as a barrister. Here it is uncertain at the date of the grant whether the determining event will ever happen.[4] The grant confers on A a determinable fee simple which, because it is not 'absolute' in the terms of section 1(1)(a) of the Law of Property Act 1925, can only

1 For the definition of the 'fee simple', see Chapter 3 (ante, p 58).
2 Law of Property Act 1925, s 1(1)(a), ante, p 68.
3 Freehold ownership of an estate in fee simple absolute in possession accounts, for instance, for 67 per cent of the country's housing stock (Central Statistical Office, *Social Trends No 22* (London 1992), p 145).
4 It is of the essence of a determinable fee that there is a possibility that the determining event may *never* happen (see *Challis*, p 251). If, however, the specified determining event is bound to occur sooner or later, no determinable fee simple can arise. For instance, a grant in fee simple to A 'until the death of B' confers on A not a determinable fee simple, but an estate *pur autre vie* (*Challis*, p 252) (ante, p 60).

be equitable.[5] As such it must take effect behind some kind of trust.[6] Throughout A's ownership of the determinable fee simple, the original grantor retains a 'possibility of reverter' in that A's estate will automatically terminate in favour of the revertee if the specified determining event occurs.[7] In this case the grantor's 'possibility of reverter' matures into a right to resume the fee simple absolute.

(a) Examples ancient and modern

No special language need be used to create a determinable fee simple so long as it is made plain that the durability of the fee simple estate is dependent on the continuance of some specified state of affairs or the non-occurrence of some specified future event.[8] The case law abounds with such curious examples as the grant of a fee simple 'during the time that such a tree shall grow',[9] or 'as long as the Church of St Paul shall stand',[10] or until X pay £100 to Y.[11] Nowadays determinable fees simple tend to be the product of statutory creation. In England and Wales, for instance, the relevant county highway authority is, in relation to the superficial and immediately subjacent soil of its public roads,[12] statutorily invested with a fee simple estate determinable on those roads ceasing to be public highways.[13]

(b) Subsequent impossibility

If the determining event indicated in the grant of a determinable fee simple later becomes impossible, the grantee's estate becomes a fee simple absolute and the grantor's possibility of reverter simply falls away.[14] If, in the example above of a grant to A in fee simple until he qualifies as a barrister, A dies without having thus qualified, his determinable fee becomes absolute and passes with his estate.

(c) Invalidity on grounds of public policy

If, although it is somewhat rare, the limiting element in a determinable fee simple is vitiated by considerations of public policy, the determinable fee is rendered void in its entirety.[15] Since the limiting words are bound

5 Law of Property Act 1925, s 1(3).
6 Post, p 612.
7 The determinable fee comes to an end without any entry or claim requiring to be made by the revertee (*Challis*, p 252).
8 *Challis*, p 252.
9 *Ayres v Falkland* (1697) 1 Ld Raym 325 at 326, 91 ER 1112 at 1113.
10 2 Plowd 557, 75 ER 820.
11 For other examples of a determinable fee, see *Challis*, p 255ff. For a more recent example of a determinable fee simple, see *In re Rowhook Mission Hall, Horsham* [1985] Ch 62.
12 See *Coverdale v Charlton* (1878) 4 QBD 104 at 116ff, 121, 126 (post, p 1049); *Sheffield City Council v Yorkshire Water Services Ltd* [1991] 1 WLR 58 at 66E-F, 67B-H.
13 See Highways Act 1980, s 263; *Foley's Charity Trustees v Dudley Corporation* [1910] 1 KB 317 at 322, 324; *Tithe Redemption Commission v Runcorn UDC* [1954] Ch 383 at 403; *Wiltshire CC v Frazer* (1984) 47 P & CR 69 at 70, 72f.
14 *Challis*, p 254. See *In re Leach* [1912] 2 Ch 422 at 429.
15 *Bl Comm*, Vol II, p 157. See *In re Moore* (1888) 39 Ch D 116 at 130, 132; *Zapletal v Wright* [1957] Tas SR 211 at 218.

into the determinable fee simple as an integral component of the estate granted, any invalidity affecting those limiting words inevitably makes the entire grant defective.

(2) The conditional fee simple

A conditional fee simple is again an estate of potentially perpetual duration which is defeasible on the satisfaction of a 'condition subsequent'. An example would occur where Blackacre is granted to A 'on condition that he shall not qualify as a barrister'. The fee simple estate vested in A is liable to forfeiture if A qualifies as a barrister and thus fulfils the condition subsequent. As is the case with the determinable fee simple, the grant of a conditional fee provides, at least in theory, a potent means by which the owner of capital in the form of land may—however capriciously—impose on the grantees of his largesse an idiosyncratic preference as to beliefs, morals or lifestyle.[16]

(a) Ancillary 'rights of entry'

It is normal to include in the grant of a conditional fee an express right of entry which entitles the grantor to forfeit the estate in the event of the fulfilment or breach of the specified condition.[17] Such rights of entry have sometimes been attached to a grant in fee simple in order to enforce payment of a rentcharge undertaken by the grantee of the land.[18] In certain parts of England[19] and Northern Ireland,[20] for instance, it has been a common conveyancing practice for land to be sold not for a capital sum but in consideration of a continuing income in the form of a perpetual rentcharge known as a 'fee farm rent'. Although such conveyances are no longer possible in England and Wales,[1] those fee farm grants which still subsist invest the grantee with merely a conditional fee simple, the estate conveyed being defeasible for non-payment of the required periodic sum.

(b) Distinction between conditional and determinable fees

It is notoriously difficult to maintain a strict distinction between the conditional and determinable forms of the fee simple.[2] At its root the

16 See eg *Jenner v Turner* (1880–81) 16 Ch D 188 at 196f per Bacon V-C: 'It is not competent to the court to inquire into the motives which may have induced the restriction. If it could be properly said they had been prompted by spite or malevolence the condition would nevertheless be valid; for the law does not prohibit testators from indulging such bad feelings, provided that no principle of public policy is thereby contravened.'

17 Post, Ante, p 73. It is now possible for the grantor in his conveyance to specify that the right of entry may be exercised by and on behalf of some person other than himself (Law of Property Act 1925, s 4(3)).

18 Rentcharges are discussed elsewhere (ante, p 72, post, p 1136).

19 Particularly in Manchester and East Lancashire, and around Bath and Bristol (see Law Commission, *Transfer of Land: Rentcharges* (Published Working Paper No 24, 1969), paras 10–14).

20 Much of the 17th and 18th Century plantation of Ulster was carried out effectively through the device of fee farm grants which still appear in chains of title to the present day (ante, p 54).

1 See Rentcharges Act 1977, s 2(1) (ante, p 72).

2 The distinction has been described as 'little short of disgraceful to our jurisprudence' (*In re King's Trusts* (1892) 29 LR Ir 401 at 410 per Porter MR).

distinction rests on the fact that in a determinable fee the limiting circumstance is integral to the formulation of the duration of the estate,[3] whereas in the conditional fee the limiting proviso operates to cut short the estate before it reaches out to its normal span.[4] The distinction is elusive in the extreme and is ultimately a matter of construction of the words used in the grant.[5] Any rationalisation of the distinction on purely semantic grounds is apt to be mocked by the almost indistinguishable duration of the estates created by the different forms of fee. An estate granted to A 'until he qualifies as a barrister' seems likely to last just as long as an estate granted 'on condition that he shall not qualify as a barrister.'

(c) The legal quality of some conditional fee simple estates

The distinction between conditional and determinable fees would be almost entirely academic but for one vital substantive difference in their characterisation as property rights. By a sort of legislative accident, the conditional fee simple ranks, in most cases, as a legal estate in land, whereas the determinable fee is clearly equitable only. In strict logic, the absence of an 'absolute' quality should have the effect of relegating all conditional fees to merely equitable status in the terms of section 1(1)(a) of the Law of Property Act 1925. However, it was considered inconvenient that fee farm grants, which were all but grants in fee simple absolute, should not enjoy legal status.[6] Accordingly, section 7(1) of the Law of Property Act 1925 was amended in 1926 to provide that fee simple grants which are subject to a right of entry or re-entry should henceforth be treated for the purpose of the Act as grants of a fee simple absolute estate.[7] Whether or not intentionally, the amending provision appears to be sufficiently widely drafted to apply not merely to fee farm grants subject to a rentcharge, but to all forms of conditional fee simple which happen to be subject to a right of entry or re-entry.[8]

3 The determinable fee 'marks the bounds or compass of the estate, and the time of its continuance' (*Preston on Estates*, Vol 1, p 49). See also *Bl Comm*, Vol II, p 155; *Challis*, p 260f; *Re Tilbury West Public School Board and Hastie* (1966) 55 DLR (2d) 407 at 410.

4 The conditional fee 'has its operation in defeating the estate before it attains the boundary or has completed the space of time described by the limitation' (*Preston on Estates*, Vol 1, p 49). See also *Bl Comm*, Vol II, p 155; *Challis*, p 261. In the words of Laskin JA in *Re North Gower Township Public School Board and Todd* (1968) 65 DLR (2d) 421 at 424, a conditional fee involves a 'superadded condition upon a grant of a fee simple rather than an integral part of the very limitation of the estate created . . .' See also *Re Essex County Roman Catholic Separate School Board and Antaya* (1978) 80 DLR (3d) 405 at 409.

5 Certain words and phrases have come to be *indicia* of a fee simple upon condition subsequent (eg 'on condition that', 'provided that') and of a fee simple determinable (eg 'while', 'until', 'as long as'), but these rules of thumb are not necessarily conclusive (see *Hopper v Liverpool Corporation* (1943) 88 SJ 213 at 214; *Re North Gower Township Public School Board and Todd* (1968) 65 DLR (2d) 421 at 424).

6 There was a danger that such grants would have come within the cumbersome provisions of the Settled Land Act 1925 (post, p 612).

7 See Law of Property (Amendment) Act 1926, Schedule. See the further amendment of section 7(1) contained in Reverter of Sites Act 1987, s 1.

8 The Law Commission recommended in 1989 that any grant of a conditional or determinable fee simple falling outside Law of Property Act 1925, s 7(1), should bring the land within the scope of the Commission's proposed 'new trust of land' (post, p 537). See *Transfer of Land: Trusts of Land* (Law Com No 181, 8 June 1989), paras 17.1, 20.4; Draft Trusts of Land Bill, clause 14 (Law Com No 181, Appendix A).

(d) Differences in the operation of conditional and determinable fees

There are also certain technical differences of operation and effect between conditional and determinable fees. *First*, whereas a determinable fee terminates automatically in favour of the revertee when the limiting event occurs, the conditional fee does not so terminate. The conditional fee continues to exist unless and until the grantor exercises his right of entry.[9] *Second*, the courts have tended to be somewhat more vigilant in applying rules of public policy to strike down undesirable conditions subsequent than has traditionally been the case with equivalent clauses contained in a determinable fee simple.[10] *Third*, if a condition subsequent is vitiated as contrary to public policy, the offending condition is merely struck out, leaving the grant as a fee simple absolute,[11] whereas in a determinable fee the grant is destroyed in its entirety.

(3) Judicial control over conditions and limitations

As indicated above, the courts have asserted a general jurisdiction to strike down certain kinds of condition or limitation attached to a grant in fee simple where the constraints concerned have been regarded as either impossible[12] or illegal[13] or as inimical to public policy on moral, social or economic grounds. In practice the courts have guarded jealously against restraints of an absolute or virtually absolute nature imposed upon the grantee of a fee simple, but have been remarkably tolerant of restraints which are merely partial or particular.

The judicial discretion to override the expressed wishes of grantors in such circumstances represents a significant diminution of the right of 'the owner' of property under English law to dispose of 'his' property in any way he will. There is in particular a disinclination to allow dispositions by which a testator seeks to direct the lives of his children from the grave.[14]

9 *Litt*, s 347; *Bl Comm*, Vol II, p 155; *Challis*, p 219. See *Matthew Manning's Case* (1609) 8 Co Rep 94b at 95b, 77 ER 618 at 620.

10 Post, p 91.

11 *Bl Comm*, Vol II, p 156f. A void condition subsequent is simply 'treated as non scriptum' (*Gower v Public Trustee* [1924] NZLR 1233 at 1257 per Salmond J). See also *Morley v Rennoldson* (1843) 2 Hare 570 at 579f, 67 ER 235 at 239; *Zapletal v Wright* [1957] Tas SR 211 at 218.

12 Blackstone held conditions to be void 'if they be impossible at the time of their creation, or afterwards become impossible by the act of God or the act of the feoffor himself' (*Bl Comm*, Vol II, p 156). See also *Sheppard's Touchstone*, p 129; *Gower v Public Trustee* [1924] NZLR 1233 at 1255 (grant to X 'on condition that he shall not become a Roman Catholic', where X is already a Roman Catholic at the date of the grant).

13 Blackstone gives the example of a grant to a man which is expressed to be defeasible 'unless he kills another' (*Bl Comm*, Vol II, p 157). The preclusion of illegality also implies that a condition subsequent cannot be allowed to frustrate the legally prescribed devolution of property. For instance, a condition subsequent cannot validly make a fee simple estate defeasible in the event of the grantee's intestacy (*In re Dixon* [1903] 2 Ch 458 at 460) or insolvency (*In re Machu* (1882) 21 Ch D 838 at 842). It is ironic that there is no objection if the offending clause appears in the form of a determinable interest (see eg *Graves v Dolphin* (1826) 1 Sim 66 at 67, 57 ER 503 at 504).

14 See *Clayton v Ramsden* [1943] AC 320 at 325 per Lord Atkin; *Re Sutcliffe* [1982] 2 NZLR 330 at 337. See also *Blathwayt v Baron Cawley* [1976] AC 397 at 427C-D; *In re Tepper's Will Trusts* [1987] Ch 358 at 370E.

The courts tend both to construe strictly any clause which purports to operate a forfeiture[15] and to exercise the equitable jurisdiction to relieve the defaulting party against the effect of forfeiture.[16]

(a) Restrictions on alienation

The common law has long held that the power of alienation is an intrinsic feature of the right of private property.[17] Any absolute restriction on the alienation of land held in fee simple is therefore, in the words of Littleton, 'against reason',[18] being wholly repugnant to the essence of ownership in fee.[19]

In view of the strong public policy in favour of free alienation, the courts have thus struck down conditions subsequent which prohibit totally any form of alienation of the estate by the grantee,[20] or which allow alienation only to a named person.[1] By contrast, however, the courts have normally been prepared to uphold clauses which prohibit alienation in favour of a specific named person[2] or which permit alienation only to a member or members of an identifiable class or group of persons.[3] Some sort of compromise is thus struck between the policy concern to render land easily commerciable

15 See *Rawson v Inhabitants of School District No 5 in Uxbridge* (1863) 89 Mass 125 at 127; *Pearson v Adams* (1912) 7 DLR 139 at 144f. The courts seem to require a greater degree of certainty in advance as to the scope of a condition subsequent than is needed when the condition is precedent (*Blathwayt v Baron Cawley* [1976] AC 397 at 424H–425A). It may be, as suggested by Lord Wright in *Clayton v Ramsden* [1943] AC 320 at 329, that the 'modern idea, perhaps, is that the beneficiary should be in a position to know beyond a peradventure what he is to do or not to do if he is to avoid a forfeiture. That must be ascertainable by him.' See *Clavering v Ellison* (1856) 3 Drew 451 at 470, 61 ER 975 at 982, (1859) 7 HL Cas 707 at 715f, 11 ER 282 at 285.

16 Post, p 812.

17 See eg *In re Ridley* (1879) 11 Ch D 645 at 648f per Jessel MR; *Hall v Busst* (1960) 104 CLR 206 at 218 per Dixon CJ; *Re Permanent Trustee Nominees (Canberra) Ltd* [1989] 1 Qd R 314 at 316.

18 *Litt*, s 360.

19 *Co Litt*, p 223a; *Bl Comm*, Vol II, p 156. See *In re Rosher* (1884) 26 Ch D 801 at 812; *In re Elliot* [1896] 2 Ch 353 at 356; *Re Winnipeg Condominium Corp No 1 and Stechley* (1979) 90 DLR (3d) 703 at 706.

20 See also *Hood v Oglander* (1865) 34 Beav 513 at 522, 55 ER 733 at 737; *Byrne v Byrne* (1953) 87 ILTR 183 at 185f. 'Alienation' for this purpose includes a mortgage (*Ware v Cann* (1830) 10 B & C 433 at 438, 109 ER 511 at 513) and a testamentary disposition (*In re Jones* [1898] 1 Ch 438 at 443).

1 *Muschamp v Bluet*, Bridgman J 132 at 137, 123 ER 1253 at 1256; *Re Cockerill* [1929] 2 Ch 131 at 134f.

2 *Litt*, s 361; *Co Litt*, p 223a/b. See, however, *In re Rosher* (1884) 26 Ch D 801 at 813f.

3 *Doe d Gill v Pearson* (1805) 6 East 173 at 180, 102 ER 1253 at 1256; *In re Macleay* (1875) LR 20 Eq 186 at 189 (alienation permitted within 'the family'). Compare, however, *Crofts v Beamish* [1905] 2 IR 349 at 356f, 360; *In re Browne* [1954] Ch 39 at 50 (condition void where alienation restricted to small and diminishing group of 'brothers'). Where the class to which alienation is permitted is defined with reference to racial or sexual characteristics, the limiting clause seems not to be unlawful by reason of statute (see Race Relations Act 1976, s 21(1); Sex Discrimination Act 1975, s 30(1)). See J.F. Garner, *Racial Restrictive Covenants in England and the United States*, (1972) 35 MLR 478; J.D.A. Brooke-Taylor, [1978] Conv 24. However, this kind of clause would seem an entirely appropriate target for invalidation under general rules of public policy.

and the countervailing impulse in favour of allowing personal control over the terms on which a private owner may dispose of his own property.[4]

(b) Restrictions on marriage

In a similar way the state of marriage is regarded as a socially approved institution and the courts have been reluctant to uphold conditions subsequent which militate against the institution in its entirety.[5] Conditions subsequent have thus been invalidated which altogether preclude marriage[6] (as distinct from remarriage[7]) on the part of the grantee, but the courts have held good partial restraints on marriage which merely prohibit the grantee's marriage with a named person[8] or with any of an ascertainable class of persons.[9]

(c) Restrictions on religious belief

The courts have not been particularly astute to restrain attempts to perpetuate religious preference—bigoted or otherwise—in the grant of a fee simple, at

4 A modern distaste for capricious restrictions is evident in *In the estate of Dunne* [1988] IR 155 at 157. Here the Irish High Court struck down a prohibition of transfer to any member of the 'Meredith families of Mountmellick' as excessively vague and also, in that it sought to 'perpetuate old family divisions', as contrary to public policy.

5 'Conditions in restraint of marriage are odious' (*Long v Dennis* (1767) 4 Burr 2052 at 2055, 98 ER 69 at 72 per Lord Mansfield). The disfavour shown towards such conditions was justified in former times on grounds both of moral paternalism and of public policy. An absolute restraint upon marriage was liable to be condemned as hindering 'a great moral and social good. . .it tends to evil and the promoting of licentiousness; it tends to depopulation, the greatest of all political sins. . .' (*Low v Peers* (1770) Wilm 364 at 372, 97 ER 138 at 141). See also *Maddox v Maddox's Administrator*, 11 Grat (52 Va) 804 at 806 (1854); O.L. Browder, *Conditions and Limitations in Restraint of Marriage*, 39 Michigan L Rev 1288 (1940-41).

6 See eg *Morley v Rennoldson* (1843) 2 Hare 570 at 579f, 583, 67 ER 235 at 239f; *Jenner v Turner* (1880-81) 16 Ch D 188 at 197; *Duddy v Gresham* (1878) 2 LR Ir 442 at 464f. The courts may exceptionally uphold a condition prohibiting marriage where there was a clear and genuine intention in the grantor to provide for the grantee while he or she remained unmarried (see *Morley v Rennoldson*, supra at 580, 239; *Low v Peers* (1770) Wilm 364 at 377, 97 ER 138 at 143; *Jones v Jones* (1875-76) 1 QBD 279 at 283; *In re Elliott* [1918] 1 IR 41 at 43f). Compare the greater willingness to tolerate the use of marriage as a limiting circumstance in a determinable fee simple (*In re King's Trusts* (1892) 29 LR Ir 401 at 410; *Oliver v Menton* [1945] IR 6 at 11f; *Stewart v Murdoch* [1969] NI 78 at 82; *In re Dolan* [1970] IR 94 at 101).

7 Grants *durante viduitate* (for the duration of widowhood) have not been struck down as offensive to any consideration of public policy (see eg *Jordan v Holkham* (1753) Amb 209, 27 ER 139). Compare, however, the more enlightened approach evident in *Duddy v Gresham* (1878) 2 LR Ir 442, where a testator had left property to his widow on condition that she should not remarry, but should 'retire immediately after my death into a convent of her own choice'!

8 *Jarvis v Duke* (1681) 1 Vern 19 at 20, 23 ER 274 ('. . . such an example of presumptuous disobedience highly meriting such a punishment; she being only prohibited to marry with one man by name, and nothing in the whole fair garden of Eden would serve her turn but this forbidden fruit'). See also *Jenner v Turner* (1880-81) 16 Ch D 188 at 196; *In re Bathe* [1925] Ch 377 at 382; *In re Hanlon* [1933] Ch 254 at 260.

9 *Duggan v Kelly* (1847) 10 Ir Eq R 295 at 301f ('a Papist'); *Perrin v Lyon* (1807) 9 East 170 at 183f, 103 ER 538 at 543 ('a Scotchman'); *Jenner v Turner* (1880-81) 16 Ch D 188 at 197 ('a domestic servant').

least where there is no vitiating degree of uncertainty attaching to the faith prescribed or proscribed by the grantor.[10] In *Blathwayt v Baron Cawley*,[11] the House of Lords upheld a condition subsequent which had the effect of forfeiting the grantee's interest if he should 'be or become a Roman Catholic.'[12]

(d) Other forms of discrimination

There has been no significant inclination to import into this context supra-national guarantees against discrimination,[13] the view being expressed that discrimination 'is not the same thing as choice' and that 'neither by express provision nor by implication has private selection yet become a matter of public policy.'[14] The deference accorded the private prejudice of the propertied class is still substantial,[15] personal caprice becoming offensive to public policy only where it imposes a comprehensive fetter upon the operation of the free market in either private property[16] or the supporting institution of bourgeois marriage.[17]

2. THE FEE SIMPLE 'IN POSSESSION'

An estate in fee simple absolute in possession confers upon its owner an immediate right to occupation and enjoyment of the land from the effective

10 See *Clayton v Ramsden* [1943] AC 320, where the House of Lords struck down as uncertain a prohibition of marriage with a person 'not of Jewish parentage and of the Jewish faith'. Compare, however, *Higgins v Bank of Ireland* [1947] IR 277 at 285f; *McCausland v Young* [1948] NI 72 at 94, [1949] NI 49 at 60; *Blathwayt v Baron Cawley* [1976] AC 397 at 425D-E, G, 429E-F; *In re Tuck's ST* [1978] Ch 49 at 62F, 65F, 66C; *In re Tepper's Will Trusts* [1987] 2 WLR 729 at 737A-C, 744G-745E.

11 [1976] AC 397. See generally J.D.A. Brooke-Taylor, [1978] Conv 24.

12 The actual grant in this case included an entailed interest, but the entail was duly barred by the tenant in tail (ante, p 59), who thereupon claimed that his fee simple was absolute and not conditional.

13 See eg The European Convention on Human Rights (1950), art 8 (right to respect for 'private and family life'), art 9 (right to freedom of religion).

14 *Blathwayt v Baron Cawley* [1976] AC 397 at 426B-C per Lord Wilberforce. See also Lord Cross of Chelsea at 429G-430A, Lord Edmund-Davies at 441D-E.

15 See eg *Re Talbot-Ponsonby's Estate* [1937] 4 All ER 309 at 313A (condition that grantee should not allow a named person to 'set foot upon' the property held valid). The private prejudices endorsed by the courts may, of course, be anti-establishment in character. See *Blathwayt v Baron Cawley* [1976] AC 397 at 442G, where Lord Fraser of Tullybelton thought that the courts would not regard as contrary to public policy a grant conditioned upon the grantee not sending his children to a fee-paying public school.

16 See the interesting statement of Lord Wilberforce in *Blathwayt v Baron Cawley* [1976] AC 397 at 426G that he found himself 'unpersuaded that, in relation to landed estates in which family attitudes and traditions may be strong and valued by testators, and moreover which may often involve close association with one or another Church, public policy requires that testators may not prefer one branch of the family to another upon religious grounds.'

17 The courts regard as void a condition which militates against the continued cohabitation of spouses (see *In re Johnson's WT* [1967] Ch 387 at 395B-C, 396C, F-G). See also *Zapletal v Wright* [1957] Tas SR 211 at 218, where a verbal condition subsequent requiring the continued cohabitation of de facto spouses was disregarded on the ground that it operated merely *in terrorem*. Compare *Andrews v Parker* [1973] Qd R 93 at 107B-D.

date of the grant to him.[18] The term 'in possession',[19] when thus used in relation to the sole freehold estate at law, distinguishes this form of fee simple from those estates in fee simple which are merely 'in remainder' or 'in reversion'.

(1) Estates 'in remainder'

An interest 'in remainder' confers a present right to future enjoyment, in the sense that the 'remainderman' is excluded from immediate enjoyment only by reason of the presence of a prior interest or prior interests vested in somebody else.[20]

An example of a fee simple absolute in remainder would occur where X grants Blackacre to A for life, with remainder to B in fee simple. Here it is A who is entitled 'in possession' as from the date of the grant; B has merely a fee simple absolute in remainder. However, it is important to realise that B, although not immediately entitled 'in possession', does indeed receive a proprietary interest at the date of the grant. He receives a present right to future enjoyment, since his remainder will 'fall into possession' on the termination of A's prior interest (ie when A dies). This incidentally brings about the important consequence that if B predeceases A, B's present right to future enjoyment (ie his interest 'in remainder') will pass to B's estate to be claimed 'in possession' by the persons entitled thereunder when A eventually dies.

Attention must be drawn to one other implication attached to a fee simple absolute in remainder. It follows with remorseless logic from section 1(1)(a) of the Law of Property Act 1925 that such an estate, not being 'in possession', cannot be a legal estate. Regardless of the manner of its creation, it can only be an equitable fee simple absolute[1] and must therefore take effect behind some form of trust.[2]

(2) Estates 'in reversion'

An estate 'in reversion' is the sum total of the rights retained throughout by a grantor who fails to exhaust the entire interest in the land in the terms of his conveyance to a stranger.[3] In other words, if a grantor fails to dispose of the fee simple absolute in his land, he himself retains a fee simple 'in

18 See *Pearson v IRC* [1981] AC 753 at 772A-D, where Viscount Dilhorne accepted the time-honoured proposition that an 'estate in possession' is one which gives 'a present right of present enjoyment'.

19 'Possession' is statutorily defined as including 'receipt of rents and profits or the right to receive the same' (Law of Property Act 1925, s 205(1)(xix)). Thus a fee simple absolute does not cease to be an estate 'in possession' merely because the owner grants a lease to a tenant. In the context of a legal lease both the landlord and the tenant have an estate 'in possession'.

20 *Bl Comm*, Vol II, p 164; *Challis*, p 78f. A fee simple in remainder must be carefully distinguished from a 'contingent' fee simple, the vesting of which is subject to a 'condition precedent' (*Bl Comm*, Vol II, p 165). See Chapter 15, post, p 612.

1 Law of Property Act 1925, s 1(3).

2 Post, p 611.

3 '... if he, who was before possessed of the whole, carves out of it any smaller estate, and grants it away, whatever is not so granted remains in him' (*Bl Comm*, Vol II, p 175). See also *Challis*, p 78.

reversion' from the moment of his non-exhaustive grant, and this fee simple estate will fall back into possession on the expiration of the limited interests which he has granted away.

An example of a fee simple absolute in reversion arises where X grants Blackacre to A for life. A clearly takes a life interest 'in possession', but X, since he has not granted away the absolute interest in the land, takes the fee simple absolute 'in reversion' himself.[4] It should be noticed that, once again, this form of fee simple can only be equitable: it falls outside the terms of section 1(1)(a) of the Law of Property Act 1925.

4 The 'reversion' which arises here by operation of law should be sharply distinguished from other forms of right which appear similar but which result from the conduct of the grantees themselves (eg the 'possibility of reverter' which rests with the grantor of a determinable fee simple and the 'right of entry' vested in the grantor of a fee simple which has been made the subject of a condition subsequent).

CHAPTER 6

Outline of the 1925 Legislation

The borderline between legal and equitable property rights in land was examined in Chapter 4.[1] The time has now come to outline the way in which both kinds of right are accommodated within the structure of the English law of real property (see generally *Fig.* 10[2]).

1. THE DISTINCTION BETWEEN REGISTERED AND UNREGISTERED LAND

For more than 60 years following the enactment of the property legislation of 1925 the primary and most fundamental classification of English land law was the distinction between *registered* and *unregistered* land. More accurately, the relevant distinction was that which existed between land in respect of which title is registered and land where title remains unregistered. This major dichotomy between two rather different regimes of title still exerts a deep impact upon the systematic organisation of land interests and the way in which these interests are protected on a transfer of title.

(1) The practical distinction

The distinction between registered and unregistered title is best seen in practical conveyancing terms.

(a) Registered title

The essence of registered title is the idea that virtually all the pertinent details of ownership relating to a plot of land falling within an area of compulsory registration of title should be recorded definitively on a central register maintained by the Land Registry.[3] This register (the 'Land Register') is kept permanently updated and the theory of registered conveyancing is that a prospective purchaser need only consult the Register in order to discover all the relevant legal information about the land which he proposes to buy.[4]

The law regulating registered titles is contained in the Land Registration Act 1925 and in the Land Registration Rules made pursuant to that Act.

1 Ante, p 67.
2 Post, p 112.
3 Post, p 170.
4 The operation of the Land Register is more fully described in Chapter 8 (post, p 166).

(b) Unregistered title

In relation to that land where title is *not* registered, none of the details of ownership appears on any central record or register (with isolated exceptions such as those in respect of 'land charges', which are centrally recorded on the Land Charges Register[5]). In unregistered land, therefore, the purchaser must investigate title by means of perusal of the historical documents of title in the hope of eliciting the legal information which he requires before he decides to purchase.[6] In order to take a good title, the purchaser must be able to find a chain of ownership which stretches over a period of at least 15 years and leads to his proposed vendor. Only if the title asserted by his vendor is verified in this way can the purchaser of unregistered land safely pay over his purchase money and complete the transaction.[7]

The law pertaining to unregistered titles is found partly in the common law and partly in provisions scattered throughout the property legislation enacted in 1925.

(2) The relationship between registered and unregistered title

Compulsory registration of title was introduced in its present form only in 1926 and even then extended merely to certain designated areas of England and Wales. Dealings in respect of land situated within these areas required thenceforth to be conducted in accordance with the Land Registration Act 1925 and to be recorded in the Land Register maintained under this Act. The residue of land in England and Wales remained land of *unregistered title* and dealings in respect of such land were governed by the much more cumbersome system of conveyancing specific to 'old system title'.[8]

It was the clear intention of Parliament that registration of title under the Land Registration Act 1925 should extend relatively quickly to cover all of England and Wales. In reality the expansion of registered title across the country proceeded much more slowly than had been anticipated,[9] but by the 1980s at least most large urban centres had been designated as areas of compulsory registration. Unregistered conveyancing was being slowly but surely displaced as, from time to time, further areas were likewise designated and more titles were introduced to the Land Register.

The movement towards universal compulsory registration of title was both inevitable and irresistible. In 1989 it was declared by Order in Council that *all* conveyances on sale taking effect on or after 1 December 1990 should conclude in the entry of the purchaser in the Land Register as the registered proprietor of the relevant title pursuant to the Land Registration Act 1925.[10]

5 Post, p 116.
6 The process of unregistered conveyancing is described in detail in Chapters 7 and 9 (post, pp 113, 245).
7 Post, p 271.
8 The term 'old system' is a borrowing from the Australian jurisdictions, where 'old system' or 'general' land law is distinguished from the nowadays more common system of registration of title under Torrens legislation (post, p 168).
9 It was initially expected that registration of title would cover the entire country within ten years of the enactment of the Land Registration Act 1925 (post, p 166).
10 See Land Registration, England and Wales: The Registration of Title Order 1989 (SI 1989/1347).

After its arrival on the Register the new title must thenceforth be transacted exclusively as a *registered title* in accordance with the terms of that Act.

The Order in Council of 1989 does not, of course, achieve an immediate or automatic conversion of all unregistered land into land of registered title. The reception of a previously unregistered title on to the Land Register will occur only with the first conveyance 'on sale'[11] next following 1 December 1990. It is therefore clear that many titles in unregistered land will remain off the Register for some appreciable period to come and that the comprehensive conversion of unregistered land into registered titles is still quite some distance away. Thus even today there remain substantial areas of England and Wales where the existing distribution of rights and obligations in land must be ascertained with reference to the 'old system' rules.[12] A substantial minority of land transactions continue to concern unregistered titles, and the law relating to such titles is not yet ready to be discarded. Unregistered land law still provides the key to determining the precise nature, allocation and priority of the land interests which, over the years, have accumulated behind unregistered titles. It is, of course, these very interests which will require to be entered on the official record when each potentially registrable title finally reaches the Land Register.

The net effect is that two approximately parallel regimes of land law still operate in this country, relating to registered and unregistered titles respectively. Diametrically opposed solutions are not infrequently thrown up when an identical factual problem arises in each of these rather different contexts. Although the system of registered title is now the pre-eminent regime of English land law, so often the starting point for an understanding of registered land is provided by 'old system' conveyancing. There is therefore an important sense in which the student of real property continues to be required to learn two slightly differing systems of land law.

2. ALIENABILITY OF LAND AND FRAGMENTATION OF BENEFIT

The organisation of property rights in English land law is profoundly influenced by the perceived need to reconcile the potentially conflicting objectives of alienability of land and fragmentation of benefit. This need is just as acute in relation to registered as unregistered land.

(1) The problem

The pervasive (and almost intractable) problem of land law revolves around the extreme difficulty involved in satisfying the twin objectives of alienability and fragmentation.

(a) Importance of alienability

On the one hand it is quite clear that land must be allowed to be freely alienable or commerciable. Transactions in respect of legal estates in land

11 Post, p 174.
12 Post, p 101.

(whether in the form of sale, lease or mortgage) must not be unduly restricted or hampered by law, for the uninhibited alienability of land is essential to the effective functioning of an exchange economy. Land is a highly marketable resource and it is vital that the market in land should not stagnate. As Lord Upjohn said in *National Provincial Bank Ltd v Ainsworth*,[13] it has been 'the policy of the law for over a hundred years to simplify and facilitate transactions in real property.'

(b) Importance of fragmented benefits

On the other hand there is a significant social interest in enabling land to be used as a means both of sharing out wealth and of allocating other kinds of benefit or utility which are incidental to land. It is highly desirable that the owner of a legal estate in land should be able to fragment, and thereby distribute, the benefits which are derived from land. These benefits may take various forms.

(i) Family interests It is important, for instance, that land should provide a convenient and flexible medium of family endowment. The owner of a legal estate may well wish to grant various kinds of 'family' interest in land to his children, or he may simply wish to share the equitable ownership of the family home with a spouse or partner. The desideratum of endowment is recognised in any society which acknowledges both private ownership and the bonds of familial relationship, for endowment is integral to the intergenerational transfer of private wealth.

(ii) Commercial interests Alternatively the owner of a legal estate in land may wish to fragment the benefit derived from the land not through the creation of 'family' equitable interests but rather through the granting away of 'commercial' equitable interests in or over the land.[14] Such rights may be of considerable commercial or practical utility. The owner may, for example, decide to grant a stranger a right of way or the benefit of a restrictive covenant over his own land, thereby conferring on the stranger a portion of the utility which otherwise he himself would have retained in the land.

(c) Apparent contradiction of objectives

The twin objectives of alienability of title and fragmentation of benefit are, in the first analysis, set against each other in irreconcilable opposition. If the legal title in land is to be freely alienable, how can rights to various forms of fragmented benefit in that land be other than transient and defeasible rights which perish when the legal title passes into the hands of a purchaser? The interest of the alienee in taking title utterly free of conflicting rights militates directly against the objective of fragmentation of benefit. The free transferability of title seems to be in conflict with the durable creation—whether for family or commercial reasons—of lesser rights in the land which are capable of surviving subsequent dealings with the legal title.

13 [1965] AC 1175 at 1233G (post, p 566).
14 Ante, p 71.

(2) The solution

Perhaps the most distinctive achievement of modern English land law lies in the way in which it has largely resolved the inherent tension between the concerns of alienation and fragmentation.[15] The accommodation of these divergent objectives of the law is made possible by a series of legislative provisions, confirmed in 1925, which simplify dealings with the legal estate in land. These provisions also ensure that fragments of benefit (which in the artificial schema of the Law of Property Act 1925 are almost always equitable interests[16]) are secured in such a way as to survive the alienation of the legal estate to a third party purchaser of the land. The outstanding success of the 1925 legislation consists in the way in which, in the context of land transfer, the law simultaneously facilitates the protection both of purchasers and of those who own various fragments of benefit.

3. PROTECTION OF PURCHASERS OF A LEGAL TITLE

The protection given to purchasers by the 1925 legislation rests upon two principal bases. *First*, the purchaser is favoured by a series of provisions which promote the free alienability of land titles. *Second*, the law now stipulates fairly narrowly the circumstances under which pre-existing rights in the land may remain binding on the purchaser after he takes his transfer.

(1) Free alienability of land titles

Two factors, above all others, have operated since 1925 to ensure the free alienability of land titles under English law. These factors operate indiscriminately in respect of both registered and unregistered land.

(a) Restriction of the number of legal estates

The present line of demarcation between legal and equitable estates, interests and charges was finalised only in the Law of Property Act 1925. Before the commencement of this legislation many kinds of limited interest in land (eg a life interest and a fee tail) constituted legal estates in land. In order that a purchaser should take a good legal title, he had to require that the conveyance to him be executed by all persons holding any legal interest in the property. In other words he had to take his conveyance not merely from the owner of the fee simple absolute but possibly also from an assortment of limited owners. The purchaser's task in investigating all the component parts of a legal title might thus be rendered a quite horrifyingly complex and protracted affair.

The difficulty caused by the multifarious nature of legal estates in land has now been removed. Section 1(1) of the Law of Property Act 1925 Now

15 See eg *City of London Building Society v Flegg* [1988] AC 54 at 73G per Lord Templeman ('One of the main objects of the legislation of 1925 was to effect a compromise between on the one hand the interests of the public in securing that land in trust is freely marketable and, on the other hand, the interests of beneficiaries in preserving their rights under the trusts').

16 Ante, p 68.

deliberately restricts the number of possible legal estates in land to two—the fee simple absolute in possession and the term of years absolute.[17] All other interests in land take effect only behind one or other of these legal estates. Thus since 1 January 1926 (the commencement date of the 1925 legislation) all purchasers have known that the only person whose conveyance is necessary to transfer a freehold estate at law is the owner of an estate in fee simple absolute in possession. A conveyance of a mere limited interest is ineffective to pass the freehold title. It is correspondingly clear that since 1 January 1926 the only vendor competent to 'assign' (or convey) a leasehold legal estate is one who owns (or claims through the owner of) a term of years absolute.

(b) Restriction of the number of owners of a legal estate

Before the enactment of the property legislation of 1925, it was possible for even an absolute legal estate (eg a fee simple estate) to be held by, and therefore fragmented between, an almost limitless number of persons, each holding a specific share or proportion of that estate. In order to take a good legal title, the purchaser had to ensure not merely that his conveyance was signed by all the legal co-owners, but also that the individual title held by each was duly investigated.[18] Such a process was cumbersome, costly and time-consuming.

This disadvantageous feature of the law was removed, or at least substantially alleviated, by the 1925 legislation. The maximum number of persons who may hold a legal estate is now limited by statute to four.[19] The number of persons from whom the conveyance of a legal title must be taken is therefore at most four, and these four are regarded as owners of one and the same legal estate, with the result that the purchaser need investigate only *one* composite title.[20] In this way a much greater degree of simplicity and convenience is introduced into the process of title transfer.

(2) Limited liability of the purchaser to pre-existing interests

A further factor which ensures substantial protection for the purchaser of a legal title is the way in which the property legislation of 1925 circumscribes fairly narrowly the conditions under which pre-existing rights in the land remain binding on him after he takes his transfer. This limited vulnerability on the part of the purchaser in respect of prior adverse interests has the consequence both of promoting the free alienability of land titles and also of securing a clear basis for decision-making about long-term investment in the land.[1]

In analysing the relative immunity of the purchaser a distinction must be drawn between registered and unregistered land. In either case the practical problem under scrutiny is whether a right acquired by B in A's land remains binding on C, a subsequent owner of A's estate (see *Fig.* 7).

17 Ante, p 68.
18 See *City of London Building Society v Flegg* [1988] AC 54 at 76H–77A per Lord Oliver of Aylmerton.
19 Law of Property Act 1925, s 34(2), (3); Trustee Act 1925, s 34(2) (post, p 512).
20 Post, p 468.
1 See R.A. Epstein, 73 Cornell L Rev 906 at 908 (1987–88).

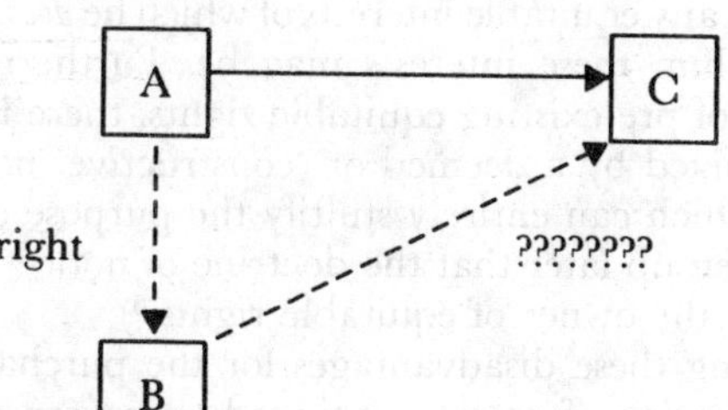

Fig. 7

(a) Legal rights in unregistered land

It is principally in relation to unregistered land or 'old system' conveyancing that the two basic axioms of English land law still retain some validity.[2] It remains almost entirely true that legal rights bind the world; with somewhat less accuracy it can be maintained that the impact of equitable rights on purchasers depends on some version of the equitable doctrine of notice.

In unregistered land legal rights, as defined with reference to section 1 of the Law of Property Act 1925, are automatically binding on and effective against all persons irrespective of notice.[3] In this sense, one of the earliest sedimentary layers of English land law is still thoroughly exposed to view in the law of unregistered title.

This means, of course, that the immunity given to purchasers of an unregistered title does not extend to immunity from pre-existing *legal* rights. The purchaser takes his title subject to these—and does so regardless of notice.[4] However, although he is bound by all legal interests affecting the land, the existence of such interests is usually obvious on physical inspection of the land or is readily apparent from the face of the documentary title investigated by him before completion of the purchase. It is unlikely in practice that the purchaser of a legal fee simple will be caught unawares by an existing legal lease or other legal interests or charges affecting the land.

(b) Equitable rights in unregistered land

The other major axiom of land law dictates that equitable rights bind all persons other than a bona fide purchaser of a legal estate for value without notice.[5] The purchaser thus takes free of any equitable interests affecting the land of which he had no notice at the date of purchase.

Although this doctrine of notice operates substantially in favour of the purchaser of unregistered land, it is not entirely satisfactory even so far as he is concerned. In the strict terms of the doctrine, the purchaser takes

2 Ante, p 75.

3 For special reasons (post, p 981), one particular legal interest relating to unregistered land—the 'puisne mortgage'—is taken outside the scope of this general rule of binding effect. The enforceability of a puisne mortgage against third parties depends on the registration of a Class C(i) land charge under Land Charges Act 1972, s 2(4).

4 Ante, p 75.

5 Ante, p 77.

his title subject to any equitable interests of which he *does* have notice, however inconvenient to him these interests may be. Furthermore, even if he has no actual notice of pre-existing equitable rights, there is always a possibility that he may be fixed by a deemed or 'constructive' notice of such rights—a consequence which can entirely stultify the purpose of his purchase. (The point will be taken up later that the doctrine of notice is equally prejudicial to the security of the owner of equitable rights.[6])

Notwithstanding these disadvantages for the purchaser of a legal estate, the equitable doctrine of notice continued to govern the binding effect of almost all equitable rights in land until the advent of the property legislation of 1925. However, the Law of Property Act 1925 sought in a rather fundamental way to modify the effect of the traditional doctrine of notice and this was done through the legislative confirmation of the device of 'overreaching'.

(i) The concept of 'overreaching' 'Overreaching' is a pivotal concept in the law of land.[7] The term is used to describe the process by which a purchaser of a legal estate in land may be given an extended immunity from various forms of pre-existing equitable (or 'beneficial') right—an immunity which goes beyond and largely supersedes the protection afforded the purchaser by the equitable doctrine of notice. To this extent the traditional doctrine of notice has now been displaced by an alternative means of guaranteeing the purchaser immunity from adverse rights.

(ii) Categories of overreaching transaction Section 2(1) of the Law of Property Act 1925 allows the purchaser of a legal estate to 'overreach' (ie deflect or take free of) many kinds of pre-existing equitable right affecting the land, 'whether or not he has notice' of these rights. This consequence is achieved through the declaration in section 2(1) that certain kinds of transaction with a legal title have a potentially 'overreaching' effect.[8] These transactions include a conveyance made under the powers conferred by the Settled Land Act 1925,[9] a conveyance made by 'trustees for sale',[10] a conveyance made by a mortgagee or personal representative,[11] and a conveyance made under court order.[12]

The effect of such conveyances of a legal estate is normally to invest the purchaser with an absolute legal title free of any pre-existing equitable rights

6 Post, p 108.
7 See Charles Harpum, [1990] CLJ 277.
8 Whether overreaching actually occurs in a given case depends on whether there has been compliance with the statutory preconditions of overreaching. These preconditions often require that the purchase moneys be paid to at least two trustees (post, p 552).
9 Law of Property Act 1925, s 2(1)(i) (post, p 631).
10 Law of Property Act 1925, s 2(1)(ii) (post, p 551). For an argument that bare trustees also have power to give an overreaching conveyance, see C. Harpum, [1990] CLJ 277 at 303f, 310. Compare, however, *Hodgson v Marks* [1971] Ch 892 (post, p 216), and see Law Commission, *Transfer of Land: Overreaching: Beneficiaries in Occupation* (Law Com No 188, 19 December 1989), para 1.4.
11 Law of Property Act 1925, s 2(1)(iii) (post, p 1006).
12 Law of Property Act 1925, s 2(1)(iv) (post, p 585).

or powers. So long as the transaction is carried out in the manner prescribed by the Law of Property Act 1925, overreaching operates by creating in the purchaser a legal estate and incidental powers which, by force of statute, 'have an absolute priority over the beneficial interests' already existing in the land.[13] As Lord Oliver of Aylmerton explained in *City of London Building Society v Flegg*,[14] each relevant disposition thus overreaches the adverse equities 'by subordinating them to the estate' taken by the purchaser. The antecedent equitable rights and powers are not thereby extinguished, but are instead deflected or 'shifted from the land'[15] so that thereafter they attach not to the land but to the capital moneys arising on the disposition.

(iii) Consequences of overreaching The device of overreaching radically extends the freedom from liability enjoyed by the purchaser of a legal estate. Provided that a potentially overreaching conveyance is conducted in the required manner,[16] the purchaser takes his title free of adverse equitable rights regardless of whether or not he had notice of such rights. However, the terms of section 2(1) of the Law of Property Act 1925 make it clear that 'overreaching' applies only to an equitable interest which is 'capable of being overreached' by the conveyance of a legal estate in the land. Not all kinds of equitable interest are thus capable.

In effect overreaching operates in relation to 'family' equitable interests, ie those equitable interests which exist behind a trust for sale or under a strict settlement of land.[17] It is a matter of extreme importance that the purchaser of a legal estate in land should take his title free of such interests. It is often coincidentally true that those who own 'family' equitable interests have no real desire to retain their interests in the land after a legal estate in that land has been conveyed to a third party purchaser; they may be just as happy that their 'family' equitable interests should thereafter attach to the money proceeds of the conveyance or that such proceeds be reinvested in the purchase of new realty.

(iv) Operation of overreaching The operation of overreaching can be illustrated in the following way. Suppose that T1 and T2 hold a legal estate in fee simple as 'trustees for sale' on behalf of A and B, who each hold beneficial one-half shares in the property.[18] (This form of legal and equitable ownership probably covers most matrimonial homes in England and Wales.) The equitable interests held by A and B behind this trust for sale are, in the contemplation of the Law of Property Act 1925, interests 'capable of being overreached'. If, as may well happen in the normal course of events, T1 and T2 sell and convey their legal estate to a purchaser, P, the overreaching mechanism normally comes into operation (see *Fig*. 8).

13 *City of London Building Society v Flegg* [1988] AC 54 at 83G-H per Lord Oliver of Aylmerton.
14 [1988] AC 54 at 91B-C.
15 *City of London Building Society v Flegg* [1988] AC 54 at 91A-B per Lord Oliver of Aylmerton.
16 Post, p 551.
17 Ante, p 98.
18 It will be seen later that it is quite possible that T1 and T2 may be the same people as A and B (post, p 521).

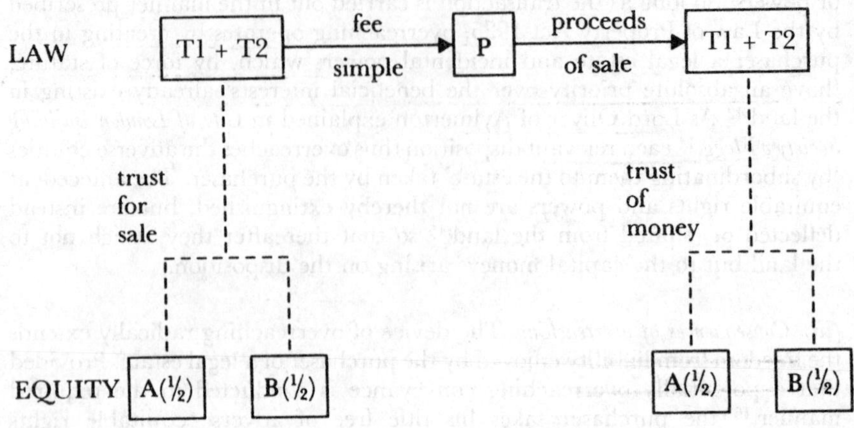

Fig. 8

In accordance with section 2(1) of the Law of Property Act 1925, the conveyance to P overreaches (and therefore enables P to take free of) the equitable rights of A and B behind the trust. This result follows whether or not P had notice actual or constructive of the rights of A and B. However, although the equitable rights of A and B are, by this means, swept off the land conveyed to P, their rights are not in fact destroyed. As against P they are, of course, no longer effective—this is the whole purpose of the overreaching device. But the equitable rights of A and B remain binding on and enforceable against the trustees, T1 and T2, who now stand possessed not of land but of the capital proceeds of sale of land. In other words, the equitable rights of A and B are automatically translated by the overreaching conveyance into exactly equivalent interests in the money proceeds achieved by the sale. Each is the beneficial owner of half of these proceeds, and T1 and T2 are now effectively trustees of a sum of money. This conclusion is highly advantageous for all parties concerned. P takes a clean and unfettered title to the land, while the equitable rights of A and B are preserved after the conveyance by being diverted into money.

(v) Diminished role of the traditional doctrine of notice It can easily be seen that the device of overreaching has revolutionised the treatment of equitable interests in land during the period since 1925. In contrast to the earlier position, when all such rights were subject to the equitable doctrine of notice, many equitable rights are now simply swept off the land by an overreaching conveyance of an unregistered title. The role left to be played by the doctrine of notice is correspondingly diminished. As will be seen later,[19] the role of notice was further displaced by the introduction in the 1925 legislation of a limited scheme of land charge registration in respect of some of the non-overreachable equitable interests.

One important effect of the reorganisation of English land law in 1925 was therefore the subdivision of the field of equitable interests in unregistered

19 Post, p 109.

land into three categories (see *Fig.* 10[20]). These categories comprise respectively (1) those equitable interests which are overreached on conveyance pursuant to the Law of Property Act 1925, (2) those equitable interests whose effect upon a purchaser depends on the registration of a land charge, and (3) those few remaining equitable interests whose impact on third parties still turns on the equitable doctrine of notice.

(c) *Registered land*

It is in relation to registered land that the twin axioms of land law have been most radically modified, to the point where the traditional starting points of the English law of real property are now scarcely recognisable.

Exactly the same kinds of legal and equitable interest exist in registered land as in unregistered land. The line of demarcation between these interests is no different in relation to registered titles, the criteria of legal (as distinct from equitable) quality being laid down in section 1 of the Law of Property Act 1925.[1] However, it is from this point onwards that the law of registered land takes a different direction, for in it the rules of unregistered land are heavily overlaid by the principle of registration. The theory of registered title requires in effect that *all* land interests, whether legal or equitable, whether 'family' or 'commercial', be entered in the Land Register.[2] The Land Register is then regularly updated in order that it should at all times reflect the totality of property interests affecting any given plot of land governed by the Land Registration Act 1925.

(i) 'Major interests' and 'minor interests' The essential details of this registration scheme are very simple. Certain legal estates in land (ie the fee simple absolute in possession and leases of at least 21 years) are substantively registered under their own respective title numbers in the Land Register.[3] These registered interests (which might well be called 'major interests') then provide a focusing point for the registration of all other kinds of subsidiary interest affecting the land in question. In other words, the other subsidiary interests (many of them called 'minor interests') are entered on the Register against the 'major interest' to which they pertain. Provided that this process of registration is accurately and comprehensively carried out, the Register offers at all times a faithful record of all the interests relevant to any piece of land whose title is maintained pursuant to the Land Registration Act 1925.

Of course the operation of the Land Register is more complicated in practice than is indicated by this introductory glimpse of its structure. Of particular difficulty is the existence of certain statutorily defined 'overriding interests' which exist outside the registration scheme but which nevertheless bind the land.[4] However, enough will have been gathered of the working of the registration scheme to make it possible to understand the way in which

20 Post, p 112.
1 Ante, p 68.
2 Registration of title must be sharply distinguished from registration of land charges under the Land Charges Acts 1925 and 1972. The latter form of registration represents an isolated form of registration available—rather confusingly—in respect of certain kinds of interest in *unregistered* land!
3 Post, p 173.
4 Post, p 197.

purchasers (or 'transferees') of a registered title are given protection in the context of a transfer of the registered title (see *Fig.* 9).

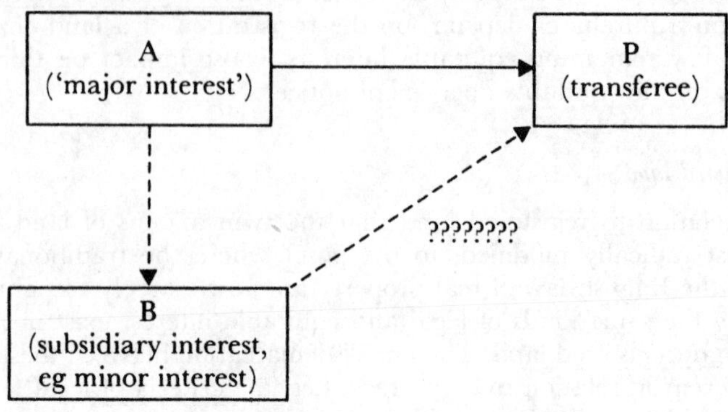

Fig. 9

(ii) Immunity of the transferee In the law of registered land the distinction between legal and equitable rights is almost insignificant—except perhaps for the purpose of defining the 'major interests' against which all other registrations require to be effected. The essence of the scheme is that all land interests—whether legal or equitable—should be recorded on the Land Register, with the now controversial exception of 'overriding interests'.

The result of a transfer of a registered freehold 'major interest' (eg by A to P in *Fig.* 9) is spelt out by statute. According to section 20(1) of the Land Registration Act 1925, a 'disposition' of A's legal estate for valuable consideration confers that estate on P subject to 'the incumbrances and other entries, if any, appearing on the register' and subject to any 'overriding interests' which affect the estate transferred.[5] However, with the exception of these two kinds of interest the estate conferred on the transferee is declared to be 'free from all other estates and interests whatsoever'. Moreover, section 59(6) of the Land Registration Act 1925 provides that a purchaser of registered land takes free of any right unprotected by entry on the Register (other than 'overriding interests') 'whether he has or has not notice thereof, express, implied, or constructive'. The equitable doctrine of notice has no obvious place within the regime of registered title.[6]

In theory therefore a very substantial degree of immunity from adverse rights is accorded to the purchaser of registered land. Apart from 'overriding interests' he is subject only to those interests positively recorded on the face of the Land Register at the date of his purchase. Moreover, it will be seen shortly that the transferee of a registered title can overreach 'family' equitable rights just as effectively as the purchaser of unregistered land, even where such interests have been entered in the Register. The overreaching mechanism

5 Post, p 186.

6 Post, p 187. In *Kemmis v Kemmis* [1988] 1 WLR 1307 at 1332E, Nourse LJ conceded that it might be 'correct, in broad terms, to describe the material provisions of the Land Registration Act 1925 as having provided a substitute for notice, which may sometimes be referred to as "statutory notice"'. He pointed out, however, that 'the substitute differs substantially from the original.'

in both contexts is identical. It is simply the case that the form of entry on the Land Register which is appropriate to 'family' equitable interests automatically ensures that the Land Registry cannot process any disposition of the 'major interest' without requiring the preconditions of overreaching to be fulfilled.[7]

(iii) 'Overriding interests' In recent years, however, it has become clear that the principal threat to the title taken by the transferee of registered land lies in the ever increasing number of 'overriding interests' which, although not contained in the Register itself, nevertheless bind transferees. It is even possible that interests in registered land which should have been protected by some form of entry on the Land Register (eg as 'minor interests') may—in the absence of such protection—rank nonetheless as overriding interests. The over-protection of such interests has become a highly controversial feature of the registration scheme and produces the absurd consequence that protective entry on the Register is unnecessary and in many instances perhaps best avoided. The most dangerous development of all has been the judicial confirmation that some of these 'overriding interests' are effective against the transferee even though the interests in question are potentially overreachable.[8]

4. PROTECTION FOR OWNERS OF FRAGMENTS OF BENEFIT

The major thrust of the English property legislation of 1925 is directed, in both registered and unregistered land, towards increased protection for the purchaser of a legal title. Yet one aspect of the remarkable achievement of this legislation is the fact that, although it confers heightened security on the purchaser, it simultaneously ensures a substantial degree of protection for those who own fragments of benefit in the land transferred. In this way the legislation facilitates both the free alienability of land titles and the durable creation of lesser entitlements in that land which are not destroyed by the act of transfer.

(1) Unregistered land

(a) Legal rights

The primary rule of unregistered land law is that legal rights bind the world. Legal rights thus require no artificial protection against third parties; their integrity is inviolable.[9] The equitable doctrine of notice has no relevance. If B, for instance, has been granted a legal term of years out of a fee simple estate owned by A in unregistered land, B's lease is wholly secure when A 'assigns the freehold reversion' (ie conveys his legal title) to a purchaser, P. Likewise if B has a legal right of way over A's land, this easement is equally binding on P, a purchaser of A's legal title.

7 Post, p 182.
8 See eg *Williams & Glyn's Bank Ltd v Boland* [1981] AC 487 (post, pp 226, 569).
9 Ante, p 75.

(b) Equitable rights

The degree of security enjoyed before 1926 by the owner of equitable interests in land was by no means so extensive as that accorded to the owner of a legal interest. Indeed, under the doctrine of notice, equitable rights are exceedingly insecure against purchasers of a legal estate, since they are liable to be destroyed if the purchaser has no notice of their existence. Equitable rights are commonly not referred to at all in the formal documents of title, and there is therefore a strong probability that a third party purchaser will not be fixed with notice and will take free of the rights in question. It may in many cases be highly inconvenient and wrong that equitable rights should be defeated in such a capricious way, especially where—as in the case of 'commercial' equitable interests—the rights have been created for valuable consideration. No equitable owner can sleep easily at night for fear that he may be confronted at any time by a purchaser of a legal estate for value who has no notice of his equitable rights.[10] And of course once 'Equity's Darling' appears on the scene, equitable rights are destroyed for ever without any form of compensation.[11]

It was inevitable by 1925 that such uncertainty could no longer be allowed to attach to equitable rights, not least because this degree of vulnerability represents the antithesis of a rational law of property. It was for this reason that from 1 January 1926 legislative changes were introduced in order to protect equitable rights in unregistered land from the eminent possibility of wanton destruction by operation of the equitable doctrine of notice. The effect of these changes was to mitigate or modify much of the force of that doctrine.

The property legislation of 1925 introduced two major means of eliminating the insecurity of equitable interests vis à vis the bona fide purchaser of a legal estate for value without notice. *First*, it provided for a limited process of statutory 'overreaching' of equitable interests. *Second*, it established a system of formal 'land charge' registration in respect of certain equitable interests in unregistered land.

(i) Overreaching It has already been seen that section 2(1) of the Law of Property Act 1925 confirmed a statutory facility of 'overreaching' in respect of 'family' equitable interests.[12] This device covers, for instance, equitable interests which arise under a strict settlement or behind a 'trust for sale', and ensures that, by complying with the statutory preconditions, the purchaser of a legal title may be guaranteed immunity from all pre-existing 'family' equitable rights. However, the beneficiaries under a settlement or trust are also protected by the overreaching process. They can, in theory at least, regard the conveyance of the legal estate with substantial indifference, since their equitable interests attach thereafter to the proceeds of the sale or other transaction. In effect, all that has happened is that the nature of the investment

10 Even if this fear never materialised, the equitable owner was still disadvantaged when he came to sell any property which carried the benefit of his equitable rights. He was in no position to command the highest price in so far as he could not assure his successor in title that the appurtenant rights were indefeasible in the event of a later transfer of the burdened land.

11 Ante, p 84.

12 Ante, p 102.

on their behalf—the character of the trust property—has undergone a transformation. With the disposition of the legal title to a third party, the beneficiaries' rights are swept off the land and on to the resulting capital proceeds. The third party takes the unregistered title free of their rights 'whether or not he has notice'. In this way security for the equitable interests is imaginatively coupled with facility for the purchaser.

(ii) Registration of land charges The second innovation of the 1925 legislation was the introduction of a limited scheme of registration of equitable interests even within the domain of 'unregistered' land. Thus, in respect of 'commercial' equitable interests in unregistered land the Land Charges Act 1925 initiated a facility by which the owners of such interests could register those interests as 'land charges' against the name of the owner of the legal estate in the land.[13]

Lest this introduction of a registration device in 'unregistered' land be thought unduly confusing, it must be borne in mind that the scheme of land charge registration seized upon only one fairly small and isolated group of equitable interests in unregistered land, making these interests alone subject to a rule of registration. The limited scope of this form of registration in the Land Charges Register contrasts markedly with the theory of comprehensive registration of all interests (whether legal or equitable) in the rather different Land Register which controls matters of 'registered title'.[14]

The Land Charges Act 1925 has now been replaced by the Land Charges Act 1972. The operation of both Acts is similar and fairly straightforward. Whereas the effect of the device of 'overreaching' is to render notice on the part of a purchaser entirely irrelevant, land charge registration renders such notice altogether inescapable.[15] The Land Charges Act modifies the traditional doctrine of notice by providing that the formal registration of certain kinds of equitable interest in the Land Charges Register 'shall be deemed to constitute actual notice. . .to all persons and for all purposes' of the existence of the right in question.[16]

In respect of 'commercial' equitable rights therefore, registration in the Land Charges Register became—from 1926 onwards—the only relevant or acceptable form of notice for the purpose of binding third parties. By registering his interest as a land charge against the estate owner, the equitable owner effectively utilises the element of publicity inherent in formal registration, immediately fixing the world with statutory notice of his interest. He thus forecloses the possibility that any subsequent purchaser can ever claim to have bought a legal estate in the encumbered land *without* notice of his equitable interest. Once registered this equitable interest remains binding on the land into whosesoever hands the legal estate may later pass.

The scheme of land charge registration clearly removes many kinds of equitable interest in unregistered land from the scope of the conventional doctrine of notice, thereby diminishing yet further the role left to be played by this doctrine in modern land law. The principle underlying the registration

13 Post, p 116.
14 Ante, p 167.
15 'With recordation, the problem of notice disappears in all but the most unusual case' (R.A. Epstein, 73 Cornell L Rev 906 at 909 (1987–88)).
16 Law of Property Act 1925, s 198(1) (post, p 118).

scheme represents an ingenious means of combining security for various kinds of equitable owner with increased facility for third parties who deal with the legal estate. The net effect is the achievement of a previously unattainable transactional efficiency in which the registration process effectively controls the 'externalities' (ie the economic costs and disincentives) which would otherwise flow from uncertainty of outcome.

Although several severe flaws will be seen later as emerging within this registration scheme,[17] its superficial advantages extend to both purchaser and equitable owner alike. By the simple act of registering his 'commercial' equitable interest, the incumbrancer effectively disables any subsequent purchaser from denying notice of his rights. At the same time the prospective purchaser is enabled, by a simple search of the Land Charges Register, to discover all the commercial equitable rights which affect his land.[18] He is further protected by the rule that a registrable but unregistered interest is statutorily declared to be void as against him,[19] with the result that he takes his legal title subject only to those interests which have in fact been protected by entry on the Register. The purchaser is put in the position of knowing exactly what he is buying; while the rights of the equitable owner are made absolutely binding on all later purchasers through the artificial but inexorable medium of notice as provided by the Register.

(iii) Equitable rights still dependent on the traditional doctrine of notice The enactment in the 1925 Acts of the devices of overreaching and land charge registration was initially thought to have rendered almost redundant the orthodox doctrine of notice in its pre-1926 form. In their combined effect it was generally considered that these devices had made notice of equitable rights either irrelevant or inescapable. However, during the period since 1925 it has become painfully obvious that the devices of overreaching and land charge registration have not exhausted the field of equitable interests in unregistered land. One of the most difficult problems to be found in modern unregistered conveyancing is the continued existence of a small, but consistently awkward, category of anomalous equitable rights which for one reason or another fall outside both major classifications of overreachable and registrable rights. To these interests the classical doctrine of notice is still applicable.[20]

(2) Registered land

The law of registered title offers, if anything, even greater protection to owners of fragments of benefit than is the case in the law of unregistered land. In registered land the significance of the distinction between legal and equitable rights is minimal. Almost all rights in registered land—of whatever kind—should be entered on the Land Register against the appropriate 'major interest'.[1] For example, 'commercial' and 'family' equitable interests are

17 Post, p 137.
18 An American commentator has aptly described the efficiency of systems of public recordation of rights as flowing precisely from the fact that such systems are 'routine and ministerial—a notable social triumph of the humdrum' (see R.A. Epstein, 73 Cornell L Rev 906 at 909 (1987-88)).
19 Land Charges Act 1972, s 4 (post, p 118).
20 Post, pp 279, 563.
1 Ante, p 105, post, p 167.

protectible as 'minor interests' by various forms of entry in the Register, and if so entered are binding upon later transferees of the registered title.[2] In particular, 'family' equitable interests are protectible primarily by the entry of a 'restriction' on the Register, which effectively ensures that any subsequent dealing with the registered title can be conducted only in such manner as will inevitably overreach the relevant equitable interests, thereby translating them into the equivalent interests in the capital proceeds received by the trustees.[3]

Thus, once again, the law of registered land strives towards a compromise between facility for the transferee and security for owners of lesser interests subordinate to the 'major' registered interest. The transferee may detect the relevant details of entitlement exposed on the face of the Land Register; the owners of such lesser interests may safeguard their rights by simple protective entry. However, as has been seen already,[4] one of the rogue developments in the modern law of registered title has been the extension of the category of 'overriding interests' which, although existing off the Register, become binding on transferees of the registered title. The over-large protection afforded such interests has recently been the subject of much anxious scrutiny. The present concern arises not least because the category of 'overriding interests' is sufficiently capacious to ensure that transferees often take title subject to rights which clearly should have been a matter of entry on the Register but which, for reasons of sheer negligence or otherwise, have not been so protected.

2 Ante, p 105, post, p 181.
3 Ante, p 107, post, p 182.
4 Ante, p 107.

Synopsis

The following diagram summarises the principal classifications and subdivisions introduced in this chapter.

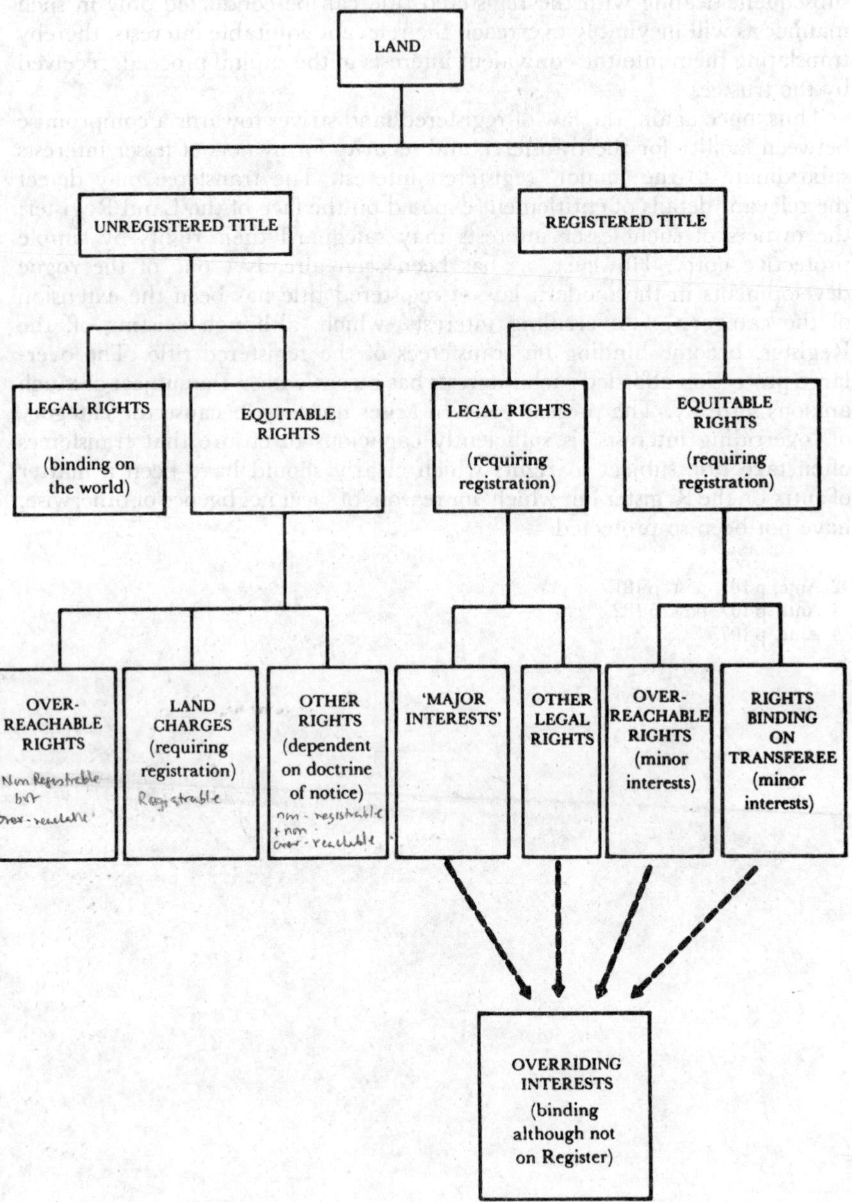

Fig 10

CHAPTER 7

Registration under the Land Charges Act

It has already been seen that the application of the raw axioms or first principles of land law was always liable to produce a considerable degree of uncertainty in unregistered or 'old system' conveyancing.[1] There remained room for both doubt and dispute as to the effectiveness against purchasers of various kinds of right which the vendor (or his predecessors) might already have granted to others. The inherent insecurity of such rights (particularly in the context of the equitable doctrine of notice) was finally removed, at least in part, by the introduction in 1925 of a partial scheme of registration in *unregistered* land.[2] The Land Charges Act 1925 (now consolidated in the Land Charges Act 1972) facilitated the public registration not merely of certain categories of equitable interest in land, but also of other matters, actions and documents relating to land.[3]

With the steady movement towards universal registration of title under the Land Registration Act 1925,[4] the role of the Land Charges Act in respect of unregistered land will of course become gradually redundant. It will nevertheless be some time before all land in England and Wales is registered pursuant to the Land Registration Act 1925,[5] and it is therefore the task of this chapter to analyse the current operation of the land charges legislation.

1. THE BASIC CONCEPT OF REGISTRATION

The concept of registration under the Land Charges Act is fundamentally very simple. A person who is interested in any claim or matter which falls within one of the registrable heads under the Land Charges Act 1972 is offered the opportunity of making an appropriate entry in the relevant division of the Register maintained pursuant to that Act.[6] The registration scheme

1 Ante, p 102.
2 Ante, p 109. On the objectives of the draftsmen of the land charges legislation, see J. Howell, [1990] Conv 250 at 252.
3 Post, p 114. Even before 1926 there had been partial systems of land charge registration. See eg Land Charges Registration and Searches Act 1888.
4 Registration of title is described in further detail in Chapter 8, post, p 166.
5 In order to ensure the comprehensive conversion of unregistered land into registered titles, there is a requirement that all conveyances on sale taking effect on or after 1 December 1990 should conclude in the entry of the purchaser as the registered proprietor of the relevant title under the Land Registration Act 1925 (see Land Registration, England and Wales: The Registration of Title Order 1989 (SI 1989/1347)). In this way old system conveyancing will gradually be replaced by registered conveyancing.
6 The Register is maintained in Plymouth by the Land Charges Department of the Land Registry, whose operations are governed in greater detail by the Land Charges Rules 1974 (SI 1974/1286) and the Land Charges (Amendment) Rules 1990 (SI 1990/485).

then proceeds on the basis of two general and somewhat blunt rules. *First*, any interest or matter—once registered—is deemed to affect all persons with notice, and therefore becomes binding for all practical purposes upon the entire world. *Second*, a registrable interest or matter—if not duly registered—is normally rendered void or ineffective in relation to third parties.

2. MATTERS AND INTERESTS REGISTRABLE UNDER THE LAND CHARGES ACT 1972

A fairly carefully defined range of matters and interests is made registrable under the Land Charges Act 1972. This range comprises the following general heads.

(1) Pending actions

The existence of certain kinds of litigation or disputed claim affecting a title to land may be the subject of a special entry in the register of pending actions which is maintained under the Land Charges Act 1972.

(a) Matters registrable as a pending action

The register of pending actions may be used for the registration of bankruptcy petitions filed on or after 1 January 1926 and for the entry of 'pending land actions'.[7] A 'pending land action' (or *lis pendens*) must comprise an action or proceeding pending in court 'relating to land or any interest in or charge on land'.[8] The definition of the matters registrable under this head thus covers most claims affecting the title to land or asserting some (even inchoate) proprietary interest in land. A pending land action may therefore include such disparate matters as a spouse's claim to a property adjustment order on divorce[9] and a claim of entitlement to an easement.[10] However, a pending land action cannot be registered in respect of a merely *monetary* claim in respect of land, with the result that registration cannot at present be used in order to protect such interests as a beneficiary's share in the proceeds of sale under a trust for sale.[11] It is possible, however, that the registration of a pending land action may provide a means of protecting

7 Land Charges Act 1972, s 5(1). See (1986) 136 NLJ 157 (H.W. Wilkinson).
8 Land Charges Act 1972, s 17(1).
9 See *Whittingham v Whittingham* [1979] Fam 9 at 13E, but compare *Sowerby v Sowerby* (1982) 44 P & CR 192 at 195ff. In *Perez-Adamson v Perez-Rivas* [1987] Fam 89 at 96D-E, 97D, the Court of Appeal held that even a general claim for property adjustment in respect of unidentified land, if registered as a lis pendens against specific property, could take priority over a mortgage charge subsequently executed by the other spouse (see [1988] Conv 58 (J.E.M.)).
10 See *Greenhi Builders Ltd v Allen* [1979] 1 WLR 156 at 159G.
11 *Taylor v Taylor* [1968] 1 WLR 378 at 384C, 385B-C.

the *occupation rights* not merely of beneficiaries under a trust for sale,[12] but also of persons who assert rights based on proprietary estoppel.[13]

(b) Effects of registration and non-registration

An entry in the register of pending actions has effect for an initial period of five years but is thereafter renewable for further periods of five years.[14] The inevitable consequence of such an entry is that any prospective purchaser of the land concerned is affected by a deemed 'actual notice' of potentially contentious issues relating to the title which he proposes to purchase.[15] However, a failure to register renders a pending land action ineffective against any purchaser 'without express notice of it'.[16] Likewise an unregistered petition in bankruptcy has no binding effect on 'a purchaser of a legal estate in good faith, for money or money's worth, without notice of an available act of bankruptcy'.[17]

(2) Writs and orders affecting land

Certain kinds of writ or order issued in the enforcement of a court order or judgment may be registered in the register of writs and orders affecting land.[18] Included within this category are charging orders,[19] orders appointing a receiver[20] or sequestrator of land,[1] and any bankruptcy order.[2] If duly registered, the writ or order is binding on all persons,[3] but if not so registered is generally ineffective against a 'purchaser of the land'.[4]

(3) Annuities

Certain annuities created between 1855 and 1926 were capable of entry in a register of annuities which was closed in 1925.[5] This register contains only anomalous annuities which by now must be almost extinct. Most modern

12 Post, p 546.
13 See *Haslemere Estates Ltd v Baker* [1982] 1 WLR 1109 at 1119H–1120A; [1983] Conv 69 at 70 (post, p 365).
14 Land Charges Act 1972, s 8.
15 Law of Property Act 1925, s 198(1) (ante, p 80).
16 Land Charges Act 1972, s 5(7).
17 Land Charges Act 1972, s 5(8).
18 As with pending actions, the registration is for a renewable period of five years (Land Charges Act 1972, s 8).
19 Land Charges Act 1972, s 6(1)(a). A *Mareva* injunction is not registrable under section 6(1)(a) (see *Stockler v Fourways Estates Ltd* [1984] 1 WLR 25 at 27B). However, following the Canadian example (see eg *Re Kumar and Kumar* (1988) 48 DLR (4th) 559), it is now open to the county court to direct that amounts unpaid under a liability order made pursuant to the Child Support Act 1991 be recoverable as a charging order (see Child Support Act 1991, s 36(1)).
20 Registration is available in respect of a receivership order made against a landlord following non-performance of repairing covenants (post, p 796). See *Clayhope Properties Ltd v Evans* [1986] 1 WLR 1223 at 1227E.
1 Land Charges Act 1972, s 6(1)(b).
2 Land Charges Act 1972, s 6(1)(c).
3 Law of Property Act 1925, s 198(1) (ante, p 80).
4 Land Charges Act 1972, s 6(4).
5 Land Charges Act 1925, s 4.

annuities are registrable as Class C(iii) or Class E land charges under the Land Charges Act 1972.[6]

(4) Deeds of arrangement

Certain deeds of arrangement entered into by a bankrupt debtor for the benefit of his creditors may be recorded in the register of deeds of arrangement affecting land.[7] If so registered, they remain valid and effective against third parties for a renewable period of five years,[8] but if unregistered are void against any purchaser of the land concerned.[9]

(5) Land charges

By far the most important form of registration under the Land Charges Act 1972 relates to the 'land charge' properly so called.[10] The process of registration of such charges (and the legal consequences of registration) provide the subject matter of the remainder of this chapter.

3. REGISTRATION OF LAND CHARGES

Certain categories of statutorily defined charge are capable of registration in the Land Charges Register which is maintained pursuant to the Land Charges Act 1972. The initial paradox of this scheme for registration of 'land charges' is that it rather confusingly facilitates the registration of interests in *unregistered* land. This apparent difficulty disappears as soon as it is realised that the scheme embraces only one fairly small group of equitable rights in unregistered land and imposes on this isolated category a systematic regime of registration.[11]

(1) Mode of entry in the register

An interest registered in the Land Charges Register must be 'registered in

6 Post, pp 141, 153.
7 Land Charges Act 1972, s 7(1).
8 Land Charges Act 1972, s 8.
9 Land Charges Act 1972, s 7(2).
10 Registration of 'land charges' must be carefully distinguished from registration of 'local land charges' (see eg J.E. Adams, (1976) 40 Conv (NS) 106). A register of local land charges (which usually relate to such public matters as planning permissions or local government activities affecting property) is maintained by the relevant local authority in respect of both registered and unregistered land situated within its area.
11 Precisely the same kinds of interest, if occurring in relation to land whose title is registered under the Land Registration Act 1925, are protected by entry in the Land Register (see Land Registration Act 1925, s 59; *Clayhope Properties Ltd v Evans* [1986] 1 WLR 1223 at 1227D-E). In the latter context, however, such interests are recorded as 'minor interests' (post, p 181), and entry usually takes the form of either a 'notice' or a 'caution' (post, p 183).

the name of the estate owner whose estate is intended to be affected.[12] This requirement causes a number of difficulties.

(a) Registration by a sub-purchaser

Not the least of the difficulties generated by a name-based register is that caused to the incumbrancer who is unaware that he is dealing with a sub-vendor. Such a difficulty occurs, for example, where A (the owner of a legal estate in fee simple in unregistered land) contracts to sell that estate to B. Before the appropriate conveyance is executed, B may well contract by way of sub-sale to convey the same legal estate to C. In this situation there are *two* land charges which qualify for registration under the terms of the Land Charges Act 1972. The first charge arises from the 'estate contract' entered into by A and B,[13] and is registrable by B against the name of the current 'estate owner', ie A. The second charge arises from a further 'estate contract', ie the contract of sub-sale between B and C.[14] Pending A's conveyance of his freehold title to B, this charge is likewise registrable against the name of A, who remains at all material times the 'estate owner'. If C, unaware that he is caught up in a sub-sale, registers *his* estate contract against B, this registration is a nullity[15] and is liable to be vacated.[16]

(b) 'Spite' registrations

The function of the Registrar in registering land charges is purely ministerial.[17]

12 Land Charges Act 1972, s 3(1). As Walton J observed in *Standard Property Investment plc v British Plastics Federation* (1985) 53 P & CR 25 at 28ff, it is important that the land charges system should operate on the footing of 'some fixed point of reference, equally available to both parties which is ... conclusive as to the name to be used.' Accordingly Walton J ruled that the name against which search should subsequently be made is the name of the estate owner 'as disclosed by the conveyance to him or her' (post, p 136). It is possible that in rare circumstances the owner of a land charge may be required to register that charge against himself. Such a case arises for instance where a purchaser of land agrees to lease back the premises to the vendor on completion of the purchase. Here the vendor has a registrable estate contract pending completion which should be registered against himself as the current estate owner (see [1980] Conv 170).

13 A registrable 'estate contract' is statutorily defined as including 'a contract by an estate owner ... to convey ... a legal estate ...' (Land Charges Act 1972, s 2(4)) (post, p 141).

14 The definition of an 'estate contract' is sufficiently wide to catch 'a contract ... by a person entitled at the date of the contract to have a legal estate conveyed to him to convey ... a legal estate ...' (Land Charges Act 1972, s 2(4)) (post, p 141).

15 Thus, if in such a case A duly conveys the legal estate to B, and B in breach of contract sells and conveys that estate not to C but to X, C's only remedy lies in damages against B in respect of breach of contract (see *Barrett v Hilton Developments Ltd* [1975] Ch 237 at 244A, F; (1975) 39 Conv (NS) 65 (F.R. Crane)). C's land charge, being void for want of proper registration, cannot bind X (Land Charges Act 1972, s 4(6), post, p 119). C's rights remain mere rights *in personam* and not *in rem* (ante, p 44). There is, of course, no strict legal duty to register a land charge (although compare Law of Property Act 1925, s 200(4)). It therefore follows that any damages recovered by C in connection with B's breach of contract will not be reduced in view of C's improper registration (see *Wright v Dean* [1948] Ch 686 at 696).

16 It has been suggested, however, that any purchaser with whom B later deals in breach of contract may, by virtue of the (albeit invalid) registration against B, have acquired sufficient notice of the contract between B and C to be liable in tort for procurement of breach of this contract. It may even be possible for C, by timely intervention, to obtain an injunction restraining further dealing between B and the other purchaser (see [1989] Conv 232 (J.E.A.)).

17 See S.M. Cretney, (1969) 32 MLR 477 at 486f.

No inquiry is made at the date of registration into the validity of the charge registered, and there is no requirement that the estate owner be informed of the application for registration.[18] It is therefore possible that land charge registration may be used for tactical reasons in order to impose an apparent (but fictitious) blot on an owner's title. Such a registration may well delay or frustrate future transactions with the property affected, requiring the estate owner to take positive action to secure a vacation of the entry on the register.[19]

(2) Effect of registration

Once a proper registration has been effected against the name of the appropriate estate owner, that registration is, in the terms of section 198(1) of the Law of Property Act 1925, 'deemed to constitute actual notice ... of the fact of such registration, to all persons and for all purposes connected with the land affected ...'

This provision has great force.[20] It has even been held, for instance, that it overrides the protection apparently afforded a lessee by section 44(5) of the Law of Property Act 1925.[1] In *White v Bijou Mansions Ltd*[2] Simonds J took the view that, by virtue of section 198(1), a land charge registered by a stranger against the superior title of a lessor is binding on even a lessee or sublessee regardless of the fact that the latter have no right to investigate the lessor's title. By reason of the statutory fiction, the due registration of any land charge is deemed (in the widest terms possible) to constitute *actual notice* of the interest so registered.

(3) Effect of non-registration

Just as the effect of registration is phrased in absolute terms in section 198(1) of the Law of Property Act 1925, so the consequence of failure to register a registrable interest is specified in similarly draconian language. The precise effect of non-registration depends on the category of land charge concerned, but the general result of failure to register is that the registrable interest is rendered void against certain kinds of purchaser.

18 See eg *Taylor v Taylor* [1968] 1 WLR 378 at 383A-B.

19 Land Charges Act 1972, s 1(6). See eg *Heywood v B.D.C. Properties Ltd* (No 2) [1963] 1 WLR 975 at 979ff; *Georgiades v Edward Wolfe & Co Ltd* [1965] Ch 487 at 503E, 506D-E; *Alpenstow Ltd v Regalian Plc* [1985] 1 WLR 721 at 727B-G, 728B-C. See also S.M. Cretney, (1968) 118 NLJ 1167; *Barnett v Hassett* [1981] 1 WLR 1385 at 1389C. In some jurisdictions compensation may be claimed by the aggrieved estate owner in respect of loss flowing from improper registrations (see eg *Ed Sinclair Construction & Supplies Ltd v Grunthaler* (1980) 105 DLR (3d) 296 at 304; *Bedford Properties Pty Ltd v Surgo Pty Ltd* [1981] 1 NSWLR 106 at 107A).

20 See H.W.R. Wade, [1954] CLJ 89.

1 Under section 44 of the Law of Property Act 1925, an intending lessee or assignee is not entitled to examine the title to the freehold or to a leasehold reversion connected with the interest which he proposes to purchase. However, section 44(5), overturning the rule in *Patman v Harland* (1881) 17 Ch D 353, provides that such a lessee or assignee 'shall not ... be deemed to be affected with notice of any matter or thing of which, if he had contracted that such title should be furnished, he might have had notice.'

2 [1937] Ch 610 at 619.

(a) Classes A, B, C(i), (ii) and (iii), and F

A land charge of Class A, Class B, Class C(i), (ii) and (iii), or Class F is made 'void' for want of registration 'as against a purchaser of the land charged with it, or of any interest in such land . . .'[3] A 'purchaser' is defined as connoting any person (including a mortgagee or lessee) who gives 'valuable consideration'.[4] S.17(1) LCA

(b) Classes C(iv) and D

An unregistered land charge of Class C(iv) or Class D is rendered 'void' against a somewhat narrower category of purchaser. Non-registration makes a charge within these Classes void merely 'as against a purchaser for money or money's worth of a legal estate in the land charged . . .'[5] An important statutory immunity is thus conferred on the purchaser, although in rare circumstances this immunity may be lost if the purchaser either fails to plead his statutory defence,[6] or is precluded from doing so by some argument based upon constructive trust[7] or estoppel.[8]

(c) Differential effects of non-registration

The different consequences attached to non-registration may have important practical results. Thus, for instance, non-registration by an incumbrancer causes a 'general equitable charge' (which belongs to Class C(iii)[9]) to become void as against a purchaser of *any* estate or interest—legal or equitable—in the land. However, a similar failure to register an 'estate contract' (which belongs to Class C(iv)[10]) makes the relevant charge void only as against a purchaser of a legal estate for money or money's worth. Unregistered land charges always remain binding upon third party donees of the land affected, that is, upon those persons who have not given any valuable consideration in respect of the transaction of transfer (eg the recipient of land under a will or on intestacy).

(4) Irrelevance of the traditional doctrine of notice

As indicated above, the statutory consequences of non-registration are spelt out with precision in the Land Charges Act 1972. Furthermore, where an unregistered charge is statutorily declared 'void' as against a purchaser, it is entirely irrelevant that at the date of the conveyance to him the purchaser

3 Land Charges Act 1972, s 4(2), (5), (8). For reference to the Classes defined in the Land Charges Act, see post, p 140.
4 Land Charges Act 1972, s 17(1).
5 Land Charges Act 1972, s 4(6).
6 See eg *Balchin v Buckle* (1982) *The Times*, 1 June, 126 Sol Jo 412.
7 Post, p 413.
8 In *Old & Campbell Ltd v Liverpool Victoria Friendly Society* [1982] QB 133 (Note) at 159A, for instance, Oliver J held that the defendants, having represented to a tenant in two documents that his unregistered estate contract was still valid and subsisting, were estopped from pleading non-registration when the tenant later incurred substantial expenditure on the faith of that representation (post, p 312). Compare, however, the unwillingness in *Topliss Showers Ltd v Gessey & Son Ltd* [1982] ICR 501 at 518D-F, to allow estoppel to avert the consequences of non-registration where 'registration is a statutory requirement imposed as a matter of public policy'.
9 Post, p 141.
10 Post, p 141.

had actual express knowledge—from another source—of the existence of the registrable but unregistered interest.[11] Once 'void' by virtue of statute, the charge cannot be revitalised by any residual application of the traditional doctrine of notice. Towards this end the courts have rigorously maintained the integrity of the rules surrounding the registration of land charges, although in the process the courts have had to address squarely some fundamental questions relating to the very nature of legal rules.

(a) Preference for certainty over justice

It has long been a characteristic inclination of the common law-trained property lawyer to prefer certainty over justice in the ascertainment of proprietary rights.[12] In this respect English law merely reflects a widely held theory that hard-edged rules of property are ultimately more efficient in that they minimise confusion over property entitlements, limit costly controversies and thereby facilitate the productive processes of commerce.[13] On this view it is far preferable that property rules maintain a clear-cut, crystalline form and do not dissolve into the 'mud' which would result from post hoc discretion-laden formulations supposedly designed to secure 'fair' outcomes in isolated cases.[14] The preservation of precision in rule systems of property promotes the efficient allocation of goods and 'encourage[s] people to plan and act carefully, knowing that no judicial cavalry will ride to their rescue later'.[15]

The property legislation of 1925 was influenced quite heavily by this policy preference for certainty—not least in the approach adopted in respect of land charge registration. The major objective of the 1925 legislation was the simplification of conveyancing, and in the context of land charges this objective is more effectively ensured if the consequences of registration and non-registration are absolutely clear-cut and conclusive.

(i) Modification of the doctrine of notice It is for this reason that the traditional doctrine of notice is displaced or, more accurately, is drastically adapted by the land charges scheme. Under the Law of Property Act 1925 and the

11 A purchaser 'shall not be prejudicially affected by notice of . . . any instrument or matter capable of registration under the Land Charges Act [1972] . . . which is void or not enforceable as against him under that Act . . . by reason of the non-registration thereof' (Law of Property Act 1925, s 199(1)(i)).

12 Thus Blackstone was prepared to categorise property rules as relating to 'things in themselves indifferent' (*Bl Comm*, Vol 1, p 55). See also *Vallejo v Wheeler* (1774) 1 Cowp 143 at 153, 98 ER 1012 at 1017 per Lord Mansfield ('In all mercantile transactions the great object should be certainty: and therefore, it is of more consequence that a rule should be certain, than whether the rule is established one way or the other. Because speculators in trade then know what ground to go upon'). See also *Ashburn Anstalt v Arnold* [1989] Ch 1 at 26D per Fox LJ ('In matters relating to the title to land, certainty is of prime importance').

13 See eg D. Baird and T. Jackson, *Information, Uncertainty and the Transfer of Property*, 13 J Legal Stud 299 (1984); C.G. Holderness, *A Legal Foundation for Exchange*, 14 J Legal Stud 321 at 344 (1985).

14 'In the absence of clear definitions around property rights, individuals dissipate resources in conflicts and bullying, or in taking precautions against being bullied. Crystalline rules, it seems, can halt this frittering away, be it public or private. Hard-edged rules define assets and their ownership in such a way that what is bought stays bought and can be safely traded to others, instead of repeatedly being put up for grabs' (C.M. Rose, *Crystals and Mud in Property Law*, 40 Stanford L Rev 577 at 591 (1987–88)).

15 C.M. Rose, 40 Stanford L Rev 577 at 592 (1987–88).

Land Charges Act 1925 the orthodox concept of notice suffered modification to the extent that registration of a land charge became the *only* recognised form of notice to third parties in respect of wide categories of commercial equitable interest. The law of land charges thus conforms to the general tendency in English property law to facilitate certainty as to outcome rather than justice as between parties. An interest which falls within the registrable heads under the Land Charges Act is *either* duly registered as a land charge and therefore rendered binding *or* is not so registered and is accordingly void against most purchasers.

(ii) Statutory incorporation of an amoral rule The overall efficiency of this system of land charge registration is significantly reinforced by the rule that the purchaser is not bound by notice of any registrable interest where such notice is obtained by him outside the register of land charges. By allowing the equitable doctrine of notice to be superseded by a 'mechanical principle of registration', the 1925 legislation thus gave effect to a 'shift from a moral to an a-moral basis' in the protection of equitable interests in land.[16] The only control upon this displacement of ethical concern lies in the over-arching prohibition of fraud.[17] The aims of efficiency and facility secured by the land charges scheme must not be attained at the price of fraud on the part of the main actors,[18] for ultimately fraud unravels all.[19]

A dramatic illustration of the ethical shift achieved by the Land Charges Act is found in *Hollington Bros Ltd v Rhodes*.[20] Here L contracted to grant a lease to T. This contract was in fact an 'estate contract' registrable as a land charge of Class C(iv),[1] but T neglected to register the charge against L. L then conveyed his legal estate in the property to P, expressly 'subject to and with the benefit of such tenancies as may affect the premises' (see *Fig.* 11).

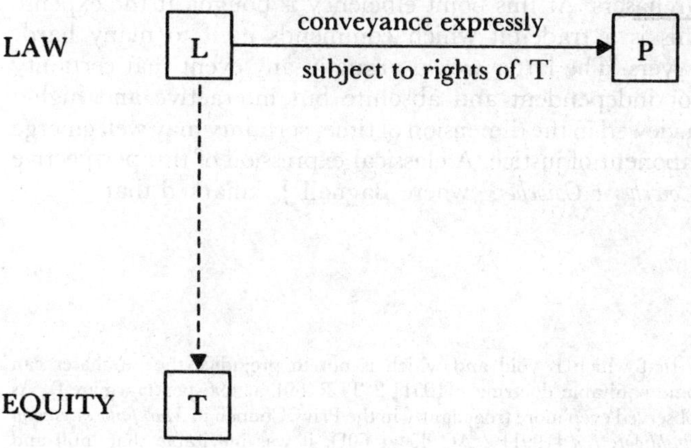

Fig. 11

16 See H.W.R. Wade, [1956] CLJ 216 at 227.
17 See *London, Chatham & Dover Railway Co v South Eastern Railway Co* [1892] 1 Ch 120 at 143 per Lindley LJ (affd [1893] AC 429).
18 See *Zelezniak v Senkiw* (1984) 2 DLR (4th) 321 at 328 per Matas JA (dissenting).
19 Post, p 128.
20 [1951] 2 TLR 691.
1 Post, p 142.

Notwithstanding that P thus had actual express knowledge of the rights of T, P subsequently gave T notice to quit the premises, thereby effectively forcing T to negotiate a new lease. In proceedings brought by T, Harman J held that T's estate contract was void as against P by reason of its non-registration and ruled moreover that it was quite irrelevant that P had actual knowledge from an extrinsic source of the existence of tenancies affecting the premises.[2] P was thus entitled to take his interest free of the adverse claims of an existing tenant—a result which was in ethical terms most unsatisfactory. The price paid by P had been calculated with reference to the existence of subsisting tenancies, but he was enabled to repudiate the existing incumbrances and coerce a re-negotiation at a new and higher rent level.[3]

(iii) Tension between certainty and justice Outcomes such as that demonstrated in *Hollington Bros Ltd v Rhodes* have, of course, been criticised as attaching a disproportionate penalty to the 'venial fault of non-registration'.[4] There is indeed a certain 'defiance of ethics' where a purchaser with actual notice is allowed to trample over a third party's rights. Nevertheless, for the traditionally minded property lawyer, this result has at least the merit that it keeps the position clear-cut. Moreover, as Mahon J observed in *Carly v Farrelly*,[5] '[n]o stable system of jurisprudence could permit a litigant's claim to justice to be consigned to the formless void of individual moral opinion.'[6]

Thus, in the land charges context, the strict application of the statute renders unnecessary any general enquiry into the state of mind or moral standing of the individual purchaser in every transaction. Either the incumbrancer has registered his interest and thereby made it binding, or he has failed to register—in which case his interest almost inevitably becomes void as against purchasers. At this point efficiency is bought at the expense of fairness, and this is a trade-off which commends itself to many hard-nosed property lawyers. The latter would argue in any event that certainty and justice are not independent and absolute but interactive and highly conditional. When viewed in the dimension of time, certainty may well emerge as an intrinsic component of justice. A classical expression of this perspective is to be found in *Cowcher v Cowcher*,[7] where Bagnall J remarked that

2 'I do not see how that which is void and which is not to prejudice the purchaser can be validated by some equitable doctrine' ([1951] 2 TLR 691 at 696 per Harman J). As Lord Templeman observed even more trenchantly in the Privy Council in *Markfaith Investment Ltd v Chiap Hua Flashlights Ltd* [1991] 2 AC 43 at 60D, it was inevitable that 'null and void was construed as meaning null and void'. See also *Coventry Permanent Economic Building Society v Jones* [1951] 1 All ER 901 at 904B-C per Harman J; *Beesly v Hallwood Estates Ltd* [1960] 1 WLR 549 at 558; *Buckley v S.R.L. Investments Ltd and Cator and Robinson* (1971) 22 P & CR 756 at 764, 768.

3 There is an argument that P's taking of title expressly 'subject to' the rights of T may raise a constructive trust in P to give effect to those rights (post, p 440).

4 H.W.R. Wade, [1956] CLJ 216 at 217.

5 [1975] 1 NZLR 356 at 367.

6 See the equivalent discussion in relation to non-registration of rights under the Land Registration Act 1925 (post, p 186).

7 [1972] 1 WLR 425 at 430A-C.

in determining rights, particularly property rights, the only justice that can be attained by mortals, who are fallible and not omniscient, is justice according to the law; the justice which flows from the application of sure and settled principles to proved or admitted facts. So in the field of equity the length of the Chancellor's foot has been measured or is capable of measurement. This does not mean that equity is past childbearing; simply that its progeny must be legitimate—by precedent out of principle. It is well that this should be so; otherwise no lawyer could safely advise on his client's title and every quarrel would lead to a law suit.[8]

(b) Attempts to reintroduce a moral criterion

In its concern for long-term certainty rather than short-term justice, the law of property (and especially the law relating to land charges) is therefore largely indifferent to the relative moral claims of litigants. Nevertheless it is difficult *in extremis* to remain entirely insensitive to the ethical aspects of the relationship between purchaser and equitable incumbrancer. For this reason an intermittent (though fiercely fought) controversy rages over where precisely the boundaries of permissible behaviour should be drawn.

Central to this controversy is the critical value of systemic efficiency—ie the price, measured in terms of the ethical quality of outcome, beyond which a mere efficiency of process proves unacceptably expensive. For the English property lawyer this critical price tends to be expressed in relation to an indefinable threshold of 'fraud': a *fraudulent* purchaser may not rely on the non-registration of adverse rights. But while all would agree that fraud cannot be allowed to succeed,[9] recognition of its presence in a transaction is never a universally shared perception. There may even be shifts or oscillations, over fairly long historical cycles, in the liminal standards of identifiable 'fraud'. There is nowadays a strong argument that judicial notions of moral neighbourhood and the courts' tolerance of exploitative unconcern for the rights of the vulnerable should be adjusted to compensate for the more general relaxation of cultural, political and religious constraints on aggressive individualism.[10]

It is with such ends in view that several means have been suggested by which more effective moral criteria can be restored to the law of land charges. At a higher level of abstraction these suggestions mirror the wider contention that absolute and hard-edged rules of property law must ultimately give way to more open-textured rules or 'standards'[11] which take some account of moral relativities. There is even an argument that, paradoxically, a more judgmental or ethically based system of property rules is itself an instrument of economic efficiency. The prospect of ex post redistributions of entitlement in accordance with moral equities may go far to dissuade the wrongdoer from even attempting bad faith manipulations of the rules and may therefore have a reassuring and stabilising general effect on the expectations of the transacting community.

8 See [1982] Conv 396.
9 Ante, p 42.
10 See eg Paul Finn, *Commerce, The Common Law and Morality*, (1989) 17 MULR 87.
11 See Duncan Kennedy, *Form and Substance in Private Law Adjudication*, 89 Harv L Rev 1685 at 1710ff (1975–76).

In the light of such considerations the law of land charges has seen a number of attempts to elevate factors of fairness in counterpoint to the policy desideratum of efficiency.[12]

(i) Protection for actual occupation It has sometimes been suggested that non-registration of a land charge should not have the effect of rendering void a registrable incumbrance belonging to a person who is *in actual occupation of the land.* Persons in actual possession of land may well have equitable interests of a fairly short-term nature in relation to which it is unrealistic to expect the vigilance of registration. The elderly widow who occupies property under an agreement for a lease has, in technical terms, a registrable estate contract. However, it seems unreasonable that the protection of her interest against third parties should rest exclusively on her registration of a Class C(iv) land charge—a registration which, in such circumstances and in the absence of legal advice, the lay person is highly unlikely to effect. It may seem much more reasonable that such a person should be able to rely for her protection upon her actual occupation of the land.[13] The fact of physical possession indicates to a purchaser just as effectively as the fact of registration that there is a possibility that the occupier has a proprietary interest of some kind in the land.

In the present state of the law, however, even the fact of actual occupation provides no protection for an incumbrancer who fails—albeit quite excusably—to register a land charge in respect of his interest. This conclusion seems not to be disturbed by section 14 of the Law of Property Act 1925, which provides that

> This Part of this Act shall not prejudicially affect the interest of any person in possession or in actual occupation of land to which he may be entitled in right of such possession or occupation.

It was once thought that this provision enabled an incumbrancer in actual occupation to escape the consequences of non-registration.[14] However, it is now generally agreed that, in spite of the prominence afforded section 14 in recent cases,[15] the section is so limited in scope as to provide no assistance in the present problem.[16] The application of section 14 is expressly restricted to Part I of the Law of Property Act 1925. The consequences of non-registration

12 These attempts alike involve what Professor Carol Rose has described as a transmutation of 'crystalline' rules into 'muddy' rules. 'A strong element of moral judgment runs through the cases in which mud supersedes crystal. These cases are often rife with human failings—sloth and forgetfulness on the one hand, greed and self-dealing on the other. These vices put pressure on our efforts to elaborate clear and distinct property specifications, and make judges and others second guess the deals that call for a pound of flesh' (see C.M. Rose, 40 Stanford L Rev 577 at 597 (1987-88)).

13 This idea is recognised, in the context of registered title, in section 70(1)(g) of the Land Registration Act 1925 (post, p 203).

14 See eg *Bendall v McWhirter* [1952] 2 QB 466 at 483.

15 See eg *City of London Building Society v Flegg* [1986] Ch 605 at 618F–620E (Court of Appeal), but compare now [1988] AC 54 at 80C-F per Lord Oliver of Aylmerton.

16 See also *Coventry Permanent Economic Building Society v Jones* [1951] 1 All ER 901 at 904A-B; R.E. Megarry, (1952) 68 LQR 379 at 385.

of land charges are spelt out in a separate statute—the Land Charges Act[17]—and these consequences cannot therefore be muted by the saving provision contained in section 14 for the benefit of persons in possession.[18]

(ii) Relevance of actual but not constructive notice Another possible means of making the operation of the land charges system more 'just' lies in a compromise proposal that a purchaser should be prejudicially affected by actual notice (as distinct from merely constructive notice) of an unregistered incumbrance.[19] On this footing, constructive notice would be relevant only where the incumbrancer is also in actual occupation of the land concerned.[20] In all other circumstances the definitive nature of the Register would hold good unless, at the date of the transaction in question, the purchaser had actual knowledge of an unregistered land charge. In such a case—it is argued—the purchaser would be acting inconsistently with the requirements of conscience and would become a fair target for a limited application of the traditional doctrine of notice.

In spite of its attractions this approach has, for the moment, been firmly rejected by the House of Lords in *Midland Bank Trust Co Ltd v Green*.[1] This decision must now be examined in greater detail.

(5) Integrity of the system of land charge registration

The operation of the Land Charges Register is now largely overshadowed by the significant decision reached by the House of Lords in *Midland Bank*

17 There is here an ironic accident of legislative history. The Law of Property Act 1922 was, of course, the authentic source of the provisions which appear in a consolidated form in the 1925 legislation. Section 14 of the Law of Property Act 1925 was precisely foreshadowed by section 33 of the 1922 Act. However, when section 33 provided that nothing in Part I of the 1922 Act should 'prejudicially affect' the rights of actual occupiers, this saving provision clearly applied to the consequences of non-registration of land charges as then laid down in section 3(5) of Part I of the 1922 Act. When the 1922 Act was later consolidated, the land charges provisions (including section 3(5)) were diverted into a separate statute—the Land Charges Act. This formal restructuring of the 1922 legislation thus brought about the almost certainly unintended result that owners of land charges were (and still are) deprived of such protection as would otherwise be afforded by section 14 of the Law of Property Act 1925. See C. Harpum, (1977) 41 Conv (NS) 415 at 419 (n 31); M. Friend and J. Newton, [1982] Conv 213 at 215ff.

18 The general effect of this inevitably restricted construction of section 14 is to generate a blatant anomaly in the treatment of land charges as compared with the treatment of the rights of persons in 'actual occupation' of registered land (see Land Registration Act 1925, s 70(1)(g), post, p 203).

19 This suggestion has been made particularly vigorously in the context of registered title, and is therefore considered in further depth in Chapter 8 (post, p 192). There are parallels in other registration areas for according relevance to actual but not constructive notice (see, eg, Land Charges Act 1972, s 5(7) (ante, p 115); Patents Act 1977, s 33(1)).

20 See eg H.W.R. Wade, [1956] CLJ 216 at 227.

1 [1981] AC 513. It is worth noting that the attempt to distinguish between actual and constructive notice in other areas of the law has not been without difficulty. Such a distinction provides a clear incentive for a purchaser to maintain a Nelsonian stance of wilful blindness in the face of the obvious. This possibility in its turn necessitates further (and more subtle) calibrations of the states of mind required to make a purchaser liable to adverse claims. See, for instance, the difficult gradations of knowledge which bear upon the imposition of constructive trusteeship on the ground of participation in a fraud perpetrated by a fiduciary (see eg *Baden, Delvaux and Lecuit v Société Générale pour Favoriser le Développement du Commerce et de l'Industrie en France SA* [1983] BCLC 325 at 407ff per Peter Gibson J).

Trust Co Ltd v Green.[2] Here W, an owner of land in fee simple, granted his son, G, an option to purchase the land at a specified price which amounted to £22,500.[3] G failed to register this option as an estate contract under Class C(iv) of the Land Charges Act.[4] Six years later, in consequence of some family discord, W sought to revoke the option which he had earlier granted to G. Upon discovering that the option had never been registered by G, W quietly and speedily conveyed the land (which was by now worth £40,000) to his own wife, E, for a consideration of £500, with the clear intention of thereby defeating the unregistered option (see *Fig.* 12). G, who had at all material times been a tenant in occupation of the land, then purported to exercise his option. His mother declined to sell him the land in accordance with the option. G began proceedings against his father and the executors of his mother's estate—his mother having meanwhile died—claiming both a declaration that the option was binding on his mother's estate and an order of specific performance of the option. G then died and his executors, the plaintiff bank, continued the action with, of course, the benefit of a large sympathy factor weighing on behalf of G's bereaved widow and children.

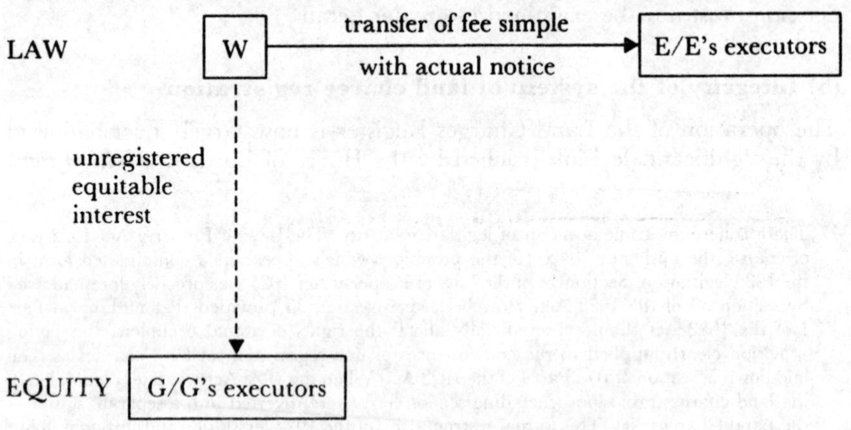

Fig. 12

By the time the action reached the courts, the value of the disputed land had inflated to over £400,000. It was plain that a decision against E's executors would effectively enable G's widow and children to buy the land for £22,500 in accordance with the option. A decision in favour of E's executors would result in a sale of the land and the division of the proceeds of sale between the five children of W and E, G's widow and children receiving in effect only 20 per cent of the value of the land.

The decision required in *Midland Bank Trust Co Ltd v Green* was essentially one relating to statutory construction. E's executors pleaded in their defence

2 [1981] AC 513, on appeal from [1980] Ch 590. See [1981] CLJ 213 (C. Harpum); [1981] Conv 361 (H.E. Johnson); (1981) 97 LQR 518 (B. Green); (1980) 96 LQR 8 (R.J. Smith).
3 G bought the option from his father for the sum of £1.
4 Post, p 142.

that the conveyance to E had been a bona fide sale and that E had been a 'purchaser for money or money's worth of a legal estate' for the purpose of what is now section 4(6) of the Land Charges Act 1972.[5] At first instance Oliver J upheld this defence and ruled that the unregistered option was not binding on E's estate.[6] This ruling was reversed by a majority decision in the Court of Appeal, only to be reinstated by the unanimous decision of the House of Lords. An analysis of the critical features emerging from this series of decisions highlights certain differences of judicial philosophy in relation to the law of property.

(a) Was there a purchase 'for money or money's worth'?

E's estate could take free of the unregistered option only if it could show that E had been a 'purchaser. . .for money or money's worth' within the meaning of the relevant provision of the Land Charges Act. This issue evoked a variety of responses at different levels in the hierarchy of courts concerned with the *Green* litigation.

(i) Requirement of 'adequate' consideration In giving judgment in the Court of Appeal in favour of G's executors, Lord Denning MR held that E had not given 'money or money's worth' within the terms of the immunity now conferred on purchasers by section 4(6). Lord Denning ruled that the statutory immunity from unregistered options presupposed the payment of 'a fair and reasonable value in money or money's worth: not an undervalue.'[7] Accordingly he regarded E's 'grotesquely small' payment of £500 as 'a gross undervalue' for this purpose and, furthermore, as providing evidence of a degree of collusion which 'would open the door to fraud of the worst description'.[8]

(ii) Rejection of the requirement of 'adequacy' Lord Denning's requirement that consideration be 'adequate' for the purpose of section 4(6) was conclusively rejected by the House of Lords. In delivering the only substantial speech in the House, Lord Wilberforce ruled that the purchaser need only show

5 Ante, p 119. The crucial provision in the *Green* litigation was of course the similarly worded predecessor provision found in Land Charges Act 1925, s 13(2). In order to aid the exposition of the provision currently in force, the courts' references in *Green* to section 13(2) are, in the following pages, rendered as references to section 4(6).

6 Oliver J confessed that he reached this conclusion 'with regret', since it seemed that G's clear rights had been 'deliberately frustrated by his parents in breach of the contract created by the option.' However, Oliver J took the view that, 'with the best will in the world', he could not allow his 'subjective moral judgment to stand in the way of . . . the clear meaning of the statutory provisions' ([1980] Ch 590 at 614D).

7 [1980] Ch 590 at 624E.

8 [1980] Ch 590 at 624D. Eveleigh LJ ([1980] Ch 590 at 628B-C) likewise thought that the true analysis of the transaction between W and E was that of 'a gift coupled with a token of £500 sought to be included to meet the requirements of [section 4] of the Land Charges Act . . .' Accordingly Eveleigh LJ held that the disputed conveyance had not been made 'for' money or money's worth within the meaning of section 4(6), the reference to payment having been inserted merely to add credibility to the claim of statutory immunity. Compare the dissenting judgment of Sir Stanley Rees ([1980] Ch 590 at 632A).

that she had provided 'valuable consideration'.[9] It was his view, moreover, that 'valuable consideration' is capable of including 'nominal consideration',[10] and that, had the decision been necessary, he would have had 'great difficulty' in any event in holding that £500 was merely a 'nominal sum of money'.[11] The House of Lords thus disposed of one of the principal bases for the decision of the majority in the Court of Appeal.

(b) Is there any requirement of good faith in section 4(6)?

The definition of 'purchaser' in the Land Charges Act does not impose any express requirement of good faith on the purchaser who claims the statutory immunity from unregistered land charges.[12] Yet the facts of *Midland Bank Trust Co Ltd v Green* offered every incentive for the infiltration of old equitable doctrines of good faith purchase into the construction of the Land Charges Act.[13] It was clearly possible to question whether E had acted in good faith in taking title from W with the deliberate object of defeating the unregistered option claimed by G. Here again divergent views were expressed by the courts.

(i) 'Fraud unravels everything' In the Court of Appeal both Lord Denning MR and Eveleigh LJ denied E's estate the protection of section 4(6) on the ground that E had not purchased in good faith. In Lord Denning's view, the statutory immunity could never avail a purchaser 'when the sale to him is done in fraud of the holder of the estate contract'.[14] In support of this conclusion Lord Denning invoked the general principle that 'fraud unravels everything', and that no court in the land 'will allow a person to keep an advantage which he has obtained by fraud'.[15] This concept of 'fraud' covered 'any dishonest dealing done so as to deprive unwary innocents of their rightful

9 A 'purchaser' within the Land Charges Act 1972 is defined in terms of one who gives 'valuable consideration' (see Land Charges Act 1972, s 17(1)). In Lord Wilberforce's view, this statutory phrase is 'a term of art which precludes any enquiry as to adequacy' ([1981] AC 513 at 531E). Indeed, the only respect in which 'valuable consideration' is wider than the phrase 'money or money's worth' is that marriage consideration is included in the former concept but excluded from the latter ([1981] AC 513 at 531E).

10 'Purchaser' is defined in Law of Property Act 1925, s 205(1)(xxi) in terms of one who gives 'valuable consideration', a concept which is in turn defined as excluding 'a nominal consideration in money'. In the Court of Appeal Eveleigh LJ ([1980] Ch 590 at 629A) had thought that this definition was made relevant to the present case by the reference to 'purchaser' in Law of Property Act 1925, s 199(1)(i) (ante, p 120). He thus held that E could not invoke the parallel immunity conferred by section 199(1)(i), since, in his view, a purchase price of £500 constituted a merely nominal consideration. In the House of Lords, however, Lord Wilberforce not only disputed the meaning of 'nominal consideration' but also declined to accept that the definition of 'purchaser' contained in the Law of Property Act could be impliedly incorporated into the Land Charges Act ([1981] AC 513 at 531G–532B).

11 [1981] AC 513 at 532B.

12 See Land Charges Act 1972, s 17(1) (formerly Land Charges Act 1925, s 20(8)).

13 See eg *Le Neve v Le Neve* (1748) 3 Atk 646 at 652, 26 ER 1172 at 1175ff, in relation to the operation of the Middlesex Registry Act 1708.

14 [1980] Ch 590 at 624F. Eveleigh LJ ([1980] Ch 590 at 627B-C) likewise imported a requirement of good faith by way of the definition of 'purchaser' in Law of Property Act 1925, s 205(1)(xxi). Compare, however, Lord Wilberforce ([1981] AC 513 at 529C-H).

15 *Lazarus Estates Ltd v Beasley* [1956] 1 QB 702 at 712.

dues', and the hallmarks of such fraud included 'transactions done stealthily and speedily in secret for no sufficient consideration.'[16]

The majority in the Court of Appeal regarded the facts in *Midland Bank Trust Co Ltd v Green* as disclosing all the characteristics of 'fraud' thus defined, in that W and E had 'hatched a plot. . .[of which] the predominant purpose was to damage [G]'.[17] An absurdly low price (one eightieth of the current market value) had been paid over in connection with a secretly and swiftly executed transaction whose clear object had been to deprive G of his unregistered option. It would, said Lord Denning, be 'most unfair to [G], his widow and children', if the fraud perpetrated by W and E were allowed to succeed.[18] This view did not commend itself, however, to the House of Lords.

(ii) Rejection of any requirement of good faith In the House of Lords Lord Wilberforce expressed the firm conviction that the omission of any requirement of 'good faith' from the land charges legislation is entirely deliberate. To read into section 4(6) a requirement of good faith purchase would introduce 'the necessity of enquiring into the purchaser's motives and state of mind'[19]—a re-emergence of the very doctrine of notice which the 1925 legislation had sought to avoid.[20] In any event, as Lord Wilberforce observed, the notion of 'good faith' is inevitably so complex that the purchaser in the instant case could not necessarily be stigmatised as having acted unequivocally in bad faith.[1] It is significant that, in reaching this conclusion, the House of Lords expressed no dissent from Lord Denning's broad principle that 'fraud unravels everything'. In itself this proposition commands universal support: a party guilty of 'fraud' can never hope to win. It is, however, the definition and practical identification of 'fraud' which elude consensus. A majority of the Court of Appeal in *Midland Bank Trust Co Ltd v Green* found 'fraud' to be present in circumstances where the House of Lords was equally clear that 'fraud' was not in issue.[2]

(iii) Differing views of the function of property law The key to these discrepant interpretations of primary fact lies in a fundamental divergence of perspective on the proper function of the law of property. The majority in the Court of Appeal effectively viewed property law as a tool of distributive justice—

16 [1980] Ch 590 at 625B. In a different context Dickson J has observed in the Supreme Court of Canada that '[c]ourts, for good reason, have been loath to attempt anything in the nature of an exhaustive definition of "defraud" but one may safely say. . .that two elements are essential, "dishonesty" and "deprivation"' (*R v Olan, Hudson and Hartnett* (1978) 86 DLR (3d) 212 at 217f).

17 [1980] Ch 590 at 622G, 625D. Compare, however, the dissenting judgment of Sir Stanley Rees ([1980] Ch 590 at 632F–633B).

18 [1980] Ch 590 at 622D.

19 [1981] AC 513 at 530A.

20 Ante, p 101.

1 'Suppose—and this may not be far from the truth—that the purchaser's motives were in part to take the farm from [G], and in part to distribute it between [G] and his brothers and sisters, but not at all to obtain any benefit for herself, is that acting in "good faith" or not?' ([1981] AC 513 at 530C-D per Lord Wilberforce).

2 Compare *Waimiha Sawmilling Co Ltd v Waione Timber Co Ltd* [1926] AC 101 at 106 per Lord Buckmaster ('If the designed object of a transfer be to cheat a man of a known existing right, that is fraudulent . . .').

in this instance as between family members competing for the largesse of their now deceased parents.[3] However, the dominant ideology of modern property law places an overwhelming emphasis upon the simple mechanics of contract and conveyance, leaving the morality of exchange largely unquestioned. According to this view, the principal purpose of the law of property is to provide clarity and procedural efficiency in the combined operation of bargain and exchange. Moreover, the law of property implicitly assumes a world of assertive individualism in which all are presumed to be equal, self-determining and competent to transact freely for the purpose of private gain. Thus to the conventional property lawyer the transaction concluded has no significant moral dimension, since the law of property so clearly expresses a preference for certainty and efficiency over the claims of fairness or moral entitlement.

(iv) It is 'not fraud to take advantage of legal rights' The decision of the House of Lords in *Midland Bank Trust Co Ltd v Green* was entirely consistent with—indeed was perhaps inevitable in the context of—the amoral approach to economic relations which infuses the market concept of property. While Lord Denning had asserted that 'fraud unravels everything', Lord Wilberforce preferred to invoke the well known principle that 'it is not fraud to take advantage of legal rights, the existence of which may be taken to be known to both parties'.[4] He pointed out that it had been perfectly open to G to protect his option by resorting to the simple mechanism of registration: this he had failed to do. In the words of Lord Wilberforce,

> If the position was simply that the purchaser had notice of the option, and decided nevertheless to buy the land, relying on the absence of notification, nobody could contend that she would be lacking in good faith. She would merely be taking advantage of a situation, which the law has provided, and the addition of a profit motive could not create an absence of good faith.[5]

In other words, the House of Lords re-asserted the crude but efficient rule that the only form of notice relevant in the land charges context is the notice constituted by due entry in the Register. While conceding the existence of an exceptional category of vitiating 'fraud', the House found no such fraud to be present on the facts of the instant case, and declined to import any general moral criterion of good faith into the operation of what is now section 4(6) of the Land Charges Act 1972. As Lord Wilberforce said.

> The case is plain: the Act is clear and definite. Intended as it was to provide a

3 It appeared in *Midland Bank Trust Co Ltd v Green* that W had treated other members of the family more generously than G, a point which did not escape the notice of Lord Denning MR.

4 *In re Monolithic Building Co* [1915] 1 Ch 643 at 663 per Lord Cozens-Hardy MR. See also *Markfaith Investment Ltd v Chiap Hua Flashlights Ltd* [1991] 2 AC 43 at 60D. Lord Wilberforce's approach is more forthrightly epitomised—even if his eventual ruling was controversial—in a playing field analogy which characterises the borderline between foul play and fair game. There may well be circumstances in which an attacking winger sells an enormous dummy to the opposing full back and has therefore deceived him. No referee, however, would whistle for a 'foul'. The score which results is in no sense vitiated by 'fraud'—precisely because all parties concerned are playing within the four corners of a game whose rules are known to all.

5 [1981] AC 513 at 530A-B.

simple and understandable system for the protection of title to land, it should not be read down or glossed: to do so would destroy the usefulness of the Act. Any attempt to remould the Act to meet the facts of the present case, on the supposition that it is a hard one and that justice requires it, is. . .removed by the consideration that the Act itself provides a simple and effective protection for persons in [G's] position—viz—by registration.[6]

There are no easy solutions to the moral dilemmas which pervade many areas of property law. The law of property is not, and in a practical world never can be, a branch of moral philosophy.[7] The decision of the House of Lords in *Midland Bank Trust Co Ltd v Green* epitomises the traditional view of the busy property lawyer that there is much to be said in favour of trading off a little justice in return for enhanced security and certainty in commercial transactions.[8] However, this pragmatic approach will never satisfy all of the people all of the time. It may well be that, in the eyes of the law, it is not fraud to take advantage of the folly of another, but it remains an uncomfortable fact of life that most fraud consists in doing precisely that. Perceptions of moral relativities are themselves relative, and it is not without significance that the Law Commission has more recently expressed the view that the outcome in *Midland Bank Trust Co Ltd v Green* does not represent an 'acceptable' resolution of the problem in hand.[9]

4. SEARCH OF THE LAND CHARGES REGISTER

Search of the Land Charges Register is governed by fairly complex rules both of statute and of judge-made law.

(1) Timing of search

It will at first sight seem somewhat strange that in unregistered or 'old system' conveyancing a prospective purchaser's investigation of title begins in earnest only after he has already entered into a contract to purchase.[10] It is, of course, only at this stage that the vendor becomes subject to any legal duty to show title to the land over the requisite period of time. During the interim between contract and conveyance, the purchaser must satisfy himself that the title offered is good. This he does by examining the deeds or documents of title relating to dispositions of the land during at least the preceding

6 [1981] AC 513 at 528A-B.

7 In *Midland Bank Trust Co Ltd v Green* the House of Lords effectively relegated G's estate to such non-proprietary remedies as might be available. The 'unfairness' of the result achieved by the House of Lords was somewhat mitigated by the fact that G's estate was held, in different proceedings before Oliver J, to be entitled to recover damages in respect of the negligence of G's solicitor in failing to register G's Class C(iv) land charge (see *Midland Bank Trust Co Ltd v Hett, Stubbs and Kemp (A Firm)* [1979] Ch 384 at 433B-D). G's estate was also successful in recovering damages against the estate of W for the tort of conspiracy (see *Midland Bank Trust Co Ltd v Green* (No 3) [1982] Ch 529 at 539H-540B, 541H-542A).

8 See *Holt, Renfrew & Co Ltd v Henry Singer Ltd* (1982) 135 DLR (3d) 391 at 399, for reference to the 'necessity of this business consideration predominating over the moral aspect'.

9 Law Commission, *Property Law: Third Report on Land Registration* (Law Com No 158, 31 March 1987), para 4.15. For further discussion of the parameters of 'fraud', see Chapter 8 (post, p 188).

10 Post, p 271.

15 years.[11] From the purchaser's point of view, this investigation must uncover a 'good root of title', ie a valid document of title which is at least 15 years old.[12] It is, however, only *after* the exchange of contracts that the purchaser enjoys any contractual right of access to the historical documents of title which alone disclose the names of previous estate owners against whom land charges may have been registered.[13] The purchaser's right of access extends to all title deeds within the scope of the statutory 15 year period (or other agreed period), but does not extend back beyond the root of title.

(2) Process of search

Shortly before the projected date of completion it is usual for the purchaser to search the Land Charges Register against the names of estate owners comprised within the relevant title. If the first conveyance relating to the property which is at least 15 years old was executed in 1930, then the relevant title commences in 1930.

Search may be personal,[14] but most purchasers take advantage of the alternative 'official search' of the Register which is available upon application and the payment of a small fee. An 'official search' takes the form of a computer-aided check of the Land Charges Register for subsisting entries against the names of the estate owners included in the purchaser's requisition for search.[15]

(3) Effect of an official search

The principal advantage of an official search of the Land Charges Register consists in the fact that the result of the search is set out in a certificate issued to the intending purchaser.[16] The issue of this certificate has important implications.

(a) Conclusive nature of the certificate of official search

According to section 10(4) of the Land Charges Act 1972, '[i]n favour of a purchaser or an intending purchaser . . . the certificate, according to its

11 Law of Property Act 1969, s 23 (ante, p 96). The title deeds are, in effect, the 'essential indicia of title to unregistered land' (see *Sen v Headley* [1991] Ch 425 at 437C per Nourse LJ, ante, p 70).

12 Post, p 137. A 'good root of title' is, in effect, any instrument which unambiguously deals with or shows title to the whole legal and equitable interest in the correctly identified property. However, it is generally considered that such instruments as leases and wills are insufficient for this purpose.

13 It is of course possible for the vendor to speed up or otherwise facilitate a transaction by affording access to the relevant documents before exchange of contracts, but this is still unusual in practice. See *Rignall Developments Ltd v Halil* [1988] Ch 190 at 201A-C.

14 Land Charges Act 1972, s 9(1).

15 Land Charges Act 1972, s 10(1), (2).

16 A further advantage attracted by official search is that the purchaser is not bound by any entry made on the Register after the issue of the certificate (other than an entry made under a 'priority notice' pursuant to Land Charges Act 1972, s 11(1)-(3), provided that completion of the purchaser's conveyance takes place within 15 working days of the date of issue of the certificate (Land Charges Act 1972, s 11(5), (6)).

tenor, shall be conclusive, affirmatively or negatively, as the case may be.'[17] Thus, even if the Registry mistakenly issues a clear or 'nil' certificate of official search in respect of a particular estate owner named in the relevant title, the certificate is *conclusive* according to its tenor. A land charge, albeit duly registered against such an estate owner, becomes utterly void.[18]

(b) Remedies in tort for any damage caused by negligent misstatement

The irrebuttable presumption contained in section 10(4) of the Land Charges Act 1972 effectively coerces the facts to accord with the fiction contained on the face of an inaccurate nil certificate. The purchaser can safely take the land free of the unnotified land charge, and the owner of the now destroyed charge is thrown back upon a remedy in damages against the Land Registry for the tort of negligence. Such an action is founded on the negligent misrepresentation which has been made by the Registry to the applicant for an official search and which has caused loss to a third party, the owner of the previously subsisting land charge.[19]

(c) Policy preference in favour of official search

It is clear that the underlying policy reflected in the Land Charges Act tends to ensure both certainty and facility in land transactions and, incidentally, to discourage personal searches of the Register. The latter point was borne out in *Oak Co-operative Building Society v Blackburn*,[20] where the Court of Appeal was concerned with the effect of a registration against an incorrect version of the name of the estate owner.[1] Russell LJ acknowledged that a personal searcher against the full correct name would not have encountered the registration in the present case and, not having the benefit of an official certificate of search, would have been affected by a 'deemed actual notice' under section 198(1) of the Law of Property Act 1925.[2] However,

17 See Land Charges Act 1925, s 17(3).

18 The effect of a clear certificate issued in error must be to extinguish (and not merely to suspend) the registered charge. Otherwise, the recipient of a clear certificate would be compelled to sell the land in his turn subject to the incumbrance, having bought the land free from the incumbrance on the strength of the clear certificate. Such a result would impose a palpable financial loss on the recipient of the certificate and would not therefore constitute an outcome 'in favour of [the] purchaser' as required by section 10(4) of the Land Charges Act 1972. In other words, the purchaser armed with an erroneously issued clear certificate of official search is a kind of statutory analogue of 'Equity's Darling'. His advent, like that of 'Equity's Darling', destroys existing incumbrances so that they cannot subsequently affect a later purchaser even though he has actual notice (see *Wilkes v Spooner* [1911] 2 KB 473 at 488, ante, p 84).

19 See *Ministry of Housing and Local Government v Sharp* [1970] 2 QB 223 (dealing with the equivalent problem in the analogous context of local land charges). An ambivalent provision in section 10(6) of the Land Charges Act 1972 purports to protect officers and employees of the Registry from personal liability for any loss arising, except where that loss is caused by an act of fraud. The clear intention is that persons aggrieved by the negligence of an officer or employee of the Registry should be able to recover damages on the basis of the vicarious liability of the Registry.

20 [1968] Ch 730.

1 Post, p 136.

2 [1968] Ch 730 at 743F-G.

Russell LJ regarded the apparent unfairness of this outcome as largely countered by the consideration that 'anyone who nowadays is foolish enough to search personally deserves what he gets'.[3] In Russell LJ's acerbic view, if the aim of the Land Charges Act is 'to arrive at a sensible working system', that aim was more effectively furthered by upholding a slightly inaccurate registration than by 'protecting a personal searcher from his folly'.[4]

(4) Consequence of discovering a registered charge

The absolute nature of a land charge registration used to cause extreme difficulty if a purchaser discovered, shortly before completion, that the Land Charges Register did in fact contain some entry prejudicial to his intended use or enjoyment of the land. In the nature of things such a discovery would usually be made only after vendor and purchaser had exchanged contracts for the purchase of the land.

(a) Literal application of Law of Property Act 1925, s 198(1)

Such is the unqualified force of section 198(1) of the Law of Property Act 1925 that it was once thought that the purchaser in such a case must be deemed to have had 'actual notice' at the date of the contract of any subsisting registration disclosed later on search of the Register. This being so, the purchaser was then obliged to complete the contract and take a conveyance of the land notwithstanding that the sale was expressed to be 'free from encumbrances' and even though the land might well be valueless to him.[5]

(b) Curative effect of amending legislation

This 'indefensible' and quite inequitable rule[6] has been displaced in relation to contracts entered into since 1969. Where search reveals the existence of a registered land charge unknown to the purchaser at the date of the contract, the purchaser is now entitled to plead his ignorance as a ground for declining to complete the contract. According to section 24(1) of the Law of Property Act 1969, the issue is no longer to be determined with reference to the fictitious 'actual notice' imposed by section 198(1) of the Law of Property Act 1925. Instead the question whether, at the time of entering into the estate contract, the purchaser had knowledge of a registered land charge 'shall be determined by reference to his actual knowledge and without regard to the provisions of section 198 . . .'

3 [1968] Ch 730 at 744A-B.

4 [1968] Ch 730 at 744A. In practical terms it would be extremely difficult in any event for the personal searcher to provide convincing proof ex post facto that he had conducted his unsupervised search against the correct name of the estate owner.

5 See eg *In re Forsey and Hollebone's Contract* [1927] 2 Ch 379 at 392f.

6 See the criticisms advanced by H.W.R. Wade, [1956] CLJ 216 at 228ff.

(5) Defective registration and defective search

To err is human. It is possible that mistakes (usually as to name[7]) may be made either in the process of registration of a land charge or in the process of search or—in rare concatenations of error—in both registration and search. The possibility of error arises from the fact that the Register of Land Charges is a register against names rather than title numbers or plots of land—a point which will be taken up later.[8]

(a) Defective registration

The correct name against which a registration should be entered on the Land Charges Register is deemed to be the full name of the 'estate owner' as recorded on his deeds of title.[9] If the incumbrancer registers against any other name, such registration will not bind a third party who subsequently requisitions an official search against the full correct name.

In *Diligent Finance Co Ltd v Alleyne*[10] the first defendant, Erskine Owen Alleyne, was the estate owner of a matrimonial home. He deserted his wife, who later registered her statutory 'rights of occupation'[11] in the matrimonial home as a Class F land charge against the name of 'Erskine Alleyne'. Two months after the registration the first defendant negotiated an increased mortgage loan from the plaintiff moneylender, which duly requisitioned an official search of the Land Charges Register before taking a new legal charge on the property and releasing the loan moneys. The plaintiff company requisitioned its search against the name of the first defendant as recorded on his title deeds, 'Erskine Owen Alleyne'. The official search certificate made no reference to the Class F charge registered by the first defendant's wife. On receiving the increased advance the first defendant left the country and the plaintiff company eventually brought possession proceedings against the wife as second defendant.[12] Foster J held that in these circumstances the Class F registration against an incomplete version of the estate owner's name could not rank ahead of the plaintiff's legal charge where the plaintiff had obtained an official search certificate against the complete and correct version of that name.[13]

7 For an ambiguity arising in relation to the precise plot of land concerned in an application for official search against a specific name, see *Du Sautoy v Symes* [1967] Ch 1146.
8 Post, p 137.
9 *Standard Property Investment plc v British Plastics Federation* (1985) 53 P & CR 25 at 32. See [1987] Conv 135 (J.E.A.).
10 (1971) 23 P & CR 346.
11 Post, p 155.
12 Foster J acknowledged that it was 'unfortunate ... that the Class F registration was not made against the proper name Erskine Owen Alleyne but only against Erskine Alleyne, but that is a mistake which I for my part cannot unfortunately rectify' ((1971) 23 P & CR 346 at 350). The debt owed to the plaintiff company amounted to only £700.
13 (1971) 23 P & CR 346 at 349f. See *Standard Property Investment plc v British Plastics Federation* (1985) 53 P & CR 25 at 33. Registration rules tend to be strictly construed in other jurisdictions also. See *Re Wilson* (1984) 8 DLR (4th) 271 at 273f (registration against 'Tom' instead of 'Thomas' held defective); *Re Gibbons* (1984) 8 DLR (4th) 316 at 317 (registration against name by which debtor commonly known in the community held inadequate). See also *Federal Business Development Bank v Registrar of Personal Property Security* (1984) 7 DLR (4th) 479 at 489f.

(b) Defective search

It is quite clear that a purchaser who requisitions an official search against an incorrect name must inevitably lose priority to an incumbrancer who has registered a land charge against the correct name of the estate owner as it appears on the title deeds.[14] By virtue of section 198(1) of the Law of Property Act 1925 such a purchaser is inescapably affected by a deemed 'actual notice' of the correct entry.

Somewhat more difficult is the issue of priority which arises where an incumbrancer has registered incorrectly, but the purchaser has likewise requisitioned an official search against the wrong name. This unlikely coincidence of error occurred in *Oak Co-operative Building Society v Blackburn*.[15] Here D1 was an estate agent whose full name was 'Francis David Blackburn'. D1 owned a dwelling-house in fee simple and he entered into an agreement to sell this property to D3. D3 was not legally represented; she agreed to pay a deposit of £100 and to pay the balance of the purchase price (£1,900) over a period of 15 years. D3 subsequently registered this estate contract as a Class C(iv) land charge against the name of 'Frank David Blackburn', 'Frank' being the name by which D1 was generally known in the locality. Several years later D1 obtained a mortgage advance of £1,300 from P on the security of the property. Before accepting a legal charge on the property, P instructed their solicitor to requisition an official search of the Land Charges Register. The solicitor mistakenly applied for an official search against the name 'Francis Davis Blackburn'.[16] The search certificate made no reference to the subsisting entry against 'Frank David Blackburn'. D1 was subsequently adjudicated bankrupt and some time later, in the words of Russell LJ, P 'roused themselves from torpor' and brought possession proceedings against D3.

Under these circumstances the Court of Appeal was called upon to decide an issue which turned ultimately on the relative gravity of two errors—an error in the initial registration and an error in the requisition of official search. Reversing the judgment of Ungoed-Thomas J, the Court of Appeal took the 'broader view that so far as possible the system should be made to work in favour of those who seek to make use of it in a sensible and practical way.'[17] The Court thus concluded that D3's registration should not be regarded as a nullity merely because D1's formal name was 'Francis' and not 'Frank'. According to Russell LJ, a registration in 'what may be fairly described as a version of the full names of the vendor' is not rendered a nullity as against 'someone who does not search at all, or who (as here) searches in the wrong name',[18] but would be a nullity as against someone

14 This conclusion follows even if the search is requisitioned not against the name of the estate owner as disclosed by his title deeds, but against some more complete version of his name (eg the full names contained in his birth certificate). See *Standard Property Investment plc v British Plastics Federation* (1985) 53 P & CR 25 at 30ff.

15 [1968] Ch 730, on appeal from [1967] Ch 1169.

16 One of the hilarious features of this case is the fact that the solicitor who requisitioned the official search was himself called 'Davis' and appears, by error, to have transposed his own name into the search application!

17 [1968] Ch 730 at 743C.

18 This generous outcome may perhaps seem excessively indulgent towards D3, given the strict tenor of the comparative case law cited in note 13, ante.

who requisitioned an official search against the full correct name as disclosed by the deeds of title.[19]

5. THE BASIC FLAW OF THE LAND CHARGES SYSTEM

Any analysis of the caselaw under the Land Charges Act makes it increasingly apparent that the present land charges scheme suffers from a rather fundamental flaw.

(1) The problem

The basic problem underlying the registration of land charges lies in the fact that registration is effected against the *name* of the estate owner whose estate is intended to be affected.[20] Names belong to people and, since people are mere mortals, their names are evanescent. As time passes, these names likewise disappear into the mists of history. The same is not true of land, which is immovable.[1]

(a) A practical example

The difficulty which unfolds itself is this. Suppose the following series of conveyances of a fee simple estate in a plot of land, Blackacre:

A conveys to B in 1930
B conveys to C in 1960
C conveys to D in 1970
D conveys to E in 1985
E conveys to F in 1990

Suppose further that in 1936 B's neighbour, N, duly registered a restrictive covenant as a Class D(ii) land charge against the name of the current estate owner, B. It is almost certain that when F searched the Land Charges Register prior to completing his purchase in 1990, he did not discover the existence of N's incumbrance. In the normal case F's investigation of the title to Blackacre will have commenced with the conveyance by C to D in 1970—

19 [1968] Ch 730 at 743E-F. See (1968) 32 Conv (NS) 284 (F.R. Crane). It is clear that the Court of Appeal had little patience with the Oak Co-operative Building Society. The Building Society was even informed by the Registry of earlier charges on the property against the name of 'Francis David Blackburn', but had not been moved to inquire further. Russell LJ denied that the Court 'need shed any tears for the plaintiffs, who could easily have protected themselves by a proper search but which owing to the error of their solicitor they never made ... [T]hey could without great trouble have caused somebody to visit the property in question, when they would have found the third defendant living there' ([1968] Ch 730 at 744B).

20 Land Charges Act 1972, s 3(1) (ante, p 117). It has been pointed out that name-registration is a perfectly suitable method of protecting land charges which have a limited expectation of life (eg estate contracts). However, other kinds of land charge (eg restrictive covenants) are commonly imposed in order to control the use of land over an indefinitely long period (see H.W.R. Wade, [1956] CLJ 216 at 222f).

1 Compare the basis of registration of title under the Land Registration Act 1925 (post, p 170).

that is, with the first conveyance which by 1990 was at least 15 years old.[2] F will have had no contractual right of access to the earlier deeds of conveyance and therefore may never have heard of B (or A). Yet, according to the draconian terms of section 198(1) of the Law of Property Act 1925, N's registration against B constitutes 'actual notice' of N's equitable interest 'to all persons and for all purposes'. F is thus fixed with actual notice of N's restrictive covenant. The fact that F received a clear certificate of official search against the names of C, D and E is quite irrelevant. Through no real fault of his own F did not obtain a certificate of search against the name of B—and that is all that matters here. F is inescapably bound by a land charge which was duly registered, albeit behind a good root of title.

(b) The 'Frankenstein's monster'

The problem disclosed here is endemic in any system of name-registration which operates on the pragmatic assumption that those investigating title can entirely ignore events anterior to an artificial and arbitrarily defined 'root of title'. The difficulty was already sufficiently apparent to the Lord Chancellor's Committee on Land Charges which reported in 1956, when the statutory period of investigation of title was still 30 years.[3] In its report this Committee (which sat under the chairmanship of Roxburgh J) confessed itself unable to suggest any remedy for the grave defect which had been exposed in the operation of the land charges scheme. The Committee conjectured that the inherently flawed name-register had been instituted in 1925 in the belief that all land in England and Wales would be covered by a system of compulsory registration of title within the following 30 years. This goal remained woefully unrealised in 1956, and the Roxburgh Committee could only recommend that the extension of compulsory registration of title should proceed apace.[4] As was said at the time, the draftsmen of the 1925 legislation 'appear to have succeeded in creating the conveyancing equivalent of a Frankenstein's monster, which with the passing years would become not only more dangerous but also more difficult to kill'.[5]

The problem of the hidden registration would still not have occasioned widespread difficulty if the minimum statutory period of investigation of title had remained as 30 years. In the example discussed above, this period would have embraced the conveyance from B to C in 1960, thus revealing to F the name of B as an earlier estate owner of Blackacre. However, in 1970 the statutory period of investigation of title was reduced to a mere 15 years,[6] and the problem was made instantly more acute. It became much more likely that purchasers would be trapped by registrations concealed behind a good root of title of whose existence they had no conceivable means

2 Law of Property Act 1969, s 23 (ante, p 132).
3 Law of Property Act 1925, s 44(1) (post, p 271).
4 Cmd 9825 (July 1956), para 22.
5 See H.W.R. Wade, [1956] CLJ 216 at 220, who pointed out that it was quite impracticable even in 1956 to convert the Land Charges Register from a name-based register into a title- or land-based register. The 'herculean labour' required to effect the transition of millions of charges already registered now makes the task utterly impossible.
6 Law of Property Act 1969, s 23 (ante, p 132).

of discovery. A partial remedy was therefore enacted in the Law of Property Act 1969.[7]

(2) A partial remedy

Section 25(1) of the Law of Property Act 1969 confers a right to compensation from public moneys on any purchaser of an estate or interest in land who suffers loss by reason of a registered land charge hidden behind a root of title. Thus, in relation to the dilemma of the concealed charge considered in the example above, the preferred legislative solution is that N's charge should remain binding on F in accordance with section 198(1) of the Law of Property Act 1925, but that any consequential loss falling on F should be assuaged by the award of money.

(a) Preconditions of statutory compensation

The availability of compensation (which is paid by the Chief Land Registrar[8]) is always subject to three statutory conditions. *First*, the completion of the transaction which occasions the loss must occur after the commencement date of the Law of Property Act 1969.[9] The compensation provision thus applies only to conveyances effected on or after 1 January 1970. *Second*, the purchaser must have no 'actual knowledge' of the charge at the date of completion of his purchase.[10] *Third*, the charge in question must have been registered 'against the name of an owner of an estate in the land who was not as owner of any such estate a party to any transaction, or concerned in any event, comprised in the relevant title.'[11] In other words, the registration in respect of which compensation is sought must be truly concealed behind the root of title.

(b) Other practical precautions

The theoretical problem of concealed registrations has been largely avoided in practice because most registered land charges tend to be referred to in later title deeds so long as there remains any possibility that these charges remain relevant.[12] It is therefore a rare purchaser who can plead complete ignorance of a charge registered behind the root of title, but it is predictable that the day is fast approaching when the compensation provisions of the Law of Property Act 1969 will assume a more vital significance.

7 See Law Commission, *Report on Land Charges affecting Unregistered Land* (Law Com No 18, 1969), para 27.
8 Law of Property Act 1969, s 25(4).
9 Law of Property Act 1969, s 25(1)(a).
10 Law of Property Act 1969, s 25(1)(b). For this purpose, 'actual knowledge' is to be determined without regard to the provisions of section 198(1) of the Law of Property Act 1925 (see Law of Property Act 1969, s 25(2)).
11 Law of Property Act 1969, s 25(1)(c).
12 The mere handing on of a series of official search certificates obtained on the occasion of purchase by each successive owner may not be enough in itself to compile an accurate or comprehensive record of all the charges affecting the land. There is, for instance, no necessary assurance that in each case the official search was requisitioned against the correct full names of former estate owners.

6. CATEGORIES OF REGISTRABLE LAND CHARGE

The categories of registrable land charge are defined in section 2 of the Land Charges Act 1972. The matters eligible for registration within these categories must, as a threshold qualification, comprise some form of 'charge on or obligation affecting land'.[13]

There are six classes of land charge registrable in unregistered land, of which the most important are Classes C, D, and F.

(1) **Class A**

Class A charges comprise various kinds of land charge which derive ultimately from statute and which arise only on the making of some statutory application.[14]

(2) **Class B**

Class B charges likewise arise by virtue of statute, and include such charges as the Law Society's charge on land recovered or preserved for a legally assisted client under the Legal Aid Act 1988 in respect of unpaid contributions to the legal aid fund.[15] Class B charges differ from Class A charges in that they originate directly in the statute concerned and do not arise merely on the chargee's application.

(3) **Class C**

Class C charges fall under four heads:

(a) Class C(i)

This class comprises the 'puisne mortgage', ie a legal mortgage which is not protected by a deposit of documents relating to the legal estate affected. A puisne mortgage is therefore a second mortgage granted by a mortgagor who has already deposited his title deeds with the first mortgagee.[16] The second mortgagee, being unable to enjoy the security provided by retention of the title deeds, is offered the alternative security of being able to register his mortgage as a land charge notwithstanding that it is *legal*. Class C(i) thus provides a rare example of a legal interest which is registrable under the Land Charges Act: land charges are almost always *equitable* rights in or over land. The puisne mortgage is, however, included amongst the registrable categories simply for reasons of convenience and because of the additional security which registration confers on a second mortgagee.

13 Land Charges Act 1972, s 2(1).
14 An example is the landlord's right to compensation under Agricultural Holdings Act 1986, s 86.
15 Legal Aid Act 1988, s 16(6).
16 Post, p 981.

(b) Class C(ii)

Class C(ii) comprises the 'limited owner's charge'. Such a charge arises where, for instance, a tenant for life of settled land[17] discharges out of his own pocket a liability to taxation attracted by the settled estate as a whole.[18] The limited owner's charge is therefore an equitable charge which, if registered, secures the right of the limited owner (ie the tenant for life) to reimbursement of the money paid by him to the Revenue.

(c) Class C(iii)

This class comprises the 'general equitable charge' and includes many kinds of equitable charge which are not otherwise registrable. Amongst the incumbrances registrable under Class C(iii) are a rentcharge granted for life (or 'equitable annuity'),[19] an equitable mortgage of a legal estate,[20] and an unpaid vendor's equitable lien on property sold. Class C(iii) does not, however, include any charge which is secured by a deposit of documents relating to the legal title affected.[1] Informal mortgages by deposit of title deeds are for this reason excluded from the registrable category.[2] Nor does Class C(iii) include any equitable charge which arises or affects an interest arising under a trust for sale or settlement of land.[3] Such charges are in any event governed by the normal process of overreaching on sale,[4] with the result that there is no reason for enforcement against a later purchaser. Furthermore, Class C(iii) does not include either an agreement to share the proceeds of sale of land[5] or an estate agent's charge on those proceeds for the purpose of securing his commission.[6] The interest of the chargee in such cases is effectively an interest in money rather than an interest in land, and Class C(iii) is appropriate only in respect of interests in land.[7]

(d) Class C(iv)

Class C(iv) comprises the 'estate contract', which is statutorily defined as

17 Post, p 616.
18 See eg Inheritance Tax Act 1984, ss 237f.
19 Ante, p 72, post, p 614. 'Equitable annuities outside trusts for sale and settlements must be extremely rare, even if only because most kinds of annuity charged upon land make it settled land' (H.W.R. Wade, [1956] CLJ 216 at 224).
20 Post, p 943. Equitable mortgages of an equitable interest under a trust for sale or strict settlement of land are normally overreached on a conveyance of that land to a third party, and are thereafter satisfied out of the proceeds of sale (see Law of Property Act 1925, s 2(1)(i), (ii); Settled Land Act 1925, s 72(2)).
1 Land Charges Act 1972, s 2(4).
2 Post, p 944.
3 Land Charges Act 1972, s 2(4).
4 Ante, pp 102, 108.
5 *Thomas v Rose* [1968] 1 WLR 1797 at 1808G-H.
6 *Georgiades v Edward Wolfe & Co Ltd* [1965] Ch 487 at 501F, 504G, 508C.
7 In 1956 the Roxburgh Committee favoured the abolition of Class C(iii) with the exception of the category of mortgages (see *Report of the Committee on Land Charges* (Cmd 9825), para 13).

LCA s.2(4)

a contract by an estate owner or by a person entitled at the date of the contract to have a legal estate conveyed to him to convey or create a legal estate, including a contract conferring either expressly or by statutory implication a valid option to purchase, a right of pre-emption or any other like right.[8]

(i) Conveyancing function of the estate contract It is integral to the conveyancing process that, from the moment of formation of a specifically enforceable contract of sale, the purchaser of a legal estate in land acquires not merely a *contractual* right but also a *proprietary* right.[9] It is for precisely this reason that the Class C(iv) land charge is designed to protect the purchaser's estate contract, ie the purchaser's right to require conveyance of the legal estate in accordance with the contract.[10] The purchaser's interest requires protection during the interim between contract and conveyance because there is always a possibility that the vendor may in breach of contract convey the legal estate to a third party who has no notice of the equitable rights created by the estate contract. Moreover, estate contracts by their very nature create merely short-term interests in land and are therefore peculiarly appropriate for protection under a system of name-registration such as the land charges scheme.[11] Ironically, however, it seems that estate contracts are in practice seldom registered by solicitors, being entered in the Land Charges Register only in cases of suspicion or delayed completion.[12]

(ii) Accepted forms of estate contract Estate contracts include not merely contracts for the sale of an estate in fee simple; they also include contracts for a lease[13] and contracts to create a mortgage of a legal estate. It matters not that the legal estate to be conveyed under the contract is greater than the estate currently vested in the estate owner,[14] although there is some doubt as to whether Class C(iv) can include an oral contract which is enforceable only on the basis of acts of part performance.[15]

(iii) Options It is also clear that the registrable category of estate contracts includes certain kinds of *option*.[16] It has been well said that the juridical nature of an option is an 'academic riddle'[17] and that an option is 'nearly

8 Land Charges Act 1972, s 2(4).
9 Post, p 263.
10 The legal estate in question may of course be either a freehold or a leasehold.
11 H.W.R. Wade, [1956] CLJ 216 at 222.
12 'Why it should be [the] collective practice [of conveyancing solicitors] to run this risk is a mystery, but the Land Registry must be grateful . . . for the volume of entries would be enormous, and "dead wood" would accumulate in the registry as fast as contracts were completed' (H.W.R. Wade, [1956] CLJ 216 at 223).
13 See *Phillips v Mobil Oil Co Ltd* [1989] 1 WLR 888 at 890H per Nicholls LJ.
14 *Sharp v Coates* [1949] 1 KB 285 at 293.
15 See eg *Mens v Wilson* (1973) 231 Estates Gazette 843.
16 See generally *Barnsley's Land Options* (2nd edn by R. Castle, London 1992).
17 *Murray v Scott* [1976] 1 NZLR 643 at 655 per Cooke J; *Alexander v Tse* [1988] 1 NZLR 318 at 324 per Somers J.

always a ticklish thing'.[18] It is, however, of the essence of an option that it entitles the grantee of the option (the *optionee*) to demand that the grantor (or *optionor*) should convey to him the agreed estate or interest at any time of the optionee's choosing,[19] provided that the latter has first satisfied any conditions as to price or otherwise to which the option was made subject.[20] The grant of an option thus imposes no obligation on the optionee, but merely confers on him a contractual right to demand to become the purchaser of land.[1] The distinguishing feature of the option is precisely that control over whether a concluded contract for sale will ever eventuate resides exclusively in the optionee.[2] The only act required of him is an act signifying his intention to exercise the option.[3]

It is trite law that the right to call for a conveyance of a legal estate in land comprises in itself an equitable interest in the land.[4] Since the right of purchase conferred by an option becomes 'crystallised immediately upon the option being granted',[5] it follows that—even before it is exercised—the

18 *Mackay v Wilson* (1947) 47 SR (NSW) 315 at 318 per Jordan CJ. An option to purchase land has been variously characterised as representing an irrevocable offer binding the optionor to sell (see *United Scientific Holdings Ltd v Burnley BC* [1978] AC 904 at 929A per Lord Diplock, 945F per Lord Simon of Glaisdale, 951A per Lord Salmon) and as a conditional contract in favour of the optionee contingently upon his exercise of the option (*Helby v Matthews* [1895] AC 471 at 482; *Griffith v Pelton* [1958] Ch 205 at 225). It may be that neither explanation is entirely satisfactory and that an option ultimately constitutes a 'relationship sui generis' (see *Spiro v Glencrown Properties Ltd* [1991] Ch 537 at 544G per Hoffmann J).

19 See *Canadian Long Island Petroleums Ltd v Irving Industries (Irving Wire Products Division) Ltd* (1975) 50 DLR (3d) 265 at 277 per Martland J.

20 It is irrelevant that the purchase price is not stipulated in the terms of the option, so long as the option provides machinery by which the price can later be objectively ascertained without the necessity of any further agreement as to price between the parties (see *Kopec v Pyret* (1983) 146 DLR (3d) 242 at 248). In *Sudbrook Trading Estate Ltd v Eggleton* [1983] 1 AC 444, for instance, the House of Lords upheld the enforceability of an option where the price was to be settled by valuers nominated by the parties or, in default, by an umpire appointed by both parties. See [1981] Conv 448 (K. Hodkinson); [1982] CLJ 233 (C. Harpum and D. Lloyd Jones); (1982) 132 NLJ 818 (H.W. Wilkinson); (1982) 98 LQR 539 (J. Murdoch); (1983) 46 MLR 493 (P. Robertshaw). See also *Re Nishi Industries Ltd* (1979) 91 DLR (3d) 321 at 323f; *Lonergan v McCartney* [1983] 3 NIJB; but compare *Van Der Waal v Goodenough* [1983] 1 NSWLR 81 at 93F.

1 See *Laybutt v Amoco Australia Pty Ltd* (1974) 132 CLR 57 at 76 per Gibbs J. The absence of a time limit on the exercise of an option does not render it void for uncertainty, since the courts can supply a reasonable time by implication. See *Reid v Moreland Timber Co Pty Ltd* (1946) 73 CLR 1 at 13 per Dixon J; *Malding Pty Ltd v Metcalfe* (1989) NSW ConvR 55-495 at 58,613. (At the other end of the scale the option in *Spiro v Glencrown Properties Ltd* [1991] Ch 537 was exercisable only before 5 pm on the day of grant!) An option which is unlimited in point of time will, however, be vitiated by perpetuity. A perpetuity period of 21 years is now imposed in respect of any disposition which confers an option to acquire for valuable consideration any interest in land (Perpetuities and Accumulations Act 1964, s 9(2)). See Chapter 16, post, p 671.

2 *Stephens v Gulf Oil Canada Ltd* (1976) 65 DLR (3d) 193 at 218.

3 *Kopec v Pyret* (1983) 146 DLR (3d) 242 at 248. On the requirements for exercise of an option, see *Mills v Haywood* (1877) 6 Ch D 196 at 200ff; *Ballas v Theophilos* (No 2) (1957) 98 CLR 193 at 204f; *Traywinds Pty Ltd v Cooper* [1989] 1 Qd R 222 at 225.

4 *London and South Western Railway Co v Gomm* (1882) 20 Ch D 562 at 581 per Jessel MR.

5 *Kopec v Pyret* (1983) 146 DLR (3d) 242 at 248. Thereafter the option can be revoked or varied only in accordance with the terms of the option itself.

option confers upon the grantee an equitable interest in the land concerned.[6] (The full equitable interest in the land will, of course, pass to the optionee on the exercise of the option,[7] at which point the optionor's estate or interest 'is taken away from him without his consent'.[8]) Meanwhile, however, the optionee's right to call for the conveyance of a legal estate is registrable as a Class C(iv) charge.[9]

An option to purchase a legal estate may take various forms apart from the obvious case of an option to purchase an estate in fee simple. The kinds of option registrable under Class C(iv) include, for example, an option to purchase a legal lease[10] and a tenant's option to renew his term[11] or to purchase a superior reversionary interest.[12] Likewise a tenant may, under Class C(iv), register a notice served by him in respect of his right under the Leasehold Reform Act 1967 to purchase the freehold reversion or to acquire an enlarged lease.[13] A Class C(iv) charge may also be registered by a landlord in respect of any right which he may have to require his tenant to surrender (rather than assign) his leasehold term.[14]

(iv) Rights of pre-emption A fundamental distinction must be drawn between an option to purchase and a 'right of pre-emption'.[15] Under an option the optionor grants to the optionee a right, solely within the optionee's control,

6 See *London and South Western Railway Co v Gomm* (1882) 20 Ch D 562 at 580f; *Webb v Pollmount* [1966] Ch 584 at 596D; *Mountford v Scott* [1975] Ch 258 at 262; *London & Blenheim Estates Ltd v Ladbroke Retail Parks Ltd* [1992] 1 WLR 1278 at 1282A; *Frobisher Ltd v Canadian Pipelines & Petroleums Ltd* (1960) 21 DLR (2d) 497 at 532; *Politzer v Metropolitan Homes Ltd* (1975) 54 DLR (3d) 376 at 382; *Stephens v Gulf Oil Canada Ltd* (1976) 65 DLR (3d) 193 at 215; *Laybutt v Amoco Australia Pty Ltd* (1974) 132 CLR 57 at 75; *Bahr v Nicolay* (No 2) (1988) 164 CLR 604 at 645f per Brennan J; *Re Davies* [1989] Qd R 48 at 51.

7 On the equitable consequences of a specifically enforceable contract for the sale of land, see Chapter 9 (post, p 263).

8 *London and South Western Railway Co v Gomm* (1882) 20 Ch D 562 at 581 per Jessel MR.

9 See eg *Midland Bank Trust Co Ltd v Green* [1981] AC 513 (ante, p 126); *Phillips v Mobil Oil Co Ltd* [1989] 1 WLR 888 at 890H per Nicholls LJ. Once an option is registered, there is no need for additional registration of any resulting contract of sale (see *Armstrong and Holmes Ltd v Holmes* (1993) *Times*, 23 June).

10 *Phillips v Mobil Oil Co Ltd* [1989] 1 WLR 888 at 890H-891A per Nicholls LJ. There is some doubt as to whether an option to purchase a lease qualifies within Class C(iv) as an 'option of purchase' or as 'any other like right' (see Land Charges Act 1972, s 2(4)(iv), ante, p 142). The former ground of eligibility seems quite adequate (see *Spiro v Glencrown Properties Ltd* [1991] Ch 537 at 545D per Hoffmann J, but compare *Phillips v Mobil Oil Co Ltd*, supra at 891A-B).

11 *Beesly v Hallwood Estates Ltd* [1960] 1 WLR 549 at 558; *Phillips v Mobil Oil Co Ltd* [1989] 1 WLR 888 at 893F, 894E-G (post, pp 323, 863). See J. Howell, [1990] Conv 169, 250. The Roxburgh Committee suggested that such options should cease to be registrable (*Report of the Committee on Land Charges* (Cmd 9825), para 15).

12 *Phillips v Mobil Oil Co Ltd* [1989] 1 WLR 888 at 891C.

13 Leasehold Reform Act 1967, s 5(5) (post, p 767). The mere service of a statutory notice by the tenant under the 1967 Act confers no priority over a transferee from the landlord: for the latter purpose the notice must be registered (see *Buckley v S.R.L. Investments Ltd and Cator and Robinson* (1971) 22 P & CR 756 at 764).

14 *Greene v Church Commissioners for England* [1974] Ch 467 at 477B.

15 In identifying whether a grant is one of option or of first refusal, the label applied by the parties themselves is not conclusive. The court may scrutinise the substance rather than the form of the transaction and need not 'adhere slavishly' to a label which misdescribes the relationship (see *Kopec v Pyret* (1983) 146 DLR (3d) 242 at 247, (1987) 36 DLR (4th) 1 at 4f).

to compel a conveyance of the optionor's land at a future date.[16] By contrast, a right of pre-emption confers upon its grantee merely a right of first refusal.[17] The decision whether to sell at all lies always within the discretion of the grantor of the right.[18] At the moment of its grant a right of pre-emption merely confirms the right of the grantee to make an offer to the grantor, which the grantor has a discretion to accept or reject. The right of pre-emption acquires substance only at such later time when it becomes 'exercisable' by the grantee.

The essential characteristic of a right of pre-emption is the intention on the part of the grantor to give to the grantee a preference over other potential buyers in the event that the grantor should decide to sell.[19] Thus, in strict terms, the right of pre-emption becomes 'exercisable' only when the grantor signifies an intention to sell on certain defined terms,[20] or is at least in receipt of a bona fide offer of purchase made by some third party.[1] In either of these events the grantee's pre-emptive right is converted into a specialised form of option.[2] The grantee may now demand to purchase on terms identical to any offer which the grantor was plainly willing to accept.[3]

16 See *Stephens v Gulf Oil Canada Ltd* (1976) 65 DLR (3d) 193 at 218. 'This feature of exclusive control by the optionee whereby he can, by his own unilateral act, compel the vendor to part with his interest in the subject-matter, does not permit the same indeterminacy of terms which characterises a right of first refusal at its inception' (*Kopec v Pyret* (1983) 146 DLR (3d) 242 at 248).

17 On one view this phrase is 'a somewhat inept term, because what the potential offeree wants is an opportunity of *accepting* an offer rather than an opportunity of refusing an offer' (see *Woodroffe v Box* (1954) 92 CLR 245 at 257 per Fullagar and Kitto JJ).

18 See *Brown v Gould* [1972] Ch 53 at 58F; *Stephens v Gulf Oil Canada Ltd* (1976) 65 DLR (3d) 193 at 217f. A right of first refusal operates in effect as a 'negative covenant on the part of the vendor not to part with his interest in the land until the first opportunity to purchase is accorded to the covenantee' (see *Canadian Long Island Petroleums Ltd v Irving Industries (Irving Wire Products Division) Ltd* (1975) 50 DLR (3d) 265 at 279f; *Kopec v Pyret* (1983) 146 DLR (3d) 242 at 247).

19 See *Kopec v Pyret* (1983) 146 DLR (3d) 242 at 247. If the original grant of the pre-emptive right stipulated a fixed purchase price which has since been rendered 'grossly inadequate' by the subsequent inflation of land values, there is a possibility that the agreement to grant the right will be struck down as void on grounds of public policy: the fixed price may be regarded as an invalid restriction upon alienation (ante, p 90). See *In re Rosher* (1884) 26 Ch D 801 at 811ff; *Hall v Busst* (1960) 104 CLR 206 at 216ff; *Saliba v Saliba* [1976] Qd R 205 at 207D-E.

20 'Rights of pre-emption do not create an interest in land, at least until activated by the potential vendor placing the land on the market' (*London & Blenheim Estates Ltd v Ladbroke Retail Parks Ltd* [1992] 1 WLR 1278 at 1282A per Judge Paul Baker QC). See also *Kling v Keston Properties Ltd* (1983) 49 P & CR 212 at 217, where Vinelott J pointed out that a vendor 'can hardly evince a desire to sell land more clearly than by contracting to sell it.' For a similar ruling, see *Kopec v Pyret* (1983) 146 DLR (3d) 242 at 252, where Scheibel J held that 'where the vendor has signified his intention to sell upon certain terms and holds himself ready to sell in the event those terms are met, the position of the preferential purchaser is transformed into that of a virtual optionholder.'

1 See *Turner v Mendenhall* 510 P2d 490 at 492 (1973); *Vancouver Key Business Machines Ltd v Teja* (1975) 57 DLR (3d) 464 at 472; *Associated Grocers Co-operative Ltd v Hubbard Properties Pty Ltd* (1986) 42 SASR 321 at 333. In advance of such an offer the right of pre-emption is not extinguished merely because the grantor offers to sell to the grantee at a price which the grantee is not prepared to pay (see *Kopec v Pyret* (1987) 36 DLR (4th) 1 at 6f).

2 See *Kopec v Pyret* (1983) 146 DLR (3d) 242 at 252 per Scheibel J. It is in this sense that a right of pre-emption has been described as a 'conditional option' (*Pata Nominees Pty Ltd v Durnsford Pty Ltd* [1988] WAR 365 at 372 per Burt CJ).

3 *Kopec v Pyret* (1987) 36 DLR (4th) 1 at 6.

It is at this time—and not before—that the grantee's personal contractual right is transformed into an interest in the land.[4] Until this point the grantee has 'a mere spes which the grantor . . . may either frustrate by choosing not to fulfil the necessary conditions or may convert into an option and thus into an equitable interest by fulfilling the conditions.'[5]

It is precisely this variable status of rights of pre-emption which has generated some confusion over their eligibility for registration under Class C(iv). The statutory definition of the Class C(iv) charge plainly includes a reference to a 'right of pre-emption'.[6] In *Pritchard v Briggs*,[7] however, the Court of Appeal held that a right of pre-emption is registrable under Class C(iv) only if and when the vendor ultimately decides to sell.[8] This ruling, although controversial,[9] is at least consistent with the theory that a right of pre-emption takes effect as an interest in land only when it becomes exercisable.[10] In its incipient form the right remains merely an unregistrable personal contractual entitlement.[11] However, the ruling in *Pritchard v Briggs* means that there is no mechanism for enforcing the incipient right against any successor in title of the grantor, with the result that if the right is never rendered exercisable by the original grantor it must fail against the successor.[12] This conclusion is driven by the dogma that only the crystallised right to call for a transfer of an estate or interest in land can create a proprietary interest in the land. It is questionable whether this dogma is worth preserving or is indeed ultimately meaningful.

(v) Conditional contracts other than options Outside the context of options and rights of pre-emption some uncertainty still attends the registrable status of contracts which remain subject to an unfulfilled condition precedent (eg the grant of a planning permission or receipt of a satisfactory survey). In practice many such conditional contracts have been registered within Class

4 See *London & Blenheim Estates Ltd v Ladbroke Retail Parks Ltd* [1992] 1 WLR 1278 at 1282A; *McFarland v Hauser* (1978) 88 DLR (3d) 449 at 461 per Martland J; *Kopec v Pyret* (1987) 36 DLR (4th) 1 at 8. The grantee's equitable interest in the land is extinguished, however, if he now refuses to purchase the land in accordance with the terms of the pre-emptive right (see *Pata Nominees Pty Ltd v Durnsford Pty Ltd* [1988] WAR 365 at 375).

5 *Pritchard v Briggs* [1980] Ch 338 at 418C-D per Templeman LJ.

6 Land Charges Act 1972, s 2(4) (ante, p 142).

7 [1980] Ch 338.

8 [1980] Ch 338 at 419F-G, 423A-B.

9 For criticism of the decision in *Pritchard v Briggs*, see [1980] CLJ 35 (C. Harpum); (1980) 96 LQR 488 (H.W.R. Wade). See also A.R. Everton, [1982] Conv 177 at 180. In so far as the ruling of the Court of Appeal seemed to contradict the pellucid wording of the statutory definition of Class C(iv), Goff LJ even ventured the view that the legislation 'proceeded on a mistaken basis as to what the law was' ([1980] Ch 338 at 398A-399E).

10 Thus, in *Kopec v Pyret* (1987) 36 DLR (4th) 1 at 7f, a right of pre-emption was properly made the subject of a caveat registered *after* the point at which it became exercisable.

11 For authority in other jurisdictions that, in advance of becoming exercisable, a right of pre-emption confers only a personal contractual right rather than a proprietary right, and cannot therefore constitute a registrable or caveatable interest in land, see *Stephens v Gulf Oil Canada Ltd* (1976) 65 DLR (3d) 193 at 217f; *Re Rutherford* [1977] 1 NZLR 504 at 510); *Kopec v Pyret* (1983) 146 DLR (3d) 242 at 247, (1987) 36 DLR (4th) 1 at 7f.

12 See eg *Peabody Donation Fund v London Residuary Body* (1988) 55 P & CR 355 at 360.

C(iv) without any objection whatsoever.[13] Registration is self-evidently appropriate where the condition in question is one which was included for the benefit of the purchaser and may be waived by him,[14] or where the relevant condition requires to be satisfied not by either of the transacting parties but by some extraneous person or event.[15] In both instances the conditional contract imposes an 'obligation affecting land' within the required statutory sense,[16] precisely because the vendor has placed entirely outside his control the fulfilment or frustration of the relevant condition.[17] There is, however, much to commend the view that Class C(iv) should be construed broadly so as to include within the registration facility all previous sale arrangements of which third parties, in the interests of saving time and money, deserve in fairness to be forewarned.[18]

(vi) Contracts of agency It is also uncertain to what extent Class C(iv) applies to contracts of agency: there are conflicting views as to whether the class of registrable estate contracts can include a *contract to create a contract* in relation to land. In *Turley v Mackay*,[19] for instance, Uthwatt J thought that Class C(iv) covered a contract 'under which one person is bound to a second person to create a legal estate in such a third person as the second person may direct.'[20] On this footing a contract by A to sell to any nominee put forward by B would itself qualify as an estate contract.

A more restrictive approach was applied in *Thomas v Rose*.[1] Here Megarry J agreed that Class C(iv) is sufficiently wide to cover a contract by A and B whereby A agrees to grant a legal estate (eg a lease) to X.[2] He was also prepared to concede that Class C(iv) includes a contract by A and B to

13 See eg *Re Longlands Farm* [1968] 3 All ER 552 at 553I. The English approach thus stands in marked contrast to the more stringent view adopted in the Australian jurisdictions. Here a purchaser under a contract subject to an unfulfilled condition precedent has been held to have no caveatable interest in the subject land (see eg *Talga Investments Pty Ltd v Tweed Canal Estates Pty Ltd* (1974) 1 BPR 9675 at 9684f; *Re Bosca Land Pty Ltd's Caveat* [1976] Qd R 119 at 122; *Re C M Group Pty Ltd's Caveat* [1986] 1 Qd R 381 at 389ff; *Re Androma Pty Ltd* [1987] 2 Qd R 134 at 150).

14 See *Wood Preservation Ltd v Prior* [1969] 1 WLR 1077 at 1094E-G (contract conditional upon purchaser obtaining planning permission 'to its entire satisfaction').

15 *Haslemere Estates Ltd v Baker* [1982] 1 WLR 1109 at 1118H–1119A (contract conditional upon the grant of planning permission and the consent of the Charity Commissioners).

16 Land Charges Act 1972, s 2(1), ante, p 140.

17 This criterion accounts quite neatly for the uneasy distinction existing between options to purchase and rights of pre-emption (ante, p 144).

18 See [1988] Conv 10 (H.W.W.).

19 [1944] Ch 37 at 40.

20 This view was justified on the ground that the object of Class C(iv) is to 'secure that obligations affecting land may be registered by persons who have a commercial interest in seeing that those obligations shall be carried out' ([1944] Ch 37 at 41).

1 [1968] 1 WLR 1797 at 1804G, where Megarry J thought that *Turley v Mackay* was not a case which ought to be extended in its ambit. 'The agent's real claim in that case was for damages, and it is possible to wonder whether his contractual rights fell within the spirit of class C(iv).'

2 '[I]t matters not that the contract is a contract to create a legal estate in favour of someone other than a contracting party' ([1968] 1 WLR 1797 at 1804A-B).

convey or create a legal estate in favour of such persons as B shall direct.[3] In the view taken by Megarry J, however, Class C(iv) is properly applicable only to those contracts 'which themselves bind the estate owner (or other person entitled) to convey or create a legal estate.'[4] No registration may be validly effected in respect of any contract which fails to impose on the estate owner a clear legal obligation to convey his estate to *somebody*.[5] In terms of this analysis Class C(iv) has no relevance to a contract 'at one remove' which merely provides 'machinery whereby such an obligation may be created by some other transaction'.[6] A contract between A and B conferring on B the power to accept 'any offer for the sale' of A's land is not a registrable estate contract: it is at most an authority to do some further act which may or may not bring an estate contract into being. In *Thomas v Rose*[7] Megarry J regarded such an agreement as constituting in essence a mere agency agreement regulating the disposal of land and providing for payment of the agent out of the proceeds of sale.

(4) Class D

Class D falls under three heads:

(a) Class D(i)

This class comprises an Inland Revenue charge for tax payable on death.

(b) Class D(ii)

This class comprises the 'restrictive covenant',[8] which for this purpose is defined as 'a covenant or agreement (other than a covenant or agreement between a lessor and a lessee) restrictive of the user of land and entered into on or after 1 January 1926'.[9]

(i) Function of the restrictive covenant A typical restrictive covenant may be taken to be an agreement between two neighbouring freeholders, A and B, to the effect that A shall not use his land, nor permit it to be used, for the purpose of any trade or business. This kind of restrictive covenant is almost invariably found in any residential context which involves multiple habitation in conditions of close proximity, the primary function of such a covenant being to preserve the essential preconditions of civilised domestic coexistence.

In all probability B will have obtained A's agreement to the restrictive

3 It is irrelevant that the contract is not a firm contract in favour of a named person or that B never in fact gives any direction ([1968] 1 WLR 1797 at 1804B).
4 [1968] 1 WLR 1797 at 1805B-C.
5 [1968] 1 WLR 1797 at 1805C.
6 [1968] 1 WLR 1797 at 1805C. The formation of commercial agreements may often be the result of two phases or processes. As Higgins J remarked in *Barrier Wharfs Ltd v W Scott Fell & Co Ltd* (1908) 5 CLR 647 at 650, '[i]t is one thing for two parties to settle what are to be the terms of an agreement, if it should be made; and quite another thing to make the agreement'. See also *Ratto v Trifid Pty Ltd* [1987] WAR 237 at 241.
7 [1968] 1 WLR 1797 at 1805F-G.
8 On restrictive covenants generally, see Chapter 22 (post, p 1136).
9 Land Charges Act 1972, s 2(5). See generally R.G. Rowley, (1956) 20 Conv (NS) 370.

covenant by the payment of money or by the offer of other valuable consideration (such as a reciprocal covenant by B himself).[10] A's undertaking clearly has contractual force and, by curtailing the potential scope of A's activities on his own property, has the general effect of promoting the amenity enjoyed by B in respect of his own property. A's covenant precludes him from using his premises as a rag merchant, bookmaker or indeed music teacher, and B plainly has a *contractual* interest in the due performance of A's promise.

(ii) Proprietary status of the restrictive covenant If the legal analysis of the relationship between A and B stopped at this point, the agreement framed between A and B would have no enduring impact upon third parties. Only the contracting parties may claim the benefit or be called upon to suffer the burden of contractual terms. No third party purchasing either A's land or B's land would be affected by a contract to which he was not privy. However, in the law of land B's interest in the performance of A's promise is not regarded as a purely contractual interest. Ever since the decision in *Tulk v Moxhay*,[11] the covenantee of a restrictive covenant has been viewed as having in some sense a *proprietary* interest in the covenantor's land to the extent that he enjoys a contractual right to control activities conducted on that land. Thus, as with the estate contract,[12] the contractual right tends to enlarge into, and to arrogate to itself the character of, a proprietary interest.

(iii) Relevance of the equitable doctrine of notice Since 1 January 1926 the proprietary interest acquired by the restrictive covenantee can take effect only as an equitable interest. It is clearly not included amongst the legal estates, interests and charges enumerated in section 1(1), (2) of the Law of Property Act 1925.[13] As such the proprietary right—the 'restrictive covenant'—is in principle fully subject to the equitable doctrine of notice. The burden of the restrictive covenant—the burden initially assumed by A—will bind all third parties who purchase A's land other than a bona fide purchaser for value of a legal estate without notice of the restrictive covenant.

(iv) Introduction of a rule of registration The equitable doctrine of notice is still relevant today in determining the binding effect of restrictive covenants which were entered into by freeholders *before 1926*. However, in relation to restrictive covenants created by freeholders *after 1925*, the traditional doctrine of notice has been modified to the extent that the only recognised form of notice of the covenantee's equitable interest is now the notice which is ensured by registration of a Class D(ii) land charge.

(v) Enforcement of restrictive covenants Let us continue to suppose that A is the covenantor and B the covenantee in relation to a restrictive covenant which precludes trade or business user on A's land. A then sells and conveys his

10 The restrictive covenant will normally be contractually enforceable even in the absence of valuable consideration. Most restrictive covenants are contained in a deed.
11 (1848) 2 Ph 774 at 777ff, 41 ER 1143 at 1144f (post, p 1137).
12 Ante, p 142.
13 Ante, p 68.

legal estate in fee simple to C, and B sells and conveys his legal estate in fee simple to D. May D now enforce the restrictive covenant against C?

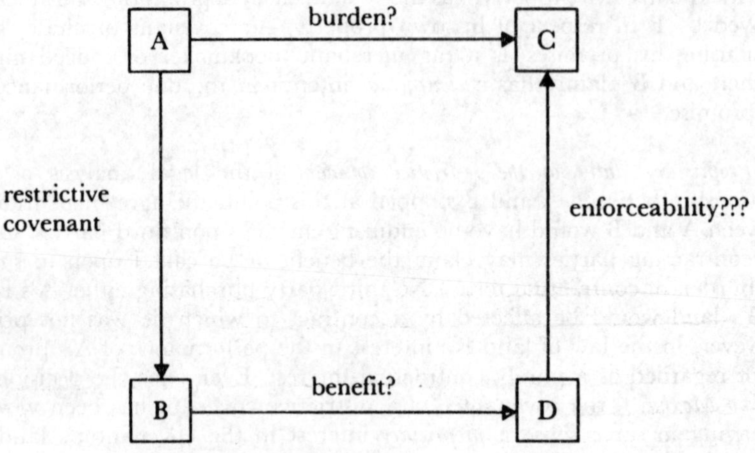

Fig. 13

The enforceability of the restrictive covenant as between C and D will turn on whether an affirmative answer can be given to two quite distinct questions.

— Has the burden of A's restrictive covenant been passed to C?
If the covenant was made after 1925 the only way in which the burden may 'run' with A's land is in consequence of the registration of a Class D(ii) land charge by B against the name of A. If such a registration was effected before A's conveyance to C, C cannot now deny that he received 'actual notice' of the restrictive covenant.[14] If B failed to register the land charge, the restrictive covenant becomes void as against C.[15]

— Has the benefit of the restrictive covenant been passed to D?
Unless the benefit of the restrictive covenant has indeed been passed to D, it will be entirely irrelevant that the land charge was duly registered against A.[16] The benefit must have been conferred on D in one or other of the methods of transmission which are discussed later in Chapter 22.[17] For the moment it is sufficient to recognise simply that the restrictive covenant in question will be enforceable against C at the behest of D only if *both* benefit *and* burden have been duly transmitted to the appropriate persons.

(vi) Exclusions from Class D(ii) Class D(ii) is so drawn as to exclude from its ambit not merely those restrictive covenants entered into before 1926

14 Law of Property Act 1925, s 198(1) (ante, p 118).
15 Land Charges Act 1972, s 4(6) (ante, p 119).
16 See eg *J Sainsbury Plc v Enfield LBC* [1989] 1 WLR 590 at 601E-F (post, p 1147).
17 Post, p 1149.

but also any restrictive covenant contained in a lease. In so far as leasehold restrictive covenants relate (or 'have reference'[18]) to the land leased, their enforcement against third parties is governed by a special framework of rules stemming from *Spencer's Case.*[19] However, it is possible that in certain circumstances a restrictive covenant between lessor and lessee may relate not to the user of the land demised but to the user of other adjoining land retained by the lessor. In such a case it is clear that the covenant undertaken by the lessor cannot be registered as a Class D(ii) charge,[20] and its enforcement against third parties in unregistered land must therefore depend on the operation of the equitable doctrine of notice.[1]

(c) Class D(iii)

This class comprises the 'equitable easement',[2] which is statutorily defined as 'an easement, right or privilege over or affecting land created or arising on or after 1 January 1926, and being merely an equitable interest.'[3] An equitable easement generally arises where a right in the nature of an easement has been created otherwise than by deed (eg by mere contract, unsealed writing or verbal grant) or has been created otherwise than for an interest equivalent to an estate in fee simple absolute in possession or a term of years absolute.[4]

(i) Uncertain coverage of Class D(iii) The Class D(iii) land charge has been the cause of much difficulty in practice. The very persons in whose favour such a charge may commonly arise are precisely those persons who will tend to be unaware of the need to secure protection by registration. Moreover the category of Class D(iii) charges is obscure and ill-defined.[5] It is far from certain which rights are registrable under this head.[6] It has been held that Class D(iii) has no application to a tenant's right to remove fixtures at the end of a lease,[7] or to an equitable right of entry for breach of a leasehold covenant.[8] Such are the difficulties connected with the registration of equitable easements that the Roxburgh Committee suggested that Class D(iii) might be abolished altogether.[9]

18 Law of Property Act 1925, ss 141(1), 142(1) (post, p 854, 859).
19 (1583) 5 Co Rep 16a, 77 ER 72 (post, p 865).
20 If, for instance, the lessor has covenanted with his lessee not to lease the adjoining premises to the latter's business rivals, it is even arguable that the covenant does not restrict 'user' so much as 'alienation', with the result that on this ground alone it falls outside Class D(ii). See eg *Re Nylar Foods Ltd and Roman Catholic Episcopal Corp of Prince Rupert* (1988) 48 DLR (4th) 175 at 179.
1 *Dartstone v Cleveland Petroleum Co Ltd* [1969] 1 WLR 1807 at 1812A.
2 Easements are discussed more fully in Chapter 21 (post, p 1043). The distinction between legal and equitable easements was outlined in Chapter 4 (ante, p 71).
3 Land Charges Act 1972, s 2(5).
4 Ante, p 71.
5 See H.W.R. Wade, [1956] CLJ 216 at 225f.
6 See *Poster v Slough Estates Ltd* [1968] 1 WLR 1515 at 1520C-D, 1521F per Cross J.
7 *Poster v Slough Estates Ltd* [1968] 1 WLR 1515 at 1521B-C. See G. McCormack, [1990] Conv 275 at 280f.
8 *Shiloh Spinners Ltd v Harding* [1973] AC 691 at 721G. See [1973] CLJ 218 (Paul Fairest). The enforceability of such a right of entry against a later purchaser of the land therefore turns on the equitable doctrine of notice (post, pp 278, 871).
9 *Report of the Committee on Land Charges*, para 16.

(ii) Estoppel-based easements Many of the problems caused by Class D(iii) were exemplified in their most pressing form in *E.R. Ives Investment Ltd v High.*[10] Here the defendant, D, and X were neighbours. X began to construct on his property a block of flats the foundations of which marginally encroached upon D's land. D agreed to ignore the unintentional incursion on condition that he was granted a right of way for his car across X's yard. This right of way was not granted by deed and therefore constituted a merely equitable easement. As such it was never registered by D as a Class D(iii) land charge against the name of X. X later conveyed the fee simple estate in his property to Y, who knew of the earlier agreement. Y also knew that D had more recently built a garage on his own land which was accessible only across X's yard.[11] Moreover D contributed part of the cost of resurfacing this yard. Y in his turn sold and conveyed the legal estate to the plaintiff, P, expressly subject to the right of way enjoyed by D across the yard. P subsequently brought an action against D for trespass to the yard, claiming that D's equitable easement should have been registered against X as a Class D(iii) land charge. Since it had not been so registered, P contended, the charge now became void notwithstanding the actual knowledge which P had received.[12]

On these facts the merits of the case pointed clearly in favour of D. As an honest but uninformed layman it had never occurred to him that the agreement informally reached with X—largely as an act of grace on D's part—required formal protection vis à vis third parties. In contrast P was an investment company which had bought with full knowledge of the agreement and was quite prepared to plead the statute in order to further its own unconscionable dealing. It was not surprising that under these circumstances the Court of Appeal strained to uphold the county court judgment at first instance in favour of D.[13]

Danckwerts and Winn LJJ agreed that D's equitable right of way was rendered statutorily void against P for non-registration notwithstanding that P had purchased with actual notice of D's rights.[14] However, both judges held that P was 'estopped' (or precluded) from pleading non-registration by D in view of the past history of acquiescence in D's expenditure on the building of a garage in a particular position and on the resurfacing of the yard which now belonged to P.[15] This acquiescence, together with the doctrine of 'mutual benefit and burden',[16] created an 'equity' in favour of D which

10 [1967] 2 QB 379. See (1967) 31 Conv (NS) 338 (F.R. Crane).
11 Compare *Sutton v O'Kane* [1973] 2 NZLR 304 at 333.
12 Ante, p 119.
13 'Could anything be more monstrous and inequitable afterwards to deprive [D] of the benefit of what he has done?' ([1967] 2 QB 379 at 399F per Danckwerts LJ).
14 [1967] 2 QB 379 at 399B-C, 403E-F.
15 For a fuller treatment of estoppel, see Chapter 11 (post, p 312). Compare *Sutton v O'Kane* [1973] 2 NZLR 304 at 334.
16 This doctrine is premised on the basis that when adjoining owners of land enter into a deed to secure continuing mutual rights and benefits, neither of them can take the benefit of the agreement and throw over the burden of it. This result, in at least one of the formulations of the doctrine of 'mutual benefit and burden', applies not only to the original parties but also to their successors in title, so that any successor who takes the continuing benefit must take it subject to the continuing burden. (There is substantial doubt as to the precise ambit which may properly be attributed to the doctrine (post, p 1136)).

bound all subsequent purchasers who took the land with actual notice.[17] The 'equity' thus raised, unlike the equitable right of way, was not liable to registration under the Land Charges Act and was therefore unaffected by D's failure to register his easement.[18]

The third member of the Court of Appeal, Lord Denning MR, went even further. He held not merely that the estoppel prevented P from asserting a legally valid answer based on want of registration, but that D's equitable easement had not even been registrable in the first place. Lord Denning took the view that Class D(iii) embraces only those equitable easements which prior to the 1925 legislation ranked as legal interests in land but which were by virtue of that legislation relegated to merely equitable status. D's rights, however, arose directly from equitable doctrines based on acquiescence and the mutuality of benefit and burden and would, even before 1925, have ranked as rights subsisting only in equity.[19] Not being caught by the registration provisions of the Land Charges Act, they were governed simply by the traditional doctrine of notice.[20]

As Lord Denning observed,[1] the decision in *E.R. Ives Investment Ltd v High* illustrates the willingness of the courts to cut back the scope of the interests registrable under Class D(iii).[2] However, Lord Denning found this restrictive tendency 'not disturbing'[3] and moreover to be wholly in keeping with the Roxburgh Committee's proposal that Class D(iii) charges should be abandoned altogether. The Court of Appeal judgments in *E.R. Ives Investment Ltd v High* underscore the vagueness of the category of charges falling within Class D(iii). It seems clear that at least some equitable easements may also be analysed in terms of non-registrable estoppel-based rights which turn on the orthodox application of the concept of notice.[4]

(5) Class E

Class E land charges comprise annuities arising before 1926 but not registered until after the Land Charges Act 1925 came into force.

(6) Class F

Class F land charges comprise charges in respect of spousal rights of occupation which arise pursuant to the Matrimonial Homes Acts 1967 and 1983. Quite

17 Post, p 365.
18 See also *Classic Communications Ltd v Lascar* (1985) 21 DLR (4th) 579 at 589f (post, p 353).
19 [1967] 2 QB 379 at 395E–396B. See C.V. Davidge, (1937) 53 LQR 259 at 260.
20 See also P.V. Baker, (1972) 88 LQR 336; D. Yates, (1974) 37 MLR 87. For reasoning similar to that of Lord Denning MR, see *Montague v Long* (1972) 24 P & CR 240 at 247f.
1 [1967] 2 QB 379 at 396C.
2 See also *Poster v Slough Estates Ltd* [1968] 1 WLR 1515 at 1521B (ante, p 18); *Shiloh Spinners Ltd v Harding* [1973] AC 691 at 721G (ante, p 73).
3 [1967] 2 QB 379 at 396C.
4 This has in turn provoked the criticism that estoppel interests fall outside the 'necessarily tidy world of the conveyancer', in that they tend to 'diminish both certainty of title and the availability of land on the market' (see F.R. Crane, (1967) 31 Conv (NS) 332 at 341f). In 1976 the Law Commission recommended that in registered land the kind of 'equity' raised in *E.R. Ives Investment Ltd v High* should be protectible by entry on the register of the title affected (see Law Commission, Published Working Paper No 67: *Land Registration (Fourth Paper)* (April 1976), paras 64ff).

independently of title or beneficial ownership,[5] the individual members of a family may well have rights of occupation in the family home which are rooted either in common law or in statute. It is with the latter kind of entitlement that Class F is concerned.

(a) Common law rights to occupy the family home

It has long been clear at common law that a wife has a right to occupy the matrimonial home.[6] Her entitlement in this respect is somewhat anomalous. If the home is owned by her husband, she resides there not as a trespasser nor even as a licensee,[7] but in virtue of her status as a wife.[8] Her common law right of occupation has often been said to be sui generis,[9] in that the right to be housed by her husband arises from the fact of marriage itself and survives today only as a residual element of some outmoded dependency-related notion of spousal maintenance.[10] Nowadays in an era of greater sex equality, it must surely be the case that the spousal right to be housed has become mutual and may therefore be claimed by either husband or wife.[11]

(i) Effect of the spousal common law right The spouse's common law right of occupation is binding only on the other spouse and is not enforceable against third parties.[12] If, however, the right of occupation is threatened by an impending disposition of the home by the homeowner-spouse, the transaction may be restrained by court injunction.[13]

(ii) Restricted scope of the common law right The common law right of occupation in the family home is available only to a de iure spouse. No similar entitlement exists in favour of any other family member, whether that person be a de facto spouse,[14] a parent or parent-in-law, or indeed any other relative or dependant of the homeowner.[15] Although the point is not entirely clear, it seems that even a minor child cannot claim any right of occupation based

5 It is now clearly established in English law that rights of occupation in land can derive from equitable entitlement under a trust for sale. A beneficial co-owner behind such a trust of the family home has, qua beneficiary, an intrinsic right to occupy that property in common with any other similarly entitled beneficiaries. See Chapter 14 (post, p 546).

6 This does not necessarily mean that the wife has any right at common law to insist on sharing residential accommodation in which her husband has set up a new home with a different partner (*Nanda v Nanda* [1968] P 351 at 354C, 357D-E). See also *Hall v King* (1988) 55 P & CR 307 at 310.

7 *National Provincial Bank Ltd v Ainsworth* [1965] AC 1175 at 1232F.

8 *Hall v King* (1988) 55 P & CR 307 at 309 per Lord Donaldson MR.

9 *National Provincial Bank Ltd v Ainsworth* [1965] AC 1175 at 1232F per Lord Upjohn.

10 See *Gurasz v Gurasz* [1970] P 11 at 16B-C.

11 See eg *Harman v Glencross* [1985] Fam 49 at 58B-C per Ewbank J.

12 *National Provincial Bank Ltd v Ainsworth* [1965] AC 1175; *Gurasz v Gurasz* [1970] P 11 at 16C. The wife's common law right cannot be enforced if the home is owned jointly by the husband and a third party (*Chaudhry v Chaudhry* [1987] 1 FLR 347 at 350G-H).

13 *Lee v Lee* [1952] 2 QB 489 at 491f. Such an injunction is available unless the husband provides his wife with reasonably suitable alternative accommodation.

14 A de facto spouse obviously cannot claim any right of occupation derived from the fact of marriage.

15 *Hall v King* (1988) 55 P & CR 307 at 309 per Lord Donaldson MR. See also (1989) 105 LQR 9 (A. Bainham).

on status. Except in cases of beneficial entitlement or court order, such rights of residence as are enjoyed by a child of the family appear to depend on the concept of revocable licence both before and after his attainment of the age of majority.[16]

(b) Statutory 'rights of occupation'

The spouse's common law right of occupation in the matrimonial home is now reinforced by statute. The Matrimonial Homes Act 1967 conferred statutory 'rights of occupation' on certain categories of spouse, and these rights are now consolidated and extended by the Matrimonial Homes Act 1983.[17] The rights created by this legislation are entirely sex-neutral, with the result that they may in appropriate cases be invoked by either husband or wife, but the statute confers no rights of occupation on family members other than a spouse.[18]

(i) Nature of the statutory 'rights of occupation' The Matrimonial Homes Act 1983 confers on specified categories of qualifying spouse a bundle of rights known collectively as statutory 'rights of occupation'. In terms of section 1(1) of the Act a qualifying spouse, if in occupation of the matrimonial home, has a 'right not to be evicted or excluded from the dwelling house or any part thereof by the other spouse' except in pursuance of a court order.[19] Furthermore, if not in occupation of the matrimonial home, a qualifying spouse has a 'right with the leave of the court . . . to enter into and occupy the dwelling house'.[20]

The statutory 'rights of occupation' are purely personal rights[1] and in

16 *Metropolitan Properties Co Ltd v Cronan* (1982) 44 P & CR 1 at 8. See also *Waterhouse v Waterhouse* (1905) 94 LT 133 at 134; *Stevens v Stevens* (1907) 24 TLR 20 at 21; *Egan v Egan* [1975] Ch 218 at 221D. The minor child's licence-based rights have been supplemented not by the common law but by statute. The notion of an enduring 'parental responsibility' confirmed by Children Act 1989, ss 2(1), (2), 3(1), provides a statutory basis of a prima facie entitlement to shelter in the home of one or other parent.

17 The Law Commission has recently recommended that the Matrimonial Homes Act 1983 be repealed, but that the framework of the existing statutory 'rights of occupation' (and the mechanism for registration thereof) should be re-enacted in virtually unmodified form (Law Commission, *Family Home: Domestic Violence and Occupation of the Family Home* (Law Com No 207, 7 May 1992), para 1.5). See Draft Family Homes and Domestic Violence Bill, clauses 4, 5 (Law Com No 207, Appendix A), in which 'rights of occupation' under the 1983 Act have been renamed 'matrimonial home rights'.

18 Compare the equivalent Scottish legislation, which does apply under certain circumstances to a 'cohabiting couple'. The Matrimonial Homes (Family Protection) (Scotland) Act 1981, s 18 empowers the court to grant 'occupancy rights' to a 'non-entitled partner' for a limited period where 'a man and a woman are living with each other as if they were man and wife'.

19 Matrimonial Homes Act 1983, s 1(1)(a). See generally O. Kahn-Freund, (1970) 33 MLR 601 at 610ff.

20 Matrimonial Homes Act 1983, s 1(1)(b). A spouse is regarded as still 'in occupation' of the matrimonial home even though temporarily absent in hospital (*Hoggett v Hoggett* (1980) 39 P & CR 121 at 128).

1 See *Wroth v Tyler* [1974] Ch 30 at 46F-G, where Megarry J described the rights as comprising 'a personal and non-assignable statutory right . . . the right may be said to be one which readily fits into no category known to conveyancers before 1967; the phrase sui generis seems apt, but of little help.'

themselves have no binding impact on purchasers of the matrimonial home unless registered in the appropriate manner.[2] The recipient of the statutory rights retains these rights for the duration of the marriage or until the other spouse himself ceases to have any beneficial, contractual or statutory right to occupy the home.[3] A spouse may at any time renounce his statutory rights in whole or part by means of a written release.[4]

(ii) Categories of spouse covered by the statutory rights The statutory 'rights of occupation' are available to any spouse who cannot claim a right of occupation by virtue of any beneficial interest or under any contract or statute, but whose spouse is entitled to occupy a dwelling house on one or other of these bases.[5] The range of the Matrimonial Homes Act 1983 is best illustrated by reference to the various patterns of ownership shown in *Fig.* 14.

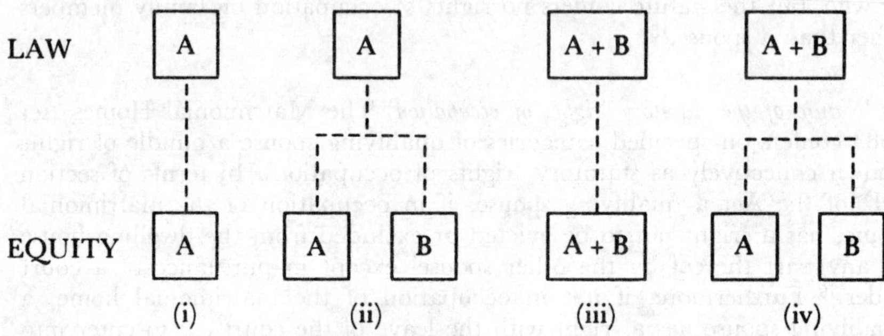

Fig. 14

In superficial terms the statutory rights are restricted by section 1(1) of the 1983 Act to those spouses who have no right to occupy the family home other than the right of occupation derived at common law from the status of marriage. Indeed the scheme of the Matrimonial Homes Act was originally directed towards the protection of 'the bare wife'[6] who was wholly denuded of all proprietary rights in the home (whether legal or equitable). Thus, if A and B are married, B will enjoy the statutory 'rights of occupation' in case (i) above (*Fig.* 14).

The initial ambit of the Matrimonial Homes Act was extended in 1970[7] to confer the statutory 'rights of occupation' on a spouse who owns an equitable

2 Post, p 159. The enforcement of one spouse's statutory rights against the other spouse does not depend on any kind of registration (*Hoggett v Hoggett* (1980) 39 P & CR 121 at 127).
3 Matrimonial Homes Act 1983, s 1(10).
4 Matrimonial Homes Act 1983, s 6(1).
5 Matrimonial Homes Act 1983, s 1(1). It is not, for instance, necessary that the entitled spouse should own the legal title in the matrimonial home, since this may be held by a third party on trust to give effect to a beneficial interest in the entitled spouse (see Matrimonial Homes Act 1983, s 1(8)). For the purpose of determining whether one spouse has an existing right to occupy a dwelling house, any right to possession conferred on a mortgagee by virtue of his mortgage is to be disregarded (Matrimonial Homes Act 1983, s 8(1)).
6 This graphic phrase was frequently used by Lord Denning MR (see *Gurasz v Gurasz* [1970] P 11 at 17D; *Williams & Glyn's Bank Ltd v Boland* [1979] Ch 312 at 328C).
7 Matrimonial Proceedings and Property Act 1970, s 38.

but not a legal interest in the home.[8] Such a spouse is brought within the framework of the parent statute through a fiction which effectively confers statutory rights by suspending existing rights. An equitable owner is, for present purposes, treated as if he or she were not entitled to occupy the dwelling house by virtue of his or her beneficial entitlement.[9] Thus denuded of any proprietary right of occupation, the equitable co-owner comes neatly within the terms of section 1(1) of the 1983 Act. Statutory 'rights of occupation' are, accordingly, enjoyed by B in case (ii) above (see *Fig.* 14).

The only cases in which 'rights of occupation' are not granted by the Matrimonial Homes Act are those in which an equitable owner is also entitled to the legal estate. Thus, for instance, no statutory rights are created for either A or B in cases (iii) and (iv) above (see *Fig.* 14), where A and B are jointly entitled to the legal estate in the matrimonial home and are respectively joint tenants and tenants in common of the equitable interest in that property. In both of these cases the occupation of A and B is already adequately protected by reason of their legal co-ownership and no further protection need be sought through the artificial intervention of statute.[10]

(iii) Property to which the statutory rights apply 'Rights of occupation' arise under the Matrimonial Homes Act 1983 only in respect of a 'dwelling house',[11] a term which is defined as including inter alia 'any building or part thereof which is occupied as a dwelling'.[12] The property in relation to which the statutory rights are claimed must have served, at least for some period, as a matrimonial home of the spouses in question.[13] However, given that these basic preconditions are fulfilled, it is irrelevant whether the matrimonial home to which the statutory rights attach is held by freehold or leasehold title, or whether, if the property is held on a tenancy, that tenancy is contractual, statutory, assured or secure.

(iv) Judicial regulation of the statutory rights Where one spouse has statutory 'rights of occupation' in the matrimonial home[14] and even where the spouses are joint tenants of the legal estate in that property,[15] it is open to either spouse to apply for a court order regulating the occupation of the home.[16]

8 See Chapter 12 (post, p 371) for an examination of the circumstances which may generate beneficial ownership in the family home.
9 Matrimonial Homes Act 1983, s 1(11).
10 See *Harman v Glencross* [1986] Fam 81 at 90D, 94A.
11 Matrimonial Homes Act 1983, s 1(1).
12 Matrimonial Homes Act 1983, s 10(1).
13 Matrimonial Homes Act 1983, s 1(10). See *Whittingham v Whittingham* [1979] Fam 9 at 16B; *Kemmis v Kemmis* [1988] 1 WLR 1307 at 1320H–1321A. The 'matrimonial home rights' proposed by the Law Commission (ante, p 155) are envisaged as having a slightly broader coverage, being applicable to a dwelling-house which at some time was *intended* by both spouses to serve as a matrimonial home even if in fact it was never so used (Law Com No 207, paras 4.4, 7.9). See Draft Family Homes and Domestic Violence Bill, clause 4(6) (Law Com No 207, Appendix A).
14 Matrimonial Homes Act 1983, s 1(2).
15 Matrimonial Homes Act 1983, s 9(1).
16 The Law Commission has recommended that a similarly expansive power of regulation should apply to the exercise of the proposed 'matrimonial home rights' (Law Com No 207, paras 4.2, 7.7). See Draft Family Homes and Domestic Violence Bill, clause 7 (Law Com No 207, Appendix A).

The court may make such order as it thinks 'just and reasonable', having regard to 'the conduct of the spouses in relation to each other and otherwise, to their respective needs and financial resources, to the needs of any children and to all the circumstances of the case'.[17] The court may declare, enforce, restrict or terminate the statutory 'rights of occupation',[18] or prohibit, suspend or restrict the exercise by either spouse of the right to occupy the home.[19] The court's power to regulate 'rights of occupation' in these ways has become both important and controversial in the context of domestic violence.[20]

(c) The 'deserted wife's equity'

It is now clear in retrospect that a spouse's common law right of occupation has never been properly capable of exerting any binding impact per se on any person except the other spouse. The purely personal nature of this right is such that it has no effect on any third party to whom the matrimonial home may be transferred or mortgaged. This, of course, raises a difficult problem where the legal owner of a matrimonial home transacts with a stranger in relation to his title in the property. It becomes very probable in such a case that the occupation right enjoyed by the legal owner's spouse will be destroyed by the dealing.

It was precisely in order to protect occupation claims in the family home against the assertion of rights by third parties that during the 1950s the Court of Appeal developed the doctrine of the 'deserted wife's equity'.

(i) The doctrine The doctrine of the 'deserted wife's equity' held that if a husband abandoned his wife, leaving her in occupation of the family home, the deserted wife acquired at the date of desertion an 'equity' which she could successfully oppose against any third party to whom her husband sold or mortgaged the home. In this way the common law rights of occupation enjoyed by deserted wives were binding on any purchaser who took with notice of those rights.[1]

(ii) Disadvantages The doctrine of the 'deserted wife's equity', although motivated by strong family considerations,[2] proved eventually to be unacceptable in terms of conventional concepts of property law. The 'deserted wife's equity' became a nightmare for practising conveyancers since it

17 Matrimonial Homes Act 1983, s 1(3). Under the proposed new scheme of 'matrimonial home rights', the court is directed to have regard to similar criteria, with particular reference to the 'respective housing needs and resources of the parties and of any relevant child' and 'the likely effect . . . on the health, safety or well-being of the parties and of any relevant child' (Law Com No 207, paras 4.33, 7.14). See Draft Family Homes and Domestic Violence Bill, clause 7(5). A child's interests assume a mandatory importance if there is any risk that the child 'is likely to suffer significant harm' (Draft Family Homes and Domestic Violence Bill, clause 7(6)).
18 Matrimonial Homes Act 1983, s 1(2)(a).
19 Matrimonial Homes Act 1983, s 1(2)(b).
20 See *Richards v Richards* [1984] AC 174.
1 For the development of this doctrine, see *Bendall v McWhirter* [1952] 2 QB 466 at 475ff; *Ferris v Weaven* [1952] 2 All ER 233 at 236F-H; *Lee v Lee* [1952] 2 QB 489 at 492; *Jess B Woodcock & Sons Ltd v Hobbs* [1955] 1 WLR 152 at 154ff; *Westminster Bank Ltd v Lee* [1956] Ch 7 at 17ff. See also F.R. Crane, (1955) 19 Conv (NS) 343.
2 Ante, p 154.

represented an unregistrable, non-overreachable incumbrance which could bind purchasers on the basis of even constructive notice.[3] In effect the doctrine imposed an embarrassing onus of enquiry on any third party entering into any transaction (eg sale, lease or mortgage) with a man whose household included a resident adult female. In order to be safe from adverse claims to occupy, the purchaser had to inquire, first, whether that woman was the wife of the vendor/lessor/mortgagor and, second, whether the marriage (if there was one) was happy and stable.[4] The problem of enquiry was far-reaching. Where a husband's bank overdraft was secured on the matrimonial home, the bank might even be required to make enquiries as to his matrimonial behaviour before honouring his cheques.[5]

(iii) Rejection of the doctrine The doctrine of the 'deserted wife's equity' was finally destroyed in *National Provincial Bank Ltd v Ainsworth.*[6] Here the House of Lords conclusively rejected the idea that the deserted wife's right of occupation in the matrimonial home was anything more than a personal right enforceable against the husband alone. Her common law right of occupation has no impact on third parties.

(d) Registration of statutory 'rights of occupation'

The almost immediate consequence of the House of Lords' ruling in *National Provincial Bank Ltd v Ainsworth* was the enactment of the Matrimonial Homes Act 1967 (now consolidated as the Matrimonial Homes Act 1983), which was designed to fulfil some of the purposes previously served by the judge-made doctrine of the 'deserted wife's equity'. The Act conferred statutory 'rights of occupation' in the matrimonial home on certain categories of spouse, but these rights are, of course, rights *in personam* and effective only against the other spouse. However, the Matrimonial Homes Act provides a process of registration by which mere rights *in personam* may effectively be transformed into rights *in rem.*[7]

(i) Process of registration Where one spouse enjoys statutory 'rights of occupation' under section 1(1) of the Matrimonial Homes Act 1983, these rights constitute a registrable charge on any beneficial estate or interest held

3 See *Rock Permanent Building Society v Kettlewell* (1956) 168 Estates Gazette 397 where Harman J described the 'equity' as 'a new terror in the surveyor's professional life' and as 'a sore subject between lawyers . . . a thorn in the flesh of the equitable branch of the law . . .'

4 See the trenchant criticisms expressed in *Westminster Bank Ltd v Lee* [1956] Ch 7 at 22; *National Provincial Bank Ltd v Hastings Car Mart Ltd* [1964] Ch 665 at 699 per Russell LJ; *National Provincial Bank Ltd v Ainsworth* [1965] AC 1175 at 1234C-E per Lord Upjohn, 1249A-B per Lord Wilberforce. See also R.E. Megarry, (1952) 68 LQR 379 at 383.

5 See *Wroth v Tyler* [1974] Ch 30 at 42G.

6 [1965] AC 1175. See O.Kahn-Freund, (1970) 33 MLR 601 at 608ff; F.R. Crane, (1965) 29 Conv (NS) 254 at 464.

7 The Matrimonial Homes Act thus 'uses the machinery of publicity in order to transform the internal right of enjoyment into a modification of title' (O. Kahn-Freund, (1970) 33 MLR 601 at 610).

by the other spouse.[8] In the case of unregistered land a Matrimonial Homes Act charge may be registered against the name of the relevant estate owner as a Class F land charge,[9] but a spouse may never register a charge in respect of more than one dwelling-house at any one time.[10] The statutory charge may be entered notwithstanding that the registering spouse is not currently in occupation (eg because he or she has been expelled from the home or has indeed left the home voluntarily).[11]

(ii) Effect of registration Once protected by entry in the appropriate register, a spouse's statutory 'rights of occupation' become binding on and enforceable against almost all third parties.[12] The one notable exception to this principle relates to a trustee in bankruptcy of the spouse against whom registration is effected. Spousal 'rights of occupation', even though duly registered, are at best effective for only a limited period against such a trustee in bankruptcy.[13] The mere registration of statutory rights cannot preclude indefinitely the possibility that the matrimonial home may have to be sold with vacant possession in order to meet the outstanding claims of the bankrupt spouse's creditors. The incidence of bankruptcy is, of course, considerably increased in circumstances of marital breakdown, not least because a husband's financial resources may be impossibly stretched by the strain of attempting to support two family units. Few men can afford successive polygamy. In the immediate context, as so often in land law, the commercial interest (as represented here by the husband's creditors) prevails over the family interest (as typically represented here by a deserted family's need of residential security).[14]

Apart from the case of insolvency, however, due registration has the universal effect of securing the registering spouse's 'rights of occupation'

8 Matrimonial Homes Act 1983, s 2(1). 'Parliament has looked with particular favour upon a spouse's right to occupy the matrimonial home and has given it the status of an equitable interest ... with consequential priority over subsequent equitable interests created by the other spouse ... provided that the owner of the subsequent interest has notice, and notice is given by the registration of a Class F land charge or the equivalent notice on the title in the case of registered land' (*Harman v Glencross* [1986] Fam 81 at 94A-B).

9 Land Charges Act 1972, s 2(1), (7). In the case of registered land the statutory 'rights of occupation' may be entered by notice as a minor interest affecting the appropriate registered title (Matrimonial Homes Act 1983, s 2(8)(a), post, p 183). Under the Draft Family Homes and Domestic Violence Bill, 'matrimonial home rights' are intended to be similarly registrable, but an order granting occupation rights to certain non-entitled applicants (post, p 163) will confer purely personal rights which are incapable of registration and cannot bind purchasers (Law Com No 207, paras 4.19, 7.13).

10 Matrimonial Homes Act 1983, s 3.

11 *Watts v Waller* [1973] QB 153 at 175G. However, it is an improper use of the registration machinery to register a charge not for the purpose of protecting and preserving a spouse's right to 'enter into and occupy' the matrimonial home, but for some ulterior motive such as to freeze the proceeds of sale of the property (see *Barnett v Hassett* [1981] 1 WLR 1385 at 1388H, 1389C).

12 Law of Property Act 1925, s 198(1) (ante, p 118). In relation to registered land the equivalent effect is secured by Land Registration Act 1925, ss 20(1), 23 (post, p 186).

13 Insolvency Act 1986, s 336(2)-(5), displacing the effect of Matrimonial Homes Act 1983, s 2(7) (post, p 603).

14 Post, pp 599, 604. There is here an irony of legislative history. The judge-made doctrine of the 'deserted wife's equity' held that the deserted wife's right of occupation was fully opposable against even her husband's trustee in bankruptcy (see *Bendall v McWhirter* [1952] 2 QB 466 at 478, but compare *National Provincial Bank Ltd v Ainsworth* [1965] AC 1175 at 1240B).

against derogation by third parties—except in one controversial situation. The court's power to regulate the exercise of spouses' statutory 'rights of occupation'[15] is expressed sufficiently widely to survive even a transfer of title to a purchaser of the matrimonial home.[16] In *Kaur v Gill,*[17] for example, it was accepted by all concerned that a purchaser was bound by a registration entered by the vendor's wife shortly before completion of the contract of sale.[18] Notwithstanding her subsisting registration, the Court of Appeal held that it still had jurisdiction to vary or terminate the exercise of the wife's rights vis à vis the new owner of the property.[19] A majority in the Court agreed, moreover, that in the exercise of this jurisdiction it was proper to take account of any special factors affecting the purchaser. Such factors comprised, in other words, an integral component of the totality of circumstance to which the court's attention is statutorily directed.[20] In balancing the respective circumstances of the parties in *Kaur v Gill*, the Court of Appeal declined to uphold the wife's registered 'rights of occupation' as against a purchaser who was blind and whose immediate need of accommodation was felt to be more pressing than hers.[1]

The decision in *Kaur v Gill* is thus a surprising reminder that the registration of a Class F charge does not operate as a permanent guarantee of security of tenure for the incumbrancer, although the circumstances in which registered rights will be varied in favour of a purchaser are likely to arise only rarely.

(iii) Consequence of non-registration It is a clear consequence of a spouse's failure to register the statutory 'rights of occupation' that these rights become ineffective against a purchaser for value of any interest in the land.[2]

(iv) Registration for ulterior motives A Matrimonial Homes Act registration can be effected quite unilaterally. The ease with which a charge can be registered, when combined with the potentially hostile impact of such a registration, has often provoked the criticism that the Matrimonial Homes Act facilitates

15 Matrimonial Homes Act 1983, s 1(3), ante, p 158.

16 Any order in favour of one spouse made pursuant to the court's powers under section 1 of the Matrimonial Homes Act 1983 normally binds third parties deriving title under the other spouse (Matrimonial Homes Act 1983, s 2(5)(a)). It seems that such third parties may themselves apply for variation or termination of a spouse's subsisting 'rights of occupation' (see Matrimonial Homes Act 1983, s 2(5)(b); *Kaur v Gill* [1988] Fam 110 at 116C, 117D-E, 120H-121A).

17 [1988] Fam 110. See [1988] CLJ 355 (C. Harpum); [1988] Conv 295 (M. Welstead); (1988) 52 MLR 110 (P. Sparkes).

18 [1988] Fam 110 at 113G-H. The purchaser failed to discover the charge prior to completion because his solicitor had carried out only a telephonic search of the register—this form of search conferring, of course, no priority period for completion of the transaction.

19 The case concerned a registered title, but the operation of the Matrimonial Homes Act 1983 would not in any relevant respect have been different in relation to unregistered land.

20 [1988] Fam 110 at 116D-117A per Dillon LJ, 117E-H per Bingham LJ. Sir Denys Buckley entered a strong dissent (see [1988] Fam 110 at 121C-D).

1 The wife was at this time housed, although not particularly satisfactorily, in local authority accommodation held by a relative ([1988] Fam 110 at 113E-F).

2 Land Charges Act 1972, s 4(8) (ante, p 119). The same result is achieved even more stringently in the context of registered title (see Land Registration Act 1925, ss 20(1), 59(6) (post, p 186)). In the latter context there is no possibility that the unprotected spousal rights may subsequently be claimed as an overriding interest even on behalf of a spouse who remains 'in actual occupation' of the matrimonial home (see Matrimonial Homes Act 1983, s 2(8)(b), post, p 211).

'spite' registrations. Megarry J observed in *Wroth v Tyler*[3] that the legislation has 'put into the hands of all spouses with statutory rights of occupation a weapon of great power and flexibility.' Particularly if registration occurs at an inconvenient moment in the process of contract and conveyance, the registering spouse is presented with a relatively simple, speedy and secret means of frustrating any proposed sale of the matrimonial home with which he does not agree.[4] The stubborn or ruthless spouse is thus enabled to force on his partner a purely private and unshared desire for domestic inertia or, even worse, is enabled to require the other spouse to buy off the charge. Considerations such as these led Megarry J in *Wroth v Tyler*[5] to condemn the Matrimonial Homes Act charge as 'a companion in obloquy for what in *Keeves v Dean*. . .Scrutton LJ stigmatised as monstrum horrendum informe ingens.'[6]

(v) Release of rights and cancellation of registration The Matrimonial Homes Act 'rights of occupation', even if registered, cease to have effect on the death of the spouse against whose estate they are registered[7] and normally come to an end on the termination of a marriage otherwise than by death.[8] There is provision for cancellation of any registration of the statutory rights in either of these events or if the court itself exercises its discretion to terminate one spouse's 'rights of occupation'.[9] A spouse may also 'release' his 'rights of occupation' in writing,[10] or may by writing agree that his 'rights of occupation' should be postponed behind some later charge on the same estate or interest.[11]

It is, moreover, an implied term of any contract for the sale of the home with vacant possession that the vendor will before completion procure the cancellation of any registration of subsisting 'rights of occupation'.[12] Considerable problems ensue if the vendor fails to secure the release of his spouse's 'rights of occupation' and the cancellation of any existing registration. In *Wroth v Tyler*,[13] for instance, a wife had secretly entered her rights on the register of her husband's title on the day following his exchange of contracts. Her action had the disastrous consequence of exposing him to liability towards his purchaser for breach of contract. The wife, who had not wanted to move house, obstinately declined to remove the entry. This refusal eventually brought about the bankruptcy of her husband (who was

3 [1974] Ch 30 at 46B.
4 See *Wroth v Tyler* [1974] Ch 30 (infra). Compare, however, *Barnett v Hassett* [1981] 1 WLR 1385 at 1388H, 1389C (ante, p 118).
5 [1974] Ch 30 at 64A-B.
6 Post, p 876.
7 Matrimonial Homes Act 1983, s 2(4)(a).
8 Matrimonial Homes Act 1983, s 2(4)(b).
9 Matrimonial Homes Act 1983, s 5(1).
10 Matrimonial Homes Act 1983, s 6(1).
11 Matrimonial Homes Act 1983, s 6(3). A mortgagee who obtains priority in this way is entitled to exercise his power of sale free of any spousal 'rights of occupation', although difficulties may arise if the mortgagee failed to warn the spouse releasing the rights of the need for independent legal advice (post, p 968).
12 Matrimonial Homes Act 1983, s 4(1). A solicitor may be liable in negligence for failing to ensure the appropriate cancellation of rights (see *Holmes v Kennard & Son* (1984) 49 P & CR 202 at 210f).
13 [1974] Ch 30.

unable to pay the contractual damages), with the ironic result that her rights were defeated in any event by her husband's trustee in bankruptcy.[14]

(e) The future of the Matrimonial Homes Act

From the very enactment of the Matrimonial Homes Act 1967 the scheme of statutory 'rights of occupation' has been fraught with difficulty. The Law Commission's recent proposal for the replacement of the Matrimonial Homes Act by a Family Homes and Domestic Violence Act does nothing to deflect the substantial criticisms which have been directed at the legislative scheme.[15] Under the Commission's recommendations, the current regime of 'rights of occupation' would simply be translated into a virtually identical regime of 'matrimonial home rights' as part of a wider regulatory scheme for the governance of domestic discord between spouses and cohabiting parties.

(i) Mass invalidation of charges The consequence of non-registration of the Matrimonial Homes Act 'rights of occupation' reveals one curious and significant feature of the benefits supposedly conferred by this legislation. In the case of most other registrable incumbrances in respect of land, the plain statutory expectation is that registration will be effected in all situations where registration is appropriate, on pain of the dire penalty that rights left unregistered will become ineffective against third parties.[16] It can hardly have been the case, however, that the legislature contemplated that there would be mass registrations in respect of all matrimonial homes, regardless of the stability of the relevant marriage relationship. Such vigilance on the part of those who enjoy Matrimonial Homes Act 'rights of occupation' would have the disastrous effect of swamping the registries with literally millions of applications for registration. In *Wroth v Tyler*[17] Megarry J thought that 'it would not be surprising if in fact the Act in the main has been operating on a basis of the mass invalidation of the statutory charges for want of registration, with registration being effected only in cases of actual or impending disputes.'

(ii) Lack of public awareness It seems anomalous that the operation of a statute of such wide social significance should depend on the ignorance or apathy of the citizens whose protection it is designed to secure. A further irony consists in the fact that the registration of spousal rights of occupation is often abused for malicious purposes by those who need protection least, but

14 Matrimonial Homes Act 1983, s 2(7), but see now Insolvency Act 1986, s 336(2)-(5) (post, p 603). As Megarry J observed ([1974] Ch 30 at 64F), 'there should be displayed in every conveyancer's office the minatory legend Cave uxorem'. The Law Commission has, however, defended the wife's exercise of her right to register her rights of occupation, arguing that such registration is 'not rendered an abuse merely because it may interfere with smooth conveyancing. It is an essential step in protecting her substantive rights and we think that to introduce restrictions on that exercise would be contrary to the policy of the Act' (see Law Commission, *Family Law: Third Report on Family Property: The Matrimonial Home (Co-ownership and Occupation Rights) and Household Goods* (Law Com No 86, June 1978), para 2.83). See also D.J. Hayton, *The Femme Fatale in Conveyancing Practice*, (1974) 38 Conv (NS) 110.

15 Ante, p 155.

16 Ante, p 118.

17 [1974] Ch 30 at 46A-B.

is frequently not effected by those who stand most clearly in need of the protection which registration provides.[18] This raises at least some question as to the desirability of legislation which in practice requires that protection of occupation should depend not only on a high level of awareness of the legal need to register rights but also on a willingness to undertake an 'essentially hostile type of proceeding'.[19] As Ormrod LJ indicated in *Williams & Glyn's Bank Ltd v Boland*,[20] the remedy offered by the Matrimonial Homes Act is 'usually "too little and too late"'.

(iii) Automatic co-ownership of the matrimonial home The fundamental difficulty associated with the Matrimonial Homes Act is the fact that an inherently worthwhile measure of reform has been substantially vitiated by the attempt to engraft family-based rights on to an existing system of registration of incumbrances governed by the general law of property. The problems which have arisen under the Matrimonial Homes Act are almost entirely attributable to the fact that this statute is not rooted unequivocally in family considerations such as those which underpin the homestead legislation in force in other parts of the Commonwealth.[1]

It is perhaps inevitable that the residential security of spouses will be assured only when the Matrimonial Homes Act 1983 finally gives way to a rule of automatic co-ownership of the legal estate in the matrimonial home during marriage—a regime not brought about by the application of commercialist principles of property law but resulting instead from the status of marriage. The social purpose of the current matrimonial homes legislation would be more effectively achieved through the statutory imposition of such a scheme of co-ownership.[2] The adoption of this solution would mean that no disposition of the legal estate could ever occur without the active participation of both spouses. Both would have to sign any document of transfer, lease or mortgage. A spouse's occupation of the matrimonial home would thus be rendered absolutely secure against hidden transactions with the title and there would be no need for any hostile registration to be effected where existing marital tension already threatens domestic harmony.

A principle of automatic co-ownership of the family home would cut clean through the difficulties which have been exposed in the operation of the Matrimonial Homes Act, but as yet no legislation incorporating this principle has been enacted in England. In 1988 the Law Commission proposed that future acquisitions of property by one spouse or by both spouses together should in the normal case result in a joint ownership of the property *in equity*, provided that the property was intended for their joint use or benefit.[3]

18 See *Williams & Glyn's Bank Ltd v Boland* [1979] Ch 312 at 328E-F per Lord Denning MR, who pointed out that the Matrimonial Homes Act 'was of precious little use to [the wife], at any rate when she was living at home in peace with her husband. She would never have heard of a Class F charge: and she would not have understood it if she had.'
19 *Williams & Glyn's Bank Ltd v Boland* [1979] Ch 312 at 339F.
20 [1979] Ch 312 at 339G.
1 For further discussion of homestead legislation, see Chapter 14, post, p 604.
2 Post, p 580.
3 Law Commission, *Family Law: Matrimonial Property* (Law Com No 175, December 1988), paras 4.1, 5.1. The Commission envisaged that the general rule of equitable co-ownership would give way to a contrary intention on the part of the spouse transferring or paying for the property, 'provided that the contrary intention is known to the other spouse'.

The major disadvantage attaching to this scheme of automatic *equitable* co-ownership is precisely the fact that the vulnerable spouse would not necessarily be a trustee of the legal estate and his or her rights as an equitable co-owner would therefore be overreachable by any later transaction in which capital moneys were paid to two trustees.[4]

4 Ante, p 102. The Law Commission, while conceding that 'in theory it would be possible to devise a scheme of statutory legal ownership', thought that such a scheme would be 'impossibly complex' (Law Com No 175, para 4.15).

CHAPTER 8

Registration of title

The present system of registration of title in England and Wales dates from the enactment of the Land Registration Act 1925. The registration scheme is administered by the Land Registry in accordance with the terms of the 1925 Act and in conformity with the Land Registration Rules prescribed pursuant to that legislation.[1] The Land Registration Act has always stood somewhat apart from the remainder of the 1925 legislation, both in style and (more obviously) in content, and it is probably fair to say that the scheme of title registration is not quite as tightly drawn as might perhaps have been desired.[2]

The operation of the Land Registration Act 1925 has become, in recent times, the subject of not only substantial criticism[3] but also a concerted programme of law reform. During the 1980s the Law Commission issued four reports directed towards a reformulation of major features of the 1925 Act. These efforts culminated in 1988 in the publication of a Draft Land Registration Bill,[4] designed to bring about a 'simplification and modernisation' of the original legislation without making any substantial alterations to the present law.[5] While this Bill has not yet been incorporated in statutory form, the movement towards change has gathered impetus from the Order in Council that all conveyances on sale taking effect in England and Wales on or after 1 December 1990 must be recorded in the Land Register pursuant to the Land Registration Act 1925.[6] The comprehensive extension of compulsory registration makes it all the more important that the scheme of title registration should operate efficiently and smoothly.

1 See Land Registration Rules 1925 (SR & O 1925/1093), as amended by Land Registration Rules 1989 (SI 1989/801).

2 While noting that the Land Registration Act 1925 has proved problematical in many respects, the Law Commission has attributed the relative lack of litigation over its provisions to the fact that the Land Registry 'has coped well with the defects in the legislation and has made the system work despite it rather than because of it.' See Law Commission, *Property Law: Fourth Report on Land Registration* (Law Com No 173, 8 November 1988), para 2.2.

3 See eg *In re White Rose Cottage* [1965] Ch 940 at 952B-E per Harman LJ; Law Com No 173, para 2.1.

4 Law Commission, Law Com No 173 (1988), Appendix.

5 Law Com No 173, para 2.3. The Draft Bill indeed managed to reduce the 148 sections of the 1925 Act to a 'much shorter statute' of 72 clauses (ibid, para 2.4).

6 See Land Registration, England and Wales: The Registration of Title Order 1989 (SI 1989/1347) (ante, p 96). Between 1925 and 1990 a number of areas of England and Wales, including most large urban centres, had been designated as areas of compulsory registration of title. It was estimated that by 1987 the Land Registration Act covered areas containing 85 per cent of the population of England and Wales (see Law Commission, *Property Law: Third Report on Land Registration: A. Overriding Interests, B. Rectification and Indemnity, C. Minor Interests* (Law Com No 158, 31 March 1987), paras 1.2 (n 8), 2.12 (n 54).

1. THE DISTINCTION BETWEEN REGISTERED AND UNREGISTERED CONVEYANCING

It is clear that registration of title now provides the primary regime of land law in England and Wales. The basic difference between registered and unregistered conveyancing consists in the fact that in unregistered conveyancing the purchaser has always been required, on each occasion of purchase, to undertake a fresh investigation of the title to be purchased. The validity of the title offered is verifiable only by means of an examination of the documents of title (ie the 'title deeds') covering at least the period of 15 years immediately preceding the proposed conveyance.[7] The basis of this practice is the pragmatic assumption that such investigation inevitably reveals all pertinent details relating to the land which the purchaser wishes to buy. In most instances this assumption is proved correct, but the principal defect of unregistered conveyancing is precisely the fact that this cumbersome investigation of title has had to be carried out on every occasion of purchase, irrespective of the length of time which has elapsed since the last transfer and investigation of title. In unregistered conveyancing the process of land transfer has thus tended to be self-perpetuating, repetitive, protracted and costly.[8]

By contrast the objective which underlies the registration scheme contained in the Land Registration Act 1925 is that the title to land should be investigated only once—by the Chief Land Registrar. All the details relevant to the ownership and enjoyment of that land (other than matters which are easily discoverable on physical inspection of the land) are then recorded on a central register—the Land Register. These details go far beyond the one isolated category of interest—the 'commercial' equitable interest—which can be made the subject of registration in the context of unregistered land.[9] Registration of title involves the registration of almost every kind of interest in the land in question—whether legal or equitable, 'family' or 'commercial'.

The aim of the registered land scheme is that the Land Register should accurately reflect the totality of estates and interests created with reference to any land falling within the coverage of the Register.[10] The Register is then kept accurate by regular up-dating of the information contained in it: there is a requirement that all subsequent transactions affecting the registered land be recorded on the Register as a condition precedent to

7 The process of unregistered conveyancing is described more fully in Chapters 7 and 9 (ante p 113, post p 245).

8 In *Williams & Glyn's Bank Ltd v Boland* [1981] AC 487 at 511D, Lord Scarman referred to unregistered conveyancing as the 'wearisome and intricate task of examining title...' For an excoriating account of the 'ritual dance' of conveyancers, see M. Joseph, *The Conveyancing Fraud* (London 1976), p 30ff.

9 It is necessary to distinguish clearly between registration of *title* in the Land Register and registration of *land charges* in the Land Charges Register. The latter form of registration relates, somewhat confusingly, to unregistered land (ante, p 113). Of course, the interests which are registrable in the Land Charges Register are also protectible when they arise in the context of *registered land*, but in the latter case they are protected as 'minor interests', and are recorded in a quite different register, the Land Register, as an integral part of a much more general process of registration.

10 See *Abbey National Building Society v Cann* [1991] 1 AC 56 at 78C per Lord Oliver of Aylmerton ('The governing principle of the Act of 1925 is that the title to land is to be regulated by and ascertainable from the register alone').

their effectiveness. The intended result is that, at any given time, a prospective purchaser of registered land should be able to verify, by a simple examination of the Register, the exact nature of all interests existing in or over the land which he proposes to buy.[11] The historic searching of title which is characteristic of unregistered conveyancing is thus rendered redundant, since the definitive record of the register has eliminated all need for retrospective investigation.

2. THE BASIC FEATURES OF REGISTRATION OF TITLE

The scheme of title registration outlined above represented for many years an aspiration of law reformers. In 1857 the Royal Commission on Land Transfer and Registration defined the problem as one of finding a means of enabling owners 'to deal with land in as simple and easy a manner, as far as the title is concerned, and the difference in the nature of the subject matter may allow, as they can now deal with moveable chattels or stock.'[12] It has long been clear that the law of conveyancing can serve the interests of the community only if it provides a secure, efficient and inexpensive mode of land transfer—an objective of ever greater importance in a mobile and industrialised society.

(1) The three central principles

The archetypal scheme of title registration was introduced during the last century in the form of the 'Torrens Title' legislation enacted in Australia and New Zealand.[13] This legislation provided in many respects a model for the English enactments which culminated in the Land Registration Act 1925.

It has been said that the fundamental features of any scheme for registration of title, whether in the form of Torrens legislation or in the form of the Land Registration Act 1925, are three in number.[14] *First*, the register of

11 See eg *Registrar of Titles (Vic) v Paterson* (1876) 2 App Cas 110 at 116f. In *Gibbs v Messer* [1891] AC 248 at 254, Lord Watson spoke of Torrens legislation (post, p 169) in terms equally apposite to the Land Registration Act 1925. He noted that the object of such legislation is 'to save persons dealing with registered proprietors from the trouble and expense of going behind the register, in order to investigate the history of their author's title, and to satisfy themselves of its validity.' See also *Re Passburg Petroleums Ltd and Landstrom Developments Ltd* (1984) 8 DLR (4th) 363 at 368 (registration system secures 'ease of dealing').

12 *Report of the Commissioners on the Registration of Title with reference to the Sale and Transfer of Land* (CP 2215, 1857-Session 2), para XL.

13 The Torrens scheme was first adopted in the Real Property Act 1858 (South Australia). There is some controversy as to whether Sir Robert Torrens was the true author of the scheme that bears his name. Torrens was accused by even his contemporaries of some degree of plagiarism (see *Sackville and Neave's Property Law: Cases and Materials* (3rd edn, Sydney 1981), para 7.33). There is evidence to suggest that the fundamental concept of the 'Torrens' scheme was formulated by Dr Ulrich Hübbe, a German lawyer living in South Australia in the 1850s, and was modelled largely on the Hanseatic system of title registration (see S. Robinson, *Transfer of Land in Victoria* (Sydney, Melbourne, Brisbane, Perth 1979), p 11ff, 20).

14 See T.B.F. Ruoff, *An Englishman Looks at the Torrens System* (Sydney, Melbourne and Brisbane 1957), p 8.

title is intended to operate as a 'mirror', reflecting accurately and incontrovertibly the totality of estates and interests which at any time affect the registered land (the 'mirror principle').[15] *Second*, trusts relating to the registered land are kept off the title, with the result that third parties may transact with the registered proprietor safe in the assurance that the interests behind any trust will be overreached (the 'curtain principle').[16] *Third*, the state itself guarantees the accuracy of the registered title, in that an indemnity is payable from public funds if a registered proprietor is deprived of his title or is otherwise prejudiced by the operation of the registration scheme (the 'insurance principle').[17]

Notwithstanding the enunciation of these clear and high-sounding principles, it will emerge in the course of this chapter that title registration under the Land Registration Act 1925 has not eliminated all problems in the transfer of land. Difficulties remain, not least in relation to the extent to which the principles governing registered land truly diverge from those governing unregistered land. Both the structure and the detailed operation of the title registration scheme have been the subject of extensive deliberation by the Law Commission. The Commission's proposals for reform, which are considered at various points throughout this chapter, are broadly aimed at bringing English law into closer accord with the three central principles referred to above.

(2) A distinctively different system of land law

For many purposes it is true to say that the system of registered title contained in the Land Registration Act 1925 utilises existing concepts of unregistered land conveyancing and simply provides more streamlined conveyancing machinery. There is, however, an important sense in which it is beginning to be realised that registration of title may achieve more than merely procedural changes in the law relating to land.

It is possible that the law of registered title will come in time to be recognised as a body of rules and concepts which is *substantively* quite different from the principles which have regulated unregistered land.[18] It may well be that the classic concepts of unregistered land (eg the distinction between legal and equitable rights and the equitable doctrine of notice) will be rendered

15 See *Re Cartlidge and Granville Savings & Mortgage Corp* (1987) 34 DLR (4th) 161 at 172 per Philp JA ('Indefeasibility is the heart of a Torrens system. The register is everything; an owner's title is conclusive and persons dealing with registered owners are not required to go behind the register').

16 See *Wolfson v Registrar General (NSW)* (1934) 51 CLR 300 at 308 per Rich and Evatt JJ.

17 See R. Stein, (1983-84) 9 Adelaide LR 267.

18 A significant step in this direction was taken by the decision of the House of Lords in *Williams & Glyn's Bank Ltd v Boland* [1981] AC 487 (post, pp 226, 569). In 1987 the Law Commission acknowledged that 'there are substantive differences between registered and unregistered land' (Law Com No 158, para 2.5). The Commission finally accepted that there was 'little justification in trying at all costs to keep the two systems in step' and, in proposing important changes in the registered land scheme, felt unconstrained by the fact that 'we might be creating or perpetuating distinctions from unregistered land. Registered land is after all to be the way forward, the new improving on the old.'

redundant by the steadily expanding coverage of registered title.[19] Under a system of registered title almost the only relevant distinction is that between 'major' and 'minor' interests; that is, between those rights which are roughly equivalent to absolute ownership of land and all other kinds of interest which diminish or qualify that ownership.[20] Interests of the latter variety are registered merely 'adjectivally', by subsidiary 'entry' on the register of the substantively registered title.

3. THE REGISTER

The Land Register is controlled by the Chief Land Registrar.[1] The Register is maintained both centrally at the Land Registry in London and regionally at nineteen district land registries.[2] It has been estimated that the Land Register currently contains over 13,500,000 separate registered titles, and is used each year to record more than 5,000,000 substantive dealings with the properties comprised in these titles.[3]

(1) The function of the Registrar and his staff

The Chief Land Registrar is statutorily required to keep a Register of Title to all freehold and leasehold land in England and Wales covered by the requirement of compulsory registration.[4] It is accordingly the function of the Registrar and his staff to record in the Land Register all details pertinent to each individual title maintained at the Registry.[5] Each title is identified by the title number assigned to the plot of land concerned,[6] thus reinforcing the point that the Land Registration Act 1925 directs that registration be effected against an area of land identified numerically rather than against the name of the current estate owner (as is the case in relation to registration in the Land Charges Register[7]).

19 On the general elimination of the doctrine of notice in registered title, see *Kemmis v Kemmis* [1988] 1 WLR 1307 at 1332E per Nourse LJ (ante, p 106). Even in this context, however, there are sporadic attempts to re-introduce something akin to the traditional doctrine (see eg *Peffer v Rigg* [1977] 1 WLR 285 (post, p 190); *Lyus v Prowsa Developments Ltd* [1982] 1 WLR 1044 (post, p 440)). See P. Sparkes, [1989] Conv 342 at 343.
20 Ante, p 105.
1 Land Registration Act 1925, s 126.
2 See The Land Registration (District Registries) Order 1991 (SI 1991/2634), Schedule.
3 Ruoff and Roper, *The Law and Practice of Registered Conveyancing* (Looseleaf edn, London 1991), para 1-12. Roughly 2,500,000 titles are contained in computerised form (ibid, para 3-03).
4 Land Registration Act 1925, s 1(1). The register need not be kept in documentary form (see Land Registration Act 1925, s 1(2), as substituted by Administration of Justice Act 1982, s 66(1)). This proviso clearly heralds the advent of a fully computerised register, and the inspection and copying of such a register are envisaged by Land Registration Act 1925, s 112(3).
5 Land Registration Act 1925, ss 126, 127. Compare *Perpetual Executors and Trustees Association of Australia Ltd v Hosken* (1912) 14 CLR 286 at 295 per Isaacs J ('. . .the Registrar is not an automaton; he has a high and responsible public duty to discharge and he has an obligation to see that the purpose of the Act is neither destroyed nor prejudicially affected').
6 Land Registration Rules 1925, r 2.
7 Ante, p 117.

The Registrar is invested with a limited quasi-judicial capacity to determine questions and difficulties arising in the day-to-day operation of the register.[8] Alternatively the Registrar may obtain from the High Court a definitive ruling on any difficult question relating to the operation of the register. The Registrar may also be required to give effect to any court order touching upon a registered title. On being served with a copy of a relevant court order, it is his function to make appropriate amendments of any register of title affected.

The Registrar and any staff acting under his authority are indemnified against any legal liability in respect of 'any act or matter done or omitted to be done in good faith in the exercise or supposed exercise' of their powers under the Land Registration Act 1925.[9]

(2) **The divisions of the Register**

The register of any individual title kept at the Land Registry is subdivided into three sections or 'parts',[10] each known itself as some sort of 'register'.

(a) The 'Property Register'

The Property Register under a particular title number records the advantageous features of the land in question. It contains a verbal description of the land and a description by reference to a filed map, and notes such matters as easements, rights, privileges and covenants over other land which enure to the benefit of the land comprised within the title number.[11] If the title is leasehold, brief details of the lease are included.[12]

(b) The 'Proprietorship Register'

The Proprietorship Register indicates the name and address of the current registered proprietor of the estate represented by a particular title number.[13] This part of the Register also indicates whether the title enjoyed by the proprietor is 'absolute', 'good leasehold', 'qualified' or 'possessory'.[14] The Proprietorship Register similarly records any restrictions, cautions or inhibitions which affect or diminish the right of the registered proprietor to dispose of the land.[15]

8 Land Registration Rules 1925, r 298(1). There is a right of appeal to the Chancery Division of the High Court (Land Registration Rules 1925, r 299). Accepted day-to-day practice in the Land Registry effectively creates the law which governs much of the business of the Registry, but Lord Denning MR warned in *Strand Securities Ltd v Caswell* [1965] Ch 958 at 977E that the Registrar is not allowed 'by his practice to make bad law'. See, however, [1981] Conv 395.
9 Land Registration Act 1925, s 131.
10 Land Registration Rules 1925, r 2.
11 Land Registration Rules 1925, r 3.
12 Land Registration Rules 1925, r 5.
13 Land Registration Rules 1925, r 6. The price paid by the registered proprietor is entered only if the proprietor has so requested (Land Registration Rules 1925, r 247, as amended by Land Registration Rules 1976 (SI 1976/1332), rr 2, 3).
14 Post, p 176.
15 Land Registration Rules 1925, r 6.

(c) *The 'Charges Register'*

The Charges Register records all the disadvantageous or negative features of the legal ownership of the estate in question. Here are entered particulars (but not the amount) of mortgages and financial charges, together with liens and notices of leases. Also included are details of other incumbrances which adversely affect the land such as restrictive covenants, easements and rights of occupation under the Matrimonial Homes Act 1983.[16]

(3) **The land certificate**

The three subdivisions of the Land Register are correlated on one index card, a copy of which is issued to the current registered proprietor and is known as the 'land certificate'.[17] This certificate provides each registered proprietor with his immediate evidence of title, and is treated in the law of registered land as the rough equivalent of the title deeds provided by unregistered conveyancing.[18] The land certificate must normally be produced to the registrar for appropriate amendment on any occasion of entry on the register of a 'restriction' or 'notice' against the relevant registered title.[19]

(4) **Public access to the Land Register**

One of the more controversial features of the Land Register used to be the fact that it was not generally open to public inspection[20]—a point not without political significance since the preclusion of access to the register ultimately frustrated any attempt to compile an accurate record of the allocation of land ownership in this country. The denial of a general right of access to the Land Register was almost without parallel in other jurisdictions,[1] and came eventually to be criticised as symptomatic of 'the obsession with unnecessary secrecy which pervades British society'.[2] In 1985 the Law Commission recommended that the Register should be made available for general public scrutiny,[3] and this proposal was realised in the

16 Land Registration Rules 1925, r 7.

17 Land Registration Act 1925, s 63(1). The certificate is, however, retained in the Land Registry if and so long as the property concerned is subject to a registered charge by way of mortgage (see Land Registration Act 1925, s 65, post, p 981).

18 See eg *Thames Guaranty Ltd v Campbell* [1985] QB 210 at 233C-D; Land Registration Act 1925, s 66 (post, p 944).

19 Land Registration Act 1925, s 64(1), (2) (post, p 183). See, however, Land Registration Act 1925, s 64(5); Housing Act 1985, Sch 9A, para 5(3), as supplied by Housing and Planning Act 1986, s 8(2), Sch 2.

20 Land Registration Act 1925, s 112(1) (original). There were inevitably several exemptions from the general prohibition of access. See eg Land Registration Act 1925, s 112(1)(i), as substituted by Administration of Justice Act 1982, s 67(1), Sch 5 (persons—such as an intending purchaser—with appropriate authority conferred by the registered proprietor).

1 See Law Commission, *Property Law: Second Report on Land Registration: Inspection of the Register* (Law Com No 148, 25 July 1985), para 18(i).

2 Comment of the National Consumer Council, as quoted in Law Com No 148, para 17(iii).

3 Law Com No 148, para 21. The Commission thought that an open register would be entirely consistent with the principle that 'in an open society there should be freedom of information and publication'. In the Commission's view, the abandonment of the rule of secrecy would not constitute any real invasion of the citizen's privacy, but would confer significant benefits particularly for the simplification of conveyancing (Ibid, para 20).

Land Registration Act 1988. Subject to the payment of a fee any person may now inspect entries on the Register and any documents (other than leases or charges) which are referred to in the Register.[4]

4. THE CLASSIFICATION OF INTERESTS IN REGISTERED LAND

The interests in land which require to be dealt with in terms of the Land Registration Act 1925 comprise largely the same kinds of interest which arise in the context of unregistered land: the only difference is one of terminology.[5] The range of possible interests in registered land includes 'registrable interests', 'minor interests',[6] 'overriding interests',[7] and 'registered charges'.[8]

5. REGISTRABLE INTERESTS

Registrable interests are those interests which are indicated in the Land Registration Act 1925 as being capable of substantive registration, ie capable of registration in their own right under an individual title number. Under section 2(1) of the Act the only interests which may be substantively registered in this manner are those estates in land which are 'capable of subsisting as legal estates.'[9] Although the term is never used in the Act, such estates provide (with slight qualifications) the 'major interests' ancillary to which all other forms of entry in the Land Register (eg 'minor interests') are effected.[10]

A distinction must be drawn here between the registration provisions which relate to 'first' or primary registration (ie the initial inclusion of a registrable interest in the Land Register) and those provisions which govern subsequent transfers of a registered estate which has already been recorded in the Register.

(1) First registration of registrable interests

First registration of a 'registrable interest' or 'major interest' has never been effected automatically by reason of the designation of a geographical district as an area of compulsory registration of title.[11] The requirement of entry

4 Land Registration Act 1925, s 112(1), as substituted by Land Registration Act 1988, s 1(1). See also Land Registration (Official Searches) Rules 1990, r 9(1) (post, p 185); Land Registration (Open Register) Rules 1991 (SI 1992/122), rr 2–4.
5 See generally D. Jackson, (1972) 88 LQR 93.
6 Post, p 181.
7 Post, p 197.
8 Post, p 228.
9 For this purpose the phrase 'legal estates' is defined by Land Registration Act 1925, s 3(xi) in terms which are sufficiently broad to catch all those 'estates', 'interests' and 'charges' referred to in Law of Property Act 1925, s 1(1), (2) (ante, p 68).
10 Ante, p 170.
11 All of England and Wales has now been so designated (see Land Registration, England and Wales: The Registration of Title Order 1989 (SI 1989/1347) (ante, p 166)).

in the Land Register begins to operate only with the first 'conveyance on sale of freehold land'[12] or grant of a lease which occurs *after* the date of such designation.[13] The estates which require substantive registration in such an event are spelt out in the Land Registration Act 1925.

(a) Freehold estates

It is clear that the interests which qualify for 'first registration' under the Land Registration Act 1925 include the legal fee simple absolute in possession. The first freehold purchaser following the effective date of compulsory registration may apply to have himself entered as the registered proprietor of the title purchased, in which case he is registered with either absolute or possessory title.[14] The registered freehold estate is thus the primary 'major interest' around which all other entries on the register are gathered.

(b) Leasehold estates

A term of years absolute may likewise be the subject of substantive registration, subject to qualifications imposed by the Land Registration Act 1925 as amended. Not every lease can constitute a registrable title.[15] It is plain, for instance, that only a legal leasehold can qualify as a 'major interest'.[16] Moreover, the registration requirement affects only leases of a certain specified duration.[17] Leases granted for more than 21 years out of an unregistered title are compulsorily registrable on grant, and existing leases with more than 21 years unexpired at the date of assignment are likewise compulsorily registrable on assignment.[18] It is now clear that a leasehold estate is registrable

12 A 'conveyance on sale' clearly excludes from first registration any transfer by way of gift or assent by personal representatives. The term 'sale' seems to require an exchange of property for a money consideration, and therefore almost certainly excludes an exchange of land for other land (see eg *In re Westminster Property Group Plc* [1985] 1 WLR 676 at 683C-D).

13 Land Registration Act 1925, s 123(1).

14 Land Registration Act 1925, s 4(a). The application for registration may be made by 'any estate owner holding an estate in fee simple', including a tenant for life (post, p 616), statutory owner, personal representative or trustee for sale. However, no application may be made by a mortgagee where there is a subsisting right of redemption or by a 'person who has merely contracted to buy land' (Land Registration Act 1925, s 4(b)).

15 See Land Registration Act 1925, s 8(1)(a). No registration may be effected in respect of a term of years which has been created as security for a mortgage loan (post, p 939), since other means exist in the scheme of registered title for protection of such interests (post, p 228).

16 Land Registration Act 1925, s 2(1).

17 Periodic tenancies, for instance, are never transferred in practice and their registration would serve no useful purpose in facilitating dealings in registered land (see Law Commission, *Property Law: Land Registration* (Law Com No 125, 26 October 1983), para 4.26(a)).

18 Land Registration Act 1925, s 123(1), as amended by Land Registration Act 1986, s 2(1). Land Registration Act 1925, s 8(1A), as supplied by Land Registration Act 1986, s 2(2), makes it clear than an application for registration can still be made if at the date of application for first registration a lease has 21 years or less to run (see Law Com No 125, paras 4.26ff). However, the amendments provided by the Land Registration Act 1986 apply only in relation to grants or assignments of leases after 1 January 1987 (see Land Registration Act 1986, s 2(5); The Land Registration Act 1986 (Commencement) Order 1986 (SI 1986/2117), para 2).

notwithstanding that it may contain an absolute prohibition on alienation or assignment.[19]

The rules in respect of registration of leaseholds demonstrate that the landlord-tenant relationship may well produce *two* (if not more) registered estates, both of which require substantive registration under different title numbers and both of which are evidenced in separate land certificates. The tenant is required to register his term of years absolute quite independently of the substantive registration effected by his landlord.[20]

(c) Easements

The existence of a legal easement benefiting land which is the subject of substantive registration may be entered in the Property Register of the relevant registered estate.[1]

(d) Consequence of failure to effect a first registration

In unregistered conveyancing the transfer of a legal estate (whether freehold or leasehold) is completed by the deed of transfer (ie the conveyance from vendor to purchaser). The same is not true of registered conveyancing. Although the same process of contract and conveyance occurs in a dealing with a registered title, the transfer of any legal estate to the purchaser is effectual and complete only when the transferee is entered on the Land Register as the new registered proprietor of the estate concerned.

This general principle is given an apparently draconian effect in the context of the requirement of first registration. The requirement of primary registration is, of course, triggered off by a conveyance or grant of some estate in land which has never yet been the subject of any entry on the register. The Land Registration Act 1925 provides accordingly that the legal title supposedly transferred by such a conveyance or grant is defeasible unless the transferee applies for a first registration of his registrable interest within two months from the date of execution of that conveyance or grant.[2] A failure by the transferee to apply for first registration renders the relevant transfer statutorily 'void so far as regards the grant or conveyance of the legal estate in the. . .land'.[3]

19 Land Registration Act 1925, s 8(2), as substituted by Land Registration Act 1986, s 3(1). See Law Com No 125, para 4.30.

20 The existence of the inferior interest must, however, be noted on the Charges Register of the superior title (see Land Registration Rules 1925, rr 7, 46).

1 Land Registration Rules 1925, rr 3(2)(c), 257.

2 Land Registration Act 1925, s 123(1). See *Buckley v S.R.L. Investments Ltd and Cator and Robinson* (1971) 22 P & CR 756 at 767. It has been made clear that section 123(1) does not apply to an omission of land from the scope of a first registration merely by reason of a defective description of the land to be registered. Section 123(1) is properly applicable only to cases which involve a 'total failure to register the conveyance on sale' (see *Proctor v Kidman* (1985) 51 P & CR 67 at 72 per Croom-Johnson LJ).

3 Land Registration Act 1925, s 123(1). In spite of the apparent ferocity of the statutory language, it seems that in practice the registrar is almost always willing to extend the period allowed for first registration, provided that 'some accident or sufficient cause' can be shown justifying the exercise of a benevolent discretion (see Land Registration Act 1925, s 123(1), proviso). Compare Ruoff and Roper, op cit, para 11-08f, and [1983] Conv 175.

(2) Possible grades of title

When the Land Registry receives an application for substantive registration of an estate in registered land, the quality of title to be accorded to the first registered proprietor must be graded within four possible classes. The class of title awarded is then indicated in the relevant Proprietorship Register.

(a) Absolute title

The highest class of title which may be granted on first registration is 'absolute title'. This form of title can be awarded in respect of both freehold and leasehold applicants.

(i) Applicant with freehold estate Where the registered land is a freehold estate, a first registration with *absolute title*[4] statutorily invests the applicant with the full legal fee simple absolute in possession in the land[5] (together with all appurtenant rights), subject only to overriding interests, those minor interests which are entered on the register[6] and certain other interests of which he has notice.[7] Absolute title is granted in the case of almost all freehold applications for first registration.

The statutory effect of first registration with absolute title is, within the limits stated above, comprehensive and far-reaching. An absolute title, once awarded to the applicant, is conclusive to override or cure any defects in the applicant's title as it existed prior to first registration. In *In re 139 High Street Deptford, ex parte British Transport Commission*,[8] for instance, it was held that a first registration with absolute title was effective to invest the successful applicant with an estate in land which was not in fact owned by the vendor and which he therefore had no power to sell.[9]

(ii) Applicant with leasehold estate Absolute title is less frequently awarded to the applicant for first registration of a leasehold estate. Here absolute title can be conferred only if the registrar is in a position to approve not only the applicant's title but also that relating to any superior freehold or leasehold estate.[10] This means that the applicant must deduce title to the registrar's

4 Absolute title cannot be awarded without the approval of the registrar (Land Registration Act 1925, s 4). However, the registrar has a discretion to approve a title as absolute notwithstanding that it is still open to objection on some score, provided that he has reason to believe that the holding under that title will not be disturbed (Land Registration Act 1925, s 13(c)).

5 Land Registration Act 1925, s 5. It has been held that section 5 invests the first registered proprietor with only the legal (and not the equitable) title (see *Epps v Esso Petroleum Co Ltd* [1973] 1 WLR 1071 at 1077E-G). This conclusion seems dubious (see *Barnsley's Conveyancing Law and Practice* (3rd edn, London 1988), p 29f).

6 Mere entry on the register cannot, however, revitalise an interest which by the date of first registration has already ceased to be enforceable (eg on the ground of non-registration as a land charge). See *Kitney v MEPC Ltd* [1977] 1 WLR 981 at 992B-C, 994H-995B. See (1977) 41 Conv (NS) 356 (F.R. Crane); [1978] CLJ 13 (D.J. Hayton).

7 Land Registration Act 1925, s 5. The vulnerability to interests of which the applicant has notice applies only where the applicant is not entitled to the land for his own benefit (eg where he holds the land on trust for another).

8 [1951] Ch 884.

9 The register was, however, rectified in favour of the former owner under Land Registration Act 1925, s 82(3)(a) ([1951] Ch 884 at 891f).

10 Land Registration Act 1925, s 8(1), proviso (i).

satisfaction not only in relation to his own leasehold but also in relation to all superior titles, unless the freehold is already registered.[11] This many lessees are unable to do, precisely because a lessee is not normally entitled to call for and investigate superior titles.[12]

If, however, absolute title is awarded to a leasehold applicant, the award operates effectively as a guarantee that the lease in question was validly granted. First registration of such a lease with absolute title is statutorily deemed to invest the successful applicant with possession of the leasehold interest together with all implied or expressed appurtenant rights and privileges.[13] The registration is subject to all the qualifications which affect a first registration of a freehold estate with absolute title,[14] with the further proviso that the applicant's new title is also subject to 'all implied and express covenants, obligations, and liabilities incident to the registered land'.[15]

(b) Good leasehold title

Even if absolute title cannot be awarded, a leasehold application for first registration will almost certainly result in the award of a *good leasehold title.* Such a title is, for all practical purposes, just as marketable as a leasehold which is registered with absolute title. The registered proprietor with good leasehold title is in exactly the same position as the recipient of an absolute title, except to the extent that a good leasehold title is held subject to any 'estate, right or interest affecting or in derogation of the title of the lessor to grant the lease'.[16] In other words, the registrar, in awarding a good leasehold title, certifies his approval of the lease, but cannot guarantee that it was validly granted by the lessor.[17]

(c) Possessory title

It is open to the registrar to grant a mere *possessory title* to any applicant for first registration who cannot produce sufficient documentary evidence of title and who therefore relies on a period of adverse possession of the land concerned. This possessory title is, however, subject to all adverse interests affecting the land which may later be shown to have existed at the date of first registration.[18]

11 A registration with absolute title is not, however, impossible where, as is increasingly frequently the case, a dispositionary lease is granted by a lessor who is himself registered with absolute title.
12 Law of Property Act 1925, s 44 (ante, p 118).
13 Land Registration Act 1925, s 9.
14 Land Registration Act 1925, s 5.
15 Land Registration Act 1925, s 9(a).
16 Land Registration Act 1925, s 10.
17 The registrar always retains a discretion to convert a good leasehold title into an absolute title if he is satisfied as to the title to the freehold and the title to any intermediate leasehold (Land Registration Act 1925, s 77(1), as amended by Land Registration Act 1986, s 1(1)).
18 Land Registration Act 1925, ss 6, 11. A possessory title may be subsequently rectified against the registered proprietor (without indemnity) for the purpose of giving effect to a superior title or if the possessory title was insufficiently grounded in a claim of adverse possession. See *Tester v Harris* (1964) 189 Estates Gazette 337 at 339, but compare *Spectrum Investment Co Ltd v Holmes* [1981] 1 WLR 221 at 230E-H.

Where freehold land is first registered with possessory title the registrar may, and on application by the proprietor must, convert the title into an absolute title if he is 'satisfied as to the title' or if the land has been registered with possessory title for at least twelve years and he is satisfied that the proprietor is in possession.[19] A possessory title registered in respect of a leasehold may similarly be upgraded to a good leasehold title if the same conditions are fulfilled.[20]

(d) *Qualified title*

In extremely rare cases the registrar may, with the applicant's consent, grant only a *qualified title* on first registration. Such cases arise where the applicant can establish title only in respect of a limited period or where there are other fundamental doubts as to the subject matter of the registration. A qualified title is highly precarious, being subject to any adverse interests which later emerge as having been in existence at the date of registration.[1]

(e) *A new statutory estate?*

Under the Land Registration Act 1925 the legal estates in registered land have now become so heavily regulated by statutory incidents that it is sometimes suggested, in the context of title registration, that the common law estates have been replaced by some new and artificial kind of statutory registered estate.[2] This view has aroused much controversy[3] and, if correct, lends some credence to the theory that the principles of registered land are evolving into a significantly different law of property which recognises only the distinction between 'major' interests (ie substantively registered titles) and 'minor' interests (ie almost everything else).[4]

(3) **Subsequent transfers of the registered estate**

The foregoing rules circumscribe the initial entry or 'first registration' of

19 Land Registration Act 1925, s 77(2), as amended by Land Registration Act 1986, s 1(1). If the relevant possessory title was registered before the commencement of the Land Registration Act 1986 on 1 January 1987, the required period of twelve years must occur *after* this commencement date, but nothing precludes the proprietor in such a case from reliance on the fifteen and ten year periods originally prescribed in Land Registration Act 1925, s 77(3)(b) (see Land Registration Act 1986, s 1(2)).

20 Land Registration Act 1925, s 77(2), as amended by Land Registration Act 1986, s 1(1).

1 Land Registration Act 1925, ss 7, 12. A qualified title may later be converted into absolute title (in the case of freehold land) or good leasehold title (in the case of leasehold land) if the registrar is 'satisfied as to the title' (Land Registration Act 1925, s 77(3), as amended by Land Registration Act 1986, s 1(1)).

2 See *Chowood Ltd v Lyall* (No 2) [1930] 2 Ch 156 at 163 per Lord Hanworth MR; H. Potter, (1942) 58 LQR 356. Compare, however, *I.A.C. (Finance) Pty Ltd v Courtenay* (1963) 110 CLR 550 at 572 per Kitto J.

3 See R.C. Connell, (1947) 11 Conv (NS) 184, 232; (1949) 12 MLR 139 at 205 (H. Potter), 477 (A.D. Hargreaves).

4 Ante, p 170.

a 'registrable interest' in the Land Register. Thereafter all transfers or assignments of the registered estate require to be recorded in the register as a condition precedent to their effectiveness at law.[5]

(a) *The requirement of registration*

The transfer of a registered estate (whether freehold or leasehold) is declared by statute to be 'completed' only when the registrar has entered on the register the name of the transferee as the proprietor of the estate transferred.[6] The accuracy of the register is thus maintained by requiring each successive transferee of a registered estate to perfect his legal title by applying to be registered as the new proprietor. In a deeper sense, however, transfer is not ultimately an act of the parties: it is an act of the state. The title of each registered proprietor comes from the fact of registration. As Windeyer J once said, registration is the 'source of the title, rather than a retrospective approbation of it as a derivative right.'[7]

(b) *Consequence of non-registration of later transfers*

Until the transferee of a registered estate has applied to be registered as the new proprietor, the transferor of that estate is deemed to remain proprietor.[8] The legal estate does not therefore pass unless and until such an application is made, but is not otherwise affected by the failure to secure registration of the transaction.[9]

In the absence of an application to register the transfer, the transferee acquires merely an equitable interest in the freehold or leasehold estate conveyed,[10] the transferor meanwhile holding the legal estate as a bare

5 In other words, the requirement of registration of all such subsequent transactions applies whether or not the transaction involves a 'conveyance on sale'. All later transfers of the registered estate—even those by way of gift or devise—thus require to be recorded in the register.

6 Land Registration Act 1925, ss 19(1), 22(1). Likewise the express grant of any legal easement or other legal interest in registered land (apart from a registered estate) must be 'completed by registration' (Land Registration Act 1925, ss 19(2), 22(2)).

7 *Breskvar v Wall* (1971) 126 CLR 376 at 400.

8 Land Registration Act 1925, ss 19(1), 22(1).

9 There is, in the context of later transactions with a registered estate, no equivalent of the rule in Land Registration Act 1925, s 123(1), which imposes a penalty of voidness for failure to apply for 'first registration' within two months (ante, p 175).

10 See *E.S. Schwab & Co Ltd v McCarthy* (1976) 31 P & CR 196 at 201 per Oliver J; *Coffey and Moylan v Brunel Construction Co Ltd* [1983] IR 36 at 40, 43; *Dalegrove Pty Ltd v Isles Parking Station Pty Ltd* (1988) 12 NSWLR 546 at 551B; *Chan v Cresdon Pty Ltd* (1989) 168 CLR 242 at 248, 256f, 261. The transferee's equitable interest follows, of course, from the fact that the transaction behind the (as yet unrecorded) instrument has created for the transferee an equitable right in the land (post, p 263). The inefficacy of the transfer at law 'cannot cut down or merge the pre-existing right which led to its execution' (*Barry v Heider* (1914) 19 CLR 197 at 216 per Isaacs J). See also *Brunker v Perpetual Trustee Co (Ltd)* (1937) 57 CLR 555 at 581 per Latham CJ; *Corin v Patton* (1990) 169 CLR 540 at 563 per Brennan J, 587f per Toohey J.

trustee.[11] Pending the registration of his transfer, however, the transferee has a right to receive mesne profits accruing from the date of his unregistered conveyance.[12] Moreover, if the transferee actually receives such profits or if he himself goes into actual occupation of the land pending registration of the transfer, his equitable interest in the land constitutes an overriding interest which will bind any future purchaser who attempts to register a later transfer adverse to his interests.[13]

(c) Effect of registration of later transfers

In the Australian High Court in *Breskvar v Wall*,[14] Barwick CJ pointed out that schemes of land registration provide 'not a system of registration of title but a system of title by registration.' In other words, the title certified by the register is not ultimately historical or derivative, but 'is the title which registration itself has vested in the proprietor.'[15] Thus, provided that the transfer of a registered estate is duly recorded in the Land Register, the title enjoyed by the transferee depends on the force of statute rather than on any intrinsic validity in the transfer itself.[16]

This truth is borne out in section 69(1) of the Land Registration Act 1925, which provides that the proprietor of land 'shall be deemed to have vested in him without any conveyance, where the registered land is freehold, the legal estate in fee simple in possession, and where the registered land is leasehold, the legal term created by the registered lease'.[17] The formula

11 See *IAC (Finance) Pty Ltd v Courtenay* (1963) 110 CLR 550 at 571; *Muswellbrook Coal Co Ltd v Minister for Mineral Resources and Energy* (1986) 6 NSWLR 654 at 657E-F; *Coffey v Brunel Construction Co Ltd* [1983] IR 36 at 40. Even here the transferee's equitable interest prior to registration depends on an underlying transaction for valuable consideration. Where a registrable transfer is purely voluntary, there is no fact or circumstance on which a court of equity might fasten as binding the conscience of the donor to hold the land on trust for the transferee. See *Corin v Patton* (1990) 169 CLR 540 at 563 per Brennan J, 588 per Toohey J, but compare 580ff per Deane J.

12 *Choudhury v Meah* (Unreported, Court of Appeal, 21 September 1981) per Lawton LJ.

13 Land Registration Act 1925, s 70(1)(g) (post, p 203). It is, of course, bizarre that the transferee can thus fail, with relative impunity, to apply for registration of his transfer. The Law Commission recommended as long ago as 1971 that section 70(1)(g) should be amended to ensure that no interest which is capable of substantive registration can ever constitute an overriding interest in default of due registration (see Law Commission, Published Working Paper No 37: *Land Registration (Second Paper)* (July 1971), para 14). More recently the Commission has declared itself to be unconvinced of any current need to discourage 'off the register' conveyancing. The Commission preferred not to withdraw the protection at present afforded in this context to transferees in actual occupation, regarding the advantages and priorities secured by registration as a generally sufficient incentive towards the due registration of the new proprietor's title (see Law Com No 158, para 2.67).

14 (1971) 126 CLR 376 at 385.

15 (1971) 126 CLR 376 at 386. See *Tessmann v Costello* [1987] 1 Qd R 283 at 296.

16 Registration cannot, however, validate a description of an interest which is not viable under the general law. See eg *Re Lehrer and the Real Property Act* (1961) SR (NSW) 365 at 376f (purported lease only a licence). See also *In re Ridgeway and Smith's Contract* [1930] VLR 111 at 117.

17 This far-reaching vesting effect is expressly subject to 'overriding interests, if any, including any mortgage term or charge by way of legal mortgage . . . which has priority to the registered estate.'

contained in section 69(1) thus operates a 'statutory magic'[18] which is sufficiently potent to invest the current registered proprietor with a full legal title even though the registered transfer to him may, for instance, have been void for irregularity[19] or even a complete forgery.[20] The mere fact of entry in the register is enough, for the time being, to confer an immediate title on the new proprietor.[1]

6. MINOR INTERESTS

A second category of interests in registered land is the category of minor interests. This category comprises a residual class of interests and includes those interests which do not otherwise rank as registrable or overriding interests or as registered charges.[2] Minor interests thus include those matters which in unregistered land are capable of protection under the Land Charges Act 1972; the rights of beneficiaries under a trust for sale or strict settlement; other equitable rights under the general law which relate to land and are not included in the foregoing categories; the rights, until registration, of those entitled to be registered in respect of a disposition to them; and leases granted prior to 1 January 1987 which contain an absolute prohibition on assignment and subletting or which were granted in consideration of a premium for a term of 21 years or less.

(1) Protection of minor interests

Minor interests qualify for protection not by means of substantive registration but by the subsidiary means of 'entry' on the register.[3] Entry of an interest operates, in effect, as a statutory substitute for the old equitable doctrine of notice[4] and ensures that later transferees of the registered title cannot wholly ignore the presence of the protected interest. Entry in the register

18 *Argyle Building Society v Hammond* (1985) 49 P & CR 148 at 153, 155 per Slade LJ. In Australia registration with a Torrens title has the same general consequence of confirming the immediate indefeasibility of the proprietor's title, even though 'indefeasibility' is 'a word that does not appear in all the Torrens statutes of this country' (*Bahr v Nicolay* (No 2) (1988) 164 CLR 604 at 637 per Wilson and Toohey JJ). See also *Frazer v Walker* [1967] 1 AC 569 at 580F–581A, 585A-C.

19 See eg *Rockhampton Permanent Building Society v Peterson* (No 2) [1989] 1 Qd R 670 at 676.

20 *Argyle Building Society v Hammond* (1985) 49 P & CR 148 at 153, 155 per Slade LJ. For other cases of transfer by forged signature, see *Registrar, Regina Land Registration District v Hermanson* (1987) 33 DLR (4th) 12 at 16ff; *Paramount Life Insurance Co v Hill* (1987) 34 DLR (4th) 150 at 154ff.

1 The vesting of a full legal title in the registering transferee does not, of course, preclude the possibility that the register may subsequently be rectified against him (post, p 229). In such cases, however, an indemnity may well be payable by way of compensation for the loss caused by rectification (post, p 237).

2 Land Registration Act 1925, s 3(xv).

3 In its latest proposals the Law Commission prefers to describe interests thus entered on the register as 'protected interests', thus reserving the term 'minor interest' for those rights which are not so entered and which do not comprise a registered or overriding interest. See Draft Land Registration Bill, clause 7(1) (Law Commission, Law Com No 173 (1988), Appendix).

4 See *Kemmis v Kemmis* [1988] 1 WLR 1307 at 1332E per Nourse LJ (ante, p 106).

may take various forms, depending to some extent on the nature of the minor interest in question.[5] Entry may be effected by way of 'restriction', 'notice', 'caution' or 'inhibition'.

(a) *Restriction*

The proprietor of any registered estate or registered charge is entitled to apply to the registrar for the entry of a 'restriction' in the relevant Proprietorship Register.[6] A restriction cannot normally be entered unless the registered proprietor's land certificate is lodged for this purpose with the registrar.[7] If the application is granted, the entry of the restriction has the effect of indicating that no disposition of, or transaction in relation to, the registered title can thenceforth be effected except in the manner expressly specified by the particular restriction. The protection provided by the entry of a restriction is peculiarly appropriate in the case of equitable interests which arise under a trust for sale[8] or strict settlement.[9] In the case of such interests the restriction effectively stipulates that no further transaction with the title shall be registered by the registrar unless all relevant capital moneys are paid to at least two trustees or to a trust corporation.[10] In this way it is ensured that the only transactions which can ever take place are those which inevitably have the effect of overreaching the beneficial interests in protection of which the restriction was entered. Enforcement of the terms of the restriction translates such interests indubitably into equivalent rights in the capital proceeds arising on the transaction.[11]

5 The registrar is not obliged to verify the substance of the entry, but (as with improperly registered land charges in unregistered land (ante, p 118)) there is jurisdiction to vacate entries made in error or motivated by unacceptable intentions. See eg *Halaga Developments Pty Ltd v Grime* (1986) 5 NSWLR 740 at 744D-E (use of multiple caveats to frustrate primary registration).

6 Land Registration Act 1925, s 58(1). The registrar has power of his own motion to enter a restriction (Land Registration Act 1925, s 58(3); Land Registration Rules 1925, r 39). A restriction may be entered at the behest of persons other than the registered proprietor (see Land Registration Act 1925, s 58(5); Land Registration Rules 1925, r 236). See also Housing Act 1985, Sch 9A, para 5(3) (as supplied by Housing and Planning Act 1986, s 8(2), Sch 2, post, p 183).

7 Land Registration Act 1925, s 64(1)(c). The Law Commission has recommended that this requirement be discontinued in all cases where a beneficiary under a trust or settlement wishes to protect his equitable rights by entry of a restriction. On this basis a beneficiary would be able to apply for the entry of a restriction without the co-operation of the registered proprietor, although the Commission proposed that the Registry be compelled to serve notice of the application on the proprietor (Law Com No 158, paras 4.53ff).

8 See eg *In re Gorman (A Bankrupt)* [1990] 1 WLR 616 at 621B.

9 The Law Commission has recommended that the restriction should henceforth become the *only* permissible form of protection for such interests (Law Com No 158, para 4.52). At present the alternative protection of a notice or caution is also available. See Draft Land Registration Bill, clause 33(5)(d), (e) (Law Commission, Law Com No 173 (1988), Appendix).

10 Land Registration Act 1925, s 58(2).

11 Ante, pp 102, 108. Of course, this result is not always welcomed by the beneficiaries whose interests are compulsorily overreached. The overreaching which is facilitated by the entry of the restriction will deprive the beneficiaries of their use value in the land, which for them may represent a matter of greater concern. Perhaps for this reason it has been suggested that the device of restriction may possibly be utilised to protect beneficiaries' rights of consultation (post, p 595) by requiring that future dealings be registered only with their consent. See M.P. Thompson, [1988] Conv 108 at 116; [1988] Conv 141 at 143 (P. Sparkes).

A desire to enforce compliance with the conditions of statutory overreaching is not necessarily the only reason for the entry of a restriction. Other kinds of restriction may be entered, as, for example, where it is wished to make the consent of a named person or body a prerequisite to any disposition of land.[12]

(b) Notice

Certain minor interests are protectible by the entry of a 'notice' on the Charges Register of the appropriate title.[13] The protection provided by such a notice extends, for instance, to almost all those categories of right which in unregistered land constitute registrable land charges.[14] Once again the registered proprietor's land certificate must normally[15] be produced before the registrar for the purpose of obtaining entry of a notice.[16]

The notice mode of protection is thus available in respect of such entitlements as a spouse's statutory 'rights of occupation' pursuant to the Matrimonial Homes Act 1983.[17] Entry by notice is likewise appropriate for a range of other rights including legal easements and legal rentcharges. A notice may also be entered to protect the recipient of a charging order made against the registered proprietor pursuant to the Charging Orders Act 1979 or the Drug Trafficking Offences Act 1986.[18] The entry of a notice (generally called a 'creditors' notice'[19]) is similarly appropriate for the purpose of protecting the interests of creditors pending the appointment of a trustee in bankruptcy in respect of the registered proprietor.[20]

12 For another example, see Housing Act 1985, Sch 9A, para 5(2)(b) (as supplied by Housing and Planning Act 1986, s 8(2), Sch 2).

13 Land Registration Act 1925, s 49(1). A notice may also be entered in respect of certain leases (s 48(1) (post, p 673)) and restrictive covenants (s 50 (post, p 1136)).

14 See Land Charges Act 1972, s 2 (ante, p 140). However, a second legal mortgage (which in unregistered land would rank as a puisne mortgage) is capable of substantive registration as a 'registered charge' in registered land (post, p 228), provided that the relevant land certificate is available to the Land Registry (see T.B.F. Ruoff and R.B. Roper, op cit, para 7.08).

15 Land Registration Act 1925, s 64(1)(c). See, however, the exception made in the case of entry of spousal rights of occupation under the Matrimonial Homes Act 1983 (Land Registration Act 1925, s 64(5)). A spouse's notice may thus be entered without the co-operation or knowledge of the other spouse (ante, p 161). A further exception to the general requirement of production of the land certificate arises with the secure tenant's 'preserved right to buy' (see Housing Act 1985, Sch 9A, para 5(3), as supplied by Housing and Planning Act 1986, s 8(2), Sch 2, post, p 775).

16 The Law Commission has recommended that 'rights of occupation' under the Matrimonial Homes Act 1983 should henceforth be protected by notice only if the registered proprietor consents to the entry, and should in all other cases be protected by the entry of a caution (*Property Law: Third Report on Land Registration* (Law Com No 158, 31 March 1987), para 4.41). See Draft Land Registration Bill, clause 33(2) (Law Commission, Law Com No 173 (1988), Appendix).

17 In relation to such rights notice is indeed the only permissible means of entry on the register. It is clearly provided that statutory 'rights of occupation' may no longer be protected by the lodging of a caution (see Matrimonial Homes Act 1983, s 2(9)).

18 Land Registration Act 1925, s 49(1)(g). The Law Commission has, however, recommended that a charging order which takes effect exclusively against the equitable interest of the debtor as a beneficiary under a trust of registered land should be capable of protection by means of restriction only (see Law Com No 158, para 4.43).

19 Land Registration Act 1925, s 61(1).

20 Land Registration Act 1925, s 49(1)(f).

The effect of any notice, once entered, is that all subsequent transferees of the registered title to which it relates take that title subject to the rights protected by the notice.[1] The entry of a notice does not, however, augment the rights thereby protected or improve the position of the incumbrancer in relation to the holder of any *earlier* incumbrance. Mere entry of the notice confers no priority over existing interests, even though the latter were themselves unprotected by entry on the register.[2] The benefit gained through entry of a notice is limited to securing priority in relation to interests granted *subsequently* which might otherwise have achieved priority by substantive registration.[3]

(c) Caution

Almost all forms of minor interest may be protected by the entry of a 'caution' in the relevant Proprietorship Register.[4] There is no requirement that the registered proprietor should co-operate by making his land certificate available to the registrar for this purpose. Although this facility for unilateral entry marks an important distinction between the caution and the notice, the caution is generally intended to achieve only a limited or temporary form of protection for some contentious matter.[5] In effect a caution operates as a species of 'statutory injunction'[6] restraining for the time being further operations of the register.

A caution may take the form of either a 'caution against first registration'[7] or a 'caution against dealings'.[8] The effect of lodging a caution in either case is that no further registration or dealing can be effected by the registrar until a notice has been served on the cautioner giving him an opportunity to object.[9] If the cautioner's objection is successful, the registrar has a broad discretion to take such action as he thinks appropriate, and this may involve

1 Land Registration Act 1925, ss 20(1)(a), 23(1)(b), 52(1).
2 Thus, in *The Mortgage Corpn Ltd v Nationwide Credit Corpn Ltd* (1992) *Times*, 27 July, a notice entered in respect of a charge over registered land could not, under Land Registration Act 1925, s 52(1), confer on the chargee any priority in relation to an earlier and wholly unprotected charge over the same land. In such a case the relevant rule governing priority is still that the charges rank in order of creation, not in order of entry on the register (post, p 186).
3 *The Mortgage Corpn Ltd v Nationwide Credit Corpn Ltd* (1992) *Times*, 27 July, per David Neuberger QC (sitting as a Deputy High Court judge).
4 See, however, Matrimonial Homes Act 1983, s 2(9) (ante, p 183). The registrar has no power to enter a caution of his own motion.
5 The means of protection for minor interests are not mutually exclusive: minor interests may often be protectible by any of several kinds of entry on the register (see *In re White Rose Cottage* [1965] Ch 940 at 949F–950B). The Law Commission has long advocated a rationalisation in this area which would draw a clear distinction between entries on the register which are contentious and those which are not. The Commission has expressed the view that an interest which is not disputed by the registered proprietor should always be protected by notice or (where appropriate) by restriction, whereas a disputed interest should always be protected by caution. See Law Commission, *Property Law: Land Registration (Fourth Paper)* (Published Working Paper No 67, April 1976), para 57f; Law Com No 158, para 4.38. See also Draft Land Registration Bill, clause 33(1), (2) (Law Commission, Law Com No 173 (1988), Appendix).
6 *Barry v Heider* (1914) 19 CLR 197 at 221 per Isaacs J.
7 Land Registration Act 1925, s 53(1).
8 Land Registration Act 1925, s 54(1).
9 Land Registration Act 1925, s 55(1). See also Land Registration Rules 1925, r 220.

the entry of a notice or restriction on the register in respect of the interest which was previously protected only by caution. If, however, the cautioner fails to substantiate his claim within 14 days, he is deemed to have been 'warned off' the register.

In practice most cautions perform the role of a holding device which is aimed at the temporary suspension of dealings in the registered land until some superior form of protection becomes available. It is clear, moreover, that the mere lodging of a caution does not in any way enhance the rights thereby protected[10] or confer on these rights any priority over other entitlements.[11] The caution merely enables the cautioner to be warned of any proposed operation of the register and gives him 'an opportunity of contending that it would be a dealing which would infringe [his] rights.'[12] The caution effectively prevents such rights from being destroyed before further protective action can be taken.

(d) Inhibition

On the application of any interested person, both the court and the registrar have power to enter an 'inhibition' on the register of title. This form of entry is made only rarely, but has the effect of precluding any dealing with the title either until the occurrence of some specified event or until further order.[13] The sorts of circumstance in which an inhibition may be appropriate include the case where the registered proprietor discovers that his land certificate has been lost or stolen, or where there has been a fraudulent dealing with the title,[14] or where a bankruptcy order has been made in respect of the proprietor and there is a need to freeze possible dealings with title.[15]

(2) Search of the register

It is open to the intending purchaser of registered land to requisition an 'official search with priority' of the Land Register for the purpose of discovering the existence of minor interests entered against the title with which he is concerned.[16] The recipient of the official search certificate then acquires a 30 day priority period during which he may take the relevant transfer and apply for its registration,[17] safe in the knowledge that his title,

10 See *FNCB-Waltons Finance Ltd v Crest Realty Pty Ltd* (1977) 10 NSWLR 621 at 631A.

11 In particular the lodgment of a caution confers no priority of any kind over already existing interests (whether or not the latter have been protected by entry on the register). See *The Mortgage Corpn Ltd v Nationwide Credit Corpn Ltd* (1992) *Times*, 27 July.

12 *Barclays Bank Ltd v Taylor* [1974] Ch 137 at 147A per Russell LJ.

13 Land Registration Act 1925, s 57(1). The Law Commission has suggested that the facility of the inhibition should be extended to cover Mareva (and other) injunctions which relate to land (see Law Com No 158, paras 4.58ff).

14 See eg *Ahmed v Kendrick* (1988) 56 P & CR 120 at 123 (post p 489).

15 Land Registration Act 1925, s 61(3), as amended by Insolvency Act 1985, Sch 8, para 5(3)(a).

16 The Land Registration (Official Searches) Rules 1990 (SI 1990/1361), r 3(1). Search applications are normally made in prescribed forms, but in some circumstances an up-dating search may be made by telephone or telex (rr 7, 8).

17 The Land Registration (Official Searches) Rules 1990, r 6. See *Watts v Waller* [1973] QB 153 at 164D-H; but compare *Howell v Montey* (1990) 61 P & CR 18 at 21; [1990] Conv 392 (P. Coughlan).

when registered, will prevail over any supervening adverse entry made during the priority period.[18] If, however, the official search fails (because of some error in the Registry) to reveal a third party interest which has been duly protected, the transferee—albeit that he is entirely blameless—takes his title subject to the prior interest,[19] but is entitled to a statutory indemnity in respect of any loss suffered.[20]

(3) Competing minor interests

In those rare circumstances where two or more competing minor interests have been duly protected by entry against the same registered title, the issue of priority between them is not dictated by the respective dates of entry, but is generally governed by the respective dates of creation. Since minor interests take effect merely as equitable interests, the problem of priority inter se is resolved in favour of the minor interest which was created first, even though it may not have been entered in the register until after the date of entry of a competing minor interest of later creation. The priority accorded earlier creation gives way only where the owner of the first minor interest has behaved fraudulently or negligently or is estopped from asserting priority by reason of conduct which induced the second owner to act to his detriment in acquiring the later minor interest.[1]

(4) Effect of failure to protect a minor interest by entry on the register

One of the fundamental objectives of a system of registered title must be to ensure that the register remains an accurate record of the interests affecting registered titles. It is 'the cardinal principle' of title registration that 'the register is everything',[2] and it is therefore important that there should be a strong incentive towards protection of minor interests by means of the appropriate entry on the register.

The Land Registration Act 1925 accordingly contains provisions which are aimed at depriving unprotected minor interests of effect in the event of a transfer of the registered title to a third party. Under section 20(1), a disposition for valuable consideration of a legal estate in registered land (whether freehold or leasehold) has the effect of conferring that estate upon

18 The Land Registration (Official Searches) Rules 1990, r 5. The Supreme Court of Canada has held that, absent special knowledge of the significance of their contents, a courier is not liable in negligence for the late delivery of registration documents to the registry (see *B.D.C. Ltd v Hofstrand Farms Ltd* (1986) 26 DLR (4th) 1 at 5, 14f).

19 *Parkash v Irani Finance Ltd* [1970] Ch 101 at 110H–111A. Compare the effect in unregistered land of Land Charges Act 1972, s 10(4) (ante, p 132), a provision which has no registered land equivalent.

20 Post, p 237.

1 See *Abigail v Lapin* [1934] AC 491 at 500ff; *Barclays Bank Ltd v Taylor* [1974] Ch 137 at 147E; *Strand Securities Ltd v Caswell* [1965] Ch 958 at 991B. The Law Commission has recommended that the existing rules as to the priority of minor interests should be reversed so that the priority of such interests inter se would normally be governed by their order of protection on the register (Law Com No 158, para 4.98). See Draft Land Registration Bill, clause 9(2) (Law Commission, Law Com No 173 (1988), Appendix).

2 See *Fels v Knowles* (1906) 26 NZLR 604 at 620; *Bunt v Hallinan* [1985] 1 NZLR 450 at 458. See also *Re Cartlidge and Granville Savings & Mortgage Corp* (1987) 34 DLR (4th) 161 at 172.

the transferee or grantee subject only 'to the incumbrances and other entries, if any, appearing on the register...and...to the overriding interests, if any, affecting the estate transferred or created'.[3] The title of the new proprietor is statutorily declared to be 'free from all other estates and interests whatsoever'.[4] The same policy appears even more plainly in section 59(6), which declares that, with several exceptions,

> a purchaser acquiring title under a registered disposition shall not be concerned with any...document, matter, or claim (not being an overriding interest...) which is not protected by a caution, or other entry on the register, whether he has or has not notice thereof, express, implied, or constructive.

Of course where a disposition is made *without* valuable consideration, unprotected minor interests remain binding on the transferee.[5] In such cases the record on the register is irrelevant because the volunteer places no reliance on it. The volunteer 'does not look to the register to decide whether or not he will accept a gift...He is happy to receive whatever interest the registered owner has to give.'[6]

(a) *The orthodox rule*

Sections 20(1) and 59(6) of the Land Registration Act 1925 seem to envisage that failure to protect a minor interest in registered land produces roughly the same consequence of voidness as that which results from a failure to register a land charge in respect of unregistered land.[7]

(i) The general irrelevance of notice Accordingly, in the context of registered land, an unprotected minor interest binds neither a 'transferee' within section 20(1) nor a 'purchaser' within section 59(6), irrespective of the state of mind of such persons.[8] As Cross J pointed out in *Strand Securities Ltd v Caswell*,[9] it is 'vital to the working of the land registration system that notice of something which is not on the register should not affect a transferee unless it is an overriding interest.'[10]

3 In subjecting land to entries appearing on the register, section 20(1) undoubtedly refers to entries so appearing at the date of registration of the title transferred (see *Abbey National Building Society v Cann* [1991] 1 AC 56 at 84B per Lord Oliver of Aylmerton).

4 See also Land Registration Act 1925, ss 23(1), 52(1). The proprietor's title is not of course free of other burdens arising by statute or under the common law which do not as such comprise an 'estate' or 'interest' in the land (eg statutorily protected tenancies and the consequences of planning laws (see Law Com No 158, para 2.1)).

5 Land Registration Act 1925, s 20(4).

6 *Re Passburg Petroleums Ltd and Landstrom Developments Ltd* (1984) 8 DLR (4th) 363 at 368 per Moir JA. Compare, however, *Bogdanovic v Koteff* (1988) 12 NSWLR 472 at 480A-B per Priestley JA.

7 In the context of unregistered land an unprotected land charge is usually void even as against a purchaser who has actual knowledge of the existence of the unregistered interest. See *Midland Bank Trust Co Ltd v Green* [1981] AC 513 (ante, p 126).

8 See *Miles v Bull* (No 2) [1969] 3 All ER 1585 at 1590D-H; *De Lusignan v Johnson* (1973) 230 Estates Gazette 499.

9 [1965] Ch 373 at 390A-B.

10 Overriding interests are discussed elsewhere (post, p 197). See *Williams & Glyn's Bank Ltd v Boland* [1981] AC 487 at 504A per Lord Wilberforce ('The only kind of notice recognised is by entry on the register').

(ii) The rationale behind the rule This general denial of effect to unprotected minor interests is of course the cornerstone of any system of title registration.[11] The provision of statutory immunity from unprotected interests 'is designed to facilitate dealings with land; and it seems to mean that a man may purchase land safely from the registered proprietor, closing his mind to the mere fact of any unregistered interest.'[12] Once again it is the plain intendment of the legislation that certainty and efficiency in the process of land transfer should prevail over short-term justice in matters of conflict between purchasers and owners of equitable interests.[13] Sections 20(1) and 59(6) of the Land Registration Act 1925 provide yet another illustration of 'the necessity of this business consideration predominating over the moral aspect'.[14] Concern for the integrity of the register ranks well above any concern for the integrity of the purchaser.

(b) The exception for fraud

Notwithstanding the general irrelevance of notice under the Land Registration Act 1925, it has always been clear that cases of fraud or bad faith constitute an exception to the integrity of the register.[15] The statutory immunity from unprotected minor interests does not extend to a purchaser who seeks *fraudulently* to take advantage of a failure to enter such interests appropriately on the register.[16] Although the system of registration of title is 'designed to provide simplicity and certitude in transfers of land', these qualities are 'amply achieved without depriving equity of the ability to exercise its jurisdiction *in personam* on grounds of conscience.'[17]

As an exception to the integrity of the register, the concept of 'fraud' has no clear definition,[18] and its identification depends on the particular

11 See *Williams & Glyn's Bank Ltd v Boland* [1981] AC 487 at 503G-H, where in relation to title registration Lord Wilberforce emphasised that '[a]bove all, the system is designed to free the purchaser from the hazards of notice—real or constructive—which, in the case of unregistered land, involved him in enquiries, often quite elaborate, failing which he might be bound by equities'. See also *Parkash v Irani Finance Ltd* [1970] Ch 101 at 108A.
12 *Wicks v Bennett* (1921) 30 CLR 80 at 95 per Higgins J.
13 Ante, p 120.
14 See *Holt, Renfrew & Co Ltd v Henry Singer Ltd* (1982) 135 DLR (3d) 391 at 399.
15 See *De Lusignan v Johnson* (1973) 230 Estates Gazette 499 per Brightman J. See generally M.P. Thompson, [1985] CLJ 280.
16 As, however, Lord Lindley said in *Assets Co Ltd v Mere Roihi* [1905] AC 176 at 210, 'fraud' is relevant only if it has been 'brought home to the person whose registered title is impeached or to his agents'. (On 'fraud' committed by an agent, see *National Commercial Banking Corpn of Australia Ltd v Hedley* (1984) 3 BPR 9477 at 9482.) There is a clear link between the quality of the 'fraud' which prejudices the statutory immunity of the registered transferee and the degree of 'fraud' relevant to justify a rectification of the transferee's title pursuant to Land Registration Act 1925, s 82(1)(d) (post, p 231). The former kind of fraud is, however, wide enough to embrace dishonesty unconnected with the *obtaining* of the registered title. See *Bahr v Nicolay* (No 2) (1988) 164 CLR 604 at 615 per Mason CJ and Dawson J; and compare Land Registration Act 1925, s 82(1)(d) (p 231).
17 *Oh Hiam v Tham Kong* (1980) 2 BPR 9451 at 9453 per Lord Russell of Killowen. See also *Frazer v Walker* [1967] 1 AC 569 at 585B-C per Lord Wilberforce; *Coles KMA Ltd v Sword Nominees Pty Ltd* (1986) 44 SASR 120 at 129.
18 'No definition of fraud can be attempted, so various are its forms and methods' (*Stuart v Kingston* (1923) 32 CLR 309 at 359). See also *Moore v Moore* (1971) 16 DLR (3d) 174 at 185; *R v Olan, Hudson and Hartnett* (1978) 86 DLR (3d) 212 at 217f per Dickson J.

circumstances of each case.[19] In the present context 'fraud' seems to require more than a mere showing of 'equitable' or 'constructive' fraud.[20] The purchaser must be guilty of 'something in the nature of personal dishonesty or moral turpitude'.[1] Dishonesty of this kind involves 'some notion of taking from someone else, literally or metaphorically, that which is his due or is due to him.'[2] Such a mental state is not easy to establish in a purchaser of a registered title, but may arise where the purchaser asserts a 'claim to hold the land for an unencumbered estate in wilful disregard of the rights to which it is known to be subject.'[3] Likewise, a fraudulent disregard of unprotected rights may be ascribed to the purchaser if 'his suspicions were aroused, and. . .he abstained from making inquiries for fear of learning the truth'.[4]

(c) Mere knowledge of the existence of unprotected rights is not fraud

It has always been vital in the present context that there should be a clear dissociation between fraud and notice: in this respect the traditional doctrine of notice must not be allowed to intrude upon the operation of the register.

(i) The historic dissociation of fraud and notice In surveying the registration schemes which were the forerunners of the Land Registration Act 1925, the Real Property Royal Commissioners of 1830 started from the premise that it is 'greatly for the public good, that civil rights should be capable of being ascertained without difficulty'. The Commissioners pointed out that a 'registered title possesses the advantages of certainty and security in a high degree, but they will be impaired, if preference be given to an unregistered over a registered deed, on the ground of notice.'[5] The Commissioners thus inveighed against the 'mischiefs' of letting in notice actual or constructive,

19 See *Bunt v Hallinan* [1985] 1 NZLR 450 at 461.

20 There must be 'actual fraud' (see *Assets Co Ltd v Mere Roihi* [1905] AC 176 at 210; *Bunt v Hallinan* [1985] 1 NZLR 450 at 458).

1 *Butler v Fairclough* (1917) 23 CLR 78 at 90; *Wicks v Bennett* (1921) 30 CLR 80 at 91; *Stuart v Kingston* (1923) 32 CLR 309 at 329 per Knox CJ. See also *Assets Co Ltd v Mere Roihi* [1905] AC 176 at 210; *Frazer v Walker* [1967] 1 AC 569 at 584C; *Whittingham v Whittingham* [1979] Fam 9 at 12F; *Bunt v Hallinan* [1985] 1 NZLR 450 at 458, 463.

2 *Sutton v O'Kane* [1973] 2 NZLR 304 at 322 per Turner P. Compare *Midland Bank Trust Co Ltd v Green* [1980] Ch 590 at 625B per Lord Denning MR (ante, p 126). See *Waimiha Sawmilling Co Ltd v Waione Timber Co Ltd* [1923] NZLR 1137 at 1175, where Salmond J indicated that 'the true test of fraud is not whether the purchaser actually knew for a certainty of the existence of the adverse right, but whether he knew enough to make it his duty as an honest man to hold his hand, and either to make further inquiries before purchasing, or to abstain from the purchase, or to purchase subject to the claimant's rights rather than in defiance of them.'

3 *Wellington City Corpn v Public Trustee* [1921] NZLR 423 at 433 per Salmond J. In the words of Salmond J in *Waimiha Sawmilling Co Ltd v Waione Timber Co Ltd* [1923] NZLR 1137 at 1173, dishonesty connotes here 'a wilful and conscious disregard and violation of the right of other persons'.

4 *Assets Co Ltd v Mere Roihi* [1905] AC 176 at 210 per Lord Lindley. There can be no 'fraud', however, if the purchaser acted on the advice of his lawyer that he was free to ignore rights which someone else claimed to have under an unregistered instrument (see *Bunt v Hallinan* [1985] 1 NZLR 450 at 462f). See also *Babcock v Carr* (1982) 127 DLR (3d) 77 at 84ff.

5 *Report*, p 37. Compare *Agra Bank Ltd v Barry* (1874) LR 7 HL 135 at 149 per Lord Cairns ('It appears to me that the object of such a statute. . .is to give a premium to diligence in registration').

and concluded that effect should always be denied to unregistered rights except 'in case of actual fraud'.[6]

These historic perceptions are now deeply embedded in the operation of most schemes of title registration throughout the common law world.[7] There is a general consensus that mere knowledge of the existence of unregistered rights does not connote 'fraud' on the part of the purchaser.[8] As the High Court of Australia observed in *Wicks v Bennett*,[9] fraud in this area requires 'something more than mere disregard of rights of which the person sought to be affected had notice.' Title registration is intended to mark a 'complete break'[10] from the equitable rules which formerly governed land law priorities. In consequence there has been a general rejection, no less so in England than elsewhere, of any temptation to qualify the system of title registration by the importing of an equitable doctrine alien to its central purpose.

(ii) The occasional re-emergence of the doctrine of notice Given the dogmatic exclusion of mere knowledge from the concept of 'fraud', it is perhaps inevitable that from time to time the case law should disclose instances where the courts have not been prepared to accept that the doctrine of actual notice has been fully extinguished in the present context.[11]

In England the clarity of the law relating to minor interests was thrown into some confusion by the decision in *Peffer v Rigg*.[12] Here B and X had married two sisters—one each—and therefore shared a common relative in the form of their mother-in-law, M. Partly in order to accommodate M during her old age, B and X joined together to buy a house. They contributed equally towards the purchase price of a property with registered title, although the property was transferred into the sole name of X. On these facts there arose an implied trust for sale, X holding the legal title as registered proprietor on behalf of himself and B as equitable tenants in common (see *Fig.* 15).

6 *Report*, p 39. The same disregard for notice except in cases of fraud was endorsed by a further Royal Commission in 1857 (see *Report of the Commissioners on the Registration of Title with reference to the Sale and Transfer of Land* (CP 2215, 1857-Session 2), para LXXIII).

7 In some jurisdictions there is specific statutory confirmation that mere knowledge on the part of a purchaser that a trust or unregistered interest is in existence 'shall not of itself be imputed as fraud' (see eg New Zealand's Land Transfer Act 1952, s 182; Alberta's Land Titles Act (RSA 1980, c L-5), s 195). See generally D.J. Whalan, *The Meaning of Fraud under the Torrens System*, (1974–75) 6 NZULR 207; P. Butt, *Notice and Fraud in the Torrens System: A Comparative Analysis*, (1977–78) 13 Univ of Western Australia LR 354.

8 See eg *Union Bank of Canada v Boulter-Waugh Ltd* (1919) 46 DLR 41 at 48; *Waimiha Sawmilling Co Ltd v Waione Timber Co Ltd* [1926] AC 101 at 106ff; *Ruptash and Lumsden v Zawick* (1956) 2 DLR (2d) 145 at 159f; *Friedmann v Barrett; Ex parte Friedmann* [1962] Qd R 498 at 504, 512; *Holt, Renfrew & Co Ltd v Henry Singer Ltd* (1982) 135 DLR (3d) 391 at 397, 408, 421f; *Re Pacific Cassiar Ltd and Esso Canada Resources Ltd* (1986) 28 DLR (4th) 104 at 117; *Bahr v Nicolay* (No 2) (1988) 164 CLR 604 at 613 per Mason CJ and Dawson J, 630f per Wilson and Toohey JJ, 652f, 655 per Brennan J.

9 (1921) 30 CLR 80 at 91.

10 See *United Trust Co v Dominion Stores Ltd* (1977) 71 DLR (3d) 72 at 75 per Laskin CJC (dissenting).

11 See eg *United Trust Co v Dominion Stores Ltd* (1977) 71 DLR (3d) 72 at 98, where Spence J voiced the opinion of the majority of the Supreme Court of Canada in holding that 'such a cardinal principle of property law cannot be considered to have been abrogated unless the legislative enactment is in the clearest and most unequivocal of terms'.

12 [1977] 1 WLR 285 (post, p 197). See (1977) 41 Conv (NS) 207 (F.R. Crane); (1977) 93 LQR 341 (R.J. Smith); [1977] CLJ 227 (D.J. Hayton); [1978] Conv 52 (J. Martin).

The circumstances of this purchase were fully known to the entire family of M. Indeed the implied trust was subsequently confirmed expressly in a formal deed of trust drawn up by B and X, although B never took steps to protect his beneficial half-share by the entry of a minor interest on the register of X's title. Some time later X's marriage to A broke down and ended in divorce. As part of the divorce settlement X transferred the legal estate in the house to A, M having died by this stage. X purported to transfer the 'whole' of the property 'as beneficial owner', in consideration of the payment of £1 by A.

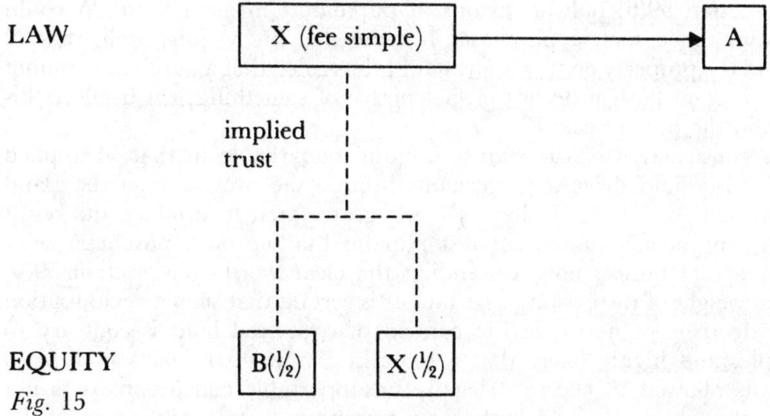

Fig. 15

A subsequently contended that the transfer invested her, as the new registered proprietor, with the legal estate in fee simple free of B's minor interest as a beneficiary behind the trust for sale. A argued that B's beneficial interest had become ineffective against her by reason of sections 20(1) and 59(6) of the Land Registration Act 1925. It was of course plain that A had at all times been perfectly well aware of the existence of B's interest in the property, since the entire family had been involved in resolving the accommodation needs posed by M. Nevertheless A was able to invoke considerable support for the proposition that, irrespective of notice, an unprotected minor interest is unenforceable against a subsequent transferee or purchaser.[13]

Notwithstanding the clear provisions of sections 20(1) and 59(6), Graham J concluded that A held the newly transferred title on trust for herself and B as equitable tenants in common.[14] He took the view, first, that A was excluded from claiming any immunity from unprotected minor interests under section 20(1), since the transfer had been described by the parties themselves as involving only a 'nominal' consideration.[15] Section 20(1) requires that there be a transfer for 'valuable consideration',[16] a phrase which for the

13 There was incidentally no question that B could claim the protection of an overriding interest by reason of 'actual occupation' (post, p 203), not least because he had never lived in the house in question.
14 [1977] 1 WLR 285 at 295E.
15 [1977] 1 WLR 285 at 293F. This ground for the decision was highly dubious. It was clear on the facts that A had also taken over a mortgage commitment in respect of the property under the terms of the divorce settlement, and her assumption of this liability must surely have constituted 'valuable consideration'.
16 See also Land Registration Act 1925, s 20(4) (ante, p 187).

purposes of the Act 'does not include a nominal consideration in money'.[17] Graham J then reinforced his decision by referring to the equitable doctrine which governs the 'knowing reception' of trust property transferred in breach of trust.[18] Since A 'knew. . .that the property was trust property when the transfer was made to her', Graham J held that she took the title 'on a constructive trust in accordance with general equitable principles'.[19]

The factor which, however, made the decision in *Peffer v Rigg* truly startling was the way in which Graham J cited the statutory definition of 'purchaser'[20] in support of his view that unprotected minor interests are rendered ineffective under section 59(6) only as against a purchaser 'in good faith'. A could not claim to be such a purchaser because she 'knew quite well' that X had held the property on trust.[1] Graham J thus ruled that a purchaser 'cannot . . . be in good faith if he has in fact notice of something which affects his title as in the present case.'[2]

This construction of the statute is quite remarkable in that, if applied broadly, it would drive a juggernaut through the provisions of the Land Registration Act 1925. Graham J's ruling appeared to produce the result that an unprotected minor interest remains binding on a purchaser with express actual notice, notwithstanding the clear wording of section 59(6) and the weight of the existing case law. It is certain that such a revitalisation of the doctrine of notice in the context of registered land is contrary to principle, and highly likely that a moralistic view of the facts in *Peffer v Rigg* was allowed to coerce a legally unsupportable conclusion. It is not usually thought to be 'bad faith' for a purchaser to take advantage of the folly of those who fail to effect the appropriate registration in protection of their interests.[3] In *De Lusignan v Johnson*,[4] for instance, Brightman J expressly indicated that to allege 'bad faith' in this situation 'would be stretching the language'. He accordingly drew a sharp distinction between 'fraud' and mere 'notice of the existence or possible existence' of unprotected rights, taking the view that only the former provides a relevant ground of complaint against a purchaser of registered land. In *Peffer v Rigg* the primary motive underlying the disputed transfer of title from X to A was not to defraud B but rather to provide A with a home in the aftermath of divorce, and

17 Land Registration Act 1925, s 3(xxxi).
18 Ante, p 125.
19 [1977] 1 WLR 285 at 294E-F. Graham J emphasised that this constructive trust was 'a new trust imposed by equity and is distinct from the trust which bound [X].' Compare *Buck v Dickinson* (1978) 79 DLR (3d) 759 at 763.
20 For the purpose of the Land Registration Act 1925, 'purchaser' is defined as a 'purchaser in good faith for valuable consideration and includes a lessee, mortgagee, or other person who for valuable consideration acquires any interest in land or in any charge on land' (Land Registration Act 1925, s 3(xxi)). The word 'transferee' is left undefined by the Land Registration Act 1925, and it is therefore unclear whether this term incorporates any requirement of good faith.
1 [1977] 1 WLR 285 at 294E.
2 [1977] 1 WLR 285 at 294C. See *Marsden v Campbell* (1897) 18 NSWR Eq 33 at 38, where a requirement of bona fides was interpreted to mean that the purchaser must take without notice of the rights of any occupant.
3 See eg *In re Monolithic Building Co* [1915] 1 Ch 643 at 663; *Midland Bank Trust Co Ltd v Green* [1981] AC 513 at 530A-B (ante, p 130).
4 (1973) 230 Estates Gazette 499.

the case should not have been stigmatised as one involving 'bad faith' in the purchaser.[5]

(d) Recognised cases of 'fraud'

In cases of manifestly dishonest transfer of the registered title, it is clear that the court may exercise an *in personam* jurisdiction to prevent the Land Registration Act being used as an instrument of fraud.[6] In such instances the transferee is deemed to take the title subject to the unprotected minor interests which he has sought to disregard. The existence of an *in personam* jurisdiction to counteract fraud is not inconsistent with the supposed indefeasibility of the title secured by the 'statutory magic' of registration.[7] Registration of title is essentially 'a system of conveyancing; it does not abrogate the principles of equity.'[8] As Brennan J observed in the Australian High Court in *Bahr v Nicolay* (No 2),[9] indefeasible title is 'designed to protect a transferee from defects in the title of the transferor, not to free him from interests with which he has burdened his own title.'

The following circumstances, which are not mutually exclusive, provide examples of the kinds of conduct which have been classified as 'fraud' for this purpose. The threshold of recognisable 'fraud' doubtless varies over time and jurisdiction, but comparative experience indicates that, while the penumbral definition of fraud may be difficult, the core notion is relatively stable.

(i) Deliberate ploy to defeat unprotected rights The term 'fraud' is applicable to a transfer of a registered title which was intended quite blatantly to defeat an incumbrancer's rights while they remained unprotected. As Lord Buckmaster said in *Waimiha Sawmilling Co Ltd v Waione Timber Co Ltd*,[10] '[i]f the designed object of a transfer be to cheat a man of a known existing right, that is fraudulent'.[11] Such a conveyance of title truly epitomises the *machinatio ad circumveniendum* which was condemned, perhaps overly broadly, by Lord Hardwicke LC in *Le Neve v Le Neve*.[12]

A label of 'fraud' is therefore liable to attach to a swiftly conducted transfer of a registered title to a friend for the deliberate purpose of defeating the equitable (and unprotected) rights of the transferor's wife.[13] Likewise a similarly motivated transfer to a company which is in reality the alter ego

5 The authority of *De Lusignan v Johnson* was preferred in *Burr v Copp* [1983] CLY 2057.
6 For a general discussion of the standard of identifiable 'fraud' in property transactions, see Chapter 7 (ante, p 123).
7 Ante, p 181. See *Bahr v Nicolay* (No 2) (1988) 164 CLR 604 at 637 per Wilson and Toohey JJ.
8 *Wilkins v Kannammal* [1951] MLJ 99 at 100 per Taylor J. See also *Boyd v Mayor of Wellington* [1924] NZLR 1174 at 1223; *Oh Hiam v Tham Kong* (1980) 2 BPR 9451 at 9454 per Lord Russell of Killowen.
9 (1988) 164 CLR 604 at 653.
10 [1926] AC 101 at 106 (ante, p 129).
11 Lord Buckmaster's dictum has been described as a 'convenient starting point' for the definition of fraud in this context. See *Bahr v Nicolay* (No 2) (1988) 164 CLR 604 at 630 per Wilson and Toohey JJ.
12 (1747) Amb 436 at 447, 27 ER 291 at 295.
13 *Efstratiou, Glantschnig and Petrovic v Glantschnig* [1972] NZLR 594 at 598f.

of the transferor is apt to be stigmatised as 'fraud'.[14] In *Jones v Lipman*,[15] for instance, Russell J held that an unprotected estate contract remained binding upon, and specifically enforceable against, the transferee of a registered title. Here the transferee was a limited company which, on closer inspection, turned out to be merely the alter ego of the transferor who had earlier granted the estate contract to the present plaintiff. In Russell J's view, the defendant company was 'the creature of the first defendant [the transferor], a device and a sham, a mask which he holds before his face in an attempt to avoid recognition by the eye of equity'.[16]

(ii) Transfer expressly 'subject to' unprotected rights If a transfer of title is expressly stipulated to be 'subject to' unprotected minor interests, it is possible that the court will impose a constructive trust upon a transferee who later reneges upon the stipulation by claiming an unencumbered legal title.[17] 'Fraud' is clearly established by the transferee's deliberate disregard of the express terms on which the bargain between transferor and transferee was allowed to take effect.[18]

Ultimately, however, there is a limiting factor. The court will not impose a constructive trust unless it is satisfied that the conscience of the transferee is affected.[19] The fact that a transfer is expressed to be 'subject to' certain rights does not necessarily imply that the transferee is in conscience bound by an obligation, not otherwise existing, to give effect to such rights. The mere incantation of the formula does not convert unenforceable rights into binding interests in land. In *Ashburn Anstalt v Arnold*,[20] for instance, there was a suggestion that a transferee had bound itself to take title 'subject to' the unprotected rights of a contractual licensee.[1] The Court of Appeal took the view that a contractual licence does not confer any proprietary interest in land[2] and therefore would not normally affect the conscience of any transferee of the land.[3] The mere recitation that the transferee takes

14 *Moore v Moore* (1971) 16 DLR (3d) 174 at 183, where the British Columbia Court of Appeal pointed out that 'incorporation of the company and the transfer by the husband to it was a device intended to defeat the rightful claims of the wife.'

15 [1962] 1 WLR 832.

16 [1962] 1 WLR 832 at 836. The transferor had in effect sought to reverse the adage 'the company *c'est moi*' (see *Pioneer Concrete Services Ltd v Yelnah Pty Ltd* (1986) 5 NSWLR 254 at 265B per Young J).

17 *Lyus v Prowsa Developments Ltd* [1982] 1 WLR 1044 at 1053F-G (post, p 440). It has even been suggested that such a stipulation may be enforceable as an *express* trust (see *Bahr v Nicolay* (No 2) (1988) 164 CLR 604 at 618f per Mason CJ and Dawson J).

18 *Lyus v Prowsa Developments Ltd* [1982] 1 WLR 1044 at 1054G-H (post, p 441). As Brennan J said in *Bahr v Nicolay* (No 2) (1988) 164 CLR 604 at 654, such a transferee 'is, in equity's eye, acting fraudulently and he may be compelled to honour the unregistered interest. A means by which equity prevents the fraud is by imposing a constructive trust on the purchaser when he repudiates the unregistered interest. . .The fraud which attracts the intervention of equity consists in the unconscionable attempt by the registered proprietor to deny the unregistered interest to which he has undertaken to subject his registered title.'

19 Post, p 415.

20 [1989] Ch 1 (post, p 920). See [1988] Conv 201 (M.P. Thompson); (1988) 51 MLR 226 (J. Hill); (1988) 104 LQR 175 (P. Sparkes).

1 The point was obiter since the Court of Appeal decided that the rights in question were in fact rights of lease not licence (post, p 690).

2 Post, p 921.

3 [1989] Ch 1 at 24D.

'subject to' such a contractual licence neither imposes any obligation on the transferee nor implies any 'fraud' by reason of repudiation, in which case no constructive trust can be raised against the transferee.[4]

It seems in consequence that the conventional (although somewhat unsatisfactory[5]) borderline between proprietary and purely personal rights in land significantly limits the vulnerability of the transferee who takes a registered title expressly 'subject to' existing rights. Any constructive trust activated by a fraudulent or unconscionable disavowal of third party rights is probably best limited to those rights which are generally accepted to be *proprietary* in quality.[6]

(iii) Collateral representation 'Fraud' is likewise present where the transfer of a registered title has been induced by a collateral representation made by the transferee that he will respect the unprotected rights of a third party. 'Fraud' may thus be found where, prior to the transfer, the transferee indicated to the transferor either verbally or in writing that he would not disturb the rights of the unprotected incumbrancer. In *Loke Yew v Port Swettenham Rubber Co Ltd*,[7] for instance, the Privy Council had no doubt that a vitiating element of fraud would be present if the transferee later repudiated the undertaking.[8] If the purchaser's representation in fact induces in the vendor 'a false sense of security as to the purchaser's intention',[9] it would be fraudulent for the purchaser later to act inconsistently with its terms.[10] In such cases the purchaser is liable to be fixed with a constructive trust in favour of the incumbrancer.[11]

4 [1989] Ch 1 at 25H-26B per Fox LJ ('The words "subject to" will, of course, impose notice. But notice is not enough to impose on somebody an obligation to give effect to a contract into which he did not enter'). Fox LJ pointed out that the use of a 'subject to' formula in a transfer may even 'be at least as consistent with an intention to protect the grantor against claims by the grantee as an intention to impose an obligation on the grantee.'

5 See *Property in Thin Air*, [1991] CLJ 252 at 292f.

6 It is notable that, in both *Lyus v Prowsa Developments Ltd* [1982] 1 WLR 1044 and *Bahr v Nicolay* (No 2) (1988) 164 CLR 604, the interest given effect under the constructive trust holding was plainly a proprietary interest in the conventional sense (ie a contractual right of purchase). See particularly *Bahr* at 655 per Brennan J. See also *Silovi Pty Ltd v Barbaro* (1988) 13 NSWLR 466 at 475F-476B.

7 [1913] AC 491 at 502ff.

8 One of the lesser ironies of legal history is the fact that Loke Yew, the unprotected incumbrancer, was not the vulnerable private citizen one might perhaps have supposed. Owning hugely valuable brothel businesses and opium import duty franchises, he controlled virtually every immoral enterprise in Selangor. It was said of him in 1896 that '[i]f he were crippled financially the revenues of the state would suffer serious loss' (see J.G. Butcher, *The Demise of the Revenue Farm System in the Federated Malay States*, (1983) 17 Modern Asian Studies 387 at 399). He petitioned in 1893 against the Women and Girls Protection Enactment on the ground that state regulation of his brothels would diminish the rents payable 'to no slight injury to Your Petitioner'. Thus it was that the man who later came to be known as the 'Carnegie of Malaya' helped to set the legal bench-mark of fraud. See J.G. Butcher, *Revenue, Morality, and the Gambling Farms in the Federated Malay States* (1988).

9 *Holt, Renfrew & Co Ltd v Henry Singer Ltd* (1982) 135 DLR (3d) 391 at 408.

10 Such a finding of 'fraud' is closely allied to the doctrine of estoppel by representation (post, p 312), and rests on clear proof of a causal link between the representation and the transfer (see eg *Holt, Renfrew & Co Ltd v Henry Singer Ltd* (1982) 135 DLR (3d) 391 at 410, 421f).

11 *Bahr v Nicolay* (No 2) (1988) 164 CLR 604 at 638 per Wilson and Toohey JJ.

(iv) Acquiescence in the exercise of unprotected rights If a transferee not merely knows of the existence of unprotected rights in the land transferred, but positively acquiesces in their continued exercise after the date of transfer, it may constitute a species of 'fraud' if the transferee subsequently claims to have taken title free of those rights.[12]

(v) Post-registration acknowledgement of unprotected rights In the present context the notion of fraud may even be sufficiently extensive to attach equitable consequence to an acknowledgement, made by the registered transferee *after* the date of registration, that he is bound by unprotected rights granted by his transferor to a third party before the transfer.[13]

In *Bahr v Nicolay* (No 2)[14] an owner of land, A, had transferred title to B, the latter having contracted for a later reconveyance of the title to A. B subsequently transferred the title to C pursuant to a contractual undertaking between B and C in which C acknowledged the existence of the repurchase agreement between A and B. Some time after the registration of C's title, C confirmed the repurchase clause in a written communication to A and recognised that C would honour its terms when A sought to exercise his rights. C later repudiated the repurchase clause as not having been protected by entry in the register. The High Court of Australia held that C was bound, either by express[15] or by constructive[16] trust, to give effect to A's unprotected interest. While C's agreement to take title subject to A's rights would probably have been enough to fix C with liability on more conventional grounds,[17] at least some members of the High Court considered it crucial that, almost immediately after taking the registered title, C had sent A written confirmation of his entitlement.[18] In this way C had 'burdened his own title' with rights which now could not in conscience be disavowed.[19]

(vi) Purchase as a fiduciary agent A further case of fraud is present where a fiduciary agent purchases land on behalf of his principal, but procures the registration of title in the name of an associate who knows of the agent's fiduciary status. Here the associate cannot properly claim, pursuant to section 20(1) of the Land Registration Act 1925, to take the registered title free of the principal's unprotected equitable interest in the land.[20]

12 See eg *Maurice Demers Transport Ltd v Fountain Tire Distributors (Edmonton) Ltd* (1974) 42 DLR (3d) 412 at 420ff; *Gough v Kiddeys Korner Ltd* [1976] BCL 62.
13 If there were evidence of detrimental reliance by the unprotected incumbrancer on this undertaking, there would, of course, be an even plainer argument based on estoppel (post, p 314).
14 (1988) 164 CLR 604.
15 (1988) 164 CLR 604 at 618f per Mason CJ and Dawson J.
16 (1988) 164 CLR 604 at 638f per Wilson and Toohey JJ, 654f per Brennan J.
17 The trial judge found that C had 'bought with the knowledge that they were bound by the terms of the Agreement' ((1988) 164 CLR 604 at 632).
18 (1988) 164 CLR 604 at 633ff per Wilson and Toohey JJ.
19 (1988) 164 CLR 604 at 653 per Brennan J (post, p 367). It is questionable whether, in the absence of evidence of estoppel, English courts would today be prepared to go quite so far as the High Court.
20 *Du Boulay v Raggett* (1989) 58 P & CR 138 at 153f. See also *Loke Yew v Port Swettenham Rubber Co Ltd* [1913] AC 491 at 504; *Bahr v Nicolay* (No 2) (1988) 164 CLR 604 at 614, 654.

(e) Proposals for reform

In recent years the Law Commission has kept under constant review the consequences of failure to protect a minor interest by appropriate entry in the register.[1] The Commission has recommended the introduction of a clear statutory requirement that all transferees and other purchasers who wish to take free from unprotected interests must take 'in good faith and for valuable consideration'.[2] The net effect of the Commission's recommendations is that a purchaser acquiring any interest in registered land should have priority over unprotected minor interests unless, for example, the purchaser has not acquired his interest 'in good faith'.[3] However, the Commission expressed the view that a transferee or purchaser is not to be 'deemed dishonest merely because he had actual knowledge of the unprotected minor interest in question'.[4] The Commission disapproved firmly of the decision in *Peffer v Rigg*,[5] and the Draft Land Registration Bill accordingly provides that, for the purpose of proving bad faith in a purchaser, it 'shall not be sufficient. . .for the owner of the minor interest to show that the person concerned was aware of' the unprotected interest.[6]

Under the Law Commission's proposals, the threshold of bad faith therefore connotes something more than mere knowledge of unprotected rights. Intriguingly the Commission has indicated that it does not consider the outcome in *Midland Bank Trust Co Ltd v Green*[7] to have been an 'acceptable' resolution of the equivalent problem in unregistered land.[8] It seems to follow that, at least in the Commission's view, the threshold of vitiating fraud is to be placed somewhere between the purchaser who is aware of, and merely indifferent to, the unprotected status of a minor interest and the purchaser who positively and quite consciously manipulates that unprotected status for the over-arching purpose of obtaining some further advantage for himself.

7. OVERRIDING INTERESTS

Overriding interests comprise a third important category of interests in registered land, being defined as including 'all the incumbrances, interests, rights, and powers not entered on the register but subject to which registered

1 Law Com No 158, paras 4.14ff; Law Com No 173, para 3.7.
2 Law Com No 158, para 4.15; Law Com No 173, para 3.7.
3 In the Commission's view, the burden of showing an absence of good faith should be on the owner of the unprotected interest (Law Com No 158, para 4.17), and such burden is given effect in the Draft Land Registration Bill, clauses 9(4), 70(1). See Law Com No 173, Appendix. If the purchaser were not a single individual but two or more persons, then an absence of good faith on the part of even one should be sufficient to enable the unprotected minor interest to prevail (Law Com No 158, para 4.16).
4 Law Com No 158, para 4.15. The Commission thought it otherwise undesirable to fetter the courts in their application of the concept of 'good faith' to the facts of each individual case.
5 [1977] 1 WLR 285 (ante, p 190).
6 Draft Land Registration Bill, clause 9(4). See Law Com No 173, Appendix.
7 [1981] AC 513 (ante, p 126).
8 Law Com No 158, para 4.15.

dispositions are by this Act to take effect.'[9] Most of the interests which fall within this 'intermediate, or hybrid, class'[10] are enumerated in section 70(1) of the Land Registration Act 1925,[11] and together represent a problematic area within the law of registered title.

(1) The function of the overriding interest

Overriding interests, as defined in the Land Registration Act 1925, are interests which bind the transferee of registered land notwithstanding that they are not recorded on the face of the register and notwithstanding that the transferee may have no actual knowledge of their existence. They are quite literally 'overriding'. Cumulatively they represent a group of interests in registered land which have been singled out either as having such distinct social importance or as involving such technical conveyancing difficulty as to merit a protection which derives not from the force of the register but from the force of statute.

(a) The conveyancing background of overriding interests

It is of the essence of the 'overriding interest' that certain kinds of right are made automatically binding on the transferee of registered land, even though they relate to matters which in unregistered conveyancing would not normally be included in title deeds or disclosed in abstracts of title. Since such matters would not therefore become apparent on an inspection of the documentary title (whether carried out by an intending purchaser or by the registrar), they are matters in relation to which it is not possible to compile a trustworthy record on the register of title.[12] As to these interests, the onus rests on persons dealing with registered land to seek information *outside* the register in the same manner and from the same sources as would persons dealing with an unregistered title. The purchaser of registered land must therefore obtain information about the possible presence of overriding interests by means of physical inspection of the land itself and by enquiries made of persons in occupation there. Overriding interests are, in large part, supposed to be rights which would become obvious to any purchaser who bothered to go and look at the property which he proposed to buy.[13]

(b) The problematic nature of overriding interests

The principal difficulty posed by overriding interests is that their existence fundamentally distorts the mirror image of the register: the register can no longer be relied upon as a comprehensive record of the totality of interests in and affecting registered land. Another factor which accentuates this

9 Land Registration Act 1925, s 3(xvi). As Lord Oliver of Aylmerton observed in *Abbey National Building Society v Cann* [1991] 1 AC 56 at 84D-E, this definition displays 'a degree of circularity' since it 'simply means "overriding interests" are "overriding interests".'

10 *Williams & Glyn's Bank Ltd v Boland* [1981] AC 487 at 503B per Lord Wilberforce.

11 See also Land Registration Rules 1925, r 258; Coal Act 1938, s 41; Coal Industry Nationalisation Act 1946, s 5; Law Com No 158, Appendix B.

12 *Lloyds Bank Plc v Rosset* [1989] Ch 350 at 370H per Nicholls LJ.

13 See eg *Lloyds Bank Plc v Rosset* [1989] Ch 350 at 394G per Mustill LJ, 402B per Purchas LJ.

difficulty is the circumstance that, in spite of the original (and vaguely comforting) theory that overriding interests will always be apparent upon physical inspection of the land, it is now quite clear that several categories of overriding interest may well remain undiscovered even by a purchaser who carefully inspects both land and title.[14] Recent decisions have tended, moreover, to increase rather than diminish the number of rights which may claim protected status as overriding interests.[15] The ultimate irony is that the transferee who is innocently ensnared by a virtually undiscoverable overriding interest does not qualify for any form of statutory compensation if the register is rectified to his prejudice in recognition of that overriding interest.[16]

It is hardly surprising, given these substantial drawbacks, that during the 1980s the Law Commission gave serious consideration to the proposal to 'close the cavernous crack in the mirror principle' by drastic amendment of the operation of overriding interests.[17] Although the Commission appeared initially to favour the virtual abolition of the entire category of overriding interests, it now seems more likely that the disadvantages created by such rights will in future be remedied in large measure by an extension of the indemnity provisions of the Land Registration Act 1925.[18] Pending such legislative intervention it is noticeable that in recent years the courts have begun to move significantly towards an ever more restrictive view of the role of certain categories of overriding interest.

(c) Loss of status as an overriding interest

It will quickly become apparent that the present state of registered land law permits some interests to enjoy a dual form of protection under the Land Registration Act 1925. In effect certain rights may be protected either by reason of their inclusion as minor interests on the register or by virtue of their status as overriding interests off the register.[19] It is quite clear, however, that an overriding interest is, by definition, an interest 'not entered on the register'.[20] If an overriding interest is at any stage the subject of some entry in the register, it ceases ipso facto to be an overriding interest and usually ranks thereafter as a minor interest.

It is also open to the registrar, on receiving satisfactory proof of an overriding interest, to enter it in the register,[1] whereupon it ranks merely as a minor interest. Likewise the registrar has discretion in appropriate cases to enter in the register a notice indicating that the land is free from overriding interests.[2] However, the powers thus vested in the registrar only partially mitigate

14 For explicit recognition of this point, see *Kling v Keston Properties Ltd* (1983) 49 P & CR 212 at 222 per Vinelott J; [1985] Conv 406 (J.E.M.).
15 See eg *Williams & Glyn's Bank Ltd v Boland* [1981] AC 487 (post, p 569).
16 Post, p 238.
17 Law Commission, *Property Law: Second Report on Land Registration (Provisional)* (November 1984), para 9.
18 Post, p 240. See Law Commission, *Property Law: Third Report on Land Registration* (Law Com No 158, 31 March 1987), para 2.7.
19 Post, p 226.
20 Land Registration Act 1925, s 3(xvi).
1 Land Registration Act 1925, s 70(3).
2 Land Registration Rules 1925, r 197.

the problems inherent in the existence of those overriding interests which never reach the state of being recorded in the register.[3]

(2) The effective date of overriding interests

The legal difficulties concerning overriding interests have been exacerbated by the fact that a transfer of a registered estate or interest is not complete at the date of disposition (ie the date of execution of the relevant document), but requires to be perfected by registration of the disposition at the Land Registry.[4] There has always been some ambivalence as to the precise date relevant for determining the existence of overriding interests.[5] The critical question is whether the categories of overriding interest are confined to those rights which were in existence and subsisting at the date of the disposition or can include rights which have emerged or been created only during the 'registration gap' which follows the date of disposition and precedes the date of registration.[6] To attach exclusive relevance to the date of registration carries the implication that the transferee of registered land may well be subjected to overriding interests which have supervened some time *after* his inspection of land and title and in respect of which he had no realistic opportunity of discovery.[7]

There is as yet no wholly satisfying resolution of this problem. One point is, however, clear. The category of overriding interest endorsed by section 70(1)(g) is now recognised as a special case and is necessarily governed by slightly different rules from those applicable to other kinds of overriding interest.[8] In *Abbey National Building Society v Cann*,[9] a majority in the House of Lords ruled that the critical date in determining the existence of overriding interests other than those protected by section 70(1)(g) is the date of

3 So grave is the danger that a transferee of registered land may be trapped unwittingly by an overriding interest that many conveyancing solicitors attempt to divert responsibility for the discovery of overriding interests to the client-purchaser himself. Illusory indeed may be the protection which the lay person imagines he buys when he employs the services of a solicitor in a purchase of registered land.

4 Ante, p 179. The problem is, if anything, intensified where the relevant disposition is one of mortgage, since the mortgagee is required to be entered on the register as proprietor of a registered charge (post, pp 229, 940).

5 'One does not. . .expect conveyancing absurdities from the pens of the skilled parliamentary draftsmen who implemented Lord Birkenhead's great scheme for the reform of English real property law embodied in the 1925 legislation, but even they occasionally may have expressed their complex interlocking concepts in forms of words which do not precisely fit every case' (*Abbey National Building Society v Cann* [1991] 1 AC 56 at 76B-C per Lord Bridge of Harwich).

6 Some clarity is provided by the rule that the date of registration of a disposition is deemed to be the date on which the application for registration of the disposition is lodged at the Land Registry (see Land Registration Rules 1925, r 83(2), as substituted by Land Registration Rules 1978, r 8).

7 See *Abbey National Building Society v Cann* [1991] 1 AC 56 at 75F-G per Lord Bridge of Harwich, 83G-84A, 88B per Lord Oliver of Aylmerton, 105A-B per Lord Jauncey of Tullichettle; *Lloyds Bank Plc v Rosset* [1989] Ch 350 at 372G-373B per Nicholls LJ. As Lord Oliver observed in *Cann*'s case ([1991] 1 AC 56 at 85C), overriding interests can come into being at any time, and some may arise without any volition on the part of the registered proprietor (eg a prescriptive easement or profit *à prendre* or rights derived from adverse possession).

8 Post, p 204.

9 [1991] 1 AC 56. See [1990] CLJ 397 (A.J. Oakley); (1990) 106 LQR 545 (R.J. Smith).

registration.[10] Admittedly this construction raises the difficulty that, between disposition and registration, a transferor might in breach of trust create overriding interests such as easements[11] or leases[12] which would then become inescapably binding upon a transferee. However, Lord Oliver of Aylmerton declined to adopt a different construction merely because of 'the theoretical possibility of so improbable an event'.[13]

(3) The categories of overriding interest

Most of the categories of overriding interest in registered land are laid down in section 70(1) of the Land Registration Act 1925.[14] By far the most controversial overriding interest is that referred to in section 70(1)(g),[15] but other significant categories of overriding interest include the following.

(a) Section 70(1)(a)

Section 70(1)(a) confers the protection of an overriding interest in relation to a number of incorporeal hereditaments including rights of common, public rights, profits *à prendre*, rights of way, and 'other easements not being equitable easements required to be protected by notice on the register'. This provision is clearly apt to give overriding protection in registered land to such rights as legal easements and profits *à prendre* (whether legal or equitable),[16] but it is not nearly so plain that the provision covers equitable easements. It was indeed assumed by many that the somewhat ambiguous wording of section 70(1)(a) had the effect of excluding all equitable easements from

10 [1991] 1 AC 56 at 87C per Lord Oliver of Aylmerton, 106C per Lord Jauncey of Tullichettle. Any other approach would incidentally mean that the effect of registration of the transferee's title could free the transferee even from overriding interests created by himself during the interval between completion and registration (see Lord Oliver of Aylmerton at 85F-G).

11 Land Registration Act 1925, s 70(1)(a), post, p 1064.

12 Land Registration Act 1925, s 70(1)(k), post, p 203.

13 [1991] 1 AC 56 at 87D. See also Lord Jauncey of Tullichettle at 105B-C, 106C-D. It was precisely this possibility which caused Lord Bridge of Harwich (at 75H-76B) to prefer the date of *disposition* as the critical date in all cases other than those involving the imposition of local land charges under section 70(1)(i).

14 The list of overriding interests in section 70(1) has been described as 'somewhat inconsequential and jumbled' (*Lloyds Bank Plc v Rosset* [1989] Ch 350 at 370F-G per Nicholls LJ). See also Land Registration Rules 1925, r 258. There is also a clear implication in Land Registration Act 1925, s 69(1) that the statutory category of overriding interests includes any mortgage or charge which has priority to the registered estate (see *Abbey National Building Society v Cann* [1991] 1 AC 56 at 85A-B per Lord Oliver of Aylmerton).

15 Post, p 203.

16 In this respect section 70(1)(a) seems to render otiose other statutory provisions which envisage that the grant of an easement or profit must be 'completed by registration' (see Land Registration Act 1925, ss 19(2), 22(2), ante, p 179). The Law Commission has recommended that the category of overriding interests should include only those easements and profits which arise by implied grant or reservation or by prescription (Law Com No 158, paras 2.26ff). This proposal, if implemented, would confer the status of a mere minor interest on expressly granted legal easements and profits which remain uncompleted by registration (ibid, para 2.26). Likewise, the Commission's recommendation would have the effect of reversing the decision in *Celsteel Ltd v Alton House Holdings Ltd* [1985] 1 WLR 204, thereby making all equitable easements protectible as minor interests only (ibid, para 2.33). See, however, Draft Land Registration Bill, clause 7(1), (2)(a) (Law Commission, Law Com No 173 (1988), Appendix).

the category of overriding interests, but this belief was shown to be unfounded in *Celsteel Ltd v Alton House Holdings Ltd.*[17] Here Scott J held that, although section 70(1)(a) does not give overriding protection to all equitable easements, it does (in conjunction with Land Registration Rules 1925, r 258[18]) confer such protection on equitable easements which are 'openly exercised and enjoyed' over the land which is the subject of the relevant transfer of title.[19]

(b) Section 70(1)(c)

Section 70(1)(c) provides that a liability to repair the chancel of a church may comprise a head of overriding interest. Liabilities of this kind have the effect of imposing on certain landowners a burden, of distinctly medieval origin, to bear the costs of repairing the chancels of probably one third of all parish churches in England and Wales.[20] The land affected by liability for chancel repairs has been estimated to cover nearly four million acres. The obligation involved is slightly quaint, but the transfer of the burdened land has in recent times exposed the transferee to an onerous and often wholly unexpected form of liability.[1] The Law Commission has now proposed that all chancel repair liability arising from the ownership of land should be phased out without compensation over a period of ten years,[2] and that failing a prompt abolition of this archaic form of liability all chancel repair obligations should become registrable local land charges.[3]

(c) Section 70(1)(f)

Pursuant to section 70(1)(f) and subject to other provisions of the Land Registration Act 1925, overriding interests also include 'rights acquired or in course of being acquired under the Limitation Acts'.[4] The operation of section 70(1)(f) was illustrated in *Bridges v Mees*.[5] Here P contracted to purchase

17 [1985] 1 WLR 204. See [1986] Conv 31 (M.P. Thompson).

18 Land Registration Rules 1925, r 258 provides that '[r]ights, privileges, and appurtenances appertaining or reputed to appertain to land or. . .enjoyed therewith or reputed or known as part or parcel of or appurtenant thereto, which adversely affect registered land, are overriding interests within section 70 of the Act. . .'

19 [1985] 1 WLR 204 at 220H–221D. The Court of Appeal subsequently confirmed the decision of Scott J without substantive comment on this point ([1986] 1 WLR 512). See Chapter 21 (post, p 1064). See also *Payne v Adnams* [1971] CLY 6486.

20 See *Property Law: Liability for Chancel Repairs* (Law Com No 152, 20 November 1985), para 1.2.

1 See eg *Chivers & Sons Ltd v Air Ministry* [1955] Ch 585 at 594ff (land sold by Queens' College Cambridge).

2 Law Com No 152, para 4.18.

3 Law Com No 152, para 5.9f. The Law Commission has recommended that, pending implementation of Law Com No 158, chancel repair liability should no longer constitute a species of overriding interest, but should subsist as a form of 'general burden' (post, p 240) on the land affected. See Law Com No 158, para 2.81.

4 On the operation of the Limitation Act 1980, see Chapter 10 (post, p 282). The Law Commission has recommended that rights already acquired by adverse possession under the general law should continue to rank as overriding interests (Law Com No 158, para 2.36), but that rights which are still in the process of acquisition by adverse possession should retain their current degree of protection under some more direct provision outside and separate from the categories of overriding interest (ibid, para 2.37). See Draft Land Registration Bill, clause 7(1), (2)(c) (Law Commission, Law Com No 173 (1988), Appendix).

5 [1957] Ch 475.

from V the fee simple estate in an area of registered land. He paid the full purchase price and entered into occupation, but never obtained from V a transfer of the registered title and never protected his estate contract by entering a minor interest on the register. When nearly 20 years later V transferred the fee simple not to P but to D instead, P was able to argue successfully before Harman J that his contractual rights were protected under section 70(1)(f)—and also for that matter under section 70(1)(g)—by reason of his adverse possession.[6] D, although registered as the new proprietor, was therefore bound by P's overriding interest.

(d) Section 70(1)(k)

The protection of an overriding interest is likewise conferred by section 70(1)(k) on leases which are granted for a term not exceeding 21 years.[7] Although this provision no longer excludes leases which are obtained on payment of a fine or premium (ie a capital sum as distinct from a periodic rent),[8] it is clear that the overriding interest protected under this head is confined to legal leases only and cannot apply to an equitable term of years.[9] However, equitable leases may, if coupled with actual occupation by the tenant or the receipt of rents and profits from a subtenant, constitute an overriding interest under section 70(1)(g).[10]

(4) Operation of section 70(1)(g)

There is no doubt that the most dramatic species of overriding interest is that referred to in section 70(1)(g) of the Land Registration Act 1925. This category comprises

6 [1957] Ch 475 at 484ff.

7 There has for a long time been a powerful argument to the effect that a lease which is not noted on the register ought not to be an overriding interest unless the tenant is in actual occupation and his existence is therefore discoverable on physical inspection of the property. This argument was, however, rejected by the Law Commission in one of its early Working Papers. The Commission expressed the view in 1971 that '[m]any short tenancies are informal and where they relate to dwelling-houses and flats are often granted without the tenant being legally represented. We cannot think that it would be desirable that a monthly tenant or even a tenant of a flat for, say, three years, who has not yet moved in, would have to register notice of this tenancy against the reversionary title at the Land Registry to protect himself against a purchaser of the reversion. . .Where there is a conflict we think that the law should incline in favour of the tenant. By not requiring occupation, the existing paragraph (k) does this and we agree with it' (Law Commission, *Property Law: Land Registration (Second Paper)* (Published Working Paper No 37, July 1971), para 89). See also Law Com No 158, paras 2.50ff; Draft Land Registration Bill, clause 7(1), (2)(b) (Law Commission, Law Com No 173 (1988), Appendix).

8 See Land Registration Act 1925, s 70(1)(k), as amended by Land Registration Act 1986, s 4(1), (4).

9 *City Permanent Building Society v Miller* [1952] Ch 840 at 853. The Law Commission has recommended that section 70(1)(k) should expressly exclude discontinuous legal leases from the category of overriding interests (Law Com No 158, para 2.46). It is clear in any event that, even if a short lease constitutes an overriding interest under section 70(1)(k), the binding effect of the covenants contained in it is still governed by the ordinary rules (post, p 845) relating to the running of the benefit and burden of leasehold covenants (see Law Com No 158, para 2.49).

10 Post, p 210.

the rights of every person in actual occupation of the land or in receipt of the rents and profits thereof, save where enquiry is made of such person and the rights are not disclosed.[11]

(a) *Purpose of section 70(1)(g)*

The object of section 70(1)(g) was described by Lord Denning MR in *Strand Securities Ltd v Caswell*[12] as being to 'protect a person in actual occupation of the land from having his rights lost in the welter of registration.' Such a person may simply 'stay there and do nothing', but will nevertheless be protected since '[n]o one can buy the land over his head and thereby take away or diminish his rights.' In other words, an onus of enquiry is placed upon the purchaser and is ignored by him at his own peril.[13]

Section 70(1)(g) was thus intended to benefit lay persons who own interests in registered land (perhaps of limited scope or duration) to whom it might not occur that protective entry in the register is required in the event of a transaction involving the registered title. In such cases it was considered that it might well be unfair to demand positive protective action in circumstances where the fact of actual occupation would signal to all prudent purchasers both the possible existence of unrecorded interests affecting the land and the necessity of further enquiry.[14]

(b) *Time at which actual occupation is required*

Prior to the litigation in *Abbey National Building Society v Cann*,[15] it was generally believed that the date on which an overriding interest crystallised by reason of 'actual occupation' was the date on which the transferee under a registered disposition was entered on the register as the new proprietor of the estate

11 The concept of 'actual possession' appears first in this context in the judgment of Lord Loughborough LC in *Taylor v Stibbert* (1794) 2 Ves 437 at 440, 30 ER 713 at 714. For the first use of the phrase 'actual occupation', see *Barnhart v Greenshields* (1853) 9 Moo PCC 18 at 34, 14 ER 204 at 210. The idea of 'actual occupation' first appears in statutory form in the list of 'overriding interests' contained in Law of Property Act 1922, Sch 16, Part I, para 5(3)(i), amending Land Transfer Act 1875, s 18. Statutory equivalents of Land Registration Act 1925, s 70(1)(g), are found in Northern Ireland's Land Registration Act 1970, Sch 5, Part I, para 15, and in the Republic of Ireland's Registration of Title Act 1964, s 72(1)(j). There is, significantly, no equivalent in the Torrens legislation of Australia (see eg Real Property Act 1900 (NSW), s 42(1)).

12 [1965] Ch 958 at 979G. See also *Lloyds Bank Plc v Rosset* [1989] Ch 350 at 402B per Purchas LJ.

13 There is an added dimension of hazard for the purchaser in that a successful claim of overriding entitlement on the part of merely one of a number of multiple occupiers effectively makes it impossible for the purchaser to assert his rights against any of the occupiers (see eg *Kemmis v Kemmis* [1988] 1 WLR 1307 at 1325D-F, 1336A). It even seems that the unfortunate purchaser is unable to recover rent from those occupiers who shelter behind an overriding interest claimed by one of their number (see *Kemmis* at 1325 E-F, 1336A-B).

14 See Law Com No 158, para 2.6. It may even be that the inclusion of section 70(1)(g) in the Land Registration Act 1925 was altogether less remarkable against the background of the conveyancing practice of former times, when it was usual for completion to take place at the premises which were the subject of the instant transaction.

15 [1991] 1 AC 56. See [1990] CLJ 397 (A.J. Oakley); [1991] Conv 116 (S. Baughen), 155 (P.F. Smith); (1990) 106 LQR 545 (R.J. Smith); (1990) 87 LSG 19, 34 (M. Beaumont).

or interest in question.[16] On this view the 'rights'—whatever they might be—of any person in 'actual occupation' of the land on this crucial day became overriding.[17]

Such a construction of the Land Registration Act was, of course, fraught with difficulty for the transferee or chargee of registered land. The vital date of registration occurs *after* completion of the contract of purchase,[18] and there was a danger that persons with adverse rights might enter into occupation of the property during the period which elapses between the completion date and the deemed date of registration. This danger was particularly acute in the context of a purchase assisted by a contemporaneous mortgage. The registered chargee was rendered vulnerable to occupiers' rights which were set up in the period between disposition and registration,[19] even though it might be wholly impossible for him to discover their existence before advancing the loan moneys.[20] By the arrival of the registration date, the mortgagee would have become irretrievably committed to the mortgage transaction and the die would be cast.[1]

In *Abbey National Building Society v Cann* D1 had purchased a leasehold dwelling-house (for occupation by D2 and D3) with the aid of a mortgage loan advanced by P. D2 later claimed to have some equitable interest in the house, largely on the basis of financial contributions made by her to an earlier home. It was D2's contention that, since she was in 'actual occupation' at the date of registration of P's mortgage charge, her equitable entitlement took priority over the registered charge. The House of Lords rejected this argument on a number of grounds, holding inter alia that the protection of section 70(1)(g) is activated only where the claimant was in 'actual occupation' at the date of disposition[2] and his or her 'rights' remained subsisting at the later date of registration.[3] In other words, a person not in actual occupation of the relevant land at the date of the disposition cannot substantiate a claim under section 70(1)(g) merely because he or she has

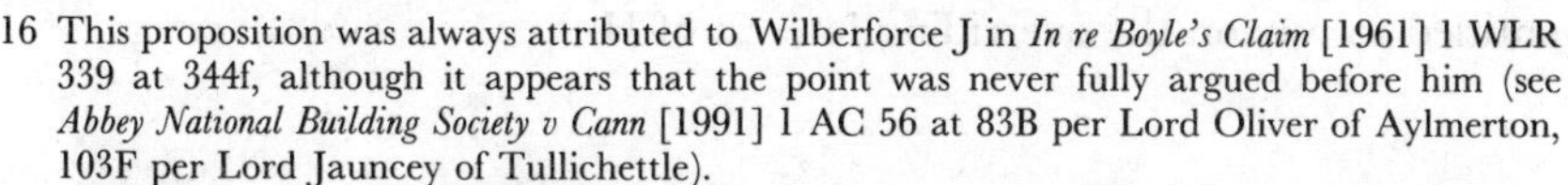

16 This proposition was always attributed to Wilberforce J in *In re Boyle's Claim* [1961] 1 WLR 339 at 344f, although it appears that the point was never fully argued before him (see *Abbey National Building Society v Cann* [1991] 1 AC 56 at 83B per Lord Oliver of Aylmerton, 103F per Lord Jauncey of Tullichettle).

17 See *E.S. Schwab & Co Ltd v McCarthy* (1976) 31 P & CR 196 at 204; *Kling v Keston Properties Ltd* (1983) 49 P & CR 212 at 218. Compare, however, *Paddington Building Society v Mendelsohn* (1985) 50 P & CR 244 at 247, and see Law Com No 158, para 2.76.

18 See Law Com No 158, para 2.57.

19 See Law Com No 158, para 2.77.

20 See *Abbey National Building Society v Cann* [1991] 1 AC 56 at 88A-B per Lord Oliver of Aylmerton.

1 See *Lloyds Bank Plc v Rosset* [1989] Ch 350 at 372G–373B per Nicholls LJ; *Abbey National Building Society v Cann* [1991] 1 AC 56 at 105B per Lord Jauncey of Tullichettle.

2 [1991] 1 AC 56 at 88C-H per Lord Oliver of Aylmerton, who referred to the date of completion of the transaction (ie disposition) and stated that 'it is at that moment that it falls to be determined whether there is an actual occupation for the purposes of paragraph (g)' ([1991] 1 AC 56 at 88F). See also [1991] 1 AC 56 at 104H–105B, 106C-D per Lord Jauncey of Tullichettle; *Lloyds Bank Plc v Rosset* [1991] 1 AC 107 at 126D per Lord Bridge of Harwich.

3 It is implicit in Land Registration Act 1925, ss 20(1)(b), 70(1) that the rights claimed as an overriding interest must be subsisting at the date of registration (see [1991] 1 AC 56 at 88D-E per Lord Oliver of Aylmerton, 104H per Lord Jauncey of Tullichettle).

assumed occupation by the date of registration.[4] In the view taken by the House of Lords, any other construction would produce a 'conveyancing absurdity',[5] since the date of disposition represents 'the only date at which the inquiry referred to in paragraph (g) could, in practice, be made and be relevant.'[6] In order that inquiry as to occupation at the disposition date should not be entirely futile, section 70(1)(g) must, by implication, be understood as 'contemplating an occupation which preceded and existed at completion of a transfer or disposition'.[7]

(c) *Continuing enforceability of the overriding interest*

Once an overriding interest has crystallised on the basis of 'actual occupation', this interest remains enforceable against the registering transferee or chargee, notwithstanding that the owner of the overriding interest ceases to occupy the land after the registration of the relevant disposition.[8] In other words, once the overriding interest materialises by virtue of actual occupation on the relevant date, its subsequent effectiveness against the transferee does not depend on continued long-term actual occupation. Of course the conditions of section 70(1)(g) must be satisfied de novo in the event of any further transfer of the registered title.

(d) *Protection of derivative interests*

A derivative interest (eg a lease) which is subsequently carved out of an overriding interest enjoys the shelter of that overriding interest against any adverse claim brought by the transferee of the registered title. In *Marks v Attallah*,[9] for instance, E, as registered proprietor, held an estate in fee simple on a bare trust for H. On the assumption[10] that H had an overriding interest vis à vis M (a transferee of the freehold from E), Ungoed-Thomas J was prepared to hold that M was also bound by the lease which H had granted to T after the effective date of registration of M's transfer (see *Fig.* 16). Although T himself could claim no overriding interest as such, he was entitled to rely on the overriding interest of H.[11]

4 [1991] 1 AC 56 at 76D per Lord Bridge of Harwich. See also *Lloyds Bank Plc v Rosset* [1989] Ch 350 at 374D-E per Nicholls LJ.

5 [1991] 1 AC 56 at 83G, 88B per Lord Oliver of Aylmerton. See also *Lloyds Bank Plc v Rosset* [1989] Ch 350 at 373B per Nicholls LJ, 402A per Purchas LJ.

6 [1991] 1 AC 56 at 88E per Lord Oliver of Aylmerton.

7 [1991] 1 AC 56 at 88C per Lord Oliver of Aylmerton. This conclusion had already been reached by the Court of Appeal in *Lloyds Bank Plc v Rosset* [1989] Ch 350 at 374B-C per Nicholls LJ.

8 *London and Cheshire Insurance Co Ltd v Laplagrene Property Co Ltd* [1971] Ch 499 at 505A-B, 509E-F.

9 (1966) 198 Estates Gazette 685; (1966) 110 SJ 709.

10 This assumption was tested and confirmed when the issue was later presented before the Court of Appeal as *Hodgson v Marks* [1971] Ch 892 (post, p 216).

11 Ungoed-Thomas J pointed out that the Land Registration Act 1925 expressly provides that transfers should be 'subject to overriding interests, and not subject to overriding interests in any particular person' ((1966) 198 Estates Gazette 685 at 687).

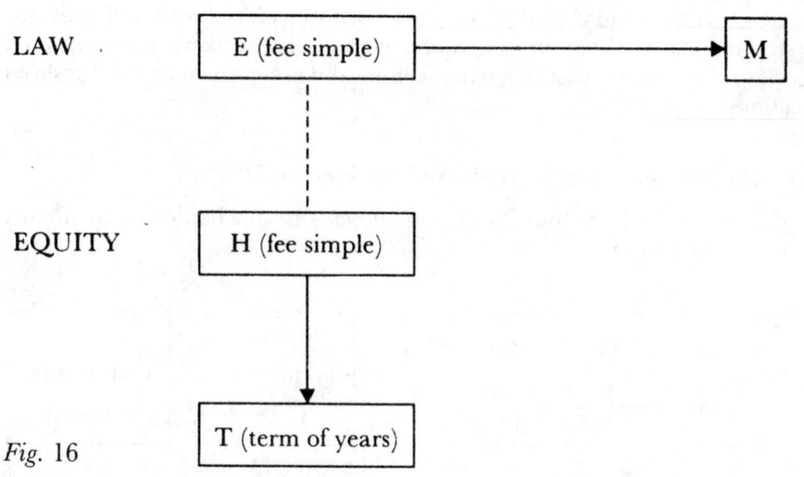

Fig. 16

(e) Protection for persons in receipt of rents and profits

In its terms section 70(1)(g) also affords the protection of an overriding interest to the rights of any person who, at the relevant date, is 'in receipt of the rents and profits' derived from the land, even though that person is not himself 'in actual occupation of the land'.[12]

(i) Protection for the commercial landlord Section 70(1)(g) thus protects the rights of a non-resident landlord as well as those of his resident tenant: the landlord is protected by virtue of his receipt of rents and profits, and the tenant by virtue of actual occupation. It seems, however, that if section 70(1)(g) is to have this effect, the landlord must be in actual receipt of those rents and profits, and not merely have an unenforced right to receive the same.[13]

(ii) No rewards for generosity Section 70(1)(g) does not apply, however, if the non-resident owner of an interest in land grants away mere rights of rent-free occupation. In such circumstances neither the licensor nor the licensee is protected. In *Strand Securities Ltd v Caswell*[14] a tenant, D, allowed his step-daughter and her children to reside rent-free in his flat while he lived elsewhere. The Court of Appeal ruled that neither D nor his step-daughter could assert an overriding interest against P, a subsequent transferee of the superior leasehold title, even though P was fully aware of the interest held by D. D was unprotected under section 70(1)(g) because at the material

12 The privilege thus accorded persons 'in receipt of the rents and profits' of land has been criticised by the Law Commission as inimical to the simplification of registered conveyancing. The Commission has recommended that the rights of such persons should no longer be made overriding by section 70(1)(g) (Law Com No 158, para 2.70). See Draft Land Registration Bill, clause 7(1), (2)(d) (Law Commission, Law Com No 173 (1988), Appendix).

13 See *E.S. Schwab & Co Ltd v McCarthy* (1976) 31 P & CR 196 at 205, 213. (Compare the more liberal definition of 'possession' in Land Registration Act 1925, s 3(xviii) and Law of Property Act 1925, s 205(1)(xix)). Even the retention of a deposit by way of security for rent appears to be inadequate to satisfy section 70(1)(g), not least since the effect of such a deposit as a deemed equivalent of rent will tend to become exhausted with the passage of time (see *E.S. Schwab & Co Ltd v McCarthy*, supra at 214 per Buckley LJ).

14 [1965] Ch 958.

date he was neither in actual occupation nor in receipt of rent and profits.[15] His step-daughter, although in actual occupation, was likewise unprotected since her rights, being those of a bare licensee, did not even enter the threshold of section 70(1)(g).[16]

(5) Nature of the 'rights' protected by section 70(1)(g)

A strict analysis of section 70(1)(g) discloses the mechanical and almost mathematical equation[17] that

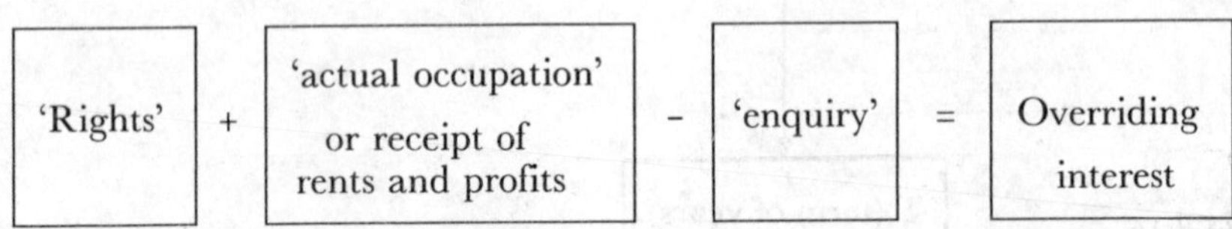

In technical terms, the 'rights' do not themselves constitute the 'overriding interest' under section 70(1)(g),[18] but those 'rights', once found in conjunction with the factual element of 'actual occupation' or receipt of rents and profits, comprise in association an 'overriding interest'.[19] The 'overriding interest' is thus an amalgam of law and fact: pre-existing rights in statutory consort with one or other of the prescribed elements of physical occupation or receipt of money.

It is clear from this analysis that what becomes binding under section 70(1)(g) is not necessarily any occupancy on the part of the person who claims 'rights' under cover of that provision but rather the 'rights' which he claims. In other words, occupation of the land is not per se one of the 'rights' referred to in section 70(1)(g).[20] It is merely a trigger which activates the statutory protection of *any rights* belonging to the actual occupier—whatever those rights may be.[1] Indeed, it may well be in a given case that the particular 'rights' protected under section 70(1)(g) are entirely unrelated to *occupation* of the land.[2] It is, however, an inescapable condition of section 70(1)(g) that the 'rights' in respect of which overriding protection is claimed

15 The Court of Appeal acknowledged that the result would have been quite different if D's step-daughter had made a 'token' payment of rent—even 'a penny a week for the privilege of remaining there' ([1965] Ch 958 at 981A-B, 983D-E).

16 Post, p 211.

17 Speaking in the immediate context of *City of London Building Society v Flegg* [1988] AC 54 at 74D, Lord Templeman emphasised that there must be 'a combination of an interest which justifies continuing occupation plus actual occupation to constitute an overriding interest'.

18 See *Blacklocks v J.B. Developments (Godalming) Ltd* [1982] Ch 183 at 196E-F.

19 '[T]here is no logical difficulty in the association of a minor interest with another factor (ie actual occupation) being, qua association, an overriding interest' (*Williams & Glyn's Bank Ltd v Boland* [1981] AC 487 at 512A per Lord Scarman). See also *Abbey National Building Society v Cann* [1991] 1 AC 56 at 84H–85A per Lord Oliver of Aylmerton.

20 'Actual occupation is not an interest in itself' (*City of London Building Society v Flegg* [1988] AC 54 at 74D per Lord Templeman).

1 See the view adopted by Lord Oliver of Aylmerton in *Abbey National Building Society v Cann* [1991] 1 AC 56 at 87E.

2 See eg *Webb v Pollmount* [1966] Ch 584 at 603C- D (specifically enforceable option to purchase land); *Kling v Keston Properties Ltd* (1983) 49 P & CR 212 at 215ff (right of pre-emption).

should relate to the land actually occupied by the claimant. Section 70(1)(g) confers no protection on rights—no matter how well founded—in respect of land not occupied by the claimant.[3]

Extensive though the sweep of section 70(1)(g) may thus appear to be, there are nevertheless certain implicit limitations on the range of interests which may come within its scope.

(a) *The 'rights' must subsist in reference to land*

Although section 70(1)(g) in broad terms attaches an overriding quality to the 'rights' of any person in actual occupation or in receipt of rents and profits, other provisions of the Land Registration Act 1925 impose implicit qualifications on the nature of the 'rights' concerned. For example, section 20(1) refers to overriding interests as interests 'affecting the estate transferred or created'. Likewise section 70(1) itself speaks of overriding interests as interests 'subsisting in reference' to 'registered land'. On the basis of these provisions, it is commonly maintained that section 70(1)(g) relates only to proprietary rights in land as already defined under the general law. In other words, section 70(1)(g) cannot apply to purely personal rights in or over land,[4] which in terms of the general law of property remain mere rights *in personam* and never have any potential for binding third parties.[5]

This restriction was adverted to in *National Provincial Bank Ltd v Hastings Car Mart Ltd*[6] by Russell LJ, who was of opinion that section 70(1)(g) deals throughout only with 'rights in reference to land which have the quality of being capable of enduring through different ownerships of the land, according to normal conceptions of title to real property.' This view was confirmed by the House of Lords in the same case,[7] Lord Wilberforce emphasising that the 'whole frame of section 70. . .shows that it is made against a background of interests or rights whose nature and whose transmissible character is known, or ascertainable, aliunde, ie, under other statutes or under the common law.'[8] Lord Wilberforce thus concluded that, in order to ascertain what 'rights' come within the ambit of section 70(1)(g),

> one must look outside the Land Registration Act and see what rights affect purchasers under the general law. To suppose that the subsection makes any right, of howsoever a personal character, which a person in occupation may have, an overriding interest by which a purchaser is bound, would involve two consequences: first that this Act is, in this respect, bringing about a substantive change in real property law by making

3 *Ashburn Anstalt v Arnold* [1989] Ch 1 at 28F-G per Fox LJ. See [1988] Conv 201 at 206 (M.P. Thompson).

4 *Ashburn Anstalt v Arnold* [1989] Ch 1 at 8F-G per Fox LJ; *Canadian Imperial Bank of Commerce v Bello* (1992) 64 P & CR 48 at 51 per Dillon LJ.

5 This view of the status of personal rights in registered land is, of course, wholly consistent with the orthodox doctrine which holds that such rights have no effect on a purchaser in the corresponding context of unregistered land.

6 [1964] Ch 665 at 696.

7 *National Provincial Bank Ltd v Ainsworth* [1965] AC 1175.

8 [1965] AC 1175 at 1261F. This statement involves a somewhat circular definition of proprietary status as being rooted in the quality of transmissibility (post, p 926). See, however, *Guckian v Brennan* [1981] IR 478 at 486, where Gannon J pointed out that the Irish equivalent of section 70 'does not create burdens: it merely classifies burdens which are created aliunde.' See also *City of London Building Society v Flegg* [1988] AC 54 at 88A-E per Lord Oliver of Aylmerton.

personal rights bind purchasers; second, that there is a difference *as to the nature of the rights by which a purchaser may be bound* between registered and unregistered land; for purely personal rights cannot affect purchasers of unregistered land even with notice. One may have to accept that there is a difference between unregistered and registered land as regards what kind of notice binds a purchaser, or what kind of inquiries a purchaser has to make. But there is no warrant in the terms of this paragraph or elsewhere in the Act for supposing that the nature of the rights which are to bind a purchaser is to be different, excluding personal rights in one case, including them in another.[9]

(b) 'Rights' accepted within the ambit of section 70(1)(g)

The orthodox reading of section 70(1)(g) is therefore that this provision refers only to 'rights' which have a recognisably proprietary character. The 'rights' capable of generating an overriding interest thus include such interests as an option to purchase a legal estate,[10] a legal tenancy,[11] an equitable lease or tenancy,[12] the equitable interest of a beneficiary under a bare trust[13] or trust for sale,[14] the right to an unpaid vendor's lien,[15] the Rent Act entitlements of protected and statutory tenants,[16] the equitable proprietary rights of an estoppel licensee,[17] the right of a tenant to deduct from future rent the cost of repairs which his landlord has wrongfully failed to effect,[18] and the right to have a conveyance rectified in equity on the ground of mistake.[19] All such rights conform sufficiently to the traditional characteristics of a proprietary interest in land to be capable of 'subsisting in reference' to registered land for the present purpose.

(c) Rights excluded from the scope of section 70(1)(g)

Correspondingly it is quite consistent that section 70(1)(g) should exclude from its ambit those rights which, although related to land in some broad

9 [1965] AC 1175 at 1261B-E. Compare, however, Law Com No 158, para 2.70 (ante, p 207).
10 *Webb v Pollmount Ltd* [1966] Ch 584 at 603C-D; *Kling v Keston Properties Ltd* (1983) 49 P & CR 212 at 217ff; [1985] Conv 406 (J.E.M.).
11 *Ashburn Anstalt v Arnold* [1989] Ch 1 at 27D; *Canadian Imperial Bank of Commerce v Bello* (1992) 64 P & CR 48 at 50ff.
12 *Grace Rymer Investments Ltd v Waite* [1958] Ch 831 at 849ff; *Greaves Organisation Ltd v Stanhope Gate Property Co Ltd* (1973) 228 Estates Gazette 725 at 729.
13 *Hodgson v Marks* [1971] Ch 892 at 934F-G (post, p 216).
14 *Williams & Glyn's Bank Ltd v Boland* [1981] AC 487 at 508A-B. See also *Winkworth v Edward Baron Development Co Ltd* (1986) 52 P & CR 67 at 78; *Kemmis v Kemmis* [1988] 1 WLR 1307 at 1325D, 1330F, 1335G.
15 *London and Cheshire Insurance Co Ltd v Laplagrene Property Co Ltd* [1971] Ch 499 at 502H.
16 *National Provincial Bank Ltd v Hastings Car Mart Ltd* [1964] Ch 665 at 689 per Lord Denning MR. On the nature of a statutory tenancy, see Chapter 18 (post, p 876). The Law Commission has pointed, however, to the difficulty that the degree of residential occupation sufficient to sustain a statutory tenancy under the Rent Act (post, p 877) may not always amount to the 'actual occupation' required for the purpose of section 70(1)(g) (see Law Com No 158, para 2.15 (n 71)).
17 *National Provincial Bank Ltd v Hastings Car Mart Ltd* [1964] Ch 665 at 689 per Lord Denning MR.
18 *Lee-Parker v Izzett* [1971] 1 WLR 1688 at 1693F-G (post, p 795).
19 *Blacklocks v J.B. Developments (Godalming) Ltd* [1982] Ch 183 at 196D-E (post, p 235).

sense, are classified either by statute or by the general law of property as mere rights *in personam*. Section 70(1)(g) does not therefore include rights which are in essence purely personal or contractual.

(i) Personal rights to occupy the matrimonial home The demarcation of the 'rights' falling within section 70(1)(g) arose most starkly when the courts were required to rule on the effect of the 'deserted wife's equity'.[20] In *National Provincial Bank Ltd v Ainsworth*,[1] the House of Lords finally, but conclusively, rejected the idea that this 'equity' could be anything more than a merely personal right effective only against the other spouse.[2] In view of its nature and origin, the wife's 'equity' could not rank under the general law as a right *in rem* and, since it therefore lacked an essential proprietary character, it fell outside the scope of section 70(1)(g).[3]

This conclusion as to the non-proprietary status of matrimonial rights of occupation was then expressly preserved in the legislation which was swiftly introduced in order to replace the ill-fated doctrine of the 'deserted wife's equity'. This legislation, now consolidated in the Matrimonial Homes Act 1983, confers statutory 'rights of occupation' on specified categories of spouse,[4] but provides quite explicitly that a spouse's 'rights of occupation' can never constitute an overriding interest even though that spouse is in 'actual occupation' of the matrimonial home.[5]

(ii) Contractual licence For some time the precise status of the contractual occupation licence has been a matter of debate.[6] Such a licence, if accorded a proprietary status in the general law of land, is clearly capable of ranking as an overriding interest under section 70(1)(g). In *National Provincial Bank Ltd v Hastings Car Mart Ltd*[7] Lord Denning MR seemed prepared to include the contractual occupation licence as one of the 'rights' covered by section 70(1)(g). However, this approach has always been controversial. It conflicts markedly with the conventional understanding of the status of the contractual

20 During the 1950s and 1960s the Court of Appeal had developed a doctrine to the effect that a wife, in the event of desertion by her husband, acquired at the date of his departure an 'equity' in the matrimonial home which she could then successfully oppose against any purchaser from her husband. Such a purchaser would be bound (in the case of unregistered land) if he had notice of the 'equity' and (in the case of registered land) if the wife remained at all material times in 'actual occupation' within the terms of section 70(1)(g). See Chapter 7 (ante, p 158).

1 [1965] AC 1175.

2 Ante, p 159.

3 It should come as no great surprise to learn that in the Court of Appeal in *National Provincial Bank Ltd v Hastings Car Mart Ltd* [1964] Ch 665 at 689, Lord Denning MR had expressed a quite contrary view.

4 See Chapter 7 (ante, p 155).

5 Matrimonial Homes Act 1983, s 2(8)(b) (post, p 569). (See Matrimonial Homes Act 1967, s 2(7)). Spousal 'rights of occupation' should of course be protected by the entry of a notice on the appropriate register of title (ante, p 183). It is clear that a spouse's right to have a prejudicial transaction set aside pursuant to Matrimonial Causes Act 1973, s 37(2) can never amount to an overriding interest under section 70(1)(g). See *Kemmis v Kemmis* [1988] 1 WLR 1307 at 1329F-G, 1332C.

6 Post, p 914.

7 [1964] Ch 665 at 688f.

licence under the general law,[8] and in *Ashburn Anstalt v Arnold*[9] the Court of Appeal expressed an overwhelming preference for the view that the conferment of a contractual licence creates no property interest.[10] On the balance of authority it now seems extremely doubtful that the rights of a contractual licensee can properly be described as 'rights' which come within the threshold of section 70(1)(g).[11]

(iii) Collateral contractual rights It seems clear that collateral contractual rights cannot rank as overriding interests under section 70(1)(g) even on behalf of a person in actual occupation of the land. This result inevitably follows even though such rights may be collateral to other rights of a proprietary nature which undoubtedly do come within the compass of section 70(1)(g). In *Eden Estates Ltd v Longman*,[12] for instance, a tenant had agreed, on taking his tenancy, to pay the landlord a substantial deposit as security against non-payment of rent or breach of other covenants in the lease. The Court of Appeal declined to hold that this collateral agreement (which appeared to be entirely verbal in origin) was binding on a subsequent assignee of the landlord's interest. The tenant's contractual right to recover his deposit could not generate an overriding interest under section 70(1)(g) even though the tenant had remained at all times in 'actual occupation'.[13]

(d) Other statutory restrictions on the range of section 70(1)(g)

The operation of section 70(1)(g) is further limited by several express statutory restrictions on the 'rights' which are capable of protection under cover of an overriding interest.

(i) Equitable rights of settled land beneficiaries There is an explicit statutory prohibition against the inclusion within the field of overriding interests of any equitable rights arising under the Settled Land Act 1925. This prohibition takes the form of a clear directive that the equitable interests of beneficiaries

8 Post, p 915. The orthodox rule is that the rights of a contractual licensee bind only the licensor, and that purchasers are never affected by a contractual licence even though they purchase with express notice of the licensee's rights (see *Clore v Theatrical Properties Ltd and Westby & Co Ltd* [1936] 3 All ER 483 at 490ff). However, Lord Denning's liberal view of section 70(1)(g) was in clear accord with his diligent efforts over many years to elevate the status of the contractual licence so that it should receive the same protection under the general law as that accorded to equitable proprietary rights (see eg *Errington v Errington and Woods* [1952] 1 KB 290 at 298ff; *Binions v Evans* [1972] Ch 359 at 367E–369C).

9 [1989] Ch 1 at 24D per Fox LJ (post, p 920).

10 The judge at first instance in *Ashburn Anstalt v Arnold* (E.C. Evans Lombe QC) had ruled that a contractual licence created a proprietary interest in land and therefore fell within the scope of section 70(1)(g). See (1988) 55 P & CR 13 at 33.

11 See, for instance, the extreme caution expressed on this point in *National Provincial Bank Ltd v Ainsworth* [1965] AC 1175 at 1239B–1240A per Lord Upjohn, 1251D–1252A per Lord Wilberforce. A non-contractual (or 'bare') licence is clearly excluded from the scope of section 70(1)(g). See *Strand Securities Ltd v Caswell* [1965] Ch 958 at 980C-D (ante, p 207); Law Com No 158, para 2.56. See also *Kemmis v Kemmis* [1988] 1 WLR 1307 at 1335B-D.

12 Unreported, 19 May 1980 ([1982] Conv 237 (P.H. Kenny)). See also *Hua Chiao Commercial Bank Ltd v Chiaphua Industries Ltd* [1987] AC 99 at 112D–113C (post, p 861).

13 See also *N.L.S. Pty Ltd v Hughes* (1966) 120 CLR 583 at 588ff.

under a strict settlement of land[14] may 'take effect as minor interests and not otherwise'.[15] There is therefore no possibility that such interests—even if coupled with actual occupation—can ever claim dual status as overriding interests under section 70(1)(g).[16]

(ii) Notice under the Leasehold Reform Act 1967 A further statutory exclusion arises under the Leasehold Reform Act 1967.[17] No overriding interest may ever be claimed in respect of any notice served by a qualifying tenant in support of his right to purchase a freehold or long leasehold title in property occupied by him.[18]

(iii) 'Preserved right to buy' On the fulfilment of certain conditions a 'secure tenant' in the public rented sector has a statutory right to purchase a freehold or a long leasehold estate in the property occupied by him.[19] In the event of any disposal of that property to a private sector landlord the tenant's 'preserved right to buy' may be protected by the entry of a minor interest against the register of the existing landlord's title.[20] However, if the 'preserved right to buy' is not duly protected in this way, it becomes ineffective against the new private sector landlord and is statutorily excluded from the category of overriding interests 'notwithstanding that the qualifying person is in actual occupation of the land'.[1]

(e) The 'rights' must have been enforceable at the date of transfer

Recent case law has also emphasised another implicit—but fairly obvious—limitation on the kinds of claim which may give rise to an overriding interest under section 70(1)(g). The operation of this paragraph necessarily presupposes some kind of transfer or dealing with a registered title, for its general effect is to render the pre-existing 'rights' of occupiers just as enforceable after the transfer as they were before. The use of the word 'rights' in this context requires not only that the relevant interest must have been in existence before the dealing, but also that it must, immediately before the dealing, have been enforceable as against the particular purchaser concerned, since otherwise it could not, quoad this purchaser, be meaningfully described as a 'right' at all for the purpose of section 70(1)(g). The operation of section 70(1)(g) does not enhance or alter the intrinsic quality of the rights which comprise the overriding interest.[2]

14 Post, p 608.
15 Land Registration Act 1925, s 86(2).
16 The Law Commission has expressed the view that the exclusion of settled land beneficial interests from section 70(1)(g) is unjustifiable, not least because a strict settlement may sometimes be created informally and quite unintentionally in the context of family arrangements (post, p 618). See Law Com No 158, para 2.69.
17 Post, p 766.
18 Leasehold Reform Act 1967, s 5(5).
19 Post, p 772.
20 Housing Act 1985, Sch 9A, para 5(2), as supplied by Housing and Planning Act 1986, s 8(2), Sch 2.
1 Housing Act 1985, Sch 9A, para 6(1(b), as supplied by Housing and Planning Act 1986, s 8(2), Sch 2.
2 See *Abbey National Building Society v Cann* [1991] 1 AC 56 at 87E-H per Lord Oliver of Aylmerton, 95F per Lord Jauncey of Tullichettle.

Thus section 70(1)(g) cannot protect an occupier's interest against a subsequent transferee or chargee if the priority otherwise accorded the occupier's interest has been waived or diminished in advance of the relevant dealing with the registered title. In *Paddington Building Society v Mendelsohn*,[3] for instance, a registered title was purchased in the name of S, the purchase moneys being provided partly by S's mother, M, and partly through a mortgage loan advanced by P. M was clearly a beneficial tenant in common behind an implied trust of the registered title (see *Fig.* 17), and she moved into joint occupation of the property with S and his girl friend during the interim between the conveyance and P's registration of its charge over the property.

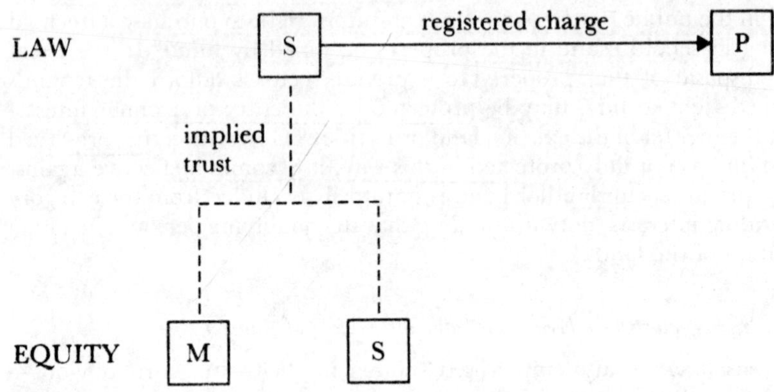

Fig. 17

M later claimed that she had thereby acquired an overriding interest under section 70(1)(g) which was binding on P.[4] The Court of Appeal held, however, that since M had both known and intended at the date of purchase that there was to be a charge in favour of P, the 'only possible intention to impute to the parties' was an intention that M's rights were to be 'subject to the rights' of P.[5] It then followed that M, having impliedly conceded priority to P, no longer retained any 'rights' adverse to P which were capable

3 (1985) 50 P & CR 244.

4 *Mendelsohn*'s case of course pre-dated the ruling of the House of Lords in *Abbey National Building Society v Cann* [1991] 1 AC 56 (ante, p 204), which fixed the date of disposition rather than registration as the relevant date for determining the existence of 'actual occupation'. However, the principle demonstrated in *Mendelsohn*'s case remains applicable today in respect of any rights claimed by a person who (for whatever reason) goes into occupation in advance of the date of disposition.

5 (1985) 50 P & CR 244 at 247. M had not signed the charge in favour of P, but as Mary Welstead has pointed out, '[i]nstead of the onus falling on the *purchaser* to investigate potential equitable claims, the onus seems to have shifted to the equitable owner to declare his rights to any purchaser of whom *he* has notice. If he does not so declare them he is deemed to have conceded priority to the purchaser...' (see [1985] CLJ 354 at 355). For evidence of the same approach in unregistered land, see *Bristol and West Building Society v Henning* [1985] 1 WLR 778 at 781G–782G (post, p 577).

of protection under section 70(1)(g).[6] As Browne-Wilkinson LJ observed, '[i]f the rights of the person in actual occupation are not under the general law such as to give any priority over the holder of the registered estate, there is nothing in section 70 which changes such rights into different and bigger rights.'[7]

(6) Nature of 'actual occupation' for the purpose of section 70(1)(g)

Section 70(1)(g) affords protection to the rights of every person in 'actual occupation' of the land transferred or charged. This critical expression is not statutorily defined, but certain guiding features emerge from the case law.[8] The acts which constitute 'actual occupation' must clearly vary in accordance with the nature of the premises concerned.[9] More than one person may be in 'actual occupation' at the same time.[10] The presence pleaded as 'actual occupation' need be in no sense adverse to that of the registered owner.[11] Perhaps most significant, it has been strongly suggested in recent cases that section 70(1)(g) is to be accorded a purposive construction, and that the internal logic of the Land Registration Act 1925 therefore imposes certain constraints upon its operation.

Contrary to earlier assertions that the equitable doctrine of notice affecting purchasers of unregistered land 'has no application even by analogy to registered land'[12], it may well be that the effect of recent judicial construction of section 70(1)(g) is in some measure to replicate the function of this equitable

6 For criticism of this application of the concept of estoppel, see Chapter 11 (post, p 330). See also the much more restrictive application of estoppel doctrine in Canada (*Re Quesnel & District Credit Union and Smith* (1988) 45 DLR (4th) 386 at 399ff). The approach in *Mendelsohn*'s case, in which rights are rendered unenforceable by virtue of a deemed participation in a subsequent registered disposition, has since received the implicit approval of the House of Lords in *Abbey National Building Society v Cann* [1991] 1 AC 56 at 82F-G, 89B, 94B-G per Lord Oliver of Aylmerton. Conversely no estoppel is raised if there is *no* prior knowledge of the relevant disposition (see *Lloyds Bank Plc v Rosset* [1991] 1 AC 107 at 127C per Lord Bridge of Harwich, [1989] Ch 350 at 387C-E per Nicholls LJ, 406B-C per Purchas LJ).

7 (1985) 50 P & CR 244 at 248. See also *E.S. Schwab & Co Ltd v McCarthy* (1976) 31 P & CR 196 at 205; *City of London Building Society v Flegg* [1988] AC 54 at 88A-B per Lord Oliver of Aylmerton. The claim asserted by M in *Mendelsohn*'s case would now be defeated on the additional ground that an acquisition mortgage allows no *scintilla temporis* to intervene between the purchase of a legal estate and the creation of the mortgage charge over it (post, p 561).

8 In *Lloyds Bank Plc v Rosset* [1989] Ch 350 at 393H, Mustill LJ pointed out, however, that no conclusive guidance could be obtained from the interpretation accorded in other branches of the law to the term 'occupation'.

9 See *Lloyds Bank Plc v Rosset* [1989] Ch 350 at 394F per Mustill LJ ('...the acts which constitute actual occupation of a dwelling house, a garage or woodland cannot all be the same'). In *Rosset*'s case there was general agreement in the Court of Appeal that differing standards of 'actual occupation' might be relevant to an ordinary dwelling house fit for habitation and a semi-derelict property. See [1989] Ch 350 at 376H–377A, 398G-H.

10 *Lloyds Bank Plc v Rosset* [1989] Ch 350 at 394D per Mustill LJ.

11 *Williams & Glyn's Bank Ltd v Boland* [1981] AC 487 at 505B per Lord Wilberforce, echoing the view of Ormrod LJ in the Court of Appeal ([1979] Ch 312 at 339A).

12 *Williams & Glyn's Bank Ltd v Boland* [1981] AC 487 at 504B per Lord Wilberforce. In *Boland* the House of Lords even rejected ([1981] AC 487 at 508E) a direct attempt to import the equitable doctrine of notice into registered land by way of Land Registration Act 1925, s 74. See also [1979] Ch 312 at 343D per Browne LJ; [1979] CLJ 254 at 256 (M.J. Prichard).

doctrine in an initially rather alien context.[13] Thus, it is increasingly said, acts constituting actual occupation must be discoverable on inspection by a purchaser who visits the premises and investigates.[14] Occupation, in order to be relevant, must be capable of disclosing the possible existence of rights adverse to the proprietor of the registered title.[15] Above all, 'conveyancing sense'[16] requires that relevant occupation must take a form and must subsist at a time which enables a purchaser to make purposeful and 'fruitful' enquiry *before* he completes the transaction under which he takes his estate or interest.[17] Once all of these links are made, 'the pieces of the jigsaw fit together reasonably well.'[18]

(a) A primarily factual criterion

The definition of 'actual occupation' arose significantly for the first time in *Hodgson v Marks*.[19] Here H had been the owner of her house in fee simple. After the death of her second husband, she took in E as her lodger and soon came to regard him as a man of substance. She entrusted him with the management of her affairs, and at his suggestion executed a voluntary transfer of her registered title in his favour. E was duly registered as proprietor, the parties having reached a verbal understanding that the transfer was simply nominal and that H should remain the real owner of the property. H and E continued to live together in the house both before and after the transfer. Some time later E dishonestly sold and transferred the legal estate to M without the knowledge or concurrence of H (see *Fig.* 18). E then

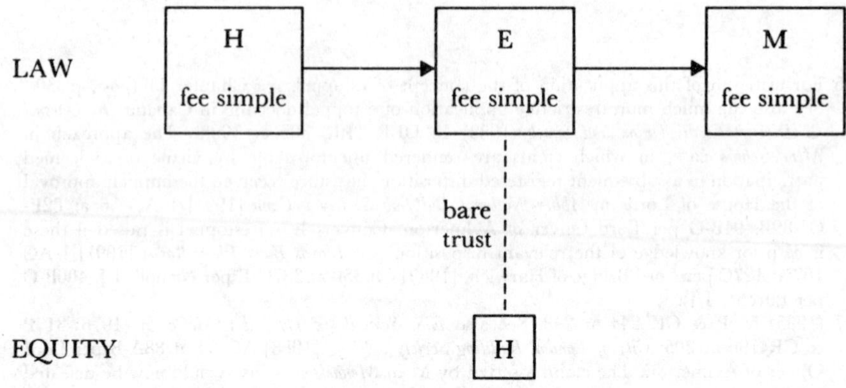

Fig. 18

13 See eg the statement of Purchas LJ in *Lloyds Bank Plc v Rosset* [1989] Ch 350 at 403B that section 70(1)(g) was 'intended to import into the law relating to registered land the equitable concept of constructive notice'. See also *National Provincial Bank Ltd v Ainsworth* [1965] AC 1175 at 1260G–1261A per Lord Wilberforce; *Hodgson v Marks* [1971] Ch 892 at 915C-G per Ungoed-Thomas J.

14 *Lloyds Bank Plc v Rosset* [1989] Ch 350 at 394G, 397A-B per Mustill LJ.

15 *Lloyds Bank Plc v Rosset* [1989] Ch 350 at 399A per Mustill LJ.

16 The phrase is that of Nicholls LJ in *Lloyds Bank Plc v Rosset* [1989] Ch 350 at 374A.

17 *Abbey National Building Society v Cann* [1991] 1 AC 56 at 88C-D per Lord Oliver of Aylmerton. See also *Lloyds Bank Plc v Rosset* [1989] Ch 350 at 374A-C per Nicholls LJ, 397A-B, 398E per Mustill LJ.

18 *Lloyds Bank Plc v Rosset* [1989] Ch 350 at 374C per Nicholls LJ.

19 [1971] Ch 892. See (1971) 35 Conv (NS) 225 (I. Leeming); (1972) 88 LQR 14 (J.L. Barton); (1973) 36 MLR 25 (R.H. Maudsley).

died, and the present litigation concerned H's claim that her rights were protected against M by virtue of section 70(1)(g). It was accepted both by Ungoed-Thomas J at first instance and by the Court of Appeal that before the transfer to M, E had held the registered title on trust for H.[20] The major question now in dispute was whether H could assert her equitable rights as a trust beneficiary against the new registered proprietor, M, it being clear that H had, at all relevant times, continued to reside in the property.

The Court of Appeal held that H's beneficial interest ranked as an overriding interest.[1] Russell LJ, while declining to 'lay down a code or catalogue of situations in which a person other than the vendor should be held to be . . . in actual occupation of registered land for the purposes of section 70(1)(g)',[2] had no doubt that on the present facts H had indeed been in 'actual occupation' of the property. The Court of Appeal construed this vital phrase quite literally, as connoting a mere physical presence on the part of persons other than the vendor.

In support of this conclusion, Russell LJ pointed to the general principle of common law and statute 'that a person in occupation is protected in his rights by that occupation'. In his view, a purchaser 'must pay heed to anyone in occupation if he is to be sure of getting a good title'. In thus placing the onus of enquiry firmly on the purchaser, Russell LJ declined to accept any sweeping proposition of law to the effect that the rights of any person who is in occupation will be overridden whenever the vendor is, or appears to be, also in occupation. It must, he said, 'depend on the circumstances, and a wise purchaser or lender will take no risks. Indeed, however wise he may be, he may have no ready opportunity of finding out; but nevertheless the law will protect the occupier.'[3]

In the aftermath of *Hodgson v Marks* it seemed therefore that for the purpose of section 70(1)(g) 'actual occupation' was to be construed largely as a matter of sheer physical fact.[4] As Lord Denning MR remarked in *Williams & Glyn's Bank Ltd v Boland*,[5] '"actual occupation" is matter of fact, not matter of law'.[6] This approach was upheld by the House of Lords in the same case, Lord Wilberforce observing that the the phrase comprised 'ordinary words of plain

20 It was found that H had intended to retain the beneficial interest in the property, and that the original transfer had therefore brought about a resulting trust of the legal estate in favour of H ([1971] Ch 892 at 906D, 933C, G). H was not precluded from asserting the existence of such a trust vis à vis E, since resulting trusts are exempted from the requirements of formality normally imposed by Law of Property Act 1925, s 53(1) (post, p 377). Compare, however, *Thwaites v Ryan* [1984] VR 65 at 93 (post, p 442).

1 [1971] Ch 892 at 934G–935A.

2 [1971] Ch 892 at 932C-D. See also *Abbey National Building Society v Cann* [1991] 1 AC 56 at 93F-G per Lord Oliver of Aylmerton.

3 [1971] Ch 892 at 932D.

4 This approach to section 70(1)(g) has sometimes been termed an 'absolutist' construction (see D.J. Hayton, *Registered Land* (3rd edn, London 1981), p 87), and contrasts strongly with a 'constitutionalist' view in which the interpretation of section 70(1)(g) accords much more harmoniously with the unregistered land doctrine of notice.

5 [1979] Ch 312 at 332E.

6 In the words used by Mustill LJ in *Lloyds Bank Plc v Rosset* [1989] Ch 350 at 397C, 398H, the real question is whether the claimant of an overriding interest pursuant to section 70(1)(g) was "there" on the property'.

English'.[7] Lord Scarman noted that, in section 70(1)(g), 'the statute has substituted a plain factual situation for the uncertainties of notice, actual or constructive, as the determinant of an overriding interest.'[8]

(b) Marginal instances of 'actual occupation'

In spite of the apparently definitive ruling in *Williams & Glyn's Bank Ltd v Boland*, the concept of 'actual occupation' is in certain respects still beset by ambiguities which may make it difficult to determine whether title is being transferred subject to the adverse claims of persons in occupation. It is by no means clear that all problems are best (or even adequately) addressed in terms of a 'plain factual' test. As Lord Oliver of Aylmerton pointed out in *Abbey National Building Society v Cann*,[9] 'even plain English may contain a variety of shades of meaning'. The case law of recent years has disclosed a judicial inclination towards restrictive definition of the scope of section 70(1)(g), and this tendency has begun to colour quite heavily the peripheral construction of 'actual occupation'.

(i) Can 'actual occupation' be symbolic or vicarious? In *Abbey National Building Society v Cann*[10] Lord Oliver of Aylmerton adverted to the fact that 'actual occupation' within the meaning of section 70(1)(g) 'does not necessarily. . .involve the personal presence of the person claiming to occupy'.[11] The courts are prepared, within fairly strict limits, to accept that 'actual occupation' can be established by symbolic or proxy occupation. In *Kling v Keston Properties Ltd*,[12] for example, P had been granted an option to purchase a garage which was later let on a long lease to D. In the dispute which followed, D parked her car across the entrance to this garage. This malicious action had the effect of trapping inside the garage a car belonging to P's wife which D plainly regarded as being wrongfully there. This being the impasse reached on the conferment of D's lease, Vinelott J held that the enforced presence of the car in the garage constituted a form of 'actual occupation' of that garage on behalf of P, thus rendering his option an overriding interest binding on D.[13]

7 [1981] AC 487 at 504F. There are, of course, some circumstances to which even this broad approach could never apply. Mere user of a right of way cannot, for instance, constitute 'actual occupation' of the land over which that right of way is exercised (*Celsteel Ltd v Alton House Holdings Ltd* [1985] 1 WLR 204 at 219E). See also Law Com No 158, para 2.57. A claim of easement necessarily implies some limited form of user (post, p 1075), and the intermittent exercise of a right of way simply lacks the intensity of user which even the minimal factual requirements of section 70(1)(g) seem to demand.

8 [1981] AC 487 at 511E-F. See also *Abbey National Building Society v Cann* [1991] 1 AC 56 at 93D per Lord Oliver of Aylmerton.

9 [1991] 1 AC 56 at 93D.

10 [1991] 1 AC 56 at 93G.

11 See also *Williams & Glyn's Bank Ltd v Boland* [1979] Ch 312 at 338D per Ormrod LJ.

12 (1983) 49 P & CR 212. See [1985] Conv 406 (J.E.M.).

13 (1983) 49 P & CR 212 at 218f. Vinelott J thought that the result would have been the same even if the car had not been trapped inside the garage. Even an intermittent user of the garage 'in the ordinary way' would have been sufficient to establish 'actual occupation'. Compare, however, *Epps v Esso Petroleum Co Ltd* [1973] 1 WLR 1071 at 1080A (regular parking of car on strip of land held not to be 'actual occupation').

Similarly, in *Abbey National Building Society v Cann*[14] itself, Lord Oliver thought that for the purpose of section 70(1)(g) a caretaker or the representative of a company could occupy on behalf of his or her employer.[15] The courts have opined on other occasions that section 70(1)(g) can be satisfied by vicarious occupation established through 'a servant'[16] or other 'agent',[17] at least so long as the occupation in question is required for and is related to the proper discharge of the function of the proxy occupier.[18] There would seem to be no reason why 'actual occupation' on the part of a claimant cannot be established through the presence of a close relative on the premises,[19] at least where such person is of full age and is capable of making a sensible response to any enquiries directed by a prospective transferee.[20]

It is clear, however, that 'actual occupation' cannot comprise the mere presence of a bare licensee.[1] Nor is section 70(1)(g) satisfied by an occupancy of the relevant premises enjoyed by casual employees who have no helpful insight to throw upon the subject matter of enquiries made by purchasers. In *Lloyds Bank Plc v Rosset*[2] a wife claimed to have an equitable entitlement in the matrimonial home which overrode the charge taken by a mortgagee of her husband's registered title. It transpired that, even before the transfer of title to the husband, the transferor had allowed the transferee's building contractors to commence work on the premises, which were at the time semi-derelict. This work was carried out largely under the direction of the wife, who for this purpose was present on the premises for lengthy periods daily. The Court of Appeal held by a majority that the presence of the builders constituted 'actual occupation' on behalf of the claimant wife, and that this occupation coupled with her own daily visits to the property made her beneficial interest overriding under section 70(1)(g).[3] However, Mustill LJ entered a strong dissent on this point, taking the view that no intending purchaser with enquiries to make as to adverse interests 'would imagine that masons and plasterers working on the fabric...could be in occupation

14 [1991] 1 AC 56 at 93G.

15 See also *Strand Securities Ltd v Caswell* [1965] Ch 958 at 981B per Lord Denning MR. Compare, however, Russell LJ (at 984D-985A), and see Law Com No 158, para 2.57.

16 *Strand Securities Ltd v Caswell* [1965] Ch 958 at 981B per Lord Denning MR.

17 *Lloyds Bank Plc v Rosset* [1989] Ch 350 at 377F-G per Nicholls LJ.

18 See *Strand Securities Ltd v Caswell* [1965] Ch 958 at 984E-G per Russell LJ; *Lloyds Bank Plc v Rosset* [1989] Ch 350 at 377G-378A per Nicholls LJ, 397H, 398B-C per Mustill LJ, 405D per Purchas LJ.

19 In *Strand Securities Ltd v Caswell* [1965] Ch 958 at 984G-985A, Russell LJ thought that the claimant of an overriding interest could establish 'actual occupation' through the presence of his spouse, although he was unwilling to extend this notion of occupation by proxy to cover the step-daughter in the instant case.

20 Post, p 223.

1 *Strand Securities Ltd v Caswell* [1965] Ch 958 at 981A-C, 984D-985A (ante, p 208). Referring to *Strand Securities*, Purchas LJ accepted in *Lloyds Bank Plc v Rosset* [1989] Ch 350 at 405E that 'occupation by a friend for her own purposes with the leave and licence of the tenant is no "actual occupation".'

2 [1991] 1 AC 107 (HL); [1989] Ch 350 (CA) (post, pp 424, 576).

3 [1989] Ch 350 at 377C-378B, 379B-C per Nicholls LJ, 405C-H per Purchas LJ. See [1988] Conv 453 at 457 (M.P. Thompson); (1988) 104 LQR 507 (R.J. Smith); [1989] CLJ 180 (P.G. McHugh).

of the site, in any relevant sense, rather than coming and going to work upon it.'[4] The House of Lords reversed the Court of Appeal's decision on other grounds,[5] but the tenor of the principal speech (delivered by Lord Bridge of Harwich) indicated a clear general preference for the view taken by the dissenting judge in the Court of Appeal.

(ii) Must 'actual occupation' be continuous? Actual occupation must involve 'some notion of continuity', since it cannot have been the statutory intention that a claimant's interest should 'override the legal estate intermittently, according to momentary changes in the proprietor's degree of actual physical connection with the land'.[6] However, the concept of 'actual occupation' within section 70(1)(g) cannot sensibly require an uninterrupted personal presence on the land by the claimant of an overriding interest.

Accordingly it is now clear that some kinds of temporary absence will not detract from the 'actual occupation' which may be asserted by a person who is normally in residence. In this context the courts have applied something akin to the notions of *corpus possessionis* and *animus revertendi* which have become familiar in the law of landlord and tenant.[7] In effect, 'actual occupation' is regarded as subsisting so long as the temporarily absent occupier can point to some physical evidence or symbol of continued residence coupled with an intention to return to the property.[8]

In *Chhokar v Chhokar*,[9] for instance, H held the registered legal title in the matrimonial home on a statutory trust for sale for himself and his wife, W, in equal shares. H agreed secretly to transfer that title at an undervalue to an acquaintance, P, H's intention being to rid himself of his wife while extracting for himself as much as he could of the outstanding equity in the matrimonial home.[10] H and P deliberately arranged that completion of the transfer should occur while W was in hospital having a baby. Immediately after the transfer of title, H disappeared with the balance of the proceeds of the sale and P advertised the property for sale at its full market value. When W emerged from hospital clutching her new-born child, she found that the locks had been changed and that she was denied access

4 [1989] Ch 350 at 398E-G. While conceding that the presence of the builders 'might add an element of continuity to a presence by somebody else, be it the husband or the wife, which was otherwise too intermittent to amount to occupation', Mustill LJ decided that the wife's daily supervisory role 'did not, any more than that of the builders, disclose anything about the possibility of interests adverse to the holder of the paper title' ([1989] Ch 350 at 399A). See also *Canadian Imperial Bank of Commerce v Bello* (1992) 64 P & CR 48 at 51 per Dillon LJ.
5 [1991] 1 AC 107 at 134A-B.
6 *Lloyds Bank Plc v Rosset* [1989] Ch 350 at 394E per Mustill LJ.
7 Post, p 760f.
8 See *Hoggett v Hoggett* (1980) 39 P & CR 121 at 130, where, in a slightly different context, 'occupation' was not regarded as necessarily interrupted merely by the fact that the occupier might have gone into hospital for a few days, or gone on a weekend visit to a friend, or gone out shopping for a few hours (post, p 761).
9 [1984] FLR 313.
10 In the words of Ewbank J, the transaction between H and P was similar to that which might have taken place 'in relation to property...asserted to have fallen off the back of a lorry' ([1984] FLR 313 at 318A-B). P was fully aware of H's fraudulent intent.

to her own home.[11] Notwithstanding that W had clearly been absent from the property when P's new title was registered, Ewbank J regarded the continuing presence of W's furniture in the house as a notional or token occupation which was quite sufficient to constitute 'actual occupation' for the purpose of section 70(1)(g). In view of W's consistent intention to resume residence, Ewbank J held without hesitation that she had an overriding interest binding on P.[12] It was somewhat ironic that, before the litigation commenced, W had managed to return into residence in the home with her two children. Her husband then reappeared and was reconciled, and the family thereafter lived together happily much to the discomfiture of P,[13] who ended up owning a house which he could neither occupy[14] nor sell[15] and from which he could derive no rental income.[16]

While temporary absence is not fatal to a claim under section 70(1)(g), the notion of 'actual occupation' does connote 'some degree of permanence and continuity which would rule out mere fleeting presence'.[17] In *Abbey National Building Society v Cann*[18] it was alleged that a trust beneficiary, D2, had acquired an overriding interest in property purchased by her son, D1. It appeared that (with the consent of the transferor) the mother's furniture had started to be unloaded on to the property from a removal van some 35 minutes prior to the execution of the relevant transfer and mortgage charge in favour of the building society, P. Lord Oliver of Aylmerton was, quite rightly, unprepared to accept that 'acts of this preparatory character carried out by courtesy of the vendor prior to completion' could ever constitute 'actual occupation' for the purpose of section 70(1)(g).[19]

(iii) Are there any persons who cannot be in 'actual occupation'? If one single issue falsifies the supposedly 'plain factual' criterion of 'actual occupation', it is

11 She later did secure a re-entry into the premises but was then violently evicted by 'heavies' employed by P. Cumming-Bruce LJ declared it difficult 'to find language which, with becoming moderation, describes the moral turpitude of every step taken by [P] throughout this transaction' ([1984] FLR 313 at 330G).

12 [1984] FLR 313 at 317F. (This conclusion was not challenged in the subsequent appeal.) Compare *Strand Securities Ltd v Caswell* [1965] Ch 958 at 985A-B, where Russell LJ was not prepared to accept that a valid claim of 'actual occupation' could be founded either on the presence of furniture or relatives or on the retention of a key by an absent occupier.

13 Cumming-Bruce LJ observed ([1984] FLR 313 at 331H) that there was no room here for the shedding of 'crocodile tears' on behalf of P merely because his unlawful enterprise had not succeeded. ('I can see no reason for giving him anything more than the court in an unreported case gave to the money-lender who had rights over a debtor. The proceedings are recorded in a play of Shakespeare'.)

14 Post, p 471.

15 Post, p 589.

16 Post, p 477.

17 *Abbey National Building Society v Cann* [1991] 1 AC 56 at 93D per Lord Oliver of Aylmerton.

18 [1991] 1 AC 56 (ante, p 200).

19 [1991] 1 AC 56 at 94A. See also Lord Oliver at 93H ('A prospective tenant or purchaser who is allowed, as a matter of indulgence, to go into property in order to plan decorations or measure for furnishings would not, in ordinary parlance, be said to be occupying it, even though he might be there for hours at a time'). For a similar view of acts preparatory to (but not constitutive of) 'actual occupation', see *Lloyds Bank Plc v Rosset* [1989] Ch 350 at 399A-B per Mustill LJ.

the question whether every individual human being present on relevant premises at a relevant time thereby attains the status of a 'person in actual occupation' for purposes of section 70(1)(g). The response to this question must be negative. It is perfectly conceivable, for instance, that a minor child may reside on the premises and hold 'rights' within the meaning of section 70(1)(g),[20] but it is nevertheless clear that such a child (at least if of tender years) can claim no overriding interest by reason of 'actual occupation'.[1] The factor which drives this conclusion is, of course, the circumstance that the child is almost certainly incapable of any adequate response to the enquiries which section 70(1)(g) clearly envisages that a purchaser may wish to make.[2] The definition of 'actual occupation' is inevitably qualified by a purposive assessment of the capacity of the individual to make intelligent and intelligible response to an inquirer.[3]

The idea that not all persons who are physically present on relevant property are necessarily persons 'in actual occupation' is far from new. There is an uncomfortable precedent in the now discredited view that a wife's residence in the family home is subordinated to, and submerged within, the occupation enjoyed by her husband. In *Bird v Syme-Thomson*,[4] for instance, Templeman J rejected a wife-beneficiary's claim that she had an overriding interest enforceable against a mortgagee who had taken a charge executed by her husband. In Templeman J's view, 'when a mortgagor is in actual occupation of the matrimonial home, it cannot be said that his wife also is in actual occupation.'[5] 'Actual occupation' in the statutory sense thus belonged exclusively to the owner of the registered title, the wife being present 'only. . .as a shadow of occupation of the owner.'[6]

This 'shadow' theory, which barely concealed a number of outdated assumptions about the significance of a woman's presence and function in the family home, was finally and convincingly refuted in *Williams & Glyn's Bank Ltd v Boland*.[7] Lord Wilberforce noted that the 'shadow' theory is now

20 A child may well be a beneficiary under a trust for sale of the family home, as for instance where part of the purchase moneys originated in a fund held on trust for that child.

1 See *Bird v Syme-Thomson* [1979] 1 WLR 440 at 444D, where Templeman J implied that the minor children of a vendor would not be able to claim the benefit of section 70(1)(g) of the Land Registration Act 1925. See also J. Martin, [1980] Conv 361 at 372.

2 It would be wholly absurd to hold that proper enquiry for the purpose of section 70(1)(g) can be made of a baby-beneficiary or that the latter's gurgling replies amount to a non-disclosure of his or her rights! It is no solution to the problem of the infant beneficiary to say that enquiry must be made of the child's parent or guardian: this may be to play into the hands of the one person who has a vested interest in not disclosing the child's beneficial entitlement.

3 The same approach may require to be adopted in relation to other persons present on premises who are affected, for instance, by senility or mental deficiency.

4 [1979] 1 WLR 440. See [1979] CLJ 23 (M.J. Prichard); [1979] Conv 72 (F.R. Crane).

5 [1979] 1 WLR 440 at 444A.

6 [1979] 1 WLR 440 at 444E. See also *Williams & Glyn's Bank Ltd v Boland* (1978) 36 P & CR 448 at 454, where Templeman J pointed to the 'wide and almost catastrophic' nature of the extensive burden of enquiry which would be forced on prospective purchasers by any other holding.

7 [1981] AC 487.

'heavily obsolete'[8] and that the statutory phrase 'actual occupation' is neutral between male and female, involving 'no question of matrimonial law, or of the rights of married women or of women as such.'[9] It was 'unacceptable' to suggest that the apparent occupation of the wife of a vendor/mortgagor could be 'satisfactorily accounted for by his',[10] and Lord Wilberforce had no difficulty in concluding that 'a spouse, living in a house, has an actual occupation capable of conferring protection, as an overriding interest, upon rights of that spouse.'[11]

(7) Enquiry under section 70(1)(g)

Pursuant to section 70(1)(g) the rights of every person in actual occupation constitute an overriding interest 'save where enquiry is made of such person and the rights are not disclosed.' Clearly it was not the intendment of the legislature that this provision should preserve rights whose existence has been concealed from an enquiring transferee or chargee of the land concerned.[12] It is equally plain, however, that section 70(1)(g) imposes on the purchaser a responsibility to ensure that any person in actual occupation is asked 'what rights he or she has in the land'.[13]

(a) Who must make the enquiry?

Section 70(1)(g) does not demand that the relevant enquiry necessarily be made by the purchaser of the registered title.[14] It seems that the relevant enquiry may be made by an agent. The terms of section 70(1)(g) are indeed

8 [1981] AC 487 at 505G. The Court of Appeal had already condemned Templeman J's approach as 'unrealistic and anachronistic' ([1979] Ch 312 at 343B per Browne LJ) and as representing the law 'a hundred years ago when the law regarded husband and wife as one: and the husband as that one' ([1979] Ch 312 at 332C per Lord Denning MR). Ormrod LJ voiced the objection that the notion of vicarious occupation through a wife 'resurrects the outmoded concept of the head of the family' ([1979] Ch 312 at 338H).

9 [1981] AC 487 at 502E. See also [1979] Ch 312 at 333D-E per Ormrod LJ.

10 [1981] AC 487 at 505G-H. According to Ormrod LJ ([1979] Ch 312 at 338F), it would be difficult to 'imagine clearer examples of "actual occupation" in the ordinary sense' than the case of a wife living with her husband in the matrimonial home. See also [1979] Ch 312 at 332D-E per Lord Denning MR.

11 [1981] AC 487 at 506C. The pre-*Boland* view of the position of a wife in the family home has now been turned on its head. In *Bird v Syme-Thomson* [1979] 1 WLR 440 at 444E Templeman J held that a wife who was physically resident in her home was not in 'actual occupation'. In *Chhokar v Chhokar* [1984] FLR 313 at 317F, a wife was unhesitatingly declared to be in 'actual occupation' notwithstanding that she was clearly absent from the property at the relevant time—she had been physically excluded from the house (ante, p 220).

12 The overriding interest will, however, remain intact if the transferee or chargee either makes no enquiry at all or is informed of the claimed rights and takes no evasive action. See *Lloyds Bank Plc v Rosset* [1989] Ch 350 at 396G-H per Mustill LJ.

13 *Winkworth v Edward Baron Development Co Ltd* (1986) 52 P & CR 67 at 77 per Nourse LJ, who added that it was not sufficient for the purpose of section 70(1)(g) merely to ask all occupiers to confirm in writing that they held 'as bare licensees and not by virtue of any tenancy or lease'. The Court of Appeal's ruling in *Winkworth* was later reversed by the House of Lords on a different point which made section 70(1)(g) irrelevant ([1986] 1 WLR 1512). See Chapter 12 (post, p 444).

14 See [1980] Conv 161.

disturbingly vague: there is no indication as to precisely when enquiry and disclosure ought to occur.[15]

(b) Of whom must the enquiry be made?

It is important to read the proviso to section 70(1)(g) with some care. In order to take the land free of overriding interests, a purchaser must make enquiry of the person whose rights would otherwise comprise an overriding interest.[16] In *Hodgson v Marks*[17] M may have made some enquiry as to the precise status or entitlement of H, but since he directed his enquiry only towards E, his enquiry was utterly irrelevant for the purpose of complying with section 70(1)(g). In order to guarantee immunity from the overriding interest, M would have had to make enquiry of H herself—and this he did not do.[18] In the words of Russell LJ, 'reliance on the untrue ipse dixit of the vendor will not suffice'.[19] A heavy onus is often placed on the purchaser since he must make enquiry of persons whose occupation may not be at all apparent.[20] However, as Russell LJ stressed, the law will protect the occupier of registered land irrespective of the difficulty facing the purchaser.[1]

(8) Has the doctrine of constructive notice any role within section 70(1)(g) ?

It is doubtless true at a general level that the old equitable doctrine of notice has been extruded from the law of registered land.[2] However, the foregoing examination of section 70(1)(g) makes it clear that, contrary to earlier indications,[3] the concept of constructive notice still exerts a continuing

15 Much criticism has been directed at the fact that the scope of the enquiry enjoined by section 70(1)(g) is not even limited, as a matter of statutory language, to any concept of 'reasonable' enquiry. The Law Commission has endorsed the view that the statutory proviso concerning enquiry 'is in practice worthless. . .[and] performs no useful function' (Law Com No 158, para 2.59). Accordingly the Commission has recommended that this proviso be discontinued and that all categories of overriding interest (whether or not arising under section 70(1)(g)) be made explicitly subject to 'the jurisdiction of the courts to postpone them as against subsequent purchasers and lenders on the general grounds of fraud or estoppel' (ibid, para 2.75). See Draft Land Registration Bill, clause 9(7) (Law Commission, Law Com No 173 (1988), Appendix).

16 In *Winkworth v Edward Baron Development Co Ltd* (1986) 52 P & CR 67 at 77, Nourse LJ was prepared to accept that in most cases enquiry may properly be made of a solicitor acting for the person in actual occupation.

17 [1971] Ch 892 (ante, p 216).

18 A purchaser may not be able to take action on the vendor's implied covenants for title if the latter has omitted to disclose overriding interests to which the land will be subject (see D. Partington, [1989] Conv 18 at 23f).

19 [1971] Ch 892 at 932D. It is not enough to make enquiry of the hall porter in a block of flats as to the potential rights of occupiers of those flats. Such a porter is the agent of the landlord rather than any of the tenants, and has no authority to make (or withhold) any relevant reply under section 70(1)(g) (see *Kling v Keston Properties Ltd* (1983) 49 P & CR 212 at 220).

20 The onus placed on the transferee or chargee becomes even greater in cases of multiple occupation in the family context. See Chapter 14 (post, p 558).

1 Ante, p 217. A purchaser of registered land is well advised to have written proof of enquiry (see [1980] Conv 361 (J. Martin)).

2 Ante, p 106.

3 Ante, p 217.

impact on the law of overriding interests.[4] It is, of course, undeniable that section 70(1)(g) diverges from the doctrine of constructive notice in certain important respects.[5] But it is equally clear that the definition of 'actual occupation' cannot rest entirely on a crude factual or physical criterion. Like the doctrine of constructive notice, section 70(1)(g) inevitably necessitates a *qualitative* assessment of the factual matrix. More abstract forms of judgment are inescapable when courts are called upon to determine whether a purchaser is to be bound by the adverse rights of persons who are present on the land.

There is therefore an unexpectedly broad equivalence between the questions whether a given presence on land is sufficiently significant (a) to fix a purchaser of unregistered land with a duty of enquiry into possible adverse rights, and (b) to constitute 'actual occupation' for the purpose of section 70(1)(g) of the Land Registration Act 1925.[6] These two forms of interrogatory lie roughly parallel,[7] and it was surely no accident that in *Lloyds Bank Plc v Rosset*[8] Mustill LJ remarked that, even if constructive notice no longer strictly applies in the field of registered title, 'the old law still gives a flavour to the new words of . . . section 70(1).'[9] The conscious recognition of the analogy with constructive notice does not, of course, promise a more liberal or generous approach towards the rights of occupiers. The position is quite the reverse. It is significant that in *Rosset*'s case Mustill LJ adverted expressly to the fact that overriding interests 'can bear harshly on the purchaser, if they are given too wide a scope'.[10] In his view, Parliament, in adding section 70(1)(g) to the list of overriding interests, must be assumed to have 'intended to produce a result which did reasonable justice to the bona fide purchaser.'[11]

The notice-oriented view of 'actual occupation' may well suggest the inherent correctness of the approach (if not the eventual ruling) at first instance in *Hodgson v Marks*.[12] Here Ungoed-Thomas J construed 'actual occupation' as connoting 'actual and apparent occupation. . .occupation by act recognisable as such'.[13] Accordingly Ungoed-Thomas J held that H had not been in 'actual occupation' for the purpose of section 70(1)(g), in that it would not have been apparent to a purchaser from the mere fact of her

4 See P. Sparkes, [1989] Conv 342, but compare (1988) 104 LQR 507 at 511 (R.J. Smith).

5 One point of divergence emerges immediately from the fact that section 70(1)(g) creates an 'overriding interest' out of the rights of any person 'in receipt of the rents and profits' of registered land. It is quite clear, by contrast, that a purchaser of unregistered land occupied by a tenant is *not* thereby fixed with constructive notice of the landlord's rights (*Hunt v Luck* [1901] 1 Ch 45 at 49, [1902] 1 Ch 428 at 432). See *Lloyds Bank Plc v Rosset* [1989] Ch 350 at 395A–396G per Mustill LJ.

6 Ante, p 82.

7 See *Lloyds Bank Plc v Rosset* [1989] Ch 350 at 403B per Purchas LJ (ante, p 216).

8 [1989] Ch 350 at 397B per Mustill LJ.

9 [1989] Ch 350 at 397B.

10 [1989] Ch 350 at 394B.

11 [1989] Ch 350 at 394C. Some impression of Mustill LJ's sympathies in this context may be gained from his concern (at 397B) lest an overly generous approach to section 70(1)(g) should bring about a 'marked, and it may be said unacceptable, contrast with the workmanlike solution arrived at for unregistered land in cases such as *Caunce v Caunce* [1969] 1 WLR 286.' See Chapter 14 (post, p 565).

12 [1971] Ch 892 (ante, p 216).

13 According to Ungoed-Thomas J, any other construction, by subjecting a purchaser to the rights of occupiers irrespective of notice, would mean that section 70(1)(g) had become 'not a form of notice at all, but its negation' ([1971] Ch 892 at 915C).

presence on the property that she was beneficially entitled.[14] The presupposition underlying section 70(1)(g) must surely be that 'actual occupation' is attributable only to those whose presence on the land is reasonably detectable and who are in any event capable of making meaningful response to enquiry.

(9) The dual status of minor and overriding interests

Most schemes for the registration of land interests operate ultimately on the basis of two simple rules. *First,* if a registrable interest has in fact been duly entered on the register, it is binding on all purchasers regardless of whether they inspect the register. *Second,* a registrable right becomes void and unenforceable against purchasers if it is not entered on the register. In the latter case it matters not that the purchaser has actual knowledge of the unprotected interest from another source.

These straightforward principles apply in the context of both registration of land charges[15] and registration of title.[16] The underlying motive is readily understandable—the rules are clear-cut and easily applicable. The medium of the public register serves as an effective form of notice. Moreover, the statutory sanction of voidness in the case of non-protection ensures that the register—whether it be the Land Charges Register or the Land Register—contains an accurate, current and comprehensive record of the interests affecting the land concerned.

(a) The existence of an overlap

It is against this background of principle that it appears particularly strange that the Land Registration Act 1925 should permit an area of overlap between minor and overriding interests in registered land. As the law of registered land currently stands, it is possible for the owners of certain kinds of equitable interest to claim a dual protected status in respect of their rights. Such equitable owners may assert priority over purchasers of the registered title *either* on the ground that they have duly protected their rights by the entry of minor interests on the register *or* on the quite different ground that their rights, taken in conjunction with 'actual occupation' under section 70(1)(g), qualify as overriding interests under that provision.[17]

The existence of this potential overlap was finally confirmed by the House of Lords in *Williams & Glyn's Bank Ltd v Boland.*[18] Here Lord Wilberforce, although impressed at first by the 'formidable' argument that the categories of minor interest and overriding interest are mutually exclusive, was finally convinced that there is no 'firm dividing line, or. . .unbridgeable gulf, between

14 Compare *Caunce v Caunce* [1969] 1 WLR 286 at 293G–294A (post, p 565). It was clear in *Hodgson v Marks* that M had known of the existence of H when he contracted to purchase the property from E; he had seen H coming up the garden path on one occasion when he visited the property prior to the transfer. He had assumed that H was E's wife and that as such she had no beneficial interest in the property. There was even some evidence to suggest that E had dishonestly attempted to implant such an impression in M's mind.
15 Ante, p 118.
16 Ante, p 186.
17 Ante, p 208.
18 [1981] AC 487 (post, pp 569, 974).

minor interests and overriding interests'.[19] He pointed to previous decisions in which potentially minor interests had found protection as overriding interests[20] and regarded these decisions as confirming that 'the fact of occupation enables protection of the latter to extend to what without it would be the former.'[1]

(b) *The undesirability of an overlap*

It is therefore quite possible that a failure to protect a minor interest by entry on the register—far from incurring the penalty of voidness—may indeed have the paradoxical result of reinforcing that interest as an overriding interest.[2] It may appear strange that a scheme of registration can so operate that rights which are left unprotected qua minor interest are, in default of such protection, preserved as overriding interests.[3] It seems to make elementary good sense that any scheme directed towards securing the registration of interests should firmly attach disadvantage to a negligent failure to register. The inappropriateness of the overlap between minor and overriding interests is intensified when comparison is made between registered and unregistered land: it is quite often the case that exactly similar problems of land law priority result in diametrically different outcomes.[4]

(c) *Future reform of section 70(1)(g)*

The implications of the overlap between minor and overriding interests have inevitably attracted the attention of the Law Commission. Some consideration was given initially to the possibility that the categories of overriding interest might be abrogated in their entirety,[5] but the Commission finally concluded in 1987 in favour of a much more limited reform of this area of the law.

Although intensely aware of the difficulties caused by the dual protection of interests within the registered land scheme, the Commission attempted

19 [1981] AC 487 at 508A.
20 See *Bridges v Mees* [1957] Ch 475 (ante, p 202) and *Hodgson v Marks* [1971] Ch 892 (ante, p 216).
1 [1981] AC 487 at 508A. Lord Scarman (at 512A) agreed that 'overriding interests and minor interests are, as categories, exclusive of each other', but found 'no logical difficulty in the association of a minor interest with another factor (ie actual occupation) being, qua association, an overriding interest.' See also *City of London Building Society v Flegg* [1988] AC 54 at 89G–90B, 90G–H per Lord Oliver of Aylmerton.
2 An overriding interest is, by definition, one which does not appear as a minor interest on the face of the register (ante, p 199).
3 See eg *Kling v Keston Properties Ltd* (1983) 49 P & CR 212 at 222 per Vinelott J ('It is disquieting that the system of land registration. . .should be so framed that a person acquiring an interest in registered land may find his interest subject to an option or right of pre-emption which has not been registered and notwithstanding that there is no person other than the vendor in apparent occupation of the property and that careful inspection and enquiry has failed to reveal anything which might give the purchaser any reason to suspect that someone other than the vendor had any interests in or rights over the property').
4 Compare eg *Hollington Brothers Ltd v Rhodes* [1951] 2 TLR 691 (ante, p 121) with *Grace Rymer Investments Ltd v Waite* [1958] Ch 831 (ante, p 210). In the former case an unregistered equitable lease in unregistered land was held to be void against a purchaser of the superior title, even though the purchaser had the clearest of express notice of the tenant's rights. In the latter case, the equivalent but unprotected estate contract was held to be an overriding interest. See generally Law Com No 158, para 2.5.
5 Ante, p 199.

to strike some kind of social balance between the integrity of the register and the legitimate claims of actual occupiers of registered land.[6] Motivated by the benevolent view that 'it is not always reasonable to expect or sensible to require protection by registration'[7], the Commission recommended the substantial retention of overriding interest protection for the rights of occupiers. The Draft Land Registration Bill accordingly recognises the 'overriding' status of 'a right of any person who is in actual occupation of, or of any part of, the land in which the right subsists'.[8] Under the Bill the existence of such an overriding interest is no longer made subject to any proviso regarding enquiry by the purchaser, but, as the Law Commission has pointed out, 'the Bill is not a charter for the unscrupulous'.[9] Failure to disclose rights when asked 'or even, in some circumstances, merely standing by' will estop a person from asserting those rights.[10] All overriding interests are expressly made subject to the application of rules relating to estoppel and fraud.[11]

By way of partial compromise the Law Commission simultaneously proposed that the range of potentially overriding interests be cut back by the exclusion of the rights of persons in receipt of the rents and profits of registered land.[12] However, the ultimate resolution of the tension between owners and occupiers of registered land was felt by the Commission to lie in a much more generous extension of statutory indemnity to those registered proprietors who are bound by overriding interests.[13]

8. REGISTERED CHARGES

A further category of right which may be created under the Land Registration Act 1925 is the 'registered charge'. Subject to any entry to the contrary on the register, the proprietor of registered land is statutorily empowered to mortgage that land by deed or otherwise in any manner which would have been permissible if the land had been unregistered.[14] The standard method of mortgaging registered land is by way of 'registered charge'. Such a charge, unless made by lease or sublease, takes effect as a 'charge by way of legal mortgage'.[15] A registered charge is therefore a legal interest which is capable of creation and disposition by means only of a 'registered disposition'.[16] As such, the registered charge can never qualify as a registrable

6 Post, p 239.
7 Law Com No 158, para 2.64 (post, p 239).
8 Clause 7(1), (2)(d) (Law Com No 173, Appendix).
9 Law Com No 173, para 3.3.
10 Law Com No 173, para 3.3.
11 See Draft Land Registration Bill, clause 9(7) (Law Com No 173 (1988), Appendix).
12 Ante, p 207. Although minded to restrict the categories of overriding interest wherever possible, the Commission felt compelled in one respect to increase the overlap between minor and overriding interests. The Commission recommended that overriding interest protection be extended to settled land beneficial interests (ante, p 213).
13 Post, p 240.
14 Land Registration Act 1925, s 106(1). Even prior to registration, a person who has acquired the right to be registered as proprietor has statutory power to deal with the land (eg by creating a charge by way of mortgage). See Land Registration Act 1925, s 37(1), (2).
15 Land Registration Act 1925, s 27(1).
16 Land Registration Act 1925, ss 3(xxii), 18(4), 21(4).

interest, minor interest or overriding interest, and becomes fully effective only when the chargee is entered as the 'proprietor' of the charge on the relevant register of title.[17] Unless and until the charge is registered as a disposition, the chargee has an equitable interest only.[18]

Upon registration the chargee is issued with a charge certificate and, while the charge remains in effect, the chargor's land certificate is deposited in the Land Registry as security against further dealings by the estate owner.[19] Subject to any contrary indication on the register, registered charges on the same land rank as between themselves according to the order in which they are entered on the register, and not according to the order in which they are created.[20]

9. RECTIFICATION AND INDEMNITY

In spite of the much vaunted claim that an 'absolute title' is the ultimately secure form of title, it is an inherent feature of the Land Registration Act 1925 that no title registered under its provisions is ever quite absolute. Even a proprietor with supposedly 'absolute title' is liable to have the register of title rectified to his prejudice in certain circumstances. A power of rectification may be exercised by the court in eight specified instances, in six of which a like power of rectification is vested in the registrar himself.[1]

There is nowadays increasing recognition of the close link which exists between rectification and the statutory categories of overriding interest. Rectification and overriding interests share the feature that they each provide a means of asserting an unregistered interest against the proprietor of registered land.[2] Together they merely represent different ways in which reliance on the register may ultimately prove to be misplaced.[3] The most important distinctions between these two large inroads into the principle of indefeasibility rest on the fact that overriding interests bind automatically whereas rectification is an essentially discretionary remedy. Moreover, rectification can affect any aspect of a registered title whilst overriding interests arise in relation only to a somewhat restricted list of rights.[4] However, even these

17 Land Registration Act 1925, s 26(1). It is a prerequisite to registration of the charge that the land certificate be produced to the Land Registry (Ruoff and Roper, *The Law and Practice of Registered Conveyancing* (Looseleaf edn, London 1991), para 3-25).

18 Land Registration Act 1925, s 106(2); *E.S. Schwab & Co Ltd v McCarthy* (1976) 31 P & CR 196 at 201, 212; *The Mortgage Corpn Ltd v Nationwide Credit Corpn Ltd* (1992) *Times*, 27 July. See also *National Commercial Banking Corpn of Australia Ltd v Hedley* (1984) 3 BPR 9477 at 9482f. Until completed by registration, the unregistered charge is a minor interest and is protectible by the entry of a notice or caution (Land Registration Act 1925, s 106(3)). A mortgage of an equitable interest (eg that of a beneficial co-owner under a trust for sale) can never constitute a registered charge, but is capable of protection by entry of a caution (see *Elias v Mitchell* [1972] Ch 652 at 664B-D, post, p 943).

19 Land Registration Act 1925, s 65.

20 Land Registration Act 1925, s 29.

1 The Law Commission has suggested that the law be amended so that the registrar and the court have identical jurisdiction in the matter of rectification (see Law Com No 158, para 3.19).

2 See Law Com No 158, para 1.4.

3 'In this respect, rectification is also a crack in the mirror principle' (Law Com No 158, para 2.10).

4 Law Com No 158, para 1.4.

differences do not obscure the reality that the future development of the law of registered land is likely to call for a greater harmonisation of the overriding interest provisions of the 1925 Act with the law relating to rectification and indemnity.[5]

It is not without significance that, just as the courts seem currently to be concerned to restrict the protection afforded by overriding interests,[6] so too there is emerging a parallel trend towards stricter construction of the court's power to rectify the register of title.

(1) Grounds of rectification

The statutory power of rectification is, without doubt, discretionary.[7] There are clearly situations in which rectification presents the only acceptable resolution of a difficulty relating to the registered title. Equally clearly the discretion to rectify should not be expressed so widely as to become exercisable merely, for instance, because a transfer has proceeded on the basis of some innocent misrepresentation or some minor misapprehension of fact.[8] The circumstances in which rectification may be obtained are therefore spelt out carefully and rectification can be ordered only if it is specifically mandated by some statutory authority.[9]

The circumstances in which the power to rectify becomes exercisable are enumerated largely in section 82(1) of the Land Registration Act 1925.[10] As soon as any one or more of the statutorily specified circumstances is shown to exist,[11] there arises 'at least theoretical discretion to rectify any part of the register, even as against innocent third parties'.[12] The relevant circumstances include the following cases.

(a) Subsisting unrecorded entitlement (section 82(1)(a))

The court alone has jurisdiction to rectify the register of title where it has been held that some person is entitled to an interest or charge which is not currently on the register. The entitlement vindicated by this form of rectification must, however, comprise an existing entitlement under the

5 Law Com No 158, para 2.10.

6 Ante, p 199.

7 *Norwich and Peterborough Building Society v Steed* [1992] 3 WLR 669 at 683B-C.

8 See *Norwich and Peterborough Building Society v Steed* [1992] 3 WLR 669 at 682H–683B.

9 As Scott LJ was at pains to emphasise in *Norwich and Peterborough Building Society v Steed* [1992] 3 WLR 669 at 683C, the mere fact that rectification is discretionary does not mean that there is in every case a general discretion to order rectification. The power to rectify must be firmly derived from one or other ground of statutory authority (see also [1992] 3 WLR 669 at 682E).

10 See also Land Registration Rules 1925, rr 13 (clerical errors), 14. It seems that the power to rectify under rule 14 is exercisable only by the registrar and not by the court (see Law Com No 158, para 3.3).

11 The grounds of rectification are not mutually exclusive, but tend instead to overlap to some degree.

12 *Argyle Building Society v Hammond* (1985) 49 P & CR 148 at 162 per Slade LJ, who also pointed out (at 157) that the jurisdiction to rectify 'plainly extends' to all the parts of register of title, ie to the Property Register, the Proprietorship Register and the Charges Register alike. See also *Norwich and Peterborough Building Society v Steed* [1992] 3 WLR 669 at 688B.

substantive law. The court's discretion to rectify pursuant to section 82(1)(a) does not give any substantive cause of action where none existed before.[13]

The most obvious application of section 82(1)(a) occurs where rectification is required in order to enter a subsisting overriding interest upon the register.[14] Further examples include rectification sought on behalf of a claimant who successfully asserts a possessory title, or who has had a transaction set aside on the ground of misrepresentation[15] or fraud[16].

(b) Interest wrongly omitted or included in the register (section 82(1)(b))

The court again has an exclusive discretion, exercisable on the application of any aggrieved person, to order rectification either for the purpose of entering on the register an interest which has been wrongly omitted by the registrar on first registration,[17] or for the purpose of excluding from the register an interest which was wrongly included.[18]

(c) Consent (section 82(1)(c))

The court or the registrar may rectify the register in any case and at any time with the consent of all persons interested.

(d) Entry obtained by fraud (section 82(1)(d))

Rectification may also be ordered where either the court or the registrar is satisfied that an existing entry in the register has been 'obtained by fraud'. The scope of this ground of rectification is perhaps more limited than at first appears. The only 'fraud' relevant under section 82(1)(d) is fraud in which the new registered proprietor has participated or colluded.[19] Moreover, as the Court of Appeal stressed in *Norwich and Peterborough Building Society v Steed*,[20] it is the obtaining of the entry in the register, rather than the procuring of the actual registrable disposition, which must be marked by fraud.

13 See *Norwich and Peterborough Building Society v Steed* [1992] 3 WLR 669 at 683D-G, 685B.
14 See eg *Chowood Ltd v Lyall* (No 2) [1930] 2 Ch 156 at 166.
15 *Norwich and Peterborough Building Society v Steed* [1992] 3 WLR 669 at 683D-F per Scott LJ.
16 *Norwich and Peterborough Building Society v Steed* [1992] 3 WLR 669 at 687D per Scott LJ.
17 See eg *Calgary and Edmonton Land Co Ltd v Discount Bank (Overseas) Ltd* [1971] 1 WLR 81 at 85A-C.
18 Once again, however, this ground of rectification provides a remedy but does not create any new substantive rights or causes of action (see *Norwich and Peterborough Building Society v Steed* [1992] 3 WLR 669 at 684B-C, 685B). See *Chowood Ltd v Lyall* (No 2) [1930] 2 Ch 156 at 168f, where Lawrence LJ thought that rights based on adverse possession might justify rectification of the register under section 82(1)(b).
19 See eg *Norwich and Peterborough Building Society v Steed* [1992] 3 WLR 669 at 684D. The rule in all Torrens legislation is that, in order to be relevant to rectification of the register, the 'fraud' must have been 'brought home to the person whose registered title is impeached or to his agents' (*Assets Co Ltd v Mere Roihi* [1905] AC 176 at 210 per Lord Lindley). See also *Frazer v Walker* [1967] 1 AC 569 at 585B-C; *National Commercial Banking Corpn of Australia Ltd v Hedley* (1984) 3 BPR 9477 at 9482 (fraud of agent); *Registrar, Regina Land Registration District v Hermanson* (1987) 33 DLR (4th) 12 at 17; *Paramount Life Insurance Co v Hill* (1987) 34 DLR (4th) 150 at 154f.
20 [1992] 3 WLR 669 at 684D per Scott LJ ('The paragraph is directed...to fraud practised on the Land Registry in order to obtain the entry in question').

Thus the innocent purchaser whose registered title is based on a disposition from a fraudster has not 'obtained' his entry in the register by fraud, and section 82(1)(d) cannot accordingly be used to remove the entry from the register.[1] By contrast 'fraud' is entirely appropriate as a ground of rectification against a transferee who has knowingly presented a forged instrument of transfer as the basis of his application for entry on the register.[2] There are other circumstances in which, arguably, fraud has been practised for the purpose of obtaining a register entry.[3] In *Re Leighton's Conveyance*,[4] for instance, a daughter had fraudulently procured and registered a disposition of land from her mother, who had been unaware of the significance of the transaction.[5] On these facts Luxmoore J was prepared to rectify the register by reinstating the mother as registered proprietor.[6] *Leighton*'s case nevertheless demonstrates the difficulties inherent in isolating, as the precondition of section 82(1)(d), a category of 'fraud practised on the Land Registry'.[7] In so far as the primary target of the fraud in *Leighton*'s case was the deceived transferor, it may be that the 'fraud' ground of rectification, as restrictively defined in *Norwich and Peterborough Building Society v Steed*, was inappropriate.[8]

(e) Double registrations (section 82(1)(e))

The court and the registrar both have power to rectify the register where two or more persons have, by mistake, been registered as proprietors of the same registered estate or charge.

(f) Wrongful registration of mortgagee (section 82(1)(f))

So long as a right of redemption currently subsists in the mortgagor, either the court or the registrar may order rectification where a mortgagee has

1 In *Norwich and Peterborough Building Society v Steed* [1992] 3 WLR 669 at 684G-H, for instance, the Court of Appeal held that, even though a mortgagor's title had been 'obtained by fraud', the registration of the charge taken in good faith by the mortgagee was not liable to rectification in favour of the party defrauded by the mortgagor. See also *Re Leighton's Conveyance* [1936] 1 All ER 667 at 673 (infra), where Luxmoore J declined to grant any rectification in respect of registered charges which the daughter had created while she was registered as proprietor.

2 *Norwich and Peterborough Building Society v Steed* [1992] 3 WLR 669 at 684G. It is questionable, however, whether section 82(1)(d) applies to a disposition which, although voidable for fraud, is registered before being avoided (see *Norwich and Peterborough Building Society* at 684G, 687D-E).

3 *Norwich and Peterborough Building Society v Steed* [1992] 3 WLR 669 at 684E. In *Peffer v Rigg* [1977] 1 WLR 285 at 294G (ante, p 190), Graham J granted rectification of the transferee's title under section 82(1), although he did not specify under which particular head he did so. It is possible that the circumstances present in this case may have constituted the case of an entry 'obtained by fraud'. See [1977] CLJ 227 at 231 (D.J. Hayton).

4 [1936] 1 All ER 667.

5 Luxmoore J expressly found that the transfer to the daughter was vitiated by fraud but not by non est factum ([1936] 1 All ER 667 at 672f).

6 [1936] 1 All ER 667 at 673. See also *Argyle Building Society v Hammond* (1985) 49 P & CR 148 at 158ff.

7 See *Norwich and Peterborough Building Society v Steed* [1992] 3 WLR 669 at 684D.

8 In *Norwich and Peterborough Building Society v Steed* [1992] 3 WLR 669 at 686G-H Scott LJ indeed thought that section 82(1)(a) would more appropriately have provided the power to rectify against the daughter in *Leighton*'s case.

been registered as proprietor of the land itself rather than merely as proprietor of a charge affecting the land.

(g) Default of title (section 82(1)(g))

Rectification may be ordered by either the court or the registrar where a legal estate has been registered in the name of a person who, if the land had not been registered, would not have been the estate owner. This ground of rectification is frequently relevant in cases of adverse possession of registered land. In *Chowood Ltd v Lyall* (No 2),[9] for example, title to an area of land had been registered in the name of a transferee, although the land in question had been adversely possessed by a third party for a sufficient period to extinguish the transferor's original title. Rectification was ordered in favour of a squatter who had acquired a good common law title by adverse possession.[10]

(h) Residual ground of rectification (section 82(1)(h))

Pursuant to section 82(1)(h) both the court and the registrar have a discretion to rectify the register where 'by reason of any error or omission in the register, or by reason of any entry made under a mistake, it may be deemed just to rectify the register'.[11] The precise ambit of this ground of rectification has become the subject of some dispute. The critical question is whether this provision contains a broad residual mandate to rectify on grounds of justice and equity.

Recent years have seen the emergence of an increasingly liberal approach to the exercise of the discretion to rectify under section 82(1)(h). In *Argyle Building Society v Hammond*,[12] for instance, the Court of Appeal seemed to confirm that the jurisdiction to rectify the register is available on an extremely broad discretionary basis.[13] This view echoed earlier statements by the Court of Appeal in *Orakpo v Manson Investments Ltd*[14] that 'if the present entries on the register do not reflect the true position, the register is open to rectification'. On this wide approach, section 82(1)(h) enables the court to order any necessary rectification 'if there is an omission in the register of some entry which ought to be there for the protection' of an applicant for rectification.[15]

In *Norwich and Peterborough Building Society v Steed*,[16] however, the Court

9 [1930] 2 Ch 156.

10 [1930] 2 Ch 156 at 168f. A further application of section 82(1)(g) arises where a registration is based on a transfer vitiated by forgery or non est factum. If title were unregistered, such a transfer would clearly be ineffective to convey a legal estate (see *Norwich and Peterborough Building Society v Steed* [1992] 3 WLR 669 at 682E-F, 686H per Scott LJ).

11 See eg *Chowood Ltd v Lyall* (No 2) [1930] 2 Ch 156 at 165ff.

12 (1985) 49 P & CR 148 at 158ff (post, p 236). See [1985] Conv 135 (A. Sydenham).

13 'On the face of it, the paragraph appears wide enough to render all the other specific paragraphs largely superfluous' (Law Com No 158, para 3.7).

14 [1977] 1 WLR 347 at 360E per Buckley LJ. See (1977) 41 Conv (NS) 210 (F.R. Crane). *Orakpo* was ultimately decided on other grounds by the House of Lords ([1978] AC 95). See (1977) 41 Conv (NS) 354 (F.R. Crane).

15 [1977] 1 WLR 347 at 361A per Buckley LJ. See also Goff LJ at [1977] 1 WLR 347 at 370B-C.

16 [1992] 3 WLR 669. See [1992] Conv 293 (C. Davis).

of Appeal took a much more restrictive view of the function of section 82(1)(h). With the concurrence of the remainder of the Court, Scott LJ rejected the 'general discretion' approach to this paragraph,[17] and ruled that the paragraph operates merely as a 'catch-all provision' authorising the rectification of any error not covered within the preceding four paragraphs of section 82(1).[18] In *Steed*'s case a building society had procured the registration of a charge which it had taken over property, title in which had been fraudulently obtained by the chargors.[19] At the date of the charge the mortgagors were holding title under a transfer which, although voidable for fraud, had not yet been set aside. On this basis the Court held that the entry in the register of the building society's charge was not therefore, in strict terms, an 'error or omission' and had not been made 'under a mistake'.[20] It followed that no rectification of the Charges Register could be ordered pursuant to section 82(1)(h),[1] and the Court was unwilling to rectify as against the building society on any supposed ground that it might be thought 'just and equitable' to make such an order.[2]

For the time being the trend of the case law under section 82(1)(h) thus seems severely to circumscribe the statutory power to rectify the register of title. However, the Law Commission recommended in 1987 that rectification should be available wherever the register (whether through error or omission) 'does not reflect. . .the title to the land according to the rules of land law which prevail apart from registration of title'.[3] This uninhibited view of the scope of rectification has now been incorporated in the Commission's Draft Land Registration Bill.[4] If enacted, this Bill would eliminate the itemised grounds of rectification contained in section 82(1). In their place the Bill would simply empower rectification in cases of error or omission either in order to give effect to an overriding interest or where 'rectification of the register would be just in all the circumstances'.[5]

17 [1992] 3 WLR 669 at 689C. See the greater hesitancy of Purchas LJ at 698D.
18 [1992] 3 WLR 669 at 685B-C.
19 It was clear that the building society was an entirely innocent third party (see [1992] 3 WLR 669 at 674A). *Steed*'s case was rooted in the same factual base as the Court of Appeal's earlier decision in *Argyle Building Society v Hammond* (1985) 49 P & CR 148 (post, p 236). In *Hammond*'s case, however, the Court had proceeded on the assumption that the mortgagors' freehold title had been obtained by reason of a forged instrument of transfer, whereas in the later case it appeared that the transfer, while engineered by fraud, was vitiated neither by forgery nor by non est factum.
20 [1992] 3 WLR 669 at 685D-E.
1 The transferor who had been defrauded by the dishonesty of the transferee/mortgagors did, of course, succeed in obtaining a rectification in his favour of the freehold title recorded in the proprietorship register (see [1992] 3 WLR 669 at 675F, 676A). The Court of Appeal's decision merely left the transferor subject to the mortgage charge taken in innocence by the building society.
2 The Court of Appeal expressed its disagreement with any portion of Slade LJ's judgment in *Argyle Building Society v Hammond* (1985) 49 P & CR 148 in which he might be construed as having espoused a wider approach to section 82(1)(h). See [1992] 3 WLR 669 at 688D-E, 689E-G.
3 Law Com No 158, para 3.34(1).
4 Law Commission, *Property Law: Fourth Report on Land Registration* (Law Com No 173, 8 November 1988), Appendix.
5 Clause 44(1).

(2) Effect of rectification

When the register is rectified by the removal of the name of the existing proprietor and the substitution of another person's name, the consequence is to vest the legal title in the new registered proprietor.[6] The former proprietor is thereafter divested of title, although it may be open to him to seek an indemnity in respect of any loss suffered by him by reason of the rectification.

Section 82(2) of the Land Registration Act 1925 provides that the register 'may be rectified. . .notwithstanding that the rectification may affect any estates, rights, charges, or interests acquired or protected by registration, or by any entry on the register, or otherwise.' This provision appears, in its express terms, to authorise orders for rectification which are not merely effective to rectify the title in question, but which also operate adversely upon the interests of innocent third parties whose rights are already duly protected by entry on the register or are supposedly overriding. However, the case law has not consistently accorded this extensive interpretation to section 82(2) and the exact scope of the provision remains unclear.

In *Freer v Unwins Ltd*,[7] for instance, a register of title was rectified by order of the Chief Land Registrar, by entering on the register notice of restrictive covenants affecting the land which had been wrongly omitted from it at the date of first registration. D was the assignee of a lease in the relevant land which had been granted prior to the rectification of the title, his lease being itself an overriding interest in the land. D had knowledge of the existence of the restrictive covenants but knew also that these covenants had not been protected by entry on the register. When P brought proceedings to enforce the restrictive covenants against D, Walton J held that D was not bound by them. According to Walton J, D's lease must, in accordance with section 19(2) of the Land Registration Act 1925, be deemed to have taken effect as if it were a registered disposition immediately on its being granted. Under section 20(1), therefore, it took effect subject to any entries appearing on the register at that date and subject to overriding interests (if any), but free from all other estates and interests.[8] The lease assigned to D was accordingly unaffected by the subsequent entry on the register of the restrictive covenant relating to the freehold title.[9] This decision thus

6 Land Registration Act 1925, s 69(1). The right to rectification may itself constitute an overriding interest pursuant to Land Registration Act 1925, s 70(1)(g) (ante, p 210), provided that it is enjoyed in association with actual occupation. See *Blacklocks v J.B. Developments (Godalming) Ltd* [1982] Ch 183 at 196E-F; [1983] Conv 169, 257.

7 [1976] Ch 288. See [1976] CLJ 211 (D.J. Hayton); (1976) 39 MLR 582 (J.M. Masson); (1976) 92 LQR 338 (R.J. Smith).

8 Ante, p 186. It seems that section 82(2) was not cited to the court (see Law Com No 158, para 3.8).

9 [1976] Ch 288 at 298G. If D had been held bound by the restrictive covenants in question, it would have received a statutory indemnity in respect of its loss, and this might have been thought to provide a good ground for holding that D took subject to the unprotected covenants. However, this pragmatic approach was not adopted and the actual decision in *Freer v Unwins Ltd* merely leaves the even more puzzling question as to why title in this case was rectified in the first place. Walton J clearly considered the registrar's decision in favour of rectification 'a very great surprise' ([1976] Ch 288 at 295B), presumably because the general scheme of the Land Registration Act 1925 is that a transferee (such as the original lessee) takes his interest in registered land free from all third party rights other than overriding interests and those interests which are duly protected by entry (Land Registration Act 1925, s 20(1)). See also [1980] CLJ 380f (D.J. Hayton).

provides a surprising instance of rectification in derogation of the rights of a freeholder but without prejudice to the rights of a leaseholder in the same land.[10]

A better example of the more likely intendment of section 82(2) is to be found in *Argyle Building Society v Hammond*.[11] In this case a former proprietor of a registered title alleged that during his absence abroad his title had been fraudulently transferred to his sister and her husband (the present defendants) by a forged instrument of which he knew nothing. The defendants had then charged the land to a building society in consideration of loan moneys which it advanced to them. The Court of Appeal was clear that, by reason of the 'statutory magic' of entry in the register,[12] the transfer (albeit forged) had been effective to vest the registered title in the defendants.[13] On the assumption, however, that there had been a forgery, the Court went on to hold that the original proprietor was entitled to rectification not only of the register of the defendants' fraudulently acquired title but also of the Charges Register containing the duly protected charge taken in all good faith by the mortgagee.[14] In the light of section 82(2), Slade LJ disregarded the objection that such a rectification of the Charges Register would deprive the innocent third party of its security.[15] The chargee, on suffering prejudice by reason of the rectification, would be entitled to an indemnity in respect of its loss.[16]

(3) Restrictions on rectification

Certain restrictions are imposed on the right to obtain rectification, largely because it is generally recognised that the unlimited availability of such a remedy would be 'productive of future uncertainty and contrary to the

10 The Law Commission has since declined to accept that the power of rectification is as limited as the decision in *Freer v Unwins Ltd* would tend to suggest. In the Commission's view, the court and the registrar must have 'as full and ample a power of rectification as is needed to achieve justice' (Law Com No 158, para 3.8). The Commission has accordingly recommended that statute should make it absolutely clear that rectification may affect estates and interests already registered or protected or any existing overriding interests (ibid, para 3.34(3)). See Draft Land Registration Bill, clause 44(2) (Law Commission, Law Com No 173 (1988), Appendix).

11 (1985) 49 P & CR 148. See [1985] Conv 135 (A. Sydenham).

12 Ante, p 181.

13 (1985) 49 P & CR 148 at 155 (ante, p 233).

14 (1985) 49 P & CR 148 at 158ff. When the assumption of forgery was later held to be unfounded, it became clear that no rectification of the Charges Register was either necessary or appropriate. See *Norwich and Peterborough Building Society v Steed* [1992] 3 WLR 669 (ante, p 233). However, in the latter case it was conceded that, had the assumed fact of forgery remained a valid finding (or if there had been a case of non est factum), rectification could have been ordered even against the mortgagee on the footing of section 82(1)(a) or (b) or (g) or even (h) (see [1992] 3 WLR 669 at 676C, 682E-F, 687D-E).

15 Slade LJ distinguished *Re Leighton's Conveyance* [1936] 1 All ER 667 (ante, p 232) on the ground that it had not involved an altogether forged disposition of title (as in *Argyle Building Society v Hammond*) but merely a disposition executed by the proprietor herself, 'albeit under a mistake induced by fraud or other sharp practice' ((1985) 49 P & CR 148 at 161ff).

16 Land Registration Act 1925, s 83(4) provides that a 'proprietor of any registered land or charge claiming in good faith under a forged disposition shall, where the register is rectified, be deemed to have suffered loss by reason of such rectification and shall be entitled to be indemnified'.

raison d'être of registration of title.'[17] It is indeed entirely correct that sympathetic consideration should be given to the reasonable expectations of transferees of registered land who have paid the full price, taken possession and become proprietors in reliance on the register of title. The motivation towards indefeasibility of the registered title is accordingly recognised in section 82(3) of the Land Registration Act 1925.[18] Pursuant to this provision, the register 'shall not be rectified, except for the purpose of giving effect to an overriding interest or an order of the court, so as to affect the title of the proprietor who is in possession...'.[19] Apart from the special cases of the overriding interest and the court order, there are two further exceptions to the general rule that the register may not be rectified to the prejudice of the proprietor 'in possession'. These additional exceptions arise where the proprietor 'has caused or substantially contributed by fraud or lack of proper care' to the error or omission in respect of which rectification is sought,[20] and where 'for any other reason, in any particular case, it is considered that it would be unjust not to rectify the register against him'.[1]

(4) Indemnity

Subject to any contrary statutory provision, 'any person suffering loss by reason of any rectification of the register...shall be entitled to be indemnified.'[2] In addition, where an 'error or omission' has occurred in the register but the register is not rectified, any person suffering loss by reason of that error or omission is likewise entitled to be indemnified.[3] These

17 Law Com No 158, para 3.5. As Lord Elwyn-Jones LC declared in Parliament, it is 'important that the entry of a person on the Land Register as the registered proprietor of a piece of land should, so far as possible, be conclusive as to his title' (*Parliamentary Debates, Official Report, House of Lords*, Vol 386 (Session 1976–77), Col 871 (26 July 1977).

18 In the words of the Law Commission, section 82(3) 'still embodies the best attempt at indefeasibility' (Law Com No 158, para 3.12).

19 The meaning of 'possession' in this context is not wholly clear (see Land Registration Act 1925, s 3(xviii)). It is likely, however, that the term applies only where there is physical possession by the registered proprietor and does not cover the case where the proprietor is merely in receipt of rents and profits derived from the land (see Law Com No 158, para 3.12). The Law Commission has suggested that it would conduce to 'greater consistency with the general and statutory principles of property law and conveyancing' if the apparent protection against rectification conferred by section 82(3) were redrafted 'so as to benefit registered proprietors who were prudent purchasers for value in good faith in actual occupation of the land' (Law Com No 158, para 3.15). See Draft Land Registration Bill, clause 44(3), (4) (Law Commission, Law Com No 173 (1988), Appendix).

20 Land Registration Act 1925, s 82(3)(a), as substituted by Administration of Justice Act 1977, s 24(b). See *In re 139 High Street Deptford, ex parte British Transport Commission* [1951] Ch 884 at 890ff; *Claridge v Tingey, In re Sea View Gardens* [1967] 1 WLR 134 at 140H–141A.

1 Land Registration Act 1925, s 82(3)(c). See *Epps v Esso Petroleum Co Ltd* [1973] 1 WLR 1071 at 1080F–1083B; [1974] CLJ 60 (S.N. Palk); *Peffer v Rigg* [1977] 1 WLR 285 at 294G. The Law Commission has criticised this exception to the principle of indefeasibility as introducing 'too great an element of uncertainty into the registration system' (Law Com No 158, para 3.16). In the Commission's view, the register should be rectified against a bona fide purchaser for value in actual occupation only in order to give effect to an overriding interest or in favour of a trustee in bankruptcy (ibid, paras 3.13, 3.16, 3.18). See Draft Land Registration Bill, clause 44(4)(b), (d) (Law Commission, Law Com No 173 (1988), Appendix).

2 Land Registration Act 1925, s 83(1).

3 Land Registration Act 1925, s 83(2). See *Argyle Building Society v Hammond* (1985) 49 P & CR 148 at 158.

provisions supply the basis for the assertion that the scheme of registered title operates on the premise of a state-guaranteed title which is backed by automatic compensation in the event of any failure in the guarantee.[4]

(a) Restrictions on indemnity

The right to receive an indemnity in cases of prejudice is not as unqualified as might at first appear. Where a registered title is rectified to give effect to a subsisting overriding interest, the proprietor is ineligible for compensation. The oddly logical rationale for this exclusion is founded in the legal (though not social or commercial) reality that in such cases the proprietor has not technically suffered any loss. The title which he purchased was at all material times subject to the overriding interest in question; the only new feature in the factual situation is that now, for the first time, the proprietor knows about the qualification on his title. Thus, according to the unsympathetic argument, there can be no compensation where there has been no loss: the rectification has merely regularised a pre-existing position.[5] The right to indemnity is also withheld in other circumstances specified in the Land Registration Act 1925, such as the case where an applicant for the statutory indemnity 'has caused or substantially contributed by fraud or lack of proper care' to the loss in respect of which he claims compensation.[6]

(b) Incidence of indemnity claims

Where a right of indemnity is recognised, the indemnity is paid by the Chief Land Registrar out of moneys provided by Parliament. It appears that few indemnity claims are ever made[7] and that, although the Land Registry collects fees from each applicant for registration, the indemnity moneys actually paid out amount to only an infinitesimal fraction of the rather vast fee income.[8] This imbalance has given rise to the observation that the indemnity scheme provided under the Land Registration Act 1925 'must be the most expensive form of insurance ever devised', making the inefficiencies of insurance for tort claims look 'positively benign'.[9]

4 Land Registration Act 1925, s 83(11) creates a six year limitation period for most claims of indemnity, the period running from the date when the claimant knew (or ought to have known) of the existence of his claim. The Law Commission has recommended that the liability to pay indemnity should rank for limitation purposes as a simple contract debt and that the period of limitation should begin to run only from the date of rectification (Law Com No 158, paras 3.31ff).

5 *In re Chowood's Registered Land* [1933] Ch 574 at 581f. The Law Commission has acknowledged the unfairness of this logic and has proposed that an indemnity be payable even where rectification is awarded on the basis of a subsisting overriding interest (post, p 240).

6 Land Registration Act 1925, s 83(5)(a), as substituted by Land Registration and Land Charges Act 1971, s 3(1).

7 According to one report (R.J. Smith, (1986) 39 CLP 111 at 117), the number of claims relating to first registration averages about 19 per year (with an average payment in each case of approximately £2,000). See also Law Com No 158, para 3.24, Appendix D.

8 The surplus accumulated by the Land Registry has been variously described as 'almost an embarrassment' ([1988] Conv 73 at 74) and as exemplifying the 'paradox of ample fees generated by indifferent performance' ((1987) 284 Estates Gazette 1437).

9 R.J. Smith, (1986) 39 CLP 111 at 116.

10. FUTURE REFORM OF REGISTRATION OF TITLE

In its Third and Fourth Reports on Land Registration,[10] the Law Commission issued a series of highly significant proposals for the future development of the law of registered titles in England and Wales. In these Reports the Commission addressed itself squarely to the difficulty of reconciling the security of property interests with the marketability of registered land. While accepting the theoretical validity of the 'ideal of a complete register of title', the Commission was not insensitive to the argument that it 'may be unjust to require that a particular interest be protected by registration on pain of deprivation.'[11] The Commission felt that the rights in question might often be readily discoverable on inspection of the land (in which case compulsory entry on the register would be unnecessary) or extremely informal or transient (in which case compulsory entry would be impracticable or undesirable).

(1) Two new guiding principles

In the light of these considerations the Commission enunciated two major principles as relevant to any reform of the law of registered land, the first principle necessarily conceding priority to the second.[12] *First*, the Commission endorsed the view that 'in the interests of certainty and of simplifying conveyancing, the class of right which may bind a purchaser otherwise than as the result of an entry in the register should be as narrow as possible.' *Second*, the Commission stipulated that 'interests should be overriding where protection against purchasers is needed, yet it is either not reasonable to expect or not sensible to require any entry on the register'. However, where operation of the second principle might threaten loss to 'honest and careful purchasers', the Commission proposed that the ordinary indemnity provisions (and the vast surplus income derived from Land Registry fees) be made available for the purpose of compensating proprietors unwittingly trapped by overriding interests.

(2) Restriction of overriding interests

In order to implement the first principle the Commission recommended that the statutory categories of overriding interest be both rationalised and simplified.[13] Towards this end the Commission proposed,[14] and the Draft Land Registration Bill provides,[15] that the present classes of overriding interest be reformulated so as to cover only (a) legal easements and profits *à prendre*[16]; (b) leases for 21 years or less[17]; (c) rights acquired by adverse possession[18];

10 Law Commission, *Property Law: Third Report on Land Registration* (Law Com No 158, 31 March 1987); *Property Law: Fourth Report on Land Registration* (Law Com No 173, 8 November 1988).
11 Law Com No 158, para 2.6.
12 Law Com No 158, para 2.6.
13 Law Com No 158, para 2.105.
14 Law Com No 158, paras 2.25ff; Law Com No 173, para 3.2.
15 Draft Land Registration Bill, clause 7(1), (2) (Law Com No 173, Appendix).
16 Ante, p 201.
17 Ante, p 203.
18 Ante, p 202.

(d) rights of persons in actual occupation of land[19]; and (e) customary rights[20]. Other rights currently recognised as overriding interests would either be reclassified under a new category as 'general burdens' on registered land[1] or be relegated to the status of minor interest and protectible as such through appropriate entry in the register.[2]

(3) More equitable compensation for loss

The formulation of the Law Commission's second principle was underpinned by a novel and imaginative approach to the provision of compensation for those who suffer loss through the emergence of overriding interests. At present, as the Commission noted, the indemnity provisions of the Land Registration Act 1925 have no application to the case of overriding interests,[3] with the inevitable result that 'one (normally) innocent party must lose without compensation.'[4] The 'all or nothing' nature of this kind of outcome seems both unattractive and discriminatory,[5] not least since the considerable surplus funds accumulated by way of the Land Registry's fee income are more than sufficient to enable all loss to be adequately compensated.[6]

The Commission therefore proposed that, in so far as it felt unable to recommend the discontinuation of all statutory protection for overriding interests, an enhanced scheme of indemnity would represent a 'second best to the complete protection of purchasers'.[7] In the view of the Commission, 'the machinery of registered conveyancing ought to be oiled by means of a "state guarantee" of title', with the consequence that a right to indemnity should arise even where an overriding interest is asserted against a registered proprietor.[8] Thus, although 'as a matter of machinery' a registered proprietor would automatically take subject to all overriding interests, he would nevertheless be eligible for compensation from public funds in respect of

19 Ante, p 203.
20 Post, p 1059.
1 Law Com No 158, para 2.15. Such 'general burdens' would include such matters as statutory tenancies under the Rent Act (ibid, para 2.53), public rights (ibid, paras 2.79ff), chancel repairs liability (ibid, para 2.81), and local land charges (ibid, para 2.94). The Commission envisaged that the Registrar would be invested with discretion to enter a note of 'general burdens' on the relevant register of title, but that, in spite of their superficial resemblance to overriding interests, 'general burdens' should never be subject to the provisions relating to rectification and indemnity (ibid, paras 2.15, 3.13). See also Law Com No 173, para 3.5; Draft Land Registration Bill, clause 5(1), (3) (Law Com No 173, Appendix).
2 Law Com No 158, para 2.108.
3 Ante, p 238.
4 Law Com No 158, para 2.10.
5 Law Com No 158, paras 2.3, 2.10.
6 Law Com No 158, paras 3.24ff.
7 Law Com No 158, para 2.12.
8 'An entirely innocent and properly careful purchaser for value of an "absolute" title, compelled and encouraged to rely upon the register, who finds his land subjected to an overriding interest might legitimately consider the system *not* to be "so far as is humanly possible, complete and perfect". He might equally legitimately look for compensation essentially because limitations of the system were accepted which still left him at some risk' (Law Com No 158, para 2.3).

his loss.[9] The availability of such an indemnity, the Commission believed, would 'go some way to enabling an acceptable balance to be achieved between competing innocent interests'.[10] In this way rectification and indemnity could be made truly complementary remedies and, if the overriding interests in question were duly entered on the register in conjunction with the award of an indemnity,[11] the general effect would ultimately be the creation of a more complete register of title.

It remains to be seen whether the Law Commission's admirable proposals will be implemented in statutory form. Already the draft Land Registration Bill has lain dormant since 1988, and there are disquieting indications that there is no overwhelming political will to institute a sensible, but considerably more expensive, reconciliation of the mutual antagonisms inherent in this (as indeed in any) scheme of title registration.

9 Law Com No 158, para 3.29. The Commission envisaged, however, that any indemnity paid under its proposals should be liable to be 'reduced where the applicant lacked proper care (ie was at fault or negligent) to such an extent as is thought just and equitable having regard to the applicant's share in the responsibility for the loss' (ibid, para 3.27). See also Law Com No 173, para 3.6; Draft Land Registration Bill, clause 45(6) (Law Com No 173, Appendix).

10 Law Com No 158, para 2.12.

11 The Commission recommended that, as a precondition of indemnity, the Registrar should have discretion to rectify the register in order to give effect to the overriding interest (Law Com No 158, para 3.29).

C. Acquisitions

CHAPTER 9

The conveyancing dimension

In England and Wales the process of land transfer is essentially a two-stage process: first contract, then conveyance (or 'completion' of the contract). In other words, when the preliminary negotiations between the prospective vendor and purchaser have taken place, the parties enter into a formal contract to execute in favour of the purchaser a conveyance of the legal estate in the land to be sold. The legal estate in question may be either an estate in fee simple (if the transaction relates to a freehold) or a term of years (if the transaction relates to a leasehold), and the transfer or assignment usually follows within twenty working days of the exchange of contracts. In unregistered land the conveyance of a legal estate has always been effective forthwith to vest that legal estate in the purchaser. The process of transferring a title in registered land is essentially similar, with the qualification that a registered title may be alienated by mere document of transfer rather than deed of conveyance and the transfer of title is not final and complete until it is recorded in the Land Register.[1] It is the concern of this chapter to trace some of the legal implications of the conveyancing process from the initiation of negotiations between vendor and purchaser to its conclusion in a completed transfer of title.[2]

1. DEALINGS BEFORE EXCHANGE OF CONTRACTS

During the period before the exchange of contracts the purchaser and vendor negotiate agreement on such matters as the purchase price to be paid for the property and the precise extent of the property to be transferred. A number of other preliminary enquiries have to be made. The parties may also want to agree a range of modalities in respect of their sale and purchase, eg whether or not certain items or fittings should pass with the realty.[3] The interval before the exchange of contracts also provides the purchaser with an opportunity to arrange the mortgage finance which he usually requires to enable him to buy the property.[4]

(1) Caveat emptor

The basic legal rule of land transfer is caveat emptor: let the buyer beware. It is essentially the responsibility of the purchaser to inform himself in all

1 Ante, p 179.
2 For an excellent description of the process of sale and purchase, see *Smith v Eric S. Bush* [1990] 1 AC 831 at 849F–850C per Lord Templeman.
3 Ante, p 11.
4 Post, p 931.

relevant respects concerning the property which he seeks to purchase.[5] Of course, the vendor must always disclose latent defects in his title[6] and, if asked by the intending purchaser for specific information, must give it accurately to the best of his ability.[7] But only relatively rarely is there any legal onus on the vendor to disclose pertinent information on his own initiative.[8]

In 1988 the Law Commission's Conveyancing Standing Committee issued a Consultation Paper in which it was provisionally proposed that the caveat emptor rule should be reversed and that vendors should be required to volunteer disclosure of 'all material facts' about properties offered for sale.[9] The response of professional bodies was, however, overwhelmingly opposed to this suggestion and in 1989 the Conveyancing Standing Committee accepted that there were 'strong countervailing disadvantages' inherent in any radical alteration of the 'well understood relationship between the parties to a sale of land'.[10] While emphasising that the 'principal aim of any reform must be to improve the likelihood of the buyer knowing in advance everything about the property which he needs to know',[11] the Conveyancing Standing Committee retreated towards the less controversial view that 'there is room for more forthcoming candour on the part of property sellers'.[12] In its opinion, the caveat emptor rule contributes to the 'adversarial atmosphere' which pervades the process of house purchase, and the Committee accordingly proposed a more co-operative model of information sharing between seller and buyer.[13] The Committee advocated the introduction of 'voluntary arrangements' under which 'standard basic information' would be volunteered to buyers without generating undesirable procedural delay.[14] These arrangements would encourage every seller to equip an intending buyer automatically with such information as up-to-date returns to local

5 In a Consultation Paper issued in 1988, the Law Commission's Conveyancing Standing Committee listed a number of exceptions to the caveat emptor rule (see *Caveat Emptor in Sales of Land* (November 1988)). Inter alia these included instances of uberrimae fidei or fiduciary relationship, circumstances where a positive representation would be distorted by silence on the part of a vendor, and cases where a vendor has deliberately concealed physical defects in the property (see eg *Gordon v Selico Co Ltd* [1986] 1 EGLR 71 at 77J (dry rot)). See also [1989] Conv 69.

6 Latent defects are incumbrances and any other adverse matters of title which a prospective purchaser could not discover for himself by inspecting the property with reasonable care (see *Yandle v Sutton* [1922] 2 Ch 199 at 207ff per Sargant J).

7 See *Terrene v Nelson* [1937] 3 All ER 739 at 744E per Farwell J. It is now, however, a criminal offence to make a 'false or misleading statement' about certain prescribed matters in the course of an estate agency business or a property development business (see Property Misdescriptions Act 1991, s 1(1)).

8 See, however, *Reed v King* 193 Cal Rptr 130 at 133 (1983), where a California court suggested that there was a duty to inform the purchaser that a decade earlier a mass murder had been committed in the house now being sold.

9 See *Caveat Emptor in Sales of Land* (November 1988).

10 *Let the buyer be well informed* (Recommendations of Conveyancing Standing Committee of the Law Commission, December 1989), paras 6, 8.

11 Ibid, para 11.

12 Ibid, para 7.

13 'We do not consider that putting the whole information onus on one party is helpful' (ibid, para 33).

14 Ibid, para 33.

authority search enquiries and replies to standard pre-contract enquiries, but not, for instance, with a copy of any survey commissioned by the seller on the condition of the property.[15]

The advance provision by the seller of basic information pertaining to the property would, of course, obviate the necessity that a number of intending purchasers may each be required, at substantial delay and expense, to gather such information for themselves. The essential thrust of the Conveyancing Standing Committee's suggestions was incorporated in 1990 in the Law Society's introduction of a 'National Protocol' governing standard steps to be taken in all domestic conveyancing transactions.[16] The National Protocol envisages that as soon as a particular property is put on the market the seller should, at his own expense, obtain local authority searches and replies to standard supplementary enquiries. The seller should also supply an extensive range of detailed information for questionnaires contained in a 'Property Information Form' and a 'Fixtures, Fittings and Contents Form'. Under the Protocol, therefore, the entire process of contract and conveyance would be expedited by a rationalisation of the way in which information is transmitted or distributed between seller and buyer. The Protocol remains, however, voluntary rather than mandatory.[17]

(2) Preliminary enquiries

Whether or not it is achieved by means of the National Protocol, it is essential for the purchaser of property to elicit certain information from his vendor before the parties reach the stage of exchanging contracts. The subject matter of such 'preliminary enquiries' (which are usually contained in standard form) relates to such issues as existing disputes concerning the property, the ownership of boundary walls, hedges and fences, the existence of mains services to the property, rights of way, planning matters, compulsory purchase orders and the ownership and maintenance of roads serving the property.[18] Although the responses to preliminary enquiries are by tradition unhelpfully vapid, the vendor bears a duty of care in relation to the accuracy of his replies.[19] An incorrect answer to a preliminary enquiry may found a liability in negligence.[20]

15 Ibid, paras 13ff.
16 See [1990] Conv 137 (H.W. Wilkinson).
17 Compare the mandatory rule in New South Wales which effectively 'shifts the obligation from the purchaser to the vendor, so that the latter has to supply certain basic information about the subject land' (see *Timanu Pty Ltd v Clurstock Pty Ltd* (1988) 15 NSWLR 338 at 339G–340A). The statutorily prescribed information must be attached by the vendor to the draft contract before signature (Conveyancing Act 1919, s 52A(2); Conveyancing (Vendor Disclosure and Warranty) Regulation 1986, regs 4(1), 5).
18 See I.S. Wickenden and S.B. Edell, (1961) 25 Conv (NS) 336.
19 Carelessness cannot be cured by an attempted exclusion of liability in the eventual terms of the contract drawn up between vendor and purchaser (Misrepresentation Act 1967, s 3, as amended by Unfair Contract Terms Act 1977, s 8(1)). See *Walker v Boyle* [1982] 1 WLR 495 at 507A-E; [1982] CLJ 231 (S. Tromans); [1982] Conv 236 (K. Hodkinson); (1983) 80 Law Soc Gaz 326 (P.H. Kenny). See also *South Western General Property Co Ltd v Marton* (1982) 263 Estates Gazette 1090 at 1092; [1983] Conv 8.
20 See eg *Wilson v Bloomfield* (1979) 123 SJ 860; [1980] Conv 401.

(3) Surveys

In advance of any exchange of formal contracts, the purchaser may also wish to commission a structural survey of the property which he proposes to buy. Moreover, any lending institution which helps to finance his purchase will certainly insist that some kind of survey is conducted on its own behalf (but at the purchaser's expense) in order that the security offered be shown to be reasonably sound.

Such surveys, if conducted negligently, provide a fertile source of legal liability. A surveyor who is careless in carrying out a survey commissioned privately by a potential purchaser before exchange of contracts is liable in negligence for the difference between the contracted purchase price and the true market value of the property at the date of purchase.[1] The damages awarded to the purchaser may also include interest on this difference in property values, together with damages for vexation and inconvenience.[2] It is also clear that a surveyor who values property for a lender owes a duty of care not only to the lender[3] but also to the mortgage applicant who proposes to purchase the property.[4] Furthermore, the lender may itself be vicariously liable to the mortgage applicant in respect of any loss caused by the negligence of the surveyor commissioned by the lender to report on the property in relation to which the mortgage loan is sought.[5]

(4) Local authority searches

It is also common practice for the purchaser to use the period before exchange of contracts to requisition a search in respect of local land charges from

1 *Perry v Sidney Phillips & Son* [1982] 1 WLR 1297 at 1302D-E, 1303F-H, 1304G, 1306C-D; [1984] Conv 60 (K. Hodkinson). The surveyor's duty of care is limited, however, to the potential purchaser who commissioned his survey. His negligence gives no cause of action in tort to potential purchasers of adjacent properties, even though their properties, when purchased, are discovered to contain the same defect (eg dry rot) which he failed to reveal in the commissioned survey (see *Shankie-Williams v Heavey* [1986] 2 EGLR 139 at 141A-C).

2 [1982] 1 WLR 1297 at 1302G-1303D, 1305F, 1307A-E. See also *Fisher v Knowles* (1982) 262 Estates Gazette 1083 at 1084; *Fryer v Bunney* (1982) 263 Estates Gazette 158 at 162ff; *Bolton v Puley* (1983) 267 Estates Gazette 1160 at 1163ff; *Treml v Ernest W. Gibson & Partners* (1984) 272 Estates Gazette 68 at 71ff; *Barrett v Dalgety New Zealand Ltd* [1979] BCL 341.

3 *London and South of England Building Society v Stone* [1983] 1 WLR 1242 at 1249H-1250A. On the quantum of damages recoverable, see *Swingcastle Ltd v Gibson* [1991] 2 AC 223 at 238F-G; *Trade Credits Ltd v Baillieu Knight Frank (NSW) Pty Ltd* (1985) 12 NSWLR 670 at 673B; *Duncan & Weller Pty Ltd v Mendelson* [1989] VR 386 at 391.

4 *Yianni v Edwin Evans & Sons* [1982] QB 438 at 456B-C; [1981] Conv 435 (M. Brazier and G. Pople); (1981) 131 NLJ 1181 (H.W. Wilkinson); *Roberts v J. Hampson & Co* [1990] 1 WLR 94 at 104D-E. See also *Smith v Eric S. Bush* [1990] 1 AC 831 at 854E-F, 859F, 874A, where the House of Lords held that it was not fair and reasonable, for the purposes of the Unfair Contract Terms Act 1977, that the surveyor of domestic property should be able to rely on general disclaimers of negligence liability contained in the survey report and mortgage application. See [1989] Conv 359 (C. Francis); (1989) 52 MLR 841 (T. Kaye).

5 See *Stevenson v Nationwide Building Society* (1984) 272 Estates Gazette 663 at 670. See also, in the case of a local authority lender, *Harris v Wyre Forest DC* [1990] 1 AC 831 at 848A-G; *Ward v McMaster* [1988] IR 338 at 351.

his local authority.[6] The authority may be liable to the purchaser in negligence in respect of any misleading replies which cause him loss.[7]

(5) Agreement 'subject to contract'

It is usual that, while pre-contractual negotiations and enquiries are being pursued, the prospective vendor and purchaser will wish to express some kind of consensus ad idem in the matter of sale. It is invariable practice for vendor and purchaser at this stage to reach an agreement for sale 'subject to contract'. However, it is generally accepted that such an agreement, albeit in written form, is not contractually binding unless and until its terms are incorporated in a formal contract of sale signed and exchanged by the parties.[8]

It is, of course, the lack of legal consequence attaching to agreements 'subject to contract' which fosters the practice of 'gazumping' at times when the property market becomes unstable and volatile.[9] With total impunity the intending vendor can choose to disregard an existing agreement for sale 'subject to contract' if it emerges that a more favourable price can be extracted from another potential purchaser.[10] In a rising property market the total absence of legal obligation until the exchange of formal contracts can lead to highly inequitable results, not least because it creates the setting for that most unseemly form of competition between would-be purchasers—the 'contract race'.[11] There is much to be said in favour of the practice in Scots law which ensures that even informal agreements for the sale of land are contractually binding.[12] Too often the 'gentleman's agreement' expressed in an agreement 'subject to contract' turns out to be merely, as Sachs J once said, 'a transaction in which each side hopes the other will act like a gentleman and neither intends so to act if it is against his material interests.'[13]

(a) Attempts to limit the 'subject to contract' proviso

In view of the inherent danger of inequity, judicial attempts were made, particularly during the 1970s, to dislodge the well-entrenched suspensive

6 Ante, p 116.

7 See *L. Shaddock & Associates Pty Ltd v Parramatta City Council* (1981) 55 ALJR 713 at 715ff (High Court of Australia).

8 *Winn v Bull* (1877) 7 Ch D 29 at 32 per Jessel MR; *Coupe v Ridout* [1921] 1 Ch 291 at 297f; *Chillingworth v Esche* [1924] 1 Ch 97 at 104f; *Lockett v Norman-Wright* [1925] Ch 56 at 62; *Keppel v Wheeler* [1927] 1 KB 577 at 592f; *Eccles v Bryant and Pollock* [1948] Ch 93 at 100f; *D'Silva v Lister House Development Ltd* [1971] Ch 17 at 28F.

9 'Gazumping' has been described as 'a practice as unattractive as its name' (see *Mulhall v Haren* [1981] IR 364 at 378 per Keane J).

10 It has even been pointed out that the duty of trustees to sell only at the best price reasonably obtainable may impose a duty to 'gazump'. See *Buttle v Saunders* [1950] 2 All ER 193 at 195C-E; [1979] Conv 451; *Cowan v Scargill* [1985] Ch 270 at 288A-C. An agent may be liable in damages to a vendor for breach of duty in failing to 'gazump' if offered a higher price (see *Keppel v Wheeler* [1927] 1 KB 577 at 585f).

11 The Law Society has attempted to control the practice of the 'contract race' by imposing a duty on the vendor's solicitor to disclose the existence of a 'contract race' to the solicitors acting for each prospective purchaser. See (1977) 74 Law Soc Gaz 834.

12 See *House Selling the Scottish Way for England and Wales* (Conveyancing Standing Committee of the Law Commission, September 1987).

13 See *Goding v Frazer* [1967] 1 WLR 286 at 293B. See also *Edward Wong Finance Co Ltd v Johnson Stokes & Master* [1984] AC 296 at 307E, where Lord Brightman observed that 'the conception of courtesy as between vendor and purchaser would be a nonsense.'

effects of the 'subject to contract' rule. Prior to 1989 it was a precondition of the actionability of contracts for the disposition of land that the relevant agreement 'or some memorandum or note thereof' be in writing signed by the party to be charged or by his authorised agent.[14] By means of creative judicial construction this requirement came to be interpreted in such a way that many documents which only remotely resembled a written memorandum of a contract of sale were treated as satisfying the statutory precondition. In this way considerable ingenuity was 'expended upon bringing about the downfall of the "gazumper"',[15] and the courts were able to limit the effectiveness of unilateral references to 'subject to contract' as a means of deflecting the onset of binding contractual commitment between vendor and purchaser.[16]

This development naturally caused much consternation in the world of conveyancers[17] but its impact was later much reduced by the decision in *Tiverton Estates Ltd v Wearwell Ltd.*[18] Here the Court of Appeal reinstated the traditional understanding of the 'subject to contract' proviso as used in normal conveyancing practice, by ruling that use of this magical phrase was apt to prevent correspondence between vendor and purchaser from satisfying the statutory requirement of a written memorandum.[19] Subsequent case law[20] was to provide ample confirmation that 'subject to contract' terminology was wholly inconsistent with the existence of a concluded agreement 'save in the most exceptional cases'.[1] The issue has now been placed beyond all doubt by the enactment of section 2(1) of the Law of Property (Miscellaneous Provisions) Act 1989,[2] which withholds contractual effect altogether from any mere memorandum of the terms of a contract

14 Law of Property Act 1925, s 40(1). See now Law of Property (Miscellaneous Provisions) Act 1989, s 2(1) (post, p 256).

15 *Mulhall v Haren* [1981] IR 364 at 378.

16 See eg *Griffiths v Young* [1970] Ch 675 at 685H–686D, 687A-E (agreement 'subject to contract' held to have been superseded by subsequent unconditional offer and acceptance made by the same parties and communicated by telephone); *Law v Jones* [1974] Ch 112 at 125H–126A ('subject to contract' correspondence held capable in itself of providing written memorandum necessary under Law of Property Act 1925, s 40(1)). See also (1971) 35 Conv (NS) 55 (F.R. Crane); [1973] CLJ 214 (C.T. Emery); (1973) 37 Conv (NS) 282 (F.R. Crane).

17 See eg *Tiverton Estates Ltd v Wearwell Ltd* [1975] Ch 146 at 159G–160B, where Lord Denning MR observed that *Law v Jones* [1974] Ch 112, by effecting a virtual repeal of the Statute of Frauds, had 'sounded an alarm bell in the offices of every solicitor in the land'. See also (1974) 38 Conv (NS) 127 (F.R. Crane); [1974] CLJ 42 (C.T. Emery); (1974) 37 MLR 695 (J.W. Tinnion); (1974) 90 LQR 1; (1974) 25 NILQ 333 (H. Wallace); *Mulhall v Haren* [1981] IR 364 at 382.

18 [1975] Ch 146 at 160F-G, 161D, 171E.

19 It was significant that the Council of the Law Society expressed its view that the traditional status of 'subject to contract' correspondence had been vindicated by the approach adopted in *Tiverton Estates Ltd v Wearwell Ltd* (see (1973) 70 Law Soc Gaz 2637).

20 See eg *Daulia Ltd v Four Millbank Nominees Ltd* [1978] Ch 231 at 249B–250D; [1978] Conv 375 (F.R. Crane); [1979] CLJ 31 (C. Harpum and D.L. Jones); (1979) 95 LQR 7 (H.W. Wilkinson); *Munton v GLC* [1976] 1 WLR 649 at 655D; *Cohen v Nessdale Ltd* [1982] 2 All ER 97 at 105a-j; [1982] Conv 71 (M.P. Thompson); *Alpenstow Ltd v Regalian Properties PLC* [1985] 1 WLR 721 at 730A-B; [1985] CLJ 356 (C. Harpum); *Devlin v Northern Ireland Housing Executive* [1982] 17 NIJB, Transcript p 13ff; *Mulhall v Haren* [1981] IR 364 at 386. See generally R.W. Clark, [1984] Conv 173, 251.

1 *Mulhall v Haren* [1981] IR 364 at 386. See *Alpenstow Ltd v Regalian Properties PLC* [1985] 1 WLR 721 at 730A-B, where Nourse J accepted that only in 'a very strong and exceptional context' will the words 'subject to contract' not be given their clear prima facie meaning.

2 Post, p 257.

for the sale of land. Such a contract, if entered into after the commencement of the 1989 Act, must itself be contained in writing signed by or on behalf of each party.

(b) Applicability of the estoppel doctrine

It is not beyond the bounds of possibility that the more inequitable effects of the 'subject to contract' proviso may be challengeable by reference to the doctrine of proprietary estoppel.[3] It is quite common for an intending purchaser to incur expenditure or other detriment in advance of a formal contract for the purchase of land. In exceptional circumstances a valid claim of estoppel may arise if the would-be purchaser has detrimentally relied on some supposed contractual commitment between the vendor and himself.[4] In *Attorney-General of Hong Kong v Humphreys Estate (Queen's Gardens) Ltd*,[5] for instance, Lord Templeman conceded that it was 'possible but unlikely that in circumstances at present unforeseeable a party to negotiations set out in a document expressed to be "subject to contract" would be able to satisfy the court that...some form of estoppel had arisen to prevent both parties from refusing to proceed with the transactions envisaged by the document.'

In an ordinary transaction of purchase, however, it is highly unlikely that a purchaser will be held to have acquired some proprietary right by estoppel prior to contract.[6] For a claim of estoppel to succeed in such a case, it must be shown that the vendor created or encouraged an expectation in the purchaser that the vendor would not withdraw from a transaction which had been agreed in principle between the parties.[7] There must also be strict proof that the purchaser relied on this expectation.[8] The claim of estoppel failed in *Attorney-General of Hong Kong v Humphreys Estate (Queen's Gardens) Ltd*[9] precisely because it was clear that the purchaser had at all times known that the vendor retained the right to resile from the agreement which had been informally reached between them.[10] As Lord Templeman pointed out,

3 See Chapter 11 (post, p 312).

4 See eg *Salvation Army Trustee Co Ltd v West Yorkshire MCC* (1981) 41 P & CR 179 (post, p 329); [1983] Conv 85.

5 [1987] AC 114 at 127H–128A.

6 *Clark v Follett* (1973) STC 240 at 263f. See also *Thwaites v Ryan* [1984] VR 65 at 96. In *Salvation Army Trustee Co Ltd v West Yorkshire MCC* (1981) 41 P & CR 179 at 199, Woolf J was careful to emphasise that his upholding of a claim of estoppel on the unusual facts of that case was not intended to 'interfere with the normal conduct of negotiations "subject to contract".'

7 See eg *Nepean District Tennis Association Inc v Council of City of Penrith* (1989) NSW ConvR 55–438 at 58,180.

8 See eg *Milchas Investments Pty Ltd v Larkin* (1989) NSW ConvR 55–487 at 58,536f, where Young J lamented the tendency for estoppel claims to be advanced 'as a back-up submission in every case where parties have failed to obtain an exchange of contracts'. Young J, in deprecating the unprincipled enforcement of *nuda pacta* by reference to estoppel, pointed out that 'generally speaking, the mere fact that a person does not keep his promise is not unconscionable. There must be something more and that something more will usually be found in looking to see what the opposing party did to his detriment...in reliance on the promise.'

9 [1987] AC 114 at 124G–125B, 127G–128A.

10 See *Waltons Stores (Interstate) Ltd v Maher* (1988) 164 CLR 387 at 423, where Brennan J pointed out that 'so long as both parties recognise that either party is at liberty to withdraw from the negotiations at any time before the contract is made, it cannot be unconscionable for one party to do so.'

no estoppel could be founded on the mere fact that the purchaser had acted 'in the confident and not unreasonable hope that the agreement in principle would come into effect.'[11]

(c) Proposed reforms

The precise status of agreements which are 'subject to contract' has been kept under constant review by the Law Commission. In 1975 the Commission accepted that the 'subject to contract' proviso 'has drawbacks and is capable of being abused in certain circumstances'.[12] The Commission nevertheless expressed itself averse to any change which would give legal effect to agreements 'subject to contract' or impose any liability (civil or criminal) on a person who withdraws from such an agreement.[13] It was the belief of the Commission that the non-legal status of 'subject to contract' agreements was 'based on a sound concept, namely that the buyer should be free from binding commitment until he has had the opportunity of obtaining legal and other advice, arranging his finance and making the necessary inspection, searches and enquiries'.

Continuing abuse of the 'subject to contract' procedure during the years since 1975 has more recently led the Law Commission to make an important and extremely sensible proposal in relation to pre-contractual dealings with land. The Commission has not advocated that legally binding effect should be given to agreements which are entered into 'subject to contract'. Instead the Commission has formulated the recommendation that the prospective vendor and purchaser should put down a 'pre-contract deposit' as soon as an offer of purchase has been made and accepted 'subject to contract'.[14] These deposits would each comprise 0.5 per cent of the purchase price of the property, and the parties would simultaneously enter into a written agreement to exchange formal contracts within four weeks. The pre-contract deposit would then be forfeited by any party who, otherwise than for good cause, withdrew or refused to exchange contracts within this period.[15]

11 [1987] AC 114 at 124F-G. It is possible that, even though a plea of estoppel is ineffective to fix the parties with a binding contract of sale, the principle of unjust enrichment may still justify a return of the intending purchaser's expenditure on the land (see *Nepean District Tennis Association Inc v Council of City of Penrith* (1989) NSW ConvR 55-438 at 58,180f).

12 Law Commission, *Report on 'Subject to Contract' Agreements* (Law Com No 65, January 1975), para 4.

13 Law Com No 65, para 4.

14 Law Commission, *Pre-Contract Deposits: A Practice Recommendation by the Conveyancing Standing Committee* (1987), para 5.

15 Ibid, para 7. The Law Commission envisaged the grounds of exception as including the case where a search or survey subsequently revealed 'nasty surprises' for the purchaser (para 8(a)). Compare the 'anti-gazumping legislation' in force in New South Wales, which requires that every contract for the sale of residential property must be preceded by a 'preliminary contract' under which the purchaser pays a deposit of 0.1 per cent of the purchase price or $100, whichever is greater (Conveyancing Act 1919, ss 66Q, 66R, 66W, as introduced by Conveyancing (Sale of Land) Amendment Act 1987; Conveyancing (Sale of Land) Regulation 1988). See *Sloane v McDonald Industries (Sales) Pty Ltd* (1989) 17 NSWLR 86 at 88ff; but compare *Molodysky v Vema Australia Pty Ltd* (1989) NSW ConvR 55-446 at 58,230ff.

The proposed 'pre-contract deposit' scheme provides an imaginative, albeit necessarily limited, form of protection against the evils of 'gazumping'.[16] The implementation of the scheme would, if nothing else, afford some compensation for the victim of 'gazumping' in respect of his wasted expenditure on professional fees connected with the abortive transaction.

2. THE EXCHANGE OF CONTRACTS

The moment of binding commitment between vendor and purchaser comes almost always with the exchange of contracts for the sale and purchase of land. The contract in question may be 'open', ie may provide expressly for nothing beyond the identification of the parties, the definition of the subject property and the price to be paid. The rights and duties of vendor and purchaser under an 'open' contract are then determined with reference to the general law of property. More common than 'open' contracts for the sale of land are 'closed' contracts which incorporate a number of standardised conditions relevant to the generality of land transactions. The most frequently used standard terms are now those contained in the Standard Conditions of Sale,[17] which, with effect from 1990, conflate the terms previously contained in the National Conditions of Sale[18] and the Law Society's Conditions of Sale.[19] The use of standard term conditions of sale substantially aids the process of land transfer.[20] The vendor, whose duty it is in any event to draw up the contract of sale, may adopt standard conditions with such modifications as may appear appropriate to the circumstances of his particular sale.

In spite of the frequent use in practice of standard written terms of contract, it used to be that there were few *legal* requirements of form in respect of the exchange of contracts. The relative informality of the contract stage has now been dramatically altered by the Law of Property (Miscellaneous Provisions) Act 1989 in relation to all contracts concluded on or after 27 September 1989.

16 The Standing Committee acknowledged, for instance, that the penalty of forfeiting the pre-contract deposit would have no deterrent effect at all in relation to a party who, by unjustified withdrawal from the 'subject to contract' agreement, stood to gain more than 0.5 per cent of the purchase price of the relevant property (para 11).

17 The Standard Conditions of Sale of 1990 are also declared to be the 21st edition of the National Conditions of Sale and the 1990 edition of the Law Society's Conditions of Sale. For a penetrating analysis of the Standard Conditions of Sale, see J.E. Adams, [1990] Conv 179.

18 20th edn (1982).

19 1984 Revision. See also the Conveyancing Lawyers' Conditions of Sale ([1981] Conv 38).

20 It is, however, a salutary fact that the small print in such standard form contracts has binding effect even in relation to 'conditions which it is probable that nobody ever read' (see *Squarey v Smith-Harris* (1981) 42 P & CR 118 at 128ff).

(1) Contracts prior to 27 September 1989

Prior to 27 September 1989 a binding contract for the sale of land could be entered into quite validly in either oral or written form, although the enforceability of the contract depended on compliance with certain minimal evidential requirements imposed by statute.[1]

(a) Requirement of a written memorandum

Pursuant to section 40(1) of the Law of Property Act 1925, no action could be brought upon any contract for the sale or other disposition of land or any interest in land unless the agreement upon which such action was brought, or 'some memorandum or note thereof', was 'in writing, and signed by the party to be charged or by some other person thereunto by him lawfully authorised.'[2] This provision derived from section 4 of the Statute of Frauds 1677 and was plainly designed to prevent dispute over oral dealings in land.[3] Section 40(1) did not render void a purely oral contract for the sale of land: it merely provided that such a contract should be unenforceable unless evidenced in some written memorandum.[4]

There were few limitations on the form or contents of the memorandum required pursuant to section 40(1). It was enough simply that some note of all the material terms of the contract was recorded in documentary form.[5] It was clearly necessary that the material terms should identify the parties beyond any possibility of later dispute.[6] These terms also had to render ascertainable both the physical subject matter of the contract[7] and the price to be paid,[8] specify a date for the handing over of possession to the purchaser,[9] and afford evidence of other expressly agreed terms.[10] According to the more generally accepted view the memorandum or note was required not merely to state the essential terms of the contract concerned, but also to incorporate

1 In so far as a binding contract for the sale of land is generally thought to vest some equitable interest in the purchaser at the date of contract (post, p 263), there is an intriguing argument that a merely oral agreement, even if supported by a memorandum or note pursuant to section 40, would still fall foul of Law of Property Act 1925, s 53(1)(a). See, however, Nicholas Seddon, *Contracts for the Sale of Land: Is a Note or Memorandum Sufficient?*, (1987) 61 ALJ 406; D. Everett, (1987) 17 U W Australia L Rev 301.

2 Although for reasons of clarity this account of section 40 is couched in the past tense, section 40 still governs the actionability of contracts entered into prior to 27 September 1989.

3 The requirement of a written memorandum had no application, however, to any contract between A and B that A should purchase land from C (*Lees v Fleming* [1980] Qd R 162 at 167E-F).

4 In practice there was little confusion as to whether section 40(1) had been satisfied by the provision of a written memorandum or note, since most contracts for the sale of land were not only evidenced in writing but were actually contained in written form.

5 *Hawkins v Price* [1947] Ch 645 at 659f; *Tiverton Estates Ltd v Wearwell Ltd* [1975] Ch 146 at 161G; *Mulhall v Haren* [1981] IR 364 at 394.

6 *Potter v Duffield* (1874) LR 18 Eq 4 at 7f; *Davies v Sweet* [1962] 2 QB 300 at 307f.

7 *Davies v Sweet* [1962] 2 QB 300 at 306.

8 See *Sudbrook Trading Estate Ltd v Eggleton* [1983] 1 AC 444 (ante, p 143).

9 *Mulhall v Haren* [1981] IR 364 at 394. See also *Walker v Bower* [1975] NZ Recent Law 138 at 139.

10 *Hawkins v Price* [1947] Ch 645 at 654.

some acknowledgement or recognition by the signatory that a contract had actually been entered into.[11]

(b) The doctrine of part performance

Irrespective of non-compliance with the provisions of section 40(1) of the Law of Property Act 1925, a contract for the sale of land remained actionable pursuant to section 40(2) if it could be shown that there had been acts of 'part performance'. For this purpose part performance generally required that the party seeking to enforce the contract had, in reliance upon that contract, undertaken some action to his own detriment or prejudice. The doctrine of part performance is thus closely related both to the doctrine of proprietary estoppel[12] and to the long-standing disinclination of the courts to allow a statute to be used as an instrument of fraud.[13]

(i) Conditions of part performance The doctrine of part performance rendered a contract enforceable, even in the absence of a written memorandum, where the plaintiff had done acts which, on a balance of probability, were referable to and explicable only in terms of the existence of the contract alleged by the plaintiff.[14] Although the acts did not need to be such as would demonstrate the precise terms of the contract,[15] the operation of the doctrine of part performance was premised on the current existence of an actual contract. Acts of reliance were irrelevant if performed on the footing of mere negotiations which might or might not ripen later into contract.[16]

(ii) Acts sufficient to constitute part performance The requirements of part performance were substantially relaxed during the 1970s and 1980s. In

11 *Tiverton Estates Ltd v Wearwell Ltd* [1975] Ch 146 at 160F-G, 171C-D. See also *Kelly v Park Hall School Ltd* [1979] IR 340 at 352; *Mulhall v Haren* [1981] IR 364 at 391; but compare the statement of Buckley LJ in *Law v Jones* [1974] Ch 112 at 124H, that it was 'not the fact of agreement but the terms agreed upon that must be found recorded in writing.' A party could not of course seek to rely on a written memorandum or note brought into existence only after the commencement of enforcement proceedings (see *Lucas v Dixon* (1889) 22 QBD 357 at 359ff; *Farr, Smith & Co Ltd v Messers Ltd* [1928] 1 KB 397 at 405; *South Coast Oils (Qld and NSW) Pty Ltd v Look Enterprises Pty Ltd* [1988] 1 Qd R 680 at 690).

12 See Chapter 11 (post, p 312).

13 Post, p 377. See *Maddison v Alderson* (1883) 8 App Cas 467 at 474 per Earl of Selborne LC; *Last v Rosenfeld* [1972] 2 NSWLR 923 at 927E-F; *Thwaites v Ryan* [1984] VR 65 at 91.

14 The doctrine was relevant, moreover, only if the plaintiff could establish a case for specific performance (*McManus v Cooke* (1887) 35 Ch D 681 at 697; *Elliott v Roberts* (1912) 28 TLR 436 at 437f). Since part performance was an equitable remedy, it was available only where the party seeking to rely on part performance had been guilty of no inequitable or unconscionable behaviour (see *Coatsworth v Johnson* (1886) 55 LJQB 220 at 222f (post, p 745)), and did not have access to any equally effective common law remedy (*Turner v Melladew* (1903) 19 TLR 273 at 274).

15 *Steadman v Steadman* [1976] AC 536 at 546F per Lord Morris of Borth-y-Gest.

16 *Thynne v Earl of Glengall* (1848) 2 HL Cas 131 at 158, 9 ER 1042 at 1052; *Ex parte Foster* (1883) 22 Ch D 797 at 811; *Biss v Hygate* [1918] 2 KB 314 at 317; *J.C. Williamson Ltd v Lukey and Mulholland* (1931) 45 CLR 282 at 300; *O'Rourke v Hoeven* [1974] 1 NSWLR 622 at 625E-F. See eg *Gely v Scobell* (1989) NSW ConvR 55-439 at 58,186f (arrangement of purchase finance constituted merely 'preparatory acts' and no part performance).

Steadman v Steadman,[17] the House of Lords departed significantly from the classic requirements of the doctrine as laid down in *Maddison v Alderson*.[18] A claim of part performance came to be supportable on the basis of any acts which could be shown to have been done in reliance on a contract, where it would in effect have constituted a fraud for the defendant to take advantage of the fact that the contract was not evidenced in writing. Relevant acts included the payment of money either to the other contracting party[19] or to some third party,[20] the entry into possession of land with the vendor's consent,[1] or the making of substantial improvements or alterations to the land.[2] In *Sutton v Sutton*[3] it was held that part performance of an oral agreement for transfer of a former matrimonial home could comprise the giving of consent to divorce on agreed financial terms. In *Steadman v Steadman*[4] it even appeared to be the majority view of the House of Lords that a sufficient act of part performance could arise where a purchaser instructed solicitors to prepare and submit a draft conveyance or transfer. Although the law lords were not agreed as to whether the acts relied upon must point to a contract in respect of *land*,[5] the view was subsequently taken that a claim of part performance must indeed indicate the existence of a contract in relation to land.[6]

(2) Contracts on or after 27 September 1989

The law relating to contracts concluded on or after 27 September 1989[7] has been fundamentally affected by the Law of Property (Miscellaneous Provisions) Act 1989, which provides that section 40 of the Law of Property Act 1925 shall cease to have effect.[8]

17 [1976] AC 536. See (1974) 90 LQR 433 (H.W.R. Wade); (1974) 38 Conv (NS) 354 (F.R. Crane); [1974] CLJ 205 (C.T. Emery).
18 (1883) 8 App Cas 467.
19 *Steadman v Steadman* [1976] AC 536 at 541B per Lord Reid, 565B per Lord Simon of Glaisdale, 570F-G per Lord Salmon. See also *In re Gonin, Decd* [1979] Ch 16 at 30G-H. Even the payment of a deposit which is retained pending the drawing up of a formal contract can constitute an act of part performance (see *Walker v Bower* [1975] NZ Recent Law 138 at 139; but compare *Gely v Scobell* (1989) NSW ConvR 55-439 at 58,186f).
20 See *Shillabeer v Diebel* (1980) 100 DLR (3d) 279 at 282.
1 *Smallwood v Sheppards* [1895] 2 QB 627 at 630; *Sharman v Sharman* (1893) 67 LT 834 at 836f; *Kingswood Estate Co Ltd v Anderson* [1963] 2 QB 169 at 181, 189, 193. See also *Wakeham v Mackenzie* [1968] 1 WLR 1175 at 1181D; *In re Gonin, Decd* [1979] Ch 16 at 31D-E; *Regent v Millett* (1976) 133 CLR 679 at 682f, affirming *Millett v Regent* [1975] 1 NSWLR 62.
2 *Lester v Foxcroft* (1701) Coll PC 108; *Reddin v Jarman* (1867) 16 LT 449 at 450; *Broughton v Snook* [1938] Ch 505 at 514ff; *Starlite Variety Stores Ltd v Cloverlawn Investments Ltd* (1979) 92 DLR (3d) 270 at 276.
3 [1984] Ch 184 at 193A-D. See [1984] Conv 152 (M.P. Thompson).
4 [1976] AC 536 at 540C per Lord Reid, 553H-554B per Viscount Dilhorne, 563A-B per Lord Simon of Glaisdale, 573D per Lord Salmon.
5 For the view that the contract need not refer to land, see [1976] AC 536 at 541C-D per Lord Reid, 554C-D per Viscount Dilhorne.
6 *In re Gonin, Decd* [1979] Ch 16 at 31B-D. See [1979] Conv 402 (M.P. Thompson).
7 Law of Property (Miscellaneous Provisions) Act 1989, s 2(7).
8 Law of Property (Miscellaneous Provisions) Act 1989, s 2(8). See P.H. Pettit, [1989] Conv 431; (1989) 105 LQR 553 (R.E. Annand).

(a) Requirement of written contract

Following upon recommendations made by the Law Commission in 1987,[9] the Law of Property (Miscellaneous Provisions) Act 1989 now imposes a requirement of written form in relation to almost all kinds of contract relating to the disposition of land. Section 2(1) of the Act provides that

> A contract for the sale or other disposition of an interest in land can only be made in writing and only by incorporating all the terms which the parties have expressly agreed in one document or, where contracts are exchanged, in each.

This statutory innovation removes what the Law Commission considered to be the 'indefensibly confusing' feature of the old law, namely that it allowed oral contracts to be binding but unenforceable.[10] Section 40 of the 1925 Act has been replaced by a 'simple, straightforward rule that contracts concerning land cannot be made orally'.[11] An unwritten contract is now not merely unenforceable but utterly void and ineffective. The 1989 Act also extends the requirement of signature. The document incorporating the terms of the contract agreed by the parties must be signed not simply 'by the party to be charged'[12] but 'by or on behalf of each party to the contract'.[13] These new requirements of signed writing have the substantial merit of establishing with greater clarity both the existence of a binding contract and the nature of the terms of that contract.[14]

Few exceptions are allowed from the general requirement of written form, but these exceptions include contracts relating to a lease for not more than three years at the best rent reasonably obtainable without taking a fine.[15] The 1989 Act preserves the pre-existing rules on the joinder of documents,[16] with the result that a number of separate and intrinsically incomplete documents may be linked in order to form a complete contract in writing.[17]

9 See Law Commission, *Transfer of Land: Formalities for Contracts for Sale etc of Land* (Law Com No 164, 29 June 1987), paras 4.1ff.

10 Law Com No 164 (1987), para 4.2.

11 Ibid.

12 See Law of Property Act 1925, s 40(1).

13 Law of Property (Miscellaneous Provisions) Act 1989, s 2(3). Where contracts are exchanged, it is sufficient that one of the relevant contractual documents (but not necessarily the same one) is signed by or on behalf of each party. In the case of an option to purchase land, it is sufficient for the purpose of section 2(1) of the 1989 Act that the agreement conferring the option complies with the requirement of writing signed by both parties. It is irrelevant that the notice under which the option is later exercised does not so comply (eg because signed only by the optionee). See *Spiro v Glencrown Properties Ltd* [1991] Ch 537 at 546E-F; [1991] CLJ 236 (A.J. Oakley); [1990] Conv 9 (J.E. Adams); [1991] Conv 140 (P.F. Smith).

14 A purchaser's acceptance of an oral warranty as to the state of the vendor's title gives rise to a collateral contract which lies outside section 2 of the 1989 Act and which is not therefore invalidated by the Act (see *Record v Bell* [1991] 1 WLR 853 at 860D, 862A-B; [1991] Conv 471 (M. Harwood)). Section 2 likewise has no application to an executed agreement supplemental to a contract (see eg *Tootal Clothing Ltd v Guinea Properties Ltd* (1992) 64 P & CR 452 at 455f (agreement to grant lease); [1993] Conv 89 (P. Luther)).

15 Law of Property (Miscellaneous Provisions) Act 1989, s 2(5)(a) (see Law of Property Act 1925, s 54(2)). Other exceptions comprise a contract made in the course of a public auction and a contract made on a recognised investment exchange regulated by the Financial Services Act 1986 (Law of Property (Miscellaneous Provisions) Act 1989, s 2(5)(b)-(c)).

16 Law of Property (Miscellaneous Provisions) Act 1989, s 2(2).

17 See *Long v Millar* (1879) 4 CPD 450 at 454ff.

However, if two or more documents are to be joined in this way, one of the documents must be signed and must contain 'some reference, express or implied, to some other document or transaction'.[18]

(b) Abolition of the doctrine of part performance

A further—and at least superficially far-reaching—effect of the 1989 Act is to abolish the equitable doctrine of part performance. This doctrine was expressly preserved by section 40(2) of the Law of Property Act 1925, but had in recent years been criticised as uncertain and unsatisfactory in its operation.[19] Accordingly in 1987 the Law Commission advocated that part performance should no longer have any role to play in contracts concerning land[20]—a consequence which now flows inevitably from the new statutory requirement of contracts in writing. Following a failure to comply with section 2 of the 1989 Act there is simply no contract in existence in relation to which, and in support of which, acts of part performance can ever occur.[1] The statutory avoidance of the unwritten contract causes a fatal detachment of the doctrine of part performance.

The destruction in this context of so venerable a contractual doctrine as that relating to part performance may not, however, achieve such wide-ranging effects as might at first be supposed. In abandoning the doctrine, the Law Commission itself predicted that any injustice caused in individual cases through an inability to plead part performance would be cured by the application of other forms of equitable principle directed towards the same end.[2] The Commission pointed in particular to the doctrine of estoppel[3] and expressed its belief that the courts would use this doctrine 'to achieve very similar results where appropriate to those of part performance.'[4]

It is therefore likely that the technical abolition of the doctrine of part performance will, in the context of non-compliance with prescribed formalities, confer a heightened emphasis upon the application of alternative equitable doctrines. The demise of part performance in no way exhausts the capacity of equity to avert an unconscionable outcome where the need demands. Even in the absence of a written contract, equity can declare in appropriate circumstances that a vendor holds property subject to equities which require him to transfer it to the purchaser as on a performance of

18 *Timmins v Moreland Street Property Co Ltd* [1958] Ch 110 at 130 per Jenkins LJ. See also *Elias v George Sahely & Co (Barbados) Ltd* [1983] 1 AC 646 at 655A-656A; [1983] Conv 78 (M.P. Thompson).

19 See eg Law Commission, *Transfer of Land: Formalities for Contracts for Sale etc of Land* (Law Com Working Paper No 92, July 1985), para 5.14. The Law Commission later condemned the doctrine as 'very confused', noting that it 'is not clear to what extent the act of part performance must relate to the contract, nor is it clear whether the act can be unilateral, without the consent or even the knowledge of the other party' (Law Com No 164 (1987), para 5.4).

20 Law Com No 164 (1987), para 4.13.

1 See P.H. Pettit, [1989] Conv 431 at 441.

2 Law Com No 164 (1987), para 5.4.

3 See Chapter 11 (post, p 312).

4 The Law Commission also referred to the possibility of other remedies founded in the law of negligence, deceit and restitution (Law Com Working Paper No 92 (1985), para 5.8; Law Com No 164 (1987), para 5.1f). There is also the possibility that the court may grant rectification of an agreement which is incomplete or incorrect (Law Com No 164 (1987), para 5.6). See P.H. Pettit, [1989] Conv 431 at 442.

the agreement. In a case of this kind, as Priestley JA explained in the New South Wales Court of Appeal in *Ash Street Properties Pty Ltd v Pollnow*,[5] equity so acts 'not in order to perform the contract as such but in order to give effect to an equity which has arisen extra the contract and as a result of what the parties have done.' In giving effect not to the agreement, which is statutorily void, but to an external equity generated by the circumstances, equity simply ensures that the statute is not used as an instrument of fraud.[6]

(3) Conditional contracts

It is possible for a binding contract for the sale of land to be made in conditional terms.[7] The courts have tended towards a generous view of the kinds of condition which may still be compatible with the existence of a binding contract for the sale and purchase of land.[8] Effect may thus be given, for instance, to a contract which is expressed to be 'subject to survey,'[9] since this condition can be construed as imposing on the purchaser an obligation to act reasonably in obtaining a surveyor's report on the property and then in deciding whether to adopt its recommendations.[10] Similarly, a binding contract may quite validly be conditioned upon the obtaining of a planning permission[11] or upon the purchaser's sale of his own property.[12]

Some conditions are, however, so vague or so general as to deprive an agreement of any genuine contractual force. Thus, for instance, a binding contract cannot be created by an acceptance of offered terms 'subject to the approval of' a named third party, although such an acceptance may constitute a counter-offer.[13] Likewise, a contract which is conditional on the availability of satisfactory mortgage finance for the purchaser is generally considered to be void for uncertainty,[14] although there are indications that the law on this point may be changing.[15]

5 (1987) 9 NSWLR 80 at 101A.

6 *Ash Street Properties Pty Ltd v Pollnow* (1987) 9 NSWLR 80 at 101C-D. See *Rochefoucauld v Boustead* [1897] 1 Ch 196 at 206 (post, p 377).

7 See A.J. Oakley, (1982) 35 CLP 151. An option to purchase land is generally viewed, not as a conditional contract of sale, but as an offer which remains open and may be accepted at any time allowed by its terms (ante, p 142).

8 No equitable interest passes, however, to the purchaser unless and until the condition precedent is met. See *McWilliam v McWilliams Wines Pty Ltd* (1964) 114 CLR 656 at 660; *Brown v Heffer* (1967) 116 CLR 344 at 350; *Re Androma Pty Ltd* [1987] 2 Qd R 134 at 150.

9 *Ee v Kakar* (1980) 255 Estates Gazette 879 at 881ff. See [1980] Conv 446 (J.E.A.); [1981] CLJ 23 (A.J. Oakley).

10 It may even be possible to exchange contracts 'subject to satisfactory searches'. See *Ganton House Investments Ltd v Corbin* [1988] 43 EG 76; but compare [1988] Conv 397 at 398 (J.E.A.).

11 *McKillop v McMullan* [1979] NI 85.

12 *Perri v Coolangatta Investments Pty Ltd* (1982) 56 ALJR 445 at 448ff; *Wiebe v Bobsien* (1985) 20 DLR (4th) 475 at 476f.

13 See *Framton v McCully* [1976] 1 NZLR 270 at 276. See also H.W. Wilkinson, [1985] Conv 90.

14 *Lee-Parker v Izzet* (No 2) [1972] 1 WLR 775 at 779F-G, 780A-B; (1976) 40 Conv (NS) 37; *Grime v Bartholomew* [1972] 2 NSWLR 827 at 837G.

15 See eg *Meehan v Jones* (1982) 42 ALR 463 at 470, 475ff (High Court of Australia); *Graham v Pitkin* [1992] 1 WLR 403 at 405F–406A per Lord Templeman. See also J. Phillips, (1975) 3 The Queensland Lawyer 113; B.H. Davis, (1977) 8 Cambrian LR 45.

(4) Manner of exchange of contracts

The exchange of contracts between vendor and purchaser is no mere matter of machinery. Exchange constitutes the 'mutual acknowledgement that the bargain has been struck',[16] and is 'the crucial and vital fact which brings the contract into existence'.[17] Until fairly recently the most common method of exchanging contracts for the sale of land, thereby rendering the contract in question legally binding, has consisted of a postal exchange of the two parts signed by vendor and purchaser respectively.

(a) Postal exchange

The general rule in the law of contract is that a postal acceptance of a contractual offer is complete when the offeree actually posts his acceptance to the offeror.[18] There has always been some doubt whether this postal rule applies to the exchange of contracts for sale of land, since the security sought by both parties in a land transaction seems to require that acceptance be complete only at the point of actual delivery of the acceptance to the offeror.[19] The legal conundrum involved here is now commonly obviated by the fact that most standardised sets of contractual conditions of sale provide that where the exchange of contracts is effected by post, the contract is made when the last part is actually posted.[20]

(b) Telephonic exchange

Just as the postal exchange of contracts has largely superseded any form of ceremonial exchange of contracts, so the postal mode of exchange is itself being gradually overtaken by telephonic exchange. The practical realities of modern 'chain transactions' increasingly require that solicitors should be able to use the medium of the telephone for the purpose of exchange. Accordingly in *Domb v Isoz*[1] the Court of Appeal recognised that the synchronised transactions which are required by such dealings often cannot be secured effectively by either physical or postal exchange. The Court therefore ruled that telephonic exchange may be used, under strictly regulated conditions,[2] where it appears both effectual and appropriate.[3] The Court took the view that an exchange of a written contract for sale is effected as soon as each part of the contract, duly signed by the appropriate party,

16 *Sindel v Georgiou* (1984) 154 CLR 661 at 666.
17 *Eccles v Bryant and Pollock* [1948] Ch 93 at 99 per Lord Greene MR. See, however, *Pitt v PHH Asset Management Ltd* (1993) *Times*, 30 July, where the Court of Appeal upheld, as an enforceable 'lock-out agreement', a prior collateral contract that during a short stipulated period the vendor would not negotiate for a higher price from other prospective purchasers.
18 *Household Fire Insurance Co (Ltd) v Grant* (1879) 4 Ex D 216 at 219f.
19 *Eccles v Bryant and Pollock* [1948] Ch 93 at 99f per Lord Greene MR.
20 See Standard Conditions of Sale (1990), Condition 2.1.1.
1 [1980] Ch 548. See [1980] Conv 227 (H.W. Wilkinson); (1980) 96 LQR 323.
2 '[A]s a matter of professional practice, exchange by telephone should only be carried out by a partner or proprietor of a firm of solicitors. . .[I]f two solicitors exchange by telephone, they should then and there agree and record identical attendance notes' ([1980] Ch 548 at 564E per Templeman LJ).
3 [1980] Ch 548 at 557G per Buckley LJ. On exchange by telex, see [1982] Conv 245. See also [1980] Conv 87ff, 227.

is in the actual or constructive possession of the other party or of his solicitor. For this purpose constructive possession can arise by way of telephonic exchange, but only in circumstances where a contract signed by a client is 'in the physical possession of his own solicitor or in the possession of the solicitor on the other side who has agreed to hold that part to the order of the despatching solicitor.'[4] Used carefully, the practice of telephonic exchange can thus serve substantially to reduce the danger that any client may lose a bargain or be left without a home.

(5) Deposits

It is customary for a deposit of 10 per cent of the purchase price to become payable by the purchaser on the exchange of contracts.[5] The requirement that such a deposit be paid is not a condition precedent to the existence of a binding contract, but is a fundamental contractual term which, if breached, entitles the injured party to sue for damages including the unpaid deposit.[6] The deposit operates effectively both as a part-payment of the contractually agreed purchase price and as a guarantee that the purchaser will complete the transaction.[7] If the purchaser breaches the contract in such a way as to relieve the vendor from any further obligation under the terms of that contract, the vendor may retain any deposit already paid by the purchaser.[8] If, however, the contract goes off by reason of the vendor's default, the purchaser is of course entitled to recover his deposit money.

(6) Remedies for breach of contract

A contract for the sale of land, if breached by either party, may lead to a range of contractual remedies.

(a) Specific performance

A contract for the sale of a legal estate in land is one in respect of which equity will generally grant specific performance. In other words, if the vendor fails to convey the legal estate according to the terms of the relevant contract, the remedy available to the frustrated purchaser will normally consist not

4 [1980] Ch 548 at 564D per Templeman LJ. The Law Society has now published various standard formulae (Formulae A, B and C) for use in telephone and telex exchange (see I.R. Storey, *Conveyancing* (3rd edn London 1990), p 329, Appendix III).

5 See Standard Conditions of Sale (1990), Condition 2.2.1. Except where he is expressly instructed so to do, it may constitute negligence on the part of a purchaser's solicitor to fail to make express provision for payment of a deposit under an open contract (see *Morris v Duke Cohan & Co* (1975) 119 SJ 826). For an attempted payment of deposit by transfer of gemstones, see *D & J Constructions Pty Ltd v Machello Pty Ltd* [1987] 2 Qd R 350 at 352f.

6 *Millichamp v Jones* [1982] 1 WLR 1422 at 1430G-H. See also *Alarm Facilities Pty Ltd v Jackson Constructions Pty Ltd* [1975] 2 NSWLR 22 at 28F-29A.

7 Against a background of recent calls for the abolition of contractual deposits, the Conveyancing Standing Committee of the Law Commission and the Law Society issued a Joint Report in 1989 which favoured continuation of the practice (*Deposits—No Time for a Change* (23 August 1989)). See [1989] Conv 377, and see also H.W. Wilkinson, *Deposits: Who Needs Them?*, (1984) 81 Law Soc Gaz 347; [1985] Conv 237.

8 The courts have an equitable jurisdiction to grant relief against forfeiture (see C. Harpum, [1984] CLJ 134). See also *Legione v Hateley* (1983) 46 ALR 1 at 12ff.

of compensatory damages, but of a court decree that the vendor do that which he promised to do, ie execute the conveyance and thus transfer the legal estate to the contractual promisee. The rationale underlying this particular form of remedy is the recognition that, since the subject matter of a sale of land is unique, breach of a contract for the sale of land cannot usually be compensated adequately by a mere award of money.[9]

Since specific performance is an intrinsically equitable remedy, it is available not of right but only at the discretion of the court. The exercise of this discretion is normally, in its turn, dependent on a showing that there was a transaction for value contained in writing.[10] Equity will not usually assist a volunteer and a contract not contained in appropriately signed written form will fail to comply with the terms of section 2 of the Law of Property (Miscellaneous Provisions) Act 1989.[11] If, however, the preconditions exacted by the equitable jurisdiction are satisfied, the remedy of specific performance is granted almost as a matter of course,[12] unless the purchaser has forfeited such help by reason of some unconscionable act or default[13] or if specific performance would prejudice the rights of third parties[14] or would cause a 'hardship amounting to injustice'.[15]

(b) Remedies in damages

In the case of failure to complete the contract, it is open to the aggrieved contracting party to rescind the contract and seek monetary compensation instead of specific performance of the contract. A failure to complete on the contractual date is remediable in damages for breach of contract or in damages in lieu of a decree for specific performance under the Supreme Court Act 1981.[16] However, no right to rescind arises until time becomes 'of the essence' by virtue of a notice to complete served by the party seeking

9 See *Hall v Warren* (1804) 9 Ves 605 at 608, 32 ER 738 at 739; *Hexter v Pearce* [1900] 1 Ch 341 at 346; *Rudd v Lascelles* [1900] 1 Ch 815 at 817.

10 See *Brunker v Perpetual Trustee Co (Ltd)* (1937) 57 CLR 555 at 599 per Dixon J.

11 Ante, p 257.

12 *Patel v Ali* [1984] Ch 283 at 286G; *Graham v Pitkin* [1992] 1 WLR 403 at 406D per Lord Templeman; *Kopec v Pyret* (1987) 36 DLR (4th) 1 at 8f.

13 See *Coatsworth v Johnson* (1886) 55 LJQB 220 at 222f (post, p 745); *Harrigan v Brown* [1967] 1 NSWR 342 at 345ff. Mere 'general naughtiness' is not enough (*FAI Insurances Ltd v Pioneer Concrete Services Ltd* (1987) 15 NSWLR 552 at 554G–555B per Young J). See eg *Carlson v Sparkes* (1981) 2 BPR 9101 at 9102f (specific performance awarded to purchaser who tortiously demolished house before completion).

14 *Warmington v Miller* [1973] QB 877 at 886F-G. There can, for instance, be no order for specific performance where the land in question has already been conveyed to a third party (see eg *Babcock v Carr* (1982) 127 DLR (3d) 77 at 85f). If, however, the third party transferee has been guilty of fraud (eg through unconscionable dealing in the face of a prior known incumbrance), he may himself be vulnerable to the remedy of specific performance. See *Potter v Sanders* (1846) 6 Hare 1 at 9ff, 67 ER 1057 at 1061f; *Canadian Long Island Petroleums Ltd v Irving Industries (Irving Wire Products Division) Ltd* (1975) 50 DLR (3d) 265 at 281 per Martland J; *Island Properties Ltd v Entertainment Enterprises Ltd* (1986) 26 DLR (4th) 347 at 351.

15 *Patel v Ali* [1984] Ch 283 at 288D-E per Goulding J. See (1984) 100 LQR 337; (1984) 134 NLJ 685 (H.W. Wilkinson). See also *Roberts v O'Neill* [1983] IR 47 at 55f; *Registered Securities Ltd v Cummins* [1983] NZ Recent Law 246 at 247; *R.D. McKinnon Holdings Pty Ltd v Hind* [1984] 2 NSWLR 121 at 126D-E; *South Coast Oils (Qld and NSW) Pty Ltd v Look Enterprises Pty Ltd* [1988] 1 Qd R 680 at 692.

16 Supreme Court Act 1981, s 50.

completion or by virtue of unreasonable delay.[17] Where an aggrieved contracting party has treated another's repudiation or breach of contract as discharging the contract, or where an order for specific performance is not complied with, damages may be recovered not only for restitution and indemnity in respect of sums paid and expenses incurred, but also for loss of bargain.[18]

(7) The interest taken by the contractual purchaser

The ultimate effect of the rules relating to specific performance is that once a contract for the sale of a legal estate in land has been entered into, the eventual conveyance of that estate is usually fairly inevitable. Either the vendor will duly convey according to his contract or the purchaser will enlist the aid of equity towards this end by means of a decree of specific performance.

The general inexorability of due transfer under a specifically enforceable contract for sale activates an equitable maxim: 'Equity looks on that as done which ought to be done'.[19] Since the contract ought (by one means or another) to eventuate in a conveyance of an estate in the land, equity regards the purchaser as having acquired, as of the date of the contract itself, certain substantial rights of a proprietary character.[20] Indeed it has sometimes been said that the existence of the contract has a 'remarkable effect' in that it 'converts the estate, so to say, in equity'.[1] That is, the contract 'actually changes the ownership of the estate in equity' and causes the land to become 'a part of the real estate of the vendee'.[2] Beneficial ownership thus passes at the point of contract to the purchaser, subject to the payment of the purchase money.[3] On this basis a specifically enforceable contract is effective to transfer the equitable ownership of the estate to the prospective purchaser, whether that estate be a fee simple or a term of years absolute.[4]

17 See *Raineri v Miles* [1981] AC 1050; [1980] CLJ 21 (D.J. Hayton); [1980] Conv 77 (A. Sydenham).

18 *Johnson v Agnew* [1980] AC 367. See also A.J. Oakley, [1980] CLJ 58; M. Hetherington, (1980) 96 LQR 403; (1979) 42 MLR 696 (G. Woodman); [1979] Conv 293 (F.R. Crane).

19 See *K.L.D.E. Pty Ltd v Commissioner of Stamp Duties (Queensland)* (1984) 155 CLR 288 at 296.

20 See *Sonenco (No 77) Pty Ltd v Silvia* (1989) 89 ALR 437 at 457 per Ryan and Gummow JJ. In *Oughtred v IRC* [1960] AC 206 at 240, Lord Jenkins spoke of the contractual purchaser as being 'treated in equity as entitled...to the property'. His interest under the contract 'is no doubt a proprietary interest of a sort, which arises...in anticipation of the execution of the transfer for which the purchaser is entitled to call.'

1 *Lysaght v Edwards* (1876) 2 Ch D 499 at 507 per Jessel MR.

2 *Lysaght v Edwards* (1876) 2 Ch D 499 at 507 per Jessel MR. See *Shaw v Foster* (1872) LR 5 HL 321 at 338 per Lord Cairns ('the purchaser was the real beneficial owner, in the eye of a Court of Equity'). See also *Raffety v Schofield* [1897] 1 Ch 937 at 943.

3 *Lysaght v Edwards* (1876) 2 Ch D 499 at 506 per Jessel MR. In *Rose v Watson* (1864) 10 HLCas 672 at 678, 11 ER 1187 at 1190, Lord Westbury LC took it to be 'very simple and very clear' that 'the ownership of the estate is, in equity, transferred by [the] contract.' See also *Legione v Hately* (1983) 152 CLR 406 at 423; *K.L.D.E. Pty Ltd v Commissioner of Stamp Duties (Queensland)* (1984) 155 CLR 288 at 297, 301.

4 See *Appleton v Aspin* [1988] 1 WLR 410 at 417D per Nourse LJ. 'Upon the exchange of contracts the purchaser acquires an equitable estate in the land' (*D.K.L.R. Holding Co (No 2) Pty Ltd v Commissioner of Stamp Duties* [1978] 1 NSWLR 268 at 279F).

(8) The vendor as trustee

If a specifically enforceable contract confers some kind of equitable ownership upon the purchaser, it becomes tempting to analyse the relationship between vendor and purchaser in terms of a trust. In *Lysaght v Edwards*,[5] Jessel MR considered it to be settled doctrine 'that the moment you have a valid contract for sale the vendor becomes in equity a trustee for the purchaser of the estate sold.'[6] Thus, if a vendor (V) and a purchaser (P) go through the process of a contract and conveyance relating to a legal estate in Blackacre, their transaction can be described, in trust terminology, as taking the course indicated in *Fig.* 19.

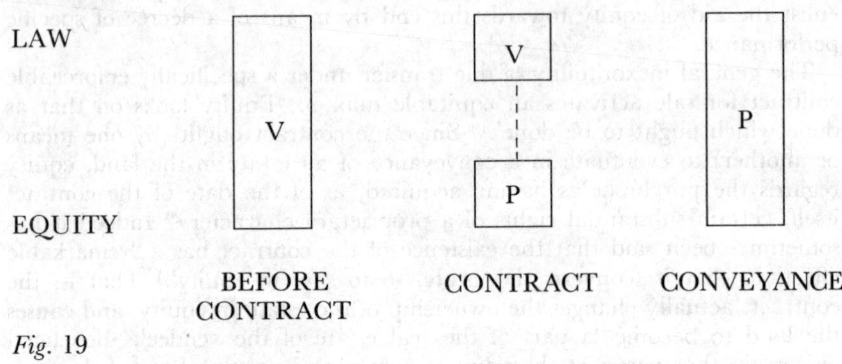

Fig. 19

(a) The pre-contractual stage

Before exchange of contracts it is clear that the entire interest in Blackacre is vested in V. Indeed, at this stage it is technically inaccurate to suppose that V's absolute ownership comprises a summation of two distinct estates, legal and equitable, both held by V.[7] Equitable doctrine resists the notion that absolute ownership requires, for all purposes and at every moment of time, the separate and concurrent existence of two different kinds of estate or interest, ie the legal and the equitable, in every form of property.[8] There

5 (1876) 2 Ch D 499 at 506.

6 See, to the same effect, *Daire v Beversham* (1661) Nels 76 at 77, 21 ER 793 at 794; *Green v Smith* (1738) 1 Atk 572 at 573, 26 ER 360; *Paine v Meller* (1801) 6 Ves 349 at 352f, 31 ER 1088 at 1089f; *Broome v Monck* (1805) 10 Ves 597 at 606, 32 ER 976 at 979; *Shaw v Foster* (1872) LR 5 HL 321 at 333 per Lord Chelmsford, 338 per Lord Cairns.

7 A man 'cannot be a trustee for himself' (*Goodright v Wells* (1781) 2 Doug KB 771 at 778, 99 ER 491 at 495 per Lord Mansfield). See also *Selby v Alston* (1797) 3 Ves 339 at 341, 30 ER 1042 at 1043; *Harmood v Oglander* (1803) 8 Ves 106 at 127, 32 ER 293 at 301 per Lord Eldon; *In re Selous* [1901] 1 Ch 921 at 922; *Re Turkington* [1937] 4 All ER 501 at 504F; *Re Heberley (deceased)* [1971] NZLR 325 at 333, 346; *D.K.L.R. Holding Co (No 2) Pty Ltd v Commissioner of Stamp Duties (N.S.W.)* (1982) 149 CLR 431 at 463.

8 See *D.K.L.R. Holding Co (No 2) Pty Ltd v Commissioner of Stamp Duties* [1978] 1 NSWLR 268 at 278B-E per Sheppard J, (1982) 149 CLR 431 at 463 per Aickin J; *Re Transphere Pty Ltd* (1986) 5 NSWLR 309 at 311D-E per McLelland J; *Oughtred v IRC* [1960] AC 206 at 216 per Wilberforce QC (arguendo).

is high authority, in the advice tendered by the Privy Council in *Commissioner of Stamp Duties (Queensland) v Livingston*,[9] that where the 'whole right of property' is vested in one person, it is strictly improper to distinguish between the legal and equitable interest in that property.[10] Merger in one absolute owner of the totality of interests, legal and beneficial, renders such a distinction unnecessary and indeed impossible.[11] The absolute owner simply holds the legal estate, together with all the rights and incidents which attach to that estate.[12] As the Privy Council pointed out in *Livingston*'s case,[13] equity 'calls into existence and protects equitable rights and interests in property only where their recognition has been found to be required in order to give effect to its doctrines.'[14]

(b) *The contractual stage*

In terms of the traditional trust analysis, as soon as a specifically enforceable contract for sale is concluded with P, the beneficial interest in Blackacre is treated as belonging to P,[15] subject to a lien for the purchase money in favour of V.[16] When subsequently the conveyance of the legal estate is executed or the registered title transferred, this beneficial interest will merge indistinguishably with the legal estate in the hands of P. Between contract and conveyance, however, it seems attractive to say that the availability of the contractual remedy of specific performance has engrafted, at least temporarily, some sort of trust relationship upon the participants in the transaction.[17] Certain consequences flow from this analysis.[18]

(i) Vendor's duty of care The vendor is, by virtue of his trusteeship, burdened by fiduciary responsibilities towards his purchaser in respect of the management and preservation of the trust property during the period between

9 [1965] AC 694 at 712C-D per Viscount Radcliffe.
10 See also *Grey v IRC* [1958] Ch 690 at 708 per Evershed MR.
11 *Corin v Patton* (1990) 169 CLR 540 at 579 per Deane J. The absolute owner has no separate equitable estate since this is 'absorbed in the legal estate' (*D.K.L.R. Holding Co (No 2) Pty Ltd v Commissioner of Stamp Duties (N.S.W.)* (1982) 149 CLR 431 at 442 per Gibbs CJ).
12 *Re Transphere Pty Ltd* (1986) 5 NSWLR 309 at 311E per McLelland J. For this reason an absolute owner is not competent to transfer a bare legal estate whilst purporting to retain the absolute beneficial interest (*D.K.L.R. Holding Co (No 2) Pty Ltd v Commissioner of Stamp Duties (N.S.W.)* (1982) 149 CLR 431 at 442 per Gibbs CJ, 463f per Aickin J, 473f per Brennan J).
13 [1965] AC 694 at 712E.
14 See also *D.K.L.R. Holding Co (No 2) Pty Ltd v Commissioner of Stamp Duties* [1978] 1 NSWLR 268 at 278D-E.
15 *Avondale Printers & Stationers Ltd v Haggie* [1979] 2 NZLR 124 at 141; *K.L.D.E. Pty Ltd v Commissioner of Stamp Duties (Queensland)* (1984) 155 CLR 288 at 297. As Deane J observed in *Kern Corporation Ltd v Walter Reid Trading Pty Ltd* (1987) 163 CLR 164 at 191, the purchaser's equitable interest in the land from the point of contract onwards 'reflects the extent to which equitable remedies are available to protect his contractual rights'.
16 See *Howard v Miller* [1915] AC 318 at 326.
17 See *Central Trust and Safe Deposit Co v Snider* [1916] 1 AC 266 at 272 per Lord Parker of Waddington; *Hoysted v Federal Commissioner of Taxation* (1920) 27 CLR 400 at 423 per Isaacs J.
18 See, however, *Lyons v Thomas* [1986] IR 666 at 675 per Murphy J.

contract and conveyance.[19] The vendor may thus be liable to the purchaser if, by reason of his negligence, the subject matter of the contract of sale is damaged during this interim by trespassers[20] or by the elements,[1] or if the property is damaged by the vendor himself[2] or is prejudiced by unfavourable transactions entered into by the vendor.[3] Moreover, if the vendor in breach of contract sells the land instead to a third party, he stands in relation to the proceeds of that sale as a trustee on behalf of the contractual purchaser.[4]

(ii) Insurable risk The trust relationship between vendor and purchaser may have one further implication of immediate practical concern to the latter. In the absence of contrary contractual provision the insurable risk in the subject matter of the contract passes concurrently with the equitable interest in the land. If this is the case, it is advisable that the purchaser buy insurance cover effective from the date of the contract, since it is generally accepted that the risk of destruction of the property passes to him as beneficial owner behind the trust of the legal estate.[5] On this basis, if a building on the land is destroyed by fire between contract and conveyance, the purchaser is still contractually bound to take the conveyance of the land and the charred remains at the full contracted purchase price.[6]

This allocation of risk between vendor and purchaser in respect of supervening physical damage has recently come under severe scrutiny. The Law Commission has condemned the present state of the law as 'fundamentally unsatisfactory and unfair', in that it imposes on the contractual purchaser a responsibility for the property at a time when he has no control over that property.[7] Accordingly the Commission has recommended that the law be reformed so that, in the absence of contrary agreement, the risk of physical damage passes to the purchaser only on completion of the contract

19 Largely because the trust concept has been 'particularly valuable in imposing duties on the vendor in the interim period' between contract and completion, the Law Commission has recommended that the relationship between vendor and contractual purchaser should continue to be analysed in terms of trusteeship (Law Commission, *Transfer of Land: Risk of Damage after Contract for Sale* (Law Com No 191, 23 April 1990), paras 2.7f).

20 *Clarke v Ramuz* [1891] 2 QB 456 at 460ff. The vendor must take reasonable steps to exclude trespassers and prevent damage by them (see *Davron Estates Ltd v Turnshire Ltd* (1982) 133 NLJ 937).

1 *Lucie-Smith v Gorman* [1981] CLY 2866.

2 *Lysaght v Edwards* (1876) 2 Ch D 499 at 507; *Cumberland Consolidated Holdings Ltd v Ireland* [1946] KB 264 at 269.

3 See *Abdulla v Shah* [1959] AC 124 at 132f (grant of unfavourable tenancies); *Sinclair-Hill v Sothcott* (1973) 226 Estates Gazette 1399 at 1401 (withdrawal of application for planning permission).

4 *Lake v Bayliss* [1974] 1 WLR 1073 at 1076D-E.

5 *Lysaght v Edwards* (1876) 2 Ch D 499 at 507 per Jessel MR.

6 See eg *Lysaght v Edwards* (1876) 2 Ch D 499 at 507; *Rayner v Preston* (1881) 18 Ch D 1 at 6; *Fletcher v Manton* (1940) 64 CLR 37 at 42, 48f; *Budhia v Wellington City Corpn* [1976] 1 NZLR 766 at 768. For a strong counter-argument, see M.P. Thompson, *Must a Purchaser buy a Charred Ruin?*, [1984] Conv 43. See also Law of Property Act 1925, s 47; *Lonsdale & Thompson Ltd v Black Arrow Group Plc* [1993] 2 WLR 815; *Kern Corporation Ltd v Walter Reid Trading Pty Ltd* (1987) 163 CLR 164.

7 Law Commission, *Transfer of Land: Risk of Damage after Contract for Sale* (Law Com No 191, 23 April 1990), para 2.9 (The purchaser 'cannot take steps physically to protect the property or to do running repairs.')

of purchase rather than at the date of exchange of contracts.[8] The Commission felt that there was no need for legislation to implement this proposal, since in practice the desired effect will almost certainly be brought about by widespread recourse to the new Standard Conditions of Sale introduced in 1990.[9] Under these Conditions the seller undertakes to transfer the property 'in the same physical state as it was at the date of the contract (except for fair wear and tear), which means that the seller retains the risk until completion'.[10]

(iii) Role of the estate contract From the moment of the exchange of contracts the purchaser of land acquires not merely a contractual right but also a proprietary right. On one far-reaching view the purchaser acquires, in the case of a freehold transaction, an equitable fee simple estate in the land. This indirectly explains why one of the most significant categories of registrable land charge or minor interest—the 'estate contract'—is designed precisely to protect the right of the purchaser to call for a conveyance in accordance with his contract.[11] By virtue of the anticipatory effect of equitable doctrine, the contractual right of the purchaser is recognised as a right in real property and (like any other commercial equitable interest) requires protection against third parties.

The same doctrine of equity applies to a contract to convey a lease or term of years. The contract itself is effective (under the doctrine in *Walsh v Lonsdale*[12]) to invest the tenant with an equitable interest in the land, ie an equitable term of years. Furthermore, a similar effect is achieved in the case of an imperfect conveyance of a leasehold interest (eg where the lease is granted in writing instead of by deed or where the lease has not been registered in the Land Register).[13] Of course, in both cases the tenant can usually obtain specific performance of the lease by means of a court order that the landlord execute a lease in the proper form. However, the tenant often has no desire to seek specific performance since in equity he is already regarded as holding a term of years on terms broadly similar (if not identical) to those contained in the original contract or imperfect lease.[14] Thus, in many instances, a contract for a lease may never eventuate in a valid conveyance of the leasehold.

(c) The conveyance stage

The final stage in the transaction between V and P (see *Fig.* 19) occurs when V's legal estate is eventually conveyed or transferred to P in due performance of their contract. At this point the legal estate in Blackacre

8 Law Com No 191 (1990), para 2.25. The Commission did not, however, envisage a similar deferment of risk in relation to other kinds of changed circumstance which, without inflicting physical damage, may affect the value of a property between contract and completion (ibid, para 2.5). Such risks include fluctuations in market value or changes in value occurring outside the parties' control (eg flowing from listed building designation).
9 Law Com No 191 (1990), paras 3.8ff.
10 Standard Conditions of Sale (1990), Condition 5.1.1. See J.E. Adams, [1990] Conv 179 at 189f.
11 Ante, pp 141, 181.
12 (1882) 21 Ch D 9 (post, p 746f).
13 *Chan v Cresdon Pty Ltd* (1989) 168 CLR 242 at 250f.
14 Post, p 749.

is effectively reunited with the beneficial interest which passed on contract.[15] The equitable estate is now 'absorbed in the legal estate', thereby confirming in P 'the whole right of property in the land'.[16]

(d) Is the trust model apt between contract and conveyance?

There has always existed some fundamental doubt whether the trust model provides an entirely apt description of the vendor-purchaser relationship between contract and conveyance.[17] Recent years have seen a distinct movement away from the indiscriminate application of trust terminology in this context.

(i) Limitations on the vendor's trusteeship It can only be in a somewhat qualified sense that a vendor ever stands as trustee for his purchaser pending completion of a specifically enforceable contract.[18] It may well be true that on contract the purchaser acquires an equitable interest, but it is also undeniable that the vendor meanwhile retains a continuing beneficial interest in the land.[19] Thus the vendor still enjoys a 'paramount right. . .to protect his own interest as vendor of the property'.[20] He still enjoys certain valuable rights in relation to the property. He has a right to remain in possession of the land until completion of the contract and payment of the purchase moneys,[1] and is beneficially entitled to the rents and profits which accrue before the date of completion.[2] Moreover, from the point of entering into a specifically enforceable contract of sale, the vendor retains an 'unpaid vendor's lien' over the property until the purchase moneys are paid in full.[3] If the purchaser enters upon the land without the vendor's permission and without authority

15 See V.G. Wellings, *The Vendor as Trustee*, (1959) 23 Conv (NS) 173; D. Waters, *Constructive Trust—Vendor and Purchaser*, (1961) 14 CLP 76.

16 *D.K.L.R. Holding Co (No 2) Pty Ltd v Commissioner of Stamp Duties (N.S.W.)* (1982) 149 CLR 431 at 442 per Gibbs CJ. See also *Brydges v Brydges* (1796) 3 Ves 120 at 126, 30 ER 926 at 929.

17 See eg *Rayner v Preston* (1881) 18 Ch D 1 at 10f per Brett LJ ('With the greatest deference, it seems wrong to say that the one is a trustee for the other').

18 *Stern v McArthur* (1988) 165 CLR 489 at 521 per Deane and Dawson JJ ('. . .the qualifications are such as to rob the proposition of much of its significance. . .').

19 See *Kern Corporation Ltd v Walter Reid Trading Pty Ltd* (1987) 163 CLR 164 at 191 per Deane J; *Stern v McArthur* (1988) 165 CLR 489 at 521f per Deane and Dawson JJ.

20 *Shaw v Foster* (1872) LR 5 HL 321 at 338 per Lord Cairns LC.

1 *Gedye v Montrose* (1858) 26 Beav 45 at 49f, 53 ER 813 at 814f; *Phillips v Silvester* (1872) 8 Ch App 173 at 176f.

2 *Cuddon v Tite* (1858) 1 Giff 395 at 399, 65 ER 971 at 973. The vendor may also retain damages recovered from a tenant in respect of breach of covenant (*In re Lyne-Stephens and Scott-Miller's Contract* [1920] 1 Ch 472 at 487). This differs from the 'inflexible rule' of equity that a trustee or fiduciary may never under any circumstances derive profit from his position of trust. See *Parker v McKenna* (1874) 10 Ch App 96 at 124 per James LJ; G.H. Jones, (1968) 84 LQR 472.

3 *Winter v Lord Anson* (1827) 3 Russ 488 at 492, 38 ER 658 at 660; *Nives v Nives* (1880) 15 Ch D 649 at 650; *Bridges v Mees* [1957] Ch 475 at 484; *In re Birmingham, Decd* [1959] Ch 523 at 528f; *London and Cheshire Insurance Co Ltd v Laplagrene Property Co Ltd* [1971] Ch 499 at 514C-D. An unpaid lender may later be subrogated to the vendor's lien after completion (see *Boodle Hatfield & Co v British Films Ltd* (1986) 2 BCC 99,221 at 99,225f (post, p 942); *Bank of Ireland Finance Ltd v D.J. Daly Ltd* [1978] IR 79 at 82).

under the contract, the vendor can maintain, for his own benefit, an action in trespass against the purchaser.[4]

(ii) Demise of the trusteeship model There thus remains considerable doubt as to the precise nature of the trust which arises in favour of the contractual purchaser and even as to the point in time at which such a trust can be said to arise.[5] In the High Court of Australia Brennan J has declared it 'inaccurate to describe as ownership' the interest which is acquired by the purchaser in advance of conveyance.[6] It may be better to acknowledge, in more guarded terms, that the making of the contract transfers beneficial ownership to the purchaser merely 'to an extent'.[7] Until the vendor is obliged on payment of the purchase moneys to convey title, the purchaser 'owns an interest in the property but he does not own the property.'[8]

With increasing scepticism as to the terminology of ownership has come greater caution in relation to the use of the model of trusteeship in this context. It is plainly impossible to transpose into the law of vendor and purchaser the general law governing the rights and duties of trustees. Where there are rights outstanding on both sides, it is becoming more generally recognised that 'the description of the vendor as a trustee tends to conceal the essentially contractual relationship which, rather than the relationship of trustee and beneficiary, governs the rights and duties of the respective parties.'[9] It may be closer to the truth to maintain, as did Sir Thomas Plumer MR in *Wall v Bright*,[10] that the vendor is 'not a mere [ie bare] trustee; he is in progress towards it'. There is accordingly a clear line of authority that the vendor becomes only a 'constructive trustee' on exchange of contracts,[11] but is converted (until the date of completion) into a 'bare trustee' for the purchaser as soon as the purchase moneys are received in full.[12] On this basis beneficial 'ownership' of land passes to the purchaser only

4 *Kern Corporation Ltd v Walter Reid Trading Pty Ltd* (1987) 163 CLR 164 at 192 per Deane J.

5 See *Chang v Registrar of Titles* (1976) 137 CLR 177 at 184 per Mason J; *Avondale Printers & Stationers Ltd v Haggie* [1979] 2 NZLR 124 at 141f. See also M.P. Thompson, [1984] Conv 43 at 44.

6 *K.L.D.E. Pty Ltd v Commissioner of Stamp Duties (Queensland)* (1984) 155 CLR 288 at 300. See also *Coffey v Brunel Construction Co Ltd* [1983] IR 36 at 43 per Griffin J.

7 *Haque v Haque* (No 2) (1965) 114 CLR 98 at 124 per Kitto J. See also *K.L.D.E. Pty Ltd v Commissioner of Stamp Duties (Queensland)* (1984) 155 CLR 288 at 301 per Brennan J.

8 *K.L.D.E. Pty Ltd v Commissioner of Stamp Duties (Queensland)* (1984) 155 CLR 288 at 300 per Brennan J. See also *Stern v McArthur* (1988) 165 CLR 489 at 522f per Deane and Dawson JJ.

9 *Chang v Registrar of Titles* (1976) 137 CLR 177 at 190 per Jacobs J. The vendor is not a trustee of the beneficial interest 'merely because he signs a contract' (*Tempany v Hynes* [1976] IR 101 at 114 per Kenny J).

10 (1820) 1 Jac & W 494 at 503, 37 ER 456 at 459.

11 *Shaw v Foster* (1872) LR 5 HL 321 at 349 per Lord O'Hagan, 356 per Lord Hatherley LC; *Lysaght v Edwards* (1876) 2 Ch D 499 at 510 per Jessel MR.

12 See eg *Bridges v Mees* [1957] Ch 475 at 484; *Weidman v McClary Man Co* (1917) 33 DLR 672 at 683; *McWilliam v McWilliams Wines Pty Ltd* (1964) 114 CLR 656 at 660; *Shanahan v Fitzgerald* [1982] 2 NSWLR 513 at 514G-515A; *Bell v Guaranty Trust Co of Canada* (1984) 4 DLR (4th) 624 at 633; *Stern v McArthur* (1988) 165 CLR 489 at 523 per Deane and Dawson JJ.

upon payment of the full purchase price,[13] and until then the vendor is merely a trustee sub modo,[14] holding by way of a trusteeship which is indeed 'unorthodox'.[15] Indeed, it has even been said, 'with due respect to some past statements of high authority to the contrary', that it is 'wrong' to characterise the position of the unpaid vendor under an uncompleted contract as that of a trustee at all.[16]

The retreat in this area from the conceptual apparatus of trusteeship may, however, have much to reveal about the essential nature of property, ownership and equitable proprietary rights. In seeking long ago to express 'what is historically the right point of view', Maitland emphasised the way in which, in equity, 'the benefit of an obligation has been so treated that it has come to look rather like a true proprietary right.'[17] What happens at the date of a specifically enforceable contract is not that the vendor has disposed of some pre-existing component of equitable ownership in the property, but rather that he has by contract allowed an obligation in favour of his purchaser to be 'impressed' upon his own legal estate.[18] Equitable rights of property are ultimately derived from some conscientious obligation to deal with property in a certain way and are always therefore in some sense commensurate with the claimant's right to relief *in personam*.[19] In the present context the right to demand due performance of the contractual obligation is constitutive of an equitable proprietary right, but one which is nevertheless 'engrafted on to' rather than 'carved out of' the vendor's legal estate.[20]

3. COMPLETION

By virtue of the exchange of contracts, vendor and purchaser are legally committed to complete the transaction. However, as Lord Erskine LC observed in *Hiern v Mill*,[1] 'no man in his senses would take an offer of a purchase from a man, merely because he stood upon the ground.' Mere

13 'When a purchaser, on payment of the price, becomes entitled to insist upon conveyance of title to the property he has contracted to purchase, he may rightly be described as the owner of it' (*K.L.D.E. Pty Ltd v Commissioner of Stamp Duties (Queensland)* (1984) 155 CLR 288 at 300f per Brennan J). See also *Rose v Watson* (1864) 10 HLCas 672 at 683, 11 ER 1187 at 1192 per Lord Cranworth; *Coffey v Brunel Construction Co Ltd* [1983] IR 36 at 43.

14 *Chang v Registrar of Titles* (1976) 137 CLR 177 at 184f per Mason J; *K.L.D.E. Pty Ltd v Commissioner of Stamp Duties (Queensland)* (1984) 155 CLR 288 at 301 per Brennan J.

15 *Lyons v Thomas* [1986] IR 666 at 676.

16 See *Kern Corporation Ltd v Walter Reid Trading Pty Ltd* (1987) 163 CLR 164 at 191f, where Deane J described the attribution of trusteeship as 'both inaccurate and misleading'. Deane J observed that it was also inaccurate to refer to the vendor as a trustee sub modo 'unless the disarming mystique of the added Latin is treated as a warrant for essential misdescription.'

17 *Equity* (2nd edn, London 1936), p 115 (ante, p 44).

18 An equitable interest 'is not carved out of a legal estate but impressed upon it' (*D.K.L.R. Holding Co (No 2) Pty Ltd v Commissioner of Stamp Duties (N.S.W.)* (1982) 149 CLR 431 at 474 per Brennan J).

19 *Glenn v Federal Comr of Land Tax* (1915) 20 CLR 490 at 503 per Isaacs J. See also *Stern v McArthur* (1988) 165 CLR 489 at 522f per Deane and Dawson JJ.

20 *Re Transphere Pty Ltd* (1986) 5 NSWLR 309 at 311E-F per McLelland J.

1 (1806) 13 Ves 114 at 122, 33 ER 237 at 240.

possession by the vendor is not sufficient; the vendor must satisfy the purchaser that he has a good title to the property and that it is subject only to the adverse interests specified in the contract. If the title is unregistered, the vendor must supply an abstract of the title of the property which discloses dealings affecting the land during at least the past 15 years.[2] In the case of a registered title, the purchaser is given authority to inspect the Land Register for entries in respect of the vendor's title.[3] If either the abstract of title or the Land Register discloses apparent defects in the title offered, the purchaser may make 'requisitions' in order to clarify matters as to which doubt exists.

When satisfied that the title is in order, the purchaser sends to the vendor a draft conveyance, or, in the case of registered land, a draft form of transfer, for approval. When this draft is approved, the purchaser makes a final search of the Land Charges Register or Land Register, as is appropriate,[4] in order to ensure that the property remains free of undisclosed adverse interests. On the date fixed for completion (which is usually 20 working days after the exchange of contracts[5]), the purchaser pays over the balance of the purchase moneys[6] and the vendor hands over the appropriate title deeds or documents.[7] The transaction is now complete, except that in the case of registered land the document of transfer must be lodged at the Land Registry in order that the purchaser may be entered in the Register as the new proprietor.[8]

The foregoing is a brief description of the process by which a title is transferred from vendor to purchaser.[9] Certain aspects of the transaction require greater emphasis.

(1) Formalities

Certain stringent requirements of form must normally be satisfied for the purpose of effecting the transfer of a legal estate in land.[10] According to section 52(1) of the Law of Property Act 1925, '[a]ll conveyances of land or of any interest therein are void for the purpose of conveying or creating

2 Law of Property Act 1969, s 23. The maximum period in respect of which (in the absence of contrary contractual stipulation) the purchaser could insist on investigating title was originally fixed by the common law as 60 years (see *Barnwell v Harris* (1809) 1 Taunt 430 at 432, 127 ER 901). This period was progressively reduced to 40 years (Vendor and Purchaser Act 1874, s 1), 30 years (Law of Property Act 1925, s 44(1)), and now 15 years.

3 Ante, p 172.

4 Ante, pp 131, 185.

5 See Standard Conditions of Sale (1990), Condition 6.1.1.

6 On the electronic transfer of funds under the CHAPS system (Clearing Houses Automatic Payment Scheme), see [1990] Conv 145 (H.W. Wilkinson).

7 The vendor's obligation to deliver a good title and the purchaser's obligation to pay the purchase money are concurrent and mutually dependent obligations in the sense that they are 'simultaneous acts to be performed interchangeably' (*Palmer v Lark* [1945] Ch 182 at 184f). See also *Foran v Wight* (1989) 168 CLR 385 at 396 per Mason CJ.

8 Ante, p 179.

9 For a fuller account of completion, see D.G. Barnsley, [1991] Conv 15, 81, 185.

10 See *Sen v Headley* [1991] Ch 425 at 440G, where the Court of Appeal recorded its strong agreement with the general proposition that 'the policy of the law in regard to the formalities for the creation and transmission of interests in land should be upheld'.

a legal estate unless made by deed.'[11] There are a number of exceptions to this rule, the most important of which relate to assents by personal representatives,[12] leases which are expressly exempted by statute from the requirement of formality,[13] and surrenders and conveyances which take effect by operation of law.[14] The formality rules relating to deeds have recently been the subject of legislative reform with effect from 31 July 1990,[15] and a careful distinction must therefore be drawn between deeds executed prior to and following this date.

The essence of a deed is that it should be 'intended by the party who does it to be the most solemn indication to the community that he really means to do what he is doing.'[16] For centuries the validity of a deed in English law has rested on compliance with the requirement that the deed be signed, sealed and delivered. The force of these ancient conditions became less compelling under modern conditions and the Law of Property (Miscellaneous Provisions) Act 1989 has now significantly altered both the constitutive elements of a deed and the formalities required for its due execution.

(a) *The constitutive elements of a deed*

At common law a deed comprised a writing on paper, vellum or parchment which was sealed and delivered.[17] To these raw elements statute law was later to add a rudimentary requirement of signature, but the constitutive elements of the deed have been profoundly affected by the Law of Property (Miscellaneous Provisions) Act 1989. Since 31 July 1990 the validity of a deed requires that it be signed, attested and delivered.[18]

(i) Material form The Law of Property (Miscellaneous Provisions) Act 1989 has abolished, with effect from 31 July 1990, any rule of law which restricts

11 Except as specified in the exceptions to the general principle in Law of Property Act 1925, s 52, an oral conveyance of a legal estate confers no interest in the land (see *Palfrey v Palfrey* (1974) 229 Estates Gazette 1593 at 1595). A parol grant has merely the force and effect of an interest at will (Law of Property Act 1925, s 54(1)). On interests at will, see Chapter 17 (post, p 680).

12 Law of Property Act 1925, s 52(2)(a). In *Sen v Headley* [1991] Ch 425 at 441B, the Court of Appeal confirmed, to the surprise of many, that the doctrine of donatio mortis causa can apply to realty. It is therefore possible that title to land may be transferred by an informal oral gift made in contemplation of death and conditional upon death, where the donor has parted with dominion over the property (eg by putting the donee in possession of keys to a box containing the title deeds). See [1991] Ch 425 at 438G–439A; [1990] Conv 132 (H.B. Parry); [1991] Conv 307 (M. Halliwell). Compare, however, *Bayliss v Public Trustee* (1988) 12 NSWLR 540 at 544G; C.E.F. Rickett, [1989] Conv 184.

13 Law of Property Act 1925, s 52(2)(d) (post, p 736).

14 Law of Property Act 1925, s 52(2)(c), (g).

15 The Law of Property (Miscellaneous Provisions) Act 1989 (Commencement) Order 1990 (SI 1990/1175), para 2. For a highly critical appraisal of the 1989 Act, see G. Virgo and C. Harpum, [1991] Lloyd's Maritime and Commercial LQ 209.

16 *Manton v Parabolic Pty Ltd* [1985] 2 NSWLR 361 at 367F-G. See also *Monarch Petroleum NL v Citco Australia Petroleum Ltd* [1986] WAR 310 at 352 ('The Latin term for a deed is factum, a thing done').

17 See R.F. Norton, *A Treatise on Deeds* (2nd edn by R.J.A. Morrison and H.J. Goolden, London 1928), p 3.

18 See (1989) 105 LQR 553 (R.E. Annand).

the substances on which a deed may be written.[19] This change gives effect to the Law Commission's recommendation that a deed should involve a requirement of writing on some durable substance, although not necessarily paper or parchment.[20] This amendment opens up the possibility that future technological innovations will dramatically change the form in which the writing of a deed is contained. However, no instrument executed on or after 31 July 1990 can constitute a deed unless 'it makes it clear on its face that it is intended to be a deed by the person making it or, as the case may be, by the parties to it'.[1] The deed must, moreover, be 'validly executed as a deed' by such person or parties.[2]

(ii) Sealing It was always said at common law that 'no writing without a seal can be a deed.'[3] The importance attached to the seal was, of course, particularly appropriate in an age when the general illiteracy of the population meant that a personal seal provided the only reliable means of authenticating legal documents. Moreover, the requirement of the seal fulfilled not only an evidentiary function but also a cautionary function: the procedure of sealing gave the parties a valuable pause for reflection before the conclusion of an irreversible transaction at law.[4] It can even be said that the seal enjoyed a significant psychological impact on the minds of the relevant actors. The presence of the seal caused the deed to be 'surrounded with a magic aura'.[5] Conveyancing, magic and sorcery have never been wholly unconnected phenomena, as is made clear by the medieval ritual and symbolism which attended the 'feoffment with livery of seisin'.[6] It is an interesting feature of the social anthropology of land law that the talismanic[7] effect of a little red wafer could be thought apt to confer upon certain transactions a legal efficacy which they would not otherwise have possessed.[8]

19 Law of Property (Miscellaneous Provisions) Act 1989, s 1(1)(a).
20 Law Commission, *Deeds and Escrows* (Law Com No 163, 29 June 1987), para 2.3.
1 Law of Property (Miscellaneous Provisions) Act 1989, s 1(2)(a). The intention towards deed may be made evident by the instrument 'describing itself as a deed or expressing itself to be executed or signed as a deed or otherwise'.
2 Law of Property (Miscellaneous Provisions) Act 1989, s 1(2)(b).
3 *Sheppard's Touchstone of Common Assurances* (8th edn by E.G. Atherley, London 1826), p 56.
4 See Duncan Kennedy, *Form and Substance in Private Law Adjudication*, 89 Harv L Rev 1685 at 1691 (1975–76).
5 *Armor Coatings (Marketing) Pty Ltd v General Credits (Finance) Pty Ltd* (1978) 17 SASR 259 at 275 per Bray CJ. This perception probably underlies the ancient common law rule (see *Pigot's Case* (1614) 11 Co Rep 26b at 27a, 77 ER 1177 at 1178) that any alteration avoids a deed: '[a]nything which violated its integrity destroyed its mana' (*Armor Coatings* at 275). See also *Monarch Petroleum NL v Citco Australia Petroleum Ltd* [1986] WAR 310 at 362; *Warburton v National Westminster Finance Australia Ltd* (1988) 15 NSWLR 238 at 243B-C per Hope JA.
6 Ante, p 61. For an historical account of the ritual solemnity attendant on transfers of land, see *Manton v Parabolic Pty Ltd* [1985] 2 NSWLR 361 at 367A–368C.
7 See *Armor Coatings (Marketing) Pty Ltd v General Credits (Finance) Pty Ltd* (1978) 17 SASR 259 at 275 per Bray CJ, for reference to the 'archaic notion of the sacrosanct and talismanic effect of the seal of the obligor on the wax on the parchment of the deed.' See also F.E. Crane, *The Magic of the Private Seal*, 15 Col L Rev 24 (1915).
8 When used today the seal tends to be merely a mass-produced red adhesive paper disc which is attached to the bottom of the document concerned: the ceremony of sealing with the aid of sealing wax has almost entirely disappeared (see Law Com No 163 (1987), para 2.4).

In modern times it was perhaps inevitable that the archaic mystique of the seal should become the subject of critical scrutiny. As long ago as 1937 Goddard J observed that 'a seal nowadays is very much in the nature of a legal fiction'.[9] It is clear that personal signatures have now acquired a far greater practical significance than the seal in establishing documentary authenticity.[10] The sealing of a document can no longer serve as a sufficient signature,[11] and in recent years the courts came to relax, almost to the point of extinction, the legal requirements of the seal.[12] In 1971 Lord Wilberforce castigated the 'medieval doctrine of the seal' and expressed the hope that 'we might have got rid of that mumbo-jumbo and aligned ourselves with most civilised countries'.[13]

In 1987 long-standing criticism of the unreality of the seal led the Law Commission to confirm its view that the seal was nowadays 'a redundant formality without substantive purpose' and to recommend that a seal should no longer be a requirement of a deed.[14] In respect of deeds executed by an individual on or after 31 July 1990 this proposal has now been given statutory force by section 1(1)(b) of the Law of Property (Miscellaneous Provisions) Act 1989.[15]

(b) Formalities of due execution

Prior to 31 July 1990 the valid execution of a deed by an individual required signature[16] and delivery of the instrument. To these requirements has now been added a further formality of attestation.

(i) Signature Section 1(3)(a) of the Law of Property (Miscellaneous Provisions) Act 1989 imposes a requirement of signature as a condition of the valid execution by an individual of an instrument as his deed.[17] It is not, however,

9 Sixth Interim Report of the Law Revision Committee on *Statute of Frauds and the Doctrine of Consideration* (Cmd 5449, 1937), p 35.

10 See *Stromdale and Ball Ltd v Burden* [1952] Ch 223 at 230, where Danckwerts J pointed out that 'with the spread of education, the signature became of importance for the authentication of documents'.

11 See Law of Property Act 1925, s 73(1).

12 Such was the diminishing mystique of the seal that in *First National Securities Ltd v Jones* [1978] Ch 109 at 118E-F, 119H, 121A-B, the Court of Appeal held that the requirement of a deed was satisfied by a signed document on which was printed a circle containing the letters 'LS'—representing *locus sigilli* (the place of a seal). See also *Commercial Credit Services v Knowles* [1978] CLY 794. See D.C. Hoath, *The Sealing of Documents—Fact or Fiction?*, (1980) 43 MLR 415; but compare *Re Smith* (1892) 67 LT 64 at 66.

13 *Parliamentary Debates, House of Lords, Official Report* (1970–71), Vol 315, Col 1213 (25 February 1971).

14 See Law Commission, *Transfer of Land: Formalities for Deeds and Escrows* (Working Paper No 93, July 1985), para 8(2)(ii); Law Com No 163 (1987), para 2.4.

15 It may well be that, notwithstanding the 1989 Act, seals continue to be used in practice to dignify documents of transfer, not least because sealing appears to provide, for the purpose of Law of Property (Miscellaneous Provisions) Act 1989, s 1(2)(a), clear evidence of an intention that an instrument should constitute a deed (see [1990] Conv 1 (H.W.W.)). A corporation is deemed to have executed a deed if its seal is affixed to the document in the presence of, and is attested by, its clerk or secretary and a member of the board of directors or other governing body (Law of Property Act 1925, s 74(1)).

16 See Law of Property Act 1925, s 73(1).

17 For the purpose of signature it is sufficient if the individual makes his mark on the instrument (Law of Property (Miscellaneous Provisions) Act 1989, s 1(4)).

necessary that the signature should be in writing. It is enough—although it is not particularly desirable[18]—that the signature should take the form of an imprint by a rubber stamp with a facsimile signature or anything similar which clearly indicates an intention to authenticate the deed.[19]

(ii) Attestation Prior to 31 July 1990 attestation of the signature on a deed, although exceedingly common in practice, was not a formal requirement in the execution of the deed. A witnessing requirement has now been imposed, however, by the provisions of the Law of Property (Miscellaneous Provisions) Act 1989.[20] An instrument is validly executed as a deed by an individual only if it is signed by him 'in the presence of a witness who attests the signature'.[1] The absence of the alleged witness at the time of signature renders the instrument ineffective as a deed[2] and a false representation attesting to signature may constitute forgery.[3]

(iii) Delivery Although the idea of 'delivery' of a deed had its origin in some manual transfer of the relevant document, it has been clear since at least the 17th century that a deed may be 'delivered by words without any act of delivery'.[4] The essential element of a deed is that it constitutes 'the most solemn act that a person can perform with respect to a particular piece of property or other right'.[5] Delivery of a deed therefore comprises any unilateral act or statement by the grantor which signifies that he adopts the deed irrevocably as his own,[6] and a deed, once delivered, is binding on its maker without any act of exchange.[7]

In 1987 the Law Commission, although declaring the present law of delivery to be 'not entirely satisfactory', somewhat reluctantly declined to recommend its abolition.[8] In the Commission's view, delivery serves at least the purpose of fixing the date at which a deed takes effect,[9] and the requirement of delivery is thus retained in the modern law.[10]

18 See eg *Goodman v J. Eban Ltd* [1954] 1 QB 550 at 561f.

19 *Bennett v Brumfitt* (1867) LR 3 CP 28 at 30f; *LCC v Agricultural Food Products Ltd* [1955] 2 QB 218 at 223ff; *R v Brentford Justices, ex parte Catlin* [1975] QB 455 at 462E-F.

20 Attestation thus becomes obligatory in unregistered conveyancing, just as it is already in registered conveyancing (see Land Registration Rules 1925, r 98 and Schedule (Form 19)).

1 Law of Property (Miscellaneous Provisions) Act 1989, s 1(3)(a)(i). Alternatively the instrument may be signed at the direction of an individual and in his presence and the presence of two attesting witnesses (Law of Property (Miscellaneous Provisions) Act 1989, s 1(3)(a)(ii)). See [1990] Conv 321.

2 *Ellison v Vukicevic* (1986) 7 NSWLR 104 at 112D-G; *Farnham v Orrell* (1989) NSW ConvR 55-443 at 58,219;

3 See *R v Brott* [1988] VR 1 at 6ff, 14ff.

4 *Co Litt*, p 36a.

5 *Manton v Parabolic Pty Ltd* [1985] 2 NSWLR 361 at 369B-C.

6 *Xenos v Wickham* (1867) LR 2 HL 296 at 312 per Blackburn J; *Re Sammon* (1979) 94 DLR (3d) 594 at 597ff; *Monarch Petroleum NL v Citco Australia Petroleum Ltd* [1986] WAR 310 at 355. See also D.E.C. Yale, [1970] CLJ 52; D.N. Clarke, [1990] Conv 85.

7 *Vincent v Premo Enterprises (Voucher Sales) Ltd* [1969] 2 QB 609 at 619D-E. See also *Ansett Transport Industries (Operations) Pty Ltd v Comptroller of Stamps* [1985] VR 70 at 76.

8 Law Com No 163 (1987), paras 2.8ff.

9 Law Com No 163 (1987), para 2.8.

10 Law of Property (Miscellaneous Provisions) Act 1989, s 1(3)(b).

(2) Conveyancing practice

The conveyancing process is normally conducted by solicitors acting for the vendor and purchaser respectively. In their hands the process has tended to appear slow and costly.[11] The interaction of supply and demand in respect of legal services was for many years distorted by the fact that solicitors enjoyed a crude monopolistic privilege in conveyancing matters.[12] In recent years, however, pressure for the removal of this monopoly became irresistible both because of increasing public disquiet about the quality of legal services and because of the modern distaste for self-interested protectionism in professional life.[13] The Administration of Justice Act 1985 accordingly makes provision for 'licensed conveyancing' to be carried out by persons who are not qualified solicitors.[14] The 1985 Act legalises the delivery of conveyancing services by 'licensed conveyancers',[15] who are subject to professional controls administered by a Council for Licensed Conveyancers.[16] Ironically, it seems in practice that the bulk of conveyancing work is still carried out by solicitors.

(3) Equitable jurisdiction to set aside unconscionable bargains

The law of real property is not a branch of moral philosophy; it is generally concerned only with the attainment of procedural efficiency in the transfer of land and not with the achievement of justice in the distribution of goods. Once the derivation of the vendor's title is clarified beyond technical dispute, the law of conveyancing raises no question either as to the substantive fairness of the fact that the vendor has land to convey or even as to the fact that the purchaser is possessed of the money consideration required for the transfer of title. This ethical neutrality is a pervasive characteristic of a capitalist system of property which is dominated both by the solid tug of money and by the inevitable advantage enjoyed by the wealthy and privileged over the poor and weak. It could not be pretended that the law of property in its traditional common law manifestation sets out either to direct or to endorse any redistribution of goods between the rich and the poor.

In only one area does the law of property make any concession to a conception of fairness as a criterion of legality in the transfer of property. There has always been an equitable jurisdiction to set aside a transaction at a considerable undervalue which has been entered into by a 'poor and

11 See *In re Stone and Saville's Contract* [1962] 1 WLR 460 at 465, where Buckley J referred to the 'stately saraband which takes place between vendor and purchaser on a purchase of land'.

12 Section 22(1) of the Solicitors Act 1974 imposed criminal liability on any 'unqualified person' who receives any 'fee, gain or reward' for the purpose of drawing or preparing any instrument of transfer or charge or any other instrument relating to real or personal estate.

13 The Royal Commission on Legal Services, which reported in 1979, vigorously resisted the introduction of a 'free-for-all' in which any person might offer conveyancing services without restriction (see *Final Report of the Royal Commission on Legal Services* (Cmnd 7648, October 1979), Vol 1, para 21.60(e)). See now Solicitors Act 1974, s 22(3), as amended by Administration of Justice Act 1985, s 6(4).

14 Administration of Justice Act 1985, s 11ff.

15 Administration of Justice Act 1985, s 11(4).

16 Administration of Justice Act 1985, s 12.

ignorant' vendor acting without independent advice.[17] The persons who nowadays fall within the purview of this classical equitable formulation are those who, in contemporary idiom, comprise members of 'the lower income group' and who may be said to 'less highly educated'.[18] The court will exercise its equitable jurisdiction to relieve such vendors of the consequences of their dealings unless the purchaser discharges an onus of proof that the transaction in question was fair, just and reasonable.[19] This merciful jurisdiction is not, however, of wide application. It cannot be invoked merely because the vendor has entered into an improvident transaction.[20] The discretion to set aside unconscionable bargains is exercised only in exceptional circumstances. In *Hart v O'Connor*,[1] for instance, Lord Brightman distinguished between transactions which are marked by 'procedural unfairness' (as, for instance, where there is an element of undue influence) and those which are adversely affected by 'contractual imbalance'. In his view, equity cannot set aside a transaction as an unconscionable bargain where 'there was no victimisation, no taking advantage of another's weakness, and the sole allegation was contractual imbalance with no undertones of constructive fraud'.[2]

4. PRIORITY OF INTERESTS AFTER THE CONVEYANCE OF A LEGAL ESTATE

One of the central questions of land law relates to the effect which the transfer of a legal estate has upon pre-existing equitable rights in the land conveyed. This issue is addressed in detail at several points in this book, but it may be helpful to summarise here some of the relevant principles.

(1) Equitable interests in unregistered land

The outline of the 1925 legislation which was contained in Chapter 6 should have made it clear that for conveyancing purposes the field of equitable interests in unregistered or 'old system' land subdivides into three distinct categories.[3] Some of these equitable interests are 'commercial' interests which

17 *How v Weldon* (1754) 2 Ves Sen 516 at 518ff, 28 ER 330 at 331f; *Fry v Lane* (1888) 40 Ch D 312 at 322. See Lord Goff of Chieveley and Gareth Jones, *The Law of Restitution* (3rd edn, London 1986), p 257ff. See also M. Cope, (1983) 57 ALJ 279; *Chrispen v Topham* (1986) 28 DLR (4th) 754 at 758f.

18 *Cresswell v Potter* (1968) [1978] 1 WLR 255 (Note) at 257F-H per Megarry J. See also *Watkin v Watson-Smith* (1986) *Times*, 3 July.

19 *Wood v Abrey* (1818) 3 Madd 417 at 423f, 56 ER 558 at 560f; *Fry v Lane* (1888) 40 Ch D 312 at 322; *Hart v O'Connor* [1985] AC 1000 at 1024B-C; *Commercial Bank of Australia Ltd v Amadio* (1983) 151 CLR 447.

20 See *Mountford v Scott* [1975] Ch 258 at 264E.

1 [1985] AC 1000 at 1017H–1018C.

2 [1985] AC 1000 at 1024D. Compare, however, the broader and arguably more humane jurisdiction exercised in Australia (*Commercial Bank of Australia Ltd v Amadio* (1983) 151 CLR 447 at 474) and New Zealand (see *Nichols v Jessup* [1986] 1 NZLR 226 at 234f), where primary emphasis is placed upon the objectively unconscionable character of 'the conduct of the stronger party in attempting to enforce, or retain the benefit of, a dealing with a person under a special disability in circumstances where it is not consistent with equity or good conscience that he should do so.'

3 Ante, p 110.

are registrable in the Land Charges Register. Others comprise 'family' interests which are statutorily overreachable on a conveyance of the land and which take effect thereafter in proceeds of sale. In a twilight zone beyond these major categories of registrable and overreachable interests there lies a third (and ultimately residual) category of equitable rights in unregistered land. Since such rights are neither registrable nor statutorily overreached, their effect on a purchaser of land falls to be determined by the equitable doctrine of notice in its traditional formulation.[4]

The interests which fall into this third category are relatively few in number, but, being anomalous, they present problems in unregistered conveyancing disproportional to their prevalence. They provide the epicentre of many a minor earthquake amidst some of the more difficult terrain of land law.[5] Collectively they constitute the nightmare of the conveyancer in that they comprise unregistrable, non-overreachable and sometimes virtually undiscoverable equitable interests which may yet bind the purchaser on a basis of constructive notice. However, the threefold division of the field of equitable interests makes it possible to adopt a schematic approach to the resolution of problems of priority wherever the owner of an equitable interest in unregistered land is confronted by a purchaser of a legal estate in that land. Such questions of priority can always be answered by asking the following questions.

(a) Could the owner of the equitable interest have protected himself against the purchaser by means of a land charge registration?

If the owner of the equitable interest had rights which were capable of registration as a land charge, then

(i) if these rights were duly registered they now bind the purchaser[6];

(ii) if these rights were not duly registered they become, for want of registration, void against most categories of purchaser—even though the purchaser may have had actual knowledge of the rights at the date of his purchase.[7]

If, however, the equitable interest in question was not registrable and does not therefore become void for non-registration, then a second question must be raised:

(b) Was the equitable interest statutorily overreached by the purchaser?

The transactions in land which attract the consequence of a statutory overreaching are detailed in section 2(1) of the Law of Property Act 1925.

4 See eg *Shiloh Spinners Ltd v Harding* [1973] AC 691 at 721D, where Lord Wilberforce declared himself prepared to accept that 'there may well be rights, of an equitable character, outside the provisions as to registration and which are incapable of being overreached.'

5 See eg *E.R. Ives Investment Ltd v High* [1967] 2 QB 379 (ante, p 152).

6 Law of Property Act 1925, s 198(1) (ante, p 118).

7 Land Charges Act 1972, s 4 (ante, p 119). See *Midland Bank Trust Co Ltd v Green* [1981] AC 513. Of course unprotected land charges are not universally void for reasons of non-registration. An unregistered estate contract remains valid, for instance, against a purchaser of an *equitable* interest in the land (see Land Charges Act 1972, s 4(6); *McCarthy and Stone Ltd v Hodge* [1971] 1 WLR 1547 at 1555D-E).

Such transactions comprise any 'conveyance'[8] to a purchaser of a legal estate in land which is effected (i) under the powers conferred by the Settled Land Act 1925, (ii) by trustees for sale, (iii) by a mortgagee or personal representative in the exercise of his paramount powers, or (iv) under an order of the court. It is clear that certain kinds of disposition of a legal estate in land (eg a conveyance by a bare trustee[9]) inherently lack any statutory overreaching capacity, for the purely artificial reason that they are not included within the statutory list of transactions which are detailed as having overreaching power. If, however, a particular equitable interest is in principle overreachable within the terms of section 2(1) of the Law of Property Act 1925, then

(i) if there was a compliance with the statutory preconditions for overreaching,[10] the equitable interest is overreached by force of statute and is henceforth satisfied out of the proceeds of the disposition;
(ii) if there was no compliance with the statutory preconditions for overreaching, the purchaser cannot properly claim that he has overreached (or taken title free of) the equitable interest.

If for any reason the equitable interest is not overreached—either because it is inherently non-overreachable or because the statutory conditions were not fulfilled—the issue of priority must turn on the answer given to the final question.

(c) Was the purchaser a bona fide purchaser of a legal estate for value without notice?

The question of priority is ultimately determined by an application of the traditional doctrine of notice:

(i) if the purchaser ranks as 'Equity's Darling', he takes the legal estate free of the equitable interest;
(ii) if the purchaser was not a bona fide purchaser of a legal estate for value without notice, he is bound by the equitable interest.

Before 1926 this application of the equitable doctrine of notice would have provided the complete answer to any question of priority arising between the owner of an equitable interest and the purchaser of a legal estate in unregistered land. But since 1925 the doctrine of notice has been overlaid by the two devices of land charge registration and statutory overreaching, thus necessitating questions (a) and (b) in advance of question (c). In effect the registration of land charges renders notice inescapable; the process of statutory overreaching renders notice irrelevant. Taken in conjunction questions (a), (b) and (c) must inevitably disclose the fate of any equitable interest in unregistered land where a legal estate is purchased by a third party. The entire field of equitable interests may thus be divided into three major categories which simply serve to exhaust all the logical possibilities affecting the issue of priority between equitable owner and purchaser. The set of *equitable interests in unregistered land* can therefore be represented in terms

8 A 'conveyance' is defined for the purpose of the Law of Property Act 1925 as including a mortgage, charge and lease of property (see Law of Property Act 1925, s 205(1)(ii)).
9 Ante, p 102. See eg *Hodgson v Marks* [1971] Ch 892 (post, p 216).
10 See eg Law of Property Act 1925, s 27(2) (ante, p 102; post, p 552).

of three sub-sets, to each of which one of the interrogatories (a) to (c) is appropriate.

SUB-SET 1	SUB-SET 2	SUB-SET 3
'COMMERCIAL' EQUITABLE INTERESTS	'FAMILY' EQUITABLE INTERESTS	UNREGISTRABLE NON-OVERREACHABLE INTERESTS
(protected by land charge registration)	(protected by effects of overreaching)	(protected by doctrine of notice)

QUESTION (a) QUESTION (b) QUESTION (c)

Fig. 20

(2) Equitable interests in registered land

In relation to registered land it is possible, in the current state of the law, to adopt a two-fold formula in the resolution of the equivalent issues of priority raised between the owners of equitable interests and a transferee of the legal title. The problem of priority can be determined by asking just two questions:

(a) Did the owner of the equitable interest have any interest capable of entry on the register as a minor interest?

If the answer to this question is in the affirmative and the right in question was duly entered as a minor interest, this entry of course prevails against the transferee.[11] If the right has not been so protected, there is some—albeit dubious—authority for the view that an unprotected minor interest is binding on a transferee who has actual knowledge of the existence of the right.[12] However, the better view is that (apart from cases of fraud) the transferee is unaffected by an unprotected minor interest 'whether he has or has not notice thereof, express, implied or constructive'.[13] If, on this view, a minor interest thus becomes ineffective as a minor interest, a further question must be posed.

(b) Can the owner of the equitable interest nevertheless claim any kind of overriding interest?

If the answer to this second question is in the affirmative, then even an

11 Land Registration Act 1925, s 20(1).
12 *Peffer v Rigg* [1977] 1 WLR 285 (ante, p 190).
13 Land Registration Act 1925, s 59(6).

unprotected minor interest may be saved as an overriding interest and may therefore be binding on the transferee of the registered title. The statutory protection afforded overriding interests may be available, for instance, on the ground that the owner of the equitable interest was at the effective date of transfer 'in actual occupation' of the land or 'in receipt of the rents and profits' thereof.[14]

The result is that the owner of an equitable interest in registered land may effectively have 'two bites at the cherry' in his claim for priority over the transferee of the registered title. He may, in some circumstances, be able to argue either that he has duly protected his interest by register entry or, in default of securing such protection, that his interest gave rise to an overriding interest which is binding on the transferee. This duplication of protection has in recent years raised profound difficulties in the conveyancing of registered titles,[15] but may become slightly less extensive if legislative effect is given to the reform proposals made by the Law Commission.[16]

14 Land Registration Act 1925, s 70(1)(g).
15 Ante, p 226; post, p 572.
16 Ante, p 239.

CHAPTER 10

Adverse possession

Almost all systems of law concede that uncontested long possession of land must ultimately confer a valid title upon the actual occupier irrespective of the formal or documentary record of ownership. Were it not so, every transfer of real property would be jeopardised by the encroachment of ancient or increasingly stale claims in derogation of the transferor's rights. Every grantor of land would be required to trace his title back to the Garden of Eden; and every 'landowner' would live under the perpetual shadow of apprehended repossession at the behest of some earlier and more meritorious claimant of title. Quite apart from the negative impact of such horrendous burdens on the process of land transfer, the connection between property and prolonged user is, as Oliver Wendell Holmes once said, 'in the nature of man's mind'.[1] In Holmes' terms, '[a] thing which you have enjoyed and used as your own for a long time. . .takes root in your being and cannot be torn away without your resenting the act and trying to defend yourself, however you came by it.' If it is complained that retention by the long possessor causes disappointment to the former owner, the inevitable response makes reference to 'his neglect having allowed the gradual dissociation between himself and what he claims, and the gradual association of it with another.'

In English law the merits of title by long possession are recognised in the body of rules which relate to 'adverse possession'. By pressing to its limit the essential relativity of title in English law,[2] the law of adverse possession effectively upholds the land rights of certain persons who have no formal ownership. The acquisition of rights by adverse possession operates in conjunction with the Limitation Act and differs markedly from any form of acquisition by conveyance or transfer. Its central feature is the idea that if the owner of property fails within a certain period to secure the eviction of a squatter or trespasser from his land, his own title is extinguished and he is thereafter statutorily barred from recovering possession of the land. Title to land being basically relative, the intruder thus acquires—as an indirect effect of the Limitation Act—a title which legitimises his continuing possession.[3]

Acquisition through adverse possession is thus founded on some notion of title by successful taking and reflects one of the oldest, yet also most

1 *The Path of the Law*, 10 Harv L Rev 457 at 477 (1897).

2 Ante, p 62.

3 Post, p 288. It has been rightly said that the law of adverse possession constitutes 'a massive common law gloss upon the basic statute' of limitations (see R.A. Epstein, *Past and Future: The Temporal Dimension in the Law of Property*, 64 Wash ULQ 667 at 680 (1986)).

imprecise and perplexing, aspects of the concept of property. The rules of adverse possession confirm that possession and title are by no means discrete concepts.[4] Possession is the root of title.[5] Possession of land serves as prima facie evidence of seisin in fee and seisin 'gives ownership good against everyone except a person who has a better, because older, title'.[6] However, where the assertion of all older titles is statute-barred, the current possessor's title becomes, for all practical purposes, an unchallengeable title to the land.

In this way the law of adverse possession ultimately causes land titles to conform to the lived boundaries—rather than the reverse—but in so doing seems to present one of the larger paradoxes of the law of property. It is plain that the application of rules of adverse possession is capable of effecting fundamental and wholly uncompensated shifts of ownership. Indeed title by adverse possession may well appear to connote 'title by theft or robbery, a primitive method of acquiring land without paying for it.'[7] Wrongful taking generates rightful title—a consequence all the more improbable because it represents a principle little adhered to in the law of personal property.[8] Seen from this perspective, the doctrine of adverse possession affords 'an anomalous instance of maturing a wrong into a right contrary to one of the most fundamental axioms of the law.'[9] Land claims, however unmeritorious, come in time to enjoy a certain self-righting quality.

1. THE RATIONALE OF ACQUISITION BY ADVERSE POSSESSION

The law of adverse possession doubtless gives effect to some pragmatic expectation, born in the more physical climate of earlier times, that a property owner will rise with rugged fortitude to assert his title against unlawful intruders. The Limitation Act thereby reflects a policy that 'those who go to sleep upon their claims should not be assisted by the courts in recovering their property'.[10] An equally potent element of policy underlying the Act is the idea that 'there shall be an end of litigation'.[11] From the earliest origins of the 'seisin-possession' concept in the common law, there has been a large social interest in 'the quieting of possession'.[12] As Lord St Leonards

4 See *Bl Comm*, vol II, p 8.
5 See *Mabo v Queensland* (1992) 107 ALR 1 at 162 per Toohey J.
6 *Newington* v *Windeyer* (1985) 3 NSWLR 555 at 563E-F per McHugh JA. See also *Peaceable d Uncle v Watson* (1811) 4 Taunt 16 at 17, 128 ER 232; *Mabo v Queensland* (1992) 107 ALR 1 at 161ff per Toohey J; C. M. Rose, *Possession as the Origin of Property*, 52 U Chi L Rev 73 (1985–86).
7 H.W. Ballantine, *Title by Adverse Possession*, 32 Harv L Rev 135 (1918–19).
8 See P. Gerstenblith, *The Adverse Possession of Personal Property*, 37 Buffalo L Rev 119 (1988–89).
9 H.W. Ballantine, 32 Harv L Rev 135 (1918–19).
10 *R.B. Policies at Lloyd's v Butler* [1950] 1 KB 76 at 81.
11 Ibid.
12 See *A'Court v Cross* (1825) 3 Bing 329 at 332f, 130 ER 540 at 541, where Best CJ pointed out that a Statute of Limitation is 'an act of peace. Long dormant claims have often more of cruelty than of justice in them'.

observed as long ago as 1852,[13] all limitation statutes are intended to prevent the 'rearing up of claims at great distances of time when evidences are lost'.[14]

(1) Varied contexts of adverse possession

Thus it has come about that the modern Limitation Act (the Limitation Act 1980) is in part directed towards extinguishing titles which have not been vindicated within the period specified by statute.[15] Yet the function of the law of adverse possession may, in reality, be more sophisticated and diverse than is suggested by the popular paradigm of the aggressive intruder whose wrongful taking of land is eventually validated by long possession. Many of the subtle difficulties and uncertainties inherent in adverse possession flow directly from overdue concentration on the crudely limited model of the self-interested 'squatter' who seizes the land of another. The typology of adverse possession is more richly varied, and it may well be that consciously wrongful seizure of land constitutes nowadays the least common form of long possession. Adverse possession rules are rather more frequently invoked to resolve ownership disputes which originate either in relatively innocent circumstances of entry under colour of title or in defective conveyancing practice. Statistically the more significant adverse possessor is one who claims that a minute sliver of land formally titled in his neighbour has been inaccurately fenced in his own favour or has been the subject of a mistaken 'double conveyance' to himself.[16] As every conveyancer is fully aware, the principle of adverse possession provides the ultimate cure or longstop remedy for defectively drawn ground plans which erroneously enclose a small portion of a neighbour's land within the claimant's boundary lines.[17] The areas of land involved in contemporary claims of long possession are rarely large tracts of uncharted wilderness but more commonly comprise a tiny slice of realty abstracted by mistake from the tenement of a neighbour.

Whatever the context of adverse possession, there are persuasive policy grounds for endorsing the principle of limitation.[18] It is widely accepted that 'certainty of title to land is a social need and occupation of land which

13 *Dundee Harbour Trustees v Dougall* (1852) 1 Macq 317 at 321.

14 The first statute of limitation was the Limitation Act 1623. The current statute, the Limitation Act 1980, came into force on 1 May 1981.

15 See *Giouroukos v Cadillac Fairview Corp Ltd* (1984) 3 DLR (4th) 595 at 604, where the Ontario Court of Appeal attributed the law of adverse possession to the 'traditional notion that it is more important that long and undisturbed possession of land be protected, even if initially wrongful, than that the law should lend its aid to the enforcement of stale claims.'

16 See eg *Bridges v Mees* [1957] Ch 475 (ante, p 202).

17 See *Belotti v Bickhardt*, 127 NE 239 at 243f (1920); *Kohua Pty Ltd v Tai Ping Trading Pty Ltd* (1985) 3 BPR 9705 at 9707. For an even more bizarre application of adverse possession, see *DeRocco v Young* (1981) 120 DLR (3d) 169 at 173, where a convicted murderer was held to be capable (after his release from prison) of acquiring a title by long possession of his victim's land, even though he was barred by public policy from claiming any interest in the victim's land by way of the beneficial interest which had been left to him in her will (ante, post, p 504).

18 See M. Dockray, *Why Do We Need Adverse Possession?* [1985] Conv 272; M.J. Radin, *Time, Possession, and Alienation*, 64 Wash ULQ 739 at 742ff (1986).

has long been unchallenged should not be disturbed.'[19] The stabilisation of title procured through the law of adverse possession confers advantage, of course, not only upon the adverse possessor himself but also upon third parties (eg purchasers, tenants and mortgagees) who deal with him in reliance on the expectations engendered by his long possession.[20] The relatively strict application of a limitation period thus operates as an important check upon immense social and legal costs which would otherwise be incurred in endless litigation over matters of title. The law of adverse possession also tends to reward, at the expense of the sluggard, the purposeful labourer who makes constructive use of available land resources.[1] Contrary to initial fears that the acquisition of title by long possession approximates to legalised theft,[2] there may be great countervailing merit in ensuring that de facto possession never diverges too markedly from de iure title.[3]

(2) Comparison with prescription

In many instances the law of adverse possession effects a shift of freehold ownership of land similar to the way in which long user of land generates the prescriptive acquisition of easements and profits *à prendre*.[4] However, one marked difference between limitation and prescription is that prescription is based upon a fiction of grant in respect of long used rights, whereas adverse possession, far from being founded on some fictional grant, operates by extinguishing prior titles.[5] Moreover, prescriptive acquisition occurs only through a user 'as of right',[6] while it has been said, quite aptly, that adverse possession under the Limitation Act is based upon 'possession as of wrong'.[7] Again, with prescription the intention of the putative grantor of rights is decisive, whereas in the context of limitation it is the intention of the adverse possessor which is profoundly significant.[8] Indeed in *Buckinghamshire CC v Moran*[9] the Court of Appeal went to some lengths to stress that in the law of adverse possession the intention of the paper owner is, in virtually every instance, 'irrelevant in practice'.

19 See Law Reform Committee, *Report on Acquisition of Easements and Profits by Prescription* (14th Report, Cmnd 3100, 1966), para 36.

20 See J.W. Singer, *The Reliance Interest in Property*, 40 Stanford L Rev 611 at 665ff (1987–88).

1 See C. M. Rose, *Possession as the Origin of Property*, 52 U Chi L Rev 73 at 81 (1985-86). The law of limitation also provides the ultimate resolution of the 'mistaken improvement' problem exposed in cases like *Pull v Barnes*, 350 P 828 (1960) (mountain cabin built on another's land). See R.J. Sutton, *What should be done for mistaken improvers?*, in P.D. Finn (ed), *Essays on Restitution* (Sydney 1990), p 245.

2 Indeed courts often go to some lengths to emphasise that the Limitation Act should not be allowed to conduce to the benefit of the dishonest or the opportunistic. As Middleton J observed in *Campeau v May* (1911) 19 OWR 751 at 752, there is 'nothing in the policy of the law which demands that it should be made easy to steal land or any hardship which requires an exception to the general rule that the way of the transgressor is hard.' See also *Giouroukos v Cadillac Fairview Corp Ltd* (1984) 3 DLR (4th) 595 at 616 per Robins JA.

3 See M. Goodman, (1970) 33 MLR 281 at 282f.

4 Post, p 1106.

5 *Buckinghamshire CC v Moran* [1990] Ch 623 at 644B-C per Nourse LJ.

6 Post, p 1108.

7 *Buckinghamshire CC v Moran* [1990] Ch 623 at 644D per Nourse LJ. See also *Bladder v Phillips* [1991] EGCS 109 per Mustill LJ.

8 *Buckinghamshire CC v Moran* [1990] Ch 623 at 644D per Nourse LJ.

9 [1990] Ch 623 at 645A per Nourse LJ.

2. THE OPERATION OF THE LIMITATION ACT 1980

The broad principle underlying the law of adverse possession is the rule that no action may be brought for the recovery of land after the expiration of a statutorily prescribed period of time running from the date when the right of action first accrued.[10] The period prescribed differs according to the nature of the particular action, but at the termination of the appropriate period the action for recovery becomes statute-barred.[11]

(1) **The period of limitation**

The Limitation Act 1980 lays down as a general rule that '[n]o action shall be brought by any person to recover any land after the expiration of twelve years from the date on which the right of action accrued to him'.[12] In respect of actions for recovery brought by the Crown the relevant limitation period is 30 years and, in respect of actions brought by the Crown to recover foreshore, is 60 years.[13]

(a) Accrual of the right of action

In order that a right of action should accrue, thereby causing the period of limitation to begin to run, the land concerned must be 'in the possession of some person in whose favour the period of limitation can run'.[14] The possession here referred to is commonly known as 'adverse possession'. Thus the limitation period begins to run from the date of the owner's dispossession by an adverse possessor[15] or from the date of the inception of adverse possession by a third party following a 'discontinuance' of possession by the original owner.[16]

(b) Aggregation of periods of adverse possession

The limitation period prescribed by statute may be established by a series

10 If proceedings are begun before the expiration of the limitation period, the right of action is unaffected by the subsequent expiration of the period while proceedings remain pending. Moreover, if a judgment for possession is obtained in an action begun in due time, the successful plaintiff has 12 years from the date of judgment in which to enforce the judgment (see *B.P. Properties Ltd v Buckler* (1988) 55 P & CR 337 at 344f).

11 For reference to a 'tenuous if picturesque' form of adverse possession, see A.R. Everton, *Built in a Night...* (1971) 35 Conv (NS) 249. See also (1972) 36 Conv (NS) 241, (1975) 39 Conv (NS) 427.

12 Limitation Act 1980, s 15(1). The generally shorter limitation periods currently in force in many parts of the United States and particularly in the American West (ranging often from six to ten years) have been attributed by some to different cultural perceptions of the length of time required to generate the relevant attachment to land. See M.J. Radin, 64 Wash ULQ 739 at 749 (1986).

13 Limitation Act 1980, Sch 1, paras 10, 11. Other provisions in the Limitation Act 1980 deal specifically with the accrual of rights of action in relation to future interests, settled land and land held on trust for sale (Limitation Act 1980, s 18, Sch 1, para 4).

14 Limitation Act 1980, Sch 1, para 8(1). Adverse possession cannot be claimed by any person who is not legally competent to hold title (eg an unincorporated association of persons). See *Afton Band of Indians v Attorney-General of Nova Scotia* (1978) 85 DLR (3d) 454 at 463ff.

15 Limitation Act 1980, Sch 1, para 1.

16 Limitation Act 1980, Sch 1, para 8(1).

of adverse possessors of land. In other words, if X (the original 'paper owner') is dispossessed of his land by A who, in his turn, is dispossessed by (or transfers his rights to) B, B may claim the period of A's adverse possession as if it were his own in defence to any action for recovery brought by X, provided that the two periods together total at least 12 years.[17] B is, however, vulnerable to any action for recovery which is brought against him by A before B's independent period of adverse possession has prevailed for at least 12 years.[18]

The adverse possession of successive trespassers can operate cumulatively to extinguish an existing title only if the periods of adverse possession are continuous. If A abandons his adverse possession within the limitation period and, after an interval, B begins adversely to possess, B cannot add to his possession the period of adverse possession earlier established by A.[19] The break in adverse possession will have restored the true owner's title to its pristine force, and the statutory limitation period starts afresh from the inception of B's possession.[20]

(2) **Special rules in respect of tenancies**

Special rules govern adverse claims in respect of land which is the subject of a term of years. No tenant can claim adverse possession against his landlord during the currency of his tenancy, not least because the tenant is estopped from denying his landlord's title.[1] The possession of a tenant cannot be considered adverse until the period covered by the last payment of rent has expired.[2]

(a) Dispossession of a tenant by a squatter

A party who seeks to acquire a possessory title to leasehold land must prove adverse possession for the requisite period of time against both the tenant and the landlord. The tenant's leasehold interest and the landlord's freehold interest must both be extinguished before an absolute possessory title can be successfully established. Thus where a tenant is dispossessed during the currency of his lease, the intruder's adverse possession begins to be effective immediately as against the tenant,[3] but the statutory limitation period does not begin to run as against the landlord until the expiry date of the lease.[4]

17 Limitation Act 1980, s 15(1). See *Willis v Earl Howe* [1893] 2 Ch 545 at 553f; *Mount Carmel Investments Ltd v Peter Thurlow Ltd* [1988] 1 WLR 1078 at 1087G–1088B; *Salter v Clark* (1904) 4 SR (NSW) 280 at 288; *Mulcahy v Curramore Pty Ltd* [1974] 2 NSWLR 464 at 476D-E.

18 See *Mount Carmel Investments Ltd v Peter Thurlow Ltd* [1988] 1 WLR 1078 at 1086E per Nicholls LJ; [1988] Conv 359 (J.E.M.).

19 Limitation Act 1980, Sch 1, para 8(2).

20 *Willis v Earl Howe* [1893] 2 Ch 545 at 554; *Mulcahy v Curramore Pty Ltd* [1974] 2 NSWLR 464 at 476E.

1 Post, p 762. See also *Shillabeer v Diebel* (1980) 100 DLR (3d) 279 at 283.

2 See *Hayward v Chaloner* [1968] 1 QB 107 at 122C-D per Russell LJ.

3 *Perry v Woodfarm Homes Ltd* [1975] IR 104 at 130.

4 Limitation Act 1980, Sch 1, para 4. For precisely this reason it has been suggested that a freeholder can acquire 'bulletproof' protection against the encroachments of adverse possessors by the simple device of granting leases of long duration (eg 999 years). See R.A. Epstein, 64 Wash ULQ 793 at 838f (1986). See also *Perry v Woodfarm Homes Ltd* [1975] IR 104 at 120; *Gioukouros v Cadillac Fairview Corp Ltd* (1984) 3 DLR (4th) 595 at 605.

Until then the landlord's freehold interest remains unaffected,[5] for it is only with the determination of the tenancy that the landlord becomes entitled to resume possession and it is only then that his independent right of action can be said to have accrued.[6] For this purpose a tenancy (otherwise than in writing) from year to year or for any other period is normally treated as being determined at the expiration of the first year or other period.[7] However, where any rent has subsequently been received in respect of such a tenancy, the right of action is treated as having accrued on the date of the last receipt of rent.[8]

(b) Surrender of a dispossessed tenant's term

Some difficulty has arisen over the question whether a dispossessed tenant can effectively surrender to his landlord a leasehold term which, from the tenant's viewpoint, has already become statute-barred against the squatter. Such a manoeuvre may be attempted in the hope of accelerating the landlord's right to possession. On the assumption that the land concerned was unregistered, the House of Lords held by a majority in *St Marylebone Property Co Ltd v Fairweather*[9] that the landlord is entitled in these circumstances to recover possession from the squatter, on the ground that the latter's possession defeated only the rights of the tenant and not the superior title of the landlord. However, this reasoning is inherently vulnerable to the objection that a tenant who has lost all his title to a leasehold estate is in no position to deal effectively with that estate, having nothing which he can either surrender or assign.[10] The highly suspect analogy of *St Marylebone Property Co Ltd v Fairweather* has been resisted in the context of registered land, where it is clear that in equivalent circumstances the squatter is entitled, after 12 years' adverse possession, to be registered as proprietor of the land.[11] Thereafter any purported surrender by the tenant is entirely ineffective to merge any leasehold interest with the landlord's superior title.[12]

(3) The extinctive effect of the Limitation Act

The operation of the Limitation Act 1980 is essentially negative in nature. The effluxion of the limitation period does not create a title in the adverse

5 *Taylor v Twinberrow* [1930] All ER Rep 342 at 344E per Scrutton LJ; *St Marylebone Property Co Ltd v Fairweather* [1963] AC 510 at 536 per Lord Radcliffe.
6 *Tichborne v Weir* (1892) 67 LT 735 at 737; *St Marylebone Property Co Ltd v Fairweather* [1963] AC 510 at 537 per Lord Radcliffe, 544, 548 per Lord Denning, 553f per Lord Morris of Borth-y-Gest. See also *Gioukouros v Cadillac Fairview Corp Ltd* (1984) 3 DLR (4th) 595 at 605ff, 609.
7 Limitation Act 1980, Sch 1, para 5(1). See *Palfrey v Palfrey* (1974) 229 Estates Gazette 1593 at 1595.
8 Limitation Act 1980, Sch 1, para 5(2).
9 [1963] AC 510 at 540ff, 548. See (1962) 78 LQR 541 (H.W.R. Wade).
10 See eg *Perry v Woodfarm Homes Ltd* [1975] IR 104 at 114, 119, 130f.
11 Land Registration Act 1925, s 75 (post, p 289).
12 *Spectrum Investment Co v Holmes* [1981] 1 WLR 221 at 230E–231C. See (1981) 32 NILQ 254 (H. Wallace); [1981] Conv 157 (C. Sydenham); [1982] Conv 201 (P.H. Kenny). The same result would follow in registered land even if the squatter did not apply to be registered as proprietor, since his possessory rights ought in any event to comprise an overriding interest pursuant to Land Registration Act 1925, s 70(1)(f) (ante, p 202).

possessor, but has the effect of extinguishing the former title of the paper owner.[13] Under section 17 of the Limitation Act 1980, the paper owner's right of action to recover his land and the title on which that right is based are alike terminated on the expiry of the limitation period.[14]

(a) Relativity of title

In English law title to land is always relative,[15] land titles being secure only if and to the extent that no other person can assert a better claim. This produces the consequence that if the paper owner whose title has been extinguished was himself a fee simple owner, the successful adverse possessor acquires a title in fee simple which is unimpeachable. Nobody can now claim a better title than the adverse possessor, since the only person who could have challenged him is now statute-barred from proceeding with any action for recovery of the land.[16]

(i) Unregistered land In unregistered land, although the adverse possessor is effectively entitled to a legal estate in fee simple absolute,[17] his long possession for 12 years does not in itself operate any *transfer* of title from the paper owner. The Limitation Act does not effect a parliamentary conveyance of the land concerned,[18] this possibility being ruled out precisely because the paper owner's title has been completely extinguished by the operation of the statute. However, when the extinguishing effect of the Limitation Act is placed in conjunction with the positive effect of adverse possession, the indirect consequence is that the adverse possessor is enabled to claim a new title of his own.

(ii) Registered land In the case of registered land, so long as the paper owner remains registered as the relevant proprietor in the Land Register, it cannot be quite true to say that his title has been extinguished by the operation of the Limitation Act. However, the Land Registration Act 1925 provides that where, if the land in question were not registered, the estate of the existing registered proprietor would have been extinguished, his estate in registered land shall be 'deemed to be held by the proprietor for the time being in trust for the person who, by virtue of the [Limitation] Acts, has acquired title against any proprietor'.[19] Moreover, the adverse possessor of

13 The effect of the Limitation Act is to extinguish the true owner's title, rather than merely to render his right of re-entry unenforceable (see *Mulcahy v Curramore Pty Ltd* [1974] 2 NSWLR 464 at 476A).

14 The extinguishment of the paper owner's title to the land also extinguishes any claim on his behalf to recover rent or mesne profits in respect of the land during the period of adverse possession. See *In re Jolly* [1900] 2 Ch 616 at 617f; *Mount Carmel Investments Ltd v Peter Thurlow Ltd* [1988] 1 WLR 1078 at 1089A-B; [1988] Conv 359 (J.E.M.).

15 Ante, p 62.

16 '[T]he squatter's title becomes impregnable, giving him a title superior to all others' (*Buckinghamshire CC v Moran* [1990] Ch 623 at 644C per Nourse LJ).

17 Post, p 291.

18 *Tichborne v Weir* (1892) 67 LT 735 at 736f. See also *St Marylebone Property Co Ltd v Fairweather* [1963] AC 510 at 535; *Perry v Woodfarm Homes Ltd* [1975] IR 104 at 122f.

19 Land Registration Act 1925, s 75(1).

registered land may apply to be registered as proprietor of that land,[20] and in the meantime his rights are regarded as an 'overriding interest' with reference to that land.[1]

(b) Rights of third parties

Precisely because there has been no transfer or assignment of title by the paper owner to the adverse possessor, the latter is not affected by certain rules of land law which impinge upon a transferee or assignee. Thus, for instance, a squatter (even after 12 years of adverse possession) cannot claim to take title free of equitable interests binding the land, because he can never establish status as a bona fide *purchaser* without notice. He has not *purchased* the land, but has instead taken title by operation of law. In this case equitable interests such as restrictive covenants will be binding upon him,[2] and this will be so regardless of whether these interests have been duly registered or protected by the incumbrancer.[3]

Where the land occupied by an adverse possessor was the subject of a lease, the squatter cannot be sued directly for rent or damages by the landlord on the ground of a breach of leasehold covenants. The squatter is not an *assignee* of any term of years and is therefore not covered by the doctrine of 'privity of estate'.[4] However, even if he is not strictly liable to observe the covenants of the lease, the adverse occupier is still vulnerable to the landlord's exercise of a right of re-entry contained in that lease in the event of non-performance of the covenants. The squatter is thus liable to suffer forfeiture and, moreover, is entirely unable to claim any right to relief against such forfeiture.[5]

(4) Inchoate rights of the squatter

An important consequence of the principle of relativity of title is the fact that, even before his possessory title has been completed, the adverse possessor acquires certain inchoate rights in the land occupied by him.

(a) Nature of the squatter's rights

Even before the paper owner becomes statute-barred from recovery, the squatter acquires incipient rights in the land which are good against all the world except those persons who (like the paper owner) are meanwhile

20 Land Registration Act 1925, s 75(2).
1 Land Registration Act 1925, s 70(1)(f) (ante, p 202).
2 *In re Nisbet and Potts' Contract* [1906] 1 Ch 386 at 402ff. See F.W. Maitland, *Equity* (2nd edn, London 1936), p 116.
3 Ante, p 79.
4 *Tichborne v Weir* (1892) 67 LT 735 at 737f (ante, p 289); *St Marylebone Property Co Ltd v Fairweather* [1963] AC 510 at 535; *Perry v Woodfarm Homes Ltd* [1975] IR 104 at 120; *Giouroukos v Cadillac Fairview Corp Ltd* (1984) 3 DLR (4th) 595 at 605. The ousted tenant continues to be contractually liable on his covenants (see *Perry v Woodfarm Homes Ltd*, supra at 130).
5 *Tickner v Buzzacott* [1965] Ch 426 at 434E-G (post, p 837). The threat of forfeiture may indirectly force the squatter to perform the leasehold covenants (see *Perry v Woodfarm Homes Ltd* [1975] IR 104 at 120).

able to assert a better title.[6] From the inception of his 'possession' the squatter is recognised as having a common law estate in fee simple, despite the fact that his possession of the land was initially tortious[7] and notwithstanding that until the 12 year period of limitation has expired he may be turned out by legal process.[8] The same land is therefore capable of yielding up a multiplicity of simultaneous legal estates in fee simple on behalf of different adverse possessors entering upon the land seriatim,[9] subject only to the vulnerability of each claimant to the unbarred rights of earlier claimants or indeed of the original paper owner.[10] Implicit in the notion of relativity of title is the recognition that mere fee simple ownership at common law does not foreclose the possibility that another person may have an older and better version of the fee simple title.

(b) *Transmissibility*

Having acquired an estate in fee simple by his own wrong, the squatter—even within the limitation period—is fully competent to assign his rights inter vivos or to dispose of them by will.[11] If he dies intestate, his rights devolve upon his next of kin. An assignee from a squatter may count the squatter's period of possession towards the period of 12 years of adverse possession which are required to establish the completion of the limitation period in favour of the *assignee*.[12] Even without any transfer of the squatter's inchoate fee simple estate,[13] the period of his possession may be added to

6 *Asher v Whitlock* (1865) LR 1 QB 1 at 5. So long, therefore, as the adverse possessor does not abandon his possession, the fact of possession—even for less than twelve years—enables him to exclude from the land anyone who does not have a better title (*Allen v Roughley* (1955) 94 CLR 98 at 109ff, 131, 135, 143; *Newington* v *Windeyer* (1985) 3 NSWLR 555 at 563F).

7 'Every fee simple is not legitimum' (*Co Litt*, p 2a). As McHugh JA observed in *Newington* v *Windeyer* (1985) 3 NSWLR 555 at 563E, 'an estate gained by wrong is nevertheless an estate in fee simple'. See also *Leach v Jay* (1878) 9 Ch D 42 at 45 per James LJ; *Mabo v Queensland* (1992) 107 ALR 1 at 161 per Toohey J.

8 See *Wheeler v Baldwin* (1934) 52 CLR 609 at 632 per Dixon CJ; *Spark v Meers* [1971] 2 NSWLR 1 at 12A-C. The squatter is even entitled to claim compensation in the event of compulsory purchase of the land before his possessory title is confirmed under the Limitation Act (see *Perry v Clissold* [1907] AC 73 at 79f). However, since his title does not derive from grant, the adverse possessor cannot claim the benefit of any easement implied, for instance, on the basis of necessity (*Wilkes v Greenway* (1890) 6 TLR 449; *North Sydney Printing Pty Ltd v Sabemo Investment Corpn Pty Ltd* [1971] 2 NSWLR 150 at 159C-D (post, p 1094)).

9 In registered land the *legal* quality of the adverse possessor's fee is, of course, dependent upon the formality of registration as proprietor (ante, p 177).

10 See eg *Heid v Connell Investments Pty Ltd and the Registrar-General* (1987) 9 NSWLR 628 at 637A-B.

11 *Asher v Whitlock* (1865) LR 1 QB 1 at 6f; *Wheeler v Baldwin* (1934) 52 CLR 609 at 632f; *Allen v Roughley* (1955) 94 CLR 98 at 108, 130ff; *Mulcahy v Curramore Pty Ltd* [1974] 2 NSWLR 464 at 476C.

12 *Asher v Whitlock* (1865) LR 1 QB 1 at 6f; *Mulcahy v Curramore Pty Ltd* [1974] 2 NSWLR 464 at 476D. A later squatter normally remains vulnerable to the recovery of possession by an earlier squatter until 12 years have elapsed since the inception of the later squatter's possession (ante, p 287). However, an assignment on gift or sale of such rights as the earlier squatter may have—insecure as they may be—would 'on ordinary principles of law' preclude any subsequent ouster of the assignee by the assignor (see *Mount Carmel Investments Ltd v Peter Thurlow Ltd* [1988] 1 WLR 1078 at 1086E-F per Nicholls LJ; [1988] Conv 359 (J.E.M.)).

13 *Willis v Earl Howe* [1893] 2 Ch 545 at 553; *Salter v Clarke* (1904) 4 SR (NSW) 280 at 288; *Mulcahy v Curramore Pty Ltd* [1974] 2 NSWLR 464 at 471A-B.

(or 'tacked' on to) the possession of the next successive squatter on the land so as to enable the latter to claim a completed possessory title after an aggregate of 12 years.[14]

3. DISPOSSESSION AND DISCONTINUANCE OF POSSESSION

It is clear law that under the Limitation Act the person claiming a possessory title to land must show either (i) a 'dispossession' (or 'ouster') of the paper owner or (ii) a 'discontinuance by the paper owner followed by possession'.[15] As Nourse LJ conceded in *Buckinghamshire CC v Moran*,[16] the distinction between these two kinds of event is 'a very fine one'. 'Dispossession' is, however, generally understood to occur where a squatter 'comes in and drives out the true owner from possession',[17] while a relevant 'discontinuance' results where the true owner 'goes out of possession and is followed in by the squatter'.[18] True cases of dispossession or ouster are nowadays somewhat rare,[19] and most of the difficulties in the law of adverse possession have arisen in the context of 'discontinuance' of possession by the paper owner followed by the inception of 'possession' on the part of an intruding squatter.

(1) 'Discontinuance' of possession by the paper owner

Except in cases of ouster or dispossession, a claim of adverse possession can succeed only if it can be shown that there was a 'discontinuance' or 'abandonment'[20] of possession by the paper owner.[1] Any claim based on an alleged 'discontinuance' of possession requires, in its turn, the rebuttal of a fairly heavy presumption that possession is retained prima facie either by the paper owner or by some person who claims through him.[2] In the absence of persuasive evidence to the contrary, the owner of the paper title is deemed to remain in possession.[3] He is regarded as maintaining a constructive possession of the land even if he is not in actual possession of the whole of it.[4] Moreover, a continuing possession may be maintained on

14 Ante, p 287.

15 *Treloar v Nute* [1976] 1 WLR 1295 at 1300E per Sir John Pennycuick. See also *Morrice v Evans* (1989) *Times*, 27 February; *Buckinghamshire CC v Moran* [1990] Ch 623 at 635H per Slade LJ, 644E per Nourse LJ.

16 [1990] Ch 623 at 644F-G. Nourse LJ referred also (at 645B) to the 'confusion' between the concepts of dispossession and discontinuance which is found in some of the decided cases.

17 Extrusion of the paper owner may sometimes occur even without his knowledge (see eg *Buckinghamshire CC v Moran* [1990] Ch 623).

18 *Buckinghamshire CC v Moran* [1990] Ch 623 at 644F per Nourse LJ, following *Rains v Buxton* (1880) 14 Ch D 537 at 539f per Fry J.

19 See, however, *Buckinghamshire CC v Moran* [1990] Ch 623 at 636B.

20 See *Milton v Proctor* (1989) NSW ConvR 55-450 at 58,254f per McHugh JA.

1 For the inevitable consequence of failure to show a 'discontinuance', see *Maguire v Browne* (1913) 17 CLR 365 at 368f.

2 *Powell v McFarlane* (1977) 38 P & CR 452 at 470. See also *Re Lundrigans Ltd and Prosper* (1982) 132 DLR (3d) 727 at 731.

3 See eg *Morrice v Evans* (1989) *Times*, 27 February.

4 See *Fletcher v Storoschuk* (1981) 128 DLR (3d) 59 at 62; *Masidon Investments Ltd v Ham* (1983) 39 OR (2d) 534 at 545d.

behalf of the paper owner through the proxy occupation of persons such as relatives.[5] There is no 'abandonment' of possession by a paper owner who persists in asserting a right to deny entry to a particular named person.[6]

(2) Retention of land for some specific future use

In the normal run of circumstances it is not difficult to determine whether there has been 'dispossession' or a 'discontinuance' of the possession of the paper owner of land. More problematic, however, is the case where a paper owner allows his land to lie dormant for the time being, while intending to put the land to some specific use in the future. It used to be thought that such circumstances were, as a matter of law, governed by a special rule adumbrated by Bramwell LJ in *Leigh v Jack*.[7] Under this rule the 'possession' of the original paper owner was regarded as wholly undisturbed by the acts of an intruder, no matter how continuous and far-reaching these acts might be, so long as the intruder's conduct did not substantially interfere with any plans which the paper owner might have for the future use of undeveloped land.[8] On this basis even extensive and significant possessory acts by the intruder were not seen as derogating from or destroying the continuing possession of the paper owner—provided only that they remained consistent with the specific future use intended by the latter.[9]

The applicability of any special rule in the present context was finally disavowed by the Court of Appeal in *Buckinghamshire CC v Moran*.[10] Here a local authority had, some 30 years earlier, acquired a plot of land which it left undeveloped for the purpose of a proposed road diversion in the future. In following years a neighbouring landowner began to maintain the plot as an extension of his garden and his successor in title installed a lock and chain which rendered the plot accessible only from his own land. The Court of Appeal ruled that this conduct, by achieving an enclosure of the disputed plot and its effective annexation to the claimant's house, constituted an assertion of 'complete and exclusive physical control' sufficient to found a plea of adverse possession.[11] In reaching this conclusion, Slade LJ thought

5 *Milton v Proctor* (1989) NSW ConvR 55-450 at 58,260.
6 *Milton v Proctor* (1989) NSW ConvR 55-450 at 58,255 per McHugh JA, 58,259 per Clarke JA.
7 (1879) 5 Ex D 264 at 273.
8 This approach was conveniently rationalised by reference to the theory that the intruder's presence could be attributed to some implied licence granted by the paper owner (post, p 296). In support of the view that possession is not necessarily lost merely because neither the paper owner nor any person claiming through him currently makes use of the land, see *Williams Brothers Direct Supply Ltd v Raftery* [1958] 1 QB 159 at 170ff; *Riley v Penttila* [1974] VR 547 at 562.
9 See eg *Wallis's Cayton Bay Holiday Camp Ltd v Shell-Mex and BP Ltd* [1975] QB 94 at 103D per Lord Denning MR; (1975) 39 Conv (NS) 57 (F.R. Crane); [1975] CLJ 32 (D. Macintyre); (1975) 91 LQR 7 (J.L. Barton). It has since been said that many of the decisions and dicta in support of *Leigh v Jack* were referable to 'a time when many plots of waste land had been brought under the spade in digging for victory during the Second World War and afterwards' (see *Buckinghamshire CC v Moran* [1990] Ch 623 at 646E-F per Nourse LJ). It may be that by 1976 Bramwell LJ's dictum had—albeit wrongly—'assumed the dignity of a special rule'.
10 [1990] Ch 623. See [1990] CLJ 23 (C. Harpum); [1989] Conv 211 (G. McCormack).
11 [1990] Ch 623 at 641B per Slade LJ.

it much too broad a proposition 'to suggest that an owner who retains a piece of land with a view to its utilisation for a specific purpose in the future can never be treated as dispossessed, however firm and obvious the intention to dispossess, and however drastic the acts of dispossession of the person seeking to dispossess him may be.'[12]

The Court of Appeal agreed in *Moran*'s case that where a paper owner has intentions of future use in relation to his land, a discontinuance of possession can be prevented 'by the slightest acts of ownership on his part, even by none at all'.[13] The paper owner can be dispossessed only if 'the squatter performs sufficient acts and has a sufficient intention to constitute adverse possession.'[14] Particularly is this the case where (as on the facts in *Moran*) the claimant possessor is at all times well aware that the paper owner has plans for the future use of undeveloped land.[15] In such circumstances 'very clear evidence' of possessory acts and intentions is required before a claim of adverse possession can succeed.[16] In *Moran*'s case, however, the squatter had indeed manifested such conduct and intentions, most relevantly and unequivocally by placing the new lock and chain on the gate to the disputed area.[17]

(3) Inception of 'possession' by a third party

In cases of adverse possession arising otherwise than by 'ouster', it is essential to show not merely that there has been a 'discontinuance' of possession by the paper owner, but also that there has been an inception of 'possession' by an adverse occupier. Without the element of a new 'possession' asserted by an intruder there would of course be no right of action in the paper owner to be statute-barred through the effluxion of time. For present purposes, however, the concept of 'possession' is given a qualified meaning. 'Possession' can be attributed to the intruder only if he can show that he has both factual possession and the requisite intention to possess (*animus possidendi*).[18]

12 [1990] Ch 623 at 639A.
13 [1990] Ch 623 at 644G per Nourse LJ.
14 [1990] Ch 623 at 644H per Nourse LJ, who went on to say that the requisite acts and intention do not differ as between cases of 'dispossession' and 'discontinuance of possession'.
15 'This factor...should make the court the more cautious before holding that the [claimant] had both a factual possession and animus possidendi sufficient to confer on him a possessory title' ([1990] Ch 623 at 640E per Slade LJ). A squatter's knowledge of the paper owner's intentions for future use 'may affect the quality of his own intention, reducing it below that which is required to constitute adverse possession' ([1990] Ch 623 at 645A-B per Nourse LJ).
16 [1990] Ch 623 at 639H-640A per Slade LJ.
17 See [1990] Ch 623 at 642D-F per Slade LJ. It may well be that, except where the claimant has actually enclosed and secured the disputed land, the courts will be 'slow to make a finding of adverse possession' in *Leigh v Jack* circumstances (ie in cases where the paper owner has reserved future intentions for use). See [1990] Ch 623 at 643G-H per Slade LJ, 645F-G, 646D per Nourse LJ.
18 See *Powell v McFarlane* (1977) 38 P & CR 452 at 470 per Slade J; *Buckinghamshire CC v Moran* [1990] Ch 623 at 636B-C per Slade LJ.

(4) Factual possession

The factual possession required in the present context is of a special kind. The possession which causes time to run under the Limitation Act must be 'open, not secret; peaceful, not by force; and adverse, not by consent of the true owner'.[19]

(a) Possession must be exclusive to the claimant

No claim of adverse possession may be founded on possession which is not exclusive to the claimant.[20] A possession which is, for instance, exercised at different times by several members of one family cannot grow into a possessory title for one of those family members alone.[1] The claimant's possession must be a 'single and conclusive possession'.[2]

(b) Possession must be 'adverse' to the paper owner

The possession which is relevant under the Limitation Act comprises only that which is truly 'adverse' to the paper owner. Any possession which is concurrent with that of the paper owner is insufficient as a foundation of possessory title.[3] Shared user cannot be 'adverse'; nor can any user which is the subject of a mandate or permission from the paper owner.[4] Thus no adverse possession arises on the basis of occupation which is exercised at the request or with the consent of the paper owner.[5] A subsisting element of leave[6] or licence[7] from the paper owner clearly negates the otherwise

19 *Mulcahy v Curramore Pty Ltd* [1974] 2 NSWLR 464 at 475D per Bowen CJ. Adverse possession 'must be peaceable and open' (*Browne v Perry* [1991] 1 WLR 1297 at 1302A per Lord Templeman).

20 *Clement v Jones* (1909) 8 CLR 133 at 139 per Griffith CJ. See also *Attorney-General of Canada v Acadia Forest Products Ltd* (1988) 41 DLR (4th) 338 at 343.

1 *Morris v Pinches* (1969) 212 Estates Gazette 1141.

2 *Powell v McFarlane* (1977) 38 P & CR 452 at 470, although Slade J conceded that 'there can be a single possession exercised by or on behalf of several persons jointly'. See eg *Newington v Windeyer* (1985) 3 NSWLR 555 at 564A-C (adverse possession by group of neighbours united by a common purpose).

3 *Treloar v Nute* [1976] 1 WLR 1295 at 1300E per Sir John Pennycuick. Thus the paper owner and the intruder cannot both be in possession at the same time (*Powell v McFarlane* (1977) 38 P & CR 452 at 470). See also *Hamson v Jones* (1989) 52 DLR (4th) 143 at 156.

4 It is a moot point whether a paper owner's permission which subsequently founds a claim of proprietary estoppel can bar the running of a limitation period. For discussion whether an estoppel claimant can enlarge his rights through a plea of adverse possession, see M. Welstead, [1991] Conv 280.

5 *Bladder v Phillips* [1991] EGCS 109 per Mustill LJ.

6 See *Canadian Pacific Ltd v Paul* (1989) 53 DLR (4th) 487 at 501 (Supreme Court of Canada). Rights granted originally as rights of way may, however, enlarge subsequently into a possessory title if the paper owner fails to challenge a more extensive user by the grantee which is no longer referable to any lawful right of easement but is wholly inconsistent with such a right (see *Thomas v Thomas* (1855) 2 K & J 79 at 83ff, 69 ER 701 at 703f; *Keefer v Arillotta* (1977) 72 DLR (3d) 182 at 188f). See also *Williams v Usherwood* (1983) 45 P & CR 235 at 251.

7 See *Blakeney v MacDonald* (1981) 116 DLR (3d) 402 at 413ff.

adverse quality of possession enjoyed by a claimant,[8] although a licensee whose licence has expired acquires the status of a trespasser in whose favour time can once again begin to run.[9] The presence of a landlord-tenant relationship between the paper owner and the occupier is likewise inconsistent with a claim of adverse possession.[10] Possession is never 'adverse' if enjoyed under a lawful title.[11] There is, moreover, a tendency to find that any possession exercised by one family member against another within the context of a loosely organised family arrangement is not in any real sense 'adverse', but is more realistically attributed to some form of licence, whether express or implied.[12]

(c) Doctrine of 'implied licence'

Until relatively recently the courts were accustomed as a matter of law to apply a doctrine of 'implied licence' in determining whether a squatter could validly claim possession of land which the paper owner, having no immediate use for the land, had left unoccupied. By invoking the notion of 'implied licence' in such circumstances, the courts effectively precluded the inception of adverse possession by strangers. In *Wallis's Cayton Bay Holiday Camp Ltd v Shell-Mex and BP Ltd*,[13] for instance, Lord Denning MR thought that it did not lie in a trespasser's mouth 'to assert that he used the land of his own wrong as a trespasser.' Instead the user exerted by the trespasser was to be ascribed to a mere 'licence or permission of the true owner',[14] such leave of course destroying any adverse quality otherwise inherent in the intruder's possession.[15]

The doctrine of 'implied licence' plainly stultified much of the law of adverse possession and this highly restrictive aspect of the law of limitation

8 *E.R. Ives Investment Ltd v High* [1967] 2 QB 379 at 396D-E per Lord Denning MR; *Hughes v Griffin* [1969] 1 WLR 23 at 30A, 31G, 32F; *Palfrey v Palfrey* (1974) 229 Estates Gazette 1593 at 1595; *Wallis's Cayton Bay Holiday Camp Ltd v Shell-Mex and BP Ltd* [1975] QB 94 at 103F-G; *Buckinghamshire CC v Moran* [1990] Ch 623 at 636G-H; *Murphy v Murphy* [1980] IR 183 at 195, 202; *Bellew v Bellew* [1982] IR 447 at 464. Any attempt by a contractual licensee to claim a possessory title may, by denying the licensor's title, constitute a fundamental breach of the contract entitling the licensor to repudiate the agreement (see *Milton v Proctor* (1989) NSW ConvR 55-450 at 58,255 per McHugh JA).

9 *Colchester BC v Smith* [1991] Ch 448 at 489E-F per Ferris J.

10 *Colchester BC v Smith* [1991] Ch 448 at 464F, 479E; *Shillabeer v Diebel* (1980) 100 DLR (3d) 279 at 283; *Sauerzweig v Feeney* [1986] IR 224 at 227.

11 *Buckinghamshire CC v Moran* [1990] Ch 623 at 636G per Slade LJ.

12 *Murphy v Murphy* [1980] IR 183 at 195. See eg *Tunley v James* (Unreported, Court of Appeal, No 81 03701, 7 April 1982); *Fruin v Fruin* [1983] Court of Appeal Bound Transcript 448; *Re Lands situate within the Townlands of Eshywilligan and Bunlougher, County Fermanagh* (Unreported, Northern Ireland High Court, 10 April 1992) per Campbell J.

13 [1975] QB 94 at 103F.

14 'By using the land, knowing that it does not belong to him, he impliedly assumes that the owner will permit it: and the owner, by not turning him off, impliedly gives permission'. See also *Gray v Wykeham Martin* (Court of Appeal Transcript No 10A of 1977), where the Court of Appeal thought that 'any sensible and neighbourly person who exercised control over a piece of land and had not any particular use for it at the time would have given a licence to anybody who wanted to use it in the way the plaintiff did.' The plaintiff must have realised that she was 'being allowed as of grace to carry on as before during these times of food shortage.'

15 See *Buckinghamshire CC v Moran* [1990] Ch 623 at 646F-G per Nourse LJ for reference to Lord Denning's 'original heresy...the implied licence theory'.

was finally amended in 1980.[16] It is now clear that, in determining whether a person occupying land is in adverse possession of the land, it is no longer to be 'assumed by implication of law that his occupation is by permission of the person entitled to the land merely by virtue of the fact that his occupation is not inconsistent with the latter's present or future enjoyment of the land.'[17] It is still, however, open to the courts to apply the concept of the implied licence—just as before 1980—but only where a finding of implied permission is 'justified on the actual facts of the case.'[18]

(d) Adverse possession need not be hostile

Adverse possession operates as an essentially objective process of law. The mere fact that possession must be 'adverse' does not mean that it must necessarily be *hostile*.[19] Possession may be objectively adverse to the interests of the paper owner without the relevant parties necessarily becoming, in any subjective sense, adversaries in respect of the possessory acts which are subsequently a matter of dispute. Thus it is quite possible that adverse possession may occur without either the paper owner or the adverse possessor having any knowledge of it at all.[20] A title may be acquired through adverse possession even though the claimant, through ignorance or mistake, was unaware of the true ownership of the property.[1] Indeed the *animus* required of the adverse possessor relates not to ownership of the land at all but rather to the assertion of a factual degree of 'complete and exclusive physical control' over the land[2]—an assertion which is wholly consistent with an erroneous assumption of entitlement. A plea of adverse possession can therefore succeed even though both parties mistakenly but genuinely believed that the claimant was the true owner of the land and that his entry on that land was therefore 'as of right'.[3] Time likewise runs under the Limitation Act even as against a paper owner who is entirely unaware that title to the land was conveyed to him long ago.[4]

(e) Possession must be open

The possession which founds a claim of adverse possession must be open,

16 See Limitation Amendment Act 1980, s 4.

17 Limitation Act 1980, Sch 1, para 8(4). See Law Reform Committee 21st Report, *Final Report on Limitation of Actions* (Cmnd 6923, 1977), para 3.47ff; (1977) 244 Estates Gazette 291, 375 (D. Brahams); *Buckinghamshire CC v Moran* [1990] Ch 623 at 637D-F, 646F-G.

18 Limitation Act 1980, Sch 1, para 8(4). See P. Jackson, (1980) 96 LQR 333 at 335f; [1986] Conv 434 (G. McCormack).

19 Indeed there may be a query as to the appropriateness of according a possessory title to one who takes land by hostile act (post, p 304).

20 *Murphy v Murphy* [1980] IR 183 at 202; *Rains v Buxton* (1880) 14 Ch D 537 at 539ff.

1 *McGugan and McNeill v Turner* [1948] 2 DLR 338 at 344ff; *Beaudoin v Aubin* (1981) 125 DLR (3d) 277 at 292; *Guild v Mallory* (1983) 144 DLR (3d) 603 at 619.

2 *Buckinghamshire CC v Moran* [1990] Ch 623 at 641B per Slade LJ (ante, p 293).

3 Entry 'as of right' is nothing to the point in the law of adverse possession, most cases of adverse possession comprising, at least objectively, possession 'as of wrong' (see *Buckinghamshire CC v Moran* [1990] Ch 623 at 644D per Nourse LJ (ante, p 285)). See also *Bladder v Phillips* [1991] EGCS 109, where Mustill LJ deliberately left open the question whether adverse possession may be claimed by one who believes he already owns the land.

4 *Palfrey v Palfrey* (1974) 229 Estates Gazette 1593 at 1595.

notorious and unconcealed.[5] The requirement of visibility ensures that the paper owner is given every opportunity of challenging the possession before it can ripen into an unimpeachable title.[6]

(f) Examples of factual possession

The requirement of factual possession signifies the necessity that adverse possession should involve some appropriate degree of exclusive physical control over the land in question. The kinds of 'possession' required for the purpose of establishing this element of physical control must depend upon the circumstances of each case.[7] The acts relied upon as evidencing the 'possession' of the claimant need not have been uninterrupted,[8] but it must be shown that 'the alleged possessor has been dealing with the land in question as an occupying owner might have been expected to deal with it and that no-one else has done so.'[9]

It is possible that adverse possession may be asserted in respect of only part of the land area titled in the paper owner, the paper owner remaining in effective possession of the remainder of his land.[10] Provided that the squatter is in exclusive factual possession of an identifiable portion of the land, it is irrelevant that the owner of the paper title has not been wholly dispossessed. Thus there can be adverse possession of a different stratum of land from that occupied by the paper owner.[11] Alternatively adverse possession may be claimed in respect of a portion of the paper owner's land which is marked off not horizontally but vertically.[12]

(i) Exclusive physical control In *Powell v McFarlane*[13] Slade J indicated that the question of 'possession' must be determined with particular reference to 'the nature of the land and the manner in which land of that nature

5 *Lord Advocate v Lord Lovat* (1880) 5 App Cas 273 at 291, 296; *McConaghy v Denmark* (1880) 4 SCR 609 at 632f; *Sherren v Pearson* (1887) 14 SCR 581 at 585; *Hamson v Jones* (1989) 52 DLR (4th) 143 at 153. The requirement of open user did not, however, prevent adverse possession of an underground cellar in *Rains v Buxton* (1880) 14 Ch D 537 at 539f. Here Fry J noted that the door into the cellar had been 'quite visible to anybody', and that there had been no concealment of user even though such user 'from its very nature. . .was not perhaps a thing at all times necessarily seen'.

6 See eg *Re Lundrigans Ltd and Prosper* (1982) 132 DLR (3d) 727 at 729ff, where the Newfoundland Court of Appeal rejected a claim of adverse possession based on the presence in a wilderness area of two log cabins which were not visible either from the ground or from the air. See also *Marengo Cave Co v Ross*, 10 NE2d 917 at 920ff (1937) (no adverse possession of underground cavern).

7 *Lord Advocate v Lord Lovat* (1880) 5 App Cas 273 at 288; *Bligh v Martin* [1968] 1 WLR 804 at 811F; *Murphy v Murphy* [1980] IR 183 at 193; *Hamson v Jones* (1989) 52 DLR (4th) 143 at 155.

8 *Bligh v Martin* [1968] 1 WLR 804 at 811F-G; *Mulcahy v Curramore Pty Ltd* [1974] 2 NSWLR 464 at 475F. In *Re Taylor and Willigar* (1980) 99 DLR (3d) 118 at 125f, it was held sufficient that the disputed property was used only in summer months and not at other times 'when the snow and ice of winter preclude their use in any practicable sense'. See also *Hamson v Jones* (1989) 52 DLR (4th) 143 at 156.

9 *Powell v McFarlane* (1977) 38 P & CR 452 at 471.

10 *Quach v Marrickville MC* (Nos 1 & 2) (1990) 22 NSWLR 55 at 67E-F, 69C.

11 See eg *Rains v Buxton* (1880) 14 Ch D 537 at 539f, where adverse possession was successfully claimed in respect of an underground cellar (supra, note 5).

12 *Quach v Marrickville MC* (Nos 1 & 2) (1990) 22 NSWLR 55 at 67E-F per Young J.

13 (1977) 38 P & CR 452 at 471.

is commonly used or enjoyed.'[14] Conduct amounting to 'possession' will be different in relation to a dwelling and to uncultivated land.[15]

Thus, in Slade J's view, absolute physical control of open land is normally impracticable 'if only because it is generally impossible to secure every part of a boundary so as to prevent intrusion'.[16] The erection of fencing is, however, 'useful evidence of occupation to the exclusion of others',[17] and it has been said that only rarely will extensive fencing fail to demonstrate the adverse possession required for a successful claim of possessory title.[18] Of course, the absence of fencing does not in itself prove a lack of possession.[19]

Relevant 'possession' can be established by a variety of other uses of the land, as for instance where the claimant has used the land for shooting[20] or for grazing and storage purposes,[1] or even where the claimant has simply erected prominent 'no trespassing'[2] or 'no dumping'[3] signs on the land. In *Newington v Windeyer*[4] the Court of Appeal of New South Wales held that a number of neighbouring owners had adversely possessed an adjoining area of open ground where, for nearly 50 years, they had maintained the area as a garden; had employed a man to mow the lawn; had used the area for parties, receptions and the display of sculpture; and had been assessed for rates in respect of the land.

(ii) Trivial or equivocal acts Trivial or equivocal acts by the adverse occupier are generally inadequate as proof of 'possession'[5] and in any event provide an exceedingly fragile foundation for claims of the requisite *animus possidendi*.[6]

14 See *Wuta-Ofei v Danquah* [1961] 1 WLR 1238 at 1243 per Lord Guest; *Newington v Windeyer* (1985) 3 NSWLR 555 at 564A per McHugh JA. See also *Kirby v Cowderoy* [1912] AC 599 at 603; *Bligh v Martin* [1968] 1 WLR 804 at 811F-H; *McDonell v Giblin* (1904) 23 NZLR 660 at 662; *Riley v Penttila* [1974] VR 547 at 561; *West Bank Estates Ltd v Arthur* [1967] 1 AC 665 at 678A-B per Lord Wilberforce.

15 *Mabo v Queensland* (1992) 107 ALR 1 at 166 per Toohey J. See also *Lord Advocate v Lord Lovat* (1880) 5 App Cas 273 at 288; *Johnston v O'Neill* [1911] AC 552 at 583.

16 (1977) 38 P & CR 452 at 471.

17 *Mulcahy v Curramore Pty Ltd* [1974] 2 NSWLR 464 at 475E. Compare, however, *Fruin v Fruin* [1983] Court of Appeal Bound Transcript 448, where the Court declined to accept as evidence of adverse possession a fence one of whose purposes had been to restrain a senile family member who was 'apt to wander'. See also *Riley v Penttila* [1974] VR 547 at 564ff, where the purpose of a fence and netting was primarily to facilitate the playing of tennis rather than to exclude the true owner.

18 *George Wimpey & Co Ltd v Sohn* [1967] Ch 487 at 511A, 512A per Russell LJ. See eg *Seddon v Smith* (1877) 36 LT 168 at 169 per Cockburn CJ ('Enclosure is the strongest possible evidence of adverse possession'). See also *Buckinghamshire CC v Moran* [1990] Ch 623 at 641H–642A. Compare, however, *Boosey v Davis* (1988) 55 P & CR 83 at 87 (incomplete fence reinforcing existing fence erected by paper owner insufficient); *Marsden v Miller* (1992) 64 P & CR 239 at 241ff (erection of fence for 24 hours insufficient).

19 *Mulcahy v Curramore Pty Ltd* [1974] 2 NSWLR 464 at 475E.

20 *Red House Farms (Thorndon) Ltd v Catchpole* (1977) 244 Estates Gazette 295 at 297ff.

1 *Treloar v Nute* [1976] 1 WLR 1295. See (1978) 41 MLR 204 (P.F. Smith).

2 *Powell v McFarlane* (1977) 38 P & CR 452 at 478. See also *Newington v Windeyer* (1985) 3 NSWLR 555 at 564C per McHugh JA.

3 *Hughes v Mulholland & McCann Ltd* [1982] 7 BNIL 72. See also *Raab v Caranci* (1980) 97 DLR (3d) 154 at 157ff, affd (1980) 104 DLR (3d) 160 (building of small wall).

4 (1985) 3 NSWLR 555 at 564B-C.

5 See *Hamson v Jones* (1989) 52 DLR (4th) 143 at 153.

6 See *Buckinghamshire CC v Moran* [1990] Ch 623 at 642E per Slade LJ.

In *Tecbild Ltd v Chamberlain*,[7] for instance, the Court of Appeal declined to attach significance to the fact that the claimant's children had been accustomed to play on the disputed plots of land as and when they wished and that the family ponies had been tethered and exercised there.[8] As the Court of Appeal confirmed, 'trivial acts of trespass' do not constitute adverse possession.[9] It must be demonstrated that the adverse occupier established a possession which was wholly inconsistent with and in denial of the rights of the paper owner as the legal owner of the land concerned.[10]

(iii) Constructive possession It is clear that acts of possession done on parts of the land to which a possessory title is sought may constitute 'evidence of possession of the whole'.[11] However, the credibility of such a claim of constructive possession of a larger whole depends vitally upon the nature of the land in question. A degree of factual possession sufficient to justify a claim over a tract of wild country[12] may be entirely inadequate to found a similar claim over urban land.[13]

(5) Intention to possess (animus possidendi)

The *animus possidendi* which is required for the inception and retention of 'possession' by an adverse occupier was defined by Slade J in *Powell v McFarlane*,[14] as comprising 'the intention, in one's own name and on one's own behalf, to exclude the world at large, including the owner with the paper title if he be not himself the possessor, so far as is reasonably practicable and so far as the processes of the law will allow.'[15]

7 (1969) 20 P & CR 633.

8 Compare *Powell v McFarlane* (1977) 38 P & CR 452 (ante, p 298).

9 (1969) 20 P & CR 633 at 644, 646. In *Boosey v Davis* (1988) 55 P & CR 83 at 86f, the Court of Appeal disallowed a claim of adverse possession which comprised a grazing use which was 'minimal' in quantity and quality. See also *Attersley v Blakely* (1970) 13 DLR (3d) 39 at 47; *Re MacEachern and MacIsaac* (1978) 81 DLR (3d) 20 at 29.

10 See *Moses v Lovegrove* [1952] 2 QB 533 at 538. See also *Bladder v Phillips* [1991] EGCS 109, where Mustill LJ disallowed a claim of adverse possession based on cleaning out parts of a ditch 'on a few brief occasions at long intervals'.

11 *Powell v McFarlane* (1977) 38 P & CR 452 at 471 ('Whether or not acts of possession done on parts of an area establish title to the whole area must, however, be a matter of degree').

12 See *Halifax County Pulp Co Ltd v Rutledge* (1982) 131 DLR (3d) 199 at 206ff; *Walker v Russell* (1966) 53 DLR (2d) 509 at 524ff. See *Weld v Scott* (1855) 12 UCQB 537 at 540, for the suggestion that the area which may be claimed by the adverse possessor is that covered by his 'pedal possession'. It may be that a consciously wrongful trespasser (as distinct from a trespasser who enters under colour of right) cannot plead a more extensive acquisition of title by reliance on constructive possession (see *Harris v Mudie* (1882) 7 OAR 414 at 427ff).

13 See *Pavledes v Ryesbridge Properties Ltd* (1989) 58 P & CR 459 at 480, where a claimant's use of a small part of an area of adjoining land as a car park was insufficient to constitute possession of the whole site. In *Williams v Usherwood* (1983) 45 P & CR 235 at 251, Cumming-Bruce LJ pointed out that, while the parking of cars on a strip of waste land might have no evidential value, such action within the enclosed curtilage of a private dwelling-house could well constitute adverse possession.

14 (1977) 38 P & CR 452 at 471f. See also *Buckinghamshire CC v Moran* [1990] Ch 623 at 640A, 641E-F per Slade LJ.

15 See also *Littledale v Liverpool College* [1900] 1 Ch 19 at 23 per Lindley MR.

(a) Intention to own is not required

It was once thought that *animus possidendi* necessarily connoted an intention to *own* or acquire *ownership* of the land or to exercise 'acts of ownership' in relation to it.[16] While the assertion of rights of ownership may well provide strong support for a claim of *animus possidendi*, it is now clear that the required mental element need not involve an intention 'to exclude the owner of the paper title in all future circumstances'. In *Buckinghamshire CC v Moran*[17] the Court of Appeal confirmed that it is sufficient that the claimant by adverse possession should demonstrate merely 'an intention for the time being to possess the land to the exclusion of all other persons, including the owner with the paper title.' In *Moran*, therefore, it was not fatal to a claim of adverse possession that the claimant had intended to continue in possession of the disputed plot of land only until such time as the paper owner activated its plans to build a proposed by-pass over it.[18] The mere fact that the statutory 12 year period had run its course against the background of a consciously limited or tentative form of intention in no way frustrated the normal operation of adverse possession.

(b) Restrictive application by the courts

There are certain respects in which it may not be easy to establish the relevant element of intention on behalf of an intruder upon another's land. The requirement of *animus possidendi* has been applied fairly restrictively by the courts.[19] As Slade J emphasised in *Powell v McFarlane*,[20] the success of any claim by a trespasser to have acquired 'possession' rests on clear and affirmative evidence that the trespasser 'not only had the requisite intention to possess, but made such intention clear to the world.' Although this intention is not necessarily incompatible with mistake or ignorance as to the true ownership of the land in question,[1] it must be shown that the claimant consciously acted in a manner which was objectively consistent with a claim to exclusive possession on his own behalf. The conduct of the adverse possessor must have been such as to demonstrate an apparent intention to exclude the paper owner from any immediate user of his property.[2] It may not be enough for this purpose that the particular manner or degree of the claimant's occupation deprived the paper owner of uses of his own property of which

16 See eg *Littledale v Liverpool College* [1900] 1 Ch 19 at 23 per Lindley MR; *George Wimpey & Co Ltd v Sohn* [1967] Ch 487 at 510G.

17 [1990] Ch 623 at 643E per Slade LJ, approving the statement of Hoffmann J at first instance ((1988) 56 P & CR 372 at 378f). See also [1990] Ch 623 at 644E per Nourse LJ. See [1990] CLJ 23 (C. Harpum); [1989] Conv 211 (G. McCormack).

18 [1990] Ch 623 at 643E-G per Slade LJ.

19 For cases in which the courts have rejected claims to possessory titles by trespassers for want of sufficient evidence of the requisite intent, see eg *Littledale v Liverpool College* [1900] 1 Ch 19 at 23ff; *George Wimpey & Co Ltd v Sohn* [1967] Ch 487 at 508F-G; *Tecbild Ltd v Chamberlain* (1969) 20 P & CR 633 at 643ff.

20 (1977) 38 P & CR 452 at 472. See generally M. Dockray, [1982] Conv 256, 345.

1 Ante, p 297.

2 *Keefer v Arillotta* (1977) 72 DLR (3d) 182 at 193.

he never intended or desired to take advantage.[3] Nor is it necessarily sufficient if the claimant's conduct indicates not so much a settled intention to exclude the true owner as an intention to confer a particular benefit upon himself.[4]

(i) Proof of intention In the absence of concealed fraud,[5] it is generally irrelevant in the law of adverse possession that the paper owner is ignorant of the fact that he has been dispossessed.[6] However, in view of the drastic results of a change of possession, a person who seeks to dispossess a paper owner must 'at least make his intentions sufficiently clear so that the owner, if present at the land, would clearly appreciate that the claimant is not merely a persistent trespasser, but is actually seeking to dispossess him'.[7] Courts will attach 'very little evidential value' to retrospective assertions of the required *animus*, because 'they are obviously easily capable of being merely self-serving, while at the same time they may be very difficult for the paper owner positively to refute'.[8] For the same reason even contemporary declarations by an adverse occupier to the effect that he is intending to assert a claim to the land provide but little support for a claim of 'possession' at the relevant time unless they are specifically brought to the attention of the true owner.[9] In general, as Sachs LJ said in *Tecbild Ltd v Chamberlain*,[10] 'intent has to be inferred from the acts themselves.'

(ii) Presumption of animus possidendi on behalf of the paper owner It is readily assumed, in the absence of clear contrary evidence, that *animus possidendi* is present in the paper owner or any other person with a right of possession of the land (eg a prior adverse possessor).[11] Thus even the slightest acts done by or on behalf of a paper owner will be found in practice to negative any supposed 'discontinuance' of his own possession.[12] The mental element required in the adverse possessor is even more obviously absent where the claimant of land has actually requested the paper owner, during the period of alleged adverse possession, to exclude trespassers from the land on behalf of the claimant.[13] A claim of adverse possession is inconsistent with a request that the *paper owner* should discharge the responsibilities normally attached to possession of land.

3 *Keefer v Arillotta* (1977) 72 DLR (3d) 182 at 193. See also *Masidon Investments Ltd v Ham* (1983) 39 OR (2d) 534 at 550ff.

4 *Murnane v Findlay* [1926] VLR 80 at 88. See eg *Riley v Penttila* [1974] VR 547 at 562ff (where a tennis court had been built on the disputed ground). See also *Masidon Investments Ltd v Ham* (1983) 39 OR (2d) 534 at 550f.

5 Post, p 304.

6 *Rains v Buxton* (1880) 14 Ch D 537 at 540f.

7 *Powell v McFarlane* (1977) 38 P & CR 452 at 480.

8 *Powell v McFarlane* (1977) 38 P & CR 452 at 476.

9 *Powell v McFarlane* (1977) 38 P & CR 452 at 476.

10 (1969) 20 P & CR 633 at 643.

11 Ante, p 292.

12 *Williams Brothers Direct Supply Ltd v Raftery* [1958] 1 QB 159 at 171; *Powell v McFarlane* (1977) 38 P & CR 452 at 472 per Slade J. See *Re St Clair Beach Estates Ltd v MacDonald* (1975) 50 DLR (3d) 650 at 656; *Masidon Investments Ltd v Ham* (1983) 39 OR (2d) 534 at 553f.

13 *Pavledes v Ryesbridge Properties Ltd* (1989) 58 P & CR 459 at 480.

(iii) Equivocal acts When the inception of 'possession' has to be inferred from equivocal acts, the intention with which those acts are performed becomes 'all-important'.[14] In *Powell v McFarlane*,[15] Slade J confirmed that 'compelling evidence' of *animus* is required where a trespasser's user of land does not by itself clearly betoken an intention on his part to possess the land to the exclusion of the true owner.[16] In this case Slade J declined to find the necessary *animus* proved on behalf of a plaintiff who, at the age of 14, had begun to use land for the purpose of grazing his cow. In Slade J's view, the conduct of one so young was 'not necessarily referable' to any intention to dispossess the paper owner and to occupy the land 'wholly as his own property'.[17]

(iv) Restrictive impact on squatters It has been said that in *Powell v McFarlane* Slade J imposed such onerous restrictions upon the notion of *animus possidendi* that 'few squatters, if any, could satisfy it'. Indeed, the heavy reliance upon a strict test of *animus* has allegedly emerged as 'yet another weapon in the armoury to be deployed against squatters'.[18] It is this interface with the law of squatting which has made the determination of *animus possidendi* so crucial and which has doubtless conduced to the restrictiveness of the courts' application of the concept of 'possession'.

It is trite law that the status of 'possession' confers on the possessor valuable privileges not only against the world at large, but also against the owner of the land concerned. It entitles even the trespasser to maintain an action in trespass against anyone who enters the land without his consent, with the sole exception of a person who has a better title to possession than himself.[19] The possessor has moreover one valuable element of protection against even the owner himself. Until 'possession' of land has actually passed to the trespasser, the owner may validly exercise the remedy of self-help against him.[20] However, once 'possession' has been taken over by the trespasser, this remedy is no longer available to the owner, and the intruder's position becomes correspondingly more secure. If he does not then leave the land voluntarily, the owner will find himself obliged to bring proceedings for possession and for this purpose to prove his title.[1]

14 *Littledale v Liverpool College* [1900] 1 Ch 19 at 23 per Lindley MR. See also *Clement v Jones* (1909) 8 CLR 133 at 140; *Riley v Penttila* [1974] VR 547 at 562.
15 (1977) 38 P & CR 452 at 476.
16 If the trespasser's acts are 'open to more than one interpretation and he has not made it perfectly plain to the world at large by his actions or words that he has intended to exclude the owner as best he can, the courts will treat him as not having had the requisite *animus possidendi* and consequently as not having dispossessed the owner' ((1977) 38 P & CR 452 at 472). See also *Buckinghamshire CC v Moran* [1990] Ch 623 at 642E-F.
17 (1977) 38 P & CR 452 at 478. See also *Re MacEachern and MacIsaac* (1978) 81 DLR (3d) 20 at 28f.
18 P. Jackson (1980) 96 LQR 333 at 334.
19 Ante, p 62; post, p 307.
20 Post, p 307.
1 See generally *Powell v McFarlane* (1977) 38 P & CR 452 at 476 per Slade J.

(v) The relevance of bad faith One of the more surprising features of the law of adverse possession is perhaps that the doctrine of long possession operates even in favour of the opportunist who is perfectly well aware that the land he occupies is not his own.[2] Although the courts are clearly not anxious to strain the law in favour of unmeritorious claimants,[3] there is in English law no general requirement of good faith in the adverse possessor.[4] Bad faith becomes relevant only if the paper owner can establish that he was the victim of a fraud perpetrated by the adverse occupier or that any fact relevant to his right of action was deliberately concealed from him by the occupier. In such circumstances the period of limitation does not begin to run until the plaintiff could with reasonable diligence have discovered the fraud or concealment.[5]

4. RECOVERY OF POSSESSION BY THE PAPER OWNER

Under the Limitation Act any action for the recovery of land from which the paper owner has been dispossessed must be brought *before* the expiration of the limitation period. After the expiration of this period the right of recovery becomes statute-barred and the title of the paper owner is extinguished. It thus becomes extremely important that the requisite steps for recovery of the land are taken by the paper owner before the end of the limitation period: the paper owner must issue his writ for possession. It is not sufficient, for instance, that within the limitation period the paper owner has sent the adverse possessor a letter demanding delivery up of possession of the relevant land. As the Court of Appeal held in *Mount Carmel Investments Ltd v Peter Thurlow Ltd*,[6] the 'possession' of the squatter is in no way terminated, nor does the owner recover a 'constructive possession' by reason of the squatter's mere receipt of a communication demanding that he should quit the land. Any contrary suggestion would be both 'distorted and novel', since in effect the relevant limitation period would start to run afresh on each occasion of a demand for possession.[7] Unless the squatter vacates the land voluntarily or gives to the paper owner a written acknowledgement of the latter's title,[8] the paper owner must initiate possession proceedings within

2 As Dean Ames once said, 'English lawyers regard not the merit of the possessor, but the demerit of the one out of possession' (J.B. Ames, *The Nature of Ownership*, in *Lectures on Legal History* (Cambridge Mass 1913), p 197).

3 See eg *Buckinghamshire CC v Moran* [1990] Ch 623 at 647A per Nourse LJ.

4 Compare, however, the good faith requirement imposed in Roman law and in most modern civilian systems (see R.H. Helmholz, *Adverse Possession and Subjective Intent*, 61 Wash ULQ 331 at 356 (1983–84)). Helmholz argues that American courts have in practice operated a test of good faith in adjudicating claims of title by long possession. See, however, R.A. Cunningham, *More on Adverse Possession: A Rejoinder to Professor Helmholz*, 64 Wash ULQ 1167 (1986).

5 See Limitation Act 1980, s 32(1). Protection is provided for innocent third parties who purchase property for valuable consideration (Limitation Act 1980, s 32(3)).

6 [1988] 1 WLR 1078 at 1084H–1085B, 1085C–1086A. See [1988] Conv 359 (J.E.M.).

7 [1988] 1 WLR 1078 at 1085H per Nicholls LJ.

8 See Limitation Act 1980, ss 29(2)(a), 30(1).

the prescribed time limit.[9] The right of recovery is otherwise barred after the expiration of 12 years.[10]

(1) No defence of necessity or social utility

In recent years the adverse possession of land has acquired new dimensions in so far as 'squatting' has commonly provided a means of coercing political action or expressing political or other protest. During the 1970s and 1980s the 'sit-in' emerged as a standard non-violent method of demonstration, whether the issue at stake was a proposed mass redundancy at the work-place, supposedly oppressive action taken by university authorities or the obscenity of empty property sitting idle at a time of severe homelessness. Even more recently the collective invasion of privately owned agricultural land by groups of 'New Age Travellers' has provided a controversial focus for the law on recovery of possession by a paper owner. It is clear, however, that the judicial reaction to squatting, sit-ins and mass trespass has taken the form of a stern reinforcement of the legal power of the paper owner of the land concerned. The courts have not been prepared to endorse any political or social justification for the dispossession of a paper owner from 'his' property. The idea that the existing distribution of land may itself express or conceal inequity is not a notion which the courts have been ready to explore.[11]

In *McPhail v Persons (Names Unknown)*,[12] a group of homeless persons secured entry to residential premises which had been left unoccupied and locked by the owner. The owner brought proceedings for the recovery of possession. In the Court of Appeal, Lord Denning MR defined a 'squatter' as 'one who, without any colour of right, enters on an unoccupied house or land, intending to stay there as long as he can.'[13] Lord Denning held that the Court could not entertain, by way of defence, a plea by a squatter that 'he was homeless and that this house or land was standing empty, doing nothing.' No such excuse could be of any avail in law, since, as Lord Denning himself had said in *Southwark LBC v Williams*,[14] if homelessness were once admitted as a defence to trespass, 'no one's house could be safe'.[15] The courts

9 [1988] 1 WLR 1078 at 1086A per Nicholls LJ.

10 In extremely rare circumstances it is possible that, even after the paper owner's rights have been extinguished by 12 years of adverse possession, his title may be revived by a later acknowledgement by the squatter. See eg *Colchester BC v Smith* [1992] Ch 421 at 435B (adverse possessor estopped from relying on Limitation Act by reason of subsequent tenancy granted by paper owner in which it was agreed that adverse possession had never occurred); [1991] Conv 397 (A.H.R. Brierley).

11 In the Republic of Ireland the Supreme Court has rejected the suggestion that the use of legal process against trespassers for the vindication of the landowner's possessory rights is an unconstitutional form of discrimination against the 'landless classes' (see *Dooley v Attorney General* [1977] IR 205 at 210).

12 [1973] Ch 447. See A.M. Prichard, (1976) 40 Conv (NS) 255; [1973] CLJ 220 (D. Macintyre).

13 [1973] Ch 447 at 456B.

14 [1971] Ch 734 at 744B-C.

15 See *Perka v The Queen* (1985) 13 DLR (4th) 1 at 34, where, in the Supreme Court of Canada, Wilson J cited *Southwark LBC v Williams* in support of the proposition that '[t]he maximisation of social utility may well be a goal of legislative policy but it is not part of the judicial task of delineating right and wrong.' As Dickson J said in *Morgentaler v The Queen* (1975) 53 DLR (3d) 161 at 209, '[n]o system of positive law can recognise any principle which would entitle a person to violate the law because on his view the law conflicted with some higher social value.' See also *Darcey v Pre-Term Foundation Clinic* [1983] 2 NSWLR 497 at 502B-D (no lawful excuse for trespass by protester against abortion).

'must, for the sake of law and order, take a firm stand. They must refuse to admit the plea of necessity to the hungry and the homeless: and trust that their distress will be relieved by the charitable and the good.'[16]

(2) Criminal liability

Far from being justifiable on grounds of a social or compassionate nature, the adverse occupation of residential premises is now in certain circumstances made a criminal offence by the Criminal Law Act 1977. Under this Act a criminal offence is committed by any person who, having entered premises as a trespasser, fails to leave those premises on being required to do so by or on behalf of either a 'displaced residential occupier'[17] or a 'protected intending occupier'[18] of those premises.[19]

Within the fairly recent past there has been a significant reinforcement of the power of the criminal law to deal with cases of trespass to private property. Public concern has been particularly aroused where a trespass takes the form of occupation by a mass motorised convoy of squatters who swarm locust-like from the land of one innocent owner to that of another or who invade ancient monuments (such as Stonehenge at midsummer). Symptomatic of the modern tightening up of the law was the introduction of a new criminal offence by the Public Order Act 1986. This legislation confers a power upon a 'senior police officer' to direct persons to leave land if the officer 'reasonably believes' that two or more such persons have entered land as trespassers and 'are present there with the common purpose of residing there for any period'.[20] In order properly to exercise this power, the senior police officer must also have reason to believe that 'reasonable steps' have been taken by or on behalf of the occupier to ask them to leave and that the trespassers have caused damage to property on the land or have used 'threatening, abusive or insulting words or behaviour' or that the trespassers 'have between them brought twelve or more vehicles on to the land'.[1] A criminal offence is committed any any person who, knowing that a direction to leave the land has been given by a senior police officer, fails to leave the land 'as soon as reasonably practicable' or who, having left, returns as a trespasser within the following three months.[2] The offence is, however,

16 [1971] Ch 734 at 744C-D. See also *Kensington and Chelsea LBC v Wells* (1974) 72 LGR 289 at 297ff per Roskill LJ; *Northern Ireland Housing Executive v Fox* [1981] 3 BNIL 62. The Court of Appeal has also ruled against the relevance in possession proceedings of matters which should properly be raised only in proceedings by way of judicial review. See *Avon CC v Buscott* [1988] QB 656 at 663F (challenge to reasonableness of local authority's failure to provide caravan site for gypsies). There may, however, be a duty to adjourn possession proceedings pending the outcome of such judicial review (see *South Hams DC v Shough* (1992) 65 P & CR 148 at 151f). See also *West Glamorgan CC v Rafferty* (1989) 57 P & CR 261 at 279ff.

17 A 'displaced residential occupier' is defined in Criminal Law Act 1977, s 12(3) (post, p 308).

18 A 'protected intending occupier' is defined in Criminal Law Act 1977, s 7(2).

19 Criminal Law Act 1977, s 7(1). Criminal trespass is punishable summarily by six months' imprisonment and/or a fine (Criminal Law Act 1977, s 7(10)). See [1978] CLJ 11.

20 Public Order Act 1986, s 39(1).

1 Public Order Act 1986, s 39(1).

2 Public Order Act 1986, s 39(2). The offence is punishable by three months' imprisonment and/or a fine. A uniformed police constable has power to arrest without warrant any person whom he 'reasonably suspects' of committing an offence under this provision (Public Order Act 1986, s 39(3)).

limited in scope in that the 'land' to which it applies does not include buildings (other than agricultural buildings or scheduled ancient monuments) and does not include land forming part of a highway.[3]

(3) Civil remedies

There are several possible civil remedies available for the purpose of assisting the paper owner to recover possession from trespassers who occupy his land.

(a) Remedy of self-help

It is quite clear that where strangers have taken over occupation of land, the paper owner of that land may exercise the remedy of self-help at any stage *before* the occupying strangers acquire 'possession' of the property in the sense currently required by the law of adverse possession.[4]

(i) Preconditions of self-help The availability of the remedy of self-help is terminated by the inception of 'possession' on the part of the trespasser, and it is for precisely this reason that the concept of 'possession' is defined so restrictively by the courts.[5] A householder who returns home from holiday to find his house occupied by squatters is entitled to throw the intruders out of his house without further ceremony. They were trespassers when they entered his house and they continued to be trespassers so long as they remained there awaiting the householder's return. The owner has not acquiesced in their presence in his house, and the vital consequence in law is that their occupation is not such as to enable them to allege that they ever gained 'possession' for the purpose of adverse possession.[6] In such a case, the owner is not obliged to go to the courts to obtain possession. He is entitled, if he so desires, to take the remedy into his own hands. As Lord Denning MR observed in *McPhail v Persons (Names Unknown)*,[7] the owner 'can go in himself and turn them out without the aid of the courts of law.' However, although Lord Denning considered the legality of this particular remedy 'beyond question', he cautioned that self-help 'is not a course to be recommended because of the disturbance which might follow'.[8]

(ii) Limitations on self-help If the owner himself uses force to secure the eviction of the trespassers, it is clear that he must use no more force than is reasonably necessary for the purpose.[9] The exercise of self-help is also subject to the

3 Public Order Act 1986, s 39(5).

4 It may have been true in the time of Bracton that the interval between wrongful entry and the inception of 'possession' was as short as four days—supposedly the period of time required for the ejected owner to ride one day in each direction of the compass in order to gather arms and friends to help in the re-ejectment (see Pollock and Maitland, *The History of English Law* (2nd edn, London 1968), Vol 2, p 50). Nowadays, however, the period may be somewhat longer and depends vitally, in any event, on the circumstances of the case.

5 Ante, p 303.

6 See Sir F. Pollock, *Torts* (15th edn, London 1951), p 292.

7 [1973] Ch 447 at 456D-E.

8 [1973] Ch 447 at 456E.

9 See *Hemmings v Stoke Poges Golf Club Ltd* [1920] 1 KB 720 at 747. Compare *R v Hussey* (1924) 18 Cr App R 160 at 161 (post, p 896).

important qualification imposed by the Criminal Law Act 1977. Under section 6(1) of this Act it is a criminal offence for any person without lawful authority to use or to threaten violence for the purpose of securing entry into any premises if, to his knowledge, there is someone present on those premises who is opposed to his entry.[10] This provision inevitably applies to some trespassers, but is not of course relevant to a squatter who enters premises by non-violent means. Simply by virtue of his de facto possession of the property, such a trespasser is entitled to resist trespass by others, although his claims must naturally give way in the face of any superior claim (eg by the real owner) to regain possession.

The Criminal Law Act 1977 provides a defence to any charge of violent entry for any person who is kept out of his own living accommodation by trespassers. Such a person has a defence to a charge under section 6 of the Act if he can prove that he was a 'displaced residential occupier' seeking to secure access to residential premises from which he had been excluded by the trespasser.[11] Apart from the case where the displaced occupier is himself a trespasser,[12] the status of 'displaced residential occupier' is defined as attaching to 'any person who was occupying any premises as a residence immediately before being excluded from occupation by anyone who entered those premises. . .as a trespasser'.[13] Such a person continues to rank as a 'displaced residential occupier' so long as he continues to be excluded from occupation of the premises by the original trespasser or by any subsequent trespasser.

The 'possession' of a lawful occupier (eg a tenant or licensee) may not be terminated by recourse to the remedy of self-help, even where the interest granted to the occupier has duly expired. Once 'possession' has been enjoyed by a tenant or licensee the occupier cannot be evicted except by due process of law. In such cases a criminal offence is committed by any person who seeks to secure the eviction of the occupier by any means other than that of court order for possession.[14]

(b) Remedy by action for possession

Although the law provides a displaced owner with the remedy of self-help in certain circumstances, this is not usually a course to be encouraged.[15] As Lord Denning MR said in *McPhail v Persons (Names Unknown)*,[16] '[i]n a civilised society, the courts should themselves provide a remedy which

10 This provision would apply, for instance, to a trespasser who breaks a door or window in order to secure entry, but not to one who merely manipulates a yale-type lock or window catch with a thin piece of metal (see Law Commission, *Report on Conspiracy and Criminal Law Reform* (Law Com No 76, 1976), para 2.61). See also (1985) LAG Bulletin (October), p 5.

11 Criminal Law Act 1977, s 6(3).

12 Criminal Law Act 1977, s 12(4).

13 Criminal Law Act 1977, s 12(3).

14 Ante, p 62, post, p 752.

15 See, in a different context, the disapproval of self-help remedies expressed in *Billson v Residential Apartments Ltd* [1992] 1 AC 494 at 524C–525C per Nicholls LJ, 536F-H per Lord Templeman (post, p 811). In Scotland private wheel clamping and the imposition of a release fee have been disallowed as a form of self-help remedy in respect of the wrongful parking of motor vehicles (see *Black v Carmichael* 1992 SLT 897.

16 [1973] Ch 447 at 457B-C.

is speedy and effective: and thus make self-help unnecessary.' For centuries therefore English law has provided a curial means by which a displaced owner can dislodge trespassers from his property. This legal process takes the form of the common law action for possession. In addition to this remedy civil damages may be recoverable in respect of trespass, the damages covering not only the diminution in the value of the land but also the cost of any works reasonably required in order to restore the owner's enjoyment of his land.[17] It is clear moreover that a landowner whose title is not in issue is prima facie entitled to an interlocutory injunction to restrain trespass on his land even though he has suffered no damage.[18]

The common law action for possession provided in many instances a potent remedy for the dispossessed paper owner. By the early 1970s, however, it had become obvious that the common law action was subject to certain disadvantages. The procedure of the action for possession was, for instance, particularly ineffective where the occupiers of premises were unidentifiable and could not therefore be named as defendants in proceedings taken against them.[19] There were also great difficulties in making a possession order where one squatter followed another in quick succession.

(c) *Remedy by summons*

Some relief from the technical defects of the common law action for possession came in 1970 when the Supreme Court Rules and County Court Rules were reformulated to provide a summary 'short-cut' procedure for the recovery of possession against trespassers. This procedure was intended to be used only in straightforward cases where there is no doubt that the occupiers of land are trespassers.

(i) The 'fast possession action' The 'fast possession action' now provided by RSC Ord 113 (in the High Court) and by CCR Ord 24 (in the county court) lends substantial assistance to landowners who are dispossessed by trespassers or squatters. The landowner may invoke a speedy remedy by summons against any person who occupies his land without his consent. He may issue an originating summons claiming possession even though he cannot identify the squatters by name.[20] The court may make an order for

17 See *Heath v Keys* (1984) *Times*, 28 May. Where a group of trespassers join in a squat, all may be made liable in negligence on a 'joint venture' basis for damage which has been caused by one member only of the group (see *Bushell v Hamilton* (1981) 113 DLR (3d) 498 at 502). See also *Lamb v Camden LBC* [1981] QB 625. A further disincentive to trespass by a group in joint and exclusive occupation of premises is the possibility that any individual member of the group may be required to discharge the entirety of the group's liability in respect of local authority charges (see *Westminster CC v Tomlin* [1989] 1 WLR 1287 at 1296B-G (total rates liability of over £27,000 for occupation of Cambodian Embassy)).

18 See *Patel v W.H. Smith (Eziot) Ltd* [1987] 1 WLR 853 at 861C-E.

19 See *In re Wykeham Terrace, Brighton, Sussex, ex Parte Territorial Auxiliary and Volunteer Reserve Association for the South East* [1971] Ch 204 at 209F.

20 See *McPhail v Persons (Names Unknown)* [1973] Ch 447 at 458E per Lord Denning MR ('A summons can be issued for possession against squatters even though they cannot be identified by name and even though, as one squatter goes, another comes in'). See also *Warwick University v de Graaf* [1975] 1 WLR 1126 at 1129H–1130B; *Wiltshire CC v Frazer* (No 1) (1984) 47 P & CR 69 at 71.

possession five days after the service of the summons,[1] and even this period may be shortened in cases of urgency.[2] The court has no discretion to withhold or suspend the order for possession once the case for possession has been established.[3] The 'short-cut' procedure is not appropriate, however, where there exists any serious triable issue eg whether the occupier is a tenant or licensee,[4] or has a defence available to him,[5] or where there is a complicated claim as to title.[6]

(ii) Extended scope The procedure by way of summons has proved to be an expeditious means of recovering possession of land from a wide variety of trespassers. It has been used successfully against such persons as students participating in a campus 'sit-in',[7] gypsies illegally camping on a roadside,[8] and residential licensees who refuse to vacate premises following the expiry of their licence.[9] Once a possession order has been granted, it can be enforced against any person who subsequently returns to the site or premises covered by the original order, provided that there is a 'plain and sufficient nexus between the original recovery of possession and the need to effect further recovery of the same land.'[10]

An order for possession under the procedure by way of summons may extend to a larger area of the owner's property than is adversely affected by the occupation in respect of which relief is initially sought. In *University of Essex v Djemal,*[11] for instance, a group of university students occupied the university's administrative offices as a protest. Faced with a summons under RSC Ord 113, they vacated the occupied premises but threatened to take further direct action if the university did not agree to their demands. The university continued with legal proceedings, and Walton J made an order for possession under RSC Ord 113, but limited the order to that part of the university premises which had been occupied.[12] The Court of Appeal

1 *Practice Direction (Chancery: Procedure)* [1983] 1 WLR 4. Once the writ of possession is granted, it must be executed by the sheriff as soon as is reasonably practicable (*Six Arlington Street Investments Ltd v Persons Unknown* [1987] 1 WLR 188 at 192G-H).
2 See RSC Ord 113, r 6(1), as substituted by *The Rules of the Supreme Court (Amendment No 3) 1986* (SI 1986/2289), post, p 311.
3 See *McPhail v Persons (Names Unknown)* [1973] Ch 447 at 458E-G per Lord Denning MR ('There is no provision for giving any time. The court cannot give any time. It must, at the behest of the owner, make an order for recovery of possession. It is then for the owner to give such time as he thinks right to the squatters. They must make their appeal to his goodwill and consideration, and not to the courts'). See also *Northern Ireland Housing Executive v McAuley* [1974] NI 233 at 235ff.
4 See *Henderson v Law* (1984) 17 HLR 237 at 241; *Crancour Ltd v Da Silvaesa* (1986) 52 P & CR 204 at 217, 226, 230f.
5 *Shah v Givert* (1983) LAG Bulletin 54. See N. Madge, (1983) LAG Bulletin 53.
6 *Cudworth v Masefield* (1984) *Times,* 16 May.
7 *University of Essex v Djemal* [1980] 1 WLR 1301.
8 *Wiltshire CC v Frazer* (No 1) (1984) 47 P & CR 69 at 75ff.
9 *GLC v Jenkins* [1975] 1 WLR 155 at 157A, 160B; *Turner v Burton* (Unreported, Court of Appeal, 12 March 1985). There was also a suggestion in 1980 that the summons procedure should be extended to the recovery of possession in respect of tenancies covered by the Rent Acts, but this proposal proved to be so controversial that it was eventually abandoned as politically unfeasible (see (1980) LAG Bulletin 201).
10 *Wiltshire CC v Frazer* (No 2) [1986] 1 WLR 109 at 113D. See also *R v Wandsworth County Court, ex parte Wandsworth LBC* [1975] 1 WLR 1314 at 1318H–1319A.
11 [1980] 1 WLR 1301. See [1981] Conv 317 (A.A. Preece).
12 The part last occupied had been Level 6 of the Social and Comparative Studies building.

took the view, however, that RSC Ord 113 confers 'a jurisdiction directed to protecting the right of the owner of property to the possession of the whole of his property, uninterfered with by unauthorised adverse possession'.[13] Because there was a threat that the students might occupy other parts of the university's premises, the Court of Appeal extended Walton J's possession order to cover the whole of the university's premises.[14]

(iii) More recent reform of RSC Ord 113 Within recent years even the 'fast possession action' has been open to criticism as a mechanism which operates too slowly and formally to provide an effective remedy when it is most needed. This criticism has been made particularly acutely in relation to much publicised cases where farmers have been unable to recover possession of their land from armies of participants in a 'hippie convoy' in time to prevent irremediable damage to growing crops or silage.

In response to this sort of concern the process of summary recovery of land was further facilitated by adjustments made to RSC Ord 113 with effect from early 1987.[15] Summary proceedings under RSC Ord 113 may now be heard and determined by a master rather than a judge.[16] The process of serving the summons is made significantly easier. Service on unnamed defendants may be effected either by affixing a copy of the summons and the accompanying affidavit to the main door or other conspicuous part of the premises occupied or by affixing a sealed transparent envelope containing the same to stakes which for this purpose are specially placed in the ground 'at conspicuous parts of the occupied land'.[17] The delay before the making of any final order for possession is also significantly reduced. Such an order may be made (in the case of residential premises) when five clear days have elapsed since the date of service and (in the case of other land) when two clear days have so elapsed.[18] These periods may be further reduced 'in case of emergency and by leave of the court'.[19] The net effect of the changes is significantly to strengthen the interests of private property against the adverse claims of intruders.

13 [1980] 1 WLR 1301 at 1304E per Buckley LJ.

14 The extension of a possession order to neighbouring areas of land is justified only if there is convincing evidence (and not merely a belief) that there is 'a real danger of actual violation' of such other areas. There need, however, be no express threat by the trespassers to extend their occupation. See *Ministry of Agriculture, Fisheries and Food v Heyman* (1990) 59 P & CR 48 at 50.

15 See *The Rules of the Supreme Court (Amendment No 3) 1986* (SI 1986/2289), which came into operation on 12 January 1987.

16 RSC Ord 113, r 1A, as introduced by SI 1986/2289. The Lord Chancellor's Department, in sponsoring the amendment of RSC Ord 113, did not accept the proposal that ex parte possession orders should be made possible under RSC Ord 113.

17 RSC Ord 113, r 4(2), as substituted by SI 1986/2289.

18 RSC Ord 113, r 6(1), as substituted by SI 1986/2289.

19 RSC Ord 113, r 6(1), as substituted by SI 1986/2289.

CHAPTER 11

Proprietary estoppel

One of the most significant movements occurring in the contemporary law of real property is the emergence of a new 'equity' based on the concept of 'estoppel'. As Browne-Wilkinson LJ observed in *Walker v Walker*,[1] the juristic basis of this 'equity' and the circumstances in which it may arise are as yet 'ill defined', but the movement 'can only be regarded as a development of the doctrine of proprietary estoppel.' It is this 'equity', and the doctrine of proprietary estoppel by which it is raised, which together form the subject matter of the present chapter. It is increasingly clear that the doctrine of estoppel, although first adumbrated by the courts over a century ago, is beginning to play a substantial role in the ordering of rights in property.[2] By identifying the circumstances in which certain claims may or may not be asserted in relation to titles in land, the doctrine has itself helped to reformulate the concept of a 'property right'—a consequence which has of course generated its own difficulties.

1. THE CENTRAL CONCERN OF PROPRIETARY ESTOPPEL

The central concern of the doctrine of proprietary estoppel is the notion of conscientious dealing in relation to land.[3] The doctrine has been explained as having its root in 'the first principle upon which all courts of equity proceed', that is, 'to prevent a person from insisting on his strict legal rights—whether arising under a contract, or on his title deeds, or by statute—when it would be inequitable for him to do so having regard to the dealings which have taken place between the parties.'[4] The core element of estoppel accordingly dictates that, in a fused system of law and equity, legally stipulated entitlements cannot be enforced in total isolation from the relational context in which relevant dealings have taken place. Against the background of

1 Unreported, Court of Appeal, 12 April 1984. See also *In re Sharpe (A Bankrupt)* [1980] 1 WLR 219 at 223D.

2 It has been suggested that many of the issues addressed in terms of the doctrines of resulting and constructive trusts could be resolved more fairly and efficiently by reference to the notion of estoppel. See Sir Nicolas Browne-Wilkinson, *Constructive Trusts and Unjust Enrichment* (Holdsworth Club of the University of Birmingham 1991), p 5f; *Gillies v Keogh* [1989] 2 NZLR 327 at 346 per Richardson J. It has also been noted elsewhere in this book (ante, p 258, post, p 1115) that the abolition of the doctrine of part performance seems likely to place a new and heightened emphasis on estoppel doctrine.

3 See eg the statement of Deane J in *Commonwealth v Verwayen* (1990) 170 CLR 394 at 440 that the doctrine of estoppel by conduct 'is founded upon good conscience'.

4 *Crabb v Arun DC* [1976] Ch 179 at 187H–188A per Lord Denning MR, citing *Hughes v Metropolitan Railway Co* (1877) 2 App Cas 439 at 448 per Lord Cairns LC.

this wider context the courts retain a form of moral scrutiny over the appropriateness of any particular assertion of rights. To this rudimentary premise can be attributed the development of estoppel in both its common law and equitable forms, the latter comprising doctrines grounded variously on estoppel by encouragement or acquiescence and upon promissory and proprietary estoppel.[5]

There is today an increasing recognition that the several historic categories of estoppel represent 'one overarching doctrine rather than a series of independent rules'.[6] This doctrine gives expression to a general judicial distaste for unconscientious departure from the basal assumptions underlying specific legal relationships.[7] The 'fundamental purpose' of the unified concept of estoppel is therefore to 'afford protection against the detriment which would flow from a party's change of position if the assumption that led to it were deserted'.[8] Indeed, the High Court of Australia has recently held that the rationale of estoppel is 'not that it is right and expedient to save persons from the consequences of their own mistake', but that 'it is right and expedient to save them from being victimised by other people.'[9] The doctrine of estoppel thus counteracts unconscionable conduct which involves 'the use of or insistence upon legal entitlement to take advantage of another's special vulnerability or misadventure. . .in a way that is unreasonable and oppressive to an extent that affronts ordinary minimum standards of fair dealing.'[10] Although starting in this way as a principle of inhibition, the doctrine has the indirect effect of creating rights on behalf of the claimant who successfully asserts an 'equity' founded upon estoppel.

2. THE GENERAL THEORY OF PROPRIETARY ESTOPPEL

To the extent that it has any separate existence, the doctrine of proprietary estoppel penalises any party who attempts unconscientiously to resile from assumptions which were previously understood to control a relevant dealing in respect of land. The doctrine has rarely been defined in one clear analytical

5 Estoppel has been described as 'a label which covers a complex array of rules spanning various categories' (*Commonwealth v Verwayen* (1990) 170 CLR 394 at 409 per Mason CJ). For a good description of the many sub-categories of estoppel doctrine, see P.D. Finn, *Equitable Estoppel*, in P.D. Finn (ed), *Essays in Equity* (Sydney 1985), p 59ff.

6 *Commonwealth v Verwayen* (1990) 170 CLR 394 at 410f per Mason CJ (Deane J agreeing at 440, 445). See also *Amalgamated Investment & Property Co Ltd v Texas Commerce International Bank Ltd* [1982] QB 84 at 122A-C; *Taylors Fashions Ltd v Liverpool Victoria Trustees Co Ltd* [1982] QB 133 (Note) at 153D; *Attorney-General of Hong Kong v Humphrey's Estate (Queen's Gardens) Ltd* [1987] AC 114 at 124A-B; *Waltons Stores (Interstate) Ltd v Maher* (1988) 164 CLR 387 at 403f per Mason CJ and Wilson J, 447ff per Deane J; *Foran v Wight* (1989) 168 CLR 385 at 411ff per Mason CJ, 434ff per Deane J. See A. Duthie, (1988) 104 LQR 362; M. Lunney, [1992] Conv 239.

7 In *Gillies v Keogh* [1989] 2 NZLR 327 at 331, Cooke P, although conceding that 'unfairness' is never 'a separate or arbitrary concept capable of being invoked in the abstract', spoke of a 'broader approach to the proprietary and promissory doctrines [which] identifies a general principle asserting the unfairness or injustice of resiling from underlying assumptions that have been acted upon.'

8 *Commonwealth v Verwayen* (1990) 170 CLR 394 at 410 per Mason CJ. See also *Waltons Stores (Interstate) Ltd v Maher* (1988) 164 CLR 387 at 419 per Brennan J.

9 *Commonwealth v Verwayen* (1990) 170 CLR 394 at 440 per Deane J.

10 *Commonwealth v Verwayen* (1990) 170 CLR 394 at 441 per Deane J.

formula, but has instead been expounded at different times by different judges in slightly divergent terms.[11] These varying formulae, although alike directed against unconscionable dealings with land, have not made for either certainty or consistency in the implementation of the fundamental premise of proprietary estoppel.[12]

(1) Essential elements of proprietary estoppel

The raw essentials of the doctrine of proprietary estoppel are threefold. In some form or other, a proprietary estoppel comprises (i) an assurance, (ii) a reliance, and (iii) a detriment.[13] If the owner of a title in land has expressly or impliedly given some assurance respecting present or future rights in his land, he cannot conscientiously withdraw that assurance if the person to whom it was given has meanwhile relied upon it to his own detriment.[14] Thus stated, the elements of assurance, reliance and detriment are interdependent and therefore capable of definition only in terms of each other. An 'assurance' is present only if the person who gives it intends it to be relied upon. 'Reliance' occurs only if the person to whom the assurance is given then takes action detrimental to his own interests. In some ultimate sense, 'detriment' results only if the assurance, once relied upon, is withdrawn.

(2) Comparison with promissory estoppel

When analysed in these terms, the doctrine of proprietary estoppel obviously shares a common origin with its contractual analogue of promissory estoppel.[15] In English law, however, the two doctrines differ in certain important respects. *First*, proprietary estoppel can arise even outside the scope of a contractual relationship,[16] although in practice proprietary estoppel and contractual relations often overlap.[17] *Second*, proprietary estoppel may be relied on as a sword and not merely as a shield, thereby conferring a right of action

11 For judicial reference to the wide variations in the formulation of the doctrine of proprietary estoppel, see *Ward v Kirkland* [1967] Ch 194 at 235D; *Cameron v Murdoch* [1983] WAR 321 at 350; *Riches v Hogben* [1986] 1 Qd R 315 at 327.

12 Ironically, the common origin of these various formulations has rather tended to impose a spurious and unnecessary uniformity on the theory of proprietary estoppel, concealing the fact that the courts have often been trying to apply a supposedly homogeneous doctrine to significantly different fact-situations. However, there are now indications that the many conceptual strands which constituted the core ideas of proprietary estoppel are in the process of being woven into one composite formula of equitable relief which, in its turn, reflects the greater underlying unity of the estoppel notion in its numerous modern manifestations.

13 See eg *Gillies v Keogh* [1989] 2 NZLR 327 at 346f per Richardson J.

14 *In re Basham, decd* [1986] 1 WLR 1498 at 1503H. See also *Brinnand v Ewens* (1987) 19 HLR 415 at 416f.

15 See G.H.Treitel, *The Law of Contract* (8th edn London 1991), p 134.

16 *Holiday Inns Inc v Broadhead* (1974) 232 Estates Gazette 951 at 1087; *Riches v Hogben* [1986] 1 Qd R 315 at 339; *Beaton v McDivitt* (1985) 13 NSWLR 134 at 150G–151B.

17 See eg *Tanner v Tanner* [1975] 1 WLR 1346 at 1350E, where Lord Denning MR described as a contractual licence something which might be more easily recognised in terms of proprietary estoppel. For conflicting views as to whether contractual licences and estoppels can logically overlap, see A. Briggs, [1981] Conv 212, [1983] Conv 285; M.P. Thompson, [1983] Conv 50. See also John Dewar, *Licences and Land Law: An Alternative View*, (1986) 49 MLR 741.

where none would otherwise exist.[18] *Third*, the equity arising in connection with proprietary estoppel may bind third parties and, in this sense, appear to constitute a substantive equitable proprietary right.[19]

(3) Controversial pressure-points

The theory of proprietary estoppel is controversial not least because, in its widest formulations, it threatens to subvert a number of hallowed doctrines or principles of law. Proprietary estoppel, in so far as it generates rights of property on behalf of a claimant, operates as an informal mechanism of rights creation which is quite inconsistent with the general requirement that the creation of land rights is dependent on compliance with certain formalities.[20] The successful assertion of proprietary estoppel often conflicts moreover with two other principles of wide application in English jurisprudence, namely, that gratuitous promises are unenforceable and that voluntarily rendered services are non-compensable.

The future development of the law of proprietary estoppel also poses several pivotal questions to which there are as yet no completely clear answers. There is a lingering debate whether the proper role of estoppel is to effectuate the legitimate expectations of parties or merely to protect against the detrimental consequences of an unconscientious insistence upon legal rights. Does estoppel effectively provide specific performance of legitimate expectations or only compensation in respect of the detriment which flows from the non-realisation of expectations? Moreover, as the critical test of estoppel relates increasingly to unconscionability, it remains uncertain whether the issue of unconscionability is to be measured in terms of conduct or in terms of outcome. Does the relevant test relate to the conscientiousness of the parties' dealings inter se or to the fairness of their outcome? How different, for that matter, is proprietary estoppel from the constructive trust? Indeed, is estoppel doctrine likely, as some fear in relation to the constructive trust,[1] to dissolve into a virtually unregulated formula of general equitable relief based upon ill-defined notions of fairness and a perceived need to prevent unjust enrichment?

Against the backdrop of these uncertainties the intrinsic elements of proprietary estoppel must be examined closely.

3. CATEGORIES IN THE CASE LAW

The concatenation of ideas underlying proprietary estoppel emerges from three broad, and not entirely distinct, categories of case. These categories comprise (1) the 'imperfect gift' cases, (2) the 'common expectation' cases, and (3) the 'unilateral mistake' cases. Irrespective of their classification, these

18 *Crabb v Arun DC* [1976] Ch 179 at 187E; *Amalgamated Investment & Property Co Ltd v Texas Commerce International Bank Ltd* [1982] QB 84 at 105D-E; *J.T. Developments Ltd v Quinn* (1991) 62 P & CR 33 at 45; *Thomas v Thomas* [1956] NZLR 785 at 793; *Classic Communications Ltd v Lascar* (1986) 21 DLR (4th) 579 at 587.

19 Post, p 364.

20 Ante, p 271. See *Sen v Headley* [1991] Ch 425 at 440G (ante, p 271); P.T. Evans, [1988] Conv 346, [1989] Conv 418.

1 See Sir Nicolas Browne-Wilkinson, *Constructive Trusts and Unjust Enrichment*, p 7.

cases all present the essential characteristics which embody the notion of proprietary estoppel, but each category of case in its turn gives a heightened emphasis to one or other of the constituent elements of assurance, reliance and detriment. As will appear later, the tendency in the modern case law is to synthesise the jurisprudence of proprietary estoppel so that it begins to compose a more unified doctrine based on a concept of 'detrimental reliance'. However, this threefold categorisation may still retain a residual importance, in that even today the response of the courts to estoppel claims seems in some respects to be graded with reference to criteria which differentiate slightly between these broad categories of circumstance.

(1) The 'imperfect gift' cases

The 'imperfect gift' cases relate typically to circumstances in which the courts, in applying the basic estoppel notion, have attached overwhelming significance to the element of 'assurance'. An assurance by X to Y that Y shall have rights in X's land is most clearly epitomised in a gift of that land by X to Y. However, a gift of an estate or interest in land must be effected in the appropriate form (eg by means of formal transfer).[2] In default of such a formality, the gift remains incomplete and it is trite law that equity will not perfect an imperfect gift.[3] Equity will not normally enforce any claim by the putative donee based on the informal gift, no matter how sincere or convincing the assurance of the would-be donor that he wished to make a gift of the land.

(a) Exceptional assistance in the perfection of a gift

There are, however, some circumstances in which equity is prepared to depart from the normal rule in order to assist the vesting of a voluntary gift of realty. These circumstances are illustrated in classic form in *Dillwyn v Llewelyn.*[4] Here a father placed his son in possession of land belonging to the father, both parties signing an informal memorandum which evidenced an intention that the land should be given to the son for the purpose of providing him with a dwelling-house. The son immediately proceeded at vast expense to build a residence for himself on that land. Lord Westbury LC recognised the imperfect (and therefore abortive) nature of the purported gift of realty, but held that 'the subsequent acts of the donor may give the donee that right or ground of claim which he did not acquire from the original gift.'[5] On the present facts, a promise of gift had been made, and 'on the strength of that promise, with the knowledge of [the father]', the son had incurred substantial expenditure on the land. Accordingly, the son was held to have acquired 'a right from the subsequent transaction to call on the donor to perform that contract and complete the imperfect donation which was made.' Lord Westbury concluded that, since 'the subsequent expenditure by the son, with the approbation of the father, supplied a valuable consideration

2 Ante, p 271. See, however, *Sen v Headley* [1991] Ch 425 (ante, p 272).
3 See *Milroy v Lord* (1862) 4 De G F & J 264 at 274, 45 ER 1185 at 1189 per Turner LJ.
4 (1862) 4 De G F & J 517, 45 ER 1285.
5 (1862) 4 De G F & J 517 at 521, 45 ER 1285 at 1286.

originally wanting',[6] the memorandum signed by both must be regarded as 'an agreement for the soil extending to the fee-simple of the land'.[7] The Court decreed that the intention to give the fee simple estate must now be performed, even though title to the land had by this stage passed to the executors of the father's estate. In other words, an unambiguous (albeit informal) assurance of entitlement must be honoured in the light of the subsequent reliance upon it.

Although the issue in *Dillwyn v Llewelyn* was considered substantially on the analogy of the doctrine of part performance, Lord Westbury LC made an important reference to the idea that the donee had an 'equity' which entitled him to claim the estate purportedly given to him by the original and informal promise.[8] The attendant circumstances left no doubt but that the original intention had been to vest a fee simple in the donee.[9] The decision thus provides authority for the proposition that where a gratuitous assurance is given that an estate or interest in land will be transferred, there arises an 'equity' in favour of the promisee based upon proprietary estoppel, provided that the promisee suffers detriment in reliance on the assurance. Under these circumstances the doctrine of proprietary estoppel not only protects the informal promisee against adverse claims to possession; it affords the promisee a ground on which he may claim the assistance of the courts towards the perfection of the intended gift. This approach to imperfect gifts of realty has been followed in other cases, the courts regarding it as irrelevant whether the original assurance of rights is contained in writing or is merely oral.[10]

(b) Far-reaching consequences

The recognition of an 'equity' raised by an informal donee's detrimental reliance can, however, produce somewhat dramatic results. In *Pascoe v Turner*,[11] it emerged that P and D had lived in a de facto relationship in a house owned by P. When P moved out in order to live with another woman elsewhere, he informed D orally that she had nothing to worry about as the house and its contents were thenceforth entirely hers. D continued to live in the house and she later effected repairs and improvements to the house costing about £230, a figure which amounted to approximately one quarter of her available capital. When P later brought possession proceedings on the basis that D had a mere revocable licence to occupy, the Court of Appeal ruled that the fee simple in the house should be conveyed by

6 In *Re Barker's Estate* (1875) 44 LJ Ch 487 at 490, Jessel MR referred to the unwillingness of courts to 'disturb voluntary deeds where consideration has been given for them, so to say, *ex post facto*'. See also *Beaton v McDivitt* (1985) 13 NSWLR 134 at 149B-C, 151A-B.

7 (1862) 4 De G F & J 517 at 522, 45 ER 1285 at 1287.

8 (1862) 4 De G F & J 517 at 522, 45 ER 1285 at 1286f. *Dillwyn v Llewelyn* has subsequently been treated as involving a case of 'equitable estoppel by acquiescence' (see *Thomas v Thomas* [1956] NZLR 785 at 793).

9 Lord Westbury declared that the 'estate was given as the site of a dwelling-house to be erected by the son...No one builds a house for his own life only, and it is absurd to suppose that it was intended by either party that the house, at the death of the son, should become the property of the father.'

10 See *Thomas v Thomas* [1956] NZLR 785 at 793f; *Raffaele v F & G Raffaele* [1962] WAR 29 at 31 (but compare *Jackson v Crosby* (No 2) (1979) 21 SASR 280 at 289).

11 [1979] 1 WLR 431. See (1979) 129 NLJ 1193 (R.D. Oughton); [1979] Conv 379.

P to D. Cumming-Bruce LJ applied *Dillwyn v Llewelyn*, holding that the circumstances raised in favour of D an 'equity', founded on proprietary estoppel, which could be satisfied only by ordering P to perfect his imperfect gift of the realty.[12]

(2) The 'common expectation' cases

Whereas the central feature of the 'imperfect gift' cases is a pellucid assurance of entitlement contained in an abortive gift of land, the element which comes to the fore in the 'common expectation' cases is the notion of 'reliance'. These cases concern not so much the situation where X has attempted to make a gift of land to Y, but rather the situation where X and Y have consistently dealt with each other in such a way as reasonably to cause Y to rely on a shared supposition that he would acquire rights of some kind in X's land. This is not to imply that the other key characteristics of proprietary estoppel are not present in such circumstances, but merely that the 'common expectation' cases particularly highlight the element of 'reliance'.

(a) Lord Kingsdown's speech in Ramsden v Dyson

The classic exposition of the 'common expectation' formulation of the doctrine of proprietary estoppel occurs in the dissenting speech of Lord Kingsdown in *Ramsden v Dyson.*[13] Here Lord Kingsdown stated that

> If a man, under a verbal agreement with a landlord for a certain interest in land, or, what amounts to the same thing, under an expectation, created or encouraged by the landlord, that he shall have a certain interest, takes possession of such land, with the consent of the landlord, and upon the faith of such promise or expectation, with the knowledge of the landlord, and without objection by him, lays out money upon the land, a Court of equity will compel the landlord to give effect to such promise or expectation.[14]

Although, for the purpose of the instant decision, Lord Kingsdown couched his observations in terms of the landlord-tenant relationship, his remarks have been accepted as having a more general role in identifying the factors which can generate a proprietary estoppel.[15] In *Taylors Fashions Ltd v Liverpool Victoria Trustees Co Ltd*,[16] Oliver J pointed out that the circumstances postulated in Lord Kingsdown's example of proprietary estoppel 'presuppose. . .the fostering of an expectation in the minds of *both* parties

12 The outcome in *Pascoe v Turner* is remarkable in that the equitable jurisdiction of the court was invoked effectively to bring about a redistribution of assets on the breakdown of a de facto marriage relationship. The manner and extent of the redistribution lay entirely within the discretion of the court, and the defendant was thereby enabled to circumvent the rule that a de facto spouse cannot claim property adjustment or financial provision from her partner on the demise of their relationship. See B. Sufrin, (1979) 42 MLR 574, and compare *McGill v S* [1979] IR 283 at 293 where Gannon J in the Irish High Court declined to follow *Pascoe v Turner*. See also *Gissing v Gissing* [1971] AC 886 at 910E-F.

13 (1866) LR 1 HL 129 at 170.

14 See also *Gregory v Mighell* (1811) 18 Ves Jun 328 at 333, 34 ER 341 at 343. The doctrine of acquiescence has been traced back into the 15th century (see Lord Goff of Chieveley and Gareth Jones, *The Law of Restitution* (3rd edn, London 1986), p 141).

15 See *Crabb v Arun DC* [1976] Ch 179 at 194D per Scarman LJ.

16 [1982] QB 133 (Note) at 147G.

at the time but from which, once it has been acted upon, it would be unconscionable to permit the landlord to depart.' This formulation of the doctrine of proprietary estoppel is sometimes known as 'estoppel by encouragement' or 'estoppel by acquiescence'.[17]

(b) Classic illustrations of 'common expectation'

A good example of this form of proprietary estoppel is found in *Plimmer v Mayor etc of Wellington.*[18] Here a licensee of land had, at the request of the owner of that land, expended considerable sums of money on the extension of a jetty and the construction of a warehouse. The Judicial Committee of the Privy Council upheld a claim on behalf of appellants claiming through the licensee that the licence, although originally revocable, had been rendered irrevocable by reason of the expenditure. Sir Arthur Hobhouse declared that the parties could not 'go on dealing with one another in the way stated in this case for a series of years, except with a sense in the minds of both that the occupant has something more than a merely precarious tenure.'[19] The Privy Council decided that the circumstances fell 'within the principle stated by Lord Kingsdown as to expectations created or encouraged by the landlord', and that the appellants therefore had an 'equity arising from expenditure on land'.[20] Accordingly they had acquired 'an indefinite, that is practically a perpetual, right' to the jetty for the purposes of the original licence.

It has been accepted in numerous cases since *Plimmer* that a common expectation engendered by encouragement from the owner of land can give rise to an 'equity' based on proprietary estoppel. The classic features of this form of estoppel were demonstrated in *Inwards v Baker.*[1] Here a father had allowed his son to build a bungalow at his own cost on the father's land, the son thereafter going into occupation of the bungalow in the belief, encouraged by his father, that he would be allowed to live there during his lifetime. The father died without making any binding contractual or other arrangements to this effect. The Court of Appeal nevertheless refused to permit the trustees under the father's will to obtain possession against the son, holding that the son had acquired by reason of his expenditure on the land an 'equity' which bound not only the father (while he was alive) but also his successors in title with notice.[2] In giving equitable relief, the Court took the view that the 'equity' could be satisfied only by holding that the son 'can remain there as long as he desires to [use it] as his home.'[3]

A similar application of the estoppel doctrine occurred in *E.R. Ives Investment*

17 The precise name given to the *Ramsden v Dyson* principle is 'really immaterial' (*Taylors Fashions Ltd v Liverpool Victoria Trustees Co Ltd* [1982] QB 133 (Note) at 151H per Oliver J).
18 (1884) 9 App Cas 699.
19 (1884) 9 App Cas 699 at 712.
20 (1884) 9 App Cas 699 at 713.
1 [1965] 2 QB 29. See (1965) 81 LQR 183 (R.H. Maudsley).
2 It has been pointed out that this decision, in conferring on the son a possessory licence for life, produced the undesirable result both of rendering the land pro tempore unsaleable and of discouraging the son from moving (see F.R. Crane, (1967) 31 Conv (NS) 332 at 342). For further criticism, see *Dodsworth v Dodsworth* (1973) 228 Estates Gazette 1115 (post, p 355).
3 [1965] 2 QB 29 at 37G. See also *Raffaele v F & G Raffaele* [1962] WAR 29 at 31.

Ltd v High.[4] Here the defendant had incurred expenditure in reliance on an agreement reached with the plaintiff's predecessor in title, under which the defendant had undertaken to raise no objection to a trespass committed upon his land by reason of the encroachment of foundations into his land, provided that the defendant could enjoy a right of way across the predecessor in title's neighbouring property. The Court of Appeal held this agreement to be binding on the plaintiff. By reason of his detrimental reliance, the defendant had acquired an 'equity' founded on the fact that the plaintiff's predecessor had 'created in [the defendant's] mind a reasonable expectation that his access over the yard would not be disturbed.'[5] A similar approach was applied by the Court of Appeal in *Crabb v Arun DC*,[6] where one party had allowed himself to become landlocked in reliance on an 'agreement in principle' that he should have a right of access and egress over land belonging to an adjacent owner.

(3) The 'unilateral mistake' cases

A significant distinction can be drawn in the jurisprudence of proprietary estoppel between the 'common expectation' cases and the 'unilateral mistake' cases. Unlike the former category, which gives pre-eminence to the shared nature of the parties' assumptions as to their mutual rights, the 'unilateral mistake' cases apply the doctrine of proprietary estoppel to circumstances in which only one party has made any error about his rights. In the 'unilateral mistake' cases, primary importance is attached to the 'detriment' which is suffered by a party who innocently relies on his mistaken supposition that he has rights in land.[7] This branch of the doctrine of proprietary estoppel regards it as unconscionable that the owner of the land should wilfully stand by and allow such a person to incur 'detriment' by relying on his own uncorrected misapprehension of the true legal position.

(a) Lord Cranworth LC's speech in Ramsden v Dyson

The foremost statement of the 'unilateral mistake' approach is found in the speech of Lord Cranworth LC in *Ramsden v Dyson.*[8] Here the Lord Chancellor gave the following instance:

> If a stranger begins to build on my land supposing it to be his own, and I, perceiving his mistake, abstain from setting him right, and leave him to persevere in his error, a Court of equity will not allow me afterwards to assert my title to the land on which he had expended money on the supposition that the land was his own. It considers that, when I saw the mistake into which he had fallen, it was my duty to be active and to state my adverse title; and that it would be dishonest in me

4 [1967] 2 QB 379 (ante, p 152). See F.R. Crane, *Estoppel Interests in Land*, (1967) 31 Conv (NS) 332.

5 [1967] 2 QB 379 at 394G.

6 [1976] Ch 179 at 189E, 192A, 198G. See (1976) 40 Conv (NS) 156 (F.R. Crane); (1976) 126 NLJ 772 (M. Vitoria); (1976) 92 LQR 174 (P.S. Atiyah), 342 (P.J. Millett).

7 The 'detriment' will often flow directly from the fact that any physical improvements effected on the land in reliance on a mistaken belief accede to the realty (ante, p 11). Such improvements normally confer no rights upon the improver (post, p 325).

8 (1866) LR 1 HL 129 at 140f.

to remain wilfully passive on such an occasion, in order afterwards to profit by the mistake which I might have prevented.

The 'unilateral mistake' cases are remarkable in that they exemplify some of the very few instances in English law where the courts have recognised a right to payment or other compensation for services rendered gratuitously.[9] True 'unilateral mistake' cases are fairly rare,[10] and the facts which require to be proved in support of this kind of estoppel claim are narrowly prescribed.

(b) *The Willmott v Barber probanda*

It was over a century ago, in *Willmott v Barber*,[11] that Fry J, without making any explicit reference to any existing case law,[12] formulated his own definition of the notion of estoppel. In his view, a man is not to be deprived of his strict legal rights 'unless he has acted in such a way as would make it fraudulent for him to set up those rights.' Fraud of this kind depended on proof of five necessary elements. *First*, the claimant of an equity based on estoppel must have made a mistake as to his legal rights. *Second*, the claimant must have 'expended some money or must have done some act. . .on the faith of his mistaken belief'. *Third*, the owner of the land must know of the existence of his own right which is inconsistent with the right claimed by the claimant. *Fourth*, the owner must know of the claimant's mistaken belief of his rights. *Fifth*, the owner must have encouraged the claimant in his expenditure of money or in the other acts which he has done, either directly or by abstaining from asserting his legal right.

The five *probanda* laid down by Fry J related quite clearly and exclusively to unilateral mistake. The very essence of the 'fraud' which is required to activate the estoppel lies in the wilful and self-interested silence of one who knows his rights and who realises that he may profit by reason of the detriment suffered by one who, not knowing his rights, acts under a mistake. Such facts were not present in *Willmott v Barber*: here both plaintiff and defendant were alike mistaken as to their true legal rights.[13] The circumstances of the instant case could not properly be categorised as a genuine example of 'unilateral mistake', and the claim of estoppel was therefore rejected.

(c) *Long-term effects of Willmott v Barber*

The observations of Fry J were, however, destined to have a much more enduring impact, for they had the perhaps unintended effect of imposing a strait-jacket on the development of proprietary estoppel during the following hundred years. Unfortunately the five *probanda*, because they were not explicitly limited to the category of 'unilateral mistake', were for a long

9 See Goff and Jones, *op cit*, p 137.

10 See, however, *Hamilton v Geraghty* (1901) 1 SRNSW (Eq) 81.

11 (1880) 15 Ch D 96 at 105f.

12 *Ramsden v Dyson* (1866) LR 1 HL 129 had been cited during argument before Fry J.

13 Neither the plaintiff assignee of a lease nor his lessor had realised that the lease prohibited assignment without the lessor's consent. In Fry J's view, the lessor could not, by acquiescing in the plaintiff's expenditure, be estopped from asserting his right to refuse consent to the assignment since at the date of the supposed acquiescence he had not realised that he had a right of veto over assignments anyway.

time regarded as applying to all claims of proprietary estoppel irrespective of the category into which they fell.[14]

The inevitable result was that the courts often attempted to force given fact-situations within Fry J's five *probanda*, even where the terminology of *Willmott v Barber* was ludicrously irrelevant or inapplicable to the circumstances in issue.[15] Likewise the courts were prone to dismiss claims based on proprietary estoppel where the *probanda* were not amply satisfied. In particular, the requirement that the estoppel claimant should have made a positive mistake as to his existing rights was apt to operate with some harshness in circumstances where the claimant was in no doubt as to the absence of any strict entitlement on his part, but had been led to expect that he would somehow and at some time acquire rights by relying upon the assurance given by the owner. The insistence on the five *probanda* thus caused special difficulty in the context of informal 'family arrangements',[16] where full awareness of the absence of any existing entitlement in strict law is not incompatible with a vague and ill-defined expectation of future entitlement.[17]

(d) *Diminishing force of* Willmott v Barber

In effect the rigid application of the *Willmott v Barber* criteria tended to attach supreme importance to the 'unilateral mistake' theory of estoppel as expounded by Lord Cranworth LC in *Ramsden v Dyson* and to divert attention away from the alternative 'common expectation' rationale found in Lord Kingsdown's judgment. Gradually it came to be recognised that the five *probanda* of Fry J did not constitute a comprehensive formula,[18] and the way was prepared for a broader restatement of the principle of estoppel. This restatement has largely reversed the balance of emphasis so that the modern law of proprietary estoppel more closely approximates to the approach adumbrated by Lord Kingsdown.

(4) The modern synthesis: 'detrimental reliance'

It fell to Oliver J in *Taylors Fashions Ltd v Liverpool Victoria Trustees Co Ltd*[19] to confirm a broader direction in the law of proprietary estoppel. The plaintiffs here were the assignees of a leasehold term granted by the predecessors in title of the defendants. Under the terms of the lease the lessee had been given an option to renew the lease at the expiration of the current term.

14 It is noteworthy that this extensive view was not taken in the early days of the development of the estoppel doctrine. Only four years after *Willmott v Barber*, the Privy Council in *Plimmer v Mayor etc of Wellington* (1884) 9 App Cas 699 at 712, was careful to distinguish clearly between the categories of 'unilateral mistake' and 'common expectation', observing that in the instant case 'the equity is not claimed because the landowner has stood by in silence while his tenant has spent money on his land.'

15 See even *Crabb v Arun DC* [1976] Ch 179 at 195F-H.

16 Post, p 906.

17 For examples of 'hard cases' both in the family arrangement context and elsewhere, see *E & L Berg Homes Ltd v Grey* (1980) 253 Estates Gazette 473; *Stilwell v Simpson* (1983) 133 NLJ 894; *Coombes v Smith* [1986] 1 WLR 808.

18 See *Electrolux Ltd v Electrix Ltd* (1953) 71 RPC 23 at 33 per Evershed MR; *Shaw v Applegate* [1977] 1 WLR 970 at 978C-D, 980B-C.

19 [1982] QB 133 (Note). See (1981) 97 LQR 513; [1982] Conv 450 (P. Jackson).

At the commencement date of the lease, such an option was generally considered to run with the land and not to require protection by registration. A few months later the original lessor conveyed the freehold reversion to the defendants. In the firm belief that the option was still valid, the plaintiffs then incurred substantial expenditure on renovations and improvements of the demised premises. Only some years later—and somewhat to the surprise of conveyancers—did the courts indicate that an option to renew a lease constitutes a registrable land charge.[20] The ineluctible result here was that the plaintiffs' option was rendered void for non-registration.[1] When the defendants subsequently declined to renew the lease, the plaintiffs argued that the defendants, by acquiescing in the expenditure, had been estopped from pleading the voidness of the option. Oliver J rejected this claim of proprietary estoppel and held the defendants entitled to refuse to renew the lease.

(a) Restricted relevance of the Willmott v Barber probanda

It was clear on the facts of *Taylors Fashions* that the plaintiffs could not establish all of the *Willmott v Barber* criteria, not least because the defendants had at all material times been unaware of their own strict rights in the matter.[2] However, Oliver J declined to succumb to a slavish application of the *Willmott v Barber probanda*, basing his dismissal of the plaintiffs' estoppel claim on different, and much wider, grounds.[3] He pointed out that Fry J's *probanda*, while arguably relevant to certain claims of estoppel, made no sense at all in other cases. He drew a broad distinction between the 'common expectation' cases and the 'unilateral mistake' cases, observing that the strict *Willmott v Barber probanda* are more properly relevant (if at all) to the latter category of case 'where all that has happened is that the party alleged to be estopped has stood by without protest while his rights have been infringed.'[4] Oliver J found it 'readily intelligible' in cases of 'pure acquiescence' or 'mere passivity' that 'there must be shown a duty to speak, protest or interfere which cannot normally arise in the absence of knowledge or at least a suspicion of the true position.'[5] However, in the 'common expectation' cases exemplified in Lord Kingsdown's dictum in *Ramsden v Dyson*, 'there is no room for the literal application of the *probanda*, for the circumstances there postulated do not presuppose a "mistake" on anybody's part, but merely the fostering

20 See *Beesly v Hallwood Estates Ltd* [1960] 1 WLR 549 (ante, p 144, post, p 863), affirmed by the Court of Appeal on different grounds ([1961] Ch 105).

1 Oliver J did not pretend that the defendants' case was 'overburdened with merit', but took the view that 'it is no part of a judge's function to seek to impose upon a party to litigation his own idiosyncratic code of commercial morality' ([1982] QB 133 (Note) at 135E-F). The option was of course still binding upon the original lessor ([1982] QB 133 (Note) at 143G).

2 They had not known that the plaintiffs were mistaken in believing that their option was still enforceable.

3 In Oliver J's view, the role of the court was not to inquire 'whether the circumstances can be fitted within the confines of some preconceived formula serving as a universal yardstick for every form of unconscionable behaviour' ([1982] QB 133 (Note) at 152A). See also *Andrews v Colonial Mutual Life Assurance Society Ltd* [1982] 2 NZLR 556 at 568.

4 [1982] QB 133 (Note) at 147B. Significantly, Oliver J thought that the strict relevance of the *probanda* even in 'unilateral mistake' cases 'must now be considered open to doubt.'

5 [1982] QB 133 (Note) at 146C, 147C.

of an expectation in the minds of *both* parties at the time but from which, once it has been acted upon, it would be unconscionable to permit the landlord to depart.'[6]

(b) A more general basis for proprietary estoppel

Having rejected the universal applicability of the *Willmott v Barber probanda*, Oliver J proceeded to find support in the case law for 'a much wider equitable jurisdiction to interfere in cases where the assertion of strict legal rights is found by the courts to be unconscionable.'[7] While the *Willmott v Barber* criteria may provide 'a valuable guide'[8] in determining the applicability of proprietary estoppel, the primary inquiry for the court is 'whether, in particular individual circumstances, it would be unconscionable for a party to be permitted to deny that which, knowingly or unknowingly, he has allowed or encouraged another to assume to his detriment'.[9] A circumstance such as the state of mind of the party alleged to be estopped thus becomes 'merely one of the relevant factors. . .in the overall inquiry.'[10]

The judgment of Oliver J in *Taylors Fashions* appears to have been a watershed in the law of proprietary estoppel. In the aftermath of *Taylors Fashions* it seems now to be accepted that 'the real question comes down simply to whether or not the assertion of strict legal rights would be unconscionable, without any detailed conditions or criteria being specified'.[11] Some categorisation of the cases will still be appropriate,[12] since, as emerges later, the requirements of estoppel continue to differentiate slightly between circumstances of 'common expectation' and 'unilateral mistake'.[13] But, in general terms, the strictures of the old *Willmott v Barber* approach have been very substantially relaxed.[14]

6 [1982] QB 133 (Note) at 147G.
7 [1982] QB 133 (Note) at 147B. The existence of this more extensive jurisdiction had already been suggested in *Shaw v Applegate* [1977] 1 WLR 970 at 980B-C per Goff LJ. (Compare, however, the cautionary remarks of Megarry V-C in *Haslemere Estates Ltd v Baker* [1982] 1 WLR 1109 at 1119G, and see the reminder in *Legione v Hateley* (1983) 152 CLR 406 at 431 per Mason and Deane JJ that the estoppel doctrine provides no 'charter for idiosyncratic concepts of justice and fairness').
8 [1982] QB 133 (Note) at 153E, quoting *Crabb v Arun DC* [1976] Ch 179 at 194E per Scarman LJ.
9 [1982] QB 133 (Note) at 151H–152A.
10 [1982] QB 133 (Note) at 152A.
11 *Appleby v Cowley* (1982) *Times*, 14 April, per Megarry V-C. See also *Amalgamated Investment & Property Co Ltd v Texas Commerce International Bank Ltd* [1982] QB 84 at 104D-E. A claim of proprietary estoppel succeeded in *In re Basham, decd* [1986] 1 WLR 1498, even though it was conceded (at 1508F-G) that the *Willmott v Barber* criteria had not been satisfied.
12 In *Taylors Fashions* [1982] QB 133 (Note) at 145ff, Oliver J undertook a meticulous analysis of the preceding case law which vindicated the view that slightly different considerations apply to the divergent categories of 'common expectation' and 'unilateral mistake'.
13 Post, p 339.
14 See, however, *Coombes v Smith* [1986] 1 WLR 808 at 817G–818B, where *Taylors Fashions Ltd v Liverpool Victoria Trustees Co Ltd* was not cited and the *Willmott v Barber* criteria were applied with full rigour. In other jurisdictions there has been a distinct trend away from the *Willmott v Barber probanda* towards the application of more flexible concepts of 'unconscionability' (*Wham-O MFG Co v Lincoln Industries* [1984] 1 NZLR 641 at 671; *Stratulatos v Stratulatos* [1988] 2 NZLR 424 at 436; *Gillies v Keogh* [1989] 2 NZLR 327 at 345 per Richardson J) and unjust enrichment (see *Carabin v Offman* (1989) 55 DLR (4th) 135 at 140ff).

4. OPERATION OF PROPRIETARY ESTOPPEL

Attention must now be turned to the way in which the modern concept of proprietary estoppel operates in the case law. A successful claim of estoppel involves a showing of three elements: (1) an assurance, (2) a reliance, and (3) a detriment.

(1) Assurance

In order to found a claim of proprietary estoppel, it is vital that there should have been some assurance of entitlement given by the person whom it is sought to estop.[15] There is in English law no doctrine akin to the Roman law concept of *negotiorum gestio*,[16] which gave the provider of a voluntary service the right to claim remuneration or reimbursement.[17] One who voluntarily improves another's land without encouragement or promise of reward does so, in English law, 'entirely at his own risk.'[18] To confer benefit gratuitously and then expect reward is, to use the blunt terms of Lord Cranworth LC, a 'folly'.[19] Thus Oliver LJ was standing on solid ground when, in *Savva v Costa and Harymode Investments Ltd*,[20] he declared himself unable to accept the proposition that 'there is some category of proprietary estoppel outside the *Ramsden v Dyson* principle, resting simply on expenditure with consent.'[1] In order to raise an equity there must have been a 'representation or expectation created by the landowner.'[2] The only

15 In the most extreme situation, it is plain that no representation can be relevant for estoppel purposes which actually *denies* that the claimant has any rights in the land. See eg *Haughan v Rutledge* [1988] IR 295 at 301 (expectation of lease rebutted by prior refusal to agree to grant lease); *Gillies v Keogh* [1989] 2 NZLR 327 at 347 per Richardson J (no encouragement of any expectation of rights where cohabitee consistently emphasised her own sole ownership of assets).

16 See W.W. Buckland and A.D. McNair, *Roman Law and Common Law* (2nd edn, London 1952), p 344.

17 See W.W. Buckland, *A Text-book of Roman Law* (3rd edn by P. Stein, Cambridge 1963), p 537ff.

18 *Stilwell v Simpson* (1983) 133 NLJ 894. 'The general principle is, beyond all question, that work and labour done or money expended by one man to preserve or benefit the property of another do not according to English law create any lien upon the property saved or benefited, nor, if standing alone, create any obligation to repay the expenditure. Liabilities are not to be forced upon people behind their backs any more than you can confer a benefit upon a man against his will' (*Falcke v Scottish Imperial Insurance Co* (1886) 34 Ch D 234 at 248 per Bowen LJ). See also *Ruabon Steamship Co v London Assurance* [1900] AC 6 at 10, 15; *Pettitt v Pettitt* [1970] AC 777 at 818B; *In re Vandervell's Trusts* (No 2) [1974] Ch 269 at 299F, H; *Avondale Printers & Stationers Ltd v Haggie* [1979] 2 NZLR 124 at 155.

19 *Ramsden v Dyson* (1866) LR 1 HL 129 at 141. In England compensation for improvements cannot be claimed under any doctrine of unjust enrichment (see *Pettitt v Pettitt* [1970] AC 777 at 795G-H per Lord Reid).

20 (1981) 131 NLJ 1114.

1 In *Milton v Proctor* (1989) NSW ConvR 55-450 at 58,258, McHugh JA pointed out that 'expenditure on improvements on land by a licensee to the licensor's knowledge does not by itself create any equity'. See also *Haughan v Rutledge* [1988] IR 295 at 301f.

2 *Savva v Costa and Harymode Investments Ltd* (1981) 131 NLJ 1114. See also *Easterbrook v The King* [1931] 1 DLR 628 at 636; *Rodgers v Moonta Town Corporation* (1981) 37 ALR 49 at 53 per Gibbs CJ (High Court of Australia).

exceptions to this principle tend to be of statutory origin[3] and are few in number.

(a) Source of the assurance

If a proprietary estoppel is effectively to restrain the exercise of rights normally incidental to a fee simple estate, the assurance on which the estoppel is based must have been given by the owner of the fee simple himself[4] or by his employees or agents.[5] It is not sufficient to raise the equity that the assurance was given by a tenant of the freehold owner.[6] The party giving the assurance need not be human. A company acting through its employees and agents can give a relevant assurance,[7] but such an assurance is not meaningful if given to a related company which is controlled by identical shareholders and management.[8]

(b) Subject matter of the assurance

The assurance required to raise an 'equity' of estoppel must confirm in its recipient *either* an understanding that he is already the owner *or* an expectation

3 See eg Matrimonial Proceedings and Property Act 1970, s 37 (ante, p 15; post, p 422). Other jurisdictions provide more general statutory relief in respect of improvements effected under mistake of title. See eg Queensland's Property Law Act 1974–82, ss 196, 197 (*Newman v Powter* [1978] Qd R 383; *Ex parte Goodlet & Smith* [1983] 2 Qd R 792); Manitoba's Law of Property Act (RSM 1970, c L90), s 27 (*Re Robertson and Saunders* (1977) 75 DLR (3d) 507); Ontario's Conveyancing and Law of Property Act (RSO 1980, c 90), s 37 (*Geldhof v Bakai* (1983) 139 DLR (3d) 527). In some jurisdictions the statutory relief available does not even require proof of mistake (see British Columbia's Property Law Act (RSBC 1979, c 340), s 32: *Re Ferguson and Lepine* (1983) 141 DLR (3d) 187).

4 *Ward v Kirkland* [1967] Ch 194 at 241D per Ungoed-Thomas J. The assurance must come from some party qua owner of the land concerned (*Western Fish Products Ltd v Penwith DC* [1981] 2 All ER 204 at 218a-b). The relevant assurance may even come from the ultimate owner of land, ie the Crown (see *Attorney-General to the Prince of Wales v Collom* [1916] 2 KB 193 at 204; *The Queen v Smith* (1981) 113 DLR (3d) 522 at 582). There is, however, no requirement that the promisor should already own the land in relation to which the assurance is made. The assurance may come, for instance, from a licensee who later acquires the legal estate (see *Watson v Goldsbrough* [1986] 1 EGLR 265 at 267F, where Browne-Wilkinson V-C held that an estoppel established against two licensees was 'fed' when they subsequently acquired a fee simple estate). See also *Riches v Hogben* [1986] 1 Qd R 315 at 321, 327, 342, where an estoppel claim was successfully based on a promise by a mother that she would purchase a house and put it in her son's name if he were prepared to emigrate to Australia to live near her.

5 That an employee or agent can give a relevant assurance was confirmed by the Court of Appeal in *Ivory v Palmer* (1976) 237 Estates Gazette 411.

6 *Ward v Kirkland* [1967] Ch 194 at 241D; *Swallow Securities Ltd v Isenberg* (1985) 274 Estates Gazette 1028 at 1030. The point appears to have been implicit in *Willmott v Barber* (1880) 15 Ch D 96.

7 In *Swallow Securities Ltd v Isenberg*, supra, the Court of Appeal was prepared, *obiter*, to hold a landlord company estopped if the relevant assurance had been mediated through its resident porter in a block of flats.

8 *Te Rama Engineering Ltd v Shortlands Properties Ltd* [1982] BCL 692 (High Court of New Zealand). Casey J thought that the identical management would act as a 'barrier to concepts of inducement, encouragement, or acquiescence'.

that he will become the owner of some interest or entitlement in the land which he would not otherwise have.[9]

(i) General nature of the rights promised The rights promised must be rights in or over land[10] and must be such as fall within the capacity of the owner to grant.[11] The assurance of entitlement must be 'clear and unequivocal'.[12] It is not sufficient that the owner should rather vaguely promise the claimant 'financial security' both before and after his death, without reference to any specific asset or assets.[13] An estoppel claim is not, however, precluded merely because the claimant's expectation did not relate to some clearly identified piece of property: a valid claim may arise from an expectation that the claimant would inherit the owner's residuary estate.[14]

The quality of the promised benefits as 'rights' may also depend rather crucially on the precise timing of their acquisition. Proprietary estoppel cannot operate if the rights promised have already passed to the claimant of the 'equity' before he incurs his expenditure or otherwise acts on the assurance given to him.[15] Doubt has been expressed whether a representation 'as to what will happen upon the representor's death or what will be in the representor's will' can be construed as an assurance that there should be a 'present acquisition of that future right by the representee.'[16] It is clear, for instance, that a mere expression of opinion as to likely future entitlement cannot rank as an assurance for the purpose of estoppel.[17] However, in *In re Basham, decd*[18] an estoppel claim was successfully founded on acts undertaken not in reliance on a belief that the claimant had any existing rights, but on the faith of an undertaking that she would be granted rights in the future. The claimant and her husband had for many years looked after the claimant's

9 For confirmation that the rights assured may be either present or future, see *Barrios v Chiabrera* (1984) 3 BPR 9276 at 9279 per Powell J. For example, in *Shaida v Kindlane Ltd* (Unreported, Chancery Division, 1976 S No 8501, 22 June 1982), Judge Baker QC upheld an estoppel claim based on an assurance that the defendants would transfer a freehold estate to the plaintiff's wife. See also *Davies v Messner* (1975) 12 SASR 333 at 341.

10 Estoppel cannot be founded on a representation that planning permission will be available for a development on the claimant's land (*Western Fish Products Ltd v Penwith DC* [1981] 2 All ER 204 at 218h).

11 *Ezekiel v Orakpo and Scott* (Unreported, Court of Appeal, 1976 E No 1773, 20 February 1980) per Brightman LJ.

12 *J.T. Developments Ltd v Quinn* (1991) 62 P & CR 33 at 46, 51 per Ralph Gibson LJ.

13 *Layton v Martin* [1986] 2 FLR 227 at 238G–239A. See also *Baumgartner v Baumgartner* [1985] 2 NSWLR 406 at 415C-D.

14 *In re Basham, decd* [1986] 1 WLR 1498 at 1510C-E.

15 *Avondale Printers & Stationers Ltd v Haggie* [1979] 2 NZLR 124 at 144. (This situation becomes problematic of course only if, as in this case, there is a subsequent re-transfer of the disputed rights to the party who gave the original assurance).

16 *Philip Lowe (Chinese Restaurant) Ltd v Sau Man Lee* (Unreported, Court of Appeal, 9 July 1985) per May LJ. See also *Layton v Martin* [1986] 2 FLR 227 at 238G–239D. *A fortiori*, if the estoppel claimant has actual knowledge that the representor has already made a will leaving the relevant property to somebody else (*Stilwell v Simpson* (1983) 133 NLJ 894). Compare, however, *Inwards v Baker* [1965] 2 QB 29 (ante, p 319), and see the way in which a Canadian court has imposed a constructive trust on the basis of the marriage vow 'With all my worldly goods I thee endow' (*Re Spears and Levy* (1975) 52 DLR (3d) 146 at 152, 154).

17 *E & L Berg Homes Ltd v Grey* (1980) 253 Estates Gazette 473 at 477 per Sir David Cairns.

18 [1986] 1 WLR 1498.

elderly step-father, having been encouraged by him to believe that his entire residuary estate would become theirs on his death. It was held to be irrelevant that the claimant's expectations were not related to any existing entitlement,[19] and that she had never enjoyed even some lesser form of right in the property promised.[20]

(ii) Examples Within the limits indicated above, the potential subject matter of the rights promised may take almost any form.[1] The courts have shown themselves willing in principle, and often in practice, to invoke the doctrine of proprietary estoppel to give effect to expectations of entitlement which vary from a fee simple interest in the land[2] to the beneficial ownership of a share in land,[3] a right of pre-emption,[4] a lease,[5] a licence,[6] and even an easement.[7] Moreover, it is not essential that the precise nature of the promised entitlement should have been spelt out in terms of recognisable property rights. There is high authority for the view that 'the equity arising from expenditure on land need not fail merely on the ground that the interest to be secured has not been expressly indicated.'[8] The expectation engendered by the assurance may simply involve a fairly inarticulate understanding that the claimant of the 'equity' will acquire some rights of some kind.[9]

(c) The manner of the assurance

The assurance which generates the 'equity' may be express or implied; it may be 'active or passive'.[10] A proprietary estoppel will arise in either case if the present claimant of the 'equity' was led to believe that he either had

19 [1986] 1 WLR 1498 at 1509B.
20 [1986] 1 WLR 1498 at 1510B-C.
1 Even the inclusion of chattels within an estate agent's printed particulars of sale may constitute a representation that those items will pass with the conveyance of the realty, with the result that the vendor can be estopped from denying that they are within the scope of the sale (see *Hamp v Bygrave* (1983) 266 Estates Gazette 720 at 726).
2 *Pascoe v Turner* [1979] 1 WLR 431 (ante, p 317).
3 *Lim Teng Huan v Ang Swee Chuan* [1992] 1 WLR 113 at 119F-G.
4 *Stilwell v Simpson* (1983) 133 NLJ 894.
5 *Watson v Goldsbrough* [1986] 1 EGLR 265 at 266F-H; *J.T. Developments Ltd v Quinn* (1991) 62 P & CR 33 at 50f.
6 *Inwards v Baker* [1965] 2 QB 29 (ante, p 319); *Greasley v Cooke* [1980] 1 WLR 1306 (post, p 353).
7 *Ward v Kirkland* [1967] Ch 194; *Crabb v Arun DC* [1976] Ch 179; *Dewhirst v Edwards* [1983] 1 NSWLR 34 (post, p 343); *Classic Communications Ltd v Lascar* (1986) 21 DLR (4th) 579 at 587ff.
8 *Plimmer v Mayor etc of Wellington* (1884) 9 App Cas 699 at 713 per Sir Arthur Hobhouse. See also *Inwards v Baker* [1965] 2 QB 29 at 37B; *Denny v Jensen* [1977] 1 NZLR 635 at 638; *Vinden v Vinden* [1982] 1 NSWLR 618 at 624E; *Cameron v Murdoch* [1983] WAR 321 at 351 (affd (1986) 63 ALR 575 at 595). Compare, however, *Coombes v Smith* [1986] 1 WLR 808 at 818C-H.
9 See, for instance, *Baumgartner v Baumgartner* [1985] 2 NSWLR 406 at 414D, 419D-E, where Kirby P held that a valid estoppel claim could be founded on oral statements made by a de facto husband. He had constantly assured his partner that the family home would be 'a security for her' and had encouraged her to continue saving for 'our house'. Such assurances gave her an 'expectation of an indefinite right of residence'. It may not be sufficient, however, that the owner merely provides a written assurance, in general terms, of emotional and financial security (see *Layton v Martin* [1986] 2 FLR 227 at 238H–239D).
10 *Warnes v Hedley* (Unreported, Court of Appeal, 31 January 1984) per May LJ.

or would acquire rights over the land in question. The determining factor in this context is the impact which the assurance had upon the mind of the claimant as a reasonable person[11]: it is irrelevant that the person giving the assurance did not himself realise the consequence or implications of the informal concession of rights.[12]

(i) Relevant forms of representation Relevant assurances may fall anywhere within the broad spectrum which ranges from a direct and positive request to incur expenditure, through encouragement and 'incitement', to mere silent abstention from the assertion of one's rights.[13] In determining the applicability of a proprietary estoppel, the courts look for evidence of 'anything done or left undone' which may have induced the detrimental reliance of the claimant.[14] It is clear that the assurance need not be made, and commonly is not made, in any manner which gives rise to contractual liability.[15] The assurance may even derive from the terms of an agreement which is, on other grounds, void for uncertainty.[16]

(ii) Representation by silence It is in relation to the role of silence that the most controversial questions arise. It is clear that an estoppel can indeed be founded on conscious silence.[17] As Lord Wensleydale said in *Ramsden v Dyson*,[18] if a stranger 'builds on my land, supposing it to be his own, and I, knowing it to be mine, do not interfere, but leave him to go on, equity considers it to be dishonest in me to remain passive and afterwards to interfere and take the profit.'[19]

The courts are reluctant, however, to attach significance to mere silence on the part of a landowner unless it is quite clear that he deliberately intended that his silence should be construed as endorsing the supposed entitlement of the estoppel claimant.[20] In *Williams v Coleman*,[1] for instance, the Court of Appeal declined to uphold a claim of proprietary estoppel against a physically disabled lady confined to a wheelchair. Fox LJ thought that her silence in the face of adverse occupation could be explained simply on the basis that she 'wanted to avoid trouble' and therefore 'made no fuss'. It

11 *Commonwealth v Verwayen* (1990) 170 CLR 394 at 445 per Deane J. See *J.T. Developments Ltd v Quinn* (1991) 62 P & CR 33 at 50, where Ralph Gibson LJ thought that the claimant's subjective belief that he has been promised rights 'cannot be decisive: he must show that the assurance given was in the circumstances such that he could reasonably so regard it.'
12 *Preston and Henderson v St Helens MBC* (1989) 58 P & CR 500 at 503. See also *Wellington CC v New Zealand Law Society* [1988] 2 NZLR 614 at 627.
13 *Ward v Kirkland* [1967] Ch 194 at 239B-C. See also *Taylors Fashions Ltd v Liverpool Victoria Trustees Co Ltd* [1982] QB 133 (Note) at 148E-F.
14 *E & L Berg Homes Ltd v Grey* (1980) 253 Estates Gazette 473 at 477 per Sir David Cairns.
15 There was, for instance, no contractual duty resting on the son in *Inwards v Baker* [1965] 2 QB 29 (ante, p 319) to take up his father's offer of land on which to build his bungalow.
16 *Lim Teng Huan v Ang Swee Chuan* [1992] 1 WLR 113 at 116F, 118B-C.
17 See *The Queen v Smith* (1981) 113 DLR (3d) 522 at 583 (Federal Court of Appeal of Canada).
18 (1866) LR 1 HL 129 at 168.
19 In *Warnes v Hedley* (Unreported, Court of Appeal, 31 January 1984), Slade LJ readily accepted that 'in some circumstances passive conduct, even if unaccompanied by any words, may suffice to constitute the relevant encouragement, if the facts are such that it is reasonable for the other party so to construe it.' See also *Denny v Jensen* [1977] 1 NZLR 635 at 638.
20 See *Salvation Army Trustee Co Ltd v West Yorkshire MCC* (1981) 41 P & CR 179 at 196 per Woolf J.
1 Unreported, Court of Appeal, 27 June 1984.

has likewise been held that inaction by a landlord in respect of past breaches of covenant by a tenant cannot constitute any assurance that the lease will not be forfeited by reason of future breaches.[2] Nor can mere inaction by a liquidator over a prolonged period during which a bankrupt improves his property be taken to connote the degree of encouragement or acquiescence required to generate a proprietary estoppel.[3] But if the owner of an interest in or over land remains wilfully silent about his interest in the knowledge that a mortgagee would otherwise be inhibited from accepting the land as security for a loan, this degree of non-disclosure may estop a future assertion of priority over the rights taken by the mortgagee.[4]

(iii) Reliance without representation There is but a blurred borderline between representation by silence and the situation where a party acts in detrimental reliance upon an assumed entitlement which has never been the subject of any representation at all whether express or implied. This troubled frontier represents one of the potential growth-points of the modern law of estoppel. At present in English law no proprietary estoppel can properly be founded on a mere legitimate expectation of rights, however reasonable the expectation, if the owner of the relevant land has failed to 'encourage or allow a belief or expectation' that the claimant would acquire rights.[5] Detrimental reliance upon a self-induced expectation cannot give rise to a valid claim of estoppel. It is at precisely this point that developments in other jurisdictions threaten to outstrip the English doctrine of estoppel. Even in the absence of any assurance or representation made by the landowner, the Australian courts have already indicated a willingness to order that the owner compensate spontaneously incurred detriment where a failure to do so would be 'unconscionable' or would lead to unjust enrichment of the owner.[6] Such a sweeping doctrine of relief seems, at least for the time being, to be unlikely to find a ready acceptance in English courts.[7]

2 *Boxbusher Properties Ltd v Graham* (1976) 240 Estates Gazette 463 at 465.

3 *Pennell v Nunn* (Unreported, Chancery Division, 1979 P No 105, 2 April 1982).

4 *Midland Bank Ltd v Farmpride Hatcheries Ltd* (1981) 260 Estates Gazette 493 at 497ff; *Ulster Bank Ltd v Shanks* [1982] NI 143 at 150A; *Bristol and West Building Society v Henning* [1985] 1 WLR 778 at 782G, 783C (post, p 577). An often quoted dictum is that of Lord Tomlin in *Greenwood v Martins Bank Ltd* [1933] AC 51 at 57: 'Mere silence cannot amount to a representation, but when there is a duty to disclose deliberate silence may become significant and amount to a representation' (see *Canadian Superior Oil Ltd v Paddon-Hughes Development Co Ltd* (1969) 3 DLR (3d) 10 at 16, (1970) 12 DLR (3d) 247 at 253; *Maurice Demers Transport Ltd v Fountain Tire Distributors (Edmonton) Ltd* (1974) 42 DLR (3d) 412 at 421).

5 See *Attorney-General of Hong Kong v Humphrey's Estate (Queen's Gardens) Ltd* [1987] AC 114 at 124F–125A, where the Privy Council declined to uphold an estoppel in favour of a party who had 'acted in the confident and not unreasonable hope' that an agreement in principle would subsequently be formalised (ante, p 251). See also *J.T. Developments Ltd v Quinn* (1991) 62 P & CR 33 at 47; *Gillies v Keogh* [1989] 2 NZLR 327 at 331 per Cooke P.

6 See eg *Nepean District Tennis Association Inc v Council of City of Penrith* (1989) NSW ConvR 55-438 at 58,180f, where the New South Wales Court of Appeal granted compensation to an estoppel claimant which had resurfaced a tennis court complex in the 'reasonable expectation', albeit unsupported by any representation, that it would acquire a long-term lease of the complex. See also *Beaton v McDivitt* (1987) 13 NSWLR 162 at 171F-G per Kirby P.

7 See eg Sir Nicolas Browne-Wilkinson, *Constructive Trusts and Unjust Enrichment*, p 7.

(d) The state of mind of the owner of the land

Certain difficulties in the application of the doctrine of proprietary estoppel relate to the state of mind which must be shown on the part of the owner of the land which is the subject of an estoppel claim.

(i) Must the owner act unconscionably in making the assurance? It is widely accepted that, for the purpose of establishing a proprietary estoppel, there is no need to show that the owner of the land acted unconscionably at the point of making the assurance of entitlement in favour of the eventual estoppel claimant.[8] The relevant element of unconscionability relates, not to the initial representation made, but to the later denial of the assumptions thereby engendered in the mind of the estoppel claimant.[9]

(ii) Must the owner know of the reliance by the claimant? In order that a proprietary estoppel be raised it is essential, however, that a certain state of knowledge should have been present in the party whose strict rights it is sought to restrain. It must be shown that that party gave the relevant assurance, whether actively or passively, with the intention that it should be relied on to another's detriment.[10] Where the assurance is repeated over a period of time, during which reliance supervenes, it must be clear that there was knowledge that the assurance was being relied upon by the eventual claimant of the 'equity'.[11] It must be proved that the party giving the assurance knew[12] or ought to have known[13] that the claimant was acting in the belief that he was acquiring some entitlement on the strength of the assurance.[14]

Usually there will be knowledge of such facts as that the claimant is engaging in expenditure on the improvement of land.[15] However, it is not necessary that the knowledge of the party sought to be estopped should extend to the precise nature of the disadvantage incurred by the claimant. In *Crabb*

8 See eg *Taylors Fashions Ltd v Liverpool Victoria Trustees Co Ltd* [1982] QB 133 (Note) at 151H–152A, where Oliver J indicated that the owner may act 'knowingly or unknowingly' in allowing or encouraging another to make assumptions to the latter's detriment (ante, p 323).

9 *Lim Teng Huan v Ang Swee Chuan* [1992] 1 WLR 113 at 117E-F per Lord Browne-Wilkinson.

10 *J.T. Developments Ltd v Quinn* (1991) 62 P & CR 33 at 46 per Ralph Gibson LJ. Mere expressions of opinion cannot amount to assurances for the purpose of proprietary estoppel (see *E & L Berg Homes Ltd v Grey* (1980) 253 Estates Gazette 473 at 477 per Sir David Cairns, ante, p 327).

11 *Griffiths v Williams* (1978) 248 Estates Gazette 947 at 949 per Goff LJ.

12 *Ward v Gold* (1969) 211 Estates Gazette 155 at 161; *Gross v French* (1976) 238 Estates Gazette 39 at 41; *Savva v Costa and Harymode Investments Ltd* (1981) 131 NLJ 1114; *Appleby v Cowley* (1982) *Times*, 14 April; *J.T. Developments Ltd v Quinn* (1991) 62 P & CR 33 at 51f. In *Shaida v Kindlane Ltd* (Unreported, Chancery Division, 1976 S No 8501, 22 June 1982), Judge Baker QC described this requirement of knowledge as 'important, though not crucial'. See also *Denny v Jensen* [1977] 1 NZLR 635 at 639.

13 *Salvation Army Trustee Co Ltd v West Yorkshire MCC* (1981) 41 P & CR 179 at 194, 196; *Swallow Securities Ltd v Isenberg* (1985) 274 Estates Gazette 1028 at 1030 per Cumming-Bruce LJ; *Watson v Goldsbrough* [1986] 1 EGLR 265 at 266M, 267E.

14 It seems to be sufficient that the giver of the assurance knew that the claimant was 'likely' to, or 'might well', undertake detrimental action in reliance on the assurance. There is no absolute obligation on the claimant to point out to the representor that he is just about to act in reliance by incurring expenditure. See *Crabb v Arun DC* [1976] Ch 179 at 198A-D per Scarman LJ; *J.T. Developments Ltd v Quinn* (1991) 62 P & CR 33 at 52ff.

15 Such knowledge may be actual or a matter of irresistible inference (see *E & L Berg Homes Ltd v Grey* (1980) 253 Estates Gazette 473 at 476, 479).

v Arun DC,[16] for instance, the Court of Appeal upheld an estoppel claim even though the defendant was unaware at the material time that the plaintiff was selling part of his land without reserving an appropriate right of way. Scarman LJ admitted that the Court was thus applying the estoppel doctrine where the defendant knew merely of the 'intention' of the plaintiff to rely on the assurance given, as distinct from having knowledge of 'the realisation of that intention'.[17] Scarman LJ nevertheless thought that a mere absence of notice of the precise prejudice incurred did not destroy the plaintiff's 'equity'. It was sufficient that the defendant had knowingly undertaken the risk that the plaintiff might act in reliance on the common expectation engendered by their mutual dealings.[18]

(iii) Must the owner know his own strict rights? It used to be the accepted view that no claim of estoppel could be established unless the person who gave the original assurance was consciously aware at the time of his own strict proprietary rights.[19] As Fry J said in *Willmott v Barber*,[20] such a person 'must know of the existence of his own right which is inconsistent with the right claimed by the plaintiff.' Without such knowledge, he is 'in the same position as the plaintiff, and the doctrine of acquiescence is founded upon conduct with a knowledge of your legal rights.' However, this requirement of knowledge is nowadays confined to cases of 'pure acquiescence', where the only assurance given has taken the form of sheer silence or, at best, passive encouragement.[1] Accordingly the owner's ignorance of his strict rights will provide no impediment to a claim of proprietary estoppel if the relevant assurance has taken a more forceful or active form.[2] Estoppel may apply if one party, although unaware of his precise rights, has by his words or conduct positively induced another party to rely on the strength of a common expectation generated by their dealings or negotiations.[3]

(iv) Must the owner know that the claimant is acting under a mistake? Again it used to be thought that, in order to establish a proprietary estoppel, a claimant must show that the owner knew that the claimant's belief in his own supposed

16 [1976] Ch 179 at 189D, 197H (ante, p 320).

17 [1976] Ch 179 at 197H–198A. However, where there is no knowledge even of an intention to rely on the assurance, the claim of proprietary estoppel must fail (see *Costagliola v English* (1969) 210 Estates Gazette 1425 at 1431). *A fortiori*, if there was a requirement (eg as a condition of grant aid) that the landowner be informed in advance of the intention to begin making improvements on the land (*Devlin v Northern Ireland Housing Executive* [1983] NI 377 at 391E per Lord Lowry LCJ).

18 See, however, *Coombes v Smith* [1986] 1 WLR 808 at 819H.

19 See eg *Ward v Kirkland* [1967] Ch 194 at 240B.

20 (1880) 15 Ch D 96 at 105.

1 *Taylors Fashions Ltd v Liverpool Victoria Trustee Co Ltd* [1982] QB 133 (Note) at 152A, 157B-C (ante, p 323).

2 It even seems to be irrelevant in such a case that the rights which the owner now seeks to enforce were not strictly pre-existing rights, but were instead rights which came into existence only upon the change of position induced by his assurance (see *Bank Negara Indonesia v Hoalim* [1973] 2 MLJ 3 at 5A-B per Lord Wilberforce).

3 That estoppel may be raised against a party who is innocently unaware of his own rights was confirmed, *obiter*, in *Canadian Superior Oil Ltd v Paddon-Hughes Development Co Ltd* (1969) 3 DLR (3d) 10 at 16f, (1970) 12 DLR (3d) 247 at 253. See also *Sarat Chunder Dey v Gopal Chunder Laha* (1892) 19 LR Ind App 203 at 215ff (Privy Council); *Cameron v Murdoch* [1983] WAR 321 at 351.

rights was erroneous or mistaken.[4] However, after *Taylors Fashions Ltd v Liverpool Victoria Trustees Co Ltd*[5] this requirement seems to have been displaced at least in relation to cases of the 'common expectation' variety,[6] although it may have a greater relevance to cases of 'unilateral mistake'. As Oliver J pointed out, 'knowledge of the true position by the party alleged to be estopped becomes merely one of the relevant factors—it may even be a determining factor in certain cases—in the overall inquiry.'[7]

(2) Reliance

In order to raise an 'equity' based on proprietary estoppel, the claimant must show that he has acted in reliance upon the assurance given by the owner of the land. The need for strict proof of reliance has sometimes been a matter of doubt. In *Greasley v Cooke*,[8] for instance, Lord Denning MR seemed to suggest that there is a presumption of reliance once it is shown that 'a representation was calculated to influence the judgment of a reasonable man'.[9] More recently, however, the Judicial Committee of the Privy Council has confirmed that reliance on the owner's representation must be clearly established[10] or at least be demonstrated to have been a matter of 'inevitable inference'.[11]

(a) The causal link between assurance and detriment

It is the element of reliance which renders it unconscionable that an assurance, once given, should be subsequently withdrawn or denied. Reliance thus provides vital evidence of the causal link between the assurance given by one party and the detriment suffered by the other.

The courts have often stressed that the assurance must be an *effective* cause of detriment. It must be proved that the assurance has 'induced'[12] the expectations of the party to whom it was given or has at least 'influenced'[13] his conduct. Accordingly, claims based on proprietary estoppel have been rejected by the courts on the ground that there was no evidence that the assurance was one of the operative causal factors bringing about the change

4 *Willmott v Barber* (1880) 15 Ch D 96 at 105.
5 [1982] QB 133 (Note) (ante, p 322).
6 [1982] QB 133 (Note) at 147B.
7 [1982] QB 133 (Note) at 152A.
8 [1980] 1 WLR 1306 at 1311C-E.
9 See also *Brikom Investments Ltd v Carr* [1979] QB 467 at 483A. Lord Denning's view was criticised as inconsistent with authority and principle (see (1981) 125 SJ 539 at 540 (M.P. Thompson)), but found a following in *Hamp v Bygrave* (1983) 266 Estates Gazette 720 at 726; *Grimison v Union Fidelity Trustee Co of Australia Ltd* (1984) 3 BPR 9469 at 9474.
10 *Attorney-General of Hong Kong v Humphrey's Estate (Queen's Gardens) Ltd* [1987] AC 114 at 124D per Lord Templeman.
11 *Lim Teng Huan v Ang Swee Chuan* [1992] 1 WLR 113 at 118D per Lord Browne-Wilkinson.
12 See *Dodsworth v Dodsworth* (1973) 228 Estates Gazette 1115 at 1117. In *Swallow Securities Ltd v Isenberg* (1985) 274 Estates Gazette 1028 at 1030, Cumming-Bruce LJ found it 'helpful to use the term "inducing an expectation" rather than the nearly synonymous verb "encouraging"...'
13 *Amalgamated Investment & Property Co Ltd v Texas Commerce International Bank Ltd* [1982] QB 84 at 105A per Goff J. See also *Coombes v Smith* [1986] 1 WLR 808 at 820A; *Layton v Martin* [1986] 2 FLR 227 at 235G.

of position in respect of which the 'equity' is claimed.[14] This has sometimes led to slightly surprising—and even harsh—decisions. The courts have on occasion declined to uphold estoppel claims in respect of improvements made to living conditions in the family home which, in the courts' view, the claimant would have effected in any case simply for reasons of domestic comfort or convenience.[15] Likewise the courts have refused to apply the doctrine of proprietary estoppel where it was felt that the claimant contributed money and labour, not in the belief that she was acquiring either an interest in the family home or a right to live there, but merely because 'she was part of the family'.[16]

(b) Change of position

The fundamental catalyst in the generation of rights by way of proprietary estoppel is the fact that there has been a change of position by the party to whom the assurance was given.[17] There must be palpable evidence that the claimant of the 'equity' has acted on the faith of the assurance given to him.[18] This requirement has often been described in the case law as predicating that the claimant has suffered some form of 'detriment',[19] a usage which is perfectly acceptable so long as it is understood as referring to a factual disadvantage which demonstrates the reality of the reliance.[20] As will be seen later,[1] the ultimate 'detriment' required to found a proprietary estoppel is the legal detriment which occurs only if the assurance initially

14 See eg *Taylors Fashions Ltd v Liverpool Victoria Trustees Co Ltd* [1982] QB 133 (Note) at 156C per Oliver J, who distinguished between action undertaken 'on the faith of' a belief that the plaintiffs had a valid right of option (ante, p 322) and action undertaken merely 'in' that belief. See also *Brinnand v Ewens* (1987) 19 HLR 415 at 417; *Avondale Printers & Stationers Ltd v Haggie* [1979] 2 NZLR 124 at 144; *Concept Projects Ltd v McKay* [1984] 1 NZLR 560 at 565.

15 See *E & L Berg Homes Ltd v Grey* (1980) 253 Estates Gazette 473 at 479 per Sir David Cairns; *Rogers v Eller* (Unreported, Court of Appeal, 20 May 1986). In *Stilwell v Simpson* (1983) 133 NLJ 894, it was considered that the claimant had effected the disputed improvements, not in response to the assurance given to him, but because it was 'natural to him to make the best of his home'.

16 *Philip Lowe (Chinese Restaurant) Ltd v Sau Man Lee* (Unreported, Court of Appeal, 9 July 1985) per May LJ. See also *Coombes v Smith* [1986] 1 WLR 808 at 820F-G; *Layton v Martin* [1986] 2 FLR 227 at 235H-236A.

17 'In cases of proprietary estoppel the factor which gives rise to the equitable obligation is A's alteration of his position on the faith of [an] understanding' (*In re Basham, decd* [1986] 1 WLR 1498 at 1504D per Edward Nugee QC). Where there is no demonstrable change of position, the claim of estoppel obviously cannot succeed (see *Beaton v McDivitt* (1985) 13 NSWLR 134 at 157C-D per Young J. On appeal estoppel was not argued, but Young J's view was upheld ((1987) 13 NSWLR 162 at 167E, 172D-E)).

18 In *Greasley v Cooke* [1980] 1 WLR 1306 at 1311H–1312A, Lord Denning MR expressed the view that there was 'no need for [the estoppel claimant] to prove that she acted to her detriment or to her prejudice'. Some later took this statement to mark an abrogation of any requirement of detriment in estoppel cases, but such an interpretation was later expressly disavowed by Dunn LJ in *Watts v Story* (Unreported, Court of Appeal, 14 July 1983). See also *Greasley v Cooke* [1980] 1 WLR 1306 at 1313H–1314A per Dunn LJ; *Coombes v Smith* [1986] 1 WLR 808 at 821B-E; [1988] Conv 59 (J.E.M.).

19 See eg *Greasley v Cooke* [1980] 1 WLR 1306 at 1314A per Dunn LJ; *Riches v Hogben* [1986] 1 Qd R 315 at 341f.

20 'Evidence of detriment must be affirmatively demonstrated' (*Commonwealth v Verwayen* (1990) 170 CLR 394 at 416 per Mason CJ).

1 Post, p 340.

given is unconscionably withdrawn.[2] It may be altogether easier and less confusing to refer to the present requirement of factual detriment in terms of a 'change of position'.

(i) Improvement of realty It is sometimes said that the improvement of land constitutes the 'classic way'[3] in which the claimant of an 'equity' can establish that he has undergone a factual detriment or change of position in reliance on an assurance. It is certainly true that reliance is most clearly and tangibly expressed in the form of expenditure on improvements to realty, provided at least that these improvements are relatively 'permanent'[4] or 'substantial'.[5] Thus proprietary estoppels have been recognised where the claimant has built a dwelling-house on another's land,[6] or has financed an addition or extension to some existing construction.[7]

(ii) Disadvantage unrelated to land It is clear, however, that 'the categories of detriment are not closed'.[8] There is no strict requirement that the change of position pleaded in support of an estoppel claim should necessarily involve any qualitative 'improvement' of land[9] or comprise expenditure on land belonging to the giver of the assurance[10] or, for that matter, comprise any form of expenditure related to land at all.[11] The disadvantage incurred by the relier may include such factors as a failure to reserve appropriate rights of way on the sale of his land.[12]

2 In *Commonwealth v Verwayen* (1990) 170 CLR 394 at 415, Mason CJ acknowledged this difference between 'two distinct types of detriment'. Mason CJ labelled as detriment 'in a broad sense' the legal detriment which follows from the denial of the correctness of a relevant assumption, and pointed to detriment 'in a narrower sense' as representing the factual disadvantage suffered by the estoppel claimant in reliance on that assumption. Compare, however, M. Lunney, [1992] Conv 239 at 246f.

3 *Shaida v Kindlane Ltd* (Unreported, Chancery Division, 1976 S No 8501, 22 June 1982) per Judge Baker QC.

4 *Griffiths v Williams* (1977) 248 Estates Gazette 947; *Taylor v Taylor* [1956] NZLR 99 at 103. In *Appleby v Cowley* (1982) *Times*, 14 April, it was argued that a proprietary estoppel could be founded on an electrical re-wiring, redecoration and damp-repair of premises. However, Megarry V-C declined to say that such expenditure should be 'ignored', but thought it carried 'little weight' in that it did 'not represent much more than keeping the building in a usable state while it was being occupied.' Compare *Beaton v McDivitt* (1985) 13 NSWLR 134 at 157C, where maintenance of a road, had it been carried out, would have been thought to be sufficient.

5 *Pascoe v Turner* [1979] 1 WLR 431 at 436B. See also *Stratulatos v Stratulatos* [1988] 2 NZLR 424 at 436; *Milton v Proctor* (1989) NSW ConvR 55-450 at 58,256ff.

6 *Inwards v Baker* [1965] 2 QB 29 (ante, p 319).

7 *Hussey v Palmer* [1972] 1 WLR 1286 (post, p 445).

8 *Watts v Story* (unreported, Court of Appeal, 14 July 1983) per Dunn LJ.

9 It is difficult, for instance, to imagine that the expenditure described in *Pennine Raceway Ltd v Kirklees MBC* [1983] QB 382 at 386B actually enhanced the utility of the land for any purpose other than that of using it for motor racing.

10 *Willmott v Barber* (1880) 15 Ch D 96 at 105; *Dewhirst v Edwards* [1983] 1 NSWLR 34 at 49F. In *Cook v Minion* (1979) 37 P & CR 58 at 65, for instance, a claim of proprietary estoppel was upheld on behalf of an owner who had installed water closets on his own land in reliance on permission received from his neighbour for ancillary rights of drainage.

11 *Holiday Inns Inc v Broadhead* (1974) 232 Estates Gazette 951 at 1087; *In re Basham, decd* [1986] 1 WLR 1498 at 1509D; *Riches v Hogben* [1986] 1 Qd R 315 at 342.

12 *Crabb v Arun DC* [1976] Ch 179 at 197G (ante, p 320). See also *Vinden v Vinden* [1982] 1 NSWLR 618 at 624F.

(iii) Personal effort and personal disadvantage The estoppel claimant's change of position may be measurable in money terms,[13] but there is ample authority that the change of position required need not involve the payment of money.[14] It may instead take the form of a contribution of labour and services in the family home,[15] the working of a farm property,[16] the abandonment of an existing job and home in order to live near the person who provides the relevant assurance,[17] or indeed, perhaps, the undergoing of any sacrifice which is not of exclusively emotional significance.[18] The disadvantage incurred may comprise a forgoing of opportunities for a career outside the home,[19] a failure to purchase other land for use as a home,[20] and even a deliberate refraining from serving a statutory notice of application for a new lease.[1]

There has been a tendency in recent years for the courts to emphasise more keenly the requirement that the estoppel claimant be shown to have incurred a 'detriment' which extends beyond mere emotional trauma or the inconvenience of a changed lifestyle.[2] In *Watts v Story*,[3] for instance, the Court of Appeal rejected a claim of estoppel in spite of substantial evidence of disadvantage suffered by the claimant. The claimant here had given up a Rent Act protected flat and had moved from a settled life in his home town in order to live with and look after his elderly grandmother. There was evidence that she had promised him that, in return for his services, her house would be his when she died. In rejecting the claim of estoppel,

13 In *Timber Top Realty Pty Ltd v Mullens* [1974] VR 312 at 318, the Supreme Court of Victoria held that reliance on an assurance was sufficiently demonstrated where the claimant of the 'equity' sold land for an inadequate consideration to the person who gave the assurance. See also *Baumgartner v Baumgartner* [1985] 2 NSWLR 406 at 419C.

14 *In re Sharpe (A Bankrupt)* [1980] 1 WLR 219 at 223E; *Greasley v Cooke* [1980] 1 WLR 1306 at 1311G, 1314A; *Watts v Story* (Unreported, Court of Appeal, 14 July 1983). Money payment in itself is no guarantee that an estoppel will be raised. Payments towards shared household expenses (such as food) or running costs (such as household bills) may more readily be seen as a mere contribution to the current living expenses of the family (see *Hannaford v Selby* (1976) 239 Estates Gazette 811 at 813; *Griffiths v Williams* (1977) 248 Estates Gazette 947).

15 *Greasley v Cooke* [1980] 1 WLR 1306 (post, p 353). See also *Hink v Lhenen* (1975) 52 DLR (3d) 301 at 315f, where what was essentially an estoppel claim was dealt with in terms of *quantum meruit*.

16 *Beech v Beech* [1982] BCL 231 (High Court of New Zealand).

17 *Jones (AE) v Jones (FW)* [1977] 1 WLR 438 at 442D. See also *Riches v Hogben* [1986] 1 Qd R 315 at 321 (where a son sold up at a loss and emigrated to Australia in order to live near his aged mother).

18 See *Christian v Christian* (1981) 131 NLJ 43 (post, p 426). See also *In re Basham, decd* [1986] 1 WLR 1498 at 1505G-H, where the claimant and her husband had 'subordinated their own interests to the wishes of the deceased'.

19 *Greasley v Cooke* [1980] 1 WLR 1306 at 1312A. Compare, however, *Coombes v Smith* [1986] 1 WLR 808 at 820H–821A.

20 *Cameron v Murdoch* [1983] WAR 321 at 360 (affirmed without comment by the Privy Council, (1986) 63 ALR 575 at 595). See also *In re Basham, decd* [1986] 1 WLR 1498 at 1505F, where the claimant and her husband had refrained from moving home in order that they could continue living near the claimant's step-father.

1 *Watkins v Emslie* (1982) 261 Estates Gazette 1192 at 1194, where the Court of Appeal rejected a claim of proprietary estoppel, not because inaction could not found the claim, but because the inaction had not been shown to have been induced by 'any assurances being given'.

2 See eg *Christian v Christian* (1981) 131 NLJ 43; *Coombes v Smith* [1986] 1 WLR 808 (ante, p 322).

3 Unreported, Court of Appeal, 14 July 1983 (ante, p 334).

Slade LJ declared that it was right in such cases to approach estoppel claims 'with a degree of caution' not least because, if successful, the plea of estoppel 'may have the drastic effect of conferring on one person a permanent, irrevocable interest in the land of another, even though he has given no consideration for such acquisition, by way of contractual arrangement, and no legally effective gift of it has been made in his favour.'[4]

Further confirmation came in *Coombes v Smith*[5] that an alteration of personal lifestyle is not necessarily a relevant change of position in the law of proprietary estoppel. Here the claimant alleged that she had left her husband to move in with the defendant, had allowed herself to become pregnant by him, and had generally looked after the child, the defendant and their shared home. Deputy Judge Jonathan Parker QC held that none of these actions was sufficient to found a claim of proprietary estoppel, but simply represented the kind of conduct to be expected of the claimant 'as occupier of the property, as the defendant's mistress, and as [the child's] mother, in the context of a continuing relationship with the defendant'.[6]

The asperity of such decisions may now be somewhat diminished by the greater willingness evident in the Court of Appeal's ruling in *Grant v Edwards*[7] to recognise intangible personal sacrifice as relevant to the foundation of an estoppel claim. Here Browne-Wilkinson V-C seemed prepared to accept that, if there was a common intention that the claimant should have an interest in the disputed property, 'any act done by her to her detriment relating to the joint lives of the parties is. . .sufficient detriment to qualify.'[8] In his view, the acts done need not be 'inherently referable to the house'.[9] They could indeed include such conduct as '[s]etting up house together, having a baby, [and] making payments to general housekeeping expenses', even though all such activity might be more accurately referable to 'the mutual love and affection of the parties and not specifically referable to the claimant's belief that she has an interest in the house.'[10] It is likely that this broader approach to ordinary acts of domestic endeavour marks the path of future developments in the law of estoppel.[11]

(iv) Shift in terminology The courts' definition of the element of reliance has become so broad that it is possible nowadays to see a subtle shift away

4 An estoppel will not be raised by reason of the mere fact that occupants have been permitted to stay in residence for an extremely long period of time without any express indication that they would ever be turned out. Something more is needed in the form of an assurance of entitlement to continue to reside (see *Rogers v Eller* (Unreported, Court of Appeal, 20 May 1986)).

5 [1986] 1 WLR 808. See [1986] CLJ 394 (D.J. Hayton); [1988] Conv 59.

6 [1986] 1 WLR 808 at 820F-G. Moreover, it could not be demonstrated in any realistic way that the claimant's conduct had been induced by 'reliance on some mistaken belief as to her legal rights' ([1986] 1 WLR 808 at 820B).

7 [1986] Ch 638. See [1986] CLJ 394 (D.J. Hayton); [1986] Conv 291 (J. Warburton).

8 [1986] Ch 638 at 657B.

9 [1986] Ch 638 at 657B.

10 [1986] Ch 638 at 657A-B.

11 The more positive approach adumbrated in *Grant v Edwards* is symptomatic of the increasing embarrassment of the English courts at the apparent inability of the law to provide satisfactory remedies for those who have devoted labours of love in the context of ultimately abortive family arrangements.

from reference to 'detriment' to the terminology of 'change of position'.[12] In *Bhimji v Salih*,[13] for instance, Brightman LJ expressed the view that the doctrine of proprietary estoppel can apply only where 'the promisee has in fact acted to his detriment in the sense that. . .the promisee has altered his position in a way which would be to his disadvantage if the strict legal position remained unqualified.'[14] Likewise in *Greasley v Cooke*[15] Lord Denning MR considered it sufficient 'if the party, to whom the assurance is given, acts on the faith of it—in such circumstances that it would be unjust and inequitable for the party making the assurance to go back on it'. This movement towards a doctrine of 'acting' on the faith of an assurance is symptomatic of the more general contemporary tendency to re-state the several elements of proprietary estoppel in terms of a composite formula of unconscionability.[16]

(c) The state of mind of the estoppel claimant

In order that the doctrine of proprietary estoppel should operate, it is clear that there must have been some kind of misapprehension by the estoppel claimant as to the extent of his own entitlement.

(i) 'Unilateral mistake' cases The requirement of misapprehension was, of course, classically expressed in the form of the first *probandum* in *Willmott v Barber*,[17] where Fry J said that the claimant 'must have made a mistake as to his legal rights.' However, this requirement of 'mistake' has led to ambiguity, and the first *probandum* of *Willmott v Barber* probably applies in strict terms only to estoppel claims which truly fall within the category of 'unilateral mistake'. It is here that the requirement of 'mistake' makes perfect and literal sense. Lord Cranworth LC's exposition in *Ramsden v Dyson*[18] bases the operation of estoppel on the premise that the person who builds upon land in reliance upon the silent acquiescence of another wrongly 'supposes himself to be building on his own land'. The 'equity' in his favour arises directly from the dishonesty implicit in the true owner's failure to correct his misapprehension. An estoppel can arise in such a case only if the claimant acted under a positive mistake as to the nature or quantum of his existing

12 For an early reference to 'change of position' as an element of proprietary estoppel, see *E.R. Ives Investment Ltd v High* [1967] 2 QB 379 at 405F per Winn LJ. See also *In re Basham, decd* [1986] 1 WLR 1498 at 1504D. In the present context the terminology of 'change' or 'alteration' of position is probably more commonly used in other jurisdictions (see eg *Maurice Demers Transport Ltd v Fountain Tire Distributors (Edmonton) Ltd* (1974) 42 DLR (3d) 412 at 423; *Mahony v Danis*, 469 A2d 31 at 36 (1983) (Supreme Court of New Jersey); *Wellington CC v New Zealand Law Society* [1988] 2 NZLR 614 at 627).

13 Unreported, Court of Appeal, 1978 B No 1099, 4 February 1981.

14 It was significant that Brightman LJ related this proposition directly to *Gissing v Gissing* [1971] AC 886 (post, p 383).

15 [1980] 1 WLR 1306 at 1311G.

16 See *Taylors Fashions Ltd v Liverpool Victoria Trustees Co Ltd* [1982] QB 133 (Note) at 155C per Oliver J (ante, p 324); *Cameron v Murdoch* [1983] WAR 321 at 351.

17 (1880) 15 Ch D 96 at 105 (ante, p 321).

18 (1866) LR 1 HL 129 at 141 (ante, p 320).

rights.[19] As Lord Cranworth said, 'if a stranger builds on my land knowing it to be mine, there is no principle of equity which would prevent my claiming the land with the benefit of all the expenditure made on it. There would be nothing in my conduct, active or passive, making it inequitable in me to assert my legal rights.'[20]

(ii) 'Common expectation' cases The requirement of mistake applies much less readily in the category of 'common expectation' cases.[1] Here the essence of the estoppel lies in the fact, not that a unilateral mistake about present entitlement has been made by someone, but that both parties have dealt with each other on the basis of a shared assumption as to their future rights. It is this important distinction between categories of estoppel claim which explains why in some cases the courts have demanded strict proof of 'mistake' on the part of the claimant,[2] while in other cases denying the necessity for proof of 'mistake' at all.[3] 'Mistake' in the *Willmott v Barber* sense is not required in the 'common expectation' category of case, except to the extent that the claimant has been induced to believe that he would receive some entitlement in the land which he would not otherwise have, and on the basis of that assurance exposed himself to recognisable legal prejudice.[4] In these circumstances it may well be that both parties originally believed and intended that the change of position should generate new rights as between themselves; the offence against conscience which attracts the operation of the estoppel is precisely the fact that subsequently one party unilaterally withdraws from that understanding.

(iii) Differentiation between mental states Many of the 'hard cases' of the past[5] can be accounted for in retrospect as exemplifying a failure to acknowledge

19 It seems that a 'unilateral mistake' can generate an estoppel even where the stranger has constructive notice of the fact that the land on which he builds is not his own. The relevant question is 'simply whether a mistake has been made, not whether the plaintiff ought to have made it' (see *Willmott v Barber* (1880) 15 Ch D 96 at 101 per Fry J). The knowledge required to bar a claim of estoppel based on 'unilateral mistake' is 'real knowledge which would involve a wilful act on the part of the party who has done the building' (*McMahon v Kerry County Council* [1981] ILRM 419 at 421).

20 See *Ezekiel v Orakpo and Scott* (Unreported, Court of Appeal, 1976 E No 1773, 20 February 1980), where Brightman LJ pointed out that the tenant, on whom had been conferred an option to purchase the freehold, had 'spent his money on that basis with his eyes open. . .His plans went awry, not because he was under any mistake or was misled by [the landlord], but because he ran out of money. . .Simply put, he was a speculator and his speculation did not pay off.'

1 As was pointed out in *Griffiths v Williams* (1977) 248 Estates Gazette 947 at 949, it is in any event difficult to pinpoint motivations in the 'common expectation' cases. Is the person who pays for improvements in her mother's home 'thinking predominantly of her own inheritance rather than the care and comfort of her mother'?

2 *Cullen v Cullen* [1962] IR 268 at 192; *Ezekiel v Orakpo and Scott* (Unreported, Court of Appeal, 1976 E No 1773, 20 February 1980) per Brightman LJ; *Salvation Army Trustee Co Ltd v West Yorkshire MCC* (1981) 41 P & CR 179 at 196; *Stilwell v Simpson* (1983) 133 NLJ 894.

3 *Ward v Kirkland* [1967] Ch 194 at 238B; *Holiday Inns Inc v Broadhead* (1974) 232 Estates Gazette 951 at 1087; *Griffiths v Williams* (1977) 248 Estates Gazette 947 at 949.

4 See eg *Griffiths v Williams* (1977) 248 Estates Gazette 947 at 949 per Goff LJ. Compare, however, *Coombes v Smith* [1986] 1 WLR 808 at 818B-H.

5 Ante, p 322. The 'hard cases' are not entirely a thing of the past: see *Coombes v Smith* [1986] 1 WLR 808.

that slightly differing mental states are required for the purpose of estoppel claims in the apparently similar categories of 'common expectation' and 'unilateral mistake'. In estoppel claims based on 'common expectation', it seems to be required merely that the owner of land has induced in the claimant a belief that he 'would receive a sufficient interest in the land to justify the expenditure' or other disadvantage undertaken by the claimant.[6] The precise nature or quantum of the interest to be received need not have been specified at this point. It is sufficient simply that there is an expectation of some future entitlement of some recognisable kind,[7] and that the disadvantage incurred by the claimant is 'referable' to his belief that he would acquire some interest in or over the land.[8] It may be over-technical in the context of informal family arrangements to expect the lay person to formulate this expectation of entitlement in other than fairly vague and non-legal terms.[9] In the 'unilateral mistake' claims, however, there seems to be required in the claimant a state of mind much more akin to total misunderstanding of his existing entitlements.[10]

(3) Detriment

The doctrine of proprietary estoppel is firmly premised on a concept of detrimental reliance and, as Dixon J observed in *Grundt v Great Boulder Pty Gold Mines Ltd*,[11] the idea of estoppel is often simply expressed in terms that 'the party asserting the estoppel must have been induced to act to his detriment.' However, Dixon J pointed out that this proposition, although substantially correct, fails to bring out clearly the 'basal purpose of the doctrine', which is 'to avoid or prevent a detriment to the party asserting the estoppel by compelling the opposite party to adhere to the assumption on which the former acted or abstained from acting.' No 'detriment' in the relevant sense ever truly arises unless and until the assurance which evoked the reliance is revoked or withdrawn.[12] As Dixon J went on to say

> the real detriment or harm from which the law seeks to give protection is that which would flow from the change of position if the assumption were deserted that led

6 *Holiday Inns Inc v Broadhead* (1974) 232 Estates Gazette 951 at 1089. However, the estoppel claim will fail if the claimant cannot show credible evidence of some 'belief or expectation that she was being offered an interest in the house of the nature which she now claims' (*Warnes v Hedley* (Unreported, Court of Appeal, 31 January 1984) per Slade LJ). Likewise in *Clayton v Singh* (Unreported, Court of Appeal, 12 April 1984), the Court of Appeal dismissed an estoppel claim for want of evidence that the expenditure pleaded by the claimant had been referable to a genuine belief in his own entitlement.

7 It need not have been clear in the mind of the claimant how precisely the entitlement would arise; it is sufficient merely that he believed that he would become entitled 'in due course of time...in some way' (see *Cameron v Murdoch* [1983] WAR 321 at 354, 360). See also *Hardwick v Johnson* [1978] 1 WLR 683 at 687G.

8 The terminology of 'referability', reminiscent of *Gissing v Gissing* [1971] AC 886 at 909F-G (post, p 432), seems to have been introduced in this context by May LJ: see *Warnes v Hedley* (Unreported, Court of Appeal, 31 January 1984); *Philip Lowe (Chinese Restaurant) Ltd v Sau Man Lee* (Unreported, Court of Appeal, 9 July 1985).

9 See the reference to 'hard cases' (ante, p 322).

10 For confirmation of this approach, see *Hastings Minor Hockey Association v Pacific National Exhibition* (1982) 129 DLR (3d) 721 at 728 (British Columbia Court of Appeal).

11 (1937) 59 CLR 641 at 674 (High Court of Australia).

12 See *Olsson v Dyson* (1969) 120 CLR 365 at 379 per Kitto J; *Grimison v Union Fidelity Trustee Co of Australia Ltd* (1984) 3 BPR 9469 at 9475.

to it. So long as the assumption is adhered to, the party who altered his situation upon the faith of it cannot complain. His complaint is that when afterwards the other party makes a different state of affairs the basis of an assertion of right against him then, if it is allowed, his own original change of position will operate as a detriment.[13]

As Dixon J indicated, the element of 'detriment' which is integral to a claim of estoppel can thus be defined in terms of whether the claimant's original act or failure to act would, in view of the changed assumption, constitute for him a 'source of prejudice'.[14] The notion of 'prejudice' itself implies some distinction between acceptable and unacceptable outcomes, and is therefore capable of definition only in terms of whether it would be 'unfair or unjust' if the party who induced the expectation or assumed state of affairs 'were left free to ignore it.'[15]

(a) Legal detriment and the criterion of unconscionability

This reductionist interpretation of the element of 'detriment' finds significant echoes as the English case law moves closer towards a more composite criterion of unconscionability as the basis of proprietary estoppel. In *Watts v Story*,[16] for instance, Slade LJ thought it neither possible nor desirable to define the required 'detriment' except in terms of such 'prejudice...that it would be inequitable to allow the party who made the relevant representation to go back on it.' Likewise, in *Amalgamated Investment and Property Co Ltd v Texas Commerce International Bank Ltd*[17] Lord Denning MR expressed the view that all forms of estoppel can now be seen to 'merge into one general principle shorn of limitations.' This principle requires that when the parties to a transaction 'proceed on the basis of an underlying assumption—either of fact or of law—whether due to misrepresentation or mistake makes no difference—on which they have conducted the dealings between them—neither of them will be allowed to go back on that assumption when it would be unfair or unjust to allow him to do so.'[18]

(b) The test of unconscionability in practice

It used to be said that this test of estoppel, depending as it does on fairness or conscience, requires a degree of 'fraud' on the part of the person sought to be estopped.[19] However, the modern tendency is to commute this stringent epithet into a requirement that the plaintiff should 'establish as a fact that the defendant, by setting up his right, is taking advantage of him in a way

13 See (1981) 44 MLR 461 at 463 (G. Woodman).
14 (1937) 59 CLR 641 at 675.
15 (1937) 59 CLR 641 at 675.
16 Unreported, Court of Appeal, 14 July 1983.
17 [1982] QB 84 at 122C.
18 Lord Denning's view was cited with apparent approval by the Privy Council in *Attorney-General of Hong Kong v Humphrey's Estate (Queen's Gardens) Ltd* [1987] AC 114 at 124A-B. See also *Dewhirst v Edwards* [1983] 1 NSWLR 34 at 49E; *Cameron v Murdoch* [1983] WAR 321 at 351.
19 *Willmott v Barber* (1880) 15 Ch D 96 at 105 (ante, p 321).

which is unconscionable, inequitable or unjust.'[20] This formula frequently demands a complex and sophisticated evaluation of all the circumstances of a given case in order to establish whether it would be 'inequitable to permit [X] to resile from the assurances given to [Y].'[1]

(i) Restrictive approach of the courts In spite of the modern acceptance of a broadly based test of unconscionable dealing, the approach of the courts when faced with claims of proprietary estoppel tends to be restrictive. The courts treat such claims 'with a degree of caution',[2] mindful of the fact that the doctrine of proprietary estoppel may have the 'drastic effect of conferring on one person a permanent, irrevocable interest in the land of another, even though he has given no consideration for such acquisition, by way of contractual arrangement, and no legally effective gift of it has been made in his favour.'[3] There are slight indications that the courts may be even more restrictive when dealing with estoppel claims based on other forms of reliance than the expenditure of money on the land of the party whom it is sought to estop.[4] Above all there seems to be a judicial anxiety lest the courts should curtail the human impulse of generosity,[5] by creating 'the impression that people are liable to be penalised for not enforcing their strict legal rights.'[6]

(ii) The measure of conscience Numerous factors affect the question whether the strict enforcement of rights is unconscionable. It is often patently obvious from the circumstances that it would be 'grossly inequitable' to leave one party without a remedy for a disadvantage which he has incurred in reliance on the basis of some legitimate expectation.[7] The courts are sometimes powerfully moved by the excessive or opulent nature of the unjust enrichment which would otherwise be conferred upon the maker of the original assurance.[8] However, each case is a matter of 'fact or degree',[9] and in evaluating the totality of the circumstances the courts have been particularly sensitive to

20 *Crabb v Arun DC* [1976] Ch 179 at 195B-C per Scarman LJ, who observed that 'fraud' was a word 'often in the mouths of those robust judges who adorned the bench in the 19th century', but is 'less often in the mouths of the more wary judicial spirits today who sit upon the bench'. See also *Swallow Securities Ltd v Isenberg* (1985) 274 Estates Gazette 1028 at 1030, where Cumming-Bruce LJ described the concept of 'taking an advantage of the defendant' as 'an essential ingredient of the equity'. It is clear, however, that a finding of 'unconscionable conduct' does not necessarily imply that the party estopped has 'acted reprehensibly' (*Salvation Army Trustee Co Ltd v West Yorkshire MCC* (1981) 41 P & CR 179 at 198).

1 *Watts v Story* (Unreported, Court of Appeal, 14 July 1983) per Slade LJ. 'The notion of unconscionability is better described than defined' (*Commonwealth v Verwayen* (1990) 170 CLR 394 at 440 per Deane J).

2 *Watts v Story*, supra, per Slade LJ.

3 Ibid, per Slade LJ.

4 Ibid, per Slade LJ.

5 See *Marcroft Wagons Ltd v Smith* [1951] 2 KB 496 at 501 per Evershed MR (post, p 712).

6 *E & L Berg Homes Ltd v Grey* (1980) 253 Estates Gazette 473 at 479 per Ormrod LJ.

7 See eg *Timber Top Realty Pty Ltd v Mullens* [1974] VR 312 at 319.

8 See *Clayton v Green* (1979) NZ Recent Law 139 at 140, where it appeared that the plaintiff's contributions of cash had indirectly enabled her son-in-law (the present defendant) to instal in his home such 'luxury items' as a swimming pool and a carpeted bar!

9 *Watts v Story* (Unreported, Court of Appeal, 14 July 1983) per Dunn LJ.

the presence of counter-balancing advantages enjoyed by the relier which may partially or completely offset the disadvantage which he has suffered. Of especial importance in this context may be the fact that the claimant of an 'equity' through improvements has meanwhile enjoyed rent-free occupation,[10] or that the party sought to be estopped has in the past shown some forbearance towards the claimant[11] or made generous gifts of money in respect of the claimant's other commitments,[12] or that the claimant has received more by way of profits drawn from a business than she ever invested in that business in the first place.[13] The courts may therefore deny an estoppel claim if of the opinion that no net disadvantage would be suffered by the claimant if the assurance originally given were allowed to be withdrawn.[14]

(c) Bars to a claim of unconscionable behaviour

Several factors may operate as a bar in any given case to the claim that considerations of conscience require a holding of proprietary estoppel. Where, for instance, the parties have already agreed a contractually binding formula for compensating extra expenditure incurred by one, 'no intervention of equity is needed' in order to bring about a fair result.[15]

(i) Infringement of statute More difficult questions arise if the expenditure on which the claim to an 'equity' is based was undertaken in breach of some statutory provision or regulation—a problem which is particularly live if the supposed 'equity' was grounded on some improvement to realty which required planning permission. In *Chalmers v Pardoe*,[16] the Privy Council decided that the aid of equity could not be lent in support of an estoppel claim based on a land transaction which contravened regulatory legislation. In this respect, an estoppel claim may be barred for want of 'clean hands'.[17] However, the courts, although recognising the force of the argument of

10 *E & L Berg Homes Ltd v Grey* (1980) 253 Estates Gazette 473 at 477 per Brandon LJ, 479 per Sir David Cairns and Ormrod LJJ; *Watts v Story* (Unreported, Court of Appeal, 14 July 1983) per Slade LJ; *Hink v Lhenen* (1975) 52 DLR (3d) 301 at 316; *Beaton v McDivitt* (1985) 13 NSWLR 134 at 158G, (1987) 13 NSWLR 162 at 172E-F.

11 *Appleby v Cowley* (1982) *Times*, 14 April 1982. Here Megarry V-C considered that, in view of a prolonged rent forbearance, the plaintiffs had received 'sufficient satisfaction' for their expenditure.

12 *Jackson v Crosby* (No 2) (1979) 21 SASR 280 at 298, 302 per Zelling J (estoppel claim abated to the extent that defendant had helped to discharge previous mortgage created by plaintiff). See also *In re Basham, decd* [1986] 1 WLR 1498 at 1505E, where it was indicated that the claim of estoppel would not have succeeded if the claimant's labour on behalf of her step-father had received any 'commensurate reward. . .during his lifetime'.

13 *Cullen v Cullen* [1962] IR 268 at 282.

14 In *Watts v Story* (Unreported, Court of Appeal, 14 July 1983), Slade LJ agreed that the claimant of the 'equity' had failed to show 'that, when the benefits derived by him from his rent-free occupation of Apple House are set against any detriments suffered by him as a result of making the move from his flat in Leeds, he has on balance suffered any detriment in financial or material terms.'

15 *Appleby v Cowley* (1982) *Times*, 14 April, per Megarry V-C.

16 [1963] 1 WLR 677 at 685.

17 See *Dewhirst v Edwards* [1983] 1 NSWLR 34 at 51B; *Jackson v Crosby* (No 2) (1979) 21 SASR 280 at 291 (Bright J).

illegality,[18] have sought almost any refuge to avoid having to sanction the unmerited retention of an unjustly received benefit by way of improvement.[19]

A lack of 'clean hands' will likewise defeat a claim to an 'equity' if the original assurance pleaded in aid by the estoppel claimant was procured by reason of his own false representations. In such a case 'it does not. . .lie in the mouth of the claimant to set up any form of estoppel.'[20]

(ii) Integrity of statutory duties and discretions It is clear that no public body or agency can be estopped from performing a duty imposed on it by statute or from exercising a discretion conferred on it by legislation.[1]

(iii) Delay It is possible[2] that a claim based on proprietary estoppel may be barred by excessive delay on the part of the claimant in seeking relief. The court will not, however, be over-ready to penalise delay by a claimant who has enjoyed unchallenged possession for a lengthy period and whose only default is that he has not taken steps to perfect an informal gift of title.[3]

5. THE EXTENT OF THE ESTOPPEL REMEDY

Once an 'equity' of estoppel has been established, the court must determine the proper scope of the remedy to be granted in the particular case.

(1) The general principle

The general principle of relief relevant to proprietary estoppel was stated over a century ago in *Plimmer v Mayor etc of Wellington.*[4] Here the Judicial Committee of the Privy Council held that when an 'equity' has been raised, 'the Court must look at the circumstances in each case to decide in what

18 See eg *Dewhirst v Edwards* [1983] 1 NSWLR 34 at 51B-C; *Wood v Browne* [1984] 2 Qd R 593 at 597ff; *Beaton v McDivitt* (1985) 13 NSWLR 134 at 157F–158C, 159B-C.

19 In *Jackson v Crosby* (No 2) (1979) 21 SASR 280 at 301, the Supreme Court of South Australia ruled that the claimant of the 'equity' did not strictly come within the terms of a licensing requirement imposed on those carrying out building work 'for fee or reward', since what he did had been done for love not money. In *Lepel v Huthnance* (1979) NZ Recent Law 269, Speight J distinguished *Chalmers v Pardoe* on the grounds that in the instant case the breach of planning control had not been 'flagrant', that the local authority had taken no action in respect of the breach, and that in any event the duty to obtain the requisite planning permit had attached technically to the defendant as owner and occupier rather than to the plaintiff as claimant of the 'equity'. See also *Beaton v McDivitt* (1985) 13 NSWLR 134 at 156A; *Silovi Pty Ltd v Barbaro* (1988) 13 NSWLR 466 at 473D–474B.

20 *Ildebrando de Franco v Stengold Ltd* (Unreported, Court of Appeal, 14 May 1985) per Parker LJ.

1 *Western Fish Products Ltd v Penwith DC* [1981] 2 All ER 204 at 219c. See [1982] Conv 450 (P. Jackson); A. Bradley, [1981] 34 CLP 1 at 12ff. Compare *Santiago v Immigration and Naturalization Service*, 526 F2d 488 at 494 (1975) per Choy J (dissenting).

2 See the suggestion made by Kirby P in the New South Wales Court of Appeal in *Beaton v McDivitt* (1987) 13 NSWLR 162 at 172G–173A.

3 *Voyce v Voyce* (1991) 62 P & CR 290 at 293 per Dillon LJ.

4 (1884) 9 App Cas 699 at 714 (ante, p 319).

way the equity can be satisfied.'[5] Although this flexibility of approach has been criticised as leading to an undesirable remedial uncertainty,[6] it is now settled law that the court 'moulds the relief to give effect to the equity'.[7] The court may therefore take into account all supervening circumstances occurring before the date of the hearing.[8] The court has an extremely wide discretion and formulates the remedy in terms of the equity required to do justice to the claimant. The remedy awarded may thus involve the grant of a recognised proprietary interest in land or may sometimes take the more limited form of an occupation licence or a money remedy or a lien for expenditure.

(a) Rationale of relief

There has long been a certain ambivalence of view as to whether the proper function of estoppel is to give belated effect to the expectations of entitlement induced in a claimant or merely to restrain the owner of land from unconscientious insistence upon his or her adverse legal rights.[9] The distinction between these remedial perspectives may dramatically affect the scope and nature of the order made by the court, as was illustrated by a graphic stereotype considered by the High Court of Australia in *Commonwealth v Verwayen.*[10] Here Deane J postulated a case in which the owner of a million dollar block of land induces a stranger to incur expenditure on the faith of a wholly gratuitous assurance of rights of ownership in the land. On the supposition that the stranger erects on the land a shed worth one hundred dollars, it is a matter of critical importance whether the estoppel remedy awarded to the stranger is aimed at the validation of his initial assumption of informal entitlement or is directed instead towards precluding the unconscientious denial of rights in the stranger without at least some restitution of his exiguous outlay of funds.

Many of the early formulations of proprietary estoppel doctrine emphasised the court's jurisdiction to ensure specific performance of the assurance or promise of rights on which the estoppel claimant had placed reliance.[11] On this basis, as soon as any convincing element of detrimental reliance was

5 See also *Chalmers v Pardoe* [1963] 1 WLR 677 at 682; *Inwards v Baker* [1965] 2 QB 29 at 37B; *E R Ives Investment Ltd v High* [1967] 2 QB 379 at 395A; *Amalgamated Investment & Property Co Ltd v Texas Commerce International Bank Ltd* [1982] QB 84 at 122D; *Voyce v Voyce* (1991) 62 P & CR 290 at 293.

6 See eg P.B.H. Birks, *An Introduction to the Law of Restitution* (Oxford 1985), p 290ff; R. P. Meagher, W.M.C. Gummow and J. Lehane, *Equity: Doctrines and Remedies* (2nd edn Sydney 1984), para 1720.

7 *Beaton v McDivitt* (1985) 13 NSWLR 134 at 158D per Young J. See also *Barrios v Chiabrera* (1984) 3 BPR 9276 at 9279; *Stratulatos v Stratulatos* [1988] 2 NZLR 424 at 438; *Milton v Proctor* (1989) NSW ConvR 55-450 at 58,265 per Clarke JA; *Commonwealth v Verwayen* (1990) 170 CLR 394 at 412 per Mason CJ.

8 *Williams v Staite* [1979] Ch 291 at 298F per Goff LJ; *Voyce v Voyce* (1991) 62 P & CR 290 at 296 per Nicholls LJ.

9 Ante, p 315. For a strong argument that the latter perspective 'provides the preferable foundation for the modern law of equitable estoppel', see P.D. Finn, *Equitable Estoppel*, in P.D. Finn (ed), *Essays in Equity* (Sydney 1985), p 61.

10 (1990) 170 CLR 394 at 441.

11 See eg Lord Kingsdown's speech in *Ramsden v Dyson* (1866) LR 1 HL 129 at 170, which indicated that 'a Court of equity will compel the [owner] to give effect to such promise or expectation' (ante, p 318).

shown, the estoppel doctrine operated effectively as a procedural mechanism for sanctioning or legitimising the informal creation of property rights in land.[12] The court would, in general terms, seek to frame the remedy in accordance with the representation on which the claimant relied, so that the outcome of the litigation would guarantee the claimant no more and no less than was actually promised in the original assurance of entitlement.[13] In Deane J's example, of course, this approach would incongruously award substantial rights in the million dollar block of land to the builder of the less than substantial hundred dollar shed.

The expectation-oriented principle of relief was always vulnerable to the objection that it subverted both the formality rule which inhibits the informal grant of rights in land and the contractual rule which renders gratuitous promises unenforceable. The breach of a voluntary promise ought not of itself to give rise to an estoppel, and indeed it is the superadded requirement of unconscionable conduct which is generally seen as the protection against undue intrusion by estoppel upon the law of contract.[14] However, the mere fact that a person does not keep his promise is not, in legal terms, an unconscionable form of behaviour.[15] As McHugh J observed in *Commonwealth v Verwayen*,[16] 'the enforcement of promises is not the object of the doctrine of equitable estoppel. The enforcement of promises is the province of contract.'

Accordingly over the years there has occurred a gradual, but not wholly uniform, drift away from the expectation-oriented basis of relief towards a more modest rationale for relief in estoppel founded upon the avoidance of unacceptable detriment for the claimant.[17] In terms of this rather different perspective the court discards any concern to make good the expectation of entitlement on which a claimant has relied,[18] and instead aims merely to provide compensation for the detriment caused by the falsification of the

12 See generally S. Moriarty, (1984) 100 LQR 376. This analysis, while interesting and challenging, does not of course explain the entirety of the case law (see eg *Griffiths v Williams* (1977) 248 Estates Gazette 947, ante, p 339), unless one simply accepts that 'perfect equity is seldom possible.' See also John Dewar, (1986) 49 MLR 741.

13 For modern articulations phrased in the language of expectations, see eg *E.R. Ives Investment Ltd v High* [1967] 2 QB 379 at 394F-395A per Lord Denning MR; *Shaida v Kindlane Ltd* (Unreported, Chancery Division, 1976 S No 8501, 22 June 1982) per Paul Baker QC, sitting as a Deputy High Court Judge.

14 See *Commonwealth v Verwayen* (1990) 170 CLR 394 at 454 per Dawson J.

15 *Milchas Investments Pty Ltd v Larkin* (1989) NSW ConvR 55-487 at 58,537 per Young J (ante, p 251). See also *Commonwealth v Verwayen* (1990) 170 CLR 394 at 416 per Mason CJ ('The breaking of a promise, without more, is morally reprehensible, but not unconscionable in the sense that equity will necessarily prevent its occurrence or remedy the consequent loss').

16 (1990) 170 CLR 394 at 501.

17 The steady progression in the case law is excellently charted in P.D. Finn, *Equitable Estoppel*, in P.D. Finn (ed), *Essays in Equity* (Sydney 1985), p 67ff.

18 See *Commonwealth v Verwayen* (1990) 170 CLR 394 at 413, where Mason CJ denied that estoppel doctrine has 'as its hallmark function the making good of assumptions.' Mason CJ expressed the view the court 'may do what is required, but no more, to prevent a person who has relied upon an assumption as to a present, past or future state of affairs (including a legal state of affairs), which assumption the party estopped has induced him to hold, from suffering detriment in reliance upon the assumption as a result of the denial of its correctness.' See also *Waltons Stores (Interstate) Ltd v Maher* (1988) 164 CLR 387 at 423 per Brennan J.

claimant's basal assumptions.[19] According to the detriment-oriented approach the appropriate estoppel remedy in the dilemma posed by Deane J may well be a simple return of the stranger's hundred dollar outlay.[20] Such a solution preserves the integrity of large doctrinal principle whilst avoiding the unconscionable outcome otherwise implicit in the incurring of uncompensated detriment.[1]

(b) Proportionality of relief

A further objection to an expectation-oriented approach to estoppel remedies is precisely the problem, highlighted in Deane J's example, that the remedial outcome may be entirely disproportionate to the degree of detrimental reliance exhibited by the estoppel claimant. As Mason CJ stated in *Commonwealth v Verwayen*,[2] a 'central element' of estoppel doctrine is that there must be 'a proportionality between the remedy and the detriment which is its purpose to avoid.'[3] Accordingly it is a recurrent theme in the case law on estoppel that the court is confined to formulating relief in terms of the 'minimum equity' required to do justice to the claimant.[4] In moulding its decree, 'the court, as a court of conscience, goes no further than is necessary to prevent unconscionable conduct.'[5] The court therefore strives to achieve only 'the minimum equity needed to avoid the relevant detriment' to the estoppel claimant.[6]

In reality the expectation- and detriment-oriented approaches do not always represent distinct or truly alternative perspectives on remedy. It is true that

19 It has been acknowledged that this detriment-oriented approach 'raises the uncomfortable prospect of a tort analogy' (see P.D. Finn, *Equitable Estoppel*, in P.D. Finn (ed), *Essays in Equity* (Sydney 1985), p 91).

20 It 'does not follow that a single act of expenditure would require a transfer of the fee simple' (*Grimison v Union Fidelity Trustee Co of Australia Ltd* (1984) 3 BPR 9469 at 9475). See also *Veitch v Caldicott* (1945) 173 LT 30 at 34 per Atkinson J.

1 Thus, although 'detriment in the broader sense' is required in order to found an estoppel (ante, p 340), the remedy provided 'will often be closer in scope to the detriment suffered in the narrower sense' (*Commonwealth v Verwayen* (1990) 170 CLR 394 at 415f per Mason CJ).

2 (1990) 170 CLR 394 at 413.

3 Mason CJ emphasised that it would be 'wholly inequitable and unjust to insist upon a disproportionate making good of the relevant assumption.' Other members of the High Court reiterated that 'a doctrine based on good conscience' should not be converted by excessively zealous application into 'an instrument of injustice or oppression' ((1990) 170 CLR 394 at 442 per Deane J).

4 *Crabb v Arun DC* [1976] Ch 179 at 198G per Scarman LJ. See also *Pascoe v Turner* [1979] 1 WLR 431 at 438A per Cumming-Bruce LJ; *Waltons Stores (Interstate) Ltd v Maher* (1988) 164 CLR 387 at 404 per Mason CJ and Wilson J. In *Cameron v Murdoch* [1983] WAR 321 at 360, Brinsden J declared it to be his 'duty. . .to do equity and no more than equity and to give relief and no more relief than is necessary to satisfy the equity created by the representation.'

5 *Waltons Stores (Interstate) Ltd v Maher* (1988) 164 CLR 387 at 419 per Brennan J. See similarly *Commonwealth v Verwayen* (1990) 170 CLR 394 at 411 per Mason CJ, 429 per Brennan J, 501 per McHugh J. In *Stratulatos v Stratulatos* [1988] 2 NZLR 424 at 438, McGechan J indicated that '[t]he relief available, broadly speaking, is that which is necessary to cure the underlying unconscionability: nothing more, and nothing less'.

6 *Commonwealth v Verwayen* (1990) 170 CLR 394 at 429 per Brennan J. See also *Silovi Pty Ltd v Barbaro* (1988) 13 NSWLR 466 at 472F per Priestley JA.

the primary focus of the estoppel remedy is no longer directed at the securing of expectations or the enforcement of promises.[7] In some cases, however, the avoidance of detriment may nevertheless 'require that the party estopped make good the assumption' on which the claimant relied, even though in other cases the relief required 'may be considerably less'.[8] It is clear that in certain situations the 'minimum equity' required will not be satisfied by anything short of an order compelling the landowner to fulfil the expectation which he or she created in the estoppel claimant.[9] Sometimes, in effect, 'the only way to prevent the promisee suffering detriment will be to enforce the promise.'[10] Even here the approach of equity remains flexible in the extreme, since the doctrine of estoppel inhibits the denial by the promisor of an assumed state of affairs only 'until the detriment is removed or the innocent party otherwise compensated.'[11] In other words, equity requires parties to act on the basis of the assumed relationship only so long as the 'equity' raised by estoppel persists. Once the detriment has 'ceased or been paid for', there is 'nothing unconscionable in a party insisting on reverting to his or her former relationship with the other party and enforcing his or her strict legal rights.'[12]

(2) Relevant criteria

The degree of discretion enjoyed by the court in fashioning the appropriate remedy is indeed substantial. As Lord Denning MR observed in *Crabb v Arun DC*,[13] here 'equity is displayed at its most flexible.'[14] It is clear that the remedy required in order to satisfy the 'equity' generated by proprietary estoppel is capable of fluctuation over the course of time. Developments subsequent to the date on which the 'equity' is initially raised may cause the court either to withhold relief from the claimant or to grant him relief in terms other than those which it would have been inclined to order at an earlier stage.[15]

7 *Commonwealth v Verwayen* (1990) 170 CLR 394 at 429 per Brennan J, 501 per McHugh J.
8 *Commonwealth v Verwayen* (1990) 170 CLR 394 at 454 per Dawson J.
9 *Commonwealth v Verwayen* (1990) 170 CLR 394 at 454 per Dawson J. See eg *Barrios v Chiabrera* (1984) 3 BPR 9276 at 9281 per Powell J.
10 *Commonwealth v Verwayen* (1990) 170 CLR 394 at 501 per McHugh J. See also Brennan J at 429, Toohey J at 475f.
11 *Commonwealth v Verwayen* (1990) 170 CLR 394 at 500 per McHugh J.
12 *Commonwealth v Verwayen* (1990) 170 CLR 394 at 501 per McHugh J.
13 [1976] Ch 179 at 189F.
14 See the approving remarks of J.D. Davies, (1979) 8 Sydney L Rev 578 at 583ff, and (1980–81) 7 Adelaide L Rev 200 at 219.
15 In *Crabb v Arun DC* [1976] Ch 179 at 189G–190A, 192E, 199C-F, the Court of Appeal satisfied the 'equity' claimed by ordering the grant of an easement without compensation, even though had the same 'equity' been asserted earlier, it would have ordered the claimant to make some payment in respect of the right of access sought. However, during the intervening period the party denying the 'equity' had acted with 'high-handedness' and had moreover sterilised the user of an industrial estate by the denial of access, and for this the Court was prepared to impose a penalty. Another case of relevant change of circumstance arose in *Dodsworth v Dodsworth* (1973) 228 Estates Gazette 1115, where the Court of Appeal had regard to the fact that the legal owner had died subsequent to the date on which the 'equity' was first raised by an assurance of accommodation.

(a) Misconduct

In some circumstances subsequent misconduct may be relevant to the court's response to a plea of proprietary estoppel.

(i) Effect on the inchoate 'equity' It seems to be accepted that an inchoate 'equity' of estoppel may be offset by misconduct on the part of the claimant which occurs after the date on which that 'equity' originates.[16] In *Williams v Staite*,[17] Cumming-Bruce LJ did not believe that 'the rights in equity of the [claimants] necessarily crystallise forever at the time when the equitable rights come into existence.' Instead the true analysis entailed that when the owner of land sought to enforce his strict legal rights against the claimant, all the relevant maxims of equity must be brought into play 'so that the court is entitled then on the facts to look at all the circumstances and decide what order should be made, if any, to satisfy the equity.' In such a case an estoppel claimant guilty of misconduct in relation to the owner of the land might well be considered to have come to the court without 'clean hands', with the result that he would be 'left with no right at all' and the legal owner would be at liberty to exercise his strict legal rights.[18]

In *Brynowen Estates Ltd v Bourne*,[19] for instance, there was clear evidence that the estoppel claimant had behaved in a 'quite extraordinarily disturbing and objectionable way', not least by swearing and making obscene gestures at visitors to the caravan park in respect of part of which she claimed an 'equity'.[20] The Court of Appeal had no hesitation in holding that any inchoate 'equity' of estoppel which might have been generated by the circumstances of the case had been amply negatived by the claimant's misconduct.

(ii) Effect on any court-ordered remedy The court is less willing to have regard to subsequent misconduct where the claimant's 'equity' of estoppel has already crystallised in the form of a remedy granted by the court.[1] In *Williams v Staite*[2] an 'equity' of estoppel had earlier resulted in the award to the claimants of a right of occupation for life. In relation to the remedy thus granted already, the Court of Appeal considered that 'subsequent excessive user or bad behaviour towards the legal owner cannot bring the equity to an end

16 Relevant misconduct may sometimes take the form of non-compliance with an agreement which underlay the estoppel in the first place. A party cannot enforce his equity of estoppel while being himself in default of such an agreement. See *E.R. Ives Investment Ltd v High* [1967] 2 QB 379 at 400A-B; *Vinden v Vinden* [1982] 1 NSWLR 618 at 625B; *Beaton v McDivitt* (1985) 13 NSWLR 134 at 157C-D, (1987) 13 NSWLR 162 at 172D.

17 [1979] Ch 291 at 300G-H. See H. Bowie, (1981) 11 VUWLR 63.

18 [1979] Ch 291 at 299D per Goff LJ. See also *Milton v Proctor* (1989) NSW ConvR 55-450 at 58,265, where Clarke JA considered misconduct by the claimant to be 'a factor, indeed a most important factor, to be weighed in the balance in determining whether the licensor should be restrained from strictly enforcing her legal rights'.

19 (1981) 131 NLJ 1212.

20 The claimant had also driven round the caravan park at speed late at night, continuously sounding her horn.

1 See *J. Willis & Son v Willis* (1986) 277 Estates Gazette 1133, where Parker LJ compared the effect of misconduct on an inchoate 'equity', and concluded that there was 'a difference between the two situations'. See [1986] Conv 406 (M.P. Thompson).

2 [1979] Ch 291.

or forfeit it'.[3] Lord Denning MR had thought that there might be extreme circumstances under which even a court-ordered licence might be revoked on the ground of subsequent misconduct by the successful estoppel claimant,[4] but this reservation has not been adopted in the subsequent case law.[5]

(b) Use of estoppel as a 'sword' or as a 'shield'

It is now a commonplace that the doctrine of proprietary estoppel can be used as a sword and not merely as a shield.[6] 'In its enlarged and elevated nature as proprietary estoppel, equity stands ready to strike or defend as and when conscience demands.'[7] However, there are some indications that when the 'equity' of estoppel is finally asserted before the court, the willingness of the court to grant a concrete remedy may be vitally affected by whether the estoppel argument is being used as a shield or as a sword.

(i) Restraint upon positive or aggressive claims In *Stilwell v Simpson*,[8] for instance, the court refused to uphold a positive claim that the plaintiff was entitled to some interest or compensation in respect of improvements effected upon the defendant's property. The court noted that the plaintiff was a protected tenant of the defendant and therefore had in any event 'a life interest by statute'. However, the court added significantly that if there had not been a protected tenancy and the defendant (or a purchaser) had 'sought to eject the plaintiff', that would have been a different matter.[9] Likewise, in *Savva v Costa and Harymode Investments Ltd*,[10] the Court of Appeal indicated that it would have regarded much more favourably the plaintiff's plea of proprietary estoppel if the litigation had been precipitated by a threat from the defendant to dispossess the plaintiff and her children from the defendant's property.[11] As it was, the plaintiff was seeking an order directing either

3 [1979] Ch 291 at 300B per Goff LJ. The Court of Appeal did, however, leave open the possibility that misconduct might give rise to an action in damages for trespass or nuisance or to an injunction restraining the misbehaviour. It appears in this case that the defendants, having already been granted an equitable licence by the county court on the ground of proprietary estoppel, informed the next purchaser of the disputed land that he was in for 'bloody trouble', which true to their word they proceeded to provide!

4 [1979] Ch 291 at 298B.

5 See eg *J. Willis & Son v Willis* (1986) 277 Estates Gazette 1133 per Parker LJ. See also the criticism in *McGill v S* [1979] IR 283 at 293 of the 'concept of a wavering licence terminable. . .upon the possibility of changeable circumstances affecting the licensee'. It would certainly be undesirable were the position of a purchaser from the licensor to depend on the relative iniquity or unpleasantness of the licensee's conduct at any particular point in time!

6 See *Crabb v Arun DC* [1976] Ch 179 at 187D-E per Lord Denning MR; *Thomas v Thomas* [1956] NZLR 785 at 793; *Dewhirst v Edwards* [1983] 1 NSWLR 34 at 49E. 'Purists may regret the use of the word "estoppel" as the name of a sword but it seems now too late to challenge the usage' (*Jackson v Crosby* (No 2) (1979) 21 SASR 280 at 287 per Bright J). Compare *Commonwealth v Verwayen* (1990) 170 CLR 394 at 437, 445 per Deane J.

7 *Classic Communications Ltd v Lascar* (1986) 21 DLR (4th) 579 at 587 per Pennell J.

8 (1983) 133 NLJ 894.

9 Ibid per Sir Douglas Frank QC.

10 (1981) 131 NLJ 1114.

11 (1981) 131 NLJ 1114, where Oliver LJ pointed out that in such circumstances the plaintiff might well have been able to claim 'an irrevocable or indefinite licence of some sort to occupy'.

a transfer of the property to herself or a reimbursement in respect of improvements effected by her. Although dismissing this claim, the Court of Appeal referred to the 'prospective potential rights' which would accrue to the plaintiff if there ever were to be any threat to deny her 'the advantage of residing' in the home in which she had sought to 'provide a proper degree of amenity for the accommodation of the children'.[12]

(ii) Greater tolerance of defensive claims Decisions like those just cited seem to show that proprietary estoppel may still be more readily accepted by the courts as a shield rather than as a sword. In other words, proprietary estoppel is sparingly used and the courts tend to apply the estoppel doctrine only where its use is quite essential in order to prevent gross injustice or where there is some immediate threat to the residential security of the claimant.

(3) Range of possible remedies

The court has virtually unlimited discretion in the matter of remedy. Over the years a range of potential relief has been recognised,[13] and the court's task is to select from a fairly well established remedial menu or repertoire. As Mason CJ confirmed in *Commonwealth v Verwayen*,[14] each case 'is one of degree'. An expectation-based measure of relief (ie relief framed on the basis of an assumed state of affairs) remains the most ample form of remedial outcome.[15] In some circumstances it may indeed be appropriate to enforce the promise upon which the claimant has relied; at the other end of the remedial spectrum there may be need for nothing more than an order for compensatory damages.[16]

Certain factors may point towards the larger and more radical forms of relief.[17] The circumstance that an assumption has been relied upon for an extended period may justify a court in requiring that the assumption be made good.[18] The same result may follow where the detriment incurred by the claimant is 'substantial and irreversible' or 'cannot satisfactorily be compensated or remedied'.[19] In different circumstances the 'equity' raised by estoppel may be wholly satisfied by a binding offer of money compensation.[20] Alternatively—particularly in cases involving an assumption about a future state of affairs—significant detriment to the claimant may be avoided altogether if he is given 'reasonable notice of the intended departure' from the relevant assumption.[1]

12 (1981) 131 NLJ 1114 per Shaw LJ.
13 See *Stratulatos v Stratulatos* [1988] 2 NZLR 424 at 438 per McGechan J.
14 (1990) 170 CLR 394 at 416.
15 Such relief 'represents the outer limits within which the relief appropriate to do justice between the parties should be framed' (*Commonwealth v Verwayen* (1990) 170 CLR 394 at 446 per Deane J).
16 *Commonwealth v Verwayen* (1990) 170 CLR 394 at 442 per Deane J.
17 See generally P.D. Finn, *Equitable Estoppel*, in P.D. Finn (ed), *Essays in Equity* (Sydney 1985), p 92f.
18 *Commonwealth v Verwayen* (1990) 170 CLR 394 at 416 per Mason CJ. See *Voyce v Voyce* (1991) 62 P & CR 290 at 293.
19 *Commonwealth v Verwayen* (1990) 170 CLR 394 at 416 per Mason CJ.
20 *Commonwealth v Verwayen* (1990) 170 CLR 394 at 441f per Deane J, who thought such relief to be the appropriate solution of the 'million dollar block' problem (ante, p 345).
1 *Commonwealth v Verwayen* (1990) 170 CLR 394 at 442 per Deane J.

The range of possible estoppel-based remedies includes the following.

(a) Grant of an unqualified estate or interest in land

It is possible, although far from inevitable,[2] that an 'equity' of estoppel can be satisfied only by a court order directing the transfer of the fee simple estate to the estoppel claimant.[3] Such orders are rare,[4] but have been made in circumstances such as those which occurred in *Pascoe v Turner*.[5] Here the Court of Appeal recognised that only the freehold title could protect the claimant from the 'ruthless' behaviour of her former lover and provide her with an interest which she might charge in order to raise finance for future repairs and improvements to the property.[6] In other cases the courts have seen fit to satisfy the 'equity' by granting or confirming a leasehold estate in land[7] or by awarding the claimant a fractional share in the relevant property.[8] In appropriate circumstances the courts have granted rights akin to an easement,[9] or have allowed the claimant to purchase the disputed land at a discount.[10]

Limitations or conditions may be attached to any interest granted by the court.[11] In *Williams v Staite*,[12] for instance, Goff LJ accepted that any right awarded to an estoppel claimant might be limited in point of time

2 See *Barrios v Chiabrera* (1984) 3 BPR 9276 at 9279 per Powell J.

3 See eg *Dillwyn v Llewelyn* (1862) 4 De G F & J 517 at 523, 45 ER 1285 at 1287 (ante, p 316); *Cameron v Cameron* (1892) 11 NZLR 642 at 659. See also *Eagleson v Public Trustee* [1922] NZLR 1054 at 1057. Compare *Stratulatos v Stratulatos* [1988] 2 NZLR 424 at 439, where McGechan J thought that it would 'offend conscience' to order a conveyance of the family home to a 'former wife now remarried and effectively a stranger to the family'.

4 The transfer of an interest in the land is often wholly 'disproportionate to the identified detriments to which the [claimant] can point' (*Beaton v McDivitt* (1987) 13 NSWLR 162 at 172F per Kirby P).

5 [1979] 1 WLR 431 at 439B (ante, p 317; post, p 359).

6 In *Riches v Hogben* [1986] 1 Qd R 315 at 321f, 327, 343 (ante, p 326), the Full Court of the Queensland Supreme Court ordered a transfer of the legal title to the estoppel claimant, subject to an equitable life interest for the maker of the relevant assurance, thereby enabling the latter to reside in a 'granny flat' associated with the property.

7 *Siew Soon Wah v Yong Tong Hong* [1973] AC 836 at 846B (Privy Council); *Andrews v Colonial Mutual Life Assurance Society Ltd* [1982] 2 NZLR 556 at 570. Compensation may be awarded if it is no longer possible or practicable to enforce a lease (see *Brownlee v Duggan* (1976) 27 NILQ 291).

8 *Barrios v Chiabrera* (1984) 3 BPR 9276 at 9280f; *Lim Teng Huan v Ang Swee Chuan* [1992] 1 WLR 113 at 119G-H. See also *Stratulatos v Stratulatos* [1988] 2 NZLR 424 at 439f, where McGechan J made an order for payment out to the claimant 'within the reasonably near future' of the value of the fractional interest, the claimant being entitled to occupy the property until payment. In *Preston and Henderson v St Helens MBC* (1989) 58 P & CR 500 at 505, the award of a fractional share in the beneficial interest confirmed the entitlement of the estoppel claimant to the owner-occupier supplement payable on compulsory purchase of a leasehold estate pursuant to the Housing Act 1985.

9 *E R Ives Investment Ltd v High* [1967] 2 QB 379 at 396E, 406B (ante, p 152); *Crabb v Arun DC* [1976] Ch 179 at 190A, 192D, 199F (ante, p 320).

10 *Cameron v Murdoch* [1983] WAR 321 at 360 (affirmed by the Judicial Committee of the Privy Council, (1986) 63 ALR 575 at 595).

11 See *Bank Negara Indonesia v Hoalim* [1973] 2 MLJ 3 at 5C.

12 [1979] Ch 291 at 300B-C.

or determinable on express conditions,[13] in which case a court might later have to rule on whether the interest had expired or the determining event had occurred.[14]

(b) Grant of a right to occupy

A more commonly granted remedy is a recognition by the court that the estoppel claimant has an irrevocable licence to occupy property rent-free either for life[15] or for some shorter period (whether fixed or not).[16] This form of order was made in *Inwards v Baker*[17] and often seems to mirror the ill-defined but nevertheless very real expectations of parties under informal family arrangements.[18]

(i) Factual foundations An interesting example of a grant of long-term occupation rights occurred in *Greasley v Cooke*.[19] Here the defendant, C had entered into occupation of a house at the age of 16 as a living-in maid to the then owner, a widower with four children. She had at first been paid a weekly wage, but after eight years of paid employment she had begun to cohabit in the house with one of the owner's sons, K. For almost the next 30 years C looked after members of the family, including a daughter who suffered from severe mental illness, but received during this period no financial reward for her services. C was later to allege that she had not asked for payment precisely because she had been encouraged by members of the family (including G, one of the present plaintiffs) to believe that she could regard the property as her home for the rest of her life. When both the original owner and his son, K, had died, the remaining members of the family brought an action for possession against C.[20] The Court of Appeal upheld C's claim of proprietary estoppel, Lord Denning MR emphasising that neither the expenditure of money nor strict proof of reliance was a necessary element in such a claim.[1] Here it was sufficient that C had 'stayed on in the house', looking after its needy occupants, 'when otherwise she might have left and got a job elsewhere.'[2] An 'equity' had been raised in favour of C in that she had acted on the faith of an assurance given to her 'in such circumstances that it would be unjust and inequitable for the

13 See eg *E R Ives Investment Ltd v High* [1967] 2 QB 379 at 395A (right of way so long as neighbour's foundations encroached); *Classic Communications Ltd v Lascar* (1986) 21 DLR (4th) 579 at 588 (easement to instal cable on hydro poles so long as hydro poles remained on land).
14 See also *Riches v Hogben* [1986] 1 Qd R 315 at 321.
15 See *Pearce v Pearce* [1977] 1 NSWLR 170 at 177F. Compare *Binions v Evans* [1972] Ch 359 (post, p 917). If it is no longer practicable to enforce such an occupation licence, money compensation may awarded in lieu (*Broughall v Hunt* (Unreported, Chancery Division, 1 February 1983)). See also (1983) 80 LSG 2198 (G. Gypps).
16 See *Silovi Pty Ltd v Barbaro* (1988) 13 NSWLR 466 at 474B-D.
17 [1965] 2 QB 29 at 37G (ante, p 319).
18 Post, p 906.
19 [1980] 1 WLR 1306. See [1981] Conv 154 (R.E. Annand); (1981) 44 MLR 461 (G. Woodman).
20 The county court judge declined to recognise that any proprietary estoppel had arisen in favour of C, holding that such a claim must fail because C had spent no money on the property.
1 [1980] 1 WLR 1306 at 1311G-1312A.
2 [1980] 1 WLR 1306 at 1312A.

party making the assurance to go back on it.'[3] The Court accordingly declared that C was entitled to occupy the house rent-free for the remainder of her life.

(ii) Difficulties The award of a right of occupation for life is, however, fraught with certain technical problems. There is a strong argument that the interest thereby conferred constitutes a 'life interest' which brings into play the cumbersome and improbable machinery of the Settled Land Act 1925.[4] In many cases it seems awkward and unlikely that the estoppel claimant should be invested with the over-large statutory powers of the 'tenant for life' under the Settled Land Act 1925.[5] In particular it is usually undesirable that the claimant should be able to call for a vesting in himself of the legal estate, and should then moreover have the legal capacity to sell, lease or mortgage that estate.[6] In order to avoid the complications of a strict settlement, the courts have tended to resolve the difficulty by making alternative kinds of order which involve either an award of monetary compensation for improvements effected by the claimant[7] or the compulsory grant of a long lease for life at a nominal rent and subject to an absolute covenant against assignment.[8]

(c) Grant of monetary compensation

There are some circumstances in which it is inappropriate to grant a remedy which involves any form of occupation right. It may, for instance, be impossible in practical terms to enforce a sharing arrangement between parties whose personal relationship has broken down.[9] Alternatively, the estoppel claimant may not have sought an occupation right in the first place[10] or may already have given up possession voluntarily.[11] In many cases it is, of course, perfectly possible for the court to satisfy the 'equity' through the award of money compensation. This remedy appears particularly appropriate where the 'equity' is founded on expenditure for improvements which are not substantial.[12] Although courts are naturally reluctant to allow a landowner to use a tender of compensation as a means of buying his way out of an

3 [1980] 1 WLR 1306 at 1311G-H.
4 See *Dodsworth v Dodsworth* (1973) 228 Estates Gazette 1115.
5 Post, p 618.
6 Settled Land Act 1925, s 19(1). See *Dodsworth v Dodsworth* (1973) 228 Estates Gazette 1115; *Griffiths v Williams* (1977) 248 Estates Gazette 947 at 949.
7 This was the solution adopted in *Dodsworth v Dodsworth* (1973) 228 Estates Gazette 1115.
8 See *Griffiths v Williams* (1977) 248 Estates Gazette 947 at 950, where Goff LJ proposed such an arrangement as a means of guaranteeing the estoppel claimant a lifelong right of occupation outside the ambit of both the Settled Land Act 1925 and the Rent Act 1977 (see F.R. Crane, (1967) 31 Conv (NS) 332 at 342). Goff LJ conceded that the nominal rent 'would be an obligation not contemplated when the representations were made to [the claimant]', but comforted himself with the thought that 'perfect equity is seldom possible'.
9 *Shaida v Kindlane Ltd* (Unreported, Chancery Division, 1976 S No 8501, 22 June 1982) per Judge Baker QC, giving the example of *Dodsworth v Dodsworth* (1973) 228 Estates Gazette 1115.
10 *Hamilton v Geraghty* (1901) 1 SRNSW (Eq) 81 at 88 per Darley CJ.
11 *Cushley v Seale* (Unreported, Court of Appeal, 28 October 1986).
12 See *Cushley v Seale* (Unreported, Court of Appeal, 28 October 1986); *Commonwealth v Verwayen* (1990) 170 CLR 394 at 441f per Deane J (ante, p 351).

estoppel claim or of forcing an inequity upon the claimant,[13] there may well be circumstances in which a simple offer of compensation negates any question of unconscionability.[14]

In *Dodsworth v Dodsworth*,[15] for instance, the owner of a bungalow had allowed the present defendants (who were her younger brother and his wife) to live with her in that property. The defendants proceeded to spend some £700 on improvements to the bungalow in the expectation that they could live in the property during the indefinite future. It was not contested that an equity of estoppel had arisen on these facts, but the Court of Appeal considered that the appropriate remedy in the circumstances comprised merely the return of the defendants' capital outlay together with some compensation for the labour invested in making the improvements.[16] The defendants' complaint had been essentially that it would be unfair to evict them in the light of their detrimental reliance on the assurances given to them, but in the Court's view this objection was easily deflected by a simple reimbursement of the money expended by them.[17]

The court's broad discretion in this area extends even to the basis adopted for assessment of compensatory payments. In some cases compensation has been fixed with reference to the enhanced value of the realty;[18] sometimes compensation has been based on the actual cost of the improvements themselves, either with[19] or without[20] payment of interest, or with some adjustment designed to counter-balance the falling value of money over time.[1] In some cases the court has ordered compensation on the basis of an intermediate figure representing a compromise between the 'enhanced value' basis and the 'actual cost' basis.[2]

(d) Grant of a right of occupation coupled with monetary compensation

A further, and rather hybrid, form of remedy lies in an award which combines an element of occupation with the grant of monetary compensation. Such

13 See *Milton v Proctor* (1989) NSW ConvR 55-450 at 58,254 per Mahoney JA.

14 *Milton v Proctor* (1989) NSW ConvR 55-450 at 58,266 per Clarke JA. See *Commonwealth v Verwayen* (1990) 170 CLR 394 at 442 per Deane J, 500f per McHugh J.

15 (1973) 228 Estates Gazette 1115 (ante, p 348).

16 (1973) 228 Estates Gazette 1115 at 1117. The defendants' occupation was secured pending their reimbursement. See also *Mayes v Mayes* (1969) 210 Estates Gazette 935 at 938.

17 Other complicating factors were the death of the owner during the hearing and the fear expressed by the Court of Appeal lest the remedy granted to the defendants should bring them within the scope of the Settled Land Act 1925 (post, p 618).

18 *Montreuil v Ontario Asphalt Co* (1922) 69 DLR 313 at 334f; *Jackson v Crosby* (No 2) (1979) 21 SASR 280 at 294f, 310; *Van den Berg v Giles* [1979] 2 NZLR 111 at 123; *The Queen v Smith* (1981) 113 DLR (3d) 522 at 583. In *Lepel v Huthnance* (1979) NZ Recent Law 269 at 270, Speight J assessed compensation in terms of the added value of the property, rather than on the basis of the cost of the improvements, not least because the plaintiff's labour had been misdirected and the end result was not up to workmanlike standards.

19 *Morris v Morris* [1982] 1 NSWLR 61 at 64F; *Grimison v Union Fidelity Trustee Co of Australia Ltd* (1984) 3 BPR 9469 at 9475.

20 *In re Whitehead* [1948] NZLR 1066 at 1071; *J.N. Elliot & Co (Farms) Ltd v Murgatroyd* (Unreported, Court of Appeal of New Zealand, CA 52/82, 12 September 1984).

1 *Cameron v Murdoch* [1983] WAR 321 at 351 (affirmed by the Judicial Committee of the Privy Council, (1986) 63 ALR 575 at 595); *Stratulatos v Stratulatos* [1988] 2 NZLR 424 at 439f.

2 *Clayton v Green* (1979) NZ Recent Law 139 at 140.

a remedy may involve the recognition that the estoppel claimant has a lien or charge on the disputed property to the appropriate value of the improvements effected[3] or of any money which has been given or loaned.[4] This lien on the property may well be coupled with a right to occupy the property until such time as the money is paid or repaid.[5]

(e) Inhibitory effect of estoppel remedies

At root all estoppel remedies involve the imposition of judicial restraint on the exercise of what would otherwise be a strict legal entitlement. Estoppel inhibits the unconscionable insistence upon legal rights in relation to the estoppel claimant, sometimes indefinitely and sometimes merely until a compensatory award or interest has been granted in satisfaction of the 'equity' raised. In effect the recognition of a proprietary estoppel is often the functional equivalent of the award of relief against forfeiture.[6] The owner of land is effectively restrained from obtaining the arbitrary eviction of the estoppel claimant or from otherwise causing him prejudice.[7]

6. THE NATURE OF A PROPRIETARY ESTOPPEL

A number of difficulties are raised in analysing the nature of the 'equity' which is protected by the doctrine of proprietary estoppel.

(1) Relationship with constructive trust

There is without doubt a close relationship between the operation of proprietary estoppel and the device of the constructive trust.[8] It is clear that the doctrine of proprietary estoppel involves 'the same general principle as that invoked in *Gissing v Gissing*. . .namely, that courts applying equitable principles will prevent a person from insisting on his strict legal rights when it would be inequitable for him to do so having regard to the dealings which

3 *Unity Joint Stock Mutual Banking Association v King* (1858) 25 Beav 72 at 78, 53 ER 563 at 565 (although foreclosure decreed against both owner and holders of lien); *Hamilton v Geraghty* (1901) 1 SRNSW (Eq) 81 at 91; *Taylor v Taylor* [1956] NZLR 99 at 103f.

4 *Hussey v Palmer* [1972] 1 WLR 1286 at 1291A-C, as explained in *In re Sharpe (A Bankrupt)* [1980] 1 WLR 219 at 222H-223A and *Savva v Costa and Harymode Investments Ltd* (1981) 131 NLJ 1114.

5 *Dodsworth v Dodsworth* (1973) 228 Estates Gazette 1115 at 1117; *In re Sharpe (A Bankrupt)* [1980] 1 WLR 219 at 224B; *Stratulatos v Stratulatos* [1988] 2 NZLR 424 at 439f.

6 See *Milton v Proctor* (1989) NSW ConvR 55-450 at 58,254 per Mahoney JA, 58,264f per Clarke JA (post, p 904).

7 Strange results may flow from a finding of estoppel. In *Cullen v Cullen* [1962] IR 268 at 292, Kenny J deliberately intended that the upholding of an estoppel claim, while not conferring any immediate right upon the estoppel claimant, would enable him to be registered as the proprietor of the land at the end of the relevant limitation period. For an interesting exploration of the link between estoppel and adverse possession, see M. Welstead, [1991] Conv 280.

8 For discussion of the constructive trust, see Chapter 12 (post, p 413). It may be that a somewhat sharper distinction may be drawn between the notion of proprietary estoppel and the operation of the resulting trust (see *Walker v Walker* (Unreported, Court of Appeal, 12 April 1984) per Browne-Wilkinson LJ).

have taken place between the parties.'[9] The estoppel doctrine likewise gives effect, at least in part, to the 'equity of expectation' generated by past dealings,[10] and for this reason claims based on estoppel tend to go hand in hand with allegations of constructive trust.[11] Further conceptual assimilation follows from the fact that the court, in concretising the 'equity' of estoppel in the grant of some interest in land, may award that interest behind a court-imposed 'constructive trust'.[12]

(a) Balance of emphasis

If there is a distinction between the doctrine of proprietary estoppel and the constructive trust as a substantive institution,[13] it may well be that 'estoppel puts weight on inducement, constructive trusts on undertakings.'[14] Expressed in another way, the constructive trust is ultimately based upon some concept of frustrated 'bargain'.[15] The 'equity' of estoppel is more clearly founded upon a concept of frustrated 'expectation', in circumstances where some 'holding out to the claimant that she had a beneficial interest' has comprised 'part of the inducement to her to do the acts relied on.'[16] Indeed the estoppel doctrine may possibly be somewhat wider in practice than the theory of constructive trust in that an estoppel claim can succeed where the claimant was promised not an equitable interest in land but the full legal interest.[17]

(b) Range of recognised contributions

There are limits upon the kinds of contributory activity which are recognised as relevant forms of 'detriment' or 'sacrifice' within even the more liberal formulations of the substantive doctrine of constructive trust.[18] It seems,

9 *Christian v Christian* (1981) 131 NLJ 43 per Brightman LJ. See also *Savva v Costa and Harymode Investments Ltd* (1981) 131 NLJ 1114 per Oliver LJ; *In re Basham, decd* [1986] 1 WLR 1498 at 1503H-1504F. Dickson J effectively used the language of estoppel in upholding a constructive trust in *Pettkus v Becker* (1981) 117 DLR (3d) 257 at 274 (post, p 451); *Sorochan v Sorochan* (1986) 29 DLR (4th) 1 at 7, 12f. See also *Hayward v Giordani* [1983] NZLR 140 at 147.

10 *Riches v Hogben* [1986] 1 Qd R 315 at 327, 339.

11 For cases in which the claimant pleaded constructive trust and estoppel in the alternative, see eg *Christian v Christian* (1981) 131 NLJ 43; *Warnes v Hedley* (Unreported, Court of Appeal, 31 January 1984); *Walker v Walker* (Unreported, Court of Appeal, 12 April 1984); *Bristol & West Building Society v Henning* [1985] 1 WLR 778; *Philip Lowe (Chinese Restaurant) Ltd v Sau Man Lee* (Unreported, Court of Appeal, 9 July 1985). It is even possible that the two forms of claim may operate cumulatively so that the claimant recovers a 50 per cent share of equitable ownership on each basis, thereby establishing entitlement to the beneficial whole (see *Preston and Henderson v St Helens MBC* (1989) 58 P & CR 500 at 505).

12 See eg *In re Sharpe (A Bankrupt)* [1980] 1 WLR 219 at 225C-D (post, p 919); *In re Basham, decd* [1986] 1 WLR 1498 at 1504A-F. See also *Sen v Headley*[1991] Ch 425 at 440A per Nourse LJ (post, p 360).

13 On the constructive trust as a substantive institution, see Chapter 12 (post, p 413). Compare the transatlantic use of the constructive trust as a remedial device (post, p 450).

14 J.D. Davies, (1980-81) 7 Adelaide L Rev 200 at 221.

15 Post, p 414.

16 *Grant v Edwards* [1986] Ch 638 at 657C per Browne-Wilkinson V-C.

17 *Riches v Hogben* [1985] 2 Qd R 292 at 299f, upheld on appeal [1986] 1 Qd R 315.

18 Post, p 426.

however, that the estoppel doctrine rests on 'wider equitable principles'[19] which provide relief in some cases where the strict application of constructive trust theory denies a remedy.[20] As was suggested by Browne-Wilkinson V-C in *Grant v Edwards*,[1] it is highly probable that the estoppel doctrine attaches significance to a somewhat broader range of contribution inclusive of the more intangible elements of domestic commitment and endeavour.[2]

(c) Onus of proof

It is also possible that the party setting up an estoppel need not have formulated in his own mind so clear a concept of his own precise entitlement as appears to be currently required in order to establish a constructive trust.[3] The onus of proof in an estoppel claim may be easier in one further respect. Where, following assurances made by the owner, an estoppel claimant has adopted a course of conduct which is prejudicial or otherwise detrimental to himself, there is a rebuttable presumption that he adopted that course of action in reliance on the assurances.[4]

(d) Extent of available remedies

It is sometimes suggested that the 'equity' comprised in a claim of proprietary estoppel is less effective than the 'equity' which is recognised when a court imposes a constructive trust on the owner of an estate in land.[5] However, this generalisation is misleading since there are respects in which the claim of proprietary estoppel is both narrower and wider than the orthodox application of constructive trust theory.

It is true that the estoppel remedy may lead in many cases to the judicial recognition of a 'lesser property right'[6] in the claimant than would normally be conferred by a constructive trust. The imposition of a constructive trust often involves, in essence, the allocation to one or other of the litigants of an aliquot share in the equitable ownership of property.[7] By contrast the recognition of a proprietary estoppel may found only 'the lesser property right of an irrevocable licence',[8] and in this sense may appear to provide an inferior or second-class form of remedy.

On the other hand, the estoppel remedy is sufficiently far-reaching that

19 *Morris v Morris* [1982] 1 NSWLR 61 at 63F-G.
20 However, for circumstances in which a claim based on constructive trust succeeded and an estoppel claim failed, see *Te Rama Engineering Ltd v Shortlands Properties Ltd* [1982] BCL 692 (ante, p 326).
1 [1986] Ch 638 at 657A-C (ante, p 337). See also *Preston and Henderson v St Helens MBC* (1989) 58 P & CR 500 at 505.
2 See eg *Greasley v Cooke* [1980] 1 WLR 1306 at 1312A (ante, p 353, post, p 909).
3 See *Bristol & West Building Society v Henning* [1985] 1 WLR 778 at 781F; *Vinden v Vinden* [1982] 1 NSWLR 618 at 623F, 625B.
4 *Coombes v Smith* [1986] 1 WLR 808 at 821E. See also *Grant v Edwards* [1986] Ch 638 at 657C; *In re Basham, decd* [1986] 1 WLR 1498 at 1507F-G.
5 *Pearce v Pearce* [1977] 1 NSWLR 170 at 177G.
6 *Bristol & West Building Society v Henning* [1985] 1 WLR 778 at 782B.
7 Post, p 413.
8 *Bristol & West Building Society v Henning* [1985] 1 WLR 778 at 782D per Browne-Wilkinson LJ.

it sometimes rivals or even surpasses the relief that is commonly provided by the imposition of a constructive trust.[9] As some of the estoppel cases demonstrate, the doctrine of proprietary estoppel is fully capable of leading to the conclusion that the claimant should be awarded not a mere partial interest in the disputed property but rather the fee simple interest itself.[10] Accordingly it is beginning to be recognised that a claim of proprietary estoppel 'may go a little further' than the kind of claim normally recognised under the head of constructive trust.[11]

(2) When does the 'equity' arise?

The 'equity' raised by proprietary estoppel is, of course, given a peculiarly concrete form when it is asserted and vindicated during the course of litigation. It is at this stage that the court, in determining the remedy required to satisfy the 'equity', recognises the claimant to be entitled to some appropriate right or interest in respect of the disputed land. However, as Browne-Wilkinson J observed in *In re Sharpe (A Bankrupt)*,[12] 'it cannot be that the interest in property arises for the first time when the court declares it to exist.' The claimant must already have a right before the court can grant a remedy in respect of its breach. Thus the 'equity' itself 'predates any order of the court', having arisen at an earlier point in the dealings of the parties.

(a) The inchoate 'equity'

It would appear that the 'equity' of estoppel arises as soon as the conscience of the landowner is affected by the transactions of the parties.[13] It is to be noted that there need not be anything fraudulent or unjust in the initial negotiations of the parties.[14] As Scarman LJ said in *Crabb v Arun DC*,[15] the 'fraud, if it be such, arises after the event, when the defendant seeks by relying on his right to defeat the expectation which he by his conduct encouraged the plaintiff to have.'[16] It is when the landowner unconscionably sets up his undoubted rights adversely to the legitimate demands of the claimant that the 'equity' comes into existence.[17] From this point onwards

9 It has been pointed out that the flexible nature of the estoppel remedy renders unnecessary the largely artificial attempt under constructive trust doctrine to quantify the interest awarded (see Sir Nicolas Browne-Wilkinson, *Constructive Trusts and Unjust Enrichment*, p 6).

10 See eg *Pascoe v Turner* [1979] 1 WLR 431 at 439B (ante, p 317); *Riches v Hogben* [1986] 1 Qd R 315 at 321f, 327, 343 (ante, p 326).

11 *Shaida v Kindlane Ltd* (Unreported, Chancery Division, 1976 S No 8501, 22 June 1982) per Judge Baker QC.

12 [1980] 1 WLR 219 at 225H, citing in support *DHN Food Distributors Ltd v Tower Hamlets LBC* [1976] 1 WLR 852.

13 See *Silovi Pty Ltd v Barbaro* (1988) 13 NSWLR 466 at 473A-B per Priestley JA.

14 *Taylors Fashions Ltd v Liverpool Victoria Trustees Co Ltd* [1982] QB 133 (Note) at 151H–152A (ante, p 331).

15 [1976] Ch 179 at 195C-D.

16 See *Taylors Fashions Ltd v Liverpool Victoria Trustees Co Ltd* [1982] QB 133 (Note) at 147H; *Olsson v Dyson* (1969) 120 CLR 365 at 379. This approach bears certain similarities to the way in which the courts have applied the company law doctrine of 'fraud on the minority' (see *Prudential Assurance Co Ltd v Newman Industries Ltd* (No 2) [1981] Ch 257 at 307D per Vinelott J).

17 *Lim Teng Huan v Ang Swee Chuan* [1992] 1 WLR 113 at 117E-F per Lord Browne-Wilkinson.

the claimant has at least some kind of inchoate right—or 'equity'—to bend the ear of the court of conscience to listen sympathetically to his tale.[18]

(b) The concretised remedy

The mere fact that a claimant has acquired an inchoate 'equity' does not mean that he already has a right to be awarded any particular interest by way of remedy: the 'equity' crystallises only when concretised in the form of a specific interest or award allocated by the court. The importance of the 'equity' is, however, precisely the fact that it opens up to the claimant the jurisdiction of the court to consider his allegation against the good conscience of the landowner and, having listened, to grant him some particular form of proprietary interest or compensatory remedy.

(c) The character of the remedial nexus

There is a certain elusive quality in the relationship between the inchoate 'equity' of estoppel and the rights to which it eventually gives birth by court decree. Nowadays there is increasing support for the idea that the 'equity' contains or represents in embryonic form the remedial award ultimately conferred by the court in satisfaction. In *Commonwealth v Verwayen*[19] Deane J envisaged that, in so far as an estoppel claim seeks to restrain an unconscientious denial of promised beneficial ownership of land (or of rights in land), the cause of action in each case is 'the ordinary one of a beneficiary against a trustee for actual or threatened breach of trust in which the estoppel was relied upon to establish the factual ingredient of [the claimant's] beneficial ownership of the alleged trust property.'

On this basis it can be maintained that the estoppel claimant's promised entitlement (whether to a freehold or leasehold estate or to some lesser interest such as an easement) comes into existence in beneficial form as soon as the ingredients of estoppel doctrine are present on the facts of a given case. Whether by virtue of some doctrine of relation back or on the footing that 'equity looks on as done that which ought to be done', the claimant can later be seen as having already acquired an equitable interest in a fee simple or in a lease or easement as the case may be.[20]

It is not insignificant that recent case law has emphasised this anticipatory dimension of the 'equity' of proprietary estoppel. In *Sen v Headley*,[1] for instance, Nourse LJ expressed the view that an estoppel-based right to call for a conveyance of land 'is the consequence of an implied or constructive trust which arises once all the requirements of the [estoppel] doctrine have been satisfied.' In *Voyce v Voyce*[2] the estoppel claimant had substantially modernised a property in reliance on an informal gift of the land from his mother.

18 See eg *Beaton v McDivitt* (1987) 13 NSWLR 162 at 172C-D, where Kirby P spoke in terms of a claimant having 'an equity which would attract the discretion of the Court'.
19 (1990) 170 CLR 394 at 437.
20 *Commonwealth v Verwayen* (1990) 170 CLR 394 at 437 per Deane J. See also *Voyce v Voyce* (1991) 62 P & CR 290 at 294, where Dillon LJ emphasised that 'the equitable rights of the defendant had accrued long before' the instant litigation.
1 [1991] Ch 425 at 440A.
2 (1991) 62 P & CR 290.

Dillon LJ went so far as to say that, during the period when the estoppel claimant remained in occupation 'under the equitable rights which were ultimately satisfied by the direction for a conveyance, he was, as is now recognised, the equitable owner' of the land.[3] These developments heavily reinforce the notion that proprietary estoppel generates anticipatory beneficial rights behind a trust which then provides the basis for the court's subsequent order of either specific performance or compensatory damages for breach.

(3) Does the 'equity' comprise a 'property interest' or 'interest in land'?

It is uncontroversial that the inchoate 'equity' generated by a claim of proprietary estoppel should be regarded as comprising an 'interest in land' for isolated purposes such as the award of compensation under the Town and Country Planning legislation.[4] However, it has been usual in the past to find such concessions closely coupled with a firm denial that the inchoate 'equity' can itself constitute a 'property interest' or 'interest in land' in the strict conveyancing sense.[5] There has been a tendency to disavow the proprietary status of this kind of 'equity',[6] not least because of the perceived difficulty of placing it within the existing canon of rights and interests recognised in the Law of Property Act 1925. At least until recently there has been a conventional, if rather half-hearted, consensus that the estoppel claimant receives no property right in the strict sense unless and until a court finally awards him one or other of the recognised property rights in satisfaction of his 'equity'.

It is precisely this denial of proprietary quality which becomes difficult to sustain as the inchoate 'equity' is increasingly closely identified behind some trust as an anticipatory version or beneficial basis of the rights ultimately recognised by the eventual court order.

(a) The modern view

Contrary to the traditional view of the status of the estoppel-based 'equity', there is nowadays gathering support for the idea that the inchoate 'equity' of the estoppel claimant can be regarded as a present right of property.[7] According to this more modern view, 'property' is not a thing but a relationship; and the essence of a 'property right' lies in the fact that it comprises a claim habitually recognised and enforced by the courts.[8] In

3 (1991) 62 P & CR 290 at 294.

4 *Pennine Raceway Ltd v Kirklees MBC* [1983] QB 382 at 389F, 391D-E. See [1983] Conv 317 (JEM). See also *Plimmer v Mayor etc of Wellington* (1884) 9 App Cas 699 at 714 (ante, p 319).

5 See eg *Pennine Raceway Ltd v Kirklees MBC* [1983] QB 382 at 391A.

6 The conventional view stems largely from the decision of the House of Lords in *National Provincial Bank Ltd v Ainsworth* [1965] AC 1175 (ante, p 159). See, however, the different view expressed by the High Court of Australia in *Latec Investments Ltd v Hotel Terrigal Pty Ltd* (1965) 113 CLR 265 (post, p 938).

7 For an interesting argument that a licence coupled with an 'equity' may fall into some intermediate category of 'quasi-property' mid-way between rights *in rem* and rights *in personam*, see A.R. Everton, *Towards A Concept Of 'Quasi-Property'?*, [1982] Conv 118 at 131f. See also S.M. Bandali, (1973) 37 Conv (NS) 402 at 409.

8 See [1991] CLJ 252 at 294f.

particular, beneficial rights and interests in property are brought into existence by equity—are indeed engrafted[9] or impressed[10] upon the relevant legal estate—only where their recognition 'has been found to be required in order to give effect to its doctrines.'[11] Equitable rights of property are therefore derived ultimately from some conscientious obligation owed to another party to deal with property in a certain way.

In terms of this analysis the 'equity' raised by a valid claim of proprietary estoppel can indeed be seen quite readily as a form of equitable proprietary right.[12] An 'equity' of estoppel denotes a clear call upon conscience to which the courts habitually respond with the granting of a remedy.[13] It is true that the particular remedy is selected at the discretion of the court, but the 'equity' of the estoppel claimant is otherwise not qualitatively different from, for instance, the 'equity' of the cestui que trust to have property dealt with as his trust requires. As Isaacs J was accustomed to point out, the latter right 'is regarded for the purposes of equity as equivalent to a right in the property itself',[14] for equitable ownership is 'always commensurate with the right to relief in a Court of Equity.'[15] The 'equity' founded on proprietary estoppel is similarly susceptible to a 'property' characterisation.[16] In *Milton v Proctor*[17] McHugh JA noted in the New South Wales Court of Appeal that the nature of the equity is 'measured by the extent to which [the court] will give the licensee protection against interference with the equity'. On this basis McHugh JA had no doubt that the 'equity' raised by a proprietary estoppel 'constitutes an interest in the land'.[18]

(b) A realist perspective

In realist terms the 'property right' *is* the recognition of the claim, and the enforceability of the claim is in fact all that is meant by the so-called

9 *Re Transphere Pty Ltd* (1986) 5 NSWLR 309 at 311E-F per McLelland J.

10 *D.K.L.R. Holding Co (No 2) Pty Ltd v Commissioner of Stamp Duties (N.S.W.)* (1982) 149 CLR 431 at 474 per Brennan J.

11 *Commissioner of Stamp Duties (Queensland) v Livingston* [1965] AC 694 at 712E per Viscount Radcliffe (ante, p 265).

12 See eg *Beaton v McDivitt* (1985) 13 NSWLR 134 at 158C, where Young J conceded that the 'equity' would constitute 'an equitable interest in the land', albeit one of 'a special idiosyncratic character'.

13 It is in this 'broader and less precise sense' that Deane J has described 'an equity' as referring to 'any entitlement or obligation. . .of which a court of equity will take cognisance' (see *Commonwealth v Verwayen* (1990) 170 CLR 394 at 435). Accordingly, in Deane J's view, 'it is permissible to speak of the operation of estoppel in equity as giving rise to "an equity".'

14 *Glenn v Federal Commissioner of Land Tax* (1915) 20 CLR 490 at 503.

15 *Trustees, Executors and Agency Co Ltd v Acting Federal Commissioner of Taxation* (1917) 23 CLR 576 at 583. See also *In re Cunliffe-Owen* [1953] Ch 545 at 557 per Evershed MR; *Stern v McArthur* (1988) 165 CLR 489 at 522f per Deane and Dawson JJ. It was no mere accident that in *Hoysted v Federal Commissioner of Taxation* (1920) 27 CLR 400 at 423, Isaacs J viewed Lord Kingsdown's judgment in *Ramsden v Dyson* as being similarly 'based on the principle that equitable property is commensurate with equitable relief.'

16 See eg *Cameron v Murdoch* [1983] WAR 321 at 360, where Brinsden J saw the plaintiffs' interest under their 'equity' as an 'equitable interest in specific assets'.

17 (1989) NSW ConvR 55-450 at 58,258.

18 See also Clarke JA's insistence in *Milton v Proctor* (1989) NSW ConvR 55-450, at 58,266f, that 'it would no longer be accurate to say that a licence never creates an interest in land'.

'property right'. It would be self-deception to regard the 'property interest' awarded by a court in satisfaction of the 'equity' of estoppel as being somehow invested with a larger 'property' significance than that which is being attributed here to the initial and inchoate 'equity' generated by the estoppel. In the last resort all that is denoted by either usage (whether the reference be to an 'equity' or to some comfortingly familiar 'property right') is that the courts will habitually enforce the claims which are so described in their respective forms of legal shorthand.

(c) The meaning of a 'property right'

It may, of course, be correctly concluded that it is not ultimately helpful to refer to anything as a 'property right'.[19] At best this usage operates merely as an abbreviated reference to certain secondary characteristics which flow from the primary fact of protection through legitimated state power. When the arrogant nonsense of the 'property right' is finally stripped away, all that remains visible to the naked eye is the raw fact of enforcement of a protected entitlement.[20] The only relevant question, in a congeries of situations involving a variety of parties, concerns who will win. True it may be that the answer is conventionally rationalised in terms of justice or conscience. But whether the 'equity' generated by proprietary estoppel is or is not a 'property right' is not in itself a particularly interesting question.[1] To attach definitive importance to some supposed talisman of 'proprietary' quality is relatively pointless, for the whole point here is that the inchoate 'equity' has a free-standing claim to protection which depends in no way upon the attribution of some more familiar, but ultimately irrelevant, title or character.

(4) Can the benefit of the 'equity' pass to a third party?

It is important to know whether an 'equity' raised by proprietary estoppel may be asserted not by the party who originally relied on the relevant assurance but by his successor in title. To ask whether the inchoate 'equity' is or is not a 'property right' does not genuinely assist in the determination of this question, since a 'property' characterisation merely states the conclusion in advance without addressing the subtlety of the central issue.[2] There seems to be some doubt as to whether an inchoate 'equity' can be asserted by successors in title. In *Fryer v Brook*,[3] for instance, Oliver LJ declined to decide

19 See *Property in Thin Air*, [1991] CLJ 252.

20 The notion of a 'property right' is, in this sense, a 'category of illusory reference' (see J. Stone, *Legal System and Lawyers' Reasonings* (London 1964), p 241ff).

1 Sometimes of course the reference to 'property' does confer a certain mechanical utility in operating those legal rules which are expressly premised on the presence or availability of 'property' (see eg *Beaton v McDivitt* (1985) 13 NSWLR 134 at 158A-B).

2 Post, p 924.

3 [1984] L S Gaz R 2856, CA.

the issue in definitive terms, but opined that the 'equity' was merely a 'personal interest' vested in the original estoppel claimant himself, and was 'rather akin to the personal right of occupation created by a statutory tenancy.'[4] As such it was not then capable of vesting in the claimant's trustee in bankruptcy.[5]

In *E.R. Ives Investment Ltd v High*,[6] however, an 'equity' based on proprietary estoppel was described by Lord Denning MR as being available also to successors in title.[7] It is possible that this statement meant only that successors in title could take advantage of the right of access which was awarded to the estoppel claimant in satisfaction of his 'equity', rather than that they could have asserted the inchoate 'equity' for the first time themselves. Only in the Australian case law is there a clear ruling that a successor in title can base an original claim to an inchoate 'equity' on the ground of an earlier assurance made to, and relied on by, his predecessor.[8] The balance of opinion in the English cases seems to incline against the transmissibility of the benefit of estoppel-based 'equities', but it may be that the Australian approach is a sign of future developments.[9]

(5) Can the burden of the 'equity' pass to a third party?

It may also be critically important to determine whether the 'equity' created by a proprietary estoppel is binding on third parties. The focus of concern here is the 'third-party impact' of the 'equity' as a mere inchoate right before it has crystallised in the form of some remedy granted by the courts.[10] It is, of course, clear that once the 'equity' has crystallised in a concrete

4 On the nature of the statutory tenancy, see Chapter 18 (post, p 876). In *Jones (A E) v Jones (F W)* [1977] 1 WLR 438 at 443D, Lord Denning MR held that the defendant had an 'equity. . .of a possessory nature entitling [him] to remain in this house, but it would not. . .extend to the defendant's wife.'

5 In any event Oliver LJ found an alternative ground for his decision in section 22(3) of the Bankruptcy Act 1914.

6 [1967] 2 QB 379 at 395A. Winn LJ (at [1967] 2 QB 379 at 403A) declined to decide the 'subsidiary but important question whether Mr High's claim, if valid, is only a personal right'.

7 See, however, F.R. Crane, (1967) 31 Conv (NS) 332 at 341.

8 *Hamilton v Geraghty* (1901) 1 SRNSW (Eq) 81 at 89; *Cameron v Murdoch* [1983] WAR 321 at 360 (affirmed (1986) 63 ALR 575 at 595). See M. Neave and M. Weinberg, *The Nature and Function of Equities*, (1978–80) 6 Tas U L Rev 24 at 30. It may be that the result of the tortuous litigation in *Neesom v Clarkson* (1842) 2 Hare 163, 67 ER 68, (1845) 4 Hare 97, 67 ER 576, can be seen as providing support for the same idea.

9 See the similar approach now adopted in relation to promissory estoppel in *Brikom Investments Ltd v Carr* [1979] QB 467 at 484G–485A per Lord Denning MR, citing in support the statement in *Co Litt*, p. 352a,b that 'every estoppel ought to be reciprocal. . .privies in estate, as the feoffee, lessee & c. . .shall be bound and take the advantage of estoppels. . .'

10 The maintenance of a distinction between the inchoate 'equity' and the eventual remedy may go some distance towards providing a solution to the problems raised by T. Bailey, [1983] Conv 99. It is all too easy to confuse the proprietary status of the inchoate 'equity' (ante, p 359) with the various kinds of property right which the courts may award in satisfaction of the 'equity'.

judicial remedy, the interest thereby recognised in the claimant can more easily be made binding on third parties.[11]

(a) Unregistered land

It seems to be agreed that the 'equity' raised by proprietary estoppel does not constitute a land charge in the context of unregistered land.[12] It follows therefore that no facility of registration can be used in order to make such an 'equity' binding upon a purchaser of the land.[13] Equally plainly an inchoate 'equity' of estoppel does not rank as an equitable interest which is capable of being overreached under section 2(1) of the Law of Property Act 1925.[14]

It is nevertheless clear that an 'equity' generated by proprietary estoppel can, under certain circumstances, run with the land,[15] so as to affect purchasers other than for value.[16] An 'equity' of this kind, albeit not yet concretised in any court-ordered remedy, has been held to bind not merely the owner of the land, but also his trustee in bankruptcy,[17] his personal representatives,[18] a donee,[19] an associated company,[20] and a successor local authority.[1]

(i) Application of the doctrine of notice There is some authority for suggesting that the impact of the inchoate 'equity' on other third parties turns on some version of the equitable doctrine of notice. It is generally thought that an 'equity' raised by an assurance given by one owner of land is enforceable against a purchaser of a legal estate in that land who has actual notice

11 This appears to be true even where the estoppel is satisfied through the recognition that the claimant has an irrevocable licence (*In re Sharpe (A Bankrupt)* [1980] 1 WLR 219 at 224G). See *Williams v Staite* [1979] Ch 291, where the point seems to have been assumed without explicit argument. Compare, however, G. Battersby, [1991] Conv 36 at 39, for a strong argument that the court-ordered remedy will bind third parties only if the right awarded by the court constitutes a conventionally recognised species of proprietary interest. While such a view has its attractions, it does not sit entirely easily alongside *Ashburn Anstalt v Arnold* [1989] Ch 1 at 24D. Here the Court of Appeal denied that a contractual licence could create a property interest, but still thought it might in certain circumstances bind a third party (post, p 922).

12 *E.R. Ives Investment Ltd v High* [1967] 2 QB 379 at 395G, 400B, 405G; *Pascoe v Turner* [1979] 1 WLR 431 at 439A; *Bristol & West Building Society v Henning* [1985] 1 WLR 778 at 781F.

13 See [1982] Conv 80 (JEM). It has been suggested, on the basis of dicta in *Haslemere Estates Ltd v Baker* [1982] 1 WLR 1109 at 1119H-1120A per Megarry V-C, that an estoppel claim may be properly registrable under the Land Charges Act 1972 as a *lis pendens* (see [1983] Conv 69 at 70 (JEM)). This may be true, but would in any event require (i) that litigation should already have commenced and (ii) that the estoppel claim should assert an interest in land (see Land Charges Act 1972, s 17(1), ante, p 114).

14 Ante, p 102. See *Shiloh Spinners Ltd v Harding* [1973] AC 693 at 721C per Lord Wilberforce. See, however, M.P. Thompson, [1988] Conv 108 at 120; and compare P.T. Evans, [1989] Conv 418 at 427.

15 The 'equity' can be traced into the proceeds of sale of the land and into further investments bought out of those proceeds (*Lepel v Huthnance* (1979) NZ Recent Law 269 at 270).

16 See *Voyce v Voyce* (1991) 62 P & CR 290 at 293f per Dillon LJ; *Torrisi v Magame Pty Ltd* [1984] 1 NSWLR 14 at 23A-C.

17 *In re Sharpe (A Bankrupt)* [1980] 1 WLR 219 at 224F.

18 *Inwards v Baker* [1965] 2 QB 29 at 37F; *Jones (A E) v Jones (F W)* [1977] 1 WLR 438 at 442F.

19 *Voyce v Voyce* (1991) 62 P & CR 290 at 293 per Dillon LJ, 296 per Nicholls LJ.

20 *E & L Berg Homes Ltd v Grey* (1980) 253 Estates Gazette 473 at 475.

1 *Salvation Army Trustee Co Ltd v West Yorkshire MCC* (1981) 41 P & CR 179 at 193.

of the circumstances which gave rise to the 'equity'.[2] It is less clear whether the 'equity' is binding on a purchaser of a legal estate with merely constructive notice.[3] If an estoppel-based 'equity' is treated as being more or less equivalent to a conventional 'equitable interest in land', there would appear to be no reason in principle why a purchaser should not be bound if he has constructive notice. However, in *In re Sharpe (A Bankrupt)*[4] Browne-Wilkinson J did remark somewhat pointedly that the 'equity' raised in the case before him might be defeated by a purchaser from a trustee in bankruptcy, provided that such purchaser did not have 'express notice'.[5] On the other hand, if the 'equity' founded on proprietary estoppel is treated on the same footing as other 'equities',[6] it would follow that an estoppel-based 'equity' could be defeated by a purchaser for value of even an equitable interest in the land, provided that he has no notice actual or constructive.[7] The law in these respects awaits clarification.

(ii) Range of remedy against successors in title It should be stressed that the precise nature of the remedy granted by the court against a successor in title may not be quite the same or as far-reaching as the remedy which the court might have granted had the 'equity' been asserted against the party who gave the initial assurance.[8]

(b) Registered land

There is less authority concerning the impact of inchoate estoppel claims on transferees of a title in registered land. There is some merit in the view that the 'equity' raised by proprietary estoppel constitutes an overriding interest under section 70(1)(g) of the Land Registration Act 1925 if coupled

2 All the members of the Court of Appeal in *E.R. Ives Investment Ltd v High* [1967] 2 QB 379 stressed the fact that the purchaser had received explicit notice of the circumstances of the claimant's 'equity' (see [1967] 2 QB 379 at 393G per Lord Denning MR, 400A, E per Danckwerts LJ, 405B per Winn LJ). See, however, *Torrisi v Magame Pty Ltd* [1984] 1 NSWLR 14 at 23B-C per Powell J, for reference to the slightly differing rationales offered as the precise basis of the decision. Of course, the impact of the 'equity' on the purchaser follows *a fortiori* if the purchaser takes only an equitable interest in the land.

3 That a purchaser of a legal estate may be bound by mere constructive notice seems to emerge from *The Duke of Beaufort v Patrick* (1853) 17 Beav 60 at 78, 51 ER 954 at 961; *Bristol & West Building Society v Henning* [1985] 1 WLR 778 at 781G. See F.R. Crane, (1967) 31 Conv (NS) 332 at 339.

4 [1980] 1 WLR 219 at 226G.

5 For an argument in favour of limiting the category of purchasers affected by an 'equity' to those with actual or express notice, see M.P. Thompson, [1983] Conv 50 at 56. Professor R.H. Maudsley proposed a resolution of the present problem which turned on whether the estoppel claimant has exclusive possession of the land. He suggested that estoppel claimants who do not enjoy exclusive possession should be protected against (i) purchasers with actual notice, and (ii) volunteers. However, estoppel claimants who have exclusive possession should be protected against *every* person coming to the land except a purchaser for value without notice, actual or constructive (see (1956) 20 Conv (NS) 281 at 291ff).

6 Ante, p 158.

7 See *Phillips v Phillips* (1861) 4 De G F & J 208 at 218, 45 ER 1164 at 1167.

8 Ante, p 351.

with actual occupation on the part of the claimant.[9] Moreover, there is a possibility that the 'equity' is protectible as a minor interest by the entry of a caution[10] (or even a notice[11]) in the land register, although it is predictable that few such cautions will be entered in practice.[12] The Law Commission has expressed the view that a requirement of registration in this context may 'add a further complication to the law'.[13]

(c) Doctrinal coherence and a conscience-based solution

The third-party impact of an 'equity' of estoppel is still a matter of some controversy. In *Ashburn Anstalt v Arnold*[14] the Court of Appeal stated a firm view that the closely analogous device of the contractual licence cannot constitute a proprietary interest in land. Yet it seems increasingly difficult to differentiate convincingly between a promise of rights based on consideration and a similar promise which induces detrimental reliance.[15] This may well be one reason why in *Canadian Imperial Bank of Commerce v Bello*[16] Dillon LJ, in endorsing the *Ashburn Anstalt* approach to the contractual licence, added his view that an estoppel could not be 'a sufficient interest in the property to be an overriding right. . .within the meaning of section 70(1)(g)' of the Land Registration Act 1925.[17]

The resolution of the present impasse is almost certainly to be found in the growing acceptance of constructive trust theory as supporting an in personam jurisdiction to restrain unconscionable conduct by third parties. In the same way in which *Ashburn Anstalt* recognised that the constructive trust might occasionally cause a purchaser to be bound by a contractual licence,[18] an 'equity' of estoppel may in certain circumstances affect a third party who has 'burdened his own title' with an independent conscientious obligation towards the estoppel claimant.[19] The 'equity' would therefore be binding, not on the basis of the notice doctrine or even because of the presence

9 See *National Provincial Bank Ltd v Hastings Car Mart Ltd* [1964] Ch 665 at 689 per Lord Denning MR (ante, p 210). For a persuasive analogy, see the approach adopted in respect of an equity of rectification in *Blacklocks v J.B. Developments (Godalming) Ltd* [1982] Ch 183 at 196E-F (ante, p 235). Compare, however, *Poster v Slough Estates Ltd* [1969] 1 Ch 495 at 507G per Cross J; *Canadian Imperial Bank of Commerce v Bello* (1992) 64 P & CR 48 at 52 per Dillon LJ.

10 See T. Bailey, [1983] Conv 99 at 103.

11 See Law Commission, *Property Law: Land Registration (Fourth Paper)* (Published Working Paper No 67, April 1976), para 50. See also para 65f.

12 See P.T. Evans [1989] Conv 418 at 428, for the suggestion that the notice doctrine may still govern the 'equity' of estoppel even in the context of registered land.

13 Law Commission, *Property Law: Second Report on Land Registration (Provisional)* (1984), para 57.

14 [1989] Ch 1 at 24D (post, p 920).

15 As Graham Battersby has said, 'it is not easy to see why a representation should be capable of binding third parties when an equivalent promise is incapable of doing so' ([1991] Conv 36 at 37).

16 (1992) 64 P & CR 48 at 52.

17 Ante, p 210. Dillon LJ referred to 'promissory estoppel', but in terms which indicated that he either meant 'proprietary estoppel' or found the notions for present purposes indistinguishable.

18 Post, p 922.

19 See *Bahr v Nicolay* (No 2) (1988) 164 CLR 604 at 653 per Brennan J (ante, p 196). See also Wilson and Toohey JJ at 638f.

of an overriding interest. The impact on the third party would follow simply from his express or implied acceptance of a transfer of land on terms whereby he voluntarily subjected himself to the 'equity' of the estoppel and which terms he cannot now in conscience be heard to disavow. In the compelling context of the in personam jurisdiction, it ceases to matter whether the rights upheld against the third party are or are not proprietary in nature. The 'policing' function achieved by the constructive trust operates regardless of the intrinsic character of the rights violated by the third party: the critical question has turned instead to focus upon the conscientiousness of the actor.

The flexibility of this approach means that the third-party impact of any inchoate 'equity' of estoppel is specific to the particular purchaser whom it is sought to bind. The mere fact that the 'equity' has binding quality as against one title holder does not preclude the possibility that another may, without injury to conscience, take free. The question of overriding conscientious obligation arises afresh on each occasion and may well admit of divergent responses on different occasions. The utility of such an approach to 'equities' of estoppel was recently confirmed by Sir Nicolas Browne-Wilkinson, as he then was. Speaking extra-judicially in 1991,[20] the Vice-Chancellor indicated that an estoppel should not impose obligations 'on outside parties who can have no sufficient information about the details of the relationship' between the landowner and the estoppel claimant. In his view '[o]nly if the third party's conduct is such as to raise an estoppel against the third party individually will the third party be affected'. If this flexible form of response accurately predicts the path of future developments, it is possible that the most appropriate protection for estoppel claimants may well lie ultimately in the general extension of existing powers of rectification under the Land Registration Act 1925.[1]

20 *Constructive Trusts and Unjust Enrichment*, p 6.
1 Ante, p 229.

D. Holdings

CHAPTER 12

Trusts

Any claim to a beneficial interest[1] in real property necessarily presupposes the existence of some kind of trust.[2] As Lord Diplock indicated in *Gissing v Gissing*,[3] it must be shown 'that the person in whom the legal estate is vested holds it as a trustee upon trust to give effect to the beneficial interest of the claimant as cestui que trust.'[4] The present chapter is therefore devoted to an account of the origin of the various kinds of trust which have a role to play in the law of land.[5]

1. ASCERTAINMENT OF BENEFICIAL OWNERSHIP

Fundamental to the ascertainment of the beneficial ownership of land is the proposition that a transfer of the legal title carries with it, prima facie, the absolute beneficial interest in the property conveyed.[6] Thus a conveyance to A of a legal title in land vests in A the whole of the beneficial interest unless some other person, B, is able to 'establish a basis upon which equity would intervene on [his or] her behalf.'[7] Equity will intervene on behalf of B only if such action is necessary in order to give effect to one or other of its doctrines.[8] Accordingly, equity's historic concern with conscience has manifested itself pre-eminently in a willingness in appropriate circumstances to call into existence some form of 'equitable' interest or ownership on behalf of B in opposition to the 'legal' title of A.[9] The recognition of such an

1 For an explanation of equitable or 'beneficial' ownership, see Chapter 2 (ante, p 34).
2 *Gissing v Gissing* [1971] AC 886 at 900B per Viscount Dilhorne; *Burns v Burns* [1984] Ch 317 at 326F, 330H-331A per Fox LJ; *Allen v Snyder* [1977] 2 NSWLR 685 at 689F; *Thwaites v Ryan* [1984] VR 65 at 69.
3 [1971] AC 886 at 904G-H.
4 The onus is on the claimant to demonstrate that the beneficial entitlement does not coincide with the legal title (*Crisp v Mullings* (1976) 239 Estates Gazette 119 per Russell LJ). See also *Bernard v Josephs* [1982] Ch 391 at 404H-405B, 407D-E; (1982) 98 LQR 518; [1982] Conv 444 (J. Warburton); [1983] CLJ 30.
5 For an excellent comparative review of the law of trusts, see Berend Hovius and Timothy Youdan, *The Law of Family Property* (Carswell 1991), Chapters 4-8.
6 *Pettitt v Pettitt* [1970] AC 777 at 813H-814A per Lord Upjohn. See also *Vandervell v IRC* [1966] Ch 261 at 287G; *Gissing v Gissing* [1971] AC 886 at 902A per Lord Pearson; *Bernard v Josephs* [1982] Ch 391 at 402D; *Burns v Burns* [1984] Ch 317 at 330H, 336D; *Currie v Hamilton* [1984] 1 NSWLR 687 at 690E; *Northern Bank Ltd v Gracey* (Unreported, High Court of Northern Ireland, 6 September 1991) per Campbell J.
7 *Allen v Snyder* [1977] 2 NSWLR 685 at 701E per Mahoney JA.
8 Ante, p 265. See *Commissioner of Stamp Duties (Queensland) v Livingston* [1965] AC 694 at 712E per Viscount Radcliffe; *Muschinski v Dodds* (1985) 160 CLR 583 at 616 per Deane J.
9 Ante, p 36.

entitlement amounts to the assertion of a trust relationship between A and B: A is conventionally described as holding his legal title on trust for B.[10]

It is the purpose of the following pages to outline the circumstances under which such a trust will come into being. Three forms of trust are relevant in this context: (1) the express trust, (2) the resulting trust, and (3) the constructive trust.[11] Sadly, however, the terminology used by courts and lawyers to refer to these different kinds of trust is lacking in uniformity and consistency.[12]

(1) Classification of trusts

Classification is arid, but confusion is worse. It may be appropriate at this point to indicate that the major classificatory distinction in the law of trusts is that between express and implied trusts. Implied trusts may be further subdivided into resulting and constructive trusts (*Fig.* 21).

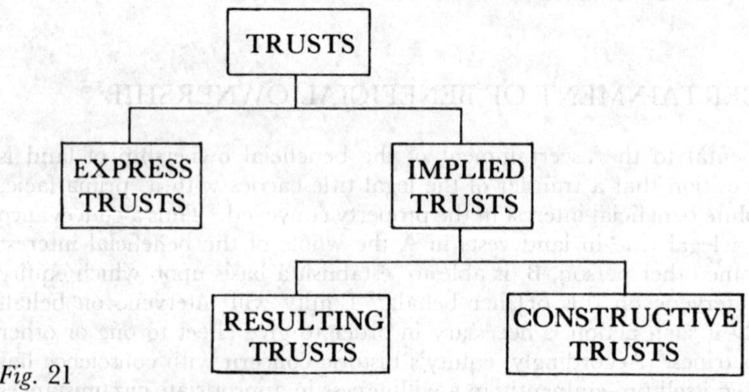

Fig. 21

It befits a jurisdiction which is less impressed by form than by substance that equity's recognition of the trust should ultimately be concerned with matters of intention. In the High Court of Australia in *Hepworth v Hepworth*,[13] Windeyer J observed that an 'intention, proved or presumed, that a trust should exist is at the base of every trust'. This proposition is borne out in the three cases of trust which are the focus of this chapter. The express

10 See *Re Transphere Pty Ltd* (1986) 5 NSWLR 309 at 311E-F, where McLelland J indicated that a legal owner who holds property on trust for another 'has at law all the rights of an absolute owner but the beneficiary has the right to compel him to hold and use those rights which the law gives him in accordance with the obligations which equity has imposed on him by virtue of the existence of the trust. Although this right of the beneficiary constitutes an equitable estate in the property, it is engrafted on to, not carved out of, the legal estate.'

11 For reference to this threefold division of the law of trusts, see *Barrios v Chiabrera* (1984) 3 BPR 9276 at 9278 per Powell J.

12 See eg *Burns v Burns* [1984] Ch 317 at 336D-F, where May LJ described as a resulting trust what would more usually be termed a constructive trust; and compare *Lloyds Bank Plc v Rosset* [1991] 1 AC 107 at 132H-133A, where Lord Bridge of Harwich referred in terms of constructive trust to circumstances which would normally be regarded as raising a resulting trust (see [1990] Conv 314 at 317 (M.P. Thompson)). See also *Allen v Snyder* [1977] 2 NSWLR 685 at 691D; *Muschinski v Dodds (1985) 160 CLR 583 at 596 per Gibbs CJ*.

13 (1963) 110 CLR 309 at 317.

trust is the very embodiment of an intention formulated by a legal owner regarding the beneficial ownership of his property; the resulting trust gives effect to an intention presumed to have been formulated with reference to the money contributions made in the context of a purchase of land; and the constructive trust arises in circumstances where it would be unconscionable not to give effect to a common intention which has provided the basis of the parties' mutual expectations and dealings.

(2) Search for intentions as to beneficial ownership

Ownership of the legal title in land is scarcely ever in doubt, since the identity of the current legal owner is usually firmly established by the last deed of conveyance (in the case of unregistered land) or by the relevant proprietorship register (in the case of registered land). In almost every case, therefore, the location of legal ownership is definitively ascertained by reference to a documentary source,[14] and indeed the primary purpose of the transfer documents which are used in conveyancing is to indicate with precision the name of the next legal owner or owners.[15] These transfer documents may, of course, go on to clarify not merely matters of legal title but also details of beneficial ownership, and such declarations of beneficial entitlement, if included in the conveyance, are generally conclusive.[16]

(a) Unexpressed beneficial ownership

It is possible, however, that the documentary title may remain silent, either completely or in part, as to the beneficial ownership of the land. In such cases it is much more difficult to ascertain the nature and quantum of the equitable interests in that land. The details of beneficial ownership following transfer are frequently not contained in any formal document or other writing, and may come into question only at some much later stage when a dispute arises.[17] When this happens it becomes necessary to render explicit that which was previously left unexpressed.[18]

14 Compare, however, the case of acquisition through adverse possession (ante, p 282).

15 See *Tinsley v Milligan* [1992] Ch 310 at 337D per Ralph Gibson LJ.

16 *Pettitt v Pettitt* [1970] AC 777 at 813E per Lord Upjohn. As Griffiths LJ said in *Bernard v Josephs* [1982] Ch 391 at 403C, the 'starting point of any inquiry into ... beneficial ownership ... must be the conveyance.' See also *In re Gorman (A Bankrupt)* [1990] 1 WLR 616 at 621C.

17 Disputes as to beneficial ownership may arise in many contexts. The issue of ownership may be precipitated by a bankruptcy or death, or in connection with tax liability, or even in unusual contexts such as arose in *Heron v Sandwell MBC* (1980) 255 Estates Gazette 65, where the question affected the payment of an owner-occupier's supplement after compulsory purchase.

18 Occasionally a silence as to the precise nature of the intended beneficial ownership can be resolved by necessary implication from the terms of a conveyance. It seems, however, that a standard declaration that the survivor of the transferees is entitled 'to give a valid receipt for capital money arising on a disposition of the land' does not constitute a declaration of trust indicating the existence of beneficial joint tenancy. See *Harwood v Harwood* [1991] 2 FLR 274 at 288E–289C per Slade LJ; *Huntingford v Hobbs* [1993] 1 FCR 45 at 51F–52C per Sir Christopher Slade, 58E–59E per Steyn LJ. See [1992] Conv 347 (H. Norman). Compare *In re Gorman (A Bankrupt)* [1990] 1 WLR 616 at 620H–621B per Vinelott J; *Huntingford v Hobbs* [1993] 1 FCR 45 at 63F-G per Dillon LJ, who later conceded to the majority view (see *Skelding v Hanson* (Unreported, Court of Appeal, 17 November 1992)).

The ascertainment of undeclared beneficial ownership becomes particularly problematic in relation to property which is acquired for family use. The legal arrangements for joint family living are usually forged in a fairly ill-defined and inarticulate fashion,[19] precise issues of beneficial entitlement emerging only years later on the termination of the relevant relationships by death or disaffection. Where the protagonists were married to each other, the courts are nowadays empowered by statute to overstep the technicalities of strict beneficial entitlement in resolving matters of dispute.[20] In dealing, for instance, with the financial consequences of divorce, the law adopts 'a forward-looking perspective in which questions of ownership yield to the higher demands of relating the means of both to the needs of each, the first consideration given to the welfare of children.'[1] Where, however, the parties were not married, their financial rights must in general be worked out according to their strict entitlements in equity—a process which, as Waite J acknowledged in *Hammond v Mitchell*,[2] 'is anything but forward-looking and involves, on the contrary, a painfully detailed retrospect.' Nor is this process aided by the recognition in English law of any law of family or community property or any special regime of 'family assets'.[3] The mere fact that persons are members of the same family has no automatic effect on their respective property entitlements.[4] Their property relations are still governed in principle by the bleak and inflexible rules of the general law of property.[5]

(b) *Extrinsic aids to the discovery of intention*

The method by which beneficial ownership is determined under such circumstances was explained in classic terms by the House of Lords in *Pettitt v Pettitt*.[6] Here Lord Upjohn pointed to the extrinsic aids which may be called into play when the documentary title performs only its minimal function of dealing with the legal ownership. Certain residual evidential devices exist to enable the court to discover the parties' intentions in respect of beneficial ownership, and the court has recourse to these devices in the following order. *First*, the court may have regard to parol evidence as to the beneficial interests intended by the parties at the date of acquisition of the legal title.[7] *Second*, if such parol evidence is lacking or inadmissible or simply inconclusive, the court may draw inferences as to intention from the conduct of the parties

19 Post, p 906.
20 See Matrimonial Causes Act 1973, ss 23–25; Inheritance (Provision for Family and Dependants) Act 1975, ss 1–3. See also Matrimonial Proceedings and Property Act 1970, s 37 (post, p 422).
1 *Hammond v Mitchell* [1991] 1 WLR 1127 at 1129D per Waite J. See Kevin Gray, *Reallocation of Property on Divorce* (Abingdon 1977), pp 278ff.
2 [1991] 1 WLR 1127 at 1129E.
3 See *Pettitt v Pettitt* [1970] AC 777 at 794G–795C per Lord Reid, 810F-G per Lord Hodson, 817A-G per Lord Upjohn; *Gissing v Gissing* [1971] AC 886 at 899G–900A per Viscount Dilhorne; *Burns v Burns* [1984] Ch 317 at 334F-G per May LJ.
4 *Grant v Edwards* [1986] Ch 638 at 651E-F per Mustill LJ.
5 *Grant v Edwards* [1986] Ch 638 at 651G per Mustill LJ.
6 [1970] AC 777 at 813F-G.
7 Parol evidence may be given not only by the parties to a transaction of purchase, but also by others who are in a position to testify to their intentions at that time eg relatives, solicitors etc (see *Hodgson v Marks* [1971] Ch 892 at 905C-E).

both before and after the conveyance of the legal estate. *Third*, if even this fails to illuminate the relevant intentions of the parties, the court may apply the equitable presumptions as to intention. These presumptions represent merely the informed speculation of lawyers over the centuries as to the type of beneficial ownership most likely to have been intended by the parties in certain stylised situations.[8] The presumptions of equity are decisive of beneficial title only in the last resort and they prevail only in the absence of other more compelling evidence of actual intention.[9]

2. EXPRESS TRUSTS

The clearest example of a trust arises where A, the owner of a legal title in land, expressly declares himself to be a trustee of that title for B. Certain rules govern the creation and enforceability of such a trust.

(1) Language creative of a trust

An express trust need not be couched in formal words; any words which plainly evince an intention to create a trust will be sufficient.[10] It is even possible that 'by the use . . . of unguarded language, a person may create a trust, as Monsieur Jourdain talked prose, without knowing it',[11] but unless an intention to create a trust is clearly to be collected from the language used and from the circumstances of the case, the courts will not be astute to discover indications of such an intention.[12]

(2) Subject matter of the trust

An express declaration of trust may extend to the entire equitable interest in the land (as where A constitutes himself a trustee for B absolutely). Alternatively, the declaration may extend merely to some limited interest in the land (as where A holds henceforth on trust to give effect to a life interest or a fractional share in B) or even to some functional equivalent of a limited interest (as where A undertakes to allow B rent-free occupation for life).[13]

No valid declaration of an express trust can be made in respect of property which does not yet exist or in which the declarant has no interest at the

8 See *Pettitt v Pettitt* [1970] AC 777 at 823H per Lord Diplock (post, p 402); *Muschinski v Dodds* (1985) 160 CLR 583 at 613.
9 Post, p 402.
10 *Cowcher v Cowcher* [1972] 1 WLR 425 at 430E; *Bloch v Bloch* (1981) 37 ALR 55 at 59.
11 *In re Schebsman, decd* [1944] Ch 83 at 104 per Du Parcq LJ. See also *Tito v Waddell* (No 2) [1977] Ch 106 at 211F.
12 Trusts affecting certain kinds of person (ie the Crown and its governmental agencies) tend not to be justiciable in the courts. See *Tito v Waddell* (No 2) [1977] Ch 106 at 222F-G; *Aboriginal Development Commission v Treka Aboriginal Arts & Crafts Ltd* [1984] 3 NSWLR 502 at 518C, 519D. There are also certain kinds of property in relation to the acquisition of which the courts seem anxious not to apply trust principles (eg barristers' chambers). See *Appleby v Cowley* (1982) *Times*, 14 April.
13 Post, p 423.

date of his purported declaration.[14] Nor, obviously, can the declarant create a trust of any larger estate than he himself owns.[15] However, with these qualifications an express trust can be declared at any time—whether on or after the declarant's acquisition of title—and in respect of any property in which the declarant is beneficially entitled.

(3) Requirement of formality

An express trust may thus take a wide variety of forms. The declaration of trust may nominate more than one beneficiary; it may allocate various kinds or sizes of equitable entitlement to numerous beneficiaries. However, irrespective of the content of the express trust, one overriding rule prevails in English law: a declaration of trust relating to land is enforceable only if evidenced in signed writing. Section 53(1)(b) of the Law of Property Act 1925 (which derives from the Statute of Frauds 1677) provides that

> a declaration of any trust respecting any land or any interest therein must be manifested and proved by some writing signed by some person who is able to declare such trust or by his will.[16]

The date of the writing is irrelevant,[17] but without written evidence a declaration of trust relating to land is valid[18] but unenforceable.[19]

(4) Exemptions from the requirement of formality

The stern rule contained in section 53(1)(b) is subject to certain important exceptions, some of which go so far as to constitute 'a drastic judicial modification' of the statutory requirement of written evidence.[20] If A, the owner of a legal title in land, attempts to deny the existence of a trust which he has already declared orally in B's favour, the only evidence of that trust is *ex hypothesi* oral or parol evidence. A's most obvious defence against B's claim is therefore that section 53(1)(b) excludes the very parol evidence which would substantiate the allegation of trust. However, there are some circumstances in which A is not entitled to shut out parol evidence of the trust in this way.

14 *Dye v Dye* (1884) 13 QBD 147 at 157; *White v Cabanas Pty Ltd* (No 2) [1970] Qd R 395 at 407E. It is possible, however, that a constructive trust may attach to property which was not owned by the declarant at the date of his declaration of trust (see *Stokes v Anderson* [1991] 1 FLR 391 at 398E-F per Nourse LJ; *Le Compte v Public Trustee* [1983] 2 NSWLR 109 at 111A, post, p 417).

15 *Dye v Dye* (1884) 13 QBD 147 at 157. A declaration of trust affecting the whole beneficial interest in co-owned land can be made only with the concurrence of all the co-owners (*Kronheim v Johnson* (1877) 7 Ch D 60 at 66).

16 This provision is the modern emanation of section 7 of the Statute of Frauds 1677 (29 Car 2, c 3). For an account of the legislative motivations underlying this famous enactment, see Tim Youdan, *Formalities for Trusts of Land, and the Doctrine in Rochefoucauld v Boustead*, [1984] CLJ 306 at 307ff.

17 *Forster v Hale* (1798) 3 Ves Jun 696 at 711, 30 ER 1226 at 1233; *Rochefoucauld v Boustead* [1897] 1 Ch 196 at 206.

18 *Gardner v Rowe* (1828) 5 Russ 258 at 262, 38 ER 1024 at 1025.

19 *Gissing v Gissing* [1969] 2 Ch 85 at 99A-B; [1971] AC 886 at 910E-F per Lord Diplock; *Cowcher v Cowcher* [1972] 1 WLR 425 at 430H-431A; *Midland Bank PLC v Dobson* [1986] 1 FLR 171 at 175C-D; *Wratten v Hunter* [1978] 2 NSWLR 367 at 371B.

20 T. Youdan, [1984] CLJ 306 at 325.

(a) Resulting, implied or constructive trusts

Certain kinds of trust are exempted from formal requirements of writing by the Law of Property Act itself. Section 53(2) provides that the requirement of formality does not affect the 'creation or operation of resulting, implied or constructive trusts'. Thus the parol nature of the evidence has no detrimental effect on B's claim against A if the same facts which underlie the express trust also give rise to a resulting or constructive trust. It is clear that the existence of an unenforceable express trust is not necessarily inconsistent with a claim alleging some other form of trust which is immune from the documentary requirements of section 53(1).[1] In this way an originally unenforceable oral declaration of trust for B may sometimes become enforceable not as an express trust, but as a resulting or constructive trust.

(b) Use of the statute as an instrument of fraud

The fundamental purpose of requiring certain formalities to be observed in the creation and operation of express trusts is the prevention of fraud which might otherwise operate against the trustee. However, this insistence on formality is not pursued to the insensate degree that reliance upon an absence of writing is allowed to facilitate the commission of fraud by the trustee himself. There is a clear doctrine to the effect that equity will never permit a statute to be used as an instrument of fraud.[2]

In the present context equity's abhorrence of fraud finds expression in the rule in *Rochefoucauld v Boustead*.[3] Here the Court of Appeal confirmed that 'the Statute of Frauds does not prevent proof of a fraud',[4] Lindley LJ holding that

> it is a fraud on the part of a person to whom land is conveyed as a trustee, and who knows it was so conveyed, to deny the trust and claim the land himself. Consequently, notwithstanding the statute, it is competent for a person claiming land conveyed to another to prove by parol evidence that it was so conveyed upon trust for the claimant, and that the grantee, knowing the facts, is denying the trust and relying upon the form of the conveyance and the statute, in order to keep the land himself.[5]

(i) Limitations of the rule in Rochefoucauld v Boustead The rule in *Rochefoucauld v Boustead* has a quite remarkable impact, but operates only within a fairly narrow range of circumstances. The rule cannot validate an express trust

1 Post, pp 402, 415.
2 *Hutchins v Lee* (1737) 1 Atk 447 at 448, 26 ER 284 at 285; *Forster v Hale* (1798) 3 Ves Jun 696 at 713, 30 ER 1226 at 1234; *Lincoln v Wright* (1859) 4 De G & J 16 at 22, 45 ER 6 at 9; *McCormick v Grogan* (1869) LR 4 HL 82 at 97; *Booth v Turle* (1873) LR 16 Eq 182 at 187; *Rochefoucauld v Boustead* [1897] 1 Ch 196 at 206; *Organ v Sandwell* [1921] VLR 622 at 630; *Last v Rosenfeld* [1972] 2 NSWLR 923 at 927E; *Barrios v Chiabrera* (1984) 3 BPR 9276 at 9278 per Powell J.
3 [1897] 1 Ch 196.
4 Ante, p 255.
5 [1897] 1 Ch 196 at 206.

which is declared by A, with supposedly immediate effect, *before* the date of his acquisition of the legal title. Such a trust fails on the ground that the relevant trust property does not yet exist.[6] Nor can the rule render enforceable an oral declaration of trust made *after* the date of acquisition by which A purports to constitute himself a trustee of property which he already owns. Such a declaration is unenforceable (in the absence of a constructive trust) since otherwise there would be no circumstances at all which came within the reach of section 53(1)(b).[7]

(ii) Application of the rule in Rochefoucauld v Boustead The rule in *Rochefoucauld v Boustead* therefore has a somewhat limited application, operating only where A acquires a title on terms of an oral undertaking that he will, from the moment of acquisition, hold on trust for B.[8] However, within this context it seems not to matter whether A acquires his legal title by conveyance from B himself[9] or by conveyance from a complete stranger, X.[10] More surprising is the fact that it seems to be irrelevant whether B has provided any consideration for A's undertaking.[11] From the date of acquisition onwards, A is affected by a fiduciary obligation towards B, and it would be fraud in equity if A were to rely on the absence of written evidence as a ground for disavowing the trust on the terms of which he acquired title.

(iii) Nature of the trust validated by the rule in Rochefoucauld v Boustead As Samuels JA pointed out in *Allen v Snyder*,[12] there is a certain ambiguity as to whether the trust which is enforced under the rule in *Rochefoucauld v Boustead* is more accurately characterised as the original express trust or as an entirely new constructive trust which is statutorily exempt from the requirement of written evidence.[13] On the one hand, it could be said that, in view of equity's utter detestation of fraud, the rule gives effect to the original express trust directly in the teeth of the statute.[14] Thus, without any attempt to surmount section 53(1)(b) by finding a resulting or constructive trust, 'equity simply enforce[s] the actual original trust upon which the person

6 Ante, p 375.
7 See *Wratten v Hunter* [1978] 2 NSWLR 367 at 371B.
8 See *Lavette v Quin* (1980) 1 BPR 9609 at 9612; *Ash Street Properties Pty Ltd v Pollnow* (1985) 3 BPR 9646 at 9651.
9 *David v Szoke* (1974) 39 DLR (3d) 707 at 717.
10 See *Chattock v Muller* (1878) 8 Ch D 177 at 181; *Pallant v Morgan* [1953] Ch 43 at 48; *Devine v Fields* (1920) 54 ILTR 101 at 103f; *Organ v Sandwell* [1921] VLR 622 at 630; *McGillicuddy v Joy* [1959] IR 189 at 212ff; *Gilmurray v Corr* [1978] NI 99 at 104E-G.
11 See T. Youdan, [1984] CLJ 306 at 331f.
12 [1977] 2 NSWLR 685 at 699D-E.
13 See T. Youdan, [1984] CLJ 306 at 330ff.
14 It is significant that in *Rochefoucauld v Boustead* [1897] 1 Ch 196 at 208, the Court of Appeal specifically referred to the trust which it enforced as an 'express trust' and emphasised that the intention to create a trust had 'existed from the first'. Later, in *Hodgson v Marks* [1971] Ch 892 at 909B, Ungoed-Thomas J noted that the circumstances in *Rochefoucauld v Boustead* had been treated as 'falling exclusively within the section corresponding to section 53(1)(b) of the Law of Property Act 1925, and the defendants did not attempt to rely on any of the other provisions of section 53 to escape the operation of the principle.' See also *Organ v Sandwell* [1921] VLR 622 at 630; *David v Szoke* (1974) 39 DLR (3d) 707 at 717; *Allen v Snyder* [1977] 2 NSWLR 685 at 689F-G, 693A-B.

accepted the property in the first place'.[15] Such an approach epitomises the blunt view that it is preferable that the plain words of a statute should be ignored than that a fraud be permitted to succeed.[16] The alternative view is that the trust which is given effect is a new constructive trust which arises as soon as A asserts his legal title in derogation of the rights to which he has agreed to take subject.[17] This analysis does less violence to section 53(1)(b), since constructive trusts are clearly a case of statutory exception under section 53(2).[18]

For most purposes, however, it matters not whether the trust enforced by the court is characterised as an express trust or as a constructive trust: both analyses result in the same conclusion. Historically, the express trust analysis seems more authentic, but the distinction remains otherwise a fairly arid issue except perhaps in one respect. In so far as the rule in *Rochefoucauld v Boustead* seems to be applicable even where B has provided no consideration at all for the benefit orally conferred by A,[19] the trust to which the rule gives effect must be express rather than constructive.[20] It has long been accepted that no constructive trust can be claimed in the absence of a showing of 'detriment' or 'sacrifice' on the part of B.[1] Thus where B has given no consideration—or indeed where the consideration has moved from some third party instead—it seems preferable to say that B is enforcing an orally declared express trust which, but for the rule in *Rochefoucauld v Boustead*, would have been entirely unenforceable.[2]

(5) Conclusive effect of a declaration of trust

It is nowadays common, but not universal, conveyancing practice to include

15 *Thwaites v Ryan* [1984] VR 65 at 91 per Fullagar J. As Fullagar J pointed out (at 93), it would be difficult to describe the trust enforced as 'implied or constructive' because it 'may often be actual and meticulously expressed'. See also *Ash Street Properties Pty Ltd v Pollnow* (1985) 3 BPR 9646 at 9651, 9656, where McLelland J leaned towards the 'express trust' analysis of the rule in *Rochefoucauld v Boustead.*

16 See *Barrios v Chiabrera* (1984) 3 BPR 9276 at 9278 per Powell J. This approach, if correct, has been described as representing 'no less than the exercise by equity of a suspending or dispensing power denied the executive branch of government since the Bill of Rights 1689' (R.P. Meagher, W.M.C. Gummow and J.R.F. Lehane, *Equity: Doctrines and Remedies* (2nd edn, Sydney 1984), para 1224). See, however, *Devine v Fields* (1920) 54 ILTR 101 at 103 per O'Connor MR: 'It is the duty of a court of equity to overcome all technicalities in order to defeat a fraud.'

17 Post, p 435. As Samuels JA said in *Allen v Snyder* [1977] 2 NSWLR 685 at 699E, the ambiguity is demonstrated most clearly in *Bannister v Bannister* [1948] 2 All ER 133 (post, p 438).

18 The 'constructive trust' analysis of the rule in *Rochefoucauld v Boustead* was favoured on appeal in *Ash Street Properties Pty Ltd v Pollnow* (1987) 9 NSWLR 80 at 84D, where Mahoney JA spoke of equity operating 'not by way of restraining reliance on the statute and so enforcing the transaction itself, but by creating equities independent of the transaction'. See also (1987) 9 NSWLR 80 at 101A per Priestley JA.

19 Ante, p 378.

20 See *Ash Street Properties Pty Ltd v Pollnow* (1985) 3 BPR 9646 at 9651 per McLelland J.

1 Post, p 425.

2 Such, however, is the vacillating character of the trust given effect by the rule that the courts have sometimes—and almost certainly incorrectly—described the trust enforced on behalf of B in these circumstances as a constructive trust. See eg *Neale v Willis* (1968) 19 P & CR 836 at 839.

an express declaration of trust in a transfer of a legal estate to co-owners.[3] Being included in the document of conveyance, this declaration of course satisfies the statutory requirement of written evidence.

(a) The general principle

It is now clearly established in the case law that a declaration of trust 'necessarily concludes the question of title . . . for all time'.[4] A declaration of trust certainly enjoys this definitive effect where it has been executed by the transferees of the legal title as well as by the transferor.[5] Even if not so executed, a declaration which has been inserted into the transfer document on the instruction of the purchasers may well be taken to provide conclusive evidence of their intentions as to beneficial ownership.[6] These rules may have surprising implications.

(i) Declaration of beneficial joint tenancy If a legal title is conveyed into the joint names of A and B, subject to an expressly declared trust for themselves as beneficial joint tenants, the equitable rights of A and B are clarified definitively as those of joint tenants.[7] In other words, either A or B could at any time exercise the unilateral right of severance enjoyed by a beneficial joint tenant.[8] Both parties would then become beneficial tenants in common

3 See the strenuous advice given to conveyancing solicitors by Bagnall J in *Cowcher v Cowcher* [1972] 1 WLR 425 at 442C, pointing out the wisdom of making an express declaration of the beneficial interests in property at the date of its acquisition. Ten years later, in *Bernard v Josephs* [1982] Ch 391 at 403E-F, Griffiths LJ expressed the wish that 'more heed had been paid' to this advice, not least because if a dispute as to beneficial ownership is later waged with the help of legal aid (as it often is), both parties may well 'see a large part of their share of the equity disappear in costs into the maw of the legal aid fund . . .' See also *Goodman v Gallant* [1986] Fam 106 at 118F-G. For evidence of the difficulties still caused by undeclared beneficial ownership, see *Springette v Defoe* [1992] 2 FLR 388 at 390E, 396A-B; *Huntingford v Hobbs* [1993] 1 FCR 45 at 58C-D; [1992] Conv 347 (H. Norman).

4 *Pettitt v Pettitt* [1970] AC 777 at 813E per Lord Upjohn. See also *Gissing v Gissing* [1971] AC 886 at 905A per Lord Diplock. An express declaration of the beneficial interests also excludes any discretionary jurisdiction of the court to value the parties' equitable shares as of the date on which they ceased to live together. The proper date for the valuation of shares in such a case is the date of realisation of the property. See *Turton v Turton* [1988] Ch 542 at 550F, 555F-H; *Passee v Passee* [1988] 1 FLR 263 at 268C-D, 272B-D; [1988] Conv 361 at 362 (J. Warburton).

5 *Robinson v Robinson* (1977) 241 Estates Gazette 153 at 155; *In re Gorman (A Bankrupt)* [1990] 1 WLR 616 at 621E. See, however, *City of London Building Society v Flegg* [1988] AC 54 at 70C-D, where Lord Templeman indicated that an express declaration of trust executed by joint transferees of a legal title could not exclude the beneficial entitlements of other contributors to the purchase price who had not executed the declaration. See M.P. Thompson, [1988] Conv 108 at 109.

6 See *Pink v Lawrence* (1978) 36 P & CR 98 at 101 per Buckley LJ; *In re Gorman (A Bankrupt)* [1990] 1 WLR 616 at 621F, 623H-624A per Vinelott J.

7 *Pettitt v Pettitt* [1970] AC 777 at 813E per Lord Upjohn. See also *Mayes v Mayes* (1969) 210 Estates Gazette 935 at 937; *In re Johns' Assignment Trusts* [1970] 1 WLR 955 at 959C; *Boydell v Gillespie* (1970) 216 Estates Gazette 1505 at 1507; *Pink v Lawrence* (1978) 36 P & CR 98 at 101; *Brykiert v Jones* (1981) 2 FLR 373 at 376A-B; *Goodman v Gallant* [1986] Fam 106 at 110H-111A; [1986] CLJ 206 (S. Juss); *Huntingford v Hobbs* [1993] 1 FCR 45 at 49F-G.

8 See the discussion of severance in Chapter 13 (post, p 485).

in equal shares, irrespective of the original proportions in which they contributed to the purchase price of the co-owned property and irrespective of the reasons which caused one party to desire a severance.[9] This result follows inexorably from the binding nature of what is effectively a settlement by the transferees designed to regulate the beneficial terms on which they agreed to hold the legal estate: the transferees committed themselves at the outset to an equitable joint tenancy.

(ii) Declaration of other forms of beneficial ownership An express declaration of trust is commonly used to stipulate for beneficial joint tenancy in the family home.[10] However, a declaration of trust may take many forms, and is conclusive in its terms regardless of which precise form of beneficial ownership it provides.[11] Thus if a legal title is vested in A, B and C on trust for themselves as tenants in common in equal shares, it is entirely irrelevant that A, B and C may have contributed the purchase moneys in unequal proportions.[12] It is clearly a matter of some importance that conveyancers should be able to rely on the face value of documents which purport to define in express terms both the legal and beneficial ownership of land.[13]

(b) Exceptions

Only extremely limited exceptions are permitted from the rule that an express declaration of trust has conclusive effect.

(i) Rescission for fraud or mistake It is always open to a party to go behind the express terms of a trust where there has been 'fraud or mistake at the time of the transaction' by which the legal title is vested.[14] This ground of exception, if proved, may lead to rescission of the declaration, but the ground is difficult to establish. Mistake, for instance, is not constituted merely by a failure on the part of a lay person to understand the precise technical

9 *Bedson v Bedson* [1965] 2 QB 666 at 689C-D; *Pettitt v Pettitt* [1970] AC 777 at 813E per Lord Upjohn; *In re Johns' Assignment Trusts* [1970] 1 WLR 955 at 959C; *Bernard v Josephs* [1982] Ch 391 at 397F; *Goodman v Gallant* [1986] Fam 106 at 108D, 119D.

10 For reference to the modern popularity of this form of ownership in relation to the family home, see Chapter 13 (post, p 466).

11 Likewise, conclusive effect must be accorded a declaration which expressly negatives the existence of a trust in favour of persons who have undoubtedly made a financial contribution towards the purchase of the property (see *Godwin v Bedwell* (1982) *Times*, 4 March (Court of Appeal)). It is also possible to provide, by way of express declaration, that joint tenancy should prevail in equity until and unless severance occurs, and that in the event of severance the parties' respective interests should be unequal (see *Goodman v Gallant* [1986] Fam 106 at 119C).

12 *Brown v Staniek* (1969) 211 Estates Gazette 283. See also *Bedson v Bedson* [1965] 2 QB 666 at 689D-E. Where A and B take a transfer of legal title and execute a declaration of trust for themselves, it may, however, be relevant that part or all of the purchase moneys came from sources other than A and B. See eg *City of London Building Society v Flegg* [1988] AC 54 at 70C-D (ante, p 103), where the House of Lords envisaged that the express trusts set out in a conveyance could be displaced by the fact that persons other than the designated beneficiaries had contributed financially towards the relevant purchase.

13 See [1979] Conv 6.

14 *Pettitt v Pettitt* [1970] AC 777 at 813E per Lord Upjohn. See also *Goodman v Gallant* [1986] Fam 106 at 116B.

significance of the declaration of trust.[15] Indeed, in *Pink v Lawrence*,[16] the appalling result was brought about that the parties were held bound by a declaration of equitable joint tenancy which they had neither read nor signed, and which (it was conceded) they probably would not have understood anyway.

(ii) Rectification Apart from cases of fraud or mistake, it is possible that a court may grant rectification of a declaration of trust in order to give effect to intentions which the parties clearly had at the date of the transaction, but which were expressed only imperfectly or not at all in the declared trust. In rare cases the court may, for instance, reinstate an original common intention that the parties should be equitable tenants in common rather than joint tenants,[17] or that one party rather than two should be beneficially entitled,[18] or even that two parties instead of one should be grantees of the legal title under the deed of conveyance.[19]

3. IMPLIED TRUSTS

Given that a conveyance of the legal title into the name of A carries prima facie the entire equitable interest too, substantial difficulties lie in the path of B, a claimant of an equitable interest, if he or she cannot base a claim of equitable entitlement on the express terms of a declaration of trust duly evidenced in writing. B's only remaining hope of making good such a claim now rests largely on the contention that there exists in his or her favour, not an express trust, but an implied trust of some variety.

(1) Classification of implied trusts

Implied trusts are of essentially two kinds, the resulting trust and the constructive trust.[20] Whereas express trusts are founded directly on the expressly declared intentions of the parties, implied trusts arise by operation of law, albeit against the background of the parties' actual or presumed intentions.[1] Moreover, section 53(2) of the Law of Property Act 1925 makes it absolutely clear that the documentary requirements imposed in respect of trusts by section 53(1) have no application to the 'creation or operation of resulting, implied or constructive trusts.'

Although similar in the sense that they are implied rather than express and are alike freed from statutory requirements of formal writing, the resulting

15 *Mayes v Mayes* (1969) 210 Estates Gazette 935 at 937; *In re Johns' Assignment Trusts* [1970] 1 WLR 955 at 958G-H; *Huntingford v Hobbs* [1993] 1 FCR 45 at 64D.
16 (1978) 36 P & CR 98 at 99.
17 See *In re Colebrook's Conveyances* [1972] 1 WLR 1397 at 1398H, but compare *Goodman v Gallant* [1986] Fam 106 at 116H–117C.
18 *Wilson v Wilson* [1969] 3 All ER 945 at 949A-B. Where the conveyance does not accurately represent the agreement of the parties, it may be possible for the court to give relief without actually employing the machinery of rectification (*Pink v Lawrence* (1978) 38 P & CR 98 at 101). See also *Gross v French* (1976) 238 Estates Gazette 39.
19 *Armstrong v Armstrong* (1979) 93 DLR (3d) 128 at 135.
20 See *Cowcher v Cowcher* [1972] 1 WLR 425 at 431A.
1 *Avondale Printers & Stationers Ltd v Haggie* [1979] 2 NZLR 124 at 145 per Mahon J.

trust and the constructive trust have largely distinct spheres of operation. They are, however, easily confused one with another. Recent years have witnessed what an Australian judge has termed, with derogatory implication, an 'apparent amalgamation of resulting and constructive trusts into one congruent class.'[2] The English Court of Appeal has on occasion asserted that resulting and constructive trusts are not mere 'inter-changeable' terms,[3] but some compression or conflation of the concepts has now emerged from the ruling of the House of Lords in *Lloyds Bank Plc v Rosset*.[4] The unavoidable outcome is a regrettable uncertainty of doctrine and it may therefore be useful to separate out the notions involved in the readily blurred classifications of resulting and constructive trust.

(2) Origin of implied trusts

Some of the ambiguity affecting this area of trust law may be traced to *Gissing v Gissing*.[5] Here, in what has become a classic point of reference in the law of trusts, Lord Diplock provided an incisive definition of the origin of implied trusts. He declared that

> A resulting, implied or constructive trust—and it is unnecessary for present purposes to distinguish between these three classes of trust—is created by a transaction between the trustee and the cestui que trust in connection with the acquisition by the trustee of a legal estate in the land, whenever the trustee has so conducted himself that it would be inequitable to allow him to deny to the cestui que trust a beneficial interest in the land acquired. And he will be held so to have conducted himself if by his words or conduct he has induced the cestui que trust to act to his own detriment in the reasonable belief that by so acting he was acquiring a beneficial interest in the land.

This dictum has been frequently applied and sometimes misapplied,[6] but it probably represents the best attempt yet to indicate the common elements which underlie both the resulting and the constructive trust.[7] Such differences as exist between these two types of trust are best explained as follows.[8] Resulting trusts are intrinsically concerned with the pattern of money contributions laid out in the purchase of property. A resulting trust thus seeks to give effect to the intentions which are presumed to underlie the way in which such moneys are put towards the acquisition of a legal title. By contrast constructive trusts are intimately concerned—not so much with money—but rather with expressly or implicitly bargained commitments

2 *Allen v Snyder* [1977] 2 NSWLR 685 at 698D per Samuels JA. See also *Avondale Printers & Stationers Ltd v Haggie* [1979] 2 NZLR 124 at 145; *Muschinski v Dodds* (1985) 160 CLR 583 at 596.

3 See eg *Walker v Walker* (Unreported 12 April 1984), where Browne-Wilkinson LJ emphasised that 'in many contexts there are crucial distinctions as to the circumstances which give rise to the existence of such trusts.' The same judge has made the point extra-judicially that '[r]esulting trusts and constructive trusts are two different animals' and that failure to distinguish them has caused 'great confusion' (see *Constructive Trusts and Unjust Enrichment* (Holdsworth Club of the University of Birmingham 1991), p 4).

4 [1991] 1 AC 107 at 132H-133A per Lord Bridge of Harwich (ante, p 372, post, p 388).

5 [1971] AC 886 at 905B-C.

6 See *Grant v Edwards* [1986] Ch 638 at 654B-C per Browne-Wilkinson V-C.

7 See *Higgins v Wingfield* [1987] VR 689 at 694f.

8 See *Avondale Printers & Stationers Ltd v Haggie* [1979] 2 NZLR 124 at 145.

respecting equitable entitlement. A constructive trust thus arises where it would be fraudulent for the owner of a legal title to assert his or her beneficial ownership in derogation of equitable rights which have already been bargained away to another. The ambivalent relationship between resulting and constructive trusts stems precisely from the fact that each is premised upon intended beneficial ownership—in one case as disclosed by the pattern of money purchase, and in the other case as embodied in some anterior bargain struck by the relevant parties.

English case law abounds with indiscriminate references to resulting and constructive trust. Any confusion of the concepts is nowadays best resolved by restricting the scope of the resulting trust narrowly to those money payments and contributions which have been channelled into the purchase of realty, thereby relegating all other forms of contributory activity to be dealt with under the law of constructive trusts.

4. RESULTING TRUSTS

A resulting trust comes into existence in certain stereotyped situations in English law, where a nominal purchaser of property (A) is deemed to hold on a trust which 'results' back to the person who has financed his or her purchase (B).[9] Under the resulting trust A takes merely the legal or paper title in the property and the equitable interest is presumed to belong to B, the 'real purchaser'.[10]

(1) Presumption of resulting trust

The origin of the resulting trust lies in a presumption as to the intended beneficial ownership of the property purchased.[11] This presumption gives way only if (and to the extent that) a contrary intention can be proved to have manifested itself in an enforceable form at the date of the purchase, or if the presumed resulting trust is itself displaced by a counter-presumption of equity.[12] In all other circumstances a resulting trust is presumed to come into existence wherever an interest in property[13] is purchased in the name

9 The word 'result' in this context is not used in any sense of causation and consequence, but rather in its root sense of 'leaping back' (Latin, *resultare*). A trust of the property springs back in favour of the real purchaser. See *Rathwell v Rathwell* (1978) 83 DLR (3d) 289 at 302 per Dickson J.

10 *Muschinski v Dodds* (1985) 160 CLR 583 at 589 per Gibbs CJ. See *Walker v Walker* (Unreported, Court of Appeal, 12 April 1984), where Browne-Wilkinson LJ held that 'a resulting trust arises where the facts alleged and proved consist of the payment of money by B to or for the benefit of A (otherwise than for the sole benefit of A) without a declaration of express trusts which fully exhaust the beneficial interest: in such a case the beneficial interest results to B to the extent that it is not exhausted by the express trust.'

11 *Gissing v Gissing* [1971] AC 886 at 902B per Lord Pearson.

12 *Calverley v Green* (1984) 155 CLR 242 at 251 per Gibbs CJ, 258 per Mason and Brennan JJ; *Muschinski v Dodds* (1985) 160 CLR 583 at 589f per Gibbs CJ, 612 per Deane J.

13 The property subject to a resulting trust may have a limited lifespan. It has been said, for instance, that there is 'no reason in principle' why a resulting trust cannot attach to a one-year tenancy, at least where—although it must happen rarely—such an estate is purchased for a premium (*Savage v Dunningham* [1974] Ch 181 at 184G).

of A, A having provided none or only part of the purchase price.[14] By operation of law,[15] a resulting trust arises in favour of B if (and to the extent that) B has provided money for the purchase.[16] In the classic terms of Eyre CB in *Dyer v Dyer*,[17] a 'trust of a legal estate . . . results to the man who advances the purchase-money.'[18] Thus, if B provides all the purchase money for a vesting of legal title in A, A is presumed (absent evidence of contrary intention) to hold the legal title on a resulting trust for B absolutely (*Fig.* 22).[19]

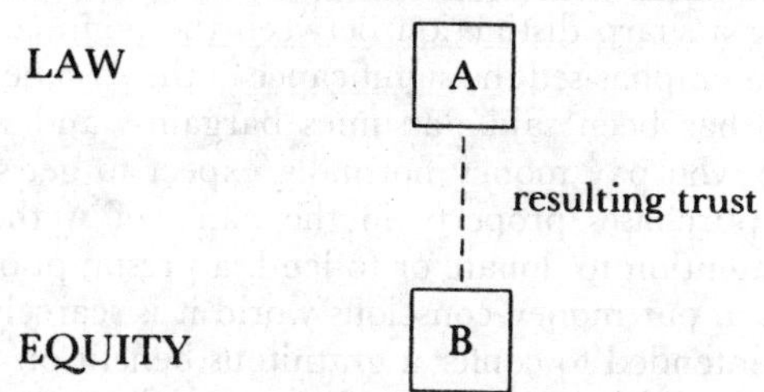

Fig. 22

The recognition that a trust relationship exists between A and B in these circumstances is a direct response to the supposed inequity of allowing A to retain property purchased in his own name without acknowledging the material assistance given in its purchase by B. It would generally be unconscionable to allow A to assert an absolute legal and beneficial title if B has paid moneys in the character of a purchaser.[20] The doctrine of

14 *Pettitt v Pettitt* [1970] AC 777 at 814A per Lord Upjohn; *Cowcher v Cowcher* [1972] 1 WLR 425 at 431B; *Wirth v Wirth* (1956) 98 CLR 228 at 235; *Goodfriend v Goodfriend* (1972) 22 DLR (3d) 699 at 702; *Allen v Snyder* [1977] 2 NSWLR 685 at 689G-690A; *Blackburn v Y V Properties Pty Ltd* [1980] VR 290 at 295, 301f; *Dullow v Dullow* (1985) 3 NSWLR 531 at 534E-F.

15 *Blackburn v Y V Properties Pty Ltd* [1980] VR 290 at 293; *Re Levy* (1982) 131 DLR (3d) 15 at 23.

16 It is not necessarily fatal to a claim of resulting trust that the funds provided by B were obtained by means of a conspiracy to defraud the Department of Social Security (*Tinsley v Milligan* [1992] Ch 310 at 326C-D per Nicholls LJ, 342A per Lloyd LJ (Ralph Gibson LJ dissenting)). See J. Martin, [1992] Conv 153.

17 (1788) 2 Cox Eq Cas 92 at 93, 30 ER 42 at 43.

18 This dictum has been frequently cited with approval (see eg *Pettitt v Pettitt* [1970] AC 777 at 814B-E per Lord Upjohn; *Gissing v Gissing* [1971] AC 886 at 902D per Lord Pearson). See also *Harwood v Harwood* [1991] 2 FLR 274 at 292B-C, where *Dyer's* case was applied to raise a presumption of resulting trust of a legal estate purchased in the names of A and B, using the moneys of A, B and C.

19 *Calverley v Green* (1984) 155 CLR 242 at 246 per Gibbs CJ, 266f per Deane J; *Stephenson Nominees Pty Ltd v Official Receiver on behalf of Official Trustee in Bankruptcy; ex parte Roberts* (1987) 76 ALR 485 at 500 per Gummow J. Money advanced by B to A on trust will, if invested by A in the acquisition of realty, produce a resulting trust for B (*McTaggart v Boffo* (1976) 64 DLR (3d) 441 at 457).

20 Post, p 390. See *Winkworth v Edward Baron Development Co Ltd* [1986] 1 WLR 1512 at 1516C-D per Lord Templeman.

resulting trust accordingly recognises an 'equity' as inhering in B[1]—an 'equity' which is founded on a perceived consensus that B will normally have been induced to finance A's purchase only by some expectation or belief that he would receive a tangible return for his contribution.[2]

(a) Ideology of the resulting trust

The resulting trust generated by the provision of purchase moneys is outstanding evidence of what Woodhouse J once termed 'the solid tug of money'.[3] In drawing a sharp distinction between the nominal and the real purchaser, equity has emphasised the significance of the cash nexus in human dealings. Equity, it has been said, 'assumes bargains, and not gifts'.[4] In crude terms, people who pay money normally expect to get something for it. Today when B purchases property in the name of A there is, in the absence of a clear intention to donate or to lend, a presumption of resulting trust in favour of B: in our money-conscious world it is scarcely conceivable that B should have intended to confer a gratuitous benefit on A.[5]

The presumption of resulting trust thus reflects a socially perceived inference as to the likely intentions of A and B regarding attributions of ownership.[6] The doctrine of resulting trust simply gives effect to the assumed intentions of the parties at the date of the acquisition of property.[7] However, resulting trusts arise ultimately by operation of law rather than with reference to the actual intentions of the parties. There is, for instance, no requirement that a resulting trustee should necessarily know that a resulting trust exists.[8] Moreover, a resulting trust will arise in favour of the provider of the purchase moneys even if the property actually purchased is not the property which he intended should be purchased (eg if A wrongfully uses B's money in purchasing Whiteacre rather than Blackacre as agreed[9]).

1 'Normally . . . the object of equitable institutions such as a resulting trust is to give the force of law to moral obligations' (*Sekhon v Alissa* [1989] 2 FLR 94 at 99C per Hoffmann J).

2 See *Taddeo v Taddeo* (1978) 19 SASR 347 at 368, where Walters J attributed the operation of the resulting trust to equity's assumption that 'independently of any fraud . . . the purchaser . . . intended to act, and . . . was acting, in pursuance of his fiduciary duty.' See also *Gissing v Gissing* [1971] AC 886 at 902B per Lord Pearson; *Pettkus v Becker* (1981) 117 DLR (3d) 257 at 263.

3 *Hofman v Hofman* [1965] NZLR 795 at 800. See also *Reid v Reid* [1979] 1 NZLR 572 at 582 per Woodhouse J.

4 *Goodfriend v Goodfriend* (1972) 22 DLR (3d) 699 at 703 per Spence J (Supreme Court of Canada), quoting D. Waters, *The Doctrine of Resulting Trusts in Common Law Canada*, (1970) 16 McGill LJ 187 at 199. See also *Gorog v Kiss* (1977) 78 DLR (3d) 690 at 694.

5 For an alternative view that the presumption of resulting trust is 'completely anachronistic', see *Dullow v Dullow* (1985) 3 NSWLR 531 at 535A.

6 See *Pettitt v Pettitt* [1970] AC 777 at 823H–824A per Lord Diplock (ante, p 375). The presumption of resulting trust is sometimes explained as 'the fact of contribution evidencing an agreement'. It has also been described as a form of 'constructive agreement' (see *Rathwell v Rathwell* (1978) 83 DLR (3d) 289 at 304 per Dickson J).

7 'Resulting trusts are as firmly grounded in the settlor's intent as are express trusts, but with this difference—that the intent is inferred, or is presumed as a matter of law from the circumstances of the case' (*Rathwell v Rathwell* (1978) 83 DLR (3d) 289 at 303 per Dickson J).

8 *Tattersfield v Tattersfield and the New Zealand Insurance Co Ltd* [1980] BCL 1110.

9 *Scott v Scott* (1963) 109 CLR 649 at 663f (High Court of Australia).

(b) Time-frame of the relevant intentions

Intrinsic to the classic theory of the resulting trust is the idea that this form of trust is based on intentions presumed to exist at the date of acquisition of the property concerned.[10] The date of acquisition is the time at which the fact of beneficial entitlement 'crystallises' under the resulting trust,[11] and the only intentions relevant to a resulting trust are supposedly those which were contemporaneous with the taking of title.[12] In very strict terms a resulting trust cannot be raised by virtue of intentions which come into existence only at some later stage.[13] It has, however, been conceded that conduct subsequent to the acquisition date may sometimes provide a basis for retrospective inference as to the actual intentions of the parties on that date[14] and that the actual quantification of the resulting beneficial interests may on occasion be deferred until a later date.[15]

The timing of the relevant intentions used to be one of the prime distinguishing features of the resulting trust when compared with the constructive trust. (It has always been clear that a constructive trust can be raised by intentions as to beneficial ownership which did not exist at the acquisition date and which were formulated or expressed only some time later.[16]) In recent years, however, a new realism has become evident in the increasing judicial acceptance that intentions may not crystallise, either in fact or by retrospective inference, at the point of acquisition of title. Particularly where the process of acquisition is elongated by a mortgage-assisted purchase,[17] the classic theory of resulting trusts that relevant intentions are formulated around the isolated moment of purchase has substantially broken down. It is now widely believed to be artificial—if not indeed untenable—to fashion such phantoms of intention in order to resolve property issues which arise perhaps many years later.[18]

One inevitable consequence of this recognition has been the gradual slippage away from resulting trust theory towards the more liberated application of the constructive trust—a process which has contributed in no small way to the recent blurring of the borderline between these two forms of trust. As it becomes increasingly unrealistic to postulate the formulation of intentions contemporaneous with the taking of title, the doctrine of resulting trust may, at least in England, have conceded some

10 See *Sekhon v Alissa* [1989] 2 FLR 94 at 95G per Hoffmann J; *Currie v Hamilton* [1984] 1 NSWLR 687 at 691D per McLelland J.

11 *Bernard v Josephs* [1982] Ch 391 at 404F.

12 *Pettitt v Pettitt* [1970] AC 777 at 800F-G per Lord Morris of Borth-y-Gest, 813D per Lord Upjohn; *Gissing v Gissing* [1971] AC 886 at 897C per Lord Reid, 900B-D per Viscount Dilhorne, 905D per Lord Diplock; *Bernard v Josephs* [1982] Ch 391 at 404C; *Burns v Burns* [1984] Ch 317 at 327A; *Hohol v Hohol* [1981] VR 221 at 225f; *Baumgartner v Baumgartner* [1985] 2 NSWLR 406 at 417F.

13 See *Jeffries v Stevens* (1982) STC 639 at 651g.

14 *Gissing v Gissing* [1971] AC 886 at 906E per Lord Diplock; *Bernard v Josephs* [1982] Ch 391 at 404F-G; *Allen v Snyder* [1977] 2 NSWLR 685 at 707E-F; *Baumgartner v Baumgartner* [1985] 2 NSWLR 406 at 417E; *Vedejs v Public Trustee* [1985] VR 569 at 573.

15 Post, p 397.

16 Post, p 417.

17 Post, p 393.

18 [1983] CLJ 30 at 33. See *Hayward v Giordani* [1983] NZLR 140 at 145 per Cooke J; *Stratulatos v Stratulatos* [1988] 2 NZLR 424 at 436 per McGechan J.

of its field of application to the doctrine of constructive trust, where the timing of intention has never been so critically defined.[19]

(c) *Mode of acquisition of title*

It matters not for the purpose of raising a resulting trust whether B purchases property with his own funds, and directs that the legal title should be conveyed by the vendor into the name of A,[20] or whether A, using funds provided by B, purchases property in his own name.[1] In either case, if the moneys have been laid out by B in the character of a purchaser, there will be a presumption of resulting trust.[2] Nor does it matter whether the title is put in the name of A or in the joint names of A and B. If, in the latter case, B has provided all of the purchase moneys, A is presumed to take no beneficial interest and he holds the legal title merely as a trustee on a resulting trust for B.[3]

All these examples are, however, to be distinguished from a rather different case which under English law is dealt with quite separately. So far we have assumed a purchase in the name of A of property previously owned by V, a vendor. No resulting trust is presumed where B is the current owner of a legal title, which he then voluntarily transfers into the name of A.[4] Under these circumstances A takes both the legal and equitable title absolutely in the absence of any evidence of contrary intention.[5]

(d) *Effect of joint contributions of money*

If A and B both contribute towards the purchase of a legal title in A's name, there is a presumed resulting trust for A and B.[6] If A and B contribute unequally, they are presumed to hold beneficially as tenants in common

19 This conceptual drift may well account for the tendency, most apparent in *Lloyds Bank Plc v Rosset* [1991] 1 AC 107 at 132H–133A per Lord Bridge of Harwich, to describe as a constructive trust what would formerly have been regarded as an example of resulting trust (ante, p 372, post, p 399).

20 *Pettitt v Pettitt* [1970] AC 777 at 814A; *Noack v Noack* [1959] VR 137 at 139; *Rathwell v Rathwell* (1978) 83 DLR (3d) 289 at 302.

1 *Bateman Television Ltd v Bateman and Thomas* [1971] NZLR 453 at 462.

2 See *Bateman Television Ltd v Bateman and Thomas* [1971] NZLR 453 at 462 per Turner J.

3 *Benger v Drew* (1721) 1 P Wms 781, 24 ER 613; *Noack v Noack* [1959] VR 137 at 139; *Calverley v Green* (1984) 155 CLR 242 at 255 per Mason and Brennan JJ, 266 per Deane J.

4 Law of Property Act 1925, s 60(3). In *Hodgson v Marks* [1971] Ch 892 at 933D, Russell LJ still thought it a 'debatable question' whether a resulting trust arises on 'a voluntary transfer by A to stranger B'. It could be argued that in such circumstances the beneficial interest never leaves the transferor at all. (Compare, however, *D.K.L.R. Holding Co (No 2) Pty Ltd v Commissioner of Stamp Duties (N.S.W.)* (1982) 149 CLR 431 at 442, 463f, 473f (ante, p 265)). The preferable view nowadays seems to be that section 60(3) simply means what it says.

5 In jurisdictions where there is no statutory equivalent of the Law of Property Act 1925, s 60(3), a gratuitous transfer of title from A to B will produce a resulting trust in favour of B (see eg *Napier v Public Trustee (Western Australia)* (1980) 32 ALR 153 at 158).

6 *Calverley v Green* (1984) 155 CLR 242 at 246 per Gibbs CJ. See the analysis of the problem of 'joint production cost allocation' in *Little v Little* (1988) 15 NSWLR 43 at 46A-C, where Bryson J thought that it was 'initially an artificial step, although characteristic of the thinking of equity lawyers, to see the beneficial ownership of money spent to acquire land as converted or transmuted into beneficial ownership of the land acquired.'

in proportion to their respective contributions (*Fig.* 23).[7] If they contribute equally, their entitlement under the resulting trust has traditionally been deemed to take the form of beneficial joint tenancy (*Fig.* 24).[8] Nowadays, however, there is increasing force in the argument that a mere equality of contribution should not automatically render the contributors joint tenants (with the rights of survivorship so disfavoured by equity[9]), but should instead produce a presumptive tenancy in common in equal shares.[10] At all events it is quite clear that any beneficial joint tenancy can be easily converted by either party into a tenancy in equal shares.[11]

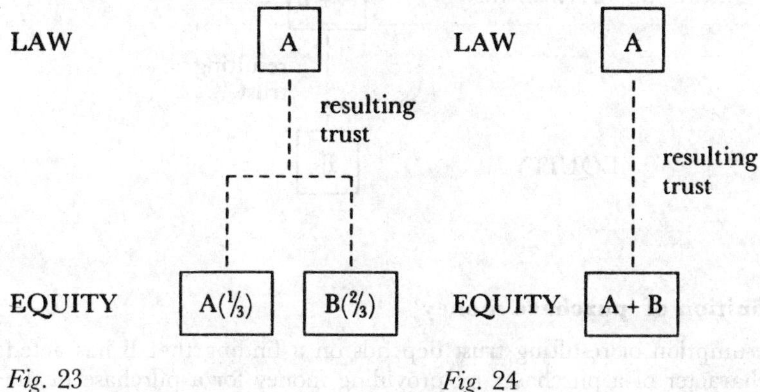

Fig. 23 *Fig.* 24

Since the ownership of the legal title is only a matter of nominal or paper title, exactly the same beneficial results follow in either of these cases if the moneys of A and B are used to purchase a legal title in the names of A and B themselves[12] or—for that matter—in the joint names of A and X,[13] or of X, Y and Z. In such circumstances, the prima facie inference

7 *Lake v Gibson* (1729) 1 Eq Cas Abr 290 at 291, 21 ER 1052 at 1053; *Aveling v Knipe* (1815) 19 Ves 441 at 444f, 34 ER 580 at 582; *Bull v Bull* [1955] 1 QB 234 at 236; *Pettitt v Pettitt* [1970] AC 777 at 814B per Lord Upjohn; *Gissing v Gissing* [1971] AC 886 at 907C per Lord Diplock; *Cowcher v Cowcher* [1972] 1 WLR 425 at 431B-C; *Williams & Glyn's Bank Ltd v Boland* [1981] AC 487 at 502F-G per Lord Wilberforce; *Goodman v Gallant* [1986] Fam 106 at 110F-H; *Harwood v Harwood* [1991] 2 FLR 274 at 292B-C; *Springette v Defoe* [1992] 2 FLR 388 at 391B-C; *Scott v Scott* (1963) 109 CLR 649 at 663; *Calverley v Green* (1984) 155 CLR 242 at 246f per Gibbs CJ, 266f per Deane J; *Currie v Hamilton* [1984] 1 NSWLR 687 at 690E-F.

8 *Lake v Gibson* (1729) 1 Eq Cas Abr 290, 21 ER 1052; *O'Connell v Harrison* [1927] IR 330 at 336; *Efstratiou, Glantschnig and Petrovic v Glantschnig* [1972] NZLR 594 at 598; *Taddeo v Taddeo* (1978) 19 SASR 347 at 365. See also *Vedejs v Public Trustee* [1985] VR 569 at 575.

9 Post, p 512.

10 See *Carmody v Delehunt* [1984] 1 NSWLR 667 at 669C, where Hutley JA found it 'wholly mysterious', in view of the equitable distaste for survivorship, that the resolution of equity should have 'faltered when it came to the rights of persons advancing equal sums of money.' See also *Tinsley v Milligan* [1992] Ch 310 at 321D, 326G per Nicholls LJ.

11 The law relating to 'severance' of beneficial joint tenancy is dealt with elsewhere (post, p 485).

12 *Crisp v Mullings* (1976) 239 Estates Gazette 119 at 121; *Walker v Hall* [1984] FLR 126 at 130C; *Re Hogg (Deceased)* (Unreported, Chancery Division, 1982 H No 2830, 11 July 1983); *Calverley v Green* (1984) 155 CLR 242 at 246 per Gibbs CJ, 258 per Mason and Brennan JJ; *Muschinski v Dodds* (1985) 160 CLR 583 at 589 per Gibbs CJ.

13 *Hoare v Hoare* (1982) *Times*, 9 November.

that equitable ownership follows the legal title is overborne by the more precise information concerning the source of the purchase money. In the absence of any contrary intention, a presumption of resulting trust is raised in favour of A and B as providers of that money. Likewise, if a legal title is purchased in the joint names of A and B, using only the moneys of B, a resulting trust is presumed in favour of B (*Fig.* 25).[14]

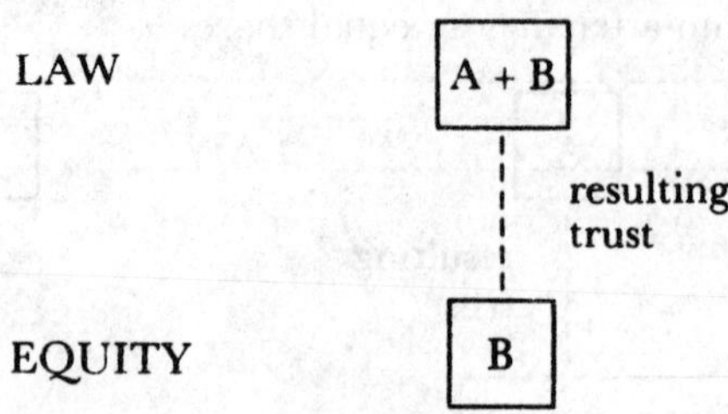

Fig. 25

(2) Definition of 'purchase money'

The presumption of resulting trust depends on a finding that B has acted in the character of a purchaser by providing money for a purchase in the name of A.[15] Difficult questions are sometimes raised as to whether various forms of financial contribution or liability constitute such a provision of 'purchase money' as to raise the presumption. Not every kind of contribution or assumption of liability can be attributed to an actual or presumed intention at the date of acquisition that beneficial ownership should result.[16] In applying the doctrine of resulting trusts, the courts attach significance only to those money contributions made by B which can fairly be said to be 'referable to' the acquisition of title by A.[17]

Among the candidates for consideration as relevant forms of 'purchase money' are the following:

(a) Direct contribution to cash price

The clearest and easiest case concerns direct contributions to the cash price at which property is purchased. Regardless of the name or names in which the legal title is purchased, those who make direct contributions of cash

14 *Wilson v Wilson* [1969] 3 All ER 945 at 949E-F; *Mellowes v Collymore* (Unreported, Court of Appeal, 27 November 1981); *Young v Young* [1984] FLR 375 at 380E; *Allied Irish Banks Ltd v McWilliams* [1982] NI 156 at 161C-D.

15 *Calverley v Green* (1984) 155 CLR 242 at 246 per Gibbs CJ. See also *Stephenson Nominees Pty Ltd v Official Receiver on behalf of Official Trustee in Bankruptcy; ex parte Roberts* (1987) 76 ALR 485 at 501 per Gummow J.

16 The lender who provides money for use in a purchase of legal title obtains, for instance, no beneficial interest by way of trust. Any presumption of resulting trust is rebutted by the intention towards loan (post, p 404).

17 *Burns v Burns* [1984] Ch 317 at 328H–329B per Fox LJ. It may be difficult to establish the 'referable' character of a payment which was made some time *after* the acquisition of a particular property and full payment of its purchase price (see eg *Winkworth v Edward Baron Development Co Ltd* [1986] 1 WLR 1512 at 1515E–1516B, post, p 444).

at the date of acquisition are presumed, in the absence of all other evidence, to have intended to take beneficial interests commensurate with their respective contributions.[18] In other words, a direct cash payment is regarded as being sufficiently 'referable to' the acquisition of title to raise a resulting trust.[19] Thus, if a legal estate is conveyed to A for £60,000, A providing £20,000 out of his own free available moneys and B £40,000 out of his own free cash resources, a resulting trust is presumed under which A takes a one-third interest and B a two-thirds interest.[20] A and B are presumed, in effect, to have formulated a 'money consensus' that their respective beneficial interests should accord with the relative proportions of their contributions.[1] This 'money consensus' is contemporaneous with, and constitutive of, the resulting trust, and therefore requires no documentary formality under section 53(1)(b) of the Law of Property Act 1925.[2]

(b) Contribution to initial deposit or legal expenses

It is now generally accepted that a money contribution by B to the initial deposit or legal expenses payable on the acquisition of a legal title will raise, in the absence of evidence of contrary intention, a resulting trust in favour of B.[3] Such a contribution casts B in the character of a purchaser,[4] and provides presumptive evidence that both parties intended from the very outset that B should have some beneficial share in the property acquired.[5] The extent of the beneficial interest earned by B's contribution is not necessarily proportional to the size of the contribution.[6] In particular, the fact that B has contributed towards the initial deposit or legal expenses may establish a framework of assumed intention in favour of beneficial co-ownership which makes it more feasible to regard subsequent payments by B as being 'referable to' the acquisition of the property.[7]

18 *Pettitt v Pettitt* [1970] AC 777 at 794A-B per Lord Reid; *Gissing v Gissing* [1971] AC 886 at 897A-B per Lord Reid; *Cowcher v Cowcher* [1972] 1 WLR 425 at 431B-C; *Williams & Glyn's Bank Ltd v Boland* [1981] AC 487 at 502F-G per Lord Wilberforce; *Bernard v Josephs* [1982] Ch 391 at 403G; *Huntingford v Hobbs* [1993] 1 FCR 45 at 54A-B.

19 *Burns v Burns* [1984] Ch 317 at 329B per Fox LJ.

20 See *Cowcher v Cowcher* [1972] 1 WLR 425 at 431E-F per Bagnall J (example (i)). See also *Gissing v Gissing* [1971] AC 886 at 907A-B per Lord Diplock.

1 *Cowcher v Cowcher* [1972] 1 WLR 425 at 436A-B per Bagnall J.

2 *Cowcher v Cowcher* [1972] 1 WLR 425 at 436C-D.

3 *Gissing v Gissing* [1971] AC 886 at 907E; *Davis v Vale* [1971] 1 WLR 1022 at 1026H; *Efstratiou, Glantschnig and Petrovic v Glantschnig* [1972] NZLR 594 at 598. Compare, however, the strongly divergent view expressed in *Little v Little* (1988) 15 NSWLR 43 at 44G-46F per Bryson J.

4 As McLelland J pointed out in *Currie v Hamilton* [1984] 1 NSWLR 687 at 691A, it is the 'aggregate cost' of purchase (ie inclusive of incidental costs, fees and disbursements)—rather than the 'mere purchase price'—which should form the basis of calculation under the resulting trust. See also *Calverley v Green* (1984) 155 CLR 242 at 265, where Murphy J spoke of 'contributions to the purchase', a phrase which may not mean the same thing as 'contributions to the purchase price' (see *Little v Little* (1988) 15 NSWLR 43 at 45E per Bryson J).

5 *Burns v Burns* [1984] Ch 317 at 344G.

6 See *Efstratiou, Glantschnig and Petrovic v Glantschnig* [1972] NZLR 594 at 598, where payment of half of the deposit was held to generate a half-share in the entire beneficial interest under a resulting trust. See also *Pearson v Pearson* [1961] VR 693 at 699; *Re Whiteley and Whiteley* (1975) 48 DLR (3d) 161 at 170.

7 *Gissing v Gissing* [1971] AC 886 at 907F-H per Lord Diplock; *Burns v Burns* [1984] Ch 317 at 344G-H.

(c) Contribution of qualifying status or eligibility

Potentially awkward questions may be posed where a legal title has been acquired partly by reason of money put up by A and partly by reason of a qualifying status or eligibility supplied by B.[8] Nowadays such circumstances arise with ever increasing frequency in the context of the 'right to buy' conferred by the Housing Act 1985 on certain categories of public sector tenant.[9] In the public housing sector a 'secure tenant' has the right, in statutorily defined circumstances, to purchase either the freehold or a long leasehold term in property which he or she has occupied during a stipulated qualifying period.[10] For this purpose the eligible tenant is entitled to receive a discount on the purchase price which varies in accordance with the duration of his or her pre-existing secure tenancy.[11] This discount may well amount to many thousands of pounds.

It is now clear that if the statutory 'right to buy' is exercised—even by A and B jointly[12]—on the basis of a qualifying period of occupation by B, the commensurate discount on the purchase price is regarded, in the absence of other evidence of intention, as a direct cash contribution by B towards the purchase price otherwise raised by A.[13] A resulting trust is presumed in favour of B to the extent that B has made a contribution of money's worth measurable in terms of the reduction in price generated by his or her status as a qualifying tenant.[14] Difficulties may arise of course if A and B, as joint occupiers under the relevant secure tenancy, can both point to qualifying periods of occupation, albeit of different duration. The Housing Act 1985 provides that the allowable discount shall be that generated by the longer of the two periods of occupation.[15] If, however, B has occupied for, say, ten years and A has occupied for five years, it seems unfair that A's period of occupation should be entirely ignored in calculating the attributable value of the discount under a resulting trust. In such circumstances it is strongly arguable that the contributory effect of the discount figure should be allocated as to one-third to A and as to two-thirds to B. It was for precisely this reason that, in *Evans v Hayward*,[16] Staughton LJ

8 These issues arose for the first time, but were left largely unresolved, in *Binmatt v Ali* (Unreported, Court of Appeal, 6 October 1981).

9 Much the same problem may arise where a private landlord sells the freehold reversion at a discount to a sitting tenant.

10 Housing Act 1985, s 118(1). See Chapter 17 (post, p 772).

11 Housing Act 1985, s 126(1).

12 Where a qualifying secure tenancy is a joint tenancy, the discount may be generated by relevant occupation on the part of one joint tenant alone (Housing Act 1985, s 119(2)), although the 'right to buy' is statutorily declared to belong to all the tenants jointly (Housing Act 1985, s 118(2)). The court is nevertheless free to attribute the discount value solely to the party whose occupation has generated the discount (see *Evans v Hayward* (Unreported, Court of Appeal, 23 June 1992) per Dillon LJ).

13 *Marsh v Von Sternberg* [1986] 1 FLR 526 at 531 per Bush J; *Springette v Defoe* [1992] 2 FLR 388 at 391D-F per Dillon LJ, 395G per Steyn LJ. See [1992] Conv 347 (H. Norman). Compare, however, *Evans v Hayward* (Unreported, Court of Appeal, 23 June 1992), where Staughton LJ found it 'difficult to say that a discount is, strictly speaking, purchase money provided by either party. It is money which is not provided by anybody.'

14 *Springette v Defoe* [1992] 2 FLR 388 at 393H-394A per Dillon LJ. In effect the discount figure is treated as a contribution towards the 'gross price' of purchase (see *Evans v Hayward* (Unreported, Court of Appeal, 23 June 1992) per Dillon LJ).

15 Housing Act 1985, s 129(3).

16 Unreported, Court of Appeal, 23 June 1992.

preferred the more flexible view that the discount is not so much an imputed money contribution but rather a 'factor capable of giving rise to an inference that [the parties] may have reached an agreement as to how it should be allocated between them'.

(d) Contribution of mortgage moneys

It is nowadays rare for purchasers of land to finance their purchases entirely from their own freely available cash reserves.[17] It is much more common that part (or all) of the purchase price should consist of moneys borrowed from a third party such as a bank or building society.[18] The provision of mortgage moneys raises peculiar difficulties in the law of resulting trusts, not least because the elongated period of repayment often places a substantial strain on the orthodox dogma that resulting trusts are based upon intentions contemporaneous with the acquisition of title.[19] In consequence the courts have been compelled to articulate an extended application of resulting trust theory.

(i) Economic reality of the instalment mortgage It was Lord Diplock in *Gissing v Gissing*[20] who conceded that it would be 'unreasonably legalistic' to treat the relevant transaction involved in a mortgage-assisted acquisition of property as restricted to the actual conveyance of title into the name of one or other party. Speaking in relation to a matrimonial home, Lord Diplock pointed out that the common intention of the spouses is 'more likely to have been concerned with the economic realities of the transaction than with the unfamiliar technicalities of the English law of legal and equitable interests in land.' In his view, the 'economic reality' underlying a mortgage-assisted acquisition is 'that the freeholder is purchasing the family home upon credit and that the purchase price is represented by the instalments by which the mortgage is repaid in addition to the initial deposit in cash.'[1] Thus the conduct of the spouses in relation to the payment of the mortgage instalments 'may be no less relevant to their common intention as to the beneficial interests in a matrimonial home acquired in this way than their conduct in relation to the payment of the cash deposit.'[2] As has been confirmed in other jurisdictions, money paid in the guise of mortgage instalments, even though removed in time from the completion of the relevant purchase, is 'difficult to exclude by any logical test from any concept of costs of acquisition.'[3]

Although economic reality may dictate that mortgage payments must be accommodated within the theory of resulting trusts, substantial difficulties remain. These difficulties are eased, but not completely resolved, by the general recognition nowadays that the conduct of relevant parties subsequent

17 *Bernard v Josephs* [1982] Ch 391 at 403G; *Burns v Burns* [1984] Ch 317 at 344D-E.
18 For an account of borrowing patterns, see Chapter 20 (post, p 932).
19 Ante, p 387.
20 [1971] AC 886 at 906F-H.
1 See *Thwaites v Ryan* [1984] VR 65 at 93, for reference to the way in which 'modern phenomena affecting the acquisition of homes by most people may prolong the period of "acquisition"'.
2 See also *Bloch v Bloch* (1981) 37 ALR 55 at 64. Compare *Calverley v Green* (1984) 155 CLR 242 at 263 per Mason and Brennan JJ.
3 *Little v Little* (1988) 15 NSWLR 43 at 45F per Bryson J.

to the date of acquisition may provide evidence of intentions contemporaneous with the initial taking of title. Inferences drawn from post-acquisition conduct may thus reflect back upon, and illuminate, intentions which must have subsisted at the date of acquisition.[4]

(ii) Primary presumption in respect of borrowed moneys Where borrowed moneys are used in the purchase of realty, there is a primary presumption that the loan moneys should be regarded as the exact equivalent of money contributed from the free available cash resources of the borrower.[5] Once money has been advanced by the lender, it is treated as being in a very real sense the borrower's own money. Thus if a legal title is taken in the name of A, the purchase price being raised by combining a direct cash contribution of £20,000 from A with a contribution of £40,000 which B has borrowed in his sole name from X, a resulting trust is normally presumed on behalf of A and B in the proportions of one-third and two-thirds.[6] The borrowed money is credited in full as a trust-generating contribution on the part of the person who has undertaken the covenant to repay.[7] If, however, the loan moneys are advanced to A and B jointly, the usual presumption is one of a resulting trust under which each is credited with having contributed half of the loan moneys towards the purchase.[8] The ultimate proportions of entitlement under this resulting trust will of course depend on whether,

4 In *Gissing v Gissing* [1971] AC 886 at 906E Lord Diplock indicated, however, that the conduct of parties subsequent to the acquisition of title is 'relevant if it is explicable only upon the basis of their having manifested to one another at the time of the acquisition some particular common intention as to how the beneficial interests should be held.' See also *Burns v Burns* [1984] Ch 317 at 327D; *Allen v Snyder* [1977] 2 NSWLR 685 at 707E-F; *Baumgartner v Baumgartner* [1985] 2 NSWLR 406 at 418B-D.

5 For a strong argument to the effect that mortgage-generated contributions of cash should not be regarded as the direct equivalent of free cash, see *Ulrich v Ulrich and Felton* [1968] 1 WLR 180 at 186E per Lord Denning MR, who maintained that in the mortgage context the asset to which the beneficial shares attach is merely 'the equity of redemption in the property' (post, p 937). Diplock LJ (at 189F-G) likewise thought that to treat a mortgage liability as the direct equivalent of cash 'ignores the economic realities of modern mortgages of owner-occupied dwelling houses.' See also J. Levin, (1972) 35 MLR 547 at 551; *Re Whiteley and Whiteley* (1975) 48 DLR (3d) 161 at 170f.

6 *Cowcher v Cowcher* [1972] 1 WLR 425 at 431E-F per Bagnall J (example (ii)). Compare, however, *Power v Brighton* (Unreported, Court of Appeal, 14 November 1984), where Dillon LJ opined in a dissenting judgment that '[e]ssentially what is held on a resulting trust is the equity of redemption in the property subject to the mortgage.' If this is so, loan moneys and their repayment are utterly irrelevant to the proportions of beneficial ownership. The party who defrays the mortgage liability is simply entitled to reimbursement out of the trust property, not to some proportionate share of the beneficial ownership. If widely accepted, this view would operate quite harshly in most cases of mortgage-assisted purchase. It is not, however, wholly without support in the case law. See *Ulrich v Ulrich and Felton* [1968] 1 WLR 180 at 186E per Lord Denning MR; *Abbey National Building Society v Cann* [1991] 1 AC 56 at 102A-B per Lord Jauncey of Tullichettle; *Calverley v Green* (1984) 155 CLR 242 at 263 per Mason and Brennan JJ. In *Equity & Law Home Loans Ltd v Prestidge* [1992] 1 WLR 137 at 142D-E, Mustill LJ hinted that there may need to be further consideration of this radically alternative (and little discussed) explanation of the operation of trust law in the context of loan repayments.

7 See *Power v Brighton* (Unreported, Court of Appeal, 14 November 1984) per Cumming-Bruce LJ and Sir Denys Buckley; *Currie v Hamilton* [1984] 1 NSWLR 687 at 691C-D per McLelland J. For an argument that, at least in the early years of a mortgage loan, such an approach devalues the significance of a mortgage deposit paid in cash, see P. Sparkes, (1991) 11 OJLS 39 at 46ff.

8 See *Springette v Defoe* [1992] 2 FLR 388 at 393H–394A.

in addition to undertaking joint liability to repay the loan, either A or B added any other form of contribution (eg from personal cash reserves) towards the purchase price, in which case the beneficial shares may be unequal.[9]

In this context, therefore, the general principle is that the proportions of equitable ownership behind a resulting trust are fixed, in the first instance, with reference to the extent to which the relevant parties have exposed themselves to a potential contractual liability vis à vis the lender of moneys. The beneficial shares thus fixed are not thereafter capable of variation merely because the loan moneys happen later to be repaid by a person other than the original borrower or in proportions different from those reflected in the original deemed contributions of joint borrowers.[10] Although a subsequent change in the pattern of anticipated repayment might under certain conditions raise a *constructive* trust,[11] the primary yardstick under a resulting trust is the idea that the assumption of personal liability to the lender of borrowed money has the same value in beneficial terms as a direct contribution of free cash.

(iii) Displacement of the primary presumption by common intention The primary presumption which fixes beneficial shares in accordance with the respective personal liabilities undertaken directly vis à vis the lender of borrowed moneys may itself be displaced by evidence of a countervailing common intention contemporaneous with the date of acquisition of title. Recent case law has emphasised that such common intention may make it clear *either* that the relevant parties have privately agreed that the formal loan liability should be informally reapportioned inter se *or* that the final quantification of beneficial credit for the repayment of borrowed moneys should be postponed until full repayment has actually occurred. In either case the countervailing common intention must be present at the date of acquisition of the legal title to which the loan relates,[12] but if proved to exist has the effect of altering the proportions of beneficial entitlement which would otherwise result under the trust.

(iv) Agreement to reapportion responsibility inter se It is always possible that the relevant parties, irrespective of their formal liability to the lender of borrowed moneys, may privately reorganise their respective liabilities inter se. The obligation as defined vis à vis the lender may be reapportioned, at the date of acquisition, in terms of quite different obligations pertaining informally inter se. While such a reorganisation of liability has no strict legal impact upon the lender, as between the parties themselves it is the privately varied

9 See eg *Springette v Defoe* [1992] 2 FLR 388 at 393H–394A, 395G-H ('right to buy' discount); *Ingram v Ingram* [1941] VLR 95 at 98ff (direct cash contribution); *Currie v Hamilton* [1984] 1 NSWLR 687 at 691D–692C. If, however, A and B have entered into an express declaration of trust for themselves as beneficial joint tenants, this declaration is conclusive irrespective of the relative proportions of financial contribution (see *Mayes v Mayes* (1969) 210 Estates Gazette 935 at 937 (ante, p 380)).

10 *Currie v Hamilton* [1984] 1 NSWLR 687 at 691C-D per McLelland J, who added, however, that the provider of uncontracted repayments may be entitled (in the absence of any evidence of gift) to an equitable contribution from the debtor and to an equitable charge over the property to secure this entitlement ([1984] 1 NSWLR 687 at 692C).

11 Post, p 448.

12 See *Huntingford v Hobbs* [1993] 1 FCR 45 at 55D-E.

allocation of responsibility for repayment which now defines the beneficial shares under the presumed resulting trust. An agreed variation of this kind can occur in at least two different ways, depending essentially upon whether the agreement has the informal effect of expanding or contracting the practical burden of repayment.

If A and B join in the purchase of property, the mere fact that B contributes money which has been borrowed from X on the strength of B's sole personal covenant to repay does not exclude the possibility that, as between themselves, A and B have nevertheless agreed to discharge the loan or mortgage liability by some combination of their joint financial efforts. If, for instance, A contributes £20,000 of his own free cash and also undertakes privately to B that he, A, will be responsible for half of the loan liability of £40,000 incurred under B's personal covenant with X, the proportions of beneficial ownership under the presumed resulting trust are the reverse of those fixed by the primary yardstick of formal liability. Under these changed circumstances A is presumed to be a beneficial tenant in common of a two-thirds share and B of only a one-third share. This altered balance flows from the fact that A's free cash, combined with his undertaking to share the loan liability, has now provided the source of £40,000 of the total purchase price of the property.[13] The proportions of resulting beneficial ownership will clearly vary in accordance with the proportion of B's loan liability which A privately agrees with B that he shall share.[14]

Some private reallocations of loan repayment have the quite different effect of concentrating rather than diffusing informal responsibility for the discharge of the debt. Thus even where A and B have purchased a joint title and formally undertaken a joint mortgage liability, there may have been a common intention that in practice A alone would assume liability for repayment.[15] Provided that this common intention was present in express or implied form at the date of acquisition of the legal title, A is treated for the purpose of the resulting trust as having contributed the whole of the sum borrowed on mortgage.[16] In the absence of such an agreement, however, it cannot be said that B should be disregarded as a mere nominee or that there is a resulting trust for A alone.[17]

13 *Cowcher v Cowcher* [1972] 1 WLR 425 at 431G-H per Bagnall J.
14 *Cowcher v Cowcher* [1972] 1 WLR 425 at 431H–432A per Bagnall J.
15 It may be, for instance, that A included B's name on the title (and therefore in the mortgage) precisely in order to harness an enhanced borrowing power for the purpose of a purchase proposed by A. Alternatively, B may have been made jointly liable on the mortgage simply because the lender of the mortgage moneys refused to proceed without the additional security of knowing that B had expressly joined in the mortgage. Such a precaution is frequently taken where B is known to be likely to enjoy joint occupation of the mortgaged property (post, p 578). See eg *Mellowes v Collymore* (Unreported, Court of Appeal, 27 November 1981) (mother-in-law in residence in family home).
16 *Huntingford v Hobbs* [1993] 1 FCR 45 at 55B–56A per Sir Christopher Slade. See also *Hoare v Hoare* (1982) *Times*, 9 November; *Bernard v Josephs* [1982] Ch 391 at 403G-H; *In re Gorman (A Bankrupt)* [1990] 1 WLR 616 at 624D; *Currie v Hamilton* [1984] 1 NSWLR 687 at 691C per McLelland J. In these circumstances no beneficial value is attached to the fact that B has technically been exposed to a potential contractual liability to the lender. In *Allied Irish Banks Ltd v McWilliams* [1982] NI 156 at 161C-D, Murray J noted that any loss suffered by a trustee could be recouped by way of reimbursement from the trust property. See also *Clooney v Clooney*, 394 A2d 313 at 316 (1978).
17 *Crisp v Mullings* (1976) 239 Estates Gazette 119; *Young v Young* [1984] FLR 375 at 378D-H; *Calverley v Green* (1984) 155 CLR 242 at 257f per Mason and Brennan JJ.

It is ultimately a question of fact whether any agreement has been reached by A and B to adjust the loan liability inter se,[18] but any agreement found to exist is immune from the requirements of section 53(1)(b) of the Law of Property Act 1925.

(v) Agreement to postpone quantification of shares It may be relatively unusual for A and B, on acquiring property with the aid of mortgage finance, to reapportion between themselves the responsibility for loan repayments. In the absence of such an agreement inter se, the beneficial shares of A and B under a resulting trust normally fall to be determined with reference to their respective formal liabilities for repayment.[19]

Under certain conditions, however, it is open to the court to find that at the date of acquisition A and B formed a common intention that their respective contributions towards acquisition should be measured not in terms of any formal liability for the discharge of the mortgage debt, but by the actual proportions in which they subsequently made repayment of the loan moneys.[20] As Lord Diplock said in the context of a family home in *Gissing v Gissing*,[1] there is 'nothing improbable' in the spouses acting on

> the understanding that the wife should be entitled to a share which was not to be quantified immediately upon the acquisition of the home but should be left to be determined when the mortgage was repaid or the property disposed of, on the basis of what would be fair having regard to the total contributions, direct or indirect, which each spouse had made by that date.

This alternative approach to the ascertainment of beneficial ownership is possible only where the court is able to detect a common intention, either express or implied, that the respective shares of A and B should not 'crystallise' on acquisition but should instead be assessed retrospectively with reference to such payments as were actually made.[2] There must, in effect, be some actual or inferable agreement at the date of acquisition to postpone the quantification of shares until a later date when account can taken of the de facto pattern of subsequent mortgage payments as between A and B.[3] In these circumstances, although the existence of the resulting trust is established at the acquisition date, the quantum of the beneficial interest

18 See *Power v Brighton* (Unreported, 14 November 1984), where a majority in the Court of Appeal found no convincing evidence of any explicit agreement between trust beneficiaries to share a mortgage liability formally undertaken by one beneficiary in her sole name, with the result that the borrowed moneys were reckoned as the full equivalent of a cash contribution originating from this beneficiary alone. See also *Harwood v Harwood* [1991] 2 FLR 274 at 294D-H.

19 See eg *Springette v Defoe* [1992] 2 FLR 388 at 393H-394A, 395G-H.

20 See *Bloch v Bloch* (1981) 37 ALR 55 at 64 per Brennan J; *Currie v Hamilton* [1984] 1 NSWLR 687 at 692D per McLelland J.

1 [1971] AC 886 at 909C-D. See also *Bernard v Josephs* [1982] Ch 391 at 407G-H per Kerr LJ; *Winkworth v Edward Baron Development Co Ltd* [1986] 1 WLR 1512 at 1516C-D; *Burns v Burns* [1984] Ch 317 at 327A-B, 344E; *Baumgartner v Baumgartner* [1985] 2 NSWLR 406 at 418C-D.

2 See *Springette v Defoe* [1992] 2 FLR 388 at 396B-D per Sir Christopher Slade; *Huntingford v Hobbs* [1993] 1 FCR 45 at 54B-C per Sir Christopher Slade.

3 For instances in which such a common intention has been found, see *Young v Young* [1984] FLR 375 at 380B-E; *Passee v Passee* [1988] 1 FLR 263 at 267G-268A, 270A-F per Nicholls LJ. Compare, however, *Springette v Defoe* [1992] 2 FLR 388 at 396D-H.

of each party remains subject to subsequent fluctuations in accordance with their relative contributions towards the discharge of the mortgage debt.[4]

Much artificiality is avoided if the court can find or infer an agreement that the quantum of beneficial ownership under a resulting trust is to be fixed by the totality of the contributions made both at acquisition and thereafter.[5] Thus, for instance, a consistent pattern of contribution by B towards mortgage payments incurred by reason of A's acquisition of title may provide evidence from which it can be inferred that there was a common intention ab initio that beneficial ownership should be shared by both A and B on a basis to be determined later.[6] Such an inference is even more readily made if there is evidence of 'regular and substantial direct contribution to the mortgage instalments'[7] or if the evidence of subsequent mortgage payments is reinforced by evidence of contribution to the initial cash deposit or legal expenses.[8] All such payments are clearly 'referable to' the acquisition of some interest in realty[9] and are therefore relevant to the ultimate calculation of beneficial entitlement.[10]

In making a global assessment of the parties' respective contributions, it is inevitable that the court should find itself 'painting with a broad brush'.[11] Where the most likely inference from the parties' conduct is that a postponed calculation of shares was intended, the court must, as Lord Diplock indicated in *Gissing v Gissing*,[12] determine what 'in all the circumstances was a fair share'.[13] The court is therefore able to respond more sensitively to the social and economic realities of mortgage-assisted purchase. In quantifying beneficial shares the court can not only have regard to payments of both mortgage capital and interest,[14] but can also take account of subsequent capital

4 *Currie v Hamilton* [1984] 1 NSWLR 687 at 692D-E per McLelland J.

5 See Nourse LJ's support in *Stokes v Anderson* [1991] 1 FLR 391 at 400B, for the 'general proposition that all payments made and acts done by the claimant are to be treated as illuminating the common intention as to the extent of the beneficial interest.'

6 *Gissing v Gissing* [1971] AC 886 at 900G per Viscount Dilhorne; *Burns v Burns* [1984] Ch 317 at 345A; *McFarlane v McFarlane* [1972] NI 59 at 74; *Allen v Snyder* [1977] 2 NSWLR 685 at 707F-G.

7 *Gissing v Gissing* [1971] AC 886 at 908B-C per Lord Diplock. See also *Burns v Burns* [1984] Ch 317 at 329B per Fox LJ, 344H-345A per May LJ.

8 *Gissing v Gissing* [1971] AC 886 at 907F-G per Lord Diplock; *Burns v Burns* [1984] Ch 317 at 344G; *C v C* [1976] IR 254 at 258.

9 See *Burns v Burns* [1984] Ch 317 at 328H-329C per Fox LJ.

10 Compare *Annen v Rattee* (1985) 273 Estates Gazette 503 at 504, where a lodger, in return for virtually exclusive occupation of a flat, paid a large part of the mortgage instalments owed by the legal owners. The Court of Appeal viewed the lodger's contributions as payments in respect merely of 'use and occupation' of the flat. They could not provide the basis for any inference of a common intention that the lodger should acquire a beneficial interest in the flat. See [1985] Conv 218, 371.

11 *Passee v Passee* [1988] 1 FLR 263 at 271H per Nicholls LJ.

12 [1971] AC 886 at 909D-E.

13 See also *Stokes v Anderson* [1991] 1 FLR 391 at 400B-C per Nourse LJ. In *Springette v Defoe* [1992] 2 FLR 388 at 392C-D, 397E-F, however, the Court of Appeal stressed that, in the absence of the requisite common intention, the mere fact that the parties have paid mortgage instalments in equal shares does not bring about the consequence that they acquire equal beneficial entitlements. There must have been a communicated belief on the part of both 'that they would be sharing benefit as well as burden equally'.

14 *Passee v Passee* [1988] 1 FLR 263 at 267G per Nicholls LJ. See [1988] Conv 361 (J. Warburton). On problems relating to the quantification of beneficial shares in mortgaged realty, see generally P. Sparkes, (1991) 11 OJLS 39.

payments towards improvements or in discharge of the mortgage debt.[15] It remains a moot point whether, in carrying out this global calculation, the court is still strictly acting in implementation of a resulting (as distinct from a constructive) trust.[16] Except in terms of the most strained of rationalisations, the open-ended nature of the common intention on which such a global assessment is premised is by now far removed from the presumed intention supposedly at the heart of the classic resulting trust.

(e) Contribution to general household expenses

Few issues have highlighted the limitations of resulting trust theory quite so clearly as the vexed question whether a trust can be raised on the footing of financial contributions made to the general expenses of a household. The problem tends to arise in the following way.

A legal title vested in the name of A alone may have been so acquired with the provision of A's own money together with a mortgage advance for which A is solely responsible. The prima facie inference disclosed by such circumstances is that A was intended to be the sole beneficial owner.[17] However, the question arises whether a resulting trust can be presumed in favour of B on the ground that B has contributed financially to the general expenses incurred by A's household, thereby freeing A *pro tanto* to discharge his mortgage commitment. This problem arises with particular acuteness in the context of a matrimonial or quasi-matrimonial home in which A and B have lived together. It is quite typical, for example, that A may have used his income to meet the mortgage payments on the property, while B has used his or her income in the payment of household bills and in the purchase of domestic consumables such as food, clothing and heating.

In this context the application of resulting trust doctrine has always proved less than satisfactory. There is, of course, a strong argument of fairness to the effect that B's financial contributions should generate for B an equitable share in the property which A has thus been freed to acquire. In the past valiant attempts have indeed been made to urge that indirect financial contributions to general household welfare should be accounted, under a resulting trust, as the *equivalent* of direct money contributions made towards the purchase price.[18] In *McFarlane v McFarlane*[19] Lord MacDermott LCJ was prepared to hold that if the parties have 'agreed to some quid pro quo in the nature of a proprietary benefit', an indirect contribution to the

15 *Passee v Passee* [1988] 1 FLR 263 at 270C–271B per Nicholls LJ.

16 Compare *Passee v Passee* [1988] 1 FLR 263 at 269H–270A (where Nicholls LJ thought the terminology of resulting trust 'probably not inappropriate') and *Lloyds Bank Plc v Rosset* [1991] 1 AC 107 at 133A (where Lord Bridge of Harwich spoke in terms of constructive trust).

17 *Bernard v Josephs* [1982] Ch 391 at 403G-H.

18 The line of authority begins with *Fribance v Fribance* (No 2) [1957] 1 WLR 384 at 387, where Denning LJ declared that the title to family assets should not depend upon fortuitous questions of family finance, upon how the spouses happened to allocate their earnings and expenditure. See also *Gissing v Gissing* [1971] AC 886 at 909E-G per Lord Diplock; *Allen v Snyder* [1977] 2 NSWLR 685 at 707F-G; *Boccalatte v Bushelle* [1980] Qd R 180 at 184B.

19 [1972] NI 59 at 70, 72.

family finances becomes 'as much the basis of a resulting trust as a direct contribution in money to the cost of acquiring a particular property.'[20]

The theory of equivalent contribution under a resulting trust has not, however, found a ready acceptance in the doctrinaire world of the orthodox property lawyer. Here the conventional approach is as simple and logical as it is also unsubtle and unrealistic. If B spends money in the purchase of item X, he will generally acquire rights in item X; but he will not normally acquire rights in item Y, which has been bought by A, even if the fact that B has purchased item X indirectly enabled A to purchase item Y.[1] Thus, in the hardened view of the property lawyer, the woman who pays the household food or electricity bills with her own money thereby acquires lots of rights in the aforementioned food and electricity; but she does not magically acquire any rights in the house which meanwhile her partner has managed to purchase with his own money.[2] Her financial contributions towards the general welfare of the family are not normally regarded as sufficiently enjoying the character of 'purchase money' to raise a resulting trust in her favour in respect of property bought by her partner.[3] The mere sharing of family living expenses does not in itself connote a joint contribution towards the acquisition of family property.[4] English law is still some distance from any realistic acknowledgement that families live in a factual community of goods and that the economic activity of family members is characterised by constructive co-operation, by partnership endeavour and often by a certain division of labour.[5]

On balance it seems preferable nowadays to regard financial contributions towards general household expenditure, not as the basis of some strained form of resulting trust, but rather as evidence of relevant detriment for the purpose of founding a constructive trust.[6] In this way the resulting trust is confined more narrowly, and perhaps more properly, to money payments which serve directly to finance the purchase of a legal title.

(f) Payment of periodic rent

In order to be relevant under the doctrine of resulting trusts, money payments must be made in connection with the acquisition rather than the use of a capital asset.[7] This has a significance, for instance, in relation to flat-sharing

20 Thus a trust was sometimes said to result if there had been some understanding between A and B that B's assumption of responsibility for more general aspects of household expenditure was part of a deliberate design to free A to discharge the acquisition cost of the home itself (see *Gissing v Gissing* [1971] AC 886 at 903B-C per Lord Pearson). The court might properly infer that a 'substantial contribution ... to family expenses' was 'referable to the acquisition of the house since, in one way or another, it enables the family to pay the mortgage instalments' (see *Burns v Burns* [1984] Ch 317 at 329A-B per Fox LJ).

1 For a prime example, see *Little v Little* (1988) 15 NSWLR 43 at 46F, where Bryson J, while recognising the 'arbitrary element' in 'joint production cost allocations', was adamant that '[w]hat one gets for paying stamp duty is a stamp, not a piece of land.'

2 *Burns v Burns* [1984] Ch 317 at 329C; *Allen v Snyder* [1977] 2 NSWLR 685 at 691C.

3 *Gissing v Gissing* [1971] AC 886 at 901B-C per Viscount Dilhorne, 910G-H per Lord Diplock.

4 *Gissing v Gissing* [1971] AC 886 at 909G-H per Lord Diplock; *McGill v S* [1979] IR 283 at 289; *Niederberger v Memnook* (1982) 130 DLR (3d) 353 at 360.

5 Post, p 450.

6 Post, p 425.

7 See eg *Passee v Passee* [1988] 1 FLR 263 at 268D-E.

arrangements, where it is common for a tenancy to be taken in the name of one of the flat-sharers, the others holding technically as contractual licensees from him. No resulting trust is presumed on the basis of money payments made by flat-sharers who contribute proportionately to the rent charged to the nominal tenant.[8] The latter stands in no fiduciary relationship to the others, and it therefore follows that if he subsequently acquires a long lease in the flat on his own behalf, this valuable asset is not held on trust for the other erstwhile flat-sharers.[9] As Plowman J pointed out in *Savage v Dunningham*,[10] serious problems would result if flat-sharing were treated not as an entirely informal arrangement but as the potential source of a trust. Each flat-sharer would, for instance, have a beneficial interest which would require written disposition within section 53(1)(c) of the Law of Property Act 1925 when he or she moved out.

(g) Contribution of domestic endeavour

It is clearly established that a contribution of domestic labour, even though performed over many years, does not constitute the equivalent of 'purchase money' for the purpose of raising a resulting trust.[11] The English law of real property notoriously refuses to attach any money value to the intangible contribution which the homemaker makes to the welfare of the family through services of domestic management and child care.[12] The courts take the view that 'the mere fact that parties live together and do the ordinary domestic tasks is . . . no indication at all that they thereby intended to alter the existing property rights of either of them.'[13] It is an enduring irony that reluctance to monetise the unquantifiable economic impact of domestic endeavour has caused an invaluable form of activity to appear valueless.[14] It must be conceded, however, that if domestic effort were accorded an imputed monetary significance in the law of resulting trusts, its impact could hardly be confined to the acquisition of an isolated asset such as the family home.[15]

8 *Savage v Dunningham* [1974] Ch 181 at 184H–185A. See also *Annen v Rattee* (1985) 273 Estates Gazette 503.

9 *Savage v Dunningham* [1974] Ch 181 at 185G. The position might be different if the flat-sharers had jointly contributed a cash premium towards the purchase of the tenancy in the name of one of their number. See also *Malayan Credit Ltd v Jack Chia-M.P.H. Ltd* [1986] AC 549 at 561D-E.

10 [1974] Ch 181 at 185D-F.

11 See eg *Burns v Burns* [1984] Ch 317 at 342G per May LJ.

12 Even the constitutional preference afforded the role of homemaker in Ireland (see Constitution of Ireland, Art 41) has not enabled the courts to award a beneficial interest to a wife and mother on the basis of domestic endeavour alone. See *L v L* [1992] ILRM 115 at 121f per Finlay CJ. McCarthy J pointed out (at 124) that there was no complementary endorsement of the domestic activities of a father 'although such a role reversal is, nowadays, by no means uncommon'. Compare *N v N and C* [1992] ILRM 127 at 131ff (wife's work in managing letting of apartments rewarded with beneficial share).

13 *Burns v Burns* [1984] Ch 317 at 331A per Fox LJ. See also *Button v Button* [1968] 1 WLR 457 at 462C (post, p 431).

14 According to Wally Seccombe, '[f]or those held spellbound by the fetishism of price theory, any operation not tagged with a price is *a priori* not economic' (*The Housewife and Her Labour under Capitalism*, (1974) 83 New Left Review 3 at 4). See Kevin Gray, *Reallocation of Property on Divorce* (Abingdon 1977), pp 22ff, 68ff.

15 As Woodhouse J once pointed out, the 'physical association of domestic effort and domestic environment' provides only an illusory nexus between cause and effect (*Aitken v Aitken* (Auckland Registry, No M 105/70 and D 697/70, 22 November 1972), Transcript pp 10f).

Domestic contributions can normally be related indiscriminately to all property acquired within the family context,[16] with the consequence that vast ranges of household asset could be found to be trammelled by the imposition of resulting trusts.[17]

(3) Relationship between express and resulting trusts

The mere existence of an unenforceable express trust of land does not foreclose the possibility that the same set of facts may also give rise to a valid resulting trust.[18] It might be thought that the explicitly declared intention contained in the express trust leaves no room for the implication of intention on which a resulting trust is supposedly based. However, this objection has not been sustained. Russell LJ observed in *Hodgson v Marks*[19] that 'if an attempted express trust fails, that seems . . . just the occasion for implication of a resulting trust, whether the failure be due to uncertainty, or perpetuity, or lack of form.'[20]

(4) Displacement of the presumption of resulting trust

As Lord Diplock noted in *Pettitt v Pettitt*,[1] the equitable presumptions as to intention are 'no more than a consensus of judicial opinion disclosed by reported cases as to the most likely inference of fact to be drawn in the absence of any evidence to the contrary.' Presumptions shift the burden of adducing evidence, in that the onus of persuasion is thrown upon the party against whom the force of the presumption operates.[2] A presumption merely allocates the 'risk of non-persuasion'.[3] However, as an American judge once said,[4] 'presumptions may be looked on as the bats of the law, flitting in the twilight but disappearing in the sunshine of actual facts.' It follows that presumptions of intention ultimately prevail only where there is no convincing evidence of the actual intentions of the parties.

The presumption of resulting trust may be rebutted by any evidence[5] (including parol evidence) which unambiguously demonstrates that B, although providing all or part of the finance for a purchase in the name

16 See *Gravina v Gravina* [1972] VR 678 at 682 per Menhennitt J.
17 Compare *E v E* [1971] NZLR 859 at 865 per Wild CJ (dissenting).
18 *Hodgson v Marks* [1971] Ch 892 at 933B (ante, p 216).
19 [1971] Ch 892 at 933C.
20 See also *Dalton v Christofis* [1978] WAR 42.
1 [1970] AC 777 at 823H.
2 See *Russell v Scott* (1936) 55 CLR 440 at 451 per Dixon and Evatt JJ. See also *Calverley v Green* (1984) 155 CLR 242 at 266 per Deane J; *Muschinski v Dodds* (1985) 160 CLR 583 at 612 per Deane J.
3 *Carkeek v Tate-Jones* [1971] VR 691 at 695 per McInerney J.
4 *Mackowik v Kansas City*, 94 SW 256 at 264 (1906) per Lamm J.
5 In determining whether the presumption of resulting trust has been rebutted, the acts and declarations of the parties forming part of the transaction are admissible as evidence either for or against the party who did the act or made the declaration. However, subsequent declarations are admissible as evidence only against the party who made them (see *Shephard v Cartwright* [1955] AC 431 at 445; *Cowcher v Cowcher* [1972] 1 WLR 425 at 436D-E; *Hepworth v Hepworth* (1963) 110 CLR 309 at 319; *Calverley v Green* (1984) 155 CLR 242 at 262 per Mason and Brennan JJ; *Muschinski v Dodds* (1985) 160 CLR 583 at 590 per Gibbs CJ).

of A, did not actually intend to take a beneficial interest in the property.[6] Where one person has contributed all of the purchase money, it is his or her intention alone which is relevant; where two persons contributed, the intentions of both are material.[7] It seems, moreover, that the presumption of resulting trust may be rebutted either in whole or in part.[8] In *Napier v Public Trustee (Western Australia)*,[9] for instance, the High Court of Australia held that the presumption had been rebutted as to the grant of a life interest in disputed property, but still operated in respect of the interest in remainder.[10]

Evidence which rebuts the presumption of resulting trust may take any of a number of forms.

(a) Gift

There may be evidence, for instance, that B intended to confer an entirely gratuitous benefit upon A in the form of the whole or part of the equitable ownership of the disputed property.[11] Evidence of a donative intention excludes any possibility of a resulting trust in favour of B.[12] Even where money changes hands under a family arrangement,[13] the arrangement itself can rest so heavily upon the presence of a gift relationship between the parties that there is no question of loan-based contractual rights or equity shareholding behind any sort of trust.[14]

The presumption of resulting trust may also be rebutted in a less obvious case of donative intent. A and B may have contributed unequally to the purchase price of property in circumstances where A, having made the greater contribution, intended that B should have a beneficial quantum other than that commensurate with his actual financial contribution (eg a half-share or even the entire beneficial interest). On these facts the resulting trust which would have arisen on the basis of actual contributions is rebutted in part by A's intention to advance B to the extent of the beneficial increment in excess of the proportion fixed by his own contribution.[15] It is likely, however, that B's enhanced beneficial entitlement, unsupported by resulting trust, can be validated only on the basis of a constructive trust.[16]

6 *Pettitt v Pettitt* [1970] AC 777 at 814F-G; *Allen v Snyder* [1977] 2 NSWLR 685 at 698F.

7 *Calverley v Green* (1984) 155 CLR 242 at 251 per Gibbs CJ; *Muschinski v Dodds* (1985) 160 CLR 583 at 590 per Gibbs CJ.

8 *In re Kerrigan; Ex parte Jones* (1947) 47 SR (NSW) 76 at 82.

9 (1980) 32 ALR 153 at 155, 158.

10 See also *Rider v Kidder* (1805) 10 Ves Jun 360 at 368, 32 ER 884 at 887; *Dullow v Dullow* (1985) 3 NSWLR 531 at 540F-541D.

11 *Cowcher v Cowcher* [1972] 1 WLR 425 at 431C. See also *Reber v Reber* (1988) 48 DLR (4th) 376 at 378.

12 *Winkworth v Edward Baron Development Co Ltd* [1986] 1 WLR 1512 at 1516D; *Taddeo v Taddeo* (1978) 19 SASR 347 at 366f (post, p 410); *Barrios v Chiabrera* (1984) 3 BPR 9276 at 9279.

13 On the law relating to family arrangements, see Chapter 19 (post, p 906).

14 See eg *Walker v Walker* (Unreported, Court of Appeal, 12 April 1984), where a father had announced at his son's wedding that he proposed to give the newly married couple money to set up a house. See also *Julian v Furby* (Unreported, Court of Appeal, No 79 15962, 24 November 1981), where a father-in-law was held to have made a gift of his labour in effecting improvements.

15 See *Springette v Defoe* [1992] 2 FLR 388 at 392E-F per Dillon LJ; *Currie v Hamilton* [1984] 1 NSWLR 687 at 690F.

16 Post, p 448.

(b) Loan

The presumption of resulting trust is likewise displaced by proof that B provided the purchase moneys by way of loan.[17] A lender does not advance money in the character of a purchaser and therefore takes no beneficial interest.[18] Were it otherwise, a lender could recover his money twice over,[19] and banks and building societies would moreover acquire a myriad of beneficial interests in the millions of homes bought on the strength of mortgage advances.

The application of a loan analysis, while clearly excluding any possibility of resulting trust, may nevertheless have other—fairly complex—implications in the context of family arrangements. In such arrangements it is quite common that money should be lent towards the purchase of property on the understanding that the lender should have some form of residential privilege in the property pending the repayment of his or her loan. It is also frequently the case in such arrangements that no term date is fixed in relation to the loan and there may be only the haziest of intentions as to how or when the money is to be repaid. Particularly where the lender is an elderly person, the provision of loan moneys returnable at some unspecified future date tends to merge obscurely with an anticipated devolution of property by way of succession. In such circumstances the courts have often recognised the primarily contractual nature of the relationship, while awarding the lender some form of occupation lien pending repayment. This form of remedy is readily coupled, in somewhat imprecise association, with related notions of irrevocable licence, constructive trust and proprietary estoppel.

Both the flexibility and the uncertainty of the law in this area were demonstrated in *In re Sharpe (A Bankrupt)*.[20] Here S had acquired a leasehold interest in a shop and maisonette, much of the purchase price of this property being contributed by S's 77-year-old aunt, J. In order to raise her contribution to the property, J had sold her existing home and had moved into the maisonette with S and his wife on the understanding that she would be able to stay there for as long as she wished. S later became bankrupt and his trustee in bankruptcy contracted to sell the leasehold premises to P with vacant possession. When S's trustee in bankruptcy moved for vacant possession, J argued that she had an interest in the premises.

17 *Winkworth v Edward Baron Development Co Ltd* [1986] 1 WLR 1512 at 1516D per Lord Templeman. See *Hussey v Palmer* [1972] 1 WLR 1286 at 1292E; *In re Sharpe (A Bankrupt)* [1980] 1 WLR 219 at 222E-F, 223A-B; *Hoare v Hoare* (1982) *Times*, 9 November; *Wear v DePutron* (Unreported, Court of Appeal, 6 March 1984); *Risch v McFee* [1991] 1 FLR 105 at 109B-C; *Avondale Printers & Stationers Ltd v Haggie* [1979] 2 NZLR 124 at 145; *Barrios v Chiabrera* (1984) 3 BPR 9276 at 9279.

18 *In re Cooke* (1857) 6 Ir Ch R 430 at 438; *Bateman Television Ltd v Bateman and Thomas* [1971] NZLR 453 at 459, 462. It is possible, however, that a money payment, made initially as a loan, may subsequently be transmuted into a trust-generating contribution of funds. Such a result will occur if the lender, acting in reliance on a promise of beneficial entitlement, never makes any attempt to recover either capital or interest. In effect the loan money is assimilated de facto into the provision of the purchase price (see *Risch v McFee* [1991] 1 FLR 105 at 110E-H).

19 *In re Sharpe (A Bankrupt)* [1980] 1 WLR 219 at 223B.

20 [1980] 1 WLR 219. See [1980] Conv 207 (J. Martin); (1980) 96 LQR 336 (G. Woodman); A.R. Everton, [1982] Conv 119 at 125ff.

Browne-Wilkinson J declined to hold that J had an interest in the property by way of resulting trust, taking the view that the moneys paid by J had been paid by way of loan.[1] However, he was inclined to agree that J had acquired 'something less than an aliquot share of the equity in the premises, namely, the right to stay on in the premises until the money she provided indirectly to acquire them has been repaid.'[2] Browne-Wilkinson J accepted that such a right had a somewhat mixed derivation which drew support from analogous concepts of proprietary estoppel, constructive trust and irrevocable licence.[3] The right generated on J's behalf, 'whether it be called a contractual licence or an equitable licence or an interest under a constructive trust',[4] was binding not only upon S but also upon S's trustee in bankruptcy, who simply stepped into the shoes of the debtor. J had a right to live in the property until her loan was repaid, and it followed that the trustee in bankruptcy took the property subject to that right.[5]

(c) Legally ineffective relationships

Similarly no resulting trust can be claimed by an occupier of property who makes payments of money to the legal owner under circumstances where those payments are more in the nature of contributions to current living

1 [1980] 1 WLR 219 at 222F. The loan analysis of the relationship was supported by the fact that, after S became bankrupt, J (acting on her solicitor's advice) obtained from him a promissory note for £15,700. The parties thereby clearly indicated that the moneys paid by J to S were to be repayable. The mere use of a promissory note is not, however, conclusive evidence of a loan relationship (see *Stokes v Anderson* [1991] 1 FLR 391 at 396F–397A).

2 [1980] 1 WLR 219 at 223B-C. It was relevant that J had 'only loaned the money as part of a wider scheme, an essential feature of which was that she was to make her home in the property to be acquired with the money loaned' ([1980] 1 WLR 219 at 223H). For other attempts to resolve the 'granny flat' problem, see *Hussey v Palmer* [1972] 1 WLR 1286 (post, p 445); *Broughall v Hunt* (Unreported, Chancery Division, 1 February 1983); *Clayton v Green* (1979) NZ Recent Law 139; *Lepel v Huthnance* (1979) NZ Recent Law 269.

3 In Browne-Wilkinson J's view the right claimed by J was based upon 'the line of recent Court of Appeal decisions which has spelt out irrevocable licences from informal family arrangements, and in some cases characterised such licences as conferring some equity or equitable interest under a constructive trust' (post, p 909). Browne-Wilkinson J thought that the principles lying behind these decisions had not yet been 'fully explored' and pointed out that 'on occasion it seems that such rights are found to exist simply on the ground that to hold otherwise would be a hardship to the plaintiff.' He was, however, of the opinion that recent authorities had established the proposition that 'if the parties have proceeded on a common assumption that the plaintiff is to enjoy a right to reside in a particular property and in reliance on that assumption the plaintiff has expended money or otherwise acted to his detriment, the defendant will not be allowed to go back on that common assumption and the court will imply an irrevocable licence or trust which will give effect to that common assumption' ([1980] 1 WLR 219 at 223C-F).

4 [1980] 1 WLR 219 at 224A.

5 [1980] 1 WLR 219 at 224F–225D (ante, p 41). Although this was sufficient to dispose of the issue between J and S's trustee in bankruptcy, Browne-Wilkinson J observed that P, who was not a party to the present proceedings, would not necessarily be bound by such rights as J might have. In fact, Browne-Wilkinson J indicated that 'as a purchaser without express notice' P might well take priority over J in any action for specific performance of his contract ([1980] 1 WLR 219 at 226G).

expenses and outgoings.[6] In such cases, where the payments are not attributable to any reasonable belief that a beneficial interest is being acquired, the contributor cannot be said to have advanced the money in the character of a purchaser.

Particularly in the domestic or familial context there is seldom any intention that recurrent payments of money made between family members should create a legally binding relationship between the parties.[7] There is instead a ready presumption that such payments represent merely a contribution towards shared household expenditure on consumables[8] rather than a contribution which generates a beneficial or other entitlement in the family home for the contributor.[9] The son who gives his mother part of his weekly wage packet while living at home does not normally acquire thereby a beneficial interest in realty. Even a pattern of regular payments into a common pool may result in no more than the minimal protection afforded under an occupation licence. In *Hannaford v Selby*,[10] for example, a young couple bought a house in their own names with the aid of a mortgage loan. They moved into this property with their children and with the wife's elderly parents. Over a substantial period of time the parents paid £5 per week into the family purse, and the wife's father indulged his 'one absorbing hobby' by working hard in the garden. When friction developed between the three generations living in the house, the wife's parents claimed to have acquired a beneficial interest in the home on the ground that their financial contributions had generated some form of trust in their favour. This argument was rejected by Goulding J, who took the view that their weekly payments had not been made with any intention of acquiring an interest in the property, but represented simply 'a contribution to expenses in consideration of being allowed to live with the plaintiffs in the house.'[11] Accordingly the parents' occupation licence was revocable on reasonable notice.[12]

(d) Onus of proof

Whether the presumption of resulting trust is rebutted in any of these ways is ultimately a matter of credibility and probability, determined with reference to the facts of each individual case. It is in general unlikely that there will not be some living person who can, by his evidence, either confirm or rebut the resulting trust presumed from the payment of moneys. However, if all the available evidence is neutral as to the purpose of the money payment by B to A, the 'prima facie inference' will be that it was the common intention

6 See eg *Hannaford v Selby* (1976) 239 Estates Gazette 811 at 813 (post, p 427); *Baumgartner v Baumgartner* [1985] 2 NSWLR 406 at 419C.
7 Post, p 907.
8 *Gross v French* (1976) 238 Estates Gazette 39 at 41; *Rogers v Eller* (Unreported, Court of Appeal, 20 May 1986); *Govorko v Vicelic* (1971) 2 BPR 9477 at 9485, 9487. See also *Springette v Defoe* [1992] 2 FLR 388 at 394A-F; *Baumgartner v Baumgartner* [1985] 2 NSWLR 406 at 419C.
9 Ante, p 385.
10 (1976) 239 Estates Gazette 811.
11 (1976) 239 Estates Gazette 811. Compare, however, *Timms v Timms* (1973) 226 Estates Gazette 1565, where the Court of Appeal preferred to find in favour of a tenancy rather than a family arrangement.
12 (1976) 239 Estates Gazette 811 at 813 (six months' notice given).

of A and B that there should be a resulting trust in proportion to the moneys contributed.[13]

(5) Presumption of advancement

In normal circumstances the onus of proving the donative intent of B falls, not unnaturally, upon A.[14] However, there is one rather distinct group of circumstances in which a different presumption of law comes into operation, thus effectively reversing the onus of proof. In these situations the presumption of resulting trust is displaced by a countervailing 'presumption of advancement' which, in a number of stereotyped situations, supports an inference of gift by supplying an all-important donative intent on the part of B. The effect of the presumption of advancement is to establish that the disputed property belongs to A both at law and in equity,[15] the onus now shifting to B to rebut the inference that he intended to 'advance' A.[16]

(a) Relationships which raise a presumption of advancement

A presumption of advancement arises where property is nominally transferred to a person whose welfare the real purchaser of the property would naturally have wished to promote or 'advance'.[17] Accordingly, a special donative intent is presumed in favour of certain persons who come within the bonds of deemed familial affection[18] and for whom the real purchaser has some 'obligation in conscience to provide'.[19] By circumscribing the field of recognised 'advancement', the presumption casts an incidental and quite interesting light on socially perceived boundaries of personal and familial responsibility. Thus, in the absence of clear evidence of contrary intention at the time of purchase,[20] the presumption of advancement infers a donative

13 *Gissing v Gissing* [1971] AC 886 at 907C per Lord Diplock. See also *Seldon v Davidson* [1968] 1 WLR 1083 at 1090F; *Crane v Davis* (Unreported, Chancery Division, 8 May 1981).

14 *Wirth v Wirth* (1956) 98 CLR 228 at 235 per Dixon CJ.

15 On the application of the presumption of advancement, 'the prima facie position remains that the equitable interest is presumed to follow the legal estate and to be at home with the legal title' (see *Calverley v Green* (1984) 155 CLR 242 at 267 per Deane J).

16 *Murless v Franklin* (1818) 1 Swan 13 at 18, 36 ER 278 at 280. See also *Sidmouth v Sidmouth* (1840) 2 Beav 447 at 454, 48 ER 1254 at 1257; *Pearson v Pearson* [1961] VR 693 at 698; *Martin v Martin* (1959) 110 CLR 297 at 303; *Pettitt v Pettitt* [1970] AC 777 at 814G per Lord Upjohn.

17 'The presumption is based on the concept that where a property is transferred to a person whom the transferor has an obligation to support, it is presumed to be an advance of the interest the dependant might reasonably expect to receive on the death of the transferor' (*Re Levy* (1982) 131 DLR (3d) 15 at 25). See also *Murless v Franklin* (1818) 1 Swans 13 at 17, 36 ER 278 at 280; *Dullow v Dullow* (1985) 3 NSWLR 531 at 535F–536A.

18 In *Wirth v Wirth* (1956) 98 CLR 228 at 237, Dixon CJ thought that 'the presumption of advancement doubtless in its inception was concerned with relationships affording "good" consideration'.

19 *Scott v Pauly* (1917) 24 CLR 274 at 281 per Isaacs J. In the words of Jessel MR in *Bennet v Bennet* (1879) 10 Ch D 474 at 477, 'the presumption of gift arises from the moral obligation to give'. See, however, *Calverley v Green* (1984) 155 CLR 242 at 247f.

20 Subsequent acts and declarations of the child (but not of the parent) may operate to rebut the presumed advancement (*Sidmouth v Sidmouth* (1840) 2 Beav 447 at 455, 48 ER 1254 at 1257). See also *Cowcher v Cowcher* [1972] 1 WLR 425 at 436D; *Charles Marshall Pty Ltd v Grimsley* (1956) 95 CLR 353 at 366; *Blackburn v Y V Properties Pty Ltd* [1980] VR 290 at 293.

intent where a father provides the consideration for a transfer into the name of his child[1] or where a person (male or female) purchases property in the name of someone in relation to whom he currently stands *in loco parentis*.[2] The presumption does not, however, apply to a purchase in the name of a sister,[3] a son-in-law[4] or a nephew.[5] Nor does it rebut the presumption of resulting trust where property is purchased in the name of a parent or parent-in-law.[6]

(b) Applicability to mothers

It seems, moreover, still to be generally accepted that the presumption of advancement does not apply, even 'in these days of sex equality',[7] to a provision of money or transfer of other benefits by a mother to her own son or daughter.[8] This distinction between the cases of a father and a mother was once rationalised on the basis that the father was supposedly 'the head of the family' and therefore 'under the primary moral obligation to provide for the children of the marriage'.[9] However, the distinction comports very

1 *Dyer v Dyer* (1788) 2 Cox Eq Cas 92 at 93f, 30 ER 42 at 43; *Sidmouth v Sidmouth* (1840) 2 Beav 447 at 454, 48 ER 1254 at 1257; *Shephard v Cartwright* [1955] AC 431 at 445; *In re Vandervell's Trusts* (No 2) [1974] Ch 269 at 289A; *Charles Marshall Pty Ltd v Grimsley* (1956) 95 CLR 353 at 364; *Goodfriend v Goodfriend* (1972) 22 DLR (3d) 699 at 703; *Napier v Public Trustee (Western Australia)* (1980) 32 ALR 153 at 158; *Calverley v Green* (1984) 155 CLR 242 at 247 per Gibbs CJ, 268 per Deane J. The presumption also applies to an illegitimate child (*Soar v Foster* (1858) 4 K & J 152 at 160, 70 ER 64 at 67) and to an adopted child (*Standing v Bowring* (1886) 31 Ch D 282 at 287). A child is, of course, competent to hold a legal estate in land only if he has attained the age of 18 (Law of Property Act 1925, s 1(6)).

2 *Shephard v Cartwright* [1955] AC 431 at 445; *In re Vandervell's Trusts* (No 2) [1974] Ch 269 at 289A; *Charles Marshall Pty Ltd v Grimsley* (1956) 95 CLR 353 at 364; *Young v Young* (1959) 15 DLR (2d) 138 at 139; *Napier v Public Trustee (Western Australia)* (1980) 32 ALR 153 at 158; *Calverley v Green* (1984) 155 CLR 242 at 247 per Gibbs CJ, 268 per Deane J. The presumption of advancement thus applies to gifts to an illegitimate child (*Beckford v Beckford* (1774) Lofft 490 at 492, 98 ER 763 at 764), a stepson (*In re Paradise Motor Co Ltd* [1968] 1 WLR 1125 at 1140A), and a grandchild whose father is dead (*Edbrand v Dancer* (1680) 2 Ch Cas 26, 22 ER 829; *Soar v Foster* (1858) 4 K & J 152 at 160, 70 ER 64 at 67).

3 *Noack v Noack* [1959] VR 137 at 140; *Gorog v Kiss* (1977) 78 DLR (3d) 690 at 694. It cannot be claimed that a brother stands *in loco parentis* to his sister (*O'Brien v Bean and Bean* (1957) 7 DLR (2d) 332 at 333).

4 *Knight v Biss* [1954] NZLR 55 at 57.

5 *Drury v Drury* (1675) 73 SS 205; *Russell v Scott* (1936) 55 CLR 440 at 451.

6 *Binmatt v Ali* (Unreported, Court of Appeal, 6 October 1981); *Groves v Christiansen* (1978) 86 DLR (3d) 296 at 301).

7 *Gross v French* (1975) 238 Estates Gazette 39 per Scarman LJ.

8 *Bennet v Bennet* (1879) 10 Ch D 474 at 478; *In re Vandervell's Trusts* (No 2) [1974] Ch 269 at 289A; *Preston v Greene* [1909] 1 IR 172 at 177f; *Lattimer v Lattimer* (1978) 82 DLR (3d) 587 at 590. Compare *Bull v Bull* [1955] 1 QB 234 at 236, and *Rupar v Rupar* (1964) 49 WWR 226 at 234, where it seems to have been thought that the presumption of advancement could, in the absence of contrary intention, apply to a mother. More recently, however, the normal presumption of resulting trust has been applied to a mother in the absence of sufficient evidence of gift or loan (see *Sekhon v Alissa* [1989] 2 FLR 94 at 100B per Hoffmann J; [1990] Conv 213 (G. Kodilinye).

9 *Scott v Pauly* (1917) 24 CLR 274 at 282 per Isaacs J. It may be, however, that the onus on the child to prove a donative intent on the part of his mother will be fairly easily satisfied (see *Bennet v Bennet* (1879) 10 Ch D 474 at 479f per Jessel MR; *Main v Main* [1939] 1 DLR 723 at 725).

uneasily with modern notions of equality,[10] and is particularly difficult to justify in relation to benefits conferred on her children by a mother who is widowed, divorced or single.[11] In such cases it must surely require little evidence to establish a donative intent.[12]

(c) Applicability to spouses

Perhaps the most controversial issue of all is whether the presumption of advancement still applies as between husband and wife.[13] It is clear that such a presumption did once operate not only in favour of a married woman,[14] but also in favour of a woman to whom property was transferred in express contemplation of a marriage which subsequently took place with the donor.[15] However, the presumption of advancement has never applied as between merely cohabiting parties.[16] Nor has it ever had any application in favour of a husband.[17] The relevance in modern conditions of the sex-discriminatory concept of 'advancement' is now highly questionable.[18] In its application in the marital context, the presumption was all too plainly an index of a former social climate in which wives enjoyed inferior status.[19] The archaic nature of the presumption was recognised by the House of Lords in *Pettitt*

10 The starkly unjustifiable nature of the distinction appears in two cases concerning the ownership of lottery moneys won on a ticket purchased in the name of a child (compare *B v B* (1976) 65 DLR (3d) 460 at 466, with *Kiddle v Afoa and Afoa* (1984) NZ Recent Law 47).

11 In *Scott v Pauly* (1917) 24 CLR 274 at 282, Isaacs J thought that the presumption of advancement might apply to a widow. It may not require very strong evidence to show that a mother is *in loco parentis* (*Re Orme* (1883) 50 LT (NS) 51 at 53). The recent Australian case law discloses a marked willingness to extend the presumption to a mother (see *Dullow v Dullow* (1985) 3 NSWLR 531 at 536C, 541D-E).

12 *Edwards v Bradley* (1957) 9 DLR (2d) 673 at 678 (Supreme Court of Canada); *Lattimer v Lattimer* (1978) 82 DLR (3d) 587 at 590; *Dullow v Dullow* (1985) 3 NSWLR 531 at 534G.

13 It appears from *In re Figgis, decd* [1969] 1 Ch 123 at 144C that the presumption of advancement may still apply in respect of a joint bank account held by husband and wife (compare, however, *Re Berry (A Bankrupt)* [1978] 2 NZLR 373 at 378).

14 *Christ's Hospital v Budgin et Ux* (1712) 2 Vern 683 at 684, 23 ER 1043 at 1044; *Martin v Martin* (1959) 110 CLR 297 at 303; *Hepworth v Hepworth* (1963) 110 CLR 309 at 317.

15 *Moate v Moate* [1948] 2 All ER 486 at 487G-H; *Wirth v Wirth* (1956) 98 CLR 228 at 237f). See also *Ibbotson v Kushner* (1978) 84 DLR (3d) 417 at 419.

16 *Rider v Kidder* (1805) 10 Ves Jun 360 at 367, 32 ER 884 at 887; *Soar v Foster* (1858) 4 K & J 152 at 162, 70 ER 64 at 68; *Collins v Sanders* (1956) 3 DLR (2d) 607 at 615; *David v Szoke* (1974) 39 DLR (3d) 707 at 716; *Allen v Snyder* [1977] 2 NSWLR 685 at 690B; *Calverley v Green* (1984) 155 CLR 242 at 248 per Gibbs CJ, 268f per Deane J. See, however, *Napier v Public Trustee (Western Australia)* (1980) 32 ALR 153 at 154 per Gibbs ACJ. It is always possible, of course, that there may be sufficient evidence of an actual donative intention to support the equitable entitlement of a cohabiting transferee (see *Murdock v Aherne* (1878) 4 VLR (E) 244 at 249; *Carkeek v Tate-Jones* [1971] VR 691 at 697ff).

17 *Pettitt v Pettitt* [1970] AC 777 at 815E-F; *Northern Bank Ltd v Henry* [1981] IR 1 at 18; *Allied Irish Banks Ltd v McWilliams* [1982] NI 156 at 161D; *Doohan v Nelson* [1973] 2 NSWLR 320 at 327D; *Brophy v Brophy* (1974) 3 ACTR 57 at 60; *Taddeo v Taddeo* (1978) 19 SASR 347 at 365, 367; *Muschinski v Dodds* (1985) 160 CLR 583 at 590 per Gibbs CJ.

18 It seems that the presumption of advancement still obtains in the Republic of Ireland (see *Heavey v Heavey* [1977] 111 ILTR 1 at 3; *M v M* [1980] 114 ILTR 46 at 49) and in Australia (see *Doohan v Nelson* [1973] 2 NSWLR 320 at 325E; *Napier v Public Trustee (Western Australia)* (1980) 32 ALR 153 at 158).

19 The presumption of advancement 'found its place in Victorian days when a wife was utterly subordinate to her husband. It has no place, or, at any rate, very little place, in our law today' (*Falconer v Falconer* [1970] 1 WLR 1333 at 1335H–1336A per Lord Denning MR).

v Pettitt,[20] where Lord Diplock thought that it would be 'an abuse of legal technique ... to apply to transactions between the post-war generation of married couples 'presumptions' which are based upon inferences of fact which an earlier generation of judges drew as to the most likely intentions of earlier generations of spouses belonging to the propertied classes of a different social era.'[1]

The contemporary disfavour for the social philosophy of advancement has led to an almost irresistible movement away from the presumption, at least in the context of spousal transactions concerning land. It would seem that the presumption of advancement can now play only an extremely marginal role in determining between living spouses questions of equitable ownership.[2] In few cases will recourse to the presumption be necessary or conclusive, for it will be a rare case in which evidence of actual intention is completely absent. Where, however, the presumption is applicable, its strength may well require to be assessed relative to the date of the disputed purchase and to the age and social outlook of the particular spouses.[3] In *Re Hogg (Deceased)*,[4] for example, the presumption was held to be more readily applicable to spouses born at the end of the last century who married in 1930 with the benefit of a marriage settlement and who each possessed substantial capital assets of his or her own. Cultural factors may also influence the court, as in *Taddeo v Taddeo*,[5] where Bray CJ declined to apply a presumption of resulting trust in favour of an Italian wife, on the ground that there was evidence that she, 'as would be normal for a wife in Italy', had trusted her Italian husband 'to perform his moral obligation to use his money as well as hers for the benefit of the family without expecting any proprietary interest for herself'.

What little force the presumption retains can of course be rebutted by evidence of a contrary intention on the part of the spouses.[6] Only where this contrary intention involves some element of fraud or illegality will the courts decline to admit evidence tending to rebut the presumption of

20 [1970] AC 777 at 824C. See also Lord Reid (at 793E-F).

1 It is notable in any event that in *Pettitt* Lord Upjohn remained unrepentant about the role of the equitable presumptions. He acknowledged that they had been 'criticised as being out of touch with the realities of today', but maintained that 'when properly understood and properly applied to the circumstances of today ... they remain as useful as ever in solving questions of title' ([1970] AC 777 at 813G-H). See also *Calverley v Green* (1984) 155 CLR 242 at 265f per Deane J.

2 *Pettitt v Pettitt* [1970] AC 777 at 811G per Lord Hodson; *Gissing v Gissing* [1971] AC 886 at 907C-D per Lord Diplock; *Re Berry (A Bankrupt)* [1978] 2 NZLR 373 at 378; *Napier v Public Trustee (Western Australia)* (1980) 32 ALR 153 at 154. See, however, *Harwood v Harwood* [1991] 2 FLR 274 at 294A-B, where Slade LJ found 'nothing sufficient to displace' the presumption of advancement, although noting that the presumption 'must be applied with caution in modern social conditions'.

3 See *Doohan v Nelson* [1973] 2 NSWLR 320 at 326A.

4 Unreported, Chancery Division, 1982 H No 2830, 11 July 1983.

5 (1978) 19 SASR 347 at 366f.

6 *Organ v Sandwell* [1921] VLR 622 at 626, 629; *Allen v Snyder* [1977] 2 NSWLR 685 at 690A. In *Doohan v Nelson* [1973] 2 NSWLR 320 at 329C, significance was attached to the fact that the husband still used the wife's house as security for borrowings for his own purposes. See generally J. Martin, [1992] Conv 153.

advancement.[7] Thus an advancement may still be presumed in favour of a married woman if the husband's motive in placing or purchasing property in her name was to defeat the potential claims of his own creditors. Such a transaction is vitiated by illegal purpose if it amounts to an agreement by the spouses to vest a title in the wife 'so that they might both pretend to anyone who became a creditor that she was the beneficial owner, but with a secret agreement that she would reconvey the interest to him when he wanted it'.[8] A husband cannot be heard to maintain as against his creditors that his family home belongs to his wife, while maintaining as against his wife that the house still belongs in equity to himself.[9] Likewise, a conveyance into a wife's name for tax reasons takes effect as a gift to her in equity too,[10] at least so long as the transaction was not merely an attempt to minimise the incidence of taxation, but involved a further element of criminal non-disclosure penalised by the relevant tax code.[11]

The combined operation of the presumptions of resulting trust and advancement in the spousal context is best explained in a number of examples.

(i) H's funds used for a purchase in the name of W Where a husband purchases a legal title in his wife's name, it may be that in the absence of all other evidence he is presumed to have intended that she should take both the legal and equitable ownership.[12] However, it is questionable whether today the presumption of advancement retains even this degree of residual strength. Its severely diminished role under modern conditions was indicated by the Privy Council in *Neo Tai Kim v Foo Stie Wah.*[13] Here Lord Brightman declared that the presumption of advancement is 'not an immutable rule to be applied blindly where there is no direct evidence as to the common intention of the spouses. It is rather a guideline to be followed by the court in an appropriate case where it searches for the intention which ought, in the absence of evidence, to be imputed to the parties.'

(ii) H's funds used for a purchase in joint names If a husband purchases a legal title in the joint names of himself and his wife, then in the total absence of all other evidence the spouses would seem to be joint tenants in equity

7 This application of the 'clean hands' doctrine was explained in terms of Lord Eldon LC's statement in *Muckleston v Brown* (1801) 6 Ves Jun 52 at 69, 31 ER 934 at 942, that the plaintiff 'coming to equity to be relieved against his own act, and the defence being dishonest, between the two species of dishonesty the Court would not act; but would say, "Let the estate lie where it falls".' See also *Goodfriend v Goodfriend* (1972) 22 DLR (3d) 699 at 703, but compare *Moody v Cox & Hatt* [1917] 2 Ch 71 at 87f. See also *Tinsley v Milligan* [1992] Ch 310 at 323F-324E per Nicholls LJ.

8 *David v Szoke* (1974) 39 DLR (3d) 707 at 719. See also *Gascoigne v Gascoigne* [1918] 1 KB 223 at 226f, but compare *Goodfriend v Goodfriend* (1972) 22 DLR (3d) 699 at 707.

9 See eg *Tinker v Tinker* [1970] P 136 at 141G-H; *Cantor v Cox* (1976) 239 Estates Gazette 121 at 123; *Maysels v Maysels* (1974) 45 DLR (3d) 337 at 345f, affd (1976) 64 DLR (3d) 765 (Supreme Court of Canada). See G. Kodilinye, (1980) 9 Anglo-Am L Rev 28.

10 *Miller v Miller* (1983) 39 OR (2d) 74 at 81. See also *Martin v Martin* (1959) 110 CLR 297 at 305f. See also *Webb v Webb* [1991] 1 WLR 1410 at 1419F-G (transfer designed to avoid exchange control), but compare *Sekhon v Alissa* [1989] 2 FLR 94 at 98A-C.

11 *In re Emery's Investment Trusts* [1959] Ch 410 at 422.

12 *Pettitt v Pettitt* [1970] AC 777 at 815E per Lord Upjohn; *Pearson v Pearson* [1961] VR 693 at 698.

13 Unreported, Privy Council No 30 of 1982, 4 March 1985. See also *McFarlane v McFarlane* [1972] NI 59 at 75.

also.[14] To this extent, again, the presumption of advancement has a residual function, but the position is more likely to be confirmed by evidence of an actual intention expressed by the spouses in favour of joint equitable ownership.[15]

(iii) W's funds used for a purchase in the name of H If a wife purchases a legal title in her husband's name, he probably holds on a resulting trust for her,[16] 'but in practice there will in almost every case be some explanation (however slight) of this (today) rather unusual course.'[17]

(iv) W's funds used for a purchase in joint names If a wife purchases a legal title in the joint names of herself and her husband, in the absence of any other evidence the inference may be that the spouses were intended to be joint owners in equity also. As Lord Upjohn once said, there seems to be 'no other reason for it.'[18] However, if this form of vesting is explicable on another footing (eg because the wife believed that she would not obtain a mortgage loan unless her husband was on the legal title), there may be a resulting trust for the wife absolutely as the sole provider of the moneys.[19]

(v) Joint funds used for acquisition of a legal title If both spouses contribute to the purchase of a legal title, there is high authority for the view that they are to be taken, in the absence of all other evidence, as having intended to be beneficial owners in the proportions contributed.[20] For this purpose, it seems to be irrelevant whether the legal title is purchased in the name of the husband or of the wife or, indeed, in the names of both.[1] Even the fact that such a purchase is put in the name of the wife appears to be insufficient to found any claim to an advancement in her favour,[2] unless perhaps the husband's financial contribution is 'very small'.[3]

It has sometimes been suggested that if, in any of these situations, the husband makes a larger financial contribution than the wife, the excess of

14 *Pettitt v Pettitt* [1970] AC 777 at 815E; *Re Hogg (Deceased)* (Unreported, Chancery Division, 1982 H No 2830, 11 July 1983); *Calverley v Green* (1984) 155 CLR 242 at 256 per Mason and Brennan JJ. Compare, however, *Pearson v Pearson* [1961] VR 693 at 698, where the Full Court of the Supreme Court of Victoria thought that, in the absence of an actual donative intent, there would be a resulting trust for the provider of the purchase moneys.

15 There is a statutory presumption in some jurisdictions that a vesting of legal title in the joint names of husband and wife is prima facie proof that each spouse is intended on severance to have a one-half beneficial interest in the property (see eg Ontario's Family Law Reform Act 1978 (RSO 1980, c 152), s 11(1)(a); Nova Scotia's Matrimonial Property Act 1980, s 21(1)(a)).

16 See eg *Northern Bank Ltd v Henry* [1981] IR 1 at 8, 18.

17 *Pettitt v Pettitt* [1970] AC 777 at 815E-F per Lord Upjohn. See also *Pearson v Pearson* [1961] VR 693 at 698.

18 *Pettitt v Pettitt* [1970] AC 777 at 815F. Compare, however, *Pearson v Pearson* [1961] VR 693 at 698, where once again the Full Court thought that, absent an actual donative intent, there would be a resulting trust for the provider of the purchase moneys.

19 *Allied Irish Banks Ltd v McWilliams* [1982] NI 156 at 160D, 161D.

20 *Pettitt v Pettitt* [1970] AC 777 at 815F-G per Lord Upjohn; *McFarlane v McFarlane* [1972] NI 59 at 67 per Lord MacDermott LCJ. See eg *Re Rogers' Question* [1948] 1 All ER 328 at 330A.

1 *Pettitt v Pettitt* [1970] AC 777 at 815G.

2 See *McFarlane v McFarlane* [1972] NI 59 at 75 per Lowry J.

3 *Pettitt v Pettitt* [1970] AC 777 at 815G; *Calverley v Green* (1984) 155 CLR 242 at 259 per Mason and Brennan JJ.

a moiety should be treated as an advancement of the wife, thereby bringing about either a beneficial joint tenancy[4] or tenancy in common in equal shares.[5] However, it seems far preferable to abandon even this residual notion of advancement in favour of saying simply that there is a presumed resulting trust for the spouses as beneficial tenants in common in arithmetic proportion to their respective contributions.[6]

5. CONSTRUCTIVE TRUSTS

The constructive trust is perhaps the most controversial and far-reaching of the devices used by equity in vindication of its own doctrines.[7] In the words of Cardozo J, the constructive trust is

> the formula through which the conscience of equity finds expression. When property has been acquired in such circumstances that the holder of the legal title may not in good conscience retain the beneficial interest, equity converts him into a trustee.[8]

Whether analysed as a 'right' or as a 'remedy',[9] the constructive trust involves a judicial finding that a person should be 'made liable in equity as trustee by the imposition or construction of the court of equity.'[10] Accordingly, the court may well acknowledge that A is the owner of the legal title in 'his' property, but still require that for reasons of consonance with equitable doctrine he should hold that title, in the character of a fiduciary, on an implied trust for B.[11] In its more dramatic manifestations, the imposition of a constructive trust on A amounts effectively to a decree of confiscation, awarding to B property which A had previously thought belonged to himself both at law and in equity. A court-ordered constructive trust which confers an absolute interest on B has the double effect of confirming both the sole equitable title of B and the absence of any beneficial ownership in A.[12]

(1) Role of intention in the creation of the constructive trust

The liability of A as a constructive trustee does not depend directly on any intention on the part of A that he should hold property on trust for B.[13]

4 *Re Hogg (Deceased)* (Unreported, Chancery Division, 1982 H No 2830, 11 July 1983).
5 See *Harwood v Harwood* [1991] 2 FLR 274 at 294A-B.
6 See *Hine v Hine* [1962] 1 WLR 1124 at 1132; *Bernard v Josephs* [1982] Ch 391 at 398A-C. See also *Pearson v Pearson* [1961] VR 693 at 698; *McFarlane v McFarlane* [1972] NI 59 at 74f; *Crisp v Mullings* (1976) 239 Estates Gazette 119 at 121.
7 'In general it may be said that the constructive trust has been a ready means of developing our property law in modern times and that the process is a continuing one' (*Sen v Headley* [1991] Ch 425 at 440B per Nourse LJ).
8 *Beatty v Guggenheim Exploration Co*, 225 NY 380 at 386 (1919), quoted in *Binions v Evans* [1972] Ch 359 at 368C per Lord Denning MR.
9 See *Chase Manhattan Bank NA v Israel-British Bank (London) Ltd* [1981] Ch 105 at 124F-G per Goulding J; *Allen v Snyder* [1977] 2 NSWLR 685 at 703C.
10 *Selangor United Rubber Estates Ltd v Cradock* (No 3) [1968] 1 WLR 1555 at 1582A-B.
11 See *Muschinski v Dodds* (1985) 160 CLR 583 at 616f per Deane J.
12 Not every constructive trust confers an absolute equitable interest on B. It is equally feasible, in certain circumstances, that a constructive trust may be imposed on A, directing him to hold on trust for some lesser equitable entitlement on the part of B (see eg *Bannister v Bannister* [1948] 2 All ER 133, post, p 438).
13 *Muschinski v Dodds* (1985) 160 CLR 583 at 613 per Deane J.

The reality is usually quite the reverse, for the imposition of trust liability is normally the last result desired or contemplated by A.[14] Indeed, in most cases, A is made a constructive trustee by intervention of the court precisely because he has sought to *avoid* liability as a fiduciary. The imposition of constructive trusteeship rests primarily not upon intention, but upon the fact that A has, by some prior agreement or bargain, taken upon himself a fiduciary role which he cannot now be heard to disavow. As Dixon J said in *Cohen v Cohen*,[15] the constructive trust represents an instance 'where the equity is fastened upon the trustee not because he intended to become the fiduciary of property but because of the character of his dealings and in spite of his intention to take the property for himself.'[16] However, although not the direct product of intention, the constructive trust operates against the background of—and indeed is ultimately premised upon—some bargain or common intention which now makes the assertion of absolute beneficial entitlement unconscionable.[17] Where the owner of a legal title has entered into an agreement, since acted upon, to share or allocate beneficial ownership in some particular way, equity will not allow him to deny the beneficial interest conceded and 'will construct a trust to give effect to it.'[18]

(2) General principle underlying the constructive trust

It is an inveterate doctrine of equity that no person who holds property in a fiduciary capacity may ever be permitted to set up an inconsistent personal claim in respect of that property.[19] The rigour of this rule is preserved with great diligence. As long ago as *Keech v Sandford*[20] it was conceded that it 'may seem hard, that the trustee is the only person of all mankind' who is debarred from deriving personal advantage from the property which he holds on trust, but, as King LC said, 'it is very proper that rule should be strictly pursued, and not in the least relaxed.' This vigilance on the part of equity provides the basis of the constructive trust.[1] A constructive trust will be imposed by the court in any case where a fiduciary seeks to deny that his title to property is qualified by his own status as a fiduciary.[2]

(a) Role of bargain

It may well be asked how, for present purposes, a fiduciary status comes to impinge at all upon the ownership of a legal title in land. This question

14 See *Rathwell v Rathwell* (1978) 83 DLR (3d) 289 at 305.
15 (1929) 42 CLR 91 at 100.
16 See also *White v Cabanas Pty Ltd* (No 2) [1970] Qd R 395 at 408A; *Allen v Snyder* [1977] 2 NSWLR 685 at 690B; *McMahon v McMahon* [1979] VR 239 at 244; *South Yarra Project Pty Ltd* v *Gentsis* [1985] VR 29 at 37.
17 See *Allen v Snyder* [1977] 2 NSWLR 685 at 693A-B; *Baumgartner v Baumgartner* [1985] 2 NSWLR 406 at 435A-B.
18 *Grant v Edwards* [1986] Ch 638 at 646H-647A per Nourse LJ.
19 *Parker v McKenna* (1874) LR 10 Ch 96 at 124; *Meinhard v Salmon*, 164 NE 545 at 546 (1928); *Malsbury v Malsbury* [1982] 1 NSWLR 226 at 231C.
20 (1726) 2 Eq Ca Abr 741, 22 ER 629, Sel Cas T King 61 at 62, 25 ER 223.
1 Ante, p 383.
2 'Strictly, constructive trusts arise where one who is already a trustee or otherwise clothed with fiduciary character seeks to retain an advantage from his trust' (*Cowcher v Cowcher* [1972] 1 WLR 425 at 431A).

was addressed directly by the House of Lords in *Gissing v Gissing*.[3] Here Lord Diplock observed that the preceding case law on constructive trusts had largely passed over the first—and critical—stage in the analysis of this form of trust, ie, 'the role of . . . agreement . . . in the creation of an equitable estate in real property.'[4] The equitable interest to which the constructive trust gives effect results invariably from some anterior bargain or agreement relating to the property, by which an owner of a legal title has undertaken to give effect to an equitable entitlement in someone else.

(b) Role of conscience

It has already been seen that an express agreement by A, conferring on B a beneficial interest in A's land, is potentially creative of an express trust in respect of that land.[5] Such a declaration of trust is enforceable by B provided that it is evidenced in writing in accordance with section 53(1)(b) of the Law of Property Act 1925.[6] But if it is not evidenced by a duly signed document, the declaration of trust remains purely oral and therefore unenforceable as an express trust.[7]

This, however, is not the end of the story: the legal effect of the oral agreement is not yet spent. As Lord Diplock pointed out in *Gissing v Gissing*,[8] the court may still give effect to the agreement as to beneficial ownership, notwithstanding the absence of written evidence of the trust thereby declared. Equity's willingness to enforce a trust in this context is attributable quite simply to the fact that A, the legal owner, may have 'so conducted himself that it would be inequitable to allow him to deny to [B] a beneficial interest'. Such circumstances will arise, characteristically, if A 'by his words or conduct has induced [B] to act to his own detriment in the reasonable belief that by so acting he was acquiring a beneficial interest in the land.'[9] If by no other means, equity will frustrate the unconscionable behaviour of A through the imposition of a constructive trust in favour of B.[10] Unlike the antecedent oral declaration of trust, this constructive trust is fully enforceable by B, precisely because constructive trusts are, by section 53(2) of the Law of Property Act 1925, exempted from any requirement of formal writing.

(3) Component elements of the constructive trust

Given this account of the general principle underlying the constructive trust, it becomes possible to say that the imposition of a constructive trust requires

3 [1971] AC 886 (ante, p 383; post, p 431).
4 [1971] AC 886 at 904G. For reference in this context to the terminology of 'bargain', see *Grant v Edwards* [1986] Ch 638 at 651G–652B, 653D per Mustill LJ. The pre-eminent significance of agreement as a factor in the formative phase of the constructive trust has since been heavily re-emphasised by the House of Lords in *Lloyds Bank Plc v Rosset* [1991] 1 AC 107 at 132E-F per Lord Bridge of Harwich.
5 Ante, p 375.
6 If the trust is declared in proper form, the doctrine of constructive trust cannot be invoked to contradict it (see *Goodman v Gallant* [1986] Fam 106 at 116F-G).
7 Post, p 418.
8 [1971] AC 886 at 905D-E.
9 [1971] AC 886 at 905B-C (ante, p 383).
10 See *Grant v Edwards* [1986] Ch 638 at 646H–647A per Nourse LJ.

proof of three elements.[11] The facts must disclose (a) a common intention, (b) a change of position, and (c) equitable fraud. These three elements are, however, almost inextricably inter-related. For the purpose of establishing a constructive trust, a common intention is recognised as relevant only if comprised within some form of 'bargain' under which one party changes his position. A change of position occurs in the relevant sense only if it is truly referable to a common intention that rights of beneficial ownership should be acknowledged by the legal owner. Equitable fraud is present only if the legal owner then tries to escape from the 'bargain' by asserting the absolute, exclusive or unqualified nature of his own rights.

Thus stated, the constituent elements of the constructive trust bear a remarkable similarity to the features of proprietary estoppel.[12] It is not uncommon to find that in many cases arguments based on constructive trust and proprietary estoppel are pleaded in the alternative.[13] The elements of the constructive trust must now be examined more closely.

(4) Common intention

In strict theory every constructive trust derives ultimately from some bargain which affects the conscience of the party who is eventually made liable as constructive trustee.[14] For instance, if A, the owner of a legal title, has made some agreement to recognise the existence of equitable rights in B, it is unconscionable for A later to disown this common intention if, in the meantime, the agreement has induced a change of position by the other party to the agreement. Likewise, if A has purchased from X land which, to the knowledge of A, is already the subject of some bargain between B and X, then A will be made to hold that land on a constructive trust for B.

(a) Parties to the agreement or common intention

It follows that no crucial importance is attached to the precise origin of the agreement or common intention which underlies constructive trust liability. It is sufficient merely that there is some anterior 'bargain' relating to equitable rights in B which affects the property in such a way as to impinge on the conscience of A, the current legal owner. It matters not whether

11 See *Ogilvie v Ryan* [1976] 2 NSWLR 504 at 516G–517A; *Hohol v Hohol* [1981] VR 221 at 225; *Butler v Craine* [1986] VR 274 at 283; *Higgins v Wingfield* [1987] VR 689 at 690, 699.

12 Post, p 428. See *Grant v Edwards* [1986] Ch 638 at 656H per Browne-Wilkinson V-C ('The two principles have been developed separately without cross-fertilisation between them: but they rest on the same foundation and have on all other matters reached the same conclusions'). In *Austin v Keele* (1987) 10 NSWLR 283 at 290F Lord Oliver of Aylmerton indicated that Lord Diplock's formulation of a doctrine of implied trusts in *Gissing v Gissing* [1971] AC 886 was '[i]n essence . . . an application of proprietary estoppel.'

13 Post, pp 424, 425.

14 See *Nemeth v Nemeth* (1978) 17 ALR 500 at 503. In this context a distinction should be maintained between the *constructive trust* (to which reference is made here) and the *constructive trusteeship* which may be imposed on those who participate by way of knowing receipt or assistance in the commission of equitable fraud.

this 'bargain' was incorporated (as it more usually is) in an agreement between A and B directly[15] or whether it took the form of an undertaking given by A to a stranger, X.[16] It is even possible that the 'bargain' may not have been made by A at all, but may have been concluded between B and X in circumstances of which A has actual or deemed knowledge.[17] In all of these examples it may well be that A's conscience is bound by the bargain in a way which makes him guilty of equitable fraud should he ever attempt to defeat the agreement.

(b) Time-frame of the agreement

Whereas a resulting trust can arise only in respect of an intention which is presumed to have been present at the date of acquisition of the trust property,[18] the precise timing of the agreement or 'bargain' which underlies the constructive trust appears much less relevant.

It matters not whether the agreement guaranteeing equitable rights for B precedes[19] or is contemporaneous with[20] the acquisition of the legal estate in the name of A. In either case A can be said to have taken his title subject to a fiduciary obligation towards B which, if breached by A, may lead to the imposition of a constructive trust. The constructive trust is, however, capable of somewhat wider application. It may be imposed in order to give effect to a 'bargain' or common intention to recognise beneficial rights in B, even though the relevant agreement between A and B occurred only some time *after* A's acquisition of title.[1] In this respect, the constructive trust is rather more flexible than the express trust. It is true that an express trust for B may be declared by A after the date on which he acquires his title to land, but the enforceability of this kind of post-acquisition trust is dependent upon compliance with the statutory requirement of written evidence.[2] However, a constructive trust arising in the same context is enforceable even though the agreement or common intention on which it is based was never statutorily evidenced.

15 See eg *Bannister v Bannister* [1948] 2 All ER 133 (post, p 438).
16 See eg *Binions v Evans* [1972] Ch 359 (post, p 917); *Lyus v Prowsa Developments Ltd* [1982] 1 WLR 1044 (post, p 440); *Anstalt v Arnold* [1989] Ch 1 (post, p 920).
17 See eg *Peffer v Rigg* [1977] 1 WLR 285; *White v Cabanas Pty Ltd* (No 2) [1970] Qd R 395 at 408B.
18 Ante, p 387.
19 This is so at least if the property concerned is specific and identifiable and was, at the time of the agreement, within the contemplation of both A and B (see *Le Compte v Public Trustee* [1983] 2 NSWLR 109 at 111A).
20 *Pettitt v Pettitt* [1970] AC 777 at 813D per Lord Upjohn.
1 In *Lloyds Bank Plc v Rosset* [1991] 1 AC 107 at 132E-F, Lord Bridge of Harwich thought that only 'exceptionally' could a constructive trust be founded upon an agreement reached at some date later than that of acquisition. (See also *Hammond v Mitchell* [1991] 1 WLR 1127 at 1129F.) This restrictive note is not, however, generally echoed in the case law. See eg *Gissing v Gissing* [1971] AC 886 at 901D per Viscount Dilhorne, 906E-F per Lord Diplock; *Bernard v Josephs* [1982] Ch 391 at 404D-E; *Burns v Burns* [1984] Ch 317 at 327D per Fox LJ; *Layton v Martin* [1986] 2 FLR 227 at 236E-F; *Grant v Edwards* [1986] Ch 638 at 651G–652A per Mustill LJ; *Gough v Fraser* [1977] 1 NZLR 279 at 283; *Allen v Snyder* [1977] 2 NSWLR 685 at 691C; *McMahon v McMahon* [1979] VR 239 at 244; *Butler v Craine* [1986] VR 274 at 285ff.
2 *Wratten v Hunter* [1978] 2 NSWLR 367 at 371B (ante, p 376).

(c) Form of the agreement or common intention

Recent developments have made it clear that the application of constructive trust doctrine in English law is closely controlled by the precise form taken by the agreement, bargain or common intention which necessarily lies at its base. The required element of common intention may be manifested in one or other of two distinct forms—either as an *express bargain* or as an *implied bargain.*[3] It now appears that these divergent forms of bargain each correlate with significantly differing standards of proof in respect of the detriment or 'change of position' which must also be shown to exist as the precondition of any constructive trust.[4]

(i) Express bargain Although it perhaps happens only rarely,[5] it is possible that an express bargain respecting beneficial ownership may have been reached between A, the owner of the legal title, and B, the claimant of an equitable interest. An express agreement of this kind must be sharply distinguished from any implied bargain which rests merely upon inferences drawn from the conduct of the parties. Where there is 'an express agreement [between A and B] as to the way in which the beneficial interest shall be held,' said Lord Diplock in *Gissing v Gissing*,[6] the court 'will give effect to it—notwithstanding the absence of any written declaration of trust.'[7] This express verbal agreement must of course be supported by some change of position on the part of B. As Lord Diplock pointed out,[8] an agreement which fails to 'provide for anything to be done' by B is 'a merely voluntary declaration of trust and unenforceable for want of writing.'[9] In the absence of writing a trust 'does not come into being merely from a gratuitous intention to transfer or create a beneficial interest.'[10] There must be some form of *bargain* struck between the parties either before the acquisition of the legal title 'or exceptionally at some later date'.[11]

In this context a premium is placed upon clear evidence that the relevant parties have 'orally declared themselves in such a way as to make plain their common intention that the claimant should have a beneficial interest

3 See the reference in *Grant v Edwards* [1986] Ch 638 at 654F-H per Browne-Wilkinson V-C to the distinction between 'direct evidence' of common intention and 'inferred common intention'.

4 It has been said that prior to the decision of the Court of Appeal in *Grant v Edwards* [1986] Ch 638 the distinction between the two categories of common intention or bargain 'had not been clearly perceived' (see *Stokes v Anderson* [1991] 1 FLR 391 at 398F-G per Nourse LJ).

5 See *Grant v Edwards* [1986] Ch 638 at 647C per Nourse LJ; *Stokes v Anderson* [1991] 1 FLR 391 at 398A per Nourse LJ. As Lord Hodson observed in *Pettitt v Pettitt* [1970] AC 777 at 810E-F, the conception of 'a normal married couple spending the long winter evenings hammering out agreements about their possessions appears grotesque'. See also *Lloyds Bank Plc v Rosset* [1991] 1 AC 107 at 127H-128A per Lord Bridge of Harwich.

6 [1971] AC 886 at 905D-E.

7 In other words, what would have been wholly unenforceable as an express trust (ante, p 376) may become effective instead as a constructive trust.

8 [1971] AC 886 at 905E.

9 Post, p 425.

10 *Austin v Keele* (1987) 10 NSWLR 283 at 291B-C per Lord Oliver of Aylmerton (Judicial Committee of the Privy Council).

11 *Lloyds Bank Plc v Rosset* [1991] 1 AC 107 at 132E-F (ante, p 417).

in the property'.[12] As Lord Bridge of Harwich held in *Lloyds Bank Plc v Rosset*,[13] there must have been some 'agreement, arrangement or understanding reached between them that the property is to be shared beneficially.' Speaking in the context of a family home, Lord Bridge went on to indicate that the finding of such an agreement or arrangement 'can only ... be based on evidence of express discussions between the partners, however imperfectly remembered and however imprecise their terms may have been.'[14] The express bargain must comprise 'a shared intention communicated between' the relevant parties.[15] The consensus ad idem must be a demonstrable reality: the required common intention is not sufficiently established even if each of the parties independently 'happened to be thinking on the same lines in his or her uncommunicated thoughts'.[16] In this respect, as Steyn LJ remarked in *Springette v Defoe*,[17] the court does not recognise communication 'at a subconscious level ... Our trust law does not allow property rights to be affected by telepathy.' In the absence of a bargain embodied in *express* negotiation and discussion,[18] claims of beneficial entitlement can be made good only under the somewhat more rigorous criteria which apply to constructive trusts founded on *implied* bargain.[19]

The 'primary emphasis' now accorded to express discussions means that 'the tenderest exchanges of a common law courtship may assume an unforeseen significance many years later when they are brought under equity's microscope'.[20] Under this analysis 'many thousands of pounds of value may be liable to turn on fine questions as to whether the relevant words were spoken in earnest or in dalliance and with or without representational intent.'[1] In *Lloyds Bank Plc v Rosset*[2] Lord Bridge instanced as outstanding examples of the 'express bargain' category of constructive trust the circumstances of *Eves v Eves*[3] and *Grant v Edwards*.[4] In both cases the claimant (the female partner in a relationship) had been explicitly led by the male partner to

12 *Stokes v Anderson* [1991] 1 FLR 391 at 398A per Nourse LJ. Such direct evidence of common intention 'need have nothing to do with the contributions made to the cost of acquisition' (see *Grant v Edwards* [1986] Ch 638 at 655D per Browne-Wilkinson V-C).

13 [1991] 1 AC 107 at 132E-F. See (1990) 106 LQR 539 (J.D. Davies); [1991] CLJ 38 (M. Dixon).

14 See also *Hammond v Mitchell* [1991] 1 WLR 1127 at 1129F.

15 *Springette v Defoe* [1992] 2 FLR 388 at 393D per Dillon LJ. See eg *Hammond v Mitchell* [1991] 1 WLR 1127 at 1137A-B, although compare [1992] Conv 218 at 220 (A. Lawson).

16 *Springette v Defoe* [1992] 2 FLR 388 at 393F-G per Dillon LJ.

17 [1992] 2 FLR 388 at 394H.

18 See eg *Springette v Defoe* [1992] 2 FLR 388 at 393G, 397B.

19 Post, p 427.

20 *Hammond v Mitchell* [1991] 1 WLR 1127 at 1139C-D per Waite J.

1 As Lord Bridge observed in *Lloyds Bank Plc v Rosset* [1991] 1 AC 107 at 127G, evidence of express discussions is now the 'vital issue' raised in pleadings in this area. It is 'of prime importance' for both parties that affidavit assertions of express agreement are made with a high degree of particularity, since the case may otherwise founder for vagueness or, alternatively, the legal owner may not know exactly what case he must meet (see *Hammond v Mitchell* [1991] 1 WLR 1127 at 1139E-F).

2 [1991] 1 AC 107 at 133C-F.

3 [1975] 1 WLR 1338 (post, p 429). See (1976) 92 LQR 489 (F. Webb); R.H. Maudsley, (1977) 28 NILQ 123 at 132f.

4 [1986] Ch 638 (post, p 420). See [1986] Conv 291 (J. Warburton); [1986] CLJ 394 (D.J. Hayton); (1986) 130 SJ 347 (P.M. Rank).

believe, when they established a home together, that the property would belong to them jointly. In *Eves* the female partner had been told that the legal title in the home was vested in her partner's sole name only because she was then under 21 years of age. Similarly in *Grant v Edwards* the male partner had informed the claimant that the only reason for not acquiring their home in joint names was the fact that she was involved in divorce proceedings and that, if the property were acquired jointly, this might operate to her prejudice in these proceedings. In both cases the evidence pointed to a clear common intention, expressly adverted to in the parties' discussions, that, when these special circumstances were displaced, some form of shared ownership would be entirely appropriate.[5]

(ii) Implied bargain In the absence of an express bargain based upon direct negotiations, a constructive trust may be founded upon an implied bargain inferred from the conduct of the relevant parties.[6] It has long been clear that the court, in eliciting common intention, may rely on inferences drawn from the conduct and mutual dealings of the parties.[7] As Lord Bridge confirmed in *Lloyds Bank Plc v Rosset*,[8] the pattern of such conduct or dealings may not only provide a 'basis from which to infer a common intention to share the property beneficially' but may also serve as evidence of the change of position required to raise the constructive trust.[9]

The process of determining whether the parties' conduct discloses evidence of any implied bargain is, of course, detailed, time-consuming and laborious. The court must engage in an 'inferential analysis involving a scrutiny of all events potentially capable of throwing evidential light on the question whether, in the absence of express discussion, a presumed intention can be spelt out of the parties' past course of dealing.'[10]

(iii) The demonstrable reality of bargain The role of bargain is central to the operation of the constructive trust and it is well established that the bargain, whether express or implied, must be a demonstrable fact. There must be evidence in all cases of an authentic agreement or common intention reached between A and B.[11] While the court may 'infer' a common intention which is plainly evidenced by the conduct of A and B, the court may not impute

5 See *Eves v Eves* [1975] 1 WLR 1338 at 1345B per Brightman J; *Grant v Edwards* [1986] Ch 638 at 649A-B per Nourse LJ.

6 In *Grant v Edwards* [1986] Ch 638 at 655F-G, Browne-Wilkinson V-C emphasised that express verbal declarations of intended co-ownership—if present on the facts—make it unnecessary for the court to have recourse to inferences based on other forms of conduct.

7 See *Gissing v Gissing* [1971] AC 886 at 900G, 902G, 908E-G; *Burns v Burns* [1984] Ch 317 at 336E-F, 344H-345A; *Allen v Snyder* [1977] 2 NSWLR 685 at 691D; *McMahon v McMahon* [1979] VR 239 at 244; *Boccalatte v Bushelle* [1980] Qd R 180 at 185F; *Hohol v Hohol* [1981] VR 221 at 226; *Hayward v Giordani* [1983] NZLR 140 at 151; *Butler v Craine* [1986] VR 274 at 285.

8 [1991] 1 AC 107 at 132H-133A.

9 Post, p 430.

10 *Hammond v Mitchell* [1991] 1 WLR 1127 at 1129H per Waite J.

11 *Allen v Snyder* [1977] 2 NSWLR 685 at 694A; *Baumgartner v Baumgartner* [1985] 2 NSWLR 406 at 435B.

to them an intention which they never actually had.[12] It is widely accepted[13] that there is no jurisdiction to impute to the parties a fictitious common intention that B should be beneficially entitled, even if it is highly probable that such an agreement would in any event have been reached by the parties had they only considered the issue[14] or would have been fair, just or reasonable in all the circumstances.[15]

The detailed substance of any bargain concluded between the parties is determined objectively.[16] In *Gissing v Gissing*[17] Lord Diplock indicated that, in so far as the law of constructive trusts rests upon a common intention, 'the relevant intention of each party is the intention which was reasonably understood by the other party to be manifested by that party's words or conduct notwithstanding that he did not consciously formulate that intention in his own mind or even acted with some different intention which he did not communicate to the other party.'[18] Effect is given to 'the inferences as to the intentions of parties to a transaction which a reasonable man would draw from their words or conduct and not to any subjective intention or absence of intention which was not made manifest at the time of the transaction itself.'[19]

(iv) The practical unrealism of the bargain requirement It is ultimately the unrealistic requirement of demonstrable bargain, now regularly confirmed by the House of Lords at twenty-year intervals,[20] which has exerted a tight stranglehold over the development of any rational law of family property in England. English courts have always seen the origin of the trust as founded in some common intention or conscious bargain directed towards the diffusion

12 See *Grant v Edwards* [1986] Ch 638 at 651G–652A per Mustill LJ; *Butler v Craine* [1986] VR 274 at 285; *Cooke v Cooke* [1987] VR 625 at 638. For recognition of 'the uncertain boundaries between inference and conjecture', see *Doohan v Nelson* [1973] 2 NSWLR 320 at 329E. For a case on the borderline, see *Eves v Eves* [1975] 1 WLR 1338 at 1345D-F (post, p 429).

13 Isolated statements to the contrary can be found (see eg Lord Reid in *Pettitt v Pettitt* [1970] AC 777 at 795C-F; *Gissing v Gissing* [1971] AC 886 at 897F-G). Such propositions have not, however, commanded general support (see *Allen v Snyder* [1977] 2 NSWLR 685 at 694B; *Muschinski v Dodds* (1985) 160 CLR 583 at 595 per Gibbs CJ).

14 *Pettitt v Pettitt* [1970] AC 777 at 804H–805A, 810F, 816D; *Gissing v Gissing* [1971] AC 886 at 898C, 900E-F, 904E-F; *In re Densham (A Bankrupt)* [1975] 1 WLR 1519 at 1524E-F; *Burns v Burns* [1984] Ch 317 at 326D, 335G; *Grant v Edwards* [1986] Ch 638 at 652F; *McFarlane v McFarlane* [1972] NI 59 at 71; *Allen v Snyder* [1977] 2 NSWLR 685 at 690F, 694A-B, 696F-G; *Avondale Printers & Stationers Ltd v Haggie* [1979] 2 NZLR 124 at 146; *McMahon v McMahon* [1979] VR 239 at 244; *Malsbury v Malsbury* [1982] 1 NSWLR 226 at 230B.

15 *Pettitt v Pettitt* [1970] AC 777 at 805A, 808B-C; *Gissing v Gissing* [1971] AC 886 at 900E-F, 904E-F; *Cowcher v Cowcher* [1972] 1 WLR 425 at 429H; *Burns v Burns* [1984] Ch 317 at 334B-C; *McFarlane v McFarlane* [1972] NI 59 at 76f; *Lloyds Bank Plc v Rosset* [1991] 1 AC 107 at 132G-H per Lord Bridge of Harwich; *Allen v Snyder* [1977] 2 NSWLR 685 at 690D, F; *Avondale Printers & Stationers Ltd v Haggie* [1979] 2 NZLR 124 at 145f; *Baumgartner v Baumgartner* [1985] 2 NSWLR 406 at 412F-G.

16 *Burns v Burns* [1984] Ch 317 at 336F per May LJ. See also *Pearson v Pearson* [1961] VR 693 at 698.

17 [1971] AC 886 at 906B-C.

18 See *Calverley v Green* (1984) 155 CLR 242 at 261; *Baumgartner v Baumgartner* [1985] 2 NSWLR 406 at 412F-G.

19 [1971] AC 886 at 906C-D per Lord Diplock. See also *Eves v Eves* [1975] 1 WLR 1338 at 1342E; *Springette v Defoe* [1992] 2 FLR 388 at 397D per Sir Christopher Slade.

20 See *Gissing v Gissing* [1971] AC 886; *Lloyds Bank Plc v Rosset* [1991] 1 AC 107.

of equitable ownership.[1] The inevitable result of this approach has been the frequent denial of equitable entitlement in the context of family arrangements, purely and simply on the ground that the relevant participants failed to advert in any precise or legalistic way to the property consequences of their relationship.[2] The application of trust doctrine in both *Gissing*'s case and *Rosset*'s case can be viewed as regrettably unsympathetic to the realities of family living, since the House of Lords effectively required that beneficial entitlement be proved on the basis of intentions which are rarely articulated or even contemplated in the daily round of domestic life. It is no great surprise that expressly bargained beneficial entitlement is rarely proved to the satisfaction of the court.

(d) Subject matter of the agreement

It is clear that a constructive trust may be raised in respect of any agreement or common intention entered into by A that a recognisable equitable right of property should be acknowledged as belonging to B. It is not necessary that 'the bargain ... should include any express stipulation that [A] is in so many words to hold as trustee.'[3] It is enough that 'the bargain should have included a stipulation under which some sufficiently defined beneficial interest in the property was to be taken by another.'[4]

(i) Origin of the rights enforced Where a constructive trust is imposed on A, the legal owner, in favour of B, the beneficial entitlement thereby confirmed tends to relate to an informal equitable right created de novo by A. It is, however, immaterial—although much less common—that the equitable rights which A undertakes to respect may be pre-existing rights conferred by a separate agreement between, say, B and X; or that B would have had a contractual right in any event to recover damages from X for breach of that separate agreement.[5] A constructive trust can arise simply by reason

1 There is, in one specific context relevant only to husband and wife, a partial relaxation of this dogma of common intention as the basis of beneficial entitlement. Matrimonial Proceedings and Property Act 1970, s 37 creates in effect a rebuttable presumption of common intention as between spouses that certain kinds of improvements made by either to the property of the other shall generate a beneficial interest (or an enlarged beneficial interest) for the 'improving' spouse. Section 37, introduced in order to reverse the approach adopted by the House of Lords in *Pettitt v Pettitt* [1970] AC 777, applies only where a spouse 'contributes in money or money's worth to the improvement' of property. The contribution, if of a 'substantial nature', generates an equitable entitlement whose quantum, in default of agreement between the spouses, is determined by the court in terms of what 'may seem in all the circumstances just'.Section 37 is a little used and not entirely happy provision, driving an uncomfortable distinction between contributions made towards the 'improvement' of property and contributions made towards the acquisition or retention of property. See, however, *In re Nicholson (Decd)* [1974] 1 WLR 476 at 482G–483C (enhanced equitable share on the basis of installation of central heating in the family home).

2 Ante, p 418.

3 *Bannister v Bannister* [1948] 2 All ER 133 at 136D. See also *White v Cabanas Pty Ltd* (No 2) [1970] Qd R 395 at 397F; *Baumgartner v Baumgartner* [1985] 2 NSWLR 406 at 444C.

4 *Bannister v Bannister* [1948] 2 All ER 133 at 136D.

5 *Binions v Evans* [1972] Ch 359 (post, p 917); *Lyus v Prowsa Developments Ltd* [1982] 1 WLR 1044 at 1051E (post, p 440); *White v Cabanas Pty Ltd* (No 2) [1970] Qd R 395 at 399B-C. Indeed, the imposition of a constructive trust on A in *Binions v Evans* has since been explained as having been necessary to save X from an unmerited, but otherwise unavoidable, liability in damages to B (see *Lyus v Prowsa Developments Ltd*, supra, at 1051F-G).

of A's agreement to be bound by X's agreement, at least so long as X's agreement conferred some kind of equitable proprietary right on B.[6]

(ii) Recognised rights Many different kinds of proprietary interest have been recognised as providing appropriate subject matter for a constructive trust. It has been held sufficient to ground constructive trust liability that A has undertaken either that B should have the entire equitable fee simple interest in A's property,[7] or merely that B should have some lesser equitable right such as a life interest,[8] an equitable share as a tenant in common,[9] an estate contract[10] (including an option to purchase[11]) or even a right to the conditional re-transfer of an interest already transferred by B to A.[12] However, the interest conferred or conceded by A—whatever its nature or quantum—must relate to a specific asset or to specific assets.[13]

(iii) Unconventional rights More controversial is the suggestion made by Lord Denning MR in *Binions v Evans*[14] that a constructive trust may give effect to an undertaking by A that B should have a right which is not conventionally acknowledged as an equitable proprietary interest. The interest recognised by way of constructive trust in this case was, in Lord Denning's view, a contractual licence,[15] even though it is generally thought improbable that such a licence can ever constitute a property right in land.[16]

Lord Denning's approach may perhaps be rationalised, as it was by Dillon J in *Lyus v Prowsa Developments Ltd*,[17] on the footing that 'even if the beneficial interest of the claimant in the property concerned has not yet been fully defined, the court may yet intervene to raise a constructive trust on appropriate terms if to leave the defendant retaining the property free from all interest of the claimant would be tantamount to sanctioning a fraud on the part of the defendant.'[18] It was this perspective which more recently influenced

6 It seems also to be irrelevant that the equitable entitlement which A's 'bargain' supposedly conferred on B is later confirmed by a purported testamentary disposition by A in B's favour (see *Hayward v Giordani* [1983] NZLR 140 at 144, 152; but compare *Thwaites v Ryan* [1984] VR 65 at 82). Such a disposition is not necessarily inconsistent with, and therefore does not negative, the reality of the preceding common intention, particularly where the parties are lay persons who lack a 'sound understanding of the nature of equitable interests' (*Napier v Public Trustee (Western Australia)* (1980) 32 ALR 153 at 160).

7 *White v Cabanas Pty Ltd* (No 2) [1970] Qd R 395 at 399B-C, 406B; *Doohan v Nelson* [1973] 2 NSWLR 320 at 329E.

8 *Bannister v Bannister* [1948] 2 All ER 133 at 137B.

9 *Malsbury v Malsbury* [1982] 1 NSWLR 226 at 231E; *Hayward v Giordani* [1983] NZLR 140 at 145.

10 See eg *Lyus v Prowsa Developments Ltd* [1982] 1 WLR 1044.

11 *Avondale Printers & Stationers Ltd v Haggie* [1979] 2 NZLR 124 at 162, 164.

12 *Last v Rosenfeld* [1972] 2 NSWLR 923 at 937B. See also *Cadd v Cadd* (1909) 9 CLR 171 at 187.

13 *Layton v Martin* [1986] 2 FLR 227 at 237A-B, 238B; *Pasi v Kamana* [1986] 1 NZLR 603 at 607 per McMullin J.

14 [1972] Ch 359 (post, p 917).

15 [1972] Ch 359 at 367C, 369D.

16 Post, p 920. See also J.D. Davies, (1979) 8 Sydney L Rev 578 at 579.

17 [1982] 1 WLR 1044 at 1053A.

18 See also *Eves v Eves* [1975] 1 WLR 1338 at 1342E-F, 1345B.

the Court of Appeal in *Ashburn Anstalt v Arnold*[19] to revive the suggestion that, in certain rigidly controlled circumstances, a constructive trust may be raised in protection of a contractual licence. Although the point was technically obiter, the Court did not dismiss the possibility that a purchaser may acquire legal title in circumstances which fasten upon him a conscientious obligation towards the contractual licensee.

(iv) Indefinite offers and joint ventures The outer margins of constructive trust doctrine are quickly reached if the subject matter of the 'bargain' between the parties is so ill-defined as not even faintly to resemble a recognised proprietary right. In *Layton v Martin*,[20] for instance, A had written a letter to B suggesting that B should come to live with him, in return for which A offered 'financial security during my life and financial security on my death.' This offer was held to be too vague to found any claim based on constructive trust (or indeed proprietary estoppel).[1]

In recent years English courts have gone to great lengths to confirm that a constructive trust cannot be founded merely on some mutual assumption that family life is to be shared as a form of joint venture.[2] In *Midland Bank PLC v Dobson*[3] the Court of Appeal had been prepared to find the necessary common intention present in evidence that the parties had treated their home as 'our house' and had always followed 'a principle of sharing everything'.[4] A much more restrictive approach has since emerged in the House of Lords' ruling in *Lloyds Bank Plc v Rosset*.[5] Here Lord Bridge of Harwich indicated that the simple and normal expectation that parties will 'share the practical benefits of occupying the matrimonial home whoever owns it' is 'something quite distinct from sharing the beneficial interest in the property asset which the matrimonial home represents.'[6] In *Rosset*'s case the House of Lords thought it entirely irrelevant that the spouses had formed a common intention that a dilapidated house should be purchased and

19 [1989] Ch 1 at 25H–26E per Fox LJ (post, p 922). See [1988] CLJ 353 (A.J. Oakley); [1988] Conv 201 (M.P. Thompson); (1988) 51 MLR 226 (J. Hill); (1988) 104 LQR 175 (P. Sparkes); [1988] All ER Rev 176 (P.J. Clarke).

20 [1986] 2 FLR 227.

1 [1986] 2 FLR 227 at 238B. Compare *Ungurian v Lesnoff* [1990] Ch 206 at 224A-D; *Malsbury v Malsbury* [1982] 1 NSWLR 226 at 230C-D; *Le Compte v Public Trustee* [1983] 2 NSWLR 109 at 111C, F. Compare, however, *Cooke v Cooke* [1987] VR 625 at 633, where Southwell J considered that expressions such as 'a house for her' might possibly be intended to import beneficial interest, whereas the expression 'a house for her to live in' imported no offer of beneficial entitlement.

2 In the heyday of the now discredited 'family assets' doctrine (ante, p 374), Lord Denning MR had been prepared to award spouses equal shares in the matrimonial home merely on the ground that there had been 'a general atmosphere of joint ownership to the income and capital of the parties' (*Smith v Baker* [1970] 1 WLR 1160 at 1162D).

3 [1986] 1 FLR 171 at 174A-E.

4 The claim to beneficial entitlement failed on another ground (post, p 434). See also *Eves v Eves* [1975] 1 WLR 1338 at 1345B-F per Brightman J; *Grant v Edwards* [1986] Ch 638 at 655G-H per Browne-Wilkinson V-C.

5 [1991] 1 AC 107 (ante, p 219).

6 [1991] 1 AC 107 at 128A. See also *Cooke v Cooke* [1987] VR 625 at 634, where the Supreme Court of Victoria held that the fact that the claimant trusted that the legal owner would not disturb her occupancy was no more 'consistent with a belief in beneficial ownership than with the existence of some licence'. The facts were entirely compatible with the status of a '"safe" licensee'.

renovated as a 'joint venture' and then 'shared by parents and children as the family home'. Lord Bridge did not believe that such evidence 'throws any light on their intentions with respect to the beneficial ownership of the property.'[7] On this basis it was held, perhaps somewhat harshly, that the wife had failed to establish any constructive trust in her favour.[8]

(5) Change of position

In order that a constructive trust should arise, it is not sufficient merely that a common intention should have been expressed or a 'bargain' made that B should have some beneficial entitlement in A's land.[9] If the assurance of beneficial entitlement is purely oral, further elements are required. One of these is that there must be a 'change of position' by the party who relies upon the 'bargain' or agreement as to beneficial ownership.[10] According to Lord Bridge of Harwich in *Lloyds Bank Plc v Rosset*,[11] 'even the clearest oral agreement' to hold property in trust would be ineffective for want of writing unless the claimant had 'altered her position in reliance on the agreement', thereby acquiring 'an enforceable interest . . . by way either of a constructive trust or of a proprietary estoppel'.[12] In the absence of such a 'change of position' the express verbal agreement would constitute a merely voluntary declaration of trust and would therefore remain unenforceable for want of writing.[13] Traditionally equity will not assist a volunteer.[14]

It seems that the required 'change of position' itself involves two features, which in broad terms relate respectively to fact and motive. *First*, there must be proof of 'detriment' or 'sacrifice' by the party who seeks to rely on the bargain; *second*, the change of position undertaken by this party must be 'referable to' the bargain.

(a) There must be a showing of 'detriment' or 'sacrifice'

In order that an unenforceable oral trust declared by A should become enforceable by B, there must have been a change of position by B. In the terms used by Lord Diplock in *Gissing v Gissing*,[15] B must have been induced by A to 'act to his [or her] own detriment'. B must show that he or she

7 *Lloyds Bank Plc v Rosset* [1991] 1 AC 107 at 130C-D. Compare the view adopted in the Court of Appeal ([1989] Ch 350 at 380F-H per Nicholls LJ).
8 Her failure to establish beneficial co-ownership inevitably frustrated the wife's further claim to an overriding interest enforceable against a chargee of the legal title (ante, p 219).
9 *Grant v Edwards* [1986] Ch 638 at 656A per Browne-Wilkinson V-C.
10 For reference to the terminology of 'change of position', see *Burns v Burns* [1984] Ch 317 at 327G-H per Fox LJ. It is indeed the change of position that constitutes the bargain by providing evidence of some 'quid pro quo moving from the claimant' (*Layton v Martin* [1986] 2 FLR 227 at 236H–237A per Scott J).
11 [1991] 1 AC 107 at 129C.
12 The close link between constructive trust and proprietary estoppel is discussed elsewhere (ante, p 356, post, p 452).
13 *Gissing v Gissing* [1971] AC 886 at 905E per Lord Diplock (ante, p 418). See also *Eves v Eves* [1975] 1 WLR 1338 at 1345B-C per Brightman J; *Grant v Edwards* [1986] Ch 638 at 656A per Browne-Wilkinson V-C; *Midland Bank PLC v Dobson* [1986] 1 FLR 171 at 175C-D per Fox LJ.
14 See *Midland Bank PLC v Dobson* [1986] 1 FLR 171 at 175E; *McFarlane v McFarlane* [1972] NI 59 at 73; *Austin v Keele* (1987) 10 NSWLR 283 at 291B-C per Lord Oliver of Aylmerton.
15 [1971] AC 886 at 905C.

has suffered some 'detriment' in reliance on A's undertaking as to the beneficial position,[16] or that he or she has otherwise made some 'material sacrifice' connected with the property.[17] This requirement of some form of 'contribution'[18] or 'consideration'[19] moving from B seems to be a strict precondition of the imposition of a constructive trust.[20] In this sense, the need to establish a change of position creates clear analogies between the constructive trust doctrine and both the doctrine of part performance[1] and the historic willingness of equity to grant specific performance of agreements for consideration.[2]

(i) Limits of 'detriment' and 'sacrifice' The forms of 'detriment' or 'sacrifice' which denote a relevant change of position are manifold.[3] The most obvious kind of 'detriment' or 'sacrifice' asserted by claimants under a constructive trust relates to financial expenditure, but a change of position may well comprise other forms of conduct or activity.[4] The outer limits of the notion of 'detriment' or 'sacrifice' are nevertheless circumscribed with some strictness. It is clear, for example, that the determination of property interests 'cannot be dealt with on the basis of sentiment'.[5] Sheer emotional commitment to a joint venture does not represent a sufficient change of position. In *Christian v Christian*,[6] for example, the claimant argued inter alia that she had suffered 'detriment' in the form of the social embarrassment caused by living with her de facto husband in a house situated in close proximity to the current home of the defendant's legal wife. Brightman LJ rejected this alleged 'detriment', observing that equity is 'concerned with the protection of property and proprietary interests, not with the protection of people's feelings.'

16 *Christian v Christian* (1981) 131 NLJ 43 (post, p 443). The legal owner's bad conscience and the claimant's disappointed expectation do not, without more, warrant equitable intervention: there must be acts of 'material detriment' (*Higgins v Wingfield* [1987] VR 689 at 695ff).

17 *Gissing v Gissing* [1971] AC 886 at 905F per Lord Diplock. As Fullagar J indicated in *Thwaites v Ryan* [1984] VR 65 at 90, 95, the claimant under a constructive trust 'must expend some money or do some other act, or omission, on the faith of his belief', and 'detriment' can be simply defined as 'so acting on the faith of an expectation or belief that, if the expectation or belief be disappointed, the actor would suffer so substantially as to make it unconscionable for the other party to disappoint him'.

18 *Allen v Snyder* [1977] 2 NSWLR 685 at 691A per Glass JA. See also *Boccalatte v Bushelle* [1980] Qd R 180 at 185E.

19 *Taddeo v Taddeo* (1978) 19 SASR 347 at 365.

20 In *Neale v Willis* (1968) 19 P & CR 836 at 839, the Court of Appeal imposed a 'constructive trust' on A in favour of B, even though the consideration for A's oral undertaking to confer beneficial rights on B seems to have been provided not by B but by B's mother. However, the decision is far better analysed not as a case of constructive trust, but as involving an express declaration of trust which was made enforceable only by reason of the rule in *Rochefoucauld v Boustead*—of which principle it is indeed a textbook illustration (ante, p 377).

1 See *Taddeo v Taddeo* (1978) 19 SASR 347 at 365.

2 See *Cowcher v Cowcher* [1972] 1 WLR 425 at 431A.

3 The required nature and quality of the acts capable of amounting to 'detriment' have not been settled (*Higgins v Wingfield* [1987] VR 689 at 695).

4 Post, p 428.

5 *Wood v Wood* (Unreported, 1979 W No 1393, 7 July 1982) per Lawton LJ. See also *Winkworth v Edward Baron Development Co Ltd* [1986] 1 WLR 1512 at 1516C, where Lord Templeman observed that 'Equity is not a computer. Equity operates on conscience but is not influenced by sentimentality.'

6 (1981) 131 NLJ 43 (ante, p 336).

In his view, 'the only contributions, detriments and sacrifices, that move the court in this field are those of a monetary or proprietary nature.'[7]

(ii) The net concept of 'detriment' or 'sacrifice' The courts seem to analyse even recognised forms of 'detriment' or 'sacrifice' in net terms. Thus a 'change of position', understood in the broadest sense, is seen as comprising the required degree of 'detriment' or 'sacrifice' only if it results in a net disadvantage to the individual concerned.[8] A claimed 'detriment' must hurt.[9] In *Hannaford v Selby*,[10] for instance, the claimant's work in cultivating vegetables in his son-in-law's garden was not accounted to be 'detriment' in the relevant sense, since he was regarded as merely indulging his 'one absorbing hobby'.[11] Likewise, in *Layton v Martin*[12] the claimant's housekeeping and other services had already been compensated at least in part by the award of a regular salary.[13] In *Thwaites v Ryan*,[14] the Supreme Court of Victoria declined to accept that the plaintiff had acted to his detriment in 'leaving his moribund marriage and moribund tenancy and going to live rent free in the pleasant home of his old friend.'[15]

(iii) Different standards of proof It used to be assumed that the same definition of recognisable 'detriment' or 'sacrifice' applied indifferently throughout the law of constructive trusts.[16] However, recent case law has confirmed emphatically that the standard of proof relating to 'changes of position' varies markedly in accordance with the nature of the bargain or agreement which it is sought to enforce by way of constructive trust. The divergent standards correlate precisely with whether the agreement in question is an *express bargain* or an *implied bargain*. As Lord Bridge of Harwich reinforced

7 '[T]he court is only entitled to look at the financial contributions or their real or substantial equivalent, to the acquisition of the house; that the husband may spend his weekends redecorating or laying a patio is neither here nor there, nor is the fact that the woman has spent so much of her time looking after the house, doing the cooking and bringing up the family' (*Burns v Burns* [1984] Ch 317 at 344E-F per May LJ).

8 Thus, somewhat unsympathetically, no 'detriment' was found in *Cooke v Cooke* [1987] VR 625 at 634, 638f, where a woman was provided with rent-free accommodation by the father of her child. (The total cost of any contributions made by her 'must have been small indeed when compared with the value of the benefits provided by [the father]'.) See also *Pasi v Kamana* [1986] 1 NZLR 603 at 604, 607 (financial contributions went towards support of claimant herself: no evidence that 'she gave or contributed without receiving, or that she suffered any deprivation'). Compare the Canadian rejection of any suggestion that the benefits of past occupation preclude a claim of constructive trust (see *Palachik v Kiss* (1983) 146 DLR (3d) 385 at 397 per Wilson J; *MacDonald v Mackenzie Estate* (1990) 64 DLR (4th) 476 at 488).

9 See eg the reference by Marks J in *Higgins v Wingfield* [1987] VR 689 at 700 to the idea that the claimant must 'suffer materially (ie not just psychologically)'.

10 (1976) 239 Estates Gazette 811 at 813.

11 See also *Pettitt v Pettitt* [1970] AC 777 at 826A per Lord Diplock.

12 [1986] 2 FLR 227 at 231F-G.

13 See also *Heyland v Heyland* (1972) *Times*, 25 January; *McPhee v McPhee* (1980) NZ Recent Law 42.

14 [1984] VR 65 at 89.

15 Compare the rejection, in the analogous area of proprietary estoppel, of arguments that detriment could be established by a woman who voluntarily left an unhappy marriage in order to live with her lover and give birth to and rear their child (*Coombes v Smith* [1986] 1 WLR 808 at 820A-F).

16 See *Stokes v Anderson* [1991] 1 FLR 391 at 398F-G per Nourse LJ.

in *Lloyds Bank Plc v Rosset*,[17] the difference between these two kinds of bargain is a 'critical distinction which [the] judge ... should always have in the forefront of his mind' since it directly controls the character of the evidence required in support of a claim of constructive trust.

(iv) Detriment required in 'express bargain' constructive trusts In delivering the only substantive speech in the House of Lords in *Lloyds Bank Plc v Rosset*,[18] Lord Bridge indicated that a much lower standard of proof applies in respect of the 'detriment' or 'sacrifice' which underlies an 'express bargain' constructive trust. Once there is evidence of an agreed beneficial entitlement based on direct negotiation or discussion, the claimant need show 'only ... that he or she has acted to his or her detriment or significantly altered his or her position in reliance on the agreement'. The court is no longer bound to look for conduct from which a common intention can be inferred;[19] the court looks only for 'conduct which amounts to an acting upon it by the claimant.'[20] The court may therefore take account of behaviour which falls 'far short of such conduct as would by itself have supported the claim in the absence of an express representation ... that [the claimant] should have ... an interest'.[1]

The change of position required in this context obviously includes the incurring of expenditure which is referable to the acquisition of a joint home,[2] but may well extend much further.[3] Evidence that a direct agreement has been 'acted upon' may be established, for instance, by a claimant's contribution of physical labour towards the renovation of a joint home,[4] or by her participation in commercial activities undertaken by her partner.[5] The precise parameters of relevant conduct are, however, still somewhat unclear. Perhaps the broadest formulation of relevant 'detriment' or 'sacrifice' is to be found in *Grant v Edwards*.[6] Here, in dealing with a partner's claim to a beneficial share in a family home, Browne-Wilkinson V-C thought that 'useful guidance' could be obtained from the principles underlying the law of proprietary estoppel.[7] This instructive analogy tended to suggest that 'any act done by [the claimant] to her detriment relating to the joint lives of the parties is ... sufficient detriment to qualify. The acts do not have to be inherently referable to the house'.

On this footing Browne-Wilkinson V-C was prepared in *Grant v Edwards*

17 [1991] 1 AC 107 at 132D-E, 133H–134A.
18 [1991] 1 AC 107 at 132F-G.
19 *Grant v Edwards* [1986] Ch 638 at 655F-G per Browne-Wilkinson V-C.
20 *Grant v Edwards* [1986] Ch 638 at 647C per Nourse LJ.
1 *Lloyds Bank Plc v Rosset* [1991] 1 AC 107 at 133F-G per Lord Bridge of Harwich.
2 See *Grant v Edwards* [1986] Ch 638 at 649F–650C per Nourse LJ; *Stokes v Anderson* [1991] 1 FLR 391 at 398A-B.
3 See *Grant v Edwards* [1986] Ch 638 at 647D per Nourse LJ.
4 *Eves v Eves* [1975] 1 WLR 1338 at 1340D-E, 1342F-G, 1344C-D, 1345C. See also *Cooke v Head* [1972] 1 WLR 518 at 519G-H, 520F-G; *Grant v Edwards* [1986] Ch 638 at 648D per Nourse LJ; *Hayward v Giordani* [1983] NZLR 140 at 142, 150, 152.
5 *Hammond v Mitchell* [1991] 1 WLR 1127 at 1137D-E. See [1992] Conv 218 (A. Lawson); (1993) 56 MLR 224 (P. O'Hagan).
6 [1986] Ch 638 at 657A-B.
7 Browne-Wilkinson V-C considered the principles of proprietary estoppel to be 'closely akin to those laid down in *Gissing v Gissing* [1971] AC 886' ([1986] Ch 638 at 656F-H). See Chapter 11 (ante, p 312).

to have regard to such activities as '[s]etting up house together, having a baby, [and] making payments to general housekeeping expenses (not strictly necessary to enable the mortgage to be paid)'.[8] Such conduct was relevant even though it might be 'referable to the mutual love and affection of the parties and not specifically referable to the claimant's belief that she has an interest in the house.'[9] In the same case, however, Nourse LJ expressed the more restrictive view that conduct is relevant only if it is 'conduct on which the woman could not reasonably have been expected to embark unless she was to have an interest in the house.'[10] Only by adopting the latter kind of conduct could the claimant be 'seen to act to her detriment on the faith of the common intention.'[11] Thus, in Nourse LJ's opinion, the mere fact that a woman moved into joint occupation of her lover's home would not normally constitute an incurring of recognisable detriment on her part, since the law is 'not so cynical as to infer that a woman will only go to live with a man to whom she is not married if she understands that she is to have an interest in their home.'[12] In *Eves v Eves*,[13] by contrast, a constructive trust had been quite correctly imposed because there, in the absence of some anticipated beneficial entitlement, the female claimant could not reasonably have been expected to undertake the arduous physical effort which in fact she devoted to the improvement of her lover's home.[14]

It therefore remains uncertain to what extent highly personal circumstances and matters of lifestyle can today support constructive trusts of the 'express bargain' or—even less likely—the 'implied bargain' variety.[15] Here some of the law's least attractive characteristics tend to find expression in a general unconcern for the special needs and vulnerabilities of women claimants. The strictures imposed by orthodox trust theory are such that 'detriment' is seldom established unless the claimant's conduct substantially oversteps boundaries of conventional expectation based on stereotyped perceptions of her appropriate gender role. As was once said of a wife's claim to a matrimonial home, 'before equity will intervene to protect the wife, her contribution must exceed that normally expected of a wife carrying out her normal matrimonial role'.[16]

This institutional lack of empathy is mirrored in other statements that beneficial ownership is not altered by the performance of 'the ordinary

8 See eg Waite J's willingness in *Hammond v Mitchell* [1991] 1 WLR 1127 at 1137A-G to hold that the claimant had 'acted to her detriment or significantly altered her position' by making a 'contribution as mother/helper/unpaid assistant and at times financial supporter to the family prosperity generated by [her partner's] dealing activities'.

9 [1986] Ch 638 at 657A.

10 [1986] Ch 638 at 648G-H.

11 [1986] Ch 638 at 648H. See also *Hohol v Hohol* [1981] VR 221 at 225.

12 [1986] Ch 638 at 648F-G.

13 [1975] 1 WLR 1338.

14 Apart from redecorating the entire house and demolishing a garden shed single-handed, it was the formidable achievement of the claimant in *Eves v Eves* that she wielded a 14lb sledgehammer to break up an area of concrete at the front of the house, dump the rubble in a skip, and prepare the garden for turfing ([1975] 1 WLR 1338 at 1340D-E). Janet Eves seems to have stimulated the emergence of a small army of women, all 'wielding a pickaxe' within the domestic curtilage in the hope of emulating her legal success (see *Ungurian v Lesnoff* [1990] Ch 206 at 223F-224A per Vinelott J).

15 Post, p 430.

16 *Lloyds Bank Plc v Rosset* [1989] Ch 350 at 402F per Purchas LJ. (Purchas LJ upheld the claim of beneficial entitlement).

domestic tasks'[17] or by the fact that the husband 'likes to occupy his leisure by laying a new lawn in the garden or building a fitted wardrobe in the bedroom while the wife does the shopping, cooks the family dinner or bathes the children'.[18] In *Cooke v Cooke*[19] the claimant even argued before the Supreme Court of Victoria that, in response to the legal owner's invitation, she had foregone an abortion, had remained 'chaste' and 'faithful' to him, had refrained from seeking outside employment and had brought up two young children in his house. Southwell J rejected her assertion of beneficial entitlement, holding that there was no reason to infer 'that had it not been for a belief in beneficial ownership she would have structured her life so differently that it would be possible to say that in living as she did she acted to her detriment in any relevant sense.'[20]

(v) Detriment required in 'implied bargain' constructive trusts Whatever the precise parameters of the 'change of position' required under an 'express bargain' constructive trust, it is now clear that 'more rigorous standards ... apply when intention has to be inferred from conduct alone.'[1] Under an 'implied bargain' constructive trust, much more exacting proof of 'detriment' or 'sacrifice' is needed not least because, as Lord Bridge pointed out in *Lloyds Bank Plc v Rosset*,[2] the claimant is attempting to rely entirely on the conduct of the parties 'both as the basis from which to infer a common intention to share the property beneficially and as the conduct relied on to give rise to a constructive trust.'[3] Accordingly, in *Rosset*'s case, Lord Bridge acknowledged that 'direct contributions to the purchase price by the partner who is not the legal owner, whether initially or by payment of mortgage instalments, will readily justify the inference necessary to the creation of a constructive trust', but concluded significantly that 'it is at least extremely doubtful whether anything less will do.'[4]

The ruling of the House of Lords in *Lloyds Bank Plc v Rosset* underlines, in the context of the 'implied bargain' constructive trust, the intense preoccupation with money payments which dominates so much of the law of trusts. In this respect the ruling is both confusing and severely restrictive. Where A is the relevant legal owner it is, of course, widely accepted that B's financial contributions may raise a constructive trust *either* where A and B agree at the outset that the beneficial ownership should be in different proportions from those in which they actually contribute the purchase money,[5] *or* where B makes some subsequent financial contribution (eg towards paying off a large part of the mortgage debt) in circumstances not foreseen at the

17 *Burns v Burns* [1984] Ch 317 at 331A per Fox LJ.
18 *Pettitt v Pettitt* [1970] AC 777 at 826A-B per Lord Diplock. See also *Burns v Burns* [1984] Ch 317 at 344E-F per May LJ (ante, p 427).
19 [1987] VR 625.
20 [1987] VR 625 at 639. Southwell J observed (at 636) that he would in any event have considered it 'contrary to public policy to hold that a woman acted to her detriment in deciding to allow a normal pregnancy to continue.'
1 *Hammond v Mitchell* [1991] 1 WLR 1127 at 1137H per Waite J.
2 [1991] 1 AC 107 at 132H-133A.
3 There is here, as Mustill LJ pointed out in *Grant v Edwards* [1986] Ch 638 at 652G-653A, 'a risk of circularity'.
4 [1991] 1 AC 107 at 133A.
5 Post, p 448.

date of A's acquisition.[6] But in so far as Lord Bridge intended to refer to other forms of money payment towards purchase, such payments would more generally be assumed to raise, not a constructive trust, but a resulting trust instead.[7]

The extreme limitations imposed by the *Rosset* ruling become more apparent on fuller realisation of the many forms of contributory activity which, in the absence of express bargain, are now excluded from the ambit of the constructive trust. Lord Bridge himself conceded that even the execution of substantial or arduous renovation works on property in such cases as *Eves v Eves*[8] fell 'far short' of the kind of conduct required.[9] Still less is any constructive trust generated by many years of faithful domestic endeavour on the part of a wife, mother and homemaker.[10] Even a pattern of prolonged contribution by the claimant to the shared general expenses of a common household raises no constructive trust in respect of the family home in the absence of an 'express representation'[11] by the legal owner that the contributor was to have a beneficial interest. In *Gissing v Gissing*,[12] for example, the claimant wife alleged that she had made indirect contributions towards the purchase of the family home through her use of her own moneys on various forms of household and other family-related expenditure. The legal title in the home had been purchased in the name of the husband and he was solely responsible for repayment of the mortgage loan secured on the realty. In the absence of any express agreement between the spouses as to how the beneficial interest should be held,[13] the House of Lords declined on the facts to infer that her expenditure had been referable to any bargain directed at beneficial co-ownership or could now be seen as reflecting any common intention that the wife should acquire an equitable share in the family home.[14] The mere fact of contribution to joint expenditure does not in itself constitute a sufficient change of position.[15]

In some respects the *Rosset* ruling appears even more restrictive in tenor than the draconian decision in *Gissing*. In the latter case the House of Lords at least left open the possibility that a pattern of indirect financial contribution by B to the general economy of a household might sometimes generate a trust entitlement in property vested in A. Such a result might occur if B's

6 See *Burns v Burns* [1984] Ch 317 at 327D, 329B; *Winkworth v Edward Baron Development Co Ltd* (1986) 52 P & CR 67 at 75, 79f.
7 Ante, p 399.
8 [1975] 1 WLR 1338 (ante, p 429).
9 [1991] 1 AC 107 at 133F-G. See also *Grant v Edwards* [1986] Ch 638 at 648D per Nourse LJ.
10 *Button v Button* [1968] 1 WLR 457 at 462A-C; *Gissing v Gissing* [1969] 2 Ch 85 at 98E-F; *Burns v Burns* [1984] Ch 317 at 327H, 331A-B, 345B-C; *Layton v Martin* [1986] 2 FLR 227 at 235H-236A, 238C-D; *C v C* [1976] IR 254 at 257. Compare *Hall v Hall* (1982) 3 FLR 379 at 381E-F per Lord Denning MR, but see now *Burns v Burns* [1984] Ch 317 at 331C-F, 342G (post, p 450).
11 [1991] 1 AC 107 at 133F-G per Lord Bridge of Harwich.
12 [1971] AC 886.
13 [1971] AC 886 at 910E.
14 [1971] AC 886 at 911B-C.
15 '[S]uch conduct is no less consistent with a common intention to share the day-to-day expenses of the household, while each spouse retains a separate interest in capital assets acquired with their own moneys or obtained by inheritance or gift' ([1971] AC 886 at 909H per Lord Diplock). See also *Grant v Edwards* [1986] Ch 638 at 657F per Browne-Wilkinson V-C.

payments were 'referable to the acquisition' of A's property,[16] in the sense that there was some conscious arrangement between A and B that their allocation of the burden of the family's financial commitments should eventuate in beneficial ownership for both.[17] Even so it required to be clearly established that B's assumption of responsibility for more general aspects of household expenditure was part of some deliberate design to free A to discharge the acquisition cost of the home itself.[18] A conscious arrangement of this kind was in practice extremely difficult to prove.[19]

It would be an ironically retrograde move if the *Rosset* ruling has effectively precluded beneficial co-ownership of the family home in circumstances of indiscriminately shared family expenditure. General economic pressures prevailing in the late 1980s and 1990s have now made the retention of many family homes a joint and somewhat dire struggle for survival which calls for the utmost combined efforts of the relevant parties and in which the conscious calculation of individual accounts has no place.

(b) The change of position must be 'referable to' the 'bargain'

Detriment or sacrifice *per se* is insufficient to support a claim of constructive trust.[20] It must be shown that the claimant's change of position was 'referable to' the earlier 'bargain' or common intention that the legal owner should acknowledge some beneficial entitlement in the claimant. There must be some causal nexus between the legal owner's agreement and the claimant's active willingness to undergo detriment or sacrifice.[1]

16 *Gissing v Gissing* [1971] AC 886 at 909E-G per Lord Diplock. See also *McFarlane v McFarlane* [1972] NI 59 at 69, 71, 75; *Allen v Snyder* [1977] 2 NSWLR 685 at 707F-G; *Boccalatte v Bushelle* [1980] Qd R 180 at 184B. Proof of a 'substantial contribution . . . to family expenses' was later held to be a ground on which the court could properly infer that such payment is 'referable to the acquisition of the house since, in one way or another, it enables the family to pay the mortgage instalments' (*Burns v Burns* [1984] Ch 317 at 329A-B).

17 In *Gissing v Gissing* [1971] AC 886 at 909F, Lord Diplock spoke of an 'adjustment to [the wife's] contribution to other expenses of the household which it can be inferred was referable to the acquisition of the house'. See also *Burns v Burns* [1984] Ch 317 at 328G-H; *Toner v Toner* (1972) 23 NILQ 208; *Allen v Snyder* [1977] 2 NSWLR 685 at 691B.

18 *Gissing v Gissing* [1971] AC 886 at 903B-C; *Burns v Burns* [1984] Ch 317 at 329B-C, 330C-D; *Toner v Toner* (1972) 23 NILQ 208; *Nemeth v Nemeth* (1977-78) 17 ALR 500 at 510; *Boccalatte v Bushelle* [1980] Qd R 180 at 185E; *Northern Bank Ltd v Beattie* [1982] 18 NIJB, p 16f. It was said to be somewhat easier to infer this kind of common intention where B has already made some direct financial contribution, for instance, to the initial deposit paid on or before acquiring the property (see *Gissing v Gissing* [1971] AC 886 at 907G-908B; *Burns v Burns* [1984] Ch 317 at 344G-H).

19 See the unsuccessful outcome of the claims pursued in *Burns v Burns* [1984] Ch 317 at 345B-D; *Richards v Dove* [1974] 1 All ER 888 at 894h-895c; *McFarlane v McFarlane* [1972] NI 59 at 73; *McKeown v McKeown* [1975] NI 139 at 142C-D; *Nemeth v Nemeth* (1977-78) 17 ALR 500 at 510; *In Re Barnes (A Bankrupt)* [1979] 4 NIJB, p 6.

20 *Pettitt v Pettitt* [1970] AC 777 at 805E; *Gissing v Gissing* [1971] AC 886 at 900H, 901B-C, 909G-H, 910G-H; *Bernard v Josephs* [1982] Ch 391 at 404E-F; *Grant v Edwards* [1986] Ch 638 at 651F; *Allen v Snyder* [1977] 2 NSWLR 685 at 691C; *McGill v S* [1979] IR 283 at 289.

1 This is the traditional view outlined in the case law, but there are already indications of a changing emphasis in this area. In *Grant v Edwards* [1986] Ch 638 at 656B-D, Browne-Wilkinson V-C declined to express 'any concluded view' on the need for 'positive evidence' of 'conscious reliance' on the common intention (ante, p 428). See also *Winkworth v Edward Baron Development Co Ltd* [1986] 1 WLR 1512 at 1515F, where the House of Lords looked (in vain) merely for some 'connection between the acquisition . . . and the payment'.

This notion of causation was stressed in Lord Diplock's classic exposition of the constructive trust in *Gissing v Gissing*.[2] Here Lord Diplock indicated that a constructive trust will arise only if the legal owner has 'induced' the claimant to act to his or her own detriment 'in the reasonable belief that by so acting he [or she] was acquiring a beneficial interest in the land.' This formulation seems to require a certain mental element or motivation on the part both of A, the legal owner, and of B, the claimant of an equitable interest. To raise a constructive trust, A's conduct must have been 'intended to induce [B] to act to his or her detriment upon the faith of the promise of a specified beneficial interest in the land', and B must have 'so acted with the intention of acquiring that beneficial interest.'[3]

Once again the precise content of the requirement of 'referability' seems to be graded according to whether the claim of constructive trust is founded on express or implied bargain.

(i) Referability under an 'express bargain' constructive trust The requirement of referability usually occasions little difficulty where A and B have reached an express agreement as to the beneficial ownership of land vested at law in the name of A. The explicit nature of the agreement obviates the need to demonstrate a positive causal connection between the verbal assurance of A and the detrimental reliance of B. Lord Diplock confirmed in *Gissing v Gissing*[4] that there need be no formal demonstration that A's conduct was intended to induce B to act to her detriment on the faith of the promise of some specified beneficial interest or that B acted with the intention of acquiring such an interest. As Browne-Wilkinson V-C suggested in *Grant v Edwards*,[5] the causal link is readily presumed to be self-evident.

In *Grant v Edwards* the claimant de facto wife had contributed financially towards household expenses, her partner having undertaken sole responsibility for the repayment of the mortgage on the family home. Browne-Wilkinson V-C noted that, without the woman's contributions, the man's means would have been 'insufficient to keep up the mortgage payments', and that her indirect contributions were therefore 'essentially linked to the payment of the mortgage instalments'.[6] The mere use of the claimant's money 'whether directly or indirectly' in the discharge of mortgage instalments provided, in Browne-Wilkinson V-C's view, 'a sufficient link between the detriment suffered by the claimant and the common intention'. The court could 'infer that she would not have made such payments were it not for her belief

2 [1971] AC 886 at 905C.

3 [1971] AC 886 at 905G-H. This means, ironically, that if the claimant is 'almost wholly unmercenary', her claim of constructive trust will fail (see *Layton v Martin* [1986] 2 FLR 227 at 235B, 239H-240A).

4 [1971] AC 886 at 905G-H. See eg *Le Compte v Public Trustee* [1983] 2 NSWLR 109 at 111C, E-F.

5 [1986] Ch 638 at 657C. Browne-Wilkinson V-C urged, on an analogy with the law of proprietary estoppel, that an express holding out to the claimant that she had a beneficial interest is 'an act of such a nature as to be part of the inducement to [the claimant] to do the acts relied on'. In the absence of contrary evidence, 'the right inference is that the claimant acted in reliance on such holding out and the burden lies on the legal owner to show that she did not do so'. For a slightly more restrictive view, compare [1986] Ch 638 at 648G-H per Nourse LJ (ante, p 429).

6 [1986] Ch 638 at 656D-E.

that she had an interest in the house.'[7] The claimant was accordingly recognised as having acquired a one-half interest in the beneficial ownership.

(ii) Referability under an 'implied bargain' constructive trust The criterion of referability is applied much more stringently to claims of constructive trust based upon implied bargain. Where the relevant common intention as to beneficial title is left to be inferred from the mutual conduct of A and B, the acts or omissions alleged as 'detriment' by B must, according to Lord Diplock in *Gissing v Gissing*,[8] be 'referable to the acquisition' of a beneficial interest in A's property.[9] Only if this test of 'referability' is satisfied can B rebut the normal legal inference that the sole title taken by A invests him also with the sole equitable interest.[10]

In *Philip Lowe (Chinese Restaurant) Ltd v Sau Man Lee*,[11] for example, May LJ indicated in the Court of Appeal that a showing of referability was 'at the very least a sine qua non of the existence of any such equity' as was asserted by the claimant. Here the claimant, a de facto wife, was not awarded any beneficial interest because it was found that the detriment she had incurred by working in the family restaurant had been undertaken, not in any belief that she was thereby acquiring an equitable interest, but 'because she was part of the family'.[12] Likewise, in *Lloyds Bank Plc v Rosset*,[13] the House of Lords declined to accept that the claimant wife had demonstrated any relevant change of position where, in the absence of an express bargain, her efforts had consisted merely of personal assistance in the renovation of the family home.[14] In the view of Lord Bridge of Harwich, her intensive efforts were explicable simply on the basis of the fact that she had been 'extremely anxious' that the home should be available for occupation as soon as possible. Her labours did not comprise work 'upon which she could not reasonably have

7 *Grant v Edwards* [1986] Ch 638 at 656E-F.

8 [1971] AC 886 at 905B-C, 909G.

9 See eg *Grant v Sanderson* [1983] Court of Appeal Unbound Transcript 862; *Burns v Burns* [1984] Ch 317 at 327G-H, 328H-329B; *Warner v Warner* (Unreported, Court of Appeal, 11 July 1984); *Grant v Edwards* [1986] Ch 638 at 651G-H; *Winkworth v Edward Baron Development Co Ltd* [1986] 1 WLR 1512 at 1515F-G.

10 [1971] AC 886 at 909H-910A.

11 Unreported, Court of Appeal, 9 July 1985.

12 See also *Coombes v Smith* [1986] 1 WLR 808 at 820F-G; *Layton v Martin* [1986] 2 FLR 227 at 235H-236A. In *Midland Bank Plc v Dobson* [1986] 1 FLR 171 at 177E, the Court of Appeal again denied beneficial entitlement, after a marriage of 34 years, to a wife who had not demonstrated that she had been 'induced to act to her detriment upon the basis of a common intention of ownership of the house or that there was otherwise any nexus between the acquisition of the property and something provided or foregone by [her]'. Compare the broader and more humane approach adopted by Sir Robin Cooke in the Judicial Committee of the Privy Council in *Maharaj v Chand* [1986] AC 898 at 907G ('... in the absence of evidence to the contrary, the right inference is that the claimant acted in the belief that she (or he) would have an interest in the house and not merely out of love and affection').

13 [1991] 1 AC 107 at 131C-G.

14 A potent reminder of the 'solid tug of money' appears in Lord Bridge's comment that 'the monetary value of [the claimant's] work expressed as a contribution to a property acquired at a cost exceeding £70,000 must have been so trifling as to be almost de minimis' ([1991] 1 AC 107 at 131G). Compare the reference to improvements of 'an ephemeral character' in *Pettitt v Pettitt* [1970] AC 777 at 796E per Lord Reid.

been expected to embark unless she was to have an interest in the house'.[15]

The application of this strict test of 'referability' has caused the failure of innumerable trust claims. In *Gissing v Gissing*,[16] for example, the wife's indirect financial contributions towards general household expenditure raised no trust in her favour in the absence of a showing that these contributions had been made in conscious response to a 'bargain' with the legal owner directed towards bringing about beneficial co-ownership in the family home.[17] The fairness of the 'referability' criterion laid down in *Gissing v Gissing* has long been the subject of criticism.[18] In particular, it is clear that the application of this criterion penalises those lay persons who, in the confused circumstances of domestic life and financial pressure, fail to advert at a sufficiently conscious mental level to the motivations and implications of their day-to-day actions.[19] Correspondingly, an unfair advantage in legal terms is conferred on those who are either more calculating in the advancement of their own self-interest or more sophisticated in their ability to provide (or fabricate) evidence *ex post facto* which bears out the claim that the detriment incurred by them was 'referable to' some agreement with the legal owner.[20]

(6) Equitable fraud

Before a constructive trust can be imposed, a third element must be established in addition to a mere 'change of position' premised on some 'bargain' between the relevant parties. This element is variously described in the case law, but in effect amounts to a requirement that 'equitable fraud'[1] be shown to exist. Such 'equitable fraud' is present 'as soon as the absolute character of the conveyance is set up for the purpose of defeating the beneficial interest' guaranteed by the parties' bargain.[2] In this sense 'equitable fraud' provides

15 Lord Bridge's dismissive approach is apparent in his observation that 'it would seem the most natural thing in the world for any wife, in the absence of her husband abroad, to spend all the time she could spare and to employ any skills she might have, such as the ability to decorate a room, in doing all she could to accelerate progress of the work quite irrespective of any expectation she might have of enjoying a beneficial interest in the property' ([1991] 1 AC 107 at 131E). Compare, however, the approach adopted in the Court of Appeal ([1989] Ch 350 at 381G–382A per Nicholls LJ).

16 [1971] AC 886.

17 Ante, p 431; post, p 449.

18 See eg *Hargrave v Newton* [1971] 1 WLR 1611 at 1613A-B; *Hazell v Hazell* [1972] 1 WLR 301 at 304C-D. However, Lord Denning MR's suggestion in *Falconer v Falconer* [1970] 1 WLR 1333 at 1336D-E that mere expenditure without the requisite intention can raise a trust has since been rejected as inconsistent with *Gissing v Gissing* (see *Savva v Costa and Harymode Investments Ltd* (1981) 131 NLJ 1114 per Ormrod LJ).

19 See eg *McKeown v McKeown* [1975] NI 139 at 142C-D.

20 The force of these criticisms was indeed recognised by Lord Reid in *Gissing v Gissing* [1971] AC 886 at 897C-E. See also *Grant v Edwards* [1986] Ch 638 at 656B-D.

1 See *Nocton v Ashburton* [1914] AC 932 at 953f per Viscount Haldane LC: 'In Chancery the term "fraud" thus came to be used to describe what fell short of deceit, but imported breach of a duty to which equity had attached its sanction ... What it really means ... is, not moral fraud in the ordinary sense, but breach of the sort of obligation which is enforced by a Court that from the beginning regarded itself as a Court of conscience.' For an early reference to 'equitable fraud', see *Lincoln v Wright* (1859) 4 De G & J 16 at 23, 45 ER 6 at 9. See also *Le Compte v Public Trustee* [1983] 2 NSWLR 109 at 111B, where Rath J thought that 'the words "the demands of justice and good conscience" should be read as exegetical of "fraud".'

2 *Bannister v Bannister* [1948] 2 All ER 133 at 136C-D. See also *Last v Rosenfeld* [1972] 2 NSWLR 923 at 934F; *Baumgartner v Baumgartner* [1985] 2 NSWLR 406 at 412A-B.

the 'common denominator' or 'connecting link' which runs through the many categories of circumstance where constructive trusts have been imposed.[3]

(a) Unconscientious use of the legal title

The essence of 'equitable fraud' lies therefore in what has been called the 'unconscientious use of the legal title'.[4] The court will not impose a constructive trust 'unless it is satisfied that the conscience of the estate owner is affected.'[5] As Lord Diplock insisted in *Gissing v Gissing*,[6] a constructive trust will arise only where the legal owner, A, 'has so conducted himself that it would be inequitable to allow him to deny to [B] a beneficial interest in the land.'[7] However, the required inequity is plainly established by any 'disclaimer by the legal owner of the obligations of conscience based upon an express agreement, or common intention of the parties.'[8] Such a disclaimer would, in the words of Viscount Dilhorne in *Gissing v Gissing*,[9] amount to a 'breach of faith'.[10] Were A's disclaimer to remain unchecked, the 'suffering which would otherwise occur' on the part of B 'makes it "a fraud on B" for A to assert his rights, that is to say, makes it unconscionable of A to assert his rights.'[11]

(b) Attempted derogation from agreed entitlements

The constructive trust comes into play primarily in order to frustrate fraudulent designs.[12] It is clear that the fraud required to activate the constructive trust need not have been present in the original agreement or 'bargain' which guaranteed some kind of beneficial interest for B.[13] A constructive trust is, however, imposed on A if he later behaves inequitably by attempting to derogate from the beneficial rights conferred on B by the earlier 'bargain'. Moreover, A cannot escape from that 'bargain' by pleading its unenforceability through want of written evidence. There is a clear doctrine of equity to the effect that any 'reliance by the trustee on the statute requiring writing would be equitable fraud' itself.[14] Equity will never allow a statute to be used as an instrument of fraud.[15]

3 *Avondale Printers & Stationers Ltd v Haggie* [1979] 2 NZLR 124 at 159. See also *South Yarra Project Pty Ltd* v *Gentsis* [1985] VR 29 at 37.
4 *Ogilvie v Ryan* [1976] 2 NSWLR 504 at 518E per Holland J. See also *Baumgartner v Baumgartner* [1985] 2 NSWLR 406 at 412A-B.
5 *Ashburn Anstalt v Arnold* [1989] Ch 1 at 25H.
6 [1971] AC 886 at 905C (post, p 449).
7 This dictum has sometimes been over-emphasised to the exclusion of the remainder of Lord Diplock's judgment (post, p 454).
8 *Allen v Snyder* [1977] 2 NSWLR 685 at 694E; *Baumgartner v Baumgartner* [1985] 2 NSWLR 406 at 435A-B.
9 [1971] AC 886 at 900B-C.
10 See also *Boccalatte v Bushelle* [1980] Qd R 180 at 186A.
11 *Thwaites v Ryan* [1984] VR 65 at 90.
12 *Avondale Printers & Stationers Ltd v Haggie* [1979] 2 NZLR 124 at 160.
13 *Bannister v Bannister* [1948] 2 All ER 133 at 136C, F-G; *Last v Rosenfeld* [1972] 2 NSWLR 923 at 934F.
14 *Allen v Snyder* [1977] 2 NSWLR 685 at 692E; *Baumgartner v Baumgartner* [1985] 2 NSWLR 406 at 435A-B.
15 Ante, p 377.

(7) Quantification of entitlements

In quantifying beneficial entitlements under a constructive trust, the court does not sit 'as under a palm tree, to exercise a general discretion to do what the man in the street, on a general overview of the case, might regard as fair.'[16] Nor is this a context in which the maxim 'equality is equity' can be applied 'unthinkingly'.[17] Once the existence of a constructive trust has been established, the mandate of the court is to 'do its best to discover from the conduct of the [parties] whether any inference can reasonably be drawn as to the probable common understanding about the amount of the share' to be taken by the claimant.[18] Under a constructive trust the interest recognised on behalf of the claimant usually takes the form of some defined fraction of the equitable ownership, but may also sometimes comprise another kind of proprietary interest such as a life interest.[19] In all cases the extent of the claimant's interest is 'prima facie . . . that which the parties intended'.[20] Only if it is impossible to ascertain the intended quantum of entitlement will the court rely on the equitable maxim for the conclusion that beneficial ownership belongs to the relevant parties in equal shares.[1]

Although the starting-point for the determination of quantum lies in the express or implied bargain struck between the parties, there is a new recognition nowadays that 'all payments made and acts done by the claimant are to be treated as illuminating the common intention as to the extent of the beneficial interest.'[2] At this stage, as Nourse LJ indicated in *Stokes v Anderson*,[3] there is 'no practicable alternative to the determination of a fair share.' The court must 'supply the common intention by reference to that which all the material circumstances have shown to be fair.' Likewise in *Grant v Edwards*[4] Browne-Wilkinson V-C drew on the analogy of proprietary estoppel to suggest that in ascertaining the quantum of entitlement under a constructive trust the court should give effect to the common intention

16 *Springette v Defoe* [1992] 2 FLR 388 at 393D per Dillon LJ. See also Sir Christopher Slade's rejection in *Huntingford v Hobbs* [1993] 1 FCR 45 at 53F of the idea that the parties' respective beneficial interests fall to be determined 'by reference to any broad concepts of justice'.
17 *Hammond v Mitchell* [1991] 1 WLR 1127 at 1137F per Waite J. See also *Gissing v Gissing* [1971] AC 886 at 897B per Lord Reid, 903A-B per Lord Hodson; *McFarlane v McFarlane* [1972] NI 59 at 67.
18 *Gissing v Gissing* [1971] AC 886 at 908F per Lord Diplock.
19 See eg *Bannister v Bannister* [1948] 2 All ER 133 at 137B (ante, p 423).
20 *Grant v Edwards* [1986] Ch 638 at 657F-G per Browne-Wilkinson V-C.
1 *Gissing v Gissing* [1971] AC 886 at 908G per Lord Diplock. In some cases, however, the finances of the parties are so inextricably intermixed that 'an equitable knife must be used to sever the Gordian Knot' (*National Provincial Bank Ltd v Ainsworth* [1965] AC 1175 at 1236B per Lord Upjohn). See also *Rimmer v Rimmer* [1953] 1 QB 63 at 73; *Pettitt v Pettitt* [1970] AC 777 at 803H–804A per Lord Morris of Borth-y-Gest; *McFarlane v McFarlane* [1972] NI 59 at 67 per Lord McDermott LCJ; *Burns v Burns* [1984] Ch 317 at 345A per May LJ.
2 *Stokes v Anderson* [1991] 1 FLR 391 at 400B per Nourse LJ. It has been said, however, that the circumstances or conduct which brought about the breakdown of a personal relationship 'cannot be relevant in principle to the basis of calculation' (*Huntingford v Hobbs* [1993] 1 FCR 45 at 61E-F). The only exceptions to the general irrelevance of misconduct arise in respect of marginal adjustments over mortgage payments (post, p 479) and where it is alleged that the claimant was coerced by domestic violence to agree to abandon her interest in property (see *Skelding v Hanson* (Unreported, Court of Appeal, 17 November 1992) per Dillon LJ).
3 [1991] 1 FLR 391 at 400B-C.
4 [1986] Ch 638 at 657G–658A.

'so far as may fairly be done between the parties.'[5] The 'fair result by which the common intention ought to be supplied'[6] may well not be equal beneficial ownership.[7] The recognition of disparate proportions of beneficial ownership may be just as common.[8] As Lord Diplock stressed in *Gissing v Gissing*,[9] each case 'must depend upon its own facts.'

(8) Sphere of operation of constructive trusts

The following examples merely illustrate some of the general kinds of circumstance in which the constructive trust may be invoked in the law of land.

(a) Agreement that B should retain a beneficial interest in land purchased from B by A

One of the classic illustrations of the constructive trust doctrine occurs where B, a vendor, conveys the legal title in his land to A, a purchaser, on the strength of some oral undertaking by A that B shall retain a beneficial entitlement in the land even after the transfer. In such circumstances conscience demands that A be held to his agreement that the beneficial title should not belong solely to himself. The imposition of a constructive trust upon A can be quite easily rationalised here on the basis that B would never have parted with the property in the absence of such an oral undertaking from A.[10]

(i) The Bannister principle In *Bannister v Bannister*[11] B, the sister-in-law of A, had conveyed her freehold interest in two cottages to A at a gross undervalue, upon A's oral undertaking that she would be allowed to live in one of the cottages rent-free for the remainder of her life. The conveyance made no reference to this oral promise. When A later sought to evict B on the ground that she was a mere tenant at will,[12] the Court of Appeal upheld the refusal of the county court to order possession against her.

In the view of the Court of Appeal, A, although the current legal owner by virtue of the conveyance, was bound by a constructive trust in favour of B. Scott LJ held that such a trust is 'raised against a person who insists on the absolute character of a conveyance to himself for the purpose of defeating a beneficial interest, which, according to the true bargain, was to belong to another.'[13] Here there had been a 'bargain', in the sense that

5 Here, said Browne-Wilkinson V-C, 'equity is displayed at its most flexible'.
6 *Stokes v Anderson* [1991] 1 FLR 391 at 400D per Nourse LJ.
7 See, however, the equal shares awarded in *Grant v Edwards* [1986] Ch 638 at 651A, 654B, 658A; *Hammond v Mitchell* [1991] 1 WLR 1127 at 1137F-G.
8 See *Gissing v Gissing* [1971] AC 886 at 909C; *Bernard v Josephs* [1982] Ch 391 at 398C; *Falconer v Falconer* [1970] 1 WLR 1333 at 1336E-F. A one-third share was awarded in *Latter v McDonald* (Unreported, Court of Appeal, 26 February 1985); a one-fourth share in *Eves v Eves* [1975] 1 WLR 1338 at 1342H, 1343E, 1346A and *Stokes v Anderson* [1991] 1 FLR 391 at 401C-D; and a one-fifth share in *Hall v Hall* (1982) 3 FLR 379 at 381H, 385C.
9 [1971] AC 886 at 907A.
10 See *Avondale Printers & Stationers Ltd v Haggie* [1979] 2 NZLR 124 at 163.
11 [1948] 2 All ER 133.
12 For a description of 'tenancy at will', see Chapter 17 (post, p 680).
13 [1948] 2 All ER 133 at 136C.

B had been induced to convey the cottages to A partly in consideration of money payment and partly on the strength of his oral undertaking that B should enjoy a life interest in one cottage. Thus, even though the initial conveyance had not been fraudulent,[14] a fatal element of fraud was introduced as soon as A attempted to set up an absolute entitlement in himself in derogation of the beneficial rights which he had already agreed should be retained by B. Equitable fraud of this kind could not be covered up by the plea that 'no written evidence of the real bargain is available'.[15]

(ii) Extensions of the Bannister principle This application of the constructive trust is firmly established in other cases where there has been an unwritten agreement between A and B that B should retain either an absolute[16] or a limited[17] beneficial interest in land which he conveys to A. The precise nature or quantum of that interest is immaterial,[18] and it is generally accepted that the statutory requirement of writing can never be employed to 'smother proof of an oral arrangement creating a trust.'[19] For this purpose, moreover, it appears to be entirely irrelevant whether the purchase price paid by A is the full market value,[20] or is reduced in the light of the oral arrangement,[1] or is indeed non-existent.[2] The key question is simply 'whether the transferor would have parted with his property but for the oral undertaking of the transferee.'[3] If that question is answered in the negative, then A's renunciation of his promise or disavowal of the common intention formulated between A and B will 'operate in equity as a fraud' on B.[4]

14 There was an express finding by the county court judge that no fraud was present in the conveyance ([1948] 2 All ER 133 at 135C).
15 [1948] 2 All ER 133 at 136D.
16 *Hutchins v Lee* (1737) 1 Atk 447 at 448, 26 ER 284 at 285; *Childers v Childers* (1857) 1 De G & J 482 at 492, 44 ER 810 at 814; *In re Duke of Marlborough* [1894] 2 Ch 133 at 146.
17 *Booth v Turle* (1873) LR 16 Eq 182 at 183, 188; *Bannister v Bannister* [1948] 2 All ER 133 at 136E-F; *Last v Rosenfeld* [1972] 2 NSWLR 923 at 936E.
18 *Bannister v Bannister* [1948] 2 All ER 133 at 136E-F; *Last v Rosenfeld* [1972] 2 NSWLR 923 at 936E; *Avondale Printers & Stationers Ltd v Haggie* [1979] 2 NZLR 124 at 163.
19 *Dalton v Christofis* [1978] WAR 42 at 46 per Smith J. See also *Organ v Sandwell* [1921] VLR 622 at 630.
20 *Last v Rosenfeld* [1972] 2 NSWLR 923 at 930B, 936B. It is arguable, however, that if A pays B the full market value there is then no element of 'detriment' or 'sacrifice' on the part of B sufficient to raise a constructive trust in his favour. Strictly speaking, this may well be true, in which case this situation is better analysed as involving an oral declaration of an express trust which, but for the rule in *Rochefoucauld v Boustead*, would have been unenforceable (ante, p 377). There is as always a lingering doubt as to the proper characterisation of the trust enforced by virtue of this rule, but it seems in accordance with principle to restrict the operation of the constructive trust to cases in which there has been a true 'change of position' by B in the shape of some 'detriment' or 'sacrifice'.
1 *Booth v Turle* (1873) LR 16 Eq 182 at 183, 188; *Bannister v Bannister* [1948] 2 All ER 133 at 134F.
2 *Hutchins v Lee* (1737) 1 Atk 447 at 448, 26 ER 284 at 285; *Childers v Childers* (1857) 1 De G & J 482 at 492, 44 ER 810 at 814; *In re Duke of Marlborough* [1894] 2 Ch 133 at 146. In some cases the transfer to the alleged trustee was expressed to be for valuable consideration, but the consideration was never in fact paid (see eg *Davies v Otty* (No 2) (1865) 35 Beav 208 at 213, 55 ER 875 at 877; *Haigh v Kaye* (1872) 7 Ch App 469 at 473f).
3 *Avondale Printers & Stationers Ltd v Haggie* [1979] 2 NZLR 124 at 163.
4 Ibid.

(b) Agreement that B should retain a beneficial interest in land purchased by A from X

Another illustration of the constructive trust in operation arises where A purchases X's legal estate in land, having first agreed with the vendor that B should retain a beneficial interest in that land even after the transfer to A.

Precisely these circumstances arose in *Lyus v Prowsa Developments Ltd*.[5] Here a development company, X, was the owner of an area of land on which it proposed to build a number of residential properties. The development was financed by a loan of money from a bank, Y, secured by way of a legal charge over X's land. Some time after the creation of this charge, X contracted with B to build a house on one plot within the development area and sell that plot to B. B paid a contractual deposit and waited for the house to be built. Before either the house or the transaction of purchase could be completed, X became insolvent and Y, in exercise of its statutory powers of sale as mortgagee, sold the property to A1, another development company (*Fig.* 26). Although the transfer of the legal title to A1 made no reference to B or his rights, the contract preceding the transfer made it quite clear that the transfer was expressly 'subject to' B's contractual rights under the estate contract between B and X. A1 later transferred the same legal title to A2, the contract for sale again stipulating that A2 should take 'subject to' B's equitable rights under the original estate contract.

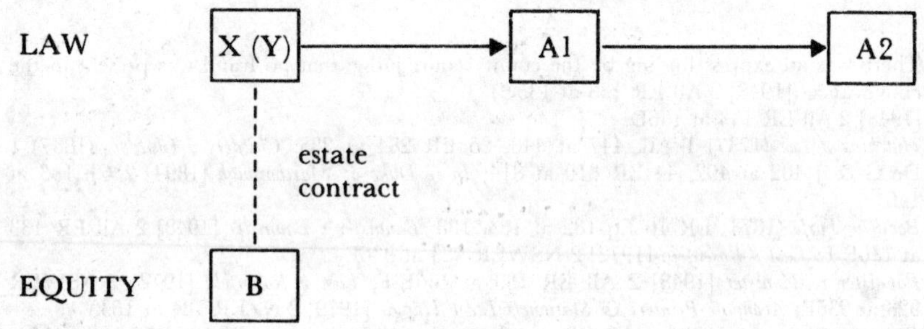

Fig. 26

B sued *inter alia* for a declaration that the estate contract was binding on A1 and A2.[6] Dillon J concluded that it had been 'a stipulation of the bargain' between Y and A1 that A1 would give effect to B's equitable rights

5 [1982] 1 WLR 1044. See [1983] CLJ 54 (C. Harpum); [1983] Conv 64 (P. Jackson); (1983) 46 MLR 96 (P.H. Kenny); (1984) 47 MLR 476 (P. Bennett).

6 The estate contract had been duly protected by entry of a caution against X's registered title. However, this protection could not avail B as against Y, the bank-mortgagee, which derived overriding rights from a mortgage charge which was clearly prior to any rights which B had acquired under the later estate contract (see also Land Registration Act 1925, s 34(4)). In effect the issue of priority between B and A1 and A2 respectively was decided as if the caution had never been entered.

under the original estate contract with X,[7] and that a similar stipulation had been made as between A1 and A2. Accordingly, Dillon J applied *Bannister v Bannister*[8] and held that both A1 and A2 had taken the legal estate on a constructive trust for B.[9] The 'fraud' present in this case lay very largely in A1 'reneging on a positive stipulation in favour of [B] in the bargain under which [A1] acquired the land.'[10] Specific performance was ordered against A2 on the terms of the original estate contract.

(c) Agreement that B should acquire a beneficial interest in land purchased by A from X

It is possible that resort may be had to the constructive trust doctrine in order to give effect to an otherwise unenforceable agreement that B should acquire a beneficial interest in land purchased by A from X.

(i) Deviation from the shares generated by money contributions No recourse to the constructive trust doctrine will, of course, be needed if the agreed or presumed beneficial ownership follows the precise proportions in which A and B contributed moneys towards a purchase in the name of A. In such cases, where 'there is a correspondence between the proportions contributed and the beneficial interests intended', the agreement is enforceable—without any requirement of formal writing—as a resulting trust.[11]

If, however, the beneficial ownership, as agreed between A and B, is unrelated to their actual contributions, there arises in favour of B an 'express trust which lacks writing'.[12] It is in this context that the constructive trust may play a valuable role. To the extent that the agreed beneficial shares deviate from the ratio of actual money contributions—even if B claims a beneficial share unsupported by any actual money contribution[13]—the arrangement may still be enforceable as a constructive trust.[14]

(ii) Fiduciary consequences of an anterior bargain Underlying the imposition of a constructive trust in this situation is the idea that it would be 'equitable fraud' for A to rely on the statutory requirement of writing in order to defeat the agreement reached between himself and B.[15] The existence of

7 [1982] 1 WLR 1044 at 1053E.
8 [1948] 2 All ER 133 (ante, p 438).
9 [1982] 1 WLR 1044 at 1053F-G. See D.J. Hayton, (1983) 133 NLJ 188; C.T. Emery and B. Smythe, (1983) 133 NLJ 798.
10 [1982] 1 WLR 1044 at 1054G-H. For another application of the same principle, see eg *Binions v Evans* [1972] Ch 359 at 368B, 370D-G (post, p 917).
11 *Allen v Snyder* [1977] 2 NSWLR 685 at 692A per Glass JA. See also *Bloch v Bloch* (1981) 37 ALR 55 at 64.
12 *Allen v Snyder* [1977] 2 NSWLR 685 at 692C-D per Glass JA, who pointed out that such an agreement, far from giving rise to a resulting trust, operates 'as a pro tanto rebuttal of the trusts resulting presumptively from the actual contributions.' See also *Cowcher v Cowcher* [1972] 1 WLR 425 at 431C, 433H; *Currie v Hamilton* [1984] 1 NSWLR 687 at 690F.
13 In such a case, however, B's claim must be supported by evidence of some other form of 'detriment' or 'sacrifice'.
14 See *Calverley v Green* (1984) 155 CLR 242 at 263 per Mason and Brennan JJ.
15 *Allen v Snyder* [1977] 2 NSWLR 685 at 692E.

an anterior 'bargain' implies that A's conscience was bound—even at the date of acquisition—by an obligation to recognise equitable rights in B. It is the fact of agreement or common intention which supplies the vital link in the argument, for the obligation created by the 'bargain' casts A in the role of a fiduciary *ab initio*. As Fullagar J said in *Thwaites v Ryan*,[16] 'the trust existed *as the trustee took the property*. To set up the statute would be to steal what was in equity never his . . . [A] person who *accepts* property in a fiduciary capacity cannot set up in himself . . . the legal estate free of the trust.' It also follows that A's character as a fiduciary at the very moment of acquisition will give rise to an allegation of 'equitable fraud' should he ever subsequently attempt to derogate from the rights in B to which he has agreed to take subject. Again in the words of Fullagar J,[17]

> If A accepts property upon trust for B absolutely and then seeks to steal B's property by invoking the statute, equity is liable to say that A has received a benefit which binds his conscience and he cannot be allowed to assert against B the existence in A of something that A never had, namely the legal estate unencumbered by the trust. By invoking the statute A would be using it to steal from B property which, so far as A is concerned, was always the property of B.[18]

The well known decision of the Supreme Court of New South Wales in *Ogilvie v Ryan*[19] provides an example of the operation of the constructive trust in circumstances of purchase by A from X. Here B, a woman aged 62, had left her existing home in order to live with A in a house which he purchased in his own name for this purpose. Before moving into this property, A and B agreed orally that if B kept house and cared for A until he died—he was then aged 82—B would be entitled to live in the house rent-free for the remainder of her life. A and B then lived together on these terms for a further two years until A died. At this point, E, the executor of A's will, took proceedings for possession against B. Holland J held that E was bound by a constructive trust to give effect to the undertaking made by his predecessor in title, on the ground that it would be 'an unconscientious use of the legal title' if E were now to assert it in derogation of an interest conferred by A.[20] Even though B had made no contribution (financial or otherwise) towards the acquisition of legal title by A, an oral declaration of trust could have been enforced, in view of B's faithful performance of her side of the 'bargain', against A (and therefore against his personal representative). A had effectively acquired the property on terms that he should hold as a trustee for B.[1] As Holland J observed,[2]

> an appropriate constructive trust will be declared in Equity to defeat a species of fraud, namely, that in which a defendant seeks to make an unconscionable use of his legal title by asserting it to defeat a beneficial interest in the property which

16 [1984] VR 65 at 92f.
17 [1984] VR 65 at 91.
18 See also *Vedejs v Public Trustee* [1985] VR 569 at 572f.
19 [1976] 2 NSWLR 504. See M.A. Neave, *The Constructive Trust as a Remedial Device*, (1977–78) 11 Melbourne ULR 343; I. Hardingham, *The Non-marital Partner as Contractual Licensee*, (1979–80) 12 Melbourne ULR 356.
20 [1976] 2 NSWLR 504 at 518E.
1 See *Last v Rosenfeld* [1972] 2 NSWLR 923 at 928B-C; *Thwaites v Ryan* [1984] VR 65 at 94.
2 [1976] 2 NSWLR 504 at 518D-E.

he ... has agreed to or promised; or which it was the common intention of the parties that the plaintiff should have, in return for benefits to be provided by, and in fact obtained from, the plaintiff in connection with their joint use or occupation of the property.[3]

(d) Agreement that B should acquire a beneficial interest in land already owned by A

A significantly different question arises where A agrees with B that B should acquire some beneficial interest in land which is already owned by A at law. A declaration of trust in B's favour made subsequently to A's acquisition of title is fully enforceable if evidenced in writing.[4] Difficulties arise, however, if some time *after* taking title A constitutes himself a trustee for B by means of purely oral declaration or agreement. In seeking to enforce his beneficial claim under these circumstances, B cannot invoke either the doctrine of resulting trust or the rule in *Rochefoucauld v Boustead*, since both of these are activated by intentions (actual or presumed) existing contemporaneously with A's acquisition of title.[5]

The same kind of objection would also be fatal to any claim based by B on constructive trust were the latter form of trust exclusively premised upon a fiduciary *acquisition* of legal title. In the circumstances now under discussion, B cannot of course argue that A acquired his legal estate as a fiduciary, since the trust alleged by B can only have come into existence, if at all, at some date subsequent to A's acquisition of the title concerned.

(i) Deferred assumption of fiduciary status It is clear, however, that the constructive trust doctrine is not dependent on a showing that A was a fiduciary at the date of his acquisition of title.[6] It is widely accepted that A's fiduciary character may arise at some much later date and that a constructive trust may be imposed in order to frustrate any attempt by A to deny that he has constituted himself a trustee for B by some act or agreement occurring subsequent to the acquisition date.[7] In such a case the constructive trust is imposed, not on the basis of any theory concerning the fiduciary acquisition of title, but on the basis of the argument that a later 'change of position' by B has conferred an advantage upon A, the beneficial effect of which he cannot now conscionably claim to retain.[8]

3 It has been suggested that justice could have been done in this case (and in similar cases) through an application of the doctrine of estoppel rather than through the invocation of a constructive trust. See eg R.H. Maudsley, *Constructive Trusts*, (1977) 28 NILQ 123 at 133, 136ff; J.D. Davies, (1979) 8 Sydney L Rev 578 at 583.

4 Ante, p 376.

5 Ante, pp 384, 377.

6 *Gissing v Gissing* [1971] AC 886 at 905B-C (ante, p 417); *Butler v Craine* [1986] VR 274 at 284f. Compare, however, *Thwaites v Ryan* [1984] VR 65 at 71, 93.

7 See eg *Gissing v Gissing* [1971] AC 886 at 901D, 906E, 908B-C; *Christian v Christian* (1981) 131 NLJ 43; *Mellowes v Collymore* (Unreported, Court of Appeal, 27 November 1981); *Burns v Burns* [1984] Ch 317 at 327D; *Warner v Warner* (Unreported, Court of Appeal, 11 July 1984); *Winkworth v Edward Baron Development Co Ltd* (1986) 52 P & CR 67 at 79f; *Grant v Edwards* [1986] Ch 638 at 651H-652A; *Butler v Craine* [1986] VR 274 at 287.

8 See *Nemeth v Nemeth* (1978) 17 ALR 500 at 506.

(ii) Reluctant recognition of post-acquisition constructive trusts The foregoing rationale closely resembles the concept of 'unjust enrichment' which provides the central feature of a much wider doctrine of the remedial constructive trust as applied, for instance, in the USA.[9] It is precisely the more open-ended nature of this application of constructive trust theory which makes the English courts fairly reluctant to admit constructive trust claims based on events occurring after the date of acquisition. However, such claims have been allowed, although usually only on strict proof that the supervening element of 'detriment' or 'sacrifice' on the part of B was truly 'referable to' some 'bargain' or common intention that a beneficial interest would be generated thereby.[10]

In *Bernard v Josephs*,[11] for example, Griffiths LJ conceded that it might 'in exceptional circumstances' be inferred that the parties had agreed to alter their beneficial interests subsequent to the acquisition of a quasi-matrimonial home. He instanced the hypothetical case in which 'the man bought the house in the first place and the woman years later used a legacy to build an extra floor to make more room for the children.' In such circumstances, 'the obvious inference' would be that the parties had agreed that the woman would acquire a share in 'the greatly increased value of the house produced by her money.' However, Griffiths LJ added ominously, 'this depends upon the court being able to infer an intention to alter the share in which the beneficial interest was previously held'. The 'mere fact' that one party 'has spent time and money on improving the property' would not normally be sufficient ground to justify such an inference.

(iii) Ambivalent judicial response An illustration of the ambivalence with which the English courts approach constructive trust claims of this kind is provided by *Winkworth v Edward Baron Development Co Ltd.*[12] Here a matrimonial home was purchased in the name of a limited company owned and controlled by H and W. All of the purchase money was provided by the company, with the result that immediately following the purchase the entire beneficial interest in the property vested in the company alone. Some time after the acquisition W paid £8,600 of her own money to the company's bank, thereby reducing the company's overdraft on its current account with that bank. A majority in the Court of Appeal decided that this supervening payment raised a constructive trust in favour of W. Nourse LJ applied the principles stated in *Gissing v Gissing*, and held that W's payment had been 'referable to the acquisition' of the property.[13] In his view, it could reasonably be inferred that W and the company had formed a common intention that

9 Post, p 450.
10 See the way in which constructive trust claims foundered for want of a proven common intention in *Grant v Sanderson* [1983] Court of Appeal Unbound Transcript 862; *Warner v Warner* (Unreported, Court of Appeal, 11 July 1984).
11 [1982] Ch 391 at 404D-F.
12 [1986] 1 WLR 1512 (House of Lords); (1986) 52 P & CR 67 (Court of Appeal).
13 (1986) 52 P & CR 67 at 74f.

a beneficial interest in the property should be conferred on W.[14] Kerr LJ dissented, however, precisely on the ground that W's payment could not be attributed to any intention that it was to be referable to or on account of the purchase price which the company had paid for the property.[15]

When *Winkworth* was appealed, the House of Lords unanimously endorsed the dissenting judgment of Kerr LJ and reversed the ruling of the Court of Appeal. While not denying that a trust may arise *after* the date of acquisition, Lord Templeman pointed out that there had been 'no connection between the acquisition of [the property] and the payment of £8,600'.[16] The supervening payment made by W could not be said to be 'referable' to the acquisition of the house, not least because the property 'had already been bought and paid for in full'.[17] In the stern view adopted by the House of Lords, the payment into the company's bank account had not manifested 'an intention on the part of [W] to offer to buy a part interest' in the house.[18] Nor, by submitting to a reduction in its overdraft, had the company manifested 'an intention to sell to [W] a bizarre proportion of [the property] at a price which had never been negotiated and could never have been justified.'[19]

A highly controversial example of the way in which the constructive trust may cover post-acquisition agreements or arrangements is found in the decision of the Court of Appeal in *Hussey v Palmer*.[20] Here B, an elderly widow, had been invited to live in a house the legal title in which was already owned by her son-in-law, A. An extra bedroom was built for her as an extension to the existing house, and the cost of this construction was paid by B. Although the purpose of the arrangement had been to provide accommodation for B during her old age, the residence of B was brought to a premature end by domestic discord and B sought a return of her capital outlay.

It was typical of this kind of informal family arrangement that the parties had never spelt out clearly the legal implications of their relationship. The Court of Appeal nevertheless decided, by a majority, that a constructive trust existed in favour of B. Lord Denning MR stated the philosophy of the constructive trust in broad terms, holding it to be

> a trust imposed by law whenever justice and good conscience require it. It is a liberal process, founded upon large principles of equity, to be applied in cases where the legal owner cannot conscientiously keep the property for himself alone, but ought to allow another to have the property or the benefit of it or a share in it. The trust may arise at the outset when the property is acquired, or later on, as the circumstances require. It is an equitable remedy by which the court can enable an aggrieved party to obtain restitution.[1]

14 (1986) 52 P & CR 67 at 73, 75. Once the requisite common intention was found, the court would 'not allow the [legal owner] to deny that interest and will construct a trust to give effect to it.'
15 (1986) 52 P & CR 67 at 83ff.
16 [1986] 1 WLR 1512 at 1515F.
17 [1986] 1 WLR 1512 at 1515E-F.
18 [1986] 1 WLR 1512 at 1516A.
19 [1986] 1 WLR 1512 at 1516B.
20 [1972] 1 WLR 1286. See (1973) 37 Conv (NS) 65 (D.J. Hayton); (1973) 89 LQR 2; (1973) 36 MLR 436 (T.C. Ridley).
1 [1972] 1 WLR 1286 at 1290A.

Lord Denning thus ruled that it would be 'entirely against conscience that [A] should retain the whole house and not allow [B] any interest in it, or any charge upon it.'[2] The Court decided that A therefore held his legal title subject to an equitable interest in B proportionate to the value of her cash investment in the extension.

As is indicated by the fact that there was a dissent in *Hussey v Palmer*,[3] the applicability of a constructive trust in such circumstances is not entirely free of doubt. Although there was clearly a recognisable 'change of position' on the part of B, it is difficult to identify the relevant 'bargain' or common intention,[4] and even more difficult to pinpoint the precise kind of interest which A, even by inference, was supposed to have agreed to confer upon B.[5] The pivotal feature of the case was probably the inequitable nature of the conduct of A, who had behaved most oppressively and unfairly towards B,[6] and it may be that the majority decision was influenced more by such factors than by the technical requirements of constructive trust theory.[7]

(e) *Agreement that B should acquire an enlarged beneficial interest in land owned by A*

Further difficulties arise where a legal title in land is already vested in A, subject to an existing trust under which B has some beneficial entitlement. These difficulties occur if B later claims to have acquired an enlarged beneficial share over and above the quantum of beneficial entitlement already enjoyed by him under the original terms of the trust. It is one of the formal proprieties

2 [1972] 1 WLR 1286 at 1291B.

3 [1972] 1 WLR 1286 at 1292C-D per Cairns LJ, who pointed out that B had herself testified in court to having merely 'lent' the money to A. In the view of Cairns LJ, 'it is going a very long way to say that ... there was some misunderstanding by her of the legal position and that she was describing as a loan something which was not a loan at all.' Where there is documentary evidence which confirms the status of a transaction as a loan, this is enough to displace the possibility that a contribution of money may have generated a trust (see eg *In re Sharpe (A Bankrupt)* [1980] 1 WLR 219 at 222G-H, ante, p 404).

4 See *Avondale Printers & Stationers Ltd v Haggie* [1979] 2 NZLR 124 at 145; M. Neave, (1978) 11 Melbourne ULR 343 at 361.

5 The interest recognised by Lord Denning MR as having been acquired by B under the court-imposed constructive trust seemed to hover ambivalently between a proportionate share in the beneficial ownership of the property and a mere lien for the money advanced by her ([1972] 1 WLR 1286 at 1291B-D). See *In re Sharpe (A Bankrupt)* [1980] 1 WLR 219 at 222H–223A. It is perhaps significant that a similar claim of constructive trust in favour of a mother-in-law was quickly brushed aside in *Broughall v Hunt* (Unreported, Chancery Division, 1 February 1983) in preference for a contractual licence solution (post, p 909). See also *Savva v Costa and Harymode Investments Ltd* (1981) 131 NLJ 1114.

6 There was evidence ([1972] 1 WLR 1286 at 1288D-E) that A had refused even to reply to a somewhat plaintive request made by B after her departure from the home for an allowance of £1 per week to help her out!

7 For a critical view of *Hussey v Palmer*, see *In re Sharpe (A Bankrupt)* [1980] 1 WLR 219 at 223A; *Avondale Printers & Stationers Ltd v Haggie* [1979] 2 NZLR 124 at 145; *Malsbury v Malsbury* [1982] 1 NSWLR 226 at 231B-C. It may be that, as was suggested in *Holiday Inns Inc v Broadhead* (1974) 232 Estates Gazette 951 at 1087 and *Savva v Costa and Harymode Investments Ltd* (1981) 131 NLJ 1114, the decision in *Hussey v Palmer* is better analysed as an illustration of the principle in *Ramsden v Dyson* (1866) LR 1 HL 129 (ante, p 318). See the application of the law of proprietary estoppel in analogous circumstances in *Clayton v Green* (1979) NZ Recent Law 139 at 140.

of a valid trust that the beneficial interests should crystallise in the intended proportions at the commencement of the trust,[8] and should not thereafter fluctuate arbitrarily or be otherwise varied except in accordance with the statutory requirements of writing.

(i) Strict application of trust principles The present problem may easily arise if B makes supervening contributions of money towards the acquisition cost of A's property. In *Cowcher v Cowcher*,[9] instance, the legal title in a matrimonial home was purchased in the name of A. However, the purchase price of £12,000 was raised effectively by means of a cash contribution of some £4,000 from B and a mortgage loan of £8,000 for repayment of which A undertook sole responsibility. These money contributions constituted what Bagnall J called a 'money consensus',[10] under which a presumed resulting trust arose for A and B in the precise proportions of their respective contributions.[11] The trust generated by this 'money consensus' was clearly immune from all requirements of writing or other formality.[12] When A's business later ran into difficulties, B used her own moneys to discharge in part A's mortgage responsibility. B claimed that, by reason of these supervening financial contributions, her beneficial share under the trust of the matrimonial home had been increased from one-third to one-half.

B's claim, although apparently justified in terms of fairness, was rejected by Bagnall J. In his view, the beneficial interests under the trust had crystallised at the point of creation of the trust as shares of two-thirds and one-third for A and B respectively. These proportions fixed by the initial 'money consensus' were capable of subsequent variation only in strict compliance with section 53(1)(c) of the Law of Property Act 1925.[13] This provision requires that 'a disposition of an equitable interest or trust subsisting at the time of the disposition must be in writing and signed by the person disposing of the same . . .'[14] In Bagnall J's analysis, any attempt to vary the beneficial shares achieved by the original 'money consensus' must be regarded as the consequence of some 'interest consensus' reached by the parties which, unlike the original 'money consensus', was not immune from the statutory requirement of writing. B's assertion of an extra beneficial entitlement necessarily involved a subsequent disposition of a one-sixth share in her favour. Bagnall J decided that her claim must fail for want of writing in compliance

8 *Bernard v Josephs* [1982] Ch 391 at 404F.
9 [1972] 1 WLR 425. See (1972) 35 MLR 547 (J. Levin).
10 Ante, p 391.
11 [1972] 1 WLR 425 at 431B-C.
12 [1972] 1 WLR 425 at 431C-D.
13 See also *Sekhon v Alissa* [1989] 2 FLR 94 at 100C per Hoffmann J.
14 Section 53(1)(c) derives ultimately from section 9 of the Statute of Frauds 1677. The object of both provisions is 'to prevent hidden oral transactions in equitable interests in fraud of those truly entitled, and making it difficult, if not impossible, for the trustees to ascertain who are in fact [their] beneficiaries' (*Vandervell v IRC* [1967] 2 AC 291 at 311B-C per Lord Upjohn). It is clear that section 53(1)(c) applies not merely to the disposition of equitable interests arising under an express trust, but also to the disposition of interests arising under a resulting trust (see *Cowcher v Cowcher* [1972] 1 WLR 425 at 432E) and also under a constructive trust (see *Oughtred v IRC* [1960] AC 206 at 230, 233; *Appleby v Cowley* (1982) *Times*, 14 April).

with section 53(1)(c).[15] B's beneficial entitlement was held to remain as a one-third share.[16]

The judgment of Bagnall J in *Cowcher v Cowcher* thus contains a stern ruling that the subsequent variation of the original beneficial shares fixed under a trust can operate only as an express disposition requiring writing.[17] This approach leads to obvious difficulties and the possibility of substantial injustice in those circumstances where parties make supervening contributions of money in a loose and informal manner, without having ever contemplated the necessity of compliance with a statutory requirement of writing. Moreover, it would seem exceedingly strange if a supervening contribution could generate a beneficial share where none existed before,[18] but could not augment a beneficial share already in existence.

(ii) Liberalising effects of the constructive trust It now seems to be agreed that the dilemma exposed in *Cowcher* is best resolved through the application of a constructive trust. In *In re Densham (A Bankrupt)*[19] Goff J expressed some disapproval of the excessively rigid view adopted by Bagnall J as to the role of section 53(1)(c). Goff J was of the opinion that the original shares of beneficial ownership as fixed by actual money contribution at the date of purchase could indeed be varied by a subsequent 'interest consensus' without the necessity of compliance with section 53(1)(c). Thus if a legal title were purchased in the name of A, and A expressly agreed that B should receive a larger beneficial share under a trust than was strictly justified by B's money contribution towards that purchase, B could justifiably claim that larger share on the footing of a constructive trust. To hold the agreement in B's favour unenforceable for want of writing would, in Goff J's terms, be 'contrary to equitable principles' since it would be 'unconscionable for a party to set up the statute and repudiate the agreement.' A would become a 'constructive trustee of the property so far as necessary to give effect to the agreement.'[20] However, the major difficulty lying in B's path is the requirement that he prove the existence of an agreement or bargain for

15 Bagnall J conceded ([1972] 1 WLR 425 at 432E-F) that, notwithstanding section 53(1)(c), 'a parole agreement for valuable consideration to vary the trusts, of which equity would grant specific performance' would have been 'as valid as an assignment in writing; for it would operate as an agreement for sale of an equitable interest upon which the vendor would become a trustee for the purchaser subject only to the payment of the consideration.' However, Bagnall J added that such an agreement could be implied from conduct 'only in the most exceptional circumstances' and that the mere payment by one beneficial owner of a mortgage instalment properly payable by the other could not normally imply an agreement to alter the beneficial interests. See also *Avondale Printers & Stationers Ltd v Haggie* [1979] 2 NZLR 124 at 142.

16 B was allowed to recover the amount of her supervening contributions (approximately £1,500) in addition to the value of her one-third equitable share (ante, p 391). However, the value of the extra one-sixth share which she unsuccessfully claimed would, by virtue of the considerable inflation of the land values involved, have been in the region of £7,000.

17 See also *Jeffries v Stevens* (1982) STC 639 at 651g for disapproval of the possibility of 'a wavering equity in . . . property'. By the same token, however, an initial beneficial entitlement cannot be forfeited merely by reason of the effluxion of time: it can normally be got out of its owner only by means of written disposition (see *Brykiert v Jones* (1981) 2 FLR 373 at 375G).

18 Ante, p 444.

19 [1975] 1 WLR 1519. See (1976) 92 LQR 489 (F. Webb).

20 [1975] 1 WLR 1519 at 1525D-E. See, however, Insolvency Act 1986, s 339(3)(c) (post, p 597).

enhanced beneficial ownership and that his financial contribution was 'referable' to it.[1]

6. THE FUTURE OF THE TRUST

The fundamental problem in the contemporary English law of trusts lies in the dogmatic requirement that some conscious intention as to beneficial title be demonstrated as the minimal condition for the creation of equitable co-ownership. In many circumstances the search for evidence of such intention is wholly unreal and the attempt to ascertain relevant intention is vitiated by artificiality. The court has no residual jurisdiction to subject disputed property to a trust merely on the ground that such a result 'would be fair in all the circumstances'.[2] Particularly in the context of the family home it has now come to be questioned whether the law of trusts can be modified or refashioned so as to reflect more accurately the social actuality in which claims of beneficial entitlement are apt to arise.

(1) The claim of social justice

If taken out of context certain passages in Lord Diplock's seminal formulation of trust doctrine in *Gissing v Gissing*[3] seem capable of endorsing the idea that the court may award a trust interest ex aequo et bono—whenever it would be 'inequitable' not to do so. However, far from supporting a liberated view of the role of the trust, Lord Diplock's approach constituted a severely restrictive application of trust doctrine.[4] The requirement of 'referability'[5] imposed by Lord Diplock served to reinforce the highly qualified nature of any suggestion that trusts arise in order to ensure fair outcomes.[6] The failure of the wife's claim in *Gissing* was not based on any perception that it was 'inequitable' to grant her a beneficial share in the matrimonial home. The decision rested simply on the fact that, in the absence of any conscious agreement to share the beneficial title, the House of Lords declined to infer that the wife's expenditure had been 'referable to' the acquisition of the family home.[7]

Yet the result in *Gissing* remains open to criticism on grounds of social

1 See Lord Diplock's reference in *Gissing v Gissing* [1971] AC 886 at 906E to the necessity for 'some subsequent fresh agreement, acted upon by the parties, to vary the original beneficial interests created when the matrimonial home was acquired'.
2 *Gissing v Gissing* [1971] AC 886 at 900F per Viscount Dilhorne.
3 [1971] AC 886 at 905B-D (ante, p 383).
4 This conclusion is confirmed by the merest glance at the actual decision reached by the House of Lords in *Gissing*. In this case the claimant wife, during a marriage of some 25 years' duration, had made indirect financial contributions towards the purchase of the family home through the use of her own moneys on various forms of household and other family-related expenditure. The House of Lords nevertheless denied her any beneficial entitlement in the property, which was vested at law solely in the name of her husband. See *Allen v Snyder* [1977] 2 NSWLR 685 at 694B-695C.
5 Ante, p 432.
6 See Lord Diplock's insistence that an implied trust arises only if the alleged trustee 'has induced the cestui que trust to act to his own detriment in the reasonable belief that by so acting he was acquiring a beneficial interest in the land' (ante, p 383).
7 Ante, p 435.

justice.[8] The claimant wife (and indeed most marital and quasi-marital partners) would doubtless have continued to make her appropriate contribution to the family partnership without regard to any anticipation of reward or tangible pay-off—and this for at least two reasons. *First*, it is seldom contemplated in advance that family relationships will break down and thereby require that the respective property rights of the parties be crystallised. *Second*, it is characteristic of most family life that the constructive contributions of family members are motivated less by the mercenary incentives of an exchange economy than by higher principles of love and duty. The requirement of 'referability' nevertheless operates as a sharp brake upon successful claims to beneficial entitlement on the part of family members. The insistence of the House of Lords in *Gissing* (and more recently in *Lloyds Bank Plc v Rosset*[9]) that equitable co-ownership be premised on some demonstrable 'common intention' has thrown almost insuperable obstacles even in the way of those who have contributed substantially to the success of a joint venture and who stand most clearly in need of legal protection. In *Burns v Burns*,[10] for example, the Court of Appeal sent away empty-handed a de facto wife who had lived with her partner for 17 years, had borne and reared two children by him, and had contributed both money and household services to the relationship. In *Wood v Wood*[11] a similar result caused Lawton LJ to observe that the outcome should provide a 'cautionary tale for women who cohabit with men without having clear understandings with them about their property dealings one with the other.' In his view, 'questions of property rights as between cohabitees cannot be dealt with on the basis of sentiment, they have got to be dealt with in accordance with the law of property.'

It is inevitable, in the face of outcomes which to many may seem inequitable, that some attention should be focused on other less restrictive interpretations of the trust model to be found in other jurisdictions.

(2) The remedial constructive trust

English law has traditionally regarded the constructive trust as a substantive institution analogous to the express trust.[12] A constructive trust arises where, in relation to defined property, some person has undertaken a fiduciary role which thereafter he cannot be heard to disavow.[13] In such circumstances, the person concerned is made liable *as though* he were a trustee. In its adherence to a substantive doctrine of constructive trusts, English law now contrasts sharply with the application of constructive trust theory in certain other jurisdictions.

(a) The North American constructive trust

In the North American model, for instance, the constructive trust is an overtly

8 Ante, p 435.
9 [1991] 1 AC 107 (ante, p 424).
10 [1984] Ch 317 (ante, p 430).
11 Unreported, Court of Appeal, 1979 W No 1393, 7 July 1982.
12 *Avondale Printers & Stationers Ltd v Haggie* [1979] 2 NZLR 124 at 147.
13 Ante, p 414.

remedial mechanism.[14] It provides a third head of civil obligation, ranking alongside but still rather distinct from, contract and tort, in which the court subjects a person holding title to property to an equitable duty to convey it to, or to hold it on trust for, another on the ground that the current title holder would be 'unjustly enriched' if he were permitted to retain the property beneficially.[15] The constructive trust in this sense is closely linked with the emergence of the law of restitution as a third major form of civil liability in the common law world.[16] This remedial perspective is not without respectable antecedents,[17] but its importance lies nowadays in the fact that it opens up a range of almost uncontrollably diverse applications.

The application of a liberal doctrine of constructive trust has, for instance, revolutionised the law of family property in Canada.[18] In *Rathwell v Rathwell*[19] the Supreme Court of Canada invoked a wide concept of remedial constructive trust in order to confer a half-share in the matrimonial property on a wife who had made substantial domestic contributions to the marriage partnership. In the words of Dickson J, the application of the constructive trust

> comprehends the imposition of trust machinery by the Court in order to achieve a result consonant with good conscience. As a matter of principle, the Court will not allow any man to appropriate to himself the value earned by the labours of another. That principle is not defeated by the existence of a matrimonial relationship between the parties; but, for the principle to succeed, the facts must display an enrichment, a corresponding deprivation, and the absence of any juristic reason—such as a contract or disposition of law—for the enrichment.[20]

This approach was taken one step further in *Pettkus v Becker*,[1] where the

14 See *Chase Manhattan Bank NA v Israel-British Bank (London) Ltd* [1981] Ch 105 at 126G-127D; *Simonds v Simonds*, 408 NYS2d 359 at 362ff (1978). See also J.L. Dewar, *The Development of the Remedial Constructive Trust*, (1982) 60 CBR 265.

15 The American *Restatement of Restitution* provides that 'a person who has been unjustly enriched at the expense of another is required to make restitution to that other' (para 1). Likewise, where 'a person holding title to property is subject to an equitable duty to convey it to another on the ground that he would be unjustly enriched if he were permitted to retain it, a constructive trust arises' (para 160). See also A.W. Scott, (1955) 71 LQR 39, *Law of Trusts* (3rd edn, Boston and Toronto 1967), Vol V, p 3413; D.W.M. Waters, *The Constructive Trust* (London 1964).

16 See Lord Goff of Chieveley and Gareth Jones, *The Law of Restitution* (3rd edn, London 1986). See also *Beatty v Guggenheim Exploration Co*, 225 NY 380 at 386 (1919), where Cardozo J described the constructive trust as 'the formula through which the conscience of equity finds expression. When property has been acquired in such circumstances that the holder may not in good faith retain the beneficial interest, equity converts him into a trustee'.

17 See eg *Moses v Macferlan* (1760) 2 Burr 1005 at 1012, 97 ER 676 at 681, where Lord Mansfield pointed out that 'the gist of this kind of action is that the defendant, upon the circumstances of the case, is obliged by the ties of natural justice and equity to refund the money . . .'

18 See generally Mary Welstead, *Domestic Contribution and Constructive Trusts: The Canadian Perspective*, (1987) 2 Denning LJ 151. See also J.D. McCamus and L. Taman, (1978) 16 Osgoode Hall LJ 741; A.J. McClean, (1982) 16 UBCLR 155.

19 (1978) 83 DLR (3d) 289.

20 (1978) 83 DLR (3d) 289 at 306. For confirmation of the three constitutive elements of the constructive trust, see *Sorochan v Sorochan* (1986) 29 DLR (4th) 1 at 5 per Dickson CJC. Compare Lord Reid's observation in *Pettitt v Pettitt* [1970] AC 777 at 795G-H that the doctrine of unjust enrichment, whilst applicable to money claims, is not necessarily appropriate in relation to real property. See also *In re Sharpe (A Bankrupt)* [1980] 1 WLR 219 at 225G, where Browne-Wilkinson J declared the 'constructive trust as a remedy' to be 'a novel concept in English law'.

1 (1980) 117 DLR (3d) 257.

Supreme Court of Canada similarly applied the remedial constructive trust for the purpose of recognising the entitlement of a de facto wife to one-half of the family assets acquired through her joint efforts with her partner in his farm business.[2] In terms which closely resembled the language of proprietary estoppel, Dickson J noted that 'where one person in a relationship tantamount to spousal prejudices herself in the reasonable expectation of receiving an interest in property and the other person in the relationship freely accepts benefits conferred by the first person in circumstances where he knows or ought to have known of that reasonable expectation, it would be unjust to allow the recipient of the benefit to retain it.'[3]

This recognition was extended yet again in *Sorochan v Sorochan*,[4] where the Supreme Court invoked the principle of 'unjust enrichment' to confer a substantial share of quasi-matrimonial property on a homemaker and mother. Dickson CJC acknowledged that the claimant's unwaged domestic endeavour had clearly conferred a 'benefit' upon her partner, resulting in a corresponding 'deprivation' to herself.[5] There being no 'juristic reason' in the form of any obligation (contractual or otherwise) to perform such household services, the claimant was awarded a constructive trust of part of her de facto husband's land plus a money sum of $20,000.[6]

The North American (and particularly the Canadian) articulation of constructive trust theory is interesting because it widens considerably the conditions which activate the imposition of a trust on the owner of a legal estate.[7] If the trigger for the traditional presumption of resulting trust is a contribution of money, it may well be that contributions of labour provide the trigger for the application of the constructive trust based on 'unjust enrichment'. Moreover, this development may be symptomatic of the contemporary emergence of the 'new property', one of the strongest features of which is the recognition that men and women have a property in their own labour. The remedial constructive trust also mirrors something of the advances which are being made in other jurisdictions through the development of the doctrine of proprietary estoppel. However, the 'unjust enrichment' constructive trust seems to incorporate a more positive and ultimately more realistic emphasis upon the element of 'benefit' conferred on the recipient of the relevant contribution of services or money. Estoppel theory is still largely dominated by the inquiry whether 'detriment' has been incurred by the contributor. It is often the case that an emphasis on the benefit conferred more accurately reveals the true value of the respective contributions made in the context of family arrangements.

2 Tragically the successful plaintiff never received her award of $150,000. She committed suicide in November 1986 (see *Montreal Gazette*, 11 November 1986), driven to despair by a legal system which had allowed her former partner to frustrate in large measure all attempts made by her to enforce the court order in her favour. The only sums paid over by the defendant, amounting to $68,000, were in fact seized by the plaintiff's lawyer for legal fees. See Mary Welstead, (1987) 2 Denning LJ 151.

3 (1980) 117 DLR (3d) 257 at 274.

4 (1986) 29 DLR (4th) 1.

5 (1986) 29 DLR (4th) 1 at 6f.

6 See also *Rawluk v Rawluk* (1990) 65 DLR (4th) 161 at 169ff per Cory J; C.E.F. Rickett, [1991] Conv 124.

7 There is, for instance, no need to relate specific contributions to particular assets (see *Nuti v Nuti* (1980) 108 DLR (3d) 587 at 603, (1982) 122 DLR (3d) 384).

(b) The English response

The remedial constructive trust has conferred a new freedom on courts in other jurisdictions to do justice in the resolution of the property rights within family arrangements.[8] The remedial trust arises quite independently of the vagaries of intentions which may or may not have been formulated by the parties.[9] It substitutes the broad principle of restitution of unjust enrichment for a sterile and ritualistic preoccupation with ultimately illusory figments of common intention. Accordingly the remedial trust relates much more sensitively to the realities of family life so grievously falsified by the English application of trust doctrine.

(i) The 'new model' constructive trust For a brief period during the 1970s it seemed that some more liberated version of constructive trust doctrine might take root and flourish in England.[10] The form of constructive trust found its foremost protagonist in the English courts in the predictable shape of Lord Denning MR. In *Cooke v Head*,[11] the former Master of the Rolls declared that the courts would 'impose or impute' a constructive trust 'whenever two parties by their joint efforts acquire property to be used for their joint benefit'.[12]

Perhaps the most clear-cut articulation of the remedial constructive trust emerged in *Eves v Eves*.[13] Here a de facto wife claimed to have effected extensive improvements to a house vested at law in the sole name of her partner.[14] The Court of Appeal awarded her one quarter of the beneficial ownership in the property, Lord Denning MR basing his reasoning on a liberal theory of constructive trust.[15] He observed that 'a few years ago even equity would not have helped' a claimant in the position of the plaintiff, but noted that 'things have altered now. Equity is not past the age of child bearing. One of her latest progeny is a constructive trust of a new model. Lord Diplock brought it into the world and we have nourished it.'[16] Lord Denning proceeded to cite in his support Lord Diplock's famous formulation in *Gissing v Gissing*,[17] suppressing however the severely limiting qualifications

8 See eg *McGrath v Hilding*, 394 NYS2d 603 at 606f(1977); *Clooney v Clooney*, 394 A2d 313 at 316 (1978); *Wright v Wright*, 311 NW2d 484 at 485f (1981); *In re Estate of Eriksen*, 337 NW2d 671 at 674 (1983); *Willits v Willits Estate* (1982) 14 Sask R 114 at 126f; *Pratt v MacLeod* (1982) 129 DLR (3d) 123 at 132ff; *Palachik v Kiss* (1983) 146 DLR (3d) 385 at 391ff; *Murray v Roty* (1983) 147 DLR (3d) 438 at 443ff; *O'Neill v Mehain* (1985) 57 BCLR 64 at 68.

9 See *Hayward v Giordani* [1983] NZLR 140 at 148, 149.

10 See also Marcia Neave, *The Constructive Trust as a Remedial Device*, (1978) 11 Melbourne ULR 343.

11 [1972] 1 WLR 518 at 520F.

12 *Cooke v Head* involved parties to a de facto relationship, but Lord Denning pointed out that the same constructive trust doctrine was applicable to 'husband and wife, to engaged couples, and to man and mistress, and maybe to other relationships too' ([1972] 1 WLR 518 at 520G).

13 [1975] 1 WLR 1338. See (1976) 92 LQR 489 (F. Webb); R.H. Maudsley, (1977) 28 NILQ 123 at 132f.

14 Ante, p 429.

15 The other judges in the Court of Appeal, Browne LJ and Brightman J, were more cautious and preferred to find a more traditional basis for reaching the same conclusion (ante, p 419).

16 [1975] 1 WLR 1338 at 1341F-G.

17 [1971] AC 886 at 905B-D (ante, p 383).

imposed by that rationale of trust doctrine.[18] Thus curtailed Lord Diplock's speech provided apparent support for the proposition that a trust arises 'whenever [a] trustee has so conducted himself that it would be inequitable to allow him to deny to the cestui que trust a beneficial interest'.[19] On this basis Lord Denning reiterated his view that a new head of inequitable conduct is disclosed whenever the court considers that it would be fair to cause beneficial ownership to be shared by two or more parties who have acquired property by joint efforts.

(ii) Objections to the remedial constructive trust Lord Denning's attempts to introduce a more liberal principle of constructive trust were evident in other cases of the 1970s.[20] However, the application of the remedial constructive trust proved to be excessively controversial in the English context,[1] and did not survive Lord Denning's retirement from the bench.[2] Such forms of trust were (and still are) vulnerable to the objection that they represent a law of 'palm-tree justice' under which past decisions are worthless as precedent and future decisions are almost entirely unpredictable.[3] As Mahon J pointed out in *Carly v Farrelly*,[4] no 'stable system of jurisprudence could permit a litigant's claim to justice to be consigned to the formless void of individual moral opinion'.[5]

It is a further objection that the remedial constructive trust serves as an improper agent for the informal creation of proprietary rights. Its operation in this way unfairly prejudices a separate category of interests which by long tradition are jealously protected by the law of property—the interests

18 Lord Denning MR consistently declined in other cases to adopt Lord Diplock's notion of 'referable' contributions (ante, p 435). See *Hargrave v Newton* [1971] 1 WLR 1611 at 1613B-D, where Lord Denning found the concept 'very difficult to apply'. See also *Hazell v Hazell* [1972] 1 WLR 301 at 304C-E. For criticism of Lord Denning's overly selective technique, see *Avondale Printers & Stationers Ltd v Haggie* [1979] 2 NZLR 124 at 146f per Mahon J.

19 Compare *Allen v Snyder* [1977] 2 NSWLR 685 at 700F-701A, where Samuels JA observed in the New South Wales Court of Appeal that in *Eves v Eves* Lord Denning had 'proclaimed the legitimacy of equity's latest progeny, plucked by Lord Diplock from her capacious womb, and it was named "a constructive trust of a new model." But I would respectfully suggest that Lord Diplock's speech in *Gissing v Gissing* gives no warrant for identifying him as midwife; his Lordship, by exemplifying the trustee's inequitable conduct as the basis of the trust, is expressing no novelty ... [T]he legitimacy of the new model is at least suspect; at best it is a mutant from which further breeding should be discouraged.'

20 See eg *Heseltine v Heseltine* [1971] 1 WLR 342 at 346D-F; *Hussey v Palmer* [1972] 1 WLR 1286 at 1289H-1290D (ante, p 445).

1 See A.J. Oakley, (1973) 26 CLP 17.

2 See P.T. Evans, *The Fall and Rise of the Remedial Constructive Trust?* [1989] Conv 418.

3 See Dillon LJ's insistence in *Springette v Defoe* [1992] 2 FLR 388 at 393D, that the court 'does not as yet sit, as under a palm tree, to exercise a general discretion to do what the man in the street, on a general overview of the case, might regard as fair.'

4 [1975] 1 NZLR 356 at 367. Compare, however, *Pasi v Kamana* [1986] 1 NZLR 603 at 607 per McMullin J.

5 One reason for the submergence of the 'new model' constructive trust in England has lain in the powerful objection that the imposition of such a trust constitutes an argument of last resort. For the hard-nosed property lawyer, the 'finding' of a remedial constructive trust is an act of intellectual bankruptcy, amounting effectively to a judicial confession that no convincing reason can be found in law for giving judgment in favour of a deserving plaintiff.

of innocent third parties.[6] Part of the problem in the present context is precisely the fact that any beneficial interest awarded by way of constructive trust gains an automatic priority over creditors of the constructive trustee in the event of any insolvency affecting the latter.[7] Furthermore, even if the constructive trustee remains perfectly solvent, there is always a danger that third parties who purchase the trust property from him may find themselves fixed with deemed notice of the constructive beneficiary's equitable interest.[8]

(3) New directions

The day is slowly coming when English courts will no longer feel bound to search for—or disingenuously to fashion—phantoms of common intention in order to resolve the property relations of disaffected participants in family arrangements.[9] There is already in some quarters a weary recognition of the 'air of unreality about the whole exercise' and it is increasingly acknowledged that the court can only view 'broadly' the conduct of the parties in its search for their 'unexpressed and probably unconsidered intentions as to . . . beneficial ownership'.[10]

(a) Antipodean developments

Any movement towards a more sympathetic application of trust law will find a ready echo in recent developments in other common law jurisdictions. In 1983 the Court of Appeal of New Zealand refused in *Hayward v Giordani*[11] to exclude the possibility that the court may properly impose a constructive trust, on the Canadian analogy, in response to an allegation of 'unjust enrichment'. Cooke J found the approach of the Canadian Supreme Court 'very helpful . . . in working out the property rights of common law spouses', and indicated that to him it seemed 'only a small step to eliminate the need to strain for proof of common intention'.[12] This step was finally taken in *Gillies v Keogh*,[13] where Cooke P led the Court of Appeal in rejecting the notion that constructive trusts arise only on the basis of 'the actual subjective intention of the parties'. Cooke P noted the practical nexus between constructive trust, unjust enrichment, imputed common intention and estoppel,[14] and observed that

> Whatever legal label or rubric cases in this field are placed under, reasonable expectations in the light of the conduct of the parties are at the heart of the matter.

6 'Third parties who have not been unjustly enriched may suffer as a result of holding that there is a constructive trust' (Sir Nicolas Browne-Wilkinson, *Constructive Trusts and Unjust Enrichment* (Holdsworth Club of the University of Birmingham 1991), p 3). For a far-reaching insight into this policy concern, see A.J. Oakley, *Constructive Trusts* (2nd edn, London 1987), p 4ff.

7 Post, p 597. See also *Re Osborn* (1989) 91 ALR 135 at 139ff.

8 Ante, p 83; post, p 564.

9 [1982] CLJ 30 at 33. See also *Hayward v Giordani* [1983] NZLR 140 at 145 per Cooke J; *Stratulatos v Stratulatos* [1988] 2 NZLR 424 at 436 per McGechan J.

10 *Bernard v Josephs* [1982] Ch 391 at 404B per Griffiths LJ. See [1983] CLJ 30.

11 [1983] NZLR 140.

12 [1983] NZLR 140 at 148.

13 [1989] 2 NZLR 327 at 332. See (1990) 106 LQR 213 (M. Bryan).

14 [1989] 2 NZLR 327 at 330.

It can be said that a party is unjustly enriched if he or she retains the entire fruits of contributions made by the other, notwithstanding that the other has suffered detriment or made a sacrifice and has reasonably expected from the conduct of the first party and all the circumstances that the contributions will carry rights. Similarly, to retain the sole benefit can be labelled unconscionable or contrary to equity or manifestly unfair ... These ideas may be seen as but the application in a particular field of the equitable jurisdiction to interfere where the assertion of strict legal rights is found by the Court to be unconscionable...[15]

These developments in New Zealand closely mirror the way in which, after observing for some time the strictures of the orthodox trust analysis,[16] the Australian courts have begun to elaborate a jurisprudence of 'unconscionability' in the resolution of claims of beneficial entitlement. In *Baumgartner v Baumgartner*,[17] a de facto wife, by pooling her income with that of her partner, had made indirect contributions towards the family home. The High Court of Australia confirmed the 'unconscionability' doctrine earlier adumbrated in *Muschinski v Dodds*[18] and awarded her a 45 per cent share in the disputed property.[19] In *Muschinski v Dodds* Deane J had taken the view that 'in its modern context, the constructive trust can properly be described as a remedial institution which equity imposes regardless of actual or presumed agreement or intention (and subsequently protects) to preclude the retention or assertion of beneficial ownership of property to the extent that such retention or assertion would be contrary to equitable principle.'[20] The recognition of the constructive trust as remedial did not, however, mean that it 'represents a medium for the indulgence of idiosyncratic notions of fairness and justice'.[1] The remedy was available 'only when warranted by established equitable principles or by the legitimate processes of legal reasoning, by analogy, induction and deduction, from the starting point of a proper understanding of the conceptual foundation of such principles.'[2] In *Baumgartner*'s case the High Court accordingly applied its

15 [1989] 2 NZLR 327 at 331. See also Sir Robin Cooke, *Fairness*, (1989) 19 VUW Law Rev 421. In *Gillies v Keogh* the Court of Appeal declined on the facts to award any beneficial interest to the claimant de facto partner. It emerged that the legal owner had consistently asserted throughout the relationship that the disputed property was hers alone. Cooke P declared that '[t]he principle of freedom to stipulate against a trust or obligation is consistent with all the theories. A constructive trust cannot arise if the conduct of the parties and the circumstances show that a reasonable person in the claimant's position would not expect a benefit' ([1989] 2 NZLR 327 at 334).

16 See eg *Allen v Snyder* [1977] 2 NSWLR 685 (Court of Appeal of New South Wales).

17 (1987) 164 CLR 137, on appeal from [1985] 2 NSWLR 406.

18 (1985) 160 CLR 583 at 620. Here Deane J applied the general equitable principle which 'operates in a case where the substratum of a joint relationship or endeavour is removed without attributable blame and where the benefit of money or other property contributed by one party on the basis and for the purposes of the relationship or endeavour would otherwise be enjoyed by the other party in circumstances in which it was not specifically intended or specially provided that that other party should so enjoy it.' In such a case, said Deane J, citing *Atwood v Maude* (1868) LR 3 Ch App 369 at 374f and *Lyon v Tweddell* (1881) 17 Ch D 529 at 531, 'equity will not permit that other party to assert or retain the benefit of the relevant property to the extent that it would be unconscionable for him to do so'.

19 This award reflected the proportions in which the parties' respective earnings had been mixed in the common pool.

20 (1985) 160 CLR 583 at 614.

1 (1985) 160 CLR 583 at 615.

2 (1985) 160 CLR 583 at 615.

understanding of equitable principle to hold that the legal owner's assertion of exclusive beneficial title amounted to 'unconscionable conduct which attracts the intervention of equity and the imposition of a constructive trust'.[3]

A standard concern caused by the broad extension of trust doctrine is, of course, that trust interests, once liberally created, may take priority over the claims of creditors of and purchasers from the trustee.[4] Conscious of this fear, Deane J was careful to emphasise in *Muschinski v Dodds*[5] that the constructive trust constitutes

> an in personam remedy attaching to property which may be moulded and adjusted to give effect to the application and interplay of equitable principles in the circumstances of the particular case. In particular, where competing common law or equitable claims are or may be involved, a declaration of constructive trust by way of remedy can properly be so framed that the consequences of its imposition are operative only from the date of judgment or formal court order or from some other specified date.

It is not impossible therefore that the 'unconscionability' doctrine can avoid undue risk of prejudice to third parties: a trust interest generated against one party on the footing of 'unconscionability' has no dogmatically predetermined or inexorable impact on any other party. Ironically the precise reverse may indeed be true. If the binding effect of jural claims is subjected to an overriding test of unconscionability, it may turn out in many circumstances to be unconscionable for a beneficiary under a remedial constructive trust to assert priority over the trustee's creditor or purchaser.[6] The price of this flexibility is, however, that the full third-party impact of a *Baumgartner* equity may ultimately depend unpredictably on a series of one-off adjudications specific to each set of circumstances. This degree of uncertainty is, for some, too high a price to pay when compared with the convenience of the ready-made conclusions compelled by the dogmas of conventional equity jurisprudence.

It is clear that the trust doctrines of Australia and New Zealand have begun to shift sharply away from their more orthodox points of departure in English law. It is but a short further step to move towards a concentration of the court's focus on unconscionability of *outcome* rather than mere

3 (1987) 164 CLR 137 at 149 per Mason CJ, Wilson and Deane JJ. Professor Paul Finn has questioned whether the law of unjust enrichment or restitution will prove to be 'the Siamese twin of the unconscionability principle' (see *Commerce, The Common Law and Morality*, (1989) 17 MULR 87 at 89). In *Baumgartner v Baumgartner* (1987) 164 CLR 137 at 152f, Toohey J went so far as to suggest that 'unconscionable conduct' and 'unjust enrichment' approaches might well be but component—if not identical—aspects of a unifying legal concept of restitution. See also *Gillies v Keogh* [1989] 2 NZLR 327 at 343 per Richardson J.

4 Ante, p 455.

5 (1985) 160 CLR 583 at 615.

6 See eg *Re Osborn* (1989) 91 ALR 135 at 141f, where the Federal Court of Australia pointed out that a husband's trustee in bankruptcy could not be said to be 'acting unconscionably in attempting to recover property which, on the face of it is recoverable'. Here a wife failed to enforce on her own behalf a claimed *Baumgartner* entitlement against the property now vested in her husband's trustee in bankruptcy. According to Pincus J, the *Baumgartner* principle did not extend to cases where there was as yet 'no unconscionable conduct alleged against the legal owner' at the time of the bankruptcy, ie the husband.

unconscionability of *conduct.* If this step is taken[7]—and it is not clear that such a move was not already implicit in *Baumgartner*—the court will be in a position to impose a constructive trust whenever the end result of the parties' mutual dealings is to leave them with economic or proprietary allocations which are considered unacceptable to the conscience of equity.[8] It is a large question whether such a far-reaching doctrine is ultimately sustainable as a principled approach to the resolution of property disputes in either the commercial or the familial context. Courts of law are not courts of morals.[9] The critical issue relates, as always, to the degree of permissible or desirable compromise to be maintained in the trade-off between the ends and the means of the adjudication process.

(b) The English reception of broader concepts of trust doctrine

Recent trends in other Commonwealth jurisdictions have plainly given English lawyers much to ponder.[10] Ultimately it may be that, in the interests of social justice, English courts will return to the approach to trusts of family property which was adumbrated by Lord Reid in *Pettitt v Pettitt*[11] and *Gissing v Gissing.*[12] Here Lord Reid, albeit a lone voice in the House of Lords, urged that the courts be free to impute to family members a 'deemed intention' with respect to beneficial ownership based on the likely intentions of reasonable persons.[13] Lord Reid made clear his sense of disquiet with any requirement of actual or inferred common intention as the necessary foundation of beneficial entitlement, noting that, if such a requirement were held to be good law, he himself 'could not contemplate the future results of such a decision with equanimity.'[14]

In the view of many, Lord Reid's prognosis has been proved broadly correct. Sir Nicolas Browne-Wilkinson (as he then was), speaking extra-

7 At least some members of the High Court were willing to contemplate this possibility at the stage of argument in *Gazzola v Gazzola* (1990) 92 ALR 45. (The case went off on other grounds.)

8 See, however, *Re Osborn* (1989) 91 ALR 135 at 142 per Pincus J.

9 Sir Nicolas Browne-Wilkinson has described the Australian approach as 'close to saying that, if the defendant's conduct in relation to property is unconscionable, he is to be treated as a constructive trustee . . . that such unconscionable conduct is actionable *per se* . . . Manifestly there is much unconscionable behaviour which does not give rise to a remedy' (*Constructive Trusts and Unjust Enrichment*, p 7).

10 See eg D.J. Hayton, *Equitable Rights of Cohabitees*, [1990] Conv 370.

11 [1970] AC 777 at 795C-G.

12 [1971] AC 886 at 897C-G.

13 Such an approach is not far removed from the statutory presumption of intention supplied, in the context of spousal impovements, by Matrimonial Proceedings and Property Act 1970, s 37 (ante, p 422). As Lord Reid was quick to point out in *Pettitt v Pettitt* [1970] AC 777 at 794A-E, the distinction between improvements and other forms of contribution is somewhat artificial in the context of the family home.

14 *Gissing v Gissing* [1971] AC 886 at 897G. In *Pasi v Kamana* [1986] 1 NZLR 603 at 605, Cooke P doubted whether there was any 'significant difference' between Lord Reid's deemed common intention and the unjust enrichment concept used by the Supreme Court of Canada. 'Unconscionability, constructive or equitable fraud, Lord Denning's "justice and good conscience" and "in all fairness": at bottom in this context these are probably different formulae for the same idea . . . One way of putting the test is to ask whether a reasonable person in the shoes of the claimant would have understood that his or her efforts would naturally result in an interest in the property.' See also *Stratulatos v Stratulatos* [1988] 2 NZLR 424 at 437 per McGechan J; *Gillies v Keogh* [1989] 2 NZLR 327 at 340 per Cooke P.

judicially in 1991, expressed the belief that 'the law took a wrong turning in *Gissing v Gissing*' and that 'the law of constructive and resulting trusts has been distorted'.[15] In the opinion of the former Vice-Chancellor, there is now a need for a 'rethink' of the common intention constructive trusts 'invented' in *Gissing*'s case.[16] Nevertheless there is a profound reluctance to embrace any over-broad formula for change. As Sir Nicolas Browne-Wilkinson indicated, there are 'great dangers in seeking to turn equity into one comprehensive law of unjust enrichment based on some sweeping fundamental concept.'[17] He suggested instead that the law of unjust enrichment and restitution should be developed 'incrementally' and that the trust doctrine expounded in *Gissing v Gissing* could 'with advantage' be refashioned on the guiding analogy of the principles of proprietary estoppel.[18] Such a redirection of the law of trusts, it was argued, could confer enormous benefit in terms of flexibility of judicial response and the need to accommodate emerging solutions to the legitimate claims of third parties.[19]

15 *Constructive Trusts and Unjust Enrichment*, p 5. Sir Nicolas Browne-Wilkinson pointed out that the members of the House of Lords sitting on *Gissing v Gissing* did not include an equity or property lawyer. Lord Upjohn, who had sat on *Pettitt v Pettitt* [1970] AC 777, died on 27 January 1971, six weeks before the House of Lords' hearing in *Gissing*.

16 Ibid, p 4.

17 Ibid, p 7. It may perhaps be observed, however, that the highly artificial reasoning present in some recent English decisions closely approaches the recognition of a general principle of 'fairness'. See eg Nourse LJ's reference in *Stokes v Anderson* [1991] 1 FLR 391 at 400D to the 'fair result by which the common intention ought to be supplied' for the purpose of a constructive trust.

18 Ante, p 312. See, however, *Stokes v Anderson* [1991] 1 FLR 391 at 399C-D per Nourse LJ, for a reminder that the law of trusts has not yet been assimilated with that of proprietary estoppel.

19 Ante, p 455.

CHAPTER 13

Co-ownership

Co-ownership is the term used to describe the form of ownership in which two or more persons are simultaneously entitled in possession to an interest or interests in the same property. Co-ownership thus connotes some form of concurrent (as distinct from successive) holding in respect of property, and is governed in English law by rules markedly different from those which regulate land which is the subject of a strict settlement under the Settled Land Act 1925.[1]

1. THE MODERN SOCIAL CONTEXT OF CO-OWNERSHIP

Concurrent ownership of an estate or interest in land has nowadays become infinitely more common than the limited forms of successive ownership which are dealt with under the Settled Land Act 1925. At the zenith of its influence the strict settlement of land was underpinned by certain assumptions concerning wealth, status and the gender of owners of property.[2] It is no accident that the demise of the strict settlement in modern times has coincided with fundamental changes in the social norms relating to such factors.[3] In particular it can be said that contract has largely displaced status as the conceptual basis of family relationships.[4] Coupled with this movement from status-dependent relationships to voluntary co-operative relationships has been the wide acknowledgement of a new egalitarian ideal. This has been evident not least in respect of the relationship between male and female, between husband and wife.[5] The modern emphasis in domestic living

1 Post, p 608.

2 Post, p 609.

3 Our own society has ceased to be regulated to the same degree by status and gender. See eg M.A. Glendon, *Power and Authority in the Family: New Legal Patterns as Reflections of Changing Ideologies*, (1975) 23 AJCL 1; M.A. Glendon, *The New Family and the New Property* (Toronto 1981), p 11ff.

4 In a former age the relation of husband and wife was strictly defined in terms of the incidents of a lifelong status. Nowadays the continuance and quality of the spousal relationship are overshadowed by the reality of liberal divorce laws which recognise that marriage has become a form of permissive cohabitation. See O.R. McGregor, *Equality, sexual values and permissive legislation: the English experience*, (1972) 1 Jnl Soc Pol 44; Kevin Gray, *Reallocation of Property on Divorce* (Abingdon 1977), p 11ff.

5 Thus we no longer accept the sex-based lines of demarcation which, in real property terms, classed married women along with infants, idiots, traitors, felons and aliens, under the general heading of 'disabilities'. See eg *European Asian of Australia Ltd v Kurland* (1985) 8 NSWLR 192 at 200B-C per Rogers J ('...in the year 1985 it seems anachronistic to be told that being a female and a wife is, by itself, sufficient qualification to enrol in the class of persons suffering from a special disadvantage...That being a female spouse should place a person shoulder to shoulder with the sick, the ignorant and the impaired is not to be tolerated').

arrangements is placed very much more on the sharing of property by persons situated in a relation of equality.

It was therefore inevitable that changing social facts should reflect themselves in our most important shared living arrangements—those which relate to the family home—with obvious implications for the law of real property and, especially, the law of co-ownership. Contemporary social patterns are far removed from those of a former age which saw the grant of patriarchal largesse epitomised in the marriage settlement. Concurrent ownership of an absolute interest in land—rather than the successive entitlement to limited interests conferred by a settlement—has become the expression of this newer social pattern. The power structure embodied in settled land arrangements of the past has been largely displaced by the shared power relationships preferred in the more democratic, egalitarian, industrial and urban society of the late 20th century.

2. TYPES OF CO-OWNERSHIP

English law has known four types of co-ownership. They are respectively (i) joint tenancy, (ii) tenancy in common, (iii) tenancy by entireties, and (iv) coparcenary. The last two forms of co-ownership are for all practical purposes archaic.

3. JOINT TENANCY

The essence of joint tenancy consists in the theory that each joint tenant is 'wholly entitled to the whole' of the estate or interest which is the subject of co-ownership.[6] No joint tenant holds any specific share in the property himself, but each is (together with the other joint tenant or tenants) invested with the total interest in the land.[7] The whole is not so much the sum of the parts, for each and every part is itself co-extensive with the whole.[8] In Bracton's expressive language, each joint tenant *totum tenet et nihil tenet*[9]; each holds everything and yet holds nothing.[10]

6 In this context, the term 'tenant' has nothing necessarily to do with the landlord-tenant relationship: it merely signifies 'owner'. However, there arises here a possibility of ambiguity in that the total interest which is subject to 'joint tenancy' may well be either an estate in fee simple, or a life interest, or even a term of years (ie a 'tenancy' in the landlord-tenant sense).

7 See *Wright v Gibbons* (1949) 78 CLR 313 at 329 per Dixon J; *In re Rushton (A Bankrupt)* [1972] Ch 197 at 203A per Goff J.

8 'Joint tenancy is based on the theory that together the joint tenants have but one estate, not a number of estates equal to the number of joint tenants' (*In Re Estate of King*, 572 SW2d 200 at 211 (1978)).

9 '*Quilibet totum tenet, et nihil tenet; scilicet, totum in communi, et nihil separatim per se*' (*Bracton*, fo 430 (Woodbine's edn), Vol 4, 336). See also *Co Litt*, p 186a; *Dawson v IRC* [1988] 1 WLR 930 at 934D, 938C. According to Pollock and Maitland, joint tenancy was already in existence by the 13th century and is 'decidedly older' than tenancy in common (*The History of English Law* (2nd edn, London 1968), Vol 2, p 20). See also *Carmody v Delehunt* [1984] 1 NSWLR 667 at 675E-G per Priestley JA.

10 See *Challis*, p 367.

(1) An undifferentiated form of co-ownership

Joint tenancy is thus an undifferentiated kind of co-ownership in which an entire estate or interest in property—rather than any defined proportion or aliquot share—is vested simultaneously in all the co-owners. The co-owned property is a single estate held by joint owners who are bound together in a 'thorough and intimate union of interest and possession'[11] and who together comprise but one composite person in the eyes of the law.[12]

(2) Absence of shareholding

Any reference to ownership in specific 'shares' (eg A owns a one-quarter interest and B a three-quarters interest) is normally sufficient to establish that A and B co-own not as joint tenants, but rather as tenants in common.[13] Even to say that A and B hold property in equal shares is, in strict terms and in the absence of any other evidence, to indicate that A and B are tenants in common.[14]

Such ambivalence as may attach to the nature of co-ownership in equal shares or half-shares is almost certainly attributable to the fact that a joint tenancy is fairly easily convertible by 'severance'[15] into a tenancy in common in equal shares. In consequence, every joint tenancy is also potentially a tenancy in common in equal shares,[16] and every joint tenant is proleptically a co-owner in equal shares and thus entitled to dispose of his aliquot share or to grant a lease or life interest out of that share.[17] There is therefore

11 *Bl Comm*, Vol II, p 182. So intimate is the union that, so far as vesting of title is concerned, it is irrelevant whether a joint tenant has made an equal (or indeed any) contribution to the purchase price of the co-owned property (see *Paluszek v Wohlrab*, 115 NE2d 764 at 766 (1953); *Brockway's Estate v CIR*, 219 F2d 400 at 403 (1954)).

12 As Lord Browne-Wilkinson explained in *Hammersmith and Fulham LBC v Monk* [1992] 1 AC 478 at 492B, a transfer of land to two or more persons as joint tenants 'operates so as to make them, vis à vis the outside world, one single owner'. See also Joshua Williams, *Principles of the Law of Real Property* (23rd edn by T.C. Williams, London 1920), p 143; *Duncan v Suhy*, 37 NE2d 826 at 828 (1941); *In Re Lorch's Estate*, 33 NYS2d 157 at 166 (1941); *Osterloh's Estate v Carpenter*, 337 SW2d 942 at 946 (1960).

13 *Cowcher v Cowcher* [1972] 1 WLR 425 at 430H; *Paluszek v Wohlrab*, 115 NE2d 764 at 766 (1953).

14 See *Martin v Martin* (1987) 54 P & CR 238 at 240 per Millett J. It may well be that Blackstone misled generations of lawyers when, in expounding Littleton's law-French (*Litt*, s 288), he taught that joint tenants are 'seised *per my et per tout*, by the half or moiety, and by all. . .' (*Bl Comm*, Vol II, p 182). See, for instance, *Doe d Aslin v Summersett* (1830) 1 B & Ad 135 at 140, 109 ER 738 at 739 per Lord Tenterden CJ. The word '*my*' is now generally agreed to have been the *mie* which in old French served as a negative expletive particle, rather than *mi* or 'half' as Blackstone seems to have believed. (So much should have been obvious in any event from the reflection that there may be more than two joint tenants; but see *Nielson-Jones v Fedden* [1975] Ch 222 at 228C). In effect, Littleton's phrase '*per my et per tout*' is merely a reiteration of Bracton's '*totum tenet et nihil tenet*'. On the 'singular infelicity' of Blackstone's translation, see Serjeant Manning's notes to *Daniel v Camplin* (1845) 7 Man & G 167 at 172, 135 ER 73 at 75 (note (c)). See also *Murray v Hall* (1849) 7 CB 441 at 455, 137 ER 175 at 180 (note (a)).

15 Post, p 485.

16 It was with this possibility in mind that Coke, while conceding that joint tenants are wholly seised of the whole, was nevertheless careful to point out that 'yet to divers purposes each of them hath but a right to a moiety, as to enfeoff, give, or demise, or to forfeit or lose by default in a *praecipe*.' (*Co Litt*, p 186a).

17 See *Challis*, p 367. Such forms of alienation automatically bring about either a total or partial severance of the joint tenancy (post, p 490).

an inevitable tendency on the part of lawyers to refer sometimes to joint tenants as being already entitled to equal shares,[18] but this merely reflects the extremely marginal nature of the legal distinction between the actual and the inchoate rights of the joint tenant.

(3) Distinguishing characteristics of joint tenancy

As Deane J observed in the High Court of Australia in *Corin v Patton*,[19] '[t]he substance of joint tenancy, while it subsists, lies in the equality and the personal character of the interests of the joint tenants in the undivided rights which constitute ownership of the whole of the relevant property'. It is commonly said, therefore, that the distinguishing characteristics of joint tenancy are two in number. *First*, joint tenants enjoy as between themselves a 'right of survivorship'. *Second*, the existence of joint tenancy always presupposes the presence of the 'four unities'.

(a) Right of survivorship (ius accrescendi)

It has been said that the right of survivorship or *ius accrescendi* is the 'grand and distinguishing' incident of joint tenancy.[20] On the death of one of two joint tenants, the surviving joint tenant becomes the sole owner by right of survivorship. This doctrine was elegantly described by Blackstone:

> [W]hen two or more persons are seised of a joint estate. . .the entire tenancy upon the decease of any of them remains to the survivors, and at length to the last survivor. . .The interest of two joint-tenants is not only equal or similar, but also is one and the same. One has not originally a distinct moiety from the other. . .but. . .each. . .has a concurrent interest in the whole; and therefore, on the death of his companion, the sole interest in the whole remains to the survivor.[1]

(i) Operation of the survivorship principle The operation of the *ius accrescendi* may be illustrated in the following way. Suppose that a fee simple estate in Blackacre was vested originally in three joint tenants, A, B and C. If C now dies, the estate remains vested in A and B as the surviving joint tenants,[2] and C's entitlement is simply extinguished.[3] Regardless of whether C dies testate or intestate, no 'share' in Blackacre can devolve with his estate[4] because

18 See eg *Bl Comm*, Vol II, p 182.

19 (1990) 169 CLR 540 at 579.

20 *De Witt v San Francisco*, 2 Cal 289 at 297 (1852). See also *In re Robertson* (1944) 44 SR (NSW) 103 at 105; *Matter of Estate of Oney*, 641 P2d 725 at 727 (1982).

1 *Bl Comm*, Vol II, p 183f. The *ius accrescendi* was described in *Wharton's Law Lexicon* (11th edn 1711), p 471, as 'a general concentration of property from more to fewer, by the accession of the part of him or them that die to the survivors or survivor, till it passes to a single hand, and the joint tenancy ceases.'

2 *Litt*, s 280; *Co Litt*, p 181a.

3 *Wright v Gibbons* (1949) 78 CLR 313 at 323 per Latham CJ; *Corin v Patton* (1990) 169 CLR 540 at 575 per Deane J. See also *Green v Skinner*, 197 P 60 at 62 (1921); *Fleming v Fleming*, 174 NW 946 at 953 (1921).

4 The operation of survivorship is frustrated only rarely. An example arises where an application is made under the Inheritance (Provision for Family and Dependants) Act 1975 for provision out of the estate of a decedent. The 'severable share' of a deceased beneficial joint tenant may be treated as part of his net estate 'to such extent as appears to the court to be just in all the circumstances of the case' (Inheritance (Provision for Family and Dependants) Act 1975, s 9(1)).

as a joint tenant C had no 'share' as such in the land.[5] He had no fraction of ownership which was capable of transmission on his death, since together with A and B he was wholly entitled to the whole. By virtue of the same argument, when C dies A and B are already fully entitled as joint tenants to the entire fee simple estate in Blackacre, and no further vesting in them as survivors is required.[6] No 'interest' passes to either of them on C's death[7]; the entire interest in the land merely 'survives' to them as the remaining joint tenants.

Similarly, if B predeceases A, the right of survivorship operates once more: B drops out of the picture, leaving A as the sole owner of the fee simple estate in Blackacre.[8] At least in strict theory, A's ownership has been enlarged throughout the entire process only to the extent that he is no longer subject to the hazard of survivorship.[9] In reality, of course, there has been a 'distinct shifting of economic interest, a decided change for the survivor's benefit'.[10] Moreover, it is irrelevant to the vesting of title in the survivor that he made little or no contribution towards the initial purchase of the property.[11]

Any doubt as to the identity of the surviving joint tenant is resolved in England by the rule governing *commorientes*. Under this rule where two or more persons have died in circumstances rendering it uncertain which survived the other or others, the deaths are presumed to have occurred in order of seniority, and the younger shall be deemed to have survived the elder.[12] The *commorientes* rule is not entirely satisfactory, and it is arguable that in the case of contemporaneous death the solution provided by the Uniform Simultaneous Death Act is much to be preferred.[13] Under this Act, which has been adopted for instance in California, the death of two or more joint

5 Administration of Estates Act 1925, s 3(4); *Challis*, p 366, citing *Litt*, s 280; *Eastgate v Equity Trustees Executors And Agency Co Ltd* (1964) 110 CLR 275 at 289f; *Dando v Dando*, 99 P2d 561 at 562 (1940).

6 'Technically, joint tenants are originally entitled to all which they ever have' (*Fadden v Deputy Federal Commissioner of Taxation* (1943) 68 CLR 76 at 84). See also *In Re Peterson's Estate*, 45 P2d 45 at 48f (1935); *Kleemann v Sheridan*, 256 P2d 553 at 555 (1953); *Williamson's Estate v Williamson*, 380 SW2d 333 at 338 (1964).

7 Except in the voracious view of the taxman, who, in defiance of the strict technicalities of land law, insists that a 'notional estate' (in the form of the appropriate aliquot share) has passed to the surviving joint tenant or tenants and is therefore chargeable to inheritance tax. See *Eastgate v Equity Trustees Executors And Agency Co Ltd* (1964) 110 CLR 275 at 284 per Kitto J, 290 per Menzies J; *United States v Jacobs*, 306 US 363 at 371, 83 L.ed 763 at 769 (1939); but compare *In Re Gerling's Estate*, 303 SW2d 915 at 919 (1957). In England it seems that for the purpose of inheritance tax, the value of a notional half-share under a joint tenancy is generally regarded by the Inland Revenue as being 45 per cent of the whole, the discount reflecting the fact that the co-owner did not enjoy complete control over the asset and that any realisation of the relevant value would have involved a transaction-cost for the vendor (see A.R. Mellows, *The Law of Succession* (4th edn, London 1983), p 196).

8 *Corin v Patton* (1990) 169 CLR 540 at 575 per Deane J.

9 See *Eastgate v Equity Trustees Executors And Agency Co Ltd* (1964) 110 CLR 275 at 283; *Craig v Federal Commissioner of Taxation* (1945) 70 CLR 441 at 452; *In Re Peterson's Estate*, 45 P2d 45 at 48f (1935); *In Re Foster's Estate*, 320 P2d 855 at 859 (1958).

10 *United States v Jacobs*, 306 US 363 at 371, 83 L.ed 763 at 769 (1939) per Black J.

11 *Wright v Bloom*, 359 P2d 1080 at 1083 (1961).

12 Law of Property Act 1925, s 184. This rule is, however, subject to any order of the court (see *In re Lindop* [1942] Ch 377 at 382; *Hickman v Peacey* [1945] AC 304 at 316). See also Administration of Estates Act 1925, s 46(3), as added by Intestates' Estates Act 1952, s 1(4).

13 See *Hickman v Peacey* [1945] AC 304 at 314, 317, where Viscount Simon LC, while conceding that time is infinitely divisible, opined that section 184 of the Law of Property Act 1925 has no application if the relevant deaths are 'absolutely simultaneous'.

tenants simultaneously is treated as a severance and an equal share of the property devolves with the estate of each decedent.[14]

(ii) Advantages of the survivorship principle Joint tenancy, with its inherent right of survivorship, may at first sight appear somewhat capricious,[15] but the undifferentiated co-ownership of joint tenancy is ideal for some purposes. Ever since 1925 co-ownership of a legal estate in land (ie of the fee simple absolute in possession or of a term of years absolute) has necessarily taken the form of joint tenancy.[16] The co-owners of a legal estate are automatically joint tenants and hold that estate as trustees. This fact has great importance both for the internal administration of the trust and for the conduct of transactions with strangers in respect of the trust property.

(iii) Avoidance of probate difficulties It would be highly inconvenient if there had to be a new vesting of the trust property on every occasion of death within the trusteeship. It is however of the essence of joint tenancy that, on the death of a trustee, the surviving trustees are *already* invested with the entire interest in the property and no further vesting in their names is required.[17]

(iv) Facility of dealings with title Similarly, it has already been seen[18] that a purchaser from joint tenants need investigate only one title—the title held by each and all of the joint tenants—with the result that co-ownership by way of joint tenancy not only facilitates the internal management of the trust, but also promotes the free alienation of land. Thus joint tenancy serves admirably the needs which arise in connection with the administration and disposition of the legal title to property. Since the legal title is only a 'paper title', authorising its owners merely to exercise fiduciary powers of management and disposition, the caprice of survivorship is usually rendered quite harmless in reality, since it in no way affects the equitable (ie beneficial)

14 See Cal Prob Code, s 296.2; *In re Estate of Meade*, 39 Cal Rptr 278 at 282 (1964).

15 The Supreme Court of California has pointed out that 'a joint tenant's right of survivorship is an expectancy that is not irrevocably fixed upon the creation of the estate; it arises only upon success in the ultimate gamble—survival—and then only if the unity of the estate has not theretofore been destroyed...' (*Tenhet v Boswell*, 133 Cal Rptr 10 at 14 (1976) per Mosk J). Another American court has observed that, while the joint tenants of a fee simple estate are alive, 'each has a specialised form of life estate, with what amounts to a contingent remainder in the fee, the contingency being dependent upon which joint tenant survives' (*Green v Skinner*, 197 P 60 at 62 (1921)).

16 Post, p 512. Joint tenancy can exist even though one of the co-owners has the potential of perpetual existence. A corporate body, being an artificial person in the eyes of the law, enjoys in theory a kind of immortality. However, it is now legally feasible for a corporate body to become a joint tenant (see Bodies Corporate (Joint Tenancy) Act 1899, s 1(1)). Moreover, survivorship operates in the sense that the jointly owned property devolves on the other joint tenant or tenants if the company is ever dissolved (see Bodies Corporate (Joint Tenancy) Act 1899, s 1(2)).

17 Moreover the appointment of new trustees may be made by the surviving trustee or trustees (Trustee Act 1925, s 36(1)) or by the court (Trustee Act 1925, s 41(1)). See also Trustee Act 1925, ss 36(7), 43. Where the appointment has been made by deed, a vesting of the land in the new trustees may be achieved by simple reliance on the vesting provisions contained in the Trustee Act 1925, s 40. There is normally no necessity for a re-conveyance of the trust property. See, however, Land Registration Act 1925, s 47(1) in relation to registered land.

18 Ante, p 100.

ownership of property. It is, of course, beneficial ownership which determines entitlements to the prospective proceeds of sale of the co-owned land.[19]

(v) Indestructibility of survivorship A unique and intimate union exists between joint tenants.[20] This identity of interest is so complete that the principal feature of their relationship—the right of survivorship—takes precedence over any testamentary disposition made by a joint tenant.[1] A disposition contained in the will of a joint tenant is entirely ineffective in respect of any land to which his joint tenancy relates, simply because a joint tenant has no specific share or interest which he can pass on his death.[2] Moreover, by the time the will takes effect survivorship has already operated.[3] The same point is expressed in the proposition that severance of a joint tenancy cannot normally be effected by will.[4] Unless a severance of the joint tenancy has occurred inter vivos, the right of survivorship is indestructible.

(vi) Utility as an estate planning device Not only does the right of survivorship override testamentary dispositions; it often has the effect of rendering testamentary gifts quite unnecessary. Where, for instance, the joint tenants are husband and wife, the operation of survivorship assumes most clearly its modern function as a simple and cost-effective estate planning device.[5] The *ius accrescendi* permits the co-owned estate to vest automatically in the survivor of the couple on the death of his or her partner—an outcome which seems in general to be desired by married couples.[6] In common with all other rules of intestate succession, survivorship is a speedy and inexpensive testamentary substitute designed to benefit a surviving partner while

19 Ante, p 108.

20 There is much evidence to suggest that joint tenancy is almost exclusively a form of matrimonial or quasi-matrimonial tenure. It has been surmised that the sharp rise in the incidence of joint tenancies from the 1940s onwards may have been stimulated both by increasing social recognition of the emancipation of married women and by the ever-present reality of death under war-time conditions (see N.W. Hines, *Real Property Joint Tenancies: Law, Fact, and Fancy*, 51 Iowa L Rev 582 at 590, 623 (1965–66)).

1 It has been postulated that there is a 'deep-rooted need for survivorship—the people want it' (N. Sterling, *Joint Tenancy and Community Property in California*, 14 Pacific LJ 927 at 929 (1982–83).

2 'The event of death does not sever the joint tenancy because the right of the survivor of the joint tenants to have the entire interest is the essence of a joint tenancy; the event which triggers this legal effect cannot at the same time be the event which would destroy it' (*Re Levy* (1982) 131 DLR (3d) 15 at 25). See also *Swift d Neale v Roberts* (1764) 3 Burr 1488 at 1496f, 97 ER 941 at 946; *In re Fritz' Estate*, 20 P2d 361 at 363 (1933); *In re Estate of Moy*, 31 Cal Rptr 374 at 377 (1963).

3 According to Coke, 'yet in consideration of Law there is a Priority of Time in an Instant, as here the Survivor is preferred before the Devise: for Littleton saith, that the Cause is that no Devise can take Effect till after the Death of the Devisor, and by his Death all the Land presently cometh by the Law to his Companion' (*Co Litt*, p 185b). See also *Bl Comm*, Vol II, p 186.

4 The law of severance is dealt with elsewhere (post, p 485), but compare the effect of mutual wills (post, p 501).

5 Survivorship may even be coupled with added taxation advantages for the survivor, as is for instance the case under New Zealand's Joint Family Homes Act 1964, s 22(1) (post, p 605). For the motivation behind this conferment of tax exemption, see Vol 292, *New Zealand Parliamentary Debates*, 3692ff; Vol 340, *New Zealand Parliamentary Debates*, 2995ff.

6 In Britain joint tenancy has become the predominant form of freehold ownership for young married couples: see J.E. Todd and L.M. Jones, *Matrimonial Property* (London 1972), p 80; A.J. Manners and I. Rauta, *Family Property in Scotland* (1981), p 5.

necessitating only minor administrative adjustments to the formerly joint title.[7]

(vii) Safety from unsecured creditors A further, and rather more dubious, benefit of the survivorship principle is that its operation renders the surviving joint tenant or tenants immune from unsecured debts incurred independently by the deceased joint tenant during his lifetime.[8] On the death of the debtor the entire co-owned property vests by operation of law in the survivor or survivors free of any claims which may be advanced by the decedent's creditors.[9] Consistently with the theory of joint tenancy,[10] the decedent's estate has no interest in the co-owned property from which outstanding unsecured claims can be satisfied.[1] Unsecured creditors are therefore unable to reach into the joint tenancy after the debtor's death unless that debtor severed the joint tenancy before he died.[2] Criticism has been directed at this rule which renders unsecured creditors extremely vulnerable when dealing with a debtor who contrives to tie up his property in joint tenancy form.[3] It is at precisely this point that 'the ineluctable logic of received property law strains in one direction while common humanity and sound public policy strain in the other.'[4]

(b) The 'four unities'

It is axiomatic that the 'four unities' must be present before a joint tenancy can be said to exist[5]; and that where all 'four unities' are present in a multiple

7 Speaking of joint tenancy, one American commentator has pointed out that 'the people want it. . .because in most instances they want the survivor to get all the property in the event of death. It is the poor man's will; it is faster and, in "no tax" cases, it is cheaper. It works well in practice for people of modest means' (see Y.B. Griffith, *Community Property in Joint Tenancy Form*, 14 Stanford L Rev 87 at 108 (1961–62)). For the criticism that survivorship is nevertheless somewhat inflexible as a quasi-testamentary device, see N.W. Hines, 51 Iowa L Rev 582 at 598.

8 The unilateral creation of a *secured* charge over jointly owned property would normally have had the effect of severance (post, p 493).

9 *Power v Grace* [1932] 2 DLR 793 at 795ff; *Re Maroukis and Maroukis* (1985) 12 DLR (4th) 321 at 325 per McIntyre J. See also *Irvine v Helvering*, 99 F2d 265 at 269 (1938); *King v King*, 236 P2d 912 at 913 (1951); *Frederick v Shorman*, 147 NW2d 478 at 484 (1966); *Schlichenmayer v Luithle*, 221 NW2d 77 at 83 (1974). The corollary is, of course, that if the *debtor* is the survivor, the creditors have access to the entire property formerly held under joint tenancy (see eg *Rupp v Kahn*, 55 Cal Rptr 108 at 112f (1966)).

10 Ante, p 463.

1 Unless a creditor can prove that the decedent deliberately put his property in joint tenancy form in order to defraud his creditors (post, p 597)

2 The effects of insolvency are examined more generally elsewhere (post, p 597).

3 The California Law Reform Commission, for instance, has castigated this aspect of joint tenancy law as 'anachronistic' and has pointed out that 'the existing rule gives the surviving joint tenant an unjustified windfall at the expense of the creditors of the deceased joint tenant'. The Commission recommended that unsecured creditors of a deceased joint tenant be allowed to reach into the severable share of the debtor to the extent that his estate is insufficient to meet their claims (*Recommendation Relating To Non-Probate Transfers*, 15 Cal Law Revision Commission Reports (1980), 1620f). This is the rule currently incorporated in the Uniform Probate Code, s 6–107.

4 See *Harris v Crowder*, 322 SE2d 854 at 855 (1984) per Neely J. See also J.W. Fisher, 91 W Va L Rev 267 at 273ff (1988–89).

5 *A.G. Securities v Vaughan* [1990] 1 AC 417 at 431H per Fox LJ

holding of land there is joint tenancy.[6] These unities—the 'hallmark inhabitants of the institution of joint tenancy'[7]—are the unities of possession, interest, title and time.[8] Only unity of possession is required as a precondition of tenancy in common.[9]

(i) Unity of possession Unity of possession means that each joint tenant is as much entitled to possession of every part of the co-owned land as the other joint tenant or tenants.[10] He may not physically delineate any part of the land as being 'his' land rather than that of any of his brethren,[11] nor prevent them from taking their appropriate share of the rents and profits derived from the land.[12] This unity of possession is only occasionally displaced by statutory intervention. Perhaps the best example of such intervention is provided by the Domestic Violence and Matrimonial Proceedings Act 1976,[13] which in cases of domestic discord empowers the court to oust a joint tenant from the family home.[14]

(ii) Unity of interest Unity of interest follows from the proposition that each joint tenant is 'wholly entitled to the whole'. The interest held by each joint tenant is therefore the same in extent, nature and duration. Joint tenancy cannot exist between persons holding interests of different natures or duration eg beween a freeholder and a leaseholder, an owner in possession and an owner in remainder, an owner of a fee simple interest and an owner of a life interest.[15] The unity of interest enjoyed by joint tenants means that a purchaser from joint tenants need investigate only one title. It also brings about the consequence that the full legal estate in jointly owned property cannot be effectually conveyed to a third party without the active participation

6 *Corin v Patton* (1990) 169 CLR 540 at 572 per Deane J.
7 *Corin v Patton* (1990) 169 CLR 540 at 572 per Deane J.
8 'This analysis has perhaps attracted attention rather by reason of its captivating appearance of symmetry and exactness, than by reason of its practical utility' (*Challis*, p 367). The requirement of the 'four unities' has not been literally adhered to in other jurisdictions: see eg *Estate of Grigsby*, 184 Cal Rptr 886 at 889 (1982). See also *Corin v Patton* (1990) 169 CLR 540 at 572f, where Deane J said that the 'traditional ritual' of the four unities 'cloaks some obscurity of precise meaning, some overlapping between the unities and some conceptual difficulties about the essential character of joint tenancy.'
9 Post, p 470.
10 *Wiseman v Simpson* [1988] 1 WLR 35 at 42E-G per Ralph Gibson LJ. The implications of unity of possession for joint tenants are the same as those for tenants in common (post, p 471).
11 *Swartzbaugh v Sampson*, 54 P2d 73 at 75 (1936). See also *Meyer v Riddick* (1990) 60 P & CR 50 at 54, where Fox LJ confirmed that no joint tenant can claim for himself an exclusive possession of the co-owned land.
12 Post, p 474.
13 Domestic Violence and Matrimonial Proceedings Act 1976, ss 1(1), (2), 4(1). See eg *Davis v Johnson* [1979] AC 264, 317. Compare *Wiseman v Simpson* [1988] 1 WLR 35 at 42E-G, where Ralph Gibson LJ pointed to the Draconian nature of an ouster order and observed that, absent any infringement of her rights, a joint tenant who simply finds the presence of another joint tenant intolerable has no remedy at law and can do nothing but leave the co-owned premises. See also *Wilde v Wilde* [1988] 2 FLR 83.
14 The Law Commission has recommended that the Domestic Violence and Matrimonial Proceedings Act 1976 be replaced by a Family Homes and Domestic Violence Act which would reformulate and reinforce the civil remedies available in respect of domestic violence and occupation of the family home. See *Family Home: Domestic Violence and Occupation of the Family Home* (Law Com No 207, 7 May 1992).
15 *Bl Comm*, Vol II, p 181.

of all the joint tenants, each of whom must put his signature to the transfer document.[16] Thus a purchaser of a legal estate owned by joint tenants takes an unimpaired title only if he receives a conveyance from all of those joint tenants,[17] since the purchaser can readily see on the face of the documentary title an explicit reference to the existence of a joint ownership.[18] It is indeed the mandatory participation of all the joint tenants in effecting dispositions of the joint property which has led in recent years to a proposal that all matrimonial homes should automatically be held by way of joint tenancy between husband and wife.[19] Only in this way can the law ultimately remove the insecurity which affects the position of one spouse if his or her partner should attempt to deal with title unilaterally or become insolvent.

(iii) Unity of title Unity of title entails that each joint tenant must derive his title to the land from the same act or document.[20] Joint tenants, it was always said, 'are in under the same feudal contract or investiture'.[1]

(iv) Unity of time Unity of time expresses the idea that the interest of each joint tenant must normally vest at the same time.[2]

4. TENANCY IN COMMON

Tenancy in common is firmly to be distinguished from joint tenancy. It is frequently said that, unlike joint tenants, tenants in common hold land in 'undivided shares'. The phrase 'undivided shares' may seem confusing at first, since it appears to conjure up a picture of the amorphous undifferentiated co-ownership which characterises joint tenancy. However, the key to the distinction between joint tenancy and tenancy in common

16 See, however, P.W. Smith, [1980] Conv 191.

17 The rules concerning the grant of a leasehold estate require slight modification. As a matter of law it seems to be possible for one of a number of joint owners to give a valid lease of the joint property without the concurrence of those others (see *Tilling v Whiteman* [1980] AC 1 at 24B per Lord Fraser of Tullybelton; [1980] CLJ 27 at 29f). The latter are, of course, bound to respect the rights of tenancy thus created. However, whereas a truly joint letting would have conferred on the tenant a right to exclusive possession vis à vis all persons (including all the co-owners), a unilateral letting by one co-owner gives the tenant a right to exclusive possession vis à vis all persons *except* the non-participating co-owners. A unilateral lease by one joint owner can never therefore preclude the right of non-participant co-owners to share possession of the leased premises in common with the tenant or even to lease those premises to another, quite different, tenant (see *Frieze v Unger* [1960] VR 230 at 245; *Beaton v McDivitt* (1985) 13 NSWLR 134 at 145F).

18 It remains in general true that, in order to be fully effective, all positive dealings with a joint tenancy require the concurrence of all the joint tenants (see *A.G. Securities v Vaughan* [1990] 1 AC 417 at 432E per Fox LJ; *Hammersmith and Fulham LBC v Monk* [1992] 1 AC 478 at 490G-H per Lord Bridge of Harwich). In the context of a leasehold estate, for instance, the co-operation of all the joint owners is required for the purpose of surrendering the lease (post, p 758), claiming a right to relief against forfeiture (post, p 813), and exercising a break clause (post, p 753) or an option to renew the lease (post, p 737). Only in the matter of giving notice to quit is unilateral action by landlord or tenant fully effective (post, p 756).

19 Post, p 580.

20 *Bl Comm*, Vol II, p 181.

1 See R. Preston, *Essay on Abstracts of Title* (1824), Vol 2, p 62.

2 *Bl Comm*, Vol II, p 181.

lies in the reference to the word 'shares'.[3] It is only in the tenancy in common that the co-owners hold distinct shares at all. It is only of tenants in common that it can be meaningful to say, for instance, that A has a one-quarter interest and B a three-quarters interest, or even that A and B are each entitled to a one-half share. The allocation of shares or proportions is not possible as between joint tenants, who are of course wholly entitled to the whole.[4] Tenants in common are however owners of distinct shares, albeit in property which has not yet been divided up physically. It is not possible to point to one parcel or area of the co-owned land rather than any other as belonging to a particular tenant in common[5]: tenants in common own specific, but undivided, shares in the land.[6]

The principal characteristics of tenancy in common are two in number: (i) there is no right of survivorship as between tenants in common, and (ii) only unity of possession is required.

(1) There is no right of survivorship

No right of survivorship obtains between tenants in common. The size of each tenant in common's share is a fixed quantum which cannot be altered by reason of the death of any other tenant in common. In the absence of a right of survivorship, the share of each passes on his death either in accordance with the terms of his will (if he died testate) or according to the rules of intestate succession.

(2) Only unity of possession is required

Of the four unities required in joint tenancy only unity of possession is an essential constitutive element of tenancy in common.[7] Unity of interest is not required; it is for precisely this reason that it is possible for one tenant in common to own, say, a one-third share in the co-owned property while another tenant in common owns a two-thirds share. Nor is unity of title or unity of time essential; as has just been seen, it is possible for the share of a tenant in common to be transmitted by will or on an intestacy to some third party. However, unity of possession is an indispensable component of tenancy in common, for without it there would exist no co-ownership

3 See eg *Re Davies* (Deceased) [1950] 1 All ER 120 at 123.

4 'A joint interest in equal shares is a contradiction in terms; the words of severance create a tenancy in common' (*Cowcher v Cowcher* [1972] 1 WLR 425 at 430H per Bagnall J). See also *Malayan Credit Ltd v Jack Chia-M.P.H. Ltd* [1986] AC 549 at 559E-G; *Bl Comm*, Vol II, p 193 (. . .'joint tenants do not take by distinct halves or moieties. . .').

5 Coke described the tenancy in common enjoyed by two co-owners as applying to property which is 'common to them both. . .and neither of them knoweth his Part in several' (*Co Litt*, p 189a). This was later amplified in Blackstone's statement that 'because none knoweth his own severalty. . .they all occupy promiscuously' (*Bl Comm*, Vol II, p 191).

6 The tenancy in common has become a pivotal concept in the legal structuring of condominium ownership. Under this (largely transatlantic) form of co-ownership it is usual for each condominium dweller to own a specific unit in fee simple, but to be a tenant in common with the other condominium dwellers in respect of shared areas and accessways. See J.E. Cribbet, *Condominium—Home Ownership For Megalopolis?*, 61 Mich L Rev 1207 at 1215 (1962-63).

7 *Bl Comm*, Vol II, p 191f.

at all.[8] There would merely be separate ownership of physically distinct areas of land.

As is true in respect of joint tenants,[9] the unity of possession enjoyed by tenants in common entails that each tenant in common is as much entitled to possession of the co-owned land as is any other tenant in common.[10] No tenant in common may physically demarcate any part of that land as his to the exclusion of his brethren.[11] Instead, each tenant in common has 'a right to exercise acts of ownership over the whole property',[12] subject to the qualification that in so doing he must not interfere with the like right of any other co-owner.[13] It follows that no tenant in common has any right to demand compensation in respect of the simultaneous enjoyment of the land by a fellow tenant in common except where the latter has received 'more than comes to his just share or proportion'.[14] However, this notion of a 'just share or proportion' has been construed so widely that in practice there is now relatively little left of the original rule that unity of possession precludes compensation claims between co-owners. The implications of unity of possession must now be explored in greater detail.

(a) Occupation and use

It has long been clear that at common law each tenant in common has 'a perfect right'[15] to possession of the entire property and to the 'use and

8 *Bl Comm*, Vol II, p 192.

9 Ante, p 468.

10 *Wight v IRC* (1982) 264 Estates Gazette 935 at 936f; *Swartzbaugh v Sampson*, 54 P2d 73 at 75 (1936); *Dimmick v Dimmick*, 24 Cal Rptr 856 at 858 (1962); *Govorko v Vicelic* (1971) 2 BPR 9477 at 9490; *Barrios v Chiabrera* (1984) 3 BPR 9276 at 9279f; *Dunkel v Izsak* (1984) 3 BPR 9668. Compare, however, *Chhokar v Chhokar* [1984] FLR 313 at 332D-F, where Cumming-Bruce LJ refused to allow a tenant in common to assert any right to occupy a house which was already occupied by a married woman and her family (ante, p 220).

11 Perhaps the most bizarre circumstances in which this principle has been applied arose in *Galasso v Del Guercio*, 276 A2d 186 at 189f (1971). Here the Superior Court of New Jersey was called upon to resolve a dispute between co-owners as to which family member should be laid to rest in precisely which location in the family mausoleum. See also *Silvia v Helger*, 67 A2d 27 at 28 (1949).

12 *Griffies v Griffies* (1863) 8 LT (NS) 758 per Kindersley V-C. See also *Goodwyn v Spray* (1786) Dick 667, 21 ER 431; *Job v Potton* (1875) LR 20 Eq 84 at 97 per Bacon V-C; *Flynn v United States*, 205 F2d 756 at 760 (1953); *Dunkel v Izsak* (1984) 3 BPR 9668 per Powell J.

13 *Saulsberry v Saulsberry*, 121 F2d 318 at 321 (1941); *Sayers v Pyland*, 161 SW2d 769 at 773 (1942); *Stevahn v Meidinger*, 57 NW2d 1 at 7 (1952); *Tompkins v Superior Court of City and County of San Francisco*, 27 Cal Rptr 889 at 892 (1963); *Nasti v Verderosa*, 342 NYS2d 40 at 41 (1973); *Jemzura v Jemzura*, 330 NE2d 414 at 419 (1975).

14 This formula was first used in a statute of 1705 (4 Anne, c.16, s 27) which gave both the joint tenant and the tenant in common an action of account in respect of profits derived from undue exploitation of the co-owned land by another cotenant. This statute has now been repealed (see Law of Property (Amendment) Act 1924, Sch 10), but the idea persists that co-owners are accountable to each other if one of them should take 'more than his proper share' (*Bull v Bull* [1955] 1 QB 234 at 237 per Denning LJ). See also *Job v Potton* (1875) LR 20 Eq 84 at 93. Even before the repeal in the 1924 Act, the notion of 'just share or proportion' was construed as referring not merely to the 'receipt of issues and profits' but more widely to any 'receiving' in excess of one's 'just share' (see *Henderson v Eason* (1851) 17 QB 701 at 719, 117 ER 1451 at 1457).

15 *Henderson v Eason* (1851) 17 QB 701 at 720, 117 ER 1451 at 1458 per Parke B. In *Hole v Thomas* (1802) 7 Ves Jun 589 at 590, 32 ER 237, Eldon LC spoke of 'one tenant in common having a right to enjoy, as he pleases'.

enjoyment of it in a proper manner'.[16] This right, existing irrespective of the quantum of the tenant in common's undivided share, has been influential in fixing the degree of mutual tolerance which the law still requires of co-owners in their dealings inter se.[17]

(i) Trespass and ouster It is now settled law, for instance, that no action will lie in trespass against a tenant in common merely because he exclusively occupies and exploits the whole or any one part rather than another of the co-owned property.[18] He is not thereby taking 'more than comes to his just share or proportion'. Thus in *Jacobs v Seward*,[19] for instance, the House of Lords rejected a claim in trespass based partly upon the allegation that one tenant in common had cut a crop of grass on the co-owned land. Lord Hatherley LC declared that it was 'idle to talk of trespass as a consequence of a man making hay upon his own field—for it is his own—or a moiety of it at least, and no definite portion of it is mapped out as his moiety.'[20]

A remedy for trespass is available against a tenant in common only in cases of 'ouster',[1] it being likewise settled law that no tenant in common may go so far as to turn another cotenant out of the property.[2] Moreover, the term 'ouster' is wide enough to cover not merely cases in which one

16 *Bull v Bull* [1955] 1 QB 234 at 237 per Denning LJ. The insistence upon use 'in a proper manner' is an echo of Lord Hatherley LC's statement in *Jacobs v Seward* (1872) LR 5 HL 464 at 474, that no action will lie against a tenant in common if he uses the co-owned property 'in an ordinary and legitimate way' or for 'a perfectly legitimate purpose'. It is less clear, however, whether Denning LJ was correct in thinking that the old authorities concerning tenancy in common at law are equally applicable after 1925 to tenancy in common in equity (post, p 549).

17 Post, p 475. There is a recurring assertion that the boundaries of the cotenant's liability are fixed with reference to whether he was adopting the only (or only reasonable) means of enjoying or exploiting his right of ownership. See eg *Job v Potton* (1875) LR 20 Eq 84 at 93, 97 per Bacon V-C.

18 *Co Litt*, p 199b; *Bl Comm*, Vol II, pp 183, 194.

19 (1872) LR 5 HL 464 at 473.

20 As counsel argued in *Job v Potton* (1875) LR 20 Eq 84 at 90, '[o]wners are not trespassers'. However, in *Jacobs v Seward* (1872) LR 5 HL 464 at 474, 478, both Lord Hatherley and Lord Westbury conceded that there might have been a legitimate case for an accounting in respect of the profit made from the harvesting of the hay (post, p 476). See also *Harper v O'Neal*, 363 So2d 930 at 932 (1978). It is clear beyond doubt that the harvesting co-owner cannot be guilty of theft (see *State v McCoy* (1883) NC 466; Annot, 17 ALR.3d 1394 at 1396).

1 *Co Litt*, p 199b; *Bl Comm*, Vol II, p 194; *Jacobs v Seward* (1872) LR 5 HL 464 at 472, 478. See also *Stedman v Smith* (1857) 8 El & Bl 1 at 6, 120 ER 1 at 3. Although the early cases often speak only of 'actual' ouster, it is probable that an action in trespass will lie even where the ouster is 'constructive', as for instance where an innocent tenant in common is just as surely caused—albeit by indirect means—to leave the co-owned property (see *Dennis v McDonald* [1982] Fam 63 at 70C, 71D). However, it seems that a statement by one tenant to the effect that the other tenant could leave if she did not like his behaviour does not constitute constructive ouster (*Diotallevi v Diotallevi* (1982) 134 DLR (3d) 477 at 479). See also *Spiller v Mackereth*, 334 So2d 859 at 862 (1976).

2 *Bull v Bull* [1955] 1 QB 234 at 237 per Denning LJ. See also *Smith v United States*, 153 F2d 655 at 661 (1946); *Zaslow v Kroenert*, 176 P2d 1 at 5 (1946).

tenant evicts or excludes another from the land,[3] but also those cases where he otherwise interferes with the common enjoyment of that land.[4] For the purpose of establishing trespass, however, this interference must be such as to tend towards the destruction of the co-owned property in its original form.[5] As Lord Hatherley LC pointed out in *Jacobs v Seward*,[6] 'where the act done by the tenant in common is right in itself, and nothing is done which destroys the benefit of the other tenant in common in the property, there no action will lie, because he can follow that property as long as it is in existence and not destroyed.'

(ii) Other forms of liability It is possible that two other forms of claim may arise from an illegitimate user exercised by a tenant in common on the co-owned land. There appears to be no reason why the tort of nuisance cannot be alleged by one tenant in common against another,[7] although it may sometimes be difficult to prove that the alleged interference with the plaintiff's beneficial use of the land is sufficiently severe to meet the criterion of 'unreasonableness' which is constitutive of the tort.[8] It is also possible that one co-owner may be guilty of 'voluntary waste' by reason of his activity on the co-owned land,[9] but again it is both necessary and difficult to demonstrate that the activity in question has tended to the destruction of the property.[10] However, where waste is proved, the remedy for the other

3 See *Bull v Bull* [1955] 1 QB 234 at 237. In *Jacobs v Seward* (1872) LR 5 HL 464 at 473, 477f, the House of Lords held that the mere putting of a lock upon a gate by one tenant in common could not constitute 'ouster', unless there was direct evidence that by this means another tenant in common had been intentionally denied entry. See also *Spiller v Mackereth*, 334 So2d 859 at 862 (1976), but compare *Zaslow v Kroenert*, 176 P2d 1 at 5f (1946), where there was manifest evidence of an intention to exclude the other cotenant, not least in the form of a change of locks and the prominent display of 'no trespassing' notices. For the suggestion that 'ouster' can occur where one co-owner unilaterally leases the property to a stranger, see *Oates v Oates* [1949] SASR 37 at 40.

4 See eg *Stedman v Smith* (1857) 8 El & Bl 1 at 7, 120 ER 1 at 3. Here D rested part of the roof of his wash-house on the top of a dividing wall which he co-owned with P. P was held to have been 'excluded from the top of the wall: he might have wished to train fruit trees there, or to amuse himself [sic] by running along the top of the wall'. See also *De La Cuesta v Bazzi*, 118 P2d 909 at 915 (1941).

5 *Cubitt v Porter* (1828) 8 B & C 257 at 268, 108 ER 1039 at 1043.

6 (1872) LR 5 HL 464 at 475. The required degree of 'ouster' was not found either in *Cubitt v Porter* (destruction of old wall and building of new and better wall) or in *Ferguson v Miller* [1978] 1 NZLR 819 at 825. For an example of 'ouster' by destruction of the common property, see *Wilkinson v Haygarth* (1847) 12 QB 837 at 845, 116 ER 1085 at 1088 (removal of turf).

7 It is no longer thought to be essential to a successful claim of nuisance that the user complained of should have emanated from land other than that of the plaintiff (see eg *Hargrave v Goldman* (1963) 110 CLR 40 at 60; *Clearlite Holdings Ltd v Auckland City Corporation* [1976] 2 NZLR 729 at 736).

8 See eg *Ferguson v Miller* [1978] 1 NZLR 819 at 828, where McMullin J declined to apply the term 'nuisance' to a property developer's proposal to widen a carriageway on a co-owned access strip and resurface the accessway in permanent materials.

9 *Co Litt*, p 200b. The definition of waste marks out, as always, the boundaries of permissible advancement of self-interest and the proper limits of entrepreneurial zeal (ante, p 57). Thus the mere cutting of timber is not destructive waste (*Arthur v Lamb* (1865) 2 Dr & Sm 428 at 430, 62 ER 683 at 684), but the cutting of saplings or felling of timber 'at unseasonable times' would be (*Hole v Thomas* (1802) 7 Ves Jun 589 at 590, 32 ER 237).

10 In *Ferguson v Miller* [1978] 1 NZLR 819 at 826, McMullin J considered the proposed development to be 'an act of repair rather than an act of waste.' See also *Jacobs v Seward* (1872) LR 5 HL 464, where the allegation of waste seems not even to have been raised.

co-owner may take the form of either an action of account[11] or an injunction[12] or both.

(b) Rents and profits received from a stranger

If a tenant in common is not himself in occupation of the land, he is entitled to share in any rents and profits derived from the land (eg by way of a lucrative letting to a stranger).[13] His rights in this respect are measured in strict proportion to the quantum of his individual share as a tenant in common,[14] so that, for instance, a tenant in common of a one-third interest is entitled to receive one third of the net rents and profits derived from the co-owned property.[15]

Tenants in common are liable to account inter se in respect of any income received by one tenant from a stranger in excess of his own 'just share or proportion'.[16] However, this liability to account applies only to actual (rather than constructive) receipts of income drawn from the property. Tenants in common are not fiduciaries one for another;[17] nor is their relationship one of partnership or agency.[18] Even if one tenant in common is left to manage

11 *Sayers v Pyland*, 161 SW2d 769 at 771f (1942).

12 See *The Durham and Sunderland Railway Co v Wawn* (1841) 3 Beav 119 at 123, 49 ER 47 at 48; *Foshee v Foshee*, 143 So2d 301 at 303f (1962), 177 So2d 99 at 101 (1965). No injunction will issue unless there is evidence of 'malicious destruction' (*Hole v Thomas* (1802) 7 Ves Jun 589 at 590, 32 ER 237) as distinct from acts done in 'the proper course of husbandry' and 'good management' (*Arthur v Lamb* (1865) 2 Dr & Sm 428 at 430, 62 ER 683 at 684). See also *Twort v Twort* (1809) 16 Ves Jun 128 at 131, 33 ER 932 at 934, 2 Ves Jun Supp 431, 34 ER 1165; *Bailey v Hobson* (1869) LR 5 Ch App 180 at 182.

13 Not all the cotenants need join in the letting, and a non-participant cotenant, precisely because he is not bound by any agreement, is entitled to an account direct from the stranger in respect of a proportionate share of the net profits drawn from the land by the latter. See *Job v Potton* (1875) LR 20 Eq 84 at 97f (where the non-participant cotenant was not limited to a share of a mining royalty agreed by the other cotenants).

14 *Henderson v Eason* (1851) 17 QB 701 at 719, 117 ER 1451 at 1458.

15 See *Job v Potton* (1875) LR 20 Eq 84 at 95ff. However, the rents and profits shared in this way must be carefully confined to 'those receipts which can properly be regarded as rents and revenue of the common property itself as distinct from profits which the defendant [who ran a caravan park] may have made by his use and occupation of the common property (eg fees for services and for use of items of equipment)' (*Squire v Rogers* (1980) 27 ALR 330 at 345).

16 *Henderson v Eason* (1851) 17 QB 701 at 719, 117 ER 1451 at 1457f; *Kennedy v De Trafford* [1897] AC 180 at 187; *Bernard v Josephs* [1982] Ch 391 at 401C, 410B; *Chhokar v Chhokar* [1984] FLR 313 at 332G. See also *Zanzonico v Zanzonico*, 2 A2d 597 at 598 (1938); *Rehfuss v McAndrew*, 33 So2d 16 at 17 (1947); *American Oil Service v Hope Oil Co*, 15 Cal Rptr 209 at 214 (1961); *Jeffress v Piatt*, 370 SW2d 383 at 386 (1963); *Squire v Rogers* (1980) 27 ALR 330 at 345; *Barrios v Chiabrera* (1984) 3 BPR 9276 at 9281. A co-owner's right to recover a share of rents and profits does not generate for him a lien for that sum upon the co-owned land (see *Brickwood v Young* (1905) 2 CLR 387 at 398; 86 CJS 417f).

17 *Kennedy v De Trafford* [1897] AC 180 at 189. See also *Pure Oil Co v Byrnes*, 57 NE2d 356 at 361 (1944); *Taylor v Brindley*, 164 F2d 235 at 240 (1947); *Britton v Green*, 325 F2d 377 at 383 (1963). In spite of this basic statement of principle, it has sometimes been argued that the legal control of co-ownership relations has developed to the point where cotenants stand in a position tantamount to a fiduciary nexus (see D. Weible, *Accountability of Cotenants*, 29 Iowa L Rev 558 at 590 (1943-44); 86 CJS 377).

18 *Leigh v Dickeson* (1884-85) 15 QBD 60 at 65. Of course, if there exists between the co-owners an agreement akin to partnership, under which one co-owner undertakes to manage the property for the common benefit, then there may arise a liability for 'wilful default' (see *Henderson v Eason* (1851) 17 QB 701 at 718f, 117 ER 1451 at 1457).

the property, he is under no duty to extract the maximum (or indeed any) rental value from the property.[19] There is therefore no liability to account for such rents or profits as might have been (but were not in fact) derived from prudent letting of the land to an outsider.[20]

(c) Profit derived from industry of one tenant in common

A different problem arises where one tenant in common enjoys sole occupation of the co-owned land and derives a profit or income from that land by reason of his own exertions.

(i) Legitimate profit In *Henderson v Eason*,[1] Parke B thought that in many such instances it would be 'impossible' to say that the occupying co-owner 'has received more than comes to his just share.' He held that there is no liability to account for profits where a co-owner 'employs his capital and industry in cultivating the whole of a piece of land. . .in a mode in which the money and labour expended greatly exceed the value of the rent or compensation for the mere occupation of the land.'[2] In a 'hazardous venture' undertaken under such circumstances,[3] the risk of which is entirely his own,[4] the co-owner is entitled to retain all the produce of the venture.[5] In a spirited endorsement of free enterprise capitalism, Parke B concluded that the co-owner, in taking all the 'fructus industriales', receives in truth merely 'the

19 Nor, in the absence of agreement, may a co-owner demand any fee for his personal services in managing the property (see *Kahnovsky v Kahnovsky*, 21 A2d 569 at 573 (1941); *Curl v Neilson*, 167 P2d 320 at 322f (1946); *Combs v Ritter*, 223 P2d 505 at 506 (1950); *Lewis v Latham*, 79 So2d 811 at 814 (1955); *In Re Estate and Guardianship of Purton*, 441 P2d 561 at 570 (1968); *Neal v Neal*, 470 SW2d 383 at 386f (1971)).

20 *Wheeler v Horne* (1740) Willes 208 at 210, 125 ER 1135 at 1136; *Henderson v Eason* (1851) 17 QB 701 at 718f, 117 ER 1451 at 1457. In *Chhokar v Chhokar* [1984] FLR 313 at 332F, the wife was not required to account for any notional rent which she should have derived from her husband whom she allowed to live with her in the co-owned property. (Presumably the husband could have claimed that he was merely exercising his statutory rights of occupation under what is now the Matrimonial Homes Act 1983 (ante, p 155)). See also *Boulter v Boulter* (1898) 19 LR (NSW) Eq 135 at 138f; *In Re Tolman's Estate* (1928) 23 Tas LR 29 at 31; *Thompson v Flynn*, 58 P2d 769 at 771 (1936); *Mastbaum v Mastbaum*, 9 A2d 51 at 54 (1939); *Riechmann v Riechmann*, 283 NE2d 734 at 736 (1972); *Thrift v Thrift* (1976) 10 ALR 332 at 339.

1 (1851) 17 QB 701 at 720, 117 ER 1451 at 1458.

2 (1851) 17 QB 701 at 720f, 117 ER 1451 at 1458.

3 Parke B gave the example of cultivating hops. Compare, however, *Jacobs v Seward* (1872) LR 5 HL 464 at 474, 478. Here the cultivation of hay was considered not to be sufficiently hazardous, nor the investment of personal energy so excessive, as to exclude a liability to account, although Lord Hatherley LC conceded (at 476) that any expense incurred in making the hay would have to be allowed for in the accounting.

4 Parke B pointed out that 'if the speculation had been a losing one altogether, he could not have called for a moiety of the losses, as he would have been enabled to do had [the land] been cultivated by the mutual agreement of the cotenants' ((1851) 17 QB 701 at 721, 117 ER 1451 at 1458). For further reference to the profit-sharing implications of a risk-sharing agreement between co-owners, see *Anon* (1684) Skinner 230, 90 ER 106.

5 This approach, correlating profit with risk, has been applied fairly widely to farming operations conducted by one co-owner (see eg *Swartzbaugh v Sampson*, 54 P2d 73 at 75 (1936); *Black v Black*, 204 P2d 950 at 953 (1949); *Reid v Reid* (1978) 87 DLR (3d) 370 at 372).

return for his own capital and labour, to which his cotenant has no right.'[6] This statement almost certainly still represents good law, at least so long as the co-owner's activities have caused no long-term destruction of the revenue potential or capital value of the land.

(ii) Liability to account In *Henderson v Eason* there is a clear implication that there may be some cases in which a co-owner will indeed have received more than his 'just share or proportion', even though his profit derives from engaging his own personal efforts in productive use of the co-owned land.[7] For instance, a co-owner may, by his industrious exploitation of the common land, have exhausted or diminished the capital value of the property through activities such as mining, quarrying or oil drilling.[8] Here, even though the co-owner has invested his own energy and risk-capital, he cannot retain the entire profit himself but must submit to a fair accounting with his cotenants.[9] His liability to account is not affected by the fact that he did not in any way exclude his cotenants from similar exploitation of the resource or even that he did not extract any more than his proportionate share of that resource.[10]

(d) Rent obligations as between tenants in common

It is often said that in the absence of agreement[11] no obligation in respect of rent or mesne profits can normally arise as between co-owners by reason merely of the fact that one tenant in common may happen to enjoy sole occupation of the entire co-owned property.[12]

(i) The general principle Since tenants in common (and, for that matter, joint tenants) enjoy unity of possession, each is equally entitled with his brethren to physical possession of the property.[13] The traditional view is that no tenant

6 See also *Pico v Columbet*, 12 Cal 414 at 421 (1859). For a modern (and very similar) defence of the same approach, see L. Berger, *An Analysis of the Economic Relations between Cotenants*, 21 Arizona L Rev 1015 (1979).

7 See eg *Jacobs v Seward* (1872) LR 5 HL 464.

8 Such activities may technically constitute waste (see 86 CJS 420). In Britain the ownership of petroleum reserves is vested by statute in the Crown (ante, p 19).

9 *Payne v Callahan*, 99 P2d 1050 at 1057 (1940). Such accounting relates only to the *net* profit derived from the operation. It allows the entrepreneur-cotenant reimbursement of the reasonable and necessary expenses incurred in extraction and marketing (see *Job v Potton* (1875) LR 20 Eq 84 at 97; *Cox v Davison*, 397 SW2d 200 at 203 (1965); *P & N Investment Corp v Florida Ranchettes Inc*, 220 So2d 451 at 454 (1968)) and recognises his right to 'reasonable compensation' for his personal services (see *White v Smyth*, 214 SW2d 967 at 975 (1948)).

10 *White v Smyth*, 214 SW2d 967 at 975 (1948) (Supreme Court of Texas).

11 *M'Mahon v Burchell* (1846) 2 Ph 127 at 135f, 41 ER 889 at 893; 1 Coop T Cott 457 at 475, 47 ER 944 at 951; *Henderson v Eason* (1851) 17 QB 701 at 720, 117 ER 1451 at 1458; *Roberts v Roberts*, 150 SW2d 236 at 237 (1941).

12 *M'Mahon v Burchell* (1846) 2 Ph 127 at 135, 41 ER 889 at 893; 1 Coop T Cott 457 at 475, 47 ER 944 at 951; *Kennedy v De Trafford* [1897] AC 180 at 190f; *Jones (A.E.) v Jones (F.W.)* [1977] 1 WLR 438 at 443B. See (1978) 41 MLR 208 at 209 (J. Alder). See also *In Re Randall's Estate*, 132 P2d 763 at 766 (1942); *Rehfuss v McAndrew*, 33 So2d 16 at 17 (1947); *Goforth v Ellis*, 300 SW2d 379 at 383 (1957); *Baird v Moore*, 141 A2d 324 at 329 (1958); *Parceluk v Knudtson*, 139 NW2d 864 at 873 (1966); *Hunter v Schultz*, 49 Cal Rptr 315 at 319f (1966); *Seesholts v Beers*, 270 So2d 434 at 436 (1972); *Barrios v Chiabrera* (1984) 3 BPR 9276 at 9280; *Dunkel v Izsak* (1984) 3 BPR 9668.

13 *Jacobs v Seward* (1872) LR 5 HL 464 at 473; *Bull v Bull* [1955] 1 QB 234 at 237.

in common should be charged a rent for the sole enjoyment of that which is his 'perfect right' and which the other tenant or tenants in common are likewise free to enjoy.[14] The unilateral decision of one co-owner to vacate the land should not 'change his status into that of a landlord over the remaining cotenant in possession.'[15]

(ii) The proliferation of exceptions There have always been several exceptions to the basic principle of rent-immunity between co-owners. These categories of exception overlap to some extent, but all involve some trauma in the personal or family relationship of the co-owners. An occupation rent is payable, for instance, by a tenant in common whose sole occupation is achieved by the ouster or violent exclusion of another tenant in common.[16] A rent obligation may also be imposed by a court on or pending the granting of a divorce.[17] Alternatively, a rent liability may arise on the termination of a personal relationship in circumstances where it has become 'unreasonable' to expect continued joint occupation.[18] These circumstances of exception have so proliferated that in *Chhokar v Chhokar*[19] the Court of Appeal simply took the view that nowadays the proper test in determining the applicability of an occupation rent is whether the imposition of such an obligation upon a co-owner would be 'fair'.[20]

The exceptions to the principle of rent-immunity between co-owners have now become so numerous that the prima facie position today may well be that rent should be paid. In *Dennis v McDonald*,[1] for instance, Purchas J, in summarising the caselaw, pointed out that '[o]nly in cases where the tenants in common not in occupation were in a position to enjoy their right to occupy but chose not to do so voluntarily, and were not excluded by any relevant factor, would the tenant in common in occupation be entitled to do so free of liability to pay an occupation rent.' It appears, moreover, that the courts have frequently imposed a rent obligation on a sole occupier effectively as a condition of postponing a sale to which another co-owner

14 *Henderson v Eason* (1851) 17 QB 701 at 720, 117 ER 1451 at 1458 per Parke B. See also *Griffies v Griffies* (1863) 8 LT (NS) 758; *McCormick v McCormick* [1921] NZLR 384 at 385; *Thompson v Flynn*, 58 P2d 769 at 771 (1936); *Reid v Reid* (1978) 87 DLR (3d) 370 at 372.

15 *Seesholts v Beers*, 270 So2d 434 at 437 (1972) per Walden J.

16 *Jones (A.E.) v Jones (F.W.)* [1977] 1 WLR 438 at 442B; *Dennis v McDonald* [1982] Fam 63 at 71D, 80A; *Bernard v Josephs* [1982] Ch 391 at 401B, 409B. See also *Mastron v Cotton* [1926] 1 DLR 767 at 768; *Luke v Luke* (1936) 36 SR (NSW) 310 at 314; *Szuba v Szuba* [1951] OWN 61 at 63; *Brunscher v Reagh*, 330 P2d 396 at 398 (1958); *Lawrence v Lawrence*, 329 SW2d 416 at 419f (1959); *Heyse v Heyse*, 176 NW2d 316 at 320 (1970); *Palmer v Protrka*, 476 P2d 185 at 190 (1970); *Spiller v Mackereth*, 334 So2d 859 at 862 (1976); *Roberts v Roberts*, 584 P2d 378 at 380 (1978); *Barrios v Chiabrera* (1984) 3 BPR 9276 at 9280; *Dunkel v Izsak* (1984) 3 BPR 9668.

17 See eg *Bedson v Bedson* [1965] 2 QB 666 at 682F; *Harvey v Harvey* [1982] Fam 83 at 89B; [1982] CLJ 228 at 230; *Brown v Brown* (1981) *Times*, 11 December.

18 *Cousins v Dzosens* (1981) *Times*, 12 December. See also *Bernard v Josephs* [1982] Ch 391 at 405F.

19 [1984] FLR 313 at 332E per Cumming-Bruce LJ.

20 The criterion of 'simple fairness' as the determinant of rent obligations between co-owners had already been propounded in New Zealand (see *Mayo v Mayo* [1966] NZLR 849 at 851). In *Chhokar* the Court considered it unfair to burden a wife with a rent obligation in favour of another tenant in common who had acted with 'moral turpitude' in conspiring with her husband to evict her from the matrimonial home (ante, p 220).

1 [1982] Fam 63 at 71A-B.

would otherwise be entitled.[2] Likewise a co-owner who claims credit for improvements, repairs or other outgoings paid on the co-owned property may have to give credit for a notional rent to be assessed in respect of any sole occupation which he has enjoyed.[3]

(iii) Quantification of rent liability There is a tendency in all cases to calculate the rent payable either on the analogy of a 'fair rent' for Rent Act purposes[4] or (more usually and more pragmatically) on the basis of a rough equation that any payment of mortgage interest by the sole occupier approximates to the appropriate rent.[5] The courts have been anxious, however, to deny that the introduction of a periodic money liability between co-owners compulsorily creates between them any relationship of landlord and tenant.[6]

The precise rationale for the payment of rent, particularly in cases of ouster, is increasingly unclear, although this uncertainty may have an impact upon the calculation of the amount payable. In *Dennis v McDonald*,[7] Purchas J envisaged the payment of rent as compensation to the non-occupying co-owner in respect of the *advantage* derived by the other co-owner from his sole occupation. However, the Court of Appeal in the same case[8] preferred to see the payment of rent more in terms of compensation for the *detriment* suffered by the ousted co-owner in consequence of the occupying co-owner's failure to discharge 'in due order' the trust behind which the co-ownership existed.[9] The distinction may appear insignificant, but the theory that rent is compensation payable by a trustee to a beneficiary was regarded by the Court of Appeal as rendering irrelevant the purpose to which the trustee then puts the property.[10] In particular, it meant that no deduction from the rent payable should be allowed merely on the ground that the payer was providing a home for the children of both co-owners.[11] Such a deduction

2 The potential to do so was pointed out in *Dennis v McDonald* [1982] Fam 63 at 74A, and *Bernard v Josephs* [1982] Ch 391 at 411C, and appears to have been realised in practice in *Bedson v Bedson* [1965] 2 QB 666 at 682F, 683C; *Eves v Eves* [1975] 1 WLR 1338 at 1343A; *Cousins v Dzosens* (1981) *Times*, 12 December. See J.E. Martin, [1982] Conv 305 at 309.

3 Post, pp 479, 481.

4 *Dennis v McDonald* [1982] Fam 63 at 75E per Purchas J, 82A per Sir John Arnold P.

5 See eg *Leake v Bruzzi* [1974] 1 WLR 1528 at 1533B, H; *Suttill v Graham* [1977] 1 WLR 819 at 822C, 823H; *Bernard v Josephs* [1982] Ch 391 at 401B, 405G; *In re Gorman* (A Bankrupt) [1990] 1 WLR 616 at 625G, 626E-G. In *Dennis v McDonald* [1982] Fam 63 at 75C, Purchas J rejected the suggestion that the occupation rent should be a rack rent, assessed in relation to half of the value of the capital asset, because 'this was not the concept behind an occupation rent.'

6 See eg *Dennis v McDonald* [1982] Fam 63 at 81C per Sir John Arnold P. It is perhaps for this reason that the courts have often been at pains to stress that the payments ordered do not strictly constitute an occupation 'rent' (see *Dennis v McDonald* [1982] Fam 63 at 81A; *Harvey v Harvey* [1982] Fam 83 at 89B).

7 [1982] Fam 63 at 70ff.

8 [1982] Fam 63 at 80G, 81F.

9 There is discussion in Chapter 14 (post, p 526) of the way in which the 1925 legislation generally superimposed a trust for sale upon the phenomenon of co-ownership.

10 [1982] Fam 63 at 81A. The 'breach of trust' approach may also create difficulties if the non-occupying co-owner was the sole trustee of the legal estate. See R. Schuz, (1982) 12 Family Law 108 at 114.

11 [1982] Fam 63 at 80B-C.

would have been more appropriate on the former view, which fastens on the net advantage derived by the occupying co-owner in the totality of the circumstances.[12]

(e) Liability for repairs and improvements

The question sometimes arises whether any liability exists between co-owners in respect of moneys voluntarily expended by one co-owner on the repair or permanent improvement of the co-owned property.[13] The problems raised by such expenditure are complex, particularly in the case of tenancy in common, which is 'a tenure of an inconvenient nature, and. . .is unfit for persons who cannot agree amongst themselves.'[14]

(i) The general principle The general principle applicable in this context was stated in *Leigh v Dickeson*.[15] Here the Court of Appeal held that no co-owner has the right to demand a contribution from his cotenants towards expenses which he has properly but voluntarily incurred in respect of repairs or improvements to the co-owned property.[16] However, this immunity from arbitrary calls for contribution does not avail the other co-owners if the repairs or improvements were effected by agreement with them[17] or at their express or implied request.[18] Nor does any immunity apply if the work was done pursuant to an existing obligation to a third party binding all the

12 For approval of the approach of Purchas J in preference to that of the Court of Appeal, see R. Schuz, *loc cit*, at 114; R. Cocks, *Co-ownership, Rights of Occupation and Obscurity*, [1984] Conv 198 at 205.

13 The payment of other forms of outgoings on the property (eg instalments payments under a mortgage) may raise similar questions as to the allowance of credits between co-owners (see *Leake v Bruzzi* [1974] 1 WLR 1528 at 1533B, H; *Suttill v Graham* [1977] 1 WLR 819 at 822C, 823H; *In re Gorman (A Bankrupt)* [1990] 1 WLR 616 at 626F–628A). Improvements made by spouses are singled out for special statutory treatment (see Matrimonial Proceedings and Property Act 1970, s 37, ante, p 422).

14 *Leigh v Dickeson* (1884–85) 15 QBD 60 at 69 per Lindley LJ.

15 (1884–85) 15 QBD 60. This decision was in its turn confirmed and applied by the Australian High Court in *Brickwood v Young* (1905) 2 CLR 387 at 394f, 400. See also *Miller v Prater*, 100 SW2d 842 at 844 (1937); *Lewis v Latham*, 79 So2d 811 at 814 (1955); *Cox v Davison*, 397 SW2d 200 at 201 (1965); *Cummings v Anderson*, 614 P2d 1283 at 1287 (1980).

16 'If the law were otherwise, a part-owner might be compelled to incur expense against his will: a house might be situate in a decaying borough, and it might be thought by one co-owner that it would be better not to repair it' (*Leigh v Dickeson* (1884–85) 15 QBD 60 at 65 per Brett MR). Compare the law in many jurisdictions in the United States, where there is power to demand contributions from cotenants in respect of repairs which are absolutely necessary, although there is no similar liability in respect of permanent improvements (see 48A CJS 364, 86 CJS 445, 449f).

17 *Anon* (1684) Skin 230, 90 ER 106; *Leigh v Dickeson* (1884–85) 15 QBD 60 at 64; *Harwood v Harwood* [1991] 2 FLR 274 at 294E-G. See also *In re Holyman* (1935) 30 Tas LR 15 at 26, 29f; *Collier v Collier*, 242 P2d 537 at 542 (1952); *Ruptash and Lumsden v Zawick* [1956] 2 DLR (2d) 145 at 158; *Young v Young*, 376 A2d 1151 at 1157 (1977). However, a covenant by one co-owner to share the cost of repairs or improvements, being a positive covenant, does not run with the land to affect the covenantor's successors in title (post, p 1133). See *Ruptash and Lumsden v Zawick* [1956] 2 DLR (2d) 145 at 160 (Supreme Court of Canada).

18 *Leigh v Dickeson* (1884–85) 15 QBD 60 at 64, 66. It seems that a request or agreement will not be implied merely from the making of improvements or from their necessity or utility (*Young v McKittrick*, 267 Ill App 267 (1932); *Currie v Hamilton* [1984] 1 NSWLR 687 at 693A-C per McLelland J).

co-owners to maintain or repair their property.[19] In such cases there is, of course, an immediate contractual liability to contribute towards the costs incurred.

Moreover, although it is impossible for a co-owner to assert an immediate and active entitlement to reimbursement as an independent head of claim against his cotenants,[20] a claim for contribution towards necessary expenditure gives rise to an 'equity' which may be vindicated defensively[1] by that co-owner when the value of the property is eventually realised or distributed between the cotenants.[2] In other words, a proportionate part of the money laid out by one co-owner on repair or improvement may be recovered later, usually from the proceeds of sale of the property, thus effectively sharing between all the co-owners the cost of any repair or improvement which has resulted in an enhanced sale price.[3] The rationale underlying this rule of reimbursement seems to be the prevention of unjust enrichment of other co-owners,[4] but this principle has no application where there was a clear intention to make a gift to the other co-owners of the value of the repair or improvement.[5]

It seems that this passive or dormant equity is available not only to a tenant in common but also to a joint tenant.[6] Thus any co-owner who is out of pocket may subsequently assert a lien upon the property (or the fund representing it) for the value of his repairs or improvements.[7] The

19 *Leigh v Dickeson* (1884–85) 15 QBD 60 at 66 per Cotton LJ. There is an indirect liability to contribute if the work was done by a co-owner who was also a trustee acting in the proper discharge of his duties (see *Gross v French* (1975) 238 Estates Gazette 39 at 41). The old writ *de reparatione facienda* (*Co Litt*, p 200b) seems to have been available only in the context of an existing obligation to third parties (see *Leigh v Dickeson* (1884–85) 15 QBD 60 at 67, 68f).

20 *Leigh v Dickeson* (1884–85) 15 QBD 60 at 65, 66; *Brickwood v Young* (1905) 2 CLR 387 at 395; *Squire v Rogers* (1980) 27 ALR 330 at 346.

1 For the original reference to a 'defensive' equity, see *Brickwood v Young* (1905) 2 CLR 387 at 395, 397.

2 *Leigh v Dickeson* (1884–85) 15 QBD 60 at 65, 67, 69; *In re Jones* [1893] 2 Ch 461 at 476; *In re Cook's Mortgage* [1896] 1 Ch 923 at 925; *Mayes v Mayes* (1969) 210 Estates Gazette 935 at 938; *Gross v French* (1975) 238 Estates Gazette 39 at 41; *Brickwood v Young* (1905) 2 CLR 387 at 395, 399; *Noack v Noack* [1959] VR 137 at 142f, 146.

3 '[O]ne party cannot take the increase in value, without making an allowance for what has been expended in order to obtain that increased value; in fact, the execution of the repairs and improvements is adopted and sanctioned by accepting the increased value' (*Leigh v Dickeson* (1884–85) 15 QBD 60 at 67).

4 See *Swan v Swan* (1820) 8 Price 518 at 519, 146 ER 1281; *Boulter v Boulter* (1898) 19 LR (NSW) Eq 135 at 137; *Re Byrne* (1906) 6 SR (NSW) 532 at 536; *Cummings v Anderson*, 614 P2d 1283 at 1287f (1980).

5 *Noack v Noack* [1959] VR 137 at 146 (Full Court): 'No principle of equity can be invoked to recall a gift once made'.

6 *Re Byrne* (1906) 6 SR (NSW) 532 at 536. See also *Noack v Noack* [1959] VR 137 at 143, 146. Profound difficulties will, however, attach to any attempt to claim this equity on behalf of a deceased joint tenant, since it would involve 'a claim against an estate in which the joint tenant's interest had entirely ceased' (*Re Byrne* (1906) 6 SR (NSW) 532 at 536f). See D. Mendes da Costa, (1961–62) 3 Melbourne ULR 137 at 146, but compare *Isaryk v Isaryk* [1955] OWN 487 at 489, where the extinction of a joint tenant's interest on death was not thought to preclude his estate from recovering from a cotenant an excess over the latter's just share of rents and profits arising from the land, provided that action for such recovery was brought within the appropriate limitation period.

7 *Brickwood v Young* (1905) 2 CLR 387 at 397.

equity of reimbursement which arises here does not immediately constitute a lien on the property, but comprises simply a right to have a lien decreed in respect of a co-owner's interest when the value of that property is ultimately realised or distributed amongst all the co-owners.[8] The better view is that the measure of compensation in such cases should be related to the actual increment in value conferred on the property by the work done, rather than to the cost of doing the work.[9] On any footing, it is probably the case that minor refurbishments are to be completely disregarded on the ground that they are merely 'in the nature of ordinary maintenance' and thus do not constitute a permanent improvement of the realty.[10]

(ii) Equitable counterclaims There is an important limitation on the right of a co-owner to assert an 'equity' based on expenditure on repairs or improvements effected by him. Such a claim is normally allowable only if he submits to payment of an occupation rent in respect of any sole occupation enjoyed by him[11] or if he accounts for any rents and profits which he may have derived from lettings of the land.[12] The relevant principle here seems

8 See *Mayes v Mayes* (1969) 210 Estates Gazette 935 at 938; *Gross v French* (1975) 238 Estates Gazette 39 at 41; *Dietsch v Long*, 43 NE2d 906 at 916f (1942); *Ruptash and Lumsden v Zawick* [1956] 2 DLR (2d) 145 at 159 (SCC); *Canada Life Assurance Co v Kennedy* (1978) 89 DLR (3d) 397 at 401.

9 *Parker v Trigg* [1884] WN 27 at 28; *Watson v Gass* (1881-82) 45 LT (NS) 582 at 585; *Williams v Williams* (1899-1900) 81 LT (NS) 163; *Gross v French* (1975) 238 Estates Gazette 39 at 41; *Brickwood v Young* (1905) 2 CLR 387 at 398; *Mastin v Mastin's Administrator*, 50 SW2d 77 at 79 (1932); *Noack v Noack* [1959] VR 137 at 146. (In *Currie v Hamilton* [1984] 1 NSWLR 687 at 693B-C, McLelland J could find no 'evidence of any quantifiable enhancement of the realizable value of the property'.) Compare, however, the more restrictive view that compensation should be limited to the amount of the actual expenditure or the extent of the increment in value generated by that expenditure, whichever is the lesser figure (*In re Jones* [1893] 2 Ch 461 at 479; *In re Cook's Mortgage* [1896] 1 Ch 923 at 925; *Boulter v Boulter* (1898) 19 LR (NSW) Eq 135 at 137; *McMahon v The Public Curator of Queensland* [1952] St R Qd 197 at 202f (although here the court was prepared to allow the 'present day equivalent in value of the sums of money actually expended. . .in making the improvements')).

10 *McMahon v The Public Curator of Queensland* [1952] St R Qd 197 at 204 (painting of house). See also *Currie v Hamilton* [1984] 1 NSWLR 687 at 693C.

11 Ante, p 478. See *Pascoe v Swan* (1859) 27 Beav 508 at 509, 54 ER 201 at 202; *Teasdale v Sanderson* (1864) 33 Beav 534, 55 ER 476; *Williams v Williams* (1899-1900) 81 LT (NS) 163; *McCormick v McCormick* [1921] NZLR 384 at 387f per Salmond J; *Roberts v Roberts*, 150 SW2d 236 at 238 (1941); *Carkeek v Tate-Jones* [1971] VR 691 at 702f; *Reid v Reid* (1978) 87 DLR (3d) 370 at 372.

12 *Attorney-General v Magdalen College, Oxford* (1854) 18 Beav 223 at 255, 52 ER 88 at 100; *Pascoe v Swan* (1859) 27 Beav 508 at 509, 54 ER 201 at 202; *In re Jones* [1893] 2 Ch 461 at 478; *Williams v Williams* (1899-1900) 81 LT (NS) 163; *Brickwood v Young* (1905) 2 CLR 387 at 398, 401; *Mastin v Mastin's Administrator*, 50 SW2d 77 at 79 (1932). The offsetting of improvement costs in an accounting in respect of rents and profits provides an example of the case referred to by Brett MR in *Leigh v Dickeson* (1884-85) 15 QBD 60 at 64f: 'Sometimes money has been expended for the benefit of another person under such circumstances that an option is allowed to him to adopt or decline the benefit: in this case, if he exercises his option to adopt the benefit, he will be liable to repay the money expended. . .' (see *Squire v Rogers* (1980) 27 ALR 330 at 348). Yet because the taking of reciprocal accounts falls so clearly within the jurisdiction of equity, the approach of the courts is flexible and is heavily determined by notions of simple fairness (see eg *Baird v Moore*, 141 A2d 324 at 330ff (1958); *Weh v Weh*, 164 A2d 508 at 513 (1960)).

to be that he who comes to equity must himself do equity.[13] Thus, when the value of the co-owned land is finally distributed amongst the co-owners, there must be a counter-balancing of various types of income and expenditure connected with that land. Only in this way can it be ensured that each co-owner receives no more and no less than his proportionate share of the net rental value derived from the land during the period of co-ownership, together with his proper share of the net increase in the capital value of the land accruing over that period. This may require relatively refined calculation particularly where, for instance, the rents and profits drawn from the land have been ploughed back into the land in the form of permanent improvements.[14]

(iii) Impact of the equity on third parties It is clear that the 'defensive' equity of a co-owner to receive compensation from his cotenants is a right which is not merely personal to the individual tenant who effects the improvements or repairs. The expenditure incurred by such a co-owner raises in his favour an equity attaching to the land, analogous to an equitable charge created by the owners for the time being, although enforceable only in the event of a later partition or distribution of the value of the land amongst the co-owners.[15] This 'equity' is fully capable of running with the land. Thus it may enure to the benefit of the successor in title of the original owner of the 'equity',[16] and may also bind the successor in title to the share of any other co-owner, except where that successor has purchased for value without notice.[17] It is by no means certain that such an 'equity' is capable of effective registration in a register of title.[18]

5. TENANCY BY ENTIRETIES

Before 1 January 1926 there existed in England a type of co-ownership known as the 'tenancy by entireties'. This type of co-ownership was restricted to

13 '[W]hile at common law...a tenant in common who occupies joint property without complaint from his cotenants is not required to account for the value of the use thereof, yet when he resorts to equity and seeks contribution from his cotenants for funds expended in the betterment of the common estate, it would seem that he should be required to do equity and allow as an offset the value of the use of the premises' (*Roberts v Roberts*, 150 SW2d 236 at 238 (1941) (Supreme Court of Texas)).

14 See eg *Squire v Rogers* (1980) 27 ALR 330 at 347.

15 *Brickwood v Young* (1905) 2 CLR 387 at 396; *Noack v Noack* [1959] VR 137 at 146.

16 *Brickwood v Young* (1905) 2 CLR 387 at 396. See also *Williams v Williams* (1899–1900) 81 LT (NS) 163, 68 LJ Ch 528 at 529; *In re Jones* [1893] 2 Ch 461 at 476ff.

17 *Dietsch v Long*, 43 NE2d 906 at 916f (1942); *Ruptash and Lumsden v Zawick* [1956] 2 DLR (2d) 145 at 159; *Squire v Rogers* (1980) 27 ALR 330 at 346. In this context the decision of the majority in the Ontario Court of Appeal in *Canada Life Assurance Co v Kennedy* (1978) 89 DLR (3d) 397 must be wrong. It was ruled that a contractual lien conferred on one tenant in common in connection with improvements effected by her took priority over a bona fide mortgagee of the share of the other tenant in common, even though the mortgagee was wholly unaware of the agreement between the two co-owners. See the strong dissent entered by Wilson JA ((1978) 89 DLR (3d) 397 at 410f).

18 See eg *Ruptash and Lumsden v Zawick* [1956] 2 DLR (2d) 145 at 159, where the Supreme Court of Canada held that even the entry of a caveat on the register of title of the co-owned property did not give notice to a purchaser of the existence of a co-owner's claim for a proportionate share of the cost of repairs effected before the sale of that property.

husband and wife, and constituted the 'most intimate union of ownership known to the law.'[19] The tenancy by entireties was in effect a species of joint tenancy,[20] and was distinguished from joint tenancy only by its characteristic incident: it was unseverable.[1] In other words, the tenancy by entireties did not differ in its essential nature from a joint tenancy except in so far as neither tenant had the capacity to reduce the co-ownership to co-ownership in distinct shares.[2] Instead tenants by entireties were for the duration of marriage rendered co-owners of the whole rather than of 'undivided shares'.[3] In this way the tenancy by entireties reflected the medieval theory of the indivisible unity of husband and wife. In terms of this theory the wife had no independent existence at law; her legal personality simply merged with that of her husband.[4] The effect of the tenancy by entireties was that any conveyance to husband and wife before 1883 rendered them compulsorily subject to this form of unseverable co-ownership.

(1) Conversion into joint tenancy

Of course the 'deeply rooted fiction' of conjugal unity could not survive the advent of more liberal views of the relationship of the sexes.[5] The creation of new tenancies by entireties was prohibited in 1882,[6] and all remaining tenancies by entireties were on 1 January 1926 converted automatically into joint tenancies.[7]

(2) Abortive revival of the tenancy by entireties

The tenancy by entireties is therefore now a mere curiosity of legal history, although more recently there has been an indirect attempt to resurrect the concept of an unseverable form of co-ownership in relation to property owned jointly by husband and wife.[8] In *Bedson v Bedson*,[9] Lord Denning MR seemed to hold that, where spouses own as joint tenants, neither can sever the joint tenancy and sell his own interest separately. In Lord Denning's view, if either spouse could sell his or her severable share, 'it would mean that the purchaser could insist on going into possession himself—with the other spouse

19 *Challis*, p 377.
20 Ante, p 461.
1 Post, p 485.
2 *Registrar-General of New South Wales v Wood* (1926) 39 CLR 46 at 54. See *Challis*, p 376 (note); *United States v Jacobs*, 306 US 363 at 370, 83 L.ed 763 at 768 (1939); *In Re Estate of King*, 572 SW2d 200 at 211 (1978).
3 Ante, p 469.
4 Post, p 570.
5 In *Registrar-General of New South Wales v Wood* (1926) 39 CLR 46 at 53, Isaacs J observed that 'for the purposes of daily life' this fiction is 'so opposed to fact and experience and to present-day habits of thought that outside the solemn precincts of a Court no one in his senses would venture to affirm it.' See also *United States v Jacobs*, 306 US 363 at 369, 83 L.ed 763 at 768 (1939).
6 Married Women's Property Act 1882, ss 1, 5. See *Challis*, p 378.
7 Law of Property Act 1925, Sch 1, Part VI.
8 A more direct attempt to revive the tenancy by entireties is to be found in New Zealand's Joint Family Homes Act 1964, s 9(2)(c)(proviso), which states that neither spouse may sever the statutory joint tenancy under which a registered joint family home is held (post, p 605).
9 [1965] 2 QB 666 at 678B.

there—which is absurd'.[10] However, this approach did not commend itself to all the members of the Court of Appeal in *Bedson*, Russell LJ considering the prohibition on unilateral severance to be 'without the slightest foundation in law or in equity'.[11] It is now clear that Lord Denning's revival of the defunct tenancy by entireties is widely regarded as heretical.[12] Marital status alone does not inhibit unilateral severance of the equitable interest in a matrimonial home. As Russell LJ said in *Bedson v Bedson*,[13] it is 'inherent in the nature of the beneficial interest created that either joint tenant may sever at any time inter vivos.'

6. COPARCENARY

Coparcenary is a form of co-ownership which is now virtually extinct.[14] It arose before 1926 where a person died intestate leaving two or more persons as his 'heir', and in most instances coparcenary embodied the pernicious theory that it took two or more females to equal one male. Normally, under the pre-1926 rule of primogeniture, the eldest son of the intestate decedent constituted the 'heir'. However, if the decedent left not sons but daughters, those daughters inherited together as 'coparceners'.[15] Coparcenary was a hybrid form of co-ownership, bearing attributes of both joint tenancy and tenancy in common: coparceners held in undivided shares without any right of survivorship,[16] even though in most cases the 'four unities' were present.[17]

In the Administration of Estates Act 1925,[18] English law abandoned the general concept of descent to the 'heir', with the consequence that no new coparcenary can now occur save in those few exceptional cases where realty still descends to an 'heir'.[19] Coparcenary can therefore still emerge in two special cases, where two or more females (or their issue) are entitled on an intestacy. The first case occurs where the intestate was a 'lunatic or defective' of full age at the end of 1925 who never recovered his testamentary capacity.[20] The second case arises where the intestate was a tenant in tail

10 In coming to this conclusion, Lord Denning purported to rely on the Law of Property Act 1925, s 36(1), (3), although, as Plowman J later pointed out in *In re Draper's Conveyance* [1969] 1 Ch 486 at 493B, these provisions appear irrelevant to the proposition put forward.

11 [1965] 2 QB 666 at 690E.

12 See eg *In re Draper's Conveyance* [1969] 1 Ch 486 at 494A; *Cowcher v Cowcher* [1972] 1 WLR 425 at 430G-H; *Fleming v Hargreaves* [1976] 1 NZLR 123 at 127; *Harris v Goddard* [1983] 1 WLR 1203 at 1208G; (1966) 82 LQR 29 (REM). However, Lord Denning's dictum in *Bedson* has the dubious merit of being consistent with other recent indications that a beneficiary in possession of land has a *right* of occupation or at least has a right not to have that occupation prejudiced by the intervention of any third party (post, p 547). See also I.A. Saunders and A. McGregor, (1973) 37 Conv (NS) 270 at 272.

13 [1965] 2 QB 666 at 689C.

14 See *Bl Comm*, Vol II, p 187ff; *Challis*, p 373ff.

15 See also *Bl Comm*, Vol II, p 187; *Challis*, p 373f.

16 *Bl Comm*, Vol II, p 188. However, at common law each parcener was entitled as against his coparceners to a compulsory partition of the property (*Litt*, s 241).

17 See *Bl Comm*, Vol II, p 188; *Challis*, p 374f.

18 Administration of Estates Act 1925, s 45(1).

19 All land in which coparcenary still existed at the end of 1925 was automatically subjected to a statutory trust for sale behind which the coparceners took equitable interests as tenants in common (Law of Property Act 1925, Sch 1, Part IV).

20 Administration of Estates Act 1925, s 51(2).

who died without barring his entail.[1] In both situations the land is now held on trust for sale for the coparceners.[2]

7. SEVERANCE

Certain acts or events cause the undifferentiated co-ownership of joint tenancy to crystallise into co-ownership in distinct and undivided shares.[3] The process by which joint tenancy may thus be converted into tenancy in common is known as severance,[4] and it is ultimately a 'mere matter of evidence' whether severance has occurred.[5]

(1) Facility of severance

Historically the common law has been willing to mitigate the hazards of survivorship by allowing severance to occur relatively easily.[6] Any act or event which is incompatible with the characteristic features of joint tenancy is apt to precipitate such a severance. Thus any dealing by a joint tenant which excludes the future operation of survivorship will result in severance. Joint tenancy depends, moreover, upon the continued existence of the three unities of possession, interest and title,[7] and the destruction of either unity of interest or unity of title will automatically bring about a severance.[8] For the purpose of severance under the common law rules the consent of

1 Law of Property Act 1925, s 130(4); Administration of Estates Act 1925, ss 45(2), 51(4).

2 Where the intestate was a lunatic or defective, the trust for sale arises under the Administration of Estates Act 1925, s 33(1). Where he was a tenant in tail, the trust for sale is imposed by the Law of Property Act 1925, s 36(1), (2).

3 See A.J. McClean, (1979) 57 Can Bar Rev 1; P. Butt, (1979–82) 9 Sydney L Rev 568.

4 See *Harris v Goddard* [1983] 1 WLR 1203 at 1210E per Dillon LJ: 'Severance is. . .the process of separating off the share of a joint tenant, so that the concurrent ownership will continue but the right of survivorship will no longer apply. The parties will hold separate shares as tenants in common.'

5 *Crooke v De Vandes* (1805) 11 Ves Jun 330 at 333, 32 ER 1115 at 1116. The onus of proof that severance has occurred rests upon the party seeking to establish severance (see *Flynn v Flynn* [1930] IR 337 at 343; *Re Denny* (1947) 116 LJR 1029 at 1031; *Greenfield v Greenfield* (1979) 38 P & CR 570 at 578; *Re Sorensen and Sorensen* (1979) 90 DLR (3d) 26 at 33; *Barton v Morris* [1985] 1 WLR 1257 at 1260G).

6 Ante, p 462. See *Cray v Willis* (1729) 2 P Wms 529, 24 ER 847 ('. . .the duration of all lives being uncertain, if either party has an ill opinion of his own life, he may sever the jointenancy. . .so that survivorship can be no hardship, where either side may at pleasure prevent it').

7 'The unity of time of vesting only applies to the original creation of the joint tenancy and cannot, therefore, be affected by any subsequent act' (*Re Murdoch and Barry* (1976) 64 DLR (3d) 222 at 225). See also *Nielson-Jones v Fedden* [1975] Ch 222 at 228F.

8 *Bl Comm*, Vol II, p 192. See *Corin v Patton* (1990) 169 CLR 540 at 548 per Mason CJ and McHugh J, 573 per Deane J. See also *Power v Grace* [1932] 2 DLR 793 at 795; *Tenhet v Boswell*, 133 Cal Rptr 10 at 14 (1976); *In Re Estate of Estelle*, 593 P2d 663 at 665 (1979); *First National Bank of Southglenn v Energy Fuels Corp*, 618 P2d 1115 at 1118 (1980); *Minouk State Bank v Grassman*, 432 NE2d 386 at 389 (1982); *Samuel v District Land Registrar* [1984] 2 NZLR 697 at 702. Destruction of unity of possession would, of course, terminate co-ownership altogether by means of 'partition' (post, p 515).

the other joint tenant or joint tenants is not necessarily required,[9] and severance may in this sense be quite unilateral.[10] The major restriction upon the availability of severance is, however, the rule that severance can be effected only inter vivos: there can be no unilateral severance by will.[11]

(2) Consequence of severance

In the absence of any contrary court order[12] or agreement between the co-owners[13] the aliquot shares which result from severance are always equal in size, irrespective of the proportions in which the joint tenants may have contributed initially towards the purchase price of the co-owned property.[14] The fact of severance, when it occurs, should be noted in a memorandum of severance signed by at least one of the joint tenants and endorsed on or annexed to the conveyance which created the joint tenancy.[15]

(3) Abolition of severance at law

Since the commencement of the Law of Property Act 1925, joint tenancy has been capable of severance only in respect of equitable interests in land: there can be no severance of a joint tenancy in a legal estate.[16] Section 36(2) of the Law of Property Act 1925 provides two major means of effecting

9 *Burke v Stevens*, 70 Cal Rptr 87 at 91 (1968). A form of unseverable joint tenancy (the 'tenancy by entireties') was available to husband and wife in England before 1926 (ante, p 482). In some jurisdictions joint tenancy has been made unseverable without the consent of all the joint tenants, with the express purpose of guaranteeing to each joint tenant the indestructibility of his right of survivorship (see eg Land Titles Act (Saskatchewan)(RSS 1978, c.L-5), s 240; *Re The Queen And Peters* (1983) 141 DLR (3d) 508 at 516).

10 See *Staples v Maurice* (1774) 4 Bro Parl Cas 580 at 585, 2 ER 395 at 399. The joint tenants may of course bind themselves by agreement inter se not to do any act which will result in the severance of the joint tenancy (see *Re Debney* (1960) 60 SR (NSW) 471 at 473). However, even if such a contractual undertaking is broken (eg if one joint tenant sells his severable share to a stranger), it can sound only in damages against the errant co-owner: the illicit severance cannot prejudice the rights of the stranger (see *Fitts v Stone*, 166 SW2d 897 at 899 (1942)). It seems also that an injunction may be available to restrain an impending dealing which threatens to sever the joint tenancy. See D. Mendes da Costa, (1961-62) 3 Melbourne ULR 137, 306, 433 at 440.

11 Ante, p 466. However, the execution of mutual wills by joint tenants may bring about a severance (post, p 501).

12 The court may, for instance, authorise an unequal division of proceeds of sale under the Matrimonial Causes Act 1973, ss 24(1), 24A, an order which would arguably have severing effect even before being duly performed (post, p 496).

13 An agreement deviating from equality of shares after severance may be present in rare cases of a partnership arrangement involving joint tenants (see eg *Barton v Morris* [1985] 1 WLR 1257 at 1262D-H), or may be incorporated in a declaration of trust (see *Goodman v Gallant* [1986] Fam 106 at 119C).

14 '[U]pon a severance the person severing will take 1/nth of the property beneficially, where "n" is the original number of the joint tenants' (*Nielson-Jones v Fedden* [1975] Ch 222 at 228E per Walton J). See also *Bedson v Bedson* [1965] 2 QB 666 at 689C; *Goodman v Gallant* [1986] Fam 106 at 119D; *Corin v Patton* (1990) 169 CLR 540 at 573, 575 per Deane J.

15 Post, p 516. In registered land a 'restriction' (ante, p 182) should be entered on the register of title (see A. Kenny and P. Kenny, (1980) 80 Law Soc Gaz 1473 at 1475).

16 Law of Property Act 1925, s 36(2), ante, p 465, post, p 512. Thus severance by a co-owner who is a joint tenant both at law and in equity cannot affect his trusteeship of the legal estate. Although after severance he becomes a tenant in common in equity, he remains as a joint tenant of the legal estate until such time as he (i) retires from the trust, or (ii) 'releases' his legal estate to the other joint tenants (post, p 515), or (iii) dies.

severance in equity, and other circumstances of severance exist under more general doctrines of law. These methods of severance must be examined in turn.

8. SEVERANCE BY WRITTEN NOTICE

Section 36(2) of the Law of Property Act 1925 enables a joint tenant to effect a severance by giving to the other joint tenants a 'notice in writing' of his 'desire' to sever the joint tenancy. Although doubt has been expressed on the point,[17] it has been said that this provision radically altered the law of severance by introducing an entirely new method of severance as regards land.[18]

(1) Advantages

The statutory method of severance by written notice is doubtless convenient.[19] It may be quite unilateral[20]: no consent is required to be forthcoming from other joint tenants.[1] The severance is effective if there is evidence that the notice was duly posted to the other joint tenants[2]; it is not necessary that the notice should have been received by them.[3] The 'notice in writing' need not be signed[4] and may even take the form of a writ or originating summons by which proceedings are commenced for a judicial determination of the rights of the joint tenants inter se.[5] In *In re Draper's Conveyance*[6] a wife applied by summons under the Married Women's Property Act 1882[7] for an order directing a sale of the jointly owned matrimonial home and equal distribution of the proceeds of sale. The husband died shortly after the court had made the order requested, and Plowman J held that severance had occurred and

17 See note 10. In *Burgess v Rawnsley* [1975] Ch 429 at 440B, Lord Denning MR thought section 36(2) merely declaratory of the pre-1926 law as to severance. See also *Hawkesley v May* [1956] 1 QB 304 at 313, as commented upon in *Davies v Davies* [1983] WAR 305 at 308 per Burt CJ.

18 See *Burgess v Rawnsley* [1975] Ch 429 at 444G per Browne LJ, 447E per Sir John Pennycuick; *Harris v Goddard* [1983] 1 WLR 1203 at 1208H per Lawton LJ.

19 The written notice method of severance has the great advantage of speed and simplicity in circumstances where much can turn on the precise sequence of rapidly occurring events (see eg *First National Securities Ltd v Hegerty* [1985] QB 850 at 865B-E). For an appropriate form of words, see *Goodman v Gallant* [1986] Fam 106 at 109B.

20 The availability of statutory severance by written notice relieves joint tenants of any necessity to undertake the charade of executing a mortgage charge or an assignment to a trustee or even a self-directed assignment (post, p 492), these being the only other means by which a joint tenant can unilaterally sever whilst retaining a proprietary right in the common property. See *Corin v Patton* (1990) 169 CLR 540 at 584 per Deane J.

1 *Harris v Goddard* [1983] 1 WLR 1203 at 1209B per Lawton LJ.

2 See Law of Property Act 1925, s 196.

3 *Re 88 Berkeley Road, NW 9* [1971] Ch 648 at 655C.

4 *In re Draper's Conveyance* [1969] 1 Ch 486 at 492A.

5 This seems to be the case at least so long as the writ or summons is coupled with a supporting affidavit, in circumstances where the two documents taken in conjunction clearly indicate a desire to sever (see *In re Draper's Conveyance* [1969] 1 Ch 486 at 492C). In *Burgess v Rawnsley* [1975] Ch 429 at 447F, Sir John Pennycuick thought that the 'notice in writing' could comprise either the writ or the summons or the affidavit.

6 [1969] 1 Ch 486. See (1968) 84 LQR 462 (P.V. Baker).

7 Compare the effect of an application under the Matrimonial Causes Act 1973 (post, p 497).

that the wife now held the legal estate (as sole surviving trustee) on trust for herself and her husband's estate in equal shares.[8]

(2) Limitations

Severance by written notice is, however, subject to certain limitations. It has no reference to settled land,[9] and may well be inapplicable to cases in which the names on the legal title are not identical to the beneficiaries behind the trust (eg where A, B and C hold the legal estate on trust for sale for A, B, C and D, or where T1 and T2 hold the legal estate on trust for sale for X, Y and Z).[10] Likewise it seems that the written notice method of severance is not available if the co-owned land has already been sold: the land is no longer 'vested in joint tenants beneficially', as seems to be required by section 36(2).[11] In such cases it may be that severance can be effected only by other means.

Perhaps the most important limitation on the scope of the written notice method of severance is that 'a desire to sever must evince an intention to bring about the wanted result immediately'.[12] Thus it is not enough that the written notice should express a desire to sever at some time in the future. It was on this ground that the Court of Appeal in *Harris v Goddard*[13] refused to find that severance had occurred where a spouse had merely included in her divorce petition a prayer that the divorce court might make such order respecting the matrimonial property 'as may be just.'[14] It is likewise insufficient that joint tenants should refer to severance in a draft separation agreement which, although sent by one party to the other, was never accepted by the recipient.[15]

8 Plowman J based his decision both on the written notice provision in section 36(2) and on the old common law of severance (see [1969] 1 Ch 486 at 492B). It has been said that *In re Draper's Conveyance* can be treated as involving an act of a joint tenant 'operating upon' her own share (post, p 496).

9 Law of Property Act 1925, s 36(2).

10 It is possible that such a construction is compelled by the strict wording of section 36(2), '...where a legal estate...is vested in joint tenants beneficially...' However, there is much to commend a more liberal and more sensible construction which would enable all equitable joint tenants to take advantage of the facility of severance by written notice. See, in favour of this wider view, *Burgess v Rawnsley* [1975] Ch 429 at 439G per Lord Denning MR, 444F per Browne LJ, 447G per Sir John Pennycuick). See, *contra*, [1976] CLJ 20 at 24 (D.J. Hayton).

11 See *Nielson-Jones v Fedden* [1975] Ch 222 at 229E. See, *contra*, *Burgess v Rawnsley* [1975] Ch 429 at 440A per Lord Denning MR.

12 *Harris v Goddard* [1983] 1 WLR 1203 at 1209B per Lawton LJ. See also *Lyons v Lyons* [1967] VR 169 at 172. For confirmation of the paramount importance of intention under section 36(2), see *Gore and Snell v Carpenter* (1990) 60 P & CR 456 at 462.

13 [1983] 1 WLR 1203. See (1984) 100 LQR 161; [1984] Conv 148 (S. Coneys); (1984) 134 NLJ 63 (H.W. Wilkinson).

14 Both Lawton LJ (at 1209D) and Dillon LJ (at 1210H) also pointed out that the general prayer in the wife's petition could have been satisfied by relief which did not involve 'severance' at all. In the exercise of its discretion under the Matrimonial Causes Act 1973, the divorce court could have made an order extinguishing the interest of one or other spouse in the property or directing a resettlement on the spouses successively and not as concurrent owners. Compare *In re Draper's Conveyance* [1969] 1 Ch 486 (ante, p 487), where the claim plainly involved a severance of the beneficial joint tenancy.

15 *Gore and Snell v Carpenter* (1990) 60 P & CR 456 at 462f (severance clause merely a 'part of the package of proposals').

9. THE *WILLIAMS V HENSMAN* METHODS OF SEVERANCE

Section 36(2) of the Law of Property Act 1925 makes it clear that severance can be effected in equity if a joint tenant does 'such other acts or things as would, in the case of personal estate, have been effectual to sever the tenancy in equity' before 1926.[16] The classic authority on the pre-1926 forms of severance in personalty was provided in *Williams v Hensman*[17] by Page Wood V-C, who laid down three categories of circumstance which result in severance.[18] These categories are now examined in turn. In general terms, in the context of a dealing between a joint tenant and a stranger the issue of severance tends to focus on whether the transaction in question has destroyed an essential unity of joint tenancy. Where, however, the context is that of a dealing of the joint tenants *inter se*, the more useful question seems to be whether any of the co-owners have evinced an intention which is clearly inconsistent with the future operation of the *ius accrescendi*.[19]

(1) Act of a joint tenant 'operating upon his own share'

According to Page Wood V-C, 'an act of any one of the persons interested operating upon his own share may create a severance as to that share.'[20] This mode of severance may be quite unilateral[1] and the 'act' of severance may be concealed—even dishonestly—from the other joint tenant or tenants.[2] However, in order to amount to severance the 'act' of the joint tenant must be 'such as to preclude him from claiming by survivorship any interest in the subject-matter of the joint tenancy.'[3] In other words, the 'act' which operates upon the joint tenant's share must have a final or irrevocable

16 In 1985 the Law Commission expressed the view that 'as time goes by, it is increasingly undesirable to have to refer to pre-1926 law' (see Law Commission, *Trusts of Land* (Law Com Working Paper No 94, September 1985), para 3.24). The Commission has, however, reserved further consideration of the law of severance for a future project (see *Transfer of Land: Trusts of Land* (Law Com No 181, 8 June 1989), para 1.3).

17 (1861) 1 John & H 546 at 557, 70 ER 862 at 867, approved by the Privy Council in *Tan Chew Hoe Neo v Chee Swee Cheng* (1929) LR 56 Ind App 112 at 115. It was confirmed by Lawton LJ in *Harris v Goddard* [1983] 1 WLR 1203 at 1208H that the reference in section 36(2) to '...such other acts or things...' merely 'put into statutory language the other ways of effecting severance to which Page Wood V-C referred in *Williams v Hensman*.'

18 *Williams v Hensman* related to personalty, but the principles enunciated there have been applied indifferently to property real and personal. See *Burgess v Rawnsley* [1975] Ch 429; *Re Murdoch and Barry* (1976) 64 DLR (3d) 222 at 224; *McNab v Earle* [1981] 2 NSWLR 673 at 675G; *Abela v Public Trustee* [1983] 1 NSWLR 308 at 316E.

19 See *Bradley v Mann*, 525 P2d 492 at 493 (1974), affd 535 P2d 213 at 214 (1975); *Mangus v Miller*, 532 P2d 368 at 369 (1975).

20 (1861) 1 John & H 546 at 557, 70 ER 862 at 867.

1 *Harris v Goddard* [1983] 1 WLR 1203 at 1209B; *Clark v Carter*, 70 Cal Rptr 923 at 925 (1968); *Gonzales v Gonzales*, 73 Cal Rptr 83 at 87 (1968).

2 See eg *First National Securities Ltd v Hegerty* [1985] QB 850 (post, p 977); *Ahmed v Kendrick* (1988) 56 P & CR 120 at 126; *Burke v Stevens*, 70 Cal Rptr 87 at 91 (1968); *Corin v Patton* (1990) 169 CLR 540 at 585f per Deane J. See also *In Re Estate of Casella*, 64 Cal Rptr 259 at 265 (1967).

3 *In re Wilks* [1891] 3 Ch 59 at 61 per Stirling J.

character which effectively estops any future claim that longevity has conferred the benefits of survivorship on that co-owner.[4]

(a) Alienation inter vivos

A sufficient 'act' for the purpose of the rule in *Williams v Hensman* typically takes the form of a total or partial alienation of a joint tenant's share.[5] That this should be so is, in one sense, entirely consistent with the theory of joint tenancy. A joint tenancy is severed if one of the 'four unities' ceases to be present, as for instance would be the case if one joint tenant were to alienate his proprietary interest in the joint tenancy to a third party.[6] In such an event the stranger, as alienee, would not enjoy unity of title with the remaining joint tenants.[7]

There is, however, a logical difficulty at this point. In terms of the definition of joint tenancy, a joint tenant does not own an interest or 'share' which is sufficiently distinct to provide the subject matter of a disposition. The only way in which the alienor can validly dispose of an 'interest' is on the assumption that severance has already occurred. The act of alienation is thus, paradoxically, both the source and the vehicle of the interest conveyed. In some curious dislocation of time and causation, the completed act of transfer brings into being the very 'interest' which purported to be the subject matter of the transfer in the first place. It is small wonder that Dixon J observed in *Wright v Gibbons*[8] that joint tenancy is 'a form of ownership bearing many traces of the scholasticism of the times in which its principles were developed.'

(i) Dealings with strangers The effect of this form of severance may be seen in the following examples. Suppose that A, B and C are joint tenants at law and in equity (see *Fig.* 27).

4 For express reference to the terminology of estoppel in this context, see *Re Murdoch and Barry* (1976) 64 DLR (3d) 222 at 229. Compare, however, A.J. McClean, (1979) 57 Can Bar Rev 1 at 29f.

5 If the relevant transfer requires registration in a register of title, such a transfer, if not for consideration, probably cannot constitute a severing 'act' unless and until it is duly registered (see *Golding v Hands, Golding and Boldt* [1969] WAR 121 at 126; *Re Murdoch and Barry* (1976) 64 DLR (3d) 222 at 228). See generally *Corin v Patton* (1990) 169 CLR 540.

6 *Litt*, s 292; *Co Litt*, p 189a. See also *Partriche v Powlet* (1740) 2 Atk 54 at 55, 26 ER 430 at 431 per Lord Hardwicke LC: '*Alienatio rei praefertur iuri accrescendi*'. This proposition is yet another expression of one of the historic premises of English property law, ie that the highest consummation of a thing lies in its alienation (ante, p 90). Even a joint tenant's ineffective attempt to convey the entire jointly held estate operates to sever his own equitable share and pass it to the transferee. See Law of Property Act 1925, s 63(1); *First National Securities Ltd v Hegerty* [1985] QB 850 at 854B, 862G-H; *Ahmed v Kendrick* (1988) 56 P & CR 120 at 126 (post, p 977).

7 *Bl Comm*, Vol II, p 185. See also *Re Murdoch and Barry* (1976) 64 DLR (3d) 222 at 225f.

8 (1949) 78 CLR 313 at 330. Dixon J sought to reconcile the 'not altogether compatible aspects of joint tenancy' by resorting to Coke's proposition that 'to divers purposes' (eg alienation) each joint tenant is conceived as being entitled to an aliquot share (ante, p 462).

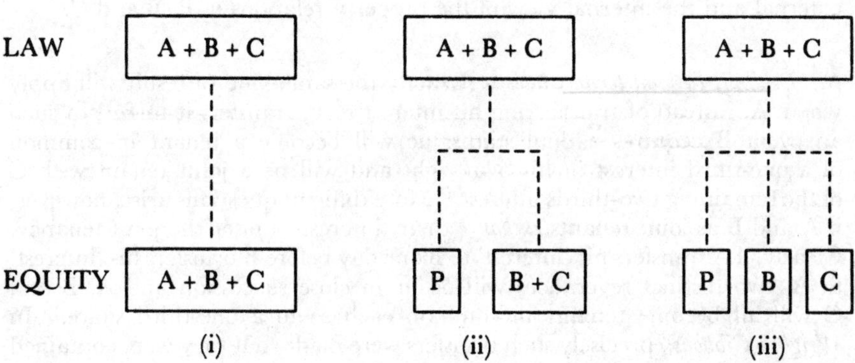

Fig. 27

If A transfers to P his 'share' or 'interest' in the joint tenancy, A thereby destroys the pre-existing unity of title and thus severs the joint tenancy.[9] This severance affects only the equitable ownership, since there can be no tenancy in common of a legal estate.[10] The result (as reflected in situation (ii) above) is that A, B and C will remain as trustees, holding the legal estate on trust for P (as a tenant in common owning a one-third share in equity) and B and C (as joint tenants inter se of the remaining two-thirds).[11]

Viewed objectively, this situation can still be described as disclosing a form of tenancy in common as between P, B and C. In strict analytical terms P is a tenant in common of a one-third share and the collective entity of (B + C) becomes a tenant in common of a two-thirds share. As between themselves, however, B and C are 'wholly entitled to the whole' of their two-thirds interest as joint tenants.[12] The right of survivorship will continue to operate between them with respect to this two-thirds interest unless and until either severs. In the event of such a severance A, B and C will still hold the legal estate as joint tenants, but will now hold it on trust for P,

9 *Corin v Patton* (1990) 169 CLR 540 at 588 per Toohey J. This result follows even if A's 'share' is transferred to P by means of an instrument executed by P under a power of attorney and without the knowledge of the other joint tenants (see *Re Mills and Andrewes* (1983) 142 DLR (3d) 294).

10 Law of Property Act 1925, ss 1(6), 36(2), post, p 512.

11 *Litt*, s 294; *Co Litt*, p 189a; *Wright v Gibbons* (1949) 78 CLR 313 at 323 per Latham CJ; *Bedson v Bedson* [1965] 2 QB 666 at 689D per Russell LJ; *Corin v Patton* (1990) 169 CLR 540 at 575 per Deane J.

12 See *Denne d Bowyer v Judge* (1809) 11 East 288 at 289, 103 ER 1014 at 1015; *Shelton v Vance*, 234 P2d 1012 at 1014 (1951); *First National Bank of Denver v Groussman*, 483 P2d 398 at 401, affd 491 P2d 1382 (1971); *First National Bank of Southglenn v Energy Fuels Corp*, 618 P2d 1115 at 1118 (1980); *Corin v Patton* (1990) 169 CLR 540 at 575 per Deane J.

B and C as tenants in common each owning a one-third share in equity (ie situation (iii) above).[13] The contradictions which appear in this context are more apparent than real, and merely mark the distinction between the external and the internal view of the property relations of P, B and C.

(ii) Dealings by joint tenants inter se Exactly the same kind of result will apply where A, instead of transferring his interest to P, transfers it to B.[14] In such an event B acquires a dual status: he will become a tenant in common of a one-third interest in his own right and will be a joint tenant with C of the remaining two-thirds interest.[15] More difficult questions arise, however, if A and B as joint tenants *exchange* their 'interests' under the joint tenancy. Clearly, if A transfers his 'interest' to B one day before B transfers his 'interest' to A, two distinct severances will occur in close succession and A, B and C will all become tenants in common each as to a one-third share.[16] In *Wright v Gibbons*[17] precisely such transfers were made, but they were contained in one and the same instrument of transfer executed simultaneously by A and B. The High Court of Australia ruled that this mutual assurance or transposition of interests likewise had the effect of rendering A, B and C tenants in common each as to a one-third interest.[18]

(b) Alienation in equity

It would make no difference to the steps outlined above if, instead of transferring his 'interest' to P outright, A merely concludes a specifically enforceable contract to transfer to P.[19] Once again, equity looks on as done that which ought to be done, and the contract will operate in equity to

13 It is entirely irrelevant to this outcome that P later transfers his share back to A (see *Palmer v Palmer*, 121 P2d 822 at 825 (1942); *Alden v Alden*, 393 P2d 5 at 6 (1964)).
14 *Hammond v McArthur*, 183 P2d 1 at 3 (1947). It has even been held that A may sever by transferring his 'share' to himself (post, p 493), at least where such a transfer is made irrevocable eg through registration or delivery of the deed of transfer (see *Re Murdoch and Barry* (1976) 64 DLR (3d) 222 at 228; *Re Sammon* (1979) 94 DLR (3d) 594 at 597; *McNab v Earle* [1981] 2 NSWLR 673 at 677A; *Re Lamanna and Lamanna* (1983) 145 DLR (3d) 117 at 119; *Re Horne and Evans* (1987) 39 DLR (4th) 416 at 421). See also *Corin v Patton* (1990) 169 CLR 540 at 562 per Mason CJ and McHugh J, and compare *Freed v Taffel* [1984] 2 NSWLR 322 at 324F, 325E. It is unlikely, however, that English courts will accept a self-dealing transfer as sufficient for severance (see *Rye v Rye* [1962] AC 496 at 514), in the absence of amending legislation such as that found in New Zealand's Property Law Act 1952, s 66A (see *Samuel v District Land Registrar* [1984] 2 NZLR 697 at 702).
15 See *Wright v Gibbons* (1949) 78 CLR 313 at 324, 332; *In re Galletto's Estate*, 171 P2d 152 at 156 (1946). B's two separate holdings will be distinguished by their different incidents: his joint tenancy of the two-thirds interest will still be subject to the right of survivorship.
16 *Wright v Gibbons* (1949) 78 CLR 313 at 324f per Latham CJ.
17 (1949) 78 CLR 313.
18 Dixon J thought that an exactly similar result would follow if A and B as joint tenants were to grant their two aliquot shares to X effectively as a trustee for A and B as tenants in common in equal shares ((1949) 78 CLR 313 at 332).
19 *Brown v Raindle* (1796) 3 Ves 256 at 257, 30 ER 998 at 999; *Gould v Kemp* (1834) 2 My & K 304 at 309, 39 ER 959 at 961; *Wilson v Bell* (1843) 5 Ir Eq R 501 at 507; *Kingsford v Ball* (1852) 2 Giff (App) i at iii, 66 ER 294 at 295; *Caldwell v Fellowes* (1870) LR 9 Eq 410 at 418; *Re Hewett* [1894] 1 Ch 362 at 367. The elements of a specifically enforceable contract are discussed elsewhere (post, p 744).

transfer A's equitable interest to P under the doctrine in *Walsh v Lonsdale*.[20] The effect will be identical to that of an actual transfer.[1]

(c) Alienation by mortgage or lease

It is clear that the 'act' of alienation necessary for the purpose of effecting severance may comprise a mortgage.[2] Thus if one joint tenant mortgages a jointly held entitlement either at law or in equity, the effect of severance follows in precisely the same way as if there had been an outright transfer of that joint tenant's 'share'.[3] Such a mortgage may, of course, be effected unilaterally without disclosure to the other cotenant or cotenants.[4] The device of mortgage therefore offers the only means (other than the cumbersome and legally dubious possibility of assignment to oneself or to a trustee[5]) of achieving a secret severance of a joint tenancy without thereby alienating the severing tenant's proprietary rights in their entirety.

The severance effect of a lease granted unilaterally by one joint tenant is a matter of some doubt.[6] There is good authority that the creation of such a lease leads not to the complete severance of a joint tenancy but merely to a partial severance or suspension of the joint tenancy during the leasehold term.[7]

20 (1882) 21 Ch D 9 (post, p 748). Severance will not be defeated by the mere fact that the contracting joint tenant dies prior to the performance of his contract to transfer (see *Thomas v Johnson*, 297 NE2d 712 at 714f (1973)).

1 See *Burgess v Rawnsley* [1975] Ch 429 at 443G; *Freed v Taffel* [1984] 2 NSWLR 322 at 325C. Severance will similarly occur if A declares himself a trustee of his own 'interest' on behalf of X (*Re Mee* (1971) 23 DLR (3d) 491 at 497; *Re Sorensen and Sorensen* (1979) 90 DLR (3d) 26 at 37; *Earl v Earl* [1979] 6 WWR 600 at 611); or if A transfers his 'interest' to T in order that T should hold on trust for A (*Cray v Willis* (1729) 2 P Wms 529, 24 ER 847; *Staples v Maurice* (1774) 4 Bro Parl Cas 580 at 585, 2 ER 395 at 399; *Clark v Carter*, 70 Cal Rptr 923 at 925f (1968); *Re Murdoch and Barry* (1976) 64 DLR (3d) 222 at 226; *In the Marriage of Badcock and Badcock* (1979) FLC 90-723 at p 78,896; *Corin v Patton* (1990) 169 CLR 540, (1988) 13 NSWLR 15 at 25D-F). However, it seems that no severance will occur if A and B merely release their legal ownership in favour of C in order that C should hold on trust for A, B and C (*Groves v Christiansen* (1978) 86 DLR (3d) 296 at 306); or if A grants P an irrevocable but as yet unexercised option to purchase A's 'interest' (*Re McKee and National Trust Co Ltd* (1975) 56 DLR (3d) 190 at 196).

2 See eg *First National Securities Ltd v Hegerty* [1985] QB 850 at 862G-H. A mortgage granted in respect of a legal estate operates either by way of charge or demise, the mortgagee in either case being regarded as having acquired a proprietary interest in the land (see Law of Property Act 1925, s 87(1), post, p 939).

3 Ante, p 490. See Law of Property Act 1925, s 63(1); *First National Securities Ltd v Hegerty* [1985] QB 850 at 854B. A specifically enforceable agreement to mortgage land will also, on the *Walsh v Lonsdale* principle, effect a severance, although a slightly wider view may have been expressed in *First National Securities Ltd* at 862G-H. Here Sir Denys Buckley thought that an application by one joint tenant for a loan secured on co-owned property might be a 'sufficient act of alienation' for the purpose of severance (post, p 495).

4 There is, of course, no severance if all the joint tenants together grant a mortgage over the joint property (see *Wollam v Barclays Bank Plc* (Unreported, 22 February 1988) per Knox J).

5 Ante, p 492.

6 The possibility of such a unilateral grant seems clear (ante, p 469).

7 See *Wright v Gibbons* (1949) 78 CLR 313 at 327 per Rich J, 330 per Dixon J; *Corin v Patton* (1990) 169 CLR 540 at 573 per Deane J.

(d) Alienation by will

The alienation of a joint tenant's 'share' by will does not normally constitute an 'act. . .operating upon his own share' for the purpose of severance.[8] Neither death nor the execution of a testamentary document before death[9] is a severing event. The *ius accrescendi* prevails over the testamentary disposition,[10] and the gift is ineffective[11] except where all the joint tenants have made mutual wills.[12]

(e) Involuntary alienation

The severing event which operates upon a joint tenant's 'share' need not be voluntary. In a weak sense, the relevant act of alienation may be coerced by external circumstances which deprive the joint tenant of any true consent to the transfer of his share.[13] In a stronger sense, a bankruptcy affecting one of the joint tenants causes an involuntary assignment of the bankrupt's aliquot 'share' in favour of his trustee in bankruptcy[14] and thereby severs the joint tenancy.[15] In such cases severance occurs without the consent of any of the joint tenants[16] and may ultimately lead to a sale of the co-owned property against their wishes.[17] It seems that severance is similarly produced by the making of a charging order under the Charging Orders Act 1979[18]

8 Ante, p 489.

9 The execution of a will disposing of a joint tenant's share, although expressive of a severing intention, remains a revocable act until the testator's death and therefore lacks the definitive quality required by the first limb of the rule in *Williams v Hensman.* For an argument favouring severance by will, see N. Sterling, (1982–83) 14 Pacific LJ 927 at 952f.

10 '*Ius accrescendi praefertur ultimae voluntati*' (*Co Litt*, p 185b). See *Moyse v Gyles* (1700) 2 Vern 385 at 386, 23 ER 846 at 847.

11 *Litt*, s 287; *Co Litt*, p 185b (ante, p 466).

12 Post, p 501.

13 See eg *Fleming v Hargreaves* [1976] 1 NZLR 123 at 126.

14 Post, p 597. See eg *In re Holliday (A Bankrupt)* [1981] Ch 405 at 411D, 421D (post, p 601). The bankrupt's property does not, however, vest in the trustee until the moment of adjudication of bankruptcy. Thus, notwithstanding that a joint tenant has committed an act of bankruptcy, survivorship may still occur pending adjudication (see *In re Dennis (A Bankrupt)* [1992] 3 WLR 204 at 206H–207C).

15 *Morgan v Marquis* (1853) 9 Exch 145 at 147f, 156 ER 62 at 63; *Re White* [1928] 1 DLR 846 at 848; *Bedson v Bedson* [1965] 2 QB 666 at 690B; *In re Rushton (A Bankrupt)* [1972] Ch 197 at 203A; *In re Gorman (A Bankrupt)* [1990] 1 WLR 616 at 624A-B; *In Re Blodgett*, 115 F.Supp 33 at 35 (1953); *Flynn v O'Dell*, 281 F2d 810 at 817 (1960); *Canada Life Assurance Co v Kennedy* (1978) 87 DLR (3d) 397 at 400. In *Paten v Cribb* (1862) 1 QSCR 40 at 41, Lutwyche J observed that, for the purpose of severance, 'it makes no difference. . .whether one joint tenant has conveyed away his own share in his lifetime, or whether the law has done it for him.'

16 In jurisdictions where some form of homestead legislation is in force (post, p 605), this involuntary assignment is not usually regarded as falling within the control of the legislation. Being more in the nature of a vesting by operation of law, it does not constitute a disposition in respect of which the bankrupt's spouse has any power of veto. See eg *Containercare (Ireland) Ltd v Wycherley* [1982] IR 143 at 150.

17 Post, p 598.

18 Post, p 495. See also Drug Trafficking Offences Act 1986, ss 9, 10.

in respect of a debtor joint tenant's beneficial interest in land,[19] or even by the imposition of a statutory charge in favour of the Law Society upon any interest 'recovered or preserved' for a joint tenant in legally aided litigation.[20]

(f) Declaration of intention

Despite isolated statements to the contrary,[1] it seems fairly clear that a mere declaration of intention to sever is ineffective towards that end.[2] Unless incorporated in a written notice[3] or contained in a specifically enforceable agreement to alienate the 'share' concerned,[4] it is difficult to see how a unilateral declaration by a joint tenant can truly be said to 'operate upon' his own share[5] or destroy the unity of title which is constitutive of joint tenancy.[6] The vice targeted by this approach to mere declarations of intention is, of course, the hazard of uncertainty. If statements of intention were effective to sever, it could become infinitely more difficult to identify the precise ownership of interests in the land covered by such statements.[7] For this reason there is an argument in favour of upholding severance by declared intent in one limited case. It may well be that severing significance should be attached to a declaration of intention which is evidenced in an irrevocable form akin to the conclusive effect achieved by the delivery of a deed[8] or the registration of a document.[9]

(g) Commencement of litigation

There is judicial support for the proposition that the formal commencement of litigation concerning a joint tenancy may constitute an 'act' operating

19 The effect of a charging order absolute is to place the creditor in the same position as an equitable chargee (Charging Orders Act 1979, s 3(4)). Compare the severing effect brought about in the Republic of Ireland by the registration of a judgment mortgage against a joint tenant under the Judgment Mortgage (Ireland) Act 1850 (see *Containercare (Ireland) Ltd v Wycherley* [1982] IR 143 at 151).

20 *Bedson v Bedson* [1965] 2 QB 666 at 690G per Russell LJ (ante, p 140).

1 See *Hawkesley v May* [1956] 1 QB 304 at 313 per Havers J; *In re Draper's Conveyance* [1969] 1 Ch 486 at 491G. Compare, however, (1976) 50 ALJ 246 at 249 (PB). Havers J's statement in *Hawkesley v May* was *obiter*, and has not been followed in other jurisdictions: see *Golding v Hands, Golding and Boldt* [1969] WAR 121 at 125f; *Re Murdoch and Barry* (1976) 64 DLR (3d) 222 at 228; *Re Sorensen and Sorensen* (1979) 90 DLR (3d) 26 at 39; *In the Marriage of Pertsoulis and Pertsoulis* (1980) FLC 90-832 at p 75,270f; *Davies v Davies* [1983] WAR 305 at 308; *Abela v Public Trustee* [1983] 1 NSWLR 308 at 314G; *Freed v Taffel* [1984] 2 NSWLR 322 at 324E.

2 To give severing effect to mere declarations of intention would render redundant the 'mutual agreement' method of severance (see *Corin v Patton* (1990) 169 CLR 540 at 548 per Mason CJ and McHugh J).

3 Law of Property Act 1925, s 36(2).

4 *Partriche v Powlet* (1740) 2 Atk 54 at 55, 26 ER 430 at 431 per Lord Hardwicke LC. See also *Moyse v Gyles* (1700) 2 Vern 385 at 386, 23 ER 846 at 847; *Nielson-Jones v Fedden* [1975] Ch 222 at 231A.

5 *Davies v Davies* [1983] WAR 305 at 307 per Burt CJ.

6 *Corin v Patton* (1990) 169 CLR 540 at 548 per Mason CJ and McHugh J, 565f per Brennan J.

7 See *Corin v Patton* (1990) 169 CLR 540 at 548 per Mason CJ and McHugh J.

8 Ante, p 275.

9 See *Re Murdoch and Barry* (1976) 64 DLR (3d) 222 at 228; *Re Knowlton and Bartlett* (1985) 16 DLR (4th) 209 at 213f.

upon the 'share' of the litigant joint tenant.[10] The objection has sometimes been raised that the mere commencement of legal proceedings is not a sufficiently conclusive 'act' upon which to found a severance since such proceedings can always be abandoned or discontinued.[11] However, the English courts have tended to regard the possibility of a discontinuance of the proceedings either as negligible[12] or as entirely irrelevant.[13]

(h) Court order

It has been suggested that, even if the commencement of litigation does not sever a joint tenancy, severance must be implicit in any court order resulting from litigation aimed at determining the rights of one joint tenant as against another. On this view, the order of the court itself effects a severance even before the order is duly carried through to performance. Support for this view in England has, however, been less than clear,[14] not least because the court order would not in any event constitute an 'act' of one of the joint tenants except in the strained sense that the proceedings were rooted in an action brought by at least one co-owner.[15]

Severance by mere court order has been justified elsewhere on the ground that an otherwise binding order (eg for sale and distribution of proceeds) would be rendered entirely abortive by the continued operation of the *ius accrescendi*: an untimely death before the court order is perfected should not have this capricious effect.[16] The solution in England may well be that

10 See *In re Draper's Conveyance* [1969] 1 Ch 486 at 492C (ante, p 487). See also *Harris v Goddard* [1983] 1 WLR 1203 at 1209H, where Lawton LJ thought that the service of the summons and the filing of the affidavit in *In re Draper's Conveyance* could have been 'acts effectual to sever' within *Williams v Hensman*.

11 See eg *In re Wilks* [1891] 3 Ch 59 at 61; *Nielson-Jones v Fedden* [1975] Ch 222 at 236C; *Munroe v Carlson* (1976) 59 DLR (3d) 763 at 765; *Rodrigue v Dufton* (1977) 72 DLR (3d) 16 at 19; *In the Marriage of Badcock and Badcock* (1979) FLC 90-723 at p 78,897; *In the Marriage of Pertsoulis and Pertsoulis* (1980) FLC 90-832 at p 75,272; *Berdal v Burns* [1990] WAR 140 at 144.

12 *In re Draper's Conveyance* [1969] 1 Ch 486 as interpreted in *Harris v Goddard* [1983] 1 WLR 1203 at 1210B. See in any event (1968) 84 LQR 463 (P.V.B.).

13 *Burgess v Rawnsley* [1975] Ch 429 at 440C, 447G. If, despite widespread doubts, *Burgess v Rawnsley* is correct in upholding the severing effect of an agreement which was later cancelled, it is difficult to see why severance is not irreversibly achieved by the mere commencement of litigation irrespective of the subsequent conduct of the parties.

14 In *Davies v Davies* [1983] WAR 305 at 306f, Burt CJ opined that the decision of Plowman J in *In re Draper's Conveyance* could have been reached on the footing that the court order in that case itself effected the severance. However, Plowman J was careful to emphasise ([1969] 1 Ch 486 at 494D) that severance had been brought about by the summons and the affidavit and 'not by any order that was made'.

15 Perhaps for this reason it has been suggested in Australia that the three categories of severance endorsed by *Williams v Hensman* have now been supplemented by a fourth, ie severance arising from 'the settlement by court order of the interests of joint tenants in the joint property in a manner inconsistent with continuation of the joint tenancy' (see *Berdal v Burns* [1990] WAR 140 at 144).

16 See *Re Johnstone* [1973] Qd R 347 at 351E; *Public Trustee v Grivas* [1974] 2 NSWLR 316 at 321E; *Gillette v Cotton* [1979] 4 WWR 515 at 525f; *In the Marriage of Pertsoulis and Pertsoulis* (1980) FLC 90-832 at p 75, 272.

severance is inherent in even an unperfected court order where the court's jurisdiction stems from legislation which empowers an alteration[17] (rather than merely a declaration[18]) of the rights of the joint tenants. This result must be the correct outcome where, for instance, a court order in respect of jointly owned property takes full effect only over an elongated period. It would be quite wrong that the postponed consequences of such court orders as a *Mesher*[19] or *Harvey*[20] order should be frustrated by the premature death of one of the co-owners.[1]

(2) Mutual agreement

The second method of severance referred to by Page Wood V-C in *Williams v Hensman*[2] was severance by 'mutual agreement' on the part of all the co-owners who currently enjoy the status of joint tenant. Although it may sometimes be difficult to distinguish this form of severance from the third method outlined by Page Wood V-C ('mutual conduct'),[3] it is clear that joint tenants by acting together may effectively agree *inter se* to sever their

17 The legislation involved in the Australian cases cited in note 16 empowered a substantive alteration of rights and these decisions may thus provide better guidance as to the effect of a court order for sale and distribution of proceeds under the similarly broad provisions of the English Matrimonial Causes Act 1973, ss 24, 24A.

18 See *In re Draper's Conveyance* [1969] 1 Ch 486 at 494D, where Plowman J accepted that the court's power under section 17 of the Married Women's Property Act 1882 is merely declaratory of the existing rights of the parties and cannot authorise a conversion of these rights into a tenancy in common. It may be that the decisive factor in this context is the scope of the judicial discretion conferred by the relevant legislation. See also *Nielson-Jones v Fedden* [1975] Ch 222 at 236E.

19 In the event of divorce a *Mesher* order enables the court to impose a trust for sale on the former family home, occupation pending sale being reserved for one or other ex-spouse as custodial parent. Sale (and the consequent division of capital proceeds in the proportions ordered by the court) is normally postponed until the youngest child of the parties reaches the age of 17 or 18 (see *Mesher v Mesher* [1980] 1 All ER 126n).

20 A *Harvey* order resembles a *Mesher* order, but postpones sale and distribution of capital proceeds until the death, remarriage, cohabitation or voluntary removal of the custodial parent (see *Harvey v Harvey* [1982] Fam 83; [1982] CLJ 228). Here, even more clearly, the reference of death as one of the contingencies conditioning sale makes it clear that no rule of survivorship can have been intended to operate.

1 See eg *Berdal v Burns* [1990] WAR 140 at 144ff, where the Supreme Court of Western Australia ruled that the Australian equivalent of a *Harvey* order had immediate severing effect. Such severance therefore prevented a surviving ex-spouse from claiming the whole of the eventual proceeds of sale of a former matrimonial home merely by reason of the death of the other ex-spouse in advance of the postponed sale and court-ordered distribution of proceeds.

2 (1861) 1 John & H 546 at 557, 70 ER 862 at 867 (ante, p 489).

3 Post, p 500. The possibility of confusion between 'mutual agreement' and 'mutual conduct' is intensified by judicial statements that the court will 'infer an agreement' to sever 'if the acts and dealings of the parties in respect to the joint property *indicate an intention* to treat it as property held in common and not jointly' (*Wilson v Bell* (1843) 5 Ir Eq R 501 at 507). See also *Mann v Bradley*, 535 P2d 213 at 214 (1975); *Corin v Patton* (1990) 169 CLR 540 at 574 per Deane J, 587 per Toohey J. For an argument which fundamentally questions the validity of the distinction between 'mutual agreement' and 'mutual conduct', see A.J. McClean, (1979) 57 Can Bar Rev 1 at 16. See also *Lyons v Lyons* [1967] VR 169 at 171.

joint tenancy.[4] In the absence of contrary intention or arrangement, such a severance will result in a tenancy in common in equal shares.[5]

(a) *Form of the agreement*

Mutual agreement provides a flexible and informal mode of severance. The agreement need not take the form of a specifically enforceable contract.[6] Although valuable consideration will have passed between the severing joint tenants,[7] the agreement need not be in written form.[8] The significance of the agreement is 'not that it binds the parties; but that it serves as an indication of a common intention to sever'.[9] There is some doubtful authority for the proposition that severance is accomplished even though the agreement is revocable and may never be carried through to performance.[10] On this view subsequent repudiation of the agreement would not detract from its severing quality. However, the better and more modern approach is to deny severing effect to negotiations which reached a mere 'agreement in principle', if there is evidence that the parties reserved the right to alter their respective bargaining positions in the light of later developments.[11]

(b) *Content of the agreement*

The agreement may either contemplate severance in express terms or comprise merely an agreement that the joint tenants should deal with the property in a manner which necessarily involves severance.[12] Severing effect has thus

4 *Staples v Maurice* (1774) 4 Bro Parl Cas 580 at 585f, 2 ER 395 at 399; *Wardlow v Pozzi*, 338 P2d 564 at 565 (1959); *Re Knowlton and Bartlett* (1985) 16 DLR (4th) 209 at 211. It seems that there must be mutuality between all the joint tenants existing at the date of the relevant agreement. There is no authority for severance where only some of those joint tenants are party to the agreement (see *Wright v Gibbons* (1949) 78 CLR 313 at 322; *Tyson v Tyson* [1960] NSWR 177 at 180; *Corin v Patton* (1990) 169 CLR 540 at 547). Compare, however, A.J. McClean, (1979) 57 Can Bar Rev 1 at 2.

5 *Paterson v Paterson* (1980) 108 DLR (3d) 234 at 236.

6 Compare the case of severance under the first rule in *Williams v Hensman* (ante, p 489), where an agreement by A to transfer his 'share' to P constitutes an 'act. . .operating upon his own share' only if the agreement is specifically enforceable (see *Burgess v Rawnsley* [1975] Ch 429 at 444B-C per Browne LJ, 446C per Sir John Pennycuick).

7 As Deane J indicated in *Corin v Patton* (1990) 169 CLR 540 at 574, 'mutual agreement' is inevitably supported by valuable consideration: 'each party agrees to relinquish the beneficial interest of a joint tenant of the common property, including the right of accretion by survivorship, in return for the share of a tenant in common.'

8 *Wilson v Bell* (1843) 5 Ir Eq R 501 at 507; *Lagar v Erickson*, 56 P2d 1287 at 1288 (1936). Of course severance follows *a fortiori* where the agreement is in written form (see *Smith v Morton*, 106 Cal Rptr 52 at 55 (1972)). For the strong contention that, for the purpose of severance by 'mutual agreement', writing is indeed required under the old Statute of Frauds (now Law of Property (Miscellaneous Provisions) Act 1989, s 2(1), ante, p 257), see A.J. McClean, (1979) 57 Can Bar Rev 1 at 16f; *Lyons v Lyons* [1967] VR 169 at 171.

9 *Burgess v Rawnsley* [1975] Ch 429 at 446C per Sir John Pennycuick). See also *Frewen v Relfe* (1787) 2 Bro CC 220 at 224, 29 ER 123 at 125; *Gebhardt v Dempster* [1914] SALR 287 at 309; *Abela v Public Trustee* [1983] 1 NSWLR 308 at 315F.

10 *Burgess v Rawnsley* [1975] Ch 429 at 444D per Browne LJ; *Abela v Public Trustee* [1983] 1 NSWLR 308 at 314C, 315F.

11 *Gore and Snell v Carpenter* (1990) 60 P & CR 456 at 461f.

12 *Burgess v Rawnsley* [1975] Ch 429 at 444A per Browne LJ, 446C per Sir John Pennycuick. See also *Wilson v Bell* (1843) 5 Ir Eq R 501 at 507; *Re Pozzi* [1982] Qd R 499 at 501C.

been attributed, for instance, to an agreement between two joint tenants that on the death of either co-owner the interest of the decedent should be passed to their daughter.[13]

(i) Illustrations Severance will not normally result simply from an agreement by co-owners to join in a sale[14] or lease[15] of the jointly owned property to a third party.[16] Such action alone does not exclude the possibility of future survivorship in respect of the capital proceeds of the transaction. However, an agreement that the proceeds of sale should be divided equally (or even unequally) between the co-owners does effect a severance, for the precise reason that further survivorship is now excluded.[17] Thus, where the joint tenants are spouses, severance may be brought about by a separation agreement which envisages a sale and distribution of the entire proceeds of sale in specific proportions,[18] or by a consent order made by a court to the same effect.[19] In *Nielson-Jones v Fedden*,[20] however, Walton J declined to find that severance had occurred by 'mutual agreement' where two spouses had signed a memorandum authorising the husband to organise a sale of the co-owned property and to employ some part of the proceeds in the purchase of a small dwelling-house for himself. This agreement was regarded as regulating only the 'use' and not the 'ownership' of the money proceeds of the sale.[1]

(ii) An extreme example An extreme (and somewhat dubious) example of severance by 'mutual agreement' was provided by the controversial decision

13 *McDonald v Morley*, 101 P2d 690 at 692 (1940).

14 *Re Hayes' Estate* [1920] 1 IR 207 at 211; *Re Allingham* [1932] VLR 469 at 472; *County of Fresno v Kahn*, 24 Cal Rptr 394 at 397 (1962); *Lyons v Lyons* [1967] VR 169 at 172; *Public Trustee v Grivas* [1974] 2 NSWLR 316 at 320C; *Abela v Public Trustee* [1983] 1 NSWLR 308 at 314B. No severance is brought about by the compulsory acquisition of jointly owned land (see *Ex Parte Railway Commissioners for NSW* (1941) 41 SR (NSW) 92 at 95).

15 *Palmer v Rich* [1897] 1 Ch 134 at 143; *Lyons v Lyons* [1967] VR 169 at 170.

16 Nor will severance be brought about by a mere agreement between the joint tenants for a splitting of the rental income derived from a joint letting (see *Flannigan v Wotherspoon* [1953] 1 DLR 768 at 775f). Such an agreement does not exclude the possibility of survivorship in respect of the freehold reversion. For the same reason an agreement allowing one joint tenant sole residence of the property does not connote a severance by 'mutual agreement' (see *Gillette v Nicolls*, 262 P2d 856 at 859 (1953); *Cole v Cole*, 294 P2d 494 at 496 (1956); *Lyons v Lyons* [1967] VR 169 at 170; *Compton v Compton*, 624 P2d 345 at 346 (1981)).

17 *Crooke v De Vandes* (1805) 11 Ves Jun 330 at 333, 32 ER 1115 at 1116; *Flannigan v Wotherspoon* [1953] 1 DLR 768 at 776.

18 *Re McKee and National Trust Co Ltd* (1975) 56 DLR (3d) 190 at 196; *Re Pozzi* [1982] Qd R 499 at 502E. It seems that severance may be implied from the fact that joint tenants have agreed to divide between themselves the deposit paid over by the purchaser at the point of contract (see *Crooke v De Vandes* (1805) 11 Ves Jun 330 at 333, 32 ER 1115 at 1116; *Flannigan v Wotherspoon* [1953] 1 DLR 768 at 776), provided that this agreement apportions the whole and not merely part of the deposit (see *Nielson-Jones v Fedden* [1975] Ch 222 at 230D).

19 *Public Trustee v Grivas* [1974] 2 NSWLR 316 at 322C; *In Re Estate of Estelle*, 593 P2d 663 at 666 (1979). A consent order may still have severing effect even though it fails to define precisely the respective shares of the parties in the proceeds of the court-ordered sale (see *Abela v Public Trustee* [1983] 1 NSWLR 308 at 316B).

20 [1975] Ch 222 at 229G.

1 See the criticism of this decision in *Burgess v Rawnsley* [1975] Ch 429 at 440B, 448B (post, p 503), but compare *Bank of British Columbia v Nelson* (1979) 17 BCLR 223.

of the Court of Appeal in *Burgess v Rawnsley*.[2] Here two parties, H and R, joined in the purchase of a dwelling-house.[3] The legal title was taken in joint names on trust for sale for themselves as beneficial joint tenants, each providing half of the purchase price. On the subsequent breakdown of the relationship, H negotiated with R to buy her out, and a county court judge found as a fact that R had orally agreed to sell her share in the house to H for a specified price. R subsequently revoked that agreement and demanded a higher price, but H died before negotiations could proceed further. The Court of Appeal held that H had indeed severed the beneficial joint tenancy before his death and that his estate was therefore entitled to a half-share in any proceeds of sale of the property. Both Browne LJ and Sir John Pennycuick reluctantly based this conclusion on the ground that severance had been effected by the agreement which the county court judge had found on the somewhat unsatisfactory evidence before him.[4]

(3) **Mutual conduct**

The third method of severance adverted to by Page Wood V-C in *Williams v Hensman* has been termed severance by the 'mutual conduct' of the existing joint tenants. In the words of Page Wood V-C, severance may be effected 'by any course of dealing sufficient to intimate that the interests of all were mutually treated as constituting a tenancy in common.'[5] In spite of the close conceptual similarity,[6] the balance of judicial opinion is now to the effect that this third category of severing circumstance is not 'a mere sub-heading of rule 2' of Page Wood V-C's categories.[7]

(a) General nature of 'mutual conduct'

'Mutual conduct' has been taken to comprise any conduct of the joint tenants which falls short of evidencing an express or implied agreement to sever but which nevertheless indicates an unambiguous common intention that

2 [1975] Ch 429. See [1976] CLJ 20 (D.J. Hayton); (1975) 39 Conv (NS) 433 (F.R. Crane); (1976) 50 ALJ 246 (PB); (1976) 40 Conv (NS) 77 (J.F. Garner); (1977) 41 Conv (NS) 243 (S.M. Bandali).

3 The judgment of Lord Denning MR ([1975] Ch 429 at 435F-H) contains an account of a love story—as poignant as any to be found in the bleak pages of the law reports—which began at a scripture rally in Trafalgar Square.

4 'The evidence upon which that finding was based appears to be rather weak . . ' ([1975] Ch 429 at 445H per Sir John Pennycuick). See also [1975] Ch 429 at 442G, 443G per Browne LJ. It has been suggested that a doctrine of temporary severance may be appropriate in cases of short-lived agreement, with a reversion to joint tenancy when the agreement is terminated or revoked (see P. Butt, (1979–82) 9 Sydney L Rev 568 at 576f).

5 (1861) 1 John & H 546 at 557, 70 ER 862 at 867 (ante, p 489).

6 The impulse towards merger of Page Wood V-C's second and third categories comes from regarding them as examples of respectively express and implied forms of agreement. See eg *Corin v Patton* (1990) 169 CLR 540 at 574 per Deane J, 587 per Toohey J (ante, p 497).

7 *Burgess v Rawnsley* [1975] Ch 429 at 447D per Sir John Pennycuick. See also [1975] Ch 429 at 439B per Lord Denning MR, 444F per Browne LJ; *Greenfield v Greenfield* (1979) 38 P & CR 570 at 577; *Gore and Snell v Carpenter* (1990) 60 P & CR 456 at 462; *Abela v Public Trustee* [1983] 1 NSWLR 308 at 315A; *Re Knowlton and Bartlett* (1985) 16 DLR (4th) 209 at 211; *Berdal v Burns* [1990] WAR 140 at 144; *Corin v Patton* (1990) 169 CLR 540 at 547f, 574. Contra, *In re Wilks* [1891] 3 Ch 59 at 61f; *Flynn v Flynn* [1930] IR 337 at 343; *Lyons v Lyons* [1967] VR 169 at 170f; *Nielson-Jones v Fedden* [1975] Ch 222 at 231B.

the joint tenancy should be severed.[8] Severance by 'mutual conduct' requires neither an express act of severance, nor a contract, nor a declaration of trust. It requires merely a consensus between the joint tenants, arising in the course of dealing with the co-owned property, which effectively excludes the future operation of a right of survivorship.[9]

(b) Examples of 'mutual conduct'

Examples of the 'course of dealing' required to establish severance are manifold and depend on the individual facts of each case. The following issues have featured near the centre of judicial concern.

(i) Long-term assumptions about ownership It is clear that severance by 'mutual conduct' occurs where co-owners, although originally joint tenants, have acted over a long period of time on the assumption that each owns a severed share as a tenant in common.[10] However, the mere fact that joint property is for tax reasons included among the assets of a partnership with separate capital accounts for the co-owners does not necessarily constitute a severing 'course of dealing'.[11]

(ii) Mutual wills The consensus required for 'mutual conduct' can be provided by the concurrent execution of mutual wills by two joint tenants, as for instance in the case of mutual wills which leave the respective share of each joint tenant to the survivor for life with remainder to some designated third party.[12]

(iii) Physical conversion of co-owned property 'Mutual conduct' is not necessarily constituted by a mere physical division of the co-owned property without partition or sale, where for reasons of convenience the joint tenants are left in sole and separate occupation of self-contained portions of the converted

8 See *Abela v Public Trustee* [1983] 1 NSWLR 308 at 315G; but compare the greater hesitancy of Deane J in *Corin v Patton* (1990) 169 CLR 540 at 574. A common intention to sever may be more readily inferred from a course of conduct where the joint tenants are married to each other (see *Harris v Goddard* [1983] 1 WLR 1203 at 1208F; *Estate of Gebert*, 157 Cal Rptr 46 at 51 (1979)) or where the personal relationship of the joint tenants has broken down (see *In the Marriage of Badcock and Badcock* (1979) FLC 90-723 at p 78,898; *Abela v Public Trustee* [1983] 1 NSWLR 308 at 315E). See also *Re Walters and Walters* (1978) 79 DLR (3d) 122 at 127.

9 See *Szabo v Boros* (1967) 64 DLR (2d) 48 at 49 per Davey CJBC.

10 See eg *Wilson v Bell* (1843) 5 Ir Eq R 501 at 507ff; *Re Denny* (1947) 116 LJR 1029 at 1037. See also *Gore and Snell v Carpenter* (1990) 60 P & CR 456 at 462, where long-term assumptions were regarded as the pre-eminent manifestation of 'mutual conduct'.

11 *Barton v Morris* [1985] 1 WLR 1257 at 1262D-H. See also *Brown v Oakshot* (1857) 24 Beav 254 at 258, 53 ER 355 at 357, but compare *Bedson v Bedson* [1965] 2 QB 666 at 690F per Russell LJ.

12 *In re Wilford's Estate* (1879) 11 Ch D 267 at 269; *In the Estate of Heys* [1914] P 192 at 195; *Szabo v Boros* (1967) 64 DLR (2d) 48 at 52. In *Re Bryan and Heath* (1980) 108 DLR (3d) 245 at 250, mutual wills distributing the respective shares of the co-owners among the surviving co-owner and the children of the family were held to constitute severance both by 'mutual agreement' and by 'mutual conduct'. See also *Re Sorensen and Sorensen* (1979) 90 DLR (3d) 26 at 38.

property.[13] A territorial realignment of this kind is not incompatible with continuing joint tenancy.[14]

(iv) Commencement of litigation It seems that severance by 'mutual conduct' is not brought about simply by reason of the fact that the joint tenants have initiated court proceedings for partition[15] of the co-owned property or for a sale and distribution of proceeds.[16] However, it may well be that the formal commencement of such litigation between joint tenants effects a severance on other grounds.[17]

(v) Negotiations between joint tenants Perhaps the most difficult issue in this area is whether a process of inconclusive negotiation between joint tenants in relation to their respective 'shares' can amount to 'mutual conduct'. Severance by 'mutual conduct' provided the ground on which Lord Denning MR preferred to rest his judgment in *Burgess v Rawnsley*.[18] In his view, this head of severance includes any 'course of dealing in which one party makes clear to the other that he desires that their shares should no longer be held jointly but be held in common.'[19]

It is likely that this approach to negotiations would today be considered rather over-broad.[20] Even in *Burgess v Rawnsley* Lord Denning's finding of 'mutual conduct' in the context of abortive negotiations for purchase did not receive support from the other members of the Court of Appeal. Both Browne LJ[1] and Sir John Pennycuick[2] doubted whether a 'course of dealing' was sufficiently clearly established here to bring into play Page Wood V-C's third category of severing circumstance. Sir John Pennycuick admitted that 'where one tenant negotiates with another for some rearrangement of interest, it may be possible to infer from the particular facts a common intention to sever even though the negotiations break down.'[3] However, he thought such an inference to be entirely dependent on the individual facts of any

13 *Greenfield v Greenfield* (1979) 38 P & CR 570 at 578; *Sanders v McDonald and Pringle* [1981] CLY 1534; *Haughabaugh v Honald*, 5 Am D 548 at 550 (1812); *Stiff v Stiff*, 168 NW2d 273 at 274 (1969). Compare *Gore and Snell v Carpenter* (1990) 60 P & CR 456 at 462, where severance might have followed from the co-owners' tentative plans for a severance of their joint tenancies of two houses and for the transfer of one property to each party. Their negotiations never crystallised sufficiently to effect a true severance (post, p 503).

14 Cp *Roche v Sheridan* (1857) 9 Ir Jur 409.

15 Post, p 515.

16 *Dando v Dando*, 99 P2d 561 at 562 (1940); *Teutenberg v Schiller*, 291 P2d 53 at 56 (1955); *Munroe v Carlson* (1976) 59 DLR (3d) 763; *Rodrigue v Dufton* (1977) 72 DLR (3d) 16.

17 Ante, p 495.

18 [1975] Ch 429 (ante, p 500).

19 [1975] Ch 429 at 439C. This description of severance seems unacceptably broad in so far as it gives effect to unilateral declarations of intention (ante, p 495). It is significant that the High Court of Australia has declined to follow *Burgess v Rawnsley* (see *Corin v Patton* (1990) 169 CLR 540 at 547f per Mason CJ and McHugh J, 565f per Brennan J, 584 per Deane J). If Lord Denning's view is defensible at all, it must be on the basis that it was the communication of the desire to sever, rather than its mere formulation, which was 'the effective act' (see *Corin* at 584f per Deane J).

20 See eg *Gore and Snell v Carpenter* (1990) 60 P & CR 456 at 462 ('...negotiations are not the same thing as a course of dealing'). See also *McDowell v Hirschfield Lipson & Rumney and Smith* [1992] 2 FLR 126 at 130C-E.

1 [1975] Ch 429 at 444E.

2 [1975] Ch 429 at 447B.

3 [1975] Ch 429 at 447A.

given case.[4] In his view, the negotiations in *Burgess v Rawnsley*, 'if they can be properly described as negotiations at all', fell far short of warranting an inference of severance: '[o]ne could not ascribe to joint tenants an intention to sever merely because one offers to buy out the other for X and the other makes a counter-offer of Y.'[5]

In other jurisdictions the courts have been more prepared to uphold severance as resulting from abortive or inconclusive negotiations between the joint tenants with respect to their individual 'shares'. This is particularly so where the negotiations have been incorporated in correspondence between the parties[6] or have been mediated through their respective legal advisers,[7] and where the parties have plainly begun to conceptualise their entitlements in terms of individualised shareholding.

(c) Limitations on 'mutual conduct'

Most of the limitations imposed on the concept of 'mutual conduct' stem from the judicial disinclination to accept that severance may be achieved by a merely unilateral and unwritten declaration of intention expressed by one of the joint tenants.[8] In this context the largely unspoken fear is that the facility of informal declaration, once admitted as a head of severance, would enable an unscrupulous joint tenant to hedge his bets in the gamble surrounding longevity. If the declarant subsequently failed to outlive his fellow co-owners, he would have ensured that a severed share devolved upon his own estate; if, however, he did survive them, he would be able simply to deny that he had ever made a severing declaration.[9] It was for this reason that in *Williams v Hensman*[10] Page Wood V-C emphasised explicitly that, in the absence of an express act of severance, 'it will not suffice to rely on an intention, with respect to the particular share, declared only behind the backs of the other persons interested.' Instead, ruled Page Wood V-C, it is imperative to 'find in this class of cases a course of dealing by which the shares of all the parties to the contest have been effected. . .'[11]

Thus while in *Burgess v Rawnsley* Sir John Pennycuick was quite ready

4 In *Gore and Snell v Carpenter* (1990) 60 P & CR 456 at 462, the court refused to infer the common intention necessary for a finding of 'mutual conduct' where 'there were simply negotiations between the husband and the wife and. . .there was no finality and there was no mutuality.' See also *Robichaud v Watson* (1983) 147 DLR (3d) 626 at 633.

5 [1975] Ch 429 at 447B. For a significant adoption of the observations of Sir John Pennycuick in preference to those of Lord Denning MR, see *Harris v Goddard* [1983] 1 WLR 1203 at 1211B per Dillon LJ.

6 *Ginn v Armstrong* (1969) 3 DLR (3d) 285 at 288. Compare *Nielson-Jones v Fedden* [1975] Ch 222 at 230C, 231A (ante, p 499); but see *Burgess v Rawnsley* [1975] Ch 429 at 440B per Lord Denning MR, who considered that *Nielson-Jones v Fedden* had been wrongly decided and that severance could instead have been upheld there on the basis of 'mutual conduct'.

7 *Re Walters and Walters* (1978) 79 DLR (3d) 122 at 127, affd (1978) 84 DLR (3d) 416n; *Robichaud v Watson* (1983) 147 DLR (3d) 626 at 636. See, however, A.J. McClean, (1979) 57 Can Bar Rev 1 at 23.

8 Ante, p 495.

9 In this context the formality of an irrevocable delivery or registration may be an all-important indication of a joint tenant's intention to exclude himself from the possibility of future survivorship (ante, pp 492, 495). See *Re Sammon* (1979) 94 DLR (3d) 594 at 600f.

10 (1861) 1 John & H 546 at 558, 70 ER 862 at 867.

11 The word 'effected' in this quotation must have the meaning of 'affected'. The latter word is used in the Law Journal report (see (1861) 30 LJ 878 at 880).

to concede that the 'policy of the law as it stands today. . .is to facilitate severance at the instance of either party',[12] neither he nor any other member of the Court of Appeal was prepared to hold that severance could be effected either by an uncommunicated declaration by one joint tenant[13] or indeed by a mere verbal notice by one joint tenant to the other joint tenant or tenants.[14] It follows, *a fortiori*, that a declaration made by a joint tenant to a third party outside the joint tenancy is likewise incapable of bringing about a severance.[15]

10. SEVERANCE IN CONSEQUENCE OF UNLAWFUL KILLING

Severance of a joint tenancy may occur on a footing quite different from any so far considered. It is possible that severance may result, not from any lawful act of a joint tenant, but rather in consequence of the unlawful killing of one joint tenant by another.[16]

(1) The general rationale

In *Cleaver v Mutual Reserve Fund Life Association*,[17] Fry LJ gave classic expression to the view that 'no system of jurisprudence can with reason include amongst the rights which it enforces rights directly resulting to the person asserting them from the crime of that person.'[18] A forfeiture rule[19] is thus applied by the courts as a rule of public policy in order to ensure that no wrongdoer shall profit from his crime[20] and, in particular, to ensure that 'a man shall

12 [1975] Ch 429 at 448A, ante, p 462.

13 [1975] Ch 429 at 439C per Lord Denning MR, 444G per Browne LJ, 448A per Sir John Pennycuick.

14 [1975] Ch 429 at 439E per Lord Denning MR, 448A per Sir John Pennycuick.

15 *Greenfield v Greenfield* (1979) 38 P & CR 570 at 578 (communication to wife of other joint tenant held ineffective).

16 See generally J.B. Ames, *Can a Murderer Acquire Title by his Crime and Keep it?*, in *Lectures on Legal History* (Cambridge Mass 1913), p 310; J. Chadwick, (1914) 30 LQR 211; J.W. Wade, 49 Harvard L Rev 715 (1935–36); J.L. Toohey, *Killing the Goose that lays the Golden Eggs*, (1958) 32 ALJ 14; Tim Youdan, *Acquisition of Property by Killing*, (1973) 89 LQR 235.

17 [1892] 1 QB 147 at 156.

18 Quoted with approval in *Beresford v Royal Insurance Co Ltd* [1938] AC 586 at 596 per Lord Atkin, and in *Helton v Allen* (1940) 63 CLR 691 at 709 (High Court of Australia). See also *Davitt v Titcumb* [1990] Ch 110 at 114D–115C; *Rosenfeldt v Olson* (1985) 16 DLR (4th) 103 at 120ff, (1986) 25 DLR (4th) 472 at 475.

19 The term 'forfeiture rule' now has legislative status, being defined for the purpose of the Forfeiture Act 1982 as comprising 'the rule of public policy which in certain circumstances precludes a person who has unlawfully killed another from acquiring a benefit in consequence of the killing' (Forfeiture Act 1982, s 1(1)).

20 This rule is a narrower formulation (see eg *Helton v Allen* (1940) 63 CLR 691 at 710) than the idea that 'no man shall profit from his own wrong', since otherwise the slightest negligence by a beneficiary resulting in the death of the benefactor would bar recovery (see *Public Trustee v Evans* (1985) 2 NSWLR 188 at 191F-G). This may be an important qualification in the present context, given the proclivity of joint tenants to inflict death on each other in car accidents caused through the negligent driving of one. See, however, Road Traffic Act 1988, s 1, as substituted by Road Traffic Act 1991, s 1.

not slay his benefactor and thereby take his bounty.'[1] This principle has a special application to joint tenants who, in fact if not in strict legal theory, derive benefit from the earlier decease of one of their number.[2]

(2) The operation of the forfeiture rule

The operation of the forfeiture rule differs according to the number of joint tenants involved.

(a) *Two joint tenants*

The forfeiture rule operates easily in the case where the joint tenancy is limited to two persons who are joint tenants both of the legal estate and the equitable interest in the co-owned property. If, for instance, X and Y are joint tenants, and X unlawfully kills Y, it seems that X will remain invested with the legal estate by survivorship, but will hold it on trust for himself and Y's estate as tenants in common in equal shares,[3] subject only to the proviso that X may not take (directly or indirectly) as a beneficiary under Y's estate.[4] In other words, the right of survivorship does not operate in an unqualified form: the killer cannot claim the benefit of the *ius accrescendi* in relation to the equitable interest. As Cardozo said,[5] 'the social interest served by refusing to permit the criminal to profit by his crime is greater than that served by the preservation and enforcement of legal rights of ownership.'

1 *In the Estate of Hall* [1914] P 1 at 7 per Hamilton LJ. See also *Re Sigsworth* [1935] Ch 89 at 92; *In re Giles, decd* [1972] Ch 544 at 552B; *Re Nordstrom* (1962) 31 DLR (2d) 255 at 263. The courts in other jurisdictions are beginning to question whether the forfeiture rule is in every circumstance an inflexible rule of public policy. See eg the refusal to apply the rule in *Public Trustee v Evans* [1985] 2 NSWLR 188 at 193B-F (where one joint tenant killed her husband while attempting to avert lethal violence directed against herself and her children).

2 Ante, p 464.

3 *Re Thorp and the Real Property Act* (1963) 80 WN (NSW) 61 at 65; *Schobelt v Barber* (1967) 60 DLR (2d) 519 at 524; *Re Pechar (Deceased)* [1969] NZLR 574 at 587; *Rasmanis v Jurewitsch* (1970) 70 SR (NSW) 407 at 411; *Re Gore* (1972) 23 DLR (3d) 534 at 536. Where, as so frequently happens, the murder of Y is followed by the suicide of X, X's estate will hold the joint property at law on trust for X's estate and Y's estate as tenants in common in equal shares (see *Re Dreger* (1976) 69 DLR (3d) 47 at 49, 60). The beneficiary under both estates may well be the same person (see eg *Whitfield v Flaherty*, 39 Cal Rptr 857 (1964)). There is much to be said in favour of treating the murder-suicide phenomenon, not in terms of rules which aim to frustrate cupidinous slaying, but rather in terms analogous to the Californian rule relating to simultaneous death (ante, p 464). See *Johansen v Pelton*, 87 Cal Rptr 784 at 789 (1970).

4 *In re K, decd* [1985] Ch 85 at 100G; *Johansen v Pelton*, 87 Cal Rptr 784 at 786, 788 (1970). This proviso is incorporated in California's Probate Code, s 258. See also *Re Pechar (Deceased)* [1969] NZLR 574 at 587. The same proviso must also preclude X from taking as a beneficiary under the estate of Z if *Z* was the beneficiary of Y's estate. See *Public Trustee v Evans* (1985) 2 NSWLR 188 at 193D; T.G Youdan, (1973) 89 LQR 235 at 236f. It seems preferable simply to regard the wrong-doing joint tenant as 'notionally not being in existence, so that the other next of kin took the estate' (*Public Trustee v Fraser* (1987) 9 NSWLR 433 at 444E). See also *Re Jane Tucker, Decd* (1920) 21 SR (NSW) 175 at 177H. There appears to be no justification for Vaisey J's suggestion in *Re Callaway* [1956] Ch 559 at 565, that the disentitled beneficiary's portion should pass to the crown as bona vacantia. See (1956) 72 LQR 475; [1956] CLJ 167 (F.J. Odgers).

5 See B.N. Cardozo, *The Nature of the Judicial Process* (New Haven and London 1969), p 43.

(i) Homicide as a severing event Although this conclusion has been accepted as correct in most jurisdictions, it is much less easy to articulate the precise legal reasoning which underlies the outcome stated above. Differing explanations have been put forward. It has sometimes been suggested that the act of killing constitutes so clear a violation of the intimate union of joint tenancy that the inherent feature of this co-ownership form—the right of survivorship—can no longer operate.[6] The rule of survivorship has, in effect, been displaced by reason of the unlawful attempt by one joint tenant to predetermine in his own favour the gamble on longevity.[7] A more widely accepted explanation is quite simply that homicide is itself a severing event.[8] However, this explanation has been criticised by some courts on the ground that it controverts the long-established principle that severance can be effected only before death.[9] Moreover, the proposition has been considered undesirable in so far as it seems to countenance the addition of homicide as an approved method of terminating joint tenancy![10]

(ii) Application of constructive trust principles Increasingly the view is taken that the forfeiture imposed on the killer is best justified in terms of the application of an equitable doctrine of constructive trust based on unjust enrichment.[11] In other words, the killer is recognised as taking the entirety by survivorship but is, by reason of his misconduct, subjected to the full rigour of equitable control: He is made to hold the legal estate on a constructive trust for himself and the victim's estate in equal shares.[12]

(iii) Unjust enrichment The constructive trust approach has major merits. The legal devolution of title is left untouched, while the principle of public policy

6 'This form of ownership implies mutual rights. Its subsistence depends upon a tacit understanding or consent to accept the risks and chances of the natural expectancy of life, but the risk that one joint tenant should feloniously slay the other is a risk which is not contemplated. This act is a repudiation of the terms on which they hold' (*In re Barrowcliff* [1927] SASR 147 at 151 per Napier J). See also *Kemp v The Public Curator of Queensland* [1969] Qd R 145 at 149; *Bradley v Fox*, 129 NE2d 699 at 705f (1955).

7 See *Re Pupkowski* (1957) 6 DLR (2d) 427 at 430. See (1957) 35 Can Bar Rev 966 (R. St J. Macdonald). In *In re K, decd* [1985] Ch 85 at 100H, Vinelott J seemed prepared to accept that the operation of the forfeiture rule simply severs the joint tenancy.

8 *In re Barrowcliff* [1927] SASR 147 at 151; *Bradley v Fox*, 129 NE2d 699 at 706 (1955); *Kemp v The Public Curator of Queensland* [1969] Qd R 145 at 149; *Johansen v Pelton*, 87 Cal Rptr 784 at 786, 788 (1970).

9 See *Re Thorp and the Real Property Act* (1963) 80 WN (NSW) 61 at 63; *Rasmanis v Jurewitsch* (1970) 70 SR (NSW) 407 at 411C; *Public Trustee v Evans* (1985) 2 NSWLR 188 at 193A-B.

10 See *In Re King's Estate*, 52 NW2d 885 at 889 (1952); *Abbey v Lord*, 336 P2d 226 at 233 (1955); *Rasmanis v Jurewitsch* (1970) 70 SR (NSW) 407 at 412A.

11 See B.N. Cardozo, *The Nature of the Judicial Process*, p 42; *Scott on Trusts*, para 493.2 (p 3516f, 3520); *Abbey v Lord*, 336 P2d 226 at 230, 231; *Re Pechar (Deceased)* [1969] NZLR 574 at 587f; Tim Youdan, (1973) 89 LQR 235 at 253f. See also the exposition of constructive trust doctrine in the context of unjust enrichment in *Rosenfeldt v Olson* (1985) 16 DLR (4th) 103 at 121ff, but see (1986) 25 DLR (4th) 472 at 476f.

12 *Bradley v Fox*, 129 NE2d 699 at 706 (1955); *Re Stone* [1989] 1 Qd R 351 at 352. In *In re K, decd* [1985] Ch 85 at 100F-H, Vinelott J noted this approach, but thought that English law already provided an easier solution.

is enforced through the medium of trust.[13] The imposition of a constructive trust efficiently prevents unjust enrichment:[14] the killer is stripped of any profit arising from his crime, but is not otherwise subjected to penalty or forfeiture in respect of his own inchoate interest under the joint tenancy.[15] Contrary to the English approach, where the courts have superficially limited their inquiry to the nature of the crime committed, the application of constructive trust principles focuses on the wider question whether the taking of a benefit by the wrongdoer would be so 'unconscionable' as to attract the operation of the public policy rule.[16] Thus, although the devolution of title is allowed to take its normal course, the relative culpability of the killer's conduct can be made relevant at this secondary stage in determining whether, and if so to what extent, a constructive trust should be imposed on the title-holder.[17] Accordingly the constructive trust approach allows a flexible grading of response by the court to the relative wrongfulness of the co-owners,[18] and where a constructive trust is actually imposed, this trust is capable of binding a third party to whom the killer has transferred the property.[19]

(iv) Form of the constructive trust remedy The precise form of the constructive trust required by public policy is open to question. Since the principal concern is that the killer should not be allowed to retain any benefit flowing to

13 See *Re Thorp and the Real Property Act* (1963) 80 WN (NSW) 61 at 65. In *Re Stone* [1989] 1 Qd R 351 at 352 McPherson J spoke of the constructive trust approach as conferring the advantage of certainty.

14 *Scott on Trusts*, para 492 (p 3495f), para 493 (p 3517); *Johansen v Pelton*, 87 Cal Rptr 784 at 787 (1970).

15 *Schobelt v Barber* (1967) 60 DLR (2d) 519 at 523f; *Re Gore* (1972) 23 DLR (3d) 534 at 536, 538; *Re Dreger* (1976) 69 DLR (3d) 47 at 60. There is a marked disinclination in the civil law area against the imposition of a double penalty where the killer has already been subjected to the censure of the criminal law. See *Schobelt v Barber*, supra at 523f; 41 Minnesota L Rev 639 at 654 (1956–57).

16 See *Public Trustee v Fraser* (1987) 9 NSWLR 433 at 443E-F, 444B per Kearney J.

17 See *Abbey v Lord*, 336 P2d 226 at 230 (1959); *Re Thorp and the Real Property Act* (1963) 80 WN (NSW) 61 at 63; *Re Stone* [1989] 1 Qd R 351 at 353. Compare *In re K, decd* [1985] Ch 85 at 98E-F, where Vinelott J declined to evaluate the degree of moral culpability once it had been established that death was 'the consequence, albeit unintended, of [a] deliberate threat'. This approach has been described as 'blinkered' (see *Public Trustee v Fraser* (1987) 9 NSWLR 433 at 444C, although Kearney J went on to say that consideration of relative culpability would displace the operation of forfeiture only in the 'most exceptional circumstances').

18 See *Re Public Trustee of Manitoba and LeClerc* (1982) 123 DLR (3d) 650 at 651, where the right of survivorship was allowed to operate freely in favour of a killer who had been found not guilty of manslaughter by reason of insanity. In strict terms the case involved no unlawful or wrongful act which could attract the imposition of a constructive trust by way of forfeiture. See also *In re Giles, decd* [1972] Ch 544 at 552A; *Re H (deceased)* [1990] 1 FLR 441 at 446G–447E. The forfeiture rule was, however, applied in *Re Stone* [1989] 1 Qd R 351 at 354 (surviving joint tenant guilty of manslaughter on ground of diminished responsibility). See also *Public Trustee v Fraser* (1987) 9 NSWLR 433 at 444C-E (paranoid schizophrenia leading to finding of diminished responsibility but no lack of moral culpability sufficient to displace forfeiture rule).

19 *Bradley v Fox*, 129 NE2d 699 at 706 (killer transferred property to defence attorney as security for legal fees). However, the bona fide purchaser without notice should be protected (see Tim Youdan, (1973) 89 LQR 235 at 255f, commenting on *In re Cash (Deceased)* (1911) 30 NZLR 577 at 580f).

him from the slaying of his cotenant,[20] any benefit coming to him must be held on trust for someone other than himself.[1] In the two-man joint tenancy, this leads fairly clearly to the designation of the victim's estate as the appropriate recipient of that which the killer may not properly retain. Few courts have gone so far as to maintain that there should be a constructive trust for the victim's estate of the entire interest in the co-owned property.[2] The balance of authority favours a solution under which the killer holds the legal title in the co-owned property on constructive trust for himself and the victim's estate in equal shares.

Even this solution has been challenged on the ground that it indirectly confers upon the killer the benefit of retaining behind the constructive trust a severed one-half share which is henceforth free from the uncertainty of survivorship.[3] Had events taken their normal course, the survivor might well have lost the gamble of longevity anyway.[4] For this reason some courts and commentators have inclined towards a more sophisticated form of constructive trust which allows the killer only a life interest in one half of the co-owned property, the entirety being otherwise held on constructive trust for the victim's estate.[5] However, even this variant of the constructive trust approach is vulnerable to criticism,[6] and the preferable view seems to be the simpler conclusion that the co-owned property is held on constructive trust for the killer and his victim's estate equally.

(v) Forfeiture Act 1982 Although the conclusion stated above almost certainly represents the current law in England, the courts have recently been given a limited discretion to override the draconian effect of this forfeiture rule

20 In strict theory the killer has not acquired by his wrongful act any larger interest in the property than he had formerly, since joint tenants are each invested with the entire estate from the very inception of the joint tenancy (ante, p 461). However, the courts have had little hesitation in ruling that this 'common law fiction' should not be allowed to blind the eyes of equity to the fact that a wrongdoer has in reality benefited by his own wrongful conduct (see *Bradley v Fox*, 129 NE2d 699 at 705 (1955); *National City Bank of Evansville v Bledsoe*, 144 NE2d 710 at 714 (1957)).

1 'Where two persons have an interest in property and the interest of one of them is enlarged by his murder of the other, to the extent to which it is enlarged he holds it upon a constructive trust for the estate of the other' (*Restatement of the Law of Restitution* (St Paul 1937), s 188 (p 773)).

2 See *Colton v Wade*, 80 A2d 923 at 926 (1951); *Neiman v Hurff*, 93 A2d 345 at 347 (1952).

3 *Scott on Trusts*, para 493.2 (p 3520f).

4 It ought for this purpose to be immaterial that because of their respective ages or states of health it is probable that the killer would have been the survivor in any event (see *Restatement of the Law of Restitution*, s 188, comment a (p 773)).

5 This is the view favoured in the *Restatement of the Law of Restitution*, s 188 (p 773f) and by Robert Goff and Gareth Jones, *The Law of Restitution* (2nd edn London 1978), p 489. (No preference is expressed in the 3rd edn 1986, p 630). See also *Colton v Wade*, 80 A2d 923 at 925 (1951).

6 The restriction of the killer to a mere life interest in half of the joint property has been criticised as concentrating undue attention on what the victim has lost in derogation of what the killer has always had at least in inchoate form (see *Johansen v Pelton*, 87 Cal Rptr 784 at 791 (1970)). The 'life interest' approach may even comprise an unconstitutional deprivation of the killer's property interest (see *In Re Estate of Hart*, 135 Cal Rptr 544 at 547 (1982)). The 'life interest' approach has no application to the phenomenon of double killing (ie murder followed by suicide) where, in any event, the public policy concern to prevent unjust enrichment of the killer is abundantly falsified by the killer's patent lack of interest in the fruits of his crime (see *Johansen v Pelton*, 87 Cal Rptr 784 at 789 (1970); *Re Gore* (1972) 23 DLR (3d) 534 at 537).

in cases other than those involving murder.[7] Section 2 of the Forfeiture Act 1982 empowers the court to modify the operation of the rule if, having regard to the conduct of the offender and of the deceased and other material circumstances, 'the justice of the case requires the effect of the rule to be so modified'.[8] The evidence available so far suggests that this discretion may not be liberally exercised.[9]

(b) *More than two joint tenants*

Where unlawful killing occurs between two joint tenants, the legal conclusion examined above is the same irrespective of whether the reasoning employed is that based on a supposed severance by reason of homicide or on an imposition of constructive trust.[10] However, the mode of legal reasoning adopted may well make a difference where the original joint tenancy comprises more than two co-owners.

Where A, B and C are joint tenants and A kills B unlawfully (C being entirely blameless), the resulting legal title is clearly vested in A and C as survivors. On the assumption that homicide effects a severance, a tenancy in common of the equitable interest would now arise between A as to one third, B's estate as to one third, and C as to one third. However, in *Rasmanis v Jurewitsch*,[11] the Court of Appeal of New South Wales preferred the constructive trust approach in ruling that any benefit flowing to the killer from his crime must be held on trust for some person other than himself. That person, decided the Court, was C. In other words, the equitable interests behind the constructive trust belong to C as a tenant in common of one-third, and to A and C as joint tenants of the remaining two-thirds. In this way any profit arising from A's wrong passes to C rather than A, and A retains merely a chance of survivorship in relation to a two-thirds interest. The justice achieved by this result may be questioned. It would be more consistent with the consensus attained in the case of two joint tenants that B's estate should take a one-third share, A and C remaining joint tenants of a two-thirds interest. While admittedly A must not be allowed to derive benefit from his crime, there is no convincing reason why C should benefit either.

11. SEVERANCE BY EQUITABLE INTERVENTION

There has been a tentative suggestion that a constructive trust may be imposed more broadly to bring about severance even in circumstances which do not involve the wrongful killing of one joint tenant by another. In *Public Trustee v Grivas*,[12] Bowen CJ in Eq did not exclude the possibility that equity might impose a constructive trust on a surviving joint tenant in a case where it would be unconscionable that such a survivor should take the entire benefit

7 Forfeiture Act 1982, s 5.
8 Forfeiture Act 1982, s 2(2).
9 See eg *In re K, decd* [1985] 1 WLR 234 at 242ff, affirming [1985] Ch 85 at 100H–102A.
10 See *Rasmanis v Jurewitsch* (1970) 70 SR (NSW) 407 at 411F.
11 (1970) 70 SR (NSW) 407 at 412B-G.
12 [1974] 2 NSWLR 316 at 322D.

of the joint property by survivorship.[13] Such an approach would render the survivor a trustee on behalf of himself and the estate of the deceased joint tenant in equal shares, and would thus in effect result in severance. This wider basis for severance awaits a more general acceptance by the courts.

12. SEVERANCE BY MERGER OF INTERESTS

Severance may also be brought about where the four unities which are characteristic of joint tenancy are destroyed by a 'merger' of interests. Such a merger occurs, for instance, where A, B and C are joint tenants for life, with remainder to D in fee simple, and A later acquires D's remainder. Such a transaction destroys unity of interest between A, B and C, in that A's life interest is seen as merging with the fee simple interest, and A's entitlement as becoming thereby distinguishable from that of B and C. Under these circumstances severence would occur in respect of the life interest, A becoming a tenant in common while B and C remain joint tenants for life. A similar result follows if A, B and C begin as joint tenants for life with remainder to A in fee simple. Oddly enough, the dual nature of A's initial entitlements seems not to connote any merger of interests which would precipitate a severance.[14] However, if C subsequently acquires A's fee simple in remainder, C's joint life interest is immediately severed.[15]

13. CONCURRENT INTERESTS IN THE PROPERTY LEGISLATION OF 1925

Integral to any understanding of concurrent interests in modern land law is the maintenance of a rigid distinction between ownership *at law* and ownership *in equity*. If this distinction is preserved, it becomes possible to view with equanimity the apparent contradiction that, for instance, the same persons may be simultaneously joint tenants at law and tenants in common in equity.

(1) Legal and equitable ownership

It is important to remember that the legal title to land, while of course it binds the whole world, is otherwise relatively unimportant. It comprises merely a 'paper title', indicating those persons who are entrusted with nominal ownership and the appropriate powers of management and disposition. In other words, the legal title is concerned with internal administration and

13 The situation before the court in *Grivas* involved the death of a joint tenant occurring after a court order for sale of the joint property but before that order could be implemented (ante, pp 496, 497). See also *Gray v Gray*, 412 A2d 1208 at 1211 (1980). It may well be that severance by equitable intervention is exactly the form of severance contemplated in the reference in *Berdal v Burns* [1990] WAR 140 at 144 to a fourth category of severance additional to the three endorsed by *Williams v Hensman* (ante, p 489).

14 *Bl Comm*, Vol II, pp 181, 186. It has been doubted whether a modern court would adhere to the logic (or illogic) of this ancient rule: see D. Mendes da Costa, (1961–62) 3 Melbourne ULR 137, 306, 433 at 444.

15 *Morgan's Case* (t Eliz 1) 2 And 202, 123 ER 620; *Wiscot's Case* (1599) 2 Co Rep 60b, 76 ER 555 at 556f.

formal transfer. The legal title in co-owned land invests the legal owner with fiduciary (and largely administrative) duties. Equitable ownership, by contrast, is concerned with actual beneficial enjoyment—enjoyment either of the residential utility conferred by occupation of the land or of the rents and profits derived from letting the land, and ultimately of course enjoyment of the proceeds resulting from any sale of the land.

Thus, if A and B hold as joint tenants *at law* (ie are joint tenants of a legal estate), all that is meant is that A and B are jointly invested with the paper title and are jointly charged with the managerial and dispositive functions connected with it. Since they are joint tenants, the right of survivorship operates between them. *In equity* A and B may also hold as joint tenants, but equally well—depending on the relevant circumstances—they may be tenants in common. There is nothing inherently inconsistent or incompatible in the proposition that A and B, although joint tenants at law, are tenants in common in equity. All that is now being said is that each has a distinct share in the fruits of beneficial enjoyment, that is, a distinct share in ultimately the money value of the co-owned property. Most importantly, when A and B (as legal joint tenants) convey their legal estate to a purchaser in execution of their trust, it is in their respective capacities as beneficial tenants in common that they may each claim a share in the capital proceeds of sale.

(2) Co-ownership at law

Historically the common law always preferred joint tenancy to tenancy in common as the medium of co-ownership, largely because the operation of survivorship tended to restrict the numbers of persons from whom feudal obligations might be due.[16] Later joint tenancy came to be preferred simply because conveyancers could more easily investigate the single title held by joint tenants than if the legal title were fragmented between tenants in common, each of whom could in turn dispose separately of his share. In short, the common law favoured the sweeping together of interests by means of survivorship and leaned away from tenancy in common. The law, said Holt CJ in 1700, 'loves not fractions of estates, nor to divide and multiply tenures'.[17]

(a) The common law presumption

The presumption at law was therefore in favour of joint tenancy, and wherever co-ownership existed in relation to a legal estate in land the co-owners were presumed to be joint tenants of that estate *except* where either one of the 'four unities' was absent or 'words of severance' had been employed in the terms of the grant to the co-owners. Words of severance could be either express or implied, and comprised any language which denoted that the grantees were intended to take distinct and identifiable shares in the land

16 *Bl Comm*, Vol II, p 193. These feudal services and their incidents, which were owed by an occupier of land to his immediate superior in the tenurial relationship (ante, p 52), were of course more effectively secured if due from persons whose number was liable to decrease with the passage of time.

17 *Fisher v Wigg* (1700) 1 Salk 391 at 392, 91 ER 339 at 340.

granted, thereby negating the presumption of joint tenancy[18] and its concomitant of survivorship.[19]

(b) The presumption becomes irrebuttable

There has already been some discussion of the way in which the property legislation of 1925 sought to resolve the tension which existed before 1925 between the conflicting objectives of alienability of land and security of endowment.[20] The aim of alienability was promoted by a series of important provisions contained in the Law of Property Act 1925. Prior to this enactment it had been possible for a legal estate to be held in undivided shares, although the presumption of the law was clearly in favour of joint tenancy. The 1925 Act extended the presumption of the law to its logical conclusion by providing that co-ownership at law must now take only the form of joint tenancy and may never take the form of tenancy in common. Section 1(6) of the Law of Property Act 1925 provides unequivocally that a legal estate 'is not capable of subsisting or of being created in an undivided share in land'.

Tenancies in common can therefore no longer exist at law, and the effect of the 1925 Act is to sweep all co-ownership in undivided shares into equity.[1] The corollary of the mandatory nature of joint tenancy at law is the provision in section 36(2) of the Law of Property Act 1925 that '[n]o severance of a joint tenancy of a legal estate, so as to create a tenancy in common in land, shall be permissible'. The cumulative effect of the 1925 Act is to facilitate the purchaser of the legal estate, who no longer faces the risk of investigating title to a fragmented legal estate.[2] His task is further eased by the fact that the maximum number of persons who may be joint tenants of any legal estate held on trust for sale is now restricted to four.[3]

(3) Co-ownership in equity

Equity, in contrast to the common law, traditionally preferred tenancy in common to joint tenancy as the medium of co-ownership. Tenancy in common represents certainty and fairness in the property relations of co-owners. Each tenant in common holds a fixed beneficial interest immune from the caprice

18 See *Robertson v Fraser* (1871) LR 6 Ch App 696 at 699 per Lord Hatherley LC ('anything which in the slightest degree indicates an intention to divide the property must be held to abrogate the idea of a joint tenancy, and to create tenancy in common'. Examples of express words of severance include the terms 'equally' (see *Lewen v Dodd* (1595) Cro Eliz 443 at 444f, 78 ER 684 at 685; *Lewen v Cox* (1595) Cro Eliz 695 at 696, 78 ER 931 at 932; *Right d Compton v Compton* (1808) 9 East 267 at 276, 103 ER 575 at 579), to 'be divided between two' (see *Peat v Chapman* (1750) 1 Ves Sen 542, 27 ER 1193; *Re Crow* (1985) 12 DLR (4th) 415 at 422), and 'among' (*Richardson v Richardson* (1845) 14 Sim 526 at 528, 60 ER 462). Words of severance would be implicit in, for instance, a direction that the co-owners should pay an annuity to a third party 'in equal shares'.

19 See the transatlantic suggestion that on this ground even a reference to taking title 'jointly' is to be construed in its 'ordinary' meaning as inclusive of tenancy in common (*Re White* (1987) 38 DLR (4th) 631 at 633f). This view may be thought to strain the limits of legal deference to popular usage, and extremely clear evidence of supporting intention should be required to sustain such a construction.

20 Ante, p 97.

1 Law of Property Act 1925, s 34(1). See also *Rothera v Nottingham City Council* (1980) 39 P & CR 613 at 617.

2 Ante, p 100; post, p 550.

3 See Trustee Act 1925, s 34(2); Law of Property Act 1925, s 34(2), (3).

of survivorship.[4] Equity thus 'avoids the gamble of the tontine',[5] and in a tenancy in common each share constitutes a distinct and indefeasible quantum of wealth which can serve as the subject of either commerce or family endowment. Thus, whereas the law leaned in favour of joint tenancy largely for reasons of convenience, equity has always leaned towards tenancy in common for reasons of fairness.[6]

(a) Equity follows the law

In consequence even prior to 1925 equity, as always following the law, was accustomed to treat co-owners as tenants in common in all cases in which they were accounted to be tenants in common in the eyes of the law. In other words, equity regarded co-owners as tenants in common in all cases where the 'four unities' were not present or where words of severance were expressed or implied.[7] However, equity went further and in a number of special cases has always been prepared to presume—quite irrespective of the position at law—that in the absence of contrary agreement the co-owners hold as equitable tenants in common. These special cases involve circumstances in which equity is anxious to avoid the caprice of survivorship, and thus leans heavily in favour of tenancy in common even though the co-owners are joint tenants at law (see *Fig.* 28).

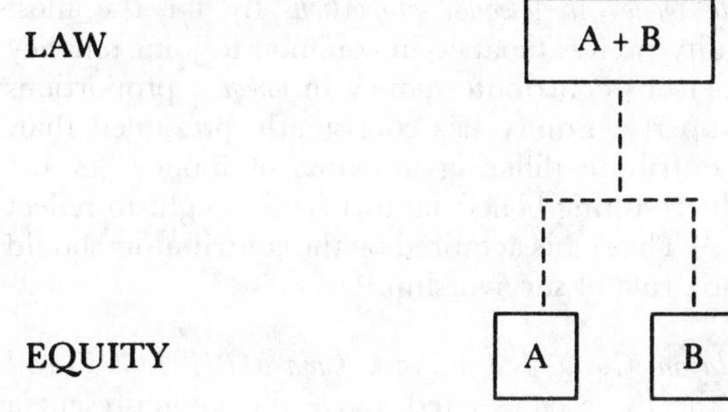

Fig. 28

4 Survivorship 'is looked upon as odious in equity' (*R v Williams* (1735) Bunb 342 at 343, 145 ER 694). See also *In re Woolley* [1903] 2 Ch 206 at 211; *Carmody v Delehunt* [1984] 1 NSWLR 667 at 669B-C per Hutley JA.

5 *Corin v Patton* (1990) 169 CLR 540 at 573 per Deane J.

6 See *Martin v Martin* (1987) 54 P & CR 238 at 240.

7 Difficulty has been occasioned by the ambivalent quality of a grant to 'A and B as beneficial joint tenants in common in equal shares'. Following *Slingsby's Case* (1587) 5 Co Rep 18b at 19a, 77 ER 77 at 78, such a grant was generally taken to confer a joint tenancy if contained in a deed inter vivos, but to create a tenancy in common if contained in a will (see eg *Joyce v Barker Bros (Builders) Ltd* (1980) 40 P & CR 512 at 513f; [1980] Conv 171 (J.E. Adams)). More recently, in *Martin v Martin* (1987) 54 P & CR 238 at 243f, Millett J considered the rule of construction in *Slingsby's Case* to be a rule of last resort. In *Martin* (unlike in *Joyce*) the purchasers had themselves executed the ambiguous declaration of trust, and it was therefore held that the 'meaningless jumble of words' in question pointed towards a beneficial tenancy in common. Millett J preferred to view the instant case as one in which the purchasers, having declared a trust for themselves as joint tenants, immediately severed that tenancy with the further reference to ownership 'in common in equal shares'. In *Joyce*, however, the grantor, having already conveyed away an estate to purchasers as beneficial joint tenants, had put it out of his power thereafter to sever the tenancy. See [1988] Conv 57 (J.E.M.)).

(b) Special cases

It is now clear that the cases in which joint tenants at law are presumed to hold as tenants in common in equity are not rigidly circumscribed by the courts.[8] The circumstances in which equity may infer an intention to create a beneficial tenancy in common include the following.

(i) Partners Where commercial partners acquire title to land for the purpose of their joint business enterprise, equity has always presumed that they hold the equitable interest in the land as tenants in common. The rationale for this equitable preference lies in the belief that the incidents of joint tenancy are inimical to commerce.[9] In particular the hazards of survivorship are alien to the essence of commercial partnership.

(ii) Mortgagees Where two or more persons lend money on the security of property, equity presumes that the mortgagees are tenants in common as between themselves, even though as against the mortgagor they may have taken their mortgage as joint tenants. The basis of this presumption is the belief that each mortgagee, irrespective of his posture towards the outside world, intended as against his co-mortgagee to 'lend his own and take back his own'.[10]

(iii) Purchasers who contribute money in unequal proportions By far the most important case in which equity prefers tenancy in common to joint tenancy arises where two or more persons contribute money in *unequal* proportions towards the purchase of property. Equity has consistently presumed that, as between persons who contribute differing amounts of money 'in the character of a purchaser', the resulting beneficial ownership ought to reflect the disparity of contribution.[11] The rights acquired by the contributors should not be regulated by the crude rule of survivorship.[12]

(iv) Business tenants In *Malayan Credit Ltd v Jack Chia-MPH Ltd*[13] Lord Brightman confirmed that the three cases cited above do not represent a definitive or exhaustive list of the special circumstances in which equity leans towards tenancy in common. There exist other cases in which equity may properly infer that, even though a legal title is held by way of joint tenancy, it was nevertheless intended that the parties should be tenants in common in equity. An example of such circumstances arose in *Malayan Credit Ltd v Jack Chia-MPH Ltd*, where the Privy Council upheld a beneficial tenancy in common where the grantees of a lease held the premises 'for their several individual business purposes'.[14]

8 See *Malayan Credit Ltd v Jack Chia-MPH Ltd* [1986] AC 549 at 560E per Lord Brightman.
9 See *Jeffereys v Small* (1683) 1 Vern 217, 23 ER 424; *Lake v Craddock* (1732) 3 P Wms 158 at 159, 24 ER 1011 at 1012. See *Co Litt*, p 182a ('Ius accrescendi inter mercatores locum non habet').
10 *Morley v Bird* (1798) 3 Ves Jun 628 at 631, 30 ER 1192 at 1193. See also *In re Jackson* (1887) 34 Ch D 732 at 737, and compare now Law of Property Act 1925, s 111.
11 Where the contributions are equal in amount there is prima facie a joint tenancy between the contributors (ante, p 389).
12 For an account of the presumption of resulting trust, see Chapter 12 (ante, p 384).
13 [1986] AC 549 at 560E-F.
14 [1986] AC 549 at 560F.

14. TERMINATION OF CO-OWNERSHIP

Severance has the effect of converting co-ownership by joint tenancy into co-ownership by tenancy in common, but co-ownership may be altogether terminated or extinguished in any of the following ways.

(1) Partition

The unity of possession which is essential to both joint tenancy and tenancy in common is destroyed if the co-owned land is physically divided up or partitioned amongst the individual co-owners. Under section 28(3) of the Law of Property Act 1925, trustees for sale are now given power to effect a partition with the consent of their beneficiaries and to convey to each his separate portion of the realty. If the trustees or any of the beneficiaries refuse to consent to a partition, it is open to any person interested to apply to the court under section 30 of the Law of Property Act 1925, in which case the court may make 'such order as it thinks fit'.[15] After partition there can be no co-ownership; there is merely separate ownership of the individual parcels of land which once comprised the co-owned realty.

(2) Union of the property in one joint tenant

Co-ownership clearly ends if a co-owned estate comes into the sole ownership of one joint tenant. In the context of a joint tenancy originally affecting both the legal and equitable interest in land, this may happen in two different ways.

(a) Release inter vivos

In strict terms a joint tenant has no interest with which he can deal unilaterally at law.[16] However, the Law of Property Act 1925 permits a joint tenant to 'release' his interest to the other joint tenant or tenants[17] and even makes provision for him to 'convey' his interest to another joint tenant.[18] It is clearly possible that the process of release may cause the entire co-owned interest to be held by only one of the original joint tenants, in which case all forms of co-ownership have been extinguished by the union in the single tenant.

15 Post, p 585. Partition is rare in England, but is more common in other jurisdictions. On the criteria relevant to the court's discretion see eg *Schnytzer v Wielunski* [1978] VR 418 at 423ff (Property Law Act 1958 (Victoria), s 223); *Hayward v Skinner* [1981] 1 NSWLR 590 at 593F–595A (Conveyancing Act 1919 (New South Wales), s 66G(1), (4)). Partition may not be sanctioned by the court if its purpose is to evade planning controls or zoning regulations which prohibit subdivision of the land (see eg *Cochrane v Cochrane* (1980) 108 DLR (3d) 395 at 397f).

16 Ante, p 490.

17 Law of Property Act 1925, s 36(2). See *Harris v Goddard* [1983] 1 WLR 1203 at 1210F. Although it is open to a joint tenant to release his joint tenancy at any time subsequent to the creation of this form of co-ownership, it seems that he may disclaim his interest ab initio only if the other joint tenants are parties to his disclaimer (see *In re Schär, Decd* [1951] Ch 280 at 285).

18 Law of Property Act 1925, s 72(4).

(b) Operation of survivorship

The same effect may be brought about by the operation of survivorship.[19] If one of two remaining joint tenants dies without having effected a severance in equity, the entire interest both at law and in equity survives to the remaining tenant. Any trust for sale which previously gave effect to the co-ownership terminates with the demise of the joint tenancy.[20]

(i) The problem with subsequent dealings It is expressly provided by section 36(2) of the Law of Property Act 1925 that nothing affects 'the right of a survivor of joint tenants, who is solely and beneficially interested, to deal with his legal estate as if it were not held on trust for sale.' There is, however, a practical difficulty here. The survivor is faced with the problem that if he should ever try to sell the property, his purchaser will require clear proof that none of the now deceased joint tenants brought about a severance of his equitable share prior to his death. In unregistered land the original joint tenancy will, of course, be obvious from the face of the vendor's title deeds, and the vendor is consequently put on proof of a negative. If severance had occurred prior to the death of a deceased joint tenant, the purchaser would stand in clear danger of receiving only part of the beneficial interest in the land since the deceased's share would have devolved with his estate.

(ii) The statutory solution The survivor can always circumvent the present difficulty by appointing another trustee to act with him in giving what is conventionally regarded as an overreaching conveyance to the purchaser. However, legislation has now intervened in order to spare the surviving joint tenant both the inconvenience of such a manoeuvre and the impossibility of proving that no severance has ever taken place. Under section 1(1) of the Law of Property (Joint Tenants) Act 1964, the surviving joint tenant is deemed to be solely and beneficially entitled if he conveys as 'beneficial owner' or if the conveyance contains a statement that he is so interested. The 1964 Act has no application to registered land,[1] and is moreover ineffective in relation to unregistered land if a memorandum of severance has been attached to the title deeds[2] or if a receiving order (or a petition for one) has been registered under the Land Charges Act.[3] In all other cases, however, it is safe for a purchaser to rely on the presumption contained in the Act, and the purchaser thus takes priority over any owner of a severed share which was not the subject of a memorandum of severance.[4]

(3) Conveyance to a single third party

Co-ownership of land plainly terminates if the co-owners convey their land to a single third party. The purchaser takes the land free of all trusts if

19 Ante, p 463.
20 See *In re Cook* [1948] Ch 212 at 215f.
1 Law of Property (Joint Tenants) Act 1964, s 3.
2 Law of Property (Joint Tenants) Act 1964, s 1(1)(a). On the 1964 Act, see (1964) 28 Conv (NS) 329; (1966) 30 Conv (NS) 27 (P. Jackson).
3 Law of Property (Joint Tenants) Act 1964, s 1(1)(b).
4 Even in the absence of a memorandum of severance, it is doubtful, however, that a purchaser with express notice of a severance can rely on the 1964 Act (see (1984) 100 LQR 149 (P. Jackson)).

he pays the purchase moneys to at least two trustees. Of course, a conveyance of the land to more than one purchaser will create a new co-ownership in the land, as will a conveyance to a single purchaser in circumstances where two or more persons have contributed to the purchase moneys.[5]

5 Ante, p 388.

CHAPTER 14

Trusts for sale

During the years since the enactment of the property legislation of 1925 the device of the 'trust for sale' has become an integral feature of the law of co-ownership of land. There are nowadays few situations in English law in which co-ownership in possession does not bring into existence either expressly or impliedly some form of trust for sale, and it is for this reason that the operation of the trust for sale provides the subject matter of this chapter.

Some of the discussion contained in this chapter is overshadowed by the increasingly prevalent recognition that the trust for sale, as defined in the Law of Property Act 1925, is an excessively complex and not wholly suitable vehicle for the expression of contemporary forms of co-ownership. During the 1970s and 1980s the Law Commission published a series of working papers and reports which proposed far-reaching reforms of certain aspects of the trust for sale.[1] The Commission's concern culminated in the issue of two draft Bills[2] which, if given statutory force, would effect changes of some significance in the operation of the trust law relating to realty. Throughout this chapter reference is made, where appropriate, to the proposed amendments of the law.

1. ORIGIN AND STRUCTURE OF THE TRUST FOR SALE

During the 20th century the English law relating to co-ownership has adopted and modified for its own artificial purposes a form of trust holding whose origin was markedly different from its present function.

(1) Historical development

In its archetypal 19th century form the 'trust for sale' provided a means by which a testator could direct trusted friends (ie his executors) to sell his property after his death and distribute the money proceeds to a number of specified beneficiaries. The duty of these 'trustees' was therefore unequivocal and immediate: they became immediately subject to a duty to convert (ie

1 See *Family Law: Third Report on Family Property: The Matrimonial Home (Co-ownership Rights) and Household Goods* (Law Com No 86, 13 June 1978); *Property Law: The Implications of Williams & Glyn's Bank Ltd v Boland* (Law Com No 115, Cmnd 8636, August 1982); *Trusts of Land* (Law Com Working Paper No 94, September 1985); *Trusts of Land: Overreaching* (Law Com Working Paper No 106, January 1988); *Transfer of Land: Trusts of Land* (Law Com No 181, 8 June 1989); *Transfer of Land: Overreaching: Beneficiaries in Occupation* (Law Com No 188, 19 December 1989).

2 Draft Trusts of Land Bill (Law Com No 181, Appendix A); Draft Law of Property (Overreaching) Bill (Law Com No 188, Appendix A).

to sell) the trust property, normally within a period of one year from the date of the testator's death (the so-called 'executor's year').

(2) Changing functions

As a legal device the trust for sale was initially more concerned with the exchange value of land than with its use value.[3] The overriding emphasis was on property as capital rather than on property as a means of utility. It was this conception of the trust for sale which was adopted in the property legislation of 1925 for the purpose of fulfilling a much broader function in regulating co-ownership of land. It is somewhat ironic that the modified version of the trust for sale which appeared so attractive in 1925 has now become—not least in the residential context—a somewhat inappropriate medium for the legal formulation of co-ownership.[4]

(3) Static features

In spite of the initially strange nomenclature, it is important to remember that a 'trust for sale' of land does in fact exhibit the classic features of the trust concept.[5] As with any trust, the 'trust for sale' separates the functions of administration and enjoyment of property. Administration is vested in the trustees for sale as owners of the legal estate in the land. It is they who exercise the appropriate powers of management and disposition in relation to this estate. Enjoyment is, however, conferred upon the beneficiaries behind the trust for sale, ie upon those who hold the equitable interests and on whose behalf the trustees are invested with the legal estate. Even so, the trust for sale is more than simply a *trust* of property: it is a trust *for sale*. Certain essential features have been superimposed on the basic trust device by the 1925 legislation, with the object of ensuring that the property held on 'trust' is ultimately converted and its money value distributed in the manner specified either by the settlor or by law.

(4) Successive and concurrent interests

It is possible to incorporate two quite different modes of beneficial entitlement within the framework of the trust for sale. A trust for sale can provide either for a succession of beneficial interests to be held in the land or for the equitable ownership of the land to be held by several persons absolutely and concurrently.

(a) The 'successive interest trust for sale'

Under a 'successive interest trust for sale' it is possible to provide for a series of beneficial interests to be held consecutively in the land, as for instance where Blackacre is conveyed to trustees for sale on behalf of 'A for life, remainder to B for life, remainder to C in fee simple' (see *Fig.* 29).

3 For adoption of the terminology of 'use value', see Law Com No 188, para 3.3.
4 Post, p 537.
5 Ante, p 35.

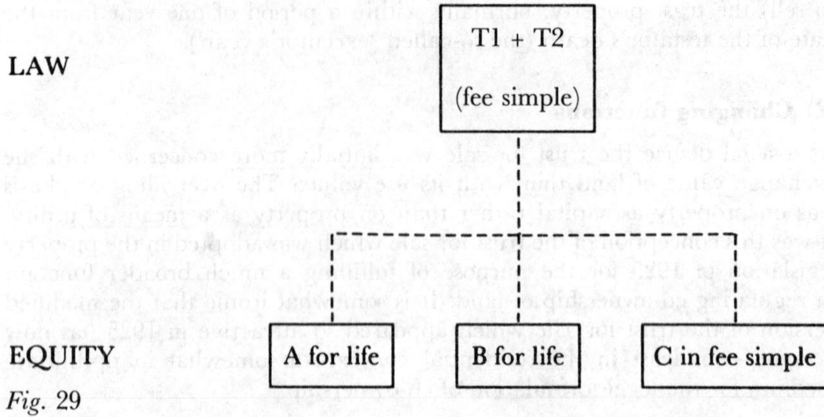

Fig. 29

(i) Location of the legal estate This use of the trust for sale produces an effect which is remarkably similar to that achieved by a strict settlement created pursuant to the Settled Land Act 1925.[6] Under a trust for sale, however, the legal estate in the land and the attendant decision-making powers are not vested, as is the case under a strict settlement,[7] in the beneficiary who is currently in possession (ie A). The essence of the trust for sale is that the legal estate in the land is placed in the hands of separate trustees (T1 and T2),[8] who thereafter exercise all the decision-making powers with regard to the administration of the land and its eventual disposition.[9]

(ii) Operation of the trust Under the trust for sale the trustees manage the property pending sale, allowing the beneficiary in possession at any given time either to reside on the land or to receive the rents and profits derived from the land. The trustees also exercise discretion as to the precise timing of sale, in which event the beneficial interests of A, B and C will normally be overreached and translated into the resulting proceeds.[10] In the absence of sale, the legal estate remains vested in the trustees and continues to be so vested regardless of death amongst the beneficiaries. If no sale occurs before C's beneficial interest falls into possession, C (if of full age) may call upon the trustees to vest the legal estate in himself, whereupon the trust for sale has terminated and C stands as absolute owner both at law and in equity.

(b) The 'co-ownership trust for sale'

A trusts for sale more usually takes the form of a 'co-ownership trust for sale'. Such a trust provides for simultaneous entitlement in possession on

6 Post, p 608.
7 Settled Land Act 1925, ss 19(1), 20(1), 38ff.
8 There is nothing, however, to preclude a beneficiary from also being a trustee (post, p 521).
9 A trust for sale in this form may be preferred to a strict settlement under the Settled Land Act 1925 precisely because it is, for some reason, thought desirable that the legal initiative in respect of management and disposition should be entrusted to persons other than the beneficiary in possession.
10 Ante, p 102, post, p 550.

the part of the beneficiaries, as where Blackacre is conveyed to trustees for sale on behalf of 'A, B and C in equal shares' (see *Fig.* 30).

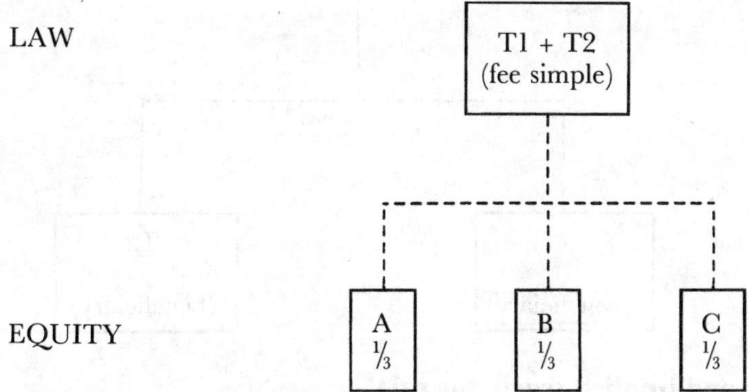

Fig. 30

(i) Location of the legal estate The primary purpose of the 'co-ownership trust for sale' is to provide for concurrent beneficial ownership of land rather than successive entitlements in equity. However, just as in the 'successive interest trust for sale' (*Fig.* 29), the legal estate is vested in 'trustees for sale', and it is they who are charged with the exercise of powers of interim management and eventual disposition on behalf of the beneficiaries.

(ii) Operation of the trust In the 'co-ownership trust for sale' the interests of the beneficiaries are held simultaneously in possession, whether in specific proportions or otherwise. Whereas in the trust for sale outlined in *Fig.* 29 the beneficial interests (other than that of the final remainderman C) are limited and consecutive, the interests enjoyed by beneficiaries behind a 'co-ownership trust for sale' are absolute and concurrent. The beneficiaries have proportional rights in the income drawn from the land before sale, and usually enjoy specific shares of the capital proceeds of sale if and when sale takes place (see *Fig.* 30).

(iii) Division of functions The co-ownership trust for sale is nowadays very much more common than the successive interest trust for sale. But whether a trust for sale gives effect to successive or concurrent beneficial entitlements, at the heart of its structure lies the firm distinction between ownership of the legal estate (which is essentially a 'paper title') and ownership of the equitable interests (which carry beneficial enjoyment). The legal title is concerned with powers of management and disposition; the beneficial interests are concerned with money and actual occupation.

There is nothing, of course, to prevent trustees and beneficiaries from being the same people. T1 and T2 may hold a legal estate on trust for sale for *themselves* as beneficiaries. But even here there remains a vital division of function: T1 and T2 wear different hats at different times—those of trustee and beneficiary respectively. In the capacity of trustee for sale, each is the owner of the legal estate. In the capacity of beneficiary, each owns an equitable interest. Their various headgear must never be confused:

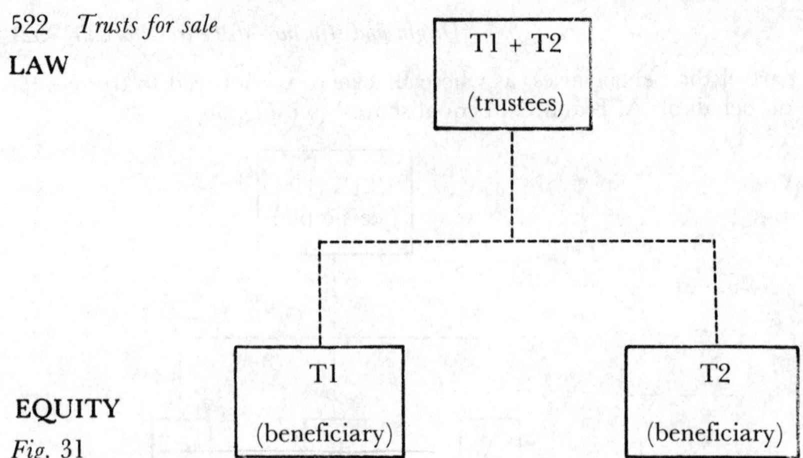

Fig. 31

(5) Express and implied trusts for sale

Trusts for sale arise either expressly or by implication. An express trust for sale arises where land is specifically vested in persons as trustees to hold 'on trust for sale' on behalf of certain beneficiaries. An implied trust for sale is normally the creation of some statutory provision, with the result that the terms 'implied trust for sale' and 'statutory trust for sale' may be used interchangeably. In the absence of an express trust for sale, an implied trust for sale arises by force of statute in almost every situation in which land is owned concurrently in possession by two or more persons.[11] A statutory trust for sale also occurs automatically on a death intestate.[12]

(a) *'Successive interest' trusts for sale*

A 'successive interest trust for sale' can be created only by *express* means. In *Fig.* 29,[13] it is precisely the explicit nature of the direction that T1 and T2 should hold 'on trust for sale' which indeed brings about a trust for sale rather than a strict settlement.[14] Thus, where successive equitable interests in land are granted to designated beneficiaries, the grant inevitably takes the form of a strict settlement under the Settled Land Act 1925 unless the accompanying legal title is expressly directed to be held 'on trust for sale'.[15]

11 An exceptional case is that of joint tenancy for life, which comprises a form of co-ownership in possession arising under a strict settlement (see Settled Land Act 1925, s 19(2), post, p 616).

12 Administration of Estates Act 1925, s 33.

13 Ante, p 520.

14 To convey a legal estate to T1 and T2 merely 'on trust for' specified beneficiaries in succession would in fact produce a strict settlement under the Settled Land Act 1925, under which the person entitled to hold the legal estate would be the beneficiary currently in possession (rather than T1 and T2). Any conveyance to the latter 'on trust' would be simply ineffective as a conveyance of the legal estate, and the legal title would remain in the grantor pending its transfer to the appropriate tenant for life.

15 See *Peach v Peach* (Unreported, Court of Appeal, 1979 P 2745, 3 November 1981). The Law Commission suggested in 1985 that the priority thus accorded to the Settled Land Act 1925 should be terminated and that any grant of land which creates successive interests should be presumed to be held on a trust for sale unless this possibility is specifically excluded (Law Commission, Working Paper No 94, para 3.3, 14.1). See now Law Com No 181, paras 4.3ff, 20.2.

Trusts for sale are nowadays much more common than strict settlements.[16] The latter are rarely created deliberately,[17] and usually come into being only where a settlor has unwisely attempted to confer a life interest by informal means.[18] Here, in default of some explicit reference to a trust 'for sale', the ill-defined arrangement of the settlor initiates an imperfect settlement with all the disadvantages which ensue under the Settled Land Act 1925.[19]

(b) 'Co-ownership' trusts for sale

A 'co-ownership trust for sale' may arise *either* expressly *or* by implication of statute. An express trust of this kind is created, for instance, by a conveyance of a legal estate explicitly to T1 and T2 'on trust for sale' for themselves in equity. An implied trust for sale of the co-ownership variety arises, for example, where the legal estate is conveyed simply 'to A and B'. In the latter case statute intervenes to supply the existence of a trust for sale, more or less as a conveyancing device, with the result that the legal estate in the land is then held by A and B as trustees for sale presumptively for themselves in equity.[20]

2. STATUTORY DEFINITION OF THE 'TRUST FOR SALE'

The Law of Property Act 1925 adopted the familiar device of the 'trust for sale' and gave to it a central role in the restructuring of property law which took effect on 1 January 1926. A 'trust for sale' within the meaning of the Act is, however, accorded a somewhat specific definition which confines the statutory reference to 'an immediate binding trust for sale, whether or not exercisable at the request or with the consent of any person, and with or without a power at discretion to postpone the sale'.[1]

(1) Imposition of a duty

It is clear from the statutory definition that a 'trust for sale' necessarily imposes a 'trust' or duty upon the trustees. The essence of this trust is the *duty to sell* which is imposed on all trustees for sale by the very nature of their trust. If a mere *power of sale* has been conferred, then there can be no 'trust for sale'.[2] The distinction is ultimately one of construction of the words used in any express grant. However, a direction which somewhat

16 As landholding devices, the trust for sale and the strict settlement are mutually exclusive (see Settled Land Act 1925, s 1(7)).

17 There are several powerful reasons nowadays for opting in favour of the more flexible arrangement of the trust for sale. The trust for sale substantially avoids the probate difficulties and quite disastrous tax implications which attach to the strict settlement of land. The strict settlement under the Settled Land Act 1925 has accordingly become extremely cumbersome and is little used under modern conditions (post, p 608). See also G.A. Grove, (1961) 24 MLR 123 at 127.

18 See Chapter 15 (post, p 608).

19 Post, p 618.

20 Post, p 528.

1 Law of Property Act 1925, s 205(1)(xxix).

2 The granting of a mere power of sale connotes the existence of a strict settlement of land, in which case that power of sale belongs properly, not to the trustees in the first instance, but to the tenant for life (post, p 616).

ambiguously imposes a 'trust either to retain or to sell the land' is now properly construed as a trust to sell the land combined with a power to postpone the sale.[3]

(2) Immediacy of the trust

In terms of the statutory definition, a 'trust for sale' must be an 'immediate' trust for sale. This requirement of immediacy attaches, however, not to the sale but to the trust.

(a) Implied power to postpone sale

The existence of a 'trust for sale' does not necessitate an instant sale of the land. Indeed, section 25(1) of the Law of Property Act 1925 provides significantly that 'a power to postpone sale shall, in the case of every trust for sale of land, be implied unless a contrary intention appears'.[4] However, the statutory definition produces the consequence that no trust for sale arises unless and until the land is impressed by a duty of sale in the trustees. If the 'trust' to sell arises only with effect from some future date, there is meanwhile no 'immediate' trust for sale. Any attempt to postpone the coming into effect of a trust for sale brings the relevant trust within the scope (at least initially) of the Settled Land Act 1925.[5]

(b) The 'trust for sale' as a device for retaining land

In effect a 'trust for sale' is in most cases a device of landholding directed not towards a *sale* but rather towards the *retention* of the land concerned—at least for the foreseeable future.[6] In imposing the (at first confusing) terminology of 'trust for sale' upon various forms of landholding, the Law of Property Act 1925 merely aims at a simplification of conveyancing. The use of a 'trust for sale' ensures that when, at some distant date, the land comes to be sold (ie when the trust to sell is eventually 'executed'), the conveyancing machinery is already at hand to guarantee facility for the purchaser and security for those who own equitable interests. The device of overreaching enables the purchaser to take an unencumbered title, while beneficial interests relating to the land purchased are thenceforth satisfied out of the proceeds of the sale.[7] However, this outcome should not disguise

3 Law of Property Act 1925, s 25(4). See also Law of Property Act 1925, s 32(1), and *In re Hanson* [1928] Ch 96 at 99.

4 For an instance of contrary intention, see *In re Atkins' Will Trusts* [1974] 1 WLR 761 at 767C-D. The Law Reform Committee observed as long ago as 1982 that '[i]n many ways the reality is that a trust for sale is a power of sale' (see Law Reform Committee, *The powers and duties of trustees* (23rd Report, Cmnd 8733, October 1982), para 3.61).

5 Thus a grant of land to A for life, with remainder to B and C on trust for sale, creates a strict settlement during the lifetime of A. The trust becomes an 'immediate trust for sale' only on A's death. Compare, however, *Re Jacobson, deceased* [1970] VR 180 at 189 ('immediate binding trust for sale' consistent with conferment on widow of rent-free occupation pending sale).

6 See *In re Evers' Trust* [1980] 1 WLR 1327 at 1330G per Ormrod LJ ('[T]he trust for sale has become a very convenient and much used conveyancing technique. Combined with the statutory power in the trustees to postpone the sale, it can be used to meet a variety of situations, in some of which an actual sale is far from the intentions of the parties at the time when the trust for sale comes into existence').

7 Post, p 550.

the fact that, in most cases, unless and until a sale takes place the presence of a 'trust for sale' is nothing other than a convenient 'legal fiction'.[8] It is largely for this reason that the Law Commission has proposed that the trust for sale be replaced by a new form of land trust which deliberately eschews the artificial and misleading terminology of 'sale'.[9]

(3) Binding nature of the trust

A 'trust for sale' must also be 'binding' in a highly specialised, but nowadays seldom crucial, sense. 'Trustees for sale' must be able, in dealing with a purchaser, to give a comprehensively overreaching conveyance of the legal estate, since otherwise the purchaser cannot acquire a clean title. A trust cannot constitute a 'binding trust for sale' where, for instance, the land subject to the trust is also the subject of legal or equitable entitlements arising *prior* to the trust which the trustees have no competence to overreach.[10] The case law on the meaning of the term 'binding' is confused,[11] but happily this aspect of the definition of a 'trust for sale' rarely causes problems in modern practice. The interpretation of the word 'binding' has an importance in demarcating the point in time at which a grant of land originally in the form of a strict settlement gives way to a trust for sale.[12] But, since strict settlements are now seldom created, the problem of construction is very much less pressing.

(4) Imposition of named consents

A trust for sale may be 'immediate' and 'binding' for the purpose of the Law of Property Act 1925 even though exercisable only at the request or with the consent of a named person or named persons. Thus, if a grantor of land wishes to render that land effectively unsaleable in the hands of his grantee, all he need do is to convey the land to trustees on trust for sale, specifying that sale is subject to the consent of some person who is extremely unlikely ever to agree to any sale.[13]

(a) Effect of an imposed consent

The technique of imposing a named consent in relation to the execution of a trust for sale may well be used for the purpose of ensuring, for instance, that a specific beneficiary under the trust is guaranteed rent-free use or occupation of the trust property for so long as he wishes.[14] Where this is

8 *Williams & Glyn's Bank Ltd v Boland* [1979] Ch 312 at 336F-G per Ormrod LJ.
9 Post, p 537.
10 Additional overreaching powers appropriate to such a case are available only if the trust is converted into an *ad hoc* trust for sale under Law of Property Act 1925, s 2(2). The essence of an *ad hoc* trust for sale is that the trustees are either a trust corporation or persons appointed or approved by the court.
11 See eg *In re Leigh's Settled Estates* [1926] Ch 852; *In re Parker's Settled Estates* [1928] Ch 247; *In re Norton* [1929] 1 Ch 84. See also M.M. Lewis, (1938) 54 LQR 576.
12 This issue is, of course, vital in determining whether a purchaser of the land should look to the tenant for life or to the trustees for sale for a good conveyance of the legal title.
13 See *In re Inns* [1947] Ch 576 at 582.
14 See *In re Herklots' Will Trusts* [1964] 2 All ER 66 at 69I, 71C-D; *Ayer v Benton* (1967) 204 Estates Gazette 359 at 360.

done, the property can be disposed of only if and when sale accords with the needs and wishes of the named beneficiary.

(b) Legality of an imposed consent

The possibility that the exercise of a trust for sale may thus be controlled by requisite (and perhaps unobtainable) consents has brought about the rather strange consequence that land held supposedly on 'trust for sale' can, in some circumstances, be effectively incapable of sale. It is debatable whether the imposition of an unobtainable consent to the execution of a trust for sale is in truth compatible with the trustees' duty to sell,[15] but no challenge on this point has yet been made in the courts. In theory the courts have jurisdiction under section 30 of the Law of Property Act 1925[16] to dispense with a requisite consent which is not forthcoming, but this jurisdiction has not yet been exercised in any reported decision.

3. THE IMPOSITION OF A TRUST FOR SALE IN ALL CASES OF CO-OWNERSHIP

It has been seen that the objectives of the property legislation of 1925 were essentially twofold: the achievement of facility for the purchaser of real property coupled with a guarantee of security for the owners of equitable interests in that property.[17] In the context of the co-ownership of land, the first objective was furthered by the prohibition of tenancies in common of the legal estate; both objectives were promoted by the policy, introduced in 1925, according to which a trust for sale was imposed upon all cases of co-ownership.

(1) The trust for sale as a conveyancing device

Under the scheme of the 1925 legislation a sale of land held on 'trust for sale' is rendered a specially efficacious method of disposing of realty. Section 2(1)(ii) of the Law of Property Act 1925 declares, as a matter of first principle, that a conveyance of the legal estate shall overreach all relevant equitable interests affecting that estate provided that the conveyance is made by 'trustees for sale'. Accordingly it became vital in 1925 that, for purposes of conveyancing simplicity, all situations of co-ownership should be enabled to attract the peculiarly advantageous overreaching consequences which the statute

15 There is, in relation to the trust for sale, no express equivalent of section 106 of the Settled Land Act 1925 (post, p 638). The analogy provided by section 106 in a parallel field has of course stimulated the suggestion that, apart from the strictures necessarily imposed by a requisite named consent or the exercise of the trustees' power to postpone sale, the competence of a trustee for sale must be likewise irreducible. It might even be argued that section 106 is impliedly incorporated in the trust for sale provisions of the Law of Property Act 1925 by means of the reference in section 28(1) of that Act (post, p 539). However, sinuously attractive though these suggestions may be, the real truth is almost certainly that the respective policies of the trust for sale and the strict settlement are simply in conflict (see Law Commission, Working Paper No 94 (1985), para 8.5).

16 Post, p 596.

17 Ante, p 99.

attaches to a sale of land held on 'trust for sale.'[18] The only way in which the 1925 legislation could secure this result was by ensuring—even artificially—that henceforth all cases of co-ownership should necessarily be brought under the umbrella of a 'trust for sale'.

(a) Comprehensive coverage of the trust for sale

In terms of the intention which lay behind the 1925 Act, it mattered not whether the co-ownership related to the legal estate in land or to the equitable interest or indeed to both. In any case of co-ownership where a trust for sale was not already provided by the express terms of the relevant conveyance, the 1925 Act aimed to supply a trust for sale by statutory implication. By and large the Law of Property Act 1925 succeeds in ensuring that all cases of co-ownership in possession are comprehensively covered by a trust for sale.[19] In several cases where the legislation fails to provide a trust for sale, the courts—by fair means or foul—have filled in the gaps.[20]

(b) Advantages of the trust for sale

The imposition of a trust for sale in all cases of co-ownership is, of course, only a conveyancing device. The trust for sale has no effect whatever on the nature or extent of the respective beneficial rights of the several persons interested.[1] The use of a trust for sale in this context brings into operation the conveyancing machinery which has already been examined,[2] thereby facilitating the process of land transfer. The existence of a trust for sale ensures that a purchaser of co-owned land need be concerned only with the legal title. He need not concern himself with the equitable interests of the co-owners (whether as joint tenants or as tenants in common), because he knows that these beneficial interests are hidden behind the trust and will be overreached upon sale.

Similarly the beneficiaries behind the trust for sale are guaranteed certain forms of protection. The inclusion of equitable co-owners within the ambit of a 'trust for sale' gives them access to those protective provisions of the Law of Property Act 1925 which relate expressly to the 'trust for sale'.[3] The statutory activation of a trust for sale ensures that upon further dealings with the legal title in the land the equitable interests of the beneficial co-owners are translated into equivalent interests in the capital proceeds arising.[4] Moreover, the beneficiaries are more generally protected throughout by the fact that the owners of the legal estate in the land are bound by strict duties of trusteeship.

The trust for sale represents the foremost legislative attempt to accommodate in the field of co-ownership the potentially conflicting interests of purchaser and co-owner. It will soon become apparent that, in view of the increased importance of residential utility during the years since 1925,

18 Post, p 550.
19 See *In re Citro (A Bankrupt)* [1991] Ch 142 at 150G per Nourse LJ.
20 Post, p 533.
1 *Goodman v Gallant* [1986] Fam 106 at 110E.
2 Ante, p 103.
3 Post, p 593.
4 See *City of London Building Society v Flegg* [1988] AC 54 at 73G–74A per Lord Templeman.

the money-oriented concepts of the 1925 legislation are sometimes less than satisfactory.[5] However, the present concern is to examine the means by which a trust for sale emerges in various cases of co-ownership.

(2) Express trusts for sale

Little difficulty is occasioned by a transfer which expressly stipulates that the legal estate in the land conveyed shall be held 'on trust for sale'. A typical example arises where a transfer document is executed in favour of A and B to hold 'on trust for sale for themselves as beneficial joint tenants'.[6] Such a declaration of trust is conclusive of the nature and quantum of beneficial entitlement, at least if the transfer was executed by the purchasers themselves.[7] The existence of a trust for sale is clearly expressed on the face of the purchase deed, and the statutory provisions relevant to trusts for sale are plainly applicable.

(3) Implied trusts for sale

Slightly more controversial are the cases in which the paper title makes no express provision for a trust for sale in the context of co-ownership. However, in almost every case of co-ownership in possession, a trust for sale is supplied by implication of statute.[8] The following are some of the more obvious instances.

(a) *Conveyance to joint tenants*

A conveyance to joint tenants may take several forms, as is illustrated in the following examples.

(i) Conveyance to 'A and B' Suppose that A and B purchase a legal estate in land and that the conveyance or transfer is simply executed in favour of 'A and B'.[9] The transfer document has performed its minimal purpose in identifying the new owners at law and there is no express stipulation as to beneficial ownership.[10] Suppose further that there is no available evidence relating to the intentions of A and B as to beneficial interest or as to the

5 See eg *In re Evers' Trust* [1980] 1 WLR 1327 at 1330G per Ormrod LJ (ante, p 524).
6 As a matter of conveyancing practice it is nowadays usual, but not invariable, practice to include an express trust for sale in cases of co-ownership. See A. Kenny and P. Kenny, (1983) 80 Law Soc Gaz 1473 at 1474.
7 Ante, p 380.
8 The precise terms of the statutory trusts are recited in Law of Property Act 1925, s 35.
9 In this case and in the following examples, it matters not whether the legal estate is a fee simple or a term of years absolute (eg a long lease). Uncomfortable and unfamiliar though the terminology may be, it seems that a statutory trust for sale is interposed even in the case of co-ownership of the tenant's interest under a periodic tenancy. The tenants hold the legal estate in the tenancy as joint tenants on trust for sale for themselves as joint tenants in equity. See *Hammersmith and Fulham LBC v Monk* [1992] 1 AC 478 at 490C-F per Lord Bridge of Harwich, 493B-F per Lord Browne-Wilkinson. See also *Savage v Dunningham* [1974] Ch 181 at 184G-H.
10 The courts have delivered frequent exhortations about the desirability of including in the conveyance an express declaration of the beneficial interests in property at the date of purchase (see *Cowcher v Cowcher* [1972] 1 WLR 425 at 442C; *Bernard v Josephs* [1982] Ch 391 at 403E).

way in which the purchase money is contributed.[11] In this situation the conveyance contains no express wording creative of a 'trust for sale'. A and B are clearly joint tenants of the legal estate,[12] and, in the absence of all other evidence, equitable ownership is left to be governed by the maxim that 'equity follows the law.'[13] A and B are therefore joint tenants in equity just as they are joint tenants at law (see *Fig.* 32).[14] The onus of proving otherwise rests on any person who would dispute that the beneficial entitlement coincides with the legal entitlement.[15]

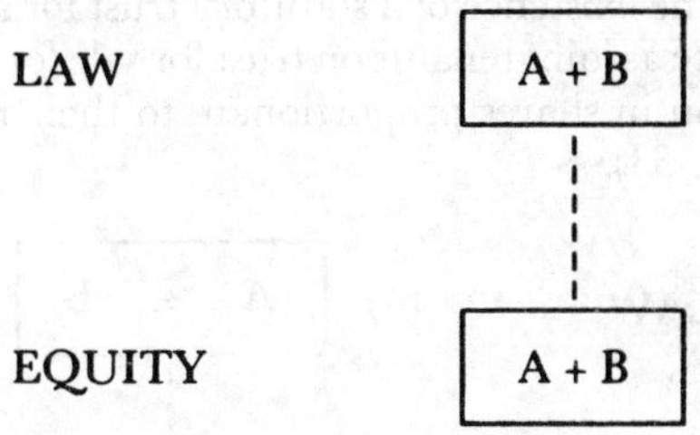

Fig. 32

Although there is no express trust for sale here, such a trust is supplied by implication of statute, and A and B are said to hold the legal estate in the land on trust for sale for themselves as beneficial joint tenants.[16]

(ii) Conveyance to 'A and B' after purchase with unequal contributions Suppose that A and B purchase a legal estate in land and that the conveyance is executed as before in favour of 'A and B'. As before, the conveyance makes reference neither to equitable ownership nor to the existence of a trust for sale, but

11 The relevance of such matters in determining beneficial ownership is discussed elsewhere (ante, pp 373, 383ff).
12 Ante, p 512.
13 However, a conveyance into joint names at law does not necessarily mean joint tenancy or equality of shares in equity. If there is no express declaration of trust which is conclusive of beneficial entitlement, but there is evidence of disparate contributions towards the purchase, there will be beneficial tenancy in common (*Goodman v Gallant* [1986] Fam 106 at 118D).
14 *Pettitt v Pettitt* [1970] AC 777 at 814A; *Cowcher v Cowcher* [1972] 1 WLR 425 at 430E; *Bernard v Josephs* [1982] Ch 391 at 402B-C.
15 *Crisp v Mullings* (1975) 239 Estates Gazette 119 per Russell LJ.
16 Law of Property Act 1925, s 36(1). This provision is sufficiently wide to generate an implied trust for sale wherever there is a joint tenancy in equity (except where the land is settled land). A trust for sale thus arises by implication of statute where (i) A and B are joint tenants of the legal estate and B and C are joint tenants of the equitable interest (see *Hoare v Hoare* (1982) *Times*, 9 November); (ii) A and B are joint tenants of the legal estate and A, B, C and D are joint tenants of the equitable interest (see *Mulley v Mulley*, Court of Appeal Unbound Transcript 1100, 28 November 1983); and—presumably—(iii) where A is sole owner of the legal estate, but A and B are joint tenants of the equitable interest (ante, p 389). Subsequent severance of an equitable joint tenancy will not displace the statutory trust for sale (see *Ali and Amer v Sandwell MBC* (1990) 60 P & CR 374 at 375).

let us suppose that there is clear evidence that A and B have contributed the purchase price in unequal proportions.

Once again A and B are necessarily joint tenants of the legal estate. In equity, however, they are tenants in common since the situation of unequal contribution is one in which equity—regardless of the position at law—leans in favour of undivided shares.[17] This kind of co-ownership is one of those cases not clearly caught by the terms of the Law of Property Act 1925, and there is thus no unequivocal statutory authority for the imposition of a trust for sale.[18] However, the courts have glossed the wording of the Act[19] in order to imply the existence of a statutory trust for sale.[20] A and B therefore hold the legal estate as joint tenants on trust for sale for themselves as beneficial tenants in common in shares proportionate to their respective contributions of money (see *Fig.* 33).

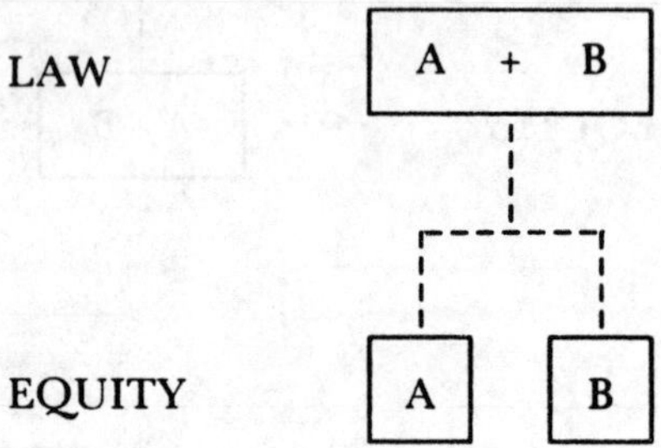

Fig. 33

(iii) Co-ownership of only the legal estate Another and somewhat unusual case of co-ownership occurs where a trust for sale, if not express, is implied by virtue of statute. This case arises where a legal estate is vested in A and B as joint tenants in circumstances where the entire equitable interest is clearly vested in A alone (see *Fig.* 34).

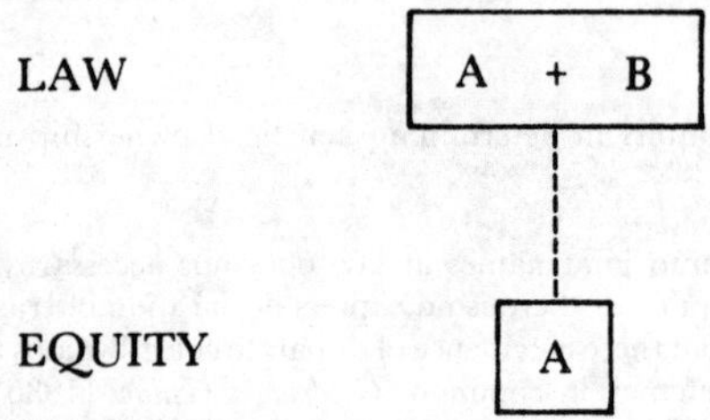

Fig. 34

17 Ante, p 514.
18 See *Concurrent interests in land,* (1944) 9 Conv (NS) 37 at 45.
19 Law of Property Act 1925, ss 34(1), 36(1).
20 *Re Buchanan-Wollaston's Conveyance* [1939] Ch 738 at 744; *Goodman v Gallant* [1986] Fam 106 at 110C-D. For a broad assertion that 'land held in undivided shares in possession must be held by trustees for sale', see *In re Hind* [1933] Ch 208 at 221 per Maugham J. See also (1944) 9 Conv (NS) 37 at 45; *City of London Building Society v Flegg* [1988] AC 54 at 77G-H per Lord Oliver of Aylmerton.

Again, it has been accepted that this situation is covered by an implied trust for sale,[1] although there seems to be no convincing statutory authority for the proposition.[2]

(iv) Conveyance to A and B on trust for C and D in equal shares Another difficult case arises where a legal estate is conveyed to 'A and B on trust for C and D in equal shares'. This conveyance is plainly intended to create undivided shares for C and D, but the 1925 legislation prohibits such creation except under the provisions of either the Settled Land Act 1925 or the Law of Property Act 1925.[3] However, not a single provision in these statutes appears either to sanction the conferment of undivided shares on C and D in this way[4] or to imply the existence of a trust for sale under these circumstances.[5] There is nevertheless general agreement that, for reasons of conveyancing simplicity, the shares of C and D as equitable tenants in common must subsist behind a statutory trust for sale, although it is unsatisfactory to be unable to demonstrate the derivation of such a trust.[6]

(b) Conveyance to tenants in common

Special problems are raised after 1925 by a conveyance of land to persons as tenants in common. Clearly no legal estate can be held in undivided shares,[7] and this unusual form of conveyance is now given effect only in equity behind a trust for sale supplied by implication of statute. If, for instance, a legal estate is conveyed to A, B and C as tenants in common in equal shares, then provided that all are of full age the transfer is construed as a grant of the legal estate to A, B and C as joint tenants, to hold on an implied trust for sale for themselves as equitable tenants in common (see *Fig.* 35).[8] A similar result follows if a legal estate is conveyed to more than four persons as tenants in common (eg to A, B, C, D, E and F in equal shares). The first four persons named in the grant become necessarily joint

1 *Wilson v Wilson* [1969] 3 All ER 945 at 949C (ante, p 390); *Young v Young* [1983] Court of Appeal Bound Transcript 466. See also *Mellowes v Collymore* (Unreported, Court of Appeal, 27 November 1981), where the Court of Appeal found a trust for sale in circumstances where A, B and C held a legal estate on trust for A and B.

2 See C. Harpum, [1990] CLJ 277 at 302f, 310, who leaves open the possibility that this situation may constitute a bare trust. This could be an awkward conclusion if bare trustees have no power to give an overreaching conveyance (post, p 536).

3 Settled Land Act 1925, s 36(4); Law of Property Act 1925, s 34(1).

4 The conveyance cannot constitute a 'trust instrument' for the purpose of the Settled Land Act 1925, s 36(4): see Settled Land Act 1925, s 117(1)(xxxi).

5 The circumstances here are not quite the same as in *Re Buchanan-Wollaston's Conveyance* [1939] Ch 738 (ante, p 530): the legal estate is not vested in the persons who are equitably entitled. The already questionable recourse to the Law of Property Act 1925, s 36(1) becomes even less tenable in the present case.

6 See (1944) 9 Conv (NS) 37 at 44. Essentially the same problem arose in *City of London Building Society v Flegg* [1986] Ch 605, [1988] AC 54 (post, p 553), where A and B held a legal estate on an implied trust for A, B, C and D as equitable tenants in common. Both the Court of Appeal and the House of Lords proceeded on the premise that C and D were beneficiaries behind a trust for sale.

7 Ante, p 512.

8 Law of Property Act 1925, s 34(2).

tenants of the legal estate,[9] thereafter holding on an implied trust for sale for all the grantees as tenants in common of the equitable interest (see *Fig.* 36).[10] In other words, the tenancy in common specified in the conveyance is given effect only in relation to the equitable interest in the property.[11]

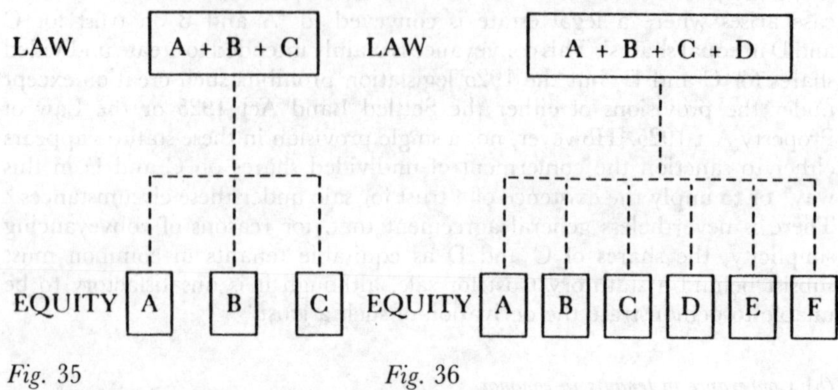

Fig. 35 *Fig.* 36

(c) Conveyance to a single co-owner

Perhaps the most problematic case of all is that which arises on a conveyance of a legal estate to a person who is recognised in equity as being either a joint tenant or a tenant in common. Suppose that A and B co-operate in the purchase of a legal estate in land, each contributing part of the purchase money, but that the legal title is taken solely in the name of A. If they contribute unequally, it is clear that, in the absence of any contrary intention, they are regarded as tenants in common of the equitable interest in the land in proportions fixed by their respective contributions (see *Fig.* 37).[12] If they contribute equally, they seem to be regarded as joint tenants of that equitable interest (see *Fig.* 38).[13] Difficulties emerge, however, if in either case the legal estate is conveyed not to A and B jointly but to A alone without any express declaration of trust for A and B as equitable co-owners. The co-ownership generated by these circumstances is undisclosed on the title: on the face of the purchase deed A appears to be solely entitled both at law and in equity. Moreover, these cases of co-ownership are plainly not covered by an express trust for sale. They are not, however, uncommon situations and if excluded from the aegis of a trust for sale would provide a particularly significant breach in the general policy of the 1925 legislation

9 The number of trustees permitted to hold a legal estate in land is restricted to four (ante, p 100).

10 Law of Property Act 1925, s 34(2). See eg *Persey and Another v Bazley* (1984) 47 P & CR 37 at 39; [1985] Conv 292 (J. Martin). 'The fact that the other owners of undivided shares are thereby excluded from any real control of the land has had to be sacrificed to the simplicity of conveyancing' (see (1944) 9 Conv (NS) 37 at 38).

11 If, in either of the cases considered here, the grant were made not by a deed inter vivos but by testamentary disposition, the legal estate would be held on an exactly similar trust for sale implied by statute, the only difference being that the legal estate would vest in the trustees of the will for the purpose of the Settled Land Act 1925 or (failing such trustees) would vest in the testator's personal representatives (Law of Property Act 1925, s 34(3)).

12 Post, p 533.

13 Post, p 533. See *Knightly v Sun Life Assurance Society Ltd* (1981) *Times*, 23 July.

that all cases of co-ownership in possession should be governed by a trust for sale.[14]

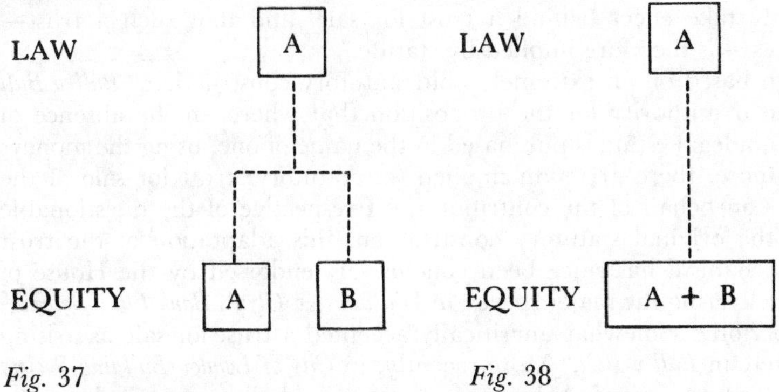

Fig. 37 *Fig.* 38

(i) A statutory omission The obvious solution is that both of these situations should be covered by an implied trust for sale supplied by statute. The 1925 legislation arguably achieves this objective in the case of equitable joint tenancy (*Fig.* 38).[15] However, the legislation altogether fails to advert to the phenomenon of equitable tenancy in common where the legal title is held by one person alone (*Fig.* 37)—an omission which has been attributed to simple legislative oversight.[16] Nowhere does the legislation provide the much needed statutory authority for the implication of a trust for sale in this context. Nevertheless the problem has not remained unresolved.

(ii) A judicial solution In *Bull v Bull*,[17] a mother and her adult son contributed unequal proportions of the purchase price of a dwelling-house which was duly conveyed into the sole name of the son. It was expressly found that the mother had not intended to make a gift of her contribution to the son.[18] They lived together in the house for some time, but in circumstances of discord following the son's marriage, the son brought proceedings for possession against his mother, arguing that she was merely a licensee and could therefore be evicted at will.

It seemed that the only way in which the courts could save the ageing mother from being thrown out of her home by her ungrateful offspring was by finding an implied trust for sale in her favour.[19] By this means the mother would be able to enjoy access to the statutory protection given to beneficial

14 It is not without interest that the Law of Property Act 1922 contained a much clearer indication that all cases of equitable co-ownership were intended to be covered by at least an implied trust for sale. Section 10 of that Act (which was not duplicated in any of the 1925 legislation) was expressly directed at 'removing the difficulties incidental to land being held in undivided shares' and at 'preventing the creation of undivided shares in land, except under a settlement and behind a trust for sale. . .'

15 Law of Property Act 1925, s 36(1), ante, p 529.

16 See *Williams & Glyn's Bank Ltd v Boland* [1979] Ch 312 at 330C per Lord Denning MR.

17 [1955] 1 QB 234. See [1955] CLJ 155 at 156 (H.W.R. Wade); (1955) 18 MLR 303 (V. Latham), 408 (H.R. Gray); (1956) 19 MLR 312 (E.A. Forrest).

18 [1955] 1 QB 234 at 236.

19 Ironically it may well be that the desired objective could have been achieved by means other than the imposition of a 'trust for sale' (post, p 534). Nowadays the mother would probably be said to be protected by proprietary estoppel (ante, p 312).

co-owners.[20] Despite the lacuna in the 1925 legislation,[1] Denning LJ in the Court of Appeal glossed the wording of section 36(4) of the Settled Land Act 1925 to produce the desired result that an equitable tenancy in common 'shall. . .only take effect behind a trust for sale' and that such a trust—if not express—is therefore implied by statute.[2]

Although based on an extremely bold statutory construction,[3] *Bull v Bull* provides clear authority for the proposition that where, in the absence of gift or loan, a legal estate is purchased in the name of one, using the moneys of two or more, there arises an implied (or statutory) trust for sale of the legal estate on behalf of the contributors.[4] Irrespective of the questionable nature of the original statutory construction, this adaptation of the trust for sale mechanism has since been conclusively endorsed by the House of Lords. In delivering the major speech in *Williams & Glyn's Bank Ltd v Boland*,[5] Lord Wilberforce somewhat uncritically accepted a trust for sale as arising appropriately in *Bull v Bull*.[6] More recently, in *City of London Building Society v Flegg*,[7] Lord Oliver of Aylmerton appeared wholly reconciled to the conclusion that the 1925 legislation had 'established the trust for sale as the conveyancing machinery through which effect is given to the interests of owners in undivided shares'.[8]

(iii) Hidden consequences It thus appears settled that a trust for sale is implied

20 Post, p 593.

1 It was thought at one time that the implication of a statutory trust for sale under analogous circumstances would involve 'straining the construction of too many of the provisions of the Property Legislation to be acceptable' ((1944) 9 Conv (NS) 37 at 46). See also M. Friend and J. Newton, [1982] Conv 213.

2 The Court's decision had the effect of making the mother a beneficiary behind a trust for sale. Thus she could not be arbitrarily evicted from the home which she had helped to buy, and the only way in which the son could effectively move her from the house was either by arranging a sale of the property (in which case the mother's interest would be translated into a share in the proceeds of sale) or by buying out her interest with cash (post, p 596).

3 Denning LJ's construction of this apparently irrelevant statutory provision does indeed seem rather strained. Section 36(4) provides that '[a]n undivided share in land shall not be capable of being created except under a trust instrument or under the Law of Property Act 1925, and shall then only take effect behind a trust for sale.' The circumstances present in *Bull v Bull* involved no trust instrument; nor were they covered by any provision in the Law of Property Act 1925 (hence the resort to the Settled Land Act 1925). However, Denning LJ read s 36(4) as if it contained no reference to such matters, thus reaching the convenient (if technically unwarranted) conclusion that a trust for sale must exist in every case of equitable tenancy in common. For a discussion of this flawed reasoning, see B. Rudden, (1963) 27 Conv (NS) 51.

4 For a suggestion that *Bull v Bull* could have been resolved by analysing the parties' rights as simply those of beneficiaries behind a 'straight' or bare trust of land, see (1970) 34 Conv (NS) 420 at 421 (F.R. Crane). On this view there would simply have been a trust of land of a character not essentially different from a trust of money or shares or other forms of property, but the trust would not be subject to the special statutory regime imposed on the artificially created 'trust for sale'. Some judicial support can be found, oddly, in the judgment of Lord Denning MR in *Williams & Glyn's Bank Ltd v Boland* [1979] Ch 312 at 330C, 331A (see also R.J. Smith, (1979) 95 LQR 501; W.J. Swadling, [1986] Conv 379). Compare, however, [1979] Ch 312 at 333G per Ormrod LJ, 340A per Browne LJ.

5 [1981] AC 487 at 503D (post, pp 545ff, 569).

6 For a similar endorsement of the 'trust for sale' approach, see [1981] AC 487 at 510G per Lord Scarman.

7 [1988] AC 54 at 77H–78A.

8 Lord Oliver made express reference, in particular, to Law of Property Act 1925, s 34(1) and Settled Land Act 1925, s 36(4).

by statute wherever a legal estate in land is vested in one owner following a joint purchase using the moneys of more than one contributor. In the context of the practical problem highlighted in the facts of *Bull v Bull*, this result represents a highly convenient solution.[9] However, for other purposes the implication of a trust for sale may prove to have less desirable consequences. The over-ready implication of a statutory trust for sale brings about the result that vast numbers of property owners are elevated to the status of trustee for sale—a status which will not only surprise the unwitting property owner but may also introduce unsuspected complications for third parties with whom he deals.[10]

(d) Conveyance to co-owners one of whom is a minor

Further problems are raised by a conveyance of a legal estate to persons who include among their number one who is a minor. Land may be conveyed, for instance, to A, B and C, under circumstances where C is not yet aged 18. If the conveyance purports to transfer a legal estate to A, B and C as joint tenants, a clear statutory solution is provided. A and B take the legal estate, holding on an implied trust for sale for A, B and C as equitable joint tenants (*Fig.* 39).[11] If, however, the conveyance transfers the legal estate to A, B and C on trust for themselves as tenants in common, it seems that once again only A and B can take the legal estate, this time holding on an implied trust for sale for A, B and C as equitable tenants in common (*Fig.* 40).[12]

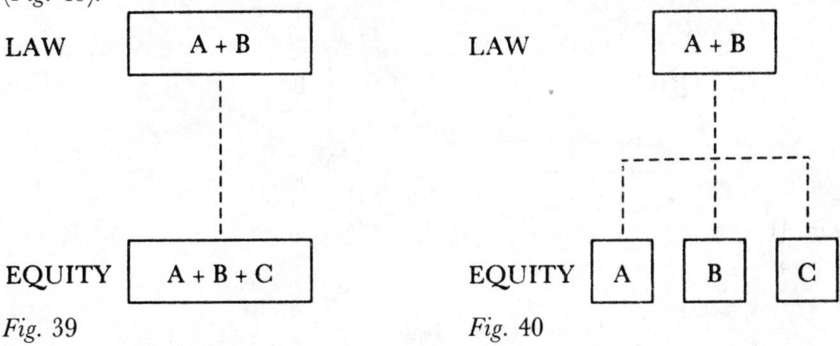

Fig. 39 *Fig.* 40

9 It could be said that in *Bull v Bull* the Court of Appeal simply used common sense and a little ingenuity in filling one of the lacunae left in the 1925 legislation (see F.R. Crane, (1955) 19 Conv (NS) 146). The result reached in *Bull v Bull* had already been applied—although without reference to section 36(4) of the Settled Land Act 1925—in *Re Rogers' Question* [1948] 1 All ER 328 at 329A, and in *Re Rayleigh Weir Stadium* [1954] 1 WLR 786 at 790. Later cases have somewhat blandly assumed the existence of a statutory trust for sale in all situations of equitable tenancy in common where the legal estate is vested in one name only. See *Brown v Robertson* (1962) 182 Estates Gazette 157; *Kent v Regan* (1964) 192 Estates Gazette 545 at 547; *Waller v Waller* [1967] 1 WLR 451 at 453B, (1967) 31 Conv (NS) 140 (F.R. Crane); *Taylor v Taylor* [1968] 1 All ER 843 at 846I. See also W.J. Swadling, [1986] Conv 379.

10 Where, as in *Bull v Bull*, a trust for sale arises by implication of statute, there will be no reference to the trust on the face of the conveyance of the legal estate to the trustee. When the trustee later comes to sell the legal estate, he will appear to be offering a good title 'as beneficial owner' (post, p 560).

11 Law of Property Act 1925, s 19(2).

12 Law of Property Act 1925, s 19(5).

(e) Conveyance to a bare trustee

Extreme difficulties of analysis present themselves where a legal title in land is conveyed to one who stands as a bare trustee. Such a case will occur if, for instance, the absolute legal entitlement is held by A, and the entire beneficial interest is, on one ground or another, isolated in B (see *Fig.* 41).[13] It is difficult to see how an implied trust for sale can be found within such a configuration of interests,[14] and even more difficult to locate any power in a bare trustee to give an overreaching conveyance of the legal estate.[15] Given, however, that the statutory trust for sale is supposed to govern cases of co-ownership in possession, it is at least consistent that no trust for sale should arise in this situation. There is here no concurrent ownership of any interest either at law or in equity.[16]

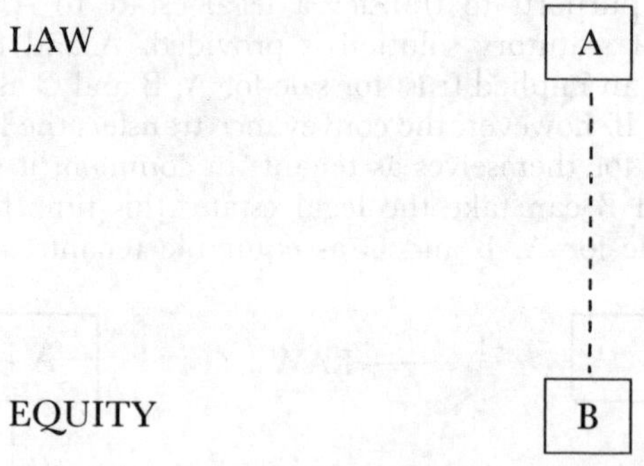

Fig. 41

13 See eg *Hodgson v Marks* [1971] Ch 892 (ante, p 216).

14 See eg Law Commission, Working Paper No 106 (1988), para 3.3; Law Com No 188, paras 1.4, 2.17.

15 See *Hodgson v Marks* [1971] Ch 892 (ante, p 216). The Law Commission has expressed the view that a beneficial interest under a bare trust is at present overreachable only through the creation of an *ad hoc* trust for sale (ante, p 525). See Law Commission, Working Paper No 106 (1988), para 3.3, but compare C. Harpum, [1990] CLJ 277 at 303f. If overreaching is not available in the normal way under a bare trust, it is likely that the impact of the bare beneficial interest on a purchaser depends (in unregistered land) on the equitable doctrine of notice and (in registered land) on whether the interest is protected as a minor interest or overriding interest.

16 The Law Commission has suggested that the normal overreaching machinery of the Law of Property Act 1925 should be extended to bare trusts in order to secure greater protection for purchasers (see Law Commission, Working Paper No 106 (1988), paras 3.3, 7.1; Law Com No 188, paras 3.10, 4.27). The Commission also envisages that bare trusts would be accommodated within the proposed new 'trust of land' (post, p 537). See Law Com No 181, paras 7.1, 20.2.

4. THE FUTURE OF THE TRUST FOR SALE

It is clear that the concept of the trust for sale was adopted and manipulated by the framers of the 1925 legislation specifically in order to serve perceived conveyancing objectives. In this respect the terminology of 'trust for sale' was an appropriate reminder that the primary responsibility of the trustees lay in the performance of their duty to sell the co-owned property and to convert the land into a money form available either for re-investment or for distribution amongst the beneficiaries.

During the years since 1925, however, it has become increasingly obvious that the language of 'trust for sale' provides a somewhat misleading description of the reality which underlies most circumstances of co-ownership of land. The conversion-oriented theory of the 1925 legislation compels co-owners of land to hold their legal title on some supposed trust 'for sale', although it is quite apparent that in practice this form of trust is more often aimed at the retention of land than at its alienation.[17] For this reason it has been proposed in recent years that the trust for sale be replaced by more realistically named devices which perform essentially the same function of modulating the rights and responsibilities inherent in co-ownership of land.

(1) A 'matrimonial home trust'

It has commonly been said that the terminology of 'trust for sale' is particularly inappropriate in relation to co-ownership of the matrimonial home. Most spouses have little interest in any immediate sale of their home but are rather more concerned—at least for the foreseeable future—to retain a secure base for themselves and their children.[18] Accordingly in 1971 the Law Commission tentatively suggested that in the family context the device of the trust for sale should be replaced by a 'matrimonial home trust', on the ground that 'this is a far more appropriate term than "trust for sale" which to the layman seems to imply that the property must be sold.'[19] Although this proposal was never implemented by legislation, it provided a preview of more wide-ranging suggestions for reform of the law.

(2) A new trust of land

The Law Commission has more recently recommended that the device of the 'trust for sale' should be abandoned altogether. In a working paper issued in 1985,[20] the Commission noted that the automatic imposition of a trust for sale on co-owners who may have purchased property for their

17 Ante, p 524.

18 See eg *Williams (J.W.) v Williams (M.A.)* [1976] Ch 278 at 285E-F, where, in relation to the matrimonial home, Lord Denning MR pointed out that the courts 'nowadays have great regard to the fact that the house is bought as a home in which the family is to brought up. It is not treated as property to be sold, nor as an investment to be realised for cash.'

19 *Family Law: Family Property Law* (Law Commission Published Working Paper No 42 (1971), para 1.115. This in turn led to the Law Commission's later proposal that all matrimonial homes should be co-owned by spouses either in consequence of an express trust for sale or by virtue of a new statutory regime of co-ownership in the matrimonial home (Law Com No 86 (1978), para 1.1).

20 *Trusts of Land* (Law Commission Working Paper No 94, September 1985), para 6.4.

own occupation 'is highly artificial and difficult to explain to a lay client.' The Commission inclined towards the view that the structure of co-ownership laid down in 1925 'is no longer suitable for modern conditions'.

In its eventual report, issued in 1989, the Law Commission proposed that the present dual system of trusts for sale and strict settlements should be replaced by an entirely new unitary 'trust of land'—much on the same basis as existing trusts of personalty—which could be used to give effect to both concurrent and successive interests in land.[1] Under such a trust, the legal estate in land would be held by trustees armed with the powers of an absolute owner to sell or to retain the land.[2] It was the Law Commission's view that, in the area of concurrent interests, the new form of land trust would correspond more closely to the perceptions of most co-owners and would, moreover, provide 'a considerably more accessible concept than that of the trust for sale'.[3] All land which would previously have been held under an implied trust for sale would be held under a 'trust of land', and 'the main purpose of the trust will no longer be the realisation of the capital value of the land'.[4] The court would be given a broad power to intervene in any dispute relating to a trust of land, and any person interested could apply to the court for an order regulating any matter arising under the trust whether in respect of sale, occupation or otherwise.[5]

The Commission envisaged that the new trust of land would retain the overreaching mechanism largely in its present form. Under the new scheme, therefore, a purchaser would be able, as under the present trust for sale, to take title from the trustees and, on condition of payment to at least two trustees, would then overreach the interests of beneficiaries in the normal way.[6] Further details of the proposed 'new trust of land' will be introduced in the course of the following pages, but it is clear that the regime recommended by the Law Commission, if implemented in statutory form, will effect a significant rationalisation of the less attractive and more artificial features of the trust for sale.[7]

5. THE RESPECTIVE ROLES OF TRUSTEE AND BENEFICIARY

The essence of most forms of the trust concept is the idea that the trustees hold the legal title to the trust property and are invested with powers of management and disposition. The beneficiaries merely benefit. The sole fact that someone is a beneficiary confers neither a right to be appointed as a trustee nor any entitlement to select or veto the appointment of any

1 See Law Com No 181, paras 1.7, 20.1. For the first reference to the possibility of introducing a 'new trust of land', see Law Commission, Working Paper No 94, para 6.1.
2 Law Com No 181, paras 3.5, 10.6. See Working Paper No 94, paras 6.1, 7.5.
3 Law Com No 181, para 3.6.
4 Law Com No 181, para 3.5. See Draft Trusts of Land Bill, clause 1 (Law Com No 181, Appendix A).
5 Law Com No 181, paras 12.6ff, 20.3. See Draft Trusts of Land Bill, clause 6 (Law Com No 181, Appendix A).
6 Law Com No 181, paras 1.7, 3.6, 6.1f, 20.2. See Working Paper No 94, para 9.1.
7 For a penetrating critique of the Law Commission's proposals, see R.J. Smith, [1990] Conv 12.

particular trustee.[8] Even if the trustees and the beneficiaries are the same persons, their functions are quite distinct.

(1) Powers of the trustees for sale

The powers exercisable by trustees for sale are defined by statute on an express analogy with the powers enjoyed by the tenant for life and settlement trustees under the Settled Land Act 1925.[9]

(a) Powers of management and disposition

The referential incorporation of Settled Land Act powers means that trustees for sale are invested with all the powers of management and disposition which would be enjoyed by a tenant for life and settlement trustees under a strict settlement.[10] Trustees for sale are therefore possessed of certain powers to grant leases[11] and mortgages[12] in respect of the land which they hold, and of course their ultimate power—that of sale[13]—is also a *duty*.

A trust for sale thus confers upon the trustees a mixture of powers and duties. The trust for sale itself imports a duty to sell coupled with a power at discretion to postpone sale.[14] In any case of conflict, where the trustees

8 In 1978 the Law Commission proposed that a beneficial owner of the matrimonial home should have statutory 'trusteeship rights'. These rights would have included a right to prevent other persons becoming trustees of the home without the consent of the spouse-beneficiary, and a right for the latter himself or herself to apply to the court for appointment as a trustee (see Law Com No 86, paras 1.295ff). These proposals have now been supplemented by the Law Commission's more recent recommendation that, under the new trust of land, beneficiaries who are ascertained, sui iuris and unanimous should be entitled to exercise, by direction to the existing trusteeship, a 'priority right of appointment' (Law Com No 181, paras 9.1, 20.3). See Draft Trusts of Land Bill, clause 18 (Law Com No 181, Appendix A).

9 Law of Property Act 1925, s 28(1). See *In re Conquest* [1929] 2 Ch 353 at 358. These powers include the powers conferred during a minority by Settled Land Act 1925, s 102, even though no minority in fact exists in the context of the relevant trust for sale (see *In re Gray* [1927] 1 Ch 242 at 248). See Chapter 15 (post, p 637).

10 The Settled Land Act powers are, however, fairly limited (infra). They may be (and very commonly are) enlarged by express provision in the trust instrument (Settled Land Act 1925, s 109(1)). See *City of London Building Society v Flegg* [1986] Ch 605 at 612H–613A).

11 In the absence of an expressly conferred extension of their power, the trustees are generally limited to granting leases for terms not exceeding 50 years (see Settled Land Act 1925, s 41). It has been recommended that the maximum term generally permissible could usefully be increased to 100 years, thereby enabling the grant of a 99 year term of years (see Law Reform Committee, *The powers and duties of trustees* (23rd Report, Cmnd 8733, October 1982), para 8.6).

12 See the limited mortgaging powers conferred on the tenant for life by Settled Land Act 1925, s 71(1). There is, for instance, no power to purchase land with the assistance of mortgage finance.

13 See Settled Land Act 1925, s 38.

14 Under the new trust of land proposed by the Law Commission, the trustees' existing duty to sell and power to postpone would be replaced by the conferment of all the powers of an absolute owner including the power either to sell or to retain the land (Law Com No 181, paras 10.4ff). See Draft Trusts of Land Bill, clause 4(1). It would remain possible, by means of express wording, to impose a duty of sale but a power to retain should be statutorily implied irrespective of contrary intention (Law Com No 181, para 3.7). In the absence of actual notice purchasers would not be affected by any express limitation on the trustees' powers (Law Com No 181, paras 10.10, 20.3). See Draft Trusts of Land Bill, clauses 4(2), 19.

cannot agree whether to sell or to postpone sale, the duty to sell overrides the power to postpone sale and is normally determinative of the controversy.[15] In the last resort the court has a statutory discretion to resolve such disagreements in respect of sale by making 'such order as it thinks fit'.[16]

(b) *Power to re-invest in land*

Upon execution of their trust to sell, the trustees are responsible either for the proper investment of the proceeds of sale or (at the request of the beneficiaries) for the due distribution of those proceeds amongst the beneficiaries. In the absence of distribution the trustees have power[17] to re-invest the proceeds of sale in the purchase of other land which is then likewise held by them on trust for sale.[18] This useful power of reinvestment is, however, liable to one possible restriction. It is arguable that the trustees' power to re-invest in land is lost if at any point the trustees do not retain at least some land on trust for sale. By selling *all* the land originally held on trust for sale, the trustees may lose their status as 'trustees for sale',[19] in which case they become ordinary trustees of mere personalty and have as such  no power to invest in realty.[20] For this reason it is sometimes said to be prudent for trustees for sale always to retain a small portion of land on trust for sale simply in order to preserve their character as 'trustees for sale'.

(2) **Delegation of certain powers**

It is open to trustees for sale to delegate certain of their statutory powers to any person of full age (other than a mere annuitant) who is currently

15 See *In re Mayo* [1943] Ch 302 at 304 (post, p 585). The Law Commission has proposed that, in the restructuring of trust powers under the new trust of land, the bias in favour of sale pursuant to section 30 should be removed (Law Com No 181, para 12.5).

16 Law of Property Act 1925, s 30 (post, p 585). The Law Commission has recommended that the broad resolution power conferred on the courts by section 30 should be extended, with certain modifications, to the trust of land proposed by the Commission (ante, p 537) (Law Com No 181, paras 12.1ff, 20.3). See Draft Trusts of Land Bill, clause 6. The Commission claimed that the court's discretion, being limited at present to a power to either order or refuse a sale, is rather 'one-dimensional' (Law Com No 181, para 12.4). The court has, for instance, no power to refuse sale and yet impose an occupation rent. It is not entirely clear that the current section 30 discretion is quite so circumscribed.

17 This power is derived from Settled Land Act 1925, s 73(1)(xi), as impliedly incorporated by Law of Property Act 1925, s 28(1).

18 Law of Property Act 1925, s 32(1).

19 By ceasing to hold *land*, it is arguable that the trustees lose their character as 'trustees for sale', as defined by Law of Property Act 1925, s 205(1)(xxix), and thereby fall outside the ambit of section 28(1). See *In re Wakeman* [1945] Ch 177 at 181f per Uthwatt J, but compare *In re Wellsted's Will Trusts* [1949] Ch 296 at 319.

20 Trustees of mere personalty have no power to invest any of their trust fund in land unless expressly authorised to do so by their trust instrument. Even where there is power to invest in land, the term 'investment' has been restrictively construed so as not to comprise the purchase of a house for the occupation of a beneficiary (see *In re Power* [1947] Ch 572 at 575). However, land is traditionally regarded as a sound form of investment, and it has been recommended that the investment powers of ordinary trustees should be extended to cover the purchase of freeholds and leaseholds (Law Com No 181, paras 10.8, 20.3). See Draft Trusts of Land Bill, clause 4(1) (Law Com No 181, Appendix A). See also Law Reform Committee, *The powers and duties of trustees* (23rd Report, Cmnd 8733, October 1982), para 3.2ff.

entitled in possession to the net rents and profits of the land.[1] The powers which may be so delegated comprise the trustees' powers of management of the land and their powers of and incidental to leasing and accepting surrenders of leases.[2] The trustees' power of sale may also be delegated for a limited period not exceeding one year.[3] The delegation must be made in writing signed by the trustees and is revocable by further signed writing.[4] If a delegation is made, the trustees cease to be liable for the acts or defaults of the delegate, since the delegate himself is thereafter deemed to have assumed the duties and liabilities of a trustee in relation to the exercise of the delegated powers.[5]

(3) Rights of the trust for sale beneficiary

Perhaps the least satisfactory feature of the contemporary law relating to the trust for sale has been its apparent inability to articulate coherently the precise nature of the rights enjoyed by the trust for sale beneficiary. In some broad sense the beneficiary is entitled, in his or her allotted proportion, to receive the benefits of the land held on trust for sale and, in particular, to claim a share in any capital moneys arising on the eventual disposition of the legal title. Less certain is the exact nature of the beneficiary's rights pending an overreaching disposition of the land. A large part of the attendant confusion is attributable to the way in which the history of the trust for sale has been coloured—albeit inconsistently—by the 'doctrine of conversion'. According to the theory of 'conversion', the equitable interests of trust for sale beneficiaries comprise rights in *personalty* rather than rights in *land*.

(a) The doctrine of conversion

It seems quite reasonable to suppose, a priori, that the equitable interests of beneficiaries under a trust for sale constitute rights of some sort in the *land* which is held on trust for sale. The net income drawn from the land

1 Law of Property Act 1925, s 29(1). A refusal by the trustees to delegate their powers in accordance with section 29 may become the subject of an application to the court under Law of Property Act 1925, s 30, which empowers the court to 'make such order as it thinks fit'. The Law Commission has recommended that under the new land trust the trustees should have a much wider power to delegate all the trust powers (without any limitation as to time) to any beneficiary of full age with a present vested interest in the land (Law Com No 181, paras 11.1, 20.3). See Draft Trusts of Land Bill, clause 5(1)).

2 Law of Property Act 1925, s 29(1). A trust for sale beneficiary, even though entitled to receive rents and profits, has no power to grant tenancies in the absence of a proper delegation under section 29, and any tenancy purportedly granted by him is not binding. In *Napier v Light* (1975) 119 SJ 166 at 167, the Court of Appeal held that two trust for sale beneficiaries, although together absolutely entitled and sui iuris, could not create a valid tenancy without the appropriate delegation. The rule in *Saunders v Vautier* ((1841) 4 Beav 115 at 116, 49 ER 282, Cr & Ph 240 at 249, 41 ER 482 at 485 (ante, p 49) gives beneficiaries authority merely to terminate the trust, not to commit their trustees to arbitrarily created tenancies.

3 Trustee Act 1925, s 25(1), as amended by Powers of Attorney Act 1971, s 9. See, however, Law Com No 181, para 11.1.

4 Law of Property Act 1925, s 29(1).

5 Law of Property Act 1925, s 29(3). The Law Commission has suggested that the immunity enjoyed by the delegating trustees should be removed (Law Com No 181, para 11.3).

is, after all, payable to any beneficiaries who are currently entitled in possession, and there has always been a possibility that the beneficiaries may be permitted to occupy the land itself. Notwithstanding these powerful indications, the law of trusts for sale has constantly been overshadowed by a doctrine which apparently insists that the equitable interest of the trust for sale beneficiary is at all times merely an interest in the prospective proceeds of sale of the land. In terms of this 'doctrine of conversion', the beneficiary holds no interest in land, but merely an interest in the money which the land represents. Quite how consistent has been the application of this theory is open to debate,[6] but there is little doubt that the doctrine of conversion has been perceived, rightly or wrongly, as having some role to play in the judicial implementation of the trust for sale.

(i) Rationale of 'conversion' The rationale behind the doctrine of conversion fastens upon the primacy of the trustees' duty to sell land held on trust for sale. Since 'equity looks on that as done which ought to be done',[7] equity anticipated the factual result brought about by the discharge of the trustees' duty to sell and converted the beneficiaries' interests into personalty from the very inception of an 'immediate, binding trust for sale'. Thus, even before sale took place—even if sale never took place—the doctrine of conversion supposedly insisted that the beneficiaries' rights be analysed proleptically as rights in *money* rather than rights in *land*.

(ii) Utility of 'conversion' It is clear that the initial and entirely proper function of the doctrine of conversion was to ensure clarity and certainty in the devolution of the beneficial interests subsisting behind an express trust for sale.[8] The great advantage conferred by the doctrine is that the devolution of such interests is not left to be determined by largely fortuitous factors such as the precise timing of sale by the trustees.[9] It would be manifestly unsatisfactory that the character of a beneficiary's interest should hover arbitrarily between realty and personalty, and it is precisely this uncertainty which the original doctrine of conversion was designed to prevent. Under the doctrine all beneficial interests behind a trust for sale of land fall to be considered—both before and after sale—as interests in the prospective money proceeds only and therefore as 'personalty'.

6 See eg S. Anderson, *The Proper, Narrow Scope of the Doctrine of Conversion*, (1984) 100 LQR 86.

7 Post, p 745.

8 See *Chandler v Pocock* (1880) 15 Ch D 491 at 496 per Jessel MR, who pointed out that the doctrine of conversion was not a rule which 'turns sovereigns into acres, or *vice versa*', but rather was a rule which 'works a conversion for the purpose of devolution.'

9 Were it not for the doctrine of conversion, the destination of a trust for sale interest left by will could well depend on whether the trustees for sale had sold the land before or after the date of the death of the testator/beneficiary. If the land had been sold the day before the testator/beneficiary died, his beneficial interest under the trust for sale would rank as 'personalty' and pass to any designated recipient of his 'personal property'. If, on the other hand, the land had been sold by the trustees the day after his death, his beneficial interest would be characterised as 'real property' and would accordingly pass to the devisee of his 'realty'. The doctrine of conversion avoided these problems but, in characterising all equitable interests behind a trust for sale as personalty, was apt to create further difficulties (see eg *In re Kempthorne* [1930] 1 Ch 268 at 286, 290ff).

(b) Misapplication of the theory of conversion

It is clear in retrospect that the true historical emphasis of the doctrine of conversion was the protection of the interests of beneficiaries within the framework of the trust for sale rather than any concern with the needs of parties outside the trust. That the doctrine should have the effect of conferring any benefit on strangers to the trust was entirely fortuitous, since the authentic purpose of the doctrine was simply to ensure the orderly and convenient characterisation of interests on the death of a beneficial owner. Yet in recent times the doctrine has commonly been applied—or misapplied—in such a way as to facilitate the protection of third parties who purchase land from trustees for sale.

(i) The nexus with overreaching So great was the concentration on securing the protection of purchasers within the statutory scheme of 1925 that the original emphasis of the doctrine of conversion has since become obscured. The process of distortion was further accentuated by the tendency—pervasive in the enactments of 1925—to confine the significance of property to its value in immediate exchangeable cash terms. The concern for the interests of purchasers and the inclination to monetise all value operated in close conjunction. Both motivations caused the legislation to focus closely upon the need to ensure unrestricted alienability of title within an efficient property market. This in turn created a need for a mechanism which would enable the purchaser of land to take title free from fragments of benefit already vested in others which might prejudice or conflict with his own interest in the land.

Just such a mechanism was offered by the statutory device for the 'overreaching' of equitable interests behind a trust for sale. Moreover, the old theory of 'conversion' now seemed to offer an additional and extremely obliging rationale for such overreaching.[10] It became tempting to suggest that a purchaser from trustees for sale need never be concerned with the rights of beneficiaries since such rights had always been detached from the land and were at all times rights merely in prospective proceeds of sale. In *Irani Finance Ltd v Singh*,[11] for example, Cross LJ went so far as to assert that the 'whole purpose of the trust for sale' is to ensure, 'by shifting the equitable interests away from the land and into the proceeds of sale, that a purchaser of the land takes free from the equitable interests.' Cross LJ thought that to recognise the beneficiaries as having rights in the land itself—even 'for a limited period' pending sale of the land—would be 'inconsistent with the trust for sale being an "immediate" trust working an immediate conversion, which is what the Law of Property Act 1925 envisages'.[12]

(ii) Supposed exceptions from the scope of 'conversion' The full rigour of this 'conversion' theory could not always be maintained without offence to

10 The misconceived nature of this supposed link has been well brought out by Charles Harpum, [1990] CLJ 277 at 278ff.

11 [1971] Ch 59 at 80A (post, p 596).

12 [1971] Ch 59 at 80A-B. Despite following a number of tortuous paths through the forest of conversion doctrine, the courts have never quite abandoned the direction pursued in *Irani Finance Ltd v Singh* (see eg *City of London Building Society v Flegg* [1988] AC 54 at 82C-83D per Lord Oliver of Aylmerton).

statutory intention. The courts allowed supposedly haphazard exceptions from the scope of an otherwise uncompromising doctrine. In *Cooper v Critchley*,[13] for instance, the Court of Appeal was of the opinion that a trust for sale beneficiary had an interest in 'land' for the purpose of section 40 of the Law of Property Act 1925.[14] Similarly, in *Elias v Mitchell*,[15] it was held that a beneficiary ranks as a 'person interested...in...land' for the purpose of protecting his beneficial interest as a minor interest by entry of a caution against a registered title.

(c) Retreat from a general theory of conversion

Although the so-called 'exceptions' to the doctrine of conversion were initially regarded as mere isolated deviations from an otherwise general doctrine, recent years have seen a marked, although not wholly consistent, judicial retreat from the theory of conversion. Even on the historically dubious assumption that equity required an automatic conversion of trust for sale interests, the courts have increasingly recognised that it is often unrealistic to relegate the rights of beneficiaries to a mere monetary interest. Such an analysis cannot be maintained with any conviction where the immediate and primary motivation underlying the trust for sale is not sale but rather retention of land.[16]

(i) Increasing importance of 'security claims' The retreat from the general doctrine of conversion has coincided, not insignificantly, with an accumulation of emphasis during recent years on the importance of residential security.[17] This changing emphasis is itself mirrored in a heightened awareness of 'security claims' in other fields of modern legislation such as those providing for employment security, social security and pension security. 'Security claims' of these kinds acquire a greatly increased importance in times of housing shortage, general economic recession, uncertain employment prospects and ever more frequent family breakdown. Consistent with the dominant need of the present age, the factor which unifies all such claims is the general quest not for dispositive power over 'things', but rather for enhanced security in the enjoyment of 'utility'.

(ii) Changing perceptions of social status The modern social ethic of equality between men and women has also had an indirect, but significant, impact on the recent development of the theory of the trust for sale. Many trusts for sale relate to the family home and the categories of trust for sale beneficiary clearly include vast numbers of women who have contributed financially

13 [1955] Ch 431 at 439. See (1955) 19 Conv (NS) 148 (F.R. Crane); (1955) 71 LQR 177 (R.E.M.); [1955] CLJ 155 (H.W.R. Wade).

14 According to this provision, a contract for sale of 'any interest in land' was generally actionable only if evidenced in a written memorandum. See now Law of Property (Miscellaneous Provisions) Act 1989, s 2(6) (ante, p 257).

15 [1972] Ch 652 at 664B-D. See (1972) 36 Conv (NS) 206 (D.J. Hayton).

16 Ante, p 524.

17 For reference to 'the modern law's attentiveness to interests of occupation', see (1988) 104 LQR 367 (S. Gardner). It is only fair, however, to note with Charles Harpum that this solicitude has waned over the last few years ([1990] CLJ 277 at 315).

and otherwise to the acquisition of their homes.[18] The doctrine of conversion of course characterises the beneficial rights of such persons as mere personalty, and it was inevitable that the opprobrium of sex-based discrimination should eventually attach to a doctrine which seemed to deny a primary category of beneficiaries any entitlement in the property actually held on trust for sale for them and so visibly occupied by them.

(iii) Reaction in the context of the family home It came therefore as no surprise that the foremost challenge to the doctrine of conversion occurred in the context of the family home. It was clearly in this context that the doctrine failed most markedly to accord with social reality.[19]

The reaction against the doctrine of conversion emerged most dramatically in *Williams & Glyn's Bank Ltd v Boland*,[20] where the courts were indirectly required to determine the status of the equitable interest of a spouse-beneficiary behind a statutory trust for sale of the matrimonial home.[1] The Court of Appeal declined to apply the received doctrine of conversion, Ormrod LJ noting that in cases involving the family home 'the object of the trust was to provide a joint home and the last thing the parties contemplated was that the house should be sold and the cash divided between them.'[2] Ormrod LJ went on to acknowledge that the imposition of a trust for sale may have been 'an inescapable consequence' of a general legislative scheme directed towards the simplification of conveyancing, but was unwilling to press 'this legal fiction to its logical conclusion'.[3] He clearly felt that, in relation to a trust for sale of the family home, the rights of a beneficiary in possession were 'not accurately described as an interest in a sum of money, simpliciter',[4] and that these rights should not therefore be 'dismissed as a mere interest in the proceeds of sale except where it is essential to the working of the scheme to do so.'[5]

This disavowal of any universal formulation of conversion enabled the Court of Appeal to hold that a spouse-beneficiary behind a trust for sale has rights 'subsisting in reference' to land for the purpose of section 70(1) of the Land Registration Act 1925.[6] The right of occupation inherent in her beneficial entitlement may therefore rank as an overriding interest, enjoying priority over a chargee of the registered title.[7] On appeal this conclusion was upheld by the House of Lords, Lord Wilberforce observing

18 Ante, p 384.
19 See, for instance, the closely related proposals to replace the trust for sale of family property by some kind of 'matrimonial home trust' or new form of land trust (ante, p 537).
20 [1981] AC 487 (House of Lords); [1979] Ch 312 (Court of Appeal).
1 The point at issue was whether an equitable interest under a trust for sale could be properly described as 'subsisting in reference to' land for the purpose of section 70(1)(g) of the Land Registration Act 1925 (ante, p 209). Such an interest, if dismissed merely as an interest in prospective proceeds of sale, would be manifestly incapable of ranking as an overriding interest binding upon the chargee of the registered title.
2 [1979] Ch 312 at 336E-F. Lord Denning MR (at 329F) observed likewise that when 'a married man and his wife buy a house, they do it so as to live in it—so that it should be a home for them both and their children—for the foreseeable future. They do not intend to sell it—at any rate not for many years hence.'
3 [1979] Ch 312 at 336G. See [1979] CLJ 254 (M.J. Prichard).
4 [1979] Ch 312 at 336D.
5 [1979] Ch 312 at 336G-H.
6 Ante, p 210.
7 Post, p 569.

that 'to describe the interests of spouses in a house jointly bought to be lived in as a matrimonial home as merely an interest in proceeds of sale, or rents and profits until sale, is just a little unreal'.[8]

(d) Present status of conversion

The present status of the equitable doctrine of conversion is nowadays a matter of some uncertainty. It seems to be generally, but not universally,[9] acknowledged that the doctrine has little (if any) relevance in the characterisation of the rights of a beneficiary behind a trust for sale of the family home. It is uncertain whether this liberated view of the doctrine extends to other forms of property (eg business or partnership property) which may equally well be held on trust for sale. It does, however, appear fairly clear that the much overworked doctrine of conversion is now tending towards its demise. It has at last been realised that the notion of conversion is by no means crucial to the operation of overreaching under the Law of Property Act 1925, and that its supposed reinforcement of the process of overreaching is neither necessary nor helpful. What is perhaps clearest of all is that the doctrine discloses no insuperable barrier in the way of asserting—at least in the context of residential property—that the trust for sale beneficiary has a right of occupation. It came therefore as no surprise when in 1989 the Law Commission finally recommended that the doctrine of conversion should be abolished in relation to all trusts, irrespective of the nature of the trust property and irrespective of the date of creation.[10] As soon as Parliament approves the Commission's Draft Trusts of Land Bill, the doctrine of conversion will cease to have any application in the law relating to co-owned land.[1]

(e) Recognition of the beneficiary's right to occupy

Perhaps the issue most deeply affected by the ambivalent history of the doctrine of conversion has been the question whether the beneficiary under a trust for sale has, qua beneficiary, any *right of occupation* of the land held on trust.[2] The received doctrine of conversion, as extended and distorted by generations of property lawyers, insisted that the beneficiary's rights were confined to

8 [1981] AC 487 at 507F. See [1980] CLJ 243 (M.J. Prichard).

9 See eg *Harman v Glencross* [1985] Fam 49 at 54A-B, 55G-56C per Ewbank J, for an uninhibited reference to the continuing force of the conversion doctrine in the context of the family home. See also J. Warburton, *The Doctrine of Conversion—Fact or Fiction?*, [1986] Conv 415.

10 Law Com No 181, paras 3.5, 20.2.

1 See Draft Trusts of Land Bill, clause 21 (Law Com No 181, Appendix A).

2 It is true, but for this purpose entirely irrelevant, that a trust for sale beneficiary may have rights of occupation derived otherwise than from his status as a beneficiary. He may well have statutory 'rights of occupation' pursuant to the Matrimonial Homes Act 1983 (ante, p 155), but such rights are a quite separate phenomenon. The Law Commission has even proposed that the courts should be statutorily empowered to grant short-term occupation rights in the family home to non-entitled persons who have been associated by marriage or cohabitation (see Law Commission, *Family Home: Domestic Violence and Occupation of the Family Home* (Law Com No 207, 7 May 1992), paras 4.18ff, 7.7f). The exercise of such a power may, of course, create new rights of occupation in respect of land which is co-owned, but the Commission's view is that these rights should be purely personal rights only and should be neither registrable nor capable of binding a purchaser (Law Com No 207, para 4.19).

personalty: the beneficiary had no interest in land. If this is so, it becomes tempting to query the location of the beneficial interest in land pending the execution of a trust for sale. It has been said that there is 'something bizarre' about the proposition 'that the legal estate in Blackacre may be held on trust without any beneficial interest in Blackacre existing anywhere or in anyone.'[3] The conundrum—as yet not wholly resolved—remains to trouble even contemporary rationalisations of the trust for sale.

The issue is not without importance. The definition of the beneficiary's rights has a significance not merely as between the beneficiary and his trustees, but also as against third parties who take a conveyance of the land from trustees for sale. If a beneficial interest under a trust for sale does indeed carry with it an implicit right of occupation, the beneficiary may be able to assert this right either in opposition to any moves towards sale taken by the trustees or in derogation of the rights enjoyed by an eventual purchaser.

(i) The traditional view There is considerable authority in the older cases for the proposition that a trust for sale beneficiary has no *right* as such to physical occupation of the land vested at law in the trustees for sale.[4] The beneficiary had, to be sure, a right to receive his due share of any rents and profits derived from the land, but could not insist on going into possession himself.[5] Possession was an attribute of the legal title. Thus, in the traditional view, occupation by a beneficiary was not a right but a privilege to be accorded or withheld by the trustees in the fiduciary exercise of their powers of management of the land.[6] This analysis survived the re-structuring of property law which culminated in the enactments of 1925.[7] In almost all cases of co-ownership the legal title was confirmed in 'trustees for sale'[8] who under their 'statutory trusts' had no express power to allow a beneficiary into occupation pending sale.[9] The orthodox view thus seemed clear that the trust for sale beneficiary had, in his capacity as beneficiary, no right to occupy the land.

(ii) The modern view In recent years the traditional denial of any right of

3 [1971] CLJ 44 at 48 (M.J. Prichard). It is 'not easy to accept that all beneficial interest in a parcel of land evaporates (*in nubibus*?) once it is held on trust for sale', presumably condensing only when the land is transferred in execution of the trust ([1979] CLJ 251 at 253 (M.J. Prichard)). See also C. Harpum, [1990] CLJ 277 at 279.

4 Even before 1926 beneficiaries with equitable interests behind trusts of land were not entitled to physical possession as of right but only at the discretion of their trustees, duly controlled by the court. See *In re Bagot's Settlement* [1894] 1 Ch 177 at 180f; *In re Earl of Stamford and Warrington* [1925] Ch 162 at 171; (1955) 19 Conv (NS) 146 at 147 (F.R. Crane).

5 See eg *Hoysted v Federal Commissioner of Taxation* (1920) 27 CLR 400 at 410 per Knox CJ and Starke J (High Court of Australia).

6 On this view the beneficiary in possession by permission of the trustees ranked as a tenant at will (post, p 680). See *Cuvet v Davis* (1883) 9 VLR 390 at 396; *DKLR Holding Co (No 2) Pty Ltd v Commr of Stamp Duties* [1980] 1 NSWLR 510 at 519A–520A per Hope JA. The tenancy was determinable at any time on the trustees' demand for possession (see *Garrard v Tuck* (1849) 8 CB 231 at 250, 137 ER 498 at 506; *Melling v Leak* (1855) 16 CB 652 at 668f, 139 ER 915 at 921).

7 See *In re Landi (Deceased)* [1939] Ch 828 at 835. The decision in *In re Landi* 'cannot. . .be reconciled with the proposition that equitable tenants in common can still claim possession as of right' ((1955) 19 Conv (NS) 146 at 147 (F.R. Crane)).

8 Ante, p 526.

9 See Law of Property Act 1925, s 35.

occupation for the trust for sale beneficiary has been modified beyond all recognition. It has become clear that, in many instances of trust for sale, the courts nowadays recognise that a right to occupy the land has necessarily become an integral component of the rights enjoyed by the beneficiary.[10] This affirmation of beneficial entitlement to the land itself is entirely consistent with the courts' increasing deference to the 'use' value of property as distinct from its 'exchange' or capital value. During the last 40 years or so the courts have begun to recognise that entitlement to unhindered enjoyment of residential property is usually more significant than entitlement to a mere cash value on sale.[11] The modern recognition of beneficial occupation as an incident of equitable entitlement is, however, still subject to the deeply unsympathetic operation of the conveyancing machinery of the 1925 legislation.[12]

The evolution of occupation rights for beneficiaries is commonly justified on at least two inter-related grounds, both reflecting a changing social consensus on the importance of residential utility and residential security. In *City of London Building Society v Flegg*,[13] Lord Oliver of Aylmerton indicated that a beneficial right of occupation under a trust for sale of land may be founded upon circumstances either of agreement or of underlying purpose. In his view, the 'enjoyment of the property in specie either alone or concurrently with other beneficiaries' may emerge as one of the 'incidents' of the equitable interest of the trust for sale beneficiary 'according to the agreement between the beneficiaries or to the purpose for which the trust was originally created'.

The first of these grounds is easily explained even in terms of the traditional view of trusts for sale. On the assumption that possession lies within the gift of the trustees for sale, it is doubtless open to the beneficiaries (being sui iuris) to join together in acquiescing in the allocation of possession to one or more or indeed all of their number.[14] In such a case there can be no question of breach of trust on the part of the trustees. Moreover, the willingness of the beneficiaries to acquiesce in an allocation of occupation rights becomes all the more obviously inferable in the light of wider contemporary perceptions of the utility of this form of enjoyment. The modern tendency for congruence between the trusteeship and the class of beneficiaries may well make agreements of this kind almost inevitable: the trustees and the beneficiaries are often exactly the same persons.

10 It is important to distinguish the beneficiary's intrinsic right of occupation from the artificial statutory 'rights of occupation' conferred on spouse-beneficiaries (and indeed on other categories of spouse) by the Matrimonial Homes Act 1983 (ante, p 569).

11 In this sense, the right to secure accommodation, free from the interventions of strangers, has itself become a species of property right, although not easily assimilated within the canon of existing proprietary interests in land. This right of residential protection begins to parallel the security of tenure or 'status of irremovability' once enjoyed, for instance, under the Rent Act (post, p 877).

12 See eg *City of London Building Society v Flegg* [1988] AC 54 at 73F, 90F–91D (post, p 555), where the House of Lords simultaneously recognised the occupation rights of trust for sale beneficiaries and held that the equitable interests of which they were incidents had been swept away by the process of overreaching.

13 [1988] AC 54 at 81D.

14 See the explanation of the mother's occupation in *Bull v Bull* [1955] 1 QB 234, as cited by Lord Oliver of Aylmerton in *Flegg*'s case [1988] AC 54 at 81G-H (mother 'permitted to occupy').

The second (and closely allied) rationale for beneficial rights of occupation is founded on the shared purpose underlying the origin of many trusts for sale. Here the crucial catalyst in the development of the case law was the decision of the Court of Appeal in *Bull v Bull*.[15] In this case Denning LJ led the Court of Appeal in according a right of occupation to a mother who, as equitable tenant in common, held beneficially behind an implied trust for sale of residential property.[16] In later cases Lord Denning MR was forced to restrict the scope of this recognition of rights, doing so by reference to differing sorts of 'prime object' underlying a trust for sale. In *Bull v Bull* the 'prime object of the trust' had been that the son and mother 'should occupy the house together'.[17]

This purposive view of trusts for sale has now been endorsed by the House of Lords, with the result that beneficiaries seem to have a right to occupy the land wherever the underlying object of the trust involves residence or shared occupation.[18] In *Williams & Glyn's Bank Ltd v Boland*,[19] for example, the House of Lords was prepared to confirm that a beneficiary under a trust for sale of the family home has a right of occupation in the property held on trust.[20] Lord Wilberforce, although observing that the beneficiary's rights in respect of occupation were 'obscure', was ultimately happy to endorse the reasoning adumbrated in *Bull v Bull*.[1] Lord Scarman declared more boldly that an equitable tenant in common 'enjoys, by reason of her interest, a present right of occupation as well as a right to a share in the proceeds of sale, if and when the house is sold'.[2]

This view later received ample confirmation in *City of London Building Society v Flegg*.[3] Here, in another situation of joint family residence, the House of

15 [1955] 1 QB 234 (ante, p 533, post, p 594).

16 [1955] 1 QB 234 at 238. Denning LJ's ruling was based on a somewhat dubious analogy between the rights of equitable tenants in common under the 1925 legislation and the concurrent rights of occupation enjoyed by legal tenants in common prior to 1926 (ante, p 472). Denning LJ was therefore able to conclude rather broadly that today every tenant in common pending sale is 'concurrently entitled' with the other beneficial co-owners 'to the possession of the land and to the use and enjoyment of it in a proper manner'.

17 See *Barclay v Barclay* [1970] 2 QB 677 at 684A. See also Edmund Davies LJ (at 684G) and Megaw LJ (at 685G-H). (Lord Denning MR (at 684B) considered the 'prime object' of the trust in *Barclay*'s case to be not joint residence but sale (post, p 596)). See also *Williams & Glyn's Bank Ltd v Boland* [1979] Ch 312 at 331A-C, 333C, where Lord Denning MR declared forthrightly that, pending sale of a family home, a spouse-beneficiary behind a trust for sale had 'an equitable interest in land'.

18 In 1989 the Law Commission proposed that under the new trust of land (ante, p 537) a beneficiary with a present vested interest should have a right to occupy trust land which has been provided or acquired for the beneficiary's occupation. It was envisaged that the trustees would be empowered to agree or impose reasonable terms as to rents, repairs and outgoings. Where there was more than one eligible beneficiary, trustees would have a discretionary power (possibly subject to the award of compensation) to exclude or restrict the occupation right of any individual beneficiary (Law Com No 181, paras 13.3f, 20.3). See Draft Trusts of Land Bill, clause 7(1).

19 [1981] AC 487 (post, p 569).

20 Indeed Lord Scarman declared ([1981] AC 487 at 511H) that in *Boland* 'the critically important right' of the spouse-beneficiary was her 'right of occupation of the land' (post, p 570).

1 [1981] AC 487 at 507B-D. See Lord Wilberforce's reference ([1981] AC 487 at 507F) to the sheer unreality of applying the conversion dogma to 'the interests of spouses in a house jointly bought to be lived in as a matrimonial home' (ante, p 546).

2 [1981] AC 487 at 510G.

3 [1988] AC 54; [1986] Ch 605 (post, p 553).

Lords accepted without hesitation the proposition that the relevant parties 'were entitled to occupy. . .as tenants in common under the trust for sale'.[4] Lord Oliver of Aylmerton spoke of the beneficiary's possession or occupation as 'no more than a method of enjoying in specie the rents and profits pending sale in which he is entitled to share'.[5] According to Lord Oliver, the right to occupy arises as one of the 'incidents' of the beneficiary's interest under the trust for sale, albeit an incident which is 'not a separate and severable right which can be regarded as. . .free standing. It is and has to be referable to the trust from which, and from which alone, it arises.'[6] Thus, in the view adopted by Lord Oliver, the right to occupy 'derives from and is. . .fathered by the interests under the trust for sale.'[7] It 'depends upon and is co-terminous with' the interest in the rents and profits under the trust for sale,[8] with the result that once the 'parent interest', by which alone occupation can be justified, has been overreached, 'nothing remains to which a right of occupation can attach'.[9] In the meantime, however, unless and until the 'parent interest' is 'displaced by the execution of the trust',[10] the right to occupy subsists as a component part of the beneficiary's entitlement under a trust for sale. In the light of this high authority it now seems that—however confused its historical antecedents—the trust for sale beneficiary's right of occupation has now finally acquired an unchallengeable status in the law of co-ownership.[11]

6. PROTECTION FOR A PURCHASER FROM TRUSTEES FOR SALE

One of the major achievements of the property legislation of 1925 was to make land generally marketable without simultaneously destroying its utility as a medium of family endowment. It is consistent with this policy that the trust for sale, as a conveyancing device, should enable a purchaser of any land held on trust for sale to acquire a good title free of the equitable interests of the beneficiaries. The legal title (whether it relates to registered or unregistered land) must be rendered freely alienable while fragments of beneficial ownership in the land are jealously safeguarded.

These twin objectives of facility for the purchaser and security for the beneficial owners are, in the context of the trust for sale, realised through the technical device of 'overreaching'.[12] This device effectively allows certain kinds of subsisting equitable interest to be swept off the land and on to the proceeds of sale, thereby affording the purchaser an absolute defence

4 [1988] AC 54 at 70D-E per Lord Templeman. See also [1986] Ch 605 at 614E, 617F-G per Dillon LJ.
5 [1988] AC 54 at 83F. See also 91A.
6 [1988] AC 54 at 81D-E.
7 [1988] AC 54 at 83F.
8 [1988] AC 54 at 84A.
9 [1988] AC 54 at 90H–91C.
10 [1988] AC 54 at 84B.
11 For similar confirmation that beneficial entitlement behind a trust for sale gives rise to a 'personal right' to occupy the land, see *Kemmis v Kemmis* [1988] 1 WLR 1307 at 1325D per Purchas LJ, 1335H–1336A per Nourse LJ. See also *Meyer v Riddick* (1990) 60 P & CR 50 at 54 per Fox LJ; *In re Citro (A Bankrupt)* [1991] Ch 142 at 158H per Nourse LJ.
12 The operation of 'overreaching' was explained in Chapter 6 (ante, p 103).

against any future claim founded on the equitable rights of trust for sale beneficiaries.

(1) Documentation in a trust for sale

Where land is held on an *express* trust for sale, the details of ownership (both legal and equitable) are often—although not necessarily—contained in two separate documents. One of these documents is a vesting document or conveyance which records the vesting of the legal title in the trustees for sale. The other document, if there is one, is a 'trust instrument' which records the equitable rights behind the trust. Normally a purchaser of the land need concern himself only with the first of these documents, since he knows that any equitable interests outlined in the trust instrument will be overreached on sale provided that he complies with the relevant statutory requirements. The primary protection for the purchaser therefore lies in his statutory claim to have overreached all subsisting beneficial interests, and it is a highly attractive incidental effect of the overreaching mechanism that these equitable rights are thereafter preserved as equivalent interests in the proceeds of sale.

(2) The statutory conditions for 'overreaching'

Before a purchaser of land held on trust for sale can properly claim to have overreached, or taken title free of, the interests of beneficiaries under that trust, he must show that certain statutory conditions for overreaching have been satisfied. Section 2(1)(ii) of the Law of Property Act 1925 provides that

> A conveyance to a purchaser of a legal estate in land shall overreach any equitable interest or power affecting that estate, whether or not he has notice thereof, if. . .the conveyance is made by trustees for sale and the equitable interest or power is at the date of the conveyance capable of being overreached by such trustees. . .and the statutory requirements respecting the payment of capital money arising under a disposition upon trust for sale are complied with. . .[13]

The conditions laid down in this provision bear detailed examination.

(a) The conveyance must be 'made by trustees for sale'

No overreaching may occur in respect of a trust for sale except in the context of a 'conveyance'[14] made by 'trustees for sale'. 'Trustees for sale' are themselves defined in terms of 'persons. . .holding land on trust for sale',[15] and a 'trust for sale' is further defined as an 'immediate binding trust for sale'.[16] If,

13 See also Law of Property Act 1925, s 28(1), which provides that an exercise by trustees for sale of their powers as conferred by this section (ante, p 539) 'shall operate to overreach any equitable interests or powers which are by virtue of this Act or otherwise made to attach to the net proceeds of sale as if created by a trust affecting those proceeds.'

14 A 'conveyance' within the Law of Property Act 1925 is defined as including, unless the context otherwise requires, 'a mortgage, charge, lease, assent, vesting declaration, vesting instrument, disclaimer, release and every other assurance of property or of an interest therein by any instrument, except a will. . .' (Law of Property Act 1925, s 205(1)(ii)).

15 Law of Property Act 1925, s 205(1)(xxix).

16 Ante, p 523.

in the event of a disposition of the land, the purchaser fails to receive a conveyance made by 'trustees for sale', the overreaching mechanism described in section 2(1) of the Law of Property Act 1925 cannot operate in his favour.

(b) The equitable interests must be 'capable of being overreached'

The equitable interests which are 'capable of being overreached' by a purchaser are, in general, the equitable proprietary interests of trust for sale beneficiaries as joint tenants or tenants in common behind the trust. A conveyance of land held on trust for sale cannot entitle the purchaser to overreach 'commercial' equitable interests (such as estate contracts and restrictive covenants).[17] Interests of the latter kind continue to bind the land after the conveyance if—but only if—they have been protected by the appropriate form of registration or entry.[18]

Apart, however, from duly protected 'commercial' equitable rights, the only type of equitable interest which cannot be overreached on an ordinary conveyance by trustees for sale is an equity created *prior* to the trust for sale itself.[19] Such equitable interests rarely arise nowadays, and can be overreached by the purchaser only if recourse is had to the special machinery of an *ad hoc* trust for sale.[20]

(c) Capital money must be paid over in the prescribed manner

It is a vital condition for overreaching under section 2(1)(ii) of the Law of Property Act 1925 that the purchaser must comply with 'the statutory requirements respecting the payment of capital money arising under a disposition upon trust for sale'. These statutory requirements are found in the provision that 'the proceeds of sale or other capital money shall not be paid to or applied by the direction of fewer than two persons as trustees for sale'.[1]

The requirement of payment to at least two trustees for sale is mandatory, overriding any contrary provision in the instrument (if any) which created the trust for sale.[2] Payment to fewer than two trustees precludes the purchaser from claiming that he has statutorily overreached the equitable interests under the trust for sale.[3] The 'two trustee' rule is therefore a principle of rigid application and admits of scarcely any exceptions. The two exceptions permitted by statute allow the purchaser to make payment to a trust

17 Ante, p 98.

18 Ante, pp 113, 181. In registered land, of course, certain rights remain binding on the transferee notwithstanding a failure to enter them on the register of title (see Land Registration Act 1925, s 70(1), ante, p 197).

19 There is, in the context of the trust for sale, no equivalent of Settled Land Act 1925, s 72(3). See *In re Ryder and Steadman's Contract* [1927] 2 Ch 62 at 82f.

20 Ante, p 525.

1 Law of Property Act 1925, s 27(2), as substituted by Law of Property (Amendment) Act 1926, Schedule.

2 Law of Property Act 1925, s 27(2).

3 In such circumstances these equitable interests remain binding on a purchaser of unregistered land unless he can show that he purchased without notice of them (post, p 563). In the case of registered land, the equitable interests may constitute overriding interests pursuant to Land Registration Act 1925, s 70(1)(g) (post, p 568).

corporation or to a sole personal representative.[4] The insistence in all other cases on strict observance of the 'two trustee' rule marks a pragmatic recognition that a payment made to two trustees for sale is much less likely to be misappropriated or misapplied than a payment made to a single individual.[5]

(3) The effects of overreaching

If the three statutory conditions for overreaching are satisfied, the purchaser of land held on trust for sale 'overreaches' the beneficial interests behind the trust entirely irrespective of whether he has notice of such entitlements.[6]

(a) *Purchaser can henceforth ignore all trusts*

There is a clear provision in section 27(1) of the Law of Property Act 1925 that the purchaser who complies with the conditions of overreaching 'shall not be concerned with the trusts affecting the proceeds of sale of land subject to a trust for sale...or affecting the rents and profits of land until sale, whether or not those trusts are declared by the same instrument by which the trust for sale is created.'[7] In other words, the equitable interests behind the trust now take effect conclusively in the capital money arising from the disposition. The purchaser takes a good legal title free from all beneficial claims, and even does so irrespective of actual occupation by the claimant beneficiaries which would otherwise have founded an overriding interest in registered land or provided constructive notice in unregistered land.[8]

During the seven decades following the enactment of the 1925 Acts it has been widely assumed that, on compliance with the 'two trustee' rule, a purchaser from trustees for sale receives a statutory immunity from trust beneficial interests even where one or more of the beneficiaries may have been in actual occupation of the property at the date of the transaction.[9] Only rarely has there been any serious challenge to this assumption. In *City of London Building Society v Flegg*[10] a registered title in a family home

4 Law of Property Act 1925, s 27(2). There is no provision for the payment of purchase money into court.

5 See Law Com No 86, para 1.250.

6 Thus even a purchaser with *express* notice of adverse equitable rights takes title free of them provided that there is compliance with the statutory conditions of overreaching (see *City of London Building Society v Flegg* [1988] AC 54 at 83E-F per Lord Oliver of Aylmerton).

7 According to Lord Oliver of Aylmerton, it is 'tolerably clear that the scheme of the Act is to enable a purchaser or mortgagee, so long as he pays the proceeds of sale or other capital moneys to not less than two trustees or to a trust corporation, to accept a conveyance or mortgage without reference at all to the beneficial interests of co-owners interested only in the proceeds of sale and rents and profits until sale, which are kept behind the curtain and do not require to be investigated' (*City of London Building Society v Flegg* [1988] AC 54 at 78H–79A). See also Law of Property Act 1925, s 10(1).

8 See *Williams & Glyn's Bank Ltd v Boland* [1981] AC 487 at 503D-E per Lord Wilberforce; *City of London Building Society v Flegg* [1988] AC 54 at 89F-G per Lord Oliver of Aylmerton. See also J. Martin, [1980] Conv 361 at 362, [1981] Conv 219. Contra, C. Sydenham, [1980] Conv 427.

9 See *City of London Building Society v Flegg* [1988] AC 54 at 76E-F per Lord Oliver of Aylmerton. See also *Owen v Williams* (Unreported, Court of Appeal, 21 November 1985) per Nourse LJ (post, p 579).

10 [1988] AC 54; [1986] Ch 605.

had been purchased in the name of A and B, the greater part of the purchase money having been provided by X and Y, the parents of B. The conveyance to A and B contained an express trust for sale and explicitly declared that the trustees for sale, A and B, were possessed of the mortgaging powers of an absolute owner. Although the conveyance made no reference to X and Y, it was perfectly clear that they were beneficiaries behind the trust for sale of the registered title[11] and indeed X and Y moved into joint occupation of the property with A and B and remained there at all material times (see *Fig.* 42).[12]

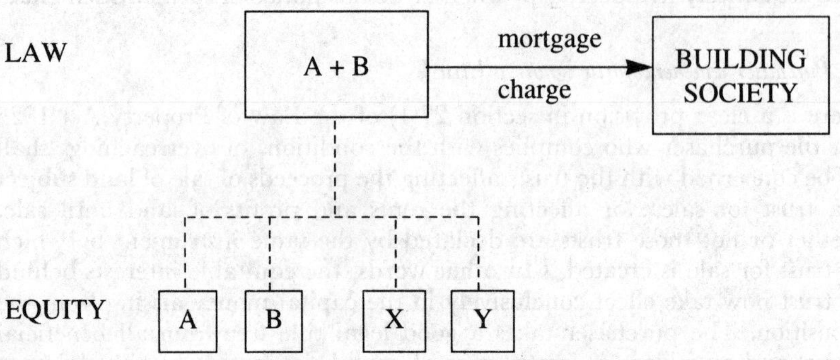

Fig. 42

Some time later, and without the knowledge or consent of either X or Y, A and B charged their legal title to a building society. A and B were subsequently made bankrupt and the building society sought to recover possession of the property, plainly assuming that the mortgage transaction executed by two trustees for sale had an unchallengeable overreaching effect on such equitable interests as might exist. X and Y claimed, however, that by reason of actual occupation at the date of the mortgagee's charge their equitable rights under the trust for sale (or at least the occupation rights incidental thereto[13]) had acquired the status of overriding interests pursuant to section 70(1)(g) of the Land Registration Act 1925.[14] Somewhat surprisingly this claim succeeded in the Court of Appeal.

In support of its conclusion, the Court of Appeal relied on *Williams & Glyn's Bank Ltd v Boland*,[15] where (according to Dillon LJ) the reasoning of Lord Wilberforce did 'not depend at all...on the fact that...there

11 Although the conveyance contained an express declaration of trust for A and B as beneficial joint tenants, the House of Lords regarded A, B, X and Y as together beneficial tenants in common (see [1988] AC 54 at 70A-E per Lord Templeman, 77G per Lord Oliver of Aylmerton). The declaration of trust, precisely because not executed by X and Y (ante, p 380), could not preclude the assertion of a competing beneficial entitlement by X and Y as contributors of value. See C. Harpum, [1990] CLJ 277 at 302; compare M.P. Thompson, [1988] Conv 108 at 109.

12 [1986] Ch 605 at 614E-F.

13 Post, p 570.

14 Ante, p 203.

15 [1981] AC 487 (post, p 569).

was only one registered proprietor of the land and therefore only one trustee for sale.'[16] In the view adopted by Dillon LJ, the protection of overriding interests under section 70(1)(g) could be founded on a simple association existing between the equitable interest of a trust for sale beneficiary and the fact of 'actual occupation' of the property held on trust.[17] Thus, in the event of a dealing effected even by two registered proprietors, 'what would otherwise have been a minor interest capable of being overridden under the Law of Property Act 1925 by two trustees for sale, is, if protected by the fact of actual occupation of the land, elevated to the status of an overriding interest.'[18] Since no enquiry had been made of X and Y before the charge was executed, the Court held that the building society must take its mortgage subject to their overriding interests.[19]

This ruling immediately threatened a number of extraordinary consequences.[20] *First*, a disposition and receipt of capital moneys by two trustees for sale would no longer automatically overreach otherwise overriding interests in registered land and probably would not overreach the equivalent equitable interests in unregistered land either.[1] *Second*, the Court of Appeal's decision had the effect of ripping apart the 'curtain' which supposedly conceals trust for sale equities from the purchaser who deals with two trustees. *Third*, a new onus was placed on the purchaser to identify all beneficiaries in possession (in either registered or unregistered land) and ensure that each gave consent to the transaction in hand.[2] In effect, as Lord Oliver of Aylmerton later observed in the House of Lords, the Court of Appeal's ruling was of 'very considerable importance not only to conveyancers but to anyone proposing to lend upon the security of property'.[3]

Much to the relief of conveyancers, the House of Lords unanimously overturned the ruling of the Court of Appeal as contrary to several structural tenets of the property legislation of 1925.[4] According to Lord Oliver of Aylmerton, the analogy with *Boland*'s case was imperfect precisely because the transaction in *Boland* resulted in a receipt of capital money by only one trustee for sale. In Lord Oliver's view, this restrictive circumstance was not 'merely part of the narrative but. . .an essential part of the reasoning'

16 [1986] Ch 605 at 616H–617D.
17 [1986] Ch 605 at 617B-C.
18 [1986] Ch 605 at 617C.
19 Dillon LJ reinforced this ruling by reference ([1986] Ch 605 at 618D–620E) to Law of Property Act 1925, s 14, which, in his view, made it clear that the operation of overreaching under section 2(1)(ii) could not 'prejudicially affect the interest of any person in possession or in actual occupation of land to which he may be entitled in right of such possession or occupation'. See (1986) 136 NLJ 83 (H. Lewis).
20 For a good summary of these consequences, recounted with an appropriate frisson of horror, see [1988] AC 54 at 76E–77A per Lord Oliver of Aylmerton. For further critical views, see [1986] CLJ 202 (C. Harpum); [1986] Conv 131 (D.J. Hayton); (1986) 136 NLJ 208 (D.J. Hayton); (1986) 49 MLR 519 (R.J. Smith); (1986) 102 LQR 349.
1 [1988] AC 54 at 77A.
2 If relevant consents were withheld, the only course available would be an application to court under section 30 of the Law of Property Act 1925 (ante, p 526).
3 [1988] AC 54 at 76G. '[F]inancial institutions advancing money on the security of land will face hitherto unsuspected hazards' ([1988] AC 54 at 77A).
4 [1988] AC 54. See [1987] Conv 451 (W.J. Swadling); [1987] CLJ 392 (C. Harpum); (1987) 103 LQR 520 (R.J. Smith); (1988) 51 MLR 365 (S. Gardner); [1988] Conv 108 (M.P. Thompson).

in *Boland*.[5] The House of Lords went on to hold that section 70(1)(g) could protect only such 'rights' of persons in actual occupation as were 'subsisting in reference' to the land on completion of the mortgage charge.[6] In the present case the 'rights' of the beneficiaries had already been overreached on the execution of the mortgage charge and payment of the mortgage moneys to two trustees.[7] The mere fact of such payment had instantly ensured that the rights of X and Y were 'shifted from the land to the capital moneys in the hands of the trustees',[8] with the result that the immunity conferred by the 'two trustee' rule was already in place. It followed inescapably that when the mortgagee came to register its charge, there would no longer exist for the purpose of section 70(1)(g) any 'rights' in the beneficiaries which, by association with their undoubted actual occupation, could found a claim of overriding interest binding on the mortgagee.[9]

There seems to be little doubt that the ruling of the House of Lords in *Flegg*'s case has conclusively reinstated the conventional understanding of overreaching and the machinery of conveyancing. Observance of the 'two trustee' rule guarantees that in registered land a purchaser may, in one sense, overreach even an overriding interest.[10] Until *Flegg* the equivalent effect in unregistered land had never really been question, and with the final outcome in *Flegg* an important part of the orthodoxy of English land law has been restored.

(b) Purchaser is not answerable for the application of the proceeds

Under the Law of Property Act 1925 the effect of overreaching is expansive, conferring many further kinds of protection on the purchaser who conforms to the statutory prescription. Thus, for instance, a receipt in writing in respect

5 [1988] AC 54 at 89C-D. In *Boland* 'it was a critical feature of the [wives'] argument that their interests were not overreached but were kept alive as against the purchaser. . .'

6 [1988] AC 54 at 91A-B per Lord Oliver of Aylmerton. Pursuant to Land Registration Act 1925, s 26(1), a charge relating to a registered title is completed only when the registrar enters the chargee as the proprietor of the charge (ante, p 229). In *Flegg*'s case the building society's charge, although executed within the priority period provided by an official search, had not yet been completed by registration. Lord Oliver took the view, however, that the chargee was still entitled to be registered and that registration was a mere formality ([1988] AC 54 at 91E-G). For a contrary view (which Lord Oliver found unpersuasive) that the issue should have been decided as a contest between two competing equities, see [1988] Conv 141 (P. Sparkes).

7 [1988] AC 54 at 91F-G per Lord Oliver of Aylmerton. It has been pointed out that payment to two trustees would not have overreached the rights of X and Y if those rights had arisen by way of a loan made to A and B, rather than by way of a contribution towards purchase price. Rights derived from a loan may well comprise some species of irrevocable and non-overreachable licence (ante, p 404). See M.P. Thompson, [1988] Conv 108 at 119f.

8 [1988] AC 54 at 91A-B per Lord Oliver of Aylmerton.

9 'If, then, one asks what were the subsisting rights of the respondents referable to their occupation, the answer must. . .be that they were rights which, vis à vis the appellants, were, eo instante with the creation of the charge, overreached and therefore subsisted only in relation to the equity of redemption' ([1988] AC 54 at 90F per Lord Oliver of Aylmerton). See also Lord Templeman at 73F.

10 A more accurate way of expressing the impact of *Flegg* would be that the case demonstrates that section 70(1)(g) requires not merely that the claimant of an overriding interest is in 'actual occupation' but also that he has 'rights' subsisting with reference to the land.

of the purchase money operates as a 'sufficient discharge' to the purchaser of land formerly held on trust for sale, and effectively exonerates him from seeing to the application of the proceeds of sale by the trustees or from being 'answerable for any loss or misapplication thereof.'[11] The combined effect of statute[12] is therefore that the purchaser who fulfils the three conditions for overreaching takes a legal title free both of the beneficial interests and of the terms of the trust.

(c) Consents

Where the execution of a trust for sale is made the subject of requisite consents to be obtained from two or more persons,[13] the consent of any two of such persons is deemed sufficient in favour of the purchaser.[14]

(d) Consultation

The purchaser is 'not concerned to see' that the trustees for sale have properly discharged any duty which they may have to consult their beneficiaries in accordance with the provisions of section 26(3) of the Law of Property Act 1925.[15]

(e) Postponement of sale

The purchaser is 'not concerned in any case with any directions respecting the postponement of a sale' contained in any instrument creative of the trust for sale.[16]

(f) Currency of the trust for sale

In order to activate all the statutory protections conferred on a purchaser from trustees for sale, the trust for sale is 'deemed to be subsisting until the land has been conveyed to or under the direction of the persons interested in the proceeds of sale'.[17]

(4) The effects of dispositions by a sole trustee for sale

It cannot now be doubted that full overreaching effect is achieved through a disposition made by trustees for sale acting in conformity with the Law

11 Trustee Act 1925, s 14(1). A valid receipt cannot be given by a sole trustee other than a trust corporation (Trustee Act 1925, s 14(2)(a)).
12 See also Law of Property Act 1925, ss 2(1)(ii), 27(2).
13 Ante, p 525.
14 Law of Property Act 1925, s 26(1).
15 Law of Property Act 1925, s 26(3) (post, p 595).
16 Law of Property Act 1925, s 25(2) (ante, p 524).
17 Law of Property Act 1925, s 23.

of Property Act 1925.[18] This important effect of the 'two trustee' rule is, of course, a pivotal feature of the protection conferred on purchasers of land by the 1925 legislation.[19] By contrast, however, an extremely awkward dilemma emerges where a disposition is made by a sole trustee acting in defiance of the 1925 Act and therefore, necessarily, in breach of his trust. It is clear that a disposition by such a trustee (other than a trust corporation[20]) enjoys no overreaching effect by virtue of statute.[1] What remains to be resolved is whether the purchaser takes a good title at law from a sole trustee and whether the purchaser is bound by the equitable interests of co-owners under the trust for sale.[2]

Nowhere does the 1925 legislation provide for the consequences of a disposition by a sole trustee for sale. Yet such dispositions may not be uncommon.[3] As Lord Wilberforce pointed out in *Williams & Glyn's Bank Ltd v Boland*,[4] the incidence of undisclosed trusts for sale concealed behind an apparently sole legal title has been dramatically increased by 'the extension, beyond the paterfamilias, of rights of ownership, itself following from the diffusion of property and earning capacity.'[5] Thus an implied (or statutory) trust for sale is often generated by a co-operative purchase of a legal title which is then transferred into the name of one person only.[6] Such a trust arises with particular frequency in the family context, where several members of a household (eg A, B and C in *Fig.* 43) may make financial contributions quite informally towards a purchase in the name of only one of their number.[7] The owner of the legal title may even be entirely unaware that he or she is in truth a trustee for sale, and the significance of this trusteeship will

18 Where there is co-ownership of the legal estate, the presence of joint tenancy on the face of the documentary title inevitably signals to any purchaser the existence of a trust for sale in respect of the property. The immediate practical consequence is that the purchaser will insist on paying any relevant capital moneys to at least two trustees, thereby overreaching all equitable interests under the trust for sale (ante, p 526).

19 It seems to have been the plain expectation of the property legislation of 1925 that all dealings with the legal title of any land held in co-ownership should be conducted by no fewer than two trustees for sale. Payment of capital moneys to at least two such trustees was intended to confer upon the purchaser a title which was statutorily declared free of pre-existing co-ownership interests, whilst providing a safeguard for the financial interests of the equitable co-owners. See *Taylor v Taylor* [1968] 1 WLR 378 at 382G per Danckwerts LJ; Law Com No 86, para 1.250.

20 Law of Property Act 1925, ss 2(1)(ii), 27(2) (ante, p 102).

1 *City of London Building Society v Flegg* [1988] AC 54 at 74C per Lord Templeman, 89A-G per Lord Oliver of Aylmerton.

2 The term 'purchaser' is used here in its extended statutory sense, which includes both a lessee and a mortgagee (see Law of Property Act 1925, s 205(1)(xxi); Land Registration Act 1925, s 3(xxi)). A chargee of a legal estate in land is statutorily declared to stand in the same position as if he had taken a legal estate (ie a long leasehold) in the land charged by way of legal mortgage (see Law of Property Act 1925, s 87(1); Land Registration Act 1925, s 3(i), ante, p 79).

3 For an informed estimate that over 75 per cent of mortgages of matrimonial homes are now in joint names, see Law Com No 115, paras 29, 60. However, as the Law Commission noted, this 'still leaves a considerable residue of existing and future purchases which have been or will be taken in the name of a sole legal owner'.

4 [1981] AC 487.

5 [1981] AC 487 at 508G.

6 Ante, p 532.

7 Ante, p 535.

emerge for the first time only when the legal title is made the subject of some later disposition to a third party, P.[8]

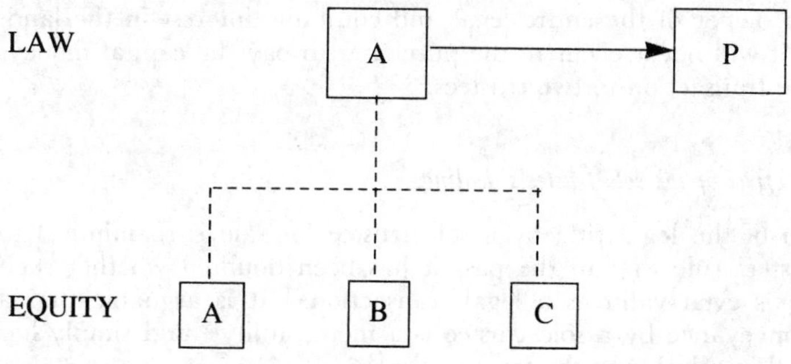

Fig. 43

In such cases protection for the purchaser can often be achieved by allowing the residential security enjoyed by members of the vendor's family to be prejudiced through dealings with the legal title of which they were unaware and to which they did not consent.[9] The conflict of interests here is both stark and inescapable.[10] An underlying tension has long existed in English property law between policy considerations of residential security and conveyancing convenience. In the present context the equitable co-ownership

8 The most insidious form of disposition in the present context may well be a post-acquisition mortgage of the legal estate in the co-owned land (post, p 562). If, for instance, the legal owner tries to sell or lease the family residence, other members of his family are more likely to be aware of the impending disposition and are therefore in a position more readily to assert such equitable rights as they may have (although see *Chhokar v Chhokar* [1984] FLR 313 (ante, p 220)). A mortgage of land is usually a much less visible transaction and the continued occupation of the home by other family members will not necessarily cause alarm to the mortgagee or precipitate disclosure of their co-ownership rights.

9 Of course few problems arise in practice if the relevant disposition is effected with the knowledge or consent of all concerned. There must be thousands of conveyances completed each year by vendors who are sole trustees for sale although neither they nor their purchasers realise this fact. However, failure to comply with the conditions of statutory overreaching usually makes no difference to anyone, since the proceeds of the sale are generally re-invested in the purchase of another family home and the beneficial co-owners can, if necessary, claim to trace their equitable rights into the new property. In 1978 the Law Commission proposed that each spouse should have rights to ensure that the other spouse's share of the proceeds of sale of the matrimonial home is used in the acquisition of a new home (see Law Com No 86, paras 1.365ff).

10 As Murray J observed in the High Court of Northern Ireland in *Northern Bank Ltd v Beattie* [1982] 18 NIJB, p 1, the phrase 'the eternal triangle' has nowadays taken on a new meaning for the judge in the Chancery Division. A typical dispute may involve 'a husband-mortgagor of his matrimonial home, a bank mortgagee of that home, an estranged wife still living in the home'. Essentially the same issues may, of course, arise in relation to a much wider range of members of the legal owner's family. The equitable co-owners of the family home may well include such persons as the legal owner's parents, his de facto partner, his child, his spinster aunt, his homosexual lover, or many other persons who may have helped to finance his purchase of the home. The application of land law principles is indifferent to the precise nature of their relationship.

of the trust for sale beneficiaries necessarily exists *dehors* the paper title offered to the purchaser, and it is quite possible that the latter will have no idea that his vendor is in fact a trustee for sale. Quite reasonably the purchaser will believe that the vendor is dealing as 'beneficial owner' of the land, ie as the sole owner of the entire legal and equitable interest in the land. Accordingly it will never occur to the purchaser to pay the capital moneys arising on the transaction to two trustees.

(a) *The legal effect of the sole trustee's dealings*

A disposition of the legal title by a sole trustee for sale is so inimical to the 'two trustee' rule that in the past it has been doubted whether such a disposition is even valid as a legal transaction.[11] It is arguable that a purported conveyance by a sole trustee is a mere nullity[12] and simply has no effect at all in relation to the legal estate.[13]

Such reservations notwithstanding, it is now generally accepted that a disposition effected by a de facto legal owner—albeit a sole trustee for sale—is unchallengeable as a valid transaction with the legal title.[14] Such a dealing is regarded as a good transaction at law, even though entered into wrongfully and in breach of trust.[15] This conclusion is even more inevitable in respect

11 There is some authority for the view that a sole statutory trustee simply lacks the competence to deal unilaterally with his own legal title by way of either sale or mortgage (see *Bull v Bull* [1955] 1 QB 234 at 238 per Denning LJ; *Waller v Waller* [1967] 1 WLR 451 at 453C; compare, however, *Tunstall v Tunstall* [1953] 1 WLR 770 at 771). In favour of the requirement of two trustees are the twin considerations that a sole trustee for sale acts in clear breach of his trust when he purports to deal with his legal title, and cannot in any event give a 'valid receipt' for any proceeds paid to him (see Trustee Act 1925, s 14(2). This provision could, at least in theory, make it difficult for a purchaser subsequently to prove that he was a 'purchaser for value'—a point which may be crucial later (post, p 563)).

12 It is significant that the penalty of voidness attaches to an irregular conveyance of a legal estate by a tenant for life of settled land who acts outside his statutory authority (see Settled Land Act 1925, s 18(1)(a); *Weston v Henshaw* [1950] Ch 510 at 519f, post, p 632). Since the powers of trustees for sale are modelled on the analogy of the Settled Land Act powers (ante, p 539), it can be argued that the settled land rule is effectively carried over into the context of the implied trust for sale (see S.M. Clayton, [1981] Conv 19). However, it seems improbable that Parliament would have preferred to achieve a comparable result in the case of the trust for sale by means of a mere tenuous inference from the Settled Land Act rather than an express provision in the Law of Property Act 1925 (see B. Rudden, (1963) 27 Conv (NS) 51 at 56).

13 There is even some indication that this result was intended by the legislature. Section 27(2) of the Law of Property Act 1925 (ante, p 552) seems to leave open the inference that, where capital money does arise on a transaction by trustees for sale, it is indeed 'necessary to have more than one trustee' and that the absence of a second trustee invalidates the disposition at law.

14 See eg *Caunce v Caunce* [1969] 1 WLR 286 (post, p 565); *Kingsnorth Finance Co Ltd v Tizard* [1986] 1 WLR 783 at 785C; *Ulster Bank Ltd v Shanks* [1982] NI 143 at 144E per Murray J (although here no trust for sale as such was involved). For a query as to the mortgaging powers of trustees for sale, see however (1986) 49 MLR 519 at 523 (R.J. Smith).

15 'The fact that a trustee acts in breach of trust does not mean that he has no capacity to do the act he wrongly did' (*Hammersmith and Fulham LBC v Monk* [1992] 1 AC 478 at 493E per Lord Browne-Wilkinson). See, however, [1979] CLJ 23 at 26 (M.J. Prichard). In *Northern Bank Ltd v Henry* [1981] IR 1 at 19, Kenny J expressly left open the question whether a disposition by a bare trustee, likewise acting wrongfully and in breach of trust, has any legal validity.

of titles which are registered under the Land Registration Act 1925.[16] Here the registration of the dealing operates by 'statutory magic'[17] to confirm the legal effect of the transaction in favour of the transferee or chargee,[18] despite any defect which may have attended the manner of disposition.[19]

(b) The equitable effect of the sole trustee's dealings

Given that a sole trustee for sale is competent to deal validly and effectively with his legal title, it now becomes vital to determine whether the purchaser takes his title free of the equitable co-ownership interests behind the trust for sale or is instead bound by them. If the purchaser enjoys priority over the beneficial co-owners, he takes free of their equitable rights (including such rights of occupation as may be comprised within their beneficial entitlements). If conversely the equitable rights remain binding on the purchaser, an important step has been taken towards guaranteeing the residential security of many kinds of family member.[20]

(i) The range of relevant disposition The problem of priority raised here can occur in relation to almost any form of disposition effected by a sole trustee for sale. However, in its decision in *Abbey National Building Society v Cann*,[1] the House of Lords has recently removed one species of transaction from the field of controversy. Where a taking of title is funded by an acquisition mortgage loan from a third party, it used to be thought that a *scintilla temporis* (or fraction of time) was interposed between the arrival of the legal title

16 The trustee has all the powers conferred by statute upon the 'proprietor' of the registered title (see Land Registration Act 1925, s 3(xx)), and these powers may include a power to transfer the fee simple interest, to grant a lease, and to charge the registered land by way of mortgage (Land Registration Act 1925, ss 18(1), 21(1), 25(1) (ante, p 539).

17 Land Registration Act 1925, ss 20(1), 69(1). See *Argyle Building Society v Hammond* (1985) 49 P & CR 148 at 155 (ante, p 236). Of course the proprietor's competence could have been limited by the entry of a 'restriction' on the register of his title (ante, p 182), but in the absence of such entry his powers remain freely exercisable if and so long as he remains registered as 'proprietor'.

18 No question was raised as to the validity as a legal transaction of the mortgage effected by a sole trustee for sale in *Williams & Glyn's Bank Ltd v Boland* [1981] AC 487 (post, p 569). In *Knightly v Sun Life Assurance Society Ltd* (1981) *Times*, 23 July, Nourse J expressly rejected an argument that such a mortgage was legally ineffective. For a similar approach in relation to the transfer of an estate in fee simple, see also *Chhokar v Chhokar* [1984] FLR 313 (post, p 562). A disposition of the registered title by a bare trustee is likewise effective at law, even though the trustee is acting in breach of trust (see *Hodgson v Marks* [1971] Ch 892 at 899C).

19 This outcome reflects a cogent public policy in favour of the protection of innocent purchasers. Any contrary holding would, of course, impose an intolerable burden of enquiry on the purchaser who takes title from an apparently single vendor. The purchaser would either have to satisfy himself of the non-existence of a trust for sale or assume the risk that in years past his vendor may have been the recipient of money contributions creative of an implied trust for sale.

20 If the purchaser is bound by the rights of equitable co-owners, he will merely have stepped into the shoes of the vendor as a sole trustee for sale, and must thereafter hold the legal estate on behalf of himself and any other beneficiary whose interest has not been overreached.

1 [1991] 1 AC 56 (ante, p 205, post, p 974). See (1990) 106 LQR 545 (R.J. Smith).

in the new title-holder and the creation by him of the mortgage charge which secured the money advance necessary for his acquisition.[2] Accordingly it was believed that, where a collaborative purchase was funded by disparate contributors in conjunction with an acquisition mortgage loan, the all-important interval of a micro-second would allow a statutory trust to engraft itself upon the newly acquired title in advance of the creation of the appropriate mortgage charge.[3] The beneficial interests of the contributing co-owners would therefore take priority—albeit by the narrowest of margins—over the charge taken by the lender.

In *Cann*'s case, however, the House of Lords denied the relevance of the *scintilla temporis*. The House ruled that, in the 'vast majority of cases' of acquisition mortgage, the acquisition of the legal title and the creation of the charge are 'not only precisely simultaneous but indissolubly bound together.'[4] In consequence the legal owner who can fund his acquisition of title only 'by borrowing money for the security of which he is contractually bound to grant a mortgage to the lender eo instante with the execution of the conveyance in his favour cannot in reality ever be said to have acquired even for a *scintilla temporis* the unencumbered fee simple or leasehold estate in land whereby he could grant interests having priority over the mortgage'.[5] In such cases the only estate taken by the legal owner is an already encumbered interest or 'equity of redemption'.[6] Any trust for sale which comes into being takes effect only against this encumbered title, and the security taken by the mortgagee under the charge therefore enjoys an inevitable priority over any beneficial interests claimed by co-owners behind the trust for sale.[7]

While acquisition mortgages no longer present a difficult issue of priority in the present context, the same cannot be said of post-acquisition mortgages. The controversy over transactions effected by a sole trustee for sale has tended to focus almost exclusively[8] on the phenomenon of the second mortgage or further advance which is granted perhaps many years after the original purchase of the property. Such a mortgage may be concluded by a sole legal owner without the knowledge or participation of any of the other beneficial co-owners behind the trust for sale.[9] In the case of a post-acquisition mortgage, beneficial co-ownership interests may already have been generated quite silently by a range of contributory activity on the part of family members

2 See *Church of England Building Society v Piskor* [1954] Ch 553 at 564f (post, p 979).

3 In other words, there was a distinct possibility that equitable co-ownership rights might have intervened before the mortgagee received his security, as for instance would be the case if part of the purchase price for the acquisition were contributed by other family members (see Law Com No 115, paras 33ff, post, p 572).

4 [1991] 1 AC 56 at 92F per Lord Oliver of Aylmerton.

5 [1991] 1 AC 56 at 102A-B per Lord Jauncey of Tullichettle.

6 Post, p 975.

7 See Chapter 20 (post, p 979).

8 See, however, *Chhokar v Chhokar* [1984] FLR 313 (ante, p 220) for an example involving the transfer of an estate in fee simple.

9 This possibility is given a strange twist where the legal title in the family home is vested in a company (see eg *Winkworth v Edward Baron Development Co Ltd* (1986) 52 P & CR 67, ante, p 444). The transaction may even comprise a purely informal mortgage of the property by deposit of title documents for the purpose of obtaining a business loan or securing a bank overdraft.

during the period since the initial acquisition of the property.[10] The question inevitably arises whether the lender takes his security subject to these undisclosed equitable rights, or whether he indeed acquires priority over equitable co-owners and can therefore in the last resort recover his loan by forcing a sale of the family home.

(ii) The competing interests The answer to the present question must be sought in the law of both registered and unregistered title. In either case the resolution of the problem is invidious. The relevant contest often involves two substantially innocent parties, one of whom must suffer the prejudicial effects of the transaction entered into by a sole trustee for sale. When the problem of priority finally surfaces, the mortgagee is usually horrified to discover the existence of adverse equities in the land[11]; the beneficial co-owners behind the trust may well be equally discomfited to realise for the first time that the land has been the subject of a disposition which, for instance, has mortgaged their home to the hilt.[12]

(c) Unregistered land

In the context of an implied trust for sale of unregistered land,[13] it is quite clear that the present issue of priority depends on the operation of the equitable doctrine of notice.[14] In other words, the purchaser from a sole statutory trustee for sale takes free of the adverse equitable interests of co-owners only if he ranks as a bona fide purchaser of a legal estate for value without notice (either actual or constructive).[15] It is plain that the process of statutory overreaching which normally protects co-ownership interests cannot have occurred; nor does the equitable interest of the trust for sale beneficiary constitute any species of registrable charge under the Land Charges Act

10 Ante, p 443.

11 See eg *Equity & Law Home Loans Ltd v Prestidge* [1992] 1 WLR 137 at 141E.

12 In the relevant case law it is a strangely recurring feature that the sole trustee of the legal estate intended, by means of his mortgage, to extract a portion of the capital value of the co-owned property in order to disappear and make a new life somewhere else (see *Caunce v Caunce* [1969] 1 WLR 286 at 289F; *Kingsnorth Finance Co Ltd v Tizard* [1986] 1 WLR 783 at 787A; *Equity & Law Home Loans Ltd v Prestidge* [1992] 1 WLR 137 at 140G, 141C-E, 145D-E).

13 The position is quite different in relation to an *express* trust for sale of the family home. Here, of course, it is quite impossible for the purchaser to disclaim notice of the trust affecting the property. If the legal title expressly reveals the existence of a trust for sale, the purchaser must deal with and pay his money to at least two trustees, even if this means that he must demand the appointment of a second trustee, since otherwise the transaction will not overreach the equities behind the trust. Furthermore, if the legal title is already vested in two or more joint tenants, any conveyance executed by only one such trustee will not even produce a good conveyance at law. An effective disposition of a jointly held legal title requires the active participation of all the joint tenants (ante, p 468).

14 *Caunce v Caunce* [1969] 1 WLR 286 at 289G per Stamp J; *Kingsnorth Finance Co Ltd v Tizard* [1986] 1 WLR 783 at 792H-793A per Judge Finlay QC. See also *Williams & Glyn's Bank Ltd v Boland* [1979] Ch 312 at 330D, 334C; J.F. Garner, (1969) 33 Conv (NS) 240.

15 The same result appears to follow even if the co-ownership is not analysed in terms of a trust for sale (see *Ulster Bank Ltd v Shanks* [1982] NI 143 at 150H; *Allied Irish Banks Ltd v McWilliams* [1982] NI 156 at 161F; *Northern Bank Ltd v Beattie* [1982] 18 NIJB, p 20).

1972.[16] There is therefore no alternative to a residual application of the equitable doctrine of notice.[17]

(i) Nature of constructive notice It is not easy either to define the factual circumstances which fix a purchaser with constructive notice or to determine whether the purchaser has indeed discharged his duty of careful enquiry.[18] It seems, however, to be settled law that a purchaser will be bound by adverse equities only if he has failed to make reasonable enquiries as to the possible existence of undisclosed co-ownership. Moreover, the traditional approach of English courts disfavours any unnecessary extension of the concept of constructive notice.[19] Purchasers are not lightly to be held to have a duty of enquiry into otherwise undisclosed rights in the land which they seek to purchase. The issue depends not upon the nature of the right but upon the individual circumstances of the case.[20]

The relevant case law reveals a pattern, at least until relatively recently, of severely restrictive applications of the doctrine of notice.[1] Thus a purchaser is not fixed with constructive notice of undisclosed co-ownership merely because he had special access to information which might have prompted the realisation that someone other than the sole trustee for sale contributed financially towards the purchase of land.[2] Nor, for instance, is there

16 In unregistered land an equitable interest behind an implied trust for sale cannot be registered under the Land Charges Act either as a land charge (see *Kingsnorth Finance Co Ltd v Tizard* [1986] 1 WLR 783 at 792H) or as a *lis pendens* (see *Taylor v Taylor* [1968] 1 WLR 378 at 384C). Some beneficial co-owners behind a trust for sale may, of course, have registrable 'rights of occupation' pursuant to the Matrimonial Homes Act 1983. These rights are not, however, proprietary in nature and in the present context are almost invariably rendered void for lack of registration (ante, pp 119, 161). In *Caunce v Caunce* [1969] 1 WLR 286, the Matrimonial Homes Act had not yet been extended to beneficial co-owners (see Matrimonial Homes Act 1983, s 1(11), introduced by Matrimonial Proceedings and Property Act 1970, s 38).

17 Most disputes centre around the issue of constructive notice. If the purchaser had had actual notice of the existence of a trust for sale or of the beneficial interests behind it, the transaction—at least in its current form—would never have been completed.

18 There may be a difference between the question whether a party is fixed with constructive notice and whether 'it is reasonable in the circumstances to pursue enquiry' (see *Midland Bank Ltd v Farmpride Hatcheries Ltd* (1981) 260 Estates Gazette 493 at 497 per Shaw LJ).

19 See *Hunt v Luck* [1901] 1 Ch 45 at 48 (ante, p 82).

20 It has been said that the 'commonness or otherwise of the right which may be disclosed by the enquiry cannot. . .affect the reasonableness or otherwise of making any enquiry' (*Midland Bank Ltd v Farmpride Hatcheries Ltd* (1981) 260 Estates Gazette 493 at 498 per Oliver LJ).

1 See eg *Caunce v Caunce* [1969] 1 WLR 286 at 291G-H per Stamp J; *Ulster Bank Ltd v Shanks* [1982] NI 143 at 150F.

2 In *Caunce v Caunce* [1969] 1 WLR 286 at 291C-H, Stamp J rejected an argument that a bank-mortgagee should have realised that the property offered as security had five years earlier been purchased in part with moneys withdrawn by the mortgagor's wife from an account at the very same branch of the very same bank. Stamp J considered that the onus of enquiry urged on behalf of the wife 'would. . .have been more appropriate to a police inquiry or that of a detective agency than to a bank manager who often no doubt arranges finances daily in the ordinary course of business' ([1969] 1 WLR 286 at 292F). Moreover, as Stamp J pointed out, such a duty of enquiry, if once accepted, could not logically be confined to the financial relations of merely the vendor/mortgagor and his spouse. The bank would be obliged to conduct similar research into the bank accounts of the borrower's father and perhaps other relatives ([1969] 1 WLR 286 at 292G).

constructive notice of a wife's beneficial interest merely because the mortgagor had requested the mortgagee to direct all correspondence to him at his business address rather than at the family home.[3]

(ii) The relevance of joint occupation of a family home In the present context it has often been crucial to determine whether a purchaser is fixed with any duty of enquiry as to possible co-ownership interests by virtue merely of the fact that, at the date of the disputed transaction,[4] the vendor/mortgagor shared joint occupation of the property with other persons.[5]

In *Caunce v Caunce*[6] Stamp J declined to accept that a wife's shared occupation of the matrimonial home had been other than 'wholly consistent with the sole title offered by the husband' to a bank as mortgagee. In Stamp J's view the wife had not been 'in apparent occupation or possession' since her presence in the family home was 'ostensibly because she was the husband's wife...' The fact of joint residence was not in itself so remarkable as to cause the bank reasonably to suspect that the wife was in residence in the capacity of a beneficial co-owner as distinct from that merely of a dutiful wife.[7] It followed therefore that the husband's mortgagee was not fixed with constructive notice of her rights merely by reason of a failure to make further enquiries on the premises. Any contrary holding, added Stamp J, would be adverse to the public interest in that bank-mortgagees would be rendered 'snoopers and busybodies in relation to wholly normal transactions of mortgages.'[8]

This restrictive application of the doctrine of notice is, of course, entirely consistent with the hard-nosed conveyancer's view of land law priorities. The conveyancing perspective places a premium on the free commerciability of land, thereby elevating the 'exchange value' of realty in preference to

3 *Northern Bank Ltd v Henry* [1981] IR 1 at 6 per McWilliam J. The point was not taken up by the Supreme Court on appeal, but both McWilliam J and Henchy J in the Supreme Court ([1981] IR 1 at 10) were prepared to hold that a bank was fixed with constructive notice by reason of its 'foolhardy' failure to enquire whether there was any litigation pending or threatened in respect of the property offered as security.

4 The clearest case of constructive notice must arise if, at the date of the transaction, the vendor/mortgagor is not himself in occupation but has left other persons in possession of the premises. Here the purchaser is confronted with 'another party whose presence demands an explanation and whose presence one ignores at one's peril' (*Caunce v Caunce* [1969] 1 WLR 286 at 294A per Stamp J). In such a case the presence of strangers is obviously inconsistent with the sole title ostensibly offered by the legal owner.

5 There is of course a duty in the purchaser to inspect the land as well as the title in respect of which he transacts (ante, p 82), but see *Northern Bank Ltd v Henry* [1981] IR 1 at 6 per McWilliam J (supra, note 3).

6 [1969] 1 WLR 286 at 293G.

7 Stamp J indicated that there might be many other persons whose presence in a family home would be similarly compatible with the sole title ostensibly vested in the vendor. Such persons would include, for instance, 'the vendor's father, his Uncle Harry or his Aunt Matilda, any of whom, be it observed, might have contributed money towards the purchase of the property' ([1969] 1 WLR 286 at 293H). In Stamp J's view, the mere fact of joint residence by any of these persons in the family home would not put a purchaser on enquiry as to the possibility of an undisclosed beneficial entitlement. Compare, however, *Nelthorpe v Holgate* (1844) 1 Collyer 203 at 212, 215, 63 ER 384 at 388f.

8 [1969] 1 WLR 286 at 294D.

its 'use value'.[9] Transactions in land are naturally facilitated by reducing the burden of enquiry imposed on purchasers and by protecting the latter from the claims of undetected beneficial co-owners.[10] The commercialist concern for smooth conveyancing practice can be promoted only by claiming priority over the social interest which favours residential protection for family members.[11]

There is a further dimension to the generally persuasive policy that the burden of enquiry fastened upon purchasers should not be increased save for good cause. It is a cogent fact of economic life that banks and other institutional lenders would not be so ready to lend money on the security of realty if the law were to impose added risks for the bona fide mortgagee.[12] In the older case law it is significant that the money interest was consistently allowed to prevail over the residential interests of family members. The 'solid tug of money',[13] coupled with a pragmatic desire not to inhibit lenders from financing home ownership and entrepreneurial endeavour, has traditionally exerted an hypnotic influence over the determination of priorities in this area.

(iii) The modern application of constructive notice Notwithstanding the traditionally stern approach to the doctrine of constructive notice, recent years have witnessed a more general recognition of the importance of residential security in the family home. Over time this shift in approach has been reflected in the ordering of priorities in the present context.[14] The idea that purchasers might be fixed with a duty of enquiry as to the possible equitable entitlements of resident family members first received significant

9 Ante, p 543. It is the traditional view of the property lawyer that 'where the equities are equal the purchaser should prevail, for the policy of the law is to favour alienability and clean titles' (H.W.R. Wade, [1956] CLJ 216 at 219). See also G. Woodman, (1980) 96 LQR 336 at 340.

10 In *Caunce v Caunce* [1969] 1 WLR 286 at 292H, Stamp J relied heavily on the famous dictum of Lord Upjohn in *National Provincial Bank Ltd v Ainsworth* [1965] AC 1175 at 1233G–1234A, that it 'has been the policy of the law for over a hundred years to simplify and facilitate transactions in real property. It is of great importance that persons should be able freely and easily to raise money on the security of their property' (ante, p 98).

11 The decision in *Caunce v Caunce* [1969] 1 WLR 286 epitomised the inveterate tradition of the property lawyer that it is virtually conclusive of any issue of priority in land law to declare the matter to be essentially a problem of conveyancing or banking practice. It was consistent with this view that the law should tend towards minimising any possible duty of enquiry as to the equitable entitlements of wives and other family members concealed behind statutory trusts. Emphasising that 'the practice of conveyancers carries great weight', Stamp J pointed out 'how unworkable and undesirable it would be if the law required such an enquiry—an enquiry. . .which would be as embarrassing to the enquirer as it would be. . .intolerable to the wife and the husband' ([1969] 1 WLR 286 at 294C).

12 See *Multiservice Bookbinding Ltd v Marden* [1979] Ch 84 at 104H (post, p 961).

13 The phrase is that of Woodhouse J in *Hofman v Hofman* [1965] NZLR 795 at 800.

14 The initial movement away from the approach confirmed in *Caunce v Caunce* came in *Hodgson v Marks* [1971] Ch 892 at 935A (ante, p 216), where Russell LJ declared himself unable to accept a 'general proposition' that enquiry need not be made of any person on the premises if the proposed vendor himself appears to be in occupation. Russell LJ was not, however, prepared to formulate any 'code or catalogue of situations in which a person other than the vendor should be held to be in occupation of unregistered land for the purpose of constructive notice of his rights' ([1971] Ch 892 at 932C-D). The matter must depend on the circumstances, although Russell LJ added ominously that 'a wise purchaser or lender will take no risks'.

support in the Irish jurisdictions.[15] In *Northern Bank Ltd v Henry*,[16] the Irish Supreme Court took the view that 'any person who was offered a title to a matrimonial home by one spouse should have been alerted to the possibility that the other spouse might have a claim. . .to at least a share in the beneficial interest in the property.'[17] This forthright approach almost immediately found a following in the High Court of Northern Ireland.[18]

In *Kingsnorth Finance Co Ltd v Tizard*[19] the English courts finally confirmed this less restrictive approach to constructive notice in the context of co-ownership of unregistered land.[20] Here the legal title in the disputed property was held by a husband on an implied trust for sale for himself and his estranged wife. The home provided a residence for the husband and two children of the family. The wife slept in the house only in the husband's absence and otherwise lived in separate accommodation nearby, usually visiting the home twice a day in order to cook meals for the children. The husband, although merely a sole statutory trustee, secretly charged the legal title to a finance company and then disappeared to America with one of the children, leaving the wife to defend the mortgagee's inevitable action for possession. It appeared that before any charge was taken over the home, the mortgagee's agent had made a pre-arranged visit to the premises on a Sunday afternoon for the purpose of the usual mortgagee's inspection and valuation. It was clear in retrospect that the time of the visit had been fixed by the husband to coincide with the wife's absence from the home and that all signs of her occupation had been 'temporarily eliminated' by the husband.[1] The agent of course discovered evidence of occupation by two teenage children, but was told by the husband that their mother had left the home some time before and lived elsewhere.

On these facts the mortgagee's action for possession was rejected by the High Court. The husband had originally described himself in his loan

15 In England the scope of *Caunce* was cut back in the context of registered land in *Williams & Glyn's Bank Ltd v Boland* [1981] AC 487. Although the House of Lords expressly declined to overrule *Caunce*, Lord Scarman indicated (at 511G) that he himself was 'by no means certain' that the case had been correctly decided. Lord Wilberforce expressed approval (at 505E) of the observations of Russell LJ in *Hodgson v Marks*, and in the Court of Appeal Ormrod LJ ([1979] Ch 312 at 335D) thought that *Caunce* might well be decided differently.

16 [1981] IR 1 (ante, p 565). See R.A. Pearce, *Joint Occupation and the Doctrine of Notice*, (1980) 15 Ir Jur (NS) 211.

17 [1981] IR 1 at 21 per Parkes J. The finding of constructive notice here was prompted in part by the the total failure of the bank-mortgagee to enquire whether persons other than the mortgagor were in occupation of the property. The bank had been 'prepared to take whatever interest in the property the husband had "warts and all"' ([1981] IR 1 at 19). See also *Somers v W* [1979] IR 94 at 111, 114f, where the mere fact that a purchaser knew that she was dealing with a family home was held to be enough to fasten upon her a duty to enquire as to the possible beneficial entitlement of the vendor's wife.

18 See *Allied Irish Banks Ltd v McWilliams* [1982] NI 156 at 161H–162A; *Northern Bank Ltd v Beattie* [1982] 18 NIJB, p 20.

19 [1986] 1 WLR 783. See (1986) 136 NLJ 771 (P. Luxton); [1986] Conv 283 (M.P. Thompson).

20 In *Bristol and West Building Society v Henning* [1985] 1 WLR 778 at 781G, Browne-Wilkinson LJ had already accepted without demur a ruling at first instance that a woman's occupation of the family home could constitute constructive notice of her equitable rights. The case was, however, decided by the Court of Appeal on different grounds (post, p 577).

1 [1986] 1 WLR 783 at 793C.

application as being 'single', and Judge Finlay QC held that the agent's reference in his report to the presence of the children should have alerted the mortgagee to the need to make further enquiry as to the possible rights of a wife.[2] Here the wife had indeed been in 'occupation' of the property in that she had been present 'virtually every day for some part of the day'.[3] The failure to make further enquiry as to her possible entitlements, coupled with a form of inspection which Judge Finlay QC condemned as unsatisfactory,[4] led the court to the conclusion that the mortgagee was fixed with constructive notice of the wife's equitable interest under the trust for sale.[5]

The decision in *Kingsnorth Finance Co Ltd v Tizard* anticipated a more general shift in the courts' application of the constructive notice doctrine in this area. The modern judicial approach recognises that the purchaser of unregistered land is nowadays subject to duty of care to examine the possibility of concealed equitable entitlement on the part of those who share occupation of the land with the vendor.[6] Particularly in the light of parallel developments in the law relating to registered titles, it is now widely acknowledged that failure to make such enquiry almost inevitably precludes the purchaser from disavowing notice of such co-ownership interests as may have lain concealed behind the statutory trust for sale at the date of the relevant disposition.[7]

(d) Registered land

Exactly the same problem of priority which has been discussed in unregistered land terms has posed itself in the law of registered title. The relevant issues reached the House of Lords in 1980 in the conjoined appeals in *Williams*

2 [1986] 1 WLR 783 at 792D.

3 Judge Finlay QC considered that 'occupation' for this purpose did not require 'continuous and uninterrupted presence; such a notion would be absurd'. In this case the relevant 'presence' of the wife was not 'negatived by regular and repeated absence' ([1986] 1 WLR 783 at 788D-E).

4 Judge Finlay QC was not satisfied that in the present circumstances a 'pre-arranged inspection on a Sunday afternoon fell within the category of "such inspections which ought reasonably to have been made," the words in section 199 of the Law of Property Act 1925...' ([1986] 1 WLR 783 at 795B).

5 [1986] 1 WLR 783 at 794E.

6 The duty of care imposed on purchasers does not, however, extend to a duty to inform a beneficial co-owner of prejudicial dealings with the legal title in sufficiently good time to enable her to enlist the aid of the Department of Social Security in keeping up instalments payments under a mortgage. The duty of alert enquiry is not so comprehensive as to penalise the purchaser for lack of vigilance in this respect. See *Equity & Law Home Loans Ltd v Prestidge* [1992] 1 WLR 137 at 144H–145B per Mustill LJ.

7 This trend is now so clear in unregistered land cases that in *Lloyds Bank Plc v Semmakie* [1993] 1 FLR 34 at 42C–D, for instance, counsel simply conceded the issue without argument. Scott LJ had no doubt that this concession was correct, noting that recent developments had caused it to be 'brought home to banks, building societies and other mortgagees that a wife in occupation of a matrimonial home might have an equitable interest which by constructive notice might become binding on mortgagees or other purchasers from her husband, the legal owner.' See also *City of London Building Society v Flegg* [1988] AC 54 at 81D, where Lord Oliver of Aylmerton readily conceded that enjoyment of land 'in specie' could 'serve to give notice to third parties of the occupier's interest under the trust'.

& Glyn's Bank Ltd v Boland and *Williams & Glyn's Bank Ltd v Brown.*[8] Both cases concerned the question whether a wife-beneficiary under an implied trust for sale could claim priority over a bank to which her husband had charged the family home by way of legal mortgage as security for a business loan (see *Fig.* 44). In both cases it was alleged (and generally accepted) that the wife had acquired an equitable share in the home by reason of her past financial contributions towards its purchase. It was likewise common ground that in neither case had the bank made any enquiry of the wife before advancing the mortgage moneys to her husband; each wife claimed that she had had no contemporary knowledge of the creation of the mortgage charge. It was also painfully clear that neither wife had protected any entitlement by appropriate entry against her husband's registered title.[9] It therefore followed that the issue of priority against the bank wholly depended on whether the equitable proprietary interest of a wife-beneficiary under a trust for sale could rank as an overriding interest pursuant to section 70(1)(g) of the Land Registration Act 1925.[10]

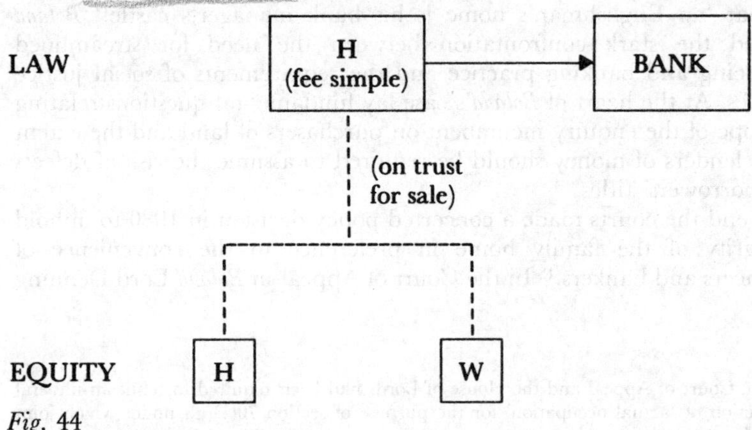

Fig. 44

To this question the House of Lords gave an affirmative answer.[11] The House held that in the absence of enquiry an equitable co-owner 'in actual

8 [1981] AC 487 (hereafter referred to collectively as *Boland*).

9 In *Boland* W could, by timely intervention, have protected *two* kinds of entitlement by entry on the register of H's title. She could have entered her equitable proprietary interest as a minor interest (ante, p 182); she could similarly have protected her spousal 'rights of occupation' under the Matrimonial Homes Act (ante, p 183). For lack of entry in the register both of these entitlements were rendered entirely ineffective against the bank-mortgagee unless they could provide the basis for an 'overriding interest' under section 70(1)(g) of the Land Registration Act 1925 (see Land Registration Act 1925, ss 20(1), 59(6)).

10 Spousal 'rights of occupation' under the Matrimonial Homes Act can never rank as an overriding interest (see Matrimonial Homes Act 1967, s 2(7), now Matrimonial Homes Act 1983, s 2(8)(b) (ante, p 211)).

11 The plaintiff bank had succeeded in its action for possession before Templeman J ((1978) 36 P & CR 448), only to lose in the Court of Appeal ([1979] Ch 312) and the House of Lords ([1981] AC 487). On the Court of Appeal's ruling, see [1979] Conv 377 (F.R. Crane); (1979) 42 MLR 567 (W.T. Murphy); [1979] CLJ 254 (M.J. Prichard); (1979) 95 LQR 501 (R.J. Smith); (1979) 129 NLJ 700 (H.W. Wilkinson). On the House of Lords' decision, see (1980) 43 MLR 692 (S. Freeman); [1980] Conv 361 (J. Martin); [1980] CLJ 243 (M.J. Prichard); (1981) 97 LQR 12 (R.J. Smith); (1980) 130 NLJ 896 (R.L. Deech).

occupation'[12] behind an implied trust for sale of the family home has an overriding interest binding those who unwittingly deal with the sole trustee for sale.[13] Since in *Boland* the right which thus became 'overriding' was the right of occupation carried by an equitable interest under a trust for sale,[14] the bank was held to be unable to exercise the mortgagee's normal right to recover possession of the property for the purpose of selling up and recouping the outstanding loan. This decision has not only clarified the law of registered land but has had a profound collateral effect in coercing the law of unregistered land towards a parallel conclusion.

(i) Reversal of the traditional property perspective The *Boland* decision was remarkable in that it reversed almost an entire ideology concerning property and financial relations in the context of the family home. Until *Boland* the courts had fairly consistently endorsed the view that those who lend money expect to be repaid in full even if that means that wives and families must be evicted from their homes—a view somewhat crudely expressed in the adage that 'an Englishman's home is his bank manager's castle!' *Boland* symbolised the stark confrontation between the need for streamlined conveyancing and banking practice and the requirements of social justice for families. At the heart of *Boland*'s case lay fundamental questions relating to the scope of the enquiry incumbent on purchasers of land and the extent to which lenders of money should be required to assume the risk of defects in their borrowers' titles.

In the end the courts made a concerted policy decision in 1980 to uphold the integrity of the family home in preference to the convenience of conveyancers and bankers.[15] In the Court of Appeal in *Boland* Lord Denning

12 Both the Court of Appeal and the House of Lords had been required to rebut an illiberal construction of 'actual occupation' for the purpose of section 70(1)(g), under which joint occupation of land—even by a spouse—was discounted as 'only. . .a shadow of occupation of the owner' (ante, p 222). As Lord Denning MR observed of the matrimonial homes in *Boland* [1979] Ch 312 at 332D-E, 'Visit the home and you will find that [the wife] is in personal occupation of it just as much as [the husband] is. She eats there and sleeps there just as he does. She is in control of all that goes on there—just as much as he. In no respect whatever does the nature of her occupation differ from his. . .'

13 The relevant principles of registered land law do not in general depend on whether the parties involved are married or related by family connection (see *Williams & Glyn's Bank Ltd v Boland* [1981] AC 487 at 502F per Lord Wilberforce). As Ormrod LJ pointed out in the Court of Appeal in *Boland*, the appellant wives were 'relying not upon their position as married women, but upon their property rights as ordinary citizens.' It was purely 'incidental' that the wives were married to the persons in whom the legal estate was vested ([1979] Ch 312 at 333D-E).

14 Ante, p 549. It has been seen elsewhere (ante, p 545), that one of the major obstacles in the way of an affirmative outcome was removed fairly early in the *Boland* litigation. It was accepted by all concerned that, despite the doctrine of conversion, an equitable interest behind a trust for sale is a right subsisting in reference to land in a sense sufficient to satisfy the definitional requirements of Land Registration Act 1925, s 70(1).

15 In *Boland* [1979] Ch 312 at 332H–333A, Lord Denning MR even went so far as to fasten an obligation of social morality upon institutional lenders: 'If a bank is to do its duty, in the society in which we live, it should recognise the integrity of the matrimonial home. It should not destroy it by disregarding the wife's interest in it—simply to ensure that it is paid the husband's debt in full—with the high interest rate now prevailing'. It is perhaps significant that in *Boland* the bank had sanctioned a sale of the mortgagor's property (valued at £22,500) for merely £1,500 ((1978) 36 P & CR 448 at 450f).

MR declared that the courts 'should not give monied might priority over social justice'.[16] He did not see that this new approach would cause any difficulty to conveyancers[17] or impair the proper conduct of businesses,[18] since

> [a]nyone who lends money on the security of a matrimonial home nowadays ought to realise that the wife may have a share in it. He ought to make sure that the wife agrees to it, or to go to the house and make inquiries of her. It seems to me utterly wrong that a lender should turn a blind eye to the wife's interest or the possibility of it—and afterwards seek to turn her and the family out—on the plea that he did not know she was in actual occupation.[19]

The House of Lords unanimously confirmed this relegation of the commercial interest of the bank-mortgagee behind the claim to family security. Lord Wilberforce acknowledged that this 'extension of the risk area' for purchasers might 'add to the burdens of purchasers, and involve them in enquiries which in some cases may be troublesome.'[20] He was not, however, unhappy to see a 'departure from an easy-going practice of dispensing with enquiries as to occupation beyond that of the vendor and accepting the risks of doing so.'[1] The intensification of the duty of enquiry was simply the inevitable concomitant of 'the widespread development of shared interests of ownership.'[2]

In practice the *Boland* ruling marked what promised to be a significant shift in the balance of risk between owners and lenders, leaving it to the latter to adopt means of self-protection. This adjustment was, moreover,

16 [1979] Ch 312 at 333A. In his view the bank was 'not entitled to throw these families out into the street—simply to get the last penny of the husband's debt' ([1979] Ch 312 at 333C).

17 See the comparable remarks of Lord Denning MR in *Brikom Investments Ltd v Carr* [1979] QB 467 at 484F: 'I prefer to see that justice is done: and let the conveyancers look after themselves'.

18 The husbands in *Boland* were both small businessmen who had gone bankrupt when Williams & Glyn's called in their respective loans. It was therefore particularly unfortunate that Williams & Glyn's chose 1979 to run a series of advertisements in the national press containing such announcements as 'Williams & Glyn's believes businesses should make their bank managers work harder for them. . .Call in and see your local Williams & Glyn's manager soon. You've nothing to lose. . .' (*Guardian*, 12 July 1979). A certain piquancy attached to the Bank's assurance (*Guardian*, 8 May 1979) that 'Williams & Glyn's believes small businesses deserve all the help a bank can give. . .we encourage managers to visit customers on their home ground. . .That's a higher degree of commitment than many banks undertake. But then Williams & Glyn's Bank is a rather different kind of bank. . .' The propensity of Williams & Glyn's Bank to call in business loans at short notice became the subject of considerable concern in 1979 (see *Economist*, 5-11 May 1979). However, in *Williams & Glyn's Bank Ltd v Barnes* [1981] Com LR 205, Gibson J upheld the bank's claim that money lent on overdraft is prima facie repayable on demand.

19 [1979] Ch 312 at 332G. See also Ormrod LJ (at 339B-C).

20 [1981] AC 487 at 508G.

1 [1981] AC 487 at 508H.

2 An even more robust unconcern for the protests of conveyancers emerged in the speech of Lord Scarman, who thought that the alleged difficulties in conveyancing and banking practice had been 'exaggerated'. In his view, 'bankers and solicitors exist to provide the service which the public needs. They can—as they have successfully done in the past—adjust their practice, if it be socially required' ([1981] AC 487 at 510B-C).

underpinned by strong judicial references to the rhetoric of social justice.[3] The decision in *Boland* was, at its roots, a statement of social ethics about the importance of providing security for the family—and in particular the married woman—in occupation of the family home.[4] In *Boland* the House of Lords effectively traded off protection for the bank against what was then perceived to be a higher social interest.

(ii) Criticism of the Boland ruling Nothwithstanding the powerful appeal to wide sentiments of social justice, the correctness of the *Boland* decision has since been questioned in both moral and practical terms.[5] Quite apart from the danger of collusive and fabricated claims of equitable co-ownership,[6] it remains at least dubious whether the wives in *Boland* should have been allowed to enjoy the prospects of their husbands' business prosperity, while retaining an immunity from the shared misfortune of their adversity.[7] More specifically, it is extremely questionable whether a beneficial co-owner deserves protection if he or she has failed to take advantage of the freely available protection provided by registration.[8] The *Boland* ruling demonstrates in a peculiarly direct way that reliance can no longer be placed on an apparently unencumbered legal title as recorded in the Land Register.[9] The purchaser of registered land must at his own risk take steps to prove a negative—that is, satisfy himself by means of further inspection and

3 In Lord Scarman's view, the 'achievement of social justice' now required that the courts give a meaning to section 70(1)(g) which militated in favour of, and not against, the preservation of those rights of co-ownership in the family home which the courts have come to recognise over the past three decades as having been earned by various kinds of family member ([1981] AC 487 at 510B-C).

4 See eg the extra-judicial statement by Lord Simon of Glaisdale that, although many of the issues were 'highly technical', running through the judgments in *Boland* was 'a strong sense of the social issues that were involved' (*Parliamentary Debates, House of Lords, Official Report*, Vol 437 (Session 1982-1983), Col 641 (15 December 1982)).

5 Even Lord Wilberforce was to confess, in an extra-judicial statement in 1985, that he had subsequently 'had some misgivings about whether or not we were right' in *Boland* (see *Parliamentary Debates, House of Lords, Official Report*, Vol 460 (Session 1984-85), Col 1271 (5 March 1985)). See also the bitter reproach delivered by Lord Templeman in *Winkworth v Edward Baron Development Co Ltd* [1986] 1 WLR 1512 at 1515C, although compare *Parliamentary Debates, House of Lords, Official Report*, Vol 437 (Session 1982-1983), Col 649 (15 December 1982).

6 Post, p 575. The wives in *Boland* were not locked in mortal matrimonial combat with their respective husbands. Rather it was the case that each husband was seeking grimly to hang on to the family home by opposing against the bank his wife's alleged equitable interest under a statutory trust for sale. The Law Commission has pointed to the danger that 'occupiers' rights may often be invoked primarily to frustrate proceedings brought by a mortgagee against the legal owner, as in fact they were in *Boland* itself' (Law Com No 115, para 30).

7 There is a powerful argument that the risks inherent in the pursuit of a financial enterprise are not fairly susceptible of a narrower allocation than its benefits (see *European Asian of Australia Ltd v Kurland* (1985) 8 NSWLR 192 at 200F per Rogers J).

8 One of the bank's counsel, Robert Reid QC, was later to condemn the decision in *Boland* as 'one of the furthest extensions of what is sometimes called "The Nanny State"; that is the state in which people are presumed incapable of taking any coherent decision for themselves about any important matter' (see *Williams & Glyn's Bank Ltd v Boland: Report of a Conference on Problems of Conflict of Interest in the Matrimonial Home* (1981), p 26).

9 The bank in *Boland* was surely entitled to wonder why, having dutifully searched the register of title, it lost priority to two wives who had wholly failed to protect any of their respective entitlements by entry in that register (ante, p 569).

enquiry that no overriding interest will impinge upon the title which he takes.[10] The imposition of such an onerous duty militates heavily against the traditionally vigorous preference of English land law for the protection of purchasers.[11]

It is little wonder that in *Boland* counsel for the bank expressed the view that the banking world desired and needed 'a workable system',[12] and that this goal would be made quite unattainable if lenders (and other purchasers) were required to make comprehensive and intrusive enquiries in every case.[13] Yet, as Lord Hailsham LC has since pointed out, it is patently undeniable that contrary to the predictions of conveyancers 'the world has not come to an end as a result of the decision in *Boland*'.[14] If a reason be sought, it lies in the way in which silently but surely the original *Boland* principle has been eroded during the past decade almost to the point of extinction.[15]

(e) Subsequent erosion of the Boland principle

In view of the intensification of risk for purchasers signalled in *Boland*, considerable energy has been invested by conveyancers in seeking ways

10 The range of persons who may claim such interests is considerable. As Lord Wilberforce indicated in *Williams & Glyn's Bank Ltd v Boland* [1981] AC 487 at 508F, the class of protected co-ownership interests extends beyond that of the spouse to include the rights of 'other members of the family or even outside it' (see also [1979] Ch 312 at 333F per Ormrod LJ). Lord Wilberforce envisaged that overriding interests could easily arise in 'the case of a man living with a mistress, or of a man and a woman—or for that matter two persons of the same sex—living in a house in separate or partially shared rooms' ([1981] AC 487 at 506B). Enquiry may have to be made of many kinds of domestic *ménage* (each of possibly intermittent or discontinuous quality) such as those involving homosexual partners, 'old cronies', platonic friends, and polygamous spouses. That property problems can and do arise within such unorthodox domestic relationships is well illustrated in *Philip Lowe (Chinese Restaurant) Ltd v Sau Man Lee* (Unreported, Court of Appeal, 9 July 1985) (ante, p 434).

11 Even the Law Commission, for some three decades the firmest advocate of family property rights, was moved to remark that *Boland*, while consistent with the 'current social policy which favours the protection of the wife in the matrimonial home', is inconsistent with 'the policy of property law which upholds the security of titles, the marketability of land and the simplification of conveyancing' (Law Com No 115, para 70).

12 The reaction to *Boland* from the banking and conveyancing world was predictably fierce. See eg *Times*, 24 June 1980 (letter from Derek Wheatley, Legal Adviser, Lloyds Bank Head Office). Speaking extra-judicially in 1982, Lord Templeman observed that 'no one has great sympathy for lenders or banks but the point is that at the end of the day it is the borrower who pays, unless there is some speedy and efficient method of conveyancing' (see *Parliamentary Debates, House of Lords, Official Report*, Vol 437 (Session 1982–1983), Col 650 (15 December 1982)).

13 [1981] AC 487 at 502C. Indeed, so anxious was the bank to obtain a declaratory ruling from the House of Lords in support of a 'workable system' that the bank undertook, in the event of a favourable judgment, not to pursue any order for possession against the respondent wives.

14 *Parliamentary Debates, House of Lords, Official Report*, Vol 437 (Session 1982–1983), Col 662 (15 December 1982).

15 This reaction against *Boland* merely realigns English law with that of other jurisdictions, where by contrast the courts have not afforded spouses protection against third parties who take a mortgage charge from the legal owner of the family home (see eg *Royal Bank of Canada v Nicholson* (1981) 112 DLR (3d) 364 at 367; *Containercare (Ireland) Ltd v Wycherley* [1982] IR 143 at 153). An Australian commentator has said that 'it would be striking at the most basic tenets of the Torrens system' to apply in the *Boland* situation any of the statutory exceptions to the Torrens principle of indefeasibility of title (see P. Butt, *Conveyancing and the Rights of Persons in Occupation*, (1981) 55 ALJ 119 at 123).

to minimise the hazards posed by undisclosed co-ownership interests in both registered and unregistered land. During recent years a mixture of means—some highly pragmatic, some judge-made—has been developed in order to cut back the scope of the *Boland* principle or, as it is sometimes put in practice, in order to 'capture the *Boland* interest'.[16]

(i) Enquiry of the vendor/mortgagor While enquiry made directly of a vendor/mortgagor cannot in itself neutralise the adverse rights of occupiers under section 70(1)(g),[17] such an enquiry, if answered both honestly and accurately,[18] will resolve the difficulties exposed by *Boland*.[19] The purchaser is put in a position to make separate approaches to each person named by the vendor/mortgagor in order to extract a release of his or her rights.[20]

(ii) Requirement of express waiver or consent from putative beneficiaries If the purchaser is aware of the identity of other persons in actual occupation of the land in question,[1] it is open to him to seek from these persons an express waiver of rights or consent to the transaction in hand.[2] Such waiver or consent can be made a condition *sine qua non* of the transaction and will preclude any future claim that an occupier has a beneficial co-ownership interest which enjoys priority over the purchaser.[3]

The participation of putative co-owners may, however, contain a latent danger for a mortgagee. There is a possibility that an occupier who supplies

16 See *Northern Bank Ltd v Gracey* (Unreported, High Court of Northern Ireland, 6 September 1991) per Campbell J. For reference to the fearsome 'Wagbol', see [1981] Conv 17.

17 Misleading or dishonest representations made by the vendor/mortgagor cannot operate to the prejudice of the rights of any equitable co-owner whose entitlement has not been disclosed. See *Hodgson v Marks* [1971] Ch 892 at 932D per Russell LJ (ante, p 224). The Law Commission has dismissed the suggestion that a declaration by the vendor should be statutorily deemed conclusive as to the existence or non-existence of co-ownership rights (Law Com No 115, Appendix 2, paras 21ff).

18 The purchaser may have a remedy in either contract or tort in respect of a misrepresentation made by the vendor, but an award of damages will be of little avail to a mortgagee if the only asset from which such an award might be satisfied is the property subject to the mortgage. This property may well have been rendered unsaleable by reason of the adverse claim of the beneficial co-owner.

19 See R.J. Smith, (1979) 95 LQR 501 at 505; [1980] Conv 85, but compare [1980] Conv 311, 313. See also Law Com No 115, Appendix 2, para 15. Vendors are normally asked in the standard Preliminary Enquiries before contract to give the full names, and ages if under 18, of all persons, other than the vendor, in actual occupation of the property.

20 Infra.

1 Physical inspection of the premises prior to completion of the transaction, while advisable, is not necessarily conclusive in favour of the purchaser and may not be realistic in the context of 'chain' transactions of sale and purchase (see Law Com No 115, paras 39f). Such an inspection may not detect all the existing occupiers and, in any event, new occupiers may arrive during the period between the inspection and the effective date of the transaction (ante, p 204).

2 In the case of a mortgage of the legal estate, this is most effectively achieved by requiring any putative beneficial co-owner to join with the sole legal owner in executing the mortgage charge. A variant on this tactic is the requirement that a putative beneficial co-owner sign a licence agreement acknowledging that his or her occupation of the land arises merely by licence (ante, p 208) and not by way of beneficial entitlement (see *Kemmis v Kemmis* [1988] 1 WLR 1307 at 1335B-C per Nourse LJ).

3 However, the release of rights operates only as against the purchaser; the rights remain intact as against the legal owner or against the proceeds of sale in his hands.

a waiver or consent may subsequently claim that he or she was the victim of undue influence and that his or her participation in the transaction is therefore vitiated.[4] In order to be unimpeachable, any waiver or consent signed by a putative co-owner should stipulate expressly and unambiguously its legal effect on such rights as the signatory may have.[5] If this is done, it is unlikely that the consent can be set aside on the ground that a purchaser such as a bank-mortgagee has exerted undue influence over the signatory.[6] Moreover, in *National Westminster Bank Plc v Morgan*,[7] the House of Lords reaffirmed that in the context of 'an ordinary banking transaction' a bank has no duty to ensure that independent legal advice is received by a wife who joins in a mortgage of the matrimonial home.[8]

(iii) Strict proof of beneficial entitlement It has become increasingly common for purchasers, when confronted by a party claiming rights as an equitable co-owner, to demand strict proof of the supposed equitable entitlement. Priority over the purchaser can be obtained only if there is in fact beneficial co-ownership of the land in question.[9] Often the only evidence of the origin of a statutory trust for sale lies in vague, unsubstantiated, self-serving and possibly even collusive claims of financial contribution towards a purchase many years before.[10] In many cases there is clearly a fear that a successful

4 The law relating to the setting aside of unconscionable bargains is discussed elsewhere (ante, p 276). Referring specifically to the cases of the mentally infirm and persons under the age of 18, the Law Commission has pointed out that some occupiers may be legally incapable of giving a valid consent to a release of their rights (see Law Com No 115, para 42(i)(b)).

5 See *Zamet v Hyman* [1961] 1 WLR 1442 at 1446 per Lord Evershed MR. In *Midland Bank Ltd v Goodall* (CA Unbound Transcript 1064, 1 November 1983), the Court of Appeal held, slightly unsatisfactorily, that such duty as a bank may have was fully satisfied by the inclusion in the letter of consent signed by the mortgagor's wife of a printed warning that the document 'should be signed only after consulting a Solicitor or other professional adviser'.

6 In *National Westminster Bank Plc v Morgan* [1985] AC 686, the House of Lords disapproved the view expressed by Lord Denning MR in *Lloyds Bank Ltd v Bundy* [1975] QB 326 at 339C that a presumption of undue influence, arising from 'inequality of bargaining power', exists between banker and customer. See C.J. Barton and P.M. Rank, *Undue Influence—A Retreat?*, [1985] Conv 387.

7 [1985] AC 686 at 709D per Lord Scarman (post, p 968). It is noteworthy that other jurisdictions have been generally unsympathetic to the suggestion that a bank has a duty to ensure that a wife should receive independent professional advice before guaranteeing her husband's mortgage debt (see eg *Royal Bank of Canada v Poisson* (1980) 103 DLR (3d) 735 at 738).

8 A mortgagee may have a special duty to insist that independent advice is obtained where the circumstances are such that a husband-mortgagor himself 'could be expected to have influence over' the signatory of the consent (see *Kings North Trust Ltd v Bell* [1986] 1 WLR 119 at 124C, 125A-B (post, p 971)). See also the fairly strict requirement of legal advice imposed by the High Court of Australia in *Bank of New Zealand v Rogers* (1941) 65 CLR 42 at 87.

9 *Williams & Glyn's Bank Ltd v Boland* itself concerned a preliminary point of law and it was therefore assumed for this purpose that W was entitled as an equitable co-owner behind a trust for sale.

10 See *Midland Bank PLC v Dobson* [1986] 1 FLR 171 at 174D, where Fox LJ observed that 'assertions made by a husband and wife as to a common intention formed 30 years ago regarding joint ownership, of which there is no contemporary evidence and which happens to accommodate their current need to defeat the claims of a creditor, must be received by the courts with caution.' Compare *Knightly v Sun Life Assurance Society Ltd* (1981) *Times*, 23 July, where a wife-mortgagor sought—unsuccessfully—to assert a beneficial entitlement on behalf of her husband who had no wish to be involved in the instant litigation and who maintained throughout that he had no equitable interest in the mortgaged property.

fabrication of joint financial contribution may enable an insolvent husband to save his matrimonial home from the hands of his creditors under cover of a fictitious beneficial interest claimed on behalf of his wife.[11] Accordingly it is entirely predictable that the purchaser's first line of attack should be a full-frontal assault on the existence of the claimed equitable entitlement. It was precisely the denial of such entitlement which devastated the assertion made by the defendant wife in *Lloyds Bank Plc v Rosset*[12] that she had an overriding interest binding upon her husband's mortgagee.[13]

(iv) Application of estoppel doctrine One of the more disarming contentions advanced on behalf of purchasers rests on a new judicial willingness to apply something akin to a doctrine of estoppel against beneficial co-owners of the family home. The courts have shown themselves disinclined to allow a beneficial co-owner deliberately to remain silent about his or her equitable rights at the date of the relevant transaction,[14] only to assert those rights later as having priority over the third party who dealt in good faith with the legal owner.[15] In such circumstances the owner of the undisclosed rights cannot be heard conscionably to raise these rights in derogation of an interest or security taken by the purchaser from a sole trustee for sale.[16]

In applying the doctrine of estoppel to security transactions with the family home, the courts have drawn a necessary distinction between those cases in which a husband has negotiated a mortgage without the knowledge of the wife-beneficiary and those cases in which the beneficial co-owner has been fully aware of the transaction and its importance for the family.[17] In

11 See eg *Williams & Glyn's Bank Ltd v Boland* (1978) 36 P & CR 448 at 454, where at first instance Templeman J was careful to say merely that the wife 'claimed' to have made the cash contributions which supposedly generated a statutory trust of the husband's legal title. Templeman J was also acutely aware that it would make a nonsense of the Matrimonial Homes Act if the spouse of a legal owner 'could say or allege at any time that he or she had contributed to the purchase price', thereby founding her protection on an overriding interest rather than on plainly unregistered spousal 'rights of occupation'.

12 [1991] 1 AC 107 at 134A-B per Lord Bridge of Harwich.

13 This line of attack has been used successfully in relation to both unregistered land (see *Midland Bank PLC v Dobson* [1986] 1 FLR 171 at 177G) and registered land (see *Anglia Building Society v Lewis* (Unreported, Court of Appeal, No 8008681, 29 January 1982); *Anand v Gill* [1983] CA Bound Transcript 302).

14 On the role of representation by silence in the law of estoppel, see Chapter 11 (ante, p 312). It is certainly questionable whether an estoppel of this kind can be raised if the purchaser merely informs an occupier that it will be assumed, in the absence of reply within seven days, that the latter claims no adverse interest in the property (but see J. Russell, (1981) 32 NILQ 3 at 21).

15 The force of this estoppel doctrine is merely intensified if the original silence as to equitable entitlement was calculated to induce the third party to enter into a transaction in which he would not otherwise have engaged.

16 See eg *Midland Bank Ltd v Farmpride Hatcheries Ltd* (1981) 260 Estates Gazette 493 at 497 per Shaw LJ, 498f per Oliver LJ. It has been suggested that a wife of the legal owner might be estopped from asserting her rights against a purchaser if she appeared to acquiesce in the sale, for example by showing the purchaser around the house and encouraging him in expenditure (see [1980] Conv 361 at 368 (J. Martin); *Spiro v Lintern* [1973] 1 WLR 1002 at 1013B-D). Compare *Hodgson v Marks* [1971] Ch 892 at 934A (resulting trust).

17 Ante, p 215 (note 6). For explicit reference to this distinction, see *Anglia Building Society v Lewis* (Unreported, Court of Appeal, No 8008681, 29 January 1982) per Dunn LJ; *Paddington Building Society v Mendelsohn* (1985) 50 P & CR 244 at 248f per Browne-Wilkinson LJ.

the former category of case the courts have not penalised the undisclosed beneficiary for her silence.[18] However, in cases falling within the latter category, the courts have been all too ready to disallow any claim by family members to override the priority apparently conferred by a mortgage upon a third party.[19] The courts have taken the view that wilful non-disclosure of an interest capable of undermining the security offered 'would be conduct which would leave the owner of the equitable interest open to the charge of coming to the court with hands that were not clean.'[20] In circumstances of this kind, the equitable owner is estopped from claiming priority: any other approach is 'unarguable' and 'would go near to saying that our system of conveyancing permits a mortgagor to obtain money under a false pretence.'[1]

The application of the estoppel approach has seriously curtailed the scope both of constructive notice in unregistered land and of overriding interests in the registered land context. In *Paddington Building Society v Mendelsohn*,[2] the Court of Appeal made it clear that section 70(1)(g) of the Land Registration Act 1925 provides protection only to those rights which, by their 'inherent quality', are enforceable rights at the date of the relevant disposition.[3] In *Mendelsohn*'s case an equitable co-owner was deemed, by non-disclosure of her rights to a mortgagee, to have conceded priority to the latter.[4] In *Equity & Law Home Loans Ltd v Prestidge*[5] this approach was extended to defeat the equitable claim of a mortgagor's wife who had certainly known of the existence of an acquisition mortgage, but who was wholly unaware that

18 Ante, p 215. The foremost example within this category is *Williams & Glyn's Bank Ltd v Boland* [1981] AC 487. See also *Winkworth v Edward Baron Development Co Ltd* (1986) 52 P & CR 67 at 77 (reversed on other grounds [1986] 1 WLR 1512, ante, p 444); *Equity & Law Home Loans Ltd v Prestidge* [1992] 1 WLR 137 at 144A.

19 See *Knightly v Sun Life Assurance Society Ltd* (1981) *Times*, 23 July; *Bristol and West Building Society v Henning* [1985] 1 WLR 778 at 782G, 783C. In *Ulster Bank Ltd v Shanks* [1982] NI 143 at 150A, it was considered highly relevant that the wife-beneficiary had been present during at least part of the negotiations between the husband-mortgagor and the bank manager.

20 *Ulster Bank Ltd v Shanks* [1982] NI 143 at 150D per Murray J. Likewise Browne-Wilkinson LJ declared in *Bristol and West Building Society v Henning* [1985] 1 WLR 778 at 782G that he 'would not impute to the parties an intention to mislead the society by purporting to offer the unencumbered fee simple of the property as security when in fact there was to be an equitable interest which would take priority to the society.' See (1986) 49 MLR 245 (M.P. Thompson).

1 *Knightly v Sun Life Assurance Society Ltd* (1981) *Times*, 23 July per Nourse J. Compare *Bristol and West Building Society v Henning* [1985] 1 WLR 778 at 781G–782A, where Browne-Wilkinson LJ observed that there was a 'risk that the common sense answer in this case may get lost in the many different technicalities which can arise. The basic fact is that the mortgage was granted to the society with the full knowledge and approval of Mrs Henning.' The judge noted that the 'logical result' of the wife's argument claiming priority was that she would be 'entitled to stay in possession indefinitely without making any payment. That would be a strange result which I would be reluctant to reach.'

2 (1985) 50 P & CR 244 at 248.

3 Ante, p 214.

4 Accordingly the Court held ((1985) 50 P & CR 244 at 248f) that her rights were no longer enforceable rights at the date of registration of the mortgage charge, even though she remained 'in actual occupation' of the family home. Her equitable rights never came within the threshold of section 70(1)(g). Nowadays, since *Mendelsohn*'s case involved an acquisition mortgage, her rights would also be defeated on the ground that no *scintilla temporis* intervened before the creation of such a mortgage (ante, p 215, post, p 979).

5 [1992] 1 WLR 137 at 143H–145B. See [1992] Conv 206 (M.P. Thompson).

this mortgage had later been replaced by a new mortgage covering an even larger loan advanced to her husband.[6] In this context, said Mustill LJ, the wife's beneficial interest was one 'which from the outset had carved out of it by anticipation a recognition of the rights of the mortgagees whose finance was intended to bring the purchase into being.'[7]

The net effect of the estoppel approach is to suspend the 'general philosophy of the decision of the House of Lords in *Williams & Glyn's Bank Ltd v Boland*'[8] in the case of the beneficial co-owner who has knowledge of (and therefore gives a deemed consent to) any dealing effected by a sole trustee for sale. Such an exclusion dramatically limits the application of *Boland* and it is questionable whether this erosion of the integrity of family property rights is truly justifiable in the name of estoppel or implied waiver.[9] Be that as it may, the present concern has now been heavily submerged in a more recent and even more drastic circumscription of the *Boland* principle.

(v) Denial of the scintilla temporis The decision of the House of Lords in *Abbey National Building Society v Cann,*[10] by eliminating the effect of the *scintilla temporis* in the creation of acquisition mortgages, has also indirectly destroyed any possibility that financial contributors towards a purchase may ever claim priority over the mortgagee in respect of their beneficial co-ownership interests. This implication of *Cann*'s case applies irrespective of any knowledge on the part of the beneficiaries behind the trust for sale that the acquisition depended vitally on mortgage finance. All that the title-holder receives on acquisition is an equity of redemption, and it is upon this already limited interest that any implied trust for sale is engrafted. By definition the beneficial interests of co-owners, being carved out of the attenuated rights of the legal owner, must be postponed to the security taken by the mortgagee.

(vi) Requirement of joint conveyance or mortgage It is clear that, somewhat as a last resort, a purchaser dealing with land which may be held on an implied trust for sale can obtain an unimpeachable title simply by insisting on taking a joint conveyance or mortgage.[11] In dealing explicitly with two

6 The wife's imputed consent to the first mortgage 'must, in common sense, apply to the creation of a new encumbrance in replacement of the old, whether [the wife] knew about it or not, provided that it did not change [her] position for the worse' ([1992] 1 WLR 137 at 144B per Mustill LJ). Thus even an undisclosed re-mortgage in the *same* amount would still have the effect of postponing the wife's equitable claim to that of the mortgagee ([1992] 1 WLR 137 at 143G-H).

7 [1992] 1 WLR 137 at 145D. Mustill LJ did, however, concede (at 144G) that the mortgagee should not be able to enforce its security against the wife in any sum larger than that of the original mortgage advance.

8 The phrase is that of Nourse LJ in *Kemmis v Kemmis* [1988] 1 WLR 1307 at 1335A-B.

9 Land Registration Act 1925, s 70(1)(g) appears, for instance, to embody a broad assumption that a purchaser will make enquiry of potential claimants of an overriding interest. See [1985] CLJ 354 (M. Welstead).

10 [1991] 1 AC 56 (ante, pp 205, 562, post, p 975).

11 This rather desperate expedient is not without precedent in the law of real property, since this solution was commonly applied to remove doubt about possible severances under a joint title before the enactment of the Law of Property (Joint Tenants) Act 1964 (ante, p 516). See [1980] Conv 458.

trustees, the purchaser is automatically assured that any sale or mortgage will overreach any equitable interests otherwise asserted by putative co-owners hidden behind an implied trust.[12] This mode of protection for the purchaser is not particularly apt to evoke enthusiastic participation from the vendor,[13] who is put to the inconvenience and expense of finding a second legal owner.[14]

(vii) Insurance An alternative way of freeing purchasers from the hazard represented by adverse equitable rights in the family home lies in the device of insurance.[15] In the area of mortgage transactions some insurance companies now offer a scheme under which the insurer contracts to take over the security, together with a transfer of the lender's mortgage, if an equitable owner emerges to assert binding rights against the mortgagee.[16]

(viii) Bankruptcy The ultimate recourse for a mortgagee who is trapped by undisclosed co-ownership interests may lie in forcing a bankruptcy. The mortgagor, if sued by the mortgagee on the repayment covenant contained in the mortgage, may be made bankrupt. The mortgagor's trustee in bankruptcy then has locus standi to apply under section 30 of the Law of Property Act 1925 for a sale of the property concerned.[17] Under the provisions of the Insolvency Act 1986 it is extremely unlikely that the court will postpone sale for more than a limited period of perhaps one year.[18] At this point the property must be sold up, releasing the cash value of the mortgagor's equitable share in at least partial satisfaction of the mortgage debt.[19]

In these circumstances the mere fact that another beneficial owner has a binding or 'overriding' interest in the property does not preclude the possibility of sale at the behest of the trustee in bankruptcy. The binding or 'overriding' nature of such an interest means not that a sale can be resisted, but only that the owner of the binding or 'overriding' interest is entitled

12 See *City of London Building Society v Flegg* [1988] AC 54 (ante, p 555). Overreaching effect will be achieved under the Law of Property Act 1925, s 2(1)(ii), even though a disposition made without due consultation (see Law of Property Act 1925, s 26(3)) will constitute a breach of trust giving rise at least in theory to a remedy in damages.

13 See Law Com No 115, para 42(ii). See, however, the suggestion by Nourse LJ in *Owen v Williams* (Unreported, Court of Appeal, 21 November 1985) that the appointment of a second trustee for sale was 'the obvious way out' of the difficulties apparent in that case.

14 See the Law Commission's proposal of statutory 'trusteeship rights' for spouses (ante, p 539).

15 It is significant that in *Williams & Glyn's Bank Ltd v Boland* [1979] Ch 312 at 332H-333A, Lord Denning MR seemed to regard the 'high interest rate now prevailing' in respect of bank loans as providing the institutional lender with an informal mechanism of insurance against the risks of security transactions.

16 See J.E. Adams, *American Title Insurance in an English Context*, [1979] Conv 322; C. Sydenham, [1980] Conv 427 at 432. Insurance is not, however, a panacea. It is predictable that insurance schemes will make it a condition of cover that the purchaser has taken all reasonable care to limit the insured risk in the first place by making enquiry as to the possible existence of undisclosed co-ownership of the property—the very burden which the purchaser seeks to minimise.

17 Post, p 597.

18 Insolvency Act 1986, s 336(5) (post, p 604).

19 Post, p 597.

on sale to be paid the value of his or her interest *in priority to* all other claims including that of the mortgagee.[20]

(5) Future reform of the law

It is not surprising that recent years have seen an intensification of concern on the part of law reformers with the proper balance to be maintained between the security of title transactions and the protection of co-ownership interests. It is highly likely that the cyclical movement of the law will at some point be intercepted by significant statutory intervention. Although most attention has focused on the special problem of adverse dealings with the family home,[1] the most recent proposals of the Law Commission have a somewhat wider reference to the entire field of co-ownership and the law of trusts for sale. It remains to be seen whether the imaginative objectives of the Law Commission will some day take legislative shape.

(a) A statutory scheme of co-ownership

In 1978 the Law Commission recommended the adoption of a statutory scheme of co-ownership,[2] under which all spouses (other than existing legal co-owners[3]) were to become joint tenants of the equitable interest in their matrimonial home.[4] In all cases the regime of mandatory co-ownership was to take effect behind a statutory trust for sale.[5] Any equitable co-owner not represented on the legal title would be able to protect his or her new statutory equitable interest either by registering a Class G land charge (in the case of unregistered land)[6] or by entering a restriction in the register of title (in the case of registered land).[7] Thus, in either context, registration

20 This was precisely the approach adopted by Murray J in the High Court of Northern Ireland in *Northern Bank Ltd v Beattie* [1982] 18 NIJB, Transcript, p 25. In technical terms such a solution probably represents the outcome which should have occurred in *Williams & Glyn's Bank Ltd v Boland* [1981] AC 487. It seems clear that if the bank in *Boland* had gone one step further and had issued a bankruptcy notice, it could then have forced a sale of the property notwithstanding the wife's cverriding interest. This was later admitted expressly by Lord Hailsham LC speaking extra-judicially in the House of Lords (see *Parliamentary Debates, House of Lords, Official Report*, Vol 437 (Session 1982–1983), Col 663 (15 December 1982)). However, it is likely that the bank, having undertaken not to press for possession if it won the case (ante, p 573), felt that it could not honourably seek a bankruptcy sale in the immediate aftermath of losing the case.

1 For a more detailed account of proposals for reform in this area, see *Elements of Land Law* (1st edn 1987), pp 862–868.

2 Law Com No 86, para 1.1.

3 The Law Commission recognised that there would be no need for 'statutory co-ownership' in cases where the spouses had already imposed co-ownership on their home in express terms eg by means of a conveyance to themselves expressly as joint tenants of the legal estate (Law Com No 86, para 1.3).

4 Law Com No 86, paras 1.18, 1.54ff. The imposition of joint tenancy would have applied even where both spouses were already equitable tenants in common behind an implied trust for sale (Law Com No 86, para 1.28).

5 Law Com No 86, para 1.62.

6 Law Com No 86, para 1.318.

7 Law Com No 86, para 1.328. The Commission proposed that the production of a registered proprietor's land certificate should not be necessary for the entry of a restriction (ibid, para 1.329).

would inevitably ensure that a purchaser was bound by the registering spouse's beneficial interest under the statutory co-ownership scheme.[8]

The Law Commission's proposed scheme was complex,[9] but its merits were clear. Registration would have the double consequence of making the consent of both spouses essential for dealings with the matrimonial home, and of safeguarding the rights of both in any capital moneys which might arise from a transaction. The visibility of formal registration would meanwhile forewarn purchasers of the need to comply with the 'two trustee rule'.[10] However, the success of the entire scheme depended vitally on an active requirement of registration and there was an obvious danger that, for reasons of ignorance or sheer inertia, qualifying spouses would neglect to register their rights.[11] The scheme of statutory co-ownership was never implemented in legislation, and has now been superseded by more general and even more innovative recommendations.

(b) Non-overreachable rights for beneficiaries in occupation

Possible directions for reform of the law of co-ownership have been taken into a new dimension in more recent proposals made by the Law Commission. In 1987 the Commission abandoned its prior emphasis on the achievement of protection through registration of rights.[12] In its *Third Report on Land Registration*,[13] the Commission suggested that the rights of persons 'in actual occupation' of land should continue to constitute an overriding interest binding on transferees and chargees. The Commission coupled this recommendation with a proposed extension of the existing statutory indemnity scheme to almost all third parties adversely affected by overriding interests.[14] In the Commission's view, this balance of competing considerations gave

8 Law Com No 86, paras 1.320, 1.331. It was envisaged that any failure by an equitable co-owner to take the necessary protective action would render the relevant interest unenforceable against third parties (Law Com No 86, paras 1.322(a), 1.332) and that such an interest could never constitute an overriding interest in registered land (Law Com No 86, para 1.333). An unregistered charge would be deemed to be void 'no matter whether the purchaser has notice of the trust, or of the beneficial interest, in other ways or from other sources' (Law Com No 86, para 1.322).

9 The Law Commission's scheme for statutory co-ownership was introduced in the House of Lords as a Private Member's Bill during the 1979–1980 session, only to founder through lack of parliamentary time. The sponsor of the Bill, Lord Simon of Glaisdale, later agreed that a Bill of this complexity had been beyond the capacity of a private Member (*Parliamentary Debates, House of Lords, Official Report*, Vol 437 (Session 1982–1983), Col 642 (15 December 1982)).

10 Once registration was effected, no third party dealing with the legal owner could ever disclaim knowledge of the trust. 'The registration facility thus remedies, for relevant land, the unsatisfactory feature of the present law about the two trustee rule in relation to land that is unregistered: that there is no satisfactory way to ensure that a purchaser has notice of the circumstances which bring the rule into play' (Law Com No 86, para 1.320).

11 In the aftermath of the ruling of the House of Lords in *Williams & Glyn's Bank Ltd v Boland*, the Law Commission re-issued in substantially unamended form the statutory co-ownership scheme of 1978 (see *Property Law: The Implications of Williams & Glyn's Bank Ltd v Boland* (Law Com No 115, Cmnd 8636, August 1982). A modified and cumbersome version of this scheme appeared in the abortive Land Registration and Law of Property Bill 1985 (see *Parliamentary Debates, House of Lords, Official Report (Fifth Series)*, Vol 460 (Session 1984–85), Cols 1270ff).

12 See also Law Com No 188, para 3.8.

13 Law Com No 158, para 2.64 (ante, p 227).

14 Ante, p 240.

appropriate weight to the fact that 'society generally (which includes purchasers and mortgagees) should recognise and respect' equitable rights of ownership in the family home.[15]

(i) The caprice of the overreaching mechanism It is significant that the Law Commission's proposals of 1987 did not derogate from the paramountcy of the overreaching mechanism in relation to co-ownership interests. The Commission's endorsement of the overriding interests of occupiers of land was limited by the recognition that a conveyance by trustees for sale in conformity with the Law of Property Act 1925 would inexorably oblige beneficial co-owners to surrender their occupation rights in favour of purely financial rights. By 1989, however, the Commission had begun seriously to question the aptness of an overreaching mechanism which turns so arbitrarily on the precise composition of the trusteeship in a trust for sale. The combined effect of the decisions in *Williams & Glyn's Bank Ltd v Boland*[16] and *City of London Building Society v Flegg*[17] is, of course, somewhat capricious. The priority accorded to beneficial co-owners in the event of a dealing with a legal title held on trust for sale may rather crucially depend on whether there is one trustee for sale or two. The beneficiary's right of occupation is certainly overreached on a disposition effected by two trustees, but may not be so dislodged in the event of a disposition by a sole trustee.[18]

(ii) Additional protection for beneficiaries in possession In 1989 the Law Commission acknowledged the unjustifiably arbitrary element implicit in the outcomes confirmed in *Boland* and *Flegg*.[19] The Commission indicated its view that the primary focus of reform should rest not on the protection of the financial interests of trust for sale beneficiaries but rather on the preservation of their security of tenure.[20] This approach represents, of course, an important recognition of the use value (as distinct from the exchange value) of residential property.[1] In the Commission's analysis,[2] the present protection accorded to the interests of equitable owners in possession is inadequate, not least because the operation of the overreaching principle may sometimes result in the peremptory and unconsented eviction of trust for sale beneficiaries.[3] Overreaching effects, at the very least, a compulsory surrender of the beneficiaries' occupation rights in exchange for mere money rights, an outcome which the Commission felt in many cases could be prejudicial and unwarranted.

15 Law Com No 158, para 2.63.
16 [1981] AC 487 (ante, p 569).
17 [1988] AC 54 (ante, p 553).
18 Ante, pp 568, 576.
19 Law Com No 188, paras 1.4, 2.28ff, 3.5. As the Commission pointed out, the dilemma here is deepened by the fact that a bare trustee seems to have no overreaching power at all (ante, pp 102, 536).
20 Pointing out that almost all other occupiers of residential property have some form of protection from arbitrary eviction, the Commission stated its wish to focus on beneficiaries' 'prospect of enjoyment of the land itself and its loss where overreaching occurs' (Law Commission, Working Paper No 106 (1988), para 6.1; Law Com No 188, para 3.4).
1 Ante, pp 543, 566.
2 Law Com No 188, para 4.1.
3 This was precisely the outcome eg in *City of London Building Society v Flegg* [1988] AC 54 (ante, p 556).

The Commission therefore concluded[4] that the Law of Property Act 1925 should be amended to confer a new form of protection on any person 'of full age and capacity who is entitled to a beneficial interest' in land and who 'has a right to occupy it and is in occupation of it at the date of the conveyance'.[5] The Commission recommended that no conveyance of a legal estate in the relevant land should overreach the interest of such a person 'unless that person consents'.[6] The relevant consent need not be expressed with any particular formality but must be 'real'.[7] There would be a residual (and unfettered) judicial discretion, where appropriate in all the circumstances of the case, to dispense with a requisite consent.[8]

The Law Commission's proposal and Draft Bill finally endorses on behalf of trust beneficiaries a right of requisite consent prior to a fully overreaching conveyance[9] and, in this important sense, envisages a fundamental shift in the balance of protection between beneficial co-owners and purchasers in both registered and unregistered land.[10] The Commission was mindful of the need to 'maintain arrangements which will not unduly interfere with conveyancing', but felt that the 'very fact of occupation can be used to alert prospective purchasers and mortgagees to the claims of the equitable owners'.[11] The Commission was, however, careful to add that the proposals for a consent requirement did not of themselves create any equitable interests or entitle anyone to an interest which he would not otherwise have had.[12] Likewise the consent requirement was not intended to 'give any new rights of priority to equitable interests.'[13] In consequence beneficial entitlements whose priority against purchasers has been cut back (eg by an express or implied waiver of rights or by the application of estoppel doctrine or by the denial of the *scintilla temporis* or otherwise) will remain so curtailed.

7. DISPUTES OVER DISPOSITIONS OF CO-OWNED LAND

Almost all forms of co-ownership in possession involve the existence of a trust for sale under the Law of Property Act 1925,[14] and it is of the essence

4 Law Com No 188, paras 4.3, 5.3(i).
5 The Commission confined the protection to a beneficiary who 'is in actual occupation of the property under a right enforceable against the person conveying the legal estate' (Law Com No 188, para 4.4).
6 See Draft Law of Property (Overreaching) Bill, clause 1(2) (Law Com No 188, Appendix A). The Commission thought that lack of consent should not invalidate the conveyance, but should cause the purchaser to take subject to the subsisting rights which had not been overreached (Law Com No 188, para 4.3 (n 1)).
7 Law Com No 188, paras 4.15f. A 'real' consent is, in the Commission's view, one which 'has truly been given'.
8 Law Com No 188, para 4.17ff. The Commission thought it likely and appropriate that the exercise of this discretion should follow the principles already adumbrated under section 30 of the Law of Property Act 1925 (post, p 593).
9 No consent would be required on the part of a beneficiary in the case of a sale effected by a personal representative or a mortgagee acting in exercise of his paramount power of sale (post, p 1003). See Law Com No 188, paras 4.20ff, 5.3.
10 The Commission envisaged, however, that it would continue to be the practice 'in many conveyancing cases' for prospective purchasers and mortgagees to require consents and waivers of rights from occupiers of property (Law Com No 188, para 4.25).
11 Law Com No 188, para 4.2. See also para 3.9.
12 Law Com No 188, para 4.5.
13 Law Com No 188, para 4.7.
14 Ante, p 526.

of a trust for sale that the trustees are the persons invested with the decision-making powers of management and disposition. Any full and complete disposition of a legal estate in the co-owned land requires the active co-operation of all the trustees for sale: all must join in the execution of the relevant document of disposition.[15] In this context difficult problems arise if there is any dispute as to whether the co-owned land should be sold, leased or mortgaged. These problems are intensified by the fact that land is a uniquely flexible form of property. By its nature land provides not merely a medium of long-term capital accumulation, investment and exchange; it also has an importance as an asset for intermediate-term use and enjoyment. The question whether land should be disposed of at any given time often highlights an underlying tension between the 'exchange value' of land (ie its potential for lucrative commercial exploitation) and its 'use value' (ie its potential for continued beneficial occupation).[16] Sooner or later the objectives of use and exchange become mutually incompatible and their respective merits emerge as matters of dispute between various interested parties. Obvious difficulties arise where the trustees for sale cannot agree inter se whether to deal with the land. These difficulties are compounded if a beneficiary under the trust for sale presses for a decision on possible dealing contrary to that favoured by the trustees. Perhaps an even deeper dilemma presents itself where some third party claims a right to *compel* a disposition of the co-owned land in defiance of the wishes both of the trustees for sale and of the beneficiaries under the trust.

(1) Dispute between the trustees themselves as to a proposed disposition

A fairly complex system of judge-made rules has developed to resolve disputes which arise between the trustees themselves as to whether a proposed disposition of the co-owned land should take place.

(a) The primary rule

The orthodox approach to trusts for sale of land holds that the prime object of a trust for sale is the conversion of the co-owned land into a monetary form in which all the beneficiaries may have equal enjoyment of their respective rights. Thus, in strict theory, a trust for sale is regarded as importing a mandatory duty to sell unless the trustees unanimously exercise their power to postpone sale.[17] In practice the trustees' duty to sell is frequently displaced

15 Ante, p 468.

16 It is true that some forms of dealing with land may reflect this tension in only an attenuated form. By means of a mortgage, for instance, owners of land may not be forced into an immediate or irrevocable choice between the realisation of the 'exchange value' and the 'use value' of their land. The mortgage transaction is commonly a device for allowing the mortgagor to enjoy both kinds of value simultaneously (post, p 933).

17 An implied power to postpone sale is supplied by statute (see Law of Property Act 1925, s 25(1), ante, p 524).

by a unanimous exercise of the power to postpone sale, with the result that trustees for sale can be said to be invested with enormous discretion as to whether sale ever takes place.[18]

The duty to sell land held on trust for sale is suspended, however, only by the unanimous decision of the trustees.[19] If even one of the trustees positively wishes to execute the trust to sell, the other trustees may be compelled to join with him in effecting a transfer of the property. In *In re Mayo*[20] Simonds J held that any disagreement between the trustees as to the desirability of sale should normally be resolved in favour of discharging the primary purpose of the trust for sale. In the event of dispute the trust to sell will thus be held to prevail in the absence of proven mala fides in the trustee who presses for sale.[1]

The rule laid down in *In re Mayo* provides a prima facie (and usually conclusive) resolution of any disagreement between trustees as to sale of the co-owned property. In rare cases, however, it may happen that, although the fiduciary duty to sell is primary and even though a majority of the beneficiaries wishes that sale should occur, one of the trustees still adamantly refuses to join in effecting a transfer of the co-owned estate to a third party. The conveyance cannot then proceed since the signature of all the trustees is required. In these circumstances, those who press for sale may apply to the court under section 30 of the Law of Property Act 1925 for an order directing the recalcitrant trustee to co-operate in the transfer of the land. Application may be made under section 30 '[i]f the trustees for sale refuse to sell. . .',[2] whereupon the court has a broad discretion to 'make such order as it thinks fit.'

(b) Exercise of discretion under Law of Property Act 1925, s 30

Although section 30 is aimed at assisting a party who wishes to compel the execution of a trust for sale, the express terms of section 30 reserve for the court a discretionary power to withhold enforcement of the trust for sale. The proper approach to this discretion was spelt out in *In re Buchanan-Wollaston's Conveyance*.[3] Here Sir Wilfred Greene MR indicated that the court of equity, when asked to enforce a trust for sale, 'must look into all the circumstances of the case and consider whether or not, at the particular moment and in the particular circumstances when the application is made to it, it is right and proper that such an order shall be made.' Above all

18 See *In re Evers' Trust* [1980] 1 WLR 1327 at 1330G (ante, p 524).

19 A proposal to introduce a rule of decision by majority vote was rejected by the Law Reform Committee in 1982 (see Law Reform Committee, *The Powers and Duties of Trustees* (23rd Report, Cmnd 8733, October 1982), paras 3.60ff).

20 [1943] Ch 302 at 304.

1 See *In re Buchanan-Wollaston's Conveyance* [1939] Ch 738 at 748, where reference was made to the argument of the plaintiff trustee to the effect that the trustees had indeed determined the question of sale by vote, in that this vote had consisted of 'a vote at a meeting which he and he alone had attended, although the [other trustees] were invited to come'.

2 Any 'person interested' may likewise invoke section 30 where the trustees refuse to exercise any of their powers under sections 28 and 29 (eg powers to grant leases and mortgages (ante, p 539)) or where any 'requisite consent' cannot be obtained.

3 [1939] Ch 738 at 747.

the court must ask itself the question 'whether or not the person applying for execution of the trust for sale is a person whose voice should be allowed to prevail.'[4]

It is clear that the test to be applied under section 30 is not 'what is reasonable'.[5] As Devlin LJ pointed out in *Jones v Challenger*,[6] it is often entirely reasonable, for instance, that one trustee (if beneficially entitled) should wish to realise his equitable share in cash while another trustee who is likewise entitled should wish to continue to enjoy the use value of the property. The exercise of discretion pursuant to section 30 must therefore be governed by criteria other than some supposed standard of 'reasonableness'. It is against this background that the courts have developed a doctrine of 'secondary or collateral objects' underlying a trust for sale which may, in some circumstances, displace the primacy of the trustees' duty of sale.[7]

(c) Circumstances displacing the primacy of the duty to sell

Although the rule in *In re Mayo* emphasises the primacy of the trustees' duty to sell, Devlin LJ indicated in *Jones v Challenger*[8] that 'this simple principle' cannot prevail 'where the trust itself or the circumstances in which it was made show that there was a secondary or collateral object besides that of sale.'[9] Acknowledging that the conveyancing device of the trust for sale may nowadays serve a multiplicity of secondary purposes, Devlin LJ stated that, even in the absence of mala fides, it is 'wrong and inequitable for one of the parties to the trust to invoke the letter of the trust in order to defeat one of its purposes, whether that purpose be written or unwritten'.[10] In his view, there is 'something akin to mala fides if one trustee tries to defeat a collateral object in the trust by arbitrarily insisting on the duty of sale'.[11]

Accordingly the courts have consistently held that certain kinds of collateral object or underlying purpose in a trust for sale may have the effect of displacing the prime object of sale. If such a collateral purpose is still capable of fulfilment, the courts, in exercising their broad discretion under section 30, generally decline to grant an order for sale.[12] In such cases the courts will not permit the enforcement of the trust for sale unless, in all the circumstances, 'it

4 See eg *Chhokar v Chhokar* [1984] FLR 313 at 329f.
5 See *Jones v Challenger* [1961] 1 QB 176 at 180, 184; *Rivett v Rivett* (1966) 200 Estates Gazette 858; *Mayes v Mayes* (1969) 210 Estates Gazette 935 at 937; *In re Turner (A Bankrupt)* [1974] 1 WLR 1556 at 1558B-C.
6 [1961] 1 QB 176 at 184.
7 The reference in this context to 'secondary or collateral objects' as underlying a trust for sale indicates—rather confusingly—the element of purpose which in a different context was described in terms of the 'prime object' underlying a trust for sale. See *Barclay v Barclay* [1970] 2 QB 677 at 684A per Lord Denning MR (ante, p 549).
8 [1961] 1 QB 176 at 181.
9 Devlin LJ stressed that *In re Mayo* had itself been 'a simple uncomplicated case of a trust for sale of freehold property, where the beneficiaries were brother and sister, and where there was no suggestion that either of them were intended to or even wished to occupy the property.'
10 [1961] 1 QB 176 at 181.
11 [1961] 1 QB 176 at 183.
12 *Rivett v Rivett* (1966) 200 Estates Gazette 858.

is right and proper to order the sale'.[13] If, however, it appears that the collateral purpose of a trust for sale is no longer capable of fulfilment, the courts regard their discretion under section 30 as being 'of a much more limited character'[14] and tend therefore to sanction the proposed sale unless it is clearly inequitable to do so.

In practice the question whether the original trust purpose has wholly failed is apt to merge with the inquiry as to whose voice should in equity be allowed to prevail. In *Cousins v Dzosens*[15] the two forms of interrogatory were said to be 'really one and the same question', in that if 'there is still some outstanding equity to be satisfied, it must necessarily follow that the trust purposes cannot yet have been wholly exhausted; and if the entire purpose of the trust has not yet been accomplished, then there must be scope for equity to determine whether or not a sale should proceed.'

There are several broad kinds of circumstance in which the courts generally decline to accede to the argument that the initial or underlying purpose of the trust for sale has been frustrated and in which therefore the courts have exercised discretion *against* ordering a sale.

(i) Covenant not to sell without the consent of all the trustees There is authority for the view that the court, in exercising jurisdiction under section 30, may not think it 'right and proper' to order sale where the trustees have already covenanted inter se not to dispose of the co-owned land without the concurrence of all the trustees.[16]

In *In re Buchanan-Wollaston's Conveyance*[17] four individuals, who each owned separate but neighbouring properties overlooking the sea, combined to purchase a piece of land which they desired to keep as an open space in order to preserve their common sea view. The land was conveyed to them as joint tenants, and they therefore held the legal estate as trustees on trust for sale for themselves in the proportions of their respective financial contributions towards the purchase.[18] The parties then entered into a deed of covenant by which they mutually undertook not to part or deal with the co-owned land except with the unanimous consent of all parties or by majority vote. One of the trustees subsequently sold his own property and thus wished, notwithstanding the opposition of the other trustees, to withdraw his investment from the jointly held open land. He brought proceedings under section 30 for a court order directing his fellow trustees to join with him in selling that property and realising the proceeds. Farwell J refused at first instance to order such a sale, taking the view that the applicant for sale 'was putting forward a claim to equitable assistance merely to enable him thereby to escape from his contractual obligations'. To facilitate this course of action 'would be to disregard the well established rule of equity

13 *Jones v Challenger* [1961] 1 QB 176 at 183.
14 *Rivett v Rivett* (1966) 200 Estates Gazette 858.
15 (1981) *Times*, 9 December (John Waite QC).
16 An agreement between co-owners postponing or displacing otherwise available powers of sale has been held not to be void as amounting to a restraint on alienation, at least where the powers can be reactivated on the giving of 12 months' notice (see *Re Permanent Trustee Nominees (Canberra) Ltd* [1989] 1 Qd R 314 at 316ff).
17 [1939] Ch 217, 738.
18 Ante, p 530.

that he who seeks equity must do equity.'[19] Farwell J's decision was upheld by the Court of Appeal, Sir Wilfred Greene MR agreeing that the plaintiff 'could not...ask the Court to act in a way inconsistent with his own contractual obligations'.[20]

Thus, if trustees for sale have contractually displaced the primacy of the duty to sell, the court will not so exercise discretion under section 30 as to facilitate a breach of that contract.[1] Sale will not be ordered while the underlying contractual purpose subsists.[2]

(ii) Estoppel operating to make sale inequitable The court may likewise lean against sale in circumstances of estoppel, where it would be inequitable to order a sale of the co-owned property.[3] In *Jones (A.E.) v Jones (F.W.)*,[4] for instance, a father had induced his son to give up his employment and to contribute money towards the purchase of the father's house on the basis of a reasonable expectation, encouraged by the father, that the son could live in that house for the rest of his life. The Court of Appeal held that the father's widow (who had succeeded to the father's interests under the relevant trust for sale) was estopped from obtaining an order for sale under section 30. The Court took the view that section 30 should not be invoked so as to defeat the purpose originally contemplated by the father and son, which was to provide long-term housing for the latter.[5]

(iii) Provision of a family home The courts have similarly adapted the collateral purpose doctrine towards the resolution of disputes between spouses or quasi-marital partners as to sale of the family home. It is, of course, extremely common for spouses or de facto partners to hold the legal estate in their family home on an express or implied trust for sale for themselves. If, as trustees for sale, the parties cannot agree whether or not to sell their home, either may invoke the court's jurisdiction under section 30. Such recourse may become necessary in a situation of crisis where one party wishes the property to be sold and the proceeds of sale distributed in the appropriate beneficial shares, while the other party simply wishes to remain living in the home with or without children of the family.[6]

19 [1939] Ch 217 at 223f.

20 [1939] Ch 738 at 745. Compare *Miller v Lakefield Estates Ltd* (1989) 57 P & CR 104 at 107ff.

1 See also *L.M. Rosen Realty Ltd v D'Amore* (1982) 132 DLR (3d) 648 at 661, (1984) 7 DLR (4th) 285 at 296.

2 In *In re Buchanan-Wollaston's Conveyance* [1939] Ch 738 at 747f, the Court of Appeal added that sale might be ordered if circumstances were to change, in that if 'all the parties died, and all their houses were sold, ...the Court, if asked to enforce a statutory trust for sale, would not be disposed to listen to arguments against such a sale adduced by people who had no real interest in keeping this land unsold.'

3 Estoppel is discussed more generally in Chapter 11 (ante, p 312).

4 [1977] 1 WLR 438.

5 [1977] 1 WLR 438 at 442D-G, 443D-E.

6 If the issue arises on the granting of a divorce, the court has of course an extensive jurisdiction under the Matrimonial Causes Act 1973 to determine the pattern of the family's future living arrangements. There are, however, several other broad categories of circumstance which do not involve a dissolution of marriage, but in which the future of the family home may likewise become a matter of dispute.

In such cases, even if it is accepted that the 'prime object' of the relevant trust is sale, the resolution of this thoroughly human impasse by reference to mere dogma has little attraction in the family context. Not surprisingly the primacy of the duty to sell has been heavily modified by the courts in order to take into account the specific needs and vulnerabilities which are present in the diffuse and complex world of family relations.[7] The courts have therefore tended to exercise their discretion under section 30 with reference to whether the original collateral purpose of the trust for sale of the family home is still, in any realistic sense, capable of fulfilment.[8]

A trust for sale of the family home almost always originates with the secondary or collateral purpose of providing a base for joint residential occupation by the members of a family. Accordingly, the courts have tended to order a sale of the family home pursuant to section 30 only where the collateral residential purpose has clearly been exhausted or frustrated,[9] but have otherwise proved unwilling to allow the trust for sale to be executed while the initial purpose remains substantially capable of fulfilment.[10] Thus section 30 cannot be invoked by one trustee for sale in order to compel a sale of the family home while the relevant family members otherwise continue to live together in amity.[11] As Devlin LJ observed in *Jones v Challenger*,[12] where property is acquired by a husband and wife for the purpose of providing a matrimonial home, 'neither party has a right to demand the sale while that purpose still exists'. By contrast, if the underlying object of the family

7 In the family context, however, it is not irrelevant that the court's refusal to order sale is sometimes tantamount to the making of a maintenance order against a non-resident co-owner in favour of a resident co-owner (see J. Martin, [1980] Conv 361 at 376). No rent is usually chargeable in respect of the latter's sole occupation of the co-owned premises (ante, p 476).

8 This approach is applicable even outside the immediate family context. See eg *Power v Brighton* (Unreported, Court of Appeal, 14 November 1984), where the court declined to order a sale of property held on an implied trust for sale. The property had been purchased for the purpose of providing a home for the new legal owner, who had funded the acquisition with contributions of money from friends. When these contributors desired to withdraw their respective cash investments, the Court of Appeal held that the 'underlying purpose of the trust' was still in existence and therefore precluded sale.

9 This inhibition has no effect where sale is sought under section by a trustee in bankruptcy of one of the co-owner/trustees. See *In re Citro (A Bankrupt)* [1991] Ch 142 at 147B, 158G–159A per Nourse LJ (post, p 601).

10 See eg *Stott v Ratcliffe* (1982) 126 SJ 310, where the original purpose of a trust for sale was to provide a home for two co-owners during their joint lifetimes and thereafter for the survivor. On the death of one of the co-owners the Court of Appeal declined to order sale at the behest of the personal representatives of the deceased tenant in common, the explicit object of the acquisition of the co-owned property having been to secure a home for the survivor. See also *Wight v IRC* (1982) 264 Estates Gazette 935 at 936f; *Jones (A.E.) v Jones (F.W.)* [1977] 1 WLR 438 at 442G.

11 See the extension of this approach in *Chhokar v Chhokar* [1984] FLR 313 at 327E-G, 328C-G, where the Court of Appeal refused to countenance an application for sale made by a third party who had purchased the family home in fraud of the beneficial entitlement of the vendor's wife (ante, p 220). The wife continued to live in the home and later became reconciled with her husband. The Court held that the 'underlying objects' of the original trust for sale were still subsisting at the date of the application for sale, and there appeared now to be no special reason for frustrating the initial intention of the spouses to use the property as their matrimonial home (ante, p 471).

12 [1961] 1 QB 176 at 182. See also *In re Citro (A Bankrupt)* [1991] Ch 142 at 147B-C, 158G per Nourse LJ.

home trust is wholly frustrated by later events and can no longer be achieved, it seems that 'some very special circumstances need to be shown to induce the court not to order a sale.'[13]

On this basis it used to be said that divorce[14] or separation[15] or the breakdown of some other relevant family relationship[16] normally marked the destruction of the collateral purpose of a trust for sale of the family home, in which case the the primacy of the duty to sell was restored. The courts thus inclined towards sale, thereby averting any risk that a refusal to order sale might either prejudice the monetary value of a beneficiary's equitable share[17] or otherwise keep this share locked up in the property for an unduly lengthy or indefinite period.[18] The more recent case law confirms, however, that the courts have nowadays moved away from this property-oriented perspective in favour of a more family-oriented view of the judicial discretion exercisable under section 30. It is by no means clear that the underlying purpose of a trust for sale is indeed truly spent when a marriage or family relationship breaks down: frequently the home may

13 *Re Holliday (A Bankrupt)* [1981] Ch 405 at 415F per Goff LJ. See also *Rivett v Rivett* (1966) 200 Estates Gazette 858. Ultimately, however, the decision whether a sale should be ordered lies within the discretion of the court and the presence or absence of the original collateral purpose of the trust for sale is merely one, albeit highly persuasive, factor influencing the exercise of this discretion. Any dogmatic assertion that the subsistence or destruction of the initial purpose of the trust is the only criterion is ultimately inconsistent with the discretionary nature of the jurisdiction conferred by section 30 (see *Luciv v Filinov* (Unreported, Court of Appeal, 15 May 1980) per Megaw LJ).

14 See *Jones v Challenger* [1961] 1 QB 176 at 183. In the words of Devlin LJ (at 184), it was not 'inequitable' in this event for one of the spouses to want to realise his investment. If the 'prime object' of the trust was to have any weight, 'the preservation of the house as a home for one of them singly is not an object at all.' Most decisions nowadays as to the future disposition of the matrimonial home on divorce are not made pursuant to Law of Property Act 1925, s 30, but under the different (and rather more specialised) jurisdiction of the divorce courts pursuant to Matrimonial Causes Act 1973, ss 23–25.

15 See *Rawlings v Rawlings* [1964] P 398 at 416, 419, but compare the vigorous dissent by Willmer LJ (at 414). See also *Bedson v Bedson* [1965] 2 QB 666 at 680A; *In re Citro (A Bankrupt)* [1991] Ch 142 at 151F-G, 158B.

16 See eg *Rivett v Rivett* (1966) 200 Estates Gazette 858, where the legal title in a family home was owned jointly by a widower and his son, the purpose of the arrangement being that both should occupy the home together. When the arrangement was disrupted by personal discord, Goff J ruled that the estrangement of father and son had terminated the original purpose of the trust, in that one of 'the two entities' for whom the home had been intended was no longer able to derive any realistic benefit. A sale of the property was thus ordered, even though the home was still required as a residence by the son, his wife and their children. See also *Luciv v Filinov* (Unreported, Court of Appeal, 15 May 1980).

17 This consideration became even more pressing where a delayed sale might dramatically affect—if not destroy—the money value of the beneficial shares (see eg *Jones v Challenger* [1961] 1 QB 176 at 187 (lease with only six years to run)). Compare *Mayes v Mayes* (1969) 210 Estates Gazette 935 at 937, where in the case of a relatively long leasehold term the urgency of sale was considerably abated, the co-owned asset not being a wasting asset but one which was liable to inflate in value.

18 This concern was apt to be all the more significant where, for instance, an excessively large family home was plainly unsuitable for sole occupation by the beneficial co-owner who resisted sale. Such circumstances could well make it just and equitable to release the cash shares of the equitable co-owners (see *Jackson v Jackson* [1971] 1 WLR 1539 at 1543G-H).

still be required as accommodation for the children of the family.[19] In terms of the more modern approach the continuing residential needs of minor children of the family serve to prolong the collateral purpose of the trust for sale beyond the termination of the mutual relationship of the trustees or beneficiaries.[20]

The controlling relevance of this more utilitarian approach was evident, for instance, in *In re Evers' Trust*.[1] Here the Court of Appeal declined a section 30 application in respect of a quasi-marital home made by a male partner on the termination of a de facto relationship. The cohabiting parties had earlier purchased a home in joint names largely with the aid of a joint mortgage loan. When the parties separated, the woman and three children (including two from an earlier union) remained in the house. In dealing with the conflicting interests of the parties, the Court of Appeal stressed the importance of the use value as distinct from the exchange value of such property as the family home. Ormrod LJ cited with approval the 'modern view' articulated by Lord Denning MR in *Williams (J. W.) v Williams (M.A.)*,[2] according to which the courts 'nowadays have great regard to the fact that the house is bought as a home in which the family is to be brought up. It is not treated as property to be sold, nor as an investment to be realised for cash.'[3] In *Evers'* case the Court of Appeal therefore refused to endorse

19 For an early realisation of this aspect, see *Rawlings v Rawlings* [1964] P 398 at 419, where Salmon LJ opined that the court would not execute the trust where there were young children, since the original purpose of the trust 'would no doubt have been to provide a home for them'. See the much more startling (and surely inaccurate) statement of Lawton LJ in *Burke v Burke* [1974] 1 WLR 1063 at 1068D: 'If the circumstances are such that the parents buy a house in which to accommodate themselves and any children of the marriage, for my part I cannot see why the children should not be beneficiaries under any implied trust which may come into existence on the purchase of the home'.

20 Compare the view formerly taken, for example by Buckley LJ in *Burke v Burke* [1974] 1 WLR 1063 at 1067D-E, that the interests of children are 'only incidentally to be taken into consideration. . .so far as they affect the equities in the matter as between the two persons entitled to the beneficial interests in the property.' To treat the children's father as being 'obliged to make provision for his children by agreeing to retain the property unsold' was to 'confuse with a problem relating to property considerations which are relevant to maintenance.' In *Williams (J. W.) v Williams (M.A.)* [1976] Ch 278 at 285E-G, Lord Denning MR was later to refer to Buckley LJ's perspective as exemplifying 'the old approach' which was 'now out-dated'. See, however, *Re Holliday (A Bankrupt)* [1981] Ch 405 at 417F-H per Goff LJ.

1 [1980] 1 WLR 1327. See [1981] Conv 79 (A. Sydenham).

2 [1976] Ch 278 at 285E-F. See also *Browne v Pritchard* [1975] 1 WLR 1366 at 1371H, where in the context of property adjustment under the Matrimonial Causes Act 1973 Ormrod LJ had dismissed an argument that a wife would be 'kept out of her money' if the court did not order an immediate sale of the former matrimonial home and division of the proceeds. He pointed out that the wife in that case was 'not being kept out of her money. If the marriage had not broken down . . . she would never have touched a penny of the value of the house, because investment in a home is the least liquid investment that one can possibly make. It cannot be converted into cash while the children are at home and often not until one spouse dies unless it is possible to move into much smaller and cheaper accommodation.'

3 Ormrod LJ observed ([1980] 1 WLR 1327 at 1332H-1333A) that the approach expressed in the judgment of Lord Denning MR in *Williams (J. W.) v Williams (M.A.)* had considerable advantages 'in these "family" cases', in that it enabled the court 'to deal with substance, that is, reality, rather than form, that is, convenience of conveyancing'. Ormrod LJ also pointed out that the family-oriented approach to section 30 'brings the exercise of discretion under this section, so far as possible, into line with the exercise of the discretion given by section 24 of the Matrimonial Causes Act 1973.'

a sale which would have allowed the applicant to evict his partner and the children from their home merely in order to extract his capital investment and apply it for other purposes. Ormrod LJ pointed out that the underlying purpose of this trust for sale had been to provide a home for the couple and their three children 'for the indefinite future' and that this purpose was still capable of substantial fulfilment.[4]

The decision in *Evers'* case reflects the way in which, in the context of section 30 applications, the bleak and normally inflexible rules of property law have been increasingly coloured by considerations much more sympathetic to the realities of family life.[5] The Court of Appeal's approach in this case illustrates a significant development in the courts' sensitivity to the balance which exists in this area between property considerations and family considerations.[6] It is not wholly impossible, however, that both of these ranges of consideration may some day be submerged more heavily by cogent issues of public housing policy. It may be that increased pressure on public housing resources will at some future date provide a ground on which the courts will decline to order the sale of co-owned homes under section 30. In *Bernard v Josephs*,[7] for instance, Kerr LJ observed that 'above all, in these times of housing shortage, a sale has the disadvantage that the property ceases to be available as a home for either of the parties.' This consideration—whether rightly or wrongly entertained—has become a dominant concern under the Matrimonial Causes Act 1973,[8] and certainly influenced the court in *Bernard v Josephs* to hold that the order for sale in that case should not be enforced if the defendant were willing and able to buy out the plaintiff's share for cash.

(d) The future of section 30

In conjunction with its proposals for a new 'trust of land', the Law Commission has recommended a reformulation of section 30 of the Law of Property Act 1925.[9] The Commission considered that the judicial construction of the existing section 30 has inevitably been overshadowed by the duty to sell which is intrinsic to the device of the trust for sale. The duty of sale would, of course, disappear from the operation of the new 'trust of land', which

4 [1980] 1 WLR 1327 at 1333E–1334D. The Court of Appeal took into account that the man now had a secure home with his own mother and had no present need to realise his investment, while the woman was prepared to accept full responsibility for the outstanding mortgage liability and would have found it extremely difficult to rehouse herself if the property had been sold. The Court therefore postponed any question of sale, but indicated that sale might become appropriate at some future stage if circumstances changed, as for instance if the woman remarried or if it became financially possible for her to buy the man out.

5 The more family-oriented approach to section 30 enables the court to respond to a wide variety of competing needs presented by members of a family. It is clear, for instance, that the court may, in its discretion, withhold a sale of the family home where a co-owner who wishes to retain the home is out of work (*Mayes v Mayes* (1969) 210 Estates Gazette 935 at 937).

6 It has been said that all section 30 applications relating to the home (whether matrimonial or quasi-matrimonial) should be dealt with by the Family Division rather than the Chancery Division (see *Bernard v Josephs* [1982] Ch 391 at 401F).

7 [1982] Ch 391 at 410D. See [1983] CLJ 30 at 33f.

8 See eg *Harvey v Harvey* [1982] Fam 83 at 88E-F; [1982] CLJ 228 at 230f.

9 Ante, p 537.

is premised on the vesting in trustees of twin (and equally balanced) powers either to sell or to retain the trust land.[10] It was the hope of the Commission that this restructuring of the trust powers, and in particular the elimination of the duty to sell, would 'clear the way for a genuinely broad and flexible approach', in consequence of which the courts would 'not be required to give a preference to sale'.[11]

The proposed reformulation of section 30 sets out certain guidelines for the exercise of the court's discretion,[12] the Commission's declared aim being to 'consolidate and rationalise the present approach'.[13] In determining whether trust land should be sold, the court is directed (where the land includes a dwelling) to have regard to 'the welfare of any minor who occupies or might reasonably be expected to occupy it as his home'.[14] Other relevant criteria would include the intentions of the settlor, the purpose for which the land was acquired, the wishes of any adults entitled to interests in possession, the interest of any creditor who has obtained a charging order under the Charging Orders Act 1979 against any trust beneficiary, and any other matters which appear to the court to be relevant. Although the recommended guidelines expressly indicate the welfare of children as an independent factor for consideration, it is unlikely that the reformulated section 30 would dramatically alter the existing pattern of discretionary decision-making in respect of trusts for sale. Indeed, as the Law Commission observed, one function of the proposed guidelines will be to put the current criteria on a statutory footing.[15]

(2) The right of a beneficiary to affect the decisions of trustees for sale

A second range of problem arises if a beneficiary under a trust for sale presses for a decision on possible dealing contrary to that favoured by the trustees. If a beneficiary is not himself one of the trustees for sale, his ability to compel any disposition of the legal title is severely limited. If the trust is a statutory trust for sale, he may be able to claim the benefit of section 26(3) of the Law of Property Act 1925 if he owns the largest share of the beneficial interest.[16] Pursuant to this provision the trustees are obliged 'so far as consistent with the general interest of the trust' to give effect to the wishes of such a person. In the absence of proper consultation of his interests, the beneficiary may of course invoke section 30 of the Law of Property

10 Ante, p 538.
11 Law Com No 181, para 12.5.
12 Law of Property Act 1925, s 30(3) (proposed version as contained in Draft Trusts of Land Bill, clause 6(1) (Law Com No 181, Appendix A)).
13 Law Com No 181, para 12.9. The Commission agreed that the present exercise of discretion under section 30 'gets the balance more or less right' and that the criteria which the courts have evolved for settling disputes over trusts for sale 'are ones which will continue to have validity in the context of the new system.' The Commission thought that 'there will be much of value in the existing body of case law, even though these cases assume that there is a duty to sell'
14 Law of Property Act 1925, s 30(3)(c) (proposed version as contained in Draft Trusts of Land Bill, clause 6(1) (Law Com No 181, Appendix A)).
15 Law Com No 181, para 12.9.
16 Post, p 595.

Act 1925. The judicial discretion conferred by this provision remains applicable on behalf of 'any person interested' in any circumstance where 'the trustees for sale refuse to sell'. Section 30 opens up the jurisdiction of the court to make 'such order as it thinks fit' with reference, if relevant, to the 'secondary or collateral objects' of the trust.[17]

More usually, however, the impasse between beneficiary and trustees presents itself in a different form. It sometimes happens that, even though the trustees for sale are unanimous in wishing to dispose of the co-owned land, some beneficiary under the trust is anxious that the land should instead be retained for his or her own occupation. Such a dispute raises problems of some complexity. So long as the rights of a trust for sale beneficiary were characterised as mere notional rights in the moneys of some future sale, it was quite consistent that decisions as to the proper management or disposition of the trust property should remain wholly within the control of the trustees for sale.[18] But as soon as the trust for sale beneficiary began to be seen as having an interest 'in' land and a correlative right to occupy that land pending sale,[19] it was inescapable that the courts should also recognise some right in the beneficiary to influence the decisions taken by the trustees for sale.

In a series of developments during the last 40 years the courts have in certain instances enabled the trust for sale beneficiary to intercept the decision-making processes of his trustees in order to ensure that his own preferences are not entirely ignored. These developments have conferred on the trust for sale beneficiary a limited measure of control over dealings by his trustees which threaten to prejudice his own enjoyment of the co-owned land.[20] In such circumstances the beneficiary, although having no vote qua trustee in the matter of sale, is effectively given an opportunity to throw 'spanners into the works', by means of several tactical manoeuvres which may delay or frustrate a proposed sale which he wishes to prevent. There must be some closer examination of the devices which may be employed to protect the occupation interests of the beneficiary.

(a) *Appointment of a second trustee*

Where a sole trustee for sale (as in *Bull v Bull*[1]) proposes to sell the land held on trust, it is open to any beneficiary to apply to the court for an injunction restraining sale until at least one other trustee has been appointed.[2] Of course the technical possibility of obtaining an injunction of this kind is of little use to a beneficiary who is unaware of an impending sale. Moreover, even an injunction will delay sale only temporarily since the sole trustee

17 Ante, p 540.
18 Ante, p 547.
19 Ante, p 548.
20 Some beneficiaries may also be entitled to protect their statutory 'rights of occupation' pursuant to the Matrimonial Homes Act 1983 (ante, p 159), thereby precluding any sale with vacant possession. See eg *Wroth v Tyler* [1974] Ch 30.
1 [1955] 1 QB 234 (ante, p 533, post, p 595).
2 See *Waller v Waller* [1967] 1 WLR 451 at 453E-F, 454C; (1967) 31 Conv (NS) 140 (F.R. Crane). On the appointment of further trustees, see Trustee Act 1925, ss 36(1), 40(1) (ante, p 465).

is free to appoint one of his cronies as co-trustee to join with him in giving a good conveyance of the legal estate.[3]

(b) Duty of consultation

The Law of Property Act 1925 contains a special provision for consultation in relation to trusts for sale which arise by implication of statute.[4] Section 26(3) provides that the statutory trustees 'shall so far as practicable consult the persons of full age for the time being beneficially interested in possession. . .and shall, so far as consistent with the general interest of the trust, give effect to the wishes of such persons, or in the case of dispute, of the majority (according to the value of their combined interests) of such persons'.[5]

If the trustees attempt to sell the land without first discharging this duty of consultation, they may be restrained by injunction from completing the transaction.[6] However, the statutory duty of consultation is hedged about by qualifications, and ultimately comprises only a duty to listen coupled with a privilege to say 'no'. There is no duty in the trustees to comply with the wishes of the beneficiaries, except where these wishes are those of the majority shareholder(s) in equity and are also 'consistent with the general interest of the trust'. In *Bull v Bull*,[7] Denning LJ accepted that the son could have forced a sale of the property against the wishes of his mother if he so desired: all he needed to do was to appoint a second trustee for sale to act with him. In Denning LJ's view, the two trustees would 'no doubt have to consider the mother's wishes, but as the son appears to have made the greater contribution, he could in theory override her wishes about a sale'.[8]

(c) Implied consent of the beneficiary in possession

In *Bull v Bull*[9] Denning LJ pointed to a further 'practical difficulty' which a trust for sale beneficiary might lay in the way of trustees for sale who

3 See the Law Commission's proposal in 1978 of 'trusteeship rights' in the matrimonial home and the more recent suggestion that beneficiaries should be able to direct the appointment of new trustees (ante, p 539).

4 Section 26(3) has no direct application to express trusts for sale, thereby providing support for Stephen Cretney's argument that in the Law of Property Act 1925 Parliament itself recognised 'the need to distinguish between cases where the trust for sale should be regarded as machinery, on the one hand, and those where it has been expressly chosen, when its logical consequences eg the conversion of the equitable interests may be implemented' ((1971) 34 MLR 441 at 442). The Law Commission has recommended that the duty of consultation under section 26(3) be extended to cover all trusts of land unless expressly excluded by the trust instrument (Law Com No 181, paras 13.5, 20.3). See Draft Trusts of Land Bill, clause 3 (Law Com No 181, Appendix A).

5 If a trust for sale beneficiary is bankrupt, the consultation pursuant to section 26(3) must not be with him, but with his trustee in bankruptcy. See *Fryer v Brooks* [1984] LS Gaz R 2856, CA.

6 See *Waller v Waller* [1967] 1 WLR 451 at 453D.

7 [1955] 1 QB 234 (ante, p 533).

8 [1955] 1 QB 234 at 238. See [1955] CLJ 158, where Professor H.W.R. Wade asked: 'What is the effect, one may wonder, of a provision of an Act of Parliament which operates only "in theory"?'

9 [1955] 1 QB 234 at 238.

had conformed with the minimal requirement of consultation stipulated by the Law of Property Act 1925. If such trustees still pressed for a sale, they would be confronted with the problem that 'so long as [the mother] is there, they could not sell with vacant possession.' Denning LJ proceeded to spell out for the beneficiary in possession under a trust for sale something akin to a 'status of irremovability'.[10] He held that by virtue of her right of occupation as an equitable tenant in common 'she could not be turned out by the trustees except with her consent.'[11]

The approach adopted by Denning LJ in *Bull v Bull* appeared to suggest that a beneficiary in possession behind a trust for sale enjoys an implied right of consent to any disposition of the land proposed by the trustees for sale.[12] If, as was the case in *Bull v Bull* itself, such a beneficiary adamantly refused to give her consent to a sale with vacant possession, she would effectively stultify the transaction proposed by the trustees.[13] The only recourse then available to the trustees would be an application to the court under section 30 of the Law of Property Act 1925 to dispense with the consent thus withheld.[14] Denning LJ anticipated that the court would make such an order only if 'satisfied that it was right and proper to do so and on such terms as to alternative accommodation as it thought fit to impose.'[15]

The decision in *Bull v Bull* seemed to confer upon the beneficiary in possession a fairly general power of veto over dealings by the trustees for sale. However, such a proposition now requires to be restricted in at least two dimensions. It is clear that no such veto or requisite consent can be claimed where the 'prime' (or underlying) object of the trust for sale is indeed sale as distinct from joint residence. In *Barclay v Barclay*[16] a testator had left his bungalow to be held on trust for sale, the proceeds of sale to be divided after his death between five members of his family. In ordering sale the Court of Appeal declined to accede to the wishes of one of the beneficiaries, who during the testator's lifetime had been allowed to occupy the property and who selfishly wished to remain in occupation permanently. The Court distinguished *Bull v Bull* on the ground that there the 'prime object of the trust' had been that the son and mother 'should occupy the house together'. In *Barclay*, according to Lord Denning MR, the facts were 'very different' since here the 'prime object of the trust was that the bungalow should be sold'.[17]

10 Post, p 877.
11 [1955] 1 QB 234 at 238.
12 For the view that in *Bull v Bull* the Court of Appeal elevated the wishes of a beneficiary to 'the status of a "requisite consent"', see [1971] CLJ 44 at 45 (M.J. Prichard).
13 'Why it should be in the power of a beneficiary with a minor interest to impede the execution of a trust for sale is something of a mystery' (H.W.R. Wade, [1955] CLJ 157). See also (1955) 18 MLR 303 (V. Latham).
14 Ante, p 526.
15 [1955] 1 QB 234 at 239. See also *City of London Building Society v Flegg* [1986] Ch 605 at 620A-B per Dillon LJ.
16 [1970] 2 QB 677. See (1970) 86 LQR 443 (P.V. Baker).
17 [1970] 2 QB 677 at 684A-B. See also Edmund Davies LJ (at 684G) and Megaw LJ (at 685G-H). Compare [1971] CLJ 44 at 46 (M.J. Prichard) for the view that *Barclay v Barclay* came 'perilously close' to drawing a line between express trusts for sale (where the 'prime object' may well be sale) and statutory trusts for sale (where the 'prime object' may in fact be continued residence). See also *Irani Finance Ltd v Singh* [1971] Ch 59 at 80 per Cross LJ.

There is a second limitation on any implied right of consent which may be claimed by a trust for sale beneficiary. In the event of a disposition effected by at least two trustees, the House of Lords has now expressly rebutted any suggestion that the trustees are unable to give an overreaching conveyance save with the consent of the beneficiaries in occupation.[18] Even in the case of a disposition by a sole trustee for sale, the real significance of any right of consent vested in a beneficiary in possession is that his beneficial entitlement may bind those who purchase from the sole trustee.[19] It is in this limited sense only that a beneficiary's wishes in the matter of disposition may ultimately impinge upon his trustees' dealings with the legal title in co-owned land.

(3) Rights of a trustee in bankruptcy

Personal bankruptcy presents yet another forum in which disputes as to the sale of land held on trust for sale may require to be resolved. When bankruptcy affects a person who is a beneficial co-owner of land, it is virtually inevitable that his or her trustee in bankruptcy will seek a sale of the co-owned property—possibly contrary to the clear wishes of all the co-owners—where such sale is likely to raise money for distribution amongst the creditors.

(a) Locus standi of the trustee in bankruptcy

Bankruptcy has, of course, no direct impact on any legal title held by the bankrupt as a trustee for sale,[20] but all property owned by the bankrupt beneficially (ie the bankrupt's 'estate'[1]) vests by operation of law in his trustee in bankruptcy.[2] The trustee in bankruptcy is then statutorily bound to 'get in, realise and distribute' that estate in satisfaction of the claims of creditors.[3] Where the bankrupt was beneficially entitled to a share in property held

18 *City of London Building Society v Flegg* [1988] AC 54 at 86H–87C per Lord Oliver of Aylmerton (ante, p 555).

19 *Williams & Glyn's Bank Ltd v Boland* [1981] AC 487 (ante, p 569).

20 See *Worrall v Harford* (1802) 8 Ves 4 at 8, 32 ER 250 at 252; *In re Morgan* (1881) 18 Ch D 93 at 104.

1 The estate which vests in the trustee in bankruptcy cannot include a mere right on the part of a bankrupt spouse to apply for property adjustment on divorce. Such a right does not constitute 'property' in any sense recognisable in bankruptcy law (see eg *Deloitte, Haskins & Sells Ltd v Graham* (1983) 144 DLR (3d) 539 at 543).

2 Insolvency Act 1986, ss 283(1)(a), (3)(a), 306. The involuntary alienation to the trustee in bankruptcy operates an automatic severance of any beneficial joint tenancy held by the bankrupt (ante, p 494).

3 Insolvency Act 1986, s 305(2). On application by a trustee in bankruptcy, the court may also review any transaction 'at an undervalue' entered into by the bankrupt within the five years immediately preceding the presentation of the bankruptcy petition (Insolvency Act 1986, ss 339(1), 341(1)(a)). The court may order that property transferred away by the bankrupt (or its money proceeds) be vested in the trustee and treated as part of the bankrupt's distributable estate (Insolvency Act 1986, s 342(1)). Transactions 'at an undervalue' include transactions by way of gift, or for marriage consideration, or for significantly less than full consideration (Insolvency Act 1986, s 339(3)). See eg *In Re Densham (A Bankrupt)* [1975] 1 WLR 1519 at 1529C per Goff J; *Elements of Land Law* (1st edn), pp 884–887. Transactions are, however, immune from review if they were entered into more than *two* years before the presentation of the bankruptcy petition and if the bankrupt can prove that he was not insolvent at the date of the transaction and did not become insolvent in consequence of it (Insolvency Act 1986, s 341(2)).

on trust for sale, it has been quite clear since *In Re Solomon (A Bankrupt)*[4] that the trustee in bankruptcy ranks as a 'person interested' within the meaning of section 30 of the Law of Property Act 1925. He may therefore apply for an order for sale of the entire co-owned property and, in determining this application, the court has discretion to make 'such order as it thinks fit'.

(b) *Exercise of the court's discretion*

Although section 30 contains no express limitation on the exercise of the court's discretion to order sale, the case law in this area evidences an extremely clear pattern. Irrespective of the nature of the co-owned property, where the court is asked by a trustee in bankruptcy to make an order of sale, the court usually does so.[5] The net proceeds released by such a sale are therefore available for the satisfaction of debts owed to creditors to a maximum value represented by the bankrupt's former beneficial share under the trust for sale.

(c) *Disputes relating to the family home*

Bankruptcy is personal financial crisis in its most extreme form, leading as it does to a severe diminution of legal capacity for the individual who is the subject of a bankruptcy order.[6] Bankruptcy tends to occur in close association with such events as redundancy, business failure or marriage breakdown,[7] and in each case the advent of bankruptcy has a potentially devastating impact on family life.[8] This impact is intensified by the fact that frequently the only substantial capital asset available to meet the claims of creditors is the family home in which the bankrupt's partner and children (and often the bankrupt himself) are still living.[9]

A peculiar poignancy therefore attaches to any application made by a trustee in bankruptcy for sale of co-owned land which comprises a family home.[10] The execution of the trust for sale is being sought not by the bankrupt or his spouse (either or both of whom may desperately wish to retain the

4 [1967] Ch 573 at 586.

5 *In re Citro (A Bankrupt)* [1991] Ch 142 at 160C, 161E per Bingham LJ. ('[T]he order sought by the trustee must be made unless there are, at least, compelling reasons, not found in the ordinary run of cases, for refusing it.')

6 See eg Insolvency Act 1986, s 284(1).

7 It is not impossible that a divorced husband may become bankrupt under the financial strain of attempting to support two families.

8 'Eviction from the family home may be a disaster not only to the debtor himself. . .but also to those who are living there as his dependants who may not, and often do not, have any legal or beneficial rights in the property which they can enforce' (*Insolvency Law and Practice* (Report of the Review Committee chaired by Sir Kenneth Cork, Cmnd 8558, June 1982), para 1116).

9 See generally C. Palley, *Wives, Creditors and the Matrimonial Home* (1969) 20 NILQ 132; C. Hand, *Bankruptcy and the Family Home*, [1983] Conv 219.

10 The Cork Committee noted quite rightly that where the family home is in the sole ownership of the debtor, section 30 of the Law of Property Act 1925 (which relates only to the execution of trusts for sale) confers no discretion upon the court to permit his family continued possession of that home for any length of time against the wishes of the trustee in bankruptcy. See *Insolvency Law and Practice* (Cmnd 8558, June 1982), para 1117.

home),[11] but by a third party who represents the claims of creditors. It is inevitable that the section 30 jurisdiction should fix a particularly sharp focus on the recurring tension between the entirely legitimate commercial interests of creditors and the competing claims of families to residential security at a time of special crisis.[12] It is at precisely this point that there emerges a cogent argument that the outcome of the discretion conferred by section 30 should never be inevitable or predetermined.

The resolution of the tension exposed here must now be sought both in the existing case law on the exercise of the section 30 discretion and in the overlay of special provisions relating to spouses which was imposed by the Insolvency Act 1986.[13]

(i) The historic record Prior to the commencement of the Insolvency Act 1986, it was consistently maintained by the courts that, even though a section 30 application was initiated by a trustee in bankruptcy, the matter remained ultimately one of discretion for the court.[14] There could not be said to be any presumption (either rebuttable or irrebuttable) in favour of the trustee in bankruptcy.[15] Notwithstanding these protestations of neutrality, a review of the case law relating to section 30 reveals that in almost every instance the question of priority between commercial and family claims has been resolved conclusively in favour of the trustee in bankruptcy.[16] The courts have been consistently ready to exercise their discretion under section 30 in favour of fairly immediate sale, even though the family home might still be required for the bankrupt's partner and their children.[17] Once again the 'solid tug of money' (as represented in the claims of creditors) has tended to prevail over the family interest.[18] Although the courts have steadily

11 Self-induced bankruptcy is, in rare cases, used in an attempt to defeat the first wife's claims for property adjustment on divorce (see eg *In re Holliday* [1981] Ch 405 at 412G, 414C-D; *In re Lowrie (A Bankrupt)* [1981] 3 All ER 353 at 355j–356a).

12 As Hoffmann J observed in *In re Citro (A Bankrupt)* [1991] Ch 142 at 150A-B, the resolution of this tension is 'by no means an easy thing...The two interests are not in any sense commensurable. On the one hand, one has the financial interests of the Crown, some banking institutions and a few traders. On the other, one has personal and human interests of these two families.'

13 The case law under section 30 remains applicable to unmarried couples (see *In re Citro (A Bankrupt)* [1991] Ch 142 at 159G-H per Nourse LJ).

14 *In re Turner (A Bankrupt)* [1974] 1 WLR 1556 at 1558A; *In re Densham (A Bankrupt)* [1975] 1 WLR 1519 at 1531E; *In re Holliday (A Bankrupt)* [1981] Ch 405 at 420C.

15 *In re Turner (A Bankrupt)* [1974] 1 WLR 1556 at 1558B per Goff J. According to the Court of Appeal in *Thames Guaranty Ltd v Campbell* [1985] QB 210 at 239A-B, the result of the contest between the family and the creditors is 'by no means a foregone conclusion.' The discretion of the court 'is a real one and in considering whether or not to order a sale, the court must weigh the conflicting legal and moral claims of the creditors on the one hand and those of the wife on the other, taking all relevant facts, including the existence of children, into account'.

16 See eg *In re Densham (A Bankrupt)* [1975] 1 WLR 1519 at 1532B; *Bird v Syme-Thomson* [1979] 1 WLR 440 at 445E-F; *In re Lowrie (A Bankrupt)* [1981] 3 All ER 353 at 358h, 359h; *In re Holliday (A Bankrupt)* [1981] Ch 405 at 425G.

17 See *Harman v Glencross* [1985] Fam 49 at 58A-B (ante, p 546) for a rare admission that under section 30 the 'only real question' is 'how long is the wife to continue to have possession and not whether there should be a sale at all.' See also *In re Citro (A Bankrupt)* [1991] Ch 142 at 147D-E, 157A-B per Nourse LJ.

18 See eg the statement of Cumming-Bruce LJ in *Chhokar v Chhokar* [1984] FLR 313 at 327G that, because he represents 'innocent creditors', the court 'will usually pay great regard to the voice of a trustee in bankruptcy'.

maintained that the relevant question is simply 'whose voice in equity ought to prevail',[19] it is impossible to find a single case in which the voice of the trustee in bankruptcy has not eventually prevailed.[20] The section 30 discretion has been exercised uniformly in favour of sale of the family home (usually within three or six months) in order that the bankrupt's share of the proceeds be released for the satisfaction of his debts.[1]

Typical of the commercialist bias of the court in section 30 applications is the decision in *In Re Bailey (A Bankrupt)*.[2] Here the Divisional Court in Bankruptcy had been requested, in the exercise of its discretion, to postpone the sale of a former matrimonial home for two years in order that the bankrupt co-owner's son might complete his studies at the local school and take his GCE 'A' level examinations. The Court declined to grant such a postponement,[3] Walton J laying emphasis on 'the purely property aspect of the matter.'[4] He pointed out that the maxim *pacta sunt servanda*, 'although somewhat out of fashion, must be borne in mind. A person must discharge his liabilities before there is any room for being generous. One's debts must be paid, and paid promptly. . .'[5]

19 *In re Turner (A Bankrupt)* [1974] 1 WLR 1556 at 1558C. See also *Chhokar v Chhokar* [1984] FLR 313 at 329F–330H.

20 The case law has tended to have a self-fulfilling quality. See eg *In re Bailey (A Bankrupt)* [1977] 1 WLR 278 at 283C, where Walton J attributed great significance to the fact that 'no case of the many referred to yet has thrown up the case where [the trustee in bankruptcy's] voice was not allowed to prevail.'

1 It seems to have been regarded as extremely relevant in the case law that the trustee in bankruptcy was statutorily *bound* (by Bankruptcy Act 1914, ss 48ff) to realise the debtor's assets (see eg *In re Turner (A Bankrupt)* [1974] 1 WLR 1556 at 1558E; *In re Densham (A Bankrupt)* [1975] 1 WLR 1519 at 1531G). It has been suggested that if section 30 is invoked not by a trustee in bankruptcy, but merely by a mortgagee, different considerations may be applicable. It may well be that sale would be less readily ordered at the behest of a mortgagee who, unlike a trustee in bankruptcy, has no statutory *duty* as such to realise the mortgagor's assets (see R.J. Smith, (1979) 95 LQR 501 at 506; J. Martin, [1980] Conv 361 at 376ff).

2 [1977] 1 WLR 278.

3 Megarry V-C distinguished the Court of Appeal's family-oriented approach in *Williams (J.W.) v Williams (M.A.)* [1976] Ch 278 (ante, p 591) on the ground that this had been 'not a bankruptcy case, but a husband and wife case' ([1977] 1 WLR 278 at 281F-G). In his view, the intervention of the trustee in bankruptcy materially altered the nature of the exercise under section 30. The 'husband and wife' cases were irrelevant for the present purpose since they 'were not cases in which matters of commercial obligation arose, as in the case of bankruptcy.' Moreover, said Megarry V-C, 'bankruptcy has, in relation to the matrimonial home, its own claim to protection.'

4 [1977] 1 WLR 278 at 283E. Walton J observed that the present decision 'may be yet another case where the sins of the father have to be visited on the children, but that is the way in which the world is constructed, and one must be just before one is generous' ([1977] 1 WLR 278 at 284E).

5 [1977] 1 WLR 278 at 283A-B. Postulating the example of a house which had been specially adapted to suit the needs of a handicapped child, Walton J conceded that there might sometimes be special circumstances where the court 'would hesitate long before making an immediate order for sale' ([1977] 1 WLR 278 at 284B-C). Compare, however, *In re Toobman (A Bankrupt)* (1982) *Times*, 3 March, where Warner J ordered the sale of the family home in exercising a similar discretion under Bankruptcy Act 1914, s 108(1). Here the bankrupt's wife suffered from severe heart disease and anxious depression and her doctor certified that her condition was largely attributable to her husband's financial problems and the constant threat of losing their home. Warner J nevertheless thought that there was 'no definite period, short of Mrs Toobman's life' for which he could 'usefully postpone the sale'. Her state of health did not justify keeping the creditors out of their money during her lifetime, 'with only statutory interest at 4 per cent per annum to compensate them.'

Only one reported decision prior to the Insolvency Act 1986 displays any aberration from the solid preference expressed throughout the case law for the claims of creditors. In *In Re Holliday (A Bankrupt)*[6] an ex-wife was still living in the former matrimonial home with three young children. Her ex-husband had been adjudicated bankrupt on his own petition,[7] but the extent of his outstanding liabilities was fairly small (in the region of £6,000). The Court of Appeal considered that the ex-wife had 'strong and justifiable grounds' for arguing that an immediate sale would be 'unfair' to her. The Court had particular regard to the bankrupt's conduct in leaving his wife for another woman, and to the fact that his ex-wife was now 'saddled with the burden of providing a proper home for her children' without the resources necessary for this purpose.[8] The Court also attached great relevance to the extreme hardship in which the ex-wife found herself and to the fact that postponed payment was highly unlikely to cause any great hardship to any of the creditors.[9] The Court thus declined to order an immediate sale of the property (in which there was in any event an ample equity of some £27,000).[10] Instead the Court postponed sale for five years (by which time the two eldest children would be over 17 years of age), while reserving the power to enforce the trust for sale on the application of any interested party should circumstances change in the meantime.[11]

It is significant that subsequent courts have gone out of their way to disavow any suggestion that the temporary concession to hardship demonstrated in *Holliday*'s case marked the beginning of a more general departure from the otherwise contrary pattern of the case law under section 30.[12] Indeed, in *In re Citro (A Bankrupt)*,[13] the Court of Appeal has more recently confirmed that the voice of the bankrupt's spouse will only 'in exceptional circumstances' prevail against that of the trustee in bankruptcy.[14] In *Citro*'s case Nourse LJ declined to accept as 'exceptional circumstances' the fact that a court-

6 [1981] Ch 405. See [1981] Conv 79 (A. Sydenham); (1981) 97 LQR 200 (C. Hand).

7 On the general irrelevance of the motive underlying a self-induced bankruptcy, see *Ex parte Painter* [1895] 1 QB 85 at 91; *In re Harry Dunn* [1949] Ch 640 at 647; *In re A Debtor* [1967] Ch 590 at 596C; *Re Mottee* (1977) 29 FLR 406 at 415.

8 [1981] Ch 405 at 424A-B.

9 In *In re Citro (A Bankrupt)* [1991] Ch 142 at 157D–158A, Nourse LJ thought the latter factor to have been the 'one special feature' decisive of *Holliday*'s case.

10 [1981] Ch 405 at 424D, 425D-E. It may be significant that Goff LJ died before the final judgments were delivered.

11 [1981] Ch 405 at 424E. See also *In re Gorman (A Bankrupt)* [1990] 1 WLR 616 at 629H–630B, where Vinelott J proposed to postpone sale for long enough to enable the bankrupt's wife to pursue a negligence action the proceeds of which could be used to buy out the trustee in bankruptcy. (The trustee was meanwhile entitled to a market rate of interest.)

12 See the statement of Balcombe LJ in *Harman v Glencross* [1986] Fam 81 at 95F-H that the decision in *Holliday* was 'very much against the run of the recent authorities' and represented a 'high water-mark for the protection of the wife and children under section 30'. See also *In re Lowrie (A Bankrupt)* [1981] 3 All ER 353 at 356a ('One can scarcely. . .imagine a more exceptional set of facts. . .'); [1982] Conv 74 (A. Sydenham).

13 [1991] Ch 142 at 157B per Nourse LJ. (Here the Insolvency Act 1986 was not yet in force at the relevant date.)

14 Bingham LJ ([1991] Ch 142 at 160E-F) was 'inclined to think that a test of exceptional circumstances was, in the absence of statutory guidance, more stringent than was warranted', but felt that, in enacting Insolvency Act 1986, s 336(5) (post, p 604), Parliament 'appears to have expressly approved it'. Sir George Waller, in a dissenting judgment, was prepared to accept as 'exceptional circumstances' the housing difficulty and educational disruption which emerged from the evidence at trial ([1991] Ch 142 at 163D).

ordered sale would cause difficulties with children's schooling and result in the eviction of a wife with young children. . .in circumstances where the realisation of her beneficial interest will not produce enough to buy a comparable home in the same neighbourhood, or indeed elsewhere.' These effects, said Nourse LJ, 'while engendering a natural sympathy in all who hear of them. . .are the melancholy consequences of debt and improvidence with which every civilised society has been familiar.'[15]

(ii) Changes introduced by the Insolvency Act 1986 Many of the shortcomings of the English law of insolvency were addressed by a Review Committee, chaired by Sir Kenneth Cork, which reported in 1982. This Committee concluded that it would be 'consonant with present social attitudes to alleviate the personal hardships of those who are dependent on the debtor but not responsible for his insolvency, if this can be achieved by delaying for an acceptable time the sale of the family home.'[16] The substance of this recommendation is now incorporated in the Insolvency Act 1986, although in a rather complex form which omits some of the more subtle refinements of the original proposal.

In the following ways the 1986 Act significantly adjusts the balance to be struck between family and commercial interests on bankruptcy.

(iii) Limited security of tenure for the bankrupt himself The 1986 Act confers on the bankrupt himself certain 'rights of occupation' as against the trustee in bankruptcy in respect of any dwelling-house in which the bankrupt was beneficially entitled.[17] These rights, although framed on the analogy of 'rights of occupation' under the Matrimonial Homes Act 1983,[18] are quite independent of such rights as the bankrupt's spouse (if any) may have under the latter statute.[19] Moreover, the bankrupt's 'rights of occupation' are expressed to be conditional on his living with some persons under the age of 18 with whom he has at some previous time occupied the dwelling-house in question.[20]

The bankrupt's 'rights of occupation' are deemed to take effect under the Matrimonial Homes Act 1983,[1] and include a right not to be evicted

15 [1991] Ch 142 at 157B-D. At first instance Hoffmann J had granted a postponement of sale until the youngest child reached the age of 16. This outcome was rejected by Nourse LJ (at 159B) as an erroneous fashioning of Hoffmann J's orders 'by reference to those which might have been made in the Family Division in a case where bankruptcy had not supervened.' In overruling the first instance decision with 'regret', Bingham LJ (at 161D-F) felt that Hoffmann J's approach, although foreclosed by authority, had been 'conducive to justice in the broadest sense', as reflecting 'the preference which the law increasingly gives to personal over property interests'.

16 *Insolvency Law and Practice* (Cmnd 8558, June 1982), para 1118.

17 Insolvency Act 1986, s 337(1), (2). The bankrupt cannot claim any right of occupation qua beneficial owner, since his own beneficial interest has of course vested in his trustee in bankruptcy (see Insolvency Act 1986, s 306(1)).

18 Ante, p 155.

19 Insolvency Act 1986, s 337(2).

20 Insolvency Act 1986, s 337(1)(b). This condition is somewhat more restrictive than the terms of the Cork Report, which recommended (para 1124f) that statutory protection should also be available where the home was currently occupied by the debtor's wife or cohabitee or by the debtor together with 'a dependant parent of the debtor or of his wife who has been living there as part of the family on the basis of a long term arrangement.'

1 Insolvency Act 1986, s 337(3)(a).

or excluded from the dwelling-house except with the leave of the court.[2] Thus any attempt by the trustee in bankruptcy to realise the cash value of the bankrupt's home necessarily involves an application to court for the termination of the bankrupt's 'rights of occupation'. This application, although treated as an application under section 1 of the 1983 Act,[3] is determined by the bankruptcy court with reference to criteria laid down in the Insolvency Act 1986. Accordingly, pursuant to section 337(5) of the 1986 Act, the court must make 'such order. . .as it thinks just and reasonable having regard to the interests of the creditors, to the bankrupt's financial resources, to the needs of the children and to all the circumstances of the case other than the needs of the bankrupt.' These statutory criteria are unranked and somewhat general in their tenor, in strong contrast with the express recommendation of the Cork Committee that, in balancing familial and commercial interests, the court should 'give primary consideration to the welfare of dependant children, to the circumstances of the wife, and to the situation of dependant parents who are resident in the family dwelling.'[4]

The significance of these provisions of the Insolvency Act 1986 lies in the fact that important elements of due legal process and judicial discretion are now necessarily interposed before any sale of the bankrupt's home may take place. Moreover, this statutory protection is available irrespective of whether the bankrupt's ownership of his home was joint or sole,[5] the only relevant precondition being that he should be living at the material time with persons under the age of 18. The bankrupt's security of tenure is, however, severely curtailed by an overriding statutory direction which relates to any case in which more than one year has elapsed since the bankrupt's estate vested in his trustee. In determining any application made at this later stage for a termination of the bankrupt's 'rights of occupation', the court is directed to assume, 'unless the circumstances of the case are exceptional, that the interests of the bankrupt's creditors outweigh all other considerations.'[6] This provision clearly signals that the bankrupt's home will rarely be immune from sale for more than a limited adjustment period of one year following his bankruptcy.

(iv) Limited security of tenure for the bankrupt's spouse The Insolvency Act 1986 also confirms a form of limited security of tenure arising by virtue of any 'rights of occupation' which the bankrupt's spouse may enjoy independently under the Matrimonial Homes Act 1983.[7] In the event of bankruptcy, such rights can now be terminated only on application to the bankruptcy court, which is statutorily directed pursuant to section 336(4) to make 'such order. . .as it thinks just and reasonable'. The court's discretion is once again structured by reference to a number of statutory criteria.[8] These criteria,

2 Insolvency Act 1986, s 337(2)(a)(i).
3 Ante, p 157.
4 *Insolvency Law and Practice* (Cmnd 8558, June 1982), para 1129.
5 See *Insolvency Law and Practice* (Cmnd 8558, June 1982), para 1117 (ante, p 598).
6 Insolvency Act 1986, s 337(6).
7 The bankrupt's spouse is expressly precluded from acquiring statutory 'rights of occupation' (eg by reason of marriage) during the period which intervenes between the presentation of the petition for a bankruptcy order and the vesting of the bankrupt's estate in a trustee (Insolvency Act 1986, s 336(1)).
8 Insolvency Act 1986, s 336(4).

which are similar to those under section 337(5) governing applications to terminate the 'rights of occupation' of the bankrupt himself,[9] are again controlled by the injunction that the interests of the bankrupt's creditors shall normally be regarded as paramount in all applications made more than one year after the vesting of the bankrupt's estate in his trustee.[10]

(v) Limited postponement of the execution of a trust for sale Where the bankrupt and his spouse (or former spouse) are trustees for sale of a dwelling-house, any application for sale made by the trustee in bankruptcy under section 30 of the Law of Property Act 1925 must now be addressed to the bankruptcy court.[11] This court is directed to determine the application with reference to precisely the same criteria,[12] contained in section 336(4) of the Insolvency Act 1986, which regulate the discretionary termination of the 'rights of occupation' enjoyed by the bankrupt's spouse under the Matrimonial Homes Act 1983.[13] Once again the court's discretion is peremptorily limited, save in 'exceptional' circumstances,[14] by the instruction that in any application made more than one year after the trustee in bankruptcy is invested with the bankrupt's estate the court must assume that 'the interests of the bankrupt's creditors outweigh all other considerations.'[15]

(vi) Comparison with homestead legislation It was one of the original purposes of the Insolvency Act 1986 to induce a better and more compassionate balance in the consideration of competing interests in the family home on bankruptcy. In particular the statutory compromise was aimed at establishing a legal mechanism which would delay rather than cancel the rights of creditors.[16] The heightened emphasis thus accorded the residential expectations of family members was intended to mark a significant advance on the pattern of decision-making evident in the antecedent case law under section 30 of the

9 The criteria are adapted to include reference also to the conduct of the spouse 'so far as contributing to the bankruptcy' (s 336(4)(b)), the needs and financial resources of the spouse (s 336(4)(c)) and, of course, the needs of any children (s 336(4)(d)).

10 Insolvency Act 1986, s 336(5).

11 Insolvency Act 1986, s 336(3).

12 The Law Commission has recommended that the provisions of Insolvency Act 1986, s 336 should be extended, with modifications, to cover all applications for sale in which a trust for sale beneficiary has been adjudged bankrupt (Law Com No 181, paras 12.12, 20.3).

13 A trustee for sale, even though a spouse, does not of course have 'rights of occupation' under the Matrimonial Homes Act 1983. Such rights are not conferred upon an owner of the legal estate (ante, p 157). The Law Commission has proposed that the criteria contained in section 336(4) should be extended to those cases in which the bankrupt has merely a beneficial interest in land held on trust for him by his spouse (Law Com No 181, para 12.11). At present the guidelines of section 336(4) are applicable only where the bankrupt is entitled (whether solely or jointly) to the legal estate in the dwelling-house.

14 This reference to a category of 'exceptional' circumstances is intended to apply the same test as that which has already evolved in the case law on bankruptcy pursuant to section 30 of the Law of Property Act 1925 (ante, p 599ff). See *In re Citro (A Bankrupt)* [1991] Ch 142 at 159G-H per Nourse LJ, 160E-F per Bingham LJ. There is therefore, as Nourse LJ pointed out (at 159H), a desirable symmetry between the criteria applicable to married and unmarried couples (ante, p 601).

15 Insolvency Act 1986, s 336(5). It is clear that the Law Commission, in proposing in 1989 a reformulation of Law of Property Act 1925, s 30, did not intend to alter this effect of insolvency. See Explanatory Note 24 to Clause 6 of the Draft Trusts of Land Bill (Law Com No 181, Appendix A).

16 See *Insolvency Law and Practice* (Cmnd 8558, June 1982), para 1118.

Law of Property Act 1925. In practice it appears that the limiting statutory formulae, coupled with strict construction by the courts, may have produced a substantial continuity with the bankruptcy case law rather than a quantum step into a new jurisprudence of insolvency.

Even at face value the innovative measures of the Insolvency Act 1986 fall short of the objectives of the 'homestead legislation' which is currently in force in New Zealand and in many of the common law jurisdictions of Canada and the United States. At the heart of each of these homestead schemes is a large presumption in favour of long-term security of tenure in the family home. By contrast, the balance of emphasis expressed in the Insolvency Act 1986 still heavily favours the recovery of creditors' claims, at most subject to a limited delay in the enforcement of those claims against family assets.

One of the oldest and most typical schemes of homestead rights is contained in New Zealand's Joint Family Homes Act 1964. Under this statute it is possible for spouses to register their home as a 'joint family home'.[17] Upon registration the spouses become legal and beneficial joint tenants,[18] and while the joint family home settlement remains registered the interests of the husband and wife are unaffected by bankruptcy or assignment for the benefit of creditors.[19] Creditors of either spouse may oppose the initial registration,[20] but may subsequently attack the joint family home settlement only on the limited grounds laid down in the Act.[1]

Under the Act the court retains a discretion to cancel any existing joint family home registration,[2] but it is clear that this discretion will not be exercised in favour of sale merely because one of the spouses has been declared bankrupt.[3] Cancellation followed by sale and distribution will be ordered only in fairly exceptional circumstances. Such circumstances may arise, however, where there has been unconscientious dealing by the debtor with his creditors,[4] or where *both* spouses have been adjudicated bankrupt and there remains a very substantial equity from which the creditors could be satisfied without undue hardship to the family.[5] Even if the court decides in a particular case that the joint family home must be sold up to meet the claims of creditors, the proceeds of that sale remain to a level specified

17 Joint Family Homes Act 1964, s 5. Registration is entirely voluntary.
18 Joint Family Homes Act 1964, s 9(1)(b).
19 Joint Family Homes Act 1964, s 9(2)(d). See *Official Assignee v Lawford* [1984] 2 NZLR 257 at 263.
20 Joint Family Homes Act 1964, s 6(1).
1 Joint Family Homes Act 1964, ss 16–20.
2 Joint Family Homes Act 1964, s 16(1).
3 See eg *Official Assignee of Pannell v Pannell* [1966] NZLR 324 at 325, where Wilson J did not think the very considerable total of the bankrupt's debts or the large number of his creditors to be 'sufficient, without more, to warrant...an order for sale.'
4 See *Official Assignee of Pannell v Pannell* [1966] NZLR 324 at 326.
5 See eg *Official Assignee v Lawford* [1984] 2 NZLR 257 at 264ff, where even after satisfaction of the creditors' claims the equity amounted to over $70,000. The Court of Appeal considered that this surplus was sufficient to enable the bankrupts to purchase a quite adequate home and that 'on an objective view the present appellants and their family cannot possibly be said to be in a situation of hardship...True, their standard of living has fallen; the home will be more modest and they no longer own a yacht...' ([1984] 2 NZLR 257 at 265). Compare *Rukat v Rukat* [1975] Fam 63 at 73F ('The rich gourmet who because of financial stringency has to drink vin ordinaire with his grouse may well think that he is suffering a hardship; but sensible people would say he was not').

by statute immune from third party claims,[6] with the result that the family salvages something from the calamity of insolvency.[7]

The priorities expressed in the Joint Family Homes Act 1964 are quite different from those which have prevailed hitherto in the English law of bankruptcy. The New Zealand legislation was enacted with the express object of promoting the stability and permanence of family life as a higher social end than that represented by commercial security for the creditor.[8] The 1964 Act indeed embodies a remarkable and imaginative attempt to strike a humane social balance between competing interests, and it is highly arguable that English law would be enriched by the enactment of similar legislation.

(d) The equity of exoneration

If and when a trustee in bankruptcy finally succeeds in obtaining a court order for the sale of jointly owned property, the division of the resulting proceeds of sale may be affected by the operation of the 'equity of exoneration'. This little known equity is founded on the general proposition that if two joint owners of property charge that property in order to secure the debts of only one of the joint owners, the other joint owner stands merely in the position of a surety and is entitled, as between the two joint owners, to have the secured indebtedness discharged so far as is possible out of the equitable interest of the debtor.[9] The equity of exoneration in effect allocates more fairly as between joint mortgagors the ultimate burden of an indebtedness which was incurred for the benefit of only one co-owner.

(i) Operation of the equitable principle of exoneration The operation of this equitable doctrine can be demonstrated in a practical context where two co-owners of a family home have jointly charged that property as security for the debts of one co-owner who is subsequently adjudicated bankrupt. Such a charge may well arise, for instance, where a bank insists on the provision of some security in respect of the husband's bank overdraft. Were it not for the equity of exoneration, the burden of this indebtedness could quite properly be thrown in exactly equal proportions upon the funds which represent the beneficial half-shares of the co-owners in the net proceeds of an enforced bankruptcy sale. However, the equity of exoneration entitles the bankrupt's co-owner to insist that the burden of the creditors' claims should be diverted

6 In the event of cancellation of a joint family home registration on the ground of bankruptcy, $61,000 must be set aside for the beneficiaries of the joint family home settlement, notwithstanding that this pro tanto defeats the claims of creditors (see Joint Family Homes Act 1964, s 16(1)(a), as amended by Joint Family Homes (Specified Sum) Order 1992 (SR 1992/96)). See, however, *Official Assignee v Noonan* [1988] 2 NZLR 252 at 255ff.

7 Similar schemes of limited immunity from the effects of bankruptcy are contained in Canadian provincial legislation. See eg Alberta's Exemptions Act (RSA 1980, c E-15), s 1(1)(k); Saskatchewan's Exemptions Act (RSS 1978, c E-14), s 2(1), para 11.

8 See Vol 292, *New Zealand Parliamentary Debates*, 3493ff (Hon T.C. Webb, Attorney-General)); Vol 340, *New Zealand Parliamentary Debates*, 2294 (Hon J.R. Hanan, Minister of Justice). In *Fairmaid v Otago District Land Registrar* [1952] NZLR 782 at 786, North J described the legislation as ensuring that 'husband and wife can live contentedly in their home in the knowledge that it is secured to them as a family home so long as they need it whatever the vicissitudes of life may bring.' See also *Sutherland v Sutherland* [1955] NZLR 689 at 691; *Official Assignee v Lawford* [1984] 2 NZLR 257 at 261; *Official Assignee v Noonan* [1988] 2 NZLR 252 at 255 per Richardson J, 255f per Somers J.

9 See *In re Pittortou (A Bankrupt)* [1985] 1 WLR 58 at 61B.

primarily on to the bankrupt's share in those proceeds. The result of this process is to enhance the proprietary interest of the bankrupt's co-owner and to augment her eventual money recovery.[10]

(ii) Relevance of intention The equity of exoneration depends upon the presumed intention of the parties.[11] The equity comes into play only if it can be inferred from the circumstances of the case that the joint mortgagors together intended that the burden of the secured indebtedness should fall primarily on the share of the actual debtor.

Thus the equity cannot operate if the indebtedness in question was incurred for the purpose of financing a higher standard of living for both co-owners and their family.[12] In other words, the equity cannot be invoked if in reality both joint mortgagors received and enjoyed the benefits of the indebtedness.[13] Thus, in *In Re Pittortou (A Bankrupt)*,[14] Scott J held that the equity of exoneration should be confined to payments other than those made for the 'joint benefit of the household'. On this basis the bankrupt's wife was not entitled to any exoneration in respect of debts arising in connection with the running of the joint family household. She was, however, entitled to require that debts incurred by her husband for purely business purposes and in supporting another woman should be treated as charged primarily on his own half-share in the mortgaged property.[15]

10 *In re Pittortou (A Bankrupt)* [1985] 1 WLR 58 at 61F. See also *In re A Debtor (No 24 of 1971)* [1976] 1 WLR 952 at 955.
11 *In re Pittortou (A Bankrupt)* [1985] 1 WLR 58 at 62A.
12 See *Paget v Paget* [1898] 1 Ch 470 at 475ff; *In re Pittortou (A Bankrupt)* [1985] 1 WLR 58 at 62G.
13 *In re Woodstock (A Bankrupt)* (Unreported, Walton J, 19 November 1979).
14 [1985] 1 WLR 58 at 62H.
15 [1985] 1 WLR 58 at 62H–63A. See also *Re Berry* [1976] 2 NZLR 449 at 451f; *Farrugia v Official Receiver in Bankruptcy* (1982) 43 ALR 700 at 703.

CHAPTER 15

Strict settlements

The term 'settlement' is a generic term which, when properly applied, covers all deliberately created trust arrangements affecting land or other property. In the context of land the term 'settlement' thus includes not only a 'strict settlement' of land (which is governed by the provisions of the Settled Land Act 1925) but also a 'trust for sale' of land (which is governed largely by the Law of Property Act 1925). Both the strict settlement and the trust for sale involve arrangements under which the legal estate in land is held on trust, in order that the benefit derived from the land should be deflected towards specified persons called 'beneficiaries'. The present chapter deals with the law relating to strict settlements of land; the institution of the trust for sale was discussed in Chapter 14.[1]

1. THE MODERN INCIDENCE OF THE STRICT SETTLEMENT

It is one of the ironies of legal development that the strict settlement in its present form is a moribund institution. Most of the circumstances caught within the terms of the Settled Land Act 1925 are archaic and are now found only rarely in practice.[2] Paradoxically the 1925 Act contains in a highly perfected form certain sophisticated devices for the legal articulation of the strict settlement. Just as the strict settlement reached its zenith of refinement as a legal institution, other factors began to operate in such a way as to render the strict settlement an unsuitable (if not fiscally disastrous) form of landholding.[3] Today the strict settlement has been almost wholly displaced by the trust for sale,[4] and the skill of lawyers is now devoted more commonly to avoiding than promoting the creation of strict settlements of land. In recent years the Law Commission has condemned the strict

1 Ante, p 518.

2 The Law Commission reported in 1989 that its consultation of practitioners had revealed the existence of very few strict settlements still currently on file, most of these having been established decades ago (see Law Commission, *Transfer of Land: Trusts of Land* (Law Com No 181, 8 June 1989), para 4.3 (n 72)).

3 The tax consequences which flow from the creation of a strict settlement are onerous in the extreme, taxation falling on the full capital value of the estate on the termination of each successive interest (see A.R. Mellows, *The Law of Succession* (4th edn, London 1983), p 304). Estate duty, the forerunner of this form of taxation, was introduced by the Finance Act 1894. The wealth retrieved by the Revenue by means of this tax was to provide the basis of the great naval rearmament in this country which immediately preceded the First World War. See F.H. Lawson, *Introduction to the Law of Property* (London 1958), p 94f.

4 See Chapter 14. The successive interests which take effect under a strict settlement can just as easily be created behind a 'successive interest' trust for sale (ante, p 519).

settlement as 'excessively complex and no longer necessary'[5] and in 1989 the Commission recommended that the creation of new strict settlements under the Settled Land Act 1925 should be prohibited and that successive interests should henceforth be assimilated within a new form of land trust.[6]

(1) The function of the strict settlement

In its classical form the strict settlement was essentially a landholding mechanism which was only gradually and with great ingenuity modified by statute in the late 19th and early 20th centuries to ensure the commerciability of the great landed estates. The strict settlement provided a structure whose overriding purpose was the protection of the interests of the beneficiaries and, ultimately, the protection of the dynastic impulse.[7] For the settled land beneficiaries, the value of the land lay not in its exchange value on the open market but rather in the fact that it provided a medium for the intergenerational transfer of wealth within the family.[8] Wealth was synonymous with land and land was retained within the family essentially by conferring limited kinds of interest on key family members and (usually) by subjecting the property to resettlement every generation. In this way 'no single individual ever acquired an unfettered power to appropriate the family capital for his individual purposes.'[9]

(2) The demise of the strict settlement

The device of the settlement evolved as a form of landholding designed primarily to satisfy the property-related aspirations of a distinctive social élite. Marriage settlements provided for patterns of landholding which gave effect to the living arrangements ordained by a patriarchal figure—a paterfamilias. The interests created under the strict settlement were heavily determined by status and gender.[10] Status was determinative in the sense that the settled land interests were graded according to status within the

5 Law Commission, *Trusts of Land* (Law Com Working Paper No 94, September 1985), para 17.1.

6 Law Com No 181 (1989), para 4.3ff. For a description of the proposed 'trust of land', see Chapter 14 (ante, p 537).

7 As Professor A.W.B. Simpson has said, the elaboration of settled land interests was 'the product of aristocratic dynastic family landholding. To the wealthy landed classes, real property was the essential endowment not of individuals but of the family . . . Land was to be exploited in the interests of the family, not the individual, but the mechanism for its exploitation was, paradoxically, a subtle manipulation of individual property rights . . . The compromise commonly employed in Blackstone's time, and evolved in the seventeenth century, was the strict settlement under which the land was managed by a succession of life tenants' (*Introduction* to W. Blackstone, *Commentaries on the Laws of England* (Facsimile edn, Chicago and London 1979), Vol 2, pp x–xi).

8 See eg Lloyd Bonfield, *Marriage, Property and the 'Affective Family'*, (1983) 1 Law and History Review 297 at 298ff.

9 See A.W.B. Simpson, loc cit, p xi.

10 For an account of the complex calibrations distinguishing the various forms of provision which could be made by a marriage settlement, see Lloyd Bonfield, *Marriage Settlements 1601–1740: The Adoption of the Strict Settlement* (Cambridge 1983).

family structure.[11] Gender was relevant inasmuch as the male of the species was commonly advanced in preference to the female.

The modern demise of the strict settlement in favour of concurrent ownership under the trust for sale owes much to the fundamental social changes which have occurred during the last two centuries. Our own society has ceased to be regulated to the same degree by status and gender.[12] Coupled with the movement from status-dependent to voluntary co-operative relationships has been the wide acknowledgement of a new egalitarian ideal. This has been particularly evident in respect of the relationship between male and female, between husband and wife.[13] The social pattern described here is far removed from that of a former age which saw the grant of patriarchal largesse epitomised in the marriage settlement. Concurrent ownership of an absolute interest in land has become the appropriate medium for the tangible expression of the new social pattern.

In the event the device of the strict settlement has now outlived its social and economic purpose. Indeed even by 1925 it had become clear that the strict settlement could no longer survive as a medium of dynastic family landholding. The Settled Land Act 1925 recognised the moribund nature of the device and, ironically, incorporated within the new statutory scheme the very mechanisms which were required to facilitate the destruction of the great settled estates of England. The keynote of the 1925 Act was the introduction of a means by which the legal title in settled land could most efficiently be sold off in a manner consistent with the securing of some degree of financial protection for the beneficial interests contained within the settlement. It is the nature of this remarkable compromise which provides the focus of much of the remainder of this chapter.

2. COVERAGE OF THE SETTLED LAND ACT 'SETTLEMENT'

A 'settlement' is, in the correct sense of the word, a document or group of documents,[14] but the term is commonly used to refer to the form of property holding expressed within these documents. A 'settlement' within the meaning of the Settled Land Act 1925 (sometimes called a 'strict settlement' or 'Settled Land Act settlement') arises in two generalised kinds of situation: (1) where limited successive equitable interests are carved out of ownership of a legal estate in land, and (2) where an absolute (as distinct from a limited) interest in land is conferred on a grantee who is subject to some disability, liability

11 'The evolution of the property object gives to property the power to create separate species within the genus homo, a power like that of an Egyptian king who establishes castes . . .'. See K. Renner, *The Institutions of Private Law and Their Social Functions* (London and Boston 1949), p 109.

12 See eg M.A. Glendon, *Power and Authority in the Family: New Legal Patterns as Reflections of Changing Ideologies*, (1975) 23 AJCL 1.

13 The literature is legion, but see particularly O.R. McGregor, *Equality, sexual values and permissive legislation: the English experience*, (1972) 1 Journal of Social Policy 44; M.A. Glendon, *The New Family and the New Property* (Toronto 1981), p 11ff.

14 Settled Land Act 1925, s 1(1).

or contingency which detracts from his capacity or entitlement to hold such an interest.

(1) Limited beneficial interests

It is the objective of the Settled Land Act 1925 to impose a special regime of estate ownership on certain statutorily defined patterns of landholding. These patterns of interests are not mutually exclusive and may overlap to some degree. The first group of situations caught within the regime of the Settled Land Act 1925 is described in section 1(1).

(a) Interests in succession

For the purpose of the 1925 Act a strict settlement arises where land 'stands . . . limited in trust for any persons by way of succession'.[15] This case neatly catches the circumstances described in *Fig.* 45 where land is granted to A for life, with remainder to B in fee simple.[16] It would also apply to a more extended series of successive interests, as for instance where land is granted to A for life, with remainders to B for life, then to C for life, and so on. All such interests are equitable only[17] and may therefore take effect successively in possession behind the trust arrangement known as the 'strict settlement'.[18]

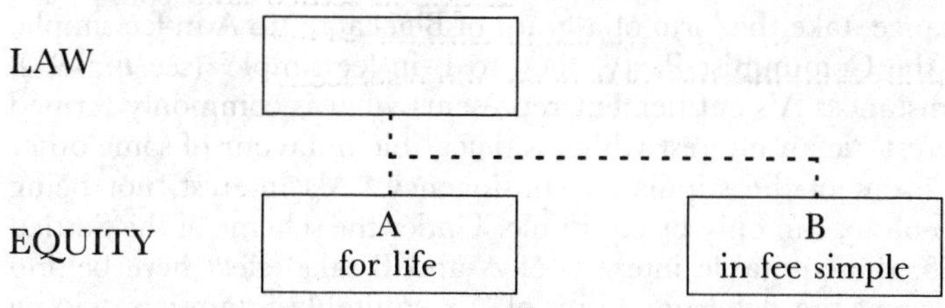

Fig. 45

(b) The entailed interest

The definition of 'settlement' is expressly widened by statute to cover the circumstances where land is 'limited in trust for any person in possession for an entailed interest . . .'[19] An entailed interest can take effect only as

15 Settled Land Act 1925, s 1(1)(i).

16 *Ungurian v Lesnoff* [1990] Ch 206 at 226B per Vinelott J.

17 The identity of the legal owner in *Fig.* 45, is revealed later (post, p 616).

18 'Possession' in this context bears a highly specialised twin meaning. The beneficiary 'in possession' need not, of course, enjoy personal occupation of the land. In this sense 'possession' may—and very commonly does—comprise the receipt of rents and profits drawn from the land (Settled Land Act 1925, s 117(1)(xix)). Entitlement 'in possession' does, however, denote that the owner of the relevant interest is not excluded from immediate enjoyment of the land (or its rents and profits) by reason of the presence of any prior interest or prior interests vested in somebody else (ante, p 93).

19 Settled Land Act 1925, s 1(1)(ii)(a).

an equitable interest,[20] and this means that the Settled Land Act has application to the following case:

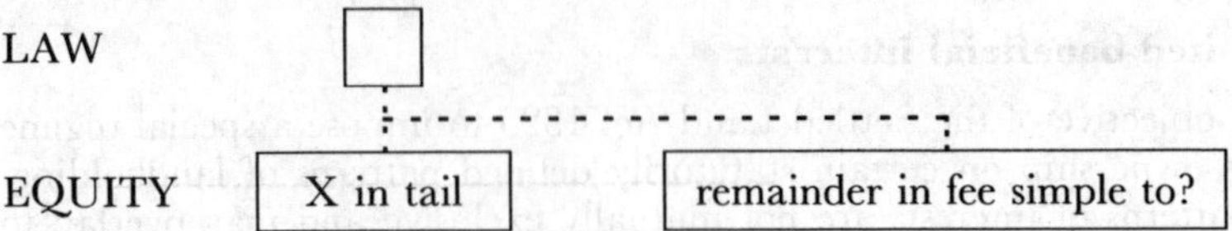

Fig. 46

Here the limited interest held beneficially by X means necessarily that there is some kind of successive interest which must fall into possession when X's interest determines.[1] If the fee simple is not otherwise disposed of, it will revert to the original grantor or to his estate.[2]

(c) *The 'shifting' interest*

In rare situations land may be limited to A in fee simple, subject to this interest divesting in favour of B in the event that some specified condition is or is not fulfilled. Here A's interest is clearly subject to a condition subsequent, and B's interest is subject to a condition precedent. An example might, for instance, take the form of a grant of Blackacre 'to A in fee simple, but if A joins the Communist Party, then to B in fee simple' (see *Fig.* 47). In these circumstances A's entitlement represents what is commonly termed a 'shifting interest', ie an interest which is defeasible in favour of some other person in the event of the stipulated contingency.[3] A's interest, not being a fee simple absolute, can only be equitable. Under the scheme of the Settled Land Act 1925, the equitable interests of A and B take effect here behind a strict settlement,[4] the determinability of A's equitable interest providing the successive element which is so characteristic of this form of landholding.[5]

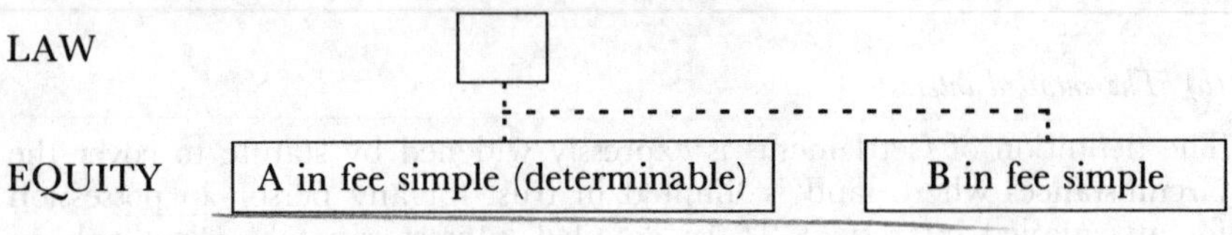

Fig. 47

20 Law of Property Act 1925, s 1(1), (2), ante, p 68.

1 Of course, it is normally fairly easy for X to frustrate the element of succession by barring the entail (ante, p 59), a step which withdraws X's entitlement altogether from the scope of the Settled Land Act (post, p 630).

2 At this stage the name of the owner of the legal estate has been left blank. His or her identity will become obvious shortly (post, p 621).

3 In this situation, however, nothing 'shifts' except the right to 'possession' in the technical sense. No actual interest in land passes from A to B.

4 Settled Land Act 1925, s 1(1)(ii)(b).

5 Once again, the identity of the legal owner in *Fig.* 47 has yet to be supplied (post, p 621).

(2) Absolute interests granted to persons subject to disability, liability or contingency

All the foregoing situations have concerned successive interests which, primarily for reasons of convenience, are brought within the ambit of the Settled Land Act 1925. However, the Act also governs a second (and slightly different) group of circumstances. This group involves not the grant of limited interests by way of succession but rather the conferment of absolute beneficial entitlement upon a recipient who is, for some reason, subject to a disability, liability or contingency which precludes his holding the absolute legal interest.

(a) The 'springing' interest

The Settled Land Act applies to the so-called 'springing interest' which arises where land is 'limited in trust for any person for an estate in fee simple or for a term of years contingently on the happening of any event'.[6] Examples of such an interest arise if land is granted to G in fee simple in the event that he should be called to the Bar or attain the age of 30, and so on. G's entitlement in fee simple is thereby made contingent upon his performing some qualifying condition, with the result that he has a 'springing interest' which may or may not materialise at a future date. Such an arrangement in relation to land can be brought about only under the aegis of a strict settlement (see *Fig.* 48), since someone has to manage and administer the land until it becomes clear whether G will or will not satisfy the contingency.[7]

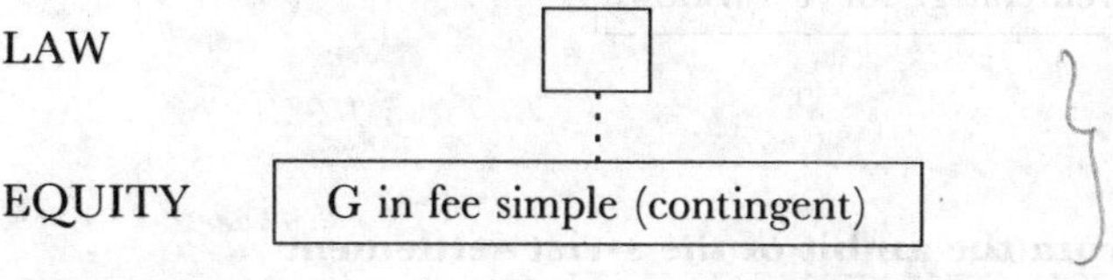

Fig. 48

(b) Grant to a minor

A 'settlement' within the meaning of the Settled Land Act 1925 is raised by the grant of a legal estate in freehold or leasehold land to a minor (ie one who has not yet attained the age of 18). A minor is never, of course, competent to hold any legal estate in land.[8] Such a grant can confer only an equitable interest, there being no equivalent objection to *equitable* entitlement on the part of a minor. During the minority, however, the legal fee simple absolute in possession must be vested in an adult nominee who is entrusted with fiduciary powers of management and disposition. This arrangement must be effected (as in *Fig.* 49) behind a strict settlement pursuant to the 1925 Act.[9]

6 Settled Land Act 1925, s 1(1)(iii).
7 Of course, if the contingency is never satisfied, the fee simple reverts to the settlor or (if he is dead) to his estate.
8 Law of Property Act 1925, s 1(6), ante, p 69.
9 Settled Land Act 1925, s 1(1)(ii)(d).

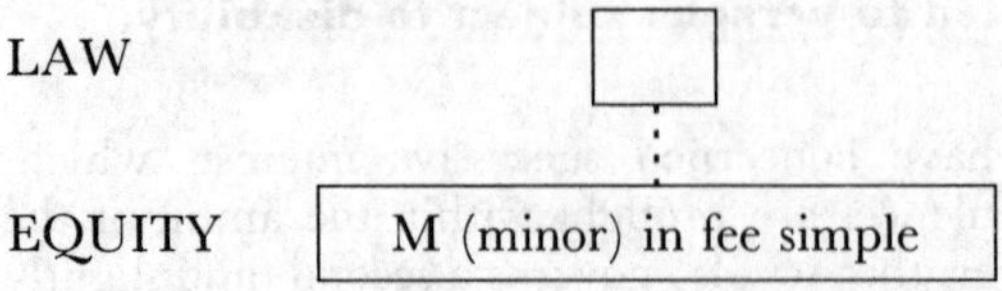

LAW

EQUITY M (minor) in fee simple

Fig. 49

(c) Family rentcharge

There is one other situation in which the Settled Land Act 1925 applies to the grant of an absolute interest in land. Where land is charged 'whether voluntarily or in consideration of marriage' with the payment of any rentcharge for the life of any person or any less period, the land is subjected to a strict settlement.[10] This would be the case, for instance, where a testator, T, left land to his eldest son, S, in fee simple subject to the payment of an annual income (derived from the rents and profits drawn from the land) to T's widow for the remainder of her life or until her remarriage (see *Fig.* 50).[11]

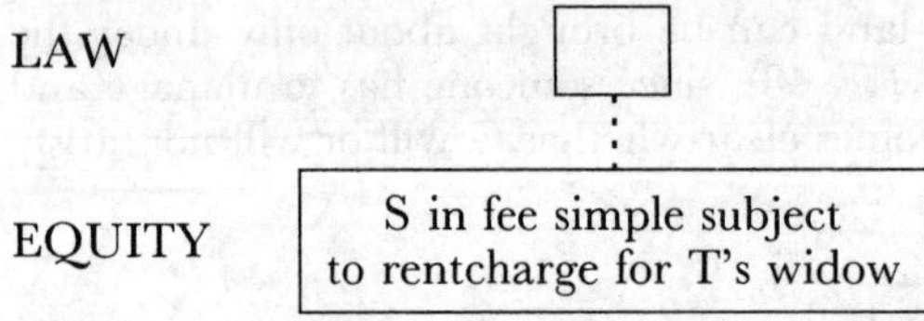

Fig. 50

(3) Exclusions from the ambit of the strict settlement

Extensive though the ambit of the Settled Land Act 1925 may be, several kinds of landholding are quite clearly excluded from its scope.

(a) Bare trust

A 'bare trust' of land falls entirely outside the scope of the Settled Land Act 1925.[12] It follows, moreover, that wherever settled land interests resolve themselves into the form of a bare trust, the land in question ceases to be the subject of a strict settlement and is no longer governed by the Act. A bare trust arises, for instance, where the legal estate in property is, at any time, vested in one person absolutely while simultaneously the whole equitable interest is held by another person absolutely (see *Fig.* 51).

10 Settled Land Act 1925, s 1(1)(v).

11 However, if S's fee simple were subject to the payment of a rentcharge which arose, not voluntarily or in consideration of marriage, but in return for money or money's worth, then the fee simple would rank technically as a conditional fee simple. Such an estate is deemed to be a legal estate and may, of course, exist without the necessity of creating a strict settlement (ante, p 87, post, p 1136).

12 Ante, p 40. A bare trust arises where a title is vested in a trustee who has no active duties to perform (*In re Cunningham and Frayling* [1891] 2 Ch 567 at 572 per Stirling J).

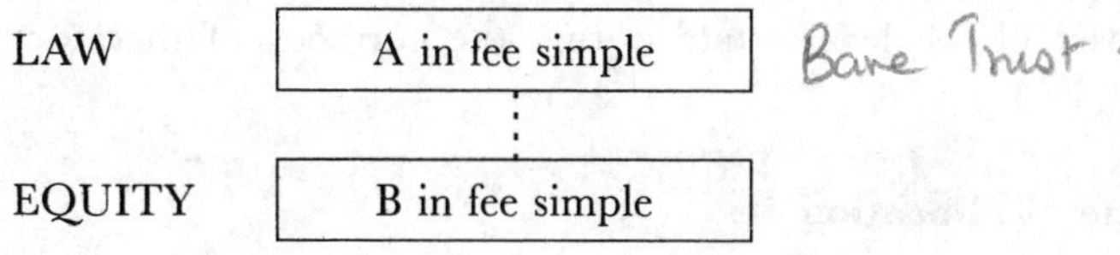

Fig. 51

It is a principle of general application to bare trusts of this kind that, since A's interest comprises a purely nominal or 'paper' title, A must convey his estate in accordance with any directions given by B.[13] B, as owner of the absolute beneficial interest is the only person with any right to enjoy the property and derive value from it. Thus, if B is *sui iuris* (ie of full age and sound mind), he may direct A to convey the legal estate to himself, B. Such a conveyance of course destroys the bare trust by constituting B the sole owner at law and in equity.[14] This indeed is what should happen in the normal course of events, because this form of bare trust is intrinsically an anomalous and unstable arrangement in respect of property. Here the bare trust connotes a state of disequilibrium: the 'paper' title is for the time being vested in one who has no beneficial stake in the property. Thus equity favours a return to a state of equilibrium, and this is most easily achieved by means of a conveyance by the legal owner to the equitable owner.[15]

(b) Trust for sale

The form of landholding known as the 'trust for sale' falls unequivocally outside the ambit of the strict settlement. The Settled Land Act 1925 has no application to 'land held on trust for sale'.[16] The essential difference between a strict settlement and a trust for sale is the fact that in the trust for sale the legal estate is vested in trustees and the beneficial interests are normally concurrent and absolute rather than successive and limited.[17]

3. ALLOCATION OF THE LEGAL ESTATE UNDER A STRICT SETTLEMENT

In each of the circumstances of 'settlement' already described in *Figs.* 45 to 50 the owner of the full legal estate in the settled land (ie of the legal fee simple absolute in possession) has been left unspecified. It is now necessary to identify the legal owner in each case, there being no possible vacuum

13 See *Christie v Ovington* (1875) 1 Ch D 279 at 281 per Hall V-C.
14 See *Commissioner of Stamp Duties (Queensland) v Livingston* [1965] AC 694 at 712C–D per Viscount Radcliffe (ante, p 265).
15 Of course, it is not impossible that the equitable owner B should direct that A convey the legal estate to a third party X. B's right so to direct is simply an application of the rule in *Saunders v Vautier* (1841) 4 Beav 115 at 116, 49 ER 282, Cr & Ph 240 at 249, 41 ER 482 at 485 (ante, p 49). However, such a conveyance would not destroy the existence of a bare trust. The transferee at law X would thenceforth hold on a bare trust for B, unless he took title as a bona fide purchaser for value without notice.
16 Settled Land Act 1925, s 1(7).
17 Ante, p 521.

or hiatus in respect of the legal estate during the currency of the strict settlement.

(1) The rationale of allocation

The allocation of legal ownership in settled land depends fundamentally upon the premise that the legal title is a merely nominal or paper title. Ownership of the legal estate in settled land confers upon the title holder no benefit at all but instead imposes on this person a number of fiduciary obligations of administration. This being so, it matters not greatly who holds the legal estate in the settled land so long as he or she is faithful in the discharge of fiduciary responsibilities of management and disposition in relation to the trust property.

The allocation of legal ownership is therefore reduced largely to a question of convenience, and it makes sense in general terms to vest the legal estate (with its attendant decision-making powers) in the beneficiary who is currently entitled to an equitable interest in possession. Almost invariably the currently entitled beneficiary has the most direct financial concern in the orderly operation of the strict settlement. He or she may reasonably be expected to discharge with care the day-to-day management of the settled property: it is, after all, the beneficiary in possession who will derive the immediate and tangible benefit of such vigilance. Moreover, the facility of land transfer is greatly enhanced if the full legal title is vested in the beneficiary currently in possession. It is generally more convenient that the eventual purchaser of the settled land should be able to transact directly with the person who has the immediate beneficial stake in the land.

(2) The 'tenant for life'

It was in the light of these considerations that the Settled Land Act 1925 confirmed the office or status of the 'tenant for life'. It is the tenant for life who, pursuant to the scheme of the Act, is competent to hold the legal estate and to exercise the concomitant powers of interim management and eventual disposition.

(a) The owner of a life interest

The Settled Land Act 1925 confers the office of 'tenant for life' upon 'the person of full age who is for the time being beneficially entitled under a settlement to possession of settled land for his life.'[18] Thus the settled land beneficiary who holds a life interest in possession[19] qualifies as the 'tenant

18 Settled Land Act 1925, s 19(1). It is, of course, possible that there may be more than one tenant for life (see Settled Land Act 1925, s 117(1)(xxviii)), for example where land is granted to A and B for their joint lives with remainder to the survivor for life. Both A and B, if of full age, occupy the position of tenant for life (Settled Land Act 1925, s 19(2)). They are entitled to hold the legal estate as joint tenants, and in the exercise of their joint powers of management and disposition must act unanimously or not at all (see *Re 90 Thornhill Road, Tolworth, Barker v Addiscott* [1970] Ch 261 at 265H, 267A). The survivor becomes, of course, a single tenant for life.

19 'Possession' bears the extended meaning discussed earlier (ante, pp 93, 611).

for life' for the purpose of the Act (see eg A in *Fig.* 45[20]). No great formality of language is required in order to constitute a tenant for life for the purpose of the Act. In the absence of express reference to the existence of a 'trust for sale',[1] an equitable life interest under the Act is denoted by the grant of a right to reside for life[2] or to receive rents and profits for life.[3] Once a person has been so designated as 'tenant for life', he is entitled to call for a vesting in his own name of the legal estate in the settled land.[4]

(b) *The dual entitlement of the tenant for life*

It is at this point that the duality of the tenant for life's interest in the settled land becomes most clearly apparent. The tenant for life usually holds two distinct interests in the land, one legal and the other equitable. His legal ownership is purely nominal and fiduciary. The quantum of the life tenant's benefit under the terms of the strict settlement is confined to the extent of his own equitable life interest. He is entitled to occupy and enjoy the land during his lifetime (or to receive the rents and profits drawn from the land during that time). As soon as there is any possibility that the tenant for life may derive personal profit from his *legal* ownership,[5] independent 'trustees of the settlement' intervene to ensure that he suffers no temptation to abandon his fiduciary role for the advancement of self-interest.[6] The intervention of the trustees of the settlement also ensures that the interests of the settled land beneficiaries are 'overreached' by a purchaser and are translated into the proceeds of sale paid over by him.[7]

20 Ante, p 611.
1 Ante, p 522.
2 *Re Carne's Settled Estates* [1899] 1 Ch 324 at 329f per North J; *In re Boyer's Settled Estates* [1916] 2 Ch 404 at 409 per Sargant J. A grantee may be sufficiently marked out as a tenant for life by the conferment of a non-exclusive right to reside until death (see *Re Potter, decd* [1970] VR 352 at 354ff) or of a right to reside for a period determinable on some earlier event (see *Ungurian v Lesnoff* [1990] Ch 206 at 226A–B). See also *In re Gibbons* [1920] 1 Ch 372 at 377ff (option to occupy and enjoy use of a house); *Bogdanovic v Koteff* (1988) 12 NSWLR 472 at 475A–C.
3 See *Peach v Peach* (Unreported, Court of Appeal No 1979 P 2475, 3 November 1981) per Cumming-Bruce LJ.
4 Settled Land Act 1925, s 9(2). See eg *Peach v Peach* (Unreported, Court of Appeal No 1979 P 2475, 3 November 1981) per Templeman LJ; *Ungurian v Lesnoff* [1990] Ch 206 at 224D–E, 226D.
5 Such a situation arises, for instance, where in the exercise of his powers of disposition under Settled Land Act 1925, ss 38ff he transacts with the settled estate and receives capital proceeds (eg from a purchaser of the legal title).
6 Post, p 638.
7 This functional analysis of the roles played by the tenant for life—whether before or after sale of the settled land—makes it plain that there is no inherent contradiction in the duality of the interests initially held by him under the characteristic strict settlement. Qua legal owner, the tenant for life is competent to administer interim management of the settled land and finally to put his signature to any deed of conveyance disposing of a legal estate in that land. Qua beneficial owner, the tenant for life is entitled to enjoy the settled land before sale (ie to live in the property or receive rents and profits therefrom for the duration of his beneficial interest). This beneficial interest is converted, on sale of the legal estate, into the equivalent right to draw the periodic income from the invested capital proceeds of sale.

(c) *The difficulties of informal grant*

The relatively broad ambit of the statutory notion of 'settlement' ensures that the Settled Land Act 1925 is sometimes applicable in circumstances where its operation is least anticipated. For instance, there is a danger, particularly in the context of family arrangements, that the Act may become relevant to a loosely worded conferment of informal rights of rent-free occupation for life.

(i) The Bannister ruling A crucial decision in this context was the ruling of the Court of Appeal in *Bannister v Bannister*.[8] Here the defendant had conveyed her freehold interest in two cottages to her brother-in-law, the present plaintiff, on his oral undertaking that she could thereafter live in one of the cottages rent-free for the remainder of her life. The conveyance failed to incorporate this oral promise, but when the plaintiff later sought possession against the defendant, the Court of Appeal held that he was bound by a constructive trust to give effect to her interest. This interest, said Scott LJ, was an equitable life interest determinable on her ceasing to live in the cottage.[9] The imposition of the constructive trust had 'the effect of making the beneficiary a tenant for life within the meaning of the Settled Land Act'.[10]

(ii) Doubts left by the Bannister ruling The Court of Appeal had no need in *Bannister*'s case to pursue the implications of holding that the defendant came within the Settled Land Act. It has since been doubted, however, whether this aspect of the Court's ruling can have been correct.[11] The inter vivos creation of a strict settlement requires the execution of at least two deeds (a trust instrument and a vesting document),[12] and it seems wholly impossible that the defendant in *Bannister* could properly have become a tenant for life by way of merely oral grant.[13] Nevertheless the decision of the Court of Appeal in *Bannister* provides an uncomfortable precedent in support of the proposition that a purely oral grant may attract the operation of the Settled Land Act.[14]

(iii) Conveyancing consequences Further doubts as to the correctness of *Bannister* are raised by the conveyancing consequences which follow if an informal

8 [1948] 2 All ER 133 (ante, p 438).
9 [1948] 2 All ER 133 at 136B.
10 [1948] 2 All ER 133 at 137B–C.
11 See A.J. Hawkins, (1966) 30 Conv (NS) 256; J.A. Hornby, (1977) 93 LQR 561.
12 Settled Land Act 1925, s 4(1) (post, p 623).
13 It has been suggested that in such cases the court order itself may be the instrument which constitutes the settlement within Settled Land Act 1925, s 1(1) (*Griffiths v Williams* (1977) 248 Estates Gazette 947 at 950 per Goff LJ). See also [1978] Conv 250 at 251.
14 The *Bannister* was recently applied in *Ungurian v Lesnoff* [1990] Ch 206 at 224A–D, where Vinelott J was able, perhaps surprisingly, to infer an intention to create a right of residence for life on the basis of the conduct and oral dealings of the relevant parties. It has since been observed that the lack of supporting documentation here would normally have been considered a fundamental flaw in any attempt to construct a strict settlement for the purposes of the Settled Land Act (see J. Hill, (1991) 107 LQR 596 at 598).

lifetime right of personal occupation is brought within the scope of the Settled Land Act 1925. So long as he is of full age, the grantee would appear to qualify as the statutory 'tenant for life'[15] and to be entitled to call for a vesting of the full legal estate in his own name.[16] In *Bannister's* case this would have involved the somewhat improbable result that the defendant, having conveyed the legal estate to her brother-in-law, would immediately have been entitled to insist that the legal estate should be reconveyed to her as tenant for life. However unattractive in the present context, this outcome merely reflects the fundamental design which lies at the root of the Settled Land Act—that the tenant for life should hold two distinct interests in the land. But it certainly seems strange that the informal grantee, consistently with the scheme of the Settled Land Act, should be empowered to sell, lease or mortgage the settled estate—consequences which may have been wholly outside the contemplation of the grantor.[17]

(iv) Avoidance of the Settled Land Act 1925 There is a general consensus that the machinery of the Settled Land Act 1925 should not, in principle, be activated by a loosely phrased grant of some limited interest or residential privilege.[18] The implausibility of such a statutory application is reinforced where the relevant parties had no conscious understanding that their dealings would attract such specific legal effects. In view of the difficulties implicit in the operation of the Settled Land Act 1925 in these circumstances, the courts have often tended to resist the over-ready application of the Act to the informal conferment of ill-defined rights of occupation for life. Indeed lawyers nowadays devote great care to avoiding the snares of the Settled Land Act rather than to the drafting of settlements which are deliberately designed to fall within its scope.

In recent years the concept of the residential licence has provided the most obvious way in which informal life interests may be diverted away from the dangerous complexities of the Settled Land Act.[19] It is not altogether clear, however, that the licence construction necessarily or properly excludes the heavy-handed operation of the Settled Land Act. The judicial ambivalence on this point was apparent in the decision of the Court of Appeal in *Binions v Evans*.[20] Here D had been granted a right of rent-free residence in a cottage

15 Settled Land Act 1925, s 19(1) (ante, p 616).

16 'This must in most cases defeat the entire object of the conferment of a life occupancy' ([1990] CLJ 25 at 27 (Mika Oldham)).

17 Nevertheless these were precisely the consequences recently attached in *Ungurian v Lesnoff* [1990] Ch 206 at 226D to the informal grant to a cohabitee of a right of residence for life. Vinelott J had little hesitation in holding the grantee to be a tenant for life who, on receiving a vesting of legal title in her favour, could sell the property and 'reinvest the proceeds in the sale of another house or . . . enjoy the income from them.' It has been pointed out that such an outcome 'would look very like an award of secured financial provision for a cohabitee, quantified without regard to the "maintenance" needs involved' ([1990] CLJ 25 at 27). See also [1990] Conv 223 (P. Sparkes); J. Hill, (1991) 107 LQR 596.

18 See eg Law Commission, *Transfer of Land: Trusts of Land* (Law Com No 181, 8 June 1989), paras 4.1f.

19 For a discussion of the law of licences, see Chapter 19 (post, p 890).

20 [1972] Ch 359. For the full facts of this case, see Chapter 19 (post, p 917).

for the remainder of her life. A majority in the Court of Appeal still felt constrained by grudging deference to *Bannister v Bannister* to hold that this grant was caught by the Settled Land Act 1925.[1] However, Lord Denning MR declined to apply *Bannister* precisely on the ground that it would have been 'entirely contrary to the true intent of the parties' that D should have acquired, by reason of the grant, a statutory power of sale or lease of the property under the Settled Land Act.[2]

Lord Denning accordingly found a ready escape route in *Binions v Evans* in the form of a severely restrictive construction of section 1(1)(i) of the Settled Land Act 1925, taking the view that the statutory reference to 'land ... limited in trust' covers only the case where land is 'expressly limited' in trust and where there is a genuine 'succession of one beneficiary after another'.[3] In an informal arrangement of the kind present in *Binions v Evans*, there was no true 'limitation' of land and therefore no 'settlement'.[4] Thus, although ultimately reaching the same result as his brethren in the majority, Lord Denning did so by way of a finding of contractual licence.[5] Subsequent decisions have echoed this disquiet with the *Bannister* ruling,[6] and there is now a divergent line of authority to the effect that there can be such a phenomenon as a licence for life which exists outside the clutches of the Settled Land Act 1925.[7] Licences for life have frequently been awarded in satisfaction of the 'equity' raised by proprietary estoppel.[8]

The approach adopted by Lord Denning in *Binions v Evans*, although heavily reinforced by common sense, is not however easily reconciled with the circumstances and the ruling in *Bannister*.[9] On the one hand it is the deliberate policy of the 1925 legislation that land should be rendered easily marketable,[10] and there is therefore a strong argument in favour of maximising the coverage of the Settled Land Act, thereby extending as widely as possible the benefits

1 'I realise that the application of the Settled Land Act 1925 may produce some odd consequences' ([1972] Ch 359 at 370D–G per Megaw LJ). See also Stephenson LJ (at 372E–G). See, however, *Ivory v Palmer* (1976) 237 Estates Gazette 411 at 413, where Cairns LJ thought that the majority view in *Binions v Evans* had 'stretched to the very limit the application of the Settled Land Act'.

2 [1972] Ch 359 at 366D. For further reference to the over-large powers which would be made available under the Settled Land Act 1925, see also *Dodsworth v Dodsworth* (1973) 228 Estates Gazette 1115; *Griffiths v Williams* (1977) 248 Estates Gazette 947 at 949.

3 [1972] Ch 359 at 366E-F.

4 In *Ungurian v Lesnoff* [1990] Ch 206 at 225C, Vinelott J noted that Lord Denning's view had not been shared by Megaw and Stephenson LJJ. Vinelott J was thus prepared, in not dissimilar circumstances, to find that a strict settlement had been been created by informal grant.

5 [1972] Ch 359 at 367C (post, p 917).

6 Such is the embarrassment caused by *Bannister* that in *Ivory v Palmer* (1976) 237 Estates Gazette 411 at 416 Browne LJ was at pains to stress that 'the court did not in fact ... base its decision on the Settled Land Act 1925, but on more general principles of the law of trusts.'

7 *Foster v Robinson* [1951] 1 KB 149 at 158ff; *Ivory v Palmer* (1976) 237 Estates Gazette 411 at 413 per Cairns LJ.

8 See eg *Inwards v Baker* [1965] 2 QB 29 at 37; *Greasley v Cooke* [1980] 1 WLR 1306 at 1312B.

9 See eg *Griffiths v Williams* (1977) 248 Estates Gazette 947 at 950, where Goff LJ questioned whether *Dodsworth v Dodsworth* (1973) 228 Estates Gazette 1115 might not have been decided per incuriam on the ground that the Court of Appeal in the latter case failed to advert to section 1 of the Settled Land Act 1925.

10 Ante, p 97. See *Ungurian v Lesnoff* [1990] Ch 206 at 226C per Vinelott J.

of its conveyancing and overreaching machinery.[11] On the other hand, there is the very real difficulty that this resolution introduces into the relationship of the parties a statutory mechanism which was never intended by them to be relevant and is usually most unwelcome to them. The law here remains in a state of some confusion, although there seems to be every incentive to avoid the complications of the Settled Land Act if at all possible.[12]

(d) The owners of beneficial interests other than a life interest

The Settled Land Act 1925 obviously aims to confer the status and powers of the 'tenant for life' on any person who, at a given point in time, holds an equitable life interest in possession in settled land. Such a description would not, however, be apt in relation to the range of beneficiaries already referred to in *Figs.* 46 to 50 inclusive,[13] none of whom held a life interest in possession. Here again, the pragmatic common sense of the Settled Land Act dictates that the legal estate and attendant powers be vested in the beneficiary currently in possession—albeit that he or she holds some beneficial interest other than a *life* interest.

Section 20(1) of the 1925 Act therefore confers the powers of the 'tenant for life' upon the holders of other limited or qualified interests in the settled land,[14] subject only to the proviso that such persons must be of full age[15] and that the beneficial interest of each is in possession. By statutory fiction the functional role of the 'tenant for life' is thereby extended to cover most settled land beneficiaries who can properly claim to be currently entitled in possession. Thus a tenant in tail who is entitled in possession is recognised for the purpose of the 1925 Act as having all the powers of the tenant for life.[16] Likewise recognised are the owner of a 'shifting interest'[17] and the owner of an estate which remains subject to a family rentcharge.[18] All are entitled within the scheme of the 1925 Act to call for a vesting of the full legal estate in the settled land and thenceforth to exercise the appropriate powers of management and disposition in respect of this nominal or 'paper' title.

11 Ante, p 102.
12 In *Griffiths v Williams* (1977) 248 Estates Gazette 947 at 950, for instance, the Court of Appeal was so anxious to escape the possible implications of the Settled Land Act that it effectively resolved the residential problems of the parties by dictating, with only the barest consent of those parties, an alternative solution in terms of the grant of a long tenancy at a nominal rent.
13 Ante, pp 612–614.
14 Settled Land Act 1925, s 20(1).
15 See Law of Property Act 1925, s 1(6).
16 Settled Land Act 1925, s 20(1)(i). See eg X in *Fig.* 46 (ante, p 612).
17 Settled Land Act 1925, s 20(1)(ii). See eg A in *Fig.* 47 (ante, p 612).
18 Settled Land Act 1925, s 20(1)(ix). See eg S in *Fig.* 50 (ante, p 614), although it is also provided that someone in the position of S may alternatively convey the land subject to a prior interest 'as if the land had not been settled land' (Law of Property (Amendment) Act 1926, s 1).

(e) Special cases

No reference has yet been made to the allocation of legal ownership in *Figs.* 48 and 49. For obvious reasons section 20(1) makes no provision for conferring the powers of the tenant for life either upon the owner of a 'springing interest' or upon a minor.

(i) The 'springing' interest In *Fig.* 48,[19] G was granted land in fee simple contingent upon the happening of some event. Until that event occurs, the contingency to which G's interest is subject remains unfulfilled and G has no vested interest in the property at all. He cannot therefore claim to have a beneficial interest in possession, and in these circumstances there is no more reason to allocate the legal estate in the settled land to G than there is to vest it in anyone else. During the interim—before it becomes clear whether or not G will satisfy the relevant contingency—the legal estate must be held by a nominee. Under the solution adopted by the Settled Land Act 1925, in the absence of a tenant for life duly qualified in terms of section 19(1) or section 20(1), the legal estate and the attendant powers require to be vested in the 'statutory owner'.[20]

(ii) Grant to a minor Section 20(1) likewise withholds the powers of the tenant for life from a minor (eg M in *Fig.* 49[1]), for the plain reason that a minor is incompetent to hold a legal estate in land.[2] Here again a nominee must step in to hold the legal estate in the settled land until the beneficially entitled minor is relieved of his disability. During the minority of the grantee, the powers of the tenant for life are conferred either upon a personal representative of the settlor (in the case of a testamentary grant) or upon the trustees of the settlement.[3] When M attains the age of 18, the legal fee simple absolute must be conveyed to him, whereupon the strict settlement will come to an end.[4]

(iii) The 'statutory owner' There can never be a vacuum in relation to the legal estate in settled land, and the Settled Land Act 1925 confirms in order of priority certain categories of persons who are competent to hold the legal estate and to exercise the relevant powers. In default of any person qualified under sections 19 and 20, the powers of the tenant for life are usually conferred upon the 'statutory owner'.[5] The 'statutory owner' is either the person of full age on whom such powers are expressly conferred by the terms of the strict settlement or, failing such a nomination, the trustees of the settlement.

19 Ante, p 613.
20 Infra. The 'trustees of the settlement' usually constitute collectively the 'statutory owner' for this purpose (post, p 623).
1 Ante, p 614.
2 Law of Property Act 1925, s 1(6).
3 Settled Land Act 1925, s 26(1).
4 Settled Land Act 1925, s 7(5).
5 Settled Land Act 1925, s 23(1).

4. TRUSTEES OF THE SETTLEMENT

It will already be clear that the trustees of the settlement play an important residual role under the Settled Land Act 1925. The settlement trustees stand normally, as it were, in the wings and look on from a distance: they exercise a general supervision of the strict settlement from afar. They dash on stage only on those rare occasions when their presence is required, as, for instance, where there is no beneficiary qualified to hold the legal estate in the settled land, or where the settled estate is about to be sold and conveyed to a third party purchaser. Normally, however, the trustees play only a back-up role, and in this respect perform a quite different function from that of the trustees in a trust for sale, who are almost always intimately involved in everything that happens to the land held on trust.[6]

In creating a strict settlement it is usual for the settlor not merely to settle the land on designated beneficiaries but also to nominate quite separate trustees of the settlement to exercise a general overseeing role.[7] In the first instance, therefore, the settlement trustees will be those persons upon whom have been conferred, by the express terms of the settlement, the various powers and consents which are characteristic of the function of such trustees. Section 30(1) of the Settled Land Act 1925 contains, in a descending order of priority, a list of the categories of person who thus qualify for the trusteeship. If the settlement arises by way of will or intestacy, then, in default of a person or persons nominated within the terms of section 30(1), the personal representatives of the deceased (ie the executors or persons holding letters of administration) exercise for the time being the functions of the trustees of the settlement.[8] If, for whatever reason, no persons qualify as the settlement trustees within any of the categories enumerated in section 30, any beneficiary or any person otherwise interested in the settlement may apply to the court for the appointment of a fit person as trustee.[9]

5. THE CREATION OF A STRICT SETTLEMENT

The basic principle with regard to the creation of strict settlements of land is that two documents are required to be executed. A settlement created by means of one document alone is imperfect—but not altogether ineffective, as will shortly appear.

6 Ante, p 539.

7 These trustees need not be, and commonly are not in fact, beneficially entitled under the settlement. The number of settlement trustees may not normally exceed four (Trustee Act 1925, s 34(2), (3)), a restriction which was endorsed in 1982 by the 23rd Report of the Law Reform Committee (see *The powers and duties of trustees* (23rd Report, Cmnd 8733, October 1982), para 2.2).

8 Settled Land Act 1925, s 30(3).

9 Settled Land Act 1925, s 34(1).

(1) The purpose of the 'two-document rule'

There is good sense in the requirement of two documents for the purpose of creating a strict settlement. One document is a 'vesting' document of some kind—a 'vesting deed' or a 'vesting instrument'. Its proper function is to vest the 'paper' title (ie the legal estate) and the administrative and decision-making functions connected with it in the person or persons qualified to exercise the powers of the tenant for life for the purpose of the particular strict settlement. Thus the vesting document operates as a conveyance of the legal estate in the settled land to the appropriate person or persons.[10] The second document is concerned, by contrast, with the beneficial interests in the settled land.[11] This second document—the 'trust instrument'—performs the entirely different function of laying out the equitable interests created under the trusts of the strict settlement.

(a) Conveyancing implications

This use of two quite separate documents is highly convenient as a matter of conveyancing practice, and indeed represents a highly significant component of the ultimate scheme of the Settled Land Act 1925. The statutory scheme is designed to enable land which is the subject of a family settlement to be freely commerciable notwithstanding the existence of beneficial interests attached to the land. By 1925 the idea that settled land must be kept within the family had long given way to a recognition that somehow the preservation of family interests in the land (the interests of endowment[12]) must be reconciled with the overall economic objective of making the land freely marketable.

The 1925 legislation sought to accommodate these potentially conflicting objectives through the device of 'overreaching'.[13] The legal estate in settled land may be conveyed to a third party, but the beneficial entitlements—representing the real wealth in the settled property—survive that transfer inasmuch as after the conveyance they adhere not to the land but to the capital proceeds of the disposition.[14] Thus, on a conveyance of the legal estate in settled land, the purchaser takes a free title and the equitable interests of the beneficiaries are translated into precisely equivalent interests in the capital money arising.[15] Where, for instance, A was formerly entitled to a life interest in the settled land (see *Fig.* 52), this interest is converted on conveyance into a life interest in the capital sum produced by the disposition. In effect A enjoys henceforth a lifelong right to receive the income generated by investment of the capital sum released by the disposition. A has, of course, no right to the capital money itself: this fund is reserved for B, who was previously entitled by way of remainder to the absolute interest in the land. B's entitlement to the corpus of the capital money will, however, fall into possession only on A's death.

10 See eg the persons entitled at LAW in *Figs.* 45 to 50, ante.
11 See eg the interests marked out in EQUITY in *Figs.* 45 to 50, ante.
12 Ante, p 98.
13 Ante, p 102.
14 A 'disposition' (or 'conveyance') of settled land may include not only a conveyance on sale but also a lease, mortgage or assent relating to the settled land (see Settled Land Act 1925, s 117(1)(v)).
15 Law of Property Act 1925, s 2(1)(i) (ante, p 102, post, p 641).

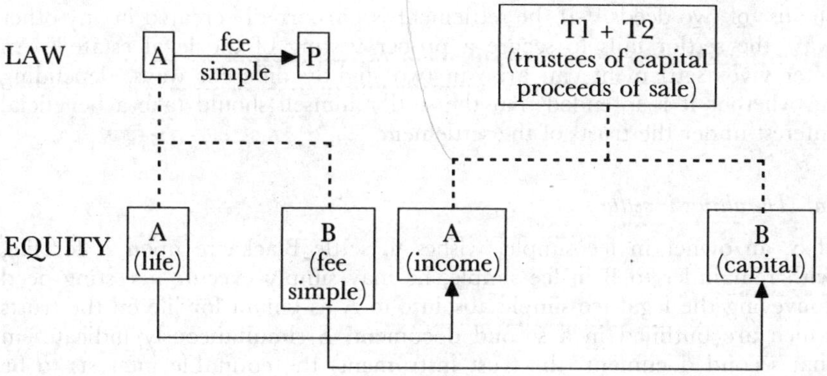

Fig. 52

(b) The 'curtain' principle

It is intrinsic to the device of overreaching that the purchaser takes the legal title to the land unencumbered by the equitable interests under the strict settlement. The beneficiaries' rights are swept off the land on to the proceeds of sale. The less the purchaser knows about the beneficial interests the better: his position is quite secure so long as overreaching takes place. He need not even inquire into the nature of the beneficiaries' rights: he is concerned only with the legal title.

These simple facts provide the rationale for the 'curtain principle' which appears at the culmination of the Settled Land Act 1925.[16] The 'curtain principle' drives a wedge between matters affecting the legal title to land and matters concerned with beneficial entitlement. On a disposition of settled land, the third party need look only at the document which relates to the legal estate. The trusts under the settlement—the beneficial interests—are kept off the title. They are concealed behind a 'curtain' and are not normally revealed to the purchaser. The purchaser has, after all, no proper concern with the precise details of the family equitable interests dispensed by the original settlor.

The successful operation of this 'curtain principle' thus depends heavily on the use of two separate documents relating to the settled land, only one of which is inspected by the intending purchaser. Under section 110(2) of the Settled Land Act 1925, a purchaser of a legal estate in settled land normally 'shall not . . . be bound or entitled to call for the production of the trust instrument . . .'. Under normal circumstances he has no right to investigate the details of the trust, precisely because overreaching will automatically sweep all beneficial interests off the land.

(2) Creation of an inter vivos settlement

In accordance with the 'two-document rule' the Settled Land Act 1925 clearly requires that the creation of a strict settlement inter vivos be effected by

16 Post, p 644.

the use of two deeds.[17] If the settlement is purportedly created in any other way, the settlor fails to secure a proper vesting of the legal estate.[18] An inter vivos settlement can arise in two slightly different ways, depending on whether it is intended that the settlor himself should take a beneficial interest under the trusts of the settlement.

(a) *The altruistic settlor*

If S, an owner in fee simple, wishes to settle Blackacre upon A for life, with remainder to B in fee simple, he may simply execute a vesting deed conveying the legal fee simple absolute to A as tenant for life on the trusts which are outlined in a second document. S simultaneously indicates in that second document (the trust instrument) the equitable interests to be enjoyed successively by A and B. The position would thus be as follows:

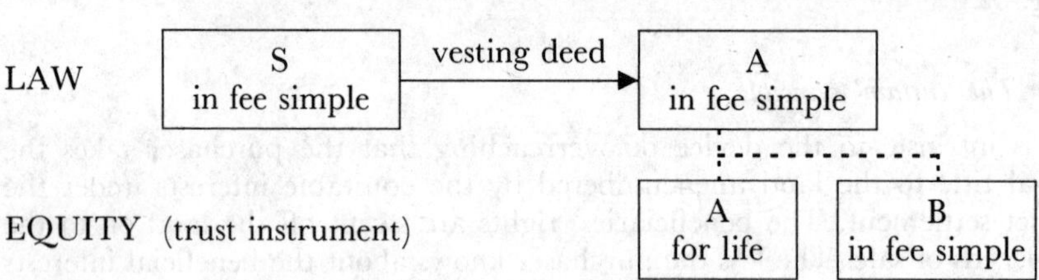

Fig. 53

A difficulty clearly presents itself if S attempts to create a strict settlement by means of only one document (eg where S signs a simple written statement granting Blackacre to A for life with remainder to B). In the absence of the appropriate vesting instrument the settlement is imperfect, but the Settled Land Act 1925 provides a remedy for the defect. Section 9(1) deems certain categories of document to be a 'trust instrument' for the purpose of the Act. Included amongst these categories is an 'instrument inter vivos intended to create a settlement of a legal estate in land which . . . does not comply with the requirements of this Act with respect to the method of effecting such a settlement'.[19] Thus the settlor's informal writing, which in its unsophisticated way spells out the beneficial entitlements just as would a proper trust instrument, is regarded as constituting one of the two documents required for the perfect creation of a strict settlement. The missing document—the vesting deed—must now be supplied by the trustees of the settlement,[20]

17 Settled Land Act 1925, s 4(1).

18 A vesting deed must contain reference to those matters with which a future purchaser is justifiably concerned. The deed must make it clear that the legal estate transferred is held on the trusts of a strict settlement (Settled Land Act 1925, s 5(1)). It should also name the persons who are to be the trustees of the settlement. The private details of the settlement trusts are, however, contained only in the trust instrument (Settled Land Act 1925, s 4(3)). A minor error in the details required to be present in a vesting deed does not invalidate the deed (Settled Land Act 1925, s 5(3)).

19 Settled Land Act 1925, s 9(1)(iii).

20 Settled Land Act 1925, s 9(2).

who leap once more into the breach to ensure that the strict settlement survives. They rectify the omission of the settlor by declaring (in a vesting deed executed by themselves) that the legal estate shall henceforth vest in the appropriate person on the trusts of the settlement.[1] As soon as the missing document is provided by this means, the settlement becomes perfect for almost all purposes.[2]

(b) The self-interested settlor

Alternatively a settlor may well wish to include himself amongst the beneficiaries of his own strict settlement. In this case, he may settle Blackacre upon himself for life, with remainders over to A and B successively as before (see *Fig.* 54). Here, since S, the first tenant for life, is already invested with the fee simple in his capacity as the original owner, there is clearly no necessity for any *conveyance* to him of the legal estate in the settled land. It is sufficient merely that there be a vesting document which 'declares' that henceforth S is to hold the legal estate on the trusts of the settlement contained in his trust instrument.[3]

LAW	S in fee simple	(confirmed by declaration in vesting document)	
EQUITY (trust instrument)	S for life	A for life	B in fee simple

Fig. 54

(3) Creation of a settlement by will

The 'two-document rule' is again given indirect effect where a settlor attempts to create a settlement of land not inter vivos but by will. In these circumstances the will is deemed, for the purposes of the Act, to be a trust instrument.[4] This fiction is convenient since the will naturally spells out the interests in the land to be taken by various designated beneficiaries. The second requisite document—the vesting document—is left to be executed in favour

1 In *Fig.* 53, this person is A. If, in the situation depicted in *Fig.* 54, the settlor omits to confirm by way of a vesting document that he himself henceforth holds the legal estate subject to the trusts of the settlement, the trustees of the settlement have a similar power to make the appropriate declaration on his behalf. If there exist no trustees of the settlement to perform these functions, the court may be asked to make a suitable appointment (Settled Land Act 1925, s 9(3)).

2 Post, p 644. There are other kinds of error or omission which may conceivably arise in the creation of a strict settlement, but the 1925 Act incorporates at almost every point of default the appropriate machinery for rectifying the initial error (see also Settled Land Act 1925, s 27, which uses the device of the settlement to deal with ineffective conveyances of the legal estate to a minor).

3 Settled Land Act 1925, s 4(2).

4 Settled Land Act 1925, s 6(a).

of the appropriate tenant for life by the testator/settlor's personal representatives.[5]

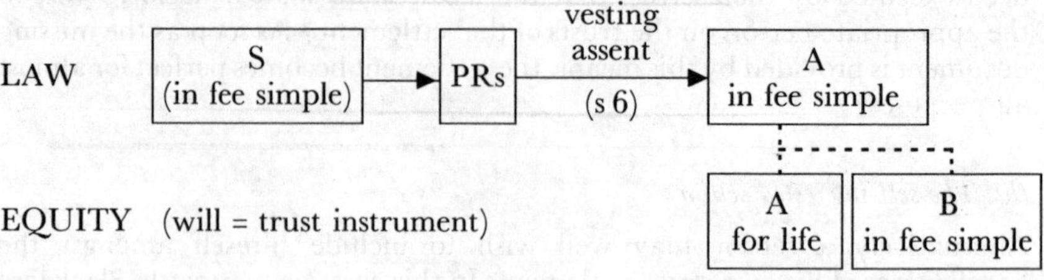

Fig. 55

6. THE EFFECTS OF PERFECT AND IMPERFECT VESTING OF THE LEGAL ESTATE

The conveyancing implications of imperfect and perfect vesting of the legal estate in settled land are contained in a notable pair of sections in the Settled Land Act 1925, sections 13 and 18. These two sections are mutually exclusive in their scope and operation. Section 18 takes over where section 13 has ceased to operate.

(1) Conveyancing implications of imperfect vesting

Section 13 relates to the situation in which a strict settlement is as yet imperfect for want of a second (ie vesting) document. In such circumstances the legal estate in the settled land has not been properly vested in the tenant for life, and only the trustees of the settlement (in the case of an inter vivos settlement) or the testator's personal representatives (in the case of a settlement by will) are now competent to cure the initial defect. The second document being essential to the full validity of the settlement, an awkward hiatus is interposed unless and until the missing document is duly provided by the responsible persons.

Section 13 of the Settled Land Act 1925 addresses the question whether, during this period of limbo, the legal estate in the settled land may be made the subject of dealings with third parties. Section 13 provides unequivocally that, during the currency of an imperfect settlement,

> any purported disposition [of the legal estate] inter vivos by any person ... shall operate only as a contract for valuable consideration to carry out the transaction after the requisite vesting instrument has been executed ...

5 Settled Land Act 1925, s 6(b). This procedure makes sense because it is in the settlor's personal representatives that his legal estate automatically vests at the moment of his death. By means of a ministerial act of signature upon a 'vesting assent', they simply shuffle the nominal legal title on to the person entitled in terms of the settlor's will. It seems that a vesting document is still required even where this person is already invested with the full legal estate (eg as the survivor of the original personal representatives). See *In re King's Will Trusts* [1964] Ch 542 at 548; *In re Edwards' Will Trusts* [1982] Ch 30 at 33C; [1982] Conv 4 (P.W. Smith). The vesting document used here need not, however, be a 'vesting deed': it may be a simple written statement or 'vesting assent' (Settled Land Act 1925, s 8(1)).

(a) Exception for Equity's Darling

Section 13 allows for certain exceptional circumstances in which a disposition of a legal estate in the settled land can, notwithstanding the imperfection, enjoy the full legal effect intended. The most important exception arises on behalf of the purchaser of a legal estate who has no notice of the fact that the person with whom he is dealing is in reality entitled to have a vesting deed or assent executed in his favour. Section 13 thus honours the general principle that an innocent purchaser of a legal estate in land receives maximum protection.

(b) Paralysing effect of section 13

The general effect of section 13 is otherwise to paralyse dealings with the legal estate for the duration of the imperfect settlement. It does not follow, however, that during this period transactions in relation to the legal estate have utterly no effect. The import of section 13 is simply that such dealings cannot usually have the full effect originally intended at law (eg the effect of fee simple transfer to a third party). The transaction in question will, however, enjoy a limited contractual effect. The purported dealing is deemed, pursuant to section 13, to constitute an *agreement* to carry out the original intention of the contracting parties if and when the settlement is later rendered perfect by the execution of a proper vesting deed.

The operation of section 13 can be seen perhaps most plainly in the situation described in *Fig.* 54.[6] Suppose that S has not yet confirmed in any vesting document the fact that henceforth he holds the legal fee simple in Blackacre on the trusts of the settlement which he has created. Even in the absence of a declaration reciting the existence of the settlement trusts, S is of course entitled to occupy Blackacre, since his beneficial life interest is currently the only equitable interest in possession. Moreover S retains his original documents of title in respect of Blackacre, and these title deeds will show him to be an owner in fee simple without any reference to the strict settlement. It is precisely where S attempts to use *these* title deeds as the basis of a transaction with some third party that section 13 comes clearly into play.

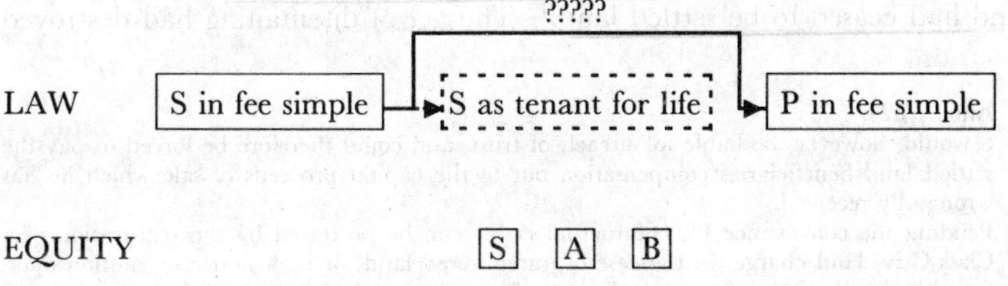

Fig. 56

S may, for instance, attempt to sidestep the existence of the imperfect strict settlement by selling the fee simple in his earlier capacity as absolute owner

6 Ante, p 627.

(see *Fig.* 56). Such manipulation of S's role as estate owner almost certainly constitutes a fraud on the other settled land beneficiaries. If successful in this ploy, S will receive for himself absolutely the capital proceeds of sale (paid over by the purchaser P). If he had sold qua tenant for life, his own beneficial interest would normally have been overreached and he would have received merely a life interest in the income drawn from the proceeds of sale.[7]

In these circumstances if P is a purchaser who has no knowledge of the existence of the strict settlement (still less of S's entitlement to a vesting instrument), then he takes the legal estate free of the settled land interests, in accordance with the principal exception embodied in section 13.[8] If, on the other hand, P is a purchaser who does not enjoy the immunity conferred by section 13 (eg where he knows of the existence of the imperfect settlement), then the result is somewhat different. At this point section 13 intervenes to frustrate the S's purported conveyance in fee simple: the transaction takes effect only as a contract by S to convey the legal estate to P at some later date when the settlement has been perfected by the provision of a vesting document. By its very nature such a document would of course compel S to convey as a tenant for life subject to the settlement trusts. A sale under these circumstances would obviously overreach the beneficial interests under the settlement (provided always that the capital money was duly paid to the trustees of the settlement).[9]

(c) Special effect of disentailing

It appears that section 13 automatically ceases to have any application if the circumstances which in the first place raise the necessity for a strict settlement themselves cease to exist. In *In re Alefounder's Will Trusts*,[10] for instance, a settlement was technically imperfect because a tenant in tail had never received a proper vesting in his favour qua tenant for life. The tenant in tail later barred his entail, thereby converting his equitable interest into a fee simple interest and destroying any remainder over. Astbury J upheld his competence at this point to convey the fee simple to a third party entirely free of the fetters imposed by section 13.[11] It was clear that the original entailed entitlement had come within the four corners of the Settled Land Act 1925, but from the moment the entail was barred the land had ceased to be settled land.[12] The act of disentailing had destroyed

7 Ante, p 624.

8 S would, however, be liable for breach of trust, and could therefore be forced to pay the settled land beneficiaries compensation out of the capital proceeds of sale which he has wrongfully received.

9 Pending the conveyance P's contractual rights can be protected by the registration of a Class C(iv) land charge (in the case of unregistered land) or by a notice or caution upon the title (in the case of registered land). P's contractual right to call for a conveyance at the later point in time when the settlement is perfected is thereby protected as a form of estate contract (Settled Land Act 1925, s 13). By the appropriate registration, P can effectively prevent S from conveying the legal estate under the perfected settlement to any other third party.

10 [1927] 1 Ch 360.

11 [1927] 1 Ch 360 at 364. The former tenant in tail happened quite fortuitously to possess title deeds which appeared to show him to be an absolute owner at law and in equity.

12 See *In re Blake's Settled Estates* [1932] IR 637 at 640, 647f.

the very premise for the application of the Settled Land Act and the former tenant in tail was now free to convey without first perfecting the imperfect settlement. Section 13 can have no application if an imperfect settlement of land is demolished before its construction is complete.

(2) Conveyancing implications of perfect vesting

Whereas section 13 of the Settled Land Act 1925 paralyses dealings before the execution of the requisite vesting instument, section 18 operates in an entirely different context. It applies only where the strict settlement is already perfect (ie where the two necessary documents have been executed—whether belatedly or not).

Section 18(1)(a) provides that where land

> is the subject of a vesting instrument and the trustees of the settlement have not been discharged . . . then any disposition of a legal estate by the tenant for life or statutory owner . . . other than a disposition authorised by this Act or any other statute . . . shall be void.

In other words, where a strict settlement is perfect, the legal estate may be dealt with only in accordance with the terms laid down in the Act. Any irregular disposition of the legal estate is void and ineffectual—a most draconian result.[13]

(a) Authorised dealings

The scope of authorised dealing with the legal estate in settled land is effectively circumscribed by section 18(1)(b), (c).[14] Section 18(1)(b) provides that a conveyance of the legal estate to a purchaser shall be effective only if the capital proceeds of sale arising are paid to or by the direction of the trustees of the settlement or into court. Section 18(1)(c) provides imperatively that the capital money 'shall not, except where the trustee is a trust corporation, be paid to or by the direction of fewer persons than two as trustees of the settlement.'

These vital provisions must be read in conjunction with section 2(1)(i) of the Law of Property Act 1925,[15] which details those transactions in real property which are generally capable of having overreaching effect. Section 2(1)(i) makes it a clear precondition of overreaching in the settled land context that 'the statutory requirements respecting the payment of capital money arising under the settlement are complied with.' Thus, exceptional instances apart, no overreaching of the settled land interests ever takes place unless the capital money arising on the relevant disposition is paid to at least two trustees. The combined effect of these provisions is, of course, to nullify any purported disposition of the legal estate in the settled land which fails to safeguard the beneficiaries' interests. Once again, it will be noticed, the trustees

13 For this purpose the term 'disposition' bears the extended meaning confirmed in Settled Land Act 1925, s 117(1)(v) (ante, p 624). Section 18 has no application to dealings with an equitable interest—it strikes only at transactions related to the legal estate in the settled land. Other minor exceptions to section 18 are contained in section 18(2).

14 The ambit of authorised dealing with the legal estate may be widened by the express words of the vesting instrument.

15 Ante, p 102.

of the settlement are called upon to play a vital role in preserving the settled land entitlements. Payment to at least two settlement trustees minimises the possibility of self-serving fraud on the part of the tenant for life (even if he is also one of the trustees), and causes the settled land interests to attach henceforth to the proceeds of sale. The settlement trustees now stand in a fiduciary position in relation not to land but to a fund of money, and the beneficiaries' rights are converted automatically into the equivalent interests in that fund.[16]

(b) Unauthorised dealings

The best known application of section 18 of the Settled Land Act 1925 occurred in *Weston v Henshaw*.[17] Here a tenant for life under a perfect strict settlement fortuitously possessed (in addition to the vesting instrument) an old set of title deeds derived from an earlier transaction. These title deeds now inaccurately made him appear to be the 'beneficial owner', ie to be absolutely entitled both at law and in equity without reference to any settlement or trust. The tenant for life wrongfully produced the earlier documents of title in order to persuade a third party to lend money on the security of an apparently unencumbered fee simple. The fraud succeeded, and the third party took a mortgage over the land as his security. Never suspecting for one moment the existence of the later deed of settlement, he paid the loan moneys to the tenant for life alone, who proceeded to dissipate the amounts advanced. On the death of the tenant for life, the remainderman discovered the fraud and argued that the mortgage granted by the dishonest tenant for life was a void disposition under section 18(1) by reason of the fact that the capital moneys arising had not been paid to at least two trustees, but had been paid merely to one tenant for life (see *Fig.* 57).

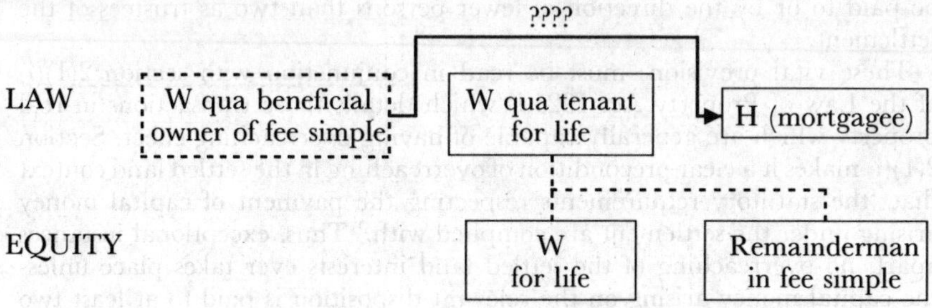

Fig. 57

Danckwerts J held that the mortgagee must indeed lose his security, since the mortgage had been unauthorised in the special sense used in the legislation and because, in the strict terms of section 18(1)(a), an unauthorised disposition

16 Ante, p 624.
17 [1950] Ch 510.

is expressly declared to be 'void.' If this decision was correct, *Weston v Henshaw* represents an exception to the general policy of English land law that the innocent purchaser should not be prejudiced or penalised.[18]

(i) Doctrinal controversy Considerable doubt has always surrounded the decision in *Weston v Henshaw*. Most significantly, the ruling seems to conflict with section 110(1) of the Settled Land Act 1925, which provides that in any transaction in which a purchaser deals 'in good faith with a tenant for life or statutory owner', the purchaser shall 'be conclusively taken . . . to have complied with all the requisitions of this Act.' On this basis it could be argued that the purchaser must be irrebuttably presumed to have paid the capital money to at least two trustees in accordance with section 18(1)(c) even though he clearly did not do so. However, in *Weston v Henshaw* Danckwerts J rejected this argument on the ground that section 110(1) applies only in favour of a purchaser who *knows* that he is dealing with a tenant for life.[19]

In *In re Morgan's Lease*[20] Ungoed-Thomas J was later to express the *obiter* view that section 110(1) is relevant irrespective of the purchaser's state of knowledge. This alternative approach has tended to attract considerable support amongst commentators,[1] not least because it introduces much needed common sense into the matter. The circumstance in which the purchaser least needs the protection conferred by section 110(1) is the case where he actually knows that he is dealing with a limited owner of settled land. It is exactly where the purchaser is *unaware* of this fact that section 110(1) appears pre-eminently apposite.

(ii) A possible reconciliation Notwithstanding the conflict between section 18(1)(a) and section 110(1) of the Settled Land Act 1925, Danckwerts J seemed in *Weston v Henshaw* to find the plain language of the former provision utterly compelling: unauthorised dispositions of the legal estate in settled land 'shall be void'. It can be argued, however, that section 18(1)(a) strikes down only those dispositions by a tenant for life which are so irregular as to be wholly ultra vires the Act itself. In *Weston v Henshaw*, not only was the capital money not paid to the trustees of the settlement, but the tenant for life acted ultra vires the Settled Land Act by using old title documents

18 Essentially the same policy dilemma emerges where an innocent purchaser buys land entirely unaware of the fact that the land is held on trust for sale (ante, p 563). In the latter context the courts have generally striven to protect the innocent purchaser. In commenting on *Weston v Henshaw*, G.A. Grove once pointed out: 'Had the borrower been instead of a tenant for life the last survivor of trustees for sale it would seem that the mortgagee would have acquired a good title as a bona fide purchaser of the legal estate without notice of the equitable interests. For the protection of purchasers it seems desirable that the law should be altered. Section 13, in avoiding dispositions of settled land made prior to the execution of a vesting instrument, expressly excludes dispositions made in favour of a purchaser of a legal estate without notice of any settlement' ((1961) 24 MLR 123 at 129).

19 [1950] Ch 510 at 519.

20 [1972] Ch 1 at 9A–C. Ungoed-Thomas J also noted that the earlier authority of the Court of Appeal in *Mogridge v Clapp* [1892] 3 Ch 382 at 400f had not been cited before Danckwerts J in *Weston v Henshaw*. See E.H. Scamell, [1957] CLP 152 at 163.

1 See R.H. Maudsley, (1973) 36 MLR 25 at 28f.

for the fraudulent purpose of deceiving the mortgagee. The Settled Land Act gives the tenant for life no authority to cheat. Indeed, in *Weston v Henshaw* the mortgagor made no attempt at all to transact in his capacity as tenant for life; he purported to act, vis à vis the mortgagee, in the capacity of sole beneficial owner.

On this basis it may be possible to reduce sections 18(1)(a) and 110(1) to some reasonable consistency. It may well be that a purchaser takes a good title under section 110(1) where the tenant for life, while remaining essentially intra vires the Act, has nevertheless violated some provision of the Act. Such would be the case, for instance, where a disposition by the tenant for life is clearly within the authority conferred upon him by the Act (ie where he has made no attempt to act otherwise than qua tenant for life), but he has failed to ensure that the capital money arising on the disposition is paid to the settlement trustees.[2] Thus the immunity conferred by section 110(1) effectively extends only to dealings by those who transact within the four corners of the Act. Conversely, as Danckwerts J indicated in *Weston v Henshaw*,[3] section 18(1) is by its very essence concerned with 'transactions which are not in pursuance of the Act and which it therefore makes void.'

This rationale, despite its attractions, still leaves certain difficulties unresolved. The protection of section 110(1) is denied to the purchaser who, unaware of the fraud perpetrated by a dishonest tenant for life, stands objectively in greatest need of protection. It may also seem slightly odd that, if the purchaser is disabled from pleading section 110(1) because of some fundamental breach of the Settled Land Act committed by his vendor, the purchaser's title should simultaneously be declared void by reference to another provision of the same Act, ie section 18(1)(a). Recent case law has done nothing to aid the ultimate reconciliation of sections 18(1)(a) and 110(1),[4] and it may be that the former provision remains, at some level, a stubborn counter-example to the major bias in English land law towards the protection of innocent purchasers.[5]

2 This rationale derives some support from Settled Land Act 1925, s 112(2), which provides that any provision in the Settled Land Act which refers to 'sale, purchase, . . . mortgaging, . . . leasing, or other disposition or dealing' shall be construed as extending only to 'transactions under this Act.'

3 [1950] Ch 510 at 519.

4 See eg *Bevan v Johnston* [1990] 2 EGLR 33 at 34H-J per Stuart-Smith LJ, where the grant of a tenancy was held to be void pursuant to section 18(1)(a) without reference to section 110(1). See, however, (1991) 107 LQR 596 (J. Hill).

5 It has been suggested (see D.W. Elliott, (1971) 87 LQR 338 at 341) that the confusion in the present context is attributable to an underlying ambivalence in the Settled Land Act 1925 as to whether the tenant for life is a mere donee of powers of disposition or is truly an estate owner in the more ample sense envisaged throughout the 1925 Act. In terms of the latter perspective, even wrongful transactions by the tenant for life take effect in favour of innocent third parties, whereas on the former view any abuse of power by the life tenant is justifiably subject to the strict sanction of voidness. According to Elliott, '[t]he legislature, having decided to simplify conveyancing by making the tenant for life an actual estate owner instead of a mere donee of a power, nevertheless balks at the logical implications of this change, and ends by making his position indistinguishable from a mere donee.' See also R.H. Maudsley, (1973) 36 MLR 25 at 28f; R. Warrington, [1985] Conv 377.

7. THE POWERS OF THE TENANT FOR LIFE AND STATUTORY OWNER

Given his characteristically dual entitlement under a strict settlement,[6] the tenant for life is empowered to deal not merely with his own equitable beneficial interest but also with the legal estate in the settled land.

(1) Powers in relation to an equitable interest

The primary rule is that a tenant for life may deal as he wishes with his own equitable interest under the strict settlement, and that such dealings normally have no effect upon the ownership of the legal estate in the settled land.[7]

(a) Disposition to a stranger

The tenant for life's freedom of action in respect of his own beneficial interest may be illustrated in the following example (see *Fig.* 58).

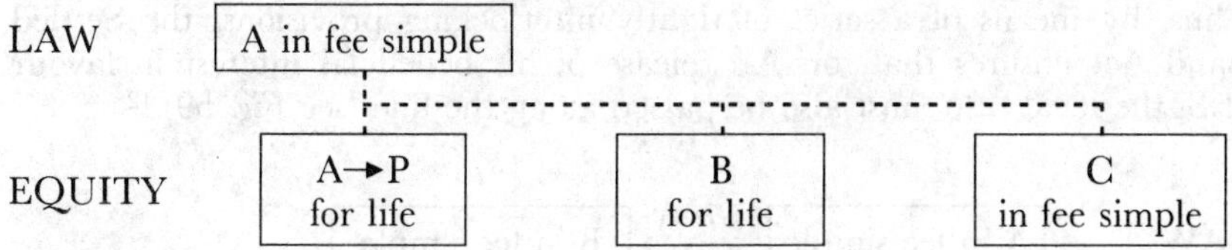

Fig. 58

Here A, a tenant for life, has sold his beneficial life interest to P. P simply takes A's place amongst the settled land beneficiaries, although P's new equitable entitlement will of course terminate on the death of A. P has simply bought that which A owned in equity, with the result that he now holds a beneficial interest *pur autre vie*.[8] However, A's dealing with his equitable interest in no way affects his holding of the legal fee simple absolute in the settled land. Notwithstanding that A has realised his beneficial share or stake in the property, he is still charged with the exercise of his fiduciary responsibilities in relation to the administration and disposition of the settled land. In this respect he is in the same position as any other fiduciary who holds property on trust without being beneficially entitled to the trust assets.[9]

6 Ante, p 60.

7 Settled Land Act 1925, s 104(1). See *In re Earl of Pembroke and Thompson's Contract* [1932] IR 493 at 501ff. See, however, Law of Property Act 1925, s 137(2)(i), (4).

8 This is clearly an imprudent purchase by P, since it represents an incautious gamble on the longevity of A.

9 On any later conveyance by A of the legal estate pursuant to the 1925 Act, the equities which, on overreaching, will attach to the proceeds of sale will be those belonging to P (for A's life), B and C.

(b) Surrender to the next remainderman

There are several minor exceptions to the basic rule that equitable dealings have no automatic effect upon the legal title to settled land, and these exceptions are of a commonsense nature. If, in *Fig.* 58, A had not sold his beneficial life interest to P, but had instead surrendered this life interest to the next remainderman, B, ownership of the legal estate would indeed have been affected. Such a transaction obviously accelerates the point at which B's equitable interest falls into possession. It therefore makes sense that the nominal ownership of the legal title should be shuffled on to B as the person now beneficially entitled in possession. Accordingly the Settled Land Act 1925 provides that where there is an assurance by a tenant for life in favour of the next remainderman, with 'intent to extinguish' the tenant for life's interest under the settlement, then the statutory powers of the tenant for life 'shall ... cease to be exercisable by him and ... shall thenceforth become exercisable as if he were dead'.[10] The corollary appears in section 7(4), according to which

> if by reason of forfeiture, surrender, or otherwise the estate owner of any settled land ceases to have the statutory powers of a tenant for life and the land remains settled land, he shall be bound forthwith to convey the settled land to the person who under the trust instrument ... becomes the tenant for life ...[11]

Thus, by means of a series of tightly interlocking provisions, the Settled Land Act ensures that, on A's release of his beneficial interest in favour of B, the legal title must also be passed along the line (see *Fig.* 59).[12]

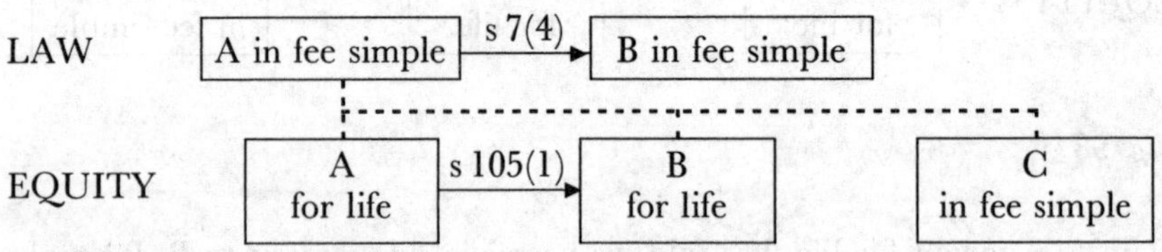

Fig. 59

(c) Unreasonable refusal to exercise powers

Equitable dealings may also impinge upon ownership of the legal estate in the rare case where a tenant for life, on alienating his equitable interest, then wilfully neglects to discharge his remaining fiduciary responsibilities in relation to the legal estate. In the situation depicted in *Fig.* 58,[13] it is

10 Settled Land Act 1925, s 105(1). See also Settled Land Act 1925, s 19(4).

11 Section 7(4) thus operates more widely than in the mere case of surrender. The provision applies wherever the estate owner of settled land ceases to have the statutory powers of the tenant for life (eg where the relevant equitable interest is forfeited for breach of condition or is otherwise determined in accordance with the terms of the settlement).

12 In the circumstances hypothesised here, the land remains settled land for the purpose of section 7(4) even after A's surrender of his life interest to B. There is still a succession of beneficial entitlements in the land which can exist only by way of a strict settlement (see Settled Land Act 1925, s 1(1)(i) and *Fig.* 45, ante, p 611).

13 Ante, p 635.

conceivable that A may take the view that, since he no longer has any beneficial stake in the property, there is no further incentive for him to devote care to the administrative responsibilities connected with legal ownership of the settled land. In cases of wilful refusal by the tenant for life to exercise his statutory powers, any person interested in the settled land may apply to the court for an order authorising the trustees of the settlement to exercise the statutory powers in the name and on behalf of the tenant for life.[14] Once again, the settlement trustees intervene to ensure that the settlement continues unprejudiced.

(2) Powers in relation to the legal estate

In relation to the legal estate in settled land the tenant for life (or, as the case may be, the 'statutory owner') has certain powers which are detailed in sections 38–75 of the Settled Land Act 1925.

(a) Content of the powers

The tenant for life is statutorily empowered to sell the settled land (or any part of it) or any easement, right or privilege over the land.[15] He has power to lease the land (or any easement, right or privilege over it) for any period not exceeding 50 years,[16] although it has been recommended that this power be extended to the grant of ordinary leases not exceeding 100 years.[17] The tenant for life also has power to raise money for certain limited purposes by mortgaging the settled estate,[18] but has, for instance, no power to purchase land with the assistance of mortgage finance.

(b) Fiduciary character of the powers

The tenant for life is, of course, a fiduciary in respect of his ownership of the legal estate and his exercise of the statutory powers of management and disposition.[19] He is subject to the draconian rule which affects all who act,

14 Settled Land Act 1925, s 24(1). See *Re Thornhill's Settlement* [1941] Ch 24 at 30f. The court may order that any documents of title in the possession of the tenant for life be delivered to the trustees. The transfer of authority to the settlement trustees may also be based on the tenant for life's consent to such an order.

15 Settled Land Act 1925, s 38(i). The sale must normally be made for the 'best consideration in money that can reasonably be obtained' (Settled Land Act 1925, s 39(1)). The tenant for life may also make an exchange of settled land (Settled Land Act 1925, s 38(iii)).

16 Settled Land Act 1925, s 41(iv). A tenant for life may also grant leases not exceeding 100 years for mining and not exceeding 999 years for building or forestry (see Settled Land Act 1925, s 41(i)–(iii)). In all cases the lease must normally be made by deed, must take effect in possession within twelve months of its date, must reserve 'the best rent that can reasonably be obtained', and must contain a condition of re-entry on the covenanted rent not being paid within a specified time not exceeding 30 days (Settled Land Act 1925, s 42(1)).

17 Law Reform Committee, *The powers and duties of trustees* (23rd Report, Cmnd 8733, October 1982), para 8.6.

18 Settled Land Act 1925, s 71(2).

19 See Settled Land Act 1925, ss 16(1)(i), 107(1). See also *In re Hunt's Settled Estates* [1905] 2 Ch 419 at 423 per Farwell J, [1906] 2 Ch 11 at 12. It is irrelevant, however, that the tenant for life acts out of ill will or caprice or because he desires to be relieved of the trouble of attending to the management of the land, provided always that he acts in good faith (*Cardigan v Curzon-Howe* (1885) 30 Ch D 531 at 539).

in this broad sense, as trustees in relation to property, in that he is not permitted to derive any unauthorised profit or personal advantage from his trusteeship.[20] Any improper exercise of the statutory powers conferred upon the tenant for life constitutes a breach of trust, in respect of which the settled land beneficiaries may seek an injunction[1] or damages.

The tenant for life must at all times consult the interests of the beneficiaries, although difficulties may present themselves simply by virtue of the fact that the tenant for life is often himself one of the beneficiaries. It seems that a tenant for life may 'legitimately exercise his powers with some, but not of course, an exclusive regard for his own personal interests'.[2] There must, however, come a point beyond which the advancement of self-interest constitutes a violation of the tenant for life's fiduciary responsibilities. Such a case arises, for instance, where, to the long-term detriment of the other beneficiaries, the tenant for life presses for an untimely sale of the settled estate at a gross under-value, simply because short-run hedonism indicates an imperative need of ready cash.[3]

(c) Self-dealing by the tenant for life

Another situation in which the tenant for life may be tempted to exercise his statutory powers improperly arises where he proposes to sell the legal estate to himself. There is a fairly stern rule of English law to the effect that a trustee is not normally allowed to 'self-deal' in this way.[4] A fiduciary may not normally purchase trust property since there is an obvious temptation for the fiduciary to offer himself exceptionally favourable terms of sale to the prejudice of the other beneficiaries. Under the Settled Land Act 1925, however, a tenant for life is permitted to purchase the settled estate provided that the negotiations preceding sale (or other disposition) are conducted not by the tenant for life as vendor but by the trustees of the settlement.[5]

(d) Unfettered nature of the Settled Land Act powers

The breadth of the discretionary powers enjoyed by the tenant for life is reinforced by section 106(1) of the Settled Land Act 1925. This subsection renders 'void' any provision which purports to prohibit, restrict or in any

20 See *Parker v McKenna* (1874) LR 10 Ch 96 at 124 per James LJ; *Bray v Ford* [1896] AC 44 at 51f per Lord Herschell; *Meinhard v Salmon* 164 NE 545 at 546, (1928) per Cardozo CJ; *Phipps v Boardman* [1964] 1 WLR 993 at 1010 per Wilberforce J.

1 See eg *Hampden v Earl of Buckinghamshire* [1893] 2 Ch 531 at 544.

2 *Re Boston's Will Trusts* [1956] Ch 395 at 405 per Vaisey J. For a discussion of Vaisey J's 'somewhat delphic answer', see [1956] CLJ 174 (H.W.R. Wade).

3 An imminent and improvident transaction by the life tenant may be restrained by injunction (see *Wheelwright v Walker* (1883) 31 WR 912; *In re Earl Somers* (1895) 11 TLR 567; *Middlemas v Stevens* [1901] 1 Ch 574 at 577). It has also been recommended that the settlement trustees would be able to control transactions more effectively if the tenant for life could be required, under Settled Land Act 1925, s 101, to provide them in advance of any transaction with an independent valuation of the land supplied by a competent valuer (see Law Reform Committee, 23rd Report (October 1982), para 8.9).

4 See *Williams v Scott* [1900] AC 499 at 503; *Wright v Morgan* [1926] AC 788 at 796f.

5 Settled Land Act 1925, s 68. See *Re Pennant's Will Trusts* [1970] Ch 75 at 81B.

way inhibit a tenant for life in relation to the exercise of the statutory powers vested in him.[6] These statutory powers are, in effect, irreducible and unavoidable.[7] They may, of course, be increased (but never diminished) by the express terms of any actual settlement[8] and may always be augmented by order of the court.[9]

Section 106(1) may well be relevant where a settled land beneficiary is granted an interest which is made expressly liable to forfeiture upon his ceasing to reside in the settled property. If the beneficiary ceases to reside precisely because he has exercised the tenant for life's statutory power to sell the settled estate, the forfeiture clause is rendered void under section 106(1). In consequence the beneficiary's interest endures in the capital proceeds of sale.[10] If, however, the cesser of residence is not attributable to the exercise of any statutory power by the tenant for life, the forfeiture clause is given its full intended effect: the beneficial interest terminates. In this case the beneficiary, being no longer in residence, is ineligible to receive the rents and profits drawn from the land and cannot participate further in the beneficial enjoyment provided by the settlement.[11]

8. THE FUNCTIONS OF THE TRUSTEES OF THE SETTLEMENT

The primary duty of the trustees of the strict settlement is to 'conserve the settled property'.[12] The trustees supervise the settlement from a distance, although they rarely hold the legal estate themselves and have no general power to control the tenant for life's decisions in effecting dispositions of the settled property.[13] The responsibilities of the trustees are fiduciary and, for the most part, residual. The trustees are, however, entitled to be served by the tenant for life with written notice of any proposed disposition of the settled estate.[14] Such a warning puts the trustees on notice that they must be ready to receive the capital money shortly to be paid over in order that the overreaching mechanism be activated and the beneficiaries' interests safeguarded.

6 Section 106(1) has no application, however, to the grant to a stranger of an option of purchase, where the exercise of the option cannot be said to have the 'effect of clogging the powers of the life tenant to sell the freehold.' See *Peach v Peach* (Unreported, Court of Appeal No 1979 P 2475, 3 November 1981) per Cumming-Bruce LJ.

7 The tenant for life cannot validly contract not to exercise the statutory powers (Settled Land Act 1925, s 104(2)).

8 Settled Land Act 1925, s 109(1).

9 Settled Land Act 1925, s 64(1)).

10 See *In re Acklom* [1929] 1 Ch 195 at 198ff; *In re Fitzgerald* [1902] 1 IR 162 at 165f.

11 See *In re Haynes* (1887) 37 Ch D 306 at 309f.

12 *Re Boston's Will Trusts* [1956] Ch 395 at 405 per Vaisey J.

13 Only in the case of a proposed sale of a 'principal mansion house' or the cutting of certain timber do the trustees have a requisite consent which must be obtained as a preliminary to a transaction entered into by the tenant for life (see Settled Land Act 1925, ss 65, 66).

14 Settled Land Act 1925, s 101.

9. CONTINUATION AND TERMINATION OF A STRICT SETTLEMENT

The Settled Land Act 1925 is without question a remarkable piece of legislation. It resembles in many ways a well oiled piece of machinery in which all the component parts operate smoothly and efficiently to achieve the statutory objective. The legislative scheme was designed to *work*: it is dynamic not static. By and large it has worked successfully. Nowhere is the smooth functioning of the Settled Land Act more clearly visible than in the provisions regulating the continuation and determination of a strict settlement.

(1) Special personal representatives

Suppose the existence of a strict settlement under which a settlor has conferred a life interest upon A, with remainders over for B for life and for C in fee simple (see Fig 60[15]). A's life interest obviously determines on his death, at which point B's life interest immediately falls into possession. The land continues, however, to be settled land since there remains an element of beneficial succession between B and C sufficient to attract the terms of section 1(1) of the Settled Land Act 1925. On A's death the legal estate in the settled land must clearly vest in somebody else. The scheme devised by the Settled Land Act ensures that where, on the determination of any interest by death, the land continues to be settled land, then the legal estate vests automatically in the deceased's 'special personal representatives'.[16] These special personal representatives 'hold the settled land on trust, if and when required so to do, to convey it to the person who . . . becomes the tenant for life.'[17] In the current example, B, the next entitled remainderman, now qualifies as the tenant for life and may require the special personal representatives to vest the legal estate in the settled land in him.[18] The transition of ownership of the settled land interests from A to B has now been completed.

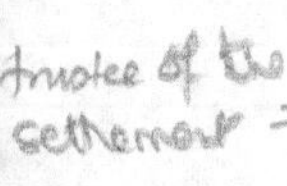

(2) Transfer to an absolute owner

The next transition occurs (perhaps many years later) when B's life interest determines. At this point C's equitable fee simple absolute falls into possession—although it still remains equitable. (C does not become owner of the *legal* fee simple absolute until there has been a proper vesting of this estate in his favour.) On B's death the legal estate vests in his ordinary

15 Post, p 641.
16 See eg *Mellor v Harpur-Crewe* (Unreported, Court of Appeal, 2 November 1992) per Dillon LJ. The settlor is normally deemed to have appointed as the 'special personal representatives' for this purpose the persons who are trustees of the settlement (see Administration of Estates Act 1925, s 22(1)). Here again recourse is had to the settlement trustees—as distinct from the deceased's ordinary personal representatives, in whom is vested all property of the deceased other than the settled land—on the ground that the former group of persons will have a special concern for the interests of the settlement.
17 Settled Land Act 1925, s 7(1).
18 The transfer may be effected by mere 'vesting assent' (ante, p 628).

personal representatives (rather than in his special personal representatives).[19] At this point C, being now absolutely entitled to the beneficial interest in the land, has a statutory right to require the personal representatives to convey the land to him.[20]

When the personal representatives duly convey the legal estate in what was formerly settled land, the absolute legal and equitable ownership will finally merge in a single person free of any settlement or trust.

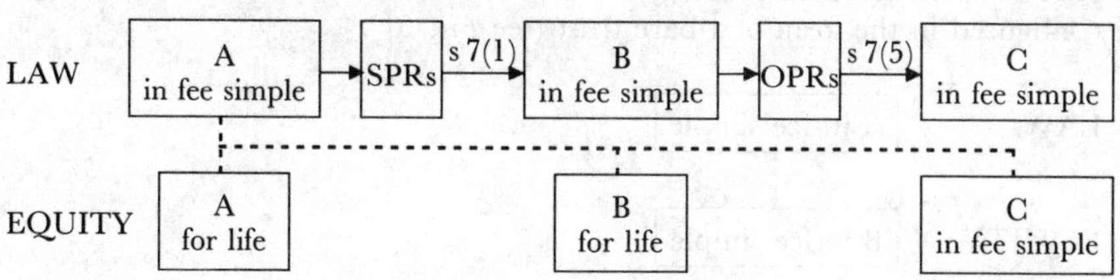

Fig. 60

10. THE CULMINATION OF THE SETTLED LAND ACT 1925

It was one of the major tasks of the property legislation of 1925 to render land commerciable without thereby destroying its utility as a medium of family endowment.[1] The outstanding merit of this legislation is that it goes a long way towards achieving its objective. The device of overreaching ensures that the land can be disposed of entirely free from the interests contained behind the settlement or trust. Simultaneously these same beneficial interests survive the disposition and endure as beneficial interests in the capital money generated by the transaction. Thus the culminating effect of the Settled Land Act 1925—and indeed the ultimate protection for both purchasers and settled land beneficiaries—lies in the overreaching effect of dispositions of the legal estate in the settled land.

The overreaching of settled land interests is, however, dependent upon compliance with certain conditions which are laid down in section 2(1)(i) of the Law of Property Act 1925. These conditions are three in number:

(1) The conveyance must be 'made under the powers conferred by the Settled Land Act 1925'

A conveyance of the legal estate in settled land will overreach the beneficial interests under the settlement only if, first, the conveyance is made under the powers conferred by the 1925 Act. This condition obviously denies overreaching effect to transactions which occur after settled land has, for some reason, been withdrawn from the ambit of the Settled Land Act 1925.

19 See *In re Bridgett and Hayes' Contract* [1928] Ch 163 at 170. The distinction here is attributable to the fact that when B's beneficial interest determines, the land ceases to be settled land: there is no longer any succession of equitable interests sufficient to bring the land within the ambit of section 1(1) of the Settled Land Act 1925.

20 Settled Land Act 1925, s 7(5).

1 Ante, p 98.

In *Fig.* 47,[2] for instance, A held the legal estate in settled land qua tenant for life by virtue of his holding an equitable determinable fee simple in possession. If the specified determining event should now occur (eg A joins the Communist Party), his equitable fee simple automatically comes to an end although he remains invested with the *legal* fee simple absolute in possession. In all normal circumstances A's legal estate remains vested in him unless or until he dies or conveys it away. With the determination of A's beneficial entitlement, however, the remaining interests are now left configured in the form of a bare trust (see *Fig.* 61).

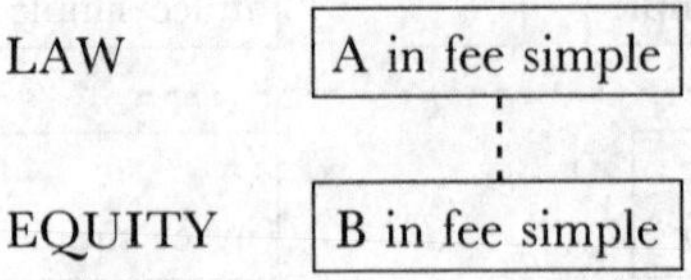

Fig. 61

At this point the strict settlement has in fact come to an end, there no longer being a succession of beneficial interests. The strict settlement has been quietly transmuted into a bare trust, and the outcome no longer falls within the four corners of the Settled Land Act 1925.[3] In this case A, the nominal owner, is now liable to convey the legal estate to or by the direction of the real owner, B. Suppose, however, that A conveys the land instead to a third party purchaser, P, in fraud of the beneficiary behind the bare trust (see *Fig.* 62).

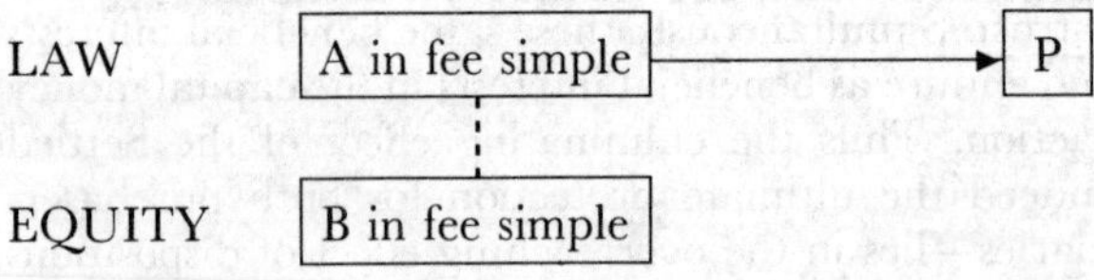

Fig. 62

It cannot be argued that such a conveyance overreaches B's equitable interest by virtue of section 2(1)(i) of the Law of Property Act 1925: the conveyance has not been effected 'under the powers conferred by the Settled Land Act 1925'.[4] A bare trustee cannot give an overreaching conveyance.[5] Moreover the beneficiary of a bare trust has no interest capable of protection either as a land charge or (in the case of registered land) as a minor interest. The fate of B's beneficial interest is therefore governed by the equitable

2 Ante, p 612.

3 Ante, p 614. An exactly similar circumstance occurs where, under the express provisions of the settlement, a life tenant's beneficial interest is duly determined on remarriage, leaving the remainderman absolutely entitled in possession. See P.A. Stone, [1984] Conv 354; R. Warrington, [1985] Conv 377.

4 By the same token P cannot claim the protection of section 110(1),(2) of the Settled Land Act 1925 as a 'purchaser of a legal estate in settled land'.

5 Ante, p 536.

doctrine of notice[6] or (in the case of registered land) by the applicability of overriding interest protection.[7] It is, of course, clear that section 18 of the Settled Land Act 1925 can have no application here. As soon as the settlement is ended by the determination of A's equitable interest (ie as soon as a bare trust arises), the situation is taken completely outside the scope of the Settled Land Act 1925, and *Weston v Henshaw* has no relevance at all.

(2) The equitable interests must be 'capable of being overreached'

A second condition of overreaching is that the equitable interests in question must be 'capable of being overreached'. 'Commercial' equitable interests are not normally capable of being overreached.[8] Overreaching is appropriate only in the case of 'family' equitable interests. By way of minor exception to this rule—and for reasons of convenience—the Settled Land Act 1925 provides that a conveyance of a legal estate in settled land overreaches certain limited categories of 'commercial' equitable interest notwithstanding their registration under the Land Charges Act 1925 or 1972.[9] The disposition of settled land will not, of course, overreach existing *legal* rights over the settled estate which have already been granted away to third parties (eg leases or mortgages). Such interests remain binding in their terms upon the new owner of the legal estate.[10] Otherwise, however, the disposition of the legal estate in the settled land is effective to overreach all subsisting beneficial interests in the land,[11] provided that the third condition of overreaching is satisfied.

(3) There must be compliance with the statutory requirements respecting the payment of capital money

A disposition of the legal estate in settled land will have overreaching effect only if certain statutory requirements respecting the payment of capital money are complied with.[12] In general this means that the capital proceeds of any disposition must be paid to at least two trustees of the settlement. If this

6 If A as vendor had produced his vesting deed under the settlement for inspection by the purchaser P, P could not subsequently disclaim notice of beneficial interests existing behind the settlement. In the present circumstances, however, it is probable that P has paid two settlement trustees anyway, and it is even possible that A made his title fraudulently as vendor on the basis of old title documents—as in *Weston v Henshaw* [1950] Ch 510. In either case the better view is that P can claim the immunity of a bona fide purchaser of a legal estate for value without notice, and may thus take free of B's equitable interest. B's only remedy at this stage lies in a claim against A for undoubted breach of trust. See P.A. Stone, [1984] Conv 354 at 360, but compare R. Warrington, [1985] Conv 377 at 378ff.

7 Ante, p 210.

8 Ante, p 103.

9 See Settled Land Act 1925, s 72(3). These interests comprise annuities, limited owner's charges and general equitable charges, all of which have a definite and easily quantifiable money value. These interests might as well be satisfied out of the capital proceeds of the relevant transaction and are therefore swept off the land at this convenient opportunity.

10 Settled Land Act 1925, s 72(2).

11 Settled Land Act 1925, s 72(1),(2).

12 Ante, p 631.

does not happen, it may well be that the disposition is entirely void.[13] The purchaser of settled land is quite safe, however, if he pays the purchase money to at least two settlement trustees, who thereafter hold the money on a trust of personalty.[14] From the moment when the purchaser obtains his receipt from the settlement trustees, he is exonerated from any liability for loss or misapplication of the funds now in the hands of those trustees.[15] Moreover the purchaser is conclusively deemed by statute to have given 'the best price, consideration, or rent' reasonably obtainable for the land and to have 'complied with all the requisitions of this Act.'[16] This ample immunity is dependent only upon the purchaser having dealt 'in good faith with a tenant for life or statutory owner', and may well confer protection on the purchaser in some situations where he has innocently failed to pay the purchase money to at least two trustees.[17]

The protection afforded the purchaser leads to the culmination of the Settled Land Act 1925—the operation of the 'curtain principle'.[18] In the normal case the purchaser is neither bound nor indeed entitled to call for the production of the trust instrument relating to the settled land.[19] The trusts of the settlement remain concealed from his view, and in this way the Act combines maximum facility for the purchaser with protection for the settled land beneficiaries. The purchaser takes a clear title and the beneficial interests are swept off the land by the device of overreaching.[20]

13 Settled Land Act 1925, s 18(1)(a) (ante, p 631).
14 As trustees they are of course under a duty to invest the capital prudently and to distribute income and capital in accordance with the terms of the original trust instrument.
15 Settled Land Act 1925, s 95.
16 Settled Land Act 1925, s 110(1).
17 See *Re Morgan's Lease* [1972] Ch 1 (ante, p 633).
18 Ante, p 625.
19 Settled Land Act 1925, s 110(2) (ante, p 625).
20 The only occasions on which the purchaser may insist upon seeing the trust instrument relate to the exceptional cases in which an originally imperfect settlement has been rendered perfect under Settled Land Act 1925, s 9 (ante, p 626). See the proviso to Settled Land Act 1925, s 110(2).

CHAPTER 16

The rule against perpetuities

An owner of property has, in principle, the right to create and dispose of whatever interests he or she may choose out of the property which is the subject of ownership. This freedom is frequently associated, however, with various forms of social and economic cost which for centuries the so-called *rule against perpetuities* has sought to minimise. It is this rule which provides the focus of attention in the present chapter.

The rule against perpetuities indirectly serves to demarcate the kinds of restriction or condition which an owner, in the exercise of dispositive power, may validly place upon the enjoyment of future interests in his or her property. In order to achieve this objective, the rule imposes an arbitrarily defined limit on the interval which is permitted to elapse between the *creation* of a future interest and its eventual *vesting*.[1] The rule then operates, supposedly in the public interest, to invalidate certain forms of grant on the ground of *excessive delay* in 'vesting'. Formulated initially at common law,[2] the rule against 'remoteness of vesting' has since been confirmed, albeit in a heavily curtailed guise, by modern legislation.[3]

The rule against perpetuities is notoriously a rule of some considerable complexity.[4] Epitomising the arid technicality of the law of property, the mysteries of the rule have bemused and irritated whole generations of lawyers and law students.[5] Although initially a very flexible principle, the rule became in due course 'one of the most rigid and mathematical of all judge-made rules'.[6] The rule dogmatically declares that legal effect may not be given

1 The concept of 'vesting' is shortly to be defined more closely (post, p 653).

2 The rule against perpetuities first emerged in the *Duke of Norfolk's* case (1683) 3 Ch Cas 1, 22 ER 931, but its development was to span 150 years until the decision in *Cadell v Palmer* (1833) 1 Cl & Fin 372, 6 ER 956. See generally G.L. Haskins, *Extending the Grasp of the Dead Hand: Reflections on the Origins of the Rule Against Perpetuities*, 126 U of Pennsylvania L Rev 19 (1977–78); G.S. Alexander, *The Dead Hand and the Law of Trusts in the Nineteenth Century*, 37 Stan L Rev 1189 (1984–85).

3 See Perpetuities and Accumulations Act 1964 (post, p 665).

4 There is high judicial authority for the proposition that, in view of the 'net which the Rule spreads for the unwary', a lawyer who omits to take account of the rule in drafting an instrument cannot be said, for the purpose of a claim in negligence, to have 'failed to use such skill, prudence and diligence as lawyers of ordinary skill and capacity commonly exercise' (*Lucas v Hamm* 15 Cal Rptr 821 at 825, 364 P 2d 685 at 689 (1961) per Gibson CJ (Supreme Court of California). See also (1965) 81 LQR 478 (R.E.M.). For an excoriating description of the impenetrable qualities of the common law rule, see W.B. Leach, *Perpetuities: Staying the Slaughter of the Innocents*, (1952) 68 LQR 35.

5 The rule against perpetuities acquired an unaccustomed prominence in the public imagination when its cynical manipulation played a critical role in the tortuous plot revealed in the film *Body Heat* (L. Kasdan dir, Warner/Ladd 1981), starring William Hurt and Kathleen Turner.

6 J.H.C. Morris and W.B. Leach, *The Rule Against Perpetuities* (1st edn, London 1956), p 12.

to certain kinds of grant or gift and, in so doing, articulates a wealth of commentary on the way in which society regards the institution of property.

1. THE POLICY UNDERLYING THE RULE AGAINST PERPETUITIES

It has long been a fundamental guiding principle of English law that land should remain freely alienable on such terms as may be chosen by the landowner.[7] It seems somehow intrinsic to the idea of ownership that, in relation to his or her property, the owner should enjoy an absolute power of disposition both inter vivos and upon death.[8] Part of the owner's overriding sovereignty comprises an ability to determine the quantum and configuration of the interests to be carved out of his or her title and transferred to others.[9] In this sense the owner enjoys a virtual legislative power: he or she may fashion in advance a regime or constitutional settlement which predicates the terms on which others may thereafter hold the property. By subtle calibrations of time and contingency the owner may seek to stipulate quite specific conditions of entitlement for future owners of interests in the land, thereby giving effect to highly personal and perhaps even idiosyncratic preferences as to lifestyle and general conduct. The dispositive powers attached to ownership become therefore a mechanism for governance.[10] Indeed this capacity of the current owner to designate in detail the future ownership of his or her property may well be thought to provide a significant incentive not only for the accumulation of wealth but also for the efficient and productive exploitation of land, capital and labour.[11]

It was precisely in order to counter the less obvious negative effects of this ideal of free alienation that the rule relating to perpetuities came into existence. The rule represents one of the most remarkable attempts made by the common law to give legal effect to a number of distinct (but not unrelated) elements of social and economic policy.[12] It is only with the declining importance of these policies in modern times that the rule against perpetuities has tended towards desuetude.

7 Ante, p 90. Blackstone defended the right to transfer property on ground that, without such a right, there would be dereliction of property followed by a free-for-all, and 'all those mischiefs and contentions would ensue, which property was introduced to prevent' (see *Bl Comm*, Vol II, p 294).

8 'Because of its centrality to the market society infrastructure, alienability is one of the most important liberal indicia of property' (M.J. Radin, *Time, Possession, and Alienation*, 64 Wash ULQ 739 at 750 (1986)).

9 The doctrine of estates provides, of course, an almost perfect medium for the realisation of this objective. Under the doctrine of estates the overall ownership of land can be fragmented or graded in temporal slices of differing durations (see Chapter 3, ante, p 56).

10 Consider for example the regulatory intent revealed in a grant of Blackacre to A for life conditional upon his qualifying at the English Bar, with remainders over for A's widow for life during her widowhood and then for such of A's children as attain the age of 21.

11 See R.C. Ellickson, *Adverse Possession and Perpetuities Law: Two Dents in the Libertarian Model of Property Rights*, 64 Wash ULQ 723 at 735f (1986).

12 See generally L.M. Simes, *Is the Rule against Perpetuities Doomed?*, 52 Michigan L Rev 179 at 190ff (1953–54); *The Policy against Perpetuities*, 103 University of Pennsylvania L Rev 707 (1954–55); *Public Policy and the Dead Hand* (Ann Arbor, Michigan 1955), p 32ff.

(1) The inherent contradiction of free alienation

Freedom of alienation confers on the alienor a comprehensive creative control over the pattern of future holdings in his or her land. The principle of unrestricted alienability contains, however, an inherent contradiction: it necessarily involves a potential freedom to impose *limits* on future alienation.[13] Indeed complete freedom of alienation is pre-eminently manifested in a grant of interests which are themselves so limited that none of the grantees can ever replicate the grantor's original exercise of dispositive freedom.[14] Free alienability of land is even more significantly cut back where the alienor, in pursuit of dispositive freedom, effectively ties the land up for generations by the conferment of highly contingent (ie conditional) future interests. Unless statute intervenes, the onward transfer of the full title in land is stultified indefinitely while it remains to be seen whether the stipulated contingencies will be fulfilled by the potential grantees. In its fullest form, therefore, freedom to alienate implies the power to suspend or destroy freedom of alienation itself.[15] The ultimate exercise of the power of free alienation is an abuse of that power—a breach of the inner morality of alienation.[16]

(2) The uncertainty of remote vestings

Additional practical complications follow from the creation of contingent interests which range out uncontrolled into the future. As Richard Epstein once pointed out,[17] the major cost associated with the passage of time is uncertainty. In the context of property law, this uncertainty generates increased litigation, high administrative costs and substantial error rates. Non-vested future entitlements must be held under the trusts of a settlement.[18] Trust administration becomes more burdensome with time; institutional trustees may perhaps be less than wholly enthusiastic managers of the trust

13 Nowhere is this contradiction more clearly demonstrated than in the fluctuating fortunes of the estate in tail (ante, p 59). The early common law era began with what Pollock and Maitland were to call 'a strong bias in favour of free alienation' (*The History of English Law* (2nd edn, London 1968), Vol 2, p 18f). This tendency towards freedom of alienation was then temporarily checked by the Statute *De Donis Conditionalibus* of 1285, which permitted the creation of unbarrable entailed interests in land (see J.H.C. Morris and W.B. Leach, op cit, p 3f). By 1472, however, the courts had discovered a method of barring even these entails by the technique of 'common recovery' (see *Taltarum*'s case (1472) YB 12 Edw IV Mich, fol 14, pl 16, fol 19, pl 25).

14 'The exercise of the power to convey by any individual cannot begin to be full unless he can limit the power to convey of the individual to whom he conveys.' See C. Donahue, 'The Future of the Concept of Property Predicted from its Past', in J.R. Pennock and J.W. Chapman (ed), *Property: Nomos XXII* (New York 1980), p 33.

15 Some commentators nevertheless accept this outcome as an inevitable component of a libertarian view of the institution of property. See eg R.A. Epstein, *Past and Future: The Temporal Dimension in the Law of Property*, 64 Wash ULQ 667 at 705 (1986), where it is argued that the only justification for restraints of private alienation is 'to prevent the infliction of external harms, either through aggression or the depletion of common-pool resources'. See also R.A. Epstein, *Why Restrain Alienation?*, 85 Col L Rev 970 (1985).

16 It may also be argued that to fetter the dispositive power of following generations of donees offends against some notion of inter-generational justice or equality (see A. Reeve, *Property* (Basingstoke 1986), p 159). Compare, however, R.A. Epstein, 64 Wash ULQ 667 at 704f (1986).

17 See R.A. Epstein, 64 Wash ULQ 667 (1986).

18 Ante, p 613.

property. Consensual escape from the grip of old restrictions on entitlement may prove extremely awkward, not least, as Robert Ellickson has observed,[19] because 'the dead are highly inflexible negotiators'. All of these factors point clearly towards the undesirability of allowing legal rights and duties to depend on events (whether past or future) which are excessively remote from the present.[20]

(3) The policy against withdrawing property from commerce

It is commonly said that the rule against perpetuities reflects a general policy preference that property should not be withdrawn indefinitely from the field of commerce. In the context of realty a principal purpose of the rule is therefore to ensure the full utilisation of land as a commerciable and therefore income-producing commodity. One of the great commentators on the rule, John Chipman Gray, declared the rule to represent one of the 'modes adopted by the Common Law for forwarding the circulation of property.'[1]

As will be seen in due course, the rule against perpetuities developed as a means of restricting the grant of future interests in specific property where such interests might 'vest' at some remote future date on the eventual fulfilment of a contingency expressly stipulated by the settlor. An example of a future interest occurs, for instance, where a settlor grants Blackacre 'to A in fee simple, but upon the condition that if none of A's children shall survive to the age of 30, then to B in fee simple.'[2] Here A's interest vests immediately, but is liable to be determined by future events over which he has no control. By contrast B's interest is not vested at the date of grant, but remains contingent until the specified contingency is fulfilled (ie until it becomes clear that no child of A has survived to the required age of 30).

It is not difficult to perceive the rationale for the rule against perpetuities in the context of such a grant. The terms of the grant operate as a disincentive to any heavy investment by A in long-term development or exploitation of the land since his ownership is liable to terminate on the happening of an uncertain event. The land is thereby rendered less productive and A's determinable fee simple, although in theory alienable, is unlikely to command a ready market. If purchased by a stranger, the interest alienated will of

19 64 Wash ULQ 723 at 736 (1986).

20 Most of the disadvantages of an unpredictably futuristic vesting were illustrated in the will of Mr Ernest Digweed, an eccentric Portsmouth schoolmaster turned recluse who died in 1976 aged 81 (see *Guardian*, 21 January 1977). The testator left his entire estate (worth £26,107) to the Public Trustee on trust to pay the invested proceeds to 'the Lord Jesus Christ' if during the next 80 years the same 'shall come to reign on Earth'. The hapless solicitor dealing with the will was reported to be taking counsel's advice on whether this gift was vitiated by anticipated difficulties in identifying the rightful donee. Ironically the inclusion of the 80 year reference (post, p 668) almost certainly rendered the gift immune from challenge on ground of perpetuity.

1 *The Rule against Perpetuities* (4th edn, Boston 1942), p 4. See also G.S. Alexander, 37 Stan L Rev 1189 at 1256ff (1984–85).

2 The creation of this kind of determinable fee simple necessarily attracts the operation of the Settled Land Act 1925 (ante, p 612).

course remain defeasible upon the stipulated contingency.[3] Likewise B's contingent fee simple, although clearly an alienable interest in the land,[4] is also in practice non-commerciable. The restrictive terms attached to the respective interests of A and B have, in other words, rendered both interests effectively unmarketable. Moreover, while the contingency remains unresolved there is no single person with competence at common law to sell (or mortgage) an entire unencumbered fee simple estate in the land.[5] Alienation is thus inhibited even in favour of a third party who might have been prepared to harness the land for constructive income-producing purposes.[6] These negative consequences are regarded as so inimical to the public interest that, as will shortly appear,[7] B's contingent interest is in fact struck down by the common law rule against perpetuities, and the fee simple vested in A is made absolute. In this way the common law imposes an important restraint upon undue protraction of the process of acquiring the absolute interest in property.[8]

(4) The policy against undue concentrations of wealth

The rule against perpetuities was not only aimed at ensuring the alienability of land for purposes of productivity. It has played an important part in countering what Professor Barton Leach called the 'urge to family aggrandisement.'[9] Lawyers of an earlier age were deeply conscious of the threat to the public welfare posed by family dynasties founded on great landed estates or great capital wealth. A vital component of the policy incorporated in the rule against perpetuities was therefore the desire to 'prevent the tying up of the soil of England in the hands of the great families.'[10] In this sense, the rule was akin to the medieval Statutes of Mortmain which were designed to prevent an excessive amount of landed wealth from coming within the sole control of the Church. A clear social interest pointed towards the curtailment of any concentration of the basic resource of land in the hands of constricted social groups. The rule accordingly tended to invalidate

3 Any interest taken by the purchaser is liable to terminate automatically in favour of B's fee simple absolute if no child of A attains the age of 30.

4 See Law of Property Act 1925, s 4(2)(a).

5 It was precisely in order to remedy this deficiency that comprehensive dispositive powers have now been conferred by statute upon the 'tenant for life' (ante, p 637, post p 664).

6 'In order to make a profit from land, one must have a type of ownership which insures enjoyment forever or for a fixed and determinate period of time. People who purchase land, whether for profit or for their own use and enjoyment, are not likely to buy unless they can secure either a fee simple absolute or a lease for a fixed term of years' (L.M. Simes, 103 University of Pennsylvania L Rev 707 at 710 (1954–55)).

7 Post, p 653.

8 In 1841 Jarman's treatise on the law of wills foresaw dire implications for 'the state of a community in which a considerable portion of the land and capital was locked up. That free and active circulation of property, which is one of the springs as well as the consequences of commerce, would be obstructed; the improvement of land checked; its acquisition rendered difficult; the capital of the country gradually withdrawn from trade; and the incentives to exertion in every branch of industry diminished. Indeed, such a state of things would be utterly inconsistent with national prosperity...' (see T. Jarman, *A Treatise on Wills* (1st edn, London 1841), Vol 1, p 219).

9 *Perpetuities: Staying the Slaughter of the Innocents*, (1952) 68 LQR 35 at 40.

10 J.H.C. Morris and W.B. Leach, op cit, p 11.

the creation of contingent future interests for family members which had the effect of withdrawing land from commerce.[11]

In more recent times the rule against perpetuities came also to ensure that the wealth inherent in trust capital was periodically freed for risk investment for the greater economic good of the community as a whole. It is fairly clear, however, that the redistributive function of the common law rule has dramatically abated with the increasing prominence of modern regimes of taxation. Undue concentrations of wealth in the world of today are more effectively restrained by the operation of the laws of income and capital taxation than by any prohibition of perpetuity.

(5) The policy in favour of the survival of the fittest

It has even been suggested[12] that the rule against perpetuities gave effect to some social evolutionary principle favouring the survival of the fittest. It is, of course, quite arguable that every society implements, perhaps unconsciously, certain basic rules of eugenic self-control. On this basis it may be thought socially undesirable that some members of society should have assured incomes and thus remain insulated or protected from the general economic struggle for existence. The brutal principle of the survival of the fittest tends to suggest that those who are unable to maintain themselves in the economic struggle should not survive. In this sense the rule against perpetuities may constitute some elementary expression of an impulse to preserve the unfettered operation of economic competition.[13] If there is indeed a strong social objection to the continuation of a line of weaklings, the rule effectively ensures that, while economic provision may be made on behalf of the unfit for one generation and during the minority of the next generation (ie during 'lives in being' plus 21 years), any attempt to extend such provision to further generations is rendered void.[14]

(6) The policy against capricious gifts

The rule against perpetuities undoubtedly limits the extent to which legal

11 It is arguable that the centrifugal force of the rule against perpetuities has played a more significant role in our social history than may appear on first reflection. Morris and Leach speculated that the rule may have 'succeeded in preventing enormous concentrations of land in the hands of a very few and thereby brought it about that England never suffered unbearably from those conditions which elsewhere have produced violent social revolution—land hunger, a class of servants or peons and widespread destitution' (op cit, p 11).

12 See L.M. Simes, 103 University of Pennsylvania L Rev 707 at 722 (1954–55).

13 Thus, for instance, the *Restatement of the Law of Property* endorses a eugenic rationale for the rule against perpetuities on the ground that 'limitations unalterably effective over a long period of time would hamper the normal operation of the competitive struggle. Persons less fit, less keen in the social struggle, might be thereby enabled to retain property disproportionate to their skills in the competitive struggle' (see American Law Institute, *Restatement of the Law of Property* (St Paul Mo 1944), p 2132).

14 The social policy which favours the survival of the fittest has, of course, become distinctly unfashionable in recent decades. In the post-industrial age of welfare capitalism there is no place for the 'social statics' of Herbert Spencer. According to Spencer, legal and social development was best left to evolve by a process of natural selection similar to that operating in the sphere of biology. See H. Spencer, *Social Statics* (London 1851).

effect is given to capricious or eccentric dispositions of property.[15] By invalidating some of the more extreme forms of contingent grant, the rule has certainly operated as a partial check upon gifts of property which might have had anti-social consequences in sterilising the use of economically valuable resources or in dissipating the substance of existing wealth. It is, however, clear in retrospect that the success of the rule in restraining capricious donation can be seriously over-estimated. Even rigorous application of the common law rule was never wholly able to eliminate eccentric gifts of property.[16]

(7) The policy in favour of limiting the control of the 'dead hand'

Perhaps the primary modern rationale for the rule against perpetuities is the concern to limit the influence exerted by the 'dead hand' of the original grantor over present-day allocations of valuable resource. Thus, whereas a person may generally do as he pleases with his property during his lifetime,[17] the same is not necessarily true after his death.[18] It is broadly deemed to be socially desirable that the wealth of the world should be controlled by its living members and not by the dead.[19] The creation of future interests in property carries the inevitable risk that, over extended stretches of time, the use and exploitation of property may be unduly restricted by the declared wishes of persons long dead. By fashioning enforceable rules for distant times, the far-reaching hand of the testator may sterilise the productive use of property under unforeseeably changed circumstances, thereby causing economic stagnation for future generations. It may also seem wrong that

15 In Galsworthy's *The Forsyte Saga*, for instance, Timothy Forsyte is recorded as having died in 1920, leaving the residue of his estate 'in trust for that male lineal descendant of my father Jolyon Forsyte who after the decease of all lineal descendants of my said father in being at the time of my death shall last attain the age of twenty-one absolutely...'

16 This is amply demonstrated by famous will of Peter Thellusson who died in 1797, leaving a fortune valued then at £30 million. The residue of his estate was left to trustees upon trust to accumulate the rents and profits during the lives of all his sons, grandsons and great-grandsons living at his death or born in due time afterwards, to invest the rents and profits in the purchase of land, and on the death of the survivor to divide it into three lots, each of which was to be strictly settled on the eldest lineal male descendant then living of each of his three sons. In the apt words of Morris and Leach (op cit, p 259), Thellusson thus 'locked his treasure in a mausoleum and flung the key to some remote descendant yet unborn, regardless of the claims which his wife and children might have had upon his bounty.' The will was upheld by the House of Lords as valid under the rule against perpetuities (see *Thellusson v Woodford* (1799) 4 Ves 227, 31 ER 117, (1805) 11 Ves 112, 32 ER 1030). A special Act of Parliament was required to prevent future exhibitions of similar posthumous greed, and the Thellusson litigation was to drag through the courts for another 50 years.

17 He may even destroy his own property (see eg *R v Denton* [1981] 1 WLR 1446 at 1148G (no offence under the Criminal Damage Act 1971 to set fire to one's own premises). This is, of course, the point where utilitarian and libertarian notions of property ownership are apt to come into conflict (see eg 64 Wash ULQ 793 at 845f (1986)).

18 See, for instance, *M'Caig v University of Glasgow* 1907 SC 231 at 242, where Lord Kyllachy thought that it would be contrary to public policy that trustees should be directed by a testator to 'turn the income of the estate into money, and throw the money yearly into the sea...'

19 See eg L.M. Simes, 103 University of Pennsylvania L Rev 707 at 723f (1954–55). See Schwartz, 64 Wash ULQ 793 at 845 (1986), for the strongly utilitarian view that welfare and efficiency are maximised if decision-making is concentrated in 'the most knowledgeable people who will bear the direct consequences...that is, the people now alive'.

norms of conduct and belief embraced by a long dead settlor should be foisted arbitrarily and under wholly different social conditions upon beneficiaries of a succeeding generation.

Not least for these reasons the rule against perpetuities imposes mandatory limits upon the extent to which wealth can be locked up under the otherwise indefinite control of the 'dead hand'. The rule significantly abridges the right of the property owner to create precisely whatever interests he or she may choose; as a matter of law it expunges long-term, objectively costly, ownership restrictions.[20] By prohibiting the creation of certain forms of future interest, the rule thus aims to maintain a balance between those future interests which will vest within the reasonably foreseeable future and those which will not. In the public interest the latter kinds of grant are struck down on grounds of remoteness and a compromise of sorts is effected between the desire of one generation to fetter the future allocation of property resources and the contrary desire of following generations to enjoy total freedom of disposition.

2. THE COMMON LAW RULE AGAINST PERPETUITIES

The common law rule against perpetuities limits the creation of future interests by discriminating against those interests which may not vest in their recipients until an excessively remote point in time.[1] For this purpose 'remoteness of vesting' is defined in terms of John Chipman Gray's classic statement of the rule:

> No interest is good unless it must vest, if at all, not later than twenty-one years after some life in being at the creation of the interest.[2]

In accordance with Gray's formula, the common law rule renders void ab initio any limitation (or grant) of property where there exists any possibility that the grantee's interest may 'vest' *outside* the perpetuity period. In the case of an inter vivos grant, the common law perpetuity period is measured from the date of the instrument of grant; in the case of a testamentary disposition, the relevant period is measured from the date of the testator's death. In either case the perpetuity period is constituted by an artificially defined period comprising all the 'lives in being' at common law plus 21 years.[3] The grant of an interest is valid only if it can be predicted with total certainty that the interest in question (if it is going to vest at all) *must vest* within the perpetuity period so defined.

In the operation of this rule the common law is concerned neither to examine the statistical probability of timely vesting nor to 'wait and see'

20 See R.C. Ellickson, 64 Wash ULQ 723 at 736 (1986).

1 The common law formulation of the rule still governs gifts taking effect before 16 July 1964 (ie the commencement date of the Perpetuities and Accumulations Act 1964), and provides the base on which gifts taking effect thereafter are tested from the point of view of perpetuity (post, p 666).

2 *The Rule against Perpetuities* (4th edn, Boston 1942), s 201.

3 This period can be extended by a further period of gestation of 9 months in respect of a life in being or of a beneficiary in the event of the birth of a posthumous child. See *Duke of Norfolk's Case* (1683) 3 Ch Cas 1, 22 ER 931; *Thellusson v Woodford* (1805) 11 Ves 112 at 143, 32 ER 1030 at 1042.

whether the grantee's interest will in fact vest within the time allowed.[4] The common law rule simply contains a formal mechanism for testing the validity of any relevant interest *in advance* of its actual vesting. The interest is struck down as void ab initio unless at the effective date of grant it can already be predicted that a vesting *must* follow within the permitted period as a matter of inevitable and logical necessity. An interest cannot escape the savagery of the common law rule merely because there is exceedingly little chance that it will actually vest outside the period allowed. The perspective of the common law rule is skewed and its logic applied to a distorted end. The consuming concern of the rule is not with practical realities or eminent probabilities but only with the strictly logical feasibility of an untimely vesting. The rigour of the common law rule is such that all contingent interests are declared irretrievably void if there is even the slightest possibility that the point of vesting may not occur until after the expiration of the perpetuity period.[5]

(1) The meaning of 'vesting'

The precise meaning of the notion of 'vesting' is, of course, critical to the operation of the common law rule. The validity of any grant depends vitally upon a 'vesting' of the relevant interest within the perpetuity period.

In general an interest is properly described as 'vested' where its recipient is an ascertainable person whose entitlement is subject to no condition precedent other than the regular termination of any existing prior interests.[6] A 'vested' interest is, by definition, no longer qualified by any element of contingency or conditionality relating to the inception of the grantee's entitlement.[7] A distinction can therefore be drawn between interests which are respectively

(a) 'vested in possession',
(b) 'vested in interest', and
(c) 'contingent'.

4 The only case in which the common law permits the 'wait and see' principle to operate is the case of alternative contingencies (see *In re Curryer's Will Trusts* [1938] Ch 952 at 956).

5 Compare, however, *Consolidated Development Pty Ltd v Holt* (1986) 6 NSWLR 607 at 617A-D, where Young J held that Torrens registration of an interest void at common law had the effect of curing the defect of remoteness and rendering the interest indefeasible. It is likely that English courts would allow the 'statutory magic' of registration (ante, p 181) to operate with similar effect, since otherwise no person could deal safely on the faith of the register. Ruoff and Roper indicate merely that the registrar may enter some notice calling attention to a defect of perpetuity (see *The Law and Practice of Registered Conveyancing* (Looseleaf edn, London 1991), para 17-46).

6 An 'executory' interest does not 'vest', however, until it falls into possession. An 'executory' interest is one which cuts off a prior interest instead of merely following it when the prior interest terminates through the effluxion of time. An example of an 'executory' interest arises in respect of B's grant under a limitation of Blackacre 'to A in fee simple, but upon the condition that if none of A's children shall survive to the age of 30, then to B in fee simple' (ante, p 648).

7 As will emerge later (p 659), the interests of donees under a *class gift* do not 'vest' for this purpose until the exact membership of the class has been definitively ascertained. A class gift thus remains contingent (ie unvested) while it remains possible that membership of the class may yet be expanded by the addition of further persons or diminished by the future exclusion of some of its present members.

This distinction may be illustrated by reference to a limitation which settles Blackacre *upon A for life, with remainder to B for life and further remainder to C in fee simple on his admission as a Solicitor of the Supreme Court.*

At the date of this grant A can be described as taking an equitable life interest 'vested in possession'. He has a right to immediate possession of the land, not being excluded from such possession by reason of any prior entitlement.[8] Again at the date of grant B takes an equitable life interest 'vested in interest'. He is excluded from immediate possession only by reason of the existence of A's prior interest. B's interest is not, in any true sense, 'contingent' since the inception of his entitlement cannot be said to depend upon his fulfilment of any qualification stipulated by the grantor.[9] His interest, if he receives it at all, is delayed merely as a matter of time and not as a matter of contingency. It is utterly irrelevant that B may not take an interest 'vested in possession' until after the expiration of the perpetuity period. It is sufficient that he takes his interest 'vested in interest' at a point which is manifestly within—indeed at the very commencement of—the perpetuity period.

By contrast C's equitable fee simple in remainder is delayed by more than merely a factor of time. It is truly 'contingent', in that even if A and B were dead, C would still be required to perform the qualifying condition to which his entitlement is subject (ie he would still be required to obtain admission as a Solicitor of the Supreme Court). Herein lies the central concern of the rule against perpetuities: *the rule strikes only at contingent interests.* As soon as an interest vests (whether 'in interest' or 'in possession'), it is safe from the ambit of the rule.[10] In the limitation considered here, it is only the entitlement taken by C which is vulnerable to scrutiny under the rule against perpetuities.

A frequently used figure which neatly illustrates the common law rule is the idea of a queue. In a series of successive interests the grantee who first enjoys possession stands at the head of the queue: his interest has already *vested in possession.* Those standing behind him in the queue hold interests *vested in interest*: their interests will eventually fall into possession as one by one they work their way to the head of the queue. Their arrival at the head of the queue is only a matter of time: they are subject to no contingency, since the element of contingency consists effectively of *getting into* the queue. It is those who stand around outside the queue—in the hope of one day joining it—whose interests are *contingent.* The rule against perpetuities thus directs its narrow focus upon the point in time at which any given interest may finally cross this crucial borderline from contingency to vesting. If it remains logically possible that a specified contingency *may* be fulfilled outside

8 Ante, p 92.

9 In this instance the apparent contingency that B, in order to take his life interest, must survive A, is treated not as a true qualifying condition laid down by the grantor, but merely as a factor intrinsic to the meaningfulness of a life interest. A contingency must, in other words, govern something not implicit in the nature of the limitation itself. Indeed, if B's grant had related not to a life interest but to a fee simple in remainder, the possibility that B might predecease A would be entirely irrelevant. In such an event B's interest, having 'vested' at the date of grant, would simply pass with his estate to his successors.

10 Where there is a timely vesting 'in interest', it is irrelevant that vesting 'in possession' does not occur until after the close of the perpetuity period.

the artificially defined perpetuity period (ie that a grantee may take too long to join the queue), then at common law the contingent interest is declared void ab initio for reasons of public policy. In consequence of the extreme rigour of the rule, the grantee is deprived of even the bare opportunity of seeing whether he might in fact have satisfied the stipulated contingency within the permitted period.

(2) The perpetuity period at common law

The perpetuity period defined by common law is the period marked out by 'lives in being' plus 21 years. Central though it is to the operation of the common law rule, there appears to be no entirely satisfactory definition of the concept of 'lives in being'.[11] Clarity in this respect has generally proved to be elusive.[12]

(a) Identification of 'lives in being'

For the purpose of the common law rule, a 'life in being' is the life of any person[13] alive at the date of the grant who is either expressly or impliedly mentioned in the grant.[14] A 'life in being' need not be related to any of the beneficiaries of the grant,[15] although the question of perpetuity is of course averted completely if a grantee is himself a 'life in being' for the purpose of the grant in question.[16] It must be possible to say of any candidate 'life in being' that his or her longevity is causally relevant in determining

11 'The proper question to ask is: Can I point to some person or persons now living and say that this interest will by the very terms of its creation be vested in an identified individual within twenty-one years after that person dies?' (See B.M. Sparks, *Perpetuities problems of the general practitioner*, 8 University of Florida L Rev 465 at 470 (1955)). For an excellent review of the competing theories as to the identification of 'lives in being', see R.L. Deech, *Lives in Being Revived*, (1981) 97 LQR 593.

12 See R.J. Lynn, *Perpetuities Literacy for the 21st Century*, 50 Ohio St LJ 219 at 227 (1989-90).

13 A 'life in being' must be *human* (*In re Dean* (1889) 41 Ch D 552 at 557f). See *Re Kelly* [1932] IR 255 at 260, where Meredith J similarly insisted that '"[l]ives" means human lives. It was suggested that the last of the dogs could in fact not outlive the testator by more than twenty-one years. I know nothing of that. The court does not enter into the question of a dog's expectation of life. In point of fact neighbours' dogs and cats are unpleasantly long-lived; but I have no knowledge of their precise expectation of life. . .[T]here can be no doubt that "lives" means lives of human beings, not of animals or trees in California.'

14 A child *en ventre sa mère* (ie an unborn child in the mother's womb) is regarded, for the purpose of the rule, as already a 'life in being' (ante, p 652).

15 See, for instance, the common use of a 'royal lives' clause, ie a clause included in an instrument of gift which selects as the measuring lives for the purpose of the gift all the descendants of a named sovereign who are living at the effective date of gift. In *In re Villar* [1928] Ch 471, a testator validly used as the 'period of restriction' the period 'ending at the expiration of 20 years from the day of the death of the last survivor of all the lineal descendants of Her Late Majesty Queen Victoria who shall be living at the time of my death.' (It was calculated that there were approximately 120 such lives in being at the date of the testator's death in 1926.) The formula contained in more recent 'royal lives' clauses has been amended to refer to King George V (see the warning note sounded by Morton J in *Re Leverhulme (No 2)* [1943] 2 All ER 274 at 280H-281A). See generally R. H. Maudsley, *The Modern Law of Perpetuities* (London 1979), p 88ff.

16 An example would be a gift to 'my son Sam if he swims the Channel'.

the latest date at which the interest under challenge can vest.[17] Thus, for instance, in relation to a disposition to 'the first child of X to attain the age of 30', X (if alive at the effective date of gift[18]) constitutes a 'life in being' since the duration of his life indirectly predetermines the latest possible date on which the gift can vest. In the absence of any 'life in being' other than X, such a gift must fail at common law precisely because vesting cannot be guaranteed to occur within 21 years of X's death.[19] The clear purpose of the common law rule was to tie the perpetuity period to the life span of an existing person or group of persons, selected by the settlor as the measuring yard-stick for his grant, and then to extend the period thus demarcated by a further 21 years.[20] The rule thus enabled a settlor or testator to use the attainment of majority as a condition precedent to entitlement under a family settlement.[1]

(b) Absence of 'lives in being'

Where, in relation to any particular grant, no relevant 'lives in being' exist at common law, the perpetuity period comprises simply a 'period in gross' of 21 years from the effective date of grant.[2] In *Palmer v Holford*,[3] for instance, a testamentary gift was made to all the children of a named person, X, living 28 years after the testator's death. Although X was manifestly alive at the date of the testator's death, he was discounted as a 'life in being' since his longevity had no impact at all on the date of vesting in his children.[4] The date of such vesting was fixed entirely independently of whether X

17 According to Professor Jesse Dukeminier, the identification of validating 'lives in being' requires a two-step process of analysis. *First*, if a validating life is found, it will necessarily be found among the lives that can affect vesting, and no others. *Second*, with respect to each person in the pool of lives that can affect vesting, 'we ask whether the interest will necessarily vest or fail within the life of such person or upon, or within twenty-one years after, such person's death. If we find a person in the pool by whom the necessary proof can be made, we have found the validating life', ie the person who enables us to prove that the interest is valid. See J. Dukeminier, *Perpetuities: The Measuring Lives*, 85 Col L Rev 1648 at 1650 (1985). Compare, however, L.W. Waggoner, *Perpetuities: A Perspective on Wait-And-See*, 85 Col L Rev 1714 (1985).

18 If X were *dead* at the date of the grant, those of his children alive at this date would all of course constitute 'lives in being', thereby validating the disposition to 'the first child of X to attain the age of 30'. In these circumstances the contingency could never be satisfied *outside* the perpetuity period.

19 X may, for instance, die leaving an only child aged 2, who will therefore require a further 28 years to attain the stipulated age. The fact that at the effective date of gift X may have serried ranks of children all aged 29 does not assist the gift at common law: it is possible that they may all perish the instant after the gift is made, with the consequence that X's sole survivor is a child born after the date of gift who is, say, only two years old on X's death. Such a sequence of events, although entirely hypothetical and indeed highly improbable, is enough to consign the gift to perpetuity.

20 'What period will take care of the normal desires of the testator who makes a family settlement by way of testamentary trust? The answer is clear enough. It is lives in being and twenty-one years. The testator may well desire to give life estates to his wife and children; he may also wish to provide for unborn grandchildren during their minority' (see L.M. Simes, 103 University of Pennsylvania L Rev 707 at 729f (1954–55)).

1 The age of majority was lowered from 21 to 18 years by s 1(1) of the Family Law Reform Act 1969, but this has not affected the operation of the rule against perpetuities.

2 *See In re Hooper* [1932] 1 Ch 38 at 40f.

3 (1828) 4 Russ 403, 38 ER 857.

4 The testator was obviously not a 'life in being' when his disposition came into effect.

survived the testator by a long or a short period. The gift was therefore declared void on the ground that vesting would occur (if at all) a full seven years after the expiration of the only measuring period remaining at common law.[5]

(3) Simple applications of the common rule

The common law rule against perpetuities may now be applied to several simple grants. For this purpose it must be borne in mind that a grant of a contingent interest in property can fail for two quite separate reasons. Such a grant may fail

either (i) because the grantee never satisfies the specified contingency,
or (ii) because, although the grantee may well satisfy the specified contingency, it is possible that he may do so at a point in time later than the close of the permitted perpetuity period.

The perpetuity question is a narrow inquiry: the focus of the rule fixes only upon whether a contingency may be met *outside* the perpetuity period. If there is any possibility that this may happen, the interest granted is immediately declared void at common law on the ground of perpetuity (ie for reason (ii) above). It is utterly irrelevant for the purpose of the rule against perpetuities that a grant may be destined to fail on the quite different ground that nobody ever qualifies in terms of the stipulated contingency (ie for reason (i) above). The mere fact that nobody qualifies simply means that the property in question remains unclaimed; it does *not* render the contingent interest void on grounds of perpetuity.

(a) *'Blackacre to my first child to be called to the English Bar'*

If this grant is contained in an inter vivos settlement, it is void at common law—unless of course at the date of grant one of the settlor's children has already qualified as a barrister (in which case his or her interest would be no longer *contingent* but *vested in possession*).[6] If, however, this grant is contained in a will it is perfectly valid under the rule against perpetuities.

(i) Inter vivos grant In applying the common law rule to an inter vivos grant, the technique is to set up the 'easy' case in which there is least likelihood of any vesting outside the perpetuity period. If even this case can be struck down because it offends the rule against remoteness, then all 'harder' cases are inevitably tainted by perpetuity and must fall with it.

In the context of the present gift, the easiest case is that in which, at the effective date of grant, the settlor has *n* existing children all of whom are on the verge of being called to the Bar. It is scarcely conceivable that within a very short period of time the stipulated contingency will not have been met by at least one of the settlor's children. The next step is to inquire whether, by adopting the most pessimistic prognosis possible, the 'easy' case thus constructed may be knocked down. Here it is possible—although

5 (1828) 4 Russ 403 at 406f, 38 ER 857 at 858 per Leach MR.
6 At common law account is, of course, taken only of legitimate issue. See now, however, Family Law Reform Act 1969, s 15; Family Law Reform Act 1987, s 1(1).

admittedly unlikely—that the instant after the settlor signs the instrument of grant all the settlor's existing children may perish in some collective disaster. If this possibility were to materialise, the only life in being left for the purpose of delimiting the perpetuity period at common law would be the life of the settlor himself. Any child who claimed the interest granted would necessarily be a future-born child (ie not a life in being), and it is quite likely that such a child might not qualify at the Bar until more than 21 years after the death of the only available life in being (ie that of the settlor). The mere logical possibility of such a conclusion is enough at common law to render the grant void ab initio, thus overriding the extreme improbability that the settlor's expressed intentions should be so comprehensively and fatefully frustrated. The common law has regard only to possibilities not probabilities, and in the present instance it is *possible* that the interest granted may not vest (ie the contingency may not be satisfied) until after the perpetuity period has elapsed.

(ii) Testamentary grant If the grant of Blackacre 'to my first child to be called to the English Bar' is contained in the will of the settlor, it is perfectly valid under the common law rule against perpetuities. In such a case the testator's children (but not of course the testator) would be the relevant lives in being. Apart from the possible addition of a child *en ventre sa mère*—for which possibility the common law expressly makes allowance—the potential recipients of the interest granted are all in being and ascertainable at the effective date of the gift (ie the date of the testator's death). Thus their own lives become the measuring lives, with the result that the gift is clearly validated. There cannot be a posthumous call to the Bar, with the result that the first child to attain the specified qualification must inevitably do so within the span of the measuring period.

(b) 'Blackacre to A [a bachelor] for life, remainder to any wife he may marry for life, and, upon their deaths, remainder to the eldest child of A then living'

There are three quite distinct gifts involved here. The first two gifts are valid under the common law rule against perpetuities, but the third is void. It is irrelevant whether the gifts in question are inter vivos or testamentary, since there is no family relationship between the settlor and the recipients of the grant.

(i) '. . .to A [a bachelor] for life. . .' This first gift vests in possession immediately and clearly no question of perpetuity arises.

(ii) '. . .to any wife he may marry for life. . .' This second gift vests in interest on A's marriage, since at this point A's wife will have satisfied the contingency of becoming A's wife. A's marriage must occur (if at all) during A's lifetime and therefore well within the perpetuity period which here consists of A's life plus 21 years.

(iii) '. . .to the eldest child of A then living' The third gift is, however, subject to a contingency which may be satisfied outside the perpetuity period. The identity of 'the eldest child of A then living' can be determined only upon the deaths of A and his wife. It is possible that A may marry a woman who is not alive at the date of the settlement. Such an 'unborn spouse' cannot rank as a 'life in being' for the purpose of the common law rule. She might, however, outlive her husband by more than 21 years, with the result that the contingency which governs the gift is not resolved until more than 21 years after the death of the only person who does rank as a 'life in being' for the purpose of this gift (ie A). Because there is a slight *possibility* that the foregoing hypothetical developments may in due course materialise, this third gift—but not the first two gifts—must be struck down at the very outset for reasons of perpetuity.[7]

(4) Applications of the rule to class gifts

So far the common law rule against perpetuities has been applied merely to gifts made in each instance to a single donee. A settlor may of course direct his gift not to a single donee but to an entire 'class'. It is an intrinsic characteristic of a so-called 'class gift' that the size of the share taken by each donee is capable of variation in accordance with the numerical membership of the class.[8]

The difficulty inherent in applying the common law rule to class gifts is compounded by the principle that no member of a class may ever be regarded as taking a 'vested' interest while the total membership of the class remains indeterminate.[9] In other words, no class gift is valid under the rule unless it is possible at the effective date of grant to predict that as a matter of logical necessity the quantum (or at least the minimum size of each share) will have been ascertained at the latest by the end of the perpetuity period. A class gift is valid only if it can be predicted with total certainty that the interest to be taken by each and every class member will have vested in interest by the end of that period. If it is possible that the interest of even one class member may not vest in interest until after the expiry of the perpetuity period, the class gift is vitiated for all members.[10] Remoteness which taints the interest of one taints the gift for all.[11]

7 See *In re Frost* (1889) 43 Ch D 246 at 253f per Kay J; *Hardebol v Perpetual Trustee Co Ltd* [1975] 1 NSWLR 221 at 225A-C per Holland J.

8 See *In re Drummond* [1988] 1 WLR 234 at 240G-H, where Sir Denys Buckley described a class gift as 'a limitation in favour of a number of persons which is uncertain in number when the limitation is created and is to be ascertained in future, such persons all coming within a common classification or description, taking one divisible subject matter in specified proportions dependent on the number of takers, all of whose interests must, it seem, vest at the same time.' See also *Pearks v Moseley* (1880) 5 App Cas 714 at 723 per Lord Selborne LC.

9 Ante, p 653. See *In re Drummond* [1988] 1 WLR 234 at 241A-B, where Sir Denys Buckley, although expressing himself not 'fully convinced' of the logic, surmised that the rule rests on the basis that 'until the precise share of the subject matter which any particular member of the class is to receive is known, what is to vest in him cannot be identified, so that there can be no vesting'.

10 See *Pearks v Moseley* (1880) 5 App Cas 714 at 723 per Lord Selborne LC; *In re Drummond* [1988] 1 WLR 234 at 241C per Sir Denys Buckley.

11 See *Leake v Robinson* (1817) 2 Mer 363 at 388f, 35 ER 979 at 988f per Grant MR.

The rigour of this rule is mitigated only by the 'class-closing presumption' permitted by the decision in *Andrews v Partington*.[12] This presumption is a presumption of convenience (designed initially to facilitate the administration of estates) which often quite fortuitously enables a class gift to avoid the vice of perpetuity.[13] In accordance with *Andrews v Partington* the donor is *presumed* to have intended that the class to whom a gift is made should *close* as soon as the first share vests in possession.[14] In other words, as soon as the first share of any member of the class vests in possession, the class is artificially closed around the potential donees who are alive at that time. Only the potential donees within this redefined class may actually go on to attempt to satisfy the specified contingency (if any) and thereby qualify for their respective shares in possession. The operation of the 'class-closing presumption' has the effect that future-born class members are arbitrarily excluded from the class. However, it often happens—entirely fortuitously—that their exclusion saves the class gift as a whole from failure on the ground of perpetuity.[15]

The application of the common law rule to class gifts may be demonstrated by reference to two such gifts.

(a) Blackacre 'to such of the children of A as attain the age of 25'

This gift is valid at common law, whether the gift is effected inter vivos or by will, *provided that* at least one of A's children has already reached the age of 25 by the effective date of the gift.[16] If this proviso is met, the presumption raised by *Andrews v Partington* comes into play (in the absence of any contrary intention expressed by the donor). Since the first share within the class (ie that of the existing 25-year-old) has already vested in possession, the class closes immediately at the date of the gift and includes only those children of A who are alive at this point.[17] Since any existing children are in being and ascertainable at the date of the gift, they themselves must constitute the measuring lives for the purpose of the common law rule. There is, of course, no possibility that any member of this artificially reduced class can attain the age of 25 posthumously, with the result that the class gift as a whole is valid.

12 (1791) 3 Bro CC 401 at 404, 29 ER 610 at 611. On the class-closing rules, see generally A. Lyall, (1985) 20 Ir Jur (NS) 66.

13 In *In re Drummond* [1988] 1 WLR 234 at 242C-D, Sir Denys Buckley referred to the presumption as more accurately representing a 'rule of construction' than a 'rule of convenience'.

14 The class-closing presumption may be rebutted, but only by expressions of contrary intention in the words of gift which point to an 'inescapable incompatibility with the operation of the rule' in *Andrews v Partington* (*In re Clifford's Settlement Trusts* [1981] Ch 63 at 67C per Megarry V-C). See also *In re Chapman's Settlement Trusts* [1977] 1 WLR 1163 at 1167F-1168A; [1978] Conv 73 (F.R. Crane).

15 See eg *Picken v Matthews* (1878) 10 Ch D 264 at 267ff per Malins V-C.

16 The gift is otherwise rendered void by the possibility that A may die leaving, say, a child aged 1 who was not alive at the effective date of the gift. Such a child would not meet the stipulated contingency (ie the attainment of the age of 25) until three years after the end of the perpetuity period, which here consists of A's life plus 21 years.

17 Where the first share has not yet vested in possession, the class remains, at common law, indefinitely open and the class gift must fail. See eg the penalty of voidness applied in *Reid v Earle* (1914) 18 CLR 493 at 508 per Isaacs and Gavan Duffy JJ (gift failed since, at the testator's death, none of the beneficiaries could yet 'call for his share').

The consequence of applying the class-closing presumption is, in effect, to eliminate from the class of potential donees precisely those children of A (ie those born after the date of the gift) who would have vitiated the entire class gift for reasons of perpetuity. Only the potential donees who remain within the class have an opportunity to satisfy the contingency and thereby qualify to receive their proportionate share of the gift. As and when each child of A within the class attains the age of 25, his or her aliquot share vests in possession.

(b) Blackacre 'to A for life, with remainder to A's grandchildren'

The gift to A is perfectly valid since it vests immediately in possession. The class gift to A's grandchildren is valid at common law *provided that* at the effective date of the gift (whether inter vivos or testamentary) at least one of the grandchildren is alive.

The reasoning which underlies the validity of the class gift is as follows. If at the date on which the settlement takes effect A already has at least one grandchild, this grandchild takes an interest vested in interest. (He is excluded from immediate possession only by reason of A's prior life interest.) This grandchild's interest must necessarily fall into possession on A's death since, even if the grandchild predeceases A, the grandchild's estate will call for his share in possession.[18] It can therefore be predicted on the very day on which the settlement takes effect that at least one share within the class will *vest in possession* on A's death. It can therefore be predicted with total certainty that, in accordance with *Andrews v Partington*, the class must close well within the perpetuity period (which here consists of A's life plus 21 years). The class, on closing, will then comprise all grandchildren of A who are alive at the date of A's death. The nature and quantum of their respective entitlements will be resolved at that point—a good 21 years in advance of the expiry of the relevant perpetuity period. Once again, the operation of the class-closing presumption eliminates precisely those potential donees (ie grandchildren born after A's death) whose presence within the class would have vitiated the class gift at common law even for those grandchildren born before A's death.

If the class gift just discussed had been made not simply to 'A's grandchildren', but to 'such of A's grandchildren as are called to the Bar', the result would have been quite different. In this instance the class would have remained indefinitely open in the absence of a grandchild of A already fully qualified at the effective date of the gift. It could not then have been predicted with certainty that the class would close within the perpetuity period (ie that at least one of A's grandchildren would necessarily qualify at the Bar within 21 years of A's death), and in this case the entire class gift would have failed at common law.

18 This merely goes to demonstrate that an interest which is vested *in interest*—as distinct from an interest which is still only *contingent*—is a sufficiently substantial right of property to pass with a deceased's estate (ante, p 653). Once again the borderline between contingency and vesting is crucial.

3. THE REACTION AGAINST THE COMMON LAW RULE

The common law rule against perpetuities was, and still is, draconian in the extreme. Most of the cases decided under the rule have involved a harsh application of what has become a mechanical, over-technical and (for the lay person) quite incomprehensible principle. It is no accident that across the common law world the last 50 years have witnessed a dramatic retreat from general applications of the rule. The fundamental motivations behind the rule have come into question. It is increasingly apparent that, largely because of its heavily formulaic character, the common law rule frequently fails to achieve its own stated objectives. Although a principal purpose of the rule is supposedly the desire to render property readily alienable, this purpose is realised only fitfully. In spite of the enormous care taken to eliminate the threat to alienability posed by contingent grants, at common law land can be quite easily and validly sterilised for up to a century at a time by the grant of *vested* interests to a series of life tenants who are all in existence at the effective date of the gift.[19] Nevertheless the common law rule blindly accepts such a consequence while continuing to tilt needlessly at the windmills of marginal contingency. Perfectly sensible conditional grants are sacrificed at common law on grounds of trivial fortuity.

(1) Unreasoned dogmatism

In declining, in particular, to have regard to realistic probabilities, the common law rule stands widely condemned of unreasoned and obdurate dogmatism. In remorseless defiance of the laws of nature and experience, things physically or practically impossible are presumed to remain legally feasible.[20] Although grudgingly prepared to concede that a deceased person cannot have children,[1] it is notorious that under the common law rule the octogenarian woman is disingenuously deemed to be fertile.[2] In *Jee v Audley*,[3] for instance, it was held that for the purpose of the rule a person should

19 Richard Epstein has pointed, by way of example, to a limitation to 'A for life, remainder to B, to C, to D, to Z, all living persons for life, remainder to the children of B now living'. Such a series of dispositions ties up the land for vast periods 'without ever running afoul of any restrictions on the creation of future interests' (64 Wash ULQ 667 at 710 (1986)).

20 Such applications of the common law rule represent what Richard Helmholz has termed 'a parade of horribles' (64 Wash ULQ 793 at 841 (1986)).

1 See eg *Re Fawaz (decd)* [1958] VR 426 at 431 per Dean J. Ironically, this certitude is now, of course, falsified by the existence of sperm and ova banks. See generally W.B. Leach, *Perpetuities in the Atomic Age: The Sperm Bank and the Fertile Decedent*, (1962) 48 ABAJ 942; C. Sappideen, *Life after Death—Sperm Banks, Wills and Perpetuities*, (1979) 53 ALJ 311.

2 As Professor W.B. Leach once pointed out, in the 'Never Never Land' of the common law rule against perpetuities, the cases on supposedly fertile octogenarians breed much more successfully than the octogenarians themselves. See (1952) 68 LQR 35 at 46. The oldest mother for who there is authenticated evidence seems to have been a Mrs R.A. Kistler of Glendale, California, who gave birth to a child on 18 October 1956 at the age of 57 years 129 days (see *Guinness Book of Records 1993* (London 1992), p 58).

3 (1787) 1 Cox Eq Cas 324 at 325f, 29 ER 1186 at 1187f. See to similar effect *Teague v Trustees, Executors & Agency Co Ltd* (1923) 32 CLR 252 at 265 per Knox CJ, 275 per Starke J.

be deemed to be capable to having further children regardless of his or her age or physical condition.[4]

Moreover, in looking only to the possibility that a gift may *not* vest in time, the common law is wholly unmoved by the possibility—or even the distinct probability—that a gift may indeed vest within the period allowed under the rule. In *In re Wood*,[5] for instance, a testator had instructed his trustees to continue the excavation of certain gravel pits until the gravel was exhausted and then to sell the land and hold the proceeds on trust for his children. The gravel pits were subsequently worked out within the six years following the testator's death, but the Court of Appeal held that the gift to his children must fail for remoteness.[6] There had been, at the effective date of the gift (ie the date of the testator's death), a vitiating degree of uncertainty that the pits would necessarily be exhausted within the perpetuity period. Contingent gifts are thus liable to be struck down at common law if there is even the slightest possibility that they may offend the rule: it is not permitted to 'wait and see' whether they do in fact offend.

Not only is the common law rule rigid and inflexible in its application. The rule frequently violates good sense in that the penalty for non-compliance falls not upon the erring grantor, but upon the innocent intended beneficiary. Indeed, in cases of testamentary grant, property clearly (but invalidly) gifted to a deliberately chosen grantee is taken away and allocated in default to some third party, supposedly on the ground that the gift might have vested too remotely and must therefore go to the person (either the next-of-kin or a residuary legatee) who would have been entitled had the invalid gift not been made at all.[7] Such a result contains the further irony that the ultimate recipient under the rule is then almost inevitably the very person from whom the settlor wished to *divert* his estate in the event of his death. Often, however, the strict application of the common law rule has led to a situation in which the person 'whom the testator clearly wished to restrict to a limited participation in his estate quitted the fray laden with the testator's money bags.'[8]

Only one outcome could be worse than this—and it is that the testator's *lawyer* should make off laden with his money bags. Yet the common law rule tends to trap not testators and settlors who have long-term designs in

4 Compare *Re Gaite's Will Trusts* [1949] 1 All ER 459 at 460A, where a gift was upheld on the ground that it was *legally* impossible, in view of the Age of Marriage Act 1929, that a five-year-old child should produce legitimate issue (who would necessarily have vitiated the gift). The court was unwilling to base its decision upon a mere factual impossibility. See, however, W.B. Leach (1952) 68 LQR 35 at 47, for an apparently well documented instance of birth given by a five-year-old girl in Peru in 1939. The case was fully discussed in a report presented to the Academy of Medicine at Lima and published in *La Reforma Medica*, No 306 (Lima, Peru, May 1939). In respect of dispositions taking effect after 1 January 1970, any reference to a child or other relative includes, in the absence of contrary intention, an illegitimate child and persons descended through illegitimate persons (see Family Law Reform Act 1969, s 15).

5 [1894] 2 Ch 310, [1894] 3 Ch 381.

6 [1894] 2 Ch 310 at 315 per Kekewich J, [1894] 3 Ch 381 at 385f per Lindley LJ, 386 per Lopes LJ, 387 per Davey LJ.

7 See eg W.B. Leach, (1952) 68 LQR 35 at 49f. Compare the statement made, with apparently unconscious irony, by Lord Dunedin in *Ward v Van der Loeff* [1924] AC 653 at 667, to the effect that a testator had framed a testamentary disposition in such manner as to offend the rule against perpetuities and 'I am afraid he must take the consequences.'

8 See W.B. Leach, (1952) 68 LQR 35 at 36.

contravention of the rule, but rather those who fall foul of the rule through the ignorance or oversight of some lawyer to whom they have entrusted their affairs.[9] The ineptitude of such a lawyer may indeed be gross since the snares laid by the common law rule can be avoided by an express clause which clearly restricts the permissible vesting of the relevant gift to the span of the perpetuity period[10] or provides that the gift becomes absolute and possessory at the latest by the end of this period.[11]

(2) Changed conditions

It was perhaps inevitable that the attractions of the highly artificial common law rule should seem greatly diminished in the context of a modern law of property. No obvious social merit attaches to a rule which so needlessly sacrifices non-culpable donees on altars of unyielding principle. Recent disenchantment with the common law rule is not, however, attributable entirely to its sheer mechanical inflexibility. The reaction which has overtaken the rule in most jurisdictions is a more general response to the fact that under changed social and economic conditions the policy motivations of the rule are no longer clearly served by its rigid and unreflecting application.

It was of course one of the professed purposes of the common law rule to facilitate the commerciability of land by restraining the creation of those highly contingent interests which would otherwise act as a clog upon the title. In England commerciability of title is nowadays achieved much more simply by use of the conveyancing apparatus confirmed in the property legislation of 1925.[12] It is no longer credible to maintain that certain kinds of contingent future interests must be struck down on grounds of abstract principle. Pursuant to the legislation of 1925, contingent interests are mandatorily swept into equity and now take effect behind some version of trust (whether in the form of a strict settlement or a trust for sale).[13] Under the Settled Land Act 1925 and the Law of Property Act 1925 there is always *some* person invested with the legal competence to market the land.[14] Moreover, this person (whether tenant for life or trustee for sale) is able, on compliance with certain statutory conditions, to give a conveyance on sale which overreaches all equitable interests subsisting behind the 'curtain' of the trust.

9 'This means that our courts in applying the Rule are not protecting the public welfare against the predatory rich but are imposing forfeitures upon some beneficiaries and awarding windfalls to others because some member of the legal profession has been inept' (W.B. Leach, (1952) 68 LQR 35 at 36).

10 It is arguable that the threat of perpetuity may be averted altogether through the incorporation of a general saving clause in the wording of any particular grant. On this basis no contingent interest would ever be vulnerable on grounds of perpetuity if it were validly stipulated as part of the contingency that the interest must so vest as not to violate the rule against perpetuities. It seems, however, that it is probably not enough merely to stipulate that vesting may be postponed only 'so far as the rules of law and equity will permit' (*Portman v Viscount Portman* [1922] 2 AC 473 at 486f per Viscount Birkenhead LC, 496f per Lord Atkinson, 504 per Lord Wrenbury. See also *Christie v Gosling* (1866) LR 1 HL 279 at 290). Compare *Re Vaux* [1939] Ch 465 at 473ff; and see Leach and Logan, *Perpetuities: Standard Saving Clause to Avoid Violations of the Rule*, 74 Harv L Rev 1141 (1961).

11 For reference to the standard use in the United States of such a 'carefully crafted perpetuities savings clause', see R.J. Lynn, 50 Ohio St LJ 219 at 227f (1989-90).

12 See also Settled Land Act 1882, ss 3(i), 22(1).

13 Ante, pp 518, 609.

14 Ante, p 539.

Overreaching transmutes the contingent entitlements into potential rights in a fund of trust moneys.[15] Thus, far from rendering land titles unmarketable, contingent equitable interests are subjected to a form of forced exchange which actually ensures the constant liquidity of the encumbered land.[16] By virtue of the 1925 legislation, contingent interests in land have effectively become interests in a 'revolving fund' held by a fiduciary owner. In this sense a 'remarkable compromise' has been effected between the desire to tie up property in the family and the policy of free alienability.[17] The net effect of the 1925 legislation has thus been to destroy one of the principal rationales of the common law rule. The policy of free alienability of land no longer requires the rigorous application of a perpetuities rule.

(3) Pressure for reform

During recent decades considerations of the kind rehearsed above generated a profound disaffection from the common law rule against perpetuities.[18] Pressure built up during the 1950s and 1960s for reform of the law, largely on the ground that the common law rule had outlived its original purpose.[19] In England this process of reaction culminated in the enactment of the Perpetuities and Accumulations Act 1964.

4. THE PERPETUITIES AND ACCUMULATIONS ACT 1964

The Perpetuities and Accumulations Act 1964 has vastly modified the operation of the rule against perpetuities in respect of all gifts of property taking effect on or after 16 July 1964.[20] The statutory rule has introduced an entirely new emphasis in the application of the rule prohibiting perpetuity, thus dramatically reflecting the way in which social and economic conditions have changed since the original formulation of the rule.[1] The principal amendments of the common law rule are the following innovations.

15 Ante, p 102.

16 Even if the land is never sold, one of the most important duties of the fiduciary owner (whether tenant for life or trustee for sale) is to meet one of the other major concerns of the common law rule against perpetuities, ie the need to make the trust property productive (ante, p 648).

17 See L.M. Simes, 103 University of Pennsylvania L Rev 707 at 717 (1954–55); R.A. Epstein, 64 Wash ULQ 667 at 714ff (1986).

18 See W.B. Leach, *Perpetuities: Staying the Slaughter of the Innocents*, (1952) 68 LQR 35; *Perpetuities in Perspective: Ending the Rule's Reign of Terror*, 65 Harv L Rev 721 (1952).

19 In the colourful terms of Professor Barton Leach, the rule persisted in personifying itself 'as an elderly female clothed in the dress of a bygone period, who obtrudes her personality into current affairs with unpredictable bursts of indecorous energy. Time was when she stood at the centre of family activity, necessary to the family welfare. A new generation with new problems has arisen, yet she persists in treating ancient issues as present realities and in applying her own familiar solutions. Asserting an authority derived from an earlier day, she insists that a stockade be built round the house to protect it from Indians even though there have been no Indians for decades, the stockade is highly uneconomical, friendly neighbours are rebuffed, and the policeman and fireman are impeded in performing their protective functions' ((1952) 68 LQR 35 at 39).

20 The common law rule applies still to gifts which took effect before the commencement date of the 1964 Act.

1 See generally S.J. Bailey [1965] CLJ 232; J.H.C. Morris and H.W.R. Wade, (1964) 80 LQR 486.

(1) The principle of 'wait and see'

The Perpetuities and Accumulations Act 1964 may be invoked only where a gift has already failed at common law.[2] One of the major criticisms of the common law rule has always been that it strikes down gifts on the ground of the merest possibility of a vesting outside the perpetuity period. Gifts have been invalidated by the remorseless application of the rule even where there has been little likelihood of any violation of the intendment of the rule.

In order to remedy this harsh consequence the 1964 Act introduces an almost unprecedented 'wait and see' principle. The Act allows judgment on the validity of a contingent gift to be postponed during a 'wait and see' period until it becomes clear whether the gift will *in fact* offend the rule against perpetuities. Only if it must so offend is the gift finally declared invalid. Section 3(1) of the Act provides that

> Where, apart from the provisions of this section and sections 4 and 5 of this Act, a disposition would be void on the ground that the interest disposed of might not become vested until too remote a time, the disposition shall be treated, until such time (if any) as it becomes established that the vesting must occur, if at all, after the end of the perpetuity period, as if the disposition were not subject to the rule against perpetuities.

This provision effectively allows the lawyer to 'wait and see' whether a gift will vest within the perpetuity period defined by the Act.[3] The gift concerned is given every opportunity of vesting within the period. It is not struck down ab initio simply because there is some fantastical possibility that it may vest outside the period.[4] It becomes invalid only if and when it is conclusively established that a vesting within the 'wait and see' period is quite impossible. In this sense the modern rule against perpetuities provides an entirely new focus on the central definition of perpetuity: gifts are invalidated not if they *may*, but only if they *must*, vest outside the allowable time span. In this respect the mechanical application of the common law has been alleviated by a much more sensibly pragmatic rule.

(2) The 'wait and see' period

For the purpose of the 'wait and see' provision in the 1964 Act, the perpetuity period (or 'wait and see' period) is defined in slightly different terms from those which delineate the perpetuity period at common law. The 'wait and see' period is calculated with reference to the statutory 'lives in being' enumerated in section 3(5) of the Act, the period consisting of these lives

2 Perpetuities and Accumulations Act 1964, s 3(1). The common law rule is the 'platform' on which the 1964 Act is based (see R.H. Maudsley, op cit, p 44).

3 Post, p 667.

4 Ironically the 'wait and see' provision is open to the criticism that it 'creates uncertainty for lawyer and client; it also tends to prolong the actual period allowed for vesting and may well validate all gifts' (see R.L. Deech, (1984) 4 OJLS 454 at 459). See also R.L. Deech, (1981) 97 LQR 593 at 597. The crystalline solutions produced by the common law rule have at least the merit that, in terms of the famous Coase theorem, clear definitions of entitlement enable parties so to rearrange their affairs as to maximise their joint product (see T.W. Merrill, 64 Wash ULQ 793 at 843f (1986)).

plus 21 years.[5] There is a general rider to the effect that the 'lives in being' used for this purpose must pertain to 'individuals in being and ascertainable at the commencement of the perpetuity period.'[6] Furthermore, it is provided that reference cannot be made to a generic category of 'lives in being' under section 3(5), if 'the number of persons of that description is such as to render it impracticable to ascertain the date of death of the survivor.'[7] The 'lives in being' for the purpose of the statutory rule are the following:

(*a*) the person by whom the disposition was made;

(*b*) a person to whom or in whose favour the disposition was made, that is to say—

(i) in the case of a disposition to a class of persons, any member or potential member of the class;

(ii) in the case of an individual disposition to a person taking only on certain conditions being satisfied, any person as to whom some of the conditions are satisfied and the remainder may in time be satisfied;

(iii) in the case of a special power of appointment exercisable in favour of members of a class, any member or potential member of the class;

(iv) in the case of a special power of appointment exercisable in favour of one person only, that person or, where the object of the power is ascertainable only on certain conditions being satisfied, any person as to whom some of the conditions are satisfied and the remainder may in time be satisfied;

(v) in the case of any power, option or other right, the person on whom the right is conferred;

(*c*) a person having a child or grandchild within sub-paragraphs (i) to (iv) of paragraph (*b*) above, or any of whose children or grandchildren, if subsequently born, would by virtue of his or her descent fall within those sub-paragraphs;

(*d*) any person on the failure or determination of whose prior interest the disposition is limited to take effect.[8]

It is clear from this provision that the statutory lives in being include those of the settlor, potential donees,[9] and parents and grandparents of potential donees. The lives in being specified by the statute exclude some lives which would have been relevant to the common law rule, eg royal lives expressly selected by the settlor as the measuring lives and to which the date of vesting is related.[10]

5 Where there are no statutory 'lives in being' relevant to a gift, the perpetuity period is a period of 21 years (see Perpetuities and Accumulations Act 1964, s 3(4)(b)).

6 Perpetuities and Accumulations Act 1964, s 3(4)(a).

7 Perpetuities and Accumulations Act 1964, s 3(4)(a). See eg *In re Moore* [1901] 1 Ch 936, where an over-ambitious testatrix attempted to use as her perpetuity period 'the longest period allowed by law, that is to say, until the end of the period of 21 years from the death of the last survivor of all the persons who shall be living at my death.' Joyce J (at 938) held this formula to be vitiated by uncertainty. See also *Hardebol v Perpetual Trustee Co Ltd* [1975] 1 NSWLR 221 at 224D-F.

8 See D.E. Allan, *Perpetuities: Who are the Lives in Being?* (1965) 81 LQR 106.

9 Potential donees must, however, be 'individuals in being and ascertainable at the commencement of the perpetuity period' (see Perpetuities and Accumulations Act 1964, s 3(4)(a)). If this were not required, no perpetuity problem could *ever* arise, since every donee would be a statutory 'life in being' for the purpose of validating his own gift.

10 See R.H. Maudsley, op cit, p 125f.

(3) An alternative perpetuity period

The Perpetuities and Accumulations Act 1964 introduced an even more significant innovation in the form of an alternative perpetuity period. Pursuant to section 1(1), an instrument of disposition may expressly provide that the applicable perpetuity period 'shall be of a duration equal to such number of years not exceeding eighty as is specified in that behalf in the instrument.'[11] It has thus become possible for a settlor to specify, in substitution for the traditional common law period of 'lives in being' plus 21 years, an alternative perpetuity period of not more than 80 years in duration.[12] This alternative period has the advantage of great simplicity, but requires to be instituted by express provision in the instrument of grant.[13] The alternative 80-year period may be used in conjunction with the principle of 'wait and see'.[14]

(4) Age reduction

The Perpetuities and Accumulations Act 1964 contains other provisions the main import of which is to reformulate the terms of a gift to make these terms conformable to the rule against perpetuities. One of the principal reasons for failure of a gift under the common law rule has tended to be the fact that the gift is contingent upon a person reaching an age in excess of 21 years. One rather obvious method of eliminating the danger of perpetuity in such cases is to cut the age contingency down to 21 years, and this indeed was the technique chosen by the draftsmen of the 1925 property legislation. Section 163 of the Law of Property Act 1925 automatically reduced to 21 years any excessive age contingency which would otherwise have caused a gift to fail under the common law rule.[15]

The 1964 Act contains a more effective and certainly more sophisticated method directed towards the same end. Where a disposition is vitiated merely by reason of the fact that it requires the attainment of a specified age exceeding twenty-one years, the disposition is treated for all purposes 'as if, instead of being limited by reference to the age in fact specified, it had been limited by reference to the age nearest to that age which would, if specified instead, have prevented the disposition from being so void.'[16] Thus if, at the end of the 'wait and see' period, a contingent beneficiary still falls short of a specified age attainment, the age stipulated in the instrument of gift may be reduced artificially in order to assist the satisfaction of the age contingency. For example, in relation to a gift to 'such of the children of A as attain the age of 30', the age of 30 may be reduced if it subsequently becomes clear that even at the end of the 'wait and see' period vesting is incomplete.

11 Compare the period of 90 years now favoured in the United States by the National Conference of Commissioners on Uniform State Laws (see Uniform Statutory Rule Against Perpetuities, s 1(a)(2) (Uniform Laws Annotated, Vol 8A (1992 Supp), p 351).
12 This alternative period need not be expressed as a specific number of years, but may instead be identified by reference to a stipulated terminal date no more than 80 years distant from the effective date of grant (see *Re Green's Will Trusts* [1985] 3 All ER 455 at 460b-f per Nourse J).
13 See R.H. Maudsley, op cit, p 113f.
14 See, however, R.H. Maudsley, op cit, p 124f.
15 This provision has now been repealed in respect of instruments coming into effect after 15 July 1976 (see Children Act 1975, s 108(1)(a), Sch 3).
16 Perpetuities and Accumulations Act 1964, s 4(1).

In such a case, the age contingency expressed may be reduced to such age between 21 years and 30 years as will enable the offending beneficiary to take a vested interest in the final moment of the 'wait and see' period.[17]

(5) Class reduction

It is clear that sometimes the operation of the common law class-closing presumption may fortuitously save a gift from the vice of perpetuity by means of an artificial reduction of the class of potential donees who then go on to attempt to satisfy the stipulated contingency.[18] In some circumstances it is possible that, even within this reduced class, the specified contingency will remain unsatisfied in respect of some members until after the conclusion of the common law perpetuity period.[19] Such an outcome of course vitiates the entire gift for all concerned. Under the 1964 Act, however, a 'wait and see' provision now operates with the result that the danger of perpetuity in such a case is effectively postponed until the end of the 'wait and see' period. If at this point it appears that some of the members of a class have not yet satisfied a stipulated contingency, the 1964 Act permits a further measure of class reduction in order to save the gift for those members who *have* qualified in time.[20] Thus, where at any time it becomes apparent that a class gift will otherwise be vitiated by the retention within the class of any claimants (whether or not yet alive), then, unless their exclusion would exhaust the class, such persons are immediately 'deemed for all the purposes of the disposition to be excluded from the class'.[1] In effect, remaining potential donees who have not yet satisfied the contingency in question are arbitrarily excluded from the class in order that the gift be saved for those who have managed to qualify within the 'wait and see' period.

Attention was directed earlier to the validity at common law of a disposition to 'A for life, with remainder to such of A's grandchildren as are called to the Bar.'[2] Where the 1964 Act applies, A's grandchildren have the entire 'wait and see' period in which to qualify as barristers (assuming that one is not already qualified at the date of the gift). The class may of course 'close' in the common law sense as soon as the first member of the class takes a share vested in possession (ie qualifies as a barrister on or after the death of A). However, whether the class 'closes' at this intermediate point or remains open until the end of the 'wait and see' period, any members

17 Age reduction cannot, however, save a gift where the specified contingency is not the attainment of a particular age but survival for a stipulated term of years after some named event.

18 Ante, p 660.

19 See *In re Drummond* [1988] 1 WLR 234 at 242A-B, where Sir Denys Buckley indicated that a mere class-closing under *Andrews v Partington* does not necessarily 'eliminate the perpetuity risk'.

20 In some circumstances there may thus be two different and successive reductions of the membership of a class. The first reduction occurs at common law (pursuant to *Andrews v Partington*) either at the commencement, or during the course, of the 'wait and see' period. The second reduction is statutory and occurs, if at all, at the conclusion of the 'wait and see' period. See P. Sparkes and R. Snape, *Class Closing and the Wait and See Rule*, [1988] Conv 339.

1 Perpetuities and Accumulations Act 1964, s 4(4). Age reduction may be combined with class reduction (see Perpetuities and Accumulations Act 1964, s 4(3)).

2 Ante, p 661.

within the class who have not qualified by the latter point are simply excluded from the class by force of statute. Their exclusion is indeed vital for the purpose of the rule against perpetuities, since their continued inclusion within the class of potential donees would postpone vesting for the entire class until a point outside the statutory perpetuity period and would therefore invalidate the entire gift.

(6) Presumptions as to fertility

The Perpetuities and Accumulations Act 1964 also attempts to introduce some much needed realism into the question whether, for the purpose of a determination of perpetuity, a given individual is capable of having a child. Section 2(1) effectively overturns decisions such as that in *Jee v Audley*,[3] by providing certain statutory presumptions regarding future parenthood. Where any question turns on the ability of a person to have a child at some future time, it is now presumed that a male can have a child at the age of fourteen years or over, but not under that age, and that a female can have a child at the age of twelve years or over, but not under that age or over the age of fifty-five years.[4] These presumptions may always be overridden, in the case of a living person, by evidence that he or she will or will not be able to have a child at the time in question.[5]

(7) The problem of the 'unborn spouse'

It was observed earlier that a problem of perpetuity arises at common law in relation to a disposition of 'Blackacre to A [a bachelor] for life, remainder to any wife he may marry for life, and, upon their deaths, remainder to the eldest child of A then living'.[6] The third gift contained in this limitation is void at common law since vesting may occur outside the period of 'lives in being' plus 21 years, as would for instance become inevitable if A's wife were a person unborn at the date of the gift and she were to survive A by more than 21 years.

The awkward implications of the 'unborn spouse' problem have now been resolved by statute. A disposition such as the third gift above to 'the eldest child of A then living' is expressly validated by the Perpetuities and Accumulations Act 1964. Where a disposition would otherwise be void on the ground that it is limited by reference to the time of death of the survivor of a person in being at the commencement of the perpetuity period and any spouse of that person 'and that time has not arrived at the end of the perpetuity period', the disposition is 'treated for all purposes. . .as if it had instead been limited by reference to the time immediately before the

3 Ante, p 662.

4 Perpetuities and Accumulations Act 1964, s 2(1)(a). Where a question as to fertility is decided by treating a person as unable to have a child at a particular time, and he or she does so, the High Court may make such order as it thinks fit for placing the persons interested in the property comprised in the disposition, so far as may be just, in the position they would have held if the question had not been so decided (see Perpetuities and Accumulations Act 1964, s 2(2)).

5 Perpetuities and Accumulations Act 1964, s 2(1)(b). Any reference in this context to 'having a child' is extended to include having a child 'by adoption, legitimation or other means' (Perpetuities and Accumulations Act 1964, s 2(4)).

6 Ante, p 658.

end of that period'.[7] In effect the statute artificially advances the date on which the remaining element of contingency is satisfied, with the result that the disposition in question can no longer fail to vest in the final moment of the 'wait and see' period.

(8) Options and the rule against perpetuities

Options to purchase land have always presented grave potential problems for the purpose of the rule against perpetuities. Section 9(2) of the Perpetuities and Accumulations Act 1964 expressly provides a perpetuity period of 21 years in respect of any disposition which confers an 'option to acquire for valuable consideration any interest in land.'[8] The rule against perpetuities has no application at all to the grant of an option to purchase an interest reversionary upon a lease provided that the option in question is exercisable only by the lessee or his successors in title and ceases to be exercisable no later than one year following the determination of the lease.[9]

6. THE NET EFFECT OF THE PERPETUITIES AND ACCUMULATIONS ACT 1964

It has been said that the Perpetuities and Accumulations Act 1964 'comes out...better...than any other Wait and See legislation in the world.'[10] Perhaps the only major technical criticism which might be made of the new statutory perpetuity rule is that it should have abrogated the old common law rule entirely. Instead the statutory rule comes into operation only where the application of the common law rule has already invalidated the disposition under review.

(1) A fundamental change of perspective

The successful operation of the law of perpetuities rests today on the fact that the contemporary rule adopts a perspective fundamentally different from that of the common law principle. Instead of destroying a disposition for fear of possible perpetuity, the modern law effectively validates the relevant disposition for those beneficiaries who actually manage to obey the rule. In practice the Perpetuities and Accumulations Act 1964 simply implies into all gifts made after 15 July 1964 the very rider which (if incorporated expressly) will probably save gifts from the vice of perpetuity at common law.[11] In this sense the rule as modified by statute preserves the ultimate rationale of a rule against perpetuities, by ensuring that some kind of balance is maintained between the dispositive control of 'the dead hand' and the dispositive control of the living.

7 Perpetuities and Accumulations Act 1964, s 5.

8 No recourse can be had to the alternative perpetuity period of 80 years (see Perpetuities and Accumulations Act 1964, s 9(2)).

9 Perpetuities and Accumulations Act 1964, s 9(1). Even at common law a covenant for renewal of a lease is perfectly valid even though it can be exercised outside the perpetuity period (see *Woodall v Clifton* [1905] 2 Ch 257 at 265 per Warrington J, 268 per Romer LJ).

10 R.H. Maudsley, op cit, p 227.

11 Ante, p 664.

(2) Does the perpetuity rule have a future?

It is nowadays questionable whether a particularly valuable function is performed by the preservation of a perpetuity rule in *any* form.[12] Even under the common law there are few kinds of donative intention which, with a little care, cannot be framed validly within the four corners of the rule. Since for all practical purposes the rule can be evaded by cautious drafting, the salutary truth is that the percentage of wealth caught by the rule has always been infinitesimal and wholly disproportionate to the in terrorem impact exerted by the rule on the minds of donors and their lawyers.[13]

The common law rule against perpetuities has now been marginalised as an obsolete and discredited principle, its shortcomings being suppressed by the substantial palliative of 'wait and see' legislation. It should not, however, be overlooked that the Perpetuities and Accumulations Act 1964 is merely a vehicle for highly artificial and disingenuous manipulations of actuality. The *legerdemain* of such devices as arbitrary age and class reduction, when placed alongside the revolutionary perspective of 'wait and see', has resulted in the virtual abandonment of any genuine commitment to a principle against perpetuity. Only the outer shell of the perpetuity rule remains, the inner core having been eviscerated by contrivances which accommodate almost every imaginable disposition of property within the procrustean dimensions of the now heavily modified rule. Dispositions are re-drafted to conform to the 'rule'; contingencies are shamelessly fiddled until they are finally 'met'; and the declared intent of grantors is subverted without a second thought—all in supposed fidelity to a principle whose underlying motivations are now largely forgotten or utterly irrelevant.

In these circumstances it inevitably becomes an open question whether there remains any major social or economic purpose in preserving the modern attenuated version of the rule against perpetuities. As Richard Epstein has aptly observed,[14] the 'wait and see' innovation has merely ensured that, instead of 99.9 per cent of dispositions being valid, the proportion is now increased to 99.95 per cent. Nevertheless, the persistence of some incredibly peripheral uncertainty as to valid vesting causes everybody 'to worry about it in a very large way.' There is much to be said for Epstein's conclusion that the continued retention of the perpetuity rule 'tends to queer all sorts of transaction, slow people up, get them apprehensive and nervous for no particular social gain. So strike the rule down.'

12 On the question whether all forms of perpetuity rule should now be abolished, see R.L. Deech, (1984) 4 OJLS 454. Compare, however, R.J. Lynn, 50 Ohio St LJ 219 at 239f (1989–90).

13 Indeed it may not be entirely futile to suggest that, for the legal profession, one of the long-term purposes of the perpetuity rule—or at any rate one of its more satisfactory by-products—has been to cause the uninformed lay person to imagine that the services of a lawyer are required in the making of all but the most simple and straightforward kinds of gift.

14 64 Wash ULQ 793 at 842 (1986).

CHAPTER 17

Leases

In the structural organisation of estates and interests confirmed in the Law of Property Act 1925, the term of years or tenancy is firmly marked out as a proprietary interest in land. Section 1(1)(b) of the 1925 Act clearly identifies the 'term of years absolute' as one of the two legal estates in land recognised today in English law.[1]

1. CONCEPTUAL ORIGINS AND PRACTICAL FUNCTIONS

A 'term of years' confers a right to occupy and enjoy land for a determinate period.[2] A term of this kind is created by a grant or 'demise' of land which confers upon the grantee a right of exclusive possession for some lesser term than that held by the grantor.[3] A 'term of years', otherwise known as a 'lease' or 'tenancy', is thus the product of an express or implied grant by a 'lessor' (or 'landlord') and has the consequence of investing the 'lessee' (or 'tenant') with some form of ownership interest in the land. Yet this proprietary attribution serves largely to obscure the fact that, by virtue of its historical origins, the 'term of years' is a curious hybrid which hovers ambiguously between the worlds of property and contract.

(1) Historical foundations of the leasehold estate

The proprietary character of the term of years is nowadays so readily assumed that it can be easily overlooked that the leasehold relationship is founded essentially on contract. The leasehold estate provides perhaps the pre-eminent historic demonstration of the transformation of contractual right into proprietary title.[4] The right to occupy another's land for a defined period of time was originally considered to confer no estate in the land, but merely to create rights *in personam*.[5] The lessee's remedies were restricted to a personal action in damages against the lessor on his covenant to give enjoyment of the land.[6] In time, however, it came to be accepted that the lessee for a

1 Ante, p 68.
2 Ante, p 69.
3 See *Javad v Mohammed Aqil* [1991] 1 WLR 1007 at 1012C per Nicholls LJ.
4 As Lord Browne-Wilkinson pointed out in *Hammersmith and Fulham LBC v Monk* [1992] 1 AC 478 at 491G-H, the lease provides a classic reminder of the fact that 'a contract between two persons can, by itself, give rise to a property interest in one of them. . .The contract of tenancy confers upon the tenant a legal estate in the land: such legal estate gives rise to rights and duties incapable of being founded in contract alone.'
5 See *Street v Mountford* [1985] AC 809 at 814E per Lord Templeman.
6 See generally A.W.B. Simpson, *A History of The Land Law* (2nd edn, Oxford 1986), p 71ff; F. Pollock and F.W. Maitland, *The History of English Law* (London 1968), Vol II, p 106ff.

term, although denied 'seisin' in the strict sense, had a right to 'possession' which could be protected against third parties. The enactment of the Statute of Gloucester 1278 and the steady development of the action of ejectment during the late Middle Ages effectively converted the personal relationship of landlord and tenant into a new category of proprietary relationship based on the recognition of some form of estate ownership vested in the tenant.[7] The tenant's rights were now vindicated by a recovery not merely of damages but of possession of the land. Commensurately with this extension of protection, the leasehold relationship began to generate an entitlement which more closely resembled a right *in rem*.

It was by virtue of this metamorphosis that, almost unnoticed, the term of years crossed the critical conventional borderline between contract and property. At this point the interest conferred by a lease could no longer be regarded as lying altogether outside the law of real property, although a lingering recollection of its contractual antecedents inhibited its full acceptance within the strict system of feudal tenements.[8] The hybrid character of the term of years, partaking as it did of the nature of both realty and personalty, caused the tenant's interest to be classified, with fitting ambiguity, as a 'chattel real'.[9] This hesitancy notwithstanding, the tenant's interest in the land came to be accepted 'as analogous to a form of feudal tenure'.[10]

(2) Conceptual ambivalence of the lease

Precisely because of the nature of its origin the lease for a term of years still possesses a 'duality of character' which, as Deane J pointed out in *Progressive Mailing House Pty Ltd v Tabali Pty Ltd*,[11] sometimes gives rise to conceptual difficulty. The lease is 'both an executory contract and an executed demise.'[12] Viewed from the perspective of property, the lease represents a conveyance of a proprietary estate in land, this conveyancing perspective being particularly apt to describe the effect of leasehold dispositions in the rural, agrarian society of a bygone era.[13] Viewed from the perspective of contract, however, the lease is manifestly different from a conveyance of a fee simple in that the conveyance of a leasehold interest does not represent a fully executed contract. Even after grant the lease is 'partly executory: rights and obligations remain outstanding on both sides throughout its

7 See T. Plucknett, *A Concise History of the Common Law* (5th edn, London 1956), p 574.
8 *Progressive Mailing House Pty Ltd v Tabali Pty Ltd* (1985) 157 CLR 17 at 51 per Deane J.
9 See *National Carriers Ltd v Panalpina (Northern) Ltd* [1981] AC 675 at 708B–C per Lord Russell of Killowen. The terminology of 'chattel real' is now archaic (see *Crago v Julian* [1992] 1 WLR 372 at 377H per Nicholls V-C).
10 *Progressive Mailing House Pty Ltd v Tabali Pty Ltd* (1985) 157 CLR 17 at 51 per Deane J.
11 (1985) 157 CLR 17 at 51 (High Court of Australia).
12 (1985) 157 CLR 17 at 51. See Kilgarlin J's reference in *Brown v RepublicBank First National Midland*, 766 SW2d 203 at 204 (1988), to the 'dual nature' of the lease as 'both a contract and a conveyance of an interest in land'. See also *Hoyt's Pty Ltd v Spencer* (1919) 27 CLR 133 at 142 per Isaacs J.
13 See *Javins v First National Realty Corporation* 428 F2d 1071 at 1074 per Judge Skelly Wright (1970) (post, p 784).

currency.'[14] There remains today a significant tension between these competing proprietary and contract-based perspectives.

Of course the notion of the term of years as a vehicle of estate ownership makes a certain conceptual sense in the context of 'broad acre' or 'green field' leases of land.[15] Yet except in the nowadays unusual case of a completely unconditional demise for a long term with no rent reserved,[16] the leasehold estate cannot be divorced from its basis in the law of contract. Especially in the context of modern forms of urban occupancy, the lease often appears more obviously as a relatively short-term commercial relationship, framed in the language of executory promises of an all-inclusive character to which the terminology of conveyance or estate ownership may seem peculiarly inappropriate. Some 60 years ago William Douglas and Jerome Frank argued that 'to assimilate leases of modern office buildings to feudal tenure in seventeenth century England is to disregard the essential elements of the bargain made, the present money economy, and the great development in contract law which has taken place since Coke wrote.'[17] In more recent times Laskin J of the Supreme Court of Canada agreed that it is 'no longer sensible to pretend that a commercial lease. . .is simply a conveyance and not also a contract.'[18] It is increasingly recognised, moreover, that the modern residential letting represents a commercial transaction which results in the sale of a package of consumer utilities of shelter and convenience.[19] In reality the urban tenant is frequently a purchaser of goods and services under a specialised form of consumer contract.[20]

This renewed acceptance of the heavily contractual dimension of the landlord–tenant relationship inevitably counteracts the conventional common law analysis of the lease as a conveyance of a proprietary estate.[1] In many

14 *National Carriers Ltd v Panalpina (Northern) Ltd* [1981] AC 675 at 705G per Lord Simon of Glaisdale.

15 *Wood Factory Pty Ltd v Kiritos Pty Ltd* (1985) 2 NSWLR 105 at 120F per Priestley JA. 'Leases acquired the character of conveyances of real property when their primary function was to govern the relationship between landowners and farmers' (*Trentacost v Brussel* 412 A2d 436 at 442 per Pashman J (1980)). See also W.M. McGovern, *The Historical Conception of a Lease for Years*, 23 UCLA L Rev 501 (1975–76).

16 See eg *Knight's Case* (1588) 5 Co Rep 54b at 55a, 77 ER 137 at 138.

17 W.O. Douglas and J. Frank, *Landlords' Claims in Reorganizations*, 42 Yale LJ 1003 at 1005 (1932–33).

18 *Highway Properties Ltd v Kelly, Douglas & Co Ltd* (1971) 17 DLR (3d) 710 at 721.

19 'When American city dwellers, both rich and poor, seek "shelter" today, they seek a well known package of goods and services—a package which includes not merely walls and ceilings, but also adequate heat, light and ventilation, serviceable plumbing facilities, secure windows and doors, proper sanitation, and proper maintenance' (*Javins v First National Realty Corporation* 428 F2d 1071 at 1074 per Judge Skelly Wright (1970)).

20 See *Green v Superior Court of City and County of San Francisco*, 517 P2d 1168 at 1175 (1974), where in the Supreme Court of California Tobriner J observed that 'in most significant respects, the modern urban tenant is in the same position as any other normal consumer of goods. . .A tenant may reasonably expect that the product he is purchasing is fit for the purpose for which it is obtained, that is, a living unit'.

1 See eg *Brown v RepublicBank First National Midland* 766 SW2d 203 at 205 (1988), where Kilgarlin J spoke in the Supreme Court of Texas of the need to abandon the 'feudal antecedents' of landlord–tenant law and to replace such 'antiquated property law concepts with more equitable and contemporary solutions in contract'. In Kilgarlin J's view, the 'property aspects' of the transaction of lease 'are now subservient to the mutual promises made by landlord and tenant'. See also *Hussein v Mehlman* [1992] 2 EGLR 87 at 88K–L per Sedley QC.

ways the modern social function of the tenancy relationship as a consumer contract marks a significant transformation from its former role as the medium of estate ownership. Recent years have accordingly seen a growing tendency to expose the law of leases to a much more comprehensive application of ordinary contract principles.[2] Such principles seemed largely irrelevant where the dominant analysis of the lease was that of an executed demise under which an estate in land had actually passed to the tenant. Nowadays it has become impossible to maintain the traditional assumption that leases lie generally beyond the reach of such contractual doctrines as those of frustration, repudiatory breach and mitigation of loss.[3] Indeed the gradual infiltration of such doctrines may seem perversely to have brought the lease almost full circle to its medieval origin as a species of essentially contractual obligation.[4]

Notwithstanding the modern 'contractualisation' of the lease,[5] the relationship between the property- and contract-based views of the leasehold nexus remains one of continuing tension.[6] In certain significant respects English law still persists in identifying the tenant in terms of proprietary ownership; leasehold tenure is still often viewed as a form of estate ownership analogous to freehold tenure.[7] Recent statutory extensions of the law relating to leasehold enfranchisement[8] serve as an inescapable reminder that leasehold status frequently provides a gateway to enlarged rights of fee simple ownership. In recent times even short-term or periodic tenancies, with their capacity for devolution upon members of the tenant's family,[9] have come to evince

2 See *Progressive Mailing House Pty Ltd v Tabali Pty Ltd* (1985) 157 CLR 17 at 29 per Mason J. In particular, in the enforcement against landlords of implied warranties of habitability and fitness for use, American courts have increasingly stressed that the contractual principles established in other areas of the law 'provide a more rational framework for the apportionment of landlord–tenant responsibilities' (see *Javins v First National Realty Corporation* 428 F2d 1071 at 1080 (1970)).

3 Post, pp 764, 763, 844. It has been recognised nevertheless that the applicability of pure contractual doctrine decreases 'the further one moves away from the case where the rights of the parties are. . .essentially defined by executory covenant or contractual promise to the case where the tenant's rights are, as a matter of substance, more properly to be viewed by reference to their character as an estate (albeit a chattel one) in land with a root of title in the executed demise' (see *Progressive Mailing House Pty Ltd v Tabali Pty Ltd* (1985) 157 CLR 17 at 53 per Deane J).

4 It has become a recurring judicial refrain that the courts see 'no reason' why a particular issue should 'receive any different answer in the context of the contractual relationship of landlord and tenant than that which it would receive in any other contractual context' (*Hammersmith and Fulham LBC v Monk* [1992] 1 AC 478 at 483B per Lord Bridge of Harwich). See also *Hadjiloucas v Crean* [1988] 1 WLR 1006 at 1022G, 1024G per Mustill LJ; *Prudential Assurance Co Ltd v London Residuary Body* (1992) 63 P & CR 386 at 399 per Scott LJ; *Hussein v Mehlman* [1992] 2 EGLR 87 at 89E per Sedley QC.

5 See eg Hicks, *The Contractual Nature of Real Property Leases*, 24 Baylor L Rev 443 (1972); J. Effron, *The Contractualisation of the Law of Leasehold: Pitfalls and Opportunities*, (1988) 14 Monash L Rev 83; K. Mackie, (1988) 62 ALJ 53; [1993] Conv 71 (S. Bright).

6 See eg Lord Browne-Wilkinson's reference in *Hammersmith and Fulham LBC v Monk* [1992] 1 AC 478 at 491E, to 'two instinctive reactions. . .which lead to diametrically opposite conclusions'.

7 Post, p 698. See eg the Law Commission's reference to the function of the lease in creating 'temporary property ownership' (*Landlord and Tenant: Privity of Contract and Estate* (Law Com No 174, 29 November 1988), para 3.26).

8 See Leasehold Reform Act 1967, s 1; Leasehold Reform, Housing and Urban Development Act 1993, s 1 (post, pp 766, 770).

9 Post, p 876.

a tantalising resemblance to a modern form of entailed estate. In these and many other ways the law of landlord and tenant remains permeated by the oscillating ambivalence of the lease as a source of both proprietary and contractual entitlement.

2. ESSENTIAL ELEMENTS IN A 'LEASE' OR 'TENANCY'

The essential ambiguity of the leasehold device as both contract and property is captured in the statement of Lord Templeman in *Prudential Assurance Co Ltd v London Residuary Body*[10] that '[a] demise for years is a contract for the exclusive possession and profit of land for some determinate period.' Some years earlier, in *Street v Mountford*,[11] Lord Templeman had indicated that '[t]o constitute a tenancy the occupier must be granted exclusive possession for a fixed or periodic term certain in consideration of a premium or periodical payments.' Neither formula entirely eliminates the difficulties inherent in the definition of the 'term of years'.[12]

(1) Types of lease or tenancy

It has been said quite correctly that a lease is 'chameleonic in both character and function'.[13] In the legal systems of the common law world the leasehold device has been adapted and manipulated for an extremely broad range of purposes. It currently provides a legal vehicle for many forms of residential, commercial and agricultural user. The lease or tenancy has come to play a vital (and not particularly comfortable) role in mediating a host of contractual, consumer, conveyancing and investment relationships. Essentially the same legal concept has had to do service for arrangements which, in their context and purpose, can differ as widely as the short-term letting for residential occupation and a leasehold term of 3,000 years used as mortgage security.[14] The multiplicity of uses to which the uniform concept of tenancy has been put only barely conceals the difficulties which are inherent in the indifferent application of the same legal rules to the periodic tenant who pays £50 per week for his bed-sit, the home-owner who has just paid £50,000 for a 99 year lease of a new flat, and the large commercial concern which rents a warehouse for £5,000 per year.[15]

The types of tenancy known to English law include the following.

(a) Fixed term lease

The concept of the lease or tenancy may apply to the grant of exclusive possession for any fixed period of time. The period may be long or short, although the longer the term the greater is the tendency to use the terminology of 'lease' rather than 'tenancy'.

10 [1992] 2 AC 386 at 390C.
11 [1985] AC 809 at 818E.
12 There is a definition of 'term of years absolute' in Law of Property Act 1925, s 205(1)(xxvii), but, being circular in nature, the statutory definition provides little assistance.
13 *219 Broadway Corp v Alexander's, Inc*, 387 NE2d 1205 at 1207 per Judge Jasen (1979).
14 Post, p 939.
15 See *Wood Factory Pty Ltd v Kiritos Pty Ltd* (1985) 2 NSWLR 105 at 120F per Priestley JA.

(i) Purchase of a long lease A long lease may well comprise the grant of a term of 99 years, in which case the purchase of such an estate begins to resemble the purchase of an estate in fee simple. The grantee under a 99 year lease of a house or flat normally purchases his or her estate in the land on payment of an initial cash sum or 'premium' not dissimilar from the purchase price of a freehold estate in equivalent realty. Like the freeholder, the leaseholder may use the estate purchased as security for a loan covering all or part of the purchase price. After acquisition the leaseholder's only remaining financial liabilities to the grantor relate to the continuing payment of what is usually a fairly nominal ground rent, together with payment of such periodic service or management charges as may be stipulated for in the covenants of the lease.

(ii) Leasehold as a marketable capital asset The proprietor of a long leasehold stands possessed of an asset which, although necessarily of a wasting nature, will still for many years command an inflating market value on alienation (or 'assignment'). In other words, it is open to the leaseholder at any time to assign the unexpired portion of the term for such price as the current market will sustain,[16] and this price will continue for some time to run ahead of the initial purchase price of the lease at the commencement of the term. The leaseholder may alternatively deal with his or her estate by way of sublease.[17]

(iii) Termination A fixed term lease automatically comes to an end on the expiration of the period stipulated. At this point the reversion to the landlord 'falls in' and the land is no longer encumbered by the lease. The superior owner is once again free to resume physical possession and to deal with the property as he wishes.[18]

(b) Periodic tenancy

A 'term of years' may also take the form of a periodic tenancy which runs from week to week, or from month to month, or from quarter to quarter, or from year to year.[19] Such tenancies may be created either expressly or impliedly. A periodic tenancy continues indefinitely until determined by the giving of the appropriate notice.[20]

(i) The old common law presumption There used to be a strong common law presumption that, in the absence of express words, a periodic tenancy was impliedly created by the payment and acceptance of a periodic sum in the

16 It is not uncommon, however, for a lease to contain a covenant prohibiting assignment except with the consent of the landlord (post, p 800).
17 Post, p 734.
18 The generality of this proposition is qualified by the possibility that, by virtue of protective legislation, the tenant may enjoy some kind of security of tenure on the expiry of his lease (post, pp 877, 885).
19 Law of Property Act 1925, s 205(1)(xxvii).
20 Post, p 753.

nature of rent.[1] Such circumstances were apt to generate a weekly, monthly, quarterly or yearly tenancy, depending on the period with reference to which the payment was calculated.[2] However, the reservation of rent and its payment on some periodic basis are not wholly incompatible with the existence of a mere tenancy *at will*.[3]

(ii) The primacy of intention In cases of dispute the court must ultimately examine the 'intentions of the parties in all the circumstances',[4] in order to determine whether it is 'right and proper to infer. . .that the parties had reached an agreement' for a periodic tenancy.[5] In *Javad v Mohammed Aqil*[6] the Court of Appeal conceded that, in the total absence of any other 'material surrounding circumstances', the inference 'sensibly and reasonably to be drawn' from the periodic payment of rent is that the parties intended to create a periodic tenancy. Nicholls LJ indicated, however, that it is relatively rare that the fact of periodic payment should stand isolated from other factors which may help to clarify the matter of intention.[7] Where other explanatory circumstances exist, the payment of rent on a periodic basis, although a 'very important' factor, is merely one of the indicators to which the court must have regard in ascertaining the nature of the parties' relationship.[8]

In *Javad*, for instance, an occupier had been allowed into possession of premises pending the conclusion of negotiations over a proposed 10 year lease. The Court of Appeal declined to find that a periodic tenancy had been created by the occupier's payment during this period of quarterly amounts of rent. According to Nicholls LJ, entry into possession while negotiations proceed is 'one of the classic circumstances in which a tenancy at will may exist'.[9] There had been credible evidence here that the parties understood that the premises were to be vacated if negotiations broke down. The Court felt unable on this basis to accede to the occupier's argument that the periodic payments had generated a tenancy which would prematurely have qualified for extended protection under Part II of the Landlord and Tenant Act 1954.[10] The lease contemplated by the parties had clearly been

1 *Doe d Lord v Crago* (1848) 6 CB 90 at 98f, 136 ER 1185 at 1188f. This presumption 'dies very hard' (see *Longrigg, Burrough & Trounson v Smith* (1979) 251 Estates Gazette 847 at 849 per Ormrod LJ), but see now *Javad v Mohammed Aqil* [1991] 1 WLR 1007 at 1011H–1012C per Nicholls LJ.

2 See *Cole v Kelly* [1920] 2 KB 106 at 132. For further discussion of the implied periodic tenancy, see p 740, post.

3 *Doe d Bastow v Cox* (1847) 11 QB 122 at 123, 116 ER 421 at 422; *Hagee (London) Ltd v A.B. Erikson and Larson* [1976] QB 209 at 214F–G. The 'tenancy at will' is discussed shortly (post, p 680).

4 *Cardiothoracic Institute v Shrewdcrest Ltd* [1986] 1 WLR 368 at 378C. See also *Doe d Cheny v Batten* (1775) 1 Cowp 243 at 245, 98 ER 1066 at 1067 per Lord Mansfield CJ; *Irish Shell and BP Ltd v John Costello Ltd* [1984] IR 511 at 517f per Henchy J.

5 *Longrigg, Burrough & Trounson v Smith* (1979) 251 Estates Gazette 847 at 849. See also *Uzun v Ramadan* [1986] 2 EGLR 255 at 257E–H.

6 [1991] 1 WLR 1007 at 1012E. See [1991] CLJ 232 (S. Bridge).

7 The typical case today 'invariably involves more than the simple facts of possession and an unexplained payment of rent' ([1991] 1 WLR 1007 at 1014H).

8 [1991] 1 WLR 1007 at 1012F–G.

9 [1991] 1 WLR 1007 at 1019E.

10 Post, p 887.

a long lease rather than any periodic tenancy. The Court was therefore reluctant, while the parties were 'in the throes of negotiating larger terms', to infer the creation of a different, and much more limited, interest on the mere basis of periodic payments of money.[11]

(iii) Relevance of statutory protection of the tenant In days of increased statutory control over the landlord's right to recover possession, there is an increasing tendency to accept that the old common law presumption of periodic tenancy is 'unsound and no longer holds'.[12] In determining whether the mere fact of payment and acceptance of rent generates an implied periodic tenancy, the courts tend nowadays to draw inferences as to the parties' likely intentions in the light of the potential effects of modern protective legislation.[13] In *Cardiothoracic Institute v Shrewdcrest Ltd*,[14] for instance, the potential impact of the protective scheme provided for business tenants by Part II of the Landlord and Tenant Act 1954 made the court unwilling to believe that the parties had intended, by mere payment and acceptance of rent, to create a periodic tenancy. It is, however, quite arguable that the common law presumption still retains its force where, for instance, a tenancy unaffected by statutory prolongation has come to an end and the parties have not yet expressly agreed on the creation of a new tenancy. Under these circumstances the continuing payment and acceptance of a periodic rent may well generate a periodic tenancy 'on the footing that that is what the parties must have intended or be taken to have intended.'[15]

(c) Tenancy at will

The phenomenon of the 'tenancy at will' occupies an obscurely defined no-man's land between the periodic tenancy and the mere licence.[16] A tenancy at will arises if, with the consent of the owner, a person enjoys occupation of land for an indefinite period in circumstances where either party may at any time terminate the arrangement at will, ie on demand.[17] No notice

11 [1991] 1 WLR 1007 at 1013B-C, 1017F–G. Likewise in *Uzun v Ramadan* [1986] 2 EGLR 255 at 257F, it was held that the parties' known intention to create a five-year term could not support an implication of periodic tenancy founded on periodic payments of rent. See [1988] Conv 17 (J.E.A.). See also *Sopwith v Stutchbury* (1983) 17 HLR 50 at 74 per Stephenson LJ; *Brent LBC v O'Bryan* (1992) 65 P & CR 258 at 262ff.

12 *Longrigg, Burrough & Trounson v Smith* (1979) 251 Estates Gazette 847 at 849 per Ormrod LJ. In *Javad v Mohammed Aqil* [1991] 1 WLR 1007 at 1017C–D, Nicholls LJ considered as a 'peculiarly arid issue' the question whether the old common law presumption from periodic payment has nowadays been overturned as unsound or simply operates only very seldom.

13 See eg *Javad v Mohammed Aqil* [1991] 1 WLR 1007 at 1014H, where the Court of Appeal saw the 'widespread intervention of statute in the landlord–tenant area' as providing one highly potent reason why few cases arise to be dealt with nowadays purely on the footing of entry into possession coupled with the tendering of a periodic rent.

14 [1986] 1 WLR 368 at 379F-G. See [1987] Conv 55 (J.E.M.); [1988] Conv 16 (J.E.A.).

15 *Cardiothoracic Institute v Shrewdcrest Ltd* [1986] 1 WLR 368 at 378B–C.

16 For a definition of 'licence', see Chapter 19 (post, p 891).

17 *Errington v Errington and Woods* [1952] 1 KB 290 at 296. See also *Doe d Groves v Groves* (1847) 10 QB 486 at 491f, 116 ER 185 at 187f; *Buck v Howarth* [1947] 1 All ER 342 at 343G. With certain exceptions (post, p 736), all interests in land created merely by parol have 'the force and effect of interests at will only (Law of Property Act 1925, s 54(1)).

to quit is required in order to determine a tenancy at will,[18] and the existence of any express stipulation relating to notice is itself inconsistent with a tenancy at will.[19] The tenancy at will thus differs from a periodic tenancy, which is terminable only by the giving of appropriate notice.[20] It is of the essence of a tenancy at will that it continues indefinitely until terminated on demand by either party or brought to an end by the death of either.[1]

Tenancies at will tend nowadays to be fairly unusual and slightly anomalous. It may be that such a tenancy 'can now serve only one legal purpose, and that is to protect the interests of an occupier during a period of transition.'[2] A tenancy at will normally confers merely some form of intermediate status, and is readily (although not always) converted into an estate in the land by way of implied periodic tenancy as soon as the tenant offers and the owner accepts some payment of rent which is referable to a year or aliquot part of a year.[3]

(i) Nature of a tenancy at will A tenancy at will is something of a hybrid and its status in law is in many respects unclear.[4] A tenancy at will is said to comprise a 'personal relation between the landlord and his tenant',[5] and a tenant at will, having no estate in the land, cannot sublet or assign his tenancy to a stranger.[6] This being so, the tenant at will closely resembles the licensee, who similarly has no estate in the land and who avoids being classified as a trespasser only because the landowner consents to his occupancy.[7] However, the status of the tenant at will differs vitally from that of the mere licensee in that, even if he has no 'estate' as such, the tenant at will is accounted to be in 'possession' of the land.[8] Unlike the

18 *Crane v Morris* [1965] 1 WLR 1104 at 1108B–C; *Cliffe v Cooper* (Unreported, Court of Appeal, 20 May 1985)). It seems that a tenancy at will may validly indicate a future date beyond which the tenancy shall not continue (*GLC v Minchin* (Unreported, Court of Appeal, 1979 G No 2837, 25 February 1981)).

19 See *Colchester BC v Smith* [1991] Ch 448 at 483C per Ferris J. Compare, however, *Uzun v Ramadan* [1986] 2 EGLR 255 at 257H; [1988] Conv 16 (J.E.A.).

20 See *Javad v Mohammed Aqil* [1991] 1 WLR 1007 at 1009A–B per Nicholls LJ.

1 *James v Dean* (1805) 11 Ves 383 at 391, 32 ER 1135 at 1138; *Wheeler v Mercer* [1957] AC 416 at 427. A tenancy at will is also terminated if the tenant commits acts of voluntary waste (see *Countess of Shrewsbury's Case* (1600) 5 Co Rep 13b, 77 ER 68 at 69; *Warren v Keen* [1954] 1 QB 15 at 21; *Nichols v R.A. Gill Ltd* (1975) 51 DLR (3d) 493 at 498). See also *Kater v Kater* (1960) 104 CLR 497 at 503.

2 *Heslop v Burns* [1974] 1 WLR 1241 at 1253A per Scarman LJ. See also *Irish Shell and BP Ltd v John Costello Ltd* [1984] IR 511 at 515 per O'Higgins CJ.

3 Post, p 740. See *Roe d Bree v Lees* (1777) 2 W Bl 1171 at 1173, 96 ER 691 at 692; *Richardson v Langridge* (1811) 4 Taunt 128 at 132, 128 ER 277 at 278; *Doe d Hull v Wood* (1845) 14 M & W 682 at 687, 153 ER 649 at 651; *Landale v Menzies* (1909) 9 CLR 89 at 129f.

4 See eg *Irish Shell and BP Ltd v John Costello Ltd* [1984] IR 511 at 523, where McCarthy J opined that a tenancy at will is 'something of a misnomer if one gives to the cognate word "tenant" the ordinary meaning rather than its limited source meaning of "holder". In truth the tenant at will is a person with a licence and no more than a licence to occupy.'

5 *Wheeler v Mercer* [1957] AC 416 at 427 per Viscount Simonds.

6 See *Murphy v Ford* (1855) 5 ICLR 19 at 23; *Anderson v Tooheys Ltd* (1937) 54 WN (NSW) 21 at 23; *Victa Sales Pty Ltd v Tucker* [1970] 1 NSWR 737 at 739. Compare, however, *Ward v Ryan* (1875) IR 10 CL 17 at 19. The tenant at will has no estate which may vest in his trustee in bankruptcy (see *Re Keith G Collins Ltd and Director, Veterans' Land Act* (1987) 35 DLR (4th) 96 at 101).

7 Post, p 891.

8 *Lynes v Snaith* [1899] 1 QB 486 at 488f. The concept of 'possession' is discussed further elsewhere (post, pp 697, 708).

licensee, who enjoys no positive (as distinct from defensive) rights,[9] the tenant at will has an 'exclusive right of occupation'.[10] It follows therefore that, unlike the licensee, the tenant at will is entitled to maintain an action in trespass against a stranger[11] (although not against the owner himself[12]).

(ii) Eligibility for statutory protection Although imprecisely drawn, the borderline between tenancy at will and periodic tenancy is sometimes disproportionately significant in defining the availability of various kinds of statutory protection. It is clear, for instance, that the tenant at will cannot invoke the code of protection applicable to business tenancies under Part II of the Landlord and Tenant Act 1954,[13] although it seems that he does come within the protection of the Rent Act.[14]

(d) Tenancy at sufferance

A tenancy at sufferance arises where a tenant who has enjoyed a perfectly valid term of years holds over at the end of his term without the consent or dissent of the landlord.[15] It is the absence of the landlord's consent which distinguishes a tenancy at sufferance from a tenancy at will.[16] A tenant at sufferance has no 'tenancy' in any true sense and is not entitled to maintain any action in trespass.[17] The tenant at sufferance is not liable to pay rent as such, but is liable to a money claim for use and occupation of the land.[18]

(2) The parties to a lease must be legally competent

Certain requirements of legal competence must be satisfied by the parties to a properly constituted term of years.

(a) Competent lessor

In order to grant a valid lease, the grantor must have legal competence to create a term of years in the subject land.[19] In a very elementary sense

9 See *Street v Mountford* [1985] AC 809 at 816C per Lord Templeman.
10 *Goldsack v Shore* [1950] 1 KB 708 at 714f per Evershed MR.
11 *Heslop v Burns* [1974] 1 WLR 1241 at 1253C; *Cuvet v Davis* (1883) 9 VLR 390 at 396; *Victa Sales Pty Ltd v Tucker* [1970] 1 NSWR 737 at 739.
12 Non-consensual entry by the owner amounts to a termination of the tenancy at will (see *Co Litt*, p 55b; *Doe d Bennett v Turner* (1840) 7 M & W 226 at 232f, 151 ER 749 at 751; *Landale v Menzies* (1909) 9 CLR 89 at 133).
13 *Wheeler v Mercer* [1957] AC 416 at 426f, 428, 435; *Hagee (London) Ltd v A.B. Erikson and Larson* [1976] QB 209 at 215C, 216F; *Cardiothoracic Institute v Shrewdcrest Ltd* [1986] 1 WLR 368 at 376E–F; *Javad v Mohammed Aqil* [1991] 1 WLR 1007 at 1009B–C.
14 *Francis Jackson Developments Ltd v Stemp* [1943] 2 All ER 601 at 603H–604A.
15 See *Co Litt*, p 57b; *Remon v City of London Real Property Co Ltd* [1921] 1 KB 49 at 58. Active dissent by the owner would render the occupier a trespasser (see *Simms v Lee* (1945) 45 SR (NSW) 352 at 354ff).
16 *Wheeler v Mercer* [1957] AC 416 at 426.
17 *Schwartz v Zamrl* [1968] 2 NSWR 51 at 53; *Victa Sales Pty Ltd v Tucker* [1970] 1 NSWR 737 at 738f. He may, however, be eligible for protection under the Rent Act (post, p 873). See *Remon v City of London Real Property Co Ltd* [1921] 1 KB 49 at 58.
18 *Bayley v Bradley* (1848) 5 CB 396 at 406, 136 ER 932 at 936.
19 For reference to the capacity of one joint owner unilaterally to grant a lease over jointly owned land, see Chapter 13 (ante, p 469).

it is clear that no lease is validly created unless the grantor himself has an estate in the land.[20] For instance, a company cannot effectively grant a term of years if title to the land in question is vested not in the company itself but in the name of the person who formed the company.[1] Nor has a corporate entity any capacity to grant leases over its land unless a leasing power has been duly included in its memorandum of association or (where applicable) within its statutory mandate.[2]

(b) Competent lessee

The grantee of a lease must likewise be legally competent to hold a term of years. The lessee must be a legal person such as an individual or a corporate body and, in the latter case, must be duly empowered by the company constitution to be the recipient of leases. No tenancy can be granted to an unincorporated association since such a body has no legal personality or status.[3] Nor can the grant be construed as one to the members of the association from time to time: a legal estate cannot be vested in a fluctuating body of persons.[4]

Problems arise only rarely as to the legal competence of the lessee. However, two of the more common issues relate to the competence of (i) a grant to a minor and (ii) a grant to the lessor himself.

(i) Lease to a minor It is clear that a minor (ie a person under the age of 18) is not competent to hold a legal estate in land,[5] and this necessarily means that a minor lacks capacity to hold any leasehold interest which ranks as a legal estate. This limitation on the competence of the lessee is seldom discussed but seems to be an inescapable conclusion of law. In strict terms a conveyance of a legal estate to a minor operates instead in the manner provided by the Settled Land Act 1925,[6] which means that the conveyance operates only as an agreement for valuable consideration to execute a settlement in favour of the minor.[7] The intending lessor meanwhile holds the estate on trust for the minor.[8]

Terms of years are not often conferred upon minors, but embarrassing consequences are introduced in those few areas where such leases are not unknown. A local authority which grants a council tenancy to a 17-year-old single mother has almost certainly no intention to activate the more

20 See *Southgate BC v Watson* [1944] KB 541 at 544; *Lewisham BC v Roberts* [1949] 2 KB 608 at 622; *Street v Mountford* [1985] AC 809 at 821B; *Royal Philanthropic Society v County* (1985) 276 Estates Gazette 1068 at 1071; *Dellneed Ltd v Chin* (1987) 53 P & CR 172 at 187. The only kind of tenancy within the competent grant of a person without a current estate in the land is a tenancy by estoppel (post, p 978). See *LB of Camden v Shortlife Community Housing Ltd* (1992) 90 LGR 358 at 381 per Millett J.
1 *Torbett v Faulkner* [1952] 2 TLR 659 at 660, 662.
2 See *LB of Camden v Shortlife Community Housing Ltd* (1992) 90 LGR 358 at 377f (any grant of tenancy by council void without consent of Secretary of State).
3 *LB of Camden v Shortlife Community Housing Ltd* (1992) 90 LGR 358 at 374 per Millett J. See eg *Congregational Christian Church v Iosefa Tauga* (1982) 8 Comm Law Bull 129 (grant to church invalid because church was an unincorporated association).
4 *Jarrott v Ackerley* (1915) 113 LT 371 at 373 per Eve J.
5 Law of Property Act 1925, s 1(6) (ante, p 69).
6 Law of Property Act 1925, s 19(1).
7 Settled Land Act 1925, s 27(1).
8 Ibid.

obscure provisions of the Settled Land Act 1925.[9] It is extremely dubious whether such a grant constitutes a 'conveyance' within the meaning of that Act,[10] but if it does it seems that the landlord authority must hold on trust for the minor. In view of these difficulties, a tenancy agreement with a minor is best analysed as creating an equitable[11] rather than a legal leasehold interest. Such a tenancy takes effect as a contract for a lease[12] and, since it relates to the supply of a 'necessary',[13] falls within one of the categories of contracts with minors which remain fully enforceable in law.[14]

(ii) Lease to the lessor himself It has been clear since 1925 that, notwithstanding the terms of section 72(3) of the Law of Property Act 1925,[15] a person cannot grant a lease to himself of land of which he is the owner.[16] The major obstacle appears to consist in the absurdity of enforcing leasehold covenants against oneself.[17]

(3) A lease must have a fixed maximum duration

As Blackstone explained,[18] the leasehold estate is commonly called a 'term' or *terminus* precisely 'because its duration or continuance is bounded, limited and determined: for every such estate must have a certain beginning, and certain end.'[19] In view of this strictly terminal aspect, the 'term of years' represents pre-eminently 'a time in the land' or 'land for a time'.[20] The grant of a lease or tenancy accordingly confers a right of exclusive possession

9 Ante, p 613.

10 The Settled Land Act 1925 does not define 'conveyance', but in the Law of Property Act 1925 the term is used only in relation to an assurance of a property interest 'by any instrument' (Law of Property Act 1925, s 205(1)(ii)).

11 Section 1(6) of the Law of Property Act 1925 does not, of course, prohibit the holding of an *equitable* interest by a minor.

12 Post, p 743.

13 See *Lowe v Griffith* (1835) 4 LJCP 94 at 96.

14 This view was endorsed by the Law Commission in 1984. The Commission sought to allay the concern expressed by some public landlord authorities, by pointing out that a minor is liable to pay the rent accruing during the currency of his contractual tenancy up to the date of any repudiation (*Law of Contract: Minors' Contracts* (Law Com No 134, 28 June 1984), para 5.15). See *Valentini v Canali* (1889) 24 QBD 166 at 167; *Davies v Beynon-Harris* (1931) 47 TLR 424. Compare *Can an under-18-year old be a contractual tenant?*, (1983) 147 Loc Gov Rev 259. See now Minors' Contracts Act 1987, s 1.

15 Section 72(3) provides that 'a person may convey land to or vest land in himself', but this has been construed as meaning merely that a sole executor may properly convey land to himself as devisee, or that a beneficial owner may convey land to himself as a trustee for charitable purposes (see *Rye v Rye* [1962] AC 496 at 514).

16 *Rye v Rye* [1962] AC 496 at 505 per Viscount Simonds, 514 per Lord Denning. See *Hocking v Kerhardy* (Unreported, Court of Appeal, 26 August 1992), where the Court of Appeal frustrated an attempt by a registered proprietor to obtain priority over a legal chargee by alleging an earlier lease of the property to a company which merely provided a trading name for his own activities.

17 Compare eg Property Law Act 1952 (New Zealand), ss 49, 66A; *Harding v Commissioner of Inland Revenue* [1977] 1 NZLR 337 at 341; *Samuel v District Land Registrar* [1984] 2 NZLR 697 at 701f.

18 *Bl Comm*, Vol II, p 143.

19 Blackstone emphasised that the leasehold estate must expire 'at a period certain and prefixed' (ibid). See also *Prudential Assurance Co Ltd v London Residuary Body* [1992] 2 AC 386 at 390D-E per Lord Templeman.

20 Ante, p 58.

of land for a quantum of time fixed in advance at the commencement date. From this proposition flow several implications.

(a) The lessor necessarily retains a reversionary interest

A lease or tenancy always comprises the grant of a lesser estate out of a larger estate in land. It is therefore an integral feature of every term of years that the landlord is left with some kind of reversionary interest in the land.[1] In other words, there must always be a reversionary interest, retained throughout by the landlord, which 'falls in' at the end of the quantum of time represented by the lease. The presence of this reversionary interest in the landlord carries the important implication that he is regarded as holding an estate 'in possession' in the land even during the currency of the lease, 'possession' being defined broadly in the Law of Property Act 1925 as including 'receipt of rents and profits or the right to receive the same'.[2] The landlord's reversion is recognised as giving him an estate in the land sufficient, for instance, to provide him with a 'dominant tenement' for the purpose of enforcing restrictive covenants against a subtenant.[3]

(b) The lease must commence at a 'time certain'

The lease must commence at a 'time certain' which is either expressly fixed by the parties or readily ascertainable before the start of the term.[4] There cannot in law be an agreement for a lease to commence at some unspecified future date. If an agreement to create a future lease does not stipulate at least an ascertainable commencement date, there is no concluded contract.[5] In other words, the lease must have a definite *terminus a quo*.[6] If the commencement date is not specified, it may in some circumstances be inferred

1 *Re British American Oil Co Ltd and DePass* (1960) 21 DLR (2d) 110 at 115.

2 Law of Property Act 1925, s 205(1)(xix). There are always therefore at least two estates concurrently in possession in the landlord-tenant relationship, since both landlord and tenant enjoy 'possession' in the extended statutory sense.

3 *Hall v Ewin* (1888) 37 Ch D 74 at 79; *Teape v Douse* (1905) 92 LT 319 at 320; *Northern Ireland Carriers Ltd v Larne Harbour Ltd* [1981] 5 NIJB, Transcript, p 10 per Murray J. The landlord has, of course, no right to possession in the sense of immediate exclusive possession, for this has been surrendered during the term to the tenant (see *Reference Re Prince Edward Island Lands Protection Act* (1988) 40 DLR (4th) 1 at 10f). Nor, during the term, is the landlord in possession for the purpose of the law of adverse possession (ante, p 287). See *Giouroukos v Cadillac Fairview Corp Ltd* (1984) 3 DLR (4th) 595 at 605f.

4 *Bl Comm*, Vol II, p 143; *Say v Smith* (1563) 1 Plowd 269 at 272, 75 ER 410 at 415.

5 *Harvey v Pratt* [1965] 1 WLR 1025 at 1026D-E, 1027C; *Dunlop Olympic Ltd v Ellis* [1986] WAR 8 at 11. The commencement date cannot simply be taken to be the date of the contract (*Marshall v Berridge* (1881) 19 Ch D 233 at 239). See also *Lace v Chantler* [1944] KB 368 at 370; *Brown v Gould* [1972] Ch 53 at 61B; *Secretary of State for Social Services v Beavington* (1982) 262 Estates Gazette 551 at 554; *Kerns v Manning* [1935] IR 869 at 880; *McQuaid v Lynam* [1965] IR 564 at 574; *Omsac Developments Ltd v Colebourne* (1980) 110 DLR (3d) 766 at 768; *South Coast Oils (Qld and NSW) Pty Ltd v Look Enterprises Pty Ltd* [1988] 1 Qd R 680 at 696.

6 Where a term is expressed to commence 'from' a specified day, the term does not, in the absence of clear contrary indication, include that day. Instead the term is normally presumed to begin at midnight following the day specified (see *Sunnyvale Services B O P Ltd v Bhana* [1986] 1 NZLR 314 at 316). A term expressed to commence 'on' a specified day is generally deemed to include that day (see *Clayton's Case* (1585) 5 Co Rep 1a, 77 ER 48). See, however, E. Cooke, [1993] Conv 206.

that the term begins immediately on the taking of possession, provided that there is no doubt as to the precise date on which this occurs.[7]

The commencement date of a lease may of course be postponed to a date considerably later than that of the instrument which creates the leasehold term, in which case the lease is known as a 'reversionary' lease.[8] However, a statutory penalty of voidness now attaches to any reversionary term granted at a rent or in consideration of a fine which is limited to take effect more than 21 years after the date of the instrument purporting to create it.[9]

(c) *The term may be of any length*

Subject to the requirement that its maximum duration be ascertainable, a term of years may relate to any length of time.

(i) Short terms The term may itself comprise merely a fraction of a year,[10] and could in theory be extremely short.[11] In *National Carriers Ltd v Panalpina (Northern) Ltd*,[12] for instance, Lord Roskill agreed that a holiday-maker may well have a legal estate in a cottage let to him for a short period as a holiday home, although 'the estate in land which he acquires has little or no meaning for him.' It is likely, however, that the shorter the supposed term, the greater the probability that the grant will be construed as conferring not a leasehold interest but a licence.[13]

(ii) Long terms Equally a term of years may well extend to vast expanses of time which begin to resemble a grant in fee simple.[14] Leases of 3,000

7 *James v Lock* (1977) 246 Estates Gazette 395 at 397. Thus there is no want of certainty where a verbal agreement for a lease is followed by an immediate taking of possession pursuant to the agreement: the agreement coupled with entry ensures a certain commencement (see *Jopling v Jopling* (1909) 8 CLR 33 at 39 per Griffith CJ).
8 In the case of an orally granted lease, the postponement of the commencement date ensures that the term does not take effect 'in possession'. It cannot therefore take the benefit of the limited exemption from requirements of formality otherwise conferred by Law of Property Act 1925, s 54(2), post, p 736 (see *Abjornson v Urban Newspapers Pty Ltd* [1989] WAR 191 at 206).
9 Law of Property Act 1925, s 149(3). However, this provision does not affect the validity of a *contract* to create a lease at some future time which, when created by instrument, will then take effect either immediately or within 21 years of the date of that instrument (Perpetuities and Accumulations Act 1964, s 9(2)). See *In re Strand and Savoy Properties Ltd* [1960] Ch 582 at 591; (1960) 76 LQR 352 (R.E.M.); *Weg Motors Ltd v Hales* [1962] Ch 49 at 68, 78.
10 Law of Property Act 1925, s 205(1)(xxvii) (ante, p 677).
11 See eg *Boylan v Mayor of Dublin* [1949] IR 60 at 73, where Black J adverted to the possibility of a lease for three days or three hours.
12 [1981] AC 675 at 714D.
13 See eg the 'coronation cases' (post, p 902). See also *Voli v Inglewood Shire Council* (1963) 110 CLR 74 at 91 per Windeyer J.
14 See *National Carriers Ltd v Panalpina (Northern) Ltd* [1981] AC 675 at 714B. The longest lease on record is an Irish lease comprising a grant for 10 million years (ante, p 70). The Irish tend to specialise in the granting of extremely long terms. Part of the Dublin cattle market was leased by John Jameson to the Dublin City Corporation on 21 January 1863 for a term of 100,000 years (see N. McWhirter (ed), *Guinness Book of Records* (27th edn Enfield, Middx, 1980), p 190). See also *In re Sergie* [1954] NI 1 (mortgage demise for 10,000 years).

years are not unknown for the purpose of creating certain kinds of mortgage.[15] Outside the context of mortgage, leases are frequently created for a term of 999 years. A term of 99 years is commonly granted in respect of leasehold flats, and local authorities are statutorily empowered to grant terms of 125 years in respect of dwelling-houses covered by the 'right to buy' provisions of the Housing Act 1985.[16]

(iii) Discontinuous terms It is not even essential that the quantum of time in respect of which possession is granted under a lease should comprise one single continuous period. The advent of the phenomenon of 'holiday timesharing'[17] has confirmed the idea that a lease may comprise an aggregate of discontinuous periods of time.[18] In *Cottage Holiday Associates Ltd v Customs and Excise Commissioners*,[19] Woolf J accepted as a lease a document which granted the lessee, in consideration of an initial premium, a right to occupy a holiday cottage for one week in each year for a term of 80 years.[20] The creation of timeshare arrangements is now regulated by statute,[1] but the conceptual limits of timesharing may be reached if and when thought is given to the enfranchisement of fragmented and discontinuous leasehold terms.[2]

(d) The maximum duration of the lease must be ascertainable

Irrespective of the length of the term granted, it is an essential characteristic of a lease that it should confer an estate in land of certain maximum duration.[3] From the very outset a finite point (or *terminus ad quem*) must be either expressed or implicit or must be capable of being rendered certain.[4] Any purported lease whose maximum duration is not ascertainable at the commencement

15 Post, p 939.
16 Housing Act 1985, s 139(1), Sch 6, Part III, para 12(1).
17 See J. Edmonds, *International Timesharing* (2nd edn, London 1984), p 9ff.
18 As early as *Smallwood v Sheppards* [1895] 2 QB 627 at 630, it was recognised that a lease granting a right of occupation for three successive bank holidays could constitute a single letting.
19 [1983] QB 735 at 739D. However, Woolf J held that the length of the 'term' granted by such a lease was 80 weeks rather than 80 years ([1983] QB 735 at 739H–740F). Woolf J ([1983] QB 735 at 738A) expressly left open the effect of Law of Property Act 1925, s 149(3) (see D. Green, (1983) 80 Law Soc Gaz 2500 at 2501).
20 It is quite common nowadays that lessees of office buildings are not entitled to occupy the demised premises at certain times eg at weekends (see *Cottage Holiday Associates Ltd v Customs and Excise Commissioners* [1983] QB 735 at 739G–H). See also [1983] Conv 319.
1 The Timeshare Act 1992 introduced various kinds of protection against oppressive dealing in relation to timeshare users. See [1992] Conv 301 (H.W. Wilkinson).
2 See R.A. Epstein, *Past and Future: The Temporal Dimension in the Law of Property*, 64 Wash ULQ 667 at 705f, 857 (1986).
3 It does not follow that a lease must stipulate a *minimum* duration. It is the outer limit of the term which must be fixed or capable of being rendered certain. Provided that the maximum duration is certain, it is irrelevant that the term is capable of an earlier determination (eg through surrender or the operation of some limiting condition or through the lessor's exercise of a right of entry). See *Co Litt*, p 45; *Bl Comm*, Vol II, p 143; *Prudential Assurance Co Ltd v London Residuary Body* [1992] 2 AC 386 at 395A per Lord Templeman.
4 For an excellent examination of the law of terminal certainty, see S. Bright, *Uncertainty in leases—Is it a vice?*, (1993) 13 Legal Studies 38.

date is void[5] in that it fails to show 'the certainty of the time for which the lessee shall have the land'.[6] The 'certainty of term' principle is fundamentally the expression of a property-oriented view of the leasehold relationship: it articulates the concern that property rights should be both discrete and defined.

(i) Applications of the 'certainty of term' principle The 'ancient and technical rule of law'[7] relating to certainty of term has been applied with rigour in the law of landlord and tenant. In *Lace v Chantler*,[8] for instance, the Court of Appeal held that no lease had been validly granted where a right of occupation was conferred 'for the duration of the war'.[9] The dogma of the common law rule has been similarly applied to strike down a letting of premises 'for so long as the lessee shall use them',[10] or 'so long as the company is trading'.[11] Likewise the courts have indicated that uncertainty of term vitiates a letting expressed to continue 'until Britain wins the Davis Cup'[12] or 'until the end of the peanut crop in 1968 or end of harvesting period or as otherwise agreed upon'.[13]

(ii) Rationales for the common law rule Although it is nowadays far from easy to provide any really convincing rationale for the continued application of the 'certainty of term' principle,[14] there may have been several related historic motivations behind the common law rule. *First*, it is clear that the common

5 *Prudential Assurance Co Ltd v London Residuary Body* [1992] 2 AC 386 at 392B per Lord Templeman. It is possible, however, that a tenant who enters under the void lease may acquire an implied periodic tenancy on the payment and acceptance of a periodic rent (post, p 692). See eg *Lace v Chantler* [1944] KB 368 at 372; *Prudential Assurance*, supra at 392B.

6 *Say v Smith* (1563) 1 Plowd 269 at 272, 75 ER 410 at 415. See also *Eton College v Bard* [1983] Ch 321 at 332A; *Re Lehrer and the Real Property Act* (1961) 61 SR (NSW) 365 at 376f.

7 *Prudential Assurance Co Ltd v London Residuary Body* [1992] 2 AC 386 at 396G per Lord Browne-Wilkinson.

8 [1944] KB 368 at 370f.

9 See also *M.W. Investments Ltd v Kilburn Envoy Ltd* [1947] Ch 370 at 376. In view of the large number of supposed lettings affected, the ruling in *Lace v Chantler* had to be reversed by retroactive legislation (see Validation of War-time Leases Act 1944, s 1(1), which converted such arrangements into determinable leases of 10 years). It has been suggested that the strict approach of *Lace v Chantler* may not properly have been applicable in cases where the terminal date of the lease, although unpredictable, was specified in much clearer words. See eg *Eker v Becker* (1946) 174 LT 410 at 411 (lease determinable on 'the cessation of...hostilities...meaning thereby the actual date of the cease fire order'); *Mrs Levin, Ltd v Wellington Co-operative Book Society* [1947] NZLR 83 at 86 (lease determinable automatically three months after the cessation of active hostilities in war). See also *Ashburn Anstalt v Arnold* [1989] Ch 1 at 11G per Fox LJ.

10 *Congregational Christian Church v Iosefa Tauga* (1982) 8 Comm Law Bull 129.

11 *Birrell v Carey* (1989) 58 P & CR 184 at 186 per Fox LJ. See [1990] Conv 288 (J.E. Martin).

12 *Prudential Assurance Co Ltd v London Residuary Body* (1992) 63 P & CR 386 at 397 per Scott LJ.

13 *Bishop v Taylor* (1968) 118 CLR 518 at 523.

14 See *Prudential Assurance Co Ltd v London Residuary Body* [1992] 2 AC 386 at 396G–H, where Lord Browne-Wilkinson declared that '[n]o one has produced any satisfactory rationale for the genesis of this rule. No one has been able to point to any useful purpose that it serves at the present day.'

law abhorred 'any such thing as a lease in perpetuity',[15] not least since such a lease, if granted imprudently, could endanger the productive exploitation of land over an indefinite period.[16] *Second*, the perpetual lease was a conceptual nonsense in that it postulated a term without a *terminus*.[17] Such a lease struck at the heart of the doctrine of estates by threatening to confound the distinction between the term of years and the one perpetual estate recognised by the common law, the estate in fee simple.[18] The perpetual lease offended against the intrinsic orderliness of the common law arrangement of estates.[19] *Third*, the open-ended nature of an uncertain term militated against the clear historic concern of the common law that the parties to a bargain should 'know where they stand'[20] and that neither party should be left in 'a state of unknowing' as to his maximum commitment.[1] *Fourth*, it may have been felt to be inherently unfair that parties who had contemplated a short, but uncertainly defined, term should find that they had mistakenly created an endless term.[2] *Fifth*, there was inevitably some fear that an obscurely defined terminal date might present insuperable problems of construction simply on grounds of linguistic, semantic or contextual uncertainty.[3]

(iii) Disenchantment with the common law rule Recent years have seen a growing disenchantment with the common law rule in respect of certainty of term. It is far from clear that the historic rationales for the rule retain today the force which they may once have enjoyed. The rule is itself open to objection on the ground that it frequently denies efficacy to consciously bargained agreements which in all reality are scarcely likely to survive as perpetuities.[4] The operation of the rule is, moreover, both arbitrary and artificial. The 'certainty of term' principle strikes arbitrarily at some attempts to create

15 *Sevenoaks, Maidstone, and Tunbridge Railway Co v London, Chatham, and Dover Railway Co* (1879) 11 Ch D 625 at 635 per Jessel MR. See also *Wotherspoon v Canadian Pacific Ltd* (1987) 39 DLR (4th) 169 at 205.

16 For reference to the economic dangers posed by perpetual grants, see Chapter 16 (ante, p 645).

17 That such a phenomenon was quite impossible appears in the rejection of a lease 'for ever' in *Doe d Roberton v Gardiner* (1852) 12 CB 319 at 333, 138 ER 927 at 933 per Jervis CJ.

18 See the reference to the fee simple as conferring 'a time in the land without end' (*Walsingham's Case* (1573) 2 Plowd 547 at 555, 75 ER 805 at 816f (ante, p 58)).

19 This may account for the anxious way in which the common law often attempted to refashion leases of uncertain duration. A lease for an unspecified term of years was long ago held to be a good lease for two years certain, in that certainty was lacking in respect of any longer term and any shorter term would falsify the wording of the grant (see *Bishop of Bath's Case* (1605) 6 Co Rep 34b at 35b/36a, 77 ER 303 at 305f). Alternatively, if all else failed, the indefinite term might be construed as a grant in fee simple subject to the payment of a rentcharge (ante, p 72). See *Doe d Roberton v Gardiner* (1852) 12 CB 319 at 333, 138 ER 927 at 933f; *Wotherspoon v Canadian Pacific Ltd* (1987) 39 DLR (4th) 169 at 205.

20 See *Ashburn Anstalt v Arnold* [1989] Ch 1 at 12E per Fox LJ ('Put another way, the court does not know what to enforce').

1 *In re Midland Railway Co's Agreement* [1971] Ch 725 at 732H–733A.

2 Such, for instance, would have been the result if the determining, but uncertain, event subsequently proved to be impossible or unlikely to occur. See *Prudential Assurance Co Ltd v London Residuary Body* (1992) 63 P & CR 386 at 400f per Scott LJ.

3 As Anthony Brown J is reported to have said, uncertain words in a lease 'are but babble' (*Say v Smith* (1563) 1 Plowd 269 at 272, 75 ER 410 at 415). See also S. Bright, (1993) 13 Legal Studies 38 at 40ff.

4 See eg *Lace v Chantler* [1944] KB 368 (ante, p 688).

a leasehold relationship, while other attempts—in themselves no less flawed—have been rescued from voidness by modern statutory intervention.[5] A high degree of artificiality is inevitably present in any rule which solemnly strikes down a term whose voidness could have been averted by a minor (and purely cosmetic) redrafting of the words of grant.[6]

Within the last few years considerations of this kind led English courts briefly to relax the requirement that the maximum duration of a term of years be ascertainable in advance of the term.[7] In effect the courts diluted the force of the common law rule by holding that certainty of term need not be predicated at the *commencement* of a supposed term of years, but could be sufficiently established with reference to the circumstances pertaining at its *termination*.[8] This short-lived departure from orthodoxy was to provide yet another vivid reflection of the continuing tension between contract- and property-oriented views of the landlord-tenant relationship.[9]

In *Ashburn Anstalt v Arnold*,[10] for example, the Court of Appeal upheld as a valid lease an agreement which granted rent-free occupancy for an indefinite period. The agreement had been made expressly subject to determination on the giving of three months' notice by the owner and on its certification of readiness to proceed with redevelopment of the property. The Court of Appeal held that the arrangement could be brought to an end by either party 'in circumstances which are free from uncertainty in the sense that there would be no doubt whether the determining event had occurred.'[11] Fox LJ distinguished the determining event in the present case from the entirely unpredictable and uncontrollable determining event stipulated in *Lace v Chantler*. In *Ashburn Anstalt* the determination of the relationship had lain essentially within the control of both the owner (who could give three months' notice and the required certificate) and the occupier (who was not obliged to occupy the premises and 'could simply walk out').[12] There was here no danger that the parties might fall into the 'vice of uncertainty' by failing to appreciate where they stood. The position was quite the reverse, and Fox LJ declared that he could see 'no reason why the court should not hold the parties to their agreement'.[13] The Court of Appeal accordingly held that the agreement had conferred possession of the premises 'for a term which was not uncertain'.[14]

5 Post, p 693.

6 It is quite clear, for instance, that whereas a lease 'until England wins the World Cup' is invalid, no objection can be raised against a lease for 99 years subject to determination on the earlier happening of this uncertain—indeed unlikely—event (see *Prudential Assurance Co Ltd v London Residuary Body* [1992] 2 AC 386 at 395A per Lord Templeman; (1992) 63 P & CR 386 at 397 per Scott LJ). The latter lease is entirely valid since it creates a determinable certain term of 99 years.

7 The relevant issues tended to arise in their most critical form in the context of rent-free occupancy. Here there is no possibility that the parties may fall back upon an implied periodic tenancy: the choice lies starkly between valid long lease and mere licence.

8 See *Canadian Imperial Bank of Commerce v Bello* (1992) 64 P & CR 48 at 56 per Staughton LJ.

9 Ante, p 674.

10 [1989] Ch 1. See [1988] CLJ 353 (A.J. Oakley).

11 [1989] Ch 1 at 12E.

12 [1989] Ch 1 at 11G–12D.

13 [1989] Ch 1 at 12E–F.

14 [1989] Ch 1 at 12H.

(iv) Reaffirmation of the common law rule The approach adopted by the Court of Appeal in *Ashburn Anstalt* and other similar cases[15] clearly marked a none too subtle shift from a prospective requirement of certainty of term to a retrospective requirement of certainty of duration. In the process the Court accorded a new primacy to clearly expressed contractual intentions in preference to the narrow property-oriented concern that asset entitlements be defined with certainty *ab initio*. These developments came, however, to a sharp halt in *Prudential Assurance Co Ltd v London Residuary Body*.[16] Here the old London County Council had in 1930 granted a 'lease' of a strip of land fronting a highway at an annual rent of £30, the tenancy being expressed to 'continue until the. . .land is required by the council for the purposes of the widening of' the highway. The council later abandoned any intention of widening the road and the freehold reversion eventually passed to the London Residuary Body (which was not a highway authority). Meanwhile shop premises had been erected by the occupier on the relevant strip of land and by the late 1980s it was clear that the current annual commercial rent was in excess of £10,000. When the London Residuary Body sought to determine the occupier's rights by giving six months' notice to quit, the occupier asserted the existence of a valid indefinite term of years determinable only in the event of a road-widening proposal.

The Court of Appeal, acknowledging that it was bound by the apparently irreconcilable precedents of *Lace v Chantler* and *Ashburn Anstalt v Arnold*,[17] strove bravely to fashion a ground of distinction based on the degree of control exercisable by relevant parties over the determining event under an indefinite term.[18] Scott LJ considered that *Lace v Chantler* continued to be the binding authority except in cases where 'the uncertain duration of the term can be controlled by both parties'.[19] In *Prudential Assurance*, however, Scott LJ held that the determining event (ie the requirement for road-widening purposes) had not been an event 'governed and controlled by the council simply according to its private interests and wishes'. The occurrence of this event had at all times been controlled by the 'proper performance by the council of its statutory duties as highway authority' and thus lay outside the control of the council 'qua landlord'.[20] On this basis the Court of Appeal ruled that the indefinite term was irretrievably void for uncertainty.

The conclusion, but not the reasoning, of the Court of Appeal was later confirmed in *Prudential Assurance* by the House of Lords.[1] The Lords, rejecting

15 In *Canadian Imperial Bank of Commerce v Bello* (1992) 64 P & CR 48 at 54ff, a differently constituted Court of Appeal held that no 'unacceptable uncertainty' was present in an arrangement for indefinite occupation which was expressed to be determinable when the owner discharged in full a debt owed to the occupier. The determining events were 'sufficiently under the control' of both parties in that the term could be brought to an end by full payment on the part of the owner or voluntary departure by the occupier.
16 [1992] 2 AC 386; (1992) 63 P & CR 386. See [1992] Conv 118 (P.F. Smith).
17 (1992) 63 P & CR 386 at 397.
18 Thus, in *Lace v Chantler*, the 'bringing to the end of the uncertainty of duration of the term was not within the control' of either party; whereas in *Ashburn Anstalt v Arnold*, the owner needed to 'consult no interests but its own' in bringing about or not bringing about the determining event 'as it might choose' ((1992) 63 P & CR 386 at 397f).
19 (1992) 63 P & CR 386 at 398.
20 (1992) 63 P & CR 386 at 398.
1 [1992] 2 AC 386 at 391B, 392B, 393G, 395G.

all casuistry founded upon relative degrees of control over determining events, preferred to hold with brutal simplicity that an agreement for indeterminate occupation can never constitute a legally recognisable term of years.[2] Lord Templeman took the straightforward view that 'principle and precedent dictate that it is beyond the power of the landlord and the tenant to create a term which is uncertain.'[3] The House of Lords thus applied the full force of the common law rule that the maximum duration of a term of years must be ascertainable at the commencement of every lease. The clear property-orientation of this approach was evident in Lord Templeman's anxiety lest a more liberal view of the certainty rule should allow loosely defined arrangements between parties to 'continue until the crack of doom' and enable them to enjoy 'in perpetuity' rights which had originally been contemplated as purely temporary.[4]

In *Prudential Assurance* the consequence of Lord Templeman's uncompromising approach was to render the occupier, in the absence of a valid indefinite term, a mere yearly tenant by virtue of his payment of an annual rent. Accordingly the London Residuary Body was entirely free to terminate his periodic tenancy by giving half a year's notice to quit.[5] This conclusion was endorsed, albeit reluctantly, by other members of the House of Lords. Lord Browne-Wilkinson noted, for instance, that this 'unsatisfactory' outcome, far from effectuating the initial contemplation and contractual intent of the parties, had brought about the 'bizarre' result that both parties would be left with premises which were incapable of use.[6] Lord Browne-Wilkinson, although accepting that a departure from a land law rule which had been established for many centuries might upset long held titles, voiced a concern that the archaic common law rule should be re-examined by the Law Commission to 'see whether there is in fact any good reason now for maintaining a rule which operates to defeat contractually agreed arrangements between the parties (of which all successors in title are aware) and which is capable of producing such an extraordinary result as that in the present case.'[7]

In the aftermath of the *Prudential Assurance* case there must be a strong argument for enacting a statutory conversion of all uncertain terms (other than those already covered by legislation[8]) into a determinable term of, say, 90 years.[9] Such a solution would preserve the integrity of the venerable

2 The House of Lords overruled both *In re Midland Railway Co's Agreement* [1971] Ch 725 and *Ashburn Anstalt v Arnold* [1989] Ch 1 as having been wrongly decided ([1992] 2 AC 386 at 395G per Lord Templeman).

3 [1992] 2 AC 386 at 394E-H ('I consider that the principle of *Lace v Chantler*. . .reaffirming 500 years of judicial acceptance of the requirement that a term must be certain applies to all leases and tenancy agreements').

4 [1992] 2 AC 386 at 394G-H. Lord Templeman referred pointedly to the fact that the agreement, if upheld as an indefinitely long term, would have entitled the occupier 'to stay there for ever and a day at the 1930 rent of £30' ([1992] 2 AC 386 at 390B).

5 [1992] 2 AC 386 at 392B-C (post, p 754).

6 [1992] 2 AC 386 at 396E-G. The tenant's remaining premises, situated behind the street frontage, would be effectively cut off from frontage to a shopping street; the use of the landlord's premises, once severed from the tenant's, would almost certainly be sterilised.

7 [1992] 2 AC 386 at 397A. Lords Griffiths and Mustill (at 396B, 397B) expressly associated themselves with this concern.

8 Post, p 693.

9 See Law of Property Act 1925, s 149(6), post, p 693.

common law principle of certainty of term, while enabling sensible effect to be given to the clearly intended bargains of contracting parties.

(e) Special difficulties

The recently reinforced common law requirement of a prefixed maximum duration leaves a number of grave difficulties in the leasehold area. Many of these difficulties would remain unresolved but for several statutory interventions which ensure that at least some of the problematic cases are forced artificially, but nevertheless effectively, within the procrustean dimensions of the rule.

(i) Lease for life Longevity being an unpredictable quality, a lease for life offends against the prescription that leases must be of fixed maximum duration.[10] A 'term of years' as defined in the Law of Property Act 1925 cannot therefore include a lease for life or a lease which is determinable on the death of some named person.[11] However, statute intervenes to reconcile the lease for life with the common law requirement.[12] If granted at a rent or in consideration of a fine,[13] a lease for life or lives or for any term of years determinable with life or lives[14] is automatically converted into a 90 year term.[15] The fixed term thus created is determinable after the death of the original lessee (or the dropping of any other specified life) by the giving of at least one month's written notice.[16]

(ii) Lease until marriage Likewise a lease terminable upon the marriage of the lessee is converted into a 90 year term, determinable after the marriage of the original lessee by the giving of at least one month's written notice.[17]

(iii) Perpetually renewable lease A perpetually renewable lease again fails, for want of a clear finite point, to qualify as a valid leasehold term. In theory

10 *Co Litt*, p 45; *Bl Comm*, Vol II, p 143.
11 Law of Property Act 1925, s 205(1)(xxvii).
12 Law of Property Act 1925, s 149(6).
13 A tenancy for life under which no rent or premium is payable may, somewhat inconveniently, fall within the Settled Land Act 1925 (see eg *Binions v Evans* [1972] Ch 359 at 370D, 372E–G (ante, p 619)). Compare, however, *Skipton Building Society v Clayton* (1993) *Times*, 25 March. Here, for one third of its current market value, a purchaser had bought out the interest held by sitting tenants, guaranteeing them instead a rent-free tenancy for life. The Court of Appeal applied section 149(6) to this life tenancy on the ground that the discounted purchase price constituted a premium or fine for the purpose of attracting the statutory conversion to a 90 year term.
14 See *Bass Holdings Ltd v Lewis* [1986] 2 EGLR 40 at 40K per Nourse LJ (example of 'lease to A for a term of 20 years if he shall live so long')
15 It has been questioned whether an automatic conversion to a 90 year term should sensibly be the result of a short-term letting conditioned upon the survival of the lessee. See *Bass Holdings Ltd v Lewis* (Unreported, 17 February 1986 (appeal: [1986] 2 EGLR 40)) per Hoffmann J (who suggested that in this respect the 'great conveyancers' who drafted the 1925 Acts may have been guilty of 'simply a mistake').
16 The statutory conversion also operates in relation to a *contract* to create a lease determinable by death or marriage (Law of Property Act 1925, s 149(6)).
17 Law of Property Act 1925, s 149(6).

LPA 1922 S145

such a grant could endure for ever, but is now converted automatically by statute into a term of 2,000 years[18] determinable only by the lessee.[19] This statutory conversion is, however, the subject of some judicial distaste, largely because it frequently operates in a highly artificial way to subvert the likely expectations of the parties.[20] There is nowadays a tendency for the courts to lean against construing a lease as perpetually renewable in the absence of an unequivocal covenant to this effect.[1]

(iv) Timeshare lease It is clear that a 'timeshare lease' can easily be drafted in such manner as to satisfy the requirement of certain maximum duration. In *Cottage Holiday Associates Ltd v Customs and Excise Commissioners*,[2] Woolf J recognised that there is a distinction between the lease which created the timeshare interest and the interest itself. The lease might continue for 80 years, but the timeshare interest conferred by it comprised a term of only 80 holiday periods of one week each. On any construction, no difficulty could arise here in respect of fixed maximum duration, not least because the rule against perpetuities ensures the imposition of a strict outer limit on all interests granted by the timesharing arrangement.[3]

(v) Periodic tenancy It is less easy to sustain the argument that a periodic tenancy satisfies the requirement of certain prefixed maximum duration. It is clear that a periodic tenancy (eg a weekly or monthly tenancy) commonly takes effect as a number of periods or units which confer on the tenant an estate in the land.[4] It is equally clear that a periodic tenancy continues indefinitely until determined by the appropriate notice.[5] It constitutes 'an open-ended term with a series of possible termination dates which will only become effective if a valid notice to quit is served'.[6]

In view of its open-ended nature the periodic tenancy is not viewed in English law as an aggregated series of distinct terms. Instead the units of time which constitute the periodic tenancy are seen as comprising (at least retrospectively) one single unbroken term[7] which, unless and until duly determined, perpetually elongates itself by the superaddition of a fresh unit

18 Law of Property Act 1922, s 145, Sch 15, para 1. See *Parkus v Greenwood* [1950] Ch 644 at 648; *Caerphilly Concrete Products Ltd v Owen* [1972] 1 WLR 372 at 375F, 378C.
19 Law of Property Act 1922, Sch 15, para 10(1).
20 See eg *Caerphilly Concrete Products Ltd v Owen* [1972] 1 WLR 372 at 376B, where Sachs LJ expressed doubt as to whether the parties ever contemplated that their renewable five-year term should be recast as a lease 'which went on ad infinitum'.
1 See eg *Marjorie Burnett Ltd v Barclay* (1981) 258 Estates Gazette 642 at 644; (1981) 131 NLJ 683 (H.W. Wilkinson)).
2 [1983] QB 735 at 740E–F.
3 See eg Perpetuities and Accumulations Act 1964, s 1(1).
4 *Commonwealth Life (Amalgamated) Assurance Ltd v Anderson* (1946) 46 SR (NSW) 47 at 49, 51; *Fink v McIntosh* [1946] VLR 290 at 292.
5 Post, p 753. By its very nature, a periodic tenancy does not expire by reason of the effluxion of time (*Queen's Club Gardens Estates Ltd v Bignell* [1924] 1 KB 117 at 130; *Mitchell v Wieriks, ex parte Wieriks* [1975] Qd R 100 at 102D).
6 Frank Webb, *Notices to quit by one joint tenant*, [1983] Conv 194 at 209.
7 See *Hammersmith and Fulham LBC v Monk* [1992] 1 AC 478 at 490B per Lord Bridge of Harwich.

or period.[8] The term simply grows period by period 'as a single term springing from the original grant.'[9] There cannot be said to be a termination of one tenancy at the end of each period, followed by the commencement of a new letting or 'renewal' of the old letting.[10] This being so, it is uncertain at the outset of a periodic tenancy what will be the maximum duration of the term created. As Russell LJ pointed out in *In re Midland Railway Co's Agreement*,[11] it 'cannot be predicated that in no circumstances will it exceed, for instance, 50 years'. In other words, the periodic tenancy has a certain *terminus a quo* but no certain or predictable *terminus ad quem*.

In spite of this difficulty there is no serious doubt as to the leasehold quality of the periodic tenancy.[12] Courts have sought in several ways to avert the doctrinal embarrassment otherwise caused by the general requirement of prefixed maximum duration. In *In re Midland Railway Co's Agreement*,[13] Russell LJ simply argued that this requirement 'cannot. . .have direct reference to periodic tenancies.' The Court of Appeal in effect preferred 'as a matter of justice to hold parties to their clearly expressed bargain' rather than extend to the periodic tenancy a land law doctrine 'so as to deny the efficacy of that bargain'.[14]

More recent case law has tended to address the doctrinal difficulty in rather different terms. In *Hammersmith and Fulham LBC v Monk*,[15] for instance, Lord Browne-Wilkinson emphasised that a periodic tenancy is 'founded on the continuing will of both landlord and tenant that the tenancy shall persist.' In the words of Lord Bridge of Harwich,[16] 'the substance of the matter is that. . .by his omission to give notice of termination. . .each party signifies the necessary positive assent to the extension of the term for a further period.'

8 *Legg v Strudwick* (1709) 2 Salk 414, 91 ER 359; *Jones v Mills* (1861) 10 CB (NS) 788 at 798, 142 ER 664 at 667; *Gandy v Jubber* (1865) 9 B & S 15 at 18, 122 ER 914 at 916; *Bowen v Anderson* [1894] 1 QB 164 at 167; *Queen's Club Gardens Estates Ltd v Bignell* [1924] 1 KB 117 at 130. For this reason it is quite possible that a weekly tenancy may 'continue from week to week quite as long as a yearly tenancy from year to year' (*Jones v Chappell* (1875) LR 20 Eq 539 at 544).

9 *In re Midland Railway Co's Agreement* [1971] Ch 725 at 732F per Russell LJ. For further recognition of the integrity of the original letting, see *Oxley v James* (1844) 13 M & W 209 at 214, 153 ER 87 at 89; *Bowen v Anderson* [1894] 1 QB 164 at 167; *Amad v Grant, Grosglik v Grant* (1947) 74 CLR 327 at 336; *In re Belajev* (1979) 22 SASR 1 at 4.

10 See *Jones v Chappell* (1875) LR 20 Eq 539 at 544. Compare, however, the careless remarks of Somervell LJ in *Leek & Moorlands Building Society v Clark* [1952] 2 QB 788 at 793. For the distinction between a periodic yearly tenancy and a perpetually renewable one-year tenancy, see *Gray v Spyer* [1922] 2 Ch 22 at 38f. It is significant (post, p 756) that the continuation of a periodic tenancy does not depend on the exercise after each unit of time of some kind of option to renew the letting. The tenancy continues as an integral term until duly determined by notice. On this basis it has been suggested that the true analogy for a notice to quit is with a break notice (see F. Webb, [1983] Conv 194 at 208), although this analysis now presents some problems in respect of unilateral exercise by one joint tenant (post, pp753, 758).

11 [1971] Ch 725 at 732F. See [1971] CLJ 198 (D. MacIntyre). Compare, however, *Centaploy Ltd v Matlodge Ltd* [1974] Ch 1 at 11C; (1973) 89 LQR 457.

12 There is, for instance, statutory recognition that a tenancy from year to year can constitute a 'term of years' (Law of Property Act 1925, s 205(1)(xxvii)).

13 [1971] Ch 725 at 732F-G.

14 [1971] Ch 725 at 733C. Russell LJ thought (at 733F-G) that the 'certainty of term' principle could affect a periodic tenancy only if in such a tenancy 'an attempt was made to prevent the lessor ever determining the tenancy' (post, p 753).

15 [1992] 1 AC 478 at 492A (post, p 756).

16 [1992] 1 AC 478 at 490H-491A.

Unless and until this power to determine the periodic tenancy is exercised, it remains the case that each occupational unit of time, as it is added to the preceding unit of time, is itself of strictly defined duration.[17] On this basis it is feasible to maintain that the periodic tenancy conforms to the general principle of certain maximum duration. In *Prudential Assurance Co Ltd v London Residuary Body*,[18] Lord Templeman was able simultaneously to affirm that the certainty of term rule 'applies to all leases and tenancy agreements' and that a tenancy from year to year is 'saved from being uncertain because each party has power by notice to determine at the end of any year. The term continues until determined as if both parties made a new agreement at the end of each year for a new term for the ensuing year.'[19] The same reasoning is, of course, applicable to preserve any other kind of periodic tenancy from falling foul of the ancient common law principle against uncertainty of term.

(vi) Service tenancy In so far as a service occupancy is simply expressed as being co-terminous with the occupier's employment by the owner of property, there may be doubt as to whether the occupancy can constitute a tenancy.[20] If the employee's employment, and therefore his occupancy of service accommodation, are of uncertain maximum duration, it may be that the common law requirement necessary for a leasehold estate is absent.[1] However, it is much more likely that where a periodic rent is paid for a service occupancy, there will arise an irresistible inference that there exists a periodic tenancy terminable by the appropriate notice in the event that the employment comes to an end.

(4) The demised premises must be identified with certainty

All lands and all interests in land 'lie in grant',[2] and may therefore be made the subject matter of a lease or tenancy.[3] Irrespective of the precise nature of the letting, it is a clear rule that the subject matter of a term of years must be described and identified with certainty.[4]

17 'Whether the tenancy be from year to year, quarter to quarter, month to month, or week to week, it is a tenancy for a definite term of a year, a quarter, a month, or a week, as the case may be, with a superadded provision that it is to continue for another definite term of the same period, unless, by proper notice to quit, it is terminated...' (*Commonwealth Life (Amalgamated) Assurance Ltd v Anderson* (1946) 46 SR (NSW) 47 at 50f per Jordan CJ).

18 [1992] 2 AC 386 at 394E–F.

19 Lord Templeman had already expressed the view that the 'term' which, in conjunction with the grant of exclusive possession, is constitutive of a tenancy can be either a 'fixed or periodic term certain' (*Street v Mountford* [1985] AC 809 at 818E). See also Lord Templeman's reference (at 826E) to a 'periodical term'.

20 Post, p 714.

1 See eg *Ball v Crawford* [1981] BCL 627 (New Zealand High Court). However, English courts seem not to have been particularly sensitive to the existence of this problem (see eg *Scrimgeour v Waller* (1981) 257 Estates Gazette 61).

2 Law of Property Act 1925, s 51(1).

3 For a definition of 'land', see Chapter 1 (ante, p 5).

4 *Goldsworthy Mining Ltd v Federal Commissioner of Taxation* (1973) 128 CLR 199 at 211. On the difficulties caused by inadequate or imprecise plans, see *Wallington v Townsend* [1939] Ch 588 (leasehold boundary appeared to run through middle of tenant's bathroom); *Kohua Pty Ltd v Tai Ping Trading Pty Ltd* (1985) 3 BPR 9705 at 9707. See also *South Coast Oils (Qld and NSW) Pty Ltd v Look Enterprises Pty Ltd* [1988] 1 Qd R 680 at 700f.

(a) Conventions of leasehold conveyancing

The requirement of certain identification is usually satisfied without excessive difficulty,[5] particularly since the boundaries of a demised property are often regarded as fixed, in the absence of contrary intention, by reference to certain conventions of leasehold conveyancing which have become rules of law. Thus, for instance, the external wall enclosing the demised premises is normally regarded as part of the demised premises.[6] A conveyance of a leasehold also passes void spaces above false ceilings in a flat.[7] In the case of a top-floor flat, the lease includes the immediately superjacent air space above the roof of the demised premises,[8] with the result that the tenant may properly seek to raise the roof and convert the loft into additional accommodation for himself.[9]

(b) Fluctuating boundaries

It is in any event sufficient that the description of the subject matter of a lease or tenancy is such as to enable the boundaries of the property to be ascertained or identified at any given time. Where, for example, the area of demised land fluctuates with changes in a littoral boundary caused by accretion,[10] the requirement of certainty is adequately met. The territorial limit of the lease is readily ascertainable, since it can simply be measured with reference to the surface as it exists from time to time.[11]

(5) A lease must confer a right of exclusive possession

It is also an essential feature of any lease or tenancy that the grantee should be given a right to 'exclusive possession' of the demised premises,[12] and no tenancy can be said to exist where such a right has not been conferred on the occupier.[13] The recipient of any lesser right can never claim to be a tenant,[14] for the right to exclusive possession is a sine qua non of the landlord–tenant relationship.

5 That two sets of premises can form the subject matter of a single tenancy is clear from *Walter v Rumbal* (1695) 1 Ld Raym 53 at 55, 91 ER 931 at 933.

6 *Sturge v Hackett* [1962] 1 WLR 1257 at 1265. A lease of a flat prima facie conveys an estate in the external walls of that flat, but not in the external walls of other flats in the same building (*Campden Hill Towers Ltd v Gardner* [1977] QB 823 at 834F–G).

7 *Graystone Property Investments Ltd v Margulies* (1983) 269 Estates Gazette 538 at 541f.

8 *Kelsen v Imperial Tobacco Co (of Great Britain and Ireland) Ltd* [1957] 2 QB 334 at 339f.

9 See *Haines v Florensa* (1990) 59 P & CR 200 at 205f; *Davies v Yadegar* (1990) 22 HLR 232 at 235ff.

10 Ante, p 26.

11 *Goldsworthy Mining Ltd v Federal Commissioner of Taxation* (1973) 128 CLR 199 at 211f.

12 See *Wright v Stavert* (1860) 2 E & E 721 at 727, 121 ER 270 at 273; *Radaich v Smith* (1959) 101 CLR 209 at 214 per McTiernan J; *Hull v Parsons* [1962] NZLR 465 at 468; *Re Villa Otthon Management and Bamboulis* (1988) 40 DLR (4th) 574 at 576.

13 *Street v Mountford* [1985] AC 809 at 818E per Lord Templeman. Thus, for example, the right to park a car in a large garage can take the form of a lease only if the right relates to an identified parking bay rather than to the entire parking area in general (see *Harley Queen v Forsyte Kerman* [1983] CLY 2077).

14 See *Street v Mountford* [1985] AC 809 at 816C per Lord Templeman; *Beaton v McDivitt* (1985) 13 NSWLR 134 at 146A–C per Young J. Such a grantee will be in most cases a mere licensee (see eg *Wilson v Tavener* [1901] 1 Ch 578 at 581; *Peakin v Peakin* [1895] 2 IR 359 at 362; *Daalman v Oosterdijk* [1973] 1 NZLR 717 at 720).

(a) Exclusive possession as territorial control

As Windeyer J declared in *Radaich v Smith*,[15] the legal right to exclusive possession is 'the proper touchstone' of a lease or tenancy.[16] In particular, it is usually this element which alone confers the degree of territorial control necessary to enable the tenant effectively to carry out the purpose (whether commercial or residential) for which he took the letting.[17] Windeyer J pointed out, for instance, that the occupier of the disputed lock-up shop in *Radaich v Smith* would have been 'astounded' to be informed that she had no right to control entry to the shop or that the freehold owner was simultaneously entitled to provide other persons with keys to the premises and to authorise them to carry on other sorts of business there.[18]

(i) Exclusory power The authority of the Australian High Court in *Radaich v Smith* was enthusiastically endorsed in *Street v Mountford*,[19] where the House of Lords pointed out that the hallmark of exclusive possession is entirely consistent with the 'elevation of a tenancy into an estate in land.' The common law requirement of 'exclusive possession' thus serves as a constant reminder of the way in which privacy and 'excludability' are seen as intrinsic components of estate ownership within the capitalist concept of property.[20]

The right of exclusive possession justifies the exercise of exclusory power. Accordingly, as Lord Templeman confirmed in *Street v Mountford*,[1] the tenant 'is able to exercise the rights of an owner of land, which is in the real sense his land albeit temporarily and subject to certain restrictions.'[2] Viewed from this perspective, estate ownership of a leasehold is not qualitatively different from estate ownership of an unencumbered freehold: the common feature of exclusive possession eliminates the false dichotomy which might otherwise suggest itself between these two forms of proprietary control. The tenant is simply owner pro tempore,[3] and one of the most dramatic indicia of his ownership is his ability to 'keep out strangers and keep out the landlord unless the landlord is exercising limited rights reserved to him by the tenancy

15 (1959) 101 CLR 209 at 223. See also *Armstrong v Armstrong* [1970] 1 NSWR 133 at 135; *Goldsworthy Mining Ltd v Federal Commissioner of Taxation* (1973) 128 CLR 199 at 212; *Hayes v Seymour-Johns* (1981) 2 BPR 9366 at 9368; *Rental Bond Board v Bayman Development Pty Ltd* (1985) 3 BPR 9670 at 9674 per Street CJ.

16 For the English adoption of this reference to the 'touchstone' of exclusive possession, see *Aslan v Murphy* (Nos 1 and 2) [1990] 1 WLR 766 at 770E–F per Lord Donaldson of Lymington MR.

17 See eg *Radaich v Smith* (1959) 101 CLR 209 at 215 per McTiernan J, 217 per Taylor J, 221 per Menzies J ('exclusive possession' clearly essential for reasonably convenient carrying on of milk bar business). See also *Hayes v Seymour-Johns* (1981) 2 BPR 9366 at 9368f.

18 (1959) 101 CLR 209 at 224f.

19 [1985] AC 809 at 814E–F, 816B. See Law of Property Act 1925, s 1(1)(b) (ante, p 69).

20 See *Property in Thin Air*, [1991] CLJ 252 at 268ff.

1 [1985] AC 809 at 816B.

2 It has always been clearly recognised that the tenant's right to exclusive possession is not inconsistent with the imposition of restrictions as to the uses to which he may put the land (see *Glenwood Lumber Co Ltd v Phillips* [1904] AC 405 at 408; *Re British American Oil Co Ltd and DePass* (1960) 21 DLR (2d) 110 at 117ff).

3 By contrast a licensee, 'lacking exclusive possession can in no sense call the land his own' (*Street v Mountford* [1985] AC 809 at 816C per Lord Templeman (post, p 891)). The licensee has 'no legal title which will permit him to exclude other persons' (see *AG Securities v Vaughan* [1990] 1 AC 417 at 471A per Lord Oliver of Aylmerton).

agreement to enter and view and repair.'[4] Whether his term of years be long or short, whether the land area be large or small,[5] the tenant has, in respect of the demised premises, a right of territorial control which he may vindicate by action in trespass even as against his own landlord.[6]

(ii) Immunity from supervisory control The tenant's intrinsic territorial prerogative does not merely confer an entitlement to exclude the rest of the world; it implies a general immunity from any detailed supervision or regulation of his activities on the demised premises. No claim of tenancy can ultimately be sustained if an overall power of supervisory control is reserved for the freehold owner. Such an explanation underlay the denial, in *Westminster CC v Clarke*,[7] of the tenant status of an occupant of a room in a council-run hostel for homeless persons. In order to facilitate the 'efficient and harmonious' administration of the hostel on behalf of its vulnerable clientèle, the council had expressly limited the accommodation rights accorded to occupants.[8] An occupant was not entitled to any particular room, could be required to share with other persons, and was forbidden to entertain visitors without permission from hostel staff. All occupants were obliged to comply with the directions of the hostel warden and with other stipulated conditions of occupation. In these circumstances the House of Lords concluded that an assertion of tenancy was incompatible with the 'totality, immediacy, and objectives of the powers exercisable by the council and the restrictions imposed on [the occupant].'[9] The curtailed nature of each occupant's rights confirmed that the council 'retained possession of all the rooms of the hostel in order to supervise and control the activities of occupiers.'[10] No individual occupier could on his own behalf assert a right of exclusive possession.

(b) 'Exclusive possession' distinguished from 'exclusive occupation'

The key element of 'overall control' later becomes vital in distinguishing between the 'exclusive possession' which is indicative of a true tenancy and the 'exclusive occupation' which often characterises many licences.[11] 'Exclusive occupation' is not synonymous with the right of 'exclusive possession' which is the attribute of a tenancy. It is often the case that persons who are allowed to enjoy sole occupation in fact are not necessarily to be

4 *Street v Mountford* [1985] AC 809 at 816B–C. See also *Lewis v Bell* [1985] 1 NSWLR 731 at 734F–G. It is widely accepted that a reservation to the landlord, either by contract or statute, of a limited right of entry for the purpose of viewing or repairing the premises, is not inconsistent with a tenant's right of exclusive possession (see eg *Radaich v Smith* (1959) 101 CLR 209 at 222 per Windeyer J). For a statutory right of entry, see Landlord and Tenant Act 1985, ss 8(2), 11(6) (post, p 803).

5 A single room can, by the grant of a tenancy, become the 'exclusive domain of a particular individual' (see *AG Securities v Vaughan* [1990] 1 AC 417 at 471B–C per Lord Oliver of Aylmerton).

6 See *Wright v Stavert* (1860) 2 E & E 721 at 728f, 121 ER 270 at 273; *Stocker v Planet Building Society* [1879] 27 WR 877 at 878.

7 [1992] 2 AC 288 (post, p 883). See [1992] JSWFL 334; [1992] Conv 113 (J. Martin), 285 (D.S. Cowan).

8 [1992] 2 AC 288 at 301A–H.

9 [1992] 2 AC 288 at 302A.

10 [1992] 2 AC 288 at 301H–302A per Lord Templeman.

11 Post, p 707.

taken as having been given a right of 'exclusive possession' in law.[12] Many contractual licensees and lodgers (eg students in university halls of residence, residents in a hotel, and persons living in an old people's home) undoubtedly enjoy sole occupation in this sense, but equally clearly have no tenancy.[13]

(c) Circumstances negating a right of exclusive possession

Certain circumstances negate the existence of any right of exclusive possession and therefore of any claim by an occupier to hold as a tenant. Thus, for instance, the existence of an unlimited right of access for the freeholder (or his agents) clearly precludes any assertion of tenancy.[14] Still less is a claim of tenancy justified where the freehold owner has genuinely reserved a contractual right to exclude the occupier from the premises for a specific portion of each day[15] or to require the occupier to transfer his occupation to other premises belonging to the freeholder.[16] Furthermore any attempt to confer a right of 'exclusive possession' on two or more persons simultaneously otherwise than as joint tenants or tenants in common[17] must inevitably be self-contradictory and meaningless.[18] It follows, *a fortiori*, that if premises are shared in joint occupation with the supposed landlord, so that exclusive possession cannot be claimed by either, there is no question of tenancy.[19]

The allocation of keys to the premises is an ambivalent guide to exclusiveness of possession. An occupier's mere possession of a key to the premises constitutes no proof of either 'exclusive possession' or 'exclusive occupation'.[20] Equally it is no requirement of a tenancy that the occupier should have exclusive possession of the keys.[1] As Lord Donaldson of Lymington MR indicated

12 *Radaich v Smith* (1959) 101 CLR 209 at 223 per Windeyer J. See eg *Smith v Northside Developments Ltd* (1988) 55 P & CR 164 at 167; [1989] Conv 55 (J.E.M.).

13 Post, p 716.

14 In *Westminster CC v Clarke* [1992] 2 AC 288 at 301F–302A (ante, p 699), the fact that hostel staff were entitled to 'enter the accommodation at any time' was destructive of any claim of tenancy. See also *Dresden Estates Ltd v Collinson* (1988) 55 P & CR 47 at 55 per Lloyd LJ; *Essex Plan Ltd v Broadminster* (1988) 56 P & CR 353 at 356f; [1989] Conv 55 (J.E.M.); *Beaton v McDivitt* (1985) 13 NSWLR 134 at 146B–C; *Rental Bond Board v Bayman Development Pty Ltd* (1985) 3 BPR 9670 at 9676 per Street CJ.

15 For cases where an owner has sought contractually to confine a resident's rights to discontinuous periods of occupation, see eg *Crancour Ltd v Da Silvaesa* (1986) 52 P & CR 204 and *Aslan v Murphy* (No 1) [1990] 1 WLR 766 (occupier supposedly excluded from premises every day between 10.30 am and 12.00 midday). Such restrictions are apt, however, to be struck down, in the light of the factual situation, as representing no part of the 'true bargain' between the parties and as being 'wholly unrealistic and. . .clearly pretences' (see *Aslan v Murphy* (No 1) [1990] 1 WLR 766 at 772H–773A per Lord Donaldson of Lymington MR).

16 *Dresden Estates Ltd v Collinson* (1988) 55 P & CR 47 at 53 per Glidewell LJ ('You cannot have a tenancy granting exclusive possession of particular premises, subject to a provision that the landlord can require the tenant to move to somewhere else. The landlord can only do that by terminating the tenancy and creating a new one in other premises'). See also *Crancour Ltd v Da Silvaesa* (1986) 52 P & CR 204 at 212ff (post, p 726).

17 Ante, p 461.

18 *Wetherby Apartments v Tootell* (Unreported, Court of Appeal, 27 October 1981); *Hindmarsh v Quinn* (1914) 17 CLR 622 at 630.

19 *Pearch v Gyucha* (1953) 73 WN (NSW) 122; *Walliker v Deveaux* (1959) 78 WN (NSW) 409 at 410; *Armstrong v Armstrong* [1970] 1 NSWR 133 at 135.

20 *Michel v Volpe* (1967) 202 Estates Gazette 213.

1 *Aslan v Murphy* (No 1) [1990] 1 WLR 766 at 773E.

in *Aslan v Murphy* (No 1),[2] the critical issue relates to the purpose underlying the provision or retention of keys. A landlord may genuinely need to retain a key in order to enter quickly in cases of emergency or to facilitate the reading of meters or the execution of repairs. The retention of a key for such purposes is not inconsistent with the existence of a tenancy.[3] The possibility of tenancy may, however, be negatived if an owner retains a key in order to enjoy occasional access to the premises for reasons of his own convenience,[4] or in order to monitor the observance of relevant conditions of occupation,[5] or to provide genuine services (eg frequent cleaning and daily bed-making) which are practicable only if access is facilitated by retention of a master key.[6] A prohibition on any interference with or changing of locks by the occupier does not in itself exclude the possibility that the occupier is a tenant, at least where there is no indication that the owner was obliged to supply services to the occupier or intended genuinely to share occupation of the premises.[7]

(6) Rent or other consideration

An obligation on the part of the tenant to pay rent or, more properly, to perform 'rent-service', was once considered to be an integral aspect of the tenurial relationship of landlord and tenant.[8] Correspondingly, the landlord's right to receive rent or 'rent-service' tended to be regarded as a normal incident annexed to his reversion in the land.[9] So long as the tenant was given exclusive possession by the conveyance of a leasehold estate, his obligation to pay rent was absolute and unqualified.[10] In recent years, however, there has been a distinct movement away from this tenurial or property-based view towards a more contractual analysis of the concept of rent. The

2 [1990] 1 WLR 766 at 773E.

3 *Aslan v Murphy* (No 1) [1990] 1 WLR 766 at 773F.

4 *Garland v Johnson* (Unreported, Court of Appeal, 24 February 1982).

5 *Oxford Overseas Student Housing Association v Mukherjee* (Unreported, Court of Appeal, 21 November 1989) per Bingham LJ.

6 *Aslan v Murphy* (No 1) [1990] 1 WLR 766 at 773F–H. The fact that virtually no services are in fact provided may reverse the balance once more in favour of tenancy (see *Aslan* at 773G–H).

7 *Duke v Wynn* [1990] 1 WLR 766 at 776A per Lord Donaldson of Lymington MR.

8 On the property-oriented view of the lease, rent simply 'issues out of the land'. See W. Holdsworth, *History of English Law* (2nd edn, London 1937), Vol VII, p 262; *Shevill v Builders Licensing Board* (1980) 2 BPR 9662 at 9672 per Mahoney JA. The common law has always been fairly ready, in the absence of an express covenant for rent, to imply a promise to pay reasonable compensation for the loss of land use caused to the landlord by reason of the occupation of the tenant (see *Dean and Chapter of Rochester v Pierce* (1808) 1 Camp 466 at 467, 170 ER 1023).

9 Thus there can in law be an assignment of the right to recover rent simpliciter (see *Knill v Prowse* (1884) 33 WR 163 at 164; *Rhodes v Allied Dunbar Pension Services Ltd* [1989] 1 WLR 800 at 806C per Nicholls LJ).

10 The tenant's rent obligation was held to survive a number of calamities. See *Paradine v Jane* (1647) Aleyn 26 at 27f, 82 ER 897 at 898 (dispossession during civil war); *Monk v Cooper* (1727) 2 Stra 763, 93 ER 833 at 834; *Belfour v Weston* (1786) 1 TR 310 at 312, 99 ER 1112 at 1113 (destruction of premises by fire). The tenant's obligation to pay rent could never, of course, survive wrongful eviction by the landlord (see *Wood Factory Pty Ltd v Kiritos Pty Ltd* (1985) 2 NSWLR 105 at 121B–C per Priestley JA).

courts have come to characterise rent not so much as the incident of a medieval tenure, but rather as the likely outcome of the bargain contracted between owner and occupier.[11] On this basis rent represents the consideration which the tenant frequently agrees to pay in return for his continuing right of exclusive possession.[12]

(a) Necessity for rent or other money payment

When seen from the viewpoint of the landlord, the lease or tenancy is nowadays primarily an instrument for the commercial exploitation of land. Most leases and tenancies are therefore granted expressly in consideration of money or money's worth. Indeed in *Street v Mountford*[13] Lord Templeman went so far as to describe the payment of rent as one of the decisive 'hallmarks' of a tenancy, thereby seeming to endorse the idea that rent payment remains a sine qua non of the conferment of a leasehold estate.[14] Such a suggestion is, however, inconsistent with modern statutory authority[15] and finds no support in other authoritative expositions of the concept of tenancy.[16] In *Ashburn Anstalt v Arnold*,[17] therefore, the Court of Appeal declined to treat Lord Templeman as having laid down a principle of 'no rent, no lease'.[18] The reference to the 'hallmark' quality of rent payment was accordingly read down as merely a positive pointer towards the existence of a tenancy and not as a negative and definitive proposition that 'you cannot have a tenancy without a rent'.[19] It thus seems to be accepted nowadays that the

11 See *Shevill v Builders Licensing Board* (1980) 2 BPR 9662 at 9672, where Mahoney JA thought that 'the modern view of leases, and of the rent paid under them, has tended away from the technicalities of the past and towards the understanding of rent as simply a payment which a tenant is bound by his contract to pay to the landlord for the use of his land'.

12 See eg *C.H. Bailey Ltd v Memorial Enterprises Ltd* [1974] 1 WLR 728 at 732B-D, 735B-C; *United Scientific Holdings Ltd v Burnley BC* [1978] AC 904 at 935A per Lord Diplock.

13 [1985] AC 809 at 826E (see also at 818C, 821B).

14 'To constitute a tenancy the occupier must be granted exclusive possession for a fixed or periodic term certain in consideration of a premium or periodical payments' ([1985] AC 809 at 818E). See also *Scrimgeour v Waller* (1981) 257 Estates Gazette 61 at 63 per Sir David Cairns.

15 The presence or absence of a rent is made expressly irrelevant in the definition of a 'term of years' in Law of Property Act 1925, s 205(1)(xxvii), although the absence of a money rent has in the past precluded a tenancy from some special forms of statutory protection (see eg Rent Act 1977, s 5(1), post, p 875).

16 See eg *Radaich v Smith* (1959) 101 CLR 209 at 222 per Windeyer J. See also *Knight's Case* (1588) 5 Co Rep 54b at 55a, 77 ER 137 at 138; *Burns v Dennis* (1948) 48 SR (NSW) 266 at 267 per Jordan CJ; *Re British American Oil Co Ltd and DePass* (1960) 21 DLR (2d) 110 at 115; *Hayes v Seymour-Johns* (1981) 2 BPR 9366 at 9369.

17 [1989] Ch 1 at 9F-10C per Fox LJ.

18 See also *AG Securities v Vaughan* [1990] 1 AC 417 at 430C-G per Fox LJ ('A lease is an estate in the land for the duration of the lease. The parties are free to create it for such considerations as they choose').

19 [1989] Ch 1 at 10C per Fox LJ. In *Ashburn Anstalt* a lease was found to exist even in the clear absence of any obligation to pay rent ([1989] Ch 1 at 12G-13B). The Court of Appeal's decision in *Ashburn Anstalt* was overruled on other grounds by the House of Lords in *Prudential Assurance Co Ltd v London Residuary Body* [1992] 2 AC 386 at 395G, but in the latter case Lord Templeman was pointedly careful (at 390C) to avoid any reference to rent payment as a necessary component of the definition of a lease (see, however, *Westminster CC v Clarke* [1992] 2 AC 288 at 299G-H per Lord Templeman).

reservation of a rent is not strictly necessary for the creation of a tenancy,[20] although it is difficult in practice to conceive of a periodic tenancy without a rent[1] and it remains likely that the absence of rent payment may point persuasively towards the existence of a mere licence.[2]

(b) Definition of 'rent'

In its ordinary or essential meaning, 'rent', where it is contractually due, comprises any payment made for the possession of realty under a lease.[3] Thus rent usually takes the form of monetary compensation paid for the tenant's use of the demised premises,[4] although there is in principle no objection to a rent which is fixed in some other way,[5] eg in the form of services in kind,[6] bottles of wine,[7] or other chattels.[8] Where a rent is fixed in money terms, nothing turns on the adequacy of the consideration.[9]

Not all money payments made by a tenant necessarily constitute 'rent'.

20 See eg *Birrell v Carey* (1989) 58 P & CR 184 at 187 per Fox LJ; *Axtell v George* (Unreported, Court of Appeal, 13 February 1991) per Lord Donaldson of Lymington MR; *Prudential Assurance Co Ltd v London Residuary Body* (1992) 63 P & CR 386 at 397 per Scott LJ; *Canadian Imperial Bank of Commerce v Bello* (1992) 64 P & CR 48 at 55 per Ralph Gibson LJ; *Skipton Building Society v Clayton* (1993) *Times*, 25 March, per Sir Christopher Slade.

1 See *Prudential Assurance Co Ltd v London Residuary Body* (1992) 63 P & CR 386 at 397 per Scott LJ. It is fair to record that in *Street v Mountford* [1985] AC 809 at 826E, Lord Templeman's reference to rent payments as a decisive 'hallmark' was made in the immediate context of 'a periodical term'.

2 See eg *Colchester BC v Smith* [1991] Ch 448 at 485B–C (upheld [1992] Ch 421). See also [1988] Conv 201 at 203 (M.P. Thompson). It does not necessarily follow, however, that a tenancy always arises wherever the landowner demands compensation for use and occupation. See *Northern Ireland Housing Executive v McCann* [1979] NI 39 at 43E; *Westminster CC v Basson* (1991) 62 P & CR 57 at 59f (regular payments demanded from squatters in initially unlawful occupation).

3 *Commr of Stamp Duties v J V (Crows Nest) Pty Ltd* (1987) 7 NSWLR 529 at 531F per Mahoney JA. See generally R.G. Lee, [1991] Conv 270.

4 See *United Scientific Holdings Ltd v Burnley BC* [1978] AC 904 at 935A per Lord Diplock, 947B per Lord Simon of Glaisdale, 963G per Lord Fraser of Tullybelton. A payment for the use of land may be 'rent' notwithstanding that there is no right of distraint (post, p 839) (see *T & E Homes Ltd v Robinson* [1979] 1 WLR 452 at 457E, 459E–F; *Commr of Stamp Duties v J V (Crows Nest) Pty Ltd* (1987) 7 NSWLR 529 at 532A per Mahoney JA).

5 *Co Litt*, p 142a. In certain restricted contexts 'rent' must nevertheless have a distinct quantifiable money value. For instance, no protected tenancy can normally arise under the Rent Act 1977 where the tenant's obligations comprise the performance of onerous services for the latter (see Rent Act 1977, s 5(1)). The statutory machinery for rent restriction would be totally inoperable if the consideration for the tenant's occupation were not ultimately expressible in terms of money (*Barnes v Barratt* [1970] 2 QB 657 at 667E per Sachs LJ; *Bostock v Bryant* (1990) 61 P & CR 23 at 26ff). See, however, *Montague v Browning* [1954] 1 WLR 1039 at 1044f.

6 *Co Litt*, p 96a; *Doe d Tucker v Morse* (1830) 1 B & Ad 365 at 369, 109 ER 822 at 824; *Duke of Marlborough v Osborn* (1864) 5 B & S 67 at 74, 122 ER 758 at 761; *Barnes v Barratt* [1970] 2 QB 657 at 666D, 670F–G. See also *Montague v Browning* [1954] 1 WLR 1039 at 1044f (employee's wages subject to regular fixed deduction in respect of his occupation under a service tenancy). Compare, however, *Scrimgeour v Waller* (1981) 257 Estates Gazette 61 at 63; *Meier v Lucas* (Unreported, Court of Appeal, 4 March 1986).

7 *Pitcher v Tovey* (1692) 4 Mod 71 at 75f, 87 ER 268 at 271.

8 *Co Litt*, p 142a. It is not impossible that the rent should be the annual rendering of one peppercorn.

9 *Royal Philanthropic Society v County* (1985) 276 Estates Gazette 1068 at 1072.

The coverage of the term 'rent' is restricted to only some of the payments which may arise as the result of a transaction of lease. In its proper sense 'rent' includes only those payments which a tenant is bound to make 'for the use of' the land in question,[10] thereby excluding those payments which are made 'merely in respect of' such use or are 'in reality only an accidental or incidental part of the transaction by which the right to use is granted.'[11]

On this basis 'rent' prima facie excludes moneys which the tenant may be obliged to expend on repairs or improvements,[12] but may well include payments which the tenant is directed to make for the purpose of indemnifying the landlord's financial obligations to third parties (eg payment of part or all of the landlord's monthly mortgage liability).[13] The definition of 'rent' may even extend to obligatory payments made by way of donation to some third party nominated by the landlord[14] or in discharge of certain unrelated liabilities of the landlord (eg periodical instalments on store account or credit cards). It is likely that exorbitant payments made in respect of furniture hire under otherwise rent-free tenancies also constitute 'rent'.[15] The parties' own description of a payment as 'rent' is persuasive but not conclusive.[16] In all cases the test of 'rent' is ultimately whether the relevant payment is made in consideration of the grant of the tenancy 'however it be described or allocated'.[17]

(c) Certainty of rent obligation

It has long been established that the reservation of rent under a lease or tenancy must be certain both as to the amount and as to the time when

10 *Bostock v Bryant* (1990) 61 P & CR 23 at 25 per Stuart-Smith LJ. 'Rent' may therefore comprise payments which were made as a matter of understood obligation, even though the landlord deposited the money in a trust account for the tenants, possibly hoping thereby to institute on their behalf a sort of involuntary 'savings scheme' (see *Ward v Warnke* (1990) 22 HLR 496 at 498ff per Fox LJ; R.G. Lee, [1991] Conv 270 at 272).

11 *Commr of Stamp Duties v J V (Crows Nest) Pty Ltd* (1987) 7 NSWLR 529 at 532C–G per Mahoney JA. McHugh JA warned (at 538D) that the relevant distinctions are 'often difficult to draw in practice', but the Court of Appeal of New South Wales had little hesitation in holding that periodical payments by a health centre franchisee in respect of administration and advertising by the franchisor did not constitute 'rent'.

12 *Commr of Stamp Duties v J V (Crows Nest) Pty Ltd* (1987) 7 NSWLR 529 at 532C per Mahoney JA.

13 A strong argument in favour of recognising obligatory payments to third parties as a form of rent lies in the fact that such payments (if disclosed) are treated for tax purposes as the equivalent of rent received by the property owner (see *Jeffries v Stevens* [1982] STC 639 at 651b per Walton J).

14 See, however, *Michel v Volpe* (1967) 202 Estates Gazette 213, where the occupier was contractually obliged to make 'donations' to a periodical supplied by the person who provided her accommodation. The Court of Appeal held that this arrangement created a licence rather than a subtenancy, even though the occupier's 'donations book' was eventually replaced by 'a kind of rent book'.

15 It is often believed, almost certainly in error, that such diversionary tactics guarantee landlords immunity from protective legislation such as the Rent Act (post, p 873).

16 See *Bostock v Bryant* (1990) 61 P & CR 23 at 25, where Stuart-Smith LJ held that the occupiers' payment of gas and electricity bills for a house which they shared with the owner represented not 'rent' but merely a reimbursement of expenses for shared consumables.

17 *Property Holding Co Ltd v Clark* [1948] 1 KB 630 at 649 per Evershed LJ. See also *Sidney Trading Co Ltd v Finsbury BC* [1952] 1 All ER 460 at 462A, where Lord Goddard CJ indicated that if 'there is a sum of money which the tenant agrees to pay as a consideration for the tenancy, it is for this purpose a rent.'

it is payable.[18] The quantum of rent payable must therefore be certain at the commencement or at least capable of being calculated with certainty[19] at the due date for payment.[20] The historic rationale for the requirement of a 'rent certain' is that the landlord's remedy of distress for unpaid rent (ie the right to remove goods to the value of the default[1]) can operate only where the rent obligation is clearly defined.[2]

(i) Variable rent Consistently with this qualified requirement of certainty, it is quite possible that the rent due from the tenant may fluctuate during the course of the term.[3] Rent may also be altered in accordance with an express rent review clause contained in the lease.[4] In such cases the variability of the rent obligation is perfectly valid so long as the rent payable can be ascertained with certainty at the due date for payment. It is less clear whether, in the absence of a rent review clause, the rent level may be validly adjusted by a wholly unilateral decision on the part of the landlord. In *Greater London Council v Connolly*[5] the Court of Appeal declined to hold void for uncertainty a provision that a council tenant's rent was 'liable to be increased or decreased on notice being given', even though such a clause admittedly rendered the rent level 'dependent...on the whim of the landlords.' More recently, in *Dresden Estates Ltd v Collinson*,[6] the Court of Appeal held that such a clause was inconsistent with the existence of a tenancy and therefore pointed clearly to a relationship of licence.

(ii) Indeterminate rent While the courts are disinclined to strike down purposeful transactions as void on the ground of uncertainty,[7] there are

18 *Parker v Harris* (1692) 1 Salk 262, 91 ER 230; *Booker Industries Pty Ltd v Wilson Parking (Qld) Pty Ltd* (1982) 149 CLR 600 at 610 per Brennan J.

19 For the rules of certainty in relation to the capital purchase price of options to renew a lease or to purchase a reversion, see Chapter 7 (ante, p 143).

20 *Greater London Council v Connolly* [1970] 2 QB 100 at 109A per Lord Denning MR; *Booker Industries Pty Ltd v Wilson Parking (Qld) Pty Ltd* (1982) 149 CLR 600 at 610 per Brennan J. If the rent, although quantifiable at the due date, has not yet been ascertained, it cannot be demanded retrospectively for periods preceding the date when it finally is quantified (*Re Essoldo (Bingo) Ltd's Underlease* (1971) 23 P & CR 1 at 4f).

1 Post, p 839.

2 See *In re Knight, ex parte Voisey* (1882) 21 Ch D 442 at 457; *Greater London Council v Connolly* [1970] 2 QB 100 at 112D; *United Scientific Holdings Ltd v Burnley BC* [1978] AC 904 at 935B–C. For evidence of the diminishing impact in this area of the conceptual restrictions imposed by the largely archaic law of distress, see *T & E Homes Ltd v Robinson* [1979] 1 WLR 452 at 456H–457A.

3 Coke gave the example of a rent-service comprising the shearing of 'all the sheep pasturing within the lord's manor' (*Co Litt*, p 96a). See also *Kendall v Baker* (1852) 11 CB 842 at 850, 138 ER 706 at 710 (rent riding on the price of wheat). A rent may be validly tied to some index of inflation (see eg *Blumenthal v Gallery Five Ltd* (1971) 220 Estates Gazette 31 at 33; *Re Collins Cartage & Storage Co Ltd and McDonald* (1981) 116 DLR (3d) 570 at 571f; *Trifid Pty Ltd v Ratto* [1985] WAR 19 at 29 (revsd on different grounds [1987] WAR 237)).

4 Rent review clauses, although now a universal feature in commercial leases, are rarely found in residential leases. See D.N. Clarke, [1989] Conv 111.

5 [1970] 2 QB 100 at 109D, 111H.

6 (1988) 55 P & CR 47 at 53.

7 *Greater London Council v Connolly* [1970] 2 QB 100 at 108F; *Brown v Gould* [1972] Ch 53 at 56F.

some circumstances in which a tenancy is liable to be invalidated by uncertainty as to the rent obligation. Although the courts' approach to such provisions may nowadays have become more liberal,[8] it has been held in the past that a tenancy 'at a rent to be agreed' is vitiated by uncertainty,[9] at least where no formula or mechanism was provided for quantifying the rent.[10] An option for renewal 'at a rental to be agreed' may, however, be valid if the option stipulated that the new rent should not exceed the existing rent and indicated a plain contractual intention in the relevant parties to be bound by the option.[11] Nor is a tenancy regarded as void for uncertainty merely because the rent is to be fixed 'having regard to the market value of the premises'[12] or is to be quantified as the current 'market rental'.[13] The concept of 'market rental' has a well known meaning in the context of landlord-tenant negotiations, and the courts will, if necessary, provide machinery for assessing the value of such a rental in any given case.[14]

3. THE DISTINCTION BETWEEN 'LEASE' AND 'LICENCE'

A lease (or tenancy) confers upon the occupier a proprietary estate to which is annexed a right of exclusive possession enforceable against all persons including the landlord.[15] By contrast, a licence confers upon the occupier not an estate in the land but merely a personal permission to occupy.[16] When described in such abstract terms, the lease appears wholly different in nature from the licence. However, the distinction has proved in practice to be more problematical,[17] not least because the factual and physical evidence of a lease 'on the ground' often seems to differ in no substantial respect from that of a contractual licence. A landowner is entirely free to make

8 See eg *Corson v Rhuddlan BC* (1990) 59 P & CR 185 at 194 per Ralph Gibson LJ.

9 *King's Motors (Oxford) Ltd v Lax* [1970] 1 WLR 426 at 429A; *King v King* (1980) 41 P&CR 311 at 314; *Young v Van Beneen* [1953] 3 DLR 702 at 704f; *Booker Industries Pty Ltd v Wilson Parking (Qld) Pty Ltd* (1982) 149 CLR 600 at 604 per Brennan J.

10 *Brown v Gould* [1972] Ch 53 at 58C. In *Beer v Bowden (Note)* [1981] 1 WLR 522, the Court of Appeal upheld a lease for 10 years which fixed an annual rent for the first five years, but provided that thereafter the rent should be such rent 'as shall...be agreed'. Geoffrey Lane LJ indicated (at [1981] 1 WLR 522 at 527G-H) that the lease was saved from voidness only by reason of the tenant's 'subsisting estate in land' and the concession by the tenant that 'some rent must be paid in respect of these premises'. The Court implied an obligation to pay a 'fair rent'.

11 See *Corson v Rhuddlan BC* (1990) 59 P & CR 185 at 194ff; [1990] Conv 290 (J.E. Martin).

12 *Brown v Gould* [1972] Ch 53 at 61F, 62C.

13 *Andrews v Colonial Mutual Life Assurance Society Ltd* [1982] 2 NZLR 556 at 565.

14 *Andrews v Colonial Mutual Life Assurance Society Ltd* [1982] 2 NZLR 556 at 565. See also *Sudbrook Trading Estate Ltd v Eggleton* [1983] 1 AC 444 at 484A per Lord Fraser of Tullybelton (ante, p 143).

15 Ante, p 697.

16 See *Street v Mountford* [1985] AC 809 at 816C. Licences are discussed in Chapter 19 (post, p 890).

17 See eg *Brooker Settled Estates Ltd v Ayers* (1987) 54 P & CR 165 at 167, where O'Connor LJ referred to 'this tortured question as to whether an occupant is in occupation as a licensee or a tenant'.

accommodation available on either basis,[18] although both lease and licence commonly involve the payment of a rent in return for the right to some form of exclusive occupancy for a prefixed period of time.

(1) Significance of the distinction

The blurred nature of the distinction between the lease and the licence has been responsible for much confusion in the law of landlord and tenant.[19] Yet the distinction—however elusive—is a vital determinant of a range of legal issues.

(a) The common law of landlord and tenant

In the common law of landlord and tenant the lease-licence distinction derives an immediate relevance from the fact that a proprietary estate in land is conferred by a lease but never by a licence. Only a tenant, for instance, has an estate in the land which is capable of assignment to a stranger.[20] Furthermore, it is orthodox teaching that leases—but not most kinds of licence—are capable of binding a transferee of land.[1] Only a tenant[2]—and not a licensee[3]—is entitled to sue a third party for nuisance or trespass. Only a tenant—and not a licensee—may properly be subject to the remedy of distress for arrears of rent.[4] A licensee—but not normally a tenant—is subject to the 'short-cut' summary procedure for the recovery of possession under RSC, Ord 113.[5]

(b) The ambit of protective legislation

The distinction between lease and licence is also vital in defining the coverage of various schemes of protective legislation. Historically the most controversial function of this conceptual divide has been to delineate the scope of full protection under the Rent Act 1977.[6] The ample benefits conferred by this

18 *Aslan v Murphy* [1990] 1 WLR 766 at 770B-C per Lord Donaldson of Lymington MR. 'It is not a crime, nor is it contrary to public policy, for a property owner to license occupiers to occupy property on terms which do not give rise to a tenancy' (*Antoniades v Villiers* [1990] 1 AC 417 at 445C-E per Bingham LJ).

19 See *National Carriers Ltd v Panalpina (Northern) Ltd* [1981] AC 675 at 714A per Lord Roskill.

20 Post, p 734. See *Richardson v Landecker* (1950) 50 SR (NSW) 250 at 255; *Lewis v Bell* [1985] 1 NSWLR 731 at 735G.

1 Post, p 859.

2 *Harper v Charlesworth*(1825) 4 B & C 574 at 585, 107 ER 1174 at 1178; *Street v Mountford* [1985] AC 809 at 816B-C (ante, p 698). It seems that, in order to maintain an action in trespass, the tenant must be in possession (see *Simpson v Knowles* [1974] VR 190 at 195).

3 See *AG Securities v Vaughan* [1990] 1 AC 417 at 454A-B per Lord Bridge of Harwich. A licensee has no right to sue a third person in respect of a disturbance of his rights (*Hill v Tupper* (1863) 2 H & C 121 at 127, 159 ER 51 at 53 (post, p 1065); *Lewisham BC v Roberts* [1949] 2 KB 608 at 622). See Chapter 19 (post, p 891).

4 The assertion by the owner of a right to distrain upon the goods of the occupier may operate virtually as an estoppel, precluding the owner from any future claim that the occupier had merely a licence (see eg *Carden v Choudhury* (Unreported, Court of Appeal, 29 February 1984)).

5 *Crancour Ltd v Da Silvaesa* (1986) 52 P & CR 204 at 226.

6 Post, p 873.

Act apply only to the tenant and not to the licensee.[7] Similarly the distinction between lease and licence serves to fix the boundaries of the statutory codes governing assured tenancies[8] and business tenancies.[9] The definitional knife-edge separating lease from licence may also affect even wider categories of problems, ranging from the level of compensation payable to a householder on compulsory purchase[10] to the allocation of legal liability for defective premises.[11]

(c) Rare instances of superior protection for the licensee

Although it is generally true that a tenancy confers on the occupier a greater degree of legal protection than does a licence in equivalent circumstances, this is not always the case. A licensee may sue the licensor in negligence for failure to exercise reasonable care in safeguarding the licensee's belongings from burglary.[12] A similar claim on behalf of a tenant founders on the fact that the tenant is the owner of an 'estate' in the land and is himself responsible for the defence of his right to exclusive possession of that land. It is also significant that various forms of licence in land—notably the 'irrevocable licence' or licence based on proprietary estoppel—are sometimes accorded a degree of security of tenure which exceeds that conferred by a tenancy.[13]

(2) Exclusive possession is the essential criterion

Since medieval times the criterion of exclusive possession has marked off the boundary between the lease and the licence.[14] In all but exceptional circumstances the conferment of a right of exclusive possession for a term has served to denote the grant of a leasehold estate in the land. This right to exclusive possession symbolises the overall territorial control characteristic of estate ownership in English law.[15] Such entitlement gives legal expression to the perception that, in some elemental sense, the tenant has a 'stake' in the land[16] and not a mere fragile permission for temporary personal occupation. It is indeed this 'stake' in the land which, in the words of Lord Templeman in *Street v Mountford*,[17] enables the tenant (unlike the licensee)

7 Rent Act 1977, s 1 (post, p 874).
8 Housing Act 1988, s 1(1) (post p 880).
9 Landlord and Tenant Act 1954, s 23(1). The distinction between tenancy and licence is now no longer vital to the operation of the protective codes regulating either secure tenancies (see Housing Act 1985, s 79(3)) or agricultural tenancies (see Agricultural Holdings Act 1986, s 2(2)(b)).
10 See *David v LB of Lewisham* (1977) 34 P & CR 112 at 115f; *McHugh v LB of Islington* (1984) 270 Estates Gazette 1095 at 1096 (post, p 713).
11 Defective Premises Act 1972, s 4(1) (post, p 791). See *Wheat v E. Lacon & Co Ltd* [1966] AC 552 at 579A-B, 579F-580A; *McDonagh v Kent AHA* (Unreported, Court of Appeal, 7 October 1985).
12 *Appah v Parncliffe Investments Ltd* [1964] 1 WLR 1064 at 1067.
13 See eg *Hardwick v Johnson* [1978] 1 WLR 683 at 689H (post, p 909).
14 See [1985] CLJ 351 at 352 (S. Tromans).
15 Ante, p 698.
16 See *Marchant v Charters* [1977] 1 WLR 1181 at 1185G per Lord Denning MR.
17 [1985] AC 809 at 816B-C.

to 'call the land his own'. It also sustains both the tenant's ability to resist intrusion by any trespasser and his capacity to transfer his rights to a stranger.[18]

In so far as exclusive possession provides 'the proper touchstone' of a lease or tenancy,[19] any circumstances which directly or indirectly negate the occupier's right of exclusive possession qua tenant fall inevitably short of establishing a tenancy. Such circumstances are often rationalised by reference to the presence of some domestic or charitable relationship[20] or the absence of any true intent to create enforceable legal relations.[1] Ultimately, however, these contra-indications of tenancy are intricately interlinked explanations which meld together in the assertion that the occupier has failed to demonstrate that he or she had a stake in or possessory control over the land.

(3) Exclusive possession is not a comprehensive criterion

While a right of exclusive possession is the sine qua non of tenancy, it does not follow that a tenancy is necessarily present wherever someone is, or seems to be, in exclusive occupation of land.[2] In some circumstances the existence of a landlord-tenant relationship may be excluded because the occupier's exclusive possession is referable to some other category of legal relationship. In other circumstances it becomes apparent on examination that the occupier's exclusive occupation of land is compatible with (and explicable by reference to) the exclusive possession of another.

(a) Exclusive possession referable to some other category of legal relationship

According to Lord Templeman in *Street v Mountford*,[3] an occupier who enjoys exclusive possession 'is not necessarily a tenant.' The landlord-tenant relationship is established only where there is exclusive possession 'for a fixed or periodic term certain'.[4] This qualification is significant since, as Lord Templeman pointed out,[5] it is quite possible to enjoy exclusive possession outside the landlord-tenant relationship.[6] The conferment of a right of exclusive possession is not inconsistent with other forms of legal status[7] (or

18 See *Barnes v Barratt* [1970] 2 QB 657 at 669G–H; *Shell-Mex and BP Ltd v Manchester Garages Ltd* [1971] 1 WLR 612 at 617H–618A. The student who lives in a bed-sitting room provided in a hostel or hall of residence has, for instance, no 'estate' which he can meaningfully transfer to a stranger.

19 *Radaich v Smith* (1959) 101 CLR 209 at 223 per Windeyer J (ante, p 698).

20 Post, p 712.

1 Post, p 720.

2 *Street v Mountford* [1985] AC 809 at 823D per Lord Templeman.

3 [1985] AC 809 at 818E.

4 See also *Prudential Assurance Co Ltd v London Residuary Body* [1992] 2 AC 386 at 390C per Lord Templeman ('exclusive possession and profit of land for some determinate period').

5 [1985] AC 809 at 818E.

6 This concern to distinguish exclusive possession as the substratum of tenancy from the exclusive posession inherent in other forms of legal status may perhaps account for Lord Templeman's unnecessary reference to the payment of some rent or premium as a 'hallmark' of tenancy (ante, p 702).

7 See *Errington v Errington and Woods* [1952] 1 KB 290 at 297f per Denning LJ.

perhaps even with a total absence of legal status[8]). That exclusive possession of land may be 'referable to a legal relationship other than a tenancy'[9] is amply demonstrated by such persons as the owner in fee simple, the trespasser,[10] the mortgagee in possession,[11] the purchaser allowed into possession before completion,[12] and the occupier who retains land pending the exercise of an option.[13] All of these categories of person enjoy an exclusiveness of possession which arises quite independently of any grant for a term at a rent, possession being ancillary in each case to some other kind of interest or status in the land.[14] Such alternative forms of status or relationship, 'although exhibiting the ordinary badges of a tenancy',[15] do not create a term of years.

It is even possible that the extrinsic relationship which prevents exclusive possession from having the character of a tenancy may result not from ownership of another interest in the land, but from the enjoyment of a statutory right. It seems that exclusive possession outside the landlord-tenant relationship may be enjoyed by an occupier whose provision of limited accommodation is referable to the fulfilment by a local housing authority of its statutory duty under the homeless persons legislation.[16] Although granted 'exclusive possession' of council accommodation pending the outcome of a 'homelessness inquiry'[17] or the securing of alternative accommodation after repossession,[18] such a person will have merely a licence unless the local authority has quite explicitly offered him a 'tenancy'.[19]

(b) Exclusive occupation compatible with the exclusive possession of another

Factual exclusiveness of occupation does not indicate unambiguously the existence of a tenancy. 'Exclusive occupation' is not the same thing as a right of 'exclusive possession' and points indifferently towards both tenancy

8 See eg *Colchester BC v Smith* [1991] Ch 448 at 484A-485D, where Ferris J thought exclusive possession wholly compatible with certain kinds of 'exceptional transaction, not intended to give rise to legal obligations on either side.'
9 [1985] AC 809 at 826H-827A.
10 Ante, p 291.
11 Post, p 981.
12 See *Essex Plan Ltd v Broadminster* (1988) 56 P & CR 353 at 355f. However, if an occupier enters into possession with the ultimate intention of negotiating a purchase of the property, and that purchase never materialises, the occupancy will still rank as a tenancy if the facts otherwise satisfy the *Street v Mountford* criteria of 'exclusive possession at a rent for a term' (see *Bretherton v Paton* [1986] 1 EGLR 172 at 174H).
13 *Essex Plan Ltd v Broadminster* (1988) 56 P & CR 353 at 355ff; [1989] Conv 55 (J.E.M.).
14 Thus, in *Essex Plan Ltd v Broadminster* (1988) 56 P & CR 353 at 356, Hoffmann J pointed out that the optionee's possession was 'ancillary and referable to' its right to call for a long lease, an entitlement which had given it 'in equity an immediate interest in the land' (ante, p 143). The same kind of analysis applies to each of the other cases of exclusive possession enjoyed otherwise than qua tenant. For instance, the owner in fee simple and the trespasser can attribute their exclusive possession, respectively, to a rightful and wrongful estate in fee (ante, p 291).
15 *Essex Plan Ltd v Broadminster* (1988) 56 P & CR 353 at 356 per Hoffmann J.
16 See Housing Act 1985, ss 63ff.
17 *South Holland DC v Keyte* (1985) 19 HLR 97 at 101ff.
18 *Ogwr BC v Dykes* [1989] 1 WLR 295 at 302H-303B per Purchas LJ. See [1989] Conv 194 (J.E.M.).
19 See *Eastleigh BC v Walsh* [1985] 1 WLR 525 at 530F-H; [1985] Conv 217.

and licence. The mere fact of exclusive occupation is not necessarily inconsistent with a right of 'exclusive possession' vested in someone else, and it is only the right to 'exclusive possession' in the full legal sense which demonstrates an unequivocal indicium of tenancy.[20] Accordingly there remains outside the landlord-tenant relationship a range of circumstance where, in reality, overall territorial control of the land is reserved not for the actual occupier but for the landowner himself. In these cases the landowner retains 'possession' in the strict legal sense, but his possession casts a shadow in the form of a factum of exclusive occupation enjoyed by the occupier. Appearances are nevertheless deceptive: mere exclusiveness of occupation can closely mimic tenancy since it frequently persists for a determinate period at a rent.

In *Street v Mountford*[1] the House of Lords confirmed the existence of certain kinds of occupancy which, although exclusive, do not constitute a tenancy. According to Lord Templeman, tenancy is excluded in these instances either on the ground that the occupier's apparent possession should be treated in law as the 'possession' of someone else,[2] or on the ground that the relevant circumstances negative the intention to enter into any legal contractual relationship at all.[3] In this context Lord Templeman referred[4] with approval to *Facchini v Bryson*,[5] where Denning LJ had indicated that tenancy might be precluded where 'there has been something in the circumstances, such as a family arrangement, an act of friendship or generosity, or such like, to negative any intention to create a tenancy.'[6] As Windeyer J was later to observe in *Radaich v Smith*,[7] these exceptional instances are probably best regarded as cases where a factual enjoyment of sole occupation falls significantly short of any conferment of a right to 'exclusive possession'.[8]

In *Street v Mountford*[9] the House of Lords seems to have revived the old '*Facchini v Bryson* categories' as representing good law today.[10] Amongst the forms of exclusive occupancy thus omitted from the ambit of the modern landlord-tenant relationship are the following inter-related categories of case.

20 Clarity in this area is not assisted by the fact that the courts have often used the terms 'exclusive possession' and 'exclusive occupation' as if they were interchangeable. Something of this confusion is present even in the speeches of Lord Templeman in *Street v Mountford* [1985] AC 809 at 826E and *Antoniades v Villiers* [1990] 1 AC 417 at 459A–B, F, 460F. See also *Aslan v Murphy* [1990] 1 WLR 766 at 770E–G, where Lord Donaldson of Lymington MR spoke of a 'spectrum of exclusivity ranging from the occupier of a detached property under a full repairing lease, who is without doubt a tenant, to the overnight occupier of a hotel bedroom who, however up-market the hotel, is without doubt a lodger.' There is a strong argument for regarding the element of 'exclusive possession' as being truly present only in a lease or tenancy (see eg [1986] JSWL 46 at 49 (D. Hoath)).

1 [1985] AC 809 at 818E per Lord Templeman.

2 [1985] AC 809 at 818F–G.

3 [1985] AC 809 at 819C, 820D.

4 [1985] AC 809 at 821H–822A. See *AG Securities v Vaughan* [1990] 1 AC 417 at 426H–427A per Fox LJ.

5 [1952] 1 TLR 1386 at 1389.

6 [1985] AC 809 at 821H–822A (post, p 720).

7 (1959) 101 CLR 209 at 223 (ante, p 700).

8 Post, p 713.

9 [1985] AC 809 at 823D–E.

10 See eg *AG Securities v Vaughan* [1990] 1 AC 417 at 431F per Fox LJ.

(i) Accommodation based on 'charity' In *Street v Mountford*[11] Lord Templeman indicated that the occupier who is 'an object of charity' will normally be excluded from the status of tenant. However dubious the analogy, this reference to 'charity' has been construed as covering accommodation provided through various socialised forms of charity underpinned by therapeutic motivations. In *Brent People's Housing Association Ltd v Winsmore*,[12] for example, the exception for charity-based accommodation was invoked in order to establish the licensee status of an occupier who lived in a house managed by a 'single homeless project group' sponsored by a registered (and necessarily charitable) housing association. The absence of any right of 'exclusive possession' vested in the occupier was underscored by the fact that all the residents in the house lived under the close supervision of local authority social workers who were employed full-time at the house to provide support, advice and general assistance.[13] As Lord Templeman later emphasised in *Westminster CC v Clarke*,[14] a claim of independent possession on the part of a resident in a hostel is incompatible with the exercise of far-reaching supervisory control by the owner or its agents.

(ii) Accommodation based on friendship or generosity The undefined and open-ended category of 'charity' tends to merge with cases of accommodation based on 'friendship or generosity'.[15] In the law of landlord and tenant generosity has never been left to be its own dubious reward. In the classic case of *Marcroft Wagons Ltd v Smith*,[16] a landlord, acting in response to 'the ordinary decencies of human life',[17] had allowed the daughter of his now deceased tenants to remain in occupation in the immediate aftermath of her double bereavement, paying the same rent as had obtained under those tenancies. The Court of Appeal was unwilling to penalise the landlord's compassionate 'indulgence' by imposing on him the strictures of Rent Act control,[18] and the Court therefore rejected the daughter's contention that she had acquired a new tenancy.[19] In *Street v Mountford*,[20] the House of Lords approved this decision as one in which the parties evidenced no intention to contract at all, but the ruling is equally explicable on the footing that

11 [1985] AC 809 at 818E.
12 Unreported, County Court, 20 November 1985. See *Rent Acts: Selected Case Law Guide* (Institute of Rent Officers Educational Trust), Vol 1, p 347; (1986) 17 Jiro (Ed Supp) No 1, p ii.
13 The denial of tenant status probably extends to many other kinds of sheltered or 'special needs' accommodation.
14 [1992] 2 AC 288 at 301H–302A (ante, p 699).
15 See Denning LJ's reference to 'friendship or generosity' in *Facchini v Bryson* [1952] 1 TLR 1386 at 1389.
16 [1951] 2 KB 496.
17 [1951] 2 KB 496 at 502.
18 Evershed MR was particularly anxious that the courts should do nothing which might inhibit or stultify the already rare human impulse towards altruism (see [1951] 2 KB 496 at 501).
19 In *Turner v Burton* (Unreported, Court of Appeal, 12 March 1985), a mere revocable licence was found where the occupier had initially asked for accommodation for 'one or two weeks at most' and was then allowed to stay on for a few more weeks because he had lost his job.
20 [1985] AC 809 at 820D.

the relevant occupation did not confer a 'stake' in the land or constitute 'exclusive possession' in any true legal sense.[1] The disputed occupancy had an entirely personal character.

The decision in *Marcroft Wagons Ltd v Smith* set the pattern for a number of cases in which occupancy motivated by altruism has been held to give rise to a mere licence.[2] On closer analysis it is not always easy to understand why the fact that a particular transaction has been induced by friendship or generosity should necessarily bring the transaction within an exceptional category. Indeed, it can be observed that until the effect of the transaction has been determined, it is impossible to appreciate the extent of the grantor's generosity or to know quite how far the ties of friendship have carried him.[3]

(iii) Occupancy of a domestic or quasi-familial character Loose informal arrangements for occupancy within a familial or quasi-familial context have always been apt to be analysed in terms of revocable licence rather than tenancy.[4] Such circumstances commonly disclose no grant of 'independent possession' to the occupier[5] and sometimes the parties may also lack any intention to form an enforceable legal relationship.[6] In *Barnes v Barratt*,[7] for instance, the Court of Appeal declined to attach the label of 'tenancy' to an arrangement under which a couple were provided with exclusive occupation of three rooms in a house in return for their performance of cooking and other domestic services and their payment of certain household bills. There existed here merely a 'personal licence to occupy', not least, as Sachs LJ emphasised, because the situation 'was closely akin to those produced by family arrangements to share a house.'[8]

1 This was the rationale advanced by Windeyer J in *Radaich v Smith* (1959) 101 CLR 209 at 223 (ante, p 711). See also R. Street, [1985] Conv 328 at 331; D.N. Clarke, [1986] Conv 39 at 43.

2 See J.W. Harris, *Licences and Tenancies—The Generosity Factor*, (1969) 32 MLR 92. It should not be assumed, however, that an occupancy coloured by circumstances of friendship or generosity always gives rise to a licence. See eg *Sopwith v Stutchbury* (1983) 17 HLR 50 at 55 (express grant of tenancy to friend in aftermath of broken marriage).

3 See *Radaich v Smith* (1959) 101 CLR 209 at 220 per Taylor J.

4 See eg *Booker v Palmer* [1942] 2 All ER 674 at 677C (evacuees); *Cobb v Lane* [1952] 1 All ER 1199 at 1201A (brother). See also *Errington v Errington and Woods* [1952] 1 KB 290 at 298.

5 See eg *Peakin v Peakin* [1895] 2 IR 359 at 361f (occupation allowed to owner's sisters was 'not an independent possession by them'). The fact of family relationship does not, however, operate any automatic bar against the creation of a tenancy (see *Nunn v Dalrymple* (1990) 59 P & CR 231 at 239f per Stocker LJ).

6 *Street v Mountford* [1985] AC 809 at 824E–F (ante, p 709).

7 [1970] 2 QB 657.

8 [1970] 2 QB 657 at 670A. Sharing between family members is apt to create merely a licence (see *David v LB of Lewisham* (1977) 34 P & CR 112 at 115f; *Armstrong v Armstrong* [1970] 1 NSWR 133 at 135). See also *Heslop v Burns* [1974] 1 WLR 1241 at 1252G, where the relationship between the owner and the occupiers was not only 'very akin to a family arrangement' but also marked by an extreme degree of generosity on the part of the former towards the latter. There seems to have been some ground for believing that the owner had formed a romantic attraction for one of the occupiers (see [1974] 1 WLR 1241 at 1244C).

The critical issue in such cases is whether the occupancy has detracted from the landowner's exercise of overall control over the premises and the conduct which takes place there. Frequently the domestic or quasi-familial character of the arrangement positively reinforces the fact that, far from possessory control having been transferred to the occupier, the latter remains intimately subject to supervision and regulation by the owner.[9] In *Oxford Overseas Student Housing Association v Mukherjee*,[10] for instance, Bingham LJ upheld the licensee status of a resident in a hostel set up with the 'laudable objective' of providing accommodation for overseas students 'arriving in a strange country and in a strange town with no friends and contacts'. The Court of Appeal attached great significance to the fact that the hostel warden retained a general power of surveillance to ensure the observance of relevant conditions of occupation.[11]

(iv) Service occupancy In *Street v Mountford*[12] the House of Lords expressly indicated service occupancy as a form of occupancy entirely personal to the occupier and therefore incompatible with the relationship of landlord and tenant. As Lord Templeman observed, 'the possession and occupation of the servant is treated as the possession and occupation of the master and the relationship of landlord and tenant is not created.'[13] It may be questioned whether this attribution of 'possession' to the 'master' as distinct from the 'servant' unduly echoes, in both terminology and ideology, a bygone age when the personality of the 'servant' was virtually suspended for the duration of his service. There is, however, surprisingly modern judicial support for the old view that occupancy granted to an employee results in a mere licence provided that the occupancy is 'strictly ancillary to the performance of the duties which the occupier has to perform' within the employment relationship.[14]

Street v Mountford confirms that where an employee is required to occupy his employer's premises for the better performance of his duties, the employee then ranks as a mere licensee.[15] In such circumstances the occupancy permitted to the employee—however exclusive in its nature—is entirely personal to him and is wholly dependent upon the specific relationship created by his

9 See eg *Abbeyfield (Harpenden) Society Ltd v Woods* [1968] 1 WLR 374 at 376G–H per Lord Denning MR ('The whole arrangement was so personal in nature that the proper inference is. . .that he was a licensee').
10 Unreported, Court of Appeal, 21 November 1989.
11 Ante, p 699.
12 [1985] AC 809 at 818E, 827A.
13 [1985] AC 809 at 818F–G. See also *Wrotham Park Settled Estates v Naylor* (1991) 62 P & CR 233 at 237 per Hoffmann J.
14 *Smith v Seghill Overseers* (1875) LR 10 QB 422 at 428. See *Dobson v Jones* (1844) 5 Man & G 112 at 120, 134 ER 502 at 506; *Scrimgeour v Waller* (1981) 257 Estates Gazette 61 at 64; *Royal Philanthropic Society v County* (1985) 276 Estates Gazette 1068 at 1072 ([1986] Conv 215 (P.F. Smith)); *Norris v Checksfield* [1991] 1 WLR 1241 at 1246A per Woolf LJ.
15 [1985] AC 809 at 818F–G. See *Glasgow Corporation v Johnstone* [1965] AC 609 at 626E–G; *Street v Mountford* [1985] AC 809 at 818G; *H.A. Warner Pty Ltd v Williams* (1946) 73 CLR 421 at 429 per Dixon J; *Gibson v Death* (Unreported, Court of Appeal, 17 June 1986).

employment.[16] The position may be different if the accommodation provided by an employer is not aimed at facilitating the better or more convenient performance of the employee's contract of service. Where the employee's occupancy is incidental to rather than contingent upon his employment—and especially if the accommodation might just as readily have been allocated to a non-employee—the courts seem much more willing to identify the status of the accommodation in terms of tenancy.[17]

(v) Occupancy of the 'lodger' In *Street v Mountford* the House of Lords provided one further, and critically important, instance of residential occupation which coexists with exclusive possession vested in another. Even if a residential occupier enjoys rights of exclusive occupation for a term, he may still be precluded from the status of tenant if he falls into the category of a *lodger*.[18] Lord Templeman drew a crucial distinction between the 'tenant' and the 'lodger' based on the location of overall control in respect of the premises which he occupies.[19] A lodger is entitled to live in the premises 'but cannot call the place his own.'[20] In all his conduct on the premises the lodger is subject to the supervisory authority of the owner, who at all times 'retains his character of master of the house, and...retains the general control and dominion over the whole house'.[1] In particular, stated Lord Templeman, an occupier is a 'lodger' if the 'landlord' provides attendance or services 'which require the landlord or his servants to exercise unrestricted access to and use of the premises.'[2] In such circumstances it is not the provision

16 See eg *Ramsbottom v Snelson* [1948] 1 KB 473 at 477 (chauffeur or gardener); *Macann v Annett* [1948] NZLR 116 at 120; *Snell v Mitchell* [1951] NZLR 1 at 3 ('live-in' housekeepers).

17 'Where the purpose of placing the employee in occupation of the premises is to give him the benefit of a dwelling place whether as a concession or as part of his recompense for his services or in consideration of a deduction from his wages, he is regarded as having an independent occupation of the premises and the relation is construed as landlord and tenant' (*H.A. Warner Pty Ltd v Williams* (1946) 73 CLR 421 at 429 per Dixon J). See also *Hughes v Overseers of Chatham* (1843) 5 Man & G 54 at 78, 134 ER 479 at 488; *Dover v Prosser* [1904] 1 KB 84 at 85f; *Facchini v Bryson* [1952] 1 TLR 1386 at 1389; *Royal Philanthropic Society v County* (1985) 276 Estates Gazette 1068 at 1072.

18 [1985] AC 809 at 817H–818D.

19 Indeed Lord Templeman went so far as to say that 'save in exceptional circumstances' the only live question in the determination of the status of a residential occupancy is henceforth the inquiry 'whether...the occupier is a lodger or a tenant' ([1985] AC 809 at 827E–F).

20 [1985] AC 809 at 818A. See *Allan v Liverpool Overseers* (1874) LR 9 QB 180 at 191f.

1 *Thompson v Ward* (1871) LR 6 CP 327 at 361 per Bovill CJ. Other early legal definitions of the term 'lodger' similarly emphasise the idea that lodgers 'submit themselves to [the owner's] control' (*Ancketill v Baylis* (1882) 10 QBD 577 at 586). In *Bradley v Baylis* (1881) 8 QBD 195 at 219, Jessel MR saw the owner of lodgings as one who 'gives to the "inmates"...merely a right of ingress and egress, and retains to himself the general control, with...a right to interfere, a right to turn out trespassers, and so on...' See also N. Madge, (1985) LAG Bulletin 77 at 78.

2 [1985] AC 809 at 818A. See also *Antoniades v Villiers* [1990] 1 AC 417 at 459F–G per Lord Templeman. This judicial emphasis on the relevance of attendance or services has led on occasion to the most fearful foisting of unwanted attendance or services upon occupiers (see eg *Crancour Ltd v Da Silvaesa*(1986) 52 P & CR 204 (promise to provide a housekeeper, cleaning and lighting of common parts, window cleaning, telephone, collection of rubbish and the laundering of bed linen)).

of services or attendance which negatives the possibility of tenancy.[3] The decisive factor is the absence of any right in the occupier to resist intrusion: it is the owner who 'retains possession' precisely in order to supply the services or attendance.[4]

The 'lodger' classification endorsed in *Street v Mountford* simply confirms existing authority relating to the status of serviced accommodation. Such circumstances disclose a mere licence since the occupancy conferred is so clearly personal to the occupier and the supervision of his activities so intrusive as to exclude any possibility that he has an 'estate' in the land.[5] Traditional examples within this category include the long-term hotel resident,[6] the lodger in a furnished room,[7] and the resident in an old people's home,[8] all of whom can be said to enjoy a mere 'exclusive occupation' as distinct from any right of 'exclusive possession'.[9] The possibility of tenancy is kept alive, however, where there is no contractual undertaking to provide the occupier with intrusive attendance or services[10] or if in practice the contracted services or attendance can be provided without the necessity of actual entry into the occupier's premises.[11] In such circumstances an express reservation of limited rights for the landlord to enter and view the state of the premises

3 See eg Rent Act 1977, s 7 (post, p 875). It appears that in exceptional cases a residential occupier may still be a licensee even though not in receipt of services or attendance (see *Brooker Settled Estates Ltd v Ayers* (1987) 54 P & CR 165 at 169f; *Nicolaou v Pitt* (1989) 21 HLR 487 at 493 per Mustill LJ).

4 *Antoniades v Villiers* [1990] 1 AC 417 at 459F-G per Lord Templeman. Tenancy is precluded by the fact that the 'owner retains control and unrestricted access' ([1990] 1 AC 417 at 467A-B per Lord Oliver of Aylmerton). The mere fact that contractually stipulated attendance is declined by the occupier or is never actually provided by the owner does not necessarily convert a licence into a tenancy (*Crancour Ltd v Da Silvaesa* (1986) 52 P & CR 204 at 212 per Ralph Gibson LJ, 230 per Purchas LJ).

5 *Antoniades v Villiers* [1990] 1 AC 417 at 459B-D per Lord Templeman, 466E-G per Lord Oliver of Aylmerton.

6 *Appah v Parncliffe Investments Ltd* [1964] 1 WLR 1064 at 1071; *Luganda v Service Hotels Ltd* [1969] 2 Ch 209 at 217D. See also *Re Canadian Pacific Hotels Ltd and Hodges* (1979) 96 DLR (3d) 313 at 318 (hotel retained 'a general, over-all control of the property').

7 *Marchant v Charters* [1977] 1 WLR 1181 at 1185G-H ('attractive bachelor service apartments', ie bed-sits each with its own gas-ring). This decision was approved in *Street v Mountford* [1985] AC 809 at 824G-825C. See also *Maxwell v Brown* (1982) 35 OR (2d) 770 at 772, where the rules and restrictions imposed by the owner of a rooming house as to cooking privileges and the number of occupants were held sufficient to deny the occupier a 'stake in the room'. Compare, however, *Guppys (Bridport) Ltd v Brookling* (1984) 269 Estates Gazette 846 at 850, where the character of the occupancy depended largely on whether the owner's 'janitor' had exercised effective control over the admission of visitors—particularly of the opposite sex.

8 *Abbeyfield (Harpenden) Society Ltd v Woods* [1968] 1 WLR 374 at 376F-H, as approved in *Street v Mountford* [1985] AC 809 at 824B.

9 It is well established that the 'exclusiveness' of the occupation enjoyed by such persons is not prejudiced or diminished by reason merely of the fact that staff may enter the room daily to make the bed and clean the room or that a landlady has a right of access at all times (see *Luganda v Service Hotels Ltd* [1969] 2 Ch 209 at 219D-F).

10 *Street v Mountford* [1985] AC 809 at 818C. (It was conceded in *Street v Mountford* [1985] AC 809 at 818D, 826B-C, that there had been no provision of attendance or services.) The mere absence of any contracted provision of attendance or services does not, however, guarantee the existence of a tenancy (see *Brooker Settled Estates Ltd v Ayers* (1987) 54 P & CR 165 at 168f (post, p 718).

11 *Crancour Ltd v Da Silvaesa* (1986) 52 P & CR 204 at 211f, 216f per Ralph Gibson LJ.

or to repair and maintain 'only serves to emphasise the fact that the grantee is entitled to exclusive possession and is a tenant.'[12]

(4) Identification of the 'nature and quality' of an occupancy

Even when the general parameters of the notion of tenancy are established, it may sometimes remain difficult to know whether a particular agreement, on its true construction, confers in strict terms a right of 'exclusive possession' referable to the existence of a tenancy.[13] The court must therefore scrutinise the 'nature and quality'[14] of any disputed occupancy in order to determine whether the occupier has been granted the right to 'exclusive possession' in the relevant sense.[15] The task of the court is to ascertain the 'true bargain between the parties'[16] and this task may prove highly elusive.[17]

(a) Irrelevant or ambivalent factors

The determination whether a given occupancy constitutes a lease or a licence is ultimately 'a question of law. . .to be decided upon the basis of the primary facts'.[18] The difficulty facing the court is that many of the 'primary facts' remain neutral or ambivalent as between tenancy and licence. It is, for instance, strictly irrelevant whether a disputed occupancy is permanent or merely temporary.[19] It is likewise irrelevant whether the premises concerned are furnished or unfurnished.[20] It is of no significance that the parties refer to the money consideration for the occupancy as 'rent' or even make use of a 'rent book'.[1] The potential application of protective legislation is entirely irrelevant to the problem of determining the legal effect of the rights granted

12 *Street v Mountford* [1985] AC 809 at 818C–D. See also *Dellneed Ltd v Chin* (1987) 53 P & CR 172 at 184; *Antoniades v Villiers* [1990] 1 AC 417 at 459G–H per Lord Templeman.

13 This much was conceded by Lord Templeman himself in *Street v Mountford* [1985] AC 809 at 826G–H. The difficulty is intensified where the relevant agreement is purely oral. Here the existence of a right of exclusive possession can be established by an examination of the 'circumstances and facts of the case' directed towards ascertaining whether the 'proper inference is that such a term was included by means of and derived from a history of such a right being recognised' (*Smith v Northside Developments Ltd* (1988) 55 P & CR 164 at 167 per Arnold P).

14 *Marchant v Charters* [1977] 1 WLR 1181 at 1185G per Lord Denning MR; *Crancour Ltd v Da Silvaesa* (1986) 52 P & CR 204 at 229 per Purchas LJ.

15 *Street v Mountford* [1985] AC 809 at 825B–C.

16 *Aslan v Murphy* [1990] 1 WLR 766 at 770C per Lord Donaldson of Lymington MR.

17 See eg *Hadjiloucas v Crean* [1988] 1 WLR 1006 at 1025B, where Mustill LJ regretted that 'this important jurisdiction, which the judges have to exercise in difficult circumstances on the basis of evidence which is often fragmentary and imprecise, should appear to be governed by rules which do not always yield a direct and unequivocal solution.'

18 *Carden v Choudhury* (Unreported, Court of Appeal, 29 February 1984) per Arnold P.

19 *Marchant v Charters* [1977] 1 WLR 1181 at 1185F. The mere effluxion of time cannot convert a licensee into a tenant (see *Crancour Ltd v Da Silvaesa* (1986) 52 P & CR 204 at 212 per Ralph Gibson LJ).

20 *Marchant v Charters* [1977] 1 WLR 1181 at 1185F.

1 Such terminology provides no more than a 'convenient means of verbal reference to the payments' (*Street v Mountford* (1984) 49 P & CR 324 at 328 per Slade LJ). See also *Lewis v Bell* [1985] 1 NSWLR 731 at 738G.

by an agreement for residential occupation.[2] No 'decisive importance' is, in general, attached to the exercise or failure to exercise rights provided for in the parties' agreement.[3] Thus, even though there has in fact been no performance of a contractual obligation to provide the occupier with 'attendance', the mere fact that such services were stipulated for in the parties' agreement may be effective to classify their status in terms of licence rather than tenancy.[4]

(b) Consideration of documents and circumstances

It is well established that, in seeking to assess whether the 'nature and quality' of an occupancy disclose a grant of 'exclusive possession' in the strict sense, the court will look to the substance of the disputed transaction and not merely to its external form.[5] In determining whether the grantee was entitled to 'exclusive possession' or merely to the use of land 'for limited purposes', the court must consider 'the purpose of the grant, the terms of the grant and the surrounding circumstances'.[6]

The written terms of any agreement are always 'of prime importance' and frequently require 'a meticulous perusal'.[7] The court should apply the techniques of construction of the ordinary law of contract,[8] although judges are reluctant to 'award marks for drafting' or to 'draw up a "shopping list" of clauses' in any given agreement which argue respectively in favour of either tenancy or licence.[9] Nevertheless a careful construction of any relevant written agreement will usually indicate whether a right of exclusive possession has been genuinely conferred on or genuinely denied to the occupier concerned. The issue is one of substance: if the agreement confers and imposes on the grantee in substance the rights and obligations of a tenant, and on

2 *Street v Mountford* [1985] AC 809 at 819G–H per Lord Templeman; *Crancour Ltd v Da Silvaesa* (1986) 52 P & CR 204 at 214f, 230; *Antoniades v Villiers* [1990] 1 AC 417 at 445E–F per Bingham LJ. See *Aldrington Garages Ltd v Fielder* (1978) 37 P & CR 461 at 468, where Geoffrey Lane LJ said that if the parties stipulate expressly for a licence rather than a tenancy 'they should not be prevented from that course by the courts bending over backwards to ensure that landlords do not manage to avoid the provisions of the Rent Acts.' In his view the mere fact that such agreements might 'result in enhanced profits for the owners does not necessarily mean that the agreements should be construed as tenancies rather than as licences.' The decision in *Aldrington Garages Ltd v Fielder* was disapproved in *Street v Mountford* [1985] AC 809 at 826A, but there was no criticism of this particular dictum. See also *Antoniades*, supra at 445C–E per Bingham LJ.

3 *Crancour Ltd v Da Silvaesa* (1986) 52 P & CR 204 at 230 per Purchas LJ. See also *Hadjiloucas v Crean* [1988] 1 WLR 1006 at 1024F–1025A per Mustill LJ.

4 *Crancour Ltd v Da Silvaesa* (1986) 52 P & CR 204 at 222 per Nicholls LJ. Compare, however, *Aslan v Murphy* (No 1) [1990] 1 WLR 766 at 773G–H per Lord Donaldson of Lymington MR.

5 *Antoniades v Villiers* [1990] 1 AC 417 at 466G–H per Lord Oliver of Aylmerton. See also *Shell-Mex & BP Ltd v Manchester Garages Ltd* [1971] 1 WLR 612 at 618D–E per Buckley LJ; *Demuren v Seal Estates Ltd* (1978) 249 Estates Gazette 440 at 444; *University of Reading v Johnson-Houghton* (1985) 276 Estates Gazette 1353 at 1355; *Gatien Motor Co Ltd v Continental Oil Co of Ireland Ltd* [1979] IR 406 at 414, 420.

6 *Street v Mountford* [1985] AC 809 at 817G–H per Lord Templeman.

7 *Hadjiloucas v Crean* [1988] 1 WLR 1006 at 1022E–F per Mustill LJ. 'Subject to the agreement on its face appearing to be a sham, the effect in law of the agreement must depend upon its construction in accordance with the normal rules in the context of its factual matrix and genesis' (*Crancour Ltd v Da Silvaesa* (1986) 52 P & CR 204 at 229 per Purchas LJ).

8 *Hadjiloucas v Crean* [1988] 1 WLR 1006 at 1022G per Mustill LJ.

9 *Crancour Ltd v Da Silvaesa* (1986) 52 P & CR 204 at 230 per Purchas LJ.

the grantor in substance the rights and obligations of a landlord, then this finding is indeed conclusive in favour of tenancy.[10] If this is not the case, the grantee must then be a licensee.

The presence or absence of a right to 'exclusive possession' may be inferable from some of the written terms of an occupancy agreement. In *Lewis v Bell*,[11] for instance, the Court of Appeal of New South Wales pointed out the special significance of any terms bearing upon the transferability of the occupier's rights. A leasehold estate is inherently assignable to third parties,[12] and a term which affirms the occupier's right to transfer his entitlement to a third party carries the clear implication that the occupier has an 'exclusive possession' sufficient to sustain such a transfer. Somewhat paradoxically, a term which expressly prohibits the assignment of the occupier's rights may likewise reinforce the occupier's claim to 'exclusive possession', since the specific restraint on transfer impliedly concedes that the occupier would otherwise have been competent to alienate his rights.[13] However, a term which stipulates merely that the occupier's rights are personal to him and are for that reason non-transferable has the effect of negativing any implication of 'exclusive possession'.[14] Similarly a term which entitles the owner at his convenience to move the occupier from one room to another within the same house fairly clearly negatives any claim of 'exclusive possession' which the occupier might otherwise have in respect of the room originally allocated to him.[15]

(c) The relevance of intention

The tenancy character of arrangements for occupation is not, except in one marginal sense, controlled by the subjective intentions of the parties. Since a tenancy comprises at its core a contractual nexus, it is clear that the parties to a tenancy must at least intend to enter into a legally binding contractual relationship. Their subjective intentions are otherwise largely irrelevant in determining the quality or legal status of the rights created by their contract.[16]

10 *Addiscombe Garden Estates Ltd v Crabbe* [1958] 1 QB 513 at 522 per Jenkins LJ. Parker LJ thought, for example, that the inclusion of a covenant for quiet enjoyment was 'inconsistent with the document being a licence' ([1958] 1 QB 513 at 529). See also *Rental Bond Board v Bayman Development Pty Ltd* (1985) 3 BPR 9670 at 9676 per Street CJ.

11 [1985] 1 NSWLR 731 at 735G–736A per Mahoney JA.

12 Post, p 734.

13 See *Dellneed Ltd v Chin* (1987) 53 P & CR 172 at 185. References to subletting may not connote quite so clearly the existence of a tenancy (see *Lewis v Bell* [1985] 1 NSWLR 731 at 738G). See, however, *Rental Bond Board v Bayman Development Pty Ltd* (1985) 3 BPR 9670 at 9676 per Street CJ (covenant not to part with possession 'more akin to a fetter on the right of possession than the absence of such a right'). Compare *Tower Hamlets LBC v Miah* [1992] 2 WLR 761 at 764G–H, where the Court of Appeal ignored the obvious implications to be drawn from a specific provision requiring that a local authority grantee do nothing to create 'any secure or other tenancy'.

14 *Dresden Estates Ltd v Collinson* (1988) 55 P & CR 47 at 53 per Glidewell LJ; *Lewis v Bell* [1985] 1 NSWLR 731 at 735G per Mahoney JA.

15 *Crancour Ltd v Da Silvaesa* (1986) 52 P & CR 204 at 222.

16 See *Crancour Ltd v Da Silvaesa* (1986) 52 P & CR 204 at 230, where Purchase LJ stressed that no decisive significance is to be attached to the 'actual subjective intention of the parties, even if they are ad idem, . . .unless they do not intend to enter into the agreement at all'.

As Lord Templeman declared in *Street v Mountford*,[17] 'the only intention which is relevant is the intention demonstrated by the agreement to grant exclusive possession for a term at a rent.' The presence of a tenancy is thus a coldly objective issue of definition,[18] and the identification of a given occupancy as a lease or a licence is ultimately 'a question of law. . .to be decided upon the basis of the primary facts'.[19] Several related consequences follow.

(i) No intention to enter into binding legal relations It has long been clear that in certain fairly rare situations a tenancy classification is ruled out precisely because the relevant parties, while agreeing on a temporary occupation of the land, lack any intention to enter into a binding legal or contractual relationship.[20] In these circumstances the occupier's status, not being that of a trespasser,[1] is simply that of a licensee.[2] Such a hiatus of contractual intent was demonstrated, for instance, in *Garland v Johnson*.[3] Here a flat-owner who had recently been the victim of a burglary reached a 'gentleman's agreement' with a casual acquaintance, under which the latter was given a temporary right to occupy the former's flat during his absence abroad. The Court of Appeal upheld the existence of a mere licence, partly on the ground that the occupancy was a personal occupancy 'in the role of a caretaker or a friend looking after the place',[4] and partly because the agreed payments to be made by the occupier were so minimal as to fall far short of an economic rent. In truth, the occupier had no 'stake in the land', but had merely been permitted, on part-payment of 'expenses', to occupy the flat 'as a precaution against burglars'.[5] The owner had not sought commercial gain but merely an occupier whom he could trust.[6]

17 [1985] AC 809 at 826G. See also *Royal Philanthropic Society v County* (1985) 276 Estates Gazette 1068 at 1072; *Lewis v Bell* [1985] 1 NSWLR 731 at 736D–737C.

18 'The question. . .is not "what did the parties intend?" The question is, "What is the effect in law of the rights which they actually created?"' (*AG Securities v Vaughan* [1990] 1 AC 417 at 431G per Fox LJ).

19 *Carden v Choudhury* (Unreported, Court of Appeal, 29 February 1984) per Arnold P. The issue is decided on a balance of probabilities (see *University of Reading v Johnson-Houghton* (1985) 276 Estates Gazette 1353 at 1356).

20 'The grant of a legal right cannot be referable to an extra-legal relationship' (*LB of Camden v Shortlife Community Housing* (1992) 90 LGR 358 at 372 per Millett J). See *Street v Mountford* [1985] AC 809 at 826H, where Lord Templeman thought it quite possible that 'surrounding circumstances' may demonstrate a plain absence of any 'intention to create legal relationships'. See also *Hadjiloucas v Crean* [1988] 1 WLR 1006 at 1019D per Mustill LJ.

1 Post, p 891.

2 See Lord Templeman's reference in *Street v Mountford* [1985] AC 809 at 821H-822A to *Facchini v Bryson* [1952] 1 TLR 1386 at 1389, where Denning LJ had indicated that tenancy might be precluded by circumstances which 'negative any intention to create a tenancy.'

3 Unreported, Court of Appeal, 24 February 1982.

4 Per Eveleigh LJ. 'Caretaker's agreements' of this kind seem to have been long accepted in Ireland as giving rise only to a licence (see *Davies v Hilliard* (1967) 101 ILTR 50 at 56; *Gatien Motor Co Ltd v Continental Oil Co of Ireland Ltd* [1979] IR 406 at 421).

5 Per Eveleigh LJ.

6 Once again, the element of overall control seems to have been a decisive factor. Eveleigh LJ noted that the parties had 'treated the place,. . .in their mutual contemplation, not as the [occupier's] flat but as the [owner's] home.'

(ii) Definitional intent is not conclusive Except in the basic sense explained above, the subjective intentions of the parties play no paramount or critical role in delimiting the legal character of their relationship.[7] There is a long-standing doctrine that the superficial label attached by the parties to their transaction is not necessarily definitive of its legal status.[8] The descriptive labels (eg 'lease', 'tenancy' or 'licence') applied by the parties themselves have only a persuasive and not a conclusive quality,[9] and the court retains an undoubted jurisdiction to override any appellation or 'false label' if it does not correspond with the inner reality of the transaction in hand.[10] It is open to the court in appropriate circumstances to regard a transaction, whether described as a 'licence',[11] 'management contract',[12] 'option agreement',[13] 'memorandum of agreement',[14] or otherwise, as constituting in substance a lease. Conversely the court may take the view that a supposed 'lease' or 'tenancy' comprises in truth a mere licence.[15]

There has always of course been some incentive for property owners to mislabel the transaction of tenancy. During the 1970s and 1980s, for instance, the significant extension of statutory control over residential[16] and business[17] tenancies made it increasingly attractive to circumvent such legislation by the grant of a 'licence' as distinct from a 'tenancy'.[18] The decision of the Court of Appeal in *Somma v Hazelhurst and Savelli*[19] gave currency to the

7 '[T]he parties' description of their transaction cannot affect the substance of it' (*Ashburn Anstalt v Arnold* [1989] Ch 1 at 13B per Fox LJ). See also *Nicolaou v Pitt* (1989) 21 HLR 487 at 492 per Mustill LJ ('the categorisation of the agreement as a licence or a tenancy is for the law to decide').

8 *Shell-Mex & BP Ltd v Manchester Garages Ltd* [1971] 1 WLR 612 at 615D, 618D–E; *Aslan v Murphy* [1990] 1 WLR 766 at 770D per Lord Donaldson of Lymington MR; *Antoniades v Villiers* [1990] 1 AC 417 at 466H–467A per Lord Oliver of Aylmerton.

9 See *Aslan v Murphy* [1990] 1 WLR 766 at 770D, where Lord Donaldson of Lymington MR stated that labels 'give no guidance at all' in circumstances in which there is 'enormous pressure on the homeless to agree to any label which will facilitate the obtaining of accommodation'. See also *Guppys (Bridport) Ltd v Brookling* (1984) 269 Estates Gazette 846 at 850.

10 'The court is concerned to enquire into what is the real relationship between the parties' (*Hayes v Seymour-Johns* (1981) 2 BPR 9366 at 9370).

11 See eg *Addiscombe Garden Estates Ltd v Crabbe* [1958] 1 QB 513 at 525; *Demuren v Seal Estates Ltd* (1978) 249 Estates Gazette 440 at 444; *O'Malley v Seymour* (1978) 250 Estates Gazette 1083 at 1088; *University of Reading v Johnson-Houghton* (1985) 276 Estates Gazette 1353 at 1356; *McDonagh v Kent AHA* (Unreported, Court of Appeal, 7 October 1985); *Ashburn Anstalt v Arnold* [1989] Ch 1 at 13B; *Irish Shell and BP Ltd v John Costello Ltd* [1981] ILRM 66 at 71.

12 *Dellneed Ltd v Chin* (1987) 53 P & CR 172 at 185ff. See also *Greenstreet v Moorchat Ltd* (Unreported, Court of Appeal, 1981 G No 3845, 12 November 1982), which concerned a 'management contract' under which the occupier agreed to pay £416,000 per annum ('payable weekly') in return for the privilege of being 'manager' of an all-night cinema in Soho. The Court of Appeal construed this as a lease.

13 *Rental Bond Board v Bayman Development Pty Ltd* (1985) 3 BPR 9670 at 9676ff.

14 *Baron Hamilton v Edgar* (1953) 162 Estates Gazette 568.

15 See eg *Taylor v Caldwell* (1863) 3 B & S 826 at 832, 122 ER 309 at 312; *Clore v Theatrical Properties Ltd and Westby & Co Ltd* [1936] 3 All ER 483 at 490, 491; *R.A. Sanson Investments Ltd v Sanson* (Unreported, Court of Appeal, 11 March 1982).

16 Post, p 873.

17 Post, p 887.

18 See *Antoniades v Villiers* [1990] 1 AC 417 at 459B–D per Lord Templeman, 466E-G per Lord Oliver of Aylmerton.

19 [1978] 1 WLR 1014. See [1979] CLJ 38.

idea that the legal character of a transaction could be stipulated (or overridden) by express agreement between the parties.[20] This meant in effect that the legal status of an occupancy could be dictated by the expressly imposed intention of the stronger bargaining party, who was almost invariably the landowner.[1] It became a fairly common practice for intending occupiers to be required to sign a declaration which expressly denied that their rights were other than those of a licensee.

In *Street v Mountford*[2] the occupier was given a right of exclusive occupancy of a self-contained flat on payment of a weekly 'licence fee'. The agreement signed by the occupier was expressly described as a 'licence agreement', and the occupier specifically and in writing disavowed any intention to take a tenancy.[3] The Court of Appeal felt constrained to hold that, while the 'fact of exclusive occupation' was 'a most important pointer' as to the intentions of the parties, 'their true intentions are the decisive consideration in determining whether an agreement creates a tenancy. . .or a licence.'[4] Here the unequivocal written acknowledgement by the occupier that no tenancy was intended was conclusive in favour of a licence characterisation.[5] This decision was overturned on appeal,[6] the House of Lords deciding that the facts of the case disclosed the existence of a tenancy and not a licence. Lord Templeman, who delivered the only substantial speech, declared that the parties 'cannot turn a tenancy into a licence merely by calling it one.'[7] In his view

> [i]f the agreement satisfied all the requirements of a tenancy, then the agreement produced a tenancy and the parties cannot alter the effect of the agreement by insisting that they only created a licence. The manufacture of a five-pronged implement

20 According to Cumming-Bruce LJ, if both parties intended to create a licence and could 'frame any written agreement in such a way as to demonstrate that it is not really an agreement for a lease masquerading as a licence', the Court could detect no 'reason in law or justice why they should be prevented from achieving that object' ([1978] 1 WLR 1014 at 1024H–1025A). This approach was applied not merely in the residential sector but also in relation to business tenancies (see *Rossvale Ltd v Green* (1979) 250 Estates Gazette 1183; *Matchams Park (Holdings) Ltd v Dommett* (1984) 272 Estates Gazette 549 at 555).

1 See eg *Aldrington Garages Ltd v Fielder* (1978) 37 P & CR 461 at 468; *Sturolson & Co v Weniz* (1984) 272 Estates Gazette 326 at 329f.

2 (1984) 49 P & CR 324, (1984) 271 Estates Gazette 1261. See (1984) 81 Law Soc Gaz 2355 (P.H. Kenny); [1984] JSWL 292 (M.A. Jones); P. Vincent-Jones, *Exclusive Possession and Exclusive Control of Private Rented Housing: A Socio-Legal Critique of the Lease-Licence Distinction*, (1987) 14 J Law and Society 445.

3 The owner of the flat—a local solicitor—later maintained that this form of agreement was explicitly framed with reference to the decisions emerging from the Court of Appeal during the period 1977–1979. He claimed to have 'decided to take the Court of Appeal at its word and drafted a document, using the simplest possible terms, expressed to be a personal non-assignable licence' (see R. Street, *Coach and Horses Trip Cancelled?*, [1985] Conv 328 at 329).

4 (1984) 49 P & CR 324 at 330 per Slade LJ.

5 (1984) 49 P & CR 324 at 331f.

6 [1985] AC 809. In the process the House of Lords overruled *Somma v Hazelhurst and Savelli* ([1985] AC 809 at 825H–826A). For the losing landlord's view, see R. Street, [1985] Conv 328. See also [1985] CLJ 351 (S. Tromans); (1985) LAG Bulletin 77; [1985] All ER Rev 190 (P.J. Clarke); [1986] JSWL 46 (D. Hoath); [1986] Conv 344 (S. Bridge).

7 [1985] AC 809 at 821C.

for manual digging results in a fork even if the manufacturer, unfamiliar with the English language, insists that he intended to make and has made a spade.[8]

Lord Templeman was plainly moved by the consideration that if exclusive possession at a rent for a term does not constitute a tenancy, then 'the distinction between a contractual tenancy and a contractual licence of land becomes wholly unidentifiable.'[9] Unless these three hallmarks are 'decisive', the task of differentiation becomes 'impossible. . .save by reference to the professed intention of the parties or by the judge awarding marks for drafting.'[10]

The ruling in *Street v Mountford* was dramatic and its outcome, on first impression, may seem quite remarkable. The decision provides an extremely powerful confirmation that the 'professed intention of the parties' does not serve as the determinant of the precise legal status of the occupancy agreed by them.[11] Although the occupier had signed a written acknowledgement that she had no tenancy, this was precisely the interest which the House of Lords held had been conferred upon her by the disputed agreement. In placing significant limits on the parties' powers of self-determination, *Street v Mountford* effectively curtails private contractual autonomy in favour of more stringent social regulation of property relationships. In holding that landlord and tenant are not free to contract into different legal categories of relationship, the decision presents an unusually significant demonstration of the constant interplay between bargained outcomes and doctrinal constraints. It illustrates the pervasive tension between the paramount will and the need for systemic conformity, and touches ultimately upon the limits of coercive control over individual freedom to stipulate contractually for a particular status at law.

(d) Shams and pretences

The strictures imposed by protective legislation provide an inevitable temptation for landlords to grant lettings which are contractually structured

8 [1985] AC 809 at 819E–F. The same point was made, perhaps even more graphically, by Bingham LJ in *Antoniades v Villiers* [1990] 1 AC 417 at 444B ('A cat does not become a dog because the parties have agreed to call it a dog'). See also *Voli v Inglewood Shire Council* (1963) 110 CLR 74 at 91 per Windeyer J ('[m]isnomers are not. . .to be used as a means for modifying law').

9 [1985] AC 809 at 825C. See also Lord Templeman at 827A–B.

10 [1985] AC 809 at 826E. Lord Templeman observed that the same realisation had already occurred, a quarter of a century before, in the High Court of Australia. In *Radaich v Smith* (1959) 101 CLR 209 at 222, Windeyer J had emphasised the 'self-contradictory and meaningless' quality of any assertion that a person legally entitled to exclusive possession for a term is a mere licensee. In his view, '[t]o say that a man who has, by agreement with a landlord, a right of exclusive possession for a term is not a tenant is simply to contradict the first proposition by the second.' See also *Goldsworthy Mining Ltd v Federal Commissioner of Taxation* (1973) 128 CLR 199 at 212; *Lapham v Orange City Council* [1968] 2 NSWR 667 at 670f; *Lewis v Bell* [1985] 1 NSWLR 731 at 734E–F.

11 [1985] AC 809 at 819G–H. See *Antoniades v Villiers* [1990] 1 AC 417 at 463H–464A per Lord Templeman ('an express statement of intention is not decisive'). See also *LB of Camden v Shortlife Community Housing* (1992) 90 LGR 358 at 371f per Millett J.

so as to circumvent statutory control.[12] The jurisprudence of landlord and tenant (in common with the law of taxation) has always attempted to maintain a strict distinction between the concepts of 'avoidance' and 'evasion'.[13] 'Avoidance' is the entirely legitimate objective of arranging legal relations so that they do not attract the operation of regulatory legislation.[14] 'Evasion' involves the use of essentially deceptive devices in order to avert the operation of regulatory legislation where it would otherwise clearly apply.[15] For the purpose of policing the often indistinct border between the two concepts, the courts have developed a distinction between 'genuine transactions' and 'shams' which still plays a significant role in the law of landlord and tenant.[16] As Lord Templeman urged in *Street v Mountford*,[17] the courts must 'be astute to detect and frustrate sham devices and artificial transactions whose only object is to disguise the grant of a tenancy and to evade the Rent Acts.'[18]

(i) Ascertainment of the reality of transactions In determining whether an agreement has sought cynically and improperly to conceal the grant of exclusive possession behind the guise of a licence, the primary duty of the court is to seek out 'the substance and reality of the transaction'.[19] In each case the court must establish the true nature of the contractual relationship and 'where the language of licence contradicts the reality of lease, the facts must prevail.'[20] Recent authority has stressed that the court should be

12 By the early 1980s evasive devices had become sufficiently prevalent to cause commentators to question whether the Rent Act had in reality become irrelevant to landlord-tenant relations (see J. Doling, *Have the Rent Acts become irrelevant?*, (1984) 270 Estates Gazette 1148).

13 That the distinction is far from easy is demonstrated by the emergence of the term 'avoision' to denote in tax law the mirky middle-ground between the concepts (see A. Seldon (ed), *Tax Avoision* (London 1979), p 4).

14 The freedom so to order one's affairs has provided a conventional starting-point for the courts in the law of taxation (see *IRC v Duke of Westminster* [1936] AC 1 at 19 per Lord Tomlin; *Helvering v Gregory*, 69 F.2d 809 (1934) at 810 per Judge Learned Hand; but compare now *Furniss v Dawson* [1984] AC 474 at 526F-527E).

15 'A property owner is entitled to arrange his affairs so as not to get his property enmeshed in the Rent Acts. What he is not entitled to do is to arrange his affairs in one way, which brings his property within the Rent Acts, and then to dress them up in another way so as to give the impression that it is outside the Rent Acts' (*O'Malley v Seymour* (1978) 250 Estates Gazette 1083 at 1088 per Lawton LJ).

16 See generally A. Nicol, *Outflanking Protective Legislation—Shams and Beyond*, (1981) 44 MLR 21; [1989] Conv 196 (C. Rodgers).

17 [1985] AC 809 at 825H.

18 See also *Facchini v Bryson*[1952] 1 TLR 1386 at 1390, where Denning LJ pointed out that if the courts were not astute to denounce sham transactions, 'we should make a hole in the Rent Acts through which could be driven—I will not in these days say a coach and four—but an articulated vehicle.'

19 *Antoniades v Villiers* [1990] 1 AC 417 at 466C per Lord Ackner. The 'critical question' is 'not simply how the arrangement is presented to the outside world in the relevant documentation, but what is the true nature of the arrangement' ([1990] 1 AC 417 at 466G-H per Lord Oliver of Aylmerton). See Mustill LJ's reference to 'camouflage' which may 'prevent the transaction from being seen for what it really is' (*Hadjiloucas v Crean* [1988] 1 WLR 1006 at 1022G).

20 *Antoniades v Villiers* [1990] 1 AC 417 at 463C per Lord Templeman. The court should not be astute to find ways of circumventing protective legislation enacted on behalf of tenants (*Hadjiloucas v Crean* [1988] 1 WLR 1006 at 1014F-G per Purchas LJ). See also *Stribling v Wickham* (1989) 21 HLR 381 at 390 per Sir Denys Buckley.

particularly sensitive to the vulnerability of those who seek residential accommodation on the open rental market.[1] As Lord Templeman indicated in *Antoniades v Villiers*,[2] such persons 'may concur in any expression of intention. . .may sign a document couched in any language. . .[and] may sign any number of documents in order to obtain. . .shelter'. Where the benefits of statutory protection cannot legally be contracted away, the language of a supposed licence must therefore be 'examined and construed. . .in order to decide whether the rights and obligations enjoyed and imposed create a licence or a tenancy.'[3] In Lord Templeman's words, any document which 'expresses the intention, genuine or bogus, of both parties or of one party to create a licence will nevertheless create a tenancy if the rights and obligations enjoyed and imposed satisfy the legal requirements of a tenancy.'

In furtherance of this task of construction, the court may have regard not only to the express terms of documents, but also to the surrounding circumstances including any relationship between prospective occupiers, the course of negotiations and the nature and extent of the accommodation together with its intended and actual mode of user.[4] Although the conduct of the parties subsequent to the date of the relevant agreement is, as a matter of contractual principle, irrelevant as an aid to construction,[5] such conduct is both admissible and highly relevant as to 'whether the documents were or were not genuine documents giving effect to the parties' true intentions.'[6] The court is entitled, and indeed obliged, to take an agreement 'otherwise than at its face value'[7] where the agreement is a 'sham'[8] or contains terms which constitute a 'pretence'.[9]

1 Contrast the approach adopted widely during the 1970s and early 1980s and epitomised in such decisions as those of the Court of Appeal in *Somma v Hazelhurst and Savelli* [1978] 1 WLR 1014 (post, p 727); *Buchmann v May* [1978] 2 All ER 993 (post, p 875); *Aldrington Garages Ltd v Fielder* (1979) 39 P & CR 461 (see [1979] CLJ 38). It may well be that during the late 1970s and early 1980s the courts allowed the boundary between legitimate avoidance and illicit evasion of the Rent Act to shift in response to some perceived need to stimulate rather than fetter the supply of rented accommodation in large urban centres. Certainly until the mid-1980s there were few bold decisions overturning the superficial labels attached to evasive devices. See, however, *Walsh v Griffiths-Jones and Durant* [1978] 2 All ER 1002 at 1010d–e (joint tenancy upheld on behalf of two young graduates of Trinity College, Cambridge); *Demuren v Seal Estates Ltd* (1978) 249 Estates Gazette 440 at 442; *O'Malley v Seymour* (1978) 250 Estates Gazette 1083 at 1087f; *R v Rent Officer for LB of Camden, ex parte Plant* (1981) 257 Estates Gazette 713 at 718 per Glidewell J.

2 [1990] 1 AC 417 at 458E–G.

3 For this purpose the court may read together, and treat as 'one single transaction', two or more separate licence agreements with different occupiers of the same premises, where it is clear that the agreements were interdependent and were executed contemporaneously ([1990] 1 AC 417 at 458G–459B, 460H per Lord Templeman, 468C per Lord Oliver of Aylmerton, 475D per Lord Jauncey of Tullichettle).

4 *Antoniades v Villiers* [1990] 1 AC 417 at 458G–H per Lord Templeman.

5 See *Hadjiloucas v Crean* [1988] 1 WLR 1006 at 1024F–1025A per Mustill LJ.

6 *Antoniades v Villiers* [1990] 1 AC 417 at 469C per Lord Oliver of Aylmerton, 475F per Lord Jauncey of Tullichettle.

7 *Hadjiloucas v Crean* [1988] 1 WLR 1006 at 1019D–F per Mustill LJ.

8 See *Snook v London and West Riding Investments Ltd* [1967] 2 QB 786 at 802E per Diplock LJ; *Hoggett v Hoggett* (1980) 39 P & CR 121 at 125.

9 The recent trend has been to move away from the terminology of 'sham devices' and 'artificial transactions' towards the terminology of 'pretence' (see *Antoniades v Villiers* [1990] 1 AC 417 at 462H per Lord Templeman). See also *Aslan v Murphy* [1990] 1 WLR 766 at 770G–H per Lord Donaldson of Lymington MR. In *Hadjiloucas v Crean* [1988] 1 WLR 1006 at 1019F, Mustill LJ drew a distinction between the 'sham' (which wilfully misrepresents the

(ii) Identification of misleading terms In *Antoniades v Villiers*,[10] Lord Templeman indicated that, in seeking to identify elements of 'pretence' in an occupation agreement, the court must look beyond the parties' expression of intention and must 'pay attention to the facts and surrounding circumstances and to what people do as well as to what people say.' Any elements of 'pretence' detected in this process may then be eliminated or discarded from the agreement as 'obviously inconsistent with the realities of the situation', thereby isolating the genuine elements of the agreement as the basis for ascertaining the true nature of the transaction.[11]

In practice the real clue to the existence of severable 'pretences' seems to be the inclusion of written terms which are so inconsistent,[12] incomprehensible or improbable[13] that they cannot seriously have been intended to be operative or effective between the parties. In *Antoniades v Villiers*,[14] for instance, an unmarried couple entered into identical contemporaneous 'licence' agreements with the owner of a small attic flat. Both agreements recited, amidst multiple references to the terminology of 'licensor' and 'licensee', that the owner was unwilling to grant exclusive possession of any part of the premises and instead reserved on his own behalf a right 'at any time' to use the premises in common with the licensee 'and such other licensees or invitees as the licensor may permit from time to time to use the said rooms.' Each 'licensee' expressly agreed to 'use his best endeavours amicably and peaceably to share the use of the rooms' with others. An addendum to the document provided that the flat was 'for single people sharing' and accordingly each 'licensee', in signing this addendum, contracted to vacate the flat on marrying 'any occupier of the flat'. The owner nevertheless supplied a double bed on the express request of the two occupiers and throughout their occupancy of the flat the owner made no attempt to use any of the rooms or to authorise their use by third parties.[15]

true agreement between the parties) and the case where, although the document 'does precisely reflect the true agreement', its language or superficial label indicates that 'it falls into one legal category, whereas when properly analysed in the light of the surrounding circumstances it can be seen to fall into another.'

10 [1990] 1 AC 417 at 463H-464A.

11 See *Hadjiloucas v Crean* [1988] 1 WLR 1006 at 1023H-1024A per Mustill LJ. See also Purchas LJ at 1013H-1014A; *Duke v Wynne* [1990] 1 WLR 766 at 775H-776A.

12 See eg *Demuren v Seal Estates Ltd* (1979) 249 Estates Gazette 440 at 443, where despite the payment of a year's rent by post-dated cheques the 'licensor' retained a right to terminate the 'licence' at any time on one week's notice. In upholding a tenancy, the Court of Appeal found these terms 'irreconcilable' and pointed out that there was 'something so badly wrong with this agreement that one is bound to look at it with the gravest suspicion.'

13 See *Aslan v Murphy (No 1)* [1990] 1 WLR 766 at 772H-773A, where the Court of Appeal held that the 'true bargain between the parties' could not sensibly include a 'wholly unrealistic' provision that the 'licensee' should vacate his rented room every day between 10.30 am and midday (see [1990] JSWL 128 (P.T. Evans)). See also *Crancour Ltd v Da Silvaesa* (1986) 52 P & CR 204 at 215, where Ralph Gibson LJ considered a similar set of conditions to be 'astonishingly extreme' and 'bizarre'. Nicholls LJ found the agreement 'so extraordinary. . .that it calls for an explanation' ((1986) 52 P & CR 204 at 224).

14 [1990] 1 AC 417. See [1989] CLJ 19 (C. Harpum); [1989] Conv 128 (P.F. Smith); (1989) 52 MLR 408 (J. Hill); (1989) 105 LQR 165 (P.V. Baker).

15 [1990] 1 AC 417 at 458B.

The agreements involved in *Antoniades v Villiers* conformed closely to the standard pattern of the 'non-exclusive occupation licence' which became prevalent in England during the 1980s. When the status of these agreements was challenged in *Antoniades v Villiers*, the House of Lords unanimously declared them to contain not a licence but a disguised tenancy within the protection of the Rent Act 1977.[16] In the view taken by the House of Lords, the agreements were riddled with 'pretence', but once the elements of 'pretence' were cut away the documents plainly revealed the existence of a term of years granted to the occupiers as joint tenants.

In the light of the intended use of the flat as a quasi-matrimonial home, the House of Lords pointed out that there was 'an air of total unreality about these documents read as separate and individual licences'.[17] No 'realistic significance' could be attached to the owner's reservation of a supposed right to share, or authorise a stranger to share, accommodation which had been 'specifically adapted for the occupation by a couple living together.'[18] The physical circumstances of the small attic flat, with its sloping roof and limited facilities, were clearly so unsuitable for multiple occupation that nobody could seriously have imagined that the parties had genuinely contemplated a sharing arrangement with either the owner or limitless numbers of strangers.[19] It was equally implausible to suppose that the young couple had each genuinely undertaken, as appeared from the express terms of their agreements, to discharge all liabilities for gas and electricity by whomsoever consumed in the flat and to accept responsibility for the defaults of other nominee occupiers over whose behaviour they could have had no control.[20] The 'bizarre results'[1] produced by the literal operation of the agreements

16 Post, p 873.

17 [1990] 1 AC 417 at 467H per Lord Oliver of Aylmerton.

18 [1990] 1 AC 417 at 468A per Lord Oliver of Aylmerton. Lord Jauncey of Tullichettle noted (at 476D–E) that, read literally, the 'common user' clause would have enabled the 'licensor' to 'pack the flat with as many people as could find some sleeping space therein.' An unlimited number of strangers could have been permitted to share the flat with the young couple 'even to the extent of sharing the joys of the double bed.' See *Somma v Hazelhurst and Savelli* [1978] 1 WLR 1014 where, at first instance, a county court judge had thought it a 'most revolting' idea that a 'licensor' should have reserved the right to introduce a substitute 'licensee' of a different sex into a context of non-exclusive sharing. (This objection cut little ice in the Court of Appeal, Cumming-Bruce LJ indicating ([1978] 1 WLR 1014 at 1028E–G) that moralistic argument on this point was somewhat irrelevant given the status of the current occupiers' relationship!)

19 In so far as the agreements reserved for the owner a right of joint occupation, Lord Templeman considered such a power incapable of lawful exercise. Without a court possession order under Rent Act 1977, s 98 (post, p 878), such entry into possession by a landlord would quite improperly constitute an ouster of the entire Rent Act scheme for the protection of tenants ([1990] 1 AC 417 at 461C–462C). This reasoning is open to query as a petitio principii (see (1989) 52 MLR 408 at 411 (J. Hill)), but Lord Templeman was certainly correct in thinking that if a right of common user 'at any time' were held legitimate, every tenancy agreement could be re-labelled a 'licence' and contracted out of the Rent Act by a simple reservation of rights of shared possession which the owner never in fact intended to exercise.

20 [1990] 1 AC 417 at 467H–468A per Lord Oliver of Aylmerton, 476B-D per Lord Jauncey of Tullichettle.

1 [1990] 1 AC 417 at 476B per Lord Jauncey of Tullichettle.

compelled the conclusion that such unrealistic clauses had not been 'seriously intended' to have any practical effect or to serve any other purpose than to avert 'the ordinary legal consequences attendant upon letting the appellants into possession at a monthly rent.'[2]

The unreality permeating the agreements was only accentuated by the owner's reservation of a right of eviction without court order[3] and by the contracted forfeiture of the couple's occupation rights 'if their double-bedded romance blossomed into wedding bells.'[4] The 'pretence' character of all these provisions was underlined by the fact that the owner had never in practice sought to enforce any of his rights in their literal terms.[5] Once these colourable elements within the agreements were stripped away as 'pro non scripto',[6] it became obvious that the residue of rights and obligations comprised a joint tenancy which had been only barely concealed behind the 'smokescreen' or 'window-dressing' of the supposed 'licences'.[7]

(5) Arrangements for multiple occupation

Difficulties of a different kind are raised in determining the character of informal arrangements for shared or multiple occupation. It is clear that the shared occupation of rented premises may give rise to alternative analyses that each occupier has exclusive possession (and therefore a tenancy) of a distinct part of the premises[8] *or* that all the occupiers are licensees[9] *or* that some of them (to a maximum of four[10]) hold as joint tenants *or* even that one or more, acting as tenant, may have granted an occupation licence

2 [1990] 1 AC 417 at 468A–B per Lord Oliver of Aylmerton. The various forms of 'pretence' contained in the agreements were explained by the fact that the owner's 'real intention was to rely on the language of the agreement to escape the Rent Acts' ([1990] 1 AC 417 at 463B per Lord Templeman).

3 [1990] 1 AC 417 at 468B per Lord Oliver of Aylmerton (who considered that this right 'cannot seriously have been thought to be effective').

4 [1990] 1 AC 417 at 463F per Lord Templeman.

5 [1990] 1 AC 417 at 458B, 463F–G per Lord Templeman, 476G–H per Lord Jauncey of Tullichettle.

6 [1990] 1 AC 417 at 477A per Lord Jauncey of Tullichettle.

7 In *Street v Mountford* [1985] AC 809 at 825G, the House of Lords had already overruled the contrary conclusion reached on almost identical facts in *Somma v Hazelhurst and Savelli* [1978] 1 WLR 1014 (where in reality the joint occupiers had taken a room in order that they might 'live together in quasi-connubial bliss making weekly payments'). See also *Caplan v Marden* (1986) Legal Action 30, 136 NLJ 131 (joint tenancy upheld where three students had been granted three identical non-exclusive occupation licences).

8 This analysis would apply where, for instance, each occupier has been granted exclusive possession of at least *some* accommodation (eg a private bed-sitting room) in an otherwise shared house. Exactly this situation is envisaged as a potential protected tenancy pursuant to Rent Act 1977, s 22 (post, p 875).

9 In extreme cases the licence conclusion is compelled simply because the sharing of premises has become so comprehensive as to preclude any claim by anybody to exclusive possession of any part of the premises (see eg *Choudhury v Meah* (Unreported, Court of Appeal, 21 September 1981), where the overcrowding of premises in Soho was so gross as to destroy any possible claims of exclusive possession).

10 Trustee Act 1925, s 34(2) (ante, p 100).

to the other occupier or occupiers.[11] In such contexts the distinction between tenancy and licence may prove problematical.

(a) Doctrinal starting-points

The fixed points of reference are few, but they seem to follow from well established doctrine. It is elementary that no form of holding which fails to display the 'four unities' of joint ownership[12] can itself comprise a joint tenancy. Where the 'four unities' are evidenced by two or more persons who hold a term of years in the same premises, they must hold together as joint tenants. Collectively such persons are entitled 'to exclude everyone other than those who have concurrent estates.'[13] Such persons, as joint owners of the leasehold estate, bear a joint and several liability for the whole rent.[14] They are vulnerable to the operation of survivorship and are subject in their dealings to all the inhibitions placed by law on unilateral action by one joint tenant. Thus, for instance, no joint tenant, acting alone and without the concurrence of the others, may validly terminate the lease[15] (unless it is a periodic tenancy[16]) or surrender the term to the landlord.[17] These rules have no parallel application to mere licensees.[18]

(b) A single occupation agreement

Where one document is used to confer concurrent rights of occupation on two or more persons, the true character of the transaction falls to be determined in the manner outlined by the House of Lords in *Street v Mountford*[19] and *Antoniades v Villiers*.[20] After the severance of any 'sham' term or 'pretence' which serves to disguise reality, the transaction must be identified as either a joint tenancy or a joint licence in accordance with ordinary principles of landlord-tenant law. A conclusion in favour of joint tenancy causes no great conceptual difficulty,[1] and may even be facilitated by the fact that only one document has been used to record the expression of joint rights and obligations. Since joint tenants comprise collectively one person in contemplation of law, the unity of possession which crucially identifies joint ownership is not inconsistent with the exclusiveness of possession which is integral to the concept of tenancy.

11 See *Baker v Turner* [1950] AC 401 at 417; *Rogers v Hyde* [1951] 2 KB 923 at 932.
12 Ante, p 467.
13 *AG Securities v Vaughan* [1990] 1 AC 417 at 471G per Lord Oliver of Aylmerton. See also Lord Oliver at 469H.
14 *AG Securities v Vaughan* [1990] 1 AC 417 at 469G-H per Lord Oliver of Aylmerton, 473E per Lord Jauncey of Tullichettle. It seems that the absence of joint obligations of payment is evidence of a disunity of interest inconsistent with a claim of joint tenancy (*Mikeover Ltd v Brady* [1989] 3 All ER 618 at 625e-f, 627a-e; (1990) 106 LQR 215 (J.L. Barton); *Stribling v Wickham* (1989) 21 HLR 381 at 390).
15 *AG Securities v Vaughan* [1990] 1 AC 417 at 473E-F per Lord Jauncey of Tullichettle.
16 Ante, p 469.
17 Ante, p 469.
18 *AG Securities v Vaughan* [1990] 1 AC 417 at 471F-472A per Lord Oliver of Aylmerton.
19 [1985] AC 809 (ante, p 722).
20 [1990] 1 AC 417 (ante, p 726).
1 There was surprisingly belated statutory recognition of the possibility that a leasehold may be co-owned (Housing Act 1980, s 27(3) [now Housing Act 1985, s 81]). See *Howson v Buxton* (1929) 139 LT 504 at 506 per Scrutton LJ; J. Martin, [1978] Conv 436.

(c) Interdependent occupation agreements

Slightly more difficulty arises where occupation rights are conferred on a number of persons by means of more than one document. In *Antoniades v Villiers*[2] Lord Templeman acknowledged the possibility of circumstances where two or more documents collectively disclose such an interdependent character that they must be read together as conferring a joint right of exclusive possession appropriate to tenancy.[3] Thus, for example, concurrent 'licences' granted to a husband and wife in respect of a one-bedroomed flat would create a joint tenancy if each 'licence' envisaged joint occupation only with the other spouse.[4] The tenancy character of such interdependent agreements is not diminished by the fact that the landlord 'may choose to require' each of the joint tenants to agree expressly to pay his or her proportionate part of the total rent.[5] Nor does it detract from the occupiers' status as joint tenants that the documents contain terms, at variance with 'the substance and reality of the transaction',[6] which purport to deny them a collective right of exclusive possession.[7]

(d) Multiple sharing by a shifting population of occupants

Problems of an insuperable nature tend to afflict any attempt to apply a tenancy classification to loose informal arrangements under which premises are shared by a constantly shifting population of occupants. Such multiple sharing—the classic flat-share prevalent amongst young urban professionals—frequently involves contemporaneous and overlapping occupation by a number of previously unconnected individuals. This context differs vitally from that envisaged by interdependent agreements, in that multiple sharers do not usually enter into occupation simultaneously in pursuance of any preconceived arrangement inter se. In *AG Securities v Vaughan*,[8] for instance, four individual occupiers shared a four-bedroom flat under four separate non-exclusive licence agreements with the owner, each of a different date at a different monthly rent and for different periods of six months. Each occupier had his own bedroom, sharing communal facilities in the flat with the other residents, and as one occupier moved out a replacement was found to take over his vacancy.

2 [1990] 1 AC 417 at 458G–459B.
3 Ante, p 726. It goes to the interdependent quality of such agreements that neither or none of the prospective occupiers would have been prepared to enter into the transaction alone. See eg *Antoniades v Villiers* [1990] 1 AC 417 at 460H per Lord Templeman ('Both would have signed or neither').
4 This in effect was the analysis accorded the two 'licence' agreements at the centre of *Antoniades v Villiers* [1990] 1 AC 417 at 460H–461B, 468C (ante, p 726).
5 *Antoniades v Villiers* [1990] 1 AC 417 at 461B per Lord Templeman. See also *Walsh v Griffiths-Jones and Durant* [1978] 2 All ER 1002 at 1010a–b or *Demuren v Seal Estates Ltd* (1978) 249 Estates Gazette 440 at 443.
6 *Antoniades v Villiers* [1990] 1 AC 417 at 466C per Lord Ackner.
7 This is the approach which, as Lord Templeman indicated in *Antoniades v Villiers* [1990] 1 AC 417 at 465D–F, should have been applied to the facts in *Hadjiloucas v Crean* [1988] 1 WLR 1006. See also *Nicolaou v Pitt* (1989) 21 HLR 487 at 491ff.
8 [1990] 1 AC 417. See [1989] Conv 128 (P.F. Smith).

In the absence of any assertion that any occupier held a separate tenancy in respect of his own individual bedroom,[9] the House of Lords held that this factual matrix did not enable the four 'licensees' in residence at any given moment collectively to claim a tenancy in respect of the entire flat.[10] As Lord Jauncey of Tullichettle pointed out, any joint tenancy asserted by them would be 'notably deficient in the four unities of interest, title, time and possession'.[11] Their rights and obligations having initially been several, they could not by some 'legal alchemy' ever become joint.[12] There was no artificiality in the terms of the licences themselves,[13] and indeed only the 'highest degree of artificiality' could force 'into the mould of a joint tenancy' contracts which had been made at different times and on different terms.[14] In particular the disunity of time could not be repaired by recourse to the 'strange and unnatural theory' that successive alterations in the membership of the flat-sharing group brought about some implied surrender of an existing tenancy followed immediately by an implied grant of a new joint tenancy to the group as most recently constituted.[15] Moreover even if some joint tenancy could be assembled from the facts it would necessarily involve the untenable assertion that a rule of survivorship would operate in the event of the death of any one occupier.[16] It would also entail the surprising consequence that any occupier could, unilaterally and without wider reference, terminate the occupation rights of all after the expiry of any six month period.[17]

(6) The lease-licence distinction in the non-residential sector

The task of distinguishing between tenancy and licence sometimes arises outside the residential sector in relation to other forms of occupancy. Although classification in the non-residential sector cannot, of course, rest upon the

9 Ironically, there are indications that such an assertion might conceivably have been more successful than the claim made to a tenancy in respect of the entire premises (see [1990] 1 AC 417 at 460E per Lord Templeman, 466B-C per Lord Ackner, 471B-C per Lord Oliver of Aylmerton, 473B per Lord Jauncey of Tullichettle).

10 See also *Stribling v Wickham* (1989) 21 HLR 381 at 389f; [1989] Conv 192 (J.E. Martin).

11 [1990] 1 AC 417 at 474F. This fatal flaw had already been exposed in Sir George Waller's dissenting judgment in the Court of Appeal ([1990] 1 AC 417 at 436F). See also 472B per Lord Oliver of Aylmerton. It is not sufficient that the occupiers have unity of possession, time and title if they do not also have unity of interest (see *Mikeover Ltd v Brady* [1989] 3 All ER 618 at 625d-f per Slade LJ).

12 [1990] 1 AC 417 at 454A per Lord Bridge of Harwich. See also *Stribling v Wickham* (1989) 21 HLR 381 at 389 per Parker LJ.

13 [1990] 1 AC 417 at 470C-D per Lord Oliver of Aylmerton.

14 [1990] 1 AC 417 at 454C. In the absence of interdependent agreements, each occupier's several liability in respect of disparate amounts of rent was regarded as highly inimical to any suggestion of joint tenancy ([1990] 1 AC 417 at 471H-472A per Lord Oliver of Aylmerton).

15 [1990] 1 AC 417 at 472A per Lord Oliver of Aylmerton, 474D-E per Lord Jauncey of Tullichettle.

16 [1990] 1 AC 417 at 460G per Lord Templeman.

17 According to Lord Jauncey of Tullichettle, any holding over would involve a 'springing interest' the continuance of which would require the consent of all parties to the lease ([1990] 1 AC 417 at 473E-F).

borderline between 'tenant' and 'lodger',[18] the courts seem to have been prepared in the context of commercial premises[19] and agricultural land[20] to refer to broadly the same indicia which identify a tenancy in the residential sphere.[1]

In the business context, for instance, the courts have tended just as consistently to invoke the criterion of 'overall control' as the determining factor in the identification of a tenancy. In *Shell-Mex and BP Ltd v Manchester Garages Ltd*,[2] the Court of Appeal construed an agreement relating to a petrol filling station as a merely personal licence. Lord Denning MR attached particular significance to a stipulation contained in the agreement that the owners should be allowed unimpeded access to the premises, observing that this clause seemed to connote that the owners 'remain in possession themselves'.[3] Everything turns, however, on 'the nature of the transaction itself' as disclosed by the written terms of the occupancy and the surrounding circumstances.[4] In *Dresden Estates Ltd v Collinson*,[5] for instance, the Court of Appeal found that a business occupancy was excluded from having tenancy character by reason of express terms which, without artifice, had entitled the owner to require the occupier to transfer his occupation to other premises belonging to the owner.[6]

4. FLEXIBILITY OF LEASEHOLD ARRANGEMENTS

The potential flexibility of leasehold arrangements may be demonstrated with reference to the following diagram:

18 See eg *Dresden Estates Ltd v Collinson* (1988) 55 P & CR 47 at 52 per Glidewell LJ.

19 See eg *London & Associated Investment Trust PLC v Calow* [1986] 2 EGLR 80 at 84D per Judge Paul Baker QC; *Dellneed Ltd v Chin* (1987) 53 P & CR 172 at 187. Results are not always uniform or consistent. Compare *Kewal Investments Ltd v Arthur Maiden Ltd* [1990] 1 EGLR 193 at 194G–H (no tenancy in respect of advertising panels) and *Rochester Poster Services Ltd v Dartford BC* (1991) 63 P & CR 88 at 93 (tenancy).

20 See eg *Colchester BC v Smith* [1991] Ch 448 at 483G–484A; *Ashdale Land & Property Co Ltd v Manners* [1992] 34 EG 76 at 78f. See, however, *McCarthy v Bence* [1990] 1 EGLR 1; [1991] Conv 58 (C. Rodgers), 207 (M. Slater).

1 There has been a suggestion that the courts may not scrutinise non-residential agreements quite so carefully in order to detect possible shams or pretence terms ((1987) 50 MLR 655 at 660 (S. Bridge)). See, however, *Dellneed Ltd v Chin* (1987) 53 P & CR 172 at 185ff.

2 [1971] 1 WLR 612.

3 [1971] 1 WLR 612 at 616B-C, approved in *Street v Mountford* [1985] AC 809 at 824D–E. See also *University of Reading v Johnson-Houghton* (1985) 276 Estates Gazette 1353, where a grant of rights to train and exercise racehorses was scrutinised most carefully in order to discover whether the grantee had acquired a right of exclusive possession. The status of the agreement as a tenancy was confirmed when it appeared that the grantee had a right to exclude even the owner from the area concerned. See [1986] Conv 275 (C.P. Rodgers).

4 See also *London & Associated Investment Trust Plc v Calow* [1986] 2 EGLR 80 at 84D.

5 (1988) 55 P & CR 47 at 53f. See [1987] Conv 220 (P.F. Smith); (1987) 50 MLR 655 (S. Bridge).

6 See also *Smith v Northside Developments Ltd* (1988) 55 P & CR 164 at 167ff; [1989] Conv 55 (J.E.M.).

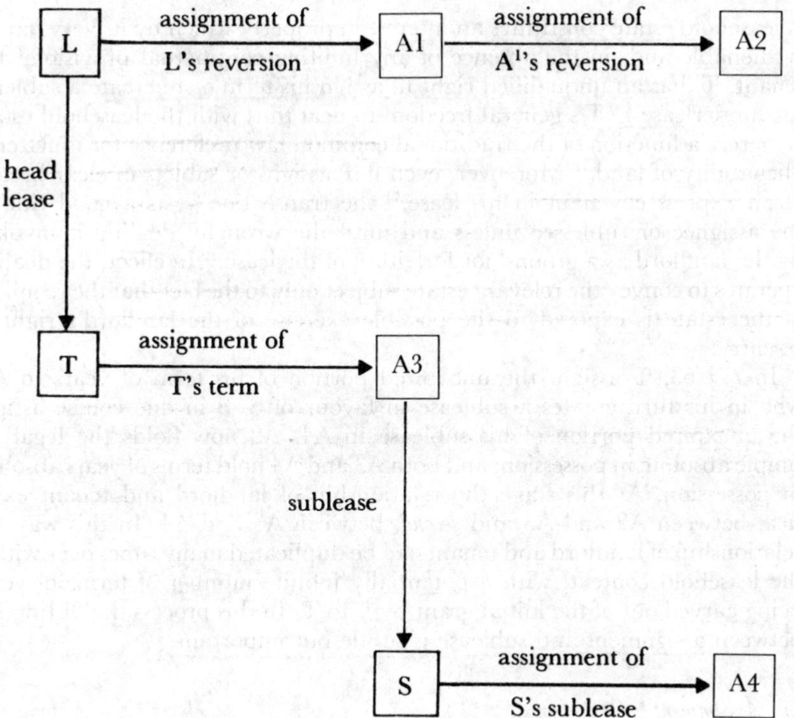

Fig. 63

The events depicted in *Fig.* 63 find their origin in the grant of a lease to T made by L, the owner of an estate in fee simple absolute. This grant invests T with an estate in the land (a 'term of years absolute'), thereby precluding L from resuming occupation of the land until the termination of the lease. The sum total of the rights meanwhile retained by L is known as a 'reversion', ie the residue of the rights reversionary upon the lease. The essence of a legal lease is that both landlord and tenant are invested with a legal estate in possession.[7] Each has an estate in the land with which—at least in theory—he may deal quite independently.

(1) Subsequent dealings by L

It is open to L subsequently to assign his 'reversion' to an assignee, A1, by conveying to him a fee simple estate in the land which is subject to the lease. A1 may thereafter execute a further assignment of the 'reversion' to A2, the 'reversion' normally increasing steadily in value as the lease approaches its expiry.

7 Ante, p 93.

(2) Subsequent dealings by T

A leasehold estate constitutes an interest in property which by its very nature is alienable and, in the absence of any limiting contractual provision,[8] the tenant, T, has an unqualified right to assign his term or to create a sublease (or 'underlease').[9] T's general freedom to deal thus with the leasehold estate is merely a function of the traditional common law preference for unfettered alienability of land.[10] Moreover, even if T assigns or sublets in clear breach of an express covenant in his lease,[11] the transaction vests a good title in the assignee or sublessee unless and until the wrongful dealing is invoked by the landlord as a ground for forfeiture of the lease.[12] In effect, the dealing operates to convey the relevant estate subject only to the fact that the recipient of the estate is exposed to the possible exercise of the landlord's right of re-entry.

In *Fig.* 63, T assigns the unexpired portion of his term of years to A3, who in his turn creates a sublease in favour of S. S in due course assigns the unexpired portion of his sublease to A4. A2 now holds the legal fee simple absolute in possession, and both A3 and A4 hold terms of years absolute in possession. At this stage the relationship of landlord and tenant exists *first*, between A2 and A3 and *second*, between A3 and A4. In this way the relationship of landlord and tenant can be duplicated many times over within the leasehold context, with a potentially infinite number of terms of years being carved out of the initial grant by L to T. In this process the distinction between assignment and sublease is subtle but important.

(a) Assignment

The distinguishing feature of an assignment is that it comprises a disposition to the assignee of the assignor's entire interest in the land,[13] thereby putting the assignee into the shoes of the assignor as henceforth the tenant under the lease. The assignor thereafter retains no interest, estate or reversion in

8 Post, p 800. Any contractual restraint upon the tenant's right to assign or sublet is strictly construed against the landlord (see *Church v Brown* (1808) 15 Ves 258 at 265, 33 ER 752 at 755; *Wilson v Rosenthal* (1906) 22 TLR 233 (post, p 800)).

9 See *Williams v Earle* (1868) LR 3 QB 739 at 750; *Garry Denning Ltd v Vickers* [1985] 1 NZLR 567 at 569 per Woodhouse P and Richardson J.

10 Ante, pp 90, 97. See generally G.E. Wall, *The Right to Sublease*, 53 Tulane L Rev 556 (1978–79).

11 It is different if the prohibition takes the form, not of a covenant against assignment or subletting, but of a proviso or condition that the head lease shall cease in the event of any unlawful dealing. In such circumstances any purported assignment or subletting is entirely nugatory and void (see *Paul v Nurse* (1828) 8 B & C 486 at 488, 108 ER 1123 at 1124; *Garry Denning Ltd v Vickers* [1985] 1 NZLR 567 at 570 per Woodhouse P and Richardson J).

12 *Williams v Earle* (1868) LR 3 QB 739 at 750; *Old Grovebury Manor Farm Ltd v W. Seymour Plant Sales and Hire Ltd* (No 2) [1979] 1 WLR 1397 at 1398G; *Governors of the Peabody Donation Fund v Higgins* [1983] 1 WLR 1091 at 1095E–G, 1097C–D; *Massart v Blight* (1951) 82 CLR 423 at 440; *South Yarra Project Pty Ltd v Gentsis* [1985] VR 29 at 34; *Garry Denning Ltd v Vickers* [1985] 1 NZLR 567 at 570, 572.

13 See *Milmo v Carreras* [1946] KB 306 at 310 per Lord Greene MR.

the land,[14] although this does not mean that his obligations under the lease are necessarily terminated at this point.[15]

(b) Sublease

By contrast the essence of a sublease consists in the fact that the sublessor retains a reversionary interest in the land, the sublease bringing into existence a new tenurial relationship between sublessor and sublessee.[16] A sublease can therefore be granted only for some lesser period of time than the term enjoyed by the sublessor.[17] Effectively the sublessor carves a subsidiary estate out of his own interest in the land,[18] meanwhile retaining a reversion on the sublease which will take effect (even if only fleetingly) at the termination of the sublease.

(c) Test of substance not form

Whether a particular dealing has produced a sublease or an assignment is ultimately a matter of substance and not of form, and the court accordingly has power to override any label erroneously attached to the transaction.[19] It is well established that any purported sublease for a term identical to[20] or greater than[1] that held by the sublessor is deemed to operate not as a sublease but as an assignment.[2]

5. FORMALITIES OF LEASES AND TENANCIES

The creation and assignment of most kinds of lease are subject to certain statutory requirements of formality. A leasehold interest in land comprises at least potentially a legal estate,[3] and therefore the creation and assignment of such an interest are subject to fairly stringent rules relating to formality.[4]

14 The assignor 'from that moment is a stranger to the land' (*Milmo v Carreras* [1946] KB 306 at 310 per Lord Greene MR).
15 Post, p 841.
16 *Garry Denning Ltd v Vickers* [1985] 1 NZLR 567 at 570.
17 '[W]hen the grant is for the residue of the term of the grantor, there must be an exception of the last day or the last hour, or of some other period of the term' (*Jameson v London and Canadian Loan Agency Co* (1897) 27 SCR 435 at 442 per Strong CJ).
18 Thus at common law a subtenancy comes automatically and simultaneously to an end when the head tenancy out of which the subtenancy was carved comes to an end by any means other than surrender by the head tenant to the head landlord (*Gisborne v Burton* [1989] QB 390 at 395E per Dillon LJ).
19 *Milmo v Carreras* [1946] KB 306 at 310 per Lord Greene MR; *Gaumont v Luz* (1980) 111 DLR (3d) 609 at 614f; *Garry Denning Ltd v Vickers* [1985] 1 NZLR 567 at 572.
20 *Parmenter v Webber* (1818) 8 Taunt 593 at 595f, 129 ER 515 at 516; *Beardman v Wilson* (1868) LR 4 CP 57 at 58; *Hallen v Spaeth* [1923] AC 684 at 687.
1 *Hicks v Downing* (1696) 1 Ld Raym 99, 91 ER 962 (tenant cannot 'by this gain any tortious reversion'); *Wollaston v Hakewill* (1841) 3 Man & G 297 at 323, 133 ER 1157 at 1167f per Tindal CJ; *Sunnyvale Services B O P Ltd v Bhana* [1986] 1 NZLR 314 at 319.
2 The sublessor has no 'property in his term. . .left after he has made what is really a transfer' (*Hallen v Spaeth* [1923] AC 684 at 687f per Viscount Haldane).
3 Law of Property Act 1925, s 1(1)(b) (ante, p 69).
4 Further rules of formal registration or register entry apply to leasehold interests in registered land (ante, p 174).

(1) Creation

The statutory requirements of formality in respect of the initial grant or creation of leasehold interests are contained in an uncoordinated series of provisions in the Law of Property Act 1925.[5] The starting point is the proposition that 'no interest in land can be created or disposed of except by writing signed by the person creating or conveying the same. .'[6] All interests created merely by parol have 'the force and effect of interests at will only.'[7] Moreover, 'all conveyances of land or of any interest therein are void for the purpose of conveying or creating a legal estate unless made by deed'.[8] The foregoing provisions are expressly made subject to contrary statutory indication. Accordingly a deed is not required for the creation at law of any 'leases or tenancies. . .not required by law to be made in writing'.[9] Further investigation of the statute reveals that no writing of any kind is required for the creation of 'leases taking effect in possession for a term not exceeding three years. . .at the best rent which can be reasonably obtained without taking a fine'.[10]

The net effect of these provisions is that a legal lease or tenancy at a full market rent for a period not exceeding three years can be created in writing or even orally.[11] In all other cases a legal lease requires to be created by deed. Special problems arise in relation to three kinds of lease or tenancy.

(a) Periodic tenancies

It follows from the provisions of the Law of Property Act 1925 that a legal periodic tenancy may be created without any kind of formality,[12] even though it is possible that the tenancy may continue indefinitely for much more than three years.[13] Such a tenancy may be created simply by verbal grant.[14]

5 These provisions stem from the Statute of Frauds 1677, ss 1, 2, and the Real Property Act 1845, s 3. See *Crago v Julian* [1992] 1 WLR 372 at 376C per Nicholls V-C ('. . .a hotchpotch of sections. . .').

6 Law of Property Act 1925, s 53(1)(a). This provision allows signature by an agent with written authority and also permits the creation and disposal of interests in land 'by will, or by operation of law'.

7 Law of Property Act 1925, s 54(1).

8 Law of Property Act 1925, s 52(1). Section 52(2) details certain exceptions to this basic principle, one of the exceptional cases relating to 'conveyances taking effect by operation of law' (s 52(2)(g)).

9 Law of Property Act 1925, s 52(2)(d).

10 Law of Property Act 1925, s 54(2). A 'fine' (or 'premium') is a lump sum payment which is sometimes demanded as part of the consideration for the grant of a term of years. The reference to a lease 'taking effect in possession' means that section 54(2) has no saving impact on the grant of a lease to commence at a future date (see *Haselhurst v Elliot* [1945] VLR 153 at 155; *Abjornson v Urban Newspapers Pty Ltd* [1989] WAR 191 at 199).

11 *Kushner v Law Society* [1952] 1 KB 264 at 272; *Crago v Julian* [1992] 1 WLR 372 at 376D-E per Nicholls V-C. The creation of a term of exactly three years requires no formality (see *Hayes v Seymour-Johns* (1981) 2 BPR 9366 at 9371). See generally P. Sparkes, [1992] Conv 252, 337.

12 *In re Knight, ex parte Voisey* (1882) 21 Ch D 442 at 456, 458; *Hammond v Farrow* [1904] 2 KB 332 at 335.

13 It seems to be determinative that, at the commencement of the periodic tenancy, it is entirely uncertain that the tenancy will continue for more than three years and eminently possible that it may come to a conclusion sooner (see *In re Knight, ex parte Voisey* (1882) 21 Ch D 442 at 456; *Duncan v Paki* [1976] 2 NZLR 563 at 565).

14 *Kushner v Law Society* [1952] 1 KB 264 at 274.

Moreover, a periodic tenancy may be created either expressly or by implication from conduct. An express periodic tenancy is one which is granted, for instance, 'from week to week' or 'from month to month'. An implied periodic tenancy often arises where a property owner accepts rent paid on a periodic basis by a 'tenant at will'[15] (ie by one who occupies land with the consent of the owner) or by a tenant under a formally invalid lease.[16] In these cases the precise nature of the tenancy is determined prima facie by the period with reference to which the rent payable is calculated, not by the frequency with which that rent is actually paid.[17] Where a landlord accepts rent paid on a periodic basis by a 'tenant at sufferance'[18] (ie one who holds over at the end of a valid tenancy), such payment may well be construed as giving rise to a weekly tenancy notwithstanding that the original tenancy comprised a fixed term of one year.[19]

(b) *Renewable leases*

The fact that a lease for a period not exceeding three years contains an option for renewal does not convert the lease into a term exceeding three years, even though the total period of possession enjoyed by the tenant may ultimately extend beyond three years.[20] The option for renewal, if exercised by the tenant,[1] merely has the effect of creating a fresh lease for a new term.[2] No formality is required in respect of either the first term or the second term, provided that the second term does not itself exceed three years.

(c) *Determinable leases*

The requirement of formal creation by deed applies to a lease which is granted for a definite term in excess of three years, notwithstanding that

15 Ante, p 678.
16 Post, p 740.
17 Thus in the absence of some express description of the precise nature of the tenancy, a tenant whose rent obligation amounts to '£520 per annum payable weekly' is presumed to hold a yearly tenancy, whereas a tenant whose rent obligation amounts to '£10 per week' is presumed to hold a weekly tenancy (see *Ladies' Hosiery & Underwear Ltd v Parker* [1930] 1 Ch 304 at 328f). See also *E.O.N. Motors Ltd v Secretary of State for the Environment* (1981) 258 Estates Gazette 1300, where there was an agreement that rent should be paid every quarter 'on the basis of £20 per week'. This agreement was held to give rise to a weekly tenancy notwithstanding that the rent was paid in quarterly instalments. Although the tenant had been in possession for four years, Sir Douglas Frank QC, sitting as a deputy High Court judge, observed that the tenancy 'continues to be a tenancy for one week, however long it may last.'
18 Ante, p 682.
19 See *Adler v Blackman* [1952] 2 All ER 41 at 44A–B, affd [1953] 1 QB 146 at 150ff.
20 *Hand v Hall* (1877) 2 Ex D 355 at 358. See also *Markfaith Investment Ltd v Chiap Hua Flashlights Ltd* [1991] 2 AC 43 at 58E per Lord Templeman.
1 Where a lease is vested in more than one tenant, an option for renewal of the term cannot be exercised unilaterally by one joint tenant (see *Newman v Keedwell* (1977) 35 P & CR 393 at 398; *Hammersmith and Fulham LBC v Monk* [1992] 1 AC 478 at 490G per Lord Bridge of Harwich).
2 *Lewis v Stephenson* (1898) 67 LJQB 296 at 300; *Rider v Ford* [1923] 1 Ch 541 at 547; *Gerraty v McGavin* (1914) 18 CLR 152 at 163f; *Minister v New South Wales Aerated Water and Confectionery Co Ltd* (1916) 22 CLR 56 at 78; *195 Crown Street Pty Ltd v Hoare* [1969] 1 NSWR 193 at 199; *Travinto Nominees Pty Ltd v Vlattas* (1973) 129 CLR 1 at 17 per Barwick CJ.

the lease may be determinable by the tenant within the first three years.[3] The determinable 90 year term into which most leases for life are converted by statute[4] is, however, immune from the requirement of formal creation since the term of 90 years takes effect by operation of law.[5]

(2) Assignment

The exemption from formality accorded by the Law of Property Act 1925 to certain kinds of lease or tenancy applies only to the *creation* of such terms of years. It is clear that the *assignment* of any legal leasehold interest must—irrespective of its duration—be effected formally by deed.[6] Thus a yearly tenancy, although perfectly capable of oral creation, must be assigned by deed if it is to invest the assignee with a legal estate in the land.[7] An assignment by mere signed writing takes effect as an equitable assignment, investing the assignee with only an equitable term, and an oral assignment is nowadays wholly ineffectual.[8]

In these respects the relevant statutory provisions doubtless compel a 'curious distinction' between the manner in which a short lease may be created and the manner in which it may be assigned, but the distinction is now too well established to be disturbed.[9]

(3) Informal and equitable leases

It has always been clear that no *legal* lease or tenancy is validly created or conferred otherwise than in appropriate compliance with the strict statutory requirements of formality relevant to the execution or assignment of a term of years.[10] Any purported conveyance of a leasehold interest in disregard

3 *Kushner v Law Society* [1952] 1 KB 264 at 274.
4 Ante, p 693.
5 Law of Property Act 1925, s 52(2)(g) (ante, p 736).
6 *Crago v Julian* [1992] 1 WLR 372 at 376C-D, 377D-E per Nicholls V-C. See [1992] Conv 375 (P. Sparkes). An assignment is a 'disposal' which requires signed writing pursuant to Law of Property Act 1925, s 53(1)(a), the excepting effect of section 54(2) being confined to the 'creation' of certain leases. Moreover, if the assignment is to take effect at law, it constitutes a 'conveyance' which requires to be made by deed pursuant to Law of Property Act 1925, s 52(1), from which requirement there is no escape in section 52(2)(d). In registered land the assignment must also be completed by registration of the new leasehold proprietor (ante, p 179).
7 *Botting v Martin* (1808) 1 Camp 317 at 319, 170 ER 970 at 971. Compare *Trustees of the Gift of Thomas Pocklington v Hill* (1989) 21 HLR 391 at 396f, where, in disregard of the statutory obstacles, the Court of Appeal proceeded on the assumption of an oral assignment of a periodic tenancy (see [1989] Conv 289 (J.E.M.)). This approach may have been justifiable on the basis of consideration and part performance, but has now been rejected as non-authoritative (see *Crago v Julian* [1992] 1 WLR 372 at 378B).
8 Prior to 27 September 1989 an oral assignment might arguably have been supported in equity on the basis of consideration and part performance (see *Crago v Julian* [1992] 1 WLR 372 at 378C-D; *Croydon LBC v Buston* (1991) 24 HLR 36 at 38. See [1992] Conv 375 at 381f (P. Sparkes)). See now Law of Property (Miscellaneous Provisions) Act 1989, s 2 (ante, p 256).
9 *Crago v Julian* [1992] 1 WLR 372 at 376F-377A per Nicholls V-C. Nicholls V-C did, however, confess (at 377B) that he saw 'common sense and practicality' in the argument that an orally created lease should be likewise capable of informal assignment. See [1992] Conv 268 (J. Martin).
10 Ante, p 736.

of these formal requirements is declared 'void for the purpose of conveying or creating a legal estate.'[11] It is equally clear, however, that certain transactions which have not resulted in any formal vesting of a legal leasehold estate may nevertheless be effective to confer an *equitable* or informal term of years.

An equitable lease may arise in various ways. Plainly, for instance, if the grantor of a lease holds only an equitable title (eg an equitable fee simple estate), any term of years granted can itself have only equitable quality.[12] More commonly, however, an equitable lease may arise where the owner of a legal estate in land enters into a specifically enforceable *contract* to create a legal lease. Although the contract never reaches performance (ie no legal lease is ever executed), equity regards the agreement as giving rise to an equitable lease. Equity is also prepared to give similar effect to an abortive attempt to create or dispose of a legal leasehold, where the relevant imperfection comprises a failure to use a deed or (in the case of registered land) to complete the disposition of the leasehold by registration of the lessee as registered proprietor. In such cases the informal or imperfect transaction is deemed to have an effect precisely equivalent to that of an unperformed contract to grant a lease.

The foregoing propositions feed at various stages into an extended chain of legal response which regulates the impact to be accorded to leases which do not proceed beyond the stage of contract or which otherwise fail to achieve their full intended effect at law. The logical progression of the courts' approach in this area is perhaps best illustrated by tracing the way in which some kind of effect is given to a lease which is either formally defective or merely contractual.

Assume for this purpose that L, an owner of a legal estate in fee simple, has set about conferring on T a legal lease for a term of 30 years, but that the envisaged grant of a legal term of years has gone no further than the exchange of contracts to create the appropriate leasehold estate in T. Alternatively assume that a purported conveyance of the legal estate to T has been vitiated by the use of mere informal writing or even by failure to secure the appropriate registration of the instrument of lease. In every case the transaction is clearly incompetent to invest T with a *legal* lease for a term of 30 years, but may nevertheless bring about the following consequences.

(a) Tenancy at will

A 'tenancy at will'[13] arises by implication where the tenant under an agreement for a future lease or a formally invalid lease enters into possession of the land with the consent of the landlord.[14] Thus T, if allowed into

11 Law of Property Act 1925, s 52(1) (ante, p 736). See eg *Rochester Poster Services Ltd v Dartford BC* (1991) 63 P & CR 88 at 93.

12 See eg *Marks v Attallah* (1966) 198 Estates Gazette 685; (1966) 110 SJ 709 (ante, p 206).

13 Ante, p 680.

14 *Braythwayte v Hitchcock* (1842) 10 M & W 494 at 497, 152 ER 565 at 567; *Moore v Dimond* (1929) 43 CLR 105 at 114f; *Progressive Mailing House Pty Ltd v Tabali Pty Ltd* (1985) 157 CLR 17 at 25f per Mason J.

occupation of the 'demised' premises, immediately acquires the status of a tenant at will.[15]

(b) Implied periodic tenancy

As soon as a periodic rent is offered by a tenant at will in virtue of his occupation of land, and such payment is accepted by the landowner, the tenancy at will is readily converted by implication of law into a periodic tenancy.[16] This result follows whether the tenant entered under an agreement to create a future lease[17] or by virtue of a formally defective lease[18] or even under a purported lease which is altogether void on other grounds (eg uncertainty of term).[19] Thus, in the present example, T becomes entitled, from the first payment of rent under his agreement or informal grant, to a 'term of years' in the full common law sense.[20]

(i) Nature of the periodic term The precise nature of this periodic tenancy is governed prima facie by the period with reference to which the rent is payable.[1] Until recently it has often been said that it takes little to raise a presumption that the implied periodic tenancy generated by the tenant's payments is a yearly tenancy.[2] The fact that rent is paid 'by reference to a year, or aliquot part of a year, affords evidence of a tenancy from year to year.'[3] Thus the payment of a quarterly rent has been held to raise a

15 Ante, p 681.

16 See *Javad v Mohammed Aqil* [1991] 1 WLR 1007 at 1012E-G per Nicholls LJ. Recent case law has stressed that, where parties are still negotiating for a lease, there is a danger that too facile an assumption of periodic tenancy may generate wholly unintended rights for the occupier (ante, p 679). Such warnings may, however, be much less pertinent where the parties have already contracted to grant a lease or have already executed a formally invalid lease.

17 *Hamerton v Stead* (1824) 3 B & C 478 at 483, 107 ER 811 at 813; *Chapman v Towner* (1840) 6 M & W 100 at 104, 151 ER 338 at 340; *Doe d Thomson v Amey* (1840) 12 Ad & El 476 at 479f, 113 ER 892 at 893; *Anderson v Midland Railway Co* (1861) 3 E & E 614 at 622, 121 ER 573 at 576; *Swain v Ayres* (1888) 21 QBD 289 at 293; *Moore v Dimond* (1929) 43 CLR 105 at 112f; *Dockrill v Cavanagh* (1944) 45 SR (NSW) 78 at 80f per Jordan CJ; *Chan v Cresdon Pty Ltd* (1989) 168 CLR 242 at 248.

18 *Doe d Rigge v Bell* (1793) 5 Term Rep 471 at 472, 101 ER 265 at 266 per Lord Kenyon CJ; *Moore v Dimond* (1929) 43 CLR 105 at 113f; *Chan v Cresdon Pty Ltd* (1989) 168 CLR 242 at 248; *Abjornson v Urban Newspapers Pty Ltd* [1989] WAR 191 at 199.

19 *Prudential Assurance Co Ltd v London Residuary Body* [1992] 2 AC 386 at 392B-C per Lord Templeman.

20 *Moore v Dimond* (1929) 43 CLR 105 at 112.

1 *Martin v Smith* (1874) LR 9 Ex 50 at 52; *Adams v Cairns* (1901) 85 LT 10 at 11.

2 Since the 18th century a consistently strong presumption persisted that a general occupation of land for which a periodic rent was paid should be construed as a tenancy from year to year (see *Doe d Martin and Jones v Watts* (1797) 7 TR 83 at 85f, 101 ER 866 at 868; *Low v Adams* [1901] 2 Ch 598 at 601; *Moore v Dimond* (1929) 43 CLR 105 at 116; *Progressive Mailing House Pty Ltd v Tabali Pty Ltd* (1985) 157 CLR 17 at 26 per Mason J). See generally *Bl Comm*, Vol II, p 147; W.S. Holdsworth, *History of English Law* (2nd edn, London 1937), Vol VII, p 244f.

3 *Moore v Dimond* (1929) 43 CLR 105 at 114. See *Braythwayte v Hitchcock* (1842) 10 M & W 494 at 497, 152 ER 565 at 567; *Landale v Menzies* (1909) 9 CLR 89 at 129f; *Rochester Poster Services Ltd v Dartford BC* (1991) 63 P & CR 88 at 93; *Prudential Assurance Co Ltd v London Residuary Body* [1992] 2 AC 386 at 392B per Lord Templeman.

presumption of a periodic tenancy from year to year,[4] although this presumption can be rebutted.

In principle even the payment of a weekly rent would not normally displace this presumption in favour of an implied yearly tenancy.[5] There is, however, some suggestion in the case law that a yearly tenancy comes about only if the tenant continues to pay a periodic rent for at least a whole year,[6] or if the premises are 'ordinarily let from year to year'[7] or if there is some other evidence that the rent was paid with reference to a yearly holding.[8] There may also be some indication that the presumption of yearly tenancy is coming to be viewed as outdated. In *Javad v Mohammed Aqil*,[9] the Court of Appeal, although emphasising the importance of inference from all the circumstances of the case, hinted that a greater realism may nowadays be applicable in this context. According to Nicholls LJ, where one party permits another to go into possession of his land on payment of a weekly or monthly rent, 'failing more the inference sensibly and reasonably to be drawn is that the parties intended that there should be a weekly or monthly tenancy.'

(ii) Duration of the periodic tenancy The common law tenancy implied from periodic payments continues only during the term originally contemplated in the contract for a lease or ineffective legal demise (ie, in the present example, for a term of 30 years). Throughout this term the periodic tenancy is, of course, vulnerable to earlier determination by due notice to quit[10] and if not so determined will simply expire, without any further notice to quit, through the effluxion of time.[11]

(iii) Terms of the implied periodic tenancy The terms on which T holds his implied periodic tenancy are governed by the rule confirmed in *Martin v Smith*.[12] T's tenancy is deemed to incorporate by implication all the originally agreed

4 See eg *Doe d Thomson v Amey* (1840) 12 Ad & El 476 at 479f, 113 ER 892 at 893; *Lee v Smith* (1854) 9 Exch 662 at 665, 156 ER 284 at 285; *Croft v William F. Blay Ltd* [1919] 2 Ch 343 at 349, 357; *Moore v Dimond* (1929) 43 CLR 105 at 117.

5 See *Moore v Dimond* (1929) 43 CLR 105 at 116f, where the High Court of Australia expressed concern lest, for instance, the fact of weekly payments under an agreed term of much greater duration should cause the tenant to be relegated to a mere 'terminable holding of a week'.

6 *Moore v Dimond* (1929) 43 CLR 105 at 122f per Isaacs J. See also *Knight v Benett* (1826) 3 Bing 361 at 364, 130 ER 552 at 553; *Arden v Sullivan* (1850) 14 QB 832 at 839, 117 ER 320 at 323; *Hunt v Allgood* (1861) 10 CB (NS) 253 at 257, 142 ER 448 at 450.

7 *Doe d Lord v Crago* (1848) 6 CB 90 at 98, 136 ER 1185 at 1188.

8 However, such evidence is not generally difficult to find. In *Moore v Dimond* (1929) 43 CLR 105 at 123, Isaacs J was prepared to accept evidence of 'relevant conduct' including 'entry upon or retention of possession upon the faith of an agreement'.

9 [1991] 1 WLR 1007 at 1012E–G.

10 *Doe d Davenish v Moffatt* (1850) 15 QB 257 at 265, 117 ER 455 at 458; *Progressive Mailing House Pty Ltd v Tabali Pty Ltd* (1985) 157 CLR 17 at 26 per Mason J; *Chan v Cresdon Pty Ltd* (1989) 168 CLR 242 at 248.

11 *Doe d Davenish v Moffatt* (1850) 15 QB 257 at 265, 117 ER 455 at 458; *Moore v Dimond* (1929) 43 CLR 105 at 113.

12 (1874) LR 9 Ex 50 at 52.

terms of the lease as contained in the contract[13] or defective grant[14] in so far as these terms are compatible with and transferable to T's periodic tenancy.[15] Thus T's periodic tenancy will be taken prima facie to include any covenant in the invalid letting which related, for instance, to restrictions on the use of the premises or to a right of entry reserved for the landlord.[16]

Some of the originally agreed terms may not, however, be so easily transferable. In *Martin v Smith*,[17] for instance a leasehold term requiring the tenant to redecorate the premises at the end of the seventh year was held to be inconsistent with a periodic tenancy which by its nature could be no more than a tenancy from year to year.[18] Moreover, the broad equivalence which is generally maintained between the terms of the original lease and those of the implied common law periodic tenancy should not obscure the fact that these two leasehold interests are quite separate legal phenomena. In a highly significant decision in *Chan v Cresdon Pty Ltd*,[19] the High Court of Australia has ruled, for instance, that a third party's guarantee of due performance under a lease which is rendered formally defective for want of registration has no application to the due performance of the tenant's obligations under the periodic tenancy implied from entry into possession and acceptance of rent. A majority in the High Court took the controversial view that the common law tenancy 'was distinct from the unregistered lease',[20] with the result that a guarantee expressly made with reference to one form of tenancy could not be arbitrarily assumed to apply to the other.

(iv) Legal quality of the implied periodic tenancy No special formality of creation is required of the periodic tenancy which arises by implication from T's entry into possession and payment of rent. Being at most a yearly tenancy, it need not be created by deed or other writing.[1] T's term of years arises by sheer implication from conduct, and takes effect as a legal estate in the land. As such it remains binding on L (and, indeed, on any assignee of L's reversion) until either the appropriate notice to quit is given or the originally contemplated period of 30 years expires.

13 *Bennett v Ireland* (1858) EB & E 326 at 334f, 120 ER 530 at 533; *Swain v Ayres* (1888) 21 QBD 289 at 293 per Lord Esher MR; *Moore v Dimond* (1929) 43 CLR 105 at 113; *Progressive Mailing House Pty Ltd v Tabali Pty Ltd* (1985) 157 CLR 17 at 26 per Mason J; *Chan v Cresdon Pty Ltd* (1989) 168 CLR 242 at 248.

14 *Progressive Mailing House Pty Ltd v Tabali Pty Ltd* (1985) 157 CLR 17 at 26 per Mason J; *Re Eastdoro Pty Ltd* [1989] 2 Qd R 182 at 184.

15 *Doe d Rigge v Bell* (1793) 5 Term Rep 471 at 472, 101 ER 265 at 266 per Lord Kenyon CJ; *Arden v Sullivan* (1850) 14 QB 832 at 839, 117 ER 320 at 323; *Croft v William F. Blay Ltd* [1919] 2 Ch 343 at 349; *Prudential Assurance Co Ltd v London Residuary Body* [1992] 2 AC 386 at 392B–C per Lord Templeman.

16 See eg *Thomas v Packer* (1857) 1 H & N 669 at 672f, 156 ER 1370 at 1371f.

17 (1874) LR 9 Exch 50 at 52.

18 Such a covenant would have been enforceable if the tenant had in fact continued to occupy, as a yearly tenant, for the originally anticipated term of seven years (*Martin v Smith* (1874) LR 9 Ex 50 at 52f).

19 (1989) 168 CLR 242.

20 (1989) 168 CLR 242 at 249f.

1 Law of Property Act 1925, ss 52(2)(d), 54(2) (ante, p 736).

(c) Contract to create a lease

In terms of the foregoing analysis, a formally invalid lease may be partially saved as a periodic tenancy at common law, thereby enjoying a certain limited effect as a legal transaction. There is, however, another quite different way in which T's abortive 30 year term may still be given force. The vitiating defect of formality strikes at the effectiveness of only the informal or unregistered instrument of grant, thereby preventing it from becoming a source of rights.[2] This denial of legal effect for T's term of years does not preclude the possibility that equitable doctrine may operate quite independently to give effect to the *contractual* rights which 'lie behind or beyond' the legal estate purportedly conferred on T.[3] In accordance with equitable principle,[4] the antecedent agreement for value to create a lease in favour of T causes T to acquire an equitable interest in the land commensurate with his ability to obtain specific performance of his contract.[5]

Thus, although effect is withheld at law from the term of years which it was intended that T should take, T may be able in equity to claim an alternative estate or interest which finds its source, not in the abortive legal grant, but in the pre-existing contract for value.[6] In such a case, T's rights following a formally defective leasehold grant may be viewed in equity as the precise equivalent of those which would have arisen had the intended conferment of a legal lease proceeded no further than a contractual agreement to grant such a lease.[7]

(d) Equitable lease

Where no legal lease has been validly created, the recourse to the contractual substratum of the parties' dealings carries important implications for the rights of L and T respectively.

(i) Protection against third parties Since T is not disabled from relying on contract as a source of entitlement, T's rights rank as an 'estate contract' which requires protection against third parties who may deal with L's reversionary title. T may register this estate contract as a Class C(iv) land charge in the case of unregistered land,[8] and may enter a minor interest on L's title in the case of registered land.[9]

2 Law of Property Act 1925, s 52(1); Land Registration Act 1925, s 123(1).
3 See *Corin v Patton* (1990) 169 CLR 540 at 572 per Deane J. The inefficacy of the transaction at law 'does not touch whatever rights are behind it' and 'cannot cut down or merge the pre-existing right' which led to the void or unregistered conveyance of the leasehold estate (see *Barry v Heider* (1914) 19 CLR 197 at 216 per Isaacs J (ante, p 179)).
4 Ante, p 263.
5 *Corin v Patton* (1990) 169 CLR 540 at 588 per Toohey J. See also *Parker v Taswell* (1858) 2 De G & J 559 at 570f, 44 ER 1106 at 1111; *Brunker v Perpetual Trustee Co (Ltd)* (1937) 57 CLR 555 at 581 per Latham CJ.
6 *Corin v Patton* (1990) 169 CLR 540 at 563 per Brennan J. See also *Chan v Cresdon Pty Ltd* (1989) 168 CLR 242 at 257.
7 Compare eg Settled Land Act 1925, ss 13, 27(1).
8 Ante, p 141.
9 Ante, p 181.

(ii) Availability of specific performance Since it is now irrelevant whether T's rights stem from a defectively performed or wholly unperformed agreement to grant a lease, his rights are effectively those which arise from a contractual agreement by L to convey a legal term of 30 years. At law such an agreement is, of course, remediable in the event of breach by an award of compensatory damages. In the view of equity, however, the agreement to create a lease carries the potential of a much more far-reaching remedial outcome. A contract for the transfer of an interest in land is a contract of which equity will usually grant specific performance.[10] In the present context, breach of L's contractual obligation to create a legal term of 30 years in T may give rise, not to a mere award of money damages, but to a court order that L do that which he promised, ie convey an effective legal lease to T. As an equitable remedy the decree of specific performance is not, of course, available as of right. Its award lies within the discretion of the court, which will normally grant specific performance only if certain conditions are fulfilled.[11]

First, there must be appropriate compliance with such formality rules as may apply to the relevant contract for a lease. This means that, in relation to a contract entered into prior to 27 September 1989, there must have been compliance with the requirement of *written evidence* (or of part performance) laid down by section 40 of the Law of Property Act 1925.[12] In the case of contracts concluded on or after 27 September 1989,[13] there must, in the absence of an estoppel, be due observance of the rather stricter requirement of *written contract* now contained in section 2 of the Law of Property (Miscellaneous Provisions) Act 1989.[14]

Second, the claimant of specific performance must have given value: 'equity will not assist a volunteer'.

Third, the claimant must not have forfeited his claim to equitable assistance through unconscionable or inequitable conduct: 'he who comes into equity must come with clean hands'.[15] In the context of an agreement for a lease, this last condition means that the court has a discretion to withhold specific performance from either party[16] if there is conduct which alienates the sympathy of equity. The circumstances in which a 'clean hands' defence may successfully be raised are, however, somewhat limited,[17] and the court

10 Ante, p 261.
11 Ante, p 262.
12 Ante, p 254.
13 An exception is made, by cross-reference to Law of Property Act 1925, s 54(2) (ante, p 736), for contracts to grant a lease or tenancy at a full market rent for a period not exceeding three years (see Law of Property (Miscellaneous Provisions) Act 1989, s 2(5)(a)).
14 Ante, p 256. Some doubt has been expressed whether, in the absence of a prior written contract, an abortive instrument of grant can itself be deemed to constitute the *contract* in writing which is required by Law of Property (Miscellaneous Provisions) Act 1989, s 2 (see J. Howell, [1990] Conv 441).
15 See P.H. Pettit, [1990] Conv 416.
16 Even the landlord may be precluded from obtaining specific performance if, by his conduct, he has forfeited the assistance of the equitable jurisdiction (*Warwick Grove Pty Ltd v Wright & Howson* [1979] 1 SR (WA) 69 at 73). In such a case the court will simply decline to compel the tenant to execute the legal lease.
17 It has been said, for instance, that 'general depravity' does not connote an absence of 'clean hands' (*Dering v Earl of Winchelsea* (1787) 1 Cox Eq Cas 318 at 319, 29 ER 1184 at 1185 per Eyre CB). See also *Attorney-General for the United Kingdom v Heinemann Publishers Australia Pty Ltd* (1987) 8 NSWLR 341 at 383B per Powell J.

will not usually refuse its aid unless the breaches alleged are 'gross and wilful'.[18] In extreme cases disqualifying conduct may include a failure to fulfil obligations fixed by the originally agreed lease[19] or dishonest concealment of a lease through non-registration in order to facilitate further mortgaging.[20] Nevertheless the courts tend not to refuse equitable assistance in circumstances where relief against forfeiture would have been granted under a legal lease.[1] Thus the court may grant specific performance to a tenant notwithstanding his breach of a term for rent payment, where the relevant arrears have since been paid to the landlord and accepted by him.[2]

(iii) The anticipatory effect of equity Provided that these preconditions of equitable relief are satisfied,[3] T has a right to compel the specific performance of his agreement for a 30 year lease by means of a court order directing the due execution or registration of a formal lease in his favour.[4] His contractual rights, being specifically enforceable, have a certain quality of inevitability: they contain the potential of irresistible enlargement into a legal lease on the terms originally agreed. At this point equitable doctrine intervenes with decisive effect.

Since 'equity looks on that as done which ought to be done', the technical availability of specific performance now enables the parties to be treated *as if* a legal lease 'had been granted and was actually in existence.'[5] Equity anticipates the due performance of the contractual obligation[6] and, in so doing, ensures that the agreement for a lease operates 'not merely to create

18 *Parker v Taswell* (1858) 2 De G & J 559 at 573, 44 ER 1106 at 1112. See also *Upper Hutt Arcade Ltd v Burrell and Burrell Properties Ltd* [1973] 2 NZLR 699 at 703.

19 *Coatsworth v Johnson* (1886) 55 LJQB 220 at 222f (breach of covenant in agreement to cultivate land in 'a good and husbandlike manner'). See also *Williams v Frayne* (1937) 57 CLR 710 at 730; *Australian Hardwoods Pty Ltd v Commissioner for Railways* [1961] 1 WLR 425 at 432. The 'clean hands' rule can also apply to unfulfilled conditions precedent where there is no waiver by the landlord (see *Cornish v Brook Green Laundry Ltd* [1959] 1 QB 394 at 407; *Euston Centre Properties Ltd v H & J Wilson Ltd* (1982) 262 Estates Gazette 1079 at 1082; *Shelley v United Artists Corpn Ltd* (1990) 60 P & CR 241 at 248).

20 See *Chan v Cresdon Pty Ltd* (1989) 168 CLR 242 at 256, 263.

1 Post, p 829. See *Parker v Taswell* (1858) 2 De G & J 559 at 573, 44 ER 1106 at 1112. A mere delay by the tenant in seeking specific performance of the contract for a lease does not fetter the equitable jurisdiction to award such relief (see *Tottenham Hotspur Football & Athletic Co Ltd v Princegrove Publishers Ltd* [1974] 1 WLR 113 at 122B–C; *Baxton v Kara* [1982] 1 NSWLR 604 at 611E).

2 *Baxton v Kara* [1982] 1 NSWLR 604 at 610D–E. See also *Kemp v Lumeah Investments Pty Ltd* (1983) 3 BPR 9203 at 9206 (specific performance conditional on payment of arrears).

3 See, however, S. Gardner, (1987) 7 OJLS 60; P. Sparkes, (1988) 8 OJLS 350.

4 *Progressive Mailing House Pty Ltd v Tabali Pty Ltd* (1985) 157 CLR 17 at 26. In the early years after the Judicature Acts there was a general expectation that specific performance would actually be obtained in such a case, the formal lease normally being decreed to extend back to the date agreed between the parties for the commencement of the term (see *McMahon v Ambrose* [1987] VR 817 at 829f).

5 *Swain v Ayres* (1888) 21 QBD 289 at 293 per Lord Esher MR. In *Lowther v Heaver* (1889) 41 Ch D 248 at 264, Cotton LJ made the point that the tenant 'being entitled in equity to have a lease granted, his rights. . .do not depend on its actually having been granted.' See also *McMahon v Ambrose* [1987] VR 817 at 830.

6 The equitable doctrine 'applies without there being an actual order for specific performance. . . When issues as to the rights of the parties have come before the courts it has usually been enough that the court, by holding that it would grant specific performance, has established the existence of equitable rights and then enforced them' (*McMahon v Ambrose* [1987] VR 817 at 830).

contractual rights and duties, but to create an equitable term of years'.[7] Thus, although the absence of a formal conveyance or registration is fatal to any claim that T has received a *legal* term of years,[8] his entitlement to specific performance enables him to assert, as against L, that he holds an *equitable* term of years for the same period and on the same covenants as those stipulated in the original agreement for a lease.[9] With its characteristic regard for substantive intent in preference to mere form,[10] equity thus views the parties' respective rights and obligations on the fictitious basis that the agreement to create a legal lease has already been duly performed.[11] In effect, the specifically enforceable rights generated behind a formally deficient or unregistered lease or an agreement for a future lease are alike treated as having given rise to the equitable equivalent of the intended legal term.[12]

This outcome, although commonly attributed to the later decision of the Court of Appeal in *Walsh v Lonsdale*,[13] is more properly credited as the doctrine in *Parker v Taswell*.[14] In the present context it enables T to maintain that he has an *equitable lease* for 30 years, and that the rights and duties of L and T are fixed in equity as though L had already conveyed a legal term to T. This assertion is, however, heavily dependent on the availability of

7 *National Trustees, Executors and Agency Co of Australasia Ltd v Boyd* (1926) 39 CLR 72 at 82. The relationship between the contracting parties 'in equity [is] that of landlord and tenant' (*Progressive Mailing House Pty Ltd v Tabali Pty Ltd* (1985) 157 CLR 17 at 26 per Mason J).

8 *Lowther v Heaver* (1889) 41 Ch D 248 at 264 per Cotton LJ; *National Trustees, Executors and Agency Co of Australasia Ltd v Boyd* (1926) 39 CLR 72 at 82; *Chan v Cresdon Pty Ltd* (1989) 168 CLR 242 at 251f.

9 *Rochester Poster Services Ltd v Dartford BC* (1991) 63 P & CR 88 at 93; *Williams v Frayne* (1937) 58 CLR 710 at 730 per Dixon J; *Progressive Mailing House Pty Ltd v Tabali Pty Ltd* (1985) 157 CLR 17 at 27 per Mason J; *Abjornson v Urban Newspapers Pty Ltd* [1989] WAR 191 at 199. The equitable lease does not, however, incorporate a third party's guarantee of the tenant's due performance of the terms contained in the pre-existing agreement for a lease: the third party's guarantee is confined to performance under the legal term envisaged in the contract (see *Chan v Cresdon Pty Ltd* (1989) 168 CLR 242 at 256ff).

10 *Chan v Cresdon Pty Ltd* (1989) 168 CLR 242 at 252. See *Gilbert v Cossey* (1912) 106 LT 607 at 608, where Darling J thought that in the present context the doctrine of specific performance had been reduced to a mere 'legal fiction'. It was now widely recognised 'that justice really demanded that a person be held to have an interest in land, although the document under which he claimed it had only a signature upon a piece of paper. . .instead of a piece of wax on parchment. . .'.

11 See *Warmington v Miller* [1973] QB 877 at 887C–E per Stamp LJ; *Rochester Poster Services Ltd v Dartford BC* (1991) 63 P & CR 88 at 93.

12 See *Swain v Ayres* (1888) 21 QBD 289 at 293 per Lord Esher MR; *York House Pty Ltd v Federal Commissioner of Taxation* (1930) 43 CLR 427 at 435f; *Chan v Cresdon Pty Ltd* (1989) 168 CLR 242 at 252. It is widely accepted that an unregistered leasehold disposition results in an equitable lease (see *National Trustees, Executors and Agency Co of Australasia Ltd v Boyd* (1926) 39 CLR 72 at 82; *Brunker v Perpetual Trustee Co (Ltd)* (1937) 57 CLR 555 at 581, 599; *Progressive Mailing House Pty Ltd v Tabali Pty Ltd* (1985) 157 CLR 17 at 27, 54).

13 (1882) 21 Ch D 9 (post, p 747). See eg the reference to the tenant's entitlement to a '*Walsh v Lonsdale* equity' in *Cornish v Brook Green Laundry Ltd* [1959] 1 QB 394 at 406f. See also *Progressive Mailing House Pty Ltd v Tabali Pty Ltd* (1985) 157 CLR 17 at 26.

14 (1858) 2 De G & J 559 at 570, 573, 44 ER 1106 at 1111f. Here Lord Chelmsford LC observed that 'the intention of the parties having been that there should be a lease. . .the aid of equity [is] only invoked to carry that intention into effect.' He therefore construed the obligations of the contracting landlord and tenant as if the stipulations of their original informal agreement had been 'converted into a covenant according to the intention of the parties'. See also *Warwick Grove Pty Ltd v Wright & Howson* [1979] 1 SR (WA) 69 at 73.

specific performance[15] and remains valid only so long as the preconditions of specific enforcement continue to be met.[16] If subsequently, by reason of some gross breach on the part of T, L becomes entitled to resist specific performance, T's term ceases to be an equitable term and reverts instead to a legal and readily terminable periodic tenancy.[17]

(4) Resolution of the conflict between law and equity

It is of course inevitable that the variety of legal and equitable response to formally defective and merely contractual leases should seem to raise a problem of conflict. Entry into possession followed by payment and acceptance of rent founds the implication of a legal periodic tenancy (perhaps from year to year). However, a party who is entitled to specific performance is also regarded as holding an equitable lease for the same period and on the same terms as originally agreed by the parties. Where the rights and obligations fixed by the periodic tenancy at common law are inconsistent with those incorporated within the equitable lease, which perspective on the leasehold relationship is to prevail?

This problem posed itself, apparently for the first time, in *Walsh v Lonsdale*.[18] Here D granted P a seven-year lease in writing, one of the terms of the tenancy being that P should pay each year's rent in advance. No lease by deed was executed, but P entered into possession and proceeded for some time to pay rent in arrear, thereby appearing to become a yearly periodic tenant at common law. D then demanded a year's rent in advance and, on P's refusal to pay rent in advance, distrained for it (by seizing P's goods). P brought an action seeking both damages for trespass and a decree of specific performance of the informal lease. These facts disclosed a clear conflict between P's yearly tenancy (under which as a matter of law rent was payable in arrear) and the seven-year equitable lease which arose in accordance with *Parker v Taswell* (in terms of which rent was expressly payable in advance). The liability of D in trespass obviously turned on the question whether the legal periodic tenancy or the equitable seven-year lease was determinative of the rights and duties of the parties.

In an historic judgment the Court of Appeal decided that, in consequence of the Judicature Acts 1873-1875, any conflict between the rules of law and equity should be resolved by an application of the rules of equity.[19] D's act in distraining upon the goods of P had therefore been perfectly lawful since D's rights were conclusively established by the terms of the equitable seven-year lease, which had expressly stipulated that rent was due in advance.

With admirable clarity the Court disposed of the problem of apparently co-existing yet incompatible estates in the land. Jessel MR declared that

> there are not two estates as there were formerly, one estate at common law by reason of the payment of rent from year to year, and an estate in equity under the agreement.

15 *Chan v Cresdon Pty Ltd* (1989) 168 CLR 242 at 252.
16 See *Euston Centre Properties Ltd v H & J Wilson Ltd* (1982) 262 Estates Gazette 1079 at 1082.
17 *Williams v Frayne* (1937) 57 CLR 710 at 730 per Dixon J.
18 (1882) 21 Ch D 9.
19 Supreme Court of Judicature Act 1873, s 25(11); see now Supreme Court Act 1981, s 49(1) (ante, p 37).

There is only one Court, and the equity rules prevail in it. The tenant holds under an agreement for a lease. He holds, therefore, under the same terms in equity as if a lease had been granted, it being a case in which both parties admit that relief is capable of being given by specific performance. That being so, he cannot complain of the exercise by the landlord of the same rights as the landlord would have had if a lease had been granted.[20]

It is thus perfectly plain that a tenant who enters into possession under a specifically enforceable contract for a lease[1] holds not a legal periodic tenancy from year to year, but rather an equitable tenancy on the same terms as those contained in the abortive informal grant.[2] If, however, the preconditions of specific enforceability cease to be met,[3] the obligations of the parties are governed by the terms appropriate to the legal periodic tenancy which is implied from the tenant's entry into possession and payment of rent.[4] An equitable tenancy cannot co-exist with a legal periodic tenancy, and the doctrine founded on the equitable jurisdiction to order specific performance effectively ensures that the terms of the equitable tenancy prevail where (and only where) the remedy of specific performance is available.[5]

In all other cases the tenant is relegated to his rights at common law. Paradoxical though it may at first appear, the periodic tenancy implied at law offers a form of protection far inferior to that ensured by an equitable lease for the originally agreed term. The common law tenancy, although technically more potent in that it binds the world, suffers from the disadvantage that it is terminable at any time by the appropriate notice to quit. Unless supplemented by special protective legislation,[6] the security of tenure afforded even by a legal tenancy from year to year[7] falls short of that available under an equitable lease (which must be allowed to run its full course except where a right of re-entry arises for breach of covenant).

The doctrine of *Walsh v Lonsdale* has come to apply to a wide range of purportedly legal transactions which are vitiated by non-compliance with some legal formality. The doctrine establishes a principle of general

20 (1882) 21 Ch D 9 at 14f. However, as Jessel MR pointed out, the tenant could not, on this premise, be turned out on six months' notice as would have been the case had he been merely a tenant from year to year. Under the equitable lease, the tenant had the right to insist that the landlord could re-enter only for breach of covenant.

1 The principle of *Walsh v Lonsdale* applies even where the agreement is embodied in a consent order of the court confirming a compromise between the parties (see *Tottenham Hotspur Football & Athletic Co Ltd v Princegrove Publishers Ltd* [1974] 1 WLR 113 at 122A).

2 See *Swain v Ayres* (1888) 21 QBD 289 at 293; *Goldstein v Sanders* [1915] 1 Ch 549 at 556; *Tottenham Hotspur Football & Athletic Co Ltd v Princegrove Publishers Ltd* [1974] 1 WLR 113 at 121G–H; *Industrial Properties (Barton Hill) Ltd v Associated Electrical Industries Ltd* [1977] QB 580 at 598B–C, 610C.

3 The doctrine in *Walsh v Lonsdale* is applicable 'only in those cases where specific performance can be obtained between the same parties in the same court, and at the same time as the subsequent legal question falls to be determined' (*Manchester Brewery Co v Coombs* [1901] 2 Ch 608 at 617 per Farwell J). This may mean that the full effect of *Walsh v Lonsdale* cannot apply as between one of the original parties and an assignee of the other (see R.J. Smith, [1978] CLJ 98 at 102).

4 *Coatsworth v Johnson* (1886) 55 LJQB 220 at 222f; *Williams v Frayne* (1937) 57 CLR 710 at 730.

5 *Swain v Ayres* (1888) 21 QBD 289 at 293 per Lord Esher MR.

6 Post, p 873. See [1988] Conv 16 (J.E.A.).

7 Such a tenancy is determinable on six months' notice (post, p 754).

application to such transactions as the granting of easements, profits and mortgages, and brings about the effect that informal grants in any of these cases are construed as contracts which, if capable of specific performance, are regarded as grants of equitable interests of the relevant kind.[8]

(5) Is a contract for a lease as good as a lease itself?

The effect of the doctrine of *Walsh v Lonsdale* is, in most cases, to convert a formally defective lease or a mere contract for a lease into a perfectly valid equitable lease on the terms of the parties' original agreement. In view of this result, it is often said that an agreement for a lease is as good as a lease itself.[9] For this reason the parties to a contract for a lease may well not seek specific performance at all and may be quite content to allow their obligations to be governed by a contract which never eventuates in the conveyance of a legal estate to the tenant.[10] For most purposes the mere contract is as efficacious as the legal lease itself. Yet the substantial truth of this proposition conceals certain significant respects in which a contract for a lease falls vitally short of the conveyance of a legal leasehold estate.[11]

(a) Parties are dependent on the availability of specific performance

The doctrine in *Walsh v Lonsdale* is entirely dependent on the availability of the discretionary remedy of specific performance.[12] It is for the party who seeks to rely on the doctrine to establish that he is entitled to specific performance of the contract for a lease. Thus the status of a tenant as an equitable tenant under *Walsh v Lonsdale* is dependent on the theoretical willingness of the court to grant the discretionary remedy of specific performance of his contract for a lease. If this contract is one in respect of which equity cannot or will not grant specific performance,[13] the tenant's position is then very different from that which would have obtained if a formal legal lease had been granted in the first place. In such a case the tenant's only remedy in respect of default by his landlord will be a mere action in damages for breach of contract, and in the meantime his rights

8 Post, pp 943, 1087.

9 See eg *In re Maughan, Ex parte Monkhouse* (1885) 14 QBD 956 at 958; *Lowther v Heaver* (1889) 41 Ch D 248 at 264 per Cotton LJ. Indeed, there are even certain respects in which a contract for a lease offers more liberal remedies than does the equivalent legal lease. Under a contract for a lease, for instance, the landlord enjoys the benefit of an *implied* right of re-entry in the event of breach by the tenant (post, p 807).

10 'Over the years there have been many cases in which the parties have relied on their equitable rights under agreements for leases. . .despite their frailties' (*McMahon v Ambrose* [1987] VR 817 at 830). See also *Re Eastdoro Pty Ltd* [1989] 2 Qd R 182 at 184.

11 'Although it has been suggested that the decision in *Walsh v Lonsdale* takes away all differences between the legal and equitable estate, it, of course, does nothing of the sort, and the limits of its applicability are really somewhat narrow' (*Manchester Brewery Co v Coombs* [1901] 2 Ch 608 at 617 per Farwell J).

12 'To that extent an equitable lease is vulnerable' (*Chan v Cresdon Pty Ltd* (1989) 168 CLR 242 at 261 per Toohey J).

13 The tenant may not, for instance, be able to enforce the contract in the county court simply because the value of the property falls outside the county court limit of jurisdiction (see County Courts Act 1984, s 23(d)).

will simply be those (much less secure) rights which exist by virtue of the periodic tenancy implied at law.[14]

(b) There is no 'privity of estate' under a contract for a lease

Certain leasehold covenants are binding on assignees of the original lessor and lessee respectively where there exists 'privity of estate'.[15] However, it is generally considered that 'privity of estate' arises only where a leasehold term is validly granted as a legal estate in the land and all subsequent assignments by either lessor or lessee are formally executed by deed. In the conventional view, no 'privity of estate' can obtain in relation to a contract for a lease quite simply because there exists no 'estate' to which anyone can be 'privy'. The net result is that leasehold covenants entered into by the original lessee under a contract for a lease may not be enforceable against his assignees—an illustration of the general rule that the benefit but not the burden of a contract is assignable. This is one important respect in which, at least from the point of view of the lessor, a contract for a lease is certainly not as good as a lease.

(c) Equitable tenant cannot claim the benefit of Law of Property Act 1925, s 62

The 'general words' provision of section 62 of the Law of Property Act 1925 is activated only by a 'conveyance' of a legal estate.[16] Section 62 cannot therefore be invoked by a tenant under a contract for a lease,[17] with the result that no easements can be implied in favour of such a tenant on the basis of the 'general words'.[18]

(d) Equitable tenant cannot plead purchase of a legal estate without notice

In the law relating to unregistered land, it is quite impossible for an equitable tenant to claim immunity from prior unregistrable, non-overreachable equitable interests. The binding effect of such interests is still governed by the equitable doctrine of notice,[19] and in advance of acquiring a legal term of years the contractual tenant cannot claim to be a bona fide purchaser of a legal estate for value without notice.[20]

(e) Equitable tenant is insecure against third parties

Perhaps the most important deficiency of a contract for a lease consists in the fact that the tenant is insecure against a third party who purchases his landlord's title (see *Fig.* 64).

14 Ante, p 742.
15 Post, p 847.
16 'Conveyance' is defined in Law of Property Act 1925, s 205(1)(ii).
17 *Borman v Griffith* [1930] 1 Ch 493 at 497f.
18 Post, p 1102.
19 Ante, p 278.
20 Ante, p 77.

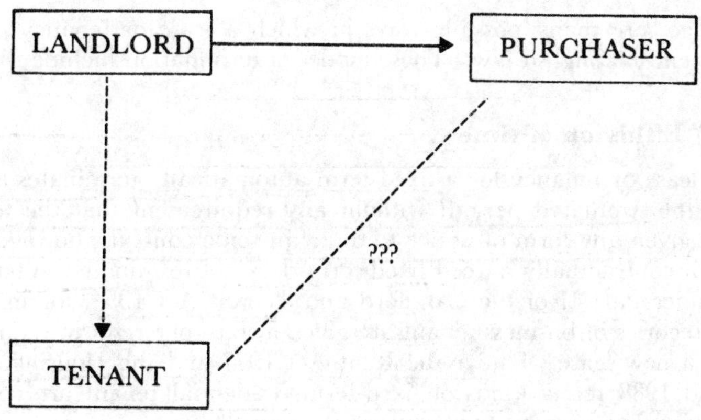

Fig. 64

(i) Unregistered land If the contract is specifically enforceable, the tenant is regarded as holding an equitable lease. Such an interest, if held in unregistered land, ought to be registered as a Class C(iv) land charge against the name of the landlord.[1] If not so registered, the equitable tenant's lease becomes void against any purchaser of a legal estate for money or money's worth irrespective of the purchaser's knowledge.[2] If for some reason the contract for a lease is not specifically enforceable, the tenant has at best a legal periodic tenancy which, although binding on the purchaser, may be determined by the appropriate notice to quit.

(ii) Registered land If a specifically enforceable contract for a lease relates to registered land, the tenant has an equitable interest which should be protected as a minor interest.[3] Such an interest, if not duly protected, is ineffective against a transferee of the landlord's registered title, subject only to the possibility that the tenant's interest may, in some circumstances, bind as an 'overriding interest'.[4]

If, conversely, the tenant's contract for a lease is not capable of specific performance, his position is that of a legal periodic tenant whose rights are binding on the transferee of the landlord's title,[5] but which may nevertheless be terminated at any time by the appropriate notice to quit.

1 Ante, p 141.
2 Land Charges Act 1972, s 4(6). See *Midland Bank Trust Co Ltd v Green* [1981] AC 513 at 527H–528A (ante, p 126).
3 Ante, p 181.
4 Land Registration Act 1925, s 70(1)(g). See *Grace Rymer Investments Ltd v Waite* [1958] Ch 831 at 849, 851 (ante, p 210).
5 Land Registration Act 1925, s 70(1)(k) as amended by Land Registration Act 1986, s 4(1) (ante, p 203).

6. TERMINATION OF LEASES AND TENANCIES

There are many possible ways in which a lease or tenancy may come to an end in English law.[6] These modes of termination include the following.

(1) Effluxion of time

A lease or tenancy for a fixed term automatically terminates on the expiry of the stipulated period[7] without any requirement that the tenant should be given any form of notice to quit.[8] In some contexts, however, the expiry of a contractually agreed fixed term does not terminate the tenant's rights. Under Part II of the Landlord and Tenant Act 1954, for instance, many categories of business tenant are given a statutory right to request the grant of a new lease.[9] Under the Rent Act 1977 and the Housing Acts of 1985 and 1988 many kinds of fixed-term residential tenant are converted into periodic tenants on the expiry of the term.[10]

(2) Notice to quit

A lease or tenancy may be determinable by notice to quit.[11] The availability of this method of termination depends to some extent on the quality of the tenancy concerned.[12]

(a) Fixed term tenancies

In the case of a fixed term of years a notice to quit is effective only if the parties have expressly agreed that this should be so, since otherwise such a lease simply continues until the expiry of the term. A long lease often

6 Until effective termination of the lease the tenant remains liable for any covenanted rent. Notwithstanding the tenant's service of a notice to quit, his liability persists if he fails to deliver up possession of the premises (eg if his wife remains in occupation). See Matrimonial Homes Act 1983, s 1(6); *Griffiths v Renfree* (1989) 21 HLR 338 at 342ff.

7 Notwithstanding expiry of a fixed term, it is not, however, lawful for a landlord to enforce his right to recover possession of premises let 'as a dwelling' by any means other than proceedings in court (Protection from Eviction Act 1977, s 3(1), as amended by Housing Act 1988, s 30). Section 3 thus prohibits re-entry without a court order except in the case of statutorily protected tenancies (which are covered by the Rent Act 1977 (post, p 873)) and 'excluded tenancies'. The latter category relates principally to accommodation shared by the tenant with a resident owner-occupier (see Protection from Eviction Act 1977, s 3A).

8 A lease which is expressly limited to continue only so long as the tenant abstains from breaching any covenant takes effect as a lease which is determinable by a proviso for re-entry on such breach (Law of Property Act 1925, s 146(7)).

9 Post, p 887.

10 Post, pp 876, 885, 881.

11 Unless the contrary is proved, service of the notice to quit is deemed to have been effected if the notice is posted. An assertion that the notice was not received does not constitute proof to the contrary (see *Lex Service Plc v Johns* (1989) 59 P & CR 427 at 432f). See also Law of Property Act 1925, s 196; Landlord and Tenant Act 1927, s 23.

12 There are also certain rules, of archaic derivation, relating to a holding over by the tenant after the expiry of a notice to quit. A tenant for years who holds over after the landlord's service of a written notice to quit becomes liable to pay the landlord double the annual value of the land in respect of the period of holding over (Landlord and Tenant Act 1730, s 1). Any holding over by any kind of tenant following notice (written or verbal) by the *tenant* is penalised by the imposition of a liability to pay double rent which is enforceable by action or distress (Distress for Rent Act 1737, s 18).

contains provision for a 'break notice' which allows either the landlord or the tenant to determine the lease by notice at any of a number of stipulated intervals in advance of the due determination of the term granted.[13]

(b) Periodic tenancies

It is intrinsic to the concept of a periodic tenancy that it should be determinable by a notice to quit given by *either* the landlord *or* the tenant.[14] As the House of Lords made clear in *Prudential Assurance Co Ltd v London Residuary Body*,[15] it is the constant and bilateral availability of this power of determination by notice which alone prevents the periodic tenancy from failing the general leasehold test of certainty of term.

(i) Contractual limitations on determination by notice In accordance with the certainty principle it is repugnant to the nature of periodic tenancy that the entitlement to give a notice to quit should be contractually confined to one or other party in the leasehold relationship.[16] Thus there can be no valid periodic tenancy (whether weekly,[17] yearly,[18] or otherwise) which contains a provision that the tenancy is determinable only by the tenant and not by the landlord. It is equally inconsistent with the concept of periodic tenancy that both parties should contractually be denied the power to give the other notice to quit.[19]

Even a partial restraint or fetter on the landlord's power of determination by notice may be enough to invalidate the arrangement as a periodic tenancy.[20] As Lord Templeman emphasised in the *Prudential Assurance* case,[1] a term of years must 'either be certain or uncertain. It cannot be partly certain because the tenant can determine it at any time and partly uncertain

13 A break clause cannot be exercised by a single joint tenant acting unilaterally (see *Hammersmith and Fulham LBC v Monk* [1992] 1 AC 478 at 490G per Lord Bridge of Harwich; *Hounslow LBC v Pilling* (1993) 25 HLR 305, per Nourse LJ).

14 Where a tenant dies intestate in mid-term, the landlord's notice to quit should be served upon the President of the Family Division of the High Court (*Practice Direction (Service of Notice to Quit)* [1965] 1 WLR 1237). The death of the tenant does not in itself terminate a tenancy, and if the tenant dies intestate the residue of his tenancy vests in the President of the Family Division (Administration of Estates Act 1925, s 9, as amended by Administration of Justice Act 1970, s 1, Sch 2). See *Wirral BC v Smith and Cooper* (1982) 4 HLR 81 at 84; (1983) 80 Law Soc Gaz 883 (M. Lee).

15 [1992] 2 AC 386 at 394F-395C per Lord Templeman (ante, p 691).

16 *Doe d Warner v Browne* (1807) 8 East 165 at 166f, 103 ER 305 at 306; *Prudential Assurance Co Ltd v London Residuary Body* [1992] 2 AC 386 at 394F per Lord Templeman. See also *Roe d Prideaux Brune v Prideaux* (1808) 10 East 158 at 187, 103 ER 735 at 746.

17 *Centaploy Ltd v Matlodge Ltd* [1974] Ch 1 at 15A–B per Whitford J.

18 *Prudential Assurance Co Ltd v London Residuary Body* [1992] 2 AC 386 at 395G per Lord Templeman.

19 *Prudential Assurance Co Ltd v London Residuary Body* [1992] 2 AC 386 at 394F per Lord Templeman.

20 See *Cheshire Lines Committee v Lewis & Co* (1880) 50 LJQB 121 at 124 per Lush J (periodic tenancy invalidated by proviso that landlord should not give notice before he required to demolish demised premises). In *Prudential Assurance Co Ltd v London Residuary Body* [1992] 2 AC 386 at 395G, the House of Lords overruled *In re Midland Railway Co's Agreement* [1971] Ch 725 at 733F–734A, where the Court of Appeal had upheld a proviso in a half-yearly tenancy which purported to inhibit the landlords from giving notice unless and until they required the premises for the purpose of their own undertaking.

1 [1992] 2 AC 386 at 395B–C.

because the landlord cannot determine it for an uncertain period.' It seems therefore that a fetter on the landlord's power of determination may be valid if limited to a defined period or portion of the lease,[2] but will otherwise cause the term to fail for uncertainty.[3]

In the *Prudential Assurance* case itself, a local authority landlord's power to determine by notice was expressly curtailed pending the landlord's need to requisition the land for the purpose of a road-widening scheme.[4] The indefinite nature of the term clearly invalidated the arrangement as a long lease, but in place of such a lease a yearly periodic tenancy had arisen by reason of the tenant's entry into possession and payment of periodic rent. The tenant unsuccessfully argued that this yearly tenancy impliedly incorporated the originally agreed fetter suspending exercise of the landlord's power of determination in the absence of a road-widening scheme.[5] The House of Lords ruled that a fetter of such uncertain duration was wholly repugnant to the notion of a periodic tenancy and could not therefore stand. According to Lord Templeman, such an inhibition on the landlord would have made 'a nonsense of the concept of a tenancy from year to year because it is of the essence of a tenancy from year to year that both the landlord and the tenant shall be entitled to give notice determining the tenancy.'[6] The yearly tenancy in this case was therefore terminable at any time by the giving of six months' notice by either party.[7]

(ii) Common law rules governing the length of notice In the absence of express agreement between landlord and tenant,[8] the length of the notice required in order to terminate a periodic tenancy is governed in the first instance by the common law and depends on the nature of the tenancy concerned.

A yearly tenancy may be determined by not less than half a year's notice expiring at the end of a year of the tenancy.[9] In the case of all other periodic

2 See *Prudential Assurance Co Ltd v London Residuary Body* [1992] 2 AC 386 at 395A, where Lord Templeman would have been prepared to uphold a yearly tenancy which was made subject to a fetter on the landlord's right to determine the tenancy 'before the expiry of five years unless the war ends'. Lord Templeman declared such a lease valid as a 'determinable certain term of five years'.

3 In *Prudential Assurance Co Ltd v London Residuary Body* [1992] 2 AC 386 at 395B, Lord Templeman indicated that the vice of uncertainty would taint a lease from year to year which fettered the landlord's right to give notice pending the occurrence of some entirely unpredictable event (eg 'the end of the war').

4 [1992] 2 AC 386 (ante, p 691).

5 The Court of Appeal had taken the view, on what it considered to be ordinary principles of contractual implication, that the parties would have been respectively 'astonished' and 'horrified' at the suggestion that the landlord's right of determination should not be so limited ((1992) 63 P & CR 386 at 399ff per Scott LJ).

6 [1992] 2 AC 386 at 392F–G.

7 [1992] 2 AC 386 at 393G–H.

8 *In re Threlfall* (1880) 16 Ch D 274 at 281f per Cotton LJ; *Ashburn Anstalt v Arnold* [1989] Ch 1 at 11F per Fox LJ; *Prudential Assurance Co Ltd v London Residuary Body* [1992] 2 AC 386 at 392C per Lord Templeman.

9 *Doe d Rigge v Bell* (1793) 5 Term Rep 471 at 472, 101 ER 265 at 266 per Lord Kenyon CJ; *Sidebotham v Holland* [1895] 1 QB 378 at 383; *Javad v Mohammed Aqil* [1991] 1 WLR 1007 at 1009B; *Prudential Assurance Co Ltd v London Residuary Body* [1992] 2 AC 386 at 392B-C per Lord Templeman. The notice need not be (but usually is) in writing (see *Doe d Lord Macartney v Crick* (1805) 5 Esp 196 at 197, 170 ER 784). For the purpose of computing the precise length of half a year's notice, the existence of a leap year is ignored (*Sunnyvale Services B O P Ltd v Bhana* [1986] 1 NZLR 314 at 317).

tenancies, the notice required at common law comprises at least one full period[10] (eg one month's notice in the case of a monthly tenancy,[11] and one week's notice in the case of a weekly tenancy[12]). In each case there is a requirement at common law that, in the absence of contrary agreement,[13] the notice should expire on the last day of a completed period of the tenancy (ie on a rent day).[14] Thus a notice to quit in relation to a weekly tenancy cannot be made to expire during the currency of a week.[15] The same approach is applicable mutatis mutandis to monthly and quarterly periodic tenancies.[16]

(iii) Statutory intervention The common law rules relating to notice must be read subject to the overriding provision contained in the Protection from Eviction Act 1977 that in the case of residential premises no notice to quit has any validity if it is given less than four weeks before the date on which it is to take effect.[17] This requirement applies irrespective of whether the notice is given by the landlord or by the tenant. In either case the notice must be in writing,[18] but a notice which is too short may be cured by an agreement on the part of the recipient to waive his strict rights.[19]

Where the landlord gives the tenant notice to quit, the written notice must include certain statutorily prescribed information[20] which assures the tenant that even after the notice has expired the landlord must take proceedings in court before the tenant can be lawfully evicted. The tenant

10 *Javad v Mohammed Aqil* [1991] 1 WLR 1007 at 1009B.

11 A month for this purpose is a calendar month (see Law of Property Act 1925, s 61(a)). Thus a month's notice should expire on the corresponding day of the next month (ie, a notice to quit given on 14 May should expire on 14 June). Where there is no 'corresponding day' (eg in relation to a month's notice given on 31 May), the notice should be made to expire on 30 June). See *Dodds v Walker* [1981] 1 WLR 1027 at 1030E–F.

12 *Queen's Club Gardens Estates Ltd v Bignell* [1924] 1 KB 117 at 124. For a suggestion that the common law rules relating to weekly and monthly tenancies are more flexible and may require the giving of *reasonable* notice, see E. Cooke, [1992] Conv 263. See also *Simmons v Crossley* [1922] 2 KB 95 at 103ff per Swift J.

13 *Soames v Nicholson* [1902] 1 KB 157 at 158. See, however, *Harler v Calder* (1988) 21 HLR 214 at 217.

14 See *Kemp v Derrett* (1814) 3 Camp 510 at 511, 170 ER 1463 at 1464; *Precious v Reedie* [1924] 2 KB 149 at 151f. The courts in England and elsewhere have refused to split hairs over the question whether a notice to quit on the anniversary date of a periodic tenancy is as effective as a notice to quit on the last day of the relevant period. In *Sidebotham v Holland* [1895] 1 QB 378 at 383, Lindley LJ observed that 'a notice to quit at the first moment of the anniversary ought to be just as good as a notice to quit on the last moment of the day before.' See also *Crate v Miller* [1947] KB 946 at 948f; *Municipality of Metropolitan Toronto v Atkinson* (1977) 78 DLR (3d) 142 at 147f per Laskin CJC.

15 *Queen's Club Gardens Estates Ltd v Bignell* [1924] 1 KB 117 at 124ff; *Lynch v Dolan* [1973] IR 319 at 328.

16 *Ex parte Maddocks; Re Brown* [1968] 3 NSWR 651 at 652.

17 Protection from Eviction Act 1977, s 5(1)(b). Section 5(1) of the 1977 Act does not apply to excluded tenancies under the Housing Act 1988 (see Protection from Eviction Act 1977, s 5(1B)(a)) but is relevant to restricted contracts (post, p 874). See *Lambeth LBC v Udechuku* (1981) 41 P & CR 200 at 208.

18 Protection from Eviction Act 1977, s 5(1)(a).

19 See *Elsden v Pick* [1980] 1 WLR 898 at 906A–B, 907H–908A, 909B. A unilateral waiver by one of a number of joint tenants cannot, however, release the landlord from the obligation to comply with section 5 of the 1977 Act (*Hounslow LBC v Pilling* (1993) 25 HLR 305).

20 Protection from Eviction Act 1977, s 5(1)(a). See The Notices to Quit (Prescribed Information) Regulations 1988 (SI 1988/2201). The landlord need not use the precise form of wording set out in these regulations, provided he transmits in substance the information required (see *Beckerman v Durling* (1981) 6 HLR 87 at 90; *Wilsher v Foster* [1981] CLY 1546).

must also be informed that he may be able to obtain free legal advice relating to his rights. In effect every effort must be made to ensure that the notice to quit does not have an intimidating impact on the occupier or inhibit his exercise of such legal rights as he may have. A notice which fails to include the prescribed information is invalid and ineffective to determine the tenancy.[1]

(iv) Notice to quit in relation to joint tenants Special problems may arise where a notice to quit is either served or received by one of a number of co-owners of an estate in land. Controversy often attaches to the unilateral action of one joint landlord or joint tenant who seeks to terminate a periodic tenancy by notice to quit.

The conceptual difficulties in this area were greatly clarified by the decision of the House of Lords in *Hammersmith and Fulham LBC v Monk*.[2] Here Lord Bridge of Harwich adverted to the long established analysis of the periodic tenancy as creating between landlord and tenant an estate in land which 'continued only so long as it was the will of both parties that it should continue'.[3] Each prolongation of the periodic tenancy is thus a positive act of continued endorsement of the leasehold relationship on both sides, no less effective because it connotes what Lord Bridge termed a 'tacit relocation' of the obligations of the tenancy during the superadded unit of time.[4] The law implies consent to this tacit relocation 'if all the parties are silent on the matter.'[5] Thus, in contemplation of law, each party 'signifies the necessary positive assent to the extension of the term for a further period' by his *omission* to give due notice of termination of the periodic tenancy.[6] Correspondingly, by the act of giving the appropriate notice to quit, either party may 'signify his unwillingness that the tenancy should continue' beyond the end of any period.[7]

Where the interest of either the landlord or the tenant is held *jointly* by two or more parties, it seems to follow from Lord Bridge's account of the logic of periodic tenancy that 'the will of all the joint parties is necessary to the continuance of the interest'[8] and that the withdrawal of any party's assent to the continuance of a periodic tenancy has terminal effect. Accordingly the House of Lords confirmed in *Hammersmith and Fulham LBC v Monk*[9] that an effective notice to quit may be given unilaterally by any one of two

1 A notice to quit is not invalidated by reason of the fact that it contains more information than is required by the Protection from Eviction Act 1977 (see *Meretune Investments v Martin* [1984] CLY 1917).
2 [1992] 1 AC 478. See [1992] Conv 279 (S. Goulding); [1992] CLJ 218 (L. Tee).
3 [1992] 1 AC 478 at 484F. See Blackstone's reference to tenancies from year to year as existing 'so long as both parties please' (*Bl Comm*, Vol II, p 147).
4 [1992] 1 AC 478 at 487H-488D.
5 See *Smith v Grayton Estates Ltd* 1960 SC 349 at 354 per Lord President Clyde.
6 [1992] 1 AC 478 at 490H-491A (ante, p 695).
7 [1992] 1 AC 478 at 484F. See also Lord Browne-Wilkinson at 492B. Obvious reasons of convenience point in favour of a rule which compels a conscious *opting out* rather than a regular *opting in* as the determinant of whether a periodic tenancy shall continue in force.
8 [1992] 1 AC 478 at 484F-G. See the statement of Lord Tenterden CJ in *Doe d Aslin v Summersett* (1830) 1 B & Ad 135 at 140, 109 ER 738 at 739, that each joint tenant 'holds the whole of all so long as he and all shall please'.
9 [1992] 1 AC 478.

or more joint landlords.[10] The notice is, in other words, no less valid because it is given, for instance, by one freeholder without the concurrence of the other freeholder or freeholders.[11]

The issue which fell for decision in *Hammersmith and Fulham LBC v Monk* concerned the related question whether a periodic tenancy may be determined by a notice given unilaterally by one of the joint owners of a *leasehold* interest. In *Monk*'s case, following a domestic dispute, one of two cohabiting joint tenants of a council flat gave the landlord authority notice to quit, thereby precipitating the homelessness of her erstwhile partner.[12] The House of Lords upheld the effectiveness of this notice, albeit that it was given without the knowledge or consent of the other cohabitee. The House declared itself clearly of the view that, in the absence of contrary provision in the tenancy agreement, the power of determination by notice may quite validly be exercised independently and without the concurrence of the other joint lessee or lessees.[13]

Once again, as Lord Browne-Wilkinson observed, the relevant legal issues highlighted the pervasive tension between the property- and contract-based analyses of the landlord-tenant relationship.[14] An 'instinctive reaction' founded on a 'property based' perspective prompted a 'revulsion' against the idea that one joint tenant could unilaterally terminate her partner's property rights in the home: his 'property rights in the home cannot be destroyed without his consent.'[15] Counterpoised against this response was a quite different 'contract based' reaction: the female cohabitee could not be 'held to a tenancy contract which is dependent for its continuance on the will of the tenant.'[16] In the view endorsed by the House of Lords, English law for at least 160 years has resolved the instant question by adoption of the 'contractual, as opposed to the property, approach'.[17]

Even this clear preference has not, however, removed all difficulty from this increasingly vexed area of the law. The House of Lords' ruling in *Hammersmith and Fulham LBC v Monk* leaves a cohabiting joint tenant exceedingly vulnerable to vindictive action by a disaffected partner. In *Hounslow LBC v Pilling*[18] a female joint tenant, acting unilaterally, purported to give her landlord authority notice to quit a shared weekly tenancy. The tenancy agreement had required written notice of four weeks 'or such lesser

10 [1992] 1 AC 478 at 485D per Lord Bridge of Harwich. In the words of Lord Browne-Wilkinson (at 492G), where there are joint lessors of a periodic tenancy, the continuing 'will' must be the 'will of all the lessors individually, not the conjoint will of all the lessors collectively.'

11 See *Doe d Aslin v Summersett* (1830) 1 B & Ad 135 at 140ff, 109 ER 738 at 739f; *Doe d Kindersley v Hughes* (1840) 7 M & W 139 at 141f, 151 ER 711 at 713; *Alford v Vickery* (1842) Car & M 280 at 283, 174 ER 507 at 508; *Parsons v Parsons* [1983] 1 WLR 1390 at 1399A; [1984] Conv 166 (J.T.F.). See generally F. Webb, [1983] Conv 194.

12 The female cohabitee had first ascertained the willingness of the council to rehouse her on termination of the tenancy.

13 [1992] 1 AC 478 at 491A per Lord Bridge of Harwich, 492H–493A per Lord Browne-Wilkinson. See *Doe d Lord Macartney v Crick* (1805) 5 Esp 196 at 197, 170 ER 784 per Lord Ellenborough; *Leek and Moorlands Building Society v Clark* [1952] 2 QB 788 at 793; *Greenwich LBC v McGrady* (1983) 46 P & CR 223 at 224.

14 Ante, p 674.

15 [1992] 1 AC 478 at 491H–492A.

16 [1992] 1 AC 478 at 492A. See also Lord Bridge of Harwich at 483B–E.

17 [1992] 1 AC 478 at 492F–G per Lord Browne-Wilkinson. See *Doe d Aslin v Summersett* (1830) 1 B & Ad 135, 109 ER 738.

18 (1993) 25 HLR 305.

period as the council may accept'. Accordingly, with the latter's consent, the departing cohabitee gave three days' notice to quit the premises. Some lingering sense of the property-oriented perspective on leasehold relationships caused the Court of Appeal to strain against this unilateral destruction of the domestic circumstances of the remaining joint tenant: the Court rejected the notice as inappropriate and therefore ineffective. Nourse LJ held that, in relying on the local authority's discretionary acceptance of a shorter period of notice, the departing cohabitee had not in fact exercised a power of determination by notice to quit but had instead sought to operate what amounted to a break clause in the tenancy agreement. It is, of course, clear law that a break clause cannot be invoked by one joint tenant unilaterally.[19] Thus, by means of a resourceful if somewhat forced construction of the facts, the Court of Appeal managed to prevent a collusive agreement between a joint tenant and her landlord authority from resulting in the arbitrary eviction of her partner.

(3) Forfeiture

In the event of a breach of covenant by the tenant, a lease may become determinable according to the rules of forfeiture. The law in relation to forfeiture is discussed in detail in the general context of remedies available to the landlord.[20]

(4) Surrender

A lease or tenancy may be determined by a surrender of the tenant's interest to his immediate landlord. If the landlord accepts the surrender, the tenant's term of years merges forthwith in the landlord's reversion and is extinguished.[1] A surrender offered by only one of two or more joint tenants is ineffective.[2] A surrender of the tenant's term may be made either expressly or impliedly by operation of law.[3]

(a) *Express surrender*

Since the surrender of a tenant's term is effectively a disposition of an estate

19 Ante, p 753.
20 Post, p 805.
1 Where a 'protected tenant' under the Rent Act remains throughout in possession of premises, he cannot, for instance, claim that a surrender of his protected tenancy converted him into a 'statutory tenant' (see *Foster v Robinson* [1951] 1 KB 149 at 158, 160) or prevented the inception of a 'protected shorthold tenancy' pursuant to Housing Act 1980, s 52(2) (see *Dibbs v Campbell* (1988) 20 HLR 374 at 380ff). In effect surrender seems to interpose a *scintilla temporis* which prevents any claim that the tenant was a protected tenant 'immediately before' the termination of the prior holding. See, however, S. Bridge, [1989] Conv 98 at 108f.
2 *Leek and Moorlands Building Society v Clark* [1952] 2 QB 788 at 795; *Greenwich LBC v McGrady* (1983) 46 P & CR 223 at 224; *Hammersmith and Fulham LBC v Monk* [1992] 1 AC 478 at 490G per Lord Bridge of Harwich.
3 *Foster v Robinson* [1951] 1 KB 149 at 155.

in the land,[4] an express surrender must be contained in a deed in order to be effective at law.[5] It is also likely that equity would be prepared to give effect to an express surrender made by mere writing.[6] However, surrender is not achieved by a document which merely manifests an intention on the part of the tenant to give up possession at some future stage.[7] Surrender must be accompanied by some (even notional) delivery up of possession[8] and cannot operate in futuro.[9] Where there is surrender by express agreement, the landlord has, of course, no claim for damages for the early termination,[10] although the surrender may command a money value payable by the tenant in the light of prevailing market factors.[11]

(b) Surrender by operation of law

Surrender occurs by operation of law where, with the landlord's concurrence or acquiescence, the tenant consciously does some act which is inconsistent with the continuance of the tenancy.[12] This form of surrender is ultimately founded on the doctrine of estoppel.[13] Implied surrender effectively requires 'a change of possession, or something that is equivalent to a change of

4 Surrender of a tenancy constitutes, for instance, a 'disposal' of assets in violation of a restraint order made in respect of the tenant pursuant to Drug Trafficking Offences Act 1986, s 8 (*In re R (Restraint Order)* [1990] 2 QB 307 at 314D–E). Somewhat surprisingly, however, a local authority landlord which accepts a surrender does not rank as an 'acquiring authority' within the Land Compensation Act 1973. Thus a tenant who surrenders a local authority tenancy on the assurance that alternative council accommodation will be provided has no entitlement to a 'disturbance payment' (see *R v Islington LBC, ex parte Knight* [1984] 1 WLR 205 at 210E–G).

5 Law of Property Act 1925, s 52(1). See *Hoggett v Hoggett* (1980) 39 P & CR 121 at 126. This requirement applies even to the surrender of an orally granted tenancy.

6 See *Hoggett v Hoggett* (1980) 39 P & CR 121 at 126. It used to be suggested that an oral surrender, if evidenced by writing or acts of part performance, might also be sufficient in equity (compare, however, *Townsend v Clifford* (1973) 228 Estates Gazette 135 at 139, 141).

7 *Re Humphrey and Ontario Housing Corporation* (1979) 96 DLR (3d) 567 at 569.

8 See *Brown v Draper* [1944] KB 309 at 313. In *Foster v Robinson* [1951] 1 KB 149 at 154, Evershed MR thought that surrender might be sufficiently established by 'either an actual yielding up of possession, or its equivalent'. Subsequent cases have seized gratefully on this reference to an 'equivalent' of delivery up of possession (see eg *Collins v Claughton* [1959] 1 WLR 145 at 148), with the result that express surrender perhaps need not involve an actual abandonment of occupation 'providing that the intention of all parties is clear'. See *Dibbs v Campbell* (1988) 20 HLR 374 at 382 per Purchas LJ (tenants did not vacate because of 'inclement weather prevailing at the time'). See S. Bridge, [1989] Conv 98 at 109.

9 *Whitehead v Clifford* (1814) 5 Taunt 518 at 519, 128 ER 791 at 792.

10 *Wood Factory Pty Ltd v Kiritos Pty Ltd* (1985) 2 NSWLR 105 at 133B per Priestley JA.

11 A tenant has been held entitled to recover from a subtenant the cost demanded by the landlord for surrender, where the surrender was precipitated by the subtenant's breach (*Morrison Lamothe Inc v Bedok* (1986) 29 DLR (4th) 255 at 291f).

12 *Fredco Estates Ltd v Bryant* [1961] 1 All ER 34 at 46G; *Mavromatis v Mavromatis* [1968] 1 NSWR 647 at 649. No formality is required in respect of a surrender by operation of law (Law of Property Act 1925, s 52(2)(c)), but it is not sufficient that the parties enter into a mere parol agreement to surrender which is unsupported by any confirmatory act of delivery of possession (see *195 Crown Street Pty Ltd v Hoare* [1969] 1 NSWR 193 at 199).

13 *Foster v Robinson* [1951] 1 KB 149 at 155 per Evershed MR. See also *Wallis v Hands* [1893] 2 Ch 75 at 82; *RT & MI Abela Pty Ltd v Esso Australia Ltd* (1989) 89 ALR 485 at 501.

possession',[14] in circumstances where it would subsequently be unconscionable to plead the absence of a formal deed of surrender.

(i) Actual delivery up of possession Where an implied surrender is premised on some claim of actual delivery up of possession by the tenant, it must be shown that the tenant has intentionally and unequivocally removed all evidence of his possession under the former tenancy. The return of the tenant's key, accompanied by the tenant's going out of occupation, represents a classic instance of surrender by operation of law,[15] although this implication may be less persuasive in the case of a commercial lease.[16] It must be clear that the tenant's actions were intended to mark the surrender of his term[17] and were accepted by the landlord as doing so.[18] The mere vacation of the rented property does not necessarily connote a surrender by the tenant, even if he discontinues his payment of rent.[19] In such a case it is always open to the landlord to regard the tenancy as subsisting and to sue for the arrears of rent. The courts may, however, be more ready to find a surrender by operation of law where a departing tenant has left behind him sizeable arrears of rent and remains absent for a substantial period of time.[20] The implication of surrender is even stronger where the absent tenant was also in substantial breach of other leasehold covenants[1] or where the landlord begins to use the vacated premises for his own purposes (eg by reletting them).[2] In such circumstances the inference must be powerful that the tenancy has been abandoned and that the landlord has finally accepted this fact.[3]

In determining whether surrender has occurred, the courts have tended to have recourse to concepts of 'corpus possessionis' and 'animus revertendi'.

14 *Hoggett v Hoggett* (1980) 39 P & CR 121 at 126. See also *Oastler v Henderson* (1877) 2 QBD 575 at 578.

15 See *E.S. Schwab & Co Ltd v McCarthy* (1976) 31 P & CR 196 at 205, although Oliver J (at 206ff) doubted whether, in the case of registered land, such a surrender could in the absence of a registered disposition be effective to vest in the landlord anything more than a mere equitable interest in the tenant's lease. See also *Palfrey v Palfrey* (1974) 229 Estates Gazette 1593 at 1595.

16 See *Oastler v Henderson* (1877) 2 QBD 575 at 578ff; *Buchanan v Byrnes* (1906) 3 CLR 704 at 722f; *Wood Factory Pty Ltd v Kiritos Pty Ltd* (1985) 2 NSWLR 105 at 137B–C per Priestley JA, 146A–B per McHugh JA.

17 See *Heath Estates Ltd v Burchell* (1979) 251 Estates Gazette 1173 at 1174.

18 See *Wood Factory Pty Ltd v Kiritos Pty Ltd* (1985) 2 NSWLR 105 at 146B per McHugh JA (continued assertion of rent liability inconsistent with acceptance of surrender).

19 *Addy v Donnelly* [1983] Court of Appeal Bound Transcript 506; *NRMA Insurance Ltd v B & B Shipping and Marine Salvage Co Pty Ltd* (1947) 47 SR (NSW) 273 at 282f. The surrender of a statutory tenancy under the Rent Act 'is no easy matter' (*Hulme v Langford* (1985) 50 P & CR 199 at 202 per Stephenson LJ), not least because the courts are disinclined to allow the protection conferred by a special statutory regime to be contracted, or still less given, away. See also *Mavromatis v Mavromatis* [1968] 1 NSWR 647 at 651.

20 *Preston BC v Fairclough* (1982) 8 HLR 70 at 73.

1 *Andrews v Hogan* (1952) 86 CLR 223 at 252 per Fullagar J; *Wood Factory Pty Ltd v Kiritos Pty Ltd* (1985) 2 NSWLR 105 at 137D–F per Priestley JA.

2 *Hughes v NLS Pty Ltd* [1966] WAR 100 at 101f; *Sandum v Holmes* (1985) 16 DLR (4th) 629 at 633; *Wood Factory Pty Ltd v Kiritos Pty Ltd* (1985) 2 NSWLR 105 at 133C–D per Priestley JA, 146A per McHugh JA.

3 *Wood Factory Pty Ltd v Kiritos Pty Ltd* (1985) 2 NSWLR 105 at 133C per Priestley JA. As the element of agreed termination becomes weaker, the concepts of surrender and repudiation tend to merge with a doctrine of abandonment. See *Stagg v Wyatt* (1838) 2 Jur 892, but compare *Sauerzweig v Feeney* [1986] IR 224 at 226f.

There is no surrender by operation of law while there remains any physical or symbolic evidence (or 'corpus') of the tenant's possession or so long as the tenant retains any intention (or 'animus') to return to the property. Thus the tenant's 'corpus' of possession can be preserved intact where the tenant has departed but his wife,[4] his furniture,[5] or his dog[6] remain at the premises. Moreover, a continuing 'corpus' of possession can be maintained vicariously where the tenant's wife, even though physically absent during the relevant period, intends to return to the property.[7]

(ii) Constructive delivery up of possession There may even be a constructive delivery up of possession, as for instance where a tenant does not relinquish his possession but accepts some new status inconsistent with that enjoyed under the former tenancy.[8] It seems, however, that where one kind of letting arrangement is supposedly replaced by another,[9] the court will not accept that there has been a valid surrender of the earlier tenancy unless there is clear evidence of the grant of a new tenancy or licence.[10] Where the parties do not have in mind the 'substantial result' of bringing about a new arrangement on terms different from those of the earlier tenancy, the court will not infer that a new relationship has been formed between the parties and will therefore decline to accept that the earlier tenancy has been surrendered by operation of law.[11]

(iii) Wrongful termination by landlord It has been suggested that another instance of surrender by operation of law occurs where a landlord wrongfully terminates a tenancy and brings about the dispossession of the tenant. If in such circumstances the tenant takes no steps to recover possession, a time must come when as a matter of fact he will be treated as having elected to accept

4 *Old Gate Estates Ltd v Alexander* [1950] 1 KB 311 at 318ff. The tenant can be said to retain a 'corpus' of possession even where, against his will, his wife insists upon exercising either her common law right to reside in the matrimonial home (see *Middleton v Baldock* [1950] 1 KB 657 at 662ff) or her statutory 'rights of occupation' under the Matrimonial Homes Act 1983 (see *Hoggett v Hoggett* (1980) 39 P & CR 121 at 126ff). See generally Chapter 7 (ante, p 155).

5 *Old Gate Estates Ltd v Alexander* [1950] 1 KB 311 at 317.

6 *Hoggett v Hoggett* (1980) 39 P & CR 121 at 126f.

7 *Hoggett v Hoggett* (1980) 39 P & CR 121 at 127f (wife in hospital for operation).

8 See *Foster v Robinson* [1951] 1 KB 149 at 159, where the tenant accepted a rent-free licence for life and Evershed MR thought it irrelevant for the purpose of this surrender that the key had not been 'handed over and then been handed back the next minute' to mark the superseding of the old relationship by a new and different one. See also *Palfrey v Palfrey* (1974) 229 Estates Gazette 1593 at 1595; *Short Bros (Plant) Ltd v Edwards* (1979) 249 Estates Gazette 539 at 542.

9 A landlord has no power to grant a new lease during the term of an existing tenancy except on the footing that the old lease has been surrendered. The tenant, by accepting the new lease, is estopped from denying such surrender (see *Jenkin R. Lewis & Son Ltd v Kerman* [1971] Ch 477 at 496B–C per Russell LJ).

10 *Hulme v Langford* (1985) 50 P & CR 199 at 203ff. Here the tenant had requested that the landlord should transfer a tenancy out of his name into that of his wife. However, the Court of Appeal held that, in order to be effective, such a surrender would necessarily have involved a 'tripartite agreement' between the tenant, the landlord and the wife.

11 *Take Harvest Ltd v Liu* [1993] 2 WLR 785 at 794F–H per Sir Christopher Slade (Judicial Committee of the Privy Council).

the landlord's wrongful act.[12] There is similarly a surrender by operation of law where the tenant gives up possession in response to an invalid notice to quit.[13]

(5) Disclaimer

A lease or tenancy may be terminated by various instances of disclaimer of the relationship of landlord and tenant.[14]

(a) *Disclaimer by denial of title*

One form of disclaimer is of medieval origin and occurs where the tenant denies or repudiates his landlord's title 'either by setting up the title of a rival claimant or by asserting a claim of ownership in himself'.[15] Such conduct breaches the implied condition in every lease that the tenant shall not do anything which may prejudice the position of his landlord.[16] The tenant's lease becomes automatically liable to forfeiture on the basis that repudiation of the superior title is incompatible with the fundamental obligations owed by the tenant to his landlord[17] and indicates an intention to be no longer bound by the contract of tenancy.[18]

In order to be effective repudiation must be clear and unambiguous.[19] Thus a disclaimer of the landlord's title to a mere part of the demised premises does not necessarily constitute a disclaimer as to the whole of the premises.[20] Any repudiation by the tenant of the leasehold relation may, of course, be ignored by the landlord, who is perfectly entitled to continue to enforce the terms of the demise.[1] Equally, however, the landlord may elect to re-enter and, by serving proceedings for possession, may accept the tenant's repudiation and bring the relationship to an end.[2]

12 See *Wood Factory Pty Ltd v Kiritos Pty Ltd* (1985) 2 NSWLR 105 at 121B–D, where Priestley JA observed that the landlord's 'offer' to the tenant to accept a surrender of the lease would take 'the form of a breach of the most important term of the lease itself.'

13 *Grimman v Legge* (1828) 8 B & C 324 at 326f, 108 ER 1063 at 1064; *Dodd and Davies v Acklom* (1843) 6 Man & G 672 at 680ff, 134 ER 1063 at 1066f; *Sandum v Holmes* (1985) 16 DLR (4th) 629 at 632f.

14 A unilateral disclaimer by one joint tenant alone is ineffective (see *Hammersmith and Fulham LBC v Monk* [1992] 1 AC 478 at 490G per Lord Bridge of Harwich).

15 *Warner v Sampson* [1959] 1 QB 297 at 318 per Hodson LJ, 324 per Ormerod LJ.

16 *W.G. Clark (Properties) Ltd v Dupre Properties Ltd* [1992] Ch 297 at 308D.

17 *Doe d Ellerbrock v Flynn* (1834) 1 CM & R 137 at 141, 149 ER 1026 at 1028; *Vivian v Moat* (1881) 16 Ch D 730 at 734; *Wisbech St Mary Parish Council v Lilley* [1956] 1 WLR 121 at 125; *Warner v Sampson* [1959] 1 QB 297 at 312f.

18 *W.G. Clark (Properties) Ltd v Dupre Properties Ltd* [1992] Ch 297 at 303C; *Milton v Proctor* (1989) NSW ConvR 55-450 at 58,262 per Clarke JA.

19 *Doe d Gray v Stanion* (1836) 1 M & W 695 at 703, 150 ER 614 at 617; *W.G. Clark (Properties) Ltd v Dupre Properties Ltd* [1992] Ch 297 at 303C per Thomas Morison QC.

20 See *W.G. Clark (Properties) Ltd v Dupre Properties Ltd* [1992] Ch 297 at 304F–G, 305C–D, where Thomas Morison QC did not rule out the possibility that a partial disclaimer may lead to a forfeiture of part of the premises.

1 *W.G. Clark (Properties) Ltd v Dupre Properties Ltd* [1992] Ch 297 at 303B.

2 *W.G. Clark (Properties) Ltd v Dupre Properties Ltd* [1992] Ch 297 at 306E–F, 307E. It may well be that the service of a notice under Law of Property Act 1925, s 146 (post, p 817) is a prerequisite to re-entry, with the result that the disclaiming tenant may be able to seek relief from forfeiture (see *W.G. Clark (Properties) Ltd*, supra at 309E per Thomas Morison QC). Compare, however, *Warner v Sampson* [1958] 1 QB 404 at 422ff.

(b) Disclaimer by the tenant's trustee in bankruptcy

Another kind of disclaimer may arise on the bankruptcy of the tenant. It is open to the tenant's trustee in bankruptcy to disclaim[3] a subsisting lease owned by the bankrupt if that lease comprises property which is 'unsaleable or not readily saleable' or is likely to give rise to a 'liability to pay money or perform any onerous act'.[4] Such a disclaimer has the effect of terminating the lease[5] and releasing both the bankrupt and his estate from all further liability in connection with it.[6]

(6) Repudiatory breach

Relatively recent developments in the law of landlord and tenant have revived the possibility that the concept of disclaimer or repudiation may have an even wider application to leases than was previously thought. Many common law jurisdictions have come to accept that the breach by either landlord or tenant of a 'fundamental term' of the lease may constitute such a repudiation of the lease as to entitle the other party, at his election, to regard the lease as terminated and to sue immediately for damages in respect of the loss of the lease.[7] This view of the contractual implications of repudiatory conduct is, of course, closely linked with the general drift away from the 'property-based approach' in respect of leasehold relationships.[8]

During the present century English courts have not been willing to accept that ordinary contractual principles relating to wrongful repudiation can apply generally in the context of a term of years.[9] In retrospect, however, it is evident that the decision of the House of Lords in *National Carriers Ltd*

3 A disclaimer of interest in a licence to assign relating to a lease operates as a disclaimer of the lease itself (see *MEPC plc v Scottish Amicable Life Assurance Society* (1993) *Times*, 6 April).

4 Insolvency Act 1986, s 315(1), (2)(b). The disclaimer may require the approval of the court (Insolvency Act 1986, s 317). Whereas a trustee in bankruptcy may disclaim a protected tenancy under the Rent Act 1977 (see *Smalley v Quarrier* [1975] 1 WLR 938 at 943E, 945D–E; *Fletcher v Davies* (1981) 257 Estates Gazette 1149), he cannot disclaim a statutory tenancy (*Sutton v Dorf* [1932] 2 KB 304 at 308). The latter form of tenancy lacks the quality of a true proprietary estate and does not therefore vest in the tenant's trustee (post, p 876). See also Insolvency Act 1986, s 283(3A)(b).

5 Exercise of the trustee's statutory right to disclaim extinguishes the tenant's interest in the property immediately without any question of acceptance by the landlord (*W.G. Clark (Properties) Ltd v Dupre Properties Ltd* [1992] Ch 297 at 303B–C).

6 Insolvency Act 1986, s 315(3)(a).

7 Landmark decisions were those of the Canadian Supreme Court in *Highway Properties Ltd v Kelly, Douglas & Co Ltd* (1971) 17 DLR (3d) 710 and the High Court of Australia in *Progressive Mailing House Pty Ltd v Tabali Pty Ltd* (1985) 157 CLR 17. See also *Wood Factory Pty Ltd v Kiritos Pty Ltd* (1985) 2 NSWLR 105 at 115E–F, 121A–B, 130A–133E, 143G–144C; *Nangus Pty Ltd v Charles Donovan Pty Ltd* [1989] VR 184 at 188f; *Lehndorff Canadian Pension Properties Ltd v Davis Management Ltd* (1989) 59 DLR (4th) 1 at 16f.

8 Ante, p 675. See *Hammersmith and Fulham LBC v Monk* [1992] 1 AC 478 at 491E–492A, 492G per Lord Browne-Wilkinson.

9 See eg *Total Oil of Great Britain Ltd v Thompson Garages (Biggin Hill) Ltd* [1972] 1 QB 318 at 324A-C per Lord Denning MR. See, however, *Hussein v Mehlman* [1992] 2 EGLR 87 at 89K, where Sedley QC pointed out that the *Total Oil* case 'silently overruled an important line of cases. . .in which, throughout the 19th century, the courts took it as axiomatic that a contract of letting could be terminated by the innocent party without notice if the other party failed to fulfil a fundamental term of the contract.'

v Panalpina (Northern) Ltd,[10] by exposing leases to the operation of the contractual doctrine of frustration, substantially opened the way for reconsideration of the issue in English law.[11] A heavily persuasive force in this direction is already provided by the tempting analogy of disclaimer of title, which enables the landlord at his election to treat the lease as terminated.[12]

In *Hussein v Mehlman*[13] the tenants under a three-year lease vacated their rented home after only 15 months on the ground of gross and persistent breaches by their landlord of his statutory obligations of repair and maintenance under the Landlord and Tenant Act 1985.[14] Declining to accept any 'major premise' that a lease of land is 'in its essence different from other contracts',[15] Sedley QC upheld the tenants' claim for damages for repudiatory breach of contract by the landlord. This important decision confirms the increasing tendency in English law to subject tenancy law to the application of general contractual doctrine.[16] It remains to be seen how far the ramifications of repudiatory breach will extend in this unfamiliar context. As Sedley QC acknowledged,[17] the acceptance of a principle of elective termination by repudiatory breach appears equally applicable to certain kinds of default by a tenant in payment of rent in so far as 'the obligation to pay rent is as fundamental as the obligation to keep the house habitable'. It seems clear that decisions such as *Hussein v Mehlman* are likely to bring about a dramatic reversal of the well established principle in at least the modern English law of landlord and tenant that performance of the parties' respective obligations is not interdependent.

(7) Merger

A lease may be determined by merger where the tenant acquires the landlord's reversion and holds both interests in the same name and in exercise of the same legal capacity.[18] Under these circumstances—at least so long as there is no contrary intention—the lease merges with the reversionary title and is extinguished.[19]

(8) Frustration

It has been recognised for a long time that the individual covenants contained

10 [1981] AC 675 (post, p 765).
11 See eg *Progressive Mailing House Pty Ltd v Tabali Pty Ltd* (1985) 157 CLR 17 at 28f per Mason J; *Wood Factory Pty Ltd v Kiritos Pty Ltd* (1985) 2 NSWLR 105 at 123G per Priestley JA.
12 See Hicks, *The Contractual Nature of Real Property Leases*, 24 Baylor L Rev 443 (1972).
13 [1992] 2 EGLR 87; Conv 71 (S. Bright); [1993] CLJ 212 (C. Harpum).
14 See Landlord and Tenant Act 1985, s 11 (post, p 789).
15 [1992] 2 EGLR 87 at 89E.
16 See also *Killick v Roberts* [1991] 1 WLR 1146 at 1149H, where the Court of Appeal held that a tenancy agreement which one party had been induced to enter into by reason of the fraud of the other could be rescinded at the innocent party's election. See [1992] CLJ 21 (L. Tee); [1992] Conv 269 (J. Martin).
17 [1992] 2 EGLR 87 at 90H-J.
18 It is not sufficient, for instance, that the tenant should have acquired the reversion merely qua personal representative (*Chambers v Kingham* (1878) 10 Ch D 743 at 746).
19 See Law of Property Act 1925, s 185.

in a lease may be suspended or discharged in so far as supervening impossibility of performance affects continuing or future obligations.[20] Only fairly recently, however, has it been accepted that the contractual doctrine of frustration may sometimes apply to the existence of the lease as a whole.[1] In *National Carriers Ltd v Panalpina (Northern) Ltd*,[2] the House of Lords ruled by a majority that a lease can be affected by frustration, although the cases in which the doctrine will be applicable are likely to be 'exceedingly rare'.[3] It must be shown that a 'supervening event' has brought about such a 'fundamental change of circumstances as to enable the court to say—"this was not the bargain which these parties made and their bargain must be treated as at an end".'[4] In the *National Carriers* case itself the only access road leading to the demised premises had been closed by the local authority for a period of 18 months during a ten-year lease. The House of Lords declined to accept that this interruption of access had been of sufficient gravity to frustrate the entire lease.[5]

(9) Enlargement

There exists a little used facility pursuant to section 153 of the Law of Property Act 1925 for the enlargement of certain long leases into a fee simple estate.[6] It is open to the tenant to execute a deed of enlargement in respect of a lease which was granted for a term in excess of 300 years, of which at least 200 years remain unexpired.[7] Qualifying leases must not be liable to be determined by re-entry for condition broken,[8] nor must any rent of money value be payable.[9] After enlargement the tenant takes the fee simple subject to all the same covenants and provisions which governed the now extinguished lease.[10]

(10) Termination on statutory grounds

Leases and tenancies may also be terminated on a number of express statutory grounds which are examined more closely in Chapter 18.[11]

20 *Cricklewood Property and Investment Trust Ltd v Leighton's Investment Trust Ltd* [1945] AC 221 at 240.
1 For the older law, see *Cricklewood Property and Investment Trust Ltd v Leighton's Investment Trust Ltd* [1945] AC 221 at 228ff.
2 [1981] AC 675. See [1981] Conv 227 (K. Hodkinson); (1981) 32 NILQ 162 (B. Dickson); [1981] CLJ 217 (S. Tromans); (1982) 60 Can Bar Rev 619 (J.T. Robertson).
3 [1981] AC 675 at 692B-D, 697A.
4 [1981] AC 675 at 717D per Lord Roskill.
5 [1981] AC 675 at 697G-698A, 707B-F, 718A. It is quite possible, however, that the answer would have been different in the case of a more lengthy interruption of access.
6 See also the operation of the Leasehold Reform Act 1967 (post, p 766).
7 Law of Property Act 1925, s 153(1). A sublease can be enlarged only if it was created out of a superior term which is itself capable of enlargement under the Law of Property Act 1925 (see Law of Property Act 1925, s 153(2)(ii)).
8 Law of Property Act 1925, s 153(2)(i).
9 Law of Property Act 1925, s 153(1)(b).
10 Law of Property Act 1925, s 153(8).
11 Post, p 873.

7. THE TENANT'S 'RIGHT TO BUY'

Recent decades have witnessed in Britain a quite remarkable shift from leasehold to freehold tenure.[12] The expansion of the so-called 'property-owning democracy'[13] has been particularly promoted by several significant legislative devices aimed at promoting domestic owner-occupation through leasehold enfranchisement.

(1) Leasehold Reform Act 1967

A controversial means of leasehold enfranchisement is contained in the Leasehold Reform Act 1967. The principal object of this legislation is to confer on certain tenants holding long leases a right compulsorily to purchase either the freehold reversion or an extended term of years in the property which they occupy.

On the expiry of a long lease the demised premises (inclusive of any construction, improvements or repairs effected by the tenant) revert to the landlord without any compensation for the tenant. In 1966 the Labour Government of the day recognised that residential long leases had 'worked very unfairly against the occupying leaseholder'[14] in that, although the freeholder had provided the land, it was the original leaseholder who in the vast majority of cases had either built the house at his own expense or had borne the cost of improvements and maintenance during the currency of the term.[15] The ensuing Leasehold Reform Act 1967 was therefore formulated on the premise that 'the land belongs in equity to the landowner and the house belongs in equity to the occupying leaseholder.'[16] The Act effectively confers on the tenant a right to acquire the freehold by compulsory purchase from the landlord.[17]

(a) Qualifying conditions

The Leasehold Reform Act 1967 applies only to premises which consist of a 'house'.[18] For this purpose a 'house' can comprise a terraced or semi-detached house or an entire house divided up into flats or maisonettes, but

12 Post, p 933.

13 See Lord Diplock's reference in *Pettitt v Pettitt* [1970] AC 777 at 824C to 'the emergence of a property-owning, particularly a real-property-mortgaged-to-a-building-society-owning, democracy.'

14 *Leasehold Reform in England and Wales* (Cmnd 2916, 1966), para 1.

15 It was acknowledged to be 'quite indefensible, if justice is to be done as between freeholder and occupying leaseholder', that property which had been cherished and improved as the home of the leaseholder should revert without compensation to the landlord at the expiry of the term (Cmnd 2916, para 1).

16 Cmnd 2916, para 4.

17 Any attempt by contractual means to exclude or modify the tenant's rights under the Leasehold Reform Act 1967 is in principle void (see Leasehold Reform Act 1967, s 23(1)). See *Buckley v S.R.L. Investments Ltd and Cator and Robinson* (1971) 22 P & CR 756 at 767; *Rennie v Proma Ltd & Byng* (1990) 22 HLR 129 at 137ff; *Woodruff v Hambro* (1991) 23 HLR 295 at 299ff.

18 Leasehold Reform Act 1967, s 2(1).

not an individual flat[19] or a tower block of flats.[20] The tenant must hold a 'long tenancy', ie a term certain which when granted was in excess of 21 years,[1] and this tenancy must be 'at a low rent'.[2] The tenant must also be able to show *either* that he has occupied the relevant house[3] as his only or main residence[4] for a period of at least three years prior to notifying his desire to exercise his statutory rights *or* that he has so occupied the house for periods together totalling three years during the ten years prior to the service of his notice.[5]

(b) The tenant's statutory rights

The Leasehold Reform Act confers on a qualifying tenant two substantive rights. *First*, the tenant has a right to require that his existing lease be replaced by a new tenancy for a term which expires 50 years after the expiry date of the existing tenancy.[6] *Second*, the tenant has an alternative right to the enfranchisement of his lease, in that he is entitled compulsorily to purchase the freehold in the demised premises.[7]

The tenant may, at any time during the original term of years,[8] serve a written notice on the landlord, indicating his desire to avail himself of one or other of his statutory entitlements.[9] The mere right to serve such a notice does not in itself constitute an interest in the land,[10] but the tenant's rights after service of the notice can be protected by registration of a Class

19 Leasehold Reform Act 1967, s 2(1)(a). See [1982] Conv 241.

20 *Lake v Bennett* [1970] 1 QB 663 at 671A. See *Tandon v Trustees of Spurgeons Homes* [1982] AC 755 at 766F-H, where the House of Lords was prepared to accept that the Act could apply to leasehold premises which comprised a shop with living accommodation above. See [1982] Conv 378. See also *Lake v Bennett* [1970] 1 QB 663 at 671C, 672D-E; *Sharpe v Duke Street Securities NV* (1988) 55 P & CR 331 at 334ff.

1 Leasehold Reform Act 1967, s 3(1). Certain categories of lease are excluded either in whole or in part from the scope of the Leasehold Reform Act 1967. Such categories include leases of National Trust property (Leasehold Reform Act 1967, s 32) and leases from a charitable housing trust (Leasehold Reform Act 1967, s 1(3), as amended by Leasehold Reform, Housing and Urban Development Act 1993, s 67).

2 Leasehold Reform Act 1967, s 1(1)(a). The 'low rent' limits have historically been defined with reference to specified rateable values and the 'letting value' of the property (Leasehold Reform Act 1967, s 4(1)). However, with effect from the commencement of the Leasehold Reform, Housing and Urban Development Act 1993, the 'low rent' criterion will effectively cease to be a precondition of the statutory right to *enfranchise* (as distinct from *extend*) a lease (see Leasehold Reform Act 1967, s 1A, as introduced by Leasehold Reform, Housing and Urban Development Act 1993, s 63).

3 It is sufficient that he has occupied only part of the house (see *Harris v Swick Securities Ltd* [1969] 1 WLR 1604 at 1607E-F).

4 See *Poland v Earl Cadogan* [1980] 3 All ER 544 at 549c-550j (tenant put himself outside the ambit of the Leasehold Reform Act by going abroad and leaving it to his daughter and Harrods to sublet his house).

5 Leasehold Reform Act 1967, s 1(1)(b), as amended by Housing Act 1980, s 141, Sch 21, para 1(1). See *Harris v Plentex* (1980) 40 P & CR 483 at 485f.

6 Leasehold Reform Act 1967, s 14(1).

7 Leasehold Reform Act 1967, s 8(1).

8 Leasehold Reform Act 1967, s 16(1)(a).

9 Leasehold Reform Act 1967, ss 8(1), 14(1), 22, Sch 3. Where the tenant has served such a notice, the landlord may not, during the currency of the tenant's claim, bring any proceedings to terminate the tenancy without the leave of the court (Leasehold Reform Act 1967, Sch 3, para 4(1)). See, however, *Central Estates (Belgravia) Ltd v Woolgar* [1972] 1 QB 48 at 55H-56A, 56G-57A.

10 See *Uddin v Birmingham CC* (1990) 59 P & CR 341 at 345.

C(iv) land charge (in the case of unregistered land)[11] and by the entry of a minor interest in the register of title (in the case of registered land).[12]

(c) *Price*

Where the tenant exercises his right to obtain a 50 year extension of his existing lease, no price or premium is payable other than the rent due under the lease.[13] Where the tenant exercises his right to purchase the freehold reversion, the price payable is fixed with reference to the value which the house, if sold on the open market by a willing seller, might be expected to realise on the basis of certain assumptions detailed in the statute.[14] In default of agreement between landlord and tenant, the price payable is determined by a local Leasehold Valuation Tribunal, with a right of appeal to the Lands Tribunal.[15] Historically the price payable to the landlord has tended to be a fairly depressed price,[16] but recent alterations in the compensation formulae made by the Leasehold Reform, Housing and Urban Development Act 1993 will almost certainly have the effect of raising the general level of consideration for the landlord's compulsory transfer.[17]

(d) *The 'human rights' challenge*

One of the underlying assumptions of the Leasehold Reform Act 1967 has been that the true investment input in a qualifying lease derives essentially from the tenant, either in the form of the capital premium for which the leasehold term was initially purchased or by way of the tenant's construction and maintenance of a dwelling-house on the site. In such cases the landlord's capital investment has either been fully compensated already or been dwarfed by the tenant's own investment of capital. Thus, on one view, the Leasehold Reform Act 1967 merely regularises the landlord-tenant relationship by recognising the tenant's moral right to be regarded as the absolute owner of the property. However, this analysis is controversial not least because

11 Ante, p 144. An unregistered notice is rendered void against a purchaser for money or money's worth, irrespective of his knowledge of the tenant's rights under the Leasehold Reform Act (see *Buckley v S.R.L. Investments Ltd and Cator and Robinson* (1971) 22 P & CR 756 at 763f, 768).

12 Ante, p 181. It is clear that the tenant's rights arising from service of his notice can never constitute an overriding interest pursuant to Land Registration Act 1925, s 70(1)(g) (Leasehold Reform Act 1967, s 5(5), ante, p 213).

13 Leasehold Reform Act 1967, s 15(2)(a). After the expiry of 25 years from the term date of the original lease a higher rent may become payable in accordance with Leasehold Reform Act 1967, s 15(2)(b).

14 See Leasehold Reform Act 1967, s 9, as amended by Leasehold Reform, Housing and Urban Development Act 1993, s 66, Sch 15.

15 Housing Act 1980, s 142, Sch 22.

16 See eg *Divis v Middleton* (1983) 268 Estates Gazette 157 (£665 for freehold of property subject to unexpired term of 89 years); *London & Winchester Properties Ltd's Appeal* (1983) 267 Estates Gazette 685 at 686, *Wilkes v Larkcroft Properties Ltd* (1983) 268 Estates Gazette 903 at 906 (£560 and £420 respectively for freeholds of properties subject to unexpired terms of 17 years); *Effra Investments Ltd v Stergios* (1982) 264 Estates Gazette 449 at 453 (£34,500 for freehold property valued at £70,000 with vacant possession where the tenant served his notice one month before expiry of 99 year lease).

17 See Leasehold Reform, Housing and Urban Development Act 1993, s 66, Sch 15.

the 1967 Act frequently brings about a compulsory transfer of an increasingly valuable capital asset, at a depressed or sometimes derisory price, just as the long leasehold term reaches towards its term date. It has been said with force that the Act 'greatly favours the tenant'[18] and is in effect 'an expropriatory Act'.[19]

In 1984 the Leasehold Reform Act 1967 was challenged in the European Court of Human Rights as a violation of the requirement in the European Convention on Human Rights that '[n]o one shall be deprived of his possessions except in the public interest...'.[20] In *James v United Kingdom*,[1] trustees acting on behalf of the Duke of Westminster, the freehold owner of large areas of Belgravia, alleged that the operation of the 1967 Act had already caused losses to the Duke's estate in excess of £2.5 million.[2] The European Court rejected the claim, holding that the compulsory transfer of property from one individual to another 'may, depending upon the circumstances, constitute a legitimate means for promoting the public interest'.[3] Although the applicants' complaint was not 'groundless',[4] the United Kingdom Parliament's belief in the existence of social injustice in 1967 'was not such as could be characterised as manifestly unreasonable' in view of the relative capital investments of landlord and tenant.[5] In the Court's view, housing represents a 'prime social need, the regulation of which cannot entirely be left to the play of market forces.' There must be legislative competence to secure 'greater social justice in the sphere of people's homes, even where such legislation interferes with existing contractual relations between private parties and confers no direct benefit on the State or the community at large.'[6]

(2) Landlord and Tenant Act 1987

Purchase by a tenant of his landlord's superior interest was further promoted by the Landlord and Tenant Act 1987, which introduced a limited right

18 *Tandon v Trustees of Spurgeons Homes* [1982] AC 755 at 761A per Lord Wilberforce (dissenting).
19 *Manson v Duke of Westminster* [1981] QB 323 at 332C per Stephenson LJ. It is often painfully clear that the benefits of the 1967 Act are not conferred on the deprived or disadvantaged. In spite of its socialist origins, the Act is primarily of benefit to those who are already possessed of sufficient capital resources or borrowing power to acquire long leases in the first place.
20 Article 1 of Protocol No 1 to the European Convention on Human Rights.
1 (1986) 8 EHRR 123.
2 Although the unencumbered freehold value of the properties so far enfranchised varied from £44,000 to £225,000, the prices paid by the tenants had ranged from £2,500 to £111,000. Many of the enfranchising tenants had since sold up their newly acquired freeholds, some at an instant profit of over £100,000.
3 (1986) 8 EHRR 123 at 140. The Court cited in support the U.S. Supreme Court's endorsement of state legislation for the compulsory transfer of title from lessors to lessees in the interests of reducing the concentration of land ownership (see *Hawaii Housing Authority v Midkiff*, 467 US 229 at 241ff, 81 L Ed 2d 186 at 198ff (1984)).
4 (1986) 8 EHRR 123 at 144.
5 (1986) 8 EHRR 123 at 144. The Court laid great emphasis on the fact that any 'windfall profits' gained through onward sales by the enfranchising tenants had been made, not at the expense of the applicants who had received the statutorily prescribed compensation, but at the expense of the predecessors in title of the enfranchising tenants (para 69).
6 (1986) 8 EHRR 123 at 143.

of pre-emption for tenants of premises contained within a block of flats.[7] Under the 1987 Act qualifying tenants are entitled to a right of first refusal in the event of any disposal of their landlord's interest in the property.[8] The landlord may not dispose of his interest without first serving on the qualifying tenants a notice indicating both his intention and the proposed sale price.[9] The notice is statutorily deemed to constitute an offer by the landlord to dispose of the property on those terms which may be accepted by the requisite majority of the qualifying tenants.[10] The tenants must then be allowed a period of not less than two months[11] within which they may accept[12] or reject the offer or make a counter-offer.[13] A binding acceptance of the landlord's offer may be made by qualifying tenants with more than 50 per cent of the 'available votes', ie by a bare majority of the qualifying tenants who own 'constituent flats' in the relevant building on the expiry date of the landlord's notice.[14] If the landlord's offer is rejected, the landlord is free during the next twelve months to dispose of his interest provided that he does so for a consideration not less than that specified in the original notice and on terms which correspond to the other terms of that notice.[15]

(3) Leasehold Reform, Housing and Urban Development Act 1993

One of the alleged shortcomings of the Leasehold Reform Act 1967 has always been that it has no application to the leasehold estate in a flat as distinct from a 'house'.[16] This deficiency is now remedied by Part I of the Leasehold Reform, Housing and Urban Development Act 1993, which confers a 'right of collective enfranchisement' on certain categories of qualifying tenants holding leases in blocks of flats.[17] Subject to compliance with certain fairly tightly drawn conditions, qualifying tenants will be able under the Act to have the freehold of the premises 'acquired on their behalf' by a person or persons nominated by them and at a price determined in accordance with the statute.[18] The professed objective of the reform is to enable flat owners to gain effective ownership and managerial control of their blocks of flats. The legislation has proved controversial partly because of the way in which it endorses yet a further process of compulsory acquisition from

7 The enactment came in response to the concern expressed by the Nugee Committee in 1985 to provide increased safeguards for the interests of long leaseholders in mansion blocks (see *Report of the Committee of Inquiry on the Management of Privately Owned Blocks of Flats* (Chairman: E.G. Nugee QC, 1985), Vol 1, para 7.9.13ff).

8 See *Denetower Ltd v Toop* [1991] 1 WLR 945 at 948B–D per Browne-Wilkinson V-C.

9 Landlord and Tenant Act 1987, s 1(1). It is sufficient if the notice is served on at least 90 per cent of the qualifying tenants (Landlord and Tenant Act 1987, s 5(4)).

10 Landlord and Tenant Act 1987, s 5(2)(b).

11 Landlord and Tenant Act 1987, s 5(2)(c).

12 Landlord and Tenant Act 1987, s 6.

13 Landlord and Tenant Act 1987, s 7.

14 Landlord and Tenant Act 1987, ss 5(6), 6(1)(b).

15 Landlord and Tenant Act 1987, s 6(3).

16 Ante, p 766.

17 Any agreement to exclude or modify the statutory entitlement is generally void (Leasehold Reform, Housing and Urban Development Act 1993, s 93).

18 Leasehold Reform, Housing and Urban Development Act 1993, s 1(1). On payment of a statutorily determined premium qualifying tenants are also given, in relation to their individual flats, certain rights to acquire in substitution of their existing lease a new lease of 90 years at a peppercorn rent (ss 39(1), 56(1), Sch 13).

existing freeholders and partly because the benefits of statutory enfranchisement are still withheld from a substantial minority of leaseholders.

(a) Eligible property

The 1993 Act applies to premises which consist of a building containing two or more flats held by 'qualifying tenants'.[19] The freehold in the building must be owned by the one and the same person.[20] Certain categories of property are significantly excluded from the scope of the Act. The legislation does not apply to premises of which more than 10 per cent of the internal floor area is designated for non-residential use, eg as shops or other commercial premises.[1] Nor does the Act cover premises where there is a resident landlord[2] and the premises do not contain more than four flats or units.[3] The 'qualifying tenants' must hold at least two-thirds of the total number of flats in the building,[4] with the consequence that the benefits of collective enfranchisement are denied to those living in blocks of flats where more than one third of the flats are rented rather than held by long lease.

(b) Qualifying tenants

Qualifying tenants must hold a 'long lease' of a flat,[5] a 'long lease' being defined essentially as a term of years certain which when granted was in excess of 21 years.[6] The lease must moreover be 'at a low rent'.[7] This restriction most controversially excludes from the scope of the 1993 Act those thousands of tenants under leases granted on or after 1 April 1990 who pay annual ground rents set at more than £1,000 in London and £250 elsewhere.[8]

A strict residence condition is attached to the status of 'qualifying tenant'. The claimant tenant must have occupied his flat 'as his only or principal home' either for the preceding twelve months or for periods amounting to three years in the preceding ten years.[9] The fear has been widely expressed that this residence condition will dramatically limit the process of enfranchisement under the 1993 Act. Many tenants who would otherwise qualify to exercise the right to collective enfranchisement will lose the opportunity simply because a significant minority of flat owners in their

19 Leasehold Reform, Housing and Urban Development Act 1993, s 3(1)(a), (b).
20 Leasehold Reform, Housing and Urban Development Act 1993, s 3(1)(a).
1 Leasehold Reform, Housing and Urban Development Act 1993, s 4(1). Garage, parking space and storage areas, if ancillary to a particular dwelling in the premises, are taken to be occupied or designated for residential purposes (s 4(2)). Common parts of the building are disregarded (s 4(3)).
2 See Leasehold Reform, Housing and Urban Development Act 1993, s 10.
3 Leasehold Reform, Housing and Urban Development Act 1993, s 4(4).
4 Leasehold Reform, Housing and Urban Development Act 1993, s 3(1)(c).
5 Leasehold Reform, Housing and Urban Development Act 1993, s 5(1).
6 Leasehold Reform, Housing and Urban Development Act 1993, s 7(1). The lease must not be a business lease (s 5(2)(a)) and the Act does not generally apply to leases held from a charitable housing trust (s 5(2)(b)).
7 Leasehold Reform, Housing and Urban Development Act 1993, s 5(1).
8 Leasehold Reform, Housing and Urban Development Act 1993, s 8(1)(c).
9 Leasehold Reform, Housing and Urban Development Act 1993, s 6(1), (2). Occupation by a company 'or other artificial person' is not regarded as relevant occupation (s 6(3)). Under a lease held by joint tenants, the residence condition need only be satisfied in respect of one joint tenant (s 6(4)).

block fail the residence condition. The benefits of the Act are therefore unavailable where, in any particular block of flats, more than one third of the flats have been purchased for investment purposes or by persons living or working abroad or who are otherwise non-resident in the required sense.[10]

(c) Exercise of the right to collective enfranchisement

The exercise of the statutory right to collective enfranchisement is initiated by the service of a notice of claim on the reversioner by not less than two thirds of the 'qualifying tenants' of the flats contained in the premises.[11] Thereafter the conduct of all proceedings on behalf of the participating tenants is in the hands of the 'nominee purchaser'.[12] These proceedings, involving a statutory routine of notice and counter-notice, are designed to lead to a conveyance to the nominee purchaser of the fee simple estate in the premises.[13] The price of this form of compulsory acquisition is fixed by reference to criteria laid down in the Act.[14] These criteria assume a sale on the open market by a willing seller[15] and incorporate elements of value designed to compensate the freeholder for his share of the 'marriage value' (ie the increased value generated by the merger of freehold and leasehold interests)[16] and for any other loss resulting to him from the enfranchisement.[17]

(4) Housing Act 1985

A significant aspect of the charter of rights conferred on the public sector tenant takes the form of his statutory 'right to buy' the home in which he lives. This right was introduced in the Housing Act 1980 and is now contained in the Housing Act 1985.[18]

(a) Nature of the 'right to buy'

The Housing Act 1985 confers on certain qualifying categories of 'secure tenant'[19] the right, in statutorily defined circumstances, to purchase either the freehold or a long leasehold term in the property in which the secure

10 It is inferable that the residence qualification will raise many of the same problems as are brought into focus under the Rent Act requirements of residence (post, p 877).
11 Leasehold Reform, Housing and Urban Development Act 1993, s 13(1), (2). No qualifying tenant may participate in giving a relevant notice of claim if at this date he is obliged to give up possession of his flat in pursuance of a court order (Leasehold Reform, Housing and Urban Development Act 1993, Sch 3, para 3(1)). A qualifying tenant is likewise debarred (except with leave of the court) where any proceedings are pending to enforce a right of re-entry or forfeiture against him (Sch 3, para 3(2)). No such proceedings may be instituted by the landlord (except with leave of the court) during the currency of any claim to exercise the right to collective enfranchisement (Sch 3, para 7(1)).
12 Leasehold Reform, Housing and Urban Development Act 1993, s 15(1).
13 Leasehold Reform, Housing and Urban Development Act 1993, s 34(1).
14 Leasehold Reform, Housing and Urban Development Act 1993, s 32(1), Sch 6.
15 Leasehold Reform, Housing and Urban Development Act 1993, Sch 6, para 3(1).
16 Leasehold Reform, Housing and Urban Development Act 1993, Sch 6, para 4.
17 Leasehold Reform, Housing and Urban Development Act 1993, Sch 6, para 5.
18 For further reference to the origins of the 'right to buy', see Chapter 20 (post, p 935).
19 Post, p 882.

tenant lives.[20] This right has been described as bearing a 'strong resemblance to an option to purchase'.[1] The secure tenant is entitled to acquire the freehold if his dwelling-house is a 'house' and his landlord owns the freehold.[2] If his dwelling-house is not a 'house' but is a flat or if his landlord is not the owner of the freehold, the secure tenant has a right to be granted a long lease for a term of usually not less than 125 years at a rent which does not exceed £10 per annum.[3]

(b) Conditions of eligibility

The 'right to buy' is conferred by the 1985 Act on any secure tenant who satisfies a complex series of statutory conditions.[4] The 'right to buy' relates only to a 'dwelling-house' within the definition of the 1985 Act.[5] A secure tenant qualifies for the 'right to buy' if he has been a secure tenant of a public sector landlord for a period of at least two years,[6] although neither the landlord nor the dwelling-house need have been the same during the whole of this period.[7] The tenant cannot, however, exercise the 'right to buy' if, at any stage before the completion of his purchase, he becomes the subject of a possession order made against him on any of the grounds which permit the landlord to recover possession under the Housing Act 1985.[8]

20 Where a qualifying secure tenancy is a joint tenancy, the 'right to buy' belongs to all the tenants jointly (Housing Act 1985, s 118(2), ante, p 392). A secure tenant may also nominate not more than three 'members of his family' to share the 'right to buy' with him, but may validly do so only if those members are not already joint tenants but occupy the dwelling-house as their 'only or principal home' (Housing Act 1985, s 123(1)). If the secure tenant dies before the completion of the purchase, the nominee or nominees may exercise the 'right to buy' by survivorship (see *Harrow LBC v Tonge* (1992) 25 HLR 99).

1 *Dance v Welwyn Hatfield DC* [1990] 1 WLR 1097 at 1100A per Nourse LJ.

2 Housing Act 1985, s 118(1)(a).

3 Housing Act 1985, s 118(1)(b), Sch 6, Part III, paras 11, 12(1).

4 Housing Act 1985, s 138(1), as amended by Leasehold Reform, Housing and Urban Development Act 1993, Sch 22). Once the statutory conditions have been satisfied, the landlord has no discretion to resist the exercise of the right to buy (see *Taylor v Newham LBC* [1993] 2 All ER 649 at 655e). As soon as all matters relating to the grant have been agreed or determined, the landlord's duty to convey becomes enforceable by injunction (Housing Act 1985, s 138(3)), and the tenant becomes immediately the equitable owner of the property (see *Dance v Welwyn Hatfield DC* [1990] 1 WLR 1097 at 1104F–1105B per Nourse LJ).

5 A dwelling-house is a 'house' if it is 'a structure reasonably so called' (s 183(2)) and a dwelling-house which is not a house is a 'flat' (s 183(3)). Where a building is divided horizontally, the resulting residential units are 'flats' rather than 'houses' (s 183(2)(a)). Certain kinds of property are excepted from the scope of the Act (Housing Act 1985, Sch 5, as amended by Leasehold Reform, Housing and Urban Development Act 1993, s 106). See *Freeman v Wansbeck DC* (1983) 82 LGR 131 at 134ff.

6 Housing Act 1985, s 119(1). This qualifying period need not be a continuous period (Housing Act 1985, Sch 4, para 1), nor need it be a period immediately preceding the tenant's exercise of his 'right to buy' (see Housing Act 1980, s 27(3); Housing Act 1985, Sch 4, para 2(a)).

7 See Housing Act 1980, s 1(3)(a). Even though a tenant has not himself resided for a period of two years, the requisite residence may include residence by a spouse with whom he was living at the date on which he claimed the 'right to buy'(Housing Act 1985, Sch 4, para 2(a)).

8 Housing Act 1985, s 121(1). See *Enfield LBC v McKeon* [1986] 1 WLR 1007 at 1015G–H, where the Court of Appeal held that a tenant's attempt to exercise her 'right to buy' had been effectively pre-empted by the Council's recovery of possession on the ground that the accommodation afforded by the house was more extensive than was required by the tenant.

If the law were not so, as Slade LJ pointed out in *Enfield LBC v McKeon*,[9] a secure tenant would always be able to frustrate the enforcement of any possession order against him—no matter how good the ground on which it was made—by the simple device of claiming the 'right to buy'. The tenant also loses the 'right to buy' if, at any point before completion of the purchase, he ceases to hold a secure tenancy.[10]

(c) *Terms of purchase*

A secure tenant exercises his 'right to buy' by serving a written notice on the landlord.[11] The qualifying tenant has a right to purchase either the freehold or a long leasehold term at the price which such an interest would achieve on the open market,[12] minus a discount which is variable in accordance with the duration of the pre-existing secure tenancy.[13] In order to prevent private profiteering at public expense, the 1985 Act imposes in cases of 'early disposal' an obligation to repay in part or whole any discount which was made in favour of the tenant on the exercise of his 'right to buy'.[14] On purchase the tenant is required to covenant to repay a statutorily prescribed portion of the discount in the event of any onward sale of the fee simple or grant of a long lease during the three years immediately following his purchase.[15]

The completion of a purchase under the 'right to buy' terminates any secure tenancy previously enjoyed by the purchasing tenant.[16] Thereafter the position of the purchaser is governed largely by the terms and covenants which are attached by the Housing Act 1985 to the conveyance of his freehold or the grant of his lease.[17]

9 [1986] 1 WLR 1007 at 1015F-G. Compare, however, *Dance v Welwyn Hatfield DC* [1990] 1 WLR 1097 at 1105G.

10 See eg *Muir Group Housing Association Ltd v Thornley* (1992) 25 HLR 89 at 97 (tenant innocently sublet whole house shortly before completion date, thereby forfeiting his status as secure tenant pursuant to Housing Act 1985, s 93(2) (post, p 884)).

11 Housing Act 1985, s 122(1).

12 Housing Act 1985, ss 126(1)(a), 127(1)-(3).

13 Housing Act 1985, s 126(1)(b). In the case of a house the appropriate discount ranges from 32 per cent to a maximum of 60 per cent after 30 years of qualifying residence (Housing Act 1985, s 129(2)(a)). In the case of a flat the relevant discount ranges from 44 per cent to a maximum of 70 per cent (Housing Act 1985, s 129(2)(b)). The maximum discount allowable is currently fixed at £50,000. See Housing Act 1985, s 131(2); The Housing (Right to Buy) (Maximum Discount) Order 1989 (SI 1989/513).

14 This obligation constitutes a charge which may be protected under Land Registration Act 1925 by entry against the purchaser's registered title (Housing Act 1985, s 156(3)). Certain disposals are exempted from the liability to repay the discount (see Housing Act 1985, s 160(1)), eg a disposal on divorce in pursuance of a property transfer order made under Matrimonial Causes Act 1973, s 24. See, however, *R v Rushmoor BC, ex parte Barrett* [1989] QB 60 at 69A-B (immunity does not therefore cover a sale ordered under Matrimonial Causes Act 1973, s 24A, where the net proceeds of sale are divided between the spouses).

15 Housing Act 1985, ss 155(1), (2), 159(1)(b).

16 Housing Act 1985, s 139(2).

17 Housing Act 1985, s 139(1). See generally Housing Act 1985, Sch 6. The conveyance or grant cannot normally exclude or restrict the general words implied under Law of Property Act 1925, s 62 (ante, p 7). See Housing Act 1985, Sch 6, para 1.

(d) The 'rent to mortgage' scheme

The secure tenant who qualifies for the exercise of the statutory 'right to buy' is entitled to purchase with the aid of mortgage finance advanced by the landlord authority. For this purpose the Leasehold Reform, Housing and Urban Development Act 1993 confers on the secure tenant a right to acquire the freehold or a long lease 'on rent to mortgage terms'.[18] Under the 'rent to mortgage' scheme the periodic payments made by the tenant, if fixed at a specified level, enable him gradually to redeem the 'landlord's share' secured by mortgage to the landlord.

The 'rent to mortgage' scheme replaces the graduated form of purchase facility previously afforded by a 'shared ownership lease' granted under the Housing Act 1985.[19] Under a 'shared ownership lease' the tenant did not purchase outright either a freehold or a leasehold estate in the entire property, but instead purchased a notional proportion (usually an 'initial share' of 50 per cent) of the property on a long lease,[20] while remaining a periodic tenant and paying a periodic rent in respect of the remainder. The 'shared ownership lease' allowed for the possibility of progressive purchase by the tenant, by conferring a right to acquire 'additional shares' in the dwelling-house (in multiples of 12.5 per cent).[1] The tenant could thus increase the proportion of his capital share in the dwelling-house by stages until he completed the acquisition of 100 per cent of the property and became eligible (where his landlord owned a fee simple estate) to have the freehold conveyed to him.[2]

The 'rent to mortgage' scheme differs from the 'shared ownership' scheme essentially in so far as it enables the qualifying tenant of a dwelling-house to make an immediate purchase of an estate in fee simple.[3] The purchaser on 'rent to mortgage' terms is otherwise subject to roughly equivalent conditions of purchase. In particular, the 'rent to mortgage' purchaser is entitled to a similar discount based on qualifying periods of residence.[4] Any pre-existing secure tenancy comes to an end on the occasion of any grant made in pursuance of the right to acquire on 'rent to mortgage' terms.[5] There is also provision for repayment of discount by the purchaser in the event of any disposal of the property within three years of purchase.[6]

(e) The 'preserved right to buy'

The Housing Act 1985 also provides measures designed to protect the tenant's 'right to buy' where the landlord's interest in his dwelling-house is 'privatised',

18 Housing Act 1985, s 143(1), as substituted by Leasehold Reform, Housing and Urban Development Act 1993, s 108.
19 See Housing Act 1985, s 143(1) (old version).
20 Housing Act 1985, s 145(2), (3), Sch 6, para 12(1).
1 Housing Act 1985, Sch 8, para 1(1).
2 Housing Act 1985, Sch 8, para 2(1).
3 Housing Act 1985, s 150(1)(a), as substituted by Leasehold Reform, Housing and Urban Development Act 1993, s 115.
4 Housing Act 1985, s 148, as substituted by Leasehold Reform, Housing and Urban Development Act 1993, s 113.
5 Housing Act 1985, s 151(2), as substituted by Leasehold Reform, Housing and Urban Development Act 1993, s 116.
6 Housing Act 1985, s 155(3), as substituted by Leasehold Reform, Housing and Urban Development Act 1993, s 120.

ie transferred from public ownership into ownership within the private sector. Where the secure tenant's dwelling-house is the subject of such a disposal to a private sector landlord, the tenant is given a 'preserved right to buy' which is effective against the new landlord in exactly the same terms as formerly against the original public sector landlord.[7] The bindingness of this 'preserved right to buy' on the new landlord depends, however, on the entry of the right against the appropriate register of title,[8] and if not duly registered in this way the 'preserved right to buy' will become entirely ineffective.[9]

7 Housing Act 1985, s 171B(1).
8 Housing Act 1985, Sch 9A, para 5(4) (see The Housing (Preservation of Right to Buy) Regulations 1989 (SI 1989/368), Reg 3, Sch 2).
9 Housing Act 1985, Sch 9A, para 6(2).

CHAPTER 18

Leasehold covenants

For most of the past century English law has adhered to the general principle that there is no interdependence between the proper performance of the covenants of landlord and tenant respectively. This rule is itself in marked contrast with the historic principle of English contract law that breach of a material covenant by one contracting party relieves the other contracting party of his obligations under the contract.[1] Yet, at least until recently, a breach of the landlord's responsibilities under a lease has not usually been considered to release the tenant or entitle him to throw up the lease.[2] Nor has the tenant any right, for instance, to take part in a 'rent strike' in order to bring pressure to bear upon a defaulting landlord.[3] In this sense the remedial rights of landlord and tenant have been distributed most unevenly: subject to certain constraints imposed by law the landlord normally retains a right to forfeit the lease in the event of misconduct by the tenant.[4] It seems likely, however, that the increasing penetration of contractual doctrine into the law of landlord and tenant will do much to reverse the traditional independence of covenanted obligations in the leasehold context.[5]

1. LEASEHOLD RIGHTS AND OBLIGATIONS

A lease characteristically contains a number of express and implied rights and obligations relevant to one or other or both of the parties.

1 *Kingston v Preston* (1773) 2 Doug 689, 99 ER 437 per Lord Mansfield). See generally W.M. McGovern, *Dependent Promises in the History of Leases and Other Contracts*, 52 Tulane L Rev 659 at 666ff (1977–78); J.A. Humbach, *The Common-Law Conception of Leasing: Mitigation, Habitability, and Dependence of Covenants*, 60 Wash Univ LQ 1213 (1982–83).

2 For partial exceptions to this rule, see *Smith v Marrable* (1843) 11 M & W 5, 152 ER 693 (post, p 783); *Lee-Parker v Izzet* [1971] 1 WLR 1688 (post, p 795). On the unsatisfactory nature of the tenant's rights under the general law, see eg *Poverty and the Residential Landlord–Tenant Relationship* (Research Report by Adrian Bradbrook, Canberra 1975), p 49.

3 See eg *Amrani v Oniah* [1984] CLY 1974; *Bishop v Moy* [1963] NSWR 468 at 469f. The tenant must instead avail himself of some existing remedy by way of damages or injunction or specific performance. If the tenant withholds rent, he is liable to be sued for arrears by the landlord and may find that his non-payment of rent affords the landlord a ground for forfeiting the lease and recovering possession. For the sad fate of a tenant who retaliated to non-repair by her landlord by withholding service charges, see *Di Palma v Victoria Square Property Co Ltd* [1984] Ch 346 (post, p 815).

4 Compare the landlord and tenant law of Ontario, where it has been enacted that 'the common law rules respecting the effect of the breach of a material covenant by one party to a contract on the obligation to perform by another party apply to tenancy agreements' (Landlord and Tenant Act (RSO 1980, c 232), s 89). Likewise the Uniform Residential Landlord and Tenant Act adopted in several American jurisdictions specifically allows the tenant to raise a breach of covenant by the landlord as a defence in any action for possession for non-payment of rent (see Uniform Residential Landlord and Tenant Act, s 4.105).

5 See eg the recent and highly significant ruling of Sedley QC in *Hussein v Mehlman* [1992] 2 EGLR 87 (post, p 794).

(1) Express obligations of the landlord

Most formal leases contain a wide range of express covenants entered into by the landlord stipulating rights and responsibilities in respect of such matters as repair, insurance, rights of access, options for renewal and the like. The precise content of these covenants is left to be determined largely by the parties themselves, although the normal balance of bargaining power as between landlord and tenant ensures that the express burdens of the leasehold relationship are usually allocated more heavily to the tenant than the landlord. Where, however, a landlord has undertaken an express obligation, the courts tend to construe the relevant covenant strictly according to its terms.[6]

(2) Implied obligations of the landlord

In the absence of express contrary agreement, the relationship of lessor and lessee impliedly imposes certain general and traditionally defined obligations on the landlord.[7] These obligations vary slightly depending on the legal or equitable nature of the lease.

(a) Legal lease

The implied obligations of the landlord under a legal lease include the following.

(i) Covenant for quiet enjoyment There is in every lease an implied covenant or contractual term[8] that the landlord shall permit the tenant 'quiet enjoyment' of the premises let.[9] The covenant has nothing to do with noise-free enjoyment of the demised premises, but impliedly guarantees that the tenant shall be immune from the exercise of adverse rights over the land.[10]

6 See eg *Posner v Scott-Lewis* [1987] Ch 25 at 33C–F (covenant to employ resident porter in block of flats).

7 These obligations may be modified or varied by specific arrangement between landlord and tenant and if a deed contains an express covenant dealing with a particular matter in respect of the demised premises, 'there is no room for an implied covenant covering the same ground or any part of it' (*Malzy v Eichholz* [1916] 2 KB 308 at 313f). See also *Line v Stephenson* (1838) 4 Bing (NC) 678 at 682ff, 132 ER 950 at 952, affd (1838) 5 Bing (NC) 183 at 186, 132 ER 1075 at 1076; *Miller v Emcer Products Ltd* [1956] Ch 304 at 319; *Lend Lease Development Pty Ltd v Zemlicka* (1985) 3 NSWLR 207 at 218D–F.

8 In strict terms a 'covenant' exists only in relation to a lease by deed, but there is an equivalent implied contractual term for quiet enjoyment in tenancies not granted by deed (see *Budd-Scott v Daniell* [1902] 2 KB 351 at 355f).

9 *Budd-Scott v Daniell* [1902] 2 KB 351 at 356f; *Markham v Paget* [1908] 1 Ch 697 at 715f; *Kenny v Preen* [1963] 1 QB 499 at 511.

10 See *Hudson v Cripps* [1896] 1 Ch 265 at 268. The covenant for quiet enjoyment has been described as being 'an ordinary incident of a tenancy...it is of the very essence of the tenancy' (*Kanizaj v Brace* [1954] NZLR 283 at 284). The fact of a demise is sufficient to create an implied condition that the landlord is entitled to grant some term in the demised premises (*Miller v Emcer Products Ltd* [1956] Ch 304 at 318f per Romer LJ), although this implied condition of title is excluded by an express covenant for quiet enjoyment which makes no promise as to title (see *W.G. Clark (Properties) Ltd v Dupre Properties Ltd* [1992] Ch 297 at 305F–H).

The landlord thus has a duty to ensure that the tenant remains free of any physical interference with or interruption of his enjoyment of the demised premises during the currency of the lease.[11] Although the landlord's obligation is not absolute, it covers not merely his own conduct (whether rightful or wrongful) but also the rightful (but not wrongful[12]) acts of any person claiming 'under' him.[13]

The covenant for quiet enjoyment does not impose on the landlord a positive obligation to perform repairs in the demised premises which otherwise would not be his responsibility.[14] There may, however, be a breach of the implied covenant for quiet enjoyment where, for instance, a burst water pipe in premises retained by the landlord causes water to flow into and damage the tenant's premises[15] or where a landlord has defaulted in his covenant to maintain the weatherproofing of other parts of a block of flats.[16]

Any harassment or unlawful eviction of the tenant constitutes a breach of the landlord's implied covenant for quiet enjoyment.[17] The landlord's conduct may thus give rise to an action in damages or to an injunction on behalf of the tenant,[18] but harassment has not traditionally entitled the tenant to terminate the tenancy.[19] Examples of a breach of the covenant for quiet possession include a changing of the locks,[20] the removal of doors

11 The implied covenant extends to 'any acts calculated to interfere with the peace or comfort of the tenant, or his family' (*McCall v Abelesz* [1976] QB 585 at 594E per Lord Denning MR). See also *Kenny v Preen* [1963] 1 QB 499 at 513, 515. The landlord's duty is construed narrowly. There is, for instance, no breach where the tenant suffers discomfort from a malfunctioning of a heating system (*B.G. Preeco 3 Ltd v Universal Explorations Ltd* (1988) 42 DLR (4th) 673 at 675).

12 In *Malzy v Eichholz* [1916] 2 KB 308 at 315f, for example, a landlord was held not to have breached the covenant for quiet enjoyment where one tenant complained of acts of nuisance committed, without the landlord's authority or concurrence, by other tenants. See also *Lend Lease Development Pty Ltd v Zemlicka* (1985) 3 NSWLR 207 at 208E-G (no breach where landlord's demolition works outside demised premises impaired security and facilitated theft from tenant).

13 See, however, *Celsteel Ltd v Alton House Holdings Ltd* (No 2) [1987] 1 WLR 291 at 294B-D (landlord not liable for disturbance of tenant's occupation through the lawful exercise of rights by persons who had earlier been granted tenancies of adjacent property by a former owner of the present landlord's reversion).

14 See *Duke of Westminster v Guild* [1985] QB 688 at 703F.

15 *Anderson v Oppenheimer* (1880) 5 QBD 602 at 607. See also *Martins Camera Corner Pty Ltd v Hotel Mayfair Ltd* [1976] 2 NSWLR 15 at 24A-C.

16 *Gordon v Selico Co Ltd* [1985] 2 EGLR 79 at 83D. It is probable, however, that no liability accrues to the landlord in the absence of some wilful or negligent omission or commission by him (see *Anderson v Oppenheimer* (1880) 5 QBD 602 at 607f; *Booth v Thomas* [1926] Ch 397 at 403, 411).

17 See R.L. Archdale, (1986) 130 SJ 601.

18 See *McCall v Abelesz* [1976] QB 585 at 594G, but compare (1979) 42 MLR 223 at 227f. An imaginative use of the criminal process (and particularly of conditions for bail) may effectively give the dispossessed tenant all the benefits of a civil injunction (post, p 809).

19 It has been suggested in this context that the courts should apply in favour of the tenant a doctrine of 'constructive eviction' (post, p 808), and this argument may have been furthered by the recent confirmation in *Hussein v Mehlman* [1992] 2 EGLR 87 at 88G that English law recognises the concept of repudiatory breach of leasehold covenants. See also A.J. Bradbrook, (1975-76) 10 Melbourne UL Rev 459 at 466.

20 *Ubhi v Nothey* (1983) LAG Bulletin 105; *Amrani v Oniah* [1984] CLY 1974; *Barnett v Djordjevic* (1984) LAG Bulletin 124 (£750 for three days out of possession); *Chukwu v Iqbal* (Unreported, Court of Appeal, 30 January 1985).

and windows,[1] the removal of the tenant's belongings,[2] the truncation of mains services[3] or central heating[4] in the tenant's home, actual or threatened violence aimed at inducing the departure of the tenant,[5] and the physical replacement of one tenant by another.[6] Even the eviction of a statutory tenant following the issue of a court order for possession, but before its execution by officers of the court, has been held to amount to a breach of the covenant for quiet enjoyment.[7]

The tenant's right to damages for breach of the covenant for quiet enjoyment is not prejudiced by the fact that he himself may be in breach of some of the terms of the letting. It is well established that the tenant's due payment of rent or performance of other covenants cannot—even by express words—be made a condition precedent of the tenant's right to quiet enjoyment of the premises.[8] The court may award not only general damages for loss suffered, but also 'aggravated' damages for injury to feelings[9] and possibly 'exemplary' or 'punitive' damages in order to 'teach the defendant that a ruthless and cynical disregard of the plaintiff's rights for his own profit is not an appropriate method of proceeding'.[10] In practice, however, the quantum of awards has tended to remain quite low.[11] Awards for a breach resulting in the wrongful eviction of a tenant have thus generally failed to reflect the tenant's true loss,[12] but this deficiency is now amply remedied by the new ground of civil liability created by the Housing Act 1988 in respect of unlawful deprivation of occupation rights.[13]

1 *Lavender v Betts* [1942] 2 All ER 72 at 73H.
2 *Chrysostomou v Georgiou* (1982) LAG Bulletin 33.
3 *Perera v Vandiyar* [1953] 1 WLR 672 at 675f.
4 *Malloy and Lunt v Alexander* [1982] CLY 1747.
5 See *McMillan v Singh* (1985) 17 HLR 120 at 123, where the landlord threw the tenant's camp bed and suitcase out into the garden and threatened to kill him if he tried to return (£500 damages).
6 *McMillan v Singh* (1985) 17 HLR 120 at 122.
7 *Kyriacou v Pandeli* [1980] CLY 1648. Such action by a landlord also gives rise to a liability in damages pursuant to Housing Act 1988, ss 27, 28 (post, p 809). See *Haniff v Robinson* [1993] 1 All ER 185 at 192d–e.
8 *Dawson v Dyer* (1833) 5 B & Ad 584 at 588, 110 ER 906 at 907f; *Edge v Boileau* (1885) 16 QBD 117 at 120; *Slater v Hoskins* [1982] 2 NZLR 541 at 551. The equitable doctrine of 'clean hands' has no application to a common law claim for damages (*McMillan v Singh* (1985) 17 HLR 120 at 124).
9 *McMillan v Singh* (1985) 17 HLR 120 at 125 (£250 aggravated damages); *Ashgar v Armed* (1984) LAG Bulletin 124 (£500 aggravated damages). Damages for breach of contract may include an element of compensation for the 'mental upset and distress' caused by the landlord's conduct (*McCall v Abelesz* [1976] QB 585 at 594E). This may include damages for inconvenience and distress caused to members of the tenant's family (*McCall v Abelesz*, supra at 594F).
10 *McMillan v Singh* (1985) 17 HLR 120 at 125 per Arnold P (£250 exemplary damages awarded in order to negative the landlord's profit from a re-letting at a higher rent). No principle of 'double jeopardy' precludes the award of exemplary damages where the landlord has already been fined heavily under the Protection from Eviction Act 1977 (*Ashgar v Armed* (1984) LAG Bulletin 124).
11 See eg *De Silva v Qureshi* (1984) LAG Bulletin 47 (£500 exemplary damages plus £500 general damages for removal of mains services).
12 See R. Clayton and H. Tomlinson, (1986) LAG Bulletin 10.
13 Housing Act 1988, ss 27, 28 (post, p 809). See *Tagro v Cafane* [1991] 1 WLR 378.

(ii) Covenant against derogation from grant A landlord has an implied obligation not to 'derogate from his grant'.[14] This obligation has been described as 'a principle which merely embodies in a legal maxim a rule of common honesty'.[15] The landlord may not grant land to the tenant on terms which effectively or substantially negative the utility of the grant.[16] Neither the landlord nor any person claiming under him[17] may engage in conduct which is inconsistent with the purpose for which the lease was granted.[18] In *Harmer v Jumbil (Nigeria) Tin Areas Ltd*,[19] for instance, the Court of Appeal held that the obligation not to derogate from grant had been breached where a landlord, having leased land for the express purpose of storing explosives, allowed adjoining land to be used for mining operations which endangered the furtherance of the tenant's enterprise.[20] The implied covenant against derogation from grant is likewise breached where a landlord carries out noisy renovations in the same building which render the demised premises unfit for the specialised purposes envisaged by the tenant[1] or which expose the demised premises to unlawful entry by burglars.[2] Most conduct which breaches the landlord's duty to afford quiet enjoyment represents also a derogation from the leasehold grant,[3] but this is not always or necessarily so.[4]

Is it the same?

(b) Equitable lease

Under an equitable lease (or contract for a lease)[5] there is an implied term, which may be displaced by contrary agreement, that the formal lease when executed should contain 'the usual covenants'.[6] These covenants include the

14 See generally D.W. Elliott, (1964) 80 LQR 244; M.A. Peel, (1965) 81 LQR 28. On the distinction between quiet enjoyment and non-derogation from grant, see *Lend Lease Development Pty Ltd v Zemlicka* (1985) 3 NSWLR 207 at 208G per Kirby P.

15 *Harmer v Jumbil (Nigeria) Tin Areas Ltd* [1921] 1 Ch 200 at 225 per Younger LJ.

16 A grantor 'having given a thing with one hand is not to take away the means of enjoying it with the other' (*Birmingham, Dudley and District Banking Co v Ross* (1888) 38 Ch D 295 at 313 per Bowen LJ). Actual physical interference with the tenant's activities need not be shown in order to prove that a derogation has occurred (see *Telex (Australasia) Pty Ltd v Thomas Cook & Son (Australasia) Pty Ltd* [1970] 2 NSWR 257 at 266).

17 *Aldin v Latimer Clark, Muirhead & Co* [1894] 2 Ch 437 at 447; *Molton Builders Ltd v City of Westminster LBC* (1975) 30 P & CR 182 at 186.

18 The benefit of the landlord's obligation not to derogate from grant may also be claimed by those who take under the tenant (see *Molton Builders Ltd v City of Westminster LBC* (1975) 30 P & CR 182 at 186).

19 [1921] 1 Ch 200 at 225.

20 See also *Mount Cook National Park Board v Mount Cook Motels Ltd* [1972] NZLR 481 at 496. Compare *Port v Griffith* [1938] 1 All ER 295 at 299E–300G.

1 *Telex (Australasia) Pty Ltd v Thomas Cook & Son (Australasia) Pty Ltd* [1970] 2 NSWR 257 at 266 (where the tenant traded in hearing aids and audiometric equipment). See also *Aldin v Latimer Clark, Muirhead & Co* [1894] 2 Ch 437 at 444.

2 *Lend Lease Development Pty Ltd v Zemlicka* (1985) 3 NSWLR 207 at 216F–G (Court of Appeal of New South Wales).

3 See *Robinson v Kilvert* (1889) 41 Ch D 88 at 95ff; *Malzy v Eichholz* [1916] 2 KB 308 at 314.

4 See eg *Grosvenor Hotel Co v Hamilton* [1894] 2 QB 836 at 840.

5 Ante, p 738.

6 *Propert v Parker* (1832) 3 My & K 280 at 281, 40 ER 107. See L. Crabb, [1992] Conv 18.

traditional qualified covenant by the landlord to permit quiet enjoyment to the contractual tenant.[7]

(3) Implied obligations of the landlord in respect of the repair and maintenance

There is in general no implied guarantee by the landlord as to the state of repair or fitness of the subject matter of any letting.[8] The broad rule is *caveat emptor*. Since historically the leasehold was conceptualised as a conveyance of an estate in land which conferred a right to exclusive possession, the tenant, so long as he was given exclusive possession at the commencement of the lease, had no right thereafter to complain about the fitness of the land for his purpose.[9] He was deemed to assume all risks attached to the condition of the land unless he had reached some contrary agreement with the lessor. The tenant hired at his peril and the landlord gave no implied undertaking as to the physical condition of the land or (in the case of a building) as to its continuing state of repair. In Erle CJ's famous remark, 'fraud apart, there is no law against letting a tumble-down house.'[10] The common law principle was clear: 'the lessee must make his objections to the condition of the premises before taking the lease.'[11]

The common law rule, so stated, still applies to most leases outside the area of residential letting. The law could not, however, remain unaffected by the social and economic changes brought about by the creation of an urbanised proletariat during the early years of the 19th century. A myriad of houses 'suitable for. . .use. . .by members of the working classes'[12] quickly formed in orderly patterns of squalid misery around the factories, textile

7 *Hampshire v Wickens* (1878) 7 Ch D 555 at 561.

8 See *Gott v Gandy* (1853) 2 El & Bl 845 at 847f, 118 ER 984 at 985; *Duke of Westminster v Guild* [1985] QB 688 at 697D–E per Slade LJ; *J.F. Hillam Pty Ltd v K.L. Mooney and P.H. Hill* (1988) 48 SASR 381 at 388. The suggestion in *Barrett v Lounova (1982) Ltd* [1990] 1 QB 348 at 356B–D per Kerr LJ that there may be an implied duty to repair is almost certainly confined to the special facts of that case (see P.F. Smith, [1988] Conv 448 at 449, [1989] Conv 216). Compare *Demetriou v Poolaction Ltd* [1991] 1 EGLR 100 at 104C–F.

9 The immunity thus conferred on the lessor was doubtless due in great measure to the fact that the subject matter of leases was more commonly agricultural land than residential dwellings (see *Siney v Corporation of Dublin* [1980] IR 400 at 408 per O'Higgins CJ). The courts were greatly concerned to prevent the extension of lessors' duties in agrarian leases (see eg *Sutton v Temple* (1843) 12 M & W 52 at 65, 152 ER 1108 at 1113 (no liability for cattle killed by lead poisoning in field)).

10 *Robbins v Jones* (1863) 15 CB (NS) 221 at 240, 143 ER 768 at 776. See *Anns v Merton LBC* [1978] AC 728 at 768E per Lord Salmon ('The immunity of a landlord who sells or lets a house which is dangerous or unfit for habitation is deeply entrenched in our law'.) The exception made for fraud may be important. See eg *Gordon v Selico Co Ltd* [1986] 1 EGLR 71 at 77J, where a vendor of a long lease was held liable in damages for the tort of deceit where he had fraudulently concealed the existence of dry rot in a flat sold to the plaintiffs.

11 H. Tiffany, *Treatise on the Law of Landlord and Tenant* (1912), p 572f. At common law there may even be 'situations in which there is no repairing obligation imposed either expressly or impliedly on anyone in relation to a lease' (*Demetriou v Poolaction Ltd* [1991] 1 EGLR 100 at 104D per Stuart-Smith LJ).

12 This terrible statutory phrase was to recur in legislation dating from the Housing of the Working Classes Act 1885 to the present day (see eg Rent Act 1977, s 101(2)). See also *Chorley BC v Barratt Developments (North West) Ltd* [1979] 3 All ER 634 at 639a–c; R.G. Lee, *The Demise of the Working Classes*, [1980] Conv 281.

mills, coal-pits and iron-works of the industrial revolution.[13] This sudden aggregation of residential dwellers in large industrial conurbations[14] inevitably gave an unprecedented prominence to the legal issue of habitability in the residential sector.[15] Gradually the abstentionism of the common law rule came to be qualified by a number of exceptions (arising both at common law and by statute) which impose on the landlord various kinds of duty in relation to the physical condition and repair of the premises leased.[16] These sporadic interventions[17] survive in modern law as a piecemeal collection of provisions rather than as any particularly coherent code of protection for tenants.

(a) The landlord's liability at common law

At common law the potential liability of the landlord has been steadily, albeit uncertainly, extended by developments in the law of contract and tort.

(i) Implied condition of fitness for human habitation A significant exception to the common law principle of *caveat emptor* in landlord–tenant relations was established in 1843 in *Smith v Marrable*.[18] Here the Court of Exchequer held it to be an *implied condition* in the letting of any furnished dwelling-house that the premises should be reasonably fit for habitation at the commencement of the term. Breach of this condition entitles the tenant to quit the letting

13 Some of the early industrialists and landowners took care to provide decent housing conditions for the workers, but all too often the new housing took the form of the back-to-back terraces, cellar dwellings or courtyard dwellings which became the slums of the future (see A. Briggs, *Victorian Cities* (Harmondsworth, Middx 1968), p 226f; J. Burnett, *A Social History of Housing 1815–1970* (London 1978), pp 11, 54ff).

14 In 1801 approximately 80 per cent of the population of England and Wales was still 'rural' and only 20 per cent lived in towns of more than 5,000 inhabitants. By 1851 54 per cent of the population had become urban dwellers, and there were already ten urban centres of more than 100,000 inhabitants each, accounting in total for a quarter of the population of the entire country (see J. Burnett, op cit, p 6f).

15 The full horror of some of the housing supposedly suitable for use by members of the working classes is apparent in the *First Report of the Royal Commission on the Housing of the Working Classes* (PP 1884–85, XXX), p 11f. The Commissioners recorded that in Bristol 'privies actually exist in living rooms'; that in Liverpool they found 'walls. . .alive with vermin'; and that in Southwark some houses had 'large cracks and holes in the walls large enough for a man to enter'. The Commissioners also referred (at p 12) to the curiously modern complaint of 'jerry building'.

16 For a more detailed account of the law in this area, see *Elements of Land Law* (1st edn 1987), pp 901–960.

17 The nature of the interest which even a supposedly enlightened 19th century landlord had in the living conditions of his tenants is apparent in the earnest statement that 'sanitary improvements lead to higher rentals being obtained and to the tenants enjoying better health, and, consequently, being in a better position to pay the said rent'. (G.H. Larmuth, *A Practical Guide to the Law of Landlord and Tenant* (Manchester 1878), p 45).

18 (1843) 11 M & W 5 at 8f, 152 ER 693 at 694 (infestation by bugs). There has always been a further special exception to the common law rule. This exception governs the liability of a lessor who sells a leasehold estate in a house still in the process of construction. The vendor is impliedly taken to warrant the suitability of materials used, the quality of the workmanship and the fitness of the house for habitation (see *Perry v Sharon Development Co Ltd* [1937] 4 All ER 390 at 393A–B; *Siney v Corporation of Dublin* [1980] IR 400 at 408).

immediately and without notice.[19] The implied condition of fitness is, however, gravely limited.[20] It relates only to the condition of the premises at the commencement of the letting.[1] It applies only to a residential tenancy,[2] has no relevance to unfurnished premises,[3] and even in relation to furnished premises does not extend to dangerous appliances or furnishings supplied by the landlord.[4] Because the landlord's liability arises *ex contractu*, no person other than the tenant can maintain an action for breach of the implied condition.[5]

The common law condition of fitness thus falls far short of the implied 'warranty of habitability' which in other jurisdictions has become a central feature of a contemporary 'revolution' in the landlord-tenant relationship.[6] In *Javins v First National Realty Corporation*,[7] the symbolic turning-point in the reorientation of this area of law in the United States, Judge Skelly Wright pointed to the modern social function of the residential tenancy as a consumer contract for the supply of a 'package of goods and services'.[8] In his view the tenant 'may legitimately expect that the apartment will be fit for habitation for the time period for which it is rented.'[9] The initiative taken in the *Javins* ruling has left a lasting mark on American landlord and tenant law[10] and has entrenched the humane principle that the residential landlord is contractually liable to supply his tenants with decent housing conditions throughout the term of the tenancy. In sharp contrast English common law

19 According to Parke B, 'if the demised premises are incumbered with a nuisance of so serious a nature that no person can reasonably be expected to live in them, the tenant is at liberty to throw them up.' See also *Collins v Barrow* (1831) 1 M & Rob 112 at 114, 174 ER 38 at 39. The tenant is under no obligation to give the landlord an opportunity to remedy the defect (*Wilson v Finch Hatton* (1877) 2 Ex D 336 at 341).

20 The implied condition does not apply to ordinary disrepair which merely renders habitation unpleasant or inconvenient as distinct from impossible (see eg *Maclean v Currie* (1884) Cab & El 361 (cracked plaster)).

1 *Hart v Windsor* (1843) 12 M & W 68 at 85f, 152 ER 1114 at 1121; *Sarson v Roberts* [1895] 2 QB 395 at 397f.

2 See *Bradford House Pty Ltd v Leroy Fashion Group Ltd* (1983) 46 ALR 305 at 313. Compare the willingness in the United States to extend a warranty of fitness to commercial leases (see *Davidow v Inwood North Professional Group—Phase 1*, 747 SW2d 373 at 376ff (Tex 1988)). See also G.G. Greenfield and M.Z. Margolies, 45 Albany L Rev 855 (1980-81); J.A. Marley, 13 Rutgers LJ 91 (1981-82).

3 *Hart v Windsor* (1843) 12 M & W 68 at 87, 152 ER 1114 at 1122; *Lane v Cox* [1897] 1 QB 415 at 417. In effect almost all council tenancies and certainly all long (eg 99 year) leases of residential flats are nowadays excluded from the scope of the condition.

4 *Pampris v Thanos* [1968] 1 NSWR 56 at 58 (tenant's wife electrocuted on contact with faulty refrigerator). There is a possibility that the landlord may be liable in negligence (see *Parker v South Australian Housing Trust* (1986) 41 SASR 493 at 509, 517, 536, 539ff).

5 *Cameron v Young* [1908] AC 176 at 180f; *Pampris v Thanos* [1968] 1 NSWR 56 at 58.

6 See E.H. Rabin, *The Revolution in Residential Landlord-Tenant Law: Causes and Consequences*, 69 Cornell L Rev 517 (1983-84); M.A. Glendon, *The Transformation of American Landlord-Tenant Law*, 23 Boston College L Rev 503 (1982).

7 428 F2d 1071 (1970).

8 428 F2d 1071 at 1074 (ante, p 675).

9 428 F2d 1071 at 1079. Some commentators have even gone so far as to support the warranty of habitability quite explicitly as a device aimed at 'a significant expropriation or redistribution away from people who are owners of low-income property.' See Duncan Kennedy, *In favor of the Warranty of Habitability, In brief* (May 1987), p 8.

10 See J.E. Cribbet (1986) U of Ill L Rev 1 at 7.

remains tethered to the limitations of *Smith v Marrable*, and has therefore been forced to seek the same goal, somewhat imperfectly, through tortuous and fragmented initiatives of common law and statute.

(ii) Implied contractual duty of care In certain circumstances English courts are willing to imply on the part of the landlord a contractual duty of care which has the indirect effect of promoting the utility enjoyed by tenants.[11] In *Liverpool City Council v Irwin*,[12] the House of Lords ruled that a local authority landlord of a high-rise block of flats had a contractual duty to 'take reasonable care to keep in reasonable repair and usability' the common parts and facilities (eg lifts, stairways and rubbish chutes).[13] Such a duty could be implied into the contract of tenancy as a matter of 'necessity'.[14] The maintenance of these facilities could not simply be regarded as 'conveniences provided at discretion: they are essentials of the tenancy without which life in the dwellings, as a tenant, is not possible.'[15]

The landlord's implied contractual duty of care, although significantly endorsed by the House of Lords, is again somewhat limited in scope. It confers rights only upon the contracting tenant (and not others such as members of his family or associates) and may always be excluded by the simple expedient of express contractual provision.[16] This implied duty of care may apply more readily to high-rise blocks designed for multiple occupation than to other kinds of tenancy.[17] Moreover the courts can easily stultify the common law duty by adopting an extremely limited view of the circumstances of 'necessity' or 'business efficacy' which activate the implication of the landlord's obligation.[18]

11 See eg *Dunster v Hollis* [1918] 2 KB 795 at 802 per Lush J.

12 [1977] AC 239.

13 [1977] AC 239 at 256G.

14 [1977] AC 239 at 254F. The House of Lords ultimately held that the council had not been shown to be in breach of its contractual obligation of care. It was clear that the council had made considerable efforts, despite the depradations committed by the local vandals, to maintain the efficiency of communal facilities in the flats ([1977] AC 239 at 256G per Lord Wilberforce, 259F–G per Lord Cross of Chelsea, 269C–D per Lord Edmund-Davies). The council's duty was not *absolute*. Lord Salmon (at 263C–G) reached his conclusion 'with some reluctance and doubt', opining that the tenants' counter-claim might well have succeeded if they had pleaded that the landlord was subject to a duty merely to take 'reasonable care'. Compare *Karaggianis v Malltown Pty Ltd* (1979) 21 SASR 381 at 3390ff.

15 [1977] AC 239 at 254F-G. As Lord Salmon asked with some force, '[c]an a pregnant woman accompanied by a young child be expected to walk up 15. . .storeys in the pitch dark to reach her home? Unless the law. . .imposes an obligation upon the council at least to use reasonable care to keep the lifts working properly and the staircase lit, the whole transaction becomes inefficacious, futile and absurd' ([1977] AC 239 at 262A–B).

16 *Liverpool City Council v Irwin* [1977] AC 239 at 259E, 260C. See eg *Coughlan v The Mayor etc of the City of Limerick* (1977) 111 ILTR 141 at 142.

17 [1977] AC 239 at 254G, 256E–F, 270B–C. See *Duke of Westminster v Guild* [1985] QB 688 at 699B–C; *Gordon v Selico Co Ltd* [1986] 1 EGLR 71L.

18 See eg *O'Leary v LB of Islington* (1983) 9 HLR 81 at 86, 89 (no duty to 'police' the behaviour of other residents on housing estate); *Collins v Northern Ireland Housing Executive* [1984] 17 NIJB, Transcript p 21 (no duty to keep heating system in working order). Carswell J held that the defect in the latter case affected only 'the quality of enjoyment of the facilities supplied, not. . .the basic ability to use the accommodation.'

(iii) The landlord's liability in negligence A landlord's duty towards a tenant may be heightened by the application of the law of negligence. Although there is authority, stemming largely from the restrictive and much criticised[19] ruling of the House of Lords in *Cavalier v Pope*,[20] to the effect that a landlord cannot be liable to a tenant in negligence by reason of the defective nature of the demised premises at the *commencement* of the tenancy,[1] it is clear that liability in negligence can arise in respect of events occurring after the commencement date.[2]

It is well established, for instance, that a claim in negligence may lie against a landlord if, by some action or omission on premises retained within his exclusive possession and control,[3] damage is caused to that part of the premises which is demised to the tenant.[4] However, in the absence of personal injury or damage to property, the landlord owes no general duty of care to avoid causing inconvenience or discomfort to his tenant.[5] The landlord's liability in negligence is, in any event, far from absolute; he is liable only to take reasonable care to ensure the safety of those persons who might reasonably be expected to be affected by his actions or defaults.[6] A landlord has, for example, no liability in negligence for malicious damage caused by a third party, unless there was some special relationship between the

19 The decision in *Cavalier v Pope* of course predates *Donoghue v Stevenson* [1932] AC 562, and has been described as 'conceptually inconsistent with the general principle of liability for negligence' enunciated in that case (see *Parker v South Australian Housing Trust* (1986) 41 SASR 493 at 516 per King CJ).

20 [1906] AC 428 at 430ff. See *Bottomley v Bannister* [1932] 1 KB 458 at 477.

1 See *Robbins v Jones* (1863) 15 CB (NS) 221 at 240, 143 ER 768 at 776; *Bottomley v Bannister* [1932] 1 KB 458 at 477; *Otto v Bolton and Norris* [1936] 2 KB 46 at 54; *Davis v Foots* [1940] 1 KB 116 at 121, 124; *McGowan v Harrison* [1941] IR 331 at 337.

2 There is always of course the possibility that one tenant may sue another tenant directly in respect of negligence which leads to loss of amenity (see *Elfassy v Sylben Investments Ltd* (1979) 91 DLR (3d) 96). However, the defendant in such an action may be able to plead successfully that he had no reason to suspect the existence of the problem which caused the damage of which the plaintiff now complains. See eg *Hawkins v Dhawan* (1987) 19 HLR 232 at 235, where the Court of Appeal held that just as every dog must be 'allowed its first bite', so a tenant's washbasin must be allowed its first flood, even though the overflow escapes to the premises of a neighbouring tenant.

3 A typical problem in this context arises where the landlord grants away tenancies of flats in a building, while retaining for himself exclusive possession over such parts of the building as the roof or the service ducts.

4 *Cockburn v Smith* [1924] 2 KB 119 at 129; *Duke of Westminster v Guild* [1985] QB 688 at 701C–E. See *Hargroves, Aronson & Co v Hartopp* [1905] 1 KB 472 at 477 (failure to clear a blocked rain-water gutter); *A. Prosser & Sons Ltd v Levy* [1955] 1 WLR 1224 at 1233 (overflow of water from a basin); *Martins Camera Corner Pty Ltd v Hotel Mayfair Ltd* [1976] 2 NSWLR 15 at 26E (failure to clear a blocked down-pipe); *Sharpe v Manchester City Council* (1977) 5 HLR 71 at 76 (invasion of cockroaches from the service ducts).

5 *Collins v Northern Ireland Housing Executive* [1984] 17 NIJB, Transcript, p 32f (ante, p 785). The 'neighbour principle' of *Donoghue v Stevenson* does not, oddly, require the landlord to exercise diligence on behalf of one tenant in selecting only civilised tenants to live in neighbouring premises (see *Smith v Scott* [1973] Ch 314 at 322A–B, E–F) or to enforce standards of good neighbourliness generally (see *O'Leary v LB of Islington* (1983) 9 HLR 81 at 88).

6 See eg *Ryan v LB of Camden* (1982) 8 HLR 75 at 78ff (no liability for unforeseeable injury caused to baby by unlagged central heating pipe). See also *McAuliffe v Moloney* [1971] IR 200 at 203, and contrast the approach of the Supreme Court of New Jersey in *Coleman v Steinberg*, 253 A.2d 167 at 170ff (1969).

landlord and the third party or the injury to the plaintiff is the inevitable and foreseeable result of the landlord's act or omission.[7]

Strong arguments of principle favour the imposition of negligence liability on a landlord in respect of defects present in the demised premises at the commencement date of the letting, particularly where the landlord (unlike the tenant) had special means of knowledge of latent defects and concealed dangers.[8] Nevertheless English courts have sternly adhered to the denial of liability laid down in *Cavalier v Pope*,[9] allowing an exception only where the landlord was also the builder of negligently constructed premises.[10] Although in broad agreement that the outmoded rule in *Cavalier v Pope* 'must be kept in close confinement',[11] English judges have resisted the trend in other jurisdictions to view the rule as inapplicable to social housing[12] or as simply wrong in general.[13] In *McNerny v LB of Lambeth*[14] the Court of Appeal took the view that only legislative intervention can finally remove this archaic but obdurate principle.

(iv) The landlord's liability for nuisance There is no doubt that a tenant, being in possession or occupation of land, has locus standi to sue in respect of the tort of nuisance.[15] An action in nuisance may lie where the acts or omissions of the landlord on his own land unduly interfere with the tenant's comfortable and convenient enjoyment of the demised premises.[16]

7 *King v Liverpool City Council* [1986] 1 WLR 890 at 901B–E, 902B–E (no liability for water damage emanating from vandalised superjacent flat). See also *Smith v Littlewoods Organisation Ltd* [1987] AC 241 at 267F–G per Lord Mackay of Clashfern, 279B per Lord Goff of Chieveley. Compare, however, *Sheppard v Northern Ireland Housing Executive* [1984] 1 NIJB, Transcript, p 4 per Lord Lowry LCJ (liability for landlord's ineffective action to prevent vandalism to soil pipes). The landlord's liability for damage emanating from the landlord's adjoining premises may be better founded on the obligation not to derogate from grant (see *Lend Lease Development Pty Ltd v Zemlicka* (1985) 3 NSWLR 207 at 216F–G (ante, p 781)).

8 For an extreme instance, see *MacDonald v Sebastian* (1988) 43 DLR (4th) 636 at 637 (arsenic in water supply).

9 [1906] AC 428 at 430ff. See eg *McNerny v LB of Lambeth* (1988) 21 HLR 188 at 192 per Dillon LJ, 195f per Taylor LJ; [1989] Conv 216 (P.F. Smith).

10 See eg *Rimmer v Liverpool City Council* [1985] QB 1 at 13G–14F (tenant injured when falling through thin glass panel in inadequately designed flat constructed by local authority landlord). Stephenson LJ distinguished *Cavalier v Pope* as a case relating only to the liability of a 'bare landlord' as distinct from that of a 'builder owner' ([1985] QB 1 at 14G). For an American parallel, see the ruling of the Supreme Court of California in *Becker v IRM Corp*, 213 Cal Rptr 213 (1985); R. Deeb, 20 Loyola of Los Angeles L Rev 323 (1987). See also *Ward v McMaster* [1985] IR 29 at 42.

11 *Rimmer v Liverpool City Council* [1985] QB 1 at 9H per Stephenson LJ. See also *Greene v Chelsea BC* [1954] 2 QB 127 at 138 per Denning LJ.

12 *Siney v Corporation of Dublin* [1980] IR 400 at 414f, 421f; *Parker v South Australian Housing Trust* (1986) 41 SASR 493 at 544. See T. Kerr and R. Clark, (1980) 15 Ir Jur (NS) 32. Compare, however, *McNerny v LB of Lambeth* (1988) 21 HLR 188 at 193 per Dillon LJ.

13 See *Basset Realty Ltd v Lindstrom* (1980) 103 DLR (3d) 654 at 670.

14 (1988) 21 HLR 188 at 193, 195 per Dillon LJ, 196 per Taylor LJ.

15 *Inchbald v Robinson* (1869) LR 4 Ch App 388 at 395ff; *Jones v Chappell* (1875) LR 20 Eq 539 at 543f. See eg *McCall v Abelesz* [1976] QB 585 at 599F; *Guppys (Bridport) Ltd v Brookling* (1984) 269 Estates Gazette 846 at 946. See M.J. Russell, (1977) 40 MLR 651.

16 *Thompson-Schwab v Costaki* [1956] 1 WLR 335 at 338. See eg *Guppys (Bridport) Ltd v Brookling* (1984) 269 Estates Gazette 846 (disconnection of water and electricity supplies and interference with washing and toilet facilities); *Sharpe v Manchester City Council* (1977) 5 HLR 71 at 75f (invasion of cockroaches from service ducts); *Sheppard v Northern Ireland Housing Executive* [1984] 1 NIJB (blocked sewage pipe) (ante, p 786).

It is clear law that a landlord is not in general liable for a nuisance committed by his tenant.[17] A landlord may, however, acquire a nuisance liability if he has either expressly or even impliedly authorised a tenant to commit nuisance.[18] A landlord's liability vis à vis one tenant may thus be founded on acts committed by other tenants in occupation of a different part of the landlord's property.[19] This may sometimes prove to be a potent mechanism of redress in disputes arising between neighbours in a crowded multiple residential context.[20]

(v) The landlord's liability under Rylands v Fletcher It is quite possible for the actions or inactions of a landlord to attract liability under the rule in *Rylands v Fletcher*.[1] The courts have declined, however, to accept that a tenant may invoke the rule in *Rylands v Fletcher* in order to make the landlord liable for the tortious acts of other tenants of his who live in the neighbourhood.[2] Noxious neighbours (and the noise created by them) may escape and do damage, but they do not constitute dangerous 'things' likely to do mischief in the sense required by *Rylands v Fletcher*.

(b) The landlord's liability under statute

A fragmented series of statutory interventions has created further grounds of potential liability for landlords in the context of residential tenancies. The obligations thus imposed are, however, of a partial and imperfect character and have proved deeply unsatisfactory for the purpose of protecting tenants from the impact of poor housing conditions.

(i) Implied terms as to fitness for human habitation Section 8(1) of the Landlord and Tenant Act 1985 imposes two implied contractual terms in the letting of a dwelling-house. These terms comprise a condition that the house is 'fit for human habitation at the commencement of the tenancy' and a further undertaking that the house 'will be kept by the landlord fit for human habitation during the tenancy'.[3] The overtly protective intent of this social

17 *Smith v Scott* [1973] Ch 314 at 321B. A landlord has thus been held to bear no liability in nuisance simply because he grants a letting to a tenant whom he knows to be nuisance-prone (*Smith v Scott*, supra at 321E–F). See, however, *Page Motors Ltd v Epsom and Ewell BC* (1982) 80 LGR 337 at 347f.

18 *Harris v James* (1876) 35 LT 240 at 241; *Hilton v James Smith & Sons (Norwood) Ltd* (1979) 251 Estates Gazette 1063 at 1067f. See *Smith v Scott* [1973] Ch 314 at 321C; *Tetley v Chitty* [1986] 1 All ER 663 at 671e–f.

19 See eg *Sampson v Hodson-Pressinger* [1981] 3 All ER 710 at 714j (landlord liable for noise penetration between adjacent tenants' properties where he purchased reversion in the knowledge of faulty construction). See [1982] Conv 155; [1982] CLJ 38 (M. Owen).

20 The express or implied reservation of a right to enter and repair the demised property may demonstrate that the landlord has retained a 'sufficient basis of control' to enable a nuisance liability to be fastened on him in respect of defects arising on the demised premises (see *Heap v Ind Coope and Allsopp Ltd* [1940] 2 KB 476 at 483; *Mint v Good* [1951] 1 KB 517 at 521, 527f; *Carter v Murray* [1981] 2 NSWLR 77 at 79F).

1 (1868) LR 3 HL 330. See eg *Martins Camera Corner Pty Ltd v Hotel Mayfair Ltd* [1976] 2 NSWLR 15 at 27B (damage caused by water overflowing from landlord's premises).

2 *Smith v Scott* [1973] Ch 314 at 321F–G.

3 On the original social purpose of section 8(1), which has antecedents extending back to Housing of the Working Classes Act 1890, s 75, see *Summers v Salford Corporation* [1943] AC 283 at 293, 297.

legislation is underscored by the fact that the implied terms cannot be excluded by express contractual provision.[4]

For the purpose of section 8(1), a house is 'unfit for human habitation' only if it is 'not reasonably suitable for occupation' by reason of one or more of a number of stated defects, which include its condition of repair, stability, freedom from damp, internal arrangement, natural lighting, ventilation, water supply, and drainage, sanitation and cooking facilities.[5] The practical scope of section 8(1) is nowadays disastrously circumscribed. The provision has no application if the property cannot be rendered fit for human habitation at reasonable expense.[6] Judicial construction has added the scarcely justifiable rider that the landlord's obligation arises only when he is notified of the relevant defect,[7] and the statutory rent limits on eligible tenancies[8] now make the section virtually ineffective except in respect of properties which are, in any event, fit only for total demolition rather than repair.[9]

(ii) Implied covenant for repair and maintenance Pursuant to section 11 of the Landlord and Tenant Act 1985,[10] certain covenants relating to repair and maintenance are impliedly undertaken by the landlord in a lease of a dwelling-house for a term of less than seven years.[11] The landlord impliedly undertakes to keep in repair the structure and exterior of the dwelling-house.[12] This obligation extends to the walls (and in some circumstances the roof[13]) of the demised premises, to drains, gutterings and external pipes, and also to any steps and flagstones giving access to the house.[14] The landlord also

4 Landlord and Tenant Act 1985, s 8(1).

5 Landlord and Tenant Act 1985, s 10. See eg *Summers v Salford Corporation* [1943] AC 283 at 297f (broken sash-cord had the effect of jamming a bedroom window). The criterion of 'unfitness' was not, however, met in *Stanton v Southwick* [1920] 2 KB 642 at 646 (infestation by rats entering house) or in *Wainwright v Leeds City Council* (1984) 270 Estates Gazette 1289 at 1290 (damp penetration).

6 *Buswell v Goodwin* [1971] 1 WLR 92 at 97A. See J.I. Reynolds, (1974) 37 MLR 377 at 384, but compare M.J. Robinson, (1976) 39 MLR 43. On the issue of 'reasonable expense', compare Housing Act 1985, s 189(1) (post, p 792).

7 *Morgan v Liverpool Corporation* [1927] 2 KB 131 at 141, 143, 150f, 153; *McCarrick v Liverpool Corporation* [1947] AC 219 at 229f.

8 In relation to tenancies granted on or after 6 July 1957, the annual rent limit is £80 in London and £52 elsewhere (Landlord and Tenant Act 1985, s 8(4)). There is an overwhelming case for a new statutory definition of 'low rent' (see *Quick v Taff Ely BC* [1986] QB 809 at 817B, 821D–E). See also *R v Cardiff City Council, ex parte Cross* (1983) 81 LGR 105 at 116; P.F. Smith, [1990] Conv 335 at 346f.

9 See also Housing Act 1985, s 302(c).

10 As amended by Housing Act 1988, s 116(1). The statutory provision cannot normally be excluded by contrary contractual provision (Landlord and Tenant Act 1985, ss 11(4), 12(1)).

11 See Landlord and Tenant Act 1985, s 13(1). The landlord's implied covenant thus has no application to a 99 year lease of a residential flat (see eg *Gordon v Selico Co Ltd* [1985] 2 EGLR 79 at 80H–J).

12 Landlord and Tenant Act 1985, s 11(1)(a). If the dwelling-house forms part only of a building (eg is a flat), the landlord's implied covenant extends to any part of the building's structure or exterior in which he has an estate or interest (Landlord and Tenant Act 1985, s 11(1A)(a)).

13 *Douglas-Scott v Scorgie* [1984] 1 WLR 716 at 721C–D; [1984] JSWL 228 (M.A. Jones); [1984] Conv 229.

14 *Brown v Liverpool Corporation* [1969] 3 All ER 1345 at 1346I. See, however, *Hopwood v Cannock Chase DC* [1975] 1 WLR 373 at 377H–378A, 378C–D (patio in the back-yard); *McAuley v Bristol CC* [1992] QB 134 at 141G (step in back garden); *King v South Northamptonshire DC* (1992) 64 P & CR 35 at 39 (path outside scope of letting).

impliedly undertakes[15] to keep in repair and 'proper working order' installations for the supply of water, gas and electricity, facilities for sanitation,[16] and installations for space heating and heating water.[17] A breach is instantly committed by any landlord who cuts off the supply of gas or electricity as a means of harassment of the tenant.[18]

As in the case of section 8(1) of the Landlord and Tenant Act 1985, no liability arises for the landlord under section 11(1) unless and until he is notified of the relevant defect.[19] The effect of this extra-statutory requirement[20] is to preclude the tenant from relief under the implied statutory covenants where injury or loss has resulted suddenly from a latent and previously invisible defect.[1] The scope of the landlord's obligations is also severely curtailed by the extremely limited interpretation given by the courts to the concept of 'disrepair'.[2] In *Quick v Taff Ely BC*[3] Dillon LJ indicated that 'disrepair is related to the physical condition of whatever has to be repaired, and not to questions of lack of amenity or inefficiency.' The Court of Appeal thus held the implied statutory covenants substantially inapplicable to a council house where 'very severe condensation' had rendered the living conditions of the tenant and his family 'appalling'.[4] In the absence of evidence of physical damage to the walls or the windows, the landlord authority was not in breach of any implied statutory covenant.[5] Here there was no damage to the tenant's walls, merely lots of mould on them.[6] Relevant disrepair does not include mere loss of amenity.[7]

The ambit of the landlord's statutory duty is further constrained by the way in which the courts have construed the obligation to 'repair' as excluding any liability to improve the demised premises beyond their condition at the commencement date of the tenancy. The landlord is not obliged to 'improve the house so that it is a different house from the house which

15 Landlord and Tenant Act 1985, s 11(1)(b), (c). If the dwelling-house forms part only of a building, the landlord's implied covenant extends to any installation which serves the tenant's residence and which is owned or controlled by the landlord (Landlord and Tenant Act 1985, s 11(1A)(b)). See, however, Landlord and Tenant Act 1985, s 11(1B), (3A).

16 It is irrelevant that the facilities, whether or not by reason of inherent design defect, have never been in 'proper working order'. See *Liverpool City Council v Irwin* [1977] AC 239 at 257E, 264C–D, 270A, C–D (£5 damages for faulty lavatory cistern).

17 See *Taylor v Knowsley BC* (1985) 17 HLR 376 (£100 awarded for loss of hot water for five months).

18 *McCall v Abelesz* [1976] QB 585 at 594C–D.

19 *O'Brien v Robinson* [1973] AC 912 at 926A, 930B. The notice need not come directly from the tenant (*McGreal v Wake* (1984) 269 Estates Gazette 1254 at 1256; *Dinefwr BC v Jones* (1987) 284 Estates Gazette 58; *Hall v Howard* (1989) 57 P & CR 226 at 230ff). See also *Sheldon v West Bromwich Corporation* (1973) 25 P & CR 360 at 363f.

20 The imposition of a notice requirement has not been thought necessary in relation to parallel legislation in other jurisdictions (see eg *Gaul v King* (1980) 103 DLR (3d) 233 at 242).

1 See eg *O'Brien v Robinson* [1973] AC 912 at 915G–926A (collapsing ceiling).

2 Under section 11(1) the landlord is under no obligation to do anything at all 'until there exists a condition which calls for repair' (*Quick v Taff Ely BC* [1986] QB 809 at 821F per Lawton LJ).

3 [1986] QB 809 at 818C–D. See [1986] Conv 45 (J.E.M.).

4 [1986] QB 809 at 815A.

5 [1986] QB 809 at 819G.

6 Compare *Stent v Monmouth DC* (1987) 54 P & CR 193 at 204ff (physical damage caused by defective door).

7 [1986] QB 809 at 817F.

[the tenant] originally took.[8] The net effect of this highly restrictive approach is to make the landlord's implied undertaking inapplicable to inherent design defects in the tenant's housing.[9] The landlord's implied repairing covenant is, in any event, relative to the 'age, character and prospective life of the dwelling-house and the locality in which it is situated.[10] This means in practice that the repairing obligation is not measured objectively and the statutory standard of repair may tend towards a minimal obligation where the dwelling-house is so severely sub-standard that its expected use is confined to the short-term only.[11]

(iii) Liability under the Defective Premises Act 1972 Section 4(1) of the Defective Premises Act 1972 imposes on the landlord a statutory duty to take reasonable care to prevent personal injury or property damage which may be caused by defects in the state of the demised premises.[12] This duty of care arises only in relation to defects which fall within the landlord's covenanted responsibilities of 'maintenance or repair'.[13] Even in the absence of any repairing obligation under the terms of the tenancy, the landlord is still taken to owe a duty of care within section 4(1) if he has expressly[14] or impliedly[15] reserved for himself 'the right to enter the premises to carry out any description of maintenance or repair'.[16]

The landlord's duty of care arises only if he actually knew or if he 'ought in all the circumstances to have known' of the relevant defect.[17] The landlord's duty is not absolute.[18] His statutory duty is owed not to the world at large, but only to 'persons who might reasonably be expected to be affected by defects in the state of the premises'.[19] In relation to such persons, the landlord

8 *Wainwright v Leeds City Council* (1984) 270 Estates Gazette 1289 at 1290 per Dunn LJ (no duty to install a new damp course).
9 See eg *McDougall v Easington DC* (1989) 58 P & CR 201 at 207 per Mustill LJ.
10 Landlord and Tenant Act 1985, s 11(3). 'The standard of repair may depend on whether the house is in a South Wales valley or in Grosvenor Square' (*Quick v Taff Ely BC* [1986] QB 809 at 821F per Lawton LJ).
11 Compare *Payne v Haine* (1847) 16 M & W 541 at 545, 153 ER 1304 at 1306; *Proudfoot v Hart* (1890) 25 QBD 42 at 51; *LB of Newham v Patel* (1978) 13 HLR 77 at 83ff. See D. Hughes, [1984] JSWL 137 at 148.
12 Any attempt in the contract of tenancy to restrict or exclude the landlord's liability is void (Defective Premises Act 1972, s 6(3)).
13 Defective Premises Act 1972, s 4(3). Such responsibilities include any duties of repair or maintenance impliedly undertaken by the landlord pursuant to Landlord and Tenant Act 1985, ss 8(1), 11(1) (ante, p 788, 789). See Defective Premises Act 1972, s 4(5).
14 See eg *Hamilton v Martell Securities Ltd* [1984] Ch 266 at 271D–F (express reservation of right to effect repairs in event of tenant's failure to do so).
15 *McAuley v Bristol CC* [1992] QB 134 at 151F–H per Ralph Gibson LJ, 154F per Neill LJ. It has been suggested that under a local authority tenancy the council always has an implied right to repair any part of its property and to enter demised premises for that purpose (see *Smith v Bradford Metropolitan Council* (1982) 4 HLR 86 at 91f). Compare, however, *McAuley v Bristol CC*, supra at 149H–150B per Ralph Gibson LJ.
16 Defective Premises Act 1972, s 4(4).
17 Defective Premises Act 1972, s 4(2). There is no requirement of notification by the tenant. Constructive knowledge of defects may attach to a local authority whose appointed officials fail to detect the relevant defects by inspection (*Clarke v Taff Ely BC* (1980) 10 HLR 44 at 52f).
18 Cf *Gaul v King* (1980) 103 DLR (3d) 233 at 243 ('The object of the legislation is to provide reasonable standards for rental premises. This does not mean that the Legislature intended the lessors should be insurers.')
19 Defective Premises Act 1972, s 4(1).

is obliged to take only 'such care as is reasonable in all the circumstances to see that they are reasonably safe from personal injury or from damage to their property caused by a relevant defect'.[20] It matters not whether the 'relevant defect' was present at the commencement of the tenancy or materialised only later.[1] However, the defect must have originated in, or continued because of, an 'act or omission by the landlord' which was a breach of his obligation to repair or maintain or would have been such if he had had the requisite knowledge.[2]

(iv) Liability under the Health and Safety at Work etc Act 1974 Section 4(2) of the Health and Safety at Work etc Act 1974 imposes a duty to take reasonable care to ensure that all means of access to and egress from the relevant premises, together with any 'plant or substance. . .provided for use' on those premises, are 'safe and without risks to health'. The duty bears only upon a person who has control of the relevant premises 'in connection with the carrying on by him of a trade, business or other undertaking (whether for profit or not)'.[3] Moreover, the statutory duty relates only to 'non-domestic premises' and only in favour of non-employees.[4] In *Westminster City Council v Select Management Ltd*,[5] it was nevertheless held that the statutory duty was fully applicable in respect of the lifts in a block of residential flats managed by the defendant company.[6] This somewhat surprising application of the 1974 Act may thus provide a useful remedy for the residential tenant who finds that the management company which controls the common parts of his block of flats persistently ignores its responsibility in respect of lifts, stairways, and electrical installations in the common parts of the buildings.

(v) Repair notice under the Housing Act 1985 Where demised premises are in a 'state of disrepair',[7] the landlord's responsibilities may be enforced indirectly through the power of the local housing authority to issue a 'repair notice' requiring the execution of appropriate repair works.[8] A 'repair notice' must also be served[9] where a dwelling-house is considered 'unfit for human

20 Defective Premises Act 1972, s 4(1). See eg *Issitt v LB of Tower Hamlets*(Unreported, Court of Appeal Unbound Transcript 1115, 6 December 1983) (landlord authority not liable for injury to child where 'any responsible parent' would have put a screw in rather than waiting for the council workman to call round).

1 Defective Premises Act 1972, s 4(3).

2 Defective Premises Act 1972, s 4(3). The landlord is not therefore liable in respect of inherent design defects, which by their very nature are not attributable to any failure by him to repair or maintain (see eg *Rimmer v Liverpool City Council* [1985] QB 1 at 7D–E; *McDonagh v Kent AHA* (Unreported, Court of Appeal, 7 October 1985)).

3 Health and Safety at Work etc Act 1974, s 4(4).

4 Health and Safety at Work etc Act 1974, s 4(1).

5 [1984] 1 WLR 1058 at 1061E-G. See (1985) 48 MLR 589 (B. Barrett); [1986] Conv 45.

6 Taylor J thought that the statutory duty would be raised in favour of workmen who came to repair the lifts or electrical installations ([1984] 1 WLR 1058 at 1061D).

7 Housing Act 1985, s 190(1), (1A), (1B), as amended by Local Government and Housing Act 1989, Sch 9, para 2.

8 Housing Act 1985, s 190(2), as amended by Housing Act 1988, Sch 15, para 2(3). See *Kenny v Kingston upon Thames Royal LBC* (1985) 274 Estates Gazette 395 at 397; *White v Barnet LBC* [1990] 2 QB 328 at 337A–B.

9 See Housing Act 1985, s 189(1), (1A). Anomalously this power does not apply to local authority tenancies (see *R v Cardiff City Council, ex parte Cross* (1983) 81 LGR 105 at 114).

habitation'[10] if the authority is satisfied that the service of such a notice 'is the most satisfactory course of action.'[11] If a repair notice is not complied with, the local housing authority may decide in its discretion to execute the necessary repairs itself[12] and to recover the cost from the defaulter.[13]

(vi) Intervention in the case of 'statutory nuisance' A 'statutory nuisance' arises, within the meaning of section 79(1) of the Environmental Protection Act 1990, where any premises are 'in such a state as to be prejudicial to health or a nuisance'.[14] The situations thus covered include such eventualities as structural defects in houses, crumbling plaster,[15] the presence of toxic blue asbestos,[16] and blocked drains and lavatories. Disrepair caused by damp can lead to a finding of 'statutory nuisance',[17] but the courts have tended to be reluctant to allow the 'statutory nuisance' jurisdiction to be used as a forum for complaints which are more closely related to design defects in housing than to 'public health' complaints arising from housing conditions.[18] The mere fact that the landlord is not in breach of any of his obligations as landlord, whether in tort or in contract,[19] constitutes 'persuasive' but by no means 'conclusive' evidence that the landlord is freed of responsibility for a statutory nuisance.[20]

A tenant's complaint relating to an alleged statutory nuisance may lead either to the service by the local authority of an 'abatement notice'[1] or to an order by a magistrates' court that the nuisance be abated and remedial

10 See Housing Act 1985, s 604(1), (2), as substituted by Local Government and Housing Act 1989, Sch 9, para 83.

11 Housing Act 1985, ss 189(1), (1A), 604A(1), as amended by Local Government and Housing Act 1989, Sch 9, paras 1(1), 84. The housing authority may ultimately make either a demolition or a closing order (Housing Act 1985, ss 264(1), 265(1), as substituted by Local Government and Housing Act 1989, Sch 9, para 14) or take steps towards the compulsory purchase of the condemned housing for the purpose of providing short-term accommodation pending demolition (Housing Act 1985, s 300(1)).

12 Housing Act 1985, s 193(1). See, however, *Elliott v Brighton BC* (1981) 258 Estates Gazette 441 at 445f.

13 Housing Act 1985, s 193(3), Sch 10, as amended by Housing Act 1988, Sch 15, para 13.

14 Environmental Protection Act 1990, s 79(1)(a) (formerly Public Health Act 1936, s 92). See also Environmental Protection Act 1990, s 79(7) (definition of 'prejudicial to health'). A 'statutory nuisance' also includes other forms of disamenity, eg the emission of smoke, fumes, gases or noise from premises 'so as to be prejudicial to health or a nuisance' (Environmental Protection Act 1990, s 79(1)(b)–(c), (g)), and 'any dust, steam, smell or effluvia' or 'accumulation or deposit' which is likewise prejudicial (Environmental Protection Act 1990, s 79(1)(d)–(e)).

15 *Coventry City Council v Quinn* [1981] 1 WLR 1325 at 1328E–F.

16 *R v Camberwell Green Magistrates, ex parte Healey* (Unreported, Queen's Bench Divisional Court, CO/305/84, 10 October 1984).

17 *Patel v Mehtab* (1980) 5 HLR 78 at 83; *Coventry City Council v Quinn* [1981] 1 WLR 1325 at 1329E; *McCorley v Chief Executive of Birmingham City Council* (Unreported, Queen's Bench Divisional Court, CO/464/83, 12 January 1984).

18 See eg *Dover DC v Farrar*(1980) 2 HLR 35 at 38, but compare *GLC v LB of Tower Hamlets* (1983) 15 HLR 54 at 61.

19 See eg Landlord and Tenant Act 1985, s 11(1) (ante, p 789).

20 *Birmingham DC v Kelly* (1985) 17 HLR 572 at 579f per Woolf J. See also *Clayton v Sale UDC* [1926] 1 KB 415 at 426.

1 Environmental Protection Act 1990, s 80(1).

works executed.[2] The local authority may itself take steps to remove the nuisance at the owner's expense.[3]

(c) The tenant's remedies for breach of landlord's repairing covenants

It has, at least until fairly recently, been a general principle underlying the landlord-tenant relationship in English law that the performance of the parties' respective obligations is not interdependent.[4] For this reason it has not usually been thought wise (and on occasion it has proved disastrous[5]) for the tenant to withhold payment of rent or service charges on the ground of his landlord's patent failure to discharge a duty to repair.[6] The tenant must seek to vindicate his rights through the legitimate channels which the law affords. The remedies open to the tenant include the following.

(i) Damages for breach of covenant It is of course clear that the tenant may sue the landlord for damages for breach of any repairing covenant expressly or impliedly undertaken by the landlord in the lease.[7] It was reiterated by the Court of Appeal in *Calabar Properties Ltd v Stitcher*[8] that in assessing the tenant's damages for breach of a landlord's repairing covenant, the court starts from 'the fundamental principle' that the purpose of such damages is 'so far as is possible by means of a monetary award, to place the plaintiff in the position which he would have occupied if he had not suffered the wrong complained of...'. The object of the award is 'not to punish the landlord but...to restore the tenant to the position he would have been in had there been no breach.'[9] Damages must therefore be assessed as the difference between the value of the property to the tenant in its condition of disrepair and the value which the property would have had if the landlord had fulfilled his repairing obligation.[10]

(ii) Order for specific performance Although the remedy of specific performance is not available for the enforcement of a *tenant*'s repairing obligation,[11] the

2 Environmental Protection Act 1990, s 82(2).
3 Environmental Protection Act 1990, s 80(3), (4). See, however, *Salford City Council v McNally* [1976] AC 379 at 390A; *Birmingham DC v Kelly* (1985) 17 HLR 572 at 581 per Woolf J.
4 Ante, p 777.
5 See eg *Di Palma v Victoria Square Property Co Ltd* [1986] Ch 150 (post, p 815).
6 See now, however, the possibility that a doctrine of repudiatory breach may entitle the tenant both to throw up the tenancy and sue for breach of the landlord's repairing obligation (*Hussein v Mehlman* [1992] 2 EGLR 87 (post, p 844)).
7 See the substantial damages awarded for breach of Landlord and Tenant Act 1985, s 11 (ante, p 789) in *Downie v LB of Lambeth* (1986) Legal Action 95. An action for damages for breach of the landlord's repairing covenant, even if coupled with an application for a mandatory injunction, cannot be registered as a pending land action within Land Charges Act 1972, s 17(1). See *Regan & Blackburn Ltd v Rogers* [1985] 1 WLR 870 at 875D–E; [1985] Conv 406; (1986) 136 NLJ 157 (H.W. Wilkinson).
8 [1984] 1 WLR 287 at 295G–H per Stephenson LJ.
9 [1984] 1 WLR 287 at 297F. See (1984) 81 Law Soc Gaz 1269 (D.W. Williams); [1984] Conv 230 (J.E.M.); (1984) LAG Bulletin 51 (N. Madge and D. Watkinson). See also *Loria v Hammer* [1989] 2 EGLR 249 at 260F–H; [1990] Conv 124 (J.E. Martin).
10 See *Calabar Properties Ltd v Stitcher* [1984] 1 WLR 287 at 296C.
11 *Hill v Barclay* (1810) 16 Ves 402 at 405f, 33 ER 1037 at 1038; *Regional Properties Ltd v City of London Real Property Co Ltd* (1981) 257 Estates Gazette 64 at 66.

courts may be prepared in appropriate circumstances to order specific performance of a *landlord's* covenant to repair.[12] This discretion to award specific performance in favour of the tenant is expressly confirmed by statute.[13] In exceptional circumstances a mandatory injunction compelling repairs may even be made at an interlocutory stage if the effect of the disrepair is to expose tenants to 'a real risk of damage to health'.[14]

(iii) Remedies of self-help and set-off Further relief in the case of disrepair lies in the form of three similar, but distinct, remedies available to the tenant on a basis of self-help.

At common law the tenant has a *right of recoupment* from future rent in respect of the cost of repairs covenanted by the landlord. The right, of ancient derivation, confers a significant remedy on the tenant where the landlord is in breach of any covenant (whether express or implied) to repair the demised premises.[15] In *Lee-Parker v Izzet*[16] Goff J confirmed that the tenant may execute the covenanted repairs himself and then deduct the cost of these repairs from future payments of rent.[17] The tenant who takes advantage of this right is *pro tanto* immune from any action by the landlord for arrears of rent and also has in the same degree an answer to any claim by the landlord to distrain upon his goods.[18] The tenant must first have given the landlord notice of the need for repair[19] and the right of recoupment applies only to such portion of the tenant's expenditure as is reasonable and proper in all the circumstances of the case.[20]

If instead of paying for necessary repairs which the landlord should have effected, the tenant cross-claims for damages for breach of the landlord's

12 See *Jeune v Queens Cross Properties Ltd* [1974] Ch 97 at 101C–D per Pennycuick V-C. See also *Francis v Cowcliffe* (1977) 33 P & CR 368 at 374ff; *Peninsular Maritime Ltd v Padseal Ltd* (1981) 259 Estates Gazette 860 at 868.

13 Landlord and Tenant Act 1985, s 17(1). See *Parker v Camden LBC* [1986] Ch 162 at 173G–H; (1982) LAG Bulletin 66 at 68 (J. Luba).

14 *Parker v Camden LBC* [1986] Ch 162 at 174C, where Donaldson MR pointed out that the failure of a local authority landlord to repair and restart boilers which supplied heating and hot water made both elderly and very young occupiers of housing on a council estate vulnerable to 'a far from fanciful risk of death'.

15 The remedy can be traced back at least as far as *Taylor v Beal* (1591) Cro Eliz 222, 78 ER 478. See also *Waters v Weigall* (1795) 2 Anst 575 at 576, 145 ER 971. The legitimacy of broad formulations of the common law doctrine has been questioned (see P.M. Rank, (1976) 40 Conv (NS) 196). However, the doctrine seems to have a good common law pedigree (see A. Waite, [1981] Conv 199).

16 [1971] 1 WLR 1688 at 1693F–G. See also *Melville v Grapelodge Developments Ltd* (1979) 39 P & CR 179 at 186.

17 See also *Asco Developments Ltd v Gordon* (1978) 248 Estates Gazette 683 (reduction of existing rent arrears); *Knockholt Proprietary Ltd v Graff* [1975] Qd R 88 at 90G–91A.

18 *Lee-Parker v Izzet* [1971] 1 WLR 1688 at 1693A–B, 1695H. See (1982) LAG Bulletin 66 at 67 (J. Luba); A. Waite, (1984) LAG Bulletin 66.

19 *Lee-Parker v Izzet* [1971] 1 WLR 1688 at 1693H; *British Anzani (Felixstowe) Ltd v International Marine Management (UK) Ltd* [1979] 2 All ER 1063 at 1070b.

20 *Lee-Parker v Izzet* [1971] 1 WLR 1688 at 1693G, 1695H–1696A. The tenant's right of recoupment ranks in registered land as an overriding interest on behalf of a tenant who remains 'in actual occupation' of the land (see *Lee-Parker v Izzet* [1971] 1 WLR 1688 at 1691G) and in unregistered land comprises a non-registrable, non-overreachable right which binds all except a purchaser for value without notice.

covenant, it seems that the tenant has an *equitable right of set-off*. He may set off his unliquidated claim for damages against a liquidated claim by the landlord in respect of any non-payment of rent.[1] This remedy may be even more valuable than the common law right to make deductions from rent, in that it can cover consequential damage flowing from the landlord's breach.[2]

'Secure tenants', as defined by the Housing Act 1985,[3] are now given a *statutory 'right to repair'* in respect of certain kinds of defect in the condition of their accommodation. This 'right to repair' is currently outlined in a statutory instrument approved under the Housing Act 1985.[4] In relation to any 'qualifying repair',[5] the secure tenant may serve on his landlord a 'tenant's repair claim'.[6] The landlord authority may refuse to accept the claim on any of a number of specified grounds[7] (or may accept the tenant's claim with modifications[8]) but must otherwise consent to the relevant repairs being effected at the landlord's expense either by some person approved by the landlord[9] or by the tenant himself.[10] If the landlord authority fails either to accept the tenant's repair claim or to provide a satisfactory ground for refusing it, the tenant may ultimately carry out the necessary repairs and claim payment for them from the landlord authority.[11]

(iv) Appointment of receiver In the event of continuing default by a corporate landlord in its obligations of repair, it may be possible for the tenants to apply to the High Court for the appointment of a receiver to receive the

1 *British Anzani (Felixstowe) Ltd v International Marine Management (UK) Ltd* [1979] 2 All ER 1063 at 1068d–h, 1074c–d. The right to a set-off arises, however, only if it would be inequitable to allow the landlord to recover the rent in the face of the tenant's claim (see (1979) LAG Bulletin 210 at 211 (A. Arden)).

2 *British Anzani (Felixstowe) Ltd v International Marine Management (UK) Ltd* [1979] 2 All ER 1063 at 1070a–c, f–g, 1076h–j. It seems, however, that the right to set-off may be effectively excluded by contrary contractual provision (see *Electricity Supply Nominees Ltd v IAF Group Ltd* [1993] 1 WLR 1059 at 1064B-C).

3 See Housing Act 1985, s 79ff (post, p 882).

4 The Secure Tenancies (Right to Repair Scheme) Regulations 1985 (SI 1985/1493). See Housing Act 1985, s 96(1).

5 A 'qualifying repair' is any repair 'which the landlord of a secure tenant is obliged by a repairing covenant to carry out, other than a repair to the structure or exterior of a flat' (SI 1985/1493, reg 1(2)).

6 SI 1985/1493, reg 3(1).

7 SI 1985/1493, reg 5, Annex B, Parts 1 and 2. It is a mandatory ground of refusal that the landlord's costs in effecting the repair would be less than £20 (Ground 1), and a discretionary ground of refusal that the landlord's costs in effecting the repair would be more than £200 (Ground 4).

8 SI 1985/1493, reg 7(1)(b), 8(1)(iv).

9 SI 1985/1493, reg 7(2).

10 SI 1985/1493, reg 7(3)(i).

11 SI 1985/1493, reg 11. The Leasehold Reform, Housing and Urban Development Act 1993 proposes the setting in place of new regulations which will replace this right of self-help and replace it by a procedure under which the landlord authority will, on application, issue the tenant with a 'repair notice' authorising qualifying repairs to be carried out by a listed contractor within a specified period (see Housing Act 1985, s 96, as substituted by Leasehold Reform, Housing and Urban Development Act 1993, s 121).

rents from the tenants and to manage the entire property in accordance with the landlord's obligations.[12]

(v) Appointment of a manager Increasing concern at the plight of long leaseholders in deteriorating mansion blocks led the Nugee Committee in 1985 to propose increased safeguards against the defaults of the negligent landlord who flagrantly ignores his repairing obligations.[13] The Landlord and Tenant Act 1987 introduced a protective procedure which is more generally effective than the High Court jurisdiction to appoint a receiver. Any tenant of a flat within a building containing two or more flats[14] may apply to a county court for an order appointing a manager to take over the management of the premises or the functions of a receiver or both.[15] The applicant must first have served a preliminary notice on the defaulting landlord, specifying the matters of complaint and giving him a reasonable time within which to remedy the default.[16] The court may normally make an order only if satisfied that the landlord is in breach of his obligations, that his breach is likely to continue, and that it is 'just and convenient' to make the order.[17]

The court ultimately has power to make an 'acquisition order' on an application by not less than two-thirds of the qualifying tenants, thereby allowing the tenants to purchase the landlord's interest without his consent.[18] Such an order can be made only if the landlord is in breach (and is likely to continue to be in breach) of his obligations[19] or where three years have elapsed since the appointment of a manager and a more permanent or far-reaching remedy is required.[20] As the Nugee Committee noted, the ultimate solution of the problems which emerge in the context of multiple leasehold occupation is likely to be achieved only with the introduction of some form of freehold or 'commonhold' ownership of flats.[1]

(4) Other statutory obligations of the landlord

Apart from their statutory responsibilities in respect of repair and fitness of premises, landlords (or their agents) are subject to other important obligations imposed by statute. These obligations include the following.

12 See *Hart v Emelkirk Ltd* [1983] 1 WLR 1289 at 1291H; *Daiches v Bluelake Investments Ltd* [1985] 2 EGLR 67 at 70A–D. This remedy may, however, have limited application and utility. See *Parker v Camden LBC* [1986] Ch 162 at 173B–D, 176E–F, 179A–D (no application to local authority tenancies); *Evans v Clayhope Properties Ltd* [1988] 1 WLR 358 at 363A–F; [1988] Conv 363 (C.P. Rodgers).

13 See *Report of the Committee of Inquiry on the Management of Privately Owned Blocks of Flats* (Chairman: E.G. Nugee QC, 1985), Vol 1, para 7.2.17.

14 Landlord and Tenant Act 1987, s 21(2), (3).

15 Landlord and Tenant Act 1987, s 24(1).

16 Landlord and Tenant Act 1987, s 22.

17 Landlord and Tenant Act 1987, s 24(2).

18 Landlord and Tenant Act 1987, ss 27(4), 28(1), as amended by Leasehold Reform, Housing and Urban Development Act 1993, s 85(3).

19 Landlord and Tenant Act 1987, s 29(2), as amended by Leasehold Reform, Housing and Urban Development Act 1993, s 85(4).

20 Landlord and Tenant Act 1987, s 29(3).

1 See *Report of the Committee of Inquiry on the Management of Privately Owned Blocks of Flats*, Vol 1, para 7.9.11. In relation to commonhold ownership, see Chapter 1 (ante, p 10).

(a) Disclosure of certain information

The landlord of premises occupied as a dwelling is now statutorily obliged to supply his tenant with certain kinds of information which may prove vital for the effective enforcement of the tenant's rights.

(i) Identity of the landlord If the tenant of 'premises occupied as a dwelling' makes a written request for the landlord's name and address *either* to any person who demands or last received rent payable under the tenancy *or* to any agent of the landlord in relation to the tenancy, that person must within 21 days supply the tenant with a written statement of the information requested.[2] In the case of a corporate landlord, the tenant may make a further written request that he be informed of the name and address of every director and of the secretary of the landlord company.[3]

(ii) Assignment by the landlord In the event of any assignment of the landlord's reversion in respect of tenanted premises which consist of or include a dwelling, the new landlord is statutorily obliged to give the tenant written notice of the assignment and of the landlord's name and address within at most two months of the date of the assignment.[4]

(b) Provision of rent book

Where a tenant has a right to occupy premises as a residence in consideration of a rent which is payable weekly, the landlord must provide a 'rent book or other similar document for use in respect of the premises'.[5] Any rent book provided in pursuance of this duty must contain such details as the name and address of the landlord,[6] and certain statutorily prescribed

2 Landlord and Tenant Act 1985, s 1(1). The period of 21 days begins with the date of receipt of the request. Non-compliance is a criminal offence (section 1(2)), but only the identity of the immediate landlord need be disclosed (section 1(3)). Any written demand (eg for rent) which is made to a residential tenant must contain the name and address of the landlord (Landlord and Tenant Act 1987, s 47(1)). The landlord of every residential tenant must furthermore furnish his tenants with written advice of an address in England or Wales at which notices (eg notices of proceedings) may be served (Landlord and Tenant Act 1987, s 48(1)). Until such an address is notified to the tenant, no rent or service charge otherwise due from the tenant can be treated as due (Landlord and Tenant Act 1987, s 48(2)).

3 Landlord and Tenant Act 1985, s 2(1). The obligations of disclosure imposed by Landlord and Tenant Act 1985, ss 1, 2, have no reference to business tenancies governed by Part II of the Landlord and Tenant Act 1954 (see Landlord and Tenant Act 1985, s 32(1)), but do apply in the case of statutory tenancies under the Rent Act (see Landlord and Tenant Act 1985, s 1(3)).

4 Landlord and Tenant Act 1985, s 3(1). This provision catches statutory tenancies, and is activated by 'any conveyance other than a mortgage or charge' of the landlord's interest (Landlord and Tenant Act 1985, s 3(4)). In default of such a notice, the former landlord remains expressly liable to the tenant on the covenants of the lease (Landlord and Tenant Act 1985, s 3A, as added by Landlord and Tenant Act 1987, s 50).

5 Landlord and Tenant Act 1985, s 4(1). This requirement does not apply, however, if the rent includes a payment in respect of board and the value of that board to the tenant forms 'a substantial proportion of the whole rent' (Landlord and Tenant Act 1985, s 4(2)).

6 Landlord and Tenant Act 1985, s 5(1), as amended by Housing Act 1988, Sch 17, para 67.

information relating to rent and other particulars of the tenancy.[7] Failure to comply with any of these requirements constitutes a criminal offence,[8] but such failure does not invalidate the tenancy or render the rent thereunder irrecoverable.[9] The statutory rules relating to rent books are often ignored by landlords, and there is a strong argument for more vigorous enforcement of this branch of the law on behalf of residential tenants.[10]

(c) Restrictions in respect of service charges

The Landlord and Tenant Act 1985 imposes certain duties on the landlord in respect of 'service charges'[11] which are payable by the tenant in a block of flats. In determining the amount of a service charge payable for a given period, account may be taken of relevant costs only to the extent that these costs (eg the costs of repairs) were 'reasonably incurred' and the services provided or works carried out were 'of a reasonable standard'.[12] No service charge can normally be based on relevant costs incurred more than 18 months before the presentation of the charge for payment.[13] Where a service charge is payable in advance of any expenditure, the landlord may demand only such amount as is 'reasonable' and must make any necessary adjustment by way of rebate after the relevant costs have been incurred.[14] In any case in which the costs of proposed works exceed a statutorily prescribed amount,[15] the landlord must obtain at least two estimates for the works[16] and must supply these together with a written notice for the tenant's observations.[17] A tenant may in writing require the landlord to supply him with a written summary of costs incurred in connection with service charges,[18] and the

7 Landlord and Tenant Act 1985, s 5(1)(a), (b). See The Rent Book (Forms of Notice) Regulations 1982 (SI 1982/1474), Schedule, as amended by SI 1988/2198 and SI 1990/1067. The prescribed information must include details of the tenant's right not to be harassed or unlawfully evicted and of his right (where necessary) to receive help with payment of his rent.

8 Landlord and Tenant Act 1985, s 7(1).

9 *Shaw v Groom* [1970] 2 QB 504 at 516E–F, 526B–D; *Lambeth LBC v Udechuku* (1981) 41 P & CR 200 at 208. A tenant is not guilty of participating in any fraud upon the Inland Revenue merely because he suspects that his landlord's refusal to supply a rent book is related to an unwillingness to leave a permanent trace of the rent payments made (see *Chukwu v Iqbal* (Unreported, Court of Appeal, 30 January 1985) per Fox LJ).

10 See D.C. Hoath, [1978–79] JSWL 3.

11 A 'service charge' is defined as an amount which is payable by a tenant of a flat, as part of or in addition to rent, in respect of 'services, repairs, maintenance, or insurance or the landlord's costs of management' and which varies in whole or part according to the relevant costs (Landlord and Tenant Act 1985, s 18(1)).

12 Landlord and Tenant Act 1985, s 19(1). Account must be taken of any grant aid received by the landlord (Landlord and Tenant Act 1985, s 20A).

13 Landlord and Tenant Act 1985, s 20B.

14 Landlord and Tenant Act 1985, s 19(2).

15 The prescribed limit is whichever is the greater of £25 multiplied by the number of flats in the building or £500 (Landlord and Tenant Act 1985, s 20(3)).

16 Landlord and Tenant Act 1985, s 20(4). At least one estimate must be provided by 'a person wholly unconnected with the landlord'.

17 Landlord and Tenant Act 1985, s 20(4)(b), (c).

18 Landlord and Tenant Act 1985, s 21(1). If there are more than four flats in the building, the summary must be certified as 'fair' by a qualified accountant (Landlord and Tenant Act 1985, s 21(6)).

tenant also has rights to inspect accounts, receipts and other documents supporting this summary.[19]

The Leasehold Reform, Housing and Urban Development Act 1993 now reinforces the tenant's protection through the conferment of a right to join with other tenants who pay a common service charge in requiring that a 'management audit' be carried out on their behalf in relation to the management of the premises.[20] This audit is directed towards ascertaining whether the landlord's obligations and management functions are being discharged in an 'efficient and effective manner' and the extent to which the tenants' service charges are being likewise applied.[1]

(5) Express obligations of the tenant

The express terms of leases both formal and informal tend to impose extensive liabilities and disabilities on the tenant. These may range from such matters as the payment of rent to an absolute undertaking by the tenant not to assign or sublet the premises.[2] If the tenant expressly covenants in a more qualified form not to assign or sublet the premises without the landlord's consent, there is a statutory implication that such consent shall not be unreasonably withheld.[3] Where, however, there have been extensive and longstanding breaches of covenant by the tenant it may not be unreasonable for a landlord to refuse to consent to an assignment unless he can be reasonably satisfied that the assignee will remedy the breaches.[4]

If the tenant expressly covenants not to make improvements or alterations to the demised premises without the landlord's consent, it is again implied by statute that such consent shall not be unreasonably withheld.[5] A covenant by the tenant not to use the premises except for a specified purpose does not, however, constitute a positive undertaking to use the premises for that

19 Landlord and Tenant Act 1985, s 22(2).

20 Leasehold Reform, Housing and Urban Development Act 1993, s 76.

1 Leasehold Reform, Housing and Urban Development Act 1993, s 78(1).

2 An absolute prohibition may be waived by the landlord, but he cannot be compelled to permit a proposed assignment or sublease even if he is acting wholly unreasonably. A covenant against assignment or subletting of 'any part of' the demised premises is breached by an assignment or subletting of the whole of the premises (*Field v Barkworth* [1986] 1 WLR 137 at 139F–G, 140E–F), but a covenant which simply relates to the whole is not broken by a transaction in respect of only a part (*Wilson v Rosenthal* (1906) 22 TLR 233).

3 Landlord and Tenant Act 1927, s 19(1). See *Bickel v Duke of Westminster* [1977] QB 517 at 524C–G; *Bocardo SA v S & M Motels Ltd* [1980] 1 WLR 17 at 23F–24G; *Bromley Park Garden Estates Ltd v Moss* [1982] 1 WLR 1019; [1983] Conv 140 (L. Crabb). Landlord and Tenant Act 1988, s 1(3) imposes on the landlord a duty, on the tenant's service of a written application for consent, to supply the consent requested 'within a reasonable time' or, failing this, to provide reasons for withholding consent. The onus of showing the reasonableness of a refusal of consent lies on the landlord (Landlord and Tenant Act 1988, s 1(6)).

4 See *Orlando Investments Ltd v Grosvenor Estate Belgravia* (1990) 59 P & CR 21 at 27ff (breach of repairing covenants). Consent may also reasonably be withheld on the ground that an assignee may claim protection under the Leasehold Reform Act 1967 (see *Norfolk Capital Group Ltd v Kitway Ltd* [1977] QB 506 at 514D, 516A, F–G), but not necessarily on the ground that the Rent Act will come into operation (see *West Layton Ltd v Ford* [1979] QB 593 at 605A–C). See also *Leeward Securities Ltd v Lilyheath Properties Ltd* (1983) 17 HLR 35 at 47ff; P.F. Smith, [1986] 6 RRLR 240.

5 Landlord and Tenant Act 1927, s 19(2).

purpose.[6] No liability attaches to the tenant if under such circumstances he makes no use of the land at all.[7]

(6) Implied obligations of the tenant

In the absence of contrary stipulation in the lease, certain obligations are imposed on the tenant by implication of law. These include a covenant to pay rent[8] and rates.[9] The tenant's implied duties are, however, limited in content and nature. The courts will, for instance, be slow to imply additional covenants such as a covenant that the tenant should not use the premises for immoral purposes.[10]

(a) Obligation not to commit waste

There is an implied duty in the tenant not to commit waste. The extent of this duty depends on the character of the tenancy concerned.

(i) Fixed term of years A tenant holding under a fixed term of years is, in the absence of contrary agreement, liable for both voluntary and permissive waste.[11] On this basis a tenant for years is liable for any repair for which his landlord is not expressly or impliedly responsible.[12]

(ii) Yearly tenancy The liability of a yearly tenant is probably somewhat different from that of other periodic tenants.[13] A yearly tenant is liable for voluntary waste,[14] but is liable for permissive waste only if he fails to weatherproof the premises.[15] He is not liable for 'fair wear and tear'.[16]

(iii) Other periodic tenancies It is of course clear that the tenant must not damage the premises wilfully or negligently,[17] but it seems that, in the absence of

6 *Marquis of Bute v Guest* (1846) 15 M & W 160 at 165, 153 ER 804 at 807; *Lacon v Laceby* [1897] WN 39.

7 See *Pulleng v Curran* (1982) 44 P & CR 58 at 68; *Australian Safeway Stores Pty Ltd v Toorak Village Development Pty Ltd* [1974] VR 268 at 273.

8 Ante, p 701.

9 *Squire v C. Brewer & Sons Ltd* (Unreported, Court of Appeal, 15 July 1983).

10 *Burfort Financial Investments Ltd v Chotard* (1976) 239 Estates Gazette 891 at 893.

11 *Yellowly v Gower* (1855) 11 Exch 274 at 293f, 156 ER 833 at 841f. On the meaning of 'waste', see Chapter 3 (ante, p 57).

12 Compare, however, *Warren v Keen* [1954] 1 QB 15 at 20, where Denning LJ seemed to say that even a tenant for years has no general duty to carry out repairs.

13 If there is a difference, it seems to be attributable historically to the fact that a tenancy from year to year tended to arise by operation of law (ante, p 740), whereas in a tenancy created by the landlord's own act it was the 'landlord's folly' not to restrain the tenant by express provisions as to waste (see *Prior v Hanna* (1988) 43 DLR (4th) 612 at 616).

14 *Marsden v Edward Heyes Ltd* [1927] 2 KB 1 at 6ff.

15 *Wedd v Porter* [1916] 2 KB 91 at 100; but see *Warren v Keen* [1954] 1 QB 15 at 20.

16 *Haskell v Marlow* [1928] 2 KB 45 at 58; *Warren v Keen* [1954] 1 QB 15 at 20. The exception for 'fair wear and tear' exempts the tenant from liability for repairs which are decorative and for remedying parts which wear out or come adrift in the course of reasonable use (*Regis Property Co Ltd v Dudley* [1959] AC 370 at 410 per Lord Denning). The tenant may, however, be liable if further damage flows from fair wear and tear and he takes no remedial action, eg if a missing slate ultimately causes structural decay through water penetration (see *Haskell v Marlow* [1928] 2 KB 45 at 59).

17 *Warren v Keen* [1954] 1 QB 15 at 20. See *Prior v Hanna* (1988) 43 DLR (4th) 612 at 618ff (monthly tenant not liable, in absence of evidence of wilful or negligent damage, when smoking guests caused fire damage).

express contract, periodic tenants other than the yearly tenant have no general duty to put and keep the premises in repair.[18] The only duty of the periodic tenant is to use the premises in a 'husbandlike' or 'tenantlike' manner.[19] As Denning LJ explained in *Warren v Keen*,[20] this means merely that the tenant 'must do the little jobs about the place which a reasonable tenant would do'. He must mend the electric light when it fuses; he must unstop the sink when it is blocked by his waste. If he goes away for any length of time during winter, he must turn off the water and empty the boiler.[1] However, the weekly or monthly tenant bears no liability for disrepair which is caused by 'fair wear and tear or lapse of time'.[2]

(b) 'Usual covenants' in an equitable lease

Under an equitable lease or contract for a lease, the obligations impliedly undertaken by the tenant are taken, in the absence of express agreement, to include 'the usual covenants'.[3] These covenants comprise[4] undertakings by the tenant to pay rent, to pay tenant's rates and taxes, to keep and deliver up the premises in repair at the end of the term, and to permit the landlord to enter and inspect the premises where the landlord is responsible for any repair. In addition, and in sharp contrast with the law of forfeiture under a legal lease, the landlord under an equitable lease has an *implied* right of re-entry at least in respect of non-payment of rent[5] and possibly also nowadays in respect of any breach of covenant.[6]

(7) Statutory obligations of the tenant

Statute provides the source for many of the obligations which are imposed on certain categories of tenant. Most of the responsibilities of the 'secure

18 *Warren v Keen* [1954] 1 QB 15 at 20.

19 *Warren v Keen* [1954] 1 QB 15 at 20; *Firstcross Ltd v Teasdale* (1984) 47 P & CR 228 at 233. See also *Bickman v Smith Motors Ltd* [1955] 5 DLR 256 at 257; *Gallo v St Cyr* (1983) 144 DLR (3d) 146 at 148f, 153.

20 [1954] 1 QB 15 at 20.

1 *Warren v Keen* [1954] 1 QB 15 at 20. See also *Policicchio v Phoenix Assurance Co of Canada* (1978) 79 DLR (3d) 453 at 461. Compare, however, *Wycombe AHA v Barnett* (1984) 264 Estates Gazette 619 at 621.

2 *Warren v Keen* [1954] 1 QB 15 at 20.

3 It was held in *Flexman v Corbett* [1930] 1 Ch 672 at 678 that the list of 'usual covenants' is neither fixed nor closed.

4 These, together with the landlord's implied covenant for quiet enjoyment (ante, p 778), are the 'usual covenants' as classically expounded by Jessel MR in *Hampshire v Wickens* (1878) 7 Ch D 555 at 561 (see *Chester v Buckingham Travel Ltd* [1981] 1 WLR 96 at 99G). It is clear, however, that other covenants may also be 'usual' in particular contexts. The content of the 'usual covenants' turns on the circumstances of each case and is influenced both by the practice of conveyancers in the relevant district (*Flexman v Corbett* [1930] 1 Ch 672 at 678) and by the character of the property concerned. See eg *Chester v Buckingham Travel Ltd* [1981] 1 WLR 96 at 101D–E.

5 *Hodgkinson v Crowe* (1875) 10 Ch App 622 at 626.

6 See *Chester v Buckingham Travel Ltd* [1981] 1 WLR 96 at 105E–F; (1981) 97 LQR 385 (G. Woodman); (1981) 131 NLJ 545 (H.W. Wilkinson).

tenant' of local authority housing are, for instance, laid down in the Housing Act 1985.[7] More generally a tenant may be subject to important rights of entry reserved by statute on behalf of his landlord. In a tenancy governed by section 8 or section 11 of the Landlord and Tenant Act 1985,[8] the landlord, on giving the tenant 24 hours' notice in writing, has a right of entry 'at reasonable times of the day' for the purpose of viewing the condition and state of repair of the demised premises.[9]

(8) Unlawful leasehold practices

Under English law there are few general restrictions on the kinds of clause or covenant which may be inserted in a tenancy agreement or lease. It is, for instance, open to the landlord, if he so chooses, to require that the demised premises should be occupied as a private residence for the use of the tenant's family only,[10] or that no children should live in the property,[11] or that the tenant should not keep a domestic pet on the premises.[12]

(a) Discrimination on grounds of race or sex

Statute only rarely interferes with the content of leasehold undertakings or with letting practices in general. It is, however, unlawful for a landlord to discriminate on grounds of race or sex either in the 'terms on which he offers...premises'[13] or in refusing altogether an application for a tenancy.[14] Likewise grounds of race or sex may not be used by a landlord in order to justify the differential provision of access to any benefits or facilities in relation to the premises,[15] or to justify the eviction or detrimental treatment

7 Post, p 884.

8 Ante, pp 788, 789.

9 Landlord and Tenant Act 1985, ss 8(2), 11(6).

10 See, however, the wide definition accorded to 'family' in *Wrotham Park Settled Estates v Naylor* (1991) 62 P & CR 233 at 237f. Here Hoffmann J declined to find any breach of a family use covenant in a 999 year lease where a husband and wife as tenants occupied the demised premises (comprising several dwellings) with their 'outdoor servants'. Hoffmann J considered this ménage 'to constitute a family provided that they are all subject to one head' (here the husband and wife collectively). This extended understanding of 'family' as 'household' has a long antecedence both in England and in the United States (see eg *Liskeard Union v Liskeard Waterworks Co* (1881) 7 QBD 505 at 509 (workhouse inmates); *Salter v Lask* [1925] 1 KB 584 at 587; *City of White Plains v Ferraioli*, 313 NE2d 756 at 758f (1974); *State of New Jersey v Baker*, 405 A2d 368 at 375 (1979); *City of Santa Barbara v Adamson*, 610 P2d 436 (1980); *Charter Township of Delta v Dinolfo*, 351 NW2d 831 at 842ff (1984). Compare, however, *Brock v Wollams* [1949] 2 KB 388 at 394; *Carega Properties SA v Sharratt* [1979] 1 WLR 928 at 931E-H per Lord Diplock, 932C per Viscount Dilhorne; *Harrogate BC v Simpson* (1984) 17 HLR 205 at 210; *Kingsland v McIndoe* [1989] VR 273 at 278f.

11 Compare *Halifax Antiques Ltd v Hildebrand* (1986) 22 DLR (4th) 289 at 291ff.

12 Compare *Re Halifax County Condominium Corp No 21 and Savage* (1984) 8 DLR (4th) 336 at 339f.

13 Race Relations Act 1976, s 21(1)(a); Sex Discrimination Act 1975, s 30(1)(a). These provisions do not apply to an owner-occupier of the premises unless he uses the services of an estate agent or otherwise advertises the vacant accommodation (see Race Relations Act 1976, s 21(3); Sex Discrimination Act 1975, s 30(3)).

14 Race Relations Act 1976, s 21(1)(b); Sex Discrimination Act 1975, s 30(1)(b). Likewise these provisions have no application to an owner-occupier of the premises unless he uses the services of an estate agent or otherwise advertises the vacant accommodation (see Race Relations Act 1976, s 21(3); Sex Discrimination Act 1975, s 30(3)).

15 Race Relations Act 1976, s 21(2)(a); Sex Discrimination Act 1975, s 30(2)(a).

of the tenant.[16] However, none of these prohibitions has any application to 'small premises'[17] where the landlord would otherwise be compelled to share accommodation (such as a bathroom or kitchen) with other occupiers.[18] Where the licence or consent of the landlord (or any other person) is required for any assignment or subletting by the tenant, it is likewise unlawful for such licence or consent to be withheld on discriminatory grounds of race or sex.[19] Once again 'small premises' are exempted from the operation of this statutory restraint.[20]

(b) Overseas comparisons

The English experience in this area lags somewhat behind that of many overseas jurisdictions, where suspect classifications have been recognised as extending well beyond race and sex. On constitutional and other grounds the courts have struck down leasehold terms which discriminate against tenants who have children[1] or who are unmarried cohabitees[2] or are single parents, or which discriminate according to other suspect criteria.

In *Marina Point Ltd v Wolfson*,[3] for instance, the printed form of lease signed by the tenants, a married couple, contained a clause prohibiting residence in the landlord's apartment complex by children under the age of 18. On the subsequent birth of the tenants' child, the landlord company refused to renew the lease and eventually took eviction proceedings. The Supreme Court of California held that the landlord's exclusion of children violated California's Unruh Act which guarantees equal treatment for all citizens 'in all business establishments of every kind whatsoever'.[4] Tobriner J ruled that the Act did not permit a business enterprise to enforce a 'blanket exclusion' of families with minor children, even if children 'as a class' are 'noisier, rowdier, more mischievous and more boisterous than adults'.[5] The Act did not sanction the exclusion of an entire class of individuals from access to facilities 'on the basis of a generalised prediction that the class

16 Race Relations Act 1976, s 21(2)(b); Sex Discrimination Act 1975, s 30(2)(b).

17 'Small premises' have a statutory definition (see Race Relations Act 1976, s 22(2); Sex Discrimination Act 1975, s 32(2)).

18 Race Relations Act 1976, s 22(1); Sex Discrimination Act 1975, s 32(1).

19 Race Relations Act 1976, s 24(1); Sex Discrimination Act 1975, s 31(1).

20 Race Relations Act 1976, s 24(2); Sex Discrimination Act 1975, s 31(2).

1 See L.D. Barnett, *Child Exclusion Policies in Housing*, 67 Ky LJ 967 (1978–79); G.M. Travalio, *Suffer the Little Children—But Not in My Neighborhood*, (1979) 40 Ohio St LJ 295; A.W. Beck, *Apartment for rent: Adults only; no children allowed*, 15 Cal W L Rev 219 (1979–80); J.D. Segal, *The Enforceability of Age Restrictive Covenants in Condominium Developments*, 54 S Cal L Rev 1397 (1980–81); *Why Johnny can't rent any more—An Examination of laws prohibiting discrimination against families in rental housing*, 94 Harv L Rev 1829 (1981); S. Schovanec, *Landlord and Tenant: Is Discrimination Against Children Permissible in Oklahoma?*, 36 Okla L Rev 361 (1983). See also S.V. MacCallum and A.J. Bradbrook, (1977–78) 6 Adelaide L Rev 439.

2 See M.G. Connolly, *The Rights of Unmarried Cohabiting Couples to Housing in New York*, 11 Fordham Urban LJ 381 (1982–83). See also *Burke v Tralaggan* [1986] EOC 92-161 (refusal to let to unmarried couple held to violate Anti-Discrimination Act 1977, s 48(1)). See G. Moens, (1989) 12 Sydney L Rev 195.

3 640 P2d 115 (1982).

4 California Civil Code, s 51. In *Halet v Wend Investment Co*, 672 F2d 1305 at 1308f (1982), an adults-only letting policy was also challenged as racially discriminatory, in that it operated with 'greater impact. . .on blacks and Hispanics because more of those households included minor children'.

5 640 P2d 115 at 124.

"as a whole" is more likely to commit misconduct than some other class of the public.'[6] Accordingly the Supreme Court, by a majority,[7] declined to allow the landlord company to recover possession, Tobriner J observing that a society which 'sanctions wholesale discrimination against its children in obtaining housing engages in suspect activity.'[8]

2. LANDLORD'S REMEDIES FOR BREACH OF COVENANT BY THE TENANT

The landlord has a number of remedies in respect of the tenant's breach of the covenants contained (either expressly or impliedly) in a lease. These remedies include the following.

(1) Forfeiture of the lease

The right to 're-enter' the demised premises and forfeit the lease or tenancy is the most draconian weapon in the armoury of the landlord whose tenant has committed a breach of covenant. Almost all well drafted leases contain a stringent forfeiture clause which provides that in the event of any breach by the tenant 'it shall be lawful for the landlord to re-enter upon the demised premises and peaceably to hold and enjoy the demised premises thenceforth as if this lease had not been made and the term hereby granted shall absolutely determine...'.

As will appear later,[9] the exercise of the landlord's right of re-entry is heavily qualified by the court's discretion to grant equitable relief against forfeiture. It is clear moreover that this discretion to relieve against forfeiture cannot be evaded by the mere insertion in a tenancy agreement of a provision which enables the landlord to terminate the tenancy in the event of breach by giving the tenant a shorter period of notice than would otherwise be required. Such a clause is regarded as the functional equivalent of a forfeiture clause,[10] although the same view is not taken in relation to a clause which permits the landlord to terminate the tenancy in the event of breach by giving the same period of notice as would have been applicable in the absence of such breach.[11]

(a) Nature of re-entry

Notwithstanding the explicit terms of most forfeiture clauses, breach by the

6 640 P2d 115 at 125. The Supreme Court did, however, concede that in a different context an age-limited admission policy would be perfectly permissible under the Unruh Act in relation to retirement communities or housing complexes reserved for the elderly (640 P2d 115 at 128). However, the Court distinguished sharply between the conditions required for meeting such specialised housing needs and the 'wholesale exclusion of children from an apartment complex otherwise open to the general public'.

7 See the interesting dissent of Richardson J (640 P2d 115 at 129ff).

8 640 P.2d 115 at 129. Compare, however, *Re Hsuen and Mah* (1987) 31 DLR (4th) 199 at 203f.

9 Post, p 812.

10 *Richard Clarke & Co Ltd v Widnall* [1976] 1 WLR 845 at 850F-G.

11 *Clays Lane Housing Co-operative Ltd v Patrick* (1985) 49 P & CR 72 at 78f.

tenant does not automatically terminate a lease.[12] In the event of breach the landlord must elect either to waive the forfeiture or to enforce it.[13] If he chooses the latter course, the only way in which he may terminate the lease—except in cases covered by some special statutory regime—is by re-entering the demised premises.[14] Re-entry must take the form of some unequivocal act showing the lessor's intention to re-enter for breach of covenant.[15] Re-entry may comprise an actual physical entry upon the demised premises.[16] In this context, however, service of possession proceedings against the tenant is regarded as the equivalent of re-entry,[17] not least because it is the policy of the law that landlords should not suffer disadvantage by electing in favour of forfeiture through legal process rather than the nowadays less preferable method of self-help by physical re-entry.[18] Forfeiture of the lease dates from the point of re-entry,[19] the tenant becoming thereafter a trespasser whose continuing presence entitles the landlord to recover mesne profits from the date of re-entry.[20]

(b) Purpose of the right of re-entry

The clear purpose of the landlord's right of re-entry is to provide the landlord with a realistic form of security in the event of the tenant's failure to discharge his obligations under the lease.[1] In other words, the landlord is not relegated to a mere monetary claim in respect of the tenant's breach,[2] but may use the threat of recovery of possession as a lever to enforce compliance with

12 Post, p 832. Where the lease contains a proviso for re-entry, breach renders the lease merely voidable at the option of the landlord (see *Bowser v Colby* (1841) 1 Hare 109 at 133, 66 ER 969 at 979; *Jardine v Attorney General for Newfoundland* [1932] AC 275 at 286). The lease is avoided only upon re-entry (*Shevill v Builders Licensing Board* (1980) 2 BPR 9662 at 9667 per Samuels JA).

13 *Billson v Residential Apartments Ltd* [1992] 1 AC 494 at 534D per Lord Templeman.

14 *Billson v Residential Apartments Ltd* [1992] 1 AC 494 at 534D–E per Lord Templeman. See also *Consolidated Development Pty Ltd v Holt* (1986) 6 NSWLR 607 at 619C–D.

15 *Serjeant v Nash, Field & Co* [1903] 2 KB 304 at 310ff. See also *Jones v Carter* (1846) 15 M & W 718 at 726, 153 ER 1040 at 1043 per Parke B. The landlord or his agent must 'obtain possession to the physical exclusion of the lessee or anyone properly claiming under him' (*Tattersall's Hotel Penrith Pty Ltd v Permanent Trustee Co of NSW Ltd* (1942) 42 SR (NSW) 104 at 110). See eg *Blue Chip Investments Inc v Hicks* (1985) 18 DLR (4th) 755 at 757 (padlocking of doors to demised premises sufficient re-entry).

16 The recognition of some person other than the tenant in occupation of the premises can be taken to be the equivalent of re-entry (*Canas Property Co Ltd v K.L. Television Services Ltd* [1970] 2 QB 433 at 443B per Megaw LJ).

17 *Billson v Residential Apartments Ltd* [1992] 1 AC 494 at 534E per Lord Templeman. See also *Canas Property Co Ltd v K.L. Television Services Ltd* [1970] 2 QB 433 at 440B; *W.G. Clark (Properties) Ltd v Dupre Properties Ltd* [1992] Ch 297 at 306F. If the defaulting tenant has assigned the term, the proper defendant in possession proceedings is the assignee (see *Canas*, supra at 441E).

18 Post, p 829. See *W.G. Clark (Properties) Ltd v Dupre Properties Ltd* [1992] Ch 297 at 307F–G.

19 *Canas Property Co Ltd v K.L. Television Services Ltd* [1970] 2 QB 433 at 440A–B per Lord Denning MR.

20 *Canas Property Co Ltd v K.L. Television Services Ltd* [1970] 2 QB 433 at 442D. See also *Capital and City Holdings Ltd v Dean Warburg Ltd* (1989) 58 P & CR 346 at 351ff.

1 See *Howard v Fanshawe* [1895] 2 Ch 581 at 588; *Di Palma v Victoria Square Property Co Ltd* [1984] Ch 346 at 360D; *Direct Food Supplies (Victoria) Pty Ltd v D.L.V. Pty Ltd* [1975] VR 358 at 359; *Jam Factory Pty Ltd v Sunny Paradise Pty Ltd* [1989] VR 584 at 590.

2 As Lord Erskine LC pointed out in *Sanders v Pope* (1806) 12 Ves 282 at 289, 33 ER 108 at 110, the landlord may come 'from time to time against an insolvent estate'.

the covenants.[3] Sometimes, however, the landlord's only substantial concern when faced with a defaulting tenant is to ensure the termination of the tenancy and the eviction of the tenant from the premises.

(c) Right of re-entry as a proprietary right in land

A landlord's right of re-entry constitutes a species of proprietary interest in the land demised to the tenant.[4] If exercisable 'over or in respect of a legal term of years absolute', the right of re-entry is itself a legal right.[5] Such a right of re-entry is enforceable against the entire world—even against persons who are not in strict terms bound by the covenants to which the right of re-entry relates.[6] If annexed to an equitable term of years, the right of re-entry is equitable only[7] and may be binding on some third parties.[8] Whether legal or equitable in quality, the right of re-entry need not be exercised immediately at the point when it arises.[9] Except in circumstances of release, abandonment or waiver,[10] the right of re-entry may be exercised at any time within the statutory limitation period of twelve years.[11]

(d) General conditions for exercise of a right of re-entry

Under a legal term of years the landlord's right to re-enter and forfeit the lease arises only if the lease itself contains an express proviso for re-entry or if the lease is phrased in such a way that the performance of the tenant's obligations is rendered a 'condition' on which the future subsistence of the lease depends.[12] A right of re-entry cannot otherwise be implied in a legal lease and, in the absence of a relevant right of re-entry, a breach of covenant by the tenant gives the landlord at common law a mere right to recover damages.[13]

By curious contrast it seems that a right of re-entry is impliedly contained in every equitable lease not merely in respect of non-payment of rent[14] but possibly also in relation to other breaches of covenant by the tenant.[15]

3 See *Ezekiel v Orakpo* [1977] QB 260 at 268E–269C; *Shevill v Builders Licensing Board* (1980) 2 BPR 9662 at 9667 per Samuels JA.
4 Ante, p 73.
5 Law of Property Act 1925, s 1(2)(e).
6 *Shiloh Spinners Ltd v Harding* [1973] AC 691 at 717C, G per Lord Wilberforce.
7 Law of Property Act 1925, s 1(3).
8 For the effect of an equitable right of re-entry on third parties, see p 871, post.
9 *Owendale Pty Ltd v Anthony* (1967) 117 CLR 539 at 557.
10 Post, p 832.
11 Limitation Act 1980, s 15. See *Matthews v Smallwood* [1910] 1 Ch 777 at 786.
12 *Doe d Henniker v Watt* (1828) 8 B & C 308 at 315f, 108 ER 1057 at 1060.
13 *Shevill v Builders Licensing Board* (1980) 2 BPR 9662 at 9667 per Samuels JA. In particular the mere fact of rent arrear gives the landlord no entitlement to re-enter against the tenant (see *Lane v Dixon* (1847) 3 CB 776 at 787ff, 136 ER 311 at 315; *Doe d Dixon v Roe* (1849) 7 CB 134 at 135, 137 ER 55).
14 A proviso for re-entry in the case of non-payment of rent constitutes one of the 'usual covenants' (ante, p 802) which will be implied into a contract for a lease (*Hodgkinson v Crowe* (1875) 10 Ch App 622 at 626).
15 *Chester v Buckingham Travel Ltd* [1981] 1 WLR 96 at 105E–G.

(e) Restrictions upon exercise of the right of re-entry

In view of the potentially far-reaching nature of the landlord's right of re-entry, its exercise is subject to certain important restrictions.[16] In the famous words of Coke, 'the law leans against forfeitures'.[17]

(i) Residential leases It is unlawful to enforce a right of re-entry under a residential lease 'other than by proceedings in court while any person is lawfully residing in the premises'.[18] It is therefore quite dangerous for the landlord to take at face value the wording of the forfeiture clause in his lease.[19] No matter how heinous the breach committed by the tenant, any re-entry against a residential tenant without a court order for possession will give rise to serious criminal liability under the Protection from Eviction Act 1977.[20] Pursuant to section 1(2) of this Act a criminal offence is committed by any person who unlawfully deprives (or attempts to deprive) a 'residential occupier'[1] of his occupation of premises,[2] 'unless he proves that he believed, and had reasonable cause to believe, that the residential occupier had ceased to reside in the premises'.[3]

Criminal liability attaches not only to unlawful eviction but also to harassment of a residential tenant. Often only a blurred borderline lies between harassment and 'constructive eviction'.[4] Under section 1(3) of the Protection from Eviction Act 1977, a criminal offence is committed by any

16 See, however, *In re R (Restraint Order)* [1990] 2 QB 307 at 314A (landlord's right to forfeit not fettered by any restraint order made in respect of the tenant pursuant to Drug Trafficking Offences Act 1986, s 8).

17 *Co Litt*, pp 201b, 202a; *Duppa v Mayho* (1669) 1 Wms Saund 282 at 287, 85 ER 366 at 375 (Note).

18 Protection from Eviction Act 1977, s 2. See also *Billson v Residential Apartments Ltd* [1992] 1 AC 494 at 524D per Nicholls LJ.

19 In the case of tenancies protected under the Rent Act 1977 or the Housing Acts 1985 and 1988, further restrictions are imposed on the landlord's recovery of possession for reasons of breach by the tenant (post, pp 877, 881, 885). See eg *Antoniades v Villiers* [1990] 1 AC 417 at 461H–462A per Lord Templeman.

20 See eg *R v Brennan and Brennan* [1979] Crim LR 603 (landlord without previous convictions used the services of a 'very large man and an alsatian dog' to evict a group of students from their rented premises: 'Loss of liberty should be the usual penalty where landlords used threats or force, in the absence of unusual mitigation'). Further criminal liability may arise in connection with the offences of using and threatening violence to secure entry to premises under Criminal Law Act 1977, s 6(1) (ante, p 308). See A.J. Ashworth, [1979] JSWL 79f.

1 This term includes any 'person occupying. . .premises as a residence, whether under a contract or by virtue of any enactment or rule of law' (Protection from Eviction Act 1977, s 1(1)) and, although clearly not referable to trespassers or casual (ie non-contractual) lodgers, includes both tenants and contractual licensees.

2 Section 1(2) applies even where the premises comprise only one room (*Thurrock UDC v Shina* (1972) 23 P & CR 205 at 207). See the fines of £1,000 imposed in *Sheffield CC v Blaskey and Salis Properties Ltd* (1986) Legal Action 135.

3 See *R v Yuthiwattana* (1984) 16 HLR 49 at 63f, where the Court of Appeal emphasised that an unlawful deprivation of occupation must for this purpose have the character of an 'eviction'. A merely temporary 'locking-out' overnight or for a short period of time is more appropriately prosecuted under section 1(3) of the 1977 Act. See [1981] Conv 377 (M. Wasik).

4 See *Tagro v Cafane* [1991] 1 WLR 378 at 382E–F per Lord Donaldson of Lymington MR.

person who does 'acts'[5] which are 'calculated to interfere with the peace or comfort of the residential occupier or members of his household', or persistently[6] withdraws or withholds 'services reasonably required for the occupation of the premises as a residence'.[7] Such is the 'serious stigma' and 'social obloquy' attached to this 'truly criminal offence',[8] that a specific intent is required in the wrongdoer. Criminal liability for harassment arises only if the wrongdoer can be shown to have acted 'with intent to cause the residential occupier. . .to give up the occupation of the premises. . .or to refrain from exercising any right or pursuing any remedy in respect of the premises.'[9]

Section 1 of the Protection from Eviction Act 1977 is merely a penal provision and, in itself, creates no statutory cause of action in damages against a landlord.[10] The victim of eviction or harassment may, however, find a civil remedy in the law of contract or tort,[11] and in this context his rights have been substantially enhanced by the Housing Act 1988. In language which closely and quite consciously mirrors that of the Protection from Eviction Act 1977, the 1988 Act creates a cause of action in damages[12] for any residential occupier who suffers wrongful eviction or harassment leading

5 The word 'acts' includes a single act (*R v Evangelos Polycarpou* (1978) 9 HLR 129 at 131), but may not include an omission to act. It has been held that no offence is committed under section 1(3) merely because the landlord fails to rectify damage caused by repair work which was itself lawfully undertaken (*R v Ahmad* (1986) 130 SJ 554 at 555). Compare, however, *R v Yuthiwattana* (1984) 16 HLR 49, where a failure to replace a tenant's missing key came within section 1(3). See also (1986) Legal Action 125.

6 On the importance of 'persistently', see *R v Abrol* (1972) 116 SJ 177.

7 Harassment may comprise the intermittent but persistent withdrawal by the landlord of such services as the domestic supply of water, gas and electricity or may extend to 'more serious threats which are tantamount to the statutory crime of blackmail' (*R v Phekoo* [1981] 1 WLR 1117 at 1126G–H).

8 *R v Phekoo* [1981] 1 WLR 1117 at 1126G per Hollings J.

9 Protection from Eviction Act 1977, s 1(3). Thus no offence is committed if the defendant landlord reasonably believed the object of his attentions to be a squatter or trespasser rather than a 'residential occupier' (*R v Phekoo* [1981] 1 WLR 1117 at 1127A–B, 1128D) or if the landlord was 'utterly indifferent to, and unconcerned for', the tenant (*McCall v Abelesz* [1976] QB 585 at 598A, G). An intention to cause purely temporary disruption of occupation while repair works are carried out does not amount to an 'intent to cause the residential occupier. . .to give up. . .occupation', but may nevertheless connote an intent to cause him to 'refrain from exercising' his rights or pursuing any appropriate remedy (see *Schon v Camden LBC* [1986] 2 EGLR 37 at 39F–H).

10 *McCall v Abelesz* [1976] QB 585 at 594C, 597F. It has always, however, been possible for the aggrieved individual to lay an information on oath concerning his eviction before magistrates, which may lead to the issue of a warrant for the arrest of the offending landlord. The landlord may then be remanded on bail, one of the conditions of which can be set as the reinstatement in possession of the evicted tenant. The criminal procedure can thus provide by indirect means an immensely practical and potent form of injunction (see (1982) LAG Bulletin, December, p 14).

11 Ante, p 779. See Protection from Eviction Act 1977, s 1(5). In *Drane v Evangelou* [1978] 1 WLR 455 at 461E–F, Lawton LJ observed that '[t]o deprive a man of a roof over his head. . .is one of the worst torts which can be committed.' The cases must be 'rare in which eviction. . .does not found claims both in contract and in tort' (*Millington v Duffy* (1984) 17 HLR 232 at 235). See also *Caruso v Owen* (1983) LAG Bulletin 106 (£3,000 damages for the tort of wrongful interference with goods where landlord burned research student's PhD notes on bonfire as part of unlawful eviction).

12 The statutory liability is declared to be 'in the nature of a liability in tort' (Housing Act 1988, s 27(4)(a)).

to the surrender of occupation of premises.[13] The defaulting landlord is liable to pay damages in respect of the loss of the right of occupation,[14] such damages being assessed as the difference between the value of the landlord's interest had the occupier continued to have the same right of occupation as previously and the value of that interest freed from any remaining right of occupation.[15] In *Tagro v Cafane*[16] a landlord who had wrongfully evicted a monthly tenant from a single room in a house was, on this basis, held liable to pay damages of £31,000.[17] The statutory measure of compensation is clearly designed to be equivalent to the overall financial benefit otherwise derived by the landlord from his wrongful actions.[18] Although the 1988 Act allows the court to reduce the award of damages in the light of any prior misconduct of the former residential occupier (or of any person living with him in the premises),[19] the general effect of the statutory liability is to make any extra-curial eviction of a residential tenant an extremely expensive activity.

(ii) Non-residential leases The requirement of legal process does not normally apply to re-entry under non-residential leases.[20] Provided that the landlord first serves any statutory notice which the tenant may be entitled to receive,[1] forfeiture by peaceable re-entry remains a perfectly viable option in response to breaches of covenant under a business lease.[2] Indeed peaceable re-entry may be particularly attractive to the landlord under a business tenancy since it avoids the delay, expense and uncertainty associated with court proceedings for possession.[3] An early re-entry by a commercial landlord often forestalls

13 Housing Act 1988, s 27(1), (2). The term 'residential occupier' has the same meaning as in Protection from Eviction Act 1977, s 1 (see Housing Act 1988, s 27(9)).
14 Housing Act 1988, s 27(3).
15 Housing Act 1988, s 28(1). The landlord may seek to avert an award of damages either in part or in full by reinstating (or making a reasonable offer to reinstate) the occupier in the premises (Housing Act 1988, s 27(6), (7)). However, the mere handing over of a useless key does not suffice for this purpose (*Tagro v Cafane* [1991] 1 WLR 378 at 383F–G) and, in so far as it is 'difficult to see how you can reinstate a tenant who does not want to be reinstated', the ousted occupier seems effectively to have an option to take the compensation (*Tagro*, supra at 383F–384B).
16 [1991] 1 WLR 378 at 387D. See [1991] Conv 297 (C. Rodgers); A. Clarke, (1992) 45 CLP 81 at 98ff.
17 The plaintiff also received an additional award in excess of £15,000 in respect of trespass to her personal belongings. Lord Donaldson of Lymington MR accepted that the damages awarded at first instance 'do seem to be high', but was obviously less than overwhelmed by sympathy for an unmeritorious defendant who had shamelessly trashed his tenant's room and its contents.
18 It is increasingly recognised in other contexts that loss of a tenancy (particularly a statutorily protected tenancy) represents an extremely significant financial deprivation. See eg *Murray v Lloyd* [1989] 1 WLR 1060 at 1065A–F (damages of £115,000 for loss of statutory tenancy).
19 Housing Act 1988, s 27(7)(a).
20 See, however, Leasehold Property (Repairs) Act 1938, s 1 (post, p 824).
1 See eg Law of Property Act 1925, s 146(1) (post, p 817).
2 That peaceable re-entry remains available is implicit in the statutory reference to the enforcement of a right of re-entry 'by action or otherwise' (Law of Property Act 1925, s 146(1)). See *In re Riggs. Ex parte Lovell* [1901] 2 KB 16 at 20; *F.G. Sweeney Ltd v Powerscourt Shopping Centre Ltd* [1984] IR 501 at 504.
3 See A. Clarke, (1992) 45 CLP 81. It is not, however, open to a landlord to effect a peaceable re-entry against a tenant by means of an agreement with a subtenant under which the latter consents to have the locks changed but otherwise to remain in occupation as a direct tenant of the landlord (see *Ashton v Sobelman* [1987] 1 WLR 177 at 187A–C).

the rapid accumulation of almost certainly unrecoverable rent arrears and serves also to prevent unscrupulous tenants from enjoying a 'free ride' in terms of rent and service charges pending a court hearing.[4] There may moreover be little purpose in issuing proceedings when, in times of deep recession, the informal abandonment of commercial tenancies is not uncommon: the defaulting tenant simply vacates the premises leaving the key behind.

In spite of the advantages conferred by the self-help remedy of peaceable re-entry, it is still relatively unusual for a landlord under a non-residential lease to re-enter without first issuing court proceedings for possession. Peaceable re-entry becomes a realistic option for the business landlord only where the demised premises are, at least temporarily, unoccupied by the tenant.[5] Care is needed since in certain circumstances the exercise of the landlord's right of re-entry may give rise to criminal liability.[6] It is an offence under the Criminal Law Act 1977 for any person without lawful authority to use or to threaten violence for the purpose of securing entry into any premises where, to his knowledge, there is someone present who is opposed to the entry.[7] Peaceable re-entry upon commercial premises is usually feasible only out of business hours or at weekends.

In consequence forfeiture by physical re-entry, unsanctioned by the court, tends to display a certain surreptitious and lawless aspect. In *Billson v Residential Apartments Ltd*,[8] for instance, the tenants of unoccupied premises undertook major works of reconstruction in blatant disregard of the landlord's express reservation of a right of prior written consent to such alterations. As Lord Templeman observed, the landlord, 'perhaps incensed' by this flagrant breach of covenant, 'conceived and carried out a dawn raid which fortunately did not result in bloodshed.'[9] The landlord's agents peaceably re-entered the vacant premises at 6 am, changed the locks and fixed notices announcing that the lease had been forfeited. Four hours later the tenants' workmen broke back into the premises and regained occupation.

Subsequent litigation concerned the question whether there remained in these circumstances any jurisdiction to grant the tenants relief against forfeiture,[10] but both the Court of Appeal and the House of Lords indicated *en passant* their distaste for what Nicholls LJ stigmatised as a 'hole-in-the-corner, self-help route' to the recovery of possession.[11] Nicholls LJ expressed the view that it cannot be right 'to encourage law-abiding citizens to embark on a course which is a sure recipe for violence', and that the policy of the law is 'to discourage self-help when confrontation and a breach of the law

4 See *F.G. Sweeney Ltd v Powerscourt Shopping Centre Ltd* [1984] IR 501 at 504 per Carroll J.

5 See M. Green, (1983) 80 Law Soc Gaz 328.

6 See *Billson v Residential Apartments Ltd* [1992] 1 AC 494 at 524E per Nicholls LJ, 536G per Lord Templeman.

7 Criminal Law Act 1977, s 6(1) (ante, p 308). Re-entry is not unlawful where premises are occupied only by the tenant's goods (see *Billson v Residential Apartments Ltd* [1992] 1 AC 494 at 536G per Lord Templeman).

8 [1992] 1 AC 494. See [1992] Conv 273 (P.F. Smith); [1991] CLJ 401 (S. Bridge).

9 [1992] 1 AC 494 at 540B.

10 Post, p 826.

11 [1992] 1 AC 494 at 524G.

are likely to follow.'[12] These thoughts were echoed in the House of Lords, where Lord Templeman referred to 'the civilised method of determining the lease by issuing and serving a writ' as representing a course of action far preferable to 'the dubious and dangerous method of determining the lease by re-entering the premises'.[13] In Lord Templeman's view, the courts should not positively encourage any means by which a landlord could 'sneak up on a shop at night, break into the shop, and install new locks so that the tenant loses his lease and can only press his nose against the shop window'.[14] Such sentiments point to a modern shift in emphasis from the endorsement of *peaceable re-entry* to the promotion of *peaceful forfeiture*.[15] There seems nowadays to be a widespread apprehension that, although forfeiture by actual re-entry remains lawful, it is in general 'undesirable to encourage landlords to self-help.'[16]

(iii) Tenant's right to relief against forfeiture The most important general limitation on the successful exercise of a landlord's right of re-entry lies in the possibility that the tenant may be able in appropriate circumstances to obtain relief against forfeiture. Whereas re-entry, either by actual entry or by the service of proceedings, has the effect of terminating and avoiding a lease, the granting of relief against forfeiture constitutes a 'revival of the lease'.[17] The consequence of such relief, if granted, is 'to do away with the forfeiture just as if there had never been any'.[18] Relief thus 'involves the coercive re-establishment of the relationship of lessor and lessee which has been effectively sundered at law.'[19]

It is clear that from the earliest times courts of equity have asserted the right to relieve against the forfeiture of rights on the ground that such a penalty is disproportionate to the breach upon which the forfeiture is premised.[20] In *Shiloh Spinners Ltd v Harding*[1] the House of Lords confirmed

12 [1992] 1 AC 494 at 525A–B ('If a landlord enters business premises without warning out of business hours, violence is all too likely when the tenant arrives the next day to reopen his shop or offices and finds that he is barred from entry').

13 [1992] 1 AC 494 at 536F. Likewise Lord Oliver of Aylmerton spoke (at 543E) of 'the more conventional course of forfeiting by means of an action for possession.'

14 [1992] 1 AC 494 at 536G.

15 See eg *W.G. Clark (Properties) Ltd v Dupre Properties Ltd* [1992] Ch 297 at 307F–G, where Thomas Morison QC opined that it 'must be the policy of the law. . .to encourage peaceful repossession' and therefore concluded that the service of proceedings for possession is 'intended to put the landlord, so far as possible, into at least as good a position as he would have been in if he had resorted to self-help.'

16 *W.G. Clark (Properties) Ltd v Dupre Properties Ltd* [1992] Ch 297 at 307F–G. For an excellent discussion of the social legitimacy of self-help remedies, see Alison Clarke, (1992) 45 CLP 81 at 94ff.

17 *Billson v Residential Apartments Ltd* [1992] 1 AC 494 at 535C per Lord Templeman.

18 *Shevill v Builders Licensing Board* (1980) 2 BPR 9662 at 9667 per Samuels JA. See *Dendy v Evans* [1910] 1 KB 263 at 267ff.

19 *Stieper v Deviot Pty Ltd* (1977) 2 BPR 9602 at 9610 per Glass JA. Thus relief will not be granted on condition that the restored lease is immediately surrendered to the landlord: '[t]he object of relief against forfeiture is the continuation of a lease and not its extinction' (*Fuller v Judy Properties Ltd* (1991) 64 P & CR 176 at 184 per Dillon LJ).

20 See *Billson v Residential Apartments Ltd* [1992] 1 AC 494 at 535B (post, p 830).

1 [1973] AC 691. See [1973] CLJ 218 (P.B. Fairest).

that this inherent equitable jurisdiction extended beyond the granting of relief for non-payment of rent to cover wilful breaches of other forms of covenant.[2] Although equity still 'expects men to carry out their bargains and will not let them buy their way out by uncovenanted payment', Lord Wilberforce emphasised that the courts retain the right 'in appropriate and limited cases' to relieve against forfeiture for breach of covenant or condition 'where the primary object of the bargain is to secure a stated result which can effectively be attained when the matter comes before the court, and where the forfeiture provision is added by way of security for the production of that result.'[3]

Although it remains debatable to what extent legislative intervention has overtaken or extinguished the inherent equitable jurisdiction, it is somewhat rare for a lease ultimately to be forfeited if the tenant's breach is capable of remedy and the purpose of the landlord-tenant relationship is still capable of fulfilment.[4] The aggressively terminal tone of most leasehold forfeiture clauses is seldom borne out against the actuality of the modern jurisdiction to grant relief. It is nowadays a judicially admitted fact that in many leases, no matter how 'diligent or even punctilious a tenant may be in carrying out his obligations', there will 'in practice inevitably be occasions' when the tenant is strictly in breach of some covenant or other contained in his tenancy.[5] The potential for relief against forfeiture is an ever-present condition of the workability of most leasehold relationships. For this reason alone the right to seek relief is a valuable incident of the landlord-tenant relationship.[6] As such the right to seek relief constitutes a transferable chose in action. It can be passed to a purchaser of the lease and can vest in the tenant's trustee in bankruptcy.[7]

The court's powers in matters of relief against forfeiture differ vitally in accordance with whether forfeiture is sought on the ground of non-payment of rent or on the ground of some other breach of covenant.

2 See *Sanders v Pope* (1806) 12 Ves 282 at 289, 33 ER 108 at 110; *Billson v Residential Apartments Ltd* [1992] 1 AC 494 at 534G-H per Lord Templeman.

3 [1973] AC 691 at 723G-H. See *Sport Internationaal Bussum B.V. v Inter-Footwear Ltd* [1984] 1 WLR 776 at 783H, 785G. See also J. Story, *Commentaries on Equity Jurisprudence* (12th edn 1877), Vol II, p 561 ('Where a penalty or forfeiture is designed merely as a security to enforce the principal obligation, it is as much against conscience to allow any party to pervert it to a different and oppressive purpose, as it would be to allow him to substitute another for the principal obligation').

4 'When the landlord can be made whole by the payment of the money, there will rarely be reason to refuse the tenant relief from re-entry or forfeiture' (*Badley v Badley* (1983) 138 DLR (3d) 493 at 502). See also *Platt v Ong* [1972] VR 197 at 198.

5 See *Bass Holdings Ltd v Morton Music Ltd* [1988] Ch 493 at 528F-G per Nicholls LJ.

6 One of a number of joint tenants cannot unilaterally apply for relief against forfeiture (see *Hammersmith and Fulham LBC v Monk* [1992] 1 AC 478 at 490G per Lord Bridge of Harwich; *T.M. Fairclough & Sons Ltd v Berliner* [1931] 1 Ch 60 at 66).

7 *Howard v Fanshawe* [1895] 2 Ch 581 at 589. The right to seek relief against forfeiture passes to assignees of the original tenant, even though the assignment is itself wrongful because made in breach of covenant (*Old Grovebury Manor Farm Ltd v W. Seymour Plant Sales & Hire Ltd* (No 2) [1979] 1 WLR 1397 at 1400F-G; *Re Hurontario Management Services Ltd and Menechella Brothers Ltd* (1983) 146 DLR (3d) 110 at 112). After assignment the original tenant loses any right to apply for relief (see *Re Francini and Canuck Properties Ltd* (1982) 132 DLR (3d) 468 at 471).

(f) Forfeiture for non-payment of rent

The precise operation of forfeiture for non-payment of rent[8] depends on whether recourse is had to the jurisdiction of the county court or of the High Court.[9] In either case the landlord's right to re-enter must be preceded by a formal demand for rent[10] unless the requirement of formal demand is obviated either by the express terms of the lease[11] or by statute. Section 210 of the Common Law Procedure Act 1852 provides that there is no requirement of formal demand if at least half a year's rent is in arrear and the goods present on the premises and available for distress are insufficient to cover the arrears due. These conditions are fairly easily met since goods are deemed unavailable for distress if contained in premises which are locked.[12]

(i) The equitable jurisdiction to grant relief Notwithstanding the existence of a right in the landlord to re-enter for non-payment of rent, the courts have traditionally restrained the exercise of this right. Since the purpose of the proviso for re-entry is merely to secure the payment of rent,[13] it follows that 'when the rent is paid, the end is obtained; and therefore the landlord shall not be permitted to take advantage of the forfeiture'.[14] Accordingly in the exercise of their equitable jurisdiction the courts have long had power to reinstate the lease, where it just and equitable so to do, provided that the tenant pays all rent owed to and costs incurred by the landlord.[15]

(ii) Statutory rights to terminate possession proceedings The equitable jurisdiction is in certain respects supplemented by statute. In possession proceedings brought in the High Court for non-payment of rent, the tenant is entitled to have the proceedings stayed if he pays all rent arrears and costs before the date of judgment.[16] Somewhat anomalously this right arises only if at

8 Difficult issues may be raised by the common practice under which the payment of a maintenance or service charge under a lease is expressly covenanted as a form of additional rent (see eg *Di Palma v Victoria Square Property Co Ltd* [1986] Ch 150 at 158C; *Blatherwick (Services) Ltd v King* [1991] Ch 218 at 224E). Such a covenant clearly makes available the remedy of distress, but it has been queried whether the relevant forfeiture regime is that applicable to non-payment of rent or that relating to other forms of breach. See [1993] Conv 11 (J.E.A.), suggesting that the usual covenant be reworded so as to facilitate only the remedy of distress.

9 A landlord who unnecessarily issues proceedings in the High Court may find that he is penalised in the matter of costs (*Lircata Properties Ltd v Jones* [1967] 1 WLR 1257 at 1261F).

10 The archaic process of 'formal demand' must be made either at an appointed place or on the demised premises and should require that the exact rent owed should be paid before sunset on the last date for due payment (see *Duppa v Mayho* (1669) 1 Wms Saund 282 at 287, 85 ER 366 at 374f (Note)).

11 Almost all professionally drafted leases today stipulate that the landlord should be exempted from making 'formal demand' for the rent.

12 *Doe d Chippendale v Dyson* (1827) Mood & M 77 at 78, 173 ER 1087; *Hammond v Mather* (1862) 3 F & F 151, 176 ER 68. See also County Courts Act 1984, s 139(1).

13 Ante, p 813.

14 *Wadman v Calcraft* (1803) 10 Ves 67 at 69, 32 ER 768 at 769; *Durell v Gread* (1914) 84 LJKB 130 at 132 per Scrutton J; *Silverman v A.F.C.O. (U.K.) Ltd* (1988) 56 P & CR 185 at 189. See also *Baxton v Kara* [1982] 1 NSWLR 604 at 609G–610C; *Badley v Badley* (1983) 138 DLR (3d) 493 at 502; *Shevill v Builders Licensing Board* (1980) 2 BPR 9662 at 9667 per Samuels JA.

15 See *Howard v Fanshawe* [1895] 2 Ch 581 at 592.

16 Common Law Procedure Act 1852, s 212. It seems that payment by a third party is not sufficient (*Matthews v Dobbins* [1963] 1 WLR 227 at 229ff).

least six months' rent is in arrear.[17] The tenant has a similar right to the automatic termination of county court possession proceedings on the payment of all rent arrears and costs not less than five days before the trial date.[18]

(iii) Other statutory access to relief against forfeiture The tenant has further access to relief even after the landlord has obtained and enforced a court order for possession. The High Court has a discretionary power to grant relief where the tenant tenders payment of all arrears and costs subsequently to the granting of a possession order, provided application for relief is made within six months of the execution of the judgment for possession.[19] The High Court's discretion may be exercised notwithstanding physical re-entry by the landlord, so long as the landlord has not yet proceeded to re-let the premises to a stranger[20] or has acted 'unreasonably or precipitously' in granting rights in the premises to third parties.[1] Where relief is granted, the tenant simply continues to hold under the old lease.

A county court, if satisfied that the landlord is entitled to enforce his right of re-entry, must postpone the execution of any possession order for at least four weeks[2] and has discretion to extend this period further.[3] The tenant[4] has an automatic right to relief if, within the period thus fixed by the court, he pays all rent arrears and costs due.[5] On the tenant's failure to pay within the relevant period, the county court possession order becomes enforceable and, if the order remains unreversed, the tenant is thereafter barred from all relief.[6] Even now, however, the tenant retains one further hope of relief. Within the six months following the landlord's recovery of possession under the court order, the court has a discretion, on application by the tenant, to grant relief on such terms as it thinks fit.[7]

The county court is given one additional statutory power to relieve against forfeiture in cases of non-payment of rent. The court is expressly given power to grant relief after a forfeiture through peaceable re-entry by the landlord,

17 *Standard Pattern Co Ltd v Ivey* [1962] Ch 432 at 438, but compare (1962) 78 LQR 168 (R.E.M.). See also *Di Palma v Victoria Square Property Co Ltd* [1984] Ch 346 at 366A–B.

18 County Courts Act 1984, s 138(2).

19 Common Law Procedure Act 1852, s 210. In strict terms this six-month period of grace is available only where the rent itself is at least six months in arrears (see *Billson v Residential Apartments Ltd* [1992] 1 AC 494 at 529C per Nicholls LJ).

20 *Stanhope v Haworth* (1886) 3 TLR 34.

1 *Silverman v A.F.C.O. (U.K.) Ltd* (1988) 56 P & CR 185 at 192 per Slade LJ. See [1992] Conv 343 (J.E. Martin).

2 County Courts Act 1984, s 138(3).

3 County Courts Act 1984, s 138(4).

4 The statutory reference to 'lessee' includes an under-lessee and any person deriving title under a lessee (County Courts Act 1984, s 140), with the result that a tenant's mortgagee has the same right to relief as does the tenant himself (see also *Grand Junction Co Ltd v Bates* [1954] 2 QB 160 at 168f).

5 County Courts Act 1984, s 138(5).

6 County Courts Act 1984, s 138(7). The tenant is thus excluded from obtaining relief even in the High Court, as was demonstrated with disastrous consequences in *Di Palma v Victoria Square Property Co Ltd* [1986] Ch 150.

7 County Courts Act 1984, s 138(9A), as introduced by Administration of Justice Act 1985, s 55(4), 139(2). This extension of the relief jurisdiction was intended to prevent any recurrence of the calamitous outcome achieved in *Di Palma v Victoria Square Property Co Ltd* [1986] Ch 150, but see the stern refusal of the Court of Appeal to grant relief where no application was made within the six-month period in *United Dominions Trust Ltd v Shellpoint Trustees Ltd* (1993) *Times*, 23 March.

provided that application is made for relief within six months of the date of the peaceable re-entry.[8]

(iv) The residual equitable discretion In cases where the tenant does not have access to statutory protection against the enforcement of the landlord's right of re-entry, the tenant is relegated to seeking the favourable exercise of the courts' general equitable discretion to grant relief against forfeiture.[9] Thus, for instance, the tenant is thrown back upon the equitable discretion where, in cases falling within the jurisdiction of the High Court, a landlord does not proceed by action but simply exercises a right of peaceable re-entry without a court order.[10] Likewise the equitable jurisdiction is vital where less than six months' rent is in arrear.[11] In such cases the court tends to apply the analogy of the statutory jurisdiction in relief,[12] and the tenant can usually avert forfeiture if he pays up all arrears and costs within six months or so of the landlord's resumption of possession.[13]

(v) Indulgence towards the defaulting tenant The jurisdiction to relieve against forfeiture is exercised with what often appears at first sight to be an over-indulgent forbearance towards the tenant.[14] It is generally possible for a tenant to stave off the effects of forfeiture by paying up arrears of rent at the last possible moment, a past record of continuous arrears[15] or breaches of other covenants[16] being normally regarded as irrelevant to the question whether discretion should be exercised in his favour.[17] Relief is usually granted if, even by belated payment, the landlord can be put in the same position which he occupied before the question of forfeiture arose.[18] No matter how

8 County Courts Act 1984, s 139(2).
9 This jurisdiction is preserved by Supreme Court Act 1981, s 38(1).
10 *Howard v Fanshawe* [1895] 2 Ch 581 at 588. See also *Lovelock v Margo* [1963] 2 QB 786 at 788; *Abbey National Building Society v Maybeech Ltd* [1985] Ch 190 at 201F-G.
11 *Billson v Residential Apartments Ltd* [1992] 1 AC 494 at 529C-D per Nicholls LJ.
12 See *Howard v Fanshawe* [1895] 2 Ch 581 at 588f per Stirling J.
13 *Thatcher v C.H. Pearce & Sons (Contractors) Ltd* [1968] 1 WLR 748 at 755G-756A; *Di Palma v Victoria Square Property Co Ltd* [1984] Ch 346 at 366C.
14 See *Ladup Ltd v Williams & Glyn's Bank Plc* [1985] 1 WLR 851 at 860E-F per Warner J.
15 See *Newbolt v Bingham* (1895) 72 LT 852 at 854 per Rigby LJ; *Gill v Lewis* [1956] 2 QB 1 at 11, 14; *Re Brompton Securities Ltd (No 2)* [1988] 3 All ER 677 at 680d-h. A 'desultory' approach to rent payment is not fatal to an application for relief (see *Jam Factory Pty Ltd v Sunny Paradise Pty Ltd* [1989] VR 584 at 591).
16 *Gill v Lewis* [1956] 2 QB 1 at 13; *Pioneer Quarries (Sydney) Pty Ltd v Permanent Trustee Co of NSW Ltd* (1970) 2 BPR 9562 at 9575f. Other forms of breach may influence against the granting of relief only in very exceptional circumstances where these other breaches have caused irremediable damage to the landlord's interests. See eg *Stieper v Deviot Pty Ltd* (1977) 2 BPR 9602 at 9607 (tenant's disregard of landlord's insurance terms caused 'black mark. . .notorious in the insurance world'); *Pioneer Quarries*, supra at 9577 (tenant's immoral use of premises).
17 Relief against forfeiture for non-payment of rent may of course be conditioned upon an undertaking by the tenant to perform other covenants (see *Public Trustee v Westbrook* [1965] 1 WLR 1160 at 1163F; *Jam Factory Pty Ltd v Sunny Paradise Pty Ltd* [1989] VR 584 at 591).
18 See *Pioneer Quarries (Sydney) Pty Ltd v Permanent Trustee Co of NSW Ltd* (1970) 2 BPR 9562 at 9571f.

'appalling' the record of the tenant, the courts habitually take the view that re-entry is a mere security for payment of the rent and that if the rent is eventually paid, there is 'nothing that the landlord can currently complain of; he can only complain of the past.'[19] Accordingly relief against forfeiture for non-payment tends to be withheld only in the 'most exceptional' circumstances.[20]

(g) *Forfeiture for breach of other covenants*

Forfeiture for breach of covenants other than the covenant to pay rent is now governed by statute. Section 146 of the Law of Property Act 1925 lays down a special notice procedure in respect of such covenants which differs markedly from the rules relating to forfeiture for non-payment of rent.[1] Apart from several exceptional instances withdrawn from its scope,[2] section 146 is mandatory and cannot be excluded even by express contrary contractual provision.[3]

(i) Contents of a 'section 146 notice' Under section 146(1) the landlord cannot enforce any right of re-entry or forfeiture, either by court action or by peaceable re-entry, unless he has first served a valid statutory notice on the tenant and the tenant has failed within a reasonable time to comply with the terms of that notice. The 'section 146 notice' must specify the particular breach of which complaint is made.[4] It must require that the tenant remedy the breach 'if the breach is capable of remedy',[5] and it must normally require that the tenant make compensation in money for the breach.[6] In addition, if the notice relates to a breach of the tenant's repairing covenants, it must make visible reference to various rights to protection enjoyed by the tenant under the Leasehold Property (Repairs) Act 1938.[7] Any notice

19 See eg *Bhimji v Salih* (Unreported, Court of Appeal, 1978 B No 1099, 4 February 1981) per Brightman LJ.

20 See eg *Public Trustee v Westbrook* [1965] 1 WLR 1160 at 1163E (no rent paid for 22 years). See also *Gill v Lewis* [1956] 2 QB 1 at 13f.

1 Section 146 does not in general apply to breaches of the covenant to pay rent (Law of Property Act 1925, s 146(11)), although see section 146(4) (post, p 835).

2 See Law of Property Act 1925, s 146(8), (9).

3 Law of Property Act 1925, s 146(12). The section 146 notice procedure applies to underleases and to specifically enforceable agreements for a lease (Law of Property Act 1925, s 146(5)(a)). It seems, however, that section 146 has no application to an agreement for a lease which takes effect only as a common law periodic tenancy (*Swain v Ayres* (1888) 21 QBD 289 at 293 per Lord Esher MR, 295 per Lindley LJ, 296 per Lopes LJ).

4 Law of Property Act 1925, s 146(1)(a). The notice must be sufficiently specific to enable the tenant to provide an effective remedy (*Fletcher v Nokes* [1897] 1 Ch 271 at 273f). In the case of disrepair by the tenant it is usual to append to the notice a schedule of dilapidations prepared by a builder or surveyor.

5 Law of Property Act 1925, s 146(1)(b).

6 Law of Property Act 1925, s 146(1)(c). It is clear, however, that the landlord need not demand monetary compensation if he does not want it (*Lock v Pearce* [1893] 2 Ch 271 at 276, 279f). In *Rugby School (Governors) v Tannahill* [1935] 1 KB 87 at 91, for instance, Rugby School was not required to demand that it share by way of compensation in income derived through prostitution!

7 Leasehold Property (Repairs) Act 1938, s 1(4) (post, p 824).

which fails to comply with section 146 is rendered invalid[8] and any purported forfeiture based upon an invalid notice is void.[9]

(ii) Service of the section 146 notice Where section 146 applies, no re-entry may properly be made in the absence of due service of the required notice.[10] A section 146 notice must be served upon the 'lessee',[11] a term which bears an extended statutory meaning inclusive of an under-lessee and 'any person deriving title under a lessee'.[12] The notice must therefore be served upon an assignee of the leasehold estate and upon any mortgagee or chargee of whom the lessor is aware. Where the lease has already been assigned (even wrongfully) to a third party, a notice served on the original tenant is insufficient to satisfy the requirement of section 146 and is therefore invalid.[13] It would seem to follow that a landlord who re-enters the demised premises after service of such an invalid notice cannot, precisely because he is now in possession, cure the defect by serving a second validating notice on the assignee.[14] In *Fuller v Judy Properties Ltd*,[15] however, the Court of Appeal was grudgingly prepared to uphold the validity of a re-entry against the assignee in slightly unusual circumstances where the assignee had received a copy of the original invalid notice and would in no way have benefited from the 'mere token formality' of a return of the keys before service of the second section 146 notice.[16]

(iii) Purpose of the notice procedure As Slade LJ pointed out in *Expert Clothing Service & Sales Ltd v Hillgate House Ltd*,[17] it is 'an important purpose' of the section 146 procedure 'to give even tenants who have hitherto lacked the will or the means to comply with their obligations one last chance to summon up that will or find the necessary means before the landlord re-enters'. The landlord may not determine the lease until it is clear that the

8 For instance, a section 146 notice is invalid if it omits to require that the tenant remedy a breach of covenant which is 'capable of remedy' in the statutory sense (see eg *Glass v Kencakes Ltd* [1966] 1 QB 611 at 622; *Expert Clothing Service & Sales Ltd v Hillgate House Ltd* [1986] Ch 340 at 362A, 365B).

9 *In re Riggs, ex parte Lovell* [1901] 2 KB 16 at 20.

10 See eg *Pioneer Quarries (Sydney) Pty Ltd v Permanent Trustee Co of NSW Ltd* (1970) 2 BPR 9562 at 9577 (in respect of the equivalent New South Wales provision). A possession judgment wrongfully obtained without prior service of a section 146 notice may be set aside (see *Jacques v Harrison* (1884) 12 QBD 165 at 167ff; *Billson v Residential Apartments Ltd* [1992] 1 AC 494 at 542G per Lord Oliver of Aylmerton). Failure to comply with section 146 does not, of course, preclude the exercise of other remedies (eg an action for damages).

11 If there is more than one tenant, the notice must be served on all (*Blewett v Blewett* [1936] 2 All ER 188 at 190).

12 Law of Property Act 1925, s 146(5)(b). As to the meaning of service, see Law of Property Act 1925, s 196. See also *Van Haarlam v Kasner* (1992) 64 P & CR 214 at 220ff.

13 *Fuller v Judy Properties Ltd* (1991) 64 P & CR 176 at 185 per Stocker LJ. (The sending of a copy of this notice to the assignee is not sufficient service upon the latter.)

14 See eg *Fuller v Judy Properties Ltd* (1991) 64 P & CR 176 at 185, where Stocker LJ confessed to 'considerable doubts whether a landlord in possession can ever serve a valid section 146 notice, since the latter by its terms must presuppose that the tenants are in possession.'

15 (1991) 64 P & CR 176. See [1992] Conv 343 (J.E. Martin).

16 Dillon LJ held that the second notice was valid ((1991) 64 P & CR 176 at 183). It was in any event clear to all concerned that the tenant's breach (in assigning without consent) was irremediable.

17 [1986] Ch 340 at 358A.

tenant has failed to comply with the requirements of remedy and compensation contained in the notice.[18]

The precise way in which this inducement operates is itself dependent on whether the breach in question is 'capable of remedy' within the meaning of section 146(1). Where a breach is 'capable of remedy', the real object of the section 146 notice procedure is to afford the tenant two opportunities before the landlord proceeds to enforce his right of re-entry.[19] *First*, the notice gives the tenant the opportunity to remedy his breach 'within a reasonable time' after the service of the notice.[20] *Second*, the notice procedure further allows the tenant to apply to the court under section 146 for relief against forfeiture. Where, however, the tenant's breach is not 'capable of remedy', there is clearly no point in providing him with the first of these opportunities,[1] and the object of the notice procedure is simply to enable the tenant to throw himself upon the court's jurisdiction to grant relief.[2] The mere fact that a breach is irremediable does not destroy the need to comply with the section 146 notice procedure.[3]

(iii) Remediable breaches of covenant In the case of a remediable breach of covenant, the section 146 notice must give the tenant a reasonable period of time within which to comply with its terms.[4] The reasonableness of the time allowed is intricately linked with the remediability of the breach,[5] but it is generally thought that a period of three months is sufficient.[6] If remedial action is taken and reasonable compensation is paid by the tenant within that time, the landlord is then unable to show that the statutory condition precedent to his ability to enforce the forfeiture has been fulfilled.[7] If, however, compliance with the notice is not forthcoming within that time, the landlord may proceed to enforce the forfeiture either in person or by action,[8] subject only to the tenant's rights to obtain relief against forfeiture.[9]

18 *Billson v Residential Apartments Ltd* [1992] 1 AC 494 at 535E per Lord Templeman.
19 *Expert Clothing Service & Sales Ltd v Hillgate House Ltd* [1986] Ch 340 at 351B.
20 Law of Property Act 1925, s 146(1).
1 *Expert Clothing Service & Sales Ltd v Hillgate House Ltd* [1986] Ch 340 at 351C.
2 The court always has jurisdiction to grant relief, but it has been described as 'a bold course' to grant relief against forfeiture in the case of a breach which is 'incapable of remedy' (*Dunraven Securities Ltd v Holloway* (1982) 264 Estates Gazette 709 at 711).
3 See eg *Fuller v Judy Properties Ltd* (1991) 64 P & CR 176 (ante, p 818).
4 A 'reasonable time' depends ultimately on the facts of the individual case (see *Hick v Raymond & Reid* [1893] AC 22 at 29).
5 See, for example, the conceptual connection made in *Expert Clothing Service & Sales Ltd v Hillgate House Ltd* [1986] Ch 340 at 357B–C.
6 In *Billson v Residential Apartments Ltd* [1992] 1 AC 494 at 508A–E, Browne-Wilkinson V-C considered that an interval of only 14 days between the service of the notice and actual re-entry was a 'reasonable time'. Here the tenants' actions in proceeding with a breach of covenant in total defiance of prior warnings had demonstrated that they 'had no intention to remedy the breach at all.' For the purpose of section 146 a 'reasonable time' has already elapsed if the defaulting tenant, by persisting in breach, makes it 'clear that he is not proposing to remedy the breaches within a reasonable time, or indeed any time'.
7 *Scala House and District Property Co Ltd v Forbes* [1974] QB 575 at 585B. See also *Pioneer Quarries (Sydney) Pty Ltd v Permanent Trustee Co of NSW Ltd* (1970) 2 BPR 9562 at 9576.
8 *Expert Clothing Service & Sales Ltd v Hillgate House Ltd* [1986] Ch 340 at 362D–E. This seems to have been the basis on which the landlord re-entered in *Billson v Residential Apartments Ltd* [1992] 1 AC 494 (ante, p 811).
9 Post, p 825.

(iv) Irremediable breaches of covenant Some breaches of covenant by a tenant are irremediable,[10] and in such cases the section 146 notice need not require that the tenant make any remedy of the breach.[11] It is sufficient merely that the landlord serves a section 146 notice which specifies that the breach has occurred and demands that money compensation be paid by the tenant.[12] After a reasonable interval[13] the landlord is then free to enforce the forfeiture, subject only to the tenant's possible rights to claim relief against the forfeiture.[14]

(v) Concept of capability of remedy In view of the 'limited guidance' to be derived from the authorities,[15] it is not necessarily easy to determine whether a particular breach of covenant is of such a character as to be incapable of remedy. There is, of course, a sense in which no breach of covenant can ever truly be remedied. The breach, once committed, cannot be undone or expunged from the record,[16] and the case law of the past has certainly applied this blunt construction at least to the breach of negative covenants relating to user of the demised premises.[17] However, since section 146(1) clearly contemplates that some breaches are 'capable of remedy', this extreme approach cannot be conclusive or definitive.[18]

It is nowadays widely accepted that the concept of 'capability of remedy' turns on 'whether the harm that has been done to the landlord by the relevant breach is for practicable purposes capable of being retrieved.'[19] Thus, by a subtle semantic shift, the test of the remediability of a *breach* has become a test of the remediability of the *damage* caused by that breach. As Slade LJ indicated in *Expert Clothing Service & Sales Ltd v Hillgate House Ltd*,[20] the 'ultimate question' is whether the 'harm' suffered by the landlord would be 'effectively remedied' if the tenant were to comply within a reasonable time with a section 146 notice demanding both remedy and compensation. Only if the answer to this question is in the negative may a section 146 notice validly omit any requirement of remedy, thereby opening the way for the landlord to enforce the forfeiture.

Accordingly the sharp point of the 'remediability issue' has moved away from judicial assessments of the intrinsic quality of the tenant's acts or defaults towards a consideration of the consequential effect of the tenant's breach

10 This is expressly envisaged in the terms of Law of Property Act 1925, s 146(1). See *Expert Clothing Service & Sales Ltd v Hillgate House Ltd* [1986] Ch 340 at 362E.

11 Such a requirement would be 'pointless' where remedy within a reasonable time is impossible (*Expert Clothing Service & Sales Ltd v Hillgate House Ltd* [1986] Ch 340 at 357A). See also *Rugby School (Governors) v Tannahill* [1935] 1 KB 87 at 91, 94; *Dunraven Securities Ltd v Holloway* (1982) 264 Estates Gazette 709.

12 It may nevertheless be prudent for the landlord to proceed cautiously by demanding that the tenant's breach be remedied if, in the statutory terminology, it is 'capable of remedy'.

13 Two days are not enough for this purpose (see *Horsey Estate Ltd v Steiger* [1899] 2 QB 79 at 91f), but fourteen days are sufficient (*Civil Service Co-operative Society Ltd v McGrigor's Trustee* [1923] 2 Ch 347 at 356; *Scala House and District Property Co Ltd v Forbes* [1974] QB 575 at 589B–D).

14 Post, p 825.

15 *Expert Clothing Service & Sales Ltd v Hillgate House Ltd* [1986] Ch 340 at 351C.

16 *Expert Clothing Service & Sales Ltd v Hillgate House Ltd* [1986] Ch 340 at 362E–F.

17 See eg *Rugby School (Governors) v Tannahill* [1934] 1 KB 695 at 701f.

18 *Hoffman v Fineberg* [1949] Ch 245 at 253.

19 *Expert Clothing Service & Sales Ltd v Hillgate House Ltd* [1986] Ch 340 at 355B–C.

20 [1986] Ch 340 at 358C–D.

as measured in terms of irretrievable long-range damage to the landlord's interests.[1] A breach is 'capable of remedy' within the meaning of the statute if, but only if, the landlord can be restored within a reasonable time to the position he would have been in if no breach had occurred.[2] In this sense, therefore, 'a breach which has been remedied has been demonstrated to have been a breach which was ab initio capable of being remedied.'[3] If, however, the effects of the tenant's default cannot be cured either within a reasonable time or at all, then his breach is not 'capable of remedy' in the relevant statutory sense.[4]

(vi) Remediability of positive covenants This pragmatic approach enables some approximate predictions to be made as to the status of certain kinds of breach under section 146(1). A breach of a positive covenant (whether it be a continuing breach or a 'once and for all' breach) will normally be capable of remedy,[5] since such a breach can usually be cured by belated performance of the covenanted action.[6] Thus in *Expert Clothing Service & Sales Ltd v Hillgate House Ltd*[7] the Court of Appeal held that the tenant's breach of a covenant to reconstruct premises within a specified time was 'capable of remedy' by performance out of time, since the landlord would not suffer irretrievable prejudice if the tenant tendered late performance of his covenant and made adequate money compensation for his breach.[8] An effective remedy can be provided for a 'once and for all' breach of covenant if that which ought to have been done can be done within a reasonable time during the subsistence of the term.[9]

It may not ultimately be possible to maintain that the breach of a positive covenant is always 'capable of remedy',[10] but it is certainly difficult to think of examples of such breaches which are not.[11]

1 The 'remediability issue', thus stated, must be examined at the date of issue of the section 146 notice (*Expert Clothing Service & Sales Ltd v Hillgate House Ltd* [1986] Ch 340 at 362E).
2 *Expert Clothing Service & Sales Ltd v Hillgate House Ltd* [1986] Ch 340 at 362 E–F.
3 *Expert Clothing Service & Sales Ltd v Hillgate House Ltd* [1986] Ch 340 at 364E–F.
4 *Expert Clothing Service & Sales Ltd v Hillgate House Ltd* [1986] Ch 340 at 362F.
5 *Expert Clothing Service & Sales Ltd v Hillgate House Ltd* [1986] Ch 340 at 355B.
6 *Rugby School (Governors) v Tannahill* [1934] 1 KB 695 at 701; *Expert Clothing Service & Sales Ltd v Hillgate House Ltd* [1986] Ch 340 at 355C. See also *Bass Holdings Ltd v Morton Music Ltd* [1988] Ch 493 at 507B per Scott J.
7 [1986] Ch 340.
8 The most substantial damage imposed on the landlord by the tenant's breach flowed from the fact that the reconstructed premises would have commanded a higher rental value. However, as the Court of Appeal indicated (at 356A), this kind of loss was amply compensable in money. The Court further pointed out (at 358A–B) that the landlord would have been entitled to include in the section 146 notice a 'tight timetable' for the fulfilment of the tenant's obligation to reconstruct.
9 *Expert Clothing Service & Sales Ltd v Hillgate House Ltd* [1986] Ch 340 at 362H–363A.
10 See *Expert Clothing Service & Sales Ltd v Hillgate House Ltd* [1986] Ch 340 at 354H–355A, 358F, where Slade LJ hypothesised that irremediability might attach, for instance, to the breach of a covenant to insure the demised property if the premises had already been burnt down without insurance cover having been obtained.
11 *Expert Clothing Service & Sales Ltd v Hillgate House Ltd* [1986] Ch 340 at 362H–363A. There seems to be no decided English case in which the breach of a positive covenant has been held incapable of remedy (see *Expert Clothing Service & Sales Ltd v Hillgate House Ltd*, supra at 358F).

(vii) Remediability of negative covenants The 'remediability issue' in relation to negative covenants may produce different results. It used to be thought that no breach of any negative covenant could ever be remedied by the tenant, even if the prohibited user ceased before the service of the section 146 notice.[12] Certainly the Court of Appeal seemed to indicate, in its decision in *Scala House and District Property Co Ltd v Forbes*,[13] that there could never be any remedy in respect of a 'once and for all' breach of a negative covenant. On this basis remedy would be impossible in respect of the breach of a covenant prohibiting the assignment or subletting of the demised premises[14] or prohibiting the unconsented alteration of the premises. As Lady Macbeth said, 'what's done is done'.[15] Irremediable breach, once proved, would lead almost inexorably to re-entry by the landlord and, almost as inevitably, to the eventual exercise of discretion against any award of relief from forfeiture.[16]

By contrast, however, it now seems to have become widely accepted that remedy is possible in relation to negative covenants where the breach does not have a 'once and for all' character, but is instead of a *continuing* nature.[17] In such cases the vital determinant is whether the harm caused to the landlord by the tenant's breach can be retrieved by the cesser of the prohibited activity. In some instances, of course, it is clear that the mere cesser by the tenant of the offending user cannot constitute an adequate remedy precisely because even a complete cesser does not remove the 'stigma' which the tenant's wrongful activities have caused to attach to the premises.[18] Thus the use of the demised premises in breach of covenant as a brothel cannot be remedied by mere cesser of the immoral user (even if accompanied by the payment of compensation).[19] As O'Connor LJ observed in *Expert Clothing Service & Sales Ltd v Hillgate House Ltd*,[20] 'the taint lingers on and will not dissipate within a reasonable time.' Likewise the involvement of the tenant in any serious criminal activity in relation to the demised premises may constitute

12 See *Rugby School (Governors) v Tannahill* [1934] 1 KB 695 at 701; *Scala House and District Property Co Ltd v Forbes* [1974] QB 575 at 588A–B. Compare, however, *Rugby School (Governors) v Tannahill* [1935] 1 KB 87 at 90.

13 *Scala House and District Property Co Ltd v Forbes* [1974] QB 575 at 588D. See (1973) 89 LQR 460; [1974] CLJ 54 (D.J. Hayton).

14 See also *Expert Clothing Service & Sales Ltd v Hillgate House Ltd* [1986] Ch 340 at 354G, 363A; *Fuller v Judy Properties Ltd* (1991) 64 P & CR 176 at 182.

15 See *Bass Holdings Ltd v Morton Music Ltd* [1988] Ch 493 at 541C per Bingham LJ.

16 Post, p 831.

17 It is well established that a breach of a covenant as to user of premises constitutes a continuing breach (see *Cooper v Henderson* (1982) 263 Estates Gazette 592 at 593).

18 *Expert Clothing Service & Sales Ltd v Hillgate House Ltd* [1986] Ch 340 at 357D–E.

19 *Rugby School (Governors) v Tannahill* [1935] 1 KB 87 at 90f, 93f; *Egerton v Esplanade Hotels, London, Ltd* [1947] 2 All ER 88 at 92A. However, it is possible that such a breach is remediable by a tenant who takes immediate action directed at forfeiture in order to terminate an immoral or illegal user by his subtenant of which he was previously unaware (see eg *Glass v Kencakes Ltd* [1966] 1 QB 611 at 629; *Re Vanek and Bomza* (1977) 74 DLR (3d) 175 at 180; but compare the doubts expressed on this point in *Scala House and District Property Co Ltd v Forbes* [1974] QB 575 at 587B–C). See also *British Petroleum Pension Trust Ltd v Behrendt* (1985) 276 Estates Gazette 199 at 202, where Purchas LJ declined to regard a breach of a covenant against immoral user as remediable, particularly since the tenant had effectively shut his eyes to the conduct of his subtenant.

20 [1986] Ch 340 at 362G.

a breach incapable of remedy.[1] In *Dunraven Securities Ltd v Holloway*[2] the Court of Appeal regarded as irremediable the conduct of a tenant who had taken a lease of shop premises in Soho supposedly for the sale of old and modern prints, books and objets d'art, but who had instead used the premises as a sex shop.[3] Likewise in *Van Haarlam v Kasner*[4] a tenant's conviction for offences committed under the Official Secrets Acts was held to be an irremediable breach of a leasehold covenant against user of the premises for illegal purposes.[5]

Equally clearly there are some continuing breaches of a negative covenant where cesser of the prohibited user accompanied by reasonable compensation can constitute a sufficient remedy.[6] If such cesser provides an adequate remedy, then if the cesser occurs before the service of the section 146 notice, that notice need not demand that remedy be made. The only issue outstanding at this stage will be the payment of compensation for the tenant's breach,[7] and the tenant can avert forfeiture simply by paying the required compensation. If cesser has not yet occurred, the section 146 notice must not only demand compensation but also require that cesser occur within such time as is reasonable.

The issue of remediability seems to depend peculiarly on the facts of the particular case, and it may even be that the courts are more prepared nowadays to contemplate that 'once and for all' breaches of negative covenants are 'capable of remedy'. In *Bass Holdings Ltd v Morton Music Ltd*[8] Bingham LJ hinted that it may be 'highly and undesirably formalistic' to attach irrevocable significance to the breach of a covenant against unconsented subletting, where the unlawful subletting has been brought to an end, suitable undertakings proffered and appropriate compensation paid, and where 'the landlord could show no continuing damage.' This more liberal approach found an echo in the Court of Appeal in *Billson v Residential Apartments Ltd*,[9] where Browne-Wilkinson V-C expressed his doubt whether breach of a covenant against unconsented alteration of the demised premises could, in every instance, be said to be 'irremediable'.[10]

1 See *Hoffman v Fineberg* [1949] Ch 245 at 257 (illicit gaming club); *Ali v Booth* (1966) 110 SJ 708 at 709 (conviction of restaurateur under food hygiene regulations); *Kelly v Purvis* (1983) 80 LSG 410 (illegal use of licensed massage parlour as brothel).

2 (1982) 264 Estates Gazette 709 at 711. See (1983) 133 NLJ 485 (H.W. Wilkinson); (1983) 127 SJ 232 (D.W. Williams).

3 Although the tenant had not been prosecuted under the Obscene Publications Act 1959, magistrates had made a forfeiture order in respect of books, magazines and films found on the premises. See also *British Petroleum Pension Trust Ltd v Behrendt* (1985) 52 P & CR 117 at 124 per Purchas LJ.

4 (1992) 64 P & CR 214 at 223.

5 There was evidence that much of the tenant's illegal activity as a spy was conducted from within his flat.

6 Examples would appear to be provided by the breach of such covenants as not to place window boxes in the windows of a residential flat (see *Expert Clothing Service & Sales Ltd v Hillgate House Ltd* [1986] Ch 340 at 362G) or not to use the demised premises for residential purposes (see *Cooper v Henderson* (1982) 263 Estates Gazette 592 at 594).

7 *Expert Clothing Service & Sales Ltd v Hillgate House Ltd* [1986] Ch 340 at 362H.

8 [1988] Ch 493 at 541F–H.

9 [1992] 1 AC 494 at 508A.

10 Further indications of a changing approach may be found in *Hagee (London) Ltd v Cooperative Insurance Society Ltd* (1991) 63 P & CR 362 at 371f; *W.G. Clark (Properties) Ltd v Dupre Properties Ltd* [1992] Ch 297 at 309E–F (where the court appeared to accept the remediable quality of a breach of the tenant's implied duty not to prejudice his landlord's interests by disclaimer or repudiation).

(viii) Forfeiture for breach of the tenant's repairing covenant Forfeiture for breach of a tenant's covenant to repair merits special attention since further limits on the enforceability of such a covenant are contained in the Leasehold Property (Repairs) Act 1938. This Act was introduced in order to counteract a prevalent mischief which enabled an unscrupulous landlord to purchase the reversion on a long lease and then harass the tenant with exaggerated lists of dilapidations, not for the purpose of protecting the landlord's reversion but rather in order to coerce an early surrender of the term.[11]

The Leasehold Property (Repairs) Act 1938 provides some degree of protection for the tenant by imposing special restrictions on the availability of certain kinds of remedy for breaches of a tenant's covenant to repair.[12] The Act applies only to leases for a term of seven years or more,[13] of which at the relevant time at least three years remain unexpired.[14] The Act requires in effect that the landlord obtain the sanction of the court before pursuing remedies of forfeiture or damages. The Act does not, however, restrict the availability to the landlord of any remedy either by way of mandatory injunction[15] or by way of action for a debt due under the lease.[16]

Where the landlord seeks either forfeiture of the lease or damages on the basis of a tenant's breach of his covenant or agreement to keep or put the demised premises in repair,[17] the landlord must first serve on the tenant a notice as specified in section 146 of the Law of Property Act 1925.[18] The tenant then has a statutory right within 28 days of the service of this notice to serve on the landlord a counter-notice claiming the benefit of the 1938 Act.[19] Where a counter-notice is duly served, no proceedings (by action or otherwise) may be taken by the landlord for the purpose of re-entry or recovery

11 See *Associated British Ports v C.H. Bailey Plc* [1990] 2 AC 703 at 714E–F per Lord Templeman; [1990] Conv 305 (P.F. Smith); [1990] CLJ 401 (S. Bridge). On the intendment of the legislation, see *Sidnell v Wilson* [1966] 2 QB 67 at 76; *Hamilton v Martell Securities Ltd* [1984] Ch 266 at 278E–F. See generally P.F. Smith, [1986] Conv 85.

12 For even more specific restrictions on the landlord's remedies for the tenant's default in respect of internal decorative repairs, see Law of Property Act 1925, s 147.

13 Leasehold Property (Repairs) Act 1938, s 7(1). A lease of an agricultural holding is excluded.

14 Leasehold Property (Repairs) Act 1938, s 1(1).

15 There is venerable authority against the granting of a mandatory injunction for the specific enforcement of a tenant's repairing obligation (post, p 845), but compare *S.E.D.A.C. Investments Ltd v Tanner* [1982] 1 WLR 1342 at 1349F, where it was suggested that such a remedy is open to the landlord (see [1983] Conv 71).

16 The 1938 Act certainly does not preclude the landlord from suing for a debt due under the lease such as legal costs and surveyor's fees incurred in the preparation of a section 146 notice (*Middlegate Properties Ltd v Gidlow-Jackson* (1977) 34 P & CR 4 at 9).

17 The 1938 Act has no application to such covenants as to take out and maintain insurance on the demised premises (*Farimani v Gates* (1984) 271 Estates Gazette 887 at 888f) or to clean toilets on the demised premises (*Starrokate Ltd v Burry* (1983) 265 Estates Gazette 871 at 872).

18 Leasehold Property (Repairs) Act 1938, s 1(1), (2). The landlord's notice directed towards forfeiture is invalid unless it indicates 'in characters not less conspicuous than those in any other part of the notice' the tenant's right to serve a counter-notice (Leasehold Property (Repairs) Act 1938, s 1(4)). A section 146 notice relating to the recovery of damages for breach of covenant must be served at least one month before the commencement of the action (Leasehold Property (Repairs) Act 1938, s 1(2)).

19 Leasehold Property (Repairs) Act 1938, s 1(1), (2).

of damages unless the court gives its leave.[20] The court's leave is available only on the grounds specified in the Act,[1] of which the most important is that the present actuality or imminent likelihood of substantial diminution of the value of the landlord's reversion makes immediate remedy of the breach imperative.[2] The court may also grant leave where 'special circumstances. . .render it just and equitable that leave should be given'.[3]

There may be one potentially serious trap for the landlord under the terms of the 1938 Act. It seems that the entire scheme of the Act contemplates that the landlord's service of a section 146 notice should precede any actual remedy of the tenant's breach of his repairing covenant.[4] Accordingly it was held in *S.E.D.A.C. Investments Ltd v Tanner*[5] that the court had no jurisdiction to grant a landlord leave to pursue a claim in damages against the tenant if, in the interests of procuring an immediate remedy,[6] the landlord had already effected the necessary repairs before purporting to serve a section 146 notice on the tenant.[7] If this decision is correct, the landlord may be unable to recover his expenditure on urgently conducted repairs.[8]

(h) Relief against forfeiture for breaches other than non-payment of rent

Irrespective of whether the covenant breached by the tenant is or is not 'capable of remedy' within section 146 of the Law of Property Act 1925, there is always a possibility that the court may grant the tenant relief against forfeiture.[9] This jurisdiction is now confirmed in section 146(2) of the Law

20 Leasehold Property (Repairs) Act 1938, s 1(3). A landlord's application for the court's leave under section 1(3) is a pending land action within Land Charges Act 1972, s 17(1) and is therefore protectible by the entry of a caution in registered land (*Selim Ltd v Bickenhall Engineering Ltd* [1981] 1 WLR 1318 at 1323H–1324A).

1 However, in order to obtain leave the landlord need only make out a prima facie case or a bona fide arguable case that at least one of the grounds is satisfied. The standards of proof are 'lowly' (*Land Securities Plc v Receiver for the Metropolitan Police District* [1983] 1 WLR 439 at 444D–E, 445A; [1983] Conv 323 (P.F. Smith)).

2 Leasehold Property (Repairs) Act 1938, s 1(5)(a).

3 Leasehold Property (Repairs) Act 1938, s 1(5)(e).

4 See *S.E.D.A.C. Investments Ltd v Tanner* [1982] 1 WLR 1342 at 1347G–H.

5 [1982] 1 WLR 1342 at 1348G–H. See [1983] Conv 72 (P.F. Smith).

6 There was evidence that the landlord feared that the premises, unless repaired as a matter of urgency, might present a danger of injury to passing pedestrians. He therefore intervened swiftly in order to protect himself from liability ([1982] 1 WLR 1342 at 1344A).

7 In effect the section 146 notice was invalid because it required a remedy for a breach which had already been remedied by the landlord's anxious and precipitate action ([1982] 1 WLR 1342 at 1348F–G).

8 The courts have since sought to curtail the highly inconvenient result produced by the *S.E.D.A.C. Investments* decision. See eg *Hamilton v Martell Securities Ltd* [1984] Ch 266 at 281B–C, where a similar claim by a landlord to recover the cost of urgently conducted repairs was held to be a claim in debt for a liquidated sum rather than a claim for unliquidated damages. On this view the landlord's claim required no judicial sanction under the 1938 Act, a decision since supported in *Colchester Estates (Cardiff) v Carlton Industries Plc* (1984) 271 Estates Gazette 778 at 779. See (1984) 100 LQR 338; [1984] Conv 231 (J.E.M.); (1984) 270 Estates Gazette 908 (S. Bickford-Smith). See also *Elite Investments Ltd v T.I. Bainbridge Silencers Ltd* [1986] 2 EGLR 43 at 49H; [1986] Conv 140 (P.F. Smith).

9 As Lord Erskine LC remarked in *Davis v West* (1806) 12 Ves 475 at 476, 33 ER 180, where 'there is no fraud, and the party is capable of giving complete compensation, it is the province of a Court of Equity to interfere, and give relief against the forfeiture for breach of other covenants, as well as that for payment of rent.'

of Property Act,[10] which provides that where a landlord 'is proceeding, by action or otherwise, to enforce [a] right of re-entry or forfeiture', the tenant may apply for relief against forfeiture, and the court has a discretion to grant or withhold relief as it thinks fit. If the court decides to grant relief, it may do so on such terms as to costs, expenses, damages, compensation or injunctions to restrain future breach or otherwise[11] as it thinks appropriate in the circumstances.[12]

(i) Availability of relief Until relatively recently there has been some uncertainty as to the availability of the curial jurisdiction to grant relief against forfeiture pursuant to section 146(2). Everything turns here on the definition of the period during which, for the purpose of section 146(2), it can be said that the landlord 'is proceeding, by action or otherwise, to enforce' his right of re-entry or forfeiture. In *Billson v Residential Apartments Ltd*[13] the House of Lords did much to clarify the law in this area. A number of circumstances must be firmly distinguished.[14]

First, it is established law that the tenant has access to the section 146(2) jurisdiction in matters of relief as soon as his landlord has served a section 146 notice on him.[15] At this point the landlord is obviously still 'proceeding...to enforce' his right of re-entry or forfeiture,[16] and the tenant may invoke the court's jurisdiction under section 146(2) for the purpose of elucidating issues raised by the notice or of 'setting in train the machinery by which the dispute...can be determined by negotiation or by the court.' The tenant's right to apply for relief is not postponed until forfeiture proceedings are actually instituted by the landlord,[17] but neither is the tenant

10 It remains an open question whether the intervention of statute has replaced and therefore extinguished the inherent equitable jurisdiction to grant relief. For the view that the equitable jurisdiction is now excluded by comprehensive statutory coverage, see *Billson v Residential Apartments Ltd* [1992] 1 AC 494 at 516D–E per Browne-Wilkinson V-C, 522G per Parker LJ. (The House of Lords did not advert to the issue.) An extremely strong contrary view was expressed in *Billson* by Nicholls LJ ([1992] 1 AC 494 at 528H–529A) and emerges also in the Full Court of the Supreme Court of Western Australia in *Esther Investments Pty Ltd v Cherrywood Park Pty Ltd* [1986] WAR 279 at 288 per Burt CJ, 297 per Wallace J, 306 per Brinsden J. See also *W.G. Clark (Properties) Ltd v Dupre Properties Ltd* [1992] Ch 297 at 309C, G.

11 See eg *McIvor v Donald* [1984] 2 NZLR 487 at 493, where in relation to a similar statutory provision the New Zealand Court of Appeal held that relief could be granted on terms that the tenant submit to a programme designed to have him remedy his defaults. Where the breach complained of is a continuing breach, relief can properly be granted only on condition that the breach shall cease (see *Wrotham Park Settled Estates v Naylor* (1991) 62 P & CR 233 at 241 per Hoffmann J).

12 Law of Property Act 1925, s 146(2). See, in relation to virtually identical provisions, *Platt v Ong* [1972] VR 197 at 201f; *Dickeson v Lipschitz* [1972] 106 ILTR 1 at 3. Relief from forfeiture may, for instance, be granted in respect of part only of the demised premises when to do so would produce a 'fair and workable result' (*G.M.S. Syndicate Ltd v Gary Elliott Ltd* [1982] Ch 1 at 12F per Nourse J).

13 [1992] 1 AC 494 (ante, p 811).

14 Each of these circumstances is premised on the assumption that a valid section 146 notice has already been served on the tenant.

15 *Billson v Residential Apartments Ltd* [1992] 1 AC 494 at 538E–F, 540D per Lord Templeman.

16 *Billson v Residential Apartments Ltd* [1992] 1 AC 494 at 538H–539B per Lord Templeman.

17 *Pakwood Transport Ltd v 15 Beauchamp Place* (1978) 36 P & CR 112 at 117.

prejudiced by the fact that he does not apply for relief at this stage.[18] In particular, the tenant's access to relief is not lost merely because he fails to invoke section 146(2) immediately after service of the landlord's notice and the landlord meanwhile takes advantage of his right to make peaceable re-entry.[19]

Second, the tenant still enjoys access to relief pursuant to section 146(2) where the landlord follows up a section 146 notice by serving a writ for possession upon the tenant and recovering a court judgment for possession against him, *provided that* the landlord has not yet executed this judgment by physical re-entry.[20]

Third, where the landlord has forfeited the lease by issuing and serving a writ for possession and has both recovered judgment *and entered into possession* pursuant to this judgment, the availability of section 146(2) has finally expired.[1] The tenant's access to section 146(2) is now definitively excluded by the fact that the landlord has obtained possession 'under a final and unassailable judgment'.[2] No longer is the landlord 'proceeding, by action or otherwise, to enforce his right of re-entry or forfeiture'. His possession 'rests now, not upon the exercise of a right under the lease, but upon a judgment of the court'.[3] Moreover, and by way of sharp contrast with the rules concerning forfeiture for non-payment of rent, the court has no jurisdiction here to grant relief during some limited period of six months immediately following the landlord's actual re-entry.[4]

Fourth, there remains the circumstance (which comprised the factual basis of *Billson*'s case itself) where the landlord elects to forfeit the lease, not by issuing court proceedings and obtaining a court order for possession but instead by exercising the landlord's simple right of peaceable re-entry upon the demised premises. There is perhaps at this point a certain semantic difficulty in the idea that, having actually succeeded in re-entering, the landlord is in any real sense still 'proceeding. . .to enforce his right of re-entry' within the meaning of section 146(2). If by this stage, as Parker LJ

18 *Billson v Residential Apartments Ltd* [1992] 1 AC 494 at 540D per Lord Templeman.

19 *Billson v Residential Apartments Ltd* [1992] 1 AC 494 at 541B per Lord Templeman. As Lord Templeman confirmed (at 538F-G), it would be absurd to maintain that when the landlord has done no more than serve a section 146 notice it is too early for the tenant to apply for relief, but that when the landlord's next step is peaceably to recover possession it is then too late for the tenant to make such an application (see also *Pakwood Transport Ltd v 15 Beauchamp Place* (1978) 36 P & CR 112 at 117 per Orr LJ).

20 *Quilter v Mapleson* (1882) 9 QBD 672 at 675ff, as construed by Lord Templeman in *Billson v Residential Apartments Ltd* [1992] 1 AC 494 at 537B-F. See also *West v Rogers* (1888) 4 TLR 229; *Egerton v Jones* [1939] 2 KB 702 at 707ff.

1 *Billson v Residential Apartments Ltd* [1992] 1 AC 494 at 538A-B, 540D-E per Lord Templeman. See also *Rogers v Rice* [1892] 2 Ch 170 at 172 per Lord Coleridge CJ. (There remains of course the possibility that the possession judgment may be successfully appealed or set aside on other grounds.)

2 *Billson v Residential Apartments Ltd* [1992] 1 AC 494 at 542G per Lord Oliver of Aylmerton.

3 *Billson v Residential Apartments Ltd* [1992] 1 AC 494 at 543F per Lord Oliver of Aylmerton ('. . .any attempt by the tenant to raise the lease against him is met by the simple plea of the judgment').

4 *Rogers v Rice* [1892] 2 Ch 170 at 172; *Abbey National Building Society v Maybeech Ltd* [1985] Ch 190 at 198E-G.

argued in the Court of Appeal in *Billson*,[5] the right of entry has *already been enforced*, it would seem to follow that the tenant is thereafter excluded from any further right to relief from forfeiture pursuant to the Law of Property Act 1925.[6]

Although some of the previous case law had long been assumed to indicate the contrary, the House of Lords ruled in *Billson*'s case that relief against forfeiture remains available to the tenant *even after* the landlord's exercise of peaceable re-entry without court order.[7] The semantic difficulty in coming to this conclusion was averted by reading the present continuous form of the relevant words in section 146(2) as equivalent to the phrase 'where a lessor *proceeds*, by action or otherwise, to enforce a right of re-entry or forfeiture'.[8] In Lord Templeman's view, Parliament intended that a tenant should have access to relief under section 146(2) 'whether the landlord has asserted his rights by a writ or by re-entering'.[9] Section 146(2) thus offers the possibility of relief irrespective of the mode of forfeiture elected by the landlord, ie whether by the issue and service of a writ for curial recovery or by the self-help procedure of peaceable physical re-entry.[10] Access to statutory relief is finally cut off only if and when the landlord regains possession in virtue of a 'final, unappealed and fully executed judgment'.[11] In the absence of an executed judgment, the landlord remains vulnerable to an application for relief,[12] although delay by the tenant in seeking relief will increasingly become relevant to the discretionary decision whether to grant relief and must at some point debar the tenant from relief altogether.[13]

The ruling in *Billson*'s case has certainly clarified the law relating to

5 [1992] 1 AC 494 at 519H–520A. See also Browne-Wilkinson V-C at 509B–E (less willingly).

6 This is, of course, why the Court of Appeal was so deeply concerned with the question whether there remains outside the Act a more general inherent jurisdiction to relieve in equity (ante, p 826).

7 [1992] 1 AC 494 at 540E–F per Lord Templeman, 543C–E Lord Oliver of Aylmerton. This conclusion had already been reached in respect of similar statutory provisions in force in other jurisdictions (see eg *In re Rexdale Investments Ltd and Gibson* [1967] 1 OR 251 at 259 per Laskin J; *F.G. Sweeney Ltd v Powerscourt Shopping Centre Ltd* [1984] IR 501 at 504 per Carroll J).

8 [1992] 1 AC 494 at 536C–D, 537A per Lord Templeman. Lord Oliver of Aylmerton thought (at 543B–D) that a landlord on peaceable re-entry can resist a tenant's allegation of trespass only 'by pointing to the forfeiture clause [in the lease] and pleading his entry under it'. So long as he remains, in this way, dependent on the leasehold provision for re-entry, the landlord is still 'proceeding. . .to enforce' it. This description does not cease to be apt 'once he has lawfully set foot on the premises'. It seems that Browne-Wilkinson V-C would have shared this view in the Court of Appeal if he had not been constrained by contrary precedent ([1992] 1 AC 494 at 509B–D).

9 [1992] 1 AC 494 at 536B.

10 'So construed, section 146(2) enables the tenant to apply for relief whenever and however the landlord claims that the lease has been determined for breach of covenant' ([1992] 1 AC 494 at 537A per Lord Templeman).

11 The House of Lords overruled any previous case law authority that peaceable re-entry was in this respect 'to be equiparated with an executed judgment' (see eg *Pakwood Transport Ltd v 15 Beauchamp Place* (1978) 36 P & CR 112).

12 [1992] 1 AC 494 at 543E per Lord Oliver of Aylmerton. Contrary authority was distinguished in the House of Lords as relating only to the effects of re-entry in pursuance of a final court judgment for possession ([1992] 1 AC 494 at 539E–H, 542B–D).

13 [1992] 1 AC 494 at 540E–F per Lord Templeman, 543D–E Lord Oliver of Aylmerton.

peaceable re-entry. As the House of Lords was fully aware, the decision also has two other effects. The mere service of a section 146 notice now clearly carries no implication that a tenant must make an immediate and possibly premature application for relief in the fear that delay might otherwise leave him 'at the mercy of an aggressive landlord' who could then, by actual re-entry, snuff out his access to relief without further warning.[14]

Furthermore, the *Billson* decision goes some distance towards ensuring that the self-help remedy of forfeiture by actual re-entry is not rendered visibly more advantageous for landlords than the alternative remedy of forfeiture by due legal process. In his dissent in the Court of Appeal, Nicholls LJ observed that to allow access to section 146(2) to be foreclosed by actual re-entry would be 'an incitement to all landlords to re-enter forcibly whenever they can do so.' The courts would in effect be 'granting a charter for forcible entry', thereby encouraging the landlord 'to keep away from court and to pounce on the property, in the evening or at the weekend, and change the locks and then sit back secure in the knowledge that forfeiture is complete'.[15] The House of Lords likewise considered it undesirable and anti-social to attach prejudicial consequence to a landlord's recovery of possession by curial process.[16] The Lords preserved the relief jurisdiction of section 146(2) even after actual re-entry by the landlord without court order, precisely in order to prevent what Lord Templeman called the 'farce' in *Billson* where it was alleged that the forcible re-entry into premises for four hours had irrevocably pre-empted all further statutory rights to relief on the part of the tenants.[17]

(ii) Guidelines for the exercise of discretion Certain guidelines have emerged in the exercise of the court's discretion to grant relief against forfeiture under section 146(2) of the Law of Property Act 1925. The court is expressly directed to have regard to 'the proceedings and conduct of the parties' and 'all the other circumstances' of the case.[18] The relevant criteria are not wholly different from those applied in the exercise of the general equitable jurisdiction to relieve from forfeiture.[19] Substantial regard is had, for instance, to the gravity of the breach and the disparity between the value of the property of which forfeiture is claimed and the extent of the damage caused by the breach. Relief will be available only if the landlord's position has not been 'irrevocably damaged' by the breach.[20] Relief is inappropriate, however, if the rights

14 Lord Templeman noted that, following the contrary decision in the Court of Appeal in *Billson*, there had been 'a proliferation of section 146 notices followed by pressure on tenants to surrender on terms favourable to the landlord'. He observed that the development in the law 'pioneered by the landlords in the present case' would help to avert such coercion ([1992] 1 AC 494 at 540C).

15 [1992] 1 AC 494 at 524D–H.

16 Ante, p 811.

17 [1992] 1 AC 494 at 536H. It is relatively clear that the House of Lords was scandalised by the 'dawn raid' executed by the landlord's agents in *Billson* (see [1992] 1 AC 494 at 540B, ante, p 811).

18 Law of Property Act 1925, s 146(2).

19 See *Shiloh Spinners Ltd v Harding* [1973] AC 691 at 723H–724A per Lord Wilberforce.

20 See *W.G. Clark (Properties) Ltd v Dupre Properties Ltd* [1992] Ch 297 at 309D–E, where Thomas Morison QC would have been prepared to grant relief.

of third parties have intervened, as is the case where the landlord has re-let the property after re-entry.[1] Mere inadvertence on the part of the tenant may not, in itself, constitute a ground for relief,[2] nor is it highly persuasive that the tenant committed the breach through thoughtlessness or because he thought the breach unimportant.[3]

Certain differences nevertheless exist between the statutory and general equitable jurisdictions in relief. In contrast to the court's general equitable jurisdiction, section 146 is apt to cover 'wilful' breaches of covenant.[4] In *Billson v Residential Apartments Ltd*,[5] for example, the tenants were in gross and deliberate breach, but Mummery J, at first instance, would have been prepared to exercise discretion to relieve against forfeiture.[6] This inclination was founded largely on the fact that the tenants had purchased the lease a year earlier for £280,000 and had already expended perhaps as much as £375,000 in the unconsented renovation of the property. There being no evidence that the value of the landlord's reversion had been diminished by this conduct, it seemed inequitable to refuse relief and to precipitate a compulsory return of such a valuable asset to the landlord.[7] It may be that, in the exercise of discretion pursuant to section 146(2), the importance of issues of proportionality has nowadays overtaken any strict concern with the degree of deliberateness or wilfulness of the relevant breach.[8]

1 See eg *Fuller v Judy Properties Ltd* (1991) 64 P & CR 176 at 184, where Dillon LJ took the view that the replacement tenant ranked as a purchaser of a legal estate without notice of the defaulting tenant's 'equity to seek relief against forfeiture'. The Court of Appeal was nevertheless prepared to grant relief to the ousted tenant, but only on the basis that the terms of relief recognised the priority of the new tenant's term. (The Court exercised discretion by placing the old tenant in the position of immediate reversioner on the new lease.)

2 *Shiloh Spinners Ltd v Harding* [1973] AC 691 at 722E per Lord Wilberforce.

3 See *Eastern Telegraph Co v Dent* [1899] 1 QB 835 at 839; *Pioneer Quarries (Sydney) Pty Ltd v Permanent Trustee Co of NSW Ltd* (1970) 2 BPR 9562 at 9577.

4 See *W.G. Clark (Properties) Ltd v Dupre Properties Ltd* [1992] Ch 297 at 309C. Compare eg *Hill v Barclay* (1810) 16 Ves 402 at 405f, 33 ER 1037 at 1038 per Lord Eldon.

5 [1992] 1 AC 494 (ante, p 811).

6 (1990) 60 P & CR 392 at 411.

7 In the Court of Appeal, however, Parker LJ was moved in a contrary direction precisely by the 'deliberate and flagrant' nature of the tenants' breach coupled with the attendant 'aggravating circumstances'. Parker LJ thought that to grant relief in the circumstances of *Billson* would have been to permit the lessee to 'buy his way out by uncovenanted payment' and to force the lessor 'to live in neighbourhood with a lessee who had no respect whatever for his contractual obligations' ([1992] 1 AC 494 at 523A–B). The effect of the House of Lords' decision in *Billson* was to remit the application for relief to the High Court ([1992] 1 AC 494 at 540G): it is not known whether the application ultimately succeeded.

8 See eg *Billson v Residential Apartments Ltd* [1992] 1 AC 494 at 535B, where Lord Templeman found the general rationale for relief from forfeiture in the consideration that 'otherwise a tenant who had paid a large premium for a 999-year lease at a low rent could lose the asset by a breach of covenant which was remediable or which caused the landlord no damage. The forfeiture of any lease, however short, may unjustly enrich the landlord at the expense of the tenant.' See also [1992] 1 AC 494 at 523F–G per Nicholls LJ. See also *Van Haarlam v Kasner* (1992) 64 P & CR 214 at 226f, where Harman J thought it disproportionate to add the double penalty of forfeiture of a flat (fairly recently purchased by the tenant for £36,000), where the tenant's illegal user of the flat for purposes of espionage had already caused him to be imprisoned for 10 years.

(iii) Irremediable breaches Relief is usually (but not always[9]) granted where the tenant's breach has been remedied.[10] Conversely, it is clear that the court will rarely grant relief where the tenant's breach is not 'capable of remedy' in terms of section 146.[11] Although the court is certainly possessed of power to grant relief even in relation to an irremediable breach,[12] the very circumstances which made the breach incapable of remedy may also provide good grounds for refusing relief against forfeiture.[13] Save in exceptional cases,[14] it is the 'established practice' of the court not to grant relief where the breach involves immoral user.[15]

(iv) Trivial breaches The tenor of the case law suggests that, whereas the wilful transgressor must commonly accept the penalty of flagrant wrongdoing,[16] the transgressor whose breach is unintentional or relatively minor may confidently expect relief against forfeiture.[17] Thus, for instance, relief may be granted where a tenant in violation of his covenant has kept a pet on the demised premises, so long as the animal has not interfered with the reasonable enjoyment of other tenants or unduly frustrated the expectations of those other tenants.[18] It would be 'absurd' if a landlord could terminate a tenancy if the tenant's breach comprises some purely trivial conduct such as the keeping of a single goldfish in a bowl or the feeding of a few crumbs of bread to one sparrow or the shaking of a duster out of the window or the placing of paper in a corridor.[19]

9 See eg *Clifford v Johnson's Personal Representatives* (1979) 251 Estates Gazette 571 at 573, where the Court of Appeal approved a holding that 'a single man. . .unemployed for two years [with] no prospect of work in his field in the area. . .does not come within any reasonable ground for relief from forfeiture.' It was also a relevant factor that the granting of relief would have meant that the landlord was saddled with a protected tenant in respect of part of the premises.

10 *Earl Bathurst v Fine* [1974] 1 WLR 905 at 908A.

11 See eg *Dunraven Securities Ltd v Holloway* (1982) 264 Estates Gazette 709 at 711 (ante, p 823).

12 *Scala House and District Property Co Ltd v Forbes* [1974] QB 575 at 589D; *McIvor v Donald* [1984] 2 NZLR 487 at 491. See eg *Fuller v Judy Properties Ltd* (1991) 64 P & CR 176 at 184ff (ante, p 818); *Van Haarlam v Kasner* (1992) 64 P & CR 214 at 226f (ante, p 823).

13 See *Ali v Booth* (1966) 110 SJ 708 at 709.

14 See eg *Central Estates (Belgravia) Ltd v Woolgar* (No 2) [1972] 1 WLR 1048 at 1053D–1054B.

15 *G.M.S. Syndicate Ltd v Gary Elliott Ltd* [1982] Ch 1 at 10D–E. The same approach may apply to instances of illegal user (see *Jam Factory Pty Ltd v Sunny Paradise Pty Ltd* [1989] VR 584 at 591).

16 See also *Shiloh Spinners Ltd v Harding* [1973] AC 691 at 725E–F per Lord Wilberforce.

17 *Re Vanek and Bomza* (1977) 74 DLR (3d) 175 at 180.

18 *Re London Housing Authority and Coulson* (1978) 82 DLR (3d) 754 at 756ff (two cats); *Re Kay and Parkway Forest Developments* (1982) 133 DLR (3d) 389 at 392f (dog).

19 *Re Miller and Zuchek* (1982) 132 DLR (3d) 142 at 149. Such actions would constitute a breach of the covenants commonly found in residential leases of even as long as 99 years in duration.

(j) Waiver of breach

The landlord's exercise of a right of re-entry for breach of the tenant's covenants is subject to the operation of the doctrine of waiver.

(i) Principle of waiver Even if a lease provides that the tenant's term of years shall be void in the event of a breach of covenant, it is clear that the lease does not ipso facto become void. The tenant is not permitted to take advantage of his own wrong[20] and the landlord has a right to elect whether to treat the lease as forfeited or as remaining in force.[1] This election need not be made immediately,[2] but once made it cannot be retracted.[3]

It is against this background that waiver of forfeiture operates. A landlord is precluded from seeking re-entry (though not in general from recovering damages or arrears[4]) if with knowledge[5] of the tenant's default he does some act which unequivocally indicates his intention to regard the lease as subsisting.[6] Both knowledge and active recognition of the subsistence of the lease are necessary. One without the other is ineffective to constitute a waiver of the landlord's right to forfeit.[7] Waiver, where it does occur, may be either express or implied.

(ii) Implied waiver of forfeiture Although an implied waiver of forfeiture can arise in many kinds of circumstance, it seems that conduct in relation to rent may 'fall into a special category'.[8] An implication of waiver is almost inevitable where a landlord, with actual or constructive knowledge that a

20 *Owendale Pty Ltd v Anthony* (1967) 117 CLR 539 at 589.
1 *Expert Clothing Service & Sales Ltd v Hillgate House Ltd* [1986] Ch 340 at 359C per Slade LJ; *Billson v Residential Apartments Ltd* [1992] 1 AC 494 at 534D per Lord Templeman.
2 *Owendale Pty Ltd v Anthony* (1967) 117 CLR 539 at 557f.
3 *Jones v Carter* (1846) 15 M & W 718 at 726, 153 ER 1040 at 1043 per Parke B. See also *Scarf v Jardine* (1882) 7 App Cas 345 at 360; *Expert Clothing Service & Sales Ltd v Hillgate House Ltd* [1986] Ch 340 at 359C; *Billson v Residential Apartments Ltd* [1992] 1 AC 494 at 534E–F.
4 *Stephens v Junior Army and Navy Stores Ltd* [1914] 2 Ch 516 at 523.
5 The knowledge required for the purpose of implied waiver is sufficiently present where the landlord or any of his agents or employees is aware of the tenant's breach of covenant. See eg *Metropolitan Properties Co Ltd v Cordery* (1980) 39 P & CR 10 at 16f, where the knowledge acquired by the landlord's porters in a block of flats was attributed to the landlord. Compare *Official Custodian for Charities v Parway Estates Developments Ltd* [1985] Ch 151 at 162F–163A, where disclosure of the tenant's breach in the *London Gazette* was held not to fix the landlord with deemed knowledge of that breach. See also *Chrisdell Ltd v Johnson* (1987) 54 P & CR 257 at 264ff; [1988] Conv 139 (J.E.M.). In *Van Haarlam v Kasner* (1992) 64 P & CR 214 at 226, a landlord was held to have waived his right of forfeiture by continuing to demand and accept rent in the face of wide newspaper coverage of the tenant's illegal activities in breach of his leasehold covenants.
6 The legal effect of an act relied on as constituting waiver must be considered objectively, without regard to the motive or intention of the landlord or the actual understanding or belief of the tenant (*Central Estates (Belgravia) Ltd v Woolgar* (No 2) [1972] 1 WLR 1048 at 1054D). As was pointed out by Slade LJ in *Expert Clothing Service & Sales Ltd v Hillgate House Ltd* [1986] Ch 340 at 360D, this means that the doctrine of waiver is 'quite capable in some instances of operating harshly, most particularly where there has been an acceptance of rent by the landlord.'
7 *Perry v Davis* (1858) 3 CB (NS) 769 at 777, 140 ER 945 at 948.
8 *Expert Clothing Service & Sales Ltd v Hillgate House Ltd* [1986] Ch 340 at 360D–E per Slade LJ.

breach has occurred, continues unambiguously to demand[9] or to accept[10] any rent which falls due after the breach.[11] The mere fact that rent is accepted 'without prejudice' to the right to forfeit[12] or is accepted by reason of clerical error[13] cannot prevent the acceptance from operating as a waiver.[14] Moreover, the act of distraining for rent waives any right to forfeit the lease on the ground of rent arrears accruing before the date of the distress.[15]

Waiver may also occur, although somewhat less automatically, in other categories of case. In matters not connected directly with the payment of rent, the courts seem to be more 'free to look at *all* the circumstances of the case'[16] in considering whether a landlord's actions are consistent with his avoiding the lease. Waiver may well arise where the landlord, with knowledge of a breach giving him a right of re-entry, engages in action so unequivocal as to be consistent only with the continued existence of the landlord-tenant relationship.[17] Such conduct includes, for instance, an agreement by the landlord to grant the tenant a new lease commencing on the normal determination of an existing letting,[18] or, in some circumstances,

9 *Segal Securities Ltd v Thoseby* [1963] 1 QB 887 at 899; *David Blackstone Ltd v Burnetts (West End) Ltd* [1973] 1 WLR 1487 at 1498E–F; *Welch v Birrane* (1975) 29 P & CR 102 at 112; *Expert Clothing Service & Sales Ltd v Hillgate House Ltd* [1986] Ch 340 at 359C–F. In order to amount to waiver, the demand for rent must be effectively communicated to the tenant. It is not enough, for instance, that it is addressed to the tenant's wife (*Trustees of Henry Smith's Charity v Willson* [1983] QB 316 at 332F–333A).

10 *Croft v Lumley* (1858) 6 HL Cas 672 at 713, 10 ER 1459 at 1475; *Davenport v The Queen* (1877) 3 App Cas 115 at 131f; *Oak Property Co Ltd v Chapman* [1947] KB 886 at 898; *Expert Clothing Service & Sales Ltd v Hillgate House Ltd* [1986] Ch 340 at 359C-D; *Larking v Great Western (Nepean) Gravel Ltd* (1940) 64 CLR 221 at 240; *Owendale Pty Ltd v Anthony* (1967) 117 CLR 539 at 557f, 588; *Baxton v Kara* [1982] 1 NSWLR 604 at 608. In *Foxell v Mendis* (Unreported, Court of Appeal, 19 May 1982), however, Stephenson LJ pointed out that it is 'not an easy thing to waive the forfeiture of a statutory tenancy by the acceptance of rent'. For the proposition that there may be a distinction between rent accepted from a statutory tenant and that accepted from a contractual tenant, see *Oak Property Co Ltd v Chapman*, supra at 898f; *Trustees of Henry Smith's Charity v Willson* [1983] QB 316 at 331C–G; [1983] Conv 248 (J. Martin).

11 There is, however, no waiver of forfeiture if money is 'received in respect of the tenant's use of the land but not in its quality as rent' (*Larking v Great Western (Nepean) Gravel Ltd* (1940) 64 CLR 221 at 240). There is therefore no waiver by the landlord if he receives payments from the tenant in the form of 'mesne profits'.

12 *Segal Securities Ltd v Thoseby* [1963] 1 QB 887 at 897f; *Central Estates (Belgravia) Ltd v Woolgar* (No 2) [1972] 1 WLR 1048 at 1054E; *Expert Clothing Service & Sales Ltd v Hillgate House Ltd* [1986] Ch 340 at 359D–E.

13 *Central Estates (Belgravia) Ltd v Woolgar* (No 2) [1972] 1 WLR 1048 at 1052F–G, 1055D–F.

14 There are indications that the courts may nowadays be less enthusiastic in their support of the almost comprehensive waiver effect of a demand and acceptance of rent (see eg *Greenwich LBC v Discreet Selling Estates Ltd* (1990) 61 P & CR 405 at 412 per Staughton LJ).

15 *Doe d Flower v Peck* (1830) 1 B & Ad 428 at 437, 109 ER 847 at 850; *Kirkland v Briancourt* (1890) 6 TLR 441. A request by a landlord that the Department of Social Security should deduct rent arrears (or even current payments for use and occupation) from statutory benefit payments made to the occupier has been held not to operate as a waiver of a demand for possession (*Northern Ireland Housing Executive v Duffin* [1985] NI 210 at 214B. Compare, however, *Northern Ireland Housing Executive v McGinn* (Unreported).

16 *Expert Clothing Service & Sales Ltd v Hillgate House Ltd* [1986] Ch 340 at 360E–F.

17 See eg *Billson v Residential Apartments Ltd* [1992] 1 AC 494 at 508C–D, where Browne-Wilkinson V-C indicated that excessive delay in following up an unproductive section 146 notice by re-entry could lead to an allegation of waiver.

18 See eg *Ward v Day* (1864) 5 B & S 359 at 363, 122 ER 865 at 866.

the proffering of a mere negotiating document which contemplates continued contractual relations.[19]

(iii) Temporal scope of the waiver In the case of a 'once and for all breach',[20] any proven waiver of forfeiture precludes any claim by the landlord to forfeit the lease on the ground of the particular breach which has occurred,[1] but does not operate as a general waiver in relation to similar breaches in the future.[2] However, waiver in respect of a continuing breach of covenant can be withdrawn at any time subsequently by the landlord, whereupon his right to claim forfeiture of the lease is revitalised.[3] In the absence of some plea based upon estoppel, the tenant is not entitled to argue that one prolonged period of waiver gives him any right or expectation that the waiver of a continuing breach should continue indefinitely.[4]

(k) Effect of forfeiture

The exercise of the landlord's right of re-entry has a number of important consequences (both actual and potential) for the tenant and for other persons.

(i) Effect on tenant The mere fact that a lease or tenancy has become liable to forfeiture does not entitle the landlord to claim trespass against the tenant if the latter remains in occupation. The landlord's right to immediate possession is not enough for this purpose. It is necessary that he should convert his right to possession into actual possession by means of re-entry,[5] but once re-entry has occurred the tenant becomes a trespasser.[6] The landlord may now use such force as is reasonably necessary to expel his former tenant, provided that the latter has been requested to leave and has been given a reasonable opportunity of doing so.[7]

19 *Expert Clothing Service & Sales Ltd v Hillgate House Ltd* [1986] Ch 340 at 360F–G.

20 For the distinction between a 'once and for all' breach and a breach of a continuing nature, see p 822, ante. It seems that breach of a covenant to insure premises is not a continuing breach (see *Farimani v Gates* (1984) 271 Estates Gazette 887 at 889; but compare *Larking v Great Western (Nepean) Gravel Ltd* (1940) 64 CLR 221 at 236 per Dixon J). See also *Church Commissioners for England v Nodjoumi* (1985) 135 NLJ 1185; (1986) 136 NLJ 255 (H.W. Wilkinson).

1 *Farimani v Gates* (1984) 271 Estates Gazette 887 at 889.

2 Law of Property Act 1925, s 148(1). See eg *Billson v Residential Apartments Ltd* [1992] 1 AC 494 at 507A–D per Browne-Wilkinson V-C.

3 *Doe d Ambler v Woodbridge* (1829) 9 B & C 376 at 377f, 109 ER 140; *Greenwich LBC v Discreet Selling Estates Ltd* (1990) 61 P & CR 405 at 412f. There is no need to serve a further section 146 notice (*Farimani v Gates* (1984) 271 Estates Gazette 887 at 888).

4 *Cooper v Henderson* (1982) 263 Estates Gazette 592 at 594.

5 *Butcher v Butcher* (1827) 7 B & C 399 at 402, 108 ER 772 at 773; *Jones v Chapman* (1849) 2 Exch 803 at 821, 154 ER 717 at 724; *Lows v Telford* (1876) 1 App Cas 414 at 426; *Hegan v Carolan* [1916] 2 IR 27 at 30f; *Haniotis v Dimitriou* [1983] 1 VR 498 at 500.

6 Ante, p 806. See also *Billson v Residential Apartments Ltd* [1992] 1 AC 494 at 536G–H per Lord Templeman.

7 *Polkinghorn v Wright* (1845) 8 QB 197 at 206f, 115 ER 849 at 853; *Haniotis v Dimitriou* [1983] 1 VR 498 at 500.

It seems unclear whether on re-entering the landlord must give notice requiring the removal within a reasonable time of any goods left on the premises by the former tenant.[8] However, if such notice is given and ignored the landlord may remove the goods from the premises without incurring any liability in trespass. This is so at least if the goods are carried 'to a convenient distance' and deposited 'in a proper and convenient place for the use of the plaintiff',[9] and if the landlord does no unnecessary damage.[10] A right of distress damage feasant may be asserted by the landlord where the presence of the tenant's belongings on the premises causes actual damage, although it is possible that the costs of removal may amount to actual damage for this purpose.[11] This latter right is, however, subject to the normal limitation that the remedy of distress may not be claimed in respect of things in actual use by their owner.[12]

(ii) Effect on subtenant It is trite law that the forfeiture of a head lease necessarily and automatically destroys any sublease created out of the head lease.[13] It is also clear, however, that a subtenant has an independent right under section 146(4) of the Law of Property Act 1925 to seek relief against forfeiture.[14] The court has a broad discretion to grant relief on such terms as it thinks fit.[15] In particular the court may invest the subtenant with an entirely new estate[16] in the demised premises on such terms as are deemed appropriate,[17] subject to the proviso that the subtenant may not require a lease to be

8 *Haniotis v Dimitriou* [1983] 1 VR 498 at 501f.

9 *Houghton v Butler* (1791) 4 Term Rep 364 at 365f, 100 ER 1066 at 1067. See also *Rea v Sheward* (1837) 2 M & W 424 at 426, 150 ER 823 at 824.

10 *Neville v Cooper* (1834) 2 Cr & M 329 at 331, 149 ER 786 at 787. In *Haniotis v Dimitriou* [1983] 1 VR 498 at 502, Brooking J left for future litigation the hypothetical case 'of the Stradivarius put out on to the footpath', suggesting that relevant arguments at that stage would include the contention that such a small object was not 'encumbering' the landlord's premises, or 'doing damage' to him, or that the law will not permit the remedy of self-help where the resulting loss to the tenant is wholly disproportionate to the injury averted by the landlord.

11 *Jamieson's Tow & Salvage Ltd v Murray* [1984] 2 NZLR 144 at 149, but compare *R v Howson* (1966) 55 DLR (2d) 582 at 597.

12 *Jamieson's Tow & Salvage Ltd v Murray* [1984] 2 NZLR 144 at 150 (illegally parked car towed away with driver still sitting resolutely at steering wheel).

13 *Great Western Railway Co v Smith* (1876) 2 Ch D 235 at 253; *G.M.S. Syndicate Ltd v Gary Elliott Ltd* [1982] Ch 1 at 8C; *Rhodes v Allied Dunbar Pension Services Ltd* [1989] 1 WLR 800 at 809C per Nicholls LJ. See generally Stephen Tromans, [1986] Conv 187.

14 Section 146(4) relates to forfeiture for breach of *any* covenant (whether or not for non-payment of rent). See (1984) 134 NLJ 717 (H.W. Wilkinson).

15 In *Chatham Empire Theatre (1955) Ltd v Ultrans* [1961] 1 WLR 817 at 820, for instance, relief was granted on condition that the subtenant paid up that proportion of the total arrears of rent which corresponded with his part of the premises comprised within the head lease.

16 The new lease is 'a quite distinct piece of property from the old' (*Cadogan v Dimovic* [1984] 1 WLR 609 at 613H). See also *Official Custodian for Charities v Mackey* [1985] Ch 168 at 183E. In effect the head lessor may be forced into privity of contract with the former sublessee, but the coercion of such a legal relationship may itself be inequitable if it is unreasonable to saddle the head lessor with a lessee whom he would never willingly have contracted to accept (see *O'Connor v J.G. Mooney & Co Ltd* [1982] ILRM 373 at 383).

17 Law of Property Act 1925, s 146(4).

granted to him for any longer term than he had under his original sublease.[18] Moreover, the court has discretion to grant relief in respect of part only of the premises comprised in the head lease. Thus, absent any express restriction of the landlord's right to re-enter on part only of those premises, the court may grant relief to a tenant in respect of one portion of the premises while refusing relief to a subtenant who has been in possession of another part of the premises,[19] or vice versa.

(iii) Effect on mortgagee Forfeiture has a potentially devastating effect on any security enjoyed by a third party who has taken a mortgage over the leasehold estate of the tenant.[20] The termination of the tenant's estate in the land destroys the mortgage.[1] It is possible, however, that the mortgagee may succeed in obtaining relief against forfeiture.[2] In cases of non-payment of rent by the tenant a legal mortgagee may seek relief either under section 146(4) of the Law of Property Act 1925[3] or under the Common Law Procedure Act 1852[4] or the County Courts Act 1984[5] (depending upon whether the High Court or county court has jurisdiction).[6] Where the tenant's breach has taken some form other than non-payment of rent, the mortgagee's right to seek relief is confined to section 146(4) of the Law of Property Act 1925.[7]

18 The term of the original sublease is taken to include any extension imposed pursuant to any relevant statutory code (eg Part II of the Landlord and Tenant Act 1954). See *Cadogan v Dimovic* [1984] 1 WLR 609 at 614D–E.
19 *G.M.S. Syndicate Ltd v Gary Elliott Ltd* [1982] Ch 1 at 12E–F, following *Dumpor's Case* (1603) 4 Co Rep 119b, 76 ER 1110. See [1981] Conv 381 (R. Griffith).
20 Post, p 939.
1 Ante, p 835.
2 Ante, p 812.
3 See *Official Custodian for Charities v Mackey* [1985] Ch 168 at 183B–C; [1985] Conv 50. The mortgagee's right to claim relief under section 146(4) may arise on the ground that the mortgagee took the security of a long sublease (post, p 940) and therefore now has standing as a subtenant. Alternatively, if the mortgage was under a charge expressed to be by way of legal mortgage, the chargee has (by virtue of Law of Property Act 1925, s 87(1)) the same right to apply for relief as if he were possessed of a sub-term less by one day than the term of the charged lease (*Abbey National Building Society v Maybeech Ltd* [1985] Ch 190 at 198C–D). See *Grand Junction Co Ltd v Bates* [1954] 2 QB 160 at 168f (ante, p 815).
4 Ante, p 814.
5 Ante, p 815. See County Courts Act 1984, s 140. On this basis the mortgagee may have access to discretionary relief for a period of up to six months following the landlord's recovery of possession under the court order (see County Courts Act 1984, s 138(9A)), but relief for the mortgagee is thereafter barred both in the county court and in the High Court (see *United Dominions Trust Ltd v Shellpoint Trustees Ltd* (1993) *Times*, 23 March).
6 Ante, p 814.
7 See *Abbey National Building Society v Maybeech Ltd* [1985] Ch 190 at 198C.

For one reason or another a mortgagee may be ineligible for such statutory forms of relief against the forfeiture of the tenant. In these circumstances it becomes vital to determine whether, apart from statute, there still exists an inherent equitable jurisdiction vested in the courts to grant relief.[8] On this question views are at present divided.[9] In *Abbey National Building Society v Maybeech Ltd*[10] Nicholls J recognised a concurrent equitable jurisdiction to grant relief to a legal mortgagee who knew nothing of the tenant's breaches and from whom the landlord deliberately concealed the existence of his forfeiture proceedings.[11] Likewise there have been indications that the courts retain an inherent jurisdiction to grant relief to an equitable mortgagee or equitable chargee of a leasehold interest.[12] It has even been suggested that this residual equitable jurisdiction may be exercised after forfeiture has been completed by judgment and execution,[13] and that the court will generally grant relief on the payment of appropriate compensation.[14]

The availability of the court's inherent jurisdiction in this context was left ultimately unclear by the decision of the House of Lords in *Billson v Residential Apartments Ltd*.[15] Two members of the Court of Appeal were of the view that, at least in cases other than breach through non-payment of rent, the court's equitable jurisdiction has been extinguished by statutory intervention.[16] Nicholls LJ was convinced of the survival of the general equitable jurisdiction[17] and the House of Lords found it strictly unnecessary to resolve the difference of approach.[18]

(iv) Effect on squatter A squatter who has acquired a title by adverse possession against a leaseholder has no sufficient interest in the lease to enable him to apply for relief against its forfeiture.[19]

8 If no such jurisdiction exists, it may be that a lease containing a forfeiture clause can no longer be viewed as an acceptable security for a mortgagee where there is any possibility that the landlord may succeed in concealing forfeiture proceedings from the mortgagee until it is too late for the latter to seek relief. On this basis the mortgaging of leasehold flats would be severely jeopardised (see (1986) 136 NLJ 254).

9 See (1986) 136 NLJ 339 (P.F. Smith).

10 [1985] Ch 190 at 204C; [1985] Conv 50. See also *Billson v Residential Apartments Ltd* [1992] 1 AC 494 at 530A–B per Nicholls LJ.

11 Compare, however, *Smith v Metropolitan City Properties Ltd* (1986) 277 Estates Gazette 753 at 754, where Walton J thought it 'quite fantastic' that, by enacting Law of Property Act 1925, s 146, Parliament could be regarded as having intended to leave the inherent equitable jurisdiction untrammelled.

12 See eg *Ladup Ltd v Williams & Glyn's Bank PLC* [1985] 1 WLR 851 at 860H–861A per Warner J; [1985] Conv 407 (J.E.M.).

13 *Hare v Elms* [1893] 1 QB 604 at 607f.

14 *Ladup Ltd v Williams & Glyn's Bank PLC* [1985] 1 WLR 851 at 860E–F. See generally Stephen Tromans, [1986] Conv 187.

15 [1992] 1 AC 494 (ante, p 811).

16 [1992] 1 AC 494 at 516D–E per Browne-Wilkinson V-C, 522G per Parker LJ. See [1991] Conv 380 (S. Goulding); P.F. Smith, [1992] Conv 32.

17 [1992] 1 AC 494 at 528F–529A.

18 Ante, p 826.

19 *Tickner v Buzzacott* [1965] Ch 426 at 434.

(l) *Proposals for reform*

In 1985 the Law Commission completed an exhaustive review of the current law relating to the forfeiture of leases and tenancies.[20] The Commission formed the view that the existing law of forfeiture is 'unnecessarily complicated, is no longer coherent and may give rise to injustice.'[1] In particular the Commission pointed to the anomalous way in which the law at present incorporates two almost entirely separate regimes, one relating to forfeiture for non-payment of rent and the other relating to all other cases.[2] The Commission accordingly recommended the abolition of the existing law of forfeiture and its replacement by a new system.[3] The key feature underlying the Commission's recommendation was the recognition that re-entry by the landlord commonly occurs nowadays in the constructive form of commencement of legal proceedings, actual re-entry being unlawful in many cases.[4] The Commission thus proposed to rationalise the present procedure by acknowledging that the landlord's proceedings, which at present have to be framed as proceedings for possession, are in reality proceedings designed to terminate the tenancy.[5]

The Commission therefore proposed the introduction by legislation of a new 'termination order scheme'.[6] Under this scheme there would be no distinction between termination for non-payment of rent and termination for other reasons, and every tenancy would remain in full force until the court made a 'termination order' fixing the date on which the tenancy should end.[7] The landlord would be able to base his application for a termination order on any of a number of 'termination order events', which would broadly cover all breaches of express or implied leasehold covenant and the bankruptcy of the tenant.[8] Termination on any of these grounds would no longer depend on the inclusion of an express forfeiture clause in the covenants of a lease,[9] and would still remain available even where the consequences of a termination order event had been remedied.[10]

The court, on hearing an application for termination, would have a discretionary power to make either an 'absolute order' for termination[11] or a 'remedial order' which would end the tenancy 'if, but only if, the tenant failed to take specified remedial action within a specified time'.[12] An absolute order would in general be appropriate only where a termination order event was either of such serious character that the tenant 'ought not

20 *Codification of the Law of Landlord and Tenant: Forfeiture of Tenancies* (Law Com No 142, 21 March 1985). See [1986] Conv 165 (P.F. Smith); (1987) 84 LSG 1042 (J. Cherryman).
1 Law Com No 142, para 1.3.
2 Law Com No 142, para 3.11.
3 Law Com No 142, para 1.3.
4 Law Com No 142, para 3.4.
5 Law Com No 142, para 3.5.
6 Law Com No 142, paras 3.7, 3.26ff.
7 Law Com No 142, para 4.1.
8 Law Com No 142, paras 5.1ff.
9 Law Com No 142, paras 5.3ff.
10 Law Com No 142, para 7.13.
11 Law Com No 142, paras 9.15ff.
12 Law Com No 142, paras 9.21ff.

in all the circumstances to remain tenant of the property',[13] or comprised a wrongful assignment or an insolvency event under circumstances in which the court was satisfied that no remedial action would be adequate and satisfactory to the landlord.[14]

The Law Commission's proposals represent a most useful reformulation of the law not least because they also incorporated a recommendation that the tenant be likewise entitled to seek termination of a tenancy on the ground of breach of covenant by his landlord.[15] This suggestion, if implemented, would conclude a rather inglorious chapter of English law in which 'not even the worst possible conduct by a landlord. . .gives the tenant the right to end the tenancy'.[16] The Law Commission's recommendation envisaged that the tenant would have the right to apply to court for a termination order based on any of a number of 'termination order events',[17] the court retaining discretion either to grant the termination requested (together with compensation for the tenant[18]) or to make a 'remedial order' requiring the landlord to take specified remedial action within a specified time.[19] It remains to be seen whether the Commission's recommendations will eventuate in legislative action.

(2) Distress

Distress is an ancient common law remedy which entitles the landlord, in appropriate circumstances, summarily to seize goods found on the demised premises, sell them up and recoup from the proceeds of sale any arrears of rent owed by the tenant.[20] Although sometimes described as an obsolete remedy,[1] distress is not infrequently used, especially by local authority landlords, as a means of recovering arrears of rent from a defaulting tenant.[2]

13 Law Com No 142, paras 9.33ff. This guideline was intended by the Law Commission to 'militate against the doctrine of "stigma"' (para 9.39).

14 Law Com No 142, paras 9.43ff.

15 *Codification of the Law of Landlord and Tenant: Forfeiture of Tenancies* (Law Com No 142, 21 March 1985), paras 17.10ff.

16 Law Com No 142, para 17.2. See now, however, *Hussein v Mehlman* [1992] 2 EGLR 87.

17 Law Com No 142, paras 18.4ff.

18 Law Com No 142, para 19.15.

19 Law Com No 142, paras 19.16ff.

20 One of the best modern accounts of the law of distress is contained in *Distress for Rent* (Law Commission Working Paper No 97, May 1986), Chapter 2. For a critique of the modern law and practice of distress, see I. Loveland, *Distress for Rent: An Archaic Remedy?*, (1990) 17 J Law and Society 363.

1 *Abingdon RDC v O'Gorman* [1968] 2 QB 811 at 819E. See the reference to distress as a 'relic of feudalism' in Law Commission, *Landlord and Tenant: Interim Report on Distress for Rent* (Law Com No 5, 1966), para 5.

2 See (1978) LAG Bulletin 57 (A. Arden); Law Commission Working Paper No 97 (May 1986), para 3.3. Distress has also been advocated as an attractive alternative to other remedies for commercial arrears (see (1980) 1 PLB 33). The argument is that distress provides a faster and less cumbersome form of remedy than re-entry, which may rebound on the landlord, leaving him with empty premises and no rent. An alternative to distress exists in the form of execution against the goods of the tenant either through the issue of a warrant of execution (CCR (1981), Ord 26, r 1) or on application to the High Court for a writ of fieri facias. Both forms of process tend to be more heavily encumbered by technical difficulty than even the remedy of distress. See [1983] Conv 444 (A. Hill-Smith); (1986) 136 NLJ 546 (M. Haley).

(a) Extra-judicial nature of distress

As a remedy founded in self-help, distress is anomalous and somewhat controversial. Except in certain limited cases defined by statute,[3] there is no requirement that any due process of law be interposed before the landlord distrains upon his tenant's goods.[4] Precisely because it is a potentially traumatic remedy, the exercise of distress is subject to a number of restrictions, some of which are rooted in statutory provisions of some antiquity.

(b) General restrictions on the right to distrain

Distress may be levied only in respect of arrears of rent.[5] No other breach of covenant entitles the landlord to distrain upon the goods of his tenant. Moreover, distress is intrinsically a landlord's remedy, and is therefore available only where there is a tenancy[6] and never where there is merely a licence.[7] The landlord must, at the date of the distress, be possessed of the immediate reversion on the tenancy in relation to which he seeks to distrain. This means, in effect, that distress cannot generally be levied against a subtenant,[8] and a subtenant's goods are in any event exempted by statute from any distress levied by a head landlord against a head tenant.[9]

The landlord's right to distrain arises as soon as any rent is in arrear during the subsistence of the tenancy,[10] and the right continues for six months after the termination of the tenancy if the former tenant is still in occupation of the same premises.[11] The remedies of distress and forfeiture are mutually

3 See eg Rent (Agriculture) Act 1976, s 8 (certain agricultural tenancies or occupancies); Rent Act 1977, s 147(1) (protected or statutory tenancy); Housing Act 1988, s 19(1) (assured tenancy); Insolvency Act 1986, s 130 (tenant company in process of being wound up by court).

4 See *Rhodes v Allied Dunbar Pension Services Ltd* [1989] 1 WLR 800 at 803E per Nicholls LJ. It is precisely this absence of legal process which allows a landlord to distrain notwithstanding that an interim order has been made under Insolvency Act 1986, s 252(2) pending approval of a voluntary arrangement with the tenant's creditors (see *McMullen & Sons Ltd v Cerrone* (1993) *Times*, 10 June). See also A. Clarke, (1992) 45 CLP 81 at 115ff.

5 The right to levy distress is limited to six years of rent arrear (Limitation Act 1980, s 19). There is no right to distrain for mesne profits (*Bridges v Smyth* (1829) 5 Bing 410 at 413, 130 ER 1119 at 1120; *Alford v Vickery* (1842) Car & M 280 at 283, 174 ER 507 at 508).

6 The corollary is that an owner who distrains on the goods of one who occupies his premises is estopped from alleging that the occupier is merely a licensee, at least if the other requirements of a lease (ante, p 677) are also present. See *Ward v Day* (1863) 4 B & S 337 at 357, 122 ER 486 at 493; *Carden v Choudhury* (Unreported, Court of Appeal, 29 February 1984) (ante, p 707).

7 *Hancock v Austin* (1863) 14 CB (NS) 634 at 639f, 143 ER 593 at 596; *Ward v Day* (1863) 4 B & S 337 at 356ff, 122 ER 486 at 493.

8 See *Wade v Marsh* (1625) Lat 211, 82 ER 350.

9 Law of Distress Amendment Act 1908, s 1.

10 This is so even if rent is payable in advance (see *Walsh v Lonsdale* (1882) 21 Ch D 9 at 14f, ante, p 747). There is no requirement at common law that the landlord should make any further demand for rent before distraining (*Kerby v Harding* (1851) 6 Exch 234 at 240f, 155 ER 527 at 530).

11 Landlord and Tenant Act 1709, ss 6, 7. Thus the right to distrain is lost if a local authority rehouses elsewhere former tenants who have been evicted for rent arrears.

exclusive.[12] Distress is premised on an affirmation of the landlord-tenant relationship, while forfeiture marks an unequivocal election by the landlord to terminate that relationship.[13] It follows therefore that distress cannot lawfully be levied where the landlord has already exercised his right to re-enter the demised premises.[14] Recourse to common law distress is likewise excluded if the landlord has already obtained a court judgment for the arrears of rent.[15]

(c) Time and manner of lawful distress

The time and manner of lawful distress are regulated by rather archaic and not always rational rules. Distress cannot be levied between sunset and sunrise[16] nor on a Sunday.[17] Entry to the premises must not be made by breaking an outer door,[18] but inner doors may be broken down once entry has been achieved.[19] Entry through an open window is permissible,[20] but not through a window which, although unlocked, is closed.[1] Having entered, the landlord may remove goods and hold them in a pound pending sale.[2]

The landlord may distrain in person, but it is more normal to employ the services of a bailiff.[3] Not only must a bailiff have the authority of the landlord (usually in the written form of a warrant of distress); he must also hold a written certificate issued by the county court which entitles him to act in this capacity.[4]

12 *Bank of Montreal v Woodtown Developments Ltd* (1980) 99 DLR (3d) 739 at 743; *Country Kitchen Ltd v Wabush Enterprises Ltd* (1981) 120 DLR (3d) 358 at 361.

13 The landlord cannot 'have its cake and eat it too' (*Country Kitchen Ltd v Wabush Enterprises Ltd* (1981) 120 DLR (3d) 358 at 362). It seems that the mutually exclusive nature of the remedies cannot be reversed even by express contractual provision (*Re Coopers & Lybrand Ltd and Royal Bank of Canada* (1982) 137 DLR (3d) 356 at 360f).

14 *Kirkland v Briancourt* (1890) 6 TLR 441. Forfeiture will be established by any 'act so inconsistent with the continuance of the [tenant's] term that [the landlords] were estopped from denying that it was at an end' (*Oastler v Henderson* (1877) 2 QBD 575 at 577). Thus the landlord's right to distrain is lost if he changes the locks on the doors of the demised premises and denies the tenant entry (*Country Kitchen Ltd v Wabush Enterprises Ltd* (1981) 120 DLR (3d) 358 at 363; *Re Coopers & Lybrand Ltd and Royal Bank of Canada* (1982) 137 DLR (3d) 356 at 359), but not if he merely sends a letter demanding payment of existing arrears of rent (*Cameron v Eldorado Properties Ltd* (1981) 113 DLR (3d) 141 at 145).

15 *Chancellor v Webster* (1893) 9 TLR 568 at 569 (even though the judgment debt remains unsatisfied).

16 *Aldenburgh v Peaple* (1834) 6 C & P 212 at 213, 172 ER 1212; *Tutton v Darke* (1860) 5 H & N 647 at 650, 157 ER 1338 at 1340.

17 *Werth v London & Westminster Loan and Discount Co* (1889) 5 TLR 521 at 522.

18 *Semayne's Case* (1605) 5 Co Rep 91a at 92b, 77 ER 194 at 198; *Hancock v Austin* (1863) 14 CB (NS) 634 at 640, 143 ER 593 at 596; *Gordon v Phelan* (1881) 15 ILTR 70 at 72; *Cassidy v Foley* [1904] 2 IR 427 at 428.

19 *Browning v Dann* (1735) Bull NP 81.

20 *Long v Clarke* [1894] 1 QB 119 at 121.

1 *Nash v Lucas* (1867) LR 2 QB 590 at 594f.

2 The landlord is also authorised by the Distress for Rent Act 1737 to secure goods otherwise than by impounding them (ie to assume 'walking possession'). See *Evans v South Ribble BC* [1992] 2 WLR 429 at 434E.

3 County Courts display the names of certificated bailiffs (who are often solicitors), and there is a Certificated Bailiffs' Association.

4 See Law of Distress (Amendment) Act 1888, s 7. The Distress for Rent Rules 1988 (SI 1988/2050) now provide for general certificates valid for a year and thereafter renewable.

(d) Exemption for privileged goods

The process of distraint involves in principle the seizure of any goods found on the demised premises,[5] subject only to certain common law[6] and statutory exceptions in respect of privileged goods. Among the categories of goods immune from seizure are clothes and bedding (to a total value of £100) and tools of trade (to a total value of £150),[7] perishable foods,[8] tenant's fixtures,[9] the property of lodgers,[10] and things in actual use. Things 'in actual use' include articles which are immune from seizure simply on the ground that a breach of the peace would otherwise almost necessarily occur.[11] It is not certain how far the last exemption extends, but it seems that a tenant can effectively resist attempts at distress simply by switching on any kind of electrical apparatus in his home before the landlord or bailiff arrives to carry out the distress (eg television set, radio, refrigerator, washing machine, cooker).[12] Distress can be levied on the goods of innocent strangers which are present on the premises,[13] subject to a right in the true owner to reclaim his property by serving a statutory declaration on the landlord or bailiff.[14]

(e) Sale

The landlord or bailiff who levies distress with the intention of selling up the goods seized must give the tenant, or leave at the demised premises, a notice which states the cause for the distress and stipulates the place of sale.[15] No sooner than five days later[16] the goods may be sold—usually by auction—and the landlord may recoup the arrears of rent from the proceeds, returning the balance (if any) minus expenses to the tenant. The landlord is not permitted to purchase the goods himself, and there is a duty to obtain

5 It is, however, unlawful for the landlord to assert any lien over goods of the tenant which already happen to be in the possession of the landlord as bailee (*Finlayson v Taylor* (1983) *Times*, 14 April).

6 At common law coins were always immune from distress unless contained in a closed purse or bag (*East India Co v Skinner* (1695) 1 Botts P L 259; Law Commission Working Paper No 97 (May 1986), para 2.40). Compare, however, the unusual form of purported distress used in *Bank of Montreal v Woodtown Developments Ltd* (1980) 99 DLR (3d) 739 (landlord placed his own representatives in charge of cash register in tenant's shop).

7 Law of Distress (Amendment) Act 1888, s 4; County Courts Act 1984, s 89(1); The Protection from Execution (Prescribed Value) Order 1980 (SI 1980/26), art 2.

8 *Morley v Pincombe* (1848) 2 Exch 101 at 102, 154 ER 423.

9 *Simpson v Hartopp* (1744) Willes 512 at 514f, 125 ER 1295 at 1296f; *Darby v Harris* (1841) 1 QB 895 at 898f, 113 ER 1374 at 1376; *Crossley Bros Ltd v Lee* [1908] 1 KB 86 at 90f.

10 See Law of Distress Amendment Act 1908, s 1.

11 *Simpson v Hartopp* (1744) Willes 512 at 516, 125 ER 1295 at 1297; *Storey v Robinson* (1795) 6 Term Rep 138 at 139, 101 ER 476 at 477; *Field v Adames* (1840) 12 Ad & El 649 at 652, 113 ER 960 at 962.

12 See (1978) LAG Bulletin 57 (A. Arden).

13 *Juson v Dixon* (1813) 1 M & S 601 at 606ff, 105 ER 225 at 227. A landlord may distrain even on goods which he knows are not the property of the defaulting tenant (*Rhodes v Allied Dunbar Pension Services Ltd* [1989] 1 WLR 800 at 803E–F per Nicholls LJ).

14 Law of Distress Amendment Act 1908, s 1. The owner of the goods may obtain an ex parte interlocutory injunction to restrain sale, even though the required declaration is made through the agency of his solicitor (see *Lawrence Chemical Co Ltd v Rubinstein* [1982] 1 WLR 284 at 291C–E, 292F–H).

15 Distress for Rent Act 1689, s 1; Distress for Rent Act 1737, s 9.

16 Distress for Rent Act 1689, s 1.

the best price possible.[17] It is generally thought that the sale of goods which have been the subject of an illegal distress does not pass a good title to the purchaser.[18]

(f) Proposed abolition of distress

The Law Commission has examined the law of distress and, finding it to be 'riddled with inconsistencies, uncertainties, anomalies and archaisms', has declared that reform is 'long overdue'.[19] In the opinion of the Commission, the defects in the present law of distress are 'so fundamental and widespread that very little purpose would be served by collecting up the existing principles from the statutes and common law and restating them in modern terms in a codifying statute.'[20] After consultation the Commission has confirmed its view that distress for rent is 'wrong in principle' and has no proper place in any modern approach to debt enforcement.[1] The Commission has now firmly proposed that this form of distress should be abolished[2] and should not be permitted even as a contractual option for landlord and tenant.[3]

(3) Damages for breach of covenant

Damages may be awarded by the court where a landlord proves breach by the tenant of any covenant other than a covenant respecting payment of rent. Except where the breach is of a repairing covenant, damages are assessed on the usual contractual basis.[4] Their purpose is to place the landlord in the position—in so far as this can be done by means of a monetary award—in which he would have been if there had been no breach by the tenant.[5] Damages for breach of a tenant's covenant to keep or put premises in repair

17 There is a duty, akin to that of a mortgagee exercising his power of sale (post, p 1009), to use reasonable care in conducting the sale. An independent appraisal of the goods is mandatory only if requested in writing by the tenant (Law of Distress (Amendment) Act 1888, s 5). Compare, however, *Cameron v Eldorado Properties Ltd* (1981) 113 DLR (3d) 141 at 147ff.

18 See the application of the principle *nemo dat quod non habet* in comparable circumstances in *Trustee of Estate of Royal Inns Canada Ltd v Bolus-Revelas-Bolus Ltd* (1982) 136 DLR (3d) 272 at 279.

19 *Distress for Rent* (Law Commission Working Paper No 97, May 1986), para 5.1(1).

20 Working Paper No 97, para 5.1(2). The Commission provisionally concluded that the remedy of distress for rent 'is a relic from the ancient laws of England which has no place in modern society' (Working Paper No 97, para 5.1(5)).

1 Law Commission, *Landlord and Tenant: Distress for Rent* (Law Com No 194, 4 February 1991), para 3.2. See also A. Clarke, (1992) 45 CLP 81 at 111ff.

2 Law Com No 194 (1991), para 3.1. See also Working Paper No 97, paras 4.66, 5.1(5). Distress has been abolished in many jurisdictions (see eg Judgments (Enforcement) Act (Northern Ireland) 1969, s 122), and is of doubtful constitutional validity in other jurisdictions (see eg Constitution of the Republic of Ireland, art 43). In 1968 the Payne Committee recommended the abolition in England of distress for rent (see *Report of Committee on the Enforcement of Judgment Debts* (Cmnd 3909, February 1969), para 924).

3 Law Com No 194 (1991), para 4.8.

4 See *Anson's Law of Contract* (26th edn by A.G. Guest, Oxford, 1984), p 491ff.

5 See eg *Costain Property Developments Ltd v Finlay & Co Ltd* (1989) 57 P & CR 345 at 355ff; *Culworth Estates Ltd v Society of Licensed Victuallers* (1991) 62 P & CR 211 at 214ff.

cannot exceed the amount by which the value of the reversion has been diminished through the breach.[6]

(4) Action for arrears of rent

The effect of the Limitation Act is that a maximum of six years' arrears of rent may be recovered in an action brought by the landlord in respect of a tenant's non-payment of rent.[7] Within the parameters set by the Limitation Act there is therefore no prescriptive right to freedom from the obligation to pay rent.

It is traditionally said that the contractual principle of mitigation of damage has no application, at least in English law, to the relationship of landlord and tenant. The landlord has supposedly no duty to mitigate loss by taking steps to re-let premises which have been abandoned by the tenant during the term.[8] This view is premised essentially on the theory that a lease confers a proprietary estate on the tenant for a term and that accordingly the landlord need not concern himself with the tenant's election to under-utilise his own property during this term.[9] On this basis the tenant is entirely free, if he wishes, to enjoy his property in absentia and the landlord remains perfectly entitled, notwithstanding the tenant's premature departure, to sue for rent as it continues to accrue.

Although this principle is deeply embedded in the common law of landlord and tenant, it becomes increasingly debatable whether it can survive the gradual contractualisation of the leasehold relationship.[10] Courts in other jurisdictions have come to accept in recent times that the law of leases cannot be permanently or substantially insulated from exposure to wider aspects of contractual doctrine.[11] It may be only a matter of time before English law recognises, as it has already done in respect of frustration,[12] unilateral notices to quit[13] and repudiatory breach[14] that the rapidly developing 'contract-based' perspective on the leasehold concept requires a departure from some long cherished features of the 'property-based' analysis. In the present context such a recognition calls for the acknowledgement of a principle

6 Landlord and Tenant Act 1927, s 18(1). See *Mather v Barclays Bank plc* [1987] 2 EGLR 254; [1988] Conv 438 (J.E.M.). See also P.F. Smith, [1990] Conv 335 at 342ff. The landlord is not entitled to damages for mental distress caused by the tenant's breach of his covenant to repair (see eg *Turner v Jatko* (1979) 93 DLR (3d) 314 at 316f). For restrictions on the landlord's recovery of damages, see Leasehold Property (Repairs) Act 1938, s 1(2) (ante, p 824).

7 Limitation Act 1980, s 19.

8 See eg *Boyer v Warbey* [1953] 1 QB 234 at 245f per Denning LJ; *Maridakis v Kouvaris* (1975) 5 ALR 197 at 199.

9 See *Brown v RepublicBank First National Midland*, 766 SW2d 203 at 205 (1988) (Supreme Court of Texas).

10 Ante, p 676.

11 See eg J. Effron, *The Contractualisation of the Law of Leasehold: Pitfalls and Opportunities*, (1988) 14 Monash L Rev 83.

12 *National Carriers Ltd v Panalpina (Northern) Ltd* [1981] AC 675 at 692B–D, 697A (ante, p 765).

13 *Hammersmith and Fulham LBC v Monk* [1992] 1 AC 478 at 491E–492A, 492G per Lord Browne-Wilkinson (ante, p 756).

14 *Hussein v Mehlman* [1992] 2 EGLR 87 at 88G.

of mitigation of loss.[15] As the Supreme Court of Texas pointed out in *Brown v RepublicBank First National Midland*,[16] this contract-based approach has the added merit that it 'recognises a public policy element that requires property to be put to beneficial use.'

(5) Injunction

It is possible in appropriate circumstances for the landlord to seek the discretionary remedy of the injunction for the purpose of restraining breaches of certain covenants in the lease.[17] However, no mandatory injunction is available to enable the landlord to compel the tenant's performance of a covenant to repair the demised premises.[18]

(6) Damages for waste

The landlord may, in appropriate cases, recover damages for the tort of waste committed by the tenant. The measure of damages is represented by the diminution in the value of the reversion less a discount which allows for the fact that payment is being made some time before the reversion falls into possession.[19]

3. PRIVITY OF CONTRACT AND PRIVITY OF ESTATE

The device of the leasehold estate offers great potential flexibility in terms of assignment and the creation of subleases.[20] The enforceability of leasehold covenants presents little problem as between the original landlord and tenant, but grows more difficult as successive assignees and subtenants become increasingly remote from the initial contractual relationship. It is nevertheless important that the law should provide a framework of liability and enforcement which ensures the effective 'policing' of the covenants of the lease in the more distant reaches of the leasehold relationship beyond the nexus of original lessor and original lessee.

In English law the precise operation of leasehold enforcement rules depends on whether the lease in question is legal or equitable.[1] Attention in the following pages is directed first to relationships of liability under a legal lease. *Fig.* 65 contains a representation of a typical network of leasehold relationships, flowing from a legal head lease, which may readily serve as

15 See the endorsement of a duty of mitigation in *Schneiker v Gordon*, 732 P2d 603 at 610f (Colo 1987); *Brown v RepublicBank First National Midland*, 766 SW2d 203 at 205f (Tex 1988); *Red Deer College v Michaels* (1975) 57 DLR (3d) 386 at 390f (Supreme Court of Canada); *Tangye v Calmonton Investments Ltd* (1989) 51 DLR (4th) 593 at 602.

16 766 SW2d 203 at 205 (1988).

17 Post, p 867. See eg *Sutton Housing Trust v Lawrence* (1988) 55 P & CR 320 at 324 (covenant against keeping of animals enforceable by injunction against tenant with multiple sclerosis who kept dog for companionship).

18 *Hill v Barclay* (1810) 16 Ves 402 at 405f, 33 ER 1037 at 1038. Compare, however, *S.E.D.A.C. Investments Ltd v Tanner* [1982] 1 WLR 1342 at 1349F (ante, p 825), where it was suggested that the remedy of mandatory injunction may be open to the landlord.

19 *Whitham v Kershaw* (1886) 16 QBD 613 at 617.

20 Ante, p 732.

1 The distinction between legal and equitable leases is discussed elsewhere (ante, p 738).

a model for the present discussion. It is assumed in the following discussion not only that the head or superior lease is legal,[2] but that all subsequent assignments are effected by deed and are likewise legal.[3] Thus, in terms of *Fig.* 65, L creates a lease in favour of T and then assigns his own reversion to A1. T later assigns his term of years to A2, who in turn assigns to A3, who finally sublets to S.

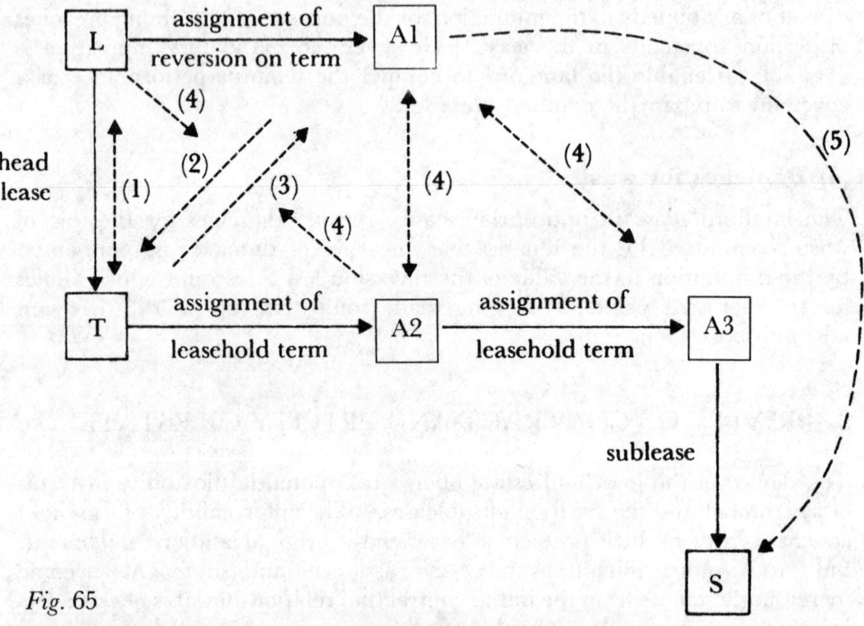

Fig. 65

(1) The duality of leasehold character

The framework of legal rules governing the enforcement of leasehold liabilities is premised upon the essential 'duality of character' implicit in the leasehold device.[4] A lease of land 'originates in contract',[5] but it also confers on the tenant an estate in the land which, like the correlative reversionary estate held by the landlord, is assignable to third parties. It is commonly said therefore that landlord and tenant may stand together in one or other of two distinct legal relationships, respectively 'privity of contract' and 'privity of estate'.[6] The first relationship denotes the ambit of contractual liability; and the second relationship indicates at any given time the precise allocation

2 It matters not for the purposes of exposition whether the lease between L and T is the head lease. Exactly the same principles, transposed as it were one octave down, would apply if L were not himself the freeholder but were instead a leaseholder holding on the covenants of a legal lease.

3 Ante, p 738.

4 *Progressive Mailing House Pty Ltd v Tabali Pty Ltd* (1985) 157 CLR 17 at 51 per Deane J (ante, p 674).

5 *City of London Corpn v Fell* [1993] 2 WLR 710 at 715C per Nourse LJ.

6 *City of London Corpn v Fell* [1993] 2 WLR 710 at 715D–E per Nourse LJ.

of the 'tenancy' of the land.[7] Thus whereas the original landlord and tenant, prior to any assignment of their respective interests, are conjoined in a privity of both contract and estate, an assignment of the estate of either will necessarily terminate the assignor's 'privity of estate', deflecting this form of privity to the assignee. As Nourse LJ observed in *City of London Corpn v Fell*,[8] an original tenant who has assigned his tenancy 'cannot properly be described as the tenant. He no longer holds the land. It is the assignee who now holds the land. It is he who has the tenancy.'[9] It is therefore the assignee who is now 'privy' to the 'estate' of the leasehold.

In English law it is the twin concepts of 'privity of contract' and 'privity of estate' which have come to regulate the complex enforcement relationships which arise in the context of leaseholds.

(2) The ambit of privity of estate

'Privity of estate' describes the relationship obtaining between any two persons who, in respect of the same leasehold estate, *currently* stand vis à vis each other in the position of landlord and tenant.[10] Privity of estate thus entails what in North America is often termed 'horizontal privity', in that the title or status of each person 'privy' to a particular leasehold estate is shuffled on with each respective assignment of the superior or inferior interest comprised within the leasehold relationship. In his turn each successive assignee can describe himself or herself, both functionally and technically, as holding as either a 'landlord' or a 'tenant' in relation to one other identified person.

In relation to the head lease depicted in *Fig.* 65,[11] 'privity of estate' potentially involves all who can trace their leasehold status directly to the 'estate' comprised within this lease. Thus L and A1 may properly claim that they have held successively as 'landlord'. Likewise in their turn T, A2 and A3 can properly describe themselves as having held as 'tenant',[12] although at any given moment the relationship of privity of estate obtains only as between those who hold their interests in possession.[13] The one person in *Fig.* 65 who is not 'privy' to the estate of the head lease is S, the sublessee. S is 'privy' not to the estate of the head lease but to the estate comprised within a different lease of which he is more immediately a party. He is, of course, 'privy' to the estate of the sublease granted him by A3.[14]

7 'A "tenant"...is someone who "holds" land of another' (*City of London Corpn v Fell* [1993] 2 WLR 710 at 715F per Nourse LJ).

8 [1993] 2 WLR 710 at 715F.

9 Equally the assignee of the superior reversionary estate ranks, after the date of assignment, as the 'landlord' (see *Hua Chiao Commercial Bank Ltd v Chiaphua Industries Ltd* [1987] AC 99 at 106G per Lord Oliver of Aylmerton).

10 Ante, p 750.

11 Ante, p 846.

12 A3 can also claim to hold as 'landlord' in relation to S as 'tenant', for a new privity of contract and estate has been generated by the sublease.

13 Each of these persons, during the currency of his tenure, can trace his position to one or other side of the notional feudal divide (or 'estate') which separates landlord from tenant.

14 In a quite graphic sense the test of 'privity of estate' turns on whether the party concerned can trace his position horizontally to the original landlord-tenant relationship to which it is claimed he is 'privy'. S cannot do this in relation to the estate of the head lease between L and T.

4. ENFORCEABILITY OF LEASEHOLD COVENANTS IN A LEGAL LEASE

The complex enforcement relationships which arise in the context of leaseholds are controlled in English law by a combination of common law and statutory rules.[15]

(1) **Liability as between L and T**

In *Fig.* 65 the relationship of L and T is aptly described, prior to assignment by either, as a privity of both contract and estate. For the present purpose, however, it is the notion of contractual privity which dominates the legal construction of their relationship. Because they enjoy this form of privity, each is contractually liable to the other on all the covenants of the lease irrespective of whether these covenants 'touch and concern' the demised land.[16] With the exception of covenants which are illegal or contrary to public policy,[17] purely personal covenants—perhaps even of an eccentric or capricious character—are fully binding and enforceable between them.

The intense contractual nexus between L and T implicates both in common law liabilities of a perhaps unexpected order of magnitude. The commencement of the lease initiates in principle a *continuing liability* on both sides throughout the entire term in the absence of some contractually agreed release.[18] Given that a term of years may be of extensive duration (eg 99 years or 999 years), the contractual liability undertaken by L and T is considerable.[19] Except in certain statutorily defined circumstances[20] both L and T have title to sue the other on all covenants of the lease for the duration of the term.

(a) T's liability survives assignment of the term

The durability of the contractual nexus is such that even the assignment of T's term to A2 (and further assignments, eg to A3) cannot relieve T

15 See generally D. Gordon, [1987] Conv 103. The Law Commission, in recommending a general reformulation of the law of positive and restrictive covenants (post, p 1166), has made it clear that its proposals are not intended to affect the traditional rules relating to the enforceability of covenants between landlord and tenant. See *Transfer of Land: The Law of Positive and Restrictive Covenants* (Law Com No 127, 26 January 1984), paras 3.9, 24.11.

16 *City of London Corpn v Fell* [1993] 2 WLR 710 at 715C-D per Nourse LJ. Reference is made elsewhere to covenants which 'touch and concern' (post, p 854).

17 Ante, p 803.

18 The liability of any surety of T also extends to the whole of the term of the lease (see *Thames Manufacturing Co Ltd v Perrotts (Nichol & Peyton) Ltd* (1984) 271 Estates Gazette 284 at 287). However, L has no right to recover from receivers appointed by T's mortgagees any moneys paid by sublessees during the period before T's lease is declared forfeit by the court (*Official Custodian for Charities v Mackey* (No 2) [1985] 1 WLR 1308 at 1313H-1314A).

19 The death of a covenanting party does not exonerate his estate from liability. In order that potential claims should not impede the winding up of estates, personal representatives are authorised to set aside a 'sufficient fund' to meet possible future liabilities and then distribute the remainder of the deceased's estate (Trustee Act 1925, s 26(1)).

20 See eg Law of Property Act 1925, s 141(1), post, p 854.

of responsibility for the due performance of his leasehold obligations.[1] After the assignment of T's term to A2, there is no longer privity of estate between L and T,[2] but there remains an enduring privity of contract which is wholly untouched by the fact of assignment.[3]

(i) T's liability on the original covenants of the lease It follows that, in the absence of contrary agreement with L,[4] T remains liable throughout the entire term of the lease irrespective of assignment.[5] As Megarry V-C held in *Warnford Investments Ltd v Duckworth*,[6] 'the assignment of the lease does nothing to disturb the direct liability of the lessee to the lessor under the lease for the whole of the term.' This enduring liability covers not merely the payment of the rent reserved by the lease,[7] but extends to all the covenants contained in the original lease.[8] Thus, if A2 or A3 defaults on any of the leasehold covenants, T is ultimately liable on the ground that he initially contracted that these covenants would be performed for the duration of the term of years granted by L.[9] T remains liable for the defaults of others, committed perhaps long after the date of assignment and long after T has ceased to have any realistic interest in or control over the demised premises. Notwithstanding lapse of time the initial contractual undertaking is liable to be honoured in full.

(ii) T's liability on the original terms as varied In that he may be made answerable for *any* breach which occurs, T is effectively rendered an insurer of the lease,

1 For rare exceptions to the general rule of T's continuing liability after assignment of his term, see Law of Property Act 1922, Sch 15, para 11 (assignment of perpetually renewable lease (ante, p 693)); Matrimonial Homes Act 1983, Sch 1, para 2(2) (court-ordered transfer of tenancy between spouses on divorce).

2 See *Milmo v Carreras* [1946] KB 306 at 310; *Picton-Warlow v Allendale Holdings Pty Ltd* [1988] WAR 107 at 110.

3 *Johnsey Estates Ltd v Lewis and Manley (Engineering) Ltd* (1987) 54 P & CR 296 at 300 per Bingham LJ; *W.E. Wagener Ltd v Photo Engravers Ltd* [1984] 1 NZLR 412 at 424.

4 It is of course open to L and T to agree contractually that T's liability should terminate with the assignment of his term. Such limitation of T's liability is unusual—a fact which the Law Commission has ascribed to the unequal bargaining power of landlords and tenants. See *Landlord and Tenant: Privity of Contract and Estate; Duration of Liability of Parties to Leases* (Law Commission Working Paper No 95, March 1986), para 7.1(c); *Landlord and Tenant: Privity of Contract and Estate* (Law Com No 174, 29 November 1988), paras 2.17, 3.3, 3.17.

5 *Walker's Case* (1587) 3 Co Rep 22a at 23a, 76 ER 676 at 680; *Baynton v Morgan* (1888) 22 QBD 74 at 82 per Lopes LJ; *Arlesford Trading Co Ltd v Servansingh* [1971] 1 WLR 1080 at 1082G. See also *195 Crown Street Pty Ltd v Hoare* [1969] 1 NSWR 193 at 195; *Francini v Canuck Properties Ltd* (1982) 35 OR (2d) 321 at 323a; *W.E. Wagener Ltd v Photo Engravers Ltd* [1984] 1 NZLR 412 at 417; *Picton-Warlow v Allendale Holdings Pty Ltd* [1988] WAR 107 at 109; *Tangye v Calmonton Investments Ltd* (1989) 51 DLR (4th) 593 at 596.

6 [1979] Ch 127 at 138C.

7 *Warnford Investments Ltd v Duckworth* [1979] Ch 127 at 138G–139A, 141H–142A. It is now a chilling fact of life for the original tenant that he may even have to pay statutory interest (under Supreme Court Act 1981, s 35A) on rent unpaid by his assignee. See eg *Allied London Investments Ltd v Hambro Life Assurance Ltd* (1984) 269 Estates Gazette 41 at 42ff, 270 Estates Gazette 948 at 950.

8 See eg *Thames Manufacturing Co Ltd v Perrotts (Nichol & Peyton) Ltd* (1984) 271 Estates Gazette 284 at 286f (T liable in damages for A2's breach of repairing and decorating covenant and breach of covenant to surrender and yield up possession); *Weaver v Mogford* [1988] 31 Estates Gazette 49 (T liable for disrepair arising during A2's tenancy).

9 *Warnford Investments Ltd v Duckworth* [1979] Ch 127 at 138H. Since T is no longer in possession, there is no purpose in any attempt by L to seek injunctive relief or forfeiture against him.

and a heavy onus of care is thereby imposed on T to select only a reliable and creditworthy assignee.[10] The burden undertaken by T is underscored by the fact that T may even be made liable on the original covenants as amended by subsequent agreement between L and A2 or A3, notwithstanding that T's liability is effectively (and involuntarily) increased by the later variation of the original terms.[11] Thus, in *Selous Street Properties Ltd v Oronel Fabrics Ltd*[12] T was held liable to pay the rent fixed under a rent review negotiated by A2 even though this rent review had proceeded on a basis different from that agreed in the terms of the original lease.[13]

This approach was evidenced in an even more extreme form in *Centrovincial Estates Plc v Bulk Storage Ltd.*[14] Here T was held liable to pay a much higher revised rent agreed between L and A2 even though the rent review had occurred without T's knowledge or consent. In Harman J's view, this result proceeded not on any footing of agency, but simply on the basis that 'each assignee is the owner of the whole estate and can deal with it so as to alter it or its terms. The estate as so altered then binds the original tenant, because the assignee has been put into the shoes of the original tenant and can do all such acts as the original tenant could have done'.[15] As Harman J pointed out, there is machinery ready to hand by which the original tenant can ensure that no rent review ever takes place without his knowledge or consent. All he need do is grant not an assignment of the whole of his unexpired term, but rather a sublease on identical terms for the same period minus two or three days.[16]

(iii) T's ultimate liability is inescapable The 'ultimate' liability of the original tenant is both inexorable and highly controversial. In the event of default by, say, A3, T has, for instance, no right to require that L first exhaust his remedies against A3.[17] L is entitled, if he so wishes, to have primary

10 In most cases L will already have made assurance doubly sure by including in the lease a covenant prohibiting any assignment or subletting without his prior consent. However, the mere fact that L has consented to T's assignment to A2 does not impliedly release T from his original liability or discharge him from responsibility for breaches occurring after the date of assignment (*Thames Manufacturing Co Ltd v Perrotts (Nichol & Peyton) Ltd* (1984) 271 Estates Gazette 284 at 286).

11 T's liability may, however, be reduced to nil by one particular subsequent event. If it appears that there has been 'some operation conducted upon the lease' (eg surrender of the whole), T's liability to pay rent is terminated (*Allied London Investments Ltd v Hambro Life Assurance Ltd* (1984) 269 Estates Gazette 41 at 46). See also *195 Crown Street Pty Ltd v Hoare* [1969] 1 NSWR 193 at 196f, 200.

12 (1984) 270 Estates Gazette 643 at 650.

13 Here the original tenant was held liable for arrears amounting to £110,000. For a critical view of the vulnerability of the original lessee who is exposed to liability on any terms which a subsequent (and possibly hard-pressed) assignee may be forced to accept, see (1984) 81 Law Soc Gaz 2214 at 2215 (K. Reynolds).

14 (1983) 46 P & CR 393 at 396ff.

15 (1983) 46 P & CR 393 at 396.

16 (1983) 46 P & CR 393 at 398. This practice of subletting has been criticised by the Law Commission (see Law Com No 174 (1988), paras 2.19, 3.21).

17 'Of course the expectation, commercially speaking, is that the assignee will pay, but the assignor does not by assignment get rid of one jot or tittle of his original liability' (*Allied London Investments Ltd v Hambro Life Assurance Ltd* (1984) 270 Estates Gazette 948 at 950 per Harman J).

recourse to the liability fixed on T.[18] T cannot complain if L has unilaterally agreed to release a third party guarantor of A3's obligations.[19] Nor if, as may frequently be the case, A3 has become insolvent, does a disclaimer of the lease by A3's trustee in bankruptcy in any way release T from liability to payment: the position is almost certainly quite the reverse.[20] It is not even open to T to argue that the landlord, in granting a licence permitting A2 to assign to A3, owed T a duty of care to assess the creditworthiness of A3 or to take timely measures to enforce the relevant covenants against A3.[1]

(iv) Increasing recourse to the 'ultimate' liability of T In realistic commercial terms the primary target for enforcement in the event of breaches occurring after assignment is usually the defaulting assignee himself. In the modern context of endemic corporate insolvency, however, it is increasingly common that a landlord should seek recourse to the ultimate contract-based liability of the original tenant. For many original tenants such enforcement comes as a wholly unanticipated (and financially disastrous) form of liability.[2] The courts have nevertheless felt bound to enforce the ultimate contractual liability of the original tenant in a surprisingly wide range of circumstances, it being entirely irrelevant that after assignment the original tenant is almost always unable to ensure compliance with the leasehold covenants.[3]

There is nevertheless one respect in which the strictly contractual origin of the tenant's liability may be beneficial. In *City of London Corpn v Fell*,[4] the Court of Appeal declined to hold an original tenant liable for rent unpaid by an assignee during a statutory extension of the latter's term pursuant to Part II of the Landlord and Tenant Act 1954.[5] In a move which may

18 'It has long been the law that the landlord may sue either the original lessee or the assignee, or both at the same time' (*Norwich Union Life Insurance Society v Low Profile Fashions Ltd* (1992) 64 P & CR 187 at 192 per Beldam LJ). The lessor cannot, of course, recover twice over for the same breach of covenant by an assignee: the remedies are alternative not cumulative (*Brett v Cumberland* (1619) Cro Jac 521 at 523, 79 ER 446 at 447).

19 See *Allied London Investments Ltd v Hambro Life Assurance Ltd* (1984) 269 Estates Gazette 41 at 42ff.

20 See *Warnford Investments Ltd v Duckworth* [1979] Ch 127 at 138G–139A; *MEPC plc v Scottish Amicable Life Assurance Society* (1993) *Times*, 6 April.

1 *Norwich Union Life Insurance Society v Low Profile Fashions Ltd* (1992) 64 P & CR 187 at 190f. Beldam LJ pointed out (at 191) that in the original lease T could have stipulated for a requirement that L must take a direct covenant from A2—as is frequently done—the result of which covenant would have been to ensure the continuing liability of A2 whose financial strength T had indeed been able to verify.

2 See eg *RPH Ltd v Mirror Group Newspapers and Mirror Group Holdings* (1992) 65 P & CR 252 at 254ff (where the original tenant was held liable for accrued rent arrears of over £2 million unpaid by Maxwell Communication Corporation plc. It was an added irony that the landlord here was another Maxwell company, itself in administrative receivership). See also Law Com No 174 (1988), paras 3.7f.

3 It is immaterial, for instance, that after his assignment to A2, T is powerless to compel A2 to carry out covenanted repairs or other obligations imposed on T by the original lease (*Thames Manufacturing Co Ltd v Perrotts (Nichol & Peyton) Ltd* (1984) 271 Estates Gazette 284 at 286).

4 [1993] 2 WLR 710 at 716E-G. See [1992] Conv 67 (D. Evans); [1993] Conv 164 (P.F. Smith).

5 Post, p 887.

be symptomatic of increasing judicial unease with the proliferating recourse to the original tenant's ultimate liability,[6] the strict contractual term was made to mark the boundary of the tenant's continuing liability.[7]

(v) T's rights to indemnity If the defaults of a subsequent assignee cause T to be made answerable in damages or arrears of rent, T has at least in theory certain rights of indemnity. It is not uncommon for each assignment of the tenant's term to contain an express covenant by the assignee to indemnify the assignor against liability for further breach.[8] A similar right of indemnity may also arise by statutory implication[9] or by way of quasi-contract.[10] The entitlement to indemnity is nevertheless apt to prove ineffective precisely because the defaulting assignee is usually insolvent.[11] Moreover, chains of indemnity covenants suffer from their obvious vulnerability to breakdown where one of the intermediate assignees becomes insolvent or disappears.[12] T may be unable to enforce the indemnity against an assignee further down the chain without having obtained an express assignment of the benefit of the particular covenant which it is sought to enforce. Such an assignment is not always forthcoming.[13] The only ray of light for T is that if the leasehold obligations taken over by a later assignee are then guaranteed by a solvent stranger, the latter's liability as guarantor is deemed to be prior to that

6 See also *RPH Ltd v Mirror Group Newspapers and Mirror Group Holdings* (1992) 65 P & CR 252 at 253 per Nicholls V-C.

7 Compare, however, *Herbert Duncan Ltd v Cluttons* [1993] 2 WLR 710 at 718E–G (express covenant to pay rent not only during contractual term but also during statutory extension).

8 There seems to have been a tendency for this practice of express indemnity to fall into desuetude because of the implied statutory covenant of indemnity (see *Johnsey Estates Ltd v Lewis and Manley (Engineering) Ltd* (1987) 54 P & CR 296 at 301).

9 Law of Property Act 1925, s 77; Land Registration Act 1925, s 24(1)(b). See *Johnsey Estates Ltd v Lewis and Manley (Engineering) Ltd* (1987) 54 P & CR 296 at 298ff.

10 *Moule v Garrett* (1872) LR 7 Exch 101 at 104; *Selous Street Properties Ltd v Oronel Fabrics Ltd* (1984) 270 Estates Gazette 643 at 747f. See Lord Goff of Chieveley and Gareth Jones, *The Law of Restitution* (3rd edn, London 1986), pp 310, 312ff. If T is made liable for the default not of A2 but of A3, T's right of indemnity is available against A3 directly (see *Moule v Garrett*, supra at 103f).

11 Insolvency on the part of the defaulting assignee is almost certainly the reason why L is suing T rather than the actual wrongdoer (see eg *Warnford Investments Ltd v Duckworth* [1979] Ch 127). T's right to indemnity usually provides only illusory comfort since T can recover no more from a man of straw than L could recover in respect of the primary liability for breach of covenant. It may therefore be prudent for the otherwise defenceless assignor, if possessed of sufficient bargaining power (but see (1983) 127 SJ 832 (G.L. Leigh)), expressly to reserve a right of re-entry against his assignee in the event of any breach by the latter for which the assignor is made liable. See eg *Shiloh Spinners Ltd v Harding* [1973] AC 691 (ante, pp 73, 151, 807).

12 In *RPH Ltd v Mirror Group Newspapers and Mirror Group Holdings* (1992) 65 P & CR 252, there had been successive assignments of the leasehold term to A2, A3 and A4. Of these assignees only A3 was now clearly solvent, but Nicholls V-C rejected an application by T that A2 be directed to enforce its right of indemnity against A3. (All the assignees here were parts of the corporate conglomerate controlled by the late Robert Maxwell.)

13 In *RPH Ltd v Mirror Group Newspapers and Mirror Group Holdings* (1992) 65 P & CR 252 at 254ff, Nicholls V-C declined to order the insolvent A2 to assign to T the benefit of A3's indemnity covenant to A2. (The only winners were presumably the receivers of L, also a Maxwell company, whose recovery from the solvent T went to diminish the appalling shortfall suffered by the Maxwell pensioners.)

of T as the original contractual tenant. In consequence T, if sued in respect of the assignee's default, is entitled to be indemnified by the guarantor.[14]

(vi) Proposals for reform The enforcement of a continuing contractual liability against the original lessee has been so widely and bitterly criticised that in 1985 the Law Commission was moved to examine the operation of the privity of contract principle in the leasehold relationship.[15] The Commission acknowledged the intrinsic unfairness of continuing liability and recognised that landlords are often given excessive protection at the expense of tenants who have long since ceased to have any interest in the leasehold property.[16] In 1988 the Commission reported its conclusion that the principle of enduring contractual privity unjustifiably duplicates the liability which arises against the original tenant's assignees by reason of privity of estate.[17] In the Commission's view, leasehold covenants should bind the parties only while they continue to own their respective interests in the property. Accordingly the Commission recommended that the law be reformed to ensure that the liability of the original tenant on the covenants of a lease (and his corresponding entitlement to the benefits of the lease) should not in general survive assignment by that tenant but should terminate at this point.[18] The Commission also proposed that the parties in the leasehold relationship should not be free, by private agreement, to reinstate the principle of enduring contractual privity.[19]

(b) L's liability survives assignment of the reversion

It follows from the contractual nature of the initial leasehold commitment that L's liability on the covenants of the lease likewise survives the assignment of his reversion to A1 (or later to A4),[20] unless the covenants in question clearly impose liability only on the person who for the time being owns the reversionary estate.[1]

14 See *Becton Dickinson U.K. Ltd v Zwebner* [1989] QB 208 at 217F–218C; [1989] Conv 292 (P. McLoughlin). See also *Kumar v Dunning* [1989] QB 193 at 200A–B per Browne-Wilkinson V-C.

15 *Landlord and Tenant: Privity of Contract and Estate; Duration of Liability of Parties to Leases* (Law Commission Working Paper No 95, March 1986).

16 Working Paper No 95, paras 3.1ff.

17 *Landlord and Tenant: Privity of Contract and Estate* (Law Com No 174, 29 November 1988), paras 3.5ff; Working Paper No 95, paras 3.17ff. See [1989] Conv 145 (H.W.W.).

18 Law Com No 174 (1988), paras 4.3ff; Working Paper No 95, para 6.2. The Commission proposed, however, that the original tenant should not be released from liability if the landlord's consent is required to the assignment and the landlord can prove that it is reasonable that the tenant should guarantee the immediate successor's liability (Law Com No 174 (1988), para 4.11).

19 Law Com No 174 (1988), paras 4.57f.

20 *Stuart v Joy* [1904] 1 KB 362 at 367f. L's vulnerability to an action based on his original covenants not only survives the assignment of his reversion to A1, but can even provide the basis for action against him by an assignee of T's term of years eg by A2 or A3 (see *Celsteel Ltd v Alton House Holdings Ltd* (No 2) [1987] 1 WLR 291 at 296D–E; [1986] 1 WLR 666 at 672G–H. See also Law of Property Act 1925, s 142(2). In such cases L is rendered liable to a party with whom he may have enjoyed neither privity of contract nor privity of estate.

1 *Bath v Bowles* (1905) 93 LT 801 at 805.

(2) Liability of T to A1

Whereas the liability inter se of L and T rests, sometimes controversially, on *privity of contract*, any assignment of the estate held by either brings into operation a series of principles based on *privity of estate.*

(a) The far-reaching effects of privity of estate

It is privity of estate which permits the contractual rights and obligations of L and T to be diffused throughout the complex of leasehold relationships which begins to emerge when either L or T assigns his interest in the land. As Nourse LJ pointed out in *City of London Corpn v Fell*,[2] these rights and obligations 'assume a wider significance, becoming. . .imprinted on the term or the reversion as the case may be, enforceable between the owners thereof for the time being as conditions of the enjoyment of their respective estates.'[3] In this sense the device of privity of estate does something which the doctrine of contractual privity is essentially concerned to prevent, ie it confers a third-party impact upon essentially contractual arrangements. Moreover, by allowing the contractual obligations of L and T to become 'imprinted' on the relevant estate, this form of privity results in the creation of a tenancy which 'is capable of existence as a species of property independently of the contract.'[4]

(b) The statutory effect of assignment of the landlord's reversion

The liability of T towards A1, although based essentially on privity of estate,[5] has for centuries been reinforced by a statutory confirmation of the rights of assignees of the landlord's reversion. Under section 141(1) of the Law of Property Act 1925,[6] the assignment of L's reversionary estate to A1 passes to A1 the benefit of all the covenants and conditions originally entered into by T in so far as these obligations have 'reference to the subject-matter' of the lease.[7]

(c) Covenants which 'touch and concern' the demised land

The reference in section 141(1) to covenants which have 'reference to the subject-matter' of the lease means in effect that A1 receives the benefit of

2 [1993] 2 WLR 710 at 715D.
3 Nourse LJ was careful to add the rider that the contractual rights and obligations enjoy this wider effect only 'so far as they touch and concern the land' (post, p 856).
4 *City of London Corpn v Fell* [1993] 2 WLR 710 at 716B per Nourse LJ.
5 Post, p 865.
6 This provision originates in the Grantees of Reversions Act 1540 (32 Hen VIII, c 34). See *Thursby v Plant* (1668) 1 Wms Saund 237 at 240, 85 ER 268 at 270, for the statement that this statute 'transferred the privity of contract'. See also *Bickford v Parson* (1848) 5 CB 920 at 930, 136 ER 1141 at 1145, where Wilde CJ held that the 1540 Act 'annexes, or rather creates, a privity of contract between those who have privity of estate'.
7 Since section 141(1) is bounded by reference to the lessee's covenants, it can clearly have no reference to undertakings entered into by a third party. A1 cannot, for instance, claim pursuant to section 141(1) to have received the benefit of a third party's surety covenant in respect of the due performance of T's obligations under the lease (see *Kumar v Dunning* [1989] QB 193 at 200A–C per Browne-Wilkinson V-C; *P. & A. Swift Investments v Combined English Stores Group Plc* [1989] AC 632 at 639G per Lord Oliver of Aylmerton (post, p 857)).

only those covenants which, in the older terminology, 'touch and concern' the demised premises.[8]

(i) Purpose of the 'touch and concern' requirement The 'touch and concern' requirement has no application to the original lessor and lessee, whose relationship is governed by the totality of their contractual stipulations. The 'touch and concern' requirement aims, by contrast, to impose some restriction on the kinds of contractual obligation which may be allowed to benefit and burden third parties who are brought within the ambit of a leasehold relationship by privity of estate. It is not clear that all of the contractual arrangements fixed by L and T should necessarily have an automatic binding effect on such participants.[9] In so far as privity of estate converts private contracts into potentially long-term arrangements for the governance of land use, the 'touch and concern' test is intended to operate as a silent filtering device for the exclusion of certain categories of covenant which are deemed not to deserve such durable impact.[10]

The practical consequence of the 'touch and concern' criterion is that not every covenant contained in a lease is enforceable outside the immediate contractual nexus of lessor and lessee.[11] The professed purpose of the 'touch and concern' test is that such extensive effect should be confined to those covenants which intrinsically affect 'the landlord in his normal capacity as landlord or the tenant in his normal capacity as tenant'.[12] By the application of this test it is thought to withhold long-term effect from leasehold rights and obligations which are of substantially personal or private significance for the parties to the lease.

(ii) Definition of 'touching and concerning' Although the general purpose of the 'touch and concern' requirement may be easily identified, more precise definitions of 'touching and concerning' have proved elusive.[13] It is notoriously difficult to propose a definition of 'touching and concerning' which is not flawed by circularity. The ascertainment of 'touching and concerning' quality is ultimately self-determining if guided only by the proposition that 'touching and concerning' covenants are those which affect parties in their generic

8 It has been accepted that the two sets of terminology are merely differing formulations of the same idea. See *Hua Chiao Commercial Bank Ltd v Chiaphua Industries Ltd* [1987] AC 99 at 106H–107A per Lord Oliver of Aylmerton; *Davis v Town Properties Investment Corporation Ltd* [1903] 1 Ch 797 at 805; *Breams Property Investment Co Ltd v Stroulger* [1948] 2 KB 1 at 7; *Dalegrove Pty Ltd v Isles Parking Station Pty Ltd* (1988) 12 NSWLR 546 at 555D; *Auscott Ltd v Panizza* (1988) NSW Conv R 55-395 at 57,666 per Bryson J.

9 'The line of cleavage between covenants which do and do not touch or concern the land has always been somewhat artificial, but it expresses the principle that not every contractual provision can be turned into an interest in land, since interests in land must be of finite and familiar character' ([1957] CLJ 148 at 149 (H.W.R. Wade)).

10 'In short, through the exercise of the touch and concern test, the judiciary is vested with power to fix the ambits of private planning' (U. Reichman, *Judicial Supervision of Servitudes*, 7 J Legal Stud 139 at 140 (1978)).

11 See *Thursby v Plant* (1668) 1 Wms Saund 237 at 239f, 85 ER 268 at 269.

12 See *Hua Chiao Commercial Bank Ltd v Chiaphua Industries Ltd* [1987] AC 99 at 107B per Lord Oliver of Aylmerton.

13 See the similar difficulties inherent in identifying the categories of rights which 'benefit' or 'accommodate' a dominant tenement in the law of easements and restrictive covenants (post, pp 1065, 1145).

character as landlord or tenant respectively. As Lord Oliver of Aylmerton put it in *Hua Chiao Commercial Bank Ltd v Chiaphua Industries Ltd*,[14] to ask whether a particular covenant 'affects the landlord qua landlord or the tenant qua tenant is an exercise which begs the question. It does so only if it runs with the reversion or with the land respectively.'[15]

In *P. & A. Swift Investments v Combined English Stores Group Plc*,[16] Lord Oliver was later to proffer his own guide to a 'satisfactory working test' for identifying 'touching and concerning' covenants.[17] *First*, such a covenant must benefit only the reversioner for the time being, so that, if separated from the reversion, it ceases to be of benefit to the covenantee. *Second*, the covenant must affect the nature, quality, mode of user or value of the land of the reversioner. *Third*, the covenant must not be expressed to be personal (ie must not have been given only to a specific reversioner or in respect of the obligations only of a specific tenant).[18]

Analysed thus, the requirement of 'touch and concern' operates largely to limit the enforcement of leasehold covenants to those promises in whose due performance the respective estate owners under a lease have a peculiar economic interest *qua estate owner*.[19] A 'touching and concerning' covenant is thus demarcated from those other covenants, albeit contained in the same lease, in whose due performance the promisee has no higher or more distinctive economic interest than he would if he were not a party to the lease.[20]

(iii) 'Touching and concerning' covenants undertaken by a tenant Although a certain artificiality may attach to the definition of 'touching and concerning' covenants, it has not in practice proved excessively difficult to identify which leasehold covenants by a tenant 'touch and concern' the demised premises.[1] Amongst the category of covenants accepted as having this quality are positive covenants such as the covenant by the tenant to pay rent[2] or to repair

14 [1987] AC 99 at 112F.
15 This vitiating factor probably also afflicts the classic test, articulated in *Mayor of Congleton v Pattison* (1808) 10 East 130 at 135, 103 ER 725 at 727, which defined a covenant as having 'touching and concerning' quality if it 'affected the nature, quality, or value of the thing demised, independently of collateral circumstances; or if it affected the mode of enjoying it.' See also *Rogers v Hosegood* [1900] 2 Ch 388 at 395.
16 [1989] AC 632 at 642E–F. See J.E. Adams, *'Touching and Concerning', from Spencer's Case to Swift* [1989] EG 24 (25 November).
17 In so doing Lord Oliver claimed not to 'expound an exhaustive guide'.
18 See also *Lang v Asemo Pty Ltd* [1989] VR 773 at 776.
19 See J.E. Stake, *Toward an Economic Understanding of Touch and Concern*, (1988) Duke LJ 925.
20 'The general principle is, that if the performance of the covenant be beneficial to the reversioner, in respect of the lessor's demand, and to no other person, his assignee may sue upon it; but if it be beneficial to the lessor, without regard to his continuing owner of the estate, it is a mere collateral covenant, upon which the assignee cannot sue' (*Vyvyan v Arthur* (1823) 1 B & C 410 at 417, 107 ER 152 at 155 per Best J).
1 Although a covenant which does not intrinsically 'touch and concern' cannot by agreement between landlord and tenant be made to run with the land, a covenant which would otherwise run can be cut back by the express terms of the lease and made purely personal to the parties (see *In re Robert Stephens & Co Ltd* [1915] 1 Ch 802 at 808; *Re Rakita's Application* [1971] Qd R 59 at 65).
2 *Parker v Webb* (1693) 3 Salk 5, 91 ER 656; *Kumar v Dunning* [1989] QB 193 at 200F–G per Browne-Wilkinson V-C; *P. & A. Swift Investments v Combined English Stores Group Plc* [1989] AC 632 at 641F–G per Lord Oliver of Aylmerton.

the premises[3] or insure them against fire,[4] or to cultivate land in a particular manner.[5] Likewise the 'touch and concern' test has been held to be satisfied by such negative covenants as the tenant's undertaking to use property for domestic purposes only[6] and not to assign the lease without the lessor's consent.[7]

(iv) Purely personal or collateral covenants In effect only covenants by the tenant which are of a purely personal or collateral nature fall outside the ambit of 'touching and concerning' covenants. Examples of such covenants would include a covenant to perform some personal service for the landlord, a covenant to pay an annual sum to a third party,[8] and a covenant for forfeiture of the lease on the criminal conviction of the tenant or any occupier of the land.[9]

(v) Surety covenants In recent times A1's remedies in respect of breach by T have been significantly enhanced in practice by the availability of recourse against a third party who has guaranteed the due performance of T's covenants. Where a guarantor has entered into a surety covenant with L, the covenant is, of course, enforceable by L on straightforward contractual principles and the guarantor's liability, unless modified, is coextensive with that of T. A difficulty arises, however, where L assigns his reversion to A1. It becomes questionable whether, in the absence of any express assignment by L to A1 of the benefit of the guarantee,[10] A1 can enforce the surety covenant against the guarantor. A1 has, of course, no privity of contract or estate with the guarantor.[11]

The problem was finally resolved in *P. & A. Swift Investments v Combined English Stores Group Plc.*[12] Here, in a case of default on the tenant's rent obligation, the House of Lords resorted to the general common law rules

3 *Matures v Westwood* (1598) Cro Eliz 599 at 600, 78 ER 842; *Williams v Earle* (1868) LR 3 QB 739 at 751f; *Kumar v Dunning* [1989] QB 193 at 200F–G; *P. & A. Swift Investments v Combined English Stores Group Plc* [1989] AC 632 at 641F–G.
4 *Vernon v Smith* (1821) 5 B & Ald 1 at 6ff, 106 ER 1094 at 1096ff.
5 *Chapman v Smith* [1907] 2 Ch 97 at 103.
6 *Wilkinson v Rogers* (1864) 2 De GJ & Sm 62 at 67ff, 46 ER 298 at 300f.
7 *Williams v Earle* (1868) LR 3 QB 739 at 749f; *Goldstein v Sanders* [1915] 1 Ch 549 at 556; *Cohen v Popular Restaurants Ltd* [1917] 1 KB 480 at 482; *Burns Philp Hardware Ltd v Howard Chia Pty Ltd* (1986) 8 NSWLR 621 at 640G.
8 *Mayho v Buckhurst* (1617) Cro Jac 438 at 439, 79 ER 374 at 375.
9 *Stevens v Copp* (1868) LR 4 Exch 20 at 24ff (sed quaere).
10 Such express assignments were relatively uncommon until the ruling in *Pinemain Ltd v Welbeck International Ltd* (1984) 272 Estates Gazette 1166 at 1169ff, where the Court of Appeal overturned the prevalent assumption in practice that the benefit of surety covenants ran generally with the reversionary estate. See [1986] Conv 50 (S. Murdoch)). See also *P. & A. Swift Investments v Combined English Stores Group Plc* [1989] AC 632 at 635H, 636H.
11 A1 cannot plead the benefit of section 141 of the Law of Property Act 1925, which applies only to covenants between landlord and tenant (see *P. & A. Swift Investments v Combined English Stores Group Plc* [1989] AC 632 at 639G-H per Lord Oliver of Aylmerton (ante, p 854)).
12 [1989] AC 632 (post, p 1128).

on the enforcement of covenants[13] in upholding the liability of the guarantor to the assignee of the landlord's reversion. Lord Templeman thought that a surety's covenant in support of a 'touching and concerning' covenant undertaken by a tenant 'must itself be a covenant which touches and concerns the land'.[14] On this basis, even in the absence of express assignment of the guarantee, the benefit of the surety's covenant must run with the landlord's reversion in favour of the assignee. In Lord Templeman's view, the tenant's surety is thus rendered a 'quasi tenant who volunteers to be a substitute or twelfth man for the tenant's team', with the result that the surety is 'subject to the same rules and regulations as the player he replaces.'[15]

Lord Oliver of Aylmerton reinforced the 'touching and concerning' quality of the surety covenant, noting that the primary obligation of the guarantor was identical to that of the tenant, 'namely that that which is covenanted to be done will be done'.[16] Provided that the other characteristics of a 'touching and concerning' covenant were present and that the covenant was 'connected with something to be done on, to or in relation to the land',[17] Lord Oliver declared that the mere fact that the surety covenant envisaged the payment of a sum of money would not prevent it from running with the landlord's reversion.[18]

Although far from free of difficulties,[19] the House of Lords' decision in *P. & A. Swift Investments v Combined English Stores Group Plc* has certainly clarified the law of surety covenants to the commercial advantage of landlords. In *Coronation Street Industrial Properties Ltd v Ingall Industries Plc*[20] the House of Lords confirmed the approach adopted in *P. & A. Swift Investments* and applied it where a guarantor had covenanted as surety to take over the unexpired term of the tenant's lease in the event of any disclaimer of the lease by a liquidator. In allowing the benefit of this covenant to be claimed by an assignee of the landlord's reversion, Lord Templeman viewed this particular form of surety covenant as 'touching and concerning' the land 'in equal measure' to a mere covenant for payment as in *P. & A. Swift Investments*. Both types of covenant simply gave 'effect to the surety's obligation to procure compliance with the terms of the old lease'.[1] Here, as a result

13 Post, p 1128.
14 [1989] AC 632 at 637H. See also Lord Oliver of Aylmerton at 641G–H; *Kumar v Dunning* [1989] QB 193 at 200H per Browne-Wilkinson V-C. See [1988] CLJ 180 (C. Harpum).
15 [1989] AC 632 at 638A.
16 [1989] AC 632 at 642C.
17 Ante, p 855.
18 [1989] AC 632 at 642F.
19 It may be difficult to reconcile *P. & A. Swift Investments* with the Privy Council's ruling in *Hua Chiao Commercial Bank Ltd v Chiaphua Industries Ltd* [1987] AC 99 (post, p 861). If a *landlord's* promise to pay money does not run with the landlord's reversion, it seems odd that a stranger's promise of payment should so run. The decision in *Hua Chiao* was expressly based, after all, on the consideration that the promise to repay the tenant's deposit was a money transaction undertaken by the landlord 'qua payee rather than qua landlord' ([1987] AC 99 at 112H–113A per Lord Oliver of Aylmerton). A further difficulty with *P. & A. Swift Investments* may be the possibility that guarantors, if made liable on a surety covenant, may seek rights to relief against forfeiture (see R.R. Sethu, (1989) 5 Australian Bar Rev 153 at 166).
20 [1989] 1 WLR 304.
1 [1989] 1 WLR 304 at 307E–F.

of the liquidator's disclaimer of the tenant's lease, the tenant retired 'mortally wounded' and the surety was 'the substitute.'[2]

(d) L's remedies after assignment of the reversion

Section 141(1) of the Law of Property Act 1925 provides explicitly that, on assignment of the landlord's reversionary estate, the benefit of all 'touching and concerning' covenants of the tenant 'shall be annexed and incident to and shall go with the reversionary estate in the land'. This wording has been held to effect a statutory transfer from L to A1 of the whole benefit of the 'touching and concerning' covenants originally made by T to L.[3] When L assigns his reversion to A1, A1 therefore acquires an exclusive right to sue in respect of all breaches of covenant whensoever committed.[4] L henceforth loses the right of action, and A1 is entitled to any appropriate remedy even in respect of breaches committed prior to the date of assignment,[5] unless these breaches were waived by L.[6]

Pursuant to section 141(1), the assignment to A1 leaves L with none of the benefit previously derived from T's leasehold covenants. This does not, however, mean that the assignment has freed L of the *burden* of his own original covenants. In the absence of contrary agreement L remains liable throughout the entire term on all the landlord's covenants contained in the lease.[7] L may therefore be sued by T in respect of defaults committed by L while T was in possession, notwithstanding that T has since assigned his term to A2.[8] L may even be sued by A2 or A3 on such covenants as 'touch and concern' the land.[9]

(3) Liability of A1 to T

The liability of A1 to T, although founded on privity of estate, also rests now on a statutory base. In accordance with section 142(1) of the Law of Property Act 1925, the assignment of L's reversionary estate to A1 passes to A1 the burden of all the covenants and conditions originally entered

2 [1989] 1 WLR 304 at 309B-C.

3 See *City and Metropolitan Properties Ltd v Greycroft Ltd* [1987] 1 WLR 1085 at 1087E.

4 It is irrelevant for this purpose that T assigned his term of years to A2 before L's assignment of the reversion in favour of A1 and that 'privity of estate' (post, p 865) never existed between A1 and T (see *Arlesford Trading Co Ltd v Servansingh* [1971] 1 WLR 1080 at 1082F-G).

5 *In re King, decd* [1963] Ch 459 at 488f, 497 (damages for L's breach of covenant to rebuild); *London & County (A. & D.) Ltd v Wilfred Sportsman Ltd* [1971] Ch 764 at 784D (right of re-entry in respect of rent arrears); *Arlesford Trading Co Ltd v Servansingh* [1971] 1 WLR 1080 at 1082E–F (right to sue for arrears of rent).

6 *London & County (A. & D.) Ltd v Wilfred Sportsman Ltd* [1971] Ch 764 at 783B.

7 In this sense there is parity between the continuing liabilities of the original landlord and tenant. The Law Commission has noted, however, that the privity of contract principle, although applying equally to both, bears more heavily on the tenant in practice simply because 'in the majority of leases the tenant undertakes many more obligations than does the landlord' (see Law Com No 174 (1988), para 2.1).

8 *City and Metropolitan Properties Ltd v Greycroft Ltd* [1987] 1 WLR 1085 at 1087F–H. See [1987] Conv 374 (P.F. Smith).

9 *Celsteel Ltd v Alton House Holdings Ltd* (No 2) [1986] 1 WLR 666 at 672H. On the danger of a multiplicity of actions against L, see *City and Metropolitan Properties Ltd v Greycroft Ltd* [1987] 1 WLR 1085 at 1087H-1088D; P.F. Smith, [1990] Conv 335 at 345.

into by L[10] in so far as the obligations contained therein 'have reference to the subject-matter of the lease'. However, as is the general rule with assignees,[11] A1's liability extends only to defaults occurring during the period of his possession as assignee of the reversionary estate. A1 cannot therefore be made liable in respect of breaches committed by L prior to the assignment.[12]

(a) *'Touching and concerning' covenants undertaken by a landlord*

Once again the obligations undertaken by L which 'have reference to the subject-matter of the lease' are those which, in the older formulation, 'touch and concern' the demised premises. 'Touching and concerning' covenants include covenants by L to renew the lease,[13] to repair or to insure the demised premises, to supply water to those premises,[14] to give T quiet possession of the premises,[15] and not to develop adjoining land.[16] L's covenant that the rent paid by T should be inclusive of rates likewise 'touches and concerns'.[17] The burden of all such covenants runs automatically with the land so as to bind the reversionary estate in the hands of A1.

(b) *Criticism of the 'touch and concern' requirement*

Recent years have seen increasing criticism of the 'touch and concern' requirement in its application to both landlord and tenant covenants.[18] The requirement seeks, of course, to identify covenants which are integral (as distinct from merely collateral) to the leasehold relationship, but the precise content of the 'touch and concern' criterion is difficult to pin down. One supporter of the 'touch and concern' test has observed that '[t]he phrase "touch and concern" continues to beguile even astute property specialists into believing that it has some objective meaning.'[19] It has been suggested that the concept ultimately concerns the 'normal expectations of society'

10 A 'covenant' within section 142(1) need not be contained in a deed or comprise a covenant under seal. It may even arise outside the document which constitutes the lease (see *Weg Motors Ltd v Hales* [1962] Ch 49 at 73, 76f; but compare *Eden Park Estates Ltd v Longman* (Unreported, Court of Appeal, 19 May 1980)). However, a covenant comes within section 142(1) only if it was actually 'entered into by a lessor'. It is not enough that it would have been inserted into the lease if the lessee had chosen to claim an equity of rectification in his favour (see *Squire v C. Brewer & Sons Ltd* (Unreported, Court of Appeal, 15 July 1983) per Slade LJ).

11 Post, p 866.

12 *Pettiward Estates v Shephard* [1986] 6 CL 173; *Duncliffe v Caerfelin Properties Ltd* [1989] 2 EGLR 38 at 39M-40B; [1990] Conv 126 (J.E. Martin). See also D. Gordon, [1987] Conv 103 at 105.

13 *Richardson v Sydenham* (1703) 2 Vern 447, 23 ER 885; *Simpson v Clayton* (1838) 4 Bing (NC) 758 at 780, 132 ER 981 at 989; *Woodall v Clifton* [1905] 2 Ch 257 at 279.

14 *Jourdain v Wilson* (1821) 4 B & Ald 266 at 267, 106 ER 935.

15 *Celsteel Ltd v Alton House Holdings Ltd* (No 2) [1986] 1 WLR 666 at 672H.

16 *Ricketts v Enfield Churchwardens* [1909] 1 Ch 544 at 555.

17 *Squire v C. Brewer & Sons Ltd* (Unreported, Court of Appeal, 15 July 1983) per Fox LJ.

18 The criticism is not new but merely intensified. See eg *Woodall v Clifton* [1905] 2 Ch 257 at 279 per Romer LJ. The 'touch and concern' requirement is found in many, but not all, common law jurisdictions. Compare, for instance, the disparaging remarks made by Gibson J in the Irish Court of Appeal in *Lyle v Smith* [1909] 2 IR 58 at 76.

19 G.S. Alexander, *Freedom, Coercion, and the Law of Servitudes*, 73 Cornell L Rev 883 at 897 (1987-88).

as to whether particular benefits or burdens are so closely related to estate ownership 'that the average person would assume that the law would decree that such benefit or burden would accompany the ownership'.[20]

On this basis the 'touch and concern' requirement may do no more than impose a trained but essentially intuitive judgment as to the kinds of benefit and burden which should be allowed to run indefinitely with land. One commentator has urged an abandonment of the 'rhetoric of touch and concern' on the ground that it merely conceals behind 'a screen of hocus pocus' the exercise of a substantive judicial discretion to terminate certain kinds of privately bargained arrangement respecting the future conduct of estate owners.[1] Other commentators take a contrary view that the operation of this constraint on the long-term private ordering of landholding is conducive to efficient and productive land management.[2]

Whatever the merits of these positions, it emerges painfully clearly that the fundamental problem with the 'touch and concern' requirement stems from the arbitrary or inconsistent outcome of its operation.[3] 'Touching and concerning' covenants have been held, for instance, to include a tenant's covenant to retail only the landlord's brand of product on the demised premises[4] but not the correlative covenant by a landlord to avoid competition with the tenant's business.[5] Just as surprising may be the fact that a covenant not to employ a named individual on business premises has been declared to run with the land,[6] while a covenant not to employ a particular class of person on the property does not so run.[7] Other conclusions, even if based faithfully on some criterion of distinctive economic interest vested in the covenantee, seem either perverse or simply contrary to justice. This appears perhaps most markedly in relation to the following kinds of leasehold covenant.

(i) Security deposits In *Hua Chiao Commercial Bank Ltd v Chiaphua Industries Ltd*[8] T paid a security deposit to L at the commencement of the lease, the deposit to be repayable, in the absence of any breach of covenant by T, at the expiration of the term. At the end of the term (and no breach having occurred) T demanded the return of the deposit from A1, which had meanwhile taken an assignment of L's reversionary estate when L went into liquidation. The Judicial Committee of the Privy Council advised that A1 was not bound

20 L. Berger, *A Policy Analysis of Promises Respecting the Use of Land*, 55 Minnesota L Rev 167 at 219f (1970–71)). See also *Abbott v Bob's U-Drive*, 352 P2d 598 at 604 (Supreme Court of Oregon, 1960).

1 S.F. French, 73 Cornell L Rev 928 at 939f (1987–88) ('[t]he "touch and concern" requirement is more in the nature of an ex post control, operating after the fact to give the court a discretionary power to terminate a servitude').

2 See U. Reichman, 55 S Cal L Rev 1177 at 1233 (1982).

3 See eg *Grant v Edmondson* [1931] 1 Ch 1 at 28 per Romer LJ ('The established rules. . .are purely arbitrary, and the distinctions, for the most part, quite illogical'). See also *Burns Philp Hardware Ltd v Howard Chia Pty Ltd* (1986) 8 NSWLR 621 at 641A per Young J; *Auscott Ltd v Panizza* (1988) NSW ConvR 55-395 at 57,665f per Bryson J.

4 *Clegg v Hands* (1890) 44 Ch D 503 at 518, 522f (beer); *Regent Oil Co Ltd v J.A. Gregory (Hatch End) Ltd* [1966] Ch 402 at 431E–F, 432F (petrol).

5 *Thomas v Hayward* (1869) LR 4 Exch 311 at 312.

6 *Lewin v American & Colonial Distributors Ltd* [1945] Ch 225 at 235.

7 *Mayor of Congleton v Pattison* (1808) 10 East 130 at 135f, 103 ER 725 at 727.

8 [1987] AC 99.

to pay the deposit sum to T, thereby relegating T to a hopeless claim against the insolvent L. The Privy Council took the view that such security deposits are merely 'collateral' to the lease and here created only rights *in personam* between T and L.[9] Lord Oliver of Aylmerton agreed that the deposit had provided security for the due performance of T's obligations during the term, but concluded that not every covenant 'which is related, however obliquely, to some other obligation which touches and concerns the land necessarily takes on from that very relationship, the same character as regards transmissibility to or against successors in title.'[10] In the Privy Council's view it was 'more realistic' to regard the obligation to return the deposit as undertaken by 'the landlord qua payee rather than qua landlord.'[11] This outcome, although perhaps consistent with the idea that T had no higher economic interest in the return of his money than any person not a party to the lease, seems both flawed and contrary to normal expectations of transmissible benefit and burden.[12]

(ii) Options conferred by L on T Allegations of arbitrary outcome may be levelled with even more justification in the context of leasehold options. The 'touching and concerning' category has been held to include a lessor's covenant to renew the lease,[13] but not a lessor's covenant to sell the freehold reversion to the lessee,[14] nor a lessee's right of pre-emption in respect of the freehold.[15] Here the relevant distinction may rest on the basis that whereas an option of renewal can possibly be seen as a matter of peculiar interest to the lessee qua lessee, neither an option of purchase nor a right of pre-emption in respect of the freehold confers any greater benefit on the lessee than on any third party.[16] Indeed such rights affect the parties not qua lessor and lessee but qua vendor and purchaser, and are therefore truly 'collateral to the relationship of landlord and tenant'.[17] A freehold option is effectively an 'option in gross',[18]

9 See also *Eden Park Estates Ltd v Longman* (Unreported, Court of Appeal, 19 May 1980) (ante, p 212); *Re Dollar Land Corporation Ltd and Solomon* (1963) 39 DLR (2d) 221 at 226.
10 [1987] AC 99 at 112C–D. The obligation to return the deposit was 'bound up with the tenant's covenant only, as it were, at one remove' ([1987] AC 99 at 111D).
11 [1987] AC 99 at 112H–113A.
12 A1 had never, of course, received T's deposit money ([1987] AC 99 at 113B), but arguably took the risk that transmissible burdens encumbered the estate assigned to it.
13 *Richardson v Sydenham* (1703) 2 Vern 447, 23 ER 885; *Simpson v Clayton* (1838) 4 Bing (NC) 758 at 780, 132 ER 981 at 989; *Mercantile Credits Ltd v Shell Co of Australia Ltd* (1976) 136 CLR 326 at 344 per Gibbs J (ante, p 860).
14 *Woodall v Clifton* [1905] 2 Ch 257 at 279 per Romer LJ.
15 *Charles Frodsham & Co Ltd v Morris* (1974) 229 Estates Gazette 961 at 962.
16 A further distinction lies in the fact that the exercise of an option for renewal results in a continuance of the leasehold relationship, whereas the exercise of an option of freehold purchase destroys this relationship. In *Woodall v Clifton* [1905] 2 Ch 257 at 279, Romer LJ invoked this difference as a ground for declaring the latter species of option to be 'concerned with something wholly outside the relationship of landlord and tenant'. It may be questioned whether this view is equally tenable nowadays when leasehold enfranchisement and the 'right to buy' have become statutorily entrenched as increasingly valuable and integral features of the leasehold relationship (ante, pp 766, 772).
17 See *Griffith v Pelton* [1958] Ch 205 at 225; *Davenport Central Service Station Ltd v O'Connell* [1975] 1 NZLR 755 at 757.
18 *Griffith v Pelton* [1958] Ch 205 at 225 per Jenkins LJ.

and has been said to lie 'outside of the terms which regulate the relations between the landlord as landlord and the tenant as tenant'.[19]

On this basis the *benefit* of freehold options or rights of freehold pre-emption, albeit conferred in a lease, cannot run with the tenant's term by virtue of the doctrine of privity of estate. Such benefits are transmissible to the tenant's successors only by express assignment.[20] This result marks an anomalous contrast with the law relating to leasehold renewal options, although even here it is said that a lessor's covenant to renew a lease is a dubious case for inclusion within the category of 'touching and concerning' covenants.[1] Often nowadays courts concede only grudgingly that the benefit of an option of renewal runs automatically with the tenant's term, blaming the disparate treatment of tenants' options on four hundred years of established practice in the matter.[2]

The transmission of the *burden* of a tenant's option of freehold purchase is clearly determined nowadays as a matter of appropriate registration,[3] eased only by the possibility that the option may constitute an overriding interest in registered land.[4] The transmission of the burden of a tenant's option to renew the lease is, however, fraught with even graver complications. It was at first thought, with the enactment of section 142(1) of the Law of Property Act 1925, that the burden of L's covenant to renew T's lease would run with the land so as automatically to bind A1, the assignee of L's reversion.[5] This may still be true in respect of registered land, since T (if in actual occupation of the land or in receipt of the rents and profits thereof) can usually claim that his option for renewal constitutes an overriding interest.[6] In *Beesly v Hallwood Estates Ltd*,[7] however, Buckley J indicated—to the surprise of many[8]—that a lessee's option to renew his lease constitutes a registrable estate contract.[9] In unregistered land such a contract requires to be registered

19 *In re Leeds and Batley Breweries Ltd and Bradbury's Lease* [1920] 2 Ch 548 at 551f per Peterson J.

20 *Griffith v Pelton* [1958] Ch 205 at 225f; *Esther Investments Pty Ltd v Cherrywood Park Pty Ltd* [1986] WAR 279 at 283, 298; *Re Meewasin Valley Authority and Olfland Land Co Ltd* (1989) 51 DLR (4th) 638 at 639. For an intriguing suggestion that the benefit of a freehold option may be carried to the tenant's assignees by the equivalent of Law of Property Act 1925, s 78, see *Esther Investments*, supra at 299f per Brinsden J.

1 See eg *Muller v Trafford* [1901] 1 Ch 54 at 60; *Woodall v Clifton* [1905] 2 Ch 257 at 279. Compare, however, (1981) 125 SJ 816 at 817 (M.P. Thompson).

2 See eg *Phillips v Mobil Oil Co Ltd* [1989] 1 WLR 888 at 891E per Nicholls LJ. Compare, however, *Alcova Holdings Pty Ltd v Pandarlo Pty Ltd* (1988) 15 NSWLR 53 at 61A–B per Bryson J.

3 Ante, pp 144, 183. See *Phillips v Mobil Oil Co Ltd* [1989] 1 WLR 888 at 892G.

4 See *Webb v Pollmount Ltd* [1966] Ch 584 at 603C–D (ante, p 208).

5 See eg *Wolstenholme & Cherry's Conveyancing Statutes* (12th edn, London 1932), p 246.

6 Land Registration Act 1925, s 70(1)(g) (ante, p 203).

7 [1960] 1 WLR 549 at 557 (ante, p 144). See also *Taylors Fashions Ltd v Liverpool Victoria Trustees Co Ltd* [1982] QB 133 (Note) at 142G–143G; *Phillips v Mobil Oil Co Ltd* [1989] 1 WLR 888 at 893F–894E.

8 See eg *Taylors Fashions Ltd v Liverpool Victoria Trustees Co Ltd* [1982] QB 133 (Note) at 138B (ante, p 322). Compare the strongly critical view expressed in (1981) 125 SJ 816 at 817f (M.P. Thompson).

9 The option for renewal is thus put effectively on a par with a lessee's option to purchase the lessor's reversion, in that both rights now constitute estate contracts registrable by the lessee.

against the lessor prior to the assignment of the reversion,[10] and if not so registered becomes statutorily void against a purchaser of a legal estate for money or money's worth.[11]

This result means that the mere circumstance that T's option for renewal 'touches and concerns' the land is not in itself sufficient to make the option binding on most assignees of the reversion.[12] In *Beesly v Hallwood Estates Ltd*[13] Buckley J rejected the argument that the tenant's renewal option had been indelibly annexed to the land by Law of Property Act 1925, s 142(1), so that the burden ran with the reversion without the requirement of registration.[14] In effect the renewal option and the lease in which it is contained are to be treated as two essentially distinct proprietary phenomena.[15] The option is not simply a term of the lease, and the fact that T's lease remains enforceable against A1 following assignment by L in no way entails the consequence that A1 is also bound by such incidents of T's lease as the renewal option which it may contain.[16] What is protected on assignment is the tenancy itself 'and not the tenancy with all its incidents'.[17]

(iii) Proposed abolition of the 'touch and concern' requirement In recent years the Law Commission has noted that it is 'hard to discern a clear guiding principle' in some of the case law on 'touching and concerning' covenants.[18] The Commission has accepted that the arbitrary and inconsistent character of many of the distinctions made in this area have now rendered it desirable that the 'touch and concern' requirement should be eliminated altogether

10 Ante, p 144. Even in registered land the option for renewal should be protected by the entry of a minor interest in the register of the lessor's title (ante, p 181). However, an unprotected option, although ineffective as a minor interest (Land Registration Act 1925, s 59(6), ante, pp 187, 226), is often valid as an overriding interest.
11 Land Charges Act 1972, s 4(6).
12 In unregistered land the 'touching and concerning' quality of the covenant is almost entirely irrelevant to the question of its impact on A1, since A1 will be bound by an unregistered option only if he is someone other than a purchaser for money or money's worth (ie a donee).
13 [1960] 1 WLR 549 at 557f.
14 Section 142(1) applies in its terms only 'if and so far as the lessor has power to bind' the reversioner. Buckley J took the view that this section does not empower a lessor to bind a reversioner 'in respect of any obligation which the legislature has said shall not be enforceable against such reversioner.' An example of such an obligation was, in Buckley J's view, an unregistered estate contract, and the effect of the Land Charges Act is therefore 'to take such an obligation out of the scope of section 142 upon a purchase of the reversion for money or money's worth taking place while the obligation is unregistered.'
15 See eg *Markfaith Investment Ltd v Chiap Hua Flashlights Ltd* [1991] 2 AC 43 at 59A per Lord Templeman ('A covenant to renew at the option of the tenant is not a lease'). Thus the new lease obtained on the tenant's exercise of his renewal option does not impliedly contain the same options (for renewal or freehold purchase) as were included in the old lease (see *Sherwood v Tucker* [1924] 2 Ch 440 at 445ff; *Re Devine and Ferguson* [1947] 1 DLR 76 at 78ff; *Palmer v Ampersand Investments Ltd* (1985) 11 DLR (4th) 295 at 304ff; *Esther Investments Pty Ltd v Cherrywood Park Pty Ltd* [1986] WAR 279 at 284, 303f). An exception arises where the original renewal covenant expressly provided for a new lease 'on the same terms and conditions in all respects' as the existing lease, in which case the new lease must faithfully replicate the old lease (see *Batchelor v Murphy* [1926] AC 63 at 68ff; *Hill v Hill* [1947] Ch 231 at 242ff).
16 See *Friedman v Barrett, Ex parte Friedman* [1962] Qd R 498 at 509ff.
17 *Mercantile Credits Ltd v Shell Co of Australia Ltd* (1976) 136 CLR 326 at 347 per Gibbs J; *Re Davies* [1989] 1 Qd R 48 at 51 per McPherson J.
18 Law Com No 174 (1988), para 2.23.

from the law of leasehold enforcement.[19] Accordingly, in a report issed in 1988, the Commission recommended legislation to ensure that henceforth there should be no distinction between lease covenants which touch and concern the land and other covenants.[20] Such a proposal, if implemented, would further the more general view endorsed by the Commission that all the terms of a lease should be regarded as 'a single bargain for letting the property'. When the interest of one of the parties changes hands the successor should 'fully take his predecessor's place as landlord or tenant, without distinguishing between different categories of covenant'.[1]

(c) T's remedies after assignment of the term

Section 142(1) of the Law of Property Act 1925 affords T an important statutory basis for enforcement of leasehold covenants against A1. However, T is in the difficult position of having virtually no access to legal remedy (other than by way of indemnity) after assigning his term to A2. After the assignment T holds no estate in the land and therefore has no standing either to apply for relief against forfeiture of the lease[2] or to sue in respect of breaches of covenant committed by L (or by any subsequent assignee of the reversion). In effect the assignment of T's term has transferred with it the right to seek legal remedies appertaining to the estate assigned, while leaving T entirely vulnerable to action brought against him on his original leasehold covenants.

(4) Other forms of liability based on 'privity of estate'

For over four centuries it has been clear in English law that liability on the covenants of a legal lease may extend even beyond those parties who are affected by privity of contract or by its statutory extension to assignees of the reversion. The doctrine of privity of estate effectively 'imprints' the contractual obligations of the original landlord and tenant upon their respective estates with the result that such obligations, so far as they 'touch and concern' the land, bind these estates in the hands of third parties.[3]

(a) Binding impact of privity of estate

This consequence of privity of estate was first clearly spelt out in the historic ruling of the Court of King's Bench in *Spencer's Case*.[4] The Court held that leasehold covenants 'run with the land' so as to affect all assignees of the

19 The Commission suggested that the uneasy delineation of 'touching and concerning' covenants would normally cause more practical difficulty, were it not for the fact the implied statutory covenants of indemnity by assignees (ante, p 852) are not limited to undertakings of a 'touching and concerning' character and effectively perpetuate a continuing contractual liability on all covenants of the lease (Law Com No 174 (1988), para 3.20).

20 Law Com No 174 (1988), para 4.46.

1 Law Com No 174 (1988), para 4.1.

2 *Re Francini and Canuck Properties Ltd* (1982) 132 DLR (3d) 468 at 471.

3 See *City of London Corpn v Fell* [1993] 2 WLR 710 at 715D per Nourse LJ. See also *Picton-Warlow v Allendale Holdings Pty Ltd* [1988] WAR 107 at 110 per Brinsden J.

4 (1583) 5 Co Rep 16a at 17b, 77 ER 72 at 75.

term who are 'privy' to the relevant estate.[5] The original covenants thus reach far outside the immediate contractual nexus of landlord and tenant and provide a basis for enforcement so long as one paramount condition is met: *Spencer's Case* applies only to those leasehold covenants which 'touch and concern' the demised premises.[6] Given, however, that this condition is satisfied, the relevant covenants can be enforced by and against any person who is privy to the leasehold estate.

Irrespective of the nature or duration of the leasehold estate concerned, *Spencer's Case* still provides the linchpin of covenant enforcement. It is ultimately by virtue of this decision that the original covenants of every legal lease are made potentially binding on all subsequent assignees of either the term[7] or the reversion.[8] In *Fig.* 65,[9] therefore, both the benefit and the burden of the 'touching and concerning' covenants of L and T become potentially enforceable as between all formal assignees of the reversionary estate or leasehold term (ie A1, A2, and A3).

(b) *Temporary nature of 'privity of estate'*

Since privity of estate denotes the relationship which exists between those who stand *pro tempore* in the shoes of the original lessor and lessee, the liability imposed by *Spencer's Case* is necessarily dependent on the duration of a given tenure in possession. Unlike the liability of the original tenant, which is unassignable and therefore coextensive with the lease,[10] the liability of each successive assignee of the term relates only to breaches committed while in possession of the land.[11] Thus, in *Fig.* 65,[12] A2 is not liable under *Spencer's Case* in respect of breaches of covenant committed prior to the assignment to himself.[13] Nor is A2 liable in respect of breaches committed by A3 after the assignment of the term to the latter,[14] unless on taking the assignment

5 In *Spencer's Case* the Court was able to draw upon the analogy of the Grantees of Reversions Act 1540, which similarly transmitted to assignees of the reversion the benefit and burden of 'touching and concerning' covenants. The 1540 Act (and its modern equivalent Law of Property Act 1925, ss 141(1), 142(1)) represent simultaneously a statutory extension of privity of contract in favour of the assignee of the reversion and an application of the idea of privity of estate.

6 *Williams v Earle* (1868) LR 3 QB 739 at 749 per Blackburn J.

7 See eg *Williams v Bosanquet* (1819) 1 Brod & Bing 238 at 262f, 129 ER 714 at 723.

8 See eg *Celsteel Ltd v Alton House Holdings Ltd* (No 2) [1986] 1 WLR 666 at 673A. (Here the application of *Spencer's Case* is simply confirmed by section 142(1) of the Law of Property Act 1925).

9 Ante, p 846.

10 Ante, p 849.

11 See *Johnsey Estates Ltd v Lewis and Manley (Engineering) Ltd* (1987) 54 P & CR 296 at 300 per Bingham LJ.

12 Ante, p 846.

13 *Grescot v Green* (1700) 1 Salk 199, 91 ER 179; *St Saviour's Southwark (Churchwardens) v Smith* (1762) 3 Burr 1271 at 1272f, 97 ER 827. This result follows even though A2 pays a lower price for the assignment deliberately in view of the prior breach (*Hawkins v Sherman* (1828) 3 C & P 459 at 461, 172 ER 500 at 502). Liability for rent unpaid by T and A2 is therefore subject to apportionment between the two with reference to the date of assignment of the term (see *Glass v Patterson* [1902] 2 IR 660 at 676ff).

14 *Onslow v Corrie* (1817) 2 Madd 330 at 340f, 56 ER 357 at 360; *Paul v Nurse* (1828) 8 B & C 486 at 488f, 108 ER 1123 at 1124. A2 is, however, liable even after the assignment to A3 in respect of breaches committed while he was himself in possession of the land (*Harley v King* (1835) 2 Cr M & R 18 at 22f, 150 ER 8 at 10).

A2 expressly covenanted to become liable for the residue of the term.[15] However, for all breaches whensoever occurring T bears an enduring liability throughout the leasehold term.[16]

(5) Liability of S to L or A1

The liability of a sublessee on the covenants of a head lease presents different kinds of problem in English law.

(a) Absence of 'privity of estate'

In *Fig.* 65[17] it is clear that S is not 'privy' to the same estate in the land as are both L and A1.[18] S's relationship of 'privity' is not with the head lease between L and T at all, but with the sublease between A3 and himself. In principle, therefore, even those covenants of the head lease which 'touch and concern' the land are unenforceable against S either by L or, after assignment of the reversion, by A1. The vital element of 'privity of estate' is not present. Neither L nor A1 may recover a money remedy directly from S (eg arrears of rent or damages for breach of covenant).[19] The proper remedy lies in an action against the person who *does* currently stand in a relationship of privity to the estate of head lease, ie S's immediate superior, A3.[20]

(b) Other remedies against S

Notwithstanding the fact that the want of 'privity of estate' renders S immune from monetary recovery on the covenants of the head lease, there are other forms of remedy which enable either L or A1 (as the case may be) to enforce leasehold covenants either directly or indirectly against S. The legal insulation of S from L and A1 is far from complete.

(i) Enforcement of restrictive covenants It is clear that L (or, after assignment of the reversion, A1) may be able to obtain an injunction restraining S from further breach of a restrictive covenant contained in the head lease, even though S is not 'privy' to that head lease. This possibility takes its origin in the decision of Lord Cottenham LC in *Tulk v Moxhay*,[1] which

15 *J. Lyons & Co Ltd v Knowles* [1943] 1 KB 366 at 368ff.
16 Ante, p 849.
17 Ante, p 846.
18 *Garry Denning Ltd v Vickers* [1985] 1 NZLR 567 at 570.
19 For the criticism that the immunity thus granted to the sublessee reinforces an unsupportable distinction between the respective positions of assignee of the term and sublessee, see W.B. Jaccard, *The Scope of Liability between Landlord and Subtenant*, 16 Col Jnl of Law and Soc Prob 364 (1980–81).
20 Where A3 is in arrear with rent it is, however, open to A1 to issue a notice under Law of Distress Amendment Act 1908, s 6, requiring S henceforth to make all his payments of rent direct to A1. In days of recession increasing use is being made of this diversion notice procedure (see [1993] Conv 11 (J.E.A.). See also *Rhodes v Allied Dunbar Pension Services Ltd* [1989] 1 WLR 800 at 805D–F, 808E–H.
1 (1848) 2 Ph 774 at 778f, 41 ER 1143 at 1144f.

effectively converted restrictive covenants into a species of proprietary interest capable of running with land and binding any purchaser other than a purchaser of a legal estate for value without notice.[2] This doctrine, when applied in the leasehold context, ensures that a restrictive covenant contained in the head lease between L and T is enforceable by way of injunction,[3] outside the area demarcated by privity of estate, against *any* occupier who takes possession of the demised premises with notice of the existence of that covenant.[4] The equitable doctrine thus represents an important limitation on the immunity of S in respect of the covenants agreed between L and T.[5]

(ii) Remedy of forfeiture There exists a further—albeit indirect—means of enforcement against S in respect of conduct in breach of covenants contained in the head lease between L and T. In the event of such conduct by S,[6] any right of re-entry which was expressly reserved by L in the head lease becomes exercisable against A3. Re-entry brings about a forfeiture of not only A3's lease but S's sublease also,[7] subject only to any rights to relief against forfeiture which may be claimed by either A3 or S.[8]

5. ENFORCEABILITY OF LEASEHOLD COVENANTS IN AN EQUITABLE LEASE

The rules governing the enforceability of covenants under an equitable (or informal) lease[9] differ in certain respects from those which obtain in relation to a legal lease. These rules will be discussed still with reference to the framework of leasehold relationships depicted in *Fig.* 65.[10]

2 Post, p 1137.
3 See the quintessentially Victorian melodrama of *Hall v Ewin* (1888) 37 Ch D 74 at 78ff (where a sub-under-lessee breached a head lease covenant prohibiting 'noisome or offensive trade, business or employment' by holding an exhibition of wild beasts in his back garden). See also *Teape v Douse* (1905) 92 LT 319 at 320; *Northern Ireland Carriers Ltd v Larne Harbour Ltd* [1981] 5 NIJB, Transcript, p 10. The restrictive covenant binds even a licensee who occupies the premises (*Mander v Falcke* [1891] 2 Ch 554 at 557f).
4 S invariably has notice of restrictive covenants contained in the head lease. Such covenants will almost certainly have been recited in identical terms in the covenants of the sublease. In any event S had the right, before taking his sublease, to call for the head lease (see *Gosling v Woolf* [1893] 1 QB 39 at 40, (1893) 68 LT 89 at 90) and is therefore affected by constructive notice of its contents (*Teape v Douse* (1905) 92 LT 319 at 320).
5 In unregistered land the equitable doctrine of notice still governs the effect on a sublessee of restrictive covenants contained in a head lease. Restrictive covenants between lessor and lessee are never registrable as a Class D(ii) land charge (Land Charges Act 1972, s 2(5), ante, p 150). In registered land such covenants are not capable of protection by the entry of a notice on the register (Land Registration Act 1925, s 50(1)), but are automatically binding on a transferee or underlessee by virtue of Land Registration Act 1925, ss 23(1)(a), (2), 24(1).
6 It is irrelevant that, for want of 'privity of estate', S was not technically bound by the covenant in question (*Shiloh Spinners Ltd v Harding* [1973] AC 691 at 717G).
7 Ante, p 835.
8 Ante, p 825.
9 Ante, p 738.
10 Ante, p 846.

(1) Liability as between L and T

Here the result is not different if the transaction concluded by L and T is not a legal lease but merely a specifically enforceable contract for a lease. L and T are still bound, now perhaps even more obviously, by a nexus of contract which endures throughout the entire term.[11] All the leasehold obligations which form part of that contract are enforceable between them, without regard to whether these obligations 'touch and concern' the demised land.

(2) Liability of T to A1

In this context the existence of a mere contract for a lease produces no difference in the liability of T to A1. Section 141(1) of the Law of Property Act 1925[12] applies equally to an equitable lease,[13] thereby ensuring that A1 can sue T in respect of those covenants which have 'reference to the subject-matter' of the lease.[14]

(3) Liability of A1 to T

The liability of A1 to T under an equitable lease is likewise governed by section 142(1) of the Law of Property Act 1925,[15] which applies indiscriminately to legal and equitable terms of years.[16] A1 is liable to T on all undertakings in the original informal lease which 'have reference to the subject-matter of the lease', subject only to one complicating factor which is primarily of importance in unregistered land.

An equitable lease constitutes an estate contract and, in the case of unregistered land, there arises a prudential requirement of registration. Therefore unless T registers the equitable lease as a Class C(iv) land charge against L, the informal term is rendered statutorily void—notwithstanding section 142(1)—against any assignee who purchases the legal reversionary estate for money or money's worth.[17] If T neglects to register his estate contract in unregistered land, his informal lease is effectively binding on A1 only if A1 is someone other than a purchaser of a legal estate for money or money's worth (eg a donee or a purchaser of an equitable interest in the land). Ironically none of these issues is relevant in relation to the same problem in registered land, since here it is clearly established that an unprotected informal lease gives rise to an overriding interest on behalf of an equitable lessee who is in actual occupation of the land or in receipt of its rents and profits.[18]

11 The ultimate liability throughout the term of the original tenant, T, is not diminished by the equitable character of the lease (see *John Betts & Sons Ltd v Price* (1924) 40 TLR 589 at 590; *Picton-Warlow v Allendale Holdings Pty Ltd* [1988] WAR 107 at 109).

12 Ante, p 854.

13 *Rickett v Green* [1910] 1 KB 253 at 259; *Rye v Purcell* [1926] 1 KB 446 at 451ff.

14 Ante, p 854.

15 Ante, p 859.

16 *Weg Motors Ltd v Hales* [1962] Ch 49 at 73.

17 Land Charges Act 1972, s 4(6). See eg *Hollington Bros Ltd v Rhodes* [1951] 2 TLR 691 at 696 (ante, p 121). Compare the reasoning in *Beesly v Hallwood Estates Ltd* [1960] 1 WLR 549 at 557f (ante, p 863).

18 Land Registration Act 1925, s 70(1)(g). See *Grace Rymer Investments Ltd v Waite* [1958] Ch 831 at 849, 851 (ante, pp 210, 227).

(4) Liability of assignees

It is well established that the benefit of an equitable lessee's covenants, so far as they 'touch and concern' the demised premises, can run with the assignment of the reversion. Thus, if *Fig.* 65[19] were taken as representing a series of transactions with an equitable head lease, A1 would be entitled to enforce 'touching and concerning' covenants against T.[20] The major distinction between the enforceability of legal and equitable leases probably emerges in relation to the liability of assignees of the equitable lease.

(a) The traditional doctrine

Orthodox doctrine holds that *Spencer's Case*[1] does not apply to an equitable lease and that therefore the burden of an equitable lessee's leasehold obligations does not pass with the assignment of his term to a third party.[2] On this view, it is impossible in *Fig.* 65 for either L or A1 (as the case may be) to recover arrears of rent or any other money remedy for breach of covenant from A2 or A3.[3] This strange result emerges most clearly from the decision of the Divisional Court in *Purchase v Lichfield Brewery Co.*[4]

The traditional view goes even further and regards the introduction of any equitable link in an otherwise legal chain of leasehold relationships as similarly having the effect that the burden of the lessee's covenants does not pass.[5] Thus, for instance, an informal or equitable assignment[6] to A2 of a legal lease granted by L to T does not effectively fasten the burden of T's leasehold obligations upon A2.[7] The equitable assignee is simply not bound.[8]

(i) Rationale of the traditional view It is generally assumed that the refusal to apply *Spencer's Case* in the context of an equitable lease is premised upon the absence of 'privity of estate' stemming from the lease between L and T. In other words, since the head lease between L and T takes the form merely of an equitable term, there exists no 'estate' in the legal sense to which anyone can be 'privy'. Thus, on this reasoning, one of the essential preconditions for enforcement against an assignee of the term is absent, and

19 Ante, p 846.
20 *Manchester Brewery Co v Coombs* [1901] 2 Ch 608 at 617ff.
1 (1583) 5 Co Rep 16a, 77 ER 72 (ante, p 865).
2 See generally R.J. Smith, *The Running of Covenants in Equitable Leases and Equitable Assignments of Legal Leases*, [1978] CLJ 98 at 113ff.
3 Money recovery can always be made from T on the basis of his original and durable contractual liability (ante, p 849). See *Camden v Batterbury* (1860) 7 CB (NS) 864 at 878ff, 141 ER 1055 at 1061.
4 [1915] 1 KB 184 at 187ff.
5 See R.J. Smith, [1978] CLJ 98 at 113ff.
6 Ante, p 738.
7 *Moores v Choat* (1839) 8 Sim 508 at 523, 59 ER 202 at 208; *Robinson v Rosher* (1841) 1 Y & C Ch Cas 7 at 11, 62 ER 767 at 768; *Moore v Greg* (1848) 2 Ph 717 at 722ff, 41 ER 1120 at 1122f; *Cox v Bishop* (1857) 8 De GM & G 815 at 822ff, 44 ER 604 at 607f; *Thornton v Thompson* [1930] SASR 310 at 313; *Chronopoulos v Caltex Oil (Australia) Pty Ltd* (1983) 45 ALR 481 at 489.
8 *Friary Holroyd and Healey's Breweries Ltd v Singleton* [1899] 1 Ch 86 at 90; *Hoskins v Dillon* (1950) 67 WN (NSW) 115 at 118; *Quadramain Pty Ltd v Sevastapol Investments Pty Ltd* (1976) 133 CLR 390 at 403 per Gibbs CJ, 405 per Stephen J, 406 per Mason J; *Government Insurance Office (N.S.W.) v K.A. Reed Services Pty Ltd* [1988] VR 829 at 837.

the issue of liability is now determined by the elementary rule that the benefit but not the burden of a contract is assignable.

(ii) Accepted qualifications of the traditional view Even if the conventional wisdom of *Purchase v Lichfield Brewery Co* is accepted, it must be remembered that this limitation on the liability of assignees excludes only the recovery of money remedies. In appropriate circumstances it remains open for either L or A1 (as the case may be) to invoke two other kinds of remedy against a defaulting assignee under an equitable lease. *First*, the owner of the reversionary estate is entitled to seek an injunction against any further breach by A2 or A3 of a restrictive covenant contained in the equitable head lease.[9] *Second*, the reversioner is likewise entitled to re-enter against a defaulting assignee of the equitable term, thereby forfeiting the lease.[10]

In the case of an equitable lease of unregistered land, the availability of both of these remedies against assignees can be explained on the basis of first principle. In such a context the restrictive covenant and the right of re-entry both constitute equitable proprietary rights which are neither overreachable nor registrable as land charges,[11] thus remaining binding on all persons other than a purchaser of a legal estate for value without notice.[12] In view of the equitable nature of the lease out of which they take their assignments, neither A2 nor A3—irrespective of the issue of notice—can claim to have purchased a legal estate. In the case of an equitable lease of registered land, it is arguable that the restrictive covenant and the right of re-entry constitute, as against A2 and A3, overriding interests on behalf of the reversioner as a person who is 'in receipt of the rents and profits' of land.[13]

(b) Alternative approaches

It is widely accepted that the result generally attributed to *Purchase v Lichfield Brewery Co* is anomalous, and for this reason various alternative approaches have been proposed as a means of ensuring the enforceability of the covenants in an equitable lease against assignees. However, it is not at all clear that any of these approaches will be readily accepted in England, and the matter awaits a more comprehensive statutory resolution.

(i) Abrogation of the distinction between law and equity By far the most radical assault yet mounted on the orthodox doctrine concerning the liability of assignees occurred in *Boyer v Warbey*.[14] Here Denning LJ appeared to suggest that the difference between legal and equitable leases was eliminated by the fusion of law and equity in the Judicature Act 1873. Thus, in Denning

9 Ante, p 867.
10 L may well have reserved an express right of re-entry for breach, but in any event it seems that a right of re-entry is implied on behalf of L in most, if not all, equitable leases (ante, p 807).
11 The restrictive covenant is not protectible by entry on any register (see Land Charges Act 1972, s 2(5); Land Registration Act 1925, s 50(1)). Likewise, in *Shiloh Spinners Ltd v Harding* [1973] AC 691 at 721D, G (ante, p 151), the House of Lords decided that an equitable right of re-entry in a lease is not registrable within any category of land charge.
12 Ante, p 868.
13 Land Registration Act 1925, s 70(1)(g) (ante, p 267). See also Land Registration Act 1925, s 23(1)(a), (2).
14 [1953] 1 QB 234 at 245f.

LJ's view, there is 'no valid reason nowadays why the doctrine of covenants running with the land—or with the reversion—should not apply equally to agreements under hand as to covenants under seal.' To this the purist is bound to object that the 1873 Act fused at most the administration of law and equity,[15] and *Boyer v Warbey* has tended to be seen as representing a somewhat maverick view of the issue. However, it has been suggested in other jurisdictions that 'privity of estate' is not necessarily confined to legal relationships, but may exist even under an equitable lease.[16] If this view were adopted, the authority of *Spencer's Case* would simply transmit the burden of the equitable lessee's covenants to assignees of the term, at least in so far as these covenants 'touched and concerned' the land.

(ii) Implied contract It has been suggested that another avenue of escape from the inconvenient result of *Purchase v Lichfield Brewery Co* lies in the argument that it may be possible to imply that a fresh contract (and therefore a new privity of contract) arises if the assignee from the original equitable lessee goes into possession, pays rent, and is accepted by the reversioner as the current tenant.[17] This possibility was left open in *Purchase v Lichfield Brewery Co* itself, where Lush J appeared rather pointedly to attribute the absence of privity of contract to the fact that the assignees 'never went into possession or were recognised by the landlord'.[18] This argument, although not entirely free of difficulty,[19] holds the most hopeful key to the resolution of the present dilemma.[20]

(iii) New periodic tenancy A further, and more debatable, approach seeks to fasten liability upon the assignee of the equitable lease on the basis that an implied legal periodic tenancy arises as soon as the assignee enters into

15 Ante, p 37.
16 See eg *Dufaur v Kenealy* (1908) 28 NZLR 269 at 295; *De Luxe Confectionery Ltd v Waddington* [1958] NZLR 272 at 278, 283f.
17 See R.J. Smith, [1978] CLJ 98 at 105f. If novation is to be pleaded successfully as a ground of action against the assignee, it may be prudent to secure a new privity of contract by arranging a tripartite agreement between reversioner, lessee and assignee, which extinguishes all liability on the part of the lessee. See *De Luxe Confectionery Ltd v Waddington* [1958] NZLR 272 at 284; R.T. Fenton, (1976–77) 7 NZULR 342 at 347, 352.
18 [1915] 1 KB 184 at 188f. In *Purchase v Lichfield Brewery Co* the assignees of the equitable lease had received their assignment by way of mortgage security and were not therefore in the same position as their assignor for the purpose of the availability of specific performance of the lease. It may be that other kinds of assignee—in relation to whom specific performance is available—are more readily subject to the doctrine of *Walsh v Lonsdale* (ante, p 746). See eg *De Luxe Confectionery Ltd v Waddington* [1958] NZLR 272 at 277. This surmise may itself be questioned (see eg p 870, ante), but if correct makes it arguable that the doctrine of *Walsh v Lonsdale* simply renders the monetary liability of such assignees equivalent to the liability which would have existed if a decree of specific performance had been granted and a legal lease had come into effect.
19 There is a substantial body of case law which denies that novation is possible through a mere entry into possession and payment of rent by the assignee (see *Camden v Batterbury* (1860) 7 CB (NS) 864 at 878ff, 141 ER 1055 at 1061; *Cox v Bishop* (1857) 8 De GM & G 815 at 822ff, 44 ER 604 at 607f; *Thornton v Thompson* [1930] SASR 310 at 313f; *Rodenhurst Estates Ltd v W.H. Barnes Ltd* [1936] 2 All ER 3 at 6). For other difficulties, see R.J. Smith, [1978] CLJ 98 at 106ff.
20 See eg *Dalegrove Pty Ltd v Isles Parking Station Pty Ltd* (1988) 12 NSWLR 546 at 552F–G per Bryson J.

possession and pays a periodic rent to the current reversioner.[1] The traditional objection to such an analysis rests on the argument that *Walsh v Lonsdale* excludes the possibility that a legal periodic tenancy may coexist with a specifically enforceable contract for a lease.[2] However, this difficulty presents no obstacle if—as some suggest—this aspect of the ruling in *Walsh v Lonsdale* is applicable only in the 'two-party situation' as between the original lessor and lessee.[3]

(iv) Other equitable techniques It is also sometimes suggested that monetary liability can be fixed upon assignees of an equitable lease by invocation of the principle of 'mutual benefit and burden'[4] or estoppel.[5] However, there is as yet little support in the case law for these techniques of imposing liability.

(5) Liability of S to L or A1

The liability of S under an equitable lease is much the same as under a legal lease. There seems to be no possibility that the owner of the reversion can obtain a money remedy against a sublessee, but he may be able to enforce a restrictive covenant by injunction.[6] Moreover, any forfeiture which takes effect against an assignee of the equitable lease automatically terminates S's sublease,[7] subject only to statutory controls such as the provision of certain rights to relief against forfeiture.[8]

6. STATUTORY INTERVENTION

Part of the complexity of the law of landlord and tenant has been generated by the statutory superimposition of special regimes of protection for designated categories of tenant. The following represents only a bare summary of the principal features of this important legislative supplement to the basic law of tenancies.

(1) Rent Act 1977

From their origins in emergency wartime legislation in 1915,[9] successive Rent Acts came to provide the mainstay of the statutory protection conferred

1 Ante, p 678.
2 See *Manchester Brewery Co v Coombs* [1901] 2 Ch 608 at 617f.
3 R.J. Smith, [1978] CLJ 98 at 108f. See, in support, *Chronopoulos v Caltex Oil (Australia) Pty Ltd* (1983) 45 ALR 481 at 489.
4 R.J. Smith, [1978] CLJ 98 at 110. See, however, *Government Insurance Office (N.S.W.) v K.A. Reed Services Pty Ltd* [1988] VR 829 at 835 per Brooking J (post, p 1136).
5 See *Rodenhurst Estates Ltd v W.H. Barnes Ltd* [1936] 2 All ER 3 at 12ff; *Government Insurance Office (N.S.W.) v K.A. Reed Services Pty Ltd* [1988] VR 829 at 835. Compare, however, *Chronopoulos v Caltex Oil (Australia) Pty Ltd* (1983) 45 ALR 481 at 488f.
6 Ante, p 867.
7 Ante, p 835.
8 Ante, p 835.
9 Increase of Rent and Mortgage Interest (War Restrictions) Act 1915. See P.Q. Watchman, *The Origin of the 1915 Rent Act*, (1980) Law and State (No 5) 20.

on residential tenants in the private rented sector.[10] The legislation imposed some measure of social control over the relationship between landlords and residential occupiers: the Rent Acts were broadly directed at preventing exploitation of the latter by the former.[11] The operation of the Rent Acts clearly restricted freedom of contract in the housing market and had the effect of inhibiting the exercise by private owners of formerly sacrosanct rights of property.[12] In their most extreme form, Rent Act legislation, by assuring qualifying tenants long-term of security of tenure at a 'fair rent', stripped the landlord's rights back to a bare reversion and caused 'an almost permanent alienation from the landlord of the right to get possession of the premises'.[13]

The significance of the Rent Act has waned dramatically with the rapid decline of the private rented sector during recent decades.[14] Successive enactments have cut back the scope of the legislation and the Housing Act 1988 finally provided that no new Rent Act tenancies could be granted on or after 15 January 1989.[15] Since there nevertheless remain significant numbers of tenants who still enjoy the protection of the Rent Act, the following provides an outline of the protective scheme of the legislation.[16]

(a) Definition of a 'protected tenancy'

The Rent Act 1977 confirms the existence of a statutory category of 'regulated tenancy', so defined as to include the sub-categories of 'protected tenancy' and 'statutory tenancy'.[17] Section 1 of the 1977 Act defines a 'protected tenancy' as 'a tenancy under which a dwelling-house (which may be a house or part of a house) is let as a separate dwelling'.[18] This definition has mandatory application in that the statutory benefits of a protected tenancy can never be bargained away by the tenant or validly disavowed by declaration or estoppel.[19]

A 'protected tenancy' comprises only those forms of occupancy which

10 For an extremely good account of this legislation and its effects, see J.E. Martin, *Residential Security* (London 1989).

11 'The Rent Acts have throughout their history constituted an interference with contract and property rights for a specific purpose—the redress of the balance of advantage enjoyed in a world of housing shortage by the landlord over those who have to rent their homes' (*Horford Investments Ltd v Lambert* [1976] Ch 39 at 52D-E per Scarman LJ).

12 See *Davis v Johnson* [1979] AC 317 at 348E-G per Lord Scarman.

13 *Blake v Attorney-General* [1982] IR 117 at 140 per O'Higgins CJ.

14 Before the First World War 90 per cent of all dwellings were privately rented (John Stanley MP, *Government Policies on Home Ownership in the 1980s*, in *Home Ownership in the 1980s* (SHAC Policy Paper 3, 1980), p 6). The most recent statistics indicate that by 1991 only 6 per cent of households in England and Wales lived in private rented accommodation (*General Household Survey 1991* (GHS No 22, London, 1993), p 55 (Table 3.26)).

15 Housing Act 1988, s 34(1).

16 For a more detailed account of the law in this area, see *Elements of Land Law* (1st edn 1987), pp 961-1044, 1062-1072.

17 Rent Act 1977, s 18(1).

18 The Rent Act 1977 also gives an extremely limited form of protection to certain residential contractual licences which qualify as a 'restricted contract' (Rent Act 1977, s 19(2)). See Rent Act 1977, ss 77ff, 103ff.

19 *Antoniades v Villiers* [1990] 1 AC 417 at 458D per Lord Templeman. See *Brown v Draper* [1944] KB 309 at 313 per Lord Greene MR; *Baxter v Eckersley* [1950] 1 KB 480 at 485. See also *Appleton v Aspin* [1988] 1 WLR 410.

have the strict character of a 'tenancy'[20] and can never extend to a licence.[1] The tenancy may, however, relate to an entire house or a self-contained flat or even a single bed-sitting room.[2] The accommodation, whatever its nature, must be let at a rent which can be given a quantifiable money value[3] and must moreover be let 'as a separate dwelling'.[4] For this reason a tenancy cannot be 'protected' unless it was intended at its commencement to provide one (and only one) unit of habitation.[5] The premises claimed as a 'separate dwelling' must be intrinsically capable of sustaining the independent domestic existence of the tenant.[6]

Certain categories of tenancy are expressly excluded from the scope of the 'protected tenancy'.[7] No tenancy can be a 'protected tenancy' if its purpose is to confer on the tenant the right to occupy a dwelling-house 'for a holiday'.[8] The Act also excludes any tenancy under which a dwelling-house is 'bona fide let at a rent which includes payments in respect of board or attendance'.[9] Nor can protection be claimed by the tenant of a 'resident landlord'.[10] The primary purpose of the last exception is plainly to permit a property

20 Ante, p 707. See *Antoniades v Villiers* [1990] 1 AC 417 at 458D–E per Lord Templeman.

1 Once a tenancy has been found to satisfy the qualifying conditions of section 1 of the 1977 Act, it is entirely irrelevant whether the tenancy is a periodic tenancy or a fixed term, a legal or an equitable tenancy, or a joint tenancy. The Rent Act exemption in respect of furnished tenancies was removed in relation to tenancies granted on or after 14 August 1974 (see Rent Act 1974, s 1(1)).

2 See *Antoniades v Villiers* [1990] 1 AC 417 at 459D per Lord Templeman.

3 See *Barnes v Barratt* [1970] 2 QB 657 at 667E per Sachs LJ; *Montague v Browning* [1954] 1 WLR 1039 at 1044f. There can be no protected tenancy if the tenant pays no rent at all or only a 'low rent' (Rent Act 1977, s 5(1)).

4 It is irrelevant that a number of tenants share certain common facilities in the same dwelling-house provided that each retains exclusive possession of at least *some* accommodation which has been let to him 'as a separate dwelling' (Rent Act 1977, s 22(1)). See, however, *Gray v Brown* (1992) 25 HLR 144 at 147ff.

5 See *Horford Investments Ltd v Lambert* [1976] Ch 39 at 47G–48D (no protection for house already converted into units for multiple residential accommodation). See also *St Catherine's College, Oxford v Dorling* [1980] 1 WLR 66 at 70F. It is irrelevant that the protected tenant never subsequently 'dwells' in the premises at all, if he sublets the entire unit to a single subtenant (see *Horford Investments Ltd v Lambert* [1976] Ch 39 at 51A).

6 *Antoniades v Villiers* [1990] 1 AC 417 at 459E per Lord Templeman. See eg *Metropolitan Properties Co (FGC) Ltd v Barder* [1968] 1 WLR 286 at 294C per Edmund Davies LJ (tiny room inadequate as 'separate dwelling'). See also *Curl v Angelo* [1948] 2 All ER 189 at 190H–191A; *Hampstead Way Investments Ltd v Lewis-Weare* [1985] 1 WLR 164 at 171H per Lord Brandon of Oakwood.

7 See Rent Act 1977, ss 13–16 (lettings by the Crown, government departments, local authorities, housing associations and housing co-operatives). Also excluded are lettings to students (s 8) or in respect of agricultural holdings (s 10) and licensed premises (s 11).

8 Rent Act 1977, s 9. See *McHale v Daneham* (1979) 123 SJ 86; *Francke v Hakmi* [1984] CLY 1906. The courts have not seemed particularly responsive to the argument that improbable holiday lets should be stigmatised as a 'sham' (see eg *Buchmann v May* [1978] 2 All ER 993 at 998h; *Tetragon Ltd v Shidasb Construction Co Ltd and Darabi* (1981) 7 HLR 113 at 117f; but compare *R v Rent Officer for LB of Camden, ex parte Plant* (1981) 257 Estates Gazette 713).

9 Rent Act 1977, s 7(1). See *Wilkes v Goodwin* [1923] 2 KB 86 at 110 per Younger LJ. A 'continental breakfast' is sufficient to constitute 'board' (*Otter v Norman* [1989] AC 129 at 146C-E). See, however, *Rita Dale v Adrahill Ltd and Ali Khan* [1982] CLY 1787; *Gavin v Lindsay* 1987 SLT (Sh Ct) 12 at 14f; *Palser v Grinling* [1948] AC 291 at 310f, 318 per Viscount Simon.

10 Rent Act 1977, s 12(1). See *Lyons v Caffery* (1983) 266 Estates Gazette 213 at 214; *Cooper v Tait* (1984) 48 P & CR 460 at 462; *Palmer v McNamara* (1990) 23 HLR 168 at 171ff.

owner to trade off some of his domestic privacy in return for the statutory assurance of substantial immunity from any possible claim to protected status on the part of the intruding tenant.[11]

(b) The statutory tenancy

Under the Rent Act a 'protected tenancy' subsists during the contractual period fixed by the terms of the relevant tenancy agreement. When this contractual period comes to an end (either by the effluxion of time or after the service of a notice to quit), it is integral to the Rent Act scheme that the tenancy continues to subsist for an indefinite period, not as a 'protected tenancy' based on the parties' contract, but as a 'statutory tenancy' which derives its legal effect from the Rent Act itself.[12] The former protected tenant thus continues to receive, by statutory extension of his or her rights, substantially the same protection under the Rent Act.[13] In clear defiance of the contractually agreed duration of the original tenancy, the statutory tenancy, unless terminated by a court or surrendered by the tenant, may then persist throughout a maximum of two or three generations.[14] On the death of a statutory (or protected) tenant, the Rent Act permits a spouse or other 'member of the original tenant's family'[15] to claim the tenancy by succession provided certain residence conditions are met.[16] This potential prolongation of a Rent Act tenancy has proved historically to be one of the most controversial features of the long-term security of tenure conferred upon the statutory tenant, since it effectively deprived the landlord of vacant possession of the rented property for a vast expanse of time.[17]

The statutory tenancy created by the Rent Act is a highly anomalous legal phenomenon.[18] It cannot be easily assimilated within the doctrine of estates, for the statutory tenant has no estate or interest known to the common

11 See *Bardrick v Haycock* (1976) 31 P & CR 420 at 424 per Scarman LJ.
12 Rent Act 1977, s 2(1)(a).
13 Rent Act 1977, s 3(1).
14 This was certainly true in respect of any Rent Act tenancy held by a tenant who died prior to 15 January 1989. The Housing Act 1988 severely curtails the operation of statutory succession in respect of any Rent Act tenant whose death occurs after this statutory commencement date (Housing Act 1988, s 39, Sch 4).
15 On the definition of membership of the family, see *Brock v Wollams* [1949] 2 KB 388 at 395; *Dyson Holdings Ltd v Fox* [1976] QB 503; *Watson v Lucas* [1980] 1 WLR 1493; *Carega Properties SA v Sharratt* [1979] 1 WLR 928; *Chios Property Investment Co Ltd v Lopez* (1988) 20 HLR 120 at 122; *Sefton Holdings Ltd v Cairns* (1988) 20 HLR 124 at 127f. See now Rent Act 1977, Sch 1, para 2(2), as inserted by Housing Act 1988, Sch 4, para 2.
16 Rent Act 1977, Sch 1, paras 2f, 6f. Where the Rent Act tenant dies on or after 15 January 1989, a surviving spouse may take the statutory tenancy by succession. However, on the death of this spouse any further succession in favour of a family member confers only an *assured* tenancy under the Housing Act 1988 and, even then, only if the relevant family member resided with the first successor in the dwelling-house for two years immediately preceding the succession (Rent Act 1977, Sch 1, para 6, as inserted by Housing Act 1988, Sch 4, para 6). If there is no surviving spouse, the number of permissible successions (of any sort) is reduced from two to one (Housing Act 1988, Sch 4, paras 3, 7).
17 See eg R. Street, [1985] Conv 328 (Street was the losing landlord in *Street v Mountford* [1985] AC 809 (ante, p 722)).
18 See *Marcroft Wagons Ltd v Smith* [1951] 2 KB 496 at 501 per Evershed MR ('*monstrum horrendum, informe, ingens*').

law.[19] All he has is a negatively expressed and largely personal right to be 'free from disturbance'[20] by his landlord unless and until some court of competent jurisdiction makes an order for the recovery of possession on behalf of that landlord.[1] It is for this reason that the statutory tenant is often referred to as having a mere 'status of irremovability'.[2]

A statutory tenancy remains in force only if and so long as the tenant 'occupies the dwelling-house as his residence'.[3] Whether in any given case the tenant can show the required continuity of personal occupation is always 'a question of fact and degree'.[4] The Rent Acts have always been concerned with the efficient allocation of private housing as a social resource and it is no purpose of the legislation to confer long-term protection on a tenant who sublets the entire dwelling-house or who cannot show substantial use of the property as a home.[5] A statutory tenancy is not, however, destroyed by short-lived or deliberate absences provided that the tenant retains an *animus revertendi* (or intention to return).[6] Nor is it fatal that the rented premises are used as merely *one* of the tenant's homes,[7] although as the House of Lords held in *Hampstead Way Investments Ltd v Lewis-Weare*,[8] the premises in relation to which a statutory tenancy is claimed must be occupied 'as a complete home in itself'.[9]

(c) Security of tenure

Under a 'regulated' tenancy (whether 'protected' or 'statutory'), the tenant acquires a certain security of tenure. If the tenant is not prepared to vacate his dwelling-house voluntarily, his landlord cannot obtain possession without (i) terminating his contractual tenancy (if such is still in force) and (ii) obtaining a court order for possession, thereby terminating the statutory tenancy which automatically arises at the end of the contractual tenancy. A court will make an order for possession against a protected or statutory

19 *Keeves v Dean* [1924] 1 KB 685 at 690, 697.
20 *Keeves v Dean* [1924] 1 KB 685 at 697.
1 Post, p 878.
2 *Keeves v Dean* [1924] 1 KB 685 at 686 per Lush J.
3 Rent Act 1977, s 2(1)(a), (3). See *Skinner v Geary* [1931] 2 KB 546 at 564; *Brown v Brash and Ambrose* [1948] 2 KB 247 at 254. A company (if genuinely constituted) cannot for this purpose assert any continuity of personal residence. See *Firstcross Ltd v East-West (Export/Import) Ltd* (1981) 41 P & CR 145 at 151ff (company let). Compare *Hilton v Plustitle Ltd* [1989] 1 WLR 149 at 153F–G, 155D.
4 *Brown v Brash and Ambrose* [1948] 2 KB 247 at 254. See eg *Skinner v Geary* [1931] 2 KB 546 at 562 per Scrutton LJ.
5 *Haskins v Lewis* [1931] 2 KB 1 at 14. See also See *Skinner v Geary* [1931] 2 KB 546 at 564 per Scrutton LJ; *Brown v Brash and Ambrose* [1948] 2 KB 247 at 254 per Asquith LJ; *Bevington v Crawford* (1974) 232 Estates Gazette 191; *Regalian Securities Ltd v Scheuer* (1982) 5 HLR 48 at 56.
6 *Skinner v Geary* [1931] 2 KB 546 at 569. See *Brown v Brash and Ambrose* [1948] 2 KB 247 at 254f; *Hallwood Estates Ltd v Flack* (1950) 155 Estates Gazette 408; *Roland House Gardens Ltd v Cravitz* (1975) 29 P & CR 432 at 436; *Brickfield Properties Ltd v Hughes* (1988) 20 HLR 108 at 113ff; *Robert Thackray's Estates Ltd v Kaye* (1989) 21 HLR 160 at 166.
7 *Kavanagh v Lyroudias* [1985] 1 All ER 560 at 562d–e; *Hampstead Way Investments Ltd v Lewis-Weare* [1985] 1 WLR 164 at 168D, 169F.
8 [1985] 1 WLR 164 at 171B. See [1985] Conv. 224 (P.F. Smith).
9 See *Kavanagh v Lyroudias* [1985] 1 All ER 560 at 562g.

tenant only on the grounds specified in the Rent Act 1977.[10] Some of these grounds are discretionary grounds for the recovery of possession; others are mandatory.

(i) Discretionary grounds for possession Pursuant to section 98(1) of the Rent Act 1977, no court order for possession can properly be made unless the court considers it 'reasonable to make such an order',[11] and

EITHER the court is satisfied that 'suitable alternative accommodation is available for the tenant or will be available for him when the possession order takes effect[12]

OR the circumstances are such as are specified in any of the Cases in Part I of Schedule 15 of the Rent Act 1977.

The most significant circumstances embraced within the Cases contained in Part I of Schedule 15 include non-payment of rent or other breach of obligation (Case 1); commission of 'a nuisance or annoyance' or immoral or illegal user (Case 2); waste, neglect or default causing the condition of the dwelling-house to deteriorate (Case 3); damage to furniture (Case 4); assignment or subletting without consent (Case 6); termination of employment to which a service tenancy is attached (Case 8); and reasonable requirement of the dwelling-house for residential occupation by the landlord or certain statutorily specified relatives (Case 9).[13]

(ii) Mandatory grounds for possession Part II of Schedule 15 of the Rent Act 1977 sets out certain grounds (Cases 11 to 20) which, if proved, lead automatically to the making of a possession order against the tenant.[14] These mandatory grounds for the recovery of possession alike require that the landlord should normally have given written notice to the tenant *before* the commencement of the tenancy that he might seek to repossess under a particular Case.[15] Cases 11 to 20 leave virtually no room for the exercise of discretion. The court may not postpone the giving up of possession to a date later than 14 days after the making of the order unless 'it appears to the court that exceptional hardship would be caused by requiring possession to be given up by that date'.[16] Even where 'exceptional hardship' is present,

10 See A. Arden, (1976) LAG Bulletin 280, (1978) LAG Bulletin 10, 186, (1979) LAG Bulletin 11; A. Harvey, (1981) LAG Bulletin 279.

11 See *Battlespring Ltd v Gates* (1983) 268 Estates Gazette 355 at 356. See also Rent Act 1977, s 100.

12 Rent Act 1977, s 98(1)(a), Sch 15, Part IV. See *Yewbright Properties Ltd v Stone* (1980) 40 P & CR 402 at 406ff; *Siddiqui v Rashid* [1980] 1 WLR 1018 at 1023E–F; *Hill v Rochard* [1983] 1 WLR 478 at 486G; *Dawncar Investments Ltd v Plews* (1993) *Times*, 28 June.

13 See eg *Kidder v Birch* (1983) 46 P & CR 362 at 364. No possession order may be made under Case 9 if the court is satisfied that, 'having regard to all the circumstances, including the question whether other accommodation is available for the landlord or the tenant, greater hardship would be caused by granting the order than by refusing to grant it' (Rent Act 1977, Sch 15, Part III, para 1).

14 Rent Act 1977, s 98(2). There is also an automatic ground of recovery for the landlord where the dwelling-house is 'overcrowded' within the meaning of the Housing Act 1985 (Rent Act 1977, s 101). Nor does the tenant have any defence against the recovery of possession after a closing order (Housing Act 1985, ss 265(1), 276). See, however, *Aslan v Murphy (No 2)* [1990] 1 WLR 766 at 776H–777H.

15 See *Bradshaw v Baldwin-Wiseman* (1985) 49 P & CR 382 at 385 per Griffiths LJ.

16 Housing Act 1980, s 89(1).

possession cannot be postponed to a date later than six weeks after the making of the court order.[17]

The most important grounds of mandatory recovery include circumstances where the landlord as the previous owner-occupier requires the dwelling-house as a residence for himself or a member of his family (Case 11)[18]; the landlord requires the dwelling-house as a residence on his retirement from regular employment (Case 12); and the landlord wishes to recover possession of property let on a 'protected shorthold tenancy' (Case 19).

(d) *Restriction of rents*

The second basic feature of the protection afforded the regulated tenant under the Rent Act 1977 lies in the measure of statutory control exercisable over the rent which may lawfully be charged by the landlord.[19] Under the scheme of the Rent Act the tenant need pay nothing more than an administratively determined 'fair rent'[20] as the price of his or her security of tenure.[1] This restriction of the rent payable not only displaces the normal operation of market forces but also cuts through the principle of sanctity of contract between landlord and tenant. A determination of 'fair rent' plainly overrides the rent agreed contractually between the parties, even though in most cases a 'fair rent' in relation to a dwelling-house is considerably less than the rent obtainable on an open and uncontrolled market.[2]

(e) *Prohibition of unlawful payments by a regulated tenant*

In order to prevent circumventions of the statutory scheme of 'fair rent' restriction, the Rent Act makes it a criminal offence for any person[3] to require or receive a premium or loan as a condition of, or in connection with, the grant, renewal or continuance of a protected tenancy,[4] and the court has power to order the repayment of any illicit premium (or 'key money') so paid.[5] The Act also prohibits certain payments made on the assignment of protected tenancies.[6]

17 Housing Act 1980, s 89(1).
18 See *Kennealy v Dunne* [1977] QB 837 at 850A–B, 851B–C; *Tilling v Whiteman* [1980] AC 1 at 18F.
19 See M.J. Radin, *Residential Rent Control*, (1986) 15 Philosophy & Public Affairs 350.
20 On the criteria relevant to a determination of 'fair rent', see Rent Act 1977, s 70(1); *Mason v Skilling* [1974] 1 WLR 1437 at 1443B–C per Lord Kilbrandon; *Metropolitan Property Holdings Ltd v Finegold* [1975] 1 WLR 349 at 354A–B.
1 Both landlord and tenant have a statutory right to apply to the local rent officer for registration of a 'fair rent' in respect of any dwelling subject to a regulated tenancy (Rent Act 1977, s 67(1)). Once registered the 'fair rent' cannot normally be varied for a period of two years (Rent Act 1977, s 67(3)).
2 In *Blake v Attorney General* [1982] IR 117 at 139, the success of the constitutional challenge mounted against the validity of the Irish Rent Act legislation (ante, p 874) was founded in part on the argument that the rent chargeable under the statutory scheme was 'oppressively uneconomic'. See also 100 Harv L Rev 1067 (1986–87); L.L. Westray, 62 S Cal L Rev 321 (1988).
3 The ambit of the criminal provision is extensive, for the term 'any person' is wide enough to include such persons as landlords, tenants, agents, middlemen and relatives (see *Farrell v Alexander* [1977] AC 59 at 71E–G, 77B–F, 96A–B).
4 Rent Act 1977, s 119(1).
5 Rent Act 1977, s 125(1).
6 Rent Act 1977, s 120(1), (2).

(f) Restriction of the right to levy distress

No distress may be levied on the goods of a regulated tenant except by leave of a county court,[7] and the court has substantial powers to adjourn, stay, suspend or postpone proceedings.[8]

(2) Housing Act 1988

Most private sector residential tenancies granted on or after 15 January 1989 constitute an 'assured tenancy' governed by the provisions of the Housing Act 1988. The assured tenancy shares some common features with the Rent Act 'regulated tenancy', which will eventually be phased out of existence if only by the passage of time. In general, however, the assured tenancy confers only a curtailed version of the amplitude of rights enjoyed by the Rent Act regulated tenant.

(a) Definition of an 'assured tenancy'

The assured tenancy provisions of the Housing Act 1988 apply to 'any tenancy under which a dwelling-house is let as a separate dwelling',[9] this formula importing by analogy the case law relating to the equivalent phrase in the Rent Act 1977.[10] The assured tenant must be an individual and must occupy the dwelling-house 'as his only or principal home'.[11] Under the scheme of the 1988 Act an assured tenancy may be either a periodic tenancy or a 'fixed term tenancy',[12] the latter term including both a tenancy at will and, more significantly, a 'shorthold tenancy' as defined by the Act. An assured 'shorthold tenancy' comprises a tenancy granted for a term certain of not less than six months,[13] the landlord having served on the tenant a notice in prescribed form prior to the entry into the tenancy.[14]

(b) Terms of the assured tenancy

An assured tenancy incorporates both terms expressly agreed by the parties and a number of terms implied by statute. The latter include a prohibition on assignment or subletting without the landlord's consent[15] and a term

7 Rent Act 1977, s 147(1).
8 See Rent Act 1977, s 100.
9 Housing Act 1988, s 1(1). Certain categories of tenancy are excluded (Housing Act 1988, Sch 1, Part I), eg tenancies at a low rent, business tenancies, lettings to students, holiday lettings, local authority tenancies and tenancies granted by a resident landlord.
10 Ante, p 875.
11 Housing Act 1988, s 1(1)(a), (b). An assured tenancy may be a joint tenancy provided that each of the joint tenants is an 'individual' and at least one of them occupies the dwelling-house as his 'only or principal home'.
12 A 'fixed term tenancy' is defined as including 'any tenancy other than a periodic tenancy' (Housing Act 1988, s 45(1)).
13 The tenancy must not be determinable by the landlord during the first six months (Housing Act 1988, s 20(1)(b)).
14 Housing Act 1988, s 20(1). The notice must state that the tenancy is to be a shorthold tenancy (Housing Act 1988, s 20(2)(d)).
15 Housing Act 1988, s 15(1).

that the tenant shall give the landlord access to the dwelling-house and 'all reasonable facilities' for the execution of any repairs which the landlord is entitled to carry out.[16] The assured tenancy may, on the death of the tenant, devolve upon his or her spouse,[17] provided that the spouse occupied the dwelling-house, immediately before the tenant's death, as his or her 'only or principal home'.[18]

Unlike the 'fair rent' control in place under the Rent Act 1977, rent levels under an assured tenancy are not in general governed by any statutory scheme of regulation. The rent payable under an assured periodic tenancy can be increased on service of a prescribed form of notice,[19] but in this case (and not before) the tenant has a right to refer the rent to a rent assessment committee for a determination of the rent at which the dwelling-house 'might reasonably be expected to be let in the open market by a willing landlord under an assured tenancy'.[20] Under an assured shorthold tenancy the tenant is entitled to refer the initial rent for consideration by a rent assessment committee,[1] but the rent cannot be varied unless there is a sufficiency of similar dwelling-houses in the locality let on assured tenancies and the rent referred is 'significantly higher' than the rent level which, in this context, the landlord 'might reasonably be expected to be able to obtain'.[2]

(c) Security of tenure

A landlord may terminate an assured tenancy only by obtaining a court order for possession on one or other of a number of statutorily specified grounds.[3] Thus an assured periodic tenancy continues notwithstanding the landlord's service of a notice to quit[4] and the expiration of a fixed-term tenancy immediately brings into effect a 'statutory periodic tenancy' on terms similar to those of the expired tenancy.[5]

The grounds justifying an order for possession are broadly similar to those contained in Parts I and II of Schedule 15 of the Rent Act 1977.[6] Some grounds are *discretionary* and enable the court to order repossession if it 'considers it reasonable to do so'.[7] These grounds are concerned essentially

16 Housing Act 1988, s 16.
17 Housing Act 1988, s 17(1). A 'spouse' for this purpose includes a person who 'was living with the tenant as his or her wife or husband' (Housing Act 1988, s 17(4)). There is no provision for succession by any 'member of the tenant's family', and the devolution under the 1988 Act applies only to an assured tenancy held by a person who was not a joint tenant and had not himself acquired the tenancy by statutory succession (Housing Act 1988, s 17(1)(a), (c)).
18 Housing Act 1988, s 17(1)(b).
19 Housing Act 1988, s 13(2). In the absence of a contrary contractual agreement, no increase is permissible during the first year of the tenancy (Housing Act 1988, s 13(1)(b), (2)).
20 Housing Act 1988, ss 13(4)(a), 14(1).
1 Housing Act 1988, s 22(1).
2 Housing Act 1988, s 22(3).
3 Housing Act 1988, s 5(1).
4 Housing Act 1988, s 5(1).
5 Housing Act 1988, s 5(2), (3). The relevant period is fixed by reference to the rental periods under the former fixed-term tenancy (Housing Act 1988, s 5(3)(d)).
6 Ante, p 878.
7 Housing Act 1988, s 7(4). The court has substantial discretion to adjourn proceedings and to stay or suspend the execution of a possession order (Housing Act 1988, s 9).

with cases of breach of covenant by the tenant,[8] but include also the case where 'suitable alternative accommodation' is available for the tenant.[9] Other grounds are *mandatory*, some requiring that the landlord should have given written notice to the tenant before the commencement of the tenancy that he might seek to repossess on a particular ground.[10] Other grounds of mandatory recovery are even more stringent, necessitating merely that the landlord have an intention to demolish or carry out substantial works on the property,[11] or show an arrear of rent payment of at least three months,[12] or require repossession of property let on a 'shorthold tenancy'.[13]

(3) Housing Act 1985

After many years of non-regulation the public rented sector was finally subjected by the Housing Act 1980 to some form of statutory protective control. The objective of this enactment (now consolidated in the Housing Act 1985) was 'the social one of giving to tenants in the public housing sector, so far as reasonably practicable, the same kind of protection from being evicted from their homes without good and sufficient cause as had been enjoyed by tenants in the private housing sector for many decades under the Rent Acts.'[14] Accordingly the 1980 and 1985 Acts seek in large measure to assimilate the rights of public and private sector tenants 'in the general interests of social equality and non-discrimination'.[15] The legislation introduces a new legal status for the public sector tenant as a 'secure tenant' and goes some distance towards establishing a 'charter of rights' in the area of public housing. This 'charter of rights' has a significant coverage in terms of the national population, extending in 1991 to some 24 per cent of all households in Britain.[16]

(a) Definition of 'secure tenancy'

In Part IV of the Housing Act 1985 the 'secure tenancy' effectively provides the analogue of the private sector 'regulated tenancy',[17] the 'secure tenant'

8 See Housing Act 1988, Sch 2, Part II, Ground 10 (unpaid rent), Ground 11 (persistent delay in payment of rent), Ground 12 (breach of obligation unrelated to payment of rent), Ground 13 (waste), Ground 14 (nuisance or annoyance), Ground 15 (damage to furniture).

9 Housing Act 1988, Sch 2, Part II, Ground 9.

10 See eg Housing Act 1988, Sch 2, Part I, Ground 1 (recovery of home formerly occupied by landlord or now required for occupation by landlord or spouse), Ground 2 (sale by mortgagee under paramount power), Ground 3 (holiday home), Ground 4 (student residence).

11 Housing Act 1988, Sch 2, Part I, Ground 6.

12 Housing Act 1988, Sch 2, Part I, Ground 8.

13 Housing Act 1988, s 21. The tenant must be given two months' notice of the intention to recover possession (Housing Act 1988, s 21(1)(b)).

14 *Harrison v Hammersmith and Fulham LBC* [1981] 1 WLR 650 at 661C per Brandon LJ.

15 [1981] 1 WLR 650 at 661D.

16 *General Household Survey 1991* (GHS No 22, London, 1993), p 55 (Table 3.26). The proportion of households falling within the public housing sector has declined from 34 per cent in 1981, this trend being largely attributable to the exercise by council tenants of their statutory 'right to buy' (ante, p 772).

17 It is inevitable that the jurisprudence elaborated under the Rent Act should provide a substantial aid to the construction of the secure tenancy provisions of the Housing Act 1985 (see *Westminster CC v Clarke* [1992] 2 AC 288 at 299B per Lord Templeman).

enjoying a relative permanence of tenure terminable only by court order.[18] The 'secure tenant' also possesses a statutory 'right to buy', which has little if any parallel in the private landlord-tenant relationship.[19] A 'secure tenancy' must always fulfil two statutorily prescribed conditions.[20] The 'landlord condition'[1] requires that the dwelling-house must belong to one or other of a number of public or quasi-public bodies.[2] The 'tenant condition'[3] requires that the tenant must be an 'individual'[4] and must occupy the relevant dwelling-house as his 'only or principal home'.[5]

In a major departure from the pattern of the Rent Act, the definition of the 'secure tenancy' is specially extended to cover not merely a tenancy in the strict sense[6] but also a licence to occupy a dwelling-house,[7] provided that the licence otherwise fulfils the conditions required of a secure tenancy.[8] A secure tenancy can arise only in relation to a 'dwelling-house'[9] which is 'let as a separate dwelling'.[10]

18 A spouse or other 'member of the tenant's family' (on satisfying a 12 month residence qualification) may succeed to the secure tenancy on the death of the tenant (Housing Act 1985, ss 87, 113). See, however, *Harrogate BC v Simpson* (1984) 17 HLR 205 at 210; *Waltham Forest LBC v Thomas* [1992] 2 AC 198 at 202E-H.

19 Ante, p 766.

20 Housing Act 1985, s 79(1). Certain lettings are expressly excluded from the scope of the 'secure tenancy'. These exceptions include long leases for a term exceeding 21 years (Housing Act 1985, s 115(1), Sch 1, para 1), tenancies granted in conjunction with some contracts of employment (Sch 1, para 2(1)), and lettings to certain students (Sch 1, para 10(1)). A tenancy granted by a local authority to a homeless person in pursuance of Part III of the Housing Act 1985 does not normally become a secure tenancy until twelve months after the local authority has notified the applicant for accommodation that it regards him as 'homeless' within the meaning of the Act (Sch 1, para 4(1); *Eastleigh BC v Walsh* [1985] 1 WLR 525 at 530F-H). Likewise no secure tenancy can be claimed in respect of a local authority letting of temporary housing accommodation provided by a third party (Sch 1, para 6; *Tower Hamlets LBC v Miah* [1992] 2 WLR 761 at 765H-766D).

1 Housing Act 1985, s 80(1).

2 These bodies include a local authority, a new town corporation, a housing action trust, an urban development corporation and certain housing co-operatives. See, however, *R v Plymouth CC and Cornwall CC, ex parte Freeman* (1987) 19 HLR 328 at 341ff.

3 Housing Act 1985, s 81.

4 A secure tenancy may be a joint tenancy provided that each of the joint tenants is an 'individual' and at least one of them occupies the dwelling-house as his 'only or principal home'.

5 This residence requirement has been construed on the analogy of the Rent Act (ante, p 877) so as to allow a person simultaneously to occupy more than one dwelling-house as his home (see *Crawley BC v Sawyer* (1988) 20 HLR 98 at 101f).

6 Ante, p 708.

7 Housing Act 1985, s 79(3).

8 A secure tenancy cannot, however, be claimed by a licensee who does not have exclusive possession (see *Westminster CC v Clarke* [1992] 2 AC 288 at 300C per Lord Templeman (ante, p 699)) or by any person who entered initially as a trespasser (Housing Act 1985, s 79(4)). See *Restormel BC v Buscombe* (1982) 14 HLR 91 at 98ff.

9 See Housing Act 1985, s 112(1).

10 Housing Act 1985, s 79(1). See the construction of the equivalent Rent Act provision (ante, p 875). See also *Central YMCA Housing Association Ltd v Saunders* (1990) 23 HLR 212 at 214ff; *Central YMCA Housing Association Ltd & St Giles Hotel Ltd v Goodman* (1991) 24 HLR 109 at 111ff.

(b) Terms of the secure tenancy

The terms of a secure tenancy comprise, in part, terms derived from the common law of landlord and tenant and, in part, terms which are stipulated by statute.[11] The residential status conferred by a secure tenancy is essentially personal, non-commerciable and non-transmissible.[12] The Housing Act 1985 thus incorporates a general prohibition of assignment except in certain specially designated circumstances.[13] Nor may the secure tenant sublet or part with possession of *part* of the dwelling-house without the written consent of the landlord.[14] If the secure tenant sublets or parts with possession of the *whole* of the dwelling-house, the tenancy ceases to be a secure tenancy and cannot subsequently become a secure tenancy.[15]

There is no formal mechanism for the control of rent levels,[16] but the secure tenant is given a statutory 'right to repair' in respect of certain kinds of defect in the condition of his accommodation.[17] The secure tenant may not make any improvement[18] without the written consent of the landlord,[19] but provision is made for an entitlement to compensation at the end of the tenancy for a secure tenant who, with consent, has made an improvement which has materially added to the likely open market price or letting value of the property.[20] The rent payable by an 'improving tenant' (or by his 'qualifying successor'[1]) must not be increased on account of the improvements made except to the extent that the rent increase corresponds to a part of the cost of the improvement which was not borne by the tenant.[2]

11 Landlord authorities must supply their tenants annually with up-to-date information which explains 'in simple terms' the express terms of a secure tenancy and the framework of ancillary statutory rights (Housing Act 1985, s 104, as amended by Leasehold Reform, Housing and Urban Development Act 1993, s 123).

12 See eg *London CC v Bown* (1990) 60 P & CR 42 at 48 (no vesting in tenant's trustee in bankruptcy). See also Insolvency Act 1986, s 283(3A)(d).

13 Housing Act 1985, s 91. See Housing Act 1985, ss 91(3)(a), 92 (assignment by way of exchange); assignment pursuant to a property transfer order on divorce (s 91(3)(b)); assignment to a potential successor (s 91(3)(c)). See, however, *Governors of the Peabody Donation Fund v Higgins* [1983] 1 WLR 1091.

14 Housing Act 1985, s 93(1)(b). Such consent must not be unreasonably withheld (Housing Act 1985, s 94(2)).

15 Housing Act 1985, s 93(2). The secure tenant has, however, an unconditional right to allow any persons to reside as 'lodgers' in his dwelling-house (Housing Act 1985, s 93(1)(a)).

16 See Housing Act 1985, s 24(1). A local authority is indeed required to fix rents broadly equivalent to private sector rents in respect of comparable housing stock (Housing Act 1985, s 24(3), (4), as added by Local Government and Housing Act 1989, s 162.

17 See Housing Act 1985, s 96(1) (ante, p 796), as substituted by Leasehold Reform, Housing and Urban Development Act 1993, s 121.

18 The term 'improvement' is defined as 'any alteration in, or addition to, a dwelling-house' and includes even such matters as the erection of a wireless or television aerial, and the carrying out of external decoration (Housing Act 1985, s 97(2)).

19 Housing Act 1985, s 97(1). The landlord must not unreasonably withhold its consent to any proposed improvement and its consent, if unreasonably withheld, is treated as having been duly given (Housing Act 1985, s 97(3). See also Housing Act 1985, s 98(2), (4)(b)).

20 Housing Act 1985, s 99A, as introduced by Leasehold Reform, Housing and Urban Development Act 1993, s 122 (referable to improvements begun after commencement of 1993 Act). See also Housing Act 1985, s 100(1) (discretionary power to reimburse cost of improvements begun on or after 3 October 1980).

1 See Housing Act 1985, s 101(3).

2 Housing Act 1985, s 101(2). The amount of any improvement, repair or other grant obtained by the tenant in connection with the carrying out of the improvement is deemed for this purpose to have been money provided by the tenant (Housing Act 1985, s 101(1)).

(c) Security of tenure

The Housing Act 1985 imposes strict limitations on the ways in which the status of the secure tenant may be terminated.[3] The landlord cannot terminate a secure tenancy otherwise than by obtaining a court order for possession or termination.[4] Where the landlord does obtain an order for possession, the secure tenancy ends only on the date which is specified in that order for the delivery up of possession.[5]

Where a dwelling-house is held on a secure tenancy, the court cannot entertain proceedings for possession or termination unless the landlord has first served on the tenant a notice in prescribed form specifying the ground on which the proceedings are being brought and giving particulars of that ground.[6] The court may not then make an order for possession of the dwelling-house except on one or more of the Grounds set out in Schedule 2 of the Housing Act 1985.[7] These Grounds fall into three main categories.

(i) Grounds coupled with a requirement of reasonableness The court may make a possession order based on any one or more of Grounds 1 to 8 in Part I of Schedule 2, provided that the court 'considers it reasonable to make the order'.[8] These Grounds include such matters as the tenant's failure to pay rent or breach of other covenants,[9] the commission of nuisance or annoyance to neighbours,[10] neglect or default by the tenant which causes deterioration in the condition of the dwelling-house or the landlord's furniture,[11] or false statements by the tenant which induced the grant of the tenancy.[12]

In the event of a secure tenant's breach of covenant under a fixed-term tenancy which is subject to re-entry or forfeiture, the court has no power to order possession in pursuance of the landlord's right of re-entry.[13] The

3 The Housing Act 1985 incorporates significant departures from the common law principles relating to the termination of contractual tenancies (see *Harrison v Hammersmith and Fulham LBC* [1981] 1 WLR 650 at 662A–C). It is always open, however, to the secure tenant to determine his or her tenancy by any of the traditional common law means, eg by notice to quit or surrender (ante, pp 752, 758).

4 Housing Act 1985, s 82(1), (3). The expiration of a fixed-term secure tenancy automatically brings into existence a periodic tenancy of the same dwelling-house on the same terms as under the expired tenancy, the relevant period being ascertainable with reference to the rental periods under the former fixed-term tenancy (Housing Act 1985, s 86(1), (2)). See *London City Corpn v Bown* (1990) 60 P & CR 42 at 46.

5 Housing Act 1985, s 82(2). A court order is thus not merely a precondition of re-entry but a precondition of the termination of the tenancy itself.

6 Housing Act 1985, s 83(1), (2). See *Torridge DC v Jones* (1985) 18 HLR 107 at 111ff.

7 Housing Act 1985, s 84(1). The Court has an extended discretion to adjourn proceedings, to stay or suspend the execution of a possession order, and to postpone the date of possession, in respect of the Grounds contained in Parts I and III of Schedule 2 (Housing Act 1985, s 85(1), (2)).

8 Housing Act 1985, s 84(2)(a). On the assessment of reasonableness, see *Woodspring DC v Taylor* (1982) 4 HLR 95 at 99.

9 Ground 1.

10 Ground 2.

11 Grounds 3 and 4.

12 Ground 5.

13 Housing Act 1985, s 82(3).

court can only make an order 'terminating the tenancy' on a specified date,[14] at which point a periodic tenancy will automatically arise on the termination of the fixed term.[15] The landlord may then elect either to allow this periodic tenancy to continue in force unless or until there is any further breach or to seek both a termination of the fixed term and a simultaneous possession order in respect of the ensuing periodic tenancy.

(ii) Grounds coupled with a requirement of suitable alternative accommodation The court may make a possession order based on any one or more of Grounds 9 to 11 in Part II of Schedule 2, provided that the court is 'satisfied that suitable accommodation will be available for the tenant when the order takes effect'.[16] These Grounds include cases of statutory 'overcrowding',[17] demolition or the carrying out of other works on the premises,[18] and conflict with the objects of a charitable landlord.[19]

(iii) Grounds coupled with both requirements The court may make a possession order based on any one or more of Grounds 12 to 16 in Part III of Schedule 2, provided that the court *both* 'considers it reasonable to make the order' *and* is 'satisfied that suitable accommodation will be available for the tenant when the order takes effect'.[20] These Grounds relate in the main to circumstances in which the premises which are the subject of a secure tenancy have been used or adapted for some special purpose which is no longer relevant in relation to the current tenant.[1] A further Ground of recovery under Part III arises where, following the death of the secure tenant, the accommodation afforded by the dwelling-house is 'more extensive than is reasonably required' by his successor.[2]

(d) Disposal to the private sector

In certain circumstances the Housing Act 1985 authorises the disposal of public sector housing into private ownership.[3] Such 'privatisation' of council estates can be effected only after a process of consultation with the tenants who are affected by any particular act of disposal,[4] and the relevant Secretary

14 Housing Act 1985, s 82(3). The provisions of section 146 of the Law of Property Act 1925 (ante, p 817) apply, with the exception of section 146(4) of that Act (see Housing Act 1985, s 82(4)).
15 Housing Act 1985, s 86(1) (ante, p 885).
16 Housing Act 1985, s 84(2)(b), Sch 2, Part IV. See eg *LB of Islington v Metcalfe and Peacock* (1983) LAG Bulletin 105; *Wandsworth LBC v Fadayomi* [1987] 1 WLR 1473.
17 Ground 9.
18 Ground 10.
19 Ground 11.
20 Housing Act 1985, s 84(2)(c).
1 Such cases arise, for instance, where the dwelling-house was let to an employee and is now required for a new employee (Ground 12) or where the premises have been adapted for disabled living or for some form of specialised or 'special needs' accommodation(Grounds 13, 14, 15).
2 Ground 16. See *Enfield LBC v French* (1985) 49 P & CR 223 at 229ff.
3 Housing Act 1985, Sch 3A, para 2, as supplied by Housing and Planning Act 1986, s 6, Sch 1.
4 Housing Act 1985, Sch 3A, para 3, as supplied by Housing and Planning Act 1986, s 6, Sch 1.

of State is prohibited from consenting to the disposal if it appears to him that a majority of those tenants do not wish the disposal to proceed.[5]

(4) Landlord and Tenant Act 1954, Part II

A certain degree of statutory protection is conferred on commercial tenants by Part II of the Landlord and Tenant Act 1954.[6] Except in certain specified cases,[7] this legislation applies to any tenant who occupies premises 'for the purposes of a business carried on by him'.[8] In this context the term 'business' is construed broadly and includes not only a 'trade, profession or employment' but also 'any activity carried on by a body of persons, whether corporate or unincorporate'.[9]

(a) Continuation of a business tenancy

The security of tenure offered by Part II of the 1954 Act operates essentially through the statutory prohibition of any termination of an eligible tenancy except in strict accordance with the provisions of the Act.[10] In the absence of a statutorily approved form of termination the tenancy continues in force indefinitely. This continuation tenancy is of uncertain duration and, apart from its legislative status, would be rendered void under the common law requirement of certainty.

(b) Termination of a business tenancy

The landlord may terminate the tenancy by serving on the tenant a notice (in prescribed form) not more than twelve months and not less than six months before the termination date specified in the notice.[11] The tenant has two months within which he may serve a written counter-notice on the landlord, notifying him whether the tenant will be willing to give up the tenancy at the date of termination.[12] A tenant who notifies his unwillingness

5 Housing Act 1985, Sch 3A, para 5(1), as supplied by Housing and Planning Act 1986, s 6, Sch 1.

6 Any agreement which purports to exclude or penalise the tenant's exercise of his statutory rights under the 1954 Act is void unless approved by the court on joint application of the parties (Landlord and Tenant Act 1954, s 38(1), (4)).

7 No protection is available under Part II of the Landlord and Tenant Act 1954 in respect of agricultural holdings (s 43(1)(a)), mining leases (s 43(1)(b)) or licensed premises (s 43(1)d)). Likewise the statute does not cover a licensee (ante, p 708), a tenant at will (ante, p 682), a service tenant (s 43(2)), or a tenant who is in breach of a leasehold covenant against business user (s 23(4)). The 1954 Act does not apply to a fixed term not exceeding 6 months unless there is a provision for renewal beyond six months or the tenant has already been in occupation for 12 months (s 43(3)). The Act does not extend to regulated or assured tenancies (see Rent Act 1977, s 24(3); Housing Act 1988, Sch 1, para 4).

8 Landlord and Tenant Act 1954, s 23(1). The tenancy may be legal or equitable, and includes a sublease (Landlord and Tenant Act 1954, s 69(1)).

9 Landlord and Tenant Act 1954, s 23(2).

10 Landlord and Tenant Act 1954, s 24(1). This prohibition does not normally prevent a termination brought about by a notice to quit or surrender by the tenant or through forfeiture of a superior letting (Landlord and Tenant Act 1954, ss 24(2), 27(2)).

11 Landlord and Tenant Act 1954, s 25(1), (2). This notice must expire not earlier than the date on which, had the 1954 Act not intervened, the tenancy could have been determined by notice to quit or by the effluxion of time (Landlord and Tenant Act 1954, s 25(3)).

12 Landlord and Tenant Act 1954, s 25(5).

may then apply to the court for a new tenancy, provided that the application is made not less than two months nor more than four months after the original notice of termination was given by the landlord.[13] Alternatively the tenant may take the initiative, in advance of any notice from the landlord, by making a formal request to the landlord for a new tenancy.[14] In this event it is the landlord who now has two months within which to serve a counter-notice informing the tenant that the landlord will oppose a court application for a new tenancy on some specified statutory ground.[15] Again the tenant may apply to the court for a new tenancy not less than two months nor more than four months after his original request.[16]

(c) Grant of a new tenancy

On application by the tenant and in the absence of agreement between the parties, the court must grant a new tenancy (on such terms as it thinks fit[17]) unless the landlord successfully opposes the grant on at least one of seven statutorily defined grounds.[18] These grounds are contained in section 30(1) of the 1954 Act and relate partly to default by the tenant[19] and partly to needs or circumstances established by the landlord.[20] The tenant is entitled to compensation from the landlord in the event that the court, on certain of these grounds,[1] fails to order a new tenancy. At the termination of his tenancy the tenant may also be able to obtain compensation in respect of certain valuable improvements effected in the premises,[2] where due notice had been given to the landlord prior to the making of the improvements.[3]

13 Landlord and Tenant Act 1954, ss 24(1)(a), 29(2), (3).

14 Landlord and Tenant Act 1954, s 26. For this purpose the tenant must hold a fixed term and not a periodic tenancy (s 26(1)).

15 Landlord and Tenant Act 1954, s 26(6).

16 Landlord and Tenant Act 1954, ss 24(1)(b), 26.

17 On renewal the court may not grant a fixed term in excess of 14 years (Landlord and Tenant Act 1954, s 33) and the rent will be an open market rent (s 34(1)).

18 Landlord and Tenant Act 1954, ss 29(1), 32-35.

19 Such grounds include breach of the tenant's repairing obligation (s 30(1)(a)), persistent delay in the payment of rent (s 30(1)(b)) and substantial breaches of other obligations of the tenant (s 30(1)(c)).

20 The landlord may establish that he has offered and is willing to provide suitable alternative accommodation for the tenant (s 30(1)(d)) or that an intervening merger of interests has made the letting of the tenant's part of the premises substantially less valuable in rental terms than a letting of the whole (s 30(1)(e)). The landlord may require possession for the purpose of demolition or reconstruction or other substantial works on the premises (s 30(1)(f)) or demonstrate that he intends to occupy the premises himself (s 30(1)(g)).

1 The relevant grounds are those contained in Landlord and Tenant Act 1954, s 30(1)(e)-(g). See Landlord and Tenant Act 1954, s 37(1), as amended by Local Government and Housing Act 1989, Sch 7.

2 Landlord and Tenant Act 1927, s 1.

3 Landlord and Tenant Act 1927, s 3.

(5) Agricultural Holdings Act 1986

The Agricultural Holdings Act 1986 confers limited statutory rights on certain categories of agricultural tenant.[4] The Act applies to an 'agricultural holding', so defined as to include the aggregate of land (whether agricultural land or not) comprised in a contract for an agricultural tenancy.[5]

The 1986 Act confers a limited right of security of tenure. A fixed-term tenancy for two years or more does not determine automatically with the effluxion of time, but continues in the form of a yearly tenancy unless either party has served written notice of termination not less than one year nor more than two years before the expiration date of the fixed term.[6] A letting for value 'for an interest less than a tenancy from year to year' is, in general, deemed to take effect as a tenancy from year to year.[7] A notice to quit an agricultural holding is normally invalid if it purports to terminate the tenancy before the expiry of twelve months from the end of the then current year of tenancy.[8] On receipt of a notice to quit the tenant may serve a counter-notice on the landlord, the consequence of which is to render the landlord's notice ineffective without a consent given by the Agricultural Land Tribunal on one of a number of statutorily specified grounds.[9] The 1986 Act also provides some protection in respect of the rent payable by a qualifying tenant. Either landlord or tenant may apply, at intervals of not less than three years, for the rent level to be submitted to arbitration.[10]

4 Certain agricultural workers may also enjoy statutory protection in respect of tied dwellings either under the Rent (Agriculture) Act 1976 or Housing Act 1988, s 24, Sch 3 ('assured agricultural occupancies').
5 Agricultural Holdings Act 1986, s 1(1).
6 Agricultural Holdings Act 1986, ss 3, 4.
7 Agricultural Holdings Act 1986, s 2(1), (2). This provision is sufficiently wide to catch certain contractual licences.
8 Agricultural Holdings Act 1986, s 25(1).
9 Agricultural Holdings Act 1986, ss 26, 27, Sch 3.
10 Agricultural Holdings Act 1986, ss 12, 84, Sch 2.

CHAPTER 19

Licences

Reference has already been made in Chapter 17[1] to the distinction between the licence and the lease. The essential difference between these two concepts lies in the fact that a lease creates an estate or proprietary interest in land, whereas, at least in the conventional understanding, a licence creates only a personal permission to be present on land.

1. THE MINIMAL FUNCTION OF THE LICENCE

'By the laws of England', declared Lord Camden CJ in *Entick v Carrington*,[2] 'every invasion of land, be it ever so minute, is a trespass. No man can set his foot upon my ground without my licence.'[3] The inviolability of privately held land from the invasion of strangers is deeply grounded in the common law[4] and is as fundamental to the concept of private property as it is to basic constitutional notions of individual freedom.[5] At common law therefore it is axiomatic that any entry upon land unsupported by consent or other justification is a trespass,[6] and such trespass is actionable per se without a showing of injury or damage to the plaintiff.[7]

1 Ante, p 706.

2 (1765) 19 Howell's State Trials 1029 at 1066, 2 Wils KB 275 at 291, 95 ER 807 at 817.

3 See also *Morris v Beardmore* [1981] AC 446 at 464C–D per Lord Scarman; *Reference re an Application for an Authorisation* (1985) 14 DLR (4th) 546 at 554 per Dickson J (dissenting); *Cadman v The Queen* (1989) 51 DLR (4th) 52 at 56f.

4 'The inviolability of private property is a fundamental principle going to the root of our social order' (*Reference re an Application for an Authorisation* (1984) 5 DLR (4th) 601 at 616 per Harradence JA).

5 See *Colet v The Queen* (1981) 119 DLR (3d) 521 at 526, where Ritchie J spoke in the Supreme Court of Canada of the 'long-standing right of a citizen . . . to the control and enjoyment of his own property, including the right to determine who shall and who shall not be permitted to invade it.' See also *Semayne's Case* (1604) 5 Co Rep 91a at 91b, 77 ER 194 at 195 (post, p 896).

6 *R v Fox* [1985] 1 WLR 1126 at 1129G-H; *DPP v Corrigan* [1986] IR 290 at 294; *DPP v McMahon* [1986] IR 393 at 398. It is just possible that there are extreme circumstances in which the sheer size of a particular land holding (and its consequent indefensibility) may affect the definition of trespass. See eg the interesting suggestion of Deane J in *Hackshaw v Shaw* (1984) 155 CLR 614 at 659, that conventional notions of trespass may not be strictly applicable to isolated stations situated within the vast expanses of the Australian outback. See *Property in Thin Air*, [1991] CLJ 252 at 286ff.

7 *Entick v Carrington* (1765) 19 Howell's State Trials 1029 at 1066, 2 Wils KB 275 at 291, 95 ER 807 at 817. Where, however, a particular user (eg of a scenic area) is only technically a trespass and inflicts no real injury, the remedy awarded may comprise merely nominal damages and no injunction (*Behrens v Richards* [1905] 2 Ch 614 at 621ff). See also *Ward v Kirkland* [1967] Ch 194 at 243C–D.

(1) A licence merely suspends liability for trespass

In the present context it is the minimal function of the licence to confer a valid defence in respect of what would otherwise be the tort of trespass.[8] In the time-honoured words of Vaughan CJ in *Thomas v Sorrell*,[9] a licence 'properly passeth no interest nor alters or transfers property in any thing, but only makes an action lawful, which without it had been unlawful.'[10] This immunity in trespass endures only so long as the licence remains unterminated[11] and connotes meanwhile neither proprietary nor possessory rights of any kind for the licensee.

Having no estate in the land, the licensee is unable to confer on a stranger any proprietary right in the land (eg a tenancy)[12] and may not even be competent to create a sub-licence.[13] Nor, in general, does a licensee have any proprietary interest in land which is assignable to third parties.[14] Unlike the tenant at will,[15] the licensee does not enjoy 'possession' of the land and therefore cannot sue in trespass or nuisance.[16] The licensee has in general no right to take action against any third party in respect of a disturbance of his rights.[17] His remedy (if any) lies only as against his licensor.

(2) Justifications for trespass

In the absence of a duly granted licence an intruder upon land is left to show justification for his or her entry in the form of some paramount right to possession, some statutory or common law right of entry, some 'involuntary and inevitable accident' arising in the absence of negligence,[18] or perhaps

8 See *Goldsack v Shore* [1950] 1 KB 708 at 714 per Evershed MR; *R v Toohey; ex parte Meneling Station Pty Ltd* (1982) 158 CLR 327 at 352 per Brennan J; *Beaton v McDivitt* (1985) 13 NSWLR 134 at 146E.

9 (1673) Vaugh 330 at 351, 124 ER 1098 at 1109.

10 See also *Street v Mountford* [1985] AC 809 at 814F–G per Lord Templeman; *Ashburn Anstalt v Arnold* [1989] Ch 1 at 13E–F; *Reid v Moreland Timber Co Pty Ltd* (1946) 73 CLR 1 at 5.

11 *Goldsack v Shore* [1950] 1 KB 708 at 714.

12 A licensee may, however, be able to create a tenancy by estoppel (ante, p 683). See *LB of Camden v Shortlife Community Housing* (1992) 90 LGR 358 at 381 per Millett J).

13 A bare licensee, for instance, cannot confer on another any right of occupation by way of sub-licence (see *Goldsack v Shore* [1950] 1 KB 708 at 714 per Evershed MR), although such competence may be available in other forms of licence.

14 See eg *Bird v Province of New Brunswick* (1988) 43 DLR (4th) 153 at 155f. If his rights are not exclusively personal in nature, it is possible that a licensor may contractually assign the benefit of these rights to a third party (see eg *Picton-Warlow v Allendale Holdings Pty Ltd* [1988] WAR 107 at 114, post, p 915), although the benefit thereby assigned does not constitute any kind of proprietary interest in land.

15 Ante, p 680.

16 *Malone v Laskey* [1907] 2 KB 141 at 151 (nuisance); *Nunn v Parkes & Co* (1924) 158 LT Jo 431 (nuisance); *Hull v Parsons* [1962] NZLR 465 at 467f (nuisance and trespass); *Simpson v Knowles* [1974] VR 190 at 195 (trespass); *Oldham v Lawson* (No 1) [1976] VR 654 at 657 (nuisance); *Moore v MacMillan* [1977] 2 NZLR 81 at 89 (trespass); *Devon Lumber Co Ltd v MacNeill* (1988) 45 DLR (4th) 300 at 308 (nuisance). See *Lyons v The Queen* (1985) 14 DLR (4th) 482 at 510 per Estey J.

17 *Hill v Tupper* (1863) 2 H & C 121 at 127, 159 ER 51 at 53 (post, p 1065).

18 *Barker v The Queen* (1983) 153 CLR 338 at 356f per Brennan and Deane JJ.

some constitutional right guaranteed by national or supra-national charter.[19] The common law has by long tradition upheld the private citizen's power to enter another's premises (and, if necessary, to break down doors for the purpose) as arising only where entry is required in order to prevent a murder or an imminent felony, or where entry is made in hot pursuit of a felon or an offender running away from an affray.[20] In the modern context these archaic[1] forms of justification should be replaced by a recognition at common law that there is a limited defence of necessity in respect of trespass. Under the American Restatement (Second) of Torts, for instance, an owner is not entitled to withhold access from a stranger where access to the owner's land 'is or reasonably appears to be necessary to prevent serious harm' to the stranger or to others.[2]

In general the common law has allowed few forms of justification to derogate from the private owner's power arbitrarily to exclude strangers from unconsented physical presence upon his land.[3] It is increasingly recognised, however, that certain limitations may have to be placed on the otherwise uninhibited nature of the owner's prerogative.[4] In extreme situations there are moral and social restrictions on the absoluteness of the owner's rights.[5]

In *State v Shack*,[6] for instance, the Supreme Court of New Jersey reversed findings of trespass in the case of an attorney and a social services worker who, in defiance of the wishes of the landowner, had entered his property in order to visit migrant farmworkers residing there.[7] Weintraub CJ led

19 See eg *Gerhardy v Brown* (1985) 159 CLR 70 at 103f, where Mason J envisaged that in 'exceptional circumstances' the 'freedom of movement' guaranteed through Australian Commonwealth legislation might indeed include unconsented access to the lands of private owners. Such derogation from the landowner's right of arbitrary exclusion would be justified if, for example, 'the purpose and effect of vesting extensive tracts of land in private ownership and denying a right of access to non-owners was to impede or defeat the individual's freedom of movement across a State or, more relevantly, to exclude persons of a particular race from exercising their freedom of movement across a State'. See [1991] CLJ 252 at 289.

20 *Swales v Cox* [1981] QB 849 at 853F-G per Donaldson LJ. Even a police officer has no common law power of entry merely because he may suspect that something is wrong (*Great Central Railway Co v Bates* [1921] 3 KB 578 at 581f). There may once have been an ancient doctrine of hot pursuit of vermin (ante, p 28), but this ground of immunity from trespass is unlikely to have survived to the present day (see *Paul v Summerhayes* (1878) 4 QBD 9 at 11).

1 The English law categories of 'felony' and 'misdemeanour' were abolished by Criminal Law Act 1967, s 1(1).

2 *Restatement of the Law, Second: Torts 2d*, (St Paul, Minn 1965), 197 (Vol 1, p 355ff).

3 See Chapter 10 (ante, p 305).

4 It has already been conceded in other jurisdictions that powers of arbitrary exclusion may no longer be an inevitable or necessary incident of 'property' in privately held land to which the public has a general or unrestricted invitation (eg shopping malls). See *Harrison v Carswell* (1976) 62 DLR (3d) 68 at 73f per Laskin CJC (dissenting); *Robins v Pruneyard Shopping Center*, 592 P2d 341 (1979), affd sub nom *Pruneyard Shopping Center v Robins*, 447 US 74, 64 L Ed 2d 741 (Supreme Court 1980). Access to such quasi-public premises may nowadays be controlled by a doctrine of reasonableness (see eg *Uston v Resorts International Hotels Inc*, 445 A2d 370 at 375 (1982)). See also *State v Schmid*, 423 A2d 615 at 629ff (1980).

5 See [1991] CLJ 252 at 297ff.

6 277 A2d 369 (1971).

7 As Weintraub CJ observed, '[p]roperty rights serve human values. They are recognised to that end, and are limited by it.' The owner of land 'must expect to find the absoluteness of his property rights curtailed by the organs of society, for the promotion of the best interests of others for whom these organs also operate as protective agencies' (277 A2d 369 at 372f (1971)).

the Supreme Court in holding that 'the employer may not deny the worker his privacy or interfere with his opportunity to live with dignity and to enjoy associations customary among our citizens. These rights are too fundamental to be denied on the basis of an interest in real property and too fragile to be left to the unequal bargaining strength of the parties'.[8]

(3) Types of licence

Although licences may assume various forms and perform a multiplicity of purposes, the law has in the past recognised four slightly overlapping categories: the bare licence, the licence coupled with the grant of an interest, the contractual licence and the licence based on proprietary estoppel.

2. BARE LICENCES

A 'bare licence' is a mere personal permission, granted otherwise than for consideration, to enter upon the land of another. Once conferred, it suspends the liability of the licensee in trespass so long as the licensee does not overstep the ambit of the licence as granted. The device of the licence thus reflects the prerogative of the owner or person in possession of land to dictate the terms on which access may be had to that land by strangers.[9] If the licensee strays beyond the geographical or temporal scope of the permission granted to him, his status becomes automatically that of trespasser.[10] Trespass is likewise constituted by any other excess of a stranger's original authority to be present on the land. Thus a person who has permission to enter land for a specific purpose commits a trespass if he enters for any other purpose[11] or if, while lawfully present on the land, he begins to pursue some alien and unauthorised purpose.[12]

8 277 A2d 369 at 374. See also the concern for freedom of association expressed in *Gerhardy v Brown* (1985) 159 CLR 70 at 133f per Brennan J, 152 per Deane J.

9 *Lyons v The Queen* (1985) 14 DLR (4th) 482 at 510 per Estey J. A licence may thus be validly conferred by any person 'in possession, using that word in its strict sense so as to include a person entitled to immediate and exclusive possession' (*Barker v The Queen* (1983) 153 CLR 338 at 341f per Mason J).

10 *Hillen and Pettigrew v ICI (Alkali) Ltd* [1936] AC 65 at 69 per Lord Atkin; *O'Keeffe v Irish Motor Inns Ltd* [1978] IR 85 at 94, 100. In the famous phrase of Scrutton LJ in *The Carlgarth* [1927] P 93 at 110, '[w]hen you invite a person into your house to use the staircase, you do not invite him to slide down the bannisters'.

11 *R v Pratt* (1855) 4 E & B 860 at 865, 868f, 119 ER 319 at 321f; *Gross v Wright* [1923] 2 DLR 171 at 185; *Farrington v Thomson & Bridgland* [1959] VR 286 at 297; *Barker v The Queen* (1983) 153 CLR 338 at 342, 346 per Mason J; *DPP v McMahon* [1986] IR 393 at 398.

12 *Hillen and Pettigrew v ICI (Alkali) Ltd* [1936] AC 65 at 69 per Lord Atkin; *Barker v The Queen* (1983) 153 CLR 338 at 357. See also *R v Jones and Smith* [1976] 1 WLR 672 at 675A–C. The old doctrine of trespass ab initio (see *The Six Carpenters' Case* (1610) 8 Co Rep 146a at 146a/b, 77 ER 695 at 696) probably applied only to an entry under the general law as distinct from by permission, and is now said to be obsolete (see *Chic Fashions (West Wales) Ltd v Jones* [1968] 2 QB 299 at 313F–G; *Barker v The Queen*, supra at 344, 363).

(1) Creation

A bare licence may be created either expressly or impliedly.[13] A common example of express conferment is the dinner or party invitation. A bare licence need not, however, be written or even oral: it can arise by implication from either circumstances or conduct.[14] A licence does not prima facie confer exclusive rights on the licensee unless exclusiveness is stipulated or necessary as a matter of implication.[15] It seems probable (but not beyond all dispute) that a valid licence can be granted unilaterally by one of two co-owners of land.[16] A doubt remains in this context since, as was said by Traynor J in *Tompkins v Superior Court of City and County of San Francisco*,[17] one joint owner's right of privacy should not be left 'completely at the mercy of another with whom he shares legal possession.'[18]

(a) Domestic premises

It is now settled law that, in the absence of a locked gate or some other notice, the occupier of a dwelling-house gives an implied licence to any member of the public to come through his garden gate (if he has one) and up to his front door in order to inquire whether he may be admitted to the house or perform some other act on the land.[19] An implied licence of this kind extends to such persons as the postman, the milkman,[20] an election canvasser[1] and a police officer,[2] provided in each case that the person concerned has a genuine and legitimate reason to be present[3] or proposes

13 It seems, for instance, that the residential status of a child in the family home rests upon a bare licence both before and after his attainment of the age of majority (ante, p 155). A bare licence is often present in many other kinds of informal arrangement for family living (ante, p 406).

14 *Faulkner v Willetts* [1982] RTR 159 at 164H. It seems that there is an implied and rebuttable authority for someone inside a dwelling-house, in response to a knock at the door, to admit a stranger to the house on behalf of the occupier (see *Robson v Hallett* [1967] 2 QB 939 at 954B–C).

15 *Reid v Moreland Timber Co Pty Ltd* (1946) 73 CLR 1 at 5.

16 See eg *Robson-Paul v Farrugia* (1969) 20 P & CR 820 at 825; *Slade v Guscott* (unreported, Court of Appeal, 28 July 1981). Compare, however, *Sanders v McDonald and Pringle* [1981] CLY 1534. See also *Jolliffe v Willmett & Co* [1971] 1 All ER 478 at 483g–484f.

17 27 Cal Rptr 889 at 892 (1963).

18 In *Tompkins* the Supreme Court of California held that a police officer could not rely on a permission to enter co-owned premises which had been given by only one of the co-owners, at least where there was no emergency and the officer did not explain to the co-owner in residence that he had the consent of an absent co-owner. See also *R v Thornley* (1980) 72 Cr App R 302 at 305.

19 *Robson v Hallett* [1967] 2 QB 939 at 951F, 953G–954A. See also *Snook v Mannion* [1982] RTR 321 at 326C–D; *Nevill v Halliday* [1983] 2 VR 553 at 556; *Halliday v Nevill* (1984) 155 CLR 1 at 7. The implied licence of the general public has been held equally applicable to an occupier's back door (see *Pamplin v Fraser* [1981] RTR 494 at 500H; *Snook v Mannion* [1982] RTR 321 at 327A-B; *Edwards v Attorney-General* [1986] 2 NZLR 232 at 237).

20 *Holden v White* [1982] QB 679 at 687D-E; [1983] CLJ 48 (J.R. Spencer).

1 *Evans v Forsyth* (1979) 90 DLR (3d) 155 at 156.

2 *Robson v Hallett* [1967] 2 QB 939 at 952A-B, 953F–954A. See also *Dobie v Pinker* [1983] WAR 48 at 51, 68.

3 *Nevill v Halliday* [1983] 2 VR 553 at 556.

to conduct 'lawful business'.[4] In all such circumstances the provision of an implied licence is designed merely to 'facilitate the practical functioning of the community'.[5]

It seems, moreover, that the implied licence which arises in this context is not ordinarily restricted to presence on the open driveway or path for the purpose of going to the entrance of the house. As the High Court of Australia pointed out in *Halliday v Nevill*,[6] a passer-by is not rendered a trespasser 'if, on passing an open driveway with no indication that entry is forbidden or unauthorised, he or she steps upon it either unintentionally or to avoid an obstruction such as a vehicle parked across the footpath.' Nor is there any trespass if the passer-by goes upon the driveway or path 'to recover some item of his or her property which has fallen or blown upon it or to lead away an errant child.' The law is 'not such an ass' that the implied or tacit licence in such a case is restricted to stepping over the item of property or around the child for the purpose of going to the entrance and asking the householder whether the item of property can be reclaimed or the child led away.[7]

There is, in general, no common law right to resist having one's land and one's activities on that land overlooked by one's neighbours or indeed by others.[8] Provided that no entry is made upon the domestic curtilage, no trespass is committed by one who merely looks across a boundary into private property[9] or who even sketches[10] or photographs[11] what he sees there.

4 *Robson v Hallett* [1967] 2 QB 939 at 954A. In *Lambert v Roberts* [1981] 2 All ER 15 at 19d, Donaldson LJ was prepared to extend this implied licence to knock on the door to all citizens (including police officers) who 'reasonably think that they have' legitimate business on the premises. The 'business' need not be with the occupier of the house (see *Brunner v Williams* [1975] Crim LR 250).

5 *Edwards v Attorney-General* [1986] 2 NZLR 232 at 237. It used to be said that, because there was no tort of harassment in English law, the court had no power at common law to throw an 'exclusion zone' around a person's home in order to prevent a named person from approaching (see *Patel v Patel* (1987) *Times*, 21 August; A. Bainham, (1989) 105 LQR 9). This view may require reconsideration following the Court of Appeal's recognition of a tort of harassment in *Khorasandjian v Bush* (1993) *Times*, 18 February.

6 (1984) 155 CLR 1 at 7.

7 (1984) 155 CLR 1 at 7. See also *Lincoln Hunt Australia Pty Ltd v Willesee* (1986) 4 NSWLR 457 at 460C–E.

8 See the Younger Committee's statement that '[i]t is not trespass to watch your neighbour's pursuits in his garden as long as you do not enter his land, even if you employ binoculars to improve your view' (*Report of the Committee on Privacy*, Cmnd 5012 (July 1972), Appendix I, para 12). See C.S. Kenny, *Cases on the English Law of Tort* (5th edn, Cambridge 1928), p 367, for an account of the unsuccessful complaint made in 1904 by the Balham dentist whose neighbours had carefully positioned large mirrors in such a way as to be able to observe operations in his surgery. See generally [1991] CLJ 252 at 259ff.

9 *In re Penny and the South Eastern Railway Co* (1857) 7 E & B 660 at 669ff, 119 ER 1390 at 1393f; *Cross v Lewis* (1824) 2 B & C 686 at 688ff, 107 ER 538 at 539f; *Turner v Spooner* (1861) 30 LJ Ch 801 at 803; *Tapling v Jones* (1865) 11 HLCas 290 at 305, 317, 11 ER 1344 at 1350, 1355. The same approach has been adopted in relation to visual intrusion into commercial premises (see *Victoria Park Racing and Recreation Grounds Co Ltd v Taylor* (1937) 58 CLR 479 at 494 per Latham CJ, 507 per Dixon J, 523 per McTiernan J).

10 *Hickman v Maisey* [1900] 1 QB 752 at 756 per A.L. Smith LJ.

11 *Bathurst City Council v Saban* (1985) 2 NSWLR 704 at 706B. See also *Aisenson v American Broadcasting Co, Inc*, 269 Cal Rptr 379 at 388 (1990).

As Lord Camden CJ observed in *Entick v Carrington*,[12] 'the eye cannot by the laws of England be guilty of a trespass.'[13]

(b) 'An Englishman's home is his castle'

In its operation within the domestic curtilage, the law of implied licences trenches peculiarly upon the general principle that 'an Englishman's home is his castle'.[14] This brocard has 'immense importance in the history of this country, and it still has immense importance.'[15] The implied licence exercised by an investigating police officer extends only to the area outside the dwelling-house.[16] Further entry may be made only with the clear licence of the occupier (or of some person acting on his behalf[17]) or in pursuance of some common law[18] or statutory police power.[19] The question whether a bare licence to *enter* premises has been granted to a police officer is ultimately one of fact, but the courts tend to assume that the owner or occupier of premises has

12 (1765) 19 Howell's State Trials 1029 at 1066.

13 There are, of course, certain exceptional circumstances in which the act of overlooking may constitute the common law nuisance of 'watching and besetting' (see *J. Lyons & Sons v Wilkins* [1899] 1 Ch 255 at 267, 271f, 276; *Ward Locke & Co (Ltd) v Operative Printers' Assistants' Society* (1906) 22 TLR 327 at 328ff). A breach of the peace may be committed where the act of 'peeping in through a slit in the curtains' of a dwelling-house during the hours of darkness 'allows the vision to penetrate into a lighted room with the hope of seeing what female modesty will properly desire to be unobserved by the public' (see *Raffaelli v Heatly* 1949 JC 101 at 104f). See also *Smith v Chief Superintendent, Woking Police Station* (1983) 76 Cr App R 234 at 237f).

14 It was affirmed as early as 1604 that 'the house of every one is to him as his castle and fortress' (see *Semayne's Case* (1604) 5 Co Rep 91a at 91b, 77 ER 194 at 195). The rule is of course subject to exceptions, but it is for the police to justify a forcible entry (*McLorie v Oxford* [1982] QB 1290 at 1296B per Donaldson LJ). For an extensive review of the maxim that 'an Englishman's home is his castle', see *Nevill v Halliday* [1983] 2 VR 553 at 561ff. It has been held that a householder may use all necessary force (including potentially lethal force) against a trespasser who invades his home (see *R v Hussey* (1924) 18 Cr App R 160 at 161). Nowadays, however, it will be rare that this principle can properly be invoked in defence of homicide.

15 *Swales v Cox* [1981] QB 849 at 855A-B per Donaldson LJ. The inviolable nature of the private dwelling was described by Estey J in *Lyons v The Queen* (1985) 14 DLR (4th) 482 at 501 as 'a basic part of our free society . . . a bulwark against tyranny of the State.' Estey J added, however, that the home 'is not a castle in isolation; it is a castle in a community and draws its support and security of existence from the community. The law has long recognised many compromises and outright intrusions on the literal sense of this concept . . . The community interest in crime detection and suppression . . . inevitably entails intrusion on the castle concept' ((1985) 14 DLR (4th) 482 at 501f).

16 *Robson v Hallett* [1967] 2 QB 939 at 951F; *Snook v Mannion* [1982] RTR 321 at 327E. The implied licence 'ends with the knock on the door' (*Edwards v Attorney-General* [1986] 2 NZLR 232 at 238).

17 *Robson v Hallett* [1967] 2 QB 939 at 954C. That a licence may be effectively granted by some person acting on the occupier's authority is clear from *Rossiter v Conway* (1893) 58 JP 350 at 351; *Jones v Lloyd* [1981] Crim LR 340 at 341; *Nevill v Halliday* [1983] 2 VR 553 at 557.

18 *Sandon v Jervis* (1858) EB&E 935 at 940f, 120 ER 758 at 760. See eg *Hart v Chief Constable of Kent* [1983] RTR 484 at 491E-F (right of 'hot pursuit').

19 See eg Police and Criminal Evidence Act 1984, ss 8(1), 17(1), 18(1). This does not, however, mean that evidence obtained by trespassing police officers is necessarily inadmissible in subsequent criminal proceedings (see *R v Fox* [1985] 1 WLR 1126 at 1131H, 1132D-E).

granted such a licence unless he has in some way manifested an intention to exclude.[20]

(c) Business and other premises

Business and other premises can be the subject of an implied licence permitting entry by members of the public, although in this context the licence is usually of a more limited nature than that which applies to domestic premises.[1] A commercial organisation may be taken to offer an implied invitation to persons who in good faith seek to acquire information or to do business.[2] There is, however, no implied licence authorising entry by investigative television journalists who, accompanied by camera crews, intrude upon the business offices of unsavoury or controversial commercial outfits.[3] There is no implied licence to enter a nuclear installation for the purpose of distributing protest literature[4] or to invade an abortion clinic in order to gather evidence relating to allegedly unlawful activities conducted there.[5] Members of the public (as distinct from parishioners[6]) have no implied right to enter a church even though the church may purport to be a place of public worship.[7] There is, however, implied authority facilitating 'unfettered access' to a police station by members of the public.[8]

(2) Revocation

The prerogative of property comprises, in the conventional analysis, the absolute right to determine who may enter or remain on land.[9] The owner or person in possession of land may arbitrarily exclude any person who lacks an entitlement, whether legal or equitable, whether by way of common law

20 *Nevill v Halliday* [1983] 2 VR 553 at 556. See eg *Faulkner v Willetts* [1982] RTR 159 at 164C–D, where the Divisional Court found an implied licence where a woman opened her front door to a police officer and walked back into the house, giving the officer the impression that he had an implied invitation to follow her into the house. Compare *R v Landry* (1982) 34 OR (2d) 697 at 704, (1986) 26 DLR (4th) 368 at 376ff.

1 On the limits of the implied licence to approach business premises, see *Great Central Railway Co v Bates* [1921] 3 KB 578 at 581f; *Mackay v Abrahams* [1916] VLR 681 at 684f; but compare *Davis v Lisle* [1936] 2 KB 434 at 438ff.

2 *Lincoln Hunt Australia Pty Ltd v Willesee* (1986) 4 NSWLR 457 at 460F per Young J, who added for the avoidance of doubt that there is, however, no implied licence for persons who wish 'to enter to hold up the premises and rob them'.

3 *Lincoln Hunt Australia Pty Ltd v Willesee* (1986) 4 NSWLR 457 at 460F. See also *Le Mistral, Inc v Columbia Broadcasting System*, 402 NYS2d 815 at 817f (1978); *Belluomo v Kake TV & Radio, Inc*, 596 P2d 832 at 844f (1979); *Emcorp Pty Ltd v Australian Broadcasting Corporation* [1988] 2 Qd R 169 at 172ff; compare *Silber v British Columbia Broadcasting System Ltd* (1986) 25 DLR (4th) 345 at 349ff.

4 *Semple v Mant* (1985) 39 SASR 282 at 287.

5 See *Darcey v Pre-Term Foundation Clinic* [1983] 2 NSWLR 497 at 500D–E, 502B–G.

6 *Cole v Police Constable 443A* [1937] 1 KB 316 at 330, 334f.

7 *Canterbury MC v Moslem Alawy Society Ltd* (1985) 1 NSWLR 525 at 541B–C.

8 *Bethune v Heffernan* [1986] VR 417 at 423f.

9 'The right to exclude strangers is an ordinary incident of ownership of land' *(Gerhardy v Brown* (1985) 159 CLR 70 at 150 per Deane J).

or under statute, to maintain a presence there.[10] A bare licence is therefore revocable at will by the licensor[11] without any necessity of prior notice.[12] In the orthodox view, no doctrine of reasonableness controls the grant by a licensor of selective access to his land.[13] Nor is there is any legal necessity that in the exercise of his discretion he should comply with rules of natural justice.[14] The licensor may exclude without assigning any reason.[15] Where a bare licence arises by implication, it may be revoked either by the owner or by some person who enjoys possession[16] or even immediate (albeit temporary) 'control'[17] of the land. Quite apart from the practicalities of the matter, there is no way in which a bare licensee, being a mere volunteer, can have his exclusion from the land restrained by the equitable remedy of injunction.[18]

(a) Mode of revocation

A bare licence is effectively revoked by any words or conduct which sufficiently indicate that a permission to be present on land has been withdrawn.[19] The crucial (and primarily factual) issue is whether the language or conduct used is such as to intimate a request to leave the property.[20] It seems that a bare licence can be validly revoked by one of two or more joint owners

10 *Forbes v New South Wales Trotting Club Ltd* (1979) 143 CLR 242 at 249, 259 per Barwick CJ, 281 per Aickin J; *Comité pour la République du Canada—Committee for the Commonwealth of Canada v The Queen in Right of Canada* (1987) 36 DLR (4th) 501 at 508 per Pratte J (dissenting); *Russo v Ontario Jockey Club* (1988) 46 DLR (4th) 359 at 361.

11 *Wood v Leadbitter* (1845) 13 M & W 838 at 844f, 153 ER 351 at 354 (even where the licence was granted by deed). See also *Mayfield Holdings Ltd v Moana Reef Ltd* [1973] 1 NZLR 309 at 315.

12 *Lambert v Roberts* [1981] 2 All ER 15 at 19d.

13 See eg *Russo v Ontario Jockey Club* (1988) 46 DLR (4th) 359 at 364; *Austin v Rescon Construction (1984) Ltd* (1989) 57 DLR (4th) 591 at 593. For a contention that the arbitrary power of exclusion may nowadays be constrained by limitations of moral and social policy, see [1991] CLJ 252 at 287ff, 297f (ante, p 892).

14 *Heatley v Tasmanian Racing and Gaming Commission* (1977) 14 ALR 519 at 538; *Russo v Ontario Jockey Club* (1988) 46 DLR (4th) 359 at 362.

15 *Russo v Ontario Jockey Club* (1988) 46 DLR (4th) 359 at 361.

16 See the reference to revocation by the 'occupier' in *Edwards v Attorney-General* [1986] 2 NZLR 232 at 238f.

17 *Bethune v Heffernan* [1986] VR 417 at 423.

18 The mere granting of a licence to go on land 'raises no equity against its subsequent revocation' (*Milton v Proctor* (1989) NSW ConvR 55-450 at 58,257 per McHugh JA).

19 See *Bethune v Heffernan* [1986] VR 417 at 423.

20 In *Gilham v Breidenbach* [1982] RTR 328n at 331E-F, a Divisional Court declined to interfere with a decision by magistrates who had decided, after hearing extracts from the *Oxford English Dictionary*, that the phrase 'fuck off' was to be interpreted as 'coarse abuse rather than a request to leave'. Donaldson LJ thought that the 'precise meaning of that observation was supremely a matter for the justices with their knowledge of the local vernacular'. See also *Snook v Mannion* [1982] RTR 321. These matters are obviously better understood in Australia. See *Halliday v Nevill* (1984) 155 CLR 1 at 19, where Brennan J declared himself 'unable to adopt the reasoning' in the English cases. 'To imply that a police officer who is pursuing a fugitive on to his home ground has the fugitive's permission to enter and remain there until the police officer's work is done is . . . contrary to the inference ordinarily to be drawn from those facts.' Compare, however, *Letts v King* [1988] WAR 76 at 81 per Brinsden J.

acting unilaterally[1] or by some person acting on behalf of the true owner or occupier.[2] A bare licence is revoked automatically by the death of the licensor or the assignment of his land.[3]

(b) Effect of revocation

Following upon the revocation of a bare licence, it becomes the duty of the licensee to leave the property 'with all reasonable speed'.[4] The licensee has a 'reasonable' time within which to vacate the licensor's premises,[5] but he becomes a trespasser unless he acts with 'reasonable expedition'.[6] It is clear, for instance, that a police officer whose implied licence has been withdrawn has a 'reasonable time to leave the premises by the most appropriate route'.[7] In relation to a bare licence enjoyed in the longer-term context of a 'family arrangement',[8] a 'reasonable' period of time for the vacation of property is determined largely by the practicalities of finding alternative accommodation. In such cases the period may perhaps be as long as twelve months.[9]

3. LICENCES COUPLED WITH THE GRANT OF AN INTEREST

Another form of licence long recognised by the common law is the 'licence coupled with the grant of an interest'. Such a licence usually comprises a permission to enter upon another's land for the specific purpose of removing something from that land (eg timber, minerals, fish, crops, or game).[10] In effect this form of licence usually combines the grant of an interest (such

1 *Robson-Paul v Farrugia* (1969) 20 P & CR 820 at 825; *Sanders v McDonald and Pringle* [1981] CLY 1534; *Annen v Rattee* (1985) 273 Estates Gazette 503 at 507. See, however, *R v Thornley* (1980) 72 Cr App R 302 at 305f.
2 In the absence of specific evidence, the authority of a casual visitor or guest to deal on the occupier's behalf with strangers coming on to the premises 'must be quite limited' (*Edwards v Attorney-General* [1986] 2 NZLR 232 at 238f).
3 Revocation in these circumstances is the inevitable consequence of the highly personal nature of the bare licence.
4 *Lambert v Roberts* [1981] 2 All ER 15 at 19c.
5 *Robson v Hallett* [1967] 2 QB 939 at 952G–953A. The licensor is bound to allow the licensee a reasonable time to remove himself, and the withdrawal of the licence becomes effective only after that period has expired (*Minister of Health v Bellotti* [1944] 1 KB 298 at 309). The expiry of this period marks the inception of a state of trespass (see *Warnes v Hedley* (Unreported, Court of Appeal, 31 January 1984)). The period allowed for removal is sometimes called 'packing up time' (see *Hounslow LBC v Twickenham Garden Developments Ltd* [1971] Ch 233 at 242B, 244E).
6 *Robson v Hallett* [1967] 2 QB 939 at 954D.
7 *Robson v Hallett* [1967] 2 QB 939 at 954D.
8 Post, p 906.
9 See eg *E. & L. Berg Homes Ltd v Grey* (1980) 253 Estates Gazette 473 at 477. See also *Hannaford v Selby* (1976) 239 Estates Gazette 811 at 813 (six months allowed).
10 *Muskett v Hill* (1839) 5 Bing (NC) 694 at 707f, 132 ER 1267 at 1272f; *Wood v Leadbitter* (1845) 13 M & W 838 at 844f, 153 ER 351 at 354f; *Hounslow LBC v Twickenham Garden Developments Ltd* [1971] Ch 233 at 243D.

as a profit *à prendre*[11]) with an ancillary permission to enter the land in order to realise or exploit that interest.[12]

(1) Types of 'interest'

It seems that no authoritative definition has yet been given by the courts of the categories of 'interest' within the present context to which a licence may be attached.[13] The types of 'interest' so far accepted for this purpose have included not merely interests in land and chattels but also—more dubiously—the 'interest' which a licensee may have in attending a creditors' meeting[14] or in seeing a cinema performance[15] or in continuing work on a building site.[16] As Megarry J pointed out in *Hounslow LBC v Twickenham Garden Developments Ltd*,[17] such cases involve 'no shred of proprietary interest in the . . . land or any chattels on it', yet, if correctly decided, make it difficult 'to see any fair stopping place in what amounts to an interest, short of any legitimate reason for being on the land.' It may therefore be best to regard the licence coupled with a grant as restricted to proprietary interests only.[18]

(2) Creation

In so far as the permission to enter on land is here the adjunct of some recognised proprietary interest, it is necessary that this proprietary interest should itself have been the subject of valid creation. In the case of a profit *à prendre*, the interest concerned must have been formally granted by deed[19] or duly acquired by prescription.[20] The same formality of grant is not required

11 Post, p 1045. The right to cut down and remove trees constitutes 'a licence as to the acts of cutting down timber but as to removing them it would be a grant' (*Reid v Moreland Timber Co Pty Ltd* (1946) 73 CLR 1 at 8 per Starke J, 13 per McTiernan J). See also *Thomas v Sorrell* (1673) Vaugh 330 at 351, 124 ER 1098 at 1109; *Muskett v Hill* (1839) 5 Bing (NC) 694 at 707f, 132 ER 1267 at 1272f.

12 See eg *Thomas v Sorrell* (1673) Vaugh 330 at 351, 124 ER 1098 at 1109; *Wood v Leadbitter* (1845) 13 M & W 838 at 844f, 153 ER 351 at 354f. A licence coupled with the grant of an interest need not always involve a profit *à prendre*: a profit *à prendre* presupposes severance from the realty. See eg *James Jones & Sons Ltd v Earl of Tankerville* [1909] 2 Ch 440 (licence to enter and take away timber which had already been felled); *Beaton v McDivitt* (1985) 13 NSWLR 134 at 146C–D.

13 *Hounslow LBC v Twickenham Garden Developments Ltd* [1971] Ch 233 at 243G per Megarry J.

14 *Vaughan v Hampson* (1875) 33 LT 15 at 16. Compare, however, *Alonso v Leichhardt Municipal Council* (1975) 1 BPR 9368 at 9371.

15 *Hurst v Picture Theatres Ltd* [1915] 1 KB 1 at 7ff.

16 *Hounslow LBC v Twickenham Garden Developments Ltd* [1971] Ch 233 at 244G, 248F.

17 [1971] Ch 233 at 244D, H.

18 See eg *Mayfield Holdings Ltd v Moana Reef Ltd* [1973] 1 NZLR 309 at 315 per Mahon J.

19 *Reid v Moreland Timber Co Pty Ltd* (1946) 73 CLR 1 at 8 per Starke J, 16 per Williams J. On the *Walsh v Lonsdale* principle (ante, p 747), equity is normally prepared to regard a profit which has been granted for value by informal writing as a specifically enforceable agreement to grant an interest (ante, p 746). See *James Jones & Sons Ltd v Earl of Tankerville* [1909] 2 Ch 440 at 443; *Reid*, supra at 16 per Williams J. Equity is therefore willing to give effect by way of injunction to a licence coupled with such an interest (*Frogley v Earl of Lovelace* (1859) Johns 333 at 339f, 70 ER 450 at 453; *Chandler v Kerley* [1978] 1 WLR 693 at 697D-E; *Woods v Donnelly* [1982] NI 257 at 263G).

20 Post, pp 1106, 1114.

where the licence is linked to a proprietary interest of a chattel character, as for instance in the case of a licence to enter on land and remove a crop of already harvested hay or cut timber.[1]

(3) Revocation

It has always been a general common law principle that a licence coupled with the grant of a proprietary interest is irrevocable during the subsistence of the proprietary interest to which it pertains.[2] So long as the proprietary interest in question was validly created,[3] the licence is co-extensive with it and enjoys the same legal character.[4] In so far as legal rights bind the world, such a licence enjoys the perpetually binding effect attributed to the proprietary interest to which it is annexed. The licence coupled with an interest is therefore not only binding on the licensor and all his successors in title,[5] but is itself capable of assignment to third parties.[6]

4. CONTRACTUAL LICENCES

A 'contractual licence' comprises a permission to be present on land which derives its force from some contract express or implied. It differs from the bare licence in that it is not granted gratuitously but is founded upon valuable consideration moving from the licensee.[7] In recent years the precise legal status of the contractual licence has proved to be a matter of some controversy, the essential dilemma being whether the contractual licence should be regarded as merely conferring rights in contract or as also having a proprietary dimension. There has been some suggestion that the law in relation to contractual licences is currently undergoing the same process of evolution which in the 19th century led to the recognition of the restrictive covenant

1 See eg *James Jones & Sons Ltd v Earl of Tankerville* [1909] 2 Ch 440 at 442; *Wood v Manley* (1839) 11 Ad & El 34 at 37, 113 ER 325 at 326.

2 *Doe d Hanley v Wood* (1819) 2 B & Ald 724 at 738ff, 106 ER 529 at 534ff; *Wood v Manley* (1839) 11 Ad & El 34 at 37, 113 ER 325 at 326; *Wood v Leadbitter* (1845) 13 M & W 838 at 845, 153 ER 351 at 354; *Reid v Moreland Timber Co Pty Ltd* (1946) 73 CLR 1 at 8, 16; *Hounslow LBC v Twickenham Garden Developments Ltd* [1971] Ch 233 at 243D; *Mayfield Holdings Ltd v Moana Reef Ltd* [1973] 1 NZLR 309 at 314; *Woods v Donnelly* [1982] NI 257 at 263A-C. The licence is irrevocable even if coupled with an informal grant of a proprietary interest effective only in equity (see *James Jones & Sons Ltd v Earl of Tankerville* [1909] 2 Ch 440 at 442f; *Reid v Moreland Timber Co Pty Ltd* (1946) 73 CLR 1 at 8, 16).

3 *Wood v Leadbitter* (1845) 13 M & W 838 at 845, 153 ER 351 at 354f.

4 See *Woods v Donnelly* [1982] NI 257 at 263C, where Hutton J held that a licence granted for life to draw sand and gravel could not be terminated without consent during the grantee's life. A 'licence coupled with an interest' is irrevocable 'so long as the term of the grant of the ancillary interest continues' (*Patel v Patel* [1983] Court of Appeal Unbound Transcript 930 per Slade LJ).

5 *Webb v Paternoster* (1619) Palm 71 at 72f, 81 ER 983 at 984; 2 Rolle 143, 81 ER 713; Popham 151, 79 ER 1250. See also *Silovi Pty Ltd v Barbaro* (1988) 13 NSWLR 466 at 475C-D per Priestley JA.

6 *Muskett v Hill* (1839) 5 Bing (NC) 694 at 710, 132 ER 1267 at 1273; *Reid v Moreland Timber Co Pty Ltd* (1946) 73 CLR 1 at 15. The assignability of the licence may be restricted by an expression of contrary intention (see *Woods v Donnelly* [1982] NI 257 at 263C).

7 *Horrocks v Forray* [1976] 1 WLR 230 at 236C-E per Megaw LJ.

as a proprietary interest of an equitable character.[8] At present, however, it seems unlikely that the contractual licence has yet acquired full proprietary status.

(1) The disparate functions of the contractual licence

The ambivalence which surrounds the contractual licence is accounted for in part by the fact that it is above all a chameleonic device which has been adapted at different times and in wildly divergent contexts in order to fill various sorts of legal hiatus.

(a) Short-term functions

At one end of the spectrum the contractual licence provides the legal medium for relationships of an extremely short-term and intensely purposive character. The contractual licence frequently supplies a personal permission to be present on another's land for the purpose of business or entertainment. It is the contractual licence which underlies the right of the cinema fan to sit in the auditorium or that of the football spectator to cheer from the terraces.[9] It was the contractual licence which provided the legal basis of the classic 'coronation cases' of 1903 where would-be spectators had hired rooms in order to watch a coronation procession which was in fact postponed by reason of the illness of King Edward VII.[10] Temporary parking in a commercial car park usually takes effect behind a contractual licence.[11]

(b) Medium-term functions

The contractual licence is also quite capable of serving a number of medium-term objectives. The building contractor who works on a construction site enjoys a contractual licence to be present on another's land.[12] 'Front of the house rights' in a theatre are commonly enjoyed by way of contractual licence.[13] On payment of his annual subscription the member of a golf club acquires a contractual licence to play on the course and to enjoy a package of benefits, privileges and club facilities.[14]

8 Post, pp 925, 1137.

9 *Winter Garden Theatre (London) Ltd v Millennium Productions Ltd* [1948] AC 173 at 189; *Hurst v Picture Theatres Ltd* [1915] 1 KB 1 at 7. In *Hurst* the Court of Appeal rationalised the licence as one coupled with the grant of an interest (ante, p 900), but it is better analysed simply as a contractual licence. For criticism of the reasoning in *Hurst*, see *Cowell v Rosehill Racecourse Co Ltd* (1937) 56 CLR 605 at 621ff, 652; *Mayfield Holdings Ltd v Moana Reef Ltd* [1973] 1 NZLR 309 at 315. Compare, however, *Hounslow LBC v Twickenham Garden Developments Ltd* [1971] Ch 233 at 244G–245A, 248F.

10 *Krell v Henry* [1903] 2 KB 740 at 750.

11 *Ashby v Tolhurst* [1937] 2 KB 242 at 249. Compare, however, the bailment analysis applied in *Davis v Pearce Parking Station Pty Ltd* (1954) 91 CLR 642 at 647; *Walton Stores Ltd v Sydney City Council* [1968] 2 NSWR 109 at 112ff. The bailment analysis may, of course, result in the imposition of a different standard of care.

12 *Hounslow LBC v Twickenham Garden Developments Ltd* [1971] Ch 233 at 246C, 247B–D; *Mayfield Holdings Ltd v Moana Reef Ltd* [1973] 1 NZLR 309 at 316.

13 *Clore v Theatrical Properties Ltd and Westby & Co Ltd* [1936] 3 All ER 483 at 490.

14 *The Banstead Downs Golf Club v The Commissioners* (1974) VATTR 219 at 227.

(c) Long-term functions

At the other end of the spectrum the contractual licence has come, during the last 40 years, to play a rather different role from any mentioned so far. Although at times scarcely distinguishable from the parallel device of tenancy,[15] the contractual licence has emerged as a common residential device peculiarly appropriate to modern social conditions. The contractual licence has acquired a wholly unaccustomed prominence as a 'possible mode of land-holding—a mode which had certainly not been developed into anything like its current maturity in the 19th century.'[16] The contractual licence thus provides the legal explanation for the social reality of occupancy enjoyed by lodgers[17] and by a wide range of family members living in informal and loosely organised 'family arrangements'.[18]

(d) Disjunctions of time and concept

The difficulties evident in the contemporary law of contractual licences are those which inevitably arise where one phrase, itself of somewhat ill-defined scope, has to do service for a range of purposes which differ broadly in context and time-scale. The formative concepts relevant to the law of contractual licences were hammered out during the 19th and early 20th centuries some time before the residential dimension of the contractual licence began properly to emerge.[19] Rules which were quite appropriate for short- or medium-term dealings have now come to appear entirely inapposite to the expectations of parties caught up in long-term residential arrangements. Conversely, ideas which would seem bizarre in the context of the 'cinema ticket' cases acquire a certain plausibility in the context of other kinds of arrangement which fall within the compass of the contractual licence.

(2) Terms of the contractual licence

A contractual licence may be created either expressly or impliedly and its terms are left to be ascertained by normal contractual principles. Some terms may be stipulated explicitly by the parties, but it is quite possible that other terms may be supplied by implication from the conduct and expectations of the parties.

15 Ante, p 706. The similarity between the long-term functions of the contractual licence and the term of years has recently been intensified by the statutory creation of 'a new animal' (see *Norris v Checksfield* [1991] 1 WLR 1241 at 1246G per Woolf LJ). Section 5(1A) of the Protection from Eviction Act 1977, as amended by Housing Act 1988, s 32, introduces the concept of the 'periodic licence' on an analogy with weekly, monthly and quarterly tenancies (see *Norris*, supra at 1248A).

16 *Heslop v Burns* [1974] 1 WLR 1241 at 1252C–D per Scarman LJ.

17 In the residential context there seems to be a presumption in favour of contractual licence rather than bare licence. The onus is on the licensor to prove that only a bare licence was present and that no monies were paid (see *Patel v Patel* [1983] Court of Appeal Unbound Transcript 930 per Slade LJ).

18 Post, p 906.

19 Even in the 1930s the Rent Acts were as yet in their infancy, and the possibility that this legislation might be circumvented through the grant of a contractual occupation licence had not been fully realised. This process of circumvention has now of course come full circle with the ruling of the House of Lords in *Street v Mountford* [1985] AC 809 (ante, p 722).

Although the express and implied terms of a contractual licence may at times resemble those contained in a lease, the assimilation of the lease and the contractual licence is far from perfect or complete. Because of the underlying ambivalence of the lease as a contractual phenomenon and as a proprietary estate,[20] it is clear that certain rules derived from contract law apply to both lease and licence. Thus, for instance, both the tenant[1] and the licensee[2] may invoke the contractual doctrine of frustration. However, the licensee cannot claim the benefit of many other rules and doctrines which presuppose ownership of an estate in the land. The contractual licensee cannot invoke on his own behalf the equitable doctrine of relief against forfeiture.[3] In the conventional view such relief is available only in respect of proprietary interests in land,[4] although in reality much the same relief may be accorded the licensee by the application of the principle of proprietary estoppel.[5] The contractual licensee enjoys no special rights in respect of the removal of fixtures from the realty.[6] The implied surrender of a contractual licence is governed by the rules on discharge of a contract by tacit abandonment[7] rather than by the principles which control the surrender of a leasehold estate.[8]

(a) *Implied term for quiet enjoyment*

It is possible that some kinds of contractual licence will be held to contain an implied undertaking by the licensor to afford quiet enjoyment to the licensee.[9] In *Smith v Nottinghamshire County Council*,[10] for instance, a number of students living in a hall of residence complained that their preparation for an examination had been prejudicially affected by noisy repairs which their university had insisted on carrying out during term time. The Court of Appeal held that there had indeed been a breach of a contractual term that the university, as a contractual licensor, should do nothing without

20 Ante, p 674.
1 Ante, p 764.
2 See *Krell v Henry* [1903] 2 KB 740 at 751ff; *National Carriers Ltd v Panalpina (Northern) Ltd* [1981] AC 675 at 690H-691A, 694A-B.
3 *Scandinavian Trading Tanker Co A.B. v Flota Petrolera Ecuatoriana* [1983] 2 AC 694 at 702A-C per Lord Diplock; *Sport Internationaal Bussum BV v Inter-Footwear Ltd* [1984] 1 WLR 776 at 794C-G.
4 Compare, however, the increasing support in the Australian jurisdictions for the proposition that equity may relieve against the forfeiture of a mere contractual licence (*Chaka Holdings Pty Ltd v Sunsim Pty Ltd* (1987) NSW ConvR 55-367; *Milton v Proctor* (1989) NSW ConvR 55-450 at 58,257 per McHugh JA). See also *Stern v McArthur* (1988) 165 CLR 489; W.M.C. Gummow, *Forfeiture and Certainty: The High Court and the House of Lords*, in P.D. Finn (ed), *Essays in Equity* (Sydney 1985), p 43f; Sir A. Mason, *Themes and Prospects*, ibid, p 248.
5 Ante, p 312. See *Milton v Proctor* (1989) NSW ConvR 55-450 at 58,254 per Mahoney JA, 58,263ff per Clarke JA.
6 *C & P Haulage v Middleton* [1983] 1 WLR 1461 at 1468B-C.
7 *Bone v Bone* [1992] EGCS 81 per Nourse LJ. See *Paal Wilson & Co A/S v Partenreederei Hannah Blumenthal* [1983] 1 AC 854 at 924D-G per Lord Brightman.
8 Ante, p 758. As Nourse LJ pointed out in *Bone v Bone* [1992] EGCS 81, the abandonment of a contractual licence requires no formalities and is not necessarily founded on estoppel. In particular, there is no need to show—as would be the case with surrender of a lease by operation of law—that the party who alleges implied abandonment has acted in detrimental reliance on some representation made by the other party.
9 On the covenant for quiet enjoyment implied in a lease, see Chapter 18 (ante, p 778).
10 (1981) *Times*, 13 November.

just cause to disturb the students from getting on with their studies with reasonable quietude in their own rooms.

(b) Implied term relating to fitness for purpose

As is demonstrated by *Smith v Nottinghamshire County Council*, the judicial implication of terms can sometimes make the contractual licence resemble the functional equivalent of a tenancy. In one respect, however, the courts have gone even further and have been willing to imply in the contractual licence a term which has never been implied in any lease. In *Wettern Electric Ltd v Welsh Development Agency*,[11] Judge John Newey QC was prepared to imply into a contractual occupation licence a term that the premises hired should be fit for the purposes envisaged by the licensee.[12] Here the plaintiffs had been unable to carry on their business in the licensed premises because, shortly after moving in, they discovered foundations defects which made the property dangerous and unusable. The defendants were found to be in breach of an implied term of fitness and were therefore liable in damages.[13] The willingness of the courts to imply such terms on the basis of 'business efficacy'[14] may well counterbalance the perceived attraction—judged from the landowner's viewpoint—which the contractual licence has seemed to enjoy over the lease.[15]

(c) Requirement of notice to quit

A fixed-term licence terminates, without any requirement of notice, on the expiration of the fixed term. Other kinds of contractual licence may, however, be terminable only upon the giving of some form of notice to quit. Such notice may, of course, be the subject of express stipulation. Moreover, in a licence of undefined duration it is possible that a requirement of reasonable notice may be implied in the light of the circumstances existing at the creation of the licence.[16] Where a contractual licence is a 'periodic licence', there is now an overriding statutory provision that no notice of termination by either party is valid unless given in writing at least four weeks before the date on which the notice is to take effect.[17]

11 [1983] QB 796. See (1983) 34 NILQ 349 (Norma Dawson); (1983) 80 Law Soc Gaz 2195 (H.W. Wilkinson); [1983] Conv 319 (J.E.M.).

12 For a discussion of the courts' reluctance to imply an equivalent term in the context of a lease, see Chapter 18 (ante, p 784).

13 [1983] QB 796 at 809A–E.

14 See *The Moorcock* (1889) 14 PD 64 at 68, cited in *Wettern Electric Ltd v Welsh Development Agency* [1983] QB 796 at 809A-B.

15 See, however, the unwillingness of the Court of Appeal to apply or extend the *Wettern Electric* ruling in *Morris-Thomas v Petticoat Lane Rentals* (1987) 53 P & CR 238 at 249ff, 255f.

16 See *Australian Blue Metal Ltd v Hughes* [1963] AC 74 at 99 per Lord Devlin. The period of notice required is not necessarily one full payment period. See the requirement of one month's notice (rather than seven or eight days) imposed by the Court of Appeal in *Smith v Northside Developments Ltd* (1988) 55 P & CR 164 at 168; [1989] Conv 55 (J.E.M.). There is no requirement of notice to quit where a service occupancy is brought to an end by the summary dismissal of an employee for employment-related misconduct (see *Norris v Checksfield* [1991] 1 WLR 1241 at 1247H per Woolf LJ).

17 Protection from Eviction Act 1977, s 5(1A), as amended by Housing Act 1988, s 32(2). A valid notice to quit must also contain 'such information as may be prescribed'.

(d) Implied terms as to residential security

In recent years there has been an increasing tendency for the courts to invoke the concept of the licence in order to resolve the legal problems generated by informal and ill-defined arrangements for communal family living.[18] In *Pettitt v Pettitt*[19] and *Gissing v Gissing*[20] the House of Lords effectively precluded the law of trusts from having much positive application to the phenomenon of the family arrangement. The required elements of conscious understanding or 'common intention' in which the House of Lords rooted the origins of trust were inevitably alien to the amorphous nature of most kinds of family arrangement.[1] The device of the licence suddenly seemed to provide the flexibility of approach to family arrangements which the clumsy and doctrinaire concepts of trust law so conspicuously lacked.

(i) Non-commercial nature of family relations Familial relations are in general non-commercial and do not often involve the prudential calculation of cash advantage which so heavily colours the relationships of strangers. It is normally the case that hard bargaining and the cold definition of legal rights are alien to the spirit in which family interaction is conducted.[2] There may, however, be a more subtle sense in which the reciprocity sought in the hard-nosed bargaining of strangers is no less effectively secured in the family context. Since family living implies at least some continuity of relationship between family members, the expected reciprocity of family transactions may take many years to be fully realised.[3] The net result is that members of family and kinship groups commonly participate in informally based living arrangements which are negotiated—if they are discussed at all—not in clearly defined terms of legal entitlement, but rather in vaguely expressed terms of anticipated mutuality.[4]

18 The problems of multiple domestic occupation are likely to emerge with increasing frequency as the proportion of old people in the general population continues to rise and as the current housing problem becomes ever more acute (see Central Statistical Office, *Social Trends 22* (1992 edn London), pp 27, 150f (Tables 1.5, 8.12)). A further dimension of difficulty is introduced by the sharing of accommodation with vulnerable or incapacitated relatives for whom 'care in the community' is now prescribed government policy.

19 [1970] AC 777 (ante, p 374).

20 [1971] AC 886 (ante, p 431).

1 See Chapter 12 (ante, p 421).

2 It is also generally true that younger members of family groups are subject to some measure of disability (both legal and economic), and are therefore more likely to be the beneficiaries of transactions motivated by a wholly non-commercial sense of generosity.

3 As William J. Goode once said, the continuity of family relationships means that husband and wife, as well as children, 'enjoy a much longer line of social credit than they would have if they were engaged in random social interaction with strangers.' This in turn means that 'an individual can give more at one time to a family member, knowing that in the long run this will not be a loss, for the other person (or someone else) is likely to reciprocate at some point' (see 'The Resistance of Family Forces to Industrialisation', in J.M. Eekelaar and S.N. Katz (ed), *Marriage and Cohabitation in Contemporary Societies* (Toronto 1980), p xiv).

4 Family arrangements are thus commonly characterised by obscure intentions, unexpressed terms, mixed motives and a high degree of mutual misunderstanding. In view of their frequently chaotic and indeterminate nature, Croom-Johnson LJ was once moved to speak of such situations as 'family non-arrangements' (*Rogers v Eller* (Unreported, Court of Appeal, 20 May 1986)). See also *Gillies v Keogh* [1989] 2 NZLR 327 at 333 per Cooke P.

(ii) The decline of non-interventionism Domestic living arrangements tend, by nature and form, to be so unlegalistic that for many years the courts declined on principle to attribute to family members any intention at all to create legally actionable relationships.[5] It was Atkin LJ who observed in *Balfour v Balfour*[6] that family arrangements

> are outside the realm of contracts altogether. The common law does not regulate the form of agreements between spouses. Their promises are not sealed with seals and sealing wax. The consideration that really obtains for them is that natural love and affection which counts for so little in these cold Courts . . . The parties themselves are advocates, judges, Courts, sheriff's officer and reporter. In respect of these promises each house is a domain into which the King's writ does not seek to run, and to which his officers do not seek to be admitted.[7]

It is, of course, clear that some family arrangements have no significant long-term legal effect other than that created by a bare licence.[8] Even where money changes hands under a family arrangement, the arrangement itself can rest so heavily upon the presence of a gift relationship between the parties that there is no question of loan-based contractual rights or equity shareholding behind any sort of resulting or constructive trust.[9] There is a ready presumption in the domestic context that payments of money merely represent contributions towards current living expenses and outgoings[10] rather than contributions which generate a beneficial or other entitlement in the family home for the contributor.[11]

It is nevertheless widely accepted nowadays that the non-interventionist view adumbrated in *Balfour v Balfour* no longer retains the force which it once had. The courts are increasingly willing to accept and to enforce some degree of contractual ordering of family relationships by the parties themselves.[12] Even where a family arrangement involves an element of de facto or non-marital cohabitation, modern courts are relatively unmoved

5 For many people, discussion of the legal implications of their living arrangements would, in any case, be inconsistent with the mutual trust on which their relationship is based (see *Doohan v Nelson* [1973] 2 NSWLR 320 at 324G–325A).

6 [1919] 2 KB 571 at 579.

7 See also *Pettitt v Pettitt* [1970] AC 777 at 796A; *Burns v Burns* [1984] Ch 317 at 335C.

8 See eg *Hoskins v Hoskins* (Unreported, 3 December 1981), where the Court of Appeal held that a deserted wife, who had been given temporary occupation of a flat belonging to her husband and his two brothers, was merely a bare licensee under 'an ad hoc short-term licence free of charge'.

9 See eg *Walker v Walker* (Unreported, Court of Appeal, 12 April 1984), where a father had announced at his son's wedding that he proposed to give the newly married couple money to set up a house. See also *Julian v Furby* (Unreported, Court of Appeal, No 79 15962, 24 November 1981), where a father-in-law was held to have made a gift of his labour in effecting improvements.

10 *Gross v French* (1976) 238 Estates Gazette 39 at 41; *Rogers v Eller* (Unreported, Court of Appeal, 20 May 1986).

11 It can only rarely be the case, for instance, that a beneficial interest in the home is acquired by the son who lives at home with his parents and gives his mother part of his weekly wage packet. The contributor here cannot usually be said to have advanced the money 'in the character of a purchaser' (ante, p 406).

12 See *Hardwick v Johnson* [1978] 1 WLR 683 at 688A–E. See also G. Temple, *Freedom of Contract and Intimate Relationships*, 8 Harvard Jnl of Law and Public Policy 121 (1985).

by the historic fear lest the conferment of rights be confused with a rewarding of supposed immorality.[13] Courts today do not, in general, regard the withholding of property or other rights as an appropriate means of manifesting an official social displeasure with unorthodox living arrangements.[14]

(iii) The implication of contractual terms The increased willingness of the courts to recognise an enforceable contractual element in at least some family arrangements has often highlighted the profound difficulties involved in determining the express and implied terms which regulate these relationships. In the early 1970s the Court of Appeal attempted to seek a resolution of the property dimension of family arrangements in some extended version of the contractual licence. The practice of contractual implication in relation to such licences was sometimes carried to controversial extremes.

In *Tanner v Tanner*,[15] for example, a young mother of twins gave up a Rent Act protected tenancy in order to move into a house bought in his own name by the father of her children. When he later evicted her from that house, the Court of Appeal awarded the woman compensation of £2,000 for the loss of a 'contractual licence'. According to Lord Denning MR, the house had obviously been 'provided for her as a house for herself and the twins for the foreseeable future'.[16] Having suffered the detriment of giving up her protected tenancy, she had acquired a contractual licence to 'have accommodation in the house for herself and the children so long as they were of school age and the accommodation was reasonably required for her and the children'.[17] The Court thus regarded the expectations of the parties as having given rise to a form of residential security which, although terminable in changed circumstances,[18] was none the less compensable by damages where the licence had already been wrongfully terminated.[19]

Although in the years following *Tanner v Tanner* the courts have occasionally implied the existence of a contractual licence from circumstances of family

13 See *Holman v Johnson* (1775) 1 Cowp 341 at 343, 98 ER 1120 at 1121. Compare now *Seidler v Schallhofer* [1982] 2 NSWLR 80 at 89G–91A; *Niederberger v Memnook* (1982) 130 DLR (3d) 353 at 356f.

14 It can be argued that this altered direction does not necessarily reflect a new judicial liberalism or even an incipient principle of moral neutrality in the courts. In many cases the modern approach is more clearly the product of a judicial desire to deprive unmarried male cohabitees of any possible haven of effective legal immunity. Alongside this motivation there has been a strong impulse to ensure that unmarried partners should not be able to contract out of legal control by opting deliberately for some autonomous or supposedly free-thinking relationship above and beyond the law (see [1982] CLJ 30 at 34). Compare, however, Cooke P's reference in *Gillies v Keogh* [1989] 2 NZLR 327 at 334 to the 'principle of freedom to stipulate against any trust or obligation'. It is not entirely impossible that widespread perceptions of a national moral decline may induce a greater willingness to penalise relationships which, by reason of instability or supposed immorality, threaten the public weal or—more crudely—tax the public purse (see eg P. Sparkes, *Morality, Amorality and Equity*, [1990] Denning LJ 91 at 102f).

15 [1975] 1 WLR 1346. See (1976) 92 LQR 168 (J.L. Barton).

16 [1975] 1 WLR 1346 at 1350B.

17 [1975] 1 WLR 1346 at 1350E.

18 [1975] 1 WLR 1346 at 1350F. For criticism of the 'concept of a wavering licence', see *McGill v S* [1979] IR 283 at 293 (ante, p 350).

19 See I.J. Hardingham, (1979–80) 12 MULR 356.

cohabitation,[20] *Tanner*'s case has been subjected to severe criticism.[1] The implied contractual undertaking found in *Tanner v Tanner* can only be described as extremely artificial,[2] and it is unlikely that the courts would nowadays be quite so ready to give contractual status to supposed undertakings whose scope and time-scale can scarcely have been present to the minds of the parties.[3] It is not perhaps surprising that the more extreme aspects of the doctrine of implied contractual licence have been disavowed in other 'family arrangement' cases.[4] As the *Tanner* approach came to appear increasingly less credible,[5] the focal point of the 'family arrangement' decisions began instead to move away from strained implications of contract towards more overtly equitable devices of licence[6] and proprietary estoppel.[7]

(3) **Revocation and termination**

From the middle of the 19th century onwards it was settled law that a contractual licence could be effectively revoked by the licensor at any time,

20 See eg *Broughall v Hunt* (Unreported, Chancery Division, 1 February 1983); (1983) 80 Law Soc Gaz 2198 (G. Gypps). The courts have even gone so far as to attribute a notional cash value to a *Tanner v Tanner* licence in the reallocation of resources between husband and wife on divorce (see *W v W* (Financial Provision: Lump Sum) [1976] Fam 107 at 113A-B).

1 See eg *McGill v S* [1979] IR 283 at 292. The factual situation present in *Tanner* could have been much better analysed in terms of proprietary estoppel (ante, p 314). It is perhaps significant that, as the contractual shortcomings of *Tanner* became increasingly evident, Lord Denning proceeded to address essentially the same problems in terms not of contractual licence but of the estoppel doctrine (see eg *Greasley v Cooke* [1980] 1 WLR 1306 (ante, p 353)).

2 Even Lord Denning MR had been forced to concede that there was 'no express contract ... but the circumstances are such that the court should imply a contract by the plaintiff—or, if need be, impose the equivalent of a contract by him ...' ([1975] 1 WLR 1346 at 1350E-F). Compare the hesitation expressed by Browne LJ (at 1351E). Lord Denning also invoked a doctrine of remedial constructive trust (ante, p 453), arguing that by his wrongful termination of the woman's licence the property owner had 'obtained an unjust benefit and should make restitution'([1975] 1 WLR 1346 at 1351B).

3 Compare eg the reluctance of a differently constituted Court of Appeal to find a contractual licence in *Horrocks v Forray* [1976] 1 WLR 230 at 238H-239C, 239E.

4 Ante, p 906. See eg *Horrocks v Forray* [1976] 1 WLR 230 at 238H-239E; *Chandler v Kerley* [1978] 1 WLR 693 at 698G-H; *Johnson v Johnson* (Unreported, Court of Appeal, 11 March 1986); *Rogers v Eller* (Unreported, Court of Appeal, 20 May 1986).

5 See eg *Chandler v Kerley* [1978] 1 WLR 693 at 698G, where the Court of Appeal declined to imply a contractual term that a de facto partner should have an occupation licence for life. Lord Scarman thought it 'wrong ... to infer, in the absence of an express promise, that the plaintiff was assuming the burden of housing another man's wife and children indefinitely, and long after his relationship with them had ended.' See [1979] Conv 184 (J.M. Masson); A.A.S. Zuckerman, (1980) 96 LQR 248 at 257.

6 See eg *Hardwick v Johnson* [1978] 1 WLR 683 at 688H, where Lord Denning MR invented the terminology of a 'personal licence ... in the nature of an equitable licence', in order to uphold an irrevocable right of occupation on behalf of a participant in a family arrangement. Lord Denning thought that the court could 'look at all the circumstances and spell out the legal relationship ... and will find the terms of that relationship according to what reason and justice require' ([1978] 1 WLR 683 at 688D), but this broad approach has subsequently been disapproved (see *Hoskins v Hoskins* (Unreported, Court of Appeal, 3 December 1981); *Rogers v Eller* (Unreported, Court of Appeal, 20 May 1986)). See also G. Battersby, [1991] Conv 36 at 46. For further reference to the 'equitable licence', see *Beaton v McDivitt* (1985) 13 NSWLR 134 at 157D-E.

7 Ante, p 353. See E. Ellis, (1979) 95 LQR 11.

notwithstanding that the revocation constituted a gross breach of contract.[8] Of course the revocation gave the licensee a right to sue for contractual damages,[9] and the measure of those damages was determined by ordinary contractual principles.[10] In *Wood v Leadbitter*,[11] however, it was accepted as clear doctrine that the breach of a contractual licence could not give rise to any further liability (whether in tort or otherwise) if, following the revocation, the licensee were forcibly ejected or barred from the land.[12] Indeed the decision in *Wood v Leadbitter* demonstrates in its most extreme historical form the private owner's paramount right to exclude.[13] Here the plaintiff had purchased a ticket of admission to the grandstand and enclosure during the four days of the Doncaster races. The owner of the racecourse knew the plaintiff to have been involved in alleged betting malpractices at another racecourse, and therefore caused him to be unceremoniously flung out of the enclosure.[14] The plaintiff's claim for damages for assault and false imprisonment was rejected by the Court of Exchequer.[15] The landowner had quite simply an unchallengeable discretion to withhold or withdraw permission to enter.[16]

While contractual damages still remain available as a remedy for breach of a contractual licence,[17] developments during the present century have

8 The licensor could enforce his paramount right by bringing possession proceedings against the erstwhile contractual licensee. Certain statutory restrictions now inhibit the power of the court to postpone the giving up of possession pursuant to a possession order (ante, p 878). Possession cannot be postponed to a date later than 14 days after the making of the order unless 'it appears to the court that exceptional hardship would be caused by requiring possession to be given up by that date'. Even where 'exceptional hardship' is present, possession cannot be postponed for more than six weeks (Housing Act 1980, s 89(1)). It seems, however, that these restrictions limit only the jurisdiction of the county court and not of the High Court (*Bain & Co v Church Commissioners for England* [1989] 1 WLR 24 at 28C-D).

9 See eg *Kerrison v Smith* [1897] 2 QB 445 at 448ff; *Milton v Proctor* (1989) NSW ConvR 55-450 at 58,257 per McHugh JA.

10 The court should not, for example, place the aggrieved party in a better financial position than if the contract had been duly performed (*C & P Haulage v Middleton* [1983] 1 WLR 1461 at 1467H-1468A). It used to be thought that the contractual damages appropriate in the 'cinema ticket' cases amounted simply to the price of the ticket, but it may be that, following *Jackson v Horizon Holidays Ltd* [1975] 1 WLR 1468 at 1472B-C, the damages will now include an element of compensation for disappointment and lost enjoyment.

11 (1845) 13 M & W 838 at 855, 153 ER 351 at 359.

12 See also *Hounslow LBC v Twickenham Garden Developments Ltd* [1971] Ch 233 at 243D-E; *Heatley v Tasmanian Racing and Gaming Commission* (1977) 14 ALR 519 at 534.

13 It was Blackstone who described the 'right of property' as 'that sole or despotic dominion which one man claims and exercises over the external things of the world, in total exclusion of the right of any other individual in the universe' (*Bl Comm*, vol II, p 2).

14 For an interesting account of the background to the litigation in this case, see P. Polden, *A Day at the Races: Wood v Leadbitter in Context*, (1993) 14 Journal of Legal History 28.

15 (1845) 13 M & W 838 at 855, 153 ER 351 at 359.

16 In *Hounslow LBC v Twickenham Garden Developments Ltd* [1971] Ch 233 at 249B-C, Megarry J referred to the 'old distinction' between the licensor's power to revoke the licence effectively and his right or liberty to do it lawfully. 'He had the power: he did it: if he did it wrongfully he may have to pay damages: but still he did it.'

17 See eg *Tanner v Tanner* [1975] 1 WLR 1346 at 1351C, where the Court of Appeal awarded compensation of £2,000 in respect of the wrongful termination of a contractual licence. See also the award of £1,500 in *Broughall v Hunt* (Unreported, Chancery Division, 1 February 1983), where in similar circumstances Judge Michael Wheeler QC admitted that he was 'frankly placed in a position of having to pluck a figure off a wall'. Compare the rather less generous quantification adopted in *Ivory v Palmer* (1976) 237 Estates Gazette 411 at 413.

made it clear that damages no longer represent the only (or even the most important) remedy available to the contractual licensee. More recent developments are deeply rooted in a new found willingness of the courts to imply a negative contractual term in restraint of revocation. The movement of the law in this area has had the indirect effect not only of altering the rules as to the revocability of contractual licences but also of adjusting the status of the contractual licence within the broader field of property concepts. As always the jural character of a right is heavily determined by the nature and extent of the remedies which the courts are prepared to award for its violation.

(a) The 'implied contract' theory

It has come to be accepted that in a contractual licence the element of licence is not a separate entity but is merely one of the manifestations of the contract in which it is contained.[18] Thus, where a contract contains a permission to occupy land for a specific purpose or period of time, it is often possible to spell out in the contract an implied negative obligation on the part of the licensor, ie, an obligation not to revoke the licence before the completion of that purpose or period. Such a term may be implied, for instance, in contractual licences which confer on the licensee a right to watch a theatre performance[19] or to carry out a building operation.[20] This development was to facilitate an even more important step in the evolution of the law.

(b) The 'licence coupled with an equity'

The implication of a negative term in restraint of revocation has revolutionised the power of the courts to govern the rights conferred by a contractual licence, not merely as between the contracting parties themselves but also—on one extreme view—even as against third parties. The crucial development in this context has come through the increased willingness of the courts to exercise their equitable jurisdiction in respect of the 'licence coupled with an equity'.

In the Court of Appeal in *National Provincial Bank Ltd v Hastings Car Mart Ltd*,[1] Lord Denning MR adverted to a long line of cases which establish the legal implications of the phenomenon known as the 'licence coupled with an equity'. Lord Denning drew an analogy between such a licence and the 'licence coupled with the grant of an interest', which has long been recognised as conferring on the licensee an irrevocable right binding on third parties.[2] He explained the 'licence coupled with an equity' as arising if

> the owner of land grants a licence to another to go upon land and occupy it for a specific period or a prescribed purpose, and on the faith of that authority the licensee enters into occupation and does work, or in some other way alters his position

18 See *Millennium Productions Ltd v Winter Garden Theatre (London) Ltd* [1946] 1 All ER 678 at 680E–H; *Hounslow LBC v Twickenham Garden Developments Ltd* [1971] Ch 233 at 246C.
19 *Hurst v Picture Theatres Ltd* [1915] 1 KB 1 at 10.
20 *Hounslow LBC v Twickenham Garden Developments Ltd* [1971] Ch 233 at 247B–C.
1 [1964] Ch 665 at 684ff.
2 Ante, p 901.

to his detriment, then the owner cannot revoke the licence at his will. He cannot revoke the licence so as to defeat the period or purpose for which it was granted. A court of equity will restrain him from so doing. Not only will it restrain him, but it will restrain any successor in title who takes the land with knowledge of the arrangement that has been made.[3]

Lord Denning then gave two further examples of the application of this rule: the doctrine of 'proprietary estoppel'[4] and the equitable approach to contractual licences.

(c) The equitable approach to contractual licences

The major modern development in the law relating to contractual licences finds its origin in the same basic idea of conscience which is embodied in the doctrine of proprietary estoppel.[5] Where a contractual licence contains, either expressly or by implication, a negative obligation binding the licensor not to revoke the licence during the currency of the contract, the courts have increasingly recognised the existence of an equitable jurisdiction to restrain the licensor by injunction from wrongful eviction of the licensee before the termination of the contract.[6] As the Court of Appeal explained in *Winter Garden Theatre (London) Ltd v Millennium Productions Ltd*,[7] the court will not assist the licensor to act in breach of his contractual undertaking.[8]

(i) The Errington decision One of the first significant demonstrations of the new equitable approach occurred in the decision of the Court of Appeal

3 [1964] Ch 665 at 686. For expositions of the doctrine that a licence, once acted upon, is irrevocable, see *Webb v Paternoster* (1619) 2 Rolle 143, 81 ER 713; Palm 71 at 72f, 81 ER 983 at 984; Popham 151, 79 ER 1250; *Tayler v Waters* (1816) 7 Taunt 374 at 384, 129 ER 150 at 153; *Liggins v Inge* (1831) 7 Bing 682 at 691f, 131 ER 263 at 267; *Feltham v Cartwright* (1839) 5 Bing (NC) 569 at 572f, 132 ER 1219 at 1220; *Wood v Manley* (1839) 11 Ad & El 34 at 37f, 113 ER 325 at 326; *Hounslow LBC v Twickenham Garden Developments Ltd* [1971] Ch 233 at 255A–F; *Woods v Donnelly* [1982] NI 257 at 266D–F; *Classic Communications Ltd v Lascar* (1986) 21 DLR (4th) 579 at 585f.

4 The estoppel dimension of the 'licence coupled with an equity' is the subject of Chapter 11 (ante, p 312).

5 The precise differences between the contractual licence and the licence associated with proprietary estoppel have been the subject of lively debate. See A. Briggs, [1981] Conv 212, [1983] Conv 285; M.P. Thompson, [1983] Conv 50. See also A.R. Everton, [1982] Conv 119, 177.

6 See *Chandler v Kerley* [1978] 1 WLR 693 at 697C per Lord Scarman ('Where the parties have contracted for a licence, equity will today provide an equitable remedy to protect the legal right ...') See also *Mayfield Holdings Ltd v Moana Reef Ltd* [1973] 1 NZLR 309 at 316. Of course, injunctive relief can be granted only where the relevant negative obligation is express or can be implied from the dealings between the parties. Where no such undertaking is present, the contractual licence is determinable on the giving of reasonable notice (see *Patel v Patel* [1983] Court of Appeal Unbound Transcript 930). If the licence is terminated in breach of contract, the licensee's remedy lies in a mere action for damages (see *Ivory v Palmer* (1976) 237 Estates Gazette 411 at 413ff).

7 [1946] 1 All ER 678 at 685 per Lord Greene MR (reversed by the House of Lords on different grounds, [1948] AC 173). See also Sir R. Evershed, (1954) 70 LQR 326 at 331ff.

8 See *Hounslow LBC v Twickenham Garden Developments Ltd* [1971] Ch 233 at 248C–E. Compare the quite different approach adopted in Australia, where the courts have preferred not to allow injunctive relief to sanction a continuing trespass. See eg *Graham H. Roberts Pty Ltd v Maurbeth Investments Pty Ltd* [1974] 1 NSWLR 93 at 102D-F, 105F-106B, 108D-G; Sir Anthony Mason, (1980) 11 U Qd LJ 121 at 129.

in *Errington v Errington and Woods*.[9] Here a father, wishing to provide a home for his son who had recently married, purchased a house in his own name with the aid of a mortgage loan. He promised that if his son and daughter-in-law continued in occupation of the house and paid all the instalments of the mortgage loan, he would then transfer the property to them absolutely. The son and his wife entered into occupation and began to make repayments of the loan to the building society. The father later died, leaving all his property (including the house) to his widow, the present plaintiff. Shortly after the father's death, the son left his wife and went to live with his widowed mother. The daughter-in-law, the defendant in the present proceedings, continued to occupy the house and to make the appropriate repayments to the building society. The plaintiff then brought an action for possession, alleging that the defendant had a mere revocable licence to occupy the house.

The Court of Appeal unanimously rejected the claim for possession and declined to eject the daughter-in-law. Denning LJ found that the father's promise was 'a unilateral contract—a promise of the house in return for their act of paying the instalments. It could not be revoked by him once the couple entered on performance of the act.'[10] This being so, the couple were licensees who enjoyed 'a permissive occupation short of a tenancy', but who also had 'a contractual right, or at any rate, an equitable right to remain so long as they paid the instalments, which would grow into a good equitable title to the house as soon as the mortgage was paid.'[11] The couple thus had a 'licence coupled with an equity', the 'equity' consisting precisely in the fact that the courts would grant equitable relief to prevent their ejection in breach of contract.[12]

(ii) The availability of injunctive relief The effect of *Errington* was to reverse the rule in *Wood v Leadbitter* that contractual licences are always de facto revocable. The position nowadays appears to be that, practicalities of time and circumstance permitting, an injunction may be available in the discretion of equity[13] to restrain a threatened breach of a contractual licence.[14] Where injunctive relief is available the court may also be prepared to grant the further remedy of specific performance in order to ensure that the terms

9 [1952] 1 KB 290. See generally H.W.R. Wade, (1948) 64 LQR 57; R.H. Maudsley, (1956) 20 Conv (NS) 281.

10 [1952] 1 KB 290 at 295.

11 [1952] 1 KB 290 at 296. See *Hardwick v Johnson* [1978] 1 WLR 683 at 689H (ante, p 909).

12 Denning LJ fully recognised that at law they had no right to remain, 'but only in equity, and equitable rights now prevail' ([1952] 1 KB 290 at 298). The case is 'a classic illustration of equity supplementing a contractual right so as to give effect to the intention of the parties to the arrangement' (*Chandler v Kerley* [1978] 1 WLR 693 at 697H–698A per Lord Scarman).

13 The court may be particularly inclined to intervene by way of injunction where (eg in the case of a large all-ticket meeting organised at an advertised venue) it is impossible to quantify in damages the inconvenience, disappointment and general disruption caused by a late cancellation. See *Alonso v Leichhardt Municipal Council* (1975) 1 BPR 9368 at 9373f.

14 *Millenium Productions Ltd v Winter Garden Theatre (London) Ltd* [1946] 1 All ER 678 at 684; *Foster v Robinson* [1951] 1 KB 149 at 156 (as cited in *Binions v Evans* [1972] Ch 359 at 367D); *Hounslow LBC v Twickenham Garden Developments Ltd* [1971] Ch 233 at 247B-C, 248F; *Piquet v Tyler* [1978] CLY Unreported Court of Appeal Case No 119. Compare, however, *Mayfield Holdings Ltd v Moana Reef Ltd* [1973] 1 NZLR 309 at 318ff.

of a contractual licence are indeed duly carried out.[15] The remedy of injunction now seems to be available in most cases in which the licensee manages to raise his complaint before a threatened revocation takes effect.[16] If, however, no application for an injunction can be made before the revocation becomes effective, the licensee is relegated to a mere action in damages for breach of contract.[17]

There may of course be certain circumstances in which equity is either unwilling or unable to grant the discretionary remedy of injunction, notwithstanding that a threatened revocation is in clear breach of contract. In *Thompson v Park*,[18] for instance, the Court of Appeal held that a highly personal sharing arrangement was not enforceable by way of injunction.[19] Equity cannot enforce 'an agreement for two people to live peaceably under the same roof.'[20] The Court thus held that under these circumstances the revocation of a contractual licence, although wrongful, was nevertheless effective, with the consequence that when the ejected licensee forcibly re-entered the premises he was guilty of trespass.[1] Although the point remains somewhat unclear, it is possible that the observations made later by the House of Lords in *Winter Garden Theatre (London) Ltd v Millennium Productions Ltd*[2] have at least the effect of relieving the contractual licensee of liability for trespass in this kind of case.

(4) Effect of the contractual licence on third parties

A vital element in any description of the modern contractual licence concerns the impact which such a licence has on third parties who deal with the affected land. In recent years this issue has proved to be a source of considerable confusion. The problem of third-party impact is, of course, fairly irrelevant where a contractual licence comprises merely a short-term permission to be present on land (eg the 'cinema ticket' case). But where a contractual licence represents a longer-term arrangement, the issue assumes a much more fundamental significance for property lawyers. For the academic there is the nice point as to the precise location of the borderline between property and contract.[3] For the conveyancer the question is one of some practical importance, for the ever-present fear of the conveyancer is that the purchaser

15 See eg *Verrall v Great Yarmouth BC* [1981] QB 202 at 216A–F, 218B, 220D–F (specific performance granted to enforce booking of public hall for National Front meeting).
16 Compare *Tanner v Tanner* [1975] 1 WLR 1346 at 1352D.
17 *Tanner v Tanner* [1975] 1 WLR 1346 at 1351A-C; *Broughall v Hunt* (Unreported, Chancery Division, 1 February 1983). It is also possible that a licensee who has been wrongfully ejected from the land in breach of his contractual licence may successfully seek damages for assault and battery (see eg *Hurst v Picture Theatres Ltd* [1915] 1 KB 1 at 11, 15).
18 [1944] KB 408.
19 Here the owners of two schools had agreed to share occupation of premises which were owned by one of them.
20 [1944] KB 408 at 409.
1 [1944] KB 408 at 411f. In *Hounslow LBC v Twickenham Garden Developments Ltd* [1971] Ch 233 at 249F-G, Megarry J confessed to 'feeling great difficulty' about the grounds given for this decision. He suggested that the case was decided 'quasi in furore' by way of heated response to the licensee's 'high-handed and riotous behaviour'.
2 [1948] AC 173. See *Verrall v Great Yarmouth BC* [1981] QB 202 at 216C–G, 219C–E.
3 See eg A. Briggs, [1981] Conv 212, [1983] Conv 285; M.P. Thompson, [1983] Conv 50. For an incisive examination of the implications of the licence debate, see John Dewar, (1986) 49 MLR 741.

of land may be trapped, and his title rendered less valuable, by an unregistrable, non-overreachable and effectively undiscoverable equitable interest.

Much of the debate in this area has tended to revolve around the Court of Appeal's decision in *Errington v Errington and Woods*.[4] The controversial feature of this ruling was not, of course, the suggestion that a landowner is bound by a licence once acted upon: it was nothing new to assert an equity against revocation in cases of detrimental reliance by the licensee. The surprising development in *Errington* was Denning LJ's endorsement of the idea that the court would restrain revocation not only by the licensor but also by 'any successor in title who takes the land with knowledge of the arrangement that has been made.'[5] Such a ruling seemed to convert the contractual licence into some form of proprietary right capable of binding all third parties claiming through the licensor other than a purchaser for value without notice.[6] It was inevitable that this proposition, albeit fortified with venerable reference to the 'licence coupled with an equity', should appear markedly in conflict with traditional views of the role and status of the contractual licence.

(a) The traditional rule

Received doctrine holds that a contractual licence confers on the licensee no proprietary interest in the land.[7] This orthodox view is founded on a firm belief that the rights of contractual licensees are at all times rights in contract only. From this it inevitably follows that the rights generated by a contractual licence bind only the licensor and licensee,[8] and cannot bind a purchaser of the land even though he may have actual notice of the licence. For these propositions there is extremely strong authority in the decisions of the House of Lords in *King v David Allen and Sons, Billposting, Ltd*[9] and of the Court of Appeal in *Clore v Theatrical Properties Ltd and Westby & Co Ltd*.[10]

4 [1952] 1 KB 290 (ante, p 912).

5 See the retrospective description of the effect of *Errington* provided by Lord Denning MR in *National Provincial Bank Ltd v Hastings Car Mart Ltd* [1964] Ch 665 at 686.

6 In *Errington v Errington and Woods* [1952] 1 KB 290 at 298f, Denning LJ pointed out that the fusion of law and equity, taken in conjunction with the new approach adumbrated in the *Winter Garden* case ([1948] AC 173, [1946] 1 All ER 678 (ante, p 912)) 'means that contractual licences now have a force and validity of their own and cannot be revoked in breach of the contract.'

7 A very typical observation is that of Slade LJ in *Patel v Patel* [1983] Court of Appeal Unbound Transcript 930, to the effect that 'it would be a heresy to suggest that the mere fact that a licence to occupy land has been given for consideration renders it irrevocable or confers any interest in the land on the licensee.'

8 The benefit of a contractual licence may, however, be the subject of an express assignment to a third party. See eg *Picton-Warlow v Allendale Holdings Pty Ltd* [1988] WAR 107 at 114 (parking bay).

9 [1916] 2 AC 54 at 59, 61f. See also the firm rulings of the Australian High Court in *Minister of State for the Army v Dalziel* (1944) 68 CLR 261 at 300; *Howie v New South Wales Lawn Tennis Ground Ltd* (1956) 95 CLR 132 at 156f.

10 [1936] 3 All ER 483 at 490ff. See also *Walton Harvey Ltd v Walker and Homfrays Ltd* [1931] 1 Ch 274 at 277.

(b) The conceptual dilemma

The orthodox view of the contractual licence of course represents sound commonsense in relation to those licences which have only a short lifespan and which are directed towards intensely purposive activity. It would be absurd, for instance, to suggest that the holder of a cinema ticket has a proprietary interest in the cinema. The Chief Justice of Australia tersely remarked on one occasion that '[f]ifty thousand people who pay to see a football match do not obtain fifty thousand interests in the football ground.'[11]

One of the pervasive problems in the law of contractual licences is, however, that the field of contractual licences also includes rights which take effect over a much longer time-scale and operate virtually indistinguishably from residential tenancies. In relation to such licences the attribution of proprietary character is not nearly so bizarre, and in the years following *Errington*'s case there were increasing indications that the emerging equitable jurisdiction to restrain premature revocation had indirectly caused at least certain kinds of contractual licence to have an extended impact upon third parties. It was no longer outrageous to contend that the protective vigour of the courts in satisfying the 'equity' of the licence had effectively converted contractual licences into rights of property.[12]

It was, of course, Lord Denning who became the foremost protagonist of the theory that the contractual licence had been elevated to the status of an equitable interest in land. Notwithstanding the suggestion that such a development could properly be achieved only by statutory intervention,[13] Lord Denning consistently maintained that in unregistered land the contractual licence was governed by the equitable doctrine of notice,[14] and that in registered land the contractual licence, although unregistrable, could generate an overriding interest if coupled with actual occupation.[15] Thus, at least in the context of those long-term arrangements where equity was prepared to protect the licensee from wrongful revocation, a contractual licence had the capacity to affect third parties who purchased the land.

11 *Cowell v Rosehill Racecourse Co Ltd* (1937) 56 CLR 605 at 616 per Latham CJ.

12 This approach did not, however, go unchallenged. Can it really be so easy, asked Professor H.W.R. Wade, 'to cross the chasm which lies between contract and property?' (see (1952) 68 LQR 337 at 348). That chasm had of course been crossed before—for example in the case of the restrictive covenant (post, p 1138)—but the courts have strictly defined the qualities which must be possessed by restrictive covenants before they cross the threshold of the law of property. A restrictive covenant qualifies as a proprietary interest only if it clearly restricts the user of one defined area of land (the 'servient tenement') for the 'benefit' of another defined area of land (the 'dominant tenement'). This imposition of constraints on the doctrine proceeding from *Tulk v Moxhay* (1848) 2 Ph 774, 41 ER 1143, represented, as Professor Wade pointed out, a 'decisive repudiation of the notion that the mere fact that an equitable remedy was available was enough to turn a contract into an interest in land binding purchasers with notice'.

13 See eg *National Provincial Bank Ltd v Hastings Car Mart Ltd* [1964] Ch 665 at 699 per Russell LJ. On appeal the House of Lords, although cautious as to the current status of the contractual licence, was less definite about the need for legislation and was not wholly unsympathetic to the idea of further judicial development (see *National Provincial Bank Ltd v Ainsworth* [1965] AC 1175 at 1239E per Lord Upjohn, 1251E per Lord Wilberforce).

14 It is clear that a contractual licence cannot be registered as any kind of land charge.

15 See *National Provincial Bank Ltd v Hastings Car Mart Ltd* [1964] Ch 665 at 688f. Compare, however, Russell LJ (at 699). It seems unlikely that a contractual licence can support a caveat under Torrens title legislation. See *Re P.T. Stevens Earthmoving Pty Ltd's Caveat* [1975] Qd R 69 at 70D, but compare *Pearce v Pearce* [1977] 1 NSWLR 170 at 179G–180A.

(c) The high-point of the Denning doctrine

The high-point of the Denning doctrine came in *Binions v Evans*.[16] Here the defendant, D, had been allowed by X, the trustees of the estate for which her late husband had worked, to reside rent-free in a cottage on that estate for the remainder of her life. This permission was granted in a written agreement which, inter alia, imposed on D an obligation to maintain the interior of the cottage and to keep the garden in good condition. It was provided that D could terminate the arrangement on giving four weeks' notice. D continued to live in the cottage (which had already been her home for some 50 years). X then conveyed the property to the present plaintiffs, P, expressly subject to the rights enjoyed by D. Notwithstanding that P had secured the purchase at a reduced price in view of D's occupation, P brought possession proceedings against D, who was by this stage 79 years of age.

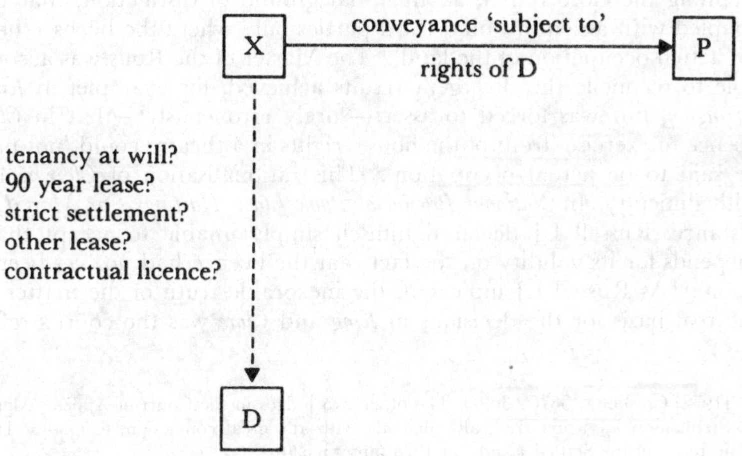

Fig. 66

The success of P's possession action clearly depended on the status of the rights held by D. In the Court of Appeal Lord Denning MR took the view that the original written agreement could not have conferred on D either a determinable 90 year lease[17] or indeed any other kind of lease.[18] Moreover, it could not be said that D was either a tenant at will[19] or a tenant for life under any kind of strict settlement.[20] Instead, Lord Denning ruled that D had been granted a contractual licence to reside in the cottage for the

16 [1972] Ch 359. See R.J. Smith, [1973] CLJ 123; (1972) 36 Conv (NS) 266 (J.E. Martin), 277 (D.J. Hayton); (1972) 88 LQR 336 (P.V. Baker); (1972) 35 MLR 551 (A.J. Oakley); (1973) 117 Sol Jo 23 (B.W. Harvey).

17 [1972] Ch 359 at 366C. D's occupation was rent-free (compare Law of Property Act 1925, s 149(6), ante, p 693).

18 [1972] Ch 359 at 366G-H. See *Lace v Chantler* [1944] KB 368 at 371 (ante, p 688).

19 [1972] Ch 359 at 366A. The right to determine the agreement was neither mutual nor at will (ante, p 680).

20 [1972] Ch 359 at 366E-G (post, p 918).

remainder of her life.[1] In accordance with authority he then held that the courts of equity would not allow the occupier under such a contract to be evicted in disregard of the contract.[2] Since P had bought the property expressly 'subject to' the contractual rights of D, they were bound by a 'constructive trust to permit the defendant to reside there during her life, or so long as she might desire.'[3] The constructive trust arose here 'for the simple reason that it would be utterly inequitable for the plaintiffs to turn the defendant out contrary to the stipulation subject to which they took the premises'.[4]

(d) Doctrinal difficulty and confusion

In concluding in *Binions v Evans* that a purchaser of unregistered land could be bound by notice of a contractual licence, Lord Denning had of course been required to distinguish the contrary precedents of *King* and *Clore*.[5] Lord Denning therefore urged, as an initial ground of distinction, that licences coupled with an equity bind third parties only where the licensee has been 'in actual occupation of the land'.[6] The Master of the Rolls was accordingly able to reconcile the divergent results achieved, for example, in *King* and *Errington*, but was forced to assert—surely erroneously[7]—that in *Clore* the licence to exercise 'front of the house' rights in a theatre could 'not properly be said to be actual occupation'.[8] This rationalisation of *Clore* is fraught with difficulty. In *National Provincial Bank Ltd v Hastings Car Mart Ltd*,[9] for instance, Russell LJ declared himself simply unable to accept that *King* 'depends for its validity on the fact that the licence had not yet been acted upon'.[10] As Russell LJ indicated, the inexorable truth of the matter is that the real basis for the decisions in *King* and *Clore* was the court's refusal in

1 [1972] Ch 359 at 367C, 369D. The other two judges in the Court of Appeal (Megaw and Stephenson LJJ) preferred, although not with any great conviction, to analyse D's rights in terms of the Settled Land Act 1925 (ante, p 620).
2 'In my opinion the defendant, by virtue of the agreement, had an equitable interest in the cottage which the court would protect by granting an injunction against the landlords restraining them from turning her out' ([1972] Ch 359 at 369C-D).
3 [1972] Ch 359 at 369D.
4 [1972] Ch 359 at 368B. See also *Errington v Errington and Woods* [1952] 1 KB 290 at 299. For further description of the operation of the constructive trust, see Chapter 12 (ante, p 413). Further support for the binding effect of a contractual licence is to be found in *DHN Food Distributors Ltd v LB of Tower Hamlets* [1976] 1 WLR 852 at 859H. See [1977] CLJ 12 (D.J. Hayton).
5 Ante, p 915.
6 [1972] Ch 359 at 369A-B. Where the licensee is not in actual occupation when the purchaser takes title, 'the position may be different' (*National Provincial Bank Ltd v Hastings Car Mart Ltd* [1964] Ch 665 at 688 per Lord Denning MR). This distinction has at least the merit that it accords with the special significance accorded in registered land to the rights of those in 'actual occupation' (see Land Registration Act 1925, s 70(1)(g), ante, p 203).
7 See eg *National Provincial Bank Ltd v Hastings Car Mart Ltd* [1964] Ch 665 at 698 per Russell LJ.
8 *National Provincial Bank Ltd v Hastings Car Mart Ltd* [1964] Ch 665 at 688.
9 [1964] Ch 665 at 697.
10 There is profound difficulty with any line of distinction drawn with reference to actual occupation by a contractual licensee. See eg R.H. Maudsley, (1956) 20 Conv (NS) 281 at 295, for confirmation that the difference between an executory and an executed licence was not relied on in *King*'s case and indeed had been regarded as irrelevant for 100 years before that.

both cases to accept that a contractual licence is anything other than a private agreement binding only the immediate parties. It creates no proprietary interest in land.[11]

In *Binions v Evans* Lord Denning therefore sought an alternative (and somewhat more powerful) ground for distinguishing the contrary precedents of *King* and *Clore*. He pointed out that in neither of these cases had there been any 'trace of a stipulation, express or implied, that the purchaser should take the property subject to the right of the contractual licensee.'[12] In *Binions v Evans*, however, the purchasers had not only taken title with actual express knowledge of the adverse rights of D; they had expressly agreed, in their contract of purchase, to take 'subject to' her rights.[13] The imposition of a constructive trust under such circumstances appears at first sight to be much more consonant with equitable principle,[14] but is vulnerable to the objection that the trust thereby gives effect to a right which is not conventionally acknowledged as an equitable proprietary interest.[15] In any event Lord Denning's views, as expounded in *Binions v Evans*, still provide no solid authority for the proposition that a contractual licence can bind third parties in the absence of a taking of title expressly 'subject to' the rights of the licensee.[16]

During the years following *Binions v Evans* it seemed that the effluxion of time, if nothing else, might give a quietus to Lord Denning's unconventional view of the third-party impact of the contractual licence. But just when the old orthodoxy appeared to be regaining its control over the conveyancing dimension, a further decision of the Court of Appeal threw the law once again into some turmoil. In *Midland Bank Ltd v Farmpride Hatcheries Ltd*[17]

11 Russell LJ was unmoved by the impact of equitable intervention following *Winter Garden Theatre (London) Ltd v Millennium Productions Ltd* [1948] AC 173. He confessed that he found it 'not easy to see, on authority, how that which has a purely contractual basis between A and B is, though on all hands it is agreed that it is not to be regarded as conferring any estate or interest in property on B, nevertheless to be treated as producing the equivalent result against a purchaser C, simply because an injunction would be granted to restrain A from breaking his contract while he is still in a position to carry it out' ([1964] Ch 665 at 698).

12 [1972] Ch 359 at 368G.

13 P were in fact supplied with a copy of the earlier agreement which conferred those rights on D.

14 Ante, p 440. It can even be argued that such a stipulation is enforceable as an *express* trust (see *Bahr v Nicolay* (No 2) (1988) 164 CLR 604 at 618f per Mason CJ and Dawson J (ante, p 194)).

15 Compare, however, *Lyus v Prowsa Developments Ltd* [1982] 1 WLR 1044 at 1053A, where Dillon J thought that 'even if the beneficial interest of the claimant in the property concerned has not yet been fully defined, the court may yet intervene to raise a constructive trust on appropriate terms if to leave the defendant retaining the property free from all interest of the claimant would be tantamount to sanctioning a fraud on the part of the defendant.' See also *Eves v Eves* [1975] 1 WLR 1338 at 1342E–F, 1345B.

16 See, for instance, the insistence of Browne-Wilkinson J in *In re Sharpe (A Bankrupt)* [1980] 1 WLR 219 at 225G-H, that an irrevocable licence can create an 'interest in land' only in association with some kind of constructive trust.

17 (1981) 260 Estates Gazette 493 (Buckley, Shaw and Oliver LJJ). See [1982] Conv 67 (R.E. Annand); (1982) 132 NLJ 68 (H.W. Wilkinson). See also *Pennine Raceway Ltd v Kirklees Metropolitan BC* [1983] QB 382 at 389F (contractual licensee recognised, in a less than 'strict conveyancing sense', as 'a person interested in land' for the purpose of statutory compensation in the event of a withdrawal of planning permission). See [1983] Conv 317 (J.E.M.).

a differently constituted Court of Appeal accepted without question that a contractual licence was fully capable of binding a purchaser of the land affected. On the facts of this case (which concerned unregistered land), the only remaining question then concerned whether the purchaser had constructive notice of the rights of the contractual licensee. As it happened the purchaser was held not to be fixed with such notice, but the significant feature of the decision was the Court's willingness to envisage that in unregistered land a contractual licence could rank alongside all other unregistrable, non-overreachable equitable rights and could ultimately be governed by the doctrine of notice.

The confusion in this area was compounded by a later decision by yet a different Court of Appeal in *Patel v Patel*.[18] Here Slade LJ, in dealing with a residential licence, reaffirmed 'the general rule . . . that a mere licence to occupy land, albeit of a contractual nature, as opposed to a lease, does not confer any interest on the licensee in the land.' Indeed Slade LJ went so far as to declare it to be a 'heresy' to suggest that 'the mere fact that a licence to occupy land has been given for consideration renders it irrevocable'.

(e) The present position

Against this background of substantial uncertainty there is generally agreed to be a need for some definitive ruling from the House of Lords on the proprietary status of the contractual licence. Pending such clarification of the law it would nevertheless appear that the balance of recent English authority has tended rather to reaffirm the orthodox view of the contractual licence.

In *Ashburn Anstalt v Arnold*[19] the Court of Appeal gave the strongest indication yet that the contractual licence generally has no binding impact on third parties.[20] It had been argued here that a transferee of a registered title, having contracted to take title 'subject to' the rights of a contractual licensee, was thus bound by an overriding interest pursuant to section 70(1)(g) of the Land Registration Act 1925.[1] The Court of Appeal rejected this contention in forthright terms.[2] Although agreeing that the actual decision

18 [1983] Court of Appeal Unbound Transcript 930 (Dunn and Slade LJJ).

19 [1989] Ch 1 (ante, p 690). See [1988] CLJ 353 (A.J. Oakley); [1988] Conv 201 (M.P. Thompson); (1988) 51 MLR 226 (J. Hill); (1988) 104 LQR 175 (P. Sparkes); [1988] All ER Rev 176 (P.J. Clarke).

20 See G. Battersby, [1991] Conv 36. The general declaratory significance of *Ashburn Anstalt* is evident in subsequent judicial comments such as that made in *Camden LBC v Shortlife Community Housing* (1992) 90 LGR 358 at 373. Here Millett J observed that in *Ashburn Anstalt* the Court of Appeal had 'finally repudiated the heretical view that a contractual licence creates an interest in land capable of binding third parties'. See also *Canadian Imperial Bank of Commerce v Bello* (1992) 64 P & CR 48 at 51 per Dillon LJ.

1 Ante, p 194. This contention had indeed been accepted at first instance by E.C. Evans Lombe QC, who sat as a Deputy High Court Judge and was constrained by Court of Appeal precedents ((1988) 55 P & CR 13 at 33ff).

2 The point was obiter since the Court of Appeal decided that the rights in issue in *Ashburn Anstalt* were in fact rights of lease not licence (ante, p 690). See also the Court of Appeal's dismissal, albeit obiter, of a similar argument in *Canadian Imperial Bank of Commerce v Bello* (1992) 64 P & CR 48 at 51.

in *Errington v Errington and Woods*[3] had been correct on the facts,[4] the Court of Appeal expressed its preference for the pre-*Errington* law, which was 'clear and well understood'.[5] According to Fox LJ, the *King/Clore* line of authority had 'rested on an important and intelligible distinction between contractual obligations which gave rise to no estate or interest in the land and proprietary rights which, by definition, did.'[6] The 'far-reaching statement of principle' in *Errington* had been unnecessary and, indeed, per incuriam. In the view firmly endorsed by the Court of Appeal in *Ashburn Anstalt*, 'a contractual licence does not create a property interest'.[7] This being so, the Court of Appeal denied that the argument was greatly furthered by a 'bare assertion' that contractual licences can achieve binding effect under a constructive trust.[8] The Court felt unable to accept 'as a general proposition' that a constructive trust could be imposed merely because a purchaser takes title under a sale which is stipulated to be 'subject to' the rights of a contractual licensee.[9]

(i) Ashburn Anstalt: a strict view The precise impact of the views expressed by the Court of Appeal in *Ashburn Anstalt* is left in some doubt, partly because these views were obiter dicta and partly because the Court appeared to oscillate between two approaches to the contractual licence. On one reading of Fox LJ's judgment, the Court could be understood to have adopted an extremely traditional approach, ie that non-proprietary rights can never be converted into binding interests in land by the mere incantation of some formula that the third party takes 'subject to' them.[10] As Fox LJ observed, the words 'subject to' will of course impose notice, '[b]ut notice is not enough to impose on somebody an obligation to give effect to a contract into which he did not enter'.[11] By reason of its intrinsically unenforceable character, a contractual licence is simply not the stuff of which a beneficial entitlement under a constructive trust can be comprised.[12] This approach has at least the merit of stern clarity, but may be vulnerable to a fatal flaw of logical circuity.[13]

3 [1952] 1 KB 290 (ante, p 912).

4 According to Fox LJ ([1989] Ch 1 at 17A-C), the outcome in *Errington* was unsupportable in its reliance on the supposedly binding effect of contractual licences, but could quite properly have been based on any of three alternative grounds: (i) that the licensor's successor in title (ie his widow) was bound, as a volunteer, by an estate contract; (ii) that she was bound by the estoppel generated by her husband's representation; and (iii) that the instalment payments made by the representees had given rise to 'direct proprietary interests by way of constructive trust'. There is even the possibility that *Errington* can be analysed in terms of the tort of interference with existing contractual rights (see *Binions v Evans* [1972] Ch 359 at 371B-D per Megaw LJ).

5 [1989] Ch 1 at 22B.

6 [1989] Ch 1 at 22B–C.

7 [1989] Ch 1 at 24D. See also *Canadian Imperial Bank of Commerce v Bello* (1992) 64 P & CR 48 at 51, where Dillon LJ confirmed that '[i]t is not every personal contract that gives an interest in land, even though the personal contract may give a right to use land.'

8 [1989] Ch 1 at 24D–E.

9 [1989] Ch 1 at 25D–E.

10 Ante, p 194.

11 [1989] Ch 1 at 26A.

12 See [1988] Conv 201 at 206 (M.P. Thompson)

13 Post, p 926.

(ii) Ashburn Anstalt: a flexible view An alternative (and more profound) reading of *Ashburn Anstalt* leaves open the possibility that a third party may *sometimes* be bound by a constructive trust to give effect to a contractual licence. In terms of this more flexible approach, the critical question relates more heavily to the conscientiousness of the third party than to the intrinsic nature of the rights which it is sought to enforce against him. Thus, in certain cases, a constructive trust operates against the third party, not because an unenforceable right is given extended vitality through some verbal formula or because the title taken by the third party is defective or already encumbered by some binding proprietary right.[14] The trust arises precisely because—and only if—the third party has 'burdened his own title' with an independent conscientious obligation towards the contractual licensee.[15] Accordingly it is a question of fact whether there are any circumstances which a court of equity may regard as binding the conscience of the third party to hold on trust for the licensee.[16]

In *Ashburn Anstalt* the Court of Appeal considered the available evidence to be plainly 'insufficient' to raise a constructive trust.[17] The mere fact that a transfer was expressed to be 'subject to' certain rights did not necessarily imply that the transferee was in conscience bound by an obligation, not otherwise existing, to give effect to such rights.[18] Fox LJ pointed out that the use of a 'subject to' formula in a transfer may even 'be at least as consistent with an intention to protect the grantor against claims by the grantee as an intention to impose an obligation on the grantee.'[19]

Significantly the Court of Appeal seemed to indicate at least three situations in which, in the present context, there may exist an *in personam* jurisdiction to counteract unconscientious conduct through the imposition of a constructive trust. *First*, a constructive trust may be appropriate to compel a third party to give effect to a contractual licence subject to which he took title and in consequence of which he paid a lower price.[20] *Second*, a constructive trust may likewise be appropriate where the contractual licence was not in fact enforceable against the third party's predecessor in title. In such a case the third party's agreement to take subject to the rights in question appears, not as an attempt to immunise his predecessor against

14 Compare, however, *Kewal Investments Ltd v Arthur Maiden Ltd* [1990] 1 EGLR 193 at 194D, H-J, where Deputy Judge Thomas Morison QC remained willing to envisage that a contractual licence might bind the conscience of a transferee by way of constructive trust. (Here the claim failed, but apparently only because the transferee had not taken title 'subject to' the rights asserted.)

15 See *Bahr v Nicolay* (No 2) (1988) 164 CLR 604 at 653 per Brennan J (ante, p 196).

16 Thus, in *Ashburn Anstalt* [1989] Ch 1 at 25H, 26D, Fox LJ accepted the negative premise that the court 'will not impose a constructive trust unless it is satisfied that the conscience of the estate owner is affected', but declared it 'undesirable' that constructive trusts of land should be imposed 'in reliance on inferences from slender materials.' See also *Canadian Imperial Bank of Commerce v Bello* (1992) 64 P & CR 48 at 51 per Dillon LJ.

17 [1989] Ch 1 at 26E.

18 [1989] Ch 1 at 25H–26A.

19 [1989] Ch 1 at 26A.

20 This view probably accounts for the outcome in *Binions v Evans* [1972] Ch 359 (ante, p 917), which the Court of Appeal in *Ashburn Anstalt* [1989] Ch 1 at 23F considered to be 'a legitimate application of the doctrine of constructive trusts'. Fox LJ ([1989] Ch 1 at 23G–H) referred somewhat confusingly, however, to *Binions v Evans* as involving a 'tenancy agreement' and not, as Lord Denning MR had assumed, a contractual licence.

contractual liability,[1] but rather as an entirely willing assumption of a new conscientious obligation towards the licensee.[2] *Third*, it may be relevant that an obligation of conscience has already been acknowledged (eg in writing) in respect of the relevant contractual entitlement.[3]

It may well be that *Ashburn Anstalt v Arnold* has given a new and subtle dimension to the question whether contractual licences comprise a form of proprietary interest.[4] The more flexible approach adumbrated in *Ashburn Anstalt* is, however, vulnerable to challenge in so far as it conduces, even in the absence of circumstances of estoppel, to the enforcement of purely gratuitous undertakings. It is also unfortunate that the constructive trust application discussed in *Ashburn Anstalt* relies heavily on previous case law in which effect was given, by way of constructive trust, to rights which plainly comprised proprietary interests in the conventional sense.[5]

The law of contractual licences now awaits an authoritative modern clarification by the House of Lords. Such clarification will, however, involve a significant consideration of the boundaries of the property concept, and this itself raises a question as to the meaning of 'property' and, in particular, of 'equitable rights of property'. There are certain movements in the contemporary jurisprudence of property which make it not at all impossible that the contractual licence will one day be recognised as a species of property interest.[6]

(5) The meaning of 'property' and 'equitable rights of property'

'Property' connotes not a thing but a relationship.[7] In effect 'property' is accurately characterised not in the form of any reification of wealth, but rather in terms of socially defined relationships and morally conditioned obligations. This point is especially true of 'equitable rights of property', and has an important implication for the issue whether a contractual licence can ever bind a purchaser of land. In *National Provincial Bank Ltd v Hastings Car Mart Ltd*,[8] Russell LJ was of the opinion that a contractual licence cannot bind third parties since, in his analysis, a contractual licence created not a right of 'property' but merely a personal right affecting the land. It followed from this premise that, since only proprietary rights have the quality of binding third parties, a contractual licence cannot affect even a third party who takes the land with actual notice.

1 See [1989] Ch 1 at 26B–C.

2 It was on this basis that the Court in *Ashburn Anstalt* [1989] Ch 1 at 24G–25A approved of *Lyus v Prowsa Developments Ltd* [1982] 1 WLR 1044 (ante, p 440) as 'a case where a constructive trust could justifiably be imposed'. *Lyus*, however, involved an estate contract and not a contractual licence.

3 [1989] Ch 1 at 26D. See also *Bahr v Nicolay* (No 2) (1988) 164 CLR 604 at 633ff per Wilson and Toohey JJ (ante, p 196).

4 See eg Clarke JA's statement in the Court of Appeal of New South Wales in *Milton v Proctor* (1989) NSW ConvR 55-450, at 58,266f, that 'the law has developed to a stage where it would no longer be accurate to say that a licence never creates an interest in land'.

5 See eg *Lyus v Prowsa Developments Ltd* [1982] 1 WLR 1044.

6 For the modern tendency in statute law to treat contractual licences indistinguishably from leases, see Housing Act 1985, s 79(3); Agricultural Holdings Act 1986, s 2(2)(b) (ante, p 708).

7 Ante, p 361.

8 [1964] Ch 665 at 697ff.

(a) Cause and effect in the characterisation of 'property'

It can, however, be argued that to approach problems of this kind in terms of a 'property' analysis is to turn the process on its head and to begin with a conclusion. Where an equitable interest is protected against third parties, the reality of the matter is not that it is protected in this way because it is 'property', but rather that it is 'property' precisely because—ultimately through the equitable intervention of the courts—it is indeed protected.[9] To address the question in terms of a 'property' analysis is to argue at one remove from the legal reality that underlies the debate, and often invites obfuscation of the issue.

(b) The priority of obligation

To say that a person is a beneficiary or has an equitable interest in property is not to say that he owns a 'thing' but to indicate that someone owes him an obligation.[10] This idea becomes a little clearer if for the unhelpful term 'beneficiary' is substituted the less modern but more literally expressive term 'cestui que trust'. Trusts, said Lindley LJ, 'are equitable obligations to deal with property in a particular way'.[11] As Isaacs J once observed, 'the right of the *cestui que trust* to have the property dealt with as the trust requires is regarded for the purpose of equity as equivalent to a right in the property itself, but only commensurate with his particular right *in personam*.'[12]

(c) Rights to relief emerge as a species of 'property'

An 'equitable right of property' is therefore simply a right to equitable relief in the face of the assertion by another of legal rights in the same 'thing'.[13] This right to relief is premised upon a perceived obligation binding the legal owner to deal with the property honestly and in good faith. An effective claim to such relief metamorphoses imperceptibly into the kind of right which, in legal shorthand, is termed a 'right of property'. As was once said in the context of the equitable rules of tracing, equitable intervention, although starting 'from a personal equity. . .ended, as was so often the case, in creating what were in effect rights of property, though not recognised as such by the common law'.[14]

9 Compare C.B. Macpherson, 'The Meaning of Property', in C.B. Macpherson (ed), *Property: Mainstream and Critical Positions* (Oxford 1978), p 3: 'Property is not thought to be a right because it is an enforceable claim: it is an enforceable claim only because and in so far as the prevailing ethical theory holds that it is a necessary human right'.

10 Ante, p 48.

11 *In re Williams* [1897] 2 Ch 12 at 18.

12 *Glenn v Federal Comr of Land Tax* (1915) 20 CLR 490 at 503 (ante, p 270).

13 For the emergence of this idea in the law of estoppel, see Chapter 11 (ante, p 362). See also *Chase Manhattan Bank NA v Israel-British Bank (London) Ltd* [1981] Ch 105 at 124F–G per Goulding J: 'Within the municipal confines of a single legal system, right and remedy are indissolubly connected and correlated, each contributing in historical dialogue to the development of the other, and save in very special circumstances it is as idle to ask whether the court vindicates the suitor's substantive right or gives the suitor a procedural remedy as to ask whether thought is a mental or a cerebral process. In fact the court does both things by one and the same act.'

14 *Sinclair v Brougham* [1914] AC 398 at 441f per Lord Parker of Waddington.

(d) The necessity of equitable relationship

Thus, in the creation of an 'equitable right of property', the existence of a moral duty is logically anterior to the recognition of a proprietary right. In the beginning was not a right but a relationship—a relationship which was enforced through the granting of a remedy. This is clear from the fact that where there is no relationship there can be no equitable right, as for instance where property is owned by one person absolutely. In *Commissioner of Stamp Duties (Queensland) v Livingston*,[15] Viscount Radcliffe spoke of the 'fallacy' contained in the assumption that for all purposes and at every moment of time the law requires the separate existence of two different kinds of estate or interest in property, the legal and the equitable. In his view such an assumption was quite unnecessary since when 'the whole right of property is in a person ... there is no need to distinguish between the legal and equitable interest in that property ... Equity in fact calls into existence and protects equitable rights and interests in property only where their recognition has been found to be required in order to give effect to its doctrines.'

(e) The analogy of intellectual property

Whole areas of equitable jurisdiction can be understood only on the basis that an equitable right of property is protected not because it has first been characterised as 'property', but because equitable intervention is imperative in order to satisfy the demands of ethical dealing within a given social or commercial relationship. This is particularly true, for example, of the law which protects the integrity of trade marks and regulates the use of confidential information. Holmes J once remarked that 'the word "property" as applied to trademarks and trade secrets is an unanalysed expression of certain secondary consequences of the primary fact that the law makes some rudimentary requirements of good faith'.[16]

(f) The analogy of the restrictive covenant

The same approach can be found at the root of the law relating to restrictive covenants. It is striking that the decision which is generally accepted as marking the conferment of proprietary character on restrictive covenants is not actually phrased in these terms at all. In *Tulk v Moxhay*,[17] Lord Cottenham LC did not hold the restrictive covenant to be binding on the third party purchaser on the ground that it was in some sense 'property', or because (as he would have expressed the same idea) it 'ran with the land'. Instead, he agreed that 'the question is not whether the covenant runs with the land, but whether a party shall be permitted to use the land in a manner inconsistent with the contract entered into by his vendor, and with notice of which he purchased.' He concluded that the restrictive covenant should be enforced against the purchaser on the morally-laden ground that 'nothing could be more inequitable than that the original purchaser should

15 [1965] AC 694 at 712C–E (ante, p 265).
16 *E.I. duPont de Nemours Powder Co v Masland*, 244 US 100 at 102, 61 L ed 1016 at 1019 (1917). See also *Jones v Bouffier* (1911) 12 CLR 579 at 613 per Isaacs J.
17 (1848) 2 Ph 774, 41 ER 1143 (post, p 1137).

be able to sell the property the next day for a greater price, in consideration of the assignee being allowed to escape from the liability which he had himself undertaken.'[18]

(g) The hallmarks of a 'property right'

The distinction between proprietary and personal rights was expounded in conventional terms by the House of Lords in *National Provincial Bank Ltd v Ainsworth.*[19] Here Lord Wilberforce declared that before a right or interest can be admitted into the 'category of property, or of a right affecting property', it must be 'definable, identifiable by third parties, capable in its nature of assumption by third parties, and have some degree of permanence or stability.'[20]

According to the traditional view a contractual licence does not sufficiently demonstrate these indicia of 'property', although it might be observed that, in so far as Lord Wilberforce's criterion of proprietary character rests upon some supposed quality of 'permanence or stability', the courts' definition of 'property' is rendered patently self-fulfilling.[1] Brief reflection reveals the horrible circularity entailed in such a reference.[2] If naively we ask which rights are proprietary, we are told that they are those rights which are assignable to and enforceable against third parties. When we then ask which rights these may be, we are told that they comprise, of course, the rights which are traditionally identified as 'proprietary'.[3]

(h) Changing perceptions of 'property'

The dogma which requires that a property interest be both identifiable by, and capable of transmission to, third parties may well represent an increasingly obsolete conception of 'property' in the context of the modern world. As a dogma it is pervaded by an image of property as something commerciable—as something belonging essentially in the world of exchange relationships. This view is not particularly apposite to many of the kinds of property which enjoy social significance today.

(i) Property as security claims The substance of the modern citizen is no longer intrinsically related to the 'ownership' of tangible and freely alienable assets, but is nowadays more readily expressed in terms of intangible, non-assignable, often non-survivable claims of an essentially personal nature. The social desire which underlies all such claims—whether in the field of employment, pensions or income maintenance—is the general quest not for dispositive power over 'things', but rather for security in the enjoyment of 'utility'.[4] The unifying

18 (1848) 2 Ph 774 at 777f, 41 ER 1143 at 1144.
19 [1965] AC 1175 at 1247G–1248A.
20 See also *National Provincial Bank Ltd v Hastings Car Mart Ltd* [1964] Ch 665 at 696 per Russell LJ.
1 Quite often—as for instance in *National Provincial Bank Ltd v Ainsworth* [1965] AC 1175 itself—the reason for asking whether a particular right is *proprietary* is precisely in order to determine whether the right is capable of binding third parties and thereby attaining just such a quality of 'permanence' and 'stability'.
2 See [1991] CLJ 252 at 292f.
3 For criticism of this kind of 'circuity', see *Colbeam Palmer Ltd v Stock Affiliates Pty Ltd* (1968) 122 CLR 25 at 34 per Windeyer J.
4 Ante, p 876.

factor here is the claim to a new dimension of security in respect of the legal bonding of home, work and family. The so-called 'new property'[5] is, of course, as profoundly related to the emerging importance of residential security as it is to employment security, pension security and social security. The definition of 'property' is constantly on the move, and in the light of current developments it may be wrong arbitrarily to exclude contractual licences from the field of 'property'.

(ii) Injunctive relief and rights of 'property' In other contexts it has become readily apparent that 'as a practical matter' the granting of injunctive relief, when 'unlimited in point of time', can be the equivalent of a property transfer order.[6] The 'status of irremovability' enjoyed, for example, by the Rent Act protected tenant was recognised in its time as 'one of the most significant rights of property' which an individual may hold.[7] Beyond a certain point procedural relief and substantive rights begin to meld, creating a protected status which is difficult to classify in traditional property law terms.

(iii) Property rights and personal rights The courts are only slowly starting to recognise that, at least in the area of residential security, property rights and personal rights are not distinct but interactive.[8] During the last two decades the judicial development of the law of licences has occurred against the backdrop of the ill-fated doctrine of the 'deserted wife's equity'.[9] Reference has since been made to the fact that in *National Provincial Bank Ltd v Ainsworth* 'the personal rights of the deserted wife were not allowed to override the property rights of the husband'.[10] In *Davis v Johnson*[11] Lord Denning MR ventured to suggest that such a concept of 'rights of property' was now 'quite out-of-date'. He declared that

> It is true that in the 19th century the law paid quite high regard to rights of property. But this gave rise to such misgivings that in modern times the law has changed course. Social justice requires that personal rights should, in a proper case, be given priority over rights of property.[12]

The immediate context of this observation was, of course, the legislative intervention contained in the Domestic Violence and Matrimonial Proceedings Act 1976.[13] It may be that the elevation of the contractual licence to proprietary status in lawyers' terms will similarly require statutory intervention.[14]

5 See C. Reich, *The New Property*, 73 Yale LJ 733 (1964).
6 See *Cantliff v Jenkins* [1978] Fam 47 (Note) at 51F-G per Stamp LJ.
7 *Mafo v Adams* [1970] 1 QB 548 at 557G-H per Widgery LJ (ante, p 877).
8 See Sir R. Evershed, (1954) 70 LQR 326 at 331, 341.
9 See Chapter 7 (ante, p 158) for a description of the way in which in *National Provincial Bank Ltd v Ainsworth* [1965] AC 1175 the House of Lords finally and conclusively determined that the 'deserted wife's equity' had no capacity to affect a purchaser.
10 *Davis v Johnson* [1979] AC 264 at 274E.
11 [1979] AC 264 at 274F.
12 See also *Williams & Glyn's Bank Ltd v Boland* [1979] Ch 312 at 333A.
13 Ante, p 468.
14 See *National Provincial Bank Ltd v Ainsworth* [1965] AC 1175 at 1239E per Lord Upjohn, 1251E per Lord Wilberforce.

E. Incumbrances

CHAPTER 20

Mortgages

In cold legal terms the device of the mortgage (and the closely related device of the 'charge') are designed to provide creditors with a valuable form of security for loan moneys advanced by them. When analysed in social and human terms, mortgage finance can be said to play a vital part in the realisation of the life chances and aspirations of a large section of the population. Quite apart from the role of mortgage finance in facilitating commercial activity, the unprecedented availability of mortgage funds has promoted a powerful ideology of home ownership in Britain. As Lord Diplock once observed,[1] the last 40 years have witnessed 'the emergence of a property-owning, particularly a real-property-mortgaged-to-a-building-society-owning, democracy.' By 1991 the proportion of owner-occupation in Great Britain had risen to 67 per cent of all households, of which in turn 62 per cent are subject to some current mortgage liability.[2] There are in Britain today more than 6.5 million mortgages on residential properties alone. When second mortgages and commercial mortgages are taken into account, it has been estimated that by mid-1992 there were almost 10 million mortgages in force over properties in the United Kingdom.[3]

1. DEFINITIONS

In the law of mortgage there exists a technical distinction between a 'mortgage' and a 'charge'.

(1) Mortgage

In strict terms a 'mortgage' is a disposition of some ownership interest in land or other property 'as a security for the payment of a debt or the discharge of some other obligation for which it is given.'[4] The 'mortgagee' (ie the lender of money) is thereby placed in the privileged position of being a secured creditor of the 'mortgagor' (ie the borrower of money), with the consequence that he enjoys priority over the latter's unsecured creditors if the latter becomes insolvent. For the purpose of recovering the amount of his loan, the mortgagee enjoys not merely a personal right based on his contract of loan with the borrower, but also a proprietary right, potentially enforceable against third parties, to realise the value of the mortgaged property

1 *Pettitt v Pettitt* [1970] AC 777 at 824C.
2 *General Household Survey 1991* (GHS No 22, London, 1993), p 55 (Table 3.26).
3 Central Statistical Office, *Social Trends 23* (1993 edn London), p 121 (Chart 8.19). This figure has more than doubled from the total of 4,506,000 mortgages in 1971.
4 *Santley v Wilde* [1899] 2 Ch 474 per Lindley LJ. See also *Swiss Bank Corpn v Lloyds Bank Ltd* [1982] AC 584 at 595C-D per Buckley LJ.

by sale. Mortgage transactions thus represent one of the safest ways of lending money since ultimately the property offered as security can be appropriated by the mortgagee and the proceeds of sale applied in the repayment of the loan.[5]

(2) Charge

Again in strict terms a 'mortgage' should be distinguished from a 'charge' over property. Whereas a mortgage actually invests the mortgagee with some form of ownership of the secured property, a charge confers no ownership,[6] but merely gives the 'chargee' certain rights (eg in respect of possession and sale) over the property charged as security for the loan.[7] Nevertheless the practical distinction between mortgages and charges is relatively unimportant and nowadays the charge may be regarded as virtually a species of mortgage.[8] The rules discussed in this chapter apply generally to both mortgages and charges.

2. THE SOCIAL SIGNIFICANCE OF MORTGAGE FINANCE

The device of the mortgage has always played an important role in business life, but during the years since the Second World War the institution of the mortgage has come to exert a new and profound effect upon the lives of ordinary people in Britain. Mortgage finance has become a central concern for vast numbers of private citizens. By mortgaging or charging realty the individual is enabled to obtain a loan of substantial capital funds which may then be applied for a number of purposes including—most significantly—the purchase of realty. The capital money is normally repayable over a long term (eg 25 years). The repayment of this loan may take the form of periodic payments of both capital and interest (as in the ordinary 'repayment' or 'instalment' mortgage).[9] Alternatively, the entire capital sum borrowed may be left outstanding during the mortgage term, the mortgagor meanwhile servicing the loan by paying periodic interest (as in the 'endowment' mortgage).[10]

The mortgage transaction will almost certainly represent the largest single form of financial indebtedness incurred by the ordinary individual during

5 *Bevham Investments Pty Ltd v Belgot Pty Ltd* (1982) 149 CLR 494 at 499.

6 See *English Scottish and Australian Bank Ltd v Phillips* (1937) 57 CLR 302 at 321.

7 An equitable charge 'does not pass either an absolute or special property to the creditor or any right of possession, but only a right of realisation by judicial process in case of non-payment of the debt' (*London County and Westminster Bank Ltd v Tompkins* [1918] 1 KB 515 at 528). See also *Weg Motors Ltd v Hales* [1962] Ch 49 at 77.

8 The distinction is finally blurred by the reference in the 1925 legislation to a 'charge by way of legal mortgage' (Law of Property Act 1925, ss 1(2)(c), 85(1)). See *Grand Junction Co Ltd v Bates* [1954] 2 QB 160 at 168f; *Regent Oil Co Ltd v J.A. Gregory (Hatch End) Ltd* [1966] Ch 402 at 431B-E.

9 During the early years of the mortgage term, most of each periodic payment will comprise interest rather than capital, the relative proportions of capital and interest altering during the course of the term.

10 Under an endowment mortgage the borrower provides additional security for the loan by assigning to the mortgagee a policy of life assurance taken out on the borrower's life. The life assurance is so calculated as to yield a capital sum equivalent to the mortgage debt on the date of its maturing or in the event of the earlier death of the mortgagor.

his or her lifetime. For the borrower the availability of mortgage finance has a multi-faceted significance.

(1) The dream of home ownership

The major impact of mortgage finance has been to make the dream of home ownership a reality for ordinary people. Mortgage finance offers the borrower an opportunity to become an owner-occupier of a dwelling-house in circumstances where he or she would not otherwise be able to afford to purchase such a property. Many institutional lenders (such as building societies, banks, local authorities and insurance companies) are prepared to advance funds on the security of a mortgage in order to facilitate home ownership for the private citizen. The individual is thereby enabled simultaneously to buy a house or flat with the borrowed money[11] and to offer the home thus purchased as security for the loan advanced.[12] The borrower retains the freehold or leasehold estate in the property throughout the mortgage term, and is enabled to acquire both a family base and a major capital asset essentially by means of instalment purchase spread over half an adult lifetime.[13]

Some impression of the social impact of mortgage finance may be gained from the steady diffusion of home-ownership in Britain during the years since the beginning of the First World War. In 1914 there were only approximately 800,000 home-owners in England, comprising some 10 per cent of all households.[14] Between 1961 and 1991 the number of owner-occupied dwellings in Britain more than doubled to a total of 15.8 million (or 66 per cent of the nation's housing stock).[15] The 20th century has, in effect, witnessed a revolutionary shift in tenure from subsistence renting to home ownership—a transformation attributable in no small measure to the unprecedented extension of mortgage facilities to broad sections of the population.

(2) The effect on life styles

The availability of mortgage finance has a significant impact on the life chances of the individual borrower. The nature of the borrower's tenure as a home-owner or occupier becomes an important determinant of social

11 Mortgagees will normally advance loans totalling 2 or 3 times the borrower's gross annual income plus half of a partner's gross annual income, but while 'negative equity' remains a prevalent fear (post, p 941) few mortgagees will lend 100 per cent of the purchase price of property.

12 Building societies are specifically empowered by Building Societies Act 1986, s 10(5) to advance money for the purchase of registered land 'notwithstanding that the advance is made before the borrower is registered as proprietor of the estate'.

13 It was Otto Kahn-Freund who so cogently pointed out that 'the social function of the building society mortgage is very closely akin to that of the urban lease. The "ownership" of a house bought with a building society mortgage (and collateral security) has the economic function of a tenancy combined with the ideological function of property' (see 'Introduction' in K. Renner, *The Institutions of Private Law and Their Social Functions* (London and Boston 1949), p 35f).

14 John Stanley MP, Minister for Housing and Construction, Department of the Environment, 'Government Policies on Home Ownership in the 1980s', in SHAC, *Home Ownership in the 1980s* (Policy Paper No 3, July 1980), p 6.

15 *Social Trends 23* (1993), p 113f (Chart 8.1).

and economic status. It may affect the individual's personal life and marriage prospects. It certainly affects creditworthiness for a number of purposes: the possession of a permanent home base is generally considered to be a good indicator of financial reliability. The nature of an individual's residential tenure may also control the timing of marriage and the arrival of children, and may well determine ultimate family size.

(3) The effect on family finance

It may well be that the availability of mortgage finance has done more than any form of taxation to redistribute private wealth in this country during the present century. Its significance can be seen in the following ways.

(a) Capital accumulation

Home ownership (even with the aid of borrowed money) has provided for most people a hitherto unparalleled means of access to capital accumulation. Given the steady increase in land values and the general effects of inflation,[16] it is probable that the ownership of realty over even short periods of time will generate a substantial capital gain for the owner. This capital may not be immediately realisable, but it nevertheless provides an asset against which further money may be borrowed for a range of domestic and other purposes.

(b) Upward mobility and commercial expansion

Capital increments, whether or not ploughed back into the realty, provide in their turn a springboard for the upwardly mobile, in that steady capital gains coupled with the borrower's increasing mortgage capacity facilitate movement to a bigger home in a better area. Alternatively, if the borrower is engaged in business, the family home may be used as security for a bank loan earmarked for the creation or extension of commercial operations.

(c) The redistribution of income over the family life-cycle

Another major, but more subtle, effect of the availability of mortgage finance is to redistribute the application of income over the average family life-cycle. Since the burden of the domestic mortgage commitment shifts housing costs from the later to the earlier stages of the family life-cycle, it has been said that the relatively new phenomenon of home ownership acts 'as an indirect subsidy paid by the young to the old, or, more precisely, forces individual households to subsidise their own old age in their late teens and twenties.'[17] This in turn means that elderly home-owners are better able to survive on minimal pension benefits than are elderly tenants, thereby diminishing (at least on the part of those who favour increased home

16 Notwithstanding the effects of recent recession in the property market, Sir Michael Kerr was able to observe in *Palk v Mortgage Services Funding Plc* [1993] 2 WLR 415 at 426E-F, that increasing value 'appears to be a long-term characteristic of all real property'.
17 J. Kemeny, *The Myth of Home Ownership* (London 1981), p 59.

ownership) any real political incentive to care effectively for the elderly. These disparities in the distribution of wealth and social welfare are then intensified by the fact that the more affluent middle-aged, who have by and large completed the payments on their homes, are in a position to use their surplus income in further personal investment or consumption or in helping their own children to realise the same ambition of home ownership.

(4) The political dimension of mortgages

Mortgage finance enjoys a certain public importance not least because the ideology of home ownership has a clear political dimension.

(a) The tendency towards preservation of the status quo

Home ownership, particularly if achieved with the aid of mortgage finance, breeds political conservatism.[18] The enlightened self-interest of the owner-occupier represents a form of political capital for those who are inclined towards the preservation of the status quo. It is also the case that the ready provision of mortgage funds effectively endorses approved patterns of life style and political demeanour. In that mortgage finance may serve either domestic or entrepreneurial purposes, the very institution of the mortgage bespeaks a flexibility of choice and self-determination which is based upon the political philosophy of the right rather than the left. It is, of course, the former influence which has moulded the English law of real property, and it should come as no surprise to note that in *National Provincial Bank Ltd v Ainsworth*[19] Lord Upjohn declared that

> It has been the policy of the law for over a hundred years to simplify and facilitate transactions in real property. It is of great importance that persons should be able freely and easily to raise money on the security of their property.

(b) The public sector tenant's 'right to buy'

In recent times the most notable political initiative in favour of home ownership has been the introduction of the council tenant's 'right to buy'.[20] The provisions of the Conservative-inspired Housing Act 1980[1] conferred

18 It was Harold Bellman, one of the leading figures in the early building society movement, who in 1927 saw clearly that the 'working man who is merely a tenant has no real anchorage, no permanent abiding place, and in certain circumstances is fair prey for breeders of faction and revolutionaries of every sort and condition. Home-ownership is a civic and national asset. The sense of citizenship is more keenly felt and appreciated, and personal independence opens up many an avenue of wide responsibility and usefulness. The benefits of home-ownership are not merely material, but ethical and moral as well. The man who has something to protect and improve—a stake of some sort in the country—naturally turns his thoughts in the direction of sane, ordered, and perforce economical government. The thrifty man is seldom or never an extremist agitator. To him revolution is anathema; and as in the earliest days Building Societies acted as a stabilising force, so today they stand ... as a "bulwark against Bolshevism and all that Bolshevism stands for".' See H. Bellman, *The Building Society Movement* (London 1927), p 53f.

19 [1965] AC 1175 at 1233G–1234A.

20 Ante, p 772.

1 These provisions are now contained in Housing Act 1985, Part V.

on qualifying council tenants a right to purchase their own homes, if necessary with the help of mortgage finance provided from public funds controlled by the Housing Corporation. The then Secretary of State for the Environment commended the scheme to Parliament as fostering 'a deeply ingrained desire for home ownership' and as stimulating 'the attitudes of independence and self-reliance that are the bedrock of a free society.'[2] In his view the 'right to buy' scheme was destined to 'transform the personal prospects of millions of our citizens, offering to turn them at their wish from tenants to owners. It will establish their rights as individuals above the bureaucracies of the State. It will come to be seen among the finest traditions and philosophies of the Conservative Party.'[3]

Between 1980 and 1991 the number of local authority and New Town Commission properties purchased under the 'right to buy' scheme totalled nearly 1.5 million.[4] It has been estimated that 8 per cent of all households in Britain today have, at some time, participated in the purchase of local authority accommodation which they had previously rented.[5] The implementation of the 'right to buy' scheme has not, however, lacked its critics. It is certain that the scheme has withdrawn badly needed housing stock from circulation within the impoverished public housing sector. It is arguable moreover that the zealous political endorsement of home ownership has caused substantial numbers of people to assume financial liabilities which under less favourable economic conditions they could never hope to discharge, with the result, for instance, that the property boom of the late 1980s was followed almost immediately by an unprecedented phase of mortgage repossession.[6]

(c) Discrimination against the rented sector

Much political vigour has been invested in the assertion of owner-occupation as a superior form of tenure to that available in the rented sector.[7] The policy of encouraging home ownership has effectively stigmatised rented housing as the preserve of the second-class citizen, and the renter, instead of enjoying the status of part-owner of housing stock, is made the subject of invidious comparisons between the 'owner' and the 'tenant'. The very fact that the public sector tenant is now given a statutory right to improve his lot by buying (ie borrowing) and therefore 'owning' his own home further underlines the negative discrimination against the renter which has so conduced to the general running-down of the rented sector.

2 Mr M. Heseltine, *Parliamentary Debates, House of Commons, Official Report*, Vol 976 (Session 1979–1980), Col 1445 (15 January 1980).
3 Ibid, Col 1460.
4 *Social Trends 23* (1993), p 114f (Chart 8.4).
5 *General Household Survey 1991* (1993), pp 36, 44 (Table 3.2).
6 The number of properties repossessed by lenders in the United Kingdom increased from 8,400 in 1983 to 75,500 in 1991 (see *Social Trends 23* (1993), p 121 (Chart 8.19). In 1991 more than 133,000 warrants were issued by courts in England and Wales for the repossession of residential premises.
7 For discussion of the 'almost mystical reverence for home-ownership', see J. Kemeny, *The Myth of Home Ownership* (London 1981), p 11.

3. THE CREATION OF LEGAL MORTGAGES

In the historical pattern of the English law of mortgage, security interests in land have been created by means of the manipulation of existing estates and interests in the land of the borrower of money. This practice has brought about the consequence that the law of mortgage is heavily marked by fiction. As Maitland said,[8] the mortgage transaction is 'one long suppressio veri and suggestio falsi'.[9] Lord Macnaghten declared in *Samuel v Jarrah Timber and Wood Paving Corpn Ltd*[10] that 'no one ... by the light of nature ever understood an English mortgage of real estate.'

(1) Pre-1926 modes of creation

In order to understand the modern law of mortgage it is necessary to bear in mind the means by which prior to 1926 a legal mortgage of land could be created. Before the commencement of the 1925 legislation, a legal mortgage of freehold land was effected by the conveyance of a fee simple estate to the mortgagee, subject to a covenant for re-conveyance on redemption of the mortgage (ie on repayment of the loan).[11] A legal mortgage of leasehold land took the form of an assignment to the mortgagee of the residue of the mortgagor's term of years in the land, subject to a proviso for re-assignment by the mortgagee on the repayment of the loan. Thus, in the case of both freehold and leasehold land, the creditor's security for the loan comprised the entire legal estate in the land currently held by the debtor. If the mortgagor failed to redeem the mortgage by the date stipulated for repayment of the capital sum (ie the 'legal date'), the mortgagee was entitled at common law to retain his security unencumbered by any further interest vested in the mortgagor.[12] Non-payment by this date triggered the absolute forfeiture of the mortgaged land.

(2) The mortgagor's equity of redemption

It was inevitable, of course, that the harsh application of the common law would prove unacceptable to the courts of equity.[13] From the seventeenth

8 *Equity* (London 1936), p 182. See also P. Jackson, *The Need to Reform the English Law of Mortgages*, (1978) 94 LQR 571.

9 The acuity of this observation is now rivalled by a more modern riposte to the notion that the rules of mortgage law do not apply fairly. In the New South Wales Court of Appeal in *General Credits Ltd v Wenham* (1989) NSW ConvR 55-492 at p 58,594, counsel had entered a submission that a particular rule 'was not cricket', a consideration, said Meagher JA, 'which enhances its attractiveness'.

10 [1904] AC 323 at 326.

11 See generally A.W.B. Simpson, *A History of The Land Law* (2nd edn Oxford 1986), p 242f.

12 As Carol Rose has said, '[e]arly common law mortgages were very crystalline indeed. They had the look of pawnshop transactions ...' (*Crystals and Mud in Property Law*, 40 Stanford L Rev 577 at 583 (1987-88)). Indeed, this feature of the common law was said by Littleton to explain the etymology of the term 'mortgage': if the debtor 'doth not pay, then the land which he puts in pledge ... is gone from him for ever, and so dead' (*Litt*, s 332).

13 See *Stocks & Enterprises Pty Ltd v McBurney* (1977) 1 BPR 9521 at 9526 per Reynolds JA (Court of Appeal of New South Wales).

century onwards the Court of Chancery began to grant significant relief to the mortgagor, although the manner of its intervention was to make the traditional method of mortgage more than slightly fictitious. Although the mortgagee was entitled to enjoy physical possession of the land, equity compelled him to account to the mortgagor in respect of any profit derived from that land in excess of the interest due under the contract of loan. Thus there ceased to be any material advantage for the mortgagee in exercising his right to possess the land and the mortgagor was commonly left in possession himself even though he no longer retained the legal title.

Furthermore, although the common law attached the drastic penalty of forfeiture for non-payment of the mortgage debt by the legal date, equity regarded the mortgagor, even *after* the due date had passed, as having a continuing right to redeem the mortgage by tendering repayment of the loan moneys. In effect, therefore, the mortgagor could ignore the date on which the debt fell strictly due, being secure in the knowledge that equity would assist him in compelling a re-conveyance or re-assignment notwithstanding that repayment was delayed until long after this date.[14] Only if the Court of Chancery in the exercise of its equitable jurisdiction considered it reasonable to grant a decree of 'foreclosure' would the mortgagor's equitable rights be terminated and the mortgagee permitted to take a free title to the land. Unless and until such a decree was granted, the mortgagor retained an 'equity to redeem' long past the expiry of his 'right to redeem' on the due date fixed at common law.

Accordingly the sum total of the mortgagor's equitable rights in the realty after the due date came to be described as his *equity of redemption.* This 'equity of redemption' simply marked the view of equity that, irrespective of the strict legal and contractual position, the mortgagor remained in substance the owner of the mortgaged land—albeit subject to the mortgage created in favour of his creditor. The inviolability in equity of the borrower's entitlement to redeem the mortgage thus inverted the legal relationship of the parties to the mortgage transaction, and the mortgagor's 'equity' came to be seen as constituting a proprietary interest in the land which could itself be bought, sold and mortgaged.[15]

14 Equity was willing to allow this forbearance in favour of the borrower since the value of the lender's security (ie the land) might greatly exceed the sum lent and it therefore seemed inequitable that the mortgagor should forfeit the entire security for failure to repay on the date fixed in the contract of loan. When it became clear that, in view of the stance adopted by equity, the contractual date of redemption was rendered academic, it became customary to fix this date a mere six months after the entry into the contract of loan. It may also be that the fixing of an early (and therefore effectively fictitious) date for repayment under the strict terms of the loan was influenced by the fact that whereas a certain spiritual opprobrium attached to the charging of interest before the loan was due for repayment, the exaction of interest thereafter was regarded by Church doctrine as constituting a wholly legitimate form of 'compensation' (*interesse*) for failure to restore the principal by the date promised. See R.H. Tawney, *Religion and the Rise of Capitalism* (Harmondsworth 1938), p 54.

15 See *Casborne v Scarfe* (1738) 1 Atk 603 at 605f, 26 ER 377 at 379, (1738) 2 Jac & W 194, 37 ER 600; *Latec Investments Ltd v Hotel Terrigal Pty Ltd (In Liquidation)* (1965) 113 CLR 265 at 277. See also A.W.B. Simpson, op cit, p 245. The proprietary status of the 'equity of redemption' is so clearly established that it may even be claimed by the crown as bona vacantia (see *Re Sir Thomas Spencer Wells* [1933] Ch 29 at 48, 55, 63).

(3) **Post-1925 modes of creation**

The developments brought about by the intervention of equity were finally rationalised in the Law of Property Act 1925, it being wholly irrelevant for present purposes whether the land concerned is registered or unregistered.[16]

(a) Legal mortgages of freehold land

Since the commencement of the Law of Property Act 1925 it has been impossible to mortgage land by the process of conveyance and re-conveyance of the fee simple estate.[17] Instead, section 85(1) of this Act provides that a legal mortgage of freehold land may be effected 'either by a demise for a term of years absolute, subject to a provision for cesser on redemption, or by a charge by deed expressed to be by way of legal mortgage.'

(i) Legal mortgage by long demise Under the first of the methods of legal mortgage envisaged by section 85(1), the security granted to the lender takes the form of a long lease in the borrower's land (usually in practice a term of 3,000 years).[18] The mortgagee is thus invested with a legal estate—a term of years absolute—in the borrower's land, and is entitled to enjoy possession of that land as a long leaseholder. Once again, a mortgage has been created by the manipulation of the existing estates which lie dormant in the land, but this method of freehold mortgage is not nowadays so commonly used as the other form introduced by section 85(1).

(ii) Legal mortgage by charge Section 85(1) also permits the freehold land to be mortgaged by means of a 'charge by deed expressed to be by way of legal mortgage'. This charge, although not conferring on the chargee any legal term or estate in the land,[19] is statutorily deemed to invest the chargee with 'the same protection, powers and remedies (including the right to take proceedings to obtain possession ...)' as if a leasehold term of 3,000 years had been created in his favour.[20]

(b) Legal mortgages of leasehold land

It has likewise been impossible since 1925 to mortgage a leasehold estate by means of assignment and re-assignment of the borrower's term of years.[1] Instead, section 86(1) of the Law of Property Act 1925 provides that a legal mortgage of leasehold land may be effected either by a subdemise for a

16 Law of Property Act 1925, ss 85(3), 86(3).

17 Any attempt after 1925 to mortgage a freehold by conveyance of a fee simple estate necessarily operates as a demise of the land to the mortgagee for a term of 3,000 years (Law of Property Act 1925, s 85(2)(a)).

18 The real value of the mortgagor's interest in the land is, of course, not so much the (fairly sterile) freehold reversion on a 3,000 year term, but rather the equity of redemption which he also still retains (ie the right to repay the loan and secure the termination of the mortgagee's technical leasehold interest).

19 *Weg Motors Ltd v Hales* [1962] Ch 49 at 74, 77.

20 Law of Property Act 1925, s 87(1).

1 Law of Property Act 1925, s 86(1). Any such assignment by way of mortgage now operates necessarily as a subdemise to the mortgagee for a term of years ten days less than the term supposedly assigned (Law of Property Act 1925, s 86(2)(a)).

term of years absolute, subject to a provision for cesser on redemption, or by a charge by deed expressed to be by way of legal mortgage.[2]

(i) Legal mortgage by long subdemise The method of subdemise requires that the borrower carve a sublease for the lender out of his own leasehold estate, the sublease being 'less by one day at least than the term vested in the mortgagor'.[3] Once again this rather cumbersome mode of mortgaging is nowadays less often used than the straightforward method of charge by way of legal mortgage.

(ii) Legal mortgage by charge Even a leasehold estate may be mortgaged by means of a 'charge by deed expressed to be by way of legal mortgage',[4] and such a charge assures the lender equivalent protection to that which would have been conferred by a mortgage subdemise.[5]

(c) Legal mortgages of registered land

The proprietor of registered land is statutorily empowered, in the absence of any contrary entry on the register, to mortgage the land by deed or otherwise in any manner which would have been permissible if the land had been unregistered.[6] The formal method of mortgaging registered land is by way of 'registered charge'.[7] Such a charge, unless made by lease or sublease, takes effect as a 'charge by way of legal mortgage'.[8]

The registered charge becomes fully effective only when the chargee is entered as the 'proprietor' of the charge on the relevant register of title,[9] and until such entry is made the chargee takes an equitable interest only.[10] Once registered as proprietor of the charge and subject to contrary entry in the register, the chargee enjoys all the powers conferred by law on the owner of a legal mortgage.[11] The registered charge is, in effect, a legal interest

2 The legal mortgagee of a leasehold estate is the reversioner expectant on any sublease (see *In re Ind, Coope & Co Ltd* [1911] 2 Ch 223 at 231) and is, in theory, entitled to receive payments of rent from the subtenant. The mortgagee may, however, permit the mortgagor to remain in possession, in which case the mortgagor remains entitled to receive and retain the income of the mortgaged property without any liability to account at law or in equity. See *Turner v Walsh* [1909] 2 KB 484 at 494; *Rhodes v Allied Dunbar Pension Services Ltd* [1989] 1 WLR 800 at 807D-F per Nicholls LJ.

3 There is a statutory proviso that where the subdemise requires the licence of the lessor, this licence shall not be unreasonably refused (Law of Property Act 1925, s 86(1)).

4 Law of Property Act 1925, s 86(1).

5 Law of Property Act 1925, s 87(1)(b).

6 Land Registration Act 1925, s 106(1).

7 For further detail, see Chapter 8 (ante, p 228).

8 Land Registration Act 1925, s 27(1). Use of the phrase, 'by way of legal mortgage', is not strictly necessary for the creation of a registered charge (see *Cityland and Property (Holdings) Ltd v Dabrah* [1968] Ch 166 at 171D-E).

9 Land Registration Act 1925, s 26(1).

10 Land Registration Act 1925, s 106(2)(a); *E.S. Schwab & Co Ltd v McCarthy* (1976) 31 P & CR 196 at 201, 212; *The Mortgage Corpn Ltd v Nationwide Credit Corpn Ltd* (1992) *Times*, 27 July. If not completed by registration, the unregistered charge is a minor interest and is protectible by the entry of a notice or caution (Land Registration Act 1925, s 106(3)).

11 Land Registration Act 1925, s 34(1).

which is capable of creation and disposition by means only of a 'registered disposition'.[12] Indeed the registered chargee may be described as holding not so much an interest *in the land* but rather a 'statutory estate or interest as chargee or mortgagee simpliciter'.[13]

(4) The overall effect of the 1925 legislation on mortgages

The changes introduced by the 1925 legislation have had the effect of injecting a much greater realism into the law and practice of mortgages.

(a) Legal title remains in the borrower

The mortgagor's continuing occupation of the land during the mortgage term is now openly acknowledged by the fact that he is permitted to retain his full legal title throughout.[14] This retention of formal title nowadays provides an important key to capital accumulation for the upwardly mobile private citizen. The mortgagor is automatically entitled to any increase in value of the mortgaged property even though initially he may have purchased the property entirely with borrowed funds. The mortgagee, in closer accord with the reality of the situation, takes merely a security interest (by way of charge or lease) over the land, and is entitled only to the return of his capital together with appropriate interest thereon.

(b) The 'equity of redemption'

The mortgagor still retains his equity of redemption, and the effective value of this right is the difference at any given point in time between the market value of the land and the sum of the mortgage debt currently outstanding.[15] Such is the significance of the mortgagor's equity of redemption that the contractual (or legal) date for repayment of the mortgage loan is rendered entirely academic. For this reason most modern mortgage deeds contain a clause—which strikes terror into the heart of only the uninformed lay person—apparently requiring repayment of the entire capital sum within a very short period (eg three or six months) of the granting of the loan.

12 Land Registration Act 1925, ss 3(xxii), 18(4), 21(4).

13 *Lai v Beem Construction Ltd* [1984] 2 NZLR 278 at 285 per Somers J.

14 That the 'owner' of the land is the mortgagor (rather than the mortgagee) is apparent from the fact that it is the former who is bound by statutory (eg tax or rating) obligations imposed on the 'owner' (see *Westminster City Council v Haymarket Publishing Ltd* [1981] 1 WLR 677 at 680C).

15 Thus, if a property has a market value of £80,000 and is currently subject to a mortgage debt of £60,000, the value of the mortgagor's equity of redemption is £20,000. The value of this equity will normally tend to increase both in consequence of the steady inflation of land values and by reason of any gradual discharge of the mortgage debt. It is not impossible, however, that the market value of the property may decline, thereby reducing the equity to a negative sum. If, for instance, the initial market value of £80,000 later slumps to £50,000, the continuing presence of a mortgage debt of £60,000 brings about a 'negative equity' of £10,000.

This 'short date' for redemption is for most purposes meaningless,[16] neither mortgagor nor mortgagee having any intention that repayment should actually be made on this date.[17]

(c) *The inescapability of statutory control*

The net effect of the provisions contained in the Law of Property Act 1925 is that all transactions which in substance secure a loan of money upon the borrower's real property must inevitably operate by way of mortgage under the terms of the Act. The courts have jurisdiction to determine whether any credit transaction (no matter in what guise presented or obscured) is in reality a mortgage transaction.[18] In *Grangeside Properties Ltd v Collingwoods Securities Ltd*[19] Harman LJ referred to

> the ancient law, which had always been, that Chancery would treat as a mortgage that which was intended to be a conveyance by way of security between A and B. Once a mortgage, always a mortgage and nothing but a mortgage, has been a principle for centuries . . . It could not be that [the 1925 Act] is intended to sweep away the view of the law which had always been that if you proved the thing was a mortgage, equity would allow you to have your equity of redemption to redeem on payment of the mortgage money, interest and costs.[20]

Thus, in a manner not unlike the way in which the courts test transactions in the rented sector,[1] the courts examine the inner substance rather than the external form of credit transactions, in order to ensure that those who borrow money on the security of land actually receive the legal protection promised by statute to mortgagors.[2]

4. THE CREATION OF EQUITABLE MORTGAGES

The possibility of an equitable mortgage or charge in respect of realty is implicit in section 1(2)(c) of the Law of Property Act 1925.[3] An equitable mortgage or charge may arise in several ways.

16 Such a clause does, however, serve the important function of accelerating the point at which the mortgagee's power of sale becomes available (post, p 1003).
17 See *Stocks & Enterprises Pty Ltd v McBurney* (1977) 1 BPR 9521 at 9526 per Reynolds JA (Court of Appeal of New South Wales).
18 See *Alliance Acceptance Co Ltd v Oakley* (1988) 48 SASR 337 at 341.
19 [1964] 1 WLR 139 at 142f.
20 'Once a mortgage always a mortgage' has been described as 'merely an expression of the general principle as to fraud in its application to mortgages' (*Last v Rosenfeld* [1972] 2 NSWLR 923 at 931E). See also *Seton v Slade* (1802) 7 Ves 265 at 273, 32 ER 108 at 111.
1 Post, p 718.
2 It is also the case that the *lender* of money is deprived of substantial protection unless his advance is secured by way of mortgage. An unsecured creditor finds himself in dire straits if the loan goes sour, although in rare circumstances such a lender may possibly rely on the equitable doctrine of subrogation. See the remarkable rescue operation successfully mounted in *Boodle Hatfield & Co v British Films Ltd* (1986) *Times*, 6 January, where a firm of solicitors had made an unsecured advance to its client in order to facilitate the completion of a purchase. See [1986] Conv 149; (1986) 136 NLJ 83, 117.
3 Ante, p 68.

(1) Mortgage of an equitable interest

A mortgage may remain equitable precisely because it is created in respect of a mere equitable interest in land (eg a beneficial interest under a trust for sale or strict settlement). The owner of an equitable interest in or subsisting in reference to land[4] may effect a mortgage of this interest by assigning it to a lender as security for moneys advanced.[5] The assignment is subject to a proviso for re-assignment on repayment of the loan.[6] Such a mortgage is necessarily equitable, and unless made by will must be in signed writing as required by section 53(1)(c) of the Law of Property Act 1925.[7]

(2) Informal mortgage of a legal interest

An equitable mortgage may also arise where the owner of a legal estate in land enters into a specifically enforceable agreement to create a legal mortgage. Equity 'looks on that as done which ought to have been done',[8] and under the doctrine in *Walsh v Lonsdale*[9] regards the agreement as an informal equitable mortgage of the legal estate.[10] The operation of this equitable doctrine demands, however, that relevant preconditions of specific enforceability be met.[11] Thus transactions undertaken prior to 27 September 1989 must be shown to comply with the requirement of written evidence or part performance contained in section 40 of the Law of Property Act 1925.[12] In respect of transactions undertaken on or after 27 September 1989, there must now be compliance with the more rigorous prescription of section 2(1) of the Law of Property (Miscellaneous Provisions) Act 1989,[13] which

4 Ante, p 545.
5 The assignee should immediately give notice to the relevant trustees in order to obtain priority under the rule in *Dearle v Hall* (post, p 1037).
6 See *Thames Guaranty Ltd v Campbell* [1985] QB 210 at 234F-G.
7 Ante, p 447. In registered land a mortgage of an equitable interest can never constitute a registered charge, but is capable of protection as a minor interest (see *Elias v Mitchell* [1972] Ch 652 at 664B-D, ante, p 229).
8 Equity has also applied the same approach to an imperfect mortgage of a legal estate (*Parker v Housefield* (1834) 2 My & K 419 at 420, 39 ER 1004). An imperfect legal mortgage occurs where the mortgagor fails to use either of the modes of legal mortgage indicated as appropriate in the Law of Property Act 1925 (ante, p 939), eg where a landowner mortgages his legal estate otherwise than by deed. In registered land the imperfection may result from a failure to complete the disposition of a legal charge by entry of the chargee as registered proprietor (see *E.S. Schwab & Co Ltd v McCarthy* (1976) 31 P & CR 196 at 201, 212; *The Mortgage Corpn Ltd v Nationwide Credit Corpn Ltd* (1992) *Times*, 27 July) or from the fact that the signature of one of the chargors has been forged (see eg *National Commercial Banking Corpn of Australia Ltd v Hedley* (1984) 3 BPR 9477 at 9482f).
9 Ante, p 746.
10 See eg *In re Beetham; Ex parte Broderick* (1887) 18 QBD 766 at 768; *Swiss Bank Corpn v Lloyds Bank Ltd* [1982] AC 584 at 594H–595A, D-E; *Hoofstetter v Rooker* (1895) 22 OAR 175 at 179; *Re Collens* (1983) 140 DLR (3d) 755 at 757f.
11 Thus, if specific performance would not be granted (eg because the agreement is to create a mortgage in breach of trust), no equitable mortgage can be said to have arisen (see *Corozo Pty Ltd v Total Australia Ltd* [1987] 2 Qd R 11 at 21).
12 Ante, p 254. See *Swiss Bank Corpn v Lloyds Bank Ltd* [1982] AC 584 at 595D-E.
13 Ante, p 257.

requires that any contract for the disposition of an interest in land must be made in writing signed by both parties.[14]

(3) Equitable mortgage by deposit of documents of title

There is a venerable doctrine, stemming from *Russel v Russel*,[15] that an equitable mortgage of land may be effected by a deposit of the title deeds relating to that land[16] coupled with an intention on the part of the owner that the depositee should hold the title deeds as his security for a loan of money.[17] Such a deposit has usually been construed as constituting a sufficient act of part performance to amount to evidence of a contract to create a mortgage,[18] although this view has never been entirely without difficulty.[19]

Today the effectiveness of equitable mortgage by deposit remains undoubted at least in relation to title documents deposited before 27 September 1989. Although such mortgages by deposit controversially ignore the historic concern for writing expressed in the Statute of Frauds 1677,[20] no further formality is required to make the equitable mortgage effective.[1] It is sufficient that there has been a mere act of deposit,[2] coupled with

14 There is considerable doubt whether, after the enactment of the Law of Property (Miscellaneous Provisions) Act 1989, it remains open to the court to deem an imperfect legal mortgage to be the equivalent of a specifically enforceable contract (see J. Howell, [1990] Conv 441).

15 (1783) 1 Bro CC 269 at 270, 28 ER 1121 at 1122. For an historical review of the doctrine, see *North West Trust Co v West* (1990) 62 DLR (4th) 749 at 755ff. See also J.H.G. Sunnucks, (1970) 33 MLR 131.

16 In relation to registered land the deposit of the land certificate has precisely the same effect (Land Registration Act 1925, s 66).

17 If this intention is present, it is probably unnecessary to deposit all of the title deeds relating to a plot of unregistered land, provided that the documents actually deposited constitute material evidence of title (see *Royal Bank of Canada v Grobman* (1978) 83 DLR (3d) 415 at 428).

18 See *Swiss Bank Corpn v Lloyds Bank Ltd* [1982] AC 584 at 594H-595A; *Thames Guaranty Ltd v Campbell* [1985] QB 210 at 218F; *Bank of Ireland Finance Ltd v D.J. Daly Ltd* [1978] IR 79 at 82. The mere delivery of documents has normally been effective without any express written or verbal agreement to mortgage, since the court has readily inferred an intention to provide security as between debtor and creditor (see eg *Shaw v Foster* (1872) LR 5 HL 321 at 339f; *In re Wallis & Simmonds (Builders) Ltd* [1974] 1 WLR 391 at 395A-E).

19 See eg *North West Trust Co v West* (1990) 62 DLR (4th) 749 at 754. It is not at all clear, for instance, why an act of part performance by the borrower (ie deposit) should entitle the lender to enforce the alleged contract. The doctrine of part performance requires that the party seeking to enforce should rely on acts of performance of his own (see Law Com No 204 (1991), para 2.9 (n 26)).

20 It has always seemed extraordinary that an equitable mortgage could be made without any writing at all. See, for instance, the regret with which Maitland was forced to accept the existence and continued force of the doctrine stemming from *Russel v Russel* (*Equity*, p 199). See also *Edge v Worthington* (1786) 1 Cox Eq Cas 211 at 212, 29 ER 1133.

1 'The right created by the deposit is not limited to keeping the deeds until the money has been paid but gives an equitable estate in the lands' (*Allied Irish Banks Ltd v Glynn* [1973] IR 188 at 192).

2 A joint owner of a freehold estate cannot validly create an equitable mortgage on that estate by means of a merely unilateral deposit of the documentary title without the consent of the other joint tenant or tenants (see *Thames Guaranty Ltd v Campbell* [1985] QB 210 at 233C-D).

the intention of thereby providing real security.[3] In this way mortgage by deposit has become, over the years, a highly convenient form of real security. In particular, an insistence upon the deposit of title documents has proved to be a powerful weapon in the hands of banks, this means being frequently used to obtain some form of security for the bank in the event that a customer's overdraft should reach a dangerously high level.

The utility of mortgage by deposit has now been thrown into grave doubt by the enactment of section 2(1) of the Law of Property (Miscellaneous Provisions) Act 1989.[4] This provision seems to bring about the inescapable, if slightly unwelcome, conclusion that, with effect from 27 September 1989, the mere deposit of title documents is ineffective to create any kind of mortgage in the absence of a written contract signed by all parties.[5] Notwithstanding the deposit of all relevant documents, an agreement to mortgage land can no longer be made orally.[6] This outcome is noticeably inconsistent with two centuries of hallowed doctrine and commercial practice, and it may just be possible to argue that oral mortgages by deposit take effect, not as contracts to mortgage, but as a species of equitable charge wholly outside the scope of the 1989 Act.[7] Until this point is clarified one way or the other, the prudent lender will obviously take care nowadays to ensure that all mortgages by deposit are supported by a written contract in conformity with the requirements of the 1989 Act.[8] In practice this is frequently done already, although following the 1989 Act there is a requirement, easily overlooked, that both lender and borrower must sign the relevant agreement.[9]

3 There must be a genuine intention that the deposit of the documentary title should operate as security for the advance. It is not sufficient that, after an agreement has been made to provide security, the documentary title happens to come into the hands of the creditor for some other purpose (*In re Beetham; Ex parte Broderick* (1887) 18 QBD 380 at 383f, 766 at 769f; *Bank of Ireland Finance Ltd v D.J. Daly Ltd* [1978] IR 79 at 82).

4 Ante, p 257.

5 This is certainly the view expressed by the Law Commission (see Law Com No 204 (1991), para 2.9). This view seems irresistible in so far as deposit can be rationalised as part performance of an agreement to mortgage. Following the commencement of Law of Property (Miscellaneous Provisions) Act 1989, s 2, there is, in the absence of a written contract, no agreement in respect of which the act of deposit can be said to provide part performance. See J. Howell, [1990] Conv 441 at 444; [1991] Conv 12 (J.E. Adams).

6 It is possible, however, that an oral agreement by A to mortgage A's land as security for a debt owed by B may be enforceable (at least in a claim in personam under the guarantee) if the agreement is evidenced by a signed memorandum or note under section 4 of the Statute of Frauds 1677. In *Deutsche Bank AG v Ibrahim* (1992) *Financial Times*, 15 January, David Neuberger QC accepted that such an agreement fell within the 1677 Act rather than section 40 of the Law of Property Act 1925 (or section 2 of the Law of Property (Miscellaneous Provisions) Act 1989). See S. Baughen, [1992] Conv 330.

7 See Law Com No 204 (1991), para 2.9 (n 26). See also (1990) 106 LQR 396 at 400 (G. Hill); S. Baughen, [1992] Conv 330 at 332. It has even been suggested that the device of mortgage by deposit is so deeply entrenched in statute (see eg Law of Property Act 1925, s 97; Land Registration Act 1925, s 66) that it survives the apparent effect of the 1989 Act (see Maudsley and Burn's *Land Law: Cases and Materials* (6th edn, London 1992), p 717).

8 If, however, a deposit of documents is accompanied by an actual written charge, it is the express terms of this charge which are definitive (see *Shaw v Foster* (1872) LR 5 HL 321 at 339f; *Thames Guaranty Ltd v Campbell* [1985] QB 210 at 241D-E).

9 See eg [1991] Conv 12, where Professor John Adams points out that, since the full impact of the 1989 Act took some time to dawn, banks and other financial institutions had to spend some time engaged in 'mopping up' potentially defective documentation for transactions effected in the interim period.

(4) Equitable charge

Although a charge differs slightly in nature from a mortgage,[10] an equitable charge may arise where land is charged in equity with some obligation such as the repayment of a debt.[11] Thus, in *Matthews v Goodday*,[12] it was accepted that a written contract by B charging his real estate to A in the sum of £500 would not constitute an 'agreement to give a legal mortgage', but would amount to 'a security by which he equitably charged his land with the payment of a sum of money.'[13] Thus, even though there is no deposit of any title document, a mere informal written agreement under which property is to be security for a debt creates an equitable charge.[14] There must, however, be a common intention to make the land a form of security as such. A mere agreement that a lender should share in the proceeds of sale in priority to the debtor is not enough to create an equitable charge over the property.[15]

5. THE DISCHARGE OF MORTGAGES

Mortgages may be discharged, and the mortgagor's equity of redemption extinguished, in a number of ways. These methods of discharge include the sale of the mortgaged property under the mortgagee's power of sale,[16] foreclosure,[17] and the operation of the Limitation Act 1980.[18] However, the simplest means of discharge arises on the repayment of all mortgage moneys owed to the mortgagee. A receipt for the outstanding moneys which is written on or annexed to the mortgage deed in the form required by statute is effective to discharge a mortgage of unregistered land.[19] A registered charge affecting registered land is normally discharged on the making of the prescribed form of application to the Land Registry under the Land Registration Rules.[20] Discharge by repayment occurs most commonly when

10 See eg *Shea v Moore* [1894] 1 IR 158 at 168.
11 'An equitable charge which is not an equitable mortgage is said to be created when property is expressly or constructively made liable, or specially appropriated, to the discharge of a debt or some other obligation, and confers on the chargee a right of realisation by judicial process, that is to say, by the appointment of a receiver or an order for sale' (*Swiss Bank Corpn v Lloyds Bank Ltd* [1982] AC 584 at 595A-B per Buckley LJ).
12 (1861) 31 LJ Ch 282 at 283.
13 See also *Freeway Mutual Pty Ltd v Taylor* (1979) 22 ALR 281 at 285.
14 *Simmons v Montague* [1909] 1 IR 87 at 95f; *Bank of Ireland Finance Ltd v D.J. Daly Ltd* [1978] IR 79 at 82.
15 *Re Sikorski and Sikorski* (1979) 89 DLR (3d) 411 at 415f.
16 Post, p 1003.
17 Post, p 1028.
18 Neither the mortgagor nor any person claiming through him may assert any right to redeem the mortgage where the mortgagee has been in possession in his capacity as mortgagee for a period of at least twelve years (Limitation Act 1980, s 16). See also *Park v Brady* [1976] 2 NSWLR 329 at 336B.
19 Law of Property Act 1925, s 115(1). The discharge of building society mortgages is expressly governed by Building Societies Act 1986, Sch 4, para 2.
20 Land Registration Rules 1925, r.151 (Form 53).

the mortgagor sells his property and makes the repayment of his mortgage debt a first call on the proceeds of sale received on the transaction.[1]

6. PROTECTION FOR THE MORTGAGOR

Two truisms about human experience have influenced the historical development of the law of mortgage. *First*, those who lend money commercially are more powerfully motivated by the wish to acquire personal profit than by any desire to render useful service to their community. *Second*, borrowers of money tend to be pictured (at least in the frozen frame of the historic stereotype) as necessitous persons who lack bargaining power and who are therefore especially vulnerable to harsh or unconscionable dealing. As Lord Henley LC declared in *Vernon v Bethell*,[2] 'necessitous men are not, truly speaking, free men, but, to answer a present exigency, will submit to any terms that the crafty may impose upon them.'

(1) Relaxation of the rules prohibiting usury

The truisms outlined above both found expression in the medieval canon law's abhorrence of usury and the sin of avarice.[3] The initially inflexible rule of the Church prescribed that no man might lawfully charge money for a loan. To do so was not only contrary to Scripture.[4] It was, in the famous words of R.H. Tawney,[5] 'contrary to nature, for it is to live without labour; it is to sell time, which belongs to God, for the advantage of wicked men; it is to rob those who use the money lent, and to whom, since they make it profitable, the profits should belong . . . ' As Tawney somewhat mischievously pointed out, 'the true descendant of the doctrines of Aquinas is the labour theory of value. The last of the Schoolmen was Karl Marx.'[6]

The practice of usury touched on another very sensitive nerve within the medieval scheme of economic ethics. This scheme regarded all commercial intercourse as subordinate in importance to the salvation of the soul, and

1 It has been a common conveyancing practice for completion to occur before the vendor's outstanding mortgage is actually discharged. The purchaser completes effectively on the basis of a mere undertaking by the vendor's solicitor that the mortgage debt will be discharged out of the proceeds of sale and the deed of discharge forwarded subsequently to the new owner. It seems that this practice (the so-called 'Hong Kong style of completion') is no longer safe and may indeed expose the purchaser's solicitor to liability in negligence (see *Edward Wong Finance Co Ltd v Johnson Stokes & Master* [1984] AC 296 at 308G).

2 (1762) 2 Eden 110 at 113, 28 ER 838 at 839.

3 See J.T. Noonan, *The Scholastic Analysis of Usury* (Cambridge Mass, 1957), p 11ff; B.N. Nelson, *The Idea of Usury* (2nd edn Princeton 1969), p 3ff; S. Homer, *A History of Interest Rates* (2nd edn, New Brunswick, NJ 1977), p 69ff.

4 Exodus xxii.25; Luke vi.35.

5 *Religion and the Rise of Capitalism* (Harmondsworth 1938), p 55.

6 Op cit, p 48.

saw all business life as but one aspect of personal conduct and therefore subject to overriding rules of personal morality. The medieval commercial ethic thus insisted on equity in bargaining, and correspondingly condemned all abuse of superior status or superior bargaining power. Usury was prohibited not least because it was often the most conspicuous kind of extortion practised against the poor and the needy.

The intellectual and doctrinal assumptions which underlay the proscription of usury were, of course, radically affected by the Protestant Reformation, the arrival of a new age of capitalism and the Calvinist acceptance of the rightness and the inevitability of commercial enterprise. But while Luther condemned even the minor fictions by which the canonists had tried to evade the laws against usury, Calvin was later to declare that the charging of interest was not intrinsically unlawful.[7] Indeed, to charge money as the price of a loan was simply to require the debtor to concede some small part of his profit to the creditor with whose capital assistance the gain had been achieved. The Calvinist doctrine held the exaction of interest to be legitimate, provided that the rate of interest did not exceed certain stated limits, provided that the creditor did not require an excessive security, and provided always that loans were extended gratis to the poor. The Protestant ethic of thrift, industry and sanctification through one's calling replaced the medieval detestation of usury, first by a qualified tolerance of certain forms of money-lending and finally by the elevation of a new ethic of investment. The lender entered into a community of risk with the borrower, and therefore rightly took his 'fair share of the profits, according to the degree in which God has blessed him by whom the money is used.'[8]

(2) The historic role of equity

Over the last three centuries the English law of mortgage has practised a cautious regulation of credit transactions related to land, and in this respect the jurisdiction of equity has played a role of pivotal importance.[9] At every stage in the evolution of the law of mortgage since the 17th century, equity has been prepared to intervene on grounds of conscience in the relationship of mortgagor and mortgagee, with the object of preventing any exploitation of the former by the latter. Equity has been particularly conscious of the possibility that the lender of money may abuse his superior bargaining strength and economic capacity by imposing on the borrower oppressive or

7 J.T. Noonan, op cit, p 365ff.

8 W. Ames, *De Conscientia et eius iure vel Casibus, Libri Quinque* (Amsterdam 1630), Book V, p 289 (Chapter XLIV, xiv, R.1), *De Contracto Usurario.* In his *Essay on Usury,* Bacon pointed out that two things 'are to be reconciled: the one that the tooth of usurie be grinded, that it bite not too much; the other that there be left open a means to invite moneyed men to lend to the merchants for the continuing and quickening of trade' (quoted in *Canada Permanent Trust Co v King Art Developments Ltd* (1985) 12 DLR (4th) 161 at 222 per Laycraft JA).

9 Equity was, in effect, beginning to take over the jurisdiction covered by the law against usury, although the usury legislation was not finally abolished until 1854 (see Usury Laws Repeal Act 1854).

unconscionable terms of dealing. The balance of legal protection in the mortgage transaction has therefore tended in favour of the mortgagor rather than the mortgagee.

(3) The modern mortgage transaction

Although equity's protective emphasis is still a potent influence in the modern law of mortgage, it could hardly be claimed that the typical mortgage of today—the granting of a legal charge over the family home—falls neatly within such historical stereotypes of the mortgage transaction as the merchant's means of raising trading credit or as the last resort of the poor in time of need. The social function of the modern mortgage has more to do with family consumption than with the needs of trade or production or even with the requirements of a rudimentary and brutal form of social security. The typical mortgage transaction of today is a means of providing residential utility for much of the population. Thus, while the law still strikes down inequitable or unconscionable dealing in the area of credit transactions,[10] the impact of legislation on the law of mortgage has in recent years been more concerned with the protection of the residential utility enjoyed by the mortgagor and his family.

(4) The rule against 'collateral advantages'

The focus of equitable concern for the mortgagor rested traditionally on the perceived need to protect the mortgagor's 'equity of redemption', since this 'equity' represents in effect the summation of the borrower's rights in the property which has been offered as security. Towards this end equity developed a loose and not always consistent amalgam of rules prohibiting a mortgagee from stipulating for any 'collateral advantage' in a mortgage transaction which might be deemed unfair or unconscionable.[11] In particular equity propounded the 'quaintly labelled'[12] doctrine which insisted that no 'clogs or fetters' should be imposed on the exercise of the mortgagor's equity of redemption.[13] The doctrine was almost a temporal expression of some notion that the debtor should always be free, by the mere act of full repayment, to be restored completely to the state of grace and perfect liberty from which he fell with the advent of the mortgage debt.[14] The right to redeem being

10 See eg Consumer Credit Act 1974, ss 137ff (post, p 964).

11 A 'collateral advantage' has been defined as embracing 'any advantage which the mortgagee obtains as a condition of the mortgagor being able to redeem' (see *Charmelyn Enterprises Pty Ltd v Klonis* (1981) 2 BPR 9527 at 9535 per Reynolds JA (Court of Appeal of New South Wales)).

12 *Bannerman Brydone Foster & Co v Murray* [1972] NZLR 411 at 429 per Woodhouse J.

13 See B. Wyman, 21 Harv L Rev 459 (1907–08); G.L. Williams, (1944) 60 LQR 190.

14 Thus a mortgagee can never sue on the mortgagor's personal covenant of payment if the mortgagee has put it out of his power to restore the mortgaged property on repayment of the debt (see *Palmer v Hendrie* (1859) 27 Beav 349 at 351, 54 ER 136 at 137; *Ellis & Co's Trustee v Dixon-Johnson* [1925] AC 489 at 491; *Cheah v Equiticorp Finance Group Ltd* [1992] 1 AC 472 at 476G-H per Lord Browne-Wilkinson).

inherent as an 'inseparable incident' of the transaction of mortgage,[15] the 'one matter that the mortgagor can insist upon is that, on redemption by payment, he gets back his security.'[16] As Walker LJ declared in *Browne v Ryan*,[17]

> When a transaction appears, or has been declared to be a mortgage . . . the mortgagor is entitled to get back his property as free as he gave it, on payment of principal, interest, and costs, and provisions inconsistent with that right cannot be enforced. The equitable rules, 'once a mortgage always a mortgage,' and that the mortgagee cannot impose any 'clog or fetter on the equity of redemption', are merely concise statements of the same rule.

(a) High-point of the 'clogs and fetters' doctrine

In its most extreme form, the prohibition against 'clogs and fetters' invalidated any condition in a mortgage transaction which tended either to inhibit the realistic possibility of redemption of the mortgage or to prevent the debtor from regaining in full his unencumbered status by mere repayment of all moneys owed.[18] Offending terms were liable simply to be struck down as null and void. Of course, the avoidance of formally agreed contractual terms represented a remarkable denial of the principle of sanctity of contract, and the history of the 'clogs and fetters' doctrine provides a fascinating account of the confrontation between the irresistible force of equity and the immovable object of traditional contract doctrine. The fluctuating fortunes of the 'clogs and fetters' prohibition epitomise the resolute opposition of the requirements of conscience and the commercial ethic of late 19th century capitalism.

(b) Retreat from the 'clogs and fetters' doctrine

Nowadays the case law on the 'clogs and fetters' doctrine seems to have a certain fin-de-siècle quality and the authorities are not wholly reconcilable. It is clear that, prior to the repeal of the usury laws in 1854 and even for some time thereafter, the courts had rigorously insisted that a mortgagee might never recover more than principal, interest and costs from the

15 *General Credits Ltd v Wenham* (1989) NSW ConvR 55-492 at p 58,592 per Meagher JA. See also *Re Shankman and Mutual Life Assurance Co of* Canada (1986) 21 DLR (4th) 131 at 134 per Cory JA.

16 *Cheah v Equiticorp Finance Group Ltd* [1992] 1 AC 472 at 476G per Lord Browne-Wilkinson (Judicial Committee of the Privy Council). The mortgagor cannot by contract waive or set aside his equitable right of redemption (see *Municipal Savings & Loan Corp v Wilson* (1982) 127 DLR (3d) 127 at 131).

17 [1901] 2 IR 653 at 676.

18 The 'clogs and fetters' principle did not, however, prevent the development of the equitable doctrine of 'consolidation', which places one important limitation on the mortgagor's entitlement to discharge all liability through repayment. Under this doctrine, if a mortgagor has charged two different properties under two separate mortgages in respect of distinct debts, and these mortgages are both vested in the same mortgagee, the mortgagor is not permitted, where the mortgage moneys have become due on both mortgages, to redeem one mortgage without also redeeming the other. The mortgagee has a right to consolidate the mortgages, in effect preventing the mortgagor from electing to redeem one mortgage on property which has increased in value, while leaving outstanding the other mortgage on land which, having depreciated in value, no longer provides adequate security. The Law of Property Act 1925 now provides that the right to consolidate is available only if expressly reserved by the mortgagee, as indeed it commonly is (see Law of Property Act 1925, s 93).

mortgagor.[19] Any additional advantage stipulated for by the mortgagee was automatically vulnerable to the stern intervention of equity. Modern courts have, however, had less occasion (and probably less desire) to apply the same censure to mortgage terms and collateral advantages which would have attracted the displeasure of judges of an earlier generation.[20] An important turning-point came in 1914 in *G. & C. Kreglinger v New Patagonia Meat and Cold Storage Co Ltd*,[1] where the House of Lords declared that 'there is now no rule in equity which precludes a mortgagee . . . from stipulating for any collateral advantage'. Such collateral advantages would henceforth be struck down only if they were, in the words of Lord Parker of Waddington, 'either (1) unfair and unconscionable, or (2) in the nature of a penalty clogging the equity of redemption, or (3) inconsistent with or repugnant to the contractual and equitable right to redeem.'

It is likely that the courts' scrutiny of mortgage terms is nowadays governed, as is suggested by the *Kreglinger* case, by a somewhat more narrow and more flexible test of fairness. Accordingly, the older case law requires to be interpreted carefully in the light of the *Kreglinger* criteria, which more clearly delineate the circumstances in which the courts will intervene in the context of mortgage transactions. Nevertheless the disfavour of oppressive terms and 'clogs' retains a residual strength in the contemporary law and now also finds expression in modern statute law. The protection afforded the mortgagor is evident primarily in the following areas.

(5) Attempted exclusion of the right to redeem

It is traditional for equity to direct its sharpest gaze upon any provision which has the effect of negating the mortgagor's 'equity of redemption'. The clearest and most conclusive form in which such a provision may appear comprises a mortgage term which potentially removes from the mortgagor the possibility of ever redeeming his mortgage.[2] What is relevant in this context is not the degree of risk that the mortgagor's equity of redemption may be excluded, but rather the fact that there exists any risk at all.

(a) *The rule*

In *Samuel v Jarrah Timber and Wood Paving Corpn Ltd*[3] the mortgagee of a quantity of debenture stock was by the terms of the mortgage given an

19 *G. & C. Kreglinger v New Patagonia Meat and Cold Storage Co Ltd* [1914] AC 25 at 58 per Lord Parker of Waddington. See also *Bluett v Charmelyn Enterprises Pty Ltd* (1976) 2 BPR 9158 at 9160; *Charmelyn Enterprises Pty Ltd v Klonis* (1981) 2 BPR 9527 at 9535.

20 See the reference by Lord Mersey in *G. & C. Kreglinger v New Patagonia Meat and Cold Storage Co Ltd* [1914] AC 25 at 46 to the doctrine of 'clogs and fetters' as being 'like an unruly dog, which, if not securely chained to its own kennel, is prone to wander into places where it ought not to be.'

1 [1914] AC 25 at 61.

2 It is a cardinal principle of the law of mortgage that the mortgagor has a *legal* right to redeem the mortgage on the redemption date fixed by the mortgage deed. Once that date has passed, the mortgagor thereafter enjoys for the indefinite future an *equitable* right to redeem until such time as his equity of redemption is finally extinguished by foreclosure or sale (post, p 1007). See *Van Den Bosch v Australian Provincial Assurance Association Ltd* [1968] 2 NSWR 550 at 552.

3 [1904] AC 323.

option to purchase the stock outright within twelve months of the date of the loan secured by the mortgage. When the mortgagee purported to exercise this option, the mortgagor sought a declaration that the option was illegal and void in that it excluded the mortgagor's equity of redemption. The House of Lords granted the declaration, somewhat reluctantly in view of the fact that in this case a 'perfectly fair bargain' had been concluded between two parties 'each of whom was quite sensible of what they were doing'.[4] However, the option was invalidated simply because 'at the same time a mortgage arrangement was made between them.' Such is the vigilance of equity to ensure that 'a mortgagee can never provide at the time of making the loan for any event or condition on which the equity of redemption shall be discharged . . .'[5]

(b) The rationale

The courts' disfavour of options for purchase which are incorporated within a mortgage transaction[6] is grounded upon the argument that such options change 'the nature of the transaction from a transfer by way of security to what is essentially a potential transfer on sale, at the option of the mortgagee.'[7] There is always a danger that this transmutation may have been the result of unfair bargaining by an unscrupulous mortgagee. However, the protective concern of equity was stretched to the limit in *Samuel v Jarrah Timber and Wood Paving Corpn Ltd*, where the House of Lords was clearly reluctant to allow the vigilance of equity to be used as 'a means of evading a fair bargain come to between persons dealing at arms' length and negotiating on equal terms.' As Lord Macnaghten pointed out,[8] the directors of a trading company in search of financial assistance 'are certainly in a very different position from that of an impecunious landowner in the toils of a crafty money-lender.'

(c) Restrictive application of the rule

The countervailing principle of freedom of contract not only underlies the House of Lords' diffidence as to the result achieved in the *Jarrah Timber* case but also explains the willingness of the House to reach a different result on the barely distinguishable facts of *Reeve v Lisle*.[9] Here an option for purchase of part of the secured property was granted to a mortgagee ten days *after* the date of execution of the mortgage transaction. The House of Lords upheld the option as valid since it derived from a transaction which was separate from and independent of the original mortgage transaction.

4 [1904] AC 323 at 325.
5 [1904] AC 323 at 327.
6 See also *Harper v Joblin* [1916] NZLR 895 at 915f; *Baker v Biddle* (1923) 33 CLR 188 at 194, 196f; *Laurin v Iron Ore Co of Canada* (1978) 82 DLR (3d) 634 at 645. The grant to the mortgagee of a mere right of pre-emption is less likely to attract equitable censure since such a grant confers on the mortgagee no right to demand the sale of the property (see *Orby v Trigg* (1722) 9 Mod Rep 2, 88 ER 276).
7 P.B. Fairest, *Mortgages* (2nd edn, London 1980), p 26.
8 [1904] AC 323 at 327.
9 [1902] AC 461.

The rationale underlying the distinction between *Jarrah Timber* and *Reeve v Lisle* is thus supposedly the idea that the mortgagor, once he has obtained the loan which he seeks, is no longer vulnerable to unconscionable dealing by his mortgagee in respect of a later and quite separate transaction.[10] However, the ultimate test turns on whether there has been, in the view of equity, unconscionable dealing between mortgagor and mortgagee. The mere fact that a mortgage and an option are contained in separate documents executed on different days does not necessarily exclude the possibility of a vitiating clog on the equity of redemption.[11] The essential issue before the court is whether the two documents represent 'in substance a single and undivided contract or two distinct contracts.'[12]

(6) Postponement of the date of redemption

It is not impossible that a mortgage, instead of excluding altogether the mortgagor's right to redeem, should merely include a contractual term which *postpones* the earliest permissible date of redemption. It is, of course, customary for a formal redemption date to be set at a relatively short distance (eg six months) from the date of the mortgage transaction, since the mortgagor retains an equity to redeem the mortgage long after this date has passed.[13] However, the contractual terms of a mortgage may sometimes defer the earliest date at which redemption may occur,[14] since the effect of such a term is to guarantee for the mortgagee a secure investment over a prolonged period at a favourable rate of interest. In certain circumstances this type of provision may operate so unilaterally in favour of the mortgagee that the courts will hold it to be invalid and unenforceable.[15] The test is ultimately one of degree as to whether contractual postponement effectively renders the equity of redemption illusory or valueless, in which case it would be unconscionable to uphold the postponement clause in its literal terms.

(a) Exceptional intervention of equity

In *Fairclough v Swan Brewery Co Ltd*[16] the mortgagor was contractually precluded from exercising his right of redemption during most of the period of the leasehold term which provided the subject matter of the mortgage. The mortgagor's leasehold estate was for a term of 17½ years, and according to the terms of the mortgage his right to redeem arose at the earliest only

10 For criticism of the logic of the distinction, see P.B. Fairest, op cit, p 27f. Compare, however, *Lewis v Frank Love Ltd* [1961] 1 WLR 261 at 271; (1961) 77 LQR 163 (P.V. Baker).

11 *Re Supreme Court Registrar to Alexander Dawson Inc* [1976] 1 NZLR 615 at 627.

12 *G. & C. Kreglinger v New Patagonia Meat and Cold Storage Co Ltd* [1914] AC 25 at 39 per Viscount Haldane LC. In *Bay of Islands Electric Power Board v Buckland* (Unreported, A No 48/1976, 10 July 1978), the Supreme Court of New Zealand upheld an option which had been granted to the mortgagee in advance of the mortgage and which was proved to be a quite separate transaction.

13 Ante, p 941.

14 Of course, in the absence of any stipulation that the mortgagor may not pay off before a specified date, there is nothing to prevent him from tendering full payment at any time and requiring that the mortgage be discharged (see *G.A. Investments Pty Ltd v Standard Insurance Co Ltd* [1964] WAR 264 at 267; *Ex parte Tori* [1977] Qd R 256 at 260D-E).

15 See E.H. Bodkin, (1941) 5 Conv (NS) 178.

16 [1912] AC 565.

six weeks before the expiry of that lease. The Judicial Committee of the Privy Council upheld a claim by the mortgagor to redeem at an earlier date, ruling that 'equity will not permit any device or contrivance being part of the mortgage transaction or contemporaneous with it to prevent or impede redemption.'[17] In this case the mortgage had been rendered 'for all practical purposes . . . irredeemable', since on redemption the effective value to the mortgagor of an almost expired lease would have been minimal.

(b) The more general approach

The facts of *Fairclough* are of course exceptional. Most modern mortgages fix a relatively early or 'short' date for repayment, and later cases have not adopted so wide a view of the inequity of agreed postponements of the due date. It is clear that the borrower has no general right either at common law or in equity to insist upon repayment of the principal debt *in advance of* the repayment date specified in the loan agreement.[18] Indeed, since the mortgagee has taken trouble to put out his moneys at interest, an express privilege of pre-payment before the contractually stipulated due date can properly be regarded as a 'valuable right'.[19] The mortgagor's entitlement to redeem before this date is essentially a matter of contract for mortgagor and mortgagee[20] and, in the absence of an expressly conferred right of early repayment, the matter does not normally fall within the purview of equity.[1]

It seems therefore that actual repayment of the mortgage moneys may be postponed quite validly until such date as may be fixed by the parties in the instrument of mortgage. Only in rare circumstances today will the court intervene in support of a mortgagor's claim to redeem earlier than the contracted date. In deference to considerations of mutuality in the parties' bargain,[2] the court will normally allow early redemption if the mortgagee

17 [1912] AC 565 at 570.

18 *Hyde Management Services Pty Ltd v F.A.I. Insurances Ltd* (1979) 144 CLR 541 at 543f per Mason J. See also *G.O. & M.J.T. Nominees Pty Ltd v Public Trustee* [1986] VR 137 at 138. It is significant that some jurisdictions confer a statutory right on the mortgagor to pay off the principal at any time during the agreed mortgage term, but only on condition that where he repays on his own initiative he also pays interest for the entirety of the originally agreed term. See eg Conveyancing Act 1919 (New South Wales), s 93(1); *Wanner v Caruana* [1974] 2 NSWLR 301 at 306C-D; *Stocks & Enterprises Pty Ltd v McBurney* (1977) 1 BPR 9521 at 9526.

19 See *Re Cloval Developments Inc and Koledin* (1984) 5 DLR (4th) 190 at 192. So important is the concern for stability of investment that, in the days before investment in shares and government securities became common, the courts even used to impose a standard term or rule of law that a mortgagor who wished to redeem after the date fixed for redemption should pay six months' interest or give six months' notice of his intention to redeem. See Kekewich J's reference in *Bovill v Endle* [1896] 1 Ch 648 at 650 to this 'equitable right' of the mortgagee.

20 See *Burrough v Cranston* (1840) 2 Ir Eq R 203 at 205; *Brown v Cole* (1845) 14 Sim 427, 60 ER 424; *West Derby Union v Metropolitan Life Assurance Society* [1897] AC 647 at 649ff; *Stansfield and Swiney v Housing Mortgage Corpn Ltd* [1964–5] NSWR 1259 at 1261f.

1 See *Stocks & Enterprises Pty Ltd v McBurney* (1977) 1 BPR 9521 at 9526 per Reynolds JA (Court of Appeal of New South Wales). Thus, even if he tendered capital plus interest for the whole of the intervening period, the mortgagor had no right, apart from express provision, to redeem before the due date (see *Brown v Cole* (1845) 14 Sim 427, 60 ER 424).

2 See *Stocks & Enterprises Pty Ltd v McBurney* (1977) 1 BPR 9521 at 9526.

was equally free under the loan terms to call in the loan moneys prematurely.[3] Alternatively the court may endorse redemption in advance of the due date if the postponement of the right to repay is in all the circumstances unconscionable or oppressive.[4]

The latter criterion of equitable intervention may nowadays be difficult to meet, as is amply demonstrated by the general approach to contractually retarded redemption dates adopted in *Knightsbridge Estates Trust Ltd v Byrne*.[5] Here the Court of Appeal was confronted with a mortgage term which stipulated that the loan moneys should not be repaid before the expiry of 40 years from the granting of the mortgage. The loan had been obtained at an interest rate of 6½ per cent per annum, and when later the mortgagor wished to avail himself of a general fall in interest rates by borrowing money elsewhere, he claimed to be entitled to redeem the mortgage before the expiration of the stipulated period. The Court of Appeal held, however, that the validity of the original loan terms was not prejudiced by the contractual postponement of the date for redemption. Sir Wilfred Greene MR made it clear that 'equity does not reform mortgage transactions because they are unreasonable.' Equity is concerned, he said, 'to see two things—one that the essential requirements of a mortgage transaction are observed, and the other that oppressive or unconscionable terms are not enforced.'[6] Thus, in the present case, the postponement of the date of redemption could not be challenged on the ground that postponement was permissible only for a 'reasonable' period. The true ground of equitable intervention arose where the contractual right of redemption was rendered 'illusory' by postponement of the right to redeem, as had occurred in *Fairclough v Swan Brewery Co Ltd*.

The Court thus declined to intervene in the *Knightsbridge Estates* case, where from the start the mortgagor had bargained at arm's length for a long-term loan of a substantial sum (£310,000) on the most advantageous terms available at the time. The resulting agreement was 'a commercial agreement between two important corporations experienced in such matters' and had 'none of the features of an oppressive bargain where the borrower is at the mercy of an unscrupulous lender.'[7] The Court of Appeal was not prepared to view the agreement made 'as anything but a proper business transaction'. Any other result would have placed 'an unfortunate restriction on the liberty of contract of competent parties who are at arm's length'.[8] Moreover, it would have led to the 'highly inequitable' consequence that whereas the mortgagor would from the outset have had the right to redeem at any time (thereby subjecting the lender to the inconvenience of profitable re-

3 See *Ex parte Tori* [1977] Qd R 256 at 257D. Of course if the mortgagee demands payment of the mortgage debt or resorts to the security (eg by taking possession), he cannot resist early or premature redemption by the mortgagor (see *Bovill v Endle* [1896] 1 Ch 648 at 650f; *Re Shankman and Mutual Life Assurance Co of Canada* (1986) 21 DLR (4th) 131 at 134).

4 See *Morgan v Jeffreys* [1910] 1 Ch 620 at 629; *G.A. Investments Pty Ltd v Standard Insurance Co Ltd* [1964] WAR 264 at 266; *Ex parte Tori* [1977] Qd R 256 at 260D.

5 [1939] Ch 441.

6 [1939] Ch 441 at 457.

7 [1939] Ch 441 at 455.

8 [1939] Ch 441 at 455.

investment[9]) the mortgagee would have had no right to require repayment of the loan otherwise than by the specified contractual instalments.[10]

(7) Solus agreements

It is not uncommon, where the mortgagor and mortgagee conduct a common trading concern, for the terms of the mortgage to require that the mortgagor refrain from any commercial competition prejudicial to the mortgagee's own business operation. These restrictions appear most frequently in the form of a 'solus tie' by which a mortgagee such as a petrol company or a brewery imposes on the mortgagor a condition that the latter shall deal only in the products manufactured or distributed by the mortgagee.

The possibility that a mortgage transaction may thus confer a collateral advantage on the mortgagee has activated the watchful concern of equity, initially because the securing of collateral benefits for the mortgagee was in the past a common means of circumventing the laws against usury.[11] More recently the vigilance of equity has been reinforced if not supplanted by another ground of concern—this time expressed by the common lawyers—that solus clauses in a mortgage agreement may offend the contractual doctrine against unreasonable restraints of trade.

(a) The equitable distaste for superadded obligations

Even after the repeal of the usury laws equity viewed the solus tie with suspicion, partly because it gave scope for coercive bargaining or commercial exploitation on the part of the mortgagee, and also because the 'advance of money with a superadded obligation' seemed so over-protective of the mortgagee as to offend against 'the settled principles of equity'.[12]

(i) The old rule of thumb The case law in this area is not wholly consistent,[13] but it seems that the courts were usually prepared to strike down as void any collateral benefit for a mortgagee which purported to remain in force *after* the redemption of the mortgage.[14] A solus tie not limited to the actual (as distinct from potential) duration of a mortgage was liable to be regarded as invalid, since such a tie—if allowed to remain in force after redemption—

9 See *Hyde Management Services Pty Ltd v F.A.I. Insurances Ltd* (1979) 144 CLR 541 at 548.

10 The decision of the Court of Appeal was affirmed by the House of Lords, but on the different ground that the mortgage in question constituted a debenture within the Companies Act 1929, ss 74, 380, and was not invalidated on the ground of postponement of the redemption date (see [1940] AC 613). However, the House of Lords threw no doubt on the reasoning applied by the Court of Appeal.

11 'A man shall not have interest for his money, and a collateral advantage besides for the loan of it, or clog the equity of redemption with any by-agreement' (*Jennings v Ward* (1705) 2 Vern 520 at 521, 23 ER 935). In view of the development of the law since 1705 (post, p 957), this statement cannot now stand unqualified (see *Biggs v Hoddinott* [1898] 2 Ch 307 at 321; *G. & C. Kreglinger v New Patagonia Meat and Cold Storage Co Ltd* [1914] AC 25 at 38; *Re Petrol Filling Station, Vauxhall Bridge Road, London* (1969) 20 P & CR 1 at 7).

12 *Noakes & Co Ltd v Rice* [1902] AC 24 at 31; *Toohey v Gunther* (1928) 41 CLR 181 at 192.

13 The difficult case is generally taken to be *Santley v Wilde* [1899] 2 Ch 474, but this decision was heavily criticised by the House of Lords in *Noakes & Co Ltd v Rice* [1902] AC 24 at 31f, 34. See also *Bevham Investments Pty Ltd v Belgot Pty Ltd* (1982) 149 CLR 494 at 501.

14 See eg *Noakes & Co Ltd v Rice* [1902] AC 24 at 29, 33; *Bradley v Carritt* [1903] AC 253 at 266.

could be seen as repugnant to the mortgagor's equity to redeem.[15] The mortgagor would be in a distinctly less favourable position after redemption than he occupied before the grant of the mortgage. Full repayment of all moneys owed would not have the effect of restoring the status quo ante, since the restrictive trading condition would still remain in operation. Conversely the courts generally upheld solus clauses whose force was in terms limited to the actual continuance of the mortgage security,[16] since in such cases there was no danger that redemption of the mortgage would leave the borrower still encumbered by some obligation towards the lender.

(ii) The qualification imposed by the Kreglinger case The distinctions outlined in the older decisions probably remain good law today, with an important qualification imposed by the decision of the House of Lords in *G. & C. Kreglinger v New Patagonia Meat and Cold Storage Co Ltd.*[17] Here Viscount Haldane LC indicated that although equity would continue to control any bargain so framed that 'the right to redeem was cut down',[18] the parties to a mortgage are entirely free to 'stipulate for a collateral undertaking, outside and clear of the mortgage'.[19] No objection can be raised against such a collateral advantage, provided that it does not comprise 'remuneration for the use of the money'[20] or constitute any 'part of the consideration given for the mortgage'.[1] If the collateral advantage is thus neither a 'part of the mortgage transaction' nor 'one of the terms of the loan',[2] but is instead 'part of another kind of transaction',[3] it falls completely outside the ambit of the equitable objection to clogs on the equity of redemption.[4] A collateral advantage included in a wholly independent transaction may therefore endure even beyond the redemption of the mortgage, provided that the advantage is not otherwise unconscionable.[5]

Thus it was that in the *Kreglinger* case itself the House of Lords upheld the validity, even after redemption of the mortgage, of an agreement that the mortgagor would not sell a specified product to any person other than the lender so long as the lender was willing to purchase at not less than the best price offered by any third party. This agreement was regarded as part of a wholly different transaction from that of the mortgage, even though it was contained in the same document and even though it may

15 See *Toohey v Gunther* (1928) 41 CLR 181 at 192.
16 *Biggs v Hoddinott* [1898] 2 Ch 307 at 313ff, 321ff.
17 [1914] AC 25.
18 See *Re Petrol Filling Station, Vauxhall Bridge Road, London* (1969) 20 P & CR 1 at 7 per Ungoed-Thomas J: 'The purpose of the [equitable] jurisdiction is to ensure that the transaction, whose "real nature and substance" was "one of mortgage simply," should be limited to a mortgage, that is, to a mortgage being "a mere security for money".'
19 [1914] AC 25 at 39.
20 *Noakes & Co Ltd v Rice* [1902] AC 24 at 34 per Lord Davey.
1 *De Beers Consolidated Mines Ltd v British South Africa Co* [1912] AC 52 at 67. See *Re Petrol Filling Station, Vauxhall Bridge Road, London* (1969) 20 P & CR 1 at 6.
2 *Samuel v Jarrah Timber and Wood Paving Corpn Ltd* [1904] AC 323 at 329 per Lord Lindley.
3 *Re Petrol Filling Station, Vauxhall Bridge Road, London* (1969) 20 P & CR 1 at 9.
4 *Re Petrol Filling Station, Vauxhall Bridge Road, London* (1969) 20 P & CR 1 at 8 per Ungoed-Thomas J.
5 *Re Petrol Filling Station, Vauxhall Bridge Road, London* (1969) 20 P & CR 1 at 7 per Ungoed-Thomas J.

have been 'in the nature of a collateral bargain the entering into which was a preliminary and separable condition of the loan'.[6]

It is not easy, however, to draw a firm distinction between, on the one hand, a collateral benefit which although apparently a sine qua non of the mortgage advance is conferred 'outside the security . . . [and] in substance independent of it',[7] and, on the other hand, a collateral agreement which is 'part of the consideration given for the mortgage'[8] and which is therefore vulnerable to the censure of equity. It may be for this reason that the more recent legal challenge to solus agreements has tended to be based on a rather different objection stemming from the law of contract.

(b) *Invalid restraints of trade*

There is a general doctrine in the law of contract that agreements which operate unreasonably in restraint of trade are void on the ground of public policy.[9] In the more recent past solus agreements by mortgagors have been subjected, with varying degrees of success,[10] to challenge on this basis.[11] In general it seems that the courts are prepared to uphold solus agreements which are limited in their stipulated duration to relatively short periods (eg five years), but would not be willing to countenance a tie which extended over a period of 21 years unless such a prolonged tie is grounded in a clear case of economic necessity.[12]

(8) Judicial control of 'oppressive and unconscionable' terms

The courts have always claimed an overriding equitable jurisdiction to strike down any term in a mortgage transaction which tends to operate in an 'oppressive or unconscionable' manner.[13] The courts' inherent supervisory function is significant, but should not be overstated since its effects are demonstrated only in exceptional cases. The areas in which judicial intervention has been most clearly evident concern the rates of interest levied on mortgage loans.

6 [1914] AC 25 at 39.

7 [1914] AC 25 at 41.

8 *De Beers Consolidated Mines Ltd v British South Africa Co* [1912] AC 52 at 67.

9 G.H. Treitel, *The Law of Contract* (8th edn, London 1991), p 401.

10 See eg *Shell UK Ltd v Lostock Garage Ltd* [1976] 1 WLR 1187 at 1199C; *Alec Lobb (Garages) Ltd v Total Oil (Great Britain) Ltd* [1985] 1 WLR 173 at 180D; *Irish Shell & BP Ltd v Ryan* [1966] IR 75 at 99; *Continental Oil Co of Ireland Ltd v Moynihan* (1977) 111 ILTR 5 at 9f.

11 The doctrine against restraint of trade has been held to have no application to restrictive covenants undertaken by persons purchasing or leasing land where those persons had no previous right to trade at all on the land in question. The doctrine applies only where a pre-existing freedom is given up (*Esso Petroleum Co Ltd v Harper's Garage (Stourport) Ltd* [1968] AC 269 at 298B-C, 309A-F, 316F-317A, 325B-F). See also *Quadramain Pty Ltd v Sevastapol Investments Pty Ltd* (1976) 133 CLR 390 at 401; *Stephens v Gulf Oil Canada Ltd* (1976) 65 DLR (3d) 193 at 203f; *Irish Shell Ltd v Elm Motors Ltd* [1984] IR 200 at 207ff.

12 *Esso Petroleum Co Ltd v Harper's Garage (Stourport) Ltd* [1968] AC 269 at 303E-304B, 320F-321E, 330B, 340C-E. See the reference to a 'rule of thumb' in *Alec Lobb (Garages) Ltd v Total Oil (Great Britain) Ltd* [1985] 1 WLR 173 at 178H-179A; [1985] Conv 141 (P. Todd).

13 See *Knightsbridge Estates Trust Ltd v Byrne* [1939] Ch 441 at 457. Issues of 'unfairness' and 'unconscionability' must be assessed as of the date of the mortgage (see *Charmelyn Enterprises Pty Ltd v Klonis* (1981) 2 BPR 9527 at 9536 per Reynolds JA (Court of Appeal of New South Wales)).

(a) Legality of variable interest rates

The modern mortgage is a quite remarkable form of transaction. In the vast majority of cases the rate of interest payable by the mortgagor is not fixed throughout the loan period or for any defined portion thereof, but fluctuates in accordance with the rate stipulated from time to time by the mortgagee.[14] The open-ended nature of this contract is little short of astonishing. The mortgagor agrees to pay *any* rate of interest demanded by the lender of the money. There is some question as to whether either party is competent to contract on this basis, or indeed as to whether the terms of such a contract of loan are sufficiently certain to support a binding legal relationship.[15]

Despite occasional suggestions that an entirely unqualified general power unilaterally to vary interest rates may 'savour of being harsh and unconscionable',[16] there has as yet been no successful legal challenge to the right of mortgagees to adjust interest rates at their discretion.[17] It is significant that most institutional lenders, when raising the interest rate, ensure that their borrowers are allowed to repay over a longer period and are free to redeem at any time. Nowadays, however, it is almost universal for mortgagees to reserve a power to increase interest rates. In the light of this modern development in lending practice, it is widely believed that 'a more robust attitude can now safely be adopted' to the validity of such powers.[18]

(b) Control of harsh interest rates

While the protection of most borrowers rests largely on the responsible exercise of power by the large institutional lenders and the underlying element of governmental regulation, no such protection is available for the individual who borrows on mortgage from another individual or from a credit company or other fringe financial institution. The protection of such borrowers depends

14 The absence of a fixed interest rate is also a feature of most mortgage loans made by institutional lenders such as banks and local authorities. Under a building society mortgage, for instance, the rules of the society are impliedly incorporated into the mortgage transaction itself (see Building Societies Act 1986, s 10(1); *Rosenberg v Northumberland Building Society* (1889) 22 QBD 373 at 380). All building societies reserve the right, on serving notice on their borrowers, to alter the rate of interest payable on mortgage loans.

15 The argument based on uncertainty has, however, been dismissed in the context of unilaterally variable interest rates in a debenture (see *ANZ Banking Group (NZ) Ltd v Gibson* [1981] 2 NZLR 513 at 525).

16 Wurtzburg and Mills, *Building Society Law* (14th edn, London 1976), p 166. The interest rates of institutional lenders tend, however, to be subject to a large element of quasi-public control in that variation of the rate is indirectly related to the general economic strategy of the government of the day.

17 Courts have even been willing to rectify contracts of loan to give effect to the parties' common (but unexpressed) intention that the relevant interest rate should be the lender's 'current rate' at any time (*Westland Savings Bank v Hancock* [1987] 2 NZLR 21 at 29). See also *Barber v Barber* [1987] 1 NZLR 426 at 428, 431, 436. Building societies tend to constitute, in any event, a rather special case. A building society which tethered itself to a rigid rate of interest in a long-term mortgage would be 'hopelessly exposed to the risk of having to pay more to its investors than it was currently receiving from its borrower' (Wurtzburg and Mills, *Building Society Law* (15th edn, London 1989), para 6.22).

18 Wurtzburg and Mills, op cit (15th edn 1989), para 6.22. (Compare Wurtzburg and Mills, op cit (14th edn 1976), p 166, which considered it to be 'open to doubt if an unlimited power simply to vary the interest rate at discretion would be legally valid').

ultimately on the important residual power of the courts to declare void any mortgage term which is 'oppressive' or 'unconscionable'.[19]

A dramatic illustration of the courts' powers in this context occurred in *Cityland and Property (Holdings) Ltd v Dabrah*.[20] Here the plaintiff company had sold a residential property to the defendant, who was the existing occupier. The balance of the purchase price was raised by a loan from the plaintiff secured upon the property in question. The mortgage granted to the plaintiff made no provision for the payment of interest as such, but required that the defendant pay by monthly instalments a sum which exceeded the loan moneys by a figure which was described by the plaintiff as a 'premium'. The plaintiff reserved the right to recover on demand the full outstanding balance of the sum payable by the defendant in the event of any default at any time. On the facts it was calculable that the premium payable by the mortgagor represented, over a three year period, an interest rate of 19 per cent per annum. Moreover, since the entire capital debt was recoverable immediately in the case of default, the 'premium' (taken as a proportion of the capital sum lent) effectively constituted a capitalised interest rate of 57 per cent. Goff J held that the imposition of this rate of interest was in the circumstances 'unfair and unconscionable',[1] and that the mortgagee was entitled to require only a 'reasonable' rate of interest, which he fixed at 7 per cent per annum.[2] The 'premium' agreed between the parties was unenforceable since it conferred an unconscionable collateral advantage in favour of the mortgagee.[3]

Dabrah's case forcefully demonstrates that the court has an inherent equitable power to rewrite the mortgage bargain. It is clear, however, that the conscionableness of a specific rate of interest will vary in accordance with the relative bargaining positions of mortgagor and mortgagee. In *Dabrah*'s case there was a plain disparity of bargaining power as between mortgagor and mortgagee, and there was also a strong suspicion that the mortgagor had agreed to disadvantageous terms only because, as the sitting tenant in the property, he had been threatened with eviction on the expiry of his lease.

The decision in *Cityland and Property (Holdings) Ltd v Dabrah* is not, however, without parallel. The courts have long exercised a similar jurisdiction under the Moneylenders Acts 1900–1927 to set aside 'harsh and unconscionable'

19 An early attempt to restrict mortgage interest rates by statute was contained in the Increase of Rent and Mortgage Interest (War Restrictions) Act 1915 (ante, p 873).
20 [1968] Ch 166.
1 See also *Banner v Berridge* (1881) 18 Ch D 254 at 279 per Kay J.
2 [1968] Ch 166 at 180D. See also *Boote v Brake* [1992] 3 NZLR 136 at 143.
3 The plaintiff was nevertheless granted an order for possession against the defendant. At first sight the approach adopted by Goff J seems to conflict with the insistence of the Court of Appeal in *Knightsbridge Estates Trust Ltd v Byrne* [1939] Ch 441 at 457 (ante, p 955) that the relevant test is not one of 'reasonableness' but rather one of 'conscionableness'. It is perhaps noteworthy that the *Knightsbridge Estates* case was not cited before Goff J. As Browne-Wilkinson J observed in *Multiservice Bookbinding Ltd v Marden* [1979] Ch 84 at 110D-E, Goff J appears to have treated the words 'unreasonable' and 'unconscionable' as being interchangeable. However, as Browne-Wilkinson J went on to say, it 'was unnecessary for [Goff J] to distinguish between the two concepts, since on either test the premium was unenforceable.' See also *Charmelyn Enterprises Pty Ltd v Klonis* (1981) 2 BPR 9527 at 9531 per Waddell J, 9542 per Mahoney JA.

transactions,[4] and disparity of bargaining strength has played an important part in determining the exercise of this discretion.[5] In *Carringtons Ltd v Smith*,[6] for instance, a borrower who was 'intelligent and a man of business' was held to be unable to upset an interest rate of 50 per cent on a transaction of loan. In *Wells v Joyce*,[7] however, the court was prepared to re-open an unfavourable loan which had been pressed on a Connemara farmer 'of rustic mind'.

(c) Index-linked interest rates

It is not unnatural, particularly in an age of inflation, that the lender of money should wish to ensure that he is compensated for any fall in the value of money occurring during the term of the loan. Unless he receives such compensation, the principal sum when finally returned to him is bound to be less valuable in real terms than the loan which was made at the beginning of the transaction. The obvious means by which a mortgagee may seek to counteract the deleterious effects of inflation lies in some index-linking of the capital and interest repayments due under a mortgage. The legality of this protective technique was once, but is no longer, a matter of considerable doubt.[8]

(i) Challenge based on grounds of public policy It used to be asserted that index-linked loans were invalidated on grounds of public policy.[9] The force of this argument was convincingly removed by the decision in *Multiservice Bookbinding Ltd v Marden*.[10] Here the terms of a mortgage of commercial premises provided that the loan could not be called in by the mortgagee, nor the mortgage redeemed by the mortgagor, within ten years of the date of the grant of the mortgage, and that interest should be payable at 2 per cent above Minimum Lending Rate on the entire capital sum throughout the duration of the loan. Furthermore, the mortgage included a provision which stipulated that any repayment of interest or capital should increase or decrease in accordance with alterations in the rate of exchange between the pound sterling and the Swiss franc subsequent to the commencement of the loan.

4 See eg *Samuel v Newbold* [1906] AC 461 at 466ff (interest rate ranging from 104 per cent to 418 per cent declared excessive). In *Wills v Wood* [1984] CCLR 7 at 11, 17, however, the Court of Appeal declined to apply the Moneylenders Acts (and the statutory requirement of a licence) to a private individual who from time to time invested his savings in the making of mortgage loans at normal interest rates to a limited number of borrowers selected by his own solicitor. However, for a more stringent view of deeply disturbing aspects of this case, see (1983) LAG Bulletin (September) 9ff; (1984) Legal Action (April), p 7. See also (1986) 136 NLJ 980.

5 See H.W. Wilkinson, (1980) 130 NLJ 749; Lord Goff of Chieveley and Gareth Jones, *The Law of Restitution* (3rd edn, London 1986), p 260f.

6 [1906] 1 KB 79 at 92ff.

7 [1905] 2 IR 134 at 142ff. See also *Kevans v Joyce* [1896] 1 IR 442 at 462ff, 485ff.

8 See eg Wurtzburg and Mills, op cit (14th edn 1976), p 167f; *Nationwide Building Society v Registry of Friendly Societies* [1983] 1 WLR 1226 at 1228B-C.

9 A further challenge on the ground of uncertainty has been dismissed (see *Charmelyn Enterprises Pty Ltd v Klonis* (1981) 2 BPR 9527 at 9529, 9539f).

10 [1979] Ch 84. See [1978] CLJ 211 (A.J. Oakley); (1978) 128 NLJ 1251 (H.W. Wilkinson); (1979) 42 MLR 338 (W.D. Bishop and B.V. Hindley); [1978] Conv 318 (F.R. Crane). See generally H.W. Wilkinson, *Index-Linked Mortgages*, [1978] Conv 346.

The clear object of these provisions was to ensure that the lender was protected against both domestic inflation and any fall in the value of the pound sterling on the international money market. Ten years after the commencement of the loan period, the mortgagor sought to redeem the mortgage on terms to be declared by the court. The mortgagor claimed that the payment clause contained in the mortgage was void and unenforceable on grounds of public policy. During the intervening period the value of the pound sterling had depreciated relative to the Swiss franc to such an extent that at the date of redemption the mortgagee would, in return for the original loan of £36,000, have received almost £133,000 by way of payments of capital and interest.

Browne-Wilkinson J gave judgment in favour of the mortgagee, holding that an index-linked money obligation could not be said to be contrary to public policy. He treated the 'Swiss franc uplift' provision as a form of index-linking, and was clearly moved by the consideration that 'unless lenders can ensure that they are repaid the real value of the money they advanced, and not merely a sum of the same nominal amount but in devalued currency, the availability of loan capital will be much diminished.' This, in Browne-Wilkinson J's view, 'would surely not be in the public interest.'[11]

(ii) Challenge based on equitable objections The mortgagor's challenge on grounds of public policy therefore failed, but the mortgagor went on to claim that the mortgage terms were in any event unenforceable on the ground that they were 'unconscionable' or 'unreasonable'. Browne-Wilkinson J took the view that such a challenge can succeed only if the mortgagor can show 'that the bargain, or some of its terms, was unfair and unconscionable: it is not enough to show that, in the eyes of the court, it was unreasonable.'[12] Moreover, a bargain is not 'unfair and unconscionable' unless one of the parties to it 'has imposed the objectionable terms in a morally reprehensible manner ... in a way which affects his conscience.'[13] Although he declined to limit the categories of unconscionable bargain, Browne-Wilkinson J gave as the classic example of such a bargain the case 'where advantage has been taken of a young, inexperienced or ignorant person to introduce such a term which no sensible well-advised person or party would have accepted.'

In the present case, however, Browne-Wilkinson J was not prepared to stigmatise the terms of the mortgage transaction as 'unconscionable' or 'oppressive', although he did concede that these terms had been 'unreasonable'.[14] The terms had not been 'imposed ... in a morally reprehensible manner', in that there had been no great inequality of bargaining power between the parties. The parties had, moreover, received

11 [1979] Ch 84 at 104G-H. For a similar conclusion in the Court of Appeal of New South Wales, see *Charmelyn Enterprises Pty Ltd v Klonis* (1981) 2 BPR 9527 at 9541 per Mahoney JA.
12 [1979] Ch 84 at 110E.
13 [1979] Ch 84 at 110F.
14 'In particular I consider that it was unreasonable both for the debt to be inflation proofed by reference to the Swiss franc and at the same time to provide for a rate of interest two per cent above bank rate—a rate which reflects at least in part the unstable state of the pound sterling. On top of this interest on the whole sum was to be paid throughout the term. The defendant made a hard bargain. But the test is not reasonableness' ([1979] Ch 84 at 112B-C).

the benefit of independent legal advice, and the loan related to commercial premises which had trebled in value during the loan period. Above all, the mortgagee was not 'a professional moneylender' and there was no evidence of 'any sharp practice of any kind' by him. Browne-Wilkinson J refused to regard the 'Swiss franc uplift' element as representing in any sense a 'premium or collateral advantage'.[15] In ensuring that he is repaid the real value of his original advance, the lender 'is not stipulating for anything beyond the repayment of principal.'[16]

(iii) Potential impact of index-linking The *Multiservice Bookbinding* case thus established that there is no objection in principle to the index-linking of mortgage commitments,[17] and the practice of index-linking has been further stimulated by the government's increasing use of this technique in borrowing money by way of issue of treasury stock.[18] This general disposition in favour of upholding the legality of index-linked mortgage payments has now been taken to the extent that even building societies, which enjoy a bargaining strength quite disproportionate to that of the individual borrower, have been allowed to take advantage of this facility for reversing the effects of the falling purchasing power of money.[19] However, the practice of index-linking building society repayments, if widely adopted, would dramatically erode the value of realty as a means of fairly rapid capital accumulation for the private citizen, who would find himself required to share with his building society a large portion of any inflated equity which he acquires during his period of ownership.[20]

(d) Penal interest rates

The courts also have power to invalidate rates of mortgage interest which are imposed for penal purposes without any consideration of whether they comprise a genuine pre-estimate of the damage suffered by the mortgagee in the event of the mortgagor's default.[1] In an area which is curiously bereft of modern English authority, it seems that the courts have tended to strike down clauses which, on default by the mortgagor, increase the interest rate

15 [1979] Ch 84 at 111C.

16 [1979] Ch 84 at 111C. Similarly, in *Charmelyn Enterprises Pty Ltd v Klonis* (1981) 2 BPR 9527 at 9536, 9541f, the Court of Appeal of New South Wales decided that, even in the context of a mortgage of domestic premises, there is in principle nothing unfair or unconscionable in stipulating for protection against inflation. Mahoney JA specifically denied (at 9541) that the indexation clause challenged in *Charmelyn* could be stigmatised as a 'clog on the equity of redemption'.

17 It has been held that there is no intrinsic objection to index-linking even though the process of indexation in a particular case produces a much greater percentage increase in the mortgage sums repayable than is reflected in the inflated value of the mortgaged property (*Charmelyn Enterprises Pty Ltd v Klonis* (1981) 2 BPR 9527 at 9532).

18 *Nationwide Building Society v Registry of Friendly Societies* [1983] 1 WLR 1226 at 1228C.

19 See *Nationwide Building Society v Registry of Friendly Societies* [1983] 1 WLR 1226 at 1231D-E.

20 See H. Cohen, (1984) 134 NLJ 437 at 439.

1 See eg *Re 459745 Ontario Ltd and Wideview Holdings Ltd* (1987) 37 DLR (4th) 765 at 767f (clause requiring three months' interest on default declared void as penalty).

beyond the primary rate normally payable.[2] Somewhat illogically the courts have declined to interfere if the mortgage agreement merely allows the mortgagor a reduction or discount from the normal or primary rate if he makes punctual payment.[3] There is, however, some authority for regarding as void a provision that, upon default by the mortgagor, a flat rate of interest becomes payable for the balance of the mortgage term on the entirety of the outstanding debt.[4] Such a clause may often bear the hallmarks of an in terrorem stipulation designed to force mortgagors to adhere to their bargains and contains none of the ingredients of a genuine pre-estimate of loss.[5]

(9) Extortionate credit bargains under the Consumer Credit Act 1974

Further protection against unconscionable dealing is now provided for mortgagors by the Consumer Credit Act 1974, which empowers the court to reopen 'extortionate' credit bargains.[6] The 1974 Act has no application to loans made by a building society or local authority,[7] but does govern loans advanced by banks and finance companies. In its application to mortgages, the legislation tends to direct its focus not upon first mortgages of residential property but upon second mortgages and short-term transactions entered into within the 'fringe area' dominated by non-institutional lenders. In this 'fringe area' borrowers stand in need of considerable legal protection, being almost by definition the 'poorer risk' borrowers who cannot obtain loan facilities from one of the institutional lenders.[8]

2 *Holles v Wyse* (1693) 2 Vern 289 at 290, 23 ER 787; *Strode v Parker* (1694) 2 Vern 316 at 317, 23 ER 804 at 805. It is possible that a provision for increased interest in the case of default on an instalment mortgage would not be regarded as penal or repugnant (see eg *C.J. Belmore Pty Ltd v A.G.C. (General Finance) Ltd* [1976] 1 NSWLR 507 at 509E). Some jurisdictions statutorily prohibit the imposition of a higher interest rate on arrears than on principal not in arrears. See eg Canada's Interest Act (RSC 1970, c I-18), s 8(1); *Vancouver City Savings Credit Union v Chambers* (1976) 59 DLR (3d) 753 at 758; *Re Weirdale Investments Ltd and Canadian Imperial Bank of Commerce* (1981) 32 OR (2d) 183 at 190; *Beauchamp v Timberland Investments Ltd* (1984) 4 DLR (4th) 485 at 487ff.

3 *Sterne v Beck* (1863) 32 LJ Ch 682 at 684f; *Wallingford v Mutual Society* (1880) 5 App Cas 685 at 702; *Re Jones's Estate* [1914] 1 IR 188 at 192ff.

4 *Wanner v Caruana* [1974] 2 NSWLR 301 at 306F.

5 The provision may not, however, be penal if it can be shown that there was an expectation that the loan interest would be paid in its entirety over the loan term and that the mortgage agreement therefore contained an absolute obligation to pay the total interest in any event albeit in instalments. (There may be a distinct commercial advantage for the mortgagee in knowing from the outset that a fixed total quantum of interest will be paid.) In such circumstances the exaction of the entire anticipated quantum of interest on default *does* represent a genuine pre-estimate of loss (see *Wanner v Caruana* [1974] 2 NSWLR 301 at 305F–306B per Street CJ). The vital question is whether the mortgage can be construed as a 'bargain for payment of a whole sum by a number of perodical instalments' (*Van Kempen v Finance & Investments Pty Ltd* (1984) 6 NSWLR 294 at 298B).

6 The court's power in this respect is not restricted, as is usual under the Consumer Credit Act 1974, to loans of less than £15,000 (see Consumer Credit Act 1974, ss 8(2), 16(7)). See The Consumer Credit (Increase of Monetary Limits) Order 1983 (SI 1983/1878).

7 Consumer Credit Act 1974, s 16(1).

8 For a general conclusion that the protective purpose of the Consumer Credit Act 1974 has not proved wholly successful and that loansharks continue to flourish, see L. Bently and G.G. Howells, [1989] Conv 164, 234.

(a) The court's powers to reopen 'extortionate' credit bargains

A court which finds a credit bargain 'extortionate' is authorised by section 137(1) of the Consumer Credit Act 1974 to 'reopen the credit agreement so as to do justice between the parties.' Once the Act is invoked by a debtor, the onus is on the creditor to prove that the credit bargain is not 'extortionate'.[9] Unless he can do this, the court may set aside in whole or part any obligation imposed by that bargain on the debtor or may otherwise alter the terms of the agreement.[10]

(b) Meaning of 'extortionate' bargain

In terms of section 138(1) of the Act, a credit bargain is 'extortionate if it ... requires the debtor or a relative of his to make payments ... which are grossly exorbitant, or ... otherwise grossly contravenes ordinary principles of fair dealing.'[11] This statutory language has been the subject of some judicial amplification.

(i) Underlying reality of 'extortionate' bargaining It has been said that the statutory jurisdiction contemplates 'at least a substantial imbalance in bargaining power of which one party has taken advantage'.[12] Despite some suggestions to the contrary,[13] it now seems likely that the word 'extortionate' is intended to demarcate much the same kind of conduct as is envisaged under the traditional rubric of 'harsh and unconscionable' dealing.[14] It has been pointed out in any event that the controlling notion in section 138(1) is that of 'extortionate' rather than merely 'unwise' transactions.[15] The borrower certainly cannot be heard to complain in retrospect that he should have been protected from undertaking an imprudent debt.[16]

(ii) Statutory criteria In determining whether a credit bargain is 'extortionate', the court must have regard to such evidence as is adduced concerning 'interest

9 Consumer Credit Act 1974, s 171(7).

10 Consumer Credit Act 1974, s 139. A debtor's trustee in bankruptcy may apply for the setting aside or variation of any 'extortionate' credit transaction which the debtor entered into within the three years preceding the commencement of his bankruptcy (Insolvency Act 1986, s 343(2)).

11 See *Davies v Directloans Ltd* [1986] 1 WLR 823 at 836G–837B.

12 *Wills v Wood* [1984] CCLR 7 at 15. Compare the reference to abuse of a 'dominant position' in Article 86 of the Treaty of Rome, and see *Matthew v Bobbins* (1981) 41 P & CR 1 at 7.

13 The term 'extortionate' is comprehensively defined in section 138 itself. For this reason, in *Davies v Directloans Ltd* [1986] 1 WLR 823 at 831C-E, Edward Nugee QC (sitting as a deputy High Court judge) thought that the old authorities on the meaning of 'harsh and unconscionable' conduct might not necessarily provide authoritative guidance in the new statutory context.

14 See *Shahabinia v Gyachi* (Unreported, Court of Appeal, 5 July 1989), where Russell LJ noted that 'it seems that the word "extortionate" is to be equated with the words "harsh and unconscionable".' See also *Castle Phillips Finance Co Ltd v Khan* [1980] CCLR 1 at 3.

15 *Wills v Wood* [1984] CCLR 7 at 15.

16 *Wills v Wood* [1984] CCLR 7 at 17; *Davies v Directloans Ltd* [1986] 1 WLR 823 at 837H. See also *Williams & Glyn's Bank Ltd v Barnes* [1981] Com LR 205 (ante, p 571).

rates prevailing at the time it was made'[17] and to 'any other relevant considerations'.[18] In particular, the court is directed,[19] in relation to the debtor, to have regard to his age, experience, business capacity,[20] state of health, and the degree to which, at the time of making the credit bargain, he was under financial pressure.[1] In relation to the creditor, the court is directed[2] to take account of the degree of risk accepted by him (having regard to the value of any security provided), his relationship with the debtor, and whether or not a colourable cash price was quoted for any goods or services included in the credit bargain.

(c) *Judicial treatment of interest rates*

Notwithstanding the legislative concern to suppress unfair or oppressive dealing in the area of consumer credit, it is difficult to find any case in which the court has regarded an interest rate as being sufficiently excessive to render a credit bargain 'extortionate' within the meaning of the Act.[3]

(i) Practical application of the statute A. Ketley Ltd v Scott[4] provided the first opportunity for the High Court to apply the terms of sections 137–140 of the Consumer Credit Act 1974. In a decision which was to become an important point of reference in this area, Foster J declined to hold that an annual rate of interest of 48 per cent was 'extortionate' in the statutory

17 Consumer Credit Act 1974, s 138(2)(a). It was finally recognised in *Davies v Directloans Ltd* [1986] 1 WLR 823 at 835D that only the annual percentage rate of interest (APR), calculable from the HMSO's Consumer Credit Tables, gives any indication of the true rate of interest charged, and that this should be the relevant figure for the purpose of section 138(2)(a). An APR of 35 per cent could well be expected in a first mortgage granted by a 'fringe' lender to a borrower unable to raise funds from a bank or building society (see *Davies v Directloans Ltd* [1986] 1 WLR 823 at 836E).

18 Consumer Credit Act 1974, s 138(2)(c).

19 Consumer Credit Act 1974, s 138(3).

20 The fact that both debtor and creditor are experienced and successful businessmen tends to rebut any allegation that their bargain was 'extortionate' (see *Arrowfield Finance v Kosmider* [1984] CCLR 38 at 49).

1 'Nearly every purchaser who borrows money in order to complete his purchase is under some degree of financial pressure. It is only if the lender takes advantage of the pressure that this factor is ... relevant in considering whether the loan is extortionate' (*Davies v Directloans Ltd* [1986] 1 WLR 823 at 832G).

2 Consumer Credit Act 1974, s 138(4).

3 For a rare instance, see *Barcabe Ltd v Edwards* [1983] CCLR 11 at 12, where a county court judge thought it '*prima facie* exorbitant' to lend money at a flat rate of 100 per cent, when other similar lenders charged approximately 20 per cent. The APR for the loan in this case was actually 319 per cent, and the court substituted a flat interest rate of 40 per cent (ie an APR of 92 per cent). Likewise, in *Shahabinia v Gyachi* (Unreported, 5 July 1989), the Court of Appeal fixed a reduced interest rate of 30 per cent in respect of three loans where the interest rates had previously stood at 156, 104 and 78 per cent per annum respectively. Compare the approach adopted in Canada, where an interest rate double that normally obtainable is regarded as prima facie harsh and unconscionable (see *Krocker v Midtown Mortgage & Loans Ltd* (1975) 52 DLR (3d) 286 at 290ff).

4 [1980] CCLR 37. See (1980) 130 NLJ 749 (H.W. Wilkinson).

sense.[5] The defendants had sought a loan from the plaintiff company at very short notice for the purpose of completing a purchase of the flat in which they lived. They signed a number of documents in great haste, including a legal charge for a loan for three months at 12 per cent interest. One of the defendants had already charged the property to secure a bank overdraft, but this fact was not disclosed to the plaintiff in the present transaction. In refusing to grant relief, Foster J had regard not only to this element of deceit[6] but also to the fact that the extraordinary nature and urgency of the transaction justified the imposition of a higher rate of interest than that normally charged by banks and building societies. The defendants had known exactly what they were doing, and had not been subject to real financial pressure. Although already entitled to a protected tenancy in the property, they simply wished to purchase that property at what was a temporary bargain price.[7]

(ii) The judicial dilemma Although no great merit attaches to the conduct of the defendants in *A. Ketley Ltd v Scott*, the facts of the case are typical of the sorts of circumstance which feature in section 137 applications. The borrower is often a person of limited means who by reason of mismanagement or misfortune has rendered himself the victim of his own overweening material ambitions. Typically, such a borrower has already exhausted the patience of institutional lenders in connection with existing loans, and is on the verge of either bankruptcy or repossession of his home. His only remaining hope of averting disaster lies in a further loan or re-mortgaging arrangement with the most shady of lenders.

These circumstances almost inevitably predetermine the conclusion that the borrower represents an exceedingly poor risk, which in turn justifies the exaction of a high rate of interest. Moreover, since the borrower would be uniformly adjudged a poor risk by the few lenders still prepared to deal with him, even a monstrous rate of interest is not discordant with the 'interest rates prevailing' generally at the bottom end of the credit market in relation to borrowers within this risk category. In *Woodstead Finance Ltd v Petrou*,[8] for instance, the defendant had charged her home in order to stave off her husband's bankruptcy. Although Browne-Wilkinson V-C confessed that to his 'untutored eye' the interest rate of 42 per cent per annum appeared 'very harsh', it could not be stigmatised as 'extortionate'. In view of the husband's 'appalling record in relation to payments' and given the 'parlous financial condition' of the couple, the loan arrangement and the rate of interest were 'normal for a risk of this kind'. Thus, somewhat ironically,

5 It was later claimed that this decision had laid down a general rule that an interest rate can never be 'extortionate' if it does not exceed 48 per cent. This suggestion was, however, vigorously denied by Dillon LJ in *Castle Phillips Finance Co Ltd v Williams* (Unreported, Court of Appeal, 25 March 1986). The borrower in this case had agreed a bridging loan at 4 per cent per month (ie at an APR of 67.7), which the Court of Appeal considered quite excessive. Although it did not reopen the transaction, the Court ordered that the conduct of the plaintiff finance company, which Dillon LJ described as 'dishonest', be referred for further action to the Director General of Fair Trading.

6 Deceit or non-disclosure of all relevant facts tends to be fatal to applications for a reopening of a credit bargain (see eg *First National Securities Ltd v Bertrand* [1980] CCLR 5 at 22; *Premier Finance Co v Gravesande* [1985] CCLR 1 at 7).

7 [1980] CCLR 37 at 43f.

8 (1986) *Times*, 23 January.

the more desperate and vulnerable the borrower, the more justified is the imposition of a high interest rate, and the less able are the courts to intervene in terms of supposedly protectionist legislation.

(10) Economic duress and unfair advantage

Much controversy in the law of credit transactions has recently concerned the degree to which the courts should strive to protect the borrower or any guarantor or surety from circumstances of economic duress and the taking of unfair advantage. During the mid-1970s the English courts developed a broad approach which placed a heavy reliance on the fashionably continental concept of 'abuse of a dominant position' in the context of an 'inequality of bargaining power' between the parties.[9] During the 1980s the balance of judicial concern moved significantly away from solicitude on behalf of borrowers, only to threaten to return during the 1990s towards a more protectionist stance.

(a) The doctrine of undue influence

A limited form of protection has always been available in the guise of the general equitable doctrine that the court may set aside, or decline to enforce, any bargain reached by means of undue influence. It was once thought that the relationship between banker and borrower was apt to raise a presumption of undue influence sufficient to vitiate loan transactions wherever it was clear that the borrower had received no independent advice as to the effect of the transaction on his rights.[10]

(i) Rejection of the liberal approach The liberal application of the notion of undue influence was finally rejected in definitive terms by the House of Lords in *National Westminster Bank Plc v Morgan.*[11] Here a husband and wife, as joint owners of their matrimonial home, had signed a charge over that property in favour of the bank in order to secure a short-term loan to tide the husband over a period of financial difficulty. The wife subsequently alleged that the bank manager had exercised undue influence in obtaining her signature during a somewhat 'tense' visit by him to their home. It was clear that both spouses had been desperately anxious not to lose their home, but the House of Lords declined to accept that these circumstances disclosed a true case of undue influence.[12]

9 Ante, p 575. English courts were in this respect some ten years behind their North American counterparts (see eg *Morrison v Coast Finance Ltd* (1966) 55 DLR (2d) 710 at 713).

10 This view is often, but somewhat inaccurately, traced back to the judgment delivered by Lord Denning MR in *Lloyds Bank Ltd v Bundy* [1975] QB 326.

11 [1985] AC 686.

12 Paradoxically the notion of 'undue influence' carries an implication that some forms of influence or pressure may be 'due' or, at least, 'not . . . sufficiently undue'. See *Barclays Bank Plc v O'Brien* [1992] 3 WLR 593 at 622C-F, where it was conceded that a wife's signature had been obtained after an 'emotional scene' in which her husband had been 'extremely insistent'. In Scott LJ's view, however, the 'heavy family pressures' (such as the danger of bankruptcy and the loss of a home) were 'not particularly unusual or sufficient . . . to overset and bear down the will' of the wife, who had signed 'because she was persuaded that it was the right thing to do, not because her husband's pressure deprived her consent of reality.'

In coming to this conclusion, Lord Scarman based the concept of undue influence on a 'victimisation of one party by the other.'[13] In order that a plea of undue influence should succeed, he held, the 'wrongfulness' of the transaction must be shown: there must be shown to be a dealing 'in which an unfair advantage has been taken of another.'[14] In Lord Scarman's view, however, the mere relationship of banker and customer is in itself insufficient to introduce any vitiating element of undue influence in the absence of evidence that the transaction concluded by them 'constituted a manifest disadvantage to the party seeking to avoid it, explicable only on the basis that undue influence has been used to procure it.'[15]

On the present facts the claim of undue influence was countered by two circumstances. *First*, the transaction had not been unfair to the wife.[16] In the context of 'an ordinary banking transaction'—albeit one directed at saving the family home from the hands of creditors—the bank had no duty to ensure that independent legal advice was received by the wife.[17] *Second*, as the judge at first instance had found, the transaction had not been 'manifestly disadvantageous' to the wife, in that it had 'provided what to her was desperately important, namely the rescue of the house'.[18]

The ruling of the House of Lords in *National Westminster Bank Plc v Morgan* severely curtailed the scope of the doctrine of undue influence, in that the absence of independent advice for the borrower (or indeed for any guarantor or surety) seemed no longer automatically fatal to the lender's claim to enforce his rights. However, as Oliver LJ added in *Coldunell Ltd v Gallon*,[19] once it is shown that the party in a dominant position has achieved a bargain in itself unconscionable, then that party is 'saddled with the burden of establishing affirmatively that no domination was practised to bring the transaction about—as for instance by demonstrating not merely the availability but the fact of separate and independent advice.'

(ii) Restrictive impact of the 'manifest disadvantage' requirement Subsequent cases have extended *Morgan* to loans advanced by finance companies and other lenders. The requirement of 'manifest disadvantage' has, however, had a severely restrictive impact on the development of the law, as is clearly demonstrated, for instance, in *Woodstead Finance Ltd v Petrou*.[20] Here Browne-Wilkinson V-C held that the issue of 'manifest disadvantage' must be analysed with reference to the position prevailing at the date of the loan transaction which it was sought to set aside. On this basis he was wholly unable to

13 [1985] AC 686 at 705A, citing *Allcard v Skinner* (1887) 36 Ch D 145 at 182f.
14 [1985] AC 686 at 707B.
15 *Coldunell Ltd v Gallon* [1986] QB 1184 at 1194G per Oliver LJ, providing a slightly more elegant version of what was said by Lord Scarman at [1985] AC 686 at 704G-H. See also *Goldsworthy v Brickell* [1987] Ch 378 at 405D-E.
16 [1985] AC 686 at 709D.
17 [1985] AC 686 at 709D.
18 [1985] AC 686 at 702A. For the continuing strength of the 'manifest disadvantage' criterion, see *Barclays Bank Plc v O'Brien* [1992] 3 WLR 593 at 636A per Purchas LJ.
19 [1986] QB 1184 at 1194H-1195A. It is clear, however, that the *Morgan* ruling provides no authority for the view that the presumption of undue influence applies only where one party to a transaction has assumed a role of dominating influence over the other (see *Goldsworthy v Brickell* [1987] Ch 378 at 406C-D per Nourse LJ, 415B-C, 416E-G per Parker LJ, 417D-E per Sir John Megaw).
20 (1986) *Times*, 23 January (ante, p 967).

accede to any plea of undue influence, precisely because the couple's finances at that stage were so overwhelmingly parlous that almost any means of warding off financial disaster would then have seemed preferable to the bankruptcy which for them lay only days away. Far from the loan representing a 'manifest disadvantage' to the borrower, it provided the only remaining straw at which she and her husband could clutch.[1]

(b) Other forms of relief

Notwithstanding the chilling effect of the ruling in *Morgan*'s case, it is clear that there remain, apart from the law of undue influence, several other means by which the courts may grant relief from the strict terms of a transaction of loan or guarantee.

(i) The banker's self-imposed duty of care In *National Westminster Bank Plc v Morgan*[2] Lord Scarman placed particular emphasis on the fact that the bank manager never 'crossed the line' between a normal banking transaction and one in which he 'goes further and advises on more general matters germane to the wisdom of the transaction'. A bank has no general duty to explain to a surety the effect of a relevant transaction,[3] but this broad proposition is likely to be true only in respect of a bank's dealings with strangers rather than with its existing customers.[4] Thus if, in the *Morgan* situation, a wife is an existing customer and the bank takes it upon itself to explain the legal implications of a mortgage or guarantee which she is required to sign, it is not impossible that the bank may become liable to her in damages if it negligently misrepresents the scope or effect of her agreement.[5] In *Cornish v Midland Bank plc*,[6] for instance, the Court of Appeal held a bank liable in negligence where it had failed to inform a wife of the vital fact that, in signing a legal charge in favour of the bank, she was signing an 'all monies' term which covered all future—and potentially unlimited—borrowings by her husband.

The recognition of such negligence liability is, of course, fraught with invidious consequence. As Scott LJ pointed out in *Barclays Bank Plc v O'Brien*,[7] it cannot be right to place the creditor on a 'Morton's fork', where his voluntary assumption of the role of advisor may generate a damages liability for carelessness whilst the threat simultaneously remains that failure to give any advice at all may render the relevant security unenforceable in equity.

1 Compare *Midland Bank Plc v Phillips* (1986) *Times*, 28 March.
2 [1985] AC 686 at 708G, 709C.
3 *O'Hara v Allied Irish Banks Ltd* [1985] BCLC 52 at 53; *Barclays Bank Plc v O'Brien* [1992] 3 WLR 593 at 613C-E per Scott LJ, 635F per Purchas LJ. It seems, for example, that there is no duty to disclose to a surety that the person for whom surety is being given has himself guaranteed the debt of a third party (see *Goodwin v National Bank of Australasia Ltd* (1968) 117 CLR 173 at 175f; *Guthrie v ANZ Banking Group Ltd* (1989) NSW ConvR 55-463 at 58,356).
4 See *Cornish v Midland Bank plc* [1985] 3 All ER 513 at 522a.
5 *Barclays Bank Plc v O'Brien* [1992] 3 WLR 593 at 635G per Purchas LJ. See also *Midland Bank Plc v Perry* (1988) 56 P & CR 202 at 206.
6 [1985] 3 All ER 513 at 520f-g, 521j.
7 [1992] 3 WLR 593 at 613E-G.

In view of the severity of this dilemma Scott LJ was minded to limit the potential of negligence liability in this area, observing that the creditor should not 'be taken to have assumed a tortious duty of care' in merely proffering to a surety some explanation of a relevant transaction or security document.[8]

(ii) Agency In recent years some courts have developed the theory that legal force may be withheld from a security transaction where some person who 'could reasonably be expected to have influence over' a prospective mortgagor or surety has acted effectively as an agent for the mortgagee in procuring the due execution of the relevant documents.[9]

In *Kings North Trust Ltd v Bell*[10] the sole legal owner of a matrimonial home fraudulently misrepresented to his wife the scope and purpose of a secured loan in order to obtain her consent to the mortgage demanded by the lender. The Court of Appeal refused to enforce the security against her. The Court held that the mortgagee had failed to ensure that she received independent advice and had simply left it to her husband to extract the required signature from her by any means he chose. Although there is in English law no presumption of undue influence as between husband and wife,[11] Dillon LJ took the view that, in the absence of independent advice, a consent obtained by means of actual undue influence on the husband's part could not be upheld. A principal (however innocent) who instructs an agent to achieve a particular end (eg the signing of a document by a mortgagor-spouse) is liable for any fraudulent misrepresentation made by the agent in achieving that end.[12]

Likewise in *Avon Finance Co Ltd v Bridger*[13] a son dishonestly persuaded his ageing parents to charge their home in order (although they were unaware of the fact) to secure a loan advanced to himself. There is no presumption of undue influence as between a son and his parents,[14] but here the son had been expressly authorised by the mortgagee to procure the execution of the mortgage. Brandon LJ considered the relationship 'between a son in the prime of life and parents in the evening of life' to be clearly 'a relationship in which it should be appreciated that the possibility of influence exists.'[15] In such circumstances the mortgagee was subject to an overriding duty to ensure that the mortgagors received independent legal advice. In default of such advice the Court of Appeal held the security to be unenforceable

8 [1992] 3 WLR 593 at 621F-G. Scott LJ conceded that if the creditor's explanation was inadequate the security might not be enforceable, but 'it would not follow that liability in damages would attach'.

9 *Kings North Trust Ltd v Bell* [1986] 1 WLR 119 at 124C, 125A-B.

10 [1986] 1 WLR 119. See [1986] Conv 213 (J.E.M.); (1986) 102 LQR 351.

11 *Bank of Montreal v Stuart* [1911] AC 120 at 137; *Kings North Trust Ltd v Bell* [1986] 1 WLR 119 at 123D-E.

12 [1986] 1 WLR 119 at 124A. It has since been pointed out that Dillon LJ made no 'explicit finding' that the debtor was acting as agent for the creditor, but spoke merely in terms of a creditor who 'entrusts to the husband the task of obtaining the execution of the relevant document' (see eg *Barclays Bank Plc v O'Brien* [1992] 3 WLR 593 at 617G-H). Dillon LJ did, however, draw a direct analogy with the approach of the general law of principal and agent in relation to fraudulent misrepresentations ([1986] 1 WLR 119 at 124A).

13 [1985] 2 All ER 281.

14 *Coldunell Ltd v Gallon* [1986] QB 1184 at 1195A. See (1986) 102 LQR 351.

15 [1985] 2 All ER 281 at 288a.

against the mortgagors where—as was manifestly the case here—their signatures had been induced by the son's undue influence and deception.[16]

(iii) A 'protected class' of sureties Although the 'agency' approach came, both in principle and in practice, to acquire some recognition as a ground of voidability in security transactions,[17] the tenor of the recent English case law indicates a strong reaction against any general application in this context of the law of principal and agent.[18]

The opportunity recently arose in *Barclays Bank Plc v O'Brien*[19] for some clarification of the nature of the duty (if any) owed by a creditor to the surety of a debt. Here a wife had executed a second mortgage of the matrimonial home as security for the bank overdraft of her husband's company. She was not made aware by the bank of the nature of the relevant documents, but signed without reading them, acting throughout in reliance on her husband's false representation that the security was limited to £60,000 and would last only three weeks. When the overdraft exceeded £154,000, the bank obtained possession of the home. The Court of Appeal held, however, that the charge was unenforceable against the wife save to the extent of £60,000.

After an exhaustive analysis of the case law, the Court of Appeal expressly disavowed the agency principle as the true or significant explanation of legal developments in this area over the past 90 years.[20] The Court resorted instead to what it believed to be the authentic equitable principles governing sureties. The Court thus reaffirmed the proposition that a creditor is not in general concerned with what has passed between debtor and surety and in particular need not concern itself with whether the surety understands the transaction in hand.[1] The Court nonetheless pointed to the historic existence of a 'protected class' of sureties, who have been treated 'differently and more tenderly' than other sureties.[2] This 'protected class' owes its existence, as

16 [1985] 2 All ER 281 at 286g. If, however, the unfair pressure emanated from a person to whom the mortgagee had given no such authority, the signatures obtained were not liable to be set aside on the ground of undue influence. In the absence of any effective agency relationship between the mortgagee and the person who actually procures the execution of the mortgage, the transaction cannot be undone even though it has been induced by thoroughly reprehensible conduct on the part of a self-interested, but wholly unauthorised, intermeddler (see eg *Coldunell Ltd v Gallon* [1986] QB 1184 at 1201C-F; [1986] Conv 213 (J.E.M.); (1986) 102 LQR 351).

17 See eg *Coldunell Ltd v Gallon* [1986] QB 1184 at 1196C–1198B per Oliver LJ; *Midland Bank Plc v Perry* (1988) 56 P & CR 202 at 207 per Fox LJ, 210 per Lloyd LJ; *Midland Bank plc v Shephard* [1988] 3 All ER 17 at 22b-h. See generally [1989] CLJ 184 (M. Oldham); [1989] Conv 63 (B. Dale).

18 For incipient signs of the disenchantment with the 'agency' approach, see *Barclays Bank Plc v Kennedy* [1989] 1 FLR 356 at 363E per Purchas LJ; *Bank of Credit and Commerce International SA v Aboody* [1990] 1 QB 923 at 972A–973A per Slade LJ. See [1990] Conv 226 (E.A. Dunbill).

19 [1992] 3 WLR 593.

20 Purchas LJ observed that '"Leaves it to the debtor" is an expression that occurs frequently in the authorities. The expression covers a wide field of positions . . . which fall far short of the creation of a formal agency' ([1992] 3 WLR 593 at 624H–625A).

1 [1992] 3 WLR 593 at 618E-F per Scott LJ, 635F per Purchas LJ. The Court agreed, however, that the creditor might, exceptionally, be affected on grounds of agency or notice in respect of any improprieties in the conduct of the debtor towards his spouse.

2 [1992] 3 WLR 593 at 619B-G per Scott LJ.

Purchas LJ observed, to the fact that '[e]quity in this jurisdiction acts upon the conscience of the creditor'.[3] For this purpose the Court adopted Dixon J's statement that the husband-wife relationship, while free of any presumption of undue influence, has 'never been divested completely of . . . equitable presumptions of an invalidating tendency.'[4] Scott LJ thought that, notwithstanding changes in the modern status of women, there still exists justification for 'the tenderness of equity' towards married women who act as sureties for their husbands.[5] Scott LJ was also prepared to extend the 'protected class' of surety beyond spouses to include 'all cases in which the relationship between the surety and the debtor is one in which influence by the debtor over the surety and reliance by the surety on the debtor are natural and probable features of the relationship.'[6]

On this basis the Court of Appeal was prepared to hold a security unenforceable against a surety within the protected class if certain additional conditions were present.[7] The creditor must know of the relationship between debtor and surety and of 'the consequent likelihood of influence and reliance.' It must be shown that the surety's consent to the impugned transaction was procured by undue influence or material misrepresentation by the debtor or that 'the surety lacked an adequate understanding of the nature and effect of the transaction'. The creditor, 'whether by leaving it to the debtor to deal with the surety or otherwise', must have failed to take reasonable steps 'to try and ensure that the surety entered into the transaction with an adequate understanding' of its nature and effect and that the surety's consent to the transaction was a true and informed one'.[8] On the facts of the present case the creditor's obligations in these respects had not, in the view of the Court of Appeal, been properly discharged.[9]

7. PROTECTION FOR THE MORTGAGEE

Important policy considerations underlie the legal protection given to mortgagees. In order that the flow of mortgage finance should be sustained, particularly for the purpose of facilitating home purchase, it is essential that certain safeguards and remedies be maintained on behalf of those who lend money on the security of real property.[10] The forms of protection or facility afforded the mortgagee include the following.

3 [1992] 3 WLR 593 at 624E.
4 *Yerkey v Jones* (1939) 63 CLR 649 at 675.
5 [1992] 3 WLR 593 at 619G-620B. Compare *European Asian of Australia Ltd v Kurland* (1985) 8 NSWLR 192 at 200A-E (ante, p 460).
6 [1992] 3 WLR 593 at 619C-D. See also Purchase LJ at 624E-H.
7 [1992] 3 WLR 593 at 619E-G per Scott LJ.
8 Purchas LJ thought that it would be 'unlikely to be sufficient if the creditor merely took steps' to ensure that the surety understood the nature of the liability accepted. Nothing less than clear and unambiguous advice to obtain independent legal advice would probably be necessary to avoid the restraining hand of equity' ([1992] 3 WLR 593 at 636B-C).
9 It now remains to be seen whether the approach adopted by the Court of Appeal will be upheld in the appeal to the House of Lords. (Hearings were held during the week of 26 April 1993.)
10 See eg the deference to public policy expressed by Browne-Wilkinson J in *Multiservice Bookbinding Ltd v Marden* [1979] Ch 84 at 104G-H (ante, p 962).

(1) Investigation of title by the mortgagee

It is customary for the lender to investigate the title offered by a borrower before taking a mortgage as security for the loan to be advanced.[11] Although such investigation normally ensures that the mortgagee takes a sound and reliable security, it is clear that lenders will do well to proceed with caution. Among the hidden dangers lying in wait for the mortgagee are the following kinds of interest, any of which may diminish or destroy the effective value of the mortgagee's security.

(a) Equitable interests of beneficiaries behind a trust for sale

A mortgage of land which is subject to an implied trust for sale[12] sometimes presents a hazard for the lender of money. The Law of Property Act 1925 provides, of course, no authority for the overreaching of equitable interests behind such a trust unless the mortgage funds are duly advanced to at least two trustees for sale.[13] Several potential problems arise in this context.

(i) Loan moneys advanced to a sole trustee for sale It is quite possible that land which is vested in the name of one person only may be held on a statutory trust for sale for a number of beneficiaries whose existence is not apparent on the face of the legal title. A mortgagee who is unaware that the land offered to him as security is governed by such a statutory trust will be equally unaware of the need to pay two trustees.[14] Being unable to claim the benefit of the statutory provision for overreaching, such a mortgagee stands in danger of losing priority to the equitable interests of beneficiaries behind the trust. There is a risk that in registered land the mortgagee may become vulnerable to the adverse claims of beneficiaries who at the material time were 'in actual occupation' of the land.[15] In unregistered land the mortgagee may likewise find that he takes his security subject to the rights of beneficiaries of whom he is deemed to have had constructive notice.[16]

The threat of prior equitable entitlements is, of course, particularly acute in a mortgage of the family home. As was said by Lord Denning MR in *Williams & Glyn's Bank Ltd v Boland*,[17] '[a]nyone who lends money on the security of a matrimonial home nowadays ought to realise that the wife may have a share in it.' In recent years, however, the risks incurred by mortgagees have subsided in consequence of a number of case law developments which culminated in the House of Lords' ruling in *Abbey National Building Society v Cann*.[18] Together these developments represent a significant judicial retreat from the marked willingness of the courts a decade or so

11 Where a building society lends on an 'acquisition mortgage', it often instructs the purchaser's solicitor to investigate title not merely on behalf of the purchaser but also on behalf of the building society itself.
12 Ante, p 528.
13 Law of Property Act 1925, ss 2(1)(ii), 27(2).
14 See Chapter 14 (ante, p 535) for a description of the way in which an implied (or statutory) trust for sale can easily come into being without anyone being aware of its existence.
15 Land Registration Act 1925, s 70(1)(g). See eg *Williams & Glyn's Bank Ltd v Boland* [1981] AC 487 (ante, p 569).
16 See eg *Kingsnorth Finance Co Ltd v Tizard* [1986] 1 WLR 783 at 792H-793A (ante, p 567).
17 [1979] Ch 312 at 332G (ante, p 571).
18 [1991] 1 AC 56 (ante, p 561).

earlier to extend residential protection to family members holding beneficial interests behind a trust of their home.

In *Cann*'s case the 75-year-old mother of a sole trustee for sale claimed that her beneficial interest ranked as an overriding interest under section 70(1)(g) of the Land Registration Act 1925. She therefore sought priority over a building society chargee which had provided her son with some of the funds needed to purchase his legal title in a leasehold property. The mother's claim to protection failed. The House of Lords confirmed, first, that an overriding interest of this kind may be asserted only if the claimant was in 'actual occupation' at the date of the relevant disposition (ie at the date of completion of the purchase and acquisition mortgage).[19] In practice few trust beneficiaries move into actual occupation in advance of the completion of a house purchase.[20] In the context of acquisition mortgages, the immediate effect of this part of the *Cann* ruling is therefore to withhold overriding interest protection from all but the most unusual cases of beneficial entitlement in registered land.[1]

The House of Lords' restrictive interpretation of 'actual occupation' of course avails only those who lend on the security of registered land. However, a further facet of the *Cann* decision tends to minimise the lender's risk in respect of *both* registered *and* unregistered land. *Cann* effectively removes the danger in either context that priorities adverse to the lender may be asserted following an 'acquisition mortgage'. The House of Lords ruled that in the 'vast majority of cases' of acquisition mortgage, the acquisition of the legal title and the creation of the relevant mortgage charge are 'not only precisely simultaneous but indissolubly bound together.'[2] In other words, no *scintilla temporis* intervenes between the two events such as could ever allow the legal owner to assert, even momentarily, that he held an unencumbered estate in the land.[3] In *Cann*, as Lord Jauncey of Tullichettle explained, it must follow that 'as a matter of reality [the son] was never vested in the unencumbered leasehold and was therefore never in a position to grant to [his mother] an interest in [the property] which prevailed over that of the society.' The interest which the mother had sought to oppose against the mortgagee 'could only be carved out of [the son's] equity of redemption.'[4]

Cann thus brings about the result that, where an acquisition mortgage is instrumental in facilitating the purchase of a legal estate, any trust for sale takes effect only against an already encumbered title and the mortgagee

19 [1991] 1 AC 56 at 88C-H per Lord Oliver of Aylmerton, 104H-105B, 106C-D per Lord Jauncey of Tullichettle. See also *Lloyds Bank Plc v Rosset* [1991] 1 AC 107 at 126D per Lord Bridge of Harwich.

20 In *Cann* the House of Lords disregarded the mother's claim to have enjoyed 'actual occupation' for 35 minutes prior to completion (ante, p 221).

1 Actual occupation which supervenes before the date of *registration* of the mortgagee's charge is irrelevant ([1991] 1 AC 56 at 76D per Lord Bridge of Harwich). See also *Lloyds Bank Plc v Rosset* [1989] Ch 350 at 374D-E per Nicholls LJ.

2 [1991] 1 AC 56 at 92F per Lord Oliver of Aylmerton (ante, p 562). For the purpose of this part of its decision, the House of Lords was obliged to overrule *Church of England Building Society v Piskor* [1954] Ch 553 (post, p 979).

3 Post, p 980. Other cases have confirmed that no *scintilla temporis* arises even on a remortgage of the property. See *Equity & Law Home Loans Ltd v Prestidge* [1992] 1 WLR 137 at 143G-144B, 145D (ante, p 577); *Walthamstow Building Society v Davies* (1990) 60 P & CR 99 at 103 (post, p 986).

4 [1991] 1 AC 56 at 102G-H.

enjoys an inevitable priority over beneficial interests behind the trust. Thus far, however, the *Cann* ruling does nothing to protect mortgagees from the dangers inherent in mortgages which are created subsequently to the acquisition of legal title. In the case of post-acquisition or second mortgages, the hazard posed by adverse equities remains a stark reality not least in view of the infinitely greater likelihood that resident beneficiaries will be able to claim 'actual occupation'.[5]

Here further relief was provided for lenders by yet another aspect of *Cann*. Although it was not strictly necessary for its decision, the House of Lords confirmed the view, already evident in the case law,[6] that certain claims of priority may be precluded by a form of estoppel. Priority for a beneficial owner will effectively be barred by any contemporaneous knowledge that the legal estate is being mortgaged. In *Cann*, for instance, Lord Oliver of Aylmerton noted that, when the son put together the funds for his purchase of the new joint family home, his mother was 'well aware that there was a shortfall which would have to be met from somewhere.'[7] She must therefore be taken as having impliedly authorised him to meet this shortfall by mortgage loan and, for this purpose, to create a charge to the lender having priority over her own interest.[8] She had permitted him to 'raise money on the security of the property without any limitation on his authority being communicated to the lender'.[9] In these circumstances, said Lord Oliver, the mother was in no position to complain, as against the lender, that too much was raised or that her own beneficial interest retained priority over the security taken by the lender.

The net effect of these recent developments is to afford significant protection for the mortgagee who lends to a borrower who is later revealed to have held the mortgaged property on trust. The only remaining case of real hazard for the lender occurs where a post-acquisition charge is taken without the knowledge of relevant beneficial owners. In such cases if further protection is required, the only practical solution may be for the mortgagee to ensure that the mortgage is executed by all the co-owners of the land (either legal or equitable) or that he receives a formal disclaimer of priority from all persons in actual occupation of the land (whether the land be held by way of registered or unregistered title).[10]

(ii) Loan moneys advanced to two trustees for sale Of course, if a mortgagee is aware of the existence of a trust for sale, he will clearly insist that the mortgage be executed jointly by the trustees for sale and that they duly give him a receipt in respect of the loan moneys paid over to them. In *City of London*

5 See Chapter 14 (ante, pp 562ff).
6 See eg *Bristol and West Building Society v Henning* [1985] 1 WLR 778 at 782G, 783C; *Paddington Building Society v Mendelsohn* (1985) 50 P & CR 244 at 248f.
7 [1991] 1 AC 56 at 94B-C. Lord Oliver discounted as 'fanciful' the possibility that the mother might have thought that her son would raise the balance (amounting to some £4,000) on unsecured loan or by access to other property.
8 This was precisely the view taken in the Court of Appeal by Dillon LJ, who pointed out that the mother had 'left it to [the son] to raise the balance' ((1989) 57 P & CR 381 at 392). In fact the son, in breach of his authority and in fraud of his mother, raised £25,000 in an abortive attempt to resolve his own financial difficulties.
9 [1991] 1 AC 56 at 94E-F.
10 Even these safeguards may not necessarily guarantee that the mortgagee's priority is altogether beyond challenge (post, p 575).

Building Society v Flegg[11] the House of Lords confirmed, after some doubt had been expressed in the Court of Appeal,[12] that this procedure will unfailingly entitle the mortgagee to overreach all beneficial interests existing behind a trust for sale affecting the land.[13] The ruling in *Flegg*'s case thus conclusively vindicates the orthodox understanding of the overreaching mechanism in the present context.

(iii) Loan moneys advanced to a fraudulent trustee for sale A further hazard for the mortgagee of land held on trust for sale lies in the possibility of a wholly fraudulent transaction with regard to a jointly held legal title. Recent developments have demonstrated, however, that even here the degree of risk for the mortgagee is not now so great as was once feared.

In *First National Securities Ltd v Hegerty*[14] a husband and wife ('H' and 'W' respectively) were joint owners of the legal and equitable interest in a dwelling-house which was held on a statutory trust for sale. H dishonestly obtained a mortgage advance on the security of this property by forging W's signature on an instrument which purported to charge the jointly owned legal estate in favour of the lender. H then left the country with the loan money and, when he defaulted on the mortgage repayments, the mortgagee brought proceedings for payment and applied ex parte for a charging order under the Charging Orders Act 1979.

In these circumstances it was clear that the fraudulently executed charge could have no operation upon the jointly owned legal title in the property, precisely because W had not in fact executed the instrument of charge.[15] Nor could the mortgagee claim to have statutorily overreached the equitable interests belonging to H and W, since there had been no true dealing with two trustees for sale. The forged charge could not affect W's equitable interest behind the trust for sale because she was wholly uninvolved in H's dishonest transaction.[16] However, the abortive legal charge had of course severed any joint tenancy which existed in equity,[17] and the only question remaining was whether that charge could now be seen as enjoying a residual effect against H's severed equitable share.

When roughly the same circumstances had arisen some years previously in *Cedar Holdings Ltd v Green*,[18] the Court of Appeal had decided that the fraudulently executed legal mortgage was not effectual to charge even H's beneficial interest in the property. This ruling was based at least in part

11 [1988] AC 54 at 73E-G per Lord Templeman, 90E–91D per Lord Oliver of Aylmerton.
12 [1986] Ch 605 at 617C-D, 619H–620A per Dillon LJ (ante, p 553).
13 A mortgagee who in good faith advances money to two trustees is statutorily exonerated of any further concern with the propriety or purpose of the mortgage or with the application of the mortgage moneys (Trustee Act 1925, s 17; Law of Property Act 1925, s 27(1)).
14 [1985] QB 850.
15 [1985] QB 850 at 863A per Sir Denys Buckley (ante, p 468). Even if the charge is registered, the entry may be said to be 'obtained by fraud' and thus liable to be rectified (Land Registration Act 1925, s 82(1)(d), ante, p 231f), provided at least that the chargee or his agent participated or colluded in the fraud. See eg *National Commercial Banking Corpn of Australia Ltd v Hedley* (1984) 3 BPR 9477 at 9481f (where an employee of the mortgagee falsely attested that the mortgage had been signed in his presence by the mortgagors 'who are personally known to me').
16 [1985] QB 850 at 863A.
17 [1985] QB 850 at 854B per Bingham J, 862G-H per Sir Denys Buckley.
18 [1981] Ch 129.

on a reluctant application of the equitable doctrine of conversion.[19] Under section 63(1) of the Law of Property Act 1925, every conveyance is declared to be 'effectual to pass all the estate, right, title, interest, claim, and demand which the conveying parties respectively have, in, to, or on the property conveyed, or expressed or intended so to be . . .' In *Cedar Holdings*, the Court of Appeal held that H's interest under the trust for sale of the co-owned property was an interest in proceeds of sale and not in 'the property' purportedly conveyed by the charge, and therefore could not be affected by section 63(1).[20]

This dogmatic approach was not followed in *First National Securities Ltd v Hegerty*. Here Bingham J pointed out that the application of the doctrine of conversion in *Cedar Holdings* had since been explicitly rejected by the House of Lords in *Williams & Glyn's Bank Ltd v Boland*.[1] Bingham J was thus in no doubt that the abortive legal charge was still effective to create a valid equitable charge in favour of the lender in relation to H's beneficial interest in the property.[2] This view was upheld by the Court of Appeal,[3] with the result that the lender was then able to apply successfully for a charging order which conferred locus standi to apply for a sale of the property pursuant to section 30 of the Law of Property Act 1925.[4] A sale, if ordered under this provision, would in effect enable a recovery of the loan money from the cash value of H's share of the proceeds.

(b) Other beneficial interests under trusts and settlements

The problems of the mortgagee are not confined to equitable rights concealed behind an implied trust for sale. Similar difficulties may afflict a lender who advances money on the security of land which is held on a bare trust not disclosed by the paper title.[5] Moreover, if the mortgagee is unaware that the land over which he takes his security is settled under the Settled Land Act 1925, the mortgage may itself be null and void.[6]

(c) Tenancies by estoppel

It used to be thought that the security taken by a mortgagee was inherently vulnerable to any tenancy agreements which might have been granted by the mortgagor before he acquired the legal title offered as security. In *Church*

19 Ante, p 541.
20 [1981] Ch 129 at 141E-F, 146C.
1 [1981] AC 487 at 507F-G per Lord Wilberforce.
2 [1985] QB 850 at 854B-C per Bingham J.
3 [1985] QB 850 at 862H-863A per Sir Denys Buckley. See *National Commercial Banking Corpn of Australia Ltd v Hedley* (1984) 3 BPR 9477 at 9482f, where a similar result was reached on the ground of either estoppel or implied agreement by the dishonest spouse.
4 Ante, p 594.
5 See eg *Hodgson v Marks* [1971] Ch 892 at 934G (ante, p 216). Here the real loser was the second defendant, the Cheltenham and Gloucester Building Society, which had advanced the purchase moneys to the first defendant, the purchaser. The Court of Appeal was not overly sympathetic towards the building society. Russell LJ observed that 'it is plain that it made no inquiries on the spot save as to repairs; it relied on [the first defendant], who lied to it; and I waste no tears on it' ([1971] Ch 892 at 932B).
6 See eg *Weston v Henshaw* [1950] Ch 510 at 520. Compare, however, *In re Morgan's Lease* [1972] Ch 1 at 9A-B (ante, p 633).

of England Building Society v Piskor,[7] for instance, a mortgagor had obtained possession of land in advance of the completion of his purchase. During the interim before completion he purported to grant periodic tenancies to two tenants who moved in before the date of the conveyance to the mortgagor. When the mortgagee later sought possession of the property on the ground of default by the mortgagor, the Court of Appeal held that the rights of the tenants took priority over the mortgage.[8] The tenancies had been mere 'leases by estoppel' during the period before completion, since the lessor had not yet acquired the legal estate out of which they might be created. However, as soon as the legal estate passed to the mortgagor/lessor on completion, these tenancies automatically became legal tenancies. The rights of the tenants crystallised as legal rights in the instant when the 'estoppel was fed' by the conveyance of the legal estate.[9]

The internal logic of the decision in *Piskor* depended vitally upon the theory that, where a taking of title is funded by an acquisition mortgage loan, a fragment of time or *scintilla temporis* intervenes between the passing of the legal estate to the mortgagor and the disposition of mortgage in favour of the lender of the purchase moneys.[10] Notwithstanding that the relevant documents of transfer and charge are executed contemporaneously, the transaction of purchase necessarily involves, in terms of this theory, conveyancing steps which in contemplation of law are regarded as taking place in a defined order. As Lord Oliver of Aylmerton was later to concede, there is 'an attractive legal logic' in the proposition that 'a person cannot charge a legal estate that he does not have'.[11] Accordingly, in *Piskor*'s case, the Court of Appeal held that the metamorphosis of the tenants' rights occurred on the feeding of their estoppel during the *scintilla temporis* between the purchaser/landlord's acquisition of his legal estate and the creation of the building society charge.

In *Abbey National Building Society v Cann*[12] the House of Lords conclusively overruled the 'successive steps' analysis[13] of *Piskor* in favour of the 'single transaction' analysis found in analogous areas of law.[14] In a purchase based on mortgage funding, declared Lord Oliver, 'the transactions of acquiring

7 [1954] Ch 553.

8 Romer LJ was notably unsympathetic towards the idea of 'enabling the [building] society to evict persons, who were already in occupation, but whose existence or rights the society had never troubled to inquire about at all' ([1954] Ch 553 at 566).

9 [1954] Ch 553 at 561, 564f. See also *Universal Permanent Building Society v Cooke* [1952] Ch 95 at 103. A similar result would have followed if title had been registered, since the tenants would have been protected by Land Registration Act 1925, s 70(1)(g), (k) (ante, pp 210, 203 however, the tenants had had a mere contract for a tenancy, their rights in unregistered land would have depended on the registration of a Class C(iv) land charge, and, in registered land, on the existence of 'actual occupation' for the purpose of Land Registration Act 1925, s 70(1)(g).

10 Ante, p 561.

11 *Abbey National Building Society v Cann* [1991] 1 AC 56 at 92E. Lord Jauncey of Tullichettle likewise noted (at 101F) that 'as a matter of strict legal analysis. . .a purchaser of property cannot grant a mortgage over it until the legal estate has vested in him.' See also *Lloyds Bank Plc v Rosset* [1989] Ch 350 at 391H–392B per Mustill LJ.

12 [1991] 1 AC 56 (ante, p 561).

13 The phrase is that of Nicholls LJ in *Lloyds Bank Plc v Rosset* [1989] Ch 350 at 384E.

14 See eg *In re Connolly Brothers Ltd (No 2)* [1912] 2 Ch 25 at 31; *Coventry Permanent Economic Building Society v Jones* [1951] 1 All ER 901 at 903; *Security Trust Co v Royal Bank of Canada* [1976] AC 503 at 519f.

the legal estate and granting the charge are, in law as in reality, one indivisible transaction.'[15] *Piskor*'s case 'flies in the face of reality' and the *scintilla temporis* is 'no more than a legal artifice'.[16] In the case of the acquisition mortgage, as Lord Oliver pointed out, the acquisition of the legal estate 'is entirely dependent upon the provision of funds which will have been provided before the conveyance can take effect and which are provided only against an agreement that the estate will be charged to secure them.'[17] The reality is that the purchaser of land who relies upon a building society or bank loan for the completion of his purchase 'never in fact acquires anything but an equity of redemption'. The land 'is, from the very inception, charged with the amount of the loan without which it could never have been transferred at all and it was never intended that it should be otherwise.'[18]

The destruction of the *scintilla temporis* theory in *Cann*'s case ensures that the acquisition mortgagor is never, even for a moment of time, in any position to deal with his legal estate as though the mortgagee had no interest therein. It is certainly clear that the mortgagor acquires no unencumbered title whereby an estoppel in favour of grantees could be fed to the prejudice of the mortgagee's security.[19]

(d) Unregistered contractual rights

A mortgagee who takes merely an equitable security over the mortgagor's property faces special difficulties. Whereas a legal mortgagee may ignore contractual rights which should have been protected by registration in the Land Charges Register or in the Land Register but which were not so protected, an equitable mortgagee is much more vulnerable. Thus an equitable mortgagee of unregistered land may be bound by a prior land charge (even if unregistered), on the basis that 'where the equities are equal, the first in time prevails'.

In *McCarthy & Stone Ltd v Julian S. Hodge & Co Ltd*[20] it was held that an unregistered estate contract should take priority over a later equitable mortgagee of the encumbered property, since the latter could not claim the immunity conferred by statute upon a 'purchaser for money or money's worth. . .of a legal estate in the land'.[1] The effect of the unregistered estate contract therefore turned on an application of the traditional doctrine that where the equities are equal, the first in time prevails. The result would not have been different if the land in question had been held by registered title, since the unprotected contractual right would have acquired protection

15 [1991] 1 AC 56 at 92D. Lord Oliver was careful to add that the 'single transaction' analysis obtains 'at least where there is a prior agreement to grant the charge on the legal estate when obtained'.

16 [1991] 1 AC 56 at 92F, 93B.

17 [1991] 1 AC 56 at 92F.

18 [1991] 1 AC 56 at 93A-B. Lord Jauncey of Tullichettle took a similar view of 'the realities of the situation' (101H). He agreed (at 102A-B) that the purchaser who can complete a transaction only by borrowing money which he is already contractually bound to secure by mortgage 'cannot in reality ever be said to have acquired even for a *scintilla temporis* the unencumbered fee simple or leasehold estate in land whereby he could grant interests having priority over the mortgage' (ante, p 975).

19 See [1991] 1 AC 56 at 102B per Lord Jauncey of Tullichettle.

20 [1971] 1 WLR 1547 at 1555D. See [1972A] CLJ 34 (P.B. Fairest).

1 See Land Charges Act 1972, s 4(6) (ante, p 119).

as an overriding interest provided that the owner of the estate contract was 'in actual occupation' at the date of the equitable mortgage.[2]

(2) **Deposit of title documents**

Various rules requiring the deposit of title documents afford the legal mortgagee a substantial safeguard against any prejudicial dealings with the legal title by the mortgagor. Section 85(1) of the Law of Property Act 1925 provides that a first mortgagee has a legal right throughout the mortgage term to retain the title deeds pertaining to the mortgaged property. This safeguard is available, of course, only to a mortgagee of unregistered land. However, much the same effect is achieved in the context of registered land by section 65 of the Land Registration Act 1925, which requires that the mortgagor's land certificate be deposited in the Land Registry until redemption of the mortgage.[3]

A second mortgagee of unregistered land obviously cannot enjoy the same security of deposit of the title deeds. However, in unregistered land a second mortgage may be protected as a Class C(i) land charge (if the mortgage is legal),[4] and as a Class C(iii) land charge (if the mortgage takes the form of an equitable charge).[5] In registered land the problem of protecting the second chargee is alleviated by the fact that the relevant land certificate is retained by the Land Registry while any charge remains registered against the title.[6]

Apart from restraining prejudicial dealings by the mortgagor, the practice of depositing title documents with the mortgagee of unregistered land facilitates any later exercise of the mortgagee's power of sale. Should that power ever become exercisable,[7] he is already equipped with the necessary documents of title for the purpose of dealing with third parties.

8. THE MORTGAGEE'S RIGHT TO POSSESSION

The English law of mortgage arms the mortgagee with a number of important rights and remedies by way of safeguard against the possibility of default by his mortgagor. Crucial in this context is the right of the mortgagee to enter into possession of the mortgaged land. This right has been the subject of some controversy, since it impinges perhaps more directly than any other right of the mortgagee upon the security of tenure enjoyed by the mortgagor, whether he be the owner of residential or commercial property.

2 Ante, p 210.
3 Ante, p 172. The mortgagor has a statutory right to inspect and make copies (at his own expense) of the title documents in the custody or power of the mortgagee (Law of Property Act 1925, s 96(1)). This right cannot be excluded by contract. On redemption of a mortgage, the mortgagee must hand the title deeds over either to the mortgagor or to the next mortgagee (see Law of Property Act 1925, s 96(2)).
4 Ante, p 140.
5 Ante, p 141.
6 Land Registration Act 1925, s 65.
7 Post, p 1004.

(1) Origin of the legal mortgagee's right to possession

A legal mortgage confers on the mortgagee a legal estate in the mortgaged property,[8] and a legal charge is statutorily deemed to have an equivalent effect.[9] It is established doctrine in the English law of mortgage that, as an incident of this estate in the land, the mortgagee has at all times 'an unqualified right to possession of the mortgaged property' in the absence of any contractual or statutory limitation.[10] This right to possession arises as soon as the mortgage is made and is not dependent on any default by the mortgagor.[11] As Harman J graphically pointed out in *Four-Maids Ltd v Dudley Marshall (Properties) Ltd*,[12] the mortgagee 'may go into possession before the ink is dry on the mortgage unless there is something in the contract, express or by implication, whereby he has contracted himself out of that right.'[13] Moreover, a mortgagor who resists his mortgagee's demand for possession automatically becomes a trespasser,[14] and, in the absence of any relevant statutory restriction, the mortgagee is then entitled to make a peaceable entry without the necessity of first obtaining a court possession order.[15]

(2) Exclusion of the mortgagee's right to possession

The mortgagee's inherent right to enter into possession may be negatived either by statutory restrictions[16] or by mortgage terms which expressly or impliedly reserve the right of possession to the mortgagor instead.[17]

(a) Express exclusion

It is not uncommon, for instance, that a building society mortgage should expressly grant the mortgagor a right of possession until default. It has been

8 Law of Property Act 1925, ss 85(1), 86(1) (ante, p 939).
9 Law of Property Act 1925, s 87(1) (ante, p 939).
10 *Mobil Oil Co Ltd v Rawlinson* (1982) 43 P & CR 221 at 223 per Nourse J. See [1982] Conv 453 (P. Jackson); (1983) 133 NLJ 247 (H.W. Wilkinson). See also to similar effect *Ashley Guarantee Plc v Zacaria* [1993] 1 WLR 62 at 69B per Nourse LJ; *National Westminster Bank Plc v Skelton (Note)* [1993] 1 WLR 72 at 77A, 81H per Slade LJ.
11 *Four-Maids Ltd v Dudley Marshall (Properties) Ltd* [1957] Ch 317 at 320; *Mobil Oil Co Ltd v Rawlinson* (1982) 43 P & CR 221 at 223f.
12 [1957] Ch 317 at 320. See (1957) 73 LQR 300 (R.E.M.).
13 See also *Alliance Perpetual Building Society v Belrum Investments Ltd* [1957] 1 WLR 720 at 723.
14 *Birch v Wright* (1786) 1 Term Rep 378 at 383, 99 ER 1148 at 1152; *Jolly v Arbuthnot* (1859) 4 De G & J 224 at 236, 45 ER 87 at 92.
15 See *McPhail v Persons, Names Unknown* [1973] Ch 447 at 456D–457B (ante, p 307). In strict terms there is no general requirement of legal process prior to the exercise of peaceable entry by a mortgagee who wishes to assert his paramount right to possession. However, there is always a danger that such entry may generate criminal liability under the Protection from Eviction Act 1977, s 1 (ante, p 808) or the Criminal Law Act 1977, s 6(1) (ante, p 308), and in practice it is highly unusual for a mortgagee to resort to peaceable entry without the benefit of a court possession order. There is also some question whether section 36 of the Administration of Justice Act 1970 has impliedly inserted a requirement of due legal process in relation to residential mortgages (post, p 997).
16 Post, p 987.
17 *Doe d Roylance v Lightfoot* (1841) 8 M & W 553 at 564f, 151 ER 1158 at 1163. Where the mortgagee's right to possession has been excluded by contract, an injunction may be granted to restrain the mortgagee from going into possession in breach of his contract (*Doe d Parsley v Day* (1842) 2 QB 147 at 156, 114 ER 58 at 62).

held that such a mortgage term constitutes an implied exclusion of the mortgagee's right to possession before default occurs.[18]

(b) Implied exclusion

It is also possible that the mortgagee's right to possession may be excluded by implication from the terms and attendant circumstances of the mortgage transaction.

(i) Instalment mortgages In *Esso Petroleum Co Ltd v Alstonbridge Properties Ltd*[19] Walton J accepted that the court will be particularly ready to find an implied term in an instalment mortgage that the mortgagor is to be entitled to remain in possession against the mortgagee unless he makes some default in payment of one of the instalments. Walton J added, however, that 'there must be something upon which to hang such a conclusion in the mortgage other than the mere fact that it is an instalment mortgage.'[20]

(ii) Other mortgages The tenor of Walton J's cautionary remark is borne out in other cases in which the courts have proved somewhat slow to find that the right to possession has been impliedly reserved to the mortgagor rather than the mortgagee.[1] In *Western Bank Ltd v Schindler*[2] the defendant mortgagor had borrowed £32,000 from the plaintiff mortgagee on the terms of an endowment mortgage which provided that no payment of capital or interest was contractually due until ten years after the date of execution of the mortgage. Notwithstanding the absence of any financial default by the mortgagor, the mortgagee subsequently claimed a right to possession, *within* the ten year period, in order to preserve the value of the security. The Court of Appeal unanimously upheld the mortgagee's claim to possession in these circumstances.[3]

The Court was unwilling to accept the argument that a contractual term excluding this right should normally be implied 'if and for so long as the terms of the mortgage preclude the mortgagee from making immediate demand for payment or otherwise immediately enforcing his security.' Buckley LJ agreed that the fact that a mortgage was an instalment mortgage might make it easier for a court to find such an implied term, but held that even this fact would not be conclusive.[4] In the present case the mortgagee's right to possession was not lightly to be held to have been excluded by implication, since only this right could effectively protect the mortgagee's legitimate interest in ensuring that at the redemption date the property would still represent a good security for a substantial debt of capital and interest. As Scarman LJ pointed out, the only way in which the mortgagee could ultimately guarantee that the mortgaged property was properly managed and

18 *Birmingham Citizens Permanent Building Society v Caunt* [1962] Ch 883 at 890 per Russell J.
19 [1975] 1 WLR 1474.
20 [1975] 1 WLR 1474 at 1484B.
1 See R.J. Smith, [1979] Conv 266 at 268ff.
2 [1977] Ch 1. See (1977) 40 MLR 356 (C. Harpum).
3 [1977] Ch 1 at 16A, 19G, 26F.
4 [1977] Ch 1 at 10C-D.

maintained, and the value of the security preserved throughout the loan term, was if the court upheld the mortgagee's claim to possession in the absence of a clear contractual exclusion of that right.[5]

(c) Attornment clauses

The *attornment clause* provides a nowadays somewhat unusual means of excluding the mortgagee's right to possession. It used to be common practice to insert in deeds of mortgage an attornment clause which had the result of creating a purely nominal landlord-tenant relationship between the parties to the mortgage.[6] Under an attornment clause the mortgagor holds effectively as a tenant of the mortgagee, and the object of the clause is to make available to the mortgagee the additional possessory remedies open to the landlord.[7] There is, however, one respect in which the inclusion of an attornment clause significantly qualifies the mortgagee's right to enter into possession. Precisely because a notional tenancy is created between mortgagor and mortgagee, the latter is required to terminate the tenancy by serving a notice to quit as a necessary preliminary to any exercise of the right to possession.[8]

The attornment clause does not, however, confer on a residential mortgagor any of the other forms of protection afforded tenants under the Rent Act legislation.[9] The mortgagor is not, for instance, entitled to the minimum period of four weeks' notice to quit which is generally applicable in the area of residential lettings.[10] In *Alliance Building Society v Pinwill*[11] Vaisey J held that the statutory requirement of a minimum period of notice protects only 'a real tenant against a real landlord under a real "residential letting"'.[12] The insertion of an attornment clause in a mortgage is now extremely rare.

(d) No exclusion by reason of mere counterclaim or cross-claim

The generally paramount quality of the legal mortgagee's right to possession is illustrated by the fact that the mortgagor cannot normally resist an action for possession by claiming an equitable set-off against the mortgagee for an unliquidated sum.[13] This proposition—the so-called '*Mobil Oil*

5 'So far from implying a term excluding the common law right, I would expect, as a matter of business efficacy, that the mortgagee would in these circumstances require its retention' ([1977] Ch 1 at 17F).

6 The rent payable under the tenancy was often a purely nominal rent such as the 2½p stipulated for in *Peckham Mutual Building Society v Registe* (1981) 42 P & CR 186 at 188.

7 Historically the attornment clause came into common use in order to give the mortgagee access to the right of distress (ante, p 839). See *Re Tuxedo Savings & Credit Union Ltd and Krusky* (1987) 35 DLR (4th) 211 at 215.

8 *Hinckley and Country Building Society v Henny* [1953] 1 WLR 352 at 355.

9 Ante, p 873.

10 See *Peckham Mutual Building Society v Registe* (1981) 42 P & CR 186 at 188f.

11 [1958] Ch 788 at 792.

12 Compare, however, P.B. Fairest, op cit, p 89, who points out that the landlord-tenant relationship created by the attornment clause has a 'quite surprising reality' in other contexts.

13 In *National Westminster Bank Plc v Skelton (Note)* [1993] 1 WLR 72 at 78C, the Court of Appeal left open the question whether the mortgagee's right to possession is affected where a mortgagor establishes that he has a claim to a quantified sum by way of equitable set-off. Slade LJ thought it possible that such a claim might actually extinguish the mortgage debt.

principle'[14]—is often justified on the basis that otherwise the mere allegation of some connected, but perhaps groundless, cross-claim by a mortgagor would have the effect of keeping the mortgagee out of his 'undoubted prima facie right to possession'.[15] Contract and statute apart, the legal mortgagee's right to possession cannot be defeated by a cross-claim on the part of the mortgagor even if it is admitted and for a sum which exceeds the mortgage debt.[16] Under the *Mobil Oil* principle, moreover, it is entirely irrelevant whether the mortgagor is himself the principal debtor of the mortgagee or merely a guarantor of the debt of a third party (eg where the mortgagor guarantees the debt of his own trading company).[17] In the latter instance, although the law is undoubted, it has been said to be 'an arresting concept' that a mortgagor could be required to give up possession of his home despite the existence of an unliquidated claim, which is admitted or shown to be likely to succeed, in an amount which either exceeds the sum due from the principal debtor or, when established, enables the debt to be paid in full.[18]

(3) Immunity from unauthorised leases created by the mortgagor

A mortgagor, while in possession, has a general statutory power to grant certain kinds of lease in respect of the mortgaged land.[19] It is customary, however, for this leasing power to be modified or excluded by the express terms of the mortgage. It is well established that the mortgagee is not bound by any lease granted by the mortgagor after the execution of the mortgage

14 The proposition is so termed following its enunciation by Nourse J in *Mobil Oil Co Ltd v Rawlinson* (1982) 43 P & CR 221 at 226f. See *National Westminster Bank Plc v Skelton (Note)* [1993] 1 WLR 72 at 78B per Slade LJ.

15 See *National Westminster Bank Plc v Skelton (Note)* [1993] 1 WLR 72 at 78A-B per Slade LJ.

16 See also *Samuel Keller (Holdings) Ltd v Martins Bank Ltd* [1971] 1 WLR 43 at 47H-48B, 51C-D; *Barclays Bank Plc v Tennet* (Unreported, Court of Appeal, 6 June 1984); *Citibank Trust Ltd v Ayivor* [1987] 1 WLR 1157 at 1161C, 1164A; *Ashley Guarantee Plc v Zacaria* [1993] 1 WLR 62 at 66C-D per Nourse LJ; *National Westminster Bank Plc v Skelton (Note)* [1993] 1 WLR 72 at 77H-78A per Slade LJ.

17 See *National Westminster Bank Plc v Skelton (Note)* [1993] 1 WLR 72 at 78F per Slade LJ; *Ashley Guarantee Plc v Zacaria* [1993] 1 WLR 62 at 69A-B per Nourse LJ.

18 See *Ashley Guarantee Plc v Zacaria* [1993] 1 WLR 62 at 70G-71B per Ralph Gibson LJ, who thought that such circumstances might, in a particular case, give rise either to an implied term excluding the mortgagee's immediate right to possession or to a stay under Administration of Justice Act 1970, s 36 (post, p 995), pending trial of the claim to the set-off. See also Woolf LJ at 71C-D, but compare *National Westminster Bank Plc v Skelton (Note)* [1993] 1 WLR 72 at 82B-C per Anthony Lincoln J.

19 The mortgagor in possession has the same leasing power as has a mortgagee in possession (Law of Property Act 1925, s 99(1), (2)). Both have statutory authority, if the mortgage was made after 1925, to lease the land for any term not exceeding 50 years (for agricultural or occupation purposes) and for any term not exceeding 999 years (for building purposes) (Law of Property Act 1925, s 99(3)). In all cases the lease must normally take effect in possession within twelve months of its date, must reserve 'the best rent that can reasonably be obtained', and must contain a condition of re-entry on the covenanted rent not being paid within a specified time not exceeding 30 days (Law of Property Act 1925, s 99(5)-(7)).

if the lease was not authorised by statute or by the mortgagee himself.[20] For this purpose it matters not whether the lease in question comprises a contractual tenancy[1] or even a statutory tenancy within the protection of the Rent Act.[2] It is also irrelevant that, subsequent to the grant of the lease, the land is re-mortgaged with the result that the first mortgage is discharged and replaced by a different mortgage.[3] In all such cases the unauthorised lease has been granted in the shadow of a prior mortgage.[4] The lease is therefore liable to be defeated by the assertion of the paramount title already conferred on the mortgagee, leaving the lessee with no remedy except against the mortgagor himself. This conclusion has a certain legal inevitability, but still operates unkindly in relation to the tenant who is entirely unaware that his or her landlord has granted a tenancy without authority and has then fallen into arrears with the mortgage payments.[5] In such an instance, however, the mortgagee simply has an unqualified right to take possession as against the tenant.[6]

(4) Exercise of the mortgagee's right to possession

It is now widely accepted that a legal mortgagee is entitled to go into possession of the mortgaged property even in the absence of default by the mortgagor and even though the date fixed for redemption has not yet passed. Entry into physical occupation is rendered impossible only where the land is subject

20 *Rogers v Humphreys* (1835) 4 Ad & E 299 at 313, 111 ER 799 at 804; *Dudley and District Benefit Building Society v Emerson* [1949] Ch 707 at 714. The mortgagee is, of course, bound by any lease created prior to the mortgage by either the mortgagor or his predecessor. There is authority that a legal mortgage of land in lease at the date of mortgage vests in the mortgagee the immediate reversion on the lease (see *Neale v Mackenzie* (1836) 1 M & W 747 at 760ff, 150 ER 635 at 640f). Under Law of Property Act 1925, s 142(1) (ante, p 859), the mortgagee may therefore be directly liable as reversioner for breaches of the covenant for quiet enjoyment if he demands possession from the tenant on the ground of default by the mortgagor (see D.G. Barnsley, *Harassment of Tenants by Mortgagees*, [1991] JSWL 220 at 223).

1 *Dudley and District Benefit Building Society v Emerson* [1949] Ch 707 at 714.

2 *Quennell v Maltby* [1979] 1 WLR 318 at 323H per Templeman LJ; *Britannia Building Society v Earl* [1990] 1 WLR 422 at 427H–428F per McCowan LJ.

3 See *Walthamstow Building Society v Davies* (1990) 60 P & CR 99 at 103, where the Court of Appeal indicated that there was no *scintilla temporis* between the two charges when it could be said that the lessee enjoyed lawful occupation as against the mortgagee. The Court expressly restricted its observations to the case where land is re-mortgaged in favour of the same mortgagee ((1990) 60 P & CR 99 at 103f per Balcombe LJ). However, the combined effect of *Abbey National Building Society v Cann* [1991] 1 AC 56 (ante, p 561) and *Equity & Law Home Loans Ltd v Prestidge* [1992] 1 WLR 137 (ante, p 577) suggests that a re-mortgage to a different mortgagee would have produced the same result.

4 In reality, the only interest with which the mortgagor can transact is his equity of redemption: all his dealings therefore take effect against this entitlement only, thereby ensuring priority for the mortgagee's paramount rights.

5 As in *Britannia Building Society v Earl* [1990] 1 WLR 422 at 424B, it is commonly the case that the tenant first learns of these circumstances when served with a notice that a warrant for possession of the premises is about to be executed. See D.G. Barnsley, *Harassment of Tenants by Mortgagees*, [1991] JSWL 220.

6 In its proposed reform of the law of mortgage (post, p 1039), the Law Commission has recommended that it should be an overriding implied term of all formal land mortgages that the mortgagor be entitled to grant any lease without the necessity of obtaining the mortgagee's consent. No lease will, however, bind the mortgagee unless it is granted with his written consent (see Law Com No 204 (1991), para 6.19).

to a lease which is binding on the mortgagee either because it was created prior to the mortgage or because it was created thereafter with the mortgagee's consent.[7] In such cases, however, the mortgagee may assume 'possession' in the sense of the right to receive the rents and profits due under the relevant lease.[8] Moreover, it is normally an implied incident of a mortgage of premises where the mortgagor is conducting a business that the mortgagee has power, on exercising his right to possession, to carry on the mortgagor's business.[9]

(a) *Factors inhibiting actual exercise of the mortgagee's right*

The principal object of most mortgages is that the mortgagor should remain in occupation of the land which forms the subject matter of the security.[10] Indeed, it is not going too far to say that, apart perhaps from the exceptional circumstances typified in *Western Bank Ltd v Schindler*,[11] a mortgagee will never nowadays seek possession unless a default has already occurred. Several factors have conduced to this result.

(i) Statutory control over residential property In the residential context the exercise of the mortgagee's right to possession has become subject to an important measure of statutory control. The court now has a discretion under section 36 of the Administration of Justice Act 1970 to regulate the recovery of possession by the mortgagee where there appears to be a realistic possibility that the mortgagor may remedy his default within a reasonable period of time.[12]

(ii) Mortgagee's strict liability to account A mortgagee who goes into possession of the mortgaged property becomes subject to the particularly stringent control of equity in his dealings with the property.[13] If, while in possession, he intercepts the rents and profits drawn from the land in order to ensure the payments due to him under the mortgage, he is liable to account strictly to the mortgagor for any income which he thus receives.[14] Furthermore,

7 See *Rogers v Humphreys* (1835) 4 Ad & El 299 at 313, 111 ER 799 at 804; *In re Ind Coope & Co Ltd* [1911] 2 Ch 223 at 231. The mortgagee himself may grant new leases (see *Chapman v Smith* [1907] 2 Ch 97 at 102), although such lessees are of course subject to the mortgagor's equity of redemption. See also Law of Property Act 1925, s 99(2).

8 *Moss v Gallimore* (1779) 1 Doug KB 279 at 283, 99 ER 182 at 184. See Law of Property Act 1925, s 205(1)(xix) (ante, p 685). The tenant may be directed to pay his rent henceforth to the mortgagee rather than to the mortgagor (*Horlock v Smith* (1842) 6 Jur 478).

9 See *Chaplin v Young* (No 1) (1864) 33 Beav 330 at 337f, 55 ER 395 at 398; *Cook v Thomas* (1876) 24 WR 427 at 428; *County of Gloucester Bank v Rudry Merthyr Steam and House Coal Colliery Co* [1895] 1 Ch 629 at 634, 638; *Mercantile Credits Ltd v Atkins* (1985) 1 NSWLR 670 at 676A-B.

10 See eg *Four-Maids Ltd v Dudley Marshall (Properties) Ltd* [1957] Ch 317 at 321, where Harman J made the point that building societies 'are not desirous of going into possession, nor would they do business if they were able to go into possession whenever they liked. The whole object of building societies is to maintain the householder in possession of his house so long as he pays the instalments to the society...'

11 [1977] Ch 1 (ante, p 983).

12 Post, p 995. See also Housing Act 1985, Sch 17, para 1(2), (3).

13 *Robertson v Norris* (1859) 1 Giff 428 at 436, 65 ER 986 at 989.

14 *Lord Trimleston v Hamill* (1810) 1 Ball & B 377 at 385. See H.E. Markson, (1979) 129 NLJ 334.

the mortgagee may not derive any profit other than the return of the principal and interest stipulated for in the terms of the mortgage.[15]

The mortgagee's duties are rendered even more onerous by the fact that he is liable on the footing of 'wilful default'.[16] The mortgagee immediately becomes responsible for the physical state of the premises.[17] As Nicholls V-C observed recently in *Palk v Mortgage Services Funding Plc*,[18] he must 'take reasonable care of the property'. He must also account to the mortgagor not only in respect of any rents and profits actually received, but also in respect of that income which he would have received if he had managed the property with due diligence.[19] Thus in *White v City of London Brewery Co*[20] a mortgagee who entered into possession and let the mortgaged property as a 'tied' public house (for the benefit of his own brewery business) was held liable to account for the greater rents which he would have received had he let the property as a 'free' house.[1] If the mortgagee himself goes into personal occupation of the property, he is chargeable with the best occupation rent obtainable on the open rental market in respect of those premises.[2] If the mortgagee takes over possession of an uncompleted building, he must act bona fide and as a provident owner, and must either sell the property or make a genuine effort to complete the building in a proper and economical way.[3]

The net result of these stringent rules is that if the mortgagee's primary concern is with the income derived from the mortgaged land, his objectives are in general much better served through the exercise of his statutory power to appoint a receiver[4] than by entry into possession subject to the strict control of equity in the matter of accounting. The handling of rents and profits by a receiver is not subject to the same rigorous surveillance of equity.[5]

15 For instance, a mortgagee in possession may not (even by an express mortgage term) impose any charge for his management of the land, since this would be to usurp the function of a receiver (*Comyns v Comyns* (1871) 5 IR Eq 583 at 587f).

16 *Lord Trimleston v Hamill* (1810) 1 Ball & B 377 at 385; *Sloane v Mahon* (1838) 1 Dr & Wal 189 at 192, 195; *Mobil Oil Co Ltd v Rawlinson* (1982) 43 P & CR 221 at 224. See also *Kennedy v General Credits Ltd* (1982) 2 BPR 9456 at 9457f per Hope JA (Court of Appeal of New South Wales).

17 See eg *Sterne v Victoria & Grey Trust Co* (1985) 14 DLR (4th) 193 at 203 (liability for negligently caused damage from frozen pipes).

18 [1993] 2 WLR 415 at 421A.

19 See *Chaplin v Young* (No 1) (1864) 33 Beav 330 at 337f, 55 ER 395 at 398. As Nicholls V-C noted in *Palk v Mortgage Services Funding Plc* [1993] 2 WLR 415 at 420H–421C, the mortgagee cannot simply leave the property empty, waiting indefinitely for an improvement in the market. He must instead let the property at a 'proper market rent'.

20 (1889) 42 Ch D 237 at 245 per Lord Esher MR, 249 per Fry LJ.

1 Similarly, a mortgagee in possession is liable to account for the notional rent of property which he has allowed to remain unoccupied and for due rent which he has failed without good cause to recover from his tenants (*Noyes v Pollock* (1886) 32 Ch D 53 at 61).

2 *Metcalf v Campion* (1828) 1 Mol 238 at 239; *Marriott v Anchor Reversionary Co* (1861) 3 De GF & J 177 at 193, 45 ER 846 at 852. If, however, there is no realistic evidence that the property could have been let out profitably, this rental value may be nil, in which case the mortgagee is not guilty of wilful default (see eg *Fyfe v Smith* [1975] 2 NSWLR 408 at 413F–414A).

3 *Penny v Walker* (1855) 24 LJ Ch 319 at 320f; *Midland Credit Ltd v Hallad Pty Ltd* (1977) 1 BPR 9570 at 9577f per Hutley JA.

4 Law of Property Act 1925, s 101(1)(iii) (post, p 1027).

5 *Refuge Assurance Co Ltd v Pearlberg* [1938] Ch 687 at 691f.

(b) Possession as an adjunct of the power of sale

It is, accordingly, extremely rare in practice for a mortgagee to exercise his right to go into possession while the mortgagor is acting in full compliance with the mortgage terms. There is in general a 'tacit agreement' between mortgagor and mortgagee that possession should be exercised de facto by the mortgagor in all cases except those of actual default.[6] While this tacit consent continues to operate, the mortgagor's possessory status has been described as effectively that of a tenant at sufferance.[7] He is, however, under no duty to account for any rents and profits derived from the land,[8] and is liable for waste only if the land ceases by reason of his waste to constitute an adequate security for the mortgage debt.[9]

In reality the mortgagee who nowadays exercises his right to possession is not concerned to attach the income drawn from the land, but rather to obtain vacant possession of the property in order that he may sell on the open market and thereby recoup the outstanding loan moneys. Possession is almost invariably sought as a preliminary to the mortgagee's exercise of his statutory power of sale.[10] It follows that in practice a mortgagee hardly ever seeks to go into possession unless and until there is actual default by the mortgagor, since it is only at this point that the mortgagee's statutory power of sale becomes exercisable.[11] Except where the mortgagee's security is threatened by an actual default, the right to possession generally remains dormant.

The close association between possession and sale has raised some question whether the right to possession is indeed an absolute and inherent right of the mortgagee or has instead dwindled into a right of access to a discretionary remedy determined by the court. The latter perspective drew considerable support from *Quennell v Maltby*,[12] where Lord Denning MR suggested that 'in modern times equity can step in so as to prevent a mortgagee, or a transferee from him, from getting possession of a house contrary to the justice of the case.' Thus, declared Lord Denning, a mortgagee could be restrained by the court from getting possession 'except where it is sought bona fide and reasonably for the purpose of enforcing the security and then only subject to such conditions as the court thinks fit to impose.'[13]

6 See *Moss v Gallimore* (1779) 1 Doug KB 279 at 283, 99 ER 182 at 184; *Christophers v Sparke* (1820) 2 Jac & W 223 at 235, 37 ER 612 at 617. See also B. Rudden, (1961) 25 Conv (NS) 278.

7 See *Green v Burns* (1879) 6 LR Ir 173 at 176 per Palles CB; *Fairclough v Marshall* (1878) 4 Ex D 37 at 48.

8 *Ex parte Calwell* (1828) 1 Mol 259; *Campion v Palmer* [1896] 2 IR 445 at 455ff; *Rhodes v Allied Dunbar Pension Services Ltd* [1989] 1 WLR 800 at 807E per Nicholls LJ.

9 *King v Smith* (1843) 2 Hare 239 at 243f, 67 ER 99 at 101f; *Harper v Aplin* (1886) 54 LT 383 at 384.

10 See *Mobil Oil Co Ltd v Rawlinson* (1982) 43 P & CR 221 at 224. The taking of possession has now become effectively 'an adjunct of the power of sale' (see R.J. Smith, [1979] Conv 266).

11 Post, p 1004.

12 [1979] 1 WLR 318 at 322G-H. See [1979] CLJ 257 (R.A. Pearce).

13 In *Quennell v Maltby* the Court of Appeal rejected a mortgagee's action for possession which, in Lord Denning's view, had been motivated not by any desire to obtain repayment of the relevant loan moneys but by the 'ulterior purpose' of recovering possession from two tenants who would otherwise have enjoyed security of tenure under the Rent Act ([1979] 1 WLR 318 at 323C).

It seems almost certain, however, that this approach does not represent good law,[14] not least because it renders otiose the protection afforded the mortgagor under section 36 of the Administration of Justice Act 1970.[15] More recent case law has tended to confirm the conventional understanding that, contractual agreement apart, a mortgagee has an absolute right to possession from the commencement of the mortgage term,[16] regardless of any default[17] and regardless even of the existence of a counterclaim by the mortgagor for a sum which exceeds the mortgage debt.[18] The better view therefore seems to be that the mortgagee's right to possession—although it generally lies dormant and may even appear a misleading fiction—is ab initio a paramount and virtually unqualified right.[19]

(5) Does the equitable mortgagee have a right to possession?

Much more doubt surrounds the question whether an equitable mortgagee or equitable chargee has an inherent right to possession similar to that enjoyed by the legal mortgagee.[20] The latter's right to possession is, of course, an incident of the legal estate which is created by the mortgage itself or implied on his behalf by statute.[1] In consequence it seems unlikely that, in the absence of some express conferment by the terms of the mortgage, a right of possession can be claimed by a mere equitable mortgagee or chargee unless and until such a right has been granted by a court.[2]

It is sometimes suggested that the doctrine in *Walsh v Lonsdale*,[3] by drawing an analogy between legal and equitable rights, has the indirect effect of conferring a right of possession upon even the equitable mortgagee.[4] Although such an end result would represent an entirely sensible extension of the common law position, recent judicial authority has tended to reinforce the

14 See *Marquis Cholmondeley v Lord Clinton* (1817) 2 Mer 171 at 359, 35 ER 905 at 976 ('A Court of Equity never interferes to prevent the Mortgagee from assuming the possession'. See also F.W. Maitland, *Equity* (2nd edn, London 1936), p 186, where it is pointed out that equity would never interfere with a claim to possession at common law except on terms of payment off of the whole principal, interest and costs, an equity which Maitland described as a 'mock equity', since it required payment in full and implied the termination of the mortgagor-mortgagee relationship itself.

15 Post, p 995. See R.J. Smith, [1979] Conv 266 at 268.

16 *Barclays Bank Plc v Tennet* (Unreported, Court of Appeal, 6 June 1984); *National Westminster Bank Plc v Jones* (Unreported, Court of Appeal, 3 December 1984). It is significant that in *Quennell v Maltby* [1979] 1 WLR 318 at 323E, 324F, Bridge and Templeman LJJ found alternative reasons for supporting the result reached by Lord Denning MR.

17 *Mobil Oil Co Ltd v Rawlinson* (1982) 43 P & CR 221 at 223f.

18 Ante, p 984.

19 See *Park v Brady* [1976] 2 NSWLR 329 at 335E.

20 For an argument that the equitable mortgagee is indeed entitled to possession, see H.W.R. Wade, (1955) 71 LQR 204 at 207.

1 Law of Property Act 1925, s 87(1) (ante, pp 939, 982).

2 See *Barclays Bank Ltd v Bird* [1954] Ch 274 at 280; *Royal Bank of Canada v Nicholson* (1980) 110 DLR (3d) 763 at 765f. The absence of a right to possession carries the further implication that the equitable mortgagee has no inherent right to receive the rents and profits derived from the land (*Finck v Tranter* [1905] 1 KB 427 at 429; *Vacuum Oil Co Ltd v Ellis* [1914] 1 KB 693 at 703, 708).

3 Ante, p 747.

4 See *General Finance, Mortgage, and Discount Co v Liberator Benefit Building Society* (1879) 10 Ch D 15 at 24 per Jessel MR; *Antrim County Land, Building, and Investment Co Ltd v Stewart* [1904] 2 IR 357 at 364 per Palles CB; *Mills v Lewis* (1985) 3 BPR 9421 at 9431.1 per Priestley JA.

orthodox view that the equitable mortgagee cannot claim possession as of right.[5] It is clear, however, that even if the equitable mortgagee or chargee has no automatic right of possession, either may nevertheless apply to the court for an order putting him into possession.[6]

(6) Averting repossession of the family home

Since the enforcement of the mortgagee's right to possession is almost always a precursor to the exercise of a power of sale, several statutory means have been developed to enable the hard-pressed mortgagor to avert the threat of dispossession. Some of these means relate specifically to residential property, where a mortgagee's recovery of possession necessarily entails particularly traumatic consequences for the mortgagor and his family.[7]

Amongst the practical limitations upon the mortgagee's right of recovery are the following.

(a) Payment of mortgage interest as income support

A mortgagor of residential property who qualifies for income support may be able, within certain prescribed limits, to claim loan interest as part of his entitlement to benefit.

(i) 'Eligible interest' as a component of 'housing costs' The 'housing costs' which are taken into account in calculating a claimant's entitlement to income support include 'mortgage interest payments'[8] and interest payments on loans for 'repairs and improvements'[9] for which the claimant is responsible.[10] The payments must relate to a dwelling which is occupied as a home by the claimant or by a member of his family.[11] Interest payments are relevant only in so far as they relate to a loan taken out for the purpose of 'acquiring

5 See eg *Ladup Ltd v Williams & Glyn's Bank Plc* [1985] 1 WLR 851 at 855B per Warner J; *Ashley Guarantee Plc v Zacaria* [1993] 1 WLR 62 at 69H per Nourse LJ.

6 The court has power under section 90(1) of the Law of Property Act 1925 to vest a legal estate in the mortgagee sufficient to enable him to assume possession (see *Ladup Ltd v Williams & Glyn's Bank Plc* [1985] 1 WLR 851 at 855B-C). The court also has an inherent jurisdiction to put an equitable mortgagee in possession (see *Re O'Neill* [1967] NI 129 at 135), not least where the mortgage contains an express covenant for entry by the mortgagee in the case of default and the court is willing to grant specific performance of the covenant (see eg *Mills v Lewis* (1985) 3 BPR 9421 at 9431.2ff per Priestley JA).

7 The number of properties repossessed by lenders in the United Kingdom increased to 75,500 in 1991. By mid-1992 nearly 200,000 borrowers had arrears of between six and twelve months in their payments (see *Social Trends 23* (1993), p 121 (Chart 8.19)).

8 Income Support (General) Regulations 1987 (SI 1987/1967), Sch 3, para 1(a). Where the claimant is aged under 60, only half of the mortgage interest due is payable during the first 16 weeks of any period of receipt of income support. Thereafter the 'eligible interest' comprises the entire interest due (para 7(1)(b)).

9 Income Support (General) Regulations 1987, Sch 3, para 1(b).

10 A former partner of the borrower may be treated as the person responsible for the relevant housing costs if the borrower is no longer making interest payments and the partner 'has to meet these costs in order to continue to live in the dwelling' (Income Support (General) Regulations 1987, Sch 3, para 3(1)(b)).

11 Income Support (General) Regulations 1987, Sch 3, para 2. It is irrelevant in either case whether the loan is a first or second mortgage loan, a bank loan or even a private or unsecured loan.

an interest in the dwelling occupied as the home'[12] or of carrying out certain prescribed and fairly basic repairs and improvements of the amenities of the dwelling.[13]

The provision of loan interest by way of income support may be a source of invaluable assistance for a family which finds itself in financial difficulty.[14] However, the interest payments thereby discharged out of public funds are liable to restriction if they are 'excessive'.[15] For this purpose amounts are deemed to be 'excessive' if and to the extent that 'the home, excluding any part which is let, is larger than is required by the claimant and his family. . .having regard, in particular, to suitable alternative accommodation occupied by a household of the same size'.[16] Interest payments are likewise 'excessive' if the 'immediate area' in which the dwelling is located 'is more expensive than other areas in which suitable alternative accommodation exists'.[17]

These restrictive provisions are, of course, a necessary safeguard against the possibility that the recently redundant executive may seek public funds to defray liabilities in respect of his country mansion or penthouse suite. In the more mundane instance the 'excessive' payment proviso may operate oppressively against the interests and wishes of an already beleaguered family unit. It is clear, however, that benefit is not to be restricted if, 'having regard to the relevant factors, it is not reasonable to expect the claimant and his family to seek alternative cheaper accommodation'.[18]

(ii) Exclusion of capital repayments from 'housing costs' The relevant regulations give effect to the broad principle that income support covers only payments of interest and not payments of capital. The official view underlying this principle seems to be the idea that, provided the claimant's accommodation is safeguarded, 'public funds ought not to be used to increase the capital assets' of those on welfare benefit.[19] It should be noted, however, that even the payment of mortgage interest will normally conduce to a degree of capital accumulation since the home-owner, if maintained in occupation, is thereby enabled to retain at least part of the inflationary increase in the capital value of his property.

12 Income Support (General) Regulations 1987, Sch 3, para 7(3)(a). Account may be taken of a replacement loan if and to the extent that the initial loan required the payment of 'eligible interest' (para 7(3)(b)).
13 Income Support (General) Regulations 1987, Sch 3, para 8 (as amended by SI 1990/547, para 18(b)). Again account may be taken of a replacement loan (para 8(1)(b)).
14 There is provision for the direct payment of mortgage interest by the Department of Social Security to the lender concerned. See Social Security (Claims and Payments) Regulations 1987 (SI 1987/1968), Sch 9A, para 3(1), as added by SI 1992/1026, para 6, Sch (effective 29 May 1992).
15 Income Support (General) Regulations 1987, Sch 3, para 10(4), as amended by SI 1988/1445, para 27, Sch 1, Part I and by SI 1990/1776, para 9(c).
16 Income Support (General) Regulations 1987, Sch 3, para 10(4)(a).
17 Income Support (General) Regulations 1987, Sch 3, para 10(4)(b).
18 Income Support (General) Regulations 1987, Sch 3, para 10(5). Even if it is reasonable to expect the unit to move to cheaper accommodation, the restriction of benefit is postponed for six months if the claimant was able to meet the mortgage commitment when it was originally entered into, and may be postponed for a further six months 'if and so long as the claimant uses his best endeavours to obtain cheaper accommodation' (para 10(6)).
19 See *Report of the Committee on One-Parent Families* (Cmnd 5629, July 1974), Vol 1, para 6.126.

(b) Right of the mortgagor's spouse to tender payment of mortgage moneys

A spouse who enjoys 'rights of occupation' under the Matrimonial Homes Act 1983[20] is entitled to tender payment in her own name of any mortgage liability affecting her dwelling-house, and such payments by her are statutorily declared to be 'as good as if made...by the other spouse.'[1] Thus the mortgagor's spouse is armed with an important right to compel the mortgagee to accept payment by her in lieu of payments by the true mortgagor, thereby withdrawing from the mortgagee a potential ground for the exercise of his power of sale.[2]

(7) The court's inherent jurisdiction to grant relief to the mortgagor

Quite apart from the foregoing means of averting repossession of residential property, more general relief may be available for mortgagors in the form of the High Court's inherent equitable jurisdiction to grant a short-term stay of possession proceedings. Irrespective of the nature of the property concerned, the exercise of this jurisdiction offers the possibility of temporary relief for the mortgagor either before or even after the making of a possession order in favour of the mortgagee.

(a) Liberal exercise of a merciful discretion

The exercise of the inherent jurisdiction has in the past enabled the court to assert some control over the enforcement of the mortgagee's right to possession, largely through the adjournment of possession proceedings in order to give more time to the mortgagor. The jurisdiction is exercisable by the Masters of the Chancery Division, and provides a temporary form of relief which may allow hard-pressed mortgagors to resolve their financial difficulties and repay overdue mortgage moneys.[3] The court's exercise of discretion in this matter is based on the convention that 'the court has never allowed a mortgagee to enforce his rights under the mortgage in the face of a concrete offer by the mortgagor to redeem.'[4]

The court's discretion to temporise was at first exercised quite liberally, one famous Chancery Master describing his function as being akin to that of a 'social worker rather than a Judge'.[5] It was the task of the Master, if matters were not altogether hopeless, to encourage the borrower to re-organise his finances and to keep his home by paying off mortgage arrears

20 Ante, p 155.

1 Matrimonial Homes Act 1983, s 1(5).

2 Post, p 1004.

3 In the celebrated words of Clauson LJ, 'the facts and the circumstances of the case were brought before the Court, and in proper cases the wind was tempered to the shorn lamb, time being given for payment and so forth...' (*Redditch Benefit Building Society v Roberts* [1940] Ch 415 at 420). This jurisdiction is exercisable both in proceedings commenced by writ and in proceedings commenced by originating summons (see RSC Ord 88, r 7).

4 *Mobil Oil Co Ltd v Rawlinson* (1982) 43 P & CR 221 at 225 per Nourse J.

5 See Master Ball, *The Chancery Master*, (1961) 77 LQR 331 at 351.

in agreed instalments.[6] It has since been said that the generous approach adopted by Chancery Masters was 'no doubt assisted by the benevolent attitude which the Legislature had by then assumed towards tenants faced with eviction by their landlords.'[7] The analogy drawn—at least tacitly—between the respective positions of the home-owner and the renter was soon to constitute a recurring cross-reference in the law relating to the protection of residential mortgagors.[8]

(b) Modern restrictions on the inherent jurisdiction

In more recent times the court's inherent jurisdiction to stay possession proceedings against mortgagors has been exercised much more sparingly.[9] In *Birmingham Citizens Permanent Building Society v Caunt*,[10] Russell J held that the inherent jurisdiction merely empowers the court to adjourn a hearing 'for a short time' in order to 'afford the mortgagor a limited opportunity to find means to pay off the mortgagee or otherwise satisfy him if there was a reasonable prospect of either of those events occurring.'[11] As Russell J indicated, however, it is unlikely that even in these circumstances an adjournment will be granted for a period of more than 28 days.[12]

(8) The court's statutory power to delay the recovery of possession

The decision in *Birmingham Citizens Permanent Building Society v Caunt* did much to restore to the mortgagee the balance of power which some imagined had been removed by the steady development of the court's inherent jurisdiction.[13] However, the net effect of the tightening-up of the court's inherent jurisdiction was to accentuate the demand for a new statutory form of relief against possession actions relating to the family home. In 1969 the Payne Committee on the Enforcement of Judgment Debts recognised that a succession of governments had 'for some years encouraged the purchase, instead of the renting, of houses by persons of modest means.' The Committee therefore concluded that where a mortgagor, because of financial difficulties, falls into arrears with his mortgage instalments, the courts should be 'empowered, subject to proper safeguards, to extend to the mortgagor the same protection in relation to the continued occupation of the house as would be given to

6 The lengths to which Chancery Masters were prepared to go appears in Master Ball's frank admission that, if necessary, the Master was generally willing to use 'time and technicality as weapons against a too stony-hearted plaintiff' ((1961) 77 LQR 331 at 351).
7 *Mobil Oil Co Ltd v Rawlinson* (1982) 43 P & CR 221 at 224 per Nourse J.
8 Post, p 995.
9 For a description of the judicial reaction against what was seen as excessive indulgence shown towards borrowers, see *Mobil Oil Co Ltd v Rawlinson* (1982) 43 P & CR 221 at 224.
10 [1962] Ch 883 at 891. See (1962) 78 LQR 171 (R.E.M.).
11 See also *London Permanent Benefit Building Society v De Baer* [1969] 1 Ch 321 at 338B, F.
12 [1962] Ch 883 at 908. See, however, *Braithwaite v Winwood* [1960] 1 WLR 1257 at 1264ff.
13 'Equity was never and should never be in the hands of the judges a sword to attack any part of the security itself, and the right to possession was an important part of that security, more particularly in the association with the ability to give vacant possession on the exercise of the power of sale' (*Birmingham Citizens Permanent Building Society v Caunt* [1962] Ch 883 at 896). See also *Robertson v Cilia* [1956] 1 WLR 1502 at 1508; (1957) 73 LQR 18 (R.E.M.).

a tenant of a property of a similar rateable value.'[14] In effect the Committee accepted that the expansion of the 'property-owning democracy' had fixed on the government of the day a broad social responsibility to assimilate mortgagors within the same kind of protective legislation as that which benefits residential tenants.[15]

The statutory relief proposed by the Payne Committee was almost immediately introduced by section 36 of the Administration of Justice Act 1970. This important legislative initiative now enables the court in the context of possession proceedings to grant relief to residential mortgagors in much the same way in which relief is granted against forfeiture in the landlord-tenant relationship.[16]

(a) *Preconditions for the exercise of the statutory discretion*

Section 36 of the Administration of Justice Act 1970 confers on the court a wide power to adjourn possession actions brought by mortgagees or to postpone the giving of possession in respect of a 'dwelling-house'[17] for such period or periods 'as the court thinks reasonable'.[18] The court's discretion is exercisable in any claim for possession of residential property in which

> it appears to the court that in the event of its exercising the power the mortgagor is likely to be able within a reasonable period to pay any sums due under the mortgage or to remedy a default consisting of a breach of any other obligation arising under or by virtue of the mortgage.[19]

14 *Report of the Committee on Judgment Debts* (Cmnd 3909, February 1969), para 1386(d). The Committee accepted (para 1386(b)) that the 'responsible building societies have proved themselves to be tolerant and understanding with those of their borrowers who have fallen into arrears with their instalments through misfortune, and not infrequently they enter into reasonable and satisfactory arrangements for the discharge of arrears without initiating or pursuing a claim for possession'. However, as the Committee went on to note, 'unfortunately all mortgagees are not responsible building societies...' See also *Report of the Committee on One-Parent Families* (Cmnd 5629, July 1974), Vol 1, para 6.116ff.

15 For a similar comparison with the protection from eviction conferred on protected and statutory tenants under the Rent Act legislation, see *Hughes v Waite* [1957] 1 WLR 713 at 715 per Harman J.

16 Ante, pp 814, 825.

17 The term 'dwelling-house' includes 'any building or part thereof which is used as a dwelling' (Administration of Justice Act 1970, s 39(1)), an extended meaning which may go too far. As Roger Smith has pointed out, section 36 thus seems capable of application to an entire office block which contains somewhere within it a caretaker's flat (see [1979] Conv 266 at 271). Moreover, it is irrelevant that part of the premises comprised in a 'dwelling-house' is used 'as a shop or office or for business, trade or professional purposes' (Administration of Justice Act 1970, s 39(2)).

18 Administration of Justice Act 1970, s 36(2). A similar power is vested in the county court in respect of any application by a local authority mortgagee for a re-vesting of a property which has been purchased by a sitting tenant with the assistance of local authority finance (Housing Act 1985, Sch 17, para 1(2), (3)). The county court may adjourn proceedings by the local authority mortgagee or postpone the date for execution of the authority's deed for 'such period as the court thinks reasonable' and on such terms with regard to mortgage payments as the court thinks fit.

19 Administration of Justice Act 1970, s 36(1). Section 89 of the Housing Act 1980 introduces certain severe restrictions on the court's exercise of discretion in making possession orders in respect of land (ante, p 910). In general the court may not postpone possession for more than 14 days from the making of a possession order, but this draconian rule does not apply in possession actions brought by mortgagees (see Housing Act 1980, s 89(2)(a)).

(i) An initial defect of drafting As it stands, the wording of section 36 contains a severe drafting imperfection which threatened initially to destroy the protective import of the provision. In *Halifax Building Society v Clark*[20] the plaintiff building society sought an order for possession against the deserted wife of the mortgagor and Pennycuick V-C ruled that it was impossible for her to satisfy the preconditions for the exercise of discretion under section 36. In the present case the mortgage instalments in arrear amounted to only £100, but the entire capital debt of over £1,400 became 'due' on the husband's default in accordance with the strict terms of the mortgage. Even if the mortgagor's wife exercised her right to tender vicarious payments,[1] it was quite obvious that there was no realistic prospect that she could raise this larger sum 'within a reasonable period'.[2] It was indeed highly unlikely that she could within a short period pay off a sum which it had been anticipated originally would take another 20 years to discharge.

This rather grave defect in the legislation was remedied by the enactment of section 8(1) of the Administration of Justice Act 1973, which redefines the phrase 'any sums due' in section 36(1) of the 1970 Act as referring only to such amounts as the mortgagor would have expected to be required to pay if the mortgage had not contained a default clause rendering the entire mortgage moneys payable in the event of any of the instalments falling into arrear.[3] Section 8(1) thus overturns the decision in *Halifax Building Society v Clark*, and effectively reinstates what was almost certainly the intention of the legislature in framing the 1970 Act.[4] The court may therefore adjourn possession proceedings or stay the execution of a possession order if there is a likelihood that during the interim the mortgagor will be able to find not only any mortgage instalments which have fallen into arrear but also any other instalments which may become due during the period of postponement.[5]

(ii) The broad coverage of section 36 As amended by the Administration of Justice Act 1973, the statutory discretion under section 36 provides valuable assistance for many mortgagors who run into temporary financial difficulties, whether by reason of unemployment, short-time working, redundancy or marital difficulties.[6] Although clearly not all judges agree on the point,[7] it has been said that the Administration of Justice Acts 1970 and 1973 together represent a form of 'social legislation' in which 'Parliament has attempted

20 [1973] Ch 307. See (1973) 89 LQR 171 (P.V. Baker); (1973) 36 MLR 550 (P. Jackson); (1973) 37 Conv (NS) 213 (F.R. Crane).

1 See Matrimonial Homes Act 1983, s 1(5) (ante, p 993).

2 [1973] Ch 307 at 313G-H. See also *Governor and Company of the Bank of Scotland v Grimes* [1985] QB 1179 at 1190C-F.

3 See Stephen Tromans, [1984] Conv 91.

4 Even before the enactment of section 8 of the Administration of Justice Act 1973, the problem addressed in *Halifax Building Society v Clark* had arisen in *First Middlesbrough Trading and Mortgage Co Ltd v Cunningham* (1974) 28 P & CR 69 at 74, and the Court of Appeal declined to adopt the construction applied in *Halifax Building Society v Clark*. For an argument that the ratio of *Cunningham*'s case may still be wider (and therefore more favourable to the mortgagor) than section 8 of the Administration of Justice Act 1973, see R.J. Smith, [1979] Conv 266 at 274f.

5 Administration of Justice Act 1973, s 8(2). See *Peckham Mutual Building Society v Registe* (1981) 42 P & CR 186 at 189.

6 For a consideration of the factors relevant to the exercise of the statutory discretion, see R.J. Smith, [1979] Conv 266 at 279f.

7 See [1983] Conv 80 (P.H. Kenny).

to give legislative shelter to a wide class of owner-occupiers'.[8] It is consistent with the nature of such legislation that the court's discretion to give relief to domestic mortgagors should be construed liberally, and indeed the courts have confirmed that the section 36 jurisdiction may be invoked not only in relation to instalment mortgages but also in relation to endowment mortgages.[9] There is also some evidence that in recent times the courts have strained to their outer limit the parameters of the protection afforded by section 36, in the full realisation that it is the external circumstance of nationwide economic recession which has been primarily responsible for plunging vast numbers of innocent homeowners into unmanageable financial crisis.[10]

(b) Does section 36 now impose a requirement of due legal process?

It is a curious feature of section 36 of the Administration of Justice Act 1970 that the protective discretion of the court arises only where 'the mortgagee. . .brings an action in which he claims possession of the mortgaged property. . .'[11] The apparent corollary is that the benevolent effect of section 36 cannot be invoked by a residential mortgagor if his mortgagee simply asserts his paramount right to possession by peaceful re-entry without court action. There is, however, a patent absurdity in the idea that section 36 should solicitously protect the mortgagor in court proceedings for possession, while leaving him hopelessly vulnerable to an extra-curial recovery of possession. This result is sufficiently anomalous to have prompted the suggestion[12] that section 36 impliedly abrogates the mortgagee's inherent common law right to go into possession at any time of his choosing without first seeking a court order.[13] There is a powerful argument in favour of the conclusion that a mortgagee may nowadays assert his right to possession only after due legal process.

This suggestion, although not without attraction, has not yet gained judicial support of any kind. Indeed, recent dicta have if anything tended to confirm the conventional view that the mortgagee may re-enter arbitrarily if he chooses.[14] In the absence of strong authority it seems difficult to maintain that the orthodox understanding of the mortgagee's paramount right to possession at common law has been subverted by a mere implication from statute.[15] On balance it seems likely that the anomaly which appears to

8 *Centrax Trustees Ltd v Ross* [1979] 2 All ER 952 at 955f per Goulding J.

9 *Governor and Company of the Bank of Scotland v Grimes* [1985] QB 1179 at 1188G, 1190G. See [1985] Conv 407 (J.E.M.), but compare *Lord Marples of Wallasey v Holmes* (1976) 31 P & CR 94 at 97. Section 36 has no application to the enforcement of charging orders, but see Charging Orders Act 1979, s 1(5). See also the refusal in the Irish Republic to apply the comparable Family Home Protection Act 1976, s 7(1) to the enforcement of a judgment mortgage in *Containercare (Ireland) Ltd v Wycherley* [1982] IR 143 at 150.

10 See eg *Target Home Loans Ltd v Clothier* (1992) 25 HLR 48 at 54 (post, p 1000), where Nolan LJ recognised that the mortgagor's difficulties were in no way caused by dishonesty, but rather by the fact that his business had suffered badly as a result of the recession.

11 Administration of Justice Act 1970, s 36(1).

12 See eg A. Clarke, [1983] Conv 293.

13 Ante, p 982.

14 Ante, p 990.

15 See, however, *Remon v City of London Real Property Co Ltd* [1921] 1 KB 49 at 59, in relation to a comparable problem under the early Rent Act legislation. See A. Clarke, [1983] Conv 293 at 296.

exist can be removed only by an express legislative provision, and that meanwhile the practical protection of residential mortgagors under section 36 is most unsatisfactorily preserved by the fact that, for one reason or another,[16] most mortgagees de facto enforce their security only after court proceedings for possession.

(c) Procedural rights for the mortgagor's spouse

Statutory intervention has conferred a number of procedural rights on the spouse of a mortgagor, for the purpose of enabling such a spouse more effectively to take advantage of the important discretion enjoyed by the court under section 36 of the Administration of Justice Act 1970. The motive behind these recent initiatives stems from the disadvantage which is inevitably suffered by a spouse who does not know that her partner's financial difficulties are beginning to jeopardise the security of the family home.

(i) No right to be informed of mortgage arrears The statutory right[17] of a mortgagor's spouse to tender mortgage payments is not of much value to a spouse who is unaware that her husband's mortgage payments have fallen into arrear. In *Hastings and Thanet Building Society v Goddard*[18] the Court of Appeal held that there is no statutory justification for requiring that a building society should inform the mortgagor's wife of her husband's default in order that she should have an opportunity to tender payments herself. Russell LJ thought that any contrary view was 'impracticable because a building society can scarcely be expected to keep track of the matrimonial status of its mortgagors.'[19] Likewise the Court refused to accept that notice of a mortgagee's possession proceedings should be served on the mortgagor's spouse (where she was not a joint tenant of the property), since her statutory rights of occupation in the matrimonial home are in no way binding on the mortgagee.[20] The only right which the spouse may assert against the mortgagee is the right to pay any moneys still owing to him and thereby prevent him from exercising his right to take possession.

The decision in *Hastings and Thanet Building Society v Goddard*, although heavily criticised,[1] remains good at common law. The ruling leads in practice to the unfortunate result that a deserted wife who discovers too late that her husband has allowed substantial mortgage arrears to accrue, may then find herself precluded from any effective argument that the court's discretion should be extended in her favour under the Administration of Justice Act.

16 Ante, p 987 (note 10).
17 Ante, p 993.
18 [1970] 1 WLR 1544. See (1971) 35 Conv (NS) 48 (F.R. Crane).
19 [1970] 1 WLR 1544 at 1548E.
20 Compare *Harman v Glencross* [1985] Fam 49 at 54G-H (ante, p 155).
1 See D.A. Nevitt and J. Levin, *Social Policy and the Matrimonial Home*, (1973) 36 MLR 345 at 349f. The Finer Committee expressed the view that 'the courts have seemed to be more concerned with reducing the administrative burdens of building societies than with safeguarding families in their homes...' (*Report of the Committee on One-Parent Families* (Cmnd 5629, July 1974), Vol 1, para 6.120).

A partial remedy for the shortcomings of the common law has now been provided in legislative form.[2]

(ii) Right to be joined as a party in possession proceedings The mortgagor's spouse, if entitled to tender vicarious mortgage payments, is now given a statutory right to apply to the court to be joined as a party in any possession proceedings brought by a mortgagee to enforce his security in respect of a dwelling-house.[3] The court must accede to her application if it sees no 'special reason' against it,[4] provided that it is satisfied that there is a realistic possibility that the spouse may be able to attract the benevolent operation of the court's discretion under section 36 of the Administration of Justice Act 1970.[5]

This statutory right at least gives the mortgagor's spouse locus standi in possession proceedings to present a case for consideration under section 36,[6] but still fails to tackle the difficulties faced by a spouse who is entirely unaware that possession proceedings are afoot against her mortgagor-husband. A compromise solution has been introduced by statute in order to meet these difficulties.

(iii) Right to be served with notice of possession proceedings It is now clear that any mortgagee who seeks to enforce his security in land which comprises a dwelling-house is statutorily obliged to serve notice of his possession action on any spouse who has protected her 'rights of occupation' in that property by registration of a Class F land charge (in unregistered land) or entry of the appropriate notice (in registered land).[7] This provision affords a further incentive towards protection of the 'rights of occupation' conferred by the Matrimonial Homes Act 1983, by guaranteeing that a spouse who duly protects her rights cannot lose her home at least without having an opportunity to be joined and heard as a party in the mortgagee's possession action. The spouse's right to notice of possession proceedings clearly imposes a burden of search on any mortgagee who intends to initiate possession proceedings, but in days of increased emphasis on residential security this result may not seem entirely unreasonable.[8]

(d) Limits of the court's discretion

The court's discretion under section 36 of the Administration of Justice Act

2 For the background to the legislation, see *Third Report on Family Property: The Matrimonial Home (Co-ownership and Occupation Rights) and Household Goods* (Law Com No 86, June 1978), para 2.25ff.
3 Matrimonial Homes Act 1983, s 8(2).
4 Matrimonial Homes Act 1983, s 8(2)(a).
5 Matrimonial Homes Act 1983, s 8(2)(b).
6 Dunn LJ recognised in *Anglia Building Society v Lewis* (Court of Appeal, No 8008681, 29 January 1982) that even if the mortgagor's spouse is unsuccessful in invoking section 36, the mere fact that the possession order is formally entered against her name also will tend to strengthen her claim to be provided with alternative accommodation by her local housing authority.
7 Matrimonial Homes Act 1983, s 8(3).
8 English law in this respect still does not go as far as, for instance, the law in Ontario, which requires that notice of mortgagees' possession actions be given to 'all persons in actual possession' in order to enable them to apply for relief (see *Canada Trustco Mortgage Co v McLean* (1983) 143 DLR (3d) 101 at 104).

1970 is subject to certain general limitations which severely cut back the protection potentially offered to the residential mortgagor.

(i) No discretion in the absence of a realistic ability to pay arrears or to remedy any other default Before the court's discretion can be properly exercised in favour of a mortgagor, it must appear to the court that the mortgagor is 'likely to be able within a reasonable period to pay any sums due under the mortgage'. Even when the effect of amending legislation is taken into account,[9] there is no scope for the exercise of *any* discretion by the court if the mortgagor (or his spouse[10]) cannot provide realistic evidence of at least some ability to pay off all the current arrears of mortgage money.[11] Simply to ask for time to pay is not enough to attract the favourable exercise of the court's discretion.

Nor is it usually sufficient for the purpose of section 36 for the mortgagor to propose that the relevant arrears should be paid out of the proceeds of sale when the property is eventually sold.[12] In *Cheltenham & Gloucester Building Society v Ensor*[13] Dillon LJ ruled that, in the absence of evidence of the availability of an immediate purchaser,[14] the requirements of section 36 were not met by this 'nebulous prospect' of paying off the arrears.[15] In *Target Home Loans Ltd v Clothier*,[16] however, the Court of Appeal was willing to defer a possession order for three months in order to enable the mortgagors to find a buyer and complete a sale. Nolan LJ referred to the 'sound commercial sense' of leaving the mortgagors in occupation of the property 'on the basis that they are in a far better position to sell it than the [mortgagee] would be'. In Nolan LJ's view, the prospect of achieving an early sale would be greatly enhanced since an occupied house 'is far more likely to look attractive and to command a buyer than one which has been repossessed by a mortgage company'.[17]

Where the mortgagor's default lies not in non-payment of moneys due

9 Administration of Justice Act 1973, s 8 (ante, p 996).
10 See Matrimonial Homes Act 1983, s 8(2), (3) (ante, p 999).
11 See eg *Williams & Glyn's Bank Ltd v Boland* [1981] AC 487 at 509C-D per Lord Wilberforce; *Peckham Mutual Building Society v Registe* (1981) 42 P & CR 186 at 189; *Town & Country Building Society v Julien* (1991) 24 HLR 312 at 316ff. Compare *Centrax Trustees Ltd v Ross* [1979] 2 All ER 952 at 954h, 957f-g. Evidence of ability to pay must relate to the entirety (and not to a mere part) of the sum currently outstanding (see *Target Home Loans Ltd v Clothier* (1992) 25 HLR 48 at 52 per Nolan LJ).
12 *Royal Trust Co of Canada v Markham* [1975] 1 WLR 1416 at 1422D-F per Sir John Pennycuick, 1423D-E per Browne LJ. A proposal that money should be raised by a letting of the mortgaged property is similarly unlikely to succeed, not least since such a letting (if unauthorised) will itself constitute a breach of the mortgage terms (see *Target Home Loans Ltd v Clothier* (1992) 25 HLR 48 at 53).
13 Unreported, Court of Appeal, 13 August 1992.
14 Compare *Palk v Mortgage Services Funding Plc* [1993] 2 WLR 415 (ante, p 988).
15 Dillon LJ considered it arguable that section 36 might be invoked by a mortgagor who could show 'active negotiation for a binding contract for sale which was likely to achieve completion within a relatively short and easily definable period.' Here the property had remained on the market for two years without attracting a buyer.
16 (1992) 25 HLR 48 at 55. There was in this case some evidence from an estate agent that the property was likely to be sold very shortly, although Nolan LJ observed mordantly that he intended 'no disrespect to the estate agency profession' in offering the suggestion that 'they would win by a distance any competition between members of different professions for optimism'.
17 (1992) 25 HLR 48 at 54.

but in some other form of breach, it is plain that the court's discretion under section 36 can be exercised only where the mortgagor's breach is capable of remedy. In *Britannia Building Society v Earl*,[18] for instance, the mortgagor had breached the terms of his mortgage by granting an unauthorised letting of the property to two joint tenants. In holding that the tenants had no independent access to discretionary relief under section 36, the Court of Appeal accepted that the mortgagor's default in this respect could not be remedied save by the departure of the tenants.[19]

(ii) No discretion to postpone proceedings indefinitely Even if the court is able to exercise discretion in favour of the mortgagor, there are substantial restrictions upon the terms on which it may do so. In *Royal Trust Co of Canada v Markham*,[20] for instance, the Court of Appeal ruled that it had no jurisdiction to order suspension of possession proceedings *sine die*.[1] The court must define the period during which the proceedings may be adjourned or any possession order stayed. In any event relief may be granted to the mortgagor only in respect of such period of time as is 'reasonable'. The Payne Committee on the Enforcement of Judgment Debts considered that a period of six months would be sufficient in most cases,[2] but the period may well be longer or shorter depending on the circumstances.[3]

(iii) No discretion before moneys have become due There is some doubt as to whether section 36 of the Administration of Justice Act 1970 can have any application where no mortgage moneys of any kind have yet become due. In *Western Bank Ltd v Schindler*,[4] two members of the Court of Appeal thought that section 36 must be applicable irrespective of the absence of actual default, since otherwise a blameless mortgagor would be put in a less advantageous position than a defaulting mortgagor who can rely on section 36. Goff LJ was, however, of the view that, on strict construction, section 36 cannot apply where there is no money due or any other default present on the facts of the case.[5] This restrictive approach has since received some confirmation in *Habib Bank Ltd v Tailor*.[6] Here the Court of Appeal ruled that the Administration of Justice Acts had no application to a mortgage given as security for a bank overdraft, under which no money was due unless and until repayment was demanded by the bank.[7]

18 [1990] 1 WLR 422 (ante, p 986).
19 [1990] 1 WLR 422 at 430B-C.
20 [1975] 1 WLR 1416 at 1423C, 1424A-B.
1 See also *National Westminster Bank Plc v Skelton (Note)* [1993] 1 WLR 72 at 81A per Slade LJ; *Cheltenham & Gloucester Building Society v Ensor* (Unreported, Court of Appeal, 13 August 1992) per Dillon LJ. Compare, however, the suggestion in *Western Bank Ltd v Schindler* [1977] Ch 1 at 14E-G.
2 *Report* (Cmnd 3909, 1969), para 1388.
3 See R.J. Smith, [1979] Conv 266 at 278f; D. McConnell, (1985) Legal Action 121; A. Brewer and S. Jarvis, (1986) Legal Action 96.
4 [1977] Ch 1 at 13D-E per Buckley LJ, 19F per Scarman LJ.
5 [1977] Ch 1 at 26E. See (1977) 40 MLR 356 (C. Harpum).
6 [1982] 1 WLR 1218. See [1983] Conv 80 (P.H. Kenny); (1983) 133 NLJ 247 (H.W. Wilkinson).
7 [1982] 1 WLR 1218 at 1225F.

(iv) No discretion available at the behest of tenants For the purpose of access to the statutory discretion pursuant to section 36, the term 'mortgagor' is given an expanded meaning to include 'any person deriving title under the original mortgagor'.[8] It appears, however, that this extended interpretation confers the potential benefit of section 36 merely upon *assignees* from the mortgagor, with the result that the court's discretion is not available to persons who hold as tenants of the original mortgagor.[9] This conclusion certainly applies in any event to statutory tenants under the Rent Act, who have no proprietary estate in the land[10] and cannot be said to 'derive title' at all.[11]

9. REMEDIES AVAILABLE TO THE LEGAL MORTGAGEE

In the event of default under a legal mortgage the mortgagee has available to him a number of remedies which operate directly against the mortgagor.[12] These remedies are in general concurrent and cumulative, but it is increasingly clear that in their exercise a mortgagee 'does owe some duties to a mortgagor.'[13] The courts do not find attractive the proposition that the mortgagee may act in a 'cavalier fashion', not least since many mortgagees nowadays carry indemnity insurance against the possibility that the mortgagor may prove unable to discharge his debt in full. Without doubt, as Nicholls V-C pointed out in *Palk v Mortgage Services Funding Plc*,[14] there is 'a legal framework which imposes constraints of fairness on a mortgagee who is exercising his remedies over his security.' The mortgagee's remedies include the following.

(1) Action on the mortgagor's personal covenant to repay

Since the mortgage transaction is ultimately founded on a contract of loan, it remains open to the mortgagee to sue the mortgagor on his personal covenant to repay the mortgage loan and interest.[15] The mortgagee cannot take action on the mortgagor's covenant before the legal redemption date stipulated by the mortgage,[16] but even a sale of the mortgaged property pursuant to his power of sale does not preclude the mortgagee from suing on the mortgagor's covenant in respect of any remaining financial loss.[17] Still less is the mortgagor's personal liability terminated by a voluntary surrender

8 Administration of Justice Act 1970, s 39(1).
9 See *Britannia Building Society v Earl* [1990] 1 WLR 422 at 429H–430B per McCowan LJ.
10 Ante, p 876.
11 *Britannia Building Society v Earl* [1990] 1 WLR 422 at 430A per McCowan LJ.
12 He may also have remedies against third parties. If, for instance, the mortgagor of a leasehold term causes his lease to become forfeit by reason of his default, the mortgagee may have access to the inherent equitable jurisdiction of the court for relief against forfeiture (ante, p 837).
13 *Palk v Mortgage Services Funding Plc* [1993] 2 WLR 415 at 420F per Nicholls V-C.
14 [1993] 2 WLR 415 at 421E-F.
15 In practice most institutional lenders are reluctant to increase the (perhaps temporary) financial difficulties of hard-pressed borrowers by suing on the personal covenant for repayment. The remedy of sale is always available if these difficulties cannot be resolved within a reasonable period.
16 *Bolton v Buckenham* [1891] 1 QB 278 at 281f; *Sinton v Dooley* [1910] 2 IR 162 at 165.
17 *Rudge v Richens* (1873) LR 8 CP 358 at 361f; *Schoole v Sall* (1803) 1 Sch & Lef 176.

of possession to the mortgagee. Contrary to popular mythology, the mortgagor gains no relief from this liability merely because he throws the keys of the premises back at his bank or building society. His indebtedness continues to grow apace unless and until the moneys owed are fully repaid. The mortgagee is, however, entitled only to simple interest upon any interest left in arrears, unless the mortgage contained an agreement (either expressly or by necessary implication) for the payment of compound interest.[18]

The recovery of arrears of interest is statute-barred six years after becoming due,[19] and the recovery of the mortgage principal is statute-barred after the expiration of twelve years from the date when the right to receive that money accrued.[20]

(2) Exercise of the power of sale

The most usual remedy invoked by the mortgagee in the event of serious default by his mortgagor is the exercise of the mortgagee's power of sale. Since vacant possession is almost inevitably an essential condition of a good sale price, the exercise of this power of sale is normally preceded by the mortgagee's recovery of possession of the mortgaged property.

(a) When the power of sale arises

The mortgagee has no common law power of sale over mortgaged property. An express power of sale is sometimes conferred by the terms of the mortgage deed, but a similar power is now supplied in any event by the provisions of the Law of Property Act 1925.[1] Under section 101 the mortgagee's statutory power of sale *arises* if three conditions are satisfied. *First*, the mortgage in question must have been effected by deed.[2] *Second*, the mortgage money must have become due.[3] Thus the mortgagee's power of sale may arise if the legal date for redemption has passed or even if any instalment of the mortgage money has become due under an instalment mortgage.[4] *Third*, the mortgage must itself contain no expression of contrary intention which would have the effect of precluding a power of sale in the foregoing circumstances.[5]

18 *Ex parte Bevan* (1803) 9 Ves 223 at 224, 32 ER 588; *Fergusson v Fyffe* (1841) 8 Cl & Fin 121 at 141, 8 ER 49 at 57; *Daniell v Sinclair* (1881) 6 App Cas 181 at 189f; *Deutsche Bank v Banque des Marchands de Moscou* (1931) 4 LDAB 293; *Domaschenz v Standfield Properties Pty Ltd* (1977) 17 SASR 56 at 61.

19 Limitation Act 1980, s 20(5). This limitation does not apply, however, if the mortgagor seeks to redeem the mortgage either in redemption proceedings (*Elvy v Norwood* (1852) 5 De G & Sm 240 at 243, 64 ER 1099 at 1100; *Holmes v Cowcher* [1970] 1 WLR 834 at 836G) or in foreclosure proceedings brought by the mortgagee (*Dingle v Coppen* [1899] 1 Ch 726 at 746). There is likewise no limitation on the arrears of interest which may be recouped from the proceeds of sale received by a mortgagee who exercises his statutory power to sell the mortgaged property (see *Holmes v Cowcher* [1970] 1 WLR 834 at 837G).

20 Limitation Act 1980, s 20(1).

1 The scope of the mortgagee's power of sale and the circumstances of its exercise may, of course, be varied or extended by the express terms of the mortgage deed (Law of Property Act 1925, s 101(3)).

2 Law of Property Act 1925, s 101(1).

3 Law of Property Act 1925, s 101(1)(i).

4 *Payne v Cardiff RDC* [1932] 1 KB 241 at 251, 253.

5 Law of Property Act 1925, s 101(4).

Section 101 of the Law of Property Act 1925 operates as a filter to section 103. If the conditions of section 101 are met, the mortgagee may proceed to exercise his power of sale in terms of section 103.[6]

(b) When the power of sale becomes exercisable

Whereas three cumulative conditions must be satisfied in order that the mortgagee's statutory power of sale should *arise*, that power becomes *exercisable* only if the mortgagee can show that any one of three conditions specified in section 103 of the Law of Property Act 1925 has been met.

(i) The three conditions In the absence of an express power of sale conferred by the mortgage instrument itself, the mortgagee may not exercise his statutory power of sale unless and until *either* the mortgagor has been in default for three months following the service upon him of a notice requiring payment of the mortgage money,[7] *or* some interest under the mortgage has remained unpaid for two months after becoming due,[8] *or* there has been a breach of some mortgage term 'other than and besides a covenant for the payment of mortgage money or interest thereon.'[9]

If any one of these conditions is satisfied, the mortgagee has statutory authority to proceed with a sale of part or all of the mortgaged property.[10] Unlike the remedy of foreclosure,[11] the exercise of the mortgagee's power of sale does not require the sanction or leave of any court.[12] Even though he is not personally invested with the mortgagor's estate, the mortgagee is statutorily clothed with full power to give a conveyance of this estate freed from all property rights over which the mortgage had priority, but subject of course to those rights which themselves rank prior to the mortgage.[13]

6 The exercise of the mortgagee's power of sale is, however, subject to the possibility that his conduct may operate as a waiver of his rights. See *Barns v Queensland National Bank Ltd* (1906) 3 CLR 925 at 939f; *Morton v Suncorp Finance Ltd* (1987) 8 NSWLR 325 at 336A.

7 Law of Property Act 1925, s 103(i). The notice requirement operates as a crude form of natural justice for the mortgagor, who is thereby given adequate warning to enable him to remedy the default (see *Bevham Investments Pty Ltd v Belgot Pty Ltd* (1982) 149 CLR 494 at 501; *Matich v United Building Society* [1987] 2 NZLR 513 at 517).

8 Law of Property Act 1925, s 103(ii).

9 Law of Property Act 1925, s 103(iii).

10 Law of Property Act 1925, s 101(1)(i). For this purpose the mortgaged property includes fixtures (ante, p 11), but in the exercise of his power of sale the mortgagee has no power to sever fixtures from the realty and sell them separately, unless such power is expressly or impliedly conferred by the instrument of mortgage (*In re Yates* (1888) 38 Ch D 112 at 120f per Cotton LJ). If, however, the mortgagee wrongly severs and sells fixtures, the property in those fixtures does not revert to the mortgagor but, subject to a damages action for actual loss, falls to be treated as proceeds of the realisation of the mortgaged property (see *In re Rogerstone Brick & Stone Co Ltd* [1919] 1 Ch 110 at 124, 127f; *Re Penning; Ex parte State Bank of South Australia* (1989) 89 ALR 417 at 433).

11 Post, p 1028.

12 If the power of sale has arisen but the mortgagor pays the due moneys before the time of exercise of the power, the court does, however, have jurisdiction to restrain sale (see *Morton v Suncorp Finance Ltd* (1987) 8 NSWLR 325 at 335B-C).

13 Law of Property Act 1925, s 104(1).

The Law of Property Act 1925 in effect confers on the mortgagee a power of compulsory sale over a title which does not belong to him at law.[14]

(ii) Premature sale It is important to distinguish between the point in time at which the statutory power of sale arises and that at which it becomes exercisable. The mortgagee has no power at all to sell until the statutory power arises. If he purports to sell the property in advance of this date, the premature transaction transfers to the purchaser merely those rights which the mortgagee enjoyed qua mortgagee, and is entirely ineffective to pass the mortgagor's legal estate.

More doubt surrounds the effect of a sale by a mortgagee in whose favour the statutory power of sale has arisen but has not yet become exercisable. The purchaser's title is statutorily declared to be unimpeachable,[15] although such a sale clearly exposes the selling mortgagee to an action in damages brought by the mortgagor.[16] It seems, however, that the purchaser cannot claim any immunity under the statute if at the time of the sale he had actual notice that the power of sale was not exercisable or that there was some other impropriety in the sale.[17] Thus the purchaser may be prejudicially affected, for instance, by actual notice that at the date of the sale the mortgagor was not in fact in default of his obligations under the mortgage. It is doubtful that the purchaser can be bound by merely constructive notice of irregularities in the matter of sale,[18] although in *Bailey v Barnes*[19] Stirling J warned that the purchaser must not 'wilfully shut his eyes and abstain from making inquiries which might have led to a knowledge of impropriety or irregularity'.

(c) Effect of sale by the mortgagee

Where a mortgagee sells under his statutory or express power of sale, his

14 Law of Property Act 1925, ss 88(1), 89(1). The mortgagee's sale is not a transaction 'by which the mortgagor, through the medium of an agent, is disposing of his own property. It is one by which his property is being divested from him' (*Forsyth v Blundell* (1973) 129 CLR 477 at 500 per Walsh J). For this reason an enforced sale, conducted under a mortgagee's paramount power, does not constitute a 'disposal' by the mortgagor thereby rendering him liable to repay discount or other grant moneys which are otherwise forfeited in whole or part by an early sale of the relevant property (see eg *Canterbury City Council v Quine* (1988) 55 P & CR 1 at 3). On the obligation to repay a local authority discount in the event of early sale of 'right to buy' property, see Chapter 17 (ante, p 774).

15 Law of Property Act 1925, s 104(2).

16 Law of Property Act 1925, s 104(2).

17 *Lord Waring v London and Manchester Assurance Co Ltd* [1935] Ch 310 at 318. To uphold such a purchaser's title would be 'to convert the provisions of the statute into an instrument of fraud' (*Bailey v Barnes* [1894] 1 Ch 25 at 30 per Stirling J). Likewise a good title may be denied to the purchaser who had actual knowledge of an irregularity in the mortgagee's exercise of an express (as distinct from statutory) power of sale (*Selwyn v Garfit* (1888) 38 Ch D 273 at 280). In default of a good title, the purchaser takes merely a transfer of the mortgage.

18 Indeed section 104(2) of the Law of Property Act 1925 seems to release the purchaser from any concern 'to see or inquire' whether the mortgagee has properly exercised his power of sale. Compare, however, the critical view expressed by P.B. Fairest, op cit, 95f, and see S. Robinson, [1989] Conv 412. See also the decision of the Court of Appeal of New Zealand in *Pasquarella v National Australia Finance Ltd* [1987] 1 NZLR 312 at 315ff, which has stimulated the comment that, where the mortgagor is in an irretrievable financial position, the purchaser may not be prejudiced merely by reason of some degree of notice of minor irregularity ([1988] Conv 317 at 319 (H.W.W.)).

19 [1894] 1 Ch 25 at 30.

conveyance is effective to vest in the purchaser the mortgagor's full legal estate (whether freehold or leasehold), subject to any mortgage which has priority to that of the selling mortgagee.[20] The conveyance otherwise operates to confer on the purchaser a good legal title, enabling him to overreach all interests which are capable of being overreached (eg subsequent mortgages, the selling mortgagee's mortgage and the mortgagor's equity of redemption).[1]

In particular it seems that the purchaser, having once taken his conveyance from the selling mortgagee, is unaffected by any estate contract entered into by the mortgagor during the course of the mortgage term. In *Duke v Robson*,[2] for example, a mortgagor of unregistered land had contracted to sell his estate to P1 for £25,000 and P1 had quite properly registered this transaction as a Class C(iv) land charge.[3] Before this contract was completed, the relevant mortgagee purported to exercise its statutory power of sale by contracting to sell the mortgaged estate to a different purchaser, P2, for £45,000 (see *Fig.* 67). The Court of Appeal refused to restrain the completion of the latter contract. The Court affirmed Plowman J's view at first instance that, while the mortgage remained unredeemed, all that the mortgagor could contract to sell was his equity of redemption.[4] This equity of redemption, together with P1's interest in it by virtue of his registered estate contract, was clearly liable to be overreached by a conveyance in pursuance of the mortgagee's paramount power of sale.[5]

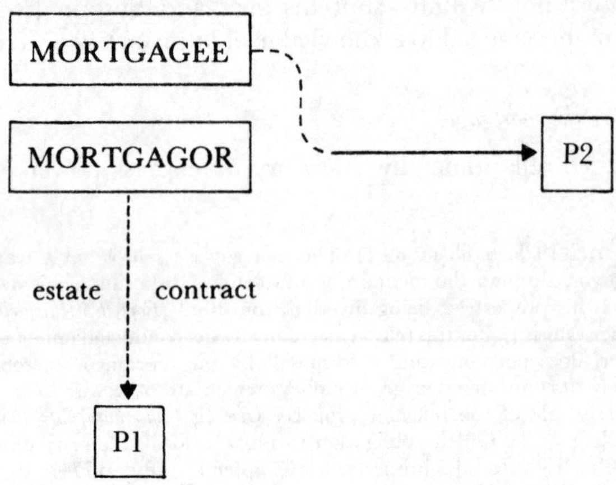

Fig. 67

20 Law of Property Act 1925, ss 88(1), 89(1).

1 Law of Property Act 1925, ss 2(1)(iii), 88(1)(b), 89(1)(b). In strict theory the mortgagee's power of sale is effectively exercised at the point of the contract to sell and not at the point of conveyance of the legal estate (post, p 1007). It follows therefore that the mortgagor's equity of redemption has already been extinguished by the contract (see *Re Sarlis and Anderson* (1984) 7 DLR (4th) 227 at 233).

2 [1973] 1 WLR 267. See (1973) 37 Conv (NS) 210 (F.R. Crane).

3 Ante, p 141.

4 [1973] 1 WLR 267 at 271D-F.

5 [1973] 1 WLR 267 at 275B-C. Russell LJ (at 275F-H) left open the possibility that P1, who had the prospect of re-selling the property for £60,000, would be able to formulate a claim in damages against the mortgagor on the ground of his inability to convey the property free from incumbrances for the contractual price of £25,000!

As *Duke v Robson* illustrates, the security taken by a legal mortgagee relates to the whole of the mortgagor's estate or interest in the land as it existed at the date of the mortgage.[6] Once the mortgage instrument is executed, all subsequent transactions of the mortgagor inevitably take place in the shadow of this security and must therefore concede priority to those rights, both immediate and inchoate, with which the mortgage has invested the lender. In the present context the mortgagor, by entering into the mortgage, has effectively subjugated his own rights in the land to the mortgagee's power of sale (whether express or statutory),[7] with the result that the mortgagee's capacity to sell is antecedent to, and remains unaffected by, the subsequent contractual dealing by the mortgagor.[8]

The solution in *Duke v Robson* is now mirrored in the resolution of the identical problem in registered land. In *Lyus v Prowsa Developments Ltd*[9] Dillon J took the view that the purchaser from the mortgagee would take free of the mortgagor's contractual commitment to sell, even though this contract had been duly protected against the mortgagor as an estate contract and even though the mortgagee had actually consented at the time to the mortgagor's dealing with a stranger.[10] In the registered land context this result is dictated even more definitively by section 34(4) of the Land Registration Act 1925, which stipulates that, on the completion of the mortgagee's sale by registration, his charge 'and all incumbrances and entries inferior thereto shall be cancelled.' The clear title thus conferred by the mortgagee follows inevitably from the fact that his initial registration as proprietor of the relevant charge effectively operated to diminish the 'totality or bundle of rights' which constituted the mortgagor's own registered title.[11] This diminution of the registered proprietor's rights can only have taken place at the date of registration of the mortgagee's charge, a point in time clearly prior to any later dealing.[12]

Upon the exercise of the mortgagee's power of sale, the mortgagor's equity of redemption is extinguished,[13] and he can bring no complaint against the mortgagee except where it can be shown that the power of sale was exercised in an improper, harsh or oppressive manner.[14] There is, in other words,

6 See *Alliance Acceptance Co Ltd v Ellison* (1986) 5 NSWLR 102 at 107D-G.

7 See *Forsyth v Blundell* (1973) 129 CLR 477 at 499 per Walsh J.

8 See also *McKean v Maloney* [1988] 1 Qd R 628 at 635f.

9 [1982] 1 WLR 1044 at 1047G–1048A (ante, p 440).

10 The actual decision in this case turned on a quite different point involving the law of constructive trusts (ante, p 413).

11 See *James v Registrar-General* (1967) 69 SR (NSW) 361 at 369, 87 WN (Pt 2) 239 at 245 per Wallace P.

12 See *Vukicevic v Alliance Acceptance Co Ltd* (1987) 9 NSWLR 13 at 15F–16A (Court of Appeal of New South Wales).

13 In strict terms the statutory power is exercised as soon as the mortgagee contracts to sell the property. In the absence of some form of equitable fraud by the mortgagee (post, p 1026), the mortgagor is from this point onwards disabled from redeeming the mortgage. He cannot frustrate the contracted sale by a belated payment of the moneys due under the mortgage (see *Lord Waring v London and Manchester Assurance Co Ltd* [1935] Ch 310 at 318; *Property & Bloodstock Ltd v Emerton* [1968] Ch 94 at 114F–115B; *Forsyth v Blundell* (1973) 129 CLR 477 at 499).

14 The court has an inherent jurisdiction to restrain the improper or oppressive exercise of the mortgagee's power of sale (see *Clark v National Mutual Life Association of Australasia Ltd* [1966] NZLR 196 at 197). The mortgagor will normally be required to give an undertaking as to damages as the price of obtaining an injunction (see *Hallifax Property Corp Pty Ltd v GIFC Ltd* (1988) NSW ConvR 55-415 at 57,799).

no general jurisdiction (as in the case of foreclosure[15]) to reopen a mortgagee's sale on grounds of mere hardship, although the sale may in rare circumstances be vitiated by fraud, mistake or other irregularity.[16]

(d) Absence of any statutory standard of fair dealing

In recent years some controversy has surrounded the nature of the duties imposed by law on the mortgagee who acts in exercise of his power of sale. The Law of Property Act 1925 clearly envisages that some exercises of the power of sale may be improper or irregular.[17] However, it may perhaps reflect the latent capitalist emphasis of the 1925 legislation that, except in relation to the application of the proceeds of the sale, this statute does not expressly impose any specific ethical standard or code of conduct on the selling mortgagee.[18] It has been left to the courts to supply an implication that the mortgagee must fulfil certain expectations of equity in his exercise of the power of sale.[19]

(e) Mortgagee's duty in relation to the application of proceeds

On the exercise of his power of sale the mortgagee is statutorily rendered a trustee of the resulting proceeds of sale. The application of these proceeds is governed by section 105 of the Law of Property Act 1925, which directs that the proceeds should be held in trust by the mortgagee, to be applied *first*, in payment of all costs, charges and expenses properly incurred by him in connection with the sale[20]; *second*, in discharge of the mortgage money and interest due under his mortgage[1]; and *third*, in payment of the residue to the mortgagor.

(f) Is the selling mortgagee a trustee for the mortgagor?

Although a selling mortgagee thus becomes a trustee of the proceeds of sale, it is commonly said that he is not strictly a trustee for the mortgagor in respect of the power of sale itself.[2] This power is given to him, not for the

15 Post, p 1030.

16 Post, p 1012. See eg *McDonald Dure Lumber Co Ltd v Marstone Holdings Ltd* (1976) 66 DLR (3d) 375 (comedy of errors in auctioneer's negligent conduct of sale).

17 See Law of Property Act 1925, s 104(2).

18 Compare eg Victoria's Transfer of Land Act 1958 (No 6399), s 77(1); Queensland's Property Law Act 1974, s 85(1).

19 See *Henry Roach (Petroleum) Pty Ltd v Credit House (Vic) Pty Ltd* [1976] VR 309 at 312.

20 The mortgagee is not, however, entitled to be reimbursed out of the mortgaged property for the costs of defending a third party's action impugning his title to the security or the enforcement or exercise of his rights under the mortgage (see *Parker-Tweedale v Dunbar Bank Plc (No 2)* [1991] Ch 26 at 33D, 47B-F).

1 The selling mortgagee is also liable to account to the holder of any subsequent mortgagee or chargee of whom he has notice. See *West London Commercial Bank v Reliance Permanent Building Society* (1885) 29 Ch D 954 at 961ff; *Kerabee Park Pty Ltd v Daley* [1978] 2 NSWLR 222 at 228F.

2 *Cuckmere Brick Co Ltd v Mutual Finance Ltd* [1971] Ch 949 at 965F per Salmon LJ; *Bishop v Bonham* [1988] 1 WLR 742 at 753F per Slade LJ; *Frost Ltd v Ralph* (1981) 115 DLR (3d) 612 at 622; *Suskind v Bank of Nova Scotia* (1984) 10 DLR (4th) 101 at 107f per Carruthers J; *Commercial and General Acceptance Ltd v Nixon* (1981) 152 CLR 491 at 494 per Gibbs CJ, 502 per Mason J, 515 per Aickin J.

benefit of another, but 'for his own benefit, to enable him the better to realise his debt.'[3] It is, in one sense, clear that the exercise of the power of sale cannot be a fiduciary exercise,[4] since the mortgagee has 'rights of his own which he is entitled to exercise adversely to the mortgagor.'[5] However, as Cross LJ pointed out in *Cuckmere Brick Co Ltd v Mutual Finance Ltd*,[6] the position of the selling mortgagee is at least 'ambiguous', since it is equally clear that he must 'pay some regard to the interests of the mortgagor when he comes to exercise the power.'

The law of mortgage thus holds somewhat inscrutably that, in exercising his power of sale, the mortgagee is entitled to give first, but not exclusive, consideration to his own interests.[7] Increasingly, as Nicholls V-C observed in *Palk v Mortgage Services Funding Plc*,[8] when the mortgagee takes steps to exercise his rights over his security, 'common law and equity alike have set bounds to the extent to which he can look after himself and ignore the mortgagor's interests.' Although the mortgagee is plainly entitled to protect his own interest, he is 'not entitled to conduct himself in a way which unfairly prejudices the mortgagor.'[9] In recent times the courts have so elevated the standard of conduct expected of the selling mortgagee that it may now be feasible to maintain, even in the face of the conventional disavowal of trustee status, that the mortgagee's duty to his mortgagor has become 'analogous to a fiduciary duty'.[10]

(g) General duty of the selling mortgagee

There has been much difference of opinion as to the proper balance to be maintained between the respective interests of the mortgagor and the mortgagee. Assessed purely in terms of immediate financial self-interest, the mortgagee's only concern in sale is to obtain with speed and efficiency a sufficient price to cover the amount of his outstanding loan. However, a sale which satisfied only this minimal purpose would almost inevitably inflict grave prejudice on the mortgagor, since any sale at an undervalue erodes the effective value of his equity of redemption. A sale price which is adequate to meet only the costs of the sale and the outstanding mortgage moneys leaves no surplus at all for the mortgagor.

3 *Warner v Jacob* (1882) 20 Ch D 220 at 224 per Kay J.
4 See Paul Finn, *Fiduciary Obligations* (Sydney 1977), p 10.
5 *Farrar v Farrars Ltd* (1888) 40 Ch D 395 at 411 per Lindley LJ. See also *Sterne v Victoria & Grey Trust Co* (1985) 14 DLR (4th) 193 at 203.
6 [1971] Ch 949 at 969F.
7 See *Palmer v Barclays Bank Ltd* (1972) 23 P & CR 30 at 35; *Palk v Mortgage Services Funding Plc* [1993] 2 WLR 415 at 420G per Nicholls V-C; *Henry Roach (Petroleum) Pty Ltd v Credit House (Vic) Pty Ltd* [1976] VR 309 at 313.
8 [1993] 2 WLR 415 at 420G.
9 [1993] 2 WLR 415 at 420H.
10 See Sir Frederick Jordan, *Chapters on Equity in New South Wales*, in *Selected Legal Papers* (Sydney 1983), p 113, cited with approval in the High Court of Australia in *Hospital Products Ltd v United States Surgical Corpn* (1984) 156 CLR 41 at 102 per Mason J. See also *Sterne v Victoria & Grey Trust Co* (1985) 14 DLR (4th) 193 at 203, where Rutherford J complained that the 'ritualistic repetition of unexamined formulas' (such as the denial that the mortgagee is a trustee) 'obscures the true nature and purpose of the contract between the two parties. The purpose of the power granted to the mortgagee by the mortgagor is to realise on the security to the extent necessary to diminish, if not eliminate, the mortgagor's debt.'

The ambiguity of the mortgagee's position was for a long time reflected in the divergent and sometimes inconsistent criteria applied by the courts in determining the propriety of a mortgagee's exercise of his power of sale.[11] It now seems clear, however, that the conduct of the selling mortgagee is to be judged with reference to two criteria, one subjective in nature and the other objective. The mortgagor must always act in good faith; he must also discharge a duty of reasonable care towards his mortgagor. The mortgagor has a valid ground for complaint if either of these criteria has not been met.

(i) Subjective criterion of good faith There is an elementary requirement of good faith in the exercise of the mortgagee's power of sale. This subjective criterion demands that the mortgagee should not deal 'wilfully and recklessly. . .with the property in such a manner that the interests of the mortgagor are sacrificed'.[12]

Equity's traditionally heavy emphasis on this requirement at first led the courts to deny that mere carelessness in the matter of sale could ever be a ground of liability for the mortgagee.[13] Thus it used to be thought that the mortgagee's only obligation to the mortgagor was simply 'not to cheat him'.[14] According to this earlier view, the court would not interfere 'even though the sale be very disadvantageous', unless the sale price was 'so low as in itself to be evidence of fraud' or there was evidence of 'corruption or collusion with the purchaser'.[15]

It is an interesting feature of the recent development of the law of mortgage throughout most of the common law world that there has been a general rejection of the idea that the subjective requirement of good faith stands alone as the exclusive criterion of the mortgagee's conduct.[16] It now seems clear that his behaviour must also measure up to an objective standard of reasonable prudence.[17]

(ii) Objective criterion of reasonable behaviour There have always been isolated statements in the case law that the selling mortgagee should 'behave. . .as a reasonable man would behave in the realisation of his own property, so that the mortgagor may receive credit for the fair value of the property

11 See *Cuckmere Brick Co Ltd v Mutual Finance Ltd* [1971] Ch 949 at 966B per Salmon LJ.

12 *Kennedy v De Trafford* [1897] AC 180 at 185 per Lord Herschell. See also *Barns v Queensland National Bank Ltd* (1906) 3 CLR 925 at 942f; *Pendlebury v Colonial Mutual Life Assurance Society Ltd* (1912) 13 CLR 676 at 680, 694, 700.

13 *Pendlebury v Colonial Mutual Life Assurance Society Ltd* (1912) 13 CLR 676 at 700; *British Columbia Land & Investment Agency v Ishitaka* (1911) 45 SCR 302 at 317.

14 *Cuckmere Brick Co Ltd v Mutual Finance Ltd* [1971] Ch 949 at 966B per Salmon LJ.

15 *Warner v Jacob* (1882) 20 Ch D 220 at 224.

16 It is unclear, however, whether the law in the Australian jurisdictions still judges the selling mortgagee merely against the subjective criterion of good faith (see eg *Barns v Queensland National Bank Ltd* (1906) 3 CLR 925 at 942f; *Pendlebury v Colonial Mutual Life Assurance Society Ltd* (1912) 13 CLR 676 at 680, 694, 700). For indications that Australian law is finally moving towards an additional test of reasonable care, see *George v Commercial Union Assurance Co of Australia Ltd* (1977) 1 BPR 9649 at 9652f; *Hospital Products Ltd v United States Surgical Corpn* (1984) 156 CLR 41 at 102 per Mason J; *National Commercial Banking Corpn of Australia v Solanowski* (1984) NSW ConvR 55-194 at 57,359f per Powell J.

17 See *Goldcell Nominees Pty Ltd v Network Finance Ltd* [1983] 2 VR 257 at 262.

sold.'[18] These statements have gathered force in recent years, and it has come to be increasingly held that the mortgagee is indeed answerable for carelessness or imprudence in the conduct of the sale.[19] Courts have drawn progressively upon the analogy that the mortgagee in possession 'must take reasonable care to maximise his return from the property'[20] and 'must take steps to preserve its value'.[1] Likewise in the exercise of his power of sale the mortgagee cannot act arbitrarily, but 'must exercise reasonable care to sell only at the proper market value.'[2] The injection of this objective criterion of reasonableness has done much to elevate the standard of dealing required of the mortgagee.

(iii) Fusion of subjective and objective criteria The conduct nowadays expected of the selling mortgagee involves a fusion of subjective and objective elements, and requires that the mortgagee should practise not only good faith but also reasonable care. As Salmon LJ said in *Cuckmere Brick Co Ltd v Mutual Finance Ltd*,[3] the mortgagee 'owes both duties'.[4] These two duties may well interact one with another. In the High Court of Australia in *Forsyth v Blundell*,[5] Menzies J likewise expressed the view that to 'take reasonable precautions to obtain a proper price is but part of the duty to act in good faith.'[6] This blending of concepts ensures that the legitimate primacy of the mortgagee's self-interest is not inconsistent with 'having regard to the interests of others or with taking reasonable care to protect the interests of others.'[7]

The precise application of the twin concepts of good faith and reasonable care depends upon the nature of the remedy sought by the mortgagor. The two tests tend to operate under 'different and mutually exclusive conditions'.[8]

18 *McHugh v Union Bank of Canada* [1913] AC 299 at 311 per Lord Moulton. See also *Falkner v Equitable Reversionary Society* (1858) 4 Drew 352 at 355, 62 ER 136 at 137; *Marriott v Anchor Reversionary Co Ltd* (1860) 7 Jur NS 155 at 156f, 2 Giff 457 at 469, 66 ER 191 at 196f, affd 3 De GF & J 177, 45 ER 846.

19 *Holohan v Friends' Provident and Century Life Office* [1966] IR 1 at 21ff, 25.

20 *Palk v Mortgage Services Funding Plc* [1993] 2 WLR 415 at 420H-421A per Nicholls V-C (the mortgagee 'cannot sell hastily at a knock-down price sufficient to pay off his debt').

1 See *Sterne v Victoria & Grey Trust Co* (1985) 14 DLR (4th) 193 at 203, where Rutherford J could see no grounds 'for distinguishing between the mortgagee's duty to preserve the physical state of the property and a duty to preserve the value at which it could be sold by ensuring that the sale takes place under conditions reasonably calculated to secure the best price under the circumstances.'

2 *Palk v Mortgage Services Funding Plc* [1993] 2 WLR 415 at 421A per Nicholls V-C.

3 [1971] Ch 949 at 966C.

4 It is significant that as long ago as *Farrar v Farrars Ltd* (1888) 40 Ch D 395 at 411, Lindley LJ had ruled that the mortgagor had no redress provided the mortgagee 'acts bona fide and takes reasonable precautions to obtain a proper price'. That the mortgagee owes both kinds of duty is now widely recognised (see eg *Canadian Imperial Bank of Commerce v Haley* (1980) 100 DLR (3d) 470 at 476f; *Bank of Montreal v Allender Investments Ltd* (1984) 4 DLR (4th) 340 at 343; *Suskind v Bank of Nova Scotia* (1984) 10 DLR (4th) 101 at 106, 108).

5 (1973) 129 CLR 477 at 481.

6 See also *Kennedy v De Trafford* [1897] AC 180 at 185 per Lord Herschell; *Sullivan v Darkin* [1986] 1 NZLR 214 at 222 per Somers J. In *Frost Ltd v Ralph* (1981) 115 DLR (3d) 612 at 617, for instance, a mortgagee's precipitate action, in selling at an undervalue one day after the mortgagor failed to redeem, was held to constitute not only a lack of reasonable care on the mortgagee's part, but also strong evidence of mala fides.

7 *Henry Roach (Petroleum) Pty Ltd v Credit House (Vic) Pty Ltd* [1976] VR 309 at 313.

8 See *Sterne v Victoria & Grey Trust Co* (1985) 14 DLR (4th) 193 at 201 per Rutherford J.

The subjective requirement of good faith relates essentially to the avoidance of conflicts of interest which might lead the court to set aside improperly transacted sales. By contrast the objective requirement of reasonable care generates, in cases of breach, a merely monetary liability in respect of any financial loss which is caused by careless or imprudent exercise of the mortgagee's power of sale. Thus, where the mortgagor brings an action against *both* the mortgagee *and* the purchaser for the setting aside of a sale, the court intervenes only if fraud or bad faith is shown to attach to the transaction. Where, however, the mortgagor seeks his remedy solely against the mortgagee and sues only for an accounting between them in respect of the sale price achieved, the court assesses the propriety of the mortgagee's conduct by reference to the rather higher standard represented by the test of reasonable care.

(h) Mortgagee's duty of objectively reasonable care

The objective requirement of reasonable care has come to exert an impact on much of the mortgagee's conduct in the exercise of his power of sale, most noticeably in relation to the price achieved by the sale. The mortgagee's duty in this respect is non-delegable[9] and the mortgagee is not relieved from responsibility merely because he entrusts the sale of the mortgaged property to an apparently competent or experienced agent.[10] It seems also that, although the duty of care may be excluded by contrary agreement between mortgagor and mortgagee,[11] the courts apply such strict construction even to widely drafted exclusion clauses that the rigour of the general duty of prudence is virtually inescapable.[12]

(i) Doctrinal basis of the mortgagee's duty The precise doctrinal foundation of the mortgagee's duty of care has proved to be a matter of some dispute. At one point in his judgment in *Cuckmere Brick Co Ltd v Mutual Finance Ltd*,[13]

9 *Wolff v Vanderzee* (1869) 20 LT 353 at 354; *Tomlin v Luce* (1889) 41 Ch D 573 at 575f, (1889) 43 Ch D 191 at 194; *Cuckmere Brick Co Ltd v Mutual Finance Ltd* [1971] Ch 949 at 969A-B, 973A. See also *Australia and New Zealand Banking Group Ltd v Bangadilly Pastoral Co Pty Ltd* (1978) 139 CLR 195 at 222 per Aickin J.

10 See *Commercial and General Acceptance Ltd v Nixon* (1981) 152 CLR 491 at 495 per Gibbs CJ, 503 per Mason J, 508 per Aickin J, 521 per Wilson J; *Sterne v Victoria & Grey Trust Co* (1985) 14 DLR (4th) 193 at 204; *McKean v Maloney* [1988] 1 Qd R 628 at 634. The non-delegable responsibility of the mortgagee is unaffected by the probability nowadays that the injured mortgagor has a valid claim in negligence directly against the mortgagee's agent (see *Cuckmere Brick Co Ltd v Mutual Finance Ltd* [1971] Ch 949 at 973C-E; *Commercial and General Acceptance Ltd v Nixon*, supra at 504f per Mason J, 516 per Aickin J).

11 *Bishop v Bonham* [1988] 1 WLR 742 at 752A per Slade LJ.

12 See eg *Bishop v Bonham* [1988] 1 WLR 742 at 753E-F, 754A, where the Court of Appeal declined to hold that an express power of sale authorising the mortgagee to sell 'in such manner and upon such terms and for such consideration. . .as you may think fit' gave the mortgagee 'carte blanche' to act as he thought fit in disregard of the duty of care. The mortgagee's exercise of his power was still constrained by the need to act as he thought fit 'within the limits of the duty of reasonable care imposed by the general law'.

13 [1971] Ch 949 at 966D-E ('The mortgagor is vitally affected by the result of the sale but its preparation and conduct is left entirely in the hands of the mortgagee. The proximity between them could scarcely be closer. Surely they are "neighbours"'). See also *Standard Chartered Bank Ltd v Walker* [1982] 1 WLR 1410 at 1415F-G per Lord Denning MR.

Salmon LJ seemed to locate the source of the mortgagee's responsibility in some version of the 'neighbour' principle adumbrated by Lord Atkin in *Donoghue v Stevenson.*[14] Salmon LJ also noted, however, that the heightened responsibility of the selling mortgagee flowed from the fact that 'many years before the modern development of the law of negligence, the courts of equity had laid down a doctrine in relation to mortgages which is entirely consonant with the general principles later evolved by the common law.'[15] There have been other suggestions that the mortgagee's duty is essentially contractual in that the mortgagor, knowing at the time of the contract of loan that he remains ultimately liable for any balance undischarged by sale, must be assumed to have conceded the mortgagee's power of sale 'only in the expectation that the mortgagee will use his best efforts to achieve the best price for the security.'[16]

Recent English case law has inclined toward the view that the duty owed by the mortgagee to the mortgagor does not derive from any analogy with tort or contract,[17] but is instead 'recognised in equity as arising out of the particular relationship between them.'[18] Nowadays the more accurate approach seems to be that the mortgagee's conduct falls to be judged with reference to venerable principles of equitable intervention. For this reason the standard expected of the selling mortgagee is perhaps better described in terms of a duty of prudence rather than a duty of reasonable care. As Knight Bruce V-C held in *Matthie v Edwards,*[19] the mortgagee must 'act in a prudent and business-like manner, with a view to obtain as large a price as may fairly and reasonably, with due diligence and attention, be under the circumstances obtainable.'[20] Thus stated, the mortgagee's responsibility begins closely to resemble Jessel MR's classic definition in *Speight v Gaunt*[1] of the quality of conduct expected of the trustee. The newly intensified

14 [1932] AC 562 at 580. For a straightforward adaptation in this context of the terminology of negligence, see *National Westminster Finance New Zealand Ltd v United Finance & Securities Ltd* [1988] 1 NZLR 226 at 237f.

15 [1971] Ch 949 at 967D. See eg *Tomlin v Luce* (1889) 43 Ch D 191 at 194f per Cotton LJ.

16 *Sterne v Victoria & Grey Trust Co* (1985) 14 DLR (4th) 193 at 203 per Rutherford J. See also *Bishop v Bonham* [1988] 1 WLR 742 at 752A-D per Slade LJ.

17 See eg *Parker-Tweedale v Dunbar Bank Plc* [1991] Ch 12 at 18H, where Nourse LJ found it 'both unnecessary and confusing' that the mortgagee's duty should be 'expressed in terms of the tort of negligence'. It has been observed that this dissociation of the law of tort and the law of mortgage may, ironically, place the mortgagor's rights on much safer ground than they would be if based on the shifting sands of liability in negligence' (L. Bently, [1990] Conv 431 at 439). See eg *Murphy v Brentwood DC* [1991] 1 AC 398.

18 *Parker-Tweedale v Dunbar Bank Plc* [1991] Ch 12 at 18H–19A per Nourse LJ. Compare, however, Purchas LJ at 24B–25D. The doctrinal distancing of mortgage law from the principle of negligence liability echoes Lord Templeman's emphatic statement in the Judicial Committee of the Privy Council in *China and South Sea Bank Ltd v Tan Soon Gin* [1990] 1 AC 536 at 543H–544A, that the tort of negligence 'has not yet subsumed all torts and does not supplant the principles of equity or contradict contractual promises or complement the remedy of judicial review or supplement statutory rights.'

19 (1846) 2 Coll 465 at 480, 63 ER 817 at 824 (reversed at (1847) 16 LJ Ch 405 at 409, but without criticism of the principle applied by Knight Bruce V-C).

20 See also *McHugh v Union Bank of Canada* [1913] AC 299 at 311 per Lord Moulton.

1 (1883) 22 Ch D 727 at 739 ('[A] trustee ought to conduct the business of the trust in the same manner that an ordinary prudent man of business would conduct his own').

equitable perspective on the dealings of mortgagees may indeed have gone some way towards modifying the conventional view that the mortgagee is never a fiduciary of his power of sale.[2]

(ii) Duty in respect of sale price Building society mortgagees have long been subject to a statutory duty to take 'reasonable care to ensure' that the price achieved on the exercise of their power of sale is 'the best price that can reasonably be obtained'.[3] Likewise a local authority mortgagee, on exercising its right to vest mortgaged property in itself,[4] must account to the mortgagor for the 'value of the house at the time of the vesting'.[5] This value is statutorily deemed to be the price which the interest vested in the authority would realise if the house, freed of the relevant incumbrance, were 'sold on the open market by a willing vendor'.[6]

It is also clear nowadays that other kinds of mortgagee owe a similar duty of prudence in respect of the price at which the mortgaged property is ultimately realised. The bench-mark of this responsibility was indicated in entirely general terms by the Court of Appeal in *Cuckmere Brick Co Ltd v Mutual Finance Ltd.*[7] Here Salmon LJ described the duty of the selling mortgagee as comprising a responsibility to 'take reasonable precautions to obtain the true market value of the mortgaged property at the date on which he decides to sell it.'[8] This duty, although expressed over the years in varying formulations,[9] comprises essentially an obligation to 'exercise reasonable care to sell only at the proper market value'.[10]

The prudent mortgagee cannot, of course, be held to any absolute obligation to realise the 'true value'[11] or to obtain the 'best price' of the mortgaged property.[12] 'Perfection is not required' of the mortgagee.[13] His duty is merely

2 Ante, p 1008.
3 See now Building Societies Act 1986, s 13(7), Sch 4, para 1(1)(a), (2). See also *Reliance Permanent Building Society v Harwood-Stamper* [1944] Ch 362 at 372ff.
4 Post, p 1024.
5 Housing Act 1985, Sch 17, para 3(1)(a).
6 Housing Act 1985, Sch 17, para 3(2).
7 [1971] Ch 949 at 968H–969A. The '*Cuckmere* principle' has been described as one of the implied primary obligations of the mortgagee (see *Bishop v Bonham* [1988] 1 WLR 742 at 752A-D per Slade LJ).
8 Salmon LJ preferred not to refer to the concepts of 'proper price' (which was 'perhaps a little nebulous') or 'best price' (which 'might suggest an exceptionally high price'). See also *Standard Chartered Bank Ltd v Walker* [1982] 1 WLR 1410 at 1415E per Lord Denning MR; *Predeth v Castle Phillips Finance Co Ltd* (1986) 279 Estates Gazette 1355 at 1356; *Bishop v Bonham* [1988] 1 WLR 742 at 750D-H per Slade LJ; *Hausman v O'Grady* (1988) 42 DLR (4th) 119 at 125, affd (1989) 57 DLR (4th) 480.
9 See *Sullivan v Darkin* [1986] 1 NZLR 214 at 218 per Davison CJ.
10 *Palk v Mortgage Services Funding Plc* [1993] 2 WLR 415 at 421A per Nicholls V-C. See also Lord Templeman's references to the duty to take 'reasonable precautions to obtain the best price reasonably obtainable at the time of sale' (*Tse Kwong Lam v Wong Chit Sen* [1983] 1 WLR 1349 at 1356G-H) and to 'sell for the current market value' (*China and South Sea Bank Ltd v Tan Soon Gin* [1990] 1 AC 536 at 545D).
11 *Bank of Nova Scotia v Barnard* (1984) 9 DLR (4th) 575 at 586.
12 *Sterne v Victoria & Grey Trust Co* (1985) 14 DLR (4th) 193 at 203.
13 *Hausman v O'Grady* (1988) 42 DLR (4th) 119 at 129 per Anderson J, affd (1989) 57 DLR (4th) 480. See also *Cuckmere Brick Co Ltd v Mutual Finance Ltd* [1971] Ch 949 at 969A, where Salmon LJ indicated that the mortgagee 'will not be adjudged to be in default unless he is plainly on the wrong side of the line'.

to invest reasonable care in the exercise of his power of sale: it is 'the effort rather than the result to which the court looks'.[14] It is readily recognised that a forced sale by a mortgagee seldom achieves the 'highest', 'best possible' or even 'market' price.[15] The 'market' for repossessed properties is inevitably a distorted and highly relative phenomenon, and cogent evidence is required to rebut the inference that the actual sale price represented the proper price in the circumstances.[16] The point remains, however, that the mortgagee is not simply entitled to adopt *any* arrangement or accept *any* price merely because it will see him paid out.[17] He has no right to sacrifice the interest of the mortgagor in the surplus of the proceeds of sale.[18]

Whether a mortgagee has fulfilled his duty of care is in each case a question of fact,[19] although the plaintiff need not discharge the perhaps impossible onus of locating and identifying prospective purchasers who would have been prepared to pay a higher price than the actual purchaser.[20] In *Cuckmere Brick Co Ltd v Mutual Finance Ltd*,[1] for instance, a mortgagee realised the mortgaged property through sale by auction. Although informed expressly of a relevant (but fairly complex) planning permission relating to the property, the mortgagee failed to make adequate reference in the auction advertisements to the full extent of the permission.[2] In consequence the land was sold at an undervalue, and the Court of Appeal held that the mortgagee was liable in damages to the mortgagor for breach of the duty of care which it owed to the latter.[3] There is, however, no necessary inference of imprudence if, as in *Palmer v Barclays Bank Ltd*,[4] the mortgagee and his agent had never

14 *Sterne v Victoria & Grey Trust Co* (1985) 14 DLR (4th) 193 at 203f per Rutherford J.

15 *Canadian Imperial Bank of Commerce v Whitman* (1985) 12 DLR (4th) 326 at 343.

16 *Hausman v O'Grady* (1988) 42 DLR (4th) 119 at 131f, affd (1989) 57 DLR (4th) 480.

17 *Henry Roach (Petroleum) Pty Ltd v Credit House (Vic) Pty Ltd* [1976] VR 309 at 313. See eg *Frost Ltd v Ralph* (1981) 115 DLR (3d) 612 at 617, 622; *Forsyth v Blundell* (1973) 129 CLR 477 at 510.

18 *Commercial and General Acceptance Ltd v Nixon* (1981) 152 CLR 491 at 494 per Gibbs CJ, 515 per Wilson J. There is some suspicion that the decisions of both the Court of Appeal and the House of Lords in *Williams & Glyn's Bank Ltd v Boland* [1981] AC 487, [1979] Ch 312 (ante, p 569) may have been influenced by the bank mortgagee's fairly ruthless sale for £1,500 of a part of the secured property which was probably worth a sum in the region of £22,500 (see (1978) 36 P & CR 448 at 451).

19 The content of this duty of care does not vary in proportion to the degree of experience possessed by the mortgagee as vendor. In other words the same standard of care is demanded of the small investor as of the institutional lender (see *Commercial and General Acceptance Ltd v Nixon* (1981) 152 CLR 491 at 503 per Mason J).

20 *McKean v Maloney* [1988] 1 Qd R 628 at 634f per McPherson J. The price achieved in a subsequent resale by the mortgagee's purchaser may have relevant evidentiary value. See *Hausman v O'Grady* (1988) 42 DLR (4th) 119 at 132, but compare *Parker-Tweedale v Dunbar Bank Plc* [1991] Ch 12 (ante, p 1013).

1 [1971] Ch 949. See (1971) 87 LQR 303.

2 See also *National Westminster Finance New Zealand Ltd v United Finance & Securities Ltd* [1988] 1 NZLR 226 at 237f (failure to publicise suitability of property for immediate subdivision).

3 Compare *Bank of Cyprus (London) Ltd v Gill* [1980] 2 Lloyds Rep 51 at 54. See (1982) 132 NLJ 883 (H.W. Wilkinson). See also *Predeth v Castle Phillips Finance Co Ltd* (1986) 279 Estates Gazette 1355 at 1358f, where the Court of Appeal held that there had been a want of reasonable care where the mortgagee authorised a 'crash sale' of the mortgaged property (see [1986] Conv 442 (M.P. Thompson)).

4 (1972) 23 P & CR 30 at 36.

been informed of the availability of any planning permission and were therefore wholly unaware of its existence.[5]

(iii) Range of the mortgagee's duty of prudence The scope of the mortgagee's duty of prudence or care, however defined, is of course fundamentally qualified by the range of persons to whom the duty is owed. The mortgagee's responsibility in respect of the sale price is clearly a duty owed primarily to the mortgagor himself.[6] It is well established, however, that second and later mortgagees[7] and any guarantor or surety of the mortgage loan[8] may also claim the benefit of the mortgagee's obligation to strive for a proper market price on sale. Such parties are entitled to an allowance in equity in respect of any financial loss occasioned through proven default by the selling mortgagee.

There is nevertheless a danger that the matrix of responsibility surrounding the selling mortgagee may become unnecessarily complex and unwieldy, and the courts have therefore set some limit on the multiplication of liabilities. In *Parker-Tweedale v Dunbar Bank Plc*,[9] for instance, the plaintiff was a beneficiary under a trust of property which had been held by his wife as sole legal owner and mortgagor. The plaintiff subsequently alleged that the mortgagee, in the exercise of its power of sale, had sold up at a price which the purchaser, on resale three weeks later, was able to better by a substantial margin of £125,000. It was conceded that the selling mortgagee had notice at all relevant times of the plaintiff's interest behind the trust. The Court of Appeal declined, however, to hold that the beneficiary was owed, in respect of the sale price, any independent duty of care additional to that already owed by the mortgagee to the mortgagor.[10] The mortgagee's duty arises from a 'particular relationship' with the mortgagor which does not extend to trust beneficiaries holding under the mortgagor.[11] Accordingly, in the view of the Court of Appeal, there was no room for the superimposition

5 It could be argued, however, that the mortgagee's failure to advertise a relevant planning permission is largely negatived by the fact that any serious prospective purchaser would normally discover the existence of the planning permission on requisitioning a local authority search (see *Goldcell Nominees Pty Ltd v Network Finance Ltd* [1983] 2 VR 257 at 277f).

6 See *Johnson v Ribbins* (1975) 235 Estates Gazette 757 at 759; *Standard Chartered Bank v Walker* [1982] 1 WLR 1410 at 1415E-G; *Clark v UDC Finance Ltd* [1985] 2 NZLR 636 at 638f.

7 *Tomlin v Luce* (1889) 41 Ch D 573 at 575f, (1889) 43 Ch D 191 at 194 per Cotton LJ; *Cuckmere Brick Co Ltd v Mutual Finance Ltd* [1971] Ch 949 at 966G per Salmon LJ; *Alliance Acceptance Co Ltd v Graham* (1974) 10 SASR 220 at 222; *Suskind v Bank of Nova Scotia* (1984) 10 DLR (4th) 101 at 112; *National Westminster Finance New Zealand Ltd v United Finance & Securities Ltd* [1988] 1 NZLR 226 at 234.

8 'Equity intervenes to protect a surety' (*China and South Sea Bank Ltd v Tan Soon Gin* [1990] 1 AC 536 at 544A per Lord Templeman). See also *Standard Chartered Bank Ltd v Walker* [1982] 1 WLR 1410 at 1415E-G; *American Express International Banking Corpn Ltd v Hurley* [1985] 3 All ER 564 at 571f; *Clark v UDC Finance Ltd* [1985] 2 NZLR 636 at 638f. A surety who repays the entire debt is entitled to a transfer of the mortgaged property in order to procure recovery from the mortgagor of the whole or part of the sum paid to the creditor (see *China and South Sea Bank Ltd v Tan Soon Gin* [1990] 1 AC 536 at 545C-E).

9 [1991] Ch 12.

10 According to Purchas LJ, the beneficiary's rights are exclusively 'against the mortgagor as trustee upon whom there is a duty to take reasonable care to preserve the assets of the trust' ([1991] Ch 12 at 25A-B).

11 [1991] Ch 12 at 19D-E per Nourse LJ.

of a further duty owed directly to the beneficiary which would enable the beneficiary to sue the mortgagee in respect of any financial loss allegedly inflicted on the trust assets in the exercise of the mortgagee's power of sale.[12]

(iv) Timing of the sale It is settled law that once his power of sale has accrued, the mortgagee is prima facie entitled to exercise it for his own purposes at any time of his own choice.[13] In *Cuckmere Brick Co Ltd v Mutual Finance Ltd*[14] Salmon LJ thought that it 'matters not that the moment may be unpropitious and that by waiting a higher price may be obtained.'[15] It was his view that the mortgagee 'has a right to realise his security by turning it into money when he likes.'[16] The mortgagee's general obligation of prudent dealing does not, in effect, extend to the timing of the proposed sale. It is broadly irrelevant that a better price would have been obtained by deferring sale,[17] or by waiting out a protracted slump in the market,[18] or by spending more money on the property prior to sale.[19] The mortgagee has interests of his own which he cannot be required to disregard. There have been occasional suggestions that the mortgagee's prerogative to determine the date of sale is qualified by his overriding duty to exercise reasonable care in the matter of sale.[20]

12 [1991] Ch 12 at 19D per Nourse LJ, 23A per Sir Michael Kerr, 25A per Purchas LJ. The Court conceded that, by way of exception, a beneficiary might maintain a direct claim against the mortgagee if the trustee/mortgagor unreasonably refuses to sue on behalf of the trust or is disabled or disqualified from so acting. Even here, however, the beneficiary is permitted to sue only in right of the trust and in the room of the trustee ([1991] Ch 12 at 19F-H, 23D-E, 25B-C).

13 See *Parker-Tweedale v Dunbar Bank Plc* [1991] Ch 12 at 18B per Nourse LJ. It is, of course, clear that a mortgagee who takes possession of a security with a view to selling it must account to the mortgagor for any loss occurring through his (or his agent's) negligence in dealing with the property between the date of his taking possession and the date of the sale (*Cuckmere Brick Co Ltd v Mutual Finance Ltd* [1971] Ch 949 at 972G per Cross LJ). See eg *Norwich General Trust v Grierson* [1984] CLY 2306.

14 [1971] Ch 949 at 965G.

15 See also *Davey v Durrant* (1857) 1 De G & J 535 at 553, 44 ER 830 at 838; *Farrar v Farrars Ltd* (1888) 40 Ch D 395 at 398, 411; *Barns v Queensland National Bank Ltd* (1906) 3 CLR 925 at 942; *Tse Kwong Lam v Wong Chit Sen* [1983] 1 WLR 1349 at 1355B, 1359F-G per Lord Templeman; *Predeth v Castle Phillips Finance Co Ltd* (1986) 279 Estates Gazette 1355 at 1356.

16 Nor has the mortgagor any valid complaint if the mortgagee, by threatening to exercise his statutory power of sale, pressurises the mortgagor into selling the mortgaged property at an unfavourable time (*Page v Barclays Bank Ltd* (Unreported, Court of Appeal, 1979 P 3253, 14 July 1980)).

17 *Hausman v O'Grady* (1988) 42 DLR (4th) 119 at 128, 130 affd (1989) 57 DLR (4th) 480 ('the mortgagees...are entitled to recover with reasonable expedition'). A mortgagee may, however, be adjudged to have acted imprudently if he fails to expose the property for sale for a reasonable period of time before sale. See *Bank of Nova Scotia v Barnard* (1984) 9 DLR (4th) 575 at 586 (14 days insufficient); *Predeth v Castle Phillips Finance Co Ltd* (1986) 279 Estates Gazette 1355 at 1356 (uninhabitable property required three months on market).

18 *Sterne v Victoria & Grey Trust Co* (1985) 14 DLR (4th) 193 at 203.

19 *Expo International Pty Ltd v Chant* [1979] 2 NSWLR 820 at 835; *Stoyanovich v National Westminster Finance* (1984) 3 BPR 9310 at 9316.

20 See eg *Standard Chartered Bank Ltd v Walker* [1982] 1 WLR 1410 at 1415G, where Lord Denning MR thought that the fact that a mortgagee may determine the timing of sale quite arbitrarily did not necessarily imply that a mortgagee 'can sell at the worst possible time. It is at least arguable that, in choosing the time, he must exercise a reasonable degree of care.' In *Wood v Bank of Nova Scotia* (1979) 10 RPR 156 at 170, affd (1981) 112 DLR (3d) 181, a bank mortgagee was held liable in damages for loss caused by a sale in the middle of the winter where there was no 'overwhelming need to sell the property quickly'. See also *Suskind v Bank of Nova Scotia* (1984) 10 DLR (4th) 101 at 112.

These suggestions were severely weakened, however, by the vigorous reassertion in *China and South Sea Bank Ltd v Tan Soon Gin*[1] of the general principle that, although the mortgagee must sell for the 'current market value', he may 'decide in his own interest if and when he should sell.'[2] In the *China and South Sea Bank* case the value of the security at the date of the mortgagor's default had clearly exceeded the repayable loan moneys, but the mortgagee delayed the exercise of its power of sale until the mortgaged asset had declined in value and become worthless. The mortgagor's surety, when pursued for the unpaid debt, argued that his own liability had been extinguished or reduced by the mortgagee's failure to realise the security whilst it still retained value.

This contention was roundly rejected by the Judicial Committee of the Privy Council, which rationalised the mortgagee's position entirely in terms of the risks implicitly assumed in the context of a guaranteed loan. In the event of default by the mortgagor, declared Lord Templeman,[3] the mortgagee 'is not obliged to do anything.'[4] By inaction, of course, the mortgagee assumes the risk of total loss should the mortgagor then decline into bankruptcy, the mortgaged assets become valueless and the surety decamp abroad. But the non-exercise of the mortgagee's power of sale in no way alters the fact that 'the surety is bound by his contract' to pay if the mortgagor does not. In a ruling deeply sympathetic towards the commercial interests of lenders, Lord Templeman pointed out that '[n]o creditor could carry on the business of lending if he could become liable to a mortgagor and to a surety or to either of them for a decline in the value of the mortgaged property'.[5] In the present case the mortgagee's inaction had not resulted in any surrender, loss, or alteration in condition of the security and the mortgagee could not be said to have engaged in any act injurious to or inconsistent with the rights of the surety. The mortgagee was simply under no duty 'to exercise his power of sale over the mortgaged securities at any particular time or at all.'[6]

Recent case law has nevertheless highlighted one potentially crucial limitation on the mortgagee's arbitrary power to determine the date of sale in defiance of the wishes of a defaulting mortgagor. Pursuant to section 91(2) of the Law of Property Act 1925, the court has a discretion to order sale at the request of either the mortgagor or the mortgagee, notwithstanding

1 [1990] 1 AC 536 at 545D per Lord Templeman. See also *Bank of Cyprus (London) Ltd v Gill* [1980] 2 Lloyds Rep 51 at 54, where the Court of Appeal approved a decision by Lloyd J that, although the mortgagee was not obliged to wait on a rising market or for a market to recover, he must nevertheless take proper steps to secure the best price available at the time in question.
2 See also *Palk v Mortgage Services Funding Plc* [1993] 2 WLR 415 at 425E-F per Sir Michael Kerr.
3 [1990] 1 AC 536 at 545E-F.
4 See also *Palk v Mortgage Services Funding Plc* [1993] 2 WLR 415 at 420F-G per Nicholls V-C ('[A] mortgagee can sit back and do nothing. He is not obliged to take steps to realise his security').
5 [1990] 1 AC 536 at 545G.
6 [1990] 1 AC 536 at 545H.

that 'any other person dissents'.[7] In appropriate circumstances the court may direct sale 'on such terms as it thinks fit'. It is thus open to a mortgagor, by invoking the favourable exercise of discretion under section 91(2), to seek an acceleration of the sale of the mortgaged property. In practice, however, the scope of this discretion has always been curtailed by the court's unwillingness to order a sale contrary to the wishes of a mortgagee in the absence of full security for the repayment of his debt.[8]

In *Palk v Mortgage Services Funding Plc*,[9] the Court of Appeal was called upon to apply section 91(2) in virtually unprecedented circumstances. Here the defaulting mortgagors, realising that they could no longer cope with mounting arrears of instalments, managed to negotiate a private sale for £283,000, although it was undisputed that the total sum required to redeem the mortgage then amounted to £358,000. The first mortgagee declined to agree to the sale. Instead it proposed simply to let the property on short-term leases until such time as the housing market improved, meanwhile crediting the mortgagors with the rental income. The mortgagors were fully aware that such action would still leave them with an income shortfall which would cause their overall debt to increase by some £30,000 each year. In desperation they sought a court-directed sale of the property in order to stem the indefinite financial haemorrhage to which they were consigned by the mortgagee's proposals. In effect the mortgagee, knowing that it could always sue on the personal covenant to repay, was prepared to speculate, at the expense of the mortgagors, on the future movement of house prices.

The Court of Appeal decided that its statutory discretion to order sale was not ousted by the fact that the mortgagors could currently show only a 'negative equity' in the property.[10] Discretion was exercised in favour of sale even though such a sale deprived the mortgagee of its contractual and statutory rights arbitrarily to decide on the disposition of its security[11] and notwithstanding that more than £75,000 of the mortgagee's debt was left unsecured and outstanding.[12] Nicholls V-C led the Court of Appeal in holding that, in the exercise of his rights over his security, 'the mortgagee must act fairly towards the mortgagor.'[13] Here the course on which the mortgagee had embarked was 'likely to be highly prejudicial to [the mortgagor's] financial position as borrower.'[14] It was contrary to 'common fairness' and

7 The discretion conferred by section 91(2) is not dependent on proof of prior breach of duty by the mortgagee. It is 'unfettered', although it must of course be exercised 'judicially' (see *Palk v Mortgage Services Funding Plc* [1993] 2 WLR 415 at 422B, G-H per Nicholls V-C, 424F per Sir Michael Kerr).

8 For this purpose security could be achieved by fixing a reserve price for the court-ordered sale sufficient to cover the outstanding debt and costs or by requiring the mortgagor to make a payment into court (see eg *Woolley v Colman* (1882) 21 Ch D 169 at 173).

9 [1993] 2 WLR 415.

10 [1993] 2 WLR 415 at 422G-H per Nicholls V-C, 425H per Sir Michael Kerr.

11 The Court of Appeal regarded section 91(2) as an 'overriding statutory power' which displaced the mortgagee's otherwise unfettered rights to determine the date of sale or decide on lettings ([1993] 2 WLR 415 at 421F-H per Nicholls V-C, 425E-G per Sir Michael Kerr).

12 By the date of the Court of Appeal hearing the total mortgage debt in *Palk* had in fact risen to £409,000 (*Times*, 1 August 1992, p 14, col 8). The husband mortgagor had become bankrupt and it was his wife, as co-mortgagor, who claimed the benefit of the section 91(2) discretion.

13 [1993] 2 WLR 415 at 420G.

14 [1993] 2 WLR 415 at 421G.

indeed 'oppressive' to compel the mortgagor to become 'an unwilling risk-taker' in an enterprise in which, short of a dramatic upward surge in the housing market, she was 'bound to suffer financially'.[15] In Nicholls V-C's view, it would be 'manifest unfairness'[16] to saddle the mortgagor with such an unattractive risk in circumstances where her liability was 'open-ended' and she remained personally liable for the ever-increasing deficit.[17] Against this background the Court of Appeal had no doubt that it should direct an immediate sale in order to protect the mortgagor from the burden of the rising debt.[18]

Although the court will direct sale in cases of negative equity 'only in exceptional circumstances',[19] it seems clear that the discretion available under section 91(2) provides in such cases a valuable and hitherto unsuspected avenue to relief for certain categories of mortgagor caught in the trap of negative equity.[20] The *Palk* decision throws the mortgagor a lifeline which may enable him or her to escape a calamitous situation in which debts increase exponentially beyond any hope of repayment from the proceeds of an eventual sale.

(v) Other preliminaries or modalities of the sale The mortgagee's duty to afford reasonable protection for the interests of his mortgagor imposes on him a duty of care in relation to other preliminaries or modalities of the sale. In organising the sale the mortgagee must act in the same way as would a 'prudent vendor' who wishes to sell property belonging to himself.[1] There is, however, no duty to incur expense in promoting a sale unless it is clear that such further expense is covered by the security.[2]

The mortgagee must, for example, take reasonable steps to ascertain the

15 [1993] 2 WLR 415 at 421H, 422E, 423B. As Nicholls V-C acutely observed (at 419G), the case revealed, as between mortgagor and mortgagee, a latent 'difference in their attitudes towards taking risks'.

16 [1993] 2 WLR 415 at 422H.

17 [1993] 2 WLR 415 at 422H, 423B-F.

18 In effect the mortgagor's liability to continuing mortgage interest was cut to approximately one twelfth of the amounts owed prior to the court-ordered sale. Nicholls V-C pointed out that the mortgagee could still, of course, pursue its preferred policy of speculating on a rising market. It could 'back its own judgment' by purchasing the property itself (post, p 1024), in which case the mortgagor would receive an immediate credit for the current market value and the mortgagee would retain the benefit of any future improvement in house prices ([1993] 2 WLR 415 at 422E-G, 423B-C).

19 [1993] 2 WLR 415 at 426B per Sir Michael Kerr, who acknowledged (at 426F-G) that the facts in *Palk* were 'extreme and exceptional'. Nicholls V-C stressed (at 423A) that the mortgagee might well have been able to justify a postponement of sale on perfectly valid grounds specific to the particular property (eg pending the outcome of an application for planning permission).

20 It is estimated that at the date of *Palk*'s case more than half a million borrowers in England and Wales were similarly trapped in properties worth less than their current mortgage debt (*Times*, 1 August 1992, p 1, col 6).

1 *Commercial and General Acceptance Ltd v Nixon* (1981) 152 CLR 491 at 503 per Mason J. See also *Tse Kwong Lam v Wong Chit Sen* [1983] 1 WLR 1349 at 1359G-H per Lord Templeman. This criterion certainly represents a tightening up of standards when compared with earlier cases (see eg *British Columbia Land & Investment Agency v Ishitaka* (1911) 45 SCR 302 at 317 per Duff J).

2 *Hallifax Property Corp Pty Ltd v GIFC Ltd* (1988) NSW ConvR 55-415 at 57,798.

value of the property before sale.[3] He must advertise the property[4] and must make a reasonable effort to bring the proposed sale to the attention of all persons likely to be interested.[5] Where the property holds appeal only for a limited market, the mortgagee must 'seek out that market and take the sale to it'.[6] There is, for instance, a want of due care where the mortgagee fails to follow up the possibility of a higher price, knowing that a prospective purchaser is prepared to pay more than an existing offer.[7] Where there are two or more interested potential purchasers, they must be brought into competition with each other so as to obtain the highest price sustainable by the available market.[8] Whether the sale is by public auction or by private treaty, the mortgagee must bring to the notice of interested parties the 'potentiality of the property to be sold'.[9] The mortgagee is under no strict duty to consult either the mortgagor or other mortgagees as to a proposed sale, but a failure to do so may in some circumstances point to a lack of good faith on his part.[10]

(vi) Sales by auction Although the mortgagee may have a duty to seek expert advice as to the method of sale,[11] there is no legal obligation to hold a sale by auction.[12] Indeed sale by public auction rather than by private treaty

3 *Pendlebury v Colonial Mutual Life Assurance Society Ltd* (1912) 13 CLR 676 at 683; *Henry Roach (Petroleum) Pty Ltd v Credit House (Vic) Pty Ltd* [1976] VR 309 at 313; *Frost Ltd v Ralph* (1981) 115 DLR (3d) 612 at 617; *Tse Kwong Lam v Wong Chit Sen* [1983] 1 WLR 1349 at 1357H–1358A. Failure to obtain a second valuation is not necessarily culpable conduct by a mortgagee (*Swerus v Central Mortgage Registry of Australia Pty Ltd* (1988) NSW ConvR 55-407 at 57,570), but a single valuation designed to ensure a 'fast sale' is not sufficient (see *Bank of Nova Scotia v Barnard* (1984) 9 DLR (4th) 575 at 586).

4 *National Westminster Finance New Zealand Ltd v United Finance & Securities Ltd* [1988] 1 NZLR 226 at 238. On the importance of advertising in a local newspaper, see *McKean v Maloney* [1988] 1 Qd R 628 at 632ff. The courts have, however, rejected the argument that the mortgagor is prejudiced by advertisements which reveal that the sale is a 'mortgagee sale' (*Hallifax Property Corp Pty Ltd v GIFC Ltd* (1988) NSW ConvR 55-415 at 57,799) or that the property 'must sell' (see *Hausman v O'Grady* (1988) 42 DLR (4th) 119 at 127, affd (1989) 57 DLR (4th) 480.

5 *Henry Roach (Petroleum) Pty Ltd v Credit House (Vic) Pty Ltd* [1976] VR 309 at 313. In *Davey v Durrant* (1857) 1 De G & J 535 at 560, 44 ER 830 at 840, Knight Bruce LJ was not prepared to hold that a mortgagee can never accept a fair offer from a private buyer until he has advertised the property for sale.

6 *National Westminster Finance New Zealand Ltd v United Finance & Securities Ltd* [1988] 1 NZLR 226 at 237f per Smellie J. See also *Sterne v Victoria & Grey Trust Co* (1985) 14 DLR (4th) 193 at 204 (hobby farm).

7 *Australia and New Zealand Banking Group Ltd v Bangadilly Pastoral Co Pty Ltd* (1978) 139 CLR 195 at 228 per Aickin J.

8 *Forsyth v Blundell* (1973) 129 CLR 477 at 509.

9 *Henry Roach (Petroleum) Pty Ltd v Credit House (Vic) Pty Ltd* [1976] VR 309 at 313; *National Westminster Finance New Zealand Ltd v United Finance & Securities Ltd* [1988] 1 NZLR 226 at 237f.

10 *Goldcell Nominees Pty Ltd v Network Finance Ltd* [1983] 2 VR 257 at 272, 278. See also *Australia and New Zealand Banking Group Ltd v Bangadilly Pastoral Co Pty Ltd* (1978) 139 CLR 195 at 202 per Jacobs J, 229 per Aickin J.

11 *Tse Kwong Lam v Wong Chit Sen* [1983] 1 WLR 1349 at 1357H, 1359G per Lord Templeman. There is, in effect, a duty to consider whether to put the property to auction (see *National Westminster Finance New Zealand Ltd v United Finance & Securities Ltd* [1988] 1 NZLR 226 at 238).

12 *Frost Ltd v Ralph* (1981) 115 DLR (3d) 612 at 624; *Swerus v Central Mortgage Registry of Australia Pty Ltd* (1988) NSW ConvR 55-407 at 57,570.

does not in itself prove the validity of a transaction,[13] particularly since an auction which produces only one bid obviously provides no guarantee that a true market value has been achieved.[14] There is, however, nothing to prevent a mortgagee from accepting the best bid obtainable at an auction, 'even though the auction is badly attended and the bidding exceptionally low', provided that none of these adverse factors is 'due to any fault of the mortgagee'.[15] Equally the mortgagee is under 'no legal duty simpliciter' to accept the highest bid at an auction,[16] particularly if this bid is made by the mortgagor.[17] Nor does the mortgagee commit any breach of his duty of care merely because prior to auction he sells the property privately without first informing the mortgagor.[18] In some cases it may be entirely consistent with the discharge of his duty that he should accept a suitably high pre-emptive bid made by a private purchaser who wishes to 'kill' the sale and withdraw the property from auction.[19]

If, however, the mortgagee chooses to sell by public auction, he has a non-delegable duty[20] to ensure that the auction is preceded by appropriate advertisement.[1] The mortgagee may be exposed to a claim in damages for negligence if a relevant newspaper advertisement was carried only once,[2] or allowed only a minimal lead time before the auction date,[3] or was hidden

13 *Tse Kwong Lam v Wong Chit Sen* [1983] 1 WLR 1349 at 1355G.

14 *Tse Kwong Lam v Wong Chit Sen* [1983] 1 WLR 1349 at 1356H–1357A. See also *Australia and New Zealand Banking Group Ltd v Bangadilly Pastoral Co Pty Ltd* (1978) 139 CLR 195 at 227 per Aickin J, who pointed out that 'there was in truth only one bidder' at the auction.

15 *Cuckmere Brick Co Ltd v Mutual Finance Ltd* [1971] Ch 949 at 965G-H per Salmon LJ. Compare, however, the truly appalling outcome in *Bank of Montreal v Allender Investments Ltd* (1984) 4 DLR (4th) 340 at 346ff, where the New Brunswick Court of Queen's Bench upheld the sole auction bid of $100 (made by the mortgagee itself!) in respect of property which had been valued at $46,000 three weeks earlier. The mortgagee was permitted to sue the mortgagor for a deficiency of some $45,700, the court holding that the mortgagee could not be faulted, in the absence of other bidders, for buying for a nominal sum at a properly advertised auction.

16 *Stoyanovich v National Westminster Finance* (1984) 3 BPR 9310 at 9315. See also *Payne v Cave* (1789) 3 Term Rep 148 at 149, 100 ER 502 at 503. Compare, however, *Australia and New Zealand Banking Group Ltd v Bangadilly Pastoral Co Pty Ltd* (1978) 139 CLR 195 at 228 per Aickin J (ante, p 1021).

17 *AGC (Advances) Ltd v McWhirter* (1977) 1 BPR 9454 at 9456ff; *Stoyanovich v National Westminster Finance* (1984) 3 BPR 9310 at 9315.

18 *Davey v Durrant* (1857) 1 De G & J 535 at 560, 44 ER 830 at 840; *Goldcell Nominees Pty Ltd v Network Finance Ltd* [1983] 2 VR 257 at 262. Such a sale may, however, indicate bad faith if the mortgagee had earlier undertaken to consult the mortgagor over any proposal to transact a private sale in advance of the auction (see *Goldcell Nominees Pty Ltd v Network Finance Ltd* [1983] 2 VR 257 at 278).

19 *Johnson v Ribbins* (1975) 235 Estates Gazette 757 at 761.

20 Ante, p 1012.

1 *Pendlebury v Colonial Mutual Life Assurance Society Ltd* (1912) 13 CLR 676 at 683ff; *Henry Roach (Petroleum) Pty Ltd v Credit House (Vic) Pty Ltd* [1976] VR 309 at 313; *Commercial and General Acceptance Ltd v Nixon* (1981) 152 CLR 491 at 500 per Mason J; *McKean v Maloney* [1988] 1 Qd R 628 at 632ff; (1989) 63 ALJ 556 (P.B.).

2 *Commercial and General Acceptance Ltd v Nixon* (1981) 152 CLR 491 at 494 per Gibbs CJ, 500f per Mason J. It was crucial here that the mortgagee failed to ensure that the advertisement appeared in the Wednesday edition of a daily newspaper which was the normal forum for each week's auction advertisements of real estate (see [1980] Qd R 153 at 156C).

3 *Commercial and General Acceptance Ltd v Nixon* (1981) 152 CLR 491 at 494, 500, [1980] Qd R 153 at 156B-C (two days). See also *Australia and New Zealand Banking Group Ltd v Bangadilly Pastoral Co Pty Ltd* (1978) 139 CLR 195 at 202 per Jacobs J, 229 per Aickin J.

'in the middle of a mixed grill of auction advertisements' ranging from sales of china and bric-à-brac to old furniture and power tools.[4] The mortgagee may also be liable for negligence if he sells properties of widely differing types and attractions in one block.[5]

The mortgagee's duty of care also renders him vicariously liable for the actual conduct of the auction sale. The precise date chosen for the day of auction may reflect prejudicially upon the price achieved on sale.[6] A reserve price should be set with the benefit of expert advice,[7] and the auctioneer informed of that price well before the commencement of the auction.[8] In some circumstances it may be a breach of the mortgagee's duty if details of the reserve price are disclosed to any individual prospective purchaser in advance of the auction,[9] or indeed are announced at the auction itself to all the potential bidders collectively.[10] Such disclosure may operate adversely by limiting the number of bidders and may even indicate that a later private sale of the property at a much lower price is not bona fide.[11] On the other hand, the announcement at the outset that there is a reserve price may reduce the chance of an abortive auction and, provided that the amount of this price is not made known until such time as bidding has stopped short, may well conduce to the achieving of the reserve price.[12]

(j) Mortgagee's duty of subjective good faith

The impact of the mortgagee's duty of good faith is nowadays most obviously apparent in the courts' response to cases where there is a potential conflict between the interest of the mortgagee as vendor in obtaining the highest price and some collateral interest of the mortgagee in achieving a lower price for the purchaser. As Jacobs J observed in *Australia and New Zealand Banking Group Ltd v Bangadilly Pastoral Co Pty Ltd*,[13] the requirement of bona fides in a mortgagee 'is concerned with a genuine primary desire to obtain for the mortgaged property the best price obtainable consistently with the right of a mortgagee to realise his security.' This goal is obviously jeopardised where the mortgagee either consciously or unconsciously grants preferment to a conflicting commercial interest on the part of the purchaser. The closer the association between mortgagee and purchaser, the less likely is the court to allow the transaction of sale to stand. The 'legitimate purpose' of the

4 *Nixon v Commercial and General Acceptance Ltd* [1980] Qd R 153 at 156C-D.
5 *Aldrich v Canada Permanent Loan & Savings Co* (1897) 24 OAR 193 at 194, 197f. See also *National Westminster Finance New Zealand Ltd v United Finance & Securities Ltd* [1988] 1 NZLR 226 at 238.
6 See eg *Australia and New Zealand Banking Group Ltd v Bangadilly Pastoral Co Pty Ltd* (1978) 139 CLR 195 at 202 per Jacobs J, 229 per Aickin J (auction two days before Christmas).
7 *Tse Kwong Lam v Wong Chit Sen* [1983] 1 WLR 1349 at 1357H.
8 *Tse Kwong Lam v Wong Chit Sen* [1983] 1 WLR 1349 at 1358A, where Lord Templeman indicated that a want of due care may be present if the auctioneer is not instructed to do more than 'put the property under the hammer'. Such a procedure 'may be appropriate to the sale of second hand furniture but is not necessarily conducive to the attainment of the best price for freehold or leasehold property'.
9 *Goldcell Nominees Pty Ltd v Network Finance Ltd* [1983] 2 VR 257 at 263, 278. See also *Tse Kwong Lam v Wong Chit Sen* [1983] 1 WLR 1349 at 1358C.
10 *Industrial Enterprises Inc v Schelstraete* (1975) 54 DLR (3d) 260 at 274.
11 *Reid v Royal Trust Corpn of Canada* (1985) 20 DLR (4th) 223 at 243.
12 *Reid v Royal Trust Corpn of Canada* (1985) 20 DLR (4th) 223 at 244.
13 (1978) 139 CLR 195 at 201 (High Court of Australia).

mortgagee's power of sale is to secure repayment of the mortgage money, and if the mortgagee 'uses the power for another purpose. . .or to serve the purposes of other individuals. . .the Court considers that to be a fraud in the exercise of the power'.[14] In such an event the appropriate remedy for the mortgagor is normally rescission of the sale and return of the security.

Conflicts of interest affecting the mortgagee tend to arise in two slightly different categories of circumstance.

(i) Sale to the mortgagee or to his representative The first category of case comprises circumstances in which any purported sale by the mortgagee is simply void and ineffective. It is, for instance, settled law that the mortgagee cannot, in exercise of his power of sale,[15] effect a valid sale of the mortgaged property either to himself alone or to himself and others.[16] A sale by a person to himself 'is no sale at all',[17] even though the sale price be the full value of the mortgaged property.[18] Precisely the same fate awaits any attempt to sell the mortgaged property to a trustee for the mortgagee,[19] or to the mortgagee's solicitor[20] or other agent.[1]

14 *Robertson v Norris* (1858) 1 Giff 421 at 424f, 65 ER 983 at 984 per Stuart V-C.

15 Compare, however, the position in relation to a sale directed by order of the court under Law of Property Act 1925, s 91(2). Here the mortgagee is indeed competent to purchase the mortgaged property, precisely because the sale is *not* a sale by a mortgagee acting in exercise of his own power of sale (see *Palk v Mortgage Services Funding Plc* [1993] 2 WLR 415 at 423C (ante, p 1020)). As Nicholls V-C pointed out in *Palk*, it may sometimes be entirely proper to allow—even to direct—a sale to the mortgagee. Such a sale may be necessary simply in order to prevent the mortgagee from unfairly saddling the mortgagor with the risk of future fluctuations in the market value of the property ([1993] 2 WLR 415 at 422D-G).

16 *Martinson v Clowes* (1882) 21 Ch D 857 at 860; *Australia and New Zealand Banking Group Ltd v Bangadilly Pastoral Co Pty Ltd* (1978) 139 CLR 195 at 225ff per Aickin J. It has been questioned whether this strict rule nowadays serves any purpose if the mortgagee is obliged in any event to act reasonably and prudently (see S. Robinson, [1989] Conv 336 at 341). If, for instance, there are no external bidders for the property, the rule may seem an unnecessary fetter on the lender's remedy of sale, although application may always be made to the court under Law of Property Act 1925, s 91(2) (ante, p 1020). Some jurisdictions confer on the mortgagee a specific statutory authority to buy in at auction (see eg New Brunswick's Property Act (RSNB 1952, c 177), s 42(1)(a); *Traders Group Ltd v Mason* (1975) 53 DLR (3d) 103 at 117).

17 *Farrar v Farrars Ltd* (1888) 40 Ch D 395 at 409 per Lindley LJ. An important exception to this principle is provided by Housing Act 1985, Sch 17, para 1(1), which allows a local authority mortgagee to vest in itself by deed any house in respect of which it is entitled to exercise a power of sale. This relaxation of the normal rule is subject both to the leave of the county court and to a statutory scheme of compensation and accounting to the mortgagor (ante, p 1014).

18 *Farrar v Farrars Ltd* (1888) 40 Ch D 395 at 409. On the practice in force in some parts of the United States, under which the mortgagee may purchase in his own name and still sue the mortgagor for any deficiency (thereby taking 'both the money and the mud'), see R.W.M. Turner, 21 Virginia L Rev 600 (1935); R.M. Washburn, 53 S Cal L Rev 843 (1980). The English practice in this respect has been described as 'far fairer to the mortgagor' (see *Canada Permanent Trust Co v King Art Developments Ltd* (1985) 12 DLR (4th) 161 at 177 per Moir JA).

19 *Downes v Grazebrook* (1817) 3 Mer 200 at 209, 36 ER 77 at 80; *Australia and New Zealand Banking Group Ltd v Bangadilly Pastoral Co Pty Ltd* (1978) 139 CLR 195 at 225 per Aickin J.

20 *Martinson v Clowes* (1882) 21 Ch D 857 at 860.

1 *Downes v Grazebrook* (1817) 3 Mer 200 at 209, 36 ER 77 at 80; *Whitcomb v Minchin* (1820) 5 Madd 91, 56 ER 830; *Martinson v Clowes* (1882) 21 Ch D 857 at 860.

(ii) Sale to an associated person A more flexible view is taken of a mortgagee's sale to a less closely associated person or entity such as a business acquaintance or a company in which the mortgagee is himself a shareholder. Such a transaction is not necessarily ineffective, but the normal onus of proof is reversed and a burden rests on the mortgagee to demonstrate positively that his 'desire to obtain the best price was given absolute preference over any desire that an associate should obtain a good bargain.'[2] It is simply the case that the court will scrutinise carefully the sale effected by the mortgagee once it appears that the circumstances surrounding that sale tend to impeach his bona fides.[3]

There is, for instance, no hard and fast rule that a mortgagee may not sell to a company in which he is interested.[4] As Lord Templeman ruled in *Tse Kwong Lam v Wong Chit Sen*,[5] the mortgagee and the company seeking to uphold the transaction 'must show that the sale was in good faith and that the mortgagee took reasonable precautions to obtain the best price reasonably obtainable at the time.' In *Tse Kwong Lam*, however, the exercise of the mortgagee's power of sale had taken the form of a public auction at which the only bidder was the mortgagee's wife, acting as the representative of the family company of which both were directors and shareholders.[6] There was no competitive bidding at the auction; the property was purchased at the reserve price which had been fixed by the mortgagee and which was, of course, clearly known to the purchaser; and the purchase was financed from funds provided by the mortgagee himself. In such circumstances the Privy Council had no doubt but that the mortgagee had failed to show that 'in all respects he acted fairly to the borrower and used his best endeavours to obtain the best price reasonably obtainable for the mortgaged property.'[7]

The critical question in every case is whether there was an independent bargain between mortgagee and purchaser.[8] It is open to the court to find that no fair bargain has been proved where, for instance, the selling mortgagee appears to have been 'either consciously or unconsciously overborne' by the fact that the purchaser was a business client and acquaintance of some commercial substance in the local community.[9]

2 *Australia and New Zealand Banking Group Ltd v Bangadilly Pastoral Co Pty Ltd* (1978) 139 CLR 195 at 201 per Jacobs J. See *Tse Kwong Lam v Wong Chit Sen* [1983] 1 WLR 1349 at 1356G-H.

3 *Goldcell Nominees Pty Ltd v Network Finance Ltd* [1983] 2 VR 257 at 263.

4 *Farrar v Farrars Ltd* (1888) 40 Ch D 395 at 409f; *Tse Kwong Lam v Wong Chit Sen* [1983] 1 WLR 1349 at 1355A. See also *Australia and New Zealand Banking Group Ltd v Bangadilly Pastoral Co Pty Ltd* (1978) 139 CLR 195 at 225f, where Aickin J indicated that such a sale 'is not necessarily invalid'.

5 [1983] 1 WLR 1349. See [1984] Conv 143 (P. Jackson).

6 See also *Australia and New Zealand Banking Group Ltd v Bangadilly Pastoral Co Pty Ltd* (1978) 139 CLR 195 (purchase at auction by an associate company controlled by the mortgagee).

7 [1983] 1 WLR 1349 at 1355F-G. 'The close relationship was not fatal but the failure to meet the standard of care required was' (*National Westminster Finance New Zealand Ltd v United Finance & Securities Ltd* [1988] 1 NZLR 226 at 235 per Smellie J).

8 *Australia and New Zealand Banking Group Ltd v Bangadilly Pastoral Co Pty Ltd* (1978) 139 CLR 195 at 227 per Aickin J.

9 *Goldcell Nominees Pty Ltd v Network Finance Ltd* [1983] 2 VR 257 at 274.

(k) Remedies for the mortgagor

The mortgagor's remedies for the improper exercise of the mortgagee's power of sale seem to depend largely on whether the irregularity falls within the category of mere imprudence or carelessness or is more accurately described in terms of bad faith.[10] The remedy of damages is appropriate primarily in the case where the mortgagee has failed to adopt 'such means as would be adopted by a prudent man to get the best price that could be obtained' for the property.[11] The remedy of rescission is usually appropriate only in narrower circumstances of equitable fraud.

(i) Damages for carelessness by the mortgagee Section 104(2) of the Law of Property Act 1925 provides a remedy in damages against the mortgagee in favour of the mortgagor who suffers loss by virtue of an improper exercise of the mortgagee's statutory power of sale. Consistently with this provision, it seems to be accepted that damages represent the appropriate remedy where the mortgagor's complaint is that the selling mortgagee failed to exercise reasonable care to obtain the true market value of the mortgaged property.[12] The measure of damages is prima facie the difference between the market value and the actual sale price,[13] but there must in all cases be clear evidence of a causal link between the mortgagee's breach of duty and the shortfall in the price received for the property.[14]

(ii) Setting aside the sale because of 'fraud on the power' It seems, however, that more far-reaching remedies may be available where the particular exercise of a mortgagee's power of sale goes beyond a case of mere carelessness and is more akin to equitable fraud or a 'fraud on the power'.[15] In this more extreme category of case the mortgagee's sale is liable to be set aside completely, with the result that the mortgagor recovers the equity of redemption of which he has been unjustly deprived.[16] The circumstances

10 In either case the mortgagor may seek an injunction to restrain the completion of any allegedly improper contract of sale entered into by the mortgagee. Some payment into court may be made a condition of this form of relief, but it is unnecessary to show that the purchaser had any knowledge of the alleged impropriety (see *George v Commercial Union Assurance Co of Australia Ltd* (1977) 1 BPR 9649 at 9652). See also *Pasquarella v National Australia Finance Ltd* [1987] 1 NZLR 312 at 315ff.

11 See *Sterne v Victoria & Grey Trust Co* (1985) 14 DLR (4th) 193 at 201f (ante, p 1014).

12 It is significant that only a money remedy was sought (and awarded) in *Cuckmere Brick Co Ltd v Mutual Finance Ltd* [1971] Ch 949 at 958B. See *Brutan Investments Pty Ltd v Underwriting and Insurance Ltd* (1980) 58 FLR 289 at 294f; *Wood v Bank of Nova Scotia* (1981) 112 DLR (3d) 181 at 183. The mortgagor's remedy for a want of 'reasonable care' resulting in a mortgagee's sale at an undervalue is sometimes described in terms of an equitable 'allowance' or account (see *Standard Chartered Bank Ltd v Walker* [1982] 1 WLR 1410 at 1416B; *General Credits (Finance) Pty Ltd v Stoyakovich* [1975] Qd R 352 at 354B-C).

13 *Sterne v Victoria & Grey Trust Co* (1985) 14 DLR (4th) 193 at 204.

14 See eg *Tomlin v Luce* (1889) 43 Ch D 191 at 194; *Cuckmere Brick Co Ltd v Mutual Finance Ltd* [1971] Ch 949 at 966F-967C per Salmon LJ, 977D, 980E-G per Cairns LJ; *Hausman v O'Grady* (1988) 42 DLR (4th) 119 at 132f, affd (1989) 57 DLR (4th) 480.

15 *Forsyth v Blundell* (1973) 129 CLR 477 at 496 per Walsh J; *George v Commercial Union Assurance Co of Australia Ltd* (1977) 1 BPR 9649 at 9652. For the suggestion that the mortgagee's sale may be impeached as a fraudulent conveyance, see J.C. McCoid, 62 Texas L Rev 639 (1983). See also *Durrett v Washington National Insurance Co*, 621 F2d 201 at 204 (1980); *Abramson v Lakewood Bank and Trust Co*, 647 F2d 547 at 549 (1981).

16 *Tse Kwong Lam v Wong Chit Sen* [1983] 1 WLR 1349 at 1359H-1360A.

which merit this more dramatic remedy do not necessarily involve any actual fraud (in the common law sense) or any collusion between the mortgagee and the purchaser,[17] but comprise those cases where the bona fides of the mortgagee has been irreparably placed in question by evidence of his 'wilful or reckless disregard of the interests of the mortgagor',[18] or by his transacting in the face of a clear conflict of interests.[19]

In *Tse Kwong Lam v Wong Chit Sen*[20] the Privy Council held that rescission of the relevant sale would, 'as a general rule', have been the appropriate remedy for the aggrieved mortgagor. However, Lord Templeman imposed the rider that the complainant will be left to a mere remedy in damages if it is 'inequitable as between the borrower and the purchaser for the sale to be set aside.'[1] In *Tse Kwong Lam* the remedy of rescission was indeed rendered inequitable because of the mortgagor's 'inexcusable delay' in prosecuting his counterclaim. The mortgagor was thus relegated to damages, which were measured as the difference between the actual sale price and the best price reasonably obtainable at the date of sale.[2]

(3) Appointment of a receiver

The option of appointing a receiver provides the mortgagee with a further remedy for default by his mortgagor which is rather different from either the remedy of action on the mortgagor's personal covenant or the remedy of forced sale.

(a) Preconditions for appointment

The mortgagee has a statutory power to appoint in writing such person as he thinks fit to act as a receiver of the income of the mortgaged property.[3] This power becomes available in the same circumstances and on the same conditions as those which cause the statutory power of sale to arise and to become exercisable.[4]

17 There must, however, be evidence that the purchaser either knew or ought to have known of the circumstances giving rise to the impropriety alleged against the mortgagee (see *Forsyth v Blundell* (1973) 129 CLR 477 at 497 per Walsh J; *George v Commercial Union Assurance Co of Australia Ltd* (1977) 1 BPR 9649 at 9652; *McKean v Maloney* [1988] 1 Qd R 628 at 635).

18 *Forsyth v Blundell* (1973) 129 CLR 477 at 496. See *Brutan Investments Pty Ltd v Underwriting and Insurance Ltd* (1980) 58 FLR 289 at 295f.

19 See eg *Goldcell Nominees Pty Ltd v Network Finance Ltd* [1983] 2 VR 257 at 278f.

20 [1983] 1 WLR 1349 at 1359H.

1 [1983] 1 WLR 1349 at 1360A.

2 [1983] 1 WLR 1360H. The damages award of HK $950,000 can only have been a fraction of the hearing-date value of the land which the mortgagor had effectively hoped to recover through an award of rescission.

3 Law of Property Act 1925, ss 101(1)(iii), 109(1).

4 Law of Property Act 1925, s 109(1). Thus a receiver cannot be appointed while the mortgagor still has a legal right to redeem the mortgage eg in advance of a legal redemption date which has been clearly stipulated in the mortgage (see *Twentieth Century Banking Corpn Ltd v Wilkinson* [1977] Ch 99 at 104D). However, the mere fact that a mortgagee has gone into possession does not preclude his appointment of a receiver (see *Refuge Assurance Co Ltd v Pearlberg* [1938] Ch 687 at 693), although in registered land the mortgagee must first be registered as the proprietor of a charge over the property (see *Lever Finance Ltd v L.N. & H.M. Needleman's Trustee* [1956] Ch 375 at 382).

(b) Functions of the receiver

The appointment of a receiver may be particularly useful if the mortgagee does not presently wish to realise his security or otherwise undertake the responsibility of going into possession of the mortgaged property.[5] The duty of the receiver is to collect all the income derived from the mortgaged land and to ensure that from that income there is payment of all sums due by way of rents, rates, taxes, his own commission, insurance premiums, repairs and, of course, interest owing under the mortgage.[6] Any surplus income is payable to the person, usually the mortgagor, who would otherwise have been entitled to the rents and profits of the property.[7]

(c) Liability for the receiver's actions

The receiver is deemed by statute to be the agent of the *mortgagor*.[8] It follows therefore that, unless the mortgage deed otherwise provides, the mortgagor becomes solely liable for any acts or defaults of the receiver even though he has had no hand in his appointment.[9] The mortgagee is not responsible for what the receiver does whilst he is the mortgagor's agent unless the mortgagee directs or interferes with the receiver's activities.[10]

(4) Foreclosure

Foreclosure is the most draconian remedy open to the mortgagee in the event of default by his mortgagor. An order for foreclosure effectively abrogates the mortgagor's equity of redemption and leaves the entire value of the mortgaged property in the hands of the mortgagee. Foreclosure is thus directed primarily at the recovery of the mortgagee's capital investment. In spite of its theoretical potency, however, resort to the remedy of foreclosure is now extremely rare in English courts. As Nicholls V-C observed in *Palk v Mortgage Services Funding Plc*,[11] 'foreclosure actions are almost unheard of today and have been so for many years'.

(a) Legal effects of foreclosure

Unlike the exercise of the statutory power of sale, the drastic remedy of foreclosure requires the interposition of some judicial control and is therefore

5 See *Visbord v Federal Commissioner of Taxation* (1943) 68 CLR 354 at 381. A receiver is not governed by the strict liability for wilful default which attaches to a mortgagee who enters into possession (ante, p 987).
6 Law of Property Act 1925, s 109(8). See *Marshall v Cottingham* [1982] Ch 82.
7 Law of Property Act 1925, s 109(8).
8 Law of Property Act 1925, s 109(2). The receiver's deemed agency is necessarily terminated by the winding up of a company mortgagor (*Gosling v Gaskell* [1897] AC 575 at 581, 585, 591f; *Thomas v Todd* [1926] 2 KB 511 at 516f). In such an event, however, the receiver may be able to continue the mortgagor's business on the basis that the mortgagee has entered into possession and given authority to the receiver to act as agent for the *mortgagee* (see *Mercantile Credits Ltd v Atkins* (1985) 1 NSWLR 670 at 679C).
9 Law of Property Act 1925, s 109(2). See eg *White v Metcalf* [1903] 2 Ch 567 at 570ff.
10 *American Express International Banking Corp v Hurley* [1985] 3 All ER 564 at 571g.
11 [1993] 2 WLR 415 at 419E.

available only on application to the court.[12] A court order for *foreclosure absolute* operates to vest the mortgagor's entire estate (whether freehold or leasehold) in the mortgagee, without compensation for the mortgagor and subject only to those legal mortgages which have priority to the mortgage in respect of which the foreclosure has been obtained.[13]

Notwithstanding that he has obtained foreclosure absolute, the mortgagee may still sue the mortgagor on his personal covenant to repay,[14] provided the mortgagee retains the mortgaged property in his possession.[15] The mortgagee is, however, precluded from such action if, having foreclosed, he then sells the property to a third party.[16] In this event it is plainly inequitable that the mortgagee should be allowed to continue to pursue the mortgagor for any deficiency resulting from the sale.[17] The mortgagee who sells following a foreclosure is not subject to the same duty of care which weighs upon the mortgagee who exercises a statutory power of sale.[18] It would therefore be grossly unfair to hold the foreclosing mortgagee to be unaccountable to the mortgagor in the matter of the price achieved by the sale yet able to recover from the latter any shortfall which supposedly remains.[19]

(b) *Preconditions of foreclosure*

The mortgagee cannot resort to foreclosure as a remedy until, at the very least, the mortgagor has ceased to have any legal right to redeem the mortgage. Only then does the mortgagor acquire his 'equity' to redeem the mortgage, and it is the possible extinguishment of this equity which is in question in foreclosure proceedings.

Where a mortgage contains an express proviso for redemption, the mortgagor's legal right to redeem is lost only when he fails to comply with the terms of that proviso.[20] The mortgagor's legal right to redeem clearly

12 *Ness v O'Neil* [1916] 1 KB 706 at 709. To the general rule there are statutory exceptions of very minor significance (see eg Small Dwellings Acquisition Act 1899, s 5(1)).

13 Law of Property Act 1925, ss 88(2), 89(2). (All subsequent mortgage terms or charges are statutorily extinguished by the foreclosure.) In registered land the order for foreclosure is completed by the cancellation of the registered charge and the registration of the former chargee as the sole proprietor of the land (Land Registration Act 1925, s 34(3)).

14 That is, he may have 'both the money and the mud' (see *Canada Permanent Trust Co v King Art Developments Ltd* (1985) 12 DLR (4th) 161 at 173 per Moir JA).

15 *Kinnaird v Trollope* (1888) 39 Ch D 636 at 642. However, such further action on the mortgagor's covenant gives the latter a new equity of redemption (see *Lockhart v Hardy* (1846) 9 Beav 349 at 356, 50 ER 378 at 380; *Palmer v Hendrie* (1859) 27 Beav 349 at 351, 54 ER 136 at 137). In some jurisdictions the mere fact of foreclosure extinguishes any further capacity to sue on the mortgagor's covenant to repay (see eg Manitoba's Mortgage Act (RSM 1970, c M200), s 16; *Manitoba Development Corp v Berkowits* (1980) 101 DLR (3d) 421 at 422ff).

16 *Perry v Barker* (1806) 13 Ves 198 at 205, 33 ER 269 at 272; *Kinnaird v Trollope* (1888) 39 Ch D 636 at 642; *Gordon Grant & Co Ltd v Boos* [1926] AC 781 at 784ff; *Lloyds and Scottish Trust Ltd v Britten* (1982) 44 P & CR 249 at 256f; *Burnham v Galt* (1869) 16 Gr 417 at 419.

17 Not only is the property no longer available in the mortgagee's hands for valuation (see *Gordon Grant & Co Ltd v Boos* [1926] AC 781 at 785 per Lord Phillimore). The mortgagee is now unable in any event to return the land on full payment by the mortgagor (see *Rushton v Industrial Development Bank* (1973) 34 DLR (3d) 582 at 589 per Laskin J; *Campbell Sharp Ltd v Caisse Populaire de St Boniface Ltee* (1984) 9 DLR (4th) 32 at 35).

18 Ante, p 1012.

19 See *Bank of Nova Scotia v Dorval* (1980) 104 DLR (3d) 121 at 125.

20 *Twentieth Century Banking Corpn Ltd v Wilkinson* [1977] Ch 99 at 105A.

ceases, for instance, if the date set at law for redemption has already passed.[1] Likewise, the mortgagor puts himself in breach of a proviso for redemption if his legal right to redeem was explicitly made conditional on the punctual payment of capital and interest and he has defaulted in this respect.[2] However, even if the mortgage contains no express proviso for redemption, the court can still order a foreclosure if the mortgagor's default is of such a nature as to bar him at law from recovering his property and to justify the court in extinguishing his equity of redemption.[3] In this respect a mortgagee may be able to obtain a foreclosure even though the circumstances fall short of those which entitle him to exercise his statutory power to sell or to appoint a receiver.[4]

(c) Procedure of foreclosure

Foreclosure proceedings are normally conducted in the High Court. If the court decides to grant an order for foreclosure, it first makes an order for *foreclosure nisi*. This order directs that accounts be taken and provides that unless the mortgagor repays the mortgage moneys due within a period stipulated by the court,[5] the mortgage will be foreclosed. If no such payment is forthcoming, the court makes an order for *foreclosure absolute*, which has the effect of transferring the mortgagor's estate to the mortgagee. However, during the interim between the order nisi and the order absolute, it is open to the mortgagor or the mortgagee to apply to the court for an order directing a sale of the property rather than foreclosure.[6] This alternative form of order may be granted in the discretion of the court,[7] and has the consequence that at least part of the value of the mortgaged property may be salvaged for the mortgagor.

Even after the court has made an order for foreclosure absolute, it is possible for the mortgagor to request the court to 're-open' the order.[8] The court thus has even further discretion to prevent the final destruction of the mortgagor's equity of redemption.[9] The remedy of foreclosure becomes statute-barred twelve years after the date when the relevant mortgage moneys fell due.[10]

1 Ante, p 941.
2 See eg *Kidderminster Mutual Benefit Building Society v Haddock* [1936] WN 158. Compare the refusal to order foreclosure in *Williams v Morgan* [1906] 1 Ch 804 at 810, where the express proviso for redemption clearly preserved the mortgagor's right to redeem at law until a stipulated date irrespective of prior default.
3 *Twentieth Century Banking Corpn Ltd v Wilkinson* [1977] Ch 99 at 105A-C.
4 See *Twentieth Century Banking Corpn Ltd v Wilkinson* [1977] Ch 99 at 104E-F. Ironically, if the mortgagee can show himself entitled to foreclosure, the court has a discretion to direct a sale anyway (Law of Property Act 1925, s 91(2)).
5 This period is usually six months.
6 Law of Property Act 1925, s 91(2).
7 In practice the court will normally direct a sale contrary to the wishes of a mortgagee only if repayment of his debt is fully secured (see *Palk v Mortgage Services Funding Plc* [1993] 2 WLR 415 at 418H-419A per Nicholls V-C).
8 A mortgagor's application to re-open an order for foreclosure absolute may be registrable as a pending land action, thereby guarding against the possibility that the mortgagee may proceed with a sale of the foreclosed property (see *Re Pacific Savings & Mortgage Corp and Can-Corp Development Ltd* (1982) 135 DLR (3d) 623 at 640).
9 See *Campbell v Holyland* (1877) 7 Ch D 166 at 172ff per Jessel MR.
10 Limitation Act 1980, s 15(1).

(d) Modern incidence of foreclosure

Foreclosure is rarely sought today, and even more rarely granted.[11] It is usually much more convenient for the mortgagee to appoint a receiver or to exercise his statutory power of sale.[12] Moreover, the court's powers to stay possession proceedings under section 36 of the Administration of Justice Act 1970 have now been extended to actions for foreclosure.[13] The courts have been increasingly reluctant to grant orders for foreclosure, particularly in the context of a rapidly rising property market, because an order for foreclosure may have the effect of transferring to the mortgagee a much more valuable property than the property over which he initially took his security. In such circumstances foreclosure would confer an increasingly valuable asset on the mortgagee at what must inevitably be a substantial undervalue.

10. REMEDIES AVAILABLE TO THE EQUITABLE MORTGAGEE

The remedies available to an equitable mortgagee differ in some respects from those which are open to a legal mortgagee, largely because the equitable mortgagee takes no legal estate or interest in the land offered as security. The equitable nature of the security, although not affecting the mortgagee's ability to sue on the mortgagor's personal covenant to repay, nevertheless has the following repercussions.

(1) Exercise of the power of sale

The statutory power of sale conferred by section 101(1) of the Law of Property Act 1925 is available in respect of any mortgage which has been effected by deed.[14] Thus some equitable mortgagees may have access to the statutory power,[15] but most equitable mortgagees are excluded from exercising the statutory power on the ground that their mortgages were effected by purely informal means.[16] Such mortgagees have no automatic right to sell, but are entitled to apply to the court under section 91 of the Law of Property Act 1925, and the court may in its discretion direct either that the mortgaged property be sold[17] or that a legal term of years be vested in the mortgagee,

11 The Law Commission has proposed that the remedy of foreclosure should be abolished (see Law Com No 204 (1991), para 7.27).

12 *Palk v Mortgage Services Funding Plc* [1993] 2 WLR 415 at 419E-F per Nicholls V-C.

13 Administration of Justice Act 1970, s 36, as amended by Administration of Justice Act 1973, s 8(2) (post, p 995).

14 Ante, p 1003. If the statutory power is available, it is possible that the equitable mortgagee is competent to convey the full *legal* estate of his mortgagor (see *In re White Rose Cottage* [1965] Ch 940 at 951C; but compare *In re Hodson and Howe's Contract* (1887) 35 Ch D 668 at 671, 673). The matter may be put beyond doubt by conferring on the mortgagee an irrevocable power of attorney to convey the mortgagor's legal estate.

15 Sale with vacant possession may, however, provide some problem since it is not entirely clear that an equitable mortgagee has the same right to possession as a legal mortgagee (ante, p 990).

16 This exclusion would not, of course, apply where the equitable mortgage was effected by a memorandum of deposit in the form of a deed (ante, p 943).

17 Law of Property Act 1925, s 91(2).

thereby converting him into a legal mortgagee for the purpose of entitlement to exercise the statutory power of sale.[18] An equitable chargee likewise has no automatic power of sale, but may nevertheless request the court for an order for sale.[19]

(2) Appointment of a receiver

The statutory power to appoint a receiver is available only in respect of mortgages created by deed,[20] but in the absence of such creation the court may be asked to appoint a receiver.[1]

(3) Foreclosure

The court has power to order foreclosure of an equitable mortgage or to order a judicial sale in lieu of foreclosure.[2] In the case of an equitable mortgage, however, foreclosure takes the form of a court order that the mortgagor convey the legal title in the mortgaged property into the name of the mortgagee.

11. PRIORITY OF MORTGAGES

There is, of course, nothing inherently improper in multiple mortgages of realty, the only limiting factor usually being the capacity for further commercial exploitation of the remaining 'equity' in the property. Sometimes, however, difficult questions of priority may arise where the same land has been mortgaged more than once to different mortgagees simultaneously. If these mortgages remain outstanding and the security eventually proves inadequate to satisfy all due financial claims, some order must be established for giving effect to the respective rights of the mortgagees. The arrangement of priorities will ultimately determine the extent to which any particular mortgagee's loan is repaid from the available money proceeds of the land.[3]

The essential issue of priority concerns the preference to be made between the claims of two mortgagees, eg M1 and M2, who have in that order taken successive mortgages over the same realty. M1 and M2 may have taken their respective mortgages over either a legal estate or an equitable interest in the mortgagor's land. A mortgage of an equitable interest generates, of course, only an equitable mortgage, but a mortgage of a legal estate may,

18 Law of Property Act 1925, s 91(7).

19 See *Matthews v Goodday* (1861) 31 LJ Ch 282 at 283; *London County and Westminster Bank Ltd v Tompkins* [1918] 1 KB 515 at 528. See also Law of Property Act 1925, s 90(1); *Ladup Ltd v Williams & Glyn's Bank Plc* [1985] 1 WLR 851 at 855B-C.

20 Law of Property Act 1925, s 101(1)(iii).

1 Supreme Court Act 1981, s 37(1), (2), formerly Supreme Court of Judicature (Consolidation) Act 1925, s 45. See *Shakel v Duke of Marlborough* (1819) 4 Madd 463, 56 ER 776.

2 *James v James* (1873) LR 16 Eq 153 at 154. However, a mere equitable chargee cannot foreclose (see *Tennant v Trenchard* (1869) 4 Ch App 537 at 542; *Ladup Ltd v Williams & Glyn's Bank Plc* [1985] 1 WLR 851 at 855B), but can only seek a court order for sale in lieu of foreclosure.

3 Perhaps surprisingly some of the problems disclosed in the law relating to priority have yet to be resolved—which may indicate that in practice the more complex issues of priority arise only infrequently.

in accordance with the precise mode of mortgage employed,[4] produce either a legal or an equitable security. To compound the potential for confusion, the mortgagor's land may be held under a registered title or may yet remain unregistered land.

The English law of priority effectively lays down two large codes or rule-systems for ascertaining priority,[5] the application of these rules depending on whether the earlier mortgagee, M1, took a mortgage over a legal estate in the mortgagor's land or merely a mortgage over an equitable interest. In other words, the definitive element in determining which rule-system should be applied is not the legal or equitable quality of the mortgage received by the lender, but rather the legal or equitable quality of the estate or interest offered as security.

(1) Mortgages of a legal estate

Where a mortgagee, M1, takes his mortgage over a legal estate of the mortgagor, the next critical distinction turns on whether the property offered as his security was unregistered or registered land.

(a) Unregistered land

As described earlier in this chapter,[6] the mortgagee of unregistered land is, in certain circumstances, entitled to the additional security of retention of the title deeds relating to the mortgagor's property. The detailed application of the priority rules now depends on whether (as may well be the case) documents of title were deposited with M1 when he took his mortgage.

(i) Deposit of title deeds with prior mortgagee Where M1's mortgage was protected by the deposit of title deeds, the next crucial variable concerns the precise quality or form of security taken by him in relation to the mortgagor's legal estate. M1 may have taken either a *legal* mortgage or an *equitable* mortgage.[7]

M1 has a legal mortgage—If M1 took a legal mortgage protected by a deposit of title documents, his mortgage is virtually inviolable by any competing claim to priority made on behalf of a later mortgagee, M2. Even if M2 likewise took a legal mortgage, M1's security binds the world and, by virtue of prior creation, must inevitably rank ahead of the security taken by M2. It is nothing to the point that M2 may not have known of the earlier mortgage, although the fact that the mortgagor no longer retained the title documents should in practice have indicated the possibility of a prior incumbrance. Legal rights have an overriding quality irrespective of notice. If, by contrast, M2 took only an *equitable* mortgage, the same priority for M1 follows a fortiori.

The only circumstances in which M1's earlier legal mortgage can lose

4 Ante, p 939.

5 Somewhat different rules govern mortgages created prior to 1926, but such mortgages are now so freakishly rare that the description here will be confined to the rules relating to mortgages made after 1925.

6 Ante, p 981.

7 The conditions which determine whether a mortgage of a legal estate is either a legal or an equitable mortgage were discussed earlier (p 939).

priority to M2 are those rare cases in which M1 can be said to have forfeited his natural priority on grounds of fraud, misrepresentation or gross negligence. Fraud would vitiate M1's claim to priority if, for instance, it emerged that M1 had colluded with the mortgagor in order to enable the latter to borrow further funds.[8] Misrepresentation may occur if M1, by leaving title deeds in the hands of the mortgagor, enabled the mortgagor to make unauthorised borrowings from later mortgagees.[9] Gross negligence may be present where, for instance, M1 fails to check that he has received all the relevant deeds and the mortgagor is thereby able to create further mortgages.[10]

M1 has an equitable mortgage — If M1 took an equitable mortgage protected by a deposit of title documents,[11] the issue of priority as against M2 depends on the legal or equitable quality of the mortgage taken by the later mortgagee. Where M2's mortgage is *legal*, the conflicting claims ought to be resolved by an application of the doctrine of notice. Although M1's mortgage is earlier in time, it should lose priority to M2's legal mortgage, provided at any rate that M2 took his mortgage without actual or constructive notice of the earlier incumbrance.[12] If the issue does indeed rest on constructive notice, much may turn on whether the mortgagor's obvious inability to give access to the relevant title deeds can be said to have put M2 on inquiry. However, the case law in this area often seems to disavow the strict relevance of constructive notice,[13] focusing instead on whether the later mortgagee, by grossly negligent investigation of the mortgagor's title, has been guilty of postponing conduct.[14] In this respect the courts have tended to treat later legal mortgagees with substantial lenience,[15] postponing claims only where it is clear that the legal mortgagee has acted with extreme imprudence.[16]

Where M1 has taken an equitable mortgage protected by a deposit of title documents and M2's later mortgage is likewise *equitable*, M1's security generally overrides that taken by M2. 'Where the equities are equal, the first in time prevails'. The chronological priority of M1's mortgage ensures that M1 must rank ahead of M2, unless M1 has forfeited this privilege by fraud, misrepresentation or gross negligence (eg in failing to retain deeds securely).[17]

8 See *Peter v Russel* (1716) 1 Eq Cas Abr 321 at 322, 21 ER 1075.
9 See *Perry Herrick v Attwood* (1857) 2 De G & J 21 at 39, 44 ER 895 at 902; *Jones v Rhind* (1869) 17 WR 1091.
10 See *Walker v Linom* [1907] 2 Ch 104 at 114ff. Compare, however, *Northern Counties of England Fire Insurance Co v Whipp* (1884) 26 Ch D 482 at 494f (no postponing conduct where mortgagor was allowed access to the safe in which the title deeds were held).
11 Ante, p 944.
12 *Brace v Duchess of Marlborough* (1728) 2 P Wms 491 at 493ff, 24 ER 829 at 830f.
13 See eg *Oliver v Hinton* [1899] 2 Ch 264 at 273 per Lindley MR.
14 See eg *Hewitt v Loosemore* (1851) 9 Hare 449 at 458, 68 ER 586 at 590, where Turner V-C considered that nothing short of 'fraud or gross and wilful negligence' in the later mortgagee would be sufficient to cause priority to be conceded to an earlier equitable mortgagee.
15 See *Hewitt v Loosemore* (1851) 9 Hare 449 at 456ff, 68 ER 586 at 589f; *Agra Bank Ltd v Barry* (1874) LR 7 HL 135 at 150ff.
16 See *Oliver v Hinton* [1899] 2 Ch 264 at 274, where Lindley MR indicated that the subsequent purchaser should lose priority only if 'guilty of such gross negligence as would render it unjust to deprive the prior incumbrancer of his priority.'
17 See *Taylor v Russell* [1891] 1 Ch 8 at 17.

(ii) No deposit of title deeds with prior mortgagee If M1 received no title documents on taking his mortgage, it matters not for priority purposes whether his mortgage is a legal mortgage or an equitable mortgage. In either case M1's mortgage, being unprotected by a deposit of deeds, depends vitally on registration under the Land Charges Act 1972.[18] A legal mortgage unaccompanied by a deposit of title documents ranks as a Class C(i) charge (or 'puisne mortgage').[19] A similar but equitable mortgage constitutes a Class C(iii) charge (or 'general equitable charge').[20]

In order to achieve priority over M2, M1 must register his mortgage appropriately under one or other head, in which case the registered charge acquires irreversible priority over any later mortgage taken by M2.[1] Any failure to secure the appropriate protection through registration renders M1's mortgage statutorily void against M2, since M2 ranks for this purpose as 'a purchaser of the land'.[2]

(b) Registered land

If M1 takes a charge over a legal estate in registered land, issues of priority will turn on whether his charge was legal or equitable.

(i) Legal charge The only formal method of mortgaging a legal estate in registered land is by way of 'registered charge'.[3] A legal mortgage of registered land is completed (ie becomes fully effective) only when the chargee is entered in the land register as the 'proprietor' of the relevant charge.[4] It is, of course, possible to create a number of registered charges in respect of the same title. However, the Land Registration Act 1925 indicates that, subject to any contrary entry on the register, registered charges 'rank according to the order in which they are entered on the register, and not according to the order in which they are created'.[5]

Thus, if M1 has been registered as proprietor of a charge, his mortgage must normally take priority over any similar registered charge which M2 subsequently enters on the register, irrespective of the chronological order in which the charges were created. M1's charge clearly takes priority over any equitable mortgage created later than the date of entry of his own

18 It is generally assumed nowadays that the registration requirements of the Land Charges Act 1972 take precedence over Law of Property Act 1925, s 97, which seems to indicate that priority as between competing mortgages unprotected by the deposit of title documents depends on the date of land charge registration. If priority were governed by section 97, M1's mortgage (if registered first) would rank ahead of M2's mortgage even if M1 had failed to register by the date on which M2's mortgage was created. Pursuant to section 4(5) of the 1972 Act, however, such failure renders M1's charge void. It is widely believed that the apparently conflicting provision in section 97 cannot have been intended to reactivate a charge which has been statutorily declared 'void'. See, however, R.E. Megarry, [1940] CLJ 243 at 255f ('the subject is not one for dogmatism'). See also J. Howell, [1993] Conv 22.

19 Ante, p 140.

20 Ante, p 141.

1 Ante, p 118.

2 Land Charges Act 1972, s 4(5). A 'purchaser' is defined as connoting any person (including a mortgagee) who gives 'valuable consideration' (Land Charges Act 1972, s 17(1)).

3 Ante, pp 228, 940.

4 Land Registration Act 1925, s 26(1).

5 Land Registration Act 1925, s 29.

registered charge and also, perhaps less obviously, over any mortgage which was created earlier but which was not protected as a minor interest[6] or under section 70(1)(g) of the Land Registration Act 1925.[7]

(ii) Equitable charge It is, of course, possible that the security taken by a mortgagee of a legal estate in registered land may comprise only an equitable charge over the land. Such a result must inevitably follow in any case where the chargee does not obtain entry in the register of title as 'proprietor' of a registered charge.[8] An equitable charge likewise arises where the mortgagor has merely contracted to charge his land or has deposited his land certificate with the chargee as security.[9]

Unless completed by registration, an equitable charge over a legal estate in registered land constitutes a minor interest and requires protection by the entry of a notice or caution in the chargor's register of title.[10] Thus if M1 duly protects his equitable charge, it acquires automatic priority over any charge (whether legal or equitable) later taken by M2. All later transactions with the mortgagor's registered title are inevitably subject to minor interests already protected by entry on the register.[11]

The position is, of course, quite different if M1 fails to secure the appropriate register entry in respect of his equitable charge. In these circumstances it is clear that M1 must lose priority if a later mortgagee, M2, takes a *legal* charge over the registered land. Such a charge can take effect only by way of a registered disposition to M2 as registered proprietor of the charge. Section 59(6) of the Land Registration Act 1925 confirms that, except in the case of fraud, a purchaser acquiring title under a registered disposition 'shall not be concerned with' any claim or interest (other than an overriding interest) which is not protected by entry on the register 'whether he has or has not notice thereof, express, implied, or constructive.'[12]

It is possible, however, that the issue of priority may arise in circumstances where both M1 and M2 have equitable charges, neither of which has yet been protected by due entry in the register. The contest between M1 and M2 is not resolved by reference to the usual rule that 'where the equities are equal, the first in time prevails'. Instead priority is given to M1's charge on the ground of its earlier creation and this priority remains entirely unaffected by the possibility that M2's charge (although created later) may at some future date be the first to reach the register.[13] The firm priority thereby accorded earlier creation gives way only if M1 has behaved fraudulently or negligently or is estopped from asserting priority by reason

6 Ante, p 181.
7 Ante, p 203. It would, of course, be highly unusual—although not impossible—for an equitable chargee to be in 'actual occupation' of the mortgagor's land.
8 Pending due entry of a registrable charge in the register, it is clear law that the charge ranks only as an equitable charge (Land Registration Act 1925, s 106(2)(a)).
9 Ante, p 943.
10 Land Registration Act 1925, s 106(3).
11 Ante, p 186.
12 Ante, p 187.
13 Ante, p 186.

of any conduct which induced M2 to act to his detriment in acquiring his later charge.[14]

(2) Mortgages of an equitable interest

A mortgage of an equitable interest in land can itself be equitable only.[15] Where the same equitable interest has been the subject of successive mortgages, it is well settled that the priority accorded to these mortgages is not governed by any rule of registration or even by the chronological order in which the mortgages were created. Instead priority is fixed in accordance with the rather different effects of the rule in *Dearle v Hall*.[16]

(a) Unregistered land

Under the rule in *Dearle v Hall* priority between competing mortgages of an equitable interest is determined essentially by the order in which notice of these mortgages is received by the trustees of the land concerned.[17] The rule applied originally only to mortgages of pure personalty, but its application was extended to mortgages of equitable interests in realty by section 137 of the Law of Property Act 1925. Under the rule, as amended by section 137, notice must now be given in writing[18] and the notice must be 'served' on the relevant trustees.[19]

The critical factor under the rule in *Dearle v Hall* concerns the order of *receipt* of notices, not the order in which notices may have been given or sent.[20] It is not even necessary that a notice of mortgage should emanate from the mortgagee himself: it is sufficient if the trustees receive a written notice from some other source.[1] It is important, however, that a notice should be served on all of the relevant trustees in existence at the time, since only

14 See *Abigail v Lapin* [1934] AC 491 at 500ff; *Barclays Bank Ltd v Taylor* [1974] Ch 137 at 147E; *Strand Securities Ltd v Caswell* [1965] Ch 958 at 991B. The Law Commission has recommended that the existing rules as to the priority of minor interests should be reversed so that the priority of such interests inter se would normally be governed by their order of protection on the register (Law Com No 158, para 4.98). See Draft Land Registration Bill, clause 9(2) (Law Commission, Law Com No 173 (1988), Appendix).

15 Ante, p 943.

16 (1823) 3 Russ 1, 38 ER 475. Mortgages of a beneficial interest under a trust for sale or strict settlement are not capable of registration under the Land Charges Act 1972 (see Land Charges Act 1972, s 2(4)(iii)(b), ante, p 141).

17 Section 137(2) of the Law of Property Act 1925 confirms that, in the case of land held on trust for sale, the relevant trustees are the trustees for sale (ante, p 538) and in the context of settled land, notice must be served on the trustees of the strict settlement (ante, p 623).

18 Law of Property Act 1925, s 137(3).

19 Law of Property Act 1925, s 137(2). If the giving of notice proves unduly difficult or cannot be achieved without 'unreasonable cost or delay', the mortgagee may require that a memorandum of the dealing be endorsed on the instrument creating the trust (Law of Property Act 1925, s 137(4). Such endorsement is acceptable as the equivalent of notice.

20 If, however, two or more notices are received simultaneously, priority is governed by the order in which the relevant mortgages were actually created (see *Calisher v Forbes* (1871) LR 7 Ch App 109 at 113f).

1 See eg *Ipswich Permanent Money Club Ltd v Arthy* [1920] 2 Ch 257 (notice sent by another mortgagee).

such a notice can guarantee priority in every event. A notice given to all the trustees remains effective notwithstanding that the recipients later die or retire without communicating the notice to those trustees who take their place.[2] A notice given to only one trustee protects any mortgage which is created during his trusteeship,[3] but normally ceases to be effective thereafter.[4]

There is one exception to the basic rule of priority established in *Dearle v Hall*. No mortgagee can ever secure priority if, at the time of making the loan, he knew (or should have known) of the existence of a prior mortgage created in favour of another creditor.[5] It would clearly be inequitable that, by the mere device of serving notice first, the later mortgagee should steal priority over an earlier mortgage of which he was (or ought to have been) fully aware. In effect, therefore, the rule in *Dearle v Hall* accords priority only to mortgagees who have no actual or constructive knowledge of prior incumbrances. It is irrelevant, however, if knowledge of an earlier mortgage reaches the later mortgagee *after* he takes his own mortgage but *before* he serves his notice on the trustees.[6]

(b) Registered land

The priority enjoyed by successive assignments of a beneficial interest in registered land used to be determined by the order of entry in the Index of Minor Interests maintained by the Land Registry.[7] This Index has now been abolished,[8] with the result that in registered land also the issue of priority as between competing mortgages of an equitable interest is now determined with reference to the rule in *Dearle v Hall*.

(3) Tacking of further advances

In some circumstances a prior mortgagee may be able to gain an enhanced priority by 'tacking' to his own original loan a further loan to the mortgagor which is not made until *after* a second mortgagee has already taken a security over the same land. The tacking of a further advance effectively increases the loan sum for which the earlier mortgagee may claim priority, thereby diminishing the real value of the security taken by the later mortgagee.

In unregistered land a prior mortgagee has a statutory right[9] to make a further advance in priority to a subsequent mortgagee (whether legal or equitable) either by agreement with that mortgagee or if the prior mortgagee

2 See *In re Wasdale* [1899] 1 Ch 163 at 166f.
3 *Ward v Duncombe* [1893] AC 369 at 382, 395. Priority for such a mortgage is retained even after the termination of the trusteeship of the recipient.
4 Notice given to only one of several trustees becomes ineffective on the recipient's death or retirement unless, in the intervening period, the notice has been communicated to at least one other surviving trustee (see *Timson v Ramsbottom* (1836) 2 Keen 35 at 52f, 48 ER 541 at 548; *In re Phillips' Trusts* [1903] 1 Ch 183 at 186f).
5 *In re Holmes* (1885) 29 Ch D 786 at 788f.
6 *Mutual Life Assurance Society v Langley* (1886) 32 Ch D 460 at 467f.
7 Land Registration Act 1925, s 102(2).
8 See Land Registration Act 1986, s 5.
9 Law of Property Act 1925, s 94(1).

had no notice of the later mortgage when making the further advance[10] or if (in any event) the prior mortgage imposes an obligation to make further advances.

In registered land, where a prior mortgage was made for securing further advances and has been substantively registered, the prior mortgagee may tack further advances until such time as the Registrar gives notice of his intention to enter in the register a later mortgage which 'would prejudicially affect the priority of any further advance'.[11] Where, however, the prior registered chargee is under an obligation, 'noted on the register', to make a further advance, any subsequent charge must take subject to any further advance which is made pursuant to that obligation.[12]

12. REFORM OF THE LAW OF MORTGAGES

In 1991 the Law Commission published a substantial report (accompanied by a Draft Bill)[13] in which was proposed a fundamental structural reform of the existing law of mortgage. In view of the Commission, the current law of mortgage is unnecessarily complex, confusing and artificial.[14] The Commission therefore recommended that all existing methods of consensual mortgage or charge over land should be abolished and replaced by two new standardised forms of mortgage, the 'formal land mortgage' and the 'informal land mortgage'.[15] Both kinds of mortgage are envisaged as having attributes expressly defined de novo by statute,[16] and, if the Commission's proposals are enacted by Parliament, will comprise the only permissible methods of mortgaging any interest in land.

(1) The guiding principle of the reformed law of mortgage

Underlying the entire new law of mortgage is the guiding principle that 'the only function of the mortgaged property is to provide security for the performance of the mortgagor's payment obligations.'[17] Thus, in the case of both the formal and the informal mortgage, the rights, remedies and powers of the mortgagee will be exercisable only in good faith and for the purpose of protecting or enforcing the security.[18]

10 Registration of the subsequent mortgage will normally constitute sufficient notice to preclude tacking (Law of Property Act 1925, s 198(1)). However, if the prior mortgage was expressed to be made for securing further advances, the prior mortgagee will not be affected by any *deemed* notice under section 198, but only by actual or constructive notice of the subsequent mortgage which arises independently of the fact of registration (Law of Property Act 1925, s 94(2)). In practice subsequent mortgagees take care to give the prior mortgagee express notice of their own mortgages, since this effectively prevents tacking.

11 Land Registration Act 1925, s 30(1).

12 Land Registration Act 1925, s 30(3).

13 Law Commission, *Transfer of Land—Land Mortgages* (Law Com No 204, 13 November 1991). The Report was preceded by *Land Mortgages* (Law Commission Working Paper No 99, August 1986).

14 Law Com No 204 (1991), paras 2.1ff.

15 Law Com No 204 (1991), para 2.30.

16 Law Com No 204 (1991), para 3.1.

17 Law Com No 204 (1991), para 3.2.

18 Law Com No 204 (1991), para 3.4.

(2) The formal land mortgage

The *formal land mortgage* is to be available for use over any interest in land whether legal or equitable, but requires to be made by deed.[19] Where the land is registered, the formal land mortgage must also be substantively registered against the relevant title in the land register,[20] and priority will be determined by the date of registration.[1] In unregistered land all formal land mortgages of a legal estate or a commercial equitable interest will rank as registrable land charges of Class C(i).[2]

(3) The informal land mortgage

By contrast an *informal land mortgage* can be created either by deed or by mere signed writing.[3] The informal land mortgage is not intended to give the mortgagee any right to enforce the security or to take other action in relation to the mortgaged property, but merely entitles the mortgagee to have the mortgage perfected by the grant of a formal land mortgage.[4] In registered land an informal land mortgage of a legal estate will be protectible by the entry of a notice or caution, priority being governed by the rules which currently apply to minor interests.[5] In unregistered land all informal land mortgages of a legal estate or a commercial equitable interest will be registrable as land charges of Class C(iii).[6]

(4) Protected mortgages

Under the Law Commission's proposals almost all mortgages (whether formal or informal) of property which includes a dwelling-house will be classified as a 'protected mortgage'.[7] Protected mortgages will be required to comply with certain rules relating to standard format.[8] Any term which postpones the mortgagor's right to redeem will generally be void,[9] and the protected mortgagor is given additional protection in respect of any 'unreasonable' action of the mortgagee in varying (or failing to vary) the interest rate payable.[10]

(5) Power of sale

It will be an implied term of all formal land mortgages that the mortgagee has power to sell the mortgagor's interest on the occurrence of an 'enforceable

19 Law Com No 204 (1991), para 3.5
20 Law Com No 204 (1991), para 3.8. Unless and until registered, the formal land mortgage will rank only as an informal land mortgage (ibid).
1 Law Com No 204 (1991), para 3.20.
2 Law Com No 204 (1991), paras 3.32f. Formal (and informal) mortgages of trust interests in both registered and unregistered land will continue to be governed by the rule in *Dearle v Hall* (paras 3.29, 3.33).
3 Law Com No 204 (1991), para 3.17.
4 Law Com No 204 (1991), paras 3.11f.
5 Law Com No 204 (1991), paras 3.21f.
6 Law Com No 204 (1991), paras 3.32f.
7 Law Com No 204 (1991), para 4.6.
8 Law Com No 204 (1991), paras 5.1ff.
9 Law Com No 204 (1991), para 6.43(a).
10 Law Com No 204 (1991), paras 6.39ff.

event' (such as a payment default or other substantial breach by the mortgagor) or even where there is some non-culpable occasion of substantial risk to the mortgagee's security (eg compulsory purchase or impending insolvency).[11] In relation to a protected mortgage the power of sale will not be exercisable without the leave of the court following the due service of an 'enforcement notice' on the mortgagor.[12] On any sale by a mortgagee or a receiver under a formal land mortgage, an overriding duty will be owed to the mortgagor (and to guarantors and subsequent mortgagees) to 'take reasonable care to ensure' that the price is 'the best price that can reasonably be obtained.'[13]

(6) Rights to possession

The Law Commission has recommended the displacement of the inherent right of possession ab initio which the legal mortgagee enjoys under the present law.[14] Instead it will be an implied and overriding provision of every formal land mortgage, that the mortgagee is entitled to take possession of the property if the taking of possession is reasonably necessary to enable the property to be sold pursuant to the mortgagee's power of sale.[15] Under a protected mortgage, however, the mortgagee will not be entitled to take possession without first serving an enforcement notice and obtaining the leave of the court.[16] The court will have discretion to order that interest payable under the protected mortgage should cease to accrue twelve weeks after the execution of any possession order or after the mortgagor voluntarily surrenders possession to the mortgagee.[17]

(7) Powers of judicial intervention

In the case of all land mortgages the Law Commission has recommended that the court should be given a new statutory jurisdiction to vary or set terms 'with a view to doing justice between the parties.' This power of intervention will be applicable if principles of fair dealing were contravened when the mortgage was granted or if the mortgage payments required are exorbitant or if the mortgagee has acquired rights substantially greater than or different from those necessary to provide him with adequate security for the mortgage debt.[18]

11 Law Com No 204 (1991), paras 7.5ff.
12 Law Com No 204 (1991), paras 7.11ff. On an application to enforce a protected formal land mortgage, the court will have powers equivalent to those currently conferred by the Administration of Justice Act 1970 (ante, p 995) and the Consumer Credit Act 1974 (ante, p 964). In addition the court will be empowered to order the mortgagee to accept a re-scheduling of payments and may vary or set aside any terms of the mortgage (paras 7.50ff).
13 Law Com No 204 (1991), para 7.23.
14 Law Com No 204 (1991), paras 6.16, 7.28.
15 Law Com No 204 (1991), para 7.28f. In a non-protected formal land mortgage the mortgagee will have, in addition, a right to take possession on the wider ground that possession is reasonably necessary for the preservation of the value of the property (para 7.36(a)).
16 Law Com No 204 (1991), para 7.32.
17 Law Com No 204 (1991), paras 7.33f.
18 Law Com No 204 (1991), para 8.5.

The Law Commission's Draft Land Mortgages Bill effectively rationalises and improves upon much of the existing law of mortgage. If and when it reaches the statute book, it is clear that the current law will have undergone a profound and long overdue transformation.

CHAPTER 21

Easements and profits *à prendre*

Any rational system of real property law is inevitably concerned to promote the efficient utilisation of land resources. This function is made rather less easy by the fact that the physical asset of land is capable of supporting an almost infinite variety of purposeful modes of exploitation. Land use can be directed towards a myriad of goals, whether social, commercial, industrial or agricultural.

The distribution of primary rights of access to this rich range of land uses is fixed by ownership of an estate in relevant land. It is the owner of the fee simple and, to the degree permitted by his leasehold covenants, the tenant for years, who have first call upon the user facilities afforded by any particular tract of land. There is no prima facie obligation that an estate owner should share these facilities with anyone else, and indeed the law does not in general mandate cooperation between neighbours.[1] Nevertheless it is often true that the most efficient utilisation of land resources occurs only where the user privileges inherent in estate ownership are shared between neighbouring landowners in some form of collaborative interaction.[2] Although A may own a fee simple estate in his land, it may make a great deal of social or commercial sense that his neighbour, B, should simultaneously have a right to use part of A's land in a certain way or indeed a right to prevent a certain kind of use of A's land. Moreover, the multiplicity of user forms sustained by A's land need not be in conflict one with another. The law of property is complex precisely because it is possible for a number of people to acquire different, but compatible, rights in or over the same thing.

While estate ownership may be said to mark out 'the default allocations of rights and obligations' in land,[3] the law of land permits owners to make permanent adjustments to these allocations through the acquisition of incorporeal user rights over the land of others. Amongst the most important rights which may be acquired in this way are easements, profits *à prendre*, and covenants.[4] The law relating to profits and covenants is of fairly ancient origin,[5] but the law of easements has developed rapidly in more recent times as a means of enabling private landowners to plan land use and to enhance the enjoyment or utility of their own land.

1 'No doctrinal rule of land law embodies the biblical command to "love thy neighbor as thyself" (S.E. Sterk, *Neighbors in American Land Law*, 87 Col L Rev 55 at 100 (1987)).

2 It can rarely be efficient to purchase an entire freehold or leasehold estate in land merely in order to secure permanent access to some valued user facility connected with that land (see, however, *Re Buchanan-Wollaston's Conveyance* [1939] Ch 738, ante, p 587).

3 S.F. French, 73 Cornell L Rev 928 (1987-88).

4 Covenants are dealt with in Chapter 22 (post, p 1123).

5 See A.W.B. Simpson, *A History of The Land Law* (2nd edn, Oxford, 1986), p 106ff.

Together the law relating to easements, profits *à prendre*, and covenants comprises a general law of 'servitudes'. Such servitudes, when created by A in favour of B, are normally binding between A and B as a matter of contract. For the land lawyer, however, the question inevitably arises whether the same rights will bind third parties such as the successors in title of A and B respectively. In reality, of course, the rights created by private agreement are usually intended to be not merely contractual but also proprietary, in the sense that they should affect all who come to the land.

Since the concern here is with the borderline of the law of property, the law has traditionally imposed certain stringent limitations both as to the kinds of user privilege which may qualify as incorporeal rights in land and also as to their modes of creation or acquisition. It is part of received wisdom that the utility and therefore the marketability of land would be gravely affected if these restrictive rules were not clear and rigorously applied. Land titles would otherwise become encumbered by useless and anti-social user-rights of dubious enforceability, vested in unspecified or unidentifiable third parties. The resulting chaos would, it is said, be inimical to the large social interest which pervades the law of property—the interest that property should be both readily alienable and capable of commercial exploitation. Even more caution is evident when the law implies or compels the compulsory creation of incorporeal rights over land, since such creation inevitably impacts upon communal definitions of the limits of altruism.

1. DEFINITIONS AND DISTINCTIONS

An easement is an incorporeal hereditament,[6] comprising in essence either a positive or a negative right of user over the land of another. In effect an easement is a right annexed to one piece of land (a 'dominant tenement') to utilise land of different ownership (a 'servient tenement') in a particular way or, indeed, to prevent the owner of that other land from utilising his own land in a particular way.[7] An easement cannot extend a right of user to the point where it becomes a right to take the natural produce of another's land or any part of his soil: such a right is classified not as an easement but as a profit *à prendre*. An easement is ultimately a privilege without profit which the owner of one tenement has over another tenement by which the servient owner permits (or refrains from) certain activities on his own land for the advantage of the dominant tenement.

The concept of the easement must be distinguished from a number of other rights which may exist over land. These include the following.

6 Ante, p 32.

7 Thus described, a negative easement differs little if at all from a restrictive covenant (post, p 1125). A restrictive covenant prohibits a specified form of user on the entirety of the servient tenement. A negative easement (eg of access to light) generally imposes no such blanket restriction on the servient owner, but merely requires that he so use his tenement that a certain facility or advantage conferred by it on the dominant tenement is not curtailed or destroyed. See J.W. Bruce and J.W. Ely, *The Law of Easements and Licences in Land* (Boston and New York, 1988), p 1-51f.

(1) Profits *à prendre*

A profit *à prendre* is a 'very peculiar type of interest'[8] which confers a right to take part of the soil, minerals or natural produce of the servient tenement.[9] A profit thus differs from an easement in that the latter right is essentially a privilege without profit.[10] A profit comprises a right to take either some part of the servient land itself (eg gravel or turf[11]) or something which grows on that land (eg grass, crops or fruit) or indeed fish[12] or wild animals[13] which are found on the servient owner's land or in his waters.[14]

A profit *à prendre* is clearly an incorporeal hereditament or proprietary interest in the servient land.[15] It is, however, the right of severance implicit in a profit *à prendre* which results in the holder of the profit acquiring title to the thing severed or gathered from the land. He does not own the subject matter of the profit while it remains in situ,[16] but has an option to sever it.[17] A profit is usually granted in conjunction with a licence to enter the servient land, in which case the licence is an incident of the grant of profit and is irrevocable during the term of the profit.[18]

(a) A profit may exist 'in gross'

A profit *à prendre* is distinguishable from an easement in that a profit may exist 'in gross', ie the owner of the profit need not be the owner of any gross

8 *Ellison v Vukicevic* (1986) 7 NSWLR 104 at 113D per Young J.

9 *Alfred F. Beckett Ltd v Lyons* [1967] Ch 449 at 482B. See also *Australian Softwood Forests Pty Ltd v Attorney-General for New South Wales; ex rel Corporate Affairs Commission* (1981) 148 CLR 121 at 130 per Mason J; *R v Toohey; ex parte Meneling Station Pty Ltd* (1982) 158 CLR 327 at 344, 352; *The Queen v Tener* (1985) 17 DLR (4th) 1 at 16f (Supreme Court of Canada); *Bolton v Forest Pest Management Institute* (1986) 21 DLR (4th) 242 at 248f.

10 The distinction between profits and easements was recognised at least as early as *Gateward's Case* (1606) 6 Co Rep 59b at 60b, 77 ER 344 at 345.

11 See *Convey v Regan* [1952] IR 56 at 61; *In re Bohan* [1957] IR 49 at 54ff.

12 See *Kerry CC v O'Sullivan* [1927] IR 26 at 29f; *Toome Eel Fishery (Northern Ireland) Ltd v Cardwell* [1966] NI 1; *Bolton v Forest Pest Management Institute* (1986) 21 DLR (4th) 242 at 248.

13 See *Finlay v Curteis* (1832) Hayes 496 at 499f.

14 The subject matter of a profit *à prendre* must be something which is capable of ownership. A right to take water itself cannot be a profit, since water is not capable of being owned (*Alfred F. Beckett Ltd v Lyons* [1967] Ch 449 at 481G–482A).

15 See *R v Toohey; ex parte Meneling Station Pty Ltd* (1982) 158 CLR 327 at 352 per Wilson J. A profit *à prendre* is sufficiently proprietary to sustain an action in nuisance on behalf of its owner (see eg *Bolton v Forest Pest Management Institute* (1986) 21 DLR (4th) 242 at 249). A profit cannot be classified as a chattel (*Cream Silver Mines Ltd v The Queen in Right of British Columbia* (1986) 27 DLR (4th) 305 at 309).

16 *The Queen v Tener* (1985) 17 DLR (4th) 1 at 17. The holder of a profit has, for instance, no property in uncaptured game (*Bolton v Forest Pest Management Institute* (1986) 21 DLR (4th) 242 at 248).

17 A profit *à prendre* exists only where the grantee has an *option* to sever. An agreement which imposes an obligation to sever something from realty confers no true profit, but creates instead a contract for the sale of goods together with a licence to go upon the land for the purpose of carrying out the contract (*Ellison v Vukicevic* (1986) 7 NSWLR 104 at 116C-E). Likewise a licence coupled with a grant need not create a profit *à prendre* (*Beaton v McDivitt* (1985) 13 NSWLR 134 at 146C-D). See eg *James Jones & Sons Ltd v Earl of Tankerville* [1909] 2 Ch 440 at 442f (right to enter and remove already felled timber).

18 Ante, p 901. See *Cowell v Rosehill Racecourse Co Ltd* (1937) 56 CLR 605 at 615 per Latham CJ.

adjoining or neighbouring land or indeed of any land at all.[19] There need not be a 'dominant tenement'.[20] The rules relating to easements are quite different, and it is an essential condition of an easement that the easement be appurtenant to 'dominant' land.[1]

(b) Scope of the profit

A profit in gross is said to be 'unstinted' in the sense that it may be exhaustive of the fruit or produce of the servient land.[2] By contrast, a 'profit appurtenant' (ie a profit which is annexed to some nearby dominant tenement) may not be exhaustive, but is limited to the needs of the dominant tenement.[3]

(c) A profit à prendre need not be exclusive

A profit *à prendre* may confer either an exclusive right or a right enjoyed in common with others (including the grantor).[4] An exclusive profit arises only where the terms of grant expressly so provide[5] or where an intention to this effect can be gathered from the language of the grant as a whole.[6] In the absence of such language the tendency to find a merely non-exclusive profit is accentuated where, for instance, the grantor would otherwise be prejudiced by having contracted to take only a fixed royalty or where the grantor would suffer if the grantee were not active or diligent in severing the subject matter of the profit.[7] Conversely a profit may be confirmed as exclusive where there would be obvious physical difficulty in several persons exercising simultaneous rights of severance in relation to a confined area of realty.[8]

(d) Duration of profits à prendre

A profit *à prendre* may be granted either in perpetuity[9] or for a fixed term[10]

19 *Bl Comm*, Vol II, p 34. See *The Queen v Tener* (1985) 17 DLR (4th) 1 at 17; *Lovett v Fairclough* (1989) 61 P & CR 385 at 396. Where a grant contains all the elements of a profit, the grant is presumed to create a profit rather than a mere licence unless there are 'strong indications that the grant was meant to be personal' (*Ellison v Vukicevic* (1986) 7 NSWLR 104 at 115A).

20 A profit in gross, once created, may be assigned and conveyed 'as a piece of real property', but does not otherwise pass on the conveyance of realty (see *Lovett v Fairclough* (1989) 61 P & CR 385 at 398).

1 Post, p 1060.

2 See eg *Staffordshire and Worcestershire Canal Navigation v Bradley* [1912] 1 Ch 91 at 103.

3 *Bailey v Stephens* (1862) 12 CB NS 91 at 108, 110, 142 ER 1077 at 1084; *Lord Chesterfield v Harris* [1908] 2 Ch 397 at 410; *Anderson v Bostock* [1976] Ch 312 at 315F-G, 318B, 318H-319A.

4 *R v Toohey; ex parte Meneling Station Pty Ltd* (1982) 158 CLR 327 at 352 per Wilson J. The fact that in given circumstances a profit is not exclusive in nature does not derogate from its proprietary character as a profit (see *Unimin Pty Ltd v Commonwealth of Australia* (1974) 2 ACTR 71 at 78; *Ellison v Vukicevic* (1986) 7 NSWLR 104 at 118B).

5 See *Duke of Sutherland v Heathcote* [1892] 1 Ch 475 at 484f.

6 *Reid v Moreland Timber Co Pty Ltd* (1946) 73 CLR 1 at 16.

7 *Ellison v Vukicevic* (1986) 7 NSWLR 104 at 118B-C.

8 *Reid v Moreland Timber Co Pty Ltd* (1946) 73 CLR 1 at 9 per Starke J.

9 A profit appurtenant is normally perpetual (see *Ex parte Florida Hills Townships Ltd* 1968 (3) SA 82 at 91H; *Ellison v Vukicevic* (1986) 7 NSWLR 104 at 113E).

10 See eg *Martyn v Williams* (1857) 1 H & N 817 at 829, 156 ER 1430 at 1436.

or indeed for any other temporal interest.[11] There is of course a danger that a perpetual and exclusive right, for instance, to cut timber would render the servient land sterile in the hands of its owner. There is thus a general (although rebuttable) implication under an interminable profit that the grantee's exercise of his rights are restricted to a 'reasonable time' following the date of grant.[12]

A non-perpetual profit may be brought to an end on the expiration of a specified term, and profits may generally be terminated[13] by abandonment, release, surrender or by the giving of an agreed notice.[14] Breach of a contractual term governing a profit may afford a remedy in damages, but probable breach of a contractual condition is not enough to enable one party to terminate the profit.[15]

(2) Licences

A licence grants a permission to do something on or affecting land which would otherwise constitute a trespass.[16] Licences are distinguishable from easements in the following respects.[17]

(a) Types of permissible user

The categories of user which are capable of recognition as easements are both relatively limited and restrictively defined. By contrast a licence may be used to permit the conduct of almost any activity on the land of the licensor (ranging from the daily delivery of milk to the holding of an open-air pop festival). A licence may in some circumstances comprise an element of exclusive occupation of land, but any claim to exclusive rights of user is incompatible with the concept of easement.[18]

(b) Creation

The creation of easements often requires compliance with rules of formality,[19] but licences may be created without any formality at all. Furthermore, an easement cannot exist in gross,[20] but a licence need not be related to the ownership of any dominant tenement.

11 See *Ex parte Henry; Re Commissioner of Stamp Duties* (1963) SR (NSW) 298 at 303ff.
12 *Reid v Moreland Timber Co Pty Ltd* (1946) 73 CLR 1 at 13 per Dixon J.
13 See *Ellison v Vukicevic* (1986) 7 NSWLR 104 at 114A-B.
14 *Unimin Pty Ltd v Commonwealth of Australia* (1974) 2 ACTR 71 at 78.
15 *Ellison v Vukicevic* (1986) 7 NSWLR 104 at 118C.
16 For an examination of the law of licences, see Chapter 19 (ante, p 890).
17 The borderline between licence and easement is easier to determine than that between licence and lease (ante, p 706). The ambiguities present in the latter context stem from the fact that a licence may confer exclusive rights in land, whereas an easement cannot generally comprise exclusive user (post, p 1076). Accordingly the courts are more ready to give an entirely literal construction to a reference to the grant of a 'licence' (see eg *IDC Group Ltd v Clark* [1992] 2 EGLR 184 at 186B-F).
18 Post, p 1078. See eg *Sunset Properties Pty Ltd v Johnston* (1975) 3 BPR 9185 at 9193 (post, p 1076).
19 Post, p 1087.
20 Post, p 1060.

(c) Effect on third parties

An easement creates a proprietary interest which is capable of benefiting and binding third parties. At least in the conventional view, a licence does not generate any similar proprietary effect.[1]

(3) Restrictive covenants

Restrictive covenants are agreements restrictive of the user of land for the benefit of other land adjoining or in the vicinity. Restrictive covenants are closely related to easements both in terminology and in substance, so much so that it has been said that restrictive covenants are in essence negative easements.[2] Certain differences nevertheless exist between the easement and the restrictive covenant. Easements are enforceable both at law and in equity. Restrictive covenants are the creature of equity and are enforceable only in equity. Moreover, easements may be acquired by prescription (ie long user),[3] while restrictive covenants may never be acquired in this way. Once again, while the permissible subject matter of an easement is relatively circumscribed, the possible content of a restrictive covenant is virtually unlimited.

(4) Public rights

Public rights are rights which are exercisable by anyone, whether he owns land or not, merely by virtue of his being a member of the public. Some public rights resemble profits *à prendre* (eg the public right of fishing). Other public rights are akin to easements (eg the public right in respect of the highway). However, all public rights are distinct from easements,[4] since they do not presuppose the existence of any dominant tenement and are never the subject of a specific grant to any individual.[5]

The more important public rights include the following.

(a) Rights of passage along the highway

Certain kinds of user of the public highway[6] are enjoyed as a matter of

1 Ante, p 915.

2 Post, p 1139. Easements were recognised much earlier in the common law. Restrictive covenants have been accorded proprietary effect only since the mid-19th century (post, p 1136).

3 Post, p 1106.

4 The public right of passage along the highway is sometimes—albeit inaccurately—referred to in somewhat loose terms as an 'easement' (see eg *Harrison v Duke of Rutland* [1893] 1 QB 142 at 154 per Lopes LJ).

5 For the best modern account of public rights, see Tim Bonyhady, *The Law of the Countryside: the Rights of the Public* (Abingdon 1987).

6 The 'highway' is defined as including not only the 'carriageway' over which there is a right of way for vehicular traffic but also the adjoining 'footway' on either side where there is merely a public right of way on foot (see Highways Act 1980, ss 328(1), 329(1)). See also *Hubbard v Pitt* [1976] QB 142 at 175D. Despite isolated statements that a navigable river is a 'public highway' (see eg *York Bros (Trading) Pty Ltd v Commr of Main Roads* [1983] 1 NSWLR 391 at 393G), the supposed analogy between rights on water and rights on land is incomplete and perhaps misleading. See *Attorney-General ex rel Yorkshire Derwent Trust Ltd v Brotherton* [1992] 1 AC 425 at 435C per Lord Oliver of Aylmerton ('I cannot. . .think that any reader of Alfred Lord Tennyson would have regarded the Lady of Shalott, as she floated down to Camelot through the noises of the night, as exercising a right of way over the subjacent soil').

public right,[7] and every highway authority has a responsibility both at common law[8] and under statute[9] to assert and protect the rights of the public to the use and enjoyment of the highways within its area.[10]

(i) Content of the citizen's rights Every citizen has a right of passage and re-passage along any highway (including the pavements,[11] footpaths[12] and bridleways) over which the public has acquired a right of way either by statute[13] or by reason of dedication and acceptance at common law.[14] It has always been the case at common law that dedication and acceptance of a highway are inferable from uninterrupted long user by the public.[15] However, the mere fact of continual trespassing cannot at common law create a public right.[16] There must be evidence that the relevant landowner intended to dedicate the highway[17] and that the proffered dedication was accepted

7 A public highway need not necessarily lead to any public place (see *Williams-Ellis v Cobb* [1935] 1 KB 310 at 320).
8 *R v Welwyn Hatfield DC, ex parte Brinkley* (1982) 80 LGR 727 at 735.
9 Highways Act 1980, s 130(1).
10 If a highway is maintainable by the relevant statutory highway authority at public expense, that authority holds a determinable fee simple interest in the surface of the highway and in so much of the subjacent land and superjacent airspace as is required for the discharge of its statutory duties (see *Coverdale v Charlton* (1878) 4 QBD 104 at 116f, 121, 126; *Foley's Charity Trustees v Dudley Corpn* [1910] 1 KB 317 at 322; *Tithe Redemption Commission v Runcorn UDC* [1954] Ch 383 at 398; *Wiltshire County Council v Frazer* (1984) 47 P & CR 69 at 72; Highways Act 1980, s 263 (ante, p 86)). See also *Attorney-General ex rel Yorkshire Derwent Trust Ltd v Brotherton* [1992] 1 AC 425 at 436A.
11 *News Group Newspapers Ltd v SOGAT '82* [1986] IRLR 337 at 346.
12 The inclusion of a footpath in a definitive map drawn up pursuant to the National Parks and Access to the Countryside Act 1949 or Wildlife and Countryside Act 1981 provides irrebuttable evidence of the existence of a footpath for the purpose of a claimed right of way (*Rubinstein v Secretary of State for the Environment* (1989) 57 P & CR 111 at 116; [1988] Conv 207 (A. Sydenham)). It is now a criminal offence to disturb the surface of a footpath, bridleway or highway (Highways Act 1980, s 131A (as added by Rights of Way Act 1990, s 1(2)), but not, except in the case of a field-edge path, to plough over a footpath or bridleway (Highways Act 1980, s 134(1), as substituted by Rights of Way Act 1990, s 1(3)). See also *Ramblers Association v Kent CC* (1990) 60 P & CR 464 at 471.
13 A public highway may be specifically designated as such by statute.
14 Both dedication and acceptance must be proved (*Dunstan v Hell's Gate Enterprises Ltd* (1988) 45 DLR (4th) 677 at 689). See also *Permanent Trustee Co of New South Wales Ltd v Campbelltown Municipal Council* (1960) 105 CLR 401 at 420 per Windeyer J; *Newington v Windeyer* (1985) 3 NSWLR 555 at 558G.
15 *Cubitt v Lady Caroline Maxse* (1873) LR 8 CP 704 at 715; *Turner v Walsh* (1881) 6 App Cas 636 at 639ff; *Folkestone Corpn v Brockman* [1914] AC 338 at 352, 362; *Newington v Windeyer* (1985) 3 NSWLR 555 at 559B-C. User by a mere section of the public (eg by neighbouring occupiers and their visitors) may not be enough (see *Newington* at 562E-F).
16 *Newington v Windeyer* (1985) 3 NSWLR 555 at 559C per McHugh JA. Evidence of continual user over a very long period may, however, generate an almost irresistible presumption of dedication (see *R v Inhabitants of the Tithing of East Mark* (1848) 11 QB 877 at 884, 116 ER 701 at 704 per Erle J (50 years)).
17 This intention must be express or capable of being implied from the conduct of the fee simple owner (*R v Inhabitants of the Tithing of East Mark* (1848) 11 QB 877 at 883, 116 ER 701 at 704). Intention on the part of a mere lessee is not enough unless the fee simple owner clearly acquiesced in the dedication (see *Pryor v Pryor* (1872) 26 LT (NS) 758 at 760; *Newington v Windeyer* (1985) 3 NSWLR 555 at 561B) or must have been aware of the general belief that dedication had occurred (*Folkestone Corpn v Brockman* [1914] AC 338 at 362f).

by the public.[18] There is now a general (although rebuttable) statutory presumption that a way is deemed to have been dedicated as a public highway where the way has been 'actually enjoyed by the public as of right and without interruption for a full period of 20 years'.[19] The intention to dedicate a way to the public is commonly rebutted by an annual and symbolic closure of the route for one day for the purpose of denying public access as of right.[20]

The public right of passage in relation to a highway is of a somewhat limited nature.[1] Citizens have a 'right to pass and repass at their pleasure for the purpose of legitimate travel'[2] and also for 'purposes incidental to passage'.[3] Any other form of user of the highway constitutes a trespass against the owner of the top-soil in the highway[4] and may well involve a criminal obstruction of the highway.[5]

(ii) Criminal obstruction of the highway The scope of the public right of passage and re-passage on the highway has tended to be defined, not so much by any positive explication given by the courts, as by the delimiting effects imposed by various forms of criminal liability derived from statute.

Of these heads of liability the most important is that created by the offence

18 The expenditure of public funds may connote acceptance. See *Village of Silverton v Hobbs* (1985) 17 DLR (4th) 518 at 521ff, but compare *Dunstan v Hell's Gate Enterprises Ltd* (1988) 45 DLR (4th) 677 at 690.

19 Highways Act 1980, s 31(1). See *Gloucestershire CC v Farrow* [1985] 1 WLR 741 at 745H–746G. See also *Dyfed CC v Secretary of State for Wales* (1990) 59 P & CR 275 at 281ff.

20 See *British Museum Trustees v Finnis* (1833) 5 C & P 460 at 465, 172 ER 1053 at 1056. See *Poole v Huskinson* (1843) 11 M & W 827 at 830, 152 ER 1039 at 1041 per Parke B ('...a single act of interruption by the owner is of much more weight, upon a question of intention, than many acts of enjoyment').

1 Adjoining landowners have no common law right to have an access constructed from their property to the public highway (*Shellharbour Municipal Council v Rovili Pty Ltd* (1989) 16 NSWLR 104 at 109F–110A). See also *Frecklington v Wellington City Council* [1988] 1 NZLR 72 at 75f.

2 *Harrison v Duke of Rutland* [1893] 1 QB 142 at 154. See also *Hickman v Maisey* [1900] 1 QB 752 at 757; *Waite v Taylor* (1985) 149 JP 551 at 553; *Thomas v National Union of Mineworkers (South Wales Area)* [1986] Ch 20 at 64A.

3 *Hubbard v Pitt* [1976] QB 142 at 149G–150A per Forbes J, who explained that '[a] tired pedestrian may sit down and rest himself. A motorist may attempt to repair a minor breakdown...[I]t is permissible to queue for tickets at a theatre or other public place of entertainment, or for a bus.' Even then such user is limited in duration to 'a reasonable while', and must be exercised 'reasonably and in such a way as not unduly to obstruct other users' ([1976] QB 142 at 150D). See also *Hadwell v Righton* [1907] 2 KB 345 at 348; *Iveagh (Earl) v Martin* [1961] 1 QB 232 at 273; *Waite v Taylor* (1985) 149 JP 551 at 553; *Cooper v Metropolitan Police Commissioner* (1985) 82 Cr App R 238 at 242.

4 *Harrison v Duke of Rutland* [1893] 1 QB 142 at 154; *Hubbard v Pitt* [1976] QB 142 at 150C-F, 175C-D. See eg *R v Pratt* (1855) 4 E & B 860 at 865, 867f, 119 ER 319 at 321f (hunting on highway); *Hickman v Maisey* [1900] 1 QB 752 at 756ff (racing tout spying on horse trials). An injunction will issue to restrain an individual who 'persistently follow[s] another on a public highway, making rude gestures or remarks in order to annoy or vex' (*Thomas v National Union of Mineworkers (South Wales Area)* [1986] Ch 20 at 64D). There is, however, no trespass by the child who chases his ball into the roadway or runs across the roadway in play (see *Culkin v McFie and Sons Ltd* [1939] 3 All ER 613 at 620F-G). See, however, Highways Act 1980, s 161(3).

5 Highways Act 1980, s 137(1). For reference to potential liability for public and private nuisance, see *Hubbard v Pitt* [1976] QB 142 at 175A, E.

of wilful obstruction of 'free passage along a highway'.[6] In the absence of 'lawful authority or excuse',[7] obstruction encompasses anything other than a passing and re-passing along the highway or activity ancillary to such passage.[8] Whether the use made of the highway by a member of the public is 'so unreasonable as to amount to obstruction' is a question of fact and degree in every case'.[9] The offence of obstruction tends in practice to catch many 'relatively minor activities which some of the public might consider to be beneficial'.[10] The offence has also been applied—somewhat dangerously—to the conduct of activities on the footpath or sidewalk which are deemed to be unpleasant, socially undesirable or obtrusive in relation to passers by.[11]

A further form of criminal liability arises where 'without lawful authority or excuse' any person deposits 'any thing whatsoever on a highway to the interruption of any user of the highway'.[12] It is a specially designated criminal offence to deposit a builder's skip on the highway without the permission of the relevant highway authority.[13] Moreover, a local authority has power to require the removal of any 'structure' erected or set up on the highway without lawful authority.[14]

(iii) Protest and demonstration on the public highway The nature of the public right of user of the highway also performs a significant function in delimiting

6 Highways Act 1980, s 137(1). 'Unless it is de minimis any stopping on the highway is prima facie an obstruction' (see *Hirst v Chief Constable of West Yorkshire* (1986) 151 JP 304). Under Highways Act 1980, s 137(2), a police constable has power to arrest without warrant any person 'whom he sees committing an offence under this section'.

7 See *Nagy v Weston* [1965] 1 WLR 280 at 284C-D. No defence can be raised on the basis that the defendant has operated a street stall in the same position for several years and has duly paid rates (*Pugh v Pidgen* (1987) 151 JP 664). In the absence of malpractice, oppression, caprice or opprobrious behaviour, it is lawful for the police to stop cars randomly on the highway for the purpose of detecting crime (including drunken driving). See *Beard v Wood* [1980] RTR 454 at 459E-H; *Chief Constable of Gwent v Dash* [1986] RTR 41 at 48G. Compare *R v Dedman* (1985) 20 DLR (4th) 321 (Supreme Court of Canada).

8 See *Waite v Taylor* (1985) 149 JP 551 at 553, where May LJ pointed out that there is no obligation 'to keep moving all the time', so long as the 'stopping is part and parcel of passing and re-passing along the highway and is ancillary to it (such as a milkman stopping to leave a milk bottle on a doorstep).' Likewise, in *Cooper v Metropolitan Police Commissioner* (1985) 82 Cr App R 238 at 242, Tudor Evans J thought that there is clearly 'a right to look in a shop window or to talk to a passing friend without committing an offence'.

9 *Nagy v Weston* [1965] 1 WLR 280 at 284D-E. See also *Fitzgerald v Montoya* (1989) 16 NSWLR 164 at 171G–172A.

10 *Waite v Taylor* (1985) 149 JP 551 at 553. Criminal liability has thus been imposed—with expressions of judicial regret—on hot dog vendors (*Nagy v Weston* [1965] 1 WLR 280 at 284F; *Pitcher v Lockett* (1966) 64 LGR 477 at 479), mobile snack bars (*Waltham Forest London Borough Council v Mills* [1980] RTR 201 at 205G-H), and street buskers juggling with lit firesticks in a pedestrian precinct (*Waite v Taylor*, supra at 553f). Compare, however, *Fitzgerald v Montoya* (1989) 16 NSWLR 164 at 166B-D (Court of Appeal of New South Wales).

11 *Cooper v Metropolitan Police Commissioner* (1985) 82 Cr App R 238 at 242ff (club tout seeking to persuade passing pedestrians to enter Soho club).

12 Highways Act 1980, s 148(c). See *Putnam v Colvin* [1984] RTR 150 at 158B-E (placing of pots with shrubs in cul-de-sac to prevent unlawful parking itself unlawful).

13 Highways Act 1980, s 139(1), (3). The criminal offence also includes leaving a skip on the highway for longer than the permitted period (*Craddock v Green* (1983) 81 LGR 235 at 239f).

14 *R v Welwyn Hatfield DC, ex parte Brinkley* (1982) 80 LGR 727 at 734ff (gypsy caravans). Possession of the highway may also be recovered under RSC Ord 113 (ante, p 309). See *Wiltshire County Council v Frazer* (1984) 47 P & CR 69 at 74ff.

the citizen's right in relation to certain forms of protest and demonstration. In *Hubbard v Pitt*[15] a majority in the Court of Appeal upheld the granting of an interlocutory injunction restraining the picketing of an estate agent's premises carried out by a local tenants' organisation. The majority decision may, however, have been based more upon an allegation of private nuisance than upon any suggestion that the demonstration on the pavement outside the estate agent's premises had constituted either a trespass or a criminal obstruction.[16] In his dissenting judgment Lord Denning MR was prepared to discharge the injunction altogether, noting specifically that the presence of half a dozen people for three hours on a Saturday morning was 'not an unreasonable use of the highway'.[17] In the words of the Master of the Rolls, 'so long as good order is maintained, the right to demonstrate must be preserved.'[18]

The liberal tenor of Lord Denning's approach has been invoked more recently in *Hirst v Chief Constable of West Yorkshire.*[19] Here a number of 'animal rights' protesters had exhibited banners and distributed leaflets in a pedestrian precinct outside a shop which sold fur coats. Their conviction on a charge of wilful obstruction of the highway was quashed by the Divisional Court of Queen's Bench, Otton J observing that the courts have long recognised the right of free speech and the right to peaceful protest on matters of public concern, subject to the need for peace and good order.[20] However, the Court confirmed the stern warning given by Lord Denning MR in *Hubbard v Pitt*[1] that any violence 'should be firmly handled and severely punished'.

(iv) Industrial protest A difficult balance requires to be maintained between the right of the citizen to use the highway as a forum for legitimate protest and the right of other citizens to enjoy uninterrupted user of the same highway for their own legitimate purposes. This issue has arisen with some force in connection with the crossing of picket lines during strikes. In *Thomas v National Union of Mineworkers (South Wales Area)*,[2] Scott J held that working miners were entitled under the general law to exercise their right to go to work 'without unreasonable harassment by others'. Since the working miners had a 'right to use the highway for the purpose of going to work',[3] they were entitled to an injunction protecting that right from 'unreasonable interference' by a group of 50 to 70 striking miners who on a daily basis hurled verbal abuse at them from the picket line.[4] In this rather special sense Scott J

15 [1976] QB 142.
16 [1976] QB 142 at 180C-D, 189C-D.
17 [1976] QB 142 at 174H–175A ('They did not interfere with the free passage of people to and fro'). Lord Denning was of the opinion (at 175C-D) that neither the aggrieved estate agent nor the local highway authority had any right of action in trespass.
18 [1976] QB 142 at 179A.
19 (1986) 151 JP 304.
20 See also *Halifax Antiques Ltd v Hildebrand* (1986) 22 DLR (4th) 289 at 298.
1 [1976] QB 142 at 178H–179A.
2 [1986] Ch 20 at 64E-F. See [1985] CLJ 374 (K.D. Ewing); A. Davidson, (1988) 18 U of W Australia L Rev 138.
3 [1986] Ch 20 at 64E.
4 [1986] Ch 20 at 65A-C. Regular picketing at the home of a working miner was held to be a common law nuisance, 'regardless of the number of people involved and regardless of the peaceful nature of their conduct' ([1986] Ch 20 at 65C-D).

seemed to suggest that unreasonable collective interference with public rights of user of the highway constitutes 'a species of private nuisance'.[5]

The decision in *Thomas v National Union of Mineworkers (South Wales Area)* also indicates that the courts may be more prepared to allow the highway to be utilised as a means of protest by private or informal interest groups (such as 'animal rights' protesters) than by more highly organised representatives of unionised labour. Whether such an approach is right or wrong, the public right of user of the highway was jeopardised by the distinctly questionable ruling given in *Moss v McLachlan*.[6] Here, in a decision which bodes ill for civil liberties, a Divisional Court upheld a supposed right in the police to turn back convoys of 'flying pickets' from proceeding along the highway towards the scene of an organised labour demonstration. Skinner J held that police officers operating on a motorway were acting within the execution of their duty when they stopped cars carrying persons 'who appeared to be striking miners'.[7] The police had sought to justify their action on the basis that the continued progress of the vehicles gave rise to a reasonable expectation that a breach of the peace would ensue in the form of a mass demonstration at a colliery some miles distant.[8] In accepting this explanation, the Divisional Court endorsed the restriction of free movement along the highway on grounds of an apprehended (but as yet unproven) unlawfulness of the ultimate objective of the journey undertaken.[9]

Moss v McLachlan sets an extremely dangerous precedent for the censoring of lawful activities of entirely innocent persons on some ground of visual similarity to other persons who are deemed inimical to an officially defined social interest.[10] Even in relation to those who look like trouble, the ill-drawn law relating to breach of the peace must be sparingly applied. The ruling in *Moss v McLachlan* has highly disturbing implications not merely for public rights in respect of the highway, but also for important freedoms of speech, association and assembly.

5 [1986] Ch 20 at 64E. In *News Group Newspapers Ltd v SOGAT '82* [1986] IRLR 337 at 346, Stuart-Smith J held that the owner of land adjoining the highway has a 'right of access to the highway from any part of his premises' (see also *Marshall v Blackpool Corpn* [1935] AC 16 at 22; *Shellharbour Municipal Council v Rovili Pty Ltd* (1989) 16 NSWLR 104 at 108F–109A). An actionable private nuisance arises in the event of interference with this right, so long as the obstruction of access amounts to 'an unreasonable use of the highway'. In this case the daily presence of 50 to 200 dismissed print workers outside Rupert Murdoch's newspaper plant at Wapping was considered to be an 'unreasonable obstruction of the highway'. See also *Thomson Electrical Works Ltd v McGraw* (1976) 61 DLR (3d) 548 at 552f; F.P. Davidson, (1982) 33 NILQ 341.

6 (1985) 149 JP 167.

7 (1985) 149 JP 167 at 168.

8 (1985) 149 JP 167 at 170ff.

9 Compare *Wills' Trustees v Cairngorm Canoeing and Sailing School Ltd*, 1976 SLT 162 at 191 where, in dealing with the analogous right of passage on navigable waters, Lord Wilberforce expressed the view that 'once a public right of passage is established, there is no warrant for making any distinction, or even for making any enquiry, as to the purpose for which it is exercised. One cannot stop a canoe, any more than one can stop a pedestrian on a highway, and ask him what is the nature of his use.'

10 Compare the statement of Wilson J in *Rouse v Bardin* (1790) 1 H Bl 351 at 355, 126 ER 206 at 208, that members of the public have a right to use the public highway 'for all purposes and at all times'.

(v) Public nuisance Some forms of user of the highway may involve the criminal offence of public nuisance.[11] It is clear, however, that not every obstruction of the highway constitutes a public nuisance. There must in addition be some 'unreasonable use of the highway by the defendant'.[12] Thus a march or procession which is conducted in an orderly manner is not a public nuisance, even though it may involve obstruction of the highway.[13] In determining the reasonableness of any particular user, the court must 'balance the rights of those who wish to demonstrate with those who wish to exercise their rights of passage.'[14] A meeting or demonstration on the highway is not necessarily unlawful,[15] although it is 'more likely to be than a procession'.[16]

Public nuisance is also actionable as a civil wrong if it 'materially affects the reasonable comfort and convenience of life of a class of Her Majesty's subjects' who come within the sphere or 'neighbourhood' of its operation.[17] The plaintiff must, moreover, show particular damage 'other than and beyond the general inconvenience suffered by the public.'[18] In *News Group Newspapers Ltd v SOGAT '82*,[19] Stuart-Smith J ruled that the holding of mass demonstrations outside Rupert Murdoch's print plant at Wapping constituted an actionable public nuisance. The demonstrations were directed by sacked print workers both against the plaintiffs' continuing employees and against lorry drivers who distributed the plaintiffs' newspapers. Stuart-Smith J held that the targets of these demonstrations comprised a sufficiently numerous 'class' for the purpose of rendering the mass show of force an actionable civil wrong.[20] The print firm had a right for its employees and visitors to pass on all roads (including pavements) approaching the plant, 'unobstructed by pickets or demonstrators acting in an abusive, insulting, threatening or violent manner.'[1] Injunctions were granted restricting the demonstrations

11 A public nuisance may arise in connection with an 'unlawful act which endangers lives. safety, health, property or comfort of the public or by which the public are obstructed in the exercise or enjoyment of any right common to all Her Majesty's subjects' (*News Group Newspapers Ltd v SOGAT '82* [1986] IRLR 337 at 346).

12 *Lowdens v Keaveney* [1903] 2 IR 82 at 87f; *R v Clark (No 2)* [1964] 2 QB 315 at 320f. It may, for instance, be reasonable to place scaffolding on the highway for the purpose of erecting or repairing a building (see *Lord Advocate v Dumbarton DC* [1990] 2 AC 580 at 599H–600A per Lord Keith of Kinkel).

13 *News Group Newspapers Ltd v SOGAT '82* [1986] IRLR 337 at 346. See now the stringent controls imposed on public processions by Public Order Act 1986, s 11ff.

14 *News Group Newspapers Ltd v SOGAT '82* [1986] IRLR 337 at 346.

15 See *Burden v Rigler* [1911] 1 KB 337 at 339f.

16 *News Group Newspapers Ltd v SOGAT '82* [1986] IRLR 337 at 346.

17 *Attorney General v P.Y.A. Quarries Ltd* [1957] 2 QB 169 at 184.

18 *News Group Newspapers Ltd v SOGAT '82* [1986] IRLR 337 at 346. The invasion of a particular city area by a group of prostitutes may constitute public nuisance (see *Attorney-General of British Columbia v Couillard* (1985) 11 DLR (4th) 567 at 572ff; but compare *Stein v Gonzales* (1985) 14 DLR (4th) 263 at 267f).

19 [1986] IRLR 337.

20 *News Group Newspapers Ltd v SOGAT '82* [1986] IRLR 337 at 346. Stuart-Smith J thought that the 'class' requirement probably does not apply at all to obstruction of the highway, since obstruction in this context can generally be presumed to affect the public at large.

1 *News Group Newspapers Ltd v SOGAT '82* [1986] IRLR 337 at 357. See now the wide formulation of the offences related to riot, violent disorder, affray, intimidation and harassment contained in Public Order Act 1986, ss 1–5.

at Wapping to a picket line consisting of no more than six workers whose function was confined to peaceful communication and persuasion.[2]

(b) Rights of passage in navigable waters

There is at common law a public right of navigation at will over all navigable tidal waters.[3] There is also a public right of passage in respect of non-tidal rivers and lakes, although this right is subject to statutory regulation,[4] and entitles the citizen to exercise only reasonable rights of user which are incidental to a right of passage and re-passage.[5] The reasonableness of any particular user is measured with reference to the 'capacity and quality of the river'.[6]

(c) Rights of fishing

From ancient times there has been a right, vested in members of the public, to fish in the sea[7] and in all tidal and salt waters.[8] There is, of course, no public right of fishing in non-tidal rivers,[9] and it is highly unlikely that any such right exists in relation to inland non-tidal lakes.[10]

(d) Rights of recreational user

Under English law members of the public have only limited public rights of recreational user in respect of land and water. There is no general right to ramble over hills and open countryside.[11] There is no public right to swim at the shore or walk upon the foreshore.[12] Such activities represent at best some form of tolerated user in respect of which the landowner by long tradition—in the generality of cases—seeks no remedy in trespass.[13]

2 *News Group Newspapers Ltd v SOGAT '82* [1986] IRLR 337 at 357.
3 See Tim Bonyhady, op cit, p 130f.
4 See eg Water Resources Act 1991, Sch 25; Countryside Act 1968, s 22(6).
5 Thus, for instance, the right of passage does not confer any entitlement to indulge in wildfowling on a river (see *Lord Fitzhardinge v Purcell* [1908] 2 Ch 139 at 166).
6 *Wills' Trustees v Cairngorm Canoeing and Sailing School Ltd*, 1976 SLT 162 at 191 per Lord Wilberforce.
7 '[E]very man may fish in the sea of common right' (1466) YB Mich 8 Edw IV, pl 30.
8 *Stephens v Snell* [1939] 3 All ER 622H; *Case of the Royal Fishery of the Banne* (1610) Dav 55, 80 ER 540 at 541. Private fisheries can exist in such waters only if created prior to Magna Carta 1215 (see *Malcomson v O'Dea* (1863) 10 HL Cas 593 at 618, 11 ER 1155 at 1165f; *Stephens v Snell*, supra at 622G).
9 Ante, p 26.
10 See *Johnston v O'Neill* [1911] AC 552 at 568, 577f, 592f. Compare, however, *Toome Eel Fishery (Northern Ireland) Ltd v Cardwell* [1966] NI 1 at 12 per Lord MacDermott CJ.
11 See *Earl of Coventry v Willes* (1863) 9 LT 384 at 385; *Hammerton v Honey* (1876) 24 WR 603 at 604. The National Parks and Access to the Countryside Act 1949, ss 60ff, brought into existence machinery for the creation of public rights of access to the countryside by means of access agreements and orders However, these procedures have ensured that no more than 0.3 per cent of the total area of England and Wales is covered by access arrangements (see Tim Bonyhady, op cit, p 150).
12 *Brinckman v Matley* [1904] 2 Ch 313 at 324; *Alfred F. Beckett Ltd v Lyons* [1967] Ch 449 at 482E-F. Such rights may be enjoyed only by way of licence.
13 Where no injury to the private landowner is caused by trespass over his property, the courts may be unwilling to issue an injunction and may order nothing more than nominal damages in respect of the tortious invasion of a deserted beauty spot (see *Behrens v Richards* [1905] 2 Ch 614 at 622f).

In *Attorney-General v Antrobus*,[14] for instance, Farwell J denied the existence of a public right of access to the megalithic monument at Stonehenge, and underlined the legal impossibility that any member of the public may acquire a *ius spatiandi*[15] (or right to wander at large) over open countryside.[16] In some circumstances, however, it is possible that a grant of a public right of recreation may be presumed from the fact of long user[17] and there does appear to be a public right to navigate at will over the surface of many non-tidal inland waters.[18]

In respect of access to the recreational outdoors, English law contrasts unfavourably with the law of other jurisdictions. There is in England no general right of access to open or uncultivated countryside, although substantial de facto access is enjoyed in a somewhat ill-defined way. The need for a more satisfactory confirmation of a general right of access is now more pressing than ever. The privatisation of water authorities is likely to frustrate the access previously enjoyed by walkers and climbers across large catchment areas in the hills. There is a very real fear that, as the price of agricultural land steadily declines, the owners of scenic open spaces will compensate either by increasing afforestation or even by imposing access charges upon those who merely wish to roam around or climb in wild and open country.[19] The American courts are, by contrast, much more willing to infer the existence of an implied licence on the part of private landowners for public access to wide areas of open space.[20] American courts have also invoked doctrines of customary right and public trust (or ius publicum[1]) in order to rationalise the public acquisition, by implied dedication, of recreational easements over beaches.[2]

14 [1905] 2 Ch 188 at 208.
15 Post, p 1068.
16 See also *In re Ellenborough Park* [1956] Ch 131 at 184 per Evershed MR. See generally Tim Bonyhady, op cit, p 123ff.
17 See eg *R v Doncaster Metropolitan BC, ex parte Braim* (1989) 57 P & CR 1 at 15; [1988] Conv 369 (J. Hill).
18 See eg *Marshall v Ulleswater Steam Navigation Co* (1871) LR 7 QB 166 at 172 (Ullswater); *Bloomfield v Johnston* (1868) IR 8 CL 68 at 87ff, 111f (Lough Erne); *Micklethwait v Vincent* (1892) 67 LT 225 at 230 (Norfolk Broads). See also *Attorney-General (ex rel Yorkshire Derwent Trust Ltd) v Brotherton* [1992] 1 AC 425 at 434D.
19 See P. Sedgwick, 'The access debate', in *High* (February 1987), p 24; W. Wright, (1990) 29 *Climber and Hill Walker* (July), p 40. Compare S. Tompkins, *The Theft of the Hills* (The Ramblers' Association, London 1986).
20 See *McKee v Gratz*, 260 US 127 at 136, 67 L Ed 167 at 170 (1922) per Holmes J ('The strict rule of English common law as to entry upon a close must be taken to be mitigated by common understanding with regard to the large expanses of uninclosed and uncultivated land in many parts, at least, of this country. Over these it is customary to wander, shoot, and fish at will until the owner sees fit to prohibit it. A licence may be implied from the habits of the country').
1 See *Shively v Bowlby*, 152 US 1 at 11ff, 38 L Ed 331 at 336ff (1894).
2 See eg *State ex rel Thornton v Hay*, 462 P2d 671 at 673ff (1969); *Gion v City of Santa Cruz*, 465 P2d 50 at 55ff (1970); *Department of Natural Resources v Ocean City*, 332 A2d 630 at 633ff (1975); *County of Los Angeles v Berk*, 605 P2d 381 at 389ff (1980). See M.L. Bryan, *Which Way to the Beach? Public Access to Beaches for Recreational Use*, 29 So Car L Rev 627 (1977-79); J.W. Singer, *The Reliance Interest in Property*, 40 Stanford L Rev 611 at 674f (1987-88).

(5) Natural rights

Landowners have certain 'natural rights' which are protected by the law of torts.[3] Natural rights are distinguishable from easements in that they come into being automatically and are not the subject of any grant.

(a) Right to support for land

The most important 'natural right' is the landowner's right to support for his land.[4] Every landowner has a right to enjoy his own land in its natural state and is therefore entitled to have his land supported by that of his neighbour.[5]

(i) Extent of the right In practical terms the landowner has a right that the lateral thrust exerted on his soil by his neighbour's land should not be removed (eg by mining or excavating operations on the neighbour's land which cause subsidence).[6] The natural right of support avails the land only in its original state unencumbered by buildings or other constructions.[7] Although the limitation has been heavily criticised as inappropriate[8] and even 'catastrophic'[9] under modern urban conditions, the natural right comprises no right to support for buildings on the land.[10] If the action of a neighbour in demolishing a contiguous and supporting building or wall causes a landowner's house to collapse, he normally has no remedy in the absence of a duly acquired easement of support.[11] If, however, the neighbour's activities

3 Violation of a natural right is actionable in the law of nuisance (see *Clerk and Lindsell on Torts* (16th edn, London 1989), para 24-56ff).

4 See generally J.F. Garner, (1948) 12 Conv (NS) 280. This natural right is an incident of ownership which passes without express provision on transfer of the land (*M.C.A. Camilleri Building & Constructions Pty Ltd v H.R. Walters Pty Ltd* (1981) 2 BPR 9277 at 9279).

5 *Backhouse v Bonomi* (1861) 9 HL Cas 503 at 512f, 11 ER 825 at 829; *Bognuda v Upton & Shearer Ltd* [1972] NZLR 741 at 760; *M.C.A. Camilleri Building & Constructions Pty Ltd v H.R. Walters Pty Ltd* (1981) 2 BPR 9277 at 9279.

6 *Dalton v Angus & Co* (1881) 6 App Cas 740 at 808; *Byrne v Judd* (1908) 27 NZLR 1106 at 1118ff. The natural right of support does not include any right to have land supported by subterranean water present in adjoining land, with the result that no action lies in respect of the extraction of such water and consequent subsidence (*Stephens v Anglian Water Authority* (1988) 55 P & CR 348 at 351).

7 *Latimer v Official Co-operative Society* (1885) 16 LR Ir 305 at 308.

8 See *Kebewar Pty Ltd v Harkin* (1987) 9 NSWLR 738 at 740G-741A (Court of Appeal of New South Wales).

9 *M.C.A. Camilleri Building & Constructions Pty Ltd v H.R. Walters Pty Ltd* (1981) 2 BPR 9277 at 9280 per Needham J.

10 *Dalton v Angus & Co* (1881) 6 App Cas 740 at 804; *Midland Bank Plc v Bardgrove Property Services Ltd* [1991] 2 EGLR 283 at 286B; *Public Trustee v Hermann* [1968] 3 NSWR 94 at 108. It is possible that if a vendor sells part of his land, knowing that the purchaser intends to erect a building, the vendor may be taken as having impliedly covenanted not to use his own adjoining land so as to injure or interfere with the purchaser's new building (*Siddons v Short, Harley & Co* (1877) 2 CPD 572 at 577). See *Kebewar Pty Ltd v Harkin* (1987) 9 NSWLR 738 at 741B-742A (post, p 1091).

11 *Peyton v London Corpn* (1829) 9 B & C 725 at 735ff, 109 ER 269 at 273f; *Ray v Fairway Motors (Barnstaple) Ltd* (1968) 20 P & CR 261 at 264; *Green v Belfast Tramways Co* (1887) 20 LR Ir 35; *Gateley v H. & J. Martin Ltd* [1900] 2 IR 269 at 272f.

on his land would have caused the subsidence of land in any event, irrespective of the presence of buildings thereon, the damages recoverable for the violation of the natural right of support for land may include damages in respect of any buildings which have been affected.[12]

(ii) Remedies Violation[13] of a landowner's natural right to support gives rise to a liability in damages and may even be the subject of a mandatory injunction.[14] However, the natural right to support is not infringed if the land which has been excavated and the adjacent land from which lateral support has thereby been removed are both, at the date of excavation, within the common ownership of one person.[15] A subsequent purchaser of the portion of land from which lateral support has been removed cannot claim any violation of his 'natural right' in the event of a later collapse of his land,[16] but may be able to sue in negligence.[17]

(b) Other natural rights

Other forms of natural right may exist. The landowner has, for instance, a natural right to water where it flows naturally in a defined channel through

12 *Stroyan v Knowles* (1861) 6 H & N 454 at 465, 158 ER 186 at 191; *Hunt v Peake* (1860) 29 LJ Ch 785 at 787; *Ray v Fairway Motors (Barnstaple) Ltd* (1968) 20 P & CR 261 at 268; *Midland Bank Plc v Bardgrove Property Services Ltd* [1991] 2 EGLR 283 at 286F; *Public Trustee v Hermann* [1968] 3 NSWR 94 at 108f. See also *Brace v South East Regional Housing Association* (1984) 270 Estates Gazette 1286. See generally E.H. Bodkin, (1962) 26 Conv (NS) 210.

13 The right is violated only where the excavation of the adjacent or subjacent land of a neighbour causes actual disturbance of the surface of the plaintiff's land (see *Darley Main Colliery Co v Mitchell* (1886) 11 App Cas 127 at 151). There is no interference with the natural right to support where the plaintiff's land suffers a mere loss of stability as distinct from actual physical damage (*Lamb v Walker* (1878) 3 QBD 389 at 400; *West Leigh Colliery Co v Tunnicliffe* [1908] AC 27 at 29; *Midland Bank Plc v Bardgrove Property Services Ltd* [1991] 2 EGLR 283 at 286F-G).

14 See *Redland Bricks Ltd v Morris* [1969] 2 All ER 576 at 579H-580F; *Economy Shipping Pty Ltd v A.D.C. Buildings Pty Ltd and Fischer Constructions Pty Ltd* [1969] 2 NSWR 97 at 106; *Grocott v Ayson* [1975] 2 NZLR 586 at 590. It seems that the withdrawal of support is not actionable in itself but only when actual damage ensues (*Taylor v Auto Trade Supply Ltd* [1972] NZLR 102 at 108; *Bognuda v Upton & Shearer Ltd* [1972] NZLR 741 at 760). Damages cannot be awarded in respect of prospective loss flowing from the infringement of a natural right, with the result that de minimis violations of the right, even if accompanied by trivial damage, are not properly the subject of any remedy (see *Hirst v Klomp* (1981) NZ Recent Law 359 at 360).

15 *Blewman v Wilkinson* [1979] 2 NZLR 208 at 211ff. See also *Jennings v Sylvania Waters Pty Ltd* [1972] 2 NSWLR 4 at 14C-D; *Soich v Sutherland SC* (1980) 2 BPR 9273 at 9275.

16 *M.C.A. Camilleri Building & Constructions Pty Ltd v H.R. Walters Pty Ltd* (1981) 2 BPR 9277 at 9281. See also *Soich v Sutherland SC* (1980) 2 BPR 9273 at 9275 per McLelland J.

17 *Blewman v Wilkinson* [1979] 2 NZLR 208 at 212, 215, 217. See also *Bognuda v Upton & Shearer Ltd* [1972] NZLR 741 at 757ff. An action for loss of support may lie against the person withdrawing support even though he has since ceased to own the land adjoining that from which support was withdrawn (*Thynne v Petrie* [1975] Qd R 260 at 262F-G). The successor in title of the person who withdrew the support is not liable for the acts of his predecessor (*Greenwell v Low Beechburn Coal Co* [1897] 2 QB 165 at 176ff; *Hall v Duke of Norfolk* [1900] 2 Ch 493 at 502f).

or past his land.[18] This natural right, being part of the fee simple estate in the land, passes without any express provision on the conveyance of that estate.[19] However, since natural rights cannot arise in respect of buildings, there is no such thing as a natural right to even 'a single ray of light'.[20] Rights to light can be created or acquired only as easements.[1]

(6) Local customary rights

Local customary rights differ from easements in that they are not necessarily appurtenant to any dominant tenement but are exercisable generally by the members of a particular local community such as a town[2] or a parish.[3] Customary rights have been held to extend to such activities as the use of an access path to the local church,[4] the playing of sports and pastimes on a piece of land,[5] the drying of fishing nets in a certain location,[6] and the holding of an annual 'fair or wake'.[7] Local customary rights can arise at common law only if they are ancient,[8] certain, reasonable and continuous.[9]

2. ESSENTIAL CHARACTERISTICS OF AN EASEMENT

An easement is an incorporeal hereditament or proprietary right, conferring on its owner (in the absence of contrary intention) such ancillary rights as are reasonably necessary to effective exercise and enjoyment of the right granted.[10] As a proprietary right an easement may even be the subject of

18 *Chasemore v Richards* (1859) 7 HL Cas 349 at 382, 11 ER 140 at 153; *Swindon Waterworks Co Ltd v Wilts and Berks Canal Navigation Co* (1875) LR 7 HL 697 at 704ff; *Jennings v Sylvania Waters Pty Ltd* [1972] 2 NSWLR 4 at 10E. There is no natural right to water which percolates underground in an undefined channel (see *Bradford Corpn v Pickles* [1895] AC 587 at 592, 595, 600). Such percolating water is 'a common reservoir or source in which nobody has any property, but of which everybody has, as far as he can, the right of appropriating the whole' (*Ballard v Tomlinson* (1885) 29 Ch D 115 at 121 per Brett MR). See also *Steadman v Erickson Gold Mining Corp* (1989) 56 DLR (4th) 577 at 579f. Strict liability attaches to any pollution of such water (*Ballard* at 121ff; *Cambridge Water Co v Eastern Counties Leather plc* [1992] EGCS 142). See also J.S. Fiennes, (1938) 2 Conv (NS) 203; P. Brett, (1950) 14 Conv (NS) 154.

19 *Jennings v Sylvania Waters Pty Ltd* [1972] 2 NSWLR 4 at 12B-D.

20 C.J. Gale, *Law of Easements* (12th edn, London 1950), p 6.

1 See *Earl Putnam Organisation Ltd v Macdonald* (1979) 91 DLR (3d) 714 at 717f.

2 *New Windsor Corporation v Mellor* [1975] Ch 380 at 391C-D.

3 *Brocklebank v Thompson* [1903] 2 Ch 344 at 354.

4 *Brocklebank v Thompson* [1903] 2 Ch 344 at 355.

5 *New Windsor Corporation v Mellor* [1975] Ch 380 at 392H.

6 *Mercer v Denne* [1905] 2 Ch 538 at 577ff.

7 *Wyld v Silver* [1963] Ch 243 at 256, 266.

8 In theory 'ancient' rights must pre-date 1189, but in practice the requirement of ancient origin is satisfied by evidence of uninterrupted long user for 20 years (or perhaps within living memory), provided always that there is no proof that the user actually originated after 1189 (see *Simpson v Wells* (1872) LR 7 QB 214 at 217; *Mercer v Denne* [1905] 2 Ch 538 at 577).

9 *Lockwood v Wood* (1844) 6 QB 50 at 64, 115 ER 19 at 24; *Daly v Cullen* (1958) 92 ILTR 127 at 130.

10 *Guth v Robinson* (1977) 1 BPR 9209 at 9215f; *Zenere v Leate* (1980) 1 BPR 9300 at 9305; *Mercantile General Life Reassurance Co of Australia Ltd v Permanent Trustee Australia Ltd* (1989) NSW ConvR 55-441 at 58,210. Trespass is committed by the owner who exceeds the express or implied scope of the rights granted (see *Mills v Silver* [1991] Ch 271 at 295A).

a trust and may therefore be held by way of legal or equitable title.[11] In view of the proprietary character of the easement, the courts have applied stringent qualifying conditions to the class of rights which may be asserted under this head. In *In re Ellenborough Park*[12] Danckwerts J defined the essential qualities of an easement in the following terms:

> (1) there must be a dominant and a servient tenement; (2) an easement must accommodate the dominant tenement, that is, be connected with its enjoyment and for its benefit; (3) the dominant and servient owners must be different persons; and (4) the right claimed must be capable of forming the subject-matter of a grant.

There is a strong tendency to accord the status of an easement to any right which satisfies these requirements,[13] irrespective of the precise label which the right in question may have been given by the parties themselves.[14]

(1) There must be a dominant tenement and a servient tenement

An easement cannot exist 'in gross' but only as appurtenant to a defined area of land.[15] An easement must in effect be linked with two parcels of land.[16] There must be a 'dominant tenement' in favour of which the easement is created or acquired,[17] and there must be a 'servient tenement' over which the easement is exercised or exercisable.[18] It is important, moreover, that at the date of grant of an easement, the grantor should own a relevant interest[19] in the servient land and the grantee a relevant interest in the dominant land.[20] As was confirmed in *London & Blenheim Estates Ltd v Ladbroke Retail Parks Ltd*,[1] there seems to be no objection to the present grant of a future estate or interest in an easement, but at the date of grant the 'essentials

11 See eg *Guth v Robinson* (1977) 1 BPR 9209 at 9213 per Powell J.
12 [1956] Ch 131 at 140.
13 See J.F. Garner, (1983) 127 SJ 95, 115. The criteria confirmed by Danckwerts J have been widely adopted (see eg *Shelf Holdings Ltd v Husky Oil Operations Ltd* (1989) 56 DLR (4th) 193 at 197f; *Canadian Pacific Ltd v Paul* (1989) 53 DLR (4th) 487 at 499 (Supreme Court of Canada)).
14 See eg *Riley v Penttila* [1974] VR 547 at 560 (a 'liberty' to use and enjoy an area of land construed as an easement).
15 *Alfred F. Beckett Ltd v Lyons* [1967] Ch 449 at 483E per Winn LJ; *Commissioner of Main Roads v North Shore Gas Co Ltd* (1967) 120 CLR 118 at 134 per Windeyer J; *Gas & Fuel Corpn of Victoria v Barba* [1976] VR 755 at 763. See generally M.F. Sturley, (1980) 96 LQR 557. Compare the law of New Zealand which has by statute dispensed with the general requirement of a dominant tenement (see Property Law Act 1952, s 122).
16 *London & Blenheim Estates Ltd v Ladbroke Retail Parks Ltd* [1992] 1 WLR 1278 at 1283B per Judge Paul Baker QC.
17 *London & Blenheim Estates Ltd v Ladbroke Retail Parks Ltd* [1992] 1 WLR 1278 at 1281F-G. Thus, for instance, a member of a golf club cannot acquire any easement to play golf, since there exists no dominant tenement in the sense required (*Banstead Downs Golf Club v The Commissioners* (1974) VATTR 219 at 226). It is sufficient—albeit rare—that the legal title to an easement should be vested in a bare trustee for the owner of the land to which the easement is intended to be appurtenant (see *Guth v Robinson* (1977) 1 BPR 9209 at 9213).
18 *Re Gordon and Regan* (1985) 15 DLR (4th) 641 at 643. It is irrelevant that the servient tenement may serve more than one dominant tenement (see eg *In re Ellenborough Park* [1956] Ch 131 at 175 (post, p 1068); *Harada v Registrar of Titles* [1981] VR 743 at 751; *Sunset Properties Pty Ltd v Johnston* (1975) 3 BPR 9185 at 9197).
19 Post, p 1070.
20 Post, p 1071.
1 [1992] 1 WLR 1278 at 1284E-F.

of an easement' must be satisfied. Thus, for instance, there can be no valid grant where the potentially servient tenement is disposed of by its owner in advance of the intended dominant owner's acquisition of the land supposed to be benefited.[2] No estate or interest in an easement can subsist in respect of a non-existent hereditament.[3]

(a) *Requirement of two tenements*

The requirement of a relationship of dominance and servience was laid down clearly by Cresswell J in *Ackroyd v Smith*.[4] Here the plaintiff and the defendant owned adjoining areas of land. The plaintiff's predecessor in title had granted to an earlier owner of the adjoining land a right to use a road across his land. When this right was subsequently claimed as an easement, Cresswell J held the right to be a mere licence on the ground that a 'right unconnected with the enjoyment or occupation of the land cannot be annexed as an incident to it.' The right concerned in the present case had been granted 'for all purposes' to the 'owners and occupiers' of the adjoining land and to 'all persons having occasion to resort thereto'. This right was held to be too ample to qualify as an easement, on the principle that a right of way cannot be granted in gross, and 'no one can have such a way but he who has the land to which it is appendant'.[5] A right granted in gross was, in the view of Cresswell J, 'personal only, and cannot be assigned'.[6] Cresswell J rationalised this rule by reference to a sentiment which pervades the early law of easements and covenants.[7] He ruled that

> It is not in the power of a vendor to create any rights not connected with the use or enjoyment of the land, and annex them to it: nor can the owner of land render it subject to a new species of burthen, so as to bind it in the hands of an assignee. 'Incidents of a novel kind cannot be devised, and attached to property, at the fancy or caprice of any owner'.[8]

Within this statement is contained the implicit concern lest an easement in gross impose 'clogs upon the title' which may render the servient land unmarketable.[9] The rationale underlying this requirement of a dominant

2 *London & Blenheim Estates Ltd v Ladbroke Retail Parks Ltd* [1992] 1 WLR 1278 at 1283B, 1284F.
3 [1992] 1 WLR 1278 at 1284F.
4 (1850) 10 CB 164 at 187ff, 138 ER 68 at 77.
5 (1850) 10 CB 164 at 188, 138 ER 68 at 77. If, however, the formal grant of the easement had been limited to the person in possession of the dominant tenement, the right of way would also have been available to other persons who had express or implied authority from the dominant tenant. See eg the reference in *Baxendale v North Lambeth Liberal and Radical Club Ltd* [1902] 2 Ch 427 at 429 to 'members of [the grantee's] family, servants, visitors, guests and tradespeople'. See also *Woodhouse and Co Ltd v Kirkland (Derby) Ltd* [1970] 1 WLR 1185 at 1190F-H; *Hammond v Prentice Brothers Ltd* [1920] 1 Ch 201 at 216; *Grinskis v Lahood* [1971] NZLR 502 at 509.
6 (1850) 10 CB 164 at 188, 138 ER 68 at 77. This case has been said to be 'not easy to understand' (*Todrick v Western National Omnibus Co Ltd* [1934] Ch 561 at 572). It is probably best explained as a case in which the purposes for which the relevant right was granted 'were to a great extent unconnected with the use of the close to which that right was claimed as appurtenant' (*Thorpe v Brumfitt* (1873) 8 Ch App 650 at 657 per Mellish LJ). See also the doubts expressed in *Guth v Robinson* (1977) 1 BPR 9209 at 9210 per Powell J.
7 Post, p 1136.
8 (1850) 10 CB 164 at 188, 138 ER 68 at 77f, quoting *Keppell v Bailey* (1834) 2 My & K 517 at 535, 39 ER 1042 at 1049.
9 See M.F. Sturley, (1980) 96 LQR 557 at 562f.

tenement is today somewhat open to challenge.[10] It may be that the abolition of the rule which forbids easements in gross would nowadays promote rather than impede the optimal utilisation of land. Sometimes, of course, this rule is effectively relaxed by statute in order to confer certain rights of use and inspection upon those bodies which operate vital public services and utilities (eg electricity, gas and water authorities).[11] In such cases the requirement of a dominant tenement is abrogated in order to further certain public or community-related purposes.[12] However, it is arguable that the requirement should also be abrogated even in relation to easements which are directed at wholly private purposes.

(b) An easement may run with both tenements

An easement is a proprietary right in the sense that, once duly created and acquired, it annexes a burden to the servient tenement and an equivalent benefit to the dominant tenement in such manner as to affect the successors in title of either tenement. The precise effects of the easement on third parties depend to some extent on the legal or equitable quality of the easement[13] and on whether it relates to unregistered or registered land. The relevant problems arise where A has granted an easement to B (see *Fig.* 68). Are C and D affected by respectively the burden and benefit of that easement?

(i) Unregistered land Where an easement is appurtenant to a dominant tenement, it becomes notionally affixed to that tenement in the same way that fixtures become annexed to realty.[14] In consequence the benefit of the

10 It has been questioned, for instance, whether a company which runs a helicopter shuttle service should be obliged to make the slightly disingenuous claim that its West End office constitutes the 'dominant tenement' in respect of some distant landing pad over which it exercises rights (see M.F. Sturley, (1980) 96 LQR 557 at 565, 567).

11 'The gas company has. . .no true easement; for there is no true dominant tenement unless it be said to be the gas works' (*Commissioner of Main Roads v North Shore Gas Co Ltd* (1967) 120 CLR 118 at 133 per Windeyer J). However loose and inaccurate the use of the term 'easement' in this context (see C. Sweet, (1916) 32 LQR 70 at 79ff), such easements seem to comprise a category of 'statutory easements' which are appurtenant only to some enterprise rather than to any particularly convincing dominant tenement (see J.F. Garner, (1956) 20 Conv (NS) 208). As Michael Sturley has said, 'land throughout England is burdened with servitudes that satisfy none of the traditional common law requirements' (55 S Cal L Rev 1417 at 1423 (1982)).

12 Alternatively it can perhaps be said that the dominant tenement relevant to such easements comprises both corporeal and incorporeal hereditaments (see *Re Salvin's Indenture* [1938] 2 All ER 498 at 506D-F), the latter being the similar rights of user which a public utility acquires in other adjoining lands. See *Gas & Fuel Corporation of Victoria v Barba* [1976] VR 755 at 763f. That a dominant tenement may consist of incorporeal property is clear from *Hanbury v Jenkins* [1901] 2 Ch 401 at 422f.

13 Ante, p 71.

14 Ante, p 11. See also Law of Property Act 1925, s 187(1). In particular, there is a prima facie inference that the easement becomes appurtenant to each and every part of the dominant tenement (see *Callard v Beeney* [1930] 1 KB 353 at 360f; *Laurie v Winch* [1952] 4 DLR 449 at 456f; *Re Maiorana and the Conveyancing Act* [1970] 1 NSWR 627 at 634; *Re Gordon and Regan* (1985) 15 DLR (4th) 641 at 645). This inference may be rebutted by contrary words of grant (see *Jennison v Traficante* (1980) 1 BPR 9657 at 9658f), but an easement is otherwise severable and is not destroyed by a later subdivision of the dominant tenement (see eg *Newcomen v Coulson* (1877) 5 Ch D 133 at 141 per Jessel MR; *Guth v Robinson* (1977) 1 BPR 9209 at 9214). In consequence the law of easements has avoided the problems which once bedevilled the law of restrictive covenants in relation to subsequent fragmentation of the dominant tenement (post, p 1152).

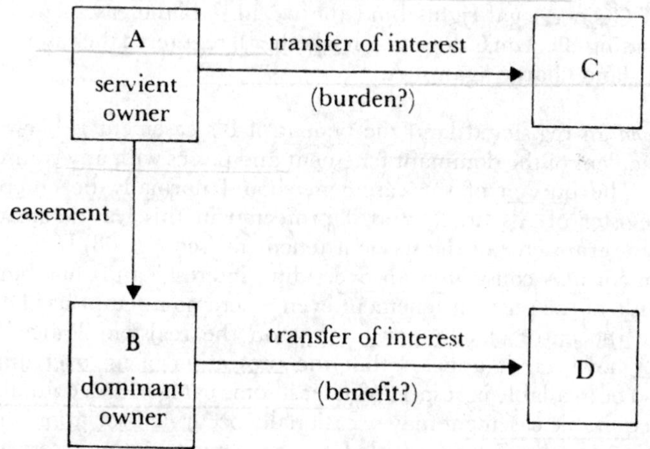

Fig. 68

easement passes with any subsequent conveyance by deed of the land concerned.[15] Thus, in *Fig.* 68, the benefit of the easement granted by A to B can be invoked by D, regardless of whether the easement was legal or equitable.

The mere fact that the benefit of an easement remains an incident of the dominant tenement in the hands of B's successor does not, however, mean that the right is enforceable against A's successor, C. This result will follow only if the burden of the easement was effectively transmitted to C under the rules which govern the binding effect of land interests in English law. There is here, of course, a difficulty for the lay person who imagines in his innocence that there can be no 'benefit' for anyone unless someone else is simultaneously subject to a correlative 'burden'.[16] However, the land lawyer approaches the issue of enforceability in an artificial manner which at first seems semantically confusing. 'Benefit' and 'burden' are treated as separate and unconnected phenomena, the transmission of which is governed by divergent principles. The apparent illogic of this approach is less bizarre when considered in the forensic context. Any action to enforce an easement will succeed only if the plaintiff can be shown to have the 'benefit', and the defendant the 'burden', of the easement in question. Thus, for the land lawyer, the real questions are whether (in *Fig.* 68) the 'benefit' of the easement concerned has been got out of B into D, and the 'burden' out of A into C.

In unregistered land, the rules governing the transmission of the burden of easements are relatively straightforward. If the easement granted by A

15 *Godwin v Schweppes Ltd* [1902] 1 Ch 926 at 932; *Wright v Macadam* [1949] 2 KB 744 at 754; *Sunset Properties Pty Ltd v Johnston* (1975) 3 BPR 9185 at 9189 (devise). See also Law of Property Act 1925, s 62(1) (post, p 1100); *Leech v Schweder* (1874) 9 Ch App 463 at 474f; *Graham v Philcox* [1984] QB 747 at 757E-F, 764F-G. The benefit of the easement may therefore be enjoyed by the occupier for the time being of the dominant land even if he is a mere lessee of that land (see *Thorpe v Brumfitt* (1873) 8 Ch App 650 at 655f).

16 See, however, *Rogers v Hosegood* [1900] 2 Ch 388 at 395 per Farwell J.

to B was legal, its burden will automatically affect the servient tenement in the hands of C since legal rights bind the world.[17] If the easement was equitable, its binding effect on C depends on whether B registered the easement as a Class D(iii) land charge against A.[18]

(ii) Registered land In registered land the benefit of B's easement is likewise a proprietary incident of the dominant tenement and passes with any transfer of B's estate.[19] The burden of the easement should normally be entered by B on the register of A's title,[20] and if protected in this way is clearly binding on C, the transferee of the servient tenement (see *Fig.* 68).[1]

A legal easement also constitutes an overriding interest,[2] and thus binds a successor in title of the servient tenement even where no attempt has been made to secure the entry of a minor interest on the register. Somewhat controversially,[3] however, it appears that the protection of an overriding interest may also be available in respect of at least some categories of equitable easement.[4] An equitable easement may occasionally occur in association with actual occupation by the person entitled to the benefit of the easement, in which case the easement is protected under the Land Registration Act 1925, s 70(1)(g).[5] In *Celsteel Ltd v Alton House Holdings Ltd*,[6] moreover, Scott J held that an equitable right of way could also be protected as an overriding interest pursuant to the Land Registration Act 1925, s 70(1)(a), where such an easement was 'openly exercised and enjoyed' as appurtenant to the dominant tenement at the date of the relevant transfer of the servient tenement.[7] In view of the confused state of the law in this area, there is

17 Ante, p 76.
18 Ante, p 151. There is some possibility in this context that an unregistered land charge may still be enforceable against C on grounds of estoppel if C had knowledge of its existence at the time of the transfer to him (see *E.R. Ives Investment Ltd v High* [1967] 2 QB 379, ante, p 152).
19 Reference to a legal easement may be entered on the property register of the relevant dominant tenement (Land Registration Rules 1925, rr 3(2)(c), 252, 254, 257 (ante, p 171)).
20 Land Registration Rules 1925, r 41. See *Celsteel Ltd v Alton House Holdings Ltd* [1985] 1 WLR 204 at 220E-F.
1 Land Registration Act 1925, ss 20(1)(a), 23(1)(b).
2 Land Registration Act 1970, s 70(1)(a); Land Registration Rules 1925, r 258 (ante, p 201).
3 See eg Law Commission, *Property Law: Third Report on Land Registration: A. Overriding Interests, B. Rectification and Indemnity, C. Minor Interests* (Law Com No 158, 31 March 1987), paras 2.31ff.
4 It had been assumed by many commentators that this possibility was excluded by the fact that Land Registration Act 1925, s 70(1)(a) expressly covers only easements other than 'equitable easements required to be protected by notice on the register' (see M.P. Thompson, [1986] Conv 31). However, this provision is ambivalent since there is no strict requirement that a person entitled to an equitable easement should necessarily protect it by entry on the register.
5 *Celsteel Ltd v Alton House Holdings Ltd* [1985] 1 WLR 204 at 220G. If, however, the easement in question is a right of way, it is unlikely that there will be actual occupation of the servient tenement (see *Celsteel* at 219E (ante, p 218)). Indeed such occupation may well be incompatible with the essentially non-exclusive character of an easement (see M.P. Thompson, [1986] Conv 31 at 36).
6 [1985] 1 WLR 204 at 220H–221D. The Court of Appeal did not subsequently interfere with this ruling ([1986] 1 WLR 512).
7 Land Registration Rules 1925, r 258 provides that rights, privileges and appurtenances 'appertaining or reputed to appertain to land...which adversely affect registered land' constitute overriding interests within Land Registration Act 1925, s 70.

a strong argument for the elimination of overriding status for any unprotected equitable easement.[8]

(2) The easement must 'accommodate' the dominant tenement

No right may qualify as an easement unless it can be shown that the right confers benefit on the dominant tenement as distinct from some merely personal advantage on the dominant owner.[9] The criterion of benefit rests ultimately on whether the dominant tenement is accommodated and its use made more beneficial by the right in question.[10]

(a) Exclusion of purely personal or commercial advantages

The classic example of a purely personal advantage which could not be claimed as an easement is the right which was alleged by the plaintiff in *Hill v Tupper*.[11] Here the owner of a canal leased land on the canal bank to the plaintiff and purported to grant him a 'sole and exclusive' right to put pleasure boats on the canal. The plaintiff subsequently contended that he had acquired an easement in respect of the canal which was enforceable against the defendant, the landlord of a nearby inn, who unlawfully interfered with the plaintiff's trade by putting rival boats on the same canal. This claim to an easement was not upheld by the court, which took the view that the plaintiff had acquired merely a licence which was, of course, unenforceable except against the licensor.

The ground for the decision in *Hill v Tupper* is somewhat unclear. Pollock CB observed that a 'new species of incorporeal hereditament cannot be created at the will and pleasure of the owner of property.'[12] Martin B held that to admit the right claimed by the plaintiff 'would lead to the creation of an infinite variety of interests in land, and an indefinite increase of possible estates.'[13] Such statements appear to be yet further expressions of the policy against imposing 'clogs' which might tend to make a title uncommerciable or inalienable. However, perhaps the most potent factor in the minds of the judges in this case was their clear apprehension that the right claimed by the plaintiff was not appurtenant to any dominant tenement. Pollock CB cited *Ackroyd v Smith*[14] in support of the proposition that it is impossible to create easements in respect of 'rights unconnected with the use and enjoyment of land.' In the present case it was scarcely realistic to argue that the plaintiff's contractual rights over the canal were such as to make his occupation of the land on the canal bank more convenient. The area

8 See M.P. Thompson, [1986] Conv 31 at 37.

9 *Dukart v District of Surrey* (1978) 86 DLR (3d) 609 at 616 (Supreme Court of Canada). There must be dominant land, but not necessarily a dominant building (see *Commonwealth v Registrar of Titles (Victoria)* (1918) 24 CLR 348 at 353, 355). See also *Waveney DC v Wholgemouth* (1985) *Times*, 11 July.

10 The criterion of accommodation must be determined at the date of grant, and it seems generally irrelevant that the benefit conferred by the easement is diminished or altogether frustrated by subsequent events (see *Huckvale v Aegean Hotels Ltd* (1989) 58 P & CR 163 at 168; [1990] Conv 292 (G. Kodilinye)).

11 (1863) 2 H & C 121, 159 ER 51.

12 (1863) 2 H & C 121 at 127, 159 ER 51 at 53.

13 (1863) 2 H & C 121 at 128, 159 ER 51 at 53.

14 (1850) 10 CB 164, 138 ER 68 (ante, p 1061).

in question included a landing stage, and it was clearly the case that this landing stage facilitated the plaintiff's use of the canal rather than vice versa.[15]

It may also be that in *Hill v Tupper* the court felt disinclined to allow a purely commercial advantage to be claimed as an easement. The plaintiff was seeking in effect to assert a commercial monopoly in respect of the business of putting pleasure boats on the canal in question. There was no sense in which the plaintiff's occupation of the alleged dominant tenement was enhanced by the easement, because his use of that land was entirely incidental to his entrepreneurial exploitation of the waterway.[16] It is also possible that the judgments in *Hill v Tupper* concealed a distaste for rights which are over-broad. It is characteristic of the easement that it should not smack of exclusiveness of possession or control.

(b) Requirement of propinquity

In order to support the claim that a given right 'accommodates' the alleged dominant tenement, there is some requirement of propinquity in relation to the servient and dominant tenements. There is no rule that the dominant and servient land must be contiguous,[17] but the servient land must at least be sufficiently closely situated to confer a practical benefit on the dominant land.[18] It is for this reason that the example is often given that there cannot be 'a right of way over land in Kent appurtenant to an estate in Northumberland'.[19]

(c) Nature of the accommodation or benefit conferred

It is an elusive task to define in positive terms the nature of the benefit which must be shown to have been conferred on the alleged dominant tenement. There is, of course, a crude sense in which in the law of easements all benefits are ultimately enjoyed by people rather than by land.[20] In *Dukart v District of Surrey*,[1] the Supreme Court of Canada spoke of the need to show that 'the dominant tenement is accommodated, serviced or supported

15 See *In re Ellenborough Park* [1956] Ch 131 at 175. It is possible that the right claimed would have been upheld as an easement if it had provided an effective means of access and egress from the plaintiff's land and the defendant's boats had interfered with that access.

16 See *In re Ellenborough Park* [1956] Ch 131 at 175, where Evershed MR said, with reference to *Hill v Tupper*, that 'it is clear that what the plaintiff was trying to do was to set up, under the guise of an easement, a monopoly which had no normal connexion with the ordinary use of his land, but which was merely an independent business enterprise. So far from the right claimed sub-serving or accommodating the land, the land was but a convenient incident to the exercise of the right.' See, however, [1956] CLJ 24 at 25 (R.N. Gooderson).

17 *Re Salvin's Indenture* [1938] 2 All ER 498 at 506G; *Guth v Robinson* (1977) 1 BPR 9209 at 9214; *Harada v Registrar of Titles* [1981] VR 743 at 751f. See also *In re Ellenborough Park* [1956] Ch 131 at 175 (where the requirement of benefit was satisfied even in respect of those houses which did not front on to the park).

18 *Bailey v Stephens* (1862) 12 CB (NS) 91 at 115, 142 ER 1077 at 1086; *Todrick v Western National Omnibus Co Ltd* [1934] Ch 561 at 572ff, 580f, 589ff; (1934) 50 LQR 313; *Pugh v Savage* [1970] 2 QB 373 at 381C-D; *Dewhirst v Edwards* [1983] 1 NSWLR 34 at 51E-F.

19 See *Bailey v Stephens* (1862) 12 CB (NS) 91 at 115, 142 ER 1077 at 1086 per Byles J; *Todrick v Western National Omnibus Co Ltd* [1934] Ch 561 at 580.

20 Post, p 1146.

1 (1978) 86 DLR (3d) 609 at 616.

by the servient tenement'. There must be between the dominant tenement and the servient tenement 'a connection of real benefit to the former . . . which is of such a character as would ordinarily be classified as a right or condition running with the land and not merely a contractual right enuring to the benefit only of persons who are parties thereto at its inception.'

(i) Enhancement of land value The test whether a particular right increases the market value of the benefited land is relevant but not conclusive.[2] There are many kinds of right which may have this effect, but not all would qualify as easements. As the Court of Appeal indicated in *In re Ellenborough Park*,[3] there must be some 'sufficient nexus between the enjoyment of the right and the use of [the dominant property].' Thus a right granted to the purchaser of a particular house to use the Zoological Gardens free of charge or to attend Lord's Cricket Ground without payment, although undoubtedly increasing the value of the property conveyed, could not at law run with the property as an easement. Such rights would be 'wholly extraneous to, and independent of, the use of a house as a house, namely as a place in which the householder and his family live and make their home.'

(ii) Exclusiveness of benefit is not necessary Such benefit as is conferred by an easement need not relate exclusively to the dominant owner. It is not fatal, for instance, to the status of an easement that it comprises a right of way which is capable of benefiting not merely the dominant tenement but also 'any passer-by, wholly unconnected with the dominant tenement, who chooses to use it as a short cut'.[4]

(iii) Benefit to trade conducted on the dominant tenement It seems to be a sufficient accommodation of the dominant tenement that the right claimed as an easement should facilitate or benefit some trade or business which is carried on in the dominant land. In *Moody v Steggles*,[5] for instance, Fry J held that the owner of a public house might claim an easement to hang a signboard on the adjoining house.[6] A commercial benefit extracted from business conducted on the servient tenement is not, however, enough to validate the claim of easement.[7]

(iv) Integral aspects of commodious domestic living In the residential context it seems that the test of accommodation requires the making of ultimately social judgments as to the kinds of benefit or advantage which are integral to the domestic arrangements required for commodious living.[8] In *In re*

2 *In re Ellenborough Park* [1956] Ch 131 at 173.
3 [1956] Ch 131 at 174. See [1956] CLJ 24 (R.N. Gooderson); (1956) 72 LQR 16 (R.E.M.).
4 *In re Ellenborough Park* [1956] Ch 131 at 172.
5 (1879) 12 Ch D 261 at 266ff. See also *Ellis v Mayor of Bridgnorth* (1863) 15 CB (NS) 52 at 78, 143 ER 702 at 712; *Leon Asper Amusements Ltd v Northmain Carwash & Enterprises Ltd* (1966) 56 DLR (2d) 173 at 176.
6 See also *William Hill (Southern) Ltd v Cabras Ltd* (1987) 54 P & CR 42 at 46.
7 See *Hill v Tupper* (1863) 2 H & C 121, 159 ER 51 (ante, p 1065).
8 Uriel Reichman has pointed out that 'what is a land use-related promise changes somewhat according to contemporary views. The striving for amenities and security in densely populated areas has already caused some changes. Matters which were looked upon in the past as indicative of hypersensitivity or extreme fine taste, and accordingly merely personal, have become a market commodity today' (7 J Legal Stud 139 at 155 (1978)).

Ellenborough Park,[9] for example, a number of owners of residential properties had been given a right of common enjoyment of a park or pleasure ground which was enclosed by their houses and which was vested in trustees. Each adjoining owner paid a proportionate part of the cost required to maintain the pleasure ground as a well stocked and carefully ordered garden. The Court of Appeal held that the right granted each purchaser of 'full enjoyment. . .of the pleasure ground' was capable of forming the subject matter of an easement. Underlying this decision was an almost unspoken value judgment that 'the use of a garden undoubtedly enhances, and is connected with, the normal enjoyment of the house to which it belongs'.[10] In the present circumstances the park had become the 'communal garden for the benefit and enjoyment of those whose houses adjoined it or were in its close proximity'[11] and as such amply satisfied the 'requirement of connexion with the dominant tenements to which it is appurtenant.'[12]

As this case demonstrates, the definition of qualifying rights in the law of easements is heavily coloured by an element of value judgment. Such judgments relate not only to the sorts of activity claimed as amounting to an easement, but also to the relative degree of merit which is thought to attach to the party advancing the claim. In *In re Ellenborough Park* the Court of Appeal had little difficulty in applying the terminology of easements to the civilised user by civilised people of a communal garden situated in an excessively bourgeois location.

(v) A purely recreational user may not be an easement There is some authority in English law for the view that a mere right of 'recreation and amusement' can never qualify as an easement since such a right lacks any capacity to confer 'utility and benefit' on land.[13] There can in short be no easement merely to have fun. Consistent with this limitation is the once widely accepted notion that the concept of an easement cannot encompass a *ius spatiandi*, ie 'a privilege of wandering at will over all and every part of another's field or park'.[14]

It is clear, however, that neither of these restrictions on the scope of easements is absolute. In *In re Ellenborough Park*[15] the Court of Appeal agreed that a *ius spatiandi*, being an 'indefinite and unregulated privilege', would indeed lack the essential qualities of an easement. The Court nevertheless considered a *ius spatiandi* to be 'substantially different' from the grant in the present case, which comprised 'the provision for a limited number of

9 [1956] Ch 131.

10 [1956] Ch 131 at 174 per Evershed MR. See also *Riley v Penttila* [1974] VR 547 at 559f ('For gracious living it has been found for a very long time. . .necessary to have space in areas around a house for the purposes of a garden and recreation, and even of a park. Undoubtedly, it adds to the enjoyment of the occupation of such house property').

11 [1956] Ch 131 at 174.

12 [1956] Ch 131 at 175. See also *Wright v Macadam* [1949] 2 KB 744 at 752, where Jenkins LJ accepted the easement character of a right to store 'such coal as might be required for the domestic purposes of the flat'.

13 *Solomon v Vintners' Company* (1859) 4 H & N 585 at 593, 157 ER 970 at 974; *Mounsey v Ismay* (1865) 3 H & C 486 at 498, 159 ER 621 at 625. See H.S. Theobald, *The Law of Land* (2nd edn, London 1929), p 263.

14 *In re Ellenborough Park* [1956] Ch 131 at 176 per Evershed MR. See *International Tea Stores Co v Hobbs* [1903] 2 Ch 165 at 172; *Attorney-General v Antrobus* [1905] 2 Ch 188 at 198ff.

15 [1956] Ch 131 at 176.

houses in a uniform crescent of one single large but private garden'.[16] Moreover, although in the view of Evershed MR 'a garden is a pleasure—on high authority, it is the purest of pleasures',[17] the right claimed here was 'appurtenant to the surrounding houses as such', and constituted 'a beneficial attribute of residence in a house as ordinarily understood.'[18] The Court of Appeal thus concluded that the use of the communal garden 'for the purposes, not only of exercise and rest but also for such domestic purposes as. . .taking out small children in perambulators or otherwise. . .is not fairly to be described as one of mere recreation or amusement, and is clearly beneficial to the premises to which it is attached.'[19]

(3) The dominant and servient tenements must be owned or occupied by different persons

An easement is by definition a right over somebody else's land. It is therefore impossible that the same person should both own *and occupy* the dominant and servient tenements, since it is a nonsense that a man should have rights against himself.[20] It is, however, quite feasible that a tenant should acquire an easement over his landlord's land, since although in this situation there is common ownership of the dominant and servient tenements, there is no common occupation.[1] Likewise a landlord may equally well acquire an easement in respect of land which is the subject of a lease to his own tenant.[2]

16 [1956] Ch 131 at 176. In *Dukart v District of Surrey* (1978) 86 DLR (3d) 609 at 616, the Supreme Court of Canada took the view that *In re Ellenborough Park* had established that some kinds of ius spatiandi are sufficiently determinate to deserve easement status. The Supreme Court pointed in particular to the fact that in *In re Ellenborough Park* Evershed MR had emphasised ([1956] Ch 131 at 179) that an easement may include a right of 'wandering at will round each and every part of the garden except of course, such parts as comprise flower beds, or are laid out for some other purpose, which renders walking impossible or unsuitable.' In *Dukart* the Supreme Court held, on similar grounds, that there can be an easement to wander at large over a beach beside a resort development. See also *Riley v Penttila* [1974] VR 547 at 559, where an easement was held to arise on the basis of a right of enjoyment of a defined area for recreation which had been given not to the public but to a limited number of lot holders.

17 [1956] Ch 131 at 179. The idea that a garden is a numinous place goes back as far as the first garden, where Adam communed with God in in the cool of the evening.

18 [1956] Ch 131 at 179.

19 [1956] Ch 131 at 179. For another instance of judicial indulgence towards perambulators, see *Behrens v Richards* [1905] 2 Ch 614 at 622.

20 *Morris v Edgington* (1810) 3 Taunt 24 at 30, 128 ER 10 at 13; *Greathead v Morley* (1841) 3 Man & G 139 at 156, 133 ER 1090 at 1097; *Bolton v Bolton* (1879) 11 Ch D 968 at 970f; *Metropolitan Railway Co v Fowler* [1892] 1 QB 165 at 171; *Wright v Macadam* [1949] 2 KB 744 at 748; *Attrill v Platt* (1884) 10 SCR 425 at 463; *Margil Pty Ltd v Stegul Pastoral Pty Ltd* [1984] 2 NSWLR 1 at 9D; *Re Lonegren and Rueben* (1987) 37 DLR (4th) 491 at 495f. See *B. & W. Investments Ltd v Ulster Scottish Friendly Society* (1969) 20 NILQ 325. It may even be that A and B, as joint freehold owners of Blackacre, can validly grant an easement to A and C, as joint freehold owners of Whiteacre (see *Re Lonegren and Rueben* (1987) 37 DLR (4th) 491 at 495f, affd (1988) 50 DLR (4th) 431 at 433) or even just to A, as sole freehold owner of Whiteacre (see *McDonald v McDougall* (1897) 30 NSR 298 at 300).

1 See *Borman v Griffith* [1930] 1 Ch 493 at 499 (post, p 1102).

2 *Beddington v Atlee* (1887) 35 Ch D 317 at 332.

(4) The easement must be capable of forming the subject matter of a grant

It is commonly said that all easements 'lie in grant'. That is, no right can successfully be claimed as an easement which could not have been granted by deed. This requirement imposes certain stringent conditions on the kinds of rights which can constitute an easement, as also on the circumstances in which a valid easement may be claimed. No easement can exist in respect of an indefinable facility or commodity whose parameters could not have been spelt out with particularity in the terms of an express grant.

(a) There must be a capable grantor and a capable grantee

It follows from the requirement of capacity for grant that the existence of any easement presupposes both a competent grantor and a competent grantee.

(i) Capable grantor The proprietary character of the easement brings into play the principle of *nemo dat quod non habet*.[3] No easement may be carved out of land except by a person who is himself entitled to a proprietary interest in the land,[4] and no such person is competent in any event to subject the land to an easement more extensive than his own proprietary interest.[5] Thus it follows that only the owner of an estate in fee simple has power to grant an easement of a fully perpetual or permanent character.[6] A tenant for years or a tenant for life is competent to make an express grant of an easement so as to bind his respective limited interest,[7] but in either case the easement so created cannot survive the termination of the limited interest.[8]

No easement can be claimed if at the date of creation of the supposed easement the servient land was owned by someone who was legally incompetent to grant an easement (eg a statutory or other corporation which has no duly constituted authority to grant away easements over its land).[9] A less obvious case of incompetent grant arises where an easement (eg a right of way) has already been validly created as appurtenant to a particular dominant tenement. In such circumstances and in the absence of contrary agreement,[10] the dominant owner has no power to grant any share of that

3 See *Rodwell v G.R. Evans & Co Pty Ltd* [1978] 1 NSWLR 448 at 452A ('The principle is that the quantum of the grantor's estate in the servient land determines the quantum of the easement').

4 A mere licensee (even under a licence coupled with an interest in land) is therefore incompetent to grant, either expressly or by implication, any easement as such over the land (see *Quicke v Chapman* [1903] 1 Ch 659 at 668, 671). A licensee is perfectly entitled, of course, to confer on a third party a purely personal right in respect of land which is effective only against himself (see *Hari v Trotter* (1958) 76 WN (NSW) 112 at 113; *Rodwell v G.R. Evans & Co Pty Ltd* (1977) 3 BPR 9114 at 9121, 9124).

5 *Booth v Alcock* (1873) 8 Ch App 663 at 666; *Beddington v Atlee* (1887) 35 Ch D 317 at 327; *Rodwell v G.R. Evans & Co Pty Ltd* (1977) 3 BPR 9114 at 9123.

6 *Rodwell v G.R. Evans & Co Pty Ltd* [1978] 1 NSWLR 448 at 452A-B (Court of Appeal of New South Wales).

7 *Simmons v Dobson* [1991] 1 WLR 720 at 723C per Fox LJ. See also *Wheaton v Maple & Co* [1893] 3 Ch 48 at 64f; *Kilgour v Gaddes* [1904] 1 KB 457 at 466.

8 *Lord Dynevor v Tennant* (1886) 32 Ch D 375 at 381.

9 *Mulliner v Midland Railway Co* (1879) 11 Ch D 611 at 619ff.

10 *Clapman v Edwards* [1938] 2 All ER 507 at 512D-H.

same easement to the owner of an adjoining tenement supposedly for the benefit of that adjoining tenement.[11]

It is possible (although not entirely clear) that an easement may be the subject of a valid unilateral grant by one of a number of joint owners of the servient tenement, provided that the encumbrance does not interfere with the rights of the other co-owners to possession and enjoyment of that land.[12] Conversely, where a person expressly grants an easement over land to which he currently has no title but to which he later acquires title, then in the period between the grant and the acquisition of the legal title the grantor is estopped as against the grantee from denying the grant.[13] The subsequent acquisition of the legal title feeds the estoppel so that thereafter, and perhaps also retrospectively, the grant operates as effectively as if the grantor had had title at the date of his grant.[14]

(ii) Capable grantee Likewise no easement may be claimed if the alleged dominant owner was at the time legally incompetent to receive such a grant (eg a company without power to acquire easements,[15] or a fluctuating body of persons such as 'the inhabitants for the time being' of a named village[16]). It is clear, however, that the dominant tenement relevant to an express grant may be held by the grantee either in fee simple or as a leaseholder.[17]

(b) The right must be sufficiently definite

In order to qualify as an easement, a right must be sufficiently definite.[18] There is, for instance, no easement such as a right to a prospect or view.[19] Such a right may be acquired only by way of a restrictive covenant which precludes the owner of the neighbouring land from building on his land

11 *Bannister v Chiene* (1902) 22 NZLR 628 at 631. See also *Classic Communications Ltd v Lascar* (1986) 21 DLR (4th) 579 at 584.

12 *Hedley v Roberts* [1977] VR 282 at 288f. Compare, however, *Paine & Co Ltd v St Neots Gas & Coke Co* [1939] 3 All ER 812 at 824A-D.

13 *Rowbotham v Wilson* (1857) 8 E & B 123 at 145, 120 ER 45 at 54, (1860) 8 HLC 348 at 364, 11 ER 463 at 470. This estoppel doctrine cannot apply to any implied grant of easement (*Quicke v Chapman* [1903] 1 Ch 659 at 668, 670) or where, in the case of an express grant, the deficiency in the grantor's title was apparent on the face of the instrument (*Bucknell v Mann* (1862) 2 NSWSCR 1 at 8; *Rodwell v G.R. Evans & Co Pty Ltd* (1977) 3 BPR 9114 at 9124).

14 *Rajapakse v Fernando* [1920] AC 892 at 897; *Universal Permanent Building Society v Cooke* [1952] Ch 95 at 101ff; *Hedley v Roberts* [1977] VR 282 at 285. A variant of the principle of 'feeding the estoppel' was adverted to in *Voyce v Voyce* (1991) 62 P & CR 290 at 294, where the Court of Appeal expressed the obiter view that a prescriptive claim to an easement of light could be built up against an adjoining occupier who had an equity founded on proprietary estoppel which was later perfected by a conveyance to him in fee simple. See [1992] Conv 56 (J.E. Martin).

15 *National Guaranteed Manure Co Ltd v Donald* (1859) 4 H & N 8 at 17f, 157 ER 737 at 741.

16 Such a body may, however, enjoy a local customary right as distinct from an easement (ante, p 1059).

17 *London & Blenheim Estates Ltd v Ladbroke Retail Parks Ltd* [1992] 1 WLR 1278 at 1284H.

18 The right claimed must not be 'too vague and uncertain' (*Bryant v Lefever* (1879) 4 CPD 172 at 178) or 'too vague and too indefinite' (*Harris v De Pinna* (1886) 33 Ch D 238 at 249f). See also *Dalton v Angus & Co* (1881) 6 App Cas 740 at 824; *Auerbach v Beck* (1985) 6 NSWLR 424 at 442C-D.

19 *William Aldred's Case* (1610) 9 Co Rep 57b at 58b, 77 ER 816 at 821; *Harris v De Pinna* (1886) 33 Ch D 238 at 262 per Bowen LJ; *Campbell v Paddington Corpn* [1911] 1 KB 869 at 875f.

in such a way as to obstruct the view which it is desired to protect.[20] Likewise there is no such easement as a right to the uninterrupted access of light or air except through defined apertures in a building.[1] There can be no claim of easement in respect of an unimpeded and general flow of air across one's neighbour's land to a windmill sited on the supposed dominant tenement[2] or for the purpose of preventing chimneys from smoking.[3] There is indeed no easement of indefinite privacy.[4] Nor does English law recognise as an easement any claim to wander at will over land.[5]

The drawing of such strict parameters around the kinds of right which may properly be asserted as easements generates a strong suspicion, particularly in relation to the 19th century case law, that objections against the indefinite nature of claimed rights may often have served to mask other—more fundamentally commercial—considerations.[6] The concession of easements of an unlimited or vague character imposes extensive limitations on the economic development and exploitation of the servient areas of land and, on this ground alone, may once have seemed contrary to the public interest.[7] It is today more questionable whether the community interest in industrial expansion is not counterbalanced by a wider concern for the preservation or enhancement of the environment.

(c) The right must be within the general nature of the rights traditionally recognised as easements

The law of easements has been generally constrained by the innately conservative principle that the categories of admissible easement must not dramatically overstep the boundaries of the kinds of easement already recognised.

(i) Novelty is not necessarily an objection It is often said that the list of easements is not closed. As Lord St Leonards observed in *Dyce v Lady James Hay*,[8] 'the category of servitudes and easements must alter and expand with the

20 See eg *Buckleigh v Brown* [1968] NZLR 647 at 651ff.

1 See *Harris v De Pinna* (1886) 33 Ch D 238 at 250f, 262; *Levet v Gas Light & Coke Co* [1919] 1 Ch 24 at 27. The High Court of Australia has recognised the right to the uninterrupted access of light and air as an easement, even though not limited to access through defined apertures (see *Commonwealth v Registrar of Titles (Victoria)* (1918) 24 CLR 348 at 353ff). The English Court of Appeal has rationalised the easement of light enjoyed by the domestic greenhouse on the ground that a greenhouse is 'not to be regarded simply as a garden under glass, but as a building with apertures, namely, the glass roof and sides'. See *Allen v Greenwood* [1980] Ch 119 at 129C per Goff LJ; [1979] Conv 298 (F.R. Crane).

2 *Webb v Bird* (1861) 10 CB (NS) 268 at 283ff, 142 ER 455 at 460f, (1863) 13 CB (NS) 841 at 843, 143 ER 332 at 333. See also *Harris v De Pinna* (1886) 33 Ch D 238 at 249f. There can be no easement to drain off surface water from dominant land except through a defined channel or watercourse (see *McPhee v Township of Plympton* (1988) 43 DLR (4th) 233 at 245).

3 *Bryant v Lefever* (1879) 4 CPD 172 at 178, 180.

4 *Browne v Flower* [1911] 1 Ch 219 at 225 per Parker J. See *Property in Thin Air*, [1991] CLJ 252 at 260ff.

5 *In re Ellenborough Park* [1956] Ch 131 at 176ff (ante, p 1068).

6 See [1991] CLJ 252 at 261ff.

7 See eg *Webb v Bird* (1861) 10 CB (NS) 268 at 284, 142 ER 455 at 461 per Erle J, (1863) 13 CB (NS) 841 at 843, 143 ER 332 at 333.

8 (1852) 1 Macq 305 at 312.

changes that take place in the circumstances of mankind.'[9] The courts are nevertheless traditionally reluctant to admit new kinds of right to the status of easement,[10] and have not usually been prepared to recognise as easements rights which lie markedly outside the range of rights which have hitherto been acknowledged as easements. A new category of right is occasionally admitted within the list of easements.[11] In many other cases, however, rights alleged to be easements have been rejected either because the rights claimed were in the nature of negative easements and therefore more appropriately created and protected as restrictive covenants or because the rights were more properly characterised as arising by way of irrevocable licence.[12]

(ii) Reluctance to accept new negative easements There is some indication that the category of negative easements is nowadays virtually closed.[13] In *Phipps v Pears*,[14] for instance, the plaintiff sought damages from the defendant on the ground that the latter had demolished his adjoining house thereby exposing the unpointed flank wall of the plaintiff's house to the rigours of the weather.[15] The plaintiff's action was based upon a supposed easement of protection from the weather, but the Court of Appeal denied that any such right could exist as an easement.[16] Lord Denning MR conceded that a right to support from an adjoining building had long been recognised as constituting a possible easement. However, such a right partakes of the nature of both positive and negative easements, in the sense that it comprises not merely a right that one's neighbour should not remove his building but also a right for the protected building to exert a sideways thrust or lean upon the adjoining building.[17] A supposed right to protection from the weather is 'entirely negative' and, in Lord Denning MR's view, is effectively 'a right to stop your neighbour pulling down his own house.' Such a right, being essentially

9 Cited with approval in *Commonwealth v Registrar of Titles (Victoria)* (1918) 24 CLR 348 at 353 per Griffith CJ.

10 See eg *Hill v Tupper* (1863) 2 H & C 121, 159 ER 51 (ante, p 1065).

11 See eg *Simpson v Godmanchester Corpn* [1897] AC 696 at 701ff, where the House of Lords held that an easement could comprise the right to enter on to another's land in order to open and shut sluice gates on a canal. See also *Attorney-General of Southern Nigeria v John Holt & Co (Liverpool) Ltd* [1915] AC 599 at 617.

12 See eg *Beard v Baulkham Hills Shire Council* (1986) 7 NSWLR 273 at 278E-G, where Young J held that an 'exclusive right to burial' in a cemetery was not a proprietary right analogous to an easement.

13 In certain circumstances a claim of negative easement may connote an exclusive possession which is inconsistent with the nature of an easement (post, p 1076). See the debate in *Shelf Holdings Ltd v Husky Oil Operations Ltd* (1987) 38 DLR (4th) 441 at 448ff, (1989) 56 DLR (4th) 193 at 201ff. See also M.M. Litman and B.H. Ziff, 57 Alta L Rev (2d) 326 (1988).

14 [1965] 1 QB 76. See [1964] CLJ 203 (K. Scott).

15 See now Building Act 1984, s 82(1)(b), under which a local authority may require the weatherproofing of surfaces exposed by demolition.

16 See also *Giltrap v Busby* (1970) 21 NILQ 342; *Marchant v Capital & Counties Property Co Ltd* (1982) 263 Estates Gazette 661; (1983) 80 Law Soc Gaz 84 (D.W. Williams).

17 It has since been noted that *Phipps v Pears* did not concern any claim to support to the gable wall, merely a claim to be protected from the weather (see *Bradburn v Lindsay* [1983] 2 All ER 408 at 414j). The courts have tended to be much more responsive where the plaintiff alleges interference with an easement of support for his building or with an easement to have a party wall kept weatherproof (see eg *Tollemache & Cobbold Breweries Ltd v Reynolds* (1983) 268 Estates Gazette 52 at 56; *Bradburn v Lindsay*, supra at 413e; *Brace v South East Regional Housing Association Ltd* (1984) 270 Estates Gazette 1286 at 1288). See [1984] Conv 54 (P. Jackson).

negative, 'must be looked at with caution' since the law 'has been very chary of creating any new negative easements'.[18]

This reluctance to recognise new negative easements was justified in *Phipps v Pears* on the ground that any contrary view would tend towards an undue restriction of the rights of neighbouring owners to enjoyment of their own land. The Court of Appeal was thus disinclined to 'hamper legitimate development', since, given the appropriate planning permissions,[19] 'every man is entitled to pull down his house if he likes.'[20] In Lord Denning's view the only way in which an owner may protect himself in such circumstances is by extracting from his neighbour a restrictive covenant that the neighbour will not take action which prejudices the owner's enjoyment of his property.[1]

(iii) Range of recognised easements Notwithstanding the clear element of judicial caution in this context, the courts have over the years accepted many widely varying kinds of right as constitutive of an easement. An easement may thus comprise a right to do something on the servient tenement (eg to use a right of way,[2] to store goods,[3] or to advertise a business[4]). An easement may also comprise a right in the dominant owner to prevent the servient owner from doing certain acts on the servient land which he would otherwise be entitled to perform, subject of course to the danger that such a right may be considered to be both negative and novel and therefore not in the nature of an easement.[5]

An easement may even sanction the performance of acts affecting the servient land which would otherwise constitute a nuisance.[6] In *Sturges v*

18 [1965] 1 QB 76 at 82G–83A. For a critical view of this rationale, see (1964) 80 LQR 318 (R.E.M.); M.A. Peel, (1964) 28 Conv (NS) 450 at 451ff. It has since been doubted whether Lord Denning's rejection of an easement of protection from the weather was intended to apply as between tenements which are separated horizontally rather than vertically (see *Sedgwick Forbes Bland Payne Group Ltd v Regional Properties Ltd* (1979) 257 Estates Gazette 64 at 70 per Oliver J).

19 Planning permission is required even for the demolition of property, if the demolition is part of a scheme of redevelopment of the site (see *London County Council v Marks & Spencer Ltd* [1953] AC 535 at 541f).

20 [1965] 1 QB 76 at 83A ('If it exposes your house to the weather, that is your misfortune. It is no wrong on his part. Likewise every man is entitled to cut down his trees if he likes, even if it leaves you without shelter from the wind or shade from the sun').

1 [1965] 1 QB 76 at 83E-F.

2 *Borman v Griffith* [1930] 1 Ch 493 at 499.

3 *Attorney-General of Southern Nigeria v John Holt & Co (Liverpool) Ltd* [1915] AC 599 at 617.

4 *Moody v Steggles* (1879) 12 Ch D 261 at 266ff; *Henry Ltd v McGlade* [1926] NI 144 at 151f.

5 Some negative rights have nevertheless been acknowledged as easements. In *Ough v King* [1967] 1 WLR 1547 at 1553A-C, for instance, the Court of Appeal upheld an easement of access to light flowing through a defined aperture. This right was effectively a right to prevent a neighbour from building on his land in such a way as to obstruct that right to light, and in the circumstances the Court of Appeal upheld an award of damages in favour of the aggrieved dominant owner (post, p 1085).

6 For the potentially dangerous doctrine that an immunity from nuisance liability may also arise by necessary implication from a statute which regulates an environmentally hazardous activity, see *Allen v Gulf Oil Refining Ltd* [1981] AC 1001 at 1014A-C, 1016F, 1024A-B; [1981] CLJ 226 (J.A. Jolowicz); (1980) 43 MLR 219 (R.A. Buckley). See also *York Bros (Trading) Pty Ltd v Commr of Main Roads* [1983] 1 NSWLR 391 at 397D–398A; but compare *City of Campbellton v Gray's Velvet Ice Cream Ltd* (1982) 127 DLR (3d) 436 at 441ff.

Bridgman[7] the defendant claimed to have acquired an easement by reason of long user to generate an excessive amount of noise and vibration in the course of his conduct of business as a confectioner. The Court of Appeal held that no easement had been acquired on the facts, but acknowledged that an easement to make noise could have been created by long user if during the period of user the noise had amounted to an actionable nuisance and the servient owner had not availed himself of the appropriate remedy in the law of tort.[8]

(iv) An easement must not impose any positive burden on the servient owner It is generally considered intrinsic to the concept of an easement that the role of the servient owner should be essentially passive. The user right acquired by the dominant owner has already shifted the boundary of altruism significantly in his favour. A true easement requires of the servient owner nothing more than an act of sufferance, in that he must either allow the dominant owner to do something on the servient land or abstain from some action of his own on that land which would otherwise be entirely legitimate.[9] In the absence of contrary agreement, an easement must not normally involve the servient owner in any expenditure of money or in any positive or onerous action.[10] Thus, for instance, no claim of easement can be based on an undertaking to maintain a supply of hot water.[11] Likewise the mere existence of a right of way imposes on the servient owner no duty to carry out necessary

7 (1879) 11 Ch D 852. See also *Miller v Jackson* [1977] QB 966 at 978G, where even Lord Denning MR held that there is 'no such easement known to the law as a right to hit cricket balls into your neighbour's land'. Compare, however, (1977) 93 LQR 481 (R.M. Goode); (1978) 41 MLR 334 (R.A. Buckley). It has been suggested, however, that the intrinsic object of the game requires a different outcome in the case of baseball (see *Bank of New Zealand v Greenwood* [1984] 1 NZLR 525 at 535)! The rights of the cricketers in *Miller v Jackson* were somewhat perversely upheld on other grounds, but other courts have been less inclined to allow the rights of neighbouring householders to be 'subordinated to the leisurely pursuits of sportsmen'. See *Kennaway v Thompson* [1981] QB 88 at 94E–95A (power boat racing) and *Banfai v Formula Fun Centre Inc* (1985) 19 DLR (4th) 683 at 692ff (automobile racing), and compare the disobliging view taken of domestic bombardment by misdirected golf balls in *Lester-Travers v City of Frankston* [1970] VR 2 at 9f; *Segal v Derrick Golf & Winter Club* (1977) 76 DLR (3d) 746 at 749f.

8 (1879) 11 Ch D 852 at 863ff. See also *In re The State Electricity Commission of Victoria & Joshua's Contract* [1940] VLR 121 at 125f; D. Wittman, (1980) 9 Jnl of Legal Studies 557.

9 See, however, A.J. Waite, [1985] CLJ 458, for the argument that this limitation on the scope of the easement is a relatively recent development in English law and that some easements of positive obligation may have survived intact to the present day.

10 See *Liverpool City Council v Irwin* [1977] AC 239 at 256D-E per Lord Wilberforce. Nor does a dominant owner have any duty to repair or maintain a facility which is the subject matter of an easement (see *Soich v Sutherland SC* (1980) 2 BPR 9273 at 9275).

11 *Regis Property Co Ltd v Redman* [1956] 2 QB 612 at 627f. A distinction must be maintained between a right to the supply of water and a right to the uninterrupted passage of water over the land of another. The former right cannot exist as an easement because it imposes on the owner of the alleged servient tenement a positive obligation to secure the supply and probably to pay for that supply. By contrast, a mere right to the uninterrupted passage of water from the land of another can constitute an easement, since it imposes an essentially negative obligation (see *Rance v Elvin* (1985) 50 P & CR 9 at 15ff).

repair or maintenance of the way.[12] A tenant's easement to use drains running through his landlord's premises imposes no duty on the landlord to keep those drains in repair.[13]

Only rarely has it been held that an easement may properly impose any positive duty on the servient owner. In *Jones v Price*,[14] however, the Court of Appeal held that a right to require a neighbour to maintain a boundary fence can be validly acquired as an easement. This fencing easement has nevertheless been described as being 'in the nature of a spurious easement',[15] and it is doubtful whether it can arise otherwise than by prescription.[16] It is also possible that a landowner whose property fronts on to the sea may be burdened by an easement to repair the sea wall.[17]

(v) An easement must not exclude reasonable alternative users of the servient tenement It has frequently been maintained that no claim can be recognised as an easement if it involves an element of exclusive possession or joint occupation of the supposedly servient land.[18] It is not, however, clear that this supposed characteristic of an easement has been enforced by the courts with any consistency or rigour. While it is quite plain that exclusive possessory rights over land are better secured by other devices such as the grant of a freehold or leasehold estate,[19] the time-honoured prohibition against exclusiveness often represents an intuitive rather than a reasoned response to the validity of certain claims of easement.[20]

12 *Jones v Pritchard* [1908] 1 Ch 630 at 637f; *Stokes v Mixconcrete (Holdings) Ltd* (1979) 38 P & CR 488 at 494, 499f; *Lawrence v Griffiths* (1987) 47 SASR 455 at 488. See also *Holden v White* [1982] QB 679 at 684A-B, 685D, 687E-F; (1982) 98 LQR 541 (K. Stanton); [1983] CLJ 48 (J.R. Spencer); [1983] Conv 58 (R. Griffith), but compare *Bartlett v Robinson* (1980) 25 SASR 552 and see now Occupiers' Liability Act 1984, s 1.

13 *Duke of Westminster v Guild* [1985] QB 688 at 702H–703C, 704A. Where the maintenance of an easement requires positive action, the dominant owner has an implied right to enter the servient land, eg for the purpose of executing repairs (see *Jones v Pritchard* [1908] 1 Ch 630 at 638).

14 [1965] 2 QB 618 at 633D-E, 639C.

15 *Lawrence v Jenkins* (1873) LR 8 QB 274 at 279.

16 Where this kind of easement exists, however, it is of some importance, for instance, in determining the respective rights and obligations of holders of grazing rights on open moorland. See *Crow v Wood* [1971] 1 QB 77 at 84E-G; *Egerton v Harding* [1975] QB 62 at 68B-F; [1975] CLJ 34 (C.F. Kolbert). See also A.J. Bradbrook, (1979) 53 ALJ 306.

17 *Keighley's Case* (1610) 10 Co Rep 139a at 139b, 77 ER 1136 at 1137.

18 In *Reilly v Booth* (1890) 44 Ch D 12 at 26, Lopes LJ observed that 'there is no easement known to the law which gives exclusive and unrestricted use of a piece of land'. See also *Metropolitan Railway Co v Fowler* [1892] 1 QB 165 at 175. It is certainly true that the limited nature of a right of easement deprives its owner of the ability to maintain an action in trespass (see *Paine & Co Ltd v St Neots Gas & Coke Co* [1939] 3 All ER 812 at 823G-H; *Simpson v Knowles* [1974] VR 190 at 195).

19 Even an easement of way gives the grantee merely a non-exclusive right of passage over the land (see *Sunset Properties Pty Ltd v Johnston* (1975) 3 BPR 9185 at 9193; *Rodwell v G.R. Evans & Co Pty Ltd* (1977) 3 BPR 9114 at 9118).

20 It may even be that the courts have in fact used the supposed requirement of non-exclusive user as a smokescreen for judicial discretion, invoking the requirement in order to strike down claims felt to be unmeritorious, while suppressing the requirement in cases where it has been thought that a remedy should be given. See eg *Wright v Macadam* [1949] 2 KB 744 at 751ff, where the Court of Appeal had no hesitation in recognising as an easement a right claimed by a hard-pressed tenant to store coal in a coal shed provided by her landlord. (The landlord had asserted a right to make an extra charge for use of the coal shed and had pulled down the coal shed before the date of the hearing.)

The case law certainly discloses no uniform application of a criterion of non-exclusive possession, and there are many instances where the courts have positively upheld the easement character of rights which comprised some form of exclusive possession or user.[1] In *Wright v Macadam*,[2] for example, the disputed use of a coal shed must surely have represented an exclusive user[3]: to some extent the definitional problem remains inevitably 'one of degree.'[4] As Judge Paul Baker QC observed in *London & Blenheim Estates Ltd v Ladbroke Retail Parks Ltd*,[5] '[a] small coal shed in a large property is one thing. The exclusive use of a large part of the alleged servient tenement is another.'

Recent years have seen increasing judicial scepticism about the weight to be accorded to the rule against possessory easements.[6] It has been suggested by some that exclusiveness of user is a vitiating circumstance only in cases of an alleged prescriptive user[7] or implied grant[8], where in reality the relevant claim amounts to an assertion that title to the land has been acquired by reason of long adverse possession.[9] It is clear that a distinction must be drawn between 'ownership of the land giving rights to the soil and to every inch of the soil' and the ownership of mere rights of enjoyment or user in respect of that land.[10] The question to be determined in every instance is whether the grantee of rights has received a *corporeal* or an *incorporeal* hereditament.[11]

Ultimately the true test is whether, 'in relation to the area over which it is to be exercisable', the right claimed as an easement is apt to 'leave the servient owner without any reasonable use of his land'.[12] It is always

1 For confirmation of this point, see *Mercantile General Life Reassurance Co of Australia Ltd v Permanent Trustee Australia Ltd* (1989) NSW ConvR 55-441 at 58,208 per Powell J. See also *Berger Bros Trading Co Pty Ltd v Bursill Enterprises Pty Ltd* [1970] 1 NSWR 137 at 140. In *Miller v Emcer Products Ltd* [1956] Ch 304 at 316, the Court of Appeal held that the right to use a lavatory on another's premises was capable of constituting an easement—although this must have involved some element of at least intermittently exclusive possession. See (1956) 72 LQR 172 (R.E.M.); *Hedley v Roberts* [1977] VR 282 at 289.

2 [1949] 2 KB 744 at 751ff. See (1959) 66 LQR 302 (R.E.M.).

3 In *Grigsby v Melville* [1972] 1 WLR 1355 at 1364F, Brightman J noted that the 'precise facts in *Wright v Macadam* in this respect are not wholly clear from the report and it is a little difficult to know whether the tenant had exclusive possession of the coal shed or of any defined portion of it.'

4 *Grigsby v Melville* [1972] 1 WLR 1355 at 1364F; *London & Blenheim Estates Ltd v Ladbroke Retail Parks Ltd* [1992] 1 WLR 1278 at 1286C.

5 [1992] 1 WLR 1278 at 1286C-D.

6 See *Mercantile General Life Reassurance Co of Australia Ltd v Permanent Trustee Australia Ltd* (1989) NSW ConvR 55-441 at 58,208 per Powell J for a warning that the supposed rule against exclusiveness 'must be scrutinised with care'.

7 Post, p 1106.

8 Post, p 1091.

9 *Mercantile General Life Reassurance Co of Australia Ltd v Permanent Trustee Australia Ltd* (1989) NSW ConvR 55-441 at 58,208 per Powell J.

10 *Saggers v Brown* (1981) 2 BPR 9329 at 9331 per Rath J. See also *Clifford v Hoare* (1874) LR 9 CP 362 at 370. A transfer of title or exclusive ownership of a building is inconsistent with the concept of easement (see *Bursill Enterprises Pty Ltd v Berger Bros Trading Co Pty Ltd* (1971) 124 CLR 73 at 91 per Windeyer J).

11 One of the pivotal issues posed by Lord Evershed MR in *In re Ellenborough Park* [1956] Ch 131 at 175f, was whether the grant was 'inconsistent with the proprietorship or possession of the alleged servient owners'.

12 *London & Blenheim Estates Ltd v Ladbroke Retail Parks Ltd* [1992] 1 WLR 1278 at 1288C per Judge Paul Baker QC (obiter).

a question of fact whether the claimed user represents such an unacceptable 'degree of invasion of the servient land'.[13] Alternatively it may be asked whether the disputed user so derogates from the totality of the grantor's rights that the grantee is left 'free to act as if [he] were the owner of the freehold'.[14] On either footing it is likely that the prohibition against exclusive possessory rights, if it ever really prevailed, has now been commuted to a recognition that the class of easements cannot comprise a user which 'substantially interferes with the whole of the servient tract'.[15] In this way the delimitation of the category of easements more effectively recognises that easements are designed, not to sterilise land, but to facilitate the purposeful, profitable and collaborative exploitation of land resources.

The adoption of a criterion of substantial interference does much to avoid the confusions apparent in any attempt to apply a general rule against exclusiveness. It also captures in a more articulate form the raw pragmatic response to circumstance which underlies much of the case law. In *Copeland v Greenhalf*,[16] for instance, the defendant was a wheelwright who had for 50 years used a narrow strip of land belonging to the plaintiff for the purpose of storing vehicles awaiting and undergoing repair. Upjohn J held that the prescriptive right claimed by the defendant was too extensive to constitute an easement in law. In his view, the right claimed went 'wholly outside any normal idea of an easement' since it amounted to a 'claim to a joint user of the land by the defendant'.[17] Indeed the defendant was arrogating to himself 'the whole beneficial user' of one strip of the land in question. Such a claim could not be established as an easement since it was 'virtually a claim to possession of the servient tenement, if necessary to the exclusion of the owner.'[18] There was, said Upjohn J, no authority in support of the idea that 'a right of this wide and undefined nature can be the proper subject-matter of an easement.'[19]

The 'substantial interference' test likewise provides a useful means of rationalising other decisions which are often presented as applications of

13 Ibid.

14 *Mercantile General Life Reassurance Co of Australia Ltd v Permanent Trustee Australia Ltd* (1989) NSW ConvR 55-441 at 58,211 per Powell J. As the Alberta Court of Appeal held in *Shelf Holdings Ltd v Husky Oil Operations Ltd* (1989) 56 DLR (4th) 193 at 202, the 'key to resolving the issue' is to balance the extent of the rights relinquished by the supposedly servient owner against the rights reserved by him. Thus in *Shelf Holdings* the grant of a right to construct an underground pipeline, coupled with a prohibition on any further building development by the grantor, did not impede the grantor's normal farming operations and thus constituted an easement.

15 See [1989] Conv 296 at 298 (Bruce Ziff and Moe Litman). For an application of the 'interference' test, see *Mercantile General Life Reassurance Co of Australia Ltd v Permanent Trustee Australia Ltd* (1989) NSW ConvR 55-441 at 58,211 per Powell J.

16 [1952] Ch 488.

17 [1952] Ch 488 at 498. Compare *V.T. Engineering Co Ltd v Richard Barland & Co Ltd* (1968) 19 P & CR 890 at 895f.

18 [1952] Ch 488 at 498. It has sometimes been supposed that *Copeland v Greenhalf* thus endorsed a criterion of non-exclusive possession, and on this basis the decision has been said to be per incuriam (see [1973] CLJ 30 at 33 (J.R. Spencer)). See, however, the refusal in *London & Blenheim Estates Ltd v Ladbroke Retail Parks Ltd* [1992] 1 WLR 1278 at 1286D to accept that *Copeland v Greenhalf* was wrongly decided.

19 [1952] Ch 488 at 498. See also *Harada v Registrar of Titles* [1981] VR 743 at 753, where the right of a public electricity authority to position pylons on private land and to prohibit the landowner from building thereon was considered to be a claim of joint user and thus inconsistent with a claim of easement.

a supposed criterion of non-exclusive possession.[20] In *Ward v Kirkland*[1] the plaintiff claimed to have a right to enter an adjoining farmyard in order to maintain the wall of his cottage abutting on to that farmyard. Ungoed-Thomas J held that the right claimed was capable of existence as an easement,[2] since the right involved no more than monthly visits to the servient land for the purposes of window-cleaning.[3] In *Grigsby v Melville*,[4] however, Brightman J doubted whether a right of storage in a cellar could constitute an easement in circumstances where the claim amounted to 'an exclusive right of user over the whole of the confined space representing the servient tenement'.[5]

Further light is thrown by the 'substantial interference' test on the proper classification of that most valuable asset of the modern urban dweller—the right to park his or her car. There is clear authority that in some circumstances the right to park a car can constitute an easement.[6] Such an easement may be validly created so long as the rights claimed do not amount to an arrogation of exclusive beneficial user of the entire servient tenement, thereby depriving the servient owner of 'any reasonable use of his land, whether for parking or anything else'.[7] Accordingly the courts have been quite ready, for instance, to uphold as easements those parking rights which are limited in point of time[8] or which relate only to a general area of land[9] rather than to a numbered or individualised parking bay.[10]

20 *Attorney-General of Southern Nigeria v John Holt & Co (Liverpool) Ltd* [1915] AC 599 at 617; *Capar v Wasylowski* (1983) 146 DLR (3d) 193 at 200f.

1 [1967] Ch 194.

2 See also *Auerbach v Beck* (1985) 6 NSWLR 424 at 442D, affd sub nom *Beck v Auerbach* (1986) 6 NSWLR 454.

3 The right could not be defeated on the ground that it comprised a user which 'would in effect exclude the defendant from the use of part of the farmyard next to the cottage, or interfere substantially with such use' ([1967] Ch 194 at 223C). The right contended for in no way resembled a claim of 'possession or joint possession of part of the defendant's property' ([1967] Ch 194 at 223E).

4 [1972] 1 WLR 1355 at 1364G.

5 Brightman J's decision was upheld by the Court of Appeal ([1974] 1 WLR 80), but without further consideration of the question of exclusive user or possession. The disinclination to uphold claims of easement in respect of confined spaces may account for the ruling in *Dikstein v Kanevsky* [1947] VLR 216 at 219, that there can be no easement to use an elevator.

6 See *London & Blenheim Estates Ltd v Ladbroke Retail Parks Ltd* [1992] 1 WLR 1278 at 1287H, citing *Le Strange v Pettefar* (1939) 161 LT 300 at 301f; *Bilkus v London Borough of Redbridge* (1968) 207 Estates Gazette 803 at 805.

7 *London & Blenheim Estates Ltd v Ladbroke Retail Parks Ltd* [1992] 1 WLR 1278 at 1288C per Judge Paul Baker QC.

8 *Leon Asper Amusements Ltd v Northmain Carwash & Enterprises Ltd* (1966) 56 DLR (2d) 173 at 176ff (parking only after 6 pm each day).

9 *Sweet & Maxwell Ltd v Michael-Michaels Advertising* [1965] CLY 2192; *Newman v Jones* (Unreported, 22 March 1982, Megarry V-C).

10 See (1973) 37 Conv (NS) 60 (D.J. Hayton). A right to park in a strictly defined space may more plausibly connote the grant of a leasehold interest (see *Harley Queen v Forsyte Kerman* [1983] CLY 2077, ante, p 697). See also (1976) 40 Conv (NS) 317. Yet another possibility is that car parking is a form of bailment (see *Walton Stores Ltd v Sydney City Council* [1968] 2 NSWR 109 at 112f, ante, p 902), although this analysis may be applicable only where custody of the vehicle has actually been transferred, eg through a handing over of car keys (see *Fred Chappell Ltd v National Car Parks Ltd* (1987) *Times*, 22 May). A claim to use a right of way as a parking lot may be too extensive to support a valid claim of easement (*Keefer v Arillotta* (1977) 72 DLR (3d) 182 at 189).

(5) Common easements

Amongst the most common easements are those which confer a right of way and those which relate to access to light. These easements deserve further consideration.

(a) Rights of way

A right of way is essentially a right to pass and re-pass along a way and to do things which are reasonably ancillary to such passage.[11] The grantee of the right of way thus has, for instance, certain ancillary rights to render the easement effective for the purposes originally contemplated.[12] In the case of an express grant the grantee is entitled not merely to repair but also to develop or improve the way in order to render it suitable for the accommodation of the dominant tenement.[13]

(i) Content of the right of way A right of way may confer not merely a right to pass and re-pass, but also a right to halt on the way for a reasonable period of time for the purpose of loading and unloading a vehicle.[14] Although a right of way does not confer any right to leave vehicles unattended on the way or to station gantries, cranes, hoists or other loading equipment on the way,[15] it does give the grantee certain rights over the superjacent airspace. The grantee can thus insist that the way remain unobstructed, not of course *usque ad coelum*, but to such height as is 'reasonable in all the circumstances'.[16]

(ii) Relation to the dominant tenement So long as a right of way is demonstrably beneficial to the occupation of the dominant tenement to which it is

11 *V.T. Engineering Ltd v Richard Barland & Co Ltd* (1968) 19 P & CR 890 at 896. Compare the public right to pass along the highway (ante, p 1048).

12 *Newcomen v Coulson* (1877) 5 Ch D 133 at 143 per Jessel MR.

13 *Gerrard v Cooke* (1806) 2 Bos & PNR 109 at 115f, 127 ER 565 at 567f; *Newcomen v Coulson* (1877) 5 Ch D 133 at 143f; *Mills v Silver* [1991] Ch 271 at 286H–287A per Dillon LJ; *Zenere v Leate* (1980) 1 BPR 9300 at 9305; *Sunset Properties Pty Ltd v Johnston* (1975) 3 BPR 9185 at 9191. Such action may involve excavating or sealing the route of the way (see *Guth v Robinson* (1977) 1 BPR 9209 at 9215f; *Lawrence v Griffiths* (1987) 47 SASR 455 at 480ff), or even carrying out alterations to meet changed conditions (see *Finlinson v Porter* (1875) LR 10 QB 188 at 193ff).

14 Whether a right of way includes ancillary rights of loading and unloading depends, in the absence of an express term, on whether such rights can be implied from the circumstances existing at the date of grant (*Zenere v Leate* (1980) 1 BPR 9300 at 9307). See *Bulstrode v Lambert* [1953] 1 WLR 1064 at 1071; *McIlwraith v Grady* [1968] 1 QB 468 at 476E; *V.T. Engineering Ltd v Richard Barland & Co Ltd* (1968) 19 P & CR 890 at 894; *Grinskis v Lahood* [1971] NZLR 502 at 509; *Deanshaw and Deanshaw v Marshall* (1978) 20 SASR 146 at 150.

15 *V.T. Engineering Ltd v Richard Barland & Co Ltd* (1968) 19 P & CR 890 at 896. A right of way normally confers no right 'permanently or indefinitely to be in occupation of the road or to use it to the exclusion of the owner of the land' (*Rodwell v G.R. Evans & Co Pty Ltd* (1977) 3 BPR 9114 at 9118).

16 *V.T. Engineering Ltd v Richard Barland & Co Ltd* (1968) 19 P & CR 890 at 895. Here the grantee was held to be entitled to a reasonable amount of 'vertical swing space' for a hoist, but Megarry J ruled that the right of way could not confer rights to a 'lateral swing space' since this would 'in effect sterilise a strip of land of indefinite depth on each side of the way'. See, however, *Reilly v Booth* (1890) 44 Ch D 12 at 17 ('You cannot have a right of way described as so many feet high').

appurtenant, it is irrelevant that other land intervenes between the dominant and servient tenements.[17] However, a right of way which is supposedly appurtenant to a particular dominant tenement may not be used colourably for the real purpose of enjoying a further access across this dominant tenement to some other property.[18] The circumstances of such a case negative any claim that benefit is conferred upon the supposed dominant tenement. Moreover, the grant of a right of way confers no right on the dominant owner to enter upon the right of way from simply *any* part of the dominant tenement adjoining the route of the right of way.[19] Provided that the right of way offers such access from the dominant tenement as is reasonable (eg by means of intermediate gateways),[20] it is entirely proper for the servient owner to erect a fence, railing or wall along the route.[1]

(iii) Construction of an express grant Where a right of way is the subject of an express grant,[2] its precise scope falls to be construed with reference to the terms of grant considered in the light of the surrounding circumstances at the date of the grant.[3] Of these circumstances one of the most material is the 'nature of the locus in quo over which the right of way is granted'.[4] Thus the sheer physical characteristics of the way granted may indicate that rights which are otherwise unlimited in their terms of grant must by necessary implication be cut back to more restricted forms of user.[5] If the terms of the grant do not sufficiently describe the extent or location of a right of way, reference may be made not only to any plan attached to a relevant conveyance but also to any planning permission which delimited the scope of the access in question.[6]

17 *Todrick v Western National Omnibus Co Ltd* [1934] Ch 561 at 572f.

18 *Allen v Gomme* (1840) 11 Ad & El 759 at 770, 113 ER 602 at 607; *Skull v Glenister* (1864) 16 CB (NS) 81 at 103, 143 ER 1055 at 1063; *Williams v James* (1867) LR 2 CP 577 at 580, 582; *Harris v Flower* (1904) 74 LJ Ch 127 at 132; *Callard v Beeney* [1930] 1 KB 353 at 359; *Bracewell v Appleby* [1975] Ch 408 at 417H–418A; *Smith v Smith* (1895) 14 NZLR 4 at 6; *Grinskis v Lahood* [1971] NZLR 502 at 509; *Re Gordon and Regan* (1985) 15 DLR (4th) 641 at 647f. An exception to this principle occurs where, at the date of the grant, the dominant tenement was itself used as a means of access to the other property (see *Nickerson v Barraclough* [1980] Ch 325 at 336D-E). See also *National Trust v White* [1987] 1 WLR 907 at 913C-D.

19 *Pettey v Parsons* [1914] 2 Ch 653 at 663f, 667, 669; *Saggers v Brown* (1981) 2 BPR 9329 at 9331.

20 *Lewis v Wakeling* (1923) 54 OLR 647 at 650ff.

1 *Pettey v Parsons* [1914] 2 Ch 653 at 663, 667, 669; *Saggers v Brown* (1981) 2 BPR 9329 at 9331f; *Dunell v Phillips* (1982) 2 BPR 9517 at 9522.

2 In the case of an implied grant, the actual user of the right is 'the only satisfactory guide' (*Milner's Safe Co Ltd v Great Northern and City Railway Co* [1907] 1 Ch 208 at 220).

3 *St Edmundsbury and Ipswich Diocesan Board of Finance v Clark* (No 2) [1975] 1 WLR 468 at 476G–477B; *Bridgwood v Keates* (Unreported, Court of Appeal, 1 November 1983); *Rodwell v G.R. Evans & Co Pty Ltd* (1977) 3 BPR 9114 at 9119; *Saggers v Brown* (1981) 2 BPR 9329 at 9331; *Andriopoulos v Marshall* (1981) 2 BPR 9391 at 9392.

4 *Cannon v Villars* (1878) 8 Ch D 415 at 420 per Jessel MR.

5 A right granted in respect of a passageway which was only 2 ft 11 in wide is necessarily restricted to foot traffic (*Bridgwood v Keates* (Unreported, Court of Appeal, 1 November 1983). See also *Milner's Safe Co Ltd v Great Northern and City Railway Co* [1907] 1 Ch 208 at 221.

6 *Scott v Martin* [1987] 1 WLR 841 at 849D–850A. A valid easement over an undefined route may also be granted where the parties agree that the route is to be fixed by some defined person (see *Talga Investments Pty Ltd v Tweed Canal Estates Pty Ltd* (1974) 1 BPR 9675 at 9681).

An express grant of a right of way must also be construed having regard to the purposes for which it was granted and which were within the reasonable contemplation of the parties at the date of grant.[7] A distinction must be maintained, however, between the present or reasonably foreseeable *purposes* of the grant and the actual *means* or *form of user* through which these purposes may be realised. Thus a right of way may not be used subsequently for a purpose wholly different from that originally envisaged by the grantor and grantee. It may well be that an easement of way granted as appurtenant to an open space cannot be invoked if that open space is subsequently built upon.[8] By contrast, a right of way granted for general purposes in respect of a house may survive the conversion of the house into a hotel,[9] although there is always the possibility that any excessive user of the original easement will be actionable as nuisance.[10]

No relevance is attached, moreover, to a mere change in the particular form of user employed in the exercise of a right of way. In the absence of any express restriction as to the form of user, the courts have been disinclined to hold that the permissible user is cut down by the past practice of the dominant owner[11] or is impliedly limited to certain kinds of person.[12] In particular an unlimited right of way may be exercised in any manner beneficial to the dominant tenement and conformable to the original purpose of the grant, even though this form of user may differ from the user at the date of the express grant.[13] Thus, for instance, a right of way which was originally used for transport by horse-drawn vehicles may quite properly extend to motorised transport for the same purpose.[14]

(iv) Fluctuations in user under an express grant While subsequent changes in the form of user under an easement are in themselves immaterial, it is clear

7 *Hamble PC v Haggard* [1992] 1 WLR 122 at 136B per Millett J.

8 *Allen v Gomme* (1840) 11 Ad & El 759 at 772, 774, 113 ER 602 at 607f. See, however, *Flavell v Lange* [1937] NZLR 444 at 449; *Grinskis v Lahood* [1971] NZLR 502 at 508f.

9 *White v Grand Hotel, Eastbourne, Ltd* [1913] 1 Ch 113 at 116f (affirmed by Court of Appeal, (1915) 84 LJ Ch 938). See also *Robinson v Bailey* [1948] 2 All ER 791 at 796B-G; *Jelbert v Davis* [1968] 1 WLR 589 at 594H–595B; *Grinskis v Lahood* [1971] NZLR 502 at 509. Compare *National Trust v White* [1987] 1 WLR 907 at 913G–914G.

10 See eg *Rosling v Pinnegar* (1986) 54 P & CR 124. Compare *Milner's Safe Co Ltd v Great Northern and City Railway Co* [1907] 1 Ch 208 at 226ff (claim of easement disallowed where access contemplated for purposes of a house, warehouse or factory on dominant land, but not for those of a railway station).

11 *Newcomen v Coulson* (1877) 5 Ch D 133 at 138f; *Bridgwood v Keates* (Unreported, Court of Appeal, 1 November 1983); *Lawrence v Griffiths* (1987) 47 SASR 455 at 479. Events subsequent to the date of grant are irrelevant to the scope of the grant, but may possibly colour the court's willingness to grant injunctive relief (see *Andriopoulos v Marshall* (1981) 2 BPR 9391 at 9392).

12 See *Bridgwood v Keates* (Unreported, Court of Appeal, 1 November 1983), where Oliver LJ refused to hold that an access to a back door was restricted by implication to 'trade visitors', thereby precluding access by the dominant owner herself or her children. In this case the real substance of the grievance expressed by the dominant owner's neighbours was the fact that she was accustomed in effect to use her back door as the principal entrance to her house. The Court of Appeal refused to intervene, although noting that if this user became 'excessive' then it would be actionable as nuisance (post, p 1083).

13 See eg *Newcomen v Coulson* (1877) 5 Ch D 133 at 138f; *Lawrence v Griffiths* (1987) 47 SASR 455 at 479.

14 *Sunset Properties Pty Ltd v Johnston* (1975) 3 BPR 9185 at 9191. See also *Lock v Abercester Ltd* [1939] Ch 861 at 863f.

that objection may be raised if the changed user imposes an excessive burden on the servient tenement relative to the burden which existed at the date of grant.[15] The courts are reluctant to allow a dominant owner to extend the exercise of a right of way substantially beyond the terms contemplated in the original grant.[16] Thus, for instance, the courts would be quick to restrain any 'abuse of the rights given to the grantee' which might occur if excessive traffic on the way caused the servient owner 'troubled days and sleepless nights'.[17]

In *Jelbert v Davis*[18] a dominant tenement had originally been used for agricultural purposes only. The dominant owner subsequently obtained planning permission to position up to 200 holiday caravans on the site. The Court of Appeal attached no significance to the change in the *form* of user of the dominant land,[19] but upheld an objection that the *volume* of user of the access route to this site was liable to become excessive. In the view of Lord Denning MR, the proposed user was likely to be 'so extensive as to be outside the reasonable contemplation of the parties at the time the grant was made'.[20] An injunction was granted.[1]

The mere alteration of a dominant tenement to which a right of way has been appurtenant does not necessarily extinguish the right of way. In *Graham v Philcox*,[2] subsequent enlargement of the original dominant tenement was held to have no effect on the existence of the easement, so long as the character and extent of the burden imposed on the servient tenement by the extended dominant tenement were not excessive.

(v) Scope of a prescriptively acquired right of way Different rules govern a right of way which has been acquired by prescription.[3] Such a right is for ever

15 Excessive user constitutes trespass and may be restrained by injunction (see *Hamble PC v Haggard* [1992] 1 WLR 122 at 133E–134E; *Mercantile General Life Reassurance Co of Australia Ltd v Permanent Trustee Australia Ltd* (1989) NSW ConvR 55-441 at 58,210ff). The servient owner is entitled to obstruct an excessive user only where the excessive user cannot be severed from a perfectly lawful user (see *Hamble* [1992] 1 WLR 122 at 134E). Otherwise it seems that excessive user does not terminate or even suspend the easement in question (see *Graham v Philcox* [1984] QB 747 at 756E-F).

16 See *Harris v Flower* (1904) 74 LJ Ch 127 at 132; *Re Gordon and Regan* (1985) 15 DLR (4th) 641 at 648.

17 *Rodwell v G.R. Evans & Co Pty Ltd* (1977) 3 BPR 9114 at 9119 per Holland J.

18 [1968] 1 WLR 589.

19 Indeed the right of way in this case had been expressly granted in respect of user 'at all times and for all purposes'.

20 [1968] 1 WLR 589 at 596A, F. See *Malden Farms Ltd v Nicholson* (1956) 3 DLR (2d) 236 at 239ff, where the dominant tenant, who had recently built a holiday beach resort, was restrained from allowing the general public (who came 'by the hundreds') to use a lake shore pathway which had originally been granted as a private right of way to an unspoilt piece of shoreline. See also *Grinskis v Lahood* [1971] NZLR 502 at 509f.

1 For further discussion of the remedy appropriate in cases of unreasonable or excessive user, see *Rosling v Pinnegar* (1986) 54 P & CR 124.

2 [1984] QB 747 at 756D–757A, 764D–765A (conversion of two flats into single dwelling-house, where one of the flats had earlier enjoyed a right of way over adjoining land). See [1985] CLJ 15 (S. Tromans); [1985] Conv 60 (P. Todd).

3 Post, p 1106. Here the relevant rules are coloured by the fact that prescriptive rights are founded on a deemed acquiescence in a user of a certain and uniform kind (see *Scott-Whitehead v National Coal Board* (1987) 53 P & CR 263 at 273).

limited to the kind of user which prevailed during the period which gave rise to the prescriptive claim.[4] It follows therefore that, although the grantees of a prescriptive right of way are entitled to repair the relevant way,[5] there is no right to improve the way (eg by constructing a made road), since such action is apt to increase significantly the burden falling on the servient tenement.[6] However, a prescriptively acquired easement is not affected merely by a subsequent increase in user as distinct from a change in the fundamental character or purpose of the original user.[7]

(vi) Interference with rights of way Any wrongful interference with a private right of way is potentially a nuisance in relation to which either damages or an injunction (or both) may be sought.[8] However, not every form of interference is actionable.[9] A right of way cannot, by definition, confer rights of exclusive user, and it necessarily follows that the threshold of actionable nuisance is reached only when there is 'substantial' interference with the way as granted[10] in a form which is plainly obstructive of its reasonable use.[11] Each case raises an issue of fact and degree, to be determined with reference to the reasonable requirements of the dominant tenement from time to time.[12] No actionable interference occurs, for example, where an adjacent building enroaches into a roadway by merely two feet,[13] but there may well be a remedy where the width of the way is more than halved.[14] The erection of a gate across the way constitutes no nuisance so long as the dominant

4 *Ballard v Dyson* (1808) 1 Taunt 279 at 286, 127 ER 841 at 844; *Williams v James* (1867) LR 2 CP 577 at 582; *Bradburn v Morris* (1876) 3 Ch D 812 at 823; *R.P.C. Holdings Ltd v Rogers* [1953] 1 All ER 1029 at 1032B-C; *Mills v Silver* [1991] Ch 271 at 287B-C. See also *Cargill v Gotts* [1981] 1 WLR 441 at 447H-448A.

5 *Mills v Silver* [1991] Ch 271 at 286F-G.

6 *Mills v Silver* [1991] Ch 271 at 287B-C.

7 *British Railways Board v Glass* [1965] Ch 538 at 562E–563A, 567G–568D (increase from 6 to 30 caravans on site); *Woodhouse & Co Ltd v Kirkland (Derby) Ltd* [1970] 1 WLR 1185 at 1190H–1191A. For the present purpose a prescriptive claim is not vitiated merely because the original easement involved user by horse-drawn vehicles, while the modern user is by way of motor car (*Lock v Abercester Ltd* [1939] Ch 861 at 863f), or because the original user has dwindled away to less onerous traffic on foot (*Davies v Stephens* (1836) 7 C & P 570 at 571, 173 ER 251 at 252). See also *Cargill v Gotts* [1981] 1 WLR 441 at 448H–449B.

8 *Saint v Jenner* [1973] Ch 275 at 280A-E; *Jalnarne Ltd v Ridewood* (1989) 61 P & CR 143 at 150; *McKellar v Guthrie* [1920] NZLR 729 at 731. Even substantial interference with an easement may be quite lawful if authorised by the express terms of the grant (see eg *Overcom Properties v Stockleigh Hall Residents Management Ltd* (1989) 58 P & CR 1 at 8ff).

9 *Celsteel Ltd v Alton House Holdings Ltd* [1985] 1 WLR 204 at 216E. See also *York Bros (Trading) Pty Ltd v Commr of Main Roads* [1983] 1 NSWLR 391 at 394D.

10 *Hutton v Hamboro* (1860) 2 F & F 218 at 219, 175 ER 1031 at 1032; *Pettey v Parsons* [1914] 2 Ch 653 at 662, 665; *Keefe v Amor* [1965] 1 QB 334 at 347D; *Overcom Properties v Stockleigh Hall Residents Management Ltd* (1989) 58 P & CR 1 at 8; *Zenere v Leate* (1980) 1 BPR 9300 at 9305; *Saggers v Brown* (1981) 2 BPR 9329 at 9331.

11 *Keefe v Amor* [1965] 1 QB 334 at 346G; *Celsteel Ltd v Alton House Holdings Ltd* [1985] 1 WLR 204 at 217B.

12 *Saggers v Brown* (1981) 2 BPR 9329 at 9332.

13 *Clifford v Hoare* (1874) LR 9 CP 362 at 370ff.

14 *Celsteel Ltd v Alton House Holdings Ltd* [1985] 1 WLR 204 at 218C-G. See also *Powell v Linney* (1983) 80 Law Soc Gaz 1982.

owner is allowed free access at all times,[15] or so long as the gate is kept open at least during the dominant owner's business hours.[16] The true test of interference here is whether the gate is 'locked against enjoyment',[17] and the locking of a gate across a right of way is not in itself inconsistent with a claim of right particularly where the dominant owner is provided with a key.[18] The installation of a large cattle grid may be a source of actionable nuisance,[19] but the courts have looked more kindly on the construction of speed ramps on a driveway.[20]

(b) *Rights of light*

In the absence of any natural right of access to light,[1] the preservation of access to sunlight must be sought by way of either a duly acquired easement of light or a restrictive covenant which precludes adverse building development. Rights of light are commonly acquired as a prescriptive easement and are often termed 'ancient lights'.[2] In English law at any rate, an easement of light can arise only in respect of light which comes through a defined aperture (such as a window)[3] and easements of light are therefore restricted to buildings.[4] The obstruction of part of the light reaching a building on the dominant tenement can constitute an actionable nuisance.

(i) Quantum of light The dominant owner is entitled to the uninterrupted access through his ancient windows of sufficient light to enable him to enjoy comfortable use of the building for the purposes of his occupancy,[5]

15 See *Flynn v Harte* [1913] 2 IR 322 at 326ff; *Sunset Properties Pty Ltd v Johnston* (1975) 3 BPR 9185 at 9194f. The existence of a right of way is not inconsistent with a duty in the dominant owner to close the gate after use (see *Lister v Rickard* (1969) 113 Sol Jo 981; *Gohl v Hender* [1930] SASR 158 at 163f).
16 *Pettey v Parsons* [1914] 2 Ch 653 at 662ff; *Lister v Rickard* (1969) 113 Sol Jo 981. See also *Healy v Ellco Farm Supplies Pty Ltd* (1986) 3 BPR 9596 at 9599.
17 See *Sunset Properties Pty Ltd v Johnston* (1975) 3 BPR 9185 at 9195 per Holland J.
18 Such action may be intended to discourage unauthorised strangers or simply to preserve the relative privacy of the servient owner (see *Sunset Properties Pty Ltd v Johnston* (1975) 3 BPR 9185 at 9195).
19 *Powell v Linney* (1983) 80 Law Soc Gaz 1982.
20 *Saint v Jenner* [1973] Ch 275 at 279D.
1 Ante, p 1059.
2 Post, p 1114.
3 Ante, p 1072. See *Levet v Gas Light & Coke Co* [1919] 1 Ch 24 at 27.
4 In other jurisdictions there has been much greater interest in the more general question of easements of solar access. See eg *Prah v Maretti*, 321 NW2d 182 at 187ff (1982); D.D. Goble, *Solar Rights: Guaranteeing a Place in the Sun*, 57 Oregon L Rev 94 (1978); P.D. Devlin, 17 Calif Western L Rev 123 (1980–81); A.J. Bradbrook, (1982) 5 Univ of New South Wales LJ 229; (1983) 15 U of W Australia L Rev 148; A.E. Blenkhorn, 32 Cleveland State L Rev 497 (1983–84).
5 *Colls v Home and Colonial Stores Ltd* [1904] AC 179 at 187, 198, 204; *Allen v Greenwood* [1980] Ch 119 at 130A-B, 135A-B. In *Carr-Saunders v Dick McNeil Associates Ltd* [1986] 1 WLR 922 at 928E-F, Millett J reiterated the 'well established' rule that no actionable wrong is committed if 'the amount of light remaining is sufficient for the comfortable enjoyment of his property by the dominant owner according to the ordinary notions of mankind.'

whether that use is residential or business.[6] Judged against the criterion of 'ordinary user',[7] the relevant issue in any alleged interference with light is not 'How much light has been taken away?' but rather 'How much light is left?'[8]

(ii) Fluctuations in user The dominant owner is not entitled to impose an increased burden on the servient tenement merely by altering either the user of his building[9] or the position or size of his windows.[10] However, an easement of light acquired under the Prescription Act 1832 relates to the building as a whole and not to a particular room within it.[11] The extent of the dominant owner's right is neither increased nor diminished by the actual use to which the dominant tenement has been put in the past[12] or by any extraordinary use to which he now chooses to put the premises or any of the rooms in them.[13] The court must therefore take account not only of present use, but also of 'other potential uses to which the dominant owner may reasonably be expected to put the premises in the future'.[14] In *Carr-Saunders v Dick McNeil Associates Ltd*,[15] for instance, it was not fatal to the dominant owner's allegation of obstruction that he had, during the prescription period, altered his premises by subdividing one large room into a number of smaller rooms. The windows had remained unchanged, even though the rooms behind them had not, and the dominant owner was therefore entitled to damages in respect of the elevation of an adjacent building which had recently obstructed the access of reasonable light to the reconstructed rooms.[16]

6 A photographic studio may be entitled to an unusually large quantity of light (see *Allen v Greenwood* [1980] Ch 119 at 133C-D, 136G-H), but a church, even if it has stained glass windows, cannot prescribe for more light than is needed in order to be 'comfortably used according to the ordinary requirements of people attending church' (see *Newham v Lawson* (1971) 22 P & CR 852 at 859f).

7 The light required for 'ordinary user' depends also on the nature of the building concerned. A greenhouse may need much more light than a warehouse (see *Allen v Greenwood* [1980] Ch 119 at 131B, 135A-B). The standard of light enjoyed by way of easement may extend beyond that which would be justified by 'ordinary user' if the servient owner has, eg during the prescription period, been aware of a specially enhanced or heightened requirement of light for the particular purposes of the dominant owner (see *Allen v Greenwood*, supra at 132D-F, 136A-B).

8 *Higgins v Betts* [1905] 2 Ch 210 at 215 per Farwell J. See also *Carr-Saunders v Dick McNeil Associates Ltd* [1986] 1 WLR 922 at 928F.

9 *Colls v Home and Colonial Stores Ltd* [1904] AC 179 at 203.

10 *Smith v Evangelization Society (Incorporated) Trust* [1933] Ch 515 at 533ff; *Scott v Goulding Properties Ltd* [1973] IR 200 at 219ff.

11 *Colls v Home and Colonial Stores Ltd* [1904] AC 179 at 204; *Price v Hilditch* [1930] 1 Ch 500 at 508; *Carr-Saunders v Dick McNeil Associates Ltd* [1986] 1 WLR 922 at 928D.

12 *Price v Hilditch* [1930] 1 Ch 500 at 506ff; *Carr-Saunders v Dick McNeil Associates Ltd* [1986] 1 WLR 922 at 928F-G.

13 *Carr-Saunders v Dick McNeil Associates Ltd* [1986] 1 WLR 922 at 928G.

14 *Carr-Saunders v Dick McNeil Associates Ltd* [1986] 1 WLR 922 at 928H. See also *Moore v Hall* (1878) 3 QBD 178 at 182.

15 [1986] 1 WLR 922 at 929F-930F.

16 It used to be said that where a building enjoying ancient lights was demolished and replaced by a new building, the ancient lights would be preserved only if the windows in the new building were in the same place and of the same number and dimensions as those in the old building (see *Cherington v Abney Mill* (1709) 2 Vern 646, 23 ER 1022). Compare, however, *Andrews v Waite* [1907] 2 Ch 500 at 510, where Neville J indicated that 'the real test. . .is identity of light, and not identity of aperture, or entrance for the light'.

(iii) Actionable interference The courts are nowadays disinclined to adopt inflexible methods of quantifying the degree of obstruction with light which gives rise to an actionable nuisance. There is no longer any '45 degrees rule',[17] and in *Carr-Saunders v Dick McNeil Associates Ltd*[18] Millett J resisted any rigid application of the '50-50 rule', under which an interference with light is actionable only where more than 50 per cent of the floor area of a room receives one lumen of light at table level. He took the view that the dominant owner is simply entitled to such access of light 'as will leave his premises adequately lit for all ordinary purposes for which they may reasonably be expected to be used.'[19]

3. CREATION OF EASEMENTS AND PROFITS

An easement or profit *à prendre* can exist *at law* only if certain conditions are fulfilled. *First*, the easement or profit must be held 'for an interest equivalent to an estate in fee simple absolute in possession or a term of years absolute'.[20] *Second*, the easement or profit must be created by statute, by deed or by prescription, and in registered land the express grant of a legal easement or profit *à prendre* must be 'completed by registration'.[1] In all other cases the easement or profit must be equitable.[2] There is no exception even in the case of an easement or profit which is granted for a period of three years or less, since there is no analogy with the rules concerning the informal creation of legal leases.[3]

(1) Informal creation

In the absence of statutory or prescriptive creation, an easement or profit which is granted *informally* has only equitable status.[4] An equitable easement or profit may therefore be created in writing otherwise than by deed, provided that the transaction is for value.[5] Likewise a specifically enforceable contract to grant an easement or profit gives rise to rights of an equitable character,[6]

17 *Colls v Home and Colonial Stores Ltd* [1904] AC 179 at 210; *Fishenden v Higgs & Hill Ltd* (1935) 153 LT 128 at 131f, 136f, 143f. This rule operated against obstructions which rose above a line extended upwards from a room at a 45 degree angle out through the centre of a window.
18 [1986] 1 WLR 922 at 927B-C.
19 [1986] 1 WLR 922 at 928G-H.
20 Law of Property Act 1925, s 1(2)(a).
1 Land Registration Act 1925, ss 19(2), 22(2) (ante, p 179).
2 See *Ellison v Vukicevic* (1986) 7 NSWLR 104 at 117E.
3 Ante, p 736.
4 See *Wood v Leadbitter* (1845) 13 M & W 838 at 843, 153 ER 351 at 354; *Mason v Clarke* [1954] 1 QB 460 at 468, 471.
5 *Frogley v Earl of Lovelace* (1859) Johns 333 at 339f, 70 ER 450 at 453; *May v Belleville* [1905] 2 Ch 605 at 613; *Reid v Moreland Timber Co Pty Ltd* (1946) 73 CLR 1 at 16. This result is merely another application of the doctrine of *Walsh v Lonsdale* (ante, p 746).
6 *Tarrant v Zandstra* (1973) 1 BPR 9381 at 9385.

so long as the contract is intended to create immediate rights.[7] It even used to be the case that an equitable easement or profit could be created by a mere oral agreement for value supported by part performance.[8] Now, however, that the doctrine of part performance can no longer affect informal agreements concerning land,[9] it is likely that a merely verbal grant can create equitable rights only if there are circumstances which justify a claim of proprietary estoppel on behalf of the intended grantee.[10]

(2) Distinction between grant and reservation

Easements and profits may be created by means of either grant or reservation. The difference between grant and reservation turns on the identity of the party in whose favour the easement or profit is created. The following examples use a right of way as a working basis for discussion.

(a) Grant

Grant arises typically where a landowner (V) disposes of part of his land to a stranger (P) as in *Fig.* 69, on terms that P shall henceforth be entitled to the benefit of an easement over the land retained by V. In this case the easement concerned is created in favour of P, the transferee of the land.

Grant need not, of course, occur only in the event of a severance or subdivision of an existing ownership, in that it is always open to a landowner to grant away easements or profits over his land. It is simply the case that grant tends to occur most frequently in cases of subdivision, where the minds of the parties are most clearly directed towards a consideration of their future needs in relation to their respective properties.[11]

(b) Reservation

Reservation arises where the original landowner (V) disposes of part of his land to P, as in *Fig.* 70, on terms that V shall nevertheless retain an easement over the land purchased by P. In this case the easement concerned is one created in favour of V, the transferor of the land.

7 Easements are subject to the rule against perpetuities (see *Dunn v Blackdown Properties Ltd* [1961] Ch 433 at 438 per Cross J, but compare G. Battersby, (1961) 25 Conv (NS) 415). There is therefore always a possibility that a grant may be rendered void on the ground of perpetuity (see eg *Newham v Lawson* (1971) 22 P & CR 852 at 855f). Where a grant is not immediate, but relates to an easement to arise in the future, it will be void unless limited to take effect only within the perpetuity period (see *Talga Investments Pty Ltd v Tweed Canal Estates Pty Ltd* (1974) 1 BPR 9675 at 9682).

8 *McManus v Cooke* (1887) 35 Ch D 681 at 697; *Bayley v Marquis Conyngham* (1863) 15 ICLR 406 at 410ff.

9 Law of Property (Miscellaneous Provisions) Act 1989, s 2(8), ante, p 256. See J. Howell, [1990] Conv 441.

10 Ante, p 312, post, p 1115.

11 If commonhold ownership schemes are introduced (ante, p 10), it will be possible for a unit holder to grant rights of easement to a third party, although it is envisaged that, if created without the consent of the commonhold association, such rights cannot survive the termination of the commonhold (see Law Commission, *Commonhold: Freehold Flats and freehold ownership of other interdependent buildings* (Cm 179, July 1987), paras 6.9ff).

GRANT

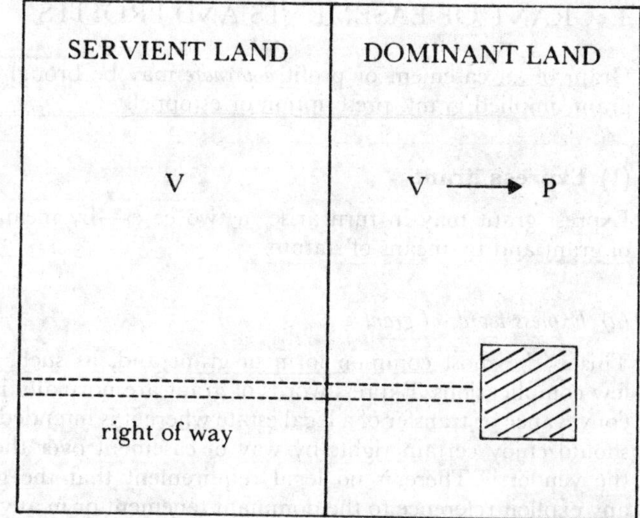

Fig. 69

RESERVATION

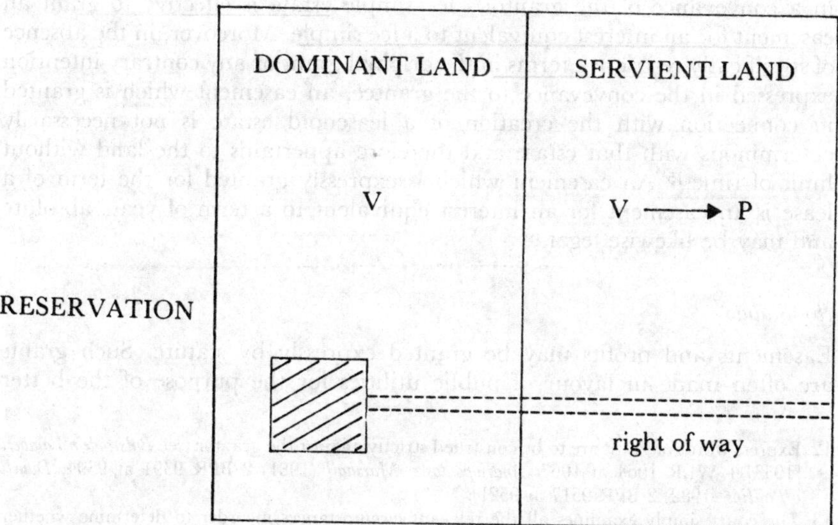

Fig. 70

The rules relating to the creation of easements and profits are made very much easier if the distinction between grant and reservation is borne in mind. The essential difference between grant and reservation is whether the right in question is granted to the transferee of the land conveyed or is reserved by the transferor in favour of the land retained. In the case of grant, the servient tenement is in the hands of V; in the case of reservation, the servient tenement is that of P.

4. GRANT OF EASEMENTS AND PROFITS

Grant of an easement or profit *à prendre* may be brought about by express grant, implied grant, prescription or estoppel.

(1) Express grant

Express grant may in turn arise in two cases—by means of express words of grant and by means of statute.

(a) Express words of grant

This is the most common form of grant and, as such, presents relatively few complications. Express words of grant are normally incorporated in the conveyance or transfer of a legal estate where it is intended that the purchaser should enjoy certain rights by way of easement over the land retained by the vendor.[12] There is no legal requirement that the grant should make any explicit reference to the dominant tenement or in any other way identify the land benefited by the easement.[13]

After 1925 the grant of an easement or profit without words of limitation confers the most ample interest which the grantor is competent to confer, unless a contrary intention is apparent.[14] Thus an easement granted expressly in a conveyance of the grantor's fee simple estate is effective to grant an easement for an interest equivalent to a fee simple. Moreover, in the absence of specifically restrictive terms in the original grant or any contrary intention expressed in the conveyance to the grantee, an easement which is granted in connection with the creation of a leasehold estate is not necessarily coterminous with that estate and therefore appertains to the land without limit of time.[15] An easement which is expressly granted for the term of a lease is an easement for an interest equivalent to a term of years absolute and may be likewise legal.[16]

(b) Statute

Easements and profits may be granted expressly by statute. Such grants are often made in favour of public utilities for the purpose of the better

12 Express words of grant are to be construed strictly against the grantor (see *Bulstrode v Lambert* [1953] 1 WLR 1064 at 1067; *Andriopoulos v Marshall* (1981) 2 BPR 9391 at 9394; *Dunell v Phillips* (1982) 2 BPR 9517 at 9521).

13 The court simply examines all the relevant circumstances in order to determine whether there was in fact a dominant tenement benefited by the supposed easement (see *Johnstone v Holdway* [1963] 1 QB 601 at 612; *The Shannon Ltd v Venner Ltd* [1965] Ch 682 at 693G-694A; *Gas & Fuel Corpn of Victoria v Barba* [1976] VR 755 at 764). The rule on this point is different in other common law jurisdictions. In New South Wales (although not in Victoria), no easement is enforceable against a third party unless the instrument which creates the interest clearly indicates both the land to which the benefit is appurtenant and the land which is subject to the burden of the easement (Conveyancing Act 1919, s 88(1)). See *Maurice Toltz Pty Ltd v Macy's Emporium Pty Ltd* (1969) 91 WN (NSW) 591 at 599D-F; *Papadopoulos v Goodwin* [1982] 1 NSWLR 413 at 417B-418E.

14 See *Reid v Moreland Timber Co Pty Ltd* (1946) 73 CLR 1 at 13 per Dixon J, but compare, however, *Ellison v Vukicevic* (1986) 7 NSWLR 104 at 114D-F.

15 *Graham v Philcox* [1984] QB 747 at 761A-D.

16 Ante, p 71.

management or execution of the function with which they are charged.[17] Thus statutorily created easements exist in favour of public utility undertakings which provide and maintain supplies of gas, electricity, water and sewerage.[18]

(2) Implied grant

There are certain cases in which, in the absence of express conferment, the grant of an easement will be implied or inferred on behalf of the purchaser of land.[19] These categories of implied grant are not wholly distinct but tend instead to merge into one another. Perhaps their most highly unifying characteristic is that they all express in slightly differing ways a general and ancient principle in English law that a grantor 'may not derogate from his grant'.[20] In other words, he must not grant land to another on terms which effectively negative the utility of the grant for the grantee.[1] Cases of implied grant fall into roughly four categories.

(a) Necessity

In certain circumstances the courts are willing to imply the grant of an easement on the ground of necessity,[2] the classic case of necessity in this context being that of the 'landlocked close'.[3] If V conveys land to P which has no legally enforceable means of access except across land retained by V,[4] it is clear that the courts will imply on behalf of P an easement of

17 See *Canadian Pacific Ltd v Paul* (1989) 53 DLR (4th) 487 at 498ff (Supreme Court of Canada).

18 Ante, p 1062.

19 Implied grant cannot occur, however, except where an express grant would have been possible (see *M.R.A. Engineering Ltd v Trimster Co Ltd* (1988) 56 P & CR 1 at 5, 7; *In re St Clement's, Leigh-on-Sea* [1988] 1 WLR 720 at 728E-H).

20 *Aldridge v Wright* [1929] 2 KB 117 at 130 per Greer LJ.

1 Ante, p 781. In the words of Bowen LJ in *Birmingham, Dudley and District Banking Co v Ross* (1888) 38 Ch D 295 at 313, 'a grantor having given a thing with one hand is not to take away the means of enjoying it with the other. And this principle will be carried out by a necessary implication of whatever fiction is required to support the origin of the right not to be interfered with by the grantor.'

2 See P. Jackson, (1981) 34 CLP 113; P.G. Glenn, 58 North Carolina L Rev 223 (1979-80). The law relating to ways of necessity has been described as 'in some respects archaic' and as needing reformulation to meet 'modern circumstances' (see *M.R.A. Engineering Ltd v Trimster Co Ltd* (1988) 56 P & CR 1 at 5 per Dillon LJ).

3 See D.A. Stroud, (1940) 56 LQR 93; A.J. Bradbrook, (1983) 10 Sydney L Rev 39. It is possible that there may be other species of easement which are implied from necessity. For the suggestion that necessity may generate an obligation of support as between adjoining terraced or semi-detached houses, see *Williams v Usherwood* (1983) 45 P & CR 235 at 254. It is also likely that in these circumstances an implied obligation of support can be founded on the rule in *Wheeldon v Burrows* (post, p 1097). See eg *Scouton & Co (Builders) Ltd v Gilyott & Scott Ltd* (1972) 221 Estates Gazette 1499; *Kebewar Pty Ltd v Harkin* (1987) 9 NSWLR 738 at 741B-742A (ante, p 1057).

4 The same principle operates on a devise of land (*Milner's Safe Co Ltd v Great Northern and City Railway Co* [1907] 1 Ch 208 at 219; *Sunset Properties Pty Ltd v Johnston* (1975) 3 BPR 9185 at 9188). Any claim of 'necessity' is rebutted by the existence of an easement impliedly available on some other basis (eg under the rule in *Wheeldon v Burrows*, post, p 1097). See *Sunset* at 9188.

access even though the conveyance or transfer to P makes no express reference to such a right.[5] This implication of rights clearly emanates from the principle against derogation from grant.[6] It is for V to select the particular route of access,[7] but once nominated this route cannot later be varied without agreement.[8] Likewise it is possible that an implied easement may arise at common law where V has conveyed to P a house one of whose external walls is sited on the common boundary with V's retained land. Here P acquires by necessity a right to enter upon V's land in order to repair or maintain his own boundary wall.[9]

(i) Criterion of 'necessity' For the present purpose the criterion of 'necessity' has generally been given a strict application in English law.[10] No 'necessity' arises on a mere showing that a particular access would be convenient or even 'reasonably necessary' for the proper enjoyment of the alleged dominant tenement,[11] although it may be that an easement founded on such grounds may be implied more easily under the head of easements of 'common intention'.[12] The claimant must establish that, without the provision of the

5 *Clark v Cogge* (1607) 2 Roll Abr 60, pl 17, Cro Jac 170, 79 ER 149; *Pomfret v Ricroft* (1669) 1 Wms Saund 321 at 323, 85 ER 454 at 460 (n 6); *Pinnington v Galland* (1853) 9 Exch 1 at 12f, 156 ER 1 at 6; *Pearson v Spencer* (1861) 1 B & S 571 at 584, 121 ER 827 at 831; *Gayford v Moffatt* (1868) 4 Ch App 133 at 135; *B. & W. Investments Ltd v Ulster Scottish Friendly Society* (1969) 20 NILQ 325.

6 Ante, p 781. See *Bolton v Bolton* (1879) 11 Ch D 968 at 971f. As Cotton LJ observed in *Birmingham, Dudley and District Banking Co v Ross* (1888) 38 Ch D 295 at 306, 'when a man grants a house, he grants that which is necessary for the existence of that house'. See also *Parish v Kelly* (1980) 1 BPR 9394 at 9400.

7 *Clark v Cogge* (1607) 2 Roll Abr 60, pl 17, Cro Jac 170, 79 ER 149; *Bolton v Bolton* (1879) 11 Ch D 968 at 971; *Deacon v South-Eastern Railway Co* (1889) 61 LT 377 at 379; *Brown v Alabaster* (1887) 37 Ch D 490 at 500; *Barba v Gas & Fuel Corpn of Victoria* (1976) 136 CLR 120 at 132. The route selected must, however, be convenient (see *Pearson v Spencer* (1861) 1 B & S 571 at 585, 121 ER 827 at 832). If the servient owner fails to point out the way, the grantee must take the nearest way possible (see *Wimbledon and Putney Commons Conservators v Dixon* (1875) 1 Ch D 362 at 369f). There is Australian authority that in default of a selection of way by the servient owner, the dominant owner has a right of selection (*Sunset Properties Pty Ltd v Johnston* (1975) 3 BPR 9185 at 9188).

8 *Pearson v Spencer* (1861) 1 B & S 571 at 584, 121 ER 827 at 832; *Deacon v South-Eastern Railway Co* (1889) 61 LT 377 at 379.

9 *Auerbach v Beck* (1985) 6 NSWLR 424 at 444D-E, affd sub nom *Beck v Auerbach* (1986) 6 NSWLR 454.

10 Compare the less exacting standard applied in Australia, where it is sufficient to show that, without an implied easement, there would be 'a substantial degree of practical difficulty of access' (*Tarrant v Zandstra* (1973) 1 BPR 9381 at 9386). See also *Torrisi v Magame Pty Ltd* [1984] 1 NSWLR 14 at 22E-G; *Lamos Pty Ltd v Hutchison* (1984) 3 BPR 9350 at 9354f. Even in Australia, however, a claim based on the mere reasonableness of the required access is not enough (*Parish v Kelly* (1980) 1 BPR 9394 at 9401).

11 Compare the position in New Zealand where there is a much more general power vested in the courts to make an order on behalf of a landlocked owner granting access through the land of neighbours with compensation to the latter (Property Law Act 1952, s 129B). Land is 'landlocked' if 'there is no reasonable access to it' as defined in Property Law Act 1952, s 129B(1)(c). See *Jacobsen Holdings Ltd v Drexel* [1986] 1 NZLR 324, [1987] 2 NZLR 52.

12 Post, p 1096. See eg *Stafford v Lee* [1992] 45 LS Gaz R 27, where the Court of Appeal imputed a common intention to create an easement which was reasonably necessary for the enjoyment of the alleged dominant tenement.

desired access or other right of user, his tenement cannot be used at all.[13] It is not fatal to the claim of necessity that some of the surrounding land belongs to third parties and not to the vendor,[14] or that there exist alternative ways open to the landlocked owner by way of precarious user.[15] It is, however, vital that the necessity pleaded by the purchaser or by his successor in title should have existed at the date of transfer of the land and not be merely a form of necessity which arose after that date.[16]

(ii) Extent of the implied right There is some authority that an implied easement of necessity confers only a right to pass and re-pass along the route of access to a landlocked dominant tenement.[17] This minimalist approach[18] derives force from a natural prejudice against the 'man who does not take the trouble to secure an actual grant of a right-of-way'.[19] Thus, for instance, it has been held that the dominant owner of a way of necessity cannot plead similar grounds of need in support of such ancillary easements as those relating to drainage, sewerage and the supply of electricity.[20] It is highly likely, however, that in modern conditions an implied grant of these auxiliary rights would nowadays be supportable on a principle of non-derogation from grant.[1]

(iii) An overriding rule of public policy? It has sometimes been suggested that implied easements of necessity rest ultimately on some rule of public policy. In *Nickerson v Barraclough*,[2] for instance, Megarry V-C referred at first instance

13 See *Union Lighterage Co v London Graving Dock Co* [1902] 2 Ch 557 at 573; *M.R.A. Engineering Ltd v Trimster Co Ltd* (1988) 56 P & CR 1 at 6. See, however, *Morris v Edgington* (1810) 3 Taunt 24 at 31, 128 ER 10 at 13, where Mansfield CJ, in dealing with a choice between alternative ways, noted that 'it would not be a great stretch to call that a necessary way, without which the most convenient and reasonable mode of enjoying the premises could not be had'. For indications that a variable threshold of 'necessity' may apply in circumstances of emergency or special need, see *St Edmundsbury and Ipswich Diocesan Board of Finance v Clark* (No 2) [1975] 1 WLR 468 at 481D; [1989] Conv 355 (J.E.M.).

14 *Serff v Acton Local Board* (1886) 31 Ch D 679 at 683f; *Barkshire v Grubb* (1881) 18 Ch D 616 at 620.

15 See *Barry v Hasseldine* [1952] Ch 835 at 839. The availability of an alternative route enjoyable as of right is, of course, destructive of any claim of necessity, even though that alternative is inconvenient (see *Titchmarsh v Royston Water Co Ltd* (1899) 81 LT 673 at 675; *Manjang v Drammeh* (1990) 61 P & CR 194 at 197 per Lord Oliver of Aylmerton).

16 *Holmes v Goring* (1824) 2 Bing 76 at 84, 130 ER 233 at 237; *Corpn of London v Riggs* (1880) 13 Ch D 798 at 806ff. See also *B.O.J. Properties Ltd v Allen's Mobile Home Park Ltd* (1980) 108 DLR (3d) 305 at 312ff; *Parish v Kelly* (1980) 1 BPR 9394 at 9400; *Torrisi v Magame Pty Ltd* [1984] 1 NSWLR 14 at 22E-G.

17 There can be no easement of necessity in respect of access to light, since land is not rendered useless without such access (see *Ray v Hazeldine* [1904] 2 Ch 17 at 20f; [1989] Conv 355 at 356 (J.E.M.).

18 See the reference in *Parish v Kelly* (1980) 1 BPR 9394 at 9400 per Rath J to 'the minimum conditions for the purpose or result'.

19 *London Corpn v Riggs* (1880) 13 Ch D 798 at 807 per Jessel MR.

20 See eg *Pryce v McGuinness* [1966] Qd R 591 at 607f (where the dominant owner successfully claimed a right of way, but was otherwise isolated in his landlocked close). See also *Union Lighterage Co v London Graving Dock Co* [1902] 2 Ch 557 at 573, but compare *Auerbach v Beck* (1985) 6 NSWLR 424 at 444E–445B.

1 Ante, p 1091, post, p 1097. See *Auerbach v Beck* (1985) 6 NSWLR 424 at 444D–445A, affd sub nom *Beck v Auerbach* (1986) 6 NSWLR 454.

2 [1980] Ch 325. See (1980) 96 LQR 187 (P. Jackson); (1980) 130 NLJ 204 (H.W. Wilkinson); [1980] Conv 95 (J.T.F.).

to a 'rule of public policy which requires that land should not be rendered unusable by being landlocked'.[3] In his view 'no transaction should, without good reason, be treated as being effectual to deprive any land of a suitable means of access.'[4] Megarry V-C thus saw no good reason to deprive the land in the present case of access to the highway, even though the terms of the relevant conveyance had seemed expressly to negative any right of way in favour of the transferee. He regarded his conclusion as being supported by the longstanding rule that a grantor may not 'derogate from his grant'.[5] In *Nickerson v Barraclough* the original vendor had sold building land as such and, according to Megarry V-C, to negative any means of access to that land in the terms of the conveyance would constitute 'a plain instance of derogation'.[6]

Megarry V-C's judgment was reversed by the Court of Appeal.[7] Here Brightman LJ ruled that 'the doctrine of way of necessity is not founded upon public policy at all but upon an implication from the circumstances.'[8] The Court held that a way of necessity can exist only in association with a grant of land[9] and rests on the implication, drawn from the circumstances of the case, that unless some way is implied a parcel of land will be inaccessible.[10] Considerations of public policy are relevant therefore only to the extent that the courts may *frustrate* a contract where the underlying intention is contrary to public policy.[11]

(iv) Access to neighbouring land for the purpose of repair English law does not normally mandate cooperation between neighbours. There has never existed any general rule of access enabling a landowner lawfully to enter neighbouring land without his neighbour's permission in order to carry

3 [1980] Ch 325 at 334D. See E.H. Bodkin, (1973) 89 LQR 87; T.A.M. Cooney, (1979) 14 Ir Jur (NS) 334. See also *Ex parte Edward Street Properties Pty Ltd* [1977] Qd R 86 at 89 per Andrews J.

4 [1980] Ch 325 at 334H–335A. Megarry V-C recognised, however, that a way of necessity will not be implied in the case of every landlocked close, since there are certain circumstances in which 'there may be good reason why the land should be deprived of all access'. He cited as examples the case where the land 'may contain large quantities of highly toxic substances with a long life' and the rather different case where it is 'desired to produce a bird sanctuary that will, as far as possible, be free from any disturbance' ([1980] Ch 325 at 334G).

5 Ante, p 1091.

6 [1980] Ch 325 at 335B.

7 [1981] Ch 426. See (1982) 98 LQR 11 (P. Jackson); L. Crabb, [1981] Conv 442.

8 See eg *North Sydney Printing Pty Ltd v Sabemo Investment Corpn Pty Ltd* [1971] 2 NSWLR 150 at 160D-E, cited in *Nickerson v Barraclough* [1981] Ch 426 at 440G.

9 It follows that no way of necessity can be implied on behalf of an owner who has acquired title to the alleged dominant tenement by adverse possession (*Wilkes v Greenway* (1890) 6 TLR 449; *North Sydney Printing Pty Ltd v Sabemo Investment Corpn Pty Ltd* [1971] 2 NSWLR 150 at 159C-D). Normally, of course, 20 years of uninterrupted user will eventually create a prescriptive right (post, p 1113).

10 Thus no way of necessity will be implied unless there is evidence from which an intention to create an easement can be inferred at the date of the transfer of the land (see *Margil Pty Ltd v Stegul Pastoral Pty Ltd* [1984] 2 NSWLR 1 at 10B-C; *Auerbach v Beck* (1985) 6 NSWLR 424 at 441E-F).

11 [1981] Ch 426 at 441A.

out necessary works on his own land.[12] In the past this legal hiatus has raised pressing problems where, for instance, a landowner needed to repair part of his property (eg a wall or roof gutter) which immediately abutted on to adjoining land. There used to be no means of legal challenge in respect of an unreasonable refusal of access by a disobliging neighbour. Nowadays, however, at least a partial remedy is provided by the Access to Neighbouring Land Act 1992.[13]

Under the 1992 Act the High Court and county court have a discretionary jurisdiction to make an 'access order'[14] on the application of any person who desires to make an unconsented entry upon 'adjoining or adjacent land' for the purpose of 'carrying out works' on his own land.[15] An access order will be made only if the court is satisfied that the works are 'reasonably necessary for the preservation' of the whole or any part of the 'dominant land' and that they cannot be carried out 'or would be substantially more difficult to carry out' without entry upon the 'servient land'.[16] The new right of access is limited to the carrying out of 'basic preservation works', which include maintenance and repair, clearance of drains and sewers, and the care of trees, hedges and shrubs.[17] However, access for the purpose of effecting demolition or of making optional improvements and alterations to the dominant property can be ordered if such works are considered by the court to be 'fair and reasonable in all the circumstances of the case'.[18] The right of access granted by the court is not, in any event, a permanent right, but is intended to provide a 'one-off' right appropriate to a particular need.[19]

The short-term easement of access authorised by the 1992 Act represents only a limited form of compulsory acquisition of user rights.[20] The 1992

12 See eg *John Trenberth Ltd v National Westminster Bank Ltd* (1979) 39 P & CR 104 at 105ff (ante, p 21). There is Australian authority that such a right may arise as an easement of necessity where the two parcels of land were formerly in common ownership (ante, p 1092).

13 The enactment of legislation was recommended in 1985 by the Law Commission. See *Rights of Access to Neighbouring Land* (Law Com No 151, Cmnd 9692, December 1985). See [1992] Conv 225.

14 This order may be entered by notice in the Land Register pursuant to Land Registration Act 1925, s 49(1)(j), or entered in the register of writs and orders affecting land under the Land Charges Act 1972, s 6(1). See Access to Neighbouring Land Act 1992, s 5(1), (2).

15 Access to Neighbouring Land Act 1992, s 1(1)(a), (2).

16 Access to Neighbouring Land Act 1992, s 1(2). Except in the case of works to residential land, compensation may be ordered in favour of the servient owner (Access to Neighbouring Land Act 1992, s 2(4)(a), (5)). The court must withhold an access order altogether where the proposed works would cause unreasonable interference with or disturbance of the servient owner or cause unreasonable hardship to any occupier (Access to Neighbouring Land Act 1992, s 1(3)).

17 Access to Neighbouring Land Act 1992, s 1(4).

18 Access to Neighbouring Land Act 1992, s 1(5). Except in the case of residential land, compensation may be payable in respect of the 'likely financial advantage' conferred by the making of the access order (Access to Neighbouring Land Act 1992, s 2(5)(a), (6)).

19 Law Com No 151, para 4.62f.

20 The compulsory acquisition of easements is already available on a more extensive scale in other jurisdictions. Compare eg Queensland's Property Law Act 1974, s 180 (see *Tipler v Fraser* [1976] Qd R 272; *Ex parte Edward Street Properties Pty Ltd* [1977] Qd R 86; *Re Seaforth Land Sales Pty Ltd's Land* (No 2) [1977] Qd R 317; *Re Worthston Pty Ltd* [1987] 1 Qd R 400; H. Tarlo, (1979) 53 ALJ 254); British Columbia's Property Law Act (RSBC 1979, c 340), s 32 (see *Re Ferguson and Lepine* (1982) 128 DLR (3d) 188).

Act thus effects a purposive and fairly successful compromise between the legitimate privacy interests of the servient owner and the wider public interest in preserving the utility of dominant land and particularly of any housing stock situated thereon.

(b) Common intention

Easements may be implied in favour of the grantee of property in order to give effect to a common intention of the grantor and grantee of that property. Such easements may not be essentially different from those implied from necessity, in that a common intention to grant a particular easement will normally be found only in cases of necessity.[1] In *Pwllbach Colliery Co Ltd v Woodman*,[2] Lord Parker of Waddington stated that the law will readily imply the grant of 'such easements as may be necessary to give effect to the common intention of the parties to a grant of real property, with reference to the manner or purposes in and for which the land granted. . .is to be used.'[3] Lord Parker added, however, that 'it is essential. . .that the parties should intend that the subject of the grant. . .should be used in some definite and particular manner'.[4]

The principle of implication from common intention was illustrated in *Wong v Beaumont Property Trust Ltd*.[5] Here the defendant's predecessor in title had leased the basement of premises to the plaintiff's predecessor in title for the express purpose of use as a restaurant. The plaintiff later bought the remainder of the lease, intending to use the premises as a Chinese restaurant. He covenanted to comply with public health regulations and to eliminate all noxious smells and odours. In fact, unknown to the parties at the date of the assignment of the lease, these obligations could be performed only by the installation of a new ventilation system leading through the upstairs premises retained by the defendant. The Court of Appeal held that the plaintiff was entitled to assert an easement of necessity in respect of the construction of the ventilation duct which would enable him to comply both with the terms of the lease and with public health regulations.[6]

1 See eg *Nickerson v Barraclough* [1980] Ch 325 at 336D, where Megarry V-C expressed the view that a 'way of necessity' should be 'more accurately referred to as a way implied from the common intention of the parties, based on a necessity apparent from the deeds'. The affinity between the grounds of necessity and common intention is again demonstrated in *B.O.J. Properties Ltd v Allen's Mobile Home Park Ltd* (1980) 108 DLR (3d) 305 at 315f. That the two categories often shade into each other is evident in *Auerbach v Beck* (1985) 6 NSWLR 424 at 444A-B. Compare, however, *M.R.A. Engineering Ltd v Trimster Co Ltd* (1988) 56 P & CR 1 at 5 per Dillon LJ.

2 [1915] AC 634 at 646f.

3 See also *Squarey v Harris-Smith* (1981) 42 P & CR 118 at 127 per Oliver LJ.

4 [1915] AC 634 at 647 ('It is not enough that the subject of the grant. . .should be intended to be used in a manner which may or may not involve this definite and particular use'). The relevant intention need not be express but may be established by implication from the surrounding circumstances. In *Stafford v Lee* [1992] 45 LS Gaz R 27, the Court of Appeal relied on conveyancing plans as evidence that the parties could not reasonably have intended that the alleged dominant tenement should be used otherwise than for residential purposes and must therefore have shared an intention to create an easement (ante, p 1092).

5 [1965] 1 QB 173. See (1964) 80 LQR 322 (R.E.M.).

6 [1965] 1 QB 173 at 181E, 183E-F. See also *In re The State Electricity Commission of Victoria & Joshua's Contract* [1940] VLR 121 at 125f (implied grant of easement to transmit noise).

(c) Quasi-easements (the rule in Wheeldon v Burrows*)*

A third category of implied grant was confirmed by the rule in *Wheeldon v Burrows*.[7] This doctrine is but another illustration of the rule that a grantor may not derogate from his grant,[8] although the presumption against derogation from grant may of course be ousted by contrary agreement.[9] By virtue of its origin in the morality of grant, the rule in *Wheeldon v Burrows* applies only to grants, and not to reservations, of easements.[10]

(i) Operation of the rule The rule in *Wheeldon v Burrows* operates characteristically in the event of a subdivision of land (see *Fig.* 71). The rule confers on P, the transferee of a part of V's land, the benefit of any user over the land retained by V, which V himself had earlier found it convenient to exercise on his own behalf during the period prior to the subdivision. However, since this user could not have been said to constitute an easement before the transfer to P—for the simple reason that both tenements were then within the common ownership and possession of V[11]—the rights impliedly granted to P under *Wheeldon v Burrows* are usually referred to as *quasi-easements*.[12] In effect P receives as quasi-easements such rights over the tenement still retained by V which V had previously found to be reasonably necessary for the proper enjoyment and utilisation of the tenement now transferred to P.[13] Thus if V, while he lived in the quasi-dominant tenement prior to subdivision of his land, had been accustomed to pass and re-pass over land which he still retains after the subdivision, this user may now be claimed by P as of right in relation to what has become a quasi-servient tenement (see *Fig.* 71).[14] The rule in *Wheeldon v Burrows* is capable, moreover, of extending

7 (1879) 12 Ch D 31. The rule has been applied throughout the common law world (see eg *United States v Thompson*, 272 F Supp 774 at 784f (1967); J.W. Bruce and J.W. Ely, *The Law of Easements and Licences in Land* (Boston and New York, 1988), pp 4–33ff).

8 Ante, p 1091. See eg *Bayley v Great Western Railway Co* (1884) 26 Ch D 434 at 453; *Aldridge v Wright* [1929] 2 KB 117 at 129f, 134; *M.R.A. Engineering Ltd v Trimster Co Ltd* (1988) 56 P & CR 1 at 7; *In re St Clement's, Leigh-on-Sea* [1988] 1 WLR 720 at 729A; *Nelson v Walker* (1910) 10 CLR 560 at 582; *Tarrant v Zandstra* (1973) 1 BPR 9381 at 9385 per Mahoney J.

9 *Borman v Griffith* [1930] 1 Ch 493 at 499; *Squarey v Harris-Smith* (1981) 42 P & CR 118 at 123, 128f.

10 *Parish v Kelly* (1980) 1 BPR 9394 at 9399f per Rath J. The rule is applicable, however, in the context not merely of conveyances on sale but also of voluntary conveyances and devises (*Sunset Properties Pty Ltd v Johnston* (1975) 3 BPR 9185 at 9188). The rule is also applicable to land held by leasehold title (*Aldridge v Wright* [1929] 2 KB 117 at 124ff).

11 Ante, p 1069. See also *Roe v Siddons* (1888) 22 QBD 224 at 236 per Fry LJ.

12 See *Nelson v Walker* (1910) 10 CLR 560 at 582, where Isaacs J explained quasi-easements as 'such things enjoyed *de facto* during unity of possession as would, had that unity not existed, have been easements.' See also *Tarrant v Zandstra* (1973) 1 BPR 9381 at 9385.

13 See *Australian Hi-Fi Publications Pty Ltd v Gehl* [1979] 2 NSWLR 618 at 621B. If, instead of retaining some land after the subdivision, V were simultaneously to convey the subdivided tenements to P and Q respectively, each purchaser would obtain by way of implied grant the same rights over the land of the other as he would have received if that other land had been retained by V (see *Swansborough v Coventry* (1832) 9 Bing 305 at 309, 131 ER 629 at 631; *Sunset Properties Pty Ltd v Johnston* (1975) 3 BPR 9185 at 9188). This result follows at least if both P and Q were 'aware of the simultaneous conveyances' (see *Aldridge v Wright* [1929] 2 KB 117 at 124ff).

14 See *Bayley v Great Western Railway Co* (1884) 26 Ch D 434 at 452f; *Borman v Griffith* [1930] 1 Ch 493 at 499.

far beyond rights of way.[15] Where, for instance, V originally owned two adjoining houses, the rule may equally well operate to imply a right of support on behalf of P if he purchases one of these houses from V.[16]

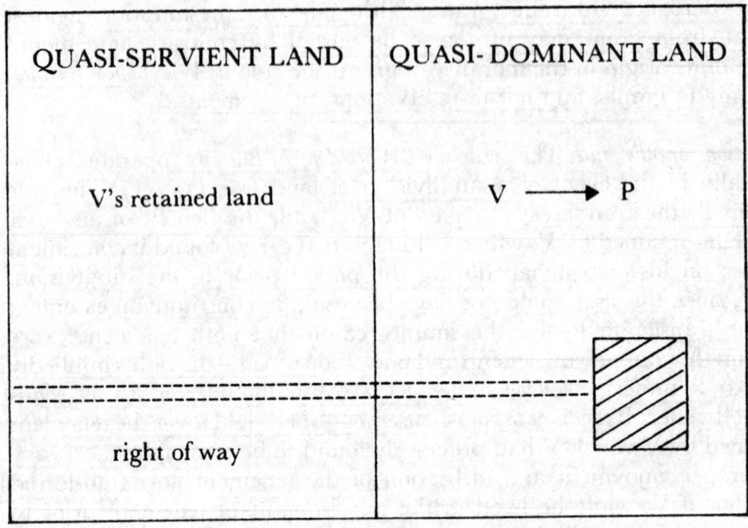

Fig. 71

An easement which arises under *Wheeldon v Burrows* as an implied incident of the transfer of a legal estate will itself share the legal quality of that estate.[17] In unregistered land such an easement is therefore enforceable against successors in title of the quasi-servient land and in registered land will constitute an overriding interest.[18]

(ii) Conditions of operation There are certain limitations upon the kinds of right which may pass to a transferee of land under the rule in *Wheeldon v Burrows.* The rule has no reference to 'mere personal conveniences',[19] but applies only to those rights which are intrinsically capable of being easements. Furthermore, in *Wheeldon v Burrows*[20] Thesiger LJ indicated that

> [O]n the grant by the owner of a tenement of part of that tenement as it is then used and enjoyed, there will pass to the grantee all those continuous and apparent easements (by which, of course, I mean *quasi* easements), or, in other words, all those easements which are necessary to the reasonable enjoyment of the property

15 See *Goldberg v Edwards* [1950] Ch 247 at 254 per Evershed MR.

16 *Scouton & Co (Builders) Ltd v Gilyott & Scott Ltd* (1972) 221 Estates Gazette 1499. See also Law of Property Act 1925, s 38. It may even be that the rule in *Wheeldon v Burrows* provides a means for a landlord to enforce a repairing obligation undertaken by a tenant even though the landlord has failed to reserve the appropriate right of entry for this purpose in the express terms of the lease (see *Sedgwick Forbes Bland Payne Group Ltd v Regional Properties Ltd* (1981) 257 Estates Gazette 64 at 68).

17 *Tarrant v Zandstra* (1973) 1 BPR 9381 at 9385 per Mahoney J.

18 Ante, p 201.

19 *Nelson v Walker* (1910) 10 CLR 560 at 584 per Isaacs J.

20 (1879) 12 Ch D 31 at 49.

granted, and which have been and are at the time of the grant used by the owners of the entirety for the benefit of the part granted.'[1]

These limiting conditions must be examined in more detail.

(iii) 'Continuous and apparent' user The requirement of 'continuous and apparent' user[2] does not appear to be applied by the courts with any great strictness.[3] The requirement has been held to be satisfied by any user which is enjoyed over substantial periods of time[4] and which is discoverable or detectable on 'a careful inspection by a person ordinarily conversant with the subject'.[5] A worn track provides evidence of 'continuous and apparent' user,[6] as indeed does an underground drain into which water runs from the eaves of a house.[7]

(iv) Reasonable necessity It has always been somewhat unclear whether, for the purpose of the rule in *Wheeldon v Burrows*, the conditions of 'reasonable necessity' and 'continuous and apparent' user are alternative or cumulative.[8] The preponderant view in the authorities seems to suggest that both conditions must be met,[9] but the two requirements tend to interact heavily, so that if a particular user is 'reasonably necessary' it will in any event be the subject

1 The *rule* in *Wheeldon v Burrows* is to be distinguished from the actual decision in that case, which concerned implied reservations (post, p 1117). A 'helpful translation' of the rule in *Wheeldon v Burrows* is to be found in *Borman v Griffith* [1930] 1 Ch 493 at 499 (see *Horn v Hiscock* (1972) 223 Estates Gazette 1437 at 1441 per Goulding J).

2 It has been suggested that the criterion of 'continuous and apparent' user was borrowed in the 19th century from the analogous concepts of continuous and apparent servitudes in French law. See *Suffield v Brown* (1864) 4 De GJ & Sm 185 at 195, 46 ER 888 at 892; *Dalton v Angus & Co* (1881) 6 App Cas 740 at 821; A.W.B. Simpson, *The Rule in Wheeldon v Burrows and the Code Civile*, (1967) 83 LQR 240.

3 The test of 'continuous and apparent' user tends to shade into the requirement of user subsisting at the date of subdivision (see *Kebewar Pty Ltd v Harkin* (1987) 9 NSWLR 738 at 741E-G).

4 'Continuous user' is not necessarily incessant user, but refers to permanent rather than merely temporary user (see Gale, *Law of Easements* (1st edn, London 1839), p 53).

5 *Pyer v Carter* (1857) 1 H & N 916 at 922, 156 ER 1472 at 1475. See also *Scouton & Co (Builders) Ltd v Gilyott & Scott Ltd* (1972) 221 Estates Gazette 1499.

6 *Hansford v Jago* [1921] 1 Ch 322 at 337ff. See also *Horn v Hiscock* (1972) 223 Estates Gazette 1437 at 1441, where Goulding J looked for a 'plainly visible road' over the property 'for the apparent use' of the alleged quasi-dominant tenement. It is not necessary that the road be made up so long as it was 'established and visible' at the date of subdivision (*Sunset Properties Pty Ltd v Johnston* (1975) 3 BPR 9185 at 9189). See also *In re St Clement's, Leigh-on-Sea* [1988] 1 WLR 720 at 729B-C.

7 *Pyer v Carter* (1857) 1 H & N 916 at 922, 156 ER 1472 at 1475.

8 The judgment of Thesiger LJ is itself ambiguous, but see (1879) 12 Ch D 31 at 58f where he seemed to regard the two requirements as 'discrete classes of case' (*Auerbach v Beck* (1985) 6 NSWLR 424 at 443B per Powell J). See also *Ward v Kirkland* [1967] Ch 194 at 224D–225A. The ambivalence on this issue is not diminished by the observations of Oliver LJ in *Squarey v Harris-Smith* (1981) 42 P & CR 118 at 124. In *Simmons v Dobson* [1991] 1 WLR 720 at 722F, Fox LJ made no reference at all to a requirement of necessity.

9 See eg *Bayley v Great Western Railway Co* (1884) 26 Ch D 434 at 452f; *Borman v Griffith* [1930] 1 Ch 493 at 499; *Horn v Hiscock* (1972) 223 Estates Gazette 1437 at 1441; *Israel v Leith* (1890) 20 OR 361 at 367; *Floyd v Heska* (1975) 50 DLR (3d) 161 at 167; *Sunset Properties Pty Ltd v Johnston* (1975) 3 BPR 9185 at 9188; *Margil Pty Ltd v Stegul Pastoral Pty Ltd* [1984] 2 NSWLR 1 at 11B; *Jones v Lockhart* (1989) 60 DLR (4th) 283 at 287f. In *Costagliola v English* (1969) 210 Estates Gazette 1425 at 1431, Megarry J applied the requirement of 'reasonable necessity' in circumstances where there was some doubt as to the continuity of the disputed user.

of 'continuous and apparent' user.[10] In so far as there is any requirement to show 'reasonable necessity',[1] it seems probable (though not absolutely clear) that this condition is not negatived by the availability of an alternative means of access.[2]

(v) User at the date of transfer The rule in *Wheeldon v Burrows* requires that the claimed form of user must have been exercised on behalf of the quasi-dominant land prior to, and must remain subsisting at the date of, the relevant transfer or subdivision of land.[3] *Wheeldon v Burrows* cannot, for instance, be invoked as the origin of an alleged easement of support for a building on a supposed quasi-dominant tenement if at the relevant date of transfer no building stood on that tenement.[4] A claim will likewise fail unless it can be linked at the relevant date to 'some continuous and apparent feature upon the alleged servient tenement designed, or appropriate, for the exercise of the easement asserted'.[5] In *Costagliola v English*,[6] however, Megarry J did not consider that an 'established means of access' was deprived of status as a quasi-easement merely because it had not been 'actively enjoyed to any great extent' during the 10 or 11 months preceding the relevant conveyance.

(vi) Application to contracts It has been clear since *Borman v Griffith*[7] that the rule in *Wheeldon v Burrows* applies not only to legal grants (eg on the conveyance of an estate in fee simple or a term of years), but also to grants which take effect only in equity (eg on a contract for a lease).[8]

(d) Law of Property Act 1925, s 62

Another form of implied grant is made possible by the operation of the 'word-saving provision' contained in section 62 of the Law of Property Act

10 This may explain why, in *Auerbach v Beck* (1985) 6 NSWLR 424 at 443A-B, Powell J was happy to regard 'continuous and apparent' user as representing the essential and irreducible precondition for a quasi-easement. In *Tarrant v Zandstra* (1973) 1 BPR 9381 at 9384f Mahoney J upheld a quasi-easement on the ground that the user was 'continuous' and would have been 'apparent as "necessary to the reasonable enjoyment"' of the dominant land.

1 In this context the standard of necessity is less stringent than that applicable to 'easements of necessity' (ante, p 1092). See *Re Standard and the Conveyancing Act 1919* (1970) 92 WN (NSW) 953 at 956A-B. It is not enough, however, to assert merely that the claimed user would be a convenient adjunct of dominant ownership (see *M.C.A. Camilleri Building & Constructions Pty Ltd v H.R. Walters Pty Ltd* (1981) 2 BPR 9277 at 9281). The test of 'reasonable necessity', if it exists, must be judged as of the date of the relevant subdivision (*Sunset Properties Pty Ltd v Johnston* (1975) 3 BPR 9185 at 9188).

2 See *Goldberg v Edwards* [1950] Ch 247 at 254f; *Costagliola v English* (1969) 210 Estates Gazette 1425 at 1431; *Horn v Hiscock* (1972) 223 Estates Gazette 1437 at 1441; *Jones v Lockhart* (1989) 60 DLR (4th) 283 at 287f.

3 See *In re St Clement's, Leigh-on-Sea* [1988] 1 WLR 720 at 729B-C.

4 *Kebewar Pty Ltd v Harkin* (1987) 9 NSWLR 738 at 741C-F per McHugh JA. See also *Auerbach v Beck* (1985) 6 NSWLR 424 at 443C-D, affd sub nom *Beck v Auerbach* (1986) 6 NSWLR 454.

5 *Auerbach v Beck* (1985) 6 NSWLR 424 at 443B-C.

6 (1969) 210 Estates Gazette 1425 at 1429.

7 [1930] 1 Ch 493 at 499. See (1930) 46 LQR 271 (H.P.); [1932] CLJ 219 (K.K.L.). See also *Horn v Hiscock* (1972) 223 Estates Gazette 1437 at 1441.

8 Ante, p 738.

1925.[9] Section 62 contains 'general words' which, unless excluded in express terms,[10] imply into any conveyance of a legal estate in land a number of rights thenceforth to be enjoyed by the transferee of that estate. Under section 62(1), every conveyance of land

> shall be deemed to include and shall by virtue of this Act operate to convey, with the land, all buildings, erections, fixtures, commons, hedges, ditches, fences, ways, waters, watercourses, liberties, privileges, easements, rights, and advantages whatsoever, appertaining or reputed to appertain to the land or any part thereof, or, at the time of conveyance, demised, occupied, or enjoyed with, or reputed or known as part or parcel of or appurtenant to the land or any part thereof.

In very similar terms section 62(2) provides that every conveyance of land which has 'houses or other buildings thereon' is deemed to include all 'cisterns, sewers, gutters, drains, ways, passages, lights, watercourses, liberties, privileges, easements, rights, and advantages' appertaining or reputed to appertain to the land or buildings.

Section 62 is an exceedingly ample provision. It has the effect of passing to the transferee of land the benefit of existing easements, profits, privileges and rights which appertain to the land conveyed, or are reputed to appertain to it, or which are at the date of the conveyance enjoyed with that land.[11] However, the provision goes even further, and under certain circumstances creates entirely new easements and profits out of many kinds of quasi-easement, right and privilege subsisting at the date of the conveyance which activates section 62.[12] It is quite possible that rights which were not easements properly so called before the conveyance may be translated to the status of easement thereafter.

In many respects section 62 of the Law of Property Act 1925 enjoys a rather wider significance than the rule in *Wheeldon v Burrows* and operates therefore as an overlay upon that rule.[13] There is, for instance, no requirement that the rights to which section 62 has reference should be 'continuous and apparent'[14] or 'necessary to the reasonable enjoyment of the land granted'[15] or perhaps even that there be evidence of actual user at the date of the

9 Formerly Conveyancing Act 1881, s 6. See generally P. Jackson, (1966) 30 Conv (NS) 340. Whether section 62 effects an *implied* form of grant is perhaps debatable. It may be more accurate to say that the use of general words, imported by statute, creates new easements and profits 'by way of express grant' (*Auerbach v Beck* (1985) 6 NSWLR 424 at 445F). See also *Broomfield v Williams* [1897] 1 Ch 602 at 610; *Goldberg v Edwards* [1950] Ch 247 at 255.

10 Law of Property Act 1925, s 62(4). See *William Hill (Southern) Ltd v Cabras Ltd* (1987) 54 P & CR 42 at 46.

11 The notion of enjoyment is not synonymous with user, and therefore section 62 may not require proof of actual user at the date of the conveyance (*In re Yateley Common* [1977] 1 WLR 840 at 850H–851A, post, p 1102).

12 See *Auerbach v Beck* (1985) 6 NSWLR 424 at 445F.

13 See *Auerbach v Beck* (1985) 6 NSWLR 424 at 445F per Powell J.

14 See *White v Williams* [1922] 1 KB 727 at 740 per Younger LJ.

15 In *Goldberg v Edwards* [1950] Ch 247 at 256, for instance, the Court of Appeal held that section 62 could apply to a way of access through a landlord's house which was clearly not necessary for the tenant in view of the fact that he had a quite separate means of access to the premises which had been let to him. See (1950) 66 LQR 302 (R.E.M.). See also *Baron Hamilton v Edgar* (1953) 162 Estates Gazette 568 at 569; *Ward v Kirkland* [1967] Ch 194 at 229G.

conveyance.[16] Section 62 seems, moreover, to provide a mode of implied grant relevant to profits,[17] which almost certainly are not covered by the rule in *Wheeldon v Burrows*.[18]

Although superficially section 62 seems to to have an extremely extensive application, its scope has been cut back by several important restrictions.

(i) Section 62 operates only on a conveyance of a legal estate The most obvious limitation on section 62 is that the 'general words' provision is activated only by a conveyance of a *legal* estate in land.[19] It is immaterial whether that legal estate be a freehold or leasehold, but section 62 can never be invoked, for instance, by a tenant who takes under a contract for a lease and who therefore holds only an equitable lease.[20]

Perhaps the classic application of section 62 arises, however, in the landlord-tenant context. In *International Tea Stores Co v Hobbs*[1] a landlord, L, owned two adjacent plots of land in fee simple, occupying one of them himself and leasing the other to a tenant, T. During the currency of the lease L permitted T, as a matter of grace and favour, to use a means of access to T's premises which ran across the plot occupied by L (see *Fig.* 72). T's

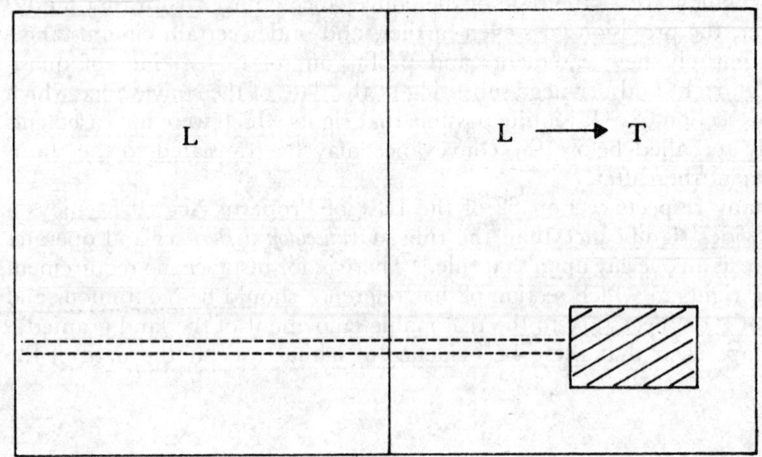

Fig. 72

16 See *In re Yateley Common* [1977] 1 WLR 840 at 850H–851A. The older authorities seem to stress the importance of actual user at the date of conveyance (see eg *Broomfield v Williams* [1897] 1 Ch 602 at 615; *Lewis v Meredith* [1913] 1 Ch 571 at 579; *Goldberg v Edwards* [1950] Ch 247 at 256), and may therefore represent the better view (see *Auerbach v Beck* (1985) 6 NSWLR 424 at 441G). See also *Re Broxhead Common, Whitehill, Hampshire* (1977) 33 P & CR 451 at 463f, where Brightman J found it impossible to say that grazing rights which had not been exercised for some 21 or 22 years prior to the relevant conveyance were 'enjoyed' or reputed to be appurtenant to the land for the purpose of section 62(1). See also *Penn v Wilkins* (1974) 236 Estates Gazette 203.

17 *White v Williams* [1922] 1 KB 727 at 737ff.

18 Ante, p 1097. See, however, *Auerbach v Beck* (1985) 6 NSWLR 424 at 445F per Powell J.

19 'Conveyance' is defined in Law of Property Act 1925, s 205(1)(ii).

20 *Borman v Griffith* [1930] 1 Ch 493 at 497f.

1 [1903] 2 Ch 165.

user of this access was clearly 'precarious' in the sense that, if he had so wished, L could at any time have revoked T's permission (or bare licence) to use this route.

Against this background in *International Tea Stores Co v Hobbs* Farwell J ruled that the statutory predecessor of section 62 was activated when L later conveyed to T the freehold reversion in the premises hitherto rented by T. This intervention of a further conveyance caused the statutory 'general words' provision to vest in T not only a freehold estate in the land purchased but also a right *by way of easement* to continue against L the user which had previously been merely precarious.[2] This slightly surprising result is supportable on the basis that section 62 of the Law of Property Act 1925 implies into the conveyance from L to T all such users as previously comprised 'privileges. . .rights, and advantages. . .appertaining. . .to the land'. What was merely a licence before the conveyance was now converted into an easement. Moreover, since T's new easement had been incorporated by implication within a conveyance of a legal estate, it was clothed with legal character and was thus enforceable against any successor in title.

Section 62 thus provides a means whereby the conveyance of a further legal estate to a sitting tenant may elevate even a purely precarious user to the status of a legal easement or profit, thereby conferring on the transferee a new right of irrevocable enjoyment.[3]

(ii) The nature of the rights caught by section 62 Section 62 is never competent to convert into an easement or profit any right which, by its very nature, is incapable of constituting an incorporeal hereditament under the general law.[4] The provision thus has no application to any claim which fails to meet the fairly stringent conditions which fix the threshold of the categories of recognised easement and profit.[5]

Moreover section 62 passes to the transferee of land only those rights which the transferor has, at the date of transfer, an intrinsic competence to confer.[6] If, for example, the transferor no longer owns any sufficient interest[7] in the supposed servient tenement at the date of the alleged operation of section 62, the general words of section 62 are entirely ineffective to create rights

2 [1903] 2 Ch 165 at 170ff. See *M.R.A. Engineering Ltd v Trimster Co Ltd* (1988) 56 P & CR 1 at 5. Exactly the same outcome would have followed upon a renewal of T's term of years (see eg *Wright v Macadam* [1949] 2 KB 744 at 747ff; *Goldberg v Edwards* [1950] Ch 247 at 257ff).

3 See *Lewis v Meredith* [1913] 1 Ch 571 at 579; *Wright v Macadam* [1949] 2 KB 744 at 751; *Goldberg v Edwards* [1950] Ch 247 at 255f; *Stafford v Pearson-Smith* (1962) 182 Estates Gazette 539 at 541. There is, incidentally, no reason why precisely the same effect should not follow a conveyance of a legal estate (whether freehold or leasehold) made in favour of someone who already occupies the quasi-dominant tenement, not by virtue of a lease, but by virtue of a mere licence to occupy.

4 See *Burrows v Lang* [1901] 2 Ch 502 at 512; *Lewis v Meredith* [1913] 1 Ch 571 at 579 per Neville J; *Wright v Macadam* [1949] 2 KB 744 at 750; *Regis Property Co Ltd v Redman* [1956] 2 QB 612 at 627f, 632; *Green v Ashco Horticulturist Ltd* [1966] 2 All ER 232 at 239C; *Auerbach v Beck* (1985) 6 NSWLR 424 at 441G.

5 Ante, p 1059ff.

6 *Quicke v Chapman* [1903] 1 Ch 659 at 668, 671f; *In re St Clement's, Leigh-on-Sea* [1988] 1 WLR 720 at 728E-H. See also Law of Property Act 1925, s 62(5).

7 Ante, p 1070.

for the transferee of the supposed dominant tenement.[8] It is a fundamental proviso of section 62 that it should not have passed out of the power of the transferor, at the date of the relevant conveyance, to create the easement or profit concerned.

There is a further possible restriction on the kinds of user which acquire a crystalline legal form pursuant to section 62. There is some authority for the view that section 62 operates only where there has been some 'diversity of ownership or occupation of the quasi-dominant and quasi-servient tenements prior to the conveyance'.[9] Such 'prior diversity of occupation' is, of course, precisely what is present in the landlord-tenant situation dealt with in *International Tea Stores Co v Hobbs*.[10] Prior to the conveyance which activated the 'general words' provision in this case there was a diversity of occupation as between L and T in respect of the two tenements concerned. Moreover, it can be argued quite plausibly that without at least some element of prior diversity of ownership or occupation of two tenements it would be difficult to point in any meaningful sense to any 'rights' or 'liberties' or 'privileges' which might be caught by the operation of section 62.[11]

The requirement of 'prior diversity of occupation' is, however, controversial.[12] If correctly applied the requirement would mean that section 62 is inapplicable in the very context where the rule in *Wheeldon v Burrows* finds its most frequent application, ie where there is a subdivision of land which was formerly subject to common ownership and occupation.[13] However, it may well be, as has been suggested in Australia, that the requirement of prior diversity of occupation is relevant only where the claimed right or privilege is 'imperceptible or non-apparent, corresponding with intermittent and non-apparent user over one of two tenements held in common ownership.'[14] On this basis the right or privilege would not pass unless there

8 Section 62 cannot operate if, prior to the transfer of the alleged dominant tenement, the common owner of the two relevant tenements has already conveyed the supposed servient tenement to a third party without an express reservation of rights in favour of the alleged dominant tenement (see *Auerbach v Beck* (1985) 6 NSWLR 424 at 445G–446A; *M.R.A. Engineering Ltd v Trimster Co Ltd* (1988) 56 P & CR 1 at 5, 7).

9 *Sovmots Investments Ltd v Secretary of State for the Environment* [1979] AC 144 at 176C per Lord Edmund-Davies, following *Long v Gowlett* [1923] 2 Ch 177 at 200 per Sargant J. See (1977) 127 NLJ 695 (H.W. Wilkinson).

10 [1903] 2 Ch 165 (ante, p 1102).

11 See *Squarey v Harris-Smith* (1981) 42 P & CR 118 at 129 per Oliver LJ. As Sargant J put it in *Long v Gowlett* [1923] 2 Ch 177 at 200, 'in order that there may be a "privilege, easement or advantage" enjoyed with Whiteacre over Blackacre so as to pass under the statute, there must be something done on Blackacre not due to or comprehended within the general rights of an occupying owner of Blackacre, but of such a nature that it is attributable to a privilege, easement, right or advantage, however precarious, which arises out of the ownership or occupation of Whiteacre, altogether apart from the ownership or occupation of Blackacre.'

12 See C. Harpum, (1977) 41 Conv (NS) 415; [1979] Conv 113. Compare P. Smith, [1978] Conv 449; [1979] Conv 311. No such requirement was raised by the Court of Appeal in *Broomfield v Williams* [1897] 1 Ch 602; nor did an absence of prior diversity of occupation prevent express (as distinct from statutory) general words from operating a grant in *Bayley v Great Western Railway Co* (1884) 26 Ch D 434.

13 Ante, p 1097.

14 *Auerbach v Beck* (1985) 6 NSWLR 424 at 445C-D per Powell J, affd sub nom *Beck v Auerbach* (1986) 6 NSWLR 454.

has been 'de facto enjoyment of it by an occupier' who is, visibly, not the owner or occupier of the servient tenement.[15]

A similar desire to cut back the ambit of section 62 is found in the idea that section 62 is apt to catch only rights or privileges of a kind 'which could readily be included in a lease or conveyance by the insertion of appropriate words in the parcels'.[16] In the past this restriction has been regarded as excluding from section 62 any privilege which was contemplated by the parties as being of a 'purely temporary' nature[17] or which was exercised on an excessively intermittent basis or on the footing of an extremely fragile permission. Thus in *Green v Ashco Horticulturist Ltd*[18] Cross J held that the tenant's intermittent consensual privilege of access through his landlord's premises was not such a user as could have been the subject of a grant of a legal right, and for this reason section 62 was inapplicable. There was evidence here that the user was extremely precarious, in that the access in question had been permitted to the tenant only at times when the landlord did not find such user inconvenient.[19] It may well be that section 62 covers only those rights which can be attributed to transferees or lessees in their capacity as such and not rights which are 'purely personal in the strict sense of that word'.[20]

(iii) Avoidance of section 62 The far reaching implication of section 62 can be averted only through the expression of contrary intention[1] or by the revocation of the relevant permission in advance of the conveyance which would otherwise activate section 62. The mere existence of an express (and more limited) grant of rights of easement in the terms of a conveyance does not necessarily exclude the acquisition by the purchaser of further and more extensive implied rights under section 62(1), if it is clear that the vendor effectively enjoyed the larger right prior to the conveyance in question.[2]

(iv) Jurisdiction to rectify The court retains an equitable jurisdiction to rectify any conveyance which mistakenly transfers to a grantee more rights than were intended in the relevant contract for sale. Thus, in *Clarke v Barnes*,[3] the court rectified a conveyance which had failed to exclude as against the purchaser the user of a right of way over other land retained by the vendor. The equitable jurisdiction was available to rectify the vendor's omission to exclude the effect of section 62, even though the purchaser maintained that

15 *Auerbach v Beck* (1985) 6 NSWLR 424 at 445D.
16 *Wright v Macadam* [1949] 2 KB 744 at 752 per Jenkins LJ. See also *Goldberg v Edwards* [1950] Ch 247 at 255f per Evershed MR.
17 *Wright v Macadam* [1949] 2 KB 744 at 752.
18 [1966] 2 All ER 232 at 239E-H.
19 See also *Goldberg v Edwards* [1950] Ch 247 at 255.
20 See *Goldberg v Edwards* [1950] Ch 247 at 257, where Evershed MR made recurring reference to rights given to persons 'qua lessees'.
1 Law of Property Act 1925, s 62(4). Section 62 is commonly excluded in standard form Conditions of Sale, although there has been some expression of judicial disquiet that this provision can be ousted by a clause buried in the small print of a contract of sale which the parties may never have read (see *Squarey v Harris-Smith* (1981) 42 P & CR 118 at 128, 130).
2 *Gregg v Richards* [1926] Ch 521 at 529ff. See also *Stafford v Pearson-Smith* (1962) 182 Estates Gazette 539 at 541.
3 [1929] 2 Ch 368 at 380ff.

he had contracted to purchase the land on the assumption that the right of way in question was included in the conveyance. However, the remedy of rectification will not be extended in order to assist any vendor who has acted otherwise than in good faith.

(3) **Prescription**

A third method of acquisition of easements and profits *à prendre* is provided by the law of prescription or long user. This area of law has become extremely complex over the years, and as long ago as 1966 the Law Reform Committee by a majority recommended the total abolition of the concept of prescriptive acquisition.[4] No reform has yet occurred, although the existing law is marked by 'much unnecessary complication and confusion'.[5] Prescriptive acquisition is something of a hybrid, since it combines elements of fictitious express grant with implications from long-term user.

(a) Rationale of prescriptive acquisition

There is in English law generally a strong policy bias in favour of the legitimacy of a user which has been exercised de facto over long periods of time.[6] This consideration underlies the law of adverse possession,[7] and likewise affords the conceptual basis of prescriptive acquisition.[8] Prescription provides the ground on which the courts may uphold as lawful the long user of any right in the nature of an easement or profit *à prendre*. Although there may be no evidence of any actual grant, the law of prescription spells an often fictitious grant out of the fact of prolonged enjoyment of rights over the land of another. As Fry J said in *Moody v Steggles*,[9] it is 'the habit, and. . .the duty, of the court, so far as it lawfully can, to clothe the fact with right'. The process of prescription must, however, be distinguished from that of adverse possession under the Limitation Act. The latter process extinguishes old titles, whereas prescription has the effect of generating new rights. Limitation thus has a negative and extinctive effect, whereas prescription is positive and creative in its mode of operation.[10]

4 *14th Report of the Law Reform Committee* (Cmnd 3100, 1966), para 32. A minority of the Committee recommended the retention of a prescription period of 12 years' user in respect of easements (see (1967) 30 MLR 189 (H.W. Wilkinson)). Among the main considerations leading to the majority proposal that prescriptive acquisition be abolished entirely was the argument that 'there is little, if any, moral justification for the acquisition of easements by prescription, a process which either involves an intention to get something for nothing or, where there is no intention to acquire any right, is purely accidental.'

5 *Tehidy Minerals Ltd v Norman* [1971] 2 QB 528 at 543F per Buckley LJ. Compare, for instance, the almost total exclusion of the prescriptive principle from the operation of Torrens title legislation (see *Dewhirst v Edwards* [1983] 1 NSWLR 34 at 48A-D).

6 Ante, p 61. See also L. Berger, *An Analysis of the Doctrine That 'First in Time is First in Right'*, 64 Nebraska L Rev 349 at 361ff (1985).

7 Post, p 282.

8 See *Clippens Oil Co Ltd v Edinburgh and District Water Trustees* [1904] AC 64 at 69f per Earl of Halsbury LC.

9 (1879) 12 Ch D 261 at 265.

10 *Lovett v Fairclough* (1989) 61 P & CR 385 at 399. See M.J. Goodman, *Adverse Possession or Prescription? Problems of Conflict*, (1968) 32 Conv (NS) 270; S. Anderson, (1975) 38 MLR 641.

(b) General principles of prescriptive acquisition

The basis of prescriptive acquisition is not merely long user per se. In order that a claim of prescription should succeed, it is necessary that there be a history of continuous user in fee simple, and that this user be a 'user as of right in which the servient owner has, with the requisite degree of knowledge,. . .acquiesced.'[11] A strong element of acquiescence or informed consent thus lies at the root of prescription.[12] The nature of the required user has traditionally been described in terms borrowed from Roman law. It is commonly said that the user must be *nec vi, nec clam, nec precario.*[13] That is, the user must have been exercised without force, without secrecy and without permission. The onus of proof lies on the claimant.[14]

(i) Continuous user as of right The user which founds a prescriptive claim must be continuous user as of right, although the degree of continuity required is dependent on the nature of the right claimed.[15] The mere fact that user is intermittent does not destroy a claim of continuous user,[16] but frequency of user may well affect the validity of the claim. Thus, for instance, a prescriptive claim to a right of way may succeed where there has been user on six to ten occasions each year for 35 years,[17] but not where there have merely three occasions of user, each separated by an interval of twelve years.[18]

Embedded in the requirement of continuous user is also the idea that the user asserted as the subject matter of a prescriptive claim must have a reasonably certain or uniform quality.[19] Thus, where the branches of a tree on Blackacre intrude into the airspace over the neighbouring Whiteacre, the incursion cannot, in view of the ever changing nature of the tree, be justified on the ground of prescription.[20] Likewise, no prescriptive right can be claimed to pollute a river where the amount of pollution introduced

11 *Mills v Silver* [1991] Ch 271 at 281G per Dillon LJ. See also *Sunset Properties Pty Ltd v Johnston* (1975) 3 BPR 9185 at 9190.

12 *Sturges v Bridgman* (1879) 11 Ch D 852 at 863 per Thesiger LJ. See also *Piromalli v Di Masi* [1980] WAR 173 at 178.

13 *Co Litt*, p 13b; *Eaton v Swansea Waterworks Co* (1851) 17 QB 267 at 275, 117 ER 1282 at 1285; *Solomon v Vintners' Co* (1859) 4 H & N 585 at 602, 157 ER 970 at 977; *Sturges v Bridgman* (1879) 11 Ch D 852 at 863; *Burrows v Lang* [1901] 2 Ch 502 at 510; *Newnham v Willison* (1988) 56 P & CR 8 at 12.

14 *Earl De La Warr v Miles* (1881) 17 Ch D 535 at 591; *Gardner v Hodgson's Kingston Brewery Co Ltd* [1903] AC 229 at 233.

15 In the case of prescriptive claims to an easement or profit appurtenant (but not a profit in gross), the continuous user pleaded in support need not be exercised by the same person throughout the entire prescription period (*Lovett v Fairclough* (1989) 61 P & CR 385 at 399).

16 *Axler v Chisholm* (1978) 79 DLR (3d) 97 at 101.

17 *Diment v N.H. Foot Ltd* [1974] 1 WLR 1427 at 1430G. Likewise the continuity of user of a roadway leading to a summer home is not vitiated by the fact that the access is closed off during winter (*Estey v Withers* (1975) 48 DLR (3d) 121 at 127f). See also *Mills v Silver* [1991] Ch 271 at 286C-D. Nor is continuity of user interrupted by an agreement between the claimant and the landowner to alter the route of access (*Davis v Whitby* [1973] 1 WLR 629 at 631C-D).

18 *Hollins v Verney* (1884) 13 QBD 304 at 315. See also *Ramsay v Cooke* [1984] 2 NZLR 680 at 687, where continuous user as of right could not be pleaded on the basis of 'merely isolated occasions when the tenant of the land had given permission by way of licence for use for a specific limited and temporary purpose'.

19 See *Hulley v Silver Springs Bleaching Co* [1922] 2 Ch 268 at 281 per Eve J.

20 *Lemmon v Webb* [1895] AC 1 at 6 (ante, p 21).

into the water has varied over time or at least has increased during the 20 years immediately preceding the claim.[1]

(ii) User as of right Prescriptive user must, moreover, be based upon an assumption of right,[2] for it is only against a background of assumed entitlement that the courts can go so far as to imply the existence of the grant from which the lawful exercise of an easement or profit is deemed to have derived. It follows that no claim of right can be premised on activity which is itself unlawful in any sense other than that necessarily involved in the trespass which is eventually cured by prescriptive acquisition.[3] It appears, however, that it is no bar to the acquisition of rights by long user that the claimant suffered from a mistaken belief that he owned the disputed land anyway[4] or that he already enjoyed rights by express grant.[5] If anything, the claimant's misapprehension confirms rather than vitiates the claim of rightful user.[6] A mere subjective mistake as to entitlement does not deprive the claimant's user of its adverse quality,[7] for the relevant focus is to be placed pre-eminently on the way 'in which that user is seen by the owner of the land over which the right is asserted'.[8]

(iii) User in fee simple Since a prescriptively acquired right is inevitably a right in perpetuity,[9] it is always said that prescription is necessarily based on user in fee simple. The user alleged must therefore be user by or on behalf of a fee simple owner against another fee simple owner.[10] Thus at

1 See *Millington v Griffiths* (1874) 30 LT 65 at 68; *Cargill v Gotts* [1981] 1 WLR 441 at 448D-E; *Scott-Whitehead v National Coal Board* (1987) 53 P & CR 263 at 273.

2 See *Earl De La Warr v Miles* (1881) 17 Ch D 535 at 591 per Brett LJ; *Hanna v Pollock* [1900] 2 IR 664 at 671; *Hamilton v Joyce* [1984] 3 NSWLR 279 at 291D-G.

3 The court 'will not recognise an easement established by unlawful activity'. See *Cargill v Gotts* [1981] 1 WLR 441 at 446H, where the Court of Appeal held that the plaintiff could not rely, for the purpose of establishing prescriptive acquisition of an easement to draw water, on his abstraction of water from a mill pond without the appropriate licence under (what was then) the Water Resources Act 1963. See (1980) 96 LQR 500, (1981) 97 LQR 382 (P. Jackson).

4 *Capar v Wasylowski* (1983) 146 DLR (3d) 193 at 200ff.

5 *Bridle v Ruby* [1989] QB 169 at 177C-E, 178F-H. See G. Kodilinye, [1989] Conv 261. To disallow user based on a mistaken belief would effectively confine prescription to someone who 'is aware that he is a wrongdoer' (*Bridle* at 177D-E per Parker LJ).

6 A mistaken belief that the claimant owns the alleged servient tenement vitiates the claim of easement only if, in reliance on his assumption, the claimant has exercised acts of ownership involving exclusive possession of that tenement. See *Attorney-General of Southern Nigeria v John Holt & Co (Liverpool) Ltd* [1915] AC 599 at 617f; *Warren v Yoell* [1944] 1 DLR 118 at 129f; *Capar v Wasylowski* (1983) 146 DLR (3d) 193 at 201; but compare *Lyell v Lord Hothfield* [1914] 3 KB 911 at 916.

7 However, a user based on a mistaken belief that it is justified on a right of limited duration, which belief is acquiesced in, cannot be made the foundation of a grant of unlimited duration (see *Chamber Colliery Co v Hopwood* (1886) 32 Ch D 549 at 556; *Bridle v Ruby* [1989] QB 169 at 177C-D).

8 *Bridle v Ruby* [1989] QB 169 at 178E per Ralph Gibson LJ.

9 *Rodwell v G.R. Evans & Co Pty Ltd* (1977) 3 BPR 9114 at 9123.

10 *Bright v Walker* (1834) 1 Cr M & R 211 at 221f, 149 ER 1057 at 1061f; *Davis v Whitby* [1973] 1 WLR 629 at 630E; *Simmons v Dobson* [1991] 1 WLR 720 at 723C. The fee simple owner of a supposed dominant tenement, if not himself in occupation, can claim the benefit of user enjoyed by the actual occupier (eg his tenant), although such a claim can equally be destroyed by a consent or licence negotiated by the latter with the alleged servient owner (*Hyman v Van den Bergh* [1907] 2 Ch 516 at 531).

common law there can be no prescriptive acquisition of an easement or profit for life or for a term of years,[11] and any claim to prescriptive acquisition at common law must inevitably fail if the user began against an occupier of the servient land who was not entitled in fee simple (eg a tenant for life or a tenant for years).[12] In such circumstances it would almost certainly be unreasonable to hold the fee simple owner bound by a prescriptive user of which he may not have been aware and which, in any event, he may have been utterly powerless to prevent.[13] Since easements can arise only where dominant and servient tenements respectively belong to different persons, it follows moreover that a tenant cannot acquire a prescriptive right against another tenant who holds under the same landlord.[14]

(iv) User nec vi It is clear that forcible user will vitiate any claim to entitlement as of right. For this purpose the notion of forcible user includes not merely a violent exercise of the user (eg the removal of an obstruction[15]), but also any insistence upon a particular user in the face of continuing protest from the supposedly servient owner.[16]

(v) User nec clam The user which founds a prescriptive claim must not be surreptitious or in any way concealed. In *Union Lighterage Co v London Graving Dock Co*,[17] for instance, the Court of Appeal declined to accept that a prescriptive claim had been established by a defendant who fixed the side of a dock to the soil of a wharf by means of underground rods which remained undetected for more than 20 years.[18] Romer LJ held that a prescriptive right to an easement over another's land could be acquired only 'when the enjoyment has been open—that is to say, of such a character that an ordinary owner of the land, diligent in the protection of his interests, would

11 *Gayford v Moffatt* (1868) 4 Ch App 133 at 135; *Wheaton v Maple & Co* [1893] 3 Ch 48 at 63; *Kilgour v Gaddes* [1904] 1 KB 457 at 460.

12 *Barker v Richardson* (1821) 4 B & Ald 579 at 582, 106 ER 1048 at 1049; *Pugh v Savage* [1970] 2 QB 373 at 383G-H. (Some of the problems connected with tenure by limited owners are eased by the Prescription Act 1832, ss 7, 8). See also A.K. Kiralfy, (1948) 13 Conv (NS) 104.

13 See *Pugh v Savage* [1970] 2 QB 373 at 383G-H per Cross LJ. Here, however, the Court of Appeal took the view (at 383H-384A, 386F) that a user which commenced against a fee simple owner is not prejudiced if the land in question is subsequently occupied by a tenant at some intermediate stage during the prescription period. See also *Rodwell v G.R. Evans & Co Pty Ltd* [1978] 1 NSWLR 448 at 451E; *Piromalli v Di Masi* [1980] WAR 173 at 176; *Connellan Nominees Pty Ltd v Camerer* [1988] 2 Qd R 248 at 256f.

14 *Kilgour v Gaddes* [1904] 1 KB 457 at 467; *Derry v Sanders* [1919] 1 KB 223 at 237; *Cory v Davies* [1923] 2 Ch 95 at 107f. The law is different in Ireland (see *Flynn v Harte* [1913] 2 IR 322 at 325f), and even English courts have remarked on the perverse nature of the anomaly which prevents, for instance, a tenant under a term of 999 years from prescribing against his neighbour who also holds a similar long lease from the same landlord (see *Simmons v Dobson* [1991] 1 WLR 720 at 724A-H). See also V.T.H. Delany, (1958) 74 LQR 82; P. Sparkes, [1992] Conv 167.

15 *Newnham v Willison* (1988) 56 P & CR 8 at 19.

16 *Dalton v Angus & Co* (1881) 6 App Cas 740 at 786. See eg *Eaton v Swansea Waterworks Co* (1851) 17 QB 267 at 275, 117 ER 1282 at 1285; *Newnham v Willison* (1988) 56 P & CR 8 at 15ff.

17 [1902] 2 Ch 557.

18 See also *Liverpool Corpn v H. Coghill and Son Ltd* [1918] 1 Ch 307 at 314 (secret discharge of factory effluent into sewer generated no easement by long user).

have, or must be taken to have, a reasonable opportunity of becoming aware of that enjoyment.'[19]

Where an access way has been used for many years, there may be a burden of proof upon the servient landowner to rebut the presumption that he had knowledge of the long user.[20] However, in cases involving other kinds of easement where the user is either less obvious[1] or extremely intermittent, the onus may be on the prescriptive claimant to prove that the alleged servient owner knew, or had reasonable means of knowledge, of the acts of user.[2]

(vi) User nec precario No prescriptive claim can be based on a user which is merely permissive, ie precariously founded on a licence or consent from the landowner.[3] User enjoyed under licence from the alleged servient owner cannot support any claim of prescription, since the element of permission inherent in such user is clearly destructive of any claim that the user was a matter of intrinsic entitlement.[4] However, a user which originates in a permission granted by the landowner may later lose its permissive character and arrogate to itself a kind of rightful quality if there is evidence that subsequent acts of user ceased to be reliant on the initial element of licence.[5]

The exclusion from the ambit of prescription of purely permissive forms of user raises the uneasy and somewhat ambivalent relationship between consent and acquiescence. A user by way of licence or consent clearly precludes any prescriptive claim, but the entire law of prescription is itself based on some notion of acquiescence in the exercise of a claimed right of user.[6] In some circumstances it may be difficult to distinguish between elements of consent and acquiescence, particularly where an alleged servient owner has tolerated a user out of good neighbourliness or because the user was too insignificant to cause him concern or inconvenience.

19 [1902] 2 Ch 557 at 571. See eg *Milne v James* (1910) 13 CLR 168 at 177f, 186f, 193f; *Capar v Wasylowski* (1983) 146 DLR (3d) 193 at 199.

20 *Diment v N.H. Foot Ltd* [1974] 1 WLR 1427 at 1434F-G.

1 See eg *Scott-Whitehead v National Coal Board* (1987) 53 P & CR 263 at 275, where Stuart-Smith J dealt with the example of river pollution, 'where there are no visible or sensible signs to be observed'.

2 *Davies v Du Paver* [1952] 2 All ER 991 at 997F-G; *Temma Realty Co Ltd v Ress Enterprises Ltd* (1968) 69 DLR (2d) 195 at 198. At the very least any onus of rebuttal which rests on the landowner in these circumstances is easily satisfied (see *Axler v Chisholm* (1978) 79 DLR (3d) 97 at 101f).

3 *Hyman v Van den Bergh* [1907] 2 Ch 516 at 530; *Henderson v Volk* (1982) 35 OR (2d) 379 at 383; *Hamilton v Joyce* [1984] 3 NSWLR 279 at 291D-G. It is fatal at common law to rest any prescriptive claim on an alleged contractual right in respect of the relevant user (see *Norton v Williams* [1939] NZLR 1051 at 1055).

4 Enjoyment merely at the will and pleasure of the owner is inconsistent with a claim of right (*Gardner v Hodgson's Kingston Brewery Co Ltd* [1903] AC 229 at 234ff). See eg *Goldsmith v Burrow Construction Co Ltd* (1987) *Times*, 31 July (locking of gate on path for substantial periods rendered user merely precarious).

5 See *Gaved v Martyn* (1865) 19 CB NS 732 at 744f, 144 ER 974 at 979f. However, the making by the claimant of periodic payments to the landowner tends to indicate that a continuing user was acknowledged to be permissive only (see *Gardner v Hodgson's Kingston Brewery Co Ltd* [1903] AC 229 at 231ff; *Bridle v Ruby* [1989] QB 169 at 177G; *Mills v Silver* [1991] Ch 271 at 292G).

6 Ante, p 1107.

It cannot be true that tolerance of a user without objection bars the creation of prescriptive rights, for such a principle would be 'fundamentally inconsistent with the whole notion of acquisition of rights by prescription'.[7] Yet a landowner's 'mere tolerance of a trespass' which continues over many years should not necessarily clothe that trespass with the character of a user as of right.[8] As the Ontario Court of Appeal held in *Henderson v Volk*,[9] 'neighbourly acquiescence' in the occasional use of a path 'during inclement weather or in times of emergency such as a last minute attempt to catch a bus' should not too readily be accepted as evidence of submission to the use.[10] It is a constant refrain in the law of easements that 'between neighbours there must be give as well as take'.[11]

The nexus between consent and acquiescence becomes less ambiguous when attention is focused on the alleged servient owner's perception of the balance of rights between himself and the claimant. Here the critical variable is the servient owner's demonstrable willingness to exclude from, or control access to, the disputed facility on his own land.[12] In *Dalton v Angus & Co*,[13] for instance, Fry J took the view that acquiescence necessarily presupposes on the part of the servient owner (1) a knowledge of the acts done[14]; (2) a power in him to stop the acts or to sue in respect of them[15]; and (3) an abstinence on his part from the exercise of such a power.[16] In this sense prescription depends on an acquiescence by the servient owner in the exercise by a dominant owner of rights which are acknowledged to be a matter of entitlement in favour of the latter.[17]

Accordingly no claim of right can be asserted where a supposed servient owner has allowed user under a purely temporary licence[18] or has retained

7 *Mills v Silver* [1991] Ch 271 at 279H–280A per Dillon LJ.

8 *Ramsay v Cooke* [1984] 2 NZLR 680 at 685f. See later *Cooke v Ramsay* [1984] 2 NZLR 689.

9 (1982) 35 OR (2d) 379 at 384.

10 As was pointed out by Cory JA, the essence of prescription is to 'subject a property owner to a burden without compensation.' The over-eager finding of successful prescriptive user 'may discourage acts of kindness and good neighbourliness; it may punish the kind and thoughtful and reward the aggressor' ((1982) 35 OR (2d) 379 at 384).

11 See *Costagliola v English* (1969) 210 Estates Gazette 1425 at 1431 per Megarry J.

12 See *Property in Thin Air*, [1991] CLJ 252 at 268ff.

13 (1881) 6 App Cas 740 at 773f.

14 Acquiescence is not, however, vitiated if the servient owner is unaware that he owns the land himself (*Capar v Wasylowski* (1983) 146 DLR (3d) 193 at 199).

15 In *Dalton v Angus & Co* the House of Lords held that the plaintiff had acquired a right of support for his building by reason of 20 years' enjoyment, and could therefore sue the defendant in respect of the damage caused by the removal of the lateral support provided by the defendant's adjoining house. It is difficult to see how in practice such a prescriptive claim could have been frustrated by the adjoining owner otherwise than by demolishing his building within the prescription period of 20 years.

16 See also *Davies v Du Paver* [1953] 1 QB 184 at 210 per Morris LJ. This statement of the principle of acquiescence closely resembles the doctrine of proprietary estoppel, particularly where the prescriptive claimant undertakes expenditure in the belief that there has been acquiescence in his assumption of right (see eg *Annally Hotel Ltd v Bergin* (1970) 104 ILTR 65 at 66ff).

17 *Hamilton v Joyce* [1984] 3 NSWLR 279 at 289B–290B. The user claimed must be 'inconsistent with any other reasonable inference than that it has been of right' (*Gardner v Hodgson's Kingston Brewery Co Ltd* [1903] AC 229 at 239 per Lord Lindley).

18 *Sturges v Bridgman* (1879) 11 Ch D 852 at 863. There can be no entitlement in circumstances of temporary licence because the servient owner has reserved the right not to renew the licence (see *Mills v Silver* [1991] Ch 271 at 282B).

control over the extent of the user (eg by means of a gate which is locked from time to time at his discretion).[19] By contrast, as Parker LJ pointed out in *Mills v Silver*,[20] a prescriptive right can be established if the user in question is 'such as to bring home to the mind of a reasonable person that a continuous right of enjoyment is being asserted'.[1] If, in these circumstances, the alleged servient owner 'does nothing', he will be 'taken to have recognised the right and not intended to resist it.' It will be no defence for him later to assert that he merely 'tolerated' the user in question.[2] The mere fact that the servient owner could have stopped the user within the prescription period 'is not inconsistent with the concept of user as of right'.[3] The critical factor will be precisely the fact that the servient owner did *not* take steps to halt the adverse user.[4] The position is, of course, very different if the relevant user is of such a nature that there were no possible or practicable means by which the servient owner could have brought it to an end.[5]

(c) Grounds of prescriptive acquisition

At common law prescription depends on the idea that long user is evidence of past grant. In other words, the fact of long user is deemed to provide evidence that the easement or profit now claimed was once duly granted in proper form, and any easement or profit established by prescription is therefore necessarily legal. The theory of prescriptive acquisition is, however, deeply marked by fiction.

19 *Lay v Wyncoll* (1966) 198 Estates Gazette 887 at 889; *Goldsmith v Burrow Construction Co Ltd* (1987) *Times*, 31 July; *Mills v Silver* [1991] Ch 271 at 282B-D. See also *Bridle v Ruby* [1989] QB 169 at 177G ('permission from time to time').

20 [1991] Ch 271 at 288D-E.

1 With many acts of neighbourly forbearance there can be no reasonable apprehension that the permitted user is generated by *entitlement*, with the result no prescription ensues (see eg *Henderson v Volk* (1982) 35 OR (2d) 379 at 384; *Bridle v Ruby* [1989] QB 169 at 177G). Likewise the casual nature of a tolerated user between neighbours may indicate that 'the user was not a user asserting a right' (*Mills v Silver* [1991] Ch 271 at 284D-E, citing *Ironside, Crabb and Crabb v Cook, Cook and Barefoot* (1978) 41 P & CR 326 at 339). In a proper case, however, the mere existence of neighbourly relations will not connote a consent or licence which frustrates prescriptive claims if there is evidence that the user was actually viewed as a matter of right (see *Sunset Properties Pty Ltd v Johnston* (1975) 3 BPR 9185 at 9191).

2 See also [1991] Ch 271 at 281G, 285E per Dillon LJ, 291B per Stocker LJ.

3 [1991] Ch 271 at 282A per Dillon LJ. At common law, for instance, a servient owner could always frustrate the prescriptive acquisition of a right of access to light by erecting a 'spite fence' to obstruct the light. Nowadays the servient owner can achieve the same objective under the Rights of Light Act 1959 by registering a notional 'spite fence' in the local land charges register (Rights of Light Act 1959, s 2).

4 See *Goldsmith v Burrow Construction Co Ltd* (1987) *Times*, 31 July, per May LJ, cited in *Mills v Silver* [1991] Ch 271 at 282C-D.

5 See eg *Webb v Bird* (1861) 10 CB (NS) 268 at 283ff, 142 ER 455 at 460f, (1863) 13 CB (NS) 841 at 843, 143 ER 332 at 333 (no easement in respect of free flow of air over alleged servient tenement in direction of claimant's windmill). See also *Bryant v Lefever* (1879) 4 CPD 172 at 178.

(i) Common law presumption from long user At common law it was presumed that a long user stemmed from a valid grant if that user had continued 'from time whereof the memory of men runneth not to the contrary',[6] a date which was somewhat arbitrarily fixed as 1189.[7] Any user which commenced before this date was apt to provide an unimpeachable basis for a claim of prescriptive acquisition. With the passage of time it came to be presumed by the courts of common law that if a user as of right for more than 20 years could be shown at any point, this user must have commenced before 1189.[8] However, this benevolent fiction was liable to be frustrated if it could be shown that a particular user could not possibly have been exercised or enjoyed at all times since 1189[9] or if there had been unity of possession between the dominant and servient tenements at any stage since 1189.[10] It is therefore usually impossible to satisfy the test of common law prescription,[11] and it is generally assumed that the ancient common law principle nowadays adds nothing to the other grounds of prescriptive claim.[12]

(ii) Lost modern grant In order to remedy the deficiencies of the common law presumption from user, the courts later developed the doctrine of 'lost modern grant'. This doctrine conceded that user dating back to 1189 could not be proved. It therefore allowed prescriptive claims to be made on the basis of a 'convenient and workable fiction'[13] that 20 years' user provided evidence of a 'modern grant' (ie a grant by deed at some date after 1189) which had since been misplaced and lost.[14] The doctrine of 'lost modern grant' was upheld by the House of Lords in *Dalton v Angus & Co*,[15] the only conditions for its application being proof of 20 years' enjoyment as

6 *Co Litt*, p 114b.

7 Statute of Westminster I, 1275, c 39. See *Dalton v Angus & Co* (1881) 6 App Cas 740 at 811 per Lord Blackburn; *Simmons v Dobson* [1991] 1 WLR 720 at 722H; *Connellan Nominees Pty Ltd v Camerer* [1988] 2 Qd R 248 at 251f.

8 *Angus & Co v Dalton* (1877) 3 QBD 85 at 105 per Cockburn CJ; *Clancy v Whelan and Considine* (1958) 92 ILTR 39 at 43f. The required period was sometimes stated to involve continuous user within living memory (*Hanna v Pollock* [1900] 2 IR 664 at 700).

9 Thus an easement of access to light could not be claimed in respect of a building which had clearly been constructed only since 1189 (*Duke of Norfolk v Arbuthnot* (1880) 5 CPD 390 at 393, 402). See also *Hanna v Pollock* [1900] 2 IR 664 at 693, 700f; *Simmons v Dobson* [1991] 1 WLR 720 at 722H–723A. For similar reasons there can be no presumption of user since before 1189 in Australia (see *Richardson v Browning* (1936) 31 Tas LR 78 at 140f; *Hamilton v Joyce* [1984] 3 NSWLR 279 at 287E) or New Zealand (see *New Zealand Loan and Mercantile Agency Co Ltd v Wellington Corpn* (1890) 9 NZLR 10 at 18f).

10 Post, p 1118.

11 *Simmons v Dobson* [1991] 1 WLR 720 at 722H per Fox LJ.

12 *Mills v Silver* [1991] Ch 271 at 278A-B.

13 *Simmons v Dobson* [1991] 1 WLR 720 at 723B per Fox LJ. Compare *Angus & Co v Dalton* (1877) 3 QBD 85 at 94, where Lush J made his classic reference to the 'revolting fiction of a lost grant'.

14 See *Bryant v Foot* (1867) LR 2 QB 161 at 181; *Dalton v Angus & Co* (1881) 6 App Cas 740 at 811ff; *Hanna v Pollock* [1900] 2 IR 664 at 694, 697f. The justification for the doctrine of 'lost modern grant' seems to be that the state of affairs which is shown to exist is otherwise unexplained (see *Attorney-General v Simpson* [1901] 2 Ch 671 at 698; *Hamilton v Joyce* [1984] 3 NSWLR 279 at 287G–288A; *Bridle v Ruby* [1989] QB 169 at 177F).

15 (1881) 6 App Cas 740.

of right,[16] coupled with an absence of any evidence that the putative grantor was legally incompetent.[17] Proof of continuous user as of right for a period of 20 years is therefore usually sufficient nowadays to found a claim of prescriptive acquisition.[18]

(iii) Prescription Act 1832 Some of the difficulties of the common law are dealt with in the Prescription Act 1832, but this statute has been castigated as 'one of the worst drafted Acts on the Statute Book'.[19] The Act is intended to supplement, rather than displace, the other grounds of prescription,[20] but its provisions are available only where some litigation has arisen in relation to an alleged incumbrance.

In respect of easements other than easements of light, the 1832 Act provides that user as of right[1] and without interruption for 20 years cannot be defeated by evidence that such user commenced after 1189.[2] An easement enjoyed for 40 years as of right and without interruption is deemed to be 'absolute and indefeasible'[3] unless enjoyed by written consent or agreement.[4]

Slightly different rules apply to the prescriptive acquisition of easements of light. Under the Prescription Act 1832, the actual enjoyment of access to light for a period of 20 years without interruption renders that access 'absolute and indefeasible'[5] unless it was enjoyed merely by reason of written

16 A claim of lost modern grant based on 20 years of actual enjoyment is not prejudiced by the fact that subsequent user may have been interrupted or discontinuous (see *Mills v Silver* [1991] Ch 271 at 278D).

17 The presumption of grant may be rebutted by evidence that the putative grantor suffered from mental incapacity or was a corporation which lacked the legal capacity to grant away rights of easement (see *Rochdale Canal Co v Radcliffe* (1852) 18 QB 287 at 314f, 118 ER 108 at 118) or did not have a full fee simple estate in the supposed servient tenement (see *Rodwell v G.R. Evans & Co Pty Ltd* (1977) 3 BPR 9114 at 9121). See also *Oakley v Boston* [1976] QB 270 at 280F–281A, 285C-E.

18 See *Tehidy Minerals Ltd v Norman* [1971] 2 QB 528 at 546A, 552A-B. It may even be that the presumption of a lost modern grant cannot be rebutted by evidence that no grant was in fact ever made (see *Angus & Co v Dalton* (1878) 4 QBD 162 at 172f, 187; *Tehidy Minerals Ltd v Norman*, supra at 552B). It has been recommended that the doctrine of lost modern grant should apply as between unit owners within the proposed commonhold ownership scheme, but not to the acquisition of rights for any unit holder over the common parts of the commonhold premises (see Law Commission, *Commonhold* (Cm 179, July 1987), paras 6.10f).

19 *14th Report of the Law Reform Committee* (Cmnd 3100, 1966), para 40.

20 See *Hyman v Van den Bergh* [1907] 2 Ch 516 at 532.

1 The user must have been *nec vi, nec clam, nec precario* (*Newnham v Willison* (1988) 56 P & CR 8 at 12, 17). See also *Jones v Price and Morgan* (1992) 64 P & CR 404 at 407.

2 Prescription Act 1832, s 2.

3 Prescription Act 1832, s 2.

4 Prescription Act 1832, s 2. In all cases under section 2 of the 1832 Act, a claim of user 'as of right' may be defeated by evidence of even verbal consent or agreement (whether given or made before or after the commencement of the statutory period), except that a consent or agreement before the commencement of the 40 year period must be by deed or writing. See *Hyman v Van den Bergh* [1907] 2 Ch 516 at 530; *Jones v Price and Morgan* (1992) 64 P & CR 404 at 407. An oral permission given before commencement of the 40 year period will bar a claim only if renewed during that period (see *Gardner v Hodgson's Kingston Brewery Co Ltd* [1903] AC 229 at 236).

5 Prescription Act 1832, s 3. There is no requirement here that the user should have been as of right; it may be merely precarious (*Colls v Home and Colonial Stores Ltd* [1904] AC 179 at 205; *Hyman v Van den Bergh* [1907] 2 Ch 516 at 530).

consent or agreement.[6] The 1832 Act also provides that a *profit à prendre* which has been enjoyed as of right and without interruption for 30 years 'next before some suit or action' cannot be defeated by proof that the profit arose only after 1189.[7] Moreover, a period of 60 years' user on the same terms makes the prescriptive claim to the profit 'absolute and indefeasible'.[8]

Any period of time pleaded in support of a claim under the Prescription Act 1832 must be the period 'next before some suit or action' in which the claim is challenged.[9] This requirement has the consequence that, however long the period of actual enjoyment, no absolute or indefeasible right can be acquired until the right is brought in question in some suit or action. Until it so crystallises, any right claimed is 'inchoate' only.[10] It follows, moreover, that irrespective of its duration, any discontinued period of long user isolated in the past cannot provide any basis of claim under the 1832 Act.[11] There is a further provision to the effect that no act of obstruction is deemed to be an interruption until it has been submitted to or acquiesced in for one year after the party interrupted had notice both of the interruption and of the person making it.[12]

(4) Estoppel

A further method of creation of easements and profits lies in the operation of the doctrine of proprietary estoppel.[13] This doctrine is the subject of an extended discussion in Chapter 11.[14] Now that the doctrine of part performance can no longer operate upon informal agreements affecting land,[15] the estoppel principle may now acquire a new significance in the present

6 A consent or agreement relevant under section 3 must be by deed or writing but may be given or made either before or after the commencement of the statutory period (*Hyman v Van den Bergh* [1907] 2 Ch 516 at 530f). The 1832 Act does not specify the persons who must be parties to the agreement, but the consent or agreement referred to in section 3 must be such as would be effectual to negative prescription at common law or under presumed grant (*Hyman* at 529f). It is possible that the prescriptive effect of section 3 may be destroyed by an agreement or consent by the tenant of the supposed dominant owner (*Hyman* at 531, ante, p 1114).

7 Prescription Act 1832, s 1.

8 Prescription Act 1832, s 1.

9 Prescription Act 1832, s 4. See *Hyman v Van den Bergh* [1907] 2 Ch 516 at 528.

10 *Hyman v Van den Bergh* [1907] 2 Ch 516 at 524f; *Newnham v Willison* (1988) 56 P & CR 8 at 17. See also *Pavledes v Ryesbridge Properties Ltd* (1989) 58 P & CR 459 at 481 (statutory period not yet elapsed).

11 See *Mills v Silver* [1991] Ch 271 at 278B-C.

12 Prescription Act 1832, s 4. See *Dance v Triplow* (1992) 64 P & CR 1; [1992] Conv 197 (Jill Martin). However, the mere fact that the Prescription Act 1832 is excluded by an interruption lasting more than one year does not preclude the possibility of a valid claim on the basis of lost modern grant (see *Ward (Helston) Ltd v Kerrier DC* (1984) 24 RVR 18 at 19).

13 See eg *Ward v Kirkland* [1967] Ch 194; *Crabb v Arun DC* [1976] Ch 179; *Dewhirst v Edwards* [1983] 1 NSWLR 34; *Classic Communications Ltd v Lascar* (1986) 21 DLR (4th) 579 at 587f (ante, pp 328, 352, 360).

14 Ante, p 312.

15 Law of Property (Miscellaneous Provisions) Act 1989, s 2(8), ante, p 256.

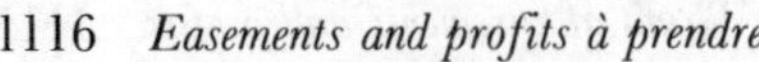

context as a means of upholding the informal grant of an easement or profit which would otherwise be wholly ineffectual.[16]

5. RESERVATION OF EASEMENTS AND PROFITS

Reservation is the converse of grant and occurs where a transferor of land reserves for himself easements or profits over the land which he transfers to another. The technique of reservation is nowadays much simpler than it used to be before the enactment of the property legislation of 1925. Once again the reservation may be either express or implied.

(1) Express reservation

If a vendor wishes to retain any right in the nature of an easement or profit *à prendre* in respect of land which he conveys to a purchaser, it is open to him to do so by means of express words contained in the document of transfer.[17] The precise extent of a reservation is ultimately a matter of construction of the words used in the light of the general principle that the terms of a grant are, in cases of doubt or ambivalence, to be construed *against* the grantor. In the past the courts were accustomed to regard the reservation of an easement or profit as constituting in law a 'regrant' of that right by the purchaser of the servient tenement, with the consequence that the *contra proferentem* rule of construction operated not in favour of the servient owner but in favour of the party who had in effect reserved the right for himself (ie the dominant owner). After 1925 it was generally considered that the balance of advantage conferred by this rule of construction had been reversed by the provision in section 65(1) of the Law of Property Act 1925 that a reservation shall 'operate at law without. . .any regrant'. However, the more recent case law seems somewhat perversely to favour the proposition that an express reservation of an easement or profit is still to be construed against the servient owner and in favour of the dominant tenant.[18]

(2) Implied reservation

It is a rule of general application that if a vendor wishes to reserve any rights over land granted away, he must do so expressly in clear and

16 See P. Pettit, [1989] Conv 431 at 442. See also Law Commission, *Transfer of Land: Formalities for Contracts for Sale etc of Land* (Law Com Working Paper No 92, July 1985), para 5.8; *Transfer of Land: Formalities for Contracts for Sale etc of Land* (Law Com No 164, 29 June 1987), para 5.4f.

17 It is even possible that a reservation in favour of C may be created by a conveyance of a legal estate by A to B which in its express terms purports to be subject to an easement (albeit not yet in existence at the date of the conveyance) for the owner or occupier of a specified dominant tenement (Law of Property Act 1925, s 65(2)). Such a conveyance creates an easement for C, to which C is entitled and which he may enforce even though he is not actually referred to by name in A's conveyance (see *Wiles v Banks* (1985) 50 P & CR 80 at 87ff).

18 See *Johnstone v Holdway* [1963] 1 QB 601 at 612f; (1963) 79 LQR 182 (R.E.M.); *St Edmundsbury and Ipswich Diocesan Board of Finance v Clark* (No 2) [1975] 1 WLR 468 at 478F-G. Compare *Cordell v Second Clanfield Properties Ltd* [1969] 2 Ch 9 at 15B–16B.

unambiguous terms.[19] In *Wheeldon v Burrows*,[20] a vendor claimed a right of access to light as impliedly reserved in his conveyance to a purchaser. This claim was denied by the Court of Appeal on the ground that reservation can arise only by reason of express stipulation in the terms of the conveyance.[1] To this rule there appear to be only two exceptions.[2]

(a) Necessity

The implication of a reservation of necessity is rare. The only circumstances in which such an implied reservation will be accepted by the courts arise where a vendor conveys away all the land adjacent to or surrounding the land retained by himself, in circumstances in which the only possible access to the land retained lies across the land conveyed away.[3] An easement of access will be implied in such a case,[4] since without such a reservation the vendor's land would be rendered unusable.[5] It is not sufficient that the easement claimed should be merely convenient or reasonably necessary for the enjoyment of the land retained.[6] It must be shown that, without the easement, the vendor's land would be completely sterilised.[7] In *Ray v Hazeldine*,[8] Kekewich J held that no easement could be impliedly reserved where the vendor retained an adjoining property which permitted a means of access. In order that an easement of necessity should arise by implied reservation, it is vital that the vendor's land should have become completely landlocked.[9]

19 *Broomfield v Williams* [1897] 1 Ch 602 at 616; *Wiles v Banks* (1985) 50 P & CR 80 at 83f.
20 (1879) 12 Ch D 31.
1 For reference to the extreme difficulty of making good a claim of implied reservation, see *Bayley v Great Western Railway Co* (1884) 26 Ch D 434 at 458 per Fry LJ; *Parish v Kelly* (1980) 1 BPR 9394 at 9399. There is no room for the contention that a reservation can be implied wherever such would be equitable in all the circumstances (see *In re Webb's Lease* [1951] Ch 808 at 817 per Evershed MR).
2 The *rule* in *Wheeldon v Burrows* applies, of course, only as a ground of implied grant, not as a means of implied reservation (see *Barton v Raine* (1981) 114 DLR (3d) 702 at 706).
3 The way of necessity is limited by the necessity at the date of grant (see *Parish v Kelly* (1980) 1 BPR 9394 at 9400).
4 It is for the transferor to select the way (*Packer v Welsted* (1657) 2 Sid 39, 82 ER 1244, *Packer v Wellstead* (1658) 2 Sid 111 at 112, 82 ER 1284 at 1285; *Pearson v Spencer* (1861) 1 B & S 571 at 584f, 121 ER 827 at 832; *Bolton v Bolton* (1879) 11 Ch D 968 at 972).
5 Ante, p 1092. See *Titchmarsh v Royston Water Co Ltd* (1899) 81 LT 673 at 675; *Barry v Hasseldine* [1952] Ch 835 at 838f; *Maude v Thornton* [1929] IR 454 at 457.
6 It has been proposed that a 'truer criterion' may be a 'negative standard of unreasonableness' (see *Parish v Kelly* (1980) 1 BPR 9394 at 9401 per Rath J).
7 *M.R.A. Engineering Ltd v Trimster Co Ltd* (1988) 56 P & CR 1 at 6.
8 [1904] 2 Ch 17 at 20f.
9 Thus no implied reservation of a right of way may be claimed where the vendor has available to him a legal entitlement (as distinct from a mere permission) to use an alternative access (*Barry v Hasseldine* [1952] Ch 835 at 839). There is some authority to the effect that a reservation of necessity is extinguished if the claimant subsequently acquires an alternative means of access (see *Holmes v Goring* (1824) 2 Bing 76 at 83ff, 130 ER 233 at 237). Compare, however, *Maude v Thornton* [1929] IR 454 at 458, and see *Proctor v Hodgson* (1855) 10 Exch 824 at 828, 156 ER 674 at 675, where both Parke B and Alderson B expressed doubt as to the correctness of *Holmes v Goring*. Parke B opined that a way of necessity ought to be 'as much a grant for ever as if expressly inserted in a deed'.

(b) Common intention

In rare circumstances an easement will be implied into a conveyance on behalf of the vendor in order to effectuate some common intention which was left unexpressed by that conveyance.[10] A heavy onus of proof rests on the vendor who wishes to show that a reservation was mutually intended.[11]

6. EXTINGUISHMENT OF EASEMENTS AND PROFITS

Since an easement or profit represents for the dominant owner an important and valuable proprietary right, it is clear that the courts have been slow to hold that such a right (if otherwise unlimited in grant) is destroyed by events subsequent to grant. There are nevertheless several ways at common law in which easements and profits may be extinguished or suspended.

(1) Unity of ownership and possession

It follows from the characteristics attributed to easements and profits that such rights are extinguished automatically if at any time the dominant and servient tenements pass into the ownership of the same person.[12] There is at least a surface logic in the proposition that 'a man cannot have an easement over his own land'.[13] The same proposition is nevertheless bounded by strong limiting factors. The extinctive merger must bring together two similar and equally perdurable estates.[14] Unity of possession without unity of ownership has merely suspensory effect on the existence of an easement.[15] There is, moreover, a highly persuasive view that the doctrine of extinguishment by merger has no application to easements of necessity.[16] In respect of such

10 *Pwllbach Colliery Co v Woodman* [1915] AC 634 at 646f (ante, p 1096).

11 See *In re Webb's Lease* [1951] Ch 808 at 820. Implied reservation has, however, been held to give a mutual right of support after the sale of one of two adjoining houses by their common owner (see *Richards v Rose* (1853) 9 Exch 218 at 221, 156 ER 93 at 94f). See also *Barton v Raine* (1981) 114 DLR (3d) 702 at 706ff.

12 *Tyrringham's Case* (1584) 4 Co Rep 36b at 38a, 76 ER 973 at 980; *The Queen v Tener* (1985) 17 DLR (4th) 1 at 17 (Supreme Court of Canada). See also J.D.A. Brooke-Taylor, (1977) 41 Conv (NS) 107. It is of interest that Torrens legislation does not necessarily take the same view of the extinguishing effect of merger (see eg Real Property Act (NSW) 1900, s 47(7)).

13 *Margil Pty Ltd v Stegul Pastoral Pty Ltd* [1984] 2 NSWLR 1 at 9D, citing *Roe v Siddons* (1888) 22 QBD 224 at 236 per Fry LJ.

14 *R v Inhabitants of Hermitage* (1692) Carth 239, 90 ER 743; *Re Cockburn* (1896) 27 OR 450 at 459f; *Re Lonegren and Rueben* (1987) 37 DLR (4th) 491 at 496f, affd (1988) 50 DLR (4th) 431 at 433. There is authority that an easement extinguished by merger can be revived by subsequent reference to that easement in a later transfer document executed by the common owner in respect of the former dominant tenement (see *Cuvet v Davis* (1883) 9 VLR 390 at 396; *Margil Pty Ltd v Stegul Pastoral Pty Ltd* [1984] 2 NSWLR 1 at 10G-11A).

15 Thus, for instance, the fact that X owns the freehold of Blackacre and simultaneously holds a lease over the adjoining Whiteacre merely suspends any easement granted earlier in respect of these two premises. The easement revives when the unity of possession is severed (see *Thomas v Thomas* (1835) 2 Cr M & R 34 at 40, 150 ER 15 at 17).

16 *Parish v Kelly* (1980) 1 BPR 9394 at 9400; *Margil Pty Ltd v Stegul Pastoral Pty Ltd* [1984] 2 NSWLR 1 at 10A-C.

easements the stringent nature of the original necessity is not normally diminished by any intervening union of title or possession.[17]

(2) Release

Release may be express or implied.

(a) Express release

The dominant owner may release his rights expressly.[18] In the case of a legal easement or profit, such a release must be contained in a deed.[19] However, in relation to an equitable easement or profit, it is sufficient if the dominant owner releases his rights by means of an informal agreement which is supported by consideration given by the servient owner or which is attended by circumstances in which it would be inequitable to revive the rights thereby abrogated.[20]

(b) Implied release

An easement or profit may be released impliedly in cases of abandonment of the exercise of the right coupled with a clear intention to release the right in question.[1] Abandonment, when it occurs, may extend to any or all of the multiple users permitted within the parcel of rights conferred by the original grant.[2] However, mere non-user of a right of way—even over a lengthy period—does not necessarily constitute abandonment,[3] since 'it is one thing not to assert an intention to use a way, and another thing to assert an intention to abandon it.'[4]

17 See *Pheysey v Vicary* (1847) 16 M & W 484 at 490, 153 ER 1280 at 1282 per Alderson B; *Margil Pty Ltd v Stegul Pastoral Pty Ltd* [1984] 2 NSWLR 1 at 9E–10C.

18 There need be no supporting evidence of non-user by the dominant owner (see *Wolfe v Freijahs' Holdings Pty Ltd* [1988] VR 1017 at 1024).

19 *Lovell v Smith* (1857) 3 CB (NS) 120 at 126f, 140 ER 685 at 687.

20 *Davies v Marshall* (1861) 10 CB (NS) 697 at 710f, 142 ER 627 at 633. There is thus the possibility that the extinguishment of an easement may be founded on the doctrine of proprietary estoppel (ante, p 312). However, there may be problems in proving the necessary elements of knowledge and reliance required in a claim of estoppel (see *Costagliola v English* (1969) 210 Estates Gazette 1425 at 1431).

1 *Swan v Sinclair* [1924] 1 Ch 254 at 266; *Tehidy Minerals Ltd v Norman* [1971] 2 QB 528 at 553D-F. Alterations to, or demolition of, a structure situated on the dominant tenement (eg a mill which enjoys an easement of water) may provide the required evidence of an intention to abandon user (see *Liggins v Inge* (1831) 7 Bing 682 at 693, 131 ER 263 at 268). In *Costagliola v English* (1969) 210 Estates Gazette 1425 at 1431, Megarry J conceded the 'undoubted similarities' between the doctrines of abandonment and proprietary estoppel, but thought it wrong to 'equate' them.

2 Thus on sufficient evidence a dominant owner of a right of way may be found to have abandoned the user of the way as a carriageway but not as a footway. See eg *Guth v Robinson* (1977) 1 BPR 9209 at 9214; compare *Bulstrode v Lambert* [1953] 1 WLR 1064 at 1068.

3 *Crossley & Sons Ltd v Lightowler* (1867) 2 Ch App 478 at 482; *Swan v Sinclair* [1924] 1 Ch 254 at 266; *Treweeke v 36 Wolseley Road Pty Ltd* (1973) 128 CLR 274 at 282ff, 302ff; *Riley v Penttila* [1974] VR 547 at 570; *Guth v Robinson* (1977) 1 BPR 9209 at 9214; *Re Kileel and Kingswood Realty Ltd* (1980) 108 DLR (3d) 562 at 565; *Barton v Raine* (1981) 114 DLR (3d) 702 at 710; *McIntyre v Porter* [1983] 2 VR 439 at 444; *Wolfe v Freijahs' Holdings Pty Ltd* [1988] VR 1017 at 1024.

4 *James v Stevenson* [1893] AC 162 at 168 per Sir Edward Fry.

The critical variable here is the showing of a 'fixed intention' on the part of the dominant owner 'never at any time thereafter to assert the right himself or to attempt to transmit it to anyone else.'[5] It takes little evidence, particularly in the case of a right conferred by express grant, to counteract any supposed intention of abandonment. Since autonomous control is of the essence of proprietary rights, a grantee 'may always, if he chooses, not exercise his rights under the grant to the full without in any way prejudicing his full right if he finds it convenient to use it.'[6] It is therefore clear that no abandonment is established by a short-lived cessation of user[7] or by the temporary suspension of a user by agreement with the servient owner.[8]

A longer suspension of user of an easement may, of course, render it necessary for the dominant owner either to provide an explanation for the non-user[9] or to show that during the period of suspension some indication was given of an intention to preserve the relevant entitlement.[10] It used to be thought, in the total absence of such evidence, that an intention to abandon could be presumed after a discontinuation of user for 20 years.[11] In more recent decisions, however, the courts have deferred markedly to the perceived long-term value of rights of easement and have proved themselves receptive to claims of latent future benefit flowing from even grossly under-used easements.[12] In *Benn v Harding*,[13] for instance, the Court of Appeal was unwilling to presume an intention to abandon a right of way even after a period of non-user of 175 years.[14] Here the non-user was met by the 'simple explanation' that throughout this period the dominant owner and his predecessors in title had enjoyed an alternative means of access to their tenement.[15]

5 *Tehidy Minerals Ltd v Norman* [1971] 2 QB 528 at 553D per Buckley LJ. See also *Huckvale v Aegean Hotels Ltd* (1989) 58 P & CR 163 at 167 per Nourse LJ, 171 per Butler-Sloss LJ; *Guth v Robinson* (1977) 1 BPR 9209 at 9214; *Jennison v Traficante* (1980) 1 BPR 9657 at 9659.

6 *Keewatin Power Co Ltd v Lake of the Woods Milling Co Ltd* [1930] AC 640 at 647 per Viscount Dunedin.

7 See *Bulstrode v Lambert* [1953] 2 WLR 1064 at 1068 (10 years); *Clark v Duckworth* [1984] 2 NZLR 58 at 64 (3 or 4 years).

8 *Payne v Sheddon* (1834) 1 Mood & R 382 at 383, 174 ER 131; *Sunset Properties Pty Ltd v Johnston* (1975) 3 BPR 9185 at 9195 (suspension of user on Sundays). Similarly, a variation of the route of an existing way by acquiescence or consent does not constitute abandonment (*Davis v Whitby* [1974] Ch 186 at 191E-192A; *Sunset Properties*, supra at 9192).

9 *Treweeke v 36 Wolseley Road Pty Ltd* (1973) 128 CLR 274 at 288 per Walsh J; *Riley v Penttila* [1974] VR 547 at 570ff; *McIntyre v Porter* [1983] 2 VR 439 at 444.

10 *Moore v Rawson* (1824) 3 B & C 332 at 337f, 107 ER 756 at 759; *Crossley & Sons Ltd v Lightowler* (1867) 2 Ch App 478 at 482; *Riley v Penttila* [1974] VR 547 at 570.

11 *Moore v Rawson* (1824) 3 B & C 332 at 339, 107 ER 756 at 759. Compare, however, *Cook v Bath Corpn* (1868) LR 6 Eq 177 at 180.

12 To permit a servient owner too readily to claim an implied release would effectively allow him to expropriate the dominant owner without compensation (see U. Reichman, *Judicial Supervision of Servitudes*, 7 J Legal Stud 139 at 157 (1978)).

13 (1992) *Times*, 13 October.

14 In the view of Hirst LJ, the abandonment of such a 'valuable latent property' should not lightly be inferred since it might be of 'considerable value in the future'. See also *Gotobed v Pridmore* (1970) 115 Sol Jo 78; *Williams v Usherwood* (1983) 45 P & CR 235 at 256; *Guth v Robinson* (1977) 1 BPR 9209 at 9214.

15 (1992) *Times*, 13 October, per Nourse LJ.

(c) Change of circumstance

It is inevitable that the problem of obsolescence should affect easements and profits, which usually arise in the context of legal arrangements with an extended or undefined time horizon.[16] There is, however, no statutory provision in English law for the discharge or modification of easements or profits which have become redundant or obstructive with the effluxion of time.[17] In the absence of such interventionist legislation there seems to be a strong argument in favour of recognising at least a limited form of 'change of circumstance' doctrine under which courts could modify or terminate obsolete forms of servitude.[18]

Although a 'change of circumstance' doctrine appears at first sight to be a novel proposition in English law, it may be neither wholly implausible nor wholly without precedent. A way of necessity is said, for instance, to be 'limited by the necessity which created it'[19] and therefore to be extinguished by changed conditions which later obviate the necessity.[20] The obsolescence issue arose recently in a more general form in *Huckvale v Aegean Hotels Ltd.*[1] Here the dominant owner's expressly granted right of way over the servient tenement became largely purposeless when that owner lost accompanying and complementary rights over other land belonging to the servient owner. The Court of Appeal felt that it could not rule out altogether the possibility that an easement may be extinguished by operation of law when it ceases to accommodate the dominant tenement.[2] Here, however, there could be no question of extinguishment since it was impossible to claim with certainty that the easement had ceased to confer a 'real and practical benefit' on the dominant land or could never be 'reasonably necessary for its better enjoyment in the future'.[3] Although agreeing that a court should be slow to hold that an easement has been 'extinguished by frustration', Slade LJ was prepared to contemplate precisely such an outcome if circumstances 'have changed so drastically since the date of the original grant of an easement

16 See S.E. Sterk, *Foresight and the Law of Servitudes*, 73 Cornell L Rev 956 (1987–88).

17 Compare Law of Property Act 1925, s 84 (post, p 1165). The New Zealand courts have power under Property Law Act 1952, s 127, to modify or extinguish an easement on the ground that it is 'obsolete' or that its continued existence 'would impede the reasonable user of the land'. See *Masters v Snell* [1979] 1 NZLR 34 at 40ff; *Armishaw v Denby Horton (NZ) Ltd* [1984] 1 NZLR 44 at 45ff. There is a similar power in New South Wales (Conveyancing Act 1919, s 89(1)). See *Manly Properties Pty Ltd v Castrisos* [1973] 2 NSWLR 420; *Pieper v Edwards* [1982] 1 NSWLR 336.

18 The possibility of such intervention undoubtedly reopens the liberal dilemma prompted by the tension between private autonomy and sensible social regulation (see G.S. Alexander, *Freedom, Coercion, and the Law of Servitudes*, 73 Cornell L Rev 883 (1987–88)). Yet the application of a 'change of circumstance' doctrine tends to inhibit undesirable 'holdout' strategies on the part of dominant owners of now pointless covenants, while reconciling foresightless private arrangements with a vastly changed present reality.

19 See *Holmes v Goring* (1824) 2 Bing 76 at 83ff, 130 ER 233 at 237 (ante, p 1117).

20 Such changed conditions would arise, for instance, with the acquisition of a hitherto unavailable alternative means of access. Alteration of a servient tenement may effect the extinguishment of a profit *à prendre*, although the profit may automatically revive if the servient property is later restored to its former condition (see *Ellison v Vukicevic* (1986) 7 NSWLR 104 at 114B-C).

1 (1989) 58 P & CR 163; [1990] Conv 292 (G. Kodilinye).

2 (1989) 58 P & CR 163 at 170 per Nourse LJ, 172 per Butler-Sloss LJ.

3 (1989) 58 P & CR 163 at 172 per Nourse LJ.

(for example by supervening illegality) that it would offend common sense and reality for the court to hold that an easement still subsisted.'[4] In the view of Slade LJ, however, the evidence must show clearly that, because of the later change of circumstance, there is 'no practical possibility' that the easement will ever again benefit the dominant tenement in the manner contemplated by the initial grant.

4 (1989) 58 P & CR 163 at 173.

CHAPTER 22

Freehold covenants

In the context of real property a 'covenant' is an agreement contained in a deed in which one party (the 'covenantor') promises another party (the 'covenantee') that he will or will not engage in some specified activity in relation to a defined area of land. As between covenantor and covenantee the covenant is then fully enforceable as a form of contract. It is the task of this chapter to examine the legal principles which give effect to *private* covenants in respect of *freehold land*.[1]

It is nowadays clear that covenants enjoy a wider significance in land law than is explained merely by their contractual effect as between covenantor and covenantee. Although initially founded in contract, covenants have come to provide a means by which certain obligations relating to land use can be made to 'run with the land' so as to benefit and burden not only the original covenanting parties but also their successors in title. By extending their operation outside the realm of contract, covenants may effectively impose controls over land use which bind all parties into whose hands the land may come at any future time.

1. THE FUNCTION OF COVENANTS IN THE PLANNING OF LAND USE

Alongside the laws relating to easements, nuisance and planning, the law of covenants provides an important means by which an external control may be asserted over the use of land. In a manner similar to the law relating to easements,[2] the law of covenants facilitates the efficient utilisation of land resources. However, whereas the law of easements is generally concerned to promote the simultaneous exercise of a range of compatible modes of land use, the law of covenants is usually more heavily concerned with the reconciliation of conflicting forms of exploitation of land. Not only does the device of the freehold covenant permit a rational and efficient allocation of responsibilities relating to land use. In an age of increasing intensification of land use, covenants also provide a means for resolving in advance the problems thrown up by potentially incompatible forms of user in adjacent land areas.

Like the law of easements, the law relating to covenants provides a highly convenient means of adjusting neighbourhood relationships in such a way as to enhance the optimal utilisation of land. The owner of Blackacre may

1 Covenants relating to leasehold land were discussed in Chapter 18 (ante, p 777).
2 Ante, p 1043.

well wish to prevent the owner of the adjoining Whiteacre from carrying out certain activities on the latter tract of land or may desire that the owner of Whiteacre should supply certain kinds of service in favour of Blackacre. However, it is rarely efficient for the owner of Blackacre to buy out the entire freehold or leasehold estate in Whiteacre simply in order to guarantee the future provision of such utilities. Such a transaction is almost always wasteful (in so far as the investment in realty is disproportionate to the benefits derived) and may not resolve the problem anyway (in so far as the rights purchased are often incomplete without the acquisition of similar rights from other adjacent landowners).[3] Without resort to such inefficient manoeuvres the law of covenants provides a means of binding adjacent landowners to a common plan for the user of their respective lands, thereby coordinating their mutual interests over several generations.[4] The device of the covenant thus facilitates entire regimes of private ordering between neighbouring landowners with the result that covenants operate effectively as a form of private legislation affecting a succession of future owners.[5]

(1) Development of private control of land use

The basic principles governing the creation and enforcement of covenants respecting land were formulated during a period when government agencies played little part in planning the use and development of the community's land resources. It was accordingly both natural and inevitable that the law should seek to give long-term effect to the agreements by which landowners attempted to regulate land use through private treaty, and the law of covenants came in this way to provide a particularly important facility for the private planning of land use.

Although this function of the covenant device has more recently been given a socialised form in planning legislation,[6] the law of private covenants still retains a broad significance. Increasingly complex schemes have been introduced in order to make private covenants widely enforceable between freeholders, not least because the existence of valid and enforceable covenants may make land much more valuable on the open market. The existence of a comprehensive scheme of restrictive covenants binding all purchasers may greatly enhance the market attraction of a particular site or area of development, in that prospective purchasers are thereby assured that local amenities or the desirable characteristics of the neighbourhood will be preserved indefinitely in the future.

3 See U. Reichman, *Judicial Supervision of Servitudes*, 7 J Legal Stud 139 at 144 (1978).

4 In this sense the law of covenants has been likened to a form of political or public constitutional document (see R.A. Epstein, *Covenants and Constitutions*, 73 Cornell L Rev 906 at 926 (1987–88)).

5 If commonhold ownership schemes are introduced (ante, p 10), a unit holder will be able to enter into covenants with a third party although any rights created thereby cannot, without the consent of the commonhold association, survive the termination of the commonhold (see Law Commission, *Commonhold: Freehold Flats and freehold ownership of other interdependent buildings* (Cm 179, July 1987), paras 6.9ff).

6 It is perhaps no mere metaphor to record that, through the medium of planning legislation, all citizens can now claim in everyone else's land a certain quantum of 'property' which is not dissimilar to the proprietary interest effectively conferred by the privately agreed restrictive covenant (post, p 1138).

(2) Positive and negative covenants

Covenants may take the form of either *positive* covenants or *negative* covenants. A positive covenant is one which imposes on the covenantor an obligation to perform some specified act or activity in relation to a defined piece of land. A positive covenant may, for instance, stipulate that the covenantor shall maintain his neighbour's boundary fence in good repair. By contrast, a negative covenant restricts disadvantageous developments on other land in the vicinity of the covenantee's property. A negative (or 'restrictive') covenant may, for example, preclude the covenantor from using his own land for the purpose of conducting trade or business. Such a covenant clearly promotes the amenity enjoyed by the covenantee on his land, by curtailing the potential scope of the activities conducted on the covenantor's land. The negative covenant may enable the covenantee to live in pleasant surroundings untroubled by the presence of nearby factories belching smoke or by neighbours who insist upon using their homes as a base for private commercial enterprise.

(3) The boundary between contract and property

As a contractual obligation a covenant is of course enforceable only as between the original covenantor and covenantee. If the legal analysis of covenants were to stop at this point, the private agreements of covenantors and covenantees would have no enduring impact upon third parties, for the doctrine of privity of contract confines the benefit and burden of contractual terms to the contracting parties alone. One of the principal targets of this privity rule is, of course, to 'curtail the social losses of destructive bargaining'.[7] It is, however, of great importance that the purposeful benefits and burdens created by a private covenant respecting land should be capable of transmission to third parties, since otherwise all obligations would be destroyed on a transfer of that land. It would, moreover, be open to any covenantor to free himself of his covenanted obligations by the simple expedient of a collusive sale and reconveyance. It is essential for ethical and commercial reasons that the benefit and burden of a covenant should run with the land to which they relate, no matter into whose hands that land may subsequently pass.

This objective of freely transmissible obligation is to some extent realised today by the law governing covenants in respect of freehold land. There is, however, a certain public interest that the law of covenants should be clear, and the law defines fairly rigidly the circumstances in which covenants may not merely have contractual force but may also impose benefits and burdens upon third parties. It has always been thought important that these rules should tend to be restrictive rather than over-broad. If covenants of *any* kind, however loose or ill-defined, were allowed to bind third parties, there is a strong possibility that the encumbered land would be rendered effectively unmarketable. No purchaser would wish to buy land under circumstances where its future use had already been fettered by trivial or

7 See R.A. Epstein, 73 Cornell L Rev 906 at 914 (1987–88)).

obscure covenants governing the activities permissible on that land.[8] It is for good reason therefore that the law of covenants has striven in the past to maintain the frontier between contract and property.[9] It is nevertheless also clear that a creative tension exists between the need to preserve alienability of land and the need to allow private ordering by consensual arrangement. The stability of land use and development ensured by running covenants often means that an enforceable covenant, far from 'clogging' or sterilising title, operates to enhance the market value of both the benefited and the burdened land.

The transmission to third parties of covenanted benefits and burdens is simultaneously governed in English law by rules of respectively common law and equitable origin. These must be examined in turn.

2. COVENANTS AT LAW

The common law rules relating to the transmission of covenants are of ancient origin.[10] It has been clear from early times that at law a covenantor need not own any estate in land.[11] The law will nevertheless enforce his covenant under certain circumstances, whether that covenant be positive or negative. These propositions were first established by *The Prior's Case*[12] in 1368, where it was held that a positive covenant to sing divine service in a chapel might be enforced at law even though the covenantor had no estate in land which could be burdened by the obligation. The approach adopted in *The Prior's Case* has been applied in more recent times, as in *Smith and Snipes Hall Farm Ltd v River Douglas Catchment Board*,[13] where the Court of Appeal enforced the defendant's positive covenant to repair and maintain the floodbanks of a river. There is, however, a requirement at common law that the *covenantee* must hold some estate in land to which the benefit of the covenant may accrue.[14]

8 For a discussion of certain difficulties in reconciling running covenants with individual freedom and the liberal concept of property, see G.S. Alexander, *Freedom, Coercion, and the Law of Servitudes*, 73 Cornell L Rev 883 at 889 (1987–88).

9 See H.W.R. Wade, (1952) 68 LQR 337 at 347f ('If there were no frontier, there would be no limit to the new incidents of property which could be invented. But rights which can bind third parties ought to be of a limited and familiar kind; for otherwise purchasers might have to investigate an infinite variety of incumbrances, and would often have no means of knowing the real effect of some fancy or imaginative transaction to which they were strangers. Therefore the law has striven to draw lines of demarcation round the special interests which, exceptionally, may be created by contract or covenant').

10 See A.W.B. Simpson, *A History of The Land Law* (2nd edn Oxford 1986), p 116ff.

11 Precisely this principle underlies the highly significant development of the law relating to surety covenants under a lease, where of course the surety owns no relevant estate in land (see eg *P. & A. Swift Investments v Combined English Stores Group Plc* [1989] AC 632, ante, p 856, post, p 1128).

12 (1368) YB 42 Edw III, pl 14, fol 3A.

13 [1949] 2 KB 500 at 506f, 514f. See (1949) 12 MLR 498 (A.K.R. Kiralfy).

14 If the covenantee parts with the land benefited by the covenant before any breach of the covenant occurs, he can recover only nominal damages in any action brought against the covenantor, since the real loss is likely to have fallen upon the person to whom he has conveyed the land.

(1) Effect of Law of Property Act 1925, s 56

Difficulties have arisen in recent years concerning the scope of the benefit conferred by covenants at law. It is clear that, on purely contractual principles, a covenant may confer an enforceable benefit upon any party who is expressly named as the covenantee in the deed of covenant.[15] At common law there was for many years a strict rule that no person could sue on a deed made inter partes[16] unless he was *named* in that deed as a party.[17] This rule was modified in the mid-19th century,[18] and the current position is elucidated in section 56(1) of the Law of Property Act 1925. According to this provision,

> A person may take an immediate or other interest in land or other property, or the benefit of any condition, right of entry, covenant or agreement over or respecting land or other property, although he may not be named as a party to the conveyance or other instrument.

(a) The doctrine of contractual privity

Few statutory provisions have generated so much confusion as section 56(1), and its effects are still not entirely clear. It was at one time thought that this section had abrogated the entire doctrine of privity of contract,[19] but the rather ambivalent utterances of the House of Lords in *Beswick v Beswick*[20] indicate on balance that this is not so. Thus, if A covenants with B to confer a benefit upon C, C is still disabled from enforcing the covenant, since he is excluded from doing so by the rules of privity.[1]

(b) Generic descriptions

The better view appears to be that section 56(1) merely removes the old rule which restricted the enforceable benefit of a covenant to those parties who were expressly referred to *by name* in the original deed of covenant. After 1925 it is no longer a precondition of a successful claim to a covenanted benefit that the claimant-beneficiary should actually have been *named* in the covenant. It is sufficient that he is designated as a covenantee under some *generic* description.[2]

15 Thus if C is *named* in the covenant as a covenantee, as for instance where A covenants expressly with B *and* C to confer benefit upon C, C is automatically entitled to sue in the event of breach, precisely because he is one of the contracting parties.

16 A deed made inter partes is to be distinguished from a *deed poll*, ie a deed executed unilaterally by one party.

17 See *Lord Southampton v Brown* (1827) 6 B & C 718 at 719f, 108 ER 615 at 616.

18 Real Property Act 1845, s 5.

19 See eg *Smith and Snipes Hall Farm Ltd v River Douglas Catchment Board* [1949] 2 KB 500 at 514ff per Denning LJ; *Beswick v Beswick* [1966] Ch 538 at 556G-557C per Lord Denning MR.

20 [1968] AC 58. See (1967) 30 MLR 687 (G.H. Treitel).

1 See *White v Bijou Mansions Ltd* [1937] Ch 610 at 624f, [1938] Ch 351 at 365.

2 It is possible that this restrictive construction of section 56(1) of the Law of Property Act 1925 has not entirely refuted the idea that a third party may sue for the benefit of a contract. In *Beswick v Beswick* [1968] AC 58 the House of Lords thought that section 56(1) could not facilitate the recovery of a contractual benefit by a non-party. However, a majority of the House formed this view on the assumption that section 56(1) is confined to real property and not because such a recovery is necessarily excluded by the contractual doctrine of privity. Only two judges in the House of Lords explicitly rejected Lord Denning's view of section 56(1) (see [1968] AC 58 at 94C-D per Lord Pearce, at 106A-E per Lord Upjohn).

Thus, for instance, a covenantor may covenant with a named party (eg the vendor of land) and also with the 'owners for the time being' of identified adjoining plots of land. In such cases the benefit of the covenant may be enforced not only by the *named* covenanting party but also by those other owners who are included in the category of covenantees, albeit that their inclusion is merely by generic reference.[3] The sole limitation on this application of section 56(1) is the requirement that those who are generically described as relevant covenantees may claim the covenanted benefit only if they are existing and identifiable individuals at the date of that covenant.[4]

(2) Transmission of the benefit of a covenant

With the foregoing qualifications, a covenant is clearly enforceable in contract by the original covenantee,[5] but greater difficulty is posed by the question whether the benefit[6] of this covenant can be transmitted at law to a third party. The common law lays down fairly strict conditions as to the passing of such a benefit.[7]

These conditions have acquired a recent prominence as the critical factor in determining the enforceability, following assignment of a leasehold reversion, of any covenant which has been made with the landlord by a surety as guarantor of the due performance of the tenant's leasehold covenants.[8] The landlord and the surety are themselves bound in a contractual nexus, but a later assignee of the landlord's reversion is, of course, unable to claim any such basis of enforcement against the surety (see *Fig.* 73). Moreover, the surety has no relevant interest in land and thus no privity of estate can be shown between him and the assignee. Nor can the assignee plead the benefit of section 141 of the Law of Property Act 1925,[9] which applies only to covenants between landlord and tenant.[10] In *P. & A. Swift Investments v Combined English Stores Group Plc*,[11] the House of Lords was therefore compelled to predicate the surety's liability to an assignee by reference to the rules which govern the enforcement of covenants between *freeholders* rather

3 See eg *Wiles v Banks* (1985) 50 P & CR 80 at 87ff (ante, p 1116).
4 See *Kelsey v Dodd* (1881) 52 LJ Ch 34 at 39; *Forster v Elvet Colliery Co Ltd* [1908] 1 KB 629 at 636f; *Grant v Edmondson* [1931] 1 Ch 1 at 27; *Bohn v Miller Bros Pty Ltd* [1953] VLR 354 at 358; *In re Ecclesiastical Comrs for England's Conveyance* [1936] Ch 430 at 441f; *Re Wilsons' Settlements* [1972] NZLR 13 at 32. Thus section 56(1) does not enable a covenant to confer benefit directly upon *future* purchasers of plots of land. A covenant which purports to be made with a named owner of land 'and with his successors in title' does not bring the successors in title within the scope of section 56(1). In such a case, only the named individual can rank as a covenantee of the promise.
5 See *P. & A. Swift Investments v Combined English Stores Group Plc* [1989] AC 632 at 639G. The covenantee's right to enforce is, of course, terminated if he assigns the benefit of the covenant to some other party. For a similar principle in the context of leaseholds, see Chapter 18 (ante, p 859).
6 For an explanation of this use of the term 'benefit' and the corresponding term 'burden', see Chapter 21 (ante, p 1063).
7 See E.H. Scamell (1954) 18 Conv (NS) 546.
8 Ante, p 857. The question is, of course, a live question only where there has been no express assignment of the benefit of the covenant as a chose in action (post, p 1132).
9 Ante, p 854.
10 See *P. & A. Swift Investments v Combined English Stores Group Plc* [1989] AC 632 at 639G per Lord Oliver of Aylmerton.
11 [1989] AC 632.

than under the rules which regulate *leasehold* covenants. As Lord Templeman noted, however, the indirect (and perhaps ironic) effect of this application of principle is to render the tenant's surety a 'quasi tenant who volunteers to be a substitute or twelfth man for the tenant's team', with the result that the surety is 'subject to the same rules and regulations as the player he replaces.'[12]

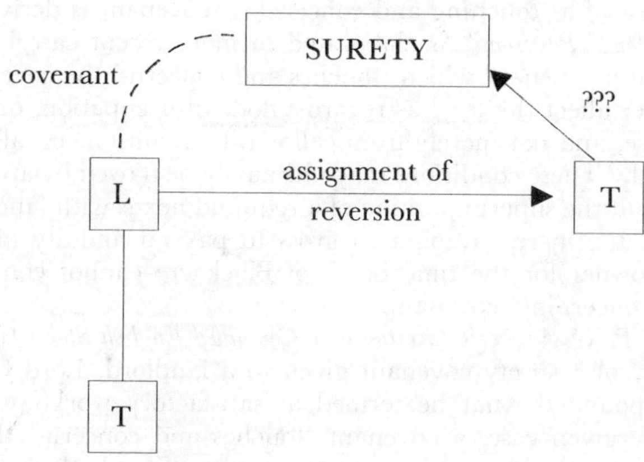

Fig. 73

In order that the benefit of a covenant should run at law with the covenantee's land, several conditions—as most recently confirmed by the House of Lords in *P. & A. Swift Investments*[13]—must be satisfied.

(a) *The covenant must 'touch and concern' the land*

It must be shown that the covenant 'touches and concerns' the land owned by the covenantee, ie that it was entered into for the benefit of the covenantee's *land* and not merely for his personal benefit.

It is, of course notoriously difficult to attribute a precise meaning to the terminology of 'touching and concerning' (or indeed to equivalent references to 'accommodation' in the law of restrictive covenants[14]). However, the clear effect of the 'touching and concerning' requirement is nowadays to limit the quasi-legislative powers of covenanting parties to objective purposes of land planning.[15] It has also been said that the limiting effect of the 'touch and concern' condition 'eliminates the possibility of creating modern variations of feudal serfdom'.[16] Whether or not this is entirely true, the requirement certainly confers upon the courts an important power to determine the permissible limits of private planning of land use.

12 [1989] AC 632 at 638A.
13 [1989] AC 632 at 639H–640A per Lord Oliver of Aylmerton.
14 Post, p 1143.
15 For a vigorous argument that the 'touch and concern' requirement should be abolished, see S.F. French, 73 Cornell L Rev 928 at 939 (1987–88). For a counter-argument that the requirement promotes the efficient allocation of the responsibilities of land management, see J.E. Stake, *Toward an Economic Understanding of Touch and Concern*, (1988) Duke LJ 925.
16 U. Reichman, 55 S Cal L Rev 1177 at 1233 (1982).

The test of whether a covenant 'touches and concerns' the land[17] is essentially the same as that which is applied in the context of leasehold covenants,[18] with the obvious qualification that the land in question here is of course the land of the covenantee rather than any land of the covenantor.[19] It must, in effect, be shown that between the covenant and the covenantee's land there is some connection which approximates to that required by the equitable rules of annexation.[20]

The classic test of a 'touching and concerning' covenant is derived from *Mayor of Congleton v Pattison*.[1] As elaborated in more recent case law,[2] this test requires that a covenant which 'touches and concerns' the covenantee's land 'must either affect the land as regards mode of occupation, or it must be such as per se, and not merely from collateral circumstances, affects the value of the land.'[3] These conditions may ultimately be flawed by an element of circularity,[4] but the superimposition of a required nexus with land means, for instance, that a mere covenant in gross to pay an annuity of £x per annum to the owner for the time being of Blackacre cannot constitute a 'touching and concerning' covenant.[5]

In dealing in *P. & A. Swift Investments v Combined English Stores Group Plc*[6] with the quality of a surety covenant given to a landlord, Lord Oliver of Aylmerton propounded what he termed a 'satisfactory working test' for whether, in any given case, a covenant 'touches and concerns' the land. *First*, a 'touching and concerning' covenant must benefit only the reversioner

17 For this purpose the covenantee's land is usually a corporeal hereditament, but may also include an incorporeal hereditament such as an easement (see *Gaw v Córas Iompair Éireann* [1953] IR 232 at 257f) or indeed may, as in the case of a surety covenant under a lease, include the covenantee's reversion on the lease (*P. & A. Swift Investments v Combined English Stores Group Plc* [1989] AC 632 at 640E per Lord Oliver of Aylmerton). See W.N. Harrison, (1957) 3 U of Qd LJ 165.

18 Ante, p 855. See *P. & A. Swift Investments v Combined English Stores Group Plc* [1989] AC 632 at 640E-F per Lord Oliver of Aylmerton. In its turn, the 'touch and concern' test is in substance the same test as that which stipulates that restrictive covenants and easements must 'accommodate' (or confer benefit upon) the land owned by their respective grantees (ante, pp 1065, 1129). See *Application of Fox* (1981) 2 BPR 9310 at 9312, 9314 per Wootten J, who pointed out that the transfer of the phrase 'touching and concerning' to freehold covenants 'has created some confusion'.

19 It is in fact irrelevant whether the covenantor has any land to be burdened. See *The Prior's Case* (1368) YB 42 Edw III, pl 14, fol 3A. The rule against perpetuities has no application to covenants which touch and concern the land (*Coronation Street Industrial Properties Ltd v Ingall Industries Ltd* [1989] 1 WLR 304 at 307H per Lord Templeman).

20 Post, p 1150.

1 (1808) 10 East 130 at 135, 103 ER 725 at 727 (ante, p 856).

2 See *Rogers v Hosegood* [1900] 2 Ch 388 at 395; *Smith and Snipes Hall Farm Ltd v River Douglas Catchment Board* [1949] 2 KB 500 at 506 per Tucker LJ; *P. & A. Swift Investments v Combined English Stores Group Plc* [1989] AC 632 at 640F.

3 In *Smith and Snipes Hall Farm Ltd v River Douglas Catchment Board* [1949] 2 KB 500 at 508, Tucker LJ ruled that the required connection between the covenant and the land concerned need not appear expressly in the terms of the covenant but may be proved by extrinsic evidence: *'Id certum est quod certum reddi potest'*.

4 Ante, p 855.

5 See *P. & A. Swift Investments v Combined English Stores Group Plc* [1989] AC 632 at 639D-E per Lord Oliver of Aylmerton. However, a surety's covenant for the due performance of a 'touching and concerning' covenant entered into by a tenant (eg a covenant to pay rent) does—necessarily—constitute a covenant which touches and concerns the land, even though it comprises a money obligation to the covenantee ([1989] AC 632 at 637H per Lord Templeman).

6 [1989] AC 632 at 642E-F.

for the time being, so that, if separated from the reversion, it ceases to be of benefit to the covenantee. *Second*, the covenant must affect the nature, quality, mode of user or value of the land of the reversioner. *Third*, the covenant must not be expressed to be personal (ie must not have been given only to a specific reversioner or in respect of the obligations only of a specific tenant). On this basis the House of Lords was able, in *P. & A. Swift Investments*, to hold that a guarantor's surety covenant sufficiently 'touched and concerned' land to run with the covenantee's reversion and become enforceable by the latter's assignee. According to Lord Oliver, the mere fact 'that a covenant is to pay a sum of money will not prevent it from touching and concerning the land so long as the three foregoing conditions are satisfied and the covenant is connected with something to be done on, to or in relation to the land'.[7]

(b) *The covenantee must have a legal estate in the land benefited*

A covenant can run with the land at law only if made with a covenantee who has a legal estate in the land benefited.[8] No benefit can pass at law where the original covenantee has a merely equitable interest in his land.

(c) *The assignee of the land must have a legal estate in the land benefited*

There used to be a rule at common law that any third party who sought to claim at law the benefit of a covenant relating to land must show that he had the *same* legal estate in that land as the original covenantee. In other words, if the original covenantee was an owner in fee simple, the benefit of the covenant could pass only to a third party who similarly owned the land in fee simple.[9] However, this requirement was not imposed in *The Prior's Case*[10] itself, and always constituted a somewhat doubtful feature of the common law rules on the passing of the benefit. In *Smith and Snipes Hall Farm Ltd v River Douglas Catchment Board*,[11] the Court of Appeal took the view the common law requirement had finally been abrogated by section 78(1) of the Law of Property Act 1925.[12] In *Smith*'s case the original covenantee had later sold his dominant tenement to P1, who in his turn leased the land to P2. The Court allowed an action for damages for breach of covenant on the suit of both P1 (the owner in fee simple) and P2 (who held merely a term of years). It was held that section 78(1) rendered the covenant in question enforceable on behalf of not only the original covenantee but all successors in title and all persons deriving title from such successors. It was sufficient merely that subsequent claimants of the covenanted benefit should hold *a* legal estate in the relevant land.[13]

7 [1989] AC 632 at 642F.
8 *Webb v Russell* (1789) 3 Term Rep 393 at 402, 100 ER 639 at 644.
9 See eg *Westhoughton UDC v Wigan Coal and Iron Co Ltd* [1919] 1 Ch 159 at 171.
10 (1368) YB 42 Edw III, pl 14, fol 3A.
11 [1949] 2 KB 500.
12 Section 78(1) of the Law of Property Act 1925 provides that a covenant 'relating to any land of the covenantee shall be deemed to be made with the covenantee and his successors in title and the persons deriving title under him or them, and shall have effect as if such successors and other persons were expressed' (post, p 1154).
13 See also *P. & A. Swift Investments v Combined English Stores Group Plc* [1989] AC 632 at 639H per Lord Oliver of Aylmerton.

(d) There must have been an intention that the benefit should run with the land owned by the covenantee at the date of the covenant

In *Smith and Snipes Hall Farm Ltd v River Douglas Catchment Board*,[14] Tucker LJ indicated that it must be shown that 'it was the intention of the parties that the benefit [of the covenant] should run with the land'. This element of intention provides perhaps the central and most important precondition for the running of a covenanted benefit at law.[15]

(e) Other means of transmitting covenanted benefits at law

If the foregoing conditions are satisfied, the benefit of a covenant (whether positive or negative) may pass at law to a third party who takes an estate in the benefited land. The legal rules for the transmission of benefit have, in the main, existed since the earliest days of the common law. Equity was later to formulate its own rules for the passing of the benefit of covenants, and did so on the assumption that it was following the rules laid down by the common law.[16] However, the common law rules continue to apply in cases which are not covered under the rules developed by equity, as for instance where the covenantor has no land upon which the burden of the covenant can be imposed.

(f) Statutory covenants for title

There is a special statutory provision in relation to the most important covenants relating to land, ie covenants in respect of title. Various covenants for title are implied by section 76 of the Law of Property Act 1925. Section 76(6) provides that the benefit of these covenants is 'annexed and incident to, and shall go with, the estate or interest of the implied covenantee, and shall be capable of being enforced by every person in whom that estate or interest is, for the whole or any part thereof, from time to time vested'.

(g) Assignment of choses in action

There exist further statutory means which facilitate the transmission of covenanted benefits at common law. The benefit of a covenant which is not exclusively personal may, for instance, be assigned as a chose in action under section 136 of the Law of Property Act 1925. In order to be effective at law, this form of assignment requires to be in writing, and express written notice of the assignment must be served upon the covenantor.

14 [1949] 2 KB 500 at 506. See, however, D.W. Elliott (1956) 20 Conv (NS) 43 at 53. *Smith and Snipes Hall Farm Ltd v River Douglas Catchment Board* was followed in *Williams v Unit Construction Co Ltd* (1955) 19 Conv (NS) 262.

15 In *Smith and Snipes Hall Farm Ltd v River Douglas Catchment Board* [1949] 2 KB 500, the deed in question showed that the object of the covenant was 'to improve the drainage of land liable to flooding and prevent future flooding'.

16 Post, p 1149.

(3) Transmission of the burden of a covenant

Whereas the benefit of a covenant can pass at law to third parties, it is a dogmatic principle of the common law that a covenanted burden cannot pass in such a way as to become directly enforceable against assigns or successors in title of the original covenantor.[17] In *Austerberry v Oldham Corpn*[18] the Court of Appeal confirmed as a clear rule of law that the burden of a covenant between freeholders cannot run with the land.[19] This rule is, of course, consonant with the general principle that the benefit, but never the burden, of a contract can be assigned to a third party.[20] It was indeed this unwillingness to hold covenants enforceable at law against the covenantor's successors in title which ultimately made it necessary for equity to provide a means by which at least the burden of restrictive covenants could be made to run with the land.[1]

(a) Modern disadvantages of non-transmissible burdens

Although the principle of *Austerberry v Oldham Corpn* was clearly motivated by a policy that land should remain unfettered for future generations, the implications of that decision are nowadays a matter of considerable disadvantage. It has been pointed out, for instance, that the principle 'impedes transactions in land which have become socially desirable.'[2] The anxiety of judges in the 19th century to limit the kinds of incumbrance which might be imposed upon the freehold estate is not particularly apposite under the vastly changed conditions of modern life where most people live in large cities. The property law of the 19th century was highly individualistic and made little provision for 'freeholders living like battery hens in urban developments' where much of the land area may consist of amenities which

17 It is one of the eternal mysteries of English land law that section 79(1) of the Law of Property Act 1925 seems never to have been invoked as a means of transmitting the burden of a positive covenant from one freeholder to another. This provision declares that a covenant relating to the covenantor's land 'is deemed to be made by the covenantor on behalf of himself his successors in title and the persons deriving title under him or them, and. . .shall have effect as if such successors or other persons were expressed'. The New Zealand equivalent of this provision (Property Law Act 1952, s 64) has been invoked in order to permit the transmission between freeholders of a positive duty to repair a right of way (see *S.J. Allen (South Island) Ltd v Crowe* (1980) NZ Recent Law 118). See also [1970] NZLJ 67 (F.M. Brookfield).

18 (1885) 29 Ch D 750 at 781. See also *Jones v Price* [1965] 2 QB 618 at 633E-F, 639G, 646D; *Rhone v Stephens* (1993) 137 Sol Jo LB 46; *Application of Fox* (1981) 2 BPR 9310 at 9311f; *Government Insurance Office (N.S.W.) v K.A. Reed Services Pty Ltd* [1988] VR 829 at 837.

19 Lindley LJ thought that the burden of a positive covenant could run with the land only if the covenant amounted, upon the true construction, 'to either a grant of an easement, or a rent-charge, or some estate or interest in the land' ((1885) 29 Ch D 750 at 781).

20 The refusal to allow the burden of a positive covenant to run with the land clearly conflicts, however, with efficiency-based arguments, under which it is clearly preferable to allocate the relevant burden to the current owner of the servient land rather than the original promisor (see J.E. Stake, (1988) Duke LJ 925 at 954f).

1 Post, p 1137.

2 See H.W.R. Wade, [1972B] CLJ 157.

belong to none personally but which are socially necessary for all.[3] The non-transmissible character of positive burdens has, moreover, made it difficult to envisage the possibility of freehold conveyancing of flats.[4]

In spite of the substantial criticism which it has attracted over the years,[5] the rule in *Austerberry v Oldham Corpn* still remains in full force. In *Rhone v Stephens*[6] the Court of Appeal, while hinting that the House of Lords might feel able to 'abolish or modify' it, expressed itself to be entirely bound by the century-old precedent. For the moment, therefore, the only relief from the obstructive aspects of the rule is to be found in various forms of avoidance device.

(b) Avoidance devices

The common law principle in respect of covenanted burdens is so profoundly inconvenient that various devices have been used to circumvent it and achieve by indirect means a result which is impossible by direct means.[7] These devices include the following:

(i) Chain of covenants Although the burden of a freehold covenant cannot be made to run with the covenantor's land, something like this result can be circuitously achieved by causing a chain of indemnity covenants to be undertaken by successive purchasers of the covenantor's land.[8] The original covenantor still remains liable, of course, on the terms of his initial covenant but, in the event of a violation by a subsequent purchaser, the original covenantor is able to sue on the indemnity covenant in order to recover any damages which he may have been required to pay to the original covenantee (or his successors in title). The chain of indemnity covenants may extend indefinitely, each succeeding purchaser of the covenantor's land entering into a covenant to indemnify his predecessor in title in respect of any future breaches.[9]

In practice, however, the utility of the chain of covenants is lessened or

3 See [1972B] CLJ 157 at 158, for the view that the rule in *Austerberry v Oldham Corpn* is inappropriate today in view of 'the tendency of an overcrowded population to live in "developments" where they are more and more dependent upon shared amenities such as roads, stairways and gardens, and where lapses by individual owners from the general standards of repair and maintenance will affect the amenity and value and even perhaps the physical stability of neighbouring homes. The law has failed to provide any mechanism by which the necessary obligations can be made to run satisfactorily with freehold land.' See also C.D. Bell, (1984) 128 SJ 323.

4 Ante, p 9.

5 The Law Commission has recommended abolition of the rule in *Austerberry v Oldham Corpn* (post, p 1167).

6 (1993) 137 Sol Jo LB 46.

7 See A. Prichard, (1973) 37 Conv (NS) 194.

8 A more effective manipulation of the device of successive covenants is the practice under which the original covenant requires that all successors in title of the covenantor enter into direct covenants with the original covenantee (see S. Bright, [1988] Conv 99 at 100). Such a requirement may be made the subject of a restriction on a registered title (ante, p 182), but the practice is still vulnerable to the possibility that the chain of responsibility may break down.

9 In *Rhone v Stephens* (1993) 137 Sol Jo LB 46, Nourse LJ expressed the view that the retention of the rule in *Austerberry v Oldham Corpn* is all the more difficult to justify where, under a chain of indemnity covenants, each successor in title has clear notice of the original covenant.

even destroyed by reason of the death or disappearance of the original covenantor or because the chain of indemnities is interrupted. A further disadvantage with the device of indemnity covenants is the fact that even if the chain of covenants remains intact, the only remedy available to the covenantor is an action in damages, whereas the remedy which he really wants is an injunction or order of specific performance.

(ii) Conversion of leasehold into freehold There are two statutory means by which a long lease may be converted into a freehold estate. Under section 153 of the Law of Property Act 1925, a long lease[10] may be enlarged into a freehold if certain conditions are fulfilled. If this occurs, the freehold becomes subject 'to all the same covenants. . .as the term would have been subject to if it had not been so enlarged'.[11] This device may be significant in the present context since the freehold is then governed by the principle which applies to leasehold covenants, ie the principle that the burden of covenants may run with the estate.[12] A similar result is brought about by the enfranchisement of a long lease under the Leasehold Reform Act 1967.[13]

(iii) Doctrine of 'mutual benefit and burden' Once again, it is possible that the burden of a freehold covenant may pass indirectly to a successor in title of the covenantor by virtue of the doctrine of 'mutual benefit and burden'.[14] On this basis a successor in title who claims the benefit of a freehold covenant would be equally subject to its burden.[15] Indeed, in *Tito v Waddell* (No 2),[16] Megarry V-C held that the doctrine covers not merely successors in title but also anybody 'whose connection with the transaction creating the benefit and burden is sufficient to show that he has some claim to the benefit whether or not he has a valid title to it.'

It is not at all clear, however, that the doctrine of 'mutual benefit and burden' has any proper application beyond its original field of application, ie where the claimant of a covenanted benefit had been named as a party in a deed containing the covenant but had not personally executed that deed.[17] The view has been forcefully put that any wider application of the

10 A long lease is defined for this purpose as a lease which was originally created for at least 300 years of which not less than 200 years are unexpired, which involves the payment of no rent or money value, and which is not liable to be determined by re-entry for condition broken (see Law of Property Act 1925, s 153(1), (2)).

11 Law of Property Act 1925, s 153(8).

12 Ante, p 854. See T.P.D. Taylor, (1958) 22 Conv (NS) 101.

13 Leasehold Reform Act 1967, s 8(3) (ante, p 767).

14 Ante, p 152. See *Halsall v Brizell* [1957] Ch 169 at 182f; (1957) 73 LQR 154 (R.E.M.); (1957) 21 Conv (NS) 160 (F.R. Crane); [1957] CLJ 35 (H.W.R. Wade); *E.R. Ives Investment Ltd v High* [1967] 2 QB 379 at 394B-E.

15 The doctrine of 'mutual benefit and burden' has been applied, for instance, to impose correlative burdens of maintenance and repair on neighbours who send their water into a common drainage system (*Hopgood v Brown* [1955] 1 WLR 213 at 226) and on purchasers of houses on a building estate who have the benefit of using the roads on that estate (*Halsall v Brizell* [1957] Ch 169 at 182f). See also *Montague v Long* (1972) 24 P & CR 240 at 247f

16 [1977] Ch 106 at 303E. See also (1977) 41 Conv (NS) 432 (F.R. Crane); E.P. Aughterson, [1985] Conv 12.

17 See *Tito v Waddell* (No 2) [1977] Ch 106 at 289D. It is to be observed that *Halsall v Brizell* [1957] Ch 169, the authority on which many assertions of the doctrine rests, was argued and decided in one day and that the reference to the doctrine was strictly obiter.

doctrine 'confounds the law relating to covenants affecting land',[18] by indiscriminately making almost any covenant an indefinitely binding incumbrance on land. Despite its initial attractions, the doctrine may be 'in truth a mere maxim masquerading as a rule of law, false and misleading. . .when read literally.'[19]

(iv) Reservation of a right of entry It is possible to reserve a right of entry in respect of land (usually annexed to an 'estate rentcharge'[20]), on terms that the right of entry becomes exercisable on events which amount to a violation of a positive covenant.[1] Such a right of entry, if duly created, becomes a legal interest in the land[2] and thus runs with the burdened land so as to affect the successors in title of the covenantor.[3]

3. COVENANTS IN EQUITY

One of the most revolutionary contributions made by equity in the area of property comprises the development during the 19th century of special equitable rules governing covenants between freeholders. This body of rules was of great importance in regulating the urban and industrial development of England before the advent of planning legislation. The new equitable regime relating to covenants has come to supplement, and indeed very largely displace, the common law rules relating to the transmission of the benefit and burden of covenants.

(1) Developments in the case law

The mid-19th century was a period of significant expansion, when the tension was greatest between the desire to keep land unfettered by private covenants (and therefore profitable for industrial development) and the conflicting desire to curb the effects of commercial and urban growth (by preserving residential amenity for the private householder). These conflicting policies were reflected in the case law of the period. In *Keppell v Bailey*,[4] for instance, Lord Brougham

18 *Government Insurance Office (N.S.W.) v K.A. Reed Services Pty Ltd* [1988] VR 829 at 840 per Brooking J.

19 *Government Insurance Office (N.S.W.) v K.A. Reed Services Pty Ltd* [1988] VR 829 at 841 per Brooking J. See *Rhone v Stephens* (1993) 137 Sol Jo LB 46, where the Court of Appeal declined to uphold the transmission of the burden of a positive covenant on the basis of the 'benefit and burden' doctrine, where the reciprocal burden claimed was 'technical or minimal'.

20 An 'estate rentcharge' (ante, p 72) is a rentcharge created specifically for the purpose of ensuring the enforceability of covenants affecting the land to which the rentcharge relates or of ensuring payments towards the provision of services or carrying out of maintenance or repairs or any other financial liability relating to the land charged (Rentcharges Act 1977, s 2(4)). See S. Bright, [1988] Conv 99 at 101ff.

1 See *Shiloh Spinners Ltd v Harding* [1973] AC 691 at 717C, G-H (ante, p 153). It is, of course, possible that relief may be granted against forfeiture (ante, p 812).

2 Ante, p 72. Compare the use of essentially fictitious rentcharges as a means of enforcing positive covenants between freeholders. See *Clem Smith Nominees Pty Ltd v Farrelly* (1980) 20 SASR 227 at 253; *Davison Properties Ltd v Manukau City Council* (1980) NZ Recent Law 225; B. Hunter, (1963–66) 2 Adelaide L Rev 208.

3 The right is not subject to the rule against perpetuities (Perpetuities and Accumulations Act 1964, s 11(1); Law of Property Act 1925, s 121).

4 (1834) 2 My & K 517 at 535, 39 ER 1042 at 1049.

refused to allow that 'incidents of a novel kind can be devised and attached to land at the fancy and caprice of any owner.' He thus declined to enforce the burden of a covenant against a successor in title of the original covenantor, taking the view that such a burden, if enforced, would fetter the use and development of the land in perpetuity.[5]

(a) *The decision in Tulk v Moxhay*

The emphasis had altered significantly by the time *Tulk v Moxhay*[6] came to be decided by the courts in 1847. The ruling of Lord Cottenham LC in this case is usually taken as marking the inception of a major development in the equitable rules concerning freehold covenants,[7] thus reversing the earlier disinclination of equity to allow land to be sterilised by the imposition of permanently binding freehold covenants.

In *Tulk v Moxhay*, the plaintiff had sold a vacant piece of land in Leicester Square to E, who covenanted on behalf of himself, his heirs and his assigns that he would keep and maintain that land 'in an open state, uncovered with any buildings, in neat and ornamental order.' The land subsequently passed by a further conveyance into the hands of the defendant. The defendant's conveyance had not contained any such covenant as that spelt out in the original conveyance from the plaintiff, but it was common ground that he had had notice of the restrictive covenant imposed in respect of the open land. When the defendant attempted to build on the open land in defiance of the covenant, the plaintiff sought an injunction to prevent him from doing so. Lord Cottenham LC upheld a decision at first instance granting the plaintiff the relief required.

Lord Cottenham took an entirely different view from that adopted earlier by Lord Brougham in *Keppell v Bailey*. In the present case, Lord Cottenham held that an injunction should be granted restraining the defendant from acting in violation of the restrictive covenant, not because the burden of such a covenant might run either at law or in equity, but rather because equity asserts a stern view on matters of conscience. The Lord Chancellor accepted the argument that the real question was

> not whether the covenant runs with the land, but whether a party shall be permitted to use the land in a manner inconsistent with the contract entered into by his vendor, and with notice of which he purchased. Of course, the price would be affected by the covenant, and nothing could be more inequitable than that the original purchaser should be able to sell the property the next day for a greater price, in consideration of the assignee being allowed to escape from the liability which he had himself undertaken.[8]

In order to preclude such an unconscionable outcome, Lord Cottenham concluded that the court should enforce the relevant covenant against any party purchasing with notice of it, 'for if an equity is attached to the property

5 (1834) 2 My & K 517 at 536f, 39 ER 1042 at 1049f.
6 (1848) 2 Ph 774, 41 ER 1143.
7 It has been pointed out that the decision reached in *Tulk v Moxhay* had been anticipated in two poorly reported cases decided by Sir Lancelot Shadwell, *Whatman v Gibson* (1838) 9 Sim 196 at 207, 59 ER 333 at 338, and *Mann v Stephens* (1846) 15 Sim 377 at 378, 60 ER 665 at 666. See A.W.B. Simpson, *A History of The Land Law* (2nd edn Oxford 1986), p 257f.
8 (1848) 2 Ph 774 at 777f, 41 ER 1143 at 1144.

by the owner, no one purchasing with notice of that equity can stand in a different situation from the party from whom he purchased.'[9]

(b) The reception of Tulk v Moxhay in the case law

The decision in *Tulk v Moxhay* was broadly based. Equity was prepared to intervene in restraint of any unconscionable conduct in respect of a contractual undertaking of which the wrongdoer—although not himself a contracting party—nevertheless had notice. The argument which had prevailed before Lord Cottenham LC was capable of wide application. Indeed, the view adopted in *Tulk v Moxhay*, far from leading to a sterilisation of land use, could even be seen as promoting the commerciability of land. As Lord Cottenham clearly recognised, unless restrictive covenants could be enforced against the covenantor's successors, 'it would be impossible for an owner of land to sell part of it without incurring the risk of rendering what he retains worthless.'[10] The ruling in *Tulk v Moxhay* was, accordingly, applied with enthusiasm during the years which followed that decision. The ruling was applied to both positive and negative covenants; it was applied on behalf of litigants who held no estate in the land benefited by the covenant; it was even applied outside the realm of real property.[11]

(c) The evolution of a new proprietary interest

The doctrine in *Tulk v Moxhay* had a dramatic effect upon both the law of contract and the law of property. The covenantee was widely regarded as having not merely a contractual interest in the performance of the covenant made with him, but also a *proprietary* interest in the land of the covenantor. Moreover, the covenantee's proprietary interest could run with the land of the covenantor, so as to bind all those into whose hands that land came, until eventually the covenantor's land was conveyed to a bona fide purchaser of a legal estate for value without notice of the covenant. The covenantee was thus given a contractual right to control activities on the land of the covenantor, and, by virtue of the equitable doctrine, this contractual right enlarged into—and arrogated to itself the status of—a proprietary right in land.[12] Because of his new power to influence user by the covenantor and his successors, the covenantee was indeed rightly viewed as having been allocated some of the 'property' in the servient land.

(d) Gradual restriction of the scope of Tulk v Moxhay

It was inevitable that, with the passage of time, the broad doctrine of *Tulk v Moxhay* should be somewhat modified. Aware of the potential scope of the doctrine, the courts had begun even during the closing decades of the 19th century to limit its application by defining precise qualities which

9 (1848) 2 Ph 774 at 778, 41 ER 1143 at 1144.
10 (1848) 2 Ph 774 at 777, 41 ER 1143 at 1144.
11 See A.W.B. Simpson, op cit, p 259.
12 See S. Gardner, (1982) 98 LQR 279 at 293ff.

required to be possessed by covenants before they could rank as equitable interests in the land of the covenantor.[13] In *London and South Western Railway Co v Gomm*,[14] Jessel MR was already re-interpreting the doctrine in *Tulk v Moxhay* as 'either an extension in equity of the doctrine of *Spencer's Case* to another line of cases, or else an extension in equity of the doctrine of negative easements.'[15] Thus the new doctrine had its 'wings clipped'.[16] Covenants began to be enforced against third parties on the same conditions as attached to the enforcement of easements, with the result that equity imposed such extra requirements as that there be a servient and a dominant tenement.[17]

Attention must now be turned to the limitations which equity thus imposed on the category of covenants capable of enforcement against successors in title.

(2) Characteristics of enforceable covenants

As the doctrine in *Tulk v Moxhay* was slowly refined, it became clear that certain requirements must be fulfilled in respect of a covenant relating to land before this covenant could be enforced in equity otherwise than between the original parties. This imposition of strict and limiting criteria was initially intended to prevent the proliferation of undesirable 'clogs upon the title' of land.[18] Tight controls were thus exerted not only over the range of social and economic interests accorded protection in the law of restrictive covenants, but also over the technical operation of the rules governing enforcement.

While something of this cautious concern still remains today at the core of the legal response, it is clear that in more recent times the courts have adopted a more sympathetic view of restrictive covenants. This relaxation of approach may in part reflect a general change in community attitudes towards the importance of preserving the attractiveness of local environments.[19] It may also owe something to increasing recognition of the availability of means for scrutiny of the contemporary merit of restrictions and, where appropriate, for the modification or discharge of unnecessary or outdated covenants.[20]

13 See H.W.R. Wade, (1952) 68 LQR 337 at 348. It has been suggested that the laissez faire approach to land obligations following *Tulk v Moxhay* was ended when it was realised that the equitable theory had been widely manipulated for the purpose of enforcing commercial monopolistic interests. 'By defeating arrangements aimed at capturing part of the market in perpetuity, title was once again salvaged from becoming a permanent carrier of all sorts of obligations' (see U. Reichman, 7 J Legal Stud 139 at 147 (1978)).

14 (1882) 20 Ch D 562 at 583. See also *In re Nisbet and Potts' Contract* [1905] 1 Ch 391 at 397 per Farwell J.

15 This did not, and does not, necessarily mean that restrictive covenants in fact *are* easements (see *Norton v Kilduff* [1974] Qd R 47 at 53E-G per Hart J). See also *White v Lauder Developments Ltd* (1976) 60 DLR (3d) 419 at 427.

16 See *Challis*, p 185.

17 See eg *Newton Abbot Co-Operative Society Ltd v Williamson & Treadgold Ltd* [1952] Ch 286 at 293 per Upjohn J.

18 Ante, p 1125.

19 See *Application of Fox* (1981) 2 BPR 9310 at 9321 per Wootten J.

20 Post, p 1165.

(a) The covenant must be negative or restrictive of the user of land

If the application of *Tulk v Moxhay* was to be limited by analogy with the doctrine of negative easements, the first limiting factor to emerge was the rule that equity would take cognisance of only those covenants which are, in their nature, truly negative or restrictive of the user of land.[1] In *Haywood v Brunswick Permanent Benefit Building Society*,[2] the Court of Appeal held that equity had no jurisdiction to enforce against an assignee from the covenantor a positive covenant to build and repair.[3] In the view of Brett LJ, equity would henceforth enforce only those covenants 'restricting the mode of using the land'.[4] Thus, from at least this point onwards, the burden of a positive covenant became unenforceable, either at law or in equity, against successors of the original covenantor. Furthermore, since the purview of equity was now confined to restrictive covenants, the remedy given by equity in respect of enforceable restrictive covenants became pre-eminently the remedy of injunction.

An additional corollary of this limiting approach was, of course, that the emerging regime applicable to restrictive covenants had no relevance to purely personal covenants which did not constrain the mode of user of a servient tenement. In a strict sense a restrictive covenant must 'control the use of the land itself and not simply control a party to the agreement',[5] even if such control has the effect of 'indirectly restricting the use of the land'.[6] It has been said, although again with some danger of beguiling circuity, that the test of a true restrictive covenant is that it must create on behalf of the covenantee 'an interest in the covenantor's land.'[7]

(i) Criterion of negative or restrictive quality The question whether a covenant is *restrictive* always involves a test of substance. A covenant phrased in a

1 See C.D. Bell, *Tulk v Moxhay Revisited*, [1981] Conv 55. For the view that the doctrine in *Tulk v Moxhay*, as originally formulated, applied only to negative covenants, compare R. Griffith, *Tulk v Moxhay Reclarified*, [1983] Conv 29, but see also [1983] Conv 327 (C.D. Bell). The idea that the original doctrine related to both positive and negative covenants seems to be supported by *Morland v Cook* (1868) LR 6 Eq 252 at 265f; *Cooke v Chilcott* (1876) 3 Ch D 694 at 701f.

2 (1881) 8 QBD 403.

3 See *Shropshire CC v Edwards* (1983) 46 P & CR 270 at 274.

4 (1881) 8 QBD 403 at 408. In Brett LJ's view, 'if we enlarged the rule as it is now contended, we should be making a new equity, which we cannot do.' So great, however, is the obloquy nowadays attached to the rule in *Austerberry v Oldham Corpn* (ante, p 1133) that, in *Rhone v Stephens* (1993) 137 Sol Jo LB 46, Nourse LJ thought it hard to see why the rule in *Tulk v Moxhay* should not apply also to positive covenants.

5 See *Re Nylar Foods Ltd and Roman Catholic Episcopal Corp of Prince Rupert* (1988) 48 DLR (4th) 175 at 179 (where a covenant not to lease land to business competitors of the covenantee was treated not as a covenant restrictive of the user of the covenantor's land, but as a personal covenant in the nature of a restriction on alienation). Such a covenant would probably also fail on the ground that it does not accommodate the covenantee's land (post, p 1143). See also *Noble v Alley* [1951] 1 DLR 321 at 326.

6 See eg *Palm Beach Lands Pty Ltd v Marshall* (1988) NSW ConvR 55-411 at 57,773, where Needham J held that a covenant restricting building without the prior written approval of the covenantee was not a covenant which runs with the land but was merely a personal covenant. Compare, however, *Cryer v Scott Brothers (Sunbury) Ltd* (1988) 55 P & CR 183.

7 *White v Lauder Developments Ltd* (1975) 60 DLR (3d) 419 at 427.

positive manner may nevertheless constitute a restrictive covenant, as is the case, for instance, with a covenant 'to use the property for residential purposes only'.[8] Conversely, a covenant 'not to let the property fall into disrepair' is, on closer examination, a positive repairing covenant. A rule of thumb commonly used to test the nature of a covenant of dubious status is the question whether the covenant requires the expenditure of money for its performance. If the covenantor is required 'to put his hand into his pocket', the covenant cannot be negative in nature.[9]

(ii) Function of restrictive covenants Restrictive covenants provide an important means of securing the segregation of land uses, and are therefore entered into for a variety of purposes both commercial and aesthetic. Particularly prior to the advent of planning legislation on a more general scale, restrictive covenants offered an appropriate method for protecting such intangible qualities as the trading interests of a covenantee or the local atmosphere or 'tone' of a community. Indeed restrictive covenants have played a vital role in the history of urban planning by shielding residential development from the undesired impact of industrial or commercial forms of land use. In this way restrictive covenants have been used widely for the purpose of preserving the residential character of particular districts or neighbourhoods.[10]

Restrictive covenants commonly require the covenantor to refrain from conducting any trade or business on his land,[11] or from using a dwelling house for any purpose other than that of a 'private dwelling house',[12] or

8 *German v Chapman* (1877) 7 Ch D 271 at 277f, 280. See also *Abbey Homesteads (Developments) Ltd v Northamptonshire CC* (1987) 53 P & CR 1 at 5, where an agreement that land should be 'reserved for school purposes' was regarded by Lawton LJ as being a 'covenant. . .just as restrictive as the seminal one in *Tulk v Moxhay*. . .'. See also Parker LJ at 7.

9 See *Haywood v Brunswick Permanent Benefit Building Society* (1881) 8 QBD 403 at 409 per Cotton LJ.

10 So successful has been the device of the restrictive covenant in securing certain uniformities of urban development that some commentators have criticised the way in which 'strait jacket' restrictions have imposed an undesirable homogeneity on housing patterns, thereby invading 'aspects of home life previously left to personal choice'. See J.L. Winokur, *The Mixed Blessings of Promissory Servitudes: Toward Optimizing Economic Utility, Individual Liberty, and Personal Identity*, (1989) Wisc L Rev 1 at 4.

11 The enforcement of a restrictive covenant against business user may provide a solution for the vexed problem of the neighbour who keeps a huge lorry parked semi-permanently on the street outside his home (see *McDonagh v Cromie* [1982] 9 BNIL 72). See also *Balchin v Buckle* (1982) 126 SJ 412 (injunction and £250 damages). A covenant against trade or business user is breached by the presence of lodgers who make fixed periodical payments but not where a person merely agrees to share part of the expenses of a single household (*Heglibiston Establishment v Heyman* (1977) 36 P & CR 351 at 360).

12 See, however, *C. & G. Homes Ltd v Secretary of State for Health* [1991] Ch 365 at 384F, 387C, 390B, where the Court of Appeal held, somewhat controversially, that such a covenant was breached where a district health authority provided supervised housing for a group of former mental in-patients who were to be cared for in the community. The fact that this form of user fell within a permissible class of use under the relevant planning legislation was relevant to, but not conclusive of, the question of breach ([1991] Ch 365 at 380D-G).

from allowing any activity which causes nuisance, annoyance, danger or detriment to his neighbours.[13] Likewise a restrictive covenant may require the covenantor to refrain, for example, from building within a certain distance from the frontage of his property or even to refrain from erecting certain kinds of construction on his land.[14] A covenant not to 'cause or permit' a certain specified form of user is not, however, breached merely because the covenantor later agrees to sell the land affected to a third party who, to his knowledge, intends to engage in one of the proscribed forms of user.[15]

In recent times a particularly prolific source of modern restrictive covenants has been the statutory power conferred on local planning authorities to enter into an agreement with 'any person interested'[16] in land in their area for the purpose of 'restricting or regulating the development or use of the land'.[17] Such agreements were frequently pressed on developers of land in order to limit the extent of the proposed development and to guarantee the preservation of existing amenities within the locality concerned.[18] A 'section 106 agreement', once reached, operates either permanently or for such period

13 In *C. & G. Homes Ltd v Secretary of State for Health* [1991] Ch 365 at 386A-E, 387E however, the Court of Appeal declined to hold that such a covenant was breached by a sheltered housing project which had allegedly inflicted a financial detriment on neighbouring properties by reason of 'impaired marketability'. Relevant 'detriment' did not comprise a financial loss suffered in the exploitation of surrounding land, but dissociated from the actual enjoyment of that land. See also D. Hubbard, *Group Homes and Restrictive Covenants*, 57 UMKC L Rev 135 (1988-89).

14 See eg *Clothier v Snell* (1966) 198 Estates Gazette 27 at 28 (restrictive covenant against any building other than bungalow). A covenant prohibiting any building other than a private dwelling-house is infringed by the construction of flats (*Carmichael v Ripley Finance Co Ltd* [1974] 1 NZLR 557 at 559), but not by the erection of a covered swimming pool in the grounds of a private house (*Harlow v Hartog* (1978) 245 Estates Gazette 140). A covenant limiting construction on a site to one house is breached by a subsequent conversion of that one house into two dwelling units (*Lawton v S.H.E.V. Pty Ltd* [1969] 2 NSWR 238 at 241f). See also *Windsor Hotel (Newquay) Ltd v Allan* (1980) 77 Law Soc Gaz 733 (large barbeque held to be a 'building').

15 *Tophams Ltd v Earl of Sefton* [1967] 1 AC 50 at 64D, 68G, 75A-76A.

16 A 'person interested' in relevant land may include a *lessee*. It has therefore been possible, in the absence of an expressly drawn prohibition in the covenants of his lease, for a lessee to conclude a 'section 106 agreement' which unilaterally restricted the utility of the demised premises—at least during the unexpired term of the lease—adversely to the interests of the lessor. (Such an agreement must in many situations prejudice the landlord's reversion, causing damage not least through the impact of the agreement upon the landlord's negotiating position in subsequent rent reviews.) There seems, surprisingly, to be no clear authority disentitling a tenant from thus derogating from the rights of his landlord—unless such conduct is actionable as a form of 'waste' (ante, p 801).

17 Town and Country Planning Act 1990, s 106(1) [formerly Town and Country Planning Act 1971, s 52(1)]. The original terms of section 106 have now been substituted by Planning and Compensation Act 1991, s 12(1). The latter provision enables 'any person interested' in land in the area of a local planning authority to enter, by agreement or otherwise, into a 'planning obligation' which restricts or regulates the development or use of that land. The 'planning obligation' remains valid for five years or such other period as is specified, and is enforceable both against the person entering into the obligation and against any person deriving title from that person (Town and Country Planning Act 1990, ss 106(3), 106A(3), (4), as substituted by Planning and Compensation Act 1991, s 12(1)).

18 See eg *Re Martin's Application* (1987) 53 P & CR 146 at 153f, (1989) 57 P & CR 119 at 124.

as might be prescribed by its terms,[19] and is enforceable by the local planning authority against the covenantor and any person deriving title under that person.[20] The agreement, although concluded in exercise of a statutory power, is 'intended in every way to operate as a true restrictive covenant as established by well-known equitable principles'.[1]

(b) The covenant must accommodate a dominant tenement

In conformity with the theory that the equitable rules about restrictive covenants merely extend the rules relating to negative easements, it has come to be accepted that equity will take cognisance only of those covenants which create a relationship of benefit between two separate plots of land.

(i) Requirement of a dominant tenement It is nowadays accepted as clear that a restrictive covenant can be enforced only if it relates to a defined servient tenement and is appurtenant to an ascertainable dominant tenement.[2] The covenantee must own an estate in the dominant tenement at the date of the making of the covenant[3] and the covenantor must likewise own an estate in the servient tenement.[4] Thus there generally cannot be any restrictive covenant in gross: there must always be an 'anchor' parcel of land to which the benefit of the restrictive covenant is tied.[5] This prohibition on restrictive covenants in gross is sometimes rationalised on the basis that there must always be some identifiable landowner with whom it is possible to bargain for a discharge or modification of the covenant.[6] Alternatively it can be

19 In the absence of express provision or cogent evidence of surrounding circumstances indicating the contrary, the agreement has permanent effect (see *Abbey Homesteads (Developments) Ltd v Northamptonshire CC* (1987) 53 P & CR 1 at 7 per Parker LJ). The modification and discharge jurisdiction of Law of Property Act 1925, s 84 (post, p 1165) is, of course, available (see eg *Re Martin's Application* (1989) 57 P & CR 119).

20 Town and Country Planning Act 1990, s 106(3).

1 *Re Martin's Application* (1987) 53 P & CR 146 at 153.

2 The terminology of dominance and servience mirrors the language of easements (ante, p 1060). In English law there is no strict requirement that the deed of covenant should positively and clearly identify the dominant and servient tenements. It is sufficient that the dominant land is ascertainable with reasonable certainty (see *Renals v Cowlishaw* (1879) 11 Ch D 866 at 868f; *Shropshire CC v Edwards* (1983) 46 P & CR 270 at 275). Compare the law of New South Wales on this point (Conveyancing Act 1919, s 88(1), ante, p 1090). See *Re Louis and the Conveyancing Act* [1971] 1 NSWLR 164 at 178A; *Clem Smith Nominees Pty Ltd v Farrelly* (1978) 20 SASR 227 at 236f.

3 *Application of Fox* (1981) 2 BPR 9310 at 9312. This rule is particularly relevant where a vendor subdivides land and takes a restrictive covenant from each respective purchaser on sale. Only under a 'scheme of development' or 'building scheme' (post, p 1159) can the vendor effectively extract a covenanted benefit on behalf of a dominant tenement in which he no longer retains any interest (*Re Mack and the Conveyancing Act* [1975] 2 NSWLR 623 at 630E). The courts are otherwise unwilling to sever away that part of a supposed dominant tenement which was not owned by the covenantee in order that the covenant remain enforceable in respect of the portion in which he did have a relevant estate (see *Application of Magney* (1981) 2 BPR 9358 at 9359).

4 A restrictive covenant is extinguished by unity of possession of the dominant and servient tenements, unless revived by their common owner in a subsequent transfer of one of those tenements (see *In re Tiltwood* [1978] Ch 269 at 280F; *Application of Caroline Chisholm Village Pty Ltd* (1980) 1 BPR 9507 at 9515). See G.M. Bates, (1980) 54 ALJ 156.

5 For an argument that the prohibition on restrictive covenants in gross should be eliminated, see S.F. French, 73 Cornell L Rev 928 at 941ff (1987-88).

6 Post, p 1165.

said that the requirement of a dominant tenement operates effectively as a test of standing, ensuring that plaintiffs must have a legitimate interest in the enforcement of particular covenants.

The party who seeks to enforce a restrictive covenant must furthermore show that his tenement—although not necessarily contiguous with—is at least reasonably proximate to the servient tenement, since otherwise the requirement of benefit is unlikely to be satisfied. As was indicated by Pollock MR in *Kelly v Barrett*[7], 'land at Clapham would be too remote and unable to carry a right to enforce. . .covenants in respect of. . .land at Hampstead.'[8]

The requirement of dominant ownership was affirmed most clearly in *London County Council v Allen*.[9] Here the Court of Appeal held that the plaintiff was unable to enforce a restrictive covenant against the covenantor's successor, on the ground that the plaintiff was not in possession of, or interested in, any land for the benefit of which the covenant had been taken.[10] The requirement that there be a dominant tenement carries the additional implication that if the covenantee parts with all the land for the benefit of which the restrictive covenant was taken, he ceases to be able to enforce the covenant except against the original covenantor.[11] Even as against the latter, his remedy is limited to the recovery of nominal damages.

There are, of course, certain exceptional cases in which the requirement of dominant ownership is modified or even entirely abrogated.[12] Following the decision in *Hall v Ewin*,[13] for instance, it has been clear that a lessor's reversion provides a sufficient dominant tenement for the enforcement of restrictive covenants contained in a lease.[14] Nowadays, moreover, many public and quasi-public bodies are dispensed by statute from any requirement of dominant ownership. In consequence of the inconvenient ruling in *London County Council v Allen*,[15] numerous bodies have been given specific authority to enforce restrictive covenants in gross, ie even though they are not possessed

7 [1924] 2 Ch 379 at 404.

8 See also *McGuigan Investments Pty Ltd v Dalwood Vineyards Pty Ltd* [1970] 1 NSWR 686 at 690f (covenant held incapable of benefiting land 17 miles distant from supposed dominant tenement); *Clem Smith Nominees Pty Ltd v Farrelly* (1978) 20 SASR 227 at 236 (covenant not enforced where tenements separated by 35 km).

9 [1914] 3 KB 642. See D.J. Hayton, (1971) 87 LQR 539 at 542f.

10 See also *Tophams Ltd v Earl of Sefton* [1967] 1 AC 50 at 81A per Lord Wilberforce; *Peabody Donation Fund v London Residuary Body* (1988) 55 P & CR 355 at 359f.

11 See *Chambers v Randall* [1923] 1 Ch 149 at 157f per Sargant J; *Formby v Barker* [1903] 2 Ch 539 at 550f; *Miles v Easter* [1933] Ch 611 at 630f; *Pirie v Registrar-General* (1963) 109 CLR 619 at 628; *Palm Beach Lands Pty Ltd v Marshall* (1988) NSW ConvR 55-411 at 57,773. In *Thompson v Potter* [1980] BCL 764, for instance, the original covenantee was held to be unable for this reason to enforce against an assignee from the original covenantor.

12 In a somewhat different context, the requirement of dominant ownership is altogether dispensed with on the last sale under a scheme of development (post, p 1159), the common vendor retaining at this point nothing which even remotely resembles a dominant tenement. See *Re Mack and the Conveyancing Act* [1975] 2 NSWLR 623 at 630E.

13 (1887) 37 Ch D 74 (ante, p 868). See also *Regent Oil Co Ltd v J.A. Gregory (Hatch End) Ltd* [1966] Ch 402 at 433A-B, F per Harman LJ.

14 Likewise a mortgagee's interest in mortgaged land is a sufficiently real interest to enable the mortgagee to enforce a restrictive covenant affecting the land (see *Regent Oil Co Ltd v J.A. Gregory (Hatch End) Ltd* [1966] Ch 402 at 433D-F (ante, p 932)).

15 [1914] 3 KB 642 (supra).

of any dominant land which might serve as a base for enforcement in the conventional sense.[16]

(ii) Criterion of 'benefit' No restrictive covenant can be enforced in equity unless the covenant in question was made for the benefit and protection of dominant land retained by the covenantee.[17] In this context a 'benefit' must be 'something affecting either the value of the land or the method of its occupation or enjoyment'.[18] Thus, for example, a covenant which forbids a covenantor to compete with a business conducted on the covenantee's land can properly be held to 'touch and concern' or 'benefit' the land in the required sense.[19]

In the past certain difficulties have afflicted the question whether a particular restrictive covenant can be said to confer true benefit upon an alleged dominant tenement which is excessively large. In *In re Ballard's Conveyance*,[20] for instance, a restrictive covenant had been made in favour of a covenantee who retained approximately 1,700 acres of land. Clauson J held that the covenant was not enforceable at the behest of the covenantee's successor in title, since it could not reasonably be maintained that the covenant in question conferred benefit upon the entirety of such an extensive dominant tenement as that claimed by the successor.[1] The strictness of this approach has since been relaxed in the more recent case law.[2] The courts tend nowadays to presume that a covenant confers benefit upon the alleged dominant

16 The dispensation extends, for instance, to local authorities (see Housing Act 1985, s 609), the National Trust (see National Trust Act 1937, s 8; *National Trust v Midlands Electricity Board* [1952] 1 All ER 298 at 302A), and the Nature Conservancy Council (Countryside Act 1968, s 15(4)). A 'section 106 agreement' is statutorily declared to be enforceable 'as if the local planning authority were possessed of adjacent land and as if the agreement had been expressed to be made for the benefit of such land' (Town and Country Planning Act 1990, s 106(3)). See *Ransom & Luck Ltd v Surbiton BC* [1949] Ch 180 at 194; *Re Martin's Application* (1987) 53 P & CR 146 at 153, (1989) 57 P & CR 119 at 124.

17 See *Formby v Barker* [1903] 2 Ch 539 at 552 per Vaughan Williams LJ. It used to be said, in the hallowed terminology of the law of covenants, that the restrictive covenant must 'touch and concern' the land of the covenantee (see eg *Rogers v Hosegood* [1900] 2 Ch 388 at 395; *In re Ballard's Conveyance* [1937] Ch 473 at 480; *Marquess of Zetland v Driver* [1939] 1 Ch 1 at 8). However, in more recent times the courts have tended to move away from the concept of covenants which 'touch and concern' the covenantee's land, in favour of a requirement that the restrictive covenant should 'benefit' the covenantee's land. The tests of 'benefit' or 'accommodation' and 'touching and concerning' quality are nevertheless substantially the same test (see *Application of Fox* (1981) 2 BPR 9310 at 9312ff (ante, p 1130).

18 *In re Gadd's Land Transfer* [1966] Ch 56 at 66B per Buckley J. Impact on land value is not, however, conclusive of the question of 'benefit' (see *Application of Fox* (1981) 2 BPR 9310 at 9314f).

19 *Newton Abbot Co-operative Society Ltd v Williamson and Treadgold Ltd* [1952] Ch 286 at 293f; *Re Quaffers Ltd's Application* (1988) 56 P & CR 142 at 152.

20 [1937] Ch 473. See G.R.Y. Radcliffe (1941) 57 LQR 203 at 210f.

1 While conceding that a breach of the covenant might well affect a portion of the successor's land in the vicinity of the covenantor's property. Clauson J was of opinion that 'far the largest part of this area of 1,700 acres could not possibly be affected by any breach of any of the stipulations'. Nor in his view did the court have jurisdiction to 'sever' the covenant and treat it as relevant to part only of the area ([1937] Ch 473 at 480f).

2 The existence of benefit to the whole of a claimed dominant tenement is nowadays rarely a matter of dispute (see eg *J. Sainsbury Plc v Enfield LBC* [1989] 1 WLR 590 at 595F-G). See also *Application of Fox* (1981) 2 BPR 9310 at 9314.

tenement unless it can be shown that such a view cannot reasonably be held.[3] In other words, it seems that the validity of a restrictive covenant will be upheld 'so long as an estate owner may reasonably take the view that the restriction remains of value to his estate.'[4] The restriction will not be discarded 'merely because others may reasonably argue that the restriction is spent.'[5]

(iii) The purpose of the 'accommodation' requirement There is a certain opaque quality in the requirement that enforceable restrictive covenants must be made for the 'benefit' or 'protection' of dominant land. As Ungoed-Thomas J once observed,[6] it is salutary to remember that '[t]he protection of land, qua land, does not have any rational or, indeed, any human significance, apart from its enjoyment by human beings, and the protection of land is for its enjoyment by human beings'. The truth is that the requirement of 'accommodation' or 'benefit', by excluding commitments of a substantially personal character, operates silently as a filter for the long-term enforcement of contractual undertakings respecting the use of land.

It is clearly undesirable that *every* promise concerning activities on or in respect of a supposed servient tenement should run with that land so as to affect third parties. Quite apart from covenants which contravene protective legislation such as the Sex Discrimination Act 1975 or the Race Relations Act 1976,[7] it would be entirely wrong that a covenantee's personal, ideological or religious prejudices should be visited indefinitely on successive owners of a servient tenement. It may be that X can validly commit himself by a contractual promise made to his neighbour Y that X's land shall never be used for the purpose of watching television or for the purpose of consuming alcohol or for the purpose of residence by children. The enforcement of conformity with a covenantee's eccentric or capricious convictions may indeed ensure a certain emotional satisfaction for the covenantee, but cannot be said in any relevant sense to confer a 'benefit' upon his land. In so far as such obligations are inimical to social values of personal liberty and identity, it is generally thought preferable that the range of enforceable land interests should be insulated from personal commitments of this kind.[8] An alternative,

3 See eg *Wrotham Park Estate Co Ltd v Parkside Homes Ltd* [1974] 1 WLR 798 at 808D, where Brightman J stated that there 'can be obvious cases where a restrictive covenant clearly is, or clearly is not, of benefit to an estate. Between these two extremes there is inevitably an area where the benefit to the estate is a matter of personal opinion, where responsible and reasonable persons can have divergent views sincerely and reasonably held. . .[I]n such cases, it is not for the court to pronounce which is the correct view. . .the court can only decide whether a particular view is one which can reasonably be held.' See [1974] CLJ 214 (C.T. Emery); *Lord Northbourne v Johnston & Son* [1922] 2 Ch 309 at 318ff.

4 The onus is on the covenantor's successor in title to show that breach of a restrictive covenant could not possibly hurt the whole of the area claimed as the dominant tenement (see *Cryer v Scott Brothers (Sunbury) Ltd* (1988) 55 P & CR 183 at 196f, 202f).

5 *Wrotham Park Estate Co Ltd v Parkside Homes Ltd* [1974] 1 WLR 798 at 808F. See G.H. Newsom, [1974] JPL 130 at 133.

6 *Stilwell v Blackman* [1968] Ch 508 at 524G–525A.

7 Ante, p 803. See J.F. Garner, *Racial Restrictive Covenants in England and the United States*, (1972) 35 MLR 478; J.D.A. Brooke-Taylor, [1978] Conv 24.

8 See U. Reichman, 7 J Legal Stud 139 at 147ff (1978); J.L. Winokur, (1989) Wisc L Rev 1 at 87f.

and not inconsistent, analysis is that the 'accommodation' requirement provides a residual legal restraint upon the deleterious social consequences otherwise flowing from the foolishness or lack of foresight which caused the original covenantor to commit himself to such miscalculated obligations.[9]

(c) The covenant must have been intended to run with the covenantor's land

A restrictive covenant may be phrased in such a way that it binds only the covenantor.[10] In all other cases, however, it is presumed that the burden of a restrictive covenant is intended to run with the land of the covenantor. This is the effect of section 79(1) of the Law of Property Act 1925, which provides that, unless a contrary intention is expressed, a covenant 'relating to any land of a covenantor or capable of being bound by him, shall be deemed to be made by the covenantor on behalf of himself his successors in title and the persons deriving title under him or them, and. . .shall have effect as if such successors and other persons were expressed'.[11]

(3) General principles of enforceability of restrictive covenants

In order that a restrictive covenant should be enforceable between parties other than the original covenantor and covenantee, it is necessary to show first that the covenant in question conforms to the characteristics which equity demands of any 'restrictive covenant'.[12] It is also essential that the party who seeks to enforce the restrictive covenant should be able to establish both that he is entitled to the *benefit* of the covenant and that the person against whom he seeks enforcement is subject to the *burden* of the covenant.[13] If he can prove only one of these requirements, his action must fail.[14] Successful enforcement depends upon an appropriate transmission of both the benefit and the burden originally taken by covenantee and covenantor respectively (see *Fig.* 74). In other words, it is essential that the plaintiff should be able to show that

(i) the benefit of the restrictive covenant has been duly transmitted to him, *and*
(ii) the burden of the restrictive covenant has been duly transmitted to the defendant.

9 See eg G.S. Alexander, 73 Cornell L Rev 883 at 895ff (1987–88); J.E. Stake, (1988) Duke LJ 925 at 934f.
10 See *In re Royal Victoria Pavilion, Ramsgate* [1961] Ch 581 at 589.
11 In this context, 'successors in title' are deemed to include the owners and occupiers for the time being of relevant land (Law of Property Act 1925, s 79(2)). Section 79 has reference only to restrictive covenants entered into on or after 1 January 1926 (Law of Property Act 1925, s 79(3)).
12 Ante, p 1139.
13 Ante, p 150.
14 See eg *J. Sainsbury Plc v Enfield LBC* [1989] 1 WLR 590 at 601E-F, where, although the burden of a restrictive covenant had duly passed to the covenantor's successors, there now remained no persons entitled to claim the benefit (post, p 1156).

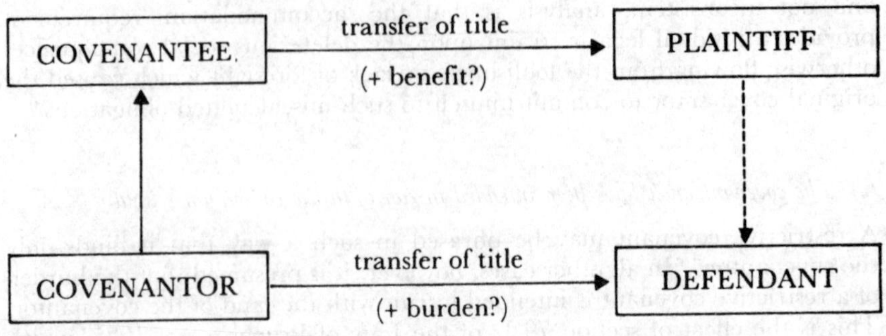

Fig. 74

(4) Transmission of the burden of a restrictive covenant

In consequence of the doctrine proceeding from *Tulk v Moxhay*,[15] the restrictive covenant has become an equitable interest in the covenantor's land. Prior to the enactment of the 1925 legislation, in common with other equitable interests in land, a restrictive covenant was binding on all persons except a bona fide purchaser for value of a legal estate without notice.[16] It was therefore unenforceable against any purchaser for value of a legal estate in the covenantor's land who had no notice of the covenant,[17] or indeed against *any* successor in title of such a person.[18] The transmission of the burden of a restrictive covenant was, in effect, governed quite simply by the equitable doctrine of notice.

(a) *Introduction of a registration requirement*

The property legislation of 1925 of course effected major alterations both in the law of restrictive covenants and, more generally, in the application of the doctrine of notice. Most kinds of restrictive covenant made after 1925 now constitute a land charge of Class D(ii).[19] The transmission of the burden of such a restrictive covenant depends upon whether (in the case of unregistered land) that covenant has been duly registered in the Land Charges Register[20] or (in the case of registered land) has been duly protected as a minor interest by entry of a notice or caution in the Land Register.[1]

Thus, in *Fig.* 74, the plaintiff will be able to enforce the restrictive covenant against the defendant as successor in title to the covenantor only if the covenantee had protected the incumbrance by the appropriate register entry

15 (1848) 2 Ph 774, 41 ER 1143 (ante, p 1137).
16 Ante, p 149.
17 A restrictive covenant does, however, bind an adverse occupier of the servient land, precisely because he is not a *purchaser* (see *In re Nisbet and Potts' Contract* [1906] 1 Ch 386 at 401ff, 408f (ante, p 79)).
18 See *Wilkes v Spooner* [1911] 2 KB 473 at 487f (ante, p 84). See also *Nottingham Patent Brick and Tile Co v Butler* (1886) 16 QBD 778 at 788.
19 Ante, p 148.
20 Ante, p 149. See *Wrotham Park Estate Co Ltd v Parkside Homes Ltd* [1974] 1 WLR 798 at 809A.
1 Ante, p 181.

prior to the transfer of title by the covenantor. If the restrictive covenant was duly protected, the defendant is now inescapably bound by it; if not, the defendant takes the freehold free of the burden of the covenant.[2]

(b) Exceptions from the registration requirement

Not all categories of restrictive covenant are governed by the provisions of the Land Charges Act 1972. A restrictive covenant made between a lessor and a lessee can never constitute a protectible Class D(ii) land charge. Such a covenant is governed instead by the rules which regulate the enforceability of leasehold covenants.[3] Furthermore, a restrictive covenant entered into by freeholders *before* 1 January 1926 is still fully subject to the equitable doctrine of notice.

(5) Transmission of the benefit of a restrictive covenant

In order that the benefit of a restrictive covenant should be transmitted in equity to a successor in title of the covenantee,[4] it is necessary not only that the covenant should 'touch and concern' or 'benefit' some dominant land, but also that the benefit be transmitted in one or more of the modes prescribed by equity. Historically, these modes of transmission have tended to be defined in fairly strict terms. Nowadays, however, there is a strong contrary tendency on the part of the courts to relax the strict requirements of equity by allowing the appurtenant quality of a covenant to be determined with reference to the intentions of the covenanting parties rather than in accordance with stipulated requirements of form.[5] This gradual movement away from technicality and heavy formalism has certainly done much to simplify the law of restrictive covenants.[6]

If the benefit of a restrictive covenant is to be transmitted in equity to a successor in title of the covenantee, it must be shown that that benefit was effectively *annexed* to the covenantee's land, or was expressly *assigned* to the successor, or has become enforceable by reason of the presence of a *building scheme* or *scheme of development*. It is sometimes said that these equitable modes of transmission of benefit are merely an elucidation of the common law rules governing the passing of the benefit of covenants.[7] It is indeed possible that the benefit of a restrictive covenant may be held to pass *at law* if the common law conditions for transmission are fulfilled, even though successful enforcement of the covenant depends ultimately on the transmission

2 Ante, p 119.

3 Ante, p 868. If the restrictive covenant—albeit contained in a lease—related to land not comprised within that lease, the position is governed by the equitable doctrine of notice (see *Dartstone Ltd v Cleveland Petroleum Co Ltd* [1969] 3 All ER 668 at 672D-G (ante, p 151)).

4 See S.J. Bailey, [1938] CLJ 339.

5 It has been pointed out that the modern tendency is 'to assimilate the law of covenants to the law of easements, where no formalities are required for establishing the right as appurtenant to the dominant tenement' (see H.W.R. Wade, [1972B] CLJ 157 at 163).

6 The trend of recent developments in this area is, however, vulnerable to the inevitable conveyancer's objection that the law now 'detracts from the vital characteristics of all property interests viz definability, ascertainability, and stability, and. . . the uncertainty thereby created casts doubt on many titles, thus inhibiting the marketability and the development of land' (see D.J. Hayton, (1971) 87 LQR 539).

7 *Rogers v Hosegood* [1900] 2 Ch 388 at 397.

of the burden in accordance with *equitable* principles.[8] There are, however, certain circumstances in which the benefit of a restrictive covenant can be claimed only by virtue of the equitable rules concerning transmission, and these cases are essentially situations in which the common law rules are not satisfied. There can be no passing of the benefit at law if, for instance, either the covenantee or his successor has merely an equitable interest in land,[9] or if the covenantee's successor takes title to part only of the original dominant tenement.[10] In such circumstances, the transmission of the benefit of a restrictive covenant rests entirely upon the operation of the equitable rules.

(6) Annexation

Annexation is the metaphorical 'nailing' of the benefit of a restrictive covenant to a clearly defined area of land belonging to the covenantee, in such a way that the benefit passes with any subsequent transfer of the covenantee's interest in that land. Annexation has traditionally comprised a formal recognition that both covenantor and covenantee intend that the benefit should run with the land so as to avail future owners of that land. Once that intention has been manifested in the express terms of the covenant, the benefit of that covenant is notionally fastened upon, or annexed to, the covenantee's land. The benefit thereafter passes automatically to all successive owners, tenants and occupiers of the land irrespective of knowledge or notice and without any specific assignment.[11] In recent years, however, the linguistic formalism required in annexation has tended to be relaxed by the courts, with the result that it is now possible to distinguish three different types of annexation.

(a) Express annexation

Express annexation is the oldest and least controversial form of annexation. Express annexation arises where the deed which contains the restrictive covenant includes some clear and formal expression of intention that the benefit of the covenant should run with the land to which the covenant is appurtenant. In other words, a formula of annexation is embedded in the very document which brings the restrictive covenant into being.

(i) Formulae of express annexation It is always a question of construction whether the benefit of any restrictive covenant is in fact intended to run with a defined piece of land. It is generally accepted that the benefit is effectively annexed to a particular piece of land if that land is sufficiently defined in

8 See eg *Rogers v Hosegood* [1900] 2 Ch 388 at 395ff.

9 See *Fairclough v Marshall* (1878) 4 Ex D 37 at 44ff.

10 See *Miles v Easter* [1933] Ch 611 at 630 per Romer LJ ('. . .at law the benefit could not be assigned in pieces. It would have to be assigned as a whole or not at all').

11 In the words of Collins LJ in *Rogers v Hosegood* [1900] 2 Ch 388 at 407, annexation is effective to make the benefit of a covenant run, 'not because the conscience of either party is affected, but because the purchaser has bought something which inhered in or was annexed to the land bought.' It is for this reason, of course, that 'the purchaser's ignorance of the existence of the covenant does not defeat the presumption [that the benefit passes on a sale of the land]' ([1900] 2 Ch 388 at 408). See also *Pirie v Registrar-General* (1963) 109 CLR 619 at 628.

the instrument containing the covenant *and* the covenant is expressed to be made 'for the benefit of the land' or 'for the benefit of the [owner] in his capacity of owner of a particular property'.[12] The use of such formulae is clearly indicative of an intention that the benefit of the relevant covenant should not be personal to the covenantee, but should enure to the advantage of future owners of the covenantee's land.

Thus in *Rogers v Hosegood*,[13] for instance, the Court of Appeal was able to find an effective annexation in the parties' clearly expressed 'intent that the covenant may enure to the benefit of the vendors [ie the covenantees] their successors and assigns and others claiming under them to all or any of their lands adjoining'.[14] In *Renals v Cowlishaw*,[15] however, a claim of annexation was rejected where a covenant had been made merely with the vendors, 'their heirs, executors, administrators, and assigns'.[16] It was fatal in this case that no reference had been made to the land which was intended to receive the benefit.[17] Annexation is essentially a conferment of benefit upon *land*, not upon *persons*, and it is therefore imperative that the covenant to be enforced should incorporate some reference to land.

(ii) Express annexation to a large dominant tenement In the past there has been some difficulty as to whether there could be an effective annexation where a restrictive covenant purported to confer benefit upon the *whole* of an excessively large dominant tenement.[18] The court in *In re Ballard's Conveyance*[19] was plainly unwilling to sever a covenanted benefit and treat it as specific only to a portion of the alleged dominant tenement. However, it has long been clear that none of the problems raised by *In re Ballard's Conveyance* have any substance if the benefit of the relevant restrictive covenant has been annexed, not to the undifferentiated whole of a large dominant tenement, but to 'each and every part' of that tenement.[20] In the case of annexation to 'each and every part', the covenantee's successors are entitled to claim

12 *Osborne v Bradley* [1903] 2 Ch 446 at 450 per Farwell J. See also *Drake v Gray* [1936] Ch 451 at 466, where Greene LJ stated that there are 'two familiar methods of indicating in a covenant of this kind the land in respect of which the benefit is to enure. One is to describe the character in which the covenantee receives the covenant. That is the form which is adopted here, a covenant with so and so, owners or owner for the time being of whatever the land may be. Another method is to state by means of an appropriate declaration that the covenant is taken "for the benefit of" whatever the lands may be.'

13 [1900] 2 Ch 388 at 408.

14 It was of no great importance that this formula of annexation defined the benefited tenement in only general terms (ante, p 1143).

15 (1878) 9 Ch D 125 at 130f (affd. (1879) 11 Ch D 866). See *Rogers v Hosegood* [1900] 2 Ch 388 at 396, 408.

16 It has been held that no annexation effect is achieved by the similar statutory wording contained in Conveyancing Act 1881, s 58 (see *J. Sainsbury Plc v Enfield LBC* [1989] 1 WLR 590 at 601D-E (post, p 1156)).

17 See also *Reid v Bickerstaff* [1909] 2 Ch 305 at 321; *Ives v Brown* [1919] 2 Ch 314 at 323f; *J. Sainsbury Plc v Enfield LBC* [1989] 1 WLR 590 at 598A-C; *Jamaica Mutual Life Assurance Society v Hillsborough Ltd* [1989] 1 WLR 1101 at 1105B-1106B per Lord Jauncey of Tullichettle.

18 These difficulties are now substantially reduced in the light of the decision of Brightman J in *Wrotham Park Estate Co Ltd v Parkside Homes Ltd* [1974] 1 WLR 798 (ante, p 1146).

19 [1937] Ch 473 (ante, p 1145).

20 See *Marquess of Zetland v Driver* [1939] Ch 1 at 10. In this case the Marquess of Zetland succeeded in depriving the citizens of Redcar in Yorkshire of the facility of 'an eating-house for the consumption of fried fish and other food' ([1939] Ch 1 at 3).

the benefit of the covenant in respect of *any* part of a large dominant tenement which is particularly adversely affected by any breach of the covenant, provided always that the successor has a proprietary interest in the portion of land in respect of which he claims the benefit.

(iii) Fragmentation of the dominant tenement Most instances of express annexation effected since *Marquess of Zetland v Driver*[1] have made clear reference to 'each and every part' of the covenantee's land or have used words of similar import. The result of such annexation is that any subsequent purchaser from the covenantee may claim the benefit of the covenant as annexed to the subject matter of *his* purchase even though he may have purchased only a part of the original dominant tenement. Fragmentation of the dominant tenement does not thus prevent the covenant from being enforceable at the behest of successors in title of the original covenantee.

Until fairly recently, however, there was a real danger that, in the absence of an annexation to 'each and every part' of the covenantee's land, a subsequent purchaser of only a part of the dominant tenement would be unable to claim a benefit which had originally been annexed to the whole of that tenement.[2] For a period technical complexity seemed to threaten good sense and to elevate arid formalism in the law of restrictive covenants.[3] However, in *Federated Homes Ltd v Mill Lodge Properties Ltd*,[4] Brightman LJ finally declared that 'if the benefit of a covenant is, on a proper construction of a document, annexed to the land, prima facie it is annexed to every part thereof, unless the contrary clearly appear'.[5] This observation, although

1 [1939] Ch 1.

2 See *Russell v Archdale* [1964] Ch 38 at 47 per Buckley J; (1962) 78 LQR 334, 482 (R.E.M.). See also *Re Arcade Hotel Pty Ltd* [1962] VR 274 at 287ff (Full Court of the Supreme Court of Victoria). There was also a risk that a successor in title of the covenantee might himself be disabled from claiming a benefit originally annexed to the undifferentiated whole if he later sold a part of that whole to a third party, on the ground that in such circumstances the vendor no longer retained the entire dominant tenement to which that benefit had been annexed. See *Stilwell v Blackman* [1968] Ch 508 at 519D-F, where, as in *Russell v Archdale*, the point was obiter because there was on the facts a valid *assignment* of the benefit of the restrictive covenant in question. See P.V. Baker (1968) 84 LQR 22, and compare *In re Selwyn's Conveyance* [1967] Ch 674 at 689A-B; (1968) 31 MLR 459 (J.W. Harris).

3 For reference to a 'somewhat muddy corner of legal history', see *Griffiths v Band* (1974) 29 P & CR 243 at 246 per Goulding J. It is noteworthy that the technical principles adumbrated in *Russell v Archdale* and *Stilwell v Blackman* have no counterpart in the law relating to assignment (post, p 1156) or, for that matter, in the law of easements (ante, p 1062).

4 [1980] 1 WLR 594 at 606G. Brightman LJ had already resolved some of the present problems in *Wrotham Park Estate Co Ltd v Parkside Homes Ltd* [1974] 1 WLR 798 at 806E, where he had held that a successor in title—albeit that he had sold away a part of the dominant tenement—might nevertheless claim the benefit if he could show that he retained 'in substance' the dominant tenement for the benefit of which the covenant was unqualifiedly taken.

5 Brightman LJ confessed to finding the 'idea of the annexation of a covenant to the whole of the land but not to a part of it a difficult conception fully to grasp' ([1980] 1 WLR 594 at 606F). See also Megaw LJ (at 608B-C). See also *Re Arcade Hotel Pty Ltd* [1962] VR 274 at 291, where Scholl J anticipated the Court of Appeal's construction by 18 years: 'Is there then some particular virtue in the addition of the words "or any part thereof" to the description of the benefited land?... why should the benefit of the covenant not be understood to be distributed over the benefited land, in the same way as the burden over the burdened land? I can see no logical reason why not; and as a mere matter of language I can see no such reason.'

technically obiter dictum,[6] clearly reflected the general relaxation during recent years of the rules relating to restrictive covenants,[7] although falling somewhat short of the simplification which has been achieved in other jurisdictions by the more direct means of statutory intervention.[8]

(b) Implied annexation

It is still somewhat uncertain to what extent annexation of a covenanted benefit may arise by implication from circumstances.[9] There is judicial support for the suggestion that annexation, although not expressed in the deed containing the restrictive covenant, may nevertheless have been so obviously intended by the covenanting parties that to ignore it would be 'not only an injustice but a departure from common sense'.[10] On this basis annexation of the benefit of a restrictive covenant may be implied from the circumstances surrounding a deed of covenant, where it is clear that the covenant had reference to a defined piece of land and that the parties themselves intended that the benefit should attach to the land rather than to the covenantee personally.[11]

The scope of implied annexation is, however, somewhat limited. If a court is to find an intention to annex, notwithstanding the absence of express words of annexation in the relevant conveyance, the required element of intention must be manifested in the conveyance, as construed in the light of the surrounding circumstances 'including any necessary implication in the conveyance from those surrounding circumstances.'[12] The primary focus is, in other words, to be placed on the language of the conveyance and

6 The remarks of the Court of Appeal in this respect have been criticised as inconsistent with earlier authorities. Compare eg *Miles v Easter* [1933] Ch 611 at 628 per Romer LJ (see G.H. Newsom (1981) 97 LQR 32 at 48f).

7 Such is the impact of the Court of Appeal's approach in *Federated Homes* that it is rarely argued today that an express annexation has other than a fully distributive effect (see eg *J. Sainsbury Plc v Enfield LBC* [1989] 1 WLR 590 at 595C-D).

8 See, for instance, s 79A of the Property Law Act 1958 (No 6344) of Victoria, as inserted by the Transfer of Land (Restrictive Covenants) Act 1964 (No 7130) in response to the ruling in *Re Arcade Hotel Pty Ltd* [1962] VR 274. Section 79A provides that when the benefit of any restrictive covenant 'purports to be annexed...to other land the benefit shall unless it is expressly provided to the contrary be deemed to be and always to have been annexed to the whole and to each and every part of such other land capable of benefiting from such restriction.' This reform vindicates the dissenting judgment of Sholl J in *Re Arcade Hotel Pty Ltd* [1962] VR 274 at 291. See also *Re Miscamble's Application* [1966] VR 596 at 598ff.

9 For the view that implied annexation is possible, see H.W.R. Wade, [1972B] CLJ 157 at 169f. The doctrine of implied annexation is, however, criticised by D.J. Hayton, (1971) 87 LQR 539; P.V. Baker (1968) 84 LQR 22 at 30. See also E.C. Ryder, (1972) 36 Conv (NS) 20.

10 *Marten v Flight Refuelling Ltd* [1962] Ch 115 at 133 per Wilberforce J. See (1962) 26 Conv (NS) 298 (J.F. Garner). Even in *Rogers v Hosegood* [1900] 2 Ch 388 at 408, Collins LJ, delivering the judgment of the Court of Appeal, held that annexation merely requires some 'indication in the original conveyance, or in the circumstances attending it, that the burden of the restrictive covenant is imposed for the benefit of the land reserved.'

11 See *Shropshire CC v Edwards* (1983) 46 P & CR 270 at 277f. It may well be that schemes of development are ultimately an instance of annexation by implication from surrounding circumstances (post, p 1159).

12 *J. Sainsbury Plc v Enfield LBC* [1989] 1 WLR 590 at 595H-596F per Morritt J.

the implications to be drawn therefrom, rather than on the surrounding circumstances together with such inferences as can be derived from the latter.

(c) Statutory annexation

One of the more dramatic developments of recent years in the area of restrictive covenants is the way in which the courts have at last begun to have recourse to long dormant provisions of the Law of Property Act 1925.[13] Section 78(1) of this Act provides that

> A covenant relating to any land of the covenantee shall be deemed to be made with the covenantee and his successors in title and the persons deriving title under him or them, and shall have effect as if such successors and other persons were expressed. For the purposes of this subsection in connexion with covenants restrictive of the user of land 'successors in title' shall be deemed to include the owners and occupiers for the time being of the land of the covenantee intended to be benefited.

At first sight, section 78(1) appears to provide, in statutory language, a formula of annexation no less efficacious than the classic formula which was upheld in *Rogers v Hosegood*.[14] Yet to the obvious puzzlement of many commentators,[15] section 78(1) was until recently never regarded as supplying a general statutory implication of the necessary words of annexation.[16]

(i) The Federated Homes ruling The spell was finally broken by the decision of the Court of Appeal in *Federated Homes Ltd v Mill Lodge Properties Ltd*.[17] The restrictive covenant involved here contained a reference to 'any adjoining or adjacent property retained by' the covenantee. One parcel of the covenantee's adjoining lands was subsequently transferred to the present plaintiff, and the question arose whether the benefit of the original restrictive covenant could be claimed by the plaintiff on the basis of a valid annexation.[18] The Court was of the opinion that it could be so claimed on the basis of

13 For the suggestion that section 62 of the Law of Property Act 1925 may be sufficient to enable the benefit of a restrictive covenant to pass on a conveyance of the dominant land, see H.W.R. Wade, [1972B] CLJ 157 at 175; D.J. Hayton, (1971) 87 LQR 539 at 567, 570. This view was endorsed by Judge John Mills QC at first instance in *Federated Homes Ltd v Mill Lodge Properties Ltd* (see [1980] 1 WLR 594 at 601C-D). Compare, however, *Rogers v Hosegood* [1900] 2 Ch 388 at 398; *Shropshire CC v Edwards* (1983) 46 P & CR 270 at 278f; *Roake v Chadha* [1984] 1 WLR 40 at 47F-G.

14 Ante, p 1151.

15 'Why the decided cases make no reference to this legislation is a mystery. . .why. . .should counsel never argue the point, judges never mention it, and textbooks not discuss it?' (H.W.R. Wade, [1972B] CLJ 157 at 171ff.) See also G.R.Y. Radcliffe, (1941) 57 LQR 203 at 205.

16 Section 78(1) could, arguably without offence to legislative intention, have been treated as implying a statutory formula of annexation in every deed containing a restrictive covenant which is clearly intended to confer a benefit upon a defined area of land. However, for many years the orthodox view of section 78(1) was that it provided merely a 'word-saving' facility, operating only when a valid annexation had *already* been established without reliance on the subsection, but nevertheless making it unnecessary to name the covenantee's successors in title (see D.J. Hayton (1971) 87 LQR 539 at 554).

17 [1980] 1 WLR 594. See (1980) 43 MLR 445 (D.J. Hayton); [1980] JPL 371 (G.H. Newsom); (1980) 130 NLJ 531 (T. Bailey); [1980] Conv 216 (A. Sydenham).

18 The restrictive covenant in issue in this case was clearly enforceable by the covenantee's successor in title on the ground of a valid chain of express assignments, but the Court nevertheless dealt with the possibility that the covenant had also been the subject of an effective annexation.

section 78(1). Brightman LJ rejected any narrow interpretation of section 78(1) as 'merely a statutory shorthand for reducing the length of legal documents'.[19] He thought that in the present case 'the benefit of [the] covenant was annexed to the retained land, and...this is a consequence of section 78...'[20] In his view, the actual wording of the restrictive covenant had been sufficient to intimate that the covenant was one 'relating to...land of the covenantee' within the sense of section 78(1). The remainder of section 78(1) was therefore activated by this conclusion, with the result that the statute supplied the words necessary to complete the required formula of annexation,[1] thereby causing the benefit of the restrictive covenant in question 'to run with the...land and therefore to be annexed to it.'[2]

(ii) Subsequent case law The views expressed by the Court of Appeal in *Federated Homes Ltd v Mill Lodge Properties Ltd* proved to be highly controversial.[3] It has been pointed out that if section 78 of the Law of Property Act 1925 indeed imposes an automatic annexation effect, this may possibly render otiose the entire device of express assignment as an alternative means of transmitting the benefit of restrictive covenants.[4] The Court of Appeal has also been criticised on the ground that, in determining a question of annexation, which 'is not a question of words but of intention', it seemed to attach paramount significance to statutory words which are 'neutral as to intention'.[5] If the decision in *Federated Homes Ltd v Mill Lodge Properties Ltd* is correct, it would seem to follow that section 78(1) has the extraordinary effect of creating an automatic annexation quite irrespective of the intentions

19 Such an interpretation seemed to Brightman LJ 'to fly in the face of the wording of the section' ([1980] 1 WLR 594 at 604D). In *Tophams Ltd v Earl of Sefton* [1967] 1 AC 50 at 73A-C, Lord Upjohn had dismissed section 79, the companion section of section 78, as having purely 'word-saving significance'. In *Federated Homes*, however, Brightman LJ referred to section 79 as a provision which 'involves quite different considerations' and which provides no 'helpful analogy' ([1980] 1 WLR 594 at 606B).

20 [1980] 1 WLR 594 at 603H.

1 'If, as the language of section 78 implies, a covenant relating to land which is restrictive of the user thereof is enforceable at the suit of (1) a successor in title of the covenantee, (2) a person deriving title under the covenantee or under his successors in title, and (3) the owner or occupier of the land intended to be benefited by the covenant, it must, in my view, follow that the covenant runs with the land, because ex hypothesi every successor in title to the land, every derivative proprietor of the land and every other owner and occupier has a right by statute to the covenant. In other words, if the condition precedent of section 78 is satisfied—that is to say, there exists a covenant which touches and concerns the land of the covenantee—that covenant runs with the land for the benefit of his successors in title, persons deriving title under him or them and other owners and occupiers' ([1980] 1 WLR 594 at 605A-C). Brightman LJ professed to find support for his view of the impact of section 78 in *Smith and Snipes Hall Farm Ltd v River Douglas Catchment Board* [1949] 2 KB 500, and *Williams v Unit Construction Co Ltd* (1955) 19 Conv (NS) 262. See, however, G.H. Newsom (1981) 97 LQR 32 at 44ff.

2 [1980] 1 WLR 594 at 607C. See also *S.J. Allen (South Island) Ltd v Crowe* (1980) NZ Recent Law 118. The liberal approach of *Federated Homes* has since been applied in *Bridges v Harrow LBC* (1981) 260 Estates Gazette 284 at 290; [1982] Conv 313 (F. Webb).

3 For the view that *Federated Homes* may be confined to much narrower limits than is generally supposed, see P.N. Todd, *Annexation After Federated Homes*, [1985] Conv 177.

4 (1980) 43 MLR 445 at 447 (D.J. Hayton).

5 See G.H. Newsom (1981) 97 LQR 32 at 34. Unlike section 79(1) (ante, p 1147), section 78(1) makes no allowance for the expression of 'a contrary intention' by the parties to the covenant.

of covenantor and covenantee.[6] In *Roake v Chadha*,[7] however, the original covenanting parties had expressly stipulated that their covenant should 'not enure for the benefit of any owner or subsequent purchaser of any part of the...estate unless the benefit...shall be expressly assigned'. Judge Paul Baker QC held that section 78 could not be applied here so as to pass the benefit of a covenant which had so clearly excluded the consequence of annexation. When construed as a whole against the background of its explicit terms, the relevant covenant simply did not relate to, and was not annexed to, the land of the covenantee. Under these circumstances section 78 was left with no proper role to play.

The only major curtailment of the liberalising influence of *Federated Homes* has concerned restrictive covenants undertaken prior to 1 January 1926. Such covenants are governed, of course, not by the wording of section 78 of the 1925 Act,[8] but by the more narrowly expressed language of section 58 of the Conveyancing Act 1881.[9] In *J. Sainsbury Plc v Enfield LBC*[10] Morritt J held that the latter formula contained significantly different terms which are not apt to supply an automatic annexation effect in the case of pre-1926 covenants.[11] The *Sainsbury* decision thereby places an extremely important limitation of the otherwise impressive span of the *Federated Homes* approach, not least since the uninhibited view of annexation adopted in *Federated Homes* is effectively withheld from restrictive covenants affecting most buildings in England and Wales which were constructed before 1926.

(7) Assignment

A second method of transmitting the benefit of a restrictive covenant in equity is provided, in the conventional view, by the device of express assignment of that benefit.[12] Thus, even though a successor in title of the covenantee cannot claim to enforce the covenant on the basis of an effective annexation, he may be able to show that the benefit of the covenant has been expressly assigned to him.

(a) *Relation between assignment and annexation*

It may well be that the broad view of annexation adopted by the Court of Appeal in *Federated Homes Ltd v Mill Lodge Properties Ltd*[13] has removed much of the scope left for the law of assignment of covenanted benefits. Nevertheless the device of assignment, to the extent that it remains a means of transmitting benefit, differs from the device of annexation in the following respects.

6 It is such considerations as these which caused the leading authority on the law of restrictive covenants to express the opinion that 'it really seems almost impossible that the view of Brightman LJ can be correct' (see G.H. Newsom (1981) 97 LQR 32 at 48). See also G.H. Newsom, (1982) 98 LQR 202.
7 [1984] 1 WLR 40 at 46B-H. See [1984] Conv 68 (P.N. Todd).
8 See Law of Property Act 1925, s 78(2).
9 Ante, p 1151.
10 [1989] 1 WLR 590 at 601D-E. See [1989] Conv 358 (J.E.M.).
11 This much had already been acknowledged in *Federated Homes Ltd v Mill Lodge Properties Ltd* [1980] 1 WLR 594 at 604H-605A per Brightman LJ.
12 See L.H. Elphinstone, (1952) 68 LQR 353.
13 [1980] 1 WLR 594 (ante, p 1152).

(i) Difference of focus Annexation and assignment are directed at quite different targets. Annexation involves the attachment of benefit to *land*; assignment involves the conferment of benefit upon a *person*.

(ii) Difference of timing Annexation and assignment occur (if at all) at different times. Annexation is effected at the date of the making of the restrictive covenant. Assignment is effected, perhaps many years later, on subsequent transfers of the covenantee's title to later purchasers of the dominant land.[14]

(iii) Difference of effect Annexation and assignment have quite different effects. Annexation has the effect of fastening the benefit of a restrictive covenant upon the dominant land for ever, with the result that the benefit passes automatically with that land on any subsequent transfer of title. Assignment is, at least according to one view, efficacious only in respect of the immediate assignee, with the result that the benefit of the restrictive covenant requires to be assigned afresh with every subsequent transfer of the dominant land.[15]

The law of assignment contrasts markedly with that of annexation, in that it was thought until relatively recently that a benefit unqualifiedly annexed to the whole of a dominant tenement could not be claimed by a successor in title of merely a portion of that land.[16] There has never been any corresponding limitation in respect of the assignment of covenanted benefits, notwithstanding that these benefits may originally have been annexed to the entirety of a dominant tenement.[17] Fragmentation of the dominant land has no prejudicial impact upon assignment since assignment is an essentially personal transaction which involves the transmission of a benefit from one individual to another.

(b) Preconditions of assignment

Assignment is usually effected by means of express words of assignment inserted into the document of transfer executed by the covenantee in favour of his successor in title or executed by that successor in favour of a later purchaser. Certain specific conditions must be fulfilled in order that assignment be effective, but in general terms the essential requirement is that assignor and assignee should express some agreement that the benefit shall pass to the latter.

14 It is not impossible that a successor in title of the covenantee may claim the benefit of a covenant on the basis of both assignment and annexation (ante, p 1152). Assignment and annexation are not, in this sense, mutually exclusive.

15 See *In re Pinewood Estate, Farnborough* [1958] Ch 280 at 287. There is, however, weighty support for the alternative view that assignment effects a 'delayed annexation'. See *Renals v Cowlishaw* (1878) 9 Ch D 125 at 130f; *Rogers v Hosegood* [1900] 2 Ch 388 at 408; *Reid v Bickerstaff* [1909] 2 Ch 305 at 320; but compare *Stilwell v Blackman* [1968] Ch 508 at 526C-E. See also S.J. Bailey, [1938] CLJ 339 at 360f; [1957] CLJ 146 (H.W.R. Wade); P.V. Baker, (1968) 84 LQR 22 at 31f; H.W.R. Wade, [1972B] CLJ 157 at 166.

16 Ante, p 1152.

17 See, for instance, the cases where assignment was held to be effective under circumstances in which supposedly annexation would not have passed the benefit to the plaintiff (*Russell v Archdale* [1964] Ch 38 at 47f; *Stilwell v Blackman* [1968] Ch 508 at 528G-529A (ante, p 1152)).

(i) The covenant must have been taken for the protection or benefit of land owned by the covenantee at the date of the covenant The assignee of the benefit of a restrictive covenant must be able to show that the covenant was originally taken for the benefit or protection of land owned by the covenantee at the date of the covenant.[18] If this were not so, the covenant would be a 'covenant in gross', and would be unenforceable except as between covenantor and covenantee. It is permissible to prove this requirement by showing that the circumstances surrounding the making of the covenant clearly establish that the covenant was intended to benefit the covenantee's land. In *Newton Abbott Co-operative Society Ltd v Williamson and Treadgold Ltd*,[19] for instance, Upjohn J was prepared to accept that the requirement of intended benefit was met by a covenant which precluded the covenantor from conducting trade in competition with the business carried by the covenantee on his nearby premises. It was quite clear here that the covenant had been taken for the protection of the covenantee's land.

(ii) The assignment must be contemporaneous with the transfer of the dominant land If the assignee of the benefit of a restrictive covenant seeks to enforce that benefit against the original covenantor, he need prove only that the benefit has been duly assigned to him as a chose in action. However, if he seeks to enforce the covenant against a successor in title to the servient land, he must show that the benefit was assigned to him contemporaneously with the transfer of the title in the dominant land. In other words, he must establish that the assignment was part of the transaction of transfer.[20] If the benefit of a restrictive covenant becomes separated from the dominant land, it ceases to be operative.[1]

(iii) The dominant tenement must be ascertainable In *Miles v Easter*[2] the Court of Appeal held that the land benefited by the restrictive covenant which the assignee seeks to enforce must be 'ascertainable' or 'certain'. As Romer LJ indicated in this case, it is impossible to ascertain the existence and location of the dominant land for this purpose unless these are 'indicated in the conveyance or have been otherwise shown with reasonable certainty'. It is clear, however, that the dominant land will be regarded as sufficiently identified if it is ascertainable with reference to extrinsic evidence.[3]

18 *Miles v Easter* [1933] Ch 611 at 625 per Bennett J. See (1933) 49 LQR 483 (H.A. Hollond). This case is sometimes known as *In re Union of London and Smith's Bank Ltd's Conveyance*.

19 [1952] Ch 286 at 293f.

20 See *Miles v Easter* [1933] Ch 611 at 632; *Newton Abbot Co-operative Society Ltd v Williamson & Treadgold Ltd* [1952] Ch 286 at 294. See also L. Elphinstone, (1952) 68 LQR 353.

1 See *Miles v Easter* [1933] Ch 611 at 632, where Romer LJ explained the assignability of a covenant as being necessary to enable the covenantee to 'dispose of his property to advantage'. This protection is not, however, necessary if he has already managed to sell the dominant land to a third party without simultaneously assigning the benefit.

2 [1933] Ch 611 at 631.

3 See eg *Newton Abbot Co-operative Society Ltd v Williamson & Treadgold Ltd* [1952] Ch 286 at 297, where Upjohn J considered that he was entitled to 'look at the attendant circumstances to see if the land to be benefited is shown "otherwise" with reasonable certainty.' See also *Re Memvale Securities Ltd's Application* (1975) 233 Estates Gazette 689 at 691, for confirmation that 'it is permissible to identify the land benefited dehors the deed'. Compare, however, D.J. Hayton, (1971) 87 LQR 539 at 568ff.

(8) Scheme of development

A third method of transmitting the benefit of restrictive covenants in equity is provided by the 'scheme of development' or 'building scheme'.[4] It is not unusual for a property developer to subdivide a large area of land into plots with the intention of selling those plots seriatim to individual purchasers. In order to preserve the value of each plot and the residential amenity of the whole area, the vendor commonly extracts certain restrictive covenants from each purchaser in turn. The object of the exercise is plainly to institute a scheme of mutually enforceable restrictive covenants which will be valid not only for the initial purchasers vis à vis each other but also as between all successors in title of the original covenantors. This aim, if duly realised, has the effect of creating a 'local law' for maintaining the character of the neighbourhood for the indefinite future.

(a) The problem

The transmission of the burden of the restrictive covenants undertaken by the original purchasers of the individual plots depends, of course, simply on the due registration against those purchasers of the relevant incumbrances created in favour of the developer of the site.[5] The transmission of the benefit received by the developer as covenantee is, however, a matter of somewhat greater difficulty. As the developer extracts restrictive covenants from each initial purchaser, the dominant tenement to which each covenant appertains is of course the area constituted by the plots of land as yet unsold by the developer, and this area inevitably shrinks with each successive sale. The dominant tenement in respect of any one covenant does not include the plots which have already been sold away,[6] and neither annexation nor assignment can enable the covenantee to distribute the benefits of later covenants to earlier purchasers.[7] Given the irreversible chronology of the transfers on sale, the enforcement of the original restrictive covenants must fairly quickly break down in the absence of some other more general mechanism for transmitting the covenanted benefits to all purchasers and their successors in title.

(b) The solution

The solution for the problem outlined above lies in the distinctly equitable rules which have evolved for the governance of 'schemes of development'. If a 'scheme of development' is present in any given circumstances, equity takes the view that the restrictive covenants appurtenant to each and every plot of land comprised within the scheme can be enforced by all who currently own land covered by the scheme.[8] If a 'scheme of development' is shown

4 According to Megarry J in *Brunner v Greenslade* [1971] Ch 993 at 999F, '"scheme of development"...is the genus; "building scheme" a species.'
5 See eg *Sawyer v Starr* [1985] 2 NZLR 540 at 551. See also (1928) 78 LJ 39 (J.M.L.).
6 See eg *Application of Magney* (1981) 2 BPR 9358 at 9359.
7 See *Re Louis and the Conveyancing Act* [1971] 1 NSWLR 164 at 178F.
8 A 'scheme of development' need not necessarily relate to the subdivision of land in a horizontal plane. Such a scheme can arise in relation to units formed by other kinds of subdivision (see *Hudson v Cripps* [1896] 1 Ch 265 at 269 (flats); *Re Spike and Rocca Group Ltd* (1980) 107 DLR (3d) 62 at 64f (tenanted units in shopping plaza)).

to exist, it matters not whether the party seeking to enforce a relevant covenant is an original covenantor or a successor in title.[9] Within a proven 'scheme of development', restrictive covenants are enforceable on a general basis, quite irrespective of the relative timing of the original covenants or of the date of purchase by either of the parties in any enforcement action.[10] The chronology of covenant and purchase is utterly irrelevant,[11] both conceding priority to the overwhelming force of an equitable principle of conscience founded upon reciprocity of obligation.[12] The 'scheme of development' thus has a special equitable character which makes it quite immune from many of the normal rules governing the enforceability of restrictive covenants.

(c) Changing criteria

The equitable consequence of a finding that there exists a 'scheme of development' is, of course, a vast simplification of the difficulties which would otherwise bedevil the enforceability of the mutual covenants of the participants in such a scheme. In view of the potent effects of a 'scheme of development', the courts used to impose severely restrictive preconditions for establishing such a scheme.

(i) The original preconditions The constituent elements of the 'scheme of development' were described in classic terms in *Elliston v Reacher*.[13] Here Parker J laid down strict requirements in relation to any enforcement of the covenants comprised within such a scheme. It must be proved (1) that both the plaintiff and defendant derive title from one common vendor, (2) that the common vendor laid out the estate in defined plots in advance of the sales of the plots now owned by plaintiff and defendant respectively, (3) that the restrictions imposed by the common vendor were intended to be for the benefit of all of the plots within the scheme, and (4) that the plaintiff and defendant (or their predecessors in title) purchased their respective plots on the footing that the restrictions imposed were mutually enforceable by the owners of all the plots within the scheme. It was further stipulated by the Court of Appeal in *Reid v Bickerstaff*[14] that the area to which the 'scheme of development' extends must be clearly defined.

9 The scheme of development 'crystallises' on the disposition of the first plot sold within the scheme, and all land comprised within the scheme is automatically bound by the terms of the scheme (*Brunner v Greenslade* [1971] Ch 993 at 1003F-G).

10 Thus, under the equity of a 'scheme of development', even prior purchasers can take the benefit of covenants entered into by later purchasers (see *Re Louis and the Conveyancing Act* [1971] 1 NSWLR 164 at 183D-E; *Application of Magney* (1981) 2 BPR 9358 at 9359).

11 As Wootten J said in *Application of Fox* (1981) 2 BPR 9310 at 9317, the 'point of a building scheme lies. . .not in the "one to one" relationship between particular blocks of land, and their effect on each other, but in the impact of the various restrictions on an area as a whole, creating a "local law" which may impinge differently on different parts of the area, but overall works to give a particular character and amenity to the area. To endeavour to pick it to pieces and examine the relationship between a lot in one corner and a lot in another corner is to miss the point of a building scheme.'

12 It is even irrelevant that, on the final sale under a 'scheme of development', the covenantee (logically) retains no dominant tenement to which the last purchaser's covenant could be said to appertain. In this case the requirement of benefit to dominant land is simply dispensed with (see *Re Mack and the Conveyancing Act* [1975] 2 NSWLR 623 at 630D-F, ante, p 1160).

13 [1908] 2 Ch 374 at 384.

14 [1909] 2 Ch 305 at 319.

(ii) Subsequent relaxation of the requirements So ferocious were the conditions thus laid down for the existence of a 'scheme of development' that between 1908 and 1965 it seems that such a scheme was upheld in only two reported English cases.[15] More recently, however, the courts have relaxed the requirements demanded of an enforceable 'scheme of development', by having regard to the equitable principles which regulated such schemes prior to *Elliston v Reacher*.[16] In the 19th century, for instance, it was much more generally recognised that the authentic basis for the enforcement of 'schemes of development' was the idea of community of interest.[17] As Lord Macnaghten said in *Spicer v Martin*,[18] 'community of interest necessarily. . . requires and imports reciprocity of obligation'.[19] The intended mutuality of the covenants created within the 'scheme of development' was seen as generating a 'local law' for the area covered by the scheme.[20] This mutuality attracted the protection of a jurisdiction founded upon notions of conscience, for it gave rise to 'an equity which is created by circumstances and is independent of contractual obligation'.[1] It is precisely a recognition of the 'equities arising from the reciprocity of obligations undertaken by purchasers'[2] which underlies the modern 'scheme of development'.

(iii) A community of interest and obligation As Megarry J observed in *Brunner v Greenslade*,[3] when the broader perspective of equity is adopted '[t]he major theoretical difficulties based on the law of covenant seem. . . to disappear.' The courts have accordingly tended to return to the authentic root of equitable obligation which underlies the 'scheme of development'.[4] In *In re Dolphin's Conveyance*,[5] for instance, the court was presented with a scheme which was defective in terms of the traditional requirements of a 'scheme of development' as laid down in *Elliston v Reacher*. The scheme lacked a single common vendor, and the vendors had not, prior to the relevant sales, laid out the estate or any defined portion of it in pre-determined lots. Stamp J nevertheless held that there was a valid 'scheme of development' in existence.[6] He noted that in the present case it had been intended 'as well by the vendors as

15 See *Newman v Real Estate Debenture Corpn Ltd and Flower Decorations Ltd* [1940] 1 All ER 131.

16 'I accordingly think that in this case I am fabricating no new equity, but merely emphasising an established equity' (see *Brunner v Greenslade* [1971] Ch 993 at 1005H per Megarry J).

17 See *Child v Douglas* (1854) Kay 560 at 572, 69 ER 237 at 242; *Renals v Cowlishaw* (1878) 9 Ch D 125 at 129 (affd (1879) 11 Ch D 866); *Nottingham Patent Brick and Tile Co v Butler* (1885) 15 QBD 261 at 268f (affd (1886) 16 QBD 778); *Collins v Castle* (1887) 36 Ch D 243 at 247.

18 (1888) 14 App Cas 12 at 25.

19 See *Re Seifeddine and Governors & Co of Hudson Bay* (1980) 108 DLR (3d) 671 at 679.

20 See *Reid v Bickerstaff* [1909] 2 Ch 305 at 319 per Cozens-Hardy MR.

1 *Lawrence v South County Freeholds Ltd* [1939] Ch 656 at 682 per Simonds J. See also *Re Mack and the Conveyancing Act* [1975] 2 NSWLR 623 at 629F–630C.

2 *Application of Fox* (1981) 2 BPR 9310 at 9316.

3 [1971] Ch 993 at 1005G.

4 See *Application of Fox* (1981) 2 BPR 9310 at 9316.

5 [1970] Ch 654. See (1970) 86 LQR 445 (P.V. Baker); (1970) 117 SJ 798 (G.H. Newsom).

6 See also *Baxter v Four Oaks Properties Ltd* [1965] Ch 816 at 828B-E; *Re Mack and the Conveyancing Act* [1975] 2 NSWLR 623 at 629C–630D. Compare, however, the stubborn adherence to *Elliston v Reacher* in Canada (*Re Lakhani and Weinstein* (1981) 118 DLR (3d) 61 at 67f) and in New Zealand (*Sawyer v Starr* [1985] 2 NZLR 540 at 544f).

the several purchasers. . .to lay down what has been referred to as a local law for the estate for the common benefit of all the several purchasers of it.'[7] There had been a clear intention that each purchaser should 'have, as against the other purchasers, in one way or another, the benefit of the restrictions to which he had made himself subject.'[8] Accordingly Stamp J found in favour of the existence of a 'scheme of development', not on the ground of any implication derived from the existence of the four points specified by Parker J in *Elliston v Reacher*, but rather on the basis of 'a wider principle'.[9] In Stamp J's view, there arose on the present facts an 'equity' which was ultimately founded on the 'common interest and the common intention actually expressed in the conveyances themselves.'[10]

(d) The modern requirements

By returning to its broad origins in obligations of reciprocity and conscience, the courts have been able to re-fashion the 'scheme of development' so that it once more becomes a useful and workable device in the enforcement of restrictive covenants.[11] The constitutive element in a 'scheme of development' is not 'the "one to one" relationship between lots, but the definition of an area within which the scheme operates to create a local environment by the application of a local law'.[12] Accordingly it is now generally accepted that a 'scheme of development' arises where there is an intention that a well defined area of land should be sold off in units or plots and that, for the benefit of the common purchasers inter se, restrictive obligations should be imposed on the user of each portion sold.[13]

It seems that ultimately there are but two requirements which are universally insisted upon,[14] and if these two requirements are fulfilled, it matters not greatly that the other requirements elucidated by Parker J in *Elliston v Reacher* are not satisfied.[15]

7 For other references to the implications of a 'local law' or 'common law' designed to govern a defined area, see *Baxter v Four Oaks Properties Ltd* [1965] Ch 816 at 826B per Cross J; *Texaco Antilles Ltd v Kernochan* [1973] AC 609 at 624E per Lord Cross of Chelsea.

8 [1970] Ch 654 at 662A.

9 See also *Re Mack and the Conveyancing Act* [1975] 2 NSWLR 623 at 634E-F.

10 [1970] Ch 654 at 664C-D, citing *Nottingham Patent Brick and Tile Co v Butler* (1885) 15 QBD 261 at 268 per Wills J.

11 For reference to the possibility that the vigilant enforcement of a 'scheme of development' may protect the character and amenity of a housing estate 'to a standard which planning control would lamentably have failed to achieve', see *Re Hornsby's Application* (1968) 20 P & CR 495 at 502. See also *Re Mack and the Conveyancing Act* [1975] 2 NSWLR 623 at 635A-B.

12 *Application of Fox* (1981) 2 BPR 9310 at 9318 per Wootten J.

13 There must be a sale and consequent acquisition of a number of lots. No 'scheme of development' can arise by reason of the mere fact that, unrelated to the acquisition of land, two persons have entered into restrictive covenants. The existence of the scheme depends upon the purchase of land by persons with the knowledge that, and in reliance upon the fact that, each will obtain the protection of covenants of a like nature entered into by others (see *Application of Caroline Chisholm Village Pty Ltd* (1980) 1 BPR 9507 at 9514).

14 These two requirements were confirmed by the Privy Council in *Jamaica Mutual Life Assurance Society v Hillsborough Ltd* [1989] 1 WLR 1101 at 1106F-G per Lord Jauncey of Tullichettle.

15 The onus of proof rests on the party who wishes to rebut the existence of a 'scheme of development' (*Application of Fox* (1981) 2 BPR 9310 at 9316).

(i) There must be an identifiable 'scheme' It is essential to a 'scheme of development' that there should be a *scheme*, and this in turn necessarily presupposes that it is possible to identify the land to which the scheme relates.[16] If the evidence presented in favour of a scheme rests upon the terms of a series of conveyances, it may well be fatal to the existence of a supposed scheme that none of those conveyances show any defined area over which reciprocal obligations are to be enforceable.[17] Although there is no requirement that the area covered by the scheme should necessarily have been subdivided into plots of uniform or predetermined size,[18] the absence of lotting may make it much more difficult to prove that there was any coherent intention to create an effective 'local law'.[19]

(ii) There must be a mutually perceived common intention The essence of a 'scheme of development' is 'reciprocity of obligations'.[20] As the Privy Council indicated in *Jamaica Mutual Life Assurance Society v Hillsborough Ltd*,[1] each respective purchaser from the original vendor must have accepted 'that the benefit of the covenants into which he has entered will enure to the vendor and to others deriving title from him and that he correspondingly will enjoy the benefit of covenants entered into by other purchasers of part of the land.' It must, in effect, be shown that the participants in the scheme alike purchased on the footing that all would be mutually bound by, and mutually entitled to enforce, a defined set of restrictions.[2]

Evidence of the required commonality of intention underpinning a 'scheme of development' may be found in the terms of the individual conveyances to the several purchasers.[3] In the absence of such evidence the court may

16 *Jamaica Mutual Life Assurance Society v Hillsborough Ltd* [1989] 1 WLR 1101 at 1106F. It is even possible that an identifiable 'scheme of development' may be constituted by a network of integrated and overlapping sub-schemes within the area of the scheme (*Application of Fox* (1981) 2 BPR 9310 at 9316).

17 *Lund v Taylor* (1975) 31 P & CR 167 at 175. The absence of any 'scheme' accounted for the failure of the claims put forward in *Harlow v Hartog* (1978) 245 Estates Gazette 140; *In re Crest Homes Plc's Application* (Unreported, Lands Tribunal, LP/19/1982, 12 January 1984); *Thompson v Potter* [1980] BCL 764.

18 *Baxter v Four Oaks Properties Ltd* [1965] Ch 816 at 828C-E; *Application of Caroline Chisholm Village Pty Ltd* (1980) 1 BPR 9507 at 9514.

19 *Baxter v Four Oaks Properties Ltd* [1965] Ch 816 at 828C; *In re Crest Homes Plc's Application* (Unreported, Lands Tribunal, LP/19/1982, 12 January 1984); *Re Worth's Application* (Unreported, Lands Tribunal, 12 July 1984).

20 *Jamaica Mutual Life Assurance Society v Hillsborough Ltd* [1989] 1 WLR 1101 at 1106G per Lord Jauncey of Tullichettle.

1 [1989] 1 WLR 1101 at 1106G.

2 It has even been said that 'the equitable doctrine of the common building scheme. . .was concerned with notice of a vendor's intention and not with the existence of a covenant in actual fact. It is possible to envisage a case where there was never one covenant contained in a conveyance and yet there might be a common building scheme, because purchasers purchased on the basis that there would be such covenants' (*Re Louis and the Conveyancing Act* [1971] 1 NSWLR 164 at 178D-E per Jacobs JA).

3 In determining the intentions of the original and subsequent purchasers, the court will have regard to as many of the relevant instruments of conveyance as possible (see C.H.S. Preston and G.H. Newsom, op cit, p 61f). See, however, *Re Worth's Application* (Unreported, Lands Tribunal, 12 July 1984), where the relevant conveyances failed to disclose evidence of any scheme.

seek out extrinsic evidence as to the circumstances of the original purchases.[4] The existence of a 'scheme of development' may be negatived if it cannot be shown, for instance, that the estate plan was brought to the attention of any of the individual purchasers.[5] Similarly, a 'scheme' cannot be established if there is no evidence that the prospective purchasers were told that the vendor was proposing to exact similar covenants, or indeed any covenants, from the purchasers of other plots.[6] The existence of a 'scheme of development' is unlikely to be inferred from the mere entry of restrictive covenants in a charges register.[7]

Where a 'scheme of development' is successfully asserted, it is, however, relatively free of many of the more technical rules relating to restrictive covenants.[8] There is, for example, no need to apply to schemes of development any 'detailed "touch and concern" requirement'.[9] An irregular distribution of benefit amongst the lots within an alleged scheme is not fatal to the existence of a valid 'scheme'. It is unnecessary to insist that every lot under the scheme is beneficially affected by every covenant or that the precise effect of each covenant was related to nominated lots when the covenants were being drafted.[10]

(9) Remedies for breach of a restrictive covenant

A range of remedies may be available to a plaintiff who successfully claims both that he is entitled to the benefit of a restrictive covenant and that the defendant is subject to its burden and in breach of its terms.[11] The court may award damages if the injury to the plaintiff's rights is small, if the damage can be estimated in money and would be adequately compensated by a small money payment, and if it would be oppressive to

4 A court would be concerned, for instance, to examine the terms of advertisement relating to the relevant sales, the nature of any representations made by the vendors to the original purchasers, and whether the latter were aware of other parallel transactions within a 'scheme' (see *Jamaica Mutual Life Assurance Society v Hillsborough Ltd* [1989] 1 WLR 1101 at 1108C).

5 *Lund v Taylor* (1975) 31 P & CR 167 at 174; *Harlow v Hartog* (1978) 245 Estates Gazette 140. In the case of an estate sold by auction, however, it may be sufficient that the covenants to be entered into by each purchaser were set out in the auction particulars. See *Lund v Taylor*, supra at 174; *In re Crest Homes Plc's Application* (Unreported, Lands Tribunal, LP/19/1982, 12 January 1984). Compare, however, *Carmichael v Ripley Finance Co Ltd* [1974] 1 NZLR 557 at 560.

6 *Lund v Taylor* (1975) 31 P & CR 167 at 174; *Jamaica Mutual Life Assurance Society v Hillsborough Ltd* [1989] 1 WLR 1101 at 1108C-D. See also *Nottingham Patent Brick and Tile Co v Butler* (1885) 15 QBD 261 at 269. The existence of a coherent common intention may also be put in doubt by any subsequent waiver of breaches or inconsistent or irregular imposition of the restrictions on other purchasers (see *Re Lakhani and Weinstein* (1981) 118 DLR (3d) 61 at 67f).

7 *In re Crest Homes Plc's Application* (Unreported, Lands Tribunal, LP/19/1982, 12 January 1984).

8 It nevertheless remains the case that a 'scheme of development' cannot be enforced if unity of seisin intervenes during the course of the scheme, although the scheme can revive if and when that unity once again disappears (see *Texaco Antilles Ltd v Kernochan* [1973] AC 609 at 625E–626D).

9 *Application of Fox* (1981) 2 BPR 9310 at 9317.

10 *Application of Fox* (1981) 2 BPR 9310 at 9318.

11 It is always open to the defendant in proceedings brought for the enforcement of a restrictive covenant to request leave to apply to the Lands Tribunal for discharge or modification of the covenant (Law of Property Act 1925, s 84(9)).

the defendant to grant a mandatory injunction.[12] In other cases, however, the court may be prepared to award a mandatory injunction. In *Wakeham v Wood*,[13] the defendant had acted in 'flagrant disregard of the plaintiff's rights' by constructing, in breach of covenant, a building which obstructed the plaintiff's view of the sea. The Court of Appeal was not inclined to enable the defendant to 'buy his way out of his wrong' and granted a mandatory order requiring the demolition of the obstruction.[14]

(10) Modification and discharge of restrictive covenants

The existence of a restrictive covenant affecting a particular piece of land clearly places a long-term fetter upon the kinds of activity which may be conducted on that land. In committing themselves to restrictive covenants, parties tend to undertake obligations over an extended time-frame without any proviso for cesser in the event of later changes of circumstance. In some cases it clearly becomes undesirable that the covenanted inhibition upon land use should continue indefinitely, and it may be in the interests of social utility that the restrictions imposed by the covenant should be abrogated or otherwise modified.

Section 84 of the Law of Property Act 1925 deals directly with the problem of obsolescence in the operation of restrictive covenants.[15] (It is indeed likely that the modern relaxation of many of the threshold requirements affecting the recognition of enforceable covenants owes much to the increasingly wide scope of the statutory power to deal with outdated or inappropriate land obligations.[16]) Section 84(1) confers a discretionary power upon the Lands Tribunal to discharge or modify any restrictive covenant (with or without compensation) on a number of grounds.[17] The Lands Tribunal may exercise this power where, for instance, by reason of changes in the character of the property concerned or the neighbourhood or otherwise, the restriction

12 *Shelfer v City of London Electric Lighting Co* [1895] 1 Ch 287 at 322. See also *Kelly v Barrett* [1924] 2 Ch 379 at 396f; *Federated Homes Ltd v Mill Lodge Properties Ltd* [1980] 1 WLR 594 at 607E-F; *Arbutus Park Estates Ltd v Fuller* (1977) 74 DLR (3d) 257 at 261ff. An award of damages compensates only for the loss sustained by the covenantee and takes no account of any gain made by the covenantor through his breach (see *Surrey CC v Bredero Homes Ltd* [1992] 3 All ER 302 at 316f; but compare [1992] Conv 457 (N.S. Price)).

13 (1982) 43 P & CR 40 at 45.

14 (1982) 43 P & CR 40 at 45, 47. See also *Wrotham Park Estate Co Ltd v Parkside Homes Ltd* [1974] 1 WLR 798 at 809D-F, 811A-C; *Lund v A.J.A. Taylor & Co Ltd* (1974) 230 Estates Gazette 363 at 367. A mandatory injunction may be refused if the plaintiff stood by while the work progressed (see *Clothier v Snell* (1966) 198 Estates Gazette 27 at 28).

15 The Law Commission has recommended that most restrictive covenants between freeholders should cease to have effect 80 years after their creation (*Transfer of Land: Obsolete Restrictive Covenants* (Law Com No 201 (July 1991), para 3.1). Any person aggrieved by the lapse would have a right to apply to the Lands Tribunal for the conversion of the relevant covenant into a 'land obligation' (post, p 1167). See [1992] Conv 2.

16 Section 84 was significantly amended and extended by Law of Property Act 1969, s 28.

17 See generally E.H. Bodkin, (1943) 7 Conv (NS) 17; Norma Dawson, (1978) 29 NILQ 223. The court has jurisdiction under section 84(2) of the Law of Property Act 1925 to declare whether given land is affected by a restrictive covenant. The court's discretion to discharge or modify under section 84 has no application to 'planning obligations' (ante, p 1142), which may be varied or discharged on application to the local planning authority (Town and Country Planning Act 1990, s 106A(1)-(6), (10), as substituted by Planning and Compensation Act 1991, s 12(1)).

is deemed 'obsolete',[18] or where the continued existence of the restriction 'would impede some reasonable user of the land for public or private purposes'.[19] In the latter case covenants may be discharged or modified where they no longer, in relation to the respective dominant owners, secure 'any practical benefits of substantial value or advantage to them'.[20]

The Lands Tribunal's power is also exercisable where the persons entitled to the benefit of the restriction have agreed expressly or by implication to its discharge or modification,[1] and where the proposed discharge or modification 'will not injure' the persons entitled to the benefit of the restriction.[2] The mere fact that planning permission has already been granted in respect of a proposed development does not necessarily indicate that the Lands Tribunal must discharge or modify a particular restrictive covenant.[3]

(11) Planning and compulsory purchase law

It has already been mentioned that much of the law relating to control of land use has been brought within the public domain by modern legislation. The field of planning law and compulsory purchase is now governed by an extremely wide range of statute law and delegated legislation. This area of law is indeed vast and lies outside the scope of this book.[4]

(12) Reform of the law of covenants

It has for long been recognised that the law of covenants in English law is in need of radical reform. As long ago as 1965 the Wilberforce Committee

18 Law of Property Act 1925, s 84(1)(a). There is inevitably great difficulty in showing that a restrictive covenant entered into in recent years is obsolete (see *Balchin v Buckle* (1982) 126 SJ 412). The test of obsoleteness is whether the original object of the restriction can still be achieved (see *In re Truman, Hanbury, Buxton & Co Ltd's Application* [1956] 1 QB 261 at 272; *Driscoll v Church Commissioners* [1957] 1 QB 330 at 341ff, 349; *Abbey Homesteads (Developments) Ltd v Northamptonshore CC* (1987) 53 P & CR 1 at 12, (1992) 64 P & CR 377 at 381). In *Re Quaffers Ltd's Application* (1988) 56 P & CR 142 at 152, for instance, a restrictive covenant was discharged on the ground that the immediate environment had been devastated through being enveloped by dual carriageway roads including the M62.

19 Law of Property Act 1925, s 84(1)(aa), as inserted by Law of Property Act 1969, s 28. See *Stannard v Issa* [1987] AC 175 at 187A-B.

20 Law of Property Act 1925, s 84(1A). The Tribunal will not, however, discharge or modify a covenant which secures a 'practical benefit' in the form of the preservation of a landscape view which is visible, not from the dominant land itself, but from land in its vicinity, and which is threatened by a proposed housing development. See *Gilbert v Spoor* [1983] Ch 27 at 33A-C, 35G-36B; [1982] Conv 452 (P.H. Kenny). See also *Re Speakman's Application* [1983] JPL 680 at 681; *Re Mercian Housing Society Ltd's Application* (1972) 23 P & CR 116 at 122ff.

1 Law of Property Act 1925, s 84(1)(b).

2 Law of Property Act 1925, s 84(1)(c). See *Re Beech's Application* (1990) 59 P & CR 502 at 509ff; [1990] Conv 455 (N.D.M. Parry). In *Re Bushell's Application* (1987) 54 P & CR 386 at 390, a proposed modification in Wimbledon was rejected where the resulting construction would have obstructed an unusually fine view from a neighbouring property (resulting in a diminution of its value by some £30,000) and would have destroyed the 'air of spaciousness' in the local environment.

3 *Re Martin's Application* (1989) 57 P & CR 119 at 125.

4 See generally P. McAuslan, *Land, Law and Planning* (London 1975); *The Ideologies of Planning Law* (Oxford 1980); M. Grant, *Urban Planning Law* (London 1982 and 2nd Cum Supp 1990); S. Tromans, *The Environmental Protection Act 1990: Text and Commentary* (London 1991).

acknowledged that many positive covenants in respect of property in this country are quite unenforceable in practice because of the unsatisfactory nature of the rules relating to the burden of those covenants.[5] The Committee agreed that the time had come for statutory intervention 'to introduce legal order and consistency into the present (inevitably) haphazard techniques of multi-unit property development'.[6]

No legislation was ever introduced to implement the proposals of the Wilberforce Committee. However, in 1984 the Law Commission issued a renewed proposal for the comprehensive reformulation of the law of freehold covenants, both positive and negative, which rested heavily on the analogy of the law of easements.[7] The Commission envisaged the creation of a new interest in land (the 'land obligation'), by means of which it would be possible to impose both positive and negative obligations on one piece of land (the 'servient land') for the benefit of another piece of land (the 'dominant land').[8] 'Land obligations' are to comprise two types of obligation. It is proposed that they should include 'neighbour obligations' (which represent the equivalents of existing positive and negative covenants)[9] and 'development obligations' (which relate to the kinds of reciprocal obligation much needed for the regulation of multi-occupied areas such as blocks of flats).[10] The Law Commision has recommended that the 'land obligation' should always be made in writing. Moreover a legal land obligation must be contained in a deed and must be made for a term equivalent to a fee simple absolute in possession or for a term of years absolute.[11] Any other 'land obligation' has merely equitable status.[12]

The Law Commission's proposed scheme, if implemented, will have the highly beneficial consequence that the extremely technical rules relating to the transmission of the benefits and burdens of covenants will disappear.[13] It is envisaged that all land obligations (including legal obligations) must be protected by the registration of a new category of Class C land charge (in the case of unregistered land) and by entry on the register of the titles of both dominant and servient tenements (in the case of registered land).[14] The benefits and burdens created by the 'land obligation' will thereafter attach to the relevant tenements and will be enforceable only as between the current owners of the respective tenements.[15] In other words, the person burdened by a land obligation will cease to be liable under it when he ceases to be owner of the relevant servient land.[16]

Although the Law Commission attached to its report a draft Land Obligations Bill, no legislation has yet been introduced in Parliament to give effect to its provisions. It is likely that the Commission's 'land obligation'

5 See *Report of the Committee of Positive Covenants Affecting Land* (Cmnd 2719, 1965).
6 Ibid, para 9.
7 *Transfer of Land: The Law of Positive and Restrictive Covenants* (Law Com No 127, 26 January 1984).
8 Law Com No 127, paras 4.21, 5.2.
9 Law Com No 127, paras 6.3ff.
10 Law Com No 127, paras 6.7ff.
11 Law Com No 127, paras 5.2, 8.8f.
12 Law Com No 127, paras 5.2, 8.8f.
13 Law Com No 127, para 4.22.
14 Law Com No 127, paras 9.4ff, 9.14ff.
15 Law Com No 127, paras 4.22, 10.2ff.
16 Law Com No 127, para 11.32.

proposals will be complemented by more recent recommendations relating to the introduction of 'commonhold' legislation.[17] The 'commonhold' proposals, if implemented, would ensure that both the benefit and the burden of a number of statutorily defined standard rights and obligations are attached indefinitely to each unit within any particular commonhold scheme.[18] The commonhold scheme would not, however, replace or render redundant the Law Commission's proposals in respect of 'land obligations'. There are still many situations in which it would be inappropriate to adopt the communal management machinery which is integral to commonhold schemes,[19] and in such cases the 'land obligation' may well provide all that is necessary for the orderly transmission of the benefit and burden of covenanted obligations between freeholders and their successors in title.[20] The commonhold scheme is principally aimed to facilitate the co-operative multi-ownership of buildings such as residential blocks of flats. There still remains a need to enable owners outside this context to create 'land obligations' inter se of a fully and permanently enforceable character.[1]

17 See Law Commission, *Commonhold: Freehold Flats and freehold ownership of other interdependent buildings* (Cm 179, July 1987), ante, pp 10, 797.
18 Law Commission, *Commonhold* (July 1987), para 7.3.
19 The Law Commission instanced the case of suburban property owners who covenant inter se to make periodic contributions towards the upkeep of a private road (ante, p 1135). Here it would be excessively burdensome to require the creation of a complex commonhold simply in order to provide a legal mechanism for the transmission of the positive burden from one individual property owner to his or her successor. See Law Commission, *Commonhold* (July 1987), para 17.2.
20 Law Commission, *Commonhold* (July 1987), paras 1.9, 17.2.
1 Law Commission, *Commonhold* (July 1987), para 17.2.

Index